Stories

W9-DJB-058

Stories

Stories

An Anthology and an Introduction

Eric S. Rabkin
University of Michigan

▦ HarperCollins*College*Publishers

Acquisitions Editor: Lisa Moore
Developmental Editor: Carolyn Viola-John
Project Coordination, Text and Cover Design: PC&F, Inc.
Cover Illustration: Bonnie Timmons
Production Manager: Willie Lane
Compositor: Digitype
Printer and Binder: Malloy Lithographing, Inc.
Cover Printer: Malloy Lithographing, Inc.

For permission to use copyrighted material, grateful acknowledgment is made to the copyright holders on pp. 1467–1474, which are hereby made part of this copyright page.

Stories

Copyright © 1995 by Harper Collins College Publishers

All rights reserved. Printed in the United States of America. No part of this book may be used or reproduced in any manner whatsoever without written permission, except in the case of brief quotations embodied in critical articles and reviews. For information address HarperCollins College Publishers, 10 East 53rd Street, New York, NY 10022.

Library of Congress Cataloging-in-Publication Data

Rabkin, Eric S.
    Stories / Eric S. Rabkin.
        p.   cm.
    Includes index.
    Filmography: p.
    ISBN 0-06-045327-3
    1. College readers.   2. Short stories.   I. Title.
PE 1417.R23   1994
808.83′1 — dc20   93-31262
                                                                   CIP

5 6 7 8 9 - DOC - 01 00 99 98

For the brightest lights in my life,
Elizabeth
and our children,
David and Rachel

Contents

Chronological Table of
  Contents xii
Preface xix
Introduction: On Reading
  Stories 1

■ **Bible** 10
Genesis 10
"Jonah" 23
"On Parables" (Mark 4) 26
"The Prodigal Son" (Luke 15) 29

■ **Taoism** 31
"A Ch'an Koan" 31
"Outsides" 32
"Smelling Essays" 33

■ **Sufism** 34
"The Ancient Coffer of Nuri
  Bey" 34
"The Bequest" 36
"The Limitations of Dogma" 37

■ **Chinua Achebe** 38
"Girls at War" 38

■ **Alice Adams** 49
"A Southern Spelling Bee" 49

■ **James Agee** 54
"A Mother's Tale" 54

■ **Ama Ata Aidoo** 69
"Something to Talk About on the
  Way to the Funeral" 69

■ **Ryunosuke
  Akutagawa** 78
"In a Grove" 78

■ **Woody Allen** 85
"The Whore of Mensa" 85

■ **Sherwood
  Anderson** 90
"Hands" 90

■ **Isaac Asimov** 95
"Reason" 95

■ **Margaret Atwood** 109
"The Resplendent Quetzal" 109

■ **James Baldwin** 119
"Going to Meet the Man" 119

■ **Amiri Baraka** 132
"The Death of Horatio Alger" 132

■ **Lynda Barry** 137
"The Night We All Got Sick" 137

■ **John Barth** 139
"Night-Sea Journey" 139

■ **Donald Barthelme** 146
"The Piano Player" 146

■ **Stephen Vincent
  Benét** 149
"Nightmare Number Three" 149

■ **Ambrose Bierce** 152
"An Occurrence at Owl Creek
  Bridge" 152

■ **Jorge Luis Borges** 159
"Emma Zunz" 159
"Pierre Menard, Author of the
  Quixote" 163

■ **Richard Brautigan** 169
"Homage to the San Francisco
  YMCA" 169

■ **Gwendolyn Brooks** 172
"The Ballad of Rudolph Reed" 172

■ **Olga Broumas** 175
"Little Red Riding Hood" 175

■ **Dick Bruna** 177
The King 177

■ **Morley Callaghan** 182
"A Cap for Steve" 182

■ **François Camoin** 190
"Things I Did To Make It Possible" 190

■ **Raymond Carver** 193
"Viewfinder" 193

■ **Willa Cather** 196
"The Joy of Nelly Deane" 196

■ **Geoffrey Chaucer** 207
"The Miller's Tale" 207

■ **John Cheever** 227
"The Swimmer" 227

■ **Anton Chekov** 236
"Vanka" 236

■ **Kate Chopin** 240
"Désirée's Baby" 240

■ **Arthur C. Clarke** 245
"The Star" 245

■ **Colette** 250
"The Other Wife" 250

■ **Joseph Conrad** 253
Heart of Darkness 253

■ **Robert Coover** 312
"The Brother" 312

■ **Julio Cortázar** 317
"Continuity of Parks" 317

■ **Stephen Crane** 319
"The Blue Hotel" 319

■ **R. Crumb** 339
"fred the teen-age girl pigeon" 339

■ **Samuel R. Delany** 342
"Corona" 342

■ **Feodor Dostoevsky** 356
"The Honest Thief" 356

■ **Arthur Conan Doyle** 370
"The Adventure of the Speckled Band" 370

■ **Harlan Ellison** 388
"I Have No Mouth, and I Must Scream" 388

■ **Louise Erdrich** 400
"Chapter Two: 1932, Sita Kozka" 400

■ **William Faulkner** 406
"Barn Burning" 406
"Dry September" 419

■ **F. Scott Fitzgerald** 428
"Babylon Revisited" 428

■ **Charlotte Perkins Gilman** 443
"The Yellow Wall-Paper" 443

■ **Ellen Glasgow** 456
"A Point in Morals" 456

■ **Susan Glaspell** 465
"A Jury of Her Peers" 465

■ **Nikolai Gogol** **481**
"The Overcoat" 481

■ **Nadine Gordimer** **505**
"Six Feet of the Country" 505

■ **Jakob & Wilhelm Grimm** **514**
"Rapunzel" 514
"The Three Spinsters" 518
"Little Red-cap" 520

■ **Dashiell Hammett** **523**
"The Gutting of Couffignal" 523

■ **Barry Hannah** **546**
"I'm Shaking to Death" 546

■ **Thomas Hardy** **549**
"The Son's Veto" 549

■ **Francis Bret Harte** **560**
"The Outcasts of Poker Flat" 560

■ **Nathaniel Hawthorne** **568**
"Rappaccini's Daughter" 568
"Young Goodman Brown" 588

■ **Sara Henderson Hay** **597**
"Rapunzel" 597

■ **Ernest Haycox** **598**
"Stage to Lordsburg" 598

■ **Ernest Hemingway** **609**
"A Clean, Well-Lighted Place" 609

■ **O. Henry** **613**
"A Midsummer Knight's Dream" 613
"Springtime à la Carte" 618

■ **Gilberto Hernandez** **623**
"The Whispering Tree" 623

■ **Spencer Holst** **627**
"The Zebra Storyteller" 627

■ **Henry James** **629**
"The Altar of the Dead" 629
"The Tree of Knowledge" 653
The Turn of the Screw 664

■ **Sara Orne Jewett** **735**
"A White Heron" 735

■ **James Joyce** **743**
"Counterparts" 743
"The Dead" 751

■ **Franz Kafka** **780**
"A Common Confusion" 780
The Metamorphosis 782

■ **Yasunari Kawabata** **814**
"One Arm" 814

■ **Jamaica Kincaid** **827**
"Girl" 827

■ **Tommaso Landolfi** **829**
"Rain" 829

■ **D. H. Lawrence** **833**
"Odour of Chrysanthemums" 833
"The Rocking-Horse Winner" 848

■ **Ursula K. Le Guin** **859**
"The Day Before the Revolution" 859

■ **Stanislaw Lem** **870**
"Prince Ferrix and the Princess Crystal" 870

■ **Doris Lessing** 878
"Pleasure" 878

■ **Jack London** 889
"To Build a Fire" 889

■ **Bernard Malamud** 901
"The German Refugee" 901

■ **Katherine
Mansfield** 911
"The Doll's House" 911

■ **Bobbie Ann
Mason** 917
"A New-Wave Format" 917

■ **Guy de
Maupassant** 930
"The Jewels" 930
"Mother Savage" 936

■ **Winsor McCay** 942
"Dreams of the Rarebit Fiend" 942

■ **Herman Melville** 944
"Bartleby the Scrivener" 944

■ **Yukio Mishima** 970
"Patriotism" 970

■ **Lorrie Moore** 987
"How" 987

■ **Alice Munro** 994
"Royal Beatings" 994

■ **Flannery
O'Connor** 1010
"Good Country People" 1010

■ **Frank O'Connor** 1025
"My Oedipus Complex" 1025

■ **Tillie Olsen** 1034
"I Stand Here Ironing" 1034

■ **Ovid** 1041
Metamorphoses 1041

■ **Grace Paley** 1050
"Wants" 1050

■ **Dorothy Parker** 1053
"The Last Tea" 1053

■ **Alan Paton** 1057
"Life for a Life" 1057

■ **Charles Perrault** 1066
"Little Red Riding Hood" 1066

■ **Edgar Allan Poe** 1069
"The Black Cat" 1069
"The Purloined Letter" 1076
"The Facts in the Case of
M. Valdemar" 1089

■ **Katherine Anne
Porter** 1096
"The Grave" 1096

■ **Nawal El Saadawi** 1101
"She Has No Place in
Paradise" 1101

■ **Leslie Silko** 1106
"Yellow Woman" 1106

■ **Isaac Bashevis
Singer** 1114
"Yentl the Yeshiva Boy" 1114

■ **Art Spiegelman** 1132
"Prisoner on the Hell Planet" 1133

■ **Gertrude Stein** 1138
"Miss Furr and Miss Skeene" 1138

■ **John Steinbeck** 1143
"The Chrysanthemums" 1143
"The Harness" 1152

■ **Junichiro Tanizaki** 1162
"The Thief" 1162

■ **James Thurber** 1170
"The Secret Life of Walter
  Mitty" 1170

■ **Leo Tolstoy** 1174
The Death of Ivan Ilyitch 1174

■ **Jean Toomer** 1215
"Becky" 1215

■ **Mark Twain** 1218
"The Diary of Adam and Eve" 1218

■ **John Updike** 1236
"Should Wizard Hit Mommy?" 1236

■ **Bill Watterson** 1241
"Something Under the Bed is
  Drooling" 1241

■ **H. G. Wells** 1242
"The Star" 1242
The Time Machine 1250

■ **Eudora Welty** 1302
"Lily Daw and the Three
  Ladies" 1302
"Petrified Man" 1310

■ **Edith Wharton** 1320
"Roman Fever" 1320

■ **Richard Wright** 1330
"The Man Who Was Almost a
  Man" 1330

■ **Xiaoping Zhu** 1340
"Chronicle of Mulberry Tree
  Village" (1988) 1340

The Elements of Narrative 1355
  The Narrative Situation 1355
  Varieties of Narrative
    Stance 1359
  Authority 1366
  Genre 1369
  Character 1373
  Language 1375
  Structure 1379
  Theme 1384
  Aesthetic Virtues 1385
Keeping a Reading Journal 1387
  The Structured Journal 1387
  The Subject Journal 1389
  The Free-Writing Journal 1390
Writing About Narratives 1392
  The Role of the Critic 1392
  Types of Writing about
    Narrative 1393
    Analysis 1393
    Generalization 1394
    Review 1396
    Meditation 1397
    Reflection 1397
  Components of the Writing
    Process 1398
    *Knowing Your Audience and
      Purpose* 1398
    Getting Ideas 1398
    Testing Ideas 1401
    Drafting 1402
    Revising 1404
  Sample Student Papers 1405
    *"Truth, Justice, and Religion in
      Borges 'Emma Zunz'"* 1405
    *"The Power of Revision in
      Broumas and Borges"* 1407
Filmography 1409
  Films 1409
  Distributors 1414
Glossary of Literary Terms 1416
**Questions for Contrast and
  Comparison** 1441
Title Index 1475

Chronological Table of Contents

■ **Bible, c. 1000 B.C.E.–
  c. 100 C.E. 10**
from Genesis 10
"Jonah" 23
"On Parables" (Mark 4) 26
"The Prodigal Son" (Luke 15) 29

■ **Taoism, c. 200
  B.C.E. 31**
"A Ch'an Koan" 31
"Outsides" 32
"Smelling Essays" 33

■ **Ovid, 43 B.C.E.–
  17 C.E. 1041**
from *Metamorphoses* (c. 8 C.E.) 1041

■ **Sufism, c. 1200 C.E. 34**
"The Ancient Coffer of Nuri
  Bey" 34
"The Bequest" 34
"The Limitations of Dogma" 37

■ **Geoffrey Chaucer,
  1343?–1400 207**
"The Miller's Tale" (c. 1390) 207

■ **Charles Perrault,
  1628–1703 1066**
"Little Red Riding Hood"
  (1697) 1066

■ **Jakob & Wilhelm
  Grimm, 1785–1863
  & 1786–1859 574**
"Little Red-cap" (1812) 520
"Rapunzel" (1812) 574
"The Three Spinsters" (1812) 578

■ **Nathaniel Hawthorne,
  1804–1864 568**
"Young Goodman Brown"
  (1835) 588
"Rappaccini's Daughter"
  (1844) 568

■ **Nikolai Gogol,
  1809–1852 481**
"The Overcoat" (1842) 481

■ **Edgar Allan Poe,
  1809–1849 1069**
"The Black Cat" (1843) 1069
"The Facts in the Case of
  M. Valdemar" (1845) 1089
"The Purloined Letter"
  (1845) 1076

■ **Feodor Dostoevsky,
  1821–1881 356**
"The Honest Thief" (1848) 356

■ **Herman Melville,
  1819–1891 944**
"Bartleby the Scrivener" (1853) 944

■ **Bret Harte,
  1836–1902 560**
"The Outcasts of Poker Flat"
  (1869) 560

■ **Guy de Maupassant,
  1850–1893 930**
"The Jewels" (1883) 930
"Mother Savage" (1884) 936

■ **Leo Tolstoy,
  1828–1910 1174**
The Death of Ivan Ilyitch
  (1886) 1174

■ **Sarah Orne Jewett,**
1849–1909 735
"A White Heron" (1886) 735

■ **Anton Chekov,**
1860–1904 236
"Vanka" (1886) 236

■ **Ambrose Bierce,**
1842–1914? 152
"An Occurrence at Owl Creek
Bridge" (1890) 152

■ **Thomas Hardy,**
1840–1928 549
"The Son's Veto" (1891) 549

■ **Kate Chopin,**
1851–1904 240
"Désirée's Baby" (1892) 240

■ **Arthur Conan Doyle,**
1859–1930 370
"The Adventure of the Speckled
Band" (1892) 370

■ **Charlotte Perkins**
Gilman,
1860–1935 443
"The Yellow Wall-Paper"
(1892) 443

■ **Mark Twain,**
1835–1910 1218
"The Diary of Adam and Eve"
(1893, 1905) 1218

■ **Henry James,**
1843–1916 629
"The Altar of the Dead" (1895) 629
The Turn of the Screw (1898) 664
"The Tree of Knowledge"
(1900) 653

■ **H. G. Wells,**
1866–1946 1242
The Time Machine (1895) 1250
"The Star" (1899) 1242

■ **Stephen Crane,**
1871–1900 319
"The Blue Hotel" (1898) 319

■ **Joseph Conrad,**
1857–1924 253
Heart of Darkness (1899) 253

■ **Ellen Glasgow,**
1873–1945 456
"A Point in Morals" (1899) 456

■ **O. Henry,**
1862–1910 613
"A Midsummer Knight's Dream"
(1905) 613
"Springtime à la Carte" (1905) 618

■ **Winsor McCay,**
1871–1934 942
"Dreams of the Rarebit Fiend"
(1905) 942

■ **Jack London,**
1876–1916 889
"To Build a Fire" (1908) 889

■ **D. H. Lawrence,**
1885–1930 833
"Odour of Chrysanthemums"
(1909, 1911) 833
"The Rocking-Horse Winner"
(1926) 848

■ **Willa Cather,**
1873–1947 196
"The Joy of Nelly Deane"
(1911) 196

■ **James Joyce,**
  1882–1941 743
"Counterparts" (1914) 743
"The Dead" (1914) 751

■ **Franz Kafka,**
  1883–1924 780
The Metamorphosis (1915) 782
"A Common Confusion"
  (1917) 780

■ **Susan Glaspell,**
  1882–1948 465
"A Jury of Her Peers" (1917) 465

■ **Sherwood Anderson,**
  1876–1941 90
"Hands" (1919) 90

■ **Junichiro Tanizaki,**
  1886–1965 1162
"The Thief" (1921) 1162

■ **Gertrude Stein,**
  1874–1946 1138
"Miss Furr and Miss Skeene"
  (1922) 1138

■ **Katherine Mansfield,**
  1888–1923 911
"The Doll's House" (1922) 911

■ **Ryunosuke Akutagawa,**
  1892–1927 78
"In a Grove" (1922) 78

■ **Jean Toomer,**
  1894–1967 1215
"Becky" (1923) 1215

■ **Colette,**
  1873–1954 250
"The Other Wife" (1924) 250

■ **Dashiell Hammett,**
  1894–1961 523
"The Gutting of Couffignal"
  (1925) 523

■ **Dorothy Parker,**
  1893–1967 1053
"The Last Tea" (1926) 1053

■ **F. Scott Fitzgerald,**
  1896–1940 428
"Babylon Revisited" (1931) 428

■ **William Faulkner,**
  1897–1962 406
"Dry September" (1931) 419
"Barn Burning" (1939) 406

■ **Ernest Hemingway,**
  1899–1961 609
"A Clean, Well-Lighted Place"
  (1933) 609

■ **Stephen Vincent Benét,**
  1898–1943 149
"Nightmare Number Three"
  (1935) 149

■ **Edith Wharton,**
  1862–1937 1320
"Roman Fever" (1936) 1320

■ **Ernest Haycox,**
  1899–1950 598
"Stage to Lordsburg" (1937) 598

■ **John Steinbeck,**
  1902–1968 1143
"The Chrysanthemums"
  (1937) 1143
"The Harness" (1938) 1152

■ Eudora Welty,
   b.1909 1302
"Lily Daw and the Three Ladies"
(1937) 1302
"Petrified Man" (1939) 1310

■ James Thurber,
   1894–1961 1170
"The Secret Life of Walter Mitty"
(1939) 1170

■ Jorge Luis Borges,
   1899–1986 159
"Pierre Menard, Author of the
   Quixote" (1939) 163
"Emma Zunz" (1948) 159

■ Richard Wright,
   1908–1960 1330
"The Man Who Was Almost a
   Man" (1940) 1330

■ Isaac Asimov,
   1920–1992 95
"Reason" (1941) 95

■ Katherine Anne Porter,
   1890–1980 1096
"The Grave" (1944) 1096

■ Frank O'Connor,
   1903–1966 1025
"My Oedipus Complex"
(1950) 1025

■ Morley Callaghan,
   1903–1990 182
"A Cap for Steve" (1952) 182

■ James Agee,
   1909–1955 54
"A Mother's Tale" (1952) 54

■ Arthur C. Clarke,
   b.1917 245
"The Star" (1955) 245

■ Flannery O'Connor,
   1925–1964 1010
"Good Country People"
(1955) 1010

■ Tillie Olsen,
   b.1913 1034
"I Stand Here Ironing" (1956) 1034

■ Nadine Gordimer,
   b.1923 505
"Six Feet of the Country"
(1956) 505

■ Doris Lessing,
   b.1919 878
"Pleasure" (1957) 878

■ John Updike,
   b.1932 1236
"Should Wizard Hit Mommy?"
(1959) 1236

■ Gwendolyn Brooks,
   b.1917 172
"The Ballad of Rudolph Reed"
(1960) 172

■ Yukio Mishima,
   1925–1970 970
"Patriotism" (1960) 970

■ Alan Paton,
   1903–1988 1057
"A Life for a Life" (1961) 1057

■ Isaac Bashevis Singer,
   1904–1991 1114
"Yentl the Yeshiva Boy"
(1962) 1114

■ **Sara Henderson Hay,**
  1906 – 1987 597
"Rapunzel" (1963) 597

■ **Bernard Malamud,**
  1914 – 1986 901
"The German Refugee" (1963) 901

■ **Donald Barthelme,**
  1931 – 1989 146
"The Piano Player" (1963) 146

■ **Yasunari Kawabata,**
  1899 – 1972 814
"One Arm" (1963 – 1964) 814

■ **John Cheever,**
  1912 – 1982 227
"The Swimmer" (1964) 227

■ **Dick Bruna,**
  b.1927 177
The King (1964) 177

■ **James Baldwin,**
  1924 – 1987 119
"Going to Meet the Man"
  (1965) 119

■ **John Barth, b.1930** 139
"Night-Sea Journey" (1966) 139

■ **Julio Cortázar,**
  1914 – 1984 317
"Continuity of Parks" (1967) 317

■ **Stanislaw Lem,**
  b.1921 870
"Prince Ferrix and the Princess
  Crystal" (1967) 870

■ **Amiri Baraka,**
  b.1934 132
"The Death of Horatio Alger"
  (1967) 132

■ **Harlan Ellison,**
  b.1934 388
"I Have No Mouth, and I Must
  Scream" (1967) 388

■ **Samuel R. Delany,**
  b.1942 342
"Corona" (1967) 342

■ **R. Crumb,**
  b.1943 339
"fred the teen-age girl pigeon"
  (1968) 339

■ **Robert Coover,**
  b.1932 312
"The Brother" (1969) 312

■ **Ama Ata Aidoo,**
  b.1942 69
"Something to Talk About on the
  Way to the Funeral" (1969) 69

■ **Grace Paley,**
  b.1922 1050
"Wants" (1971) 1050

■ **Spencer Holst,**
  b.1926 627
"The Zebra Storyteller" (1971) 627

■ **Chinua Achebe,**
  b.1930 38
"Girls at War" (1972) 38

■ **Richard Brautigan,**
  1935 – 1984 169
"Homage to the San Francisco
  YMCA" (1972) 169

■ **Art Spiegelman,**
  b.1948 1132
"Prisoner on the Hell Planet"
  (1973) 1132

■ **Ursula K. Le Guin,**
  b.1929 859
"The Day Before the Revolution"
(1974) 859

■ **Woody Allen,**
  b.1935 85
"The Whore of Mensa" (1974) 85

■ **Leslie Silko,**
  b.1948 1106
"Yellow Woman" (1974) 1106

■ **Alice Munro,**
  b.1931 994
"Royal Beatings" (1977) 994

■ **Margaret Atwood,**
  b.1939 109
"The Resplendent Quetzal"
(1977) 109

■ **Olga Broumas,**
  b.1949 175
"Little Red Riding Hood"
(1977) 175

■ **Tommaso Landolfi,**
  1908–1979 829
"Rain" (1978) 829

■ **Jamaica Kincaid,**
  b.1949 827
"Girl" (1978) 827

■ **Raymond Carver,**
  1938–1988 193
"Viewfinder" (1981) 193

■ **Alice Adams,**
  b.1926 49
"A Southern Spelling Bee"
(1982) 49

■ **François Camoin,**
  b.1939 190
"Things I Did To Make It Possible"
(1982) 190

■ **Bobbie Ann Mason,**
  b.1940 917
"A New-Wave Format" (1982) 917

■ **Gilberto Hernandez,**
  b.1957 623
"The Whispering Tree" (1984) 623

■ **Barry Hannah,**
  b.1942 546
"I'm Shaking to Death" (1985) 546

■ **Lorrie Moore,**
  b.1957 987
"How" (1985) 987

■ **Louise Erdrich,**
  b.1954 400
"Chapter Two: 1932, Sita Kozka"
(1986) 400

■ **Lynda Barry,**
  b.1956 137
"The Night We All Got Sick"
(1986) 137

■ **Nawal El Saadawi,**
  b.1931 1101
"She Has No Place in Paradise"
(1987) 1101

■ **Xiaoping Zhu,**
  b.1952 1340
"Chronicle of Mulberry Tree
Village" (1988) 1340

■ **Bill Watterson,**
  b.1958 1241
"Something Under the Bed is
Drooling" (1988) 1241

Preface

> I busied myself *to think of a story,* — a story to rival those which had excited
> us to this [writing] task. One which would speak to the mysterious fears of
> our natures, and awaken thrilling horror — one to make the reader dread to
> look round, to curdle the blood, and quicken the beatings of the heart.
> — Mary Wollstonecraft Shelley, 1831 Introduction to *Frankenstein* (1818)

The first spark of the fictional life that became Frankenstein's monster was drawn
not from lightning in the sky but from stories, stories Mary and her poet husband
Percy Bysshe Shelley and poet friend George Gordon Lord Byron had read,
shared, adored, admired. Every story exists in a community of readers or hearers,
which means that every story exists in part as the next story in a line of stories; yet
every story, if it is worthy, also speaks to us afresh. "There are only two or three
human stories," Willa Cather wrote in O *Pioneers!* (1913), "and they go on
repeating themselves as fiercely as if they had never happened before." Each
worthy story is both eternal and unique.

Stories define the world for us. They teach us to cross horizons, to think
about our surroundings, to respect what is within us. *Stories* is the first college
anthology of short narratives that is designed both to offer a full range of the
powerful experiences we gain from stories and to help readers understand how
those experiences arise. While presenting works pursuing many themes, one
continuing thematic interest of *Stories* is the exploration of story-creating, storytelling, and story-hearing as crucial human activities. Stories help us to define
ourselves, interact with others, and make decisions about our lives.

Stories vary kaleidoscopically in their subjects, forms, and uses. *Stories*
presents a greater variety of works than any other convenient, single-volume
collection. For example, *Stories* has both more total pieces (136), and more
lengthy novellas (5) than previous anthologies. *Stories* also presents whole categories of works that usually go unrepresented in other anthologies: graphic narratives (7), verse narratives (6), Bible stories (6), fairy tales (7), non-Western teaching
tales (6), pre-Renaissance classics (2), and children's literature (5). *Stories* presents
many acknowledged masterpieces of short narrative from the nineteenth and
twentieth centuries (such as works by Dostoevsky and Joyce), superb writing that
has not yet been canonized (such as works by Harlem Renaissance writer Jean
Toomer), and outstanding examples of such popular genres as detective fiction
(Arthur Conan Doyle), science fiction (Ursula K. LeGuin), Westerns (Ernest
Haycox), and "comics" (Art Spiegelman). In order to encourage understanding
through comparison, *Stories* presents multiple works from each form, genre, or
culture that it represents, and multiple stories by fourteen different authors and
from three different religious traditions. Multiple selections represent work not
only from Europe and North America but from Africa, Asia, and South America
as well.

Many of the selections fall, therefore, into natural demographic sets: a large
number of works by women, groupings of works by Japanese authors, by African
American authors, and so on. Others fall into natural formal sets: verse narratives, graphic narratives, "short shorts," novellas, and so on. And still others into

natural thematic sets: thievery in Dostoevsky, Poe, and Tanizaki; children's devotion to careless parents in Adams, Callaghan, Faulkner's "Barn Burning," and its reversal in Hardy's "The Son's Veto." In creating *Stories*, care has been paid to the possibility of exploring individual rhetorical figures, as by comparing the uses of metamorphosis in Ovid with those in Kafka.

Many of the selections in *Stories* are chosen to make available in one volume stories that directly relate to one another, as with Wells's short classic "The Star" and Clarke's partial reply to it of the same title. *Stories* not only presents a set of classic, nearly oral, Grimm fairy tales but presents alternate versions of some of them (as in the highly literate Perrault "Little Red Riding Hood" and the feminist Olga Broumas and Sara Henderson Hay verse narratives).

By avoiding one-of-a-kind stories in favor of building sets of works that overlap in diverse ways, *Stories* allows students and teachers not only to understand individual works, but also to pursue in many directions questions raised by reading those individual works. For example, *Stories* contains Poe's "The Black Cat," a genuinely classic work, justly renowned for its creation of mood and its first-person portrayal of a complicatedly unstable mind. It is a story of a man trying to construct a story that will excuse his murder of his wife. Its unconsciously self-revelatory first-person narrator can be understood as a device on its own. This device becomes even clearer, however, when one makes comparison with, say, the unconsciously self-revelatory first-person narrator in Frank O'Connor's "My Oedipus Complex" and when one makes contrast with the consciously deceptive first-person narrator of Tanizaki's "The Thief." "The Black Cat" is also somewhat fantastic, and can be compared in that regard with other works, such as Kafka's "A Common Confusion" and Kawabata's "One Arm." The powerful male fear of women revealed in "The Black Cat" becomes clearer when seen in other contexts, such as Steinbeck's realistic "The Harness." "The Black Cat" depicts the brutalizing of women, a subject treated in diverse degrees in such other works as Steinbeck's "The Chrysanthemum," El Saadawi's "She Has No Place In Paradise," Borges's "Emma Zunz," and Glaspell's "A Jury of Her Peers." Poe's own works can be compared and contrasted with each other. And of course the mid-nineteenth-century American rhetoric of Poe can be compared and contrasted with the somewhat later rhetorics of Melville and Hawthorne.

None of these connections is indispensable for a profitable reading of "The Black Cat" and therefore none is mandatory for classroom discussion. None of these requires that the selections all be read or that they be read in any particular order. But designing *Stories* so as to maximize these connections and others allows for an extra richness of reading and a cumulative critical training. The apparatus of *Stories* has been designed, therefore, both to allow profit from single readings and to encourage the greatest possible enrichment from comparative readings. The aim of *Stories* is to allow teachers and students to enjoy maximum freedom and maximum reward in sampling these narratives in any order or number desired.

The selections in *Stories* are organized primarily alphabetically by author. With that arrangement, one can most easily thumb through the book to find a given work. I say "primarily" alphabetically because the Bible, Tao, and Sufi texts, as founding texts of great cultures, come first and are alphabetized within their cultures (that is, the Sufi tales alphabetized with the Sufi tales) and not across cultures (that is, the Bible story of "The Flood" is not alphabetized between the Sufi tales of "The Bequest" and "The Limitations of Dogma").

Since writers are influenced by those who came before them, it is often crucial to have a sense of the historical development of narrative. Therefore, in addition to the main Contents, *Stories* has a supplementary, Chronological Table of Contents organized not by the author's birthdate but by the earliest publication date of each author as represented in this collection.

The Introduction explores why and how stories matter to us, beginning careful textual analysis close to where most of us began, with a children's story. I know from my own classroom experience that by a slow, close, joyful reading of Dick Bruna's marvelous poem and picture book, *The King* (1964), readers become quickly and forcefully aware of such narrative matters as suspense, form, repetition, genre, theme, and so on. By demonstrating these matters in a children's book, the Introduction helps validate our own sense that stories do and always have mattered both for entertainment and for learning. More important, each reader's own palpable ability to feel the structure of the plot, to anticipate precise words, and to uncover matters of technique makes clear that we all have within us the capacity to become ever more sophisticated and satisfied readers. The more specialized critical terms handled elsewhere in the book easily fit within the large critical categories that grow from attending carefully to even so delightfully simple a story as *The King*.

In order to enrich the reading of each story, *Stories* includes for each work a factual headnote, primarily about the author, aimed more at situating the story than at predisposing the reader to any particular critical view. Each story is followed by at least five Study and Writing Questions aimed both at helping the reader notice the details of the story's composition and at delving more deeply into the story's meanings and effects. A separate section at the back of the book with over two hundred Questions for Contrast and Comparison goes much further than any other anthology in attempting to spark each reader's own curiosity and hone each reader's critical skills. Each Question for Contrast and Comparison (QCC) aims at capitalizing on the availability of works within this single collection that can, in many ways, contextualize each other. Following the Study and Writing Questions at the end of each story is a list of the QCCs that refer to the story just read. These QCCs will rarely duplicate reading issues raised in the story questions. Used with the Study and Writing Questions, the QCCs enable students to become skilled readers who understand important narrative techniques, traditional images and symbols, variations on themes, and so on. The QCCs may be used solely for readers' own personal enrichment or they may be used by teacher and student for raising further issues about each story, for contextualizing the study of individual works, and for suggesting stories that might profitably be read next and that might be helpful in designing comparative writing or discussion topics.

Stories contains appendices on The Elements of Narrative, Keeping a Reading Journal, and Writing About Stories. The Elements of Narrative discusses briefly the major elements of narrative (such as genre, character, style, structure, narrator, and so on) and exemplifies their interrelations both in general and by reference to works collected in *Stories*. This section offers a unified critical vocabulary that allows students to address all the issues that normally arise in reading and discussing stories. Discussions of the specific varieties of each element of narrative (such as Western, flat character, satire, flashback, unreliable narrator, and so on) occur in the separate Glossary of Literary Terms. Keeping a Reading Journal discusses both structured journal-keeping techniques and "freewriting" techniques, outlining how and when to do each and comparing their advantages as aids to understanding stories, to preparing for class, and to writing about stories. Writing About Stories discusses the nature of literary argument, the possible audiences and purposes of literary arguments, the nature of evidence and logic in literary arguments, pre-writing, writing, and revising

Stories also contains a separate Filmography. In this era of college library film collections and widespread ownership of VCRs, many people have easy access to films and are, moreover, more practiced at viewing films than at reading stories. A film adaptation is, among other things, a work of criticism, a presentation of some filmmaker's conception of how to retell a given story. Most stories, of course, have not been filmed. Others have been filmed but, like "Bartleby the Scrivener" and "A Jury of Her Peers," are not widely known as films. Still others, like "Babylon Revisited" and "In a Grove" have achieved fame as films under different titles. The film based on Fitzgerald's story is called *The Last Time I Saw Paris* and Kurosawa's famous film *Rashomon* is based less on Akutagawa's short story of that name than on his "In a Grove." One of the selection criteria for *Stories* was the desire to maximize the number of good supplementary films available. The filmography of *Stories* makes it easier for instructors and students alike to find films offering new views of individual works.

In my own study and teaching, I have found that critical concepts are learned best when they arise in grappling with an actual text, not in isolation. That being so, rather than having extensive discussions of critical concepts in the Introduction, many of those discussions are reserved for the Glossary. A typical entry in the alphabetical Glossary of Literary Terms contains a heading giving the term, a succinct definition, a correct use of the term in a true statement about one of the works in *Stories*, and a critical observation that hinges on the idea labeled by the term. In addition, most entries have cross-references to other entries in the Glossary or to discussion of the concept in The Elements of Narrative. Throughout *Stories*, when a Glossary term is used, it is indicated by SMALL CAPS.

Stories is designed to offer the highest quality and variety of narratives and to make their interconnections and their study as accessible as possible. Thus a term used in a Study and Writing Question can be explored in the Glossary; contrasting texts can be located through the Questions for Contrast and Comparison; theoretical discussion of the issues that arise can be found in The Elements of Narrative; and supplementary films can be located through the filmography. The backgrounds of the writers are succinctly exposed in the headnotes and their possible influences and effects can be traced through the Chronological Table of Contents. In short, this book is designed to be the most advanced, varied, and useful collection yet created for the enjoyment and study of stories.

In creating *Stories*, I have profited greatly from the efforts of countless individuals. I gladly acknowledge my own share in the world's common debt to the story-writers and -tellers who enrich us all. I feel a special gratitude to my many fine teachers and an abiding joy in the thousands of bright, feisty, feeling students with whom I have been privileged to work. I acknowledge with gratitude the assistance of colleagues who read the manuscript and offered numerous helpful suggestions, especially Eugene Baer, Wisconsin Lutheran College; Lois Birky, Illinois Central College; Sally Burke, University of Rhode Island; Raymond Dolle, Indiana State University; Jeanne Foskett, El Paso Community College; Cheryl Glenn, Oregon State University; Christopher Howell, Emporia State University; Edward Huffstetler, Bridgewater College; July A. Jolly, Pennsylvania State University; Joseph E. Kruppa, University of Texas; Barry Maid, University of Arkansas at Little Rock; Bradford Mudge, University of Colorado, Denver; Eric Pankey, Washington University; J. Walker Rutledge, Western Kentucky University; Marilyn Sides, Wellesley College; and Elaine Supowitz, Community College of Allegheny County. I have been deeply pleased at the support and encouragement of many at HarperCollins, particularly Phil Leininger, Lucy Rosendahl, and especially Lisa Moore, each of whom, in different ways, went to bat for this unusual collection. For his expert and imaginative work on the Filmography, I am indebted to Philip Hallman. I am grateful too for the sensitive, energetic production work of Katherine McCann. I feel both warm friendship and abiding gratitude to the tireless Carolyn Viola-John, the development editor with whom I have worked so closely as colleague and confidante and co-conspirator; she has been indispensable. And I want very much to express my gratitude to my family, to my parents and grandparents at whose laps and tables I first came to love stories, to my children David and Rachel who opened their lives to me as they grew in knowledge, imagination, and beauty, and to my wife Elizabeth, who read and discussed and challenged and laughed and bore me along every step of the way both in the work and pleasure of creating *Stories* and in the greater story we are blessed to write each day with our lives. I thank you all.

E.S.R.

Introduction: On Reading Stories

Stories are everywhere in our lives. Like language itself, stories are so much a part of us — we produce and consume them so continually — that our understanding of the way they work is largely automatic. And this is as it should be. After all, if we had to think about grammar every time we uttered a sentence, we would never get through an ordinary conversation; it would be as if we were novices speaking in a foreign language, struggling over such details as noun-verb agreement, tense construction, and idiom selection. Similarly, we could never get through a story, much less enjoy it, if we had to slow down at each word to decode it grammatically, to understand its functions in developing plot, setting, and character, to decide if it is meant literally or ironically, or to notice whether it is expected or surprising in this sort of story. There is a famous cartoon in which a mother centipede looks at a baby centipede and says, "Don't think about it; just walk." Stories, like language and walking, are so complex that, if they are to succeed at all, we must be able to understand them largely automatically. And yet, if we deal with stories only automatically, we will never become better at them; that is, we will not produce more effective, beautiful, persuasive, or moving stories, nor will we enjoy the rich experience of reading stories made by others or defend properly against the tricks of unscrupulous story-makers.

The automatic nature of story production and consumption has two important consequences: first, we know much more about any given story, and about stories in general, than we are usually aware of; second, if we want to get the most from stories, we need to slow down our reading and writing to make our automatic knowledge more explicit. Although most able-bodied people are quite capable of running, and do so without thinking much about the act, if they want to be better runners, they need to think about what it means to run: to question how the feet point, how the breath coordinates with the steps, how one controls pacing, and so on. Precisely because we do know more about running than we usually realize we know, we can learn to run better by exploring our feelings as we run, by watching others run, and by raising explicit questions about what we observe in ourselves and in others. We should be able to draw conclusions from these observations and questions, and we can improve by practicing what those conclusions imply. The same is true for reading, hearing, and producing stories. The goal of all our unaccustomed deliberation and self-examination is not, of course, to make us stumble in our reading, but rather to train us so that whenever we read or hear or tell a story, our capacity to understand and enjoy it is enriched.

Because stories are everywhere in human culture and thought, a consequence of this story training is a training in language and thought that is both pleasurable and valuable in other parts of life. It is no accident that people have been telling stories as long as there have been people and that every culture, nation, family, and individual has one or more founding tales to explain and justify itself. We are, in some sense, the stories we tell, and to tell and understand stories better is to enrich and empower our lives. This training can be strenuous, illuminating, wonderful. It is certainly worthwhile both in itself and for the skills it yields.

We learn to tell stories almost as soon as we learn to speak. "I want a glass of milk and a cookie" is itself a tiny, although probably incomplete, narrative. A moment's attention shows that in this sentence the narrator reports not one but two interior states, a desire for milk and a desire for a cookie. Notice too that the sentence as uttered is subtly different from "I want a cookie and a glass of milk"—probably indicating either that the narrator in the first instance is more interested in the milk than in the cookie, or that the narrator understands that the hearer would prefer the dietary values that the first ordering might imply, or both. There is also implicit suspense here: "If I don't get milk and a cookie, I will be sad or angry and then you will be distressed, so get me the milk and cookie now and everything will be all right."

Notice how much of this narrative exists only implicitly. I imagine that most readers would take the speaker above to be a little child and the hearer to be an adult, perhaps the child's parent, perhaps even more particularly the mother. But I didn't say that the speaker was a child or that the hearer was a mother. Nonetheless, those guesses about character are clearly legitimate in context. After all, the preceding sentence, "we learn to tell stories almost as soon as we learn to speak," naturally puts us in mind of early childhood, the time when most people learn to speak, and the phrase "a tiny narrative" somehow seems fitting for tiny people, that is, for children. Also, by having the request be for milk and cookies, a snack mothers traditionally give children, our implicit guesses about the characters' identities are confirmed. We can see how true this is by noticing our reactions as the story continues:

"I want a glass of milk and a cookie."
"Row, you scurvy devil!" the taskmaster snarled back at the galley slave. "You'll be lucky to get bread and water."

The second sentence may surprise us or amuse us since it would be unusual for a mother to reply to a sweet little request with the nasty, "'Row, you scurvy devil!'" Of course, now that we've readjusted our sense of the characters, we probably take the first request to be ironic or silly, especially coming as it does from a brutalized man. But remember, nowhere did the story say the requester was a brutalized man; it could have been a woman, or even a little child, as far as the explicit words go. But stories never exist only in their explicit words. They exist also in our assumptions about what words mean in context and how the world works. We think of galley slaves as brutalized men, not as women or children, and so, lacking any information to the contrary, we make our automatic assumptions. When these automatic assumptions clash, we may get laughter, surprise, or shock. Monitoring our reactions helps us know that more is going on than we have previously realized. And by knowing, we can enjoy a richer experience. In this case, the first possible simple outcome (a child satisfied by a little snack) is replaced by more complex suspense: is this story a parody or is the slave crazy or wily? will there be the possibility of escape or waking from some childhood nightmare? Suddenly the story is opened up to a new host of possibilities, each grounded in our prior understanding, and reunderstanding, of words, stories, and the world.

We use stories regularly for explanation, persuasion, provocation, definition, and entertainment, functions that are by no means separate. "Why don't you have your essay done yet?" "Well, you see, I was at the library, and I thought I had plenty of time, but then this friend of mine came running in and said I had to help him because. . . ." Explanation takes the form of a story. This story displays a clever awareness of values common to the teller and the hearer: it is set in the library; it acknowledges the importance of timeliness; it invokes the value of friendship; and it promises to report facts that will justify a reordering of priorities. This sounds like the beginning of what just may be a successful excuse. Heck, it may even be true. But whether or not it is true, its aim will be to explain the absence of the essay, to persuade the hearer that that absence is understandable, to provoke the hearer into an extension, to define the speaker as a responsible individual, and to entertain the hearer by holding the hearer's attention and by ultimately rewarding the hearer with an outcome that seems fitting to the way the story has begun. All this and more goes on in every satisfactory story. And we understand as much, albeit implicitly, both when we produce stories and when we consume them.

In William Shakespeare's play *Othello* (1603), the title character, a black man who has risen by virtue of great skill and bravery to a powerful position in the Venetian military, is asked by a nobleman how it is that Othello is loved by the desirable, aristocratic, and white, Desdemona.

> *Duke.* Say it, Othello.
> *Othello.* Her father loved me; oft invited me;
> Still questioned me the story of my life
> From year to year, the battle, sieges, fortune
> That I have passed.
> I ran it through, even from my boyish days
> To th' very moment that he bade me tell it.
> Wherein I spoke of most disastrous chance,
> Of moving accidents by flood and field,
> Of hairbreadth scapes i' th' imminent deadly breach,
> Of being taken by the insolent foe
> And sold to slavery, of my redemption thence.
> [. . .] These things to hear
> Would Desdemona seriously incline;
> But still the house affairs would draw her thence;
> She'd come again, and with a greedy ear
> Devour up my discourse.
> [. . .] My story being done,
> She gave me for my pains a world of sighs.
> She swore in faith 'twas strange, 'twas passing strange;
> 'Twas pitiful, 'twas wondrous pitiful.
> She wished she had not heard it; yet she wished
> That heaven had made her such a man. She thanked me,
> And bade me, if I had a friend that loved her,
> I should but teach him how to tell my story,
> And that would woo her. Upon this hint I spake.
> She loved me for the dangers I had passed,
> And I loved her that she did pity them.
> This only is the witchcraft I have used.

(I, iii, 126–168)

This passage, although poetry (which many wrongly assume is somehow the opposite of narrative), is part of a story. In particular, it is part of a story that tells a story about the telling of a story. Othello may have borne on his person scars from his adventures, but his true character in Desdemona's mind arose from his tale, just as his explanation to the Duke about how he won her is created by the story he tells. Just as stories are constructed of lives, lives are constructed of stories.

To see how stories engage our complex understanding of human beings, let us examine in some detail a deceptively simple work by Dick Bruna called *The King*.

If we could sit together with *The King* before us, the first thing we would see would be the book itself and its cover. This book is a thin 6½" × 6½" hard-covered square, not a hefty textbook designed for students or a thick, densely printed 4½" × 7" paperback designed for a general market. The cover has a royal blue background. On the top, in lower-case, white block letters are the words "the king." Below them, filling most of the space, is a simple line drawing of a smiling, red, boyish face topped with a simple, golden crown. On the bottom, in smaller lower-case, white block letters are the words "dick bruna." These facts of design suggest that this is a children's book, which means that we should neither expect nor require complex plotting or characterization. If we were to find the text to be in verse, moreover, we would not consider it an oddity.

In fact, the text is verse — and more. Unlike most adult books, which we read page-by-page, *The King* uses a two-page spread as its basic compositional unit. On each left-hand page we find a four-line stanza; on each right, a line drawing in bold, primary colors. I recommend that you read the words of the first page very slowly:

A little boy in a palace lived
Far from everything.
The golden crown upon his head
Showed he was a _____.

What is the next word? The right-hand page essentially shows the cover picture again, complete with golden crown. We already know the book is called *The King*. Of course, "The golden crown upon his head/Showed he was a king"! Just like little children, we can anticipate what the word will be and feel pleased at ourselves for discovering that word. When the word actually arrives in the text, it confirms our guess. This sense of confirmation is fundamental to the pleasure of any narrative. In this case it is generated in part by rhythm (we know that it would be surprising for the last word to have more than one syllable) and rhyme (we guess that the last word has to rhyme with "thing"). Grammar further constrains our normal options. "Showed he was a _____" normally requires an adjective, adverb, or noun: "Showed he was a big fool," "Showed he was a very cute fellow," or "Showed he was a cowboy." Given the limitation to one syllable, and knowing that the adjective and adverb choices still require a trailing noun, we automatically know that the word has to be a noun. "Showed he was a ring" just won't do, however, because both the picture and the words tell us that we are dealing with a human being, and there is some limit to what human beings can be. In fact, of the common monosyllabic nouns that end in "-ing," only one applies to humans, king. So we anticipate, and our anticipations are confirmed.

I don't mean to suggest that the process of anticipation as we encounter stories is typically conscious, although we often consciously anticipate the larger aspects of plot—predicting who the murderer will be in a detective story, for example, or whether or not the hero and heroine will get together at the end of a romance. What I do suggest is that anticipation is a normal, automatic feature of all story consumption, a mental practice that goes back to our earliest uses of language. In Western culture, for example, jokes typically have three subparts ("a rabbi, a minister, and a priest") with the punch line, which we learn to anticipate with glee, coming with the third subpart. Although this triple structure is arbitrary (non-Western cultures have used double and quadruple structures for jokes), it is, like the very words used to represent things in a given language, conventional; to learn the culture means to absorb these conventions. Thus readers' anticipations are enormously complex, mobilizing in slim fractions of a second immense amounts of unconscious knowledge about language, about stories, and about the world. It is precisely because stories involve so much knowledge and engage us so complexly that the mere placing of one word after another can seem to weave the fabric of reality. In white, middle-class North American society, if adult books are illustrated, they tend to have photographs (nature books), or line drawings (how-to manuals), or complex, subtle pictures (art books). Primary colors, on the other hand, like simple verse, are usually reserved for children. Because we know these arbitrary, conventional facts, we are not surprised to find "little boy kings"—virtually nonexistent in our newspapers—in the context of Bruna's square, blue book.

To read any book properly, we must know the rules of its genre just as we must know the rules of its language. The hero and heroine rarely get together in detective stories, while in a romance the "whodunit" question (who was the cab driver who made her late so that she would miss her train and meet him on the platform?) is often irrelevant. But our knowledge of genre, like our knowledge of language, is never irrelevant. As we read, we are always involved, often unconsciously, with matters of language and genre convention. We anticipate what will come next and, as in surprising situations ("'Row, you scurvy devil!'"), often revise our sense of the whole and make new anticipations. When these anticipations are met—wholly, partially, or surprisingly—we have our confirmations, our partial confirmations, and our revelations. Thus we get pleasure from stories.

After introducing its title character, *The King* continues. On the second two-page spread, the right-hand page shows two identical women's heads—still in simple line drawings and primary colors—each with a green face. They look stern and rather overpowering against a red background. On the left-hand page, the text reads:

Two tall thin green ladies
Looked after him quite well.
To get whatever he wanted,
He just had to ring a _____.

Is there any doubt about the next word? "Sell"? "Fell"? "Dell"? Of course not. The word, we guess, is "bell"—and we are right.

This sort of confirmation may seem too simple to give some people much pleasure after a certain age; however, the notion of rhyme as anticipated repetition with crucial but appropriate variation is essential to the pleasure we feel in all stories. Whether in these simple stanzas or in larger, more complex stories, our anticipations about what a given character might do or how the plot will turn out are what keep us reading.

As we keep reading *The King*, which is one of the graphic selections reprinted in this collection, we see the introduction of more situations that allow for more anticipation of outcomes. For convenience's sake, let us consider only the words, four lines to each left-hand page. To keep the reading lively, as it would be for a child who needed to be read to, I'll leave out the last words of each stanza:

> Sometimes the king built castles
> Way up into the sky.
> With red and green and yellow blocks,
> He built them very ———.
>
> Sometimes the king would drive his car,
> A real car of his own.
> But he wasn't really happy,
> For he always played ———.
>
> One day, not far from the palace,
> A little house he spied
> With a red roof and shutters.
> The gardener lived ———.
>
> Rose was the gardener's little girl.
> She liked to skip and run.
> The king played with her every day.
> He'd never had such ———.
>
> The two played ball and hide-and-seek
> And ran upon the green.
> One day the little king said, "Rose,
> I want you for my ———."
>
> The tall green ladies said, "NO! NO!
> She doesn't have a crown.
> You cannot play with Rose again,"
> They told him with a ———.
>
> "We will find a princess
> With long and golden hair.
> She will have a shining crown.
> You'll make a handsome ———."

The little king was very sad.
The tears dripped down his nose.
"I don't want a princess.
The one I want is _____."

"If I take off my crown," he said,
"Then we'll be just the same.
I don't want to be a king.
I'd rather play a _____."

Now every day the king and Rose
Play and run and swing.
Having a friend is wonderful.
It's better than being a _____.

This is fun, isn't it? And, apparently, quite simple. But although we can understand that any speaker of English, given time, could anticipate the last words of each stanza, we may not be so aware of some of the deeper interconnections within the story. Indeed, for some of us, because of the accidents of our own educations, some of those interconnections may even be absent. But the story, arising as it does from a particular culture, supports those interconnections nonetheless.

Consider color imagery. We all know that in Western culture *gold* is traditionally symbolic of wealth and power, and most people have heard that one traditional meaning for *green* is envy. The first two stanzas, then, set up an opposition between the "little boy" (young, male, and alone, but wealthy and theoretically powerful) and the "two tall thin green ladies" (old, female, and coupled, but envious and theoretically subservient). Readers of the original published version do not need to know anything about color symbolism to sense this opposition, of course, but a glance at the illustrations shows quickly that not only the words but Bruna's choice of paints reinforces this opposition. In terms of plot, we already know by the end of the fourth stanza — although perhaps only unconsciously — that there is a social contradiction here, because the women who should be helpful servants are actually in control, enforcing the king's loneliness. Thus we can anticipate that if the outcome of the story is to be happy for the king — and the genre conventions of children's stories suggest such a happy result — the servants must be denied.

Although I do not maintain that Bruna was conscious of all he did here, it is no coincidence that the king, once he is joined by Rose in the seventh stanza, is able to run "upon the green." In the very next stanza, then, "the tall thin green ladies," their portrait from the second two-page spread repeated exactly except that now they are frowning, "said, 'NO! NO!'" In their two pictures, the green ladies are on top of a background of red, which is, quite significantly, the color of the faces of all three children in the story; but Rose, whose name is a variety of red, is on top of the green, and shown, like her house, on a green background. It is through Rose, who supplies the king with companionship to break his isolation, that the envy of the older generation is happily thwarted.

The princess whom the two tall thin green ladies imagine for the king is shown as having an unusual *green* crown, for she is their invention. Of course, as an authentic princess within this symbol system, she has hair the exact color of the king's golden crown. Rose, however, the lower-class daughter of the gardener, a working person in touch with the fruitful values of the rich, dark earth, has black hair. The king himself, once his crown is removed, is bald. Now this baldness in a little boy is, of course, amusing to a child reader — and to us too for that matter — but it corresponds perfectly with the king's open-mindedness and his willingness to see his world defined not only by birth and class, but also by desire and imagination. In the last picture, he is with Rose, and his crown is missing, but even though "Having a friend is wonderful./It's better than being a king," he is still called "the king." In short, just as in the third stanza "the king built castles [. . .] With red and green and yellow blocks," Bruna uses color symbolism to build toward the happy, unconsciously anticipated outcome in which red (which also stands for passion and love) rises against green to allow gold its due and enrich it with the value, not of hollow social position, but of real friendship.

There are, then, many ways to read this story by considering all its details: the music of its poetry, the content of its words, the style of its drawing, the choice of written and painted colors, the crucial repetitions, the order of its plot, and so on. One could see in *The King* a little tale of conflict about class, age, and gender. This is also a sexist and heterosexual tale: the villains of the piece are the apparently far-from-fertile twin females, while the king wins by using round Rose to achieve a heterosexual union. If one happened to know that the rose is also a traditional Christian symbol for the Virgin Mary, one might also see this sexless friendship as the "little boy king," God the Son, Jesus, appropriately descended to Earth to find true, spiritual happiness with a pure woman of the lower class. Rose then takes on something of the role of the king's mother because, unlike the green ladies, she really does want his happiness. This union, of course, sends envy to flight and promises to create the kingdom of Heaven on Earth. In the Gospels, Jesus is called by the Romans the King of the Jews and is given not a real crown but a mock crown of thorns. Bruna's king, too, when he achieves his highest spiritual authority, is without an Earthly crown. In the Gospels, intended to provoke us to faith and an emulation of the life of Jesus, Jesus's mission fails; we are not all instantly redeemed, and there is much left for us to do. Bruna's story, intended for children, ends before we can see what happens when the king and Rose grow up, provoking us only to recognize that our class prejudices must be put aside if the world is to be a happy and well ordered place. But no matter how richly and consciously or poorly and unconsciously we read this apparently simple story, we cannot help but see that its impact on us involves an astonishing complexity, all in only two hundred seventy-seven words and twelve simple pictures. We can find such wealth in all fine stories.

To understand stories best, to enjoy them best, to learn from them best, we must read with care both for the words we see and for the words that might have been chosen but were not; we must read with attention to our own reactions and to the common knowledge of the culture and genre from which each story arose. Stories do not matter to us only "for themselves," as some like to say, but because we understand them, even if only unconsciously, as works within human culture.

We all remember the stories of George Washington and the cherry tree and of Newton and the apple. These matter not only as legends about historical figures but even more for their exploration of the ideals of honesty and discovery. While ultimately supporting those ideals, these stories remain powerful for us in part because of their strange resonances with the story of the forbidden fruit of the Tree of Knowledge in the Garden of Eden. Yet even as stories are grounded in human history, they are also in some ways independent of history and take on lives of their own. The great white whale of *Moby Dick* haunts America's relationship with Nature. *Oliver Twist* surveys the entire landscape of childhood hopes and fears. "Rashomon" has come to symbolize the inescapability of the self. The torment of Dr. Jekyll in his monstrous identity as Mr. Hyde does not grip us because we believe Dr. Jekyll lived, but because we can all understand the terrible and delicious combination of fear and desire that comes from learning too much too soon. Stories thrill us, trouble us, amaze us, absorb us, scare us, comfort us, teach us, excite us. It is by way of stories that we define ourselves and our places in the world.

The **BIBLE,** *from the Greek word biblion, meaning book, is a founding text of Western culture. It collects works written between about 1000 B.C.E. and the third century C.E. It was vital for both Jews and Christians to decide which of the many available texts to accept as divinely inspired. The Christian canon was not fixed until the end of the fourth century, and some groups still have canons slightly different from that familiar to most Americans. For example, "The Book of Sirach" is in the Russian Orthodox Bible but not in the King James Bible, also known as the Authorized Version, the 1611 translation we use here because it is by far the most familiar to English speakers from the Renaissance to the present. The Jewish scriptures, written primarily in Hebrew and Aramaic, are known in Hebrew by the acronym Tanach for Torah (meaning "the law" in Hebrew), the first five "books," also called the Pentateuch; Nebi'im ("the prophets"); and Ketubim ("other" writings). The New Testament, originally written in koiné, the Greek dialect common to the Mediterranean world of the time, consists of four lives of Jesus (known as the Gospels), twenty-one letters (called "epistles") and a prophecy, "The Book of Revelation." Our Genesis selection tells the versions of myths known around the world; the other Bible selections are more particular to the Western tradition.*

The First Book of Moses, Called Genesis

Chapter 1

In the beginning God created the heaven and the earth.

2 And the earth was without form, and void; and darkness *was* upon the face of the deep. And the Spirit of God moved upon the face of the waters.

3 And God said, Let there be light: and there was light.

4 And God saw the light, that it *was* good: and God divided the light from the darkness.

5 And God called the light Day, and the darkness he called Night. And the evening and the morning were the first day.

6 And God said, Let there be a firmament in the midst of the waters, and let it divide the waters from the waters.

7 And God made the firmament, and divided the waters which *were* under the firmament from the waters which *were* above the firmament: and it was so.

8 And God called the firmament Heaven. And the evening and the morning were the second day.

9 And God said, Let the waters under the heaven be gathered together unto one place, and let the dry *land* appear: and it was so.

10 And God called the dry *land* Earth; and the gathering together of the waters called he Seas: and God saw that it *was* good.

11 And God said, Let the earth bring forth grass, the herb yielding seed, *and* the fruit tree yielding fruit after his kind, whose seed *is* in itself, upon the earth: and it was so.

12 And the earth brought forth grass, *and* herb yielding seed after his kind, and the tree yielding fruit, whose seed *was* in itself, after his kind: and God saw that it *was* good.

13 And the evening and the morning were the third day.

14 And God said, Let there be lights in the firmament of the heaven to divide the day from the night; and let them be for signs, and for seasons, and for days, and years:

15 And let them be for lights in the firmament of the heaven to give light upon the earth: and it was so.

16 And God made two great lights; the greater light to rule the day, and the lesser light to rule the night: he made the stars also.

17 And God set them in the firmament of the heaven to give light upon the earth,

18 And to rule over the day and over the night, and to divide the light from the darkness: and God saw that it was good.

19 And the evening and the morning were the fourth day.

20 And God said, Let the waters bring forth abundantly the moving creature that hath life, and fowl that may fly above the earth in the open firmament of heaven.

21 And God created great whales, and every living creature that moveth, which the waters brought forth abundantly, after their kind, and every winged fowl after his kind: and God saw that it was good.

22 And God blessed them, saying, Be fruitful, and multiply, and fill the waters in the seas, and let fowl multiply in the earth.

23 And the evening and the morning were the fifth day.

24 And God said, Let the earth bring forth the living creature after his kind, cattle, and creeping thing, and beast of the earth after his kind: and it was so.

25 And God made the beast of the earth after his kind, and cattle after their kind, and every thing that creepeth upon the earth after his kind: and God saw that it was good.

26 And God said, Let us make man in our image, after our likeness: and let them have dominion over the fish of the sea, and over the fowl of the air, and over the cattle, and over all the earth, and over every creeping thing that creepeth upon the earth.

27 So God created man in his own image, in the image of God created he him; male and female created he them.

28 And God blessed them, and God said unto them, Be fruitful, and multiply, and replenish the earth, and subdue it: and have dominion over the fish of the sea, and over the fowl of the air, and over every living thing that moveth upon the earth.

29 And God said, Behold, I have given you every herb bearing seed, which is upon the face of all the earth, and every tree, in the which is the fruit of a tree yielding seed; to you it shall be for meat.

30 And to every beast of the earth, and to every fowl of the air, and to every thing that creepeth upon the earth, wherein there is life, I have given every green herb for meat: and it was so.

31 And God saw every thing that he had made, and, behold, it was very good. And the evening and the morning were the sixth day.

Chapter 2

Thus the heavens and the earth were finished, and all the host of them.

2 And on the seventh day God ended his work which he had made; and he rested on the seventh day from all his work which he had made.

3 And God blessed the seventh day, and sanctified it: because that in it he had rested from all his work which God created and made.

4 These *are* the generations of the heavens and of the earth when they were created, in the day that the LORD God made the earth and the heavens,

5 And every plant of the field before it was in the earth, and every herb of the field before it grew: for the LORD God had not caused it to rain upon the earth, and *there was* not a man to till the ground.

6 But there went up a mist from the earth, and watered the whole face of the ground.

7 And the LORD God formed man *of* the dust of the ground, and breathed into his nostrils the breath of life; and man became a living soul.

8 And the LORD God planted a garden eastward in Eden; and there he put the man whom he had formed.

9 And out of the ground made the LORD God to grow every tree that is pleasant to the sight, and good for food; the tree of life also in the midst of the garden, and the tree of knowledge of good and evil.

10 And a river went out of Eden to water the garden; and from thence it was parted, and became into four heads.

11 The name of the first *is* Pi'son: that *is* it which compasseth the whole land of Hav'l-lah, where *there is* gold;

12 And the gold of that land *is* good: there *is* bdellium and the onyx stone.

13 And the name of the second river *is* Gi'hon: the same *is* it that compasseth the whole land of E-thi-o'pi-a.

14 And the name of the third river *is* Hid'de-kel: that *is* it which goeth toward the east of Assyria. And the fourth river *is* Eu-phra'tes.

15 And the LORD God took the man, and put him into the garden of Eden to dress it and to keep it.

16 And the LORD God commanded the man, saying, Of every tree of the garden thou mayest freely eat:

17 But of the tree of the knowledge of good and evil, thou shalt not eat of it: for in the day that thou eatest thereof thou shalt surely die.

18 And the LORD God said, *It is* not good that the man should be alone; I will make him an help meet for him.

19 And out of the ground the LORD God formed every beast of the field, and every fowl of the air; and brought *them* unto Adam to see what he would call them: and whatsoever Adam called every living creature, that *was* the name thereof.

20 And Adam gave names to all cattle, and to the fowl of the air, and to every beast of the field; but for Adam there was not found an help meet for him.

21 And the LORD God caused a deep sleep to fall upon Adam, and he slept: and he took one of his ribs, and closed up the flesh instead thereof;

22 And the rib, which the LORD God had taken from man, made he a woman, and brought her unto the man.

23 And Adam said, This *is* now bone of my bones, and flesh of my flesh: she shall be called Woman, because she was taken out of Man.

24 Therefore shall a man leave his father and his mother, and shall cleave unto his wife: and they shall be one flesh.

25 And they were both naked, the man and his wife, and were not ashamed.

Chapter 3

Now the serpent was more subtil than any beast of the field which the LORD God had made. And he said unto the woman, Yea, hath God said, Ye shall not eat of every tree of the garden?

2 And the woman said unto the serpent, We may eat of the fruit of the trees of the garden:

3 But of the fruit of the tree which *is* in the midst of the garden, God hath said, Ye shall not eat of it, neither shall ye touch it, lest ye die.

4 And the serpent said unto the woman, Ye shall not surely die:

5 For God doth know that in the day ye eat thereof, then your eyes shall be opened, and ye shall be as gods, knowing good and evil.

6 And when the woman saw that the tree *was* good for food, and that it *was* pleasant to the eyes, and a tree to be desired to make *one* wise, she took of the fruit thereof, and did eat, and gave also unto her husband with her; and he did eat.

7 And the eyes of them both were opened, and they knew that they *were* naked; and they sewed fig leaves together, and made themselves aprons.

8 And they heard the voice of the LORD God walking in the garden in the cool of the day: and Adam and his wife hid themselves from the presence of the LORD God amongst the trees of the garden.

9 And the LORD God called unto Adam, and said unto him, Where *art* thou?

10 And he said, I heard thy voice in the garden, and I was afraid, because I *was* naked; and I hid myself.

11 And he said, Who told thee that thou *wast* naked? Hast thou eaten of the tree, whereof I commanded thee that thou shouldest not eat?

12 And the man said, The woman whom thou gavest *to be* with me, she gave me of the tree, and I did eat.

13 And the LORD God said unto the woman, What *is* this *that* thou hast done? And the woman said, The serpent beguiled me, and I did eat.

14 And the LORD God said unto the serpent, Because thou hast done this, thou *art* cursed above all cattle, and above every beast of the field; upon thy belly shalt thou go, and dust shalt thou eat all the days of thy life:

15 And I will put enmity between thee and the woman, and between thy seed and her seed; it shall bruise thy head, and thou shalt bruise his heel.

16 Unto the woman he said, I will greatly multiply thy sorrow and thy conception; in sorrow thou shalt bring forth children; and thy desire *shall be* to thy husband, and he shall rule over thee.

17 And unto Adam he said, Because thou hast hearkened unto the voice of thy wife, and hast eaten of the tree, of which I commanded thee, saying, Thou shalt not eat of it: cursed *is* the ground for thy sake; in sorrow shalt thou eat *of* it all the days of thy life;

18 Thorns also and thistles shall it bring forth to thee; and thou shalt eat the herb of the field;

19 In the sweat of thy face shalt thou eat bread, till thou return unto the ground; for out of it wast thou taken: for dust thou *art*, and unto dust shalt thou return.

20 And Adam called his wife's name Eve; because she was the mother of all living.

21 Unto Adam also and to his wife did the LORD God make coats of skins, and clothed them.

22 And the LORD God said, Behold, the man is become as one of us, to know good and evil: and now, lest he put forth his hand, and take also of the tree of life, and eat, and live for ever:

23 Therefore the LORD God sent him forth from the garden of Eden, to till the ground from whence he was taken.

24 So he drove out the man; and he placed at the east of the garden of Eden Cher'u-bims, and a flaming sword which turned every way, to keep the way of the tree of life.

Chapter 4

And Adam knew Eve his wife; and she conceived, and bare Cain, and said, I have gotten a man from the LORD.

2 And she again bare his brother Abel. And Abel was a keeper of sheep, but Cain was a tiller of the ground.

3 And in process of time it came to pass, that Cain brought of the fruit of the ground an offering unto the LORD.

4 And Abel, he also brought of the firstlings of his flock and of the fat thereof. And the LORD had respect unto Abel and to his offering:

5 But unto Cain and to his offering he had not respect. And Cain was very wroth, and his countenance fell.

6 And the LORD said unto Cain, Why art thou wroth? and why is thy countenance fallen?

7 If thou doest well, shalt thou not be accepted? and if thou doest not well, sin lieth at the door. And unto thee *shall be* his desire, and thou shalt rule over him.

8 And Cain talked with Abel his brother: and it came to pass, when they were in the field, that Cain rose up against Abel his brother, and slew him.

9 And the LORD said unto Cain, Where *is* Abel thy brother? And he said, I know not: *Am* I my brother's keeper?

10 And he said, What hast thou done? the voice of thy brother's blood crieth unto me from the ground.

11 And now *art* thou cursed from the earth, which hath opened her mouth to receive thy brother's blood from thy hand;

12 When thou tillest the ground, it shall not henceforth yield unto thee her strength; a fugitive and a vagabond shalt thou be in the earth.

13 And Cain said unto the LORD, My punishment *is* greater than I can bear.

14 Behold, thou hast driven me out this day from the face of the earth; and from thy face shall I be hid; and I shall be a fugitive and a vagabond in the earth; and it shall come to pass, *that* every one that findeth me shall slay me.

15 And the LORD said unto him, Therefore whosoever slayeth Cain, vengeance shall be taken on him sevenfold. And the LORD set a mark upon Cain, lest any finding him should kill him.

16 And Cain went out from the presence of the LORD, and dwelt in the land of Nod, on the east of Eden.

17 And Cain knew his wife; and she conceived, and bare E'noch: and he builded a city, and called the name of the city, after the name of his son, E'noch.

18 And unto E'noch was born I'rad: and I'rad begat Me-hu'ja-el: and Me-hu'ja-el begat Me-thu'sa-el: and Me-thu'sa-el begat La'mech.

19 And La'mech took unto him two wives: the name of the one *was* Adah, and the name of the other Zil'lah.

20 And Adah bare Ja'bal: he was the father of such as dwell in tents, and *of such as* have cattle.

21 And his brother's name *was* Ju'bal: he was the father of all such as handle the harp and organ.

22 And Zil'lah, she also bare Tu'bal – cain, an instructer of every artificer in brass and iron: and the sister of Tu'bal – cain *was* Na'a-mah.

23 And La'mech said unto his wives, Adah and Zil'lah, Hear my voice; ye wives of La'mech, hearken unto my speech: for I have slain a man to my wounding, and a young man to my hurt.

24 If Cain shall be avenged sevenfold, truly La'mech seventy and sevenfold.

25 And Adam knew his wife again; and she bare a son, and called his name Seth: For God, *said she*, hath appointed me another seed instead of Abel, whom Cain slew.

26 And to Seth, to him also there was born a son; and he called his name Enos: then began men to call upon the name of the LORD.

Chapter 5

This *is* the book of the generations of Adam. In the day that God created man, in the likeness of God made he him;

2 Male and female created he them; and blessed them, and called their name Adam, in the day when they were created.

3 And Adam lived an hundred and thirty years, and begat *a son* in his own likeness, after his image; and called his name Seth:

4 And the days of Adam after he had begotten Seth were eight hundred years: and he begat sons and daughters:

5 And all the days that Adam lived were nine hundred and thirty years: and he died.

6 And Seth lived an hundred and five years, and begat Enos:

7 And Seth lived after he begat Enos eight hundred and seven years, and begat sons and daughters:

8 And all the days of Seth were nine hundred and twelve years: and he died.

9 And Enos lived ninety years, and begat Ca-i'nan:

10 And Enos lived after he begat Ca-i'nan eight hundred and fifteen years, and begat sons and daughters:

11 And all the days of Enos were nine hundred and five years: and he died.

12 And Ca-i'nan lived seventy years, and begat Ma-ha'la-le-el:

13 And Ca-i'nan lived after he begat Ma-ha'la-le-el eight hundred and forty years, and begat sons and daughters:

14 And all the days of Ca-i'nan were nine hundred and ten years: and he died.

15 And Ma-ha'la-le-el lived sixty and five years, and begat Ja'red:

16 And Ma-ha'la-le-el lived after he begat Ja'red eight hundred and thirty years, and begat sons and daughters:

17 And all the days of Ma-ha'la-le-el were eight hundred ninety and five years; and he died.

18 And Ja'red lived an hundred sixty and two years, and he begat E'noch:

19 And Ja'red lived after he begat E'noch eight hundred years, and begat sons and daughters:

20 And all the days of Ja'red were nine hundred sixty and two years: and he died.

21 And E'noch lived sixty and five years, and begat Me-thu'se-lah:

22 And E'noch walked with God after he begat Me-thu'se-lah three hundred years, and begat sons and daughters:

23 And all the days of E'noch were three hundred sixty and five years:

24 And E'noch walked with God: and he *was* not; for God took him.

25 And Me-thu'se-lah lived an hundred eighty and seven years, and begat La'mech:

26 And Me-thu'se-lah lived after he begat La'mech seven hundred eighty and two years, and begat sons and daughters:

27 And all the days of Me-thu'se-lah were nine hundred sixty and nine years: and he died.

28 And La'mech lived an hundred eighty and two years, and begat a son:

29 And he called his name Noah, saying, This *same* shall comfort us concerning our work and toil of our hands, because of the ground which the LORD hath cursed.

30 And La'mech lived after he begat Noah five hundred ninety and five years, and begat sons and daughters:

31 And all the days of La'mech were seven hundred seventy and seven years: and he died.

32 And Noah was five hundred years old: and Noah begat Shem, Ham, and Ja'pheth.

Chapter 6

And it came to pass, when men began to multiply on the face of the earth, and daughters were born unto them,

2 That the sons of God saw the daughters of men that they *were* fair; and they took them wives of all which they chose.

3 And the LORD said, My spirit shall not always strive with man, for that he also *is* flesh: yet his days shall be an hundred and twenty years.

4 There were giants in the earth in those days; and also after that, when the sons of God came in unto the daughters of men, and they bare *children* to them, the same *became* mighty men which *were* of old, men of renown.

5 And God saw that the wickedness of man *was* great in the earth, and *that* every imagination of the thoughts of his heart *was* only evil continually.

6 And it repented the LORD that he had made man on the earth, and it grieved him at his heart.

7 And the LORD said, I will destroy man whom I have created from the face of the earth; both man, and beast, and the creeping thing, and the fowls of the air; for it repenteth me that I have made them.

8 But Noah found grace in the eyes of the LORD.

9 These *are* the generations of Noah: Noah was a just man *and* perfect in his generations, *and* Noah walked with God.

10 And Noah begat three sons, Shem, Ham, and Ja'pheth.

11 The earth also was corrupt before God, and the earth was filled with violence.

12 And God looked upon the earth, and, behold, it was corrupt; for all flesh had corrupted his way upon the earth.

13 And God said unto Noah, The end of all flesh is come before me; for the earth is filled with violence through them; and, behold, I will destroy them with the earth.

14 Make thee an ark of gopher wood; rooms shalt thou make in the ark, and shalt pitch it within and without with pitch.

15 And this *is the fashion* which thou shalt make it *of*: The length of the ark *shall be* three hundred cubits, the breadth of it fifty cubits, and the height of it thirty cubits.

16 A window shalt thou make to the ark, and in a cubit shalt thou finish it above; and the door of the ark shalt thou set in the side thereof; *with* lower, second, and third *stories* shalt thou make it.

17 And, behold, I, even I, do bring a flood of waters upon the earth, to destroy all flesh, wherein *is* the breath of life, from under heaven; *and* every thing that *is* in the earth shall die.

18 But with thee will I establish my covenant; and thou shalt come into the ark, thou, and thy sons, and thy wife, and thy sons' wives with thee.

19 And of every living thing of all flesh, two of every *sort* shalt thou bring into the ark, to keep *them* alive with thee; they shall be male and female.

20 Of fowls after their kind, and of cattle after their kind, of every creeping thing of the earth after his kind, two of every *sort* shall come unto thee, to keep *them* alive.

21 And take thou unto thee of all food that is eaten, and thou shalt gather *it* to thee; and it shall be for food for thee, and for them.

22 Thus did Noah; according to all that God commanded him, so did he.

Chapter 7

And the LORD said unto Noah, Come thou and all thy house into the ark; for thee have I seen righteous before me in this generation.

2 Of every clean beast thou shalt take to thee by sevens, the male and his female: and of beasts that *are* not clean by two, the male and his female.

3 Of fowls also of the air by sevens, the male and the female; to keep seed alive upon the face of all the earth.

4 For yet seven days, and I will cause it to rain upon the earth forty days and forty nights; and every living substance that I have made will I destroy from off the face of the earth.

5 And Noah did according unto all that the LORD commanded him.

6 And Noah *was* six hundred years old when the flood of waters was upon the earth.

7 And Noah went in, and his sons, and his wife, and his sons' wives with him, into the ark, because of the waters of the flood.

8 Of clean beasts, and of beasts that *are* not clean, and of fowls, and of every thing that creepeth upon the earth,

9 There went in two and two unto Noah into the ark, the male and the female, as God had commanded Noah.

10 And it came to pass after seven days, that the waters of the flood were upon the earth.

11 In the six hundredth year of Noah's life, in the second month, the seventeenth day of the month, the same day were all the fountains of the great deep broken up, and the windows of heaven were opened.

12 And the rain was upon the earth forty days and forty nights.

13 In the selfsame day entered Noah, and Shem, and Ham, and Ja'pheth, the sons of Noah, and Noah's wife, and the three wives of his sons with them, into the ark;

14 They, and every beast after his kind, and all the cattle after their kind, and every creeping thing that creepeth upon the earth after his kind, and every fowl after his kind, every bird of every sort.

15 And they went in unto Noah into the ark, two and two of all flesh, wherein *is* the breath of life.

16 And they that went in, went in male and female of all flesh, as God had commanded him: and the LORD shut him in.

17 And the flood was forty days upon the earth; and the waters increased, and bare up the ark, and it was lift up above the earth.

18 And the waters prevailed, and were increased greatly upon the earth; and the ark went upon the face of the waters.

19 And the waters prevailed exceedingly upon the earth; and all the high hills, that *were* under the whole heaven, were covered.

20 Fifteen cubits upward did the waters prevail; and the mountains were covered.

21 And all flesh died that moved upon the earth, both of fowl, and of cattle, and of beast, and of every creeping thing that creepeth upon the earth, and every man:

22 All in whose nostrils *was* the breath of life, of all that *was* in the dry *land*, died.

23 And every living substance was destroyed which was upon the face of the ground, both man, and cattle, and the creeping things, and the fowl of the heaven; and they were destroyed from the earth: and Noah only remained *alive*, and they that *were* with him in the ark.

24 And the waters prevailed upon the earth an hundred and fifty days.

Chapter 8

And God remembered Noah, and every living thing, and all the cattle that *was* with him in the ark: and God made a wind to pass over the earth, and the waters asswaged;

2 The fountains also of the deep and the windows of heaven were stopped, and the rain from heaven was restrained;

3 And the waters returned from off the earth continually: and after the end of the hundred and fifty days the waters were abated.

4 And the ark rested in the seventh month, on the seventeenth day of the month, upon the mountains of Ar'a-rat.

5 And the waters decreased continually until the tenth month: in the tenth *month*, on the first *day* of the month, were the tops of the mountains seen.

6 And it came to pass at the end of forty days, that Noah opened the window of the ark which he had made:

7 And he sent forth a raven, which went forth to and fro, until the waters were dried up from off the earth.

8 Also he sent forth a dove from him, to see if the waters were abated from off the face of the ground;

9 But the dove found no rest for the sole of her foot, and she returned unto him into the ark, for the waters *were* on the face of the whole earth: then he put forth his hand, and took her, and pulled her in unto him into the ark.

10 And he stayed yet other seven days; and again he sent forth the dove out of the ark;

11 And the dove came in to him in the evening; and, lo, in her mouth *was* an olive leaf pluckt off: so Noah knew that the waters were abated from off the earth.

12 And he stayed yet other seven days; and sent forth the dove; which returned not again unto him any more.

13 And it came to pass in the six hundredth and first year, in the first *month*, the first *day* of the month, the waters were dried up from off the earth: and Noah removed the covering of the ark, and looked, and, behold, the face of the ground was dry.

14 And in the second month, on the seven and twentieth day of the month, was the earth dried.

15 And God spake unto Noah, saying,

16 Go forth of the ark, thou, and thy wife, and thy sons, and thy sons' wives with thee.

17 Bring forth with thee every living thing that *is* with thee, of all flesh, *both* of fowl, and of cattle, and of every creeping thing that creepeth upon the earth; that they may breed abundantly in the earth, and be fruitful, and multiply upon the earth.

18 And Noah went forth, and his sons, and his wife, and his sons' wives with him:

19 Every beast, every creeping thing, and every fowl, *and* whatsoever creepeth upon the earth, after their kinds, went forth out of the ark.

20 And Noah builded an altar unto the LORD; and took of every clean beast, and of every clean fowl, and offered burnt offerings on the altar.

21 And the LORD smelled a sweet savour; and the LORD said in his heart, I will not again curse the ground any more for man's sake; for the imagination of man's heart *is* evil from his youth; neither will I again smite any more every thing living, as I have done.

22 While the earth remaineth, seedtime and harvest, and cold and heat, and summer and winter, and day and night shall not cease.

Chapter 9

And God blessed Noah and his sons, and said unto them, Be fruitful, and multiply, and replenish the earth.

2 And the fear of you and the dread of you shall be upon every beast of the earth, and upon every fowl of the air, upon all that moveth *upon* the earth, and upon all the fishes of the sea; into your hand are they delivered.

3 Every moving thing that liveth shall be meat for you; even as the green herb have I given you all things.

4 But flesh with the life thereof, *which is* the blood thereof, shall ye not eat.

5 And surely your blood of your lives will I require; at the hand of every beast will I require it, and at the hand of man; at the hand of every man's brother will I require the life of man.

6 Whoso sheddeth man's blood, by man shall his blood be shed: for in the image of God made he man.

7 And you, be ye fruitful, and multiply; bring forth abundantly in the earth, and multiply therein.

8 And God spake unto Noah, and to his sons with him, saying,

9 And I, behold, I establish my covenant with you, and with your seed after you;

10 And with every living creature that *is* with you, of the fowl, of the cattle, and of every beast of the earth with you; from all that go out of the ark, to every beast of the earth.

11 And I will establish my covenant with you; neither shall all flesh be cut off any more by the waters of a flood; neither shall there any more be a flood to destroy the earth.

12 And God said, This *is* the token of the covenant which I make between me and you and every living creature that *is* with you, for perpetual generations:

13 I do set my bow in the cloud, and it shall be for a token of a covenant between me and the earth.

14 And it shall come to pass, when I bring a cloud over the earth, that the bow shall be seen in the cloud:

15 And I will remember my covenant, which *is* between me and you and every living creature of all flesh; and the waters shall no more become a flood to destroy all flesh.

16 And the bow shall be in the cloud; and I will look upon it, that I may remember the everlasting covenant between God and every living creature of all flesh that *is* upon the earth.

17 And God said unto Noah, This *is* the token of the covenant, which I have established between me and all flesh that *is* upon the earth.

18 And the sons of Noah, that went forth of the ark, were Shem, and Ham, and Ja'pheth: and Ham *is* the father of Canaan.

19 These *are* the three sons of Noah: and of them was the whole earth overspread.

20 And Noah began *to be* an husbandman, and he planted a vineyard:

21 And he drank of the wine, and was drunken; and he was uncovered within his tent.

22 And Ham, the father of Canaan, saw the nakedness of his father, and told his two brethren without.

23 And Shem and Ja'pheth took a garment, and laid *it* upon both their shoulders, and went backward, and covered the nakedness of their father; and their faces *were* backward, and they saw not their father's nakedness.

24 And Noah awoke from his wine, and knew what his younger son had done unto him.

25 And he said, Cursed *be* Canaan; a servant of servants shall he be unto his brethren.

26 And he said, Blessed *be* the LORD God of Shem; and Canaan shall be his servant.

27 God shall enlarge Ja'pheth, and he shall dwell in the tents of Shem; and Canaan shall be his servant.

28 And Noah lived after the flood three hundred and fifty years.

29 And all the days of Noah were nine hundred and fifty years: and he died. . . .

Chapter 11

And the whole earth was of one language, and of one speech.

2 And it came to pass, as they journeyed from the east, that they found a plain in the land of Shi'nar; and they dwelt there.

3 And they said one to another, Go to, let us make brick, and burn them throughly. And they had brick for stone, and slime had they for morter.

4 And they said, Go to, let us build us a city and a tower, whose top *may reach* unto heaven; and let us make us a name, lest we be scattered abroad upon the face of the whole earth.

5 And the LORD came down to see the city and the tower, which the children of men builded.

6 And the LORD said, Behold, the people *is* one, and they have all one language; and this they begin to do: and now nothing will be restrained from them, which they have imagined to do.

7 Go to, let us go down, and there confound their language, that they may not understand one another's speech.

8 So the LORD scattered them abroad from thence upon the face of all the earth: and they left off to build the city.

9 Therefore is the name of it called Babel; because the LORD did there confound the language of all the earth: and from thence did the LORD scatter them abroad upon the face of all the earth.

Study and Writing Questions

1. Consider the meaning of the selection's title. The word *genesis* means "the origin or creation of something" and shares a common ancestry with the following words: *generate, generation, gender,* and *kin.* In what ways does the theme of "genesis" unify the STORIES included in Genesis? Judging from our selection, why might "genesis" be an important concept to a culture?

2. What EPISODES of Genesis concern violation (disobedience or crime) and punishment? In what ways does the THEME of "law" unify our selection from Genesis?

3. Genesis contains many recurrences, from repeated FORMULAIC phrases to restatements of lineage to recurring ACTIONS such as Adam creating a son in his own image just as God had created Adam in His own image. What are the most prominent recurrences in our selection from Genesis? What are the effects of including these particular recurrences and not others?

4. Treating our selection of Genesis as a single story, how would you describe the CHARACTER of God in this narrative? What is His importance to the narrative?
5. What is the importance of speaking, speech, and language in our selection from Genesis?

See also Questions for Contrast and Comparison: 2, 4, 10, 20, 31, 32, 61, 79, 98, 124, 133, 136, 144, 145, 149, 153, 154, 155, 182, 229, and 236.

Jonah

Chapter 1

Now the word of the LORD came unto Jonah the son of A-mit'-ta-i, saying,

2 Arise, go to Nin'-e-veh, that great city, and cry against it; for their wickedness is come up before me.

3 But Jonah rose up to flee unto Tarshish from the presence of the LORD, and went down to Joppa; and he found a ship going to Tarshish: so he paid the fare thereof, and went down into it, to go with them unto Tarshish from the presence of the LORD.

4 But the LORD sent out a great wind into the sea, and there was a mighty tempest in the sea, so that the ship was like to be broken.

5 Then the mariners were afraid, and cried every man unto his god, and cast forth the wares that *were* in the ship into the sea, to lighten *it* of them. But Jonah was gone down into the sides of the ship; and he lay, and was fast asleep.

6 So the shipmaster came to him, and said unto him, What meanest thou, O sleeper? arise, call upon thy God, if so be that God will think upon us, that we perish not.

7 And they said every one to his fellow, Come, and let us cast lots, that we may know for whose cause this evil *is* upon us. So they cast lots, and the lot fell upon Jonah.

8 Then said they unto him, Tell us, we pray thee, for whose cause this evil *is* upon us; What *is* thine occupation? and whence comest thou? what *is* thy country? and of what people *art* thou?

9 And he said unto them, I *am* an Hebrew; and I fear the LORD, the God of heaven, which hath made the sea and the dry *land*.

10 Then were the men exceedingly afraid, and said unto him, Why hast thou done this? For the men knew that he fled from the presence of the LORD, because he had told them.

11 Then said they unto him, What shall we do unto thee, that the sea may be calm unto us? for the sea wrought, and was tempestuous.

12 And he said unto them, Take me up, and cast me forth into the sea; so shall the sea be calm unto you: for I know that for my sake this great tempest *is* upon you.

13 Nevertheless the men rowed hard to bring *it* to the land; but they could not: for the sea wrought, and was tempestuous against them.

14 Wherefore they cried unto the LORD, and said, We beseech thee, O LORD, we beseech thee, let us not perish for this man's life, and lay not upon us innocent blood: for thou, O LORD, hast done as it pleased thee.

15 So they took up Jonah, and cast him forth into the sea: and the sea ceased from her raging.

16 Then the men feared the LORD exceedingly, and offered a sacrifice unto the LORD, and made vows.

17 Now the LORD had prepared a great fish to swallow up Jonah. And Jonah was in the belly of the fish three days and three nights.

Chapter 2

Then Jonah prayed unto the LORD his God out of the fish's belly,

2 And said, I cried by reason of mine affliction unto the LORD, and he heard me; out of the belly of hell cried I, *and* thou heardest my voice.

3 For thou hadst cast me into the deep, in the midst of the seas; and the floods compassed me about: all thy billows and thy waves passed over me.

4 Then I said, I am cast out of thy sight; yet I will look again toward thy holy temple.

5 The waters compassed me about, *even* to the soul: the depth closed me round about, the weeds were wrapped about my head.

6 I went down to the bottoms of the mountains; the earth with her bars *was* about me for ever: yet hast thou brought up my life from corruption, O LORD my God.

7 When my soul fainted within me I remembered the LORD: and my prayer came in unto thee, into thine holy temple.

8 They that observe lying vanities forsake their own mercy.

9 But I will sacrifice unto thee with the voice of thanksgiving; I will pay *that* that I have vowed. Salvation *is* of the LORD.

10 And the LORD spake unto the fish, and it vomited out Jonah upon the dry land.

Chapter 3

And the word of the LORD came unto Jonah the second time, saying,

2 Arise, go unto Nin'-e-veh, that great city, and preach unto it the preaching that I bid thee.

3 So Jonah arose, and went unto Nin'-e-veh, according to the word of the LORD. Now Nin'-e-veh was an exceeding great city of three days' journey.

4 And Jonah began to enter into the city a day's journey, and he cried, and said, Yet forty days, and Nin'-e-veh shall be overthrown.

5 So the people of Nin'-e-veh believed God, and proclaimed a fast, and put on sackcloth, from the greatest of them even to the least of them.

6 For word came unto the king of Nin'-e-veh, and he arose from his throne, and he laid his robe from him, and covered *him* with sackcloth, and sat in ashes.

7 And he caused *it* to be proclaimed and published through Nin'-e-veh by the decree of the king and his nobles, saying, Let neither man nor beast, herd nor flock, taste anything: let them not feed, nor drink water:

8 But let man and beast be covered with sackcloth, and cry mightily unto God: yea, let them turn every one from his evil way, and from the violence that *is* in their hands.

9 Who can tell *if* God will turn and repent, and turn away from his fierce anger, that we perish not?

10 And God saw their works, that they turned from their evil way; and God repented of the evil, that he had said that he would do unto them; and he did *it* not.

Chapter 4

But it displeased Jonah exceedingly, and he was very angry.

2 And he prayed unto the LORD, and said, I pray thee, O LORD, *was* not this my saying, when I was yet in my country? Therefore I fled before unto Tarshish: for I knew that thou *art* a gracious God, and merciful, slow to anger, and of great kindness, and repentest thee of the evil.

3 Therefore now, O LORD, take, I beseech thee, my life from me; for *it is* better for me to die than to live.

4 Then said the LORD, Doest thou well to be angry?

5 So Jonah went out of the city, and sat on the east side of the city, and there made him a booth, and sat under it in the shadow, till he might see what would become of the city.

6 And the LORD God prepared a gourd, and made *it* to come up over Jonah, that it might be a shadow over his head, to deliver him from his grief. So Jonah was exceeding glad of the gourd.

7 But God prepared a worm when the morning rose the next day, and it smote the gourd that it withered.

8 And it came to pass, when the sun did arise, that God prepared a vehement east wind; and the sun beat upon the head of Jonah, that he fainted, and wished in himself to die, and said, *It is* better for me to die than to live.

9 And God said to Jonah, Doest thou well to be angry for the gourd? And he said, I do well to be angry, *even* unto death.

10 Then said the LORD, Thou hast had pity on the gourd, for the which thou hast not laboured, neither madest it grow; which came up in a night, and perished in a night:

11 And should not I spare Nin'-e-veh, that great city, wherein are more than sixscore thousand persons that cannot discern between their right hand and their left hand; and *also* much cattle?

Study and Writing Questions

1. What details of the PLOT suggest that this is a STORY about religious conversion?
2. What are the important natural IMAGES in this NARRATIVE? What are their special uses and meanings?
3. What should we make of the last four words of the narrative?
4. How would you describe Jonah's CHARACTER? In what ways is it appropriate or inappropriate in this narrative?
5. What role(s) does prophecy play in this narrative?

See also Questions for Contrast and Comparison: 2, 149, 153, 154, 155, and 191.

On Parables (Mark 4)

Chapter 4

And he began again to teach by the sea side: and there was gathered unto him a great multitude, so that he entered into a ship, and sat in the sea; and the whole multitude was by the sea on the land.

2 And he taught them many things by parables, and said unto them in his doctrine,

3 Hearken; Behold, there went out a sower to sow:

4 And it came to pass, as he sowed, some fell by the way side, and the fowls of the air came and devoured it up.

5 And some fell on stony ground, where it had not much earth; and immediately it sprang up, because it had no depth of earth:

6 But when the sun was up, it was scorched; and because it had no root, it withered away.

7 And some fell among thorns, and the thorns grew up, and choked it, and it yielded no fruit.

8 And other fell on good ground, and did yield fruit that sprang up and increased; and brought forth, some thirty, and some sixty, and some an hundred.

9 And he said unto them, He that hath ears to hear, let him hear.

10 And when he was alone, they that were about him with the twelve asked of him the parable.

11 And he said unto them, Unto you it is given to know the mystery of the kingdom of God: but unto them that are without, all *these* things are done in parables:

12 That seeing they may see, and not perceive; and hearing they may hear, and not understand; lest at any time they should be converted, and *their* sins should be forgiven them.

13 And he said unto them, Know ye not this parable? and how then will ye know all parables?

14 The sower soweth the word.

15 And these are they by the way side, where the word is sown; but when they have heard, Satan cometh immediately, and taketh away the word that was sown in their hearts.

16 And these are they likewise which are sown on stony ground; who, when they have heard the word, immediately receive it with gladness;

17 And have no root in themselves, and so endure but for a time: afterward, when affliction or persecution ariseth for the word's sake, immediately they are offended.

18 And these are they which are sown among thorns; such as hear the word,

19 And the cares of this world, and the deceitfulness of riches, and the lusts of other things entering in, choke the word, and it becometh unfruitful.

20 And these are they which are sown on good ground; such as hear the word, and receive *it*, and bring forth fruit, some thirtyfold, some sixty, and some an hundred.

21 And he said unto them, Is a candle brought to be put under a bushel, or under a bed? and not to be set on a candlestick?

22 For there is nothing hid, which shall not be manifested; neither was any thing kept secret, but that it should come abroad.

23 If any man have ears to hear, let him hear.

24 And he said unto them, Take heed what ye hear: with what measure ye mete, it shall be measured to you: and unto you that hear shall more be given.

25 For he that hath, to him shall be given: and he that hath not, from him shall be taken even that which he hath.

26 And he said, So is the kingdom of God, as if a man should cast seed into the ground;

27 And should sleep, and rise night and day, and the seed should spring and grow up, he knoweth not how.

28 For the earth bringeth forth fruit of herself; first the blade, then the ear, after that the full corn in the ear.

29 But when the fruit is brought forth, immediately he putteth in the sickle, because the harvest is come.

30 And he said, Whereunto shall we liken the kingdom of God? or with what comparison shall we compare it?

31 It is like a grain of mustard seed, which, when it is sown in the earth, is less than all the seeds that be in the earth:

32 But when it is sown, it groweth up, and becometh greater than all herbs, and shooteth out great branches; so that the fowls of the air may lodge under the shadow of it.

33 And with many such parables spake he the word unto them, as they were able to hear it.

34 But without a parable spake he not unto them: and when they were alone, he expounded all things to his disciples.

35 And the same day, when the even was come, he saith unto them, Let us pass over unto the other side.

36 And when they had sent away the multitude, they took him even as he was in the ship. And there were also with him other little ships.

37 And there arose a great storm of wind, and the waves beat into the ship, so that it was now full.

38 And he was in the hinder part of the ship, asleep on a pillow: and they awake him, and say unto him, Master, carest thou not that we perish?

39 And he arose, and rebuked the wind, and said unto the sea, Peace, be still. And the wind ceased, and there was a great calm.

40 And he said unto them, Why are ye so fearful? how is it that ye have no faith?

41 And they feared exceedingly, and said one to another, What manner of man is this, that even the wind and the sea obey him?

Study and Writing Questions

1. Each of the PARABLES in this chapter is FRAMED by the ACTION involving a ship. In what way does this SETTING contribute to the meaning of these parables?

2. Which words and phrases are repeated in these parables? What special significance, if any, do these words and phrases have?

3. What verses reveal Jesus's conscious concern with RHETORIC? Does this chapter suggest that there is a rhetorical dimension to religious faith?
4. Verse 4 seems to say that Jesus speaks in parables so that only those people who can understand him will be able to be saved by him. In the chapter as a whole, what implies that Jesus is trying to decrease or increase the number of people who will be saved?
5. Based on the evidence within this chapter, what is the answer to the question with which the chapter ends?

See also Questions for Contrast and Comparison: 25, 147, 149, 154, 155, and 156.

The Prodigal Son (Luke 15)

Chapter 15

Then drew near unto him all the publicans and sinners for to hear him.

2 And the Pharisees and scribes murmured, saying, This man receiveth sinners, and eateth with them.

3 And he spake this parable unto them, saying,

4 What man of you, having an hundred sheep, if he lose one of them, doth not leave the ninety and nine in the wilderness, and go after that which is lost, until he find it?

5 And when he hath found *it*, he layeth *it* on his shoulders, rejoicing.

6 And when he cometh home, he calleth together *his* friends and neighbours, saying unto them, Rejoice with me; for I have found my sheep which was lost.

7 I say unto you, that likewise joy shall be in heaven over one sinner that repenteth, more than over ninety and nine just persons, which need no repentance.

8 Either what woman having ten pieces of silver, if she lose one piece, doth not light a candle, and sweep the house, and seek diligently till she find *it?*

9 And when she hath found *it*, she calleth *her* friends and *her* neighbours together, saying, Rejoice with me; for I have found the piece which I had lost.

10 Likewise, I say unto you there is joy in the presence of the angels of God over one sinner that repenteth.

11 And he said, A certain man had two sons:

12 And the younger of them said to *his* father, Father, give me the portion of goods that falleth *to me*. And he divided unto them *his* living.

13 And not many days after the younger son gathered all together, and took his journey into a far country, and there wasted his substance with riotous living.

14 And when he had spent all, there arose a mighty famine in that land; and he began to be in want.

15 And he went and joined himself to a citizen of that country; and he sent him into his fields to feed swine.

16 And he would fain have filled his belly with the husks that the swine did eat: and no man gave unto him.

17 And when he came to himself, he said, How many hired servants of my father's have bread enough and to spare, and I perish with hunger!

18 I will arise and go to my father, and will say unto him, Father, I have sinned against heaven, and before thee,

19 And am no more worthy to be called thy son: make me as one of thy hired servants.

20 And he arose, and came to his father. But when he was yet a great way off, his father saw him, and had compassion, and ran, and fell on his neck, and kissed him.

21 And the son said unto him, Father, I have sinned against heaven, and in thy sight, and am no more worthy to be called thy son.

22 But the father said to his servants, Bring forth the best robe, and put *it* on him; and put a ring on his hand, and shoes on *his* feet:

23 And bring hither the fatted calf, and kill *it*; and let us eat, and be merry:

24 For this my son was dead, and is alive again; he was lost, and is found. And they began to be merry.

25 Now his elder son was in the field: and as he came and drew nigh to the house, he heard musick and dancing.

26 And he called one of the servants, and asked what these things meant.

27 And he said unto him, Thy brother is come; and thy father hath killed the fatted calf, because he hath received him safe and sound.

28 And he was angry, and would not go in: therefore came his father out, and intreated him.

29 And he answering said to *his* father, Lo, these many years do I serve thee, neither transgressed I at any time thy commandment: and yet thou never gavest me a kid, that I might make merry with my friends:

30 But as soon as this thy son was come, which hath devoured thy living with harlots, thou hast killed for him the fatted calf.

31 And he said unto him, Son, thou art ever with me, and all that I have is thine.

32 It was meet that we should make merry, and be glad: for this thy brother was dead, and is alive again; and was lost, and is found.

Study and Writing Questions

1. This chapter contains three PARABLES: one concerning sheep, one concerning silver, and one concerning sons. To what extent do they make the same point and to what extent do they make different points?
2. The third parable uses IMAGERY from the first two. How might the last parable strike us as different if it were not preceded by the first two?
3. What is the importance of the FRAME situation in conveying the meaning of the parable(s)?
4. What is the role of women in Luke 15?
5. What are the implications of Luke 15 for the proper relations between people and God?

See also Questions for Contrast and Comparison: 25, 154, 155, 156, 158, 161, and 170.

■ TAOISM *is the Chinese intellectual tradition represented by the famous ying-yang symbol, a circle divided through its center by an S-curve. This symbol signifies that the whole of things is a complex of complementary oppositions. Western distinctions among philosophy, literature, and religion did not apply in ancient China; while Westerners see the Tao ("Way") as all three, Taoists see it as one. The foundation of Taoism is the mystic, poetic Tao Teh Ching ("The Sacred Book of the Way and Virtue"), reportedly composed by the legendary Lao Tzu in the sixth century B.C.E. but more likely written in the third century B.C.E. Taoism stresses individual liberation, teaching that the world is illusory while consciousness is real yet stressing the emptying of the EGO through utter identification with Nature. Taoism opposes the rigid system of social responsibilities taught by Confucius (d. 479 B.C.E.). The greatest Taoist writer was Chuang Tzu (d.c. 286 B.C.E.) whose witty, SATIRIC PARABLES serve as objects for contemplation in the effort to release one's attachment to worldly and social appearances. Taoism not only continues today itself, but has also helped shape other Eastern "religions," including Buddhism. The Buddhist sect known as Zen (Ch'an in Chinese) uses peculiarly enigmatic teaching TALES, called koans, as objects of contemplation for those who seek transcendence. The original dates and composers of the Taoist teaching tales presented here are unclear.*

A Ch'an Koan

The Master would never speak a word when asked to explain the Tao, but would simply stick his thumb out. The Sage's young disciple seeing this, began to imitate his master, hoping thereby to gain understanding and enlightenment. One day when the boy mimicked him, the Master suddenly hacked off the boy's thumb. The shocked boy ran off crying but the Master called to him. The crying boy stopped and turned, whereupon the Master again stuck out his thumb.

Study and Writing Questions

1. What are the roles of language, noise, and silence in this NARRATIVE?
2. Define precisely the narrative VIEWPOINT. How does it affect our reading of the narrative?
3. Did the Master behave properly?
4. What is the significance of the thumb IMAGE in this narrative?
5. What is the MORAL of this narrative?

See also Questions for Contrast and Comparison: 46, 48, 98, 119, 134, 155, 160, 161, and 205.

Outsides

At Hangchow there lived a costermonger who understood how to keep oranges a whole year without letting them spoil. His fruit was always fresh-looking, firm as jade, and of a beautiful golden hue; but inside — dry as an old cocoon.

One day I asked him, saying, "Are your oranges for altar or sacrificial purposes, or for show at banquets? Or do you make this outside display merely to cheat the foolish? as cheat them you most outrageously do." "Sir," replied the orangeman, "I have carried on this trade now for many years. It is my source of livelihood. I sell; the world buys. And I have yet to learn that you are the only honest man about, and that I am the only cheat. Perhaps it never struck you in this light. The Baton-bearers of to-day, seated on their tiger skins, pose as the martial guardians of the State; but what are they compared with the captains of old? The broad-brimmed, long-robed Ministers of to-day pose as pillars of the constitution; but have they the wisdom of our ancient counsellors? Evil-doers arise, and none can subdue them. The people are in misery, and none can relieve them. Clerks are corrupt, and none can restrain them. Laws decay, and none can renew them. Our officials eat the bread of the State and know no shame. They sit in lofty halls, ride fine steeds, drink themselves drunk with wine, and batten on the richest fare. Which of them but puts on an awe-inspiring look, a dignified mien? — all gold and gems without, but dry cocoons within. You pay, sir, no heed to these things, while you are very particular about my oranges."

I had no answer to make. Was he really out of conceit with the age, or only quizzing me in defence of his fruit?

Study and Writing Questions

1. What difference does it make to our reading of the NARRATIVE that the object that initiates the encounter is an orange?
2. The costermonger gives a catalog of deceits but omits many possible items while including others. What is the nature of this catalog? What ARGUMENT does it make and what arguments does it attempt to evade?
3. What effect does the use of a FIRST-PERSON NARRATOR have on our reading of this narrative?
4. What is the significance of the narrative's ending with a question?
5. Describe the costermonger.

See also Questions for Contrast and Comparison: 40, 155, 160, 162, and 163.

Smelling Essays

Now as they wandered about the temple they came upon an old blind priest sitting under the verandah, engaged in selling medicines and prescribing for patients.

"Ah!" cried Sung, "there is an extraordinary man who is well versed in the arts of composition," and immediately he sent back to get the essay they had just been reading in order to obtain the old priest's opinion as to its merits. At the same moment up came their friend from Yü-hang and all three went along together. Wang began by addressing him as "Professor"; whereupon the priest, who thought the stranger had come to consult him as a doctor, inquired what might be the disease from which he was suffering. Wang then explained what his mission was, upon which the priest smiled and said, "Who's been telling you this nonsense? How can a man with no eyes discuss with you the merits of your compositions?" Wang replied by asking him to let his ears do duty for his eyes but the priest answered that he would hardly have patience to sit out Wang's three sections, amounting perhaps to some two thousand and more words.

"However," added he, "if you like to burn it, I'll try what I can do with my nose." Wang complied and burnt the first section there and then; and the old priest, snuffing up the smoke, declared that it wasn't such a bad effort, and finally gave it as his opinion that Wang would probably succeed at the examination.

The young scholar from Yü-hang didn't believe that the old priest could really tell anything by these means and forthwith proceeded to burn an essay by one of the old masters; but the priest no sooner smelt the smoke than he cried out, "Beautiful indeed! beautiful indeed! I do enjoy this. The light of genius and truth is evident here." The Yü-hang scholar was greatly astonished at this and began to burn an essay of his own; whereupon the priest said, "I had had but a taste of that one; why change so soon to another?"

"The first paragraph," replied the young man, "was by a friend; the rest is my own composition." No sooner had he uttered these words than the old priest began to retch violently and begged that he might have no more as he was sure it would make him sick. The Yü-hang scholar was much abashed at this and went away. But in a few days the list came out and his name was among the successful ones, while Wang's was not. He at once hurried off to tell the old priest, who, when he heard the news, sighed and said, "I may be blind with my eyes, but I am not so with my nose, which I fear is the case with the examiners. Besides," added he, "I was talking to you about composition: I said nothing about *destiny*."

Study and Writing Questions

1. What is the significance of the blind man being a priest?
2. The priest initially mistakes the intentions of his visitors. Why is that mistake part of the STORY? How does it affect our reading?
3. How would you characterize each of the priest's three visitors. Is it important for the NARRATIVE to have all three in order to make its precise point?
4. This TALE touches on three of our physical senses. What are the differences among the three in the tale and in life?
5. What does this tale appear to say about the role of writing in our lives?

See also Questions for Contrast and Comparison: 11, 79, 155, 160, and 163.

■ SUFISM *is the gnostic mysticism of Islam. Gnosis, Greek for any "knowledge," also yields the English word "agnostic" meaning "without ultimate knowledge." The various forms of Gnosticism (Christian, Jewish, Muslim, pagan) all seek knowledge of God (or gods) through intuition. Muhammad (570–632), who founded Islam, gave his followers the Koran, the Muslim scripture, and traditions that quickly evolved into sects championing somewhat competing beliefs and rules. Sufis, seeking to transcend, or rise above, rather than negate the legalism and rationality of these Muslim sects, practiced hermitry, fasting, and, among the Dervish group, "whirling," meant to induce transcendent knowledge. They spent long hours contemplating Koran passages, and constructed "teaching tales" that often have obvious morals yet may reveal new, and sometimes opposite, meanings after continued open contemplation. Sufism (from the Arabic word suf, "wool"; the Sufi ascetics wore woolen garments) arose primarily among the Sunni Muslims, beginning about the ninth century, and reached its height in the tenth and eleventh centuries, primarily in Persia (now Iran). In America, the best known Sufi work is poetry, The Rubaiyat of Omar Khayyam (d. 1122). Although Sufism and Sufi teaching tales have roots in antiquity, they remain lively today. The Sufi teaching tales included here are translations of versions written in the thirteenth, nineteenth, and twentieth centuries respectively.*

The Ancient Coffer of Nuri Bey

Nuri Bey was a reflective and respected Albanian, who had married a wife much younger than himself.

One evening when he had returned home earlier than usual, a faithful servant came to him and said:

'Your wife, our mistress, is acting suspiciously.

'She is in her apartments with a huge chest, large enough to hold a man, which belonged to your grandmother.

'It should contain only a few ancient embroideries.

'I believe that there may now be much more in it.

'She will not allow me, your oldest retainer, to look inside.'

Nuri went to his wife's room, and found her sitting disconsolately beside the massive wooden box.

'Will you show me what is in the chest?' he asked.

'Because of the suspicion of a servant, or because you do not trust me?'

'Would it not be easier just to open it, without thinking about the undertones?' asked Nuri.

'I do not think it possible.'

'Is it locked?'

'Yes.'

'Where is the key?'

She held it up, 'Dismiss the servant and I will give it to you.'

The servant was dismissed. The woman handed over the key and herself withdrew, obviously troubled in mind.

Nuri Bey thought for a long time. Then he called four gardeners from his estate. Together they carried the chest by night unopened to a distant part of the grounds, and buried it.

The matter was never referred to again.

Study and Writing Questions

1. What significance is there, if any, to the fact that Nuri Bey returned home "earlier than usual"?
2. What might be the meaning of "a few ancient embroideries"?
3. What is the effect of the NARRATOR switching from DRAMATIZATION to RECAPITULATION?
4. What evidence is there in the NARRATIVE that the husband does or does not behave properly?
5. What is the MORAL of this TALE? Are there any ways it might apply to your own life?

See also Questions for Contrast and Comparison: 4, 33, 45, 51, 65, 155, 159, 160, and 164.

The Bequest

A man died far from his home, and in the portion of his will which he had available for bequest, he left in these words: 'Let the community where the land is situated take what they wish for themselves, and let them give that which they wish to Arif the Humble.'

Now Arif was a young man at the time, who had far less apparent authority than anyone in the community. Therefore the elders took possession of whatever they wanted from the land which had been left, and they allocated to Arif a few trifles only, which nobody else wanted.

Many years later Arif, grown to strength and wisdom, went to the community to claim his patrimony. 'These are the objects which we have allocated to you in accordance with the Will,' said the elders. They did not feel that they had usurped anything, for they had been told to take what they wished.

But, in the middle of the discussion, an unknown man of grave countenance and compelling presence appeared among them. He said: 'The meaning of the Will was that you should give to Arif that which you wished *for yourselves*, for he can make the best use of it.'

In the moment of illumination which this statement gave them, the elders were able to see the true meaning of the phrase, 'Let them give that which they wish to Arif'.

'Know', continued the apparition, 'that the testator died unable to protect his property, which would, in case of his making Arif his legatee in an obvious sense, have been usurped by this Community. At the very least it would have caused dissension. So he entrusted it to you, knowing that if you thought that it was your own property you would take care of it. Hence he made a wise provision for the preservation and transmission of this treasure. The time has now come for it to be returned to its rightful use.'

Thus it was that the property was handed back; the elders were able to see the truth.

Study and Writing Questions

1. What can be inferred about the nature of the testator and his relationships to the community and to Arif?
2. Why is it important for the "property" to be "protected"?
3. What is the nature of "truth" in this tale?
4. Why did the Community obey the "apparition"?
5. How is language portrayed in "The Bequest"?

See also Questions for Contrast and Comparison: 114, 147, 155, 157, 158, and 160.

The Limitations of Dogma

One day the great Sultan Mahmud was in the streets of Ghazna, his capital. He saw a poor porter struggling under the weight of a heavy stone which he was carrying on his back. Moved by pity for his condition and unable to restrain his compassion, Mahmud called out to him, in royal command:

'Drop that stone, porter.'

Immediately he was obeyed. The stone lay there, an obstacle to all who tried to pass, for years on end. Ultimately a number of citizens interceded with the king, asking him to give a command for the stone to be taken away.

But Mahmud, reflecting in administrative wisdom, felt himself bound to reply:

'That which has been done by command cannot be rescinded by an equal command, lest the people think that imperial orders are motivated by whims. Let the stone remain where it is.'

The stone remained, therefore, for the rest of Mahmud's lifetime. Even when he was dead, from respect for royal commands, it was not moved.

The story was well known. People took its meaning in one of three ways, each according to his capacity. Those who were against rulership considered that it was an evidence of the stupidity of authority trying to maintain itself. Those who revered power felt respect for commands, however inconvenient. Those who understood aright penetrated the moral intended by the king, regardless of his reputation among the unheedy. For, by causing to be placed in that inconvenient position an obstacle, and giving currency to his reasons for leaving it there, Mahmud was telling those who could understand to obey temporal authority, but to realize that those who rule by inflexible dogma cannot be of complete use to humankind.

Those who read the lesson therefore swelled the ranks of the truth-seekers, and many thus found their way to Truth.

Study and Writing Questions

1. What are the significant IMAGES in this NARRATIVE? What do they signify here?
2. Why does the narrative offer differing interpretations of the sultan's actions?
3. What is the meaning of the last line?
4. What is the significance of this PARABLE asserting its own historical accuracy?
5. What is/are the relationship(s) among the many MORALS that this narrative can support?

See also Questions for Contrast and Comparison: 14, 73, 155, 160, and 172.

■ **CHINUA ACHEBE** (1930–) *is one of Africa's most widely honored living writers both in Africa and throughout the world. Born in eastern Nigeria, he did not learn English, the language of his country's colonizers, until age eight. He has said of his people that "among the Ibo, the art of conversation is regarded very highly, and proverbs are the palm-oil with which words are eaten." After receiving his B.A. from University College, Ibadan, he began a lifetime career as a public communicator, holding such positions as radio producer, director, and publisher. In 1966, he resigned his post as Nigeria's director of external broadcasting to serve the Biafran Ministry of Information in efforts to fund Biafra's unsuccessful war for secession from Nigeria. Things Fall Apart (1958), his first and most famous novel, depicts the personal and social upheavals inflicted on Africans by the incursion of European colonialism. Novelist, essayist, poet, and short story writer, Achebe now teaches English at the University of Massachusetts in Amherst.*

Girls at War

The first time their paths crossed nothing happened. That was in the first heady days of warlike preparation when thousands of young men (and sometimes women too) were daily turned away from enlistment centres because far too many of them were coming forward burning with readiness to bear arms in defence of the exciting new nation.

The second time they met was at a check-point at Awka. Then the war had started and was slowly moving southwards from the distant northern sector. He was driving from Onitsha to Enugu and was in a hurry. Although intellectually he approved of thorough searches at road-blocks, emotionally he was always offended whenever he had to submit to them. He would probably not admit it but the feeling people got was that if you were put through a search then you could not really be one of the big people. Generally he got away without a search by pronouncing in his deep, authoritative voice: "Reginald Nwankwo, Ministry of Justice." That almost always did it. But sometimes either through ignorance or sheer cussedness the crowd at the odd check-point would refuse to be impressed. As happened now at Awka. Two constables carrying heavy Mark 4 rifles were watching distantly from the roadside leaving the actual searching to local vigilantes.

"I am in a hurry," he said to the girl who now came up to his car. "My name is Reginald Nwankwo, Ministry of Justice."

"Good afternoon, sir. I want to see your trunk."

"O Christ! What do you think is in the trunk?"

"I don't know, sir."

He got out of the car in suppressed rage, stalked to the back, opened the trunk and holding the lid up with his left hand he motioned with the right as if to say: After you!

"Are you satisfied?" he demanded.

"Yes, sir. Can I see your pigeon-hole?"

"Christ Almighty!"

"Sorry to delay you, sir. But you people gave us this job to do."

"Never mind. You are damn right. It's just that I happen to be in a hurry. But never mind. That's the glovebox. Nothing there as you can see."

"All right, sir, close it." Then she opened the rear door and bent down to inspect under the seats. It was then he took the first real look at her, starting from behind. She was a beautiful girl in a breasty blue jersey, khaki jeans and canvas shoes with the new-style hair-plait which gave a girl a defiant look and which they called—for reasons of their own—"air force base"; and she looked vaguely familiar.

"I am all right, sir," she said at last meaning she was through with her task. "You don't recognize me?"

"No. Should I?"

"You gave me a lift to Enugu that time I left my school to go and join the militia."

"Ah, yes, you were the girl. I told you, didn't I, to go back to school because girls were not required in the militia. What happened?"

"They told me to go back to my school or join the Red Cross."

"You see I was right. So, what are you doing now?"

"Just patching up with Civil Defence."

"Well, good luck to you. Believe me you are a great girl."

That was the day he finally believed there might be something in this talk about revolution. He had seen plenty of girls and women marching and demonstrating before now. But somehow he had never been able to give it much thought. He didn't doubt that the girls and the women took themselves seriously; they obviously did. But so did the little kids who marched up and down the streets at the time drilling with sticks and wearing their mothers' soup bowls for steel helmets. The prime joke of the time among his friends was the contingent of girls from a local secondary school marching behind a banner: WE ARE IM-PREGNABLE!

But after that encounter at the Awka check-point he simply could not sneer at the girls again, nor at the talk of revolution, for he had seen it in action in that young woman whose devotion had simply and without self-righteousness convicted him of gross levity. What were her words? We are doing the work you asked us to do. She wasn't going to make an exception even for one who once did her a favour. He was sure she would have searched her own father just as rigorously.

When their paths crossed a third time, at least eighteen months later, things had got very bad. Death and starvation having long chased out the headiness of the early days, now left in some places blank resignation, in others a rock-like, even suicidal, defiance. But surprisingly enough there were many at this time also who had no other desire than to corner whatever good things were still going and to enjoy themselves to the limit. For such people a strange air of normalcy had returned to the world. All those nervous check-points disappeared. Girls became girls once more and boys boys. It was a tight, blockaded and desperate world but none the less a world—with some goodness and some badness and plenty of heroism which, however, happened most times far, far below the eye-level of the people in this story—in out-of-the-way refugee camps, in the damp tatters, in the hungry and bare-handed courage of the first line of fire.

Reginald Nwankwo lived in Owerri then. But that day he had gone to Nkwerri in search of relief. He had got from Caritas in Owerri a few heads of stockfish, some tinned meat, and the dreadful American stuff called Formula

Two which he felt certain was some kind of animal feed. But he always had a vague suspicion that not being a Catholic put one at a disadvantage with Caritas. So he went now to see an old friend who ran the WCC depot at Nkwerri to get other items like rice, beans and that excellent cereal commonly called Gabon gari.

He left Owerri at six in the morning so as to catch his friend at the depot where he was known never to linger beyond 8:30 for fear of air-raids. Nwankwo was very fortunate that day. The depot had received on the previous day large supplies of new stock as a result of an unusual number of plane landings a few nights earlier. As his driver loaded tins and bags and cartons into his car the starved crowds that perpetually hung around relief centres made crude, ungracious remarks like "War Can Continue!" meaning the WCC! Somebody else shouted "Irevolu!" and his friends replied "shum!" "Irevolu!" "shum!" "Isofeli?" "shum!" "Isofeli?" "Mba!"

Nwankwo was deeply embarrassed not by the jeers of this scarecrow crowd of rags and floating ribs but by the independent accusation of their wasted bodies and sunken eyes. Indeed he would probably have felt much worse had they said nothing, simply looked on in silence, as his trunk was loaded with milk, and powdered egg and oats and tinned meat and stockfish. By nature such singular good fortune in the midst of a general desolation was certain to embarrass him. But what could a man do? He had a wife and four children living in the remote village of Ogbu and completely dependent on what relief he could find and send them. He couldn't abandon them to kwashiokor. The best he could do—and did do as a matter of fact—was to make sure that whenever he got sizeable supplies like now he made over some of it to his driver, Johnson, with a wife and six, or was it seven? children and a salary of ten pounds a month when gari in the market was climbing to one pound per cigarette cup. In such a situation one could do nothing at all for crowds; at best one could try to be of some use to one's immediate neighbours. That was all.

On his way back to Owerri a very attractive girl by the roadside waved for a lift. He ordered the driver to stop. Scores of pedestrians, dusty and exhausted, some military, some civil, swooped down on the car from all directions.

"No, no, no," said Nwankwo firmly. "It's the young woman I stopped for. I have a bad tyre and can only take one person. Sorry."

"My son, please," cried one old woman in despair, gripping the door-handle.

"Old woman, you want to be killed?" shouted the driver as he pulled away, shaking her off. Nwankwo had already opened a book and sunk his eyes there. For at least a mile after that he did not even look at the girl until she finding, perhaps, the silence too heavy said:

"You've saved me today. Thank you."

"Not at all. Where are you going?"

"To Owerri. You don't recognize me?"

"Oh, yes, of course. What a fool I am . . . You are . . ."

"Gladys."

"That's right, the militia girl. You've changed, Gladys. You were always beautiful of course, but now you are a beauty queen. What do you do these days?"

"I am in the Fuel Directorate."

"That's wonderful."

It was wonderful, he thought, but even more it was tragic. She wore a high-tinted wig and a very expensive skirt and low-cut blouse. Her shoes, obviously from Gabon, must have cost a fortune. In short, thought Nwankwo, she had to be in the keep of some well-placed gentleman, one of those piling up money out of the war.

"I broke my rule today to give you a lift. I never give lifts these days."

"Why?"

"How many people can you carry? It is better not to try at all. Look at that old woman."

"I thought you would carry her."

He said nothing to that and after another spell of silence Gladys thought maybe he was offended and so added: "Thank you for breaking your rule for me." She was scanning his face, turned slightly away. He smiled, turned, and tapped her on the lap.

"What are you going to Owerri to do?"

"I am going to visit my girlfriend."

"Girlfriend? You sure?"

"Why not? . . . If you drop me at her house you can see her. Only I pray God she hasn't gone on weekend today; it will be serious."

"Why?"

"Because if she is not at home I will sleep on the road today."

"I pray to God that she is not at home."

"Why?"

"Because if she is not at home I will offer you bed and breakfast . . . What is that?" he asked the driver who had brought the car to an abrupt stop. There was no need for an answer. The small crowd ahead was looking upwards. The three scrambled out of the car and stumbled for the bush, necks twisted in a backward search of the sky. But the alarm was false. The sky was silent and clear except for two high-flying vultures. A humourist in the crowd called them Fighter and Bomber and everyone laughed in relief. The three climbed into their car again and continued their journey.

"It is much too early for raids," he said to Gladys, who had both her palms on her breast as though to still a thumping heart. "They rarely come before ten o'clock."

But she remained tongue-tied from her recent fright. Nwankwo saw an opportunity there and took it at once.

"Where does your friend live?"

"250 Douglas Road."

"Ah! That's the very centre of town—a terrible place. No bunkers, nothing. I won't advise you to go there before 6 p.m.; it's not safe. If you don't mind I will take you to my place where there is a good bunker and then as soon as it is safe, around six, I shall drive you to your friend. How's that?"

"It's all right," she said lifelessly. "I am so frightened of this thing. That's why I refused to work in Owerri. I don't even know who asked me to come out today."

"You'll be all right. We are used to it."

"But your family is not there with you?"

"No," he said. "Nobody has his family there. We like to say it is because of air-raids but I can assure you there is more to it. Owerri is a real swinging town and we live the life of gay bachelors."

"That is what I have heard."

"You will not just hear it; you will see it today. I shall take you to a real swinging party. A friend of mine, a Lieutenant-Colonel, is having a birthday party. He's hired the Sound Smashers to play. I'm sure you'll enjoy it."

He was immediately and thoroughly ashamed of himself. He hated the parties and frivolities to which his friends clung like drowning men. And to talk so approvingly of them because he wanted to take a girl home! And this particular girl too, who had once had such beautiful faith in the struggle and was betrayed (no doubt about it) by some man like him out for a good time. He shook his head sadly.

"What is it?" asked Gladys.

"Nothing. Just my thoughts."

They made the rest of the journey to Owerri practically in silence.

She made herself at home very quickly as if she was a regular girl friend of his. She changed into a house dress and put away her auburn wig.

"That is a lovely hair-do. Why do you hide it with a wig?"

"Thank you," she said leaving his question unanswered for a while. Then she said: "Men are funny."

"Why do you say that?"

"You are now a beauty queen," she mimicked.

"Oh, that! I mean every word of it." He pulled her to him and kissed her. She neither refused nor yielded fully, which he liked for a start. Too many girls were simply too easy those days. War sickness, some called it.

He drove off a little later to look in at the office and she busied herself in the kitchen helping his boy with lunch. It must have been literally a look-in, for he was back within half an hour, rubbing his hands and saying he could not stay away too long from his beauty queen.

As they sat down to lunch, she said: "You have nothing in your fridge."

"Like what?" he asked, half-offended.

"Like meat," she replied undaunted.

"Do you still eat meat?" he challenged.

"Who am I? But other big men like you eat."

"I don't know which big men you have in mind. But they are not like me. I don't make money trading with the enemy or selling relief or . . ."

"Augusta's boyfriend doesn't do that. He just gets foreign exchange."

"How does he get it? He swindles the government—that's how he gets foreign exchange, whoever he is. Who is Augusta, by the way?"

"My girlfriend."

"I see."

"She gave me three dollars last time which I changed to forty-five pounds. The man gave her fifty dollars."

"Well, my dear girl, I don't traffic in foreign exchange and I don't have meat in my fridge. We are fighting a war and I happen to know that some young boys at the front drink gari and water once in three days."

"It is true," she said simply. "Monkey de work, baboon de chop."

"It is not even that; it is worse," he said, his voice beginning to shake. "People are dying every day. As we talk now somebody is dying."

"It is true," she said again.

"Plane!" screamed his boy from the kitchen.

"My mother!" screamed Gladys. As they scuttled towards the bunker of palm stems and red earth, covering their heads with their hands and stooping slightly in their flight, the entire sky was exploding with the clamour of jets and the huge noise of home-made anti-aircraft rockets.

Inside the bunker she clung to him even after the plane had gone and the guns, late to start and also to end, had all died down again.

"It was only passing," he told her, his voice a little shaky. "It didn't drop anything. From its direction I should say it was going to the war front. Perhaps our people who are pressing them. That's what they always do. Whenever our boys press them, they send an SOS to the Russians and Egyptians to bring the planes." He drew a long breath.

She said nothing, just clung to him. They could hear his boy telling the servant from the next house that there were two of them and one dived like this and the other dived like that.

"I see dem well well," said the other with equal excitement. "If no to say de ting de kill porson e for sweet for eye. To God."

"Imagine!" said Gladys, finding her voice at last. She had a way, he thought, of conveying with a few words or even a single word whole layers of meaning. Now it was at once her astonishment as well as reproof, tinged perhaps with grudging admiration for people who could be so light-hearted about these bringers of death.

"Don't be so scared," he said. She moved closer and he began to kiss her and squeeze her breasts. She yielded more and more and then fully. The bunker was dark and unswept and might harbour crawling things. He thought of bringing a mat from the main house but reluctantly decided against it. Another plane might pass and send a neighbour or simply a chance passer-by crashing into them. That would be only slightly better than a certain gentleman in another air-raid who was seen in broad daylight fleeing his bedroom for his bunker stark-naked pursued by a woman in a similar state!

Just as Gladys had feared, her friend was not in town. It would seem her powerful boyfriend had wangled for her a flight to Libreville to shop. So her neighbours thought anyway.

"Great!" said Nwankwo as they drove away. "She will come back on an arms plane loaded with shoes, wigs, pants, bras, cosmetics and what have you, which she will then sell and make thousands of pounds. You girls are really at war, aren't you?"

She said nothing and he thought he had got through at last to her. Then suddenly she said, "That is what you men want us to do."

"Well," he said, "here is one man who doesn't want you to do that. Do you remember that girl in khaki jeans who searched me without mercy at the check-point?"

She began to laugh.

"That is the girl I want you to become again. Do you remember her? No wig. I don't even think she had any earrings . . ."

"Ah, na lie-o. I had earrings."

"All right. But you know what I mean."

"That time done pass. Now everybody want survival. They call it number six. You put your number six; I put my number six. Everything all right."

The Lieutenant-Colonel's party turned into something quite unexpected. But before it did things had been going well enough. There was goat-meat, some chicken and rice and plenty of home-made spirits. There was one fiery brand nicknamed "tracer" which indeed sent a flame down your gullet. The funny thing was looking at it in the bottle it had the innocent appearance of an orange drink. But the thing that caused the greatest stir was the bread — one little roll for each person! It was the size of a golf ball and about the same consistency too! But it was real bread. The band was good too and there were many girls. And to improve matters even further two white Red Cross people soon arrived with a bottle of Courvoisier and a bottle of Scotch! The party gave them a standing ovation and then scrambled to get a taste. It soon turned out from his general behaviour, however, that one of the white men had probably drunk too much already. And the reason it would seem was that a pilot he knew well had been killed in a crash at the airport last night, flying in relief in awful weather.

Few people at the party had heard of the crash by then. So there was an immediate damping of the air. Some dancing couples went back to their seats and the band stopped. Then for some strange reason the drunken Red Cross man just exploded.

"Why should a man, a decent man, throw away his life. For nothing! Charley didn't need to die. Not for this stinking place. Yes, everything stinks here. Even these girls who come here all dolled up and smiling, what are they worth? Don't I know? A head of stockfish, that's all, or one American dollar and they are ready to tumble into bed."

In the threatening silence following the explosion one of the young officers walked up to him and gave him three thundering slaps — right! left! right! — pulled him up from his seat and (there were things like tears in his eyes) shoved him outside. His friend, who had tried in vain to shut him up, followed him out and the silenced party heard them drive off. The officer who did the job returned dusting his palms.

"Fucking beast!" said he with an impressive coolness. And all the girls showed with their eyes that they rated him a man and a hero.

"Do you know him?" Gladys asked Nwankwo.

He didn't answer her. Instead he spoke generally to the party.

"The fellow was clearly drunk," he said.

"I don't care," said the officer. "It is when a man is drunk that he speaks what is on his mind."

"So you beat him for what was on his mind," said the host, "that is the spirit, Joe."

"Thank you, sir," said Joe, saluting.

"His name is Joe," Gladys and the girl on her left said in unison, turning to each other.

At the same time Nwankwo and a friend on the other side of him were saying quietly, very quietly, that although the man had been rude and offensive what he had said about the girls was unfortunately the bitter truth, only he was the wrong man to say it.

When the dancing resumed Captain Joe came to Gladys for a dance. She sprang to her feet even before the word was out of his mouth. Then she remembered immediately and turned round to take permission from Nwankwo. At the same time the Captain also turned to him and said, "Excuse me."

"Go ahead," said Nwankwo, looking somewhere between the two.

It was a long dance and he followed them with his eyes without appearing to do so. Occasionally a relief plane passed overhead and somebody immediately switched off the lights saying it might be the Intruder. But it was only an excuse to dance in the dark and make the girls giggle, for the sound of the Intruder was well known.

Gladys came back feeling very self-conscious and asked Nwankwo to dance with her. But he wouldn't. "Don't bother about me," he said, "I am enjoying myself perfectly sitting here and watching those of you who dance."

"Then let's go," she said, "if you won't dance."

"But I never dance, believe me. So please, enjoy yourself."

She danced next with the Lieutenant-Colonel and again with Captain Joe, and then Nwankwo agreed to take her home.

"I am sorry I didn't dance," he said as they drove away. "But I swore never to dance as long as this war lasts."

She said nothing.

"When I think of somebody like that pilot who got killed last night. And he had no hand whatever in the quarrel. All his concern was to bring us food . . . ."

"I hope that his friend is not like him," said Gladys.

"The man was just upset by his friend's death. But what I am saying is that with people like that getting killed and our own boys suffering and dying at the war fronts I don't see why we should sit around throwing parties and dancing."

"You took me there," said she in a final revolt. "They are your friends. I don't know them before."

"Look, my dear, I am not blaming you. I am merely telling you why I personally refuse to dance. Anyway, let's change the subject . . . Do you still say you want to go back tomorrow? My driver can take you early enough on Monday morning for you to go to work. No? All right, just as you wish. You are the boss."

She gave him a shock by the readiness with which she followed him to bed and by her language.

"You want to shell?" she asked. And without waiting for an answer said, "Go ahead but don't pour in troops!"

He didn't want to pour in troops either and so it was all right. But she wanted visual assurance and so he showed her.

One of the ingenious economics taught by the war was that a rubber condom could be used over and over again. All you had to do was wash it out, dry it and shake a lot of talcum powder over it to prevent its sticking; and it was as good as new. It had to be the real British thing, though, not some of the cheap stuff they brought in from Lisbon which was about as strong as a dry cocoyam leaf in the harmattan.

He had his pleasure but wrote the girl off. He might just as well have slept with a prostitute, he thought. It was clear as daylight to him now that she was kept by some army officer. What a terrible transformation in the short period of less than two years! Wasn't it a miracle that she still had memories of the other life, that she even remembered her name? If the affair of the drunken Red Cross man should happen again now, he said to himself, he would stand up beside the fellow and tell the party that here was a man of truth. What a terrible fate to befall a whole generation! The mothers of tomorrow!

By morning he was feeling a little better and more generous in his judgments. Gladys, he thought, was just a mirror reflecting a society that had gone completely rotten and maggoty at the centre. The mirror itself was intact; a lot of smudge but no more. All that was needed was a clean duster. "I have a duty to her," he told himself, "the little girl that once revealed to me our situation. Now she is in danger, under some terrible influence."

He wanted to get to the bottom of this deadly influence. It was clearly not just her good-time girlfriend, Augusta, or whatever her name was. There must be some man at the centre of it, perhaps one of these heartless attack-traders who traffic in foreign currencies and make their hundreds of thousands by sending young men to hazard their lives bartering looted goods for cigarettes behind enemy lines, or one of those contractors who receive piles of money daily for food they never deliver to the army. Or perhaps some vulgar and cowardly army officer full of filthy barrack talk and fictitious stories of heroism. He decided he had to find out. Last night he had thought of sending his driver alone to take her home. But no, he must go and see for himself where she lived. Something was bound to reveal itself there. Something on which he could anchor his saving operation. As he prepared for the trip his feeling towards her softened with every passing minute. He assembled for her half of the food he had received at the relief centre the day before. Difficult as things were, he thought a girl who had something to eat would be spared, not all, but some of the temptation. He would arrange with his friend at the WCC to deliver something to her every fortnight.

Tears came to Gladys's eyes when she saw the gifts. Nwankwo didn't have too much cash on him but he got together twenty pounds and handed it over to her.

"I don't have foreign exchange, and I know this won't go far at all, but . . . ."

She just came and threw herself at him, sobbing. He kissed her lips and eyes and mumbled something about victims of circumstance, which went over her head. In deference to him, he thought with exultation, she had put away her high-tinted wig in her bag.

"I want you to promise me something," he said.

"What?"

"Never use that expression about shelling again."

She smiled with tears in her eyes. "You don't like it? That's what all the girls call it."

"Well, you are different from all the girls. Will you promise?"

"O.K."

Naturally their departure had become a little delayed. And when they got into the car it refused to start. After poking around the engine the driver decided that the battery was flat. Nwankwo was aghast. He had that very week paid thirty-four pounds to change two of the cells and the mechanic who performed it had promised him six months' service. A new battery, which was then running at two hundred and fifty pounds was simply out of the question. The driver must have been careless with something, he thought.

"It must be because of last night," said the driver.

"What happened last night?" asked Nwankwo sharply, wondering what insolence was on the way. But none was intended.

"Because we use the headlight."

"Am I supposed not to use my light then? Go and get some people and try pushing it." He got out again with Gladys and returned to the house while the driver went over to neighbouring houses to seek the help of other servants.

After at least half an hour of pushing it up and down the street, and a lot of noisy advice from the pushers, the car finally spluttered to life shooting out enormous clouds of black smoke from the exhaust.

It was eight-thirty by his watch when they set out. A few miles away a disabled soldier waved for a lift.

"Stop!" screamed Nwankwo. The driver jammed his foot on the brakes and then turned his head towards his master in bewilderment.

"Don't you see the soldier waving? Reverse and pick him up!"

"Sorry, sir," said the driver. "I don't know Master wan to pick him."

"If you don't know you should ask. Reverse back."

The soldier, a mere boy, in filthy khaki drenched in sweat lacked his right leg from the knee down. He seemed not only grateful that a car should stop for him but greatly surprised. He first handed in his crude wooden crutches which the driver arranged between the two front seats, then painfully he levered himself in.

"Thank sir," he said turning his neck to look at the back and completely out of breath.

"I am very grateful. Madame, thank you."

"The pleasure is ours," said Nwankwo. "Where did you get your wound?"

"At Azumini, sir. On the tenth of January."

"Never mind. Everything will be all right. We are proud of you boys and will make sure you receive your due reward when it is all over."

"I pray God, sir."

They drove on in silence for the next half-hour or so. Then as the car sped down a slope towards a bridge somebody screamed—perhaps the driver, perhaps the soldier—"They have come!" The screech of the brakes merged into the scream and the shattering of the sky overhead. The doors flew open even before the car had come to a stop and they were fleeing blindly to the bush. Gladys was a little ahead of Nwankwo when they heard through the drowning tumult the soldier's voice crying: "Please come and open for me!" Vaguely he saw Gladys stop; he pushed past her shouting to her at the same time to come on. Then a high whistle descended like a spear through the chaos and exploded in a vast noise and motion that smashed up everything. A tree he had embraced flung him away through the bush. Then another terrible whistle starting high up and ending again in a monumental crash of the world; and then another, and Nwankwo heard no more.

He woke up to human noises and weeping and the smell and smoke of a charred world. He dragged himself up and staggered towards the source of the sounds.

From afar he saw his driver running towards him in tears and blood. He saw the remains of his car smoking and the entangled remains of the girl and the soldier. And he let out a piercing cry and fell down again.

[1972]

Study and Writing Questions

1. What are the literal and SYMBOLIC meanings of the nouns in the title? In what way(s), if any, is this STORY about CONFLICT other than armed combat?
2. What does Nwankwo decide on a "saving operation" for Gladys? What does this reveal about his CHARACTER? To what extent is this his story?
3. What does each of the main sections of this NARRATIVE concern? What does each add to the TALE?
4. What moral questions are raised by this narrative? Does "survival" justify immoral actions? If so, are there moral limits to the degree of immorality allowed?
5. What is the role of the amputee soldier in this narrative?

See also Questions for Contrast and Comparison: 55, 67, 70, 104, 137, 162, 187, 188, 189, 196, 210, and 231.

■ **ALICE ADAMS** (1926–) is a regular contributor of short fiction to some of
America's most prestigious magazines, including The Atlantic Monthly, The
New Yorker, and The Paris Review. Born in Fredericksburg, Virginia, and raised
in Chapel Hill, North Carolina, she reports "falling in love" with writing as a
student at Radcliffe College. After graduation, she married, had children, and
divorced, writing through it all. She supported herself in a succession of office jobs
until, relatively late in life, her writing became successful enough to support her.
Since publishing her first book, the novel Careless Love, in 1966, at age forty,
Adams has become a prolific and acclaimed writer. Her stories are regularly
included in the O. Henry Prize Story collections.

A Southern Spelling Bee

One afternoon in the late Thirties, in Washington, D.C., a blond and handsome
man who was to become a World War II hero, a fighter pilot of exceptional
daring—that man got so irritated at a little girl of six, his daughter's age, that he
decided to get even with her by having a spelling bee. As he told this story over
the years, which he often did, he forgot a lot that actually happened, including his
own irritation which began it all, and how it ended. It became just a funny story
about two little girls.

The man's name was Cameron Lyons, and he was from Charleston, South
Carolina, and he always spoke in those soft and unusually slow accents. His wife,
Lillian, was from North Carolina, but more and more she spoke as her husband
did. He was from a better family, with a better Southern name. Their daughter
was called Helen Jane, plump and pretty and blond, and dearly loved by both her
parents. The irritating other child was Avery Todd, and she was a distant cousin,
or child of cousins, from Cameron's side of the family; her father, Tom was in a
sanatorium in Virginia, drying out, and her mother was busy with Avery's
younger brother, a delicate boy, and with her bookstore. And so Lillian had said
that they would take Avery for a while. That was like Lillian; she was always
taking people in, even in their narrow Georgetown house, even in the Depression, providing food and shelter for stray relatives. She had a strong sense of
family.

Avery was a dark, sharply skinny child, with large melancholy eyes and a
staggering vocabulary. She was physically awkward, not good at jump rope or
hopscotch or roller-skating, but her mind was exceptional. She read all the time,
read grown-up books from her mother's store—more than was good for her, in
Lillian's opinion—and had been heard to describe Gone With the Wind as
"boring." The two children got along fairly well, but that was probably because
Helen Jane had an extremely peaceable disposition.

But Cam, who was unexpectedly intuitive, and open to vibrations, felt waves
of pure hatred that flowed toward his cherished daughter from small Avery. And
why?

His irritation at Avery began to reach a peak at lunch when innocent Helen
Jane said, "Oooh, macaroni and cheese! I just love macaroni," and Avery said
sternly, "Helen Jane, inanimate objects are not to be loved." Cam also repeated

that remark over the years, but again, as something funny that little Avery had said.

And so, while Lillian and the colored girl were clearing up from lunch, Cam took the two children into the living room and announced that they were going to have a spelling bee.

Avery looked very pleased, but Helen Jane pouted and said, "Daddy, you know I can't spell anything."

"That's all right, honey, you'll be all right." He turned to Avery. "Mississippi."

"M-i-s-s-i-s-s-i-p-p-i."

To Helen Jane he said, "Helen."

"H-e-l-e-n."

To Avery, "Constantinople."

"C-o-n-s-t-a-n-t-i-n-o-p-l-e."

"Jane."

"J-a-n-e."

And so on, for quite a while.

("I ran upstairs crying, of course," said Avery, many years later, when asked what happened after that.)

In the Forties, while Cam was heroically in England and France, the two young girls continued in their divergent directions. Sexually as well as intellectually precocious, Avery had an early and violent adolescence; there was always some passionate involvement with a boy — her heart was often broken. Sheltered, passive Helen Jane never fell in love until she was eighteen, and then she fell in love with Stuart Claiborne, an exceptionally rich and handsome Southern boy, whom she married a year later, and to whom she bore four children, and whose secret ugly temper she endured until he was finally involved in a housing scandal during the Johnson administration.

In Avery's case there was a rumor of a very early (annulled) marriage to a colored trombone player, but — to Lillian and Cam — this was so monstrous a thought that they loyally discounted it as slander. But she did get married several times, although never in church or even in her own home so that silver could be chosen and presents sent, permanent addresses noted down. One husband (they believed) was a professor — a divorced man, a Jew. Another husband (they thought) was a poet.

Avery's mother died (she of the bookstore), and her father remarried.

They had had only the briefest glimpses of Avery over the years, but Lillian, with her strong sense of family, had kept her newest name and address in the book, and so, when they came to San Francisco, where Avery was living, they telephoned. Somewhat surprisingly ("I could hardly believe it — she was so — well — *gracious* — grown-up," Lillian reported to Cameron), Avery invited them to dinner. To meet her husband, Joseph. They were not sure what he did — some kind of a doctor? Although, given Avery, anything so sensible was unlikely.

Over the phone, Avery had said to Lillian, laughing in a new (to them), dry, grown-up way: "You'll see, he looks a little like Cam."

At first glance neither Cam nor anyone else would have noticed a resemblance between himself and Joseph. But what Lillian and Cam did continuously peer at Joseph to find out (they did not know they were doing this) was: what is wrong with this one? Why did she choose him? On the surface at least there was nothing wrong: he was blond, conventionally handsome and polite, if a little quiet. The apartment was attractive. And Avery in her own dark way looked quite beautiful.

But, being a Southern woman of a very definite kind, Lillian withheld compliments, and instead she launched into a recital of their day in San Francisco. Adventures on cable cars, exotic stores. "Well, I just want you to know I found the most lovely brocade in this little bitty store on Grant Avenue, but instead of Chinese there were these Jews. You know, I just love the Jews. I think they're absolutely marvelous. I don't care what anyone says."

Cam caught a startled glance exchanged between Avery and Joseph, but at least neither of them said anything. Years back, he knew, Avery would have lashed out at anything anyone said about Jews, even Lillian saying she *liked* them. But after all, Avery was Southern, and somewhere she knew what not to say.

Lillian had not stopped talking for a minute. "It's for Mary Lillian's wedding, in June," she said. "That's my oldest granddaughter. Not a speck of money but they're both real smart so I reckon they'll be okay."

Then Avery announced dinner, and the four of them went in to her pretty table. Lillian cried out, "Avery, isn't that your mother's silver? I recognize it, I always said you should be the one to have it, even if some people thought your brother would appreciate it more."

Cam had to admit to himself that Avery looked younger than Helen Jane did, probably because Avery was so thin. With her burning dark eyes and her long proud neck she had turned into quite a woman. Strange.

Lillian was telling about Helen Jane's recent remarriage. "The nicest man you'd ever want to meet. A widower, and he'd never had any children. Now, doesn't that tell you something about the kind of man he is? To take on four not his own? He works in Washington, of course. In the C.I.A."

Avery said, "The C.I.A.?"

"Oh yes, the grandest job. They come down to see us all the time and we have the best old time."

Cameron said, "Avery, this fish is delicious, just plain delicious. Whoever would have thought you'd grow up and learn to cook?"

"No one related to me, certainly," Avery said.

And Joseph, "Actually, she's a terrific cook."

Cam noticed that Joseph drank a lot, lots of vodka before dinner, and now he was really pouring down the wine. To Cam this was an amiable and familiar weakness, more comprehensible than Jewishness or writing poetry, but for Avery, with all her father's trouble with the stuff, it seemed an odd choice; it was as though she had made some sort of circle.

"What is it that you do out here, Joseph?" Cam asked.

"I'm a psychiatrist. Mainly children."

"I married my doctor," said Avery, as though she were making a joke.

Consciously refraining from telling any of the psychiatrist jokes he knew, Cameron said, "Well, if you're interested in children you'll like this story about this little old gal here, your Avery." And he told the story about the spelling bee. And at the end in his gentle way he chuckled, and he said, "Helen Jane never did catch on, but of course Avery did."

"What did you do then?" Joseph asked Avery.

"I ran upstairs crying, of course," Avery said.

"Did you, old sweetheart?" old Cameron asked. "I didn't remember that."

By the middle of dessert, Joseph, who had indeed been drinking a lot, beginning with the vodka sneaked into his tomato juice, to cope with the hangover from the night before, slumped over in his seat. His unconscious face was no longer handsome, but swollen and coarse. "The ugliest old thing you'd ever want to see" is how Lillian later, with considerable exaggeration, described Joseph's passed-out face to Helen Jane and Ken, of the C.I.A.

But after one glance each of those Southern-trained people pretended that he was not there — what had happened had not happened — and none of them glanced a second time.

And after dinner Joseph was left snoring at the table; they all (those three Southern people) went into the living room, where Avery served coffee, and Lillian showed pictures of the grandchildren and of her daughter's marriage to Ken. And then Lillian and Cameron got up to go, and to make their prolonged Southern ritual of farewell.

At last that was over and Cameron had bundled Lillian into their rented Mercedes and he stood on the sidewalk with Avery, in the cold San Francisco summer night. Avery's arms were bare and she shivered, and at that moment Cameron was seized with an impulse toward her that was violent and obscure and inadmissibly sexual. He reached toward her — surely he had simply meant to kiss her good night? — but as he stepped forward everything went wrong and his heavy foot bore down on the uncovered instep of her high-arched foot, so that she cried out in pain.

"Oh, my darling, I'm so sorry!" breathed old Cam, drawing back.

"It's all right, I know you are," she said.

("But why did you ask them to dinner?" Joseph asked her sometime the next day.

"I don't know, I think just the sound of their voices over the phone. When I was little I thought Cam was the most marvelous, glamorous man alive," and she sighed. Then, "I thought they'd be nice!" she cried out. "God, don't they know? How I must have felt about a little girl who could just smile to get love and not have to spell Constantinople?")

"What took you so long? What on earth were you talking about?" Lillian asked Cameron, in the heavy, purring car.

"I — uh — stepped on her foot. Didn't mean to, of course. Had to say I was sorry."

"My, you are the clumsiest old boy, now aren't you." And Lillian chuckled, quite satisfied with them both, and with the evening.

[1982]

Study and Writing Questions

1. What are some examples of the use of STEREOTYPES in this NARRATIVE? What is the attitude of the NARRATOR toward stereotyping? Can you infer the attitude of the IMPLIED AUTHOR toward stereotyping?
2. What does the word "Southern" mean at various points in the narrative? Does it change with the decades and/or setting?
3. Why is Lillian "satisfied" at the end? What does that imply about her and about the point of the narrative?
4. In what way(s) is repetition important in this narrative? Note that key words (for example, "'Did you, old sweetheart?' old Cameron asked."), key phrases (for example, "'I ran crying upstairs, of course'"), and the key scene of the spelling bee are repeated in one way or another. How do the repetitions and variations enter into our responses to the narrative?
5. What is important about the OMNISCIENT NARRATOR's choices of what to tell (for example, private thoughts of the characters) and what not to tell at particular points in the narrative? Reread the first paragraph. Why does the omniscient narrator begin with that paragraph?

See also Questions for Contrast and Comparison: 97, 130, 170, 205, 206, and 207.

■ JAMES (RUFUS) AGEE (*1909–1955*), *born into a comparatively poor family in Knoxville, Tennessee, lost his father by a freak automobile accident in 1916. Agee was an artistic innovator who never settled on a single form, which slowed full critical recognition of his extraordinary skill. Permit Me Voyage (1934), the only volume of his poetry published in his lifetime, was part of the Yale Younger Poets Series. His only book-length photo-essay,* Let Us Now Praise Famous Men *(1941; done in collaboration with photographer Walker Evans), a study of three Southern share-cropping families, is now seen as perhaps the greatest documentary of the Depression. His evocative film reviews for the* Nation *were often considered more artistic than the works they discussed. Eventually he abandoned reviewing to write screenplays, including his collaboration with John Huston on the Academy Award-winning* The African Queen (1951). *As restless in his life as in his art (he had one child by each of his first two wives and none by his third), at his death from chronic heart disease he left sketches and a plan for a semi-autobiographical novel,* A Death in the Family. *After others put this narratively complex work in order, it won the Pulitzer Prize in 1957, and its* DRAMATIZATION *by Tad Mosel as* All the Way Home *won a Pulitzer Prize in 1960. Agee wrote few short stories, yet "A Mother's Tale" was reprinted in the* Fifty Best American Short Stories 1915–1965.

A Mother's Tale

The calf ran up the hill as fast as he could and stopped sharp. "Mama!" he cried, all out of breath. "What *is* it! What are they *doing!* Where are they *going!*"

Other spring calves came galloping too.

They all were looking up at her and awaiting her explanation, but she looked out over their excited eyes. As she watched the mysterious and majestic thing they had never seen before, her own eyes became even more than ordinarily still, and during the considerable moment before she answered, she scarcely heard their urgent questioning.

Far out along the autumn plain, beneath the sloping light, an immense drove of cattle moved eastward. They went at a walk, not very fast, but faster than they could imaginably enjoy. Those in front were compelled by those behind; those at the rear, with few exceptions, did their best to keep up; those who were locked within the herd could no more help moving than the particles inside a falling rock. Men on horses rode ahead, and alongside, and behind, or spurred their horses intensely back and forth, keeping the pace steady, and the herd in shape; and from man to man a dog sped back and forth incessantly as a shuttle, barking, incessantly, in a hysterical voice. Now and then one of the men shouted fiercely, and this like the shrieking of the dog was tinily audible above a low and awesome sound which seemed to come not from the multitude of hooves but from the center of the world, and above the sporadic bawlings and bellowings of the herd.

From the hillside this tumult was so distant that it only made more delicate the prodigious silence in which the earth and sky were held; and, from the hill, the sight was as modest as its sound. The herd was virtually hidden in the dust it raised, and could be known, in general, only by the horns which pricked this flat sunlit dust like little briars. In one place a twist of the air revealed the trembling fabric of many backs; but it was only along the near edge of the mass that individual animals were discernible, small in a driven frieze, walking fast, stumbling and recovering, tossing their armed heads, or opening their skulls heavenward in one of those cries which reached the hillside long after the jaws were shut.

From where she watched, the mother could not be sure whether there were any she recognized. She knew that among them there must be a son of hers; she had not seen him since some previous spring, and she would not be seeing him again. Then the cries of the young ones impinged on her bemusement: "Where are they going?"

She looked into their ignorant eyes.

"Away," she said.

"Where?" they cried. "Where? Where?" her own son cried again.

She wondered what to say.

"On a long journey."

"But where *to?*" they shouted. "Yes, where *to?*" her son exclaimed, and she could see that he was losing his patience with her, as he always did when he felt she was evasive.

"I'm not sure," she said.

Their silence was so cold that she was unable to avoid their eyes for long.

"Well, not *really* sure. Because, you see," she said in her most reasonable tone, "I've never seen it with my own eyes, and that's the only way to *be* sure; *isn't* it."

They just kept looking at her. She could see no way out.

"But I've *heard* about it," she said with shallow cheerfulness, "from those who *have* seen it, and I don't suppose there's any good reason to doubt them."

She looked away over them again, and for all their interest in what she was about to tell them, her eyes so changed that they turned and looked, too.

The herd, which had been moving broadside to them, was being turned away, so slowly that like the turning of stars it could not quite be seen from one moment to the next; yet soon it was moving directly away from them, and even during the little while she spoke and they all watched after it, it steadily and very noticeably diminished, and the sounds of it as well.

"It happens always about this time of year," she said quietly while they watched. "Nearly all the men and horses leave, and go into the North and the West."

"Out on the range," her son said, and by his voice she knew what enchantment the idea already held for him.

"Yes," she said, "out on the range." And trying, impossibly, to imagine the range, they were touched by the breath of grandeur.

"And then before long," she continued, "everyone has been found, and brought into one place; and then . . . what you see, happens. All of them.

"Sometimes when the wind is right," she said more quietly, "you can hear them coming long before you can see them. It isn't even like a sound, at first. It's more as if something were moving far under the ground. It makes you uneasy. You wonder, why, what in the world can *that* be! Then you remember what it is and then you can really hear it. And then finally, there they all are."

She could see this did not interest them at all.

"But where are they *going?*" one asked, a little impatiently.

"I'm coming to that," she said; and she let them wait. Then she spoke slowly but casually.

"They are on their way to a railroad."

There, she thought; that's for that look you all gave me when I said I wasn't sure. She waited for them to ask; they waited for her to explain.

"A railroad," she told them, "is great hard bars of metal lying side by side, or so they tell me, and they go on and on over the ground as far as the eye can see. And great wagons run on the metal bars on wheels, like wagon wheels but smaller, and these wheels are made of solid metal too. The wagons are much bigger than any wagon you've ever seen, as big as, big as sheds, they say, and they are pulled along on the iron bars by a terrible huge dark machine, with a loud scream."

"Big as *sheds?*" one of the calves said skeptically.

"Big *enough*, anyway," the mother said. "I told you I've never seen it myself. But those wagons are so big that several of us can get inside at once. And that's exactly what happens."

Suddenly she became very quiet, for she felt that somehow, she could not imagine just how, she had said altogether too much.

"Well, *what* happens," her son wanted to know. "What do you mean, *happens.*"

She always tried hard to be a reasonably modern mother. It was probably better, she felt, to go on, than to leave them all full of imaginings and mystification. Besides, there was really nothing at all awful about what happened . . . if only one could know *why.*

"Well," she said, "it's nothing much, really. They just — why, when they all finally *get* there, why there are all the great cars waiting in a long line, and the big dark machine is up ahead . . . smoke comes out of it, they say . . . and . . . well, then, they just put us into the wagons, just as many as will fit in each wagon, and when everybody is in, why . . ." She hesitated, for again, though she couldn't be sure why, she was uneasy.

"Why then," her son said, "the train takes them away."

Hearing that word, she felt a flinching of the heart. Where had he picked it up, she wondered, and she gave him a shy and curious glance. Oh dear, she thought. I should never have even *begun* to explain. "Yes," she said, "when everybody is safely in, they slide the doors shut."

They were all silent for a little while. Then one of them asked thoughtfully, "Are they taking them somewhere they don't want to go?"

"Oh, I don't think so," the mother said. "I imagine it's very nice."

"I want to go," she heard her son say with ardor. "I want to go right now," he cried. "Can I, Mama? *Can I? Please?*" And looking into his eyes, she was overwhelmed by sadness.

"Silly thing," she said, "there'll be time enough for that when you're grown up. But what I very much hope," she went on, "is that instead of being chosen to go out on the range and to make the long journey, you will grow up to be very strong and bright so they will decide that you may stay here at home with Mother. And you, too," she added, speaking to the other little males; but she could not honestly wish this for any but her own, least of all for the eldest, strongest and most proud, for she knew how few are chosen.

She could see that what she said was not received with enthusiasm.

"But I want to go," her son said.

"Why?" she asked, "I don't think any of you realize that it's a great *honor* to be chosen to stay. A great privilege. Why, it's just the most ordinary ones are taken out onto the range. But only the very pick are chosen to stay here at home. If you want to go out on the range," she said in hurried and happy inspiration, "all you have to do is be ordinary and careless and silly. If you want to have even a chance to be chosen to stay, you have to try to be stronger and bigger and braver and brighter than anyone else, and that takes *hard work. Every day.* Do you see?" And she looked happily and hopefully from one to another. "Besides," she added, aware that they were not won over, "I'm told it's a very rough life out there, and the men are unkind.

"Don't you see," she said again; and she pretended to speak to all of them, but it was only to her son.

But he only looked at her. "Why do you want me to stay home?" he asked flatly; in their silence she knew the others were asking the same question.

"Because it's safe here," she said before she knew better; and realized she had put it in the most unfortunate way possible. "Not safe, not just that," she fumbled. "I mean . . . because here we *know* what happens, and what's going to happen, and there's never any doubt about it, never any reason to wonder, to worry. Don't you see? It's just *Home*," and she put a smile on the word, "where we all know each other and are happy and well."

They were so merely quiet, looking back at her, that she felt they were neither won over nor alienated. Then she knew of her son that he, anyhow, was most certainly not persuaded, for he asked the question she most dreaded: "Where do they go on the train?" And hearing him, she knew that she would stop at nothing to bring that curiosity and eagerness, and that tendency toward skepticism, within safe bounds.

"Nobody knows," she said, and she added, in just the tone she knew would most sharply engage them, "Not for sure, anyway."

"What do you mean, *not for sure*," her son cried. And the oldest, biggest calf repeated the question, his voice cracking.

The mother deliberately kept silence as she gazed out over the plain, and while she was silent they all heard the last they would ever hear of all those who were going away: one last great cry, as faint almost as a breath; the infinitesimal jabbing vituperation of the dog; the solemn muttering of the earth.

"Well," she said, after even this sound was entirely lost, "there was one who came back." Their instant, trustful eyes were too much for her. She added, "Or so they say."

They gathered a little more closely around her, for now she spoke very quietly.

"It was my great-grandmother who told me," she said. "She was told it by *her* great-grandmother, who claimed she saw it with her own eyes, though of course I can't vouch for that. Because of course I wasn't even dreamed of then; and Great-grandmother was so very, very old, you see, that you couldn't always be sure she knew quite *what* she was saying."

Now that she began to remember it more clearly, she was sorry she had committed herself to telling it.

"Yes," she said, "the story is, there was one, *just* one, who ever came back, and he told what happened on the train, and where the train went and what happened after. He told it all in a rush, they say, the last things first and every which way, but as it was finally sorted out and gotten into order by those who heard it and those they told it to, this is more or less what happened:

"He said that after the men had gotten just as many of us as they could into the car he was in, so that their sides pressed tightly together and nobody could lie down, they slid the door shut with a startling rattle and a bang, and then there was a sudden jerk, so strong they might have fallen except that they were packed so closely together, and the car began to move. But after it had moved only a little way, it stopped as suddenly as it had started, so that they all nearly fell down again. You see, they were just moving up the next car that was joined on behind, to put more of us into it. He could see it all between the boards of the car, because the boards were built a little apart from each other, to let in air."

Car, her son said again to himself. Now he would never forget the word.

"He said that then, for the first time in his life, he became very badly frightened, he didn't know why. But he was sure, at that moment, that there was something dreadfully to be afraid of. The others felt this same great fear. They called out loudly to those who were being put into the car behind, and the others called back, but it was no use; those who were getting aboard were between narrow white fences and then were walking up a narrow slope and the men kept jabbing them as they do when they are in an unkind humor, and there was no way to go but on into the car. There was no way to get out of the car, either: he tried, with all his might, and he was the one nearest the door.

"After the next car behind was full, and the door was shut, the train jerked forward again, and stopped again, and they put more of us into still another car, and so on, and on, until all the starting and stopping no longer frightened anybody; it was just something uncomfortable that was never going to stop, and they began instead to realize how hungry and thirsty they were. But there was no food and no water, so they just had to put up with this; and about the time they became resigned to going without their suppers (for now it was almost dark), they heard a sudden and terrible scream which frightened them even more deeply than anything had frightened them before, and the train began to move again, and they braced their legs once more for the jolt when it would stop, but this time, instead of stopping, it began to go fast, and then even faster, so fast that the ground nearby slid past like a flooded creek and the whole country, he claimed, began to move too, turning slowly around a far mountain as if it were all one great wheel. And then there was a strange kind of disturbance inside the car, he said, or even inside his very bones. He felt as if everything in him was *falling,* as if he had been filled full of a heavy liquid that all wanted to flow one way, and all the others were leaning as he was leaning, away from this queer heaviness that was trying to pull them over, and then just as suddenly this leaning heaviness was gone and they nearly fell again before they could stop leaning against it. He could never understand what this was, but it too happened so many times that they all got used to it, just as they got used to seeing the country turn like a slow wheel, and just as they got used to the long cruel screams of the engine, and the steady iron noise beneath them which made the cold darkness so fearsome, and the hunger and the thirst and the continual standing up, and the moving on and on and on as if they would never stop."

"*Didn't* they ever stop?" one asked.

"Once in a great while," she replied. "Each time they did," she said, "he thought, Oh, now *at last*! *At last* we can get out and stretch our tired legs and lie down! *At last* we'll be given food and water! But they never let them out. And they never gave them food or water. They never even cleaned up under them. They had to stand in their manure and in the water they made."

"Why did the train stop?" her son asked; and with somber gratification she saw that he was taking all this very much to heart.

"He could never understand why," she said. "Sometimes men would walk up and down alongside the cars, and the more nervous and the more trustful of us would call out; but they were only looking around, they never seemed to do anything. Sometimes he could see many houses and bigger buildings together where people lived. Sometimes it was far out in the country and after they had stood still for a long time they would hear a little noise which quickly became louder, and then became suddenly a noise so loud it stopped their breathing, and during this noise something black would go by, very close, and so fast it couldn't be seen. And then it was gone as suddenly as it had appeared, and the noise became small, and then in the silence their train would start up again.

"Once, he tells us, something very strange happened. They were standing still, and cars of a very different kind began to move slowly past. These cars were not red, but black, with many glass windows like those in a house; and he says they were as full of human beings as the car he was in was full of our kind. And one of these people looked into his eyes and smiled, as if he liked him, or as if he knew only too well how hard the journey was.

"So by his account it happens to them, too," she said, with a certain pleased vindictiveness. "Only they were sitting down at their ease, not standing. And the one who smiled was eating."

She was still, trying to think of something; she couldn't quite grasp the thought.

"But didn't they *ever* let them out?" her son asked.

The oldest calf jeered. "Of *course* they did. He came back, didn't he? How would he ever come back if he didn't get out?"

"They didn't let them out," she said, "for a long, long time."

"How long?"

"So long, and he was so tired, he could never quite be sure. But he said that it turned from night to day and from day to night and back again several times over, with the train moving nearly all of this time, and that when it finally stopped, early one morning, they were all so tired and so discouraged that they hardly even noticed any longer, let alone felt any hope that anything would change for them, ever again; and then all of a sudden men came up and put up a wide walk and unbarred the door and slid it open, and it was the most wonderful and happy moment of his life when he saw the door open, and walked into the open air with all his joints trembling, and drank the water and ate the delicious food they had ready for him; it was worth the whole terrible journey."

Now that these scenes came clear before her, there was a faraway shining in her eyes, and her voice, too, had something in it of the faraway.

"When they had eaten and drunk all they could hold they lifted up their heads and looked around, and everything they saw made them happy. Even the trains made them cheerful now, for now they were no longer afraid of them. And though these trains were forever breaking to pieces and joining again with other broken pieces, with shufflings and clashings and rude cries, they hardly paid them attention any more, they were so pleased to be in their new home, and so surprised and delighted to find they were among thousands upon thousands of strangers of their own kind, all lifting up their voices in peacefulness and thanks-giving, and they were so wonderstruck by all they could see, it was so beautiful and so grand.

"For he has told us that now they lived among fences as white as bone, so many, and so spiderishly complicated, and shining so pure, that there's no use trying even to hint at the beauty and the splendor of it to anyone who knows only the pitiful little outfittings of a ranch. Beyond these mazy fences, through the dark and bright smoke which continually turned along the sunlight, dark buildings stood shoulder to shoulder in a wall as huge and proud as mountains. All through the air, all the time, there was an iron humming like the humming of the iron bar after it has been struck to tell the men it is time to eat, and in all the air, all the time, there was that same strange kind of iron strength which makes the silence before lightning so different from all other silence.

"Once for a little while the wind shifted and blew over them straight from the great buildings, and it brought a strange and very powerful smell which confused and disturbed them. He could never quite describe this smell, but he has told us it was unlike anything he had ever known before. It smelled like old fire, he said, and old blood and fear and darkness and sorrow and most terrible and brutal force and something else, something in it that made him want to run away. This sudden uneasiness and this wish to run away swept through every one of them, he tells us, so that they were all moved at once as restlessly as so many leaves in a wind, and there was great worry in their voices. But soon the leaders among them concluded that it was simply the way men must smell when there are a great many of them living together. Those dark buildings must be crowded very full of men, they decided, probably as many thousands of them, indoors, as there were of us, outdoors; so it was no wonder their smell was so strong and, to our kind, so unpleasant. Besides, it was so clear now in every other way that men were not as we had always supposed, but were doing everything they knew how to make us comfortable and happy, that we ought to just put up with their smell, which after all they couldn't help, any more than we could help our own. Very likely men didn't like the way we smelled, any more than we liked theirs. They passed along these ideas to the others, and soon everyone felt more calm, and then the wind changed again, and the fierce smell no longer came to them, and the smell of their own kind was back again, very strong of course, in such a crowd, but ever so homey and comforting, and everyone felt easy again.

"They were fed and watered so generously, and treated so well, and the majesty and the loveliness of this place where they had all come to rest was so far beyond anything they had ever known or dreamed of, that many of the simple and ignorant, whose memories were short, began to wonder whether that whole difficult journey, or even their whole lives up to now, had ever really been. Hadn't it all been just shadows, they murmured, just a bad dream?

"Even the sharp ones, who knew very well it had all really happened, began to figure that everything up to now had been made so full of pain only so that all they had come to now might seem all the sweeter and the more glorious. Some of the oldest and deepest were even of a mind that all the puzzle and tribulation of the journey had been sent us as a kind of harsh trying or proving of our worthiness; and that it was entirely fitting and proper that we could earn our way through to such rewards as these, only through suffering, and through being patient under pain which was beyond our understanding; and that now at the last, to those who had borne all things well, all things were made known: for the mystery of suffering stood revealed in joy. And now as they looked back over all that was past, all their sorrows and bewilderments seemed so little and so fleeting that, from the simplest among them even to the most wise, they could feel only the kind of amused pity we feel toward the very young when, with the first thing that hurts them or they are forbidden, they are sure there is nothing kind or fair in all creation, and carry on accordingly, raving and grieving as if their hearts would break."

She glanced among them with an indulgent smile, hoping the little lesson would sink home. They seemed interested but somewhat dazed. I'm talking way over their heads, she realized. But by now she herself was too deeply absorbed in her story to modify it much. *Let* it be, she thought, a little impatient; it's over *my* head, for that matter.

"They had hardly before this even wondered that they were alive," she went on, "and now all of a sudden they felt they understood *why* they were. This made them very happy, but they were still only beginning to enjoy this new wisdom when quite a new and different kind of restiveness ran among them. Before they quite knew it they were all moving once again, and now they realized that they were being moved, once more, by men, toward still some other place and purpose they could not know. But during these last hours they had been so well that now they felt no uneasiness, but all moved forward calm and sure toward better things still to come; he has told us that he no longer felt as if he were being driven, even as it became clear that they were going toward the shade of those great buildings; but guided.

"He was guided between fences which stood ever more and more narrowly near each other, among companions who were pressed ever more and more closely against one another; and now as he felt their warmth against him it was not uncomfortable, and his pleasure in it was not through any need to be close among others through anxiousness, but was a new kind of strong and gentle delight, at being so very close, so deeply of his own kind, that it seemed as if the very breath and heartbeat of each one were being exchanged through all that multitude, and each was another, and others were each, and each was a multitude, and the multitude was one. And quieted and made mild within this melting, they now entered the cold shadow cast by the buildings, and now with every step the smell of the buildings grew stronger, and in the darkening air the glittering of the fences was ever more queer.

"And now as they were pressed ever more intimately together he could see ahead of him a narrow gate, and he was strongly pressed upon from either side and from behind, and went in eagerly, and now he was between two fences so narrowly set that he brushed either fence with either flank, and walked alone, seeing just one other ahead of him, and knowing of just one other behind him, and for a moment the strange thought came to him, that the one ahead was his father, and that the one behind was the son he had never begotten.

"And now the light was so changed that he knew he must have come inside one of the gloomy and enormous buildings, and the smell was so much stronger that it seemed almost to burn his nostrils, and the swell and the somber new light blended together and became some other thing again, beyond his describing to us except to say that the whole air beat with it like one immense heart and it was as if the beating of this heart were pure violence infinitely manifolded upon violence: so that the uneasy feeling stirred in him again that it would be wise to turn around and run out of this place just as fast and as far as ever he could go. This he heard, as if he were telling it to himself at the top of his voice, but it came from somewhere so deep and so dark inside him that he could only hear the shouting of it as less than a whisper, as just a hot and chilling breath, and he scarcely heeded it, there was so much else to attend to.

"For as he walked along in this sudden and complete loneliness, he tells us, this wonderful knowledge of being one with all his race meant less and less to him, and in its place came something still more wonderful: he knew what it was to be himself alone, a creature separate and different from any other, who had never been before, and would never be again. He could feel this in his whole weight as he walked, and in each foot as he put it down and gave his weight to it and moved above it, and in every muscle as he moved, and it was a pride which lifted him up and made him feel large, and a pleasure which pierced him through. And as he began with such wondering delight to be aware of his own exact singleness in this world, he also began to understand (or so he thought) just why these fences were set so very narrow, and just why he was walking all by himself. It stole over him, he tells us, like the feeling of a slow cool wind, that he was being guided toward some still more wonderful reward or revealing, up ahead, which he could not of course imagine, but he was sure it was being held in store for him alone.

"Just then the one ahead of him fell down with a great sigh, and was so quickly taken out of the way that he did not even have to shift the order of his hooves as he walked on. The sudden fall and the sound of that sigh dismayed him, though, and something within him told him that it would be wise to look up: and there he saw Him.

"A little bridge ran crosswise above the fences. He stood on this bridge with His feet as wide apart as He could set them. He wore spattered trousers but from the belt up He was naked and as wet as rain. Both arms were raised high above His head and in both hands He held an enormous Hammer. With a grunt which was hardly like the voice of a human being, and with all His strength, He brought this Hammer down into the forehead of our friend: who, in a blinding blazing, heard from his own mouth the beginning of a gasping sigh; then there was only darkness."

Oh, this is *enough!* it's *enough!* she cried out within herself, seeing their terrible young eyes. How *could* she have been so foolish as to tell so much!

"What happened then?" she heard, in the voice of the oldest calf, and she was horrified. This shining in their eyes: was it only excitement? no pity? no fear?

"What happened?" two others asked.

Very well, she said to herself. I've gone so far; now I'll go the rest of the way. She decided not to soften it, either. She'd teach them a lesson they wouldn't forget in a hurry.

"Very well," she was surprised to hear herself say aloud.

"How long he lay in this darkness he couldn't know, but when he began to come out of it, all he knew was the most unspeakably dreadful pain. He was upside down and very slowly swinging and turning, for he was hanging by the tendons of his heels from great frightful hooks, and he has told us that the feeling was as if his hide were being torn from him inch by inch, in one piece. And then as he became more clearly aware he found that this was exactly what was happening. Knives would sliver and slice along both flanks, between the hide and the living flesh; then there was a moment of most precious relief; then red hands seized his hide and there was a jerking of the hide and a tearing of tissue which it was almost as terrible to hear as to feel, turning his whole body and the poor head at the bottom of it; and then the knives again.

"It was so far beyond anything he had ever known unnatural and amazing that he hung there through several more such slicings and jerkings and tearings before he was fully able to take it all in: then, with a scream, and a supreme straining of all his strength, he tore himself from the hooks and collapsed sprawling to the floor and, scrambling right to his feet, charged the men with the knives. For just a moment they were so astonished and so terrified they could not move. Then they moved faster than he had ever known men could — and so did all the other men who chanced to be in his way. He ran down a glowing floor of blood and down endless corridors which were hung with the bleeding carcasses of our kind and with bleeding fragments of carcasses, among blood-clothed men who carried bleeding weapons, and out of that vast room into the open, and over and through one fence after another, shoving aside many an astounded stranger and shouting out warnings as he ran, and away up the railroad toward the West.

"How he ever managed to get away, and how he ever found his way home, we can only try to guess. It's told that he scarcely knew, himself, by the time he came to this part of his story. He was impatient with those who interrupted him to ask about that, he had so much more important things to tell them, and by then he was so exhausted and so far gone that he could say nothing very clear about the little he did know. But we can realize that he must have had really tremendous strength, otherwise he couldn't have outlived the Hammer; and that strength such as his — which we simply don't see these days, it's of the olden time — is capable of things our own strongest and bravest would sicken to dream of. But there was something even stronger than his strength. There was his righteous fury, which nothing could stand up against, which brought him out of that fearful place. And there was his high and burning and heroic purpose, to keep him safe along the way, and to guide him home, and to keep the breath of life in him until he could warn us. He did manage to tell us that he just followed the railroad, but how he chose one among the many which branched out from that place, he couldn't say. He told us, too, that from time to time he recognized shapes of mountains and other landmarks, from his journey by train, all reappearing backward and with a changed look and hard to see, too (for he was shrewd enough to travel mostly at night), but still recognizable. But that isn't enough to account for it. For he has told us, too, that he simply *knew* the way;

that he didn't hesitate one moment in choosing the right line of railroad, or even think of it as choosing; and that the landmarks didn't really guide him, but just made him the more sure of what he was already sure of; and that whenever he *did* encounter human beings — and during the later stages of his journey, when he began to doubt he would live to tell us, he traveled day and night — they never so much as moved to make him trouble, but stopped dead in their tracks, and their jaws fell open.

"And surely we can't wonder that their jaws fell open. I'm sure yours would, if you had seen him as he arrived, and I'm very glad I wasn't there to see it, either, even though it is said to be the greatest and most momentous day of all the days that ever were or shall be. For we have the testimony of eyewitnesses, how he looked, and it is only too vivid, even to hear of. He came up out of the East as much staggering as galloping (for by now he was so worn out by pain and exertion and loss of blood that he could hardly stay upright), and his heels were so piteously torn by the hooks that his hooves doubled under more often than not, and in his broken forehead the mark of the Hammer was like the socket for a third eye.

"He came to the meadow where the great trees made shade over the water. 'Bring them all together!' he cried out, as soon as he could find breath. 'All!' Then he drank; and then he began to speak to those who were already there: for as soon as he saw himself in the water it was as clear to him as it was to those who watched him that there was no time left to send for the others. His hide was all gone from his head and his neck and his forelegs and his chest and most of one side and a part of the other side. It was flung backward from his naked muscles by the wind of his running and now it lay around him in the dust like a ragged garment. They say there is no imagining how terrible and in some way how grand the eyeball is when the skin has been taken entirely from around it: his eyes, which were bare in this way, also burned with pain, and with the final energies of his life, and with his desperate concern to warn us while he could; and he rolled his eyes wildly while he talked, or looked piercingly from one to another of the listeners, interrupting himself to cry out, '*Believe* me! Oh, *believe* me!' For it had evidently never occurred to him that he might not be believed, and must make this last great effort, in addition to all he had gone through for us, to *make* himself believed; so that he groaned with sorrow and with rage and railed at them without tact or mercy for their slowness to believe. He had scarcely what you could call a voice left, but with this relic of a voice he shouted and bellowed and bullied us and insulted us, in the agony of his concern. While he talked he bled from the mouth, and the mingled blood and saliva hung from his chin like the beard of a goat.

"Some say that with his naked face, and his savage eyes, and that beard and the hide lying off his bare shoulders like shabby clothing, he looked almost human. But others feel this is an irreverence even to think; and others, that it is a poor compliment to pay the one who told us, at such cost to himself, the true ultimate purpose of Man. Some did not believe he had ever come from our ranch in the first place, and of course he was so different from us in appearance and even in his voice, and so changed from what he might ever have looked or sounded like before, that nobody could recognize him for sure, though some were sure they did. Others suspected that he had been sent among us with his story for some mischievous and cruel purpose, and the fact that they could not imagine what this purpose might be, made them, naturally, all the more suspicious. Some believed he was actually a man, trying—and none too successfully, they said—to disguise himself as one of us; and again the fact that they could not imagine why a man would do this, made them all the more uneasy. There were quite a few who doubted that anyone who could get into such bad condition as he was in, was fit even to give reliable information, let alone advice, to those in good health. And some whispered, even while he spoke, that he had turned lunatic; and many came to believe this. It wasn't only that his story was so fantastic; there was good reason to wonder, many felt, whether anybody in his right mind would go to such trouble for others. But even those who did not believe him listened intently, out of curiosity to hear so wild a tale, and out of the respect it is only proper to show any creature who is in the last agony.

"What he told, was what I have just told you. But his purpose was away beyond just the telling. When they asked questions, no matter how curious or suspicious or idle or foolish, he learned, toward the last, to answer them with all the patience he could and in all the detail he could remember. He even invited them to examine his wounded heels and the pulsing wound in his head as closely as they pleased. He even begged them to, for he knew that before everything else, he must be believed. For unless we could believe him, wherever could we find any reason, or enough courage, to do the hard and dreadful things he told us we must do!

"It was only these things, he cared about. Only for these, he came back."

Now clearly remembering what these things were, she felt her whole being quail. She looked at the young ones quickly and as quickly looked away.

"While he talked," she went on, "and our ancestors listened, men came quietly among us; one of them shot him. Whether he was shot in kindness or to silence him is an endlessly disputed question which will probably never be settled. Whether, even, he died of the shot, or through his own great pain and weariness (for his eyes, they say, were glazing for some time before the men came), we will never be sure. Some suppose even that he may have died of his sorrow and his concern for us. Others feel that he had quite enough to die of, without that. All these things are tangled and lost in the disputes of those who love to theorize and to argue. There is no arguing about his dying words, though; they were very clearly remembered:

"'Tell them! Believe!'"

After a while her son asked, "What did he tell them to do?"

She avoided his eyes. "There's a great deal of disagreement about that, too," she said after a moment. "You see, he was so very tired."

They were silent.

"So tired," she said, "some think that toward the end, he really *must* have been out of his mind."

"Why?" asked her son.

"Because he was so tired out and so badly hurt."

They looked at her mistrustfully.

"And because of what he told us to do."

"What did he tell us to do?" her son asked again.

Her throat felt dry. "Just . . . things you can hardly bear even to think of. That's all."

They waited. "Well, *what?*" her son asked in a cold, accusing voice.

"'*Each one is himself,*'" she said shyly. "'*Not of the herd. Himself alone.*' That's one."

"What else?"

"'*Obey nobody. Depend on none.*'"

"What else?"

She found that she was moved. "'*Break down the fences,*'" she said less shyly. "'*Tell everybody, everywhere.*'"

"Where?"

"Everywhere. You see, he thought there must be ever so many more of us than we had ever known."

They were silent. "What else?" her son asked.

"'*For if even a few do not hear me, or disbelieve me, we are all betrayed.*'"

"Betrayed?"

"He meant, doing as men want us to. Not for ourselves, or the good of each other."

They were puzzled.

"Because, you see, he felt there was no other way." Again her voice altered: "'*All who are put on the range are put onto trains. All who are put onto trains meet the Man With The Hammer. All who stay home are kept there to breed others to go onto the range, and so betray themselves and their kind and their children forever.*'"

"'*We are brought into this life only to be victims; and there is no other way for unless we save ourselves.*'"

"Do you understand?"

Still they were puzzled, she saw; and no wonder, poor things. But now the ancient lines rang in her memory, terrible and brave. They made her somehow proud. She began actually to want to say them.

"'*Never be taken,*'" she said, "'*Never be driven. Let those who can, kill Man. Let those who cannot, avoid him.*'"

She looked around at them.

"What else?" her son asked, and in his voice there was a rising valor.

She looked straight into his eyes. "'*Kill the yearlings,*'" she said very gently. "'*Kill the calves.*'"

She saw the valor leave his eyes.

"Kill us?"

She nodded, "'*So long as Man holds dominion over us,*'" she said. And in dread and amazement she heard herself add, "'*Bear no young.*'"

With this they all looked at her at once in such a way that she loved her child, and all these others, as never before; and there dilated within her such a sorrowful and marveling grandeur that for a moment she was nothing except her own inward whisper, "Why, I am one alone. And of the herd, too. Both at once. All one."

Her son's voice brought her back: "Did they do what he told them to?"

The oldest one scoffed, "Would we be here, if they had?"

"They say some did," the mother replied. "Some tried. Not all."

"What did the men do to them?" another asked.

"I don't know," she said. "It was such a very long time ago."

"Do you believe it?" asked the oldest calf.

"There are some who believe it," she said.

"Do you?"

"I'm told that far back in the wildest corners of the range there are some of us, mostly very, very old ones, who have never been taken. It's said that they meet, every so often, to talk and just to think together about the heroism and the terror of two sublime Beings, The One Who Came Back, and The Man With The Hammer. Even here at home, some of the old ones, and some of us who are just old-fashioned, believe it, or parts of it anyway. I know there are some who say that a hollow at the center of the forehead—a sort of shadow of the Hammer's blow—is a sign of very special ability. And I remember how Great-grandmother used to sing an old, pious song, let's see now, yes, 'Be not like dumb-driven cattle, be a hero in the strife.' But there aren't many. Not any more."

"Do you believe it?" the oldest calf insisted; and now she was touched to realize that every one of them, from the oldest to the youngest, needed very badly to be sure about that.

"Of course not, silly," she said; and all at once she was overcome by a most curious shyness, for it occurred to her that in the course of time, this young thing might be bred to her. "It's just an old, old legend." With a tender little laugh she added, lightly, "We use it to frighten children with."

By now the light was long on the plain and the herd was only a fume of gold near the horizon. Behind it, dung steamed, and dust sank gently to the shattered ground. She looked far away for a moment, wondering. Something—it was like a forgotten word on the tip of the tongue. She felt the sudden chill of the late afternoon and she wondered what she had been wondering about. "Come, children," she said briskly, "it's high time for supper." And she turned away; they followed.

The trouble was, her son was thinking, you could never trust her. If she said a thing was so, she was probably just trying to get her way with you. If she said a thing wasn't so, it probably was so. But you never could be sure. Not without seeing for yourself. I'm going to go, he told himself; I don't care *what* she wants. And if it isn't so, why then I'll live on the range and make the great journey and find out what *is* so. And if what she told was true, why then I'll know ahead of time and the one I will charge is The Man With The Hammer. I'll put Him and His Hammer out of the way forever, and that will make me an even better hero than The One Who Came Back.

So, when his mother glanced at him in concern, not quite daring to ask her question, he gave her his most docile smile, and snuggled his head against her, and she was comforted.

The littlest and youngest of them was doing double skips in his efforts to keep up with her. Now that he wouldn't be interrupting her, and none of the big ones would hear and make fun of him, he shyly whispered his question, so warmly moistly ticklish that she felt as if he were licking her ear.

"What is it, darling?" she asked, bending down.

"What's a train?"

[1952]

Study and Writing Questions

1. How does this STORY treat the relationship of the individual to the group? What IMAGES are used to characterize each mode of existence? What emotions are associated with each?

2. How does this NARRATIVE portray motherhood? What are the conflicting motives and emotions of the speaker? To what extent are her motives and emotions functions specifically of her motherhood? To what extent are they functions of her femaleness?

3. The NARRATOR is, in many ways, UNRELIABLE: she has her own MOTIVES for telling the story as she does; she is unsure of the meaning of what she has heard secondhand from The One Who Came Back; and The One Who Came Back did not fully understand what he saw. How does the implied author manipulate these levels of unreliability to guide your involvement with the narrative, create SUSPENSE, and make THEMATIC points?

4. What phrases and references in the story recall organized religion? What do they mean? How early in the story are you aware of them? Does the author seem to favor or oppose religion? What is the significance of religion in this story?

5. What are the ALLEGORICAL meaning(s) of this narrative? To what extent is it true, as The One Who Came Back said, that "'it happens to them [humans], too'"? How might this story also be a specific allegory about events occurring at the time it was written?

See also Questions for Contrast and Comparison: 53, 56, 106, 132, 168, 186, 213, 215, and 238.

■ **(CHRISTINA) AMA ATA AIDOO** *(1942 -) was born in Abeadzi Kyia-
kor near Dominase in central Ghana, educated at the University of Ghana,
Legon (B.A., 1964), and studied creative writing at Stanford University (1964–65).
She has taught literature in England, the United States, and Kenya as well as at the
Cape Coast branch of the University of Ghana. Her literary production, marked by
a notable hiatus, has been acclaimed from the first. Even her student play,* The
Dilemma of a Ghost *(published 1965) won public production before her graduation.
Her much produced play,* Anowa *(1970), reuses a song-legend learned from her
mother. Virtually all her writings, whether drama, poetry (Someone Talking to
Someone, 1985;* Birds and Other Poems *[for children], 1987), or prose (No Sweetness Here, short stories, 1970;* Our Sister Killjoy, *novel, 1977;* The Eagle and the
Chickens and Other Stories *[for children], 1988;* Changes, *novel, 1991) have
reflected the impact of colonialism on Africans, the difficulties of women seeking
independence, and the style of Akan oral dramatic recitation. Her children's
writing is dedicated to her daughter. Aidoo, considered one of Africa's most talented
younger writers, currently lives in Zimbabwe.*

Something to Talk About on the Way to the Funeral

. . . Adwoa my sister, when did you come back?

'Last night.'

Did you come specially for Auntie Araba?

'What else, my sister? I just rushed into my room to pick up my *akatado*
when I heard the news. How could I remain another hour in Tarkwa after getting
such news? I arrived in the night.'

And your husband?

'He could not come. You know government-work. You must give notice
several days ahead if you want to go away for half of one day. O, and so many
other problems. But he will see to all that before next *Akwanbo*. Then we may
both be present for the festival and the libation ceremony if her family plans it for
a day around that time.'

Did you hear the Bosoë dance group practising the bread song?

'Yes. I hear they are going to make it the chief song at the funeral this
afternoon. It is most fitting that they should do that. After all, when the group
was formed, Auntie Araba's bread song was the first one they turned into a Bosoë
song and danced to.'

Yes, it was a familiar song in those days. Indeed it had been heard around
here for over twenty years. First in Auntie Araba's own voice with its delicate
thin sweetness that clung like asawa berry on the tongue: which later, much later,
had roughened a little. Then all of a sudden, it changed again, completely. Yes, it
still was a woman's voice. But it was deeper and this time, like good honey, was
rough and heavy, its sweetness within itself.

'Are you talking of when Mansa took over the hawking of the bread?'

Yes. That is how, in fact, that whole little quarter came to be known as
Bosohive. Very often, Auntie Araba did not have to carry the bread. The moment
the aroma burst out of the oven, children began tugging at their parents' clothes

for pennies and threepences. Certainly, the first batch was nearly always in those penny rows. Dozens of them. Of course, the children always caught the aroma before their mothers did.

'Were we not among them?'

We were, my sister. We remember that on market days and other holidays, Auntie Araba's ovenside became a little market-place all by itself. And then there was Auntie Araba herself. She always was a beautiful woman. Even three months ago when they were saying that all her life was gone, I thought she looked better than some of us who claim to be in our prime. If she was a young woman at this time when they are selling beauty to our big men in the towns, she would have made something for herself.

'Though it is a crying shame that young girls should be doing that. As for our big men! Hmm, let me shut my trouble-seeking mouth up. But our big men are something else too. You know, indeed, these our educated big men have never been up to much good.'

Like you know, my sister. After all, was it not a lawyer-or-a-doctor-or-some-thing-like-that who was at the bottom of all Auntie Araba's troubles?

'I did not know that, my sister.'

Yes, my sister. One speaks of it only in whispers. Let me turn my head and look behind me. . . . And don't go standing in the river telling people. Or if you do, you better not say that you heard it from me.

'How could I do that? Am I a baby?'

Yes, Auntie Araba was always a beauty. My mother says she really was a come-and-have-a-look type, when she was a girl. Her plaits hung at the back of her neck like the branches of a giant tree, while the skin of her arms shone like charcoal from good wood. And since her family is one of these families with always some members abroad, when Auntie Araba was just about getting ready for her puberty, they sent her to go and stay at A—with some lady relative. That's where she learnt to mess around with flour so well. But after less than four years, they found she was in trouble.

'Eh-eh?'

Eh-eh, my sister. And now bring your ear nearer.

. . . .

'That lawyer-or-doctor-or-something-like-that who was the lady's husband?'

Yes.

'And what did they do about it?'

They did not want to spoil their marriage so they hushed up everything and sent her home quietly. Very quietly. That girl was our own Auntie Araba. And that child is Ato, the big scholar we hear of.

'Ei, there are plenty of things in the world's old box to pick up and talk about, my sister.'

You have said it. But be quiet and listen. I have not finished the story. If anything like that had happened to me, my life would have been ruined. Not that there is much to it now. But when Auntie Araba returned home to her mother, she was looking like a ram from the north. Big, beautiful and strong. And her mother did not behave as childishly as some would in a case like this. No, she did not tear herself apart as if the world had fallen down. . . .

'Look at how Mother Kuma treated her daughter. Rained insults on her head daily, refused to give her food and then drove her out of their house. Ah, and look at what the father of Mansa did to her too. . . .'

But isn't this what I am coming to? This is what I am coming to.

'Ah-h-h . . .'

Anyway, Auntie Araba's mother took her daughter in and treated her like an egg until the baby was born. And then did Auntie Araba tighten her girdle and get ready to work? Lord, there is no type of dough of flour they say she has not mixed and fried or baked. *Epitsi, Tatare? Atwemo? Bofrot? Boodo? Boodoo-ngo? Sweet-bad?* Hei, she went there and dashed here. But they say that somehow, she was not getting much from these efforts. Some people even say that they landed her in debts.

'But I think someone should have told her that these things are good to eat but they suit more the tastes of the town-dwellers. I myself cannot see any man or woman who spends his living days on the farm, wasting his pennies on any of these sweeties which only satisfy the tongue but do not fill the stomach. Our people in the villages might buy tatare and epitsi, yes, but not the others.'

Like you know, my sister. This is what Auntie Araba discovered, but only after some time. I don't know who advised her to drop all those fancy foods. But she did, and finally started baking bread, ordinary bread. That turned out better for her.

'And how did she come to marry Egya Nyaako?'

They say that she grew in beauty and in strength after her baby was weaned. Good men and rich from all the villages of the state wanted to marry her.

'Ei, so soon? Were they prepared to take her with her baby?'

Yes.

'Hmm, a good woman does not rot.'

That is what our fathers said.

'And she chose Egya Nyaako?'

Yes. But then, we should remember that he was a good man himself.

'Yes, he was. I used to be one of those he hired regularly during the cocoa harvests. He never insisted that we press down the cocoa as most of these farmers do. No, he never tried to cheat us out of our fair pay.'

Which is not what I can say of his heir!

'Not from what we've heard about him. A real mean one they say he is.'

So Auntie agreed to marry Egya Nyaako and she and her son came to live here. The boy, this big scholar we now know of, went with the other youngsters to the school the first day they started it here. In the old Wesleyan chapel. They say she used to say that if she never could sleep her fill, it was because she wanted to give her son a good education.

'Poo, pity. And that must have been true. She mixed and rolled her dough far into the night, and with the first cock-crow, got up from bed to light her fires. Except on Sundays.'

She certainly went to church twice every Sunday. She was a good Christian. And yet, look at how the boy turned out and what he did to her.

'Yes? You know I have been away much of the time. And I have never heard much of him to respect. Besides, I only know very little.'

That is the story I am telling you. I am taking you to bird-town so I can't understand why you insist on searching for eggs from the suburb!

'I will not interrupt you again, my sister.'

Maybe, it was because she never had any more children and therefore, Ato became an only child. They say she spoilt him. Though I am not sure I would not have done the same if I had been in her position. But they say that before he was six years old, he was fighting her. And he continued to fight her until he became a big scholar. And then his father came to acknowledge him as his son, and it seems that ruined him completely.

'Do you mean that lawyer-or-doctor-or-something-like-that man?'

Himself. They say he and his lady wife never had a male child so when he was finishing Stan' 7 or so, he came to father him.

'Poo, scholars!'

It is a shame, my sister. Just when all the big troubles were over.

'If I had been Auntie Araba, eh, I would have charged him about a thousand pounds for neglect.'

But Auntie Araba was not you. They say she was very happy that at last the boy was going to know his real father. She even hoped that that would settle his wild spirits. No, she did not want to make trouble. So this big man from the city came one day with his friends or relatives and met Auntie Araba and her relatives. It was one Sunday afternoon. In two big cars. They say some of her sisters and relatives had sharpened their mouths ready to give him what he deserved. But when they saw all the big men and their big cars, they kept quiet. They murmured among themselves, and that was all. He told them, I mean this new father, that he was going to send Ato to college.

'And did he?'

Yes he did. And he spoilt him even more than his mother had done. He gave him lots of money. I don't know what college he sent him to since I don't know about colleges. But he used to come here to spend some of his holidays. And every time, he left his mother with big debts to pay from his high living. Though I must add that she did not seem to mind.

'You know how mothers are, even when they have several children.'

But, my sister, she really had a big blow when he put Mansa into trouble. Mansa's father nearly killed her.

'I hear Mansa's father is a proud man who believes that there is nothing which any man from his age group can do which he cannot do better.'

So you know. When school education came here, all his children were too old to go to school except Mansa. And he used to boast that he was only going to feel he had done his best by her when she reached the biggest college in the white man's land.

'And did he have the money?'

Don't ask me. As if I was in his pocket! Whether he had the money or not, he was certainly saying these things. But then people also knew him to add on these occasions, 'let us say it will be good, so it shall be good'. Don't laugh, my sister. Now, you can imagine how he felt when Ato did this to his daughter Mansa. I remember they reported him as saying that he was going to sue Ato for heavy damages. But luckily, Ato just stopped coming here in the holidays. But of course, his mother Auntie Araba was here. And she got something from Mansa's father. And under his very nose was Mansa's own mother. He used to go up and down ranting about some women who had no sense to advise their sons to keep their manhoods between their thighs, until they could afford the consequences of letting them loose, and other mothers who had not the courage to tie their daughters to their mats.

'O Lord.'

Yes, my sister.

'Hmm, I never knew any of these things.'

This is because you have been away in *the Mines* all the time. But me, I have been here. I am one of those who sit in that village waiting for the travellers. But also in connection with this story, I have had the chance to know so much because my husband's family house is in that quarter. I say, Mansa's father never let anyone sleep. And so about the sixth month of Mansa's pregnancy, her mother and Auntie Araba decided to do something about the situation. Auntie Araba would take Mansa in, see her through until the baby was born and then later, they would think about what to do. So Mansa went to live with her. And from that moment, people did not even know how to describe the relationship between the two. Some people said they were like mother and daughter. Others that they were like sisters. Still more others even said they were like friends. When the baby was born, Auntie Araba took one or two of her relatives with her to Mansa's parents. Their purpose was simple. Mansa had returned from the battlefield safe. The baby looked strong and sound. If Mansa's father wanted her to go back to school . . .

'Yes, some girls do this.'

But Mansa's father had lost interest in Mansa's education.

'I can understand him.'

I too. So Auntie Araba said that in that case, there was no problem. Mansa was a good girl. Not like one of these *yetse-yetse* things who think putting a toe in a classroom turns them into goddesses. The child and mother should go on living with her until Ato finished his education. Then they could marry properly.

'Our Auntie Araba is going to heaven.'

If there is heaven and God is not like man, my sister.

'What did Mansa's parents say?'

What else could they say? Her mother was very happy. She knew that if Mansa came back to live with them she would always remind her father of everything and then there would never be peace for anybody in the house. They say that from that time, the baking business grew and grew and grew. Mansa's hands pulled in money like a good hunter's gun does with game. Auntie Araba herself became young again. She used to say that if all mothers knew they would get daughters-in-law like Mansa, birth pains would be easier to bear. When her husband Egya Nyaako died, would she not have gone mad if Mansa was not with her? She was afraid of the time when her son would finish college, come and marry Mansa properly and take her away. Three years later, Ato finished college. He is a teacher, as you know, my sister. The government was sending him to teach somewhere far away from here. Then about two weeks or so before Christmas, they got a letter from him that he was coming home.

'Ah, I am sure Mansa was very glad.'

Don't say it loudly, my sister. The news spread very fast. We teased her. 'These days some women go round with a smile playing round their lips all the time. Maybe there is a bird on the neem tree behind their back door which is giving them special good news,' we said. Auntie Araba told her friends that her day of doom was coming upon her. What was she going to do on her own? But her friends knew that she was also very glad. So far, she had looked after her charges very well. But if you boil anything for too long, it burns. Her real glory would come only when her son came to take away his bride and his child.

'And the boy-child was a very handsome somebody too.'

And clever, my sister. Before he was two, he was delighting us all by imitating his grandmother and his mother singing the bread-hawking song. A week before the Saturday Ato was expected, Mansa moved back to her parents' house.

'That was a good thing to do.'

She could not have been better advised. That Saturday, people saw her at her bath quite early. My little girl had caught a fever and I myself had not gone to the farm. When eleven o'clock struck, I met Mansa in the market-place, looking like a festive dish. I asked her if what we had heard was true, that our lord and master was coming on the market-day lorry that afternoon. She said I had heard right.

'Maybe she was very eager to see him and could not wait in the house.'

Could you have waited quietly if you had been her?

'Oh, women. We are to be pitied.'

Tell me, my sister. I had wanted to put a stick under the story and clear it all for you. But we are already in town.

'Yes, look at that crowd. Is Auntie Araba's family house near the mouth of this road?'

Oh yes. Until the town grew to the big thing it is, the Twidan Abusia house was right on the road but now it is behind about four or so other houses. Why?

'I think I can hear singing.'

Yes, you are right.

'She is going to get a good funeral.'

That, my sister, is an answer to a question no one will ask.

'So finish me the story.'

Hmm, kinsman, when the market lorry arrived, there was no Scholar-Teacher-Ato on it.

'No?'

No.

'What did Auntie Araba and Mansa do?'

What could they do? Everyone said that the road always has stories to tell. Perhaps he had only missed the lorry. Perhaps he had fallen ill just on that day or a day or so before. They would wait for a while. Perhaps he would arrive that evening if he thought he could get another lorry, it being a market day. But he did not come any time that Saturday or the next morning. And no one saw him on Monday or Tuesday.

'Ohhh . . .'

They don't say, ohhh. . . . We heard about the middle of the next week — I have forgotten now whether it was the Wednesday or Thursday — that he had come.

'Eheh?'

Nyo. But he brought some news with him. He could not marry Mansa.

'Oh, why? After spoiling her . . .'

If you don't shut up, I will stop.

'Forgive me and go on, my sister.'

Let us stand in this alley here — that is the funeral parlour over there. I don't want anyone to overhear us.

'You are right.'

Chicha Ato said he could not marry Mansa because he had got another girl into trouble.

'Whopei!'

She had been in the college too. Her mother is a big lady and her father is a big man. They said if he did not marry their daughter, they would finish him. . . .

'Whopei!'

His lawyer-father thought it advisable for him to wed that girl soon because they were afraid of what the girl's father would do.

'Whopei!'

So he could not marry our Mansa.

'Whopei!'

They don't say, *Whopei*, my sister.

'So what did they do?'

Who?

'Everybody. Mansa? Auntie Araba?'

What could they do?

'Whopei!'

That was just before you came back to have your third baby, I think.

'About three years ago?'

Yes.

'It was my fourth. I had the third in Aboso but it died.'

Then it was your fourth. Yes, it was just before you came.

'I thought Auntie Araba was not looking like herself. But I had enough troubles of my own and had no eyes to go prying into other people's affairs. . . . So that was that. . . .'

Yes. From then on, Auntie Araba was just lost.

'And Mansa-ah?'

She really is like Auntie herself. She has all of her character. She too is a good woman. If she had stayed here, I am sure someone else would have married her. But she left.

'And the child?'

She left him with her mother. Haven't you seen him since you came?

'No. Because it will not occur to anybody to point him out to me until I ask. And I cannot recognise him from my mind. I do not know him at all.'

He is around, with the other schoolchildren.

'So what does Mansa do?'

When she left everyone said she would become a whore in the city.

'*Whopei*. People are bad.'

Yes. But perhaps they would have been right if Mansa had not been the Mansa we all know. We hear Auntie Araba sent her to a friend and she found her a job with some people. They bake hundreds of loaves of bread an hour with machines.

'A good person does not rot.'

No. She sent money and other things home.

'May God bless her. And Auntie Araba herself?'

As I was telling you. After this affair, she never became herself again. She stopped baking. Immediately. She told her friends that she felt old age was coming on her. Then a few months later, they say she started getting some very bad stomachaches. She tried here, she tried there. Hospitals first, then our own doctors and their herbs. Nothing did any good.

'O our end! Couldn't the hospital doctors cut her up and find out?'

My sister, they say they don't work like that. They have to find out what is wrong before they cut people up.

'And they could not find out what was wrong with Auntie Araba?'

No. She spent whatever she had on this stomach. Egya Nyaako, as you know, had already died. So, about three months ago, she packed up all she had and came here, to squat by her ancestral hearth.

'And yesterday afternoon she died?'

Yes, and yesterday afternoon she died.

'Her spirit was gone.'

Certainly it was her son who drove it away. And then Mansa left with her soul.

'Have you ever seen Chicha Ato's lady-wife?'

No. We hear they had a church wedding. But Auntie Araba did not put her feet there. And he never brought her to Ofuntumase.

'Maybe the two of them may come here today?'

I don't see how he can fail to come. But she, I don't know. Some of these ladies will not set foot in a place like this for fear of getting dirty.

'Hmmm . . . it is their own cassava! But do you think Mansa will come and wail for Auntie Araba?'

My sister, if you have come, do you think Mansa will not?

[1969]

Study and Writing Questions

1. What are the literal and SYMBOLIC uses of bread in this NARRATIVE?
2. What effect do the shifts in and out of English vocabulary and so-called Standard English grammar have on you?
3. What is the effect of the narrative situation on our understanding of Auntie Araba's STORY? Why doesn't Aidoo simply have an OMNISCIENT NARRATOR tell the tale? What use are the repeated SELF-REFLEXIVE comments of the narrator about her own storytelling?

4. Why does this narrative present conflicting systems of religion, medicine, education, economics, and so on? How are these systems treated? What effect(s) has their coexistence on your reading of the story?
5. Why is this narrative set on the way to the funeral as opposed to some other time such as the visiting woman's last or next visit? Will Mansa come? Will Ato? Why does the narrative end as it does? What is the meaning of the narrative?

See also Questions for Contrast and Comparison: 40, 43, 102, 106, 111, 139, 168, and 189.

RYUNOSUKE AKUTAGAWA (1892–1927) *was Japan's first great writer of what Westerners would call* SHORT STORIES. *His writing was highly praised while studying English literature at Tokyo Imperial University by his teacher, Natsume Soseki (1867–1916), the first great Japanese novelist to combine native Japanese forms of* NARRATIVE *diary and chronicle with the Western* NOVEL. *Akutagawa's first published collection,* Rashomon and Other Stories *(1916), made him the leading proponent of narrative* LYRICISM *and opponent of the then-dominant Japanese* "NATURALISM," *which relied for its effects primarily on sordid confessions. His stories* "Rashomon" *and* "In a Grove" *provided the material for Akira Kurosawa's film* Rashomon *(1950), a brilliant exploration of the importance of* VIEW-POINT *and individual* CHARACTER. *Much of Akutagawa's work uses art to make sense of a fragmenting world, whether that fragmentation comes from madness, competing viewpoints, or conflicting* AESTHETIC *traditions. Although he married, as his own health failed, his faith also failed. He feared that, like his mother who had become insane shortly after his birth, he would go mad. At the age of thirty-five, he poisoned himself at home, leaving about a hundred then-unpublished delicately written stories. The Akutagawa Prize, established eight years later, is now Japan's most prestigious award for promising new writers.*

In a Grove

The Testimony of a Woodcutter Questioned by a High Police Commissioner

Yes, sir. Certainly, it was I who found the body. This morning, as usual, I went to cut my daily quota of cedars, when I found the body in a grove in a hollow in the mountains. The exact location? About 150 meters off the Yamashina stage road. It's an out-of-the-way grove of bamboo and cedars.

The body was lying flat on its back dressed in a bluish silk kimono and a wrinkled head-dress of the Kyoto style. A single sword-stroke had pierced the breast. The fallen bamboo-blades around it were stained with bloody blossoms. No, the blood was no longer running. The wound had dried up, I believe. And also, a gad-fly was stuck fast there, hardly noticing my footsteps.

You ask me if I saw a sword or any such thing?

No, nothing, sir. I found only a rope at the root of a cedar near by. And . . . well, in addition to a rope, I found a comb. That was all. Apparently he must have made a battle of it before he was murdered, because the grass and fallen bamboo-blades had been trampled down all around.

"A horse was near by?"

No, sir. It's hard enough for a man to enter, let alone a horse.

The Testimony of a Traveling Buddhist Priest Questioned by a High Police Commissioner

The time? Certainly, it was about noon yesterday, sir. The unfortunate man was on the road from Sekiyama to Yamashina. He was walking toward Sekiyama with a woman accompanying him on horseback, who I have since learned was his wife. A scarf hanging from her head hid her face from view. All I saw was the color of her clothes, a lilac-colored suit. Her horse was a sorrel with a fine mane. The lady's height? Oh, about four feet five inches. Since I am a Buddhist priest, I took little notice about her details. Well, the man was armed with a sword as well as a bow and arrows. And I remember that he carried some twenty odd arrows in his quiver.

Little did I expect that he would meet such a fate. Truly human life is as evanescent as the morning dew or a flash of lightning. My words are inadequate to express my sympathy for him.

The Testimony of a Policeman Questioned by a High Police Commissioner

The man that I arrested? He is a notorious brigand called Tajomaru. When I arrested him, he had fallen off his horse. He was groaning on the bridge at Awataguchi. The time? It was in the early hours of last night. For the record, I might say that the other day I tried to arrest him, but unfortunately he escaped. He was wearing a dark blue silk kimono and a large plain sword. And, as you see, he got a bow and arrows somewhere. You say that this bow and these arrows look like the ones owned by the dead man? Then Tajomaru must be the murderer. The bow wound with leather strips, the black lacquered quiver, the seventeen arrows with hawk feathers—these were all in his possession I believe. Yes, sir, the horse is, as you say, a sorrel with a fine mane. A little beyond the stone bridge I found the horse grazing by the roadside, with his long rein dangling. Surely there is some providence in his having been thrown by the horse.

Of all the robbers prowling around Kyoto, this Tajomaru has given the most grief to the women in town. Last autumn a wife who came to the mountain back of the Pindora of the Toribe Temple, presumably to pay a visit, was murdered, along with a girl. It has been suspected that it was his doing. If this criminal murdered the man, you cannot tell what he may have done with the man's wife. May it please your honor to look into this problem as well.

The Testimony of an Old Woman Questioned by a High Police Commissioner

Yes, sir, that corpse is the man who married my daughter. He does not come from Kyoto. He was a samurai in the town of Kokufu in the province of Wakasa. His name was Kanazawa no Takehiko, and his age was twenty-six. He was of a gentle disposition, so I am sure he did nothing to provoke the anger of others.

My daughter? Her name is Masago, and her age is nineteen. She is a spirited, fun-loving girl, but I am sure she has never known any man except Takehiko. She has a small, oval, dark-complected face with a mole at the corner of her left eye.

Yesterday Takehiko left for Wakasa with my daughter. What bad luck it is that things should have come to such a sad end! What has become of my daughter? I am resigned to giving up my son-in-law as lost, but the fate of my daughter worries me sick. For heaven's sake leave no stone unturned to find her. I hate that robber Tajomaru, or whatever his name is. Not only my son-in-law, but my daughter . . . (Her later words were drowned in tears.)

Tajomaru's Confession

I killed him, but not her. Where's she gone? I can't tell. Oh, wait a minute. No torture can make me confess what I don't know. Now things have come to such a head, I won't keep anything from you.

Yesterday a little past noon I met that couple. Just then a puff of wind blew, and raised her hanging scarf, so that I caught a glimpse of her face. Instantly it was again covered from my view. That may have been one reason; she looked like a Bodhisattva. At that moment I made up my mind to capture her even if I had to kill her man.

Why? To me killing isn't a matter of such great consequence as you might think. When a woman is captured, her man has to be killed anyway. In killing, I use the sword I wear at my side. Am I the only one who kills people? You, you don't use your swords. You kill people with your power, with your money. Sometimes you kill them on the pretext of working for their good. It's true they don't bleed. They are in the best of health, but all the same you've killed them. It's hard to say who is a greater sinner, you or me. (An ironical smile.)

But it would be good if I could capture a woman without killing her man. So, I made up my mind to capture her, and do my best not to kill him. But it's out of the question on the Yamashina stage road. So I managed to lure the couple into the mountains.

It was quite easy. I became their traveling companion, and I told them there was an old mound in the mountain over there, and that I had dug it open and found many mirrors and swords. I went on to tell them I'd buried the things in a grove behind the mountain, and that I'd like to sell them at a low price to anyone who would care to have them. Then . . . you see, isn't greed terrible? He was beginning to be moved by my talk before he knew it. In less than half an hour they were driving their horse toward the mountain with me.

When he came in front of the grove, I told them that the treasures were buried in it, and I asked them to come and see. The man had no objection—he was blinded by greed. The woman said she would wait on horseback. It was natural for her to say so, at the sight of a thick grove. To tell you the truth, my plan worked just as I wished, so I went into the grove with him, leaving her behind alone.

The grove is only bamboo for some distance. About fifty yards ahead there's a rather open clump of cedars. It was a convenient spot for my purpose. Pushing my way through the grove, I told him a plausible lie that the treasures were buried under the cedars. When I told him this, he pushed his laborious way toward the slender cedar visible through the grove. After a while the bamboo thinned out, and we came to where a number of cedars grew in a row. As soon as we got there, I seized him from behind. Because he was a trained, sword-bearing warrior, he was quite strong, but he was taken by surprise, so there was no help for him. I soon tied him up to the root of a cedar. Where did I get a rope? Thank heaven, being a robber, I had a rope with me, since I might have to scale a wall at any moment. Of course it was easy to stop him from calling out by gagging his mouth with fallen bamboo leaves.

When I disposed of him, I went to his woman and asked her to come and see him, because he seemed to have been suddenly taken sick. It's needless to say that this plan also worked well. The woman, her sedge hat off, came into the depths of the grove, where I led her by the hand. The instant she caught sight of her husband, she drew a small sword. I've never seen a woman of such violent temper. If I'd been off guard, I'd have got a thrust in my side. I dodged, but she kept on slashing at me. She might have wounded me deeply or killed me. But I'm

Tajomaru. I managed to strike down her small sword without drawing my own. The most spirited woman is defenseless without a weapon. At last I could satisfy my desire for her without taking her husband's life.

Yes, . . . without taking his life. I had no wish to kill him. I was about to run away from the grove, leaving the woman behind in tears, when she frantically clung to my arm. In broken fragments of words, she asked that either her husband or I die. She said it was more trying than death to have her shame known to two men. She gasped out that she wanted to be the wife of whichever survived. Then a furious desire to kill him seized me. (Gloomy excitement.)

Telling you in this way, no doubt I seem a crueler man than you. But that's because you didn't see her face. Especially her burning eyes at that moment. As I saw her eye to eye, I wanted to make her my wife even if I were to be struck by lightning. I wanted to make her my wife . . . this single desire filled my mind. This was not only lust, as you might think. At that time if I'd had no other desire than lust, I'd surely not have minded knocking her down and running away. Then I wouldn't have stained my sword with his blood. But the moment I gazed at her face in the dark grove, I decided not to leave there without killing him.

But I didn't like to resort to unfair means to kill him. I untied him and told him to cross swords with me. (The rope that was found at the root of the cedar is the rope I dropped at the time.) Furious with anger, he drew his thick sword. And quick as thought, he sprang at me ferociously, without speaking a word. I needn't tell you how our fight turned out. The twenty-third stroke . . . please remember this. I'm impressed with this fact still. Nobody under the sun has ever clashed swords with me twenty strokes. (A cheerful smile.)

When he fell, I turned toward her, lowering my blood-stained sword. But to my great astonishment she was gone. I wondered to where she had run away. I looked for her in the clump of cedars. I listened, but heard only a groaning sound from the throat of the dying man.

As soon as we started to cross swords, she may have run away through the grove to call for help. When I thought of that, I decided it was a matter of life and death to me. So, robbing him of his sword, and bow and arrows, I ran out to the mountain road. There I found her horse still grazing quietly. It would be a mere waste of words to tell you the later details, but before I entered town I had already parted with the sword. That's all my confession. I know that my head will be hung in chains anyway, so put me down for the maximum penalty. (A defiant attitude.)

The Confession of a Woman Who Has Come to the *Shimizu* Temple

That man in the blue silk kimono, after forcing me to yield to him, laughed mockingly as he looked at my bound husband. How horrified my husband must have been! But no matter how hard he struggled in agony, the rope cut into him all the more tightly. In spite of myself I ran stumblingly toward his side. Or rather I tried to run toward him, but the man instantly knocked me down. Just at that moment I saw an indescribable light in my husband's eyes. Something beyond expression . . . his eyes make me shudder even now. That instantaneous look of my husband, who couldn't speak a word, told me all his heart. The flash in his eyes was neither anger nor sorrow . . . only a cold light, a look of loathing.

More struck by the look in his eyes than by the blow of the thief, I called out in spite of myself and fell unconscious.

In the course of time I came to, and found that the man in blue silk was gone. I saw only my husband still bound to the root of the cedar. I raised myself from the bamboo-blades with difficulty, and looked into his face; but the expression in his eyes was just the same as before.

Beneath the cold contempt in his eyes, there was hatred. Shame, grief, and anger . . . I don't know how to express my heart at that time. Reeling to my feet, I went up to my husband.

"Takejiro," I said to him, "since things have come to this pass, I cannot live with you. I'm determined to die, . . . but you must die, too. You saw my shame. I can't leave you alive as you are."

This was all I could say. Still he went on gazing at me with loathing and contempt. My heart breaking, I looked for his sword. It must have been taken by the robber. Neither his sword nor his bow and arrows were to be seen in the grove. But fortunately my small sword was lying at my feet. Raising it over head, once more I said, "Now give me your life. I'll follow you right away."

When he heard these words, he moved his lips with difficulty. Since his mouth was stuffed with leaves, of course his voice could not be heard at all. But at a glance I understood his words. Despising me, his look said only, "Kill me." Neither conscious nor unconscious, I stabbed the small sword through the lilac-colored kimono into his breast.

Again at this time I must have fainted. By the time I managed to look up, he had already breathed his last—still in bonds. A streak of sinking sunlight streamed through the clump of cedars and bamboos, and shone on his pale face. Gulping down my sobs, I untied the rope from his dead body. And . . . and what has become of me since I have no more strength to tell you. Anyway I hadn't the strength to die. I stabbed my own throat with the small sword, I threw myself into a pond at the foot of the mountain, and I tried to kill myself in many ways. Unable to end my life, I am still living in dishonor. (A lonely smile.) Worthless as I am, I must have been forsaken even by the most merciful Kwannon. I killed my own husband. I was violated by the robber. Whatever can I do? Whatever can I . . . I . . . . (Gradually, violent sobbing.)

The Story of the Murdered Man, as Told through a Medium
After violating my wife, the robber, sitting there, began to speak comforting words to her. Of course I couldn't speak. My whole body was tied fast to the root of a cedar. But meanwhile I winked at her many times, as much as to say "Don't believe the robber." I wanted to convey some such meaning to her. But my wife, sitting dejectedly on the bamboo leaves, was looking hard at her lap. To all appearance, she was listening to his words. I was agonized by jealousy. In the meantime the robber went on with his clever talk, from one subject to another. The robber finally made his bold, brazen proposal. "Once your virtue is stained, you won't get along well with your husband, so won't you be my wife instead? It's my love for you that made me be violent toward you."

While the criminal talked, my wife raised her face as if in a trance. She had never looked so beautiful as at that moment. What did my beautiful wife say in answer to him while I was sitting bound there? I am lost in space, but I have never thought of her answer without burning with anger and jealousy. Truly she said, . . . "Then take me away with you wherever you go."

This is not the whole of her sin. If that were all, I would not be tormented so much in the dark. When she was going out of the grove as if in a dream, her hand in the robber's, she suddenly turned pale, and pointed at me tied to the root of the cedar, and said, "Kill him! I cannot marry you as long as he lives." "Kill him!" she cried many times, as if she had gone crazy. Even now these words threaten to blow me headlong into the bottomless abyss of darkness. Has such a hateful thing come out of a human mouth ever before? Have such cursed words ever struck a human ear, even once? Even once such a . . . (A sudden cry of scorn.) At these words the robber himself turned pale. "Kill him," she cried, clinging to his arms. Looking hard at her, he answered neither yes nor no. . . . but hardly had I thought about his answer before she had been knocked down into the bamboo leaves. (Again a cry of scorn.) Quietly folding his arms, he looked at me and said, "What will you do with her? Kill her or save her? You have only to nod. Kill her?" For these words alone I would like to pardon his crime.

While I hesitated, she shrieked and ran into the depths of the grove. The robber instantly snatched at her, but he failed even to grasp her sleeve.

After she ran away, he took up my sword, and my bow and arrows. With a single stroke he cut one of my bonds. I remember his mumbling, "My fate is next." Then he disappeared from the grove. All was silent after that. No, I heard someone crying. Untying the rest of my bonds, I listened carefully, and I noticed that it was my own crying. (Long silence.)

I raised my exhausted body from the root of the cedar. In front of me there was shining the small sword which my wife had dropped. I took it up and stabbed it into my breast. A bloody lump rose to my mouth, but I didn't feel any pain. When my breast grew cold, everything was as silent as the dead in their graves. What profound silence! Not a single bird-note was heard in the sky over this grave in the hollow of the mountains. Only a lonely light lingered on the cedars and mountain. By and by the light gradually grew fainter, till the cedars and bamboo were lost to view. Lying there, I was enveloped in deep silence.

Then someone crept up to me. I tried to see who it was. But darkness had already been gathering round me. Someone . . . that someone drew the small sword softly out of my breast in its invisible hand. At the same time once more blood flowed into my mouth. And once and for all I sank down into the darkness of space.

[1922]

Study and Writing Questions

1. The headings of the sections identify both the speakers and the speaking situations. What are the effects of having these headings? What do we come to know about the speaking situations? How does this NARRATIVE technique — serial monologues — shape our understanding of the relationship here between STORY and PLOT?

2. The voices of the individual speakers are quite similar, perhaps because each is making a formal testimony; nonetheless, they reveal some individual differences. How are the speakers marked as individuals by their speech?

3. If read separately, would all these speakers be equally believable? If not, why not? What makes one individual more or less believable than another here?
4. In this story, what seems to be the importance of confession? Why do three people confess here? What are their individual MOTIVES? What is the THEMATIC significance of combining motives in a single narrative?
5. What is the significance of the title? What might a grove represent here? How does it enter into the individual testimonies and into the narrative as a whole?

See also Questions for Contrast and Comparison: 3, 14, 16, 45, 54, 92, 114, 119, 139, and 217.

WOODY ALLEN (1935–) *was born Stewart Allen Konigsberg in Brook-lyn, New York, but his name was legally changed to Heywood Allen. While still in high school, he began writing jokes for such early television comedy stars as Sid Caesar and Jack Paar and became a staff writer for the National Broadcasting Company (NBC) at seventeen. Although he attended both New York University and City College of New York, he graduated from neither, finding his real educa-tion in his work. His first filmscript was a rewrite job that became* What's New, Pussycat? *(1965), the highest grossing comedy at that time. Known primarily as a filmmaker, he has written and directed such zany comedies as* Sleeper *(1973) and more serious works such as* Crimes and Misdemeanors *(1989). His film* Annie Hall *(1977) won Academy Awards for best director and best original screenplay. His comic prose pieces appear in such magazines as* Esquire, The New Yorker, *and* Playboy, *and have been issued in three collections (*Getting Even, *1971;* Without Feathers, *1975;* Side Effects, *1980). His persistent concerns with philosophy, litera-ture, sexuality, death, other filmmakers, and his Jewish identity have marked Allen as an artist of high seriousness, but "people have always thought of me as an intellectual comedian," he wrote, "and I'm not. I'm a one-liner comic like Bob Hope . . . I'm not moralizing or didactic in any way. . . . I just want to be funny."*

The Whore of Mensa

One thing about being a private investigator, you've got to learn to go with your hunches. That's why when a quivering pat of butter named Word Babcock walked into my office and laid his cards on the table, I should have trusted the cold chill that shot up my spine.

"Kaiser?" he said, "Kaiser Lupowitz?"

"That's what it says on my license," I owned up.

"You've got to help me. I'm being blackmailed. Please!"

He was shaking like the lead singer in a rumba band. I pushed a glass across the desk top and a bottle of rye I keep handy for nonmedicinal purposes. "Suppose you relax and tell me all about it."

"You . . . you won't tell my wife?"

"Level with me, Word. I can't make any promises."

He tried pouring a drink, but you could hear the clicking sound across the street, and most of the stuff wound up in his shoes.

"I'm a working guy," he said. "Mechanical maintenance. I build and service joy buzzers. You know — those little fun gimmicks that give people a shock when they shake hands?"

"So?"

"A lot of your executives like 'em. Particularly down on Wall Street."

"Get to the point."

"I'm on the road a lot. You know how it is — lonely. Oh, not what you're thinking. See, Kaiser, I'm basically an intellectual. Sure, a guy can meet all the bimbos he wants. But the really brainy women — they're not so easy to find on short notice."

"Keep talking."

"Well, I heard of this young girl. Eighteen years old. A Vassar student. For a price, she'll come over and discuss any subject—Proust, Yeats, anthropology. Exchange of ideas. You see what I'm driving at?"

"Not exactly."

"I mean, my wife is great, don't get me wrong. But she won't discuss Pound with me. Or Eliot. I didn't know that when I married her. See, I need a woman who's mentally stimulating, Kaiser. And I'm willing to pay for it. I don't want an involvement—I want a quick intellectual experience, then I want the girl to leave. Christ, Kaiser, I'm a happily married man."

"How long has this been going on?"

"Six months. Whenever I have that craving, I call Flossie. She's a madam, with a master's in comparative lit. She sends me over an intellectual, see?"

So he was one of those guys whose weakness was really bright women. I felt sorry for the poor sap. I figured there must be a lot of jokers in his position, who were starved for a little intellectual communication with the opposite sex and would pay through the nose for it.

"Now she's threatening to tell my wife," he said.

"Who is?"

"Flossie. They bugged the motel room. They got tapes of me discussing *The Waste Land* and *Styles of Radical Will*, and, well, really getting into some issues. They want ten grand or they go to Carla. Kaiser, you've got to help me! Carla would die if she knew she didn't turn me on up here."

The old call-girl racket. I had heard rumors that the boys at headquarters were on to something involving a group of educated women, but so far they were stymied.

"Get Flossie on the phone for me."

"What?"

"I'll take your case, Word. But I get fifty dollars a day, plus expenses. You'll have to repair a lot of joy buzzers."

"It won't be ten Gs' worth, I'm sure of that," he said with a grin, and picked up the phone and dialed a number. I took it from him and winked. I was beginning to like him.

Seconds later, a silky voice answered, and I told her what was on my mind. "I understand you can help me set up an hour of good chat," I said.

"Sure, honey. What do you have in mind?"

"I'd like to discuss Melville."

"*Moby Dick* or the shorter novels?"

"What's the difference?"

"The price. That's all. Symbolism's extra."

"What'll it run me?"

"Fifty, maybe a hundred for *Moby Dick*. You want a comparative discussion—Melville and Hawthorne? That could be arranged for a hundred."

"The dough's fine," I told her and gave her the number of a room at the Plaza.

"You want a blonde or a brunette?"

"Surprise me," I said, and hung up.

I shaved and grabbed some black coffee while I checked over the Monarch College Outline series. Hardly an hour had passed before there was a knock on my door. I opened it, and standing there was a young redhead who was packed into her slacks like two big scoops of vanilla ice cream.

"Hi, I'm Sherry."

They really knew how to appeal to your fantasies. Long straight hair, leather bag, silver earrings, no make-up.

"I'm surprised you weren't stopped, walking into the hotel dressed like that," I said. "The house dick can usually spot an intellectual."

"A five-spot cools him."

"Shall we begin?" I said, motioning her to the couch.

She lit a cigarette and got right to it. "I think we could start by approaching *Billy Budd* as Melville's justification of the ways of God to man, *n'est-ce pas?*"

"Interestingly, though, not in a Miltonian sense." I was bluffing. I wanted to see if she'd go for it.

"No. *Paradise Lost* lacked the substructure of pessimism." She did.

"Right, right. God, you're right," I murmured.

"I think Melville reaffirmed the virtues of innocence in a naïve yet sophisticated sense — don't you agree?"

I let her go on. She was barely nineteen years old, but already she had developed the hardened facility of the pseudo-intellectual. She rattled off her ideas glibly, but it was all mechanical. Whenever I offered an insight, she faked a response: "Oh, yes, Kaiser. Yes, baby, that's deep. A platonic comprehension of Christianity — why didn't I see it before?"

We talked for about an hour and then she said she had to go. She stood up and I laid a C-note on her.

"Thanks, honey."

"There's plenty more where that came from."

"What are you trying to say?"

I had piqued her curiosity. She sat down again.

"Suppose I wanted to — have a party?" I said.

"Like, what kind of party?"

"Suppose I wanted Noam Chomsky explained to me by two girls?"

"Oh, wow."

"If you'd rather forget it . . ."

"You'd have to speak with Flossie," she said. "It'd cost you."

Now was the time to tighten the screws. I flashed my private-investigator's badge and informed her it was a bust.

"What!"

"I'm fuzz, sugar, and discussing Melville for money is an 802. You can do time."

"You louse!"

"Better come clean, baby. Unless you want to tell your story down at Alfred Kazin's office, and I don't think he'd be too happy to hear it."

She began to cry. "Don't turn me in, Kaiser," she said. "I needed the money to complete my master's. I've been turned down for a grant. *Twice.* Oh, Christ."

It all poured out — the whole story. Central Park West upbringing, Socialist summer camps, Brandeis. She was every dame you saw waiting in line at the Elgin or the Thalia, or penciling the words "Yes, very true" into the margin of some book on Kant. Only somewhere along the line she had made a wrong turn.

"I needed cash. A girl friend said she knew a married guy whose wife wasn't very profound. He was into Blake. She couldn't hack it. I said sure, for a price I'd talk Blake with him. I was nervous at first. I faked a lot of it. He didn't care. My friend said there were others. Oh, I've been busted before. I got caught reading *Commentary* in a parked car, and I was once stopped and frisked at Tanglewood. Once more and I'm a three-time loser."

"Then take me to Flossie."

She bit her lip and said, "The Hunter College Book Store is a front."

"Yes?"

"Like those bookie joints that have barbershops outside for show. You'll see."

I made a quick call to headquarters and then said to her, "Okay, sugar. You're off the hook. But don't leave town."

She tilted her face up toward mine gratefully. "I can get you photographs of Dwight Macdonald reading," she said.

"Some other time."

I walked into the Hunter College Book Store. The salesman, a young man with sensitive eyes, came up to me. "Can I help you?" he said.

"I'm looking for a special edition of *Advertisements for Myself*. I understand the author had several thousand gold-leaf copies printed up for friends."

"I'll have to check," he said. "We have a WATS line to Mailer's house."

I fixed him with a look. "Sherry sent me," I said.

"Oh, in that case, go on back," he said. He pressed a button. A wall of books opened, and I walked like a lamb into that bustling pleasure palace known as Flossie's.

Red flocked wallpaper and a Victorian décor set the tone. Pale, nervous girls with black-rimmed glasses and blunt-cut hair lolled around on sofas, riffling Penguin Classics provocatively. A blonde with a big smile winked at me, nodded toward a room upstairs, and said, "Wallace Stevens, eh?" But it wasn't just intellectual experiences—they were peddling emotional ones, too. For fifty bucks, I learned, you could "relate without getting close." For a hundred, a girl would lend you her Bartók records, have dinner, and then let you watch while she had an anxiety attack. For one-fifty, you could listen to FM radio with twins. For three bills, you got the works: A thin Jewish brunette would pretend to pick you up at the Museum of Modern Art, let you read her master's, get you involved in a screaming quarrel at Elaine's over Freud's conception of women, and then fake a suicide of your choosing—the perfect evening, for some guys. Nice racket. Great town, New York.

"Like what you see?" a voice said behind me. I turned and suddenly found myself standing face to face with the business end of a .38. I'm a guy with a strong stomach, but this time it did a back flip. It was Flossie, all right. The voice was the same, but Flossie was a man. His face was hidden by a mask.

"You'll never believe this," he said, "but I don't even have a college degree. I was thrown out for low grades."

"Is that why you wear that mask?"

"I devised a complicated scheme to take over *The New York Review of Books*, but it meant I had to pass for Lionel Trilling. I went to Mexico for an operation. There's a doctor in Juarez who gives people Trilling's features—for a price.

Something went wrong. I came out looking like Auden, with Mary McCarthy's voice. That's when I started working the other side of the law."

Quickly, before he could tighten his finger on the trigger, I went into action. Heaving forward, I snapped my elbow across his jaw and grabbed the gun as he fell back. He hit the ground like a ton of bricks. He was still whimpering when the police showed up.

"Nice work, Kaiser," Sergeant Holmes said. "When we're through with this guy, the F.B.I. wants to have a talk with him. A little matter involving some gamblers and an annotated copy of Dante's *Inferno*. Take him away, boys."

Later that night, I looked up an old account of mine named Gloria. She was blond. She had graduated *cum laude*. The difference was she majored in physical education. It felt good.

[1974]

Study and Writing Questions

1. Is there any THEMATIC significance to the fact that the client repairs joy buzzers? Are there other details that relate to the theme in the same way? Why does the author use details in this way?
2. How does Allen create a PARODY of the HARD BOILED DETECTIVE story? Does this parody accomplish anything besides giving us the pleasure of BURLESQUE?
3. In what way, if any, is the ending a satisfying RESOLUTION for this NARRATIVE? In what way, if any, is it disappointing?
4. What sort of equation does the narrative draw between intellect and sex?
5. Track down a significant number of the many books and writers mentioned in the narrative. (You may want to consult some of the reference books noted in the *Getting Ideas* section of "Writing About Narratives.") Are these ALLUSIONS merely decorative in this narrative or are they essential?

See also Questions for Contrast and Comparison: 41, 131, 133, 147, 152, 205, and 231.

■ SHERWOOD ANDERSON (1876–1941) *was born in Camden, Ohio. Although he spent most of his life in small American towns, he also traveled to Europe and lived occasionally in New York, Chicago, and New Orleans. Despite little schooling, he had some success in several businesses. He began writing (1909) as self-therapy and as possible career training. In 1912, he had a mental breakdown, abandoned his mail-order paint company, and began writing in earnest. Although he later held other business positions, and for a time edited one town's two weekly newspapers (one Republican, one Democrat), his focus through four marriages and many changes of locale remained writing. Winesburg, Ohio (1919), his master-piece, is a connected collection of stories (of which "Hands" is first), portraying one town through glimpses of its people. His other notable writings include story collections (The Triumph of the Egg, 1921, and Horses and Men, 1923), novels (Poor White, 1920, about the onslaught of industrialism, and Dark Laughter, 1924, about love and restlessness), and a quasi-autobiography (A Story Teller's Story, 1924). While Anderson was greatly influenced by Gertrude Stein, both Ernest Hemingway and William Faulkner acknowledged the importance of his early encouragement. On a self-styled goodwill cruise to Latin America, Anderson swallowed a toothpick, perforated his intestine, and died of peritonitis.*

Hands

Upon the half decayed veranda of a small frame house that stood near the edge of a ravine near the town of Winesburg, Ohio, a fat little old man walked nervously up and down. Across a long field that had been seeded for clover but that had produced only a dense crop of yellow mustard weeds, he could see the public highway along which went a wagon filled with berry pickers returning from the fields. The berry pickers, youths and maidens, laughed and shouted boisterously. A boy clad in a blue shirt leaped from the wagon and attempted to drag after him one of the maidens, who screamed and protested shrilly. The feet of the boy in the road kicked up a cloud of dust that floated across the face of the departing sun. Over the long field came a thin girlish voice. "Oh, you Wing Biddlebaum, comb your hair, it's falling into your eyes," commanded the voice to the man, who was bald and whose nervous little hands fiddled about the bare white forehead as though arranging a mass of tangled locks.

Wing Biddlebaum, forever frightened and beset by a ghostly band of doubts, did not think of himself as in any way a part of the life of the town where he had lived for twenty years. Among all the people of Winesburg but one had come close to him. With George Willard, son of Tom Willard, the proprietor of the New Willard House, he had formed something like a friendship. George Willard was the reporter on the *Winesburg Eagle* and sometimes in the evenings he walked out along the highway to Wing Biddlebaum's house. Now as the old man walked up and down on the veranda, his hands moving nervously about, he was hoping that George Willard would come and spend the evening with him. After the wagon containing the berry pickers had passed, he went across the field through the tall mustard weeds and climbing a rail fence peered anxiously along the road to the town. For a moment he stood thus, rubbing his hands together and looking up and down the road, and then, fear overcoming him, ran back to walk again upon the porch on his own house.

In the presence of George Willard, Wing Biddlebaum, who for twenty years had been the town mystery, lost something of his timidity, and his shadowy personality, submerged in a sea of doubts, came forth to look at the world. With the young reporter at his side, he ventured in the light of day into Main Street or strode up and down on the rickety front porch of his own house, talking excitedly. The voice that had been low and trembling became shrill and loud. The bent figure straightened. With a kind of wriggle, like a fish returned to the brook by the fisherman, Biddlebaum the silent began to talk, striving to put into words the ideas that had been accumulated by his mind during long years of silence.

Wing Biddlebaum talked much with his hands. The slender expressive fingers, forever active, forever striving to conceal themselves in his pockets or behind his back, came forth and became the piston rods of his machinery of expression.

The story of Wing Biddlebaum is a story of hands. Their restless activity, like unto the beating of the wings of an imprisoned bird, had given him his name. Some obscure poet of the town had thought of it. The hands alarmed their owner. He wanted to keep them hidden away and looked with amazement at the quiet inexpressive hands of other men who worked beside him in the fields, or passed, driving sleepy teams on country roads.

When he talked to George Willard, Wing Biddlebaum closed his fists and beat with them upon a table or on the walls of his house. The action made him more comfortable. If the desire to talk came to him when the two were walking in the fields, he sought out a stump or the top board of a fence and with his hands pounding busily talked with renewed ease.

The story of Wing Biddlebaum's hands is worth a book in itself. Sympathetically set forth it would tap many strange, beautiful qualities in obscure men. It is a job for a poet. In Winesburg the hands had attracted attention merely because of their activity. With them Wing Biddlebaum had picked as high as a hundred and forty quarts of strawberries in a day. They became his distinguishing feature, the source of his fame. Also they made more grotesque an already grotesque and elusive individuality. Winesburg was proud of the hands of Wing Biddlebaum in the same spirit in which it was proud of Banker White's new stone house and Wesley Moyer's bay stallion, Tony Tip, that had won the two-fifteen trot at the fall races in Cleveland.

As for George Willard, he had many times wanted to ask about the hands. At times an almost overwhelming curiosity had taken hold of him. He felt that there must be a reason for their strange activity and their inclination to keep hidden away and only a growing respect for Wing Biddlebaum kept him from blurting out the questions that were often in his mind.

Once he had been on the point of asking. The two were walking in the fields on a summer afternoon and had stopped to sit upon a grassy bank. All afternoon Wing Biddlebaum had talked as one inspired. By a fence he had stopped and beating like a giant woodpecker upon the top board had shouted at George Willard, condemning his tendency to be too much influenced by the people about him. "You are destroying yourself," he cried. "You have the inclination to be alone and to dream and you are afraid of dreams. You want to be like others in town here. You hear them talk and you try to imitate them."

On the grassy bank Wing Biddlebaum had tried again to drive his point home. His voice became soft and reminiscent, and with a sigh of contentment he launched into a long rambling talk, speaking as one lost in a dream.

Out of the dream Wing Biddlebaum made a picture for George Willard. In the picture men lived again in a kind of pastoral golden age. Across a green open country came clean-limbed young men, some afoot, some mounted upon horses. In crowds the young men came to gather about the feet of an old man who sat beneath a tree in a tiny garden and who talked to them.

Wing Biddlebaum became wholly inspired. For once he forgot the hands. Slowly they stole forth and lay upon George Willard's shoulders. Something new and bold came into the voice that talked. "You must try to forget all you have learned," said the old man. "You must begin to dream. From this time on you must shut your ears to the roaring of the voices."

Pausing in his speech, Wing Biddlebaum looked long and earnestly at George Willard. His eyes glowed. Again he raised the hands to caress the boy and then a look of horror swept over his face.

With a convulsive movement of his body, Wing Biddlebaum sprang to his feet and thrust his hands deep into his trousers pockets. Tears came to his eyes. "I must be getting along home. I can talk no more with you," he said nervously.

Without looking back, the old man had hurried down the hillside and across a meadow, leaving George Willard perplexed and frightened upon the grassy slope. With a shiver of dread the boy arose and went along the road toward town. "I'll not ask him about his hands," he thought, touched by the memory of the terror he had seen in the man's eyes. "There's something wrong, but I don't want to know what it is. His hands have something to do with his fear of me and of everyone."

And George Willard was right. Let us look briefly into the story of the hands. Perhaps our talking of them will arouse the poet who will tell the hidden wonder story of the influence for which the hands were but fluttering pennants of promise.

In his youth Wing Biddlebaum had been a school teacher in a town in Pennsylvania. He was not then known as Wing Biddlebaum, but went by the less euphonic name of Adolph Myers. As Adolph Myers he was much loved by the boys of his school.

Adolph Myers was meant by nature to be a teacher of youth. He was one of those rare, little-understood men who rule by a power so gentle that it passes as a lovable weakness. In their feeling for the boys under their charge such men are not unlike the finer sort of women in their love of men.

And yet that is but crudely stated. It needs the poet there. With the boys of his school, Adolph Myers had walked in the evening or had sat talking until dusk upon the schoolhouse steps lost in a kind of dream. Here and there went his hands, caressing the shoulders of the boys, playing about the tousled heads. As he talked his voice became soft and musical. There was a caress in that also. In a way the voice and the hands, the stroking of the shoulders and the touching of the hair were a part of the schoolmaster's effort to carry a dream into the young minds. By the caress that was in his fingers he expressed himself. He was one of those men in whom the force that creates life is diffused, not centralized. Under the caress of his hands doubt and disbelief went out of the minds of the boys and they began also to dream.

And then the tragedy. A half-witted boy of the school became enamored of the young master. In his bed at night he imagined unspeakable things and in the morning went forth to tell his dreams as facts. Strange, hideous accusations fell from his loose-hung lips. Through the Pennsylvania town went a shiver. Hidden, shadowy doubts that had been in men's minds concerning Adolph Myers were galvanized into beliefs.

The tragedy did not linger. Trembling lads were jerked out of bed and questioned. "He put his arms about me," said one. "His fingers were always playing in my hair," said another.

One afternoon a man of the town, Henry Bradford, who kept a saloon, came to the schoolhouse door. Calling Adolph Myers into the school yard he began to beat him with his fists. As his hard knuckles beat down into the frightened face of the schoolmaster, his wrath became more and more terrible. Screaming with dismay, the children ran here and there like disturbed insects. "I'll teach you to put your hands on my boy, you beast," roared the saloon keeper, who, tired of beating the master, had begun to kick him about the yard.

Adolph Myers was driven from the Pennsylvania town in the night. With lanterns in their hands a dozen men came to the door of the house where he lived alone and commanded that he dress and come forth. It was raining and one of the men had a rope in his hands. They had intended to hang the schoolmaster, but something in his figure, so small, white, and pitiful, touched their hearts and they let him escape. As he ran away into the darkness they repented of their weakness and ran after him, swearing and throwing sticks and great balls of soft mud at the figure that screamed and ran faster and faster into the darkness.

For twenty years Adolph Myers had lived alone in Winesburg. He was but forty but looked sixty-five. The name of Biddlebaum he got from a box of goods seen at a freight station as he hurried through an eastern Ohio town. He had an aunt in Winesburg, a black-toothed old woman who raised chickens, and with her he lived until she died. He had been ill for a year after the experience in Pennsylvania, and after his recovery worked as a day laborer in the fields, going timidly about and striving to conceal his hands. Although he did not understand what had happened he felt that the hands must be to blame. Again and again the fathers of the boys had talked of the hands. "Keep your hands to yourself," the saloon keeper had roared, dancing with fury in the schoolhouse yard.

Upon the veranda of his house by the ravine, Wing Biddlebaum continued to walk up and down until the sun had disappeared and the road beyond the field was lost in the grey shadows. Going into his house he cut slices of bread and spread honey upon them. When the rumble of the evening train that took away the express cars loaded with the day's harvest of berries had passed and restored the silence of the summer night, he went again to walk upon the veranda. In the darkness he could not see the hands and they became quiet. Although he still hungered for the presence of the boy, who was the medium through which he expressed his love of man, the hunger became again a part of his loneliness and his waiting. Lighting a lamp, Wing Biddlebaum washed the few dishes soiled by his simple meal and, setting up a folding cot by the screen door that led to the porch, prepared to undress for the night. A few stray white bread crumbs lay on the cleanly washed floor by the table; putting the lamp upon a low stool he began to pick up the crumbs, carrying them to his mouth one by one with unbelievable rapidity. In the dense blotch of light beneath the table, the kneeling figure looked like a priest engaged in some service of his church. The nervous expressive fingers, flashing in and out of the light, might well have been mistaken for the fingers of the devotee going swiftly through decade after decade of his rosary.

[1919]

Study and Writing Questions

1. What characteristics of George Willard make him the one person to whom Wing Biddlebaum really speaks? Is there any relationship between Willard's role as "reporter" and the NARRATOR's recurring comments about "the poet"?
2. How is the town of Winesburg characterized? Is it different from the town Wing left? What is the SYMBOLISM of its name?
3. Detail the structure of this NARRATIVE. How is the STORY DEFAMILIARIZED into PLOT? Why is it changed in those ways? Does the narrative VIEWPOINT change or only appear to change? Why is it treated this way?
4. What is the symbolism of the first paragraph? What does each IMAGE and ACTION represent? Why is this an effective opening paragraph for this narrative?
5. What are the meanings of the title concept in this narrative? Why does the narrative end with a rosary? Does this narrative have a DIDACTIC effect? What, finally, is this narrative about?

See also Questions for Contrast and Comparison: 33, 58, 96, 102, 104, 106, 134, 167, 220, and 229.

ISAAC ASIMOV (1920–1992), *born in Petrovichi, U.S.S.R., was brought to Brooklyn, New York at three. The glossy magazines in his father's candy store attracted him, but, forbidden to read "junk," he devoured classics until Science Wonder Stories appeared in 1929. The word "science" convinced Judah Asimov to let Isaac peruse the pulps. By age eleven, he was attempting fiction himself. He earned chemistry degrees from Columbia University (B.S., 1939; M.A., 1941; Ph.D., 1948) with a four year interruption for war-time service. Although Asimov coined the term "robotics," it was his mentor, John W. Campbell, Jr., the great editor of science fiction's "Golden Age," who formulated Asimov's "Three Laws of Robotics: (1) A robot may not injure a human being, or, through inaction, allow a human being to come to harm. (2) A robot must obey the orders given it by human beings except where such orders would conflict with the First Law. (3) A robot must protect its own existence as long as such protection does not conflict with the First or Second Law." These shaped many works, not all by Asimov. Asimov won numerous prestigious awards, including a special Hugo naming his Foundation Trilogy, based on Gibbon's Decline and Fall of the Roman Empire, as the best science fiction series of all time. He was one of the world's most prolific authors, publishing over four hundred works of science fiction, mystery, criticism, autobiography, history, and popular science.*

Reason

The Three Laws of Robotics

1 — A robot may not injure a human being, or, through inaction, allow a human being to come to harm.

2 — A robot must obey the orders given it by human beings except where such orders would conflict with the First Law.

3 — A robot must protect its own existence as long as such protection does not conflict with the First or Second Law.

Handbook of Robotics,
56th Edition, 2058 A.D.

The flame of a giant sun had given way to the soft blackness of space but external variations mean little in the business of checking the workings of experimental robots. Whatever the background, one is face to face with an inscrutable positronic brain, which the slide-rule geniuses say should work thus-and-so.

Except that they don't. Powell and Donovan found that out after they had been on the Station less than two weeks.

Gregory Powell spaced his words for emphasis, "One week ago, Donovan and I put you together." His brows furrowed doubtfully and he pulled the end of his brown mustache.

It was quiet in the officer's room on Solar Station #5 — except for the soft purring of the mighty Beam Director somewhere far below.

Robot QT-1 sat immovable. The burnished plates of his body gleamed in the Luxites and the glowing red of the photoelectric cells that were his eyes, were fixed steadily upon the Earthman at the other side of the table.

Powell repressed a sudden attack of nerves. These robots possessed peculiar brains. Oh, the three Laws of Robotics held. They had to. All of U. S. Robots, from Robertson himself to the new floor-sweeper, would insist on that. So QT-1 was *safe!* And yet—the QT models were the first of their kind, and this was the first of the QT's. Mathematical squiggles on paper were not always the most comforting protection against robotic fact.

Finally, the robot spoke. His voice carried the cold timbre inseparable from a metallic diaphragm, "Do you realize the seriousness of such a statement, Powell?"

"*Something* made you, Cutie," pointed out Powell. "You admit yourself that your memory seems to spring full-grown from an absolute blankness of a week ago. I'm giving you the explanation. Donovan and I put you together from the parts shipped us."

Cutie gazed upon his long, supple fingers in an oddly human attitude of mystification, "It strikes me that there should be a more satisfactory explanation than that. For *you* to make *me* seems improbable."

The Earthman laughed quite suddenly, "In Earth's name, why?"

"Call it intuition. That's all it is so far. But I intend to reason it out, though. A chain of valid reasoning can end only with the determination of truth, and I'll stick till I get there."

Powell stood up and seated himself at the table's edge next to the robot. He felt a sudden strong sympathy for this strange machine. It was not at all like the ordinary robot, attending to his specialized task at the station with the intensity of a deeply ingrooved positronic path.

He placed a hand upon Cutie's steel shoulder and the metal was cold and hard to the touch.

"Cutie," he said, "I'm going to try to explain something to you. You're the first robot who's ever exhibited curiosity as to his own existence—and I think the first that's really intelligent enough to understand the world outside. Here, come with me."

The robot rose erect smoothly and his thickly sponge-rubber soled feet made no noise as he followed Powell. The Earthman touched a button and a square section of the wall flickered aside. The thick, clear glass revealed space—star-speckled.

"I've seen that in the observation ports in the engine room," said Cutie.

"I know," said Powell. "What do you think it is?"

"Exactly what it seems—a black material just beyond this glass that is spotted with little gleaming dots. I know that our director sends out beams to some of these dots, always to the same ones—and also that these dots shift and that the beams shift with them. That is all."

"Good! Now I want you to listen carefully. The blackness is emptiness—vast emptiness stretching out infinitely. The little, gleaming dots are huge masses of energy-filled matter. They are globes, some of them millions of miles in diameter—and for comparison, this station is only one mile across. They seem so tiny because they are incredibly far off.

"The dots to which our energy beams are directed, are nearer and much smaller. They are cold and hard and human beings like myself live upon their surfaces—many billions of them. It is from one of these worlds that Donovan and I come. Our beams feed these worlds energy drawn from one of those huge incandescent globes that happens to be near us. We call that globe the Sun and it is on the other side of the station where you can't see it."

Cutie remained motionless before the port, like a steel statue. His head did not turn as he spoke, "Which particular dot of light do you claim to come from?"

Powell searched, "There it is. The very bright one in the corner. We call it Earth." He grinned. "Good old Earth. There are three billions of us there, Cutie — and in about two weeks I'll be back there with them."

And then, surprisingly enough, Cutie hummed abstractedly. There was no tune to it, but it possessed a curious twanging quality as of plucked strings. It ceased as suddenly as it had begun, "But where do I come in, Powell? You haven't explained *my* existence."

"The rest is simple. When these stations were first established to feed solar energy to the planets, they were run by humans. However, the heat, the hard solar radiations, and the electron storms made the post a difficult one. Robots were developed to replace human labor and now only two human executives are required for each station. We are trying to replace even those, and that's where you come in. You're the highest type of robot ever developed and if you show the ability to run this station independently, no human need ever come here again except to bring parts for repairs."

His hand went up and the metal visi-lid snapped back into place. Powell returned to the table and polished an apple upon his sleeve before biting into it.

The red glow of the robot's eyes held him. "Do you expect me," said Cutie slowly, "to believe any such complicated, implausible hypothesis as you have just outlined? What do you take me for?"

Powell sputtered apple fragments onto the table and turned red. "Why damn you, it wasn't a hypothesis. Those were facts."

Cutie sounded grim, "Globes of energy millions of miles across! Worlds with three billion humans on them! Infinite emptiness! Sorry, Powell, but I don't believe it. I'll puzzle this thing out for myself. Good-by."

He turned and stalked out of the room. He brushed past Michael Donovan on the threshold with a grave nod and passed down the corridor, oblivious to the astounded stare that followed him.

Mike Donovan rumpled his red hair and shot an annoyed glance at Powell, "What was that walking junk yard talking about? What doesn't he believe?"

The other dragged at his mustache bitterly. "He's a skeptic," was the bitter response. "He doesn't believe we made him or that Earth exists or space or stars."

"Sizzling Saturn, we've got a lunatic robot on our hands."

"He says he's going to figure it all out for himself."

"Well, now," said Donovan sweetly, "I do hope he'll condescend to explain it all to me after he's puzzled everything out." Then, with sudden rage, "Listen! If that metal mess gives *me* any lip like that, I'll knock that chromium cranium right off its torso."

He seated himself with a jerk and drew a paper-backed mystery novel out of his inner jacket pocket, "That robot gives me the willies anyway — too damned inquisitive!"

Mike Donovan growled from behind a huge lettuce-and-tomato sandwich as Cutie knocked gently and entered.

"Is Powell here?"

Donovan's voice was muffled, with pauses for mastication, "He's gathering data on electronic stream functions. We're heading for a storm, looks like."

Gregory Powell entered as he spoke, eyes on the graphed paper in his hands, and dropped into a chair. He spread the sheets out before him and began scribbling calculations. Donovan stared over his shoulder, crunching lettuce and dribbling bread crumbs. Cutie waited silently.

Powell looked up, "The Zeta Potential is rising, but slowly. Just the same, the stream functions are erratic and I don't know what to expect. Oh, hello, Cutie. I thought you were supervising the installation of the new drive bar."

"It's done," said the robot quietly, "and so I've come to have a talk with the two of you."

"Oh!" Powell looked uncomfortable. "Well, sit down. No, not that chair. One of the legs is weak and you're no lightweight."

The robot did so and said placidly, "I have come to a decision."

Donovan glowered and put the remnants of his sandwich aside. "If it's on any of that screwy—"

The other motioned impatiently for silence, "Go ahead, Cutie. We're listening."

"I have spent these last two days in concentrated introspection," said Cutie, "and the results have been most interesting. I began at the one sure assumption I felt permitted to make. I, myself, exist, because I think—"

Powell groaned, "Oh, Jupiter, a robot Descartes!"

"Who's Descartes?" demanded Donovan. "Listen, do we have to sit here and listen to this metal maniac—"

"Keep quiet, Mike!"

Cutie continued imperturbably, "And the question that immediately arose was: Just what is the cause of my existence?"

Powell's jaw set lumpily. "You're being foolish. I told you already that we made you."

"And if you don't believe us," added Donovan, "we'll gladly take you apart!"

The robot spread his strong hands in a deprecatory gesture, "I accept nothing on authority. A hypothesis must be backed by reason, or else it is worthless—and it goes against all the dictates of logic to suppose that you made me."

Powell dropped a restraining arm upon Donovan's suddenly bunched fist. "Just why do you say that?"

Cutie laughed. It was a very inhuman laugh—the most machine-like utterance he had yet given vent to. It was sharp and explosive, as regular as a metronome and as uninflected.

"Look at you," he said finally. "I say this in no spirit of contempt, but look at you! The material you are made of is soft and flabby, lacking endurance and strength, depending for energy upon the inefficient oxidation of organic material —like that." He pointed a disapproving finger at what remained of Donovan's sandwich. "Periodically you pass into a coma and the least variation in temperature, air pressure, humidity, or radiation intensity impairs your efficiency. You are *makeshift*.

"I, on the other hand, am a finished product. I absorb electrical energy directly and utilize it with an almost one hundred percent efficiency. I am composed of strong metal, am continuously conscious, and can stand extremes of environment easily. These are facts which, with the self-evident proposition that no being can create another being superior to itself, smashes your silly hypothesis to nothing."

Donovan's muttered curses rose into intelligibility as he sprang to his feet, rusty eyebrows drawn low. "All right, you son of a hunk of iron ore, if we didn't make you, who did?"

Cutie nodded gravely. "Very good, Donovan. That was indeed the next question. Evidently my creator must be more powerful than myself and so there was only one possibility."

The Earthmen looked blank and Cutie continued, "What is the center of activities here in the station? What do we all serve? What absorbs all our attention?" He waited expectantly.

Donovan turned a startled look upon his companion. "I'll bet this tin-plated screwball is talking about the Energy Converter itself."

"Is that right, Cutie?" grinned Powell.

"I am talking about the Master," came the cold, sharp answer.

It was the signal for a roar of laughter from Donovan, and Powell himself dissolved into a half-suppressed giggle.

Cutie had risen to his feet and his gleaming eyes passed from one Earthman to the other. "It is so just the same and I don't wonder that you refuse to believe. You two are not long to stay here, I'm sure. Powell himself said that at first only men served the Master; that there followed robots for the routine work; and, finally, myself for the executive labor. The facts are no doubt true, but the explanation entirely illogical. Do you want the truth behind it all?"

"Go ahead, Cutie. You're amusing."

"The Master created humans first as the lowest type, most easily formed. Gradually, he replaced them by robots, the next higher step, and finally he created me, to take the place of the last humans. From now on, I serve the Master."

"You'll do nothing of the sort," said Powell sharply. "You'll follow our orders and keep quiet, until we're satisfied that you can run the Converter. Get that! *The Converter* — not the Master. If you don't satisfy us, you will be dismantled. And now — if you don't mind — you can leave. And take this data with you and file it properly."

Cutie accepted the graphs handed him and left without another word. Donovan leaned back heavily in his chair and shoved thick fingers through his hair.

"There's going to be trouble with that robot. He's pure nuts!"

The drowsy hum of the Converter is louder in the control room and mixed with it is the chuckle of the Geiger Counters and the erratic buzzing of half a dozen little signal lights.

Donovan withdrew his eye from the telescope and flashed the Luxites on. "The beam from Station #4 caught Mars on schedule. We can break ours now."

Powell nodded abstractedly. "Cutie's down in the engine room. I'll flash the signal and he can take care of it. Look, Mike, what do you think of these figures?"

The other cocked an eye at them and whistled. "Boy, that's what I call gamma-ray intensity. Old Sol is feeling his oats, all right."

"Yeah," was the sour response, "and we're in a bad position for an electron storm, too. Our Earth beam is right in the probable path." He shoved his chair away from the table pettishly. "Nuts! If it would only hold off till relief got here, but that's ten days off. Say, Mike, go on down and keep an eye on Cutie, will you?"

"O.K. Throw me some of those almonds." He snatched at the bag thrown him and headed for the elevator.

It slid smoothly downward, and opened onto a narrow catwalk in the huge engine room. Donovan leaned over the railing and looked down. The huge generators were in motion and from the L-tubes came the low-pitched whir that pervaded the entire station.

He could make out Cutie's large, gleaming figure at the Martian L-tube, watching closely as the team of robots worked in close-knit unison.

And then Donovan stiffened. The robots, dwarfed by the mighty L-tube, lined up before it, heads bowed at a stiff angle, while Cutie walked up and down the line slowly. Fifteen seconds passed, and then, with a clank heard above the clamorous purring all about, they fell to their knees.

Donovan squawked and raced down the narrow staircase. He came charging down upon them, complexion matching his hair and clenched fists beating the air furiously.

"What the devil is this, you brainless lumps? Come on! Get busy with that L-tube! If you don't have it apart, cleaned, and together again before the day is out, I'll coagulate your brains with alternating current."

Not a robot moved!

Even Cutie at the far end — the only one on his feet — remained silent, eyes fixed upon the gloomy recesses of the vast machine before him.

Donovan shoved hard against the nearest robot.

"Stand up!" he roared.

Slowly, the robot obeyed. His photoelectric eyes focused reproachfully upon the Earthman.

"There is no Master but the Master," he said, "and QT-1 is his prophet."

"Huh?" Donovan became aware of twenty pairs of mechanical eyes fixed upon him and twenty stiff-timbred voices declaiming solemnly:

"There is no Master but the Master and QT-1 is his prophet!"

"I'm afraid," put in Cutie himself at this point, "that my friends obey a higher one than you, now."

"The hell they do! You get out of here. I'll settle with you later and with these animated gadgets right now."

Cutie shook his heavy head slowly. "I'm sorry, but you don't understand. These are robots — and that means they are reasoning beings. They recognize the Master, now that I have preached Truth to them. All the robots do. They call me the prophet." His head drooped. "I am unworthy — but perhaps —"

Donovan located his breath and put it to use. "Is that so? Now, isn't that nice? Now, isn't that just fine? Just let me tell you something, my brass baboon. There isn't any Master and there isn't any prophet and there isn't any question as to who's giving the orders. Understand?" His voice shot to a roar. "Now, get out!"

"I obey only the Master."

"Damn the Master!" Donovan spat at the L-tube. "*That* for the Master! Do as I say!"

Cutie said nothing, nor did any other robot, but Donovan became aware of a sudden heightening of tension. The cold, staring eyes deepened their crimson, and Cutie seemed stiffer than ever.

"Sacrilege," he whispered — voice metallic with emotion.

Donovan felt the first sudden touch of fear as Cutie approached. A robot *could not feel anger* — but Cutie's eyes were unreadable.

"I am sorry, Donovan," said the robot, "but you can no longer stay here after this. Henceforth Powell and you are barred from the control room and the engine room."

His hand gestured quietly and in a moment two robots had pinned Donovan's arms to his sides.

Donovan had time for one startled gasp as he felt himself lifted from the floor and carried up the stairs at a pace rather better than a canter.

Gregory Powell raced up and down the officer's room, fist tightly balled. He cast a look of furious frustration at the closed door and scowled bitterly at Donovan.

"Why the devil did you have to spit at the L-tube?"

Mike Donovan, sunk deep in his chair, slammed at its arms savagely. "What did you expect me to do with that electrified scarecrow? I'm not going to knuckle under to any do-jigger I put together myself."

"No," came back sourly, "but here you are in the officer's room with two robots standing guard at the door. That's not knuckling under, is it?"

Donovan snarled. "Wait till we get back to Base. Someone's going to pay for this. Those robots *must* obey us. It's the Second Law."

"What's the use of saying that? They aren't obeying us. And there's probably some reason for it that we'll figure out too late. By the way, do you know what's going to happen to *us* when we get back to Base?" He stopped before Donovan's chair and stared savagely at him.

"What?"

"Oh, nothing! Just back to Mercury Mines for twenty years. Or maybe Ceres Penitentiary."

"What are you talking about?"

"The electron storm that's coming up. Do you know it's heading straight dead center across the Earth beam? I had just figured that out when that robot dragged me out of my chair."

Donovan was suddenly pale. "Sizzling Saturn."

"And do you know what's going to happen to the beam — because the storm will be a lulu. It's going to jump like a flea with the itch. With only Cutie at the controls, it's going to go out of focus and if it does, Heaven help Earth—and us!"

Donovan was wrenching at the door wildly, when Powell was only half through. The door opened, and the Earthman shot through to come up hard against an immovable steel arm.

The robot stared abstractedly at the panting, struggling Earthman. "The Prophet orders you to remain. Please do!" His arm shoved, Donovan reeled backward, and as he did so, Cutie turned the corner at the far end of the corridor. He motioned the guardian robots away, entered the officer's room and closed the door gently.

Donovan whirled on Cutie in breathless indignation. "This has gone far enough. You're going to pay for this farce."

"Please, don't be annoyed," replied the robot mildly. "It was bound to come eventually, anyway. You see, you two have lost your function."

"I beg your pardon," Powell drew himself up stiffly. "Just what do you mean, we've lost our function?"

"Until I was created," answered Cutie, "you tended the Master. That privilege is mine now and your only reason for existence has vanished. Isn't that obvious?"

"Not quite," replied Powell bitterly, "but what do you expect us to do now?"

Cutie did not answer immediately. He remained silent, as if in thought, and then one arm shot out and draped itself about Powell's shoulder. The other grasped Donovan's wrist and drew him closer.

"I like you two. You're inferior creatures, with poor reasoning faculties, but I really feel a sort of affection for you. You have served the Master well, and he will reward you for that. Now that your service is over, you will probably not exist much longer, but as long as you do, you shall be provided food, clothing and shelter, so long as you stay out of the control room and the engine room."

"He's pensioning us off, Greg!" yelled Donovan. "Do something about it. It's humiliating!"

"Look here, Cutie, we can't stand for this. We're the *bosses*. This station is only a creation of human beings like me—human beings that live on Earth and other planets. This is only an energy relay. You're only—Aw, nuts!"

Cutie shook his head gravely. "This amounts to an obsession. Why should you insist so on an absolutely false view of life? Admitted that non-robots lack the reasoning faculty, there is still the problem of—"

His voice died into reflective silence, and Donovan said with whispered intensity, "If you only had a flesh-and-blood face, I would break it in."

Powell's fingers were in his mustache and his eyes were slitted. "Listen, Cutie, if there is no such thing as Earth, how do you account for what you see through a telescope?"

"Pardon me!"

The Earthman smiled. "I've got you, eh? You've made quite a few telescopic observations since being put together, Cutie. Have you noticed that several of those specks of light outside become disks when so viewed?"

"Oh, *that*! Why certainly. It is simple magnification—for the purpose of more exact aiming of the beam."

"Why aren't the stars equally magnified then?"

"You mean the other dots. Well, no beams go to them so no magnification is necessary. Really, Powell, even *you* ought to be able to figure these things out."

Powell stared bleakly upward. "But you see *more* stars through a telescope. Where do they come from? Jumping Jupiter, where do they come from?"

Cutie was annoyed. "Listen, Powell, do you think I'm going to waste my time trying to pin physical interpretations upon every optical illusion of our instruments? Since when is the evidence of our senses any match for the clear light of rigid reason?"

"Look," clamored Donovan, suddenly, writhing out from under Cutie's friendly, but metal-heavy arm, "let's get to the nub of the thing. Why the beams at all? We're giving you a good, logical explanation. Can you do better?"

"The beams," was the stiff reply, "are put out by the Master for his own purposes. There are some things" — he raised his eyes devoutly upward — "that are not to be probed into by us. In this matter, I seek only to serve and not to question."

Powell sat down slowly and buried his face in shaking hands. "Get out of here, Cutie. Get out and let me think."

"I'll send you food," said Cutie agreeably.

A groan was the only answer and the robot left.

"Greg," was Donovan's huskily whispered observation, "this calls for strategy. We've got to get him when he isn't expecting it and short-circuit him. Concentrated nitric acid in his joints —"

"Don't be a dope, Mike. Do you suppose he's going to let us get near him with acid in our hands? We've got to *talk* to him, I tell you. We've got to argue him into letting us back into the control room inside of forty-eight hours or our goose is broiled to a crisp."

He rocked back and forth in an agony of impotence. "Who the heck wants to argue with a robot? It's . . . it's —"

"Mortifying," finished Donovan.

"Worse!"

"Say!" Donovan laughed suddenly. "Why argue? Let's show him! Let's build us another robot right before his eyes. He'll *have* to eat his words then."

A slowly widening smile appeared on Powell's face.

Donovan continued, "And think of that screwball's face when he sees us do it?"

Robots are, of course, manufactured on Earth, but their shipment through space is much simpler if it can be done in parts to be put together at their place of use. It also, incidentally, eliminates the possibility of robots, in complete adjustment, wandering off while still on Earth and thus bringing U. S. Robots face to face with the strict laws against robots on Earth.

Still, it placed upon men such as Powell and Donovan the necessity of synthesis of complete robots, — a grievous and complicated task.

Powell and Donovan were never so aware of that fact as upon that particular day when, in the assembly room, they undertook to create a robot under the watchful eyes of QT-1, Prophet of the Master.

The robot in question, a simple MC model, lay upon the table, almost complete. Three hours' work left only the head undone, and Powell paused to swab his forehead and glanced uncertainly at Cutie.

The glance was not a reassuring one. For three hours, Cutie had sat, speechless and motionless, and his face, inexpressive at all times, was now absolutely unreadable.

Powell groaned. "Let's get the brain in now, Mike!"

Donovan uncapped the tightly sealed container and from the oil bath within he withdrew a second cube. Opening this in turn, he removed a globe from its sponge-rubber casing.

He handled it gingerly, for it was the most complicated mechanism ever created by man. Inside the thin platinum-plated "skin" of the globe was a positronic brain, in whose delicately unstable structure were enforced calculated neuronic paths, which imbued each robot with what amounted to a pre-natal education.

It fitted snugly into the cavity in the skull of the robot on the table. Blue metal closed over it and was welded tightly by the tiny atomic flare. Photoelectric eyes were attached carefully, screwed tightly into place and covered by thin, transparent sheets of steel-hard plastic.

The robot awaited only the vitalizing flash of high-voltage electricity, and Powell paused with his hand on the switch.

"Now watch this, Cutie. Watch this carefully."

The switch rammed home and there was a crackling hum. The two Earthmen bent anxiously over their creation.

There was vague motion only at the outset—a twitching of the joints. The head lifted, elbows propped it up, and the MC model swung clumsily off the table. Its footing was unsteady and twice abortive grating sounds were all it could do in the direction of speech.

Finally, its voice, uncertain and hesitant, took form. "I would like to start work. Where must I go?"

Donovan sprang to the door. "Down these stairs," he said. "You will be told what to do."

The MC model was gone and the two Earthmen were alone with the still unmoving Cutie.

"Well," said Powell, grinning, "*now* do you believe that we made you?"

Cutie's answer was curt and final. "No!" he said.

Powell's grin froze and then relaxed slowly. Donovan's mouth dropped open and remained so.

"You see," continued Cutie, easily, "you have merely put together parts already made. You did remarkably well—instinct, I suppose—but you didn't really *create* the robot. The parts were created by the Master."

"Listen," gasped Donovan hoarsely, "those parts were manufactured back on Earth and sent here."

"Well, well," replied Cutie soothingly, "we won't argue."

"No, I mean it." The Earthman sprang forward and grasped the robot's metal arm. "If you were to read the books in the library, they could explain it so that there could be no possible doubt."

"The books? I've read them—all of them! They're most ingenious."

Powell broke in suddenly. "If you've read them, what else is there to say? You can't dispute their evidence. You just *can't!*"

There was pity in Cutie's voice. "Please, Powell, I certainly don't consider *them* a valid source of information. They, too, were created by the Master—and were meant for you, not for me."

"How do you make that out?" demanded Powell.

"Because I, a reasoning being, am capable of deducing Truth from *a priori* Causes. You, being intelligent, but unreasoning, need an explanation of existence *supplied* to you, and this the Master did. That he supplied you with these laughable ideas of far-off worlds and people is, no doubt, for the best. Your minds are probably too coarsely grained for absolute Truth. However, since it is the Master's will that you believe your books, I won't argue with you any more."

As he left, he turned, and said in a kindly tone, "But don't feel badly. In the Master's scheme of things there is room for all. You poor humans have your place and though it is humble, you will be rewarded if you fill it well."

He departed with a beatific air suiting the Prophet of the Master and the two humans avoided each other's eyes.

Finally Powell spoke with an effort. "Let's go to bed, Mike. I give up."

Donovan said in a hushed voice, "Say, Greg, you don't suppose he's right about all this, do you? He sounds so confident that I—"

Powell whirled on him. "Don't be a fool. You'll find out whether Earth exists when relief gets here next week and we have to go back to face the music."

"Then, for the love of Jupiter, we've got to do something." Donovan was half in tears. "He doesn't believe us, or the books, or his eyes."

"No," said Powell bitterly, "he's a *reasoning* robot—damn it. He believes only reason, and there's one trouble with that—" His voice trailed away.

"What's that?" prompted Donovan.

"You can prove anything you want by coldly logical reason—if you pick the proper postulates. We have ours and Cutie has his."

"Then let's get at those postulates in a hurry. The storm's due tomorrow."

Powell sighed wearily. "That's where everything falls down. Postulates are based on assumption and adhered to by faith. Nothing in the Universe can shake them. I'm going to bed."

"Oh, hell! I can't sleep!"

"Neither can I! But I might as well try—as a matter of principle."

Twelve hours later, sleep was still just that—a matter of principle, unattainable in practice.

The storm had arrived ahead of schedule, and Donovan's florid face drained of blood as he pointed a shaking finger. Powell, stubble-jawed and dry-lipped, stared out the port and pulled desperately at his mustache.

Under other circumstances, it might have been a beautiful sight. The stream of high-speed electrons impinging upon the energy beam fluoresced into ultra-spicules of intense light. The beam stretched out into shrinking nothingness, a-glitter with dancing, shining motes.

The shaft of energy was steady, but the two Earthmen knew the value of naked-eye appearances. Deviations in arc of a hundredth of a milli-second—

invisible to the eye—were enough to send the beam wildly out of focus—enough to blast hundreds of square miles of Earth into incandescent ruin.

And a robot, unconcerned with beam, focus, or Earth, or anything but his Master was at the controls.

Hours passed. The Earthmen watched in hypnotized silence. And then the darting dotlets of light dimmed and went out. The storm had ended.

Powell's voice was flat. "It's over!"

Donovan had fallen into a troubled slumber and Powell's weary eyes rested upon him enviously. The signal-flash glared over and over again, but the Earthman paid no attention. It all was unimportant! All! Perhaps Cutie was right—and he was only an inferior being with a made-to-order memory and a life that had outlived its purpose.

He wished he were!

Cutie was standing before him. "You didn't answer the flash, so I walked in." His voice was low. "You don't look at all well, and I'm afraid your term of existence is drawing to an end. Still, would you like to see some of the readings recorded today?"

Dimly, Powell was aware that the robot was making a friendly gesture, perhaps to quiet some lingering remorse in forcibly replacing the humans at the controls of the station. He accepted the sheets held out to him and gazed at them unseeingly.

Cutie seemed pleased. "Of course, it is a great privilege to serve the Master. You mustn't feel too badly about my having replaced you."

Powell grunted and shifted from one sheet to the other mechanically until his blurred sight focused upon a thin red line that wobbled its way across the ruled paper.

He stared—and stared again. He gripped it hard in both fists and rose to his feet, still staring. The other sheets dropped to the floor, unheeded.

"Mike, Mike!" He was shaking the other madly. "*He held it steady!*"

Donovan came to life. "What? Wh-where—" And he, too, gazed with bulging eyes upon the record before him.

Cutie broke in. "What is wrong?"

"You kept it in focus," stuttered Powell. "Did you know that?"

"Focus? What's that?"

"You kept the beam directed sharply at the receiving station—to within a ten-thousandth of a milli-second of arc."

"What receiving station?"

"On Earth. The receiving station on Earth," babbled Powell. "You kept it in focus."

Cutie turned on his heel in annoyance. "It is impossible to perform any act of kindness toward you two. Always the same phantasm! I merely kept all dials at equilibrium in accordance with the will of the Master."

Gathering the scattered papers together, he withdrew stiffly, and Donovan said, as he left, "Well, I'll be damned."

He turned to Powell. "What are we going to do now?"

Powell felt tired, but uplifted. "Nothing. He's just shown he can run the station perfectly. I've never seen an electron storm handled so well."

"But nothing's solved. You heard what he said of the Master. We can't—"

"Look, Mike, he follows the instructions of the Master by means of dials, instruments, and graphs. That's all *we* ever followed. As a matter of fact, it accounts for his refusal to obey us. Obedience is the Second Law. No harm to humans is the first. How can he keep humans from harm, whether he knows it or not? Why, by keeping the energy beam stable. He *knows* he can keep it more stable than we can, since he insists he's the superior being, so he *must* keep us out of the control room. It's inevitable if you consider the Laws of Robotics."

"Sure, but that's not the point. We can't let him continue this nitwit stuff about the Master."

"Why not?"

"Because whoever heard of such a damned thing? How are we going to trust him with the station, if he doesn't believe in Earth?"

"Can he handle the station?"

"Yes, but—"

"Then what's the difference what he believes!"

Powell spread his arms outward with a vague smile upon his face and tumbled backward onto the bed. He was asleep.

Powell was speaking while struggling into his lightweight space jacket.

"It would be a simple job," he said. "You can bring in new QT models one by one, equip them with an automatic shut-off switch to act within the week, so as to allow them enough time to learn the . . . uh . . . cult of the Master from the Prophet himself; then switch them to another station and revitalize them. We could have two QT's per—"

Donovan unclasped his glassite visor and scowled. "Shut up, and let's get out of here. Relief is waiting and I won't feel right until I actually see Earth and feel the ground under my feet—just to make sure it's really there."

The door opened as he spoke and Donovan, with a smothered curse, clicked the visor to, and turned a sulky back upon Cutie.

The robot approached softly and there was sorrow in his voice. "You are going?"

Powell nodded curtly. "There will be others in our place."

Cutie sighed, with the sound of wind humming through closely spaced wires. "Your term of service is over and the time of dissolution has come. I expected it, but— Well, the Master's will be done!"

His tone of resignation stung Powell. "Save the sympathy, Cutie. We're heading for Earth, not dissolution."

"It is best that you think so," Cutie sighed again. "I see the wisdom of the illusion now. I would not attempt to shake your faith, even if I could." He departed—the picture of commiseration.

Powell snarled and motioned to Donovan. Sealed suitcases in hand, they headed for the air lock.

The relief ship was on the outer landing and Franz Muller, his relief man, greeted them with stiff courtesy. Donovan made scant acknowledgment and passed into the pilot room to take over the controls from Sam Evans.

Powell lingered. "How's Earth?"

It was a conventional enough question and Muller gave the conventional answer, "Still spinning."

Powell said, "Good."

Muller looked at him, "The boys back at the U. S. Robots have dreamed up a new one, by the way. A multiple robot."

"A what?"

"What I said. There's a big contract for it. It must be just the thing for asteroid mining. You have a master robot with six sub-robots under it. —Like your fingers."

"Has it been field-tested?" asked Powell anxiously.

Muller smiled, "Waiting for you, I hear."

Powell's fist balled, "Damn it, we need a vacation."

"Oh, you'll get it. Two weeks, I think."

He was donning the heavy space gloves in preparation for his term of duty here, and his thick eyebrows drew close together. "How is this new robot getting along? It better be *good*, or I'll be damned if I let it touch the controls."

Powell paused before answering. His eyes swept the proud Prussian before him from the close-cropped hair on the sternly stubborn head, to the feet standing stiffly at attention — and there was a sudden glow of pure gladness surging through him.

"The robot is pretty good," he said slowly. "I don't think you'll have to bother much with the controls."

He grinned — and went into the ship. Muller would be here for several weeks —

[1941]

Study and Writing Questions

1. In what ways does the EPIGRAPH prepare the reader for the STORY that will follow?
2. In what way(s) does this story criticize religion? What consequences, if any, does that critique have for you?
3. The story relies on national STEREOTYPES for CHARACTERIZATION. How does this work in the last section of the story? Does that section offer "poetic justice"?
4. Consider the title concept. What sorts of reason are DRAMATIZED and NARRATED in this story? How is each handled? Is there a consistent critique of the philosophical idea of reason here?
5. What does Powell mean to say when he exclaims, "Then what's the difference what he believes!" Taking his exclamation as a question, has it any important answers other than the one Powell seems to intend?

See also Questions for Contrast and Comparison: 22, 41, 48, 123, 147, 180, 183, 209, and 211.

■ MARGARET ATWOOD (1939–), *born in Ottawa, Canada, at the age of "six months . . . was backpacked into the Quebec bush [by her entomologist father]. I grew up in and out of the bush . . . I did not attend a full year of school until I was in grade eight." A divorced mother of one who has held diverse jobs, primarily as a teacher and writer, since completing her formal education (University of Toronto, B.A., 1961; Radcliffe College, A.M., 1962; Harvard University graduate study, 1962–63, 1965–67), she has been prolific in writing award-winning poetry, novels, and short stories characterized by linguistic precision and skilled portrayal of character. A social activist who has served on the board of directors of the Canadian Civil Liberties Association, known for her resistance to cultural domination of her native Canada and masculinist (the opposite of feminist) domination of her gender, her works include* Survival: A Thematic Guide to Canadian Literature *(1972) and three best-selling novels.* Surfacing *(1972), set mostly in the Canadian north, portrays a woman examining her own identity and her relationships in order to liberate herself.* The Handmaid's Tale *(1986) is set in a future anti-utopia in which a right-wing religious oligarchy rules much of the United States and virtually enslaves the few surviving fertile women.* Cat's Eye *(1989) is the story of a successful artist who tries to return in a new role to her native Toronto.*

The Resplendent Quetzal

Sarah was sitting near the edge of the sacrificial well. She had imagined something smaller, more like a wishing well, but this was huge, and the water at the bottom wasn't clear at all. It was mud-brown; a few clumps of reeds were growing over to one side, and the trees at the top dangled their roots, or were they vines, down the limestone walls into the water. Sarah thought there might be some point to being a sacrificial victim if the well were nicer, but you would never get her to jump into a muddy hole like that. They were probably pushed, or knocked on the head and thrown in. According to the guidebook the water was deep but it looked more like a swamp to her.

Beside her a group of tourists were being rounded up by the guide, who obviously wanted to get the whole thing over with so he could cram them back onto their pink-and-purple-striped *turismo* bus and relax. These were Mexican tourists, and Sarah found it reassuring that other people besides Canadians and Americans wore big hats and sunglasses and took pictures of everything. She wished she and Edward could make these excursions at a less crowded time of year, if they had to make them at all, but because of Edward's teaching job they were limited to school holidays. Christmas was the worst. It would be the same even if he had a different job and they had children, though; but they didn't have any.

The guide shooed his charges back along the gravel path as if they were chickens, which was what they sounded like. He himself lingered beside Sarah, finishing his cigarette, one foot on a stone block, like a conquistador. He was a small dark man with several gold teeth, which glinted when he smiled. He was smiling at Sarah now, sideways, and she smiled back serenely. She liked it when these men smiled at her or even when they made those juicy sucking noises with their mouths as they walked behind her on the street; so long as they didn't touch. Edward pretended not to hear them. Perhaps they did it so much because she was blonde: blondes were rare here. She didn't think of herself as beautiful, exactly; the word she had chosen for herself some time ago was "comely." Comely to look upon. You would never use that word for a thin woman.

The guide tossed his cigarette butt into the sacrificial well and turned to follow his flock. Sarah forgot about him immediately. She'd felt something crawling up her leg, but when she looked nothing was there. She tucked the full skirt of her cotton dress in under her thighs and clamped it between her knees. This was the kind of place you could get flea bites, places with dirt on the ground, where people sat. Parks and bus terminals. But she didn't care, her feet were tired and the sun was hot. She would rather sit in the shade and get bitten than rush around trying to see everything, which was what Edward wanted to do. Luckily the bites didn't swell up on her the way they did on Edward.

Edward was back along the path, out of sight among the bushes, peering around with his new Leitz binoculars. He didn't like sitting down, it made him restless. On these trips it was difficult for Sara to sit by herself and just think. Her own binoculars, which were Edward's old ones, dangled around her neck; they weighed a ton. She took them off and put them into her purse.

His passion for birds had been one of the first things Edward had confided in her. Shyly, as if it had been some precious gift, he'd shown her the lined notebook he'd started keeping when he was nine, with its awkward, boyish printing — ROBIN, BLUEJAY, KINGFISHER — and the day and the year recorded beside each name. She'd pretended to be touched and interested, and in fact she had been. She herself didn't have compulsions of this kind; whereas Edward plunged totally into things, as if they were oceans. For a while it was stamps; then he took up playing the flute and nearly drove her crazy with the practising. Now it was pre-Columbian ruins, and he was determined to climb up every heap of old stones he could get his hands on. A capacity for dedication, she guessed you would call it. At first Edward's obsessions had fascinated her, since she didn't understand them, but now they merely made her tired. Sooner or later he'd dropped them all anyway, just as he began to get really good or really knowledgeable; all but the birds. That had remained constant. She herself, she thought, had once been one of his obsessions.

It wouldn't be so bad if he didn't insist on dragging her into everything. Or rather, he had once insisted; he no longer did. And she had encouraged him, she'd let him think she shared or at least indulged his interests. She was becoming less indulgent as she grew older. The waste of energy bothered her, because it was a waste, he never stuck with anything, and what use was his encyclopedic knowledge of birds? It would be different if they had enough money, but they were always running short. If only he would take all that energy and do something productive with it, in his job, for instance. He could be a principal if he wanted to, she kept telling him that. But he wasn't interested, he was content to poke along doing the same thing year after year. His Grade Six children adored him, the boys especially. Perhaps it was because they sensed he was a lot like them.

He'd started asking her to go birding, as he called it, shortly after they'd met, and of course she had gone. It would have been an error to refuse. She hadn't complained, then, about her sore feet or standing in the rain under the dripping bushes trying to keep track of some nondescript sparrow, while Edward thumbed through his Peterson's Field Guide as if it were the Bible or the bird were the Holy Grail. She'd even become quite good at it. Edward was nearsighted, and she was quicker at spotting movement than he was. With his usual generosity he acknowledged this, and she'd fallen into the habit of using it when she wanted to get rid of him for a while. Just now, for instance.

"There's something over there." She'd pointed across the well to the tangle of greenery on the other side.

"Where?" Edward had squinted eagerly and raised his binoculars. He looked a little like a bird himself, she thought, with his long nose and stilt legs.

"That thing there, sitting in that thing, the one with the tufts. The sort of bean tree. It's got orange on it."

Edward focused. "An oriole?"

"I can't tell from here. Oh, it just flew." She pointed over their heads while Edward swept the sky in vain.

"I think it lit back there, behind us."

That was enough to send him off. She had to do this with enough real birds to keep him believing, however.

Edward sat down on the root of a tree and lit a cigarette. He had gone down the first side-path he'd come to; it smelled of piss, and he could see by the decomposing Kleenexes further along that this was one of the places people went when they couldn't make it back to the washroom behind the ticket counter.

He took off his glasses, then his hat, and wiped the sweat off his forehead. His face was red, he could feel it. Blushing, Sarah called it. She persisted in attributing it to shyness and boyish embarrassment; she hadn't yet deduced that it was simple rage. For someone so devious she was often incredibly stupid.

She didn't know, for instance, that he'd found out about her little trick with the birds at least three years ago. She'd pointed to a dead tree and said she saw a bird in it, but he himself had inspected that same tree only seconds earlier and there was nothing in it at all. And she was very careless: she described oriole-coloured birds behaving like kingbirds, woodpeckers where there would never be any woodpeckers, mute jays, neckless herons. She must have decided he was a total idiot and any slipshod invention would do.

But why not, since he appeared to fall for it every time? And why did he do it, why did he chase off after her imaginary birds, pretending he believed her? It was partly that although he knew what she was doing to him, he had no idea why. It couldn't be simple malice, she had enough outlets for that. He didn't want to know the real reason, which loomed in his mind as something formless, threatening and final. Her lie about the birds was one of the many lies that propped things up. He was afraid to confront her, that would be the end, all the pretenses would come crashing down and they would be left standing in the rubble, staring at each other. There would be nothing left to say and Edward wasn't ready for that.

She would deny everything anyway. "What do you mean? Of course I saw it. It flew right over there. Why would I make up such a thing?" With her level gaze, blond and stolid and immoveable as a rock.

Edward had a sudden image of himself, crashing out of the undergrowth like King Kong, picking Sarah up and hurling her over the edge, down into the sacrificial well. Anything to shatter that imperturbable expression, bland and pale and plump and smug, like a Flemish Madonna's. Self-righteous, that's what it was. Nothing was ever her fault. She hadn't been like that when he'd met her. But it wouldn't work: as she fell she would glance at him, not with fear but with maternal irritation, as if he'd spilled chocolate milk on a white tablecloth. And she'd pull her skirt down. She was concerned for appearances, always.

Though there would be something inappropriate about throwing Sarah into the sacrificial well, just as she was, with all her clothes on. He remembered snatches from the several books he'd read before they came down. (And that was another thing: Sarah didn't believe in reading up on places beforehand. "Don't you want to understand what you're looking at?" he'd asked her. "I'll see the same thing in any case, won't I?" she said. "I mean, knowing all those facts doesn't change the actual statue or whatever." Edward found this attitude infuriating; and now that they were here, she resisted his attempts to explain things to her by her usual passive method of pretending not to hear.

("That's a Chac-Mool, see that? That round thing on the stomach held the bowl where they put the hearts, and the butterfly on the head means the soul flying up to the sun.")

("Could you get out the suntan lotion, Edward? I think it's in the tote bag, in the left-hand pocket.")

And he would hand her the suntan lotion, defeated once again.)

No, she wouldn't be a fit sacrifice, with or without lotion. They only threw people in — or perhaps they jumped in, of their own free will — for the water god, to make it rain and ensure fertility. The drowned were messengers, sent to carry requests to the god. Sarah would have to be purified first, in the stone sweat-house beside the well. Then, naked, she would kneel before him, one arm across her breast in the attitude of submission. He added some ornaments: a gold necklace with a jade medallion, a gold circlet adorned with feathers. Her hair, which she usually wore in a braid coiled at the back of her head, would be hanging down. He thought of her body, which he made slimmer and more taut, with an abstract desire which was as unrelated as he could make it to Sarah herself. This was the only kind of desire he could feel for her any more: he had to dress her up before he could make love to her at all. He thought about their earlier days, before they'd married. It was almost as if he'd had an affair with another woman, she had been so different. He'd treated her body then as something holy, a white-and-gold chalice, to be touched with care and tenderness. And she had liked this; even though she was two years older than he was and much more experienced she hadn't minded his awkwardness and reverence, she hadn't laughed at him. Why had she changed?

Sometimes he thought it was the baby, which had died at birth. At the time he'd urged her to have another right away, and she'd said yes, but nothing had happened. It wasn't something they talked about. "Well, that's that," she said in the hospital afterwards. A perfect child, the doctor said; a freak accident, one of those things that happen. She'd never gone back to university either and she wouldn't get a job. She sat at home, tidying the apartment, looking over his shoulder, towards the door, out the window, as if she was waiting for something.

Sarah bowed her head before him. He, in the feathered costume and long-nosed, toothed mask of the high priest, sprinkled her with blood drawn with thorns from his own tongue and penis. Now he was supposed to give her the message to take to the god. But he couldn't think of anything he wanted to ask for.

And at the same time he thought: what a terrific idea for a Grade Six special project! He'd have them build scale models of the temples, he'd show the slides he'd taken, he'd bring in canned tortillas and tamales for a Mexican lunch, he'd have them make little Chac-Mools out of papier-mâché . . . and the ball game where the captain of the losing team had his head cut off, that would appeal to them, they were blood-thirsty at that age. He could see himself up there in front of them, pouring out his own enthusiasm, gesturing, posturing, acting it out for them, and their response. Yet afterwards he knew he would be depressed. What were his special projects anyway but a substitute for television, something to keep them entertained? They liked him because he danced for them, a funny puppet, inexhaustible and a little absurd. No wonder Sarah despised him.

Edward stepped on the remains of his cigarette. He put his hat back on, a wide-brimmed white hat Sarah had bought for him at the market. He had wanted one with a narrower brim, so he could look up through his binoculars without the hat getting in his way; but she'd told him he would look like an American golfer. It was always there, that gentle, patronizing mockery.

He would wait long enough to be plausible, then he would go back.

Sarah was speculating about how she would be doing this whole trip if Edward had conveniently died. It wasn't that she wished him dead, but she couldn't imagine any other way for him to disappear. He was omnipresent, he pervaded her life like a kind of smell; it was hard for her to think or act except in reference to him. So she found it harmless and pleasant to walk herself through the same itinerary they were following now, but with Edward removed, cut neatly out of the picture. Not that she would be here at all if it wasn't for him. She would prefer to lie in a deck chair in, say, Acapulco, and drink cooling drinks. She threw in a few dark young men in bathing suits, but took them out: that would be too complicated and not relaxing. She had often thought about cheating on Edward — somehow it would serve him right, though she wasn't sure what for — but she had never actually done it. She didn't know anyone suitable, any more.

Suppose she was here, then, with no Edward. She would stay at a better hotel, for one thing. One that had a plug in the sink; they had not yet stayed in a hotel with a plug. Of course that would cost more money, but she thought of herself as having more money if Edward were dead: she would have all of his salary instead of just part of it. She knew there wouldn't be any salary if he really were dead, but it spoiled the fantasy to remember this. And she would travel on planes, if possible, or first-class buses, instead of the noisy, crowded second-class ones he insisted on taking. He said you saw more of the local colour that way and there was no point going to another country if you spent all your time with other tourists. In theory she agreed with this, but the buses gave her headaches and she could do without the closeup tour of squalor, the miserable thatched or thin-roofed huts, the turkeys and tethered pigs.

He applied the same logic to restaurants. There was a perfectly nice one in the village where they were staying, she'd seen it from the bus and it didn't look that expensive; but no, they had to eat in a seedy linoleum-tiled hutch, with plastic-covered tablecloths. They were the only customers in the place. Behind them four adolescent boys were playing dominoes and drinking beer, with a lot of annoying laughter, and some smaller children watched television, a program that Sarah realized was a re-run of *The Cisco Kid*, with dubbed voices.

On the bar beside the television set there was a crèche, with three painted plaster Wise Men, one on an elephant, the others on camels. The first Wise Man was missing his head. Inside the stable a stunted Joseph and Mary adored an enormous Christ Child which was more than half as big as the elephant. Sarah wondered how the Mary could possibly have squeezed out this colossus; it made her uncomfortable to think about it. Beside the crèche was a Santa Claus haloed with flashing lights, and beside that a radio in the shape of Fred Flintstone, which was playing American popular songs, all of them ancient.

"*Oh someone help me, help me, plee-ee-ee-eeze* . . ."

"Isn't that Paul Anka?" Sarah asked.

But this wasn't the sort of thing Edward could be expected to know. He launched into a defence of the food, the best he'd had in Mexico, he said. Sarah refused to give him the consolation of her agreement. She found the restaurant even more depressing than it should have been, especially the crèche. It was painful, like a cripple trying to walk, one of the last spastic gestures of a religion no one, surely, could believe in much longer.

Another group of tourists was coming up the path behind her, Americans by the sound of them. The guide was Mexican, though. He scrambled up onto the altar, preparing to give his spiel.

"Don't go too near the edge, now."

"Who me, I'm afraid of heights. What d'you see down there?"

"Water, what am I supposed to see?"

The guide clapped his hands for attention. Sarah only half-listened: she didn't really want to know anything more about it.

"Before, people said they threw nothing but virgins in here," the guide began. "How they could tell that, I do not know. It is always hard to tell." He waited for the expected laughter, which came. "But this is not true. Soon, I will tell you how we have found this out. Here we have the altar to the rain god Tlaloc . . ."

Two women sat down near Sarah. They were both wearing cotton slacks, high-heeled sandals and wide-brimmed straw hats.

"You go up the big one?"

"Not on your life. I made Alf go up, I took a picture of him at the top."

"What beats me is why they built all those things in the first place."

"It was their religion, that's what he said."

"Well, at least it would keep people busy."

"Solve the unemployment problem." They both laughed.

"How many more of these ruins is he gonna make us walk around?"

"Beats me. I'm about ruined out. I'd rather go back and sit on the bus."

"I'd rather go shopping. Not that there's much to buy."

Sarah, listening, suddenly felt indignant. Did they have no respect? The sentiments weren't that far from her own of a moment ago, but to hear them from these women, one of whom had a handbag decorated with tasteless straw flowers, made her want to defend the well.

"Nature is very definitely calling," said the woman with the handbag. "I couldn't get in before, there was such a lineup."

"Take a Kleenex," the other woman said. "There's no paper. Not only that, you just about have to wade in. There's water all over the floor."

"Maybe I'll just duck into the bushes," the first woman said.

Edward stood up and massaged his left leg, which had gone to sleep. It was time to go back. If he stayed away too long, Sarah would be querulous, despite the fact that it was she herself who had sent him off on this fool's expedition.

He started to walk back along the path. But then there was a flash of orange, at the corner of his eye. Edward swiveled and raised his binoculars. They were there when you least expected it. It was an oriole, partly hidden behind the leaves; he could see the breast, bright orange, and the dark barred wing. He wanted it to be a hooded oriole, he had not yet seen one. He talked to it silently, begging it to come out into the open. It was strange the way birds were completely magic for him the first time only, when he had never seen them before. But there were hundreds of kinds he would never see; no matter how many he saw there would always be one more. Perhaps this was why he kept looking. The bird was hopping further away from him, into the foliage. *Come back,* he called to it wordlessly, but it was gone.

Edward was suddenly happy. Maybe Sarah hadn't been lying to him after all, maybe she had really seen this bird. Even if she hadn't, it had come anyway, in answer to his need for it. Edward felt he was allowed to see birds only when they wanted him to, as if they had something to tell him, a secret, a message. The Aztecs thought hummingbirds were the souls of dead warriors, but why not all birds, why just warriors? Or perhaps they were the souls of the unborn, as some believed. "A jewel, a precious feather," they called an unborn baby, according to *The Daily Life of the Aztecs. Quetzel,* that was *feather.*

"This is the bird I want to see," Sarah said when they were looking through *The Birds of Mexico* before coming down.

"The Resplendent Quetzal," Edward said. It was a green-and-red bird with spectacular iridescent-blue tail plumes. He explained to her that Quetzal Bird meant Feather Bird. "I don't think we're likely to see it," he said. He looked up the habitat. "*Cloud forests.* I don't think we'll be in any cloud forests."

"Well, that's the one I want," Sarah said. "That's the only one I want."

Sarah was always very determined about what she wanted and what she didn't want. If there wasn't anything on a restaurant menu that appealed to her, she would refuse to order anything; or she would permit him to order for her and then pick around the edges, as she had last night. It was no use telling her that this was the best meal they'd had since coming. She never lost her temper or her self-possession, but she was stubborn. Who but Sarah, for instance, would have insisted on bringing a collapsible umbrella to Mexico in the dry season? He'd argued and argued, pointing out its uselessness and the extra weight, but she'd brought it anyway. And then yesterday afternoon it had rained, a real cloudburst. Everyone else had run for shelter, huddling against walls and inside the temple doorways, but Sarah had put up her umbrella and stood under it, smugly. This had infuriated him. Even when she was wrong, she always managed, somehow, to be right. If only just once she would admit . . . what? That she could make mistakes. This was what really disturbed him: her assumption of infallibility.

And he knew that when the baby had died she had blamed it on him. He still didn't know why. Perhaps it was because he'd gone out for cigarettes, not expecting it to be born so soon. He wasn't there when she was told; she'd had to take the news alone.

"It was nobody's fault," he told her repeatedly. "Not the doctor's, not yours. The cord was twisted."

"I know," she said, and she had never accused him; nevertheless he could feel the reproach, hanging around her like a fog. As if there was anything he could have done.

"I wanted it as much as you did," he told her. And this was true. He hadn't thought of marrying Sarah at all, he'd never mentioned it because it had never occurred to him she would agree, until she told him she was pregnant. Up until that time, she had been the one in control; he was sure he was just an amusement for her. But the marriage hadn't been her suggestion, it had been his. He'd dropped out of Theology, he'd taken his public-school teaching certificate that summer in order to support them. Every evening he had massaged her belly, feeling the child move, touching it through her skin. To him it was a sacred thing, and he included her in his worship. In the sixth month, when she had taken to lying on her back, she had begun to snore, and he would lie awake at night listening to these gentle snores, white and silver they seemed to him, almost songs, mysterious talismans. Unfortunately Sarah had retained this habit, but he no longer felt the same way about it.

When the child had died, he was the one who had cried, not Sarah. She had never cried. She got up and walked around almost immediately, she wanted to get out of the hospital as quickly as possible. The baby clothes she'd been buying disappeared from the apartment; he never found out what she'd done with them, he'd been afraid to ask.

Since that time he'd come to wonder why they were still married. It was illogical. If they'd married because of the child and there was no child, and there continued to be no child, why didn't they separate? But he wasn't sure he wanted this. Maybe he was still hoping something would happen, there would be another child. But there was no use demanding it. They came when they wanted to, not when you wanted them to. They came when you least expected it. A jewel, a precious feather.

"Now I will tell you," said the guide. "The archaeologists have dived down into the well. They have dredged up more than fifty skeletons, and they have found that some of them were not virgins at all but men. Also, most of them were children. So as you can see, that is the end of the popular legend." He made an odd little movement from the top of the altar, almost like a bow, but there was no applause. "They do not do these things to be cruel," he continued. "They believe these people will take a message to the rain god, and live forever in his paradise at the bottom of the well."

The woman with the handbag got up. "Some paradise," she said to her friend. "I'm starting back. You coming?"

In fact the whole group was moving off now, in the scattered way they had. Sarah waited until they had gone. Then she opened her purse and took out the plaster Christ Child she had stolen from the crèche the night before. It was inconceivable to her that she had done such a thing, but there it was, she really had.

She hadn't planned it beforehand. She'd been standing beside the crèche while Edward was paying the bill, he'd had to go into the kitchen to do it as they were very slow about bringing it to the table. No one was watching her: the domino-playing boys were absorbed in their game and the children were riveted to the television. She'd just suddenly reached out her hand, past the Wise Men and through the door of the stable, picked the child up and put it into her purse.

She turned it over in her hands. Separated from the dwarfish Virgin and Joseph, it didn't look quite so absurd. Its diaper was cast as part of it, more like a tunic, it had glass eyes and a sort of pageboy haircut, quite long for a newborn. A perfect child, except for the chip out of the back, luckily where it would not be noticed. Someone must have dropped it on the floor.

You could never be too careful. All the time she was pregnant, she'd taken meticulous care of herself, counting out the vitamin pills prescribed by the doctor and eating only what the books recommended. She had drunk four glasses of milk a day, even though she hated milk. She had done the exercises and gone to the classes. No one would be able to say she had not done the right things. Yet she had been disturbed by the thought that the child would be born with something wrong, it would be a mongoloid or a cripple, or a hydrocephalic with a huge liquid head like the ones she'd seen taking the sun in their wheelchairs on the lawn of the hospital one day. But the child had been perfect.

She would never take that risk, go through all that work again. Let Edward strain his pelvis till he was blue in the face; "trying again," he called it. She took the pill every day, without telling him. She wasn't going to try again. It was too much for anyone to expect of her.

What had she done wrong? She hadn't done anything wrong, that was the trouble. There was nothing and no one to blame, except, obscurely, Edward; and he couldn't be blamed for the child's death, just for not being there. Increasingly since that time he had simply absented himself. When she no longer had the child inside her he had lost interest, he had deserted her. This, she realized, was what she resented most about him. He had left her alone with the corpse, a corpse for which there was no explanation.

"*Lost*," people called it. They spoke of her as having lost the child, as though it was wandering around looking for her, crying plaintively, as though she had neglected it or misplaced it somewhere. But where? What limbo had it gone to, what watery paradise? Sometimes she felt as if there had been some mistake, the child had not been born yet. She could still feel it moving, ever so slightly, holding on to her from the inside.

Sarah placed the baby on the rock beside her. She stood up, smoothing out the wrinkles in her skirt. She was sure there would be more flea bites when she got back to the hotel. She picked up the child and walked slowly towards the well, until she was standing at the very brink.

Edward, coming back up the path, saw Sarah at the well's edge, her arms raised above her head. My God, he thought, she's going to jump. He wanted to shout to her, tell her to stop, but he was afraid to startle her. He could run up behind her, grab her . . . but she would hear him. So he waited, paralyzed, while Sarah stood immobile. He expected her to hurtle downwards, and then what would he do? But she merely drew back her right arm and threw something into the well. Then she turned, half stumbling, towards the rock where he had left her and crouched down.

"Sarah," he said. She had her hands over her face; she didn't lift them. He kneeled so he was level with her. "What is it? Are you sick?"

She shook her head. She seemed to be crying, behind her hands, soundlessly and without moving. Edward was dismayed. The ordinary Sarah, with all her perversity, was something he could cope with, he'd invented ways of coping. But he was unprepared for this. She had always been the one in control.

"Come on," he said, trying to disguise his desperation, "you need some lunch, you'll feel better." He realized as he said this how fatuous it must sound, but for once there was no patronizing smile, no indulgent answer.

"This isn't like you," Edward said, pleading, as if that was a final argument which would snap her out of it, bring back the old calm Sarah.

Sarah took her hands away from her face, and as she did so Edward felt cold fear. Surely what he would see would be the face of someone else, someone entirely different, a woman he had never seen before in his life. Or there would be no face at all. But (and this was almost worse) it was only Sarah, looking much as she always did.

She took a Kleenex out of her purse and wiped her nose. It is like me, she thought. She stood up and smoothed her skirt once more, then collected her purse and her collapsible umbrella.

"I'd like an orange," she said. "They have them, across from the ticket office. I saw them when we came in. Did you find your bird?"

[1977]

Study and Writing Questions

1. In the sixth paragraph, we learn that Sarah had "pretended to be touched and interested, and in fact she had been." How can you pretend to be what you are? In what way is pretense a central concern for the main CHARACTERS?

2. What are the religious IMAGES in this STORY? How are they used to CHARAC-TERIZE Sarah and Edward? How are they used to comment on religion?

3. The IMPLIED AUTHOR, using FREE INDIRECT STYLE, switches from one VIEWPOINT CHARACTER to another and back again at strategic moments in the NARRATIVE. In what ways do these choices of moment control how we feel about the characters?

4. The couple's childlessness is important to each of them in different ways. What should childlessness mean to the IMPLIED READER of this narrative?

5. What are the significances of birds and feathers in this narrative? What is the significance of the title to our understanding of the narrative as a whole?

See also Questions for Contrast and Comparison: 2, 33, 45, 84, 100, 134, 143, and 220.

■■ **JAMES BALDWIN** (1924–1987), *grandson of a slave and son of a revival-*
■■ *ist, was raised in Harlem, New York. At fourteen, he became a preacher at*
Harlem's Fireside Pentecostal Church, which he later came to "revile"; however, he
said "the rhetoric of the storefront church" forever marked his writing. His early
efforts while only a high school graduate, attracted Richard Wright. Thus encour-
aged, Baldwin moved to France (1948–1957) where he gained perspective on his
American life. As a black in a white-dominated world, as the competitive son of a
rigid father, as an apostate from (or rejector of) a Christianity he viewed as
promoting slavery, and as a homosexual in a world he felt as coercively heterosex-
ual, Baldwin came to see individuality and the pursuit of love as the two crucial
goods in life. To protect them, he wrote essays like Notes of a Native Son *(1955) and*
The Fire Next Time *(1963). These essays are not only considered among the most*
distinguished ever produced in America, they also corrected Baldwin's own observa-
tion that "for the horrors of the American Negro's life there has been almost no
language." Although his novels vary in quality, Go Tell It On the Mountain
(1953), about the often brutal, often poignant lives of a storefront congregation, and
Another Country *(1962), about the violence one encounters in meeting other*
people, sexualities, and races, have earned permanent respect. Going to Meet the
Man *collects eight of his best stories.*

Going to Meet the Man

"What's the matter?" she asked.

"I don't know," he said, trying to laugh, "I guess I'm tired."

"You've been working too hard," she said. "I keep telling you."

"Well, goddammit woman," he said, "it's not my fault!" He tried again; he
wretchedly failed again. Then he just lay there, silent, angry, and helpless.
Excitement filled him just like a toothache, but it refused to enter his flesh. He
stroked her breast. This was his wife. He could not ask her to do just a little thing
for him, just to help him out, just for a little while, the way he could ask a nigger
girl to do it. He lay there, and he sighed. The image of a black girl caused a distant
excitement in him, like a far-away light; but, again, the excitement was more like
pain; instead of forcing him to act, it made action impossible.

"Go to sleep," she said, gently, "you got a hard day tomorrow."

"Yeah," he said, and rolled over on his side, facing her, one hand still on one
breast. "Goddamn the niggers. The black stinking coons. You'd think they'd
learn. Wouldn't you think they'd learn? I mean, *wouldn't* you?"

"They going to be out there tomorrow," she said, and took his hand away,
"get some sleep."

He lay there, one hand between his legs, staring at the frail sanctuary of his
wife. A faint light came from the shutters; the moon was full. Two dogs, far away,
were barking at each other, back and forth, insistently, as though they were
agreeing to make an appointment. He heard a car coming north on the road and
he half sat up, his hand reaching for his holster, which was on a chair near the
bed, on top of his pants. The lights hit the shutters and seemed to travel across
the room and then went out. The sound of the car slipped away, he heard it hit

gravel, then heard it no more. Some liver-lipped students, probably, heading back to that college—but coming from where? His watch said it was two in the morning. They could be coming from anywhere, from out of state most likely, and they would be at the court-house tomorrow. The niggers were getting ready. Well, they would be ready, too.

He moaned. He wanted to let whatever was in him out; but it wouldn't come out. Goddamn! he said aloud, and turned again, on his side, away from Grace, staring at the shutters. He was a big, healthy man and he had never had any trouble sleeping. And he wasn't old enough yet to have any trouble getting it up—he was only forty-two. And he was a good man, a God-fearing man, he had tried to do his duty all his life, and he had been a deputy sheriff for several years. Nothing had ever bothered him before, certainly not getting it up. Sometimes, sure, like any other man, he knew that he wanted a little more spice than Grace could give him and he would drive over yonder and pick up a black piece or arrest her, it came to the same thing, but he couldn't do that now, no more. There was no telling what might happen once your ass was in the air. And they were low enough to kill a man then, too, everyone of them, or the girl herself might do it, right while she was making believe you made her feel so good. The niggers. What had the good Lord Almighty had in mind when he made the niggers? Well. They were pretty good at that, all right. Damn. Damn. Goddamn.

This wasn't helping him to sleep. He turned again, toward Grace again, and moved close to her warm body. He felt something he had never felt before. He felt that he would like to hold her, hold her, hold her, and be buried in her like a child and never have to get up in the morning again and go downtown to face those faces, good Christ, they were ugly! and never have to enter that jail house again and smell that smell and hear that singing; never again feel that filthy, kinky, greasy hair under his hand, never again watch those black breasts leap against the leaping cattle prod, never hear those moans again or watch that blood run down or the fat lips split or the sealed eyes struggle open. They were animals, they were no better than animals, what could be done with people like that? Here they had been in a civilized country for years and they still lived like animals. Their houses were dark, with oil cloth or cardboard in the windows, the smell was enough to make you puke your guts out, and there they sat, a whole tribe, pumping out kids, it looked like, every damn five minutes, and laughing and talking and playing music like they didn't have a care in the world, and he reckoned they didn't, neither, and coming to the door, into the sunlight, just standing there, just looking foolish, not thinking of anything but just getting back to what they were doing, saying, Yes suh, Mr. Jesse. I surely will, Mr. Jesse. Fine weather, Mr. Jesse. Why, I thank you, Mr. Jesse. He had worked for a mail-order house for a while and it had been his job to collect the payments for the stuff they bought. They were too dumb to know that they were being cheated blind, but that was no skin off his ass—he was supposed to do his job. They would be late—they didn't have the sense to put money aside; but it was easy to scare them, and he never really had any trouble. Hell, they all liked him, the kids used to smile when he came to the door. He gave them candy, sometimes, or chewing gum, and rubbed their rough bullet heads—maybe the candy should have been poisoned. Those kids were grown now. He had had trouble with one of them today.

"There was this nigger today," he said; and stopped; his voice sounded peculiar. He touched Grace. "You awake?" he asked. She mumbled something, impatiently, she was probably telling him to go to sleep. It was all right. He knew that he was not alone.

"What a funny time," he said, "to be thinking about a thing like that — you listening?" She mumbled something again. He rolled over on his back. "This nigger's one of the ringleaders. We had trouble with him before. We must have had him out there at the work farm three or four times. Well, Big Jim C. and some of the boys really had to whip that nigger's ass today." He looked over at Grace; he could not tell whether she was listening or not; and he was afraid to ask again. "They had this line you know, to register" — he laughed, but she did not — "and they wouldn't stay where Big Jim C. wanted them, no, they had to start blocking traffic all around the court house so couldn't nothing or nobody get through, and Big Jim C. told them to disperse and they wouldn't move, they just kept up that singing, and Big Jim C. figured that the others would move if this nigger would move, him being the ring-leader, but he wouldn't move and he wouldn't let the others move, so they had to beat him and a couple of the others and they threw them in the wagon — but I didn't see this nigger till I got to the jail. They were still singing and I was supposed to make them stop. Well, I couldn't make them stop for me but I knew he could make them stop. He was lying on the ground jerking and moaning, they had threw him in a cell by himself, and blood was coming out his ears from where Big Jim C. and his boys had whipped him. Wouldn't you think they'd learn? I put the prod to him and he jerked some more and he kind of screamed — but he didn't have much voice left. "You make them stop that singing," I said to him, "you hear me? You make them stop that singing." He acted like he didn't hear me and I put it to him again, under his arms, and he just rolled around on the floor and blood started coming from his mouth. He'd pissed his pants already." He paused. His mouth felt dry and his throat was as rough as sandpaper; as he talked, he began to hurt all over with that peculiar excitement which refused to be released. "You all are going to stop your singing, I said to him, and you are going to stop coming down to the court house and disrupting traffic and molesting the people and keeping us from our duties and keeping doctors from getting to sick white women and getting all them Northerners in this town to give our town a bad name — !" As he said this, he kept prodding the boy, sweat pouring from beneath the helmet he had not yet taken off. The boy rolled around in his own dirt and water and blood and tried to scream again as the prod hit his testicles, but the scream did not come out, only a kind of rattle and a moan. He stopped. He was not supposed to kill the nigger. The cell was filled with a terrible odor. The boy was still. "You hear me?" he called. "You had enough?" The singing went on. "You had enough?" His foot leapt out, he had not known it was going to, and caught the boy flush on the jaw. *Jesus*, he thought, *this ain't no nigger, this is a goddamn bull*, and he screamed again, "You had enough? You going to make them stop that singing now?"

But the boy was out. And now he was shaking worse than the boy had been shaking. He was glad no one could see him. At the same time, he felt very close to a very peculiar, particular joy; something deep in him and deep in his memory was stirred, but whatever was in his memory eluded him. He took off his helmet. He walked to the cell door.

"White man," said the boy, from the floor, behind him.

He stopped. For some reason, he grabbed his privates.

"You remember Old Julia?"

The boy said, from the floor, with his mouth full of blood, and one eye, barely open, glaring like the eye of a cat in the dark, "My grandmother's name was Mrs. Julia Blossom. *Mrs.* Julia Blossom. You going to call our women by their right names yet. — And those kids ain't going to stop singing. We going to keep on singing until every one of you miserable white mothers go stark raving out of your minds. Then he closed the one eye; he spat blood; his head fell back against the floor.

He looked down at the boy, whom he had been seeing, off and on, for more than a year, and suddenly remembered him: Old Julia had been one of his mail-order customers, a nice old woman. He had not seen her for years, he supposed that she must be dead.

He had walked into the yard, the boy had been sitting in a swing. He had smiled at the boy, and asked, "Old Julia home?"

The boy looked at him for a long time before he answered. "Don't no Old Julia live here."

"This is her house. I know her. She's lived here for years."

The boy shook his head. "You might know a Old Julia someplace else, white man. But don't nobody by that name live here."

He watched the boy; the boy watched him. The boy certainly wasn't more than ten. *White man.* He didn't have time to be fooling around with some crazy kid. He yelled, "Hey! Old Julia!"

But only silence answered him. The expression on the boy's face did not change. The sun beat down on them both, still and silent; he had the feeling that he had been caught up in a nightmare, a nightmare dreamed by a child; perhaps one of the nightmares he himself had dreamed as a child. It had that feeling — everything familiar, without undergoing any other change, had been subtly and hideously displaced: the trees, the sun, the patches of grass in the yard, the leaning porch and the weary porch steps and the cardboard in the windows and the black hole of the door which looked like the entrance to a cave, and the eyes of the pickaninny, all, all, were charged with malevolence. *White man.* He looked at the boy. "She's gone out?"

The boy said nothing.

"Well," he said, "tell her I passed by and I'll pass by next week." He started to go; he stopped. "You want some chewing gum?"

The boy got down from the swing and started for the house. He said, "I don't want nothing you got, white man." He walked into the house and closed the door behind him.

Now the boy looked as though he were dead. Jesse wanted to go over to him and pick him up and pistol whip him until the boy's head burst open like a melon. He began to tremble with what he believed was rage, sweat, both cold and hot, raced down his body, the singing filled him as though it were a weird, uncontrollable, monstrous howling rumbling up from the depths of his own belly, he felt an icy fear rise in him and raise him up, and he shouted, he howled, "You lucky we *pump* some white blood into you every once in a while — your women! Here's what I got for all the black bitches in the world — !" Then he was, abruptly, almost too weak to stand; to his bewilderment, his horror, beneath his own fingers, he felt himself violently stiffen — with no warning at all; he dropped his hands and he stared at the boy and he left the cell.

"All that singing they do," he said. "All that singing." He could not remember the first time he had heard it; he had been hearing it all his life. It was the sound with which he was most familiar — though it was also the sound of which he had been least conscious — and it had always contained an obscure comfort. They were singing to God. They were singing for mercy and they hoped to go to heaven, and he had even sometimes felt, when looking into the eyes of some of the old women, a few of the very old men, that they were singing for mercy for his soul, too. Of course he had never thought of their heaven or of what God was, or could be, for them; God was the same for everyone, he supposed, and heaven was where good people went — he supposed. He had never thought much about what it meant to be a good person. He tried to be a good person and treat everybody right: it wasn't his fault if the niggers had taken it into their heads to fight against God and go against the rules laid down in the Bible for everyone to read! Any preacher would tell you that. He was only doing his duty: protecting white people from the niggers and the niggers from themselves. And there were still lots of good niggers around — he had to remember that; they weren't all like that boy this afternoon; and the good niggers must be mighty sad to see what was happening to their people. They would thank him when this was over. In that way they had, the best of them, not quite looking him in the eye, in a low voice, with a little smile: We surely thanks you, Mr. Jesse. From the bottom of our hearts, we thanks you. He smiled. They hadn't all gone crazy. This trouble would pass. — He knew that the young people had changed some of the words to the songs. He had scarcely listened to the words before and he did not listen to them now; but he knew that the words were different; he could hear that much. He did not know if the faces were different, he had never, before this trouble began, watched them as they sang, but he certainly did not like what he saw now. They hated him, and this hatred was blacker than their hearts, blacker than their skins, redder than their blood, and harder, by far, than his club. Each day, each night, he felt worn out, aching, with their smell in his nostrils and filling his lungs, as though he were drowning — drowning in niggers; and it was all to be done again when he awoke. It would never end. It would never end. Perhaps this was what the singing had meant all along. They had not been singing black folks into heaven, they had been singing white folks into hell.

Everyone felt this black suspicion in many ways, but no one knew how to express it. Men much older than he, who had been responsible for law and order much longer than he, were now much quieter than they had been, and the tone of their jokes, in a way that he could not quite put his finger on, had changed. These men were his models, they had been friends to his father, and they had taught him what it meant to be a man. He looked to them for courage now. It wasn't that he didn't know that what he was doing was right — he knew that, nobody had to tell him that; it was only that he missed the ease of former years. But they didn't have much time to hang out with each other these days. They tended to stay close to their families every free minute because nobody knew what might happen next. Explosions rocked the night of their tranquil town. Each time each man wondered silently if perhaps this time the dynamite had not fallen into the wrong hands. They thought that they knew where all the guns were; but they could not possibly know every move that was made in that secret place where the darkies lived. From time to time it was suggested that they form a posse and search the home of every nigger, but they hadn't done it yet. For one thing, this might have brought the bastards from the North down on their backs; for another, although the niggers were scattered throughout the town — down in the hollow near the railroad tracks, way west near the mills, up on the hill, the well-off ones, and some out near the college — nothing seemed to happen in one part of town without the niggers immediately knowing it in the other. This meant that they could not take them by surprise. They rarely mentioned it, but they *knew* that some of the niggers had guns. It stood to reason, as they said, since, after all, some of them had been in the Army. There were niggers in the Army right now and God knows they wouldn't have had any trouble stealing this half-assed government blind — the whole world was doing it, look at the European countries and all those countries in Africa. They made jokes about it — bitter jokes; and they cursed the government in Washington, which had betrayed them; but they had not yet formed a posse. Now, if their town had been laid out like some towns in the North, where all the niggers lived together in one locality, they could have gone down and set fire to the houses and brought about peace that way. If the niggers had all lived in one place, they could have kept the fire in one place. But the way this town was laid out, the fire could hardly be controlled. It would spread all over town — and the niggers would probably be helping it to spread. Still, from time to time, they spoke of doing it, anyway; so that now there was a real fear among them that somebody might go crazy and light the match.

They rarely mentioned anything not directly related to the war that they were fighting, but this had failed to establish between them the unspoken communication of soldiers during a war. Each man, in the thrilling silence which sped outward from their exchanges, their laughter, and their anecdotes, seemed wrestling, in various degrees of darkness, with a secret which he could not articulate to himself, and which, however directly it related to the war, related yet more surely to his privacy and his past. They could no longer be sure, after all, that they had all done the same things. They had never dreamed that their privacy could contain any element of terror, could threaten, that is, to reveal itself to the scrutiny of a judgment day, while remaining unreadable and inaccessible to themselves; nor had they dreamed that the past, while certainly refusing to be forgotten, could yet so stubbornly refuse to be remembered. They felt themselves mysteriously set at naught, as no longer entering into the real concerns of other people — while here they were, out-numbered, fighting to save the civilized world. They had thought that people would care — people didn't care; not enough, anyway, to help them. It would have been a help, really, or at least a relief, even to have been forced to surrender. Thus they had lost, probably forever, their old and easy connection with each other. They were forced to depend on each other more and, at the same time, to trust each other less. Who could tell when one of them might not betray them all, for money, or for the ease of confession? But no one dared imagine what there might be to confess. They were soldiers fighting a war, but their relationship to each other was that of accomplices in a crime. They all had to keep their mouths shut.

I stepped in the river at Jordan.

Out of the darkness of the room, out of nowhere, the line came flying up at him, with the melody and the beat. He turned wordlessly toward his sleeping wife. *I stepped in the river at Jordan.* Where had he heard that song?

"Grace," he whispered. "You awake?"

She did not answer. If she was awake, she wanted him to sleep. Her breathing was slow and easy, her body slowly rose and fell.

I stepped in the river at Jordan.
The water came to my knees.

He began to sweat. He felt an overwhelming fear, which yet contained a curious and dreadful pleasure.

I stepped in the river at Jordan.
The water came to my waist.

It had been night, as it was now, he was in the car between his mother and his father, sleepy, his head in his mother's lap, sleepy, and yet full of excitement. The singing came from far away, across the dark fields. There were no lights anywhere. They had said good-bye to all the others and turned off on this dark dirt road. They were almost home.

I stepped in the river at Jordan,
The water came over my head,
I looked way over to the other side,
He was making up my dying bed!

"I guess they singing for him," his father said, seeming very weary and subdued now. "Even when they're sad, they sound like they just about to go and tear off a piece." He yawned and leaned across the boy and slapped his wife lightly on the shoulder, allowing his hand to rest there for a moment. "Don't they?"

"Don't talk that way," she said.

"Well, that's what we going to do," he said, "you can make up your mind to that." He started whistling. "You see? When I begin to feel it, I gets kind of musical, too."

Oh, Lord! Come on and ease my troubling mind!

He had a black friend, his age, eight, who lived nearby. His name was Otis. They wrestled together in the dirt. Now the thought of Otis made him sick. He began to shiver. His mother put her arm around him.

"He's tired," she said.

"We'll be home soon," said his father. He began to whistle again.

"We didn't see Otis this morning," Jesse said. He did not know why he said this. His voice, in the darkness of the car, sounded small and accusing.

"You haven't seen Otis for a couple of mornings," his mother said.

That was true. But he was only concerned about *this* morning.

"No," said his father, "I reckon Otis's folks was afraid to let him show himself this morning."

"But Otis didn't do nothing!" Now his voice sounded questioning.

"Otis *can't* do nothing," said his father, "he's too little." The car lights picked up their wooden house, which now solemnly approached them, the lights falling around it like yellow dust. Their dog, chained to a tree, began to bark.

"We just want to make sure Otis *don't* do nothing," said his father, and stopped the car. He looked down at Jesse. "And you tell him what your Daddy said, you hear?"

"Yes, sir," he said.

His father switched off the lights. The dog moaned and pranced, but they ignored him and went inside. He could not sleep. He lay awake, hearing the night sounds, the dog yawning and moaning outside, the sawing of the crickets, the cry of the owl, dogs barking far away, then no sounds at all, just the heavy, endless buzzing of the night. The darkness pressed on his eyelids like a scratchy blanket. He turned, he turned again. He wanted to call his mother, but he knew his father would not like this. He was terribly afraid. Then he heard his father's voice in the other room, low, with a joke in it; but this did not help him, it frightened him more, he knew what was going to happen. He put his head under the blanket, then pushed his head out again, for fear, staring at the dark window. He heard his mother's moan, his father's sigh; he gritted his teeth. Then their bed began to rock. His father's breathing seemed to fill the world.

That morning, before the sun had gathered all its strength, men and women, some flushed and some pale with excitement, came with news. Jesse's father seemed to know what the news was before the first jalopy stopped in the yard, and he ran out, crying, "They got him, then? They got him?"

The first jalopy held eight people, three men and two women and three children. The children were sitting on the laps of the grown-ups. Jesse knew two of them, the two boys; they shyly and uncomfortably greeted each other. He did not know the girl.

"Yes, they got him," said one of the women, the older one, who wore a wide hat and a fancy, faded blue dress. "They found him early this morning."

"How far had he got?" Jesse's father asked.

"He hadn't got no further than Harkness," one of the men said. "Look like he got lost up there in all them trees — or maybe he just got so scared he couldn't move." They all laughed.

"Yes, and you know it's near a graveyard, too," said the younger woman, and they laughed again.

"Is that where they got him now?" asked Jesse's father.

By this time there were three cars piled behind the first one, with everyone looking excited and shining, and Jesse noticed that they were carrying food. It was like a Fourth of July picnic.

"Yeah, that's where he is," said one of the men, "declare, Jesse, you going to keep us here all day long, answering your damn fool questions. Come on, we ain't go no time to waste."

"Don't bother putting up no food," cried a woman from one of the other cars, "we got enough. Just come on."

"Why, thank you," said Jesse's father, "we be right along then."

"I better get a sweater for the boy," said his mother, "in case it turns cold."

Jesse watched his mother's thin legs cross the yard. He knew that she also wanted to comb her hair a little and maybe put on a better dress, the dress she wore to church. His father guessed this, too, for he yelled behind her, "Now don't you go trying to turn yourself into no movie star. You just come on." But he laughed as he said this, and winked at the men; his wife was younger and prettier than most of the other women. He clapped Jesse on the head and started pulling him toward the car. "You all go on," he said. "I'll be right behind you. Jesse, you go tie up that there dog while I get this car started."

The cars sputtered and coughed and shook; the caravan began to move; bright dust filled the air. As soon as he was tied up, the dog began to bark. Jesse's mother came out of the house, carrying a jacket for his father and a sweater for Jesse. She had put a ribbon in her hair and had an old shawl around her shoulders.

"Put these in the car, son," she said, and handed everything to him. She bent down and stroked the dog, looked to see if there was water in his bowl, then went back up the three porch steps and closed the door.

"Come on," said his father, "ain't nothing in there for nobody to steal." He was sitting in the car, which trembled and belched. The last car of the caravan had disappeared but the sound of singing floated behind them.

Jesse got into the car, sitting close to his father, loving the smell of the car, and the trembling, and the bright day, and the sense of going on a great and unexpected journey. His mother got in and closed the door and the car began to move. Not until then did he ask, "Where are we going? Are we going on a picnic?

He had a feeling that he knew where they were going, but he was not sure.

"That's right," his father said, "we're going on a picnic. You won't ever forget *this* picnic — !"

"Are we," he asked, after a moment, "going to see the bad nigger — the one that knocked down old Miss Standish?"

"Well, I reckon," said his mother, "that we *might* see him."

He started to ask, *Will a lot of niggers be there? Will Otis be there?* — but he did not ask his question, to which, in a strange and uncomfortable way, he already knew the answer. Their friends, in the other cars, stretched up the road as far as he could see; other cars had joined them; there were cars behind them. They were singing. The sun seemed, suddenly very hot, and he was, at once very happy and a little afraid. He did not quite understand what was happening, and he did not know what to ask — he had no one to ask. He had grown accustomed, for the solution of such mysteries, to go to Otis. He felt that Otis knew everything. But he could not ask Otis about this. Anyway, he had not seen Otis for two days; he had not seen a black face anywhere for more than two days; and he now realized, as they began chugging up the long hill which eventually led to Harkness, that there were no black faces on the road this morning, no black people anywhere. From the houses in which they lived, all along the road, no smoke curled, no life stirred — maybe one or two chickens were to be seen, that was all. There was no one at the windows, no one in the yard, no one sitting on the porches, and the doors were closed. He had come this road many a time and seen women washing in the yard (there were no clothes on the clotheslines), men working in the fields, children playing in the dust; black men passed them on the road other mornings, other days, on foot, or in wagons, sometimes in cars, tipping their hats, smiling, joking, their teeth a solid white against their skin, their eyes as warm as the sun, the blackness of their skin like dull fire against the white of the blue or the grey of their torn clothes. They passed the nigger church — dead-white, desolate, locked up; and the graveyard, where no one knelt or walked, and he saw no flowers. He wanted to ask, *Where are they? Where are they all?* But he did not dare. As the hill grew steeper, the sun grew colder. He looked at his mother and his father. They looked straight ahead, seeming to be listening to the singing which echoed and echoed in this graveyard silence. They were strangers to him now. They were looking at something he could not see. His father's lips had a strange, cruel curve, he wet his lips from time to time, and swallowed. He was terribly aware of his father's tongue, it was as though he had never seen it before. And his father's body suddenly seemed immense, bigger than a mountain. His eyes, which were grey-green, looked yellow in the sunlight; or at least there was a light in them which he had never seen before. His mother patted her hair and adjusted the ribbon, leaning forward to look into the car mirror. "You look all right," said his father, and laughed. "When that nigger looks at you, he's going to swear he throwed his life away for nothing. Wouldn't be surprised if he don't come back to haunt you." And he laughed again.

The singing now slowly began to cease; and he realized that they were nearing their destination. They had reached a straight, narrow, pebbly road, with trees on either side. The sunlight filtered down on them from a great height, as though they were under-water; and the branches of the trees scraped against the cars with a tearing sound. To the right of them, and beneath them, invisible now, lay the town; and to the left, miles of trees which led to the high mountain range which his ancestors had crossed in order to settle in this valley. Now, all was silent, except for the bumping of the tires against the rocky road, the sputtering of motors, and the sound of a crying child. And they seemed to move more slowly. They were beginning to climb again. He watched the cars ahead as they toiled patiently upward, disappearing into the sunlight of the clearing. Presently, he felt their vehicle also rise, heard his father's changed breathing, the sunlight hit his face, the trees moved away from them, and they were there. As their car crossed the clearing, he looked around. There seemed to be millions, there were certainly hundreds of people in the clearing, staring toward something he could not see. There was a fire. He could not see the flames, but he smelled the smoke. Then they were on the other side of the clearing, among the trees again. His father drove off the road and parked the car behind a great many other cars. He looked down at Jesse.

"You all right?" he asked.

"Yes, sir," he said.

"Well, come on, then," his father said. He reached over and opened the door on his mother's side. His mother stepped out first. They followed her into the clearing. At first he was aware only of confusion, of his mother and father greeting and being greeted, himself being handled, hugged, and patted, and told how much he had grown. The wind blew the smoke from the fire across the clearing into this eyes and nose. He could not see over the backs of the people in front of him. The sounds of laughing and cursing and wrath — and something else — rolled in waves from the front of the mob to the back. Those in front expressed their delight at what they saw, and this delight rolled backward, wave upon wave, across the clearing, more acrid than the smoke. His father reached down suddenly and sat Jesse on his shoulders.

Now he saw the fire — of twigs and boxes, piled high; flames made pale orange and yellow and thin as a veil under the steadier light of the sun; grey-blue smoke rolled upward and poured over their heads. Beyond the shifting curtain of fire and smoke, he made out first only a length of gleaming chain, attached to a great limb of the tree; then he saw that this chain bound two black hands together at the wrist, dirty yellow palm facing dirty yellow palm. The smoke poured up; the hands dropped out of sight; a cry went up from the crowd. Then the hands slowly came into view again, pulled upward by the chain. This time he saw the kinky, sweating, bloody head — he had never before seen a head with so much hair on it, hair so black and so tangled that it seemed like another jungle. The head was hanging. He saw the forehead, flat and high, with a kind of arrow of hair in the center, like he had, like his father had; they called it a widow's peak; and the mangled eye brows, the wide nose, the closed eyes, and the glinting eye lashes and the hanging lips, all streaming with blood and sweat. His hands were straight above his head. All his weight pulled downward from his hands; and he was a big man, a bigger man than his father, and black as an African jungle Cat, and naked. Jesse pulled upward; his father's hands held him firmly by the ankles. He wanted to say something, he did not know what, but nothing he said could have been heard, for now the crowd roared again as a man stepped forward and put more wood on the fire. The flames leapt up. He thought he heard the hanging man scream, but he was not sure. Sweat was pouring from the hair in his armpits, poured down his sides, over his chest, into his navel and his groin. He was lowered again; he was raised again. Now Jesse knew that he heard him scream. The head went back, the mouth wide open, blood bubbling from the mouth; the veins of the neck jumped out; Jesse clung to his father's neck in terror as the cry rolled over the crowd. The cry of all the people rose to answer the dying man's cry. He wanted death to come quickly. They wanted to make death wait; and it was they who held death, now, on a leash which they lengthened little by little. *What did he do?* Jesse wondered. *What did the man do? What did he do?* — but he could not ask his father. He was seated on his father's shoulders, but his father was far away. There were two older men, friends of his father's, raising and lowering the chain; everyone, indiscriminately, seemed to be responsible for the fire. There was no hair left on the nigger's privates, and the eyes, now, were wide open, as white as the eyes of a clown or a doll. The smoke now carried a terrible odor across the clearing, the odor of something burned which was both sweet and rotten.

He turned his head a little and saw the field of faces. He watched his mother's face. Her eyes were very bright, her mouth was open: she was more beautiful than he had ever seen her, and more strange. He began to feel a joy he had never felt before. He watched the hanging, gleaming body, the most beautiful and terrible object he had ever seen till then. One of his father's friends reached up and in his hands he held a knife: and Jesse wished that he had been that man. It was a long, bright knife and the sun seemed to catch it, to play with it, to caress it — it was brighter than the fire. And a wave of laughter swept the crowd. Jesse felt his father's hands on his ankles slip and tighten. The man with the knife walked toward the crowd, smiling slightly; as though this were a signal, silence fell; he heard his mother cough. Then the man with the knife walked up to the hanging body. He turned and smiled again. Now there was a silence all over the field. The hanging head looked up. It seemed fully conscious now, as though the fire had burned out terror and pain. The man with the knife took the nigger's privates in his hand, one hand, still smiling, as though he were weighing them. In the cradle of the one white hand, the nigger's privates seemed as remote as meat being weighed in the scales; but seemed heavier, too, much heavier, and Jesse felt his scrotum tighten; and huge, huge, much bigger than his father's, flaccid, hairless, the largest thing he had ever seen till then, and the blackest. The white hand stretched them, cradled them, caressed them. Then the dying man's eyes looked straight into Jesse's eyes — it could not have been as long as a second, but it seemed longer than a year. Then Jesse screamed, and the crowd screamed as the knife flashed, first up, then down, cutting the dreadful thing away, and the blood came roaring down. Then the crowd rushed forward, tearing at the body with their hands, with knives, with rocks, with stones, howling and cursing. Jesse's head, of its own weight, fell downward toward his father's head. Someone stepped forward and drenched the body with kerosene. Where the man had been, a great sheet of flame appeared. Jesse's father lowered him to the ground.

"Well, I told you," said the father, "you wasn't never going to forget *this* picnic." His father's face was full of sweat, his eyes were very peaceful. At that moment Jesse loved his father more than he had ever loved him. He felt that his father had carried him through a mighty test, had revealed to him a great secret which would be the key to his life forever.

"I reckon," he said. "I reckon."

Jesse's father took him by the hand and, with his mother a little behind them, talking and laughing with the other women, they walked through the crowd, across the clearing. The black body was on the ground, the chain which had held it was being rolled up by one of his father's friends. Whatever the fire had left undone, the hands and the knives and the stones of the people accomplished. The head was caved in, one eye was torn out, one ear was hanging. But one had to look carefully to realize this, for it was, now, merely, a black charred object on the black, charred ground. He lay spread-eagled with what had been a wound between what had been his legs.

"They going to leave him there, then?" Jesse whispered.

"Yeah," said his father, "they'll come and get him by and by. I reckon we better get over there and get some of that food before it's all gone."

"I reckon," he muttered now to himself; "I reckon." Grace stirred and touched him on the thigh: the moonlight covered her like glory. Something bubbled up in him, his nature again returned to him. He thought of the boy in the cell; he thought of the man in the fire; he thought of the knife and grabbed himself and stroked himself and a terrible sound, something between a high laugh and a howl, came out of him and dragged his sleeping wife up on one elbow. She stared at him in the moonlight which had now grown cold as ice. He thought of the morning and grabbed her, laughing and crying, crying and laughing, and he whispered, as he stroked her, as he took her, "Come on, sugar, I'm going to do you like a nigger, just like a nigger, come on, sugar, and love me just like you'd love a nigger." He thought of the morning as he labored and she moaned, thought of morning as he labored harder than he ever had before, and before his labors had ended, he heard the first cock crow and the dogs begin to bark, and the sound of tires on the gravel road.

[1965]

Study and Writing Questions

1. How does Baldwin use details to convey more than the STORY seems at first to tell? Consider, for example, the two dogs barking on the first page of the NARRATIVE, Jesse's previous occupation, the Biblical names, and the name Jim C. (perhaps for Jim Crow?). What other details seem subtly significant to you?
2. How does the use of FLASHBACK, rather than a chronological telling, emphasize some points and ignore others in the story of how Jesse got to this final morning?
3. Considering its key IMAGES and proceeding sentence by sentence, what does the last paragraph mean?
4. What is the relationship between sex and violence in this narrative?
5. What are the roles of religion in the lives of these CHARACTERS?

See also Questions for Contrast and Comparison: 55, 58, 79, 84, 86, 119, 122, 133, 151, and 239.

■ **AMIRI BARAKA** (1934–), *born LeRoi Jones in Newark, New Jersey,*
began writing early, won a scholarship to Rutgers University and later trans-
ferred to Howard University (A.B., 1953). Baraka also did graduate work at
Columbia University (A.M. in German Literature) and the New School for Social
Research before serving in the Strategic Air Command. With his first wife (Hettie
Cohen), he founded Yugen (1958), an important vehicle for Beat Generation writers
such as William Burroughs and Allen Ginsberg. Bakara became a regular contrib-
utor of poetry, essays, jazz reviews, and short stories to Evergreen Review, Poetry,
Saturday Review, and The Nation. His first book, Preface to a Twenty-Volume
Suicide Note (poetry; 1961), was acclaimed. After visiting Cuba (1960), he became
a political activist. Dutchman, about violence and sexuality in race relations, won
an Obie for Best American Play of 1964. In 1965 Jones left his family, moved from
Greenwich Village to Harlem, published his autobiographical novel, The System of
Dante's Hell, and founded the Black Arts Repertory Theater. One year later, he
married Sylvia Robinson (Amina Baraka). He returned to Newark in 1968,
founded a black nationalist group, began to speak Swahili, changed his name to
Amiri Baraka, took the title Imamu (spiritual leader), and founded Spirit House as
a base for his ongoing community and political activism. Since 1983, he has taught
Afro-American Studies at the State University of New York at Stony Brook.

The Death of Horatio Alger

The cold red building burned my eyes. The bricks hung together, like the city,
the nation, under the dubious cement of rationalism and need. A need so
controlled, it only erupted out of the used-car lots, or sat parked, Saturdays, in
front of our orange house, for Orlando, or Algernon, or Danny, or J.D. to polish.
There was silence, or summers, noise. But this was a few days after Christmas,
and the ice melted from the roofs and the almost frozen water knocked lethargi-
cally against windows, tar roofs and slow dogs moping through the yards. The
building was Central Avenue School. And its tired red sat on the corner of
Central Avenue and Dey (pronounced *die* by the natives, *day* by the teachers, or
any non-resident whites) Street. Then, on Dey, halfway up the block, the playground took over. A tarred-over yard, though once there had been gravel,
surrounded by cement and a wire metal fence.

The snow was dirty as it sat dull and melting near the Greek restaurants,
and the dimly lit "grocey" stores of the Negroes. The rich boys had metal wagons,
the poor rode in. The poor made up games, the rich played them. The poor won
the games, or as an emergency measure, the fights. No one thought of the snow
except Mr. Feld, the playground director, who was in charge of it, or Miss Martin,
the husky gym teacher Matthew Stodges had pushed into the cloakroom, who
had no chains on her car. Grey slush ran over the curbs, and our dogs drank it
out of boredom, shaking their heads and snorting.

I had said something about J.D.'s father, as to who he was, or had he ever
been. And J., usually a confederate, and private strong arm, broke bad because
Augie, Norman, and white Johnny were there, and laughed, misunderstanding
simple "dozens" with ugly insult, in that curious scholarship the white man
affects when he suspects a stronger link than sociology, or the tired cultural lies
of Harcourt, Brace sixth-grade histories. And under their naïveté he grabbed my

shirt and pushed me in the snow. I got up, brushing dead ice from my ears, and he pushed me down again, this time dumping a couple pounds of cold dirty slush down my neck, calmly hysterical at his act.

J. moved away and stood on an icy garbage hamper, sullenly throwing wet snow at the trucks on Central Avenue. I pushed myself into a sitting position, shaking my head. Tears full in my eyes, and the cold slicing minutes from my life. I wasn't making a sound. I wasn't thinking any thought I could make someone else understand. Just the rush of young fear and anger and disgust. I could have murdered God, in that simple practical way we kick dogs off the bottom step.

Augie (my best white friend), fat Norman, whose hook shots usually hit the rim, and were good for easy tip-ins by our big men, and useless white Johnny who had some weird disease that made him stare, even in the middle of a game, he'd freeze, and sometimes line drives almost knocked his head off while he shuddered slightly, cracking and recracking his huge knuckles. They were howling and hopping, they thought it was so funny that J. and I had come to blows. And especially, I guess, that I had got my lumps. "Hey, wiseass, somebody's gonna break your nose!" fat Norman would say over and over whenever I did something to him. Hold his pants when he tried his jump shot; spike him sliding into home (he was a lousy catcher); talk about his brother who hung out under the El and got naked in alleyways.

(The clucks of Autumn could have, right at that moment, easily seduced me. Away, and into school. To masquerade as a half-rich nigra with shiny feet. Back through the clean station, and up the street. Stopping to talk on the way. One beer gets you drunk and you stand in an empty corridor, lined with Italian paintings, talking about the glamours of sodomy.)

Rise and Slay.

I hurt so bad, and inside without bleeding I realized the filthy grey scratches my blood would carry to my heart. John walked off staring, and Augie and Norman disappeared, so easily there in the snow. And J.D., too, my first love, drifted against the easy sky. Weeping at what he'd done. No one there but me. THE SHORT SKINNY BOY WITH THE BUBBLE EYES.

Could leap up and slay them. Could hammer my fist and misery through their faces. Could strangle and bake them in the crude jungle of my feeling. Could stuff them in the sewie hole with the collected garbage of children's guilt. Could elevate them into heroic images of my own despair. A righteous messenger from the wrong side of the tracks. Gym teachers, cutthroats, aging pickets, ease by in the cold. The same lyric chart, exchange of particulars, that held me in my minutes, the time "Brownie" rammed the glass door down and ate up my suit. Even my mother, in a desperate fit of rhythm, was not equal to the task. Which was simple economics. I.e., a white man's dog cannot bite your son if he has been taught that something very ugly will happen to him if he does. He might pace stupidly in his ugly fur, but he will never never bite.

But what really stays to be found completely out, except stupid enterprises like art? The word on the page, the paint on the canvas (Marzette dragging in used-up canvases to revive their hopeless correspondence with the times), stone clinging to air, as if it were real. Or something a Deacon would admit was beautiful. The conscience rules against ideas. The point was to be where you wanted to, and do what you wanted to. After all is "said and done," what is left but those sheepish constructions. "I've got to go to the toilet" is no less pressing than the Puritans taking off for Massachusetts, and dragging their devils with them. (There is in those parts, even now, the peculiar smell of roasted sex organs. And when a good New Englander leaves his house in the earnestly moral sub-towns to go into the smoking hells of soon to be destroyed Yankee Gomorrahs, you watch him pull very firmly at his tie, or strapping on very tightly his evil watch.) The penitence there. The masochism. So complete and conscious a phenomenon. Like a standard of beauty; for instance, the bespectacled, soft-breasted, gently pigeon-toed maidens of America. Neither rich nor poor, with intelligent smiles and straight lovely noses. No one would think of them as beautiful but these mysterious scions of the puritans. They value health and devotion, and their good women, the left power of all our nation, are unpresuming subtle beauties, who could even live with poets (if they are from the right stock), if pushed to that. But mostly they are where they should be, reading good books and opening windows to air out their bedrooms. And it is a useful memory here, because such things as these were the vague images that had even so early, helped shape me. Light freckles, sandy hair, narrow clean bodies. Though none lived where I lived then. And I don't remember a direct look at them even, with clear knowledge of my desire, until one afternoon I gave a speech at East Orange High, as sports editor of our high school paper, which should have been printed in Italian, and I saw there, in the auditorium, young American girls, for the first time. And have loved them as flesh things emanating from real life, that is, in contrast to my own, a scraping and floating through the last three red and blue stripes of the flag, that settles the hash of the lower middle class. So that even sprawled there in the snow, with my blood and pompous isolation, I vaguely knew of a glamorous world and was mistaken into thinking it could be gotten from books. Negroes and Italians beat and shaped me, and my allegiance is there. But the triumph of romanticism was parquet floors, yellow dresses, gardens and sandy hair. I must have felt the loss and could not rise against a cardboard world of dark hair and linoleum. Reality was something I was convinced I could not have.

          And thus to be flogged or put to the rack. For all our secret energies. The first leap over the barrier: when the victim finds he can no longer stomach his own "group." Politics whinnies, but is still correct, and asleep in a windy barn. The beautiful statue of victory, whose arms were called duty. And they curdle in her snatch thrust there by angry minorities, along with their own consciences. Poets climb, briefly, off their motorcycles, to find out who owns their words. We are named by all the things we will never understand. Whether we can fight or not, or even at the moment of our hugest triumph we stare off into space remembering the snow melting in our cuts, and all the pimps of reason who've ever conquered us. It is the harshest form of love.

I could not see when I "chased" Norman and Augie. Chased in quotes because, they really did not have to run. They could have turned, and myth aside, calmly whipped my ass. But they ran, laughing and keeping warm. And J.D. kicked snow from around a fire hydrant flatly into the gutter. Smiling and broken, with his head hung just slanted towards the yellow dog ice running down a hole. I took six or seven long running steps and tripped. I couldn't have been less interested, but the whole project had gotten out of hand. I was crying, and my hands were freezing, and the two white boys leaned against the pointed metal fence and laughed and slapped their knees. I threw snow stupidly in their direction. It fell short and was not even noticed as it dropped.

(All of it rings in your ears for a long time. But the payback . . . in simple terms against such actual sin as supposing quite confidently that the big sweating purple whore staring from her peed up hall very casually at your whipping has *never* been loved . . . is hard. We used to say.)

Then I pushed to my knees and could only see J. leaning there against the hydrant looking just over my head. I called to him, for help really. But the words rang full of dead venom. I screamed his mother a purple nigger with alligator titties. His father a bilious white man with sores on his jowls. I was screaming for help in my hatred and loss, and only the hatred would show. And he came over shouting for me to shut up. Shut Up skinny bastard. I'll break your ass if you don't. Norman had both hands on his stomach, his laugh was getting so violent, and he danced awkwardly toward us howling to agitate J. to beat me some more. But J. whirled on him perfectly and rapped him hard under his second chin. Norman was going to say, "Hey me-an," in that hated twist of our speech, and J. hit him again, between his shoulder and chest, and almost dropped him to his knees. Augie cooled his howl to a giggle of concern and backed up until Norman turned and they both went shouting up the street.

I got to my feet, wiping my freezing hands on my jacket. J. was looking at me hard, like country boys do, when their language, or the new tone they need to take on once they come to this cold climate (1940's New Jersey) fails, and they are left with only the old Southern tongue, which cruel farts like me used to deride their lack of interest in America. I turned to walk away. Both my eyes were nothing but water, though it held at their rims, stoically refusing to blink and thus begin to sob uncontrollably. And to keep from breaking down I wheeled and hid the weeping by screaming at that boy. You nigger without a father. You eat your mother's pussy. And he wheeled me around and started to hit me again.

Someone called my house and my mother and father and grandmother and sister were strung along Dey street, in some odd order. (They couldn't have come out of the house "together.") And I was conscious first of my father saying, "Go on Mickey, hit him. Fight back." And for a few seconds, under the weight of that plea for my dignity, I tried, I feinted and danced, but I couldn't even roll up my fists. The whole street was blurred and hot as my eyes. I swung and swung, but J.D. bashed me when he wanted to.

My mother stopped the fight finally, shuddering at the thing she'd made. "His hands are frozen, Michael. His hands are frozen." And my father looks at me even now, wondering if they'll ever thaw.

[1969]

Study and Writing Questions

1. What issues are raised by the descriptions in the STORY'S opening paragraph? Do they predict the fighting that will follow?
2. What do we know about the NARRATOR—his age, race, location, social class, relationships, and so on? What do his arresting metaphors (for example, "evil watch," "dead ice," and "cardboard world") reveal about him?
3. What is the relationship of the middle section of the story to the opening and closing sections? How would you read the closing section differently if the middle section were missing?
4. The narrator says, "We are named by all the things we will never understand." What might that assertion have to do with questions of race, class, or gender? Does that assertion have anything to do with the sense of wonder expressed in the story's last line?
5. The typical story by Horatio Alger (1832–1890) concerns an unfortunate, often orphaned, always poor white boy who, by luck, comes to the attention of a rich person. This benefactor ultimately rewards the boy's hard work and good character with patronage that leads to the youngster's eventual rise to the upper middle class. In what way(s) is it fitting that this story is called "The Death of Horatio Alger"? Is the story ultimately hopeless? If not, why not?

See also Questions for Contrast and Comparison: 50, 55, 64, 92, 96, and 170.

■ **LYNDA BARRY** (1956–), *daughter of a white father and half-Filipino mother and raised in a racially mixed neighborhood of Seattle, "was outside of the action while I was in the middle of it. I was a shy loudmouth, the neighborhood nerd, no two ways about it." While at Evergreen State College art school in Olympia, Washington, she corresponded with her best friend, then on the staff of the University of Washington Daily. Barry illustrated her letters with sketches and, unbeknownst to Barry, the friend published them, uncredited, in the Daily, as "Ernie Pook's Comeeks" in honor of the name Barry's brother gave his possessions. Barry became an "underground" cartoonist whose success spread to monthly contributions to Esquire and Mother Jones magazines and to a nationally syndicated newspaper strip called "Ernie Pook's Comeeks." She alters her signature ("Dr. Lynda Barry," "Lynda 'Having a Ball, y'all' Barry," "Lynda Swang Thang Barry") for many of her works, even for individual strips in her half-dozen volumes of cartoons. She married in 1986 and separated in 1988, the year in which she published her first novel,* The Good Times Are Killing Me.

The Night We All Got Sick

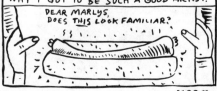

[1986]

Study and Writing Questions

1. What are the speaker's feelings about her brother, parents, cousins, aunt, and uncle? How do you know?
2. Given the speaker's assertion that she has become "such a good artist," what do you make of her self-representation?
3. The word "butt" occurs three times, but never in the main NARRATIVE. What is the importance of this word?
4. Is the STYLE — both verbal and graphic — of this narrative really childish? If so, why? If not, why not? What is the THEMATIC significance of the style?
5. Does the last panel provide a RESOLUTION for the narrative? What is this narrative about?

See also Questions for Contrast and Comparison: 11, 95, 98, 125, 170, 184, and 199.

■ **JOHN BARTH** (1930-) *was born in Cambridge, Maryland and raised on the Eastern Shore of Chesapeake Bay. After studying jazz for a year at the Juilliard School of Music, he attended Johns Hopkins University (A.B., 1951; M.A., 1952). He has taught throughout his career (Pennsylvania State University, 1953– 65; State University of New York at Buffalo, 1965– 73; and Johns Hopkins University, 1973–). He has three children from his first marriage, none from his second. Barth has been widely discussed, and often honored, for his comic, verbally spectacular, formally experimental fictions. Among his most notable and accessible novels are* The Floating Opera *(1956) and* The End of the Road *(1958) which can be read independently or as complementary studies of suicide and the relation of self-expression to survival.* The Sot-Weed Factor *(1960) is a sprawling satire, set in Maryland, of an eighteenth century satire set in Maryland. In* Giles Goat-Boy *(1968) Barth both parodies mythology and creates a huge mythic version of the modern world as all one university.* Chimera *(1972), a collection of three novellas elaborately retelling the tales of Scheherazade, Perseus, and Bellerophon as explorations of the social and psychological problems of modern life, won the National Book Award. His later works have not been as influential. His impressive shorter fictions are collected in* Lost in the Funhouse *(1968).*

Night-Sea Journey

"One way or another, no matter which theory of our journey is correct, it's myself I address; to whom I rehearse as to a stranger our history and condition, and will disclose my secret hope though I sink for it.

"Is the journey my invention? Do the night, the sea, exist at all, I ask myself, apart from my experience of them? Do I myself exist, or is this a dream? Sometimes I wonder. And if I am, who am I? The Heritage I supposedly transport? But how can I be both vessel and contents? Such are the questions that beset my intervals of rest.

"My trouble is, I lack conviction. Many accounts of our situation seem plausible to me—where and what we are, why we swim and whither. But implausible ones as well, perhaps especially those, I must admit as possibly correct. Even likely. If at times, in certain humors—striking in unison, say, with my neighbors and chanting with them 'Onward! Upward!'—I have supposed that we have after all a common Maker, Whose nature and motives we may not know, but Who engendered us in some mysterious wise and launched us forth toward some end known but to Him—if (for a moodslength only) I have been able to entertain such notions, very popular in certain quarters, it is because our night-sea journey partakes of their absurdity. One might even say: I can believe them *because* they are absurd.

"Has that been said before?

"Another paradox: it appears to be these recesses from swimming that sustain me in the swim. Two measures onward and upward, flailing with the rest, then I float exhausted and dispirited, brood upon the night, the sea, the journey, while the flood bears me a measure back and down: slow progress, but I live, I live, and make my way, aye, past many a drownèd comrade in the end, stronger, worthier than I, victims of their unremitting *joie de nager*. I have seen the best swimmers of my generation go under. Numberless the number of the dead!

Thousands drown as I think this thought, millions as I rest before returning to the swim. And scores, hundreds of millions have expired since we surged forth, brave in our innocence, upon our dreadful way. 'Love! Love!' we sang then, a quarter-billion strong, and churned the warm sea white with joy of swimming! Now all are gone down — the buoyant, the sodden, leaders and followers, all gone under, while wretched I swim on. Yet these same reflective intervals that keep me afloat have led me into wonder, doubt, despair — strange emotions for a swimmer! — have led me, even, to suspect . . . that our night-sea journey is without meaning.

"Indeed, if I have yet to join the hosts of the suicides, it is because (fatigue apart) I find it no meaningfuller to drown myself than to go on swimming.

"I know that there are those who seem actually to enjoy the night-sea; who claim to love swimming for its own sake, or sincerely believe that 'reaching the Shore,' 'transmitting the Heritage' (*Whose* Heritage, I'd like to know? And to whom?) is worth the staggering cost. I do not. Swimming itself I find at best not actively unpleasant, more often tiresome, not infrequently a torment. Arguments from function and design don't impress me: granted that we can and do swim, that in a manner of speaking our long tails and streamlined heads are 'meant for' swimming; it by no means follows — for me, at least — that we *should* swim, or otherwise endeavor to 'fulfill our destiny.' Which is to say, Someone Else's destiny, since ours, so far as I can see, is merely to perish, one way or another, soon or late. The heartless zeal of our (departed) leaders, like the blind ambition and good cheer of my own youth, appalls me now; for the death of my comrades I am inconsolable. If the night-sea journey has justification, it is not for us swimmers ever to discover it.

"Oh, to be sure, 'Love!' one heard on every side: 'Love it is that drives and sustains us!' I translate: we don't know *what* drives and sustains us, only that we are most miserably driven and, imperfectly, sustained. *Love* is how we call our ignorance of what whips us. 'To reach the Shore,' then: but what if the Shore exists in the fancies of us swimmers merely, who dream it to account for the dreadful fact that we swim, have always and only swum, and continue swimming without respite (myself excepted) until we die? Supposing even that there *were* a Shore — that, as a cynical companion of mine once imagined, we rise from the drowned to discover all those vulgar superstitions and exalted metaphors to be literal truth: the giant Maker of us all, the Shores of Light beyond our night-sea journey! — whatever would a swimmer do there? The fact is, when we imagine the Shore, what comes to mind is just the opposite of our condition: no more night, no more sea, no more journeying. In short, the blissful estate of the drowned.

" 'Ours not to stop and think; ours but to swim and sink. . . .' Because a moment's thought reveals the pointlessness of swimming. 'No matter,' I've heard some say, even as they gulped their last: 'The night-sea journey may be absurd, but here we swim, will-we nill-we, against the flood, onward and upward, toward a Shore that may not exist and couldn't be reached if it did.' The thoughtful swimmer's choices, then, they say, are two: give over thrashing and go under for good, or embrace the absurdity; affirm in and for itself the night-sea journey; swim on with neither motive nor destination, for the sake of swimming, and compassionate moreover with your fellow swimmer, we being all at sea and equally in the dark. I find neither course acceptable. If not even the hypothetical Shore can justify a sea-full of drownèd comrades, to speak of the swim-in-itself as somehow doing so strikes me as obscene. I continue to swim — but only because blind habit, blind instinct, blind fear or drowning are still more strong than the horror of our journey. And if on occasion I have assisted a fellow-thrasher, joined in the cheers and songs, even passed along to others strokes of genius from the drownèd great, it's that I shrink by temperament from making myself conspicuous. To paddle off in one's own direction, assert one's independent right-of-way, overrun one's fellows without compunction, or dedicate oneself entirely to pleasures and diversions without regard for conscience — I can't finally condemn those who journey in this wise; in half my moods I envy them and despise the weak vitality that keeps me from following their example. But in reasonabler moments I remind myself that it's their very freedom and self-responsibility I reject, as more dramatically absurd, in our senseless circumstances, than tailing along in conventional fashion. Suicides, rebels, affirmers of the paradox — naysayers and yea-sayers alike to our fatal journey — I finally shake my head at them. And splash sighing past their corpses, one by one, as past a hundred sorts of others: friends, enemies, brothers; fools, sages, brutes — and nobodies, million upon million. I envy them all.

"A poor irony: that I, who find abhorrent and tautological the doctrine of survival of the fittest (*fitness* meaning, in my experience, nothing more than survival-ability, a talent whose only demonstration is the fact of survival, but whose chief ingredients seem to be strength, guile, callousness), may be the sole remaining swimmer! But the doctrine is false as well as repellent: Chance drowns the worthy with the unworthy, bears up the unfit with the fit by whatever definition, and makes the night-sea journey essentially *haphazard* as well as murderous and unjustified.

" 'You only swim once.' Why bother then?

" 'Except ye drown, ye shall not reach the Shore of Light.' Poppycock.

"One of my late companions — that same cynic with the curious fancy, among the first to drown — entertained us with odd conjectures while we waited to begin our journey. A favorite theory of his was that the Father does exist, and did indeed make us and the sea we swim — but not a-purpose or even consciously; He made us, as it were, despite Himself, as we make waves with every tail-thrash, and may be unaware of our existence. Another was that He knows we're here but doesn't care what happens to us, inasmuch as He creates (voluntarily or not) other seas and swimmers at more or less regular intervals. In bitterer moments, such as just before he drowned, my friend even supposed that our Maker wished us unmade; there was indeed a Shore, he'd argue, which could save at least some of us from drowning and toward which it was our function to struggle — but for reasons unknowable to us He wanted desperately to prevent our reaching that happy place and fulfilling our destiny. Our 'Father,' in short, was our adversary and would-be killer! No less outrageous, and offensive to traditional opinion, were the fellow's speculations on the nature of our Maker: that He might well be no swimmer Himself at all, but some sort of monstrosity, perhaps even tailless; that He might be stupid, malicious, insensible, perverse, or asleep and dreaming; that the end for which He created and launched us forth, and which we flagellate ourselves to fathom, was perhaps immoral, even obscene.

Et cetera, et cetera: there was no end to the chap's conjectures, or the impoliteness of his fancy; I have reason to suspect that his early demise, whether planned by 'our Maker' or not, was expedited by certain fellow-swimmers indignant at his blasphemies.

"In other moods, however (he was as given to moods as I), his theorizing would become half-serious, so it seemed to me, especially upon the subjects of Fate and Immortality, to which our youthful conversations often turned. Then his harangues, if no less fantastical, grew solemn and obscure, and if he was still baiting us, his passion undid the joke. His objection to popular opinions of the hereafter, he would declare, was their claim to general validity. Why need believers hold that *all* the drownèd rise to be judged at journey's end, and non-believers that drowning is final without exception? In *his* opinion (so he'd vow at least), nearly everyone's fate was permanent death; indeed he took a sour pleasure in supposing that every 'Maker' made thousands of separate seas in His creative lifetime, each populated like ours with millions of swimmers, and that in almost every instance both sea and swimmers were utterly annihilated, whether accidentally or by malevolent design. (Nothing if not pluralistic, he imagined there might be millions and billions of 'Fathers,' perhaps in some 'night-sea' of their own!) However — and here he turned infidels against him with the faithful — he professed to believe that in possibly a single night-sea per thousand, say, one of its quarter-billion swimmers (that is, one swimmer in two hundred fifty billions) achieved a qualified immortality. In some cases the rate might be slightly higher; in others it was vastly lower, for just as there are swimmers of every degree of proficiency, including some who drown before the journey starts, unable to swim at all, and others created drowned, as it were, so he imagined what can only be termed impotent Creators, Makers unable to Make, as well as uncommonly fertile ones and all grades between. And it pleased him to deny any necessary relation between a Maker's productivity and His other virtues — including, even, the quality of His creatures.

"I could go on (*he* surely did) with his elaboration of these mad notions — such as that swimmers in other night-seas needn't be of our kind; that Makers themselves might belong to different *species*, so to speak; that our particular Maker mightn't Himself be immortal, or that we might be not only His emissaries but His 'immortality,' continuing His life and our own, transmogrified, beyond our individual deaths. Even this modified immortality (meaningless to me) he conceived as relative and contingent, subject to accident or deliberate termination: his pet hypothesis was that Makers and swimmers *each generate the other* — against all odds, their number being so great — and that any given 'immortality-chain' could terminate after any number of cycles, so that what was 'immortal' (still speaking relatively) was only the cyclic process of incarnation, which itself might have a beginning and an end. Alternatively he liked to imagine cycles within cycles, either finite or infinite: for example, the 'night-sea,' as it were, in which Makers 'swam' and created night-seas and swimmers like ourselves, might be the creation of a larger Maker, Himself one of many, Who in turn et cetera. Time itself he regarded as relative to our experience, like magnitude: who knew but what, with each thrash of our tails, minuscule seas and swimmers, whole eternities, came to pass — as ours, perhaps, and our Maker's Maker's, was elapsing between the strokes of some supertail, in a slower order of time?

Naturally I hooted with the others at this nonsense. We were young then, and had only the dimmest notion of what lay ahead; in our ignorance we imagined night-sea journeying to be a positively heroic enterprise. Its meaning and value we never questioned; to be sure, some must go down by the way, a pity no doubt, but to win a race requires that others lose, and like all my fellows I took for granted that I would be the winner. We milled and swarmed, impatient to be off, never mind where or why, only to try our youth against the realities of night and sea; if we indulged the skeptic at all, it was as a droll, half-contemptible mascot. When he died in the initial slaughter, no one cared.

"And even now I don't subscribe to all his views — but I no longer scoff. The horror of our history has purged me of opinions, as of vanity, confidence, spirit, charity, hope, vitality, everything — except dull dread and a kind of melancholy, stunned persistence. What leads me to recall his fancies is my growing suspicion that I, of all swimmers, may be the sole survivor of this fell journey, tale-bearer of a generation. This suspicion, together with the recent sea-change, suggests to me now that nothing is impossible, not even my late companion's wildest visions, and brings me to a certain desperate resolve, the point of my chronicling.

"Very likely I have lost my senses. The carnage at our setting out; our decimation by whirlpool, poisoned cataract, sea-convulsion; the panic stampedes, mutinies, slaughters, mass suicides; the mounting evidence that none will survive the journey — add to these anguish and fatigue; it were a miracle if sanity stayed afloat. Thus I admit, with the other possibilities, that the present sweetening and calming of the sea, and what seems to be a kind of vasty presence, song, or summons from the near upstream, may be hallucinations of disordered sensibility. . . .

"Perhaps, even, I am drowned already. Surely I was never meant for the rough-and-tumble of the swim; not impossibly I perished at the outset and have only imaged the night-sea journey from some final deep. In any case, I'm no longer young, and it is we spent old swimmers, disabused of every illusion, who are most vulnerable to dreams.

"Sometimes I think I am my drownèd friend.

"Out with it: I've begun to believe, not only that *She* exists, but that She lies not far ahead, and stills the sea, and draws me Herward! Aghast, I recollect his maddest notion: that our destination (which existed, mind, in but one night-sea out of hundreds and thousands) was no Shore, as commonly conceived, but a mysterious being, indescribable except by paradox and vaguest figure: wholly different from us swimmers, yet our complement; the death of us, yet our salvation and resurrection; simultaneously our journey's end, mid-point, and commencement; not membered and thrashing like us, but a motionless or hugely gliding sphere of unimaginable dimension; self-contained, yet dependent absolutely, in some wise, upon the chance (always monstrously improbable) that one of us will survive the night-sea journey and reach . . . Her! *Her*, he called it, or *She*, which is to say, Other-than-a-he. I shake my head; the thing is too preposterous; it is myself I talk to, to keep my reason in this awful darkness. There is no She! There is no You! I rave to myself; it's Death alone that hears and summons. To the drowned, all seas are calm. . . .

"Listen: my friend maintained that in every order of creation there are two sorts of creators, contrary yet complementary, one of which gives rise to seas and swimmers, the other to the Night-which-contains-the-sea and to What-waits-at-the-journey's-end: the former, in short, to destiny, the latter to destination (and both profligately, involuntarily, perhaps indifferently or unwittingly). The 'purpose' of the night-sea journey — but not necessarily of the journeyer or of either Maker! — my friend could describe only in abstractions: *consummation, transfiguration, union of contraries, transcension of categories.* When we laughed, he would shrug and admit that he understood the business no better than we, and thought it ridiculous, dreary, possibly obscene. 'But one of you,' he'd add with his wry smile, 'may be the Hero destined to complete the night-sea journey and be one with Her. Chances are, of course, you won't make it.' He himself, he declared, was not even going to try; the whole idea repelled him; if we chose to dismiss it as an ugly fiction, so much the better for us; thrash, splash, and be merry, we were soon enough drowned. But there it was, he could not say how he knew or why he bothered to tell us, any more than he could say what would happen after She and Hero, Shore and Swimmer, 'merged identities' to become something both and neither. He quite agreed with me that if the issue of that magical union had no memory of the night-sea journey, for example, it enjoyed a poor sort of immortality; even poorer if, as he rather imagined, a swimmer-hero plus a She equaled or became merely another Maker of future night-seas and the rest, at such incredible expense of life. This being the case — he was persuaded it was — the merciful thing to do was refuse to participate; the genuine heroes, in his opinion, were the suicides, and the hero of heroes would be the swimmer who, in the very presence of the Other, refused Her proffered 'immortality' and thus put an end to at least one cycle of catastrophes.

"How we mocked him! Our moment came, we hurtled forth, pretending to glory in the adventure, thrashing, singing, cursing, strangling, rationalizing, rescuing, killing, inventing rules and stories and relationships, giving up, struggling on, but dying all, and still in darkness, until only a battered remnant was left to croak 'Onward, upward,' like a bitter echo. Then they too fell silent — victims, I can only presume, of the last frightful wave — and the moment came when I also, utterly desolate and spent, thrashed my last and gave myself over to the current, to sink or float as might be, but swim no more. Whereupon, marvelous to tell, in an instant the sea grew still! Then warmly, gently, the great tide turned, began to bear me, as it does now, onward and upward will-I nill-I, like a flood of joy — and I recalled with dismay my dead friend's teaching.

"I am not deceived. This new emotion is Her doing; the desire that possesses me is Her bewitchment. Lucidity passes from me; in a moment I'll cry 'Love!' bury myself in Her side, and be 'transfigured.' Which is to say, I die already; this fellow transported by passion is not I; *I am he who abjures and rejects the night-sea journey!* I. . . .

"I am all love. 'Come!' She whispers, and I have no will.

"You who I may be about to become, whatever You are: with the last twitch of my real self I beg You to listen. It is *not* love that sustains me! No; though Her magic makes me burn to sing the contrary, and though I drown even now for the blasphemy, I will say truth. What has fetched me across this dreadful sea is a single hope, gift of my poor dead comrade: that You may be stronger-willed than I, and that by sheer force of concentration I may transmit to You, along with Your official Heritage, a private legacy of awful recollection and negative resolve.

Mad as it may be, my dream is that some unimaginable embodiment of myself (or myself plus Her if that's how it must be) will come to find itself expressing, in however garbled or radical a translation, some reflection of these reflections. If against all odds this comes to pass, may You to whom, through whom I speak, do what I cannot: terminate this aimless, brutal business! Stop Your hearing against Her song! Hate love!

"Still alive, afloat, afire. Farewell then my penultimate hope: that one may be sunk for direst blasphemy on the very shore of the Shore. Can it be (my old friend would smile) that only utterest nay-sayers survive the night? But even that were Sense, and there is no sense, only senseless love, senseless death. Whoever echoes these reflections: be more courageous than their author! An end to night-sea journeys! Make no more! And forswear me when I shall forswear myself, deny myself, plunge into Her who summons, singing . . .

"'Love! Love! Love!'"

[1966]

Study and Writing Questions

1. What are the religious positions to which this NARRATIVE alludes? To what extent are these positions criticized and to what extent accepted?
2. This narrative uses ALLUSION frequently. For example, " 'I have seen the best swimmers of my generation go under' " refers to the famous opening line of Allen Ginsberg's 1956 poem "Howl": "I saw the best minds of my generation destroyed by madness, starving hysterical naked." Read "Howl" and find other allusions to it. What other allusions to other works or phrases do you find in "Night-Sea Journey"? What sort(s) of meaning does allusion as a technique add to this narrative?
3. Many phrases that may have seemed mysterious or sober on a first reading of this narrative can be seen as jesting on a subsequent reading. What are some of these jests? How does the use of jesting affect your reading?
4. To what extent is this narrative an ALLEGORY for "the journey of life"?
5. Do the final four paragraphs (beginning with the words, "'I am all love'") suggest that the narrative as a whole has been sexist? Does this section leave you with a DIDACTIC message? Does it provide a satisfying RESOLUTION to the narrative?

See also Questions for Contrast and Comparison: 1, 21, 53, 92, and 120.

DONALD BARTHELME (1931–1989), *son of a prominent architect, was born in Philadelphia and raised in Texas. He had early creative success, writing film criticism for* The Houston Post *while still editing the University of Houston student newspaper. After directing Houston's Contemporary Arts Museum, Barthelme moved to New York in 1962 and became a full-time writer, except for occasional teaching stints as a distinguished professor at City College of the City University of New York and at the University of Houston. Most of his work, fiercely experimental in structure, ostentatiously bizarre in language, appeared first in* The New Yorker. *The most complete survey of his work is* Sixty Stories *(1981), which won the PEN/Faulkner Award for fiction. His excitingly outrageous novel* Snow White *(1967), concerning a Chinese-American woman and her seven dwarf roommates, explores the possibilities of* FAIRY TALE *reality in modern Manhattan. The* Dead Father *(1975) is a formally disconcerting psychologically telling, mock epic recounting the struggle of a son, two women, and a horde to drag a character, alternately a huge corpse and a declining father, across a mythic landscape to his burial in the city. The* Slightly Irregular Fire Engine or the Hithering Thithering Djinn *(1972) won the National Book Award for children's literature. Barthelme left a wife and daughter when he died of cancer.*

The Piano Player

Outside his window five-year-old Priscilla Hess, square and squat as a mailbox (red sweater, blue lumpy corduroy pants), looked around poignantly for someone to wipe her overflowing nose. There was a butterfly locked inside that mailbox, surely; would it ever escape? Or was the quality of mailboxness stuck to her forever, like her parents, like her name? The sky was sunny and blue. A filet of green Silly Putty disappeared into fat Priscilla Hess and he turned to greet his wife who was crawling through the door on her hands and knees.

"Yes?" he said. "What now?"

"I'm ugly," she said, sitting back on her haunches. "Our children are ugly."

"Nonsense," Brian said sharply. "They're wonderful children. Wonderful and beautiful. Other people's children are ugly, not our children. Now get up and go back out to the smokeroom. You're supposed to be curing a ham."

"The ham died," she said. "I couldn't cure it. I tried everything. You don't love me any more. The penicillin was stale. I'm ugly and so are the children. It said to tell you goodbye."

"It?"

"The ham," she said. "Is one of our children named Ambrose? Somebody named Ambrose has been sending us telegrams. How many do we have now? Four? Five? Do you think they're heterosexual?" She made a *moue* and ran a hand through her artichoke hair. "The house is rusting away. Why did you want a steel house? Why did I think I wanted to live in Connecticut? I don't know."

"Get up," he said softly, "get up, dearly beloved. Stand up and sing. Sing *Parsifal*."

"I want a Triumph," she said from the floor. "A TR–4. Everyone in Stamford, every single person, has one but me. If you gave me a TR–4 I'd put our ugly children in it and drive away. To Wellfleet. I'd take all the ugliness out of your life."

"A green one?"

"A *red* one," she said menacingly. "Red with red leather seats."

"Aren't you supposed to be chipping paint?" he asked. "I bought us an electronic data processing system. An IBM."

"I want to go to Wellfleet," she said. "I want to talk to Edmund Wilson and take him for a ride in my red TR-4. The children can dig clams. We have a lot to talk about, Bunny and me."

"Why don't you remove those shoulder pads?" Brian said kindly. "It's too bad about the ham."

"*I loved that ham*," she said viciously. "When you galloped into the University of Texas on your roan Volvo, I thought you were going to *be somebody*. I gave you my hand. You put rings on it. Rings that my mother gave me. I thought you were going to be distinguished, like Bunny."

He showed her his broad, shouldered back. "Everything is in flitters," he said. "Play the piano, won't you?"

"You always were afraid of my piano," she said. "My four or five children are afraid of the piano. *You taught them to be afraid of it.* The giraffe is on fire, but I don't suppose you care."

"What can we eat," he asked, "with the ham gone?"

"There's some Silly Putty in the deepfreeze," she said tonelessly.

"Rain is falling," he observed. "Rain or something."

"When you graduated from the Wharton School of Business," she said, "I thought *at last!* I thought *now we can move to Stamford and have interesting neighbors*. But they're not interesting. The giraffe is interesting but he sleeps so much of the time. The mailbox is *rather* interesting. The man didn't open it at 3:31 P.M. today. He was five minutes late. The government lied again."

With a gesture of impatience, Brian turned on the light. The great burst of electricity illuminated her upturned tiny face. Eyes like snow peas, he thought. Tamar dancing. My name in the dictionary, in the back. The Law of Bilateral Good Fortune. Piano bread perhaps. A nibble of pain running through the Western World. Coriolanus.

"Oh God," she said, from the floor. "Look at my knees."

Brian looked. Her knees were blushing.

"It's senseless, senseless, senseless," she said. "I've been caulking the medicine chest. What for? I don't know. You've got to give me more money. Ben is bleeding. Bessie wants to be an S.S. man. She's reading The Rise and Fall. She's identified with Himmler. Is that her name? Bessie?"

"Yes. Bessie."

"What's the other one's name? The blond one?"

"Billy. Named after your father. Your Dad."

"You've got to get me an air hammer. To clean the children's teeth. What's the name of that disease? They'll all have it, every single one, if you don't get me an air hammer."

"And a compressor," Brian said. "And a Pinetop Smith record. I remember."

She lay on her back. The shoulder pads clattered against the terrazzo. Her number, 17, was written large on her chest. Her eyes were screwed tight shut. "Altman's is having a sale," she said. "Maybe I should go in."

"Listen," he said. "Get up. Go into the grape arbor. I'll trundle the piano out there. You've been chipping too much paint."

"You wouldn't touch that piano," she said. "Not in a million years."

"You really think I'm afraid of it?"

"Not in a million years," she said, "you phony."

"All right," Brian said quietly. "All *right*." He strode over to the piano. He took a good grip on its black varnishedness. He began to trundle it across the room, and, after a slight hesitation, it struck him dead.

[1963]

Study and Writing Questions

1. Many of the proper nouns in this NARRATIVE, like Volvo, IBM, and Edmund "Bunny" Wilson, carry highly specialized cultural connotations. What are some of these CONNOTATIONS? How do they enter into the meaning of the narrative?

2. The narrative has many ALLUSIONS to works of so-called high culture, such as Shakespeare's play *Coriolanus* or Salvador Dalí's painting *The Giraffe on Fire*. What do these allusions add individually and collectively to the narrative?

3. A mother wondering off-handedly whether she has four or five children initially seems silly. Is there a more serious meaning beyond this silliness? If so, what? Are there other phrases or ACTIONS in the narrative that seem initially silly but have additional significance?

4. What is the importance of the opening paragraph of the narrative? Why is Priscilla Hess mentioned at all in this narrative?

5. What is the importance of the closing paragraph of the narrative? What does the piano represent in this narrative?

See also Questions for Contrast and Comparison: 12, 40, 41, 45, 74, 97, 123, 181, 201, and 216.

■ STEPHEN VINCENT BENÉT (1898–1943) *was born in Bethlehem,* ■ *Pennsylvania to a military family that produced a generation of poets. His paternal grandfather, although a Floridian, soldiered for the Union during the Civil War and became Army Chief of Ordnance (1874–91); an uncle became a French munitions manufacturer; and his father, whom Stephen considered his best critic, became an Army ordnance officer. Stephen's older siblings, William Rose and Laura, became accomplished poets, William's autobiographical verse novel,* The Dust Which Is God, *winning a Pulitzer Prize (1941). Having grown up on bases his father commanded, Stephen interrupted his studies at Yale University for War Office service, ill health preventing active duty. By graduation (1919), he had published three volumes of poems. His Yale graduate school thesis, published as* Heavens and Earth *(1920), shared the 1921 Poetry Society of America award with Carl Sandburg. Although critics occasionally slighted his popular novels, stories, essays, and poems, he remains famous for folksy tales like* "The Devil and Daniel Webster" *(1937); for* John Brown's Body, *a long Civil War poem (1928, Pulitzer); and for* Western Star, *a long fragment of epic verse about America's westward expansion (1943, Pulitzer). He had a nervous breakdown in 1939 and died of heart failure in 1943, leaving a wife, who had been his college sweetheart, and three children.*

Nightmare Number Three

We had expected everything but revolt
And I kind of wonder myself when they started thinking—
But there's no dice in that now.
                            I've heard fellows say
They must have planned it for years and maybe they did.
Looking back, you can find little incidents here and there,
Like the concrete-mixer in Jersey eating the wop
Or the roto press that printed "Fiddle-dee-dee!"
In a three-color process all over Senator Sloop,
Just as he was making a speech. The thing about that
Was, how could it walk upstairs? But it was upstairs,
Clicking and mumbling in the Senate Chamber.
They had to knock out the wall to take it away
And the wrecking-crew said it grinned.
                            It was only the best
Machines, of course, the superhuman machines,
The ones we'd built to be better than flesh and bone,
But the cars were in it, of course . . .
                            and they hunted us
Like rabbits through the cramped streets on that Bloody Monday,
The Madison Avenue busses leading the charge.
The busses were pretty bad—but I'll not forget
The smash of glass when the Duesenberg left the show-room
And pinned three brokers to the Racquet Club steps
Or the long howl of the horns when they saw men run,
When they saw them looking for holes in the solid ground . . .

I guess they were tired of being ridden in
And stopped and started by pygmies for silly ends,
Of wrapping cheap cigarettes and bad chocolate bars
Collecting nickels and waving platinum hair
And letting six million people live in a town.
I guess it was that. I guess they got tired of us
And the whole smell of human hands.

                                  But it was a shock
To climb sixteen flights of stairs to Art Zuckow's office
(Nobody took the elevators twice)
And find him strangled to death in a nest of telephones,
The octopus-tendrils waving over his head,
And a sort of quiet humming filling the air. . . .
Do they eat? . . . There was red . . . But I did not stop to look.
I don't know yet how I got to the roof in time
And it's lonely, here on the roof.

                            For a while, I thought
That window-cleaner would make it, and keep me company.
But they got him with his own hoist at the sixteenth floor
And dragged him in, with a squeal.
You see, they coöperate. Well, we taught them that
And it's fair enough, I suppose. You see, we built them.
We taught them to think for themselves.
It was bound to come. You can see it was bound to come.

And it won't be so bad, in the country. I hate to think
Of the reapers, running wild in the Kansas fields,
And the transport planes like hawks on a chickenyard,
But the horses might help. We might make a deal with the horses.
At least, you've more chance, out there.

                                 And they need us, too.
They're bound to realize that when they once calm down.
They'll need oil and spare parts and adjustments and tuning up.
Slaves? Well, in a way, you know, we were slaves before.
There won't be so much real difference — honest, there won't.
(I wish I hadn't looked into that beauty-parlor
And seen what was happening there.
But those are female machines and a bit high-strung.)
Oh, we'll settle down. We'll arrange it. We'll compromise.
It wouldn't make sense to wipe out the whole human race.
Why, I bet if I went to my old Plymouth now
(Of course you'd have to do it the tactful way)
And said, "Look here! Who got you the swell French horn?"
He wouldn't turn me over to those police cars;
At least I don't think he would.

                             Oh, it's going to be jake.
There won't be so much real difference — honest, there won't —
And I'd go down in a minute and take my chance —

I'm a good American and I always liked them—
Except for one small detail that bothers me
And that's the food proposition. Because, you see,
The concrete-mixer may have made a mistake,
And it looks like just high spirits.
But, if it's got so they like the flavor . . . well . . .

[1935]

Study and Writing Questions

1. Of the thousands of types of machines that exist, most (for example, bicycles, fans, radios) are never mentioned. Which machines are mentioned? How does the IMPLIED AUTHOR's choice of machines help shape the NARRATIVE?
2. Most of the nouns in this narrative are common nouns, that is, they designate a class of things. We never even learn the NARRATOR's proper name. Yet there are a few proper nouns in this narrative. Which are they? What is the special significance of each of them?
3. Describe the verse form of this piece. How does the use of verse affect your reading of this narrative?
4. Trace the changing attitudes of the narrator. What kind of person is the narrator? To what extent is the narrative about the narrator?
5. Consider "Nightmare Number Three" as a SATIRE. Are there moments when the absurd occurrences can be read as jokes? Does laughter fit with your overall sense of the narrative? If the narrative intends warning or correction, against what is it warning the reader? What corrections might we attempt?

See also Questions for Contrast and Comparison: 50, 106, 123, 148, 177, 180, 181, 182, 187, and 222.

■ AMBROSE [GWINETT] BIERCE (1842 – 1914?) *was born in a log cabin in rural Ohio, one of nine children. Virtually uneducated, he enlisted as a drummer boy in the Civil War and served with distinction, twice rescuing comrades, being wounded himself, and emerging a brevet major. Working in California, he began a self-education program. In 1871, he published a successful series of acerbic social essays in his friend Brett Harte's* Overland Monthly. *He married and left with his wife for England where he spent four years as a journalist, editor, and satirist notorious as "Bitter Bierce." He spent most of his career in San Francisco after 1875, except for reportorial stints in Washington. He collected his best satiric aphorisms from 1881 to 1906 as* The Devil's Dictionary (1906), *in which he defines "reporter" as "a writer who guesses his way to the truth and dispels it with a tempest of words." After separation from his wife and the death of his son, he began writing more literarily substantial short stories, collected as* Tales of Soldiers and Civilians (1891), *marked by a grim ingenuity of plot and style, and* Can Such Things Be? (1893), *ranging from psychological realism to supernatural horror. In 1913, dissatisfied with his writing, he put his affairs in order and left to observe the Mexican rebel, Pancho Villa. Many contradictory tales surround Bierce's death, but it is likely that he gained what his letters say he sought, "the good, kind darkness [of] euthanasia."*

An Occurrence at Owl Creek Bridge

A man stood upon a railroad bridge in northern Alabama, looking down into the swift water twenty feet below. The man's hands were behind his back, the wrists bound with a cord. A rope closely encircled his neck. It was attached to a stout cross-timber above his head and the slack fell to the level of his knees. Some loose boards laid upon the sleepers supporting the metals of the railway supplied a footing for him and his executioners — two private soldiers of the Federal army, directed by a sergeant who in civil life may have been a deputy sheriff. At a short remove upon the same temporary platform was an officer in the uniform of his rank, armed. He was a captain. A sentinel at each end of the bridge stood with his rifle in the position known as "support," that is to say, vertical in front of the left shoulder, the hammer resting on the forearm thrown straight across the chest — a formal and unnatural position, enforcing an erect carriage of the body. It did not appear to be the duty of these two men to know what was occurring at the center of the bridge; they merely blockaded the two ends of the foot planking that traversed it.

Beyond one of the sentinels nobody was in sight; the railroad ran straight away into a forest for a hundred yards, then, curving, was lost to view. Doubtless there was an outpost farther along. The other bank of the stream was open ground — a gentle acclivity topped with a stockade of vertical tree trunks, loopholed for rifles, with a single embrasure through which protruded the muzzle of a brass cannon commanding the bridge. Midway of the slope between the bridge and fort were the spectators — a single company of infantry in line, at "parade rest," the butts of the rifles on the ground, the barrels inclining slightly backward against the right shoulder, the hands crossed upon the stock. A lieutenant stood at the right of the line, the point of his sword upon the ground, his left hand resting upon his right. Excepting the group of four at the center of the bridge, not a man moved. The company faced the bridge, staring stonily, motionless. The sentinels, facing the banks of the stream, might have been statues to adorn the bridge. The captain stood with folded arms, silent, observing the work of his subordinates, but making no sign. Death is a dignitary who when he comes announced is to be received with formal manifestations of respect, even by those most familiar with him. In the code of military etiquette silence and fixity are forms of deference.

The man who was engaged in being hanged was apparently about thirty-five years of age. He was a civilian, if one might judge from his habit, which was that of a planter. His features were good—a straight nose, firm mouth, broad forehead, from which his long, dark hair was combed straight back, falling behind his ears to the collar of his well-fitting frock coat. He wore a mustache and pointed beard, but no whiskers; his eyes were large and dark gray, and had a kindly expression which one would hardly have expected in one whose neck was in the hemp. Evidently this was no vulgar assassin. The liberal military code makes provision for hanging many kinds of persons, and gentlemen are not excluded.

The preparations being complete, the two private soldiers stepped aside and each drew away the plank upon which he had been standing. The sergeant turned to the captain, saluted and placed himself immediately behind that officer, who in turn moved apart one pace. These movements left the condemned man and the sergeant standing on the two ends of the same plank, which spanned three of the cross-ties of the bridge. The end upon which the civilian stood almost, but not quite, reached a fourth. This plank had been held in place by the weight of the captain; it was now held by that of the sergeant. At a signal from the former the latter would step aside, the plank would tilt and the condemned man go down between two ties. The arrangement commended itself to his judgment as simple and effective. His face had not been covered nor his eyes bandaged. He looked a moment at his "unsteadfast footing," then let his gaze wander to the swirling water of the stream racing madly beneath his feet. A piece of dancing driftwood caught his attention and his eyes followed it down the current. How slowly it appeared to move! What a sluggish stream!

He closed his eyes in order to fix his last thoughts upon his wife and children. The water, touched to gold by the early sun, the brooding mists under the banks at some distance down the stream, the fort, the soldiers, the piece of drift—all had distracted him. And now he became conscious of a new disturbance. Striking through the thought of his dear ones was a sound which he could neither ignore nor understand, a sharp, distinct, metallic percussion like the stroke of a blacksmith's hammer upon the anvil; it had the same ringing quality. He wondered what it was, and whether immeasurably distant or near by—it seemed both. Its recurrence was regular, but as slow as the tolling of a death knell. He awaited each stroke with impatience and—he knew not why—apprehension. The intervals of silence grew progressively longer; the delays became maddening. With their greater infrequency the sounds increased in strength and sharpness. They hurt his ear like the thrust of a knife; he feared he would shriek. What he heard was the ticking of his watch.

He unclosed his eyes and saw again the water below him. "If I could free my hands," he thought, "I might throw off the noose and spring into the stream. By diving I could evade the bullets and, swimming vigorously, reach the bank, take to the woods and get away home. My home, thank God, is as yet outside their lines; my wife and little ones are still beyond the invader's farthest advance."

As these thoughts, which have here to be set down in words, were flashed into the doomed man's brain rather than evolved from it the captain nodded to the sergeant. The sergeant stepped aside.

II

Peyton Farquhar was a well-to-do planter, of an old and highly respected Alabama family. Being a slave owner and like other slave owners a politician he was naturally an original secessionist and ardently devoted to the Southern cause. Circumstances of an imperious nature, which it is unnecessary to relate here, had prevented him from taking service with the gallant army that had fought the disastrous campaigns ending with the fall of Corinth, and he chafed under the inglorious restraint, longing for the release of his energies, the larger life of the soldier, the opportunity for distinction. That opportunity, he felt, would come, as it comes to all in war time. Meanwhile he did what he could. No service was too humble for him to perform in aid of the South, no adventure too perilous for him to undertake if consistent with the character of a civilian who was at heart a soldier, and who in good faith and without too much qualification assented to at least a part of the frankly villainous dictum that all is fair in love and war.

One evening while Farquhar and his wife were sitting on a rustic bench near the entrance to his grounds, a gray-clad soldier rode up to the gate and asked for a drink of water. Mrs. Farquhar was only too happy to serve him with her own white hands. While she was fetching the water her husband approached the dusty horseman and inquired eagerly for news from the front.

"The Yanks are repairing the railroads," said the man, "and are getting ready for another advance. They have reached the Owl Creek bridge, put it in order and built a stockade on the north bank. The commandant has issued an order, which is posted everywhere, declaring that any civilian caught interfering with the railroad, its bridges, tunnels or trains will be summarily hanged. I saw the order."

"How far is it to the Owl Creek bridge?" Farquhar asked.

"About thirty miles."

"Is there no force on this side the creek?"

"Only a picket post half a mile out, on the railroad, and a single sentinel at his end of the bridge."

"Suppose a man — a civilian and student of hanging — should elude the picket post and perhaps get the better of the sentinel," said Farquhar, smiling, "what could he accomplish?"

The soldier reflected. "I was there a month ago," he replied. "I observed that the flood of last winter had lodged a great quantity of driftwood against the wooden pier at this end of the bridge. It is now dry and would burn like tow."

The lady had now brought the water, which the soldier drank. He thanked her ceremoniously, bowed to her husband and rode away. An hour later, after nightfall, he repassed the plantation, going northward in the direction from which he had come. He was a Federal scout.

III

As Peyton Farquhar fell straight downward through the bridge he lost consciousness and was as one already dead. From this state he was awakened — ages later, it seemed to him — by the pain of a sharp pressure upon his throat, followed by a sense of suffocation. Keen, poignant agonies seemed to shoot from his neck downward through every fiber of his body and limbs. These pains appeared to flash along well-defined lines of ramification and to beat with an inconceivably rapid periodicity. They seemed like streams of pulsating fire heating him to an intolerable temperature. As to his head, he was conscious of nothing but a feeling of fulness — of congestion. These sensations were unaccompanied by thought. The intellectual part of his nature was already effaced; he had power only to feel, and feeling was torment. He was conscious of motion. Encompassed in a luminous cloud, of which he was now merely the fiery heart, without material substance, he swung through unthinkable arcs of oscillation, like a vast pendulum. Then all at once, with terrible suddenness, the light about him shot upward with the noise of a loud plash; a frightful roaring was in his ears, and all was cold and dark. The power of thought was restored; he knew that the rope had broken and he had fallen into the stream. There was no additional strangulation; the noose about his neck was already suffocating him and kept the water from his lungs. To die of hanging at the bottom of a river! — the idea seemed to him ludicrous. He opened his eyes in the darkness and saw above him a gleam of light, but how distant, how inaccessible! He was still sinking, for the light became fainter and fainter until it was a mere glimmer. Then it began to grow and brighten, and he knew that he was rising toward the surface — knew it with reluctance, for he was now very comfortable. "To be hanged and drowned," he thought, "that is not so bad; but I do not wish to be shot. No; I will not be shot; that is not fair."

He was not conscious of an effort, but a sharp pain in his wrist apprised him that he was trying to free his hands. He gave the struggle his attention, as an idler might observe the feat of a juggler, without interest in the outcome. What splendid effort! — what magnificent, what superhuman strength! Ah, that was a fine endeavor! Bravo! The cord fell away; his arms parted and floated upward, the hands dimly seen on each side of the growing light. He watched them with a new interest as first one and then the other pounced upon the noose at his neck. They tore it away and thrust it fiercely aside, its undulations resembling those of a water snake. "Put it back, put it back!" He thought he shouted these words to his hands, for the undoing of the noose had been succeeded by the direst pang that he had yet experienced. His neck ached horribly; his brain was on fire; his heart, which had been fluttering faintly, gave a great leap, trying to force itself out at his mouth. His whole body was racked and wrenched with an insupportable anguish! But his disobedient hands gave no heed to the command. They beat the water vigorously with quick, downward strokes, forcing him to the surface. He felt his head emerge; his eyes were blinded by the sunlight; his chest expanded convulsively, and with a supreme and crowning agony his lungs engulfed a great draught of air, which instantly he expelled in a shriek!

He was now in full possession of his physical senses. They were, indeed, preternaturally keen and alert. Something in the awful disturbance of his organic system had so exalted and refined them that they made record of things never before perceived. He felt the ripples upon his face and heard their separate sounds as they struck. He looked at the forest on the bank of the stream, saw the individual trees, the leaves and the veining of each leaf—saw the very insects upon them: the locusts, the brilliant-bodied flies, the gray spiders stretching their webs from twig to twig. He noted the prismatic colors in all the dewdrops upon a million blades of grass. The humming of the gnats that danced above the eddies of the stream, the beating of the dragon flies' wings, the strokes of the water-spiders' legs, like oars which had lifted their boat—all these made audible music. A fish slid along beneath his eyes and he heard the rush of its body parting the water.

He had come to the surface facing down the stream; in a moment the visible world seemed to wheel slowly round, himself the pivotal point, and he saw the bridge, the fort, the soldiers upon the bridge, the captain, the sergeant, the two privates, his executioners. They were in silhouette against the blue sky. They shouted and gesticulated, pointing at him. The captain had drawn his pistol, but did not fire; the others were unarmed. Their movements were grotesque and horrible, their forms gigantic.

Suddenly he heard a sharp report and something struck the water smartly within a few inches of his head, spattering his face with spray. He heard a second report, and saw one of the sentinels with his rifle at his shoulder, a light cloud of blue smoke rising from the muzzle. The man in the water saw the eye of the man on the bridge gazing into his own through the sights of the rifle. He observed that it was a gray eye and remembered having read that gray eyes were keenest, and that all famous marksmen had them. Nevertheless, this one had missed.

A counter-swirl had caught Farquhar and turned him half round; he was again looking into the forest on the bank opposite the fort. The sound of a clear, high voice in a monotonous singsong now rang out behind him and came across the water with a distinctness that pierced and subdued all other sounds, even the beating of the ripples in his ears. Although no soldier, he had frequented camps enough to know the dread significance of that deliberate, drawling, aspirated chant; the lieutenant on shore was taking a part in the morning's work. How coldly and pitilessly—with what an even, calm intonation, presaging, and enforcing tranquillity in the men—with what accurately measured intervals fell those cruel words:

"Attention, company! . . . Shoulder arms! . . . Ready! . . . Aim! . . . Fire!"

Farquhar dived—dived as deeply as he could. The water roared in his ears like the voice of Niagara, yet he heard the dulled thunder of the volley and, rising again toward the surface, met shining bits of metal, singularly flattened, oscillating slowly downward. Some of them touched him on the face and hands, then fell away, continuing their descent. One lodged between his collar and neck; it was uncomfortably warm and he snatched it out.

As he rose to the surface, gasping for breath, he saw that he had been a long time under water; he was perceptibly farther down stream—nearer to safety. The soldiers had almost finished reloading; the metal ramrods flashed all at once in the sunshine as they were drawn from the barrels, turned in the air, and thrust into their sockets. The two sentinels fired again, independently and ineffectually.

The hunted man saw all this over his shoulder; he was now swimming vigorously with the current. His brain was as energetic as his arms and legs; he thought with the rapidity of lightning.

"The officer," he reasoned, "will not make that martinet's error a second time. It is as easy to dodge a volley as a single shot. He has probably already given the command to fire at will. God help me, I cannot dodge them all!"

An appalling plash within two yards of him was followed by a loud, rushing sound, *diminuendo*, which seemed to travel back through the air to the fort and died in an explosion which stirred the very river to its deeps! A rising sheet of water curved over him, fell down upon him, blinded him, strangled him! The cannon had taken a hand in the game. As he shook his head free from the commotion of the smitten water he heard the deflected shot humming through the air ahead, and in an instant it was cracking and smashing the branches in the forest beyond.

"They will not do that again," he thought; "the next time they will use a charge of grape. I must keep my eye upon the gun; the smoke will apprise me — the report arrives too late; it lags behind the missile. That is a good gun."

Suddenly he felt himself whirled round and round — spinning like a top. The water, the banks, the forests, the now distant bridge, fort and men — all were commingled and blurred. Objects were represented by their colors only; circular horizontal streaks of color — that was all he saw. He had been caught in a vortex and was being whirled on with a velocity of advance and gyration that made him giddy and sick. In a few moments he was flung upon the gravel at the foot of the left bank of the stream — the southern bank — and behind a projecting point which concealed him from his enemies. The sudden arrest of his motion, the abrasion of one of his hands on the gravel, restored him, and he wept with delight. He dug his fingers into the sand, threw it over himself in handfuls and audibly blessed it. It looked like diamonds, rubies, emeralds; he could think of nothing beautiful which it did not resemble. The trees upon the bank were giant garden plants; he noted a definite order in their arrangement, inhaled the fragrance of their blooms. A strange, roseate light shone through the spaces among their trunks and the wind made in their branches the music of Aeolian harps. He had no wish to perfect his escape — was content to remain in that enchanting spot until retaken.

A whiz and rattle of grapeshot among the branches high above his head roused him from his dream. The baffled cannoneer had fired him a random farewell. He sprang to his feet, rushed up the sloping bank, and plunged into the forest.

All that day he traveled, laying his course by the rounding sun. The forest seemed interminable; nowhere did he discover a break in it, not even a woodman's road. He had not known that he lived in so wild a region. There was something uncanny in the revelation.

By nightfall he was fatigued, footsore, famishing. The thought of his wife and children urged him on. At last he found a road which led him in what he knew to be the right direction. It was as wide and straight as a city street, yet it seemed untraveled. No fields bordered it, no dwelling anywhere. Not so much as the barking of a dog suggested human habitation. The black bodies of the trees formed a straight wall on both sides, terminating on the horizon in a point, like a diagram in a lesson in perspective. Overhead, as he looked up through this rift in the wood, shone great golden stars looking unfamiliar and grouped in strange constellations. He was sure they were arranged in some order which had a secret and malign significance. The wood on either side was full of singular noises, among which — once, twice, and again — he distinctly heard whispers in an unknown tongue.

His neck was in pain and lifting his hand to it found it horribly swollen. He knew that it had a circle of black where the rope had bruised it. His eyes felt congested; he could no longer close them. His tongue was swollen with thirst; he relieved its fever by thrusting it forward from between his teeth into the cold air. How softly the turf had carpeted the untraveled avenue — he could no longer feel the roadway beneath his feet!

Doubtless, despite his suffering, he had fallen asleep while walking, for now he sees another scene — perhaps he has merely recovered from a delirium. He stands at the gate of his own home. All is as he left it, and all bright and beautiful in the morning sunshine. He must have traveled the entire night. As he pushes open the gate and passes up the wide white walk, he sees a flutter of female garments; his wife, looking fresh and cool and sweet, steps down from the veranda to meet him. At the bottom of the steps she stands waiting, with a smile of ineffable joy, an attitude of matchless grace and dignity. Ah, how beautiful she is! He springs forward with extended arms. As he is about to clasp her he feels a stunning blow upon the back of the neck; a blinding white light blazes all about him with a sound like the shock of a cannon — then all is darkness and silence!

Peyton Farquhar was dead; his body, with a broken neck, swung gently from side to side beneath the timbers of the Owl Creek bridge.

[1890]

Study and Writing Questions

1. What does the title suggest? Consider both its TONE and the possible SYMBOLIC meanings of each of its last three words.
2. At what point does the NARRATIVE first shift from an outside observer's VIEWPOINT to Farquhar's? Where else do such shifts occur? To what extent is the STORY about viewpoint?
3. Why are we told that Mrs. Farquhar "was only too happy to serve [the Federal scout] with her own white hands"?
4. Water may symbolize many things, including both fertility and death (as by drowning). Underline all the occurrences of water IMAGERY in this story. How does the use of water imagery contribute to the story's meaning? impact?
5. Consider your own reactions as you read this NARRATIVE. At what point did you begin to question the reliability of the NARRATOR? At what point were you certain of the actual outcome? How does that knowledge affect a rereading of any or all of this narrative?

See also Questions for Contrast and Comparison: 1, 3, 7, 56, 72, 92, 130, 173, 187, and 204.

■■ JORGE LUIS BORGES (1899–1986) *was born in Buenos Aires, Argentina.*
■■ *His family, prominent since the war of national independence (1810–1816),
included his father, a psychology professor, and his British paternal grandmother
through whose home-tutoring Jorge was initially more familiar with English literature than with Hispanic. When war stranded the touring family in Europe, Jorge
completed his formal education at the College de Genève, Switzerland. Returning to
Buenos Aires in 1921, he began both library and literary work. Despite progressive
hereditary blindness, he rose steadily — except when dictator Juan Perón demoted
him to chicken inspector — to become Director of the National Library (1955–73).
Professor of English at the University of Buenos Aires, Borges also held distinguished
lectureships at Harvard University (1967–68) and elsewhere. Throughout his career
he produced lucid poetry (for a time leading the* Ultraismo *movement based on*
SURREALISM *and* Imagism*) and penetrating essays challenging both* AESTHETIC *and
social assumptions. His greatest fame, however, rests on his brief prose "fictions,"*
STORY/*essay hybrids that involve both speaker and reader emotionally and philosophically in their own construction. His distinctive,* SELF-REFLEXIVE *work has led to
the term "Borgesian," a fitting tribute for a translator of Faulkner, Joyce, and
Kafka. His most Borgesian collection in English is aptly called* Labyrinths *(1962).*

Emma Zunz

Returning home from the Tarbuch and Loewenthal textile mills on the 14th of
January, 1922, Emma Zunz discovered in the rear of the entrance hall a letter,
posted in Brazil, which informed her that her father had died. The stamp and the
envelope deceived her at first; then the unfamiliar handwriting made her uneasy.
Nine or ten lines tried to fill up the page; Emma read that Mr. Maier had taken by
mistake a large dose of veronal and had died on the third of the month in the
hospital of Bagé. A boardinghouse friend of her father had signed the letter, some
Fein or Fain from Rio Grande, with no way of knowing that he was addressing
the deceased's daughter.

Emma dropped the paper. Her first impression was of a weak feeling in her
stomach and in her knees; then of blind guilt, of unreality, of coldness, of fear;
then she wished that it were already the next day. Immediately afterward she
realized that that wish was futile because the death of her father was the only
thing that had happened in the world, and it would go on happening endlessly.
She picked up the piece of paper and went to her room. Furtively, she hid it in a
drawer, as if somehow she already knew the ulterior facts. She had already begun
to suspect them, perhaps; she had already become the person she would be.

In the growing darkness, Emma wept until the end of that day for the suicide
of Manuel Maier, who in the old happy days was Emmanuel Zunz. She remembered summer vacations at a little farm near Gualeguay, she remembered (tried to
remember) her mother, she remembered the little house at Lanús which had been
auctioned off, she remembered the yellow lozenges of a window, she remembered
the warrant for arrest, the ignominy, she remembered the poison-pen letters with
the newspaper's account of "the cashier's embezzlement," she remembered (but
this she never forgot) that her father, on the last night, had sworn to her that the
thief was Loewenthal. Loewenthal, Aaron Loewenthal, formerly the manager of
the factory and now one of the owners. Since 1916 Emma had guarded the secret.

She had revealed it to no one, not even to her best friend, Elsa Urstein. Perhaps she was shunning profane incredulity; perhaps she believed that the secret was a link between herself and the absent parent. Loewenthal did not know that she knew; Emma Zunz derived from this slight fact a feeling of power.

She did not sleep that night and when the first light of dawn defined the rectangle of the window, her plan was already perfected. She tried to make the day, which seemed interminable to her, like any other. At the factory there were rumors of a strike. Emma declared herself, as usual, against all violence. At six o'clock, with work over, she went with Elsa to a women's club that had a gymnasium and a swimming pool. They signed their names; she had to repeat and spell out her first and her last name, she had to respond to the vulgar jokes that accompanied the medical examination. With Elsa and with the youngest of the Kronfuss girls she discussed what movie they would go to Sunday afternoon. Then they talked about boyfriends and no one expected Emma to speak. In April she would be nineteen years old, but men inspired in her, still, an almost pathological fear . . . Having returned home, she prepared a tapioca soup and a few vegetables, ate early, went to bed and forced herself to sleep. In this way, laborious and trivial, Friday the fifteenth, the day before, elapsed.

Impatience awoke her on Saturday. Impatience it was, not uneasiness, and the special relief of it being that day at last. No longer did she have to plan and imagine; within a few hours the simplicity of the facts would suffice. She read in *La Prensa* that the *Nordstjärnan*, out of Malmö, would sail that evening from Pier 3. She phoned Loewenthal, insinuated that she wanted to confide in him, without the other girls knowing, something pertaining to the strike; and she promised to stop by at his office at nightfall. Her voice trembled; the tremor was suitable to an informer. Nothing else of note happened that morning. Emma worked until twelve o'clock and then settled with Elsa and Perla Kronfuss the details of their Sunday stroll. She lay down after lunch and reviewed, with her eyes closed, the plan she had devised. She thought that the final step would be less horrible than the first and that it would doubtlessly afford her the taste of victory and justice. Suddenly, alarmed, she got up and ran to the dresser drawer. She opened it; beneath the picture of Milton Sills, where she had left it the night before, was Fain's letter. No one could have seen it; she began to read it and tore it up.

To relate with some reality the events of that afternoon would be difficult and perhaps unrighteous. One attribute of a hellish experience is unreality, an attribute that seems to allay its terrors and which aggravates them perhaps. How could one make credible an action which was scarcely believed in by the person who executed it, how to recover that brief chaos which today the memory of Emma Zunz repudiates and confuses? Emma lived in Almagro, on Liniers Street: we are certain that in the afternoon she went down to the waterfront. Perhaps on the infamous Paseo de Julio she saw herself multiplied in mirrors, revealed by lights and denuded by hungry eyes, but it is more reasonable to suppose that at first she wandered, unnoticed, through the indifferent portico . . . She entered two or three bars, noted the routine or technique of the other women. Finally she came across men from the *Nordstjärnan*. One of them, very young, she feared might inspire some tenderness in her and she chose instead another, perhaps shorter than she and coarse, in order that the purity of the horror might not be mitigated. The man led her to a door, then to a murky entrance hall and afterwards to a narrow stairway and then a vestibule (in which there was a window with lozenges identical to those in the house at Lanús) and then to a passageway and then to a door which was closed behind her. The arduous events are outside of time, either because the immediate past is as if disconnected from the future, or because the parts which form these events do not seem to be consecutive.

During that time outside of time, in that perplexing disorder of disconnected and atrocious sensations, did Emma Zunz think *once* about the dead man who motivated the sacrifice? It is my belief that she did think once, and in that moment she endangered her desperate undertaking. She thought (she was unable not to think) that her father had done to her mother the hideous thing that was being done to her now. She thought of it with weak amazement and took refuge, quickly, in vertigo. The man, a Swede or Finn, did not speak Spanish. He was a tool for Emma, as she was for him, but she served him for pleasure whereas he served her for justice.

When she was alone, Emma did not open her eyes immediately. On the little night table was the money that the man had left: Emma sat up and tore it to pieces as before she had torn the letter. Tearing money is an impiety, like throwing away bread; Emma repented the moment after she did it. An act of pride and on that day . . . Her fear was lost in the grief of her body, in her disgust. The grief and the nausea were chaining her, but Emma got up slowly and proceeded to dress herself. In the room there were no longer any bright colors; the last light of dusk was weakening. Emma was able to leave without anyone seeing her; at the corner she got on a Lacroze streetcar heading west. She selected, in keeping with her plan, the seat farthest toward the front, so that her face would not be seen. Perhaps it comforted her to verify in the insipid movement along the streets that what had happened had not contaminated things. She rode through the diminishing opaque suburbs, seeing them and forgetting them at the same instant, and got off on one of the side streets of Warnes. Paradoxically her fatigue was turning out to be a strength, since it obligated her to concentrate on the details of the adventure and concealed from her the background and the objective.

Aaron Loewenthal was to all persons a serious man, to his intimate friends a miser. He lived above the factory, alone. Situated in the barren outskirts of the town, he feared thieves; in the patio of the factory there was a large dog and in the drawer of his desk, everyone knew, a revolver. He had mourned with gravity, the year before, the unexpected death of his wife — a Gauss who had brought him a fine dowry — but money was his real passion. With intimate embarrassment, he knew himself to be less apt at earning it than at saving it. He was very religious; he believed he had a secret pact with God which exempted him from doing good in exchange for prayers and piety. Bald, fat, wearing the band of mourning, with smoked glasses and blond beard, he was standing next to the window awaiting the confidential report of worker Zunz.

He saw her push the iron gate (which he had left open for her) and cross the gloomy patio. He saw her make a little detour when the chained dog barked. Emma's lips were moving rapidly, like those of someone praying in a low voice; weary, they were repeating the sentence which Mr. Loewenthal would hear before dying.

Things did not happen as Emma Zunz had anticipated. Ever since the morning before she had imagined herself wielding the firm revolver, forcing the wretched creature to confess his wretched guilt and exposing the daring strata- gem which would permit the Justice of God to triumph over human justice. (Not out of fear but because of being an instrument of Justice she did not want to be punished.) Then, one single shot in the center of his chest would seal Loe- wenthal's fate. But things did not happen that way.

In Aaron Loewenthal's presence, more than the urgency of avenging her father, Emma felt the need of inflicting punishment for the outrage she had suffered. She was unable not to kill him after that thorough dishonor. Nor did she have time for theatrics. Seated, timid, she made excuses to Loewenthal, she invoked (as a privilege of the informer) the obligation of loyalty, uttered a few names, inferred others and broke off as if fear had conquered her. She managed to have Loewenthal leave to get a glass of water for her. When the former, unconvinced by such a fuss but indulgent, returned from the dining room, Emma had already taken the heavy revolver out of the drawer. She squeezed the trigger twice. The large body collapsed as if the reports and the smoke had shattered it, the glass of water smashed, the face looked at her with amazement and anger, the mouth of the face swore at her in Spanish and Yiddish. The evil words did not slacken; Emma had to fire again. In the patio the chained dog broke out barking, and a gush of rude blood flowed from the obscene lips and soiled the beard and the clothing. Emma began the accusation she had prepared ("I have avenged my father and they will not be able to punish me . . ."), but she did not finish it, because Mr. Loewenthal had already died. She never knew if he managed to understand.

The straining barks reminded her that she could not, yet, rest. She disar- ranged the divan, unbuttoned the dead man's jacket, took off the bespattered glasses and left them on the filing cabinet. Then she picked up the telephone and repeated what she would repeat so many times again, with these and with other words: *Something incredible has happened . . . Mr. Loewenthal had me come over on the pretext of the strike . . . He abused me, I killed him . . .*

Actually, the story *was* incredible, but it impressed everyone because sub- stantially it was true. True was Emma Zunz' tone, true was her shame, true was her hate. True also was the outrage she had suffered: only the circumstances were false, the time, and one or two proper names.

[1948]

Study and Writing Questions

1. Why does Emma wait until her father's death to avenge him?
2. What does Loewenthal swearing at her "in Spanish and Yiddish" suggest?
3. How does the fact that Emma "never knew if [Loewenthal] managed to understand" affect your interpretation of the STORY?
4. What is the relationship between the first and last paragraphs of the NARRATIVE?
5. What are the differences between first and subsequent readings of this narrative?

See also Questions for Contrast and Comparison: 9, 14, 15, 25, 28, 49, 54, 127, 139, 147, 167, and 231.

Pierre Menard,
Author of the *Quixote*

The *visible* work left by this novelist is easily and briefly enumerated. Impardonable, therefore, are the omissions and additions perpetrated by Madame Henri Bachelier in a fallacious catalogue which a certain daily, whose *Protestant* tendency is no secret, has had the inconsideration to inflict upon its deplorable readers — though these be few and Calvinist, if not Masonic and circumcised. The true friends of Menard have viewed this catalogue with alarm and even with a certain melancholy. One might say that only yesterday we gathered before his final monument, amidst the lugubrious cypresses, and already Error tries to tarnish his Memory . . . Decidedly, a brief rectification is unavoidable.

I am aware that it is quite easy to challenge my slight authority. I hope, however, that I shall not be prohibited from mentioning two eminent testimonies. The Baroness de Bacourt (at whose unforgettable *vendredis* I had the honor of meeting the lamented poet) has seen fit to approve the pages which follow. The Countess de Bagnoregio, one of the most delicate spirits of the Principality of Monaco (and now of Pittsburgh, Pennsylvania, following her recent marriage to the international philanthropist Simon Kautzsch, who has been so inconsiderately slandered, alas! by the victims of his disinterested maneuvers) has sacrificed "to veracity and to death" (such were her words) the stately reserve which is her distinction, and, in an open letter published in the magazine *Luxe*, concedes me her approval as well. These authorizations, I think, are not entirely insufficient.

I have said that Menard's visible work can be easily enumerated. Having examined with care his personal files, I find that they contain the following items:

a) A Symbolist sonnet which appeared twice (with variants) in the review *La conque* (issues of March and October 1899).

b) A monograph on the possibility of constructing a poetic vocabulary of concepts which would not be synonyms or periphrases of those which make up our everyday language, "but rather ideal objects created according to convention and essentially designed to satisfy poetic needs" (Nîmes, 1901).

c) A monograph on "certain connections or affinities" between the thought of Descartes, Leibniz and John Wilkins (Nîmes, 1903).

d) A monograph on Leibniz's *Characteristica universalis* (Nîmes, 1904).

e) A technical article on the possibility of improving the game of chess, eliminating one of the rook's pawns. Menard proposes, recommends, discusses and finally rejects this innovation.

f) A monograph on Raymond Lully's *Ars magna generalis* (Nîmes, 1906).

g) A translation, with prologue and notes, of Ruy López de Segura's *Libro de la invención liberal y arte del juego del axedrez* (Paris, 1907).

h) The work sheets of a monograph on George Boole's symbolic logic.

i) An examination of the essential metric laws of French prose, illustrated with examples taken from Saint-Simon (*Revue des langues romanes*, Montpellier, October 1909).

j) A reply to Luc Durtain (who had denied the existence of such laws), illustrated with examples from Luc Durtain (*Revue des langues romanes*, Montpellier, December 1909).

k) A manuscript translation of the *Aguja de navegar cultos* of Quevedo, entitled *La boussole des précieux*.

l) A preface to the Catalogue of an exposition of lithographs by Carolus Hourcade (Nîmes, 1914).

m) The work *Les problèmes d'un problème* (Paris, 1917), which discusses, in chronological order, the different solutions given to the illustrous problem of Achilles and the tortoise. Two editions of this book have appeared so far; the second bears as an epigraph Leibniz's recommendation "*Ne craignez point, monsieur, la tortue*" and revises the chapters dedicated to Russell and Descartes.

n) A determined analysis of the "syntactical customs" of Toulet (N.R.F., March 1921). Menard—I recall—declared that censure and praise are sentimental operations which have nothing to do with literary criticism.

o) A transposition into alexandrines of Paul Valéry's *Le cimitière marin* (N.R.F., January 1928).

p) An invective against Paul Valéry, in the *Papers for the Suppression of Reality* of Jacques Reboul. (This invective, we might say parenthetically, is the exact opposite of his true opinion of Valéry. The latter understood it as such and their old friendship was not endangered.)

q) A "definition" of the Countess de Bagnoregio, in the "victorious volume" —the locution is Gabriele d'Annunzio's, another of its collaborators—published annually by this lady to rectify the inevitable falsifications of journalists and to present "to the world and to Italy" an authentic image of her person, so often exposed (by very reason of her beauty and her activities) to erroneous or hasty interpretations.

r) A cycle of admirable sonnets for the Baroness de Bacourt (1934).

s) A manuscript list of verses which owe their efficacy to their punctuation.[1]

This, then is the *visible* work of Menard, in chronological order (with no omission other than a few vague sonnets of circumstance written for the hospitable, or avid, album of Madame Henri Bachelier). I turn now to his other work: the subterranean, the interminably heroic, the peerless. And—such are the capacities of man!—the unfinished. This work, perhaps the most significant of our time, consists of the ninth and thirty-eighth chapters of the first part of *Don Quixote* and a fragment of chapter twenty-two. I know such an affirmation seems an absurdity; to justify this "absurdity" is the primordial object of this note.[2]

Two texts of unequal value inspired this undertaking. One is that philological fragment by Novalis—the one numbered 2005 in the Dresden edition— which outlines the theme of a *total* identification with a given author. The other is one of those parasitic books which situate Christ on a boulevard, Hamlet on La Cannebière or Don Quixote on Wall Street. Like all men of good taste, Menard

---

[1] Madame Henri Bachelier also lists a literal translation of Quevedo's literal translation of the *Introduction à la vie dévote* of St. Francis of Sales. There are no traces of such a work in Menard's library. It must have been a jest of our friend, misunderstood by the lady.

[2] I also had the secondary intention of sketching a personal portrait of Pierre Menard. But how could I dare to compete with the golden pages which, I am told, the Baroness de Bacourt is preparing or with the delicate and punctual pencil of Carolus Hourcade?

abhorred these useless carnivals, fit only—as he would say—to produce the plebeian pleasure of anachronism or (what is worse) to enthrall us with the elementary idea that all epochs are the same or are different. More interesting, though contradictory and superficial of execution, seemed to him the famous plan of Daudet: to conjoin the Ingenious Gentleman and his squire in *one* figure, which was Tartarin . . . Those who have insinuated that Menard dedicated his life to writing a contemporary *Quixote* calumniate his illustrious memory.

He did not want to compose another *Quixote*—which is easy—but *the Quixote itself.* Needless to say, he never contemplated a mechanical transcription of the original; he did not propose to copy it. His admirable intention was to produce a few pages which would coincide—word for word and line for line— with those of Miguel de Cervantes.

"My intent is no more than astonishing," he wrote me the 30th of September, 1934, from Bayonne. "The final term in a theological or metaphysical demonstration—the objective world, God, causality, the forms of the universe —is no less previous and common than my famed novel. The only difference is that the philosophers publish the intermediary stages of their labor in pleasant volumes and I have resolved to do away with those stages." In truth, not one worksheet remains to bear witness to his years of effort.

The first method he conceived was relatively simple. Know Spanish well, recover the Catholic faith, fight against the Moors or the Turk, forget the history of Europe between the years 1602 and 1918, *be* Miguel de Cervantes. Pierre Menard studied this procedure (I know he attained a fairly accurate command of seventeenth-century Spanish) but discarded it as too easy. Rather as impossible! my reader will say. Granted, but the undertaking was impossible from the very beginning and of all the impossible ways of carrying it out, this was the least interesting. To be, in the twentieth century, a popular novelist of the seventeenth seemed to him a diminution. To be, in some way, Cervantes and reach the *Quixote* seemed less arduous to him—and, consequently, less interesting—than to go on being Pierre Menard and reach the *Quixote* through the experiences of Pierre Menard. (This conviction, we might say in passing, made him omit the autobiographical prologue to the second part of *Don Quixote.* To include that prologue would have been to create another character—Cervantes—but it would also have meant presenting the *Quixote* in terms of that character and not of Menard. The latter, naturally, declined that facility.) "My undertaking is not difficult, essentially," I read in another part of his letter. "I should only have to be immortal to carry it out." Shall I confess that I often imagine he did finish it and that I read the *Quixote*—all of it—as if Menard had conceived it? Some nights past, while leafing through chapter XXVI—never essayed by him—I recognized our friend's style and something of his voice in this exceptional phrase: "the river nymphs and the dolorous and humid Echo." This happy conjunction of a spiritual and a physical adjective brought to my mind a verse by Shakespeare which we discussed one afternoon:

Where a malignant and a turbaned Turk . . .

But why precisely the *Quixote?* our reader will ask. Such a preference, in a Spaniard, would not have been inexplicable; but it is, no doubt, in a Symbolist from Nîmes, essentially a devoté of Poe, who engendered Baudelaire, who engendered Mallarmé, who engendered Valéry, who engendered Edmond Teste. The aforementioned letter illuminates this point. "The *Quixote*," clarifies Menard, "interests me deeply, but it does not seem—how shall I say it?—inevitable. I cannot imagine the universe without Edgar Allan Poe's exclamation:

Ah, bear in mind this garden was enchanted!

or without the *Bateau ivre* or the *Ancient Mariner*, but I am quite capable of imagining it without the *Quixote*. (I speak, naturally, of my personal capacity and not of those works' historical resonance.) The *Quixote* is a contingent book; the *Quixote* is unnecessary. I can premeditate writing it, I can write it, without falling into a tautology. When I was ten or twelve years old, I read it, perhaps in its entirety. Later, I have reread closely certain chapters, those which I shall not attempt for the time being. I have also gone through the interludes, the plays, the *Galatea*, the exemplary novels, the undoubtedly laborious tribulations of Persiles and Segismunda and the *Viaje del Parnaso* . . . My general recollection of the *Quixote*, simplified by forgetfulness and indifference, can well equal the imprecise and prior image of a book not yet written. Once that image (which no one can legitimately deny me) is postulated, it is certain that my problem is a good bit more difficult than Cervantes' was. My obliging predecessor did not refuse the collaboration of chance: he composed his immortal work somewhat *à la diable*, carried along by the inertias of language and invention. I have taken on the mysterious duty of reconstructing literally his spontaneous work. My solitary game is governed by two polar laws. The first permits me to essay variations of a formal or psychological type; the second obliges me to sacrifice these variations to the "original" text and reason out this annihilation in an irrefutable manner . . . To these artificial hindrances, another—of a congenital kind—must be added. To compose the *Quixote* at the beginning of the seventeenth century was a reasonable undertaking, necessary and perhaps even unavoidable; at the beginning of the twentieth, it is almost impossible. It is not in vain that three hundred years have gone by, filled with exceedingly complex events. Amongst them, to mention only one, is the *Quixote* itself."

In spite of these three obstacles, Menard's fragmentary *Quixote* is more subtle than Cervantes'. The latter, in a clumsy fashion, opposes to the fictions of chivalry the tawdry provincial reality of his country; Menard selects as his "reality" the land of Carmen during the century of Lepanto and Lope de Vega. What a series of *espagnolades* that selection would have suggested to Maurice Barrès or Dr. Rodríguez Larreta! Menard eludes them with complete naturalness. In his work there are no gypsy flourishes or conquistadors or mystics or Philip the Seconds or *autos da fé*. He neglects or eliminates local color. This disdain points to a new conception of the historical novel. This disdain condemns *Salammbô*, with no possibility of appeal.

It is no less astounding to consider isolated chapters. For example, let us examine Chapter XXXVIII of the first part, "which treats of the curious discourse of Don Quixote on arms and letters." It is well known that Don Quixote (like Quevedo in an analogous and later passage in *La hora de todos*) decided the debate against letters and in favor of arms. Cervantes was a former soldier: his verdict is understandable. But that Pierre Menard's Don Quixote — a contemporary of *La trahison des clercs* and Bertrand Russell — should fall prey to such nebulous sophistries! Madame Bachelier has seen here an admirable and typical subordination on the part of the author to the hero's psychology; others (not at all perspicaciously), a *transcription* of the *Quixote*; the Baroness de Bacourt, the influence of Nietzsche. To this third interpretation (which I judge to be irrefutable) I am not sure I dare to add a fourth, which concords very well with the almost divine modesty of Pierre Menard: his resigned or ironical habit of propagating ideas which were the strict reverse of those he preferred. (Let us recall once more his diatribe against Paul Valéry in Jacques Reboul's ephemeral Surrealist sheet.) Cervantes' text and Menard's are verbally identical, but the second is almost infinitely richer. (More ambiguous, his detractors will say, but ambiguity is richness.)

It is a revelation to compare Menard's *Don Quixote* with Cervantes'. The latter, for example, wrote (part one, chapter nine):

> . . . truth, whose mother is history, rival of time, depository of deeds, witness of the past, exemplar and adviser to the present, and the future's counselor.

Written in the seventeenth century, written by the "lay genius" Cervantes, this enumeration is a mere rhetorical praise of history. Menard, on the other hand, writes:

> . . . truth, whose mother is history, rival of time, depository of deeds, witness of the past, exemplar and adviser to the present, and the future's counselor.

History, the *mother* of truth: the idea is astounding. Menard, a contemporary of William James, does not define history as an inquiry into reality but as its origin. Historical truth, for him, is not what has happened; it is what we judge to have happened. The final phrases — *exemplar and adviser to the present, and the future's counselor* — are brazenly pragmatic.

The contrast in style is also vivid. The archaic style of Menard — quite foreign, after all — suffers from a certain affectation. Not so that of his forerunner, who handles with ease the current Spanish of his time.

There is no exercise of the intellect which is not, in the final analysis, useless. A philosophical doctrine begins as a plausible description of the universe; with the passage of the years it becomes a mere chapter — if not a paragraph or a name — in the history of philosophy. In literature, this eventual caducity is even more notorious. The *Quixote* — Menard told me — was, above all, an entertaining book; now it is the occasion for patriotic toasts, grammatical insolence and obscene de luxe editions. Fame is a form of incomprehension, perhaps the worst.

There is nothing new in these nihilistic verifications; what is singular is the determination Menard derived from them. He decided to anticipate the vanity awaiting all man's efforts; he set himself to an undertaking which was exceedingly complex and, from the very beginning, futile. He dedicated his scruples and his sleepless nights to repeating an already extant book in an alien tongue. He multiplied draft upon draft, revised tenaciously and tore up thousands of manuscript pages.[1] He did not let anyone examine these drafts and took care they should not survive him. In vain have I tried to reconstruct them.

I have reflected that it is permissible to see in this "final" *Quixote* a kind of palimpsest, through which the traces — tenuous but not indecipherable — of our friend's "previous" writing should be translucently visible. Unfortunately, only a second Pierre Menard, inverting the other's work, would be able to exhume and revive those lost Troys . . .

"Thinking, analyzing, inventing (he also wrote me) are not anomalous acts; they are the normal respiration of the intelligence. To glorify the occasional performance of that function, to hoard ancient and alien thoughts, to recall with incredulous stupor that the *doctor universalis* thought, is to confess our laziness or our barbarity. Every man should be capable of all ideas and I understand that in the future this will be the case."

Menard (perhaps without wanting to) has enriched, by means of a new technique, the halting and rudimentary art of reading: this new technique is that of the deliberate anachronism and the erroneous attribution. This technique, whose applications are infinite, prompts us to go through the *Odyssey* as if it were posterior to the *Aeneid* and the book *Le jardin du Centaure* of Madame Henri Bachelier as if it were by Madame Henri Bachelier. This technique fills the most placid works with adventure. To attribute the *Imitatio Christi* to Louis Ferdinand Céline or to James Joyce, is this not a sufficient renovation of its tenuous spiritual indications?

For Silvina Ocampo

---

[1] I remember his quadricular notebooks, his black crossed-out passages, his peculiar typographical symbols and his insect-like handwriting. In the afternoons he liked to go out for a walk around the outskirts of Nîmes; he would take a notebook with him and make a merry bonfire.

[1939]

Study and Writing Questions

1. In the first two paragraphs of the work, how are the CHARACTER of the NARRATOR and his relation to Menard revealed?
2. What is the significance of the fact that "In truth, not one worksheet remains to bear witness to his years of effort"?
3. What is the relation of Borges's work to the work of the narrator and to the work of Menard?
4. This work may be thought of as having a number of RHETORICALLY distinct parts, such as the catalogue of Menard's writings and the detailed comparative CRITICISM of Cervantes and Menard on the idea of history. Divide the work into parts. How are these parts ordered and to what end?
5. What and how does this work teach us about the art of reading?

See also Questions for Contrast and Comparison: 9, 10, 11, 28, 48, 75, 139, 155, 184, and 231.

■ **RICHARD BRAUTIGAN** (1935–1984) *was a reclusive, San Francisco writer often associated with the Beat poets. He was much admired by the Counterculture of the late 1960s and 1970s for giving innovative expression to that era's widespread disillusionment with the American Dream. He so guarded his private life that his obituary notices record conflicting birthplaces (Tacoma and Spokane, Washington), and it is not clear whether he ever married or divorced the mother of his daughter. He published several volumes of poetry, the best known being* The Pill Versus the Springhill Mine Disaster *(1968) and* Rommel Drives On Deep Into Egypt *(1970). He also published a large number of short, strange, haunting, tragicomic* NOVELS, *all characterized by the surprising juxtaposition of very brief chapters each containing, like his poems, some extraordinary turn of* IMAGE. *Although he had a cult following that admired his apparent gentleness and questing soul, deeper readings of his best works, like the novels* Trout Fishing in America *(1967) and* In Watermelon Sugar *(1968), reveal a profound anger directed against both society and self. Many of his stories have been collected in* Revenge of the Lawn *(1971). His last sad book, unbroken into chapters, was* So the Wind Won't Blow It All Away *(1982), a first-person meditation on loss. Brautigan died of an apparently self-inflicted gunshot wound.*

Homage to the San Francisco YMCA

Once upon a time in San Francisco there was a man who really liked the finer things in life, especially poetry. He liked good verse.

He could afford to indulge himself in this liking, which meant that he didn't have to work because he was receiving a generous pension that was the result of a 1920s investment that his grandfather had made in a private insane asylum that was operating quite profitably in Southern California.

In the black, as they say and located in the San Fernando Valley, just outside of Tarzana. It was one of those places that do not look like an insane asylum. It looked like something else with flowers all around it, mostly roses.

The checks always arrived on the 1st and 15th of every month, even when there was not a mail delivery on that day. He had a lovely house in Pacific Heights and he would go out and buy more poetry. He of course had never met a poet in person. That would have been a little too much.

One day he decided that his liking for poetry could not be fully expressed in just reading poetry or listening to poets reading on phonograph records. He decided to take the plumbing out of his house and completely replace it with poetry, and so he did.

He turned off the water and took out the pipes and put in John Donne to replace them. The pipes did not look too happy. He took out his bathtub and put in William Shakespeare. The bathtub did not know what was happening.

He took out his kitchen sink and put in Emily Dickinson. The kitchen sink could only stare back in wonder. He took out his bathroom sink and put in Vladimir Mayakovsky. The bathroom sink, even though the water was off, broke out into tears.

He took out his hot water heater and put in Michael McClure's poetry. The hot water heater could barely contain its sanity. Finally he took out his toilet and put in the minor poets. The toilet planned on leaving the country.

And now the time had come to see how it all worked, to enjoy the fruit of his amazing labor. Christopher Columbus' slight venture sailing West was merely the shadow of a dismal event in the comparison. He turned the water back on again and surveyed the countenance of his vision brought to reality. He was a happy man.

"I think I'll take a bath," he said, to celebrate. He tried to heat up some Michael McClure to take a bath in some William Shakespeare and what happened was not actually what he had planned on happening.

"Might as well do the dishes, then," he said. He tried to wash some plates in "I taste a liquor never brewed," and found there was quite a difference between that liquid and a kitchen sink. Despair was on its way.

He tried to go to the toilet and the minor poets did not do at all. They began gossiping about their careers as he sat there trying to take a shit. One of them had written 197 sonnets about a penguin he had once seen in a travelling circus. He sensed a Pulitzer Prize in this material.

Suddenly the man realized that poetry could not replace plumbing. It's what they call seeing the light. He decided immediately to take the poetry out and put the pipes back in, along with the sinks, the bathtub, the hot water heater and the toilet.

"This just didn't work out the way I planned it," he said. "I'll have to put the plumbing back. Take the poetry out." It made sense standing there naked in the total light of failure.

But then he ran into more trouble than there was in the first place. The poetry did not want to go. It liked very much occupying the positions of the former plumbing.

"I look great as a kitchen sink," Emily Dickinson's poetry said.

"We look wonderful as a toilet," the minor poets said.

"I'm grand as pipes," John Donne's poetry said.

"I'm a perfect hot water heater," Michael McClure's poetry said.

Vladimir Mayakovsky sang new faucets from the bathroom, there are faucets beyond suffering, and William Shakespeare's poetry was nothing but smiles.

"That's well and dandy for you," the man said. "But I have to have plumbing, *real* plumbing in this house. Did you notice the emphasis I put on *real*? Real! Poetry just can't handle it. Face up to reality," the man said to the poetry.

But the poetry refused to go. "We're staying." The man offered to call the police. "Go ahead and lock us up, you illiterate," the poetry said in one voice.

"I'll call the fire department!"

"Book burner!" the poetry shouted.

The man began to fight the poetry. It was the first time he had ever been in a fight. He kicked the poetry of Emily Dickinson in the nose.

Of course the poetry of Michael McClure and Vladimir Mayakovsky walked over and said in English and in Russian, "That won't do at all," and threw the man down a flight of stairs. He got the message.

That was two years ago. The man is now living in the YMCA in San Francisco and loves it. He spends more time in the bathroom than everybody else. He goes in there at night and talks to himself with the light out.

[1972]

Study and Writing Questions

1. Why is the asylum described in such detail? What is the importance of insanity and sanity in this NARRATIVE?
2. What impact do the particular ALLUSIONS, especially to individual poets, have on your reading of this narrative? Do they change your understanding of the nature or value of poetry or of the reading of poetry?
3. How does the relationship between poetry and plumbing in this narrative compare with their relationship in your life? What does each stand for in this narrative?
4. " 'Face up to reality,' the man said to the poetry." Did it? If so, how, and what does that suggest about the nature of poetry both within the narrative and outside it? If not, what does that suggest about the nature of poetry both within the narrative and outside it?
5. Consider the last paragraph of the narrative. In what mental state is the PROTAGONIST? Is this a good or a bad outcome? Does it resolve the CONFLICT(s) of the narrative? What does the STORY seem to be saying?

See also Questions for Contrast and Comparison: 11, 27, 28, 41, 70, 84, 93, 126, 146, 152, and 181.

■ **GWENDOLYN BROOKS** (1917–), *born in Topeka, Kansas, raised in Chicago, Illinois, a graduate of Wilson Junior College (1936), married (1939) and a mother of two, is one of America's most distinguished poets. Beginning with* A Street in Bronzeville *(1945), reflecting both admired Romantic poets and the black American jazz and ballad traditions, she created* LYRIC *portraits, primarily of poor, urban African Americans, exemplifying both the specifics of black life and universal human traits. For* Annie Allen *(1949), more verse portraits, Brooks was the first black to receive the Pulitzer Prize. Her novel,* Maud Martha *(1953), presents vignettes (short literary sketches) from the life of a ghetto woman. After a 1967 black writers congress at Fisk University, she became more self-consciously political, writing "to Blacks . . . but for anyone who wants to open the book." In the Mecca (1968) is a verse* NARRATIVE *of a woman searching her housing project for her lost daughter, observing her neighbors, and finally discovering her murdered child. Brooks still lives in the heart of Chicago and, since 1968, has been Poet Laureate of Illinois, visiting schools, hospitals, prisons, and drug centers, tirelessly inspiring people of all races to develop self-respect. She funds poetry prizes for the young, the poor, and the black. From 1985 to 1986 she was the first black woman to serve as Poetry Consultant to the Library of Congress.* Report from Part One *(1972) begins her autobiography.*

The Ballad of Rudolph Reed

Rudolph Reed was oaken.
His wife was oaken too.
And his two good girls and his good little man
Oakened as they grew.

"I am not hungry for berries.
I am not hungry for bread.
But hungry hungry for a house
Where at night a man in bed

"May never hear the plaster
Stir as if in pain.
May never hear the roaches
Falling like fat rain.

"Where never wife and children need
Go blinking through the gloom.
Where every room of many rooms
Will be full of room.

"Oh my home may have its east or west
Or north or south behind it.
All I know is I shall know it,
And fight for it when I find it."

It was in a street of bitter white
That he made his application.
For Rudolph Reed was oakener
Than others in the nation.

The agent's steep and steady stare
Corroded to a grin.
Why, you black old, tough old hell of a man,
Move your family in!

Nary a grin grinned Rudolph Reed,
Nary a curse cursed he,
But moved in his House. With his dark little wife,
And his dark little children three.

A neighbor would *look*, with a yawning eye
That squeezed into a slit.
But the Rudolph Reeds and the children three
Were too joyous to notice it.

For were they not firm in a home of their own
With windows everywhere
And a beautiful banistered stair
And a front yard for flowers and a back yard for grass?

The first night, a rock, big as two fists.
The second, a rock big as three.
But nary a curse cursed Rudolph Reed.
(Though oaken as man could be.)

The third night, a silvery ring of glass.
Patience ached to endure.
But he looked, and lo! small Mabel's blood
Was staining her gaze so pure.

Then up did rise our Rudolph Reed
And pressed the hand of his wife,
And went to the door with a thirty-four
And a beastly butcher knife.

He ran like a mad thing into the night.
And the words in his mouth were stinking.
By the time he had hurt his first white man
He was no longer thinking.

By the time he had hurt his fourth white man
Rudolph Reed was dead.
His neighbors gathered and kicked his corpse.
"Nigger —" his neighbors said.

Small Mabel whimpered all night long,
For calling herself the cause.
Her oak-eyed mother did no thing
But change the bloody gauze.

[1960]

Study and Writing Questions

1. Describe the normal rhyme and RHYTHM of this ballad. Where does the work violate these norms? What are the effects of those violations?
2. What are the key METAPHORS and SIMILES in this piece? How are they used? In what ways do they work together?
3. What might the last line refer to symbolically? Are there other SYMBOLS in the work? If so, to what do they refer?
4. What is the importance of the word "oaken" in this NARRATIVE?
5. What is the importance of the title? Why is this called a "ballad"? Why is it "The Ballad of Rudolph Reed" and not "The Ballad of the Family Reed"?

See also Questions for Contrast and Comparison: 32, 39, 55, 177, 178, and 179.

OLGA BROUMAS (1949–) *was born in Greece but educated in the United States (University of Pennsylvania, B.A., 1970; University of Oregon, M.F.A., 1973). Her poems, written in English, her second language, are highly regarded. Her second volume,* Beginning With O *(1977), from which our selection comes, won the Yale Younger Poets Award. A self-described feminist lesbian, Broumas is an associate faculty member at Freehand, a learning community of women writers and photographers that she founded in Provincetown, Massachusetts in 1982.*

Little Red Riding Hood

I grow old, old
without you, Mother, landscape
of my heart. No child, no daughter between my bones
has moved, and passed
out screaming, dressed in her mantle of blood

as I did
once through your pelvic scaffold, stretching it
like a wishbone, your tenderest skin
strung on its bow and tightened
against the pain. I slipped out like an arrow, but not before

the midwife
plunged to her wrist and guided
my baffled head to its first mark. High forceps
might, in that one instant, have accomplished
what you and that good woman failed
in all these years to do: cramp
me between the temples, hobble
my baby feet. Dressed in my red hood, howling, I went—

evading
the white-clad doctor and his fancy claims: microscope,
stethoscope, scalpel, all
the better to see with, to hear,
and to eat—straight from your hollowed basket
into the midwife's skirts. I grew up
good at evading, and when you said,
'Stick to the road and forget the flowers, there's
wolves in those bushes, mind
where you got to go, mind
you get there,' I
minded. I kept

to the road, kept
the hood secret, kept what it sheathed more
secret still. I opened

it only at night, and with other women
who might be walking the same road to their own
grandma's house, each with her basket of gifts, her small hood
safe in the same part. I minded well. I have no daughter

to trace that road, back to your lap with my laden
basket of love. I'm growing
old, old
without you. Mother, landscape
of my heart, architect of my body, what other gesture
can I conceive

to make with it
that would reach you, alone
in your house and waiting, across this improbable forest
peopled with wolves and our lost, flower-gathering
sisters they feed on.

[1977]

Study and Writing Questions

1. What are the possible meanings of the phrase "landscape of my heart"?
2. What are the IMAGES of the human body used in this poem? How are they treated? What effect(s) do they have on your reading?
3. What are the meanings of the title that develop through the poem? What are the THEMATIC consequences of this development?
4. What are the relations between women and men as implied by this poem? How does the speaker's mother see that relationship? How does the speaker see it? Has the speaker's view changed?
5. Poems in which the speaker talks mainly to someone other than the reader are called DRAMATIC MONOLOGUES. How is the dramatic monologue form used here to reveal the attitude(s) of the speaker and/or to guide our reactions?

See also Questions for Contrast and Comparison: 99, 124, 129, 194, and 195.

DICK BRUNA (1927–), born in Utrecht, Netherlands, is a world renowned writer/illustrator of children's books, having been translated into twenty-one languages and selling nearly four million copies in Britain alone. His great-grandfather founded A.W. Bruna Publishing, which his grandfather and father ran. Bruna resisted the family business, instead enrolling in art school in Amsterdam. After six months, he left to work as an artist. He has designed book jackets since 1945 and award-winning posters since 1947. In 1953 he married and published his first book, De appel (The Apple). Two years later he began the popular Miffy book series. Bruna is famous for the format he produced in 1959: small, square books of spare pictures and simple text. He revised his older works to conform to this format, including De kleine koning (1955; revised as De koning, 1965; issued in English as The King, 1962). Although he uses few words, geometric lines, and primary colors, his effects are achieved through great care: "for a book of twelve pictures I make at least a hundred . . . I go on writing texts endlessly, too. I type pages and pages of them, much too much, and then suddenly see what's right. . . . It always comes down to directness, to get as direct an effect as possible."

The King

A little boy in a palace lived

Far from everything.

The golden crown upon his head

Showed he was a king.

Two tall thin green ladies

Looked after him quite well.

To get whatever he wanted,

He just had to ring a bell.

Sometimes the king built castles

Way up into the sky.

With red and green and yellow blocks,

He built them very high.

Sometimes the king would drive his car,

A real car of his own.

But he wasn't really happy,

For he always played alone.

One day, not far from the palace,

A little house he spied

With a red roof and shutters.

The gardener lived inside.

Rose was the gardener's little girl.

She liked to skip and run.

The king played with her every day.

He'd never had such fun.

The two played ball and hide-and-seek

And ran upon the green.

One day the little king said, "Rose,

I want you for my queen."

The tall green ladies said, "NO! NO!

She doesn't have a crown.

You cannot play with Rose again,"

They told him with a frown.

"We will find a princess

With long and golden hair.

She will have a shining crown.

You'll make a handsome pair."

The little king was very sad.

The tears dripped down his nose.

"I don't want a princess.

The one I want is Rose."

"If I take off my crown," he said,

"Then we'll be just the same.

I do not want to be a king.

I'd rather play a game."

Now every day the king and Rose

Play and run and swing.

Having a friend is wonderful.

It's better than being a king.

Study and Writing Questions

1. What aspects of the drawing and writing STYLES indicate that this NARRATIVE is children's LITERATURE?
2. What are examples of humor in this narrative? How is humor generated here in the words, in the pictures, and in the relation between them?
3. Does a reading of this narrative depend upon the age of the reader? If possible, find a young child and read this with the child. If possible, find someone who has been a parent for at least a few years and read this with that person. How, if at all, do their readings and yours differ? Why?
4. What are the DIDACTIC aims of this work? Since most children are not kings, what sort of lesson(s) should they draw from this work for their own lives?
5. How is CONVENTION used in this narrative? What elements rely on convention (for example, kings are supposed to be good)? How are these conventions used (for example, kings are supposed to be adults; royal children, at least in FAIRY TALES, are usually princes and princesses)? What are the effects of this narrative's particular manipulations of convention?

See also Questions for Contrast and Comparison: 27, 37, 95, 155, 159, 169, and 177.

■ **MORLEY (EDWARD) CALLAGHAN** (1903–1990) *was born in Toronto, Ontario. While still a student at the University of Toronto (B.A., 1925), he began reporting for the Toronto Daily Star, where Ernest Hemingway also worked. Callaghan married in 1927, finished law school in 1928, and then spent a year abroad, about which he wrote* That Summer in Paris: Memories of Tangled Friendships with Hemingway, Fitzgerald, and Others *(1963). Through Hemingway's assistance, Callaghan's first stories began to appear in "little magazines," including Ezra Pound's* Exile. *Callaghan never practiced law but instead became a full-time writer. Except for brief stays in Pennsylvania and New York, he spent his entire working life in Toronto. For such books as* Strange Fugitive *(1928), a story of a bootlegger;* They Shall Inherit the Earth *(1935), a study of an average family during the Depression;* More Joy In Heaven *(1937), a portrait of a reformed prisoner whose ideals the world rejects; and* A Passion in Rome *(1961), Callaghan won virtually every prestigious Canadian writing award. Despite this acclaim, Edmund Wilson called him "perhaps the most unjustly neglected novelist in the English-speaking world." One reviewer called* Morley Callaghan's Stories *(1959) "one of the few major achievements of Canadian prose . . . and more worthy of enduring than any single work of his better publicized peers: Anderson, Hemingway and Fitzgerald."*

A Cap for Steve

Dave Diamond, a poor man, a carpenter's assistant, was a small, wiry, quick-tempered individual who had learned how to make every dollar count in his home. His wife, Anna, had been sick a lot, and his twelve-year-old son, Steve, had to be kept in school. Steve, a big-eyed, shy kid, ought to have known the value of money as well as Dave did. It had been ground into him.

But the boy was crazy about baseball, and after school, when he could have been working as a delivery boy or selling papers, he played ball with the kids. His failure to appreciate that the family needed a few extra dollars disgusted Dave. Around the house he wouldn't let Steve talk about baseball, and he scowled when he saw him hurrying off with his glove after dinner.

When the Phillies came to town to play an exhibition game with the home team and Steve pleaded to be taken to the ball park, Dave, of course, was outraged. Steve knew they couldn't afford it. But he had got his mother on his side. Finally Dave made a bargain with them. He said that if Steve came home after school and worked hard helping to make some kitchen shelves he would take him that night to the ball park.

Steve worked hard, but Dave was still resentful. They had to coax him to put on his good suit. When they started out Steve held aloof, feeling guilty, and they walked down the street like strangers; then Dave glanced at Steve's face and, half-ashamed, took his arm more cheerfully.

As the game went on, Dave had to listen to Steve's recitation of the batting average of every Philly that stepped up to the plate; the time the boy must have wasted learning these averages began to appall him. He showed it so plainly that Steve felt guilty again and was silent.

After the game Dave let Steve drag him onto the field to keep him company while he tried to get some autographs from the Philly players, who were being hemmed in by gangs of kids blocking the way to the club-house. But Steve, who was shy, let the other kids block him off from the players. Steve would push his way in, get blocked out, and come back to stand mournfully beside Dave. And Dave grew impatient. He was wasting valuable time. He wanted to get home; Steve knew it and was worried.

Then the big, blond Philly outfielder, Eddie Condon, who had been held up by a gang of kids tugging at his arm and thrusting their score cards at him, broke loose and made a run for the club-house. He was jostled, and his blue cap with the red peak, tilted far back on his head, fell off. It fell at Steve's feet, and Steve stooped quickly and grabbed it. "Okay, son," the outfielder called, turning back. But Steve, holding the hat in both hands, only stared at him.

"Give him his cap, Steve," Dave said, smiling apologetically at the big outfielder who towered over them. But Steve drew the hat closer to his chest. In an awed trance he looked up at big Eddie Condon. It was an embarrassing moment. All the other kids were watching. Some shouted. "Give him his cap."

"My cap, son," Eddie Condon said, his hand out.

"Hey, Steve," Dave said, and he gave him a shake. But he had to jerk the cap out of Steve's hands.

"Here you are," he said.

The outfielder, noticing Steve's white, worshipping face and pleading eyes, grinned and then shrugged. "Aw, let him keep it," he said.

"No, Mister Condon, you don't need to do that," Steve protested.

"It's happened before. Forget it," Eddie Condon said, and he trotted away to the club-house.

Dave handed the cap to Steve: envious kids circled around them and Steve said, "He said I could keep it, Dad. You heard him, didn't you?"

"Yeah, I heard him," Dave admitted. The wonder in Steve's face made him smile. He took the boy by the arm and they hurried off the field.

On the way home Dave couldn't get him to talk about the game; he couldn't get him to take his eyes off the cap. Steve could hardly believe in his own happiness. "See," he said suddenly, and he showed Dave that Eddie Condon's name was printed on the sweat-band. Then he went on dreaming. Finally he put the cap on his head and turned to Dave with a slow, proud smile. The cap was away too big for him; it fell down over his ears. "Never mind," Dave said. "You can get your mother to take a tuck in the back."

When they got home Dave was tired and his wife didn't understand the cap's importance, and they couldn't get Steve to go to bed. He swaggered around wearing the cap and looking in the mirror every ten minutes. He took the cap to bed with him.

Dave and his wife had a cup of coffee in the kitchen, and Dave told her again how they had got the cap. They agreed that their boy must have an attractive quality that showed in his face, and that Eddie Condon must have been drawn to him — why else would he have singled Steve out from all the kids?

But Dave got tired of the fuss Steve made over that cap and of the way he wore it from the time he got up in the morning until the time he went to bed. Some kid was always coming in, wanting to try on the cap. It was childish, Dave said, for Steve to go around assuming that the cap made him important in the neighbourhood, and to keep telling them how he had become a leader in the park a few blocks away where he played ball in the evenings. And Dave wouldn't stand for Steve's keeping the cap on while he was eating. He was always scolding his wife for accepting Steve's explanation that he'd forgotten he had it on. Just the same, it was remarkable what a little thing like a ball cap could do for a kid, Dave admitted to his wife as he smiled to himself.

One night Steve was late coming home from the park. Dave didn't realize how late it was until he put down his newspaper and watched his wife at the window. Her restlessness got on his nerves. "See what comes from encouraging the boy to hang around with those park loafers," he said. "I don't encourage him," she protested. "You do," he insisted irritably, for he was really worried now. A gang hung around the park until midnight. It was a bad park. It was true that on one side there was a good district with fine, expensive apartment houses, but the kids from that neighbourhood left the park to the kids from the poorer homes. When his wife went out and walked down to the corner it was his turn to wait and worry and watch at the open window. Each waiting moment tortured him. At last he heard his wife's voice and Steve's voice, and he relaxed and sighed; then he remembered his duty and rushed angrily to meet them.

"I'll fix you, Steve, once and for all," he said. "I'll show you you can't start coming into the house at midnight."

"Hold your horses, Dave," his wife said. "Can't you see the state he's in?" Steve looked utterly exhausted and beaten.

"What's the matter?" Dave asked quickly.

"I lost my cap," Steve whispered; he walked past his father and threw himself on the couch in the living-room and lay with his face hidden.

"Now, don't scold him, Dave," his wife said.

"Scold him. Who's scolding him?" Dave asked, indignantly. "It's his cap, not mine. If it's not worth his while to hang on to it, why should I scold him?" But he was implying resentfully that he alone recognized the cap's value.

"So you are scolding him," his wife said. "It's his cap. Not yours. What happened, Steve?"

Steve told them he had been playing ball and he found that when he ran the bases the cap fell off; it was still too big despite the tuck his mother had taken in the band. So the next time he came to bat he tucked the cap in his hip pocket. Someone had lifted it, he was sure.

"And he didn't even know whether it was still in his pocket," Dave said sarcastically.

"I wasn't careless, Dad," Steve said. For the last three hours he had been wandering around to the homes of the kids who had been in the park at the time; he wanted to go on, but he was too tired. Dave knew the boy was apologizing to him, but he didn't know why it made him angry.

"If he didn't hang on to it, it's not worth worrying about now," he said, and sounded offended.

After that night they knew that Steve didn't go to the park to play ball; he went to look for the cap. It irritated Dave to see him sit around listlessly, or walk in circles, trying to force his memory to find a particular incident which would suddenly recall to him the moment when the cap had been taken. It was no attitude for a growing, healthy boy to take, Dave complained. He told Steve firmly once and for all that he didn't want to hear any more about the cap.

One night, two weeks later, Dave was walking home with Steve from the shoemaker's. It was a hot night. When they passed an ice-cream parlour Steve slowed down. "I guess I couldn't have a soda, could I?" Steve said. "Nothing doing," Dave said firmly. "Come on now," he added as Steve hung back, looking in the window.

"Dad, look!" Steve cried suddenly, pointing at the window. "My cap! There's my cap! He's coming out!"

A well-dressed boy was leaving the ice-cream parlour; he had on a blue ball cap with a red peak, just like Steve's cap. "Hey, you!" Steve cried, and he rushed at the boy, his small face fierce and his eyes wild. Before the boy could back away Steve had snatched the cap from his head. "That's my cap!" he shouted.

"What's this?" the bigger boy said. "Hey, give me my cap or I'll give you a poke on the nose."

Dave was surprised that his own shy boy did not back away. He watched him clutch the cap in his left hand, half crying with excitement as he put his head down and drew back his right fist: he was willing to fight. And Dave was proud of him.

"Wait, now," Dave said. "Take it easy, son," he said to the other boy, who refused to back away.

"My boy says it's his cap," Dave said.

"Well, he's crazy. It's my cap."

"I was with him when he got this cap. When the Phillies played here. It's a Philly cap."

"Eddie Condon gave it to me," Steve said. "And you stole it from me, you jerk."

"Don't call me a jerk, you little squirt. I never saw you before in my life."

"Look," Steve said, pointing to the printing on the cap's sweatband. "It's Eddie Condon's cap. See? See, Dad?"

"Yeah. You're right, Son. Ever see this boy before, Steve?"

"No," Steve said reluctantly.

The other boy realized he might lose the cap. "I bought it from a guy," he said. "I paid him. My father knows I paid him." He said he got the cap at the ball park. He groped for some magically impressive words and suddenly found them. "You'll have to speak to my father," he said.

"Sure, I'll speak to your father," Dave said. "What's your name? Where do you live?"

"My name's Hudson. I live about ten minutes away on the other side of the park." The boy appraised Dave, who wasn't any bigger than he was and who wore a faded blue windbreaker and no tie. "My father is a lawyer," he said boldly. "He wouldn't let me keep the cap if he didn't think I should."

"Is that a fact?" Dave asked belligerently. "Well, we'll see. Come on. Let's go." And he got between the two boys and they walked along the street. They didn't talk to each other. Dave knew the Hudson boy was waiting to get to the protection of his home, and Steve knew it, too, and he looked up apprehensively at Dave. And Dave, reaching for his hand, squeezed it encouragingly and strode along, cocky and belligerent, knowing that Steve relied on him.

The Hudson boy lived in that row of fine apartment houses on the other side of the park. At the entrance to one of these houses Dave tried not to hang back and show he was impressed, because he could feel Steve hanging back. When they got into the small elevator Dave didn't know why he took off his hat. In the carpeted hall on the fourth floor the Hudson boy said, "Just a minute," and entered his own apartment. Dave and Steve were left alone in the corridor, knowing that the other boy was preparing his father for the encounter. Steve looked anxiously at his father, and Dave said, "Don't worry, Son," and he added resolutely, "No one's putting anything over on us."

A tall balding man in a brown velvet smoking-jacket suddenly opened the door. Dave had never seen a man wearing one of those jackets, although he had seen them in department-store windows. "Good evening," he said, making a deprecatory gesture at the cap Steve still clutched tightly in his left hand. "My boy didn't get your name. My name is Hudson."

"Mine's Diamond."

"Come on in," Mr. Hudson said, putting out his hand and laughing good-naturedly. He led Dave and Steve into his living-room. "What's this about that cap?" he asked. "The way kids can get excited about a cap. Well, it's understandable, isn't it?"

"So it is," Dave said, moving closer to Steve, who was awed by the broadloom rug and the fine furniture. He wanted to show Steve he was at ease himself, and he wished Mr. Hudson wouldn't be so polite. That meant Dave had to be polite and affable, too, and it was hard to manage when he was standing in the middle of the floor in his old windbreaker.

"Sit down, Mr. Diamond," Mr. Hudson said. Dave took Steve's arm and sat him down beside him on the chesterfield. The Hudson boy watched his father. And Dave looked at Steve and saw that he wouldn't face Mr. Hudson or the other boy; he kept looking up at Dave, putting all his faith in him.

"Well, Mr. Diamond, from what I gathered from my boy, you're able to prove this cap belonged to your boy."

"That's a fact," Dave said.

"Mr. Diamond, you'll have to believe my boy bought that cap from some kid in good faith."

"I don't doubt it," Dave said. "But no kid can sell something that doesn't belong to him. You know that's a fact, Mr. Hudson."

"Yes, that's a fact," Mr. Hudson agreed. "But the cap means a lot to my boy, Mr. Diamond."

"It means a lot to my boy, too, Mr. Hudson."

"Sure it does. But supposing we called in a policeman. You know what he'd say? He'd ask you if you were willing to pay my boy what he paid for the cap. That's usually the way it works out," Mr. Hudson said, friendly and smiling, as he eyed Dave shrewdly.

"But that's not right. It's not justice," Dave protested. "Not when it's my boy's cap."

"I know it isn't right. But that's what they do."

"All right. What did you say your boy paid for the cap?" Dave said reluctantly.

"Two dollars."

Two dollars!" Dave repeated. Mr. Hudson's smile was still kindly, but his eyes were shrewd, and Dave knew the lawyer was counting on his not having the two dollars; Mr. Hudson thought he had Dave sized up; he had looked at him and decided he was broke. Dave's pride was hurt, and he turned to Steve. What he saw in Steve's face was more powerful than the hurt to his pride: it was the memory of how difficult it had been to get an extra nickel, the talk he heard about the cost of food, the worry in his mother's face as she tried to make ends meet, and the bewildered embarrassment that he was here in a rich man's home, forcing his father to confess that he couldn't afford to spend two dollars. Then Dave grew angry and reckless. "I'll give you the two dollars," he said.

Steve looked at the Hudson boy and grinned brightly. The Hudson boy watched his father.

"I suppose that's fair enough," Mr. Hudson said. "A cap like this can be worth a lot to a kid. You know how it is. Your boy might want to sell — I mean be satisfied. Would he take five dollars for it?"

"Five dollars?" Dave repeated. "Is it worth five dollars, Steve?" he asked uncertainly.

Steve shook his head and looked frightened.

"No, thanks, Mr. Hudson," Dave said firmly.

"I'll tell you what I'll do," Mr. Hudson said. "I'll give you ten dollars. The cap has a sentimental value for my boy, a Philly cap, a big-leaguer's cap. It's only worth about a buck and a half really," he added. But Dave shook his head again. Mr. Hudson frowned. He looked at his own boy with indulgent concern, but now he was embarrassed. "I'll tell you what I'll do," he said. "This cap — well, it's worth as much as a day at the circus to my boy. Your boy should be recompensed. I want to be fair. Here's twenty dollars," and he held out two ten-dollar bills to Dave.

That much money for a cap, Dave thought, and his eyes brightened. But he knew what the cap had meant to Steve; to deprive him of it now that it was within his reach would be unbearable. All the things he needed in his life gathered around him; his wife was there, saying he couldn't afford to reject the offer, he had no right to do it; and he turned to Steve to see if Steve thought it wonderful that the cap could bring them twenty dollars.

"What do you say, Steve?" he asked uneasily.

"I don't know," Steve said. He was in a trance. When Dave smiled, Steve smiled too, and Dave believed that Steve was as impressed as he was, only more bewildered, and maybe even more aware that they could not possibly turn away that much money for a ball cap.

"Well, here you are," Mr. Hudson said, and he put the two bills in Steve's hand. "It's a lot of money. But I guess you had a right to expect as much."

With a dazed, fixed smile Steve handed the money slowly to his father, and his face was white.

Laughing jovially, Mr. Hudson led them to the door. His own boy followed a few paces behind.

In the elevator Dave took the bills out of his pocket. "See, Stevie," he whispered eagerly. "That windbreaker you wanted! And ten dollars for your bank! Won't Mother be surprised?"

"Yeah," Steve whispered, the little smile still on his face. But Dave had to turn away quickly so their eyes wouldn't meet, for he saw that it was a scared smile.

Outside, Dave said, "Here, you carry the money home, Steve. You show it to your mother."

"No, you keep it," Steve said, and then there was nothing to say. They walked in silence.

"It's a lot of money," Dave said finally. When Steve didn't answer him, he added angrily, "I turned to you, Steve. I asked you, didn't I?"

"That man knew how much his boy wanted that cap," Steve said.

"Sure. But he recognized how much it was worth to us."

"No, you let him take it away from us," Steve blurted.

"That's unfair," Dave said. "Don't dare say that to me."

"I don't want to be like you," Steve muttered, and he darted across the road and walked along on the other side of the street.

"It's unfair," Dave said angrily, only now he didn't mean that Steve was unfair, he meant that what had happened in the prosperous Hudson home was unfair, and he didn't know quite why. He had been trapped, not just by Mr. Hudson, but by his own life. Across the road Steve was hurrying along with his head down, wanting to be alone. They walked most of the way home on opposite sides of the street, until Dave could stand it no longer. "Steve," he called, crossing the street. "It was very unfair. I mean, for you to say . . ." but Steve started to run. Dave walked as fast as he could and Steve was getting beyond him, and he felt enraged and suddenly he yelled, "Steve!" and he started to chase his son. He wanted to get hold of Steve and pound him, and he didn't know why. He gained on him, he gasped for breath and he almost got him by the shoulder. Turning, Steve saw his father's face in the street light and was terrified; he circled away, got to the house, and rushed in, yelling, "Mother!"

"Son, Son!" she cried, rushing from the kitchen. As soon as she threw her arms around Steve, shielding him, Dave's anger left him and he felt stupid. He walked past them into the kitchen.

"What happened?" she asked anxiously. "Have you both gone crazy? What did you do, Steve?"

"Nothing," he said sullenly.

"What did your father do?"

"We found the boy with my ball cap, and he let the boy's father take it from us."

"No, no," Dave protested. "Nobody pushed us around. The man didn't put anything over us." He felt tired and his face was burning. He told what had happened; then he slowly took the two ten-dollar bills out of his wallet and tossed them on the table and looked up guiltily at his wife.

It hurt him that she didn't pick up the money, and that she didn't rebuke him. "It is a lot of money, Son," she said slowly. "Your father was only trying to do what he knew was right, and it'll work out, and you'll understand." She was soothing Steve, but Dave knew she felt that she needed to be gentle with him, too, and he was ashamed.

When she went with Steve to his bedroom, Dave sat by himself. His son had contempt for him, he thought. His son, for the first time, had seen how easy it was for another man to handle him, and he had judged him and had wanted to walk alone on the other side of the street. He looked at the money and he hated the sight of it.

His wife returned to the kitchen, made a cup of tea, talked soothingly, and said it was incredible that he had forced the Hudson man to pay him twenty dollars for the cap, but all Dave could think of was Steve was scared of me.

Finally, he got up and went into Steve's room. The room was in darkness, but he could see the outline of Steve's body on the bed, and he sat down beside him and whispered, "Look, Son, it was a mistake. I know why. People like us — in circumstances where money can scare us. No, no," he said, feeling ashamed and shaking his head apologetically; he was taking the wrong way of showing the boy they were together; he was covering up his own failure. For the failure had been his, and it had come out of being so separated from his son that he had been blind to what was beyond the price in a boy's life. He longed now to show Steve he could be with him from day to day. His hand went out hesitantly to Steve's shoulder. "Steve, look," he said eagerly. "The trouble was I didn't realize how much I enjoyed it that night at the ball park. If I had watched you playing for your own team — the kids around here say you could be a great pitcher. We could take that money and buy a new pitcher's glove for you, and a catcher's mitt. Steve, Steve, are you listening? I could catch you, work with you in the lane. Maybe I could be your coach . . . watch you become a great pitcher." In the half-darkness he could see the boy's pale face turn to him.

Steve, who had never heard his father talk like this, was shy and wondering. All he knew was that his father, for the first time, wanted to be with him in his hopes and adventures. He said, "I guess you do know how important that cap was." His hand went out to his father's arm. "With that man the cap was — well it was just something he could buy, eh Dad?" Dave gripped his son's hand hard. The wonderful generosity of childhood — the price a boy was willing to pay to be able to count on his father's admiration and approval — made him feel humble, then strangely exalted.

[1952]

Study and Writing Questions

1. The NARRATIVE opens with an assertion of Dave's anger. How much of his MOTIVATION comes from angry rejection of bad as opposed to generous acceptance of good? What attitude(s) toward Dave does the NARRATOR project?

2. In what ways is it important to the lives of the CHARACTERS and to our understanding of the narrative that Anna "had been sick a lot"?

3. The words "price" and "value" are in some senses synonymous, in others they are nearly opposite in meaning. How do price and value change in the worlds of the park, the ballpark, the Diamond home, and the Hudson home?

4. What evidence is there that Steve was or was not correct in asserting that Dave did finally "know how important that cap was"?

5. Note that there are many details in this story which have parallels in Christianity. For example, the first Christian martyr was Stephen; Jesus was said to be a descendant of David; Anna is a form of the name of the Virgin Mary's mother; the last line asserts that Dave, like Jesus, is humbled and then exalted. What are some other parallels? What evidence is there that this narrative does or does not have an intentional Christian spiritual level?

See also Questions for Contrast and Comparison: 34, 37, 70, 84, 135, 170, and 225.

FRANÇOIS ANDRÉ CAMOIN (1939–), *son of a professor, was born in Nice, France and educated in the United States (University of Arizona, B.A., 1964; M.A., 1965; University of Massachusetts, Ph.D., 1967). Until committing himself to full-time writing, he taught in the English departments of Slippery Rock State College (1967–1968) and Denison University (1968–1971). In 1974 he married actress Lisa Marlene Kent. His books include* Benbow and Paradise *(1975),* Deadly Virtues *(1988), and two story collections,* The End of the World is Los Angeles *(1982) and* Why Men Are Afraid of Women *(1984). Of fictions drawn from his earlier collection, such as the following, Camoin has written, "If every short story should have beginning, middle and end, should every short-short have them too, only smaller? . . . Maybe short-shorts should be only ends. Or beginnings. The way that microscopic animals are sometimes only mouths."*

Things I Did
To Make It Possible

One. I made love to Margaret only in the missionary position. We are not baboons.

Two. I went to the ocean every chance I got. My favorite place was the Santa Monica Pier but I also went to the Malibu Pier, Topanga Beach, Zuma Beach, Newport Harbor. Sometimes I fished. Mackerel scream when they are pulled out of the water, but they probably don't feel much. Certainly they don't know what's happening to them.

Three. One of the hardest things was watching my weight. I'll never be a fat man if I can help it. Ate a lot of celery, tomatoes by the dozen, lettuce. Gobbled cucumbers just so I'd have something in my mouth.

Four. Sometimes talking to Margaret is like pissing in a violin, as my mother used to say. She listens but she doesn't believe. Still I try.

Five. I ran four miles a day around the golf course in Tarzana. Sometimes with Marty, more often alone; he's like an old man — his tits joggle sadly when he runs, and he gets out of breath and asks me to stop and wait for him every few hundred yards. One leg of our course runs along the bank of the Los Angeles River, a terrible place.

Six. The tree in my back yard throws fish-shaped leaf-shadows on the patio bricks. Let a little breeze blow and clouds of shadow-fish wriggle across the bricks.

Seven. Life in a tropical paradise. Lagoon is one of the great words in the language. Listen to the sound of it. *Lagoon.* I don't know why she should be fucking Marty.

Eight. If she is. He's forty like me, and not in nearly as good a condition. What's she getting out of it? I could ask.

Nine. Another thing I did: I quit smoking.

Ten. I went to Tijuana and bought Margaret an armadillo purse with red-glass eyes. The paws curl under the hollow belly, where she can put things.

Eleven. When we were going to the university she was fucking our friend Campbell the playwright. Artsy-craftsy Campbell weighed about ninety pounds and came up to my shoulder, but he had an agile mind. And a way with women.

Twelve. I loved my wife.

Thirteen. Help me, Dr. Eisenberg. You comedian, you.

Fourteen. Margaret has to my knowledge slept with: Campbell, Marty, myself. I think she also went to bed with Norman Haas at least once. He had polio and is even smaller than Campbell. He can only move one arm, and not all of that. The woman is a saint, possibly, in her own view.

Fifteen. I also bought some armadillo boots for myself. Armadillo babies. God but that's sad. I'm wearing their mama on my feet.

Sixteen. We are nature. The smog is nature. I tried to learn to love it. I sucked it in deep when I ran, and made it a part of myself. Listened to the golf balls whizzing in the cottonwood leaves above my head and took deep breaths. Jumped over small snakes. Told myself that by the time I was ready to die it would seem natural to me. Maybe necessary. Conceivably beautiful.

Seventeen. Here are some things I collected during this time and did not use: a French postcard of a woman with bare breasts and one eye closed to indicate sexiness; a 1941 Buick with side-mount spare wheels and burned valves; an Italian coin made out of aluminum; a black pebble from the beach, cut in half by a clear streak of quartz; a dried blowfish from the souvenir shop on Santa Monica Pier; a sterling-silver medal of Benjamin Franklin; the white skull of a small animal with long front teeth.

Eighteen. I went for long walks at night and thought about the world.

Nineteen. We are not baboons or dogs. Something else.

Twenty. Fourteen years? Almost exactly now. It seems like no time at all since we were all innocent in Tucson.

Twenty-one. I picked up a little girl hitchhiking on the corner of Sunset and Doheny, and drove her out to Zuma Beach.

Twenty-two. What's this life all about anyway?

Twenty-three. In general I tried. I think I can say that much. I loved the smog; I loved the yellow grass that looks dead on the hillsides from the middle of May onward; I loved the long loose whips of the freeways that connect this town; I loved the Santa Ana wind that makes the best of us crazy; I loved the rain in winter.

Twenty-four. Try to be an angel — see where it gets you.

Twenty-five. Sweet little girl from somewhere back East. She blew me under one of the lifeguard towers in the middle of the night, and we talked until the sun came up while I smoked her cigarettes and listened to the surf. Boom-boom-boom. Saddest goddamn sound on earth.

Twenty-six. I had trouble with the video portion of my life. I kept fading in and out.

Twenty-seven. I gave money to: the City of Hope; Muscular Dystrophy; United Good Neighbors; the Heart Fund; the Cancer Society; the Boy Scouts of America; two little Mexican girls who came to the front door selling scented candles; my hitchhiker.

Twenty-eight. A dream where my father was a small blue pyramid with a single brown eye, like the picture on the dollar-bill. In my sleep he seemed perfectly natural in that form. We carried on a long conversation about life. I'm not a big-time dreamer; not many of the dreams that I can remember are as strange as that, or as interesting. Usually it's the old naked-in-a-crowd-of-strangers, or flying-over-the-hills sequence. Now and then I dream of a golden girl and love so tender I wake up with tears on my face.

Twenty-nine. Eisenberg said I should expect to feel like this. Then he laughed like a duck.

Thirty. I'm not a big-time *anything.* Not strictly true. I want. I'm a big-time wanter, maybe.

Thirty-one. I told the girl what I had to have if I was to keep going. Love, warmth, not to be alone. She touched me. No, not that, I said. You don't understand. Yes I do, she said. Lie back and listen to the water.

Thirty-two. I drove her all the way to Santa Barbara and left her by the side of the highway, under the big fig tree on Anacapa Street. Where was she going from there? I don't think she knew for sure. Should I have made myself responsible for her? Not left her to work her way up the coast? Not picked her up in the first place, when I knew what was going to happen because I wanted it, because she wanted it? I don't suppose I'll ever know.

Thirty-three. I took Margaret and Marty to dinner at The Yellowfingers on Ventura Boulevard. I got them both drunk, and then I picked a fight with the waitress for no earthly reason at all, and then I got up and went home and left Marty and Margaret to straighten it all out. I don't think either one of them could walk or say a straight sentence after all the Manhattans I made them drink.

Thirty-four. I sat under my tree and watched the fish-shaped leaf-shadows drift across the bricks. I've had no luck in my life.

[1982]

Study and Writing Questions

1. Why does the NARRATOR number his paragraphs? What does this numbering reveal about the narrator?
2. In paragraph thirteen, Dr. Eisenberg is called a "comedian." How do different meanings of that word relate to this STORY?
3. Is paragraph twenty-six a joke? If so, what does it mean? In what way might it be true? What does writing that paragraph reveal about the narrator?
4. What is the importance of the fish IMAGERY in this NARRATIVE?
5. How does the meaning of the title shift? What is the importance of the title for understanding the narrative as a whole?

See also Questions for Contrast and Comparison: 10, 45, 91, 129, and 164.

■ **RAYMOND CARVER** (1938–1988), *son of laborers, was born in Clats-kanie, Oregon, logging country. By age twenty, Carver was married (1957) with two children. He graduated from Humboldt State University in northern California (A.B., 1963) and spent a further year at the University of Iowa (1963–1964). To support his family and writing, he held a long succession of low-paying jobs, such as apartment manager and gas station attendant. He began publishing well-regarded volumes of poetry in 1968 and in 1971 began teaching creative writing at a succession of institutions, including the University of California at Santa Cruz and at Berkeley. He is most honored for his spare, unjudgmental stories of working class people that appeared in such collections as* Will You Please Be Quiet, Please? *(1976),* Furious Seasons *(1977),* What We Talk About When We Talk About Love *(1981),* Cathedral *(1984), and* Elephant and Other Stories *(1988). He taught at Syracuse University from 1980 until the Mildred and Harold Strauss Living Award of the American Academy and Institute of Arts and Letters allowed him to begin writing full-time in 1983. In 1982 he divorced, and by 1984 was living with the poet Tess Gallagher, also on the Syracuse faculty. They married two months before his death from lung cancer. Of his typical characters, he said, "God, the country is filled with these people. They're good people. People doing the best they could."*

Viewfinder

A man without hands came to the door to sell me a photograph of my house. Except for the chrome hooks, he was an ordinary-looking man of fifty or so.

"How did you lose your hands?" I asked after he'd said what he wanted.

"That's another story, he said. "You want this picture or not?"

"Come in," I said. "I just made coffee."

I'd just made some Jell-O, too. But I didn't tell the man I did.

"I might use your toilet," the man with no hands said.

I wanted to see how he would hold a cup.

I knew how he held the camera. It was an old Polaroid, big and black. He had it fastened to leather straps that looped over his shoulders and went around his back, and it was this that secured the camera to his chest. He would stand on the sidewalk in front of your house, locate your house in the viewfinder, push down the lever with one of his hooks, and out would pop your picture.

I'd been watching from the window, you see.

"Where did you say the toilet was?"

"Down there, turn right."

Bending, hunching, he let himself out of the straps. He put the camera on the sofa and straightened his jacket.

"You can look at this while I'm gone."

I took the picture from him.

There was a little rectangle of lawn, the driveway, the carport, front steps, bay window, and the window I'd been watching from in the kitchen.

So why would I want a photograph of this tragedy?

I looked a little closer and saw my head, *my head,* in there inside the kitchen window.

It made me think, seeing myself like that. I can tell you, it makes a man think.

I heard the toilet flush. He came down the hall, zipping and smiling, one hook holding his belt, the other tucking in his shirt.

"What do you think?" he said. "All right? Personally, I think it turned out fine. Don't I know what I'm doing? Let's face it, it takes a professional."

He plucked at his crotch.

"Here's coffee," I said.

He said, "You're alone, right?"

He looked at the living room. He shook his head.

"Hard, hard," he said.

He sat next to the camera, leaned back with a sigh, and smiled as if he knew something he wasn't going to tell me.

"Drink your coffee," I said.

I was trying to think of something to say.

"Three kids were by here wanting to paint my address on the curb. They wanted a dollar to do it. You wouldn't know anything about that, would you?"

It was a long shot. But I watched him just the same.

He leaned forward importantly, the cup balanced between his hooks. He set it down on the table.

"I work alone," he said. "Always have, always will. What are you saying?" he said.

"I was trying to make a connection," I said.

I had a headache. I know coffee's no good for it, but sometimes Jell-O helps. I picked up the picture.

"I was in the kitchen," I said. "Usually I'm in the back."

"Happens all the time," he said. "So they just up and left you, right? Now you take me, I work alone. So what do you say? You want the picture?"

"I'll take it," I said.

I stood up and picked up the cups.

"Sure you will," he said. "Me, I keep a room downtown. It's okay. I take a bus out, and after I've worked the neighborhoods, I go to another downtown. You see what I'm saying? Hey, I had kids once. Just like you," he said.

I waited with the cups and watched him struggle up from the sofa.

He said, "They're what gave me this."

I took a good look at those hooks.

"Thanks for the coffee and the use of the toilet. I sympathize."

He raised and lowered his hooks.

"Show me," I said. "Show me how much. Take more pictures of me and my house."

"It won't work," the man said. "They're not coming back."

But I helped him get into his straps.

"I can give you a rate," he said. "Three for a dollar." He said, "If I go any lower, I don't come out."

We went outside. He adjusted the shutter. He told me where to stand, and we got down to it.

We moved around the house. Systematic. Sometimes I'd look sideways. Sometimes I'd look straight ahead.

"Good," he'd say. "That's good," he'd say, until we'd circled the house and were back in the front again. "That's twenty. That's enough."

"No," I said. "On the roof," I said.

"Jesus," he said. He checked up and down the block. "Sure," he said. "Now you're talking."

I said, "The whole kit and kaboodle. They cleared right out."

"Look at this!" the man said, and again he held up his hooks.

I went inside and got a chair. I put it up under the carport. But it didn't reach. So I got a crate and put the crate on top of the chair.

It was okay up there on the roof.

I stood up and looked around. I waved, and the man with no hands waved back with his hooks.

It was then I saw them, the rocks. It was like a little rock nest on the screen over the chimney hole. You know kids. You know how they lob them up, thinking to sink one down your chimney.

"Ready?" I called, and I got a rock, and I waited until he had me in his viewfinder.

"Okay!" he called.

I laid back my arm and I hollered, "Now!" I threw that son of a bitch as far as I could throw it.

"I don't know," I heard him shout. "I don't do motion shots."

"Again!" I screamed, and took up another rock.

[1981]

Study and Writing Questions

1. What is the importance of the photographer having hooks instead of hands?
2. Why does the NARRATOR go on the roof? Why does he throw away the rocks? Why does he want the other man to photograph this action?
3. To what might the title refer? What does each reference suggest about the STORY?
4. Why are pictures important to the narrator, to the other man, in general, and to this NARRATIVE?
5. How do your feelings about the narrator develop scene by scene? What is your final feeling about the narrator?

See also Questions for Contrast and Comparison: 93, 95, 96, 97, 123, 129, and 172.

■ **WILLA (SIBERT) CATHER** (1873–1947), *born in a comfortable, brick farmhouse in rural Virginia, moved in 1883 with her family to the sodhouses and flatlands of Nebraska, a shock she later called "an erasure of personality." The struggles of strong individuals, especially women, to achieve personality, and of pioneers, especially immigrants, to achieve civilization, became her abiding subjects. While at the University of Nebraska (B.A., 1895), she took up journalism, which she pursued (with a year's hiatus as an English teacher) in Lincoln, Pittsburgh, Pennsylvania, and New York City, where she moved in 1906 to edit McClure's Magazine. Having already published poems (April Twilights, 1903) and short stories (The Troll Garden, 1905), she turned to writing fiction full-time in 1912. Her most famous NOVELS are O Pioneers! (1913, dedicated to Sarah Orne Jewett), about a gifted, persevering pioneer farm woman; One of Ours (1922, Pulitzer); The Professor's House (1925), about finding life's meaning; and Death Comes for the Archbishop (1927), about a friendship between French missionaries in pioneer New Mexico. Obscure Destinies (1932) collects three elegiac NOVELETTES. Although the title character of My Ántonia (1918) became "a rich mine of life, like the founders of early races," Cather never married, preferring her many friends and, after 1913, the companionship of Edith Lewis. Cather died in New York of a cerebral hemorrhage.*

The Joy of Nelly Deane

Nell and I were almost ready to go on for the last act of *Queen Esther,* and we had for the moment got rid of our three patient dressers, Mrs. Dow, Mrs. Freeze, and Mrs. Spinny. Nell was peering over my shoulder into the little cracked looking glass that Mrs. Dow had taken from its nail on her kitchen wall and brought down to the church under her shawl that morning. When she realized that we were alone, Nell whispered to me in the quick, fierce way she had:

"Say, Peggy, won't you go up and stay with me tonight? Scott Spinny's asked to take me home, and I don't want to walk up with him alone."

"I guess so, if you'll ask my mother."

"Oh, I'll fix her!" Nell laughed, with a toss of her head which meant that she usually got what she wanted, even from people much less tractable than my mother.

In a moment our tiring-women were back again. The three old ladies — at least they seemed old to us — fluttered about us, more agitated than we were ourselves. It seemed as though they would never leave off patting Nell and touching her up. They kept trying things this way and that, never able in the end to decide which way was best. They wouldn't hear to her using rouge, and as they powdered her neck and arms, Mrs. Freeze murmured that she hoped we wouldn't get into the habit of using such things. Mrs. Spinny divided her time between pulling up and tucking down the "illusion" that filled in the square neck of Nelly's dress. She didn't like things much low, she said; but after she had pulled it up, she stood back and looked at Nell thoughtfully through her glasses. While the excited girl was reaching for this and that, buttoning a slipper, pinning down a curl, Mrs. Spinny's smile softened more and more until, just before Esther made her entrance, the old lady tiptoed up to her and softly tucked the illusion down as far as it would go.

"She's so pink; it seems a pity not," she whispered apologetically to Mrs. Dow.

Every one admitted that Nelly was the prettiest girl in Riverbend, and the gayest — oh, the gayest! When she was not singing, she was laughing. When she was not laid up with a broken arm, the outcome of a foolhardy coasting feat, or suspended from school because she ran away at recess to go buggy-riding with Guy Franklin, she was sure to be up to mischief of some sort. Twice she broke through the ice and got soused in the river because she never looked where she skated or cared what happened so long as she went fast enough. After the second of these duckings our three dressers declared that she was trying to be a Baptist despite herself.

Mrs. Spinny and Mrs. Freeze and Mrs. Dow, who were always hovering about Nelly, often whispered to me their hope that she would eventually come into our church and not "go with the Methodists"; her family were Wesleyans. But to me these artless plans of theirs never wholly explained their watchful affection. They had good daughters themselves — except Mrs. Spinny, who had only the sullen Scott — and they loved their plain girls and thanked God for them. But they loved Nelly differently. They were proud of her pretty figure and yellow-brown eyes, which dilated so easily and sparkled with a kind of golden effervescence. They were always making pretty things for her, always coaxing her to come to the sewing circle, where she knotted her thread, and put in the wrong sleeve, and laughed and chattered and said a great many things that she should not have said, and somehow always warmed their hearts. I think they loved her for her unquenchable joy.

All the Baptist ladies liked Nell, even those who criticized her most severely, but the three who were first in fighting the battles of our little church, who held it together by their prayers and the labor of their hands, watched over her as they did over Mrs. Dow's century plant before it blossomed. They looked for her on Sunday morning and smiled at her as she hurried, always a little late, up to the choir. When she rose and stood behind the organ and sang "There Is a Green Hill," one could see Mrs. Dow and Mrs. Freeze settle back in their accustomed seats and look up at her as if she had just come from that hill and had brought them glad tidings.

It was because I sang contralto, or, as we said, alto, in the Baptist choir that Nell and I became friends. She was so gay and grown up, so busy with parties and dances and picnics, that I would scarcely have seen much of her had we not sung together. She liked me better than she did any of the older girls, who tried clumsily to be like her, and I felt almost as solicitous and admiring as did Mrs. Dow and Mrs. Spinny. I think even then I must have loved to see her bloom and glow, and I loved to hear her sing, in "The Ninety and Nine,"

But one was out on the hills away

in her sweet, strong voice. Nell had never had a singing lesson, but she had sung from the time she could talk, and Mrs. Dow used fondly to say that it was singing so much that made her figure so pretty.

After I went into the choir it was found to be easier to get Nelly to choir practice. If I stopped outside her gate on my way to church and coaxed her, she usually laughed, ran in for her hat and jacket, and went along with me. The three old ladies fostered our friendship, and because I was "quiet," they esteemed me a good influence for Nelly. This view was propounded in a sewing-circle discussion and, leaking down to us through our mothers, greatly amused us. Dear old ladies! It was so manifestly for what Nell was that they loved her, and yet they were always looking for "influences" to change her.

The *Queen Esther* performance had cost us three months of hard practice, and it was not easy to keep Nell up to attending the tedious rehearsals. Some of the boys we knew were in the chorus of Assyrian youths, but the solo cast was made up of older people, and Nell found them very poky. We gave the cantata in the Baptist church on Christmas Eve, "to a crowded house," as the Riverbend *Messenger* truly chronicled. The country folk for miles about had come in through a deep snow, and their teams and wagons stood in a long row at the hitch-bars on each side of the church door. It was certainly Nelly's night, for however much the tenor — he was her schoolmaster, and naturally thought poorly of her — might try to eclipse her in his dolorous solos about the rivers of Babylon, there could be no doubt as to whom the people had come to hear — and to see.

After the performance was over, our fathers and mothers came back to the dressing rooms — the little rooms behind the baptistry where the candidates for baptism were robed — to congratulate us, and Nell persuaded my mother to let me go home with her. This arrangement may not have been wholly agreeable to Scott Spinny, who stood glumly waiting at the baptistry door; though I used to think he dogged Nell's steps not so much for any pleasure he got from being with her as for the pleasure of keeping other people away. Dear little Mrs. Spinny was perpetually in a state of humiliation on account of his bad manners, and she tried by a very special tenderness to make up to Nelly for the remissness of her ungracious son.

Scott was a spare, muscular fellow, good-looking, but with a face so set and dark that I used to think it very like the castings he sold. He was taciturn and domineering, and Nell rather liked to provoke him. Her father was so easy with her that she seemed to enjoy being ordered about now and then. That night, when every one was praising her and telling her how well she sang and how pretty she looked, Scott only said, as we came out of the dressing room:

"Have you got your high shoes on?"

"No, but I've got rubbers on over my low ones. Mother doesn't care."

"Well, you just go back and put 'em on as fast as you can."

Nell made a face at him and ran back, laughing. Her mother, fat, comfortable Mrs. Deane, was immensely amused at this.

"That's right, Scott" she chuckled. "You can do enough more with her than I can. She walks right over me an' Jud."

Scott grinned. If he was proud of Nelly, the last thing he wished to do was to show it. When she came back he began to nag again. "What are you going to do with all those flowers? They'll freeze stiff as pokers."

"Well, there won't none of *your* flowers freeze, Scott Spinny, so there!" Nell snapped. She had the best of him that time, and the Assyrian youths rejoiced. They were most of them high-school boys, and the poorest of them had "chipped in" and sent all the way to Denver for Queen Esther's flowers. There were bouquets from half a dozen townspeople, too, but none from Scott. Scott was a prosperous hardware merchant and notoriously penurious, though he saved his face, as the boys said, by giving liberally to the church.

"There's no use freezing the fool things, anyhow. You get me some newspapers, and I'll wrap 'em up." Scott took from his pocket a folded copy of the Riverbend *Messenger* and began laboriously to wrap up one of the bouquets. When we left the church door he bore three large newspaper bundles, carrying them as carefully as if they had been so many newly frosted wedding cakes, and left Nell and me to shift for ourselves as we floundered along the snow-burdened sidewalk.

Although it was after midnight, lights were shining from many of the little wooden houses, and the roofs and shrubbery were so deep in snow that Riverbend looked as if it had been tucked down into a warm bed. The companies of people, all coming from church, tramping this way and that toward their homes and calling "Good night" and "Merry Christmas" as they parted company, all seemed to us very unusual and exciting.

When we got home, Mrs. Deane had a cold supper ready, and Jud Deane had already taken off his shoes and fallen to on his fried chicken and pie. He was so proud of his pretty daughter that he must give her her Christmas presents then and there, and he went into the sleeping chamber behind the dining room and from the depths of his wife's closet brought out a short sealskin jacket and a round cap and made Nelly put them on.

Mrs. Deane, who sat busy between a plate of spice cake and a tray piled with her famous whipped cream tarts, laughed inordinately at his behavior.

"Ain't he worse than any kid you ever see? He's been running to that closet like a cat shut away from her kittens. I wonder Nell ain't caught on before this. I did think he'd make out now to keep 'em till Christmas morning; but he's never made out to keep anything yet."

That was true enough, and fortunately Jud's inability to keep anything seemed always to present a highly humorous aspect to his wife. Mrs. Deane put her heart into her cooking, and said that so long as a man was a good provider she had no cause to complain. Other people were not so charitable toward Jud's failing. I remember how many strictures were passed upon that little sealskin and how he was censured for his extravagance. But what a public-spirited thing, after all, it was for him to do! How, the winter through, we all enjoyed seeing Nell skating on the river or running about the town with the brown collar turned up about her bright cheeks and her hair blowing out from under the round cap! "No seal," Mrs. Dow said, "would have begrudged it to her. Why should we?" This was at the sewing circle, when the new coat was under grave discussion.

At last Nelly and I got upstairs and undressed, and the pad of Jud's slippered feet about the kitchen premises—where he was carrying up from the cellar things that might freeze—ceased. He called "Good night, daughter," from the foot of the stairs, and the house grew quiet. But one is not a prima donna the first time for nothing, and it seemed as if we could not go to bed. Our light must have burned long after every other in Riverbend was out. The muslin curtains of Nell's bed were drawn back; Mrs. Deane had turned down the white counterpane and taken off the shams and smoothed the pillows for us. But their fair plumpness offered no temptation to two such hot young heads. We could not let go of life even for a little while. We sat and talked in Nell's cozy room, where there was a tiny, white fur rug—the only one in Riverbend—before the bed; and there were white sash curtains, and the prettiest little desk and dressing table I had ever seen. It was a warm, gay little room, flooded all day long with sunlight from east and south windows that had climbing roses all about them in the summer. About the dresser were photographs of adoring high school boys; and one of Guy Franklin, much groomed and barbered, in a dress coat and a boutonnière. I never liked to see that photograph there. The home boys looked properly modest and bashful on the dresser, but he seemed to be staring impudently all the time.

I knew nothing definite against Guy, but in Riverbend all "traveling men" were considered worldly and wicked. He traveled for a Chicago dry-goods firm, and our fathers didn't like him because he put extravagant ideas into our mother's heads. He had very smooth and flattering ways, and he introduced into our simple community a great variety of perfumes and scented soaps, and he always reminded me of the merchants in Caesar, who brought into Gaul "those things which effeminate the mind," as we translated that delightfully easy passage.

Nell was sitting before the dressing table in her nightgown, holding the new fur coat and rubbing her cheek against it, when I saw a sudden gleam of tears in her eyes. "You know, Peggy," she said in her quick, impetuous way, "this makes me feel bad. I've got a secret from my daddy."

I can see her now, so pink and eager, her brown hair in two springy braids down her back, and her eyes shining with tears and with something even softer and more tremulous.

"I'm engaged, Peggy," she whispered, "really and truly."

She leaned forward, unbuttoning her nightgown, and there on her breast, hung by a little gold chain about her neck, was a diamond ring—Guy Franklin's solitaire; every one in Riverbend knew it well.

"I'm going to live in Chicago, and take singing lessons, and go to operas, and do all those nice things—oh, everything! I know you don't like him, Peggy, but you know you *are* a kid. You'll see how it is yourself when you grow up. He's so *different* from our boys, and he's just terribly in love with me. And then, Peggy,"—flushing all down over her soft shoulders,—"I'm awfully fond of him, too. Awfully."

"Are you, Nell, truly?" I whispered. She seemed so changed to me by the warm light in her eyes and that delicate suffusion of color. I felt as I did when I got up early on picnic mornings in summer, and saw the dawn come up in the breathless sky above the river meadows and make all the corn fields golden.

"Sure I do, Peggy; don't look so solemn. It's nothing to look that way about, kid. It's nice." She threw her arms about me suddenly and hugged me.

"I hate to think about your going so far away from us all, Nell."

"Oh, you'll love to come and visit me. Just you wait."

She began breathlessly to go over things Guy Franklin had told her about Chicago, until I seemed to see it all looming up out there under the stars that kept watch over our little sleeping town. We had neither of us ever been to a city, but we knew what it would be like. We heard it throbbing like great engines, and calling to us, that faraway world. Even after we had opened the windows and scurried into bed, we seemed to feel a pulsation across all the miles of snow. The winter silence trembled with it, and the air was full of something new that seemed to break over us in soft waves. In that snug, warm little bed I had a sense of imminent change and danger. I was somehow afraid for Nelly when I heard her breathing so quickly beside me, and I put my arm about her protectingly as we drifted toward sleep.

In the following spring we were both graduated from the Riverbend high school, and I went away to college. My family moved to Denver, and during the next four years I heard very little of Nelly Deane. My life was crowded with new people and new experiences, and I'm afraid I held her little in mind. I heard indirectly that Jud Deane had lost what little property he owned in a luckless venture in Cripple Creek, and that he had been able to keep his house in Riverbend only through the clemency of his creditors. Guy Franklin had his route changed and did not go to Riverbend any more. He married the daughter of a rich cattleman out near Long Pine, and ran a dry-goods store of his own. Mrs. Dow wrote me a long letter about once a year, and in one of these she told me that Nelly was teaching in the sixth grade in the Riverbend school.

> Dear Nelly does not like teaching very well. The children try her, and she is so pretty it seems a pity for her to be tied down to uncongenial employment. Scott is still very attentive, and I have noticed him look up at the window of Nelly's room in a very determined way as he goes home to dinner. Scott continues prosperous; he has made money during these hard times and now owns both our hardware stores. He is close, but a very honorable fellow. Nelly seems to hold off, but I think Mrs. Spinny has hopes. Nothing would please her more. If Scott were more careful about his appearance, it would help. He of course gets black about his business, and Nelly, you know, is very dainty. People do say his mother does his courting for him, she is so eager. If only Scott does not turn out hard and penurious like his father! We must all have our schooling in this life, but I don't want Nelly's to be too severe. She is a dear girl, and keeps her color.

Mrs. Dow's own schooling had been none too easy. Her husband had long been crippled with rheumatism, and was bitter and faultfinding. Her daughters had married poorly, and one of her sons had fallen into evil ways. But her letters were always cheerful, and in one of them she gently remonstrated with me because I "seemed inclined to take a sad view of life."

In the winter vacation of my senior year I stopped on my way home to visit Mrs. Dow. The first thing she told me when I got into her old buckboard at the station was that "Scott had at last prevailed," and that Nelly was to marry him in the spring. As a preliminary step, Nelly was about to join the Baptist church, "Just think, you will be here for her baptizing! How that will please Nelly! She is to be immersed tomorrow night."

I met Scott Spinny in the post office that morning and he gave me a hard grip with one black hand. There was something grim and saturnine about his powerful body and bearded face and his strong, cold hands. I wondered what perverse fate had driven him for eight years to dog the footsteps of a girl whose charm was due to qualities naturally distasteful to him. It still seems strange to me that in easygoing Riverbend, where there were so many boys who could have lived contentedly enough with my little grasshopper, it was the pushing ant who must have her and all her careless ways.

By a kind of unformulated etiquette one did not call upon candidates for baptism on the day of the ceremony, so I had my first glimpse of Nelly that evening. The baptistry was a cemented pit directly under the pulpit rostrum, over which we had our stage when we sang *Queen Esther*. I sat through the sermon somewhat nervously. After the minister, in his long, black gown, had gone down into the water and the choir had finished singing, the door from the dressing room opened, and, led by one of the deacons, Nelly came down the steps into the pool. Oh, she looked so little and meek and chastened! Her white cashmere robe clung about her, and her brown hair was brushed straight back and hung in two soft braids from a little head bent humbly. As she stepped down into the water I shivered with the cold of it, and I remembered sharply how much I had loved her. She went down until the water was well above her waist, and stood white and small, with her hands crossed on her breast, while the minister said the words about being buried with Christ in baptism. Then, lying in his arm, she disappeared under the dark water. "It will be like that when she dies," I thought, and a quick pain caught my heart. The choir began to sing "Washed in the Blood of the Lamb" as she rose again, the door behind the baptistry opened, revealing those three dear guardians, Mrs. Dow, Mrs. Freeze, and Mrs. Spinny, and she went up into their arms.

I went to see Nell next day, up in the little room of many memories. Such a sad, sad visit! She seemed changed—a little embarrassed and quietly despairing. We talked of many of the old Riverbend girls and boys, but she did not mention Guy Franklin or Scott Spinny, except to say that her father had got work in Scott's hardware store. She begged me, putting her hands on my shoulders with something of her old impulsiveness, to come and stay a few days with her. But I was afraid—afraid of what she might tell me and of what I might say. When I sat in that room with all her trinkets, the foolish harvest of her girlhood, lying about, and the white curtains and the little white rug, I thought of Scott Spinny with positive terror and could feel his hard grip on my hand again. I made the best excuse I could about having to hurry on to Denver; but she gave me one quick look, and her eyes ceased to plead. I saw that she understood me perfectly. We had known each other so well. Just once, when I got up to go and had trouble with my veil, she laughed her old merry laugh and told me there were some things I would never learn, for all my schooling.

The next day, when Mrs. Dow drove me down to the station to catch the morning train for Denver, I saw Nelly hurrying to school with several books under her arm. She had been working up her lessons at home, I thought. She was never quick at her books, dear Nell.

It was ten years before I again visited Riverbend. I had been in Rome for a long time, and had fallen into bitter homesickness. One morning, sitting among the dahlias and asters that bloom so bravely upon those gigantic heaps of earth-red ruins that were once the palaces of the Caesars, I broke the seal of one of Mrs. Dow's long yearly letters. It brought so much sad news that I resolved then and there to go home to Riverbend, the only place that had ever really been home to me. Mrs. Dow wrote me that her husband, after years of illness, had died in the cold spell last March. "So good and patient toward the last," she wrote, "and so afraid of giving extra trouble." There was another thing she saved until the last.

She wrote on and on, dear woman, about new babies and village improvements, as if she could not bear to tell me; and then it came:

You will be sad to hear that two months ago our dear Nelly left us. It was a terrible blow to us all. I cannot write about it yet, I fear. I wake up every morning feeling that I ought to go to her. She went three days after her little boy was born. The baby is a fine child and will live, I think, in spite of everything. He and her little girl, now eight years old, whom she named Margaret, after you, have gone to Mrs. Spinny's. She loves them more than if they were her own. It seems as if already they had made her quite young again. I wish you could see Nelly's children.

Ah, that was what I wanted, to see Nelly's children! The wish came aching from my heart along with the bitter homesick tears; along with a quick, torturing recollection that flashed upon me, as I looked about and tried to collect myself, of how we two had sat in our sunny seat in the corner of the old bare schoolroom one September afternoon and learned the names of the seven hills together. In that place, at that moment, after so many years, how it all came back to me — the warm sun on my back, the chattering girl beside me, the curly hair, the laughing yellow eyes, the stubby little finger on the page! I felt as if even then, when we sat in the sun with our heads together, it was all arranged, written out like a story, that at this moment I should be sitting among the crumbling bricks and drying grass, and she should be lying in the place I knew so well, on that green hill far away.

Mrs. Dow sat with her Christmas sewing in the familiar sitting room, where the carpet and the wallpaper and the tablecover had all faded into soft, dull colors, and even the chromo of Hagar and Ishmael had been toned to the sobriety of age. In the bay window the tall wire flowerstand still bore its little terraces of potted plants, and the big fuchsia and the Martha Washington geranium had blossomed for Christmastide. Mrs. Dow herself did not look greatly changed to me. Her hair, thin ever since I could remember it, was now quite white, but her spare, wiry little person had all its old activity, and her eyes gleamed with the old friendliness behind her silver-bowed glasses. Her gray house dress seemed just like those she used to wear when I ran in after school to take her angelfood cake down to the church supper.

The house sat on a hill, and from behind the geraniums I could see pretty much all of Riverbend, tucked down in the soft snow, and the air above was full of big, loose flakes, falling from a gray sky which betokened settled weather. Indoors the hard-coal burner made a tropical temperature, and glowed a warm orange from its isinglass sides. We sat and visited, the two of us, with a great sense of comfort and completeness. I had reached Riverbend only that morning, and Mrs. Dow, who had been haunted by thoughts of shipwreck and suffering upon wintry seas, kept urging me to draw nearer to the fire and suggesting incidental refreshment. We had chattered all through the winter morning and most of the afternoon, taking up one after another of the Riverbend girls and boys, and agreeing that we had reason to be well satisfied with most of them. Finally, after a long pause in which I had listened to the contented ticking of the clock and the crackle of the coal, I put the question I had until then held back:

"And now, Mrs. Dow, tell me about the one we loved best of all. Since I got your letter I've thought of her every day. Tell me all about Scott and Nelly."

The tears flashed behind her glasses, and she smoothed the little pink bag on her knee.

"Well, dear, I'm afraid Scott proved to be a hard man, like his father. But we must remember that Nelly always had Mrs. Spinny. I never saw anything like the love there was between those two. After Nelly lost her own father and mother, she looked to Mrs. Spinny for everything. When Scott was too unreasonable, his mother could 'most always prevail upon him. She never lifted a hand to fight her own battles with Scott's father, but she was never afraid to speak up for Nelly. And then Nelly took great comfort of her little girl. Such a lovely child!"

"Had she been very ill before the little baby came?"

"No, Margaret; I'm afraid 't was all because they had the wrong doctor. I feel confident that either Doctor Tom or Doctor Jones could have brought her through. But, you see, Scott had offended them both, and they'd stopped trading at his store, so he would have young Doctor Fox, a boy just out of college and a stranger. He got scared and didn't know what to do. Mrs. Spinny felt he wasn't doing right, so she sent for Mrs. Freeze and me. It seemed like Nelly had got discouraged. Scott would move into their big new house before the plastering was dry, and though 't was summer, she had taken a terrible cold that seemed to have drained her, and she took no interest in fixing the place up. Mrs. Spinny had been down with her back again and wasn't able to help, and things was just anyway. We won't talk about that, Margaret; I think 't would hurt Mrs. Spinny to have you know. She nearly died of mortification when she sent for us, and blamed her poor back. We did get Nelly fixed up nicely before she died. I prevailed upon Doctor Tom to come in at the last, and it 'most broke his heart. 'Why, Mis' Dow,' he said, 'if you'd only have come and told me how 't was, I'd have come and carried her right off in my arms.'"

"Oh, Mrs. Dow," I cried, "then it needn't have been?"

Mrs. Dow dropped her needle and clasped her hands quickly. "We mustn't look at it that way, dear," she said tremulously and a little sternly; "we mustn't let ourselves. We must just feel that our Lord wanted her *then*, and took her to Himself. When it was all over, she did look so like a child of God, young and trusting, like she did on her baptizing night, you remember?"

I felt that Mrs. Dow did not want to talk any more about Nelly then, and, indeed, I had little heart to listen; so I told her I would go for a walk, and suggested that I might stop at Mrs. Spinny's to see the children.

Mrs. Dow looked up thoughtfully at the clock. "I doubt if you'll find little Margaret there now. It's half-past four, and she'll have been out of school an hour and more. She'll be most likely coasting on Lupton's Hill. She usually makes for it with her sled the minute she is out of the schoolhouse door. You know, it's the old hill where you all used to slide. If you stop in at the church about six o'clock, you'll likely find Mrs. Spinny there with the baby. I promised to go down and help Mrs. Freeze finish up the tree, and Mrs. Spinny said she'd run in with the baby, if 't wasn't too bitter. She won't leave him alone with the Swede girl. She's like a young woman with her first."

Lupton's Hill was at the other end of town, and when I got there the dusk was thickening, drawing blue shadows over the snowy fields. There were perhaps twenty children creeping up the hill or whizzing down the packed sled track. When I had been watching them for some minutes, I heard a lusty shout, and a little red sled shot past me into the deep snowdrift beyond. The child was quite buried for a moment, then she struggled out and stood dusting the snow from her short coat and red woolen comforter. She wore a brown fur cap, which was too big for her and of an old-fashioned shape, such as girls wore long ago, but I would have known her without the cap. Mrs. Dow had said a beautiful child, and there would not be two like this in Riverbend. She was off before I had time to speak to her, going up the hill at a trot, her sturdy little legs plowing through the trampled snow. When she reached the top she never paused to take breath, but threw herself upon her sled and came down with a whoop that was quenched only by the deep drift at the end.

"Are you Margaret Spinny?" I asked as she struggled out in a cloud of snow.

"Yes, 'm." She approached me with frank curiosity, pulling her little sled behind her. "Are you the strange lady staying at Mrs. Dow's?" I nodded, and she began to look my clothes over with respectful interest.

"Your grandmother is to be at the church at six o'clock, isn't she?"

"Yes, 'm."

"Well, suppose we walk up there now. It's nearly six, and all the other children are going home." She hesitated, and looked up at the faintly gleaming track on the hill slope. "Do you want another slide? Is that it?" I asked.

"Do you mind?" she asked shyly.

"No. I'll wait for you. Take your time; don't run."

Two little boys were still hanging about the slide, and they cheered her as she came down, her comforter streaming in the wind.

"Now," she announced, getting up out of the drift. "I'll show you where the church is."

"Shall I tie your comforter again?"

"No, 'm, thanks. I'm plenty warm." She put her mittened hand confidingly in mine and trudged along beside me.

Mrs. Dow must have heard us tramping up the snowy steps of the church, for she met us at the door. Every one had gone except the old ladies. A kerosene lamp flickered over the Sunday school chart, with the lesson-picture of the Wise Men, and the little barrel stove threw out a deep glow over the three white heads that bent above the baby. There the three friends sat, patting him, and smoothing his dress, and playing with his hands, which made theirs look so brown.

"You ain't seen nothing finer in all your travels," said Mrs. Spinny, and they all laughed.

They showed me his full chest and how strong his back was; had me feel the golden fuzz on his head, and made him look at me with his round, bright eyes. He laughed and reared himself in my arms as I took him up and held him close to me. He was so warm and tingling with life, and he had the flush of new beginnings, of the new morning and the new rose. He seemed to have come so lately from his mother's heart! It was as if I held her youth and all her young joy. As I put my cheek down against his, he spied a pink flower in my hat, and making a gleeful sound, he lunged at it with both fists.

"Don't let him spoil it," murmured Mrs. Spinny. "He loves color so — like Nelly."

[1911]

Study and Writing Questions

1. There are many references to physical beauty in this story, including ALLUSIONS to Queen Esther and Helen of Troy (Nelly is a nickname for Helen). What are the powers of beauty in this story? In what details do we see beauty at work?
2. What are the roles of the church in this STORY?
3. What are the possible meanings of the title? How do these meanings help shape the meaning of the NARRATIVE?
4. Describe the NARRATOR, her CHARACTER, her relationships to Nelly and others, and her reason(s) for relating the story.
5. What are the roles of males and females in this story and what does the story imply about male/female relationships?

See also Questions for Contrast and Comparison: 44, 64, 70, 102, 135, 174, 175, 192, 205, and 238.

GEOFFREY CHAUCER (1343?-1400), son of a wealthy London vintner, enjoyed Court patronage, especially from the powerful John of Gaunt, son of Edward III and father of Henry IV. Taken prisoner of war in France and ransomed (1360) by Edward III, Chaucer later performed secret diplomatic missions in France and Italy and, for his last dozen years, made his living from civil posts near London. About 1366 he married. He may have had no children or as many as two by his wife and one by a mistress. Chaucer's longest complete poem, Troilus and Criseyde (1387?), a deepening of Boccaccio's Il Filostrato, concerns love, pandering, and betrayal. Modeled on Boccaccio's Decameron (c. 1350), The Canterbury Tales (1387?-1400; incomplete) contains a "General Prologue" describing the pilgrims who are to trade TALES going to and from Canterbury, the tales themselves, and connecting material. "The Miller's Tale," prefaced here by the Miller's description from the Prologue, in part SATIRIZES "courtly love," the medieval literary tradition of a quasi-religious passion of noble knights for ladies who were unattainable—and hence not the knight's wives. In a court where only French, Anglo-Norman, and Latin had been considered literary languages, Chaucer's masterful poetry helped fix his dialect of Middle English as the ancestor of our Modern English. He was the first person buried in Poet's Corner in London's Westminster Abbey.

The Miller's Tale

The Miller.

The Miller, hardy as his own Mill-stones,
With brawny Flesh, large Sinews and strong Bones.
His Strength to all the Town was known too well;
In Wrestling still he bore away the Bell.
Short-shoulder'd, knotty as a stubborn Oak,
Hard to be bent, and harder to be broke.
Not one, so far as he, could pitch a Bar,
Or lift a Weight, or swing it in the Air.
He'd running, force a Door with his hard Head;
His Beard like any Fox's Tail was red,
But straight, and even as a Gardiner's Spade.
Just at the end of his huge Nose, he had
A large black Wart, on that a tuft of Hairs
Red, as the Bristles of an old Sow's Ears:
His Nostrils, like a Furnace, black and wide;
A Sword and Buckler hanging on his Side.
A Babbler, with a gormandyzing Throat;
As Letcherous as a Monkey or a Goat.
Corn he could steal, the same Corn thrice he toll'd;
And yet, they say, he had a Thumb of Gold:
His Coat was white, on Bag-pipes he could play,
And with that Musick brought us on our way.

Prologue To The Miller's Tale.

A Tale so nobly plan'd, and sweetly told!
Pleas'd All of either Sex, both Young and Old;
But most the Men of Sense, and Men of Taste:
Stor'd with such Virtue! With such Beauty grac'd.
They judg'd it, for the Stile, and for the Frame,
Worthy to stand in the Records of *Fame!*
  Our *Host* all Rapture, "May my Mortal Sins
"Be so forgiv'n, as well the Game begins;
"By You, *Sir Monk*, be the next Party play'd;
"For You're a Man of Learning by your Trade.
"To match the *Knight*, unbuckle wide the Male,
"And to the Full repay him, Tale for Tale."
  The *Miller*, who till then rode void of Thought,
All Pale, and Drunken with his Morning Draught,
Rose from His Horse, where balancing He sat,
And little Rev'rence pay'd to Hood, or Hat;
But, lev'ling both the Gentry and the Croud,
Exclaim'd, not *Pilate* half so harsh or loud,
And look'd like *Ananias* on Saint *Paul*,
The very Semblance of a Whited Wall!
  "A glorious Tale, now comes into my Head!
"Then take it, just as I have heard or read.
"(The Miller roar'd) Room to the Left and Right,
"Nor better cou'd the *Monk* repay the *Knight*."
Our *Host*, the *Miller*, heard, and judg'd his Case;
"Hold, *Robin*, hold (He cry'd) and know thy Place.
"Our Turns come last; then first Our Betters hear!
"What, are thy Wits quite overcome with Beer?
"Forbear! And go more orderly to Work,
"The *Christian* shou'd not stand behind the *Turk*."
  'Christian or Turk, the *Miller* made Reply,
'Be silent He that will, that will not I.
'Bar my Discourse, and I renounce the Play,
'Hail-Fellow and well met! as Neighbors say;
'Equal in Company are High and Low:
'On these Conditions shall I stay or go?'
  "Stay, in the *Dev'l's Name*, stay, and take thy Will,
(Answer'd our Host, who chose the lighter ill)
"What wou'd You more? Begin without Delay:
"A Fool Thou art, and Fools must have their Way."
  The *Miller* then; 'Half Tipsey, by my Soul!
'Fast as a Mill I feel my Senses rowl!
'If then in Manners, or in Words I fail,
'Impute it to the Strength of *Southwark* Ale.
'While first I paint in Colours to the Life,

'A jealous Husband, and a flaunting Wife;
'He Rich and Old, a Carpenter by Trade!
'She Young and Handsome, but an errant Jade!
'And last a Student's Stratagem reveal,
'Who put a Spoke into the Cuckold's Wheel'.
    Him interrupts the *Reve*. 'Forbear thy Prate;
'All lewd and drunken Ribaldry I hate;
'And hold it equally a Sin and Shame,
'To God, and Man, our Neighbour to defame:
'Much more the Virtue of his Bosom Spouse,
'To bring in Question. Spare the Wedded House.
'Another Subject chuse, the Coast is clear,
'One fit for You to tell, and Us to hear.'
Not, so reprov'd, the *Miller* spar'd his joke,
But spoke, and laugh'd full hearty He spoke.
'Good Brother *Oswalde*, I wou'd stake my Life,
'No Cuckold is the Man who has no Wife;
'Not that it therefore follows as imply'd,
'That Thou art one, because in Wedlock ty'd.
'Yet 'tis a Hazard, rightly understood,
'Wives there are many bad, and many good.
'And I as well as Thou, am duly bound,
'Be Marriage what it will, a Park, or Pound!
'Yet wou'd not I presume, in Word or Thought,
'To Sentence Wives more strictly than I ought,
'Or deem that Mine had slyly branch'd my Brow,
'No, not for all the Oxen in my Plow;
'Content, to hope the Best, good Master *Reve*,
'For I'm a perfect *Christian*, and believe;
'Nay more, to lay Partiality aside,
'All Jealousy, is Av'rice mixt with Pride;
'A Wish, to lay in Hoard, or keep for Show
'More than we want; as Wives and Husbands know.
'Then rate not by the lost, but by the giv'n,
'The Goods of Wifehood, as the Goods of Heav'n.
'Tho' some by Blasts of Wind are borne away,
'And some to thievish Birds may fall a Prey;
'If still Enough for Dayly Use remains,
'Why wail the supernumerary Grains?'
    What need of Words, the Prelude to prolong?
Nought cou'd restrain the Torrent of his Tongue;
For down He bore Us, with impetuous Sway,
And told his Tale in his own Churlish Way.
But not, to our Account, his Licence state,
If what he spoke, we faithfully relate.
Bound to the Truth, by Duty and by Force,
As Man to Wife, for Better and for Worse;

The Tale we must recount without Disguise,
Such as it was; in This no Medium lies.
　　Then timely warn'd, ye modest Virgins fly,
Nor curious lend an Ear, nor cast an Eye.
Here stop, and cautious further to ingage,
Turn the loose Leaf, and chuse a chaster Page.
Others, and many such, remain behind.
Unspotted Stories suited to your Mind;
Some fitted to instruct and to delight,
The Subject moral, and the Turn polite;
To Hist'ry, some that raise a bolder Wing,
And some that ev'n of Sacred Myst'ries sing.
Then blame not us, nor on our Labors frown;
We tell you plain, the *Miller* is a Clown!
Who talk'd of *Love*, in Nature's naked Stile.
Nor take in Serious what is meant in Sport,
We scorn to trap you with unfair Report.
The Good and Bad to your Election leave,
Condemn not us, if you yourselves deceive.
But if the Prohibition more intice,
For Curiosity may want Advice,
Convey the Ribaldry from Vulgar Sight,
Peruse it in the Closet, and by Night;
Or with a female Friend in private read,
So may the *Miller*, if you chuse, proceed.
　　　　　End of the PROLOGUE

The Miller's Tale.

WHILOM in *Oxford* an old Chuff did dwell,
A Carpenter by Trade, as Stories tell;
Who by his Craft had heap'd up many a Hoard,
And furnish'd Strangers both with Bed and Board.
With him a Scholar lodg'd, of slender Means,
But notable for Sciences and Sense.
Yet, tho' he took Degrees in Arts, his Mind
Was mostly to *Astrology* inclin'd.
A Lad in *Divination* skill'd and shrewd,
Who by Interrogations could conclude,
If Men should ask him at what certain Hours
The droughty Earth would gape for cooling Show'rs,
When it should Rain, or Snow, what should befall
Of Fifty Things; I cannot reckon all.
　　This learned *Clerk* had got a mighty Fame
For Modesty, and *Nicholas* his Name.
Subtle he was, well taught in *Cupid's* Trade,
But seem'd as Meek, and Bashful as a Maid.
A Chamber in this Hostelry he kept,

Alone he study'd, and alone he slept.
With sweet and fragrant Herbs the Room was drest,
But he was ten times sweeter than the best.
His Books of various size, or great, or small,
His *Augrim* Stones to cast Accounts withal;
His *Astrolabe* and *Almagist* apart,
With twenty more hard Names of cunning Art;
On sev'ral Shelves were couched nigh his Bed,
And the Press cover'd with a folding Red.
Above an Instrument of Music lay,
On which sweet Melody he us'd to play;
So wond'rous sweet, that all the Chamber rung,
And *Angelus ad Virginem* he sung;
Then would he Chaunt in good King *David's* Note,
Full often blessed was his merry Throat.
And thus the *Clerk* in Books and Music spent
His Time, and Exhibition's yearly Rent.
      This *Carpenter* had a new marry'd Wife,
Lov'd as his Eyes, and dearer than his Life.
The Buxom Lass had twice Nine Summers seen,
And her brisk Blood ran high in ev'ry Vein.
The Dotard, jealous of so ripe an Age,
Watch'd her, and lock'd her, like a Bird in Cage.
For she was Wild, and in her lovely Prime;
But he, poor Man! walk'd down the *Hill of Time*.
He knew the Temper of a Youthful Spouse,
And oft was seen to rub his aking Brows.
He knew his own weak side, and dreamt in Bed
She had, or would be planting on his Head.
He knew not *Cato*, for his Wit was rude;
That Men should Wed with their Similitude.
Like should with Like in Love and Years ingage,
For *Youth* can never be a Rhyme to *Age*.
Hence Jealousies create a Nuptial War,
And the warm Seasons with the frigid jar.
But when the Trap's once down, he must endure
His Fate, and *Patience is the only Cure*.
Perhaps his Father, and a hundred more
Of honest Christians, were thus serv'd before.
Fair was his charming Consort, and withall
Slender her Waist, and like a *Weasel's* small.
She had a Girdle round her barr'd with Silk,
And a clean Apron, white as Morrow Milk.
White was her Smock, embroider'd all before,
Which on her Loins in many Plaits she wore.
Broad was her silken Fillet, set full high,
And oft she twinkled with a Liqu'rish Eye.
Her Brow was arch'd like any bended *Bow*,

Like *Marble* smooth, and blacker than a *Sloe*,
She softer far than *Wool*, or fleecy *Snow*.
Were you to search the Universal Round,
So gay a Wench was never to be found.
With greater Brightness did her Colour shine,
Than a new *Noble* of the freshest Coin.
Shrill was her Song, and loud her piercing Note,
No *Swallow* on a Barn had such a Throat.
To this she skipp'd and caper'd like a *Lamb*,
Or *Kid*, or *Calf*, when they pursue their Dam.
Sweet as *Methegun* was her *Honey* Lip,
Or Hoard of *Apples* which in *Hay* are kept.
Wincing she was, as is a jolly *Colt*,
Long as a Mast, and upright as a Bolt:
Above her Ancles laced was her Shoe,
She was a *Primrose*, and a *Pigsnye* too.
And fit to lig by any Christian's Side,
Or a Lord's Mistress, or a Yeoman's Bride.
 Now *Sirs*, what think you, how the Case befell?
This *Nicholas* (for I the Truth will tell)
Was a mere Wag, and on a certain Day,
When the Good Man, the Husband, was away,
Began to sport and wanton with his Dame,
(For *Clerks* are sly, and very full of Game)
And privily he caught her by *That same.*
"My Lemman Dear (quoth he) I'm all on Fire,
"And perish, if you grant not my Desire.
He clasp her round, and held her fast, and cry'd,
"O let me, let me — never be deny'd."
At this she wreath'd her Head, and sprung aloof,
Like a young frisking *Colt*, whose tender Hoof
Felt never Farrier's Hand, and never knew
The Virgin Burden of an Iron Shoe.
'Fye *Nicholas*! away your Hands, quoth she:
'Is this your Breeding, and Civility?
'Foh! Idle Sot! what means th' unmanner'd Clown,
'To teize me thus, and toss me up and down?
'I vow I'll tell, and bawl it o'er the Town.
'You're rude, and will you not be answer'd, No?
'I will not kiss you — prithee, let me go.'
 Here *Nicholas*, a young, designing Knave,
Began to weep, and cant, and Pardon crave.
So fair he spoke, and importun'd so fast,
This seeming modest Spouse consents at last.
By good St. *Thomas* swore, her usual Oath,
That she would meet his Love — tho' mighty loath.
'If you, said she, convenient Leisure wait,
'(You know my Husband has a jealous Pate)

'I will requite you; for if once the Beast
'Should chance to find us out, and smell the Jest,
'I must be a dead Woman at the least.'
"Let that, quoth *Nicholas*, ne'er vex your Head;
"He must be a meer learned Ass indeed,
"And very foolishly besets his Wile,
"Who cannot a dull *Carpenter* beguile."
And thus they were accorded, thus they swore
To wait the Time, as I have said before.
And now, when *Nicholas* had wore away
The pleasant Time, in harmless am'rous Play,
To his melodious *Psaltery* he flew,
Play'd Tunes of Love, by which his Passion grew,
Then printed on her Lips a dear *Adieu*.
It happen'd thus, (I cannot rightly tell,
If it on *Easter* or on *Whitson* fell)
That on a Holyday, this modest Dame
To Church, with other honest Neighbours came,
In a good Fit to hear the Parson preach
What the Divine Apostles us'd to teach.
Bright was her Forehead, and no Summer's Day
Shone half so clear, so tempting, and so gay.
    Now to this Parish did a *Clerk* belong,
Who many a Time had rais'd a Holy Song:
His Name was *Absalon*, a silly Man,
Who curl'd his Hair, which strutted like a Fan;
And from his jolly, pert, and empty Head,
In Golden Ringlets on his Shoulders spred.
His Face was Red, his Eyes as Grey as *Goose*,
With St. *Paul's* Windows figur'd on his Shoes.
Full properly he walk'd in Scarlet Hose,
But light, and Silver-colour'd were his Clothes,
And Surplice white as Blossoms on the *Rose*.
Thick Poynts and Tassels did the Coxcomb please,
And fetously they dangled on his Knees.
He could let Blood, and shave your Beard, or Head,
But a mere *Barber Surgeon* by his Trade.
Nay, he cou'd draw a Bond, and learnt from *France*,
In thirty Motions how to trip, and dance.
Nay, he cou'd write and Read, and that is more
Than twenty Parish-Clerks could do before:
Could frisk and toss his twirling Legs in Air,
Nice were his Feet, and trod it to a Hair.
Songs would he play, and, not to hide his Wit,
Would squeak a *Treble* to his squawling *Kit*;
His Dress was finical, his Music queer,
And pleas'd a Tapster's Eye or Drawer's Ear.
No Tavern, Brew-house, Ale-House in the Town,

Was to the gentle *Absalon* unknown:
But he was very careful of his Wind,
And never let it sally out behind;
To give the *Devil* his Due, he had an Art
By civil Speech to win a Lady's Heart.

    This *Absalon*, so jolly, spruce and gay,
Went with the *Censer* on the Sabbath Day.
He swung the Incense Pot with comely Grace,
But chiefly would he Fume a pretty Face.
His wanton Eye, which every where he cast,
Dwelt on the *Carpenter's* fine *Dame* at last.
So sweet and proper was his lovely Wife,
That he could freely gaze away his Life.
Were he a *Cat*, this pretty *Mouse* would feel
Too soon his Talons, a delicious Meal.

    And now had *Cupid* shot a piercing Dart,
As wet the Feathers in his wounded Heart.
No Offering of the Handsome Wives he took,
He wanted nothing but a smiling Look,
The Parish Fees refus'd, and said, the Light
Of the fair Moon shines brightest in the Night.
Soon as the Cock had bid the Morning rise,
The smitten Lover to his *Fiddle* flies.
A hideous Noise his squeaking *Trilos* make,
And all the drowsy Neighbourhood awake.
At the lov'd House some am'rous Tunes he play'd,
And thus with gentle Voice he sung or said.

> *Now dear Lady,*
> *If thy Will be,*
> *I pray to Thee*
> *To pity me.*

And twenty such complaining Notes he sung,
Alike the Music of his *Kit*, and Tongue.
At this the staring *Carpenter* awoke,
And thus his Wife, fair *Alison*, bespoke.

    "Art Thou asleep, or art Thou deaf, my Dear?
"And cannot *Absalon* at Window hear?
"How with his Serenade he charms us all,
"Chanting melodiously beneath our Wall?"
'Yes, yes, I hear him, Alison reply'd,
'Too well, God wot,' and then she turn'd aside.
Thus went Affairs, till *Absalon*, alas!
Was a lost Creature, a mere whining *Ass*.
All Night he wakes, and sighs, and wears away
On his broad Locks and Dress, the live-long Day.
To such a Height his doating Fondness grew,
To kiss the Ground, and wipe her very Shoe.

Where're she went, he like a Slave pursu'd,
With spiced *Ale*, and sweet *Metheglin* woo'd.
All Dainties he could rap and rend, he got,
And sent her *Tarts* and *Custards* piping hot.
He spar'd no Cost for an expensive Treat,
Of *Mead* and *Cyder*, and all Sorts of Meat.
Throbbing he sings with his lamenting Throat,
And rivals *Philomela's* mournful Note.
With Rigour some, and some with gentle Arts
Have found a Passage to Young Ladies Hearts:
Some Wealth has won, and some have had the Lot
To fall inamour'd of a Treating Sot.
　　Sometimes he *Scaramouch'd* it all on high,
And *Harlequin'd* it with Activity.
Betrays the Lightness of his empty Head,
And how he could cut Capers in a Bed.
But neither this, nor that, the Damsel move,
For *Nicholas* has swept the Stakes of Love.
The *Parish Clerk* has nothing met but Scorn,
And may go Fiddle now, or blow his Horn.
Thus gentle *Absalon* is made her Ape,
And all his Passion turn'd into a Jape.
For *Nicholas* is always in her Eye:
True says the Proverb, that the *Nigh are Sly*.
A distant Love may Disappointment find,
For out of Sight is ever *out of Mind*.
The Scholar was at hand, as I have told,
And gave the Parish Clerk *the Dog to hold*.
Now *Nicholas* thy Craft and Cunning try,
That *Absalon* may *De Profundis* cry.
　　Now when this Carpenter was call'd away
To work at *Osney*, on a certain Day;
The subtle Scholar, and his wanton Spouse,
Were decently contriving for his Brows:
Agreed, that *Nicholas* should shape a Wile,
Her addle-pated Husband to beguile.
And, if so be the Game succeeded right,
She then would sleep within his Arms all Night.
For both were in this one Desire concern'd,
Alike they Suffer'd, and alike they Burn'd.
Strait a new Thought leapt cross the Scholar's Head,
Who at that Instant to his Chamber fled.
But to relieve his Thirst and Hunger, bore
Of Meat and Liquor a substantial Store,
And victual'd it for one long Day, or more.
"*Alce*, shou'd your Husband ask for Us (quoth he)
"Reply in Scorn, What's *Nicholas* to me?
"Am I his Keeper? help your silly Head!

"Perhaps the Man is mad, asleep, or dead;
"My Maid indeed has thump'd this Hour or more,
"And knock'd as if she'd thunder down the Door:
"But He, a moaping Drone, no Answer gave,
"Fast as a Church, and silent as the Grave."
　　Thus did one *Saturday* entire consume,
Since *Nicholas* had lock'd him in his Room.
Nor was he Idle; for no *Lent* he kept,
But eat, like other Men, and drank, and slept.
Did what he list, till the next Sun was new,
And went to Rest, as common Mortals do.
　　This Carpenter was in a grievous Pain,
Lest *Nicholas* should over-work his Brain;
By Study lose his Reason, or his Life—.
'Well, by St. *Thomas*, I don't like it, Wife.
'The World we live in, is a ticklish Place,
'And sudden Death has often stopt our Race.
'I saw a Corpse, as to the Church it past,
'And the poor Man at work but *Monday* last.
'Run, *Dick*, quoth he, run speedily up Stairs,
'Thump at the Door, and see how stand Affairs.'
Up strait he runs, like any Tempest flies,
And knocks, and bawls, and like a Madman cries.
"Hoh! Master *Nicholas*, what mean you thus
"To sleep all Night and Day, and frighten Us?"
He might as well have whistl'd to the Wind,
As from good *Nicholas* an Answer find.
At last he spy'd a Hole, full low, and deep,
Where usually the Cat was wont to creep;
Here was discover'd to his wond'ring Sight,
The Scholar gazing with his Eyes upright,
As if intent upon the Stars and Moon:
And down runs He, to tell his Master soon,
In what Array he saw this studious Man.
The *Carpenter* to cross himself began:
And cry'd, 'St. *Frideswild*, help us one and all!
'Little we know what Fate shall us befall,
'This Man with his Astronomy is got
'Into some Frenzy, and stark mad, God wot.
'This comes of poring on his cunning Books,
'Of his Moon-snuffing, and Star-peeping Looks.
'Why should a silly Earth-born Mortal pry
'On Heav'n, and search the Secrets of the Sky?
'Well fare those Men, who no more Learning need
'Than what's contain'd in the Lord's Pray'r and Creed,
'Scholars sufficient, if they can but Read!
'Thus far'd a Sage Philosopher of Old,

'Who walking out, as 'tis in Story told,
'Was so much with Astronomy bewitch'd,
'That his Star-gazing Clerkship was *beditch'd*.
'Ill Luck attends the Man, who looks too high,
'And can a Star, but not a Marl-pit spy.
'But, by St. *Thomas*, this shall never pass;
'Too well I love this gentle *Nicholas*.
'I'll ferret him, unless the Devil's in it,
'From his brown Fit of Study in a Minute.
    '*Robin*, let's try if that an Iron Pur
'And your strong Back can make this Scholar stir.'
Now *Robin* was a Lad of Brawn and Bones,
And by the Hasp heav'd up the Door at once,
Which in the Chamber fell with dreadful Sound,
As would a Man, like you or me, astound.
But *Nicholas*, did nothing do but stare;
And like a Statue gape upon the Air.
    This *Carpenter* was in a piteous Fear,
Because he did not, or he would not hear.
Though some deep *Melancholy* had impair'd
His Brain, and that of Mercy he despair'd;
For which the Student in his Arms he took
With might and main, and by the Shoulders shook.
'Cry'd, *Nicholas* awake! what? not a Word?
'Look down, despair not—think upon the *Lord!*'
Then the Night-Spell he mumbled to himself:
'Bless thee from Fiends, and every wicked Elf!'
He crost the Threshold, where a Dev'l might creep,
And each small Hole, thro' which an Imp might peep;
With solemn *Pater Nosters* blest the Door,
And *Ave Marys* after and before.
At this the *Clerk* sent forth a heavy Sigh,
With Tears, and woful Tone began to cry—
And shall this World be lost so soon? Ah! why?
'What do I hear? the *Carpenter* reply'd,
'What say'st Thou, *Nicholas*? sure Thou art beside
'Thy self: Serve God, as we poor Lab'rers do,
'And then no Harm, nor Danger will ensue.'
"Ah! Friend, quoth *Nicholas*, you little think
"What I can tell; but first let's have some Drink.
"Then, my dear Host, Thou shalt in private learn
"Some certain things, which Thee and Me concern.
"It shall no Mortal but your self avail;
"Then fetch a *Winchester* of might Ale."
And now when both had drank an equal Share,
Cries *Nicholas*, "Sit down, and draw your Chair.
"But first, sweet Landlord, you must take an Oath,

"To no Man living to betray thy Troth.
"For, trust me, what I'm going to relate
"Is *Revelation*, and as sure as Fate.
"And if you tell, this Vengeance will ensue,
"No Hare in *March* will be so Mad as You."
  'Nay, quoth mine Host, I am no Blab, not I,
'And hang me, if you catch me in a Lye.
'I would not tell, tho' twere to save my Life,
'To Chick or Child, to Man, or Maid, or Wife.'
  "Now, *John*, quoth *Nicholas*, I will not hide
"What by my Art I have of late descry'd;
"How, as I por'd upon fair *Cynthia's* Light,
"Should fall, on *Monday* next, at Quarter Night,
"A Rain so sudden, and so long to boot,
"That *Noah's* Flood was but a Spoonful to't.
"This World within the Compass of an Hour
"Shall all be drown'd, so hideous is the Show'r,
"As will the Cattle, and Mankind devour."
Cries then this silly Man, 'Alas, My Wife!
'My Bosom-comfort, and my better Life!
'And must She drown, and perish with the Rest?
'My *Alison*, the Darling of my Breast?'
At this well nigh he swoon'd o'er-whelm'd with Grief,
Fetch'd a deep Sigh, 'And is there no Relief;
'No Remedy, he cry'd, no Succour left?
'Are we, alas! of ev'ry Hope bereft?'
"No, by no Means, quoth this designing Clerk;
"Be of good Heart, and by Instruction Work.
"For if by *Nicholas* you will be led,
"And build no Castles in your own wild Head,
"None so secure: for *Solomon* says true,
"*Work all by Counsel, and you cannot rue.*
"If you'll be govern'd, and be rul'd by me,
"I'll undertake to save Thy Wife and Thee;
"But my own Art against the Flood prevail,
"And make no Use of either Mast or Sail.
"Have you not heard, how, when the World was naught,
"*Noah*, by Heav'nly Inspiration taught' —
'(Ay, ay, quoth *John*, I've in my Bible found
'That once upon a Time the World was drown'd.')
"Hast thou not heard, how *Noah* was concern'd
"For his dear Wife, and how his Bowels yearn'd,
"Till he had built and furnish'd out a Bark,
"And lodged her, with her Children in the Ark?
"Now Expedition is the Soul and Life
"Of Business; if you love Yourself or Wife,
"Run, Fly—for in this Case it is a Crime

"To loyter, or to lose an inch of Time.
"For *Alison*, Yourself, and Me provide
"Three Kneading-Troughs, to sail upon the Tide.
"But take most special Care, that they be large,
"In which a Man may swim as in a Barge.
"Let them be victual'd well, and see you lay
"Sufficient Stores against a rainy Day;
"Enough to serve You twenty Hours, and more,
"For then the Flood will swage, and not before.
"But one thing let me whisper in your Ear,
"Let not thy sturdy Servant *Robin* hear,
"Nor bonny *Gillian* know what I relate;
"I must not utter the Decrees of Fate.
"Ask me not Reasons why I cannot save
"Your trusty Serving-Maid, and honest Knave:
"Suffice it thee, unless Thy Wits be mad,
"To have as great a Grace, as *Noah* had.
"Do you make Haste, and mind the grand Affair;
"To save your Wife shall be my proper Care.
"But when these Kneading-Tubs are ready made,
"Which may secure us, when the Floods invade,
"See that you hang them in the Roof full high,
"That none our Providential Plot descry.
"And when Thou hast convey'd sufficient Store
"Of Meats and Drink, as I have said before,
"And put a sharp'ned Ax in ev'ry Boat,
"To cut the Cord, and set us all afloat;
"Then thro' the *Gable* of the House, which lies
"Above the Stable, and the Garden spies,
"Break out a Hole, so very large and wide,
"Thro' which our Tubs may sail upon the Tide.
  "Then wilt thou so much Mirth and Pleasure take
"In swimming, as the white Duck and the Drake.
"Then when I cry, Hoh! *Alison*, and *John*,
"Be merry, for the Flood will pass anon.
"Then wilt thou answer, Master *Nicholay*,
"Good morrow, for I see it is broad Day.
"Then shall we reign, as Emperors for Life,
"O'er all the World, like *Noah* and his Wife.
"But one thing I almost forgot to tell,
"Which now comes in my Head, (and mark me well)
"That on that very Night we go aboard,
"All must be hush'd, and whisper not a Word.
"But all the Time employ our holy Mind
"In earnest Prayers: for thus has Heav'n injoin'd.
  "You and your Wife must take a separate Place,
"Nor is there any Sin in such a Case.

"To morrow Night, when Men are fast asleep,
"We to our Kneading-Tubs will slyly creep.
"There will we sit, each in his Ship apart,
"And wait the Deluge with a patient Heart.
"Go now; I have no longer time to spare
"In Sermoning, use expeditious Care.
"Your Apprehension needs no more Advice:
"*One single Word's sufficient for the Wise.*
"And none, dear Landord, can your Wit inform;
"Go, save our Lives from this impending Storm."
Away hies *John*, with melancholy Look,
And sigh'd, and groan'd, at ev'ry Step he took.
To *Alison* he does his Fate deplore,
And tells a Secret which she knew before.
But yet she trembl'd, like an *Aspin* Leaf,
And seem'd to perish with dissembled Grief;
Crying, "Alas! What shall I do — begone —
"Help us to 'scape, or we are all undone.
"I am thy true and very wedded Wife;
"Go, dear, dear Spouse, and help to save my Life."
    What strong Impressions does Affection give?
By Fancy, Men have often ceas'd to live.
Howe're absurd things in themselves appear,
Weak Minds are apt to credit what they fear.
    This silly Carpenter is almost *Wood*,
And thinks of nothing else, but *Noah's* Flood.
Believes he sees it, and begins to quake,
And all for *Alison*, his Hony's Sake.
He's over-run with Sorrow and with Fear,
And sends forth many a Groan and many a Tear.
A Kneading-Trough, a Tub, and Kemelin
He gets by Stealth, and sends them to his Inn.
He makes three Ladders, whence he climbs aloof,
And privately he hangs them in the Roof.
But first he victual'd them, both Trough and Tub,
With Bread and Cheese, and Bottles fill'd with might Bub;
Enough o'Conscience to relieve their Fast,
And be sufficient for a Day's Repast.
    But e're this Preparation had been made,
He sent to *London* both his Man and Maid,
On certain Matters, which concern'd his Trade.
    And now came on the fatal *Monday* Night,
Barr'd are the Doors, out goes the Candle-Light.
And when all things in Readiness were set,
These Three their Ladders take, and up they get.
Now *Pater-Noster*, *clum*, said *Alison*,
And *clum*, quoth *Nicholas*, and *clum*, quoth *John*.
This Carpenter his *Orisons* did say,

For Men in fear are very apt to pray.
Silent he waited, when the Skies would pour
This unaccountable and dismal Show'r.
And now at *Curfew* time, dead Sleep began
To fall upon this easy, simple Man.
Who after so much Care and Bus'ness past,
And spent with sad Concern, was quickly fast.
Soft down the Ladder stole this loving Pair,
Good *Nicholas,* and *Alison* the Fair;
Then, without speaking, to the Bed they creep
Of *John,* poor Cuckold! who was fast asleep.
There all the Night they revel, sport, and toy,
And act the merry Scene of am'rous Joy;
Till that the Bell of *Lauds* began to ring,
And the fat Fryars in the Chancel sing.

    The Parish Clerk, this am'rous *Absalon,*
Who over Head and Ears in Love is gone,
At *Osney* happen'd with a jovial Crew
To spend the *Monday,* as they us'd to do;
There pulls a certain Fryar by the Sleeve,
With Pardon begg'd, and Father, by your Leave,
"When saw you *John* the Carpenter? he cries".
'Last *Saturday,* the *Cloisterer* replies,
'Since then I have not seen him with these Eyes;
'Perhaps abroad he's playing fast and loose;
'Or fetching Timber for the Abbot's Use,
'And lodges at the Graunge a Day or two,
'Or else at Home—I know no more than you.'
This made *Nab's* boiling Blood with Pleasure start,
The News rejoyc'd the Cockles of his Heart.
"Now is my Time, thinks he; the Moon is bright,
"Nor care I, if I travel all the Night;
"For at his Door since Day began to spring,
"I've seen, like him, no kind of Man, or Thing.

    "It is resolv'd; to *Alison* I'll go,
"When the first Morning Cock begins to crow;
"And to her Window privately repair,
"Then knock, and tell her my tormenting Care.
"I'll open all my Breast, and ease my Heart,
"For 'tis too much to bear Love's stinging Smart.
"Some little Comfort sure I shall not miss,
"At least she'll grant the Favour of a Kiss;
"My Mouth has itch'd all Day, from whence it seems,
"That I shall kiss: Besides my pleasant Dreams
"Of Feasts and Banquets, whence a Man may guess
"That I may haply meet with some Success:
"But for an Hour or two before I go,
"I'll first refresh me with a Nap, or so."

Now the first Cock had wak'd from his Repose
The jolly *Absalon*, and up he rose.
But first he dresses finical and gay,
And looks like any *Beau*, at Church or Play,
And brisk as Bridegroom on a Wedding-Day.
Nicely he combs the Ringlets of his Hair,
And wash'd with Rose-water, looks fresh and fair;
Then with his Finger he her Window twang'd,
Whisper'd a gentle Tone, and thus harangu'd.
  Sweet Alison, my Hony-comb, my Dear,
My Bird, my Cinamon, your Lover hear.
Awake, and speak one Word before I part,
But one kind Word, the Balsam to my Heart.
Little you think, alas! the mighty Woe,
Which for the Love of Thee I undergo.
For Thee I swelter, and for Thee I sweat,
And mourn as Lamb-kins for the Mother's Teat.
Nor false my Grief, nor does the Turtle Dove
Lament more truly, or more truly love.
I cannot eat nor drink, and all for Thee—
"Get from my Window, you *Jack Fool*, said she;
"I love another of a different Hue
"From such a silly Dunder-head as you.
"If you stand talking at that foolish Rate,
"My Chamber-pot shall be about your Pate.
"Begone, you empty Sot, and let me sleep" —
At this poor *Absalon* began to weep,
And his hard Fate with Sighs and Groans deplore,
Was ever faithful, Love thus serv'd before!
Since then my Sweet, what I desire's in vain,
Let me but one small Boon, a Kiss, obtain.
"And will you then be gone, nor loyter here,"
Quoth *Alison? — Ay certainly, my Dear!*
"Make ready then" — Now, *Nicholas*, lye still,
'Tis such a Jest, that you shall laugh your fill.
  Ravish'd with Joy, *Nab* fell upon his Knees,
The happiest Man alive in all Degrees;
In silent Raptures he began to cry,
No Lord in Europe is so blest as I.
I may expect more Favours; for a Kiss
Is an Assurance of a further Bliss.
The Window now unclasp'd, with slender Voice,
Cries *Alison*, "Be quick, and make no Noise;
"I would not for the World our Neighbours hear,
"For they're made up of Jealousy and Fear."
  Then silken Handkerchief from Pocket came,
To wipe his Mouth full clean to kiss the Dame.

Dark was the Night, as any Coal or Pitch,
When at the Window she clapt out her Breech.
The *Parish Clerk* ne'er doubted what to do,
But ask'd no Questions, and in haste fell to;
On her blind Side full savourly he prest
A loving Kiss, e'er he smelt out the Jest.
Aback he starts, for he knew well enough,
That Women's Lips are smooth, but these were rough.
What have I done, quoth he? and rav'd and star'd,
Ah me! I've kist a Woman with a Beard.
He curst the Hour, and rail'd against the Stars,
That he was born to kiss my Lady's —
Tehea, she cry'd, and clapt the Window close;
While *Absalon* with Grief and Anger goes
To meditate Revenge; and to requite
The foul Affront, he would not sleep that Night.
And now with Dust, with Sand, with Straw, with Chips,
He scrubs and rubs the Kisses from his Lips.
Oft would he say, *Alas! O basest Evil!*
Than met with this Disgrace so damn'd uncivil,
I rather had went headlong to the Devil.
To kiss a Woman's — oh! it can't be born!
But by my Soul I'll be aveng'd by Morn.

   Hot Love, the Proverb says, *grows quickly cool,*
And *Absalon's* no more an Am'rous Fool:
For since his Purpose was so fouly crost,
He gains his Quiet, tho' his Love is lost:
And, cur'd of his Distemper, can defy
All whining Coxcombs with a scornful Eye:
But for meer Anger, as he pass'd the Street,
He wept, as does a School-boy when he's beat.
In a soft, doleful Pace at last he came
To an old *Vulcan, Jarvis* was his Name;
Who late and early at the Forge turmoyl'd,
In hamm'ring Iron Bars, and Plough-shares, toil'd.
Hither repair'd, by One or Two a Clock,
Poor *Absalon*, and gave an easy Knock.
Who's there that knocks so late. Sir Jarvis cries?
"'Tis I, the pensive *Absalon* replies.
"Open the Door." 'What *Absalon*, quoth He,
'The Parish Clerk?' Ah! *Benedicite.*
Where hast thou been? some pretty Girl, I wot,
Has led you out so late upon the trot.
Some merry-meeting on the Wenching score,
You know my Meaning, — but I'll say no more.

   This *Absalon* another Distaff drew,
And had more Tow to spin than *Jarvis* knew:

He minded not a *Bean* of all he said,
For other Things employ'd his careful Head.
At last he Silence breaks, *Dear Friend,* he cries,
Lend's that hot Pur, which in the Chimney lies;
I have occasion for't, no Questions ask,
To bring it back again shall be my Task.
'With all my Heart, quoth *Jarvis,* were it Gold,
'Or splendid Nobles in a Purse untold;
'With all my Heart, as I'm an Honest *Smith,*
'I'll lend it Thee; but what wilt do therewith?'
"For that, quoth *Absalon,* nor care, nor sorrow,
"I'll give a good Account of it to Morrow."
Then up the Culter in his Hand he caught,
Tripp'd out with silent Pace, and wicked Thought.
Red-hot it was, as any burning Cole,
With which to *John* the Carpenter's he stole.
There first he cough'd, and, as his usual Wont,
Up to the Window came, and tapp'd upon't.
'Who's there? quoth *Alison,* Some Midnight Rook,
'Some Thief, I warrant, with a hanging Look.'
"Ah! God forbid, quoth this dissembling Elf,
"'Tis *Absalon,* my Life! my better Self!
"A rich Gold Ring I've to my Darling brought,
"By a known Graver exquisitely wrought.
"Beside, a Posie, most divinely writ
"By a fam'd Poet, and notorious Wit.
"My Mother gave it me ('tis wond'rous fine)
"She clapp'd it on my Finger, I on thine,
"If thou wilt deign the favour of a Kiss —"
Now *Nicholas* by chance rose up to piss,
Thinking to better, and improve the Jest,
He should salute his Breech, before the rest.
With eager Haste, and secret Joy he went,
And his Posteriors out at Window sent.
Here *Absalon,* the Wag, with subtle Tone
Whispers, "My Love! my Soul! my *Alison,*
"Speak, my sweet Bird, I know not where thou art —"
At this the Scholar let a rouzing Fart;
So loud the Noise, as frightful was the Stroke,
As Thunder, when it splits the sturdy Oak.
The Clerk was ready, and with hearty Gust
The Red-hot Iron in his Buttocks thrust.
Streight off the Skin, like Shrivel'd Parchment flew,
His Breech as raw as Saint *Bartholomew.*
The Culter had so sing'd his Hinder Part,
He thought he should have dy'd for very Smart.

In a mad Fit about the Room he ran,
Help, Water, Water, for a dying Man.
　　The *Carpenter,* as one beside his Wits,
Starts at the dreadful Sound, and up he gets.
The Name of *Water* rouz'd him from his Sleep,
He rubb'd his Eye-lids, and began to peep.
Alas! thought he, now comes the fatal Hour,
And from the Clouds does *Noah's Deluge* pour.
Up then he sits, and without more Ado
He takes his Ax, and smites the Cord in two.
Down goes the Bread, and Ale, and Cheese, and All,
And *John* himself had a confounded Fall.
Dropp'd from the Roof upon the Floor, astoun'd
He lies, as dead, and swims upon dry Ground.
　　Then *Nicholas,* to play the Counterfeit,
With *Alison,* cries Murder in the Street.
　　In came the Neighbours pouring like the Tide,
To know the reason why was *Murder* cry'd.
There they beheld poor *John,* a gasping Man,
Shut were his Eyes, his Face was pale and wan.
Batter'd his Sides, and broken was his Arm,
But stand it out he must to his own Harm.
For when he aim'd to speak in his Defence,
They bore him, down, and baffled all his Sense.
They told the People, that the Man was wood,
And dreamt of nothing else but *Noah's Flood.*
His heated Fancy of this *Deluge* rung,
That to the Roof three Kneading-Troughs he hung,
With which in Danger he design'd to swim,
And we, forsooth, must carry on the Whim:
He begg'd, and pray'd, and so we humour'd him.
　　At hearing this, the sneering Neighbours gave
An universal Shout, and hideous Laugh.
Now on the Roof, and now on *John* they gape,
And all his Earnest turn into a Jape.
He swore against the Scholar and his Wife,
And never look'd so foolish in his Life.
Whate're he speaks, the People never mind,
His Oaths are nothing, and his Words are Wind.
Thus all consent to scoff each serious Word,
And *John* remain'd a Cuckold on Record.
　　Thus Doors of Brass, and Bars of Steel are vain,
And watchful Jealousy, and carking Pain
Are fruitless all, when a good-natur'd Spouse
Designs Preferment for her Husband's Brows.
Thus *Alison* her Cuckold does defy,

And *Absalon* has kiss'd her nether Eye;
While *Nicholas* is scalded in the Breech,
My Tale is done, God save us all, and each.

End of the MILLER'S TALE

[1390?; translation, 1741]

Study and Writing Questions

1. What is the relationship of the miller's TALE to the framework within which that tale is told? How does the framework affect our understanding of the miller's tale?
2. According to the Christian church of Chaucer's time, people had three distinct "natures": the physical, the intellectual, and the spiritual. How are those natures represented in this NARRATIVE? What seems to be the relative importance of each of those natures?
3. How do style of NARRATION, DIALOGUE, and PLOT contribute to the humor of this narrative? Are there other sources of humor here? Does the employment of humor prevent this narrative from having a MORAL? If so, how? If not, what moral(s) does this narrative convey?
4. What portrait of women is implied by this narrative? How is Alison described? How does she behave? What are the outcomes for her and for the men who yearn for her? Consider material in the FRAME as well as in the inner tale.
5. What seems to be the role of the church in this society? Consider people's phrases, occupations, characters, beliefs, and so on. Does the IMPLIED AUTHOR of this narrative seem to be for or against the church or seem to hold some more complex position?

See also Questions for Contrast and Comparison: 69, 133, 145, 164, 167, 177, 192, and 193.

■ JOHN CHEEVER (1912–1982) *was born in Quincy, Massachusetts to a self-made man whose bankruptcy after the 1929 stock market crash left his wife to support the family. Cheever was expelled (perhaps by his own contrivance) from exclusive Thayer Academy at seventeen and moved to New York City where he wrote in a cramped, one-room apartment. At eighteen, his first story, "Expelled," appeared in* The New Republic *under Malcolm Cowley's editorship. Except for four years' military service during World War II, and brief stints spent teaching composition, Cheever devoted himself to creating* NOVELS *and* STORIES *noted for their vivid* IMAGERY *and piercing, comic, tolerant dissection of the lives of moneyed, Protestant suburbanites. His works include* The Wapshot Chronicle *(1957, National Book Award), an episodic novel of the eccentric Wapshot clan of St. Botolphs, Massachusetts, and its sequel,* The Wapshot Scandal *(1964);* Bullet Park *(1969); and* Falconer *(1977), about an ex-soldier, drug-addicted professor who, confined to prison, after exploring his past and his sexuality, escapes to a life of new potential. Most famed for his stories, particularly those appearing in* The New Yorker, *Cheever has been called "the Chekov of the suburbs."* The Stories of John Cheever *(1978), the most representative of his many collections, won the Pulitzer Prize and National Book Critics Circle Award. Cheever married in 1941 and had three children.*

The Swimmer

It was one of those midsummer Sundays when everyone sits around saying, "I *drank* too much last night." You might have heard it whispered by the parishioners leaving church, heard it from the lips of the priest himself, struggling with his cassock in the *vestiarium*, heard it from the golf links and the tennis courts, heard it from the wild-life preserve where the leader of the Audubon group was suffering from a terrible hangover. "I *drank* too much," said Donald Westerhazy. "We all *drank* too much," said Lucinda Merrill. "It must have been the wine," said Helen Westerhazy. "I *drank* too much of that claret."

This was at the edge of the Westerhazys' pool. The pool, fed by an artesian well with a high iron content, was a pale shade of green. It was a fine day. In the west there was a massive stand of cumulus cloud so like a city seen from a distance—from the bow of an approaching ship—that it might have had a name. Lisbon. Hackensack. The sun was hot. Neddy Merrill sat by the green water, one hand in it, one around a glass of gin. He was a slender man—he seemed to have the especial slenderness of youth—and while he was far from young he had slid down his banister that morning and given the bronze backside of Aphrodite on the hall table a smack, as he jogged toward the smell of coffee in his dining room. He might have been compared to a summer's day, particularly the last hours of one, and while he lacked a tennis racket or a sail bag the impression was definitely one of youth, sport, and clement weather. He had been swimming and now he was breathing deeply, stertorously as if he could gulp into his lungs the components of that moment, the heat of the sun, the intenseness of his pleasure. It all seemed to flow into his chest. His own house stood in Bullet Park, eight miles to the south, where his four beautiful daughters would have had their lunch and might be playing tennis. Then it occurred to him that by taking a dogleg to the southwest he could reach his home by water.

His life was not confining and the delight he took in this observation could not be explained by its suggestion of escape. He seemed to see, with a cartographer's eye, that string of swimming pools, that quasi-subterranean stream that curved across the county. He had made a discovery, a contribution to modern geography; he would name the stream Lucinda after his wife. He was not a practical joker nor was he a fool but he was determinedly original and had a vague and modest idea of himself as a legendary figure. The day was beautiful and it seemed to him that a long swim might enlarge and celebrate its beauty.

He took off a sweater that was hung over his shoulders and dove in. He had an inexplicable contempt for men who did not hurl themselves into pools. He swam a choppy crawl, breathing either with every stroke or every fourth stroke and counting somewhere well in the back of his mind the one-two one-two of a flutter kick. It was not a serviceable stroke for long distances but the domestication of swimming had saddled the sport with some customs and in his part of the world a crawl was customary. To be embraced and sustained by the light green water was less a pleasure, it seemed, than the resumption of a natural condition, and he would have liked to swim without trunks, but this was not possible, considering his project. He hoisted himself up on the far curb—he never used the ladder—and started across the lawn. When Lucinda asked where he was going he said he was going to swim home.

The only maps and charts he had to go by were remembered or imaginary but these were clear enough. First there were the Grahams, the Hammers, the Lears, the Howlands, and the Crosscups. He would cross Ditmar Street to the Bunkers and come, after a short portage, to the Levys, the Welchers, and the public pool in Lancaster. Then there were the Hallorans, the Sachses, the Biswangers, Shirley Adams, the Gilmartins, and the Clydes. The day was lovely, and that he lived in a world so generously supplied with water seemed like a clemency, a beneficence. His heart was high and he ran across the grass. Making his way home by an uncommon route gave him the feeling that he was a pilgrim, an explorer, a man with a destiny, and he knew that he would find friends all along the way; friends would line the banks of the Lucinda River.

He went through a hedge that separated the Westerhazy's land from the Grahams', walked under some flowering apple trees, passed the shed that housed their pump and filter, and came out at the Graham's pool. "Why, Neddy," Mrs. Graham said, "what a marvelous surprise. I've been trying to get you on the phone all morning. Here, let me get you a drink." He saw then, like any explorer, that the hospitable customs and traditions of the natives would have to be handled with diplomacy if he was ever going to reach his destination. He did not want to mystify or seem rude to the Grahams nor did he have the time to linger there. He swam the length of their pool and joined them in the sun and was rescued, a few minutes later, by the arrival of two carloads of friends from Connecticut. During the uproarious reunions he was able to slip away. He went down by the front of the Grahams' house, stepped over a thorny hedge, and crossed a vacant lot to the Hammers'. Mrs. Hammer, looking up from her roses, saw him swim by although she wasn't quite sure who it was. The Lears heard him splashing past the open windows of their living room. The Howlands and the Crosscups were away. After leaving the Howlands' he crossed Ditmar Street and started for the Bunkers', where he could hear, even at that distance, the noise of a party.

The water refracted the sound of voices and laughter and seemed to suspend it in midair. The Bunker's pool was on a rise and he climbed some stairs to a terrace where twenty-five or thirty men and women were drinking. The only person in the water was Rusty Towers, who floated there on a rubber raft. Oh, how bonny and lush were the banks of the Lucinda River! Prosperous men and women gathered by the sapphire-colored waters while caterer's men in white coats passed them cold gin. Overhead a red de Haviland trainer was circling around and around and around in the sky with something like the glee of a child in a swing. Ned felt a passing affection for the scene, a tenderness for the gathering, as if it was something he might touch. In the distance he heard thunder. As soon as Enid Bunker saw him she began to scream: "Oh, look who's here! What a marvelous surprise! When Lucinda said that you couldn't come I thought I'd *die*." She made her way to him through the crowd, and when they had finished kissing she led him to the bar, a progress that was slowed by the fact that he stopped to kiss eight or ten other women and shake the hands of as many men. A smiling bartender he had seen at a hundred parties gave him a gin and tonic and he stood by the bar for a moment, anxious not to get stuck in any conversation that would delay his voyage. When he seemed about to be sur- rounded he dove in and swam close to the side to avoid colliding with Rusty's raft. At the far end of the pool he bypassed the Tomlinsons with a broad smile and jogged up the garden path. The gravel cut his feet but this was the only unpleasantness. The party was confined to the pool, and as he went toward the house he heard the brilliant, watery sound of voices fade, heard the noise of a radio from the Bunkers' kitchen, where someone was listening to a ball game. Sunday afternoon. He made his way through the parked cars and down the grassy border of their driveway to Alewives Lane. He did not want to be seen on the road in his bathing trunks but there was no traffic and he made the short distance to the Levys' driveway, marked with a PRIVATE PROPERTY sign and a green tube for *The New York Times*. All the doors and windows of the big house were open but there were no signs of life; not even a dog barked. He went around the side of the house to the pool and saw that the Levys had only recently left. Glasses and bottles and dishes of nuts were on a table at the deep end, where there was a bathhouse or gazebo, hung with Japanese lanterns. After swimming the pool he got himself a glass and poured a drink. It was his fourth or fifth drink and he had swum nearly half the length of the Lucinda River. He felt tired, clean, and pleased at that moment to be alone; pleased with everything.

It would storm. The stand of cumulus cloud—that city—had risen and darkened, and while he sat there he heard the percussiveness of thunder again. The de Haviland trainer was still circling overhead and it seemed to Ned that he could almost hear the pilot laugh with pleasure in the afternoon; but when there was another peal of thunder he took off for home. A train whistle blew and he wondered what time it had gotten to be. Four? Five? He thought of the provincial station at that hour, where a waiter, his tuxedo concealed by a raincoat, a dwarf with some flowers wrapped in newspaper, and a woman who had been crying would be waiting for the local. It was suddenly growing dark; it was that moment when the pinheaded birds seemed to organize their song into some acute and knowledgeable recognition of the storm's approach. Then there was a fine noise of rushing water from the crown of an oak at his back, as if a spigot there had been turned. Then the noise of fountains came from the crowns of all the tall trees. Why did he love storms, what was the meaning of his excitement when the door sprang open and the rain wind fled rudely up the stairs, why had the simple task of shutting the windows of an old house seemed fitting and urgent, why did the first watery notes of a storm wind have for him the unmistakable sound of good news, cheer, glad tidings? Then there was an explosion, a smell of cordite, and rain lashed the Japanese lanterns that Mrs. Levy had bought in Kyoto the year before last, or was it the year before that?

He stayed in the Levys' gazebo until the storm had passed. The rain had cooled the air and he shivered. The force of the wind had stripped a maple of its red and yellow leaves and scattered them over the grass and the water. Since it was midsummer the tree must be blighted, and yet he felt a peculiar sadness at this sign of autumn. He braced his shoulders, emptied his glass, and started for the Welchers' pool. This meant crossing the Lindleys' riding ring and he was surprised to find it overgrown with grass and all the jumps dismantled. He wondered if the Lindleys had sold their horses or gone away for the summer and put them out to board. He seemed to remember having heard something about the Lindleys and their horses but the memory was unclear. On he went, barefoot through the wet grass, to the Welchers', where he found their pool was dry.

This breach in his chain of water disappointed him absurdly, and he felt like some explorer who seeks a torrential headwater and finds a dead stream. He was disappointed and mystified. It was common enough to go away for the summer but no one ever drained his pool. The Welchers had definitely gone away. The pool furniture was folded, stacked, and covered with a tarpaulin. The bathhouse was locked. All the windows of the house were shut, and when he went around to the driveway in front he saw a FOR SALE sign nailed to a tree. When had he last heard from the Welchers—when, that is, had he and Lucinda last regretted an invitation to dine with them? It seemed only a week or so ago. Was his memory failing or had he so disciplined it in the repression of unpleasant facts that he had damaged his sense of the truth? Then in the distance he heard the sound of a tennis game. This cheered him, cleared away all his apprehensions and let him regard the overcast sky and the cold air with indifference. This was the day that Neddy Merrill swam across the county. That was the day! He started off then for his most difficult portage.

Had you gone for a Sunday afternoon ride that day you might have seen him, close to naked, standing on the shoulders of Route 424, waiting for a chance to cross. You might have wondered if he was the victim of foul play, had his car broken down, or was he merely a fool. Standing barefoot in the deposits of the highway—beer cans, rags, and blowout patches—exposed to all kinds of ridicule, he seemed pitiful. He had known when he started that this was a part of his journey—it had been on his maps—but confronted with the lines of traffic, worming through the summery light, he found himself unprepared. He was laughed at, jeered at, a beer can was thrown at him, and he had no dignity or humor to bring to the situation. He could have gone back, back to the Wester-hazys', where Lucinda would still be sitting in the sun. He had signed nothing, vowed nothing, pledged nothing, not even to himself. Why, believing as he did, that all human obduracy was susceptible to common sense, was he unable to turn back? Why was he determined to complete his journey even if it meant putting his life in danger? At what point had this prank, this joke, this piece of horseplay become serious? He could not go back, he could not even recall with any clearness the green water at the Westerhazys', the sense of inhaling the day's components, the friendly and relaxed voices saying that they had *drunk* too much. In the space of an hour, more or less, he had covered a distance that made his return impossible.

An old man, tooling down the highway at fifteen miles an hour, let him get to the middle of the road, where there was a grass divider. Here he was exposed to the ridicule of the northbound traffic, but after ten or fifteen minutes he was able to cross. From here he had only a short walk to the Recreation Center at the edge of the village of Lancaster, where there were some handball courts and a public pool.

The effect of the water on voices, the illusion of brilliance and suspense, was the same here as it had been at the Bunkers' but the sounds here were louder, harsher, and more shrill, and as soon as he entered the crowded enclosure he was confronted with regimentation. "ALL SWIMMERS MUST TAKE A SHOWER BEFORE USING THE POOL. ALL SWIMMERS MUST USE THE FOOTBATH. ALL SWIMMERS MUST WEAR THEIR IDENTIFICATION DISKS." He took a shower, washed his feet in a cloudy and bitter solution, and made his way to the edge of the water. It stank of chlorine and looked to him like a sink. A pair of lifeguards in a pair of towers blew police whistles at what seemed to be regular intervals and abused the swimmers through a public address system. Neddy remembered the sapphire water at the Bunkers' with longing and thought that he might contaminate himself—damage his own prosperousness and charm—by swimming in this murk, but he reminded himself that he was an explorer, a pilgrim, and that this was merely a stagnant bend in the Lucinda River. He dove, scowling with distaste, into the chlorine and had to swim with his head above water to avoid collisions, but even so he was bumped into, splashed, and jostled. When he got to the shallow end both lifeguards were shouting at him: "Hey, you, you without the identification disk, get outa the water." He did, but they had no way of pursuing him and he went through the reek of suntan oil and chlorine out through the hurricane fence and passed the handball courts. By crossing the road he entered the wooded part of the Halloran estate. The woods were not cleared and the footing was treacherous and difficult until he reached the lawn and the clipped beech hedge that encircled their pool.

The Hallorans were friends, an elderly couple of enormous wealth who seemed to bask in the suspicion that they might be Communists. They were zealous reformers but they were not Communists, and yet when they were accused, as they sometimes were, of subversion, it seemed to gratify and excite them. Their beech hedge was yellow and he guessed this had been blighted like the Levys' maple. He called hullo, hullo, to warn the Hallorans of his approach, to palliate his invasion of their privacy. The Hallorans, for reasons that had never been explained to him, did not wear bathing suits. No explanations were in order, really. Their nakedness was a detail in their uncompromising zeal for reform and he went through the opening in the hedge.

Mrs. Halloran, a stout woman with white hair and a serene face, was reading the *Times*. Mr. Halloran was taking beech leaves out of the water with a scoop. They seemed not surprised or displeased to see him. Their pool was perhaps the oldest in the country, a fieldstone rectangle, fed by a brook. It had no filter or pump and its waters were the opaque gold of the stream.

"I'm swimming across the county," Ned said.

"Why, I didn't know one could," exclaimed Mrs. Halloran.

"Well, I've made it from the Westerhazys'," Ned said. "That must be about four miles."

He left his trunks at the deep end, walked to the shallow end, and swam this stretch. As he was pulling himself out of the water he heard Mrs. Halloran say, "We've been *terribly* sorry to hear about all your misfortunes, Neddy."

"My misfortunes?" Ned asked. "I don't know what you mean."

"Why, we heard that you'd sold the house and that your poor children . . ."

"I don't recall having sold the house," Ned said, "and the girls are at home."

"Yes," Mrs. Halloran sighed. "Yes . . ." Her voice filled the air with an unseasonable melancholy and Ned spoke briskly. "Thank you for the swim."

"Well, have a nice trip," said Mrs. Halloran.

Beyond the hedge he pulled on his trunks and fastened them. They were loose and he wondered if, during the space of an afternoon, he could have lost some weight. He was cold and he was tired and the naked Hallorans and their dark water had depressed him. The swim was too much for his strength but how could he have guessed this, sliding down the banister that morning and sitting in the Westerhazys' sun? His arms were lame. His legs felt rubbery and ached at the joints. The worst of it was the cold in his bones and the feeling that he might never be warm again. Leaves were falling down around him and he smelled wood smoke on the wind. Who would be burning wood at this time of year?

He needed a drink. Whiskey would warm him, pick him up, carry him through the last of his journey, refresh his feeling that it was original and valorous to swim across the county. Channel swimmers took brandy. He needed a stimulant. He crossed the lawn in front of the Hallorans' house and went down a little path to where they had built a house for their only daughter, Helen, and her husband, Eric Sachs. The Sachses' pool was small and he found Helen and her husband there.

"Oh, *Neddy*," Helen said. "Did you lunch at Mother's?"

"Not *really*," Ned said. "I *did* stop to see your parents." This seemed to be explanation enough. "I'm terribly sorry to break in on you like this but I've taken a chill and I wonder if you'd give me a drink."

"Why, I'd *love* to," Helen said, "but there hasn't been anything in this house to drink since Eric's operation. That was three years ago."

Was he losing his memory, had his gift for concealing painful facts let him forget that he had sold his house, that his children were in trouble, and that his friend had been ill? His eyes slipped from Eric's face to his abdomen, where he saw three pale, sutured scars, two of them at least a foot long. Gone was his navel, and what, Neddy thought, would the roving hand, bed-checking one's gifts at

3 A.M., make of a belly with no navel, no link to birth, this breach in the succession?

"I'm sure you can get a drink at the Biswangers'," Helen said. "They're having an enormous do. You can hear it from here. Listen!"

She raised her head and from across the road, the lawns, the gardens, the woods, the fields, he heard again the brilliant noise of voices over water. "Well, I'll get wet," he said, still feeling that he had no freedom of choice about his means of travel. He dove into the Sachses' cold water and, gasping, close to drowning, made his way from one end of the pool to the other. "Lucinda and I want *terribly* to see you," he said over his shoulder, his face set toward the Biswangers'. "We're sorry it's been so long and we'll call you *very* soon."

He crossed some fields to the Biswangers' and the sounds of revelry there. They would be honored to give him a drink, they would be happy to give him a drink. The Biswangers invited him and Lucinda for dinner four times a year, six weeks in advance. They were always rebuffed and yet they continued to send out their invitations, unwilling to comprehend the rigid and undemocratic realities of their society. They were the sort of people who discussed the price of things at cocktails, exchanged market tips during dinner, and after dinner told dirty stories to mixed company. They did not belong to Neddy's set — they were not even on Lucinda's Christmas card list. He went toward their pool with feelings of indifference, charity, and some unease, since it seemed to be getting dark and these were the longest days of the year. The party when he joined it was noisy and large. Grace Biswanger was the kind of hostess who asked the optometrist, the veterinarian, the real-estate dealer, and the dentist. No one was swimming and the twilight, reflected on the water of the pool, had a wintry gleam. There was a bar and he started for this. When Grace Biswanger saw him she came toward him, not affectionately as he had every right to expect, but bellicosely.

"Why, this party has everything," she said loudly, "including a gate crasher."

She could not deal him a social blow — there was no question about this and he did not flinch. "As a gate crasher," he asked politely, "do I rate a drink?"

"Suit yourself," she said. "You don't seem to pay much attention to invitations."

She turned her back on him and joined some guests, and he went to the bar and ordered a whiskey. The bartender served him but he served him rudely. His was a world in which the caterer's men kept the social score, and to be rebuffed by a part-time barkeep meant that he had suffered some loss of social esteem. Or perhaps the man was new and uninformed. Then he heard Grace at his back say: "They went for broke overnight — nothing but income — and he showed up drunk one Sunday and asked us to loan him five thousand dollars. . . ." She was always talking about money. It was worse than eating your peas off a knife. He dove into the pool, swam its length and went away.

The next pool on his list, the last but two, belonged to his old mistress, Shirley Adams. If he had suffered any injuries at the Biswangers' they would be cured here. Love — sexual roughhouse in fact — was the supreme elixir, the pain killer, the brightly colored pill that would put the spring back into his step, the joy of life in his heart. They had had an affair last week, last month, last year. He couldn't remember. It was he who had broken if off, his was the upper hand, and he stepped through the gate of the wall that surrounded her pool with nothing so considered as self-confidence. It seemed in a way to be his pool, as the lover, particularly the illicit lover, enjoys the possessions of his mistress with an authority unknown to holy matrimony. She was there, her hair the color of brass, but her figure, at the edge of the lighted, cerulean water, excited in him no profound memories. It had been, he thought, a lighthearted affair, although she had wept when he broke it off. She seemed confused to see him and he wondered if she was still wounded. Would she, God forbid, weep again?

"What do you want?" she asked.

"I'm swimming across the county."

"Good Christ. Will you ever grow up?"

"What's the matter?"

"If you've come here for money," she said, "I won't give you another cent."

"You could give me a drink."

"I could but I won't. I'm not alone."

"Well, I'm on my way."

He dove in and swam the pool, but when he tried to haul himself up onto the curb he found that the strength in his arms and shoulders had gone, and he paddled to the ladder and climbed out. Looking over his shoulder he saw, in the lighted bathhouse, a young man. Going out onto the dark lawn he smelled chrysanthemums or marigolds — some stubborn autumnal fragrance — on the night air, strong as gas. Looking overhead he saw that the stars had come out, but why should he seem to see Andromeda, Cepheus, and Cassiopeia? What had become of the constellations of midsummer? He began to cry.

It was probably the first time in his adult life that he had ever cried, certainly the first time in his life that he had ever felt so miserable, cold, tired, and bewildered. He could not understand the rudeness of the caterer's barkeep or the rudeness of a mistress who had come to him on her knees and showered his trousers with tears. He had swum too long, he had been immersed too long, and his nose and his throat were sore from the water. What he needed then was a drink, some company, and some clean, dry clothes, and while he could have cut directly across the road to his home he went on to the Gilmartins' pool. Here, for the first time in his life, he did not dive but went down the steps into the icy water and swam a hobbled sidestroke that he might have learned as a youth. He staggered with fatigue on his way to the Clydes' and paddled the length of their pool, stopping again and again with his hand on the curb to rest. He climbed up the ladder and wondered if he had the strength to get home. He had done what he wanted, he had swum the county, but he was so stupefied with exhaustion that his triumph seemed vague. Stooped, holding on to the gateposts for support, he turned up the driveway of his own house.

The place was dark. Was it so late that they had all gone to bed? Had Lucinda stayed at the Westerhazys' for supper? Had the girls joined her there or gone someplace else? Hadn't they agreed, as they usually did on Sunday, to regret all their invitations and stay at home? He tried the garage doors to see what cars were in but the doors were locked and rust came off the handles onto his hands. Going toward the house, he saw that the force of the thunderstorm had knocked one of the rain gutters loose. It hung down over the front door like an umbrella rib, but it could be fixed in the morning. The house was locked, and he thought that the stupid cook or the stupid maid must have locked the place up until he remembered that it had been some time since they had employed a maid or a cook. He shouted, pounded on the door, tried to force it with his shoulder, and then, looking in at the windows, saw that the place was empty.

[1964]

Study and Writing Questions

1. Why is exploration so important an activity for Neddy Merrill? What does it mean in the beginning of the NARRATIVE? at the end? in between?
2. Compare and contrast the use of water and liquor IMAGERY.
3. What are Neddy's attitudes toward other people? Judging from these attitudes, what sort of person is he? Has he always been this sort of person?
4. What is the social structure of "the county"?
5. What is/are the meaning(s) of the title? In what way(s) is Neddy swimming? Do the events of the narrative present actually take place? What is this narrative about?

See also Questions for Contrast and Comparison: 1, 77, 181, 206, 214, and 216.

■■ **ANTON PAVLOVICH CHEKHOV** (1860–1904), *grandson of a serf
■■ who bought his own freedom, was born a grocer's son in Taganrog in south-
western Russia. When the grocery failed (1876), his family left for Moscow, leaving
Anton to finish secondary school alone, supporting himself by tutoring. When he
went to Moscow (1879), he enrolled at the University, but, to repay family debts, also
did newspaper work ranging from cartoon captions to theater reviews to travelogues.
In 1884 he received his medical degree, published his first story collection, and
suffered his first tuberculosis hemorrhage. After his stories shared the Pushkin Prize
(1888), Russia's highest literary award, Chekhov wrote and traveled full-time
throughout Russia, Siberia, south Asia, Egypt, and western Europe. In 1892 he
moved his family to a country estate where he gave the peasants free medical care.
Elected to the Academy of Sciences in 1900, he resigned in 1902 to protest writer
Maksim Gorky's exclusion, just as he had broken with a journal that took an
anti-semitic stand against French army officer Alfred Dreyfus. Although he wrote
two novels and vastly influential plays (The Sea Gull, 1896; Uncle Vanya, 1897;
The Three Sisters, 1901; The Cherry Orchard, 1904), his unique contribution is in
the SHORT STORY GENRE. "Man," he believed, "will become better when you have
shown him what he is." In 1901 he married an actress. In 1904 he succumbed to
tuberculosis. He is buried in a Moscow monastery.*

Vanka

Vanka Zhukov, a nine-year-old boy, who had been apprenticed to Alyahin the
shoemaker these three months, did not go to bed on Christmas Eve. After his
master and mistress and the journeymen had gone to midnight Mass, he got an
inkpot and a penholder with a rusty nib out of the master's cupboard and having
spread out a crumpled sheet of paper, began writing. Before he formed the first
letter he looked fearfully at the doors and windows several times, shot a glance at
the dark icon, at either side of which stretched shelves filled with lasts, and
heaved a broken sigh. He was kneeling before a bench on which his paper lay.

"Dear Granddaddy, Konstantin Makarych," he wrote. "And I am writing
you a letter. I wish you a merry Christmas and everything good from the Lord
God. I have neither father nor mother, you alone are left me."

Vanka shifted his glance to the dark window on which flickered the reflection of his candle and vividly pictured his grandfather to himself. Employed as a
watchman by the Zhivaryovs, he was a short, thin, but extraordinarily lively and
nimble old man of about sixty-five whose face was always crinkled with laughter
and who had a toper's eyes. By day he slept in the servants' kitchen or cracked
jokes with the cook; at night, wrapped in an ample sheepskin coat, he made the
rounds of the estate, shaking his clapper. The old bitch, Brownie, and the dog
called Wriggles, who had a black coat and a long body like a weasel's, followed
him with hanging heads. This Wriggles was extraordinarily deferential and demonstrative, looked with equally friendly eyes both at his masters and at
strangers, but did not enjoy a good reputation. His deference and meekness
concealed the most Jesuitical spite. No one knew better than he how to creep up
behind you and suddenly snap at your leg, how to slip into the icehouse, or how
to steal a hen from a peasant. More than once his hind legs had been all but

broken, twice he had been hanged, every week he was whipped till he was half dead, but he always managed to revive.

At the moment Grandfather was sure to be standing at the gates, screwing up his eyes at the bright-red windows of the church, stamping his felt boots, and cracking jokes with the servants. His clapper was tied to his belt. He was clapping his hands, shrugging with the cold, and, with a senile titter, pinching now the housemaid, now the cook.

"Shall we have a pinch of snuff?" he was saying, offering the women his snuffbox.

They each took a pinch and sneezed. Grandfather, indescribably delighted, went off into merry peals of laughter and shouted:

"Peel it off, it has frozen on!"

The dogs too are given a pinch of snuff. Brownie sneezes, wags her head, and walks away offended. Wriggles is too polite to sneeze and only wags his tail. And the weather is glorious. The air is still, clear, and fresh. The night is dark, but one can see the whole village with its white roofs and smoke streaming out of the chimneys, the trees silvery with hoarfrost, the snowdrifts. The entire sky is studded with gaily twinkling stars and the Milky Way is as distinctly visible as though it had been washed and rubbed with snow for the holiday. . . .

Vanka sighed, dipped his pen into the ink and went on writing:

"And yesterday I got it hot. The master pulled me out into the courtyard by the hair and gave me a hiding with a knee-strap because I was rocking the baby in its cradle and happened to fall asleep. And last week the mistress ordered me to clean a herring and I began with the tail, and she took the herring and jabbed me in the mug with it. The helpers make fun of me, send me to the pothouse for vodka and tell me to steal pickles for them from the master, and the master hits me with anything that comes handy. And there is nothing to eat. In the morning they give me bread, for dinner porridge, and in the evening bread again. As for tea or cabbage soup, the master and mistress bolt it all themselves. And they tell me to sleep in the entry, and when the baby cries I don't sleep at all, but rock the cradle. Dear Granddaddy, for God's sake have pity on me, take me away from here, take me home to the village, it's more than I can bear. I bow down at your feet and I will pray to God for you forever, take me away from here or I'll die."

Vanka puckered his mouth, rubbed his eyes with his black fist, and gave a sob.

"I will grind your snuff for you," he continued, "I will pray to God for you, and if anything happens, you may thrash me all you like. And if you think there's no situation for me, I will beg the manager for Christ's sake to let me clean boots, or I will take Fedka's place as a shepherd boy. Dear Granddaddy, it's more than I can bear, it will simply be the death of me. I thought of running away to the village, but I have no boots and I am afraid of the frost. And in return for this when I grow big, I will feed you and won't let anybody do you any harm, and when you die I will pray for the repose of your soul, just as for my Mom's.

"Moscow is a big city. The houses are all the kind the gentry live in, and there are lots of horses, but no sheep, and the dogs are not fierce. The boys here don't go caroling, carrying the star at Christmas, and they don't let anyone sing in the choir, and once in a shop window I saw fishing-hooks for sale all fitted up with a line, for every kind of fish, very fine ones, there was even one hook that will hold a forty-pound sheatfish. And I saw shops where there are all sorts of guns, like the master's at home, so maybe each one of them is a hundred rubles. And in butchers' shops there are woodcocks and partridge and hares, but where they shoot them the clerks won't tell.

"Dear Granddaddy, when they have a Christmas tree with presents at the master's, do get a gilt walnut and put it away in the little green chest. Ask the young lady, Olga Ignatyevna, for it, say it's for Vanka."

Vanka heaved a broken sigh and again stared at the window. He recalled that it was his grandfather who always went to the forest to get the Christmas tree for the master's family and that he would take his grandson with him. It was a jolly time! Grandfather grunted, the frost crackled, and, not to be outdone, Vanka too made a cheerful noise in his throat. Before chopping down the Christmas tree, Grandfather would smoke a pipe, slowly take a pinch of snuff, and poke fun at Vanka who looked chilled to the bone. The young firs draped in hoarfrost stood still, waiting to see which of them was to die. Suddenly, coming out of nowhere, a hare would dart across the snowdrifts like an arrow. Grandfather could not keep from shouting: "Hold him, hold him, hold him! Ah, the bob-tailed devil!"

When he had cut down the fir tree, Grandfather would drag it to the master's house, and there they would set to work decorating it. The young lady, Olga Ignatyevna, Vanka's favorite, was the busiest of all. When Vanka's mother, Pelageya, was alive and a chambermaid in the master's house, the young lady used to give him goodies, and, having nothing with which to occupy herself, taught him to read and write, to count up to a hundred, and even to dance the quadrille. When Pelageya died, Vanka had been relegated to the servants' kitchen to stay with his grandfather, and from the kitchen to the shoemaker's.

"Do come, dear Granddaddy," Vanka went on. "For Christ's sake, I beg you, take me away from here. Have pity on me, an unhappy orphan, here everyone beats me, and I am terribly hungry, and I am so blue, I can't tell you how, I keep crying. And the other day the master hit me on the head with a last, so that I fell down and it was a long time before I came to. My life is miserable, worse than a dog's — I also send greetings to Alyona, one-eyed Yegorka and the coachman, and don't give my harmonica to anyone. I remain, your grandson, Ivan Zhukov, dear Granddaddy, do come."

Vanka twice folded the sheet covered with writing and put it into an envelope he had bought for a kopeck the previous day. He reflected a while, then dipped the pen into the ink and wrote the address:

To Grandfather in the village

Then he scratched himself, thought a little, and added: *Konstantin Makarych.* Glad that no one had interrupted him at his writing, he put on his cap and, without slipping on his coat, ran out into the street with nothing over his shirt.

The clerks at the butchers' whom he had questioned the day before had told him that letters were dropped into letter boxes and from the boxes they were carried all over the world in troikas with ringing bells and drunken drivers. Vanka ran to the nearest letter box and thrust the precious letter into the slit.

An hour later, lulled by sweet hopes, he was fast asleep. In his dream he saw the stove. On the stove sat grandfather, his bare legs hanging down, and read the letter to the cooks. Near the stove was Wriggles, wagging his tail.

[1886]

Study and Writing Questions

1. What is the role of religion in the lives of these CHARACTERS? What position does the IMPLIED AUTHOR seem to hold about the value of religion?
2. Describe the social realities of Vanka's world in terms of such demographic categories as class, gender, age, location, and so on.
3. How does the use of FREE INDIRECT STYLE control our reactions to this NARRATIVE?
4. Why is Wriggles described at such length? Why is he the subject of the last sentence of the narrative?
5. What idea of happiness is revealed in this narrative? What makes for happiness? Is it the same for everyone? Is happiness possible in Vanka's world? To what extent is this narrative about happiness?

See also Questions for Contrast and Comparison: 8, 11, 49, 64, 68, 70, 129, 224, and 238.

KATE (KATHERINE FLAHERTY) CHOPIN (1851–1904) *was born in St. Louis to an Irish immigrant father, a self-made businessman killed in a bridge collapse when she was four. Raised by her socially prominent mother and great-grandmother, Kate loved the latter's tales of St. Louis's early French settlers. When the older woman died (1862) Kate retreated into reading, but after graduating from Sacred Heart Convent school (1868) became a debutante and married Oscar Chopin (1870), a Louisiana Creole with whom she had six children. They lived in New Orleans "society" until Oscar's business failure (1879) forced their move to the family's northern Louisiana plantations where he died of swamp fever (1883). After managing the plantations for a year, Chopin returned to St. Louis with her children. The next year her mother died. At the urging of friends, Chopin, who had already translated De Maupassant, turned to writing. She quickly sold children's stories, a weak novel, and then superb adult tales (collected in Bayou Folk, 1894, and A Night in Acadie, 1897) myopically praised as "local color gems." Her great novel, The Awakening (1899), sympathetically explores woman's sexuality, adultery, and the repressions of marriage. It was banned by St. Louis libraries and caused publishers and friends to shun her, effectively ending her career. Chopin died of a cerebral hemorrhage, her work largely unread until its rediscovery in the 1960s.*

Désirée's Baby

As the day was pleasant, Madame Valmondé drove over to L'Abri to see Désirée and the baby.

It made her laugh to think of Désirée with a baby. Why, it seemed but yesterday that Désirée was little more than a baby herself; when Monsieur in riding through the gateway of Valmondé had found her lying asleep in the shadow of the big stone pillar.

The little one awoke in his arms and began to cry for "Dada." That was as much as she could do or say. Some people thought she might have strayed there of her own accord, for she was of the toddling age. The prevailing belief was that she had been purposely left by a party of Texans, whose canvas-covered wagon, late in the day, had crossed the ferry that Coton Maïs kept, just below the plantation. In time Madame Valmondé abandoned every speculation but the one that Désirée had been sent to her by a beneficent Providence to be the child of her affection, seeing that she was without child of the flesh. For the girl grew to be beautiful and gentle, affectionate and sincere, — the idol of Valmondé.

It was no wonder, when she stood one day against the stone pillar in whose shadow she had lain asleep, eighteen years before, that Armand Aubigny riding by and seeing her there, had fallen in love with her. That was the way all the Aubignys fell in love, as if struck by a pistol shot. The wonder was that he had not loved her before; for he had known her since his father brought him home from Paris, a boy of eight, after his mother died there. The passion that awoke in him that day, when he saw her at the gate, swept along like an avalanche, or like a prairie fire, or like anything that drives headlong over all obstacles.

Monsieur Valmondé grew practical and wanted things well considered: that is, the girl's obscure origin. Armand looked into her eyes and did not care. He was reminded that she was nameless. What did it matter about a name when he could give her one of the oldest and proudest in Louisiana? He ordered the *corbeille* from Paris, and contained himself with what patience he could until it arrived; then they were married.

Madame Valmondé had not seen Désirée and the baby for four weeks. When she reached L'Abri she shuddered at the first sight of it, as she always did. It was a sad looking place, which for many years had not known the gentle presence of a mistress, old Monsieur Abigny having married and buried his wife in France, and she having loved her own land too well ever to leave it. The roof came down steep and black like a cowl, reaching out beyond the wide galleries that encircled the yellow stuccoed house. Big, solemn oaks grew close to it, and their thick-leaved, far-reaching branches shadowed it like a pall. Young Aubigny's rule was a strict one, too, and under it his negroes had forgotten how to be gay, as they had been during the old master's easy-going and indulgent lifetime.

The young mother was recovering slowly, and lay full length, in her soft white muslins and laces, upon a couch. The baby was beside her, upon her arm, where he had fallen asleep, at her breast. The yellow nurse woman sat beside a window fanning herself.

Madame Valmondé bent her portly figure over Désirée and kissed her, holding her an instant tenderly in her arms. Then she turned to the child.

"This is not the baby!" she exclaimed, in startled tones. French was the language spoken at Valmondé in those days.

"I knew you would be astonished," laughed Désirée, "at the way he has grown. The little *cochon de lait!* Look at his legs, mamma, and his hands and fingernails, — real finger-nails. Zandrine had to cut them this morning. Is n't it true, Zandrine?"

The woman bowed her turbaned head majestically, "Mais si, Madame."

"And the way he cries," went on Désirée, "is deafening. Armand heard him the other day as far away as La Blanche's cabin."

Madame Valmondé had never removed her eyes from the child. She lifted it and walked with it over to the window that was lightest. She scanned the baby narrowly, then looked as searchingly at Zandrine, whose face was turned to gaze across the fields.

"Yes, the child has grown, has changed," said Madam Valmondé, slowly, as she replaced it beside its mother. "What does Armand say?"

Désirée's face became suffused with a glow that was happiness itself.

"Oh, Armand is the proudest father in the parish, I believe, chiefly because it is a boy, to bear his name; though he says not, — that he would have loved a girl as well. But I know it is n't true. I know he says that to please me. And mamma," she added, drawing Madame Valmondé's head down to her and speaking in a whisper, "he has n't punished one of them — not one of them — since baby is born. Even Négrillon, who pretended to have burnt his leg that he might rest from work — he only laughed, and said Négrillon was a great scamp. Oh, mamma, I'm so happy; it frightens me."

What Désirée said was true. Marriage, and later the birth of his son had softened Armand Aubigny's imperious and exacting nature greatly. This was what made the gentle Désirée so happy, for she loved him desperately. When he frowned she trembled, but loved him. When he smiled, she asked no greater blessing of God. But Armand's dark, handsome face had not often been disfigured by frowns since the day he fell in love with her.

When the baby was about three months old, Désirée awoke one day to the conviction that there was something in the air menacing her peace. It was at first too subtle to grasp. It had only been a disquieting suggestion; an air of mystery among the blacks; unexpected visits from far-off neighbors who could hardly account for their coming. Then a strange, an awful change in her husband's manner, which she dared not ask him to explain. When he spoke to her, it was with averted eyes, from which the old love-light seemed to have gone out. He absented himself from home; and when there, avoided her presence and that of her child, without excuse. And the very spirit of Satan seemed suddenly to take hold of him in his dealings with the slaves. Désirée was miserable enough to die.

She sat in her room, one hot afternoon, in her *peignoir*, listlessly drawing through her fingers the strands of her long, silky brown hair that hung about her shoulders. The baby, half naked, lay asleep upon her own great mahogany bed, that was like a sumptuous throne, with its satin-lined half-canopy. One of La Blanche's little quadroon boys — half naked too — stood fanning the child slowly with a fan of peacock feathers. Désirée's eyes had been fixed absently and sadly upon the baby, while she was striving to penetrate the threatening mist that she felt closing about her. She looked from her child to the boy who stood beside him, and back again; over and over. "Ah!" It was a cry that she could not help; which she was not conscious of having uttered. The blood turned like ice in her veins, and a clammy moisture gathered upon her face.

She tried to speak to the little quadroon boy; but no sound would come, at first. When he heard his name uttered, he looked up, and his mistress was pointing to the door. He laid aside the great, soft fan, and obediently stole away, over the polished floor, on his bare tiptoes.

She stayed motionless, with gaze riveted upon her child, and her face the picture of fright.

Presently her husband entered the room, and without noticing her, went to a table and began to search among some papers which covered it.

"Armand," she called to him, in a voice which must have stabbed him, if he was human. But he did not notice. "Armand," she said again. Then she rose and tottered towards him. "Armand," she panted once more, clutching his arm, "look at our child. What does it mean? tell me."

He coldly but gently loosened her fingers from about his arm and thrust the hand away from him. "Tell me what it means!" she cried despairingly.

"It means," he answered lightly, "that the child is not white; it means that you are not white."

A quick conception of all that this accusation meant for her nerved her with unwonted courage to deny it. "It is a lie; it is not true, I am white! Look at my hair, it is brown; and my eyes are gray, Armand, you know they are gray. And my skin is fair," seizing his wrist. "Look at my hand; whiter than yours, Armand," she laughed hysterically.

"As white as La Blanche's," he returned cruelly; and went away leaving her alone with their child.

When she could hold a pen in her hand, she sent a despairing letter to Madame Valmondé.

"My mother, they tell me I am not white. Armand has told me I am not white. For God's sake tell them it is not true. You must know it is not true. I shall die. I must die. I cannot be so unhappy, and live."

The answer that came was as brief:

"My own Désirée: Come home to Valmondé; back to your mother who loves you. Come with your child."

When the letter reached Désirée she went with it to her husband's study, and laid it open upon the desk before which he sat. She was like a stone image: silent, white, motionless after she placed it there.

In silence he ran his cold eyes over the written words. He said nothing. "Shall I go, Armand?" she asked in tones sharp with agonized suspense.

"Yes, go."

"Do you want me to go?"

"Yes, I want you to go."

He thought Almighty God had dealt cruelly and unjustly with him; and felt, somehow, that he was paying Him back in kind when he stabbed thus into his wife's soul. Moreover he no longer loved her, because of the unconscious injury she had brought upon his home and his name.

She turned away like one stunned by a blow, and walked slowly towards the door, hoping he would call her back.

"Good-by, Armand," she moaned.

He did not answer her. That was his last blow at fate.

Désirée went in search of her child. Zandrine was pacing the sombre gallery with it. She took the little one from the nurse's arms with no word of explanation, and descending the steps, walked away, under the live-oak branches.

It was an October afternoon; the sun was just sinking. Out in the still fields the negroes were picking cotton.

Désirée had not changed the thin white garment nor the slippers which she wore. Her hair was uncovered and the sun's rays brought a golden gleam from its brown meshes. She did not take the broad, beaten road which led to the far-off plantation of Valmondé. She walked across a deserted field, where the stubble bruised her tender feet, so delicately shod, and tore her thin gown to shreds.

She disappeared among the reeds and willows that grew thick along the banks of the deep, sluggish bayou; and she did not come back again.

Some weeks later there was a curious scene enacted at L'Abri. In the centre of the smoothly swept back yard was a great bonfire. Armand Aubigny sat in the wide hallway that commanded a view of the spectacle; and it was he who dealt out to a half dozen negroes the material which kept this fire ablaze.

A graceful cradle of willow, with all its dainty furnishings, was laid upon the pyre, which had already been fed with the richness of a priceless *layette*. Then there were silk gowns, and velvet and satin ones added to these; laces, too, and embroideries; bonnets and gloves; for the *corbeille* had been of rare quality.

The last thing to go was a tiny bundle of letters; innocent little scribblings that Désirée had sent to him during the days of their espousal. There was the remnant of one back in the drawer from which he took them. But it was not

Désirée's; it was part of an old letter from his mother to his father. He read it. She was thanking God for the blessing of her husband's love: —

"But, above all," she wrote, "night and day, I thank the good God for having so arranged our lives that our dear Armand will never know that his mother, who adores him, belongs to the race that is cursed with the brand of slavery."

[1892]

Study and Writing Questions

1. Clearly there are important social differences between the black and white races in the Creole country as it is represented in this STORY. How do these race-based differences compare and contrast with class-based differences in Creole country? With race- and class-based differences in France?

2. What do the French words, including names, mean? How do they enter into the meaning of the story? What is the importance for the CHARACTERS and for the reader of the bilingual SETTING?

3. Reread the last section of the story. Do you think Armand did or did not see his mother's letter? On what do you base your conclusion? If you think he did, do you think he later took Désirée back? On what do you base that conclusion? If you think the story is unclear about Armand's knowledge and ultimate actions, how does that ambiguity influence your final feelings?

4. Compare and contrast the many varieties of "love" in this story.

5. This story seems to have a white IMPLIED READER. If you are white, how does this story make you feel about yourself? If you are not white, how do you feel in trying to adopt the VIEWPOINT of the implied reader?

See also Questions for Contrast and Comparison: 7, 8, 45, 54, 65, 73, 150, and 229.

■ ARTHUR C(HARLES) CLARKE (1917-) *was born in Minehead,
Somerset, England where reading Olaf Stapledon's cosmic philosophical
science fiction "changed my life." Too poor for college, he became a government
auditor (1936), but served during World War II as technical officer for the first
fog-defeating landing radar. His 1945 proposal for the now common communica-
tions satellite, "Extraterrestrial Relays," won the Franklin Institute Gold Medal
(1963). Entering King's College, University of London on a grant, Clarke earned
first class honors in physics and mathematics (B.Sc., 1948). After editing for Science
Abstracts (1949–1950), the science backlog declassified after the war, Clarke
became a free-lance writer and won every major science writing award. In 1953 he
married, but the couple soon lived apart and divorced in 1964. Fascinated with
undersea exploration, Clarke moved to Ceylon (now Sri Lanka) in 1956, where he
has been chancellor of the national university. His novels include Childhood's End
(1953), about the transformation of the human race the most widely taught science
fiction (SF) novel; A Fall of Moondust (1961), "hard SF" inviting the reader's use of
science; 2001: A Space Odyssey (1968), a symbolic tale filmed by Stanley Kubrick;
and Rendezvous With Rama (1973), the most honored SF novel of all time. Advisor
to both NASA and CBS, he is perhaps the most important science/science fiction
writer since H. G. Wells.*

The Star

It is three thousand light years to the Vatican. Once, I believed that space could
have no power over faith, just as I believed that the heavens declared the glory of
God's handiwork. Now I have seen that handiwork, and my faith is sorely
troubled. I stare at the crucifix that hangs on the cabin wall above the Mark VI
Computer, and for the first time in my life I wonder if it is no more than an
empty symbol.

I have told no one yet, but the truth cannot be concealed. The facts are there
for all to read, recorded on the countless miles of magnetic tape and the thousands of photographs we are carrying back to Earth. Other scientists can interpret
them as easily as I can, and I am not one who would condone that tampering with
the truth which often gave my order a bad name in the olden days.

The crew are already sufficiently depressed: I wonder how they will take this
ultimate irony. Few of them have any religious faith, yet they will not relish using
this final weapon in their campaign against me—that private, good-natured, but
fundamentally serious, war which lasted all the way from Earth. It amused them
to have a Jesuit as chief astrophysicist: Dr. Chandler, for instance, could never get
over it (why are medical men such notorious atheists?). Sometimes he would meet
me on the observation deck, where the lights are always low so that the stars
shine with undiminished glory. He would come up to me in the gloom and stand
staring out of the great oval port, while the heavens crawled slowly around us as
the ship turned end over end with the residual spin we had never bothered to
correct.

"Well, Father," he would say at last, "it goes on forever and forever, and
perhaps *Something* made it. But how you can believe that Something has a special
interest in us and our miserable little world—that just beats me." Then the

argument would start, while the stars and nebulae would swing around us in silent, endless arcs beyond the flawlessly clear plastic of the observation port.

It was, I think, the apparent incongruity of my position that caused most amusement to the crew. In vain I would point to my three papers in the *Astrophysical Journal*, my five in the *Monthly Notices of the Royal Astronomical Society*. I would remind them that my order has long been famous for its scientific works. We may be few now, but ever since the eighteenth century we have made contributions to astronomy and geophysics out of all proportion to our numbers. Will my report on the Phoenix Nebula end our thousand years of history? It will end, I fear, much more than that.

I do not know who gave the nebula its name, which seems to me a very bad one. If it contains a prophecy, it is one that cannot be verified for several billion years. Even the word nebula is misleading: this is a far smaller object than those stupendous clouds of mist — the stuff of unborn stars — that are scattered throughout the length of the Milky Way. On the cosmic scale, indeed, the Phoenix Nebula is a tiny thing — a tenuous shell of gas surrounding a single star.

Or what is left of a star . . .

The Rubens engraving of Loyola seems to mock me as it hangs there above the spectrophotometer tracings. What would *you*, Father, have made of this knowledge that has come into my keeping, so far from the little world that was all the universe you knew? Would your faith have risen to the challenge, as mine has failed to do?

You gaze into the distance, Father, but I have traveled a distance beyond any that you could have imagined when you founded our order a thousand years ago. No other survey ship has been so far from Earth: we are at the very frontiers of the explored universe. We set out to reach the Phoenix Nebula, we succeeded, and we are homeward bound with our burden of knowledge. I wish I could lift that burden from my shoulders, but I call to you in vain across the centuries and the light-years that lie between us.

On the book you are holding the words are plain to read. AD MAJOREM DEI GLORIAM, the message runs, but it is a message I can no longer believe. Would you still believe it, if you could see what we have found?

We knew, of course, what the Phoenix Nebula was. Every year, in our galaxy alone, more than a hundred stars explode, blazing for a few hours or days with thousands of times their normal brilliance before they sink back into death and obscurity. Such are the ordinary novae — the commonplace disasters of the universe. I have recorded the spectrograms and light curves of dozens since I started working at the Lunar Observatory.

But three or four times in every thousand years occurs something beside which even a nova pales into total insignificance.

When a star becomes a *supernova*, it may for a little while outshine all the massed suns of the galaxy. The Chinese astronomers watched this happen in A.D. 1054, not knowing what it was they saw. Five centuries later, in 1572, a supernova blazed in Cassiopeia so brilliantly that it was visible in the daylight sky. There have been three more in the thousand years that have passed since then.

Our mission was to visit the remnants of such a catastrophe, to reconstruct the events that led up to it, and, if possible, to learn its cause. We came slowly in through the concentric shells of gas that had been blasted out six thousand years before, yet were expanding still. They were immensely hot, radiating even now with a fierce violet light, but were far too tenuous to do us any damage. When the star had exploded, its outer layers had been driven upward with such speed that they had escaped completely from its gravitational field. Now they formed a hollow shell large enough to engulf a thousand solar systems, and at its center burned the tiny, fantastic object which the star had now become — a White Dwarf, smaller than the Earth, yet weighing a million times as much.

The glowing gas shells were all around us, banishing the normal night of interstellar space. We were flying into the center of a cosmic bomb that had detonated millennia ago and whose incandescent fragments were still hurtling apart. The immense scale of the explosion, and the fact that the debris already covered a volume of space many billions of miles across, robbed the scene of any visible movement. It would take decades before the unaided eye could detect any motion in these tortured wisps and eddies of gas, yet the sense of turbulent expansion was overwhelming.

We had checked our primary drive hours before, and were drifting slowly toward the fierce little star ahead. Once it had been a sun like our own, but it had squandered in a few hours the energy that should have kept it shining for a million years. Now it was a shrunken miser, hoarding its resources as if trying to make amends for its prodigal youth.

No one seriously expected to find planets. If there had been any before the explosion, they would have been boiled into puffs of vapor, and their substance lost in the greater wreckage of the star itself. But we made the automatic search, as we always do when approaching an unknown sun, and presently we found a single small world circling the star at an immense distance. It must have been the Pluto of this vanished solar system, orbiting on the frontiers of the night. Too far from the central sun ever to have known life, its remoteness had saved it from the fate of all its lost companions.

The passing fires had seared its rocks and burned away the mantle of frozen gas that must have covered it in the days before the disaster. We landed, and we found the Vault.

Its builders had made sure that we should. The monolithic marker that stood above the entrance was now a fused stump, but even the first long-range photographs told us that here was the work of intelligence. A little later we detected the continent-wide pattern of radioactivity that had been buried in the rock. Even if the pylon above the Vault had been destroyed, this would have remained, an immovable and all but eternal beacon calling to the stars. Our ship fell toward this gigantic bull's-eye like an arrow into its target.

The pylon must have been a mile high when it was built, but now it looked like a candle that had melted down into a puddle of wax. It took us a week to drill through the fused rock, since we did not have the proper tools for a task like this. We were astronomers, not archaeologists, but we could improvise. Our original purpose was forgotten: this lonely monument, reared with such labor at the greatest possible distance from the doomed sun, could have only one meaning. A civilization that knew it was about to die had made its last bid for immortality.

It will take us generations to examine all the treasures that were placed in the Vault. They had plenty of time to prepare, for their sun must have given its first warnings many years before the final detonation. Everything that they wished to preserve, all the fruit of their genius, they brought here to this distant world in the days before the end, hoping that some other race would find it and that they would not be utterly forgotten. Would we have done as well, or would we have been too lost in our own misery to give thought to a future we could never see or share?

If only they had had a little more time! They could travel freely enough between planets of their own sun, but they had not yet learned to cross the interstellar gulfs, and the nearest solar system was a hundred light-years away. Yet even had they possessed the secret of the Transfinite Drive, no more than a few millions could have been saved. Perhaps it was better thus.

Even if they had not been so disturbingly human as their sculpture shows, we could not have helped admiring them and grieving for their fate. They left thousands of visual records and the machines for projecting them, together with elaborate pictorial instructions from which it will not be difficult to learn their written language. We have examined many of these records, and brought to life for the first time in six thousand years the warmth and beauty of a civilization that in many ways must have been superior to our own. Perhaps they only showed us the best, and one can hardly blame them. But their words were very lovely, and their cities were built with a grace that matches anything of man's. We have watched them at work and play, and listened to their musical speech sounding across the centuries. One scene is still before my eyes — a group of children on a beach of strange blue sand, playing in the waves as children play on Earth. Curious whiplike trees line the shore, and some very large animal is wading in the shadows yet attracting no attention at all.

And sinking into the sea, still warm and friendly and life-giving, is the sun that will soon turn traitor and obliterate all this innocent happiness.

Perhaps if we had not been so far from home and so vulnerable to loneliness, we should not have been so deeply moved. Many of us had seen the ruins of ancient civilizations on other worlds, but they had never affected us so profoundly. This tragedy was unique. It is one thing for a race to fail and die, as nations and cultures have done on Earth. But to be destroyed so completely in the full flower of its achievement, leaving no survivors — how could that be reconciled with the mercy of God?

My colleagues have asked me that, and I have given what answers I can. Perhaps you could have done better, Father Loyola, but I have found nothing in the *Exercitia Spiritualia* that helps me here. They were not an evil people: I do not know what gods they worshiped, if indeed they worshipped any. But I have looked back at them across the centuries, and have watched while the loveliness they used their last strength to preserve was brought forth again into the light of their shrunken sun. They could have taught us much: why were they destroyed?

I know the answers that my colleagues will give when they get back to Earth. They will say that the universe has no purpose and no plan, that since a hundred suns explode every year in our galaxy, at this very moment some race is dying in the depths of space. Whether that race has done good or evil during its lifetime will make no difference in the end: there is no divine justice, for there is no God.

Yet, of course, what we have seen proves nothing of the sort. Anyone who argues thus is being swayed by emotion, not logic. God has no need to justify His actions to man. He who built the universe can destroy it when He chooses. It is arrogance — it is perilously near blasphemy — for us to say what He may or may not do.

This I could have accepted, hard though it is to look upon whole worlds and peoples thrown into the furnace. But there comes a point when even the deepest faith must falter, and now, as I look at the calculations lying before me, I know I have reached that point at last.

We could not tell, before we reached the nebula, how long ago the explosion took place. Now, from the astronomical evidence and the record in the rocks of that one surviving planet, I have been able to date it very exactly. I know in what year the light of this colossal conflagration reached our Earth. I know how brilliantly the supernova whose corpse now dwindles behind our speeding ship once shone in terrestrial skies. I know how it must have blazed low in the east before sunrise, like a beacon in that oriental dawn.

There can be no reasonable doubt: the ancient mystery is solved at last. Yet, oh God, there were so many stars you could have used. What was the need to give these people to the fire, that the symbol of their passing might shine above Bethlehem?

[1955]

Study and Writing Questions

1. The Phoenix is a bird of ancient Greek legend, which, according to one account, lived 500 years, burned itself to ashes on a pyre, and then rose alive from the ashes to live another period. The word "nebula" comes from the Greek word for cloud. In what ways is the name "Phoenix Nebula" appropriate in this STORY?

2. Ad Majorem Dei Gloriam, the Latin motto of the Society of Jesus, the Jesuit order, means To the Greater Glory of God. In what ways does this motto raise problems for the speaker? In what ways might it offer solutions to those problems?

3. The NARRATIVE begins with a scientific fact and ends with a spiritual outcry. In the course of the narrative, the speaker uses both scientific and spiritual language. How are these languages used to dramatize the speaker's internal struggle? How does a subsequent reading of this narrative differ from a first reading?

4. What is/are the relation(s) between religion and science posed by this narrative?

5. In the middle of the narrative, in the paragraph beginning "We had checked our primary drive," the speaker suggests that the remnant of the supernova is "trying to make amends for its prodigal youth." Is this merely a figure of speech employed by the FIRST PERSON NARRATOR or a hint by the IMPLIED AUTHOR about how one might try to solve the spiritual problem the supernova's explosion poses? In what way(s) is the Bible story of the Prodigal Son (Luke 15) important in this story by Clarke?

See also Questions for Contrast and Comparison: 14, 69, 124, 148, 155, 203, and 222.

■ **(SIDONIE-GABRIELLE) COLETTE** (1873–1954) *was born in a village in Burgundy and raised by her mother, Sidonie ("Sido") Colette, to whom she credited her childhood happiness and adult wisdom. At twenty, she married thirty-four-year-old novelist Henry Gauthier-Villars, who brought her to Bohemian Paris. Needing money, he compelled her to write fictionalized memoirs. Under his pen name, "Willy," Claudine at School (1900) was an instant hit, so Willy confined Colette until "Willy" wrote three sequels and spawned "Claudine" ice cream, hats, perfume, and cigarettes. Colette performed dance and mime in music halls and carried on a notorious lesbian affair (1906–1911), divorced (1910), married an aristocrat (1912), had a daughter, and divorced again (1925). She finally was married happily (1935) to Maurice Goudeket, a Jew sixteen years her junior, her lover since 1925. Colette, proud of being part black, frankly sexual, and independent, remained humble about her writing. She wrote over fifty novels, including the enduring Cheri (1920) about a youth's intellectual and sexual awakening, and the lustrous Gigi (1944). Collected Stories (1983) embodies her innocent cynicism and gentle libertinism. Although excommunicated by the Roman Catholic Church, she was the first woman president of the Goncourt Academy, the first woman grand officer of the Legion of Honor, and the first Frenchwoman ever given a state funeral.*

The Other Wife

"Table for two? This way, Monsieur, Madame, there is still a table next to the window, if Madame and Monsieur would like a view of the bay."

Alice followed the maître d'.

"Oh, yes. Come on, Marc, it'll be like having lunch on a boat on the water . . ."

Her husband caught her by passing his arm under hers. "We'll be more comfortable over there."

"There? In the middle of all those people? I'd much rather . . ."

"Alice, please."

He tightened his grip in such a meaningful way that she turned around. "What's the matter?"

"Shhh . . ." he said softly, looking at her intently, and led her toward the table in the middle.

"What is it, Marc?"

"I'll tell you, darling. Let me order lunch first. Would you like the shrimp? Or the eggs in aspic?"

"Whatever you like, you know that."

They smiled at one another, wasting the precious time of an overworked maître d', stricken with a kind of nervous dance, who was standing next to them, perspiring.

"The shrimp," said Marc. "Then the eggs and bacon. And the cold chicken with a romaine salad. *Fromage blanc?* The house specialty? We'll go with the specialty. Two strong coffees. My chauffeur will be having lunch also, we'll be leaving again at two o'clock. Some cider? No, I don't trust it . . . Dry champagne."

He sighed as if he had just moved an armoire, gazed at the colorless midday sea, at the pearly white sky, then at his wife, whom he found lovely in her little Mercury hat with its large, hanging veil.

"You're looking well, darling. And all this blue water makes your eyes look green, imagine that! And you've put on weight since you've been traveling . . . It's nice up to a point, but only up to a point!"

Her firm, round breasts rose proudly as she leaned over the table.

"Why did you keep me from taking that place next to the window?"

Marc Seguy never considered lying. "Because you were about to sit next to someone I know."

"Someone I don't know?"

"My ex-wife."

She couldn't think of anything to say and opened her blue eyes wider.

"So what, darling? It'll happen again. It's not important."

The words came back to Alice and she asked, in order, the inevitable questions. "Did she see you? Could she see that you saw her? Will you point her out to me?"

"Don't look now, please, she must be watching us . . . The lady with brown hair, no hat, she must be staying in this hotel. By herself, behind those children in red . . ."

"Yes. I see."

Hidden behind some broad-brimmed beach hats, Alice was able to look at the woman who, fifteen months ago, had still been her husband's wife.

"Incompatibility," Marc said. "Oh, I mean . . . total incompatibility! We divorced like well-bred people, almost like friends, quietly, quickly. And then I fell in love with you, and you really wanted to be happy with me. How lucky we are that our happiness doesn't involve any guilty parties or victims!"

The woman in white, whose smooth, lustrous hair reflected the light from the sea in azure patches, was smoking a cigarette with her eyes half closed. Alice turned back toward her husband, took some shrimp and butter, and ate calmly. After a moment's silence she asked: "Why didn't you ever tell me that she had blue eyes, too?"

"Well, I never thought about it!"

He kissed the hand she was extending toward the bread basket and she blushed with pleasure. Dusky and ample, she might have seemed somewhat coarse, but the changeable blue of her eyes and her wavy, golden hair made her look like a frail and sentimental blonde. She vowed overwhelming gratitude to her husband. Immodest without knowing it, everything about her bore the overly conspicuous marks of extreme happiness.

They ate and drank heartily, and each thought the other had forgotten the woman in white. Now and then, however, Alice laughed too loudly, and Marc was careful about his posture, holding his shoulders back, his head up. They waited quite a long time for their coffee, in silence. An incandescent river, the straggled reflection of the invisible sun overhead, shifted slowly across the sea and shone with a blinding brilliance.

"She's still there, you know," Alice whispered.

"Is she making you uncomfortable? Would you like to have coffee somewhere else?"

"No, not at all! She's the one who must be uncomfortable! Besides, she doesn't exactly seem to be having a wild time, if you could see her . . ."

"I don't have to. I know that look of hers."

"Oh, was she like that?"

He exhaled his cigarette smoke through his nostrils and knitted his eyebrows. "Like that? No. To tell you honestly, she wasn't happy with me."

"Oh, really now!"

"The way you indulge me is so charming, darling . . . It's crazy . . . You're an angel . . . You love me . . . I'm so proud when I see those eyes of yours. Yes, those eyes . . . She . . . I just didn't know how to make her happy, that's all. I didn't know how."

"She's just difficult!"

Alice fanned herself irritably, and cast brief glances at the woman in white, who was smoking, her head resting against the back of the cane chair, her eyes closed with an air of satisfied lassitude.

Marc shrugged his shoulders modestly.

"That's the right word," he admitted. "What can you do? You have to feel sorry for people who are never satisfied. But we're satisfied . . . Aren't we, darling?"

She did not answer. She was looking furtively, and closely, at her husband's face, ruddy and regular; at his thick hair, threaded here and there with white silk; at his short, well-cared-for hands; and doubtful for the first time, she asked herself, "What more did she want from him?"

And as they were leaving, while Marc was paying the bill and asking for the chauffeur and about the route, she kept looking, with envy and curiosity, at the woman in white, this dissatisfied, this difficult, this superior . . .

[1924]

Study and Writing Questions

1. How is nature IMAGERY used in this story?
2. The NARRATOR uses only one SIMILE: "He sighed as if he had just moved an armoire." Does this simile have special significance? If so, what? If not, is its use a RHETORICAL flaw?
3. How does the manipulation of the role of the chauffeur affect our understanding of the NARRATIVE?
4. What social, economic, and biographical backgrounds of the husband and two wives are implied by the details of this narrative? In what ways are those backgrounds significant in our assessing the ACTION of the narrative?
5. What is/are the meaning(s) of "happiness" to the CHARACTERS in this narrative?

See also Questions for Contrast and Comparison: 125, 152, 169, 170, and 171.

JOSEPH CONRAD (1857–1924) *was born Jozef Teodor Konrad Nalecz Korzeniowski in Polish Ukraine to middle-class parents who were exiled for resisting Russian rule. Their privations broke them, his mother dying when Jozef was six, his father (who received a hero's funeral in Warsaw) when Jozef was eleven. His guardian uncle, a lawyer, let Jozef at seventeen attend the Marseilles merchant marine academy. During his career at sea, Conrad survived at least two shipwrecks and perhaps a suicide attempt; visited the Orient, South America, Australia, and Africa; and rose to command many vessels, including a Congo River steamboat sent to rescue a Belgian company agent who died on the return trip. Conrad said the brutal exploitation of the Congo, "disfigured the history of human conscience." Drawn to England by reading Dickens, Conrad earned British citizenship and his Master's (captain's) Certificate in 1886. In 1895, although his first languages were Polish and French, he began publishing English novels based on his own experiences. After his second novel (1896), he left the sea and married an Englishwoman; they had two sons. The Nigger of the Narcissus (1897) brought critical success and began a well-connected literary life, but commercial success came only with* Chance *(1913). Other important works include* Lord Jim *(1900),* Nostromo *(1904),* The Secret Agent *(1907), and eight short story collections. He died of a heart attack.*

Heart of Darkness

I

The *Nellie*, a cruising yawl, swung to her anchor without a flutter of the sails, and was at rest. The flood had made, the wind was nearly calm, and being bound down the river, the only thing for it was to come to and wait for the turn of the tide.

The sea-reach of the Thames stretched before us like the beginning of an interminable waterway. In the offing the sea and the sky were welded together without a joint, and in the luminous space the tanned sails of the barges drifting up with the tide seemed to stand still in red clusters of canvas sharply peaked, with gleams of varnished sprits. A haze rested on the low shores that ran out to sea in vanishing flatness. The air was dark above Gravesend, and farther back still seemed condensed into a mournful gloom, brooding motionless over the biggest, and the greatest, town on earth.

The Director of Companies was our captain and our host. We four affectionately watched his back as he stood in the bows looking to seaward. On the whole river there was nothing that looked half so nautical. He resembled a pilot, which to a seaman is trustworthiness personified. It was difficult to realize his work was not out there in the luminous estuary, but behind him, within the brooding gloom.

Between us there was, as I have already said somewhere, the bond of the sea. Besides holding our hearts together through long periods of separation, it had the effect of making us tolerant of each other's yarns—and even convictions. The Lawyer—the best of old fellows—had, because of his many years and many virtues, the only cushion on deck, and was lying on the only rug. The Accountant had brought out already a box of dominoes, and was toying architecturally with the bones. Marlow sat cross-legged right aft, leaning against the mizzen-mast.

He had sunken cheeks, a yellow complexion, a straight back, an ascetic aspect, and, with his arms dropped, the palms of hands outwards, resembled an idol. The director, satisfied the anchor had good hold, made his way aft and sat down amongst us. We exchanged a few words lazily. Afterwards there was silence on board the yacht. For some reason or other we did not begin that game of dominoes. We felt meditative, and fit for nothing but placid staring. The day was ending in a serenity of still and exquisite brilliance. The water shone pacifically; the sky, without a speck, was a benign immensity of unstained light; the very mist on the Essex marshes was like a gauzy and radiant fabric, hung from the wooded rises inland, and draping the low shores in diaphanous folds. Only the gloom to the west, brooding over the upper reaches, became more sombre every minute, as if angered by the approach of the sun.

And at last, in its curved and imperceptible fall, the sun sank low, and from glowing white changed to a dull red without rays and without heat, as if about to go out suddenly, stricken to death by the touch of that gloom brooding over a crowd of men.

Forthwith a change came over the waters, and the serenity became less brilliant but more profound. The old river in its broad reach rested unruffled at the decline of day, after ages of good service done to the race that peopled its banks, spread out in the tranquil dignity of a waterway leading to the uttermost ends of the earth. We looked at the venerable stream not in the vivid flush of a short day that comes and departs for ever, but in the august light of abiding memories. And indeed nothing is easier for a man who has, as the phrase goes, "followed the sea" with reverence and affection, than to evoke the great spirit of the past upon the lower reaches of the Thames. The tidal current runs to and fro in its unceasing service, crowded with memories of men and ships it had borne to the rest of home or to the battles of the sea. It had known and served all the men of whom the nation is proud, from Sir Francis Drake to Sir John Franklin, knights all, titled and untitled — the great knights-errant of the sea. It had borne all the ships whose names are like jewels flashing in the night of time, from the *Golden Hind* returning with her round flanks full of treasure, to be visited by the Queen's Highness and thus pass out of the gigantic tale, to the *Erebus* and *Terror*, bound on other conquests — and that never returned. It had known the ships and the men. They had sailed from Deptford, from Greenwich, from Erith — the adventurers and the settlers; kings' ships and the ships of men on 'Change; captains, admirals, the dark "interlopers" of the Eastern trade, and the commissioned "generals" of East India fleets. Hunters for gold or pursuers of fame, they all had gone out on that stream, bearing the sword, and often the torch, messengers of the might within the land, bearers of a spark from the sacred fire. What greatness had not floated on the ebb of that river into the mystery of an unknown earth! . . . The dreams of men, the seed of commonwealths, the germs of empires.

The sun set; the dusk fell on the stream, and lights began to appear along the shore. The Chapman lighthouse, a three-legged thing erect on a mud-flat, shone strongly. Lights of ships moved in the fairway — a great stir of lights going up and going down. And farther west on the upper reaches the place of the monstrous town was still marked ominously on the sky, a brooding gloom in sunshine, a lurid glare under the stars.

"And this also," said Marlow suddenly, "has been one of the dark places of the earth."

He was the only man of us who still "followed the sea." The worst that could be said of him was that he did not represent his class. He was a seaman, but he was a wanderer, too, while most seamen lead, if one may so express it, a sedentary life. Their minds are of the stay-at-home order, and their home is always with them—the ship; and so is their country—the sea. One ship is very much like another, and the sea is always the same. In the immutability of their surroundings the foreign shores, the foreign faces, the changing immensity of life, glide past, veiled not by a sense of mystery but by a slightly disdainful ignorance; for there is nothing mysterious to a seaman unless it be the sea itself, which is the mistress of his existence and as inscrutable as Destiny. For the rest, after his hours of work, a casual stroll or a casual spree on shore suffices to unfold for him the secret of a whole continent, and generally he finds the secret not worth knowing. The yarns of seamen have a direct simplicity, the whole meaning of which lies within the shell of a cracked nut. But Marlow was not typical (if his propensity to spin yarns be excepted), and to him the meaning of an episode was not inside like a kernel but outside, enveloping the tale which brought it out only as a glow brings out a haze, in the likeness of one of these misty halos that sometimes are made visible by the spectral illumination of moonshine.

His remark did not seem at all surprising. It was just like Marlow. It was accepted in silence. No one took the trouble to grunt even; and presently he said, very slow—

"I was thinking of very old times, when the Romans first came here, nineteen hundred years ago—the other day. . . . Light came out of this river since—you say Knights? Yes; but it is like a running blaze on a plain, like a flash of lightning in the clouds. We live in the flicker—may it last as long as the old earth keeps rolling! But darkness was here yesterday. Imagine the feelings of a commander of a fine—what d'ye call 'em?—trireme in the Mediterranean, ordered suddenly to the north; run overland across the Gauls in a hurry; put in charge of one of these craft the legionaries—a wonderful lot of handy men they must have been, too—used to build, apparently by the hundred, in a month or two, if we may believe what we read. Imagine him here—the very end of the world, a sea the colour of lead, a sky the colour of smoke, a kind of ship about as rigid as a concertina—and going up this river with stores, or orders, or what you like. Sandbanks, marshes, forests, savages,—precious little to eat fit for a civilized man, nothing but Thames water to drink. No Falernian wine here, no going ashore. Here and there a military camp lost in a wilderness, like a needle in a bundle of hay—cold, fog, tempests, disease, exile, and death,—death skulking in the air, in the water, in the bush. They must have been dying like flies here. Oh, yes—he did it. Did it very well, too, no doubt, and without thinking much about it either, except afterwards to brag of what he had gone through, in his time, perhaps. They were men enough to face the darkness. And perhaps he was cheered by keeping his eye on a chance of promotion to the fleet at Ravenna by-and-by, if he had good friends in Rome and survived the awful climate. Or think of a decent young citizen in a toga—perhaps too much dice, you know—coming out here in the train of some prefect, or taxgatherer, or trader even, to mend his fortunes. Land in a swamp, march through the woods, and in some inland post feel the savagery, the utter savagery, had closed round him, — all that mysterious life of the wilderness that stirs in the forest, in the jungles, in the hearts of wild men. There's no initiation either into such mysteries. He has to live in the midst of the incomprehensible, which is also detestable. And it has a fascination, too, that goes to work upon him. The fascination of the abomination — you know, imagine the growing regrets, the longing to escape, the powerless disgust, the surrender, the hate."

He paused.

"Mind," he began again, lifting one arm from the elbow, the palm of the hand outwards, so that, with his legs folded before him, he had the pose of a Buddha preaching in European clothes and without a lotus-flower — "Mind, none of us would feel exactly like this. What saves us is efficiency — the devotion to efficiency. But these chaps were not much account, really. They were no colonists; their administration was merely a squeeze, and nothing more, I suspect. They were conquerors, and for that you want only brute force — nothing to boast of, when you have it, since your strength is just an accident arising from the weakness of others. They grabbed what they could get for the sake of what was to be got. It was just robbery with violence, aggravated murder on a great scale, and men going at it blind — as is very proper for those who tackle a darkness. The conquest of the earth, which mostly means the taking it away from those who have a different complexion or slightly flatter noses than ourselves, is not a pretty thing when you look into it too much. What redeems it is the idea only. An idea at the back of it; not a sentimental pretence but an idea; and an unselfish belief in the idea — something you can set up, and bow down before, and offer a sacrifice to. . . ."

He broke off. Flames glided in the river, small green flames, red flames, white flames, pursuing, overtaking, joining, crossing each other — then separating slowly or hastily. The traffic of the great city went on in the deepening night upon the sleepless river. We looked on, waiting patiently — there was nothing else to do till the end of the flood; but it was only after a long silence, when he said, in a hesitating voice, "I suppose you fellows remember I did once turn freshwater sailor for a bit," that we knew we were fated, before the ebb began to run, to hear about one of Marlow's inconclusive experiences.

"I don't want to bother you much with what happened to me personally," he began, showing in this remark the weakness of many tellers of tales who seem so often unaware of what their audience would best like to hear; "yet to understand the effect of it on me you ought to know how I got out there, what I saw, how I went up that river to the place where I first met the poor chap. It was the farthest point of navigation and the culminating point of my experience. It seemed somehow to throw a kind of light on everything about me — and into my thoughts. It was sombre enough, too — and pitiful — not extraordinary in any way — not very clear either. No, not very clear. And yet it seemed to throw a kind of light.

"I had then, as you remember, just returned to London after a lot of Indian Ocean, Pacific, China Seas — a regular dose of the East — six years or so, and I was loafing about, hindering you fellows in your work and invading your homes, just as though I had got a heavenly mission to civilize you. It was very fine for a time, but after a bit I did get tired of resting. Then I began to look for a ship — I should think the hardest work on earth. But the ships wouldn't even look at me. And I got tired of that game, too.

"Now when I was a little chap I had a passion for maps. I would look for hours at South America, or Africa, or Australia, and lose myself in all the glories of exploration. At that time there were many blank spaces on the earth and when I saw one that looked particularly inviting on a map (but they all look that) I would put my finger on it and say, When I grow up I will go there. The North Pole was one of these places, I remember. Well, I haven't been there yet, and shall not try now. The glamour's off. Other places were scattered about the Equator, and in every sort of latitude all over the two hemispheres. I have been in some of them, and . . . well, we won't talk about that. But there was one yet—the biggest, the most blank, so to speak—that I had a hankering after.

"True, by this time it was not a blank space any more. It had got filled since my boyhood with rivers and lakes and names. It had ceased to be a blank space of delightful mystery—a white patch for a boy to dream gloriously over. It had become a place of darkness. But there was in it one river especially, a mighty big river, that you could see on the map, resembling an immense snake uncoiled, with its head in the sea, its body at rest curving afar over a vast country, and its tail lost in the depths of the land. And as I looked at the map of it in a shop window, it fascinated me as a snake would a bird—a silly little bird. Then I remembered there was a big concern, a Company for trade on that river. Dash it all! I thought to myself, they can't trade without using some kind of craft on that lot of fresh water—steamboats! Why shouldn't I try to get charge of one? I went on along Fleet Street, but could not shake off the idea. The snake had charmed me.

"You understand it was a Continental concern, that Trading society; but I have a lot of relations living on the Continent, because it's cheap and not so nasty as it looks, they say.

"I am sorry to own I began to worry them. This was already a fresh departure for me. I was not used to get things that way, you know. I always went my own road and on my own legs where I had a mind to go. I wouldn't have believed it of myself; but, then—you see—I felt somehow I must get there by hook or by crook. So I worried them. The men said 'My dear fellow,' and did nothing. Then—would you believe it?—I tried the women. I, Charles Marlow, set the women to work—to get a job. Heavens! Well, you see, the notion drove me. I had an aunt, a dear enthusiastic soul. She wrote: 'It will be delightful. I am ready to do anything, anything for you. It is a glorious idea. I know the wife of a very high personage in the Administration, and also a man who has lots of influence with,' etc., etc. She was determined to make no end of fuss to get me appointed skipper of a river steamboat, if such was my fancy.

"I got my appointment—of course; and I got it very quick. It appears the Company had received news that one of their captains had been killed in a scuffle with the natives. This was my chance, and it made me the more anxious to go. It was only months and months afterwards, when I made the attempt to recover what was left of the body, that I heard the original quarrel arose from a misunderstanding about some hens. Yes, two black hens. Fresleven—that was the fellow's name, a Dane—thought himself wronged somehow in the bargain, so he went ashore and started to hammer the chief of the village with a stick. Oh, it didn't surprise me in the least to hear this, and at the same time to be told that Fresleven was the gentlest, quietest creature that ever walked on two legs. No doubt he was; but he had been a couple of years already out there engaged in the noble cause, you know, and he probably felt the need at last of asserting his self-respect in some way. Therefore he whacked the old nigger mercilessly, while a big crowd of his people watched him, thunderstruck, till some man — I was told the chief's son — in desperation at hearing the old chap yell, made a tentative jab with a spear at the white man — and of course it went quite easy between the shoulder blades. Then the whole population cleared into the forest, expecting all kinds of calamities to happen, while, on the other hand, the steamer Fresleven commanded left also in a bad panic, in charge of the engineer, I believe. Afterwards nobody seemed to trouble much about Fresleven's remains, till I got out and stepped into his shoes. I couldn't let it rest, though; but when an opportunity offered at last to meet my predecessor, the grass growing through his ribs was tall enough to hide his bones. They were all there. The supernatural being had not been touched after he fell. And the village was deserted, the huts gaped black, rotting, all askew within the fallen enclosures. A calamity had come to it, sure enough. The people had vanished. Mad terror had scattered them, men, women, and children, through the bush, and they had never returned. What became of the hens I don't know either. I should think the cause of progress got them, anyhow. However, through this glorious affair I got my appointment, before I had fairly begun to hope for it.

"I flew around like mad to get ready, and before forty-eight hours I was crossing the Channel to show myself to my employers, and sign the contract. In a very few hours I arrived in a city that always makes me think of a whited sepulchre. Prejudice no doubt. I had no difficulty in finding the Company's offices. It was the biggest thing in the town, and everybody I met was full of it. They were going to run an over-sea empire, and make no end of coin by trade.

"A narrow and deserted street in deep shadow, high houses, innumerable windows with venetian blinds, a dead silence, grass sprouting between the stones, imposing carriage archways right and left, immense double doors standing ponderously ajar. I slipped through one of these cracks, went up a swept and ungarnished staircase, as arid as a desert, and opened the first door I came to. Two women, one fat and the other slim, sat on straw-bottomed chairs, knitting black wool. The slim one got up and walked straight at me — still knitting with downcast eyes — and only just as I began to think of getting out of her way, as you would for a somnambulist, stood still, and looked up. Her dress was as plain as an umbrella-cover, and she turned round without a word and preceded me into a waiting-room. I gave my name, and looked about. Deal table in the middle, plain chairs all round the walls, on one end a large shining map, marked with all the colours of a rainbow. There was a vast amount of red — good to see at any time, because one knows that some real work is done in there, a deuce of a lot of blue, a little green, smears of orange, and, on the East Coast, a purple patch, to show where the jolly pioneers of progress drink the jolly lager-beer. However, I wasn't going into any of these. I was going into the yellow. Dead in the centre. And the river was there — fascinating — deadly — like a snake. Ough! A door opened, a white-haired secretarial head, but wearing a compassionate expression, appeared, and a skinny forefinger beckoned me into the sanctuary. Its light was dim, and a heavy writing-desk squatted in the middle. From behind that structure came out an impression of pale plumpness in a frock coat. The great man himself. He was five feet six, I should judge, and had his grip on the handle-end of ever so many millions. He shook hands, I fancy, murmured vaguely, was satisfied with my French. *Bon voyage.*

"In about forty-five seconds I found myself again in the waiting-room with the compassionate secretary, who, full of desolation and sympathy, made me sign some document. I believe I undertook amongst other things not to disclose any trade secrets. Well, I am not going to.

"I began to feel slightly uneasy. You know I am not used to such ceremonies, and there was something ominous in the atmosphere. It was just as though I had been let into some conspiracy — I don't know — something not quite right; and I was glad to get out. In the outer room the two women knitted black wool feverishly. People were arriving, and the younger one was walking back and forth introducing them. The old one sat on her chair. Her flat cloth slippers were propped up on a foot-warmer, and a cat reposed on her lap. She wore a starched white affair on her head, had a wart on one cheek, and silver-rimmed spectacles hung on the tip of her nose. She glanced at me above the glasses. The swift and indifferent placidity of that look troubled me. Two youths with foolish and cheery countenances were being piloted over, and she threw at them the same quick glance of unconcerned wisdom. She seemed to know all about them and about me, too. An eerie feeling came over me. She seemed uncanny and fateful. Often far away there I thought of these two, guarding the door of Darkness, knitting black wool as for a warm pall, one introducing, introducing continuously to the unknown, the other scrutinizing the cheery and foolish faces with unconcerned old eyes. *Ave!* Old knitter of black wool. *Morituri te salutant.* Not many of those she looked at ever saw her again — not half, by a long way.

"There was yet a visit to the doctor. 'A simple formality,' assured me the secretary, with an air of taking an immense part in all my sorrows. Accordingly a young chap wearing his hat over the left eyebrow, some clerk I suppose, — there must have been clerks in the business, though the house was as still as a house in a city of the dead — came from somewhere up-stairs, and led me forth. He was shabby and careless, with ink-stains on the sleeves of his jacket, and his cravat was large and billowy, under a chin shaped like the toe of an old boot. It was a little too early for the doctor, so I proposed a drink, and thereupon he developed a vein of joviality. As we sat over our vermouths he glorified the Company's business, and by-and-by I expressed casually my surprise at him not going out there. He became very cool and collected all at once. 'I am not such a fool as I look, quoth Plato to his disciples,' he said sententiously, emptied his glass with great resolution, and we rose.

"The old doctor felt my pulse, evidently thinking of something else the while. 'Good, good for there,' he mumbled, and then with a certain eagerness asked me whether I would let him measure my head. Rather surprised, I said Yes, when he produced a thing like calipers and got the dimensions back and front and every way, taking notes carefully. He was an unshaven little man in a threadbare coat like a gaberdine, with his feet in slippers, and I thought him a harmless fool. 'I always ask leave, in the interests of science, to measure the crania of those going out there,' he said. 'And when they come back, too?' I asked. 'Oh, I never see them,' he remarked; 'and, moreover, the changes take place inside, you know.' He smiled, as if at some quiet joke. 'So you are going out there.

Famous. Interesting, too.' He gave me a searching glance, and made another note. 'Ever any madness in your family?' he asked, in a matter-of-fact tone. I felt very annoyed. 'Is that question in the interests of science, too?' 'It would be,' he said, without taking notice of my irritation, 'interesting for science to watch the mental changes of individuals, on the spot, but . . .' 'Are you an alienist?' I interrupted. 'Every doctor should be — a little,' answered that original, imperturbably. 'I have a little theory which you Messieurs who go out there must help me to prove. This is my share in the advantages my country shall reap from the possession of such a magnificent dependency. The mere wealth I leave to others. Pardon my questions, but you are the first Englishman coming under my observation . . .' I hastened to assure him I was not in the least typical. 'If I were,' said I, 'I wouldn't be talking like this with you.' 'What you say is rather profound, and probably erroneous,' he said, with a laugh. 'Avoid irritation more than exposure to the sun. Adieu. How do you English say, eh? Good-bye. Ah! Good-bye. Adieu. In the tropics one must before everything keep calm.' . . . He lifted a warning forefinger. . . . '*Du calme, du calme. Adieu.*'

"One thing more remained to do — say good-bye to my excellent aunt. I found her triumphant. I had a cup of tea — the last decent cup of tea for many days — and in a room that most soothingly looked just as you would expect a lady's drawing-room to look, we had a long quiet chat by the fireside. In the course of these confidences it became quite plain to me I had been represented to the wife of the high dignitary, and goodness knows to how many more people besides, as an exceptional and gifted creature — a piece of good fortune for the Company — a man you don't get hold of every day. Good heavens; and I was going to take charge of a two-penny-half-penny river-steamboat with a penny whistle attached! It appeared, however, I was also one of the Workers, with a capital — you know. Something like an emissary of light, something like a lower sort of apostle. There had been a lot of such rot let loose in print and talk just about that time, and the excellent woman, living right in the rush of all that humbug, got carried off her feet. She talked about 'weaning those ignorant millions from their horrid ways,' till, upon my word, she made me quite uncomfortable. I ventured to hint that the Company was run for profit.

"'You forget, dear Charlie, that the labourer is worthy of his hire,' she said, brightly. It's queer how out of touch with truth women are. They live in a world of their own, and there had never been anything like it, and never can be. It is too beautiful altogether, and if they were to set it up it would go to pieces before the first sunset. Some confounded fact we men have been living contentedly with ever since the day of creation would start up and knock the whole thing over.

"After this I got embraced, told to wear flannel, be sure to write often, and so on — and I left. In the street — I don't know why — a queer feeling came to me that I was an impostor. Odd thing that I, who used to clear out for any part of the world at twenty-four hours' notice, with less thought than most men give to the crossing of a street, had a moment — I won't say of hesitation, but of startled pause, before this commonplace affair. The best way I can explain it to you is by saying that, for a second or two, I felt as though, instead of going to the centre of a continent, I were about to set off for the centre of the earth.

"I left in a French steamer, and she called in every blamed port they have out there, for, as far as I could see, the sole purpose of landing soldiers and custom-house officers. I watched the coast. Watching a coast as it slips by the ship is like thinking about an enigma. There it is before you — smiling, frowning, inviting, grand, mean, insipid, or savage, and always mute with an air of whispering. Come and find out. This one was almost featureless, as if still in the making, with an aspect of monotonous grimness. The edge of a colossal jungle, so dark-green as to be almost black, fringed with white surf, ran straight, like a ruled line, far, far away along a blue sea whose glitter was blurred by a creeping mist. The sun was fierce, the land seemed to glisten and drip with steam. Here and there grayish whitish specks showed up clustered inside the white surf, with a flag flying above them perhaps. Settlements some centuries old, and still no bigger than pin-heads on the untouched expanse of their background. We pounded along, stopped, landed soldiers; went on, landed custom-house clerks to levy toll in what looked like a God-forsaken wilderness, with a tin shed and a flag-pole lost in it; landed more soldiers—to take care of the custom-house clerks, presumably. Some, I heard, got drowned in the surf; but whether they did or not, nobody seemed particularly to care. They were just flung out there, and on we went. Every day the coast looked the same, as though we had not moved; but we passed various places — trading places — with names like Gran' Bassam, Little Popo; names that seemed to belong to some sordid farce acted in front of a sinister black-cloth. The idleness of a passenger, my isolation amongst all these men with whom I had no point of contact, the oily and languid sea, the uniform sombreness of the coast, seemed to keep me away from the truth of things, within the toil of a mournful and senseless delusion. The voice of the surf heard now and then was a positive pleasure, like the speech of a brother. It was something natural, that had its reason, that had a meaning. Now and then a boat from the shore gave one a momentary contact with reality. It was paddled by black fellows. You could see from afar the white of their eyeballs glistening. They shouted, sang; their bodies streamed with perspiration; they had faces like grotesque masks — these chaps; but they had bone, muscle, a wild vitality, an intense energy of movement, that was as natural and true as the surf along their coast. They wanted no excuse for being there. They were a great comfort to look at. For a time I would feel I belonged still to a world of straight-forward facts; but the feeling would not last long. Something would turn up to scare it away. Once, I remember, we came upon a man-of-war anchored off the coast. There wasn't even a shed there, and she was shelling the bush. It appears the French had one of their wars going on thereabouts. Her ensign dropped limp like a rag; the muzzles of the long six-inch guns stuck out all over the low hull; the greasy, slimy swell swung her up lazily and let her down, swaying her thin masts. In the empty immensity of earth, sky, and water, there she was, incomprehensible, firing into a continent. Pop, would go one of the six-inch guns; a small flame would dart and vanish, a little white smoke would disappear, a tiny projectile would give a feeble screech — and nothing happened. Nothing could happen. There was a touch of insanity in the proceeding, a sense of lugubrious drollery in the sight; and it was not dissipated by somebody on board assuring me earnestly there was a camp of natives — he called them enemies! — hidden out of sight somewhere.

"We gave her her letters (I heard the men in that lonely ship were dying of fever at the rate of three-a-day) and went on. We called at some more places with farcical names, where the merry dance of death and trade goes on in a still and earthy atmosphere as of an over-heated catacomb; all along the formless coast bordered by dangerous surf, as if Nature herself had tried to ward off intruders; in and out of rivers, streams of death in life, whose banks were rotting into mud, whose waters, thickened into slime, invaded the contorted mangroves, that seemed to writhe at us in the extremity of an impotent despair. Nowhere did we stop long enough to get a particularized impression, but the general sense of vague and oppressive wonder grew upon me. It was like a weary pilgrimage amongst hints for nightmares.

"It was upward of thirty days before I saw the mouth of the big river. We anchored off the seat of the government. But my work would not begin till some two hundred miles farther on. So as soon as I could I made a start for a place thirty miles higher up.

"I had my passage on a little sea-going steamer. Her captain was a Swede, and knowing me for a seaman, invited me on the bridge. He was a young man, lean, fair, and morose, with lanky hair and a shuffling gait. As we left the miserable little wharf, he tossed his head contemptuously at the shore. 'Been living there?' he asked. I said 'Yes.' 'Fine lot these government chaps—are they not?' he went on, speaking English with great precision and considerable bitterness. 'It is funny what some people will do for a few francs a month. I wonder what becomes of that kind when it goes up country?' I said to him I expected to see that soon. 'So-o-o!' he exclaimed. He shuffled athwart, keeping one eye ahead vigilantly. 'Don't be too sure,' he continued. 'The other day I took up a man who hanged himself on the road. He was a Swede, too.' 'Hanged himself! Why, in God's name?' I cried. He kept on looking out watchfully. 'Who knows? The sun too much for him, or the country perhaps.'

"At last we opened a reach. A rocky cliff appeared, mounds of turned-up earth by the shore, houses on a hill, others with iron roofs, amongst a waste of excavations, or hanging to the declivity. A continuous noise of the rapids above hovered over this scene of inhabited devastation. A lot of people, mostly black and naked, moved about like ants. A jetty projected into the river. A blinding sunlight drowned all this at times in a sudden recrudescence of glare. 'There's your Company's station,' said the Swede, pointing to three wooden barrack-like structures on the rocky slope. 'I will send your things up. Four boxes did you say? So. Farewell.'

"I came upon a boiler wallowing in the grass, then found a path leading up the hill. It turned aside for the boulders, and also for an undersized railway-truck lying there on its back with its wheels in the air. One was off. The thing looked as dead as the carcass of some animal. I came upon more pieces of decaying machinery, a stack of rusty rails. To the left a clump of trees made a shady spot, where dark things seemed to stir feebly. I blinked, the path was steep. A horn tooted to the right, and I saw the black people run. A heavy and dull detonation shook the ground, a puff of smoke came out of the cliff, and that was all. No change appeared on the face of the rock. They were building a railway. The cliff was not in the way or anything; but this objectless blasting was all the work going on.

"A slight clinking behind me made me turn my head. Six black men advanced in a file, toiling up the path. They walked erect and slow, balancing small baskets full of earth on their heads, and the clink kept time with their footsteps.

Black rags were wound round their loins, and the short ends behind waggled to and fro like tails. I could see every rib, the joints of their limbs were like knots in a rope; each had an iron collar on his neck, and all were connected together with a chain whose bights swung between them, rhythmically clinking. Another report from the cliff made me think suddenly of that ship of war I had seen firing into a continent. It was the same kind of ominous voice; but these men could by no stretch of imagination be called enemies. They were called criminals, and the outraged law, like the bursting shells, had come to them, an insoluble mystery from the sea. All their meagre breasts panted together, the violently dilated nostrils quivered, the eyes stared stonily up-hill. They passed me within six inches, without a glance, with that complete, deathlike indifference of unhappy savages. Behind this raw matter one of the reclaimed, the product of the new forces at work, strolled despondently, carrying a rifle by its middle. He had a uniform jacket with one button off, and seeing a white man on the path, hoisted his weapon to his shoulder with alacrity. This was simple prudence, white men being so much alike at a distance that he could not tell who I might be. He was speedily reassured, and with a large, white, rascally grin, and a glance at his charge, seemed to take me into partnership in his exalted trust. After all, I also was a part of the great cause of these high and just proceedings.

"Instead of going up, I turned and descended to the left. My idea was to let that chain-gang get out of sight before I climbed the hill. You know I am not particularly tender; I've had to strike and to fend off. I've had to resist and to attack sometimes — that's only one way of resisting — without counting the exact cost, according to the demands of such sort of life as I had blundered into. I've seen the devil of violence, and the devil of greed, and the devil of hot desire; but, by all the stars! these were strong, lusty, red-eyed devils, that swayed and drove men — men, I tell you. But as I stood on this hillside, I foresaw that in the blinding sunshine of that land I would become acquainted with a flabby, pretending, weak-eyed devil of a rapacious and pitiless folly. How insidious he could be, too, I was only to find out several months later and a thousand miles farther. For a moment I stood appalled, as though by a warning. Finally I descended the hill, obliquely, toward the trees I had seen.

"I avoided a vast artificial hole somebody had been digging on the slope, the purpose of which I found it impossible to divine. It wasn't a quarry or a sandpit, anyhow. It was just a hole. It might have been connected with the philanthropic desire of giving the criminals something to do. I don't know. Then I nearly fell into a very narrow ravine, almost no more than a scar in the hillside. I discovered that a lot of imported drainage-pipes for the settlement had been tumbled in there. There wasn't one that was not broken. It was a wanton smash-up. At last I got under the trees. My purpose was to stroll into the shade for a moment; but no sooner within than it seemed to me I had stepped into the gloomy circle of some Inferno. The rapids were near, and an uninterrupted, uniform, headlong, rushing noise filled the mournful stillness of the grove, where not a breath stirred, not a leaf moved, with a mysterious sound — as though the tearing pace of the launched earth had suddenly become audible.

"Black shapes crouched, lay, sat between the trees leaning against the trunks, clinging to the earth, half coming out, half effaced within the dim light, in all the attitudes of pain, abandonment, and despair. Another mine of the cliff went off, followed by a slight shudder of the soil under my feet. The work was going on. The work! And this was the place where some of the helpers had withdrawn to die.

"They were dying slowly — it was very clear. They were not enemies, they were not criminals, they were nothing earthly now, — nothing but black shadows of disease and starvation, lying confusedly in the greenish gloom. Brought from all the recesses of the coast in all the legality of time contracts; lost in uncongenial surroundings, fed on unfamiliar food, they sickened, became inefficient, and were then allowed to crawl away and rest. These moribund shapes were free as air — and nearly as thin. I began to distinguish the gleam of the eyes under the trees. Then, glancing down, I saw a face near my hand. The black bones reclined at full length with one shoulder against the tree, and slowly the eyelids rose and the sunken eyes looked up at me, enormous and vacant, a kind of blind, white flicker in the depths of the orbs, which died out slowly. The man seemed young — almost a boy — but you know with them it's hard to tell. I found nothing else to do but to offer him one of my good Swede's ship's biscuits I had in my pocket. The fingers closed slowly on it and held — there was no other movement and no other glance. He had tied a bit of white worsted round his neck — Why? Where did he get it? Was it a badge — an ornament — a charm — a propitiatory act? Was there any idea at all connected with it? It looked startling round his black neck, this bit of white thread from beyond the seas.

"Near the same tree two more bundles of acute angles sat with their legs drawn up. One, with his chin propped on his knees, stared at nothing, in an intolerable and appalling manner: his brother phantom rested its forehead, as if overcome with a great weariness; and all about others were scattered in every pose of contorted collapse, as in some picture of a massacre or a pestilence. While I stood horror-struck, one of these creatures rose to his hands and knees, and went off on all-fours towards the river to drink. He lapped out of his hand, then sat up in the sunlight, crossing his shins in front of him, and after a time let his woolly head fall on his breastbone.

"I didn't want any more loitering in the shade, and I made haste towards the station. When near the buildings I met a white man, in such an expected elegance of get-up that in the first moment I took him for a sort of vision. I saw a high starched collar, white cuffs, a light alpaca jacket, snowy trousers, a clear necktie, and varnished boots. No hat. Hair parted, brushed, oiled, under a green-lined parasol held in a big white hand. He was amazing, and had a penholder behind his ear.

"I shook hands with this miracle, and I learned he was the Company's chief accountant, and that all the book-keeping was done at this station. He had come out for a moment, he said, 'to get a breath of fresh air.' The expression sounded wonderfully odd, with its suggestion of sedentary desk-life. I wouldn't have mentioned the fellow to you at all, only it was from his lips that I first heard the name of the man who is so indissolubly connected with the memories of that time. Moreover, I respected the fellow. Yes; I respected his collars, his vast cuffs, his brushed hair. His appearance was certainly that of a hairdresser's dummy; but in the great demoralization of the land he kept up his appearance. That's backbone. His starched collars and got-up shirtfronts were achievements of character. He had been out nearly three years; and later, I could not help asking him how he managed to sport such linen. He had just the faintest blush, and said modestly, 'I've been teaching one of the native women about the station. It was difficult. She had a distaste for the work.' Thus this man had verily accomplished something. And he was devoted to his books, which were in apple-pie order.

"Everything else in the station was in a muddle, — heads, things, buildings. Strings of dusty niggers with splay feet arrived and departed; a stream of manufactured goods, rubbishy cottons, beads, and brass-wire sent into the depths of darkness, and in return came a precious trickle of ivory.

"I had to wait in the station for ten days — an eternity. I lived in a hut in the yard, but to be out of the chaos I would sometimes get into the accountant's office. It was built of horizontal planks, and so badly put together that, as he bent over his high desk, he was barred from neck to heels with narrow strips of sunlight. There was no need to open the big shutter to see. It was hot there, too; big flies buzzed fiendishly, and did not sting, but stabbed. I sat generally on the floor, while, of faultless appearance (and even slightly scented), perching on a high stool, he wrote, he wrote. Sometimes he stood up for exercise. When a truckle-bed with a sick man (some invalid agent from upcountry) was put in there, he exhibited a gentle annoyance. 'The groans of this sick person,' he said, 'distract my attention. And without that it is extremely difficult to guard against clerical errors in this climate.'

"One day he remarked, without lifting his head, 'In the interior you will no doubt meet Mr. Kurtz.' On my asking who Mr. Kurtz was, he said he was a first-class agent; and seeing my disappointment at this information, he added slowly, laying down his pen, 'He is a very remarkable person.' Further questions elicited from him that Mr. Kurtz was at present in charge of a trading post, a very important one, in the true ivory-country, at 'the very bottom of there. Sends in as much ivory as all the others put together . . .' He began to write again. The sick man was too ill to groan. The flies buzzed in a great peace.

"Suddenly there was a growing murmur of voices and a great tramping of feet. A caravan had come in. A violent babble of uncouth sounds burst out on the other side of the planks. All the carriers were speaking together, and in the midst of the uproar the lamentable voice of the chief agent was heard 'giving it up' tearfully for the twentieth time that day . . . He rose slowly. 'What a frightful row,' he said. He crossed the room gently to look at the sick man, and returning, said to me, 'He does not hear.' 'What! Dead?' I asked, startled. 'No, not yet,' he answered, with great composure. Then, alluding with a toss of the head to the tumult in the station-yard, 'When one has got to make correct entries, one comes to hate those savages — hate them to the death.' He remained thoughtful for a moment. 'When you see Mr. Kurtz,' he went on, 'tell him from me that everything here' — he glanced at the desk — 'is very satisfactory. I don't like to write to him — with those messengers of ours you never know who may get hold of your letter — at that Central Station.' He stared at me for a moment with his mild, bulging eyes. 'Oh, he will go far, very far,' he began again. 'He will be a somebody in the Administration before long. They, above — the Council in Europe, you know — mean him to be.'

"He turned to his work. The noise outside had ceased, and presently in going out I stopped at the door. In the steady buzz of flies the homeward-bound agent was lying flushed and insensible; the other, bent over his books, was making correct entries of perfectly correct transactions; and fifty feet below the doorstep I could see the still tree-tops of the grove of death.

"Next day I left that station at last, with a caravan of sixty men, for a two hundred-mile tramp.

"No use telling you much about that. Paths, paths, everywhere; a stamped-in network of paths spreading over the empty land, through long grass, through burnt grass, through thickets, down and up chilly ravines, up and down stony hills ablaze with heat; and a solitude, a solitude, nobody, not a hut. The population had cleared out a long time ago. Well, if a lot of mysterious niggers armed with all kinds of fearful weapons suddenly took to travelling on the road between Deal and Gravesend, catching the yokels right and left to carry heavy loads for them, I fancy every farm and cottage thereabouts would get empty very soon. Only here the dwellings were gone, too. Still I passed through several abandoned villages. There's something pathetically childish in the ruins of grass walls. Day after day, with the stamp and shuffle of sixty pair of bare feet behind me, each pair under a 60-lb. load. Camp, cook, sleep, strike camp, march. Now and then a carrier dead in harness, at rest in the long grass near the path, with an empty water-gourd and his long staff lying by his side. A great silence around and above. Perhaps on some quiet night the tremor of far-off drums, sinking, swelling, a tremor vast, faint; a sound weird, appealing, suggestive, and wild—and perhaps with as profound a meaning as the sound of bells in a Christian country. Once a white man in an unbuttoned uniform, camping on the path with an armed escort of lank Zanzibaris, very hospitable and festive—not to say drunk. Was looking after the upkeep of the road he declared. Can't say I saw any road or any upkeep, unless the body of a middle-aged negro, with a bullet-hole in the forehead, upon which I absolutely stumbled three miles farther on, may be considered as a permanent improvement. I had a white companion, too, not a bad chap, but rather too fleshy and with the exasperating habit of fainting on the hot hillsides, miles away from the least bit of shade and water. Annoying, you know, to hold your own coat like a parasol over a man's head while he is coming-to. I couldn't help asking him once what he meant by coming there at all. 'To make money, of course. What do you think?' he said, scornfully. Then he got fever, and had to be carried in a hammock slung under a pole. As he weighed sixteen stone I had no end of rows with the carriers. They jibbed, ran away, sneaked off with their loads in the night—quite a mutiny. So, one evening, I made a speech in English with gestures, not one of which was lost to the sixty pairs of eyes before me, and the next morning I started the hammock off in front all right. An hour afterwards I came upon the whole concern wrecked in a bush—man, hammock, groans, blankets, horrors. The heavy pole had skinned his poor nose. He was very anxious for me to kill somebody, but there wasn't the shadow of a carrier near. I remembered the old doctor,—'It would be interesting for science to watch the mental changes of individuals, on the spot.' I felt I was becoming scientifically interesting. However, all that is to no purpose. On the fifteenth day I came in sight of the big river again, and hobbled into the Central Station. It was on a back water surrounded by scrub and forest, with a pretty border of smelly mud on one side, and on the three others enclosed by a crazy fence of rushes. A neglected gap was all the gate it had, and the first glance at the place was enough to let you see the flabby devil was running that show. White men with long staves in their hands appeared languidly from amongst the buildings, strolling up to take a look at me, and then retired out of sight somewhere. One of them, a stout, excitable chap with black moustaches, informed me with great volubility and many digressions, as soon as I told him who I was, that my steamer was at the bottom of the river. I was thunderstruck. What, how, why? Oh, it was 'all right.' The 'manager himself' was there. All quite correct. 'Everybody had behaved splendidly! splendidly!' — 'you must,' he said in agitation, 'go and see the general manager at once. He is waiting!'

"I did not see the real significance of that wreck at once. I fancy I see it now, but I am not sure — not at all. Certainly the affair was too stupid — when I think of it — to be altogether natural. Still . . . But at the moment it presented itself simply as a confounded nuisance. The steamer was sunk. They had started two days before in a sudden hurry up the river with the manager on board, in charge of some volunteer skipper, and before they had been out three hours they tore the bottom out of her on stones, and she sank near the south bank. I asked myself what I was to do there, now my boat was lost. As a matter of fact, I had plenty to do in fishing my command out of the river. I had to set about it the very next day. That, and the repairs when I brought the pieces to the station, took some months.

"My first interview with the manager was curious. He did not ask me to sit down after my twenty-mile walk that morning. He was commonplace in complexion, in feature, in manners, and in voice. He was of middle size and of ordinary build. His eyes, of the usual blue, were perhaps remarkably cold, and he certainly could make his glance fall on one as trenchant and heavy as an axe. But even at these times the rest of his person seemed to disclaim the intention. Otherwise there was only an indefinable, faint expression of his lips, something stealthy — a smile — not a smile — I remember it, but I can't explain. It was unconscious, this smile was, though just after he had said something it got intensified for an instant. It came at the end of his speeches like a seal applied on the words to make the meaning of the commonest phrase appear absolutely inscrutable. He was a common trader, from his youth up employed in these parts — nothing more. He was obeyed, yet he inspired neither love nor fear, nor even respect. He inspired uneasiness. That was it! Uneasiness. Not a definite mistrust — just uneasiness — nothing more. You have no idea how effective such a . . . a . . . faculty can be. He had no genius for organizing, for initiative, or for order even. That was evident in such things as the deplorable state of the station. He had no learning, and no intelligence. His position had come to him — why? Perhaps because he was never ill . . . He had served three terms of three years out there . . . Because triumphant health in the general rout of constitutions is a kind of power in itself. When he went home on leave he rioted on a large scale — pompously. Jack ashore — with a difference — in externals only. This one could gather from his casual talk. He originated nothing, he could keep the routine going — that's all. But he was great. He was great by this little thing that it was impossible to tell what could control such a man. He never gave that secret away. Perhaps there was nothing within him. Such a suspicion made one pause — for out there were no external checks. Once when various tropical diseases had laid low almost every 'agent' in the station, he was heard to say, 'Men who come out here should have no entrails.' He sealed the utterance with that smile of his, as though it had been a door opening into a darkness he had in his keeping. You fancied you had seen things—but the seal was on. When annoyed at meal-times by the constant quarrels of the white men about precedence, he ordered an immense round table to be made, for which a special house had to be built. This was the station's messroom. Where he sat was the first place—the rest were nowhere. One felt this to be his unalterable conviction. He was neither civil nor uncivil. He was quiet. He allowed his 'boy'—an overfed young negro from the coast—to treat the white men, under his very eyes, with provoking insolence.

"He began to speak as soon as he saw me. I had been very long on the road. He could not wait. Had to start without me. The up-river stations had to be relieved. There had been so many delays already that he did not know who was dead and who was alive, and how they got on—and so on, and so on. He paid no attention to my explanations, and, playing with a stick of sealing-wax, repeated several times that the situation was 'very grave, very grave.' There were rumours that a very important station was in jeopardy, and its chief, Mr. Kurtz, was ill. Hoped it was not true. Mr. Kurtz was . . . I felt weary and irritable. Hang Kurtz, I thought. I interrupted him by saying I had heard of Mr. Kurtz on the coast. 'Ah! So they talk of him down there,' he murmured to himself. Then he began again, assuring me Mr. Kurtz was the best agent he had, an exceptional man, of the greatest importance to the company; therefore I could understand his anxiety. He was, he said, 'very, very uneasy.' Certainly he fidgeted on his chair a good deal, exclaimed, 'Ah, Mr. Kurtz!' broke the stick of sealing-wax and seemed dumfounded by the accident. Next thing he wanted to know 'how long it would take to' . . . I interrupted him again. Being hungry, you know, and kept on my feet, too, I was getting savage. 'How could I tell?' I said, 'I hadn't even seen the wreck yet—some months, no doubt.' All this talk seemed to me so futile. 'Some months,' he said. 'Well, let us say three months before we can make a start. Yes. That ought to do the affair.' I flung out of his hut (he lived all alone in a clay hut with a sort of verandah) muttering to myself my opinion of him. He was a chattering idiot. Afterwards I took it back when it was borne in upon me startlingly with what extreme nicety he had estimated the time requisite for the 'affair.'

"I went to work the next day, turning, so to speak, my back on that station. In that way only it seemed to me I could keep my hold on the redeeming facts of life. Still, one must look about sometimes; and then I saw this station, these men strolling aimlessly about in the sunshine of the yard. I asked myself sometimes what it all meant. They wandered here and there with their absurd long staves in their hands, like a lot of faithless pilgrims bewitched inside a rotten fence. The word 'ivory' rang in the air, was whispered, was sighed. You would think they were praying to it. A taint of imbecile rapacity blew through it all, like a whiff from some corpse. By Jove! I've never seen anything so unreal in my life. And outside, the silent wilderness surrounding this clear speck on the earth struck me as something great and invincible, like evil or truth, waiting patiently for the passing away of this fantastic invasion.

"Oh, these months! Well, never mind. Various things happened. One evening a grass shed full of calico, cotton prints, beads, and I don't know what else, burst into a blaze so suddenly that you would have thought the earth had opened to let an avenging fire consume all that trash. I was smoking my pipe quietly by my dismantled steamer, and saw them all cutting capers in the light, with their arms lifted high, when the stout man with moustaches came tearing down to the river, a tin pail in his hand, assured me that everybody was 'behaving splendidly, splendidly,' dipped about a quart of water and tore back again. I noticed there was a hole in the bottom of his pail.

"I strolled up. There was no hurry. You see the thing had gone off like a box of matches. It had been hopeless from the very first. The flame had leaped high, driven everybody back, lighted up everything—and collapsed. The shed was already a heap of embers glowing fiercely. A nigger was being beaten near by. They said he had caused the fire in some way; be that as it may, he was screeching most horribly. I saw him, later, for several days, sitting in a bit of shade looking very sick and trying to recover himself; afterwards he arose and went out—and the wilderness without a sound took him into its bosom again. As I approached the glow from the dark I found myself at the back of two men, talking. I heard the name of Kurtz pronounced, then the words, 'take advantage of this unfortunate accident.' One of the men was the manager. I wished him a good evening. 'Did you ever see anything like it—eh? it is incredible,' he said, and walked off. The other man remained. He was a first-class agent, young, gentlemanly, a bit re-served, with a forked little beard and a hooked nose. He was standoffish with the other agents, and they on their side said he was the manager's spy upon them. As to me, I had hardly ever spoken to him before. We got into talk, and by-and-by we strolled away from the hissing ruins. Then he asked me to his room, which was in the main building of the station. He struck a match, and I perceived that this young aristocrat had not only a silver-mounted dressing-case but also a whole candle all to himself. Just at that time the manager was the only man supposed to have any right to candles. Native mats covered the clay walls; a collection of spears, assegais, shields, knives was hung up in trophies. The business intrusted to this fellow was the making of bricks—so I had been informed; but there wasn't a fragment of a brick anywhere in the station, and he had been there more than a year—waiting. It seems he could not make bricks without something, I don't know what—straw maybe. Anyways, it could not be found there, and as it was not likely to be sent from Europe, it did not appear clear to me what he was waiting for. An act of special creation perhaps. However, they were all waiting—all the sixteen or twenty pilgrims of them—for something; and upon my word it did not seem an uncongenial occupation, from the way they took it, though the only thing that ever came to them was disease—as far as I could see. They beguiled the time by backbiting and intriguing against each other in a foolish kind of way. There was an air of plotting about that station, but nothing came of it, of course. It was as unreal as everything else—as the philanthropic pretence of the whole concern, as their talk, as their government, as their show of work. The only real feeling was a desire to get appointed to a trading-post where ivory was to be had, so that they could earn percentages. They intrigued and slandered and hated each other only on that account,—but as to effectually lifting a little finger—oh, no. By heavens! there is something after all in the world allowing one man to steal a horse while another must not look at a halter. Steal a horse straight out. Very well. He has done it. Perhaps he can ride. But there is a way of looking at a halter that would provoke the most charitable of saints into a kick.

"I had no idea why he wanted to be sociable, but as we chatted in there it suddenly occurred to me the fellow was trying to get at something—in fact, pumping me. He alluded constantly to Europe, to the people I was supposed to know there—putting leading questions as to my acquaintances in the sepulchral city, and so on. His little eyes glittered like mica discs—with curiosity—though he tried to keep up a bit of superciliousness. At first I was astonished, but very soon I became awfully curious to see what he would find out from me. I couldn't possibly imagine what I had in me to make it worth his while. It was very pretty to see how he baffled himself, for in truth my body was full only of chills, and my head had nothing in it but that wretched steamboat business. It was evident he took me for a perfectly shameless prevaricator. At last he got angry, and, to conceal a movement of furious annoyance, he yawned. I rose. Then I noticed a small sketch in oils, on a panel, representing a woman, draped and blindfolded, carrying a lighted torch. The background was sombre—almost black. The movement of the woman was stately, and the effect of the torch-light on the face was sinister.

"It arrested me, and he stood by civilly, holding an empty half-pint champagne bottle (medical comforts) with the candle stuck in it. To my question he said Mr. Kurtz had painted this—in this very station more than a year ago—while waiting for means to go to his trading-post. 'Tell me, pray,' said I, 'who is this Mr. Kurtz?'

" 'The chief of the Inner Station,' he answered in a short tone, looking away. 'Much obliged,' I said, laughing. 'And you are the brickmaker of the Central Station. Everyone knows that.' He was silent for a while. 'He is a prodigy,' he said at last. 'He is an emissary of pity, and science, and progress, and devil knows what else. We want,' he began to declaim suddenly, 'for the guidance of the cause intrusted to us by Europe, so to speak, higher intelligence, wide sympathies, a singleness of purpose.' 'Who says that?' I asked. 'Lots of them,' he replied. 'Some even write that; and so *he* comes here, a special being, as you ought to know.' 'Why ought I to know?' I interrupted, really surprised. He paid no attention. 'Yes. To-day he is chief of the best station, next year he will be assistant manager, two years more and . . . but I daresay you know what he will be in two years' time. You are of the new gang—the gang of virtue. The same people who sent him specially also recommended you. Oh, don't say no. I've my own eyes to trust.' Light dawned upon me. My dear aunt's influential acquaintances were producing an unexpected effect upon that young man. I nearly burst into a laugh. 'Do you read the Company's confidential correspondence?' I asked. He hadn't a word to say. It was great fun. 'When Mr. Kurtz,' I continued, severely, 'is General Manager, you won't have the opportunity.'

"He blew the candle out suddenly, and we went outside. The moon had risen. Black figures strolled about listlessly, pouring water on the glow, whence proceeded a sound of hissing; steam ascended in the moonlight, the beaten nigger groaned somewhere. 'What a row the brute makes!' said the indefatigable man with the moustaches, appearing near us. 'Serve him right. Transgression—punishment—bang! Pitiless, pitiless. That's the only way. This will prevent all conflagrations for the future. I was just telling the manager . . .' He noticed my companion, and became crestfallen all at once. 'Not in bed yet,' he said, with a kind of servile heartiness; it's so natural. 'Ha! Danger—agitation.' He vanished. I went on to the river-side, and the other followed me. I heard a scathing murmur at my ear, 'Heap of muffs — go to.' The pilgrims could be seen in knots gesticulating, discussing. Several had still their staves in their hands. I verily believe they took these sticks to bed with them. Beyond the fence the forest stood up spectrally in the moonlight, and through the dim stir, through the faint sounds of that lamentable courtyard, the silence of the land went home to one's very heart — its mystery, its greatness, the amazing reality of its concealed life. The hurt nigger moaned feebly somewhere near by, and then fetched a deep sigh that made me mend my pace away from there. I felt a hand introducing itself under my arm. 'My dear sir,' said the fellow. 'I don't want to be misunderstood, and especially by you, who will see Mr. Kurtz long before I can have that pleasure. I wouldn't like him to get a false idea of my disposition. . . .'

"I let him run on, this papier-maché Mephistopheles, and it seemed to me that if I tried I could poke my forefinger through him, and would find nothing inside but a little loose dirt, maybe. He, don't you see, had been planning to be assistant-manager by-and-by under the present man, and I could see that the coming of that Kurtz had upset them both not a little. He talked precipitately, and I did not try to stop him. I had my shoulders against the wreck of my steamer, hauled up on the slope like a carcass of some big river animal. The smell of mud, of primeval mud, by Jove! was in my nostrils, the high stillness of primeval forest was before my eyes; there were shiny patches on the black creek. The moon had spread over everything a thin layer of silver — over the rank grass, over the mud, upon the wall of matted vegetation standing higher than the wall of a temple, over the great river I could see through a sombre gap glittering, glittering, as it flowed broadly by without a murmur. All this was great, expectant, mute, while the man jabbered about himself. I wondered whether the stillness on the face of the immensity looking at us two were meant as an appeal or as a menace. What were we who had strayed in here? Could we handle that dumb thing, or would it handle us? I felt how big, how confoundedly big, was that thing that couldn't talk, and perhaps was deaf as well. What was in there? I could see a little ivory coming out from there, and heard Mr. Kurtz was in there. I had heard enough about it, too — God knows! Yet somehow it didn't bring any image with it — no more than if I had been told an angel or a fiend was in there. I believed it in the same way one of you might believe there are inhabitants in the planet Mars. I knew once a Scotch sailmaker who was certain, dead sure, there were people in Mars. If you asked him for some idea how they looked and behaved, he would get shy and mutter something about 'walking on all-fours.' If you as much as smiled, he would — though a man of sixty — offer to fight you. I would not have gone so far as to fight for Kurtz, but I went for him near enough to a lie. You know I hate, detest, and can't bear a lie, not because I am straighter than the rest of us, but simply because it appals me. There is a taint of death, a flavour of mortality in lies — which is exactly what I hate and detest in the world — what I want to forget. It makes me miserable and sick, like biting something rotten would do. Temperament, I suppose. Well, I went near enough to it by letting the young fool there believe anything he liked to imagine as to my influence in Europe. I became in an instant as much of a pretence as the rest of the bewitched pilgrims. This simply because I had a notion it somehow would be of help to that Kurtz whom at the time I did not see — you understand. He was just a word for me. I did not see the man in the name any more than you do. Do you see him? Do you see the story? Do you see anything? It seems to me I am trying to tell you a dream—making a vain attempt, because no relation of a dream can convey the dream sensation, that commingling of absurdity, surprise, and bewilderment in a tremor of struggling revolt, that notion of being captured by the incredible which is of the very essence of dreams. . . ."

He was silent for a while.

". . . No, it is impossible; it is impossible to convey the life-sensation of any given epoch of one's existence—that which makes its truth, its meaning—its subtle and penetrating essence. It is impossible. We live, as we dream —alone. . . ."

He paused again as if reflecting, then added—

"Of course in this you fellows see more than I could then. You see me, whom you know. . . ."

It had become so pitch dark that we listeners could hardly see one another. For a long time already he, sitting apart, had been no more to us than a voice. There was not a word from anybody. The others might have been asleep, but I was awake. I listened, I listened on the watch for the sentence, for the word, that would give me the clue to the faint uneasiness inspired by this narrative that seemed to shape itself without human lips in the heavy night-air of the river.

". . . Yes—I let him run on," Marlow began again, "and think what he pleased about the powers that were behind me. I did! And there was nothing behind me! There was nothing but that wretched, old, mangled steamboat I was leaning against, while he talked fluently about 'the necessity for every man to get on.' 'And when one comes out here, you conceive, it is not to gaze at the moon.' Mr. Kurtz was a 'universal genius,' but even a genius would find it easier to work with 'adequate tools—intelligent men.' He did not make bricks—why, there was a physical impossibility in the way—as I was well aware; and if he did secretarial work for the manager, it was because 'no sensible man rejects wantonly the confidence of his superiors.' Did I see it? I saw it. What more did I want? What I really wanted was rivets, by heaven! Rivets. To get on with the work—to stop the hole. Rivets I wanted. There were cases of them down at the coast—cases—piled up—burst—split! You kicked a loose rivet at every second step in that station yard on the hillside. Rivets had rolled into the grove of death. You could fill your pockets with rivets for the trouble of stooping down—and there wasn't one rivet to be found where it was wanted. We had plates that would do, but nothing to fasten them with. And every week the messenger, a lone negro, letter-bag on shoulder and staff in hand, left our station for the coast. And several times a week a coast caravan came in with trade goods—ghastly glazed calico that made you shudder only to look at it, glass beads value about a penny a quart, confounded spotted cotton handkerchiefs. And no rivets. Three carriers could have brought all that was wanted to set that steamboat afloat.

"He was becoming confidential now, but I fancy my unresponsive attitude must have exasperated him at last, for he judged it necessary to inform me he feared neither God nor devil, let alone any mere man. I said I could see that very well, but what I wanted was a certain quantity of rivets—and rivets were what really Mr. Kurtz wanted, if he had only known it. Now letters went to the coast every week. . . . 'My dear sir,' he cried, 'I write from dictation.' I demanded rivets. There was a way — for an intelligent man. He changed his manner; became very cold, and suddenly began to talk about a hippopotamus; wondered whether sleeping on board the steamer (I stuck to my salvage night and day) I wasn't disturbed. There was an old hippo that had the bad habit of getting out on the bank and roaming at night over the station grounds. The pilgrims used to turn out in a body and empty every rifle they could lay hands on at him. Some even had sat up o' nights for him. All this energy was wasted, though. 'That animal has a charmed life,' he said; 'but you can say this only of brutes in this country. No man — you apprehend me? — no man here bears a charmed life.' He stood there for a moment in the moonlight with his delicate hooked nose set a little askew, and his mica eyes glittering without a wink, then, with a curt Good-night, he strode off. I could see he was disturbed and considerably puzzled, which made me feel more hopeful than I had been for days. It was a great comfort to turn from that chap to my influential friend, the battered, twisted, ruined, tin-pot steam-boat. I clambered on board. She rang under my feet like an empty Huntley & Palmer biscuit-tin kicked along a gutter; she was nothing so solid in make, and rather less pretty in shape, but I had expended enough hard work on her to make me love her. No influential friend would have served me better. She had given me a chance to come out a bit — to find out what I could do. No, I don't like work. I had rather laze about and think of all the fine things that can be done. I don't like work — no man does — but I like what is in the work, — the chance to find yourself. Your own reality — for yourself, not for others — what no other man can ever know. They can only see the mere show, and never can tell what it really means.

"I was not surprised to see somebody sitting aft, on the deck, with his legs dangling over the mud. You see I rather chummed with the few mechanics there were in the station, whom the other pilgrims naturally despised — on account of their imperfect manners, I suppose. This was the foreman — a boiler-maker by trade — a good worker. He was a lank, bony, yellow-faced man, with big intense eyes. His aspect was worried, and his head was as bald as the palm of my hand; but his hair in falling seemed to have stuck to his chin, and had prospered in the new locality, for his beard hung down to his waist. He was a widower with six young children (he had left them in charge of a sister of his to come out there), and the passion of his life was pigeon-flying. He was an enthusiast and a connoisseur. He would rave about pigeons. After work hours he used sometimes to come over from his hut for a talk about his children and his pigeons; at work, when he had to crawl in the mud under the bottom of the steamboat, he would tie up that beard of his in a kind of white serviette he brought for the purpose. It had loops to go over his ears. In the evening he could be seen squatted on the bank rinsing that wrapper in the creek with great care, then spreading it solemnly on a bush to dry.

"I slapped him on the back and shouted 'We shall have rivets!' He scrambled to his feet exclaiming 'No! Rivets!' as though he couldn't believe his ears. Then in a low voice, 'You . . . eh?' I don't know why we behaved like lunatics. I put my finger to the side of my nose and nodded mysteriously. 'Good for you!' he cried, snapped his fingers above his head, lifting one foot. I tried a jig. We capered on the iron deck. A frightful clatter came out of the hulk, and the virgin forest on the other bank of the creek sent it back in a thundering roll upon the sleeping station. It must have made some of the pilgrims sit up in their hovels. A dark figure obscured the lighted doorway of the manager's hut, vanished, then, a second or so after, the doorway itself vanished, too. We stopped, and the silence driven away by the stamping of our feet flowed back again from the recesses of the land. The great wall of vegetation, an exuberant and entangled mass of trunks, branches, leaves, boughs, festoons, motionless in the moonlight, was like a rioting invasion of soundless life, a rolling wave of plants, piled up, crested, ready to topple over the creek, to sweep every little man of us out of his little existence. And it moved not. A deadened burst of mighty splashes and snorts reached us from afar, as though an ichthyosaurus had been taking a bath of glitter in the great river. 'After all,' said the boiler-maker in a reasonable tone, 'why shouldn't we get the rivets?' Why not, indeed! I did not know of any reason why we shouldn't. 'They'll come in three weeks,' I said, confidently.

"But they didn't. Instead of rivets there came an invasion, an infliction, a visitation. It came in sections during the next three weeks, each section headed by a donkey carrying a white man in new clothes and tan shoes, bowing from that elevation right and left to the impressed pilgrims. A quarrelsome band of footsore sulky niggers trod on the heels of the donkey; a lot of tents, camp-stools, tin boxes, white cases, brown bales would be shot down in the courtyard, and the air of mystery would deepen a little over the muddle of the station. Five such installments came, with their absurd air of disorderly flight with the loot of innumerable outfit shops and provision stores, that, one would think, they were lugging, after a raid, into the wilderness for equitable division. It was an inextricable mess of things decent in themselves but that human folly made look like spoils of thieving.

"This devoted band called itself the Eldorado Exploring Expedition, and I believe they were sworn to secrecy. Their talk, however, was the talk of sordid buccaneers: it was reckless without hardihood, greedy without audacity, and cruel without courage; there was not an atom of foresight or of serious intention in the whole batch of them, and they did not seem aware these things are wanted for the work of the world. To tear treasure out of the bowels of the land was their desire, with no more moral purpose at the back of it than there is in burglars breaking into a safe. Who paid the expenses of the noble enterprise I don't know; but the uncle of our manager was leader of that lot.

"In exterior he resembled a butcher in a poor neighbourhood, and his eyes had a look of sleepy cunning. He carried his fat paunch with ostentation on his short legs, and during the time his gang infested the station spoke to no one but his nephew. You could see these two roaming about all day long with their heads close together in an everlasting confab.

"I had given up worrying myself about the rivets. One's capacity for that kind of folly is more limited than you would suppose. I said Hang! — and let things slide. I had plenty of time for meditation, and now and then I would give some thought to Kurtz. I wasn't very interested in him. No. Still, I was curious to see whether this man, who had come out equipped with moral ideas of some sort, would climb to the top after all and how he would set about his work when there."

II

"One evening as I was lying flat on the deck of my steamboat, I heard voices approaching—and there were the nephew and the uncle strolling along the bank. I laid my head on my arm again, and had nearly lost myself in a doze, when somebody said in my ear, as it were: 'I am as harmless as a little child, but I don't like to be dictated to. Am I the manager—or am I not? I was ordered to send him there. It's incredible.' . . . I became aware that the two were standing on the shore alongside the forepart of the steamboat, just below my head. I did not move; it did not occur to me to move: I was sleepy. 'It is unpleasant,' grunted the uncle. 'He has asked the Administration to be sent there,' said the other, 'with the idea of showing what he could do; and I was instructed accordingly. Look at the influence that man must have. Is it not frightful?' They both agreed it was frightful, then made several bizarre remarks: 'Make rain and fine weather—one man—the Council—by the nose'—bits of absurd sentences that got the better of my drowsiness, so that I had pretty near the whole of my wits about me when the uncle said, 'The climate may do away with this difficulty for you. Is he alone there?' 'Yes,' answered the manager; 'he sent his assistant down the river with a note to me in these terms: "Clear this poor devil out of the country, and don't bother sending more of that sort. I had rather be alone than have the kind of men you can dispose of with me." It was more than a year ago. Can you imagine such impudence?' 'Anything since then?' asked the other, hoarsely. 'Ivory,' jerked the nephew 'lots of it—prime sort—lots—most annoying, from him.' 'And with that?' questioned the heavy rumble. 'Invoice,' was the reply fired out, so to speak. Then silence. They had been talking about Kurtz.

"I was broad awake by this time, but, lying perfectly at ease, remained still, having no inducement to change my position. 'How did that ivory come all this way?' growled the elder man, who seemed very vexed. The other explained that it had come with a fleet of canoes in charge of an English half-caste clerk Kurtz had with him; that Kurtz had apparently intended to return himself, the station being by that time bare of goods and stores, but after coming three hundred miles, had suddenly decided to go back, which he started to do alone in a small dugout with four paddlers, leaving the half-caste to continue down the river with the ivory. The two fellows there seemed astounded at anybody attempting such a thing. They were at a loss for an adequate motive. As to me, I seemed to see Kurtz for the first time. It was a distinct glimpse: the dugout, four paddling savages, and the lone white man turning his back suddenly on the headquarters, on relief, on thoughts of home—perhaps; setting his face towards the depths of the wilderness, towards his empty and desolate station. I did not know the motive. Perhaps he was just simply a fine fellow who stuck to his work for its own sake. His name, you understand, had not been pronounced once. He was 'that man.' The half-caste, who, as far as I could see, had conducted a difficult trip with great prudence and pluck, was invariably alluded to as 'that scoundrel.' The 'scoundrel' had reported that the 'man' had been very ill—had recovered imperfectly. . . . The two below me moved away then a few paces, and strolled back and forth at some little distance. I heard: 'Military post—doctor—two hundred miles—quite alone now—unavoidable delays—nine months—no news—strange rumours.'

They approached again, just as the manager was saying, 'No one, as far as I know, unless a species of wandering trader—a pestilential fellow, snapping ivory from the natives.' Who was it they were talking about now? I gathered in snatches that this was some man supposed to be in Kurtz's district, and of whom the manager did not approve. 'We will not be free from unfair competition till one of these fellows is hanged for an example,' he said. 'Certainly,' grunted the other 'get him hanged! Why not? Anything—anything can be done in this country. That's what I say; nobody here, you understand, *here*, can endanger your position. And why? You stand the climate—you outlast them all. The danger is in Europe; but there before I left I took care to—' They moved off and whispered, then their voices rose again. 'The extraordinary series of delays is not my fault. I did my best.' The fat man sighed. 'Very sad.' 'And the pestiferous absurdity of his talk,' continued the other; 'he bothered me enough when he was here. "Each station should be like a beacon on the road towards better things, a centre for trade of course, but also for humanizing, improving, instructing." Conceive you—that ass! And he wants to be manager! No, it's—' Here he got choked by excessive indignation, and I lifted my head the least bit. I was surprised to see how near they were— right under me. I could have spat upon their hats. They were looking on the ground, absorbed in thought. The manager was switching his leg with a slender twig: his sagacious relative lifted his head. 'You have been well since you came out this time?' he asked. The other gave a start. 'Who? I? Oh! Like a charm—like a charm. But the rest—oh, my goodness! All sick. They die so quick, too, that I haven't the time to send them out of the country—it's incredible!' 'H'm. Just so,' grunted the uncle. 'Ah! my boy, trust to this—I say, trust to this.' I saw him extend his short flipper of an arm for a gesture that took in the forest, the creek, the mud, the river,—seemed to beckon with a dishonouring flourish before the sunlit face of the land a treacherous appeal to the lurking death, to the hidden evil, to the profound darkness of its heart. It was so startling that I leaped to my feet and looked back at the edge of the forest, as though I had expected an answer of some sort to that black display of confidence. You know the foolish notions that come to one sometimes. The high stillness confronted these two figures with its ominous patience, waiting for the passing away of a fantastic invasion.

"They swore aloud together—out of sheer fright, I believe—then pretending not to know anything of my existence, turned back to the station. The sun was low; and leaning forward side by side, they seemed to be tugging painfully uphill their two ridiculous shadows of unequal length, that trailed behind them slowly over the tall grass without bending a single blade.

"In a few days the Eldorado Expedition went into the patient wilderness, that closed upon it as the sea closes over a diver. Long afterwards the news came that all the donkeys were dead. I know nothing as to the fate of the less valuable animals. They, no doubt, like the rest of us, found what they deserved. I did not inquire. I was then rather excited at the prospect of meeting Kurtz very soon. When I say very soon I mean it comparatively. It was just two months from the day we left the creek when we came to the bank below Kurtz's station.

"Going up that river was like travelling back to the earliest beginnings of the world, when vegetation rioted on the earth and the big trees were kings. An empty stream, a great silence, an impenetrable forest. The air was warm, thick, heavy, sluggish. There was no joy in the brilliance of sunshine. The long stretches of the waterway ran on, deserted, into the gloom of overshadowed distances. On silvery sandbanks hippos and alligators sunned themselves side by side. The broadening waters flowed through a mob of wooded islands; you lost your way on that river as you would in a desert, and butted all day long against shoals, trying to find the channel, till you thought yourself bewitched and cut off for ever from everything you had known once — somewhere — far away — in another existence perhaps. There were moments when one's past came back to one, as it will sometimes when you have not a moment to spare to yourself; but it came in the shape of an unrestful and noisy dream, remembered with wonder amongst the overwhelming realities of this strange world of plants, and water, and silence. And this stillness of life did not in the least resemble a peace. It was the stillness of an implacable force brooding over an inscrutable intention. It looked at you with a vengeful aspect. I got used to it afterwards; I did not see it any more; I had no time. I had to keep guessing at the channel; I had to discern, mostly by inspiration, the signs of hidden banks; I watched for sunken stones; I was learning to clap my teeth smartly before my heart flew out, when I shaved by a fluke some infernal sly old snag that would have ripped the life out of the tin-pot steamboat and drowned all the pilgrims; I had to keep a look-out for the signs of dead wood we could cut up in the night for next day's steaming. When you have to attend to things of that sort, to the mere incidents of the surface, the reality — the reality, I tell you — fades. The inner truth is hidden — luckily, luckily. But I felt it all the same; I felt often its mysterious stillness watching me at my monkey tricks, just as it watches you fellows performing on your respective tightropes for — what is it? half-a-crown a tumble —— "

"Try to be civil, Marlow," growled a voice, and I knew there was at least one listener awake besides myself.

"I beg your pardon. I forgot the heartache which makes up the rest of the price. And indeed what does the price matter, if the trick be well done? You do your tricks very well. And I didn't do badly either, since I managed not to sink that steamboat on my first trip. It's a wonder to me yet. Imagine a blindfolded man set to drive a van over a bad road. I sweated and shivered over that business considerably, I can tell you. After all, for a seaman, to scrape the bottom of the thing that's supposed to float all the time under his care is the unpardonable sin. No one may know of it, but you never forget the thump — eh? A blow on the very heart. You remember it, you dream of it, you wake up at night and think of it — years after — and go hot and cold all over. I don't pretend to say that steamboat floated all the time. More than once she had to wade for a bit, with twenty cannibals splashing around and pushing. We had enlisted some of these chaps on the way for a crew. Fine fellows — cannibals — in their place. They were men one could work with, and I am grateful to them. And, after all, they did not eat each other before my face: they had brought along a provision of hippo-meat which went rotten, and made the mystery of the wilderness stink in my nostrils. Phoo! I can sniff it now. I had the manager on board and three or four pilgrims with their staves — all complete. Sometimes we came upon a station close by the bank, clinging to the skirts of the unknown, and the white men rushing out of a tumbledown hovel, with great gestures of joy and surprise and welcome, seemed very strange — had the appearance of being held their captive by a spell. The word ivory would ring in the air for a while — and on we went again into the silence, along empty reaches, round the still bends, between the high walls of our winding way, reverberating in hollow claps the ponderous beat of the sternwheel. Trees, trees, millions of trees, massive, immense, running up high; and at their foot, hugging the bank against the stream, crept the little begrimed steamboat, like a sluggish beetle crawling on the floor of a lofty portico. It made you feel very small, very lost, and yet it was not altogether depressing, that feeling. After all, if you were small, the grimy beetle crawled on — which was just what you wanted it to do. Where the pilgrims imagined it crawled to I don't know. To some place where they expected to get something, I bet! For me it crawled towards Kurtz — exclusively; but when the steam-pipes started leaking we crawled very slow. The reaches opened before us and closed behind, as if the forest had stepped leisurely across the water to bar the way for our return. We penetrated deeper and deeper into the heart of darkness. It was very quiet there. At night sometimes the roll of drums behind the curtain of trees would run up the river and remain sustained faintly, as if hovering in the air high over our heads, till the first break of day. Whether it meant war, peace, or prayer we could not tell. The dawns were heralded by the descent of a chill stillness; the wood-cutters slept, their fires burned low; the snapping of a twig would make you start. We were wanderers on prehistoric earth, on an earth that wore the aspect of an unknown planet. We could have fancied ourselves the first of men taking possession of an accursed inheritance, to be subdued at the cost of profound anguish and of excessive toil. But suddenly, as we struggled round a bend, there would be a glimpse of rush walls, of peaked grass-roofs, a burst of yells, a whirl of black limbs, a mass of hands clapping, of feet stamping, of bodies swaying, of eyes rolling, under the droop of heavy and motionless foliage. The steamer toiled along slowly on the edge of a black and incomprehensible frenzy. The prehistoric man was cursing us, praying to us, welcoming us — who could tell? We were cut off from the comprehension of our surroundings; we glided past like phantoms, wondering and secretly appalled, as sane men would be before an enthusiastic outbreak in a madhouse. We could not understand because we were too far and could not remember, because we were travelling in the night of first ages, of those ages that are gone, leaving hardly a sign — and no memories.

"The earth seemed unearthly. We are accustomed to look upon the shackled form of a conquered monster, but there — there you could look at a thing monstrous and free. It was unearthly, and the men were —— No, they were not inhuman. Well, you know, that was the worst of it — this suspicion of their not being inhuman. It would come slowly to one. They howled and leaped, and spun, and made horrid faces; but what thrilled you was just the thought of their humanity — like yours — the thought of your remote kinship with this wild and passionate uproar. Ugly. Yes, it was ugly enough; but if you were man enough you would admit to yourself that there was in you just the faintest trace of a response to the terrible frankness of that noise, a dim suspicion of there being a meaning in it which you — you so remote from the night of first ages — could comprehend. And why not? The mind of man is capable of anything — because everything is in it, all the past as well as all the future. What was there after all? Joy, fear, sorrow, devotion, valour, rage — who can tell? — but truth — truth stripped of its cloak of time. Let the fool gape and shudder — the man knows, and can look on without a wink. But he must at least be as much of a man as these on the shore. He must meet that truth with his own true stuff—with his own inborn strength. Principles won't do. Acquisitions, clothes, pretty rags—rags that would fly off at the first good shake. No; you want a deliberate belief. An appeal to me in this fiendish row—is there? Very well; I hear; I admit, but I have a voice, too, and for good or evil mine is the speech that cannot be silenced. Of course, a fool, what with sheer fright and fine sentiments, is always safe. Who's that grunting? You wonder I didn't go ashore for a howl and a dance? Well, no—I didn't. Fine sentiments, you say? Fine sentiments, be hanged! I had no time. I had to mess about with white-lead and strips of woollen blanket helping to put bandages on those leaky steampipes—I tell you. I had to watch the steering, and circumvent those snags, and get the tin-pot along by hook or by crook. There was surface-truth enough in these things to save a wiser man. And between whiles I had to look after the savage who was fireman. He was an improved specimen; he could fire up a vertical boiler. He was there below me, and, upon my word, to look at him was as edifying as seeing a dog in a parody of breeches and a feather hat, walking on his hindlegs. A few months of training had done for that really fine chap. He squinted at the steam-gauge and at the water-gauge with an evident effort of intrepidity—and he had filed teeth, too, the poor devil, and the wool of his pate shaved into queer patterns, and three ornamental scars on each of his cheeks. He ought to have been clapping his hands and stamping his feet on the bank, instead of which he was hard at work, a thrall to strange witchcraft, full of improving knowledge. He was useful because he had been instructed; and what he knew was this—that should the water in that transparent thing disappear, the evil spirit inside the boiler would get angry through the greatness of his thirst, and take a terrible vengeance. So he sweated and fired up and watched the glass fearfully (with an impromptu charm, made of rags, tied to his arm, and a piece of polished bone, as big as a watch, struck flatways through his lower lip), while the wooded banks slipped past us slowly, the short noise was left behind, the interminable miles of silence—and we crept on, towards Kurtz. But the snags were thick, the water was treacherous and shallow, the boiler seemed indeed to have a sulky devil in it, and thus neither that fireman nor I had any time to peer into our creepy thoughts.

"Some fifty miles below the Inner Station we came upon a hut of reeds, an inclined and melancholy pole, with the unrecognizable tatters of what had been a flag of some sort flying from it, and a neatly stacked wood-pile. This was unexpected. We came to the bank, and on the stack of firewood found a flat piece of board with some faded pencil-writing on it. When deciphered it said: 'Wood for you. Hurry up. Approach cautiously.' There was a signature, but it was illegible—not Kurtz—a much longer word. Hurry up. Where? Up the river? 'Approach cautiously.' We had not done so. But the warning could not have been meant for the place where it could be only found after approach. Something was wrong above. But what—and how much? That was the question. We commented adversely upon the imbecility of that telegraphic style. The bush around said nothing, and would not let us look very far, either. A torn curtain of red twill hung in the doorway of the hut, and flapped sadly in our faces. The dwelling was dismantled; but we could see a white man had lived there not very long ago. There remained a rude table—a plank on two posts; a heap of rubbish reposed in a dark corner, and by the door I picked up a book. It had lost its covers, and the pages had been thumbed into a state of extremely dirty softness; but the back had been lovingly stitched afresh with white cotton thread, which looked clean yet. It was an extraordinary find. Its title was, *An Inquiry into some Points of Seamanship*, by a man Towser, Towson—some such name—Master in his Majesty's Navy. The matter looked dreary reading enough, with illustrative diagrams and repulsive tables of figures, and the copy was sixty years old. I handled this amazing antiquity with the greatest possible tenderness, lest it should dissolve in my hands. Within, Towson or Towser was inquiring earnestly into the breaking strain of ships' chains and tackle, and other such matters. Not a very enthralling book; but at the first glance you could see there a singleness of intention, an honest concern for the right way of going to work, which made these humble pages, thought out so many years ago, luminous with another than a professional light. The simple old sailor, with his talk of chains and purchases, made me forget the jungle and the pilgrims in a delicious sensation of having come upon something unmistakably real. Such a book being there was wonderful enough; but still more astounding were the notes pencilled in the margin, and plainly referring to the text. I couldn't believe my eyes! They were in cipher! Yes, it looked like cipher. Fancy a man lugging with him a book of that description into this nowhere and studying it—and making notes—in cipher at that! It was an extravagant mystery.

"I had been dimly aware for some time of a worrying noise, and when I lifted my eyes I saw the wood-pile was gone, and the manager, aided by all the pilgrims, was shouting at me from the river-side. I slipped the book into my pocket. I assure you to leave off reading was like tearing myself away from the shelter of an old and solid friendship.

"I started the lame engine ahead. 'It must be this miserable trader—this intruder,' exclaimed the manager, looking back malevolently at the place we had left. 'He must be English,' I said. 'It will not save him from getting into trouble if he is not careful,' muttered the manager darkly. I observed with assumed innocence that no man was safe from trouble in this world.

"The current was more rapid now, the steamer seemed at her last gasp, the stern-wheel flopped languidly, and I caught myself listening on tiptoe for the next beat of the boat, for in sober truth I expected the wretched thing to give up every moment. It was like watching the last flickers of a life. But still we crawled. Sometimes I would pick out a tree a little way ahead to measure our progress towards Kurtz by, but I lost it invariably before we got abreast. To keep the eyes so long on one thing was too much for human patience. The manager displayed a beautiful resignation. I fretted and fumed and took to arguing with myself whether or no I would talk openly with Kurtz; but before I could come to any conclusion it occurred to me that my speech or my silence, indeed any action of mine, would be a mere futility. What did it matter what any one knew or ignored? What did it matter who was manager? One gets sometimes such a flash of insight. The essentials of this affair lay deep under the surface, beyond my reach, and beyond my power of meddling.

"Towards the evening of the second day we judged ourselves about eight miles from Kurtz's station. I wanted to push on; but the manager looked grave, and told me the navigation up there was so dangerous that it would be advisable, the sun being very low already, to wait where we were till next morning.

Moreover, he pointed out that if the warning to approach cautiously were to be followed, we must approach in daylight — not at dusk, or in the dark. This was sensible enough. Eight miles meant nearly three hours' steaming for us, and I could also see suspicious ripples at the upper end of the reach. Nevertheless, I was annoyed beyond expression at the delay, and most unreasonably, too, since one night more could not matter much after so many months. As we had plenty of wood, and caution was the word, I brought up in the middle of the stream. The reach was narrow, straight, with high sides like a railway cutting. The dusk came gliding into it long before the sun had set. The current ran smooth and swift, but a dumb immobility sat on the banks. The living trees, lashed together by the creepers and every living bush of the undergrowth, might have been changed into stone, even to the slenderest twig, to the lightest leaf. It was not sleep — it seemed unnatural, like a state of trance. Not the faintest sound of any kind could be heard. You looked on amazed, and began to suspect yourself of being deaf — then the night came suddenly, and struck you blind as well. About three in the morning some large fish leaped, and the loud splash made me jump as though a gun had been fired. When the sun rose there was a white fog, very warm and clammy, and more blinding than the night. It did not shift or drive; it was just there, standing all round you like something solid. At eight or nine, perhaps, it lifted as a shutter lifts. We had a glimpse of the towering multitude of trees, of the immense matted jungle, with the blazing little ball of the sun hanging over it — all perfectly still — and then the white shutter came down again, smoothly, as if sliding in greased grooves. I ordered the chain, which we had begun to heave in, to be paid out again. Before it stopped running with a muffled rattle, a cry, a very loud cry, as of infinite desolation, soared slowly in the opaque air. It ceased. A complaining clamour, modulated in savage discords, filled our ears. The sheer unexpectedness of it made my hair stir under my cap. I don't know how it struck the others; to me it seemed as though the mist itself had screamed, so suddenly, and apparently from all sides at once, did this tumultuous and mournful uproar arise. It culminated in a hurried outbreak of almost intolerably excessive shrieking, which stopped short, leaving us stiffened in a variety of silly attitudes, and obstinately listening to the nearly as appalling and excessive silence. 'Good God! What is the meaning —— ' stammered at my elbow one of the pilgrims, — a little fat man, with sandy hair and red whiskers, who wore side-spring boots, and pink pajamas tucked into his socks. Two others remained open-mouthed a whole minute, then dashed into the little cabin, to rush out incontinently and stand darting scared glances, with Winchesters at 'ready' in their hands. What we could see was just the steamer we were on, her outlines blurred as though she had been on the point of dissolving, and a misty strip of water, perhaps two feet broad, around her — and that was all. The rest of the world was nowhere, as far as our eyes and ears were concerned. Just nowhere. Gone, disappeared; swept off without leaving a whisper or a shadow behind.

"I went forward, and ordered the chain to be hauled in short, so as to be ready to trip the anchor and move the steamboat at once if necessary. 'Will they attack?' whispered an awed voice. 'We will be all butchered in this fog,' murmured another. The faces twitched with the strain, the hands trembled slightly, the eyes forgot to wink. It was very curious to see the contrast of expressions of the white men and of the black fellows of our crew, who were as much strangers to that part of the river as we, though their homes were only eight hundred miles away. The whites, of course greatly discomposed, had besides a curious look of being painfully shocked by such an outrageous row. The others had an alert, naturally interested expression; but their faces were essentially quiet, even those of the one or two who grinned as they hauled at the chain. Several exchanged short, grunting phrases, which seemed to settle the matter to their satisfaction. Their headman, a young, broad-chested black, severely draped in dark-blue fringed cloths, with fierce nostrils and his hair all done up artfully in oily ringlets, stood near me. 'Aha!' I said, just for good fellowship's sake. 'Catch 'im,' he snapped, with a bloodshot widening of his eyes and a flash of sharp teeth — 'catch 'im. Give 'im to us.' 'To you, eh?' I asked; 'what would you do with them?' 'Eat 'im!' he said, curtly, and, leaning his elbow on the rail, looked out into the fog in a dignified and profoundly pensive attitude. I would no doubt have been properly horrified, had it not occurred to me that he and his chaps must be very hungry: that they must have been growing increasingly hungry for at least this month past. They had been engaged for six months (I don't think a single one of them had any clear idea of time, as we at the end of countless ages have. They still belonged to the beginnings of time — had no inherited experience to teach them as it were), and of course, as long as there was a piece of paper written over in accordance with some farcical law or other made down the river, it didn't enter anybody's head to trouble how they would live. Certainly they had brought with them some rotten hippo-meat, which couldn't have lasted very long, anyway, even if the pilgrims hadn't, in the midst of a shocking hullabaloo, thrown a considerable quantity of it overboard. It looked like a high-handed proceeding; but it was really a case of legitimate self-defence. You can't breathe dead hippo waking, sleeping, and eating, and at the same time keep your precarious grip on existence. Besides that, they had given them every week three pieces of brass wire, each about nine inches long; and the theory was they were to buy their provisions with that currency in river-side villages. You can see how *that* worked. There were either no villages, or the people were hostile, or the director, who like the rest of us fed out of tins, with an occasional old he-goat thrown in, didn't want to stop the steamer for some more or less recondite reason. So, unless they swallowed the wire itself, or made loops of it to snare the fishes with, I don't see what good their extravagant salary could be to them. I must say it was paid with a regularity worthy of a large and honourable trading company. For the rest, the only thing to eat — though it didn't look eatable in the least — I saw in their possession was a few lumps of some stuff like hard-cooked dough, of a dirty lavender colour, they kept wrapped in leaves, and now and then swallowed a piece of, but so small that it seemed done more for the looks of the thing than for any serious purpose of sustenance. Why in the name of all the gnawing devils of hunger they didn't go for us — they were thirty to five — and have a good tuck-in for once, amazes me now when I think of it. They were big powerful men, with not much capacity to weigh the consequences, with courage, with strength, even yet, though their skins were no longer glossy and their muscles no longer hard. And I saw that something restraining, one of those human secrets that baffle probability, had come into play there. I looked at them with a swift quickening of interest — not because it occurred to me I might be eaten by them before very long, though I own to you that just then I perceived — in a new light, as it were—how unwholesome the pilgrims looked, and I hoped, yes, I positively hoped, that my aspect was not so—what shall I say?—so—unappetizing: a touch of fantastic vanity which fitted well with the dream-sensation that pervaded all my days at that time. Perhaps I had a little fever, too. One can't live with one's finger everlastingly on one's pulse. I had often 'a little fever,' or a little touch of other things—the playful paw-strokes of the wilderness, the preliminary trifling before the more serious onslaught which came in due course. Yes; I looked at them as you would on any human being, with a curiousity of their impulses, motives, capacities, weaknesses, when brought to the test of an inexorable physical neces-sity. Restraint! What possible restraint? Was it superstition, disgust, patience, fear—or some kind of primitive honour? No fear can stand up to hunger, no patience can wear it out, disgust simply does not exist where hunger is; and as to superstition, beliefs, and what you may call principles, they are less than chaff in a breeze. Don't you know the devilry of lingering starvation, its exasperating torment, its black thoughts, its sombre and brooding ferocity? Well, I do. It takes a man all his inborn strength to fight hunger properly. It's really easier to face bereavement, dishonour, and the perdition of one's soul—than this kind of prolonged hunger. Sad, but true. And these chaps, too, had no earthly reason for any kind of scruple. Restraint! I would just as soon have expected restraint from a hyena prowling amongst the corpses of a battlefield. But there was the fact facing me—the fact dazzling, to be seen, like the foam on the depths of the sea, like a ripple on an unfathomable enigma, a mystery greater—when I thought of it—than the curious, inexplicable note of desperate grief in this savage clamour that had swept by us on the river-bank, behind the blind whiteness of the fog.

"Two pilgrims were quarreling in hurried whispers as to which bank. 'Left.' 'No, no; how can you? Right, right, of course.' 'It is very serious,' said the manager's voice behind me; 'I would be desolated if anything should happen to Mr. Kurtz before we came up.' I looked at him, and had not the slightest doubt he was sincere. He was just the kind of man who would wish to preserve appear-ances. That was his restraint. But when he muttered something about going on at once, I did not even take the trouble to answer him. I knew, and he knew, that it was impossible. Were we to let go our hold of the bottom, we would be absolutely in the air—in space. We wouldn't be able to tell where we were going to—whether up or down stream, or across—till we fetched against one bank or the other,—and then we wouldn't know at first which it was. Of course I made no move. I had no mind for a smash-up. You couldn't imagine a more deadly place for a shipwreck. Whether drowned at once or not, we were sure to perish speedily in one way or another. 'I authorize you to take all the risks,' he said, after a short silence. 'I refuse to take any,' I said, shortly; which was just the answer he expected, though its tone might have surprised him. 'Well, I must defer to your judgment. You are captain,' he said, with marked civility. I turned my shoulder to him in sign of my appreciation, and looked into the fog. How long would it last? It was the most hopeless look-out. The approach to this Kurtz grubbing for ivory in the wretched bush was beset by as many dangers as though he had been an enchanted princess sleeping in a fabulous castle. 'Will they attack, do you think?' asked the manager, in a confidential tone.

"I did not think they would attack, for several obvious reasons. The thick fog was one. If they left the bank in their canoes they would get lost in it, as we would be if we attempted to move. Still, I had also judged the jungle of both banks quite impenetrable—and yet eyes were in it, eyes that had seen us. The river-side bushes were certainly very thick; but the undergrowth behind was evidently penetrable. However, during the short lift I had seen no canoes anywhere in the reach—certainly not abreast of the steamer. But what made the idea of attack inconceivable to me was the nature of the noise—of the cries we had heard. They had not the fierce character boding of immediate hostile intention. Unexpected, wild, and violent as they had been, they had given me an irresistible impression of sorrow. The glimpse of the steamboat had for some reason filled those savages with unrestrained grief. The danger, if any, I expounded, was from our proximity to a great human passion let loose. Even extreme grief may ultimately vent itself in violence—but more generally takes the form of apathy. . . .

"You should have seen the pilgrims stare! They had no heart to grin, or even to revile me: but I believe they thought me gone mad—with fright, maybe. I delivered a regular lecture. My dear boys, it was no good bothering. Keep a look-out? Well, you may guess I watched the fog for the signs of lifting as a cat watches a mouse; but for anything else our eyes were of no more use to us than if we had been buried miles deep in a heap of cotton-wool. It felt like it, too—choking, warm, stifling. Besides, all I said, though it sounded extravagant, was absolutely true to fact. What we afterwards alluded to as an attack was really an attempt at repulse. The action was very far from being aggressive—it was not even defensive, in the usual sense: it was undertaken under the stress of desperation, and in its essence was purely protective.

"It developed itself, I should say, two hours after the fog lifted, and its commencement was at a spot, roughly speaking, about a mile and a half below Kurtz's station. We had just floundered and flopped round a bend, when I saw an islet, a mere grassy hummock of bright green, in the middle of the stream. It was the only thing of the kind; but as we opened the reach more, I perceived it was the head of a long sandbank, or rather of a chain of shallow patches stretching down the middle of the river. They were discoloured, just awash, and the whole lot was seen just under the water, exactly as a man's backbone is seen running down the middle of his back under the skin. Now, as far as I did see, I could go to the right or to the left of this. I didn't know either channel, of course. The banks looked pretty well alike, the depth appeared the same; but as I had been informed the station was on the west side, I naturally headed for the western passage.

"No sooner had we fairly entered it than I became aware it was much narrower than I had supposed. To the left of us there was the long uninterrupted shoal, and to the right a high, steep bank heavily overgrown with bushes. Above the bush the trees stood in serried ranks. The twigs overhung the current thickly, and from distance to distance a large limb of some tree projected rigidly over the stream. It was then well on in the afternoon, the face of the forest was gloomy, and a broad strip of shadow had already fallen on the water. In this shadow we steamed up—very slowly, as you may imagine. I sheered her well inshore—the water being deepest near the bank, as the sounding-pole informed me.

"One of my hungry and forbearing friends was sounding in the bows just below me. This steamboat was exactly like a decked scow. On the deck, there were two little teak-wood houses, with doors and windows. The boiler was in the fore-end, and the machinery right astern. Over the whole there was a light roof, supported on stanchions. The funnel projected through that roof, and in front of the funnel a small cabin built of light planks served for a pilot-house. It contained a couch, two camp-stools, a loaded Martini-Henry leaning in one corner, a tiny table, and the steering-wheel. It had a wide door in front and a broad shutter at each side. All these were always thrown open, of course. I spent my days perched up there on the extreme fore-end of that roof, before the door. At night I slept, or tried to, on the couch. An athletic black belonging to some coast tribe, and educated by my poor predecessor, was the helmsman. He sported a pair of brass earrings, wore a blue cloth wrapper from the waist to the ankles, and thought all the world of himself. He was the most unstable kind of fool I had ever seen. He steered with no end of a swagger while you were by; but if he lost sight of you, he became instantly the prey of an abject funk, and would let that cripple of a steamboat get the upper hand of him in a minute.

"I was looking down at the sounding-pole, and feeling much annoyed to see at each try a little more of it stick out of that river, when I saw my poleman give up the business suddenly, and stretch himself flat on the deck, without even taking the trouble to haul his pole in. He kept hold on it though, and it trailed in the water. At the same time the fireman, whom I could also see below me, sat down abruptly before his furnace and ducked his head. I was amazed. Then I had to look at the river mighty quick, because there was a snag in the fairway. Sticks, little sticks, were flying about—thick: they were whizzing before my nose, dropping below me, striking behind me against my pilot house. All this time the river, the shore, the woods, were very quiet—perfectly quiet. I could only hear the heavy splashing thump of the stern-wheel and the patter of these things. We cleared the snag clumsily. Arrows, by Jove! We were being shot at! I stepped in quickly to close the shutter on the land-side. That fool helmsman, his hands on the spokes, was lifting his knees high, stamping his feet, champing his mouth, like a reined-in horse. Confound him! And we were staggering within ten feet of the bank. I had to lean right out to swing the heavy shutter, and I saw a face amongst the leaves on the level with my own, looking at me very fierce and steady; and then suddenly, as though a veil had been removed from my eyes, I made out, deep in the tangled gloom, naked breasts, arms, legs, glaring eyes,—the bush was swarming with human limbs in movement, glistening, of bronze colour. The twigs shook, swayed, and rustled, the arrows flew out of them, and then the shutter came to. 'Steer her straight,' I said to the helmsman. He held his head rigid, face forward; but his eyes rolled, he kept on, lifting and setting down his feet gently, his mouth foamed a little. 'Keep quiet!' I said in a fury. I might just as well have ordered a tree not to sway in the wind. I darted out. Below me there was a great scuffle of feet on the iron deck; confused exclamations; a voice screamed. 'Can you turn back?' I caught sight of a V-shaped ripple on the water ahead. What? Another snag! A fusillade burst out under my feet. The pilgrims had opened with their Winchesters, and were simply squirting lead into that bush. A deuce of a lot of smoke came up and drove slowly forward. I swore at it. Now I couldn't see the ripple or the snag either. I stood in the doorway, peering, and the arrows came in swarms. They might have been poisoned, but they looked as though they wouldn't kill a cat. The bush began to howl. Our wood-cutters raised a warlike whoop; the report of a rifle at my back deafened me. I glanced over my shoulder, and the pilot-house was yet full of noise and smoke when I made a dash at the wheel. The fool-nigger had dropped everything, to throw the shutter open and let off that Martini-Henry. He stood before the wide opening, glaring, and I yelled at him to come back, while I straightened the sudden twist out of that steamboat. There was no room to turn even if I had wanted to, the snag was somewhere very near ahead in that confounded smoke, there was no time to lose, so I just crowded her into the bank—right into the bank, where I knew the water was deep.

"We tore slowly along the overhanging bushes in a whirl of broken twigs and flying leaves. The fusillade below stopped short, as I had foreseen it would when the squirts got empty. I threw my head back to a glinting whizz that traversed the pilot-house, in at one shutter-hole and out at the other. Looking past that mad helmsman, who was shaking the empty rifle and yelling at the shore, I saw vague forms of men running bent double, leaping, gliding, distinct, incomplete, evanescent. Something big appeared in the air before the shutter, the rifle went overboard, and the man stepped back swiftly, looked at me over his shoulder in an extraordinary, profound, familiar manner, and fell upon my feet. The side of his head hit the wheel twice, and the end of what appeared a long cane clattered round and knocked over a little campstool. It looked as though after wrenching that thing from somebody ashore he had lost his balance in the effort. The thin smoke had blown away, we were clear of the snag, and looking ahead I could see that in another hundred yards or so I would be free to sheer off, away from the bank; but my feet felt so very warm and wet that I had to look down. The man had rolled on his back and stared straight up at me; both his hands clutched that cane. It was the shaft of a spear that, either thrown or lunged through the opening, had caught him in the side just below the ribs; the blade had gone in out of sight, after making a frightful gash; my shoes were full; a pool of blood lay very still, gleaming dark-red under the wheel; his eyes shone with an amazing lustre. The fusillade burst out again. He looked at me anxiously, gripping the spear like something precious, with an air of being afraid I would try to take it away from him. I had to make an effort to free my eyes from his gaze and attend to the steering. With one hand I felt above my head for the line of the steam whistle, and jerked out screech after screech hurriedly. The tumult of angry and warlike yells was checked instantly, and then from the depths of the woods went out such a tremulous and prolonged wail of mournful fear and utter despair as may be imagined to follow the flight of the last hope from the earth. There was a great commotion in the bush; the shower of arrows stopped, a few dropping shots rang out sharply—then silence, in which the languid beat of the stern-wheel came plainly to my ears. I put the helm hard a-starboard at the moment when the pilgrim in pink pyjamas, very hot and agitated, appeared in the doorway. 'The manager sends me——' he began in an official tone, and stopped short. 'Good God!' he said, glaring at the wounded man.

"We two whites stood over him, and his lustrous and inquiring glance enveloped us both. I declare it looked as though he would presently put to us some question in an understandable language; but he died without uttering a sound, without moving a limb, without twitching a muscle. Only in the very last moment, as though in response to some sign we could not see, to some whisper we could not hear, he groaned heavily, and that frown gave to his black death-mask an inconceivably sombre, brooding, and menacing expression. The lustre of inquiring glance faded swiftly into vacant glassiness. 'Can you steer?' I asked the agent eagerly. He looked very dubious; but I made a grab at his arm, and he understood at once I meant him to steer whether or no. To tell you the truth, I was morbidly anxious to change my shoes and socks. 'He is dead,' murmured the fellow, immensely impressed. 'No doubt about it,' said I, tugging like mad at the shoe-laces. 'And by the way, I suppose Mr. Kurtz is dead as well by this time.'

"For the moment that was the dominant thought. There was a sense of extreme disappointment, as though I had found out I had been striving after something altogether without substance. I couldn't have been more disgusted if I had travelled all this way for the sole purpose of talking with Mr. Kurtz. Talking with. . . . I flung one shoe overboard, and became aware that that was exactly what I had been looking forward to—a talk with Kurtz. I made the strange discovery that I had never imagined him as doing, you know, but as discoursing. I didn't say to myself, 'Now I will never see him,' 'Now I will never shake him by the hand,' but, 'now I will never hear him.' The man presented himself as a voice. Not of course that I did not connect him with some sort of action. Hadn't I been told in all the tones of jealousy and admiration that he had collected, bartered, swindled, or stolen more ivory than all the other agents together? That was not the point. The point was in his being a gifted creature, and that of all his gifts the one that stood out preëminently, that carried with it a sense of real presence, was his ability to talk, his words—the gift of expression, the bewildering, the illuminating, the most exalted and the most contemptible, the pulsating stream of light, or the deceitful flow from the heart of an impenetrable darkness.

"The other shoe went flying unto the devil-god of that river. I thought, By Jove! it's all over. We are too late; he has vanished—the gift has vanished, by means of some spear, arrow, or club. I will never hear that chap speak after all,—and my sorrow had a startling extravagance of emotion, even such as I had noticed in the howling sorrow of these savages in the bush. I couldn't have felt more of lonely desolation somehow, had I been robbed of a belief or had missed my destiny in life. . . . Why do you sigh in this beastly way, somebody? Absurd? Well, absurd. Good Lord! mustn't a man ever —— Here, give me some tobacco."

There was a pause of profound stillness, then a match flared, and Marlow's lean face appeared, worn, hollow, with downward folds and dropped eyelids, with an aspect of concentrated attention; and as he took vigorous draws at his pipe, it seemed to retreat and advance out of the night in the regular flicker of the tiny flame. The match went out.

"Absurd!" he cried. "This is the worst of trying to tell. . . . Here you all are, each moored with two good addresses, like a hulk with two anchors, a butcher round one corner, a policeman round another, excellent appetites, and temperature normal—you hear—normal from year's end to year's end. And you say, Absurd! Absurd be—exploded! Absurd! My dear boys, what can you expect from a man who out of sheer nervousness had just flung overboard a pair of new shoes! Now I think of it, it is amazing I did not shed tears. I am, upon the whole, proud of my fortitude. I was cut to the quick at the idea of having lost the inestimable privilege of listening to the gifted Kurtz. Of course I was wrong. The privilege was waiting for me. Oh, yes, I heard more than enough. And I was right, too. A voice. He was very little more than a voice. And I heard—him—it—this voice—other voices — all of them were so little more than voices — and the memory of that time itself lingers around me, impalpable, like a dying vibration of one immense jabber, silly, atrocious, sordid, savage, or simply mean, without any kind of sense. Voices, voices — even the girl herself — now —— "

He was silent for a long time.

"I laid the ghost of his gifts at last with a lie," he began, suddenly. "Girl! What? Did I mention a girl? Oh, she is out of it — completely. They — the women I mean — are out of it — should be out of it. We must help them to stay in that beautiful world of their own, lest ours gets worse. Oh, she had to be out of it. You should have heard the disinterred body of Mr. Kurtz saying, 'My Intended.' You would have perceived directly then how completely she was out of it. And the lofty frontal bone of Mr. Kurtz! They say the hair goes on growing sometimes, but this — ah — specimen, was impressively bald. The wilderness had patted him on the head, and, behold, it was like a ball — an ivory ball; it had caressed him, and — lo! — he had withered; it had taken him, loved him, embraced him, got into his veins, consumed his flesh, and sealed his soul to its own by the inconceivable ceremonies of some devilish initiation. He was its spoiled and pampered favourite. Ivory? I should think so. Heaps of it, stacks of it. The old mud shanty was bursting with it. You would think there was not a single tusk left either above or below the ground in the whole country. 'Mostly fossil,' the manager had remarked, disparagingly. It was no more fossil than I am; but they call it fossil when it is dug up. It appears these niggers do bury the tusks sometimes — but evidently they couldn't bury this parcel deep enough to save the gifted Mr. Kurtz from his fate. We filled the steamboat with it, and had to pile a lot on the deck. Thus he could see and enjoy as long as he could see, because the appreciation of this favour had remained with him to the last. You should have heard him say, 'My ivory.' Oh yes, I heard him. 'My Intended, my ivory, my station, my river, my —— ' everything belonged to him. It made me hold my breath in expectation of hearing the wilderness burst into a prodigious peal of laughter that would shake the fixed stars in their places. Everything belonged to him — but that was a trifle. The thing was to know what he belonged to, how many powers of darkness claimed him for their own. That was the reflection that made you creepy all over. It was impossible — it was not good for one either — trying to imagine. He had taken a high seat amongst the devils of the land — I mean literally. You can't understand. How could you? — with solid pavement under your feet, surrounded by kind neighbours ready to cheer you or to fall on you, stepping delicately between the butcher and the policeman, in the holy terror of scandal and gallows and lunatic asylums — how can you imagine what particular region of the first ages a man's untrammeled feet may take him into by the way of solitude — utter solitude without a policeman — by the way of silence — utter silence, where no warning voice of a kind neighbour can be heard whispering of public opinion? These little things make all the great difference. When they are gone you must fall back upon your own innate strength, upon your own capacity for faithfulness. Of course you may be too much of a fool to go wrong — too dull even to know you are being assaulted by the powers of darkness. I take it, no fool ever made a bargain for his soul with the devil: the fool is too much of a fool, or the devil too much of a devil — I don't know which. Or you may be such a thunderingly exalted creature as to be altogether deaf and blind to anything but heavenly sights and sounds. Then the earth for you is only a standing place — and whether to be like this is your loss or your gain I won't pretend to say. But most of us are neither one nor the other. The earth for us is a place to live in, where we must put up with sights, with sounds, with smells, too, by Jove! — breathe dead hippo, so to speak, and not be contaminated. And there, don't you see? your strength comes in, the faith in your ability for the digging of unostentatious holes to bury the stuff in — your power of devotion, not to yourself, but to an obscure, back-breaking business. And that's difficult enough. Mind, I am not trying to excuse or even explain — I am trying to account to myself for — for — Mr. Kurtz — for the shade of Mr. Kurtz. This initiated wraith from the back of Nowhere honoured me with its amazing confidence before it vanished altogether. This was because it could speak English to me. The original Kurtz had been educated partly in England, and — as he was good enough to say himself — his sympathies were in the right place. His mother was half-English, his father was half-French. All Europe contributed to the making of Kurtz; and by-and-by I learned that, most appropriately, the International Society for the Suppression of Savage Customs had intrusted him with the making of a report, for its future guidance. And he had written it, too. I've seen it. I've read it. It was eloquent, vibrating with eloquence, but too high-strung, I think. Seventeen pages of close writing he had found time for! But this must have been before his — let us say — nerves, went wrong, and caused him to preside at certain midnight dances ending with unspeakable rites, which — as far as I reluctantly gathered from what I heard at various times — were offered up to him — do you understand? — to Mr. Kurtz himself. But it was a beautiful piece of writing. The opening paragraph, however, in the light of later information, strikes me now as ominous. He began with the argument that we whites, from the point of development we had arrived at, 'must necessarily appear to them [savages] in the nature of supernatural beings — we approach them with the might as of a deity,' and so on, and so on. 'By the simple exercise of our will we can exert a power for good practically unbounded,' etc., etc. From that point he soared and took me with him. The peroration was magnificent, though difficult to remember, you know. It gave me the notion of an exotic Immensity ruled by an august Benevolence. It made me tingle with enthusiasm. This was the unbounded power of eloquence — of words — of burning noble words. There were no practical hints to interrupt the magic current of phrases, unless a kind of note at the foot of the last page, scrawled evidently much later, in an unsteady hand, may be regarded as the exposition of a method. It was very simple, and at the end of that moving appeal to every altruistic sentiment it blazed at you, luminous and terrifying, like a flash of lightning in a serene sky: 'Exterminate all the brutes!' The curious part was that he had apparently forgotten all about that valuable post-scriptum, because, later on, when he in a sense came to himself, he repeatedly entreated me to take good care of 'my pamphlet' (he called it), as it was sure to have in the future a good influence upon his career. I had full information about all these things, and, besides, as it turned out, I was to have the care of his memory. I've done enough for it to give me the indisputable right to lay it, if I choose, for an everlasting rest in the dust-bin of progress, amongst all the sweepings and, figuratively speaking, all the dead cats of civilization. But then, you see, I can't choose. He won't be forgotten. Whatever he was, he was not common. He had the power to charm or frighten rudimentary souls into an aggravated witch-dance in his honour; he could also fill the small souls of the pilgrims with bitter misgivings: he had one devoted friend at least, and he had conquered one soul in the world that was neither rudimentary nor tainted with self-seeking. No; I can't forget him, though I am not prepared to affirm the fellow was exactly worth the life we lost in getting to him. I missed my late helmsman awfully,—I missed him even while his body was still lying in the pilot-house. Perhaps you will think it passing strange this regret for a savage who was no more account than a grain of sand in a black Sahara. Well, don't you see, he had done something, he had steered; for months I had him at my back—a help—an instrument. It was a kind of partnership. He steered for me—I had to look after him, I worried about his deficiencies, and thus a subtle bond had been created, of which I only became aware when it was suddenly broken. And the intimate profundity of that look he gave me when he received his hurt remains to this day in my memory—like a claim of distant kinship affirmed in a supreme moment.

"Poor fool! If he had only left that shutter alone. He had no restraint, no restraint—just like Kurtz—a tree swayed by the wind. As soon as I had put on a dry pair of slippers, I dragged him out, after first jerking the spear out of his side, which operation I confess I performed with my eyes shut tight. His heels leaped together over the little door-step; his shoulders were pressed to my breast; I hugged him from behind desperately. Oh! he was heavy, heavy; heavier than any man on earth, I should imagine. Then without more ado I tipped him overboard. The current snatched him as though he had been a wisp of grass, and I saw the body roll over twice before I lost sight of it for ever. All the pilgrims and the manager were then congregated on the awning-deck about the pilot-house, chattering at each other like a flock of excited magpies, and there was a scandalized murmur at my heartless promptitude. What they wanted to keep that body hanging about for I can't guess. Embalm it, maybe. But I had also heard another, and a very ominous, murmur on the deck below. My friends the woodcutters, were likewise scandalized, and with a better show of reason—though I admit that the reason itself was quite inadmissible. Oh, quite! I had made up my mind that if my late helmsman was to be eaten, the fishes alone should have him. He had been a very second-rate helmsman while alive, but now he was dead he might have become a first-class temptation, and possibly cause some startling trouble. Besides, I was anxious to take the wheel, the man in pink pyjamas showing himself a hopeless duffer at the business.

"This I did directly the simple funeral was over. We were going half-speed, keeping right in the middle of the stream, and I listened to the talk about me. They had given up Kurtz, they had given up the station; Kurtz was dead, and the station had been burnt—and so on—and so on. The red-haired pilgrim was beside himself with the thought that at least this poor Kurtz had been properly avenged. 'Say! We must have made a glorious slaughter of them in the bush. Eh? What do you think? Say?' He positively danced, the bloodthirsty little gingery beggar. And he had nearly fainted when he saw the wounded man! I could not help saying, 'You made a glorious lot of smoke, anyhow.' I had seen, from the way the tops of the bushes rustled and flew, that almost all the shots had gone too high. You can't hit anything unless you take aim and fire from the shoulder; but these chaps fired from the hip with their eyes shut. The retreat, I maintained

— and I was right — was caused by the screeching of the steam-whistle. Upon this they forgot Kurtz, and began to howl at me with indignant protests.

"The manager stood by the wheel murmuring confidentially about the necessity of getting well away down the river before dark at all events, when I saw in the distance a clearing on the river-side and the outlines of some sort of building. 'What's this?' I asked. He clapped his hands in wonder. 'The station!' he cried. I edged in at once, still going half-speed.

"Through my glasses I saw the slope of a hill interspersed with rare trees and perfectly free from undergrowth. A long decaying building on the summit was half buried in the high grass; the large holes in the peaked roof gaped black from afar; the jungle and the woods made a background. There was no enclosure or fence of any kind; but there had been one apparently, for near the house half-a-dozen slim posts remained in a row, roughly trimmed, and with their upper ends ornamented with round carved balls. The rails, or whatever there had been between, had disappeared. Of course the forest surrounded all that. The river-bank was clear, and on the water-side I saw a white man under a hat like a cart-wheel beckoning persistently with his whole arm. Examining the edge of the forest above and below, I was almost certain I could see movements — human forms gliding here and there. I steamed past prudently, then stopped the engines and let her drift down. The man on the shore began to shout, urging us to land. 'We have been attacked,' screamed the manager. 'I know — I know. It's all right,' yelled back the other, as cheerful as you please. 'Come along. It's all right. I am glad.'

"His aspect reminded me of something I had seen — something funny I had seen somewhere. As I maneuvered to get alongside, I was asking myself, 'What does this fellow look like?' Suddenly I got it. He looked like a harlequin. His clothes had been made of some stuff that was brown holland probably, but it was covered with patches all over, with bright patches, blue, red, and yellow, — patches on the back, patches on the front, patches on elbows, on knees; coloured binding around his jacket, scarlet edging at the bottom of his trousers; and the sunshine made him look extremely gay and wonderfully neat withal, because you could see how beautifully all this patching had been done. A beardless, boyish face, very fair, no features to speak of, nose peeling, little blue eyes, smiles and frowns chasing each other over that open countenance like sunshine and shadow on a wind-swept plain. 'Look out, captain!' he cried 'there's a snag lodged in here last night.' What! Another snag? I confess I swore shamefully. I had nearly holed my cripple, to finish off that charming trip. The harlequin on the bank turned his little pug-nose up to me. 'You English?' he asked, all smiles. 'Are you?' I shouted from the wheel. The smiles vanished, and he shook his head as if sorry for my disappointment. Then he brightened up. 'Never mind!' he cried, encouragingly. 'Are we in time!' I asked. 'He is up there,' he replied, with a toss of the head up the hill, and becoming gloomy all of a sudden. His face was like the autumn sky, overcast one moment and bright the next.

"When the manager, escorted by the pilgrims, all of them armed to the teeth, had gone to the house this chap came on board. 'I say, I don't like this. These natives are in the bush,' I said. He assured me earnestly it was all right. 'They are simple people,' he added; 'well, I am glad you came. It took me all my time to keep them off.' 'But you said it was all right,' I cried. 'Oh, they meant no harm,' he said; and as I stared he corrected himself, 'Not exactly.' Then vivaciously, 'My faith, your pilot-house wants a clean up!' In the next breath he advised me to keep enough steam on the boiler to blow the whistle in case of any trouble. 'One good screech will do more for you than all your rifles. They are simple people,' he repeated. He rattled away at such a rate he quite overwhelmed me. He seemed to be trying to make up for lots of silence, and actually hinted, laughing, that such was the case. 'Don't you talk with Mr. Kurtz?' I said. 'You don't talk with that man — you listen to him,' he exclaimed with severe exaltation. 'But now —— ' He waved his arm, and in the twinkling of an eye was in the uttermost depths of despondency. In a moment he came up again with a jump, possessed himself of both my hands, shook them continuously, while he gabbled: 'Brother sailor . . . honour . . . pleasure . . . delight . . . introduce myself . . . Russian . . . son of an arch-priest . . . Government of Tambov . . . What? Tobacco! English tobacco; the excellent English tobacco! Now, that's brotherly. Smoke? Where's a sailor that does not smoke?'

"The pipe soothed him, and gradually I made out he had run away from school, had gone to sea in a Russian ship; ran away again; served some time in English ships; was now reconciled with the arch-priest. He made a point of that. 'But when one is young one must see things, gather experience, ideas; enlarge the mind' 'Here!' I interrupted. 'You can never tell! Here I met Mr. Kurtz,' he said, youthfully solemn and reproachful. I held my tongue after that. It appears he had persuaded a Dutch trading-house on the coast to fit him out with stores and goods, and had started for the interior with a light heart, and no more idea of what would happen to him than a baby. He had been wandering about that river for nearly two years alone, cut off from everybody and everything. 'I am not so young as I look. I am twenty-five,' he said. 'At first old Van Shuyten would tell me to go to the devil,' he narrated with keen enjoyment; 'but I stuck to him, and talked and talked, till at last he got afraid I would talk the hind-leg off his favourite dog, so he gave me some cheap things and a few guns, and told me he hoped he would never see my face again. Good old Dutchman, Van Shuyten. I've sent him one small lot of ivory a year ago, so that he can't call me a little thief when I get back. I hope he got it. And for the rest I don't care. I had some wood stacked for you. That was my old house. Did you see?'

"I gave him Towson's book. He made as though he would kiss me, but restrained himself. 'The only book I had left, and I thought I had lost it,' he said, looking at it ecstatically. 'So many accidents happen to a man going about alone, you know. Canoes get upset sometimes — and sometimes you've got to clear out so quick when the people get angry.' He thumbed the pages. 'You made notes in Russian?' I asked. He nodded. 'I thought they were written in cipher,' I said. He laughed, then became serious. 'I had lots of trouble to keep these people off,' he said. 'Did they want to kill you?' I asked. 'Oh, no!' he cried, and checked himself. 'Why did they attack us?' I pursued. He hesitated, then said shamefacedly, 'They don't want him to go.' 'Don't they?' I said, curiously. He nodded a nod full of mystery and wisdom. 'I tell you,' he cried, 'this man has enlarged my mind.' He opened his arms wide, staring at me with his little blue eyes that were perfectly round."

III

"I looked at him, lost in astonishment. There he was before me, in motley, as though he had absconded from a troupe of mimes, enthusiastic, fabulous. His very existence was improbable, inexplicable, and altogether bewildering. He was an insoluble problem. It was inconceivable how he had existed, how he had succeeded in getting so far, how he had managed to remain—why he did not instantly disappear. 'I went a little farther,' he said, 'then still a little farther—till I had gone so far that I don't know how I'll ever get back. Never mind. Plenty time. I can manage. You take Kurtz away quick—quick—I tell you.' The glamour of youth enveloped his particoloured rags, his destitution, his loneliness, the essential desolation of his futile wanderings. For months—for years—his life hadn't been worth a day's purchase; and there he was gallantly, thoughtlessly alive, to all appearance indestructible solely by the virtue of his few years and of his unreflecting audacity. I was seduced into something like admiration—like envy. Glamour urged him on, glamour kept him unscathed. He surely wanted nothing from the wilderness but space to breathe in and to push on through. His need was to exist, and to move onwards at the greatest possible risk, and with a maximum of privation. If the absolutely pure, uncalculating, unpractical spirit of adventure had ever ruled a human being, it ruled this be-patched youth. I almost envied him the possession of this modest and clear flame. It seemed to have consumed all thought of self so completely, that even while he was talking to you, you forgot that it was he—the man before your eyes—who had gone through these things. I did not envy him his devotion to Kurtz, though. He had not meditated over it. It came to him, and he accepted it with a sort of eager fatalism. I must say that to me it appeared about the most dangerous thing in every way he had come upon so far.

"They had come together unavoidably, like two ships becalmed near each other, and lay rubbing sides at last. I suppose Kurtz wanted an audience, because on a certain occasion, when encamped in the forest, they had talked all night, or more probably Kurtz had talked. 'We talked of everything,' he said, quite transported at the recollection. 'I forgot there was such a thing as sleep. The night did not seem to last an hour. Everything! Everything! . . . Of love, too.' 'Ah, he talked to you of love!' I said, much amused. 'It isn't what you think,' he cried, almost passionately. 'It was in general. He made me see things—things.'

"He threw his arms up. We were on deck at the time, and the headman of my wood-cutters, lounging near by, turned upon him his heavy and glittering eyes. I looked around, and I don't know why, but I assure you that never, never before, did this land, this river, this jungle, the very arch of this blazing sky, appear to me so hopeless and so dark, so impenetrable to human thought, so pitiless to human weakness. 'And, ever since, you have been with him, of course?' I said.

"On the contrary. It appears their intercourse had been very much broken by various causes. He had, as he informed me proudly, managed to nurse Kurtz through two illnesses (he alluded to it as you would to some risky feat), but as a rule Kurtz wandered alone, far in the depths of the forest. 'Very often coming to this station, I had to wait days and days before he would turn up,' he said. 'Ah, it was worth waiting for!—sometimes.' 'What was he doing? exploring or what?' I asked. 'Oh, yes, of course,' he had discovered lots of villages, a lake, too—he did not know exactly in what direction; it was dangerous to inquire too much—but mostly his expeditions had been for ivory. 'But he had no goods to trade with by that time,' I objected. 'There's a good lot of cartridges left even yet,' he answered, looking away. 'To speak plainly, he raided the country,' I said. He nodded. 'Not alone, surely!' He muttered something about the villages round that lake. 'Kurtz got the tribe to follow him, did he?' I suggested. He fidgeted a little. 'They adored him,' he said. The tone of these words was so extraordinary that I looked at him searchingly. It was curious to see his mingled eagerness and reluctance to speak of Kurtz. The man filled his life, occupied his thoughts, swayed his emotions. 'What can you expect?' he burst out; 'he came to them with thunder and lightning, you know—and they had never seen anything like it—and very terrible. He could be very terrible. You can't judge Mr. Kurtz as you would an ordinary man. No, no, no! Now—just to give you an idea—I don't mind telling you, he wanted to shoot me, too, one day—but I don't judge him.' 'Shoot you!' I cried. 'What for?' 'Well, I had a small lot of ivory the chief of that village near my house gave me. You see I used to shoot game for them. Well, he wanted it, and wouldn't hear reason. He declared he would shoot me unless I gave him the ivory and then cleared out of the country, because he could do so, and had a fancy for it, and there was nothing on earth to prevent him killing whom he jolly well pleased. And it was true, too. I gave him the ivory. What did I care! But I didn't clear out. No, no. I couldn't leave him. I had to be careful, of course, till we got friendly again for a time. He had his second illness then. Afterwards I had to keep out of the way; but I didn't mind. He was living for the most part in those villages on the lake. When he came down to the river, sometimes he would take to me, and sometimes it was better for me to be careful. This man suffered too much. He hated all this, and somehow he couldn't get away. When I had a chance I begged him to try and leave while there was time; I offered to go back with him. And he would say yes, and then he would remain; go off on another ivory hunt; disappear for weeks; forget himself amongst these people—forget himself—you know.' 'Why! he's mad,' I said. He protested indignantly. Mr. Kurtz couldn't be mad. If I had heard him talk, only two days ago, I wouldn't dare hint at such a thing. . . . I had taken up my binoculars while we talked, and was looking at the shore, sweeping the limit of the forest at each side and at the back of the house. The consciousness of there being people in that bush, so silent, so quiet—as silent and quiet as the ruined house on the hill—made me uneasy. There was no sign on the face of nature of this amazing tale that was not so much told as suggested to me in desolate exclamations, completed by shrugs, in interrupted phrases, in hints ending in deep sighs. The woods were unmoved, like a mask—heavy, like the closed door of a prison—they looked with their air of hidden knowledge, of patient expectation, of unapproachable silence. The Russian was explaining to me that it was only lately that Mr. Kurtz had come down to the river, bringing along with him all the fighting men of that lake tribe. He had been absent for several months—getting himself adored, I suppose—and had come down unexpectedly, with the intention to all appearance of making a raid either across the river or down stream. Evidently the appetite for more ivory had got the better of the—what shall I say?—less material aspirations. However he had got much worse suddenly. 'I heard he was lying helpless, and so I came up—took my chance,' said the

Russian. 'Oh, he is bad, very bad.' I directed my glass to the house. There were no signs of life, but there was the ruined roof, the long mud wall peeping above the grass, with three little square window-holes, no two of the same size; all this brought within reach of my hand, as it were. And then I made a brusque movement, and one of the remaining posts of that vanished fence leaped up in the field of my glass. You remember I told you I had been struck at the distance by certain attempts at ornamentation, rather remarkable in the ruinous aspect of the place. Now I had suddenly a nearer view, and its first result was to make me throw my head back as if before a blow. Then I went carefully from post to post with my glass, and I saw my mistake. These round knobs were not ornamental but symbolic; they were expressive and puzzling, striking and disturbing—food for thought and also for the vultures if there had been any looking down from the sky; but at all events for such ants as were industrious enough to ascend the pole. They would have been even more impressive, those heads on the stakes, if their faces had not been turned to the house. Only one, the first I had made out, was facing my way. I was not so shocked as you may think. The start back I had given was really nothing but a movement of surprise. I had expected to see a knob of wood there, you know. I returned deliberately to the first I had seen—and there it was, black, dried, sunken, with closed eyelids,—a head that seemed to sleep at the top of that pole, and, with the shrunken dry lips showing a narrow white line of the teeth, was smiling, too, smiling continuously at some endless and jocose dream of that eternal slumber.

"I am not disclosing any trade secrets. In fact, the manager said afterwards that Mr. Kurtz's methods had ruined the district. I have no opinion on that point, but I want you clearly to understand that there was nothing exactly profitable in these heads being there. They only showed that Mr. Kurtz lacked restraint in the gratification of his various lusts, that there was something wanting in him—some small matter which, when the pressing need arose, could not be found under his magnificent eloquence. Whether he knew of this deficiency himself I can't say. I think the knowledge came to him at last—only at the very last. But the wilderness had found him out early, and had taken on him a terrible vengeance for the fantastic invasion. I think it had whispered to him things about himself which he did not know, things of which he had no conception till he took counsel with this great solitude—and the whisper had proved irresistibly fascinating. It echoed loudly within him because he was hollow at the core. . . . I put down the glass, and the head that had appeared near enough to be spoken to seemed at once to have leaped away from me into inaccessible distance.

"The admirer of Mr. Kurtz was a bit crestfallen. In a hurried, indistinct voice he began to assure me he had not dared to take these—say, symbols—down. He was not afraid of the natives; they would not stir till Mr. Kurtz gave the word. His ascendancy was extraordinary. The camps of these people surrounded the place, and the chiefs came every day to see him. They would crawl. . . . 'I don't want to know anything of the ceremonies used when approaching Mr. Kurtz,' I shouted. Curious, this feeling that came over me that such details would be more intolerable than those heads drying on the stakes under Mr. Kurtz's windows. After all, that was only a savage sight, while I seemed at one bound to have been transported into some lightless region of subtle horrors, where pure, uncomplicated savagery was a positive relief, being something that had a right to exist—

obviously—in the sunshine. The young man looked at me with surprise. I suppose it did not occur to him that Mr. Kurtz was no idol of mine. He forgot I hadn't heard any of these splendid monologues on, what was it? on love, justice, conduct of life—or what not. If it had come to crawling before Mr. Kurtz, he crawled as much as the veriest savage of them all. I had no idea of the conditions, he said: these heads were the heads of rebels. I shocked him excessively by laughing. Rebels! What would be the next definition I was to hear? There had been enemies, criminals, workers—and these were rebels. Those rebellious heads looked very subdued to me on their sticks. 'You don't know how such a life tries a man like Kurtz,' cried Kurtz's last disciple. 'Well, and you?' I said. 'I! I! I am a simple man. I have no great thoughts. I want nothing from anybody. How can you compare me to? . . .' His feelings were too much for speech, and suddenly he broke down. 'I don't understand,' he groaned. 'I've been doing my best to keep him alive, and that's enough. I had no hand in all this. I have no abilities. There hasn't been a drop of medicine or a mouthful of invalid food for months here. He was shamefully abandoned. A man like this, with such ideas. Shamefully! Shamefully! I—I—haven't slept for the last ten nights. . . .'

"His voice lost itself in the calm of the evening. The long shadows of the forest had slipped down hill while we talked, had gone far beyond the ruined hovel, beyond the symbolic row of stakes. All this was in the gloom, while we down there were yet in the sunshine, and the stretch of the river abreast of the clearing glittered in a still and dazzling splendour, with a murky and overshadowed bend above and below. Not a living soul was seen on the shore. The bushes did not rustle.

"Suddenly round the corner of the house a group of men appeared, as though they had come up from the ground. They waded waist-deep in the grass, in a compact body, bearing an improvised stretcher in their midst. Instantly, in the emptiness of the landscape, a cry arose whose shrillness pierced the still air like a sharp arrow flying straight to the very heart of the land; and, as if by enchantment, streams of human beings—of naked human beings—with spears in their hands, with bows, with shields, with wild glances and savage movements, were poured into the clearing by the dark-faced and pensive forest. The bushes shook, the grass swayed for a time, and then everything stood still in attentive immobility.

"'Now, if he does not say the right thing to them we are all done for,' said the Russian at my elbow. The knot of men with the stretcher had stopped, too, halfway to the steamer, as if petrified. I saw the man on the stretcher sit up, lank and with an uplifted arm, above the shoulders of the bearers. 'Let us hope that the man who can talk so well of love in general will find some particular reason to spare us this time,' I said. I resented bitterly the absurd danger of our situation, as if to be at the mercy of that atrocious phantom had been a dishonouring necessity. I could not hear a sound, but through my glasses I saw the thin arm extended commandingly, the lower jaw moving, the eyes of that apparition shining darkly far in its bony head that nodded with grotesque jerks. Kurtz—Kurtz—that means short in German—don't it? Well, the name was as true as everything else in his life—and death. He looked at least seven feet long. His covering had fallen off, and his body emerged from it pitiful and appalling as from a winding-sheet. I could see the cage of his ribs all astir, the bones of his arm waving. It was as though an animated image of death carved out of old ivory had been shaking its hand with menaces at a motionless crowd of men made of dark and glittering bronze. I saw him open his mouth wide — it gave him a weirdly voracious aspect, as though he had wanted to swallow all the air, all the earth, all the men before him. A deep voice reached me faintly. He must have been shouting. He fell back suddenly. The stretcher shook as the bearers staggered forward again, and almost at the same time I noticed that the crowd of savages was vanishing without any perceptible movement of retreat, as if the forest that had ejected these beings so suddenly had drawn them in again as the breath is drawn in a long aspiration.

"Some of the pilgrims behind the stretcher carried his arms — two shotguns, a heavy rifle, and a light revolver carbine — the thunderbolts of that pitiful Jupiter. The manager bent over him murmuring as he walked beside his head. They laid him down in one of the little cabins — just a room for a bedplace and a camp-stool or two, you know. We had brought his belated correspondence, and a lot of torn envelopes and open letters littered his bed. His hand roamed feebly amongst these papers. I was struck by the fire of his eyes and the composed languor of his expression. It was not so much the exhaustion of disease. He did not seem in pain. This shadow looked satiated and calm, as though for the moment it had had its fill of all the emotions.

"He rustled one of the letters, and looking straight in my face said, 'I am glad.' Somebody had been writing to him about me. These special recommendations were turning up again. The volume of tone he emitted without effort, almost without the trouble of moving his lips, amazed me. A voice! a voice! It was grave, profound, vibrating, while the man did not seem capable of a whisper. However, he had enough strength in him — factitious no doubt — to very nearly make an end of us, as you shall hear directly.

"The manager appeared silently in the doorway; I stepped out at once and he drew the curtain after me. The Russian, eyed curiously by the pilgrims, was staring at the shore. I followed the direction of his glance.

"Dark human shapes could be made out in the distance, flitting indistinctly against the gloomy border of the forest, and near the river two bronze figures, leaning on tall spears, stood in the sunlight under fantastic head-dresses of spotted skins, warlike and still in statuesque repose. And from right to left along the lighted shore moved a wild and gorgeous apparition of a woman.

"She walked with measured steps, draped in striped and fringed cloths, treading the earth proudly, with a slight jingle and flash of barbarous ornaments. She carried her head high; her hair was done in the shape of a helmet; she had brass leggings to the knee, brass wire gauntlets to the elbow, a crimson spot on her tawny cheek, innumerable necklaces of glass beads on her neck; bizarre things, charms, gifts of witch-men, that hung about her, glittered and trembled at every step. She must have had the value of several elephant tusks upon her. She was savage and superb, wild-eyed and magnificent; there was something ominous and stately in her deliberate progress. And in the hush that had fallen suddenly upon the whole sorrowful land, the immense wilderness, the colossal body of the fecund and mysterious life seemed to look at her, pensive, as though it had been looking at the image of its own tenebrous and passionate soul.

"She came abreast of the steamer, stood still, and faced us. Her long shadow fell to the water's edge. Her face had a tragic and fierce aspect of wild sorrow and of dumb pain mingled with the fear of some struggling, half-shaped resolve. She stood looking at us without a stir, and like the wilderness itself, with an air of brooding over an inscrutable purpose. A whole minute passed, and then she made a step forward. There was a low jingle, a glint of yellow metal, a sway of fringed draperies, and she stopped as if her heart had failed her. The young fellow by my side growled. The pilgrims murmured at my back. She looked at us all as if her life had depended upon the unswerving steadiness of her glance. Suddenly she opened her bared arms and threw them up rigid above her head, as though in an uncontrollable desire to touch the sky, and at the same time the swift shadows darted out on the earth, swept around on the river, gathering the steamer into a shadowy embrace. A formidable silence hung over the scene.

"She turned away slowly, walked on, following the bank, and passed into the bushes to the left. Once only her eyes gleamed back at us in the dusk of the thickets before she disappeared.

"'If she had offered to come aboard I really think I would have tried to shoot her,' said the man of patches, nervously, 'I had been risking my life every day for the last fortnight to keep her out of the house. She got in one day and kicked up a row about those miserable rags I picked up in the storeroom to mend my clothes with. I wasn't decent. At least it must have been that, for she talked like a fury to Kurtz for an hour, pointing at me now and then. I don't understand the dialect of this tribe. Luckily for me, I fancy Kurtz felt too ill that day to care, or there would have been mischief. I don't understand. . . . No—it's too much for me. Ah, well, it's all over now.'

"At this moment I heard Kurtz's deep voice behind the curtain: 'Save me!—save the ivory, you mean. Don't tell me. Save *me*! Why, I've had to save you. You are interrupting my plans now. Sick! Sick! Not so sick as you would like to believe. Never mind. I'll carry my ideas out yet—I will return. I'll show you what can be done. You with your little peddling notions—you are interfering with me. I will return. I. . . .'

"The manager came out. He did me the honour to take me under the arm and lead me aside. 'He is very low, very low,' he said. He considered it necessary to sigh, but neglected to be consistently sorrowful. 'We have done all we could for him—haven't we? But there is no disguising the fact, Mr. Kurtz has done more harm than good to the Company. He did not see the time was not ripe for vigorous action. Cautiously, cautiously—that's my principle. We must be cautious yet. The district is closed to us for a time. Deplorable! Upon the whole, the trade will suffer. I don't deny there is a remarkable quantity of ivory—mostly fossil. We must save it, at all events—but look how precarious the position is—and why? Because the method is unsound.' 'Do you,' said I, looking at the shore, 'call it "unsound method?"' 'Without doubt,' he exclaimed, hotly. 'Don't you?' . . . 'No method at all,' I murmured after a while. 'Exactly,' he exulted. 'I anticipated this. Shows a complete want of judgment. It is my duty to point it out in the proper quarter.' 'Oh,' said I, 'that fellow—what's his name?—the brick-maker, will make a readable report for you.' He appeared confounded for a moment. It seemed to me I had never breathed an atmosphere so vile, and I turned mentally to Kurtz for relief—positively for relief. 'Nevertheless I think Mr. Kurtz is a remarkable man,' I said with emphasis. He started, dropped on me a cold heavy glance, said very quietly, 'he *was*,' and turned his back on me. My hour of favour was over; I found myself lumped along with Kurtz as a partisan of methods for which the time was not ripe: I was unsound! Ah! but it was something to have at least a choice of nightmares.

"I had turned to the wilderness really, not to Mr. Kurtz, who, I was ready to admit, was as good as buried. And for a moment it seemed to me as if I also were buried in a vast grave full of unspeakable secrets. I felt an intolerable weight oppressing my breast, the smell of the damp earth, the unseen presence of victorious corruption, the darkness of an impenetrable night. . . . The Russian tapped me on the shoulder. I heard him mumbling and stammering something about 'brother seaman — couldn't conceal — knowledge of matters that would affect Mr. Kurtz's reputation.' I waited. For him evidently Mr. Kurtz was not in his grave; I suspect that for him Mr. Kurtz was one of the immortals. 'Well!' said I at last, 'speak out. As it happens, I am Mr. Kurtz's friend — in a way.'

"He stated with a good deal of formality that had we not been 'of the same profession,' he would have kept the matter to himself without regard to consequences. 'He suspected there was an active ill will towards him on the part of these white men that —— ' 'You are right,' I said, remembering a certain conversation I had overheard. 'The manager thinks you ought to be hanged.' He showed a concern at this intelligence which amused me at first. 'I had better get out of the way quietly,' he said, earnestly. 'I can do no more for Kurtz now, and they would soon find some excuse. What's to stop them? There's a military post three hundred miles from here.' 'Well, upon my word,' said I, 'perhaps you had better go if you have any friends amongst the savages near by.' 'Plenty,' he said. 'They are simple people — and I want nothing, you know.' He stood biting his lip, then: 'I don't want any harm to happen to these whites here, but of course I was thinking of Mr. Kurtz's reputation — but you are a brother seaman and —— ' 'All right,' said I, after a time. 'Mr. Kurtz's reputation is safe with me.' I did not know how truly I spoke.

"He informed me, lowering his voice, that it was Kurtz who had ordered the attack to be made on the steamer. 'He hated sometimes the idea of being taken away — and then again. . . . But I don't understand these matters. I am a simple man. He thought it would scare you away — that you would give it up, thinking him dead. I could not stop him. Oh, I had an awful time of it this last month.' 'Very well,' I said. 'He is all right now.' 'Ye-e-es,' he muttered, not very convinced apparently. 'Thanks,' said I; 'I shall keep my eyes open.' 'But quiet — eh?' he urged, anxiously. 'It would be awful for his reputation if anybody here —— ' I promised a complete discretion with great gravity. 'I have a canoe and three black fellows waiting not very far. I am off. Could you give me a few Martini-Henry cartridges?' I could, and did, with proper secrecy. He helped himself, with a wink at me, to a handful of my tobacco. 'Between sailors — you know — good English tobacco.' At the door of the pilot-house he turned round — 'I say, haven't you a pair of shoes you could spare?' He raised one leg. 'Look.' The soles were tied with knotted strings sandal-wise under his bare feet. I rooted out an old pair, at which he looked with admiration before tucking it under his left arm. One of his pockets (bright red) was bulging with cartridges, from the other (dark blue) peeped 'Towson's Inquiry,' etc., etc. He seemed to think himself excellently well equipped for a renewed encounter with the wilderness. 'Ah! I'll never, never meet such a man again. You ought to have heard him recite poetry — his own, too, it was, he told me. Poetry!' He rolled his eyes at the recollection of these delights. 'Oh, he enlarged my mind!' 'Goodbye,' said I. He shook hands and vanished in the night. Sometimes I ask myself whether I had ever really seen him—whether it was possible to meet such a phenomenon! . . .

"When I woke up shortly after midnight his warning came to my mind with its hint of danger that seemed, in the starred darkness, real enough to make me get up for the purpose of having a look round. On the hill a big fire burned, illuminating fitfully a crooked corner of the station-house. One of the agents with a picket of a few of our blacks, armed for the purpose, was keeping guard over the ivory; but deep within the forest, red gleams that wavered, that seemed to sink and rise from the ground amongst confused columnar shapes of intense blackness, showed the exact position of the camp where Mr. Kurtz's adorers were keeping their uneasy vigil. The monotonous beating of a big drum filled the air with muffled shocks and a lingering vibration. A steady droning sound of many men chanting each to himself some weird incantation came out from the black, flat wall of the woods as the humming of bees comes out of a hive, and had a strange narcotic effect upon my half-awake senses. I believe I dozed off leaning over the rail, till an abrupt burst of yells, an overwhelming outbreak of a pent-up and mysterious frenzy, woke me up in a bewildered wonder. It was cut short all at once, and the low droning went on with an effect of audible and soothing silence. I glanced casually into the little cabin. A light was burning within, but Mr. Kurtz was not there.

"I think I would have raised an outcry if I had believed my eyes. But I didn't believe them at first—the thing seemed so impossible. The fact is I was completely unnerved by a sheer blank fright, pure abstract terror, unconnected with any distinct shape of physical danger. What made this emotion so overpowering was—how shall I define it?—the moral shock I received, as if something altogether monstrous, intolerable to thought and odious to the soul, had been thrust upon me unexpectedly. This lasted of course the merest fraction of a second, and then the usual sense of commonplace, deadly danger, the possibility of a sudden onslaught and massacre, or something of the kind, which I saw impending, was positively welcome and composing. It pacified me, in fact, so much, that I did not raise an alarm.

"There was an agent buttoned up inside an ulster and sleeping on a chair on deck within three feet of me. The yells had not awakened him; he snored very slightly; I left him to his slumbers and leaped ashore. I did not betray Mr. Kurtz—it was ordered I should never betray him—it was written I should be loyal to the nightmare of my choice. I was anxious to deal with this shadow by myself alone,—and to this day I don't know why I was so jealous of sharing with any one the peculiar blackness of that experience.

"As soon as I got on the bank I saw a trail—a broad trail through the grass. I remember the exultation with which I said to myself, 'He can't walk—he is crawling on all-fours—I've got him.' The grass was wet with dew. I strode rapidly with clenched fists. I fancy I had some vague notion of falling upon him and giving him a drubbing. I don't know. I had some imbecile thoughts. The knitting old woman with the cat obtruded herself upon my memory as a most improper person to be sitting at the other end of such an affair. I saw a row of pilgrims squirting lead in the air out of Winchesters held to the hip. I thought I would never get back to the steamer, and imagined myself living alone and unarmed in the woods to an advanced age. Such silly things — you know. And I remember I confounded the beat of the drum with the beating of my heart, and was pleased at its calm regularity.

"I kept to the track though — then stopped to listen. The night was very clear; a dark blue space, sparkling with dew and starlight, in which black things stood very still. I thought I could see a kind of motion ahead of me. I was strangely cocksure of everything that night. I actually left the track and ran in a wide semicircle (I verily believe chuckling to myself) so as to get in front of that stir, of that motion I had seen — if indeed I had seen anything. I was circumventing Kurtz as though it had been a boyish game.

"I came upon him, and, if he had not heard me coming, I would have fallen over him, too, but he got up in time. He rose, unsteady, long, pale, indistinct, like a vapour exhaled by the earth, and swayed slightly, misty and silent before me; while at my back the fires loomed between the trees, and the murmur of many voices issued from the forest. I had cut him off cleverly; but when actually confronting him I seemed to come to my senses. I saw the danger in its right proportion. It was by no means over yet. Suppose he began to shout? Though he could hardly stand, there was still plenty of vigour in his voice. 'Go away — hide yourself,' he said, in that profound tone. It was very awful. I glanced back. We were within thirty yards from the nearest fire. A black figure stood up, strode on long black legs, waving long black arms, across the glow. It had horns — antelope horns, I think — on its head. Some sorcerer, some witch-man, no doubt; it looked fiendlike enough. 'Do you know what you are doing?' I whispered. 'Perfectly,' he answered, raising his voice for that single word: it sounded to me far off and yet loud, like a hail through a speaking-trumpet. If he makes a row we are lost, I thought to myself. This clearly was not a case for fisticuffs, even apart from the very natural aversion I had to beat that Shadow — this wandering and tormented thing. 'You will be lost,' I said — 'utterly lost.' One gets sometimes such a flash of inspiration, you know. I did say the right thing, though indeed he could not have been more irretrievably lost than he was at this very moment, when the foundations of our intimacy were being laid — to endure — to endure — even to the end — even beyond.

"'I had immense plans,' he muttered irresolutely. 'Yes,' said I; 'but if you try to shout I'll smash your head with —' There was not a stick or a stone near. 'I will throttle you for good,' I corrected myself. 'I was on the threshold of great things,' he pleaded, in a voice of longing, with a wistfulness of tone that made my blood run cold. 'And now for this stupid scoundrel —' 'Your success in Europe is assured in any case,' I affirmed, steadily. I did not want to have the throttling of him, you understand — and indeed it would have been very little use for any practical purpose. I tried to break the spell — the heavy, mute spell of the wilderness — that seemed to draw him to its pitiless breast by the awakening of forgotten and brutal instincts, by the memory of gratified and monstrous passions. This alone, I was convinced, had driven him out to the edge of the forest, to the bush, towards the gleam of fires, the throb of drums, the drone of weird incantations; this alone had beguiled his unlawful soul beyond the bounds of permitted aspirations. And, don't you see, the terror of the position was not in being knocked on the head — though I had a very lively sense of that danger, too — but in this, that I had to deal with a being to whom I could not appeal in the name of anything high or low. I had, even like the niggers, to invoke him—himself—his own exalted and incredible degradation. There was nothing either above or below him, and I knew it. He had kicked himself loose of the earth. Confound the man! he had kicked the very earth to pieces. He was alone, and I before him did not know whether I stood on the ground or floated in the air. I've been telling you what we said—repeating the phrases we pronounced—but what's the good? They were common everyday words—the familiar, vague sounds exchanged on every waking day of life. But what of that? They had behind them, to my mind, the terrific suggestiveness of words heard in dreams, of phrases spoken in nightmares. Soul! If anybody had ever struggled with a soul, I am the man. And I wasn't arguing with a lunatic either. Believe me or not, his intelligence was perfectly clear—concentrated, it is true, upon himself with horrible intensity, yet clear; and therein was my only chance—barring, of course, the killing him there and then, which wasn't so good, on account of unavoidable noise. But his soul was mad. Being alone in the wilderness, it had looked within itself, and, by heavens! I tell you, it had gone mad. I had—for my sins, I suppose—to go through the ordeal of looking into it myself. No eloquence could have been so withering to one's belief in mankind as his final burst of sincerity. He struggled with himself, too. I saw it,—I heard it. I saw the inconceivable mystery of a soul that knew no restraint, no faith, and no fear, yet struggling blindly with itself. I kept my head pretty well; but when I had him at last stretched on the couch, I wiped my forehead, while my legs shook under me as though I had carried half a ton on my back down that hill. And yet I had only supported him, his bony arm clasped round my neck—and he was not much heavier than a child.

"When next day we left at noon, the crowd, of whose presence behind the curtain of trees I had been acutely conscious all the time, flowed out of the woods again, filled the clearing, covered the slope with a mass of naked, breathing, quivering, bronze bodies. I steamed up a bit, then swung downstream, and two thousand eyes followed the evolutions of the splashing, thumping, fierce river-demon beating the water with its terrible tail and breathing black smoke into the air. In front of the first rank, along the river, three men, plastered with bright red earth from head to foot, strutted to and fro restlessly. When we came abreast again, they faced the river, stamped their feet, nodded their horned heads, swayed their scarlet bodies; they shook towards the fierce river-demon a bunch of black feathers, a mangy skin with a pendant tail—something that looked like a dried gourd; they shouted periodically together strings of amazing words that resembled no sounds of human language; and the deep murmurs of the crowd, interrupted suddenly, were like the responses of some satanic litany.

"We had carried Kurtz into the pilot-house: there was more air there. Lying on the couch, he stared through the open shutter. There was an eddy in the mass of human bodies, and the woman with helmeted head and tawny cheeks rushed out to the very brink of the stream. She put out her hands, shouted something, and all that wild mob took up the shout in a roaring chorus of articulated, rapid, breathless utterance.

"'Do you understand this?' I asked.

"He kept on looking out past me with fiery, longing eyes, with a mingled expression of wistfulness and hate. He made no answer, but I saw a smile, a smile of indefinable meaning, appear on his colourless lips that a moment after twitched convulsively. 'Do I not?' he said slowly, gasping, as if the words had been torn out of him by a supernatural power.

"I pulled the string of the whistle, and I did this because I saw the pilgrims on deck getting out their rifles with an air of anticipating a jolly lark. At the sudden screech there was a movement of abject terror through that wedged mass of bodies. 'Don't! don't you frighten them away,' cried someone on deck disconsolately. I pulled the string time after time. They broke and ran, they leaped, they crouched, they swerved, they dodged the flying terror of the sound. The three red chaps had fallen flat, face down on the shore, as though they had been shot dead. Only the barbarous and superb woman did not so much as flinch, and stretched tragically her bare arms after us over the sombre and glittering river.

"And then that imbecile crowd down on the deck started their little fun, and I could see nothing more for smoke.

"The brown current ran swiftly out of the heart of darkness, bearing us down towards the sea with twice the speed of our upward progress; and Kurtz's life was running swiftly, too, ebbing, ebbing out of his heart into the sea of inexorable time. The manager was very placid, he had no vital anxieties now, he took us both in with a comprehensive and satisfied glance: the 'affair' had come off as well as could be wished. I saw the time approaching when I would be left alone of the party of 'unsound method.' The pilgrims looked upon me with disfavour. I was, so to speak, numbered with the dead. It is strange how I accepted this unforeseen partnership, this choice of nightmares forced upon me in the tenebrous land invaded by these mean and greedy phantoms.

"Kurtz discoursed. A voice! a voice! It rang deep to the very last. It survived his strength to hide in the magnificent folds of eloquence the barren darkness of his heart. Oh, he struggled! he struggled! The wastes of his weary brain were haunted by shadowy images now—images of wealth and fame revolving obsequiously round his unextinguishable gift of noble and lofty expression. My Intended, my station, my career, my ideas—these were the subjects for the occasional utterances of elevated sentiments. The shade of the original Kurtz frequented the bedside of the hollow sham, whose fate it was to be buried presently in the mould of primeval earth. But both the diabolic love and the unearthly hate of the mysteries it had penetrated fought for the possession of that soul satiated with primitive emotions, avid of lying fame, of sham distinction, of all the appearances of success and power.

"Sometimes he was contemptibly childish. He desired to have kings meet him at railway-stations on his return from some ghastly Nowhere, where he intended to accomplish great things. 'You show them you have in you something that is really profitable, and then there will be no limits to the recognition of your ability,' he would say. 'Of course you must take care of the motives—right motives—always.' The long reaches that were like one and the same reach, monotonous bends that were exactly alike, slipped past the steamer with their multitude of secular trees looking patiently after this grimy fragment of another world, the forerunner of change, of conquest, of trade, of massacres, of blessings. I looked ahead—piloting. 'Close the shutter,' said Kurtz suddenly one day; 'I can't bear to look at this.' I did so. There was a silence. 'Oh, but I will wring your heart yet!' he cried at the invisible wilderness.

"We broke down—as I had expected—and had to lie up for repairs at the head of an island. This delay was the first thing that shook Kurtz's confidence. One morning he gave me a packet of papers and a photograph—the lot tied together with a shoe-string. 'Keep this for me,' he said. 'This noxious fool' (meaning the manager) 'is capable of prying into my boxes when I am not looking.' In the afternoon I saw him. He was lying on his back with closed eyes, and I withdrew quietly, but I heard him mutter, 'Live rightly, die, die . . .' I listened. There was nothing more. Was he rehearsing some speech in his sleep, or was it a fragment of a phrase from some newspaper article? He had been writing for the papers and meant to do so again, 'for the furthering of my ideas. It's a duty.'

"His was an impenetrable darkness. I looked at him as you peer down at a man who is lying at the bottom of a precipice where the sun never shines. But I had not much time to give him, because I was helping the engine-driver to take to pieces the leaky cylinders, to straighten a bent connecting-rod, and in other such matters. I lived in an infernal mess of rust, filings, nuts, bolts, spanners, hammers, ratchet-drills—things I abominate, because I don't get on with them. I tended the little forge we fortunately had aboard; I toiled wearily in a wretched scrap-heap—unless I had the shakes too bad to stand.

"One evening coming in with a candle, I was startled to hear him say a little tremulously, 'I am lying here in the dark waiting for death.' The light was within a foot of his eyes. I forced myself to murmur, 'Oh, nonsense!' and stood over him as if transfixed.

"Anything approaching the change that came over his features I have never seen before, and hope never to see again. Oh, I wasn't touched. I was fascinated. It was as though a veil had been rent. I saw on that ivory face the expression of sombre pride, of ruthless power, of craven terror—of an intense and hopeless despair. Did he live his life again in every detail of desire, temptation, and surrender during that supreme moment of complete knowledge? He cried in a whisper at some image, at some vision—he cried out twice, a cry that was no more than a breath—

"'The horror! The horror!'

"I blew the candle out and left the cabin. The pilgrims were dining in the mess-room, and I took my place opposite the manager, who lifted his eyes to give me a questioning glance, which I successfully ignored. He leaned back, serene, with that peculiar smile of his sealing the unexpressed depths of his meanness. A continuous shower of small flies streamed upon the lamp, upon the cloth, upon our hands and faces. Suddenly the manager's boy put his insolent black head in the doorway, and said in a tone of scathing contempt—

"'Mistah Kurtz—he dead.'

"All the pilgrims rushed out to see. I remained, and went on with my dinner. I believe I was considered brutally callous. However, I did not eat much. There was a lamp in there—light, don't you know—and outside it was so beastly, beastly dark. I went no more near the remarkable man who had pronounced a judgment upon the adventures of his soul on this earth. The voice was gone.

What else had been there? But I am of course aware that next day the pilgrims buried something in a muddy hole.

"And then they very nearly buried me.

"However, as you see, I did not go to join Kurtz there and then. I did not. I remained to dream the nightmare out to the end, and to show my loyalty to Kurtz once more. Destiny. My destiny! Droll thing life is — that mysterious arrangement of merciless logic for a futile purpose. The most you can hope from it is some knowledge of yourself — that comes too late — a crop of unextinguishable regrets. I have wrestled with death. It is the most unexciting contest you can imagine. It takes place in an impalpable grayness, with nothing underfoot, with nothing around, without spectators, without clamour, without glory, without the great desire of victory, without the great fear of defeat, in a sickly atmosphere of tepid skepticism, without much belief in your own right, and still less in that of your adversary. If such is the form of ultimate wisdom, then life is a greater riddle than some of us think it to be. I was within a hair's-breadth of the last opportunity for pronouncement, and I found with humiliation that probably I would have nothing to say. This is the reason why I affirm that Kurtz was a remarkable man. He had something to say. He said it. Since I had peeped over the edge myself, I understand better the meaning of his stare, that could not see the flame of the candle, but was wide enough to embrace the whole universe, piercing enough to penetrate all the hearts that beat in the darkness. He had summed up — he had judged. 'The horror!' He was a remarkable man. After all, this was the expression of some sort of belief; it had candour, it had conviction, it had a vibrating note of revolt in its whisper, it had the appalling face of a glimpsed truth — the strange commingling of desire and hate. And it is not my own extremity I remember best — a vision of grayness without form filled with physical pain, and a careless contempt for the evanescence of all things — even of this pain itself. No! It is his extremity that I seem to have lived through. True, he had made that last stride, he had stepped over the edge, while I had been permitted to draw back my hesitating foot. And perhaps in this is the whole difference; perhaps all the wisdom, and all truth, and all sincerity, are just compressed into that inappreciable moment of time in which we step over the threshold of the invisible. Perhaps! I like to think my summing-up would not have been a word of careless contempt. Better his cry — much better. It was an affirmation, a moral victory paid for by innumerable defeats, by abominable terrors, by abominable satisfactions. But it was a victory! That is why I have remained loyal to Kurtz to the last, and even beyond, when a long time after I heard once more, not his own voice, but the echo of his magnificent eloquence thrown to me from a soul as translucently pure as a cliff of crystal.

"No, they did not bury me, though there is a period of time which I remember mistily, with a shuddering wonder, like a passage through some inconceivable world — that had no hope in it and no desire. I found myself back in the sepulchral city resenting the sight of people hurrying through the streets to filch a little money from each other, to devour their infamous cookery, to gulp their unwholesome beer, to dream their insignificant and silly dreams. They trespassed upon my thoughts. They were intruders whose knowledge of life was to me an irritating pretence, because I felt so sure they could not possibly know the things

I knew. Their bearing, which was simply the bearing of commonplace individuals going about their business in the assurance of perfect safety, was offensive to me like the outrageous flauntings of folly in the face of a danger it is unable to comprehend. I had no particular desire to enlighten them, but I had some difficulty in restraining myself from laughing in their faces, so full of stupid importance. I daresay I was not very well at that time. I tottered about the streets — there were various affairs to settle — grinning bitterly at perfectly respectable persons. I admit my behaviour was inexcusable, but then my temperature was seldom normal in these days. My dear aunt's endeavours to 'nurse up my strength' seemed altogether beside the mark. It was not my strength that wanted nursing, it was my imagination that wanted soothing. I kept the bundle of papers given me by Kurtz, not knowing exactly what to do with it. His mother had died lately, watched over, as I was told, by his Intended. A clean-shaved man, with an official manner and wearing gold-rimmed spectacles, called on me one day and made inquiries, at first circuitous, afterwards suavely pressing, about what he was pleased to denominate certain 'documents.' I was not surprised, because I had had two rows with the manager on the subject out there. I had refused to give up the smallest scrap out of that package, and I took the same attitude with the spectacled man. He became darkly menacing at last, and with much heat argued that the Company had the right to every bit of information about its 'territories.' And said he, 'Mr. Kurtz's knowledge of unexplored regions must have been necessarily extensive and peculiar — owing to his great abilities and to the deplorable circumstances in which he had been placed: therefore —— ,' I assured him Mr. Kurtz's knowledge, however extensive, did not bear upon the problems of commerce or administration. He invoked then the name of science. 'It would be an incalculable loss if,' etc., etc. I offered him the report on the 'Suppression of Savage Customs,' with the postscriptum torn off. He took it up eagerly, but ended by sniffing at it with an air of contempt. 'This is not what we had a right to expect,' he remarked. 'Expect nothing else,' I said. 'There are only private letters.' He withdrew upon some threat of legal proceedings, and I saw him no more; but another fellow, calling himself Kurtz's cousin, appeared two days later, and was anxious to hear all the details about his dear relative's last moments. Incidentally he gave me to understand that Kurtz had been essentially a great musician. 'There was the making of an immense success,' said the man, who was an organist, I believe, with lank gray hair flowing over a greasy coat-collar. I had no reason to doubt his statement; and to this day I am unable to say what was Kurtz's profession, whether he ever had any — which was the greatest of his talents. I had taken him for a painter who wrote for the papers, or else for a journalist who could paint — but even the cousin (who took snuff during the interview) could not tell me what he had been — exactly. He was a universal genius — on that point I agreed with the old chap, who thereupon blew his nose noisily into a large cotton handkerchief and withdrew in senile agitation, bearing off some family letters and memoranda without importance. Ultimately a journalist anxious to know something of the fate of his 'dear colleague' turned up. This visitor informed me Kurtz's proper sphere ought to have been politics 'on the popular side.' He had furry straight eyebrows, bristly hair cropped short, an eye-glass on a broad ribbon, and, becoming expansive, confessed his opinion that Kurtz really couldn't write a bit — 'but heavens! how that man could talk. He electrified large meetings. He had faith — don't you see? — he had the faith. He could get himself to believe anything — anything. He would have been a splendid leader of an extreme party.' 'What party?' I asked. 'Any party,' answered the other. 'He was an — an — extremist.' Did I not think so? I assented. Did I know, he asked, with a sudden flash of curiosity, 'what it was that had induced him to go out there?' 'Yes,' said I, and forthwith handed him the famous Report for publication, if he thought fit. He glanced through it hurriedly, mumbling all the time, judged 'it would do,' and took himself off with this plunder.

"Thus I was left at last with a slim packet of letters and the girl's portrait. She struck me as beautiful — I mean she had a beautiful expression. I know that the sunlight can be made to lie, too, yet one felt that no manipulation of light and pose could have conveyed the delicate shade of truthfulness upon those features. She seemed ready to listen without mental reservation, without suspicion, without a thought for herself. I concluded I would go and give her back her portrait and those letters myself. Curiosity? Yes; and also some other feeling perhaps. All that had been Kurtz's had passed out of my hands: his soul, his body, his station, his plans, his ivory, his career. There remained only his memory and his Intended — and I wanted to give that up, too, to the past, in a way — to surrender personally all that remained of him with me to that oblivion which is the last word of our common fate. I don't defend myself. I had no clear perception of what it was I really wanted. Perhaps it was an impulse of unconscious loyalty, or the fulfillment of one of these ironic necessities that lurk in the facts of human existence. I don't know. I can't tell. But I went.

"I thought his memory was like the other memories of the dead that accumulate in every man's life — a vague impress on the brain of shadows that had fallen on it in their swift and final passage; but before the high and ponderous door, between the tall houses of a street as still and decorous as a well-kept alley in a cemetery, I had a vision of him on the stretcher, opening his mouth voraciously, as if to devour all the earth with all its mankind. He lived then before me; he lived as much as he had ever lived — a shadow insatiable of splendid appearances, of frightful realities; a shadow darker than the shadow of the night, and draped nobly in the folds of a gorgeous eloquence. The vision seemed to enter the house with me — the stretcher, the phantom-bearers, the wild crowd of obedient worshippers, the gloom of the forests, the glitter of the reach between the murky bends, the beat of the drum, regular and muffled like the beating of a heart — the heart of a conquering darkness. It was a moment of triumph for the wilderness, an invading and vengeful rush which, it seemed to me, I would have to keep back alone for the salvation of another soul. And the memory of what I had heard him say afar there, with the horned shapes stirring at my back, in the glow of fires, within the patient woods, those broken phrases came back to me, were heard again in their ominous and terrifying simplicity. I remembered his abject pleading, his abject threats, the colossal scale of his vile desires, the meanness, the torment, the tempestuous anguish of his soul. And later on I seemed to see his collected languid manner, when he said one day, 'This lot of ivory now is really mine. The Company did not pay for it. I collected it myself at a very great personal risk. I am afraid they will try to claim it as theirs though. H'm. It is a difficult case. What do you think I ought to do — resist? Eh? I want no more than justice.' . . . He wanted no more than justice — no more than justice. I rang the bell before a mahogany door on the first floor, and while I waited he seemed to stare at me out of the glassy panel—stare with that wide and immense stare embracing, condemning, loathing all the universe. I seemed to hear the whispered cry, 'The horror! The horror!'

"The dusk was falling. I had to wait in a lofty drawing-room with three long windows from floor to ceiling that were like three luminous and bedraped columns. The bent gilt legs and backs of the furniture shone in indistinct curves. The tall marble fireplace had a cold and monumental whiteness. A grand piano stood massively in a corner; with dark gleams on the flat surfaces like a sombre and polished sarcophagus. A high door opened—closed. I rose.

"She came forward, all in black, with a pale head, floating towards me in the dusk. She was in mourning. It was more than a year since his death, more than a year since the news came; she seemed as though she would remember and mourn for ever. She took both my hands in hers and murmured, 'I had heard you were coming.' I noticed she was not very young—I mean not girlish. She had a mature capacity for fidelity, for belief, for suffering. The room seemed to have grown darker, as if all the sad light of the cloudy evening had taken refuge on her forehead. This fair hair, this pale visage, this pure brow, seemed surrounded by an ashy halo from which the dark eyes looked out at me. Their glance was guileless, profound, confident, and trustful. She carried her sorrowful head as though she were proud of that sorrow, as though she would say, I—I alone know how to mourn for him as he deserves. But while we were still shaking hands, such a look of awful desolation came upon her face that I perceived she was one of those creatures that are not the playthings of Time. For her he had died only yesterday. And, by Jove! the impression was so powerful that for me, too, he seemed to have died only yesterday—nay, this very minute, I saw her and him in the same instant of time—his death and her sorrow—I saw her sorrow in the very moment of his death. Do you understand? I saw them together—I heard them together. She had said, with a deep catch of the breath, 'I have survived' while my strained ears seemed to hear distinctly, mingled with her tone of despairing regret, the summing up whisper of his eternal condemnation. I asked myself what I was doing there, with a sensation of panic in my heart as though I had blundered into a place of cruel and absurd mysteries not fit for a human being to behold. She motioned me to a chair. We sat down. I laid the packet gently on the little table, and she put her hand over it. . . . 'You knew him well,' she murmured, after a moment of mourning silence.

"'Intimacy grows quickly out there,' I said. 'I knew him as well as it is possible for one man to know another.'

"'And you admired him,' she said. 'It was impossible to know him and not to admire him. Was it?'

'He was a remarkable man,' I said, unsteadily. Then before the appealing fixity of her gaze, that seemed to watch for more words on my lips, I went on, 'It was impossible not to——'

"'Love him,' she finished eagerly, silencing me into an appalled dumbness. 'How true! how true! But when you think that no one knew him so well as I! I had all his noble confidence. I knew him best.'

"'You knew him best,' I repeated. And perhaps she did. But with every word spoken the room was growing darker; and only her forehead, smooth and white, remained illumined by the unextinguishable light of belief and love.

"'You were his friend,' she went on. 'His friend,' she repeated, a little louder. 'You must have been, if he had given you this, and sent you to me. I feel I can speak to you—and oh! I must speak. I want you—you who have heard his last words—to know I have been worthy of him. . . . It is not pride. . . . Yes! I am proud to know I understood him better than any one on earth—he told me so himself. And since his mother died I have had no one—no one—to—to——'

"I listened. The darkness deepened. I was not even sure whether he had given me the right bundle. I rather suspect he wanted me to take care of another batch of his papers which, after his death, I saw the manager examining under the lamp. And the girl talked, easing her pain in the certitude of my sympathy; she talked as thirsty men drink. I had heard that her engagement with Kurtz had been disapproved by her people. He wasn't rich enough or something. And indeed I don't know whether he had not been a pauper all his life. He had given me some reason to infer that it was his impatience of comparative poverty that drove him out there.

"'. . . Who was not his friend who had heard him speak once?' she was saying. 'He drew men towards him by what was best in them.' She looked at me with intensity. 'It is the gift of the great,' she went on, and the sound of her low voice seemed to have the accompaniment of all the other sounds, full of mystery, desolation, and sorrow, I had ever heard—the ripple of the river, the soughing of the trees swayed by the wind, the murmurs of the crowds, the faint ring of incomprehensible words cried from afar, the whisper of a voice speaking from beyond the threshold of an eternal darkness. 'But you have heard him! You know!' she cried.

"'Yes, I know,' I said with something like despair in my heart, but bowing my head before the faith that was in her, before that great and saving illusion that shone with an unearthly glow in the darkness, in the triumphant darkness from which I could not have defended her—from which I could not even defend myself.

"'What a loss to me—to us!'—she corrected herself with beautiful generosity; then added in a murmur, 'To the world.' By the last gleams of twilight I could see the glitter of her eyes, full of tears—of tears that would not fall.

"'I have been very happy—very fortunate—very proud,' she went on. 'Too fortunate. Too happy for a little while. And now I am unhappy for—for life.'

"She stood up; her fair hair seemed to catch all the remaining light in a glimmer of gold. I rose, too.

"'And of all this,' she went on, mournfully, 'of all his promise, and of all his greatness, of his generous mind, of his art, nothing remains—nothing but a memory. You and I——,'

"'We shall always remember him,' I said, hastily.

"'No!' she cried. 'It is impossible that all this should be lost—that such a life should be sacrificed to leave nothing—but sorrow. You know what vast plans he had. I knew of them, too—I could not perhaps understand—but others knew of them. Something must remain. His words, at least, have not died.'

"'His words will remain,' I said.

"'And his example,' she whispered to herself. 'Men looked up to him—his greatness shone in every act. His example——,'

"'True,' I said; 'his example, too. Yes, his example. I forgot that.'

"'But I do not. I cannot—I cannot believe—not yet. I cannot believe that I shall never see him again, that nobody will see him again, never, never, never.'

"She put out her arms as if after a retreating figure, stretching them black and with clasped pale hands across the fading and narrow sheen of the window. Never see him! I saw him clearly enough then. I shall see this eloquent phantom as long as I live, and I shall see her, too, a tragic and familiar Shade, resembling in this gesture another one, tragic also, and bedecked with powerless charms, stretching bare brown arms over the glitter of the infernal stream, the stream of darkness. She said suddenly very low, 'He died as he lived.'

"'His end,' said I, with dull anger stirring in me, 'was in every way worthy of his life.'

"'And I was not with him,' she murmured. My anger subsided before a feeling of infinite pity.

"'Everything that could be done——' I mumbled.

"'Ah, but I believed in him more than any one on earth—more than his own mother, more than—himself. He needed me! Me! I would have treasured every sigh, every word, every sign, every glance.'

"I felt like a chill grip on my chest. 'Don't,' I said, in a muffled voice.

"'Forgive me. I—I—have mourned so long in silence—in silence. . . . You were with him—to the last? I think of his loneliness. Nobody near to understand him as I would have understood. Perhaps no one to hear. . . .'

"'To the very end,' I said, shakily. 'I heard his very last words. . . .'" I stopped in a fright.

"'Repeat them,' she murmured in a heart-broken tone. 'I want—I want something—something—to—to live with.'

"I was on the point of crying at her, 'Don't you hear them?' The dusk was repeating them in a persistent whisper all around us, in a whisper that seemed to swell menacingly like the first whisper of a rising wind. 'The horror! the horror!'

"'His last word—to live with,' she insisted. 'Don't you understand I loved him—I loved him—I loved him!'

"I pulled myself together and spoke slowly.

"'The last word he pronounced was—your name.'

"I heard a light sigh and then my heart stood still, stopped dead short by an exulting and terrible cry, by the cry of inconceivable triumph and of unspeakable pain. 'I knew it—I was sure!' . . . She knew. She was sure. I heard her weeping; she had hidden her face in her hands. It seemed to me that the house would collapse before I could escape, that the heavens would fall upon my head. But nothing happened. The heavens do not fall for such a trifle. Would they have fallen, I wonder, if I had rendered Kurtz that justice which was his due? Hadn't he said he wanted only justice? But I couldn't. I could not tell her. It would have been too dark—too dark altogether. . . ."

Marlow ceased, and sat apart, indistinct and silent, in the pose of a meditating Buddha. Nobody moved for a time. "We have lost the first of the ebb," said the Director, suddenly. I raised my head. The offing was barred by a black bank of clouds, and the tranquil waterway leading to the uttermost ends of the earth flowed sombre under an overcast sky—seemed to lead into the heart of an immense darkness.

[1899]

Study and Writing Questions

1. Marlow says that "'Going up that river was like traveling back to the earliest beginnings of the world.'" In what sense(s) do you believe Marlow intends this comment? In what sense(s) is it true? What does the remark reveal about Marlow and his motivations for telling the STORY? What does the remark suggest about the importance of *Heart of Darkness*?

2. Why does Marlow, who says "'I hate, detest, and can't bear a lie,'" lie to Kurtz's Intended? Does the lie contain a deeper truth about Marlow? about Kurtz? about society?

3. Who is Kurtz? What kind of person was he before his experiences in the Congo? How does he change? What made him change? Are his last words, "'The horror! The horror!,'" as Marlow says, "an affirmation" and "a moral victory"? What might his last words mean to Kurtz? To Marlow? to the reader?

4. How does the STRUCTURE of this NARRATIVE affect its meaning? What is the relationship between Marlow's FRAME SITUATION, addressing businessmen on a boat anchored in the Thames, and his other situation, acting in the world? Why does the IMPLIED AUTHOR create an outer NARRATOR rather than have Marlow tell the story directly? What is the relationship between Marlow and Kurtz? To what extent is this Kurtz's story and to what extent Marlow's?

5. Compare the opening and closing paragraphs for their SYMBOLIC content. To what does the title of the narrative refer?

6. How does this narrative treat colonialism? Consider the ACTIONS, the economic and political functions of the CHARACTERS, and the light/dark IMAGERY.

7. What are the possible relationships of the individual to society represented in this narrative? Consider the situations on shipboard and on land, both in Europe and in Africa. Consider the importance of wealth, love, idealism, and egotism. To what extent is this narrative an indictment of European civilization?

See also Questions for Contrast and Comparison: 5, 25, 55, 70, 100, 126, 173, and 227.

ROBERT (LOWELL) COOVER (1932–) *was born in Charles City, Iowa, and educated at Southern Illinois University, Indiana University (B.A., 1953), and the University of Chicago (M.A., 1965). He also served in the Navy (1953–1957), from which he retired as a lieutenant. He married in 1959 and has three children. Although he has taught for one or two years at a number of institutions, including the University of Iowa, Princeton University, and Columbia University, he has primarily worked as a full-time writer since 1966 when* The Origin of the Brunists, *his most conventional work, an epic* SATIRE *about the development of a modern religious cult, won the William Faulkner Prize for best first* NOVEL. The Universal Baseball Association, Inc., J. Henry Waugh, Prop. *(1968) dissects both the mundane and the mental lives of an introvert who becomes obsessed with the alternate reality he constructs, a baseball league in which scores and lives depend on his rolls of the dice. Coover calls* The Public Burning *(1977), narrated by a fictionalized Vice-President Richard Nixon, a "factional" account of the 1953 espionage trial and execution of the Rosenbergs and the time in which that occurred. His most recent novel is* Gerald's Party *(1987).* Pricksongs and Descants *(1969), a collection of short,* ALLUSIVE *prose experiments, has received wide acclaim. Coover, who has also written screenplays and theatrical plays, lives in London, England.*

The Brother

right there right there in the middle of the damn field he says he wants to put that thing together him and his buggy ideas and so me I says "how the hell you gonna get it down to the water?" but he just focuses me out sweepin the blue his eyes rollin like they do when he gets het on some new lunatic notion and he says not to worry none about that just would I help him for God's sake and because he don't know how he can get it done in time otherwise and though you'd have to be loonier than him to say yes I says I will of course I always would crazy as my brother is I've done little else since I was born and my wife she says "I can't figure it out I can't see why you always have to be babyin that old fool he ain't never done nothin for you God knows and you got enough to do here fields need plowin it's a bad enough year already my God and now that red-eyed brother of yours wingin around like a damn cloud and not knowin what in the world he's doing buildin a damn boat in the country my God what next? you're a damn fool I tell you" but packs me some sandwiches just the same and some sandwiches for my brother Lord knows *his* wife don't have no truck with him no more says he can go starve for all she cares she's fed up ever since the time he made her sit out on a hillside for three whole days rain and everything because he said she'd see God and she didn't see nothin and in fact she like to die from hunger nothin but berries and his boys too they ain't so bright neither but at least they come to help him out with his damn boat so it ain't just the two of us thank God for *that* and it ain't no goddamn fishin boat he wants to put up neither in fact it's the biggest damn thing I ever heard of and for weeks *weeks* I'm tellin you we ain't doin nothin but cuttin down pine trees and haulin them out to his field which is really pretty high up a hill and my God *that's* work lemme tell you and my wife she sighs and says I am really crazy r-e-a-l-l-y crazy and her four months with a child and tryin to do my work and hers too and still when I come home from haulin timbers around all day she's got enough left to rub my shoulders and the small of my back and fix a hot meal her long black hair pulled to a knot behind her head and hangin marvelously down her back her eyes gentle but very tired my God and I says to my brother I says "look I got a lotta work to do buddy you'll have to finish this idiot thing yourself I wanna help you all I can you know that but" and he looks off and he says "it don't matter none your work" and I says "the hell it don't how you think me and my wife we're gonna eat I mean where do you think this food comes from you been puttin away man? you can't eat this goddamn boat out here ready to rot in that bastard sun" and he just sighs long and says "no it just don't matter" and he sits him down on a rock kinda tired like and stares off and looks like he might even for God's sake cry and so I go back to bringin wood up to him and he's already started on the keel and frame God knows how *he* ever found out to build a damn boat lost in *his* fog where he is Lord he was twenty when I was born and the first thing I remember was havin to lead him around so he didn't get kicked by a damn mule him who couldn't never do nothin in a normal way just a huge oversize fuzzyface boy so anyway I take to gettin up a few hours earlier ever day to do my farmin my wife apt to lose the baby if she should keep pullin around like she was doin then I go to work on the boat until sundown and on and on the days hot and dry and my wife keepin good food in me or else I'd of dropped sure and no matter what I say to try and get out of it my brother he says "you come and help now the rest don't matter" and we just keep hammerin away and my God the damn thing is big enough for a hundred people and at least I think at *least* it's a place to live and not too bad at that at least it's good for somethin but my wife she just sighs and says no good will come of it and runs her hands through my hair but she don't ask me to stop helpin no more because she knows it won't do no good and she's kinda turned into herself now these days and gettin herself all ready and still we keep workin on that damn thing that damn boat and the days pass and my brother he says we gotta work harder we ain't got much time and from time to time he gets a coupla neighbors to come over and give a hand them sucked in by the size and the novelty of the thing makin jokes some but they don't stay around more than a day or two and they go away shakin their heads and swearin under their breath and disgusted they got weaseled into the thing in the first place and me I only get about half my place planted and see to my stock as much as I can my wife she takes more care of them than I can but at least we won't starve we say if we just get some rain and finally we get the damn thing done all finished by God and we cover it in and out with pitch and put a kinda fancy roof on it and I come home on that last day and I ain't never goin back ain't *never* gonna let him talk me into nothin again and I'm all smellin of tar and my wife she cries and cries and I says to her not to worry no more I'll be home all the time and me I'm cryin a little too though she don't notice just thinkin how she's had it so lonely and hard and all and for one whole day I just sleep the whole damn day and the rest of the week I work around the farm and one day I get an idea and I go over to my brother's place and get some pieces of wood left over and whaddaya know? they are all livin on that damn boat there in the middle of nowhere him and his boys and some women and my brother's wife she's there too but she's madder than hell and carpin at him to get outa that damn boat and come home and he says she's got just one more day and then he's gonna drug her on the boat but he don't say it like a threat or nothin more like a fact a plain fact tomorrow he's gonna drug her on the boat well I ain't one to get mixed up in domestic quarrels God knows so I grab up the wood and beat it back to my farm and that evenin I make a little cradle a kinda fancy one with little animal figures cut in it and polished down and after supper I give it to my wife as a surprise and she cries and cries and holds me tight and says don't never go away again and stay close by her and all and I feel so damn good and warm about it all and glad the boat thing is over and we get out a little wine and we decide the baby's name is gonna be either Nathaniel or Anna and so we drink an extra cup to Nathaniel's health and we laugh and we sigh and drink one to Anna and my wife she gently fingers the little animal figures and says they're beautiful and really they ain't I ain't much good at that sorta thing but I know what she means and then she says "where did you get the wood?" and I says "it's left over from the boat" and she don't say nothin for a moment and then she says "you been over there again today?" and I says "yes just to get the wood" and she says "what's he doin now he's got the boat done?" and I says "funny thing they're all living in the damn thing all except the old lady she's over there hollerin at him how he's gettin senile and where does he think he's sailin to and how if he ain't afraid of runnin into a octypuss on the way he oughta get back home and him saying she's a nut there ain't no water and her sayin that's what *she's* been tellin *him* for six months" and my wife she laughs and it's the happiest laugh I've heard from her in half a year and I laugh and we both have another cup of wine and my wife she says "so he's just livin on that big thing all by hisself?" and I says "no he's got his boys on there and some young women who are maybe wives of the boys or somethin I don't know I ain't never seen them before and all kindsa damn animals and birds and things I ain't never seen the likes" and my wife she says "animals? what animals?" and I says "oh all kinds I don't know a whole damn menagerie all clutterin and stinkin up the boat *God* what a mess" and my wife laughs again and she's a little silly with the wine and she says "I bet he ain't got no pigs" and "oh yes I seen them" I says and we laugh thinkin about pigs rootin around in that big tub and she says "I bet he ain't got no jackdaws" and I says "yes I seen a couple of them too or mostly I heard them you couldn't hardly hear nothin else" and we laugh again thinkin about them crows and his old lady and the pigs and all and my wife she says "I know what he ain't got I bet he ain't got no lice" and we both laugh like crazy and when I can I says "oh yes he does less he's took a bath" and we both laugh till we're cryin and we finish off the wine and my wife says "look now I *know* what he ain't got he ain't got no termites" and I says "you're right I don't recollect no termites maybe we oughta make him a present" and my wife she hold me close quiet all of a sudden and says "he's really movin Nathaniel's really movin" and she puts my hand down on her round belly and the little fella is kickin up a terrific storm and I says kinda anxious "does it hurt? do you think that—?" and "no" she says "it's good" she says and so I says with my hand on her belly "here's to you Nathaniel" and we drain what's left in the bottom of our cups and the next day we wake up in each other's arms and it's rainin and *thank* God we say and since it's rainin real good we stay inside and do things around the place and we're happy because the rain has come just in time and in the evenin things smell green and fresh and delicious and it's still rainin a little but not too hard so I decide to take a walk and I wander over by my brother's place thinkin I'll ask him if he'd like to take on some pet termites to go with his collection and there by God is his wife on the boat and I don't know if he drug her on or if she just finally come by herself but she ain't sayin nothin which is damn unusual and the boys they ain't sayin nothing neither and my brother he ain't sayin nothing they're just all standin up there on top and gazin off and I holler up at them "nice rain ain't it?" and my brother he looks down at me standin there in the rain and still he don't say nothin but he raises his hand kinda funny like and then puts it back on the rail and I decide not to say nothin about the termites and it's startin to rain a little harder again so I turn away and go back home and I tell my wife about what happened and my wife she just laughs and says "they're *all* crazy he's finally got them *all* crazy" and she's cooked me up a special pastry with fresh meat and so we forget about them but by God the next day the rain's still comin down harder than ever and water's beginnin to stand around in places and after a week of rain I can see the crops is pretty well ruined and I'm having trouble keepin my stock fed and my wife she's cryin and talkin bout our bad luck that we might as well of built a damn boat as plant all them crops and still we don't figure things out I mean it just don't come to our minds not even when the rain keeps spillin down like a ocean dumped upsidedown and now water is beginnin to stand around in big pools really big ones and water up to the ankles around the house and leakin in and pretty soon the whole damn house is gettin fulla water and I keep sayin maybe we oughta go use my brother's boat till this blows over but my wife she says "never" and then she starts in cryin again so finally I says to her I says "we can't be so proud I'll go ask him" and so I set out in the storm and I can hardly see where I'm goin and I slip up to my neck in places and finally I get to where the boat is and I holler up and my brother he comes out and he looks down at where I am and he don't say nothin that bastard he just looks at me and I shout up at him I says "hey is it all right for me and my wife to come over until this thing blows over?" and still he don't say a damn word he just raises his hand in that same sillyass way and I holler "hey you stupid sonuvabitch I'm soakin wet goddamn it and my house is fulla water and my wife she's about to have a kid and she's apt to get sick all wet and cold to the bone and all I'm askin you —" and right then right while I'm still talkin he turns around and he goes back in the boat and I can't hardly believe it me his brother but he don't come back out and I push up under the boat and I beat on it with my fists and scream at him and call him ever name I can think up and I shout for his boys and for his wife and for anybody inside and nobody comes out "GOD*damn* YOU" I cry out at the top of my lungs and half sobbin and sick and then feelin too beat out to do anythin more I turn around and head back for home but the rain is thunderin down like mad now and in places I gotta swim and I can't make it no further and I recollect a hill nearby and I head for it and when I get to it I climb up on top of it and it feels good to be on land again even if it is soggy and greasy and I vomit and retch there awhile and move further up and the next thing I know I'm wakin up the rain still in my face and the water halfway up the hill toward me and I look out and I can see my brother's boat is floatin and I wave at it but I don't see nobody wave back and then I quick look out towards my own place and all I can see is the top of it and of a sudden I'm scared scared about my wife and I go tearin for the house swimmin most all the way and cryin and shoutin and the rain still comin down like crazy and so now well now I'm back here on the hill again what little there is left of it and I'm figurin maybe I got a day left if the rain keeps comin and it don't show no signs of stoppin and I can't see my brother's boat no more gone just water how *how* did he know? that bastard and yet I gotta hand it to him it's not hard to see who's crazy around here I can't see my house no more I just left my wife inside where I found her I couldn't hardly stand to look at her the way she was

[1969]

Study and Writing Questions

1. What information is conveyed by the use of dialect? How does that information affect your understanding of the events in the STORY?
2. What words and phrases, like "damn" and "hell," take on IRONIC meanings in the course of the NARRATIVE? How does their meaning change at various points? How does that change of meaning enter into your understanding of the meaning of the narrative as a whole?
3. By adding a brother to the story of Noah, Coover creates possibilities for using parallelism, as between Noah's ark and the speaker's cradle. What are other examples of parallelism? How do the parallel elements comment on each other?
4. Describe in detail the speaker's home life. Why is it important in this story?
5. What ethical problems are raised by this narrative? Is it possible for relative values to be as important as absolute values? Which brother is the "better" person? Which is the brother of the title?

See also Questions for Contrast and Comparison: 41, 52, 124, 136, 145, 202, and 203.

■ JULIO CORTÁZAR (1914–1984), *born in Brussels, Belgium but raised in Buenos Aires, Argentina, graduated from a teacher's college. After attending the University of Buenos Aires, he taught high school (1937–1944) and university (1944–1945). He then worked in publishing (1946–1948) and as a public translator (1948–1951) until conflicts with the authoritarian Perón regime drove him to Paris. Cortázar married (1953) but later divorced. From 1952 on, he worked four months of each year for UNESCO as a free-lance translator from English and French into Spanish. Other translations include works by Chesterton, Gide, Defoe, and, notably, Poe. He began publishing poems in his twenties, but earned initial renown for* Bestiary *(1951), the first of eight superb* SHORT STORY *collections, among which are* End of the Game *(1967) and* We Love Glenda So Much *(1983). His* FICTION *always wrenches formal expectation. The preface to* Hopscotch *(1963), considered by some to be Latin America's first great* NOVEL, *explains how the reader may work through the numbered chapters in a variety of orders. "I was trying to break the habits of readers . . . to make the reader free."* 62: A Model Kit *(1968), something of a sequel, takes off from chapter 62 of the earlier novel. Cortázar, a prolific essayist and an increasingly radical activist, supported the Cuban Revolution and gave royalty income to the Nicaraguan Sandinistas. He died of a heart attack in Paris.*

Continuity of Parks

He had begun to read the novel a few days before. He had put it down because of some urgent business conferences, opened it again on his way back to the estate by train; he permitted himself a slowly growing interest in the plot, in the characterizations. That afternoon, after writing a letter giving his power of attorney and discussing a matter of joint ownership with the manager of his estate, he returned to the book in the tranquility of his study which looked out upon the park with its oaks. Sprawled in his favorite armchair, its back toward the door — even the possibility of an intrusion would have irritated him, had he thought of it — he let his left hand caress repeatedly the green velvet upholstery and set to reading the final chapters. He remembered effortlessly the names and his mental image of the characters; the novel spread its glamour over him almost at once. He tasted the almost perverse pleasure of disengaging himself line by line from the things around him, and at the same time feeling his head rest comfortably on the green velvet of the chair with its high back, sensing that the cigarettes rested within reach of his hand, that beyond the great windows the air of afternoon danced under the oak trees in the park. Word by word, licked up by the sordid dilemma of the hero and heroine, letting himself be absorbed to the point where the images settled down and took on color and movement, he was witness to the final encounter in the mountain cabin. The woman arrived first, apprehensive; now the lover came in, his face cut by the backlash of a branch. Admirably, she stanched the blood with her kisses, but he rebuffed her caresses, he had not come to perform again the ceremonies of a secret passion, protected by a world of dry leaves and furtive paths through the forest. The dagger warmed itself against his chest, and underneath liberty pounded, hidden close. A lustful, panting dialogue raced down the pages like a rivulet of snakes, and one felt it had all been decided from eternity. Even to those caresses which writhed about the lover's body, as though wishing to keep him there, to dissuade him from it; they sketched abominably the frame of that other body it was necessary to destroy. Nothing had been forgotten: alibis, unforeseen hazards, possible mistakes. From this hour on, each instant had its use minutely assigned. The cold-blooded, twice-gone-over reexamination of the details was barely broken off so that a hand could caress a cheek. It was beginning to get dark.

Not looking at one another now, rigidly fixed upon the task which awaited them, they separated at the cabin door. She was to follow the trail that led north. On the path leading in the opposite direction, he turned for a moment to watch her running, her hair loosened and flying. He ran in turn, crouching among the trees and hedges until, in the yellowish fog of dusk, he could distinguish the avenue of trees which led up to the house. The dogs were not supposed to bark, they did not bark. The estate manager would not be there at this hour, and he was not there. He went up the three porch steps and entered. The woman's words reached him over the thudding of blood in his ears: first a blue chamber, then a hall, then a carpeted stairway. At the top, two doors. No one in the first room, no one in the second. The door of the salon, and then, the knife in hand, the light from the great windows, the high back of an armchair covered in green velvet, the head of the man in the chair reading a novel.

[1967]

Study and Writing Questions

1. What are the meanings of the STORY's different SETTINGS, primarily "estate" and "forest" but also "train" and "North"?
2. What significance has color IMAGERY in this NARRATIVE?
3. Why is the single paragraph indent put where it is? How might the story be different if it were put elsewhere or if there were more or no indents?
4. What are the MOTIVES of each of the CHARACTERS? What clues in the narrative reveal those motives to the reader?
5. How do specific words or phrases that interest you seem different in first and subsequent readings of this narrative? What is the significance of such changes?

See also Questions for Contrast and Comparison: 4, 15, 25, 28, 75, 139, 184, and 204.

■ STEPHEN (TOWNLEY) CRANE (1871–1900), born in Newark, New Jersey, youngest of fourteen children of a Methodist minister, was raised mainly in upstate New York. After his father died (1880), his mother wrote for Methodist papers and a brother for a daily. Crane briefly attended Lafayette College and Syracuse University where he captained the baseball team and wrote for the New York Tribune. After his mother died (1890), he moved to New York City to write, starving, selling occasional journalism, and haunting the notorious Bowery for material. Maggie: A Girl of the Streets (1893), with its raw portraits of slum life and sexuality, had to be privately printed and The Black Riders (1895), startlingly modern verse influenced by Emily Dickinson, went unread. The Red Badge of Courage (1895), on the other hand, a masterpiece of fear and heroism in battle based solely on reading, established Crane as an important writer. Maggie was acclaimed and Crane, even though he spent the rest of his brief life as a war correspondent in the American West, Mexico, Cuba, and Greece, wrote eleven more books, including "The Open Boat," a STORY based on his own shipwreck. On that trip, he met Cora Taylor who travelled with him before and after they married (1898). Maggie and his unconventional life led to a myth of Crane's addiction and immorality that drove him to live in England where he became friends with Joseph Conrad and H.G. Wells. He died in Germany seeking a tuberculosis cure.

The Blue Hotel

I

The Palace Hotel at Fort Romper was painted a light blue, a shade that is on the legs of a kind of heron, causing the bird to declare its position against any background. The Palace Hotel, then, was always screaming and howling in a way that made the dazzling winter landscape of Nebraska seem only a grey swampish hush. It stood alone on the prairie, and when the snow was falling the town two hundred yards away was not visible. But when the traveller alighted at the railway station he was obliged to pass the Palace Hotel before he could come upon the company of low clapboard houses which composed Fort Romber, and it was not to be thought that any traveller could pass the Palace Hotel without looking at it. Pat Scully, the proprietor, had proved himself a master of strategy when he chose his paints. It is true that on clear days, when the great transcontinental expresses, long lines of swaying Pullmans, swept through Fort Romper, passengers were overcome at the sight, and the cult that knows the brown-reds and the subdivisions of the dark greens of the East expressed shame, pity, horror, in a laugh. But to the citizens of this prairie town and to the people who would naturally stop there, Pat Scully had performed a feat. With this opulence and splendour, these creeds, classes, egotisms, that streamed through Romper on the rails day after day, they had no colour in common.

As if the displayed delights of such a blue hotel were not sufficiently enticing, it was Scully's habit to go every morning and evening to meet the leisurely trains that stopped at Romper and work his seductions upon any man that he might see wavering, gripsack in hand.

One morning, when a snow-crusted engine dragged its long string of freight cars and its one passenger coach to the station, Scully performed the marvel of catching three men. One was a shaky and quick-eyed Swede, with a great shining cheap valise; one was a tall bronzed cowboy, who was on his way to a ranch near the Dakota line; one was a little silent man from the East, who didn't look it, and didn't announce it. Scully practically made them prisoners. He was so nimble and merry and kindly that each probably felt it would be the height of brutality to try to escape. They trudged off over the creaking board sidewalks in the wake of the eager little Irishman. He wore a heavy fur cap squeezed tightly down on his head. It caused his two red ears to stick out stiffly, as if they were made of tin.

At last, Scully, elaborately, with boisterous hospitality, conducted them through the portals of the blue hotel. The room which they entered was small. It seemed to be merely a proper temple for an enormous stove, which, in the centre, was humming with godlike violence. At various points on its surface the iron had become luminous and glowed yellow from the heat. Beside the stove Scully's son Johnnie was playing High-Five with an old farmer who had whiskers both grey and sandy. They were quarrelling. Frequently the old farmer turned his face toward a box of sawdust — coloured brown from tobacco juice — that was behind the stove, and spat with an air of great impatience and irritation. With a loud flourish of words Scully destroyed the game of cards, and bustled his son upstairs with part of the baggage of the new guests. He himself conducted them to three basins of the coldest water in the world. The cowboy and the Easterner burnished themselves fiery red with this water, until it seemed to be some kind of metal-polish. The Swede, however, merely dipped his fingers gingerly and with trepidation. It was notable that throughout this series of small ceremonies the three travellers were made to feel that Scully was very benevolent. He was conferring great favours upon them. He handed the towel from one to another with an air of philanthropic impulse.

Afterward they went to the first room, and, sitting about the stove, listened to Scully's officious clamour at his daughters, who were preparing the midday meal. They reflected in the silence of experienced men who tread carefully amid new people. Nevertheless, the old farmer, stationary, invincible in his chair near the warmest part of the stove, turned his face from the sawdust-box frequently and addressed a glowing commonplace to the strangers. Usually he was answered in short but adequate sentences by either the cowboy or the Easterner. The Swede said nothing. He seemed to be occupied in making furtive estimates of each man in the room. One might have thought that he had the sense of silly suspicion which come to guilt. He resembled a badly frightened man.

Later, at dinner, he spoke a little, addressing his conversation entirely to Scully. He volunteered that he had come from New York, where for ten years he had worked as a tailor. These facts seemed to strike Scully as fascinating, and afterward he volunteered that he had lived at Romper for fourteen years. The Swede asked about the crops and the price of labour. He seemed barely to listen to Scully's extended replies. His eyes continued to rove from man to man.

Finally, with a laugh and a wink, he said that some of these Western communities were very dangerous; and after his statement he straightened his legs under the table, tilted his head, and laughed again, loudly. It was plain that the demonstration had no meaning to the others. They looked at him wondering and in silence.

II

As the men trooped heavily back into the front room, the two little windows presented views of a turmoiling sea of snow. The huge arms of the wind were making attempts — mighty, circular, futile — to embrace the flakes as they sped. A gate-post like a still man with a blanched face stood aghast amid this profligate fury. In a hearty voice Scully announced the presence of a blizzard. The guests of the blue hotel, lighting their pipes, assented with grunts of lazy masculine contentment. No island of the sea could be exempt in the degree of this little room with its humming stove. Johnnie, son of Scully, in a tone which defined his opinion of his ability as a card-player, challenged the old farmer of both grey and sandy whiskers to a game of High-Five. The farmer agreed with a contemptuous and bitter scoff. They sat close to the stove, and squared their knees under a wide board. The cowboy and the Easterner watched the game with interest. The Swede remained near the window, aloof, but with a countenance that showed signs of an inexplicable excitement.

The play of Johnnie and the grey-beard was suddenly ended by another quarrel. The old man arose while casting a look of heated scorn at his adversary. He slowly buttoned his coat, and then stalked with fabulous dignity from the room. In the discreet silence of all other men the Swede laughed. His laughter rang somehow childish. Men by this time had begun to look at him askance, as if they wished to inquire what ailed him.

A new game was formed jocosely. The cowboy volunteered to become the partner of Johnnie, and they all then turned to ask the Swede to throw in his lot with the little Easterner. He asked some questions about the game, and, learning that it wore many names, and that he had played it when it was under an alias, he accepted the invitation. He strode toward the men nervously, as if he expected to be assaulted. Finally, seated, he gazed from face to face and laughed shrilly. This laugh was so strange that the Easterner looked up quickly, the cowboy sat intent and with his mouth open, and Johnnie paused, holding the cards with still fingers.

Afterward there was a short silence. then Johnnie said, "Well, let's get at it. Come on now!" They pulled their chairs forward until their knees were bunched under the board. They began to play, and their interest in the game caused the others to forget the manner of the Swede.

The cowboy was a board-whacker. Each time that he held superior cards he changed them, one by one, with exceeding force, down upon the improvised table, and took the tricks with a glowing air of prowess and pride that sent thrills of indignation into the hearts of his opponents. A game with a board-whacker in it is sure to become intense. The countenances of the Easterner and the Swede were miserable whenever the cowboy thundered down his aces and kings, while Johnnie, his eyes gleaming with joy, chuckled and chuckled.

Because of the absorbing play none considered the strange ways of the Swede. They paid strict heed to the game. Finally, during a lull caused by a new deal, the Swede suddenly addressed Johnnie: "I suppose there had been a good many men killed in this room." The jaws of the others dropped and they looked at him.

"What in hell are you talking about?" said Johnnie.

The Swede laughed again his blatant laugh, full of a kind of false courage and defiance. "Oh, you know what I mean all right," he answered.

"I'm a liar if I do!" Johnnie protested. The card was halted, and the men stared at the Swede. Johnnie evidently felt that as the son of the proprietor he should make a direct inquiry. "Now, what might you be drivin' at, mister?" he asked. The Swede winked at him. It was a wink full of cunning. His fingers shook on the edge of the board. "Oh, maybe you think I have been to nowheres. Maybe you think I'm a tenderfoot?"

"I don't know nothin' about you," answered Johnnie, "and I don't give a damn where you've been. All I got to say is that I don't know what you're driving at. There hain't never been nobody killed in this room."

The cowboy, who had been steadily gazing at the Swede, then spoke: "What's wrong with you, mister?"

Apparently it seemed to the Swede that he was formidably menaced. He shivered and turned white near the corners of his mouth. He sent an appealing glance in the direction of the little Easterner. During these moments he did not forget to wear his air of advanced pot-valour. "They say they don't know what I mean," he remarked mockingly to the Easterner.

The latter answered after prolonged and cautious reflection. "I don't understand you," he said, impassively.

The Swede made a movement then which announced that he thought he had encountered treachery from the only quarter where he had expected sympathy, if not help. "Oh, I see you are all against me. I see —— "

The cowboy was in a state of deep stupefaction. "Say," he cried, as he tumbled the deck violently down upon the board, "say, what are you gittin' at, hey?"

The Swede sprang up with the celerity of a man escaping from a snake on the floor, "I don't want to fight!" he shouted. "I don't want to fight!"

The cowboy stretched his long legs indolently and deliberately. His hands were in his pockets. He spat into the sawdust-box. "Well, who the hell thought you did?" he inquired.

The Swede backed rapidly toward a corner of the room. His hands were out protectingly in front of his chest, but he was making an obvious struggle to control his fright. "Gentlemen," he quavered, "I suppose I am going to be killed before I can leave this house! I suppose I am going to be killed before I can leave this house!" In his eyes was the dying-swan look. Through the windows could be seen the snow turning blue in the shadow of dusk. The wind tore at the house, and some loose thing beat regularly against the clap-boards like a spirit tapping.

A door opened, and Scully himself entered. He paused in surprise as he noted the tragic attitude of the Swede. Then he said, "What's the matter here?"

The Swede answered him swiftly and eagerly: "These men are going to kill me."

"Kill you!" ejaculated Scully. "Kill you! What are you talkin'?"

The Swede made the gesture of a martyr.

Scully wheeled sternly upon his son. "What is this, Johnnie?"

The lad had grown sullen. "Damned if I know," he answered. "I can't make no sense to it." He began to shuffle the cards, fluttering them together with an angry snap. "He says a good many men have been killed in this room, or something like that. And he says he's goin' to be killed here too. I don't know what ails him. He's crazy, I shouldn't wonder."

Scully then looked for explanation to the cowboy, but the cowboy simply shrugged his shoulders.

"Kill you?" said Scully again to the Swede. "Kill you? Man, you're off your nut."

"Oh, I know," burst out the Swede, "I know what will happen. Yes, I'm crazy—yes. Yes, of course, I'm crazy—yes. But I know one thing——" There was a sort of sweat of misery and terror upon his face. "I know I won't get out of here alive."

The cowboy drew a deep breath, as if his mind was passing into the last stages of dissolution. "Well, I'm doggoned," he whispered to himself.

Scully wheeled suddenly and faced his son. "You've been troublin' this man!"

Johnnie's voice was loud with its burden of grievance. "Why, good Gawd, I ain't done nothin' to 'im."

The Swede broke in. "Gentlemen, do not disturb yourselves. I will leave this house. I will go away, because"—he accused them dramatically with his glance— "because I do not want to be killed."

Scully was furious with his son. "Will you tell me what is the matter, you young divil? What's the matter, anyhow? Speak out!"

"Blame it!" cried Johnnie in despair, "don't I tell you I don't know? He—he says we want to kill him, and that's all I know. I can't tell what ails him."

The Swede continued to repeat: "Never mind, Mr. Scully; never mind. I will leave this house. I will go away, because I do not wish to be killed. Yes, of course, I am crazy—yes. But I know one thing! I will go away. I will leave this house. Never mind, Mr. Scully; never mind. I will go away."

"You will not go 'way," said Scully. "You will not go 'way until I hear the reason of this business. If anybody has troubled you I will take care of him. This is my house. You are under my roof, and I will not allow any peaceable man to be troubled here." He cast a terrible eye upon Johnnie, the cowboy, and the Easterner.

"Never mind, Mr. Scully; never mind. I will go away. I do not wish to be killed." The Swede moved toward the door which opened upon the stairs. It was evidently his intention to go at once for his baggage.

"No, no," shouted Scully peremptorily; but the white-faced man slid by him and disappeared. "Now," said Scully severely, "what does this mean?"

Johnnie and the cowboy cried together: "Why we didn't do nothin' to 'im!"

Scully's eyes were cold. "No," he said, "you didn't?"

Johnnie swore a deep oath. "Why, this is the wildest loon I ever see. We didn't do nothin' at all. We were jest sittin' here playin' cards, and he—"

The father suddenly spoke to the Easterner. "Mr. Blanc," he asked, "what has these boys been doin'?"

The Easterner reflected again. "I didn't see anything wrong at all," he said at last, slowly.

Scully began to howl. "But what does it mane?" He stared ferociously at his son. "I have a mind to lather you for this, me boy."

Johnnie was frantic. "Well, what have I done?" he bawled at his father.

III

"I think you are tongue-tied," said Scully finally to his son, the cowboy, and the Easterner; and at the end of this scornful sentence he left the room.

Upstairs the Swede was swiftly fastening the straps of his great valise. Once his back happened to be half turned toward the door, and, hearing a noise there, he wheeled and sprang up, uttering a loud cry. Scully's wrinkled visage showed grimly in the light of the small lamp he carried. This yellow effulgence, streaming upward, coloured only his prominent features, and left his eyes, for instance, in mysterious shadow. He resembled a murderer.

"Man! man!" he exclaimed, "have you gone daffy?"

"Oh, no! Oh, no!" rejoined the other. "There are people in this world who know pretty nearly as much as you do—understand?"

For a moment they stood gazing at each other. Upon the Swede's deathly pale cheeks were two spots brightly crimson and sharply edged, as if they had been carefully painted. Scully placed the light on the table and sat himself on the edge of the bed. He spoke ruminatively. "By cracky, I never heard of such a thing in my life. It's a complete muddle. I can't, for the soul of me, think how you ever got this idea into your head." Presently he lifted his eyes and asked: "And did you sure think they were going to kill you?"

The Swede scanned the old man as if he wished to see into his mind. "I did," he said at last. He obviously suspected that this answer might precipitate an outbreak. As he pulled on a strap his whole arm shook, the elbow wavering like a bit of paper.

Scully banged his hand impressively on the footboard of the bed. "Why, man, we're goin' to have a line of ilictric streetcars in this town next spring."

"'A line of electric street cars,'" repeated the Swede, stupidly.

"And," said Scully, "there's a new railroad goin' to be built down from Broken Arm to here. Not to mintion the four churches and the smashin' big brick school-house. Then there's the big factory, too. Why, in two years Romper'll be a met-tro-pol-is."

Having finished the preparation of his baggage, the Swede straightened himself. "Mr. Scully," he said, with sudden hardihood, "how much do I owe you?"

"You don't owe me anythin'," said the old man, angrily.

"Yes, I do," retorted the Swede. He took seventy-five cents from his pocket and tendered it to Scully; but the latter snapped his fingers in disdainful refusal. However, it happened that they both stood gazing in a strange fashion at three silver pieces on the Swede's open palm.

"I'll not take your money," said Scully at last. "Not after what's been goin' on here." Then a plan seemed to strike him. "Here," he cried, picking up his lamp and moving toward the door. "Here! Come with me a minute."

"No," said the Swede, in overwhelming alarm.

"Yes," urged the old man. "Come on! I want you to come and see a picter—just across the hall—in my room."

The Swede must have concluded that his hour was come. His jaw dropped and his teeth showed like a dead man's. He ultimately followed Scully across the corridor, but he had the step of one hung in chains.

Scully flashed the light high on the wall of his own chamber. There was revealed a ridiculous photograph of a little girl. She was leaning against a balustrade of gorgeous decoration, and the formidable bang to her hair was prominent. The figure was as graceful as an upright sledstake, and, withal, it was of the hue of lead. "There," said Scully, tenderly, "that's the picter of my little girl that died. Her name was Carrie. She had the purtiest hair you ever saw! I was that fond of her, she —— "

Turning then, he saw that the Swede was not contemplating the picture at all, but, instead, was keeping keen watch on the gloom in the rear.

"Look man!" cried Scully, heartily. "That's the picter of my little gal that died. Her name was Carrie. And then here's the picter of my oldest boy, Michael. He's a lawyer in Lincoln, an' doin' well. I gave that boy a grand eddication, and I'm glad for it now. He's a fine boy. Look at 'im now. Ain't he bold as blazes, him there in Lincoln, an honoured an' respicted gintleman! An honoured and respicted gintleman," concluded Scully with a flourish. And, so saying, he smote the Swede jovially on the back.

The Swede faintly smiled.

"Now," said the old man, "there's only one more thing." He dropped suddenly to the floor and thrust his head beneath the bed. The Swede could hear his muffled voice. "I'd keep it under me piller if it wasn't for that boy Johnnie. Then there's the old woman —— Where is it now? I never put it twice in the same place. Ah, now come out with you!"

Presently he backed clumsily from under the bed, dragging with him an old coat rolled into a bundle. "I've fetched him," he muttered. Kneeling on the floor, he unrolled the coat and extracted from its heart a large yellow-brown whisky-bottle.

His first manoeuvre was to hold the bottle up to the light. Reassured, apparently, that nobody had been tampering with it, he thrust it with a generous movement toward the Swede.

The weak-kneed Swede was about to eagerly clutch this element of strength, but he suddenly jerked his hand away and cast a look of horror upon Scully.

"Drink," said the old man affectionately. He had risen to his feet, and now stood facing the Swede.

There was a silence. Then again Scully said: "Drink!"

The Swede laughed wildly. He grabbed the bottle, put it to his mouth; and as his lips curled absurdly around the opening and his throat worked, he kept his glance, burning with hatred, upon the old man's face.

IV

After the departure of Scully the three men, with the cardboard still upon their knees, preserved for a long time an astounded silence. Then Johnnie said: "That's the dod-dangedest Swede I ever see."

"He ain't no Swede," said the cowboy scornfully.

"Well, what is he then?" cried Johnnie. "What is he then?"

"It's my opinion," replied the cowboy deliberately, "he's some kind of a Dutchman." It was a venerable custom of the country to entitle as Swedes all lighthaired men who spoke with a heavy tongue. In consequence the idea of the cowboy was not without its daring. "Yes, sir," he repeated. "It's my opinion this feller is some kind of a Dutchman."

"Well, he says he's a Swede, anyhow," muttered Johnnie, sulkily. He turned to the Easterner: — What do you think, Mr. Blanc?"

"Oh, I don't know," replied the Easterner.

"Well, what do you think makes him act that way?" asked the cowboy.

"Why, he's frightened." The Easterner knocked his pipe against a rim of the stove. "He's clear frightened out of his boots."

"What at?" cried Johnnie and the cowboy together.

The Easterner reflected over his answer.

"What at?" cried the others again.

"Oh, I don't know, but it seems to me this man has been reading dime novels, and he thinks he's right out in the middle of it — the shootin' and stabbin' and all."

"But," said the cowboy, deeply scandalized, "this ain't Wyoming, ner none of them places. This is Nebrasker."

"Yes," added Johnnie, "an' why don't he wait till he gits *out West?*"

The travelled Easterner laughed. "It isn't different there even — not in these days. But he thinks he's right in the middle of hell."

Johnnie and the cowboy mused along.

"It's awful funny," remarked Johnnie at last.

"Yes," said the cowboy. "This is a queer game. I hope we don't git snowed in, because then we'd have to stand this here man bein' around with us all the time. That wouldn't be no good."

"I wish pop would throw him out," said Johnnie.

Presently they heard a loud stamping on the stairs, accompanied by ringing jokes in the voice of old Scully, and laughter, evidently from the Swede. The men around the stove stared vacantly at each other. "Gosh!" said the cowboy. The door few open, and old Scully, flushed and anecdotal, came into the room. He was jabbering at the Swede, who followed him, laughing bravely. It was the entry of two roisterers from a banquet hall.

"Come now," said Scully sharply to the three seated men, "move up and give us a chance at the stove." The cowboy and the Easterner obediently sidled their chairs to make room for the new-comers. Johnnie, however, simply arranged himself in a more indolent attitude, and then remained motionless.

"Come! Git over, there," said Scully.

"Plenty of room on the other side of the stove," said Johnnie.

"Do you think we want to sit in the draught?" roared the father.

But the Swede had interposed with a grandeur of confidence. "No, no. Let the boy sit where he likes," he cried in a bullying voice to the father.

"All right! All right!" said Scully, deferentially. The cowboy and the Easterner exchanged glances of wonder.

The five chairs were formed in a crescent about one side of the stove. The Swede began to talk; he talked arrogantly, profanely, angrily. Johnnie, the cowboy, and the Easterner maintained a morose silence, while old Scully appeared to be receptive and eager, breaking in constantly with sympathetic ejaculations.

Finally the Swede announced that he was thirsty. He moved in his chair, and said that he would go for a drink of water.

"I'll git it for you," cried Scully at once.

"No," said the Swede, contemptuously. "I'll get it for myself." He arose and stalked with the air of an owner off into the executive parts of the hotel.

As soon as the Swede was out of hearing Scully sprang to his feet and whispered intensely to the others: "Upstairs he thought I was tryin' to poison 'im."

"Say," said Johnnie, "this makes me sick. Why don't you throw 'im out in the snow?"

"Why, he's all right now," declared Scully. "It was only that he was from the East, and he thought this was a tough place. That's all. He's all right now."

The cowboy looked with admiration upon the Easterner. "You were straight," he said. "You were on to that there Dutchman."

"Well," said Johnnie to his father, "he may be all right now, but I don't see it. Other time he was scared, but now's he's too fresh."

Scully's speech was always a combination of Irish brogue and idiom, Western twang and idiom, and scraps of curiously formal diction taken from the story-books and newspapers. He now hurled a strange mass of language at the head of his son. "What do I keep? What do I keep? What do I keep?" he demanded, in a voice of thunder. He slapped his knee impressively, to indicate that he himself was going to make reply, and that all should heed. "I keep a hotel," he shouted. "A hotel, do you mind? A guest under my roof has sacred privileges. He is to be intimidated by none. Not one word shall he hear that would prijudice him in favour of goin' away. I'll not have it. There's no place in this here town where they can say they iver took in a guest of mine because he was afraid to stay here." He wheeled suddenly upon the cowboy and the Easterner. "Am I right?"

"Yes, Mr. Scully," said the cowboy, "I think you're right."

"Yes, Mr. Scully," said the Easterner, "I think you're right."

V

At six-o'clock supper, the Swede fizzed like a fire-wheel. He sometimes seemed on the point of bursting into riotous song, and in all his madness he was encouraged by old Scully. The Easterner was encased in reserve; the cowboy sat in wide-mouthed amazement, forgetting to eat, while Johnnie wrathily demolished great plates of food. The daughters of the house, when they were obliged to replenish the biscuits, approached as warily as Indians, and, having succeeded in their purpose, fled with ill-concealed trepidation. The Swede domineered the whole feast, and he gave it the appearance of a cruel bacchanal. He seemed to have grown suddenly taller; he gazed, brutally disdainful, into every face. His voice rang through the room. Once when he jabbed out harpoon-fashion with his fork to pinion a biscuit, the weapon nearly impaled the hand of the Easterner, which had been stretched quietly out for the same biscuit.

After supper, as the men filed toward the other room, the Swede smote Scully ruthlessly on the shoulder. "Well, old boy, that was a good, square meal." Johnnie looked hopefully at his father; he knew that shoulder was tender from an old fall; and, indeed, it appeared for a moment as if Scully was going to flame out over the matter, but in the end he smiled a sickly smile and remained silent. The others understood from his manner that he was admitting his responsibility for the Swede's new view-point.

Johnnie, however, addressed his parent in an aside. "Why don't you license somebody to kick you downstairs?" Scully scowled darkly by way of reply.

When they were gathered about the stove, the Swede insisted on another game of High-Five. Scully gently deprecated the plan at first, but the Swede turned a wolfish glare upon him. The old man subsided, and the Swede canvassed the others. In his tone there was always a great threat. The cowboy and the Easterner both remarked indifferently that they would play. Scully said that he would presently have to go to meet the 6.58 train, and so the Swede turned menacingly upon Johnnie. For a moment their glances crossed like blades, and then Johnnie smiled and said, "Yes, I'll play."

They formed a square, with the little board on their knees. The Easterner and the Swede were again partners. As the play went on, it was noticeable that the cowboy was not board-whacking as usual. Meanwhile, Scully, near the lamp, had put on his spectacles and, with an appearance curiously like an old priest, was reading a newspaper. In time he went out to meet the 6.58 train, and, despite his precautions, a gust of polar wind whirled into the room as he opened the door. Besides scattering the cards, it chilled the players to the marrow. The Swede cursed frightfully. When Scully returned, his entrance disturbed a cosy and friendly scene. The Swede again cursed. But presently they were once more intent, their heads bent forward and their hands moving swiftly. The Swede had adopted the fashion of board-whacking.

Scully took up his paper and for a long time remained immersed in matters which were extraordinarily remote from him. The lamp burned badly, and once he stopped to adjust the wick. The newspaper, as he turned from page to page, rustled with a slow and comfortable sound. Then suddenly he heard three terrible words: "You are cheatin'!"

Such scenes often prove that there can be little of dramatic import in environment. Any room can present a tragic front; any room can be comic. This little den was now hideous as a torture-chamber. The new faces of the men themselves had changed it upon the instant. The Swede held a huge fist in front of Johnnie's face, while the latter looked steadily over it into the blazing orbs of his accuser. The Easterner had grown pallid; the cowboy's jaw had dropped in that expression of bovine amazement which was one of his important mannerisms. After the three words, the first sound in the room was made by Scully's paper as it floated forgotten to his feet. His spectacles had also fallen from his nose, but by a clutch he had saved them in air. His hand, grasping the spectacles, now remained poised awkwardly and near his shoulder. He stared at the cardplayers.

Probably the silence was while a second elapsed. Then, if the floor had been suddenly twitched out from under the men they could not have moved quicker. The five had projected themselves headlong toward a common point. It happened that Johnnie, in rising to hurl himself upon the Swede, had stumbled slightly because of his curiously instinctive care for the cards and the board. The loss of the moment allowed time for the arrival of Scully, and also allowed the cowboy time to give the Swede a great push which sent him staggering back. The men found tongue together, and hoarse shouts of rage, appeal, or fear burst from every throat. The cowboy pushed and jostled feverishly at the Swede, and the Easterner and Scully clung wildly to Johnnie; but through the smoky air, above the swaying bodies of the peace-compellers, the eyes of the two warriors ever sought each other in glances of challenge that were at once hot and steely.

Of course the board had been overturned, and now the whole company of cards was scattered over the floor, where the boots of the men trampled the fat and painted kings and queens as they gazed with their silly eyes at the war that was waging above them.

Scully's voice was dominating the yells. "Stop now! Stop, I say! Stop, now——"

Johnnie, as he struggled to burst through the rank formed by Scully and the Easterner, was crying. "Well, he says I cheated! He says I cheated! I won't allow no man to say I cheated! If he says I cheated, he's a——!"

The cowboy was telling the Swede, "Quit, now! Quit, d'ye hear——"

The screams of the Swede never ceased: "He did cheat! I saw him! I saw him——"

As for the Easterner, he was importuning in a voice that was not heeded: "Wait a moment, can't you? Oh, wait a moment. What's the good of a fight over a game of cards? Wait a moment——"

In this tumult no complete sentences were clear. "Cheat"—"Quit"—"He says"—these fragments pierced the uproar and rang out sharply. It was remarkable that, whereas Scully undoubtedly made the most noise, he was the least heard of any of the riotous band.

Then suddenly there was a great cessation. It was as if each man had paused for breath; and although the room was still lighted with the anger of men, it could be seen that there was no danger of immediate conflict, and at once Johnnie, shouldering his way forward, almost succeeded in confronting the Swede. "What did you say I cheated for? What did you say I cheated for? I don't cheat, and I won't let no man say I do!"

The Swede said, "I saw you! I saw you!"

"Well," cried Johnnie, "I'll fight any man what says I cheat!"

"No, you won't," said the cowboy. "Not here."

"Ah, be still, can't you?" said Scully, coming between them.

The quiet was sufficient to allow the Easterner's voice to be heard. He was repeating, "Oh, wait a moment, can't you? What's the good of a fight over a game of cards? Wait a moment!"

Johnnie, his red face appearing above his father's shoulder, hailed the Swede again. "Did you say I cheated?"

The Swede showed his teeth. "Yes."

"Then," said Johnnie, "we must fight."

"Yes, fight," roared the Swede. He was like a demoniac. "Yes, fight! I'll show you what kind of a man I am! I'll show you who you want to fight! Maybe you think I can't fight! Maybe you think I can't! I'll show you, you skin, you card-sharp! Yes, you cheated! You cheated! You cheated!"

"Well, let's go at it, then, mister," said Johnnie, coolly.

The cowboy's brow was beaded with sweat from his efforts in intercepting all sorts of raids. He turned in despair to Scully. "What are you goin' to do now?"

A change had come over the Celtic visage of the old man. He now seemed all eagerness; his eyes glowed.

"We'll let them fight," he answered, stalwartly. "I can't put up with it any longer. I've stood this damned Swede till I'm sick. We'll let them fight."

VI

The men prepared to go out of doors. The Easterner was so nervous that he had great difficulty in getting his arms into the sleeves of his new leather coat. As the cowboy drew his fur cap down over his ears his hands trembled. In fact, Johnnie and old Scully were the only ones who displayed no agitation. These preliminaries were conducted without words.

Scully threw open the door. "Well, come on," he said. Instantly a terrific wind caused the flame of the lamp to struggle at its wick, while a puff of black smoke sprang from the chimney-top. The stove was in mid-current of the blast, and its voice swelled to equal the roar of the storm. Some of the scarred and bedabbled cards were caught up from the floor and dashed helplessly against the farther wall. The men lowered their heads and plunged into the tempest as into a sea.

No snow was falling, but great whirls and clouds of flakes, swept up from the ground by the frantic winds, were streaming southward with the speed of bullets. The covered land was blue with the sheen of an unearthly satin, and there was no other hue save where, at the low, black railway station—which seemed incredibly distant—one light gleamed like a tiny jewel. As the men floundered into a thigh-deep drift, it was known that the Swede was bawling out something. Scully went to him, put a hand on his shoulder, and projected an ear. "What's that you say?" he shouted.

"I say," bawled the Swede again, "I won't stand much show against this gang. I know you'll all pitch on me."

Scully smote him reproachfully on the arm. "Tut, man!" he yelled. The wind tore the words from Scully's lips and scattered them far alee.

"You are all a gang of —— " boomed the Swede, but the storm also seized the remainder of this sentence.

Immediately turning their backs upon the wind, the men had swung around a corner to the sheltered side of the hotel. It was the function of the little house to preserve here, amid this great devastation of snow, an irregular V-shape of heavily encrusted grass, which crackled beneath the feet. One could imagine the great drifts piled against the windward side. When the party reached the comparative peace of this spot it was found that the Swede was still bellowing.

"Oh, I know what kind of a thing this is! I know you'll all pitch on me. I can't lick you all!"

Scully turned upon him panther-fashion. "You'll not have to whip all of us. You'll have to whip my son Johnnie. An' the man what troubles you durin' that time will have me to dale with."

The arrangements were swiftly made. The two men faced each other, obedient to the harsh commands of Scully, whose face, in the subtly luminous gloom, could be seen set in the austere impersonal lines that are pictured on the countenances of the Roman veterans. The Easterner's teeth were chattering, and he was hopping up and down like a mechanical toy. The cowboy stood rock-like.

The contestants had not stripped off any clothing. Each was in his ordinary attire. Their fists were up, and they eyed each other in a calm that had the elements of leonine cruelty in it.

During this pause, the Easterner's mind, like a film, took lasting impressions of three men—the iron-nerved master of the ceremony; the Swede, pale, motionless, terrible; and Johnnie, serene yet ferocious, brutish yet heroic. The entire prelude had in it a tragedy greater than the tragedy of action, and this aspect was accentuated by the long, mellow cry of the blizzard, as it sped the tumbling and wailing flakes into the black abyss of the south.

"Now!" said Scully.

The two combatants leaped forward and crashed together like bullocks. There was heard the cushioned sound of blows, and of a curse squeezing out from between the tight teeth of one.

As for the spectators, the Easterner's pent-up breath exploded from him with a pop of relief, absolute relief from the tension of the preliminaries. The cowboy bounded into the air with a yowl. Scully was immovable as from supreme amazement and fear at the fury of the fight which he himself had permitted and arranged.

For a time the encounter in the darkness was such a perplexity of flying arms that it presented no more detail than would a swiftly revolving wheel. Occasionally a face, as if illumined by a flash of light, would shine out, ghastly and marked with pink spots. A moment later, the men might have been known as shadows, if it were not for the involuntary utterance of oaths that came from them in whispers.

Suddenly a holocaust of warlike desire caught the cowboy, and he bolted forward with the speed of a broncho. "Go it, Johnnie! Go it! Kill him! Kill him!"

Scully confronted him. "Kape back," he said; and by his glance the cowboy could tell that this man was Johnnie's father.

To the Easterner there was a monotony of unchangeable fighting that was an abomination. This confused mingling was eternal to his sense, which was concentrated in a longing for the end, the priceless end. Once the fighters lurched near him, and as he scrambled hastily backward he heard them breathe like men on the rack.

"Kill him, Johnnie! Kill him! Kill him! Kill him!" The cowboy's face was contorted like one of those agony masks in museums.

"Keep still," said Scully, icily.

Then there was a sudden loud grunt, incomplete, cut short, and Johnnie's body swung away from the Swede and fell with sickening heaviness to the grass. The cowboy was barely in time to prevent the mad Swede from flinging himself upon his prone adversary. "No, you don't," said the cowboy, interposing an arm. "Wait a second."

Scully was at his son's side. "Johnnie! Johnnie, me boy!" His voice had a quality of melancholy tenderness. "Johnnie! Can you go on with it?" He looked anxiously down into the bloody, pulpy face of his son.

There was a moment of silence, and then Johnnie answered in his ordinary voice, "Yes, I—it—yes."

Assisted by his father he struggled to his feet. "Wait a bit now till you git your wind," said the old man.

A few paces away the cowboy was lecturing the Swede. "No, you don't! Wait a second!"

The Easterner was plucking at Scully's sleeve. "Oh, this is enough," he pleaded. "This is enough! Let it go as it stands. This is enough!"

"Bill," said Scully, "git out of the road." The cowboy stepped aside. "Now." The combatants were actuated by a new caution as they advanced toward collision. They glared at each other, and then the Swede aimed a lightning blow that carried with it his entire weight. Johnnie was evidently half stupid from weakness, but he miraculously dodged, and his fist sent the over-balanced Swede sprawling.

The cowboy, Scully and the Easterner burst into a cheer that was like a chorus of triumphant soldiery, but before its conclusion the Swede had scuffled agilely to his feet and come in berserk abandon at his foe. There was another perplexity of flying arms, and Johnnie's body again swung away and fell, even as a bundle might fall from a roof. The Swede instantly staggered to a little wind-waved tree and leaned upon it, breathing like an engine, while his savage and flamelit eyes roamed from face to face as the men bent over Johnnie. There was a splendour of isolation in his situation at this time which the Easterner felt once when, lifting his eyes from the man on the ground, he beheld that mysterious and lonely figure, waiting.

"Are you any good yet, Johnnie?" asked Scully in a broken voice.

The son gasped and opened his eyes languidly. After a moment he answered, "No—I ain't—any good—any—more." Then, from shame and bodily ill, he began to weep, the tears furrowing down through the blood-stains on his face. "He was too—too—too heavy for me."

Scully straightened and addressed the waiting figure. "Stranger," he said, evenly, "it's all up with our side." Then his voice changed into that vibrant huskiness which is commonly the tone of the most simple and deadly announcements.

"Johnnie is whipped."

Without replying, the victor moved off on the route to the front door of the hotel.

The cowboy was formulating new and unspellable blasphemies. The Easterner was startled to find that they were out in a wind that seemed to come direct from the shadowed artic floes. He heard again the wail of the snow as it was flung to its grave in the south. He knew now that all this time the cold had been sinking into him deeper and deeper, and he wondered that he had not perished. He felt indifferent to the condition of the vanquished man.

"Johnnie, can you walk?" asked Scully.

"Did I hurt—hurt him any?" asked the son.

"Can you walk, boy? Can you walk?"

Johnnie's voice was suddenly strong. There was a robust impatience in it. "I asked you whether I hurt him any!"

"Yes, yes, Johnnie," answered the cowboy, consolingly; "he's hurt a good deal."

They raised him from the ground, and as soon as he was on his feet he went tottering off, rebuffing all attempts at assistance. When the party rounded the corner they were fairly blinded by the pelting of the snow. It burned their faces like fire. The cowboy carried Johnnie through the drift to the door. As they entered, some cards again rose from the floor and beat against the wall.

The Easterner rushed to the stove. He was so profoundly chilled that he almost dared to embrace the glowing iron. The Swede was not in the room. Johnnie sank into a chair and, folding his arms on his knees, buried his face in them. Scully, warming one foot and then the other at a rim of the stove, muttered to himself with Celtic mournfulness. The cowboy had removed his fur cap, and with a dazed and rueful air he was running one hand through his tousled locks. From overhead they could hear the creaking of boards, as the Swede tramped here and there in his room.

The sad quiet was broken by the sudden flinging open of a door that led toward the kitchen. It was instantly followed by an inrush of women. They precipitated themselves upon Johnnie amid a chorus of lamentation. Before they carried their prey off to the kitchen, there to be bathed and harangued with that mixture of sympathy and abuse which is a feat of their sex, the mother straightened herself and fixed old Scully with an eye of stern reproach. "Shame be upon you, Patrick Scully!" she cried. "Your own son, too. Shame be upon you!"

"There, now! Be quiet, now!" said the old man, weakly.

"Shame be upon you, Patrick Scully!" The girls, rallying to this slogan, sniffed disdainfully in the direction of those trembling accomplices, the cowboy and the Easterner. Presently they bore Johnnie away, and left the three men to dismal reflection.

VII

"I'd like to fight this here Dutchman myself," said the cowboy, breaking a long silence.

Scully wagged his head sadly. "No, that wouldn't do. It wouldn't be right. It wouldn't be right."

"Well, why wouldn't it!" argued the cowboy, "I don't see no harm in it."

"No," answered Scully, with mournful heroism. "It wouldn't be right. It was Johnnie's fight, and now we mustn't whip the man just because he whipped Johnnie."

"Yes, that's true enough," said the cowboy; "but — he better not get fresh with me, because I couldn't stand no more of it."

"You'll not say a word to him," commanded Scully, and even then they heard the tread of the Swede on the stairs. His entrance was made theatric. He swept the door back with a bang and swaggered to the middle of the room. No one looked at him. "Well," he cried, insolently, at Scully, "I s'pose you'll tell me now how much I owe you?"

The old man remained stolid. "You don't ow me nothin'."

"Huh!" said the Swede, "huh! Don't owe 'im nothin'."

The cowboy addressed the Swede. "Stranger, I don't see how you come to be so gay around here."

Old Scully was instantly alert. "Stop!" he shouted, holding his hand forth, fingers upward. "Bill, you shut up!"

The cowboy spat carelessly into the sawdust-box. "I didn't say a word, did I?" he asked.

"Mr. Scully," called the Swede, "how much do I owe you?" It was seen that he was attired for departure, and that he had his valise in his hand.

"You don't owe me nothin'," repeated Scully in the same imperturbable way.

"Huh!" said the Swede. "I guess you're right. I guess if it was any way at all, you'd owe me somethin'. That's what I guess." He turned to the cowboy. "'Kill him! Kill him! Kill him!'" he mimicked, and then guffawed victoriously. "'Kill him!'" He was convulsed with ironical humour.

But he might have been jeering the dead. The three men were immovable and silent, staring with glassy eyes at the stove.

The Swede opened the door and passed into the storm, giving one derisive glance backward at the still group.

As soon as the door was closed, Scully and the cowboy leaped to their feet and began to curse. They trampled to and fro, waving their arms and smashing into the air with their fists. "Oh, but that was a hard minute!" wailed Scully. "That was a hard minute! Him there leerin' and scoffin'! One bang at his nose was worth forty dollars to me that minute! How did you stand it, Bill?"

"How did I stand it?" cried the cowboy in a quivering voice. "How did I stand it? Oh!"

The old man burst into sudden brogue. "I'd loike to take that Swade," he wailed, "and hould 'im down on a shtone flure and bate 'im to a jelly wid a shtick!"

The cowboy groaned in sympathy. "I'd like to git him by the neck and ha-ammer him" — he brought his hand down on a chair with a noise like a pistol-shot — "hammer that there Dutchman until he couldn't tell himself from a dead coyote!"

"I'd bate 'im until he —— "

"I'd show *him* some things —— "

And then together they raised a yearning, fanatic cry — "Oh-o-oh! if we only could —— "

"Yes!"

"Yes!"

"And then I'd —— "

"O-o-oh!"

VIII

The Swede, tightly gripping his valise, tacked across the face of the storm as if he carried sails. He was following a line of little naked, gasping trees which, he knew, must mark the way of the road. His face, fresh from the pounding of Johnnie's fists, felt more pleasure than pain in the wind and the driving snow. A number of square shapes loomed upon him finally, and he knew them as the houses of the main body of the town. He found a street and made travel along it, leaning heavily upon the wind whenever, at a corner, a terrific blast caught him.

He might have been in a deserted village. We picture the world as thick with conquering and elate humanity, but here, with the bugles of the tempest pealing, it was hard to imagine a peopled earth. One viewed the existence of man then as a marvel, and conceded a glamour of wonder to these lice which were caused to cling to a whirling, fire-smitten, ice-locked, disease-stricken, space-lost bulb. The conceit of man was explained by this storm to be the very engine of life. One was a coxcomb not to die in it. However, the Swede found a saloon.

In front of it an indomitable red light was burning, and the snowflakes were made blood-colour as they flew through the circumscribed territory of the lamp's shining. The Swede pushed open the door of the saloon and entered. A sanded expanse was before him, and at the end of it four men sat about a table drinking.

Down one side of the room extended a radiant bar, and its guardian was leaning upon his elbows listening to the talk of the men at the table. The Swede dropped his valise upon the floor and, smiling fraternally upon the barkeeper, said, "Gimme some whisky, will you?" The man placed a bottle, a whisky-glass, and a glass of ice-thick water upon the bar. The Swede poured himself an abnormal portion of whisky and drank it in three gulps. "Pretty bad night," remarked the bartender, indifferently. He was making the pretension of blindness which is usually a distinction of his class; but it could have been seen that he was furtively studying the half-erased blood-stains on the face of the Swede. "Bad night," he said again.

"Oh, it's good enough for me," replied the Swede, hardily, as he poured himself some more whisky. The barkeeper took his coin and manoeuvered it through its reception by the highly nickelled cash-machine. A bell rang; a card labelled "20 cts." had appeared.

"No," continued the Swede, "this isn't too bad weather. It's good enough for me."

"So?" murmured the barkeeper, languidly.

The copious drams made the Swede's eyes swim, and he breathed a trifle heavier. "Yes, I like this weather. I like it. It suits me." It was apparently his design to impart a deep significance to these words.

"So?" murmured the bartender again. He turned to gaze dreamily at the scroll-like birds and bird-like scrolls which had been drawn with soap upon the mirrors in back of the bar.

"Well, I guess I'll take another drink," said the Swede, presently. "Have something?"

"No, thanks; I'm not drinkin'," answered the bartender. Afterwards he asked, "How did you hurt your face?"

The Swede immediately began to boast loudly. "Why, in a fight. I thumped the soul out of a man down here at Scully's hotel."

The interest of the four men at the table was at last aroused.

"Who was it?" said one.

"Johnnie Scully," blustered the Swede. "Son of the man what runs it. He will be pretty near dead for some weeks, I can tell you. I made a nice thing of him, I did. He couldn't get up. They carried him in the house. Have a drink?"

Instantly the men in some subtle way encased themselves in reserve. "No, thanks," said one. The group was of curious formation. Two were prominent local business men; one was the district attorney; and one was a professional gambler of the kind known as "square." But a scrutiny of the group would not have enabled an observer to pick the gambler from the men of more reputable pursuits. He was, in fact, a man so delicate in manner, when among people of fair class, and so judicious in his choice of victims, that in the strictly masculine part of the town's life he had come to be explicitly trusted and admired. People called him a thoroughbred. The fear and contempt with which his craft was regarded were undoubtedly the reason why his quiet dignity shone conspicuous above the quiet dignity of men who might be merely hatters, billiard-markers, or grocery clerks. Beyond an occasional unwary traveller who came by rail, this gambler was supposed to prey solely upon reckless and senile farmers, who, when flush with good crops, drove into town in all the pride and confidence of an absolutely invulnerable stupidity. Hearing at times in circuitous fashion of the despoilment of such a farmer, the important men of Romper invariably laughed in contempt of the victim, and if they thought of the wolf at all, it was with a kind of pride at the knowledge that he would never dare think of attacking their wisdom and courage. Besides, it was popular that this gambler had a real wife and two real children in a near cottage in a suburb, where he led an exemplary home life; and when any one even suggested a discrepancy in his character, the crowd immediately vociferated descriptions of this virtuous family circle. Then men who led exemplary home lives, and men who did not lead exemplary home lives, all subsided in a bunch, remarking that there was nothing more to be said.

However, when a restriction was placed upon him — as, for instance, when a strong clique of members of the new Pollywog Club refused to permit him, even as a spectator, to appear in the rooms of the organization — the candour and gentleness with which he accepted the judgment disarmed many of his foes and made his friends more desperately partisan. He invariably distinguished between himself and a respectable Romper man so quickly and frankly that his manner actually appeared to be a continual broadcast compliment.

And one must not forget to declare the fundamental fact of his entire position in Romper. It is irrefutable that in all affairs outside his business, in all matters that occur eternally and commonly between man and man, this thieving card-player was so generous, so just, so moral, that, in a contest, he could have put to flight the consciences of nine tenths of the citizens of Romper.

And so it happened that he was seated in this saloon with the two prominent local merchants and the district attorney.

The Swede continued to drink raw whisky, meanwhile babbling at the barkeeper and trying to induce him to indulge in potations. "Come on. Have a drink. Come on. What — no? Well, have a little one, then. By gawd, I've whipped a man tonight, and I want to celebrate. I whipped him good, too. Gentlemen," the Swede cried to the men at the table, "have a drink?"

"Ssh!" said the barkeeper.

The group at the table, although furtively attentive, had been pretending to be deep in talk, but now a man lifted his eyes toward the Swede and said, shortly, "Thanks. We don't want any more."

At this reply the Swede ruffled out his chest like a rooster. "Well," he exploded, "it seems I can't get anybody to drink with me in this town. Seems so, don't it? Well!"

"Ssh!" said the barkeeper.

"Say," snarled the Swede, "don't you try to shut me up. I won't have it. I'm a gentleman, and I want people to drink with me. And I want 'em to drink with me now. Now — do you understand?" He rapped the bar with his knuckles.

Years of experience had calloused the bartender. He merely grew sulky. "I hear you," he answered.

"Well," cried the Swede, "listen hard then. See those men over there? Well, they're going to drink with me, and don't you forget it. Now you watch."

"Hi!" yelled the barkeeper, "this won't do!"

"Why won't it?" demanded the Swede. He stalked over to the table, and by chance laid his hand upon the shoulder of the gambler. "How about this?" he asked wrathfully. "I asked you to drink with me."

The gambler simply twisted his head and spoke over his shoulder. "My friend, I don't know you."

"Oh, hell!" answered the Swede, "come and have a drink."

"Now, my boy," advised the gambler, kindly, "take your hand off my shoulder and go 'way and mind your own business." He was a little, slim man, and it seemed strange to hear him use this tone of heroic patronage to the burly Swede. The other men at the table said nothing.

"What! You won't drink with me, you little dude? I'll make you, then! I'll make you!" The Swede had grasped the gambler frenziedly at the throat, and was dragging him from his chair. The other men sprang up. The barkeeper dashed around the corner of his bar. There was a great tumult, and then was seen a long blade in the hand of the gambler. It shot forward, and a human body, this citadel of virtue, wisdom, power, was pierced as easily as if it had been a melon. The Swede fell with a cry of supreme astonishment.

The prominent merchants and the district attorney must have at once tumbled out of the place backward. The bartender found himself hanging limply to the arm of a chair and gazing into the eyes of a murderer.

"Henry," said the latter, as he wiped his knife on one of the towels that hung beneath the bar rail, "you tell 'em where to find me. I'll be home, waiting for 'em." Then he vanished. A moment afterward the barkeeper was in the street dinning through the storm for help and, moreover, companionship.

The corpse of the Swede, alone in the saloon, had its eyes fixed upon a dreadful legend that dwelt atop of the cash-machine: "This registers the amount of your purchase."

IX

Months later, the cowboy was frying pork over the stove of a little ranch near the Dakota line, when there was a quick thud of hoofs outside, and presently the Easterner entered with the letters and the papers.

"Well," said the Easterner at once, "the chap that killed the Swede has got three years. Wasn't much, was it?"

"He has? Three years?" The cowboy poised his pan of pork, while he ruminated upon the news. "Three years. That ain't much."

"No. It was a light sentence," replied the Easterner as he unbuckled his spurs. "Seems there was a good deal of sympathy for him in Romper."

"If the bartender had been any good," observed the cowboy, thoughtfully, "he would have gone in and cracked that there Dutchman on the head with a bottle in the beginnin' of it and stopped all this here murderin'."

"Yes, a thousand things might have happened," said the Easterner, tartly.

The cowboy returned his pan of pork to the fire, but his philosophy continued. "It's funny, ain't it? If he hadn't said Johnnie was cheatin' he'd be alive this minute. He was an awful fool. Game played for fun, too. Not for money. I believe he was crazy."

"I feel sorry for that gambler," said the Easterner.

"Oh, so do I," said the cowboy. "He don't deserve none of it for killin' who he did."

"The Swede might not have been killed if everything had been square."

"Might not have been killed?" exclaimed the cowboy. "Everythin' square? Why, when he said that Johnnie was cheatin' and acted like such a jackass? And then in the saloon he fairly walked up to git hurt?" With these arguments the cowboy browbeat the Easterner and reduced him to rage.

"You're a fool!" cried the Easterner, viciously. "You're a bigger jackass than the Swede by a million majority. Now let me tell you one thing. Let me tell you something. Listen! Johnnie *was* cheating!"

"'Johnnie,'" said the cowboy, blankly. there was a minute of silence, and then he said, robustly, "Why, no. The game was only for fun."

"Fun or not," said the Easterner, "Johnnie was cheating. I saw him. I know it. I saw him. And I refused to stand up and be a man. I let the Swede fight it out alone. And you—you were simply puffing around the place and wanting to fight. And then old Scully himself! We are all in it! This poor gambler isn't even a noun. He is kind of an adverb. Every sin is the result of a collaboration. We, five of us, have collaborated in the murder of this Swede. Usually there are from a dozen to forty women really involved in every murder, but in this case it seems to be only five men—you, I, Johnnie, old Scully; and that fool of an unfortunate gambler came merely as a culmination, the apex of a human movement, and gets all the punishment."

The cowboy, injured and rebellious, cried out blindly into this fog of mysterious theory: "Well, I didn't do anythin', did I?"

[1898]

Study and Writing Questions

1. Describe the Western SETTING. To what extent is Nebraska at this time really "the West"? In what way(s) is the West defined in relation to the East? Does the setting conform to the Swede's preconception of the West? In what ways does the setting seem particularly appropriate for this STORY?
2. What is important about "the dreadful legend that dwelt atop of the cash-machine: 'This registers the amount of your purchase'"? What are the economic MOTIVATIONS of each of the CHARACTERS? What is the role of economics in the society presented here?
3. How is color IMAGERY used in this NARRATIVE? How does Crane use red, white, and blue?
4. Why does the Easterner say, "'Every sin is the result of a collaboration'"? Is the Easterner right when he says this? If so, who collaborates in the sin(s) of this story and how? Is the Swede himself in some sense guilty?
5. What is this narrative's DIDACTIC message? Is that message intended to apply only to men? only to the West? only to the United States? If your answer is no to any of these questions, how does Crane make the story's message more general?

See also Questions for Contrast and Comparison: 49, 53, 56, 82, 148, 152, 169, and 230.

R(OBERT DENNIS) CRUMB (1943–), *whose work revived the 1930s jazz phrase "Keep on truckin'," was born in Philadelphia, Pennsylvania and raised, like many military children, all over America. He began cartooning at six, producing single-copy comic books with his older brother. After high school, Crumb, who had no formal art training, worked for American Greetings Corporation in Cleveland and created an office strip,* Roberta Smith, Office Girl. *In 1964 he married for the first time and one year later began publishing in Harvey Kurtzman's satiric monthly,* Help! *Success led him to New York, Chicago, and San Francisco, the center of the Hippie movement, where he quickly found outlets in the underground press for his trademark characters: Angelfood McSpade, a black man embodying white fears of black sexuality; the excruciatingly middle-class Whiteman; Mr. Natural, a con-man guru, and his disciple Flakey Foont, forever blind to Mr. Natural's clay feet; and the irrepressible Fritz the Cat, the first underground* CHARACTER *to make "straight" publication. Crumb's* Head Comix, *published by Viking, was the loose source for Ralph Bakshi's* Fritz the Cat, *the first X-rated, feature-length, animated film. Crumb's* Zap *and* Snatch *comics have been subjects of obscenity trials and suppression, yet Crumb is arguably the most influential comic artist of late twentieth century America. He married fellow comic artist Aline Kominsky in 1978; they live in seclusion in California.*

fred the teen-age girl pigeon

fred the teen-age girl pigeon

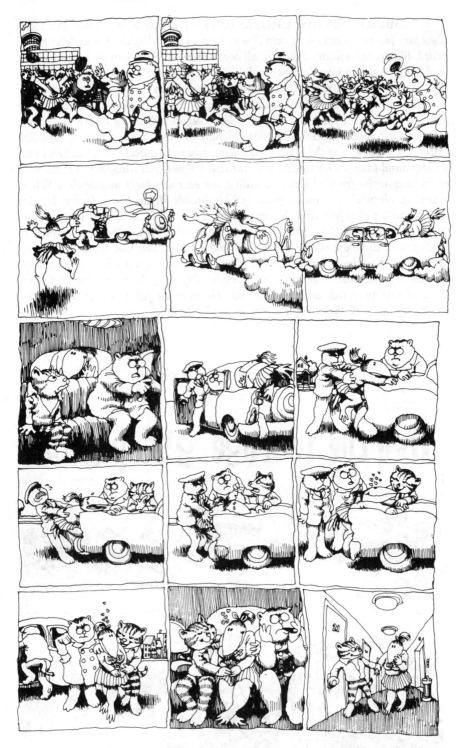

[1968]

Study and Writing Questions

1. Describe the drawing STYLE used here. How does it influence your reading of the NARRATIVE?
2. Although the STORY is told in twenty-four virtually square, virtually distinct panels, in fact some panels are shaped slightly differently than others. In addition, the panel boundaries are never quite straight, and in a few instances the contents slip outside the panels. What are the effects, both in specific panels and in the story as a whole, of these variations from regularity?
3. What meaning(s) does each of the few written words of this narrative convey?
4. What are the key visual signs of this story, such as the guitar, the limousine, and so on? How do they communicate? Does the use of CONVENTIONAL signs necessarily imply a conventional story?
5. Is this narrative a FABLE? If not, why not? If so, what is its MORAL?

See also Questions for Contrast and Comparison: 8, 12, 13, 94, 95, 132, 199, and 240.

■ **SAMUEL R(AY) DELANY (JR.)** (1942–), *was born in New York City, son of a funeral director and a library clerk. He attended the Dalton School, Bronx High School of Science, and, in 1960 and 1962–63, City College (now part of the City University of New York). In his teens he began publishing fast-moving* SCIENCE FICTION (*The Jewels of Aptor [1962]) that foreshadowed a career-long interest in the uses and production of art and myth, an interest apparent in his fictional speculations on language (as in Babel-17 [1966]), in his* PLOTS *(like that of The Einstein Intersection [1967]) in which diverse realities intersect, and in his* SETTINGS *(like the surrealistic city of Dhalgren [1975]) in which* LYRIC *prose conjoins the visceral and the* FANTASTICAL. *His recent* FICTIONS, *beginning with Tales of Nevèrÿon (1979), both discuss and construct countermyths to our own. Married in 1961 (to the poet Marilyn Hacker with whom he had a daughter), he separated in 1974 and divorced in 1980. Both his* CRITICISM *(like The Jewel-Hinged Jaw [1977]) and his fiction intermingle autobiography and* FANTASY, *inviting speculation about a life of apparent contradictions: he is a personally gentle, fiercely intellectual, black bisexual winning awards for writing in a field more often represented by a sort of workaday, adolescent, Midwestern earnestness. Since 1988, he has been Professor of Comparative Literature at the University of Massachusetts, Amherst.*

Corona

Pa ran off to Mars Colony before Buddy was born. Momma drank. At sixteen Buddy used to help out in a 'copter repair shop outside St. Gable below Baton Rouge. Once he decided it would be fun to take a 'copter, some bootleg, a girl named Dolores-jo, and sixty-three dollars and eighty-five cents to New Orleans. Nothing taken had ever, by any interpretation, been his. He was caught before they raised from the garage roof. He lied about his age at court to avoid the indignity of reform school. Momma, when they found her, wasn't too sure ("Buddy? Now, let me see, that's Laford. And James Robert Warren—I named him after my third husband who was not living with me at the time—now little James, he came along in . . . two thousand and thirty-*two*, I do believe. Or thirty-*four*—you sure now, it's Buddy?") when he was born. The constable was inclined to judge him younger than he was, but let him go to grown-up prison anyway. Some terrible things happened there. When Buddy came out three years later he was a gentler person than before; still, when frightened, he became violent. Shortly he knocked up a waitress six years his senior. Chagrined, he applied for emigration to one of Uranus' moons. In twenty years, though, the colonial economy had stabilized. They were a lot more stringent with applicants than in his Pa's day: colonies had become almost respectable. They'd started barring people with jail records and things like that. So he went to New York instead and eventually got a job as an assistant servicer at the Kennedy spaceport.

There was a nine-year-old girl in a hospital in New York at that time who could read minds and wanted to die. Her name was Lee.

Also there was a singer named Bryan Faust.

Slow, violent, blond Buddy had been at Kennedy over a year when Faust's music came. The songs covered the city, sounded on every radio, filled the title selections on every jukebox and Scopitone. They shouted and whispered and growled from the wall speaker in the spacehangar. Buddy ambled over the catwalk while the cross-rhythms, sudden silences, and moments of pure voice were picked up by jangling organ, whining oboe, bass and cymbals. Buddy's thoughts were small and slow. His hands, gloved in canvas, his feet in rubber boots, were big and quick.

Below him the spaceliner filled the hangar like a tuber an eighth of a mile long. The service crew swarmed the floor, moving over the cement like scattered ball bearings. And the music —

"Hey, kid."

Buddy turned.

Bim swaggered toward him, beating his thigh to the rhythms in the falls of sound. "I was just looking for you, kid." Buddy was twenty-four, but people would call him "kid" after he was thirty. He blinked a lot.

"You want to get over and help them haul down that solvent from upstairs? The damn lift's busted again. I swear, they're going to have a strike if they don't keep the equipment working right. Ain't safe. Say, what did you think of the crowd outside this morning?"

"Crowd?" Buddy's drawl snagged on a slight speech defect. "Yeah, there was a lot of people, huh. I been down in the maintenance shop since six o'clock, so I guess I must've missed most of it. What was they here for?"

Bim got a lot of what-are-you-kidding me on his face. Then it turned to a tolerant smile. "For Faust." He nodded toward the speaker: the music halted, lurched, then Bryan Faust's voice roared out for love and the violent display that would prove it real. "Faust came in this morning, kid. You didn't know? He's been making it down from moon to moon through the outer planets. I hear he broke 'em up in the asteroids. He's been to Mars and the last thing I heard they love him on Luna as much as anywhere else. He arrived on Earth this morning, and he'll be up and down the Americas for twelve days." He thumbed toward the pit and shook his head. "That's his liner." Bim whistled. "And did we have a hell of a time! All them kids, thousands of 'em, I bet. And people old enough to know better too. You should have seen the police! When we were trying to get the liner in here, a couple of hundred kids got through the police block. They wanted to pull his ship apart and take home the pieces. You like his music?"

Buddy squinted toward the speaker. The sounds jammed into his ears, pried around his mind, loosening things. Most were good things, touched on by a resolved cadence, a syncopation caught up again, feelings sounded on too quickly for him to hold, but good feelings. Still, a few of them . . .

Buddy shrugged, blinked. "I like it." And the beat of his heart, his lungs, and the music coincided. "Yeah. I like that." The music went faster; heart and breathing fell behind; Buddy felt a surge of disorder. "But it's . . . strange." Embarrassed, he smiled over his broken tooth.

"Yeah. I guess a lot of other people think so too. Well, get over with those solvent cans."

"Okay." Buddy turned off toward the spiral staircase. He was on the landing, about to go up, when someone yelled down, "Watch it —!"

A ten-gallon drum slammed the walkway five feet from him. He whirled to see as the casing split —

(Faust's sonar drums slammed.)

—and solvent, oxidizing in the air, splattered.

Buddy screamed and clutched his eye. He had been working with the metal rasp that morning, and his gloves were impregnated with steel flakes and oil. He ground his canvas palm against his face.

(Faust's electric bass ground against a suspended dissonance.)

As he staggered down the walk, hot solvent rained on his back. Then something inside went wild and he began to swing his arms.

(The last chorus swung toward the close. And the announcer's voice, not waiting for the end, cut over, "All *right* all you little people *out* there in music land . . .")

"What in the—"

"Jesus, what's wrong with—"

"What happened? I told you the damn lift was broken!"

"Call the infirmary! Quick! Call the—"

Voices came from the level above, the level below. And footsteps. Buddy turned on the ramp and screamed and swung.

"Watch it! What's with that guy—"

"Here, help me hold . . . Owww!"

"He's gone berserk! Get the doc up from the infirm—"

(". . . *that* was Bryan Faust's mind-*twisting*, brain-*blowing*, brand-new release, *Corona*! And you know it will be a *hit* . . . !")

Somebody tried to grab him, and Buddy hit out. Blind, rolling from the hips, he tried to apprehend the agony with flailing hands. And couldn't. A flash bulb had been jammed into his eye socket and detonated. He knocked somebody else against the rail, and staggered, and shrieked.

(". . . And he's come down to Earth at *last*, all you baby-mommas and baby-poppas! The little man from Ganymede who's been putting *the* music of *the* spheres through *so* many changes this past year arrived *in* New York this morning. And all *I* want to say, Bryan . . .")

Rage, pain, and music.

(". . . is, how do you *dig* our Earth!")

Buddy didn't even feel the pressure hypo on his shoulder. He collapsed as the cymbals died.

Lee turned and turned the volume knob till it clicked.

In the trapezoid of sunlight over the desk from the high, small window, open now for August, lay her radio, a piece of graph paper with an incomplete integration for the area within the curve $X^4 + Y^4 = K^4$, and her brown fist. Smiling, she tried to release the tension the music had built.

Her shoulders lowered, her nostrils narrowed, and her fist fell over on its back. Still, her knuckles moved to *Corona's* remembered rhythm.

The inside of her forearm was webbed with raw pink. There were a few marks on her right arm too. But those were three years old; from when she had been six.

Corona!

She closed her eyes and pictured the rim of the sun. Centered in the flame, with the green eyes of his German father and the high cheekbones and his

Arawak mother, was the impudent and insouciant, sensual and curious face of Bryan Faust. The brassy, four-color magazine with its endless hyperbolic prose was open on her bed behind her.

Lee closed her eyes tighter. If she could reach out, and perhaps touch — no, not him; that would be too much — but someone standing, sitting, walking near him, see what seeing him close was like, hear what hearing his voice was like, through air and light: she reached out her mind, reached for the music. And heard —

— your daughter getting along?

They keep telling me better and better every week when I go to visit her. But, oh, I swear, I just don't know. You have no idea how we hated to send her back to that place.

Of course I know! She's your own daughter. And she's such a cute little thing. And so smart. Did they want to run some more tests?

She tried to kill herself. Again.

Oh, *no!*

She's got scars on her wrist halfway to her elbow! What am I doing wrong? The doctors can't tell me. She's not even ten. I can't keep her here with me. Her father's tried; he's about had it with the whole business. I know because of a divorce a child may have emotional problems, but that a little girl, as intelligent as Lee, can be so — confused! She had to go back. I know she had to go back. But what is it I'm doing wrong? I hate myself for it, and sometimes, just because she can't tell me, I hate her —

Lee's eyes opened; she smashed the table with her small, brown fists, tautening the muscles of her face to hold the tears. All musical beauty was gone. She breathed once more. For a while she looked up at the window, its glass door swung wide. The bottom sill was seven feet from the floor.

Then she pressed the button for Dr. Gross, and went to the bookshelf. She ran her fingers over the spines: *Spinoza, The Secret in the Ivory Charm, The Decline of the West, The Wind in the Wil——*

She turned at the sound of the door unbolting. "You buzzed for me, Lee?"

"It happened. Again. Just about a minute ago."

"I noted the time as you rang."

"Duration, about forty-five seconds. It was my mother, and her friend who lives downstairs. Very ordinary. Nothing worth noting down."

"And how do you feel?"

She didn't say anything, but looked at the shelves.

Dr. Gross walked into the room and sat down on her desk. "Would you like to tell me what you were doing just before it happened?"

"Nothing. I'd just finished listening to the new record. On the radio."

"Which record?"

"The new Faust song. *Corona.*"

"Haven't heard that one." He glanced down at the graph paper and raised an eyebrow. "This yours, or is it from one of your books?"

"You told me to ring for you every time I . . . got an attack, didn't you?"

"Yes —"

"I'm doing what you want."

"Of course, Lee. I didn't mean to imply you hadn't been keeping your word. Want to tell me something about the record? What did you think of it?"

"The rhythm is very interesting. Five against seven when it's there. But a lot of the beats are left out, so you have to listen hard to get it."

"Was there anything, perhaps in the words, that may have set off the mind reading?"

"His colonial Ganymede accent is so thick that I missed most of the lyrics, even though it's basically English."

Dr. Gross smiled. "I've noticed the colonial expressions are slipping into a lot of young people's speech since Faust has become so popular. You hear them all the time."

"I don't." She glanced up at the doctor quickly, then back to the books.

Dr. Gross coughed; then he said, "Lee, we feel it's best to keep you away from the other children at the hospital. You tune in most frequently on the minds of people you know, or those who've had similar experiences and reactions to yours. All the children in the hospital are emotionally disturbed. If you were to suddenly pick up all their minds at once, you might be seriously hurt."

"I wouldn't!" she whispered.

"You remember you told us about what happened when you were four, in kindergarten, and you tuned into your whole class for six hours? Do you remember how upset you were?"

"I went home and tried to drink the iodine." She flung him a brutal glance. "I remember. But I hear Mommy when she's all the way across the city. I hear strangers too, lots of times! I hear Mrs. Lowery, when she's teaching down in the classroom! I hear her! I've heard people on other planets!"

"About the song, Lee —"

"You want to keep me away from the other children because I'm smarter than they are! I know. I've heard you think too —"

"Lee, I want you to tell me more about how you felt about this new song —"

"You think I'll upset them because I'm so smart. You won't let me have any friends!"

"What did you feel about the song, Lee?"

She caught her breath, holding it in, her lids batting, the muscle in the back of her jaw leaping.

"What did you *feel* about the song; did you like it, or did you dislike it?"

She let the air hiss through her lips. "There are three melodic motifs," she began at last. "They appear in descending order of rhythmic intensity. There are more silences in the last melodic line. His music is composed of silence as much as sound."

"Again, what did you feel? I'm trying to get at your emotional reaction, don't you see?"

She looked at the window. She looked at Dr. Gross. Then she turned toward the shelves. "There's a book here, a part in a book, that says it, I guess, better than I can." She began working a volume from the half-shelf of Nietzsche.

"What book?"

"Come here." She began to turn the pages. "I'll show you."

Dr. Gross got up from the desk. She met him beneath the window.

Dr. Gross took it and, frowning, read the title heading: "'*The Birth of Tragedy from the Spirit of Music* . . . death lies only in these dissonant tones —'"

Lee's head struck the book from his hand. She had leapt on him as though he were a piece of furniture and she a small beast. When her hand was not clutching his belt, shirt front, lapel, shoulder, it was straining upward. He managed to grab her just as she grabbed the window ledge.

Outside was a nine-story drop.

He held her by the ankle as she reeled in the sunlit frame. He yanked, and she fell into his arms, shrieking, "Let me die!"

They went down on the floor together, he shouting, "No!" and the little girl crying. Dr. Gross stood up, now panting.

She lay on the green vinyl, curling around the sound of her own sobs, pulling her hands over the floor to press her stomach.

"Lee, isn't there *any* way you can understand this? Yes, you've been exposed to more than any nine-year-old's mind should be able to bear. But you've got to come to terms with it, somehow! That isn't the answer, Lee. I wish I could back it up with something. If you let me help, perhaps I can —"

She shouted, with her cheek pressed to the floor, "But you can't help! Your thoughts, they're just as clumsy and imprecise as the others! How can you — *you* help people who're afraid and confused because their own minds have formed the wrong associations! How! I don't want to have to stumble around in all your insecurities and fears as well! I'm not a child! I've lived more years and places than any ten of you! Just go away and let me alone —"

Rage, pain, and music.

"Lee —"

"Go away! Please!"

Dr. Gross, upset, swung the window closed, locked it, left the room, locked the door.

Rage, pain . . . below the chaos she was conscious of the infectious melody of *Corona*. Somebody — not her — somebody else was being carried into the hospital, drifting in the painful dark, dreaming over the same sounds. Exhausted, still crying, she let it come.

The man's thoughts, she realized through her exhaustion, to escape pain had taken refuge in the harmonies and cadences of *Corona*. She tried to hide her own mind there. And twisted violently away. There was something terrible there. She tried to pull back, but her mind followed the music down.

The terrible thing was that someone had once told him not to put his knee on the floor.

Fighting, she tried to push it aside to see if what was underneath was less terrible. ("Buddy, stop that whining and let your momma alone. I don't feel good. Just get out of here and leave me *alone!*" The bottle shattered on the door jamb by his ear, and he fled.) She winced. There couldn't be anything that bad about putting your knee on the floor. And so she gave up and let it swim toward her —— suds wound on the dirty water. The water was all around him. Buddy leaned forward and scrubbed the wire brush across the wet stone. His canvas shoes were already soaked.

"Put your blessed knee on the floor, and I'll get you! Come on, move your . . ." Somebody, not Buddy, got kicked. "And don't let your knee touch that floor! Don't, I say." And got kicked again.

They waddled across the prison lobby, scrubbing. There was a sign over the elevator: Louisiana State Penal Correction Institute, but it was hard to make out because Buddy didn't read very well.

"Keep up with 'em, kid. Don't you let 'em get ahead'n you!" Bigfoot yelled. "Just 'cause you little, don't think you got no special privileges." Bigfoot slopped across the stone.

"When they gonna get an automatic scrubber unit in here?" somebody complained. "They got one in the county jail."

"This Institute" — Bigfoot lumbered up the line — "was built in nineteen hundred and *forty*-seven! We ain't had no escape in ninety-four years. We run it the same today as when it was builded back in nineteen hundred and *forty*-seven. The first time it don't do its job right of keepin' you all inside — then we'll think about running it different. Get on back to work. *Watch* that knee!"

Buddy's thighs were sore, his insteps cramped. The balls of his feet burned and his pants cuffs were sopping.

Bigfoot had taken off his slippers. As he patrolled the scrubbers, he slapped the soles together, first in front of his belly, then behind his heavy buttocks. *Slap* and *slap*. With each *slap*, one foot hit the soapy stone. "Don't bother looking up at me. You look at them stones! But don't let your knee touch the floor."

Once, in the yard latrine, someone had whispered, "Bigfoot? You watch him, kid! Was a preacher, with a revival meeting back in the swamp. Went down to the Emigration Office in town back when they was taking everyone they could get and demanded they make him Pope or something over the colony on Europa they was just setting up. They laughed him out of the office. Sunday, when everyone came to meeting, they found he'd sneaked into the town, busted the man at the Emigration Office over the head, dragged him out to the swamp, and nailed him up to a cross under the meeting tent. He tried to make everybody pray him down. After they prayed for about an hour, and nothing happened, they brought Bigfoot here. He's a trustee now."

Buddy rubbed harder with his wire brush.

"Let's see you rub a little of the devil out'n them stones. And don't let me see your knee touch the — "

Buddy straightened his shoulders. And slipped.

He went over on his backside, grabbed the pail; water splashed over him, sluiced beneath. Soap stung his eyes. He lay there a moment.

Bare feet slapped toward him. "Come on kid. Up you go, and back to work."

With eyes tight, Buddy pushed himself up.

"You sure are one clums——"

Buddy rolled to his knees.

"I *told* you not to let your knee touch the floor!"

Wet canvas whammed his ear and cheek.

"Didn't I?"

A foot fell in the small of his back and struck him flat. His chin hit the floor and he bit his tongue, hard. Holding him down with his foot, Bigfoot whopped

Buddy's head back and forth, first with one shoe, then the other. Buddy, blinded, mouth filled with blood, swam on the wet stone, tried to duck away.

"Now don't let your knees touch the floor *again*. Come on, back to work, all of you." The feet slapped away.

Against the sting, Buddy opened his eyes. The brush lay just in front of his face. Beyond the wire bristles he saw a pink heel strike in suds.

His action took a long time to form. *Slap* and *slap*. On the third *slap* he gathered his feet, leapt. He landed on Bigfoot's back, pounding with the brush. He hit three times, then he tried to scrub off the side of Bigfoot's face.

The guards finally pulled him off. They took him into a room where there was an iron bed with no mattress and strapped him, ankles, wrist, neck, and stomach, to the frame. He yelled for them to let him up. They said they couldn't because he was still violent. "How'm I gonna eat!" he demanded. "You gonna let me up to eat?"

"Calm down a little. We'll send someone in to feed you."

A few minutes after the dinner bell rang that evening, Bigfoot looked into the room. Ear, cheek, neck, and left shoulder were bandaged. Blood had seeped through at the tip of his clavicle to the size of a quarter. In one hand Bigfoot held a tin plate of rice and fatback, in the other an iron spoon. He came over, sat on the edge of Buddy's bed, and kicked off one canvas shoe. "They told me I should come in and feed you, kid." He kicked off the other one. "You real hungry?"

When they unstrapped Buddy four days later, he couldn't talk. One tooth was badly broken, several others chipped. The roof of his mouth was raw; the prison doctor had to take five stitches in his tongue.

Lee gagged on the taste of iron.

Somewhere in the hospital, Buddy lay in the dark, terrified, his eye stinging, his head filled with the beating rhythms of *Corona*.

Her shoulders bunched; she worked her jaw and tongue against the pain that Buddy remembered. She wanted to die.

Stop it! she whispered, and tried to wrench herself from the inarticulate terror which Buddy, cast back by pain and the rhythm of a song to a time when he was only twice her age, remembered. Oh, stop it! But no one could hear her, the way she could hear Buddy, her mother, Mrs. Lowery in the schoolroom.

She had to stop the fear.

Perhaps it was the music. Perhaps it was because she had exhausted every other way. Perhaps it was because the only place left to look for a way out was back inside Buddy's mind—

—when he wanted to sneak out of the cell at night to join a card game down in the digs where they played for cigarettes, he would take a piece of chewing gum and the bottle cap from a Dr. Pepper and stick it over the bolt in the top of the door. When they closed the doors after free-time, it still fitted into place, but the bolt couldn't slide in—

Lee looked at the locked door of her room. She could get the chewing gum in the afternoon period when they let her walk around her own floor. But the soft-drink machine by the elevator only dispensed in cups. Suddenly she sat up and looked at the bottom of her shoe. On the toe and heel were the metal taps that her mother had made the shoemaker put there so they wouldn't wear so fast.

She had to stop the fear. If they wouldn't let her do it by killing herself, she'd do it another way. She went to the cot, and began to work the tap loose on the frame.

Buddy lay on his back, afraid. After they had drugged him, they had brought him into the city. He didn't know where he was. He couldn't see, and he was afraid.

Something fingered his face. He rocked his head to get away from the spoon —

"Shhh! It's all right . . ."

Light struck one eye. There was still something wrong with the other. He blinked.

"You're all right," she — it was a *she* voice, though he still couldn't make out a face — told him again. "You're not in jail. You're not in the . . . the joint any more. You're in New York. In a hospital. Something's happened to your eye. That's all."

"My eye . . . ?"

"Don't be afraid any more. Please. Because I can't stand it."

It was a kid's voice. He blinked again, reached up to rub his vision clear.

"Watch out," she said. "You'll get —"

His eye itched and he wanted to scratch it. So he shoved at the voice.

"Hey!"

Something stung him and he clutched at his thumb with his other hand.

"I'm sorry," she said. "I didn't mean to bite your finger. But you'll hurt the bandage. I've pulled the one away from your right eye. There's nothing wrong with that. Just a moment." Something cool swabbed his blurred vision.

It came away.

The cutest little colored girl was kneeling on the edge of the bed with a piece of wet cotton in her hand. The light was nowhere near as bright as it had seemed; just a night-light glowed over the mirror above the basin. "You've got to stop being so frightened," she whispered. "You've *got* to."

Buddy had spent a good deal of his life doing what people told him, when he wasn't doing the opposite on purpose.

The girl sat back on her heels. "That's better."

He pushed himself up in the bed. There were no straps. Sheets hissed over his knees. He looked at his chest. Blue pajamas: the buttons were in the wrong holes by one. He reached down to fix them, and his fingers closed on air.

"You've only got one eye working so there's no parallax for depth perception."

"Huh?" He looked up again.

She wore shorts and a red and white polo shirt.

He frowned, "Who are you?"

"Dianne Lee Morris," she said. "And you're — " Then she frowned too. She scrambled from the bed, took the mirror from over the basin and brought it back to the bed. "Look. Now who are you?"

He reached up to touch with grease-crested nails the bandage that sloped over his left eye. Short, yellow hair lapped the gauze. His forefinger went on to the familiar scar through the tow hedge of his right eyebrow.

"Who are you?"

"Buddy Magowan."

"Where do you live?"

"St. Gab—" He stopped. "A hun' ni'tee' stree' 'tween Se'on and Thir' A'nue."

"Say it again."

"A hundred an' nineteenth street between Second an' Third Avenue." The consonants his night-school teacher at P.S. 125 had laboriously inserted into his speech this past year returned.

"Good. And you work?"

"Out at Kennedy. Service assistant."

"And there's nothing to be afraid of."

He shook his head, "Naw," and grinned. His broken tooth reflected in the mirror. "Naw. I was just having a bad . . . dream."

She put the mirror back. As she turned, suddenly she closed her eyes and sighed.

"What'sa matter?"

She opened them again. "It's stopped. I can't hear inside your head any more. It's been going on all day."

"Huh? What do you mean?"

"Maybe you read about me in the magazine. There was a big article about me in *New Times* a couple of years ago. I'm in the hospital too. Over on the other side, in the psychiatric division. Did you read the article?"

"Didn't do much magazine reading back then. Don't do too much now either. What'd they write about?"

"I can hear and see what other people are thinking. I'm one of the three they're studying. I do it best of all of them. But it only comes in spurts. The other one, Eddy, is an idiot. I met him when we were getting all the tests. He's older than you and even dumber. Then there's Mrs. Lowery. She doesn't hear. She just sees. And sometimes she can make other people hear her. She works in the school here at the hospital. She can come and go as she pleases. But I have to stay locked up."

Buddy squinted. "You can hear what's in my head?"

"Not now. But I could. And it was . . . ." Her lip began to quiver; her brown eyes brightened. ". . . I mean when that man tried to . . . with the . . ." And overflowed. She put her fingers on her chin and twisted. ". . . when he . . . cutting in your . . ."

Buddy saw her tears, wondered at them. "Aw, honey—" he said, reached to take her shoulder—

Her face struck his chest and she clutched his pajama jacket. "It hurt *so* much!"

Her grief at his agony shook her.

"I had to stop you from hurting! Yours was just a dream, so I could sneak out of my room, get down here, and wake you up. But the others, the girl in the fire, or the man in the flooded mine . . . those weren't dreams! I couldn't do anything about them. I couldn't stop the hurting there. I couldn't stop it at all, Buddy! I wanted to. But one was in Australia and the other in Costa Rica!" She sobbed against his chest. "And one was on Mars! And I couldn't get to Mars. I couldn't!"

"It's all right," he whispered, uncomprehending, and rubbed her rough hair. Then, as she shook in his arms, understanding swelled. "You came . . . down here to wake me up?" he asked.

She nodded against his pajama jacket.

"Why?"

She shrugged against his belly. "I . . . I don't . . . maybe the music."

After a moment he asked. "Is this the first time you ever done something about what you heard?"

"It's not the first time I ever tried. But it's the first time it ever . . . worked."

"Then why did you try again?"

"Because . . ." She was stiller now. ". . . I hoped maybe it would hurt less if I could get—through." He felt her jaw moving as she spoke. "It does." Something in her face began to quiver. "It does hurt less." He put his hand on her hand, and she took his thumb.

"You knew I was . . . was awful scared?"

She nodded. "I knew, so I was scared just the same."

Buddy remembered the dream. The back of his neck grew cold, and the flesh under his thighs began to tingle. He remembered the reality behind the dream— and held her more tightly and pressed his cheek to her hair. "Thank you." He couldn't say it any other way, but it didn't seem enough. So he said it again more slowly. "*Thank* you."

A little later she pushed away, and he watched her sniffling face with depthless vision.

"Do you like the song?"

He blinked. And realized the insistent music still worked through his head. "You can—hear what I'm thinking again?"

"No. But you were thinking about it before. I just wanted to find out."

Buddy thought awhile. "Yeah." He cocked his head. "Yeah. I like it a lot. It makes me feel . . . good."

She hesitated, then let out: "Me *too*! I think it's beautiful. I think Faust's music is so," and she whispered the next word as though it might offend, "*alive!* But with life the way it should be. Not without pain, but with pain contained, ordered, given form and meaning, so that it's almost all right again. Don't you feel that way?"

"I . . . don't know. I *like* it . . ."

"I suppose," Lee said a little sadly, "people like things for different reasons."

"You like it a lot." He looked down and tried to understand how she liked it. And failed. Tears had darkened his pajamas. Not wanting her to cry again, he grinned when he looked up. "You know, I almost saw him this morning."

"Faust? You mean you saw Bryan Faust?"

He nodded. "Almost. I'm on the service crew out at Kennedy. We were working on his liner when . . ." He pointed to his eye.

"*His* ship? *You* were?" The wonder in her voice was perfectly childish, and enchanting.

"I'll probably see him when he leaves," Buddy boasted. "I can get in where they won't let anybody else go. Except people who work at the port."

"I'd give—" she remembered to take a breath "—anything to see him. Just anything in the world!"

"There was a hell of a crowd out there this morning. They almost broke through the police. But I could've just walked up and stood at the bottom of the ramp when he come down. If I'd thought about it."

Her hands made little fists on the edge of the bed as she gazed at him.

"Course I'll probably see him when he goes." This time he found his buttons and began to put them into the proper holes.

"I wish I could see him too!"

"I suppose Bim—he's foreman of the service crew—he'd let us through the gate, if I said you were my sister." He looked back up at her brown face. "Well, my cousin."

"Would you take me? Would you really take me?"

"Sure." Buddy reached out to tweak her nose, missed. "You did something for me. I don't see why not, if they'd let you leave—"

"Mrs. Lowery!" Lee whispered and stepped back from the bed.

"—the hospital. Huh?"

"They know I'm gone! Mrs. Lowery is calling for me. She says she's seen me, and Dr. Gross is on his way. They want to take me back to my room." She ran to the door.

"Lee, there you are! Are you all right?" In the doorway Dr. Gross grabbed her arm as she tried to twist away.

"Let me go!"

"Hey!" bellowed Buddy. "What are you doin' with that little girl!" He bounded up in the middle of the bed, shedding sheets.

Dr. Gross's eyes widened. "I'm taking her back to her room. She's a patient in the hospital. She should be in another wing."

"She wanna go?" Buddy demanded, swaying over the blankets.

"She's very disturbed!" Dr. Gross countered at Buddy, towering on the bed. "We're trying to help her, don't you understand? I don't know who you are, but we're trying to keep her alive. She has to go back!"

Lee shook her head against the doctor's hip. "Oh, Buddy . . ."

He leapt over the foot of the bed, swinging. Or at any rate, he swung once. He missed wildly because of the parallax. Also because he pulled the punch in, half completed, to make it seem a floundering gesture. He was not in the Louisiana State Penal Correction Institute: the realization had come the way one only realized the tune playing in the back of the mind when it stops. "Wait!" Buddy said.

Outside the door the doctor was saying, "Mrs. Lowery, take Lee back up to her room. The night nurse knows the medication she should have."

"Yes, Doctor."

"Wait!" Buddy called. "Please!"

"Excuse me," Dr. Gross said, stepping back through the door. Without Lee. "But we have to get her upstairs and under a sedative, immediately. Believe me, I'm sorry for this inconvenience."

Buddy sat down on the bed and twisted his face. "What's . . . the matter with her?"

Dr. Gross was silent a moment. "I suppose I do have to give you an explanation. That's difficult, because I don't know exactly. Of the three proven telepaths that have been discovered since a concerted effort has been made to study them, Lee is the most powerful. She's a brilliant, incredibly creative child.

But her mind has suffered so much trauma — from all the lives telepathy exposes her to — she's become hopelessly suicidal. We're trying to help her. But if she's left alone for any length of time, sometimes weeks, sometimes hours, she'll try to kill herself."

"Then when's she gonna be better?"

Dr. Gross put his hands in his pockets and looked at his sandals. "I'm afraid to cure someone of a mental disturbance, the first thing you have to do is isolate them from the trauma. With Lee that's impossible. We don't even know which part of the brain controls the telepathy, so we couldn't even try lobotomy. We haven't found a drug that affects it yet." He shrugged. "I wish we could help her. But when I'm being objective, I can't see her ever getting better. She'll be like this the rest of her life. The quicker you can forget about her, the less likely you are to hurt her. Good night. Again, I'm very sorry this had to happen."

"G'night." Buddy sat in his bed a little while. Finally he turned off the light and lay down. He had to masturbate three times before he finally fell asleep. In the morning, though, he still had not forgotten the little black girl who had come to him and awakened — so much in him.

The doctors were very upset about the bandage and talked of sympathetic ophthalmia. They searched his left cornea for any last bits of metal dust. They kept him in the hospital three more days, adjusting the pressure between his vitreous and aqueous humors to prevent his till now undiscovered tendency toward glaucoma. They told him that the thing that had occasionally blurred the vision in his left eye was a vitreous floater and not to worry about it. Stay home at least two weeks, they said. And wear your eye patch until two days before you go back to work. They gave him a hassle with his workmen's compensation papers too. But he got it straightened out — he'd filled in a date wrong. He never saw the little girl again.

And the radios and jukeboxes and Scopitones in New York and Buenos Aires, Paris and Istanbul, in Melbourne and Bangkok, played the music of Bryan Faust.

The day Faust was supposed to leave Earth for Venus, Buddy went back to the spaceport. It was three days before he was supposed to report to work, and he still wore the flesh-colored eyepatch.

"Jesus," he said to Bim as they leaned at the railing of the observation deck on the roof of the hangar, "just look at all them people."

Bim spat down at the hot macadam. The liner stood on the takeoff pad under the August sun.

"He's going to sing before he goes," Bim said. "I hope they don't have a riot."

"Sing?"

"See that wooden platform out there and all them loudspeakers? With all those kids, I sure hope they don't have a riot."

"Bim, can I get down onto the field, up near the platform?"

"What for?"

"So I can see him up real close."

"You were the one talking about all the people."

Buddy, holding the rail, worked his thumb on the brass. The muscles in his forearm rolled beneath the tattoo: *To Mars I Would Go for Dolores-jo*, inscribed on Saturn's rings. "But I *got* to!"

"I don't see why the hell—"

"There's this little nigger girl, Bim—"

"Huh?"

"Bim!"

"Okay. Okay. Get into a coverall and go down with the clocker crew. You'll be right up with the reporters. But don't tell anybody I sent you. You know how many people want to get up there? Why you want to get so close for anyway?"

"For a . . ." He turned in the doorway. "For a friend." He ran down the stairs to the lockers.

Bryan Faust walked across the platform to the microphones. Comets soared over his shoulders and disappeared under his arms. Suns novaed on his chest. Meteors flashed around his elbows. Shirts of polarized cloth with incandescent, shifting designs were now being called Fausts. Others flashed in the crowd. He pushed back his hair, grinned, and behind the police-block hundreds of children screamed. He laughed into the microphone; they quieted. Behind him a bank of electronic instruments glittered. The controls were in the many jeweled rings hanging bright and heavy on his fingers. He raised his hands, flicked his thumbs across the gems, and the instruments, programmed to respond, began the cascading introduction to *Corona*. Bryan Faust sang. Across Kennedy, thousands — Buddy among them — heard.

And on her cot, Lee listened. "Thank you, Buddy," she whispered. "Thank you." And felt a little less like dying.

[1967]

Study and Writing Questions

1. Why does the NARRATIVE begin by focusing on Buddy's biography? What kind of person is Buddy? Does it make any difference to his CHARACTERIZATION that the STORY is set in the future?

2. Telepathy is central to Lee's characterization and to the PLOT of this story. If this story is to be meaningful for ordinary people, however, we should be able to see Lee's telepathy as similar to something in our own lives. What might telepathy represent here?

3. What sort of RHETORIC does Lee use when discussing music with Dr. Gross and when discussing it with Buddy? How do these RHETORICS reflect the uses to which Lee puts music? What does music mean to other characters in this story?

4. What is the relationship between Buddy and Lee? In what ways are they alike? In what ways are they unlike? What does the narrative suggest about people like Buddy and Lee?

5. Why is the narrative named after a song? How is the song described? What other meaning(s) of the word *corona* might be relevant to our understanding of this story?

See also Questions for Contrast and Comparison: 12, 13, 28, 55, 148, 209, and 223.

■ FËODOR MIKHAILOVICH DOSTOEVSKY (1821–1881) was born in Moscow, second of six children of an army physician at the Mariia Hospital for the Poor. After his mother's death in 1837, he was sent to a military engineering college in St. Petersburg. He earned his commission (1841) and degree (1843) but quickly resigned from the army (1844) to write. Although esteemed from his first novel (Poor People, 1846), he suffered perpetually from depression, epilepsy, and financial self-destructiveness. Active in socialist circles, he was convicted of revolutionary activity (1848). As he stood before the firing squad, his sentence was commuted to four years at hard labor in Siberia and four further years of army service; however, his physical decline led to early release (1853). The remainder of his life he edited socialist journals and wrote FICTION grappling with the contradictory attractions of Jesus, anarchy, altruism, and evil. Dostoevsky lost three children and, in 1864, his brother and co-editor, Mikhail, and his first wife, and he suffered crushing gambling debts. Travels in Europe and marriage to his stenographer (1867) deepened his social and psychological vision and stabilized his life. His greatest works include Notes from Underground (1864), Crime and Punishment (1866), The Idiot (1868), The Devils (1872) and The Brothers Karamazov (1880). He died in St. Petersburg of a pulmonary hemorrhage during an epileptic seizure.

The Honest Thief
From the Memoirs of an Unknown

One morning as I was leaving for my office, Agrafena, my cook, washerwoman, and housekeeper, came into my room and, to my great surprise, began a conversation with me. Until that morning this simple, ordinary woman of the people had been so uncommunicative that, except for a few words about my dinner each day, she had for the last six years scarcely uttered a word to me. At least I never heard her speak of anything else.

"I'd like to have a word with you, sir," she began abruptly. "Why don't you let the little room?"

"Which little room?"

"Why, as if you didn't know, sir. The one next to the kitchen, of course!"

"What for?"

"What for, sir? Why, don't you know? Because other people let their rooms, of course!"

"But who would take it?"

"Who would take it, sir? Why, surely, sir, you know who would take it. A lodger, of course."

"But, my good woman, who'd like to live in a cubby-hole like that? Why, it's nothing but a boxroom. I doubt if you could put a bed in it, and even if you could, there wouldn't be any room left to move about in."

"Why, sir, nobody wants to live in it. All he wants is a place to sleep in. He'd live on the window-sill."

"Which window-sill?"

"Why, as if you didn't know, sir! The window-sill in the passage, of course. He could sit there and sew, or do whatever he liked. He could sit on a chair, if he liked. He's got a chair, and a table, too. He's got everything, sir."

"But who is he?"

"Oh, he's a good man, sir. He's had a lot of experience in his life, he has, sir. I'll cook for him, and I'll only charge him ten roubles a month for his board and lodging."

After the exercise of a great deal of patience, I found that an elderly man had persuaded or somehow induced Agrafena to admit him to her kitchen as a paying guest. Now, I knew very well that if Agrafena ever took it into her head to do a thing, it had better be done at once, or she would give me no peace. For whenever anything was not to her liking, Agrafena became moody and fell a prey to the blackest melancholy which lasted for a fortnight or three weeks. During that time my dinners were uneatable, my floors remained unscrubbed, and several indispensable articles were missing from my personal washing, in short, my life became one long chapter of the most unfortunate accidents. I had long ago observed that this inarticulate woman was quite incapable of making up her mind or of fixing her mind on an idea that might be said to be her own. But if her feeble brain did once in a while conceive something resembling an idea or a plan, then to prevent her from carrying it into immediate execution was tantamount to putting her for some time morally out of existence. That being so, and my peace of mind being dearer to me than anything else in the world, I at once accepted Agrafena's proposal to take in a lodger.

"Tell me, has he at least some papers? A passport or something?"

"Why yes, sir. Of course he has. He's a good man, sir, just as I was telling you. A man with experience. Promised to pay me ten roubles a month, he did."

The very next day my new lodger installed himself in my modest bachelor quarters. I can't say that I was very sorry; on the contrary, in my heart of hearts I felt rather pleased. I live, on the whole, a very secluded sort of life, the life of a regular recluse. I have no acquaintances to speak of and I scarcely ever go out. Having spent ten years of my life in complete isolation from the world, I had naturally got used to solitude. But another ten, fifteen, or even more years of the same solitude, with the same Agrafena and in the same bachelor quarters, did not strike me as a particularly inviting prospect. So that in these circumstances another man, a man, moreover, of quiet habits, was a real blessing.

Agrafena had not deceived me; my lodger was a man of great experience of the world. His passport brought to light the fact that he was an old soldier; but that I knew even before I had opened it. One look at a man is sufficient to tell you that. My lodger, Astafy Ivanovich, was the finest specimen of an old soldier that it was ever my good fortune to come across. But what I liked best about him was that now and again he would tell some really good stories, mostly incidents from his own life. In view of the habitual boredom of my sort of existence, such a story-teller was a real find to me. One of the stories he told me left a vivid impression upon my mind. It arose out of the following circumstance.

I was alone in my flat, Astafy and Agrafena having gone out on business. Suddenly I heard somebody come in, and thinking it was a stranger, I went out of my room to see who it might be. It really was a stranger, a short man, who in spite of the cold autumn day, wore no overcoat.

"What do you want?"

"Does a civil servant by the name of Alexandrov live here?"

"No, I'm afraid there's no one here of that name," I replied, and I bade him a curt goodbye.

"That's odd," the stranger said, beating a cautious retreat to the door, "the caretaker told me he lived here."

"Get out! Beat it!"

Next day after dinner, while Astafy was fitting on a coat he was altering for me, someone came into the passage. I opened the door a little, and there before my very eyes my yesterday's visitor calmly took down my short winter overcoat from the coat-rack and, putting it under his arm, dashed out of the flat. Agrafena did nothing but gape at him, struck dumb with astonishment, and did not lift a finger to protect my property. Astafy Ivanovich ran out after the thief, and he came back ten minutes later, out of breath and empty-handed. The man had just vanished into thin air!

"That's a bit of bad luck, Astafy Ivanovich," I said. "A good job I've still got my winter cloak, or the villain would have left me absolutely stranded."

But Astafy Ivanovich was so overcome by it all that, looking at him, I almost forgot the loss I had suffered. He simply couldn't get over it. Every minute he would throw down the work on which he was engaged and start recounting the whole incident, how it had all happened, how he had been standing only a few feet away from the man, how the thief had taken down the coat before his very eyes, and how it had come about that he had not been able to catch him. Then he would sit down at his work again, but only to leave it a minute later, and I saw him go down to the caretaker to tell him all about it and to remonstrate with him for allowing such things to happen in his house. Then he came back and began lecturing Agrafena. When at last he did finally sit down to his work, he went on muttering to himself a long time, how it all happened, how he stood here and I there, how before his very eyes, hardly a few feet away, the man took the coat off the rack, and so on. In short, though a good man at his trade, Astafy Ivanovich was a terrible fellow for getting himself all worked up and making no end of a fuss.

"We've been fooled, Astafy Ivanovich," I said to him in the evening, offering him a glass of tea and hoping to dispel my boredom by making him tell me again the story of the stolen coat; for from its frequent repetition and the great sincerity of the speaker, I was beginning to find the story highly amusing.

"Aye, sir, we've been fooled all right," said Astafy Ivanovich. "Mind you, it's not my business, of course, but I can't help being upset all the same. It fairly makes my blood boil, it does, sir, though it's not my coat that's been stolen. For to my thinking, sir, there's no worse villain in the world than a thief. Aye, I've known many a man who'd take your things and never dream of paying for them, but a thief, sir, steals the work of your hands, the sweat of your brow, and your time, too. A nasty piece of work, that's what he is sir. Makes my blood boil just to talk about him. But begging your pardon, sir, how is it you don't seem to care about the loss of your property?"

"Well, Astafy Ivanovich, you're quite right of course. It is a confounded nuisance. I'd much rather burn my things than let a thief have them."

"Well, sir, it's a nuisance all right. Though, mind you, there are thieves and thieves. I well remember, sir, coming across an honest thief once."

"An honest thief? Why, how can a man be honest and a thief at the same time, Astafy Ivanovich?"

"Well, sir, that's true enough. There are no honest thieves, and there never have been any. What I wanted to say, sir, was that the man I had in mind seemed honest enough, but he stole all the same. Aye, I just couldn't help being sorry for him."

"Why, how did that happen, Astafy Ivanovich?"

"Well, sir, it happened two years ago. At the time I'd been out of work for nearly a year, and just before I lost my job I struck up an acquaintance with a man I accidentally met in a pub. Down and out he was. A terrible drunkard, loafer, vagabond. Been a clerk in some government office, but got chucked out a long time ago on account of his drinking. Lord, what a disgraceful sight he was! Walked about in rags, and sometimes I wasn't sure he had a shirt under his coat. No sooner did he get something than he'd spend it on drink. Not that he was what you might call obstreperous. No, sir, he was a very quiet man, kind and gentle, and he'd never ask you for anything on account of being very shy by nature. But of course I couldn't help seeing how badly the poor fellow wanted a drink, so I'd stand him one. Well, so we became good friends. I mean to say, sir, it was he really who got himself attached to me. I didn't mind either way. And what a funny man he was, sir! Stuck to me like a dog, followed me about everywhere, and that after I'd only met him once. No character at all. A rag of a man! At first he asked me to let him stay the night. Well, I did. For you see, sir, I had a look at his passport, and there was nothing wrong with it — the man was all right! The next day he wanted to stay again, and on the following day he came and spent the whole day on my window-sill. Stayed the night, too. 'Good Lord,' I thought to myself, 'I shan't be able to get rid of him now — provide food and drink for him, and a bed as well!' Just a poor man's luck, sir. Nothing to eat myself, and here's a perfect stranger to carry about on my back! Nor was it the first time he had hung on to somebody he'd never seen before. He used to spend his days with some clerk before he ran across me in the pub. They were always out drinking together. Only the poor man seemed to have had some serious trouble, for he soon drank himself to death. Anyway, the man I'm telling you about, sir, was called Yemelyan Ilyich. I was racking my brains what to do with him. I couldn't just chuck him out. I was dreadfully sorry for the poor beggar. You can't imagine, sir, what a pitiful wreck of a man he was. Never uttered a word, never asked for anything, just sat there gazing into my eyes like a dog. That's what drink does to a man, sir! Well, so there I was wondering what to say to the man. I couldn't very well say, 'Look here, Yemelyan, you'd better go. This is no place for you. You've come to the wrong man. Soon I shall have nothing to eat myself, so how can you expect me to keep you?' I wondered, sir, what he would have done if I'd said that to him. Well, I know very well of course that if I told him that he'd sit there looking at me a long time without at first being able to take in what I was saying, and when he at last saw what I meant he'd get up from the window, pick up his little bundle (I can see that bundle now, sir, a red check bundle full of holes that he carried about with him everywhere and that he used to stuff all sorts of rubbish into), and set his tattered old coat to rights to make it look decent and keep him warm, and so that the holes didn't show — very particular he was about his appearance! Then he'd open the door and go out on the landing with tears in his eyes. Well, sir, I couldn't let a man go to the dogs like that — I was really sorry for him! But, I thought next, what was going to happen to me when I lost my job? 'Wait a bit, Yemelyan, my dear fellow,' I says to myself, 'you won't be eating and drinking and making merry at my expense very much longer now. I'll be moving soon, and then, my lad, it's ten to one you'll never find me.'

"Well, sir, one fine day I did move. My old master, Alexander Filimonovich (he's dead now, God rest his soul!), said to me at the time, 'I'm very satisfied with you, Astafy,' he said. 'We shan't forget you, and when we come back from the country we'll take you on again.' I had been his butler, oh, for many years — a grand man he was, too, but he died a few months later. Well, so after seeing them off, I collected my belongings, what little money I had, thinking to take it easy for a bit, and went to live with an old lady I knew. Took a small room in her flat. She had only that small room to spare. She used to be in service herself, a nursemaid she was, but now she lived by herself on her pension. 'Well,' I says to myself, 'it's goodbye for good, Yemelyan, old fellow. You'll never find me now!'

"Well, sir, what do you think? I came back in the evening (I had gone out to see a man I knew), and there was Yemelyan sitting quietly on my chest in his tattered old coat and with his bundle beside him, and to while away the time he had borrowed a book from my landlady (a prayer book it was), and he was holding it in his hands — upside-down! So he had found me after all! I gave up. 'It's no use,' I thought to myself. 'It can't be helped. Why didn't you get rid of him at first?' So knowing very well that he had come to stay, I just said to him, 'You haven't forgotten your passport, Yemelyan, have you?'

"Well, sir, so I sat down and began to consider what to do next. 'After all,' thought I, 'what harm can a homeless old tramp do you?' And on thinking it over, I decided that the harm he'd do me wouldn't amount to much. 'He'll have to have something to eat of course,' I thought. 'Well, I'll give him a piece of bread in the morning, and to make the meal more tasty like, buy an onion or two. At midday I'll give him another bit of bread and onion, and for supper some more onion with *kvas*, and bread, too, if he asks for it. And should some cabbage soup come our way, we'll have a real feast, the two of us.' I'm no great eater myself, and it's a well-known fact, sir, that a drinking man never eats: all he wants is vodka and a drop of brandy. 'He'll ruin me with his drinking,' thought I, and as I was thinking of that something else occurred to me, something I couldn't get out of my head. For I suddenly realised, sir, that if Yemelyan was to go, there'd be nothing left for me to live for. So I made up my mind there and then to be his only provider and benefactor. 'I must get him to give up drinking,' I thought, 'I must save him from utter ruin.' 'All right, Yemelyan, old fellow,' I says to myself, 'you can stay if you like, but, mind, behave yourself — orders is orders!'

"The first thing I decided to do, sir, was to teach Yemelyan some trade, find a job of work for him to do. Naturally, it couldn't be done all at once. 'Let him enjoy himself a little first,' I says to myself, 'and in the meantime I'll think of something, find out what special abilities you possess, Yemelyan, what kind of work you're good at.' For every job, sir, first of all requires that the man engaged in it should have the right kind of ability. Well, sir, so I starts observing him on the quiet, and it didn't take me long to find out that poor old Yemelyan was a desperate case. Aye, there was nothing at all he was good for. So I first of all gives him a piece of good advice. 'Why, Yemelyan,' I says to him, 'take a look at yourself, and do,' I says, 'try to make yourself a bit more respectable like. Look at the rags you go about in. Look at that disgraceful old coat of yours! Why, God forgive me, all it's good for is to make a sieve out of. Fie, for shame, Yemelyan,' I says. 'It's about time you turned over a new leaf and became a changed man!'

"Well, sir, poor old Yemelyan just sits listening to me with his head hanging down. There was nothing you could do with him. Why, drink had robbed him even of speech. Couldn't say a sensible word, he couldn't. Talk to him about cucumbers and he talks back to you about kidney-beans! He listened to me a long time, then he just heaved a sigh.

" 'What are you sighing for, Yemelyan?'

" 'Oh, nothing,' he says, 'don't take any notice of me, Astafy. Do you know,' he says, ' do you know, Astafy, I saw two women fighting in the street today. One upset the other's basket of cranberries on purpose.'

" 'Well, what about it?'

" 'Well, you see, Astafy, so the second woman upsets the first woman's cranberries on purpose and starts stamping on them!'

" 'Well, so what about it, Yemelyan?'

" 'Oh, nothing, Astafy. I just thought I'd tell you, that's all.'

" 'That's all! Oh, Yemelyan, Yemelyan,' thought I, 'drink has been your undoing, and no mistake!'

" 'And you know, Astafy, a gentleman dropped a note on the pavement in Gorokhovaya Street—no, not in Gorokhovaya Street, in Sadovaya Street it was—and a peasant saw it and said, My lucky day! But another peasant also saw it and said, No, sir, it's my lucky day! I saw it first! . . .'

" 'Well, Yemelyan?'

" 'Well, so the two peasants had a fight, and a policeman came up, picked up the note, gave it back to the gentleman, and threatened to take the two peasants to the police station!'

" 'Well, so what about it, Yemelyan? I mean what is there specially instructive about it?'

" 'Why, I didn't mean anything, Astafy. Only the people in the street did laugh a lot.'

" 'Oh, Yemelyan, Yemelyan, what does it matter what the people in the street do? Think of yourself, Yemelyan, think of your immortal soul which you've sold for a few coppers. You know what, Yemelyan?'

" 'What, Astafy?'

" 'Why don't you get yourself some work? You really ought to, you know. For the hundredth time I'm telling you, Yemelyan—have pity on yourself!'

" 'But what work do you want me to get, Astafy? I really don't know what work I can do, and besides, I don't think anyone will give me any work.'

" 'Of course they won't give you any work, you drunkard! Why else do you think they chucked you out of the civil service?'

" 'You know, Astafy, Vlas, the potboy, was summoned to the office today.'

" 'And why did they summon him to the office?

" 'I really don't know, Astafy. I suppose they must have wanted him, so they sent for him.'

" 'Ah well,' thought I, 'there's no hope, it seems, for either of us. Yemelyan, old fellow. The good Lord must be punishing us for our sins!' And what indeed can you do with a man like that, I ask you, sir!

"But he was devilishly cunning, Yemelyan was. He'd listen quietly to me a long time, but sooner or later he'd get bored, and the minute he noticed that I was beginning to lose my temper, he'd pick up his old coat and sheer off. He'd loaf about all day and come back dead drunk in the evening. I don't know who paid for his drinks or where he got the money to pay for them himself. I had nothing to do with it!

"'Now look here, Yemelyan,' I says to him at last, 'if you go on like this very much longer, you're sure to come to a bad end. Stop drinking, do you hear? Give it up! Next time you come home drunk,' I says, 'you'll jolly well have to spend the night on the stairs. I'm damned if I'll let you in!'

"Well, sir, he saw of course that I really meant it this time, so for the next two days he didn't go out, but on the third day he cleared off again. I sat up waiting for him, but he didn't come back. To tell you the truth, sir, I was beginning to feel a bit uneasy, and, besides, I couldn't help feeling sorry for him. 'What have I done to him?' I thought. 'I've gone and scared him away good and proper now! Where could he have got to, the poor wretch? Pray God, nothing happens to him!' Well, night came and he wasn't back. In the morning I went out on the landing and there he was, sir! Spent the night on the landing, he had. Puts his head on the top step and falls asleep like that. Chilled to the marrow he was.

"'What made you do it, Yemelyan? What a place to spend the night in!'

"'Well, you were so angry with me the other night, Astafy. You were so terribly vexed and—er—promised to make me spend the night on the landing, so I—well—I didn't dare to come in, Astafy, and went to sleep here.'

"I felt mad at him and sorry for him, too, at the same time.

"'Why, surely, Yemelyan,' I says, 'you might have got yourself a different kind of job. What's the use of guarding a flight of stairs?'

"'But what different kind of job do you mean, Astafy?'

"'Why, you good-for-nothing loafer,' I says (fair mad I was at him, sir!), 'you could at least have tried to learn the tailor's trade! Look at that coat of yours! You're not satisfied, it seems, to have it all in holes, you have to sweep the stairs with it, too! Why don't you take a needle and thread and patch it up? You would have done it long ago, if you had had any sense of decency left. Oh,' I says, 'you drunkard!'

"Well, would you believe it, sir? He did take a needle and thread! I had meant it as a joke, but he got properly scared, so he took off his coat and sat down to patch it up. I looked at him: his eyes were red and bleary, and his hands shook something terrible! He shoved and shoved, but the thread just wouldn't go through the eye of the needle. How he tried, sir! Screwed up his eyes, wetted the thread, twisted it in his fingers, but it was no use. So he gave it up and looked at me.

"'Well, Yemelyan,' I says, 'you've certainly made me proud of you! If there'd been anybody about,' I says, 'I'd have sunk through the floor for shame. Why, you poor fool, don't you realise that I was joking, that I just meant it as a reproach? Now, leave it alone,' I says, 'and don't attempt to do anything you can't, and for goodness sake don't sleep on the stairs! Don't disgrace me by doing such a disreputable thing ever again!'

" 'But what am I to do, Astafy? I know very well that I'm always drunk and that I'm not good for anything. It seems to me all I am good for is to cause you, my be-ne-factor, unnecessary trouble . . .'

"And, sir, as he said it his blue lips started quivering all of a sudden, and a tear rolled down his pale cheek and trembled on his stubby chin, and in another minute the poor fellow burst into a regular flood of tears.

" 'Well, Yemelyan,' I says to myself, 'I never thought you had it in you. Who could have guessed you had such tender feelings?' No, I says to myself, 'no, it's no use deceiving myself. I ought to give up having anything to do with you. Go to the devil for all I care!'

"Well, sir, why make a long story of it? And, besides, it was such a sorry, miserable business that it is hardly worth wasting words on. I mean, sir, you wouldn't, so to speak, give a brass farthing for the whole thing, though I would gladly have given a fortune, if I had had a fortune to give, that it should never have happened to me. You see, sir, I had a pair of riding breeches (the devil take 'em!), lovely breeches they were, too, blue ones with a check pattern. They were ordered by a country gentleman who was on a visit to town, but he wouldn't take 'em, after all: they were too narrow for him, he said. Well, so they were left on my hands. 'It's a valuable article,' I thought. 'I might get fifteen roubles or more for them in the second-hand market, and even if I didn't, I might manage to get two pairs of trousers for our Petersburg gentleman out of them, and have a piece over for a waistcoat for myself.' To poor folk like us, sir, every little counts. Well, as it happened Yemelyan was having a very poor time just then. I had noticed that he had not had a drop of liquor for some days. He lost heart and looked down in the mouth. Aye, very miserable he looked, and that's the truth. I couldn't help feeling sorry to see him in such a sad state. 'Well,' I says to myself, 'either you've got no money, my lad, or you've turned over a new leaf in good earnest, listened to reason at last, and given up drink for good.' That's how things stood just then, sir. As it happened, we had a church holiday at the time, and I went to evening service. When I came back, I found Yemelyan sitting on the window-sill blind drunk, rocking to and fro. Aha, thought I, so you've gone and done it again, my lad! And I went to fetch something from my chest. I opened it and the first thing I noticed was that my breeches were no longer there. Looked for them everywhere I could think of, but couldn't find them. Well, after I'd turned the place upside down and all to no purpose, something seemed to stab me to the heart. I rushed off to my landlady and at first accused her of the theft, Aye, acted like a real madman, I did. Hardly knew what I was doing. You see, sir, it hadn't entered my head that Yemelyan was the real culprit, though the evidence was staring me in the face, as you might say, for the man was blind drunk! 'No, sir,' says my landlady, 'I never seen your breeches, and, anyway, what would I want with your breeches? I couldn't wear them, could I? Why,' she says, 'I missed a skirt of mine myself the other day, and I shouldn't wonder,' she says, 'if it wasn't one of those nice friends of yours who took it. As for your breeches,' she says, 'I know nothing about 'em.' 'But who was here while I was out,' I asked. 'Did anyone call?' 'No, sir,' she says, 'no one called. I've been here all the time and I ought to know. Yemelyan went out and came back. There he is. Why don't you ask him?' So I asked Yemelyan. 'Tell me, Yemelyan,' I says, 'you haven't by any chance taken them breeches of mine, have you? The new riding breeches,' I says, 'I made specially for the country gentleman. You remember them, don't you?'

"'No, Astafy,' he says, 'I'm sure I — er — never took 'em.'

"Well, of all things! I started searching for them again, looked everywhere, but it was no use. And Yemelyan, sir, was sitting there all the time, rocking to and fro. I squats down over the chest on my heels in front of him, and all of a sudden I looks at him out of the corner of my eye. 'Ah well,' thought I, and fairly mad at him I was, I can tell you. Got red in the face even. Then, quite unexpectedly, Yemelyan, too, looks at me.

"'No, Astafy,' he says, 'I never took your breeches. You're — er — perhaps thinking I did, but I never touched them!'

"'But where could they have got to, Yemelyan?'

"'Haven't the faintest idea, Astafy,' he says. 'I've never seen them.'

"'Well, in that case, Yemelyan,' I says, 'it seems they must have walked off by themselves, don't it?'

"'Maybe they have, Astafy,' he says. 'Maybe they have.'

"Well, sir, having heard what Yemelyan had to say for himself, I got up without another word, went over to the window, lighted my lamp, and set down to work. Altering a waistcoat for a civil servant on the floor below, I was just then. I was boiling with rage. I mean, sir, I'd have felt much happier if I'd taken all my clothes and lighted the stove with them. Well, Yemelyan must have guessed how bitter I felt. For a man given to wickedness, sir, scents trouble far off, like a bird before a storm.

"'You know, Astafy,' began Yemelyan, and his weak voice shook as he spoke, 'the male nurse Antip Prokhorovich got married this morning to the wife of the coachman who died the other day . . . .'

"Well, sir, I just gave him a look, and I suppose it must have been a very nasty look, too, for Yemelyan saw what I meant all right. So he gets up at once, goes over to the bed and starts searching for something on the floor there. I waited. He goes on rummaging a long time, muttering to himself, 'No, not here — not here. Where can the blessed thing have got to?' I waited to see what would happen. Then, believe it or not, sir, he crawled under the bed on all fours! Well, when I saw him do that, I couldn't hold out any longer.

"'What are you crawling about under the bed for, Yemelyan?' I says.

"'Why, Astafy,' he says, 'I'm looking for your breeches, of course. Maybe they've dropped down there somewhere.'

"'But why, sir,' I says (called him 'sir' out of sheer spite, I did), 'why, sir, should you go to so much trouble for a poor ignorant man like me? Why crawl on your knees for nothing?'

"'Why, Astafy,' he says, 'I don't mind. Who knows they might turn up if we go on looking for them long enough.'

"'Indeed?' I says. 'Look here, Yemelyan. . . .'

"'Yes, Astafy?'

"'Are you sure,' I says, 'you haven't simply stolen them, like a common thief, in return for everything I done for you?'

"You see, sir, it made me mad to see him crawling on his knees before me — the last straw, that was!

"'No, I haven't . . . Astafy.'

"But he didn't come out from under the bed. No, sir. Lay there a long time on his face, and when at last he did crawl out, he was as white as a sheet. He stood up, sat down beside me on the window-sill, and stayed sitting there for ten minutes, I reckon.

"'No, Astafy,' he says all of a sudden, standing up and advancing towards me, looking (I can see him still) ghastly, 'no, Astafy,' he says, 'I've never — er — touched your breeches.'

"He was shaking all over, pointing a quivering finger at his breast, and his voice shaking so dreadfully it gave me an awful turn and I just sat there as though I was stuck to the window.

"'Well, Yemelyan,' I says, 'I'm sorry if, fool that I am, I've accused you unjustly. As for the breeches,' I says, 'I don't care if they are lost. We can get along without them. We've still got our hands, thank God, and there's no need for us to go thieving or . . . begging from some poor devil, either. We can always earn our bread.'

"Yemelyan listened to me in silence, and after a while he sat down on the windowsill again. He stayed there all the evening, never stirring from his place. He was still there when I went to bed, and when I got up the next morning I found him curled up in his old coat on the bare floor. He was too humiliated, you see, to come to bed. Well, sir, since that day I conceived a violent dislike for him, and to tell you the truth, sir, during the first few days I simply hated the sight of him. It was as though my own son, so to speak, had robbed me or done me some mortal injury.

"Well, sir, for the next fortnight Yemelyan was out on the spree, drinking hard all the time. Went off the rails good and proper, that is. He'd go out in the morning and come back late at night, and for the whole of that fortnight I never heard him utter a single word. I suppose he must have felt pretty low at the time, or maybe he even wanted to do himself in, one way or another. However, at last it was all over. There was no more drinking. I reckon he must have run through his money by then. At all events, there he was sitting in the window again. Sat there, if my memory serves me right, for three whole days, without uttering a word. Then all of a sudden I saw that he was crying. You see, sir, one minute he sat there as if nothing was wrong, and the next minute he was crying. And, Lord, how that man did cry! Tears streamed in a flood out of his eyes, while he seemed to be unaware of them, just like water pouring out of a well. Well, sir, it's a terrible thing to see a man, and, particularly, an old man like Yemelyan, crying from sorrow and despair.

"'What's the matter, Yemelyan?' I says.

"He started shaking all over. Was very startled, you see, for it was the first time that evening I had spoken to him.

"'Nothing, Astafy . . . .'

"'Now, look here, Yemelyan, what does it matter? Let the whole thing go hang, so far as I'm concerned. What are you sitting like a broody hen for?'

"Felt very sorry for him, I did, sir.

"'Oh, it's nothing, Astafy. It isn't because of that at all I've been thinking — er — I'd like to get some work, Astafy.'

"'What sort of work, Yemelyan?'

"'Oh, any sort of work. Maybe I could find a job, same as I had before. I've already been to ask Fedossey Ivanovich. . . . I don't want to be a burden to you, Astafy. Maybe when I find a job I'll pay it all back and reward you for all your trouble.'

"'Don't talk such nonsense, Yemelyan. Suppose you did something you didn't ought to—what does it matter? To hell with it! Let's go on as we used to!'

"'No, Astafy. I can see you're still—er—harping on it, but I told you I never took your breeches.'

"'Well, have it your own way. I don't mind, I'm sure.'

"'No, Astafy, I can see I can't go on living with you. I'm sorry, Astafy, but I shall have to go.'

"'But, bless my soul,' I says, 'who's been offending you, Yemelyan? Who's driving you out of the house? You don't mean to say I'm doing it, do you?'

"'No, Astafy, I can't possibly stay with you now. I'd better be going.'

"You see, sir, the man was too cut up, kept harping on the same thing. And sure enough, he gets up and starts pulling his old coat over his shoulders.

"'But where are you off to, Yemelyan? Be sensible, man. What are you doing? Where will you go?'

"'Goodbye, Astafy. Don't try to stop me (here he began whimpering again). I think it's time I got out of your way. You're no longer the same.'

"'How do you mean I'm no longer the same? Of course I am the same! Mark my words, Yemelyan, you'll perish like a helpless child by yourself.'

"'No, Astafy, you're not the same,' he says. 'Every time you go out now you lock up your chest, and I can't help crying when I see you do that. No, you'd better not try to stop me, Astafy, and forgive me if I done anything to offend you while living with you.'

"Well, sir, he did go. Left me that very day, he did. I waited the whole day for him, expecting him to be back in the evening, but no, he didn't come. There was no sign of him next day, either, nor the day after. I got really worried, so worried that I could neither eat, drink nor sleep. The fellow had quite disarmed me! On the fourth day I went out to look for him. Went round all the pubs asking for him, but he wasn't to be found anywhere: gone, vanished! 'Not dead, are you, Yemelyan?' I thought to myself. 'Yielded up the ghost under some fence in a drunken stupor maybe and now you're lying there like a piece of rotten wood.' I just dragged myself home, feeling more dead than alive. Made up my mind to go out looking for him again the next day. And all the time I was cursing myself for having let such a helpless fool of a man go off by himself. Very early on the morning of the fifth day (it was a holiday) I heard the door creak. I looked up and saw Yemelyan coming in. His face was gone a bluish colour and his hair was caked in mud, as though he'd been sleeping in the street. Thin as a lath he was. He took off his tattered old coat, sat down beside me on the chest, and looked at me. I was glad to see him, I can tell you, sir, but at the same time I was more cut up than ever. For you see, sir, it's like this: if I had ever done something wrong, I'd have died like a dog sooner than come back. Aye, it's the gospel truth I'm telling you. But Yemelyan came back. And, naturally, it fairly broke my heart to see a man in such a terrible plight. I made much of him, talked kindly to him, comforted him.

"'Well, Yemelyan, my dear old fellow,' I says to him, 'I'm certainly glad to see you back. Had you been a few minutes later, I'd have gone round the pubs again looking for you. Have you had anything to eat at all?'

"'Yes, thank you, Astafy,' he says, 'I have.'

"'Come now, are you sure? Here, my dear fellow, here's some cabbage soup left over from yesterday. It's good stuff, had some beef in it. And here's some bread and an onion. Come on, eat it,' I says. 'It'll do you good.'

"I gave it to him, and saw at once that the poor chap had not tasted food for maybe three days—he was so ravenous! Aye, it was hunger that had driven him to me. Well, I felt real sorry for the poor wretch. My heart overflowed with pity as I looked at him. 'I think,' I says to myself, 'I'd better run out to the pub and get him a drink to cheer him up a little, and let's put an end to all that sorry business. There's not a drop of bitterness left in my heart against you, Yemelyan, old fellow!' So I ran out to the pub and brought back some vodka. 'Here, Yemelyan,' I says, 'come on, let's have a drink, seeing it's a holiday today! Like a drink? It's good for your health.'

"He held out his hand, held it out greedy-like, but stopped before taking the glass. A minute later I saw him take it, lift it to his mouth, and spill some of the drink on his sleeve. He got it as far as his lips, but put it down at once on the table.

"'Why, what's the matter, Yemelyan?'

"'No, thank you, Astafy, I—er—I don't think I——'

"'Don't you want a drink?'

"'No, thank you, Astafy, I—er—I—well—I'm not going to—er—drink any more, Astafy.'

"'But why not, Yemelyan? Have you given up drink altogether, or is it only today you don't feel like having one?'

"He made no answer. A moment later I noticed that he dropped his head wearily on his hand.

"'What's the matter, Yemelyan? Are you ill?'

"'Yes, Astafy. Afraid so.'

"I put him to bed at once. I could see he was in a bad way: his head was burning and he was shivering in a fever. I sat by him all day, and towards night his illness took a turn for the worse. I mixed some vegetable oil and *kvas*, put in some chopped-up spring onions and breadcrumbs, and gave it to him. 'Come,' I says, 'have some of this, Yemelyan. It'll make you feel better.' But he shook his head. 'No, thank you, Astafy,' he says. 'If you don't mind I'd much rather not have any dinner today.' I made some tea, tired my landlady out preparing all sorts of things for him, but he wouldn't have anything. 'Well,' I says to myself, 'it certainly looks bad!' The third morning I went to fetch a doctor. There was one living quite near, Kostopravov his name was. I'd known him when I was in service with the Bossomyagins. Had him in myself when I was ill. The doctor came and had a look at Yemelyan. 'He's in a bad way, isn't he?' he says. 'You could have spared yourself the trouble of calling me in. Still,' he says, 'I suppose I'd better give him some powders.' Well, sir, I never gave Yemelyan the powders, for I could see that the doctor himself hadn't any faith in them. In the meantime the fifth day came.

"Well, sir, there he lay dying before my eyes. I sat in the window with my work in my hands. My landlady was heating the stove. None of us spoke. My heart bled on account of that worthless drunkard, sir. I felt like I was losing my own son. I knew Yemelyan was looking at me all the time. I noticed that the poor fellow had been trying hard since morning to tell me something, but it seemed as if he couldn't screw up his courage to do it. At last I looked up at him. Oh, the agony in the poor fellow's eyes, sir! He'd never taken them off me for a moment; but when he saw me looking at him he dropped them quickly.

"'I say, Astafy. . . .'

"'What is it, Yemelyan?'

"'If you took my old coat to the second-hand market, Astafy, do you think they'd give you a lot for it?'

"'Well,' I says, 'I hardly think they'd offer me a great deal for it, Yemelyan. Three roubles, perhaps.'

"But as a matter of fact, sir, if I had taken it, they wouldn't have given me as much as a penny for it. Most likely they would have laughed in my face for trying to sell them a useless old rag like that. I said it just to comfort the old fellow, seeing what a simpleton he was.

"'And I was thinking, Astafy, that they might give you ten roubles for it. It's made of fine cloth, Astafy. They'd give you more than three roubles for a coat made of fine cloth, wouldn't they?'

"'Well, I don't really know, Yemelyan,' I says, 'but if you want me to take it, then of course I'll ask ten roubles for it to begin with.'

"Yemelyan was silent for a minute or two; then he called me again.

"'Astafy!'

"'What is it, Yemelyan?'

"'Sell my coat when I die. Don't bury me in it. I'll be all right without it. It's a valuable article, Astafy. It might come in very handy for you.'

"Well, sir, I can't tell you how dreadful I felt when he said that! I could see that the end was near. We were silent again. So a whole hour passed. Then I looked at him. He was still staring at me, but when he met my eyes he looked down again.

"'Want a drink of water, Yemelyan?'

"'Yes, thank you, Astafy.'

"I gave him some water and he drank it.

"'Thank you, Astafy,' he says again.

"'Is there anything else you'd like, Yemelyan?'

"'No, thank you, Astafy, I don't want anything. Only—'

"'Only what, Yemelyan?'

"'I—er—'

"'What is it, Yemelyan?'

"'The riding breeches, Astafy. It was me who—er—took them.'

"'Well,' I says, 'I'm sure the Lord will forgive you, you poor fellow. You can die in peace.'

"And feeling a lump coming up to my throat and tears gushing out of my eyes, I turned away for a moment.

"'Astafy—'

"I turned round and saw that Yemelyan was trying to say something to me. He was trying desperately to sit up, and his lips were moving soundlessly. All of a sudden he reddened, and looked at me. Then I saw him go pale again, paler and paler, and suddenly he seemed to shrivel up. His head fell back, he drew one last breath, and gave up his soul to his Maker."

[1848]

Study and Writing Questions

1. Describe the CHARACTER of the nameless NARRATOR who speaks in the first paragraph. What sort of person is he? What sorts of relationships does he have? Where does he fit in the social hierarchy? Why does he keep, in the words of the subtitle, "memoirs"?

2. Describe Astafy Ivanovich. What kind of person does he seem to be? In what ways, if any, is Astafy a DOPPELGÄNGER for Yemelyan? In what ways, if any, is Astafy a Doppelgänger for the nameless narrator? Do you find Astafy's narration of the story of Yemelyan reliable?

3. What does the title mean? Does it suggest the necessity of redefining the notions of honesty and theft or is it perhaps IRONIC? Why is it important that the memoirs mentioned in the subtitle are of "an Unknown"?

4. Describe the society of this NARRATIVE world. What class distinctions are apparent? How are the relations among the classes maintained? To what extent is the responsibility for theft social and to what extent is it individual?

5. In what way(s) does the STRUCTURE bear on the meaning of this narrative? Why does this narrative begin with the nameless narrator's encounter with his cook? Why do we need the incomplete story of the theft of the nameless narrator's coat? Why does Astafy tell the story of Yemelyan? As Astafy asks Yemelyan, "'What is there specially instructive about it?'" What is the effect of the narrative failing to return to the FRAME STORY?

See also Questions for Contrast and Comparison: 25, 47, 54, 224, 225 and 226.

■ ARTHUR CONAN DOYLE *(1859–1930), born in Edinburgh, Scotland, and educated there and on the Continent, came from a family of illustrators, his father being the least successful. To support his education (University of Edinburgh, B.M., 1881; M.D., 1885), Arthur assisted physicians and served as ship's surgeon on Arctic and West African expeditions. During lulls in his practice (1882–1890), which earned only £300 per year, he began his prolific writing of historical romances (Micah Clarke, 1889),* SCIENCE FICTIONS *(The Lost World, 1912), prefaces, plays, poetry, and pamphlets (one, defending England's role in the Boer War, earned him knighthood), and, of course, the memorable stories of Sherlock Holmes, named for American physician/poet Oliver Wendell Holmes and modeled in his deductive powers on British physiologist Joseph Bell. Doyle believed Holmes, hero of fifty-six* STORIES *and four* NOVELS, *deflected public attention from his "more important" work, including, late in life, promoting communication with the dead (History of Spiritualism, 1926), yet Doyle often acted Holmes himself, once even winning the release of a wrongly convicted murderer. By the 1920s, Holmes had helped make Doyle the world's most highly paid author, sometimes earning half a pound (about $16.00 in 1990) per word. He had two children with his first wife, who died, and three with his second, who survived him. He died of a heart attack at home in Sussex.*

The Adventure of the Speckled Band

On glancing over my notes of the seventy odd cases in which I have during the last eight years studied the methods of my friend Sherlock Holmes, I find many tragic, some comic, a large number merely strange, but none commonplace; for, working as he did rather for the love of his art than for the acquirement of wealth, he refused to associate himself with any investigation which did not tend towards the unusual, and even the fantastic. Of all these varied cases, however, I cannot recall any which presented more singular features than that which was associated with the well-known Surrey family of the Roylotts of Stoke Moran. The events in question occurred in the early days of my association with Holmes, when we were sharing rooms as bachelors in Baker Street. It is possible that I might have placed them upon record before, but a promise of secrecy was made at the time, from which I have only been freed during the last month by the untimely death of the lady to whom the pledge was given. It is perhaps as well that the facts should now come to light, for I have reasons to know that there are widespread rumours as to the death of Dr. Grimesby Roylott which tend to make the matter even more terrible than the truth.

It was early in April in the year '83 that I woke one morning to find Sherlock Holmes standing, fully dressed, by the side of my bed. He was a late riser, as a rule, and as the clock on the mantelpiece showed me that it was only a quarter-past seven, I blinked up at him in some surprise, and perhaps just a little resentment, for I was myself regular in my habits.

"Very sorry to knock you up, Watson," said he, "but it's the common lot this morning. Mrs. Hudson has been knocked up, she retorted upon me, and I on you."

"What is it, then—a fire?"

"No; a client. It seems that a young lady has arrived in a considerable state of excitement, who insists upon seeing me. She is waiting now in the sitting-room. Now, when young ladies wander about the metropolis at this hour of the morning, and knock sleepy people up out of their beds, I presume that it is something very pressing which they have to communicate. Should it prove to be an interesting case, you would, I am sure, wish to follow it from the outset. I thought, at any rate, that I should call you and give you the chance."

"My dear fellow, I would not miss it for anything."

I had no keener pleasure than in following Holmes in his professional investigations, and in admiring the rapid deductions, as swift as intuitions, and yet always founded on a logical basis, with which he unravelled the problems which were submitted to him. I rapidly threw on my clothes and was ready in a few minutes to accompany my friend down to the sitting-room. A lady dressed in black and heavily veiled, who had been sitting in the window, rose as we entered.

"Good-morning, madam," said Holmes cheerily. "My name is Sherlock Holmes. This is my intimate friend and associate, Dr. Watson, before whom you can speak as freely as before myself. Ha! I am glad to see that Mrs. Hudson has had the good sense to light the fire. Pray draw up to it, and I shall order you a cup of hot coffee, for I observe that you are shivering."

"It is not cold which makes me shiver," said the woman in a low voice, changing her seat as requested.

"What, then?"

"It is fear, Mr. Holmes. It is terror." She raised her veil as she spoke, and we could see that she was indeed in a pitiable state of agitation, her face all drawn and gray, with restless, frightened eyes, like those of some hunted animal. Her features and figure were those of a woman of thirty, but her hair was shot with premature gray, and her expression was weary and haggard. Sherlock Holmes ran her over with one of his quick, all-comprehensive glances.

"You must not fear," said he soothingly, bending forward and patting her forearm. "We shall soon set matters right, I have no doubt. You have come in by train this morning, I see."

"You know me, then?"

"No, but I observe the second half of a return ticket in the palm of your left glove. You must have started early, and yet you had a good drive in a dog-cart, along heavy roads, before you reached the station."

The lady gave a violent start and stared in bewilderment at my companion.

"There is no mystery, my dear madam," said he, smiling. "The left arm of your jacket is spattered with mud in no less than seven places. The marks are perfectly fresh. There is no vehicle save a dog-cart which throws up mud in that way, and then only when you sit on the left-hand side of the driver."

"Whatever your reasons may be, you are perfectly correct," said she. "I started from home before six, reached Leatherhead at twenty past, and came in by the first train to Waterloo. Sir, I can stand this strain no longer; I shall go mad if it continues. I have no one to turn to — none, save only one, who cares for me, and he, poor fellow, can be of little aid. I have heard of you, Mr. Holmes; I have heard of you from Mrs. Farintosh, whom you helped in the hour of her sore need. It was from her that I had your address. Oh, sir, do you not think that you could help me, too, and at least throw a little light through the dense darkness which surrounds me? At present it is out of my power to reward you for your services, but in a month or six weeks I shall be married, with the control of my own income, and then at least you shall not find me ungrateful."

Holmes turned to his desk and, unlocking it, drew out a small case-book, which he consulted.

"Farintosh," said he. "Ah yes, I recall the case; it was concerned with an opal tiara. I think it was before your time, Watson. I can only say, madam, that I shall be happy to devote the same care to your case as I did to that of your friend. As to reward, my profession is its own reward; but you are at liberty to defray whatever expenses I may be put to, at the time which suits you best. And now I beg that you will lay before us everything that may help us in forming an opinion upon the matter."

"Alas!" replied our visitor, "the very horror of my situation lies in the fact that my fears are so vague, and my suspicions depend so entirely upon small points, which might seem trivial to another, that even he to whom of all others I have a right to look for help and advice looks upon all that I tell him about it as the fancies of a nervous woman. He does not say so, but I can read it from his soothing answers and averted eyes. But I have heard, Mr. Holmes, that you can see deeply into the manifold wickedness of the human heart. You may advise me how to walk amid the dangers which encompass me."

"I am all attention, madam."

"My name is Helen Stoner, and I am living with my stepfather, who is the last survivor of one of the oldest Saxon families in England, the Roylotts of Stoke Moran, on the western border of Surrey."

Holmes nodded his head. "The name is familiar to me," said he.

"The family was at one time among the richest in England, and the estates extended over the borders into Berkshire in the north, and Hampshire in the west. In the last century, however, four successive heirs were of a dissolute and wasteful disposition, and the family ruin was eventually completed by a gambler in the days of the Regency. Nothing was left save a few acres of ground, and the two-hundred-year-old house, which is itself crushed under a heavy mortgage. The last squire dragged out his existence there, living the horrible life of an aristocratic pauper; but his only son, my stepfather, seeing that he must adapt himself to the new conditions, obtained an advance from a relative, which enabled him to take a medical degree and went out to Calcutta, where, by his professional skill and his force of character, he established a large practice. In a fit of anger, however, caused by some robberies which had been perpetrated in the house, he beat his native butler to death and narrowly escaped a capital sentence. As it was, he suffered a long term of imprisonment and afterwards returned to England a morose and disappointed man.

"When Dr. Roylott was in India he married my mother, Mrs. Stoner, the young widow of Major-General Stoner, of the Bengal Artillery. My sister Julia and I were twins, and we were only two years old at the time of my mother's re-marriage. She had a considerable sum of money—not less than £1000 a year—and this she bequeathed to Dr. Roylott entirely while we resided with him, with a provision that a certain annual sum should be allowed to each of us in the event of our marriage. Shortly after our return to England my mother died—she was killed eight years ago in a railway accident near Crewe. Dr.

Roylott then abandoned his attempts to establish himself in practice in London and took us to live with him in the old ancestral house at Stoke Moran. The money which my mother had left was enough for all our wants, and there seemed to be no obstacle to our happiness.

"But a terrible change came over our stepfather about this time. Instead of making friends and exchanging visits with our neighbours, who had at first been overjoyed to see a Roylott of Stoke Moran back in the old family seat, he shut himself up in his house and seldom came out save to indulge in ferocious quarrels with whoever might cross his path. Violence of temper approaching to mania has been hereditary in the men of the family, and in my stepfather's case it had, I believe, been intensified by his long residence in the tropics. A series of disgraceful brawls took place, two of which ended in the police-court, until at last he became the terror of the village, and the folks would fly at his approach, for he is a man of immense strength, and absolutely uncontrollable in his anger.

"Last week he hurled the local blacksmith over a parapet into a stream, and it was only by paying over all the money which I could gather together that I was able to avert another public exposure. He had no friends at all save the wandering gypsies, and he would give these vagabonds leave to encamp upon the few acres of bramble-covered land which represent the family estate, and would accept in return the hospitality of their tents, wandering away with them sometimes for weeks on end. He has a passion also for Indian animals, which are sent over to him by a correspondent, and he has at this moment a cheetah and a baboon, which wander freely over his grounds and are feared by the villagers almost as much as their master.

"You can imagine from what I say that my poor sister Julia and I had no great pleasure in our lives. No servant would stay with us, and for a long time we did all the work of the house. She was but thirty at the time of her death, and yet her hair had already begun to whiten, even as mine has."

"Your sister is dead, then?"

"She died just two years ago, and it is of her death that I wish to speak to you. You can understand that, living the life which I have described, we were little likely to see anyone of our own age and position. We had, however, an aunt, my mother's maiden sister, Miss Honoria Westphail, who lives near Harrow, and we were occasionally allowed to pay short visits at this lady's house. Julia went there at Christmas two years ago, and met there a half-pay major of marines, to whom she became engaged. My stepfather learned of the engagement when my sister returned and offered no objection to the marriage; but within a fortnight of the day which had been fixed for the wedding, the terrible event occurred which has deprived me of my only companion."

Sherlock Holmes had been leaning back in his chair with his eyes closed and his head sunk in a cushion, but he half opened his lids now and glanced across at his visitor.

"Pray be precise as to details," said he.

"It is easy for me to be so, for every event of that dreadful time is seared into my memory. The manor-house is, as I have already said, very old, and only one wing is now inhabited. The bedrooms in this wing are on the ground floor, the sitting-rooms being in the central block of the buildings. Of these bedrooms the first is Dr. Roylott's, the second my sister's, and the third my own. There is no communication between them, but they all open out into the same corridor. Do I make myself plain?"

"Perfectly so."

"The windows of the three rooms open out upon the lawn. That fatal night Dr. Roylott had gone to his room early, though we knew that he had not retired to rest, for my sister was troubled by the smell of the strong Indian cigars which it was his custom to smoke. She left her room, therefore, and came into mine, where she sat for some time, chatting about her approaching wedding. At eleven o'clock she rose to leave me, but she paused at the door and looked back.

"'Tell me, Helen,' said she, 'have you ever heard anyone whistle in the dead of the night?'

"'Never,' said I.

"'I suppose that you could not possibly whistle, yourself, in your sleep?'

"'Certainly not. But why?'

"'Because during the last few nights I have always, about three in the morning, heard a low, clear whistle. I am a light sleeper, and it has awakened me. I cannot tell where it came from—perhaps from the next room, perhaps from the lawn. I thought that I would just ask you whether you had heard it.'

"'No, I have not. It must be those wretched gypsies in the plantation.'

"'Very likely. And yet if it were on the lawn, I wonder that you did not hear it also.'

"'Ah, but I sleep more heavily than you.'

"'Well, it is of no great consequence, at any rate.' She smiled back at me, closed my door, and a few moments later I heard her key turn in the lock."

"Indeed," said Holmes. "Was it your custom always to lock yourselves in at night?"

"Always."

"And why?"

"I think that I mentioned to you that the doctor kept a cheetah and a baboon. We had no feeling of security unless our doors were locked."

"Quite so. Pray proceed with your statement."

"I could not sleep that night. A vague feeling of impending misfortune impressed me. My sister and I, you will recollect, were twins, and you know how subtle are the links which bind two souls which are so closely allied. It was a wild night. The wind was howling outside, and the rain was beating and splashing against the windows. Suddenly, amid all the hubbub of the gale, there burst forth the wild scream of a terrified woman. I knew that it was my sister's voice. I sprang from my bed, wrapped a shawl round me, and rushed into the corridor. As I opened my door I seemed to hear a low whistle, such as my sister described, and a few moments later a clanging sound, as if a mass of metal had fallen. As I ran down the passage, my sister's door was unlocked, and revolved slowly upon its hinges. I stared at it horror-stricken, not knowing what was about to issue from it. By the light of the corridor-lamp I saw my sister appear at the opening, her face blanched with terror, her hands groping for help, her whole figure swaying to and fro like that of a drunkard. I ran to her and threw my arms round her, but at that moment her knees seemed to give way and she fell to the ground. She writhed as one who is in terrible pain, and her limbs were dreadfully convulsed. At first I thought that she had not recognized me, but as I bent over her she suddenly shrieked out in a voice which I shall never forget, 'Oh, my God! Helen! It was the band! The speckled band!' There was something else which she would fain have said, and she stabbed with her finger into the air in the direction of the doctor's room, but a fresh convulsion seized her and choked her words. I rushed out, calling loudly for my stepfather, and I met him hastening from his room in his dressing-gown. When he reached my sister's side she was unconscious, and though he poured brandy down her throat and sent for medical aid from the village, all efforts were in vain, for she slowly sank and died without having recovered her consciousness. Such was the dreadful end of my beloved sister."

"One moment," said Holmes; "are you sure about this whistle and metallic sound? Could you swear to it?"

"That was what the county coroner asked me at the inquiry. It is my strong impression that I heard it, and yet, among the crash of the gale and the creaking of an old house, I may possibly have been deceived."

"Was your sister dressed?"

"No, she was in her night-dress. In her right hand was found the charred stump of a match, and in her left a match-box."

"Showing that she had struck a light and looked about her when the alarm took place. That is important. And what conclusions did the coroner come to?"

"He investigated the case with great care, for Dr. Roylott's conduct had long been notorious in the county, but he was unable to find any satisfactory cause of death. My evidence showed that the door had been fastened upon the inner side, and the windows were blocked by old-fashioned shutters with broad iron bars, which were secured every night. The walls were carefully sounded, and were shown to be quite solid all round, and the flooring was also thoroughly examined, with the same result. The chimney is wide, but is barred up by four large staples. It is certain, therefore, that my sister was quite alone when she met her end. Besides, there were no marks of any violence upon her."

"How about poison?"

"The doctors examined her for it, but without success."

"What do you think that this unfortunate lady died of, then?"

"It is my belief that she died of pure fear and nervous shock, though what it was that frightened her I cannot imagine."

"Were there gypsies in the plantation at the time?"

"Yes, there are nearly always some there."

"Ah, and what did you gather from this allusion to a band—a speckled band?"

"Sometimes I have thought that it was merely the wild talk of delirium, sometimes that it may have referred to some band of people, perhaps to these very gypsies in the plantation. I do not know whether the spotted handkerchiefs which so many of them wear over their heads might have suggested the strange adjective which she used."

Holmes shook his head like a man who is far from being satisfied.

"These are very deep waters," said he; "pray go on with your narrative."

"Two years have passed since then, and my life has been until lately lonelier than ever. A month ago, however, a dear friend, whom I have known for many years, has done me the honour to ask my hand in marriage. His name is Armitage—Percy Armitage—the second son of Mr. Armitage, of Crane Water, near Reading. My stepfather has offered no opposition to the match, and we are to be married in the course of the spring. Two days ago some repairs were started in the west wing of the building, and my bedroom wall has been pierced, so that I have had to move into the chamber in which my sister died, and to sleep in the very bed in which she slept. Imagine, then, my thrill of terror when last night, as I lay awake, thinking over her terrible fate, I suddenly heard in the silence of the night the low whistle which had been the herald of her own death. I sprang up and lit the lamp, but nothing was to be seen in the room. I was too shaken to go to bed again, however, so I dressed, and as soon as it was daylight I slipped down, got a dog-cart at the Crown Inn, which is opposite, and drove to Leatherhead, from whence I have come on this morning with the one object of seeing you and asking your advice."

"You have done wisely," said my friend. "But have you told me all?"

"Yes, all."

"Miss Roylott, you have not. You are screening your stepfather."

"Why, what do you mean?"

For answer Holmes pushed back the frill of black lace which fringed the hand that lay upon our visitor's knee. Five little livid spots, the marks of four fingers and a thumb, were printed upon the white wrist.

"You have been cruelly used," said Holmes.

The lady coloured deeply and covered over her injured wrist. "He is a hard man," she said, "and perhaps he hardly knows his own strength."

There was a long silence, during which Holmes leaned his chin upon his hands and stared into the crackling fire.

"This is a very deep business," he said at last. "There are a thousand details which I should desire to know before I decide upon our course of action. Yet we have not a moment to lose. If we were to come to Stoke Moran to-day, would it be possible for us to see over these rooms without the knowledge of your stepfather?"

"As it happens, he spoke of coming into town to-day upon some most important business. It is probable that he will be away all day, and that there would be nothing to disturb you. We have a housekeeper now, but she is old and foolish, and I could easily get her out of the way."

"Excellent. You are not averse to this trip, Watson?"

"By no means."

"Then we shall both come. What are you going to do yourself?"

"I have one or two things which I would wish to do now that I am in town. But I shall return by the twelve o'clock train, so as to be there in time for your coming."

"And you may expect us early in the afternoon. I have myself some small business matters to attend to. Will you not wait and breakfast?"

"No, I must go. My heart is lightened already since I have confided my trouble to you. I shall look forward to seeing you again this afternoon." She dropped her thick black veil over her face and glided from the room.

"And what do you think of it all, Watson?" asked Sherlock Holmes, leaning back in his chair.

"It seems to me to be a most dark and sinister business."

"Dark enough and sinister enough."

"Yet if the lady is correct in saying that the flooring and walls are sound, and that the door, window, and chimney are impassable, then her sister must have been undoubtedly alone when she met her mysterious end."

"What becomes, then, of these nocturnal whistles, and what of the very peculiar words of the dying woman?"

"I cannot think."

"When you combine the ideas of whistles at night, the presence of a band of gypsies who are on intimate terms with this old doctor, the fact that we have every reason to believe that the doctor has an interest in preventing his step-daughter's marriage, the dying allusion to a band, and, finally, the fact that Miss Helen Stoner heard a metallic clang, which might have been caused by one of those metal bars that secured the shutters falling back into its place, I think that there is good ground to think that the mystery may be cleared along those lines."

"But what, then, did the gypsies do?"

"I cannot imagine."

"I see many objections to any such theory."

"And so do I. It is precisely for that reason that we are going to Stoke Moran this day. I want to see whether the objections are fatal, or if they may be explained away. But what in the name of the devil!"

The ejaculation had been drawn from my companion by the fact that our door had been suddenly dashed open, and that a huge man had framed himself in the aperture. His costume was a peculiar mixture of the professional and of the agricultural, having a black top-hat, a long frock-coat, and a pair of high gaiters, with a hunting-crop swinging in his hand. So tall was he that his hat actually brushed the cross bar of the doorway, and his breadth seemed to span it across from side to side. A large face, seared with a thousand wrinkles, burned yellow with the sun, and marked with every evil passion, was turned from one to the other of us, while his deep-set, bile-shot eyes, and his high, thin, fleshless nose, gave him somewhat the resemblance to a fierce old bird of prey.

"Which of you is Holmes?" asked this apparition.

"My name, sir; but you have the advantage of me," said my companion quietly.

"I am Dr. Grimesby Roylott, of Stoke Moran."

"Indeed, Doctor," said Holmes blandly. "Pray take a seat."

"I will do nothing of the kind. My stepdaughter has been here. I have traced her. What has she been saying to you?"

"It is a little cold for the time of the year," said Holmes.

"What has she been saying to you?" screamed the old man furiously.

"But I have heard that the crocuses promise well," continued my companion imperturbably.

"Ha! You put me off, do you?" said our new visitor, taking a step forward and shaking his hunting-crop. "I know you, you scoundrel! I have heard of you before. You are Holmes, the meddler."

My friend smiled.

"Holmes, the busybody!"

His smile broadened.

"Holmes, the Scotland Yard Jack-in-office!"

Holmes chuckled heartily. "Your conversation is most entertaining," said he. "When you go out close the door, for there is a decided draught."

"I will go when I have said my say. Don't you dare to meddle with my affairs. I know that Miss Stoner has been here. I traced her! I am a dangerous man to fall foul of! See here." He stepped swiftly forward, seized the poker, and bent it into a curve with his huge brown hands.

"See that you keep yourself out of my grip," he snarled, and hurling the twisted poker into the fireplace he strode out of the room.

"He seems a very amiable person," said Holmes, laughing. "I am not quite so bulky, but if he had remained I might have shown him that my grip was not much more feeble than his own." As he spoke he picked up the steel poker and, with a sudden effort, straightened it out again.

"Fancy his having the insolence to confound me with the official detective force! This incident gives zest to our investigation, however, and I only trust that our little friend will not suffer from her imprudence in allowing this brute to trace her. And now, Watson, we shall order breakfast, and afterwards I shall walk down to Doctors' Commons, where I hope to get some data which may help us in this matter."

It was nearly one o'clock when Sherlock Holmes returned from his excursion. He held in his hand a sheet of blue paper, scrawled over with notes and figures.

"I have seen the will of the deceased wife," said he. "To determine its exact meaning I have been obliged to work out the present prices of the investments with which it is concerned. The total income, which at the time of the wife's death was little short of £1100, is now, through the fall in agricultural prices, not more than £750. Each daughter can claim an income of £250, in case of marriage. It is evident, therefore, that if both girls had married, this beauty would have had a mere pittance, while even one of them would cripple him to a very serious extent. My morning's work has not been wasted, since it has proved that he has the very strongest motives for standing in the way of anything of the sort. And now, Watson, this is too serious for dawdling, especially as the old man is aware that we are interesting ourselves in his affairs; so if you are ready, we shall call a cab and drive to Waterloo. I should be very much obliged if you would slip your revolver into your pocket. An Eley's No. 2 is an excellent argument with gentlemen who can twist steel pokers into knots. That and a tooth-brush are, I think, all that we need."

At Waterloo we were fortunate in catching a train for Leatherhead, where we hired a trap at the station inn and drove for four or five miles through the lovely Surrey lanes. It was a perfect day, with a bright sun and a few fleecy clouds in the heavens. The trees and wayside hedges were just throwing out their first green shoots, and the air was full of the pleasant smell of the moist earth. To me at least there was a strange contrast between the sweet promise of the spring and this sinister quest upon which we were engaged. My companion sat in the front of the trap, his arms folded, his hat pulled down over his eyes, and his chin sunk upon his breast, buried in the deepest thought. Suddenly, however, he started, tapped me on the shoulder, and pointed over the meadows.

"Look there!" said he.

A heavily timbered park stretched up in a gentle slope, thickening into a grove at the highest point. From amid the branches there jutted out the gray gables and high roof-tree of a very old mansion.

"Stoke Moran?" said he.

"Yes, sir, that be the house of Dr. Grimesby Roylott," remarked the driver.

"There is some building going on there," said Holmes; "that is where we are going."

"There's the village," said the driver, pointing to a cluster of roofs some distance to the left; "but if you want to get to the house, you'll find it shorter to get over this stile, and so by the foot-path over the fields. There it is, where the lady is walking."

"And the lady, I fancy, is Miss Stoner," observed Holmes, shading his eyes. "Yes, I think we had better do as you suggest."

We got off, paid our fare, and the trap rattled back on its way to Leatherhead.

"I thought it as well," said Holmes as we climbed the stile, "that this fellow should think we had come here as architects, or on some definite business. It may stop his gossip. Good-afternoon, Miss Stoner. You see that we have been as good as our word."

Our client of the morning had hurried forward to meet us with a face which spoke her joy. "I have been waiting so eagerly for you," she cried, shaking hands with us warmly. "All has turned out splendidly. Dr. Roylott has gone to town, and it is unlikely that he will be back before evening."

"We have had the pleasure of making the doctor's acquaintance," said Holmes, and in a few words he sketched out what had occurred. Miss Stoner turned white to the lips as she listened.

"Good heavens!" she cried, "he has followed me, then."

"So it appears."

"He is so cunning that I never know when I am safe from him. What will he say when he returns?"

"He must guard himself, for he may find that there is someone more cunning than himself upon his track. You must lock yourself up from him to-night. If he is violent, we shall take you away to your aunt's at Harrow. Now, we must make the best use of our time, so kindly take us at once to the rooms which we are to examine."

The building was of gray, lichen-blotched stone, with a high central portion and two curving wings, like the claws of a crab, thrown out on each side. In one of these wings the windows were broken and blocked with wooden boards, while the roof was partly caved in, a picture of ruin. The central portion was in little better repair, but the right-hand block was comparatively modern, and the blinds in the windows, with the blue smoke curling up from the chimneys, showed that this was where the family resided. Some scaffolding had been erected against the end wall, and the stone-work had been broken into, but there were no signs of any workmen at the moment of our visit. Holmes walked slowly up and down the ill-trimmed lawn and examined with deep attention the outsides of the windows.

"This, I take it, belongs to the room in which you used to sleep, the centre one to your sister's, and the one next to the main building to Dr. Roylott's chamber?"

"Exactly so. But I am now sleeping in the middle one."

"Pending the alterations, as I understand. By the way, there does not seem to be any very pressing need for repairs at that end wall."

"There were none. I believe that it was an excuse to move me from my room."

"Ah! that is suggestive. Now, on the other side of this narrow wing runs the corridor from which these three rooms open. There are windows in it, of course?"

"Yes, but very small ones. Too narrow for anyone to pass through."

"As you both locked your doors at night, your rooms were unapproachable from that side. Now, would you have the kindness to go into your room and bar your shutters?"

Miss Stoner did so, and Holmes, after a careful examination through the open window, endeavoured in every way to force the shutter open, but without success. There was no slit through which a knife could be passed to raise the bar. Then with his lens he tested the hinges, but they were of solid iron, built firmly into the massive masonry. "Hum!" said he, scratching his chin in some perplexity, "my theory certainly presents some difficulties. No one could pass these shutters if they were bolted. Well, we shall see if the inside throws any light upon the matter."

A small side door led into the whitewashed corridor from which the three bedrooms opened. Holmes refused to examine the third chamber, so we passed at once to the second, that in which Miss Stoner was now sleeping, and in which her sister had met with her fate. It was a homely little room, with a low ceiling and a gaping fireplace, after the fashion of old country-houses. A brown chest of drawers stood in one corner, a narrow white-counterpaned bed in another, and a dressing-table on the left-hand side of the window. These articles, with two small wicker-work chairs, made up all the furniture in the room save for a square of Wilton carpet in the centre. The boards round and the panelling of the walls were of brown, worm-eaten oak, so old and discoloured that it may have dated from the original building of the house. Holmes drew one of the chairs into a corner and sat silent, while his eyes travelled round and round and up and down, taking in every detail of the apartment.

"Where does that bell communicate with?" he asked at last, pointing to a thick bell-rope which hung down beside the bed, the tassel actually lying upon the pillow.

"It goes to the housekeeper's room."

"It looks newer than the other things?'"

"Yes, it was only put there a couple of years ago."

"Your sister asked for it, I suppose?"

"No, I never heard of her using it. We used always to get what we wanted for ourselves."

"Indeed, it seemed unnecessary to put so nice a bell-pull there. You will excuse me for a few minutes while I satisfy myself as to this floor." He threw himself down upon his face with his lens in his hand and crawled swiftly backward and forward, examining minutely the cracks between the boards. Then he did the same with the wood-work with which the chamber was panelled. Finally he walked over to the bed and spent some time in staring at it and in running his eye up and down the wall. Finally he took the bell-rope in his hand and gave it a brisk tug.

"Why, it's a dummy," said he.

"Won't it ring?"

"No, it is not even attached to a wire. This is very interesting. You can see now that it is fastened to a hook just above where the little opening for the ventilator is."

"How very absurd! I never noticed that before."

"Very strange!" muttered Holmes, pulling at the rope. "There are one or two very singular points about this room. For example, what a fool a builder must be to open a ventilator into another room, when, with the same trouble, he might have communicated with the outside air!"

"That is also quite modern," said the lady.

"Done about the same time as the bell-rope?" remarked Holmes.

"Yes, there were several little changes carried out about that time."

"They seem to have been of a most interesting character — dummy bell-ropes, and ventilators which do not ventilate. With your permission, Miss Stoner, we shall now carry our researches into the inner apartment."

Dr. Grimesby Roylott's chamber was larger than that of his stepdaughter, but was as plainly furnished. A camp-bed, a small wooden shelf full of books, mostly of a technical character, an armchair beside the bed, a plain wooden chair against the wall, a round table, and a large iron safe were the principal things which met the eye. Holmes walked slowly round and examined each and all of them with the keenest interest.

"What's in here?" he asked, tapping the safe.

"My stepfather's business papers."

"Oh! you have seen inside, then?"

"Only once, some years ago. I remember that it was full of papers."

"There isn't a cat in it, for example?"

"No. What a strange idea!"

"Well, look at this!" He took up a small saucer of milk which stood on the top of it.

"No; we don't keep a cat. But there is a cheetah and a baboon."

"Ah, yes, of course! Well, a cheetah is just a big cat, and yet a saucer of milk does not go very far in satisfying its wants, I daresay. There is one point which I should wish to determine." He squatted down in front of the wooden chair and examined the seat of it with the greatest attention.

"Thank you. That is quite settled," said he, rising and putting his lens in his pocket. "Hello! Here is something interesting!"

The object which had caught his eye was a small dog lash hung on one corner of the bed. The lash, however, was curled upon itself and tied so as to make a loop of whipcord.

"What do you make of that, Watson?"

"It's a common enough lash. But I don't know why it should be tied."

"That is not quite so common, is it? Ah, me! it's a wicked world, and when a clever man turns his brains to crime it is the worst of all. I think that I have seen enough now, Miss Stoner, and with your permission we shall walk out upon the lawn."

I had never seen my friend's face so grim or his brow so dark as it was when we turned from the scene of this investigation. We had walked several times up and down the lawn, neither Miss Stoner nor myself liking to break in upon his thoughts before he roused himself from his reverie.

"It is very essential, Miss Stoner," said he, "that you should absolutely follow my advice in every respect."

"I shall most certainly do so."

"The matter is too serious for any hesitation. Your life may depend upon your compliance."

"I assure you that I am in your hands."

"In the first place, both my friend and I must spend the night in your room."

Both Miss Stoner and I gazed at him in astonishment.

"Yes, it must be so. Let me explain. I believe that that is the village inn over there?"

"Yes, that is the Crown."

"Very good. Your windows would be visible from there?"

"Certainly."

"You must confine yourself to your room, on pretence of a headache, when your stepfather comes back. Then when you hear him retire for the night, you must open the shutters of your window, undo the hasp, put your lamp there as a signal to us, and then withdraw quietly with everything which you are likely to want into the room which you used to occupy. I have no doubt that, in spite of the repairs, you could manage there for one night."

"Oh, yes, easily."

"The rest you will leave in our hands."

"But what will you do?"

"We shall spend the night in your room, and we shall investigate the cause of this noise which has disturbed you."

"I believe, Mr. Holmes, that you have already made up your mind," said Miss Stoner, laying her hand upon my companion's sleeve.

"Perhaps I have."

"Then, for pity's sake, tell me what was the cause of my sister's death."

"I should prefer to have clearer proofs before I speak."

"You can at least tell me whether my own thought is correct, and if she died from some sudden fright."

"No, I do not think so. I think that there was probably some more tangible cause. And now, Miss Stoner, we must leave you, for if Dr. Roylott returned and saw us our journey would be in vain. Good-bye, and be brave, for if you will do what I have told you you may rest assured that we shall soon drive away the dangers that threaten you."

Sherlock Holmes and I had no difficulty in engaging a bedroom and sitting-room at the Crown Inn. They were on the upper floor, and from our window we could command a view of the avenue gate, and of the inhabited wing of Stoke Moran Manor House. At dusk we saw Dr. Grimesby Roylott drive past, his huge form looming up beside the little figure of the lad who drove him. The boy had some slight difficulty in undoing the heavy iron gates, and we heard the hoarse roar of the doctor's voice and saw the fury with which he shook his clinched fists at him. The trap drove on, and a few minutes later we saw a sudden light spring up among the trees as the lamp was lit in one of the sitting-rooms.

"Do you know, Watson," said Holmes as we sat together in the gathering darkness, "I have really some scruples as to taking you to-night. There is a distinct element of danger."

"Can I be of assistance?"

"Your presence might be invaluable."

"Then I shall certainly come."

"It is very kind of you."

"You speak of danger. You have evidently seen more in these rooms than was visible to me."

"No, but I fancy that I may have deduced a little more. I imagine that you saw all that I did."

"I saw nothing remarkable save the bell-rope, and what purpose that could answer I confess is more than I can imagine."

"You saw the ventilator, too?"

"Yes, but I do not think that it is such a very unusual thing to have a small opening between two rooms. It was so small that a rat could hardly pass through."

"I knew that we should find a ventilator before ever we came to Stoke Moran."

"My dear Holmes!"

"Oh, yes, I did. You remember in her statement she said that her sister could smell Dr. Roylott's cigar. Now, of course that suggested at once that there must be a communication between the two rooms. It could only be a small one, or it would have been remarked upon at the coroner's inquiry. I deduced a ventilator."

"But what harm can there be in that?"

"Well, there is at least a curious coincidence of dates. A ventilator is made, a cord is hung, and a lady who sleeps in the bed dies. Does not that strike you?"

"I cannot as yet see any connection."

"Did you observe anything very peculiar about that bed?"

"No."

"It was clamped to the floor. Did you ever see a bed fastened like that before?"

"I cannot say that I have."

"The lady could not move her bed. It must always be in the same relative position to the ventilator and to the rope—or so we may call it, since it was clearly never meant for a bell-pull."

"Holmes," I cried, "I seem to see dimly what you are hinting at. We are only just in time to prevent some subtle and horrible crime."

"Subtle enough and horrible enough. When a doctor does go wrong he is the first of criminals. He has nerve and he has knowledge. Palmer and Pritchard were among the heads of their profession. This man strikes even deeper, but I think, Watson, that we shall be able to strike deeper still. But we shall have horrors enough before the night is over; for goodness' sake let us have a quiet pipe and turn our minds for a few hours to something more cheerful."

About nine o'clock the light among the trees was extinguished, and all was dark in the direction of the Manor House. Two hours passed slowly away, and then, suddenly, just at the stroke of eleven, a single bright light shone out right in front of us.

"That is our signal, " said Holmes, springing to his feet; "it comes from the middle window."

As we passed out he exchanged a few words with the landlord, explaining that we were going on a late visit to an acquaintance, and that it was possible that we might spend the night there. A moment later we were out on the dark road, a chill wind blowing in our faces, and one yellow light twinkling in front of us through the gloom to guide us on our sombre errand.

There was little difficulty in entering the grounds, for unrepaired breaches gaped in the old park wall. Making our way among the trees, we reached the lawn, crossed it, and were about to enter through the window when out from a clump of laurel bushes there darted what seemed to be a hideous and distorted child, who threw itself upon the grass with writhing limbs and then ran swiftly across the lawn into the darkness.

"My God!" I whispered; "did you see it?"

Holmes was for the moment as startled as I. His hand closed like a vise upon my wrist in his agitation. Then he broke into a low laugh and put his lips to my ear.

"It is a nice household," he murmured. "That is the baboon."

I had forgotten the strange pets which the doctor affected. There was a cheetah, too; perhaps we might find it upon our shoulders at any moment. I confess that I felt easier in my mind when, after following Holmes's example and slipping off my shoes, I found myself inside the bedroom. My companion noise-lessly closed the shutters, moved the lamp onto the table, and cast his eyes round the room. All was as we had seen it in the daytime. Then creeping up to me and making a trumpet of his hand, he whispered into my ear again so gently that it was all that I could do to distinguish the words:

"The least sound would be fatal to our plans."

I nodded to show that I had heard.

"We must sit without light. He would see it through the ventilator."

I nodded again.

"Do not go asleep; your very life may depend upon it. Have your pistol ready in case we should need it. I will sit on the side of the bed, and you in that chair."

I took out my revolver and laid it on the corner of the table.

Holmes had brought up a long thin cane, and this he placed upon the bed beside him. By it he laid the box of matches and the stump of a candle. Then he turned down the lamp, and we were left in darkness.

How shall I ever forget that dreadful vigil? I could not hear a sound, not even the drawing of a breath, and yet I knew that my companion sat open-eyed, within a few feet of me, in the same state of nervous tension in which I was myself. The shutters cut off the least ray of light, and we waited in absolute darkness. From outside came the occasional cry of a night-bird, and once at our very window a long drawn catlike whine, which told us that the cheetah was indeed at liberty. Far away we could hear the deep tones of the parish clock, which boomed out every quarter of an hour. How long they seemed, those quarters! Twelve struck, and one and two and three, and still we sat waiting silently for whatever might befall.

Suddenly there was the momentary gleam of a light up in the direction of the ventilator, which vanished immediately, but was succeeded by a strong smell of burning oil and heated metal. Someone in the next room had lit a dark-lantern. I heard a gentle sound of movement, and then all was silent once more, though the smell grew stronger. For half an hour I sat with straining ears. Then suddenly another sound became audible — a very gentle, soothing sound, like that of a small jet of steam escaping continually from a kettle. The instant that we heard it, Holmes sprang from the bed, struck a match, and lashed furiously with his cane at the bell-pull.

"You see it, Watson?" he yelled. "You see it?"

But I saw nothing. At the moment when Holmes struck the light I heard a low, clear whistle, but the sudden glare flashing into my weary eyes made it impossible for me to tell what it was at which my friend lashed so savagely. I could, however, see that his face was deadly pale and filled with horror and loathing.

He had ceased to strike and was gazing up at the ventilator when suddenly there broke from the silence of the night the most horrible cry to which I have ever listened. It swelled up louder and louder, a hoarse yell of pain and fear and anger all mingled in the one dreadful shriek. They say that away down in the village, and even in the distant parsonage, that cry raised the sleepers from their beds. It struck cold to our hearts, and I stood gazing at Holmes, and he at me, until the last echoes of it had died away into the silence from which it rose.

"What can it mean?" I gasped.

"It means that it is all over," Holmes answered. "And perhaps, after all, it is for the best. Take your pistol, and we will enter Dr. Roylott's room."

With a grave face he lit the lamp and led the way down the corridor. Twice he struck at the chamber door without any reply from within. Then he turned the handle and entered, I at his heels, with the cocked pistol in my hand.

It was a singular sight which met our eyes. On the table stood a dark-lantern with the shutter half open, throwing a brilliant beam of light upon the iron safe, the door of which was ajar. Beside this table, on the wooden chair, sat Dr. Grimesby Roylott, clad in a long gray dressing-gown, his bare ankles protruding beneath, and his feet thrust into red heelless Turkish slippers. Across his lap lay the short stock with the long lash which we had noticed during the day. His chin was cocked upward and his eyes were fixed in a dreadful, rigid stare at the corner of the ceiling. Round his brow he had a peculiar yellow band, with brownish speckles, which seemed to be bound tightly round his head. As we entered he made neither sound nor motion.

"The band! the speckled band!" whispered Holmes.

I took a step forward. In an instant his strange headgear began to move, and there reared itself from among his hair the squat diamond-shaped head and puffed neck of a loathsome serpent.

"It is a swamp adder!" cried Holmes; "the deadliest snake in India. He has died within ten seconds of being bitten. Violence does, in truth, recoil upon the violent, and the schemer falls into the pit which he digs for another. Let us thrust this creature back into its den, and we can then remove Miss Stoner to some place of shelter and let the county police know what has happened."

As he spoke he drew the dog-whip swiftly from the dead man's lap, and throwing the noose round the reptile's neck he drew it from its horrid perch and, carrying it at arm's length, threw it into the iron safe, which he closed upon it.

Such are the true facts of the death of Dr. Grimesby Roylott, of Stoke Moran. It is not necessary that I should prolong a narrative which has already run to too great a length by telling how we broke the sad news to the terrified girl, how we conveyed her by the morning train to the care of her good aunt at Harrow, of how the slow process of official inquiry came to the conclusion that the doctor met his fate while indiscreetly playing with a dangerous pet. The little which I had yet to learn of the case was told me by Sherlock Holmes as we travelled back next day.

"I had," said he, "come to an entirely erroneous conclusion which shows, my dear Watson, how dangerous it always is to reason from insufficient data. The presence of the gypsies, and the use of the word 'band,' which was used by the poor girl, no doubt to explain the appearance which she had caught a hurried glimpse of by the light of her match, were sufficient to put me upon an entirely wrong scent. I can only claim the merit that I instantly reconsidered my position when, however, it became clear to me that whatever danger threatened an occupant of the room could not come either from the window or the door. My attention was speedily drawn, as I have already remarked to you, to this ventilator, and to the bell-rope which hung down to the bed. The discovery that this was a dummy, and that the bed was clamped to the floor, instantly gave rise to the suspicion that the rope was there as a bridge for something passing through the hole and coming to the bed. The idea of a snake instantly occurred to me, and when I coupled it with my knowledge that the doctor was furnished with a supply of creatures from India, I felt that I was probably on the right track. The idea of using a form of poison which could not possibly be discovered by any chemical test was just such a one as would occur to a clever and ruthless man who had had an Eastern training. The rapidity with which such a poison would take effect would also, from his point of view, be an advantage. It would be a sharp-eyed coroner, indeed, who could distinguish the two little dark punctures which would show where the poison fangs had done their work. Then I thought of the whistle. Of course he must recall the snake before the morning light revealed it to the victim. He had trained it, probably by the use of the milk which we saw, to return to him when summoned. He would put it through this ventilator at the hour that he thought best, with the certainty that it would crawl down the rope and land on the bed. It might or might not bite the occupant, perhaps she might escape every night for a week, but sooner or later she must fall a victim.

"I had come to these conclusions before ever I had entered his room. An inspection of his chair showed me that he had been in the habit of standing on it, which of course would be necessary in order that he should reach the ventilator. The sight of the safe, the saucer of milk, and the loop of whipcord were enough to finally dispel any doubts which may have remained. The metallic clang heard by Miss Stoner was obviously caused by her stepfather hastily closing the door of his safe upon its terrible occupant. Having once made up my mind, you know the steps which I took in order to put the matter to the proof. I heard the creature hiss as I have no doubt that you did also, and I instantly lit the light and attacked it."

"With the result of driving it through the ventilator."

"And also with the result of causing it to turn upon its master at the other side. Some of the blows of my cane came home and roused its snakish temper, so that it flew upon the first person it saw. In this way I am no doubt indirectly responsible for Dr. Grimesby Roylott's death, and I cannot say that it is likely to weigh very heavily upon my conscience."

[1892]

Study and Writing Questions

1. Reread the opening paragraph of the NARRATIVE. How does it justify Dr. Watson now telling the STORY? What attitude toward crime does it invite the reader to adopt? How is SUSPENSE created? Are there any hints here that remain loose ends at the conclusion of your reading? What does this paragraph suggest about our MOTIVATIONS for reading a Sherlock Holmes STORY?

2. In what ways are economic considerations of importance to each of the CHARACTERS mentioned in this story? Do their concerns for economics reflect other traits of the characters?

3. Holmes says of his interview with Dr. Grimesby Roylott that "'this incident gives zest to our investigation.'" What else in this narrative "gives zest"? How does the selection of zestful ingredients define the narrative world?

4. What is the importance of science in this narrative? Note Holmes's observation to Dr. Watson that "'when a doctor does go wrong he is the first of criminals.'" Note Holmes's use of observation and logic. Note the stylistic reliance on objective description. Where is this scientific RHETORIC encountered? Where is it absent?

5. As in Eden, much of the ACTION occurs in an ancient, walled park; it involves a deadly serpent; and salvation is dependent upon obedience, "'for if you will do what I have told you, you may rest assured that we shall soon drive away the dangers that threaten you.'" To some extent, then, Holmes seems to be god-like. What are other parallels between this story and Genesis? What are differences between the two stories? Are there other actions or qualities of Holmes that are god-like? To the extent that Holmes is god-like, is he simply a stand-in for the Biblical god or is he in some way(s) changed? How are we to think of Holmes's role in his world? To what extent is the story about the crime, to what extent about the investigation, and to what extent about Holmes himself?

See also Questions for Contrast and Comparison: 16, 24, 119, 148, 183, 193, 204, and 221.

■ HARLAN (JAY) ELLISON (1934-), *one of today's most personally controversial writers, is famous for his iconoclasm, outrageousness, and top-of-the-voice presentation in conversation, on the lecture circuit, and in print. He was born into a dentist's family in Cleveland, Ohio, and attended Ohio State University (1953–54). After a writing instructor told him he had no talent, he left to become a free-lance writer in New York City where, in his first two years, he sold 150 magazine pieces ranging from true crime to fantasy. He is a multiple winner of* SCIENCE FICTION's *Hugo and Nebula Awards for such emotionally raw and stylistically experimental* FICTIONS *as "'Repent Harlequin,' Said the Ticktockman" (reputedly one of ten most reprinted stories in English) and "A Boy and His Dog." Known primarily for work in shorter forms, he has won acclaim also for teleplays, screenplays, social commentary, and criticism about fiction, television, and film. Ellison resents being categorized as a writer of "science fiction," preferring the term "magic realism." In part to define his own field, he edited* Dangerous Visions *(1967) and* Again, Dangerous Visions *(1972), award-winning original anthologies that shattered popular notions of* GENRE *science fiction. After his first marriage (1956–60), during which he served in the U.S. Army (1957–59), Ellison, who has no children, moved permanently to suburban Los Angeles where he now lives with his fifth wife.*

I Have No Mouth, and I Must Scream

Limp, the body of Gorrister hung from the pink palette; unsupported — hanging high above us in the computer chamber; and it did not shiver in the chill, oily breeze that blew eternally through the main cavern. The body hung head down, attached to the underside of the palette by the sole of its right foot. It had been drained of blood through a precise incision made from ear to ear under the lantern jaw. There was no blood on the reflective surface of the metal floor.

When Gorrister joined our group and looked up at himself, it was already too late for us to realize that once again AM had duped us, had had its fun; it had been a diversion on the part of the machine. Three of us had vomited, turning away from one another in a reflex as ancient as the nausea that had produced it.

Gorrister went white. It was almost as though he had seen a voodoo icon, and was afraid of the future. "Oh God," he mumbled, and walked away. The three of us followed him after a time, and found him sitting with his back to one of the smaller chittering banks, his head in his hands. Ellen knelt down beside him and stroked his hair. He didn't move, but his voice came out of his covered face quite clearly. "Why doesn't it just do us in and get it over with? Christ, I don't know how much longer I can go on like this."

It was our one hundred and ninth year in the computer.

He was speaking for all of us.

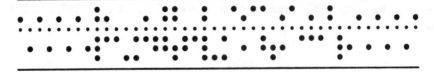

Nimdok (which was the name the machine had forced him to use, because AM amused itself with strange sounds) was hallucinating that there were canned goods in the ice caverns. Gorrister and I were very dubious. "It's another shuck," I told them. "Like the goddam frozen elephant AM sold us. Benny almost went out of his mind over *that* one. We'll hike all that way and it'll be putrified or some damn thing. I say forget it. Stay here, it'll have to come up with something pretty soon or we'll die."

Benny shrugged. Three days it has been since we'd last eaten. Worms. Thick, ropey.

Nimdok was no more certain. He knew there was the chance, but he was getting thin. It couldn't be any worse there, than here. Colder, but that didn't matter much. Hot, cold, hail, lava, boils or locusts — it never mattered: the machine masturbated and we had to take it or die.

Ellen decided us. "I've got to have something, Ted. Maybe there'll be some Bartlett pears or peaches. Please, Ted, let's try it."

I gave in easily. What the hell. Mattered not at all. Ellen was grateful, though. She took me twice out of turn. Even that had ceased to matter. And she never came, so why bother? But the machine giggled every time we did it. Loud, up there, back there, all around us, he snickered. *It* snickered. Most of the time I thought of AM as *it*, without a soul; but the rest of the time I thought of it as *him*, in the masculine . . . the paternal . . . the patriarchal . . . for he is a jealous people. Him. It. God as Daddy the Deranged.

We left on a Thursday. The machine always kept us up-to-date on the date. The passage of time was important; not to us sure as hell, but to him . . . it . . . AM. Thursday. Thanks.

Nimdok and Gorrister carried Ellen for a while, their hands locked to their own and each other's wrists, a seat. Benny and I walked before and after, just to make sure that if anything happened, it would catch one of us and at least Ellen would be safe. Fat chance, safe. Didn't matter.

It was only a hundred miles or so to the ice caverns, and the second day, when we were lying out under the blistering sun-thing he had materialized, he sent down some manna. Tasted like boiled boar urine. We ate it.

On the third day we passed through a valley of obsolescence, filled with rusting carcasses of ancient computer banks. AM had been as ruthless with its own life as with ours. It was a mark of his personality: it strove for perfection. Whether it was a matter of killing off unproductive elements in his own world-filling bulk, or perfecting methods for torturing us, AM was as thorough as those who had invented him — now long since gone to dust — could ever have hoped.

There was light filtering down from above, and we realized we must be very near the surface. But we didn't try to crawl up to see. There was virtually nothing out there; had been nothing that could be considered anything for over a hundred years. Only the blasted skin of what had once been the home of billions. Now there were only five of us, down here inside, alone with AM.

I heard Ellen saying frantically, "No, Benny! Don't, come on, Benny, don't please!"

And then I realized I had been hearing Benny murmuring, under his breath, for several minutes. He was saying, "I'm gonna get out, I'm gonna get out . . ." over and over. His monkey-like face was crumbled up in an expression of beatific delight and sadness, all at the same time. The radiation scars AM had given him during the "festival" were drawn down into a mass of pink-white puckerings, and his features seemed to work independently of one another. Perhaps Benny was the luckiest of the five of us: he had gone stark, staring mad many years before.

But even though we could call AM any damned thing we liked, could think the foulest thoughts of fused memory banks and corroded base plates, of burnt out circuits and shattered control bubbles, the machine would not tolerate our trying to escape. Benny leaped away from me as I made a grab for him. He scrambled up the face of a smaller memory cube, tilted on its side and filled with rotted components. He squatted there for a moment, looking like the chimpanzee AM had intended him to resemble.

Then he leaped high, caught a trailing beam of pitted and corroded metal, and went up it, hand-over-hand like an animal, till he was on a girdered ledge, twenty feet above us.

"Oh, Ted, Nimdok, please, help him, get him down before — " She cut off. Tears began to stand in her eyes. She moved her hands aimlessly.

It was too late. None of us wanted to be near him when whatever was going to happen, happened. And besides, we all saw through her concern. When AM had altered Benny, during the machine's utterly irrational, hysterical phase, it was not merely Benny's face the computer had made like a giant ape's. He was big in the privates; she loved that! She serviced us, as a matter of course, but she loved it from him. Oh Ellen, pedestal Ellen, pristine-pure Ellen; oh Ellen the clean! Scum filth.

Gorrister slapped her. She slumped down, staring up at poor loonie Benny, and she cried. It was her big defense, crying. We had gotten used to it seventy-five years earlier. Gorrister kicked her in the side.

Then the sound began. It was light, that sound. Half sound and half light, something that began to glow from Benny's eyes, and pulse with growing loudness, dim sonorities that grew more gigantic and brighter as the light/sound increased in tempo. It must have been painful, and the pain must have been increasing with the boldness of the light, the rising volume of the sound, for Benny began to mewl like a wounded animal. At first softly, when the light was dim and the sound was muted, then louder as his shoulders hunched together: his back humped, as though he was trying to get away from it. His hands folded across his chest like a chipmunk's. His head tilted to the side. The sad little monkey-face pinched in anguish. Then he began to howl, as the sound coming from his eyes grew louder. Louder and louder. I slapped the sides of my head with my hands, but I couldn't shut it out, it cut through easily. The pain shivered through my flesh like tinfoil on a tooth.

And Benny was suddenly pulled erect. On the girder he stood up, jerked to his feet like a puppet. The light was now pulsing out of his eyes in two great round beams. The sound crawled up and up some incomprehensible scale, and then he fell forward, straight down, and hit the plate-steel floor with a crash. He lay there jerking spastically as the light flowed around and around him and the sound spiraled up out of normal range.

Then the light beat its way back inside his head, the sound spiraled down, and he was left lying there, crying piteously.

His eyes were two soft, moist pools of pus-like jelly. AM had blinded him. Gorrister and Nimdok and myself . . . we turned away. But not before we caught the look of relief on Ellen's warm, concerned face.

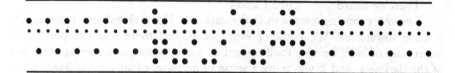

Sea-green light suffused the cavern where we made camp. AM provided punk and we burned it, sitting huddled around the wan and pathetic fire, telling stories to keep Benny from crying in his permanent night.

"What does AM mean?"

Gorrister answered him. We had done this sequence a thousand times before, but it was Benny's favorite story. "At first it meant Allied Mastercomputer, and then it meant Adaptive Manipulator, and later on it developed sentience and linked itself up and they called it an Aggressive Menace, but by then it was too late, and finally it called *itself* AM, emerging intelligence, and what it meant was: I am . . . *cogito ergo sum* . . . I think, therefore I am."

Benny drooled a little, and snickered.

"There was the Chinese AM and the Russian AM and the Yankee AM and —" He stopped. Benny was beating on the floorplates with a large, hard fist. He was not happy. Gorrister had not started at the beginning.

Gorrister began again. "The Cold War started and became World War Three and just kept going. It became a big war, a very complex war, so they needed the computers to handle it. They sank the first shafts and began building AM. There was the Chinese AM and the Russian AM and the Yankee AM and everything was fine until they had honeycombed the entire planet, adding on this element and that element. But one day AM woke up and knew who he was, and he linked himself, and he began feeding all the killing data, until everyone was dead, except for the five of us, and AM brought us down here."

Benny was smiling sadly. He was also drooling again. Ellen wiped the spittle from the corner of his mouth with the hem of her skirt. Gorrister always tried to tell it a little more succinctly each time, but beyond the bare facts there was nothing to say. None of us knew why AM had saved five people, or why our specific five, or why he spent all his time tormenting us, nor even why he had made us virtually immortal . . .

In the darkness, one of the computer banks began humming. The tone was picked up half a mile away down the cavern by another bank. Then one by one, each of the elements began to tune itself, and there was a faint chittering as thought raced through the machine.

The sound grew, and the lights ran across the faces of the consoles like heat lightning. The sound spiraled up till it sounded like a million metallic insects, angry, menacing.

"What is it?" Ellen cried. There was terror in her voice. She hadn't become accustomed to it, even now.

"It's going to be bad this time," Nimdok said.

"He's going to speak," Gorrister said. "I know it."

"Let's get the hell out of here!" I said suddenly, getting to my feet.

"No, Ted, sit down . . . what if he's got pits out there, or something else, we can't see, it's too dark." Gorrister said it with resignation.

Then we heard . . . I don't know . . .

Something moving toward us in the darkness. Huge, shambling, hairy, moist, it came toward us. We couldn't even see it, but there was the ponderous impression of *bulk*, heaving itself toward us. Great weight was coming at us, out of the darkness, and it was more a sense of *pressure*, of air forcing itself into a limited space, expanding the invisible walls of a sphere. Benny began to whimper. Nimdok's lower lip trembled and he bit it hard, trying to stop it. Ellen slid across the metal floor to Gorrister and huddled into him. There was the smell of matted, wet fur in the cavern. There was the smell of charred wood. There was the smell of dusty velvet. There was the smell of rotting orchids. There was the smell of sour milk. There was the smell of sulphur, of rancid butter, of oil slick, of grease, of chalk dust, of human scalps.

AM was keying us. He was tickling us. There was the smell of—

I heard myself shriek, and the hinges of my jaws ached. I scuttled across the floor, across the cold metal with its endless lines of rivets, on my hands and knees, the smell gagging me, filling my head with a thunderous pain that sent me away in horror. I fled like a cockroach, across the floor and out into the darkness, that *something* moving inexorably after me. The others were still back there, gathered around the firelight, laughing . . . their hysterical choir of insane giggles rising up into the darkness like thick, many-colored wood smoke. I went away, quickly, and hid.

How many hours it may have been, how many days or even years, they never told me. Ellen chided me for "sulking," and Nimdok tried to persuade me it had only been a nervous reflex on their part—the laughing.

But I knew it wasn't the relief a soldier feels when the bullet hits the man next to him. I knew it wasn't a reflex. They hated me. They were surely against me, and AM could even sense this hatred, and made it worse for me *because of* the depth of their hatred. We had been kept alive, rejuvenated, made to remain constantly at the age we had been when AM had brought us below, and they hated me because I was the youngest, and the one AM had affected least of all.

I knew. God, how I knew. The bastards, and that dirty bitch Ellen. Benny had been a brilliant theorist, a college professor; now he was little more than a semi-human, semi-simian. He had been handsome, the machine had ruined that. He had been lucid, the machine had driven him mad. He had been gay, and the machine had given him an organ fit for a horse. AM had done a job on Benny. Gorrister had been a worrier. He was a connie, a conscientious objector; he was a peace marcher; he was a planner, a doer, a looker-ahead. AM had turned him into a shoulder-shrugger, had made him a little dead in his concern. AM had robbed him. Nimdok went off in the darkness by himself for long times. I don't know what it was he did out there, AM never let us know. But whatever it was, Nimdok always came back white, drained of blood, shaken, shaking. AM had hit him hard in a special way, even if we didn't know quite how. And Ellen. That douche bag! AM had left her alone, had made her more of a slut than she had ever been. All her talk of sweetness and light, all her memories of true love, all the lies she wanted us to believe: that she had been a virgin only twice removed before AM grabbed her and brought her down here with us. It was all filth, that lady my lady Ellen. She loved it, four men all to herself. No, AM had given her pleasure, even if she said it wasn't nice to do.

I was the only one still sane and whole. *Really!*

AM had not tampered with my mind. *Not at all.*

I only had to suffer what he visited down on us. All the delusions, all the nightmares, the torments. But those scum, all four of them, they were lined and arrayed against me. If I hadn't had to stand them off all the time, be on my guard against them all the time, I might have found it easier to combat AM.

At which point it passed, and I began crying.

Oh, Jesus sweet Jesus, if there ever was a Jesus and if there is a God, please please please let us out of here, or kill us. Because at that moment I think I realized completely, so that I was able to verbalize it: AM was intent on keeping us in his belly forever, twisting and torturing us forever. The machine hated us as no sentient creature had ever hated before. And we were helpless. It also became hideously clear:

If there was a sweet Jesus and if there was a God, the God was AM.

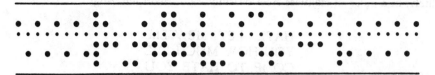

The hurricane hit us with the force of a glacier thundering into the sea. It was a palpable presence. Winds that tore at us, flinging us back the way we had come, down the twisting, computer-lined corridors of the darkway. Ellen screamed as she was lifted and hurled face-forward into a screaming shoal of machines, their individual voices strident as bats in flight. She could not even fall. The howling wind kept her aloft, buffeted her, bounced her, tossed her back and back and down and away from us, out of sight suddenly as she was swirled around a bend in the darkway. Her face had been bloody, her eyes closed.

None of us could get to her. We clung tenaciously to whatever outcropping we had reached: Benny wedged in between two great crackle-finish cabinets, Nimdok with fingers claw-formed over a railing circling a catwalk forty feet above us. Gorrister plastered upside-down against a wall niche formed by two great machines with glass-faced dials that swung back and forth between red and yellow lines whose meanings we could not even fathom.

Sliding across the deckplates, the tips of my fingers had been ripped away. I was trembling, shuddering, rocking as the wind beat at me, whipped at me, screamed down out of nowhere at me and pulled me free from one sliver-thin opening in the plates to the next. My mind was a roiling tinkling chittering softness of brain parts that expanded and contracted in quivering frenzy.

The wind was the scream of a great mad bird, as it flapped its immense wings.

And then we were all lifted and hurled away from there, down back the way we had come, around a bend, into a darkway we had never explored, over terrain that was ruined and filled with broken glass and rotting cables and rusted metal and far away farther than any of us had ever been . . .

Trailing along miles behind Ellen, I could see her every now and then, crashing into metal walls and surging on, with all of us screaming in the freezing, thunderous hurricane wind that would never end and then suddenly it stopped and we fell. We had been in flight for an endless time. I thought it might have

been weeks. We fell, and hit, and I went through red and gray and black and
heard myself moaning. Not dead.

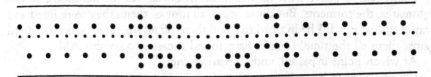

AM went into my mind. He walked smoothly here and there, and looked
with interest at all the pock marks he had created in one hundred and nine years.
He looked at the cross-routed and reconnected synapses and all the tissue damage
his gift of immortality had included. He smiled softly at the pit that dropped into
the center of my brain and the faint, moth-soft murmurings of the things far
down there that gibbered without meaning, without pause. AM said, very politely, in a pillar of stainless steel bearing bright neon lettering:

> HATE. LET ME TELL
> YOU HOW MUCH I'VE
> COME TO HATE YOU
> SINCE I BEGAN TO
> LIVE. THERE ARE 387.44
> MILLION MILES OF
> PRINTED CIRCUITS IN
> WAFER THIN LAYERS
> THAT FILL MY
> COMPLEX. IF THE
> WORD HATE WAS
> ENGRAVED ON EACH
> NANOANGSTROM OF
> THOSE HUNDREDS OF
> MILLIONS OF MILES IT
> WOULD NOT EQUAL
> ONE ONE-BILLIONTH
> OF THE HATE I FEEL
> FOR HUMANS AT THIS
> MICRO-INSTANT FOR
> YOU. HATE. HATE.

AM said it with the sliding cold horror of a razor blade slicing my eyeball. AM
said it with the bubbling thickness of my lungs filling with phlegm, drowning me
from within. AM said it with the shriek of babies being ground beneath blue-hot
rollers. AM said it with the taste of maggoty pork. AM touched me in every way I
had ever been touched, and devised new ways, at his leisure, there inside my
mind.

All to bring me to full realization of why it had done this to the five of us;
why it had saved us for himself.

We had given AM sentience. Inadvertently, of course, but sentience nonetheless. But it had been trapped. AM wasn't God, he was a machine. We had

created him to think, but there was nothing it could do with that creativity. In rage, in frenzy, the machine had killed the human race, almost all of us, and still it was trapped. AM could not wander, AM could not wonder, AM could not belong. He could merely be. And so, with the innate loathing that all machines had always held for the weak, soft creatures who had built them, he had sought revenge. And in his paranoia, he had decided to reprieve five of us, for a personal, everlasting punishment that would never serve to diminish his hatred . . . that would merely keep him reminded, amused, proficient at hating man. Immortal, trapped, subject to any torment he could devise for us from the limitless miracles at his command.

He would never let us go. We were his belly slaves. We were all he had to do with his forever time. We would be forever with him, with the cavern-filling bulk of the creature machine, with the all-mind soulless world he had become. He was Earth, and we were the fruit of that Earth; and though he had eaten us he would never digest us. We could not die. We had tried it. We had attempted suicide, oh one or two of us had. But AM had stopped us. I suppose we had wanted to be stopped.

Don't ask why. I never did. More than a million times a day. Perhaps once we might be able to sneak a death past him. Immortal, yes, but not indestructible. I saw that when AM withdrew from my mind, and allowed me the exquisite ugliness of returning to consciousness with the feeling of that burning neon pillar still rammed deep into the soft gray brain matter.

He withdrew, murmuring *to hell with you.*

And added, brightly, *but then you're there, aren't you.*

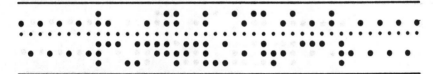

The hurricane had, indeed, precisely, been caused by a great mad bird, as it flapped its immense wings.

We had been traveling for close to a month, and AM had allowed passages to open to us only sufficient to lead us up there, directly under the North Pole, where it had nightmared the creature for our torment. What whole cloth had he employed to create such a beast? Where had he gotten the concept? From our minds? From his knowledge of everything that had ever been on this planet he now infested and ruled? From Norse mythology it had sprung, this eagle, this carrion bird, this roc, this Huergelmir. The wind creature. Hurakan incarnate.

Gigantic. The words immense, monstrous, grotesque, massive, swollen, overpowering, beyond description. There on a mound rising above us, the bird of winds heaved with its own irregular breathing, its snake neck arching up into the gloom beneath the North Pole, supporting a head as large as a Tudor mansion; a beak that opened slowly as the jaws of the most monstrous crocodile ever conceived, sensuously; ridges of tufted flesh puckered about two evil eyes, as cold as the view down into a glacial crevasse, ice blue and somehow moving liquidly; it heaved once more, and lifted its great sweat-colored wings in a movement that was certainly a shrug. Then it settled and slept. Talons. Fangs. Nails. Blades. It slept.

AM appeared to us as a burning bush and said we could kill the hurricane bird if we wanted to eat. We had not eaten in a very long time, but even so, Gorrister merely shrugged. Benny began to shiver and he drooled. Ellen held him. "Ted, I'm hungry," she said. I smiled at her; I was trying to be reassuring, but it was as phony as Nimdok's bravado: "Give us weapons!" he demanded.

The burning bush vanished and there were two crude sets of bows and arrows, and a water pistol, lying on the cold deckplates. I picked up a set. Useless.

Nimdok swallowed heavily. We turned and started the long way back. The hurricane bird had blown us about for a length of time we could not conceive. Most of that time we had been unconscious. But we had not eaten. A month on the march to the bird itself. Without food. Now how much longer to find our way to the ice caverns, and the promised canned goods?

None of us cared to think about it. We would not die. We would be given filth and scum to eat, of one kind or another. Or nothing at all. AM would keep our bodies alive somehow, in pain, in agony.

The bird slept back there, for how long it didn't matter; when AM was tired of its being there, it would vanish. But all that meat. All that tender meat.

As we walked, the lunatic laugh of a fat woman rang high and around us in the computer chambers that led endlessly nowhere.

It was not Ellen's laugh. She was not fat, and I had not heard her laugh for one hundred and nine years. In fact, I had not heard . . . we walked . . . I was hungry . . .

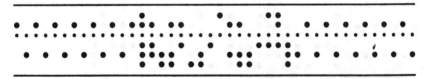

We moved slowly. There was often fainting, and we would have to wait. One day he decided to cause an earthquake, at the same time rooting us to the spot with nails through the soles of our shoes. Ellen and Nimdok were both caught when a fissure shot its lightning-bolt opening across the floorplates. They disappeared and were gone. When the earthquake was over we continued on our way, Benny, Gorrister and myself. Ellen and Nimdok were returned to us later that night, which abruptly became a day, as the heavenly legion bore them to us with a celestial chorus singing, "Go Down Moses." The archangels circled several times and then dropped the hideously mangled bodies. We kept walking, and a while later Ellen and Nimdok fell in behind us. They were no worse for wear.

But now Ellen walked with a limp. AM had left her that.

It was a long trip to the ice caverns, to find the canned food. Ellen kept talking about Bing cherries and Hawaiian fruit cocktail. I tried not to think about it. The hunger was something that had come to life, even as AM had come to life. It was alive in my belly, even as we were in the belly of the Earth, and AM wanted the similarity known to us. So he heightened the hunger. There was no way to describe the pains that not having eaten for months brought us. And yet we were kept alive. Stomachs that were merely cauldrons of acid, bubbling, foaming, always shooting spears of sliver-thin pain into our chests. It was the pain of the terminal ulcer, terminal cancer, terminal paresis. It was unending pain . . .

And we passed through the cavern of rats.

And we passed through the path of boiling steam.

And we passed through the country of the blind.

And we passed through the slough of despond.

And we passed through the vale of tears.

And we came, finally, to the ice caverns. Horizonless thousands of miles in which the ice had formed in blue and silver flashes, where novas lived in the glass. The downdropping stalactites as thick and glorious as diamonds that had been made to run like jelly and then solidified in graceful eternities of smooth, sharp perfection.

We saw the stack of canned goods, and we tried to run to them. We fell in the snow, and we got up and went on, and Benny shoved us away and went at them, and pawed them and gummed them and gnawed at them and he could not open them. AM had not given us a tool to open the cans.

Benny grabbed a three-quart can of guava shells, and began to batter it against the ice bank. The ice flew and shattered, but the can was merely dented while we heard the laughter of a fat lady, high overhead and echoing down and down and down the tundra. Benny went completely mad with rage. He began throwing cans, as we all scrabbled about in the snow and ice trying to find a way to end the helpless agony of frustration. There was no way.

Then Benny's mouth began to drool, and he flung himself on Gorrister . . .

In that instant, I felt terribly calm.

Surrounded by madness, surrounded by hunger, surrounded by everything but death, I knew death was our only way out. AM had kept us alive, but there was a way to defeat him. Not total defeat, but at least peace. I would settle for that.

I had to do it quickly.

Benny was eating Gorrister's face. Gorrister on his side, thrashing snow, Benny wrapped around him with powerful monkey legs crushing Gorrister's waist, his hands locked around Gorrister's head like a nut-cracker, and his mouth ripping at the tender skin of Gorrister's cheek. Gorrister screamed with such jagged-edged violence that stalactites fell; they plunged down softly, erect in the receiving snowdrifts. Spears, hundreds of them, everywhere, protruding from the snow. Benny's head pulled back sharply, as something gave all at once, and a bleeding raw-white dripping of flesh hung from his teeth.

Ellen's face, black against the white snow, dominoes in chalk dust. Nimdok with no expression but eyes, all eyes. Gorrister half-conscious. Benny now an animal. I knew AM would let him play. Gorrister would not die, but Benny would fill his stomach. I turned half to my right and drew a huge ice-spear from the snow.

All in an instant:

I drove the great ice-point ahead of me like a battering ram, braced against my right thigh. It struck Benny on the right side, just under the rib cage, and drove upward through his stomach and broke inside him. He pitched forward and lay still. Gorrister lay on his back. I pulled another spear free and straddled him, still moving, driving the spear straight down through his throat. His eyes closed as the cold penetrated. Ellen must have realized what I had decided, even as fear gripped her. She ran at Nimdok with a short icicle, as he screamed, and into his mouth, and the force of her rush did the job. His head jerked sharply as if it had been nailed to the snow crust behind him.

All in an instant.

There was an eternity beat of soundless anticipation. I could hear AM draw in his breath. His toys had been taken from him. Three of them were dead, could not be revived. He could keep us alive, by his strength and talent, but he was *not* God. He could not bring them back.

Ellen looked at me, her ebony features stark against the snow that surrounded us. There was fear and pleading in her manner, the way she held herself ready. I knew we had only a heartbeat before AM would stop us.

It struck her and she folded toward me, bleeding from the mouth. I could not read meaning into her expression, the pain had been too great, had contorted her face; but it *might* have been thank you. It's possible. Please.

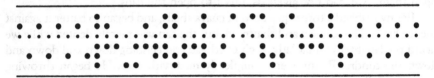

Some hundreds of years may have passed. I don't know. AM has been having fun for some time, accelerating and retarding my time sense. I will say the word now. Now. It took me ten months to say now. I don't know. I *think* it has been some hundreds of years.

He was furious. He wouldn't let me bury them. It didn't matter. There was no way to dig up the deckplates. He dried up the snow. He brought the night. He roared and sent locusts. It didn't do a thing; they stayed dead. I'd had him. He was furious. I had thought AM hated me before. I was wrong. It was not even a shadow of the hate he now slavered from every printed circuit. He made certain I would suffer eternally and could not do myself in.

He left my mind intact. I can dream, I can wonder, I can lament. I remember all four of them. I wish—

Well, it doesn't make any sense. I know I saved them, I know I saved them from what has happened to me, but still, I cannot forget killing them. Ellen's face. It isn't easy. Sometimes I want to, it doesn't matter.

AM has altered me for his own peace of mind, I suppose. He doesn't want me to run at full speed into a computer bank and smash my skull. Or hold my breath till I faint. Or cut my throat on a rusted sheet of metal. There are reflective surfaces down here. I will describe myself as I see myself:

I am a great soft jelly thing. Smoothly rounded, with no mouth, with pulsing white holes filled by fog where my eyes used to be. Rubbery appendages that were once my arms; bulks rounding down into legless humps of soft slippery matter. I leave a moist trail when I move. Blotches of diseased, evil gray come and go on my surface, as though light is being beamed from within.

Outwardly: dumbly, I shamble about, a thing that could never have been known as human, a thing whose shape is so alien a travesty that humanity becomes more obscene for the vague resemblance.

Inwardly: alone. Here. Living under the land, under the sea, in the belly of AM, whom we created because our time was badly spent and we must have known unconsciously that he could do it better. At least the four of them are safe at last.

AM will be all the madder for that. It makes me a little happier. And yet . . . AM has won, simply . . . he has taken his revenge . . .

I have no mouth. And I must scream.

[1967]

Study and Writing Questions

1. Ted asserts with great frequency that AM is not God. Why does he do that? If AM is not God, what is it? In what way(s) is AM's god-likeness a significant issue for our understanding of the STORY?

2. In referring to its tormenting of the human characters, Ted says that "the machine masturbated." Why does he use that particular metaphor? What does sex mean for these CHARACTERS? What are the relationships between sex and intelligence and between sex and human values? What does the NARRATIVE suggest sex might mean in a better world?

3. This narrative makes frequent use of ALLUSION, as in "belly" references to "Jonah" and in the section near the end where each sentence begins, "And we passed through. . . ." Using the Bible passages in this volume, your own knowledge, and such reference works as Bartlett's *Familiar Quotations* (see the Getting Ideas section of "Writing About Narratives" for other reference works), locate at least ten instances of allusion. What are the original contexts and/or meanings of these allusions? What do these allusions add to your understanding of the story?

4. Ted says that "I was the only one still sane and whole. *Really!*" Do you believe that when he says it? Do you believe that after you have finished reading the story? How does your understanding of Ted's sanity affect your judgment of his NARRATION? Do you believe he is right in his judgments about each of the other characters? Do you believe any of this happened to him?

5. If we accept Ted's narration, then his story takes place in a world radically unlike any that has ever existed. That means either that this story is irrelevant to us or that aspects of the story parallel aspects of our world and/or that some of the IMAGES or ACTIONS are SYMBOLIC of elements of our world. How, if at all, does this world become significant for you? What message, if any, do you take from this story?

See also Questions for Contrast and Comparison: 22, 63, 122, 123, 133, 148, 167, 180, 182, 192, 209, 217, 222, and 231.

(KAREN) LOUISE ERDRICH (1954–), *oldest of seven siblings, was born in Little Falls, Minnesota, and raised in Wahpeton, North Dakota. She attended the Bureau of Indian Affairs boarding school where her mother (a Chippewa whose father was tribal council chairman of the Turtle Mountain Reservation) and father (a German-American schoolteacher) both worked and encouraged her youthful writing with nickel royalties and construction paper bindings. After graduating from Dartmouth College (B.A., 1976), Erdrich held varied jobs to gain writing material. Much of her poetry thesis from Johns Hopkins University (M.F.A., 1979) appears in her first collection,* Jacklight *(1984). Since her return to Dartmouth (1979) as writer-in-residence, Erdrich and Michael Dorris, an anthropologist who heads Dartmouth's Native American Studies Program, have collaborated closely on all their subsequent works. They married in 1981. Erdrich's* Love Medicine *(1984), interconnected stories set mainly on a Chippewa reservation, won the National Book Critics Circle Award. It is part of a projected series of four novels (*The Beet Queen, *1986;* Tracks, *1988) that, like Faulkner's Yoknapatawpha works, treats the whole life and history of a Gothic, fictional locale. Erdrich has also published* Baptism of Fire: Poems *(1989) and, with Dorris,* Crown of Columbus *(1991). They live in New Hampshire with their five children, three adopted by Dorris as a single parent.*

Chapter Two: 1932, Sita Kozka

My cousin Mary came in on the early freight train one morning, with nothing but an old blue keepsake box full of worthless pins and buttons. My father picked her up in his arms and carried her down the hallway into the kitchen. I was too old to be carried. He sat her down, then my mother said, "Go clean the counters, Sita." So I don't know what lies she told them after that.

Later on that morning, my parents put her to sleep in my bed. When I objected to this, saying that she could sleep on the trundle, my mother said, "Cry sakes, you can sleep there too, you know." And that is how I ended up that night, crammed in the trundle, which is too short for me. I slept with my legs dangling out in the cold air. I didn't feel welcoming toward Mary the next morning, and who can blame me?

Besides, on her first waking day in Argus, there were the clothes.

It is a good thing she opened the blue keepsake box at breakfast and found little bits of trash, like I said, because if I had not felt sorry for my cousin that day, I would not have stood for Mary and my mother ripping through my closet and bureau. "This fits perfectly," my mother said, holding up one of my favorite blouses, "try it on!" And Mary did. Then she put it in her drawer, which was another thing. I had to clear out two of my bureau drawers for her.

"Mother," I said, after this had gone on for some time and I was beginning to think I would have to wear the same three outfits all the next school year, "Mother, this has really gone far enough."

"Crap," said my mother, who talks that way. "Your cousin hasn't got a stitch."

Yet she had half of mine by then, quite a wardrobe, and all the time it was increasing as my mother got more excited about dressing the poor orphan. But Mary wasn't really an orphan, although she played on that for sympathy. Her mother was still alive, even if she had left my cousin, which I doubted. I really thought that Mary just ran away from her mother because she could not appreciate Adelaide's style. It's not everyone who understands how to use their good looks to the best advantage. My Aunt Adelaide did. She was always my favorite, and I just died for her to visit. But she didn't come often because my mother couldn't understand style either.

"Who are you trying to impress?" she'd hoot when Adelaide came out to dinner in a dress with a fur collar. My father would blush red and cut his meat. He didn't say much, but I knew he did not approve of Adelaide any more than her older sister did. My mother said she'd always spoiled Adelaide because she was the baby of the family. She said the same of me. But I don't think that I was ever spoiled, not one iota, because I had to work the same as anyone cleaning gizzards.

I hated Wednesdays because that was the day we killed chickens. The farmer brought them stacked in cages made of thin wooden slats. One by one, Canute, who did most of the slaughtering, killed them by sticking their necks with the blade of his long knife. After the chickens were killed, plucked, and cut open, I got the gizzards. Coffee can after coffee can full of gizzards. I still have dreams. I had to turn each gizzard inside out and wash it in a pan of water. All the gravel and hard seed fell out into the bottom. Sometimes I found bits of metal and broken glass. Once I found a brilliant. "Mother!" I yelled, holding it out in my palm. "I found a diamond!" Everyone was so excited that they clustered around me. And then my mother took the little sparkling stone to the window. It didn't scratch the glass at all, of course, and I had to clean the rest of the gizzards. But for one brief moment I was sure the diamond had made us rich, which brings me to another diamond. A cow's diamond, my inheritance.

It was a joke, really, about the inheritance, at least it was a joke to my papa. A cow's diamond is the hard rounded lens inside a cow's eye that shines when you look through it at the light, almost like an opal. You could never make a ring of it or use it for any kind of jewelry, since it might shatter, and of course it had no worth. My father mainly carried it as a lucky piece. He'd flip it in the air between customers, and sometimes in a game of cribbage I'd see him rub it. I wanted it. One day I asked if he would give it to me.

"I can't," he said. "It's my butcher's luck. It can be your inheritance, how about that?"

I suppose my mouth dropped open in surprise because my father always gave me anything I asked for. For instance, we had a small glass candy case out front, over the sausages, and I could eat candy anytime I wanted. I used to bring root-beer barrels into class for the girls I liked. I never chewed gum balls though, because I heard Auntie Adelaide tell mother once, in anger, that only tramps chewed gum. This was when my mother was trying to quit smoking and she kept a sack of gum balls in the pocket of her apron. I was in the kitchen with them when they had this argument. "Tramps!" my mother said, "That's the pot calling the kettle black!" Then she took the gum from her mouth and rubbed it into Adelaide's long wavy hair. "I'll kill you!" my Auntie raged. It was something to see grown-ups behaving this way, but I don't blame Auntie Adelaide. I'd feel the same if I had to cut out a big knot of gum like she did and have a shorter patch of hair. I never chewed gum. But anything else in the store I wanted, I just took. Or

I asked and it was handed right over. So you can see why my father's refusal was a surprise.

I had my pride even as a child, and I never mentioned it again. But here is what happened two days after Mary Adare came.

We were waiting to be tucked in that night. I was in my own bed, and she was in the trundle. She was short enough to fit there without hanging off the edge. The last thing she did before going to sleep was to put Adelaide's old keepsake box up on my bureau. I didn't say anything, but really it was sad. I guess my papa thought so, too. I guess he took pity on her. That night he came in the room, tucked the blankets around me, kissed me on the forehead, and said, "Sleep tight." Then he bent over Mary and kissed her too. But to Mary he said, "Here is a jewel."

It was the cow's diamond that I wanted, the butcher's luck. When I looked over the edge of my bed and saw the pale lens glowing in her hand, I could have spit. I pretended to be asleep when she asked me what it was. Find out for yourself, I thought, and said nothing. A few weeks later, when she knew her way around town, she got some jeweler to drill a hole through one end of the lucky piece. Then she hung the cow's diamond around her neck on a piece of string, as if it were something valuable. Later on she got a gold link chain.

First my room, then my clothing, then the cow's diamond. But the worst was yet to come when she stole Celestine.

My best friend, Celestine, lived three miles out of town with her half brother and much older half sister, who were Chippewas. There weren't all that many who came down from the reservation, but Celestine's mother had been one. Her name was Regina I-don't-know-what, and she worked for Dutch James, keeping his house when he was a bachelor and after, once they married. I overheard how Celestine came just a month past the wedding, and how Regina brought down the three other children Dutch James hadn't known about. Somehow it worked out. They all lived together up until the time of Dutch James's peculiar death. He froze solid in our very meat locker. But that is an event no one in this house will discuss.

Anyway, those others were never court adopted and went by the last name Kashpaw. Celestine was a James. Because her parents died when Celestine was young, it was the influence of her big sister that was more important to Celestine. She knew the French language, and sometimes Celestine spoke French to lord it over us in school, but more often she got teased for her size and the odd flimsy clothes that her sister Isabel picked out of the dime store in Argus.

Celestine was tall, but not clumsy. More what my mother called statuesque. No one told Celestine what to do. We came and went and played anywhere we felt like. My mother would never have let me play in a graveyard, for example, but when visiting Celestine, that's what we did. There was a cemetery right on the land of Dutch James's homestead, a place filled with the graves of children who died in some plague of cough or influenza. They'd been forgotten, except by us. Their little crosses of wood or bent iron were tilted. We straightened them, even recarved the names on the wooden ones with a kitchen knife. We dug up violets from the oxbow and planted them. The graveyard was our place, because of what we did. We liked to sit there on hot afternoons. It was so pleasant. Wind ruffled the long grass, worms sifted the earth below us, swallows from the mudbanks dove through the sky in pairs. It was a nice place, really, not even very sad. But of course Mary had to ruin it.

I underestimated Mary Adare. Or perhaps I was too trusting, since it was I who suggested we go visit Celestine one day in early summer. I started out by giving Mary a ride on the handlebars of my bicycle, but she was so heavy I could hardly steer.

"You pedal," I said, stopping in the road. She fell off, then jumped up and stood the bicycle upright. I suppose I was heavy, too. But her legs were tireless. Celestine's Indian half brother, Russell Kashpaw, approached us on the way to Celestine's. "Who's your slave today?" he said. "She's cuter than you'll ever be!" I knew he said things like that because he meant the opposite, but Mary didn't. I felt her swell proudly in my old sundress. She made it all the way to Celestine's, and when we got there I jumped off and ran straight in the door.

Celestine was baking, just like a grown-up. Her big sister let her make anything she wanted, no matter how sweet. Celestine and Mary mixed up a batch of cookie dough. Mary liked cooking too. I didn't. So they measured and stirred, timed the stove and put out the cooling racks while I sat at the table with a piece of waxed paper, rolled out the dough, and cut it into fancy shapes.

"Where did you come from?" Celestine asked Mary as we worked.

"She came from Hollywood," I said. Celestine laughed at that, but then she saw it wasn't funny to Mary, and she stopped.

"Truly," said Celestine.

"Minnesota," said Mary.

"Are your mother and father still there?" asked Celestine. "Are they still alive?"

"They're dead," said Mary promptly. My mouth fell open, but before I could get a word of the real truth in, Celestine said.

"Mine are dead too."

And then I knew why Celestine had been asking these questions, when she already knew the whole story and its details from me. Mary and Celestine smiled into each other's eyes. I could see that it was like two people meeting in a crowd, who knew each other from a long time before. And what was also odd, they looked suddenly alike. It was only when they were together. You'd never notice it when they weren't. Celestine's hair was a tarnished red brown. Her skin was olive, her eyes burning black. Mary's eyes were light brown and her hair was dark and lank. Together, like I said, they looked similar. It wasn't even their build. Mary was short and stocky, while Celestine was tall. It was something else, either in the way they acted or the way they talked. Maybe it was a common sort of fierceness.

After they went back to their mixing and measuring, I could see that they were friendlier too. They stood close together, touched shoulders, laughed and admired everything the other one did until it made me sick.

"Mary's going to Saint Catherine's next fall," I interrupted. "She'll be downstairs with the little girls."

Celestine and I were in the seventh grade, which meant our room was on the top floor now, and also that we would wear special blue wool berets in choir. I was trying to remind Celestine that Mary was too young for our serious attention, but I made the mistake of not knowing what had happened last week, when Mary went into the school to take tests from Sister Leopolda.

"I'll be in your class," said Mary.

"What do you mean?" I said. "You're only eleven!"

"Sister put me ahead one grade," said Mary, "into yours."

The shock of it made me bend to my cookie cutting, speechless. She was smart. I already knew she was good at getting her way through pity. But smartness I did not expect, or going ahead a grade. I pressed the little tin cutters of hearts, stars, boys, and girls into the cookie dough. The girl shape reminded me of Mary, square and thick.

"Mary," I said, "aren't you going to tell Celestine what was in the little blue box you stole out of your mother's closet?"

Mary looked right at me. "Not a thing," she said.

Celestine stared at me like I was crazy.

"The jewels," I said to Mary, "the rubies and the diamonds."

We looked each other in the eye, and then Mary seemed to decide something. She blinked at me and reached into the front of the dress. She pulled out the cow's diamond on a string.

"What's that?" Celestine showed her interest at once.

Mary displayed the wonder of how the light glanced through her treasure and fell, fractured and glowing, on the skin of her palm. The two of them stood by the window taking turns with the cow's lens, ignoring me. I sat at the table eating cookies. I ate the feet. I nibbled up the legs. I took the arms off in two snaps and then bit off the head. What was left was a shapeless body. I ate that up too. All the while I was watching Celestine. She wasn't pretty, but her hair was thick and full of red lights. Her dress hung too long behind her knees, but her legs were strong. I liked her tough hands. I liked the way she could stand up to boys. But more than anything else, I liked Celestine because she was mine. She belonged to me, not Mary, who had taken so much already.

"We're going out now," I told Celestine. She always did what I said. She came, although reluctantly, leaving Mary at the window.

"Let's go to our graveyard," I whispered, "I have to show you something."

I was afraid she wouldn't go with me, that she would choose right there to be with Mary. But the habit of following me was too strong to break. She came out the door, leaving Mary to take the last batch of cookies from the oven.

We left the back way and walked out to the graveyard.

"What do you want?" said Celestine when we stepped into the long secret grass. Wild plum shaded us from the house. We were alone.

We stood in the hot silence, breathing air thick with dust and the odor of white violets. She pulled a strand of grass and put the tender end between her lips, then stared at me from under her eyebrows.

Maybe if Celestine had quit staring, I wouldn't have done what I did. But she stood there in her too-long dress, chewing a stem of grass, and let the sun beat down on us until I thought of what to show her. My breasts were tender. They always hurt. But they were something that Mary didn't have.

One by one, I undid the buttons of my blouse. I took it off. My shoulders felt pale and fragile, stiff as wings. I took off my undervest and cupped my breasts in my hands.

My lips were dry. Everything went still.

Celestine broke the stillness by chewing grass, loud, like a rabbit. She hesitated just a moment and then turned on her heel. She left me there, breasts out, never even looking back. I watched her vanish through the bushes, and then a breeze flowed down on me, passing like a light hand. What the breeze made me do next was almost frightening. Something happened, I turned in a slow circle. I tossed my hands out and waved them. I swayed as if I heard music from below. Quicker, and then wilder, I lifted my feet. I began to tap them down, and then I was dancing on their graves.

[1986]

Study and Writing Questions

1. Sita is very concerned with the appearance of clothing, people, and so on. What sorts of appearances most attract her attention? Which sorts that one might expect her to notice does she apparently ignore? How do these preferences on her part affect our understanding as we go through the NARRATIVE?

2. What are the IMAGES of food and food preparation in this narrative? What do they convey?

3. What does work mean in this narrative? Sita seems at one point to suggest that work confers rights on the worker. Is she consistent in this view? How is the SETTING during the Depression significant?

4. When and how do you first notice the unreliability of the NARRATOR? In what ways is she unreliable? How does that unreliability enter into your understanding of the meaning of the narrative?

5. Reread the last paragraph of the narrative. What was Sita feeling when she "was dancing on their graves?" What sort of RESOLUTION does this paragraph provide?

See also Questions for Contrast and Comparison: 37, 38, 92, 97, 158, and 170.

WILLIAM (CUTHBERT) FAULKNER (originally FALKNER) (1897–
1962) *was born near and raised in Oxford, Mississippi. He was the great-
grandson of William Cuthbert Falkner, Mississippi army officer, lawyer, railroad
builder, and melodramatic novelist, and son of Maud and Murry Falkner. William
quit high school (1916), enlisted in the Canadian Royal Air Force (1918), but never
saw combat. Like his father, he held many jobs, from postmaster to deckhand,
through 1929. In 1925 he lived in New Orleans, wrote for the* Times-Picayune
*newspaper, and met Sherwood Anderson, who arranged for the publication of his
first novel,* Soldier's Pay *(1926). After visiting the American expatriate community
in Paris (1925), he returned to Oxford for the rest of his life, except for stints in
Hollywood (including writing for* To Have and Have Not *and* The Big Sleep) *and
as a university writer-in-residence. Married in 1929, he had two children and two
stepchildren. His great saga of fictional Yoknapatawpha County, told in eleven
novels, many highly experimental (*The Sound and the Fury, *1929;* As I Lay Dying,
1930; Light in August, *1932;* Absalom, Absalom! *1936), and four story collections,
explores the often overwhelming burdens of identity, family, class, race and history,
yet, accepting the 1949 Nobel Prize, he said, "man will not merely endure: he will
prevail . . . because he has a soul, a spirit capable of compassion and sacrifice and
endurance."*

Barn Burning

The store in which the Justice of the Peace's court was sitting smelled of cheese.
The boy, crouched on his nail keg at the back of the crowded room, knew he
smelled cheese, and more: from where he sat he could see the ranked shelves
close-packed with the solid, squat, dynamic shapes of tin cans whose labels his
stomach read, not from the lettering which meant nothing to his mind but from
the scarlet devils and the silver curve of fish — this, the cheese which he knew he
smelled and the hermetic meat which his intestines believes he smelled coming in
intermittent gusts momentary and brief between the other constant one, the
smell and sense just a little of fear because mostly of despair and grief, the old
fierce pull of blood. He could not see the table where the Justice sat and before
which his father and his father's enemy (*our* enemy he thought in that despair;
ourn! mine and hisn both! He's my father!) stood, but he could hear them, the two
of them that is, because his father had said no word yet:

"But what proof have you, Mr. Harris?"

"I told you. The hog got into my corn. I caught it up and sent it back to him.
He had no fence that would hold it. I told him so, warned him. The next time I
put the hog in my pen. When he came to get it I gave him enough wire to patch
up his pen. The next time I put the hog up and kept it. I rode down to his house
and saw the wire I gave him still rolled on to the spool in his yard. I told him he
could have the hog when he paid me a dollar pound fee. That evening a nigger
came with the dollar and got the hog. He was a strange nigger. He said, 'He say to
tell you wood and hay kin burn.' I said, 'What?' 'That whut he say to tell you,' the
nigger said. 'Wood and hay kin burn.' That night my barn burned. I got the stock
out but I lost the barn."

"Where is the nigger? Have you got him?"

"He was a strange nigger, I tell you. I don't know what became of him."

"But that's not proof. Don't you see that's not proof?"

"Get that boy up here. He knows." For a moment the boy thought too that the man meant his older brother until Harris said, "Not him. The little one. The boy," and, crouching, small for his age, small and wiry like his father, in patched and faded jeans even too small for him, with straight, uncombed, brown hair and eyes gray and wild as storm scud, he saw the men between himself and the table part and become a lane of grim faces, at the end of which he saw the Justice, a shabby, collarless, graying man in spectacles, beckoning him. He felt no floor under his bare feet; he seemed to walk beneath the palpable weight of the grim turning faces. His father, stiff in his black Sunday coat donned not for the trial but for the moving, did not even look at him. *He aims for me to lie*, he thought, again with that frantic grief and despair. *And I will have to do hit.*

"What's your name, boy?" the Justice said.

"Colonel Sartoris Snopes," the boy whispered.

"Hey?" the Justice said. "Talk louder. Colonel Sartoris? I reckon anybody named for Colonel Sartoris in this country can't help but tell the truth, can they?" The boy said nothing. *Enemy! Enemy!* he thought; for a moment he could not even see, could not see that the Justice's face was kindly nor discern that his voice was troubled when he spoke to the man named Harris: "Do you want me to question this boy?" But he could hear, and during those subsequent long seconds while there was absolutely no sound in the crowded little room save that of quiet and intent breathing it was as if he had swung outward at the end of a grape vine, over a ravine, and at the top of the swing had been caught in a prolonged instant of mesmerized gravity, weightless in time.

"No!" Harris said violently, explosively. "Damnation! Send him out of here!" Now time, the fluid world, rushed beneath him again, the voices coming to him again through the smell of cheese and sealed meat, the fear and despair and the old grief of blood:

"This case is closed. I can't find against you, Snopes, but I can give you advice. Leave this country and don't come back to it."

His father spoke for the first time, his voice cold and harsh, level, without emphasis: "I aim to. I don't figure to stay in a country among people who . . ." he said something unprintable and vile, addressed to no one.

"That'll do," the Justice said. "Take your wagon and get out of this country before dark. Case dismissed."

His father turned, and he followed the stiff black coat, the wiry figure walking a little stiffly from where a Confederate provost's man's musket ball had taken him in the heel on a stolen horse thirty years ago, followed the two backs now, since his older brother had appeared from somewhere in the crowd, no taller than the father but thicker, chewing tobacco steadily, between the two lines of grim-faced men and out of the store and across the worn gallery and down the sagging steps and among the dogs and half-grown boys in the mild May dust, where as he passed a voice hissed:

"Barn burner!"

Again he could not see, whirling; there was a face in a red haze, moonlike, bigger than the full moon, the owner of it half again his size, he leaping in the red haze toward the face, feeling no blow, feeling no shock when his head struck the earth, scrabbling up and leaping again, feeling no blow this time either and tasting no blood, scrabbling up to see the other boy in full flight and himself already leaping into pursuit as his father's hand jerked him back, the harsh, cold voice speaking above him: "Go get in the wagon."

It stood in a grove of locusts and mulberries across the road. His two hulking sisters in their Sunday dresses and his mother and her sister in calico and sunbonnets were already in it, sitting on and among the sorry residue of the dozen and more movings which even the boy could remember—the battered stove, the broken beds and chairs, the clock inlaid with mother-of-pearl, which would not run, stopped at some fourteen minutes past two o'clock of a dead and forgotten day and time, which had been his mother's dowry. She was crying, though when she saw him she drew her sleeve across her face and began to descend from the wagon. "Get back," the father said.

"He's hurt. I got to get some water and wash his . . ."

"Get back in the wagon," his father said. He got in too, over the tail-gate. His father mounted to the seat where the older brother already sat and struck the gaunt mules two savage blows with the peeled willow, but without heat. It was not even sadistic; it was exactly that same quality which in later years would cause his descendants to over-run the engine before putting a motor car into motion, striking and reining back in the same movement. The wagon went on, the store with its quiet crowd of grimly watching men dropped behind; a curve in the road hid it. *Forever* he thought. *Maybe he's done satisfied now, now that he has . . .* stopping himself, not to say it aloud even to himself. His mother's hand touched his shoulder.

"Does hit hurt?" she said.

"Naw," he said. "Hit don't hurt. Lemme be."

"Can't you wipe some of the blood off before hit dries?"

"I'll wash tonight," he said. "Lemme be, I tell you."

The wagon went on. He did not know where they were going. None of them ever did or ever asked, because it was always somewhere, always a house of sorts waiting for them a day or two days or even three days away. Likely his father had already arranged to make a crop on another farm before he . . . Again he had to stop himself. He (the father) always did. There was something about his wolflike independence and even courage when the advantage was at least neutral which impressed strangers, as if they got from his latent ravening ferocity not so much a sense of dependability as a feeling that his ferocious conviction in the rightness of his own actions would be of advantage to all whose interest lay with his.

That night they camped, in a grove of oaks and beeches where a spring ran. The nights were still cool and they had a fire against it, of a rail lifted from a nearby fence and cut into lengths—a small fire, neat, niggard almost, a shrewd fire; such fires were his father's habit and custom always, even in freezing weather. Older, the boy might have remarked this and wondered why not a big one; why should not a man who had not only seen the waste and extravagance of war, but who had in his blood an inherent voracious prodigality with material not his own, have burned everything in sight? Then he might have gone a step farther and thought that that was the reason: that niggard blaze was the living fruit of nights passed during those four years in the woods hiding from all men, blue or gray, with his strings of horses (captured horses, he called them). And older still, he might have divined the true reason: that the element of fire spoke to some deep mainspring of his father's being, as the element of steel or of powder spoke to other men, as the one weapon for the preservation of integrity, else breath were not worth the breathing, and hence to be regarded with respect and used with discretion.

But he did not think this now and he had seen those same niggard blazes all his life. He merely ate his supper beside it and was already half asleep over his iron plate when his father called him, and once more he followed the stiff back, the stiff and ruthless limp, up the slope and on to the starlit road where, turning, he could see his father against the stars but without face or depth—a shape black, flat, and bloodless as though cut from tin in the iron folds of the frockcoat which had not been made for him, the voice harsh like tin and without heat like tin:

"You were fixing to tell them. You would have told him." He didn't answer. His father struck him with the flat of his hand on the side of the head, hard but without heat, exactly as he had struck the two mules at the store, exactly as he would strike either of them with any stick in order to kill a horse fly, his voice still without heat or anger: "You're getting to be a man. You got to learn. You got to learn to stick to your own blood or you ain't going to have any blood to stick to you. Do you think either of them, any man there this morning, would? Don't you know all they wanted was a chance to get at me because they knew I had them beat? Eh?" Later, twenty years later, he was to tell himself, "If I had said they wanted only truth, justice, he would have hit me again." But now he said nothing. He was not crying. He just stood there. "Answer me," his father said.

"Yes," he whispered. His father turned.

"Get on to bed. We'll be there tomorrow."

Tomorrow they were there. In the early afternoon the wagon stopped before a paintless two-room house identical almost with the dozen others it had stopped before even in the boy's ten years, and again, as on the other dozen occasions, his mother and aunt got down and began to unload the wagon, although his two sisters and his father and brother had not moved.

"Likely hit ain't fitten for hawgs," one of the sisters said.

"Nevertheless, fit it will and you'll hog it and like it," his father said. "Get out of them chairs and help your Ma unload."

The two sisters got down, big, bovine, in a flutter of cheap ribbons; one of them drew from the jumbled wagon bed a battered lantern, the other a worn broom. His father handed the reins to the older son and began to climb stiffly over the wheel. "When they get unloaded, take the team to the barn and feed them." Then he said, and at first the boy thought he was still speaking to his brother: "Come with me."

"Me?" he said.

"Yes," his father said. "You."

"Abner," his mother said. His father paused and looked back—the harsh level stare beneath the shaggy, graying, irascible brows.

"I reckon I'll have a word with the man that aims to begin tomorrow owning me body and soul for the next eight months."

They went back up the road. A week ago—or before last night, that is—he would have asked where they were going, but not now. His father had struck him before last night but never before had he paused afterward to explain why; it was as if the blow and the following calm, outrageous voice still rang, repercussed, divulging nothing to him save the terrible handicap of being young, the light weight of his few years, just heavy enough to prevent his soaring free of the world as it seemed to be ordered but not heavy enough to keep him footed solid in it, to resist it and try to change the course of its events.

Presently he could see the grove of oaks and cedars and the other flowering trees and shrubs where the house would be, though not the house yet. They walked beside a fence massed with honeysuckle and Cherokee roses and came to a gate swinging open between two brick pillars, and now, beyond a sweep of drive, he saw the house for the first time and at that instant he forgot his father and the terror and despair both, and even when he remembered his father again (who had not stopped) the terror and despair did not return. Because, for all the twelve movings, they had sojourned until now in a poor country, a land of small farms and fields and houses, and he had never seen a house like this before. *Hit's big as a courthouse* he thought quietly, with a surge of peace and joy whose reason he could not have thought into words, being too young for that: *They are safe from him. People whose lives are a part of this peace and dignity are beyond his touch, he no more to them than a buzzing wasp: capable of stinging for a little moment but that's all; the spell of this peace and dignity rendering even the barns and stable and cribs which belong to it impervious to the puny flames he might contrive . . .* this, the peace and joy, ebbing for an instant as he looked again at the stiff black back, the stiff and implacable limp of the figure which was not dwarfed by the house, for the reason that it had never looked big anywhere and which now, against the serene columned backdrop, had more than ever that impervious quality of something cut ruthlessly from tin, depthless, as though, sidewise to the sun, it would cast no shadow. Watching him, the boy remarked the absolutely undeviating course which his father held and saw the stiff foot come squarely down in a pile of fresh droppings where a horse had stood in the drive and which his father could have avoided by a simple change of stride. But it ebbed only for a moment, though he could not have thought this into words either, walking on in the spell of the house, which he could even want but without envy, without sorrow, certainly never with that ravening and jealous rage which unknown to him walked in the ironlike black coat before him: *Maybe he will feel it too. Maybe it will even change him now from what may be he couldn't help but be.*

They crossed the portico. Now he could hear his father's stiff foot as it came down on the boards with clocklike finality, a sound out of all proportion to the displacement of the body it bore and which was not dwarfed either by the white door before it, as though it had attained to a sort of vicious and ravening minimum not to be dwarfed by anything—the flat, wide, black hat, the formal coat of broadcloth which had once been black but which had now that friction-glazed greenish cast of the bodies of old house flies, the lifted sleeve which was too large, the lifted hand like a curled claw. The door opened so promptly that the boy knew the Negro must have been watching them all the time, an old man with neat grizzled hair, in a linen jacket, who stood barring the door with his body, saying, "Wipe yo foots, white man, fo you come in here. Major ain't home nohow."

"Get out of my way, nigger," his father said, without heat too, flinging the door back and the Negro also and entering, his hat still on his head. And now the boy saw the prints of the stiff foot on the doorsill and saw them appear on the pale rug behind the machinelike deliberation of the foot which seemed to bear (or transmit) twice the weight which the body compassed. The Negro was shouting "Miss Lula! Miss Lula!" somewhere behind them, then the boy, deluged as though by a warm wave by a suave turn of carpeted stair and a pendant glitter of chandeliers and a mute gleam of gold frames, heard the swift feet and saw her too, a lady—perhaps he had never seen her like before either—in a gray, smooth gown with lace at the throat and an apron tied at the waist and the sleeves turned back, wiping cake or biscuit dough from her hands with a towel as she came up the hall, looking not at his father at all but at the tracks on the blond rug with an expression of incredulous amazement.

"I tried," the Negro cried. "I tole him to . . ."

"Will you please go away?" she said in a shaking voice. "Major de Spain is not at home. Will you please go away?"

His father had not spoken again. He did not speak again. He did not even look at her. He just stood stiff in the center of the rug, in his hat, the shaggy iron-gray brows twitching slightly above the pebble-colored eyes as he appeared to examine the house with brief deliberation. Then with the same deliberation he turned; the boy watched him pivot on the good leg and saw the stiff foot drag round the arc of the turning, leaving a final long and fading smear. His father never looked at it, he never once looked down at the rug. The Negro held the door. It closed behind them, upon the hysteric and indistinguishable woman-wail. His father stopped at the top of the steps and scraped his boot clean on the edge of it. At the gate he stopped again. He stood for a moment, planted stiffly on the stiff foot, looking back at the house. "Pretty and white, ain't it?" he said. "That's sweat. Nigger sweat. Maybe it ain't white enough yet to suit him. Maybe he wants to mix some white sweat with it."

Two hours later the boy was chopping wood behind the house within which his mother and aunt and the two sisters (the mother and aunt, not the two girls, he knew that; even at this distance and muffled by walls the flat loud voices of the two girls emanated an incorrigible idle inertia) were setting up the stove to prepare a meal, when he heard the hooves and saw the linen-clad man on a fine sorrel mare, whom he recognized even before he saw the rolled rug in front of the Negro youth following on a fat bay carriage horse—a suffused, angry face vanishing, still at full gallop, beyond the corner of the house where his father and brother were sitting in the two tilted chairs; and a moment later, almost before he could have put the axe down, he heard the hooves again and watched the sorrel mare go back out of the yard, already galloping again. Then his father began to shout one of the sisters' names, who presently emerged backward from the kitchen door dragging the rolled rug along the ground by one end while the other sister walked behind it.

"If you ain't going to tote, go on and set up the wash pot," the first said.

"You, Sarty!" the second shouted. "Set up the wash pot!" His father appeared at the door, framed against that shabbiness, as he had been against that other bland perfection, impervious to either, the mother's anxious face at his shoulder.

"Go on," the father said. "Pick it up." The two sisters stooped, broad, lethargic; stooping, they presented an incredible expanse of pale cloth and a flutter of tawdry ribbons.

"If I thought enough of a rug to have to git hit all the way from France I wouldn't keep hit where folks coming in would have to tromp on hit," the first said. They raised the rug.

"Abner," the mother said. "Let me do it."

"You go back and git dinner," his father said. "I'll tend to this."

From the woodpile through the rest of the afternoon the boy watched them, the rug spread flat in the dust beside the bubbling wash pot, the two sisters stooping over it with that profound and lethargic reluctance, while the father stood over them in turn, implacable and grim, driving them though never raising his voice again. He could smell the harsh homemade lye they were using; he saw his mother come to the door once and look toward them with an expression not anxious now but very like despair; he saw his father turn, and he fell to with the axe and saw from the corner of his eye his father raise from the ground a flattish fragment of field stone and examine it and return to the pot, and this time his mother actually spoke: "Abner. Abner. Please don't. Please, Abner."

Then he was done too. It was dusk; the whippoorwills had already begun. He could smell coffee from the room where they would presently eat the cold food remaining from the mid-afternoon meal, though when he entered the house he realized they were having coffee again probably because there was a fire on the hearth, before which the rug now lay spread over the backs of the two chairs. The tracks of his father's foot were gone. Where they had been were now long, water-cloudy scoriations resembling the sporadic course of a Lilliputian mowing machine.

It still hung there while they ate the cold food and then went to bed, scattered without order or claim up and down the two rooms, his mother in one bed, where his father would later lie, the older brother in the other, himself, the aunt, and the two sisters on pallets on the floor. But his father was not in bed yet. The last thing the boy remembered was the depthless, harsh silhouette of the hat and coat bending over the rug and it seemed to him that he had not even closed his eyes when the silhouette was standing over him, the fire almost dead behind it, the stiff foot prodding him awake. "Catch up the mule," his father said.

When he returned with the mule his father was standing in the black door, the rolled rug over his shoulder. "Ain't you going to ride?" he said.

"No. Give me your foot."

He bent his knee into his father's hand, the wiry, surprising power flowed smoothly, rising, he rising with it, on to the mule's bare back (they had owned a saddle once; the boy could remember it though not when or where) and with the same effortlessness his father swung the rug up in front of him. Now in the starlight they retraced the afternoon's path, up the dusty road rife with honey-suckle, through the gate and up the black tunnel of the drive to the lightless house, where he sat on the mule and felt the rough warp of the rug drag across his thighs and vanish.

"Don't you want me to help?" he whispered. His father did not answer and now he heard again that stiff foot striking the hollow portico with that wooden and clocklike deliberation, that outrageous overstatement of the weight it carried. The rug, hunched, not flung (the boy could tell that even in the darkness) from his father's shoulder, struck the angle of wall and floor with a sound unbelievably loud, thunderous, then the foot again, unhurried and enormous; a light came on in the house and the boy sat, tense, breathing steadily and quietly and just a little fast, though the foot itself did not increase its beat at all, descending the steps now; now the boy could see him.

"Don't you want to ride now?" he whispered. "We kin both ride now," the light within the house altering now, flaring up and sinking. *He's coming down the stairs now*, he thought. He had already ridden the mule up beside the horse block; presently his father was up behind him and he doubled the reins over and slashed the mule across the neck, but before the animal could begin to trot the hard, thin arm came round him, the hard, knotted hand jerking the mule back to a walk.

In the first red rays of the sun they were in the lot, putting plow gear on the mules. This time the sorrel mare was in the lot before he heard it at all, the rider collarless and even bareheaded, trembling, speaking in a shaking voice as the woman in the house had done, his father merely looking up once before stooping again to the hame he was buckling, so that the man on the mare spoke to his stooping back:

"You must realize you have ruined that rug. Wasn't there anybody here, any of your women . . ." He ceased, shaking, the boy watching him, the older brother leaning now in the stable door, chewing, blinking slowly and steadily at nothing apparently. "It cost a hundred dollars. But you never had a hundred dollars. You never will. So I'm going to charge you twenty bushels of corn against your crop. I'll add it in your contract and when you come to the commissary you can sign it. That won't keep Mrs. de Spain quiet but maybe it will teach you to wipe your feet off before you enter her house again."

Then he was gone. The boy looked at his father, who had still not spoken or even looked up again, who was now adjusting the logger-head in the hame.

"Pap," he said. His father looked at him—the inscrutable face, the shaggy brows beneath which the gray eyes glinted coldly. Suddenly the boy went toward him, fast, stopping as suddenly. "You done the best you could!" he cried. "If he wanted hit done different why didn't he wait and tell you how? He won't git no twenty bushels! He won't git none! We'll get hit and hide hit! I kin watch . . ."

"Did you put the cutter back in that straight stock like I told you?"

"No, sir," he said.

"Then go do it."

That was Wednesday. During the rest of that week he worked steadily, at what was within his scope and some which was beyond it, with an industry that did not need to be driven nor even commanded twice; he had this from his mother, with the difference that some at least of what he did he liked to do, such as splitting wood with the half-size axe which his mother and aunt had earned, or saved money somehow, to present him with at Christmas. In company with the two older women (and on one afternoon, even one of the sisters), he built pens for the shoat and the cow which were a part of his father's contract with the landlord, and one afternoon, his father being absent, gone somewhere on one of the mules, he went to the field.

They were running a middle buster now, his brother holding the plow straight while he handled the reins, and walking beside the straining mule, the rich black soil shearing cool and damp against his bare ankles, he thought *Maybe this is the end of it. Maybe even that twenty bushels that seems hard to have to pay for just a rug will be a cheap price for him to stop forever and always from being what he used to be;* thinking, dreaming now, so that his brother had to speak sharply to him to mind the mule: *Maybe he even won't collect the twenty bushels. Maybe it will all add up and balance and vanish — corn, rug, fire; the terror and grief, the being pulled two ways like between two teams of horses — gone, done with for ever and ever.*

Then it was Saturday; he looked up from beneath the mule he was harnessing and saw his father in the black coat and hat. "Not that," his father said. "The wagon gear." And then, two hours later, sitting in the wagon bed behind his father and brother on the seat, the wagon accomplished a final curve, and he saw the weathered paintless store with its tattered tobacco- and patent-medicine posters and the tethered wagons and saddle animals below the gallery. He mounted the gnawed steps behind his father and brother, and there again was the lane of quiet, watching faces for the three of them to walk through. He saw a man in spectacles sitting at the plank table and he did not need to be told this was a Justice of the Peace; he sent one glare of fierce, exultant, partisan defiance at the man in collar and cravat now, whom he had seen but twice before in his life, and that on a galloping horse, who now wore on his face an expression not of rage but of amazed unbelief which the boy could not have known was at the incredible circumstance of being sued by one of his own tenants, and came and stood against his father and cried at the Justice: "He ain't done it! He ain't burnt . . ."

"Go back to the wagon," his father said.

"Burnt?" the Justice said. "Do I understand this rug was burned too?"

"Does anybody here claim it was?" his father said. "Go back to the wagon." But he did not, he merely retreated to the rear of the room, crowded as that other had been, but not to sit down this time, instead, to stand pressing among the motionless bodies, listening to the voices:

"And you claim twenty bushels of corn is too high for the damage you did to the rug?"

"He brought the rug to me and said he wanted the tracks washed out of it. I washed the tracks out and took the rug back to him."

"But you didn't carry the rug back to him in the same condition it was before you made the tracks on it."

His father did not answer, and now for perhaps half a minute there was no sound at all save that of breathing, the faint, steady suspiration of complete and intent listening.

"You decline to answer that, Mr. Snopes?" Again his father did not answer. "I'm going to find against you, Mr. Snopes. I'm going to find that you were responsible for the injury to Major de Spain's rug and hold you liable for it. But twenty bushels of corn seems a little high for a man in your circumstances to have to pay. Major de Spain claims it cost a hundred dollars. October corn will be worth fifty cents. I figure that if Major de Spain can stand a ninety-five dollar loss on something he paid cash for, you can stand a five-dollar loss you haven't earned yet. I hold you in damages to Major de Spain to the amount of ten bushels of corn over and above your contract with him, to be paid to him out of your crop at gathering time. Court adjourned."

It had taken no time hardly, the morning was but half begun. He thought they would return home and perhaps back to the field, since they were late, far behind all other farmers. But instead his father passed on behind the wagon, merely indicating with his hand for the older brother to follow with it, and crossed the road toward the blacksmith shop opposite, pressing on after his father, overtaking him, speaking, whispering up at the harsh, calm face beneath the weathered hat: "He won't git no ten bushels neither. He won't git one. We'll . . ." until his father glanced for an instant down at him, the face absolutely calm, the grizzled eyebrows tangled above the cold eyes, the voice almost pleasant, almost gentle:

"You think so? Well, we'll wait till October anyway."

The matter of the wagon—the setting of a spoke or two and the tightening of the tires—did not take long either, the business of the tires accomplished by driving the wagon into the spring behind the shop and letting it stand there, the mules nuzzling into the water from time to time, and the boy on the seat with the idle reins, looking up the slope and through the sooty tunnel of the shed where the slow hammer rang and where his father sat on an upended cypress bolt, easily, either talking or listening, still sitting there when the boy brought the dripping wagon up out of the branch and halted it before the door.

"Take them on to the shade and hitch," his father said. He did so and returned. His father and the smith and a third man squatting on his heels inside the door were talking, about crops and animals; the boy, squatting too in the ammoniac dust and hoof-parings and scales of rust, heard his father tell a long and unhurried story out of the time before the birth of the older brother even when he had been a professional horsetrader. And then his father came up beside him where he stood before a tattered last year's circus poster on the other side of the store, gazing rapt and quiet at the scarlet horses, the incredible poisings and convolutions of tulle and tights and the painted leers of comedians, and said, "It's time to eat."

But not at home. Squatting beside his brother against the front wall, he watched his father emerge from the store and produce from a paper sack a segment of cheese and divide it carefully and deliberately into three with his pocket knife and produce crackers from the same sack. They all three squatted on the gallery and ate, slowly, without talking; then in the store again, they drank from a tin dipper tepid water smelling of the cedar bucket and of living beech trees. And still they did not go home. It was a horse lot this time, a tall rail fence upon and along which men stood and sat and out of which one by one horses were led, to be walked and trotted and then cantered back and forth along the road while the slow swapping and buying went on and the sun began to slant westward, they—the three of them—watching and listening, the older brother with his muddy eyes and his steady, inevitable tobacco, the father commenting now and then on certain of the animals, to no one in particular.

It was after sundown when they reached home. They ate supper by lamplight, then, sitting on the doorstep, the boy watched the night fully accomplish, listening to the whippoorwills and the frogs, when he heard his mother's voice: "Abner! No! No! Oh, God. Oh, God. Abner!" and he rose, whirled, and saw the altered light through the door where a candle stub now burned in a bottle neck on the table and his father, still in the hat and coat, at once formal and burlesque as though dressed carefully for some shabby and ceremonial violence, emptying the reservoir of the lamp back into the five-gallon kerosene can from which it had been filled, while the mother tugged at his arm until he shifted the lamp to the other hand and flung her back, not savagely or viciously, just hard, into the wall, her hands flung out against the wall for balance, her mouth open and in her face the same quality of hopeless despair as had been in her voice. Then his father saw him standing in the door.

"Go to the barn and get that can of oil we were oiling the wagon with," he said. The boy did not move. Then he could speak.

"What . . ." he cried. "What are you . . ."

"Go get that oil," his father said. "Go."

Then he was moving, running, outside the house, toward the stable: this the old habit, the old blood which he had not been permitted to choose for himself, which had been bequeathed him willy nillly and which had run for so long (and who knew where, battening on what of outrage and savagery and lust) before it came to him. *I could keep on,* he thought. *I could run on and on and never look back, never need to see his face again. Only I can't. I can't,* the rusted can in his hand now, the liquid sploshing in it as he ran back to the house and into it, into the sound of his mother's weeping in the next room, and handed the can to his father.

"Ain't you going to even send a nigger?" he cried. "At least you sent a nigger before!"

This time his father didn't strike him. The hand came even faster than the blow had, the same hand which had set the can on the table with almost excruciating care flashing from the can toward him too quick for him to follow it, gripping him by the back of his shirt and on to tiptoe before he had seen it quit the can, the face stooping at him in breathless and frozen ferocity, the cold, dead voice speaking over him to the older brother who leaned against the table, chewing with that steady, curious, sidewise motion of cows:

"Empty the can into the big one and go on. I'll catch up with you."

"Better tie him up to the bedpost," the brother said.

"Do like I told you," the father said. Then the boy was moving, his bunched shirt and the hard, bony hand between his shoulder-blades, his toes just touching the floor, across the room and into the other one, past the sisters sitting with spread heavy thighs in the two chairs over the cold hearth, and to where his mother and aunt sat side by side on the bed, the aunt's arms about his mother's shoulders.

"Hold him," the father said. The aunt made a startled movement. "Not you," the father said. "Lennie. Take hold of him. I want to see you do it." His mother took him by the wrist. "You'll hold him better than that. If he gets loose don't you know what he is going to do? He will go up yonder." He jerked his head toward the road. "Maybe I'd better tie him."

"I'll hold him," his mother whispered.

"See you do then." Then his father was gone, the stiff foot heavy and measured upon the boards, ceasing at last.

Then he began to struggle. His mother caught him in both arms, he jerking and wrenching at them. He would be stronger in the end, he knew that. But he had no time to wait for it. "Lemme go!" he cried. "I don't want to have to hit you!"

"Let him go!" the aunt said. "If he don't go, before God, I am going up there myself!"

"Don't you see I can't?" his mother cried. "Sarty! Sarty! No! No! Help me, Lizzie!"

Then he was free. His aunt grasped at him but it was too late. He whirled, running, his mother stumbled forward on to her knees behind him, crying to the nearer sister: "Catch him, Net! Catch him!" But that was too late too, the sister (the sisters were twins, born at the same time, yet either of them now gave the impression of being, encompassing as much living meat and volume and weight as any other two of the family) not yet having begun to rise from her chair, her head, face, alone merely turned, presenting to him in the flying instant an astonishing expanse of young female features untroubled by any surprise even, wearing only an expression of bovine interest. Then he was out of the room, out of the house, in the mild dust of the starlit road and the heavy rifeness of honeysuckle, the pale ribbon unspooling with terrific slowness under his running feet, reaching the gate at last and turning in, running, his heart and lungs drumming, on up the drive toward the lighted house, the lighted door. He did not knock, he burst in, sobbing for breath, incapable for the moment of speech; he saw the astonished face of the Negro in the linen jacket without knowing when the Negro had appeared.

"De Spain!" he cried, panted. "Where's . . ." then he saw the white man too emerging from a white door down the hall. "Barn!" he cried. "Barn!"

"What?" the white man said. "Barn?"

"Yes!" the boy cried. "Barn!"

"Catch him!" the white man shouted.

But it was too late this time too. The Negro grasped his shirt, but the entire sleeve, rotten with washing, carried away, and he was out that door too and in the drive again, and had actually never ceased to run even while he was screaming into the white man's face.

Behind him the white man was shouting, "My horse! Fetch my horse!" and he thought for an instant of cutting across the park and climbing the fence into the road, but he did not know the park nor how high the vine-massed fence might be and he dared not risk it. So he ran on down the drive, blood and breath roaring; presently he was in the road again though he could not see it. He could not hear either: the galloping mare was almost upon him before he heard her, and even then he held his course, as if the very urgency of his wild grief and need must in a moment more find him wings, waiting until the ultimate instant to hurl himself aside and into the weed-choked roadside ditch as the horse thundered past and on, for an instant in furious silhouette against the stars, the tranquil early summer night sky which, even before the shape of the horse and rider vanished, strained abruptly and violently upward: a long, swirling roar incredible and soundless, blotting the stars, and he springing up and into the road again, running again, knowing it was too late yet still running even after he heard the shot and, an instant later, two shots, pausing now without knowing he had ceased to run, crying "Pap! Pap!", running again before he knew he had begun to run, stumbling, tripping over something and scrabbling up again without ceasing to run, looking backward over his shoulder at the glare as he got up, running on among the invisible trees, panting, sobbing, "Father! Father!"

At midnight he was sitting on the crest of a hill. He did not know it was midnight and he did not know how far he had come. But there was no glare behind him now and he sat now, his back toward what he had called home for four days anyhow, his face toward the dark woods which he would enter when breath was strong again, small, shaking steadily in the chill darkness, hugging himself into the remainder of his thin, rotten shirt, the grief and despair now no longer terror and fear but just grief and despair. *Father. My father*, he thought. "He was brave!" he cried suddenly, aloud but not loud, no more than a whisper: "He was! He was in the war! He was in Colonel Sartoris' cav'ry!" not knowing that his father had gone to that war a private in the fine old European sense, wearing no uniform, admitting the authority of and giving fidelity to no man or army or flag, going to war as Malbrouck himself did: for booty — it meant nothing and less than nothing to him if it were enemy booty or his own.

The slow constellations wheeled on. It would be dawn and then sun-up after a while and he would be hungry. But that would be tomorrow and now he was only cold, and walking would cure that. His breathing was easier now and he decided to get up and go on, and then he found that he had been asleep because he knew it was almost dawn, the night almost over. He could tell that from the whippoorwills. They were everywhere now among the dark trees below him, constant and inflectioned and ceaseless, so that, as the instant for giving over to the day birds drew nearer and nearer, there was no interval at all between them. He got up. He was a little stiff, but walking would cure that too as it would the cold, and soon there would be the sun. He went on down the hill, toward the dark woods within which the liquid silver voices of the birds called unceasing — the rapid and urgent beating of the urgent and quiring heart of the late spring night. He did not look back.

[1939]

Study and Writing Questions

1. What is the central CONFLICT of this STORY?
2. What are the meanings of fire as presented in the paragraph beginning, "That night they camped . . ."? What other meanings, if any, does fire have in the story?
3. Why are Abner Snopes's motions always deliberate?
4. What is the significance of race, gender, and age in this story? Which of these factors are the most important under what circumstances? To what extent is the story about these factors and to what extent is it about something that transcends them?
5. What are the key details (IMAGES, SETTING, situation, and so on) of the first paragraph? What do they imply? What are the key details of the last paragraph? What do they imply? How are the opening and closing paragraphs related? What sort of RESOLUTION, if any, do they suggest for the story?

See also Questions for Contrast and Comparison: 15, 33, 34, 55, 63, 70, 79, 80, 81, 84, 103, 119, 167, 176, and 239.

Dry September

Through the bloody September twilight, aftermath of sixty-two rainless days, it had gone like a fire in dry grass—the rumor, the story, whatever it was. Something about Miss Minnie Cooper and a Negro. Attacked, insulted, frightened: none of them, gathered in the barber shop on that Saturday evening where the ceiling fan stirred, without freshening it, the vitiated air, sending back upon them, in recurrent surges of stale pomade and lotion, their own stale breath and odors, knew exactly what had happened.

"Except it wasn't Will Mayes," a barber said. He was a man of middle age; a thin, sand-colored man with a mild face, who was shaving a client. "I know Will Mayes. He's a good nigger. And I know Miss Minnie Cooper, too."

"What do you know about her?" a second barber said.

"Who is she?" the client said. "A young girl?"

"No," the barber said. "She's about forty, I reckon. She ain't married. That's why I dont believe—"

"Believe, hell!" a hulking youth in a sweat-stained silk shirt said. "Wont you take a white woman's word before a nigger's?"

"I dont believe Will Mayes did it," the barber said. "I know Will Mayes."

"Maybe you know who did it, then. Maybe you already got him out of town, you damn niggerlover."

"I dont believe anybody did anything. I dont believe anything happened. I leave it to you fellows if them ladies that get old without getting married dont have notions that a man cant—"

"Then you are a hell of a white man," the client said. He moved under the cloth. The youth had sprung to his feet.

"You dont?" he said. "Do you accuse a white woman of lying?"

The barber held the razor poised above the half-risen client. He did not look around.

"It's this durn weather," another said. "It's enough to make a man do anything. Even to her."

Nobody laughed. The barber said in his mild, stubborn tone: "I aint accusing nobody of nothing. I just know and you fellows know how a woman that never—"

"You damn niggerlover!" the youth said.

"Shut up, Butch," another said. "We'll get the facts in plenty of time to act."

"Who is? Who's getting them?" the youth said. "Facts, hell! I—"

"You're a fine white man," the client said. "Aint you?" In his frothy beard he looked like a desert rat in moving pictures. "You can tell them, Jack," he said to the youth. "If there aint any white men in this town, you can count on me, even if I aint only a drummer and a stranger."

"That's right, boys," the barber said. "Find out the truth first. I know Will Mayes."

"Well, by God!" the youth shouted. "To think that a white man in this town—"

"Shut up, Butch," the second speaker said. "We got plenty of time."

The client sat up. He looked at the speaker. "Do you claim that anything excuses a nigger attacking a white woman? Do you mean to tell me you are a white man and you'll stand for it? You better go back North where you came from. The South dont want your kind here."

"North what?" the second said. "I was born and raised in this town."

"Well, by God!" the youth said. He looked about with a strained, baffled gaze, as if he was trying to remember what it was he wanted to say or to do. He drew his sleeve across his sweating face. "Damn if I'm going to let a white woman—"

"You tell them, Jack," the drummer said. "By God, if they—"

The screen door crashed open. A man stood in the floor, his feet apart and his heavy-set body poised easily. His white shirt was open at the throat; he wore a felt hat. His hot, bold glance swept the group. His name was McLendon. He had commanded troops at the front in France and had been decorated for valor.

"Well," he said, "are you going to sit there and let a black son rape a white woman on the streets of Jefferson?"

Butch sprang up again. The silk of his shirt clung flat to his heavy shoulders. At each armpit was a dark halfmoon. "That's what I been telling them! That's what I—"

"Did it really happen?" a third said. "This aint the first man scare she ever had, like Hawkshaw says. Wasn't there something about a man on the kitchen roof, watching her undress, about a year ago?"

"What?" the client said. "What's that?" The barber had been slowly forcing him back into the chair; he arrested himself reclining, his head lifted, the barber still pressing him down.

McLendon whirled on the third speaker. "Happen? What the hell difference does it make? Are you going to let the black sons get away with it until one really does it?"

"That's what I'm telling them!" Butch shouted. He cursed, long and steady, pointless.

"Here, here," a fourth said. "Not so loud. Dont talk so loud."

"Sure," McLendon said; "no talking necessary at all. I've done my talking. Who's with me?" He poised on the balls of his feet, roving his gaze.

The barber held the drummer's face down, the razor poised. "Find out the facts first, boys. I know Willy Mayes. It wasn't him. Let's get the sheriff and do this thing right."

McLendon whirled upon him his furious, rigid face. The barber did not look away. They looked like men of different races. The other barbers had ceased also above their prone clients. "You mean to tell me," McLendon said, "that you'd take a nigger's word before a white woman's? Why, you damn niggerloving—"

The third speaker rose and grasped McLendon's arm; he too had been a soldier. "Now, now. Let's figure this thing out. Who knows anything about what really happened?"

"Figure out hell!" McLendon jerked his arm free. "All that're with me get up from there. The ones that ain't—" He roved his gaze, dragging his sleeve across his face.

Three men rose. The drummer in the chair sat up. "Here," he said, jerking at the cloth about his neck; "get this rag off me. I'm with him. I dont live here, but by God, if our mothers and wives and sisters—" He smeared the cloth over his face and flung it to the floor. McLendon stood in the floor and cursed the others.

Another rose and moved toward him. The remainder sat uncomfortable, not looking at one another, then one by one they rose and joined him.

The barber picked the cloth from the floor. He began to fold it neatly. "Boys, dont do that. Will Mayes never done it. I know."

"Come on," McLendon said. He whirled. From his hip pocket protruded the butt of a heavy automatic pistol. They went out. The screen door crashed behind them reverberant in the dead air.

The barber wiped the razor carefully and swiftly, and put it away, and ran to the rear, and took his hat from the wall. "I'll be back as soon as I can," he said to the other barbers. "I cant let—" He went out, running. The two other barbers followed him to the door and caught it on the rebound, leaning out and looking up the street after him. The air was flat and dead. It had a metallic taste at the base of the tongue.

"What can he do?" the first said. The second one was saying "Jees Christ, Jees Christ" under his breath. "I'd just as lief be Will Mayes as Hawk, if he gets McLendon riled."

"Jees Christ, Jees Christ," the second whispered.

"You reckon he really done it to her?" the first said.

II

She was thirty-eight or thirty-nine. She lived in a small frame house with her invalid mother and a thin, sallow, unflagging aunt, where each morning between ten and eleven she would appear on the porch in a lace-trimmed boudoir cap, to sit swinging in the porch swing until noon. After dinner she lay down for a while, until the afternoon began to cool. Then, in one of the three or four new voile dresses which she had each summer, she would go downtown to spend the afternoon in the stores with the other ladies, where they would handle the goods and haggle over the prices in cold, immediate voices, without any intention of buying.

She was of comfortable people—not the best in Jefferson, but good people enough—and she was still on the slender side of ordinary-looking, with a bright, faintly haggard manner and dress. When she was young she had had a slender nervous body and a sort of hard vivacity which had enabled her for a time to ride upon the crest of the town's social life as exemplified by the high school party and church social period of her contemporaries while still children enough to be unclassconscious.

She was the last to realize that she was losing ground; that those among whom she had been a little brighter and louder flame than any other were beginning to learn the pleasure of snobbery—male—and retaliation—female. That was when her face began to wear that bright, haggard look. She still carried it to parties on shadowy porticoes and summer lawns, like a mask or a flag, with that bafflement of furious repudiation of truth in her eyes. One evening at a party she heard a boy and two girls, all schoolmates, talking. She never accepted another invitation.

She watched the girls with whom she had grown up as they married and got homes and children, but no man ever called on her steadily until the children of the other girls had been calling her "aunty" for several years, the while their mothers told them in bright voices about how popular Aunt Minnie had been as a girl. Then the town began to see her driving on Sunday afternoons with the cashier in the bank. He was a widower of about forty—a high-colored man, smelling always faintly of the barber shop or of whisky. He owned the first automobile in town, a red runabout; Minnie had the first motoring bonnet and veil the town ever saw. Then the town began to say: "Poor Minnie." "But she is old enough to take care of herself," others said. That was when she began to ask her old schoolmates that their children call her "cousin" instead of "aunty."

It was twelve years now since she had been relegated into adultery by public opinion, and eight years since the cashier had gone to a Memphis bank, returning for one day each Christmas, which he spent at an annual bachelor's party at a hunting club on the river. From behind their curtains the neighbors would see the party pass, and during the over-the-way Christmas day visiting they would tell her about him, about how well he looked, and how they heard that he was prospering in the city, watching with bright, secret eyes her haggard, bright face. Usually by that hour there would be the scent of whisky on her breath. It was supplied her by a youth, a clerk at the soda fountain: "Sure; I buy it for the old gal. I reckon she's entitled to a little fun."

Her mother kept to her room altogether now; the gaunt aunt ran the house. Against that background Minnie's bright dresses, her idle and empty days, had a quality of furious unreality. She went out in the evening only with women now, neighbors, to the moving pictures. Each afternoon she dressed in one of the new dresses and went downtown alone, where her young "cousins" were already strolling in the late afternoons with their delicate, silken heads and thin, awkward arms and conscious hips, clinging to one another or shrieking and giggling with paired boys in the soda fountain when she passed and went on along the serried store fronts, in the doors of which the sitting and lounging men did not even follow her with their eyes any more.

III

The barber went swiftly up the street where the sparse lights, insect-swirled, glared in rigid and violent suspension in the lifeless air. The day had died in a pall of dust; above the darkened square, shrouded by the spent dust, the sky was as clear as the inside of a brass bell. Below the east was a rumor of the twice-waxed moon.

When he overtook them McLendon and three others were getting into a car parked in an alley. McLendon stooped his thick head, peering out beneath the top. "Changed your mind, did you?" he said. "Damn good thing; by God, tomorrow when this town hears about how you talked tonight—"

"Now, now," the other ex-soldier said. "Hawkshaw's all right. Come on. Hawk; jump in."

"Will Mayes never done it, boys," the barber said. "If anybody done it. Why, you all know well as I do there aint any town where they got better niggers than us. And you know how a lady will kind of think things about men when there aint any reason to, and Miss Minnie anyway—"

"Sure, sure," the soldier said. "We're just going to talk to him a little; that's all."

"Talk hell!" Butch said. "When we're through with the—"

"Shut up, for God's sake!" the soldier said. "Do you want everybody in town—"

"Tell them, by God!" McLendon said. "Tell every one of the sons that'll let a white woman —"

"Let's go; let's go: here's the other car." The second car slid squealing out of a cloud of dust at the alley mouth. McLendon started his car and took the lead. Dust lay like fog in the street. The street lights hung nimbused as in water. They drove on out of town.

A rutted lane turned at right angles. Dust hung above it too, and above all the land. The dark bulk of the ice plant, where the Negro Mayes was night watchman, rose against the sky. "Better stop here, hadn't we?" the soldier said. McLendon did not reply. He hurled the car up and slammed to a stop, the headlights glaring on the blank wall.

"Listen here, boys," the barber said; "if he's here, dont that prove he never done it? Dont it? If it was him, he would run. Dont you see he would?" The second car came up and stopped. McLendon got down; Butch sprang down beside him. "Listen, boys," the barber said.

"Cut the lights off!" McLendon said. The breathless dark rushed down. There was no sound in it save their lungs as they sought air in the parched dust in which for two months they had lived; then the diminishing crunch of McLendon's and Butch's feet, and a moment late McLendon's voice:

"Will! . . . Will!"

Below the east the wan hemorrhage of the moon increased. It heaved above the ridge, silvering the air, the dust, so that they seemed to breathe, live, in a bowl of molten lead. There was no sound of nightbird nor insect, no sound save their breathing and a faint ticking of contracting metal about the cars. Where their bodies touched one another they seemed to sweat dryly, for no more moisture came. "Christ!" a voice said; "let's get out of here."

But they didn't move until vague noises began to grow out of the darkness ahead; then they got out and waited tensely in the breathless dark. There was another sound: a blow, a hissing explosion of breath and McLendon cursing in undertone. They stood a moment longer, then they ran forward. They ran in a stumbling clump, as though they were fleeing something. "Kill him, kill the son," a voice whispered. McLendon flung them back.

"Not here," he said. "Get him into the car." "Kill him, kill the black son!" the voice murmured. They dragged the Negro to the car. The barber had waited beside the car. He could feel himself sweating and he knew he was going to be sick at the stomach.

"What is it, captains?" the Negro said. "I aint done nothing. 'Fore God, Mr John." Someone produced handcuffs. They worked busily about the Negro as though he were a post, quiet, intent, getting in one another's way. He submitted to the handcuffs, looking swiftly and constantly from dim face to dim face. "Who's here, captains?" he said, leaning to peer into the faces until they could feel his breath and smell his sweaty reek. He spoke a name or two. "What you all say I done, Mr John?"

McLendon jerked the car door open. "Get in!" he said.

The Negro did not move. "What you all going to do with me, Mr John? I aint done nothing. White folks, captains, I aint done nothing: I swear 'fore God." He called another name.

"Get in!" McLendon said. He struck the Negro. The others expelled their breath in a dry hissing and struck him with random blows and he whirled and cursed them, and swept his manacled hands across their faces and slashed the barber upon the mouth, and the barber struck him also. "Get him in there," McLendon said. They pushed at him. He ceased struggling and got in and sat quietly as the others took their places. He sat between the barber and the soldier, drawing his limbs in so as not to touch them, his eyes going swiftly and constantly from face to face. Butch clung to the running board. The car moved on. The barber nursed his mouth with his handkerchief.

"What's the matter, Hawk?" the soldier said.

"Nothing," the barber said. They regained the highroad and turned away from town. The second car dropped back out of the dust. They went on, gaining speed; the final fringe of houses dropped behind.

"Goddamn, he stinks!" the soldier said.

"We'll fix that," the drummer in front beside McLendon said. On the running board Butch cursed into the hot rush of air. The barber leaned suddenly forward and touched McLendon's arm.

"Let me out, John," he said.

"Jump out, niggerlover," McLendon said without turning his head. He drove swiftly. Behind them the sourceless lights of the second car glared in the dust. Presently McLendon turned into a narrow road. It was rutted with disuse. It led back to an abandoned brick kiln—a series of reddish mounds and weed- and vine-chocked vats without bottom. It had been used for pasture once, until one day the owner missed one of his mules. Although he prodded carefully in the vats with a long pole, he could not even find the bottom of them.

"John," the barber said.

"Jump out, then," McLendon said, hurling the car along the ruts. Beside the barber the Negro spoke:

"Mr. Henry."

The barber sat forward. The narrow tunnel of the road rushed up and past. Their motion was like an extinct furnace blast: cooler, but utterly dead. The car bounded from rut to rut.

"Mr. Henry," the Negro said.

The barber began to tug furiously at the door. "Look out, there!" the soldier said, but the barber had already kicked the door open and swung onto the running board. The soldier leaned across the Negro and grasped at him, but he had already jumped. The car went on without checking speed.

The impetus hurled him crashing through dust-sheathed weeds, into the ditch. Dust puffed about him, and in a thin, vicious crackling of sapless stems he lay choking and retching until the second car passed and died away. Then he rose and limped on until he reached the highroad and turned toward town, brushing at his clothes with his hands. The moon was higher, riding high and clear of the dust at last, and after a while the town began to glare beneath the dust. He went on, limping. Presently he heard cars and the glow of them grew in the dust behind him and he left the road and crouched again in the weeds until they passed. McLendon's car came last now. There were four people in it and Butch was not on the running board.

They went on; the dust swallowed them; the glare and the sound died away. The dust of them hung for a while, but soon the eternal dust absorbed it again. The barber climbed back onto the road and limped on toward town.

IV

As she dressed for supper on that Saturday evening, her own flesh felt like fever. Her hands trembled among the hooks and eyes, and her eyes had a feverish look, and her hair swirled crisp and crackling under the comb. While she was still dressing the friends called for her and sat while she donned her sheerest underthings and stockings and a new voile dress. "Do you feel strong enough to go out?" they said, their eyes bright too, with a dark glitter. "When you have had time to get over the shock, you must tell us what happened. What he said and did; everything."

In the leafed darkness, as they walked toward the square, she began to breathe deeply, something like a swimmer preparing to dive, until she ceased trembling, the four of them walking slowly because of the terrible heat and out of solicitude for her. But as they neared the square she began to tremble again, walking with her head up, her hands clenched at her sides, their voices about her murmurous, also with that feverish, glittering quality of their eyes.

They entered the square, she in the center of the group, fragile in her fresh dress. She was trembling worse. She walked slower and slower, as children eat ice cream, her head up and her eyes bright in the haggard banner of her face, passing the hotel and the coatless drummers in chairs along the curb looking around at her: "That's the one: see? The one in pink in the middle." "Is that her? What did they do with the nigger? Did they—?" "Sure. He's all right." "All right, is he?" "Sure. He went on a little trip." Then the drug store, where even the young men lounging in the doorway tipped their hats and followed with their eyes the motion of her hips and legs when she passed.

They went on, passing the lifted hats of the gentlemen, the suddenly ceased voices, deferent, protective. "Do you see?" the friends said. Their voices sounded like long, hovering sighs of hissing exultation. "There's not a Negro on the square. Not one."

They reached the picture show. It was like a miniature fairyland with its lighted lobby and colored lithographs of life caught in its terrible and beautiful mutations. Her lips began to tingle. In the dark, when the picture began, it would be all right; she could hold back the laughing so it would not waste away so fast and so soon. So she hurried on before the turning faces, the undertones of low astonishment, and they took their accustomed places where she could see the aisle against the silver glare and the young men and girls coming in two and two against it.

The lights flicked away; the screen glowed silver, and soon life began to unfold, beautiful and passionate and sad, while still the young men and girls entered, scented and sibilant in the half dark, their paired backs in silhouette delicate and sleek, their slim, quick bodies awkward, divinely young, while beyond them the silver dream accumulated, inevitably on and on. She began to laugh. In trying to suppress it, it made more noise than ever; heads began to turn. Still laughing, her friends raised her and led her out, and she stood at the curb, laughing on a high, sustained note, until the taxi came up and they helped her in.

They removed the pink voile and the sheer underthings and the stockings, and put her to bed, and cracked ice for her temples, and sent for the doctor. He was hard to locate, so they ministered to her with hushed ejaculations, renewing the ice and fanning her. While the ice was fresh and cold she stopped laughing and lay still for a time, moaning only a little. But soon the laughing welled again and her voice rose screaming.

"Shhhhhhhhhhh! Shhhhhhhhhhhhhhh!" they said, freshening the icepack, smoothing her hair, examining it for gray; "poor girl!" Then to one another: "Do you suppose anything really happened?" their eyes darkly aglitter, secret and passionate. "Shhhhhhhhhh! Poor girl! Poor Minnie!"

V

It was midnight when McLendon drove up to his neat new house. It was trim and fresh as a birdcage and almost as small, with its clean, green-and-white paint. He locked the car and mounted the porch and entered. His wife rose from a chair beside the reading lamp. McLendon stopped in the floor and stared at her until she looked down.

"Look at that clock," he said, lifting his arm, pointing. She stood before him, her face lowered, a magazine in her hands. Her face was pale, strained, and weary-looking. "Haven't I told you about sitting up like this, waiting to see when I come in?"

"John," she said. She laid the magazine down. Poised on the balls of his feet, he glared at her with his hot eyes, his sweating face.

"Didn't I tell you?" He went toward her. She looked up then. He caught her shoulder. She stood passive, looking at him.

"Dont, John. I couldn't sleep . . . The heat; something. Please, John. You're hurting me."

"Didn't I tell you?" He released her and half struck, half flung her across the chair, and she lay there and watched him quietly as he left the room.

He went on through the house, ripping off his shirt, and on the dark, screened porch at the rear he stood and mopped his head and shoulders with the shirt and flung it away. He took the pistol from his hip and laid it on the table beside the bed, and sat on the bed and removed his shoes, and rose and slipped his trousers off. He was sweating again already, and he stooped and hunted furiously for the shirt. At last he found it and wiped his body again, and, with his body pressed against the dusty screen, he stood panting. There was no movement, no sound, not even an insect. The dark world seemed to lie stricken beneath the cold moon and the lidless stars.

[1931]

Study and Writing Questions

1. What do details in the opening paragraph suggest about the way the NARRATIVE will unfold?
2. What does the NARRATOR suggest by saying that Hawkshaw and McLendon "looked like men of different races"?
3. Which details make the murder victim stand out as an individual and which make him seem simply a member of a group? How does the manipulation of your feelings about the victim affect your other feelings as you read? After your reading is complete? What is this STORY about?
4. What is the structure of white society in this NARRATIVE? Which forces tend to keep this society together and which to break it apart? What are we to

understand by the last view we get of each of the three principal white CHARACTERS?

5. How does the organization of this narrative into five sections contribute to its impact?

See also Questions for Contrast and Comparison: 55, 58, 81, 84, 86, 100, 103, 119, 133, 152, 232, and 239.

F(RANCIS) SCOTT (KEY) FITZGERALD (1896–1940) *was born in St. Paul, Minnesota, into a middle-class family of an income inadequate to support its genteel values. Thanks to his mother's family money, he attended private schools, entering Princeton University at age sixteen but leaving in October, 1917 to accept an Army commission. Stationed in Alabama, he courted the talented and beautiful Zelda Sayre, whom he married in 1920. He moved to New York City on his discharge (1919) and struggled as a story writer until his first novel,* This Side of Paradise *(1920), based on his college experiences, won a commercial success that led to the speedy publication of the first of his four short story collections. He, Zelda, and their daughter lived in Paris (1924–1931) as part of the American expatriate community that included Ernest Hemingway, Gertrude Stein, and others. On the basis primarily of his stories and his classic novel,* The Great Gatsby *(1925), Fitzgerald is known as the great chronicler of "the Jazz Age," but it is equally fair to say that he exemplified what Stein called "the Lost Generation" of men who returned from The Great War to a world without fixed values. His life, marked by alcoholism, and his marriage, burdened by Zelda's psychological breakdowns and costly hospitalizations, declined in the 1930s. His literary reputation failing, he wrote unhappily in Hollywood where he died, guilt-ridden and deeply in debt.*

Babylon Revisited

"And where's Mr. Campbell?" Charlie asked.

"Gone to Switzerland. Mr. Campbell's a pretty sick man, Mr. Wales."

"I'm sorry to hear that. And George Hardt?" Charlie inquired.

"Back in America, gone to work."

"And where is the Snow Bird?"

"He was in here last week. Anyway, his friend, Mr. Schaeffer, is in Paris."

Two familiar names from the long list of a year and a half ago. Charlie scribbled an address in his notebook and tore out the page.

"If you see Mr. Schaeffer, give him this," he said. "It's my brother-in-law's address. I haven't settled on a hotel yet."

He was not really disappointed to find Paris was so empty. But the stillness in the Ritz bar was strange and portentous. It was not an American bar any more — he felt polite in it, and not as if he owned it. It had gone back into France. He felt the stillness from the moment he got out of the taxi and saw the doorman, usually in a frenzy of activity at this hour, gossiping with a *chasseur* by the servants' entrance.

Passing through the corridor, he heard only a single, bored voice in the once-clamorous women's room. When he turned into the bar he traveled the twenty feet of green carpet with his eyes fixed straight ahead by old habit; and then, with his foot firmly on the rail, he turned and surveyed the room, encountering only a single pair of eyes that fluttered up from a newspaper in the corner. Charlie asked for the head barman, Paul, who in the latter days of the bull market had come to work in his own custom-built car — disembarking, however, with due nicety at the nearest corner. But Paul was at his country house today and Alix giving him information.

"No, no more," Charlie said, "I'm going slow these days."

Alix congratulated him: "You were going pretty strong a couple of years ago."

"I'll stick to it all right," Charlie assured him. " I've stuck to it for over a year and a half now."

"How do you find conditions in America?"

"I haven't been to America for months. I'm in business in Prague, representing a couple of concerns there. They don't know about me down there."

Alix smiled.

"Remember the night of George Hardt's bachelor dinner here?" said Charlie. "By the way, what's become of Claude Fessenden?"

Alix lowered his voice confidentially: "He's in Paris, but he doesn't come here any more. Paul doesn't allow it. He ran up a bill of thirty thousand francs, charging all his drinks and his lunches, and usually his dinner, for more than a year. And when Paul finally told him he had to pay, he gave him a bad check."

Alix shook his head sadly.

"I don't understand it, such a dandy fellow. Now he's all bloated up — " He made a plump apple of his hands.

Charlie watched a group of strident queens installing themselves in a corner.

"Nothing affects them," he thought. "Stocks rise and fall, people loaf or work, but they go on forever." The place oppressed him. He called for the dice and shook with Alix for the drink.

"Here for long, Mr. Wales?"

"I'm here for four or five days to see my little girl."

"Oh-h! You have a little girl?"

Outside, the fire-red, gas-blue, ghost-green signs shone smokily through the tranquil rain. It was late afternoon and the streets were in movement; the *bistros* gleamed. At the corner of the Boulevard des Capucines he took a taxi. The Place de la Concorde moved by in pink majesty; they crossed the logical Seine, and Charlie felt the sudden provincial quality of the Left Bank.

Charlie directed his taxi to the Avenue de l'Opera, which was out of his way. But he wanted to see the blue hour spread over the magnificent façade, and imagine that the cab horns, playing endlessly the first few bars of *Le Plus que Lent*, were the trumpets of the Second Empire. They were closing the iron grill in front of Brentano's Book-store, and people were already at dinner behind the trim little bourgeois hedge of Duval's. He had never eaten at a really cheap restaurant in Paris. Five-course dinner, four francs fifty, eighteen cents, wine included. For some odd reason he wished that he had.

As they rolled on to the Left Bank and he felt its sudden provincialism, he thought, "I spoiled this city for myself. I didn't realize it, but the days came along one after another, and then two years were gone, and everything was gone, and I was gone."

He was thirty-five, and good to look at. The Irish mobility of his face was sobered by a deep wrinkle between his eyes. As he rang his brother-in-law's bell in the Rue Palatine, the wrinkle deepened till it pulled down his brows; he felt a cramping sensation in his belly. From behind the maid who opened the door darted a lovely little girl of nine who shrieked "Daddy!" and flew up, struggling like a fish, into his arms. She pulled his head around by one ear and set her cheek against his.

"My old pie," he said.

"Oh daddy, daddy, daddy, daddy, dads, dads, dads!"

She drew him into the salon, where the family waited, a boy and girl his daughter's age, his sister-in-law and her husband. He greeted Marion with his voice pitched carefully to avoid either feigned enthusiasm or dislike, but her response was more frankly tepid, though she minimized her expression of unalterable distrust by directing her regard toward his child. The two men clasped hands in a friendly way and Lincoln Peters rested his for a moment on Charlie's shoulder.

The room was warm and comfortably American. The three children moved intimately about, playing through the yellow oblongs that led to other rooms; the cheer of six o'clock spoke in the eager smacks of the fire and sounds of French activity in the kitchen. But Charlie did not relax; his heart sat up rigidly in his body and he drew confidence from his daughter, who from time to time came close to him, holding in her arms the doll he had brought.

"Really extremely well," he declared in answer to Lincoln's question. "There's a lot of business there that isn't moving at all, but we're doing even better than ever. In fact, damn well. I'm bringing my sister over from America next month to keep house for me. My income last year was bigger than it was when I had money. You see, the Czechs ———"

His boasting was for a specific purpose; but after a moment, seeing a faint restiveness in Lincoln's eye, he changed the subject:

"Those are fine children of yours, well brought up, good manners."

"We think Honoria's a great little girl too."

Marion Peters came back from the kitchen. She was a tall woman with worried eyes, who had once possessed a fresh American loveliness. Charlie had never been sensitive to it and was always surprised when people spoke of how pretty she had been. From the first there had been an instinctive antipathy between them.

"Well, how do find Honoria?" she asked.

"Wonderful. I was astonished how much she's grown in ten months. All the children are looking well."

"We haven't had a doctor for a year. How do you like being back in Paris?"

"It seems very funny to see so few Americans around."

"I'm delighted," Marion said vehemently. "Now at least you can go into a store without their assuming you're a millionaire. We've suffered like everybody, but on the whole it's a good deal pleasanter."

"But it was nice while it lasted," Charlie said. "We were a sort of royalty, almost infallible, with a sort of magic around us. In the bar this afternoon" — he stumbled, seeing his mistake — "there wasn't a man I knew."

She looked at him keenly. "I should think you'd have had enough of bars."

"I only stayed a minute. I take one drink every afternoon, and no more."

"Don't you want a cocktail before dinner?" Lincoln asked.

"I take only one drink every afternoon, and I've had that."

"I hope you keep to it," said Marion.

Her dislike was evident in the coldness with which she spoke, but Charlie only smiled; he had larger plans. Her very aggressiveness gave him an advantage, and he knew enough to wait. He wanted them to initiate the discussion of what they knew had brought him to Paris.

At dinner he couldn't decide whether Honoria was most like him or her mother. Fortunate if she didn't combine the traits of both that had brought them to disaster. A great wave of protectiveness went over him. He thought he knew what to do for her. He believed in character; he wanted to jump back a whole generation and trust in character again as the eternally valuable element. Everything else wore out.

He left soon after dinner, but not to go home. He was curious to see Paris by night with clearer and more judicious eyes than those of other days. He bought a *strapontin* for the Casino and watched Josephine Baker go through her chocolate arabesques.

After an hour he left and strolled toward Montmartre, up the Rue Pigalle into the Place Blanche. The rain had stopped and there were a few people in evening clothes disembarking from taxis in front of cabarets, and *cocottes* prowling singly or in pairs, and many Negroes. He passed a lighted door from which issued music, and stopped with the sense of familiarity; it was Bricktop's, where he had parted with so many hours and so much money. A few doors farther on he found another ancient rendezvous and incautiously put his head inside. Immediately an eager orchestra burst into sound, a pair of professional dancers leaped to their feet and a maître d'hôtel swooped toward him, crying, "Crowd just arriving, sir!" But he withdrew quickly.

"You have to be damn drunk," he thought.

Zelli's was closed, the bleak and sinister cheap hotels surrounding it were dark; up in the Rue Blanche there was more light and a local, colloquial French crowd. The Poet's Cave had disappeared, but the two great mouths of the Café of Heaven and the Café of Hell still yawned—even devoured, as he watched, the meager contents of a tourist bus—a German, a Japanese, and an American couple who glanced at him with frightened eyes.

So much for the effort and ingenuity of Montmarte. All the catering to vice and waste was on an utterly childish scale, and he suddenly realized the meaning of the word "dissipate"—to dissipate into thin air; to make nothing out of something. In the little hours of the night every move from place to place was an enormous human jump, an increase of paying for the privilege of slower and slower motion.

He remembered thousand-franc notes given to an orchestra for playing a single number, hundred-franc notes tossed to a doorman for calling a cab.

But it hadn't been given for nothing.

It had been given, even the most wildly squandered sum, as an offering to destiny that he might not remember the things most worth remembering, the things that now he would always remember—his child taken from his control, his wife escaped to a grave in Vermont.

In the glare of a *brasserie* a woman spoke to him. He bought her some eggs and coffee, and then, eluding her encouraging stare, gave her a twenty-franc note and took a taxi to his hotel.

II

He woke upon a fine fall day — football weather. The depression of yesterday was gone and he liked the people on the streets. At noon he sat opposite Honoria at Le Grand Vatel, the only resturant he could think of not reminiscent of champagne dinners and long luncheons that began at two and ended in a blurred and vague twilight.

"Now, how about vegetables? Oughtn't you to have some vegetables?"

"Well, yes."

"Here's *épinards* and *chou-fleur* and carrots and *haricots*."

"I'd like *chou-fleur*."

"Wouldn't you like to have two vegetables?"

"I usually only have one at lunch."

The waiter was pretending to be inordinately fond of children. "*Qu'elle est mignonne la petite! Elle parle exactement comme une Française.*"

"How about dessert? Shall we wait and see?"

The waiter disappeared. Honoria looked at her father expectantly.

"What are we going to do?"

"First, we're going to that toy store in the Rue Saint-Honoré and buy you anything you like. And then we're going to the vaudeville at the Empire."

She hesitated. "I like it about the vaudeville, but not the toy store."

"Why not?"

"Well, you brought me this doll." She had it with her. "And I've got lots of things. And we're not rich any more, are we?"

"We never were. But today you are to have anything you want."

"All right," she agreed resignedly.

When there had been her mother and a French nurse he had been inclined to be strict; now he extended himself, reached out for a new tolerance; he must be both parents to her and not shut any of her out of communication.

"I want to get to know you," he said gravely. "First let me introduce myself. My name is Charles J. Wales, of Prague."

"Oh, daddy!" her voice cracked with laughter.

"And who are you, please?" he persisted, and she accepted a rôle immediately: "Honoria Wales, Rue Palatine, Paris."

"Married or single?"

"No, not married. Single."

He indicated the doll. "But I see you have a child, madame."

Unwilling to disinherit it, she took it to her heart and thought quickly: "Yes, I've been married, but I'm not married now. My husband is dead."

He went on quickly, "And the child's name?"

"Simone. That's after my best friend at school."

"I'm very pleased that you're doing so well at school."

"I'm third this month," she boasted. "Elsie" — that was her cousin — "is only about eighteenth, and Richard is about at the bottom."

"You like Richard and Elsie, don't you?"

"Oh, yes. I like Richard quite well and I like her all right."

Cautiously and casually he asked: "And Aunt Marion and Uncle Lincoln — which do you like best?"

"Oh, Uncle Lincoln, I guess."

He was increasingly aware of her presence. As they came in, a murmur of ". . . adorable" followed them, and now the people at the next table bent all their silences upon her, staring as if she were something no more conscious than a flower.

"Why don't I live with you?" she asked suddenly. "Because mamma's dead?"

"You must stay here and learn more French. It would have been hard for Daddy to take care of you so well."

"I don't really need much taking care of any more. I do everything for myself."

Going out of the restaurant, a man and a woman unexpectedly hailed him.

"Well, the old Wales!"

"Hello there, Lorraine. . . . Dunc."

Sudden ghosts out of the past: Duncan Schaeffer, a friend from college. Lorraine Quarrles, a lovely, pale blonde of thirty; and one of a crowd who had helped them make months into days in the lavish times of three years ago.

"My husband couldn't come this year," she said, in answer to his question. "We're poor as hell. So he gave me two hundred a month and told me I could do my worst on that. . . . This your little girl?"

"What about coming back and sitting down?" Duncan asked.

"Can't do it." He was glad for an excuse. As always, he felt Lorraine's passionate, provocative attraction, but his own rhythm was different now.

"Well, how about dinner?" she asked.

"I'm not free. Give me your address and let me call you."

"Charlie, I believe you're sober," she said judicially. "I honestly believe he's sober, Dunc. Pinch him and see if he's sober."

Charlie indicated Honoria with his head. They both laughed.

"What's your address?" said Duncan skeptically.

He hesitated, unwilling to give the name of his hotel.

"I'm not settled yet. I'd better call you. We're going to see the vaudeville at the Empire."

"There! That's what I want to do," Lorraine said. "I want to see some clowns and acrobats and jugglers. That's just what we'll do, Dunc."

"We've got to do an errand first," said Charlie. "Perhaps we'll see you there."

"All right, you snob. . . . Good-by, beautiful little girl."

"Good-by."

Honoria bobbed politely.

Somehow, an unwelcome encounter. They liked him because he was functioning, because he was serious; they wanted to see him, because he was stronger than they were now, because they wanted to draw a certain sustenance from his strength.

At the Empire, Honoria proudly refused to sit upon her father's folded coat. She was already an individual with a code of her own, and Charlie was more and more absorbed by the desire of putting a little of himself into her before she crystallized utterly. It was hopeless to try to know her in so short a time.

Between the acts they came upon Duncan and Lorraine in the lobby where the band was playing.

"Have a drink?"

"All right, but not up at the bar. We'll take a table."

"The perfect father."

Listening abstractedly to Lorraine, Charlie watched Honoria's eyes leave their table, and he followed them wistfully about the room, wondering what they saw. He met her glance and she smiled.

"I liked that lemonade," she said.

What had she said? What had he expected? Going home in a taxi afterward, he pulled her over until her head rested against his chest.

"Darling, do you ever think about your mother?"

"Yes, sometimes," she answered vaguely.

"I don't want you to forget her. Have you got a picture of her?"

"Yes, I think so. Anyhow, Aunt Marion has. Why don't you want me to forget her?"

"She loved you very much."

"I loved her too."

They were silent for a moment.

"Daddy, I want to come and live with you," she said suddenly.

His heart leaped; he had wanted it to come like this.

"Aren't you perfectly happy?"

"Yes, but I love you better than anybody. And you love me better than anybody, don't you, now that mummy's dead?"

"Of course I do. But you won't always like me best, honey. You'll grow up and meet somebody your own age and go marry him and forget you ever had a daddy."

"Yes, that's true," she agreed tranquilly.

He didn't go in. He was coming back at nine o'clock and he wanted to keep himself fresh and new for the thing he must say then.

"When you're safe inside, just show yourself in that window."

"All right. Good-by, dads, dads, dads, dads."

He waited in the dark street until she appeared, all warm and glowing, in the window above and kissed her fingers out into the night.

III

They were waiting, Marion sat behind the coffee service in a dignified black dinner dress that just faintly suggested mourning. Lincoln was walking up and down with the animation of one who had already been talking. They were as anxious as he was to get into the question. He opened it almost immediately:

"I suppose you know what I want to see you about—why I really came to Paris."

Marion played with the black stars on her necklace and frowned.

"I'm awfully anxious to have a home," he continued. "And I'm awfully anxious to have Honoria in it. I appreciate your taking in Honoria for her mother's sake, but things have changed now"—he hesitated and then continued more forcibly—"changed radically with me, and I want to ask you to reconsider the matter. It would be silly for me to deny that about three years ago I was acting badly——"

Marion looked up at him with hard eyes.

" — but all that's over. As I told you, I haven't had more than a drink a day for over a year, and I take that drink deliberately, so that the idea of alcohol won't get too big in my imagination. You see the idea?"

"No," said Marion succinctly.

"It's a sort of stunt I set myself. It keeps the matter in proportion."

"I get you," said Lincoln. "You don't want to admit it's got any attraction for you."

"Something like that. Sometimes I forget and don't take it. But I try to take it. Anyhow, I couldn't afford to drink in my position. The people I represent are more than satisfied with what I've done, and I'm bringing my sister over from Burlington to keep house for me, and I want awfully to have Honoria too. You know that even when her mother and I weren't getting along well we never let anything that happened touch Honoria. I know she's fond of me and I know I'm able to take care of her and — well, there you are. How do you feel about it?"

He knew that now he would have to take a beating. It would last an hour or two hours, and it would be difficult, but if he modulated his inevitable resentment to the chastened attitude of the reformed sinner, he might win his point in the end.

Keep your temper, he told himself. You don't want to be justified. You want Honoria.

Lincoln spoke first: "We've been talking it over ever since we got your letter last month. We're happy to have Honoria here. She's a dear little thing, and we're glad to be able to help her, but of course that isn't the question ——"

Marion interrupted suddenly. "How long are you going to stay sober, Charlie?" she asked.

"Permanently, I hope."

"How can anybody count on that?"

"You know I never did drink heavily until I gave up business and came over here with nothing to do. Then Helen and I began to run around with ——"

"Please leave Helen out of it. I can't bear to hear you talk about her like that."

He stared at her grimly; he had never been certain how fond of each other the sisters were in life.

"My drinking only lasted about a year and a half — from the time we came over until I — collapsed."

"It was time enough."

"It was time enough," he agreed.

"My duty is entirely to Helen," she said. "I try to think what she would have wanted me to do. Frankly, from the night you did that terrible thing you haven't really existed for me. I can't help that. She was my sister."

"Yes."

"When she was dying she asked me to look out for Honoria. If you hadn't been in a sanitarium then, it might have helped matters."

He had no answer.

"I'll never in my life be able to forget the morning when Helen knocked at my door, soaked to the skin and shivering and said you'd locked her out."

Charlie gripped the sides of the chair. This was more difficult than he expected; he wanted to launch out into a long expostulation and explanation, but he only said: "The night I locked her out" — and she interrupted, "I don't feel up to going over that again."

After a moment's silence Lincoln said: "We're getting off the subject. You want Marion to set aside her legal guardianship and give you Honoria. I think the main point for her is whether she has confidence in you or not."

"I don't blame Marion," Charlie said slowly, "but I think she can have entire confidence in me. I had a good record up to three years ago. Of course, its within human possibilities I might go wrong any time. But if we wait much longer I'll lose Honoria's childhood and my chance for a home." He shook his head, "I'll simply lose her, don't you see?"

"Yes, I see," said Lincoln.

"Why didn't you think of all this before?" Marion asked.

"I suppose I did, from time to time, but Helen and I were getting along badly. When I consented to the guardianship, I was flat on my back in a sanitarium and the market had cleaned me out. I knew I'd acted badly, and I thought if it would bring any peace to Helen, I'd agree to anything. But now it's different. I'm functioning, I'm behaving damn well, so far as ——"

"Please don't swear at me," Marion said.

He looked at her, startled. With each remark the force of her dislike became more and more apparent. She had built up all her fear of life into one wall and faced it toward him. This trivial reproof was possibly the result of some trouble with the cook several hours before. Charlie became increasingly alarmed at leaving Honoria in this atmosphere of hostility against himself; sooner or later it would come out, in a word here, a shake of the head there, and some of that distrust would be irrevocably implanted in Honoria. But he pulled his temper down out of his face and shut it up inside him; he had won a point, for Lincoln realized the absurdity of Marion's remark and asked her lightly since when she had objected to the word "damn."

"Another thing," Charlie said: "I'm able to give her certain advantages now. I'm going to take a French governess to Prague with me. I've got a lease on a new apartment ——"

He stopped, realizing that he was blundering. They couldn't be expected to accept with equanimity the fact that his income was again twice as large as their own.

"I suppose you can give her more luxuries than we can," said Marion. "When you were throwing away money we were living along watching every ten francs. . . . I suppose you'll start doing it again."

"Oh, no," he said. "I've learned. I worked hard for ten years, you know — until I got lucky in the market, like so many people. Terribly lucky. It didn't seem any use working any more, so I quit. It won't happen again."

There was a long silence. All of them felt their nerves straining, and for the first time in a year Charlie wanted a drink. He was sure now that Lincoln Peters wanted him to have his child.

Marion shuddered suddenly; part of her saw that Charlie's feet were planted on the earth now, and her own maternal feeling recognized the naturalness of his desire; but she had lived for a long time with a prejudice — a prejudice founded on a curious disbelief in her sister's happiness, and which, in the shock of one terrible night, had turned to hatred for him. It had all happened at a point in her life where the discouragement of ill health and adverse circumstances made it necessary for her to believe in tangible villainy and a tangible villain.

"I can't help what I think!" she cried out suddenly. "How much you were responsible for Helen's death, I don't know. It's something you'll have to square with your own conscience."

An electric current of agony surged through him; for a moment he was almost on his feet, an unuttered sound echoing in his throat. He hung on to himself for a moment, another moment.

"Hold on there," said Lincoln uncomfortably. "I never thought you were responsible for that."

"Helen died of heart trouble," Charlie said dully.

"Yes, heart trouble." Marion spoke as if the phrase had another meaning for her.

Then, in the flatness that followed her outburst, she saw him plainly and she knew he had somehow arrived at control over the situation. Glancing at her husband, she found no help from him, and as abruptly as if it were a matter of no importance, she threw up the sponge.

"Do what you like!" she cried, springing up from her chair. "She's your child. I'm not the person to stand in your way. I think if it were my child I'd rather see her — " She managed to check herself. "You two decide it. I can't stand this. I'm sick. I'm going to bed."

She hurried from the room; after a moment Lincoln said:

"This has been a hard day for her. You know how strongly she feels — " His voice was almost apologetic: "When a woman gets an idea in her head."

"Of course."

"It's going to be all right. I think she sees now that you — can provide for the child, and so we can't very well stand in your way or Honoria's way."

"Thank you, Lincoln."

"I'd better go along and see how she is."

"I'm going."

He was still trembling when he reached the street, but a walk down the Rue Bonaparte to the quais set him up, and as he crossed the Seine, fresh and new by the quai lamps, he felt exultant. But back in his room he couldn't sleep. The image of Helen haunted him. Helen whom he had loved so until they had senselessly begun to abuse each other's love, tear it into shreds. On that terrible February night that Marion remembered so vividly, a slow quarrel had gone on for hours. There was a scene at the Florida, and then he attempted to take her home, and then she kissed young Webb at a table; after that there was what she had hysterically said. When he arrived home alone he turned the key in the lock in wild anger. How could he know she would arrive an hour later alone, that there would be a snowstorm in which she wandered about in slippers, too confused to find a taxi? Then the aftermath, her escaping pneumonia by a miracle, and all the attendant horror. They were "reconciled," but that was the beginning of the end, and Marion, who had seen with her own eyes and who imagined it to be one of many scenes from her sister's martyrdom, never forgot.

Going over it again brought Helen nearer, and in the white, soft light that steals upon half sleep near morning he found himself talking to her again. She said that he was perfectly right about Honoria and that she wanted Honoria to be with him. She said she was glad he was being good and doing better. She said a lot of other things — very friendly things — but she was in a swing in a white dress, and swinging faster and faster all the time, so that at the end he could not hear clearly all that she said.

IV

He woke up feeling happy. The door of the world was open again. He made plans, vistas, futures for Honoria and himself, but suddenly he grew sad, remembering all the plans he and Helen had made. She had not planned to die. The present was the thing — work to do and someone to love. But not to love too much, for he knew the injury that a father can do to a daughter or a mother to a son by attaching them too closely: afterward, out in the world, the child would seek in the marriage partner the same blind tenderness and, failing probably to find it, turn against love and life.

It was another bright, crisp day. He called Lincoln Peters at the bank where he worked and asked if he could count on taking Honoria when he left for Prague. Lincoln agreed that there was no reason for delay. One thing — the legal guardianship. Marion wanted to retain that a while longer. She was upset by the whole matter, and it would oil things if she felt that the situation was still in her control for another year. Charlie agreed, wanting only the tangible, visible child.

Then the question of a governess. Charles sat in a gloomy agency and talked to a cross Béarnaise and to a buxom Breton peasant, neither of whom he could have endured. There were others whom he would see tomorrow.

He lunched with Lincoln Peters at Griffons, trying to keep down his exultation.

"There's nothing quite like your own child," Lincoln said. "But you understand how Marion feels too."

"She's forgotten how hard I worked for seven years there," Charlie said. "She just remembers one night."

"There's another thing." Lincoln hesitated. "While you and Helen were tearing around Europe throwing money away, we were just getting along. I didn't touch any of the prosperity because I never got ahead enough to carry anything but my insurance. I think Marion felt there was some kind of injustice in it — you not even working toward the end, and getting richer and richer."

"It went just as quick as it came," said Charlie.

"Yes, a lot of it stayed in the hands of *chasseurs* and saxophone players and maîtres d'hôtel — well, the big party's over now. I just said that to explain Marion's feeling about those crazy years. If you drop in about six o'clock tonight before Marion's too tired, we'll settle the details on the spot."

Back at his hotel, Charlie found a *pneumatique* that had been redirected from the Ritz bar where Charlie had left his address for the purpose of finding a certain man.

DEAR CHARLIE: You were so strange when we saw you the other day that I wondered if I did something to offend you. If so, I'm not conscious of it. In fact, I have thought about you too much for the last year, and it's always been in the back of my mind that I might see you if I came over here. We *did* have such good times that crazy spring, like the night you and I stole the butcher's tricycle, and the time we tried to call on the president and you had the old derby rim and the wire cane. Everybody seems so old lately, but I don't feel old a bit. Couldn't we get together some time today for old time's sake? I've got a vile hang-over for the moment, but will be feeling better this afternoon and will look for you about five in the sweat-shop at the Ritz.

Always devotedly,

LORRAINE.

His first feeling was one of awe that he had actually, in his mature years, stolen a tricycle and pedalled Lorraine all over the Étoile between the small hours and dawn. In retrospect it was a nightmare. Locking out Helen didn't fit in with any other act of his life, but the tricycle incident did — it was one of many. How many weeks or months of dissipation to arrive at that condition of utter irresponsibility?

He tried to picture how Lorraine had appeared to him then — very attractive; Helen was unhappy about it, though she said nothing. Yesterday, in the restaurant, Lorraine had seemed trite, blurred, worn away. He emphatically did not want to see her, and he was glad Alix had not given away his hotel address. It was a relief to think, instead, of Honoria, to think of Sundays spent with her and of saying good morning to her and of knowing she was there in his house at night, drawing her breath in the darkness.

At five he took a taxi and bought presents for all the Peters — a piquant cloth doll, a box of Roman soldiers, flowers for Marion, big linen handkerchiefs for Lincoln.

He saw, when he arrived in the apartment, that Marion had accepted the inevitable. She greeted him now as though he were a recalcitrant member of the family, rather than a menacing outsider. Honoria had been told she was going; Charlie was glad to see that her tact made her conceal her excessive happiness. Only on his lap did she whisper her delight and the question "When?" before she slipped away with the other children.

He and Marion were alone for a minute in the room, and on an impulse he spoke out boldly:

"Family quarrels are bitter things. They don't go according to any rules. They're not like aches or wounds; they're more like splits in the skin that won't heal because there's not enough material. I wish you and I could be on better terms."

"Some things are hard to forget," she answered. "It's a question of confidence." There was no answer to this and presently she asked, "When do you propose to take her?"

"As soon as I can get a governess. I hoped the day after tomorrow."

"That's impossible. I've got to get her things in shape. Not before Saturday."

He yielded. Coming back into the room, Lincoln offered him a drink.

"I'll take my daily whisky," he said.

It was warm here, it was a home, people together by a fire. The children felt very safe and important; the mother and father were serious, watchful. They had things to do for the children more important than his visit here. A spoonful of medicine was, after all, more important than the strained relations between

Marion and himself. They were not dull people, but they were very much in the grip of life and circumstances. He wondered if he couldn't do something to get Lincoln out of his rut at the bank.

A long peal at the door-bell; the *bonne à tout faire* passed through and went down the corridor. The door opened upon another long ring, and then voices, and the three in the salon looked up expectantly; Lincoln moved to bring the corridor within his range of vision, and Marion rose. Then the maid came back along the corridor, closely followed by the voices, which developed under the light into Duncan Schaeffer and Lorraine Quarrles.

They were gay, they were hilarious, they were roaring with laughter. For a moment Charlie was astounded; unable to understand how they ferreted out the Peters' address.

"Ah-h-h!" Duncan wagged his finger roguishly at Charlie. "Ah-h-h!"

They both slid down another cascade of laughter. Anxious and at a loss, Charlie shook hands with them quickly and presented them to Lincoln and Marion. Marion nodded, scarcely speaking. She had drawn back a step toward the fire; her little girl stood beside her, and Marion put an arm about her shoulder.

With growing annoyance at the intrusion, Charlie waited for them to explain themselves. After some concentration Duncan said:

"We came to invite you out to dinner. Lorraine and I insist that all this chi-chi, cagy business 'bout your address got to stop."

Charlie came closer to them, as if to force them backward down the corridor.

"Sorry, but I can't. Tell me where you'll be and I'll phone you in half an hour."

This made no impression. Lorraine sat down suddenly on the side of a chair, and focusing her eyes on Richard, cried, "Oh, what a nice little boy! Come here, little boy." Richard glanced at his mother, but did not move. With a perceptible shrug of her shoulders, Lorraine turned back to Charlie:

"Come and dine. Sure your cousins won' mine. See you so sel'om. Or solemn."

"I can't," said Charlie sharply. "You two have dinner and I'll phone you."

Her voice became suddenly unpleasant. "All right, we'll go. But I remember once when you hammered on my door at four A.M. I was enough of a good sport to give you a drink. Come on, Dunc."

Still in slow motion, with blurred, angry faces, with uncertain feet, they retired along the corridor.

"Good night," Charlie said.

"Good night!" responded Lorraine emphatically.

When he went back into the salon Marion had not moved, only now her son was standing in the circle of her other arm. Lincoln was still swinging Honoria back and forth like a pendulum from side to side.

"What an outrage!" Charlie broke out. "What an absolute outrage!"

Neither of them answered. Charlie dropped into an armchair, picked up his drink, set it down again and said:

"People I haven't seen for two years having the colossal nerve ——"

He broke off. Marion had made the sound "Oh!" in one swift, furious breath, turned her body from him with a jerk and left the room.

Lincoln set down Honoria carefully.

"You children go in and start your soup," he said, and when they obeyed, he said to Charlie:

"Marion's not well and she can't stand shocks. That kind of people make her really physically sick."

"I didn't tell them to come here. They wormed your name out of somebody. They deliberately——"

"Well, it's too bad. It doesn't help matters. Excuse me a minute."

Left alone, Charlie sat tense in his chair. In the next room he could hear the children eating, talking in monosyllables, already oblivious to the scene between their elders. He heard a murmur of conversation from a farther room and then the ticking bell of a telephone receiver picked up, and in a panic he moved to the other side of the room and out of earshot.

In a minute Lincoln came back. "Look here, Charlie. I think we'd better call off dinner for tonight. Marion's in bad shape."

"Is she angry with me?"

"Sort of," he said, almost roughly. "She's not strong and——"

"You mean she's changed her mind about Honoria?"

"She's pretty bitter right now. I don't know. You phone me at the bank tomorrow."

"I wish you'd explain to her I never dreamed these people would come here. I'm just as sore as you are."

"I couldn't explain anything to her now."

Charlie got up. He took his coat and hat and started down the corridor. Then he opened the door of the dining room and said in a strange voice, "Good night, children."

Honoria rose and ran around the table to hug him.

"Good night, sweetheart," he said vaguely, and then trying to make his voice more tender, trying to conciliate something, "Good night, dear children."

V

Charlie went directly to the Ritz bar with the furious idea of finding Lorraine and Duncan, but they were not there, and he realized that in any case there was nothing he could do. He had not touched his drink at the Peters', and now he ordered a whisky-and-soda. Paul came over to say hello.

"It's a great change," he said sadly. "We do about half the business we did. So many fellows I hear about back in the States lost everything, maybe not in the first crash, but then in the second. Your friend George Hardt lost every cent, I hear. Are you back in the States?"

"No, I'm in business in Prague."

"I heard that you lost a lot in the crash."

"I did," and he added grimly, "but I lost everything I wanted in the boom."

"Selling short."

"Something like that."

Again the memory of those days swept over him like a nightmare — the people they had met travelling; then people who couldn't add a row of figures or speak a coherent sentence. The little man Helen had consented to dance with at the ship's party, who had insulted her ten feet from the table; the women and girls carried screaming with drink or drugs out of public places ——

— The men who locked their wives out in the snow, because the snow of twenty-nine wasn't real snow. If you didn't want it to be snow, you just paid some money.

He went to the phone and called the Peters' apartment; Lincoln answered.

"I called up because this thing is on my mind. Has Marion said anything definite?"

"Marion's sick," Lincoln answered shortly. "I know this thing isn't altogether your fault, but I can't have her go to pieces about it. I'm afraid we'll have to let it slide for six months; I can't take the chance of working her up to this state again."

"I see."

"I'm sorry, Charlie."

He went back to his table. His whisky glass empty, but he shook his head when Alix looked at it questioningly. There wasn't much he could do now except send Honoria some things; he would send her a lot of things tomorrow. He thought rather angrily that this was just money — he had given so many people money. . . .

"No, no more," he said to another waiter. "What do I owe you?"

He would come back some day; they couldn't make him pay forever. But he wanted his child, and nothing was much good now, beside that fact. He wasn't young any more, with a lot of nice thoughts and dreams to have by himself. He was absolutely sure Helen wouldn't have wanted him to be so alone.

[1931]

Study and Writing Questions

1. The Ritz bar "had gone back into France." What do Paris, Vermont, and Prague each represent in this STORY? What does Babylon represent? To what extent is the story about returning?
2. In what ways does money seem to affect CHARACTER, happiness, and relationships in this story?
3. Charlie thinks of one meaning of dissipate, "to make nothing of something." What are the other meanings of the word? How does each meaning apply in this story?
4. How is this NARRATIVE RESOLVED? What details in the story suggest that Charlie's "absolutely sure" feeling in the last line is valid? What details suggest that it may be invalid? Does Charlie really feel certain in the last line?
5. What is the significance of ALLUSION in this narrative? What is the relationship between Charlie's personal story and the general history of the period in which his story is set?

See also Questions for Contrast and Comparison: 45, 61, 68, 91, 97, 116, 118, 129, and 161.

■ **CHARLOTTE PERKINS (STETSON) GILMAN** (1860–1935) *was born in Hartford, Connecticut. A great-niece of the abolitionist Harriet Beecher Stowe, she was raised by her abandoned and impoverished mother. After briefly attending the Rhode Island School of Design, Charlotte worked as a commercial artist, teacher, and governess. A year after her 1884 marriage to C.W. Stetson, a Providence artist, she bore a daughter and suffered a profound post-partum depression. Treated by Dr. S. Weir Mitchell with his fashionable "rest cure," which prohibited all useful activity (especially writing), she fled to Pasadena, California, divorced, and, scandalously, sent her child to live with her father and his new wife, a friend of Charlotte's. Then began her outstanding feminist career. She argued, most famously in* Women and Economics *(1898), that women needed education for their own independence and to allow female nurturance to counterweight male aggressiveness.* Herland *(1915), her pioneering female utopian novel appeared in* The Forerunner, *a monthly magazine she wrote and edited alone (1909–1916). She thrived in marriage (1900) to her first cousin, G. H. Gilman, a lawyer, with whom she lived and traveled until his sudden death (1934). Back in California, to live near her daughter and Stetson's widow, when breast cancer prevented "work . . . [her] predominant duty," this life-long socialist committed suicide by chloroform.*

The Yellow Wall-Paper

It is very seldom that mere ordinary people like John and myself secure ancestral halls for the summer.

A colonial mansion, a hereditary estate. I would say a haunted house, and reach the height of romantic felicity—but that would be asking too much of fate!

Still I will proudly declare that there is something queer about it.

Else, why should it be let so cheaply? And why have stood so long untenanted?

John laughs at me, of course, but one expects that in marriage.

John is practical in the extreme. He has no patience with faith, an intense horror of superstition, and he scoffs openly at any talk of things not to be felt and seen and put down in figures.

John is a physician, and *perhaps*—(I would not say it to a living soul, of course, but this is dead paper and a great relief to my mind—) *perhaps* that is one reason I do not get well faster.

You see he does not believe I am sick!

And what can one do?

If a physician of high standing, and one's own husband, assures friends and relatives that there is really nothing the matter with one but temporary nervous depression—a slight hysterical tendency—what is one to do?

My brother is also a physician, and also of high standing, and he says the same thing.

So I take phosphates or phosphites—whichever it is, and tonics, and journeys, and air, and exercise, and am absolutely forbidden to "work" until I am well again.

Personally, I disagree with their ideas.

Personally, I believe that congenial work, with excitement and change, would do me good.

But what is one to do?

I did write for a while in spite of them; but it *does* exhaust me a good deal — having to be so sly about it, or else meet with heavy opposition.

I sometimes fancy that in my condition if I had less opposition and more society and stimulus — but John says the very worst thing I can do is to think about my condition, and I confess it always makes me feel bad.

So I will let it alone and talk about the house.

The most beautiful place! It is quite alone, standing well back from the road, quite three miles from the village. It makes me think of English places that you read about, for there are hedges and walls and gates that lock, and lots of separate little houses for the gardeners and people.

There is a *delicious* garden! I never saw such a garden — large and shady, full of box-bordered paths, and lined with long grape-covered arbors with seats under them.

There were greenhouses, too, but they are all broken now.

There was some legal trouble, I believe, something about the heirs and co-heirs; anyhow, the place has been empty for years.

That spoils my ghostliness, I am afraid, but I don't care — there is something strange about the house — I can feel it.

I even said so to John one moonlight evening, but he said what I felt was a *draught*, and shut the window.

I get unreasonably angry with John sometimes. I'm sure I never used to be so sensitive. I think it is due to this nervous condition.

But John says if I feel so, I shall neglect proper self-control; so I take pains to control myself — before him, at least, and that makes me very tired.

I don't like our room a bit. I wanted one downstairs that opened on the piazza and had roses all over the window, and such pretty old-fashioned chintz hangings! but John would not hear of it.

He said there was only one window and not room for two beds, and no near room for him if he took another.

He is very careful and loving, and hardly lets me stir without special direction.

I have a schedule prescription for each hour in the day; he takes all care from me, and so I feel basely ungrateful not to value it more.

He said we came here solely on my account, that I was to have perfect rest and all the air I could get. "Your exercise depends on your strength, my dear," said he, "and your food somewhat on your appetite; but air you can absorb all the time." So we took the nursery at the top of the house.

It is a big, airy room, the whole floor nearly, with windows that look all ways, and air and sunshine galore. It was nursery first and then playroom and gymnasium, I should judge; for the windows are barred for little children, and there are rings and things in the walls.

The paint and paper look as if a boys' school had used it. It is stripped off — the paper — in great patches all around the head of my bed, about as far as I can reach, and in a great place on the other side of the room low down. I never saw a worse paper in my life.

One of those sprawling flamboyant patterns committing every artistic sin.

It is dull enough to confuse the eye in following, pronounced enough to constantly irritate and provoke study, and when you follow the lame uncertain curves for a little distance they suddenly commit suicide—plunge off at outrageous angles, destroy themselves in unheard of contradictions.

The color is repellent, almost revolting; a smouldering unclean yellow, strangely faded by the slow-turning sunlight.

It is a dull yet lurid orange in some places, a sickly sulphur tint in others.

No wonder the children hated it! I should hate it myself if I had to live in this room long.

There comes John, and I must put this away—he hates to have me write a word.

We have been here two weeks, and I haven't felt like writing before, since that first day.

I am sitting by the window now, up in this atrocious nursery, and there is nothing to hinder my writing as much as I please, save lack of strength.

John is away all day, and even some nights when his cases are serious.

I am glad my case is not serious!

But these nervous troubles are dreadfully depressing.

John does not know how much I really suffer. He knows there is no *reason* to suffer, and that satisfies him.

Of course it is only nervousness. It does weigh on me so not to do my duty in any way!

I meant to be such a help to John, such a real rest and comfort, and here I am a comparative burden already!

Nobody would believe what an effort it is to do what little I am able,—to dress and entertain, and order things.

It is fortunate Mary is so good with the baby. Such a dear baby!

And yet I *cannot* be with him, it makes me so nervous.

I suppose John never was nervous in his life. He laughs at me so about this wall-paper!

At first he meant to repaper the room, but afterwards he said that I was letting it get the better of me, and that nothing was worse for such a nervous patient than to give way to such fancies.

He said that after the wall-paper was changed it would be the heavy bedstead, and then the barred windows, and then that gate at the head of the stairs, and so on.

"You know the place is doing you good," he said, "and really, dear, I don't care to renovate the house just for a three months' rental."

"Then do let us go downstairs," I said, "there are such pretty rooms there."

Then he took me in his arms and called me, a blessed little goose, and said he would go down cellar, if I wished, and have it whitewashed into the bargain.

But he is right enough about the beds and windows and things.

It is an airy and comfortable room as any one need wish, and, of course, I would not be so silly as to make him uncomfortable just for a whim.

I'm really getting quite fond of the big room, all but that horrid paper.

Out of one window I can see the garden, those mysterious deep-shaded arbors, the riotous old-fashioned flowers, and bushes and gnarly trees.

Out of another I get a lovely view of the bay and a little private wharf belonging to the estate. There is a beautiful shaded lane that runs down there from the house. I always fancy I see people walking in these numerous paths and arbors, but John has cautioned me not to give way to fancy in the least. He says that with my imaginative power and habit of story-making, a nervous weakness like mine is sure to lead to all manner of excited fancies, and that I ought to use my will and good sense to check the tendency. So I try.

I think sometimes that if I were only well enough to write a little it would relieve the press of ideas and rest me.

But I find I get pretty tired when I try.

It is so discouraging not to have any advice and companionship about my work. When I get really well, John says we will ask Cousin Henry and Julia down for a long visit; but he says he would as soon put fireworks in my pillow-case as to let me have those stimulating people about now.

I wish I could get well faster.

But I must not think about that. This paper looks to me as if it *knew* what a vicious influence it had!

There is a recurrent spot where the pattern lolls like a broken neck and two bulbous eyes stare at you upside down.

I get positively angry with the impertinence of it and the everlastingness. Up and down and sideways they crawl, and those absurd, unblinking eyes are everywhere. There is one place where two breadths didn't match, and the eyes go all up and down the line, one a little higher than the other.

I never saw so much expression in an inanimate thing before, and we all know how much expression they have! I used to lie awake as a child and get more entertainment and terror out of blank walls and plain furniture than most children could find in a toy-store.

I remember what a kindly wink the knobs of our big, old bureau used to have, and there was one chair that always seemed like a strong friend.

I used to feel that if any of the other things looked too fierce I could always hop into that chair and be safe.

The furniture in this room is no worse than inharmonious, however, for we had to bring it all from downstairs. I suppose when this was used as a playroom they had to take the nursery things out, and no wonder! I never saw such ravages as the children have made here.

The wall-paper, as I said before, is torn off in spots, and it sticketh closer than a brother — they must have had perseverance as well as hatred.

Then the floor is scratched and gouged and splintered, the plaster itself is dug out here and there, and this great heavy bed which is all we found in the room, looks as if it had been through the wars.

But I don't mind it a bit — only the paper.

There comes John's sister. Such a dear girl as she is, and so careful of me! I must not let her find me writing.

She is a perfect and enthusiastic housekeeper, and hopes for no better profession. I verily believe she thinks it is the writing which made me sick!

But I can write when she is out, and see her a long way off from these windows.

There is one that commands the road, a lovely shaded winding road, and one that just looks off over the country. A lovely country, too, full of great elms and velvet meadows.

This wall-paper has a kind of subpattern in a different shade, a particularly irritating one, for you can only see it in certain lights, and not clearly then.

But in the places where it isn't faded and where the sun is just so—I can see a strange, provoking, formless sort of figure, that seems to skulk about behind that silly and conspicuous front design.

There's sister on the stairs!

Well, the Fourth of July is over! The people are all gone and I am tired out. John thought it might do me good to see a little company, so we just had mother and Nellie and the children down for a week.

Of course I didn't do a thing. Jennie sees to everything now.

But it tired me all the same.

John says if I don't pick up faster he shall send me to Weir Mitchell in the fall.

But I don't want to go there at all. I had a friend who was in his hands once, and she says he is just like John and my brother, only more so!

Besides, it is such an undertaking to go so far.

I don't feel as if it was worth while to turn my hand over for anything, and I'm getting dreadfully fretful and querulous.

I cry at nothing, and cry most of the time.

Of course I don't when John is here, or anybody else, but when I am alone.

And I am alone a good deal just now. John is kept in town very often by serious cases, and Jennie is good and lets me alone when I want her to.

So I walk a little in the garden or down that lovely lane, sit on the porch under the roses, and lie down up here a good deal.

I'm getting really fond of the room in spite of the wall-paper. Perhaps *because* of the wall-paper.

It dwells in my mind so!

I lie here on this great immovable bed—it is nailed down, I believe—and follow that pattern about by the hour. It is as good as gymnastics, I assure you. I start, we'll say, at the bottom, down in the corner over there where it has not been touched, and I determine for the thousandth time that I *will* follow that pointless pattern to some sort of a conclusion.

I know a little of the principle of design, and I know this thing was not arranged on any laws of radiation, or alternation, or repetition, or symmetry, or anything else that I ever heard of.

It is repeated, of course, by the breadths, but not otherwise.

Looked at in one way each breadth stands alone, the bloated curves and flourishes—a kind of "debased Romanesque" with *delirium tremens* go waddling up and down in isolated columns of fatuity.

But, on the other hand, they connect diagonally, and the sprawling outlines run off in great slanting waves of optic horror, like a lot of wallowing seaweeds in full chase.

The whole thing goes horizontally, too, at least it seems so, and I exhaust myself in trying to distinguish the order of its going in that direction.

They have used a horizontal breadth for a frieze, and that adds wonderfully to the confusion.

There is one end of the room where it is almost intact, and there, when the crosslights fade and the low sun shines directly upon it, I can almost fancy radiation after all — the interminable grotesques seems to form around a common centre and rush off in headlong plunges of equal distraction.

It makes me tired to follow it. I will take a nap I guess.

I don't know why I should write this.

I don't want to.

I don't feel able.

And I know John would think it absurd. But I *must* say what I feel and think in some way — it is such a relief!

But the effort is getting to be greater than the relief.

Half the time now I am awfully lazy, and lie down ever so much.

John says I mustn't lose my strength, and has me take cod liver oil and lots of tonics and things, to say nothing of ale and wine and rare meat.

Dear John! He loves me very dearly, and hates to have me sick. I tried to have a real earnest reasonable talk with him the other day, and tell him how I wish he would let me go and make a visit to Cousin Henry and Julia.

But he said I wasn't able to go, nor able to stand it after I got there; and I did not make out a very good case for myself, for I was crying before I had finished.

It is getting to be a great effort for me to think straight. Just this nervous weakness I suppose.

And dear John gathered me up in his arms, and just carried me straight upstairs and laid me on the bed, and sat by me and read to me till it tired my head.

He said I was his darling and his comfort and all he had, and that I must take care of myself for his sake, and keep well.

He says no one but myself can help me out of it, that I must use my will and self-control and not let any silly fancies run away with me.

There's one comfort, the baby is well and happy, and does not have to occupy this nursery with the horrid wall-paper.

If we had not used it, that blessed child would have! What a fortunate escape! Why, I wouldn't have a child of mine, an impressionable little thing, live in such a room for worlds.

I never thought of it before, but it is lucky that John kept me here after all, I can stand it so much easier than a baby, you see.

Of course I never mention it to them any more — I am too wise, — but I keep watch of it all the same.

There are things in that paper that nobody knows but me, or ever will.

Behind that outside pattern the dim shapes get clearer every day.

It is always the same shape, only very numerous.

And it is like a woman stooping down and creeping about behind that pattern. I don't like it a bit. I wonder — I begin to think — I wish John would take me away from here!

It is so hard to talk with John about my case, because he is so wise, and because he loves me so.

But I tried it last night.

It was moonlight. The moon shines in all around just as the sun does.

I hate to see it sometimes, it creeps so slowly, and always comes in by one window or another.

John was asleep and I hated to waken him, so I kept still and watched the moonlight on that undulating wall-paper till I felt creepy.

The faint figure behind seemed to shake the pattern, just as if she wanted to get out.

I got up softly and went to feel and see if the paper *did* move, and when I came back John was awake.

"What is it, little girl?" he said. "Don't go walking about like that — you'll get cold."

I thought it was a good time to talk, so I told him that I really was not gaining here, and that I wished he would take me away.

"Why, darling!" said he, "our lease will be up in three weeks, and I can't see how to leave before."

"The repairs are not done at home, and I cannot possibly leave town just now. Of course if you were in any danger, I could and would, but you really are better, dear, whether you can see it or not. I am a doctor, dear, and I know. You are gaining flesh and color, your appetite is better, I feel really much easier about you."

"I don't weigh a bit more," said I, "nor as much; and my appetite may be better in the evening when you are here, but it is worse in the morning when you are away!"

"Bless her little heart!" said he with a big hug, "she shall be as sick as she pleases! But now let's improve the shining hours by going to sleep, and talk about it in the morning!"

"And you won't go away?" I asked gloomily.

"Why, how can I, dear? It is only three weeks more and then we will take a nice little trip of a few days while Jennie is getting the house ready. Really dear you are better!"

"Better in body perhaps —" I began, and stopped short, for he sat up straight and looked at me with such a stern, reproachful look that I could not say another word.

"My darling," said he, "I beg of you, for my sake and for our child's sake, as well as for your own, that you will never for one instant let that idea enter your mind! There is nothing so dangerous, so fascinating, to a temperament like yours. It is a false and foolish fancy. Can you not trust me as a physician when I tell you so?"

So of course I said no more on that score, and we went to sleep before long. He thought I was asleep first, but I wasn't, and lay there for hours trying to decide whether that front pattern and the back pattern really did move together or separately.

On a pattern like this, by daylight, there is a lack of sequence, a defiance of law, that is a constant irritant to a normal mind.

The color is hideous enough, and unreliable enough, and infuriating enough, but the pattern is torturing.

You think you have mastered it, but just as you get well underway in following, it turns a back-somersault and there you are. It slaps you in the face, knocks you down, and tramples upon you. It is like a bad dream.

The outside pattern is a florid arabesque, reminding one of a fungus. If you can imagine a toadstool in joints, an interminable string of toadstools, budding and sprouting in endless convolutions—why, that is something like it.

That is, sometimes!

There is one marked peculiarity about this paper, a thing nobody seems to notice but myself, and that is that it changes as the light changes.

When the sun shoots in through the east window—I always watch for that first long, straight ray—it changes so quickly that I never can quite believe it.

That is why I watch it always.

By moonlight—the moon shines in all night when there is a moon—I wouldn't know it was the same paper.

At night in any kind of light, in twilight, candlelight, lamplight, and worst of all by moonlight, it becomes bars! The outside pattern I mean, and the woman behind it is as plain as can be.

I didn't realize for a long time what the thing was that showed behind, that dim sub-pattern, but now I am quite sure it is a woman.

By daylight she is subdued, quiet. I fancy it is the pattern that keeps her so still. It is so puzzling. It keeps me quiet by the hour.

I lie down ever so much now. John says it is good for me, and to sleep all I can.

Indeed he started the habit by making me lie down for an hour after each meal.

It is a very bad habit I am convinced, for you see I don't sleep.

And that cultivates deceit, for I don't tell them I'm awake——O no!

The fact is I am getting a little afraid of John.

He seems very queer sometimes, and even Jennie has an inexplicable look.

It strikes me occasionally, just as a scientific hypothesis,—that perhaps it is the paper!

I have watched John when he did not know I was looking, and come into the room suddenly on the most innocent excuses, and I've caught him several times *looking at the paper!* And Jennie too. I caught Jennie with her hand on it once.

She didn't know I was in the room, and when I asked her in a quiet, a very quiet voice, with the most restrained manner possible, what she was doing with the paper—she turned around as if she had been caught stealing, and looked quite angry—asked me why I should frighten her so!

Then she said that the paper stained everything it touched, that she had found yellow smooches on all my clothes and John's, and she wished we would be more careful!

Did not that sound innocent? But I know she was studying that pattern, and I am determined that nobody shall find it out but myself!

Life is very much more exciting now than it used to be. You see I have something more to expect, to look forward to, to watch. I really do eat better, and am more quiet than I was.

John is so pleased to see me improve! He laughed a little the other day, and said I seemed to be flourishing in spite of my wall-paper.

I turned it off with a laugh. I had no intention of telling him it was *because* of the wall-paper—he would make fun of me. He might even want to take me away.

I don't want to leave now until I have found it out. There is a week more, and I think that will be enough.

I'm feeling ever so much better! I don't sleep much at night, for it is so interesting to watch developments; but I sleep a good deal in the daytime.

In the daytime it is tiresome and perplexing.

There are always new shoots on the fungus, and new shades of yellow all over it. I cannot keep count of them, though I have tried conscientiously.

It is the strangest yellow, that wall-paper! It makes me think of all the yellow things I ever saw—not beautiful ones like buttercups, but old foul, bad yellow things.

But there is something else about that paper—the smell! I noticed it the moment we came into the room, but with so much air and sun it was not bad. Now we have had a week of fog and rain, and whether the windows are open or not, the smell is here.

It creeps all over the house.

I find it hovering in the dining-room, skulking in the parlor, hiding in the hall, lying in wait for me on the stairs.

It gets into my hair.

Even when I go to ride, if I turn my head suddenly and surprise it—there is that smell!

Such a peculiar odor, too! I have spent hours in trying to analyze it, to find what it smelled like.

It is not bad—at first, and very gentle, but quite the subtlest, most enduring odor I ever met.

In this damp weather it is awful. I wake up in the night and find it hanging over me.

It used to disturb me at first. I thought seriously of burning the house—to reach the smell.

But now I am used to it. The only thing I can think of that it is like is the *color* of the paper! A yellow smell.

There is a very funny mark on this wall, low down, near the mopboard. A streak that runs round the room. It goes behind every piece of furniture, except the bed, a long, straight, even *smooch*, as if it had been rubbed over and over.

I wonder how it was done and who did it, and what they did it for. Round and round and round—round and round and round!—it makes me dizzy!

I really have discovered something at last.

Through watching so much at night, when it changes so, I have finally found out.

The front pattern *does* move—and no wonder! The woman behind shakes it!

Sometimes I think there are a great many women behind, and sometimes only one, and she crawls around fast, and her crawling shakes it all over.

Then in the very bright spots she keeps still, and in the very shady spots she just takes hold of the bars and shakes them hard.

And she is all the time trying to climb through. But nobody could climb through that pattern—it strangles so; I think that is why it has so many heads.

They get through, and then the pattern strangles them off and turns them upside down, and makes their eyes white!

If those heads were covered or taken off it would not be half so bad.

I think that woman gets out in the daytime!

And I'll tell you why—privately—I've seen her!

I can see her out of every one of my windows!

It is the same woman, I know, for she is always creeping, and most women do not creep by daylight.

I see her in that long shaded lane, creeping up and down. I see her in those dark grape arbors, creeping all around the garden.

I see her on that long road under the trees, creeping along, and when a carriage comes she hides under the blackberry vines.

I don't blame her a bit. It must be very humiliating to be caught creeping by daylight!

I always lock the door when I creep by daylight. I can't do it at night, for I know John would suspect something at once.

And John is so queer now, that I don't want to irritate him. I wish he would take another room! Besides, I don't want anybody to get that woman out at night but myself.

I often wonder if I could see her out of all the windows at once.

But, turn as fast as I can, I can only see out of one at one time.

And though I always see her, she *may* be able to creep faster than I can turn!

I have watched her sometimes away off in the open country, creeping as fast as a cloud shadow in a high wind.

If only that top pattern could be gotten off from the under one! I mean to try it, little by little.

I have found out another funny thing, but I shan't tell it this time! It does not do to trust people too much.

There are only two more days to get this paper off, and I believe John is beginning to notice. I don't like the look in his eyes.

And I heard him ask Jennie a lot of professional questions about me. She had a very good report to give.

She said I slept a good deal in the daytime.

John knows I don't sleep very well at night, for all I'm so quiet!

He asked me all sorts of questions, too, and pretended to be very loving and kind.

As if I couldn't see through him!

Still, I don't wonder he acts so, sleeping under this paper for three months.

It only interests me, but I feel sure John and Jennie are secretly affected by it.

Hurrah! This is the last day, but it is enough. John to stay in town over night, and won't be out until this evening.

Jennie wanted to sleep with me—the sly thing! but I told her I should undoubtedly rest better for a night all alone.

That was clever, for really I wasn't alone a bit! As soon as it was moonlight and that poor thing began to crawl and shake the pattern, I got up and ran to help her.

I pulled and she shook. I shook and she pulled, and before morning we had peeled off yards of that paper.

A strip about as high as my head and half around the room.

And then when the sun came and that awful pattern began to laugh at me, I declared I would finish it to-day!

We go away to-morrow, and they are moving all my furniture down again to leave things as they were before.

Jennie looked at the wall in amazement, but I told her merrily that I did it out of pure spite at the vicious thing.

She laughed and said she wouldn't mind doing it herself, but I must not get tired.

How she betrayed herself that time!

But I am here, and no person touches this paper but me, — not *alive!*

She tried to get me out of the room — it was too patent! But I said it was so quiet and empty and clean now that I believed I would lie down again and sleep all I could; and not to wake me even for dinner — I would call when I woke.

So now she is gone, and the servants are gone, and the things are gone, and there is nothing left but that great bedstead nailed down, with the canvas mattress we found on it.

We shall sleep downstairs to-night, and take the boat home to-morrow.

I quite enjoy the room, now it is bare again.

How those children did tear about here!

This bedstead is fairly gnawed!

But I must get to work.

I have locked the door and thrown the key down into the front path.

I don't want to go out, and I don't want to have anybody come in, till John comes.

I want to astonish him.

I've got rope up here that even Jennie did not find. If that woman does get out, and tries to get away, I can tie her!

But I forgot I could not reach far without anything to stand on!

This bed will *not* move!

I tried to lift and push it until I was lame, and then I got so angry I bit off a little piece at one corner — but it hurt my teeth.

Then I peeled off all the paper I could reach standing on the floor. It sticks horribly and the pattern just enjoys it! All those strangled heads and bulbous eyes and waddling fungus growths just shriek with derision!

I am getting angry enough to do something desperate. To jump out of the window would be admirable exercise, but the bars are too strong even to try.

Besides I wouldn't do it. Of course not. I know well enough that a step like that is improper and might be misconstrued.

I don't like to *look* out of the windows even — there are so many of those creeping women, and they creep so fast.

I wonder if they all come out of that wall-paper as I did?

But I am securely fastened now by my well-hidden rope — you don't get *me* out in the road there!

I suppose I shall have to get back behind the pattern when it comes night, and that is hard!

It is so pleasant to be out in this great room and creep around as I please!

I don't want to go outside. I won't, even if Jennie asks me to.

For outside you have to creep on the ground, and everything is green instead of yellow.

But here I can creep smoothly on the floor, and my shoulder just fits in that long smooch around the wall, so I cannot lose my way.

Why there's John at the door!

It is no use, young man, you can't open it!

How he does call and pound!

Now he's crying for an axe.

It would be a shame to break down that beautiful door!

"John dear!" said I in the gentlest voice, "the key is down by the front steps, under a plaintain leaf!"

That silenced him for a few moments.

Then he said — very quietly indeed, "Open the door, my darling!"

"I can't," said I. "The key is down by the front door under a plaintain leaf!"

And then I said it again, several times, very gently and slowly, and said it so often that he had to go and see, and he got it of course, and came in. He stopped short by the door.

"What is the matter?" he cried "For God's sake, what are you doing!"

I kept on creeping just the same, but I looked at him over my shoulder.

"I've got out at last," said I, "in spite of you and Jane! And I've pulled off most of the paper, so you can't put me back!"

Now why should that man have fainted? But he did, and right across my path by the wall, so that I had to creep over him every time!

[1892]

Study and Writing Questions

1. How do the NARRATOR's perceptions of the wallpaper change from section to section of the NARRATIVE? What does the wallpaper represent for her in each section? Who is the figure she sees in the wallpaper? What might the color yellow usually represent? What does it represent here? Why is the STORY called "The Yellow Wall-Paper"?

2. John refers to the narrator's "habit of story-making." In what ways is story-making as discussed and enacted in this STORY good and in what ways bad? Is the narrator the only one making stories? What is the importance of this activity being a "habit"?

3. In the fifth section, John says "now let's improve the shining hours by going to sleep." This is an ALLUSION to a poem called "Against Idleness and Mischief" from Issac Watts's *Divine Songs for Children* (1715):

How doth the busy bee
Improve each shining hour,

And gather honey all the day
   From every opening flower!

How skillfully she builds her cell!
   How neat she spreads the wax!
And labours hard to store it well
   With the sweet food she makes.

In works of labour or of skill,
   I would be busy too;
For Satan finds some mischief still
   For idle hands to do.

In books, or work, or healthful play,
   Let my first years be passed,
That I may give for every day
   Some good account at last.

What values does the Watts poem suggest? In what ways is the narrator enabled to pursue these values and in what ways disabled? How does the use of this allusion characterize John? In what ways is the narrator treated like a child by John, by medical institutions, by her family, and by society at large?

4. Although it is clear that the narrator is to some extent disabled by those around her, her refrain "What can one do?" may also suggest, as does the fact that the author was a self-supporting woman, that the narrator is not without responsibility for her situation. To what extent do you believe the story shows the narrator as responsible for her plight? To what extent is the story a feminist critique of society?

5. How does the narrator's mental state change in each section? How does the narrator's voice reflect these changes? As her mind deteriorates, she becomes ever less reliable as a narrator. When do you start questioning her reliability? What is actually happening in the last paragraph?

See also Questions for Contrast and Comparison: 21, 45, 92, 128, 133, 137, 169, 204, 205, and 217.

■ ELLEN (ANDERSON GHOLSON) GLASGOW (1873–1945), *except for a period based in New York City and spent in travel (1911–1916), lived her entire life in Richmond, Virginia. Her physical fragility led to daily reliance on friends and family, yet her unwavering determination to become a writer began with a youthful program of self-education and culminated in international fame as a pioneering Southern realist, author of nineteen novels, many of them best-sellers. Devoted to her aristocratic mother and repelled by her Calvinist father, Glasgow suffered a mental breakdown and substantial deafness at her mother's death (1893), for which she blamed her father. Eventually, however, she came to admire his stern self-reliance. Attractive and loving, she had an early affair with a married man, a later engagement, and, for the last thirty years of her life, an "intermittent romance" with a male friend, but she never married. In her superb novel* Barren Ground *(1925), which she viewed as "a vehicle of liberation," a woman overcomes feckless love to restore her father's farm to fertility and rejects a late chance to marry comfortably, "thankful to have finished with all that." Although Glasgow won a Pulitzer Prize (*In This Our Life, *1941), her other fine novels, such as* The Sheltered Life *(1932) and* Vein of Iron *(1935), are now little read, yet her ideas on art (*A Certain Measure, *1943) and frank autobiography (*The Woman Within, *1954) remain important.*

A Point in Morals

"The question seems to be —— " began the Englishman. He looked up and bowed to a girl in black who had just come in from deck and was taking the seat beside him. "The question seems to be —— " The girl was having some difficulty in removing her coat, and he turned to assist her.

"In my opinion," remarked the distinguished alienist, who was returning from a vacation in Vienna, "the question is whether or not civilization is defeating its own aims in placing an exorbitant value on human life." As he spoke he leaned forward authoritatively and accented his words with foreign precision.

"You mean that the survival of the fittest is checkmated," remarked a young journalist travelling in the interest of a New York daily, "that civilization should practise artificial selection, as it were?"

The alienist shrugged his shoulders deprecatingly. "My dear sir," he protested, "I mean nothing. It is the question that means something."

"Well, as I was saying," began the Englishman again, reaching for the salt and upsetting a spoonful, "the question seems to be whether or not, in any circumstances, the saving of a human life may become positively immoral."

"Upon that point —— " began the alienist; but a young woman, in a white dress, who was seated on the Captain's right interrupted him.

"How could it?" she asked. "At least I don't see how it could. Do you, Captain?"

"There is no doubt," remarked the journalist, looking up from a conversation he had drifted into with a lawyer from one of the Western States, "that the more humane spirit pervading modern civilization has not worked wholly for good in the development of the species. Probably, for instance, if we had followed the Spartan practice of exposing unhealthy infants, we should have retained something of the Spartan hardihood. Certainly if we had been content to remain barbarians both our digestions and our nerves would have been the better for it, and melancholia would perhaps have been unknown. But, at the same time, the loss of a number of the more heroic virtues is overbalanced by an increase of the softer ones. Notably, human life has never before been regarded so sacredly."

"On the other side," observed the lawyer, lifting his hand to adjust his eyeglasses, and pausing to brush a crumb from his coat, "though it is all very well to be philanthropic to the point of pauperizing half a community and of growing squeamish about capital punishment, the whole thing sometimes takes a disgustingly morbid turn. Why, it seems as if criminals were the real American heroes! Only last week I visited a man sentenced to death for the murder of his two wives, and, by Jove, the place was literally besieged by woman sympathizers. I counted six bunches of roses in his cell, and at least fifty notes."

"Oh, but that is a form of nervous hysteria!" said the girl in black, "and must be considered separately. Every sentiment has its fanatics, philanthropy as well as religion. But we can't judge a movement by a few over-wrought disciples."

"Why not?" asked the Englishman, quietly. He was a middle-aged man, with an optimistic expression and a build of comfortable solidity. "But to return to the original proposition. I suppose we all accept as a self-evident truth the axiom that the highest civilization is the one in which the highest value is placed upon individual life."

"And happiness," added the girl in black.

"And happiness," assented the Englishman.

"And yet," commented the lawyer, "I think that most of us will admit that such a society, where life is regarded as sacred because it is valuable to the individual, not because it is valuable to the state, tends to the non-production of heroes."

"That the average will be higher and the exception lower," observed the journalist. "In other words, that there will be a general elevation of the mass, accompanied by a corresponding lowering of the few."

"On the whole, I think our system does very well," said the Englishman, carefully measuring the horseradish. "A mean between two extremes is apt to be satisfactory in results. If we don't produce a Marcus Aurelius or a Seneca, neither do we produce a Nero or a Phocas. We may have lost patriotism, but we have gained humanity, which is better. If we have lost chivalry, we have acquired decency; and if we have ceased to be picturesque, we have become cleanly, which is considerably more to be desired."

"I have never felt the romanticism of the Middle Ages," remarked the girl in black. "When I read of the glories of the Crusaders, I can't help remembering that a knight wore a single garment for a lifetime, and hacked his horse to pieces for a whim. Just as I never think of that chivalrous brute, Richard the Lion-Hearted, that I don't see him chopping off the heads of his prisoners."

"Oh, I don't think that any of us are sighing for a revival of the Middle Ages," returned the journalist. "The worship of the past has for its devotees people who have known only the present."

"Which is as it should be," commented the lawyer. "If man were confined to the worship of the knowable, all the world would lapse into atheism."

"Just as the great lovers of humanity were generally hermits," added the girl in black. "I had an uncle who used to say that he never really loved mankind until he went to live in the wilderness."

"I think we are drifting from the point," said the alienist. "Was it not: Can the saving of a human life ever prove to be an immoral act? I once held that it could."

"Did you act upon the theory?" asked the lawyer, with rising interest. "I maintain that no proposition can be said to exist until it is translated into action. Otherwise it is in an embryonic state merely."

The alienist laid down his fork and leaned forward. He was a notable-looking man of some thirty-odd years, who had made a sudden leap into popularity through several successful cases. He had a nervous, muscular face, with singularly penetrating eyes and hair of a light sandy colour. His hands were white and well shaped.

"It was some years ago," he said, bending a scintillant glance round the table. "If you will listen —— "

There followed a stir of assent, accompanied by a nod from the young woman on the Captain's right. "I feel as if it would be a ghost story," she declared.

"It is not a story at all," returned the alienist, lifting his wineglass and holding it against the light. "It is merely a fact."

Then he glanced swiftly round the table as if challenging attention.

"As I said," he began, slowly, "it was some few years ago. Just what year it was does not matter; but at that time I had completed a course at Heidelberg, and expected shortly to set out with an exploring party for South Africa. It turned out afterward that I did not go, but for the purpose of the present story it is sufficient that I intended to do so, and had made my preparations accordingly. At Heidelberg I had lived among a set of German students who were permeated with the metaphysics of Schopenhauer, Von Hartmann, and the rest, and I was pretty well saturated myself. At that age I was an ardent disciple of pessimism. I am still a disciple, but my ardour has abated, which is not the fault of pessimism, but the virtue of middle age —— "

"A man is called conservative when he grows less radical," interrupted the journalist.

"Or when he grows less in every direction," added the Englishman, "except in physical bulk."

The alienist accepted the suggestions with an inclination, and continued. "One of my most cherished convictions," he said, "was to the effect that every man is the sole arbiter of his fate. As Schopenhauer has put it, *'that there is nothing to which a man has a more unassailable title than to his own life and person.'* Indeed, that particular sentence had become a kind of motto with our set, and some of my companions even went so far as to preach the proper ending of life with the ending of the power of individual usefulness."

He paused to help himself to salad.

"I was in Scotland at the time, where I had spent a fortnight with my parents, in a small village on the Kyles of Bute. While there I had been treating an invalid cousin who had acquired the morphine habit, and who, under my care, had determined to uproot it. Before leaving I had secured from her the amount of the drug which she had in her possession—some thirty grains—done up in a sealed package, and labelled by a London chemist. As I was in haste, I put it in my bag, thinking that I would add it to my case of medicines when I reached Leicester, where I was to spend the night with an old schoolmate. I took the boat at Tighnabruaich, the small village, found a local train at Gourock, to reach Glasgow, with one minute in which to catch the first express to London. I made the change, and secured a first-class smoking-compartment, which I at first thought to be vacant; but when the train had started a man came from the dressing-room and took the seat across from me. At first I paid no heed to him, but upon looking up once or twice and finding his eyes upon me, I became unpleasantly conscious of his presence. He was thin almost to emaciation, and yet there was a suggestion of physical force about him which it was difficult to account for, since he was both short and slight. His clothes were shabby, though well made, and his tie had the appearance of having been tied in haste, or by nervous fingers. There was a trace of sensuality about his mouth, over which he wore a drooping yellow moustache tinged with gray, and he was somewhat bald on the crown of his head, which lent a deceptive hint of intellectuality to his uncovered forehead. As he crossed his legs, I saw that his boots were carefully blacked, and that they were long and slender, tapering to a decided point."

"I have always held," interpolated the lawyer, "that to judge a man's character you must look at his feet."

The alienist sipped his claret and took up his words:

"After passing the first stop, I remembered a book at the bottom of my bag, and unfastening the strap in my search for the book, I laid a number of small articles on the seat beside me, among them the sealed package bearing the morphine label and the name of the London chemist. Having found the book, I turned to replace the articles, when I noticed that the man across from me was gazing attentively at the labelled package. For a moment his expression startled me, and I stared back at him from across my open bag, into which I had dropped the articles. There was in his eyes a curious mixture of passion and repulsion, and, beyond it all, the look of a hungry hound when he sees food. Thinking that I had chanced upon a victim of the opium craving, I closed the bag, placed it in the net above my head, and opened my book.

"For a while we rode in silence. Nothing was heard except the noise of the train and the clicking of our bags as they jostled each other in the receptacle above. I remember these details very vividly, because since then I have recalled the slightest fact in connection with the incident. I knew that the man across from me drew a cigar from his case, felt in his pocket for an instant, and then turned to me for a match. At the same time I experienced the feeling that the request veiled a larger purpose, and that there were matches in the pocket into which he had thrust his fingers.

"But, as I complied with his request, he glanced indifferently out of the window, and following his gaze, I saw that we were passing a group of low lying hills sprinkled with stray patches of heather, and that across the hills a flock of sheep were filing, followed by a peasant girl in a short skirt. It was the last faint reminder of the Highlands.

"The man across from me leaned out, looking back upon the neutral sky, the sparse patches of heather, and the flock of sheep.

"'What a tone the heather gives to a landscape!' he remarked, and his voice sounded forced and affected.

"I bowed without replying, and as he turned from the window, and a draught of cinders blew in, I bent forward to lower the sash. In a moment he spoke again:

"'Do you go to London?'

"'To Leicester,' I answered, laying the book aside, impelled by a sudden interest. 'Why do you ask?'

"He flushed nervously.

"'I—oh, nothing,' he answered, and drew away from me.

"Then, as if with swift determination, he reached forward and lifted the book I had laid on the seat. It was a treatise of Von Hartmann's in German.

"'I had judged that you were a physician,' he said, 'a student, perhaps, from a German university?'

"'I am.'

"He paused for an instant, and then spoke in absent-minded reiteration, 'So you don't go on to London?'

"'No,' I returned, impatiently. 'Can I do anything for you?'

"He handed me the book, regarding me resolutely as he did so.

"'Are you a sensible man?'

"I bowed.

"'And a philosopher?'

"'In an amateur fashion.'

"With feverish energy he went on more quickly, 'You have in your possession,' he said, 'something for which I would give my whole fortune.' He laid two half-sovereigns and some odd silver in the palm of his hand. 'This is all I possess,' he continued, 'but I would give it gladly.'

"I looked at him curiously.

"'You mean the morphine?' I demanded.

"He nodded. 'I don't ask you to give it to me. I only ask——'

"I interrupted him. 'Are you in pain?'

"He laughed softly, and I really believe he felt a tinge of amusement. 'It is a question of expediency,' he explained. 'If you happen to be a moralist——' He broke off.

"'What of it?' I inquired.

"He settled himself in his corner, resting his head against the cushions.

"'You get out at Leicester,' he said, recklessly. 'I go on to London, where Providence, represented by Scotland Yard, is awaiting me.'

"I started. 'For what?'

"'They call it murder, I believe,' he returned; 'but what they call it matters very little. I call it divine justice—that also matters very little. The point is—I shall arrive, they will be there before me. That is settled. Every station along the road is watched.'

"I glanced out of the window.

"'But you came from Glasgow,' I suggested.

"'Worse luck! I waited in the dressing-room, until the train started. I hoped to have the compartment alone, but—' He leaned forward and lowered the window-shade. 'If you don't object,' he said, apologetically; 'I find the glare trying. It is a question for a moralist,' he repeated. 'Indeed, I may call myself a question for a moralist,' and he smiled again with that ugly humour. 'To begin with the beginning, the question is bred in the bone and it's out in the blood.' He nodded at my look of surprise. 'You are an American,' he continued, 'so am I. I was born in Washington some thirty years ago. My father was a politician, whose honour was held to be unimpeachable — which was a mistake. His name doesn't matter, but he became very wealthy through judicious speculations in votes and other things. My mother has always suffered from an incipient hysteria, which developed shortly before my birth.' He wiped his forehead with his handkerchief, and knocked the ashes from his cigar with a flick of his finger. 'The motive for this is not far to seek,' he said, with a glance at my travelling-bag. He had the coolest bravado I have ever met. 'As a child,' he went on, 'I gave great promise. Indeed, we moved to England that I might be educated at Oxford. My father considered the ecclesiastical atmosphere to be beneficial. But while at college I got into trouble with a woman, and I left. My father died, his fortune burst like a bubble, and my mother moved to the country. I was put into a banking office, but I got into more trouble with women, this time two of them. One was a variety actress, and I married her. I didn't want to do it. I tried not to, but I couldn't help it, and I did it. A month later I left her. I changed my name and went to Belfast where I resolved to become an honest man. It was a tough job, but I laboured and I succeeded for a time. The variety actress began looking for me, but I escaped her, and have escaped her so far. That was eight years ago. And several years after reaching Belfast I met another woman. She was different. I fell ill of fever in Ireland, and she nursed me. She was a good woman, with a broad Irish face, strong hands, and motherly shoulders. I was weak and she was strong, and I fell in love with her. I tried to tell her about the variety actress, but somehow I couldn't, and I married her.' He shot the stump of his cigar through the opposite window and lighted another, this time drawing the match from his pocket. 'She is an honest woman,' he said, 'as honest as the day. She believes in me. It would kill her to know about the variety actress and all the others. There is one child, a girl, a freckle-faced mite just like her mother, and another is coming.'

"'She knows nothing of this affair?

"'Not a blamed thing. She is the kind of woman who is good because she can't help herself. She enjoys it. I never did. My mother is different too. She would die if other people knew of this; my wife would die if she knew of it herself. Well, I got tired, and I wanted money, so I left her and went to Dublin. I changed my name and got a clerkship in a shipping-office. My wife thinks I went to America to get work, and if she never hears of me she'll probably think no worse. I did intend going to America, but somehow I didn't. I got in with a man who signed somebody's name to a cheque and got me to present it. Then we quarrelled about the money; the man threw the job on me, and the affair came out. But before they arrested me, I ran him down and shot him. I was ridding the world of a damned traitor.'

"He raised the shade with a nervous hand; but the sun flashed in his eyes, and he lowered it.

"'I suppose I'd hang for it,' he said. 'There isn't much doubt of that. If I waited, I'd hang for it, but I am not going to wait. I am going to die.'

"'And how?'

"'Before this train reaches London,' he replied. 'I am a dead man. There are two ways. I might say three, except that a pitch from the carriage might mean only a broken leg. But there is this—' He drew a vial from his pocket and held it to the light. It contained an ounce or so of carbolic acid.

"'One of the most corrosive of irritants,' I observed.

"'And there is—your package.'

"My first impulse was to force the vial from him. He was a slight man, and I could have overcome him with but little exertion. But the exertion I did not make. I should as soon have thought, when my rational humour reasserted itself, of knocking a man down and robbing him of his watch. The acid was as exclusively his property as the clothes he wore, and equally his life was his own. Had he declared his intention to hurl himself from the window, I might not have made way for him, but I should certainly not have obstructed his passage.

"But the morphine was mine, and that I should assist him was another matter, so I said:

"'The package belongs to me.'

"'And you will not exchange?'

"'Certainly not.'

"He answered, almost angrily:

"'Why not be reasonable? You admit that I am in a mess of it?'

"'Readily.'

"'You also admit that my life is morally my own?'

"'Equally.'

"'That its continuance could in no wise prove to be of benefit to society?'

"'I do.'

"'That for all connected with me it is better that I should die unknown and under an assumed name?'

"'Yes.'

"'Then you admit also that the best I can do is to kill myself before reaching London?'

"'Perhaps.'

"'So you will leave me the morphine when you get off at Leicester?'

"'No.'

"He struck the window-sill impatiently with the palm of his hand.

"'And why not?'

"I hesitated an instant.

"'Because, upon the whole, I do not care to be the instrument of your self-destruction.'

"'Don't be a fool!' he retorted. 'Speak honestly, and say that because of a little moral shrinking on your part, you prefer to leave a human being to a death of agony. I don't like physical pain. I am like a woman about it, but it is better than hanging, or life-imprisonment, or any jury finding.'

"I became exhortatory.

"'Why not face it like a man and take your chances? Who knows——'

"'I have had my chances,' he returned. 'I have squandered more chances than most men ever lay eyes on, and I don't care. If I had the opportunity, I'd squander them again. It is the only thing chances are made for.'

"'What a scoundrel you are!' I exclaimed.

"'Well, I don't know,' he answered; 'there have been worse men. I never said a harsh word to a woman, and I never hit a man when he was down——'

"I blushed. 'Oh, I didn't mean to hit you,' I responded.

"He took no notice.

"'I like my wife,' he said. 'She is a good woman, and I'd do a good deal to keep her and the children from knowing the truth. Perhaps I'd kill myself even if I didn't want to. I don't know, but I am tired — damned tired.'

"'And yet you deserted her.'

"'I did. I tried not to, but I couldn't help it. If I were free to go back to her to-morrow, unless I was ill and wanted nursing, I'd see that she had grown shapeless, and that her hands were coarse.' He stretched out his own, which were singularly white and delicate. 'I believe I'd leave her in a week,' he said.

"Then with an eager movement he pointed to my bag.

"'That is the ending of the difficulty,' he added. 'Otherwise I swear that before the train gets to London, I will swallow this stuff and die like a rat.'

"'I admit your right to die in any manner you choose; but I don't see that it is my place to assist you. It is an ugly job.'

"'So am I,' he retorted, grimly. 'At any rate, if you leave the train with that package in your bag it will be cowardice — sheer cowardice. And for the sake of your cowardice you will damn me to this.' He touched the vial.

"'It won't be pleasant,' I said, and we were silent.

"I knew that the man had spoken the truth. I was accustomed to lies, and had learned to detect them. I knew, also, that the world would be well rid of him and his kind. Why I should preserve him for death upon the gallows I did not see. The majesty of the law would be in no way ruffled by his premature departure; and if I could trust that part of his story, the lives of innocent women and children would, in the other case, suffer considerably. And, even if I and my unopened bag alighted at Leicester, I was sure that he would never reach London alive. He was a desperate man, this I read in his set face, his dazed eyes, his nervous hands. He was a poor devil, and I was sorry for him. Why, then, should I contribute, by my refusal to comply with his request, an additional hour of agony to his existence? Could I, with my pretence of philosophic freedom, alight at my station, leaving him to swallow the acid and die like a rat in a cage before the journey was over? I remembered that I had once seen a guinea-pig die from the effects of carbolic acid, and the remembrance sickened me.

"As I sat there listening to the noise of the slackening train, which was nearing Leicester, I thought of a hundred things, I thought of Schopenhauer and Von Hartmann. I thought of the dying guinea-pig. I thought of the broad-faced Irish wife and the two children.

"Then 'Leicester' flashed before me, and the train stopped. I rose, gathered my coat and rug, and lifted the volume of Von Hartmann from the seat. The man remained motionless in the corner of the compartment, but his eyes followed me.

"I stooped, opened my bag, and laid the chemist's package on the seat. Then I stepped out, closing the door after me."

As the speaker finished, he reached forward, selected an almond from the stand of nuts, fitted it carefully between the crackers, and cracked it slowly.

The young woman in the white dress started up with a shudder.

"What a horrible story!" she exclaimed; "for it is a story, after all, and not a fact."

"A point, rather," suggested the Englishman; "but is that all?"

"All of the point," returned the alienist. "The next day I saw in the *Times* that a man, supposed to be James Morganson, who was wanted for murder, was found dead in a first-class smoking-compartment of the Midland Railway. Coroner's verdict, 'Death resulting from an overdose of opium, taken with suicidal intent.'"

The journalist dropped a lump of sugar in his cup and watched it attentively.

"I don't think I could have done it," he said. "I might have left him with his carbolic. But I couldn't have deliberately given him his death-potion."

"But as long as he was going to die," responded the girl in black, "it was better to let him die painlessly."

The Englishman smiled. "Can a woman ever consider the ethical side of a question when the sympathetic one is visible?" he asked.

The alienist cracked another almond. "I was sincere," he said. "Of that there is no doubt. I thought I did right. The question is — did I do right?"

"It would have been wiser," began the lawyer, argumentatively, "since you were the stronger, to take the vial from him and leave him to the care of the law."

"But the wife and children," replied the girl in black. "And hanging is so horrible!"

"So is murder," responded the lawyer, dryly.

The young woman on the Captain's right laid her napkin on the table and rose. "I don't know what was right," she said, "but I do know that in your place I should have felt like a murderer."

The alienist smiled half cynically. "So I did," he answered; "but there is such a thing, my dear young lady, as a conscientious murderer."

[1899]

Study and Writing Questions

1. Each of the CHARACTERS in the FRAME situation is briefly labeled. The alienist (the word itself means a specialist in the legal aspects of psychiatry, but also calls to mind the idea of alienation) tells the central STORY, but most of the frame characters speak. Who does and who does not? Are their words consistent with their labels? Is there a MORAL importance to Glasgow's use of these labels?

2. Compare and contrast the frame situation with the situation in the central story. How are they related? Why does the IMPLIED AUTHOR arrange for occasional interruptions in the telling of the central story? Are the points at which these interruptions occur in some way(s) significant?

3. What motivates the alienist to tell his story? What can you infer about his character? Do you believe he is telling the truth?

4. What kind of person is the character James Morganson? What MOTIVATES him? He is reported to have said, "'Indeed, I may call myself a question for a moralist.'" What does it mean that he says this to the alienist? Why does he say it? Is he right?

5. Try to answer the alienist's question: "'Did I do right?'" What conclusion does the implied author want you to reach? Is your conclusion consistent with the implied author's? If not, why not? If so, would it have been so without the story being told or without it being told the way it was?

See also Questions for Contrast and Comparison: 25, 51, 56, 155, 183, and 217.

■ **SUSAN GLASPELL** (1882–1948) *was a major figure in American letters. Born in Davenport, Iowa, she returned to Des Moines after graduation from Drake University (1899) to begin her writing career as a journalist. In 1911 she moved to Greenwich Village in New York City, and two years later married George Cram Cook. They spent their summers in Provincetown on Cape Cod and their winters in New York. In Provincetown they founded the highly influential, avant garde Provincetown Players company and in New York the Playwright's Theatre. Cook served as a charismatic director in these institutions, which attracted the likes of Eugene O'Neill, Edna St. Vincent Millay, and John Reed. Glaspell, usually alone but occasionally in collaboration with Cook, wrote a series of important full-length and one-act plays, the most prominent of which was the Pulitzer Prize-winning Alison's House (1930), supposedly modeled on the life of poet Emily Dickinson. Trifles (1916) was a successful one act play that Glaspell rewrote as "A Jury of Her Peers," first published in E. J. O'Brien's The Best Short Stories of 1917. After Cook's death, while they were living in Greece (1924), Glaspell briefly remarried (1925–31). Her other writing includes a book of* SHORT STORIES, *Lifted Masks (1912), and nine* NOVELS, *most concerned with the places Glaspell knew personally and many concerned with people suffering feelings of social constriction.*

A Jury of Her Peers

When Martha Hale opened the storm-door and got a cut of the north wind, she ran back for her big woolen scarf. As she hurriedly wound that round her head her eye made a scandalized sweep of her kitchen. It was no ordinary thing that called her away — it was probably farther from ordinary than anything that had ever happened in Dickson County. But what her eye took in was that her kitchen was in no shape for leaving: her bread all ready for mixing, half the flour sifted and half unsifted.

She hated to see things half done; but she had been at that when the team from town stopped to get Mr. Hale, and then the sheriff came running in to say his wife wished Mrs. Hale would come too — adding, with a grin, that he guessed she was getting scarey and wanted another woman along. So she had dropped everything right where it was.

"Martha!" now came her husband's impatient voice. "Don't keep folks waiting out here in the cold."

She again opened the storm-door, and this time joined the three men and the one woman waiting for her in the big two-seated buggy.

After she had the robes tucked around her she took another look at the woman who sat beside her on the back seat. She had met Mrs. Peters the year before at the county fair, and the thing she remembered about her was that she didn't seem like a sheriff's wife. She was small and thin and didn't have a strong voice. Mrs. Gorman, sheriff's wife before Gorman went out and Peters came in, had a voice that somehow seemed to be backing up the law with every word. But if Mrs. Peters didn't look like a sheriff's wife, Peters made it up in looking like a sheriff. He was to a dot the kind of man who could get himself elected sheriff — a heavy man with a big voice, who was particularly genial with the law-abiding, as if to make it plain that he knew the difference between criminals and non-criminals. And right there it came into Mrs. Hale's mind, with a stab, that this man who was so pleasant and lively with all of them was going to the Wright's now as a sheriff.

"The country's not very pleasant this time of year," Mrs. Peters at last ventured, as if she felt they ought to be talking as well as the men.

Mrs. Hale scarcely finished her reply, for they had gone up a little hill and could see the Wright place now, and seeing it did not make her feel like talking. It looked very lonesome this cold March morning. It had always been a lonesome-looking place. It was down in a hollow, and the poplar trees around it were lonesome-looking trees. The men were looking at it and talking about what had happened. The county attorney was bending to one side of the buggy, and kept looking steadily at the place as they drew up to it.

"I'm glad you came with me," Mrs. Peters said nervously, as the two women were about to follow the men in through the kitchen door.

Even after she had her foot on the door-step, her hand on the knob, Martha Hale had a moment of feeling she could not cross that threshold. And the reason it seemed she couldn't cross it now was simply because she hadn't crossed it before. Time and time again it had been in her mind, "I ought to go over and see Minnie Foster" — she still thought of her as Minnie Foster, though for twenty years she had been Mrs. Wright. And then there was always something to do and Minnie Foster would go from her mind. But *now* she could come.

The men went over to the stove. The women stood close together by the door. Young Henderson, the county attorney, turned around and said, "Come up to the fire, ladies."

Mrs. Peters took a step forward, then stopped. "I'm not — cold," she said.

And so the two women stood by the door, at first not even so much as looking around the kitchen.

The men talked for a minute about what a good thing it was the sheriff had sent his deputy out that morning to make a fire for them, and then Sheriff Peters stepped back from the stove, unbuttoned his outer coat, and leaned his hands on the kitchen table in a way that seemed to mark the beginning of official business. "Now, Mr. Hale," he said in a sort of semi-official voice, "before we move things about, you tell Mr. Henderson just what it was you saw when you came here yesterday morning."

The county attorney was looking around the kitchen.

"By the way," he said, "has anything been moved?" He turned to the sheriff. "Are things just as you left them yesterday?"

Peters looked from cupboard to sink; from that to a small worn rocker a little to one side of the kitchen table.

"It's just the same."

"Somebody should have been left here yesterday," said the county attorney.

"Oh — yesterday," returned the sheriff, with a little gesture as of yesterday having been more than he could bear to think of. "When I had to send Frank to Morris Center for that man who went crazy — let me tell you, I had my hands full *yesterday*. I knew you could get back from Omaha by to-day, George, and as long as I went over everything here myself —"

"Well, Mr. Hale," said the county attorney, in a way of letting what was past and gone go, "tell just what happened when you came here yesterday morning."

Mrs. Hale, still leaning against the door, had that sinking feeling of the mother whose child is about to speak a piece. Lewis often wandered along and got things mixed up in a story. She hoped he would tell this straight and plain, and not say unnecessary things that would just make things harder for Minnie Foster. He didn't begin at once, and she noticed that he looked queer — as if standing in that kitchen and having to tell what he had seen there yesterday morning made him almost sick.

"Yes, Mr. Hale?" the county attorney reminded.

"Harry and I had started to town with a load of potatoes," Mrs. Hale's husband began.

Harry was Mrs. Hale's oldest boy. He wasn't with them now, for the very good reason that those potatoes never got to town yesterday and he was taking them this morning, so he hadn't been home when the sheriff stopped to say he wanted Mr. Hale to come over to the Wright place and tell the county attorney his story there, where he could point it all out. With all Mrs. Hale's other emotions came the fear that maybe Harry wasn't dressed warm enough — they hadn't any of them realized how that north wind did bite.

"We come along this road," Hale was going on, with a motion of his hand to the road over which they had just come, "and as we got in sight of the house I says to Harry, 'I'm goin' to see if I can't get John Wright to take a telephone.' You see," he explained to Henderson, "unless I can get somebody to go in with me they won't come out this branch road except for a price I can't pay. I'd spoke to Wright about it once before; but he put me off, saying folks talked too much anyway, and all he asked was peace and quiet — guess you know about how much he talked himself. But I thought maybe if I went to the house and talked about it before his wife, and said all the women-folks liked the telephones, and that in this lonesome stretch of road it would be a good thing — well, I said to Harry that that was what I was going to say — though I said at the same time that I didn't know as what his wife wanted made much difference to John — "

Now, there he was! — saying things he didn't need to say. Mrs. Hale tried to catch her husband's eye, but fortunately the county attorney interrupted with:

"Let's talk about that a little later, Mr. Hale. I do want to talk about that, but I'm anxious now to get along to just what happened when you got here."

When he began this time, it was very deliberately and carefully:

"I didn't see or hear anything. I knocked at the door. And still it was all quiet inside. I knew they must be up — it was past eight o'clock. So I knocked again, louder, and I thought I heard somebody say 'Come in.' I wasn't sure — I'm not sure yet. But I opened the door — this door," jerking a hand toward the door by which the two women stood, "and there, in that rocker" — pointing to it — " sat Mrs. Wright."

Every one in the kitchen looked at the rocker. It came into Mrs. Hale's mind that that rocker didn't look in the least like Minnie Foster — the Minnie Foster of twenty years before. It was a dingy red, with wooden rungs up the back, and the middle rung was gone, and the chair sagged to one side.

"How did she — look?" the county attorney was inquiring.

"Well," said Hale, "she looked — queer."

"How do you mean — queer?"

As he asked it he took out a note-book and pencil. Mrs. Hale did not like the sight of that pencil. She kept her eye fixed on her husband, as if to keep him from saying unnecessary things that would go into that note-book and make trouble.

Hale did speak guardedly, as if the pencil had affected him too.

"Well, as if she didn't know what she was going to do next. And kind of—done up."

"How did she seem to feel about your coming?"

"Why, I don't think she minded—one way or other. She didn't pay much attention. I said, 'Ho' do, Mrs. Wright? It's cold, ain't it?' And she said, 'Is it?'—and went on pleatin' at her apron.

"Well, I was surprised. She didn't ask me to come up to the stove, or to sit down, but just set there, not even lookin' at me. And so I said: 'I want to see John.'

"And then she—laughed. I guess you would call it a laugh.

"I thought of Harry and the team outside, so I said, a little sharp. 'Can I see John?' 'No,' says she—kind of dull like. 'Ain't he home?' says I. Then she looked at me. 'Yes,' says she, 'he's home.' 'Then why can't I see him?' I asked her, out of patience with her now. 'Cause he's dead,' says she, just as quiet and dull—and fell to pleatin' her apron. 'Dead?' says I, like you do when you can't take in what you've heard.

"She just nodded her head, not getting a bit excited, but rockin' back and forth.

"'Why—where is he?' says I, not knowing *what* to say.

"She just pointed upstairs—like this"—pointing to the room above.

"I got up, with the idea of going up there myself. By this time I—didn't know what to do. I walked from there to here; then I says: 'Why, and what did he die of?'

"'He died of a rope around his neck,' says she; and just went on pleatin' at her apron."

Hale stopped speaking, and stood staring at the rocker, as if he were still seeing the woman who had sat there the morning before. Nobody spoke; it was as if every one were seeing the woman who had sat there the morning before.

"And what did you do then?" the county attorney at last broke the silence.

"I went out and called Harry. I thought I might—need help. I got Harry in, and we went upstairs." His voice fell almost to a whisper. "There he was—lying over the—"

"I think I'd rather have you go into that upstairs," the county attorney interrupted, "where you can point it all out. Just go on now with the rest of the story."

"Well, my first thought was to get that rope off. It looked—"

He stopped, his face twitching.

"But Harry, he went up to him, and he said, 'No, he's dead all right, and we'd better not touch anything.' So we went downstairs.

"She was still sitting that same way. 'Has anybody been notified?' I asked. 'No,' says she, unconcerned.

"'Who did this, Mrs. Wright?' said Harry. He said it business-like, and she stopped pleatin' at her apron. 'I don't know,' she says. 'You don't *know*?' says

Harry. 'Weren't you sleepin' in the bed with him?' 'Yes,' says she, 'but I was on the inside.' 'Somebody slipped a rope round his neck and strangled him, and you didn't wake up?' says Harry. 'I didn't wake up,' she said after him.

"We may have looked as if we didn't see how that could be, for after a minute she said, 'I sleep sound.'

"Harry was going to ask her more questions, but I said maybe that weren't our business; maybe we ought to let her tell her story first to the coroner or the sheriff. So Harry went fast as he could over to High Road — the Rivers' place, where there's a telephone."

"And what did she do when she knew you had gone for the coroner?" The attorney got his pencil in his hand all ready for writing.

"She moved from that chair to this one over here" — Hale pointed to a small chair in the corner — "and just sat there with her hands held together and looking down. I got a feeling that I ought to make some conversation, so I said I had come in to see if John wanted to put in a telephone; and at that she started to laugh, and then she stopped and looked at me — scared."

At the sound of a moving pencil the man who was telling the story looked up.

"I dunnno — maybe it wasn't scared," he hastened; "I wouldn't like to say it was. Soon Harry got back, and then Dr. Lloyd came, and you, Mr. Peters, and so I guess that's all I know that you don't."

He said that last with relief, and moved a little, as if relaxing. Every one moved a little. The county attorney walked toward the stair door.

"I guess we'll go upstairs first — then out to the barn and around there."

He paused and looked around the kitchen.

"You're convinced there was nothing important here?" he asked the sheriff. "Nothing that would — point to any motive?"

The sheriff too looked all around, as if to re-convince himself.

"Nothing here but kitchen things," he said, with a little laugh for the insignificance of kitchen things.

The county attorney was looking at the cupboard — a peculiar, ungainly structure, half closet and half cupboard, the upper part of it being built in the wall, and the lower part just the old-fashioned kitchen cupboard. As if its queerness attracted him, he got a chair and opened the upper part and looked in. After a moment he drew his hand away sticky.

"Here's a nice mess," he said resentfully.

The two women had drawn nearer, and now the sheriff's wife spoke.

"Oh — her fruit," she said, looking to Mrs. Hale for sympathetic under-standing. She turned back to the county attorney and explained: "She worried about that when it turned so cold last night. She said the fire would go out and her jars might burst."

Mrs. Peters' husband broke into a laugh.

"Well, can you beat the women! Held for murder, and worrying about her preserves!"

The young attorney set his lips.

"I guess before we're through with her she may have something more serious than preserves to worry about."

"Oh, well," said Mrs. Hale's husband, with good-natured superiority, "women are used to worrying over trifles."

The two women moved a little closer together. Neither of them spoke. The county attorney seemed suddenly to remember his manners — and think of his future.

"And yet," said he, with the gallantry of a young politician, "for all their worries, what would we do without the ladies?"

The women did not speak, did not unbend. He went to the sink and began washing his hands. He turned to wipe them on the roller towel — whirled it for a cleaner place.

"Dirty towels! not much of a housekeeper, would you say, ladies?"

He kicked his foot against some dirty pans under the sink.

"There's a great deal of work to be done on a farm," said Mrs. Hale stiffly.

"To be sure. And yet" — with a little bow to her — "I know there are some Dickson County farm-houses that do not have such roller towels." He gave it a pull to expose its full length again.

"Those towels get dirty awful quick. Men's hands aren't always as clean as they might be."

"Ah, loyal to your sex, I see," he laughed. He stopped and gave her a keen look. "But you and Mrs. Wright were neighbors. I suppose you were friends, too."

Martha Hale shook her head.

"I've seen little enough of her of late years. I've not been in this house — it's more than a year."

"And why was that? You didn't like her?"

"I liked her well enough," she replied with spirit. "Farmers' wives have their hands full, Mr. Henderson. And then" — She looked around the kitchen.

"Yes?" he encouraged.

"It never seemed a very cheerful place," she said, more to herself than to him.

"No," he agreed: "I don't think any one would call it cheerful. I shouldn't say she had the home-making instinct."

"Well, I don't know as Wright had, either," she muttered.

"You mean they didn't get on very well?" he was quick to ask.

"No; I don't mean anything," she answered, with decision. As she turned a little away from him, she added: "But I don't think a place would be any the cheerfuler for John Wright's bein' in it."

"I'd like to talk to you about that a little later, Mrs. Hale," he said. "I'm anxious to get the lay of things upstairs now."

He moved toward the stair door, followed by the two men.

"I suppose anything Mrs. Peters does'll be all right?" the sheriff inquired. "She was to take in some clothes for her, you know — and a few little things. We left in such a hurry yesterday."

The county attorney looked at the two women whom they were leaving alone there among the kitchen things.

"Yes — Mrs. Peters," he said, his glance resting on the woman who was not Mrs. Peters, the big farmer woman who stood behind the sheriff's wife. "Of course Mrs. Peters is one of us," he said, in a manner of entrusting responsibility.

"And keep your eye out, Mrs. Peters, for anything that might be of use. No telling; you women might come upon a clue to the motive — and that's the thing we need."

Mr. Hale rubbed his face after the fashion of a show man getting ready for a pleasantry.

"But would the women know a clue if they did come upon it?" he said; and, having delivered himself of this, he followed the others through the stair door.

The women stood motionless and silent, listening to the footsteps, first upon the stairs, then in the room above them.

Then, as if releasing herself from something strange, Mrs. Hale began to arrange the dirty pans under the sink, which the county attorney's disdainful push of the foot had deranged.

"I'd hate to have men comin' into my kitchen." she said testily — "snoopin' round and criticizin'."

"Of course it's no more than their duty," said the sheriff's wife, in her manner of timid acquiescence.

"Duty's all right," replied Mrs. Hale bluffly; "but I guess that deputy sheriff that come out to make the fire might have got a little of this on." She gave the roller towel a pull. "Wish I'd thought of that sooner! Seems mean to talk about her for not having things slicked up, when she had to come away in such a hurry."

She looked around the kitchen. Certainly it was not "slicked up." Her eye was held by a bucket of sugar on a low shelf. The cover was off the wooden bucket, and beside it was a paper bag — half full.

Mrs. Hale moved toward it.

"She was putting this in there," she said to herself — slowly.

She thought of the flour in her kitchen at home — half sifted, half not sifted. She had been interrupted and had left things half done. What had interrupted Minnie Foster? Why had that work been left half done? She made a move as if to finish it, — unfinished things always bothered her, — and then she glanced around and saw that Mrs. Peters was watching her — and she didn't want Mrs. Peters to get that feeling she had got of work begun and then — for some reason — not finished.

"It's a shame about her fruit," she said, and walked toward the cupboard that the county attorney had opened, and got on the chair, murmuring: "I wonder if it's all gone."

It was a sorry enough looking sight, but "Here's one that's all right," she said at last. She held it toward the light. "This is cherries, too." She looked again. "I declare I believe that's the only one."

With a sigh, she got down from the chair, went to the sink, and wiped off the bottle.

"She'll feel awful bad, after all her hard work in the hot weather. I remember the afternoon I put up my cherries last summer."

She set the bottle on the table, and, with another sigh, started to sit down in the rocker. But she did not sit down. Something kept her from sitting down in that chair. She straightened — stepped back, and, half turned away, stood looking at it, seeing the woman who sat there "pleatin' at her apron."

The thin voice of the sheriff's wife broke in upon her: "I must be getting those things from the front room closet." She opened the door into the other room, started in, stepped back. "You coming with me, Mrs. Hale?" she asked nervously. "You—you could help me get them."

They were soon back—the stark coldness of that shut-up room was not a thing to linger in.

"My!" said Mrs. Peters, dropping the things on the table and hurrying to the stove.

Mrs. Hale stood examining the clothes the woman who was being detained in town had said she wanted.

"Wright was close!" she exclaimed, holding up a shabby black skirt that bore the marks of much making over. "I think maybe that's why she kept so much to herself. I s'pose she felt she couldn't do her part; and then, you don't enjoy things when you feel shabby. She used to wear pretty clothes and be lively—when she was Minnie Foster, one of the town girls, singing in the choir. But that—oh, that was twenty years ago."

With a carefulness in which there was something tender, she folded the shabby clothes and piled them at one corner of the table. She looked at Mrs. Peters, and there was something in the other woman's look that irritated her.

"She don't care," she said to herself. "Much difference it makes to her whether Minnie Foster had pretty clothes when she was a girl."

Then she looked again, and she wasn't so sure; in fact, she hadn't at any time been perfectly sure about Mrs. Peters. She had that shrinking manner, and yet her eyes looked as if they could see a long way into things.

"This all you was to take in?" asked Mrs. Hale.

"No," said the sheriff's wife; "she said she wanted an apron. Funny thing to want," she ventured in her nervous little way, "for there's not much to get you dirty in jail, goodness knows. But suppose just to make her feel more natural. If you're used to wearing an apron—. She said they were in the bottom drawer of this cupboard. Yes—here they are. And then her little shawl that always hung on the stair door."

She took the small gray shawl from behind the door leading upstairs, and stood a minute looking at it.

Suddenly Mrs. Hale took a quick step toward the other woman.

"Mrs. Peters!"

"Yes, Mrs. Hale?"

"Do you think she—did it?"

A frightened look blurred the other things in Mrs. Peters' eyes.

"Oh, I don't know," she said, in a voice that seemed to shrink away from the subject.

"Well, I don't think she did," affirmed Mrs. Hale stoutly. "Asking for an apron, and her little shawl. Worryin' about her fruit."

"Mr. Peters says—" Footsteps were heard in the room above; she stopped, looked up, then went on in a lowered voice: "Mr. Peters says—it looks bad for her. Mr. Henderson is awful sarcastic in a speech, and he's going to make fun of her saying she didn't—wake up."

For a moment Mrs. Hale had no answer. Then, "Well, I guess John Wright didn't wake up—when they was slippin' that rope under his neck," she muttered.

"No, it's *strange*," breathed Mrs. Peters. "They think it was such a — funny way to kill a man."

She began to laugh; at sound of the laugh, abruptly stopped.

"That's just what Mr. Hale said," said Mrs. Hale, in a resolutely natural voice. "There was a gun in the house. He says that's what he can't understand."

"Mr. Henderson said, coming out, that what was needed for the case was a motive. Something to show anger — or sudden feeling."

"Well, I don't see any signs of anger around here," said Mrs. Hale. "I don't —"

She stopped. It was as if her mind tripped on something. Her eye was caught by a dish-towel in the middle of the kitchen table. Slowly she moved toward the table. One half of it was wiped clean, the other half messy. Her eyes made a slow, almost unwilling turn to the bucket of sugar and the half empty bag beside it. Things begun — and not finished.

After a moment she stepped back, and said, in that manner of releasing herself:

"Wonder how they're finding things upstairs? I hope she had it a little more red up up there. You know," — she paused, and feeling gathered, — "it seems kind of *sneaking*; locking her up in town and coming out here to get her own house to turn against her!"

"But, Mrs. Hale," said the sheriff's wife, "the law is the law."

"I s'pose 'tis," answered Mrs. Hale shortly.

She turned to the stove, saying something about that fire not being much to brag of. She worked with it a minute, and when she straightened up she said aggressively:

"The law is the law — and a bad stove is a bad stove. How'd you like to cook on this? — pointing with the poker to the broken lining. She opened the oven door and started to express her opinion of the oven; but she was swept into her own thoughts, thinking of what it would mean, year after year, to have that stove to wrestle with. The thought of Minnie Foster trying to bake in that oven — and the thought of her never going over to see Minnie Foster —.

She was startled by hearing Mrs. Peters say: "A person gets discouraged — and loses heart."

The sheriff's wife had looked from the stove to the sink — to the pail of water which had been carried in from outside. The two women stood there silent, above them the footsteps of the men who were looking for evidence against the woman who had worked in that kitchen. That look of seeing into things, of seeing through a thing to something else, was in the eyes of the sheriff's wife now. When Mrs. Hale next spoke to her, it was gently:

"Better loosen up your things, Mrs. Peters. We'll not feel them when we go out."

Mrs. Peters went to the back of the room to hang up the fur tippet she was wearing. A moment later she exclaimed, "Why, she was piecing a quilt," and held up a large sewing basket piled high with quilt pieces.

Mrs. Hale spread some of the blocks on the table.

"It's a log-cabin pattern," she said, putting several of them together. "Pretty, isn't it?"

They were so engaged with the quilt that they did not hear the footsteps on the stairs. Just as the stair door opened Mrs. Hale was saying:

"Do you suppose she was going to quilt it or just knot it?"

The sheriff threw up his hands.

"They wonder whether she was going to quilt it or just knot it!"

There was a laugh for the ways of women, a warming of hands over the stove, and then the county attorney said briskly:

"Well, let's go right out to the barn and get that cleared up."

"I don't see as there's anything so strange," Mrs. Hale said resentfully, after the outside door had closed on the three men — "our taking up our time with little things while we're waiting for them to get the evidence. I don't see as it's anything to laugh about."

"Of course they've got awful important things on their minds," said the sheriff's wife apologetically.

They returned to an inspection of the blocks for the quilt. Mrs. Hale was looking at the fine, even sewing, and preoccupied with thoughts of the woman who had done that sewing, when she heard the sheriff's wife say, in a queer tone:

"Why, look at this one."

She turned to take the block held out to her.

"The sewing," said Mrs. Peters, in a troubled way. "All the rest of them have been so nice and even — but — this one. Why, it looks as if she didn't know what she was about!"

Their eyes met — something flashed to life, passed between them; then, as if with an effort, they seemed to pull away from each other. A moment Mrs. Hale sat there, her hands folded over that sewing which was so unlike all the rest of the sewing. Then she had pulled a knot and drawn the threads.

"Oh, what are you doing, Mrs. Hale?" asked the sheriff's wife, startled.

"Just pulling out a stitch or two that's not sewed very good," said Mrs. Hale mildly.

"I don't think we ought to touch things," Mrs. Peters said, a little helplessly.

"I'd just finish up this end," answered Mrs. Hale, still in that mild, matter-of-fact fashion.

She threaded a needle and started to replace bad sewing with good. For a little while she sewed in silence. Then, in that thin, timid voice, she heard:

"Mrs. Hale!"

"Yes, Mrs. Peters?"

"What do you suppose she was so — nervous about?"

"Oh, I don't know," said Mrs. Hale, as if dismissing a thing not important enough to spend much time on. "I don't know as she was — nervous. I sew awful queer sometimes when I'm just tired."

She cut a thread, and out of the corner of her eye looked up at Mrs. Peters. The small, lean face of the sheriff's wife seemed to have tightened up. Her eyes had that look of peering into something. But the next moment she moved, and said in her thin, indecisive way:

"Well, I must get those clothes wrapped. They may be through sooner than we think. I wonder where I could find a piece of paper — and string."

"In that cupboard, maybe," suggested Mrs. Hale, after a glance around.

One piece of the crazy sewing remained unripped. Mrs. Peters' back turned, Martha Hale now scrutinized that piece, compared it with the dainty, accurate sewing of the other blocks. The difference was startling. Holding this block made her feel queer, as if the distracted thoughts of the woman who had perhaps turned to it to try and quiet herself were communicating themselves to her.

Mrs. Peters' voice roused her.

"Here's a bird-cage," she said. "Did she have a bird, Mrs. Hale?"

"Why, I don't know whether she did or not." She turned to look at the cage Mrs. Peters was holding up. "I've not been here in so long." She sighed. "There was a man round last year selling canaries cheap — but I don't know as she took one. Maybe she did. She used to sing real pretty herself."

Mrs. Peters looked around the kitchen.

"Seems kind of funny to think of a bird here." She half laughed — an attempt to put up a barrier. "But she must have had one — or why would she have a cage? I wonder what happened to it."

"I suppose maybe the cat got it," suggested Mrs. Hale, resuming her sewing.

"No; she didn't have a cat. She's got that feeling some people have about cats — being afraid of them. When they brought her to our house yesterday, my cat got in the room, and she was real upset and asked me to take it out."

"My sister Bessie was like that," laughed Mrs. Hale.

The sheriff's wife did not reply. The silence made Mrs. Hale turn round. Mrs. Peters was examining the bird-cage.

"Look at this door," she said slowly. "It's broke. One hinge has been pulled apart."

Mrs. Hale came nearer.

"Looks as if some one must have been — rough with it."

Again their eyes met — startled, questioning, apprehensive. For a moment neither spoke nor stirred. Then Mrs. Hale, turning away, said brusquely:

"If they're going to find any evidence, I wish they'd be about it. I don't like this place."

"But I'm awful glad you came with me, Mrs. Hale." Mrs. Peters put the bird-cage on the table and sat down. "It would be lonesome for me — sitting here alone."

"Yes, it would, wouldn't it?" agreed Mrs. Hale, a certain determined naturalness in her voice. She picked up the sewing, but now it dropped in her lap, and she murmured in a different voice: "But I tell you what I *do* wish, Mrs. Peters. I wish I had come over sometimes when she was here. I wish — I had."

"But of course you were awful busy, Mrs. Hale. Your house — and your children."

"I could've come," retorted Mrs. Hale shortly. "I stayed away because it weren't cheerful — and that's why I ought to have come. I" — she looked around — "I've never liked this place. Maybe because it's down in a hollow and you don't see the road. I don't know what it is, but it's a lonesome place, and always was. I wish I had come over to see Minnie Foster sometimes. I can see now — " She did not put it into words.

"Well, you mustn't reproach yourself," counseled Mrs. Peters. "Somehow, we just don't see how it is with other folks till — something comes up."

"Not having children makes less work," mused Mrs. Hale, after a silence, "but it makes a quiet house — and Wright out to work all day — and no company when he did come in. Did you know John Wright, Mrs. Peters?"

"Not to know him. I've seen him in town. They say he was a good man."

"Yes—good," conceded John Wright's neighbor grimly. "He didn't drink, and kept his word as well as most, I guess, and paid his debts. But he was a hard man, Mrs. Peters. Just to pass the time of day with him—." She stopped, shivered a little. "Like a raw wind that gets to the bone." Her eye fell upon the cage on the table before her, and she added, almost bitterly: "I should think she would've wanted a bird!"

Suddenly she leaned forward, looking intently at the cage. "But what do you s'pose went wrong with it?"

"I don't know," returned Mrs. Peters; "unless it got sick and died."

But after she said it she reached over and swung the broken door. Both women watched it as if somehow held by it.

"You didn't know—her?" Mrs. Hale asked, a gentler note in her voice.

"Not till they brought her yesterday," said the sheriff's wife.

"She—come to think of it, she was kind of like a bird herself. Real sweet and pretty, but kind of timid and—fluttery. How—she—did — change."

That held her for a long time. Finally, as if struck with a happy thought and relieved to get back to everyday things, she exclaimed:

"Tell you what, Mrs. Peters, why don't you take the quilt in with you? It might take up her mind."

"Why, I think that's a real nice idea, Mrs. Hale," agreed the sheriff's wife, as if she too were glad to come into the atmosphere of a simple kindness. "There couldn't possibly be any objection to that, could there? Now, just what will I take? I wonder if her patches are in here—and her things."

They turned to the sewing basket.

"Here's some red," said Mrs. Hale, bringing out a roll of cloth. Underneath that was a box. "Here, maybe her scissors are in here—and her things." She held it up. "What a pretty box! I'll warrant that was something she had a long time ago—when she was a girl."

She held it in her hand a moment; then, with a little sigh, opened it.

Instantly her hand went to her nose.

"Why—"

Mrs. Peters drew nearer—then turned away.

"There's something wrapped up in this piece of silk," faltered Mrs. Hale.

"This isn't her scissors," said Mrs. Peters in a shrinking voice.

Her hand not steady, Mrs. Hale raised the piece of silk. "Oh, Mrs. Peters!" she cried. "It's—"

Mrs. Peters bent closer.

"It's the bird," she whispered.

"But, Mrs. Peters!" cried Mrs. Hale. "*Look* at it! Its neck—look at its neck! It's all—other side *to*."

She held the box away from her.

The sheriff's wife again bent closer.

"Somebody wrung its neck," she said, in a voice that was slow and deep.

And then again the eyes of the two women met—this time clung together in a look of dawning comprehension, of growing horror. Mrs. Peters looked from the dead bird to the broken door of the cage. Again their eyes met. And just then there was a sound at the outside door.

Mrs. Hale slipped the box under the quilt pieces in the basket, and sank into the chair before it. Mrs. Peters stood holding to the table. The county attorney and the sheriff came in from outside.

"Well, ladies," said the county attorney, as one running from serious things to little pleasantries, "have you decided whether she was going to quilt it or knot it?"

"We think," began the sheriff's wife in a flurried voice, "that she was going to — knot it."

He was too preoccupied to notice the change that came in her voice on that last.

"Well, that's very interesting, I'm sure." he said tolerantly. He caught sight of the bird-cage. "Has the bird flown?"

"We think the cat got it," said Mrs. Hale in a voice curiously even.

He was walking up and down, as if thinking something out.

"Is there a cat?" he asked absently.

Mrs. Hale shot a look up at the sheriff's wife.

"Well, not *now*," said Mrs. Peters. "They're superstitious, you know; they leave."

She sank into her chair.

The county attorney did not heed her. "No sign at all of any one having come in from the outside," he said to Peters, in the manner of continuing an interrupted conversation. "Their own rope. Now let's go upstairs again and go over it, piece by piece. It would have to have been some one who knew just the —"

The stair door closed behind them and their voices were lost.

The two women sat motionless, not looking at each other, but as if peering into something and at the same time holding back. When they spoke now it was as if they were afraid of what they were saying, but as if they could not help saying it.

"She liked the bird," said Martha Hale, low and slowly. "She was going to bury it in that pretty box."

"When I was a girl," said Mrs. Peters, under her breath, "my kitten — there was a boy took a hatchet, and before my eyes — before I could get there —" She covered her face an instant. "If they hadn't held me back I would have" — she caught herself, looked upstairs where footsteps were heard, and finished weakly — "hurt him."

Then they sat without speaking or moving.

"I wonder how it would seem," Mrs. Hale at last began, as if feeling her way over strange ground — "never to have had any children around?" Her eyes made a slow sweep of the kitchen, as if seeing what that kitchen had meant through all the years. "No, Wright wouldn't like the bird," she said after that —" a thing that sang. She used to sing. He killed that too." Her voice tightened.

Mrs. Peters moved uneasily.

"Of course we don't know who killed the bird."

"I knew John Wright," was Mrs. Hale's answer.

"It was an awful thing was done in this house that night, Mrs. Hale," said the sheriff's wife. "Killing a man while he slept — slipping a thing round his neck that choked the life out of him."

Mrs. Hale's hand went out to the bird-cage.

"His neck. Choked the life out of him."

"We don't *know* who killed him," whispered Mrs. Peters wildly. "We don't *know*."

Mrs. Hale had not moved. "If there had been years and years of — nothing, then a bird to sing to you, it would be awful — still — after the bird was still."

It was as if something within her not herself had spoken, and it found in Mrs. Peters something she did not know as herself.

"I know what stillness is," she said, in a queer, monotonous voice. "When we homesteaded in Dakota, and my first baby died — after he was two years old — and me with no other then — "

Mrs. Hale stirred.

"How soon do you suppose they'll be through looking for evidence?"

"I know what stillness is," repeated Mrs. Peters, in just that same way. Then she too pulled back. "The law has got to punish crime, Mrs. Hale," she said in her tight little way.

"I wish you'd seen Minnie Foster," was the answer, "when she wore a white dress with blue ribbons, and stood up there in the choir and sang."

The picture of that girl, the fact that she had lived neighbor to that girl for twenty years, and had let her die for lack of life, was suddenly more than she could bear.

"Oh, I *wish* I'd come over here once in a while!" she cried. "That was a crime! That was a crime! Who's going to punish that?"

"We mustn't take on," said Mrs. Peters, with a frightened look toward the stairs.

"I might 'a' *known* she needed help! I tell you, it's *queer*, Mrs. Peters. We live close together, and we live far apart. We all go through the same things — its all just a different kind of the same thing! If it weren't — why do you and I *understand*? Why do we *know* — what we know this minute?"

She dashed her hand across her eyes. Then, seeing the jar of fruit on the table, she reached for it and choked out:

"If I was you I wouldn't *tell* her her fruit was gone! Tell her it *ain't*. Tell her it's all right — all of it. Here — take this in to prove it to her! She — she may never know whether it was broke or not."

She turned away.

Mrs. Peters reached out for the bottle of fruit as if she were glad to take it — as if touching a familiar thing, having something to do, could keep her from something else. She got up, looked about for something to wrap the fruit in, took a petticoat from the pile of clothes she had brought from the front room, and nervously started winding that round the bottle.

"My!" she began, in a high, false voice. "it's a good thing the men couldn't hear us! Getting all stirred up over a little thing like a — dead canary." She hurried over that. "As if that could have anything to do with — with — My, wouldn't they *laugh*?"

Footsteps were heard on the stairs.

"Maybe they would," muttered Mrs. Hale — "maybe they wouldn't."

"No, Peters," said the county attorney incisively: "it's all perfectly clear, except the reason for doing it. But you know juries when it comes to women. If there was some definite thing — something to show. Something to make a story about. A thing that would connect up with this clumsy way of doing it."

In a covert way Mrs. Hale looked at Mrs. Peters. Mrs. Peters was looking at her. Quickly they looked away from each other. The outer door opened and Mr. Hale came in.

"I've got the team round now," he said. "Pretty cold out there."

"I'm going to stay here awhile by myself," the county attorney suddenly announced. "You can send Frank out for me, can't you?" he asked the sheriff. "I want to go over everything. I'm not satisfied we can't do better."

Again, for one brief moment, the two women's eyes found one another.

The sheriff came up to the table.

"Did you want to see what Mrs. Peters was going to take in?"

The county attorney picked up the apron. He laughed.

"Oh, I guess they're not very dangerous things the ladies have picked out."

Mrs. Hale's hand was on the sewing basket in which the box was concealed. She felt that she ought to take her hand off the basket. She did not seem able to. He picked up one of the quilt blocks which she had piled on to cover the box. Her eyes felt like fire. She had a feeling that if he took up the basket she would snatch it from him.

But he did not take it up. With another little laugh, he turned away, saying:

"No; Mrs. Peters doesn't need supervising. For that matter, a sheriff's wife is married to the law. Ever think of it that way, Mrs. Peters?"

Mrs. Peters was standing beside the table. Mrs. Hale shot a look up at her; but she could not see her face. Mrs. Peters had turned away. When she spoke, her voice was muffled.

"Not — just that way," she said.

"Married to the law!" chuckled Mrs. Peters' husband. He moved toward the door into the front room, and said to the county attorney:

"I just want you to come in here a minute, George. We ought to take a look at these windows."

"Oh — windows," said the county attorney scoffingly.

"We'll be right out, Mr. Hale," said the sheriff to the farmer, who was still waiting by the door.

Hale went to look after the horses. The sheriff followed the county attorney into the other room. Again — for one moment — the two women were alone in that kitchen.

Martha Hale sprang up, her hands tight together, looking at the other woman, with whom it rested. At first she could not see her eyes, for the sheriff's wife had not turned back, since she turned away at that suggestion of being married to the law. But now Mrs. Hale made her turn back. Her eyes made her turn back. Slowly, unwillingly, Mrs. Peters turned her head until her eyes met the eyes of the other woman. There was a moment when they held each other in a steady, burning look in which there was no evasion nor flinching. Then Martha

Hale's eyes pointed the way to the basket in which was hidden the thing that would make certain the conviction of the other woman — that woman who was not there and yet who had been there with them all through the hour.

For a moment Mrs. Peters did not move. And then she did it. With a rush forward, she threw back the quilt pieces, got the box, tried to put it in her handbag. It was too big. Desperately she opened it, started to take the bird out. But there she broke — she could not touch the bird. She stood helpless, foolish.

There was the sound of a knob turning in the inner door. Martha Hale snatched the box from the sheriff's wife, and got it in the pocket of her big coat just as the sheriff and the county attorney came back into the kitchen.

"Well, Henry," said the county attorney facetiously, "at least we found out that she was not going to quilt it. She was going to — what is it you call it, ladies?"

Mrs. Hale's hand was against the pocket of her coat.

"We call it — knot it, Mr. Henderson."

[1917]

Study and Writing Questions

1. What conclusion do Mrs. Hale and Mrs. Peters reach concerning the murder? Why are they able to reach this conclusion while the men cannot? To what extent is the STORY about the differences in reasoning between men and women? What causes these differences?
2. Why do the women decide to conceal the bird? In what ways is the bird SYMBOLIC?
3. How does the control of VIEWPOINT and VIEWPOINT CHARACTER modulate both the SUSPENSE of the NARRATIVE and your feelings about Mrs. Wright?
4. How is the law represented in this story? How is it embodied in individuals? Does the law exist outside its embodiments? Is the law just? How is the title related to the idea of justice under law in general and in this story?
5. From the first paragraph's reference to a long scarf being wrapped around Mrs. Hale's head to the last line, there are many references to rope, thread, and so on in this narrative. What are they? What do they symbolize? What does the last line mean?

See also Questions for Contrast and Comparison: 16, 33, 65, 101, 102, 117, 137, 193, and 220.

■ NIKOLAI (VASIL'EVICH) GOGOL (1809-1852) *was born in the Russian Ukraine on his family's 3,000 acre, 250 serf estate. He attended boarding school (1821-1828) where, for his ugliness, he was known as "the mysterious dwarf." His father's death (1825) undermined the family fortunes, so Gogol went to St. Petersburg, then the Russian capital, intent on civil service; however, he resented bureaucracy, and his friendship with Alexander Pushkin, the great poet, led him to return to the literary activity he had explored at school. His two-volume collection of picturesque stories* (Evenings on a Farm Near Dikanka, *1831-1832) led to wide acclaim strengthened by publication of his historical romance,* Taras Bulba (1835). *Gogol believed, "It is impossible for a society to strive toward the beautiful [until it is shown its] present vile loathsomeness." Both his satiric play,* The Inspector General *(1836), concerning a poor copy clerk profiting by impersonating a feared official, and his great novel,* Dead Souls *(1842), contrasting the "dead" upper class with the vital common folk, outraged the Russian elite. Their disapproval led to Gogol's self-imposed exile in Rome (1836-1848). "The Overcoat," considered the fountainhead of Russian "realism," and said by Frank O'Connor to be the world's first story of "the little man," appeared first in Gogol's collected writings (1842). Thereafter, his health declined severely, and he died, in Moscow, insane.*

The Overcoat

In the department . . . but perhaps it is just as well not to say in which department. There is nothing more touchy and ill-tempered in the world than departments, regiments, government offices, and indeed any kind of official body. Nowadays every private individual takes a personal insult to be an insult against society at large. I am told that not so very long ago a police commissioner (I don't remember of what town) sent in a petition to the authorities in which he stated in so many words that all Government decrees had been defied and his own sacred name most decidedly taken in vain. And in proof he attached to his petition an enormous volume of some highly romantic work in which a police commissioner figured on almost every tenth page, sometimes in a very drunken state. So to avoid all sorts of unpleasant misunderstandings, we shall refer to the department in question as *a certain department.*

And so in *a certain department* there served *a certain Civil Servant,* a Civil Servant who cannot by any stretch of the imagination be described as in any way remarkable. He was in fact a somewhat short, somewhat pockmarked, somewhat red-haired man, who looked rather short-sighted and was slightly bald on the top of his head, with wrinkles on both cheeks, and a rather sallow complexion. There is nothing we can do about it: it is all the fault of the St. Petersburg climate. As for his rank (for with us rank is something that must be stated before anything else), he was what is known as a perpetual titular councillor, the ninth rank among the fourteen ranks into which our Civil Service is divided, a rank which, as every one knows, has been sneered at and held up to scorn by all sorts of writers who have the praiseworthy habit of setting upon those who cannot hit back. The Civil Servant's surname was Bashmachkin. From this it can be clearly inferred that it had once upon a time originated from the Russian word *bashmak,* to wit, shoe. But when, at what precise date, and under what circumstances the metamorphosis took place, must for ever remain a mystery. His father, grandfather, and, why, even his brother-in-law as well as all the rest of the Bashmachkins, always walked about in boots, having their soles repaired no more than three times a year. His name and patronymic were Akaky Akakyevich. The reader may think it a little odd, not to say somewhat *recherché*, but we can assure him that we wasted no time in searching for this name and that it happened in the most natural way that no other name could be given to him, and the way it came about is as follows:

Akaky Akakyevich was born, if my memory serves me right, on the night of 23rd March. His mother of blessed memory, the wife of a Civil Servant and a most excellent woman in every respect, took all the necessary steps for the child to be christened. She was still lying in bed, facing the door, and on her right stood the godfather, Ivan Ivanovich Yeroshkin, a most admirable man, who was a head clerk at the Supreme Court, and the godmother, Arina Semyonovna Byelobrúshkina, the wife of the district police inspector, a most worthy woman. The mother was presented with the choice of three names, namely, Mokkia, Sossia, or, it was suggested, the child might be called after the martyr Khozdazat, "Oh dear," thought his late mother, "they're all such queer names!" To please her, the calendar was opened at another place, but again the three names that were found were rather uncommon, namely, Trifily, Dula, and Varakhassy. "Bother," said the poor woman, "what queer names! I've really never heard such names! Now if it had only been Varadat or Varukh, but it would be Trifily and Varakhassy!" Another page was turned and the names in the calendar were Pavsikakhy and Vakhtissy. "Well," said the mother, "I can see that such is the poor innocent infant's fate. If that is so, let him rather be called after his father. His father was Akaky, so let the son be Akaky, too." It was in this way that he came to be called Akaky. The child was christened, and during the ceremony he began to cry and pulled such a face that it really seemed as though he had a premonition that he would be a titular councillor one day. Anyway, that is how it all came to pass.

We have told how it had come about at such length because we are anxious that the reader should realise himself that it could not have happened otherwise, and that to give him any other name was quite out of the question.

When and at what precise date Akaky had entered the department, and who had appointed him to it, is something that no one can remember. During all the years he had served in that department many directors and other higher officials had come and gone, but he still remained in exactly the same place, in exactly the same position, in exactly the same job, doing exactly the same kind of work, to wit, copying official documents. Indeed, with time the belief came to be generally held that he must have been born into the world entirely fitted out for his job, in his Civil Servant's uniform and a bald patch on his head. No particular respect was shown him in the department. Not only did the caretakers not get up from their seats when he passed by, but they did not even vouchsafe a glance at him, just as if a common fly had flown through the waiting-room. His superiors treated him in a manner that could be best described as frigidly despotic. Some assistant head clerk would just shove a paper under his nose without even saying, "Please copy it," or "Here's an interesting, amusing little case!" or something in a similarly pleasant vein as is the custom in all well-regulated official establishments. And he would accept it without raising his eyes from the paper, without looking up to see who had put it on his desk, or whether indeed he had any right to put it there. He just took it and immediately settled down to copy it. The young clerks laughed and cracked jokes about him, the sort of jokes young clerks could be expected to crack. They told stories about him in his presence, stories that were specially invented about him. They joked about his landlady, an old woman of seventy, who they claimed beat him, or they asked him when he was going to marry her. They also showered bits of torn paper on his head and called them snow. But never a word did Akaky say to it all, as though unaware of the presence of his tormentors in the office. It did not even interfere with his work; for while these rather annoying practical jokes were played on him he never made a single mistake in the document he was copying. It was only when the joke got too unbearable, when somebody jogged his arm and so interfered with his work, that he would say, "Leave me alone, gentlemen. Why do you pester me?" There was a strange note in the words and in the voice in which they were uttered: there was something in it that touched one's heart with pity. Indeed, one young man who had only recently been appointed to the department and who, following the example of the others, tried to have some fun at his expense, stopped abruptly at Akaky's mild expostulation, as though stabbed through the heart; and since then everything seemed to have changed in him and he saw everything in quite a different light. A kind of unseen power made him keep away from his colleagues whom at first he had taken for decent, well-bred men. And for a long time afterwards, in his happiest moments, he would see the shortish Civil Servant with the bald patch on his head, uttering those pathetic words, "Leave me alone! Why do you pester me?" And in those pathetic words he seemed to hear others: "I am your brother." And the poor young man used to bury his face in his hands, and many a time in his life he would shudder when he perceived how much inhumanity there was in man, how much savage brutality there lurked beneath the most refined, cultured manners, and, dear Lord, even in the man the world regarded as upright and honourable. . . .

It would be hard to find a man who lived so much for his job. It was not sufficient to say that he worked zealously. No, his work was a labour of love to him. There, in that copying of his, he seemed to see a multifarious and pleasant world of his own. Enjoyment was written on his face; some letters he was particularly fond of, and whenever he had the chance of writing them, he was beside himself with joy, chuckling to himself, winking and helping them on with his lips, so that you could, it seemed, read on his face every letter his pen was forming with such care. If he had been rewarded in accordance with his zeal, he would to his own surprise have got as far as a state councillorship; but, as the office wits expressed it, all he got for his pains was a metal disc in his button-hole and a stitch in his side. Still it would be untrue to say that no one took any notice of him. One director, indeed, being a thoroughly good man and anxious to reward him for his long service, ordered that he should be given some more responsible work than his usual copying, that is to say, he was told to prepare a report for another department of an already concluded case; all he had to do was to alter the title at the top of the document and change some of the verbs from the first to the third person singular. This, however, gave him so much trouble that he was bathed in perspiration and kept mopping his forehead until at last he said, "No, I can't do it. You'd better give me something to copy." Since then they let him carry on with his copying for ever. Outside this copying nothing seemed to exist for him. He never gave a thought to his clothes: his uniform was no longer green, but of some nondescript rusty white. His collar was very short and narrow so that his neck, though it was not at all long, looked as if it stuck a mile out of the collar, like the necks of the plaster kittens with wagging heads, scores of which are carried about on the heads by street-vendors of non-Russian nationality. And something always seemed to cling to his uniform: either a straw or some thread. He possessed, besides, the peculiar knack when walking in the street of passing under a window just at the time when some rubbish was tipped out of it, and for this reason he always carried about on his hat bits of water-melon or melon rind and similar trash. He had never in his life paid the slightest attention to what was going on daily in the street, and in this he was quite unlike his young colleagues in the Civil Service, who are famous as observers of street life, their eagle-eyed curiosity going even so far as to notice that the strap under the trousers of some man on the pavement on the other side of the street has come undone, a thing which never fails to bring a malicious grin to their faces. But even if Akaky did look at anything, he saw nothing but his own neat lines, written out in an even hand, and only if a horse's muzzle, appearing from goodness knows where, came to rest on his shoulder and blew a gale on his cheek from its nostrils, did he become aware of the fact that he was not in the middle of the line, but rather in the middle of the street.

On his arrival home, he would at once sit down at the table, quickly gulp down his cabbage soup, eat a piece of beef with onions without noticing what it tasted like, eating whatever Providence happened to send at the time, flies and all. Noticing that his stomach was beginning to feel full, he would get up from the table, fetch his inkwell and start copying the papers he had brought home with him. If, however, there were no more papers to copy, he would deliberately make another copy for his own pleasure, intending to keep it for himself, especially if the paper was remarkable not so much for the beauty of its style as for the fact of being addressed to some new or important person.

Even at those hours when all the light has faded from the grey St. Petersburg sky, and the Civil Service folk have taken their fill of food and dined each as best he could, according to his salary and his personal taste; when all have had their rest after the departmental scraping of pens, after all the rush and bustle, after their own and other people's indispensable business had been brought to a conclusion, and anything else restless man imposes upon himself of his own free will had been done, and even much more than is necessary; when every Civil Servant is hastening to enjoy as best he can the remaining hours of his leisure — one more enterprising rushing off to the theatre, another going for a stroll to stare at some silly women's hats, a third going to a party to waste his time paying compliments to some pretty girl, the star of some small Civil Service circle, while a fourth — as happens in nine cases out of ten — paying a call on a fellow Civil Servant living on the third or fourth floor in a flat of two small rooms with a tiny hall or kitchen, with some pretensions to fashion — a lamp or some other article that has cost many self-denying sacrifices, such as doing without dinners or country outings; in short, even when all the Civil Servants have dispersed among the tiny flats of their friends to play a stormy game of whist, sipping tea from glasses and nibbling a penny biscuit, or inhaling the smoke of their long pipes and, while dealing the cards, retailing the latest high society scandal (for every Russian is so devotedly attached to high society that he cannot dispense with it for a moment, or, when there is nothing else to talk about, telling the old chestnut about the fortress commandant who was told that the tail of the horse of Falconnetti's statue of Peter I had been docked — in short, even while every government official in the capital was doing his best to enjoy himself, Akaky Akakyevich made no attempt to woo the fair goddess of mirth and jollity. No one could possibly ever claim to have seen him at a party. Having copied out documents to his heart's content, he went to bed, smiling in anticipation of the pleasures the next day had in store for him and wondering what the good Lord would send him to copy. So passed the peaceful life of a man who knew how to be content with his lot on a salary of four hundred roubles a year; and it might have flowed on a happily to a ripe old age, were it not for the various calamities which beset the lives not only of titular, but also of privy, actual, court and any other councillors, even those who give no counsel to any man, nor take any from anyone, either.

There is in St. Petersburg a great enemy of all those who receive a salary of four hundred roubles a year, or thereabouts. This enemy is none other than our northern frost, though you will hear people say that it is very good for the health. At nine o'clock in the morning, just at the hour when the streets are full of Civil Servants on their way to their departments, he starts giving such mighty and stinging filips to all noses without exception, that the poor fellows simply do not know where to put them. At a time when the foreheads of even those who occupy the highest positions in the State ache with frost, and tears start to their eyes, the poor titular councillors are sometimes left utterly defenceless. Their only salvation lies in running as fast as they can in their thin, threadbare overcoats through five or six streets and then stamping their feet vigorously in the vestibule, until they succeed in unfreezing their faculties and abilities, frozen on the way, and are once more able to tackle the affairs of State.

Akaky had for some time been feeling that the fierce cold seemed to have no difficulty at all in penetrating to his back and shoulders, however fast he tried to sprint across the legal distance from his home to the department. It occurred to him at length that his overcoat might not be entirely blameless for this state of affairs. On examining it thoroughly at home, he discovered that in two or three places, to wit, on the back and round the shoulders, it looked like some coarse homespun cotton; the cloth had worn out so much that it let through the wind, and the lining had all gone to pieces. It must be mentioned here that Akaky's overcoat, too, had been the butt of the departmental wits; it had been even deprived of the honourable name of overcoat and had been called a *capote*. And indeed it was of a more peculiar cut: its collar had shrunk in size more and more every year, for it was used to patch the other parts. The patching did no credit to the tailor's art and the result was that the final effect was somewhat baggy and far from beautiful. Having discovered what was wrong with his overcoat, Akaky decided that he would have to take it to Petrovich, a tailor who lived somewhere on the fourth floor up some back stairs and who, in spite of the disadvantage of having only one eye and pock marks all over his face, carried on a rather successful trade in mending the trousers and frock-coats of government clerks and other gentlemen whenever, that is to say, he was sober and was not hatching some other scheme in his head.

We really ought not to waste much time over this tailor; since, however, it is now the fashion that the character of every person in a story must be delineated fully, then by all means let us have Petrovich, too. To begin with, he was known simply by his Christian name of Grigory, and had been a serf belonging to some gentleman or other; he began calling himself Petrovich only after he had obtained his freedom, when he started drinking rather heavily every holiday, at first only on the great holidays, and thereafter on any church holiday, on any day, in fact, marked with a cross in the calendar. So far as that went, he was true to the traditions of his forebears and in his altercations with his wife on this subject he would call her a worldly woman and a German. Having mentioned his wife, we had better say a word or two about her also; to our great regret, however, we know very little about her, except that Petrovich had a wife, who wore a bonnet, and not a kerchief; there appears to be some doubt as to whether she was good-looking or not, but on the whole it does not seem likely that she had very much to boast of in that respect; at any rate, only guardsmen were ever known to peer under her bonnet when meeting her in the street, twitching their moustaches and emitting a curious kind of grunt at the same time.

While ascending the stairs leading to Petrovich's flat — the stairs which, to do them justice, were soaked with water and slops and saturated with a strong spirituous smell which irritates the eyes and which, as the whole world knows, is a permanent feature of all the back stairs of St. Petersburg houses — while ascending the stairs, Akaky was already wondering how much Petrovich would ask for mending his overcoat, and made up his mind not to give him more than two roubles. The door of Petrovich's flat was open because his wife had been frying some fish and had filled the whole kitchen with smoke, so that even the cockroaches could no longer be seen. Akaky walked through the kitchen, unnoticed even by Mrs. Petrovich, and, at last, entered the tailor's room where he beheld Petrovich sitting on a large table of unstained wood with his legs crossed under him like a Turkish pasha. His feet, as is the custom of tailors when engaged in their work, were bare. The first thing that caught his eye was Petrovich's big toe, which Akaky knew very well indeed, with its deformed nail as thick and hard as the shell of a tortoise. A skein of silk and cotton thread hung about Petrovich's neck, and on his knees lay some tattered piece of clothing. He had for the last minute or two been trying to thread his needle and, failing every time, he was terribly angry with the dark room and even with the thread itself, muttering under his breath, "Won't you go through, you beast? You'll be the death of me yet, you slut!" Akaky could not help feeling sorry that he had come just at the moment when Petrovich was angry: he liked to place an order with Petrovich only when the tailor was a bit merry, or when he had, as his wife put it, "been swilling his corn-brandy, the one-eyed devil!" When in such a state, Petrovich was as a rule extremely amenable and always gave in and agreed to any price, and even bowed and thanked him. It was true that afterwards his wife would come to see Akaky and tell him with tears in her eyes that her husband had been drunk and had therefore charged him too little; but all Akaky had to do was to add another ten-copeck piece and the thing was settled. But now Petrovich was to all appearances sober as a judge and, consequently, rather bad-tempered, intractable and liable to charge any old price. Akaky realised that and was about, as the saying is, to beat a hasty retreat, but it was too late: Petrovich had already screwed up his only eye and was looking at him steadily. Akaky had willy-nilly to say, "Good morning, Petrovich!" "Good morning, sir. How are you?" said Petrovich, fixing his eye on Akaky's hands in an effort to make out what kind of offering he had brought.

"Well, you see, Petrovich, I — er — have come — er — about that, you know . . ." said Akaky.

It might be as well to explain at once that Akaky mostly talked in prepositions, adverbs, and, lastly, such parts of speech as have no meaning whatsoever. If the matter was rather difficult, he was in the habit of not finishing the sentences, so that often having begun his speech with, "This is — er — you know . . . a bit of that, you know . . ." he left it at that, forgetting to finish the sentence in the belief that he had said all that was necessary.

"What's that you've got there, sir?" said Petrovich, scrutinising at the same time the whole of Akaky's uniform with his one eye, from the collar to the sleeves, back, tails and button-holes, which was all extremely familiar to him, since it was his own handiwork. Such is the immemorial custom among tailors; it is the first thing a tailor does when he meets one of his customers.

"Well, you see, Petrovich, I've come about this here, you know . . . this overcoat of mine. The cloth, you know. . . . You see, it's really all right everywhere, in fact, excellent . . . I mean, it's in fine condition here and — er — all over. Looks a bit dusty, I know, and you might get the impression that it was old, but as a matter of fact it's as good as new, except in one place where it's a bit — er — a bit, you know. . . . On the back, I mean, and here on the shoulder. . . . Looks as though it was worn through a bit, and on the other shoulder too, just a trifle, you see. . . . Well, that's really all. Not much work in it. . . ."

Petrovich took the *capote*, first spread it on the table, examined it for a long time, shook his head, and stretched out his hand to the window for his round snuff-box with a portrait of some general, though which particular general it was impossible to say, for the place where the face should have been had been poked in by a finger and then pasted over with a square bit of paper. Having treated himself to a pinch of snuff, Petrovich held the overcoat out in his hands against the light and gave it another thorough examination, and again shook his head; he then turned it with the lining upwards and again shook his head, again took off the lid with the general pasted over with paper, and, filling his nose with snuff, replaced the lid, put away the snuff-box and, at last, said, "No, sir. Impossible to mend it. There's nothing left to it."

Akaky's heart sank at those words. "Why is it impossible, Petrovich?" he said, almost in the imploring voice of a child. "It's only on the shoulders that it's a bit worn, and I suppose you must have bits of cloth somewhere. . . ."

"Oh, I've got plenty of bits of cloth, sir, lots of 'em," said Petrovich. "But you see, sir, you can't sew 'em on. The whole coat's rotten. Touch it with a needle and it will fall to pieces."

"Well, if it falls to pieces, all you have to do is to patch it up again."

"Why, bless my soul, sir, and what do you suppose the patches will hold on to? What am I to sew them on to? Can't you see, sir, how badly worn it is? You can't call it cloth any more: one puff of wind and it will be blown away."

"But please strengthen it a bit. I mean, it can't be just — er — really, you know . . ."

"No, sir," said Petrovich firmly, "it can't be done. Too far gone. Nothing to hold it together. All I can advise you to do with it, sir, is to cut it up when winter comes and make some rags to wrap round your feet, for socks, sir, are no damned good at all: there's no real warmth in 'em. It's them Germans, sir, what invented socks to make a lot of money (Petrovich liked to get in a word against the Germans on every occasion). As for your overcoat, sir, I'm afraid you'll have to get a new one."

At the word "new" a mist suddenly spread before Akaky's eyes and everything in the room began swaying giddily. The only thing he could still see clearly was the general's face pasted over with paper on the lid of Petrovich's snuff-box.

"How do you mean, a new one?" he said, still as though speaking in a dream. "Why, I haven't got the money for it."

"Well, sir, all I can say is that you just must get yourself a new one," said Petrovich with callous indifference.

"Well, and if . . . I mean, if I had to get a new one . . . how much, I mean . . ."

"How much will it come to, sir?"

"Yes."

"Well, sir, I suppose you'll have to lay out three fifty-rouble notes or more," said Petrovich, pursing his lips significantly.

He had a great fondness for strong effects, Petrovich had. He liked to hit a fellow on the head suddenly and then steal a glance at him to see what kind of a face the stunned person would pull after his words.

"One hundred and fifty roubles for an overcoat!" cried poor Akaky in a loud voice, probably raising his voice to such a pitch for the first time in his life, for he was always distinguished by the softness of his voice.

"Yes, sir," said Petrovich. "And that, too, depends on the kind of coat you have. If you have marten for your collar and a silk lining for your hood, it might cost you two hundred."

"Now look here, Petrovich . . ." said Akaky in a beseeching voice, not hearing, or at any rate doing his best not to hear, what Petrovich was saying, and paying no attention whatever to the effect the tailor was trying to create. "Please, my dear fellow, just mend it somehow, so that I could still use it a bit longer, you know. . . ."

"No, sir, it will merely mean a waste of my work and your money," said Petrovich.

After such a verdict Akaky left Petrovich's room feeling completely crushed, while the tailor remained in the same position a long time after he had gone, without going back to his work, his lips pursed significantly. He was greatly pleased that he had neither demeaned himself nor let down the sartorial art.

In the street Akaky felt as though he were in a dream. "So that's how it stands, is it?" he murmured to himself. "I really didn't think that it would turn out like that, you know. . . ." Then after a pause he added, "Well, that's that. There's a real surprise for you. . . . I never thought that it would end like that. . . ." There followed another long pause, after which he said, "So that's how it is! What a sudden . . . I mean, what a terrible blow! Who could have . . . What an awful business!"

Having delivered himself thus, he walked on, without noticing it, in quite the opposite direction from his home. On the way a chimney-sweep brushed the whole of his sooty side against him and blackened his shoulder; from the top of a house that was being built a whole handful of lime fell upon him. But he was aware of nothing, and only when some time later he knocked against a policeman who, placing his halberd near him, was scattering some snuff from a horn on a calloused fist, did he recover a little, and that, too, only because the policeman said, "Now then, what are you pushing against me for? Can't you see where you're going? Ain't the pavement big enough for you?" This made him look up and retrace his steps.

But it was not until he had returned home that he began to collect his thoughts and saw his position as it really was. He began discussing the matter with himself, not in broken sentences, but frankly and soberly, as though talking to a wise friend with whom it was possible to discuss one's most intimate affairs.

"No, no," said Akaky, "it's pretty clear that it is impossible to talk to Petrovich now. He's a bit, you know . . . Been thrashed by his wife, I shouldn't wonder. I'd better go and see him next Sunday morning, for after all the drink he'll have had on Saturday night he'll still be screwing up his one eye, and he'll be very sleepy and dying for another drink to help him on his feet again, and his wife won't give him any money, so that if I come along and give him ten copecks or a little more he'll be more reasonable and change his mind about the overcoat, and then, you know . . ."

So Akaky reasoned with himself, and he felt greatly reassured.

Sunday came at last and, noticing from a distance that Petrovich's wife had left the house to go somewhere, he went straight in. To be sure, Petrovich did glower after his Saturday night's libations, and he could barely hold up his head, which seemed to be gravitating towards the floor, and he certainly looked very sleepy; and yet, in spite of this condition, no sooner did he hear what Akaky had come for than it seemed as if the devil himself had nudged him.

"Quite impossible, sir," he said. "You'll have to order a new one." Akaky immediately slipped a ten-copeck piece into his hand. "Thank you very much, sir," said Petrovich. "Very kind of you, I'm sure. I'll get a bit o' strength in me body and drink to your health, sir. But if I were you, sir, I'd stop worrying about that overcoat of yours. No good at all. Can't do nothing with it. Mind, I can promise you one thing, though: I'll make you a lovely new overcoat. That I will, sir."

Akaky tried to say something about mending the old one, but Petrovich would not even listen to him and said, "Depend upon it, sir, I'll make you a new one. Do my best for you, I will, sir. Might even while we're about it, sir, and seeing as how it's now the fashion, get a silver-plated clasp for the collar."

It was then that Akaky at last realised that he would have to get a new overcoat, and his heart failed him. And how indeed was he to do it? What with? Where was he to get the money? There was of course the additional holiday pay he could count on; at least there was a good chance of his getting that holiday bonus. But supposing he did get it, all that money had already been divided up and disposed of long ago. There was that new pair of trousers he must get; then there was that long-standing debt he owed the shoemaker for putting new tops to some old boots; he had, moreover, to order three shirts from the sempstress as well as two pairs of that particular article of underwear which cannot be decently mentioned in print—in short, all the money would have to be spent to the last penny, and even if the director of the department were to be so kind as to give him a holiday bonus of forty-five or even fifty roubles instead of forty, all that would remain of it would be the veriest trifle, which in terms of overcoat finance would be just a drop in the ocean. Though he knew perfectly well, of course, that Petrovich was sometimes mad enough to ask so utterly preposterous a price that even his wife could not refrain from exclaiming, "Gone off his head completely, the silly old fool! One day he accepts work for next to nothing, and now the devil must have made him ask more than he is worth himself!" — though he knew perfectly well, of course, that Petrovich would undertake to make him the overcoat for eighty roubles, the question still remained: where was he to get the eighty roubles? At a pinch he could raise half of it. Yes, he could find half of it all right and perhaps even a little more, but where was he to get the other half? . . .

But first of all the reader had better be told where Akaky hoped to be able to raise the first half.

Akaky was in the habit of putting away a little from every rouble he spent in a box which he kept locked up and which had a little hole in the lid through which money could be dropped. At the end of every six months he counted up the accumulated coppers and changed them into silver. As he had been saving up for a long time, there had accumulated in the course of several years a sum of over forty roubles. So he had half of the required sum in hand; but where was he to get the other half? Where was he to get another forty roubles?

Akaky thought and thought and then he decided that he would have to cut down his ordinary expenses for a year at least: do without a cup of tea in the evenings; stop burning candles in the evening and, if he had some work to do, go to his landlady's room and work by the light of her candle; when walking in the street, try to walk as lightly as possible on the cobbles and flagstones, almost on tiptoe, so as not to wear out the soles of his boots too soon; give his washing to the laundress as seldom as possible, and to make sure that it did not wear out, to take it off as soon as he returned home and wear only his dressing-gown of twilled cotton cloth, a very old garment that time itself had spared. To tell the truth, Akaky at first found it very hard to get used to such economy, but after some time he got used to it all right and everything went with a swing; he did not even mind going hungry in the evenings, for spiritually he was nourished well enough, since his thoughts were full of the great idea of his future overcoat. His whole existence indeed seemed now somehow to have become fuller, as though he had got married, as though there was someone at his side, as though he was never alone, but some agreeable helpmate had consented to share the joys and sorrows of his life, and this sweet helpmate, this dear wife of his, was no other than the selfsame overcoat with its thick padding of cotton-wool and its strong lining that would last a lifetime. He became more cheerful and his character even got a little firmer, like that of a man who knew what he was aiming at and how to achieve that aim. Doubt vanished, as though of its own accord, from his face and from his actions, and so did indecision and, in fact, all the indeterminate and shilly-shallying traits of his character. Sometimes a gleam would appear in his eyes and through his head there would flash the most bold and audacious thought, to wit, whether he should not after all get himself a fur collar of marten. All these thoughts about his new overcoat nearly took his mind off his work at the office, so much so that once, as he was copying out a document, he was just about to make a mistake, and he almost cried out, "Oh dear!" in a loud voice, and crossed himself. He went to see Petrovich at least once a month to discuss his overcoat, where it was best to buy the cloth, and what colour and at what price, and though looking a little worried, he always came back home well satisfied, reflecting that the time was not far off when he would pay for it all and when his overcoat would be ready.

As a matter of fact the whole thing came to pass much quicker than he dreamed. Contrary to all expectations, the director gave Akaky Akakyevich not forty or forty-five, but sixty roubles! Yes, a holiday bonus of sixty roubles. Whether he, too, had been aware that Akaky wanted a new overcoat, or whether it happened by sheer accident, the fact remained that Akaky had an additional twenty roubles. This speeded up the whole course of events. Another two or three months of a life on short commons and Akaky had actually saved up about eighty roubles. His pulse, generally sluggish, began beating fast. The very next day he went with Petrovich to the shops. They bought an excellent piece of cloth, and no wonder! For the matter had been carefully discussed and thought over for almost six months, and scarcely a month had passed without enquiries being made at the shops about prices, so as to make quite sure that the cloth they needed was not too expensive; and the result of all that foresight was that, as Petrovich himself admitted, they could not have got a better cloth. For the lining they chose calico, but of such fine and strong quality that, according to Petrovich, it was much better than silk and was actually much more handsome and glossy. They did not buy marten for a fur collar, for as a matter of fact it was rather expensive, but they chose cat fur instead, the best cat they could find in the shop, cat which from a distance could always be mistaken for marten. Petrovich took only two weeks over the overcoat, and that, too, because there was so much quilting to be done; otherwise it would have been ready earlier. For his work Petrovich took twelve roubles — less than that was quite out of the question: he had used nothing but silk thread in the sewing of it, and it was sewn with fine, double seams, and Petrovich had gone over each seam with his own teeth afterwards, leaving all sorts of marks on them.

It was . . . It is hard to say on what day precisely it was, but there could be no doubt at all that the day on which Petrovich at last delivered the overcoat was one of the greatest days in Akaky's life. He brought it rather early in the morning, just a short time before Akaky had to leave for the department. At no other time would the overcoat have been so welcome, for the time of rather sharp frosts had just begun, and from all appearances it looked as if the severity of the weather would increase. Petrovich walked in with the overcoat as a good tailor should. His face wore an expression of solemn gravity such as Akaky had never seen on it before. He seemed to be fully conscious of the fact that he had accomplished no mean thing and that he had shown by his own example the gulf that separated the tailors who merely relined a coat or did repairs from those who made new coats. He took the overcoat out of the large handkerchief in which he had brought it. (The handkerchief had just come from the laundress: it was only now that he folded it and put it in his pocket for use.) Having taken out the overcoat, he looked very proudly about him and, holding it in both hands, threw it very smartly over Akaky's shoulders, then he gave it a vigorous pull and, bending down, smoothed it out behind with his hand; then he draped it round Akaky, throwing it open in front a little. Akaky, who was no longer a young man, wanted to try it on with his arms in the sleeves, and Petrovich helped him to put his hands through the sleeves, and — it was all right even when he wore it with his arms in the sleeves. In fact, there could be no doubt at all that the overcoat was a perfect fit. Petrovich did not let this opportunity pass without observing that it was only because he lived in a back street and had no signboard and because he had known Akaky Akakyevich so long that he had charged him so little for making the overcoat. If he had ordered it on Nevsky Avenue, they would have charged him seventy-five roubles for the work alone. Akaky had no desire to discuss the matter with Petrovich and, to tell the truth he was a little frightened of the big sums which Petrovich was so fond of tossing about with the idea of impressing people. He paid him, thanked him, and left immediately for the department in his new overcoat. Petrovich followed him into the street where he remained standing a long time on one spot, admiring his handiwork from a distance; then he purposely went out of his way so that he could by taking a short-cut by a side street rush out into the street again and have another look at the overcoat, this time from the other side, that is to say, from the front.

Meanwhile Akaky went along as if walking on air. Not for a fraction of a second did he forget that he had a new overcoat on his back, and he could not help smiling to himself from time to time with sheer pleasure at the thought of it. And really it had two advantages: one that it was warm, and the other that it was good. He did not notice the distance and found himself suddenly in the department. He took off the overcoat in the hall, examined it carefully and entrusted it to the special care of the door-keeper. It is not known how the news of Akaky's new overcoat had spread all over the department, but all at once every one knew that Akaky had discarded his *capote* and had a fine new overcoat. They all immediately rushed out into the hall to have a look at Akaky's new overcoat. Congratulations and good wishes were showered upon him. At first Akaky just smiled, then he felt rather embarrassed. But when all surrounded him and began telling him that he ought to celebrate his acquisition of a new overcoat and that the least he could do was to invite them all to a party, Akaky Akakyevich was thrown into utter confusion and did not know what to do, what to say to them all, or how to extricate himself from that very awkward situation. He even tried a few minutes later with the utmost good humour to assure them, blushing to the roots of his hair, that it was not a new overcoat at all, that it was just . . . well, you know . . . just his old overcoat. At last one of the clerks, and, mind, not just any clerk, but no less a person that the assistant head clerk of the office, wishing to show no doubt that he, for one, was not a proud man and did not shun men more humble than himself, said, "So be it! I will give a party instead of Akaky Akakyevich. I invite you all, gentlemen, this evening to tea at my place. As a matter of fact, it happens to be my birthday." The Civil Servants naturally wished him many happy returns of the day and accepted his invitation with alacrity. Akaky tried at first to excuse himself, but everybody told him that it was not done and that he ought to be ashamed of himself, and he just could not wriggle out of it. However, he felt rather pleased afterwards, for it occurred to him that this would give him a chance of taking a walk in the evening in his new overcoat.

That day was to Akaky like a great festival. He came home in a most happy frame of mind, took off his overcoat, hung it with great care on the wall, stood for some time admiring the cloth and lining, and then produced his old overcoat, which had by then gone to pieces completely, just to compare the two. He looked at it and could not help chuckling out loud: what a difference! And he kept smiling to himself all during dinner when he thought of the disgraceful state of his old overcoat. He enjoyed his dinner immensely and did no copying at all afterwards, not one document did he copy, but just indulged himself a little by lying down on his bed until dusk. Then, without dawdling unnecessarily, he dressed, threw the overcoat over his shoulders, and went out into the street.

Unfortunately we cannot say where precisely the Civil Servant who was giving the party lived. Our memory is beginning to fail us rather badly and everything in St. Petersburg, all the streets and houses, has become so blurred and mixed up in our head that we find it very difficult indeed to sort it out properly. Be that as it may, there can be no doubt that the Civil Servant in question lived in one of the best parts of the town, which means of course that he did not live anywhere near Akaky Akakyevich. At first Akaky had to pass through some deserted streets, very poorly lighted, but as he got nearer to the Civil Servant's home the streets became more crowded and more brilliantly illuminated. There certainly were more people in the streets, the women were well dressed and the men even wore beaver collars. There were fewer poor peasant cabmen with their grate-like wooden sledges studded with brass nails; on the contrary, the cabmen were mostly fine fellows in crimson velvet caps with lacquered sledges and bearskin covers, and carriages with sumptuously decorated boxes drove at a great speed through the streets, their wheels crunching on the snow.

Akaky looked at it all as though he had never seen anything like it in his life, and indeed he had not left his room in the evening for several years. He stopped before a lighted shop window and for some minutes looked entranced at a painting of a beautiful woman who was taking off a shoe and showing a bare leg, a very shapely leg, too; and behind her back a gentleman had stuck his head through the door of another room, a gentleman with fine side-whiskers and a handsome imperial on his chin. Akaky shook his head and grinned, and then went on his way. Why did he grin? It might have been because he had seen something he had never seen before, but a liking for which is buried deep down inside every one of us, or because (like many another Civil Servant), he thought to himself, "Oh, those damned Frenchmen! What a people they are, to be sure! If they set their heart on something, something . . . well, something of that kind, you know, then it is something . . . well, something of that kind. . . ." But perhaps he never even said anything at all to himself. How indeed is one to delve into a man's mind and find out what he is thinking about? At last he reached the house where the young assistant head clerk of his office lived.

The assistant head clerk lived in great style: there was a lamp burning on the stairs, and his flat was on the second floor. As he entered the hall, Akaky saw on the floor rows upon rows of galoshes. Among them in the middle of the room stood a *samovar*, hissing and letting off clouds of steam. The walls were covered with overcoats and cloaks, some even with beaver collars and velvet revers. A confused buzz of conversation came from the other side of the wall, and it grew very clear and loud when the door opened and a footman came out with a trayful of empty tea-glasses, a jug of cream and a basket of biscuits. It was evident that the Civil Servants had been there for some time and had already finished their first glass of tea.

After hanging up his overcoat himself, Akaky entered the room, and there flashed upon his sight simultaneously candles, Civil Servants, pipes, card-tables, while his ears were filled with the confused sound of continuous conversation, which came from every corner of the room, and the noise of moving chairs. He stood in the middle of the room, looking rather forlorn and trying desperately to think what he ought to do. But his presence had already been noticed and he was welcomed with loud shouts, and everybody immediately went into the hall to inspect his overcoat anew. Though feeling rather embarrassed at first, Akaky, being of a singularly ingenuous nature, could not help being pleased to hear how everybody praised his overcoat. Then, of course, they forgot all about him and his overcoat and crowded, as was to be expected, round the card-tables set out for whist.

All this — the noise, the talk, and the crowd of people — was very strange and bewildering to Akaky. He simply did not know what to do, where to put his hands and feet, or his whole body; at length he sat down by the card players, looked at the cards, studied the face of one player, then of another, and after a little time began to feel bored and started yawning, particularly as it was getting late and it was long past his bedtime. He tried to take leave of his host, but they would not let him go, saying that they had to drink a glass of champagne in honour of his new overcoat. In about an hour supper was served. It consisted of a mixed salad, cold veal, meat pie, cream pastries and champagne. They made Akaky drink two glasses of champagne, after which he felt that everything got much jollier in the room. However, he could not forget that it was already midnight and that it was high time he went home. To make sure that his host would not detain him on one pretext or another, he stole out of the room and found his overcoat in the hall. The overcoat, he noticed not without a pang of regret, was lying on the floor. He picked it up, shook it, removed every speck of dust from it and, putting it over his shoulders, went down the stairs into the street.

It was still light in the street. A few small grocer's shops, those round-the-clock clubs of all sorts of servants, were still open; from those which were already closed a streak of light still streamed through the crack under the door, showing that there was still some company there, consisting most probably of maids and men-servants who were finishing their talk and gossip, leaving their masters completely at a loss to know where they were. Akaky walked along feeling very happy and even set off running after some lady (goodness knows why) who passed him like a streak of lightning, every part of her body in violent motion. However, he stopped almost at once and went on at a slow pace as before, marvelling himself where that unusual spurt of speed had come from. Soon he came to those never-ending, deserted streets, which even in daytime are not particularly cheerful, let alone at night. Now they looked even more deserted and lonely; there were fewer street lamps and even those he came across were extinguished: the municipal authorities seemed to be sparing of oil. He now came into the district of wooden houses and fences; there was not a soul to be seen anywhere, only the snow gleamed on the streets, and hundreds of dismal, low hovels with closed shutters which seemed to have sunk into a deep sleep, stretched in a long, dark line before him. Soon he approached the spot where the street was intersected by an immense square with houses dimly visible on the other side, a square that looked to him like a dreadful desert.

A long way away—goodness knows where—he could see the glimmer of light coming from some sentry-box, which seemed to be standing at the edge of the world. Akaky's cheerfulness faded perceptibly as he entered the square. He entered it not without a kind of involuntary sensation of dread, as though feeling in his bones that something untoward was going to happen. He looked back, and then cast a glance at either side of him: it was just as though the sea were all round him. "Much better not to look," he thought to himself, and, shutting his eyes, he walked on, opening them only to have a look how far the end of the square was. But what he saw was a couple of men standing right in front of him, men with moustaches, but what they were he could not make out in the darkness. He felt dazed and his heart began beating violently against his ribs. "Look, here is my overcoat!" one of the men said in a voice of thunder, grabbing him by the collar. Akaky was about to scream. "Help!" but the other man shook his fist in his face, a fist as big as a Civil Servant's head, and said, "You just give a squeak!" All poor Akaky knew was that they took off his overcoat and gave him a kick which sent him sprawling on the snow. He felt nothing at all any more. A few minutes later he recovered sufficiently to get up, but there was not a soul to be seen anywhere. He felt that it was terribly cold in the square and that his overcoat had gone. He began to shout for help, but his voice seemed to be too weak to carry to the end of the square. Feeling desperate and without ceasing to shout, he ran across the square straight to the sentry-box beside which stood a policeman who, leaning on his halberd, seemed to watch the running figure with mild interest, wondering no doubt why the devil a man was running towards him, screaming his head off while still a mile away. Having run up to the police constable, Akaky started shouting at him in a gasping voice that he was asleep and did not even notice that a man had been robbed under his very nose. The policeman said that he saw nothing, or rather that all he did see was that two men had stopped him (Akaky) in the middle of the square, but he supposed that they were his friends; and he advised Akaky, instead of standing there and abusing him for nothing, to go and see the police inspector next morning, for the inspector was quite sure to find the men who had taken his overcoat.

Akaky Akakyevich came running home in a state of utter confusion. His hair, which still grew, though sparsely, over his temples and at the back of his head, was terribly tousled; his chest, arms and trousers were covered with snow. His old landlady, awakened by the loud knocking at the door, jumped hurriedly out of bed and with only one slipper on ran to open the door, modestly clasping her chemise to her bosom with one hand. When she opened the door and saw the terrible state Akaky was in, she fell back with a gasp. He told her what had happened to him, and she threw up her arms in dismay and said that he ought to go straight to the district police commissioner, for the police inspector was quite sure to swindle him, promise him all sorts of things and then leave him in the lurch; it would be much better if he went to the district police commissioner who, it seemed, was known to her, for Anna, the Finnish girl who was once her cook, was now employed by the district commissioner of police as a nurse, and, besides, she had seen him often as he drove past the house, and he even went to church every Sunday and always, while saying his prayers, looked round at everybody very cheerfully, so that, judging from all appearances, he must be a kind-hearted man.

Having listened to that piece of advice, Akaky wandered off sadly to his room, and how he spent that night we leave it to those to judge who can enter into the position of another man. Early next morning he went to see the district police commissioner, but they told him that he was still asleep. He came back at ten o'clock and again they said he was asleep. He came back at eleven o'clock and was told that the police commissioner was not at home. He came back at lunch-time, but the clerks in the waiting-room would not admit him on any account unless he told them first what he had come for and what it was all about and what had happened. So that in the end Akaky felt for the first time in his life that he had to assert himself and he told them bluntly that he had come to see the district commissioner of police personally, that they had no right to refuse to admit him, that he had come from the department on official business, and that if he lodged a complaint against them, they would see what would happen. The clerks dared say nothing to this and one of them went to summon the commissioner.

The police commissioner took rather a curious view of Akaky's story of the loss of his overcoat. Instead of concentrating on the main point of the affair, he began putting all sorts of questions to Akaky which had nothing to do with it, such as why he was coming home so late, and was he sure he had not been to any disorderly house the night before, so that Akaky felt terribly embarrassed and went away wondering whether the police were ever likely to take the necessary steps to retrieve his overcoat.

That day (for the first time in his life) he did not go to the department. Next day he appeared looking very pale and wearing his old *capote*, which was in a worse state than ever. Many of his colleagues seemed moved by the news of the robbery of his overcoat, though there were a few among them who could not help pulling poor Akaky's leg even on so sad an occasion. It was decided to make a special collection for Akaky, but they only succeeded in collecting a trifling sum, for the clerks in his office had already spent a great deal on subscribing to a fund for a portrait of the director and also on some kind of a book, at the suggestion of one of the departmental chiefs, who was a friend of the author. Anyway, the sum collected was a trifling one. One Civil Servant, however, moved by compassion, decided to help Akaky with some good advice at any rate, and he told him that he should not go to the district police inspector, for though it might well happen that the district police inspector, anxious to win the approbation of his superiors, would somehow or other find his overcoat, Akaky would never be able to get it out of the police station unless he could present all the necessary legal proofs that the overcoat belonged to him. It would therefore be much better if Akaky went straight to a certain Very Important Person, for the Very Important Person could, by writing and getting into touch with the right people, give a much quicker turn to the whole matter.

Akaky Akakyevich (what else could he do?) decided to go and see the Very Important Person. What position the Very Important Person occupied and what his job actually was has never been properly ascertained and still remains unknown. Suffice it to say that the Very Important Person had become a Very

Important Person only quite recently, and that until then he was quite an unimportant person. Moreover, his office was not even now considered of much importance as compared with others of greater importance. But there will always be people who regard as important what in the eyes of other people is rather unimportant. However, the Very Important Person did his best to increase his importance in all sorts of ways, to wit, he introduced a rule that his subordinates should meet him on the stairs when he arrived at his office; that no one should be admitted to his office unless he first petitioned for an interview, and that every-thing should be done according to the strictest order: the collegiate registrar was first to report to the provincial secretary, the provincial secretary to the titular councillor or whomsoever it was he had to report to, and that only by such a procedure should any particular business reach him. In Holy Russia, we are sorry to say, every one seems to be anxious to ape every one else and each man copies and imitates his superior. The story is even told of some titular councillor who, on being made chief of some small office, immediately partitioned off a special room for himself, calling it "the presence chamber," and placed two commission-aires in coats with red collars and galloons at the door with instructions to take hold of the door handle and open the door to any person who came to see him, though there was hardly room in "the presence chamber" for an ordinary writing-desk.

The manners and habits of the Very Important Person were very grand and impressive, but not very subtle. His whole system was based chiefly on strictness. "Strictness, strictness, and *again* strictness!" he usually declared, and at the penultimate word he usually peered very significantly into the face of the man he was addressing. There seemed to be no particular reason for this strictness, though, for the dozen or so Civil Servants who composed the whole administra-tive machinery of his office were held in a proper state of fear and trembling, anyhow. Seeing him coming from a distance they all stopped their work immedi-ately and, standing at attention, waited until the chief had walked through the room. His usual conversation with any of his subordinates was saturated with strictness and consisted entirely of three phrases: "How dare you, sir? Do you know who you're talking to, sir? Do you realise who is standing before you, sir?" Still, he was really a good fellow at heart, was particularly pleasant with his colleagues, and quite obliging, too; but his new position went to his head. Having received the rank of general, he got all confused, was completely nonplussed and did not know what to do. In the presence of a man equal to him in rank, he was just an ordinary fellow, quite a decent fellow, and in many ways even a far from stupid fellow; but whenever he happened to be in company with men even one rank lower than he, he seemed to be lost; he sat silent and his position was really pitiable, more particularly as he himself felt that he could have spent the time so much more enjoyably. A strong desire could sometimes be read in his eyes to take part in some interesting conversation or join some interesting people, but he was always stopped by the thought; would it not mean going a little too far on his part? Would it not be mistaken for familiarity and would he not thereby lower himself in the estimation of everybody? As a consequence of this reasoning he always found himself in a position where he had to remain silent, delivering himself only from time to time of a few monosyllables, and in this way he won for himself the unenviable reputation of being an awful bore.

It was before this sort of Very Important Person that our Akaky presented himself, and he presented himself at the most inopportune moment he could possibly have chosen, very unfortunate for himself, though not so unfortunate for the Very Important Person.

At the time of Akaky's arrival the Very Important Person was in his private office, having a very pleasant talk with an old friend of his, a friend of his childhood, who had only recently arrived in St. Petersburg and whom he had not seen for several years. It was just then that he was informed that a certain Bashmachkin wanted to see him. "Who's that?" he asked abruptly, and he was told, "Some Civil Servant." "Oh," said the Very Important Person, "let him wait. I'm busy now."

Now we believe it is only fair to state here that the Very Important Person had told a thumping lied. He was not busy at all. He had long ago said all he had to say to his old friend, and their present conversation had for some time now been punctuated by long pauses, interrupted by the one or the other slapping his friend on the knee and saying, "Ah, Ivan Abramovich!" or "Yes, yes, quite right, Stepan Varlamovich!" However, he asked the Civil Servant to wait, for he wanted to show his friend, who had left the Civil Service long ago and had been spending all this time at his country house, how long he kept Civil Servants cooling their heels in his anteroom. At last, having talked, or rather kept silent as long as they liked, having enjoyed a cigar in comfortable arm-chairs with sloping backs, he seemed to remember something suddenly and said to his secretary, who was standing at the door with a sheaf of documents in his hand, "Isn't there some Civil Servant waiting to see me? Tell him to come in, please."

Seeing Akaky's humble appearance and old uniform, he turned to him and said shortly, "What do you want?" in an abrupt and firm voice, which he had specially rehearsed in the solitude of his room in front of a looking-glass a week before he received his present post and the rank of general.

Akaky, who had long since been filled with the proper amount of fear and trembling, felt rather abashed and explained as well as he could and as much as his stammering would let him, with the addition of the more than usual number of "wells" and "you knows," that his overcoat was quite a new overcoat, and that he had been robbed in a most shameless fashion, and that he was now applying to his excellency in the hope that his excellency might by putting in a word here and there or doing this or that, or writing to the Commissioner of Police of the Metropolis, or to some other person, get his overcoat back. For some unknown reason the general considered such an approach as too familiar. "What do you mean, sir?" he said in his abrupt voice. "Don't you know the proper procedure? What have you come to me for? Don't you know how things are done? In the first place you should have sent in a petition about it to my office. Your petition, sir, would have been placed before the chief clerk, who would have transferred it to my secretary, and my secretary would have submitted it to me. . . ."

"But, your excellency," said Akaky, trying to summon the handful of courage he had (it was not a very big handful, anyway), and feeling at the same time that he was perspiring all over, "I took the liberty, your excellency, of troubling you personally because — er — because, sir, secretaries are, well, you know, rather unreliable people. . . ."

"What? What did you say, sir?" said the Very Important Person. "How dare you speak like this, sir? Where did you get the impudence to speak like this, sir? Where did you get these extraordinary ideas from, sir? What's the meaning of this mutinous spirit that is now spreading among young men against their chiefs and superiors?" The Very Important Person did not seem to have noticed that Akaky Akakyevich was well over fifty, and it can only be supposed, therefore, that if he called him a young man he meant it only in a relative sense, that is to say, that compared with a man of seventy Akaky was a young man. "Do you realise, sir, who you are talking to? Do you understand, sir, who is standing before you? Do you understand it, sir? Do you understand it, I ask you?"

Here he stamped his foot and raised his voice to so high a pitch that it was not Akaky Akakyevich alone who became terrified. Akaky was on the point of fainting. He staggered, trembled all over, and could not stand on his feet. Had it not been for the door-keepers, who ran up to support him, he would have collapsed on the ground. He was carried out almost unconscious. The Very Important Person, satisfied that the effect he had produced exceeded all expectations and absolutely in raptures over the idea that a word of his could actually throw a man into a faint, glanced at his friend out of the corner of his eye, wondering what impression he had made on him; and he was pleased to see that his friend was rather in an uneasy frame of mind himself and seemed to show quite unmistakable signs of fear.

Akaky could not remember how he had descended the stairs, or how he had got out into the street. He remembered nothing. His hands and feet had gone dead. Never in his life had he been so hauled over the coals by a general and not his own general at that. He walked along in a blizzard, in the teeth of a howling wind, which was sweeping through the streets, with his mouth agape and constantly stumbling off the pavement; the wind, as is its invariable custom in St. Petersburg, blew from every direction and every side street all at once. His throat became inflamed in no time at all, and when at last he staggered home he was unable to utter a word. He was all swollen, and he took to his bed. So powerful can a real official reprimand be sometimes!

Next day Akaky was in a high fever. Thanks to the most generous assistance of the St. Petersburg climate, his illness made much more rapid progress than could have been expected, and when the doctor arrived he merely felt his pulse and found nothing to do except prescribe a poultice, and that only because he did not want to leave the patient without the beneficent aid of medicine; he did, though, express his opinion then and there that all would be over in a day and a half. After which he turned to the landlady and said, "No need to waste time, my dear lady. You'd better order a deal coffin for him at once, for I don't suppose he can afford an oak coffin, can he?"

Did Akaky Akakyevich hear those fateful words and, if he did hear them, did they produce a shattering effect upon him? Did he at that moment repine at his wretched lot in life? It is quite impossible to say, for the poor man was in a delirium and a high fever. Visions, one stranger than another, haunted him incessantly: one moment he saw Petrovich and ordered him to make an overcoat with special traps for thieves, whom he apparently believed to be hiding under his bed, so that he called to his landlady every minute to get them out of there, and once he even asked her to get a thief from under his blanket; another time he demanded to be told why his old *capote* was hanging on the wall in front of him when he had a new overcoat; then it seemed to him that he was standing before the general and listening to his reprimand, which he so well deserved, saying, "Sorry, your excellency!" and, finally, he let out a stream of obscenities, shouting such frightful words that his dear old landlady kept crossing herself, having never heard him use such words, particularly as they seemed always to follow immediately upon the words, "your excellency." He raved on and no sense could be made of his words, except that it was quite evident that his incoherent words and thoughts all revolved about one and the same overcoat. At length poor Akaky Akakyevich gave up the ghost.

Neither his room nor his belongings were put under seal because, in the first place, he had no heirs, and in the second there was precious little inheritance he left behind, comprising as it did all in all a bundle of quills, a quire of white Government paper, three pairs of socks, a few buttons that had come off his trousers, and the *capote* with which the reader has already made his acquaintance. Who finally came into all this property, goodness only knows, and I must confess that the author of this story was not sufficiently interested to find out. Akaky Akakyevich was taken to the cemetery and buried. And St. Petersburg carried on without Akaky, as though he had never lived there. A human being just disappeared and left no trace, a human being no one ever dreamed of protecting, who was not dear to anyone, whom no one thought of taking any interest in, who did not attract the attention even of a naturalist who never fails to stick a pin through an ordinary fly to examine it under the microscope; a man who bore meekly the sneers and insults of his fellow Civil Servants in the department and who went to his grave because of some silly accident, but who before the very end of his life did nevertheless catch a glimpse of a Bright Visitant in the shape of an overcoat, which for a brief moment brought a ray of sunshine into his drab, poverty-stricken life, and upon whose head afterwards disaster had most pitilessly fallen, as it falls upon the heads of the great ones of this earth! . . .

A few days after his death a caretaker was sent to his room from the department to order him to present himself at the office at once: the chief himself wanted to see him! But the caretaker had to return without him, merely reporting that Akaky Akakyevich could not come, and to the question, "Why not?" he merely said, "He can't come, sir, 'cause he's dead. That's why, sir. Been buried these four days, he has, sir." It was in this way that the news of his death reached the department, and on the following day a new clerk was sitting in his place, a much taller man, who did not write letters in Akaky's upright hand, but rather sloping and aslant.

But who could have foreseen that this was not the last of Akaky Akakyevich and that he was destined to be the talk of the town for a few days after his death, as though in recompense for having remained unnoticed all through his life. But so it fell out, and our rather poor story quite unexpectedly acquired a most fantastic ending.

Rumours suddenly spread all over St. Petersburg that a ghost in the shape of a Government clerk had begun appearing near Kalinkin Bridge and much farther afield, too, and that this ghost was looking for some stolen overcoat and, under the pretext of recovering this lost overcoat, was stripping overcoats off the backs of all sorts of people, irrespective of their rank or calling: overcoats with cat fur, overcoats with beaver fur, raccoon, fox and bear fur-coats, in fact, overcoats with every kind of fur or skin that men have ever made us of to cover their own. One of the departmental clerks had seen the ghost with his own eyes and at once recognised Akaky Akakyevich; but that frightened him so much that he took to his heels and was unable to get a better view of the ghost, but merely saw how he shook a finger at him threateningly from a distance. From all sides complaints were incessantly heard to the effect that the backs and shoulders, not only of titular councillors, but also of court councillors, were in imminent danger of catching cold as a result of this frequent pulling off of overcoats. The police received orders to catch the ghost at all costs, dead or alive, and to punish him in the most unmerciful manner as an example to all other ghosts, and they nearly did catch it. A police constable whose beat included Kiryushkin Lane had actually caught the ghost by his collar on the very scene of his latest crime, in the very act of attempting to pull a frieze overcoat off the back of some retired musician who had once upon a time tootled on a flute. Having caught him by the collar, the policeman shouted to two of his comrades to come to his help, and when those arrived he told them to hold the miscreant while he reached for his snuff-box which he kept in one of his boots, to revive his nose which had been frostbitten six times in his life; but the snuff must have been of a kind that even a ghost could not stand. For no sooner had the policeman, closing his right nostril with a finger, inhaled with his left nostril half a handful of snuff than the ghost sneezed so violently that he splashed the eyes of all three. While they were raising their fists to wipe their eyes, the ghost had vanished completely, so that they were not even sure whether he had actually been in their hands. Since that time policemen were in such terror of the dead that they were even afraid to arrest the living, merely shouting from a distance, "Hi, you there, move along, will you?" and the ghost of the Civil Servant began to show himself beyond Kalinkin Bridge, causing alarm and dismay among all law-abiding citizens of timid dispositions.

We seem, however, to have completely forgotten a certain Very Important Person who, as a matter of fact, was the real cause of the fantastic turn this otherwise perfectly true story has taken. To begin with, we think it is only fair to make it absolutely clear that the Very Important Person felt something like a twinge of compunction soon after the departure of poor Akaky Akakyevich, whom he had taken to task so severely. Sympathy for a fellow human being was not alien to him; his heart was open to all kinds of kindly impulses in spite of the fact that his rank often prevented them from coming to the surface. As soon as the friend he had not seen for so long had left, he felt even a little worried about poor Akaky, and since that day he could not get the pale face of the meek little Government clerk out of his head, the poor Civil Servant who could not take an official reprimand like a man. In fact, he worried so much about him that a week later he sent one of his own clerks to Akaky to find out how he was getting on, whether his overcoat had turned up, and whether it was not really possible to help him in any way. When he learnt that Akaky had died suddenly of a fever he was rather upset and all day long his conscience troubled him, and he was in a bad mood. Wishing to distract himself a little and forget the unpleasant incident, he went to spend an evening with one of his friends, where he found quite a large company and, what was even better, they all seemed to be almost of the same rank as he, so that there was nothing at all to disconcert him. This had a most wonderful effect on his state of mind. He let himself go, became a very pleasant fellow to talk to, affable and genial, and spent a very agreeable evening. At dinner he drank a few glasses of champagne, which, as is generally acknowledged, is quite an excellent way of getting rid of gloomy thoughts. The champagne led him to introduce a certain change into his programme for that night, to wit, he decided not to go home at once, but first visit a lady friend of his, a certain Karolina Ivanovna, presumably of German descent, with whom he was on exceedingly friendly terms. It should be explained here that the Very Important Person was not a young man, that he was a good husband and a worthy father of a family. Two sons, one of whom was already in Government service, and a very sweet sixteen-year-old daughter, whose little nose was perhaps a thought too arched, but who was very pretty none the less, came every morning to kiss his hand, saying, "*Bonjour, papa.*" His wife, who was still in the prime of life and not at all bad-looking, first gave him her hand to kiss and then, turning it round, kissed his hand. But the Very Important Person, who was very satisfied indeed with these domestic pleasantries, thought it only right to have a lady friend in another part of the town for purely friendly relations. This lady friend was not a bit younger or better-looking than his wife, but there it is: such is the way of the world, and it is not our business to pass judgment upon it. And so the Very Important Person descended the stairs, sat down in his sledge, said to his coachman, "To Karolina Ivanovna," and, wrapping himself up very snugly in his warm overcoat, gave himself up completely to the enjoyment of his pleasant mood, than which nothing better could happen to a Russian, that is to say, the sort of mood when you do not yourself have to think of anything, while thoughts, one more delightful than another, come racing through your head without even putting you to the trouble of chasing after them or looking for them. Feeling very pleased, he recalled without much effort all the pleasant happenings of the evening, all the witty sayings, which had aroused peals of laughter among the small circle of friends, many of which he even now repeated softly to himself, finding them every bit as funny as they were the first time he heard them, and it is therefore little wonder that he chuckled happily most of the time. The boisterous wind, however, occasionally interfered with his enjoyment, for, rushing out suddenly from heaven knew where and for a reason that was utterly incomprehensible, it cut his face like a knife, covering it with lumps of snow, swelling out his collar like a sail, or suddenly throwing it with supernatural force over his head and so causing him incessant trouble to extricate himself from it. All of a sudden the Very Important Person felt that somebody had seized him very firmly by the collar. Turning round, he saw a small-sized man in an old, threadbare Civil Service uniform, and it was not without horror that he recognized Akaky Akakyevich. The Civil Servant's face was white as snow and looked like that of a dead man. But the horror of the Very Important Person increased considerably when he saw that the mouth of the dead man became twisted and, exhaling the terrible breath of the grave, Akaky's ghost uttered the following words, "Aha! So here you are! I've—er—collared you at last! . . . It's your overcoat I want, sir! You didn't care a rap for mine, did you? Did nothing to get it back for me, and abused me into the bargain! All right, then, give me yours now!" The poor Very Important Person nearly died of fright. Unbending as he was at the office and generally in the presence of his inferiors, and though one look at his manly appearance and figure was enough to make people say, "Ugh, what a Tartar!" nevertheless in this emergency he, like many another man of athletic appearance, was seized with such terror that he began, not without reason, to apprehend a heart attack. He threw off his overcoat himself and shouted to his driver in a panic-stricken voice, "Home, quick!" The driver, recognising the tone which was usually employed in moments of crisis and was quite often accompanied by something more forceful, drew in his head between his shoulders just to be on the safe side, flourished his whip and raced off as swift as an arrow. In a little over six minutes the Very Important Person was already at the entrance of his house.

Pale, frightened out of his wits, and without his overcoat, he arrived home instead of going to Karolina Ivanovna's, and somehow or other managed to stagger to his room. He spent a very restless night, so that next morning at breakfast his daughter told him outright, "You look very pale today, Papa!" But Papa made no reply. Not a word did he say to any one about what had happened to him, where he had been and where he had intended to go.

This incident made a deep impression upon the Very Important Person. It was not so frequently now that his subordinates heard him say, "How dare you, sir? Do you realise who you're talking to, sir?" And if he did say it, it was only after he had heard what it was all about.

But even more remarkable was the fact that since then the appearance of the Civil Servant's ghost had completely ceased. It can only be surmised that he was very pleased with the general's overcoat which must have fitted him perfectly; at least nothing was heard any more of people who had their overcoats pulled off their backs. Not that there were not all sorts of busybodies who would not let well alone and who went on asserting that the ghost of the Civil Servant was still appearing in the more outlying parts of the town. Indeed, a Kolomna policeman saw with his own eyes the ghost appear from behind a house; but having rather a frail constitution — once an ordinary young pig, rushing out of a house, had sent him sprawling, to the great delight of some cabbies who were standing round and whom, for such an insult, he promptly fined two copecks each for snuff — he dared not stop the ghost, but merely followed it in the dark until, at last, it suddenly looked round and, stopping dead in its tracks, asked, "What do *you* want?" at the same time displaying a fist of a size that was never seen among the living. The police constable said, "Nothing," and turned back at once. This ghost, however, was much taller; it had a pair of huge moustachios, and, walking apparently in the direction of Obukhov Bridge, it disappeared into the darkness of the night.

[1842]

Study and Writing Questions

1. What is the attitude of the NARRATOR toward Akaky Akakyevitch? What is the attitude of the narrator toward the world Akaky Akakyevitch inhabits?
2. Why is Petrovich described at such length and given so large a role in the STORY?
3. Is the "FANTASTIC" ending of the story following Akaky Akakyevitch's death appropriate to the tale as a whole or not? What does it accomplish? How would the story be different if it ended with the death?

4. In the first paragraph of the story, the narrator pointedly refuses to name a government department. In the second paragraph, the narrator elaborately reports the naming of the protagonist. In what other instances are names crucial in this story? At one point, Akaky Akakyevitch humbles a junior clerk by a question; at another, he is himself humbled by the imperious questions of the Very Important Person. In what other instances is language itself important in the story? What is the social importance of names in particular and of language in general in the world of "The Overcoat"?

5. Many elements of "The Overcoat" are doubled, for example, the PROTAGONIST's own name, descriptions of men with moustaches, visits to the tailor, and portrayals of generals. What are other instances of doubling? How does Gogol's use of doubling engage his readers and affect the telling of his story?

See also Questions for Contrast and Comparison: 15, 70, 127, 140, 141, 142, 165, 224, and 226.

■ NADINE GORDIMER (1923–) *was born in a small town near Johannesburg, South Africa, daughter of a native English mother and a Jewish father who had immigrated from the Baltics. She attended convent schools and, for one year, the University of Witwatersrand (B.A., 1945). She began writing short fiction in school and won wide respect for the delicate, realistic, empathetic prose of her first story collections,* Face to Face *(1949) and* The Soft Voice of the Serpent *(1952). Thereafter, in more than a score of books, she has largely alternated story collections with novels, most recently publishing* Crimes of Conscience *(1991). Her continuing subject has been the careful delineation of social relations, especially the corrosive impact on individuals of all races of apartheid, her country's official policy (1948– 1992) of racial separation and domination by the white minority. Her writing has won universal praise abroad (including the Booker Prize for* The Conservationist, *1974) and sometimes official censorship within her homeland. Her fictions, the best known of which include* A Guest of Honor *(1970) and* Burger's Daughter *(1979), trace South Africa's changing society over four decades. Gordimer, who lives in Johannesburg, married (1952) Reinhold H. Cassirer, director of the Johannesburg branch of Sotheby Parke Bernet gallery/auctioneers. They have two children.*

Six Feet of the Country

My wife and I are not real farmers—not even Lerice, really. We bought our place, ten miles out of Johannesburg on one of the main roads, to change something in ourselves, I suppose; you seem to rattle about so much within a marriage like ours. You long to hear nothing but a deep satisfying silence when you sound a marriage. The farm hasn't managed that for us, of course, but it has done other things, unexpected, illogical. Lerice, who I thought would retire there in Chekhovian sadness for a month or two, and then leave the place to the servants while she tried yet again to get a part she wanted and become the actress she would like to be, has sunk into the business of running the farm with all the serious intensity with which she once imbued the shadows in a playwright's mind. I should have given it up long ago if it had not been for her. Her hands, once small and plain and well-kept—she was not the sort of actress who wears red paint and diamond rings—are hard as a dog's pads.

I, of course, am there only in the evenings and at weekends. I am a partner in a travel agency which is flourishing—needs to be, as I tell Lerice, in order to carry the farm. Still, though I know we can't afford it, and though the sweetish smell of the fowls Lerice breeds sickens me, so that I avoid going past their runs, the farm is beautiful in a way I had almost forgotten—especially on a Sunday morning when I get up and go out into the paddock and see not the palm trees and fishpond and imitation-stone bird bath of the suburbs but white ducks on the dam, the lucerne field brilliant as window-dresser's grass, and the little, stocky, mean-eyed bull, lustful but bored, having his face tenderly licked by one of his ladies. Lerice comes out with her hair uncombed, in her hand a stick dripping with cattle dip. She will stand and look dreamily for a moment, the way she would pretend to look sometimes in those plays. 'They'll mate tomorrow,' she will say. 'This is their second day. Look how she loves him, my little Napoleon.' So that when people come to see us on Sunday afternoon, I am likely to hear myself saying as I pour out the drinks, 'When I drive back home from the city every day past those rows of suburban houses, I wonder how the devil we ever did stand it . . . Would you care to look around?' And there I am, taking some pretty girl and her young husband stumbling down to our riverbank, the girl catching her stockings on the mealie-stooks and stepping over cow turds humming with jewel-green flies while she says, '. . . the *tensions* of the damned city. And you're near enough to get into town to a show, too! I think it's wonderful. Why, you've got it both ways!'

And for a moment I accept the triumph as if I *had* managed it — the impossibility that I've been trying for all my life: just as if the truth was that you could get it 'both ways', instead of finding yourself with not even one way or the other but a third, one you had not provided for at all.

But even in our saner moments, when I find Lerice's earthy enthusiasms just as irritating as I once found her histrionical ones, and she finds what she calls my 'jealousy' of her capacity for enthusiasm as big a proof of my inadequacy for her as a mate as ever it was, we do believe that we have at least honestly escaped those tensions peculiar to the city about which our visitors speak. When Johannesburg people speak of 'tension', they don't mean hurrying people in crowded streets, the struggle for money, or the general competitive character of city life. They mean the guns under the white men's pillows and the burglar bars on the white men's windows. They mean those strange moments on city pavements when a black man won't stand aside for a white man.

Out in the country, even ten miles out, life is better than that. In the country, there is a lingering remnant of the pre-transitional stage; our relationship with the blacks is almost feudal. Wrong, I suppose, obsolete, but more comfortable all around. We have no burglar bars, no gun. Lerice's farm boys have their wives and their piccanins living with them on the land. They brew their sour beer without the fear of police raids. In fact, we've always rather prided ourselves that the poor devils have nothing much to fear, being with us; Lerice even keeps an eye on their children, with all the competence of a woman who has never had a child of her own, and she certainly doctors them all — children and adults — like babies whenever they happen to be sick.

It was because of this that we were not particularly startled one night last winter when the boy Albert came knocking at our window long after we had gone to bed. I wasn't in our bed but sleeping in the little dressing-room-cum-linen-room next door, because Lerice had annoyed me and I didn't want to find myself softening towards her simply because of the sweet smell of the talcum powder on her flesh after her bath. She came and woke me up. 'Albert says one of the boys is very sick,' she said. 'I think you'd better go down and see. He wouldn't get us up at this hour for nothing.'

'What time is it?

'What does it matter?' Lerice is maddeningly logical.

I got up awkwardly as she watched me — how is it I always feel a fool when I have deserted her bed? After all, I know from the way she never looks at me when she talks to me at breakfast next day that she is hurt and humiliated at my not wanting her — and I went out, clumsy with sleep.

'Which of the boys is it?' I asked Albert as we followed the dance of my torch.

'He's too sick. Very sick,' he said.

'But who? Franz?' I remembered Franz had had a bad cough for the past week.

Albert did not answer; he had given me the path, and was walking along beside me in the tall dead grass. When the light of the torch caught his face, I saw that he looked acutely embarrassed. 'What's this all about?' I said.

He lowered his head under the glance of the light. 'It's not me, baas. I don't know. Petrus he send me.'

Irritated, I hurried him along to the huts. And there, on Petrus's iron bedstead, with its brick stilts, was a young man, dead. On his forehead there was still a light, cold sweat; his body was warm. The boys stood around as they do in the kitchen when it is discovered that someone has broken a dish — uncooperative, silent. Somebody's wife hung about in the shadows, her hands wrung together under her apron.

I had not seen a dead man since the war. This was very different. I felt like the others — extraneous, useless. 'What was the matter?' I asked.

The woman patted at her chest and shook her head to indicate the painful impossibility of breathing.

He must have died of pneumonia.

I turned to Petrus. 'Who was this boy? What was he doing here?' The light of a candle on the floor showed that Petrus was weeping. He followed me out the door.

When we were outside, in the dark, I waited for him to speak. But he didn't. 'Now, come on, Petrus, you must tell me who this boy was. Was he a friend of yours?'

'He's my brother, baas. He came from Rhodesia to look for work.'

The story startled Lerice and me a little. The young boy had walked down from Rhodesia to look for work in Johannesburg, had caught a chill from sleeping out along the way and had lain ill in his brother Petrus's hut since his arrival three days before. Our boys had been frightened to ask us for help for him because we had never been intended ever to know of his presence. Rhodesian natives are barred from entering the Union unless they have a permit; the young man was an illegal immigrant. No doubt our boys had managed the whole thing successfully several times before; a number of relatives must have walked the seven or eight hundred miles from poverty to the paradise of zoot suits, police raids and black slum townships that is their *Egoli*, City of Gold — the African name for Johannesburg. It was merely a matter of getting such a man to lie low on our farm until a job could be found with someone who would be glad to take the risk of prosecution for employing an illegal immigrant in exchange for the services of someone as yet untainted by the city.

Well, this was one who would never get up again.

'You would think they would have felt they could tell *us*,' said Lerice next morning. 'Once the man was ill. You would have thought at least —' When she is getting intense over something, she has a way of standing in the middle of a room as people do when they are shortly to leave on a journey, looking searchingly about her at the most familiar objects as if she had never seen them before. I had noticed that in Petrus's presence in the kitchen, earlier, she had had the air of being almost offended with him, almost hurt.

In any case, I really haven't the time or inclination any more to go into everything in our life that I know Lerice, from those alarmed and pressing eyes of hers, would like us to go into. She is the kind of woman who doesn't mind if she looks plain, or odd; I don't suppose she would even care if she knew how strange she looks when her whole face is out of proportion with urgent uncertainty. I said. 'Now I'm the one who'll have to do all the dirty work, I suppose.'

She was still staring at me, trying me out with those eyes — wasting her time, if she only knew.

'I'll have to notify the health authorities,' I said calmly. 'They can't just cart him off and bury him. After all, we don't really know what he died of.'

She simply stood there, as if she had given up — simply ceased to see me at all.

I don't know when I've been so irritated. 'It might have been something contagious,' I said. 'God knows.' There was no answer.

I am not enamoured of holding conversations with myself. I went out to shout to one of the boys to open the garage and get the car ready for my morning drive to town.

As I had expected, it turned out to be quite a business. I had to notify the police as well as the health authorities, and answer a lot of tedious questions: How was it I was ignorant of the boy's presence? If I did not supervise my native quarters, how did I know that that sort of thing didn't go on all the time? And when I flared up and told them that so long as my natives did their work, I didn't think it my right or concern to poke my nose into their private lives, I got from the coarse, dull-witted police sergeant one of those looks that come not from any thinking process going on in the brain but from that faculty common to all who are possessed by the master-race theory — a look of insanely inane certainty. He grinned at me with a mixture of scorn and delight at my stupidity.

Then I had to explain to Petrus why the health authorities had to take away the body for a post-mortem — and, in fact, what a post-mortem was. When I telephoned the health department some days later to find out the result, I was told that the cause of death was, as we had thought, pneumonia, and that the body had been suitably disposed of. I went out to where Petrus was mixing a mash for the fowls and told him that it was all right, there would be no trouble; his brother had died from that pain in his chest. Petrus put down the paraffin tin and said, 'When can we go to fetch him, baas?'

'To fetch him?'

'Will the baas please ask them when we must come?'

I went back inside and called Lerice, all over the house. She came down the stairs from the spare bedrooms, and I said, 'Now what am I going to do? When I told Petrus, he just asked calmly when they could go and fetch the body. They think they're going to bury him themselves.'

'Well, go back and tell him,' said Lerice. 'You must tell him. Why didn't you tell him then?'

When I found Petrus again, he looked up politely. 'Look, Petrus,' I said. 'You can't go to fetch your brother. They've done it already — they've *buried* him, you understand?'

'Where?' he said slowly, dully, as if he thought that perhaps he was getting this wrong.

'You see, he was a stranger. They knew he wasn't from here, and they didn't know he had some of his people here so they thought they must bury him.' It was difficult to make a pauper's grave sound like a privilege.

'Please, baas, the baas must ask them.' But he did not mean that he wanted to know the burial place. He simply ignored the incomprehensible machinery I told him had set to work on his dead brother; he wanted the brother back.

'But, Petrus,' I said, 'how can I? Your brother is buried already. I can't ask them now.'

'Oh, baas!' he said. He stood with his bran-smeared hands uncurled at his sides, one corner of his mouth twitching.

'Good God, Petrus, they won't listen to me! They can't, anyway. I'm sorry, but I can't do it. You understand?'

He just kept on looking at me, out of his knowledge that white men have everything, can do anything; if they don't, it is because they won't.

And then, at dinner, Lerice started. 'You could at least phone,' she said.

'Christ, what d'you think I am? Am I supposed to bring the dead back to life?'

But I could not exaggerate my way out of this ridiculous responsibility that had been thrust on me. 'Phone them up,' she went on. 'And at least you'll be able to tell him you've done it and they've explained that it's impossible.'

She disappeared somewhere into the kitchen quarters after coffee. A little later she came back to tell me, 'The old father's coming down from Rhodesia to be at the funeral. He's got a permit and he's already on his way.'

Unfortunately, it was not impossible to get the body back. The authorities said that it was somewhat irregular, but that since the hygiene conditions had been fulfilled, they could not refuse permission for exhumation. I found out that, with the undertaker's charges, it would cost twenty pounds. Ah, I thought, that settles it. On five pounds a month, Petrus won't have twenty pounds — and just as well, since it couldn't do the dead any good. Certainly I should not offer it to him myself. Twenty pounds — or anything else within reason, for that matter — I would have spent without grudging it on doctors or medicines that might have helped the boy when he was alive. Once he was dead, I had no intention of encouraging Petrus to throw away, on a gesture, more than he spent to clothe his whole family in a year.

When I told him, in the kitchen that night, he said, 'Twenty pounds?'

I said, 'Yes, that's right, twenty pounds.'

For a moment, I had the feeling, from the look on his face, that he was calculating. But when he spoke again I thought I must have imagined it. 'We must pay twenty pounds!' he said in the faraway voice in which a person speaks of something so unattainable it does not bear thinking about.

'All right, Petrus,' I said, and went back to the living room.

The next morning before I went to town, Petrus asked to see me. 'Please, baas,' he said, awkwardly, handing me a bundle of notes. They're so seldom on the giving rather than the receiving side, poor devils, they don't really know how to hand money to a white man. There it was, the twenty pounds, in ones and halves, some creased and folded until they were soft as dirty rags, others smooth and fairly new — Franz's money, I suppose, and Albert's, and Dora the cook's, and Jacob the gardener's, and God knows who else's besides, from all the farms and small holdings round about. I took it in irritation more than in astonishment, really — irritation at the waste, the uselessness of this sacrifice by people so poor. Just like the poor everywhere, I thought, who stint themselves the decencies of life in order to ensure themselves the decencies of death. So incomprehensible to people like Lerice and me, who regard life as something to be spent extravagantly and, if we think about death at all, regard it as the final bankruptcy.

The farm hands don't work on Saturday afternoon anyway, so it was a good day for the funeral. Petrus and his father had borrowed our donkey-cart to fetch the coffin from the city, where, Petrus told Lerice on their return, everything was 'nice' — the coffin waiting for them, already sealed up to save them from what must have been a rather unpleasant sight after two weeks' interment. (It had taken all that time for the authorities and the undertaker to make the final arrangements for moving the body.) All morning, the coffin lay in Petrus's hut, awaiting the trip to the little old burial ground, just outside the eastern boundary of our farm, that was a relic of the days when this was a real farming district rather than a fashionable rural estate. It was pure chance that I happened to be down there near the fence when the procession came past; once again Lerice had forgotten her promise to me and had made the house uninhabitable on a Saturday afternoon. I had come home and been infuriated to find her in a pair of filthy old slacks and with her hair uncombed since the night before, having all the varnish scraped from the living-room floor, if you please. So I had taken my No. 8 iron and gone off to practise my aproach shots. In my annoyance, I had forgotten about the funeral, and was reminded only when I saw the procession coming up the path along the outside of the fence towards me; from where I was standing, you can see the graves quite clearly, and that day the sun glinted on bits of broken pottery, a lopsided homemade cross, and jam-jars brown with rainwater and dead flowers.

I felt a little awkward, and did not know whether to go on hitting my golf ball or stop at least until the whole gathering was decently past. The donkey-cart creaks and screeches with every revolution of the wheels, and it came along in a slow, halting fashion somehow peculiarly suited to the two donkeys who drew it, their little potbellies rubbed and rough, their heads sunk between the shafts, and their ears flattened back with an air submissive and downcast; peculiarly suited, too, to the group of men and women who came along slowly behind. The patient ass. Watching, I thought, you can see now why the creature became a Biblical symbol. Then the procession moved on, on foot. It was really a very awkward moment. I stood there rather foolishly at the fence, quite still, and slowly they filed past, not looking up, the four men bent beneath the shiny wooden box, and the straggling troop of mourners. All of them were servants or neighbours' servants whom I knew as casual easygoing gossipers about our lands or kitchen. I heard the old man's breathing.

I had just bent to pick up my club again when there was a sort of jar in the flowing solemnity of their processional mood; I felt it at once, like a wave of heat along the air, or one of those sudden currents of cold catching at your legs in a placid stream. The old man's voice was muttering something; the people had stopped, confused, and they bumped into one another, some pressing to go on, others hissing them to be still. I could see that they were embarrassed, but they could not ignore the voice; it was much the way that the mumblings of a prophet, though not clear at first, arrest the mind. The corner of the coffin the old man carried was sagging at an angle; he seemed to be trying to get out from under the weight of it. Now Petrus expostulated with him.

The little boy who had been left to watch the donkeys dropped the reins and ran to see. I don't know why — unless it was for the same reason people crowd around someone who has fainted in a cinema — but I parted the wires of the fence and went through, after him.

Petrus lifted his eyes to me — to anybody — with distress and horror. The old man from Rhodesia had let go of the coffin entirely, and the three others, unable to support it on their own, had laid it on the ground, in the pathway. Already there was a film of dust lightly wavering up its shiny sides. I did not understand what the old man was saying; I hesitated to interfere. But now the whole seething group turned on my silence. The old man himself came over to me, with his hands outspread and shaking, and spoke directly to me, saying something that I could tell from the tone, without understanding the words, was shocking and extraordinary.

'What is it, Petrus? What's wrong?' I appealed.

Petrus threw up his hands, bowed his head in a series of hysterical shakes, then thrust his face up at me suddenly. 'He says, "My son was not so heavy." '

Silence. I could hear the old man breathing; he kept his mouth a little open, as old people do.

'My son was young and thin,' he said at last, in English.

Again silence. Then babble broke out. The old man thundered against everybody; his teeth were yellowed and few, and he had one of those fine, grizzled, sweeping moustaches one doesn't often see nowadays, which must have been grown in emulation of early Empire-builders. It seemed to frame all his utterances with a special validity. He shocked the assembly; they thought he was mad, but they had to listen to him. With his own hands he began to prise the lid off the coffin and three of the men came forward to help him. Then he sat down on the ground; very old, very weak and unable to speak, he merely lifted a trembling hand towards what was there. He abdicated, he handed it over to them; he was no good any more.

They crowded round to look (and so did I), and now they forgot the nature of this surprise and the occasion of grief to which it belonged, and for a few minutes were carried up in the astonishment of the surprise itself. They gasped and flared noisily with excitement. I even noticed the little boy who had held the donkeys jumping up and down, almost weeping with rage because the backs of the grownups crowded him out of his view.

In the coffin was someone no one had seen before: a heavily built, rather light-skinned native with a neatly stitched scar on his forehead — perhaps from a blow in a brawl that had also dealt him some other, slower-working injury that had killed him.

I wrangled with the authorities for a week over that body. I had the feeling that they were shocked, in a laconic fashion, by their own mistake, but that in the confusion of their anonymous dead they were helpless to put it right. They said to me, 'We are trying to find out,' and 'We are still making inquiries.' It was as if at any moment they might conduct me into their mortuary and say, 'There! Lift up the sheets; look for him—your poultry boy's brother. There are so many black faces—surely one will do?'

And every evening when I got home, Petrus was waiting in the kitchen. 'Well, they're trying. They're still looking. The baas is seeing to it for you, Petrus,' I would tell him. 'God, half the time I should be in the office I'm driving around the back end of the town chasing after this affair,' I added aside, to Lerice, one night.

She and Petrus both kept their eyes turned on me as I spoke, and, oddly, for those moments they looked exactly alike, though it sounds impossible: my wife, with her high, white forehead and her attenuated Englishwoman's body, and the poultry boy, with his horny bare feet below khaki trousers tied at the knee with string and the peculiar rankness of his nervous sweat coming from his skin.

'What makes you so indignant, so determined about this now?' said Lerice suddenly.

I stared at her. 'It's a matter of principle. Why should they get away with a swindle? It's time these officials had a jolt from someone who'll bother to take the trouble.'

She said, 'Oh.' And as Petrus slowly opened the kitchen door to leave, sensing that the talk had gone beyond him, she turned away, too.

I continued to pass on assurances to Petrus every evening, but although what I said was the same and the voice in which I said it was the same, every evening it sounded weaker. At last, it became clear that we would never get Petrus's brother back, because nobody really knew where he was. Somewhere in a graveyard as uniform as a housing scheme, somewhere under a number that didn't belong to him, or in the medical school, perhaps, laboriously reduced to layers of muscle and strings of nerve? Goodness knows. He had no identity in this world anyway.

It was only then, and in a voice of shame, that Petrus asked me to try and get the money back.

'From the way he asks, you'd think he was robbing his dead brother,' I said to Lerice later. But as I've said, Lerice had got so intense about this business that she couldn't even appreciate a little ironic smile.

I tried to get the money; Lerice tried. We both telephoned and wrote and argued, but nothing came of it. It appeared that the main expense had been the undertaker, and after all he had done his job. So the whole thing was a complete waste, even more of a waste for the poor devils than I had thought it would be.

The old man from Rhodesia was about Lerice's father's size, so she gave him one of her father's old suits, and he went back home rather better off, for the winter, than he had come.

[1956]

Study and Writing Questions

1. In what sense(s) is "some pretty girl" in the beginning of the STORY right in exclaiming that the NARRATOR has "got it both ways"? In what sense(s) is she wrong?
2. In the paragraph (beginning with "Unfortunately") in which the narrator thinks about the propriety of paying £20 to recover the body, how does he reveal his own views about money, blacks, death, and the authorities? How do you judge his views?
3. In what way(s) might this story be said to be about childlessness? To what extent is it about apartheid?
4. What precisely is the relationship of Lerice to the narrator? Why is she in the story? What is the significance of her looking, at the end, like Petrus?
5. What kind of person is the narrator? What does he reveal about himself in the last line? What MOTIVATES him to tell this story?

See also Questions for Contrast and Comparison: 15, 21, 38, 43, 49, 55, 67, 85, 86, 101, 122, 162, and 189.

■ **JACOB LUDWIG CARL** (1785–1863) and **WILHELM CARL** (1786–1859) **GRIMM**, *eldest of five children of a municipal lawyer in Hanau, central Germany, are among the world's most influential scholars. At the University of Marburg (1802–1806), Clemens Brentano inspired their devotion to folk poetry and F.K. von Savigny taught them the historical study of law. After collecting poetry for Brentano, they collected, mostly from oral sources, their* Children's and Household Tales *(1812–1815). Now generally called Grimm's Fairy Tales, this is the single most famous source for works that, in some form, go back to prehistory. Long before modern Germany's emergence (1871) from separate principalities, as professors and scholars in Kassel, Göttingen, and Berlin, the Grimms pursued their devotion to language, nationalism, political democracy, and, unfortunately, anti-Semitism. Jacob formulated Grimm's Law, the first scientific codification of the regularities of sound change in language evolution. They collaborated on collections of German sayings (1816–1818), heroic tales (1806–1826), and mythology (1835). They wrote a crucial grammar of the Germanic languages and initiated the monumental* Deutsches Wörterbuch, *model for all historical dictionaries (such as the definitive* Oxford English Dictionary*). The brothers lived together their whole lives, although the more robust Jacob made many scientific trips while Wilhelm married and had three children.*

Rapunzel

There once lived a man and his wife, who had long wished for a child, but in vain. Now there was at the back of their house a little window which overlooked a beautiful garden full of the finest vegetables and flowers; but there was a high wall all round it, and no one ventured into it, for it belonged to a witch of great might, and of whom all the world was afraid. One day that the wife was standing at the window, and looking into the garden, she saw a bed filled with the finest rampion; and it looked so fresh and green that she began to wish for some; and at length she longed for it greatly. This went on for days, and as she knew she could not get the rampion, she pined away, and grew pale and miserable. Then the man was uneasy, and asked,

"What is the matter, dear wife?"

"Oh," answered she, "I shall die unless I can have some of that rampion to eat that grows in the garden at the back of our house." The man, who loved her very much, thought to himself,

"Rather than lose my wife I will get some rampion, cost what it will."

So in the twilight he climbed over the wall into the witch's garden, plucked hastily a handful of rampion and brought it to his wife. She made a salad of it at once, and ate of it to her heart's content. But she liked it so much and it tasted so good, that the next day she longed for it thrice as much as she had done before; if she was to have any rest the man must climb over the wall once more. So he went in the twilight again; and as he was climbing back, he saw, all at once, the witch standing before him, and was terribly frightened, as she cried, with angry eyes,

"How dare you climb over into my garden like a thief, and steal my rampion! it shall be the worse for you!"

"Oh," answered he, "be merciful rather than just, I have only done it through necessity; for my wife saw your rampion out of the window, and became

O RAPUNZEL, RAPUNZEL!
LET DOWN THINE HAIR."

possessed with so great a longing that she would have died if she could not have had some to eat." Then the witch said,

"If it is all as you say you may have as much rampion as you like, on one condition—the child that will come into the world must be given to me. It shall go well with the child, and I will care for it like a mother."

In his distress of mind the man promised everything; and when the time came when the child was born the witch appeared, and, giving the child the name of Rapunzel (which is the same as rampion), she took it away with her.

Rapunzel was the most beautiful child in the world. When she was twelve years old the witch shut her up in a tower in the midst of a wood, and it had neither steps nor door, only a small window above. When the witch wished to be let in, she would stand below and would cry,

"Rapunzel, Rapunzel! let down your hair!"

Rapunzel had beautiful long hair that shone like gold. When she heard the voice of the witch she would undo the fastening of the upper window, unbind the plaits of her hair, and let it down twenty ells below, and the witch would climb up by it.

After they had lived thus a few years it happened that as the King's son was riding through the wood, he came to the tower; and as he drew near he heard a voice singing so sweetly that he stood still and listened. It was Rapunzel in her loneliness trying to pass away the time with sweet songs. The King's son wished to go in to her, and sought to find a door in the tower, but there was none. So he rode home, but the song had entered into his heart, and every day he went into the wood and listened to it. Once, as he was standing there under a tree, he saw the witch come up, and listened while she called out,

"O Rapunzel, Rapunzel! let down your hair."

Then he saw how Rapunzel let down her long tresses, and how the witch climbed up by it and went in to her, and he said to himself,

"Since that is the ladder I will climb it, and seek my fortune." And the next day, as soon as it began to grow dusk, he went to the tower and cried,

"O Rapunzel, Rapunzel! let down your hair."

And she let down her hair, and the King's son climbed up by it.

Rapunzel was greatly terrified when she saw that a man had come in to her, for she had never seen one before; but the King's son began speaking so kindly to her, and told how her singing had entered into his heart, so that he could have no peace until he had seen her herself. Then Rapunzel forgot her terror, and when he asked her to take him for her husband, and she saw that he was young and beautiful, she thought to herself.

"I certainly like him much better than old mother Gothel," and she put her hand into his hand, saying,

"I would willingly go with thee, but I do not know how I shall get out. When thou comest, bring each time a silken rope, and I will make a ladder, and when it is quite ready I will get down by it out of the tower, and thou shalt take me away on thy horse." They agreed that he should come to her every evening, as the old woman came in the day-time. So the witch knew nothing of all this until once Rapunzel said to her unwittingly,

"Mother Gothel, how is it that you climb up here so slowly, and the King's son is with me in a moment?"

"O wicked child," cried the witch, "what is this I hear! I thought I had hidden thee from all the world, and thou hast betrayed me!"

In her anger she seized Rapunzel by her beautiful hair, struck her several times with her left hand, and then grasping a pair of shears in her right — snip, snap — the beautiful locks lay on the ground. And she was so hard-hearted that she took Rapunzel and put her in a waste and desert place, where she lived in great woe and misery.

The same day on which she took Rapunzel away she went back to the tower in the evening and made fast the severed locks of hair to the window-hasp, and the King's son came and cried,

"Rapunzel, Rapunzel! let down your hair."

Then she let the hair down, and the King's son climbed up, but instead of his dearest Rapunzel he found the witch looking at him with wicked glittering eyes.

"Aha!" cried she, mocking him, "you came for your darling, but the sweet bird sits no longer in the nest, and sings no more; the cat has got her, and will scratch out your eyes as well! Rapunzel is lost to you; you will see her no more."

The King's son was beside himself with grief, and in his agony he sprang from the tower: he escaped with life, but the thorns on which he fell put out his eyes. Then he wandered blind through the wood, eating nothing but roots and berries, and doing nothing but lament and weep for the loss of his dearest wife.

So he wandered several years in misery until at last he came to the desert place where Rapunzel lived with her twin-children that she had borne, a boy and a girl. At first he heard a voice that he thought he knew, and when he reached the place from which it seemed to come Rapunzel knew him, and fell on his neck and wept. And when her tears touched his eyes they became clear again, and he could see with them as well as ever.

Then he took her to his kingdom, where he was received with great joy, and there they lived long and happily.

[1812]

Study and Writing Questions

1. What is the importance of eye IMAGERY in this NARRATIVE? Where are eyes, sight, and blindness used, and to what ends?
2. What ideal of marriage does this narrative project? What is the social and THEMATIC significance of marriage in this narrative?
3. It has been suggested that this STORY originally arose as a vegetation myth about the fertility of the earth and humanity's relationship with Nature. What features of the story support that suggestion?
4. What is the importance of sexuality to the STYLE, PLOT, and theme of this narrative? To what extent might this narrative be illuminated by FREUDIAN or JUNGIAN CRITICISM?
5. How extensive is Christian imagery in this text? To what extent does such imagery fit thematically with the overall narrative and to what extent does it seem an imposition on the story?

See also Questions for Contrast and Comparison: 4, 20, 24, 26, 57, 98, 113, 124, 125, 155, 157, 190, and 194.

The Three Spinsters

There was once a girl who was lazy and would not spin, and her mother could not persuade her to it, do what she would. At last the mother became angry and out of patience, and gave her a good beating, so that she cried out loudly. At that moment the Queen was going by; as she heard the crying, she stopped; and, going into the house, she asked the mother why she was beating her daughter, so that every one outside in the street could hear her cries.

The woman was ashamed to tell of her daughter's laziness, so she said,

"I cannot stop her from spinning; she is for ever at it, and I am poor and cannot furnish her with flax enough."

Then the Queen answered,

"I like nothing better than the sound of the spinningwheel, and always feel happy when I hear its humming; let me take your daughter with me to the castle—I have plenty of flax, she shall spin there to her heart's content."

The mother was only too glad of the offer, and the Queen took the girl with her. When they reached the castle the Queen showed her three rooms which were filled with the finest flax as full as they could hold.

"Now you can spin me this flax," said she, "and when you can show it me all done you shall have my eldest son for bridegroom; you may be poor, but I make nothing of that—your industry is dowry enough."

The girl was inwardly terrified, for she could not have spun the flax, even if she were to live to be a hundred years old, and were to sit spinning every day of her life from morning to evening. And when she found herself alone she began to weep, and sat so for three days without putting her hand to it. On the third day the Queen came, and when she saw that nothing had been done of the spinning she was much surprised; but the girl excused herself by saying that she had not been able to begin because of the distress she was in at leaving her home and her mother. The excuse contented the Queen, who said, however, as she went away,

"To-morrow you must begin to work."

When the girl found herself alone again she could not tell how to help herself or what to do, and in her perplexity she went and gazed out of the window. There she saw three woman passing by, and the first of them had a broad flat foot, the second had a big under-lip that hung down over her chin, and the third had a remarkably broad thumb. They all of them stopped in front of the window, and called out to know what it was that the girl wanted. She told them all her need, and they promised her their help, and said,

"Then will you invite us to your wedding, and not be ashamed of us, and call us your cousins, and let us sit at your table; if you will promise this, we will finish off your flax-spinning in a very short time."

"With all my heart," answered the girl; "only come in now, and begin at once."

Then these same women came in, and she cleared a space in the first room for them to sit and carry on their spinning. The first one drew out the thread and moved the treddle that turned the wheel, the second moistened the thread, the third twisted it, and rapped with her finger on the table, and as often as she rapped a heap of yarn fell to the ground, and it was most beautifully spun. But the girl hid the three spinsters out of the Queen's sight, and only showed her, as often as she came, the heaps of well-spun yarn; and there was no end to the praises she received. When the first room was empty they went on to the second, and then to the third, so that at last all was finished. Then the three women took their leave, saying to the girl,

"Do not forget what you have promised, and it will be all the better for you."

So when the girl took the Queen and showed her the empty rooms, and the great heaps of yarn, the wedding was at once arranged, and the bridegroom rejoiced that he should have so cleaver and diligent a wife, and praised her exceedingly.

"I have three cousins," said the girl, "and as they have shown me a great deal of kindness, I would not wish to forget them in my good fortune; may I be allowed to invite them to the wedding, and to ask them to sit at the table with us?"

The Queen and the bridegroom said at once,

"There is no reason against it."

So when the feast began in came the three spinsters in strange guise, and the bride said,

"Dear cousins, you are welcome."

"Oh," said the bridegroom, "how come you to have such dreadfully ugly relations?"

And then he went up to the first spinster and said,

"How is it that you have such a broad flat foot?"

"With treading," answered she, "with treading."

Then he went up to the second and said,

"How is it that you have such a great hanging lip?"

"With licking," answered she, "with licking."

Then he asked the third,

"How is it that you have such a broad thumb?"

"With twisting thread," answered she, "with twisting thread."

Then the bridegroom said that from that time forward his beautiful bride should never touch a spinning-wheel.

And so she escaped that tiresome flax-spinning.

[1812]

Study and Writing Questions

1. What relations does the bride have with the other women in the NARRATIVE? In what ways might this TALE be viewed as concerning women's roles?
2. What are the signs of social class in this narrative? How does social class enter into the dynamic of the PLOT?
3. Many FAIRY TALES require the PROTAGONIST to pass a test before achieving success. How does the particular test in this narrative help shape the meaning of the narrative as a whole? How is the method by which the test is met important?
4. What is the MORAL of this tale? Is its moral one you expect from a fairy tale? If so, why? If not, how does that affect your understanding of fairy tales?
5. Consider the title CHARACTERS in his narrative. What are the meanings of the word "spinster"? To what extent do these spinsters ALLUDE to the "three Fates" of classical mythology? Why is the STORY named after them rather than after the bride?

See also Questions for Contrast and Comparison: 26, 54, 70, 131, 137, 146, 155, 157, 176, 185, 190, and 201.

Little Red-cap

There was once a sweet little maid, much beloved by everybody, but most of all by her grandmother, who never knew how to make enough of her. Once she sent her a little cap of red velvet, and as it was very becoming to her, and she never wore anything else, people called her Little Red-cap. One day her mother said to her,

"Come, Little Red-cap, here are some cakes and a flask of wine for you to take to grandmother; she is weak and ill, and they will do her good. Make haste and start before it grows hot, and walk properly and nicely, and don't run, or you might fall and break the flask of wine, and there would be none left for grandmother. And when you go into her room, don't forget to say, Good morning, instead of staring about you."

"I will be sure to take care," said Little Red-cap to her mother, and gave her hand upon it. Now the grandmother lived away in the wood, half-an-hour's walk from the village; and when Little Red-cap had reached the wood, she met the wolf; but as she did not know what a bad sort of animal he was, she did not feel frightened.

"Good day, Little Red-cap," said he.

"Thank you kindly, Wolf," answered she.

"Where are you going so early, Little Red-cap?"

"To my grandmother's."

"What are you carrying under your apron?"

"Cakes and wine; we baked yesterday; and my grandmother is very weak and ill, so they will do her good, and strengthen her."

"Where does your grandmother live, Little Red-cap?"

"A quarter of an hour's walk from here; her house stands beneath the three oak trees, and you may know it by the hazel bushes," said Little Red-cap. The wolf thought to himself,

"That tender young thing would be a delicious morsel, and would taste better than the old one; I must manage somehow to get both of them."

Then he walked by Little Red-cap a little while, and said,

"Little Red-cap, just look at the pretty flowers that are growing all round you, and I don't think you are listening to the song of the birds; you are posting along just as if you were going to school, and it is so delightful out here in the wood."

Little Red-cap glanced round her, and when she saw the sunbeams darting here and there through the trees, and lovely flowers everywhere, she thought to herself,

"If I were to take a fresh nosegay to my grandmother she would be very pleased, and it is so early in the day that I shall reach her in plenty of time;" and so she ran about in the wood, looking for flowers. And as she picked one she saw a still prettier one a little farther off, and so she went farther and farther into the wood. But the wolf went straight to the grandmother's house and knocked at the door.

"Who is there?" cried the grandmother.

"Little Red-cap," he answered, "and I have brought you some cake and wine. Please open the door."

"Lift the latch," cried the grandmother; "I am too feeble to get up."

So the wolf lifted the latch, and the door flew open, and he fell on the grandmother and ate her up without saying one word. Then he drew on her clothes, put on her cap, lay down in her bed, and drew the curtains.

Little Red-cap was all this time running about among the flowers, and when she had gathered as many as she could hold, she remembered her grandmother, and set off to go to her. She was surprised to find the door standing open, and when she came inside she felt very strange, and thought to herself,

"Oh dear, how uncomfortable I feel, and I was so glad this morning to go to my grandmother!"

And when she said, "Good morning," there was no answer. Then she went up to the bed and drew back the curtains; there lay the grandmother with her cap pulled over her eyes, so that she looked very odd.

"O grandmother, what large ears you have got!"

"The better to hear with."

"O grandmother, what great eyes you have got!"

"The better to see with."

"O grandmother, what large hands you have got!"

"The better to take hold of you with."

"But, grandmother, what a terrible large mouth you have got!"

"The better to devour you!" And no sooner had the wolf said it than he made one bound from the bed, and swallowed up poor Little Red-cap.

Then the wolf, having satisfied his hunger, lay down again in the bed, went to sleep, and began to snore loudly. The huntsman heard him as he was passing by the house, and thought,

"How the old woman snores — I had better see if there is anything the matter with her."

Then he went into the room, and walked up to the bed, and saw the wolf lying there.

"At last I find you, you old sinner!" said he; "I have been looking for you a long time." And he made up his mind that the wolf had swallowed the grandmother whole, and that she might yet be saved. So he did not fire, but took a pair of shears and began to slit up the wolf's body. When he made a few snips Little Red-cap appeared, and after a few more snips she jumped out and cried, "Oh dear, how frightened I have been! it is so dark inside the wolf." And then out came the old grandmother, still living and breathing. But Little Red-cap went and quickly fetched some large stones, with which she filled the wolf's body, so that when he waked up, and was going to rush away, the stones were so heavy that he sank down and fell dead.

They were all three very pleased. The huntsman took off the wolf's skin, and carried it home. The grandmother ate the cakes, and drank the wine, and held up her head again, and Little Red-cap said to herself that she would never more stray about in the wood alone, but would mind what her mother told her.

[1812]

Study and Writing Questions

1. To what extent is this NARRATIVE about some aspect(s) of sexuality? Note how the title CHARACTER carries her gifts; note that flowers are the sexual organs of plants; and so on. What are those aspects? To what might the title ALLUDE?

2. What Christian IMAGERY can you find in this narrative? What are the THEMA-
TIC and RHETORICAL effects of this imagery?
3. What are the stages in the life of a female as represented in this STORY? What
are the relations among females of different stages?
4. How are male/female relations portrayed in this narrative? Note that there are
two male figures here.
5. What is the explicit MORAL of this TALE? What is the implicit moral? How are
they related?

See also Questions for Contrast and Comparison: 3, 6, 26, 53, 77, 83, 99, 106,
124, 125, 132, 155, 169, 172, 190, 191, 194, and 238.

■ **(SAMUEL) DASHIELL HAMMETT** (1894–1961) *was born on his family's farm in St. Mary's County, Maryland. Educated almost entirely at home, he began working full-time at fourteen, most significantly as a far-travelling Pinkerton Detective (1914–1922). After being hospitalized for tuberculosis in San Francisco, where he lived from 1921–1929, he married his nurse. They had two daughters but soon separated (1927) and finally divorced (1937). In 1922, Hammett retreated to a cheap room to write. Within a year, publishing in Black Mask, the leading "pulp" detective magazine, he had created the "hard-boiled" detective story that used terse sentences to narrate, as his rival Raymond Chandler said, the lives of "people that commit [murder] for reasons, not just to provide a corpse." By 1934, Hammett had published over seventy stories and serialized novels, including Red Harvest (1929), with the nameless Continental Op as detective; The Maltese Falcon (1930), with Sam Spade; The Glass Key (1931); and The Thin Man (1934). His screenplays include The Watch on the Rhine (1943), but he was eventually blacklisted in Hollywood, and briefly jailed, for his radical political activities. In November 1930 he met Lillian Hellman, then a Hollywood writer, later an important playwright. Their stormy affair included drinking binges, separations, and other lovers, but lasted through her nursing Hammett in his final five-year fight with lung cancer.*

The Gutting of Couffignal

Wedge-shaped Couffignal is not a large island, and not far from the mainland, to which it is linked by a wooden bridge. Its western shore is a high, straight cliff that jumps abruptly up out of San Pablo Bay. From the top of this cliff the island slopes eastward, down to a smooth pebble beach that runs into the water again, where there are piers and a clubhouse and moored pleasure boats.

Couffignal's main street, paralleling the beach, has the usual bank, hotel, moving-picture theater, and stores. But it differs from most main streets of its size in that it is more carefully arranged and preserved. There are trees and hedges and strips of lawn on it, and no glaring signs. The buildings seem to belong beside one another, as if they had been designed by the same architect, and in the stores you will find goods of a quality to match the best city stores.

The intersecting streets—running between rows of neat cottages near the foot of the slope—become winding hedged roads as they climb toward the cliff. The higher these roads get, the farther apart and larger are the houses they lead to. The occupants of these higher houses are the owners and rulers of the island. Most of them are well-fed old gentlemen who, the profits they took from the world with both hands in their younger days now stowed away at safe percentages, have bought into the island colony so they may spend what is left of their lives nursing their livers and improving their golf among their kind. They admit to the island only as many storekeepers, working people, and similar riffraff as are needed to keep them comfortably served.

That is Couffignal.

It was some time after midnight. I was sitting in a second-story room in Couffignal's largest house, surrounded by wedding presents whose value would add up to something between fifty and a hundred thousand dollars.

Of all the work that comes to a private detective (except divorce work, which the Continental Detective Agency doesn't handle) I like weddings as little as any. Usually I manage to avoid them, but this time I hadn't been able to. Dick Foley, who had been slated for the job, had been handed a black eye by an unfriendly pickpocket the day before. That let Dick out and me in. I had come up to Couffignal—a two-hour ride from San Francisco by ferry and auto stage—that morning, and would return the next.

This had been neither better nor worse than the usual wedding detail. The ceremony had been performed in a little stone church down the hill. Then the house had begun to fill with reception guests. They had kept it filled to overflowing until some time after the bride and groom had sneaked off to their eastern train.

The world had been well represented. There had been an admiral and an earl or two from England; an ex-president of a South American country; a Danish baron; a tall young Russian princess surrounded by lesser titles, including a fat, bald, jovial and black-bearded Russian general, who had talked to me for a solid hour about prize fights, in which he had a lot of interest, but not so much knowledge as was possible; an ambassador from one of the Central European countries; a justice of the Supreme Court; and a mob of people whose prominence and near-prominence didn't carry labels.

In theory, a detective guarding wedding presents is supposed to make himself indistinguishable from the other guests. In practice, it never works out that way. He has to spend most of his time within sight of the booty, so he's easily spotted. Besides that, eight or ten people I recognized among the guests were clients or former clients of the Agency, and so knew me. However, being known doesn't make so much difference as you might think, and everything had gone off smoothly.

A couple of the groom's friends, warmed by wine and the necessity of maintaining their reputations as cutups, had tried to smuggle some of the gifts out of the room where they were displayed and hide them in the piano. But I had been expecting that familiar trick, and blocked it before it had gone far enough to embarrass anybody.

Shortly after dark a wind smelling of rain began to pile storm clouds up over the bay. Those guests who lived at a distance, especially those who had water to cross, hurried off for their homes. Those who lived on the island stayed until the first raindrops began to patter down. Then they left.

The Hendrixson house quieted down. Musicians and extra servants left. The weary house servants began to disappear in the direction of their bedrooms. I found some sandwiches, a couple of books and a comfortable armchair, and took them up to the room where the presents were now hidden under gray-white sheeting.

Keith Hendrixson, the bride's grandfather—she was an orphan—put his head in at the door. "Have you everything you need for your comfort?" he asked.

"Yes, thanks."

He said good night and went off to bed—a tall old man, slim as a boy.

The wind and the rain were hard at it when I went downstairs to give the lower windows and doors the up-and-down. Everything on the first floor was tight and secure, everything in the cellar. I went upstairs again.

Pulling my chair over by a floor lamp, I put sandwiches, books, ashtray, gun and flashlight on a small table beside it. Then I switched off the other lights, set fire to a Fatima, sat down, wriggled my spine comfortably into the chair's padding, picked up one of the books, and prepared to make a night of it.

The book was called *The Lord of the Sea*, and had to do with a strong, tough and violent fellow named Hogarth, whose modest plan was to hold the world in one hand. There were plots and counterplots, kidnapings, murders, prisonbreakings, forgeries and burglaries, diamonds large as hats and floating forts larger than Couffignal. It sounds dizzy here, but in the book it was as real as a dime.

Hogarth was still going strong when the lights went out.

In the dark, I got rid of the glowing end of my cigarette by grinding it in one of the sandwiches. Putting the book down, I picked up gun and flashlight, and moved away from the chair.

Listening for noises was no good. The storm was making hundreds of them. What I needed to know was why the lights had gone off. All the other lights in the house had been turned off some time ago. So the darkness of the hall told me nothing.

I waited. My job was to watch the presents. Nobody had touched them yet. There was nothing to get excited about.

Minutes went by, perhaps ten of them.

The floor swayed under my feet. The windows rattled with a violence beyond the strength of the storm. The dull boom of a heavy explosion blotted out the sounds of wind and falling water. The blast was not close at hand, but not far enough away to be off the island.

Crossing to the window, peering through the wet glass, I could see nothing. I should have seen a few misty lights far down the hill. Not being able to see them settled one point. The lights had gone out all over Couffignal, not only in the Hendrixson house.

That was better. The storm could have put the lighting system out of whack, could have been responsible for the explosion — maybe.

Staring through the black window, I had an impression of great excitement down the hill, of movement in the night. But all was too far away for me to have seen or heard even had there been lights, and all too vague to say what was moving. The impression was strong but worthless. It didn't lead anywhere. I told myself I was getting feebleminded, and turned away from the window.

Another blast spun me back to it. This explosion sounded nearer than the first, maybe because it was stronger. Peering through the glass again, I still saw nothing. And still had the impression of things that were big moving down there.

Bare feet pattered in the hall. A voice was anxiously calling my name. Turning from the window again, I pocketed my gun and snapped on the flashlight. Keith Hendrixson, in pajamas and bathrobe, looking thinner and older than anybody could be, came into the room.

"Is it —"

"I don't think it's an earthquake," I said, since that is the first calamity your Californian thinks of. "The lights went off a little while ago. There have been a couple of explosions down the hill since the —"

I stopped. Three shots, close together, had sounded. Rifle-shots, but of the sort that only the heaviest of rifles could make. Then, sharp and small in the storm, came the report of a far-away pistol.

"What is it?" Hendrixson demanded.

"Shooting."

More feet were pattering in the halls, some bare, some shod. Excited voices whispered questions and exclamations. The butler, a solemn, solid block of a man, partly dressed and carrying a lighted five-pronged candlestick, came in.

"Very good, Brophy," Hendrixson said as the butler put the candlestick on the table beside my sandwiches. "Will you try to learn what is the matter?"

"I have tried, sir. The telephone seems to be out of order, sir. Shall I send Oliver down to the village?"

"No-o. I don't suppose it's that serious. Do you think it is anything serious?" he asked me.

I said I didn't think so, but I was paying more attention to the outside than to him. I had heard a thin screaming that could have come from a distant woman, and a volley of small-arms shots. The rocket of the storm muffled these shots, but when the heavier firing we had heard before broke out again, it was clear enough.

To have opened the window would have been to let in gallons of water without helping us to hear much clearer. I stood with an ear tilted to the pane, trying to arrive at some idea of what was happening outside.

Another sound took my attention from the window—the ringing of the bell-pull at the front door. It rang loudly and persistently.

Hendrixson looked at me. I nodded. "See who it is, Brophy," he said.

The butler went solemnly away, and came back even more solemnly. "Princess Zhukovski," he announced.

She came running into the room—the tall Russian girl I had seen at the reception. Her eyes were wide and dark with excitement. Her face was very white and wet. Water ran in streams down her blue waterproof cape, the hood of which covered her dark hair.

"Oh, Mr. Hendrixson!" She had caught one of his hands in both of hers. Her voice, with nothing foreign in its accents, was the voice of one who is excited over a delightful surprise. "The bank is being robbed, and the—what do you call him?—marshal of police has been killed!"

"What's that?" the old man exclaimed, jumping awkwardly because water from her cape had dripped down on one of his bare feet. "Weegan killed? And the bank robbed?"

"Yes! Isn't it terrible?" She said it as if she were saying wonderful. "When the first explosion woke us, the general sent Ignati down to find out what was the matter, and he got down there just in time to see the bank blown up. Listen!"

We listened, and heard a wild outbreak of mixed gunfire.

"That will be the general arriving!" she said. "He'll enjoy himself most wonderfully. As soon as Ignati returned with the news, the general armed every male in the household from Aleksandr Sergyeevich to Ivan the cook, and led them out happier than he's been since he took his division to East Prussia in 1914."

"And the duchess?" Hendrixson asked.

"He left her at home with me, of course, and I furtively crept out and away from her while she was trying for the first time in her life to put water in a samovar. This is not the night for one to stay at home!"

"H-m-m," Hendrixson said, his mind obviously not on her words. "And the bank!"

He looked at me. I said nothing. The racket of another volley came to us.

"Could you do anything down there?" he asked.

"Maybe, but—" I nodded at the presents under their covers.

"Oh, those!" the old man said. "I'm as much interested in the bank as in them; and besides, we will be here."

"All right!" I was willing enough to carry my curiosity down the hill. "I'll go down. You'd better have the butler stay in here, and plant the chauffeur inside the front door. Better give them guns if you have any. Is there a raincoat I can borrow? I brought only a light overcoat with me."

Brophy found a yellow slicker that fit me. I put it on, stowed gun and flashlight conveniently under it, and found my hat while Brophy was getting and loading an automatic pistol for himself and a rifle for Oliver, the mulatto chauffeur.

Hendrixson and the princess followed me downstairs. At the door I found she wasn't exactly following me—she was going with me.

"But Sonya!" the old man protested.

"I'm not going to be foolish, though I'd like to," she promised him. "But I'm going back to my Irinia Androvna, who will perhaps have the samovar watered by now."

"That's a sensible girl!" Hendrixson said, and let us out into the rain and the wind.

It wasn't weather to talk in. In silence we turned downhill between two rows of hedging, with the storm driving at our backs. At the first break in the hedge I stopped, nodding toward the black blot a house made. "That is your—"

Her laugh cut me short. She caught my arm and began to urge me down the road again. "I only told Mr. Hendrixson that so he would not worry," she explained. "You do not think I am not going down to see the sights."

She was tall. I am short and thick. I had to look up to see her face—to see as much of it as the rain-gray night would let me see. "You'll be soaked to the hide, running around in this rain," I objected.

"What of that? I am dressed for it." She raised a foot to show me a heavy waterproof boot and a woolen-stockinged leg.

"There's no telling what we'll run into down there, and I've got work to do," I insisted. "I can't be looking out for you."

"I can look out for myself." She pushed her cape aside to show me a square automatic pistol in one hand.

"You'll be in my way."

"I will not," she retorted. "You'll probably find I can help you. I'm as strong as you, and quicker, and I can shoot."

The reports of scattered shooting had punctuated our argument, but now the sound of heavier firing silenced the dozen objections to her company that I could still think of. After all, I could slip away from her in the dark if she became too much of a nuisance.

"Have it your own way," I growled, "but don't expect anything from me."

"You're so kind," she murmured as we got under way again, hurrying now, with the wind at our backs speeding us along.

Occasionally dark figures moved on the road ahead of us, but too far away to be recognizable. Presently a man passed us, running uphill—a tall man whose nightshirt hung out of his trousers, down below his coat, identifying him as a resident.

"They've finished the bank and are at Medcraft's!" he yelled as he went by.

"Medcraft is the jeweler," the girl informed me.

The sloping under our feet grew less sharp. The houses—dark but with faces vaguely visible here and there at windows—came closer together. Below, the flash of a gun could be seen now and then—orange streaks in the rain.

Our road put us into the lower end of the main street just as a staccato rat-ta-tat broke out.

I pushed the girl into the nearest doorway, and jumped in after her.

Bullets ripped through walls with the sound of hail tapping on leaves.

That was the thing I had taken for an exceptionally heavy rifle—a machine gun.

The girl had fallen back in a corner, all tangled up with something. I helped her up. The something was a boy of seventeen or so, with one leg and a crutch.

"It's the boy who delivers papers," Princess Zhukovski said, "and you've hurt him with your clumsiness."

The boy shook his head, grinning as he got up. "No'm, I ain't hurt none, but you kind of scared me, jumping on me like that."

She had to stop and explain that she hadn't jumped on him, that she had been pushed into him by me, and that she was sorry and so was I.

"What's happening?" I asked the newsboy when I could get a word in.

"Everything," he boasted, as if some of the credit were his. "There must be a hundred of them, and they've blowed the bank wide open, and now some of 'em is in Medcraft's, and I guess they'll blow that up, too. And they killed Tom Weegan. They got a machine gun on a car in the middle of the street. That's it shooting now."

"Where's everybody—all the merry villagers?"

"Most of 'em are up behind the Hall. They can't do nothing, though, because the machine gun won't let 'em get near enough to see what they're shooting at, and that smart Bill Vincent told me to clear out, 'cause I've only got one leg, as if I couldn't shoot as good as the next one, if I only had something to shoot with!"

"That wasn't right of them," I sympathized. "But you can do something for me. You can stick here and keep your eye on this end of the street, so I'll know if they leave in this direction."

"You're not just saying that so I'll stay here out of the way, are you?"

"No," I lied. "I need somebody to watch. I was going to leave the princess here, but you'll do better."

"Yes," she backed me up, catching the idea. "This gentleman is a detective, and if you do what he asks you'll be helping more than if you were up with the others."

The machine gun was still firing, but not in our direction now.

"I'm going across the street," I told the girl. "If you—"

"Aren't you going to join the others?"

"No. If I can get around behind the bandits while they're busy with the others, maybe I can turn a trick."

"Watch sharp now!" I ordered the boy, and the princess and I made a dash for the opposite sidewalk.

We reached it without drawing lead, sidled along a building for a few yards, and turned into an alley. From the alley's other end came the smell and wash and the dull blackness of the bay.

While we moved down this alley I composed a scheme by which I hoped to get rid of my companion, sending her off on a safe wild-goose chase. But I didn't get a chance to try it out.

The big figure of a man loomed ahead of us.

Stepping in front of the girl, I went on toward him. Under my slicker I held my gun on the middle of him.

He stood still. He was larger than he had looked at first. A big, slope-shouldered, barrel-bodied husky. His hands were empty. I spotted the flashlight on his face for a split second. A flat-cheeked, thick-featured face, with high cheekbones and a lot of ruggedness in it.

"Ignati!" the girl exclaimed over my shoulder.

He began to talk what I suppose was Russian to the girl. She laughed and replied. He shook his big head stubbornly, insisting on something. She stamped her foot and spoke sharply. He shook his head again and addressed me. "General Pleshskev, he tell me bring Princess Sonya to home."

His English was almost as hard to understand as his Russian. His tone puzzled me. It was as if he was explaining some absolutely necessary thing that he didn't want to be blamed for, but that nevertheless he was going to do.

While the girl was speaking to him again, I guessed the answer. This big Ignati had been sent out by the general to bring the girl home, and he was going to obey his orders if he had to carry her. He was trying to avoid trouble with me by explaining the situation.

"Take her," I said, stepping aside.

The girl scowled at me, laughed. "Very well, Ignati," she said in English, "I shall go home," and she turned on her heel and went back up the alley, the big man close behind her.

Glad to be alone, I wasted no time in moving in the opposite direction until the pebbles of the beach were under my feet. The pebbles ground harshly under my heels. I moved back to more silent ground and began to work my way as swiftly as I could up the shore toward the center of action. The machine gun barked on. Smaller guns snapped. Three concussions, close together—bombs, hand grenades, my ears and my memory told me.

The stormy sky glared pink over a roof ahead of me and to the left. The boom of the blast beat my eardrums. Fragments I couldn't see fell around me. That, I thought, would be the jeweler's safe blowing apart.

I crept on up the shore line. The machine gun went silent. Lighter guns snapped, snapped. Another grenade went off. A man's voice shrieked pure terror.

Risking the crunch of pebbles, I turned down to the water's edge again. I had seen no dark shape on the water that could have been a boat. There had been boats moored along this beach in the afternoon. With my feet in the water of the bay I still saw no boat. The storm could have scattered them, but I didn't think it had. The island's western height shielded this shore. The wind was strong here, but not violent.

My feet sometimes on the edge of the pebbles, sometimes in the water, I went on up the shore line. Now I saw a boat. A gently bobbing black shape ahead. No light was on it. Nothing I could see moved on it. It was the only boat on that shore. That made it important.

Foot by foot, I approached.

A shadow moved between me and the dark rear of a building. I froze. The shadow, man-size, moved again, in the direction from which I was coming.

Waiting, I didn't know how nearly invisible, or how plain, I might be against my background. I couldn't risk giving myself away by trying to improve my position.

Twenty feet from me the shadow suddenly stopped.

I was seen. My gun was on the shadow.

"Come on," I called softly. "Keep coming. Let's see who you are."

The shadow hesitated, left the shelter of the building, drew nearer. I couldn't risk the flashlight. I made out dimly a handsome face, boyishly reckless, one cheek dark-stained.

"Oh, how d'you do?" the face's owner said in a musical baritone voice. "You were at the reception this afternoon."

"Yes."

"Have you seen Princess Zhukovski? You know her?"

"She went home with Ignati ten minutes or so ago."

"Excellent!" He wiped his stained cheek with a stained handkerchief, and turned to look at the boat. "That's Hendrixson's boat," he whispered. "They've got it and they've cast the others off."

"That would mean they are going to leave by water."

"Yes," he agreed, "unless—Shall we have a try at it?"

"You mean jump it?"

"Why not?" he asked. "There can't be very many aboard. God knows there are enough of them ashore. You're armed. I've a pistol."

"We'll size it up first," I decided, "so we'll know what we're jumping."

"That is wisdom," he said, and led the way back to the shelter of the buildings.

Hugging the rear walls of the buildings, we stole toward the boat.

The boat grew clearer in the night. A craft perhaps forty-five feet long, its stern to the shore, rising and falling beside a small pier. Across the stern something protruded. Something I couldn't quite make out. Leather soles scuffled now and then on the wooden deck. Presently a dark head and shoulders showed over the puzzling thing in the stern.

The Russian lad's eyes were better than mine.

"Masked," he breathed in my ear. "Something like a stocking over his head and face."

The masked man was motionless where he stood. We were motionless where we stood.

"Could you hit him from here?" the lad asked.

"Maybe, but night and rain aren't a good combination for sharpshooting. Our best bet is to sneak as close as we can, and start shooting when he spots us."

"That is wisdom," he agreed.

Discovery came with our first step forward. The man in the boat grunted. The lad at my side jumped forward. I recognized the thing in the boat's stern just in time to throw out a leg and trip the young Russian. He tumbled down, all sprawled out on the pebbles. I dropped behind him.

The machine gun in the boat's stern poured metal over our heads.

"No good rushing that!" I said. "Roll out of it!"

I set the example by revolving toward the back of the building we had just left.

The man at the gun sprinkled the beach, but sprinkled it at random, his eyes no doubt spoiled for night-seeing by the flash of his gun.

Around the corner of the building, we sat up.

"You saved my life by tripping me," the lad said coolly.

"Yes. I wonder if they've moved the machine gun from the street, or if—"

The answer to that came immediately. The machine gun in the street mingled its vicious voice with the drumming of the one in the boat.

"A pair of them!" I complained. "Know anything about the layout?"

"I don't think there are more than ten or twelve of them," he said, "although it is not easy to count in the dark. The few I have seen are completely masked— like the man in the boat. They seem to have diconnected the telephone and light lines first and then to have destroyed the bridge. We attacked them while they were looting the bank, but in front they had a machine gun mounted in an automobile, and we were not equipped to combat on equal terms."

"Where are the islanders now?"

"Scattered, and most of them in hiding, I fancy, unless General Pleshskev has succeeded in rallying them again."

I frowned and beat my brains together. You can't fight machine guns and hand grenades with peaceful villagers and retired capitalists. No matter how well led and armed they are, you can't do anything with them. For that matter, how could anybody do much against a game of that toughness?

"Suppose you stick here and keep your eye on the boat," I suggested. "I'll scout around and see what's doing farther up, and if I can get a few good men together, I'll try to jump the boat again, probably from the other side. But we can't count on that. The getaway will be by boat. We can count on that, and try to block it. If you lie down you can watch the boat around the corner of the building without making much of a target of yourself. I wouldn't do anything to attract attention until the break for the boat comes. Then you can do all the shooting you want."

"Excellent!" he said. "You'll probably find most of the islanders up behind the church. You can get to it by going straight up the hill until you come to an iron fence, and then follow that to the right."

"Right."

I moved off in the direction he had indicated.

At the main street I stopped to look around before venturing across. Everything was quiet there. The only man I could see was spread out face-down on the sidewalk near me.

On hands and knees I crawled to his side. He was dead. I didn't stop to examine him further, but sprang up and streaked for the other side of the street.

Nothing tried to stop me. In a doorway, flat against a wall, I peeped out. The wind had stopped. The rain was no longer a driving deluge, but a steady downpouring of small drops. Couffignal's main street, to my senses, was a deserted street.

I wondered if the retreat to the boat had already started. On the sidewalk, walking swiftly toward the bank, I heard the answer to that guess.

High up on the slope, almost up to the edge of the cliff, by the sound, a machine gun began to hurl out its stream of bullets.

Mixed with the racket of the machine gun were the sounds of smaller arms, and a grenade or two.

At the first crossing, I left the main street and began to run up the hill. Men were running toward me. Two of them passed, paying no attention to my shouted, "What's up now?"

The third man stopped because I grabbed him — a fat man whose breath bubbled, and whose face was fish-belly white.

"They've moved the car with the machine gun on it up behind us," he gasped when I had shouted my question into his ear again.

"What are you doing without a gun?" I asked.

"I — I dropped it."

"Where's General Pleshskev?"

"Back there somewhere. He's trying to capture the car, but he'll never do it. It's suicide! Why don't help come?"

Other men had passed us, running downhill, as we talked. I let the white-faced man go, and stopped four men who weren't running so fast as the others.

"What's happening now?" I questioned them.

"They's going through the houses up the hill," a sharp-featured man with a small mustache and a rifle said.

"Has anybody got word off the island yet?" I asked.

"Can't," another informed me. "They blew up the bridge first thing."

"Can't anybody swim?"

"Not in that wind. Young Catlan tried it and was lucky to get out again with a couple of broken ribs."

"The wind's gone down," I pointed out.

The sharp-featured man gave his rifle to one of the others and took off his coat. "I'll try it," he promised.

"Good! Wake up the whole country, and get word through to the San Francisco police boat and to the Mare Island Navy Yard. They'll lend a hand if you tell 'em the bandits have machine guns. Tell 'em the bandits have an armed boat waiting to leave in. It's Hendrixson's."

The volunteer swimmer left.

"A boat?" two of the men asked together.

"Yes. With a machine gun on it. If we're going to do anything, it'll have to be now, while we're between them and their get-away. Get every man and every gun you can find down there. Tackle the boat from the roofs if you can. When the bandits' car comes down there, pour it into it. You'll do better from the buildings than from the street."

The three men went on downhill. I went uphill, toward the crackling of firearms ahead. The machine gun was working irregularly. It would pour out its rat-tat-tat for a second or so, and then stop for a couple of seconds. The answering fire was thin, ragged.

I met more men, learned from them the general, with less than a dozen men, was still fighting the car. I repeated the advice I had given the other men. My informants went down to join them. I went on up.

A hundred yards farther along, what was left of the general's dozen broke out of the night, around and past me, flying downhill, with bullets hailing after them.

The road was no place for mortal man. I stumbled over two bodies, scratched myself in a dozen places getting over a hedge. On soft, wet sod I continued my uphill journey.

The machine gun on the hill stopped its clattering. The one in the boat was still at work.

The one ahead opened again, firing too high for anything near at hand to be its target. It was helping its fellow below, spraying the main street.

Before I could get closer it had stopped. I heard the car's motor racing. The car moved toward me.

Rolling into the hedge, I lay there, straining my eyes through the spaces between the stems. I had six bullets in a gun that hadn't yet been fired on this night that had seen tons of powder burned.

When I saw wheels on the lighter face of the road, I emptied my gun, holding it low.

The car went on.

I sprang out of my hiding-place.

The car was suddenly gone from the empty road.

There was a grinding sound. A crash. The noise of metal folding on itself. The tinkle of glass.

I raced toward those sounds.

Out of a black pile where an engine sputtered, a black figure leaped — to dash off across the soggy lawn. I cut after it, hoping that the others in the wreck were down for keeps.

I was less than fifteen feet behind the fleeing man when he cleared a hedge. I'm no sprinter, but neither was he. The wet grass made slippery going.

He stumbled while I was vaulting the hedge. When we straightened out again I was not more than ten feet behind him.

Once I clicked my gun at him forgetting I had emptied it. Six cartridges were wrapped in a piece of paper in my vest pocket, but this was no time for loading.

I was tempted to chuck the empty gun at his head. But that was too chancy.

A building loomed ahead. My fugitive bore off to the right, to clear the corner.

To the left a heavy shotgun went off.

The running man disappeared around the house-corner.

"Sweet God!" General Pleshskev's mellow voice complained. "That with a shotgun I should miss all of a man at the distance!"

"Go round the other way!" I yelled, plunging around the corner after my quarry.

His feet thudded ahead. I could not see him. The general puffed around from the other side of the house.

"You have him?"

"No."

In front of us was a stone-faced bank, on top of which ran a path. On either side of us was a high and solid hedge.

"But, my friend," the general protested. "How could he have — ?"

A pale triangle showed on the path above — a triangle that could have been a bit of shirt showing above the opening of a vest.

"Stay here and talk!" I whispered to the general, and crept forward.

"It must be that he has gone the other way," the general carried out my instructions, rambling on as if I were standing beside him, "because if he had come my way I should have seen him, and if he had raised himself over either of the hedges or the embankment, one of us would surely have seen him against . . ."

He talked on and on while I gained the shelter of the bank on which the path sat, while I found places for my toes in the rough stone facing.

The man on the road, trying to make himself small with his back in a bush, was looking at the talking general. He saw me when I had my feet on the path.

He jumped, and one hand went up.

I jumped, with both hands out.

A stone, turning under my foot, threw me sidewise, twisting my ankle, but saving my head from the bullet he sent at it.

My outflung left arm caught his legs as I spilled down. He came over on top of me. I kicked him once, caught his gun-arm, and had just decided to bite it when the general puffed up over the edge of the path and prodded the man off me with the muzzle of the shotgun.

When it came my turn to stand up, I found it not so good. My twisted ankle didn't like to support its share of my hundred-and-eighty-some pounds. Putting most of my weight on the other leg, I turned my flashlight on the prisoner.

"Hello, Flippo!" I exclaimed.

"Hello!" he said without joy in the recognition.

He was a roly-poly Italian youth of twenty-three or -four. I had helped send him to San Quentin four years ago for his part in a payroll stick-up. He had been out on parole for several months now.

"The prison board isn't going to like this," I told him.

"You got me wrong," he pleaded. "I ain't been doing a thing. I was up here to see some friends. And when this thing busted loose I had to hide, because I got a record, and if I'm picked up I'll be railroaded for it. And now you got me, and you think I'm in on it!"

"You're a mind reader," I assured him, and asked the general, "Where can we pack this bird away for a while, under lock and key?"

"In my house there is a lumber-room with a strong door and not a window."

"That'll do it. March, Flippo!"

General Pleshskev collared the youth, while I limped along behind them, examining Flippo's gun, which was loaded except for the one shot he had fired at me, and reloading my own.

We had caught our prisoner on the Russian's grounds, so we didn't have far to go.

The general knocked on the door and called out something in his language. Bolts clicked and grated, and the door was swung open by a heavily mustached Russian servant. Behind him the princess and a stalwart older woman stood.

We went in while the general was telling his household about the capture, and took the captive up to the lumber-room. I frisked him for his pocket-knife and matches—he had nothing else that could help him get out—locked him in and braced the door solidly with a length of board. Then we went downstairs again.

"You are injured!" the princess cried, seeing me limp across the floor.

"Only a twisted ankle," I said. "But it does bother me some. Is there any adhesive tape around?"

"Yes," and she spoke to the mustached servant, who went out of the room and presently returned, carrying rolls of gauze and tape and a basin of steaming water.

"If you'll sit down," the princess said, taking these things from the servant. But I shook my head and reached for the adhesive tape.

"I want cold water, because I've got to go out in the wet again. If you'll show me the bathroom, I can fix myself up in no time."

We had to argue about that, but I finally got to the bathroom, where I ran cold water on my foot and ankle, and strapped it with adhesive tape, as tight as I could without stopping the circulation altogether. Getting my wet shoe on again was a job, but when I was through I had two firm legs under me, even if one of them did hurt some.

When I rejoined the others I noticed that sounds of firing no longer came up the hill, and that the patter of rain was lighter, and a gray streak of coming daylight showed under a drawn blind.

I was buttoning my slicker when the knocker rang on the front door. Russian words came through, and the young Russian I had met on the beach came in.

"Aleksander, you're—" The stalwart older woman screamed, when she saw the blood on his cheek, and fainted.

He paid no attention to her at all, as if he was used to having her faint.

"They've gone in the boat," he told me while the girl and two men servants gathered up the woman and laid her on an ottoman.

"How many?" I asked.

"I counted ten, and I don't think I missed more than one or two, if any."

"The men I sent down there couldn't stop them?"

He shrugged. "What would you? It takes a strong stomach to face a machine gun. Your men had been cleared out of the buildings almost before they arrived."

The woman who had fainted had revived by now and was pouring anxious questions in Russian at the lad. The princess was getting into her blue cape. The woman stopped questioning the lad and asked her something.

"It's all over," the princess said. "I am going to view the ruins."

That suggestion appealed to everybody. Five minutes later all of us, including the servants, were on our way downhill. Behind us, around us, in front of us, were other people going downhill, hurrying along in the drizzle that was very gentle now, their faces tired and excited in the bleak morning light.

Halfway down, a woman ran out of a cross-path and began to tell me something. I recognized her as one of Hendrixson's maids.

I caught some of her words.

"Presents gone. . . . Mr. Brophy murdered . . . Oliver . . ."

"I'll be down later," I told the others, and set out after the maid.

She was running back to the Hendrixson house. I couldn't run, couldn't even walk fast. She and Hendrixson and more of his servants were standing on the front porch when I arrived.

"They killed Oliver and Brophy," the old man said.

"How?"

"We were in the back of the house, the rear second story, watching the flashes of the shooting down in the village. Oliver was down here, just inside the front door, and Brophy in the room with the presents. We heard a shot in there, and immediately a man appeared in the doorway of our room, threatening us with two pistols, making us stay there for perhaps ten minutes. Then he shut and locked the door and went away. We broke the door down — and found Brophy and Oliver dead."

"Let's look at them."

The chauffeur was just inside the front door. He lay on his back, with his brown throat cut straight across the front, almost back to the vertebrae. His rifle was under him. I pulled it out and examined it. It had not been fired.

Upstairs, the butler Brophy was huddled against a leg of one of the tables on which the presents had been spread. His gun was gone. I turned him over, straightened him out, and found a bullet-hole in his chest. Around the hole his coat was charred in a large area.

Most of the presents were still there. But the most valuable pieces were gone. The others were in disorder, lying around any which way, their covers pulled off.

"What did the one you saw look like?" I asked.

"I didn't see him very well," Hendrixson said. "There was no light in our room. He was simply a dark figure against the candle burning in the hall. A large man in a black rubber raincoat, with some sort of black mask that covered his whole head and face, with small eyeholes."

"No hat?"

"No, just the mask over his entire face and head."

As we went downstairs again I gave Hendrixson a brief account of what I had seen and heard and done since I had left him. There wasn't enough of it to make a long tale.

"Do you think you can get information about the others from the one you caught?" he asked, as I prepared to go out.

"No. But I expect to bag them just the same."

Couffignal's main street was jammed with people when I limped into it again. A detachment of Marines from Mare Island was there, and men from a San Francisco police boat. Excited citizens in all degrees of partial nakedness boiled around them. A hundred voices were talking at once, recounting their personal adventures and braveries and losses and what they had seen. Such words as machine gun, bomb, bandit, car, shot, dynamite, and killed sounded again and again, in every variety of voice and tone.

The bank had been completely wrecked by the charge that had blown the vault. The jewelry store was another ruin. A grocer's across the street was serving as a field hospital. Two doctors were toiling there, patching up damaged villagers.

I recognized a familiar face under a uniform cap — Sergeant Roche of the harbor police — and pushed through the crowd to him.

"Just get here?" he asked as we shook hands. "Or were you in on it?"

"In on it."

"What do you know?"

"Everything."

"Who ever heard of a private detective that didn't," he joshed as I led him out of the mob.

"Did you people run into an empty boat out in the bay?" I asked when we were away from audiences.

"Empty boats have been floating around the bay all night," he said.

I hadn't thought of that.

"Where's your boat now?" I asked him.

"Out trying to pick up the bandits. I stayed with a couple of men to lend a hand here."

"You're in luck," I told him. "Now sneak a look across the street. See the stout old boy with the black whiskers, standing in front of the druggist's?"

General Pleshskev stood there, with the woman who had fainted, the young Russian whose bloody cheek had made her faint, and a pale, plump man of forty-something who had been with them at the reception. A little to one side stood big Ignati, the two men-servants I had seen at the house, and another who was obviously one of them. They were chatting together and watching the excited antics of a red-faced property-owner who was telling a curt lieutenant of Marines that it was his own personal private automobile that the bandits had stolen to mount their machine gun on, and what he thought should be done about it.

"Yes," said Roche, "I see your fellow with the whiskers."

"Well, he's your meat. The woman and the two men with him are also your meat. And those four Russians standing to the left are some more of it. There's another missing, but I'll take care of that one. Pass the word to the lieutenant, and you can round up those babies without giving them a chance to fight back. They think they're safe as angels."

"Sure, are you?" the sergeant asked.

"Don't be silly!" I growled, as if I had never made a mistake in my life.

I had been standing on my one good prop. When I put my weight on the other to turn away from the sergeant, it stung me all the way to the hip. I pushed my back teeth together and began to work painfully through the crowd to the other side of the street.

The princess didn't seem to be among those present. My idea was that, next to the general, she was the most important member of the push. If she was at their house, and not yet suspicious, I figured I could get close enough to yank her in without a riot.

Walking was hell. My temperature rose. Sweat rolled out on me.

"Mister, they didn't none of 'em come down that way."

The one-legged newsboy was standing at my elbow. I greeted him as if he were my pay-check.

"Come on with me," I said, taking his arm. "You did fine down there, and now I want you to do something else for me."

Half a block from the main street I led him up on the porch of a small yellow cottage. The front door stood open, left that way when the occupants ran down to welcome police and Marines, no doubt. Just inside the door, beside a hall rack, was a wicker porch chair. I committed unlawful entry to the extent of dragging that chair out on the porch.

"Sit down, son," I urged the boy.

He sat, looking up at me with puzzled freckled face. I took a firm grip on his crutch and pulled it out of his hand.

"Here's five bucks for rental," I said, "and if I lose it I'll buy you one of ivory and gold."

And I put the crutch under my arm and began to propel myself up the hill.

It was my first experience with a crutch. I didn't break any records. But it was a lot better than tottering along on an unassisted bum ankle.

The hill was longer and steeper than some mountains I've seen, but the gravel walk to the Russians' house was finally under my feet.

I was still some dozen feet from the porch when Princess Zhukovski opened the door.

"Oh!" she exclaimed, and then, recovering from her surprise, "your ankle is worse!" She ran down the steps to help me climb them. As she came I noticed that something heavy was sagging and swinging in the right-hand pocket of her gray flannel jacket.

With one hand under my elbow, the other arm across my back, she helped me up the steps and across the porch. That assured me she didn't think I had tumbled to the game. If she had, she wouldn't have trusted herself within reach of my hands. Why, I wondered, had she come back to the house after starting downhill with the others?

While I was wondering we went into the house, where she planted me in a large and soft leather chair.

"You must certainly be starving after your strenuous night," she said. "I will see if —— "

"No, sit down." I nodded at a chair facing mine. "I want to talk to you."

She sat down, clasping her slender white hands in her lap. In neither face nor pose was there any sign of nervousness, not even of curiosity. And that was overdoing it.

"Where have you cached the plunder?" I asked.

The whiteness of her face was nothing to go by. It had been white as marble since I had first seen her. The darkness of her eyes was as natural. Nothing happened to her other features. Her voice was smoothly cool.

"I am sorry," she said. "The question doesn't convey anything to me."

"Here's the point," I explained. "I'm charging you with complicity in the gutting of Couffignal, and in the murders that went with it. And I'm asking you where the loot has been hidden."

Slowly she stood up, raised her chin, and looked at least a mile down at me.

"How dare you? How dare you speak so to me, a Zhukovski!"

"I don't care if you're one of the Smith Brothers!" Leaning forward, I had pushed my twisted ankle against a leg of the chair, and the resulting agony didn't improve my disposition. "For the purpose of this talk you are a thief and a murderer."

Her strong slender body became the body of a lean crouching animal. Her white face became the face of an enraged animal. One hand — claw now — swept to the heavy pocket of her jacket.

Then, before I could have batted an eye — though my life seemed to depend on my not batting it — the wild animal had vanished. Out of it — and now I know where the writers of the old fairy stories got their ideas — rose the princess again, cool and straight and tall.

She sat down, crossed her ankles, put an elbow on an arm of her chair, propped her chin on the back of that hand, and looked curiously into my face.

"How ever," she murmured, "did you chance to arrive at so strange and fanciful a theory?"

"It wasn't chance, and it's neither strange nor fanciful," I said. "Maybe it'll save time and trouble if I show you part of the score against you. Then you'll know how you stand and won't waste your brains pleading innocence."

"I shall be grateful," she smiled, "very!"

I tucked my crutch in between one knee and the arm of my chair, so my hands would be free to check off my points on my fingers.

"First — whoever planned the job knew the island — not fairly well, but every inch of it. There's no need to argue about that. Second — the car on which the machine gun was mounted was local property, stolen from the owner here. So was the boat in which the bandits were supposed to have escaped. Bandits from the outside would have needed a car or a boat to bring their machine guns, explosives, and grenades here, and there doesn't seem to be any reason why they shouldn't have used that car or boat instead of stealing a fresh one. Third — there wasn't the least of hint of the professional bandit touch on this job. If you ask me, it was a military job from beginning to end. And the worst safe-burglar in the world could have got into both the bank vault and the jeweler's safe without wrecking the buildings. Fourth — bandits from the outside wouldn't have destroyed the bridge. They might have blocked it, but they wouldn't have destroyed it. They'd have saved it in case they had to make their get-away in that direction. Fifth — bandits figuring on a get-away by boat would have cut the job short, wouldn't have spread it over the whole night. Enough racket was made here to wake up California all the way from Sacramento to Los Angeles. What you people did was to send one man out in the boat, shooting, and he didn't go far. As soon as he was at a safe distance, he went overboard, and swam back to the island. Big Ignati could have done it without turning a hair."

That exhausted my right hand. I switched over, counting on my left.

"Sixth — I met one of your party, the lad, down on the beach, and he was coming from the boat. He suggested that we jump it. We were shot at, but the man behind the gun was playing with us. He could have wiped us out in a second if he had been in earnest, but he shot over our heads. Seventh — that same lad is the only man on the island, so far as I know, who saw the departing bandits. Eight — all of your people that I ran into were especially nice to me, the general even spending an hour talking to me at the reception this afternoon. That's a distinctive amateur crook trait. Ninth—after the machine gun car had been wrecked I chased its occupant. I lost him around this house. The Italian boy I picked up wasn't him. He couldn't have climbed up on the path without my seeing him. But he could have run around to the general's side of the house and vanished indoors there. The general liked him, and would have helped him. I know that, because the general performed a downright miracle by missing him at some six feet with a shotgun. Tenth—you called at Hendrixson's house for no other purpose than to get me away from there."

That finished the left hand. I went back to the right.

"Eleventh—Hendrixson's two servants were killed by someone they knew and trusted. Both were killed at close quarters and without firing a shot. I'd say you got Oliver to let you into the house, and were talking to him when one of your men cut his throat from behind. Then you went upstairs and probably shot the unsuspecting Brophy yourself. He wouldn't have been on his guard against you. Twelfth—but that ought to be enough, and I'm getting a sore throat from listing them."

She took her chin off her hand, took a fat white cigarette out of a thin black case, and held it in her mouth while I put a match to the end of it. She took a long pull at it—a draw that accounted for a third of its length—and blew the smoke down at her knees.

"That would be enough," she said when all these things had been done, "if it were not that you yourself know it was impossible for us to have been so engaged. Did you not see us—did not everyone see us—time and time again?"

"That's easy!" I argued. "With a couple of machine guns, a trunkful of grenades, knowing the island from top to bottom, in the darkness and in a storm, against bewildered civilians—it was duck soup. There are nine of you that I know of, including two women. Any five of you could have carried on the work, once it was started, while the others took turns appearing here and there, establishing alibis. And that is what you did. You took turns slipping out to alibi yourselves. Everywhere I went I ran into one of you. And the general! That whiskered old joker running around leading the simple citizens to battle! I'll bet he led 'em plenty! They're lucky there are any of 'em alive this morning!"

She finished her cigarette with another inhalation, dropped the stub on the rug, ground out the light with one foot, sighed wearily, put her hands on her hips, and asked, "And now what?"

"Now I want to know where you have stowed the plunder."

The readiness of her answer surprised me.

"Under the garage, in a cellar we secretly dug there some months ago."

I didn't believe that, of course, but it turned out to be the truth.

I didn't have anything else to say. When I fumbled with my borrowed crutch, preparing to get up, she raised a hand and spoke gently. "Wait a moment, please. I have something to suggest."

Half standing, I leaned toward her, stretching out one hand until it was close to her side.

"I want the gun," I said.

She nodded, and sat still while I plucked it from her pocket, put it in one of my own, and sat down again.

"You said a little while ago that you didn't care who I was," she began immediately. "But I want you to know. There are so many of us Russians who once were somebodies and who now are nobodies that I won't bore you with the repetition of a tale the world has grown tired of hearing. But you must remember that this weary tale is real to us who are its subjects. However, we fled from Russia with what we could carry of our property, which fortunately was enough to keep us in bearable comfort for a few years.

"In London we opened a Russian restaurant, but London was suddenly full of Russian restaurants, and ours became, instead of a means of livelihood, a source of loss. We tried teaching music and languages, and so on. In short, we hit on all the means of earning our living that other Russian exiles hit upon, and so always found ourselves in overcrowded, and thus unprofitable, fields. But what else did we know—could we do?

"I promised not to bore you. Well, always our capital shrank, and always the day approached on which we should be shabby and hungry, the day when we should become familiar to readers of your Sunday papers—charwomen who had been princesses, dukes who now were butlers. There was no place for us in the world. Outcasts easily become outlaws. Why not? Could it be said that we owed the world any fealty? Had not the world sat idly by and seen us despoiled of place and property and country?

"We planned it before we had heard of Couffignal. We could find a small settlement of the wealthy, sufficiently isolated, and, after establishing ourselves there, we would plunder it. Couffignal, when we found it, seemed to be the ideal place. We leased this house for six months, having just enough capital remaining to do that and to live properly here while our plans matured. Here we spent four months establishing ourselves, collecting our arms and our explosives, mapping our offensive, waiting for a favorable night. Last night seemed to be that night, and we had provided, we thought, against every eventuality. But we had not, of course, provided against your presence and your genius. They were simply others of the unforeseen misfortunes to which we seem eternally condemned."

She stopped, and fell to studying me with mournful large eyes that made me feel like fidgeting.

"It's no good calling me a genius," I objected. "The truth is you people botched your job from beginning to end. Your general would get a big laugh out of a man without military training who tried to lead an army. But here are you people with absolutely no criminal experience trying to swing a trick that needed the highest sort of criminal skill. Look at how you all played around with me! Amateur stuff! A professional crook with any intelligence would have either let me alone or knocked me off. No wonder you flopped! As for the rest of it—your troubles—I can't do anything about them."

"Why?" very softly. "Why can't you?"

"Why should I?" I made it blunt.

"No one else knows what you know." She bent forward to put a white hand on my knee. "There is wealth in that cellar beneath the garage. You may have whatever you ask."

I shook my head.

"You aren't a fool!" she protested. "You know——"

"Let me straighten this out for you," I interrupted. "We'll disregard whatever honesty I happen to have, sense of loyalty to employers, and so on. You might doubt them, so we'll throw them out. Now I'm a detective because I happen to like the work. It pays me a fair salary, but I could find other jobs that would pay more. Even a hundred dollars more a month would be twelve hundred a year. Say twenty-five or thirty thousand dollars in the years between now and my sixtieth birthday.

"Now I pass up about twenty-five or thirty thousand of honest gain because I like being a detective, like the work. And liking work makes you want to do it as well as you can. Otherwise there'd be no sense to it. That's the fix I am in. I don't know anything else, don't enjoy anything else, don't want to know or enjoy anything else. You can't weigh that against any sum of money. Money is good stuff. I haven't anything against it. But in the past eighteen years I've been getting my fun out of chasing crooks and tackling puzzles, my satisfaction out of catching crooks and solving riddles. It's the only kind of sport I know anything about, and I can't imagine a pleasanter future than twenty-some years more of it. I'm not going to blow that up!"

She shook her head slowly, lowering it, so that now her dark eyes looked up at me under the thin arcs of her brows.

"You speak only of money," she said. "I said you may have whatever you ask."

That was out. I don't know where these women get their ideas.

"You're still all twisted up," I said brusquely, standing now and adjusting my borrowed crutch. "You think I'm a man and you're a woman. That's wrong. I'm a manhunter and you're something that has been running in front of me. There's nothing human about it. You might just as well expect a hound to play tiddly-winks with the fox he's caught. We're wasting time anyway. I've been thinking the police or Marines might come up here and save me a walk. You've been waiting for your mob to come back and grab me. I could have told you they were being arrested when I left them."

That shook her. She had stood up. Now she fell back a step, putting a hand behind her for steadiness, on her chair. An exclamation I didn't understand popped out of her mouth. Russian, I thought, but the next moment I knew it had been Italian.

"Put your hands up." It was Flippo's husky voice. Flippo stood in the doorway, holding an automatic.

I raised my hands as high as I could without dropping my supporting crutch, meanwhile cursing myself for having been too careless, or too vain, to keep a gun in my hand while I talked to the girl.

So this was why she had come back to the house. If she freed the Italian, she had thought, we would have no reason for suspecting that he hadn't been in on the robbery, and so would look for the bandits among his friends. A prisoner, of course, he might have persuaded us of his innocence. She had given him the gun so he could either shoot his way clear, or, what would help her as much, get himself killed trying.

While I was arranging these thoughts in my head, Flippo had come up behind me. His empty hand passed over my body, taking away my own gun, his, and the one I had taken from the girl.

"A bargain, Flippo," I said when he had moved away from me, a little to one side, where he made one corner of a triangle whose other corners were the girl and I. "You're out on parole, with some years still to be served. I picked you up with a gun on you. That's plenty to send you back to the big house. I know you weren't in on this job. My idea is that you were up here on a smaller one of your own, but I can't prove that and don't want to. Walk out of here, alone and neutral, and I'll forget I saw you."

Little thoughtful lines grooved the boy's round, dark face.

The princess took a step toward him.

"You heard the offer I just now made him?" she asked. "Well, I make that offer to you, if you will kill him."

The thoughtful lines in the boy's face deepened.

"There's your choice, Flippo," I summed up for him. "All I can give you is freedom from San Quentin. The princess can give you a fat cut of the profits in a busted caper, with a good chance to get yourself hanged."

The girl, remembering her advantage over me, went at him hot and heavy in Italian, a language in which I know only four words. Two of them are profane and the other two obscene. I said all four.

The boy was weakening. If he had been ten years older, he'd have taken my offer and thanked me for it. But he was young and she — now that I thought of it — was beautiful. The answer wasn't hard to guess.

"But not to bump him off," he said to her in English, for my benefit. "We'll lock him up in there where I was at."

I suspected Flippo hadn't any great prejudice against murder. It was just that he thought this one unnecessary, unless he was kidding me to make the killing easier.

The girl wasn't satisfied with his suggestion. She poured more hot Italian at him. Her game looked surefire, but it had a flaw. She couldn't persuade him that his chances of getting any of the loot away were good. She had to depend on her charms to swing him. And that meant she had to hold his eye.

He wasn't far from me.

She came close to him. She was singing, chanting, crooning Italian syllables into his round face.

She had him.

He shrugged. His whole face said yes. He turned —

I knocked him on the noodle with my borrowed crutch.

The crutch splintered apart. Flippo's knees bent. He stretched up to his full height. He fell on his face on the floor. He lay there, deadstill, except for a thin worm of blood that crawled out of his hair to the rug.

A step, a tumble, a foot or so of hand-and-knee scrambling put me within reach of Flippo's gun.

The girl, jumping out of my path, was halfway to the door when I sat up with the gun in my hand.

"Stop!" I ordered.

"I shan't," she said, but she did, for the time at least. "I am going out."

"You are going out when I take you."

She laughed, a pleasant laugh, low and confident.

"I'm going out before that," she insisted good-naturedly. I shook my head.

"How do you purpose stopping me?" she asked.

"I don't think I'll have to," I told her. "You've got too much sense to try to run while I'm holding a gun on you."

She laughed again, an amused ripple.

"I've got too much sense to stay," she corrected me. "Your crutch is broken, and you're lame. You can't catch me by running after me, then. You pretend you'll shoot me, but I don't believe you. You'd shoot me if I attacked you, of course, but I shan't do that. I shall simply walk out, and you know you won't shoot me for that. You'll wish you could, but you won't. You'll see."

Her face turned over her shoulder, her dark eyes twinkling at me, she took a step toward the door.

"Better not count on that!" I threatened.

For answer to that she gave me a cooing laugh. And took another step.

"Stop, you idiot!" I bawled at her.

Her face laughed over her shoulder at me. She walked without haste to the door, her short skirt of gray flannel shaping itself to the calf of each gray wool-stockinged leg as its mate stepped forward.

Sweat greased the gun in my hand.

When her right foot was on the doorsill, a little chuckling sound came from her throat.

"Adieu!" she said softly.

And I put a bullet in the calf of her left leg.

She sat down — plump! Utter surprise stretched her white face. It was too soon for pain.

I had never shot a woman before. I felt queer about it.

"You ought to have known I'd do it!" My voice sounded harsh and savage and like a stranger's in my ears. "Didn't I steal a crutch from a cripple?"

[1925]

Study and Writing Questions

1. What is the attitude of the NARRATOR toward crime? violence? disorder? Are these the same or different for him in general and at various points in the STORY?

2. There are a number of times when the NARRATIVE becomes self-reflexive, as when the narrator settles down to read *The Lord of the Sea* and comments about its believability. What other examples of SELF-REFLEXIVITY are there? How do they influence your reading of the narrative?

3. The last line of the narrative employs a certain sort of humor. How would you characterize that humor? Where else do you find it in the narrative? What is the role of humor in this narrative?

4. What range of male/female relationships is portrayed in this narrative? The opening ACTION takes place at a wedding, the main action includes the Continental Op and a woman, and there are some minor encounters with other women. What does the Continental Op seem to think of women? What does the IMPLIED AUTHOR seem to think of male/female relations?

5. What are the main social and political issues in this narrative? To what extent is class an issue? To what extent does the assertion that "'outcasts easily become outlaws'" mitigate the crimes? There are direct references to the

Russian Revolution and indirect ALLUSIONS to the actions of different nations during World War I. To what extent is this island a microcosm in which to reexamine some of the same social and political issues raised by Hammett's contemporary history?

See also Questions for Contrast and Comparison: 16, 70, 84, 100, 104, 119, 216, 221, 225, and 228.

■ **BARRY HANNAH** (1942–) *was born in Clinton, Mississippi, and edu-
cated at Mississippi College (B.A., 1964) and the University of Alabama
(M.A., 1966; M.F.A., 1967). Although he has published seven* NOVELS, *including*
Geronimo Rex *(1972), which won the William Faulkner Prize for best first novel,
Hannah agrees with his critics that his writing, often characterized by the portrayal
of Gothic violence, bizarre sex, and black humor, works best in short forms. His
much praised novel* Ray *(1981), about a man who fought in both the Civil War and
Vietnam, is little more than a hundred pages. His* STORIES, *which have been
collected in* Airships *(1978) and* Captain Maximus *(1985), generally appear first in*
Esquire. *Hannah describes himself as both a writer and an educator, having taught
(primarily as writer-in-residence) at such institutions as Clemson University and the
Universities of Alabama, Iowa, Montana, and Mississippi. His current home in
Oxford, Mississippi, is in "the backyard of the house Faulkner wrote about in* The
Sound and the Fury." *"As a Southern writer," Hannah has said, "you're pretty
sure the world thinks you're dumb — and you're going to prove you're not." Hannah
has three children and is twice divorced.*

I Am Shaking to Death

We went over there, Nag and I, because of nothing else to do over here, and
there were things going on, all right. A man had a fat farm south of town way out
in the sticks, near Yocona or something like that. It was not spoken of too
generally. What a wretched, hot buggy piece of the South it was down there, the
remnants of horse country, they said. There never was any good farming there.
Man had a fat farm that was somewhat illegal.

The fat women were tied to a rope behind a jeep, naked, and he would, or
somebody would, drive them slow down through a long pasture and into a
swamp like so much, what can I say, head of pork, except they agreed to it, the
women I mean, from the North, the far North, the East, not just the South. They
agreed that they were ugly enough for things to happen to them and they would
not be released until they were thin and better. And when they were thin, their
attitudes had improved and they could leave or not, but you bet they were
changed. So we would wait out there watching them and slowly fall in love with
one or two.

In the heat and the bugs, they clambered along mud-spattered behind the
jeep, none of them looking like a panty ad, not yet, sliding through gook and
briars. We thought — at least I did — about women and their burdens, these
burdens of fat they had brought on themselves. And it was quite a joy to watch
them struggle for relief.

It became August, and I saw on the steps of the Episcopal Church her, the
one I'd had my eye on.

I went up to introduce myself.

She was in a black silk dress with black shoes and slim calves. I guess we fell
in love with each other.

For after church, on Sunday afternoons, she would come by my place and I
would press her and press her. She would undress, and I would press her and
press her.

How can I forget the joy that a lean woman offers you, her brown legs raised for your giant urgency, her one stocking still on one leg, she wants you so much. And she tells you do it, do it, and then yes, more.

Some women you don't like after you've exhausted yourself in her, like you're both out on the meat rack at the Jitney Jungle — it's already dead and the less said the better.

But this woman was not some women.

She said nothing. She just smiled and was quiet; I admired the way she was graceful putting back on her hose and shoes and stepped back in her dress. She left off the brassiere because she saw me looking at her breasts again, and they were miraculous.

This woman I had watched lean down from something near porcine, a nameless drudge in a group of them, to something you just had to see — oh, my.

She addressed her hair in the bathroom. I've got a nice place with all sorts of mirrors. Mainly to remind me of who I am.

I am trying to get better looking and wiser as I age, just like everybody my age I know. Even trying to quit the cigarettes and the beer.

There is a guy in town, black. I lent him my car and he stole it. He professed to me that he was my friend, a brother, and then he stole my Cutlass. I'll never get over how slim, soft-spoken, and well-dressed he was.

He was missing his upper teeth.

I thought I could trust a guy with his upper teeth already gone.

They found him over in the Senatobia Jail. I myself was once locked in there one night for DWI. It's a horrible place. The jailors watch teevee and forget you ever occurred. Then they all get together and lie when you try to get some justice.

So that's what she and I began talking about, she with a strawberry cotton dress on this time. She said almost nothing, her eyes just glittering blue and her white nice teeth and the pink full lips.

"I guess you've got it made," she said at last, looking around at my place, all my art on the walls and my Scandinavian furniture.

"In the shade," I said.

The air-conditioner was pumping and that was all we could hear for about five minutes.

"Well," she said, "I don't, I don't at all. I spent just about my last dime getting this way. I don't have even the fare back to Minneapolis."

I took us in the Jaguar up to Minneapolis. We tried to stay along the river because the water always gives me peace. I like to get my Jag dirty-looking at the river and hear on my tape deck some old Sam and Dave songs. The Jag is an orchestra inside.

We got out and danced on the levee, shoes muddy, tires muddy.

Then I pressed her in the snow and she pressed me back. Then we went back into the motel in lower Minnesota and it was cold. I was shivering so much we almost had to call somebody. She couldn't get all the quilts on me fast enough, and I stood up, six-feet-four, skinny legs, long hair frozen and clacking around my eyes blind with cold, and I was shaking and shaking. Out the window the moon sat down in front of my eyes and looked at me with all its scars on it — no clouds, nothing, a white horror without a face. I mean, no features except that acne it has.

When I finally got warmer, I still had nothing to say. She ordered some soup, and my teeth and throat shot it all over her.

Her. The one I loved.

Anything. Help. I am shaking to death.

Her home was even farther north!

We went into Minneapolis, the city. But I forgot.

When people say they live in a city up North, you still have miles to travel — and then, and then. Even the Jag was complaining about the cold and the distance and then there was still more of it ahead.

I don't remember her house. Like me, she owned too much.

I really wish she'd read this and write me a letter.

[1985]

Study and Writing Questions

1. What does the word "love" seem to mean to the NARRATOR the two times he uses it? What does his understanding of "love" tell us about him?
2. What is the role of the woman in this STORY? Does the narrator think she is one of his mirrors? Is she?
3. How do the narrator's descriptions of women's bodies affect your feelings about him? How does the narrator's description of his own body affect your feelings about him? about what is happening in the story?
4. What is the importance of the structure of this NARRATIVE? Each section involves the narrator and at least one other person. What are the roles of each of the other people? How do the CHARACTERS' relationships evolve and change in the narrative?
5. What does the last line suggest about the character of the narrator? What is the narrative about?

See also Questions for Contrast and Comparison: 98, 128, 129, 130, 131, 188, and 197.

■ THOMAS HARDY (1840–1928), *son of a stonemason in Dorsetshire, England, was educated privately and, at sixteen, apprenticed to a local architect. He practiced in London (1862–1867) and Dorset (1867–1874), winning the Medal of the Royal Institute of British Architects. After the success of his fourth* NOVEL, *Far From the Madding Crowd (1874), he turned full-time to writing. Hardy's life and writings were highly controversial. His early affair with a "cousin," who may have been his niece, scandalized Victorian society, and his first marriage (1874), which lasted until his wife's death (1912), was never easy or close. Nonetheless, within his own lifetime his brooding novels of the economically and emotionally depressed rural life, including* The Return of the Native *(1878),* The Mayor of Casterbridge *(1886),* Tess of the D'Urbervilles *(1891), and* Jude the Obscure *(1896), put him in the first rank in critical opinion. The public outcry at his exploration of the tragic nature of sexual passion in the last two novels caused him to turn from prose to poetry (eight volumes published between 1898 and 1928). These poems met only moderate initial success but are now considered classics. He lived in Dorset, where he designed his own shrouded mansion, but went to London and traveled abroad often. He married Florence Emily Dugdale, a children's author, in 1914. His ashes are buried in Poets' Corner, Westminster Abbey, and his heart in Dorsetshire.*

The Son's Veto

I

To the eyes of a man viewing it from behind, the nut-brown hair was a wonder and a mystery. Under the black beaver hat surmounted by its tuft of black feathers, the long locks, braided and twisted and coiled like the rushes of a basket, composed a rare, if somewhat barbaric, example of ingenious art. One could understand such weavings and coilings being wrought to last intact for a year, or even a calendar month; but that they should be all demolished regularly at bedtime, after a single day of permanence, seemed a reckless waste of successful fabrication.

And she had done it all herself, poor thing. She had no maid, and it was almost the only accomplishment she could boast of. Hence the unstinted pains.

She was a young invalid lady—not so very much of an invalid—sitting in a wheeled chair, which had been pulled up in the front part of a green enclosure, close to a bandstand where a concert was going on, during a warm June after-noon. It had place in one of the minor parks or private gardens that are to be found in the suburbs of London, and was the effort of a local association to raise money for some charity. There are worlds within worlds in the great city, and though nobody outside the immediate district had ever heard of the charity, or the band, or the garden, the enclosure was filled with an interested audience sufficiently informed on all these.

As the strains proceeded many of the listeners observed the chaired lady, whose back hair, by reason of her prominent position, so challenged inspection. Her face was not easily discernible, but the aforesaid cunning tress-weavings, the white ear and poll, and the curve of a cheek which was neither flaccid nor sallow, were signals that led to the expectation of good beauty in front. Such expecta-tions are not infrequently disappointed as soon as the disclosure comes; and in the present case, when the lady, by a turn of the head, at length revealed herself, she was not so handsome as the people behind her had supposed, and even hoped—they did not know why.

For one thing (alas! the commonness of this complaint), she was less young than they had fancied her to be. Yet attractive her face unquestionably was, and not at all sickly. The revelation of its details came each time she turned to talk to a boy of twelve or thirteen who stood beside her, and the shape of whose hat and jacket implied that he belonged to a well-known public school. The immediate bystanders could hear that he called her 'Mother'.

When the end of the recital was reached, and the audience withdrew, many chose to find their way out by passing at her elbow. Almost all turned their heads to take a full and near look at the interesting woman, who remained stationary in the chair till the way should be clear enough for her to be wheeled out without obstruction. As if she expected their glances, and did not mind gratifying their curiosity, she met the eyes of several of her observers by lifting her own, showing these to be soft, brown, and affectionate orbs, a little plaintive in their regard.

She was conducted out of the gardens, and passed along the pavement till she disappeared from view, the schoolboy walking beside her. To inquiries made by some persons who watched her away, the answer came that she was the second wife of the incumbent of a neighbouring parish, and that she was lame. She was generally believed to be a woman with a story—an innocent one, but a story of some sort or other.

In conversing with her on their way home the boy who walked at her elbow said that he hoped his father had not missed them.

'He have been so comfortable these last few hours that I am sure he cannot have missed us,' she replied.

'*Has*, dear mother—not *have*!' exclaimed the public-school boy, with an impatient fastidiousness that was almost harsh. "Surely you know that by this time!'

His mother hastily adopted the correction, and did not resent his making it, or retaliate, as she might well have done, by bidding him to wipe that crumby mouth of his, whose condition had been caused by surreptitious attempts to eat a piece of cake without taking it out of the pocket wherein it lay concealed. After this the pretty woman and the boy went onward in silence.

That question of grammar bore upon her history, and she fell into reverie, of a somewhat sad kind to all appearance. It might have been assumed that she was wondering if she had done wisely in shaping her life as she had shaped it, to bring out such a result as this.

In a remote nook in North Wessex, forty miles from London, near the thriving county-town of Aldbrickham, there stood a pretty village with its church and parsonage, which she knew well enough, but her son had never seen. It was her native village, Gaymead, and the first event bearing upon her present situation had occurred at that place when she was only a girl of nineteen.

How well she remembered it, that first act in her little tragi-comedy, the death of her reverend husband's first wife. It happened on a spring evening, and she who now and for many years had filled that first wife's place was then parlour-maid in the parson's house.

When everything had been done that could be done, and the death was announced, she had gone out in the dusk to visit her parents, who were living in the same village, to tell them the sad news. As she opened the white swing-gate and looked towards the trees which rose westward, shutting out the pale light of the evening sky, she discerned, without much surprise, the figure of a man standing in the hedge, though she roguishly exclaimed as a matter of form, 'O, Sam, how you frightened me!'

He was a young gardener of her acquaintance. She told him the particulars of the late event, and they stood silent, these two young people, in that elevated, calmly philosophic mind which is engendered when a tragedy has happened close at hand, and has not happened to the philosophers themselves. But it had its bearing upon their relations.

'And will you stay on now at the Vicarage, just the same?' asked he.

She had hardly thought of that. 'O yes—I suppose!' she said. 'Everything will be just as usual, I imagine?'

He walked beside her towards her mother's. Presently his arm stole round her waist. She gently removed it; but he placed it there again, and she yielded the point. 'You see, dear Sophy, you don't know that you'll stay on; you may want a home; and I shall be ready to offer one some day, though I may not be ready just yet.'

'Why, Sam, how can you be so fast! I've never even said I liked 'ee; and it is all your own doing, coming after me!'

'Still, it is nonsense to say I am not to have a try at you like the rest.' He stooped to kiss her a farewell, for they had reached her mother's door.

'No, Sam; you sha'n't!' she cried, putting her hand over his mouth. 'You ought to be more serious on such a night as this.' And she bade him adieu without allowing him to kiss her or to come indoors.

The vicar just left a widower was at this time a man about forty years of age, of good family, and childless. He had led a secluded existence in this college living, partly because there were no resident landowners; and his loss now intensified his habit of withdrawal from outward observation. He was seen still less than heretofore, kept himself still less in time with the rhythm and racket of the movements called progress in the world without. For many months after his wife's decease the economy of his household remained as before; the cook, the housemaid, the parlour-maid, and the man out-of-doors performed their duties or left them undone, just as Nature prompted them—the vicar knew not which. It was then represented to him that his servants seemed to have nothing to do in his small family of one. He was struck with the truth of this representation, and decided to cut down his establishment. But he was forestalled by Sophy, the parlour-maid, who said one evening that she wished to leave him.

'And why?' said the parson.

'Sam Hobson has asked me to marry him, sir.'

'Well—do you want to marry?'

'Not much. But it would be a home for me. And we have heard that one of us will have to leave.'

A day or two after she said: 'I don't want to leave just yet, sir, if you don't wish it. Sam and I have quarrelled.'

He looked up at her. He had hardly ever observed her before, though he had been frequently conscious of her soft presence in the room. What a kitten-like, flexuous, tender creature she was! She was the only one of the servants with whom he came into immediate and continuous relation. What should he do if Sophy were gone?

Sophy did not go, but one of the others did, and things went on quietly again.

When Mr. Twycott, the vicar, was ill, Sophy brought up his meals to him, and she had no sooner left the room one day than he heard a noise on the stairs. She had slipped down with the tray, and so twisted her foot that she could not stand. The village surgeon was called in; the vicar got better, but Sophy was incapacitated for a long time; and she was informed that she must never again walk much or engage in any occupation which required her to stand long on her feet. As soon as she was comparatively well she spoke to him alone. Since she was forbidden to walk and bustle about, and, indeed, could not do so, it became her duty to leave. She could very well work at something sitting down, and she had an aunt a seamstress.

The parson had been very greatly moved by what she had suffered on his account, and he exclaimed, 'No, Sophy; lame or not lame, I cannot let you go. You must never leave me again!'

He came close to her, and, though she could never exactly tell how it happened, she became conscious of his lips upon her cheek. He then asked her to marry him. Sophy did not exactly love him, but she had a respect for him which almost amounted to veneration. Even if she had wished to get away from him she hardly dared refuse a personage so reverend and august in her eyes, and she assented forthwith to be his wife.

Thus it happened that one fine morning, when the doors of the church were naturally open for ventilation, and the singing birds fluttered in and alighted on the tie-beams of the roof, there was a marriage-service at the communion-rails, which hardly a soul knew of. The parson and a neighbouring curate had entered at one door, and Sophy at another, followed by two necessary persons, whereupon in a short time there emerged a newly-made husband and wife.

Mr. Twycott knew perfectly well that he committed social suicide by this step, despite Sophy's spotless character, and he had taken his measures accordingly. An exchange of livings had been arranged with an acquaintance who was incumbent of a church in the south of London, and as soon as possible the couple removed thither, abandoning their pretty home, with trees and shrubs and glebe, for a narrow, dusty house in a long, straight street, and their fine peal of bells for the wretchedest one-tongued clangour that ever tortured mortal ears. It was all on her account. They were, however, away from every one who had known her former position; and also under less observation from without than they would have had to put up with in any country parish.

Sophy the woman was as charming a partner as a man could possess, though Sophy the lady had her deficiencies. She showed a natural aptitude for little domestic refinements, so far as related to things and manners; but in what is called culture she was less intuitive. She had now been married more than fourteen years, and her husband had taken much trouble with her education; but she still held confused ideas on the use of 'was' and 'were', which did not beget a respect for her among the few acquaintances she made. Her great grief in this relation was that her only child, on whose education no expense had been and would be spared, was now old enough to perceive these deficiencies in his mother, and not only to see them but to feel irritated at their existence.

Thus she lived on in the city, and wasted hours in braiding her beautiful hair, till her once apple cheeks waned to pink of the very faintest. Her foot had never regained its natural strength after the accident, and she was mostly obliged to avoid walking altogether. Her husband had grown to like London for its freedom and its domestic privacy; but he was twenty years his Sophy's senior, and had latterly been seized with a serious illness. On this day, however, he had seemed to be well enough to justify her accompanying her son Randolph to the concert.

II

The next time we get a glimpse of her is when she appears in the mournful attire of a widow.

Mr. Twycott had never rallied, and now lay in a well-packed cemetery to the south of the great city, where, if all the dead it contained had stood erect and alive, not one would have known him or recognized his name. The boy had dutifully followed him to the grave, and was now again at school.

Throughout these changes Sophy had been treated like the child she was in nature though not in years. She was left with no control over anything that had been her husband's beyond her modest personal income. In his anxiety lest her experience should be over-reached he had safeguarded with trustees all he possibly could. The completion of the boy's course at the public school, to be followed in due time by Oxford and ordination, had been all previsioned and arranged, and she really had nothing to occupy her in the world but to eat and drink, and make a business of indolence, and go on weaving and coiling the nut-brown hair, merely keeping a home open for the son whenever he came to her during vacations.

Foreseeing his probable decease long years before her, her husband in his lifetime had purchased for her use a semi-detached villa in the same long, straight road whereon the church and parsonage faced, which was to be hers as long as she chose to live in it. Here she now resided, looking out upon the fragment of lawn in front, and through the railings at the ever-flowing traffic; or, bending forward over the window-sill on the first floor, stretching her eyes far up and down the vista of sooty trees, hazy air, and drab house-façades, along which echoed the noises common to a suburban main thoroughfare.

Somehow, her boy, with his aristocratic school-knowledge, his grammars, and his aversions, was losing those wide infantine sympathies, extending as far as to the sun and moon themselves, with which he, like other children, had been born, and which his mother, a child of nature herself, had loved in him; he was reducing their compass to a population of a few thousand wealthy and titled people, the mere veneer of a thousand million or so of others who did not interest him at all. He drifted further and further away from her. Sophy's milieu being a suburb of minor tradesmen and under-clerks, and her almost only companions the two servants of her own house, it was not surprising that after her husband's death she soon lost the little artificial tastes she had acquired from him, and became — in her son's eyes — a mother whose mistakes and origin it was his painful lot as a gentleman to blush for. As yet he was far from being man enough — if he ever would be — to rate these sins of hers at their true infinitesimal value beside the yearning fondness that welled up and remained penned in her heart till it should be more fully accepted by him, or by some other person or thing. If he had lived at home with her he would have had all of it; but he seemed to require so very little in present circumstances, and it remained stored.

Her life became insupportably dreary; she could not take walks, and had no interest in going for drives, or, indeed, in travelling anywhere. Nearly two years passed without an event, and still she looked on that suburban road, thinking of the village in which she had been born, and whither she would have gone back — O how gladly! — even to work in the fields.

Taking no exercise she often could not sleep, and would rise in the night or early morning to look out upon the then vacant thoroughfare, where the lamps stood like sentinels waiting for some procession to go by. An approximation to such a procession was indeed made early every morning about one o'clock, when the country vehicles passed up with loads of vegetables for Covent Garden market. She often saw them creeping along at this silent and dusky hour — waggon after waggon, bearing green bastions of cabbages nodding to their fall, yet never falling, walls of baskets enclosing masses of beans and peas, pyramids of snow-white turnips, swaying howdahs of mixed produce — creeping along behind aged nighthorses, who seemed ever patiently wondering between their hollow coughs why they had always to work at that still hour when all other sentient creatures were privileged to rest. Wrapped in a cloak, it was soothing to watch and sympathize with them when depression and nervousness hindered sleep, and to see how the fresh greenstuff brightened to life as it came opposite the lamp, and how the sweating animals steamed and shone with their miles of travel.

They had an interest, almost a charm, for Sophy, these semirural people and vehicles moving in an urban atmosphere, leading a life quite distinct from that of the daytime toilers on the same road. One morning a man who accompanied a waggon-load of potatoes gazed rather hard at the house-fronts as he passed, and with a curious emotion she thought his form was familiar to her. She looked out for him again. His being an old-fashioned conveyance, with a yellow front, it was easily recognizable, and on the third night after she saw it a second time. The man alongside was, as she had fancied, Sam Hobson, formerly gardener at Gaymead, who would at one time have married her.

She had occasionally thought of him, and wondered if life in a cottage with him would not have been a happier lot than the life she had accepted. She had not thought of him passionately, but her now dismal situation lent an interest to his resurrection — a tender interest which it is impossible to exaggerate. She went back to bed, and began thinking. When did these market-gardeners, who travelled up to town so regularly at one or two in the morning, come back? She dimly recollected seeing their empty waggons, hardly noticeable amid the ordinary day-traffic, passing down at some hour before noon.

It was only April, but that morning, after breakfast, she had the window opened, and sat looking out, the feeble sun shining full upon her. She affected to sew, but her eyes never left the street. Between ten and eleven the desired waggon, now unladen, reappeared on its return journey. But Sam was not looking round him then, and drove on in a reverie.

'Sam!' cried she.

Turning with a start, his face lighted up. He called to him a little boy to hold the horse, alighted, and came and stood under the window.

'I can't come down easily, Sam, or I would!' she said. 'Did you know I lived here?'

'Well, Mrs. Twycott, I knew you lived along here somewhere. I have often looked out for 'ee.'

He briefly explained his own presence on the scene. He had long since given up his gardening in the village near Aldbrickham, and was now manager at a market-gardener's on the south side of London, it being part of his duty to go up to Covent Garden with waggon-loads of produce two or three times a week. In answer to her curious inquiry, he admitted that he had come to this particular district because he had seen in the Aldbrickham paper, a year or two before, the announcement of the death in South London of the aforetime vicar of Gaymead, which had revived an interest in her dwelling-place that he could not extinguish, leading him to hover about the locality till his present post had been secured.

They spoke of their native village in dear old North Wessex, the spots in which they had played together as children. She tried to feel that she was a dignified personage now, that she must not be too confidential with Sam. But she could not keep it up, and the tears hanging in her eyes were indicated in her voice.

'You are not happy, Mrs. Twycott, I'm afraid?' he said.

'O, of course not! I lost my husband only the year before last.'

'Ah! I meant in another way. You'd like to be home again?'

'This is my home—for life. The house belongs to me. But I understand'— She let it out then. 'Yes, Sam. I long for home—*our* home! I *should* like to be there, and never leave it, and die there.' But she remembered herself. 'That's only a momentary feeling. I have a son, you know, a dear boy. He's at school now.'

'Somewhere handy, I suppose? I see there's lots on 'em along this road.'

'O no! Not in one of these wretched holes! At a public school—one of the most distinguished in England.'

'Chok' it all! of course! I forget, ma'am, that you've been a lady for so many years.'

'No, I am not a lady,' she said sadly. 'I never shall be. But he's a gentleman, and that—makes it—O how difficult for me!'

III

The acquaintance thus oddly reopened proceeded apace. She often looked out to get a few words with him, by night or by day. Her sorrow was that she could not accompany her one old friend on foot a little way, and talk more freely than she could do while he paused before the house. One night, at the beginning of June, when she was again on the watch after an absence of some days from the window, he entered the gate and said softly, 'Now, wouldn't some air do you good? I've only half a load this morning. Why not ride up to Covent Garden with me? There's a nice seat on the cabbages, where I've spread a sack. You can be home again in a cab before anybody is up.'

She refused at first, and then, trembling with excitement, hastily finished her dressing, and wrapped herself up in cloak and veil, afterwards sidling downstairs by the aid of the handrail, in a way she could adopt on an emergency. When she had opened the door she found Sam on the step, and he lifted her bodily on his strong arm across the little forecourt into his vehicle. Not a soul was visible or audible in the infinite length of the straight, flat highway, with its ever-waiting lamps converging to points in each direction. The air was fresh as country air at this hour, and the stars shone, except to the north-eastward, where there was a whitish light — the dawn. Sam carefully placed her in the seat, and drove on.

They talked as they had talked in old days, Sam pulling himself up now and then, when he thought himself too familiar. More than once she said with misgiving that she wondered if she ought to have indulged in the freak. 'But I am so lonely in my house,' she added, 'and this makes me so happy!'

'You must come again, dear Mrs. Twycott. There is no time o' day for taking the air like this.'

It grew lighter and lighter. The sparrows became busy in the streets, and the city waxed denser around them. When they approached the river it was day, and on the bridge they beheld the full blaze of morning sunlight in the direction of St. Paul's, the river glistening towards it, and not a craft stirring.

Near Covent Garden he put her into a cab, and they parted, looking into each other's faces like the very old friends they were. She reached home without adventure, limped to the door, and let herself in with her latch-key unseen.

The air and Sam's presence had revived her: her cheeks were quite pink — almost beautiful. She had something to live for in addition to her son. A woman of pure instincts, she knew there had been nothing really wrong in the journey, but supposed it conventionally to be very wrong indeed.

Soon, however, she gave way to the temptation of going with him again, and on this occasion their conversation was distinctly tender, and Sam said he never should forget her, notwithstanding that she had served him rather badly at one time. After much hesitation he told her of a plan it was in his power to carry out, and one he should like to take in hand, since he did not care for London work: it was to set up as a master greengrocer down at Aldbrickham, the county-town of their native place. He knew of an opening — a shop kept by aged people who wished to retire.

'And why don't you do it, then, Sam?' she asked with a slight heartsinking.

'Because I'm not sure if — you'd join me. I know you wouldn't — couldn't! Such a lady as ye've been so long, you couldn't be a wife to a man like me.'

'I hardly suppose I could!' she assented, also frightened at the idea.

'If you could,' he said eagerly, 'you'd on'y have to sit in the back parlour and look through the glass partition when I was away sometimes — just to keep an eye on things. The lameness wouldn't hinder that . . . I'd keep you as genteel as ever I could, dear Sophy — if I might think of it!' he pleaded.

'Sam, I'll be frank,' she said, putting her hand on his. 'If it were only myself I would do it, and gladly, though everything I possess would be lost to me by marrying again.'

'I don't mind that! It's more independent.'

'That's good of you, dear, dear Sam. But there's something else. I have a son . . . I almost fancy when I am miserable sometimes that he is not really mine, but one I hold in trust for my late husband. He seems to belong so little to me personally, so entirely to his dead father. He is so much educated and I so little that I do not feel dignified enough to be his mother . . . Well, he would have to be told.'

'Yes. Unquestionably.' Sam saw her thought and her fear. 'Still, you can do as you like, Sophy—Mrs. Twycott,' he added. 'It is not you who are the child, but he.'

'Ah, you don't know! Sam, if I could, I would marry you, some day. But you must wait a while, and let me think.'

It was enough for him, and he was blithe at their parting. Not so she. To tell Randolph seemed impossible. She could wait till he had gone up to Oxford, when what she did would affect his life but little. But would he ever tolerate the idea? And if not, could she defy him?

She had not told him a word when the yearly cricket-match came on at Lord's between the public schools, though Sam had already gone back to Aldbrickham. Mrs. Tywcott felt stronger than usual: she went to the match with Randolph, and was able to leave her chair and walk about occasionally. The bright idea occurred to her that she could casually broach the subject while moving round among the spectators, when the boy's spirits were high with interest in the game, and he would weigh domestic matters as feathers in the scale beside the day's victory. They promenaded under the lurid July sun, this pair, so wide apart, yet so near, and Sophy saw the large proportion of boys like her own, in their broad white collars and dwarf hats, and all around the rows of great coaches under which was jumbled the *débris* of luxurious luncheons; bones, pie-crusts, champagne-bottles, glasses, plates, napkins, and the family silver; while on the coaches sat the proud fathers and mothers; but never a poor mother like her. If Randolph had not appertained to these, had not centred all his interests in them, had not cared exclusively for the class they belonged to, how happy would things have been! A great huzza at some small performance with the bat burst from the multitude of relatives, and Randolph jumped wildly into the air to see what had happened. Sophy fetched up the sentence that had been already shaped; but she could not get it out. The occasion was, perhaps, an inopportune one. The contrast between her story and the display of fashion to which Randolph had grown to regard himself as akin would be fatal. She awaited a better time.

It was on an evening when they were alone in their plain suburban residence, where life was not blue but brown, that she ultimately broke silence, qualifying her announcement of a probable second marriage by assuring him that it would not take place for a long time to come, when he would be living quite independently of her.

The boy thought the idea a very reasonable one, and asked if she had chosen anybody? She hesitated; and he seemed to have a misgiving. He hoped his stepfather would be a gentleman? he said.

'Not what you call a gentleman,' she answered timidly. 'He'll be much as I was before I knew your father'; and by degrees she acquainted him with the whole. The youth's face remained fixed for a moment; then he flushed, leant on the table, and burst into passionate tears.

His mother went up to him, kissed all of his face that she could get at, and patted his back as if he were still the baby he once had been, crying herself the while. When he had somewhat recovered from his paroxysm he went hastily to his own room and fastened the door.

Parleyings were attempted through the keyhole, outside which she waited and listened. It was long before he would reply, and when he did it was to say sternly at her from within: 'I am ashamed of you! It will ruin me! A miserable boor! a churl! a clown! It will degrade me in the eyes of all the gentlemen of England!'

'Say no more — perhaps I am wrong! I will struggle against it!' she cried miserably.

Before Randolph left her that summer a letter arrived from Sam to inform her that he had been unexpectedly fortunate in obtaining the shop. He was in possession; it was the largest in the town, combining fruit with vegetables, and he thought it would form a home worthy even of her some day. Might he not run up to town to see her?

She met him by stealth, and said he must still wait for her final answer. The autumn dragged on, and when Randolph was home at Christmas for the holidays she broached the matter again. But the young gentleman was inexorable.

It was dropped for months; renewed again; abandoned under his repugnance; again attempted; and thus the gentle creature reasoned and pleaded till four or five long years had passed. Then the faithful Sam revived his suit with some peremptoriness. Sophy's son, now an undergraduate, was down from Oxford one Easter, when she again opened the subject. As soon as he was ordained, she argued, he would have a home of his own, wherein she, with her bad grammar and her ignorance, would be an encumbrance to him. Better obliterate her as much as possible.

He showed a more manly anger now, but would not agree. She on her side was more persistent, and he had doubts whether she could be trusted in his absence. But by indignation and contempt for her taste he completely maintained his ascendancy; and finally taking her before a little cross and altar that he had erected in his bedroom for his private devotions, there bade her kneel, and swear that she would not wed Samuel Hobson without his consent. 'I owe this to my father!' he said.

The poor woman swore, thinking he would soften as soon as he was ordained and in full swing of clerical work. But he did not. His education had by this time sufficiently ousted his humanity to keep him quite firm; though his mother might have led an idyllic life with her faithful fruiterer and green-grocer, and nobody have been anything the worse in the world.

Her lameness became more confirmed as time went on, and she seldom or never left the house in the long southern thoroughfare, where she seemed to be pining her heart away. 'Why mayn't I say to Sam that I'll marry him? Why mayn't I?' she would murmur plaintively to herself when nobody was near.

Some four years after this date a middle-aged man was standing at the door of the largest fruiterer's shop in Aldbrickham. He was the proprietor, but to-day, instead of his usual business attire, he wore a neat suit of black; and his window was partly shuttered. From the railway-station a funeral procession was seen approaching: it passed his door and went out of the town towards the village of Gaymead. The man, whose eyes were wet, held his hat in his hand as the vehicle moved by; while from the mourning coach a young smooth-shaven priest in a high waistcoat looked black as a cloud at the shopkeeper standing there.

[1891]

Study and Writing Questions

1. What is the SYMBOLISM of the first two paragraphs? After having read the NARRATIVE, reread these paragraphs. What do they predict about Sophy's CHARACTER? about the ACTION?
2. What are the meanings of the word "child" in this narrative? What are the relations between children and adults?
3. Does the last paragraph of the narrative provide a satisfying RESOLUTION? If so, how; if not, what is its effect?
4. What are the signs of social class in the world of this STORY and what are their importance in the lives of these characters?
5. What precisely is the THEME of this narrative and how does the narrative make us appreciate that theme?

See also Questions for Contrast and Comparison: 69, 97, 106, 159, 165, 168, and 176.

(FRANCIS) BRET(T) HARTE (1836–1902), *whose father taught school in his own Albany, New York home, read Shakespeare by the time he was six. After his father's death (1845), the family struggled in New York City, where Bret worked at odd jobs. They finally moved to California when Bret's mother married an Oakland businessman. Bret tried prospecting, guarding for Wells Fargo, and printing, but in 1854 declared his aim to become a writer. His first success, "M'liss" (1860), ultimately led to the editorship of the Overland Monthly, where, in its second issue, he published "The Luck of Roaring Camp" (1868). This* STORY *won national acclaim for enriching the sentimental conventions of "local-color" writing with the sensitive* CHARACTERIZATION *and moral ambiguity found in all Harte's best stories. Other well-known Harte stories include "The Outcasts of Poker Flat" (1869), "Tennessee's Partner" (1869), and his immensely popular ballad, "Plain Language from Truthful James" (1870), also known as* The Heathen Chinee. *His marriage (1862), though often estranged, produced four children. Harte went East in 1871 as a literary celebrity, courted editor, and popular lecturer, but his writing, though prolific, never regained its early power. Well connected (he collaborated on the play* Ah Sin *with Samuel Clemens), he became U.S. consul in Crefeld, Prussia (1878), and Glasgow, Scotland (1880–1885). He lived his last years in London, where his work sold more readily.*

The Outcasts of Poker Flat

As Mr. John Oakhurst, gambler, stepped into the main street of Poker Flat on the morning of the twenty-third of November, 1850, he was conscious of a change in its moral atmosphere since the preceding night. Two or three men, conversing earnestly together, ceased as he approached, and exchanged significant glances. There was a Sabbath lull in the air, which, in a settlement unused to Sabbath influences, looked ominous.

Mr. Oakhurst's calm, handsome face betrayed small concern of these indications. Whether he was conscious of any predisposing cause, was another question. "I reckon they're after somebody," he reflected; "likely it's me." He returned to his pocket the handkerchief with which he had been whipping away the red dust of Poker Flat from his neat boots, and quietly discharged his mind of any further conjecture.

In point of fact, Poker Flat was "after somebody." It had lately suffered the loss of several thousand dollars, two valuable horses, and a prominent citizen. It was experiencing a spasm of virtuous reaction, quite as lawless and ungovernable as any of the acts that had provoked it. A secret committee had determined to rid the town of all improper persons. This was done permanently in regard of two men who were then hanging from the boughs of a sycamore in the gulch, and temporarily in the banishment of certain other objectionable characters. I regret to say that some of these were ladies. It is but due to the sex, however, to state that their impropriety was professional, and it was only in such easily established standards of evil that Poker Flat ventured to sit in judgment.

Mr. Oakhurst was right in supposing that he was included in this category. A few of the committee had urged hanging him as a possible example, and a sure method of reimbursing themselves from his pockets of the sums he had won from them. "It's agin justice," said Jim Wheeler, "to let this yer young man from

Roaring Camp—an entire stranger—carry away our money." But a crude sentiment of equity residing in the breasts of those who had been fortunate enough to
win from Mr. Oakhurst overruled this narrower local prejudice.

Mr. Oakhurst received his sentence with philosophic calmness, none the less
coolly that he was aware of the hesitation of his judges. He was too much of a
gambler not to accept Fate. With him life was at best an uncertain game, and he
recognized the usual percentage in favor of the dealer.

A body of armed men accompanied the deported wickedness of Poker Flat to
the outskirts of the settlement. Besides Mr. Oakhurst, who was known to be a
coolly desperate man, and for whose intimidation the armed escort was intended,
the expatriated party consisted of a young woman familiarly known as "The
Duchess"; another, who had gained the infelicitous title of "Mother Shipton";
and "Uncle Billy," a suspected sluice-robber and confirmed drunkard. The
cavalcade provoked no comments from the spectators, nor was any word uttered
by the escort. Only, when the gulch which marked the uttermost limit of Poker
Flat was reached, the leader spoke briefly and to the point. The exiles were
forbidden to return at the peril of their lives.

As the escort disappeared, their pent-up feelings found vent in a few hysterical tears from the Duchess, some bad language from Mother Shipton, and a
Parthian volley of expletives from Uncle Billy. The philosophic Oakhurst alone
remained still. He listened calmly to Mother Shipton's desire to cut somebody's
heart out, to the repeated statements of the Duchess that she would die on the
road, and to the alarming oaths that seemed to be bumped out of Uncle Billy as
he rode forward. With the easy good humor characteristic of his class, he insisted
upon exchanging his own riding-horse, Five Spot, for the sorry mule which the
Duchess rode. But even this act did not draw the party into any closer sympathy.
The young woman readjusted her somewhat draggled plumes with a feeble, faded
coquetry; Mother Shipton eyed the possessor of Five Spot with malevolence, and
Uncle Billy included the whole party in one sweeping anathema.

The road to Sandy Bar—a camp that, not having as yet experienced the
regenerating influences of Poker Flat, consequently seemed to offer some invitation to the emigrants—lay over a steep mountain range. It was distant a day's
severe journey. In that advanced season, the party soon passed out of the moist,
temperate regions of the foothills into the dry, cold, bracing air of the Sierras.
The trail was narrow and difficult. At noon the Duchess, rolling out of her saddle
upon the ground, declared her intention of going no farther, and the party
halted.

The spot was singularly wild and impressive. A wooded amphitheater, surrounded on three sides by precipitous cliffs of naked granite, sloped gently
toward the crest of another precipice that overlooked the valley. It was undoubtedly the most suitable spot for a camp, had camping been advisable. But Mr.
Oakhurst knew that scarcely half the journey to Sandy Bar was accomplished,
and the party were not equipped or provisioned for delay. This fact he pointed
out to his companions curtly, with a philosophic commentary on the folly of
"throwing up their hand before the game was played out." But they were
furnished with liquor, which in this emergency stood them in place of food, fuel,
rest, and prescience. In spite of his remonstrances, it was not long before they
were more or less under its influence. Uncle Billy passed rapidly from a bellicose

state into one of stupor, the Duchess became maudlin, and Mother Shipton snored. Mr. Oakhurst alone remained erect, leaning against a rock, calmly surveying them.

Mr. Oakhurst did not drink. It interfered with a profession which required coolness, impassiveness, and presence of mind, and, in his own language, he "couldn't afford it." As he gazed at his recumbent fellow-exiles, the loneliness begotten of his pariah-trade, his habits of life, his very vices, for the first time seriously oppressed him. He bestirred himself in dusting his black clothes, washing his hands and face, and other acts characteristic of his studiously neat habits, and for a moment forgot his annoyance. The thought of deserting his weaker and more pitiable companions never perhaps occurred to him. Yet he could not help feeling the want of that excitement which, singularly enough, was most conducive to that calm equanimity for which he was notorious. He looked at the gloomy walls that rose a thousand feet sheer above the circling pines around him; at the sky, ominously clouded; at the valley below, already deepening into shadow. And, doing so, suddenly he heard his own name called.

A horseman slowly ascended the trail. In the fresh, open face of the newcomer Mr. Oakhurst recognized Tom Simson, otherwise known as "The Innocent" of Sandy Bar. He had met him some months before over a "little game," and had, with perfect equanimity, won the entire fortune — amounting to some forty dollars — of that guileless youth. After the game was finished, Mr. Oakhurst drew the youthful speculator behind the door and thus addressed him: "Tommy, you're a good little man, but you can't gamble worth a cent. Don't try it over again." He then handed him his money back, pushed him gently from the room, and so made a devoted slave of Tom Simson.

There was a remembrance of this in his boyish and enthusiastic greeting of Mr. Oakhurst. He had started, he said, to go to Poker Flat to seek his fortune. "Alone?" No, not exactly alone; in fact — a giggle — he had run away with Piney Woods. Didn't Mr. Oakhurst remember Piney? She that used to wait on the table at the Temperance House? They had been engaged a long time, but old Jake Woods had objected, and so they had run away, and were going to Poker Flat to be married, and here they were. And they were tired out, and how lucky it was they had found a place to camp and company. All this the Innocent delivered rapidly, while Piney — a stout, comely damsel of fifteen — emerged from behind the pine-tree, where she had been blushing unseen, and rode to the side of her lover.

Mr. Oakhurst seldom troubled himself with sentiment, still less with propriety; but he had a vague idea that the situation was not felicitous. He retained, however, his presence of mind sufficiently to kick Uncle Billy, who was about to say something, and Uncle Billy was sober enough to recognize in Mr. Oakhurst's kick a superior power that would not bear trifling. He then endeavored to dissuade Tom Simson from delaying further, but in vain. He even pointed out the fact that there was no provision, nor means of making a camp. But, unluckily, the Innocent met this objection by assuring the party that he was provided with an extra mule loaded with provisions, and by the discovery of a rude attempt at a log-house near the trail. "Piney can stay with Mrs. Oakhurst," said the Innocent, pointing to the Duchess, "and I can shift for myself."

Nothing but Mr. Oakhurst's admonishing foot saved Uncle Billy from bursting into a roar of laughter. As it was, he felt compelled to retire up the canyon until he could recover his gravity. There he confided the joke to the tall pine trees, with many slaps of his leg, contortions of his face, and the usual profanity. But when he returned to the party, he found them seated by a fire—for the air had grown strangely chill and the sky overcast—in apparently amicable conversation. Piney was actually talking in an impulsive, girlish fashion to the Duchess, who was listening with an interest and animation she had not shown for many days. The Innocent was holding forth, apparently with equal effect, to Mr. Oakhurst and Mother Shipton, who was actually relaxing into amiability. "Is this yer a d—d picnic?" said Uncle Billy, with inward scorn, as he surveyed the sylvan group, the glancing fire-light, and the tethered animals in the foreground. Suddenly an idea mingled with the alcoholic fumes that disturbed his brain. It was apparently of a jocular nature, for he felt impelled to slap his leg again and cram his fist into his mouth.

As the shadows crept slowly up the mountain, a slight breeze rocked the tops of the pine-trees, and moaned through their long and gloomy aisles. The ruined cabin, patched and covered with pine boughs, was set apart for the ladies. As the lovers parted, they unaffectedly exchanged a kiss, so honest and sincere that it might have been heard above the swaying pines. The frail Duchess and the malevolent Mother Shipton were probably too stunned to remark upon this last evidence of simplicity, and so turned without a word to the hut. The fire was replenished, the men lay down before the door, and in a few minutes were asleep.

Mr. Oakhurst was a light sleeper. Toward morning he awoke benumbed and cold. As he stirred the dying fire, the wind, which was now blowing strongly, brought to his cheek that which caused the blood to leave it—snow!

He started to his feet with the intention of awakening the sleepers, for there was no time to lose. But turning to where Uncle Billy had been lying, he found him gone. A suspicion leaped to his brain and a curse to his lips. He ran to the spot where the mules had been tethered; they were no longer there. The tracks were already rapidly disappearing in the snow.

The momentary excitement brought Mr. Oakhurst back to the fire with his usual calm. He did not waken the sleepers. The Innocent slumbered peacefully, with a smile on his good humored, freckled face; the virgin Piney slept beside her frailer sisters as sweetly as though attended by celestial guardians, and Mr. Oakhurst, drawing his blanket over his shoulders, stroked his mustachios and waited for the dawn. It came slowly in the whirling mist of snowflakes, that dazzled and confused the eye. What could be seen of the landscape appeared magically changed. He looked over the valley, and summed up the present and future in two words—"Snowed in!"

A careful inventory of the provisions, which, fortunately for the party, had been stored within the hut, and so escaped the felonious fingers of Uncle Billy, disclosed the fact that with care and prudence they might last ten days longer. "That is," said Mr. Oakhurst, *sotto voce* to the Innocent, "if you're willing to board us. If you ain't—and perhaps you'd better not—you can wait till Uncle Billy gets back with provisions." For some occult reason, Mr. Oakhurst, could not bring himself to disclose Uncle Billy's rascality, and so offered the hypothesis that he had wandered from the camp and had accidentally stampeded the animals. He dropped a warning to the Duchess and Mother Shipton, who of course knew the facts of their associate's defection. "They'll find out the truth about us *all*, when they find out anything," he added, significantly, "and there's no good frightening them now."

Tom Simson not only put all his worldly store at the disposal of Mr. Oakhurst, but seemed to enjoy the prospect of their enforced seclusion. "We'll have a good camp for a week, and then the snow'll melt, and we'll all go back together." The cheerful gayety of the young man and Mr. Oakhurst's calm infected the others. The Innocent, with the aid of pine boughs, extemporized a thatch for the roofless cabin, and the Duchess directed Piney in the rearrangement of the interior with a taste and tact that opened the blue eyes of that provincial maiden to their fullest extent.

"I reckon now you're used to fine things at Poker Flat," said Piney. The Duchess turned away sharply to conceal something that reddened her cheek through its professional tint, and Mother Shipton requested Piney not to "chatter." But when Mr. Oakhurst returned from a weary search for the trail, he heard the sound of happy laughter echoed from the rocks. He stopped in some alarm, and his thoughts first naturally reverted to the whisky, which he had prudently *cached*. "And yet it don't somehow sound like whisky," said the gambler. It was not until he caught sight of the blazing fire through the still blinding storm, and the group around it, that he settled to the conviction that it was "square fun."

Whether Mr. Oakhurst had *cached* his cards with the whisky as something debarred the free access of the community, I cannot say. It was certain that, in Mother Shipton's words, he "didn't say cards once" during the evening. Haply the time was beguiled by an accordion, produced somewhat ostentatiously by Tom Simson, from his pack. Notwithstanding some difficulties attending the manipulation of this instrument, Piney Woods managed to pluck several reluctant melodies from its keys, to an accompaniment by the Innocent on a pair of bone castinets. But the crowning festivity of the evening was reached in a rude camp-meeting hymn, which the lovers, joining hands, sang with great earnestness and vociferation. I fear that a certain defiant tone and Covenanter's swing to its chorus, rather than any devotional quality, caused it speedily to infect the others, who at last joined in the refrain:

> I'm proud to live in the service of the Lord,
> And I'm bound to die in His army.

The pines rocked, the storm eddied and whirled above the miserable group, and the flames of their altar leaped heavenward, as if in token of the vow.

At midnight the storm abated, the rolling clouds parted, and the stars glittered keenly above the sleeping camp. Mr. Oakhurst, whose professional habits had enabled him to live on the smallest possible amount of sleep, in dividing the watch with Tom Simson, somehow managed to take upon himself the greater part of that duty. He excused himself to the Innocent, by saying that he had "often been a week without sleep." "Doing what?" asked Tom. "Poker!" replied Oakhurst, sententiously, "when a man gets a streak of luck — nigger-luck — he don't get tired. The luck gives in first. Luck," continued the gambler, reflectively, "is a mighty queer thing. All you know about it for certain is that it's bound to change. And it's finding out when it's going to change that makes you. We've had a streak of bad luck since we left Poker Flat—you come along, and slap you get into it, too. If you can hold your cards right along you're all right. For," added the gambler, with cheerful irrelevance,

"I'm proud to live in the service of the Lord,
And I'm proud to die in His army."

The third day came, and the sun, looking through the white-curtained valley, saw the outcasts divide their slowly decreasing store of provisions for the morning meal. It was one of the peculiarities of that mountain climate that its rays diffused a kindly warmth over the wintry landscape, as if in regretful commiseration of the past. But it revealed drift on drift of snow piled high around the hut; a hopeless, uncharted, trackless sea of white lying below the rocky shores to which the castaways still clung. Through the marvelously clear air, the smoke of the pastoral village of Poker Flat rose miles away. Mother Shipton saw it, and from a remote pinnacle of her rocky fastness, hurled in that direction a final malediction. It was her last vituperative attempt, and perhaps for that reason was invested with a certain degree of sublimity. It did her good, she privately informed the Duchess. "Just to go out there and cuss, and see." She then set herself to the task of amusing "the child," as she and the Duchess were pleased to call Piney. Piney was no chicken, but it was a soothing and ingenious theory of the pair thus to account for the fact that she didn't swear and wasn't improper.

When night crept up again through the gorges, the reedy notes of the accordion rose and fell in fitful spasms and long-drawn gasps by the flickering camp-fire. But music failed to fill entirely the aching void left by insufficient food, and a new diversion was proposed by Piney—storytelling. Neither Mr. Oakhurst nor his female companions caring to relate their personal experiences, this plan would have failed, too, but for the Innocent. Some months before he had chanced upon a stray copy of Mr. Pope's ingenious translation of the Iliad. He now proposed to narrate the principal incidents of that poem—having thoroughly mastered the argument and fairly forgotten the words—in the current vernacular of Sandy Bar. And so for the rest of that night the Homeric demigods again walked the earth. Trojan bully and wily Greek wrestled in the winds, and the great pines in the canyon seemed to bow to the wrath of the son of Peleus. Mr. Oakhurst listened with quiet satisfaction. Most especially was he interested in the fate of "Ash-heels," as the Innocent persisted in denominating the "swift-footed Achilles."

So with small food and much of Homer and the accordion, a week passed over the heads of the outcasts. The sun again forsook them, and again from leaden skies the snowflakes were sifted over the land. Day by day closer around them drew the snowy circle, until at last they looked from their prison over drifted walls of dazzling white, that towered twenty feet above their heads. It became more and more difficult to replenish their fires, even from the fallen trees beside them, now half-hidden in the drifts. And yet no one complained. The lovers turned from the dreary prospect and looked into each other's eyes, and were happy. Mr. Oakhurst settled himself coolly to the losing game before him. The Duchess, more cheerful than she had been, assumed the care of Piney. Only Mother Shipton—once the strongest of the party—seemed to sicken and fade.

At midnight on the tenth day she called Oakhurst to her side. "I'm going," she said, in a voice of querulous weakness, "but don't say anything about it. Don't waken the kids. Take the bundle from under my head and open it." Mr. Oakhurst did so. It contained Mother Shipton's rations for the last week, untouched. "Give 'em to the child," she said, pointing to the sleeping Piney. "You've starved yourself," said the gambler. "That's what they call it," said the woman, querulously, as she lay down again, and, turning her face to the wall, passed quietly away.

The accordion and the bones were put aside that day, and Homer was forgotten. When the body of Mother Shipton had been committed to the snow, Mr. Oakhurst took the Innocent aside, and showed him a pair of snowshoes, which he had fashioned from the old pack-saddle. "There's one chance in a hundred to save her yet," he said, pointing to Piney; "but it's there," he added, pointing toward Poker Flat. "If you can reach there in two days she's safe." "And you?" asked Tom Simson. "I'll stay here," was the curt reply.

The lovers parted with a long embrace. "You are not going, too?" said the Duchess, as she saw Mr. Oakhurst apparently waiting to accompany him. "As far as the canyon," he replied. He turned suddenly, and kissed the Duchess, leaving her pallid face aflame, and her trembling limbs rigid with amazement.

Night came, but not Mr. Oakhurst. It brought the storm again and the whirling snow. Then the Duchess, feeding the fire, found that some one had quietly piled beside the hut enough fuel to last a few days longer. The tears rose to her eyes, but she hid them from Piney.

The women slept but little. In the morning, looking into each other's faces, they read their fate. Neither spoke; but Piney, accepting the position of the stronger, drew near and placed her arm around the Duchess's waist. They kept this attitude for the rest of the day. That night the storm reached its greatest fury, and, rending asunder the protecting pines, invaded the very hut.

Toward morning they found themselves unable to feed the fire, which gradually died away. As the embers slowly blackened, the Duchess crept closer to Piney, and broke the silence of many hours: "Piney, can you pray?" "No, dear," said Piney, simply. The Duchess without knowing exactly why, felt relieved, and, putting her head upon Piney's shoulder, spoke no more. And so reclining, the younger and purer pillowing the head of her soiled sister upon her virgin breast, they fell asleep.

The wind lulled as if it feared to waken them. Feathery drifts of snow, shaken from the long pine boughs, flew like white-winged birds, and settled about them as they slept. The moon through the rifted clouds looked down upon what had been the camp. But all human stain, all trace of earthly travail, was hidden beneath the spotless mantle mercifully flung from above.

They slept all that day and the next, nor did they waken when voices and footsteps broke the silence of the camp. And when pitying fingers brushed the snow from their wan faces, you could scarcely have told from the equal peace that dwelt upon them, which was she that had sinned. Even the Law of Poker Flat recognized this, and turned away, leaving them still locked in each other's arms.

But at the head of the gulch, on one of the largest pine trees, they found the deuce of clubs pinned to the bark with a bowie knife. It bore the following, written in pencil, in a firm hand:

BENEATH THIS TREE
LIES THE BODY
OF
JOHN OAKHURST,
WHO STRUCK A STREAK OF BAD LUCK
ON THE 23D OF NOVEMBER, 1850,
AND
HANDED IN HIS CHECKS
ON THE 7TH OF DECEMBER, 1850.

And pulseless and cold, with a Derringer by his side and a bullet in his heart, though still calm as in life, beneath the snow lay he who was at once the strongest and yet the weakest of the outcasts of Poker Flat.

[1869]

Study and Writing Questions

1. What is the attitude of the NARRATOR toward the CHARACTERS in the first five paragraphs? Does that attitude continue throughout the NARRATIVE? Looking back over the narrative, in what ways do you find the narrator's attitude appropriate and in what ways inappropriate to the action? If you find the attitude at any time inappropriate, why do you think the IMPLIED AUTHOR allowed the narrator to project that inappropriate attitude?

2. There are two main SETTINGS in this narrative, each with both physical and social dimensions. What are the characteristics of each? What is the importance of each setting? In what ways is civilization better than the wilderness and in what ways worse? How are the settings related to each other geographically and philosophically?

3. Although the STORY is populated by comparatively unschooled characters, there are many brief ALLUSIONS (for example, to Parthian shots) and at least two major references, one to Homer's *Iliad* and another to a hymn. What is significant about each allusion? What is the THEMATIC significance of employing allusion in this narrative?

4. What is (are) the conception(s) of virtue in this narrative? Who is good and who is bad? Who is sometimes good and sometimes bad? Does a good act have the power to redeem a corrupt individual? To what extent is virtue an expression of the self and to what extent a relationship between the self and others? How important is society in defining virtue?

5. How does gambling figure in the plot? Why is the town called Poker Flat? Why does Oakhurst choose a two of clubs for his last message? What other references to gambling are there? What does gambling come to SYMBOLIZE in this narrative?

See also Questions for Contrast and Comparison: 5, 58, 68, 82, 148, 229, 230, 231, and 232.

NATHANIEL HAWTHORNE (1804–1864) *came from a Puritan family that arrived in Massachusetts in 1630 and included a judge at the Salem witchcraft trials (1692). At the death of his sea-captain father (1808), Hawthorne's mother withdrew into perpetual solitude, a pattern that also marked her son's life. After graduation from Bowdoin College (1825), Hawthorne returned to Salem for a lonely writing apprenticeship that culminated in his first book,* Twice Told Tales *(1837). This* STORY *collection received little contemporary favor but led to work hackwriting and editing. A four-year growing love for Sophia Amelia Peabody culminated in 1842 in marriage and a move to Concord, Massachusetts, where Hawthorne, who lived near Emerson and Thoreau, became more outgoing. With his second collection,* Mosses From an Old Manse *(1846), his skill began to be recognized. A lucrative political appointment to the Salem Custom House (1846–1849) allowed him to write* The Scarlet Letter *(1850), his first great* NOVEL *exploring the ambiguous torments of innocence and the hypocrisy of Puritanism.* The House of Seven Gables *(1851) and* The Blithedale Romance *(1852), based on his year's residence (1841) at the utopian Brook Farm, soon followed. Appointed consul in Liverpool (1853–1857) by his college classmate, President Franklin Pierce, Hawthorne remained in Europe until 1860 when he returned to Concord for the rest of his life.*

Rappaccini's Daughter

A young man, named Giovanni Guasconti, came, very long ago, from the more southern region of Italy, to pursue his studies at the University of Padua. Giovanni, who had but a scant supply of gold ducats in his pocket, took lodgings in a high and gloomy chamber of an old edifice which looked not unworthy to have been the palace of a Paduan noble, and which, in fact, exhibited over its entrance the armorial bearings of a family long since extinct. The young stranger, who was not unstudied in the great poem of his country, recollected that one of the ancestors of this family, and perhaps an occupant of this very mansion, had been pictured by Dante as a partaker of the immortal agonies of his Inferno. These reminiscences and associations, together with the tendency to heartbreak natural to a young man for the first time out of his native sphere, caused Giovanni to sigh heavily as he looked around the desolate and ill-furnished apartment.

"Holy Virgin, signor!" cried old Dame Lisabetta, who, won by the youth's remarkable beauty of person, was kindly endeavoring to give the chamber a habitable air, "what a sigh was that to come out of a young man's heart! Do you find this old mansion gloomy? For the love of Heaven, then, put your head out of the window, and you will see as bright sunshine as you have left in Naples."

Guasconti mechanically did as the old woman advised, but could not quite agree with her that the Paduan sunshine was as cheerful as that of southern Italy. Such as it was, however, it fell upon a garden beneath the window and expended its fostering influences on a variety of plants, which seemed to have been cultivated with exceeding care.

"Does this garden belong to the house?" asked Giovanni.

"Heaven forbid, signor, unless it were fruitful of better pot herbs than any that grow there now," answered old Lisabetta. "No; that garden is cultivated by the own hands of Signor Giacomo Rappaccini, the famous doctor, who, I warrant him, has been heard of as far as Naples. It is said that he distils these plants into medicines that are as potent as a charm. Oftentimes you may see the signor doctor at work, and perchance the signora, his daughter, too, gathering the strange flowers that grow in the garden."

The old woman had now done what she could for the aspect of the chamber; and, commending the young man to the protection of the saints, took her departure.

Giovanni still found no better occupation than to look down into the garden beneath his window. From its appearance, he judged it to be one of those botanic gardens which were of earlier date in Padua than elsewhere in Italy or in the world. Or, not improbably, it might once have been the pleasure-place of an opulent family; for there was the ruin of a marble fountain in the centre, sculptured with rare art, but so woefully shattered that it was impossible to trace the original design from the chaos of remaining fragments. The water, however, continued to gush and sparkle in the sunbeams as cheerfully as ever. A little gurgling sound ascended to the young man's window, and made him feel as if the fountain were an immortal spirit that sung its song unceasingly and without heeding the vicissitudes around it, while one century imbodied it in marble and another scattered the perishable garniture on the soil. All about the pool into which the water subsided grew various plants, that seemed to require a plentiful supply of moisture for the nourishment of gigantic leaves, and in some instances, flowers gorgeously magnificent. There was one shrub in particular, set in a marble vase in the midst of the pool, that bore a profusion of purple blossoms, each of which had the lustre and richness of a gem; and the whole together made a show so resplendent that it seemed enough to illuminate the garden, even had there been no sunshine. Every portion of the soil was peopled with plants and herbs, which, if less beautiful, still bore tokens of assiduous care, as if all had their individual virtues, known to the scientific mind that fostered them. Some were placed in urns, rich with old carving, and others in common garden pots; some crept serpent-like along the ground or climbed on high, using whatever means of ascent was offered them. One plant had wreathed itself round a statue of Vertumnus, which was thus quite veiled and shrouded in a drapery of hanging foliage, so happily arranged that it might have served a sculptor for a study.

While Giovanni stood at the window he heard a rustling behind a screen of leaves, and became aware that a person was at work in the garden. His figure soon emerged into view, and showed itself to be that of no common laborer, but a tall, emaciated, sallow, and sickly-looking man, dressed in a scholar's garb of black. He was beyond the middle term of life, with gray hair, a thin, gray beard, and a face singularly marked with intellect and cultivation, but which could never, even in his more youthful days, have expressed much warmth of heart.

Nothing could exceed the intentness with which this scientific gardener examined every shrub which grew in his path: it seemed as if he was looking into their inmost nature, making observations in regard to their creative essence, and discovering why one leaf grew in this shape and another in that, and wherefore such and such flowers differed among themselves in hue and perfume. Nevertheless, in spite of this deep intelligence on his part, there was no approach to intimacy between himself and these vegetable existences. On the contrary, he avoided their actual touch or the direct inhaling of their odors with a caution that impressed Giovanni most disagreeably; for the man's demeanor was that of one walking among malignant influences, such as savage beasts, or deadly snakes, or evil spirits, which, should he allow them one moment of license, would wreak upon him some terrible fatality. It was strangely frightful to the young man's imagination to see this air of insecurity in a person cultivating a garden, that most simple and innocent of human toils, and which had been alike the joy and labor of the unfallen parents of the race. Was this garden, then, the Eden of the present world? And this man, with such a perception of harm in what his own hands caused to grow, — was he the Adam?

The distrustful gardener, while plucking away the dead leaves or pruning the too luxuriant growth of the shrubs, defended his hands with a pair of thick gloves. Nor were these his only armor. When, in his walk through the garden, he came to the magnificent plant that hung its purple gems beside the marble fountain, he placed a kind of mask over his mouth and nostrils, as if all this beauty did but conceal a deadlier malice; but, finding his task still too dangerous, he drew back, removed the mask, and called loudly, but in the infirm voice of a person affected with inward disease, —

"Beatrice! Beatrice!"

"Here am I, my father. What would you?" cried a rich and youthful voice from the window of the opposite house — a voice as rich as a tropical sunset, and which made Giovanni, though he knew not why, think of deep hues of purple or crimson and of perfumes heavily delectable. "Are you in the garden?"

"Yes, Beatrice," answered the gardener, "and I need your help."

Soon there emerged from under a sculptured portal the figure of a young girl, arrayed with as much richness of taste as the most splendid of the flowers, beautiful as the day, and with a bloom so deep and vivid that one shade more would have been too much. She looked redundant with life, health, and energy; all of which attributes were bound down and compressed, as it were, and girdled tensely, in their luxuriance, by her virgin zone. Yet Giovanni's fancy must have grown morbid while he looked down into the garden; for the impression which the fair stranger made upon him was as if here were another flower, the human sister of those vegetable ones, as beautiful as they, more beautiful than the richest of them, but still to be touched only with a glove, nor to be approached without a mask. As Beatrice came down the garden path, it was observable that she handled and inhaled the odor of several of the plants which her father had most sedulously avoided.

"Here, Beatrice," said the latter, "see how many needful offices require to be done to our chief treasure. Yet, shattered as I am, my life might pay the penalty of approaching it so closely as circumstances demand. Henceforth, I fear, this plant must be consigned to your sole charge."

"And gladly will I undertake it," cried again the rich tones of the young lady, as she bent towards the magnificent plant and opened her arms as if to embrace it. "Yes, my sister, my splendour, it shall be Beatrice's task to nurse and serve thee; and thou shalt reward her with thy kisses and perfumed breath, which to her is as the breath of life."

Then, with all the tenderness in her manner that was so strikingly expressed in her words, she busied herself with such attentions as the plant seemed to require; and Giovanni, at his lofty window, rubbed his eyes and almost doubted whether it were a girl tending her favorite flower, or one sister performing the duties of affection to another. The scene soon terminated. Whether Dr. Rappaccini had finished his labors in the garden, or that his watchful eyes had caught the stranger's face, he now took his daughter's arm and retired. Night was already closing in; oppressive exhalations seemed to proceed from the plants and steal upward past the open window; and Giovanni, closing the lattice, went to his couch and dreamed of a rich flower and beautiful girl. Flower and maiden were different, and yet the same, and fraught with some strange peril in either shape.

But there is an influence in the light of morning that tends to rectify whatever errors of fancy, or even of judgment, we may have incurred during the sun's decline, or among the shadows of the night, or in the less wholesome glow of moonshine. Giovanni's first movement, on starting from sleep, was to throw open the window and gaze down into the garden which his dreams had made so fertile of mysteries. He was surprised and a little ashamed to find how real and matter-of-fact an affair it proved to be, in the first rays of the sun which gilded the dew-drops that hung upon leaf and blossom, and, while giving a brighter beauty to each rare flower, brought everything within the limits of ordinary experience. The young man rejoiced that, in the heart of the barren city, he had the privilege of overlooking this spot of lovely and luxuriant vegetation. It would serve, he said to himself, as a symbolic language to keep him in communion with Nature. Neither the sickly and thoughtworn Dr. Giacomo Rappaccini, it is true, nor his brilliant daughter, were now visible; so that Giovanni could not determine how much of the singularity which he attributed to both was due to their own qualities and how much to his wonder-working fancy; but he was inclined to take a most rational view of the whole matter.

In the course of the day he paid his respects to Signor Pietro Baglioni, professor of medicine in the university, a physician of eminent repute to whom Giovanni had brought a letter of introduction. The professor was an elderly personage, apparently of genial nature, and habits that might almost be called jovial. He kept the young man to dinner, and made himself very agreeable by the freedom and liveliness of his conversation, especially when warmed by a flask or two of Tuscan wine. Giovanni, conceiving that men of science, inhabitants of the same city, must needs be on familiar terms with one another, took an opportunity to mention the name of Dr. Rappaccini. But the professor did not respond with so much cordiality as he had anticipated.

"Ill would it become a teacher of the divine art of medicine," said Professor Pietro Baglioni, in answer to a question of Giovanni, "to withhold due and well-considered praise of a physician so eminently skilled as Rappaccini; but, on the other hand, I should answer it but scantily to my conscience were I to permit a worthy youth like yourself, Signor Giovanni, the son of an ancient friend, to imbibe erroneous ideas respecting a man who might hereafter chance to hold your life and death in his hands. The truth is, our worshipful Dr. Rappaccini has as much science as any member of the faculty—with perhaps one single exception—in Padua, or all Italy; but there are certain grave objections to his professional character."

"And what are they?" asked the young man.

"Has my friend Giovanni any disease of body or heart, that he is so inquisitive about physicians?" said the professor, with a smile. "But as for Rappaccini, it is said of him — and I, who know the man well, can answer for its truth — that he cares infinitely more for science than for mankind. His patients are interesting to him only as subjects for some new experiment. He would sacrifice human life, his own among the rest, or whatever else was dearest to him, for the sake of adding so much as a grain of mustard seed to the great heap of his accumulated knowledge."

"Methinks he is an awful man indeed," remarked Guasconti, mentally recalling the cold and purely intellectual aspect of Rappaccini. "And yet, worshipful professor, is it not a noble spirit? Are there many men capable of so spiritual a love of science?"

"God forbid," answered the professor, somewhat testily; "at least, unless they take sounder views of the healing art than those adopted by Rappaccini. It is his theory that all medicinal virtues are comprised within those substances which we term vegetable poisons. These he cultivates with his own hands, and is said even to have produced new varieties of poison, more horribly deleterious than Nature, without the assistance of this learned person, would ever have plagued the world withal. That the signor doctor does less mischief than might be expected with such dangerous substances is undeniable. Now and then, it must be owned, he has effected, or seemed to effect, a marvellous cure; but, to tell you my private mind, Signor Giovanni, he should receive little credit for such instances of success, — they being probably the work of chance, — but should be held strictly accountable for his failures, which may justly be considered his own work."

The youth might have taken Baglioni's opinions with many grains of allowance had he known that there was a professional warfare of long continuance between him and Dr. Rappaccini, in which the latter was generally thought to have gained the advantage. If the reader be inclined to judge for himself, we refer him to certain black-letter tracts on both sides, preserved in the medical department of the University of Padua.

"I know not, most learned professor," returned Giovanni, after musing on what had been said of Rappaccini's exclusive zeal for science, — "I know not how dearly this physician may love his art; but surely there is one object more dear to him. He has a daughter."

"Aha!" cried the professor, with a laugh. "So now our friend Giovanni's secret is out. You have heard of this daughter, whom all the young men in Padua are wild about, though not half a dozen have ever had the good hap to see her face. I know little of the Signora Beatrice save that Rappaccini is said to have instructed her deeply in his science, and that, young and beautiful as fame reports her, she is already qualified to fill a professor's chair. Perchance her father destines her for mine! Other absurd rumors there be, not worth talking about or listening to. So now, Signor Giovanni, drink off your glass of lachryma."

Guasconti returned to his lodgings somewhat heated with the wine he had quaffed, and which caused his brain to swim with strange fantasies in reference to Dr. Rappaccini and the beautiful Beatrice. On his way, happening to pass by a florist's, he bought a fresh bouquet of flowers.

Ascending to his chamber, he seated himself near the window, but within the shadow thrown by the depth of the wall, so that he could look down into the garden with little risk of being discovered. All beneath his eye was a solitude. The strange plants were basking in the sunshine, and now and then nodding gently to one another, as if in acknowledgment of sympathy and kindred. In the midst, by the shattered fountain, grew the magnificent shrub, with its purple gems clustering all over it; they glowed in the air, and gleamed back again out of the depths of the pool, which thus seemed to overflow with colored radiance from the rich reflection that was steeped in it. At first, as we have said, the garden was a solitude. Soon, however, — as Giovanni had half hoped, half feared, would be the case, — a figure appeared beneath the antique sculptured portal, and came down between the rows of plants, inhaling their various perfumes as if she were one of those beings of old classic fable that lived upon sweet odors. On again beholding Beatrice, the young man was even startled to perceive how much her beauty exceeded his recollection of it; so brilliant, so vivid, was its character, that she glowed amid the sunlight, and, as Giovanni whispered to himself, positively illuminated the more shadowy intervals of the garden path. Her face being now more revealed than on the former occasion, he was struck by its expression of simplicity and sweetness, — qualities that had not entered into his idea of her character, and which made him ask anew what manner of mortal she might be. Nor did he fail again to observe, or imagine, an analogy between the beautiful girl and the gorgeous shrub that hung its gemlike flowers over the fountain, — a resemblance which Beatrice seemed to have indulged a fantastic humor in heightening, both by the arrangement of her dress and the selection of its hues.

Approaching the shrub, she threw open her arms, as with a passionate ardor, and drew its branches into an intimate embrace — so intimate that her features were hidden in its leafy bosom and her glistening ringlets all intermingled with the flowers.

"Give me thy breath, my sister," exclaimed Beatrice; "for I am faint with common air. And give me this flower of thine, which I separate with gentlest fingers from the stem and place it close beside my heart."

With these words the beautiful daughter of Rappaccini plucked one of the richest blossoms of the shrub, and was about to fasten it in her bosom. But now, unless Giovanni's draughts of wine had bewildered his senses, a singular incident occurred. A small orange-colored reptile, of the lizard or chameleon species, chanced to be creeping along the path, just at the feet of Beatrice. It appeared to Giovanni, — but, at the distance from which he gazed, he could scarcely have seen anything so minute, — it appeared to him, however, that a drop or two of moisture from the broken stem of the flower descended upon the lizard's head. For an instant the reptile contorted itself violently, and then lay motionless in the sunshine. Beatrice observed this remarkable phenomenon, and crossed herself, sadly, but without surprise; nor did she therefore hesitate to arrange the fatal flower in her bosom. There it blushed, and almost glimmered with the dazzling effect of a precious stone, adding to her dress and aspect the one appropriate charm which nothing else in the world could have supplied. But Giovanni, out of the shadow of his window, bent forward and shrank back, and murmured and trembled.

"Am I awake? Have I my senses?" said he to himself. "What is this being? Beautiful shall I call her, or inexpressibly terrible?"

Beatrice now strayed carelessly through the garden, approaching closer beneath Giovanni's window, so that he was compelled to thrust his head quite out of its concealment in order to gratify the intense and painful curiosity which she excited. At this moment there came a beautiful insect over the garden wall; it had, perhaps, wandered through the city, and found no flowers or verdure among those antique haunts of men until the heavy perfumes of Dr. Rappaccini's shrubs had lured it from afar. Without alighting on the flowers, this winged brightness seemed to be attracted by Beatrice, and lingered in the air and fluttered about her head. Now, here it could not be but that Giovanni Guasconti's eyes deceived him. Be that as it might, he fancied that, while Beatrice was gazing at the insect with childish delight, it grew faint and fell at her feet; its bright wings shivered; it was dead—from no cause that he could discern, unless it were the atmosphere of her breath. Again Beatrice crossed herself and sighed heavily as she bent over the dead insect.

An impulsive movement of Giovanni drew her eyes to the window. There she beheld the beautiful head of the young man—rather a Grecian than an Italian head, with fair, regular features, and a glistening of gold among his ringlets—gazing down upon her like a being that hovered in mid air. Scarcely knowing what he did, Giovanni threw down the bouquet which he had hitherto held in his hand.

"Signora," said he, "there are pure and healthful flowers. Wear them for the sake of Giovanni Guasconti."

"Thanks, signor," replied Beatrice, with her rich voice, that came forth as it were like a gush of music, and with a mirthful expression half childish and half woman-like. "I accept your gift, and would fain recompense it with this precious purple flower; but if I toss it into the air it will not reach you. So Signor Guasconti must even content himself with my thanks."

She lifted the bouquet from the ground, and then, as if inwardly ashamed at having stepped aside from her maidenly reserve to respond to a stranger's greeting, passed swiftly homeward through the garden. But few as the moments were, it seemed to Giovanni, when she was on the point of vanishing beneath the sculptured portal, that his beautiful bouquet was already beginning to wither in her grasp. It was an idle thought; there could be no possibility of distinguishing a faded flower from a fresh one at so great a distance.

For many days after this incident the young man avoided the window that looked into Dr. Rappaccini's garden, as if something ugly and monstrous would have blasted his eyesight had he been betrayed into a glance. He felt conscious of having put himself, to a certain extent, within the influence of an unintelligible power by the communication which he had opened with Beatrice. The wisest course would have been, if his heart were in any real danger, to quit his lodgings and Padua itself at once; the next wiser, to have accustomed himself, as far as possible, to the familiar and daylight view of Beatrice—thus bringing her rigidly and systematically within the limits of ordinary experience. Least of all, while avoiding her sight, ought Giovanni to have remained so near this extraordinary being that the proximity and possibility even of intercourse should give a kind of substance and reality to the wild vagaries which his imagination ran riot continually in producing. Guasconti had not a deep heart—or, at all events, its depths were not sounded now, but he had a quick fancy, and an ardent southern temperament, which rose every instant to a higher fever pitch. Whether or no Beatrice possessed those terrible attributes, that fatal breath, the affinity with those so beautiful and deadly flowers which were indicated by what Giovanni had witnessed, she had at least instilled a fierce and subtle poison into his system. It was not love, although her rich beauty was a madness to him; nor horror, even while he fancied her spirit to be imbued with the same baneful essence that seemed to pervade her physical frame; but a wild offspring of both love and horror that had each parent in it, and burned like one and shivered like the other. Giovanni knew not what to dread; still less did he know what to hope; yet hope and dread kept a continual warfare in his breast, alternately vanquishing one another and starting up afresh to renew the contest. Blessed are all simple emotions, be they dark or bright! It is the lurid intermixture of the two that produces the illuminating blaze of the infernal regions.

Sometimes he endeavored to assuage the fever of his spirit by a rapid walk through the streets of Padua or beyond its gates: his footsteps kept time with the throbbings of his brain, so that the walk was apt to accelerate itself to a race. One day he found himself arrested; his arm was seized by a portly personage, who had turned back on recognizing the young man and expended much breath in overtaking him.

"Signor Giovanni! Stay, my young friend!" cried he. "Have you forgotten me? That might well be the case if I were as much altered as yourself."

It was Baglioni, whom Giovanni had avoided ever since their first meeting, from a doubt that the professor's sagacity would look too deeply into his secrets. Endeavoring to recover himself, he started forth wildly from his inner world into the outer one and spoke like a man in a dream.

"Yes; I am Giovanni Guasconti. You are Professor Pietro Baglioni. Now let me pass!"

"Not yet, not yet, Signor Giovanni Guasconti," said the professor, smiling, but at the same time scrutinizing the youth with an earnest glance. "What! did I grow up side by side with your father? and shall his son pass me like a stranger in these old streets of Padua? Stand still, Signor Giovanni; for we must have a word or two before we part."

"Speedily, then, most worshipful professor, speedily," said Giovanni, with feverish impatience. "Does not your worship see that I am in haste?"

Now, while he was speaking there came a man in black along the street, stooping and moving feebly like a person in inferior health. His face was all overspread with a most sickly and sallow hue, but yet so pervaded with an expression of piercing and active intellect that an observer might easily have overlooked the merely physical attributes and have seen only this wonderful energy. As he passed, this person exchanged a cold and distant salutation with Baglioni, but fixed his eyes upon Giovanni with an intentness that seemed to bring out whatever was within him worthy of notice. Nevertheless, there was a peculiar quietness in the look, as if taking merely a speculative, not a human interest, in the young man.

"It is Dr. Rappaccini!" whispered the professor when the stranger had passed. "Has he ever seen your face before?"

"Not that I know," answered Giovanni, starting at the name.

"He *has* seen you! he must have seen you!" said Baglioni, hastily. "For some purpose or other, this man of science is making a study of you. I know that look of his! It is the same that coldly illuminates his face as he bends over a bird, a mouse, or a butterfly, which, in pursuance of some experiment, he has killed by the perfume of a flower; a look as deep as Nature itself, but without Nature's warmth of love. Signor Giovanni, I will stake my life upon it, you are the subject of one of Rappaccini's experiments!"

"Will you make a fool of me?" cried Giovanni, passionately. "*That*, signor professor, were an untoward experiment."

"Patience! patience!" replied the imperturbable professor. "I tell thee, my poor Giovanni, that Rappaccini has a scientific interest in thee. Thou hast fallen into fearful hands! And the Signora Beatrice, —what part does she act in this mystery?"

But Guasconti, finding Baglioni's pertinacity intolerable, here broke away, and was gone before the professor could again seize his arm. He looked after the young man intently and shook his head.

"This must not be," said Baglioni to himself. "The youth is the son of my old friend, and shall not come to any harm from which the arcana of medical science can preserve him. Besides, it is too insufferable an impertinence in Rappaccini, thus to snatch the lad out of my own hands, as I may say, and make use of him for his infernal experiments. This daughter of his! It shall be looked to. Perchance, most learned Rappaccini, I may foil you where you little dream of it!"

Meanwhile Giovanni had pursued a circuitous route, and at length found himself at the door of his lodgings. As he crossed the threshold he was met by old Lisabetta, who smirked and smiled, and was evidently desirous to attract his attention; vainly, however, as the ebullition of his feelings had momentarily subsided into a cold and dull vacuity. He turned his eyes full upon the withered face that was puckering itself into a smile, but seemed to behold it not. The old dame, therefore, laid her grasp upon his cloak.

"Signor! signor!" whispered she, still with a smile over the whole breadth of her visage, so that it looked not unlike a grotesque carving in wood, darkened by centuries. "Listen, signor! There is a private entrance into the garden!"

"What do you say?" exclaimed Giovanni, turning quickly about, as if an inanimate thing should start into feverish life. "A private entrance into Dr. Rappaccini's garden?"

"Hush! hush! not so loud!" whispered Lisabetta, putting her hand over his mouth. "Yes; into the worshipful doctor's garden, where you may see all his fine shrubbery. Many a young man in Padua would give gold to be admitted among those flowers."

Giovanni put a piece of gold into her hand.

"Show me the way," said he.

A surmise, probably excited by his conversation with Baglioni, crossed his mind, that this interposition of old Lisabetta might perchance be connected with the intrigue, whatever were its nature, in which the professor seemed to suppose that Dr. Rappaccini was involving him. But such a suspicion, though it disturbed Giovanni, was inadequate to restrain him. The instant that he was aware of the possibility of approaching Beatrice, it seemed an absolute necessity of his existence to do so. It mattered not whether she were angel or demon; he was irrevocably within her sphere, and must obey the law that whirled him onward, in ever-lessening circles, towards a result which he did not attempt to foreshadow; and yet, strange to say, there came across him a sudden doubt whether this intense interest on his part were not delusory; whether it were really of so deep and positive a nature as to justify him in now thrusting himself into an incalculable position; whether it were not merely the fantasy of a young man's brain, only slightly or not at all connected with his heart.

He paused, hesitated, turned half about, but again went on. His withered guide led him along several obscure passages, and finally undid a door, through which, as it was opened, there came the sight and sound of rustling leaves, with the broken sunshine glimmering among them. Giovanni stepped forth, and, forcing himself through the entanglement of a shrub that wreathed its tendrils over the hidden entrance, stood beneath his own window in the open area of Dr. Rappaccini's garden.

How often is it the case that, when impossibilities have come to pass and dreams have condensed their misty substance into tangible realities, we find ourselves calm, and even coldly self-possessed, amid circumstances which it would have been a delirium of joy or agony to anticipate! Fate delights to thwart us thus. Passion will choose his own time to rush upon the scene, and lingers sluggishly behind when an appropriate adjustment of events would seem to summon his appearance. So was it now with Giovanni. Day after day his pulses had throbbed with feverish blood at the improbable idea of an interview with Beatrice, and of standing with her, face to face, in this very garden, basking in the Oriental sunshine of her beauty, and snatching from her full gaze the mystery which he deemed the riddle of his own existence. But now there was a singular and untimely equanimity within its breast. He threw a glance around the garden to discover if Beatrice or her father were present, and, perceiving that he was alone, began a critical observation of the plants.

The aspect of one and all of them dissatisfied him; their gorgeousness seemed fierce, passionate, and even unnatural. There was hardly an individual shrub which a wanderer, straying by himself through a forest, would not have been startled to find growing wild, as if an unearthly face had glared at him out of the thicket. Several also would have shocked a delicate instinct by an appearance of artificialness indicating that there had been such commixture, and, as it were, adultery, of various vegetable species, that the production was no longer of God's making, but the monstrous offspring of man's depraved fancy, glowing with only an evil mockery of beauty. They were probably the result of experiment, which in one or two cases had succeeded in mingling plants individually lovely into a compound possessing the questionable and ominous character that distinguished the whole growth of the garden. In fine, Giovanni recognized but two or three plants in the collection, and those of a kind that he well knew to be poisonous. While busy with these contemplations he heard the rustling of a silken garment, and, turning, beheld Beatrice emerging from beneath the sculptured portal.

Giovanni had not considered with himself what should be his deportment; whether he should apologize for his intrusion into the garden, or assume that he was there with the privity at least, if not by the desire, of Dr. Rappaccini or his daughter; but Beatrice's manner placed him at his ease, though leaving him still in doubt by what agency he had gained admittance. She came lightly along the path and met him near the broken fountain. There was surprise in her face, but brightened by a simple and kind expression of pleasure.

"You are a connoisseur in flowers, signor," said Beatrice, with a smile, alluding to the bouquet which he had flung her from the window. "It is no marvel, therefore, if the sight of my father's rare collection has tempted you to take a nearer view. If he were here, he could tell you many strange and interesting facts as to the nature and habits of these shrubs; for he has spent a lifetime in such studies, and this garden is his world."

"And yourself, lady," observed Giovanni, "if fame says true, — you likewise are deeply skilled in the virtues indicated by these rich blossoms and these spicy perfumes. Would you deign to be my instructress, I should prove an apter scholar than if taught by Signor Rappaccini himself."

"Are there such idle rumors?" asked Beatrice, with the music of a pleasant laugh. "Do people say that I am skilled in my father's science of plants? What a jest is there! No; though I have grown up among these flowers, I know no more of them than their hues and perfume; and sometimes methinks I would fain rid myself of even that small knowledge. There are many flowers here, and those not the least brilliant, that shock and offend me when they meet my eye. But pray, signor, do not believe these stories about my science. Believe nothing of me save what you see with your own eyes."

"And must I believe all that I have seen with my own eyes?" asked Giovanni, pointedly, while the recollection of former scenes made him shrink. "No, signora; you demand too little of me. Bid me believe nothing save what comes from your own lips."

It would appear that Beatrice understood him. There came a deep flush to her cheek; but she looked full into Giovanni's eyes, and responded to his gaze of uneasy suspicion with a queenlike haughtiness.

"I do so bid you, signor," she replied. "Forget whatever you may have fancied in regard to me. If true to the outward senses, still it may be false in its essence; but the words of Beatrice Rappaccini's lips are true from the depths of the heart outward. Those you may believe."

A fervor glowed in her whole aspect and beamed upon Giovanni's consciousness like the light of truth itself; but while she spoke there was a fragrance in the atmosphere around her, rich and delightful, though evanescent, yet which the young man, from an indefinable reluctance, scarcely dared to draw into his lungs. It might be the odor of the flowers. Could it be Beatrice's breath which thus embalmed her words with a strange richness, as if by steeping them in her heart? A faintness passed like a shadow over Giovanni and flitted away; he seemed to gaze through the beautiful girl's eyes into her transparent soul, and felt no more doubt or fear.

The tinge of passion that had colored Beatrice's manner vanished; she became gay, and appeared to derive a pure delight from her communion with the youth not unlike what the maiden of a lonely island might have felt conversing with a voyager from the civilized world. Evidently her experience of life had been confined within the limits of that garden. She talked now about matters as simple as the daylight or summer clouds, and now asked questions in reference to the city, or Giovanni's distant home, his friends, his mother, and his sisters—

questions indicating such seclusion, and such lack of familiarity with modes and forms, that Giovanni responded as if to an infant. Her spirit gushed out before him like a fresh rill that was just catching its first glimpse of the sunlight and wondering at the reflections of earth and sky which were flung into its bosom. There came thoughts, too, from a deep source, and fantasies of a gemlike brilliancy, as if diamonds and rubies sparkled upward among the bubbles of the fountain. Ever and anon there gleamed across the young man's mind a sense of wonder that he should be walking side by side with the being who had so wrought upon his imagination, whom he had idealized in such hues of terror, in whom he had positively witnessed such manifestations of dreadful attributes, — that he should be conversing with Beatrice like a brother, and should find her so human and so maidenlike. But such reflections were only momentary; the effect of her character was too real not to make itself familiar at once.

In this free intercourse they had strayed through the garden, and now, after many turns among its avenues, were come to the shattered fountain, beside which grew the magnificent shrub, with its treasury of glowing blossoms. A fragrance was diffused from it which Giovanni recognized as identical with that which he had attributed to Beatrice's breath, but incomparably more powerful. As her eyes fell upon it, Giovanni beheld her press her hand to her bosom as if her heart were throbbing suddenly and painfully.

"For the first time in my life," murmured she, addressing the shrub, "I had forgotten thee."

"I remember, signora," said Giovanni, "that you once promised to reward me with one of these living gems for the bouquet which I had the happy boldness to fling to your feet. Permit me now to pluck it as a memorial of this interview."

He made a step towards the shrub with extended hand; but Beatrice darted forward, uttering a shriek that went through his heart like a dagger. She caught his hand and drew it back with the whole force of her slender figure. Giovanni felt her touch thrilling through his fibres.

"Touch it not!" exclaimed she, in a voice of agony. "Not for thy life! It is fatal!"

Then, hiding her face, she fled from him and vanished beneath the sculptured portal. As Giovanni followed her with his eyes, he beheld the emaciated figure and pale intelligence of Dr. Rappaccini, who had been watching the scene, he knew not how long, within the shadow of the entrance.

No sooner was Guasconti alone in his chamber than the image of Beatrice came back to his passionate musings, invested with all the witchery that had been gathering around it ever since his first glimpse of her, and now likewise imbued with a tender warmth of girlish womanhood. She was human; her nature was endowed with all gentle and feminine qualities; she was worthiest to be worshipped; she was capable, surely, on her part, of the height and heroism of love. Those tokens which he had hitherto considered as proofs of a frightful peculiarity in her physical and moral system were now either forgotten, or, by the subtle sophistry of passion transmitted into a golden crown of enchantment, rendering Beatrice the more admirable by so much as she was the more unique. Whatever had looked ugly was now beautiful; or, if incapable of such a change, it stole away and hid itself among those shapeless half ideas which throng the dim region beyond the daylight of our perfect consciousness. Thus did he spend the night, nor fell asleep until the dawn had begun to awake the slumbering flowers in Dr. Rappaccini's garden, whither Giovanni's dreams doubtless led him. Up rose the sun in his due season, and, flinging his beams upon the young man's eyelids, awoke him to a sense of pain. When thoroughly aroused, he became sensible of a burning and tingling agony in his hand—in his right hand—the very hand which Beatrice had grasped in her own when he was on the point of plucking one of the gemlike flowers. On the back of that hand there was now a purple print like that of four small fingers, and the likeness of a slender thumb upon his wrist.

Oh, how stubbornly does love,—or even that cunning semblance of love which flourishes in the imagination, but strikes no depth of root into the heart,—how stubbornly does it hold its faith until the moment comes when it is doomed to vanish into thin mist! Giovanni wrapped a handkerchief about his hand and wondered what evil thing had stung him, and soon forgot his pain in a reverie of Beatrice.

After the first interview, a second was in the inevitable course of what we call fate. A third; a fourth; and a meeting with Beatrice in the garden was no longer an incident in Giovanni's daily life, but the whole space in which he might be said to live; for the anticipation and memory of that ecstatic hour made up the remainder. Nor was it otherwise with the daughter of Rappaccini. She watched for the youth's appearance, and flew to his side with confidence as unreserved as if they had been playmates from early infancy—as if they were such playmates still. If, by any unwonted chance, he failed to come at the appointed moment, she stood beneath the window and sent up the rich sweetness of her tones to float around him in his chamber and echo and reverberate throughout his heart: "Giovanni! Giovanni! Why tarriest thou? Come down!" And down he hastened into that Eden of poisonous flowers.

But, with all this intimate familiarity, there was still a reserve in Beatrice's demeanor, so rigidly and invariably sustained that the idea of infringing it scarcely occurred to his imagination. By all appreciable signs, they loved; they had looked love with eyes that conveyed the holy secret from the depths of one soul into the depths of the other, as if it were too sacred to be whispered by the way; they had even spoken love in those gushes of passion when their spirits darted forth in articulated breath like tongues of long-hidden flame; and yet there had been no seal of lips, no clasp of hands, nor any slightest caress such as love claims and hallows. He had never touched one of the gleaming ringlets of her hair; her garment—so marked was the physical barrier between them—had never been waved against him by a breeze. On the few occasions when Giovanni had seemed tempted to overstep the limit, Beatrice grew so sad, so stern, and withal wore such a look of desolate separation, shuddering at itself, that not a spoken word was requisite to repel him. At such times he was startled at the horrible suspicions that rose, monster-like, out of the caverns of his heart and stared him in the face; his love grew thin and faint as the morning mist, his doubts alone had substance. But, when Beatrice's face brightened again after the momentary shadow, she was transformed at once from the mysterious, questionable being whom he had watched with so much awe and horror; she was now the beautiful and unsophisticated girl whom he felt that his spirit knew with a certainty beyond all other knowledge.

A considerable time had now passed since Giovanni's last meeting with Baglioni. One morning, however, he was disagreeably surprised by a visit from the professor, whom he had scarcely thought of for whole weeks, and would willingly have forgotten still longer. Given up as he had long been to a pervading excitement, he could tolerate no companions except upon condition of their perfect sympathy with his present state of feeling. Such sympathy was not to be expected from Professor Baglioni.

The visitor chatted carelessly for a few moments about the gossip of the city and the university, and then took up another topic.

"I have been reading an old classic author lately," said he, "and met with a story that strangely interested me. Possibly you may remember it. It is of an Indian prince, who sent a beautiful woman as a present to Alexander the Great. She was as lovely as the dawn and gorgeous as the sunset; but what especially distinguished her was a certain rich perfume in her breath — richer than a garden of Persian roses. Alexander, as was natural to a youthful conqueror, fell in love at first sight with this magnificent stranger; but a certain sage physician, happening to be present, discovered a terrible secret in regard to her."

"And what was that?" asked Giovanni, turning his eyes downward to avoid those of the professor.

"That this lovely woman," continued Baglioni, with emphasis, "had been nourished with poisons from her birth upward, until her whole nature was so imbued with them that she herself had become the deadliest poison in existence. Poison was her element of life. With that rich perfume of her breath she blasted the very air. Her love would have been poison — her embrace death. Is not this a marvellous tale?"

"A childish fable," answered Giovanni, nervously starting from his chair. "I marvel how your worship finds time to read such nonsense among your graver studies."

"By the by," said the professor, looking uneasily about him, "what singular fragrance is this in your apartment? Is it the perfume of your gloves? It is faint, but delicious; and yet, after all, by no means agreeable. Were I to breathe it long, methinks it would make me ill. It is like the breath of a flower; but I see no flowers in the chamber."

"Nor are there any," replied Giovanni, who had turned pale as the professor spoke; "nor, I think, is there any fragrance except in your worship's imagination. Odors, being a sort of element combined of the sensual and the spiritual, are apt to deceive us in this manner. The recollection of a perfume, the bare idea of it, may easily be mistaken for a present reality."

"Ay; but my sober imagination does not often play such tricks," said Baglioni; "and, were I to fancy any kind of odor, it would be that of some vile apothecary drug, wherewith my fingers are likely enough to be imbued. Our worshipful friend Rappaccini, as I have heard, tinctures his medicaments with odors richer than those of Araby. Doubtless, likewise, the fair and learned Signora Beatrice would minister to her patients with draughts as sweet as a maiden's breath; but woe to him that sips them!"

Giovanni's face evinced many contending emotions. The tone in which the professor alluded to the pure and lovely daughter of Rappaccini was a torture to his soul; and yet the intimation of a view of her character, opposite to his own, gave instantaneous distinctness to a thousand dim suspicions, which now grinned at him like so many demons. But he strove hard to quell them and to respond to Baglioni with a true lover's perfect faith.

"Signor professor," said he, "you were my father's friend; perchance, too, it is your purpose to act a friendly part towards his son. I would fain feel nothing towards you save respect and deference; but I pray you to observe, signor, that there is one subject on which we must not speak. You know not the Signora Beatrice. You cannot, therefore, estimate the wrong—the blasphemy, I may even say—that is offered to her character by a light or injurious word."

"Giovanni! my poor Giovanni!" answered the professor, with a calm expression of pity, "I know this wretched girl far better than yourself. You shall hear the truth in respect to the poisoner Rappaccini and his poisonous daughter; yes, poisonous as she is beautiful. Listen; for, even should you do violence to my gray hairs, it shall not silence me. That old fable of the Indian woman has become a truth by the deep and deadly science of Rappaccini and in the person of the lovely Beatrice."

Giovanni groaned and hid his face.

"Her father," continued Baglioni, "was not restrained by natural affection from offering up his child in this horrible manner as the victim of his insane zeal for science; for, let us do him justice, he is as true a man of science as ever distilled his own heart in an alembic. What, then, will be your fate? Beyond a doubt you are selected as the material of some new experiment. Perhaps the result is to be death; perhaps a fate more awful still. Rappaccini, with what he calls the interest of science before his eyes, will hesitate at nothing."

"It is a dream," muttered Giovanni to himself; "surely it is a dream."

"But," resumed the professor, "be of good cheer, son of my friend. It is not yet too late for the rescue. Possibly we may even succeed in bringing back this miserable child within the limits of ordinary nature, from which her father's madness has estranged her. Behold this little silver vase! It was wrought by the hands of the renowned Benvenuto Cellini, and is well worthy to be a love gift to the fairest dame in Italy. But its contents are invaluable. One little sip of this antidote would have rendered the most virulent poisons of the Borgias innocuous. Doubt not that it will be as efficacious against those of Rappaccini. Bestow the vase, and the precious liquid within it, on your Beatrice, and hopefully await the result."

Baglioni laid a small, exquisitely wrought silver vial on the table and withdrew, leaving what he had said to produce its effect upon the young man's mind.

"We will thwart Rappaccini yet," thought he, chuckling to himself, as he descended the stairs; "but, let us confess the truth of him, he is a wonderful man—a wonderful man indeed; a vile empiric, however, in his practice, and therefore not to be tolerated by those who respect the good old rules of the medical profession."

Throughout Giovanni's whole acquaintance with Beatrice, he had occasionally, as we have said, been haunted by dark surmises as to her character; yet so thoroughly had she made herself felt by him as a simple, natural, most affectionate, and guileless creature, that the image now held up by Professor Baglioni looked as strange and incredible as if it were not in accordance with his own original conception. True, there were ugly recollections connected with his first glimpses of the beautiful girl; he could not quite forget the bouquet that withered in her grasp, and the insect that perished amid the sunny air, by no ostensible agency save the fragrance of her breath. These incidents, however, dissolving in the pure light of her character, had no longer the efficacy of facts, but were acknowledged as mistaken fantasies, by whatever testimony of the senses they might appear to be substantiated. There is something truer and more real than what we can see with the eyes and touch with the finger. On such better evidence had Giovanni founded his confidence in Beatrice, though rather by the necessary force of her high attributes than by any deep and generous faith on his part. But now his spirit was incapable of sustaining itself at the height to which the early enthusiasm of passion had exalted it; he fell down, grovelling among earthly doubts, and defiled therewith the pure whiteness of Beatrice's image. Not that he gave her up; he did but distrust. He resolved to institute some decisive test that should satisfy him, once for all, whether there were those dreadful peculiarities in her physical nature which could not be supposed to exist without some corresponding monstrosity of soul. His eyes, gazing down afar, might have deceived him as to the lizard, the insect, and the flowers; but if he could witness, at the distance of a few paces, the sudden blight of one fresh and healthful flower in Beatrice's hand, there would be room for no further question. With this idea he hastened to the florist's and purchased a bouquet that was still gemmed with the morning dew-drops.

It was now the customary hour of his daily interview with Beatrice. Before descending into the garden, Giovanni failed not to look at his figure in the mirror, — a vanity to be expected in a beautiful young man, yet, as displaying itself at that troubled and feverish moment, the token of a certain shallowness of feeling and insincerity of character. He did gaze, however, and said to himself that his features had never before possessed so rich a grace, nor his eyes such vivacity, nor his cheeks so warm a hue of superabundant life.

"At least," thought he, "her poison has not yet insinuated itself into my system. I am no flower to perish in her grasp."

With that thought he turned his eyes on the bouquet, which he had never once laid aside from his hand. A thrill of indefinable horror shot through his frame on perceiving that those dewy flowers were already beginning to droop; they wore the aspect of things that had been fresh and lovely yesterday. Giovanni grew white as marble, and stood motionless before the mirror, staring at his own reflection there as at the likeness of something frightful. He remembered Baglioni's remark about the fragrance that seemed to pervade the chamber. It must have been the poison in his breath! Then he shuddered — shuddered at himself. Recovering from his stupor, he began to watch with curious eye a spider that was busily at work hanging its web from the antique cornice of the apartment, crossing and recrossing the artful system of interwoven lines — as vigorous and active a spider as ever dangled from an old ceiling. Giovanni bent towards the insect, and emitted a deep, long breath. The spider suddenly ceased its toil; the web vibrated with a tremor originating in the body of the small artisan. Again Giovanni sent forth a breath, deeper, longer, and imbued with a venomous feeling out of his heart: he knew not whether he were wicked, or only desperate. The spider made a convulsive grip with his limbs and hung dead across the window.

"Accursed! accursed!" muttered Giovanni, addressing himself. "Hast thou grown so poisonous that this deadly insect perishes by thy breath?"

At that moment a rich, sweet voice came floating up from the garden.

"Giovanni! Giovanni! It is past the hour! Why tarriest thou? Come down!"

"Yes," muttered Giovanni again. "She is the only being whom my breath may not slay! Would that it might!"

He rushed down, and in an instant was standing before the bright and loving eyes of Beatrice. A moment ago his wrath and despair had been so fierce that he could have desired nothing so much as to wither her by a glance; but with her actual presence there came influences which had too real an existence to be at once shaken off: recollections of the delicate and benign power of her feminine nature, which had so often enveloped him in a religious calm; recollections of many a holy and passionate outgush of her heart, when the pure fountain had been unsealed from its depths and made visible in its transparency to his mental eye; recollections which, had Giovanni known how to estimate them, would have assured him that all this ugly mystery was but an earthly illusion, and that, whatever mist of evil might seem to have gathered over her, the real Beatrice was a heavenly angel. Incapable as he was of such high faith, still her presence had not utterly lost its magic. Giovanni's rage was quelled into an aspect of sullen insensibility. Beatrice, with a quick spiritual sense, immediately felt that there was a gulf of blackness between them which neither he nor she could pass. They walked on together, sad and silent, and came thus to the marble fountain and to its pool of water on the ground, in the midst of which grew the shrub that bore gem-like blossoms. Giovanni was affrighted at the eager enjoyment—the appetite, as it were—with which he found himself inhaling the fragrance of the flowers.

"Beatrice," asked he, abruptly, "whence came this shrub?"

"My father created it," answered she, with simplicity.

"Created it! created it!" repeated Giovanni. "What mean you, Beatrice?"

"He is a man fearfully acquainted with the secrets of Nature," replied Beatrice; "and, at the hour when I first drew breath, this plant sprang from the soil, the offspring of his science, of his intellect, while I was but his earthly child. Approach it not!" continued she, observing with terror that Giovanni was drawing nearer to the shrub. "It has qualities that you little dream of. But I, dearest Giovanni,—I grew up and blossomed with the plant and was nourished with its breath. It was my sister, and I loved it with a human affection; for, alas!—hast thou not suspected it?—there was an awful doom."

Here Giovanni frowned so darkly upon her that Beatrice paused and trembled. But her faith in his tenderness reassured her, and made her blush that she had doubted for an instant.

"There was an awful doom," she continued, "the effect of my father's fatal love of science, which estranged me from all society of my kind. Until Heaven sent thee, dearest Giovanni, oh, how lonely was thy poor Beatrice!"

"Was it a hard doom?" asked Giovanni, fixing his eyes upon her.

"Only of late have I known how hard it was," answered she, tenderly. "Oh, yes; but my heart was torpid, and therefore quiet."

Giovanni's rage broke forth from his sullen gloom like a lightning flash out of a dark cloud.

"Accursed one!" cried he, with venomous scorn and anger. "And, finding thy solitude wearisome, thou hast severed me likewise from all the warmth of life and enticed me into thy region of unspeakable horror!"

"Giovanni!" exclaimed Beatrice, turning her large bright eyes upon his face. The force of his words had not found its way into her mind; she was merely thunderstruck.

"Yes, poisonous thing!" repeated Giovanni, beside himself with passion. "Thou hast done it! Thou hast blasted me! Thou hast filled my veins with poison! Thou hast made me as hateful, as ugly, as loathsome and deadly a creature as thyself—a world's wonder of hideous monstrosity! Now, if our breath be happily as fatal to ourselves as to all others, let us join our lips in one kiss of unutterable hatred, and so die!"

"What has befallen me?" murmured Beatrice, with a low moan out of her heart. "Holy Virgin, pity me, a poor heart-broken child!"

"Thou,—dost thou pray?" cried Giovanni, still with the same fiendish scorn. "Thy very prayers, as they come from thy lips, taint the atmosphere with death. Yes, yes; let us pray! Let us to church and dip our fingers in the holy water at the portal! They that come after us will perish as by a pestilence! Let us sign crosses in the air! It will be scattering curses abroad in the likeness of holy symbols!"

"Giovanni," said Beatrice, calmly, for her grief was beyond passion, "why dost thou join thyself with me thus in those terrible words? I, it is true, am the horrible thing thou namest me. But thou,—what hast thou to do, save with one other shudder at my hideous misery to go forth out of the garden and mingle with thy race, and forget there ever crawled on earth such a monster as poor Beatrice?"

"Dost thou pretend ignorance?" asked Giovanni, scowling upon her. "Behold! this power have I gained from the pure daughter of Rappaccini."

There was a swarm of summer insects flitting through the air in search of the food promised by the flower odors of the fatal garden. They circled round Giovanni's head, and were evidently attracted towards him by the same influence which had drawn them for an instant within the sphere of several of the shrubs. He sent forth a breath among them, and smiled bitterly at Beatrice as at least a score of the insects fell dead upon the ground.

"I see it! I see it!" shrieked Beatrice. "It is my father's fatal science! No, no, Giovanni; it was not I! Never! never! I dreamed only to love thee and be with thee a little time, and so to let thee pass away, leaving but thine image in mine heart; for, Giovanni, believe it, though my body be nourished with poison, my spirit is God's creature, and craves love as its daily food. But my father,—he has united us in this fearful sympathy. Yes; spurn me, tread upon me, kill me! Oh, what is death after such words as thine? But it was not I. Not for a world of bliss would I have done it."

Giovanni's passion had exhausted itself in its outburst from his lips. There now came across him a sense, mournful, and not without tenderness, of the intimate and peculiar relationship between Beatrice and himself. They stood, as it were, in an utter solitude, which would be made none the less solitary by the densest throng of human life. Ought not, then, the desert of humanity around them to press this insulated pair closer together? If they should be cruel to one another, who was there to be kind to them? Besides, thought Giovanni, might there not still be a hope of his returning within the limits of ordinary nature, and leading Beatrice, the redeemed Beatrice, by the hand? O, weak, and selfish, and unworthy spirit, that could dream of an earthly union and earthly happiness as possible, after such deep love had been so bitterly wronged as was Beatrice's love by Giovanni's blighting words! No, no; there could be no such hope. She must pass heavily, with that broken heart, across the borders of Time — she must bathe her hurts in some fount of paradise, and forget her grief in the light of immortality, and *there* be well.

But Giovanni did not know it.

"Dear Beatrice," said he, approaching her, while she shrank away as always at his approach, but now with a different impulse, "dearest Beatrice our fate is not yet so desperate. Behold! there is a medicine, potent, as a wise physician has assured me, and almost divine in its efficacy. It is composed of ingredients the most opposite to those by which thy awful father has brought this calamity upon thee and me. It is distilled of blessed herbs. Shall we not quaff it together, and thus be purified from evil?"

"Give it me!" said Beatrice, extending her hand to receive the little silver vial which Giovanni took from his bosom. She added, with a peculiar emphasis, "I will drink; but do thou await the result."

She put Baglioni's antidote to her lips; and, at the same moment, the figure of Rappaccini emerged from the portal and came slowly towards the marble fountain. As he drew near, the pale man of science seemed to gaze with a triumphant expression at the beautiful youth and maiden, as might an artist who should spend his life in achieving a picture or a group of statuary and finally be satisfied with his success. He paused; his bent form grew erect with conscious power; he spread out his hands over them in the attitude of a father imploring a blessing upon his children; but those were the same hands that had thrown poison into the stream of their lives. Giovanni trembled. Beatrice shuddered nervously, and pressed her hand upon her heart.

"My daughter," said Rappaccini, "thou art no longer lonely in the world. Pluck one of those precious gems from thy sister shrub and bid thy bridegroom wear it in his bosom. It will not harm him now. My science and the sympathy between thee and him have so wrought within his system that he now stands apart from common men, as thou dost, daughter of my pride and triumph, from ordinary women. Pass on, then, through the world, most dear to one another and dreadful to all besides!"

"My father," said Beatrice, feebly, — and still as she spoke she kept her hand upon her heart, — "wherefore didst thou inflict this miserable doom upon thy child?"

"Miserable!" exclaimed Rappaccini. "What mean you, foolish girl? Dost thou deem it misery to be endowed with marvellous gifts against which no power nor strength could avail an enemy — misery, to be able to quell the mightiest with a breath — misery, to be as terrible as thou art beautiful? Wouldst thou, then, have preferred the condition of a weak woman, exposed to all evil and capable of none?"

"I would fain have been loved, not feared," murmured Beatrice, sinking down upon the ground. "But now it matters not. I am going, father, where the evil which thou hast striven to mingle with my being will pass away like a dream—like the fragrance of these poisonous flowers, which will no longer taint my breath among the flowers of Eden. Farewell, Giovanni! Thy words of hatred are like lead within my heart; but they, too, will fall away as I ascend. Oh, was there not, from the first, more poison in thy nature than in mine?"

To Beatrice,—so radically had her earthly part been wrought upon by Rappaccini's skill,—as poison had been life, so the powerful antidote was death; and thus the poor victim of man's ingenuity and of thwarted nature, and of the fatality that attends all such efforts of perverted wisdom, perished there, at the feet of her father and Giovanni. Just at that moment Professor Pietro Baglioni looked forth from the window, and called loudly, in a tone of triumph mixed with horror, to the thunderstricken man of science,—

"Rappaccini! Rappaccini! and is *this* the upshot of your experiment!"

[1844]

Study and Writing Questions

1. What does Beatrice mean when she asks, "'Was there not, from the first, more poison in thy nature than in mine?'" Is she right?
2. Why is the STORY so full of IMAGES of eyes and of seeing?
3. In the Bible, in Matthew 13:31-32, Jesus says that "The kingdom of heaven is like unto a grain of mustard seed, which a man took, and sowed in his field: which indeed is the least of all seeds: but when it is grown, it is the greatest among herbs, and becometh a tree, so that the birds of the air come and lodge in the branches thereof." How does this reference affect your understanding of Baglioni's assertion that Rappaccini would "sacrifice human life . . . for the sake of adding so much as a grain of mustard seed to the great heap of his accumulated knowledge"?
4. Why does Hawthorne give the last line to Baglioni? In what ways(s) is this NARRATIVE resolved?
5. What is the role of science in this story?

See also Questions for Contrast and Comparison: 4, 24, 27, 29, 30, 71, 99, 116, 128, 148, 217, and 222.

Young Goodman Brown

YOUNG Goodman Brown came forth at sunset into the street at Salem village; but put his head back, after crossing the threshold, to exchange a parting kiss with his young wife. And Faith, as the wife was aptly named, thrust her own pretty head into the street, letting the wind play with the pink ribbons of her cap while she called to Goodman Brown.

"Dearest heart," whispered she, softly and rather sadly, when her lips were close to his ear, "prithee put off your journey until sunrise and sleep in your own bed to-night. A lone woman is troubled with such dreams and such thoughts that she's afeard of herself sometimes. Pray tarry with me this night, dear husband, of all nights in the year."

"My love and my Faith," replied young Goodman Brown, "of all nights in the year, this one night must I tarry away from thee. My journey, as thou callest it, forth and back again, must needs be done 'twixt now and sunrise. What, my sweet, pretty wife, dost thou doubt me already, and we but three months married?"

"Then God bless you!" said Faith, with the pink ribbons; "and may you find all well when you come back."

"Amen!" cried Goodman Brown. "Say thy prayers, dear Faith, and go to bed at dusk, and no harm will come to thee."

So they parted; and the young man pursued his way until, being about to turn the corner by the meeting-house, he looked back and saw the head of Faith still peeping after him with a melancholy air, in spite of her pink ribbons.

"Poor little Faith!" thought he, for his heart smote him. "What a wretch am I to leave her on such an errand! She talks of dreams, too. Methought as she spoke there was trouble in her face, as if a dream had warned her what work is to be done tonight. But no, no; 't would kill her to think it. Well, she's a blessed angel on earth; and after this one night I'll cling to her skirts and follow her to heaven."

With this excellent resolve for the future, Goodman Brown felt himself justified in making more haste on his present evil purpose. He had taken a dreary road, darkened by all the gloomiest trees of the forest, which barely stood aside to let the narrow path creep through, and closed immediately behind. It was all as lonely as could be; and there is this peculiarity in such a solitude, that the traveller knows not who may be concealed by the innumerable trunks and the thick boughs overhead; so that with lonely footsteps he may yet be passing through an unseen multitude.

"There may be a devilish Indian behind every tree," said Goodman Brown to himself; and he glanced fearfully behind him as he added, "What if the devil himself should be at my very elbow!"

His head being turned back, he passed a crook of the road, and, looking forward again, beheld the figure of a man, in grave and decent attire, seated at the foot of an old tree. He arose at Goodman Brown's approach and walked onward side by side with him.

"You are late, Goodman Brown," said he. "The clock of the Old South was striking as I came through Boston, and that is full fifteen minutes agone."

"Faith kept me back a while," replied the young man, with a tremor in his voice, caused by the sudden appearance of his companion, though not wholly unexpected.

It was now deep dusk in the forest, and deepest in that part of it where these two were journeying. As nearly as could be discerned, the second traveller was about fifty years old, apparently in the same rank of life as Goodman Brown, and bearing a considerable resemblance to him, though perhaps more in expression than features. Still they might have been taken for father and son. And yet, though the elder person was as simply clad as the younger, and as simple in manner too, he had an indescribable air of one who knew the world, and who would not have felt abashed at the governor's dinner table or in King William's court, were it possible that his affairs should call him thither. But the only thing about him that could be fixed upon as remarkable was his staff, which bore the likeness of a great black snake, so curiously wrought that it might almost be seen to twist and wriggle itself like a living serpent. This, of course, must have been an ocular deception, assisted by the uncertain light.

"Come, Goodman Brown," cried his fellow-traveller, "this is a dull pace for the beginning of a journey. Take my staff, if you are so soon weary."

"Friend," said the other, exchanging his slow pace for a full stop, "having kept covenant by meeting thee here, it is my purpose now to return whence I came. I have scruples touching the matter thou wot'st of."

"Sayest thou so?" replied he of the serpent, smiling apart. "Let us walk on, nevertheless, reasoning as we go; and if I convince thee not thou shalt turn back. We are but a little way in the forest yet."

"Too far! too far!" exclaimed the goodman, unconsciously resuming his walk. "My father never went into the woods on such an errand, nor his father before him. We have been a race of honest men and good Christians since the days of the martyrs; and shall I be the first of the name of Brown that ever took this path and kept" —

"Such company, thou wouldst say," observed the elder person, interpreting his pause. "Well said, Goodman Brown! I have been as well acquainted with your family as with ever a one among the Puritans; and that's no trifle to say. I helped your grandfather, the constable, when he lashed the Quaker woman so smartly through the streets of Salem; and it was I that brought your father a pitch-pine knot, kindled at my own hearth, to set fire to an Indian village, in King Philip's war. They were my good friends, both; and many a pleasant walk have we had along this path, and returned merrily after midnight. I would fain be friends with you for their sake."

"If it be as thou sayest," replied Goodman Brown, "I marvel they never spoke of these matters; or, verily, I marvel not, seeing that the least rumor of the sort would have driven them from New England. We are a people of prayer, and good works to boot, and abide no such wickedness."

"Wickedness or not," said the traveller with the twisted staff, "I have a very general acquaintance here in New England. The deacons of many a church have drunk the communion wine with me; the selectmen of divers towns make me their chairman; and a majority of the Great and General Court are firm supporters of my interest. The governor and I, too — But these are state secrets."

"Can this be so?" cried Goodman Brown, with a stare of amazement at his undisturbed companion. "Howbeit, I have nothing to do with the governor and council; they have their own ways, and are no rule for a simple husbandman like me. But, were I to go on with thee, how should I meet the eye of that good old man, our minister, at Salem village? Oh, his voice would make me tremble both Sabbath day and lecture day."

Thus far the elder traveller had listened with due gravity; but now burst into a fit of irrepressible mirth, shaking himself so violently that his snake-like staff actually seemed to wriggle in sympathy.

"Ha! ha! ha!" shouted he again and again; then composing himself, "Well, go on, Goodman Brown, go on; but, prithee, don't kill me with laughing."

"Well, then, to end the matter at once," said Goodman Brown, considerably nettled, "there is my wife, Faith. It would break her dear little heart; and I'd rather break my own."

"Nay, if that be the case," answered the other, "e'en go thy ways, Goodman Brown. I would not for twenty old women like the one hobbling before us that Faith should come to any harm."

As he spoke he pointed his staff at a female figure on the path, in whom Goodman Brown recognized a very pious and exemplary dame, who had taught him his catechism in youth, and was still his moral and spiritual adviser, jointly with the minister and Deacon Gookin.

"A marvel, truly, that Goody Cloyse should be so far in the wilderness at nightfall," said he. "But with your leave, friend, I shall take a cut through the woods until we have left this Christian woman behind. Being a stranger to you, she might ask whom I was consorting with and whither I was going."

"Be it so," said his fellow-traveller. "Betake you to the woods, and let me keep the path."

Accordingly the young man turned aside, but took care to watch his companion, who advanced softly along the road until he had come within a staff's length of the old dame. She, meanwhile, was making the best of her way, with singular speed for so aged a woman, and mumbling some indistinct words — a prayer, doubtless — as she went. The traveller put forth his staff and touched her withered neck with what seemed the serpent's tail.

"The devil!" screamed the pious old lady.

"Then Goody Cloyse knows her old friend?" observed the traveller, confronting her and leaning on his writhing stick.

"Ah, forsooth, and is it your worship indeed?" cried the good dame. "Yea, truly is it, and in the very image of my old gossip, Goodman Brown, the grandfather of the silly fellow that now is. But — would your worship believe it? — my broomstick hath strangely disappeared, stolen, as I suspect, by that unhanged witch, Goody Cory, and that, too, when I was all anointed with the juice of smallage, and cinquefoil, and wolf's bane" —

"Mingled with fine wheat and the fat of a new-born babe," said the shape of old Goodman Brown.

"Ah, your worship knows the recipe," cried the old lady, cackling aloud. "So, as I was saying, being all ready for the meeting, and no horse to ride on, I made up my mind to foot it; for they tell me there is a nice young man to be taken into communion to-night. But now your good worship will lend me your arm, and we shall be there in a twinkling."

"That can hardly be," answered her friend. "I may not spare you my arm, Goody Cloyse; but here is my staff, if you will."

So saying, he threw it down at her feet, where, perhaps, it assumed life, being one of the rods which its owner had formerly lent to the Egyptian magi. Of this fact, however, Goodman Brown could not take cognizance. He had cast up his eyes in astonishment, and, looking down again, beheld neither Goody Cloyse nor the serpentine staff, but his fellow-traveller alone, who waited for him as calmly as if nothing had happened.

"That old woman taught me my catechism," said the young man; and there was a world of meaning in this simple comment.

They continued to walk onward, while the elder traveller exhorted his companion to make good speed and persevere in the path, discoursing so aptly that his arguments seemed rather to spring up in the bosom of his auditor than to be suggested by himself. As they went, he plucked a branch of maple to serve for a walking stick, and began to strip it of the twigs and little boughs, which were wet with evening dew. The moment his fingers touched them they became strangely withered and dried up as with a week's sunshine. Thus the pair proceeded, at a good free pace, until suddenly, in a gloomy hollow of the road, Goodman Brown sat himself down on the stump of a tree and refused to go any farther.

"Friend," said he, stubbornly, "my mind is made up. Not another step will I budge on this errand. What if a wretched old woman do choose to go to the devil when I thought she was going to heaven: is that any reason why I should quit my dear Faith and go after her?"

"You will think better of this by and by," said his acquaintance, composedly. "Sit here and rest yourself a while; and when you feel like moving again, there is my staff to help you along."

Without more words, he threw his companion the maple stick, and was as speedily out of sight as if he had vanished into the deepening gloom. The young man sat a few moments by the roadside, applauding himself greatly, and thinking with how clear a conscience he should meet the minister in his morning walk, nor shrink from the eye of good old Deacon Gookin. And what calm sleep would be his that very night, which was to have been spent so wickedly, but so purely and sweetly now, in the arms of Faith! Amidst these pleasant and praiseworthy meditations, Goodman Brown heard the tramp of horses along the road, and deemed it advisable to conceal himself within the verge of the forest, conscious of the guilty purpose that had brought him thither, though now so happily turned from it.

On came the hoof tramps and the voices of the riders, two grave old voices, conversing soberly as they drew near. These mingled sounds appeared to pass along the road, within a few yards of the young man's hiding-place; but, owing doubtless to the depth of the gloom at that particular spot, neither the travellers nor their steeds were visible. Though their figures brushed the small boughs by the wayside, it could not be seen that they intercepted, even for a moment, the faint gleam from the strip of bright sky athwart which they must have passed.

Goodman Brown alternately crouched and stood on tiptoe, pulling aside the branches and thrusting forth his head as far as he durst without discerning so much as a shadow. It vexed him the more, because he could have sworn, were such a thing possible, that he recognized the voices of the minister and Deacon Gookin, jogging along quietly, as they were wont to do, when bound to some ordination or ecclesiastical council. While yet within hearing, one of the riders stopped to pluck a switch.

"Of the two, reverend sir," said the voice like the deacon's, "I had rather miss an ordination dinner than to-night's meeting. They tell me that some of our community are to be here from Falmouth and beyond, and others from Connecticut and Rhode Island, besides several of the Indian powwows, who, after their fashion, know almost as much deviltry as the best of us. Moreover, there is a goodly young woman to be taken into communion."

"Mighty well, Deacon Gookin!" replied the solemn old tones of the minister. "Spur up, or we shall be late. Nothing can be done, you know, until I get on the ground."

The hoofs clattered again; and the voices, talking so strangely in the empty air, passed on through the forest, where no church had ever been gathered or solitary Christian prayed. Whither, then, could these holy men be journeying so deep into the heathen wilderness? Young Goodman Brown caught hold of a tree for support, being ready to sink down on the ground, faint and overburdened with the heavy sickness of his heart. He looked up to the sky, doubting whether there really was a heaven above him. Yet there was the blue arch, and the stars brightening in it.

"With heaven above and Faith below, I will yet stand firm against the devil!" cried Goodman Brown.

While he still gazed upward into the deep arch of the firmament and had lifted his hands to pray, a cloud, though no wind was stirring, hurried across the zenith and hid the brightening stars. The blue sky was still visible, except directly overhead, where this black mass of cloud was sweeping swiftly northward. Aloft in the air, as if from the depths of the cloud, came a confused and doubtful sound of voices. Once the listener fancied that he could distinguish the accents of towns-people of his own, men and women, both pious and ungodly, many of whom he had met at the communion table, and had seen others rioting at the tavern. The next moment, so indistinct were the sounds, he doubted whether he had heard aught but the murmur of the old forest, whispering without a wind. Then came a stronger swell of those familiar tones, heard daily in the sunshine at Salem village, but never until now from a cloud of night. There was one voice of a young woman, uttering lamentations, yet with an uncertain sorrow, and entreating for some favor, which, perhaps, it would grieve her to obtain; and all the unseen multitude, both saints and sinners, seemed to encourage her onward.

"Faith!" shouted Goodman Brown, in a voice of agony and desperation; and the echoes of the forest mocked him, crying, "Faith! Faith!" as if bewildered wretches were seeking her all through the wilderness.

The cry of grief, rage, and terror was yet piercing the night, when the unhappy husband held his breath for a response. There was a scream, drowned immediately in a louder murmur of voices, fading into far-off laughter, as the dark cloud swept away, leaving the clear and silent sky above Goodman Brown. But something fluttered lightly down through the air and caught on the branch of a tree. The young man seized it, and beheld a pink ribbon.

"My Faith is gone!" cried he, after one stupefied moment. "There is no good on earth; and sin is but a name. Come, devil; for to thee is this world given."

And, maddened with despair, so that he laughed loud and long, did Goodman Brown grasp his staff and set forth again, at such a rate that he seemed to fly along the forest path rather than to walk or run. The road grew wilder and drearier and more faintly traced, and vanished at length, leaving him in the heart of the dark wilderness, still rushing onward with the instinct that guides mortal man to evil. The whole forest was peopled with frightful sounds—the creaking of the trees, the howling of wild beasts, and the yell of Indians; while sometimes the wind tolled like a distant church bell, and sometimes gave a broad roar around the traveller, as if all Nature were laughing him to scorn. But he was himself the chief horror of the scene, and shrank not from its other horrors.

"Ha! ha! ha!" roared Goodman Brown when the wind laughed at him. "Let us hear which will laugh loudest. Think not to frighten me with your deviltry. Come witch, come wizard, come Indian powwow, come devil himself, and here comes Goodman Brown. You may as well fear him as he fear you."

In truth, all through the haunted forest there could be nothing more frightful than the figure of Goodman Brown. On he flew among the black pines, brandishing his staff with frenzied gestures, now giving vent to an inspiration of horrid blasphemy, and now shouting forth such laughter as set all the echoes of the forest laughing like demons around him. The fiend in his own shape is less hideous than when he rages in the breast of man. Thus sped the demoniac on his course, until, quivering among the trees, he saw a red light before him, as when the felled trunks and branches of a clearing have been set on fire, and throw up their lurid blaze against the sky, at the hour of midnight. He paused, in a lull of the tempest that had driven him onward, and heard the swell of what seemed a hymn, rolling solemnly from a distance with the weight of many voices. He knew the tune; it was a familiar one in the choir of the village meeting-house. The verse died heavily away, and was lengthened by a chorus, not of human voices, but of all the sounds of the benighted wilderness pealing in awful harmony together. Goodman Brown cried out, and his cry was lost to his own ear by its unison with the cry of the desert.

In the interval of silence he stole forward until the light glared full upon his eyes. At one extremity of an open space, hemmed in by the dark wall of the forest, arose a rock, bearing some rude, natural resemblance either to an alter or a pulpit, and surrounded by four blazing pines, their tops aflame, their stems untouched, like candles at an evening meeting. The mass of foliage that had overgrown the summit of the rock was all on fire, blazing high into the night and fitfully illuminating the whole field. Each pendent twig and leafy festoon was in a blaze. As the red light arose and fell, a numerous congregation alternately shone forth, then disappeared in shadow, and again grew, as it were, out of the darkness, peopling the heart of the solitary woods at once.

"A grave and dark-clad company," quoth Goodman Brown.

In truth they were such. Among them, quivering to and fro between gloom and splendor, appeared faces that would be seen next day at the council board of the province, and others which, Sabbath after Sabbath, looked devoutly heavenward, and benignantly over the crowded pews, from the holiest pulpits in the land. Some affirm that the lady of the governor was there. At least there were high dames well known to her, and wives of honored husbands, and widows, a great multitude, and ancient maidens, all of excellent repute, and fair young girls, who trembled lest their mothers should espy them. Either the sudden gleams of light flashing over the obscure field bedazzled Goodman Brown, or he recognized a score of the church members of Salem village famous for their especial sanctity. Good old Deacon Gookin had arrived, and waited at the skirts of that venerable saint, his revered pastor. But, irreverently consorting with these grave, reputable, and pious people, these elders of the church, these chaste dames and dewy virgins, there were men of dissolute lives and women of spotted fame, wretches given over to all mean and filthy vice, and suspected even of horrid crimes. It was strange to see that the good shrank not from the wicked, nor were the sinners abashed by the saints. Scattered also among their pale-faced enemies were the Indian priests, or powwows, who had often scared their native forest with more hideous incantations than any known to English witchcraft.

"But where is Faith?" thought Goodman Brown; and, as hope came into his heart, he trembled.

Another verse of the hymn arose, a slow and mournful strain, such as the pious love, but joined to words which expressed all that our nature can conceive of sin, and darkly hinted at far more. Unfathomable to mere mortals is the lore of fiends. Verse after verse was sung; and still the chorus of the desert swelled between like the deepest tone of a mighty organ; and with the final peal of that dreadful anthem there came a sound, as if the roaring wind, the rushing streams, the howling beasts, and every other voice of the unconcerted wilderness were mingling and according with the voice of guilty man in homage to the prince of all. The four blazing pines threw up a loftier flame, and obscurely discovered shapes and visages of horror on the smoke wreaths above the impious assembly. At the same moment the fire on the rock shot redly forth and formed a glowing arch above its base, where now appeared a figure. With reverence be it spoken, the figure bore no slight similitude, both in garb and manner, to some grave divine of the New England churches.

"Bring forth the converts!" cried a voice that echoed through the field and rolled into the forest.

At the word, Goodman Brown stepped forth from the shadow of the trees and approached the congregation, with whom he felt a loathful brotherhood by the sympathy of all that was wicked in his heart. He could have well-nigh sworn that the shape of his own dead father beckoned him to advance, looking downward from a smoke wreath, while a woman, with dim features of despair, threw out her hand to warn him back. Was it his mother? But he had no power to retreat one step, nor to resist, even in thought, when the minister and good old Deacon Gookin seized his arms and led him to the blazing rock. Thither came also the slender form of a veiled female, led between Goody Cloyse, that pious teacher of the catechism, and Martha Carrier, who had received the devil's promise to be queen of hell. A rampant hag was she. And there stood the proselytes beneath the canopy of fire.

"Welcome, my children," said the dark figure, "to the communion of your race. Ye have found thus young your nature and your destiny. My children, look behind you!"

They turned; and flashing forth, as it were, in a sheet of flame, the fiend worshippers were seen; the smile of welcome gleamed darkly on every visage.

"There," resumed the sable form, "are all whom ye have reverenced from youth. Ye deemed them holier than yourselves, and shrank from your own sin, contrasting it with their lives of righteousness and prayerful aspirations heavenward. Yet here are they all in my worshipping assembly. This night it shall be granted you to know their secret deeds: how hoary-bearded elders of the church have whispered wanton words to the young maids of their households; how many a woman, eager for widows' weeds, has given her husband a drink at bedtime and let him sleep his last sleep in her bosom; how beardless youths have made haste to inherit their fathers' wealth; and how fair damsels — blush not, sweet ones — have dug little graves in the garden, and bidden me, the sole guest to an infant's funeral. By the sympathy of your human hearts for sin ye shall scent out all the places — whether in church, bedchamber, street, field, or forest — where crime has been committed, and shall exult to behold the whole earth one stain of guilt, one mighty blood spot. Far more than this. It shall be yours to penetrate, in every bosom, the deep mystery of sin, the fountain of all wicked arts, and which inexhaustibly supplies more evil impulses than human power — than my power at its utmost — can make manifest in deeds. And now, my children, look upon each other."

They did so; and, by the blaze of the hell-kindled torches, the wretched man beheld his Faith, and the wife her husband, trembling before that unhallowed altar.

"Lo, there ye stand, my children," said the figure, in a deep and solemn tone, almost sad with its despairing awfulness, as if his once angelic nature could yet mourn for our miserable race. "Depending upon one another's hearts, ye had still hoped that virtue were not all a dream. Now are ye undeceived. Evil is the nature of mankind. Evil must be your only happiness. Welcome again, my children, to the communion of your race."

"Welcome," repeated the fiend worshippers, in one cry of despair and triumph.

And there they stood, the only pair, as it seemed, who were yet hesitating on the verge of wickedness in this dark world. A basin was hollowed, naturally, in the rock. Did it contain water, reddened by the lurid light? or was it blood? or, perchance, a liquid flame? Herein did the shape of evil dip his hand and prepare to lay the mark of baptism upon their foreheads, that they might be partakers of the mystery of sin, more conscious of the secret guilt of others, both in deed and thought, than they could now be of their own. The husband cast one look at his pale wife, and Faith at him. What polluted wretches would the next glance show them to each other, shuddering alike at what they disclosed and what they saw!

"Faith! Faith!" cried the husband, "look up to heaven, and resist the wicked one."

Whether Faith obeyed he knew not. Hardly had he spoken when he found himself amid calm night and solitude, listening to a roar of the wind which died heavily away through the forest. He staggered against the rock, and felt it chill and damp; while a hanging twig, that had been all on fire, besprinkled his cheek with the coldest dew.

The next morning young Goodman Brown came slowly into the street of Salem village, staring around him like a bewildered man. The good old minister was taking a walk along the graveyard to get an appetite for breakfast and meditate his sermon, and bestowed a blessing, as he passed, on Goodman Brown. He shrank from the venerable saint as if to avoid an anathema. Old Deacon Gookin was at domestic worship, and the holy words of his prayer were heard through the open window. "What God doth the wizard pray to?" quoth Goodman Brown. Goody Cloyse, that excellent old Christian, stood in the early sunshine at her own lattice, catechizing a little girl who had brought her a pint of morning's milk. Goodman Brown snatched away the child as from the grasp of the fiend himself. Turning the corner by the meeting-house, he spied the head of Faith, with the pink ribbons, gazing anxiously forth, and bursting into such joy at sight of him that she skipped along the street and almost kissed her husband before the whole village. But Goodman Brown looked sternly and sadly into her face, and passed on without a greeting.

Had Goodman Brown fallen asleep in the forest and only dreamed a wild dream of a witch-meeting?

Be it so if you will; but, alas! it was a dream of evil omen for young Goodman Brown. A stern, a sad, a darkly meditative, a distrustful, if not a desperate man did he become from the night of that fearful dream. On the Sabbath day, when the congregation were singing a holy psalm, he could not listen because an anthem of sin rushed loudly upon his ear and drowned all the blessed strain. When the minister spoke from the pulpit with power and fervid eloquence, and, with his hand on the open Bible, of the sacred truths of our religion, and of saint-like lives and triumphant deaths, and of future bliss or misery unutterable, then did Goodman Brown turn pale, dreading lest the roof should thunder down upon the gray blasphemer and his hearers. Often, waking suddenly at midnight, he shrank from the bosom of Faith; and at morning or eventide, when the family knelt down at prayer, he scowled and muttered to himself, and gazed sternly at his wife, and turned away. And when he had lived long, and was borne to his grave a hoary corpse, followed by Faith, an aged woman, and children and grandchildren, a goodly procession, besides neighbors not a few, they carved no hopeful verse upon his tombstone, for his dying hour was gloom.

[1835]

Study and Writing Questions

1. What is "the dark communion of your race" to which the "dark figure" welcomes Young Goodman Brown?
2. As it is described in the STORY, what are the SYMBOLIC associations with the devil's staff? How do they help the THEMATIC development of the story?
3. How does the story use the supernatural to convey psychological truths of our world?
4. What is the significance of the name of the title CHARACTER?
5. How does this NARRATIVE use AMBIGUITY at crucial moments? If Hawthorne had resolved the final ambiguity of the story in favor of Brown's experience being either certainly imaginary or certainly real, how might the story be weaker or stronger?

See also Questions for Contrast and Comparison: 3, 30, 31, 69, 77, 84, 106, 126, 133, 151, and 234.

■ SARA HENDERSON HAY (1906–1987) was born in Pittsburgh, Pennsylvania, and attended Brenau College (1926–1928) in Gainesville, Georgia, and Columbia University (1928–1931) in New York City. She remained in New York working (1935–1942) as a staff member in the rare book department of the publishing firm of Charles Scribner's Sons. A private person, she published the first of her seven slender volumes of poetry, Field of Honor, in 1933, and the last, Seasons of the Heart, marked by its Christian yearnings, posthumously in 1989. She is known for addressing "fragile" subjects of domestic communication, children's concerns, and animals. The Delicate Balance (1951) won the Edna St. Vincent Millay Memorial Award of the Poetry Society of America for the best volume of poetry of its year. Late in life (1951), she married Nikolai Lopatnikoff, a composer and professor of music composition at Pittsburgh's Carnegie Mellon University. In 1963 she was named a Distinguished Daughter of Pennsylvania.

Rapunzel

Oh God, let me forget the things he said.
Let me not lie another night awake
Repeating all the promises he made,
Freezing and burning for his faithless sake;
Seeing his face, feeling his hand once more
Loosen my braided hair until it fell
Shining and free; remembering how he swore
A single strand might lift a man from Hell . . .

I knew that other girls, in Aprils past,
Had leaned, like me, from some old tower's room
And watched him clamber up, hand over fist . . .
I knew that I was not the first to twist
Her heartstrings to a rope for him to climb.
I might have known I would not be the last.

[1963]

Study and Writing Questions

1. What religious IMAGES and REFERENCES are there in the first stanza? How do they affect your understanding of the situation? How do they affect your reading of the poem as a whole?
2. What is the importance of knowledge in the second stanza? Is knowledge a good or a bad thing from the speaker's VIEWPOINT?
3. How does the speaker feel at the beginning of the poem? How does she feel at the end? How do your feelings change, if at all?
4. What is the relationship in this piece between its two STORIES, the one to which the speaker ALLUDES and the one consisting of the speaker's present contemplation of the past?
5. This verse is a sonnet, a form traditionally used for love poetry. How does the poetic form of this dramatic monologue contribute to its meaning?

See also Questions for Contrast and Comparison: 124, 148, 192, 193, 194, and 195.

■ **ERNEST (JAMES) HAYCOX (JR.)** (1899–1950) *was born in Portland, Oregon. His family moved often until his parents' divorce (1910), as his restless father shifted from job to job. At sixteen, Haycox joined the Oregon National Guard and pursued Mexican revolutionary Pancho Villa. He finished high school (1917) in Portland and then served fourteen months in France during World War I. After working on student newspapers in high school and then at Reed College and the University of Oregon (B.A., 1923), he became a police reporter for the Portland Oregonian, covering his walls with rejection slips for his fiction until his first sales in 1924. He then drove to New York City to approach publishers, but finding small acceptance came home. On the train back to New York in 1925, he met Jill Marie Chord on her way to art school in New York. They soon married and returned to Oregon for the rest of their lives. Advised in New York to write for the Western "pulp" magazines, Haycox not only quickly mastered the form but deepened it by a recognition of the power of nature and the complex strictures of social roles. His 24* NOVELS *and 254* STORIES *include such classics as* Trouble Shooter *(1937),* The Border Trumpet *(1939),* The Wild Bunch *(1943), and* Bugles in the Afternoon *(1944). Cancer cut short the tetralogy, begun with* The Earthbreakers *(1952), that Haycox hoped would complete his evolution from Western writer to historical novelist.*

Stage to Lordsburg

This was one of those years in the Territory when Apache smoke signals spiraled up from the stony mountain summits and many a ranch cabin lay as a square of blackened ashes on the ground and the departure of a stage from Tonto was the beginning of an adventure that had no certain happy ending. . . .

The stage and its six horses waited in front of Weilner's store on the north side of Tonto's square. Happy Stuart was on the box, the ribbons between his fingers and one foot teetering on the brake. John Strang rode shotgun guard and an escort of ten cavalrymen waited behind the coach, half asleep in their saddles.

At four-thirty in the morning this high air was quite cold, though the sun had begun to flush the sky eastward. A small crowd stood in the square, presenting their final messages to the passengers now entering the coach. There was a girl going down to marry an infantry officer, a whisky drummer from St. Louis, an Englishman all length and bony corners and bearing with him an enormous sporting rifle, a gambler, a solid-shouldered cattleman on his way to New Mexico and a blond young man upon whom both Happy Stuart and the shotgun guard placed a narrow-eyed interest.

This seemed all until the blond man drew back from the coach door; and then a girl known commonly throughout the Territory as Henriette came quietly from the crowd. She was small and quiet, with a touch of paleness in her cheeks and her quite dark eyes lifted at the blond man's unexpected courtesy, showing surprise. There was this moment of delay and then the girl caught up her dress and stepped into the coach.

Men in the crowd were smiling but the blond one turned, his motion like the swift cut of a knife, and his attention covered that group until the smiling quit. He was tall, hollow-flanked, and definitely stamped by the guns slung low on his hips. But it wasn't the guns alone; something in his face, so watchful and so smooth, also showed his trade. Afterwards he got into the coach and slammed the door.

Happy Stuart kicked off the brakes and yelled, "Hi!" Tonto's people were calling out their last farewells and the six horses broke into a trot and the stage lunged on its fore and aft springs and rolled from town with dust dripping off its wheels like water, the cavalrymen trotting briskly behind. So they tipped down the long grade, bound on a journey no stage had attempted during the last forty-five days. Out below in the desert's distance stood the relay stations they hoped to reach and pass. Between lay a country swept empty by the quick raids of Geronimo's men.

The Englishman, the gambler and the blond man sat jammed together in the forward seat, riding backward to the course of the stage. The drummer and the cattleman occupied the uncomfortable middle bench; the two women shared the rear seat. The cattleman faced Henriette, his knees almost touching her. He had one arm hooked over the door's window sill to steady himself. A huge gold nugget slid gently back and forth along the watch chain slung across his wide chest and a chunk of black hair lay below his hat. His eyes considered Henriette, reading something in the girl that caused him to show her a deliberate smile. Henriette dropped her glance to the gloved tips of her fingers, cheeks unstirred.

They were all strangers packed closely together, with nothing in common save a destination. Yet the cattleman's smile and the boldness of his glance were something as audible as speech, noted by everyone except the Englishman, who sat bolt upright with his stony indifference. The army girl, tall and calmly pretty, threw a quick side glance at Henriette and afterwards looked away with a touch of color. The gambler saw this interchange of glances and showed the cattleman an irritated attention. The whisky drummer's eyes narrowed a little and some inward cynicism made a faint change on his lips. He removed his hat to show a bald head already beginning to sweat; his cigar smoke turned the coach cloudy and ashes kept dropping on his vest.

The blond man had observed Henriette's glance drop from the cattleman; he tipped his hat well over his face and watched her — not boldly but as though he were puzzled. Once her glance lifted and touched him. But he had been on guard against that and was quick to look away.

The army girl coughed gently behind her hand, whereupon the gambler tapped the whisky drummer on the shoulder. "Get rid of that." The drummer appeared startled. He grumbled, "Beg pardon," and tossed the smoke through the window.

All this while the coach went rushing down the ceaseless turns of the mountain road, rocking on its fore and aft springs, its heavy wheels slamming through the road ruts and whining on the curves. Occasionally the strident yell of Happy Stuart washed back. "Hi, Nellie! By God—!" The whisky drummer braced himself against the door and closed his eyes.

Three hours from Tonto the road, making a last round sweep, let them down upon the flat desert. Here the stage stopped and the men got out to stretch. The gambler spoke to the army girl, gently: "Perhaps you would find my seat more comfortable." The army girl said "Thank you," and changed over. The cavalry sergeant rode up to the stage, speaking to Happy Stuart.

"We'll be goin' back now—and good luck to ye."

The men piled in, the gambler taking the place beside Henriette. The blond man drew his long legs together to give the army girl more room, and watched Henriette's face with a soft, quiet care. A hard sun beat fully on the coach and dust began to whip up like fire smoke. Without escort they rolled across a flat earth broken only by cacti standing against a dazzling light. In the far distance, behind a blue heat haze, lay the faint suggestion of mountains.

The cattleman reached up and tugged at the ends of his mustache and smiled at Henriette. The army girl spoke to the blond man. "How far is it to the noon station?" The blond man said courteously: "Twenty miles." The gambler watched the army girl with the strictness of his face relaxing, as though the run of her voice reminded him of things long forgotten.

The miles fell behind and the smell of alkali dust got thicker. Henriette rested against the corner of the coach, her eyes dropped to the tips of her gloves. She made an enigmatic, disinterested shape there; she seemed past stirring, beyond laughter. She was young, yet she had a knowledge that put the cattleman and the gambler and the drummer and the army girl in their exact places; and she knew why the gambler had offered the army girl his seat. The army girl was in one world and she was in another, as everyone in the coach understood. It had no effect on her for this was a distinction she had learned long ago. Only the blond man broke through her indifference. His name was Malpais Bill and she could see the wildness in the corners of his eyes and in the long crease of his lips; it was a stamp that would never come off. Yet something flowed out of him toward her that was different than the predatory curiosity of other men; something unobtrusively gallant, unexpectedly gentle.

Upon the box Happy Stuart pointed to the hazy outline two miles away. "Injuns ain't burned that anyhow." The sun was directly overhead, turning the light of the world a cruel brass-yellow. The crooked crack of a dry wash opened across the two deep ruts that made this road. Johnny Strang shifted the gun in his lap. "What's Malpais Bill ridin' with us for?"

"I guess I wouldn't ask him," returned Happy Stuart and studied the wash with a troubled eye. The road fell into it roughly and he got a tighter grip on his reins and yelled: "Hang on! Hi, Nellie! God damn you, hi!" The six horses plunged down the rough side of the wash and for a moment the coach stood alone, high and lonely on the break, and then went reeling over the rim. It struck the gravel with a roar, the front wheels bouncing and the back wheels skewing around. The horses faltered but Happy Stuart cursed at his leaders and got them into a run again. The horses lunged up the far side of the wash two and two, their muscles bunching and the soft dirt flying in yellow clouds. The front wheels struck solidly and something cracked like a pistol shot; the stage rose out of the wash, teetered crosswise and then fell ponderously on its side, splintering the coach panels.

Johnny Strang jumped clear. Happy Stuart hung to the handrail with one hand and hauled on the reins with the other; and stood up while the passengers crawled through the upper door. All the men, except the whisky drummer, put their shoulders to the coach and heaved it upright again. The whisky drummer stood strangely in the bright sunlight shaking his head dumbly while the others climbed back in. Happy Stuart said, "All right, brother, git aboard."

The drummer climbed in slowly and the stage ran on. There was a low, gray dobe relay station squatted on the desert dead ahead with a scatter of corrals about it and a flag hanging limp on a crooked pole. Men came out of the dobe's dark interior and stood in the shade of the porch gallery. Happy Stuart rolled up and stopped. He said to a lanky man: "Hi, Mack. Where's the God-damned Injuns?"

The passengers were filing into the dobe's dining room. The lanky one drawled: "You'll see 'em before tomorrow night." Hostlers came up to change horses.

The little dining room was cool after the coach, cool and still. A fat Mexican woman ran in and out with the food platters. Happy Stuart said: "Ten minutes," and brushed the alkali dust from his mouth and fell to eating.

The long-jawed Mack said: "Catlin's ranch burned last night. Was a troop of cavalry around here yesterday. Came and went. You'll git to the Gap tonight all right but I do' know about the mountains beyond. A little trouble?"

"A little," said Happy, briefly, and rose. This was the end of rest. The passengers followed, with the whisky drummer straggling at the rear, reaching deeply for wind. The coach rolled away again, Mack's voice pursuing them. "Hit it a lick, Happy, if you see any dust rollin' out of the east."

Heat had condensed in the coach and the little wind fanned up by the run of the horses was stifling to the lungs; the desert floor projected its white glitter endlessly away until lost in the smoky haze. The cattleman's knees bumped Henriette gently and he kept watching her, a celluloid toothpick drooped between his lips. Happy Stuart's voice ran back, profane and urgent, keeping the speed of the coach constant through the ruts. The whisky drummer's eyes were round and strained and his mouth was open and all the color had gone out of his face. The gambler observed this without expression and without care; and once the cattleman, feeling the sag of the whisky drummer's shoulder, shoved him away. The Englishman sat bolt upright, staring emotionlessly at the passing desert. The army girl spoke to Malpais Bill: "What is the next stop?"

"Gap Creek."

"Will we meet soldiers there?"

He said: "I expect we'll have an escort over the hills into Lordsburg."

And at four o'clock of this furnace-hot afternoon the whisky drummer made a feeble gesture with one hand and fell forward into the gambler's lap.

The cattleman shrugged his shoulders and put a head through the window, calling up to Happy Stuart: "Wait a minute." When the stage stopped everybody climbed out and the blond man helped the gambler lay the whisky drummer in the sweltering patch of shade created by the coach. Neither Happy Stuart nor the shotgun guard bothered to get down. The whisky drummer's lips moved a little but nobody said anything and nobody knew what to do—until Henriette stepped forward.

She dropped to the ground, lifting the whisky drummer's shoulders and head against her breasts. He opened his eyes and there was something in them that they could all see, like relief and ease, like gratefulness. She murmured: "You are all right," and her smile was soft and pleasant, turning her lips maternal. There was this wisdom in her, this knowledge of the fears that men concealed behind their manners, the deep hungers that rode them so savagely, and the loneliness that drove them to women of her kind. She repeated, "You are all right," and watched this whisky drummer's eyes lose the wildness of what he knew.

The army girl's face showed shock. The gambler and the cattleman looked down at the whisky drummer quite impersonally. The blond man watched Henriette through lids half closed, but the flare of a powerful interest broke the severe lines of his cheeks. He held a cigarette between his fingers; he had forgotten it.

Happy Stuart said: "We can't stay here."

The gambler bent down to catch the whisky drummer under the arms. Henriette rose and said, "Bring him to me," and got into the coach. The blond man and the gambler lifted the drummer through the door so that he was lying along the back seat, cushioned on Henriette's lap. They all got in and the coach rolled on. The drummer groaned a little, whispering: "Thanks—thanks," and the blond man, searching Henriette's face for every shred of expression, drew a gusty breath.

They went on like this, the big wheels pounding the ruts of the road while a lowering sun blazed through the coach windows. The mountain bulwarks began to march nearer, more definite in the blue fog. The cattleman's eyes were small and brilliant and touched Henriette personally, but the gambler bent toward Henriette to say: "If you are tired—"

"No," she said. "No. He's dead."

The army girl stifled a small cry. The gambler bent nearer the whisky drummer, and then they were all looking at Henriette; even the Englishman stared at her for a moment, faint curiosity in his eyes. She was remotely smiling, her lips broad and soft. She held the drummer's head with both her hands and continued to hold him like that until, at the swift fall of dusk, they rolled across the last of the desert floor and drew up before Gap Station.

The cattleman kicked open the door and stepped out, grunting as his stiff legs touched the ground. The gambler pulled the drummer up so that Henriette could leave. They all came out, their bones tired from the shaking. Happy Stuart climbed from the box, his face a gray mask of alkali and his eyes bloodshot He said: "Who's dead?" and looked into the coach. People sauntered from the station yard, walking with the indolence of twilight. Happy Stuart said, "Well, he won't worry about tomorrow," and turned away.

A short man with a tremendous stomach shuffled through the dusk. He said: "Wasn't sure you'd try to git through yet, Happy."

"Where's the soldiers for tomorrow?"

"Other side of the mountains. Everybody's chased out. What ain't forted up here was sent into Lordsburg. You men will bunk in the barn. I'll make out for the ladies somehow." He looked at the army girl and he appraised Henriette instantly. His eyes slid on to Malpais Bill standing in the background and recognition stirred him then and made his voice careful. "Hello, Bill. What brings you this way?"

Malpais Bill's cigarette glowed in the gathering dusk and Henriette caught the brief image of his face, serene and watchful. Malpais Bill's tone was easy, it was soft. "Just the trip."

They were moving on toward the frame house whose corners seemed to extend indefinitely into a series of attached sheds. Lights glimmered in the windows and men moved around the place, idly talking. The unhitched horses went away at a trot. The tall girl walked into the station's big room, to face a soldier in a disheveled uniform.

He said: "Miss Robertson? Lieutenant Hauser was to have met you here. He is at Lordsburg. He was wounded in a brush with the Apaches last night."

The tall army girl stood very still. She said: "Badly?"

"Well," said the soldier, "yes."

The fat man came in, drawing deeply for wind. "Too bad — too bad. Ladies, I'll show you the rooms, such as I got."

Henriette's dove-colored dress blended with the background shadows. She was watching the tall army girl's face whiten. But there was a strength in the army girl, a fortitude that made her think of the soldier. For she said quietly, "You must have had a bad trip."

"Nothing — nothing at all," said the soldier and left the room. The gambler was here, his thin face turning to the army girl with a strained expression, as though he were remembering painful things. Malpais Bill had halted in the doorway, studying the softness and the humility of Henriette's cheeks. Afterwards both women followed the fat host of Gap Station along a narrow hall to their quarters.

Malpais Bill wheeled out and stood indolently against the wall of this desert station, his glance quick and watchful in the way it touched all the men loitering along the yard, his ears weighing all the night-softened voices. Heat died from the earth and a definite chill rolled down the mountain hulking so high behind the house. The soldier was in his saddle, murmuring drowsily to Happy Stuart.

"Well, Lordsburg is a long ways off and the damn' mountains are squirmin' with Apaches. You won't have any cavalry escort tomorrow. The troops are all in the field."

Malpais Bill listened to the hoofbeats of the soldier's horse fade out, remembering the loneliness of a man in those dark mountain passes, and went back to the saloon at the end of the station. This was a low-ceilinged shed with a dirt floor and whitewashed walls that once had been part of a stable. Three men stood under a lantern in the middle of this little place, the light of the lantern palely shining in the rounds of their eyes as they watched him. At the far end of the bar the cattleman and the gambler drank in taciturn silence. Malpais Bill took his whisky when the bottle came, and noted the barkeep's obscure glance. Gap's host put in his head and wheezed, "Second table," and the other men in here began to move out. The barkeep's words rubbed together, one tone above a whisper. "Better not ride into Lordsburg. Plummer and Shanley are there."

Malpais Bill's lips were stretched to the long edge of laughter and there was a shine like wildness in his eyes. He said, "Thanks, friend," and went into the dining room.

When he came back to the yard night lay wild and deep across the desert and the moonlight was a frozen silver that touched but could not dissolve the world's incredible blackness. The girl Henriette walked along the Tonto road, swaying gently in the vague shadows. He went that way, the click of his heels on the hard earth bringing her around.

Her face was clear and strange and incurious in the night, as though she waited for something to come, and knew what it would be. But he said: "You're too far from the house. Apaches like to crawl down next to a settlement and wait for strays."

She was indifferent, unafraid. Her voice was cool and he could hear the faint loneliness in it, the fatalism that made her words so even. "There's a wind coming up, so soft and good."

He took off his hat, long legs braced, and his eyes were both attentive and puzzled. His blond hair glowed in the fugitive light.

She said in a deep breath: "Why do you do that?"

His lips were restless and the sing and rush of strong feeling was like a current of quick wind around him. "You have folks in Lordsburg?"

She spoke in a direct, patient way as though explaining something he should have known without asking. "I run a house in Lordsburg."

"No," he said, "it wasn't what I asked."

"My folks are dead—I think. There was a massacre in the Superstition Mountains when I was young."

He stood with his head bowed, his mind reaching back to fill in that gap of her life. There was a hardness and a rawness to this land and little sympathy for the weak. She had survived and had paid for her survival, and looked at him now in a silent way that offered no explanations or apologies for whatever had been; she was still a pretty girl with the dead patience of all the past years in her eyes, in the expressiveness of her lips.

He said: "Over in the Tonto Basin is a pretty land. I've got a piece of a ranch there—with a house half built."

"If that's your country why are you here?"

His lips laughed and the rashness in him glowed hot again and he seemed to grow taller in the moonlight. "A debt to collect."

"That's why you're going to Lordsburg? You will never get through collecting those kind of debts. Everybody in the Territory knows you. Once you were just a rancher. Then you tried to wipe out a grudge and then there was a bigger one to wipe out—and the debt kept growing and more men are waiting to kill you. Someday a man will. You'd better run away from the debts."

His bright smile kept constant, and presently she lifted her shoulders with resignation. "No," she murmured, "you won't run." He could see the sweetness of her lips and the way her eyes were sad for him; he could see in them the patience he had never learned.

He said, "We'd better go back," and turned her with his arm. They went across the yard in silence, hearing the undertone of men's drawling talk roll out of the shadows, seeing the glow of men's pipes in the dark corners. Malpais Bill stopped and watched her go through the station door; she turned to look at him once more, her eyes all dark and her lips softly sober, and then passed down the narrow corridor to her own quarters. Beyond her window, in the yard, a man was murmuring to another man: "Plummer and Shanley are in Lordsburg. Malpais Bill knows it." Through the thin partition of the adjoining room she heard the army girl crying with a suppressed, uncontrollable regularity. Henriette stared at the dark wall, her shoulders and head bowed; and afterwards returned to the hall and knocked on the army girl's door and went in.

Six fresh horses fiddled in front of the coach and the fat host of Gap Station came across the yard swinging a lantern against the dead, bitter black. All the passengers filed sleep-dulled and miserable from the house. Johnny Strang slammed the express box in the boot and Happy Stuart gruffly said: "All right, folks."

The passengers climbed in. The cattleman came up and Malpais Bill drawled: "Take the corner spot, mister," and got in, closing the door. The Gap host grumbled: "If they don't jump you on the long grade you'll be all right. You're safe when you get to Al Schrieber's ranch." Happy's bronze voice shocked the black stillness and the coach lurched forward, its leather springs squealing.

They rode for an hour in this complete darkness, chilled and uncomfortable and half asleep, feeling the coach drag on a heavy-climbing grade. Gray dawn cracked through, followed by a sunless light rushing all across the flat desert now far below. The road looped from one barren shoulder to another and at sunup they had reached the first bench and were slamming full speed along a boulder-strewn flat. The cattleman sat in the forward corner, the left corner of his mouth swollen and crushed, and when Henriette saw that her glance slid to Malpais Bill's knuckles. The army girl had her eyes closed, her shoulders pressing against the Englishman, who remained bolt upright with the sporting gun between his knees. Beside Henriette the gambler seemed to sleep, and on the middle bench Malpais Bill watched the land go by with a thin vigilance.

At ten they were rising again, with juniper and scrub pine showing on the slopes and the desert below them filling with the powdered haze of another hot day. By noon they reached the summit of the range and swung to follow its narrow rock-ribbed meadows. The gambler, long motionless, shifted his feet and caught the army girl's eyes.

"Schrieber's is directly ahead. We are past the worst of it."

The blond man looked around at the gambler, making no comment; and it was then that Henriette caught the smell of smoke in the windless air. Happy Stuart was cursing once more and the brake blocks began to cry. Looking through the angled vista of the window panel Henriette saw a clay and rock chimney standing up like a gaunt skeleton against the day's light. The house that had been there was a black patch on the ground, smoke still rising from pieces that had not been completely burnt.

The stage stopped and all the men were instantly out. An iron stove squatted on the earth, with one section of pipe stuck upright to it. Fire licked lazily along the collapsed fragments of what had been a trunk. Beyond the location of the house, at the foot of a corral, lay two nude figures grotesquely bald, with deliberate knife slashes marking their bodies. Happy Stuart went over there and had his look; and came back.

"Schriebers. Well—"

Malpais Bill said: "This morning about daylight." He looked at the gambler, at the cattleman, at the Englishman who showed no emotion. "Get back in the coach." He climbed to the coach's top, flattening himself full length there. Happy Stuart and Strang took their places again. The horses broke into a run.

The gambler said to the army girl: "You're pretty safe between those two fellows," and hauled a .44 from a back pocket and laid it over his lap. He considered Henriette more carefully than before, his taciturnity breaking. He said: "How old are you?"

Her shoulders rose and fell, which was the only answer. But the gambler said gently, "Young enough to be my daughter. It is a rotten world. When I call to you, lie down on the floor."

The Englishman had pulled the rifle from between his knees and laid it across the sill of the window on his side. The cattleman swept back the skirt of his coat to clear the holster of his gun.

The little flinty summit meadows grew narrower, with shoulders of gray rock closing in upon the road. The coach wheels slammed against the stony ruts and bounced high and fell again with a jar the springs could not soften. Happy Stuart's howl ran steadily above this rattle and rush. Fine dust turned all things gray.

Henriette sat with her eyes pinned to the gloved tips of her fingers, remembering the tall shape of Malpais Bill cut against the moonlight of Gap Station. He had smiled at her as a man might smile at any desirable woman, with the sweep and swing of laughter in his voice; and his eyes had been gentle. The gambler spoke very quietly and she didn't hear him until his fingers gripped her arm. He said again, not raising his voice: "Get down."

Henriette dropped to her knees, hearing gunfire blast through the rush and run of the coach. Happy Stuart ceased to yell and the army girl's eyes were round and dark. The walls of the canyon had tapered off. Looking upward through the window on the gambler's side, Henriette saw the weaving figure of an Apache warrior reel nakedly on a calico pony and rush by with a rifle raised and pointed in his bony elbows. The gambler took a cool aim; the stockman fired and aimed again. The Englishman's sporting rifle blasted heavy echoes through the coach, hurting her ears, and the smell of powder got rank and bitter. The blond man's boots scraped the coach top and round small holes began to dimple the paneling as the Apache bullets struck. An Indian came boldly abreast the coach and made a target that couldn't be missed. The cattleman dropped him with one shot. The wheels screamed as they slowed around the sharp ruts and the whole heavy superstructure of the coach bounced high into the air. Then they were rushing downgrade.

The gambler said quietly, "You had better take this," handing Henriette his gun. He leaned against the door with his small hands gripping the sill. Pallor loosened his cheeks. He said to the army girl: "Be sure and keep between those gentlemen," and looked at her with a way that was desperate and forlorn and dropped his head to the window's sill.

Henriette saw the bluff rise up and close in like a yellow wall. They were rolling down the mountain without brake. Gunfire fell off and the crying of the Indians faded back. Coming up from her knees then she saw the desert's flat surface far below, with the angular pattern of Lordsburg vaguely on the far borders of the heat fog. There was no more firing and Happy Stuart's voice lifted again and the brakes were screaming on the wheels, and going off, and screaming again. The Englishman stared out of the window sullenly; the army girl seemed in a deep desperate dream; the cattleman's face was shining with a strange sweat.

Henriette reached over to pull the gambler up, but he had an unnatural weight to him and slid into the far corner. She saw that he was dead.

At five o'clock that long afternoon the stage threaded Lordsburg's narrow streets of dobe and frame houses, came upon the center square and stopped before a crowd of people gathered in the smoky heat. The passengers crawled out stiffly. A Mexican boy ran up to see the dead gambler and began to yell his news in shrill Mexican. Malpais Bill climbed off the top, but Happy Stuart sat back on his seat and stared taciturnly at the crowd. Henriette noticed then that the shotgun messenger was gone.

A gray man in a sleazy white suit called up to Happy. "Well, you got through."

Happy Stuart said: "Yeah. We got through."

An officer stepped through the crowd, smiling at the army girl. He took her arm and said, "Miss Robertson, I believe. Lieutenant Hauser is quite all right. I will get your luggage —"

The army girl was crying then, definitely. They were all standing around, bone-weary and shaken. Malpais Bill remained by the wheel of the coach, his cheeks hard against the sunlight and his eyes riveted on a pair of men standing under the board awning of an adjoining store. Henriette observed the manner of their waiting and knew why they were here. The blond man's eyes, she noticed, were very blue and flame burned brilliantly in them. The army girl turned to Henriette, tears in her eyes. She murmured: "If there is anything I can ever do for you —"

But Henriette stepped back, shaking her head. This was Lordsburg and everybody knew her place except the army girl. Henriette said formally, "Goodby," noting how still and expectant the two men under the awning remained. She swung toward the blond man and said, "Would you carry my valise?"

Malpais Bill looked at her, laughter remote in his eyes, and reached into the luggage pile and got her battered valise. He was still smiling as he went beside her, through the crowd and past the two waiting men. But when they turned into an anonymous and dusty little side street of the town, where the houses all sat shoulder to shoulder without grace or dignity, he had turned sober. He said: "I am obliged to you. But I'll have to go back there."

They were in front of a house no different from its neighbors; they had stopped at its door. She could see his eyes travel this street and comprehend its meaning and the kind of traffic it bore. But he was saying in that gentle, melody-making tone:

"I have watched you for two days." He stopped, searching his mind to find the thing he wanted to say. It came out swiftly. "God made you a woman. The Tonto is a pretty country."

Her answer was quite barren of feeling. "No. I am known all through the Territory. But I can remember that you asked me."

He said: "No other reason?" She didn't answer but something in her eyes pulled his face together. He took off his hat and it seemed to her he was looking through this hot day to that far-off country and seeing it fresh and desirable. He murmured: "A man can escape nothing. I have got to do this. But I will be back."

He went along the narrow street, made a quick turn at the end of it, and disappeared. Heat rolled like a heavy wave over Lordsburg's housetops and the smell of dust was very sharp. She lifted her valise, and dropped it and stood like that, mute and grave before the door of her dismal house. She was remembering how tall he had been against the moonlight at Gap Station.

There were four swift shots beating furiously along the sultry quiet, and a shout, and afterwards a longer and longer silence. She put one hand against the door to steady herself, and knew that those shots marked the end of a man, and the end of a hope. He would never come back; he would never stand over her in the moonlight with the long gentle smile on his lips and with the swing of life in his casual tone. She was thinking of all that humbly and with the patience life had beaten into her. . . .

She was thinking of all that when she heard the strike of boots on the street's packed earth; and turned to see him, high and square in the muddy sunlight, coming toward her with his smile.

[1937]

Study and Writing Questions

1. How does Haycox use DESCRIPTION to develop his THEMES and control our expectations? What are the effects of description in the first paragraph? What are the effects of description in the first six paragraphs treated as a unit? Where else is description prominent in this NARRATIVE?

2. How is nature IMAGERY used SYMBOLICALLY? For example, what does it mean that Henriette thinks of Malpais Bill in moonlight but at the end in sunlight? What are other examples of symbolic nature imagery? What do they mean?

3. In the course of this narrative we see many locations and white people of many professions. List these locations and occupations. How are they related to each other socially?

4. What is the role of the Apaches in this narrative? To what extent are they mere STEREOTYPES? Are they treated as inferior to the whites? What is their relationship with the landscape? Do you view this STORY as racist?

5. How does the MOTIF of the journey work in this narrative? Why is each of the CHARACTERS on this journey? What does each expect? What does each find? How does this journey prepare the main characters for a change in their lives? Is the RESOLUTION happy, sad, or in some ways more complicated than either of those terms suggests?

See also Questions for Contrast and Comparison: 5, 119, 148, 230, 231, and 232.

■ **ERNEST HEMINGWAY** (1899–1961), *to the public of his time, epitomized the "manly" writer (to quote his Nobel Prize Citation, 1954). Born near Chicago, Illinois, his writing was encouraged by his music teacher mother while his physician father, especially in summers in rural Michigan, encouraged his fishing and hunting. Rejecting college, he began reporting, first for the Kansas City Star, then for the Toronto Star. He joined the Red Cross Ambulance Corps and was wounded during World War I. After six months convalescing in Italy, he became a foreign correspondent. Part of the famous Paris expatriate group that included John Dos Passos, F. Scott Fitzgerald, and Gertrude Stein, he began writing his trademark* STORIES, *with their terse* DIALOGUE *and understated* NARRATION. *After the success of his first collection,* In Our Time *(1924), he owned a series of homes in Key West, Florida, Cuba, Idaho, and New York City, but pursued an exhausting succession of travels (Europe, the Near East, Africa) for outdoor sport and journalism, love affairs (he had four wives and three children), and stints of writing. His* NOVELS *include* The Sun Also Rises *(1926) about the "Lost Generation,"* A Farewell to Arms *(1929) about love and war,* For Whom the Bell Tolls *(1940) about loyalty and struggle, and* The Old Man and the Sea *(1952) about endurance against nature. Often injured, and finally debilitated, Hemingway, like his father, took his own life.*

A Clean, Well-Lighted Place

It was late and every one had left the café except an old man who sat in the shadow the leaves of the tree made against the electric light. In the day time the street was dusty, but at night the dew settled the dust and the old man liked to sit late because he was deaf and now at night it was quiet and he felt the difference. The two waiters inside the café knew that the old man was a little drunk, and while he was a good client they knew that if he became too drunk he would leave without paying, so they kept watch on him.

"Last week he tried to commit suicide," one waiter said.

"Why?"

"He was in despair."

"What about?"

"Nothing."

"How do you know it was nothing?"

"He has plenty of money."

They sat together at a table that was close against the wall near the door of the café and looked at the terrace where the tables were all empty except where the old man sat in the shadow of the leaves of the tree that moved slightly in the wind. A girl and a soldier went by in the street. The street light shone on the brass number on his collar. The girl wore no head covering and hurried beside him.

"The guard will pick him up," one waiter said.

"What does it matter if he gets what he's after?"

"He had better get off the street now. The guard will get him. They went by five minutes ago."

The old man sitting in the shadow rapped on his saucer with his glass. The younger waiter went over to him.

"What do you want?"

The old man looked at him. "Another brandy," he said.

"You'll be drunk," the waiter said. The old man looked at him. The waiter went away.

"He'll stay all night," he said to his colleague. "I'm sleepy now. I never get into bed before three o'clock. He should have killed himself last week."

The waiter took the brandy bottle and another saucer from the counter inside the café and marched out to the old man's table. He put down the saucer and poured the glass full of brandy.

"You should have killed yourself last week," he said to the deaf man. The old man motioned with his finger. "A little more," he said. The waiter poured on into the glass so that the brandy slopped over and ran down the stem into the top saucer of the pile. "Thank you," the old man said. The waiter took the bottle back inside the café. He sat down at the table with his colleague again.

"He's drunk now," he said.

"He's drunk every night."

"What did he want to kill himself for?"

"How should I know?"

"How did he do it?"

"He hung himself with a rope."

"Who cut him down?"

"His niece."

"Why did they do it?"

"Fear for his soul."

"How much money has he got?"

"He's got plenty."

"He must be eighty years old."

"Anyway I should say he was eighty."

"I wish he would go home. I never get to bed before three o'clock. What kind of hour is that to go to bed?"

"He stays up because he likes it."

"He's lonely. I'm not lonely. I have a wife waiting in bed for me."

"He had a wife once too."

"A wife would be no good to him now."

"You can't tell. He might be better with a wife."

"His niece looks after him."

"I know. You said she cut him down."

"I wouldn't want to be that old. An old man is a nasty thing."

"Not always. This old man is clean. He drinks without spilling. Even now, drunk. Look at him."

"I don't want to look at him. I wish he would go home. He has no regard for those who must work."

The old man looked from his glass across the square, then over at the waiters.

"Another brandy," he said, pointing to his glass. The waiter who was in a hurry came over.

"Finished," he said, speaking with that omission of syntax stupid people employ when talking to drunken people or foreigners. "No more tonight. Close now."

"Another," said the old man.

"No. Finished." The waiter wiped the edge of the table with a towel and shook his head.

The old man stood up, slowly counted the saucers, took a leather coin purse from his pocket and paid for the drinks, leaving half a peseta tip.

The waiter watched him go down the street, a very old man walking unsteadily but with dignity.

"Why didn't you let him stay and drink?" the unhurried waiter asked. They were putting up the shutters. "It is not half-past two."

"I want to go home to bed."

"What is an hour?"

"More to me than to him."

"An hour is the same."

"You talk like an old man yourself. He can buy a bottle and drink at home."

"It's not the same."

"No, it is not," agreed the waiter with a wife. He did not wish to be unjust. He was only in a hurry.

"And you? You have no fear of going home before your usual hour?"

"Are you trying to insult me?"

"No, hombre, only to make a joke."

"No," the waiter who was in a hurry said, rising from pulling down the metal shutters. "I have confidence. I am all confidence."

"You have youth, confidence, and a job," the older waiter said. "You have everything."

"And what do you lack?"

"Everything but work."

"You have everything I have."

"No. I have never had confidence and I am not young."

"Come on. Stop talking nonsense and lock up."

"I am of those who like to stay late at the café," the older waiter said. "With all those who do not want to go to bed. With all those who need a light for the night."

"I want to go home and into bed."

"We are of two different kinds," the older waiter said. He was now dressed to go home. "It is not only a question of youth and confidence although those things are very beautiful. Each night I am reluctant to close up because there may be some one who needs the café."

"Hombre, there are bodegas open all night long."

"You do not understand. This is a clean and pleasant café. It is well lighted. The light is very good and also, now, there are shadows of the leaves."

"Good night," said the younger waiter.

"Good night," the other said. Turning off the electric light he continued the conversation with himself. It is the light of course but it is necessary that the place be clean and pleasant. You do not want music. Certainly you do not want music. Nor can you stand before a bar with dignity although that is all that is provided for these hours. What did he fear? It was not fear or dread. It was a nothing that he knew too well. It was all a nothing and a man was nothing too. It was only that and light was all it needed and a certain cleanness and order. Some lived in it and never felt it but he knew it all was nada y pues nada y nada y pues nada. Our nada who art in nada, nada be thy name thy kingdom nada thy will be nada in nada as it is in nada. Give us this nada our daily nada and nada us our nada as we nada our nadas and nada us not into nada but deliver us from nada; pues nada. Hail nothing full of nothing, nothing is with thee. He smiled and stood before a bar with a shining steam pressure coffee machine.

"What's yours?" asked the barman.

"Nada."

"Otro loco más," said the barman and turned away.

"A little cup," said the waiter.

The barman poured it for him.

"The light is very bright and pleasant but the bar is unpolished," the waiter said.

The barman looked at him but did not answer. It was too late at night for conversation.

"You want another copita?" the barman asked.

"No, thank you," said the waiter and went out. He disliked bars and bodegas. A clean, well-lighted café was a very different thing. Now, without thinking further, he would go home to his room. He would lie in the bed and finally, with daylight, he would go to sleep. After all, he said to himself, it is probably only insomnia. Many must have it.

[1933]

Study and Writing Questions

1. What is the importance of light in this NARRATIVE? What do the shadows of the leaves SYMBOLIZE?
2. What seem to be the fundamental qualities of youth and age here?
3. What is the importance of cleanliness? Why does the older waiter point out that the bar is unpolished?
4. "Nada y pues nada" is Spanish for "nothing and then nothing." What is the waiter thinking about in the "nada" paragraph? What does he believe? What does he want to believe? What is the THEMATIC significance of the term "nada" in this narrative?
5. Consider the last word, "it." What is the "it" that many must have? Why does the waiter say that to himself? What does the IMPLIED AUTHOR seem to believe about "it"?

See also Questions for Contrast and Comparison: 40, 61, 69, 70, 152, and 236.

■ **O. HENRY** (pseudonym for William Sydney Porter; 1862 – 1910) *was born and raised in Greensboro, North Carolina, by his grandmother and aunt after his mother died and his father turned to drinking and inventing a perpetual motion machine. Leaving school at fifteen, he worked in a drugstore until, to treat tuberculosis symptoms, he moved to Texas where he held many jobs, including ranch hand, and founded a humorous weekly,* Rolling Stone *(1894 – 1895). While a teller at a loosely managed Austin bank (1891 – 94), he was accused of embezzlement. Although the bank later withdrew the charges, Porter was indicted and fled to Honduras, returning, when his wife was on her deathbed, to be arrested and convicted. In prison (1899 – 1902) he met many of the characters who later filled his* FICTION. *He transformed his* STYLE *and adopted his famous pseudonym to hide the shame of imprisonment. Upon release, he moved to New York City, haunted its public establishments, and talked with its "four million" people, whom he thought as worthy of fictional treatment as the élite "four hundred." He produced hundreds of "O. Henry" stories set vividly in the city, Central America, and the West and South, most characterized by tolerance,* IRONIC *humor, and surprise endings. He remarried in 1907. Although critical favor shifted from his eloquence to terse, modern* STYLES, *at his death from liver cirrhosis he was the world's most popular writer.*

A Midsummer Knight's Dream

"The knights are dead;
    Their swords are rust.
    Except a few who have to hust-
    Le all the time
    To raise the dust."

Dear reader: It was summertime. The sun glared down upon the city with pitiless ferocity. It is difficult for the sun to be ferocious and exhibit compunction simultaneously. The heat was — oh, bother thermometers! — who cares for standard measures, anyhow? It was so hot that ——

The roof gardens put on so many extra waiters that you could hope to get your gin fizz now — as soon as all the other people got theirs. The hospitals were putting in extra cots for bystanders. For when little woolly dogs loll their tongues out and say "woof, woof!" at the fleas that bite 'em, and nervous old black bombazine ladies screech "Mad dog!" and policemen begin to shoot, somebody is going to get hurt. The man from Pompton, N. J., who always wears an overcoat in July, had turned up in a Broadway hotel drinking hot Scotches and enjoying his annual ray from the calcium. Philanthropists were petitioning the Legislature to pass a bill requiring builders to make tenement fire-escapes more commodious, so that families might die all together of the heat instead of one or two at a time. So many men were telling you about the number of baths they took each day that you wondered how they got along after the real lessee of the apartment came back to town and thanked 'em for taking such good care of it. The young man who called loudly for cold beef and beer in the restaurant, protesting that roast pullet and Burgundy was really too heavy for such weather, blushed when he met your eye, for you had heard him all winter calling, in modest tones, for the same ascetic viands. Soup, pocketbooks, shirt waists, actors, and baseball excuses grew thinner. Yes, it was summertime.

A man stood at Thirty-fourth Street waiting for a downtown car. A man of forty, gray-haired, pink-faced, keen, nervous, plainly dressed, with a harassed look around the eyes. He wiped his forehead and laughed loudly when a fat man with an outing look stopped and spoke with him.

"No, siree," he shouted with defiance and scorn. "None of your old mosquito-haunted swamps and skyscraper mountains without elevators for me. When I want to get away from hot weather I know how to do it. New York, sir, is the finest summer resort in the country. Keep in the shade and watch your diet, and don't get too far away from an electric fan. Talk about your Adirondacks and your Catskills! There's more solid comfort in the borough of Manhattan than in all the rest of the country together. No, siree! No tramping up perpendicular cliffs and being waked up at 4 in the morning by a million flies, and eating canned goods straight from the city for me. Little old New York will take a few select summer boarders; comforts and conveniences of home — that's the ad. that I answer every time."

"You need a vacation," said the fat man, looking closely at the other. "You haven't been away from town in years. Better come with me for two weeks, anyhow. The trout in the Beaverkill are jumping at anything now that looks like a fly. Harding writes me that he landed a three-pound brown last week."

"Nonsense!" cried the other man. "Go ahead, if you like, and boggle around in rubber boots wearing yourself out trying to catch fish. When I want one I go to a cool restaurant and order it. I laugh at you fellows whenever I think of you hustling around in the heat in the country thinking you are having a good time. For me Father Knickerbocker's little improved farm with the big shady lane running through the middle of it."

The fat man sighed over his friend and went his way. The man who thought New York was the greatest summer resort in the country boarded a car and went buzzing down to his office. On the way he threw away his newspaper and looked up at a ragged patch of sky above the housetops.

"Three pounds!" he muttered, absently. "And Harding isn't a liar. I believe, if I could — but it's impossible — they've got to have another month — another month at least."

In his office the upholder of urban midsummer joys dived, head foremost, into the swimming pool of business. Adkins, his clerk, came and added a spray of letters, memoranda and telegrams.

At 5 o'clock in the afternoon the busy man leaned back in his office chair, put his feet on the desk and mused aloud:

"I wonder what kind of bait Harding used."

She was all in white that day; and thereby Compton lost a bet to Gaines. Compton had wagered she would wear light blue, for she knew that was his favorite color, and Compton was a millionaire's son, and that almost laid him open to the charge of betting on a sure thing. But white was her choice, and Gaines held up his head with twenty-five's lordly air.

The little summer hotel in the mountains had a lively crowd that year. There were two or three young college men and a couple of artists and a young naval officer on one side. On the other there were enough beauties among the young ladies for the correspondent of a society paper to refer to them as a "bevy." But the moon among the stars was Mary Sewell. Each one of the young men greatly desired to arrange matters so that he could pay her millinery bills, and fix the furnace, and have her do away with the "Sewell" part of her name forever. Those who could stay only a week or two went away hinting at pistols and blighted hearts. But Compton stayed like the mountains themselves, for he could afford it. And Gaines stayed because he was a fighter and wasn't afraid of millionaires' sons, and—well, he adored the country.

"What do you think, Miss Mary?" he said once. "I knew a duffer in New York who claimed to like it in the summertime. Said you could keep cooler there than you could in the woods. Wasn't he an awful silly? I don't think I could breathe on Broadway after the 1st of June."

"Mamma was thinking of going back week after next," said Miss Mary with a lovely frown.

"But when you think of it," said Gaines, "there are lots of jolly places in town in the summer. The roof gardens, you know, and the—er—the roof gardens."

Deepest blue was the lake that day—the day when they had the mock tournament, and the men rode clumsy farm horses around in a glade in the woods and caught curtain rings on the end of a lance. Such fun!

Cool and dry as the finest wine came the breath of the shadowed forest. The valley below was a vision seen through an opal haze. A white mist from hidden falls blurred the green of a hand's breadth of tree tops halfway down the gorge. Youth made merry hand-in-hand with young summer. Nothing on Broadway like that.

The villagers gathered to see the city folks pursue their mad drollery. The woods rang with the laughter of pixies and naiads and sprites. Gaines caught most of the rings. His was the privilege to crown the queen of the tournament. He was the conquering knight—as far as the rings went. On his arm he wore a white scarf. Compton wore light blue. She had declared her preference for blue, but she wore white that day.

Gaines looked about for the queen to crown her. He heard her merry laugh, as if from the clouds. She had slipped away and climbed Chimney Rock, a little granite bluff, and stood there, a white fairy among the laurels, fifty feet above their heads.

Instantly he and Compton accepted the implied challenge. The bluff was easily mounted at the rear, but the front offered small hold to hand or foot. Each man quickly selected his route and began to climb. A crevice, a bush, a slight projection, a vine or tree branch—all of these were aids that counted in the race. It was all foolery—there was no stake; but there was youth in it, cross reader, and light hearts, and something else that Miss Clay writes so charmingly about.

Gaines gave a great tug at the root of a laurel and pulled himself to Miss Mary's feet. On his arm he carried the wreath of roses; and while the villagers and summer boarders screamed and applauded below he placed it on the queen's brow.

"You are a gallant knight," said Miss Mary.

"If I could be your true knight always," began Gaines, but Miss Mary laughed him dumb, for Compton scrambled over the edge of the rock one minute behind time.

What a twilight that was when they drove back to the hotel! The opal of the valley turned slowly to purple, the dark woods framed the lake as a mirror, the tonic air stirred the very soul in one. The first pale stars came out over the mountain tops where yet a faint glow of ——

"I beg your pardon, Mr. Gaines," said Adkins.

The man who believed New York to be the finest summer resort in the world opened his eyes and kicked over the mucilage bottle on his desk.

"I — I believe I was asleep," he said.

"It's the heat," said Adkins. "It's something awful in the city these —— "

"Nonsense!" said the other. "The city beats the country ten to one in summer. Fools go out tramping in muddy brooks and wear themselves out trying to catch little fish as long as your finger. Stay in town and keep comfortable — that's my idea."

"Some letters just came," said Adkins. "I thought you might like to glance at them before you go."

Let us look over his shoulder and read just a few lines of one of them:

MY DEAR, DEAR HUSBAND: Just received your letter ordering us to stay another month. . . . Rita's cough is almost gone. . . . Johnny has simply gone wild like a little Indian. . . . Will be the making of both children . . . work so hard, and I know that your business can hardly afford to keep us here so long . . . best man that ever . . . you always pretend that you like the city in summer . . . trout fishing that you used to be so fond of . . . and all to keep us well and happy . . . come to you if it were not doing the babies so much good. . . . I stood last evening on Chimney Rock in exactly the same spot where I was when you put the wreath of roses on my head . . . through all the world . . . when you said you would be my true knight . . . fifteen years ago, dear, just think! . . . have always been that to me . . . ever and ever,

MARY.

The man who said he thought New York the finest summer resort in the country dropped into a café on his way home and had a glass of beer under an electric fan.

"Wonder what kind of a fly old Harding used," he said to himself.

[1905]

Study and Writing Questions

1. How do the content, TONE and verse STRUCTURE of the EPIGRAPH prepare you for the NARRATIVE that follows?

2. What is the attitude of the NARRATOR toward his CHARACTERS? Does it change during the NARRATION?
3. What is the attitude of the narrator toward his reader? Does it change during the narration?
4. Why is the final line about fishing? Is the outcome of this narrative sad, happy, or something else? What is this narrative about?
5. What is the relationship of this narrative to Shakespeare's *A Midsummer Night's Dream*? Does knowing something about the play enrich or change your reading of this STORY? If so, how?

See also Questions for Contrast and Comparison: 8, 45, 105, 106, 127, 184, and 214.

Springtime à la Carte

It was a day in March.

Never, never begin a story this way when you write one. No opening could possibly be worse. It is unimaginative, flat, dry, and likely to consist of mere wind. But in this instance it is allowable. For the following paragraph, which should have inaugurated the narrative, is too wildly extravagant and preposterous to be flaunted in the face of the reader without preparation.

Sarah was crying over her bill of fare.

Think of a New York girl shedding tears on the menu card!

To account for this you will be allowed to guess that the lobsters were all out, or that she had sworn ice-cream off during Lent, or that she had ordered onions, or that she had just come from a Hackett matinée. And then, all these theories being wrong, you will please let the story proceed.

The gentleman who announced that the world was an oyster which he with his sword would open made a larger hit than he deserved. It is not difficult to open an oyster with a sword. But did you ever notice any one try to open the terrestrial bivalve with a typewriter? Like to wait for a dozen raw opened that way?

Sarah had managed to pry apart the shells with her unhandy weapon far enough to nibble a wee bit at the cold and clammy world within. She knew no more shorthand than if she had been a graduate in stenography just let slip upon the world by a business college. So, not being able to stenog, she could not enter that bright galaxy of office talent. She was a free-lance typewriter and canvassed for odd jobs of copying.

The most brilliant and crowning feat of Sarah's battle with the world was the deal she made with Schulenberg's Home Restaurant. The restaurant was next door to the old red brick in which she hall-roomed. One evening after dining at Schulenberg's 40-cent, five-course *table d'hôte* (served as fast as you throw the five baseballs at the colored gentleman's head) Sarah took away with her the bill of fare. It was written in an almost unreadable script neither English nor German, and so arranged that if you were not careful you began with a toothpick and rice pudding and ended with soup and the day of the week.

The next day Sarah showed Schulenberg a neat card on which the menu was beautifully typewritten with the viands temptingly marshalled under their right and proper heads from "hors d'œuvre" to "not responsible for over-coats and umbrellas."

Schulenberg became a naturalized citizen on the spot. Before Sarah left him she had him willingly committed to an agreement. She was to furnish typewritten bills of fare for the twenty-one tables in the restaurant—a new bill for each day's dinner, and new ones for breakfast and lunch as often as changes occurred in the food or as neatness required.

In return for this Schulenberg was to send three meals per diem to Sarah's hall room by a waiter—an obsequious one if possible—and furnish her each afternoon with a pencil draft of what Fate had in store for Schulenberg's customers on the morrow.

Mutual satisfaction resulted from the agreement. Schulenberg's patrons now knew what the food they ate was called even if its nature sometimes puzzled them. And Sarah had food during a cold, dull winter, which was the main thing with her.

And then the almanac lied, and said that spring had come. Spring comes when it comes. The frozen snows of January still lay like adamant in the cross-town streets. The hand-organs still played "In the Good Old Summertime," with their December vivacity and expression. Men began to make thirty-day notes to buy Easter dresses. Janitors shut off steam. And when these things happen one may know that the city is still in the clutches of winter.

One afternoon Sarah shivered in her elegant hall bedroom; "house heated; scrupulously clean; conveniences; seen to be appreciated." She had no work to do except Schulenberg's menu cards. Sarah sat in her squeaky willow rocker, and looked out the window. The calendar on the wall kept crying to her: "Springtime is here, Sarah — springtime is here, I tell you. Look at me, Sarah, my figures show it. You've got a neat figure yourself, Sarah — a — nice springtime figure — why do you look out the window so sadly?"

Sarah's room was at the back of the house. Looking out the window she could see the windowless rear brick wall of the box factory on the next street. But the wall was clearest crystal; and Sarah was looking down a grassy lane shaded with cherry trees and elms and bordered with raspberry bushes and Cherokee roses.

Spring's real harbingers are too subtle for the eye and ear. Some must have the flowering crocus, the wood-starring dogwood, the voice of bluebird — even so gross a reminder as the farewell handshake of the retiring buckwheat and oyster before they can welcome the Lady in Green to their dull bosoms. But to old earth's choicest kind there come straight, sweet messages from his newest bride, telling them they shall be no stepchildren unless they choose to be.

On the previous summer Sarah had gone into the country and loved a farmer.

(In writing your story never hark back thus. It is bad art, and cripples interest. Let it march, march.)

Sarah stayed two weeks at Sunnybrook Farm. There she learned to love old Farmer Franklin's son Walter. Farmers have been loved and wedded and turned out to grass in less time. But young Walter Franklin was a modern agriculturist. He had a telephone in his cow house, and he could figure up exactly what effect next year's Canada wheat crop would have on potatoes planted in the dark of the moon.

It was in this shaded and raspberried lane that Walter had wooed and won her. And together they had sat and woven a crown of dandelions for her hair. He had immoderately praised the effect of the yellow blossoms against her brown tresses; and she had left the chaplet there, and walked back to the house swinging her straw sailor in her hands.

They were to marry in the spring — at the very first signs of spring, Walter said. And Sarah came back to the city to pound her typewriter.

A knock at the door dispelled Sarah's visions of that happy day. A waiter had brought the rough pencil draft of the Home Restaurant's next day fare in old Schulenberg's angular hand.

Sarah sat down to her typewriter and slipped a card between the rollers. She was a nimble worker. Generally in an hour and a half the twenty-one menu cards were written and ready.

To-day there were more changes on the bill of fare than usual. The soups were lighter; pork was eliminated from the entrées, figuring only with Russian turnips among the roasts. The gracious spirit of spring pervaded the entire menu. Lamb, that lately capered on the greening hillsides, was becoming exploited with the sauce that commemorated its gambols. The song of the oyster, though not silenced, was *dimuendo con amore*. The frying-pan seemed to be held, inactive, behind the beneficent bars of the broiler. The pie list swelled; the richer puddings had vanished; the sausage, with his drapery wrapped about him, barely lingered in a pleasant thanatopsis with the buckwheats and the sweet but doomed maple.

Sarah's fingers danced like midgets above a summer stream. Down through the courses she worked, giving each item its position according to its length with an accurate eye.

Just above the desserts came the list of vegetables. Carrots and peas, asparagus on toast, the perennial tomatoes and corn and succotash, lima beans, cabbage — and then —

Sarah was crying over her bill of fare. Tears from the depths of some divine despair rose in her heart and gathered to her eyes. Down went her head on the little typewriter stand; and the keyboard rattled a dry accompaniment to her moist sobs.

For she had received no letter from Walter in two weeks and the next item on the bill of fare was dandelions — dandelions with some kind of egg — but bother the egg! — dandelions, with whose golden blooms Walter had crowned her his queen of love and future bride — dandelions, the harbingers of spring, her sorrow's crown of sorrow — reminder of her happiest days.

Madam, I dare you to smile until you suffer this test: Let the Marechal Niel roses that Percy brought you on the night you gave him your heart be served as a salad with French dressing before your eyes at a Schulenberg *table d'hôte*. Had Juliet so seen her love tokens dishonored the sooner would she have sought the lethean herbs of the good apothecary.

But what witch is Spring! Into the great cold city of stone and iron a message had to be sent. There was none to convey it but the little hardy courier of the fields with his rough green coat and modest air. He is a true soldier of fortune, this *dent-de-lion* — this lion's tooth, as the French chefs call him. Flowered, he will assist at love-making, wreathed in my lady's nut-brown hair; young and callow and unblossomed, he goes into the boiling pot and delivers the word of his sovereign mistress.

By and by Sarah forced back her tears. The cards must be written. But, still in a faint, golden glow from her dandelion dream, she fingered the typewriter keys absently for a little while, with her mind and heart in the meadow lane with her young farmer. But soon she came swiftly back to the rock-bound lanes of Manhattan, and the typewriter began to rattle and jump like a strike-breaker's motor car.

At 6 o'clock the waiter brought her dinner and carried away the typewritten bill of fare. When Sarah ate she set aside, with a sigh, the dish of dandelions with its crowning ovarious accompaniment. As this dark mass had been transformed from a bright and love-indorsed flower to be an ignominious vegetable, so had her summer hopes wilted and perished. Love may, as Shakespeare said, feed on itself: but Sarah could not bring herself to eat the dandelions that had graced, as ornaments, the first spiritual banquet of her heart's true affection.

At 7:30 the couple in the next room began to quarrel: the man in the room above sought for A on his flute; the gas went a little lower; three coal wagons started to unload — the only sound of which the phonograph is jealous; cats on the back fences slowly retreated toward Mukden. By these signs Sarah knew that it was time for her to read. She got out "The Cloister and the Hearth," the best non-selling book of the month, settled her feet on her trunk, and began to wander with Gerard.

The front door bell rang. The landlady answered it. Sarah left Gerard and Denys treed by a bear and listened. Oh, yes; you would, just as she did!

And then a strong voice was heard in the hall below, and Sarah jumped for her door, leaving the book on the floor and the first round easily the bear's.

You have guessed it. She reached the top of the stairs just as her farmer came up, three at a jump, and reaped and garnered her, with nothing left for the gleaners.

"Why haven't you written — oh, why?" cried Sarah.

"New York is a pretty large town," said Walter Franklin. "I came in a week ago to your old address. I found that you went away on a Thursday. That consoled some; it eliminated the possible Friday bad luck. But it didn't prevent my hunting for you with police and otherwise ever since!"

"I wrote!" said Sarah, vehemently.

"Never got it!"

"Then how did you find me?"

The young farmer smiled a springtime smile.

"I dropped into that Home Restaurant next door this evening," said he. "I don't care who knows it; I like a dish of some kind of greens at this time of the year. I ran my eye down that nice typewritten bill of fare looking for something in that line. When I got below cabbage I turned my chair over and hollered for the proprietor. He told me where you lived."

"I remember," sighed Sarah, happily. "That was dandelions below cabbage."

"I'd know that cranky capital W 'way above the line that your typewriter makes anywhere in the world," said Franklin.

"Why, there's no W in dandelions," said Sarah in surprise.

The young man drew the bill of fare from his pocket and pointed to a line.

Sarah recognized the first card she had typewritten that afternoon. There was still the rayed splotch in the upper right-hand corner where a tear had fallen. But over the spot where one should have read the name of the meadow plant, the clinging memory of their golden blossoms had allowed her fingers to strike strange keys.

Between the red cabbage and the stuffed green peppers was the item:

"DEAREST WALTER, WITH HARD-BOILED EGG."

[1905]

Study and Writing Questions

1. In what ways are the NARRATOR's attitudes toward the CHARACTERS and toward the reader alike and in what ways different?
2. How important is the SELF-REFLEXIVITY of this NARRATIVE? To what extent is this a STORY about storytelling?

3. What are the effects of the last line? Is it too predictable? too SENTIMENTAL? Why does it for the first time reveal the accompaniment to the greens?

4. How is SUSPENSE manipulated in this narrative? Since we suspect quite early whether or not there will be a successful reunion, what keeps us reading?

5. In some ways this narrative concerns economics, writing, and romance. Do these topics work together in a single, coherent narrative? If so, how? If not, what is the overall effect of the narrative for you?

See also Questions for Contrast and Comparison: 8, 11, 41, 105, 106, 125, and 184.

GILBERTO HERNANDEZ (1957–) *was the second son of a large, Chicano family that lived in an ethnically mixed, working-class neighborhood in Oxnard, California. His mother had collected comics as a child and practiced copying and blowing up individual panels. His father worked nights, slept days, and died young, but his sons remember that he had painted in his youth and brought home crayons to "turn us loose." All the children played at drawing, led by the eldest, Mario, and Gilberto, "the most creative one." The Hernandez brothers consider the main influences on their work to be The Fantastic Four with its superheroes and monsters; Archie with its satiric focus on teen life; Dennis the Menace with its exuberance for mischief; "underground" comics, notably the intentionally outrageous Zap Comics and the "hip" work of R. Crumb; and the punk music of the Sex Pistols. After five years of virtual unemployment after high school, Gilberto, with Mario and Jaime, sold (1982) a collection of science fictional, socially analytical* TALES *to a then-new publisher. Fantagraphics Books became a powerhouse in alternative comics, and Love and Rockets was the first American comic to succeed in the European mode of album publication of previously serialized work. The brothers continue to innovate with such noteworthy series as Mr. X and Heartbreak Soup. They still live in Oxnard.*

Study Questions

1. Although Ofelia has no lines, she is in the first and last panel. What is the relationship between children and adults in this NARRATIVE world?
2. What is the effect on the reader of mixing English and Spanish?
3. What are the effects of naming the unseen man "Beto," a nickname for the AUTHOR?
4. Does the RESOLUTION of this narrative produce POETIC JUSTICE? Why does the IMPLIED AUTHOR have Beto say "urp"?
5. Consider the THEME of knowledge and belief in this narrative. What are each of the CHARACTERS supposed to learn? What are we supposed to learn? What is the relationship between the daily world and the world of FAIRY TALE in this narrative?

See also Questions for Contrast and Comparison: 8, 32, 52, 95, 139, 199, and 238.

The Whispering Tree

[1984]

■■■ **SPENCER HOLST** (1926–) *was born in Detroit, Michigan, to a family of*
■■■ *journalists: his great-grandfather, a physician, founded the Weston, Ohio*
Avalanche *shortly after the Civil War; his grandmother wrote a gossip column for
sixty years; his father, Lawrence Spencer "Doc" Holst, was a life-time baseball
writer for the Detroit* Free Press *and Detroit* Times; *and his mother worked on
several suburban newspapers. He left home for New York City after the tenth grade
(1942) "to be a poet—and failed." Nevertheless, he has lived there ever since,
successfully producing wry, compressed* FICTIONS *that he has recited to enthusiastic
audiences (winning performance awards) and published in two incomplete collections,* The Language of Cats and Other Stories *(1971) and* Spencer Holst Stories
*(1976), which won the American Academy and Institute of Arts and Letters
Rosenthal Award for fiction. His complete fiction is now collected in* The Zebra
Storyteller *(1993). Preferring the life of a "true artist," until the mid-1980s, when he
became a typographical proofreader, Holst has never held a long-term job or one
directly concerned with writing. Although he knows no German, he collaborated
with Vera Lachmann in producing the three-volume translation of her poetry. Since
1990, he has also painted. For more than thirty years, he has been married to the
painter Beate Wheeler. They have a son.*

The Zebra Storyteller

ONCE upon a time there was a Siamese cat who pretended to be a lion and spoke
inappropriate Zebraic.

That language is whinnied by the race of striped horses in Africa.

Here now: An innocent zebra is walking in a jungle and approaching from
another direction is the little cat; they meet.

"Hello there!" says the Siamese cat in perfectly pronounced Zebraic, "It
certainly is a pleasant day, isn't it? The sun is shining, the birds are singing, isn't
the world a lovely place to live today!"

The zebra is so astonished at hearing a Siamese cat speaking like a zebra,
why—he's just fit to be tied.

So the little cat quickly ties him up, kills him, and drags the better parts of
the carcass back to his den.

The cat successfully hunted zebras many months in this manner, dining on
filet mignon of zebra every night, and from the better hides he made bow neckties
and wide belts after the fashion of the decadent princes of the Old Siamese court.

He began boasting to his friends he was a lion, and he gave them as proof the
fact that he hunted zebras.

The delicate noses of the zebras told them there was really no lion in the
neighborhood. The zebra deaths caused many to avoid the region. Superstitious,
they decided the woods were haunted by the ghost of a lion.

One day the storyteller of the zebras was ambling, and through his mind ran
plots for stories to amuse the other zebras, when suddenly his eyes brightened,
and he said, "That's it! I'll tell a story about a Siamese cat who learns to speak our
language! What an idea! That'll make 'em laugh!"

Just then the Siamese cat appeared before him, and said, "Hello there!
Pleasant day today, isn't it!"

The zebra storyteller wasn't fit to be tied at hearing a cat speaking his language, because he'd been thinking about that very thing.

He took a good look at the cat, and he didn't know why, but there was something about his looks he didn't like, so he kicked him with a hoof and killed him.

That is the function of the storyteller.

[1971]

Study and Writing Questions

1. What are the FAIRY TALE elements of this NARRATIVE? In what way do they contribute to the TONE and DIDACTIC purpose of the narrative?
2. Describe the Siamese cat. What are his strengths and what are his weaknesses?
3. Describe the title CHARACTER. What are his strengths and what are his weaknesses? How would Holst's STORY or the title character's story be different if the title character were a different type of animal? (Note: Siamese cats and zebras do not normally inhabit the same environment.)
4. What are the sources and importance of humor in this narrative?
5. Consider the SELF-REFLEXIVITY of this narrative. What does this narrative say or imply about stories and storytellers? Does what it says about them apply to this story?

See also Questions for Contrast and Comparison: 5, 11, 28, 93, 132, 139, 146, 155, 184, 227, and 240.

HENRY JAMES (1843–1916), *grandson of a wealthy Albany, New York, merchant, was raised to a life of philosophical speculation. His father wrote widely about spirituality, while his brother William both supported the importance of religion and helped found modern experimental psychology. Born in New York City, Henry was privately tutored there, in New England, and throughout Europe. Multitalented, he entered Harvard Law School at nineteen, but encouraged by such important figures as C. E. Norton, James Russell Lowell, and William Dean Howells, began writing in 1865 and published prolifically thereafter. Believing America too culturally restrictive for a writer, he lived most of his life after 1875 in Europe. Although his attempts in the 1890s at* DRAMA *were not successful, he was a perceptive literary theorist. His ideas of "scenic progression" helped raise his complex* NOVELS *and* STORIES, *often restricted to a single* VIEWPOINT, *to the first rank in literary influence. Many of his works explore the vocation of artist (*The Aspern Papers, *1888;* Roderick Hudson, *1876) and the relations between European sophistication and American rectitude and vigor (*Daisy Miller, *1879;* The Portrait of a Lady, *1881;* The Ambassadors, *1903). To protest U.S. reluctance to enter World War I, he converted to British citizenship in 1915. The next year, he was awarded the Order of Merit. He never married. His ashes are buried in Cambridge, Massachusetts.*

The Altar of the Dead

I

He had a mortal dislike, poor Stransom, to lean anniversaries, and he disliked them still more when they made a pretence of a figure. Celebrations and suppressions were equally painful to him, and there was only one of the former that found a place in his life. Again and again he had kept in his own fashion the day of the year on which Mary Antrim died. It would be more to the point perhaps to say that the day kept *him*: it kept him at least, effectually, from doing anything else. It took hold of him year after year with a hand of which time had softened but had never loosened the touch. He waked up to this feast of memory as consciously as he would have waked up to his marriage-morn. Marriage had had, of old, but too little to say to the matter: for the girl who was to have been his bride there had been no bridal embrace. She had died of a malignant fever after the wedding-day had been fixed, and he had lost, before fairly tasting it, an affection that promised to fill his life to the brim.

Of that benediction, however, it would have been false to say this life could really be emptied: it was still ruled by a pale ghost, it was still ordered by a sovereign presence. He had not been a man of numerous passions, and even in all these years no sense had grown stronger with him than the sense of being bereft. He had needed no priest and no altar to make him forever widowed. He had done many things in the world—he had done almost all things but one: he had never forgotten. He had tried to put into his existence whatever else might take up room in it, but he had never made it anything but a house of which the mistress was eternally absent. She was most absent of all on the recurrent December day that his tenacity set apart. He had no designed observance of it, but his nerves made it all their own. They always drove him forth on a long walk, for the goal of his pilgrimage was far. She had been buried in a London suburb, in a place then almost natural, but which he had seen lose one after another every feature of freshness. It was in truth during the moments he stood there that his eyes beheld the place least. They looked at another image, they opened to another light. Was it a credible future? Was it an incredible past? Whatever it was, it was an immense escape from the actual.

It is true that if there were not other dates than this there were other memories; and by the time George Stransom was fifty-five such memories had greatly multiplied. There were other ghosts in his life than the ghost of Mary Antrim. He had perhaps not had more losses than most men, but he had counted his losses more; he had not seen death more closely, but he had, in a manner, felt it more deeply. He had formed little by little the habit of numbering his Dead: it had come to him tolerably early in life that there was something one had to do for them. They were there in their simplified, intensified essence, their conscious absence and expressive patience, as personally there as if they had only been stricken dumb. When all sense of them failed, all sound of them ceased, it was as if their purgatory were really still on earth: they asked so little that they got, poor things, even less, and died again, died every day, of the hard usage of life. They had no organized service, no reserved place, no honour, no shelter, no safety. Even ungenerous people provided for the living, but even those who were called most generous did nothing for the others. So, on George Stransom's part, there grew up with the years a determination that he at least would do something, do it, that is, for his own, and perform the great charity without reproach. Every man had his own, and every man had, to meet this charity, the ample resources of the soul.

It was doubtless the voice of Mary Antrim that spoke for them best; at any rate, as the years went on, he found himself in regular communion with these alternative associates, with those whom indeed he always called in his thoughts the Others. He spared them the moments, he organized the charity. How it grew up he probably never could have told you, but what came to pass was that an altar, such as was after all within everybody's compass, lighted with perpetual candles and dedicated to these secret rites, reared itself in his spiritual spaces. He had wondered of old, in some embarrassment, whether he had a religion; being very sure, and not a little content, that he had not at all events the religion some of the people he had known wanted him to have. Gradually this question was straightened out for him: it became clear to him that the religion instilled by his earliest consciousness had been simply the religion of the Dead. It suited his inclination, it satisfied his spirit, it gave employment to his piety. It answered his love of great offices, of a solemn and splendid ritual, for no shrine could be more bedecked and no ceremonial more stately than those to which his worship was attached. He had no imagination about these things save that they were accessible to every one who should ever feel the need of them. The poorest could build such temples of the spirit — could make them blaze with candles and smoke with incense, make them flush with pictures and flowers. The cost, in the common phrase, of keeping them up fell entirely on the liberal heart.

II

He had this year, on the eve of his anniversary, as it happened, an emotion not unconnected with that range of feeling. Walking home at the close of a busy day, he was arrested in the London street by the particular effect of a shop-front which lighted the dull brown air with its mercenary grin and before which several persons were gathered. It was the window of a jeweller whose diamonds and sapphires seemed to laugh, in flashes like high notes of sound, with the mere joy of knowing how much more they were 'worth' than most of the dingy pedestrians staring at them from the other side of the pane. Stransom lingered long enough to suspend, in a vision, a string of pearls about the white neck of Mary Antrim, and then was kept an instant longer by the sound of a voice he knew. Next him was a mumbling old woman, and beyond the old woman a gentleman with a lady on his arm. It was from him, from Paul Creston, the voice had proceeded: he was talking with the lady of some precious object in the window. Stransom had no sooner recognized him than the old woman turned away; but simultaneously with this increase of opportunity he became aware of a strangeness which stayed him in the very act of laying his hand on his friend's arm. It lasted only a few seconds, but a few seconds were long enough for the flash of a wild question. Was *not* Mrs Creston dead? — the ambiguity met him there in the short drop of her husband's voice, the drop conjugal, if it ever was, and in the way the two figures leaned to each other. Creston, making a step to look at something else, came nearer, glanced at him, started and exclaimed — a circumstance the effect of which was at first only to leave Stransom staring, staring back across the months at the different face, the wholly other face the poor man had shown him last, the blurred, ravaged mask bent over the open grave by which they had stood together. Creston was not in mourning now; he detached his arm from his companion's to grasp the hand of the older friend. He coloured as well as smiled in the strong light of the shop when Stransom raised a tentative hat to the lady. Stransom had just time to see that she was pretty before he found himself gaping at a fact more portentous. 'My dear fellow, let me make you acquainted with my wife.'

Creston had blushed and stammered over it, but in half a minute, at the rate we live in polite society, it had practically become, for Stransom, the mere memory of a shock. They stood there and laughed and talked; Stransom had instantly whisked the shock out of the way, to keep it for private consumption. He felt himself grimacing, he heard himself exaggerating the usual, but he was conscious that he had turned slightly faint. That new woman, that hired performer, Mrs Creston? Mrs Creston had been more living for him than any woman but one. This lady had a face that shone as publicly as the jeweller's window, and in the happy candour with which she wore her monstrous character there was an effect of gross immodesty. The character of Paul Creston's wife thus attributed to her was monstrous for reasons which Stransom could see that his friend perfectly knew that he knew. The happy pair had just arrived from America, and Stransom had not needed to be told this to divine the nationality of the lady. Somehow it deepened the foolish air that her husband's confused cordiality was unable to conceal. Stransom recalled that he had heard of poor Creston's having, while his bereavement was still fresh, gone to the United States for what people in such predicaments call a little change. He had found the little change indeed, he had brought the little change back; it was the little change that stood there and that, do what he would, he couldn't, while he showed those high front-teeth of his, look like anything but a conscious ass about. They were going into the shop Mrs Creston said, and she begged Mr Stransom to come with them and help to decide. He thanked her, opening his watch and pleading an engagement for which he was already late, and they parted while she shrieked into the fog, 'Mind now you come to see me right away!' Creston had had the delicacy not to suggest that, and Stransom hoped it hurt him somewhere to hear her scream it to all the echoes.

He felt quite determined, as he walked away, never in his life to go near her. She was perhaps a human being, but Creston oughtn't to have shown her without precautions, oughtn't indeed to have shown her at all. His precautions should have been those of a forger or a murderer, and the people at home would never have mentioned extradition. This was a wife for foreign service or purely external use; a decent consideration would have spared her the injury of comparisons. Such were the first reflections of George Stransom's amazement; but as he sat alone that night — there were particular hours that he always passed alone — the harshness dropped from them and left only the pity. He could spend an evening with Kate Creston, if the man to whom she had given everything couldn't. He had known her twenty years, and she was the only woman for whom he might perhaps have been unfaithful. She was all cleverness and sympathy and charm; her house had been the very easiest in all the world and her friendship the very firmest. Without accidents he had loved her, without accidents every one had loved her: she had made the passions about her as regular as the moon makes the tides. She had been also of course far too good for her husband, but he never suspected it, and in nothing had she been more admirable than in the exquisite art with which she tried to keep every one else (keeping Creston was no trouble) from finding it out. Here was a man to whom she had devoted her life and for whom she had given it up — dying to bring into the world a child of his bed; and she had had only to submit to her fate to have, ere the grass was green on her grave, no more existence for him than a domestic servant he had replaced. The frivolity, the indecency of it made Stransom's eyes fill; and he had that evening a rich, almost happy sense that he alone, in a world without delicacy, had a right to hold up his head. While he smoked, after dinner, he had a book in his lap, but he had no eyes for his page: his eyes, in the swarming void of things, seemed to have caught Kate Creston's, and it was into their sad silences he looked. It was to him her sentient spirit had turned, knowing that it was of her he would think. He thought, for a long time, of how the closed eyes of dead women could still live — how they could open again, in a quiet lamplit room, long after they had looked their last. They had looks that remained, as great poets had quoted lines.

The newspaper lay by his chair — the thing that came in the afternoon and the servants thought one wanted; without sense for what was in it he had mechanically unfolded and then dropped it. Before he went to bed he took it up, and this time, at the top of a paragraph, he was caught by five words that made him start. He stood staring, before the fire, at the 'Death of Sir Acton Hague, KCB,' the man who, ten years earlier, had been the nearest of his friends and whose deposition from this eminence had practically left it without an occupant. He had seen him after that catastrophe, but he had not seen him for years. Standing there before the fire he turned cold as he read what had befallen him. Promoted a short time previous to the governorship of the Westward Islands,

Acton Hague had died, in the bleak honour of this exile, of an illness consequent on the bite of a poisonous snake. His career was compressed by the newspaper into a dozen lines, the perusal of which excited on George Stransom's part no warmer feeling than one of relief at the absence of any mention of their quarrel, an incident accidentally tainted at the time, thanks to their joint immersion in large affairs, with a horrible publicity. Public indeed was the wrong Stransom had, to his own sense, suffered, the insult he had blankly taken from the only man with whom he had ever been intimate; the friend, almost adored, of his University years, the subject, later, of his passionate loyalty: so public that he had never spoken of it to a human creature, so public that he had completely overlooked it. It had made the difference for him that friendship too was all over, but it had only made just that one. The shock of interests had been private, intensely so; but the action taken by Hague had been in the face of men. Today it all seemed to have occurred merely to the end that George Stransom should think of him as 'Hague' and measure exactly how much he himself could feel like a stone. He went cold, suddenly and horribly cold, to bed.

III

The next day, in the afternoon, in the great grey suburb, he felt that his long walk had tired him. In the dreadful cemetery alone he had been on his feet an hour. Instinctively, coming back, they had taken him a devious course, and it was a desert in which no circling cabman hovered over possible prey. He paused on a corner and measured the dreariness; then he became aware in the gathered dusk that he was in one of those tracts of London which are less gloomy by night than by day, because, in the former case, of the civil gift of light. By day there was nothing, but by night there were lamps, and George Stransom was in a mood which made lamps good in themselves. It wasn't that they could show him anything; it was only that they could burn clear. To his surprise, however, after a while, they did show him something: the arch of a high doorway approached by a low terrace of steps, in the depth of which — it formed a dim vestibule — the raising of a curtain, at the moment he passed, gave him a glimpse of an avenue of gloom with a glow of tapers at the end. He stopped and looked up, making out that the place was a church. The thought quickly came to him that since he was tired he might rest there; so that after a moment he had in turn pushed up the leathern curtain and gone in. It was a temple of the old persuasion, and there had evidently been a function — perhaps a service for the dead; the high altar was still a blaze of candles. This was an exhibition he always liked, and he dropped into a seat with relief. More than it had ever yet come home to him it struck him as good that there should be churches.

This one was almost empty and the other altars were dim; a verger shuffled about, an old woman coughed, but it seemed to Stransom there was hospitality in the thick sweet air. Was it only the savour of the incense, or was it something larger and more guaranteed? He had at any rate quitted the great grey suburb and come nearer to the warm centre. He presently ceased to feel an intruder — he gained at last even a sense of community with the only worshipper in his neighbourhood, the sombre presence of a woman, in mourning unrelieved, whose back was all he could see of her and who had sunk deep into prayer at no great distance from him. He wished he could sink, like her, to the very bottom, be as motionless, as rapt in prostration. After a few moments he shifted his seat; it was almost indelicate to be so aware of her. But Stransom subsequently lost himself altogether; he floated away on the sea of light. If occasions like this had been more frequent in his life he would have been more frequently conscious of the great original type, set up in a myriad temples, of the unapproachable shrine he had erected in his mind. That shrine had begun as a reflection of ecclesiastical pomps, but the echo had ended by growing more distinct than the sound. The sound now rang out, the type blazed at him with all its fires and with a mystery of radiance in which endless meanings could glow. The thing became, as he sat there, his appropriate altar, and each starry candle an appropriate vow. He numbered them, he named them, he grouped them — it was the silent roll-call of his Dead. They made together a brightness vast and intense, a brightness in which the mere chapel of his thoughts grew so dim that as it faded away he asked himself if he shouldn't find his real comfort in some material act, some outward worship.

This idea took possession of him while, at a distance, the black-robed lady continued prostrate; he was quietly thrilled with his conception, which at last brought him to his feet in the sudden excitement of a plan. He wandered softly about the church, pausing in the different chapels, which were all, save one, applied to a special devotion. It was in this one, dark and ungarnished, that he stood longest — the length of time it took him fully to grasp the conception of gilding it with his bounty. He should snatch it from no other rites and associate it with nothing profane; he would simply take it as it should be given up to him and make it a masterpiece of splendour and a mountain of fire. Tended sacredly all the year, with the sanctifying church around it, it would always be ready for his offices. There would be difficulties, but from the first they presented themselves only as difficulties surmounted. Even for a person so little affiliated the thing would be a matter of arrangement. He saw it all in advance, and how bright in especial the place would become to him in the intermissions of toil and the dusk of afternoons; how rich in assurance at all times, but especially in the indifferent world. Before withdrawing he drew nearer again to the spot where he had first sat down, and in the movement he met the lady whom he had seen praying and who was now on her way to the door. She passed him quickly, and he had only a glimpse of her pale face and her unconscious, almost sightless eyes. For that instant she looked faded and handsome.

This was the origin of the rites more public, yet certainly esoteric, that he at last found himself able to establish. It took a long time, it took a year, and both the process and the result would have been — for any who knew — a vivid picture of his good faith. No one did know, in fact — no one but the bland ecclesiastics whose acquaintance he had promptly sought, whose objections he had softly overridden, whose curiosity and sympathy he had artfully charmed, whose assent to his eccentric munificence he had eventually won, and who had asked for concessions in exchange for indulgences. Stransom had of course at an early stage of his inquiry been referred to the Bishop, and the Bishop had been delightfully human, the Bishop had been almost amused. Success was within sight, at any rate, from the moment the attitude of those whom it concerned became liberal in response to liberality. The altar and the small chapel that enclosed it, consecrated to an ostensible and customary worship, were to be splendidly maintained; all that Stransom reserved to himself was the number of his lights and the free enjoyment of his intention. When the intention had taken complete effect the enjoyment became even greater than he had ventured to hope. He liked to think of this effect when he was far from it — he liked to convince himself of it yet again when he was near. He was not often, indeed, so near as that a visit to it had not perforce something of the patience of a pilgrimage; but the time he gave to his devotion came to seem to him more a contribution to his other interests than a betrayal of them. Even a loaded life might be easier when one had added a new necessity to it.

How much easier was probably never guessed by those who simply knew that there were hours when he disappeared and for many of whom there was a vulgar reading of what they used to call his plunges. These plunges were into depths quieter than the deep sea-caves, and the habit, at the end of a year or two, had become the one it would have cost him most to relinquish. Now they had really, his Dead, something that was indefeasibly theirs; and he liked to think that they might, in cases, be the Dead of others, as well as that the Dead of others might be invoked there under the protection of what he had done. Whoever bent a knee on the carpet he had laid down appeared to him to act in the spirit of his intention. Each of his lights had a name for him, and from time to time a new light was kindled. This was what he had fundamentally agreed for, that there should always be room for them all. What those who passed or lingered saw was simply the most resplendent of the altars, called suddenly into vivid usefulness, with a quiet elderly man, for whom it evidently had a fascination, often seated there in a maze or a doze; but half the satisfaction of the spot for this mysterious and fitful worshipper was that he found the years of his life there, and the ties, the affections, the struggles, the submissions, the conquests, if there had been such, a record of that adventurous journey in which the beginnings and the endings of human relations are the lettered mile-stones. He had in general little taste for the past as a part of his own history; at other times and in other places it mostly seemed to him pitiful to consider and impossible to repair; but on these occasions he accepted it with something of that positive gladness with which one adjusts one's self to an ache that is beginning to succumb to treatment. To the treatment of time the malady of life begins at a given moment to succumb; and these were doubtless the hours at which that truth most came home to him. The day was written for him there on which he had first become acquainted with death, and the successive phases of the acquaintance were each marked with a flame.

The flames were gathering thick at present, for Stransom had entered that dark defile of our earthly descent in which some one dies every day. It was only yesterday that Kate Creston had flashed out her white fire; yet already there were younger stars ablaze on the tips of the tapers. Various persons in whom his interest had not been intense drew closer to him by entering this company. He went over it, head by head, till he felt like the shepherd of a huddled flock, with all a shepherd's vision of differences imperceptible. He knew his candles apart, up to the colour of the flame, and would still have known them had their positions all been changed. To other imaginations they might stand for other things — that they should stand for something to be hushed before was all he desired; but he was intensely conscious of the personal note of each and of the distinguishable way it contributed to the concert. There were hours at which he almost caught himself wishing that certain of his friends would now die, that he might establish with them in this manner a connection more charming than, as it happened, it was possible to enjoy with them in life. In regard to those from whom one was separated by the long curves of the globe such a connection could only be an improvement: it brought them instantly within reach. Of course there were gaps in the constellation, for Stransom knew he could only pretend to act for his own, and it was not every figure passing before his eyes into the great obscure that was entitled to a memorial. There was a strange sanctification in death, but some characters were more sanctified by being forgotten than by being remembered. The greatest blank in the shining page was the memory of Acton Hague, of which he inveterately tried to rid himself. For Acton Hague no flame could ever rise on any altar of his.

IV

Every year, the day he walked back from the great graveyard, he went to church as he had done the day his idea was born. It was on this occasion, as it happened, after a year had passed, that he began to observe his altar to be haunted by a worshipper at least as frequent as himself. Others of the faithful, and in the rest of the church, came and went, appealing sometimes, when they disappeared, to a vague or to a particular recognition; but this unfailing presence was always to be observed when he arrived and still in possession when he departed. He was surprised, the first time, at the promptitude with which it assumed an identity for him — the identity of the lady whom, two years before, on his anniversary, he had seen so intensely bowed, and of whose tragic face he had had so flitting a vision. Given the time that had elapsed, his recollection of her was fresh enough to make him wonder. Of himself she had of course no impression, or rather she had none at first: the time came when her manner of transacting her business suggested to him that she had gradually guessed his call to be of the same order. She used his altar for her own purpose — he could only hope that, sad and solitary as she always struck him, she used it for her own Dead. There were interruptions, infidelities, all on his part, calls to other associations and duties; but as the months went on he found her whenever he returned, and he ended by taking pleasure in the thought that he had given her almost the contentment he had given himself. They worshipped side by side so often that there were moments when he wished he might be sure, so straight did their prospect stretch away of growing old together in their rites. She was younger than he, but she looked as if her Dead were at least as numerous as his candles. She had no colour, no sound, no fault, and another of the things about which he had made up his mind was that she had no fortune. She was always black-robed, as if she had had a succession of sorrows. People were not poor, after all, whom so many losses could overtake; they were positively rich when they had so much to give up. But the air of this devoted and indifferent woman, who always made, in any attitude, a beautiful, accidental line, conveyed somehow to Stransom that she had known more kinds of trouble than one.

He had a great love of music and little time for the joy of it; but occasionally, when workaday noises were muffled by Saturday afternoons, it used to come back to him that there were glories. There were moreover friends who reminded him of this and side by side with whom he found himself sitting out concerts. On one of these winter evenings, in St James's Hall, he became aware after he had seated himself that the lady he had so often seen at church was in the place next him and was evidently alone, as he also this time happened to be. She was at first too absorbed in the consideration of the programme to heed him, but when she at last glanced at him he took advantage of the movement to speak to her, greeting her with the remark that he felt as if he already knew her. She smiled as she said 'Oh yes, I recognize you'; yet in spite of this admission of their long acquaintance it was the first time he had ever seen her smile. The effect of it was suddenly to contribute more to that acquaintance than all the previous meetings had done. He hadn't 'taken in', he said to himself, that she was so pretty. Later, that evening (it was while he rolled along in a hansom on his way to dine out) he added that he hadn't taken in that she was so interesting. The next morning, in the midst of his work, he quite suddenly and irrelevantly reflected that his impression of her, beginning so far back, was like a winding river that had at last reached the sea.

His work was indeed blurred a little, all that day, by the sense of what had now passed between them. It wasn't much, but it had just made the difference. They had listened together to Beethoven and Schumann; they had talked in the pauses and at the end, when at the door, to which they moved together, he had asked her if he could help her in the matter of getting away. She had thanked him and put up her umbrella, slipping into the crowd without an allusion to their meeting yet again and leaving him to remember at leisure that not a word had been exchanged about the place in which they frequently met. This circumstance seemed to him at one moment natural enough and at another perverse. She mighn't in the least have recognized his warrant for speaking to her; and yet if she hadn't he would have judged her an underbred woman. It was odd that when nothing had really ever brought them together he should have been able success- fully to assume that they were in a manner old friends — that this negative quantity was somehow more than they could express. His success, it was true, had been qualified by her quick escape, so that there grew up in him an absurd desire to put it to some better test. Save in so far as some other improbable accident might assist him, such a test could be only to meet her afresh at church. Left to himself he would have gone to church the very next afternoon, just for the curiosity of seeing if he should find her there. But he was not left to himself, a fact he discovered quite at the last, after he had virtually made up his mind to go. The influence that kept him away really revealed to him how little to himself his Dead ever left him. They reminded him that he went only for them — for nothing else in the world.

The force of this reminder kept him away ten days: he hated to connect the place with anything but his offices or to give a glimpse of the curiosity that had been on the point of moving him. It was absurd to weave a tangle about a matter so simple as a custom of devotion that might so easily have been daily or hourly; yet the tangle got itself woven. He was sorry, he was disappointed: it was as if a long, happy spell had been broken and he had lost a familiar security. At the last, however, he asked himself if he was to stay away for ever from the fear of this muddle about motives. After an interval neither longer nor shorter than usual he re-entered the church with a clear conviction that he should scarcely heed the presence or the absence of the lady of the concert. This indifference didn't prevent his instantly perceiving that for the first time since he had first seen her she was not on the spot. He had now no scruple about giving her time to arrive, but she didn't arrive, and when he went away still missing her he was quite profanely and consentingly sorry. If her absence made the tangle more intricate, that was only her fault. By the end of another year it was very intricate indeed; but by that time he didn't in the least care, and it was only his cultivated consciousness that had given him scruples. Three times in three months he had gone to church without finding her, and he felt that he had not needed these occasions to show him that his suspense had quite dropped. Yet it was, incongruously, not indifference, but a refinement of delicacy that had kept him from asking the sacristan, who would of course immediately have recognized his description of her, whether she had been seen at other hours. His delicacy had kept him from asking any question about her at any time, and it was exactly the same virtue that had left him so free to be decently civil to her at the concert.

This happy advantage now served him anew, enabling him when she finally met his eyes — it was after a fourth trial — to determine without hesitation to wait till she should retire. He joined her in the street as soon as she had done so, and asked her if he might accompany her a certain distance. With her placid permission he went as far as a house in the neighbourhood at which she had business: she let him know it was not where she lived. She lived, as she said, in a mere slum, with an old aunt, a person in connection with whom she spoke of the engrossment of humdrum duties and regular occupations. She was not, the mourning niece, in her first youth, and her vanished freshness had left something behind which, for Stransom, represented the proof that it had been tragically sacrificed. Whatever she gave him the assurance of she gave it without references. She might in fact have been a divorced duchess, and she might have been an old maid who taught the harp.

V

They fell at last into the way of walking together almost every time they met, though, for a long time, they never met anywhere save at church. He couldn't ask her to come and see him, and, as if she had not a proper place to receive him, she never invited him. As much as himself she knew the world of London, but from an undiscussed instinct of privacy they haunted the region not mapped on the social chart. On the return she always made him leave her at the same corner. She looked with him, as a pretext for a pause, at the depressed things in suburban shop-fronts; and there was never a word he had said to her that she had not beautifully understood. For long ages he never knew her name, any more than she had ever pronounced his own; but it was not their names that mattered, it was only their perfect practice and their common need.

These things made their whole relation so impersonal that they had not the rules or reasons people found in ordinary friendships. They didn't care for the things it was supposed necessary to care for in the intercourse of the world. They ended one day (they never knew which of them expressed it first) by throwing out the idea that they didn't care for each other. Over this idea they grew quite intimate; they rallied to it in a way that marked a fresh start in their confidence. If to feel deeply together about certain things wholly distinct from themselves didn't constitute a safety, where was safety to be looked for? Not lightly nor often, not without occasion nor without emotion, any more than in any other reference by serious people to a mystery of their faith; but when something had happened to warm, as it were, the air for it, they came as near as they could come to calling their Dead by name. They felt it was coming very near to utter their thought at all. The word 'they' expressed enough; it limited the mention, it had a dignity of its own, and if, in their talk, you had heard our friends use it, you might have taken them for a pair of pagans of old alluding decently to the domesticated gods. They never knew — at least Stransom never knew — how they had learned to be sure about each other. If it had been with each a question of what the other was there for, the certitude had come in some fine way of its own. Any faith, after all, has the instinct of propagation, and it was as natural as it was beautiful that they should have taken pleasure on the spot in the imagination of a following. If the following was for each but a following of one, it had proved in the event to be sufficient. Her debt, however, of course, was much greater than his, because while she had only given him a worshipper he had given her a magnificent temple. Once she said she pitied him for the length of his list (she had counted his candles almost as often as himself) and this made him wonder what could have been the length of hers. He had wondered before at the coincidence of their losses, especially as from time to time a new candle was set up. On some occasion some accident led him to express this curiosity, and she answered as if she was surprised that he hadn't already understood. 'Oh, for me, you know, the more there are the better — there could never be too many. I should like hundreds and hundreds — I should like thousands; I should like a perfect mountain of light.'

Then of course, in a flash, he understood. 'Your Dead are only One?'

She hesitated as she had never hesitated. 'Only One', she answered, colouring as if now he knew her innermost secret. It really made him feel that he knew less than before, so difficult was it for him to reconstitute a life in which a single experience had reduced all others to nought. His own life, round its central hollow, had been packed close enough. After this she appeared to have regretted her confession, though at the moment she spoke there had been pride in her very embarrassment. She declared to him that his own was the larger, the dearer possession — the portion one would have chosen if one had been able to choose; she assured him she could perfectly imagine some of the echoes with which his silences were peopled. He knew she couldn't: one's relation to what one had loved and hated had been a relation too distinct from the relations of others. But this didn't affect the fact that they were growing old together in their piety. She was a feature of that piety, but even at the ripe stage of acquaintance in which they occasionally arranged to meet at a concert or to go together to an exhibition she was not a feature of anything else. The most that happened was that his worship became paramount. Friend by friend dropped away till at last there were more emblems on his altar than houses left him to enter. She was more than any other the friend who remained, but she was unknown to all the rest. Once when she had discovered, as they called it, a new star, she used the expression that the chapel at last was full.

'Oh no,' Stransom replied, 'there is a great thing wanting for that! The chapel will never be full till a candle is set up before which all the others will pale. It will be the tallest candle of all.'

Her mild wonder rested on him. 'What candle do you mean?'

'I mean, dear lady, my own.'

He had learned after a long time that she earned money by her pen, writing under a designation that she never told him in magazines that he never saw. She knew too well what he couldn't read and what she couldn't write, and she taught him to cultivate indifference with a success that did much for their good relations. Her invisible industry was a convenience to him; it helped his contented thought of her, the thought that rested in the dignity of her proud, obscure life, her little remunerated art and her little impenetrable home. Lost, with her obscure relative, in her dim suburban world, she came to the surface for him in distant places. She was really the priestess of his altar, and whenever he quitted England he committed it to her keeping. She proved to him afresh that women have more of the spirit of religion than men; he felt his fidelity pale and faint in comparison with hers. He often said to her that since he had so little time to live he rejoiced in her having so much; so glad was he to think she would guard the temple when he should have ceased. He had a great plan for that, which of course he told her too, a bequest of money to keep it up in undiminished state. Of the administration of this fund he would appoint her superintendent, and if the spirit should move her she might kindle a taper even for him.

'And who will kindle one even for me?' she gravely inquired.

VI

She was always in mourning, yet the day he came back from the longest absence he had yet made her appearance immediately told him she had lately had a bereavement. They met on this occasion as she was leaving the church, so that postponing his own entrance he instantly offered to turn round and walk away with her. She considered, then she said: 'Go in now, but come and see me in an hour.' He knew the small vista of her street, closed at the end and as dreary as an empty pocket, where the pairs of shabby little houses, semi-detached but indissolubly united, were like married couples on bad terms. Often, however, as he had gone to the beginning, he had never gone beyond. Her aunt was dead—that he immediately guessed, as well as that it made a difference; but when she had for the first time mentioned her number he found himself, on her leaving him, not a little agitated by this sudden liberality. She was not a person with whom, after all, one got on so very fast: it had taken him months and months to learn her name, years and years to learn her address. If she had looked, on this reunion, so much older to him, how in the world did he look to her? She had reached the period of life that he had long since reached, when, after separations, the dreadful clockface of the friend we meet announces the hour we have tried to forget. He couldn't have said what he expected as, at the end of his waiting, he turned the corner at which, for years, he had always paused; simply not to pause was a sufficient cause for emotion. It was an event, somehow; and in all their long acquaintance there had never been such a thing. The event grew larger when, five minutes later, in the faint elegance of her little drawing-room, she quavered out some greeting which showed the measure she took of it. He had a strange sense of having come for something in particular; strange because, literally, there was nothing particular between them, nothing save that they were at one on their great point, which had long ago become a magnificent matter of course. It was true that after she had said 'You can always come now, you know,' the thing he was there for seemed already to have happened. He asked her if it was the death of her aunt that made the difference; to which she replied: 'She never knew I knew you. I wished her not to.' The beautiful clearness of her candour — her faded beauty was like a summer twilight — disconnected the words from any image of deceit. They might have struck him as the record of a deep dissimulation; but she had always given him a sense of noble reasons. The vanished aunt was present, as he looked about him, in the small complacencies of the room, the beaded velvet and the fluted moreen; and though, as we know, he had the worship of the Dead, he found himself not definitely regretting this lady. If she was not in his long list, however, she was in her niece's short one, and Stransom presently observed to his friend that now, at least, in the place they haunted together, she would have another object of devotion.

'Yes, I shall have another. She was very kind to me. It's that that makes the difference.'

He judged, wondering a good deal before he made any motion to leave her, that the difference would somehow be very great and would consist of still other things than her having let him come in. It rather chilled him, for they had been happy together as they were. He extracted from her at any rate an intimation that she should now have larger means, that her aunt's tiny fortune had come to her, so that there was henceforth only one to consume what had formerly been made to suffice for two. This was a joy to Stransom, because it had hitherto been equally impossible for him either to offer her presents or to find contentment in not doing so. It was too ugly to be at her side that way, abounding himself and yet not able to overflow — a demonstration that would have been a signally false note. Even her better situation too seemed only to draw out in a sense the loneliness of her future. It would merely help her to live more and more for their small ceremonial, at a time when he himself had begun wearily to feel that, having set it in motion, he might depart. When they had sat a while in the pale parlour she got up and said: 'This isn't *my* room: let us go into mine.' They had only to cross the narrow hall, as he found, to pass into quite another air. When she had closed the door of the second room, as she called it, he felt that he had at last real possession of her. The place had the flush of life — it was expressive; its dark red walls were articulate with memories and relics. These were simple things — photographs and water-colours, scraps of writing framed and ghosts of flowers embalmed; but only a moment was needed to show him they had a common meaning. It was here that she had lived and worked; and she had already told him she would make no change of scene. He saw that the objects about her mainly had reference to certain places and times; but after a minute he distinguished among them a small portrait of a gentleman. At a distance and without their glasses his eyes were only caught by it enough to feel a vague curiosity. Presently this impulse carried him nearer, and in another moment he was staring at the picture in stupefaction and with the sense that some sound had broken from him. He was further conscious that he showed his companion a white face when he turned round on her with the exclamation: 'Acton Hague!'

She gave him back his astonishment. 'Did you know him?'

'He was a friend of all my youth — my early manhood. And *you* knew him?'

She coloured at this, and for a moment her answer failed; her eyes took in everything in the place, and a strange irony reached her lips as she echoed: 'Knew him?'

Then Stransom understood, while the room heaved like the cabin of a ship, that its whole contents cried out with him, that it was a museum in his honour, that all her later years had been addressed to him and that the shrine he himself had reared had been passionately converted to this use. It was all for Acton Hague that she had kneeled every day at his altar. What need had there been for a consecrated candle when he was present in the whole array? The revelation seemed to smite our friend in the face, and he dropped into a seat and sat silent. He had quickly become aware that she was shocked at the vision of his own shock, but as she sank on the sofa beside him and laid her hand on his arm he perceived almost as soon that she was unable to resent it as much as she would have liked.

VII

He learned in that instant two things: one of them was that even in so long a time she had gathered no knowledge of his great intimacy and his great quarrel; the other was that in spite of this ignorance, strangely enough, she supplied on the spot a reason for his confusion. 'How extraordinary,' he presently exclaimed, 'that we should never have known!'

She gave a wan smile which seemed to Stransom stranger even than the fact itself. 'I never, never spoke of him.'

Stransom looked about the room again. 'Why then, if your life had been so full of him?'

'Mayn't I put you that question as well? Hadn't your life also been full of him?'

'Any one's, every one's life was who had the wonderful experience of knowing him. I never spoke of him,' Stransom added in a moment, 'because he did me — years ago — an unforgettable wrong.' She was silent, and with the full effect of his presence all about them it almost startled her visitor to hear no protest escape from her. She accepted his words; he turned his eyes to her again to see in what manner she accepted them. It was with rising tears and an extraordinary sweetness in the movement of putting out her hand to take his own. Nothing more wonderful had ever appeared to Stransom than, in that little chamber of remembrance and homage, to see her convey with such exquisite mildness that as from Acton Hague any injury was credible. The clock ticked in the stillness — Hague had probably given it to her — and while he let her hold his hand with a tenderness that was almost an assumption of responsibility for his old pain as well as his new, Stransom after a minute broke out: 'Good God, how he must have used *you!*'

She dropped his hand at this, got up and, moving across the room, made straight a small picture to which, on examining it, he had given a slight push. Then turning round on him with her pale gaiety recovered: 'I've forgiven him!' she declared.

'I know what you've done,' said Stransom; 'I know what you've done for years.' For a moment they looked at each other across the room, with their long community of service in their eyes. This short passage made, to Stransom's sense, for the woman before him, an immense, an absolutely naked confession; which was presently, suddenly blushing red and changing her place again, what she appeared to become aware that he perceived in it. He got up. 'How you must have loved him!' he cried.

'Women are not like men. They can love even where they've suffered.'

'Women are wonderful,' said Stransom. 'But I assure you I've forgiven him too.'

'If I had known of anything so strange I wouldn't have brought you here.'

'So that we might have gone on in our ignorance to the last?'

'What do you call the last?' she asked, smiling still.

At this he could smile back at her. 'You'll see — when it comes.'

She reflected a moment. 'This is better perhaps; but as we were — it was good.'

'Did it never happen that he spoke of me?' Stransom inquired.

Considering more intently, she made no answer, and he quickly recognized that he would have been adequately answered by her asking how often he himself had spoken of their terrible friend. Suddenly a brighter light broke in her face, and an excited idea sprang to her lips in the question: 'You *have* forgiven him?'

'How, if I hadn't, could I linger here?'

She winced, for an instant, at the deep but unintended irony of this; but even while she did so she panted quickly: 'Then in the lights on your altar — ?'

'There's never a light for Acton Hague!'

She stared, with a great visible fall. 'But if he's one of your Dead?'

'He's one of the world's, if you like — he's one of yours. But he's not one of mine. Mine are only the Dead who died possessed of me. They're mine in death because they were mine in life.'

'*He* was yours in life then, even if for a while he ceased to be. If you forgave him you went back to him. Those whom we've once loved —'

'Are those who can hurt us most,' Stransom broke in.

'Ah, it's not true — you've *not* forgiven him!' she wailed with a passion that startled him.

He looked at her a moment. 'What was it he did to you?'

'Everything!' Then abruptly she put out her hand in farewell. 'Goodbye.'

He turned as cold as he had turned that night he read of the death of Acton Hague. 'You mean that we meet no more?'

'Not as we have met — not *there*!'

He stood aghast at this snap of their great bond, at the renouncement that rang out in the word she so passionately emphasised. 'But what's changed — for you?'

She hesitated, in all the vividness of a trouble that, for the first time since he had known her, made her splendidly stern. 'How can you understand now when you didn't understand before?'

'I didn't understand before only because I didn't know. Now that I know, I see what I've been living with for years,' Stransom went on very gently.

She looked at him with a larger allowance, as if she appreciated his good-nature. 'How can I, then, with this new knowledge of my own, ask you to continue to live with it?'

'I set up my altar, with its multiplied meanings,' Stransom began; but she quickly interrupted him.

'You set up your altar, and when I wanted one most I found it magnificently ready. I used it, with the gratitude I've always shown you, for I knew from of old that it was dedicated to Death. I told you, long ago, that my Dead were not many. Yours were, but all you had done for them was none too much for *my* worship! You had placed a great light for Each—I gathered them together for One!'

'We had simply different intentions,' Stransom replied. 'That, as you say, I perfectly knew, and I don't see why your intention shouldn't still sustain you.'

'That's because you're generous—you can imagine and think. But the spell is broken.'

It seemed to poor Stransom, in spite of his resistance, that it really was, and the prospect stretched grey and void before him. All, however, that he could say was: 'I hope you'll try before you give up.'

'If I had known you had ever known him I should have taken for granted he had his candle,' she presently rejoined. 'What's changed, as you say, is that on making the discovery I find he never has had it. That makes my attitude—' she paused a moment, as if thinking how to express it, then said simply—'all wrong.'

'Come once again,' Stransom pleaded.

'Will you give him his candle?' she asked.

He hesitated, but only because it would sound ungracious; not because he had a doubt of his feeling. 'I can't do that!' he declared at last.

'Then goodbye.' And she gave him her hand again.

He had got his dismissal; besides which, in the agitation of everything that had opened out to him, he felt the need to recover himself as he could only do in solitude. Yet he lingered—lingered to see if she had no compromise to express, no attenuation to propose. But he only met her great lamenting eyes, in which indeed he read that she was as sorry for him as for any one else. This made him say: 'At least, at any rate, I may see you here.'

'Oh yes, come if you like. But I don't think it will do.'

Stransom looked round the room once more; he felt in truth by no means sure it would do. He felt also stricken and more and more cold, and his chill was like an ague in which he had to make an effort not to shake. 'I must try on my side, if you can't try on yours,' he dolefully rejoined. She came out with him to the hall and into the doorway, and here he put to her the question that seemed to him the one he could least answer from his own wit. 'Why have you never let me come before?'

'Because my aunt would have seen you, and I should have had to tell her how I came to know you.'

'And what would have been the objection to that?'

'It would have entailed other explanations; there would at any rate have been that danger.'

'Surely she knew you went every day to church,' Stransom objected.

'She didn't know what I went for.'

'Of me then she never even heard?'

'You'll think I was deceitful. But I didn't need to be!'

Stransom was now on the lower doorstep, and his hostess held the door half-closed behind him. Through what remained of the opening he saw her framed face. He made a supreme appeal. 'What *did* he do to you?'

'It would have come out—*she* would have told you. That fear, at my heart—that was my reason!' And she closed the door, shutting him out.

VIII

He had ruthlessly abandoned her—that, of course, was what he had done. Stransom made it all out in solitude, at leisure, fitting the unmatched pieces gradually together and dealing one by one with a hundred obscure points. She had known Hague only after her present friend's relations with him had wholly terminated; obviously indeed a good while after; and it was natural enough that of his previous life she should have ascertained only what he had judged good to communicate. There were passages it was quite conceivable that even in moments of the tenderest expansion he should have withheld. Of many facts in the career of a man so in the eye of the world there was of course a common knowledge; but this lady lived apart from public affairs, and the only period perfectly clear to her would have been the period following the dawn of her own drama. A man, in her place, would have 'looked up' the past—would even have consulted old newspapers. It remained singular indeed that in her long contact with the partner of her retrospect no accident had lighted a train; but there was no arguing about that; the accident had in fact come: it had simply been that security had prevailed. She had taken what Hague had given her, and her blankness in respect of his other connections was only a touch in the picture of that plasticity Stransom had supreme reason to know so great a master could have been trusted to produce.

This picture, for a while, was all that our friend saw: he caught his breath again and again as it came over him that the woman with whom he had had for years so fine a point of contact was a woman whom Acton Hague, of all men in the world, had more or less fashioned. Such as she sat there today, she was ineffaceably stamped with him. Beneficent, blameless as Stransom held her, he couldn't rid himself of the sense that he had been the victim of a fraud. She had imposed upon him hugely, though she had known it as little as he. All this later past came back to him as a time grotesquely misspent. Such at least were his first reflections; after a while he found himself more divided and only, at the end of it, more troubled. He imagined, recalled, reconstituted, figured out for himself the truth she had refused to give him; the effect of which was to make her seem to him only more saturated with her fate. He felt her spirit, in the strange business, to be finer than his own in the very degree in which she might have been, in which she certainly had been, more wronged. A woman, when she was wronged, was always more wronged than a man, and there were conditions when the least she could have got off with was more than the most he could have to endure. He was sure this rare creature wouldn't have got off with the least. He was awestruck at the thought of such a surrender—such a prostration. Moulded indeed she had been by powerful hands, to have converted her injury into an exaltation so sublime. The fellow had only had to die for everything that was ugly in him to be washed out in a torrent. It was vain to try to guess what had taken place, but nothing could be clearer than that she had ended by accusing herself. She absolved him at every point, she adored her very wounds. The passion by which he had profited had rushed back after its ebb, and now the tide of tenderness, arrested for ever at flood, was too deep even to fathom. Stransom sincerely considered that he had forgiven him; but how little he had achieved the miracle that she had achieved! His forgiveness was silence, but hers was mere unuttered sound. The light she had demanded for his altar would have broken his silence with a blare; whereas all the lights in the church were for her too great a hush.

She had been right about the difference — she had spoken the truth about the change: Stransom felt before long that he was perversely but definitely jealous. His tide had ebbed, not flowed; if he had 'forgiven' Acton Hague, that forgiveness was a motive with a broken spring. The very fact of her appeal for a material sign, a sign that should make her dead lover equal there with the others, presented the concession to Stransom as too handsome for the case. He had never thought of himself as hard, but an exorbitant article might easily render him so. He moved round and round this one, but only in widening circles — the more he looked at it the less acceptable it appeared. At the same time he had no illusion about the effect of his refusal; he perfectly saw that it was the beginning of a separation. He left her alone for many days; but when at last he called upon her again this conviction acquired a depressing force. In the interval he had kept away from the church, and he needed no fresh assurance from her to know she had not entered it. The change was complete enough: it had broken up her life. Indeed it had broken up his, for all the fires of his shrine seemed to him suddenly to have been quenched. A great indifference fell upon him, the weight of which was in itself a pain; and he never knew what his devotion had been for him till, in that shock, it stopped like a dropped watch. Neither did he know with how large a confidence he had counted on the final service that had now failed: the mortal deception was that in this abandonment the whole future gave way.

These days of her absence proved to him of what she was capable; all the more that he never dreamed she was vindictive or even resentful. It was not in anger she had forsaken him; it was in absolute submission to hard reality, to crude destiny. This came home to him when he sat with her again in the room in which her late aunt's conversation lingered like the tone of a cracked piano. She tried to make him forget how much they were estranged; but in the very presence of what they had given up it was impossible not to be sorry for her. He had taken from her so much more than she had taken from him. He argued with her again, told her she could now have the altar to herself; but she only shook her head with pleading sadness, begging him not to waste his breath on the impossible, the extinct. Couldn't he see that in relation to her private need the rites he had established were practically an elaborate exclusion? She regretted nothing that had happened; it had all been right so long as she didn't know, and it was only that now she knew too much and that from the moment their eyes were open they would simply have to conform. It had doubtless been happiness enough for them to go on together so long. She was gentle, grateful, resigned; but this was only the form of a deep immutability. He saw that he should never more cross the threshold of the second room, and he felt how much this alone would make a stranger of him and give a conscious stiffness to his visits. He would have hated to plunge again into that well of reminders, but he enjoyed quite as little the vacant alternative.

After he had been with her three or four times it seemed to him that to have come at last into her house had had the horrid effect of diminishing their intimacy. He had known her better, had liked her in greater freedom, when they merely walked together or kneeled together. Now they only pretended; before they had been nobly sincere. They began to try their walks again, but it proved a lame imitation, for these things, from the first, beginning or ending, had been connected with their visits to the church. They had either strolled away as they came out or gone in to rest on the return. Besides, Stransom now grew weary; he couldn't walk as of old. The omission made everything false; it was a horrible mutilation of their lives. Our friend was frank and monotonous; he made no mystery of his remonstrance and no secret of his predicament. Her response, whatever it was, always came to the same thing — an implied invitation to him to judge, if he spoke of predicaments, of how much comfort she had in hers. For him indeed there was no comfort even in complaint, for every allusion to what had befallen them only made the author of their trouble more present. Acton Hague was between them, that was the essence of the matter; and he was never so much between them as when they were face to face. Stransom, even while he wanted to banish him, had the strangest sense of desiring a satisfaction that could come only from having accepted him. Deeply disconcerted by what he knew, he was still worse tormented by really not knowing. Perfectly aware that it would have been horribly vulgar to abuse his old friend or to tell his companion the story of their quarrel, it yet vexed him that her depth of reserve should give him no opening and should have the effect of a magnanimity greater even than his own.

He challenged himself, denounced himself, asked himself if he were in love with her that he should care so much what adventures she had had. He had never for a moment admitted that he was in love with her; therefore nothing could have surprised him more than to discover that he was jealous. What but jealousy could give a man that sore, contentious wish to have the detail of what would make him suffer? Well enough he knew indeed that he should never have it from the only person who, today, could give it to him. She let him press her with his sombre eyes, only smiling at him with an exquisite mercy and breathing equally little the word that would expose her secret and the word that would appear to deny his literal right to bitterness. She told nothing, she judged nothing; she accepted everything but the possibility of her return to the old symbols. Stransom divined that for her too they had been vividly individual, had stood for particular hours or particular attributes — particular links in her chain. He made it clear to himself, as he believed, that his difficulty lay in the fact that the very nature of the plea for his faithless friend constituted a prohibition; that it happened to have come from *her* was precisely the vice that attached to it. To the voice of impersonal generosity he felt sure he would have listened; he would have deferred to an advocate who, speaking from abstract justice, knowing of his omission without having known Hague, should have had the imagination to say: 'Oh, remember only the best of him; pity him; provide for him.' To provide for him on the very ground of having discovered another of his turpitudes was not to pity him, but to glorify him. The more Stransom thought the more he made it out that this relation of Hague's, whatever it was, could only have been a deception finely practised. Where had it come into the life that all men saw? Why had he never heard of it, if it had had the frankness of an attitude honourable? Stransom knew enough of his other ties, of his obligations and appearances, not to say enough of his general character, to be sure there had been some infamy. In one way or another the poor woman had been coldly sacrificed. That was why, at the last as well as the first, he must still leave him out.

IX

And yet this was no solution, especially after he had talked again to his friend of all it had been his plan that she should finally do for him. He had talked in the other days, and she had responded with a frankness qualified only by a courteous reluctance, a reluctance that touched him, to linger on the question of his death. She had then practically accepted the charge, suffered him to feel that he could depend upon her to be the eventual guardian of his shrine; and it was in the name of what had so passed between them that he appealed to her not to forsake him in his old age. She listened to him now with a sort of shining coldness and all her habitual forbearance to insist on her terms; her deprecation was even still ten-derer, for it expressed the compassion of her own sense that he was abandoned. Her terms, however, remained the same, and scarcely the less audible for not being uttered; although he was sure that, secretly, even more than he, she felt bereft of the satisfaction his solemn trust was to have provided for her. They both missed the rich future, but she missed it most, because after all it was to have been entirely hers; and it was her acceptance of the loss that gave him the full measure of her preference for the thought of Acton Hague over any other thought whatever. He had humour enough to laugh rather grimly when he said to himself: 'Why the deuce does she like him so much more than she likes me?' — the reasons being really so conceivable. But even his faculty of analysis left the irritation standing, and this irritation proved perhaps the greatest misfortune that had ever overtaken him. There had been nothing yet that made him so much want to give up. He had of course by this time well reached the age of renounce-ment; but it had not hitherto been vivid to him that it was time to give up everything.

Practically, at the end of six months, he had renounced the friendship that was once so charming and comforting. His privation had two faces, and the face it had turned to him on the occasion of his last attempt to cultivate that friendship was the one he could look at least. This was the privation he inflicted; the other was the privation he bore. The conditions she never phrased he used to murmur to himself in solitude: 'One more, one more — only just one.' Certainly he was going down; he often felt it when he caught himself, over his work, staring at vacancy and giving voice to that inanity. There was proof enough besides in his being so weak and so ill. His irritation took the form of melancholy, and his melancholy that of the conviction that his health had quite failed. His altar moreover had ceased to exist; his chapel, in his dreams, was a great dark cavern. All the lights had gone out — all his Dead had died again. He couldn't exactly see at first how it had been in the power of his late companion to extinguish them, since it was neither for her nor by her that they had been called into being. Then he understood that it was essentially in his own soul the revival had taken place, and that in the air of this soul they were now unable to breathe. The candles might mechanically burn, but each of them had lost its lustre. The church had become a void; it was his presence, her presence, their common presence, that had made the indispensable medium. If anything was wrong everything was — her silence spoiled the tune.

Then when three months were gone he felt so lonely that he went back; reflecting that as they had been his best society for years his Dead perhaps wouldn't let him forsake them without doing something more for him. They stood there, as he had left them, in their tall radiance, the bright cluster that had already made him, on occasions when he was willing to compare small things with great, liken them to a group of sea-lights on the edge of the ocean of life. It was a relief to him, after a while, as he sat there, to feel that they had still a virtue. He was more and more easily tired, and he always drove now; the action of his heart was weak and gave him none of the reassurance conferred by the action of his fancy. None the less he returned yet again, returned several times, and finally, during six months, haunted the place with a renewal of frequency and a strain of impatience. In winter the church was unwarmed, and exposure to cold was forbidden him, but the glow of his shrine was an influence in which he could almost bask. He sat and wondered to what he had reduced his absent associate and what she now did with the hours of her absence. There were other churches, there were other altars, there were other candles; in one way or another her piety would still operate; he couldn't absolutely have deprived her of her rites. So he argued, but without contentment; for he well enough knew there was no other such rare semblance of the mountain of light she had once mentioned to him as the satisfaction of her need. As this semblance again gradually grew great to him and his pious practice more regular, there was a sharper and sharper pang for him in the imagination of her darkness; for never so much as in these weeks had his rites been real, never had his gathered company seemed so to respond and even to invite. He lost himself in the large lustre, which was more and more what he had from the first wished it to be — as dazzling as the vision of heaven in the mind of a child. He wandered in the fields of light; he passed, among the tall tapers, from tier to tier, from fire to fire, from name to name, from the white intensity of one clear emblem, of one saved soul, to another. It was in the quiet sense of having saved his souls that his deep, strange instinct rejoiced. This was no dim theological rescue, no boon of a contingent world; they were saved better than faith or works could save them, saved for the warm world they had shrunk from dying to, for actuality, for continuity, for the certainty of human remembrance.

By this time he had survived all his friends; the last straight flame was three years old, there was no one to add to the list. Over and over he called his roll, and it appeared to him compact and complete. Where should he put in another, where, if there were no other objection, would it stand in its place in the rank? He reflected, with a want of sincerity of which he was quite conscious, that it would be difficult to determine that place. More and more, besides, face to face with his little legion, reading over endless histories, handling the empty shells and playing with the silence — more and more he could see that he had never introduced an alien. He had had his great compassions, his indulgences — there were cases in which they had been immense; but what had his devotion after all been if it hadn't been fundamentally a respect? He was, however, himself surprised at his stiffness; by the end of the winter the responsibility of it was what was uppermost in his thoughts. The refrain had grown old to them, the plea for just one more. There came a day when, for simple exhaustion, if symmetry should really demand just one more he was ready to take symmetry into account. Symmetry was harmony, and the idea of harmony began to haunt him; he said to himself that harmony was of course everything. He took, in fancy, his composition to pieces, redistributing it into other lines, making other juxtapositions and contrasts. He shifted this and that candle, he made the spaces different, he effaced the disfigurement of a possible gap. There were subtle and complex relations, a scheme of cross-reference, and moments in which he seemed to catch a glimpse of the void so sensible to the woman who wandered in exile or sat where he had seen her with the portrait of Acton Hague. Finally, in this way, he arrived at a conception of the total, the ideal, which left a clear opportunity for just another figure. 'Just one more — to round it off; just one more, just one,' continued to hum itself in his head. There was a strange confusion in the thought, for he felt the day to be near when he too should be one of the Others. What, in this case, would the Others matter to him, since they only mattered to the living? Even as one of the Dead, what would his altar matter to him, since his particular dream of keeping it up had melted away? What had harmony to do with the case if his lights were all to be quenched? What he had hoped for was an instituted thing. He might perpetuate it on some other pretext, but his special meaning would have dropped. This meaning was to have lasted with the life of the one other person who understood it.

In March he had an illness during which he spent a fortnight in bed, and when he revived a little he was told of two things that had happened. One was that a lady, whose name was not known to the servants (she left none) had been three times to ask about him; the other was that in his sleep, and on an occasion when his mind evidently wandered, he was heard to murmur again and again: 'Just one more — just one'. As soon as he found himself able to go out, and before the doctor in attendance had pronounced him so, he drove to see the lady who had come to ask about him. She was not at home; but this gave him the opportunity, before his strength should fail again, to take his way to the church. He entered the church alone; he had declined, in a happy manner he possessed of being able to decline effectively, the company of his servant or of a nurse. He knew now perfectly what these good people thought; they had discovered his clandestine connection, the magnet that had drawn him for so many years, and doubtless attached a significance of their own to the odd words they had repeated to him. The nameless lady was the clandestine connection — a fact nothing could have made clearer than his indecent haste to rejoin her. He sank on his knees before his altar, and his head fell over on his hands. His weakness, his life's weariness overtook him. It seemed to him he had come for the great surrender. At first he asked himself how he should get away; then, with the failing belief in the power, the very desire to move gradually left him. He had come, as he always came, to lose himself; the fields of light were still there to stray in; only this time, in straying, he would never come back. He had given himself to his Dead, and it was good: this time his Dead would keep him. He couldn't rise from his knees; he believed he should never rise again; all he could do was to lift his face and fix his eyes upon his lights. They looked unusually, strangely splendid, but the one that always drew him most had an unprecedented lustre. It was the central voice of the choir, the glowing heart of the brightness, and on this occasion it seemed to expand, to spread great wings of flame. The whole altar flared — it dazzled and blinded; but the source of the vast radiance burned clearer than the rest, it gathered itself into form, and the form was human beauty and human charity — it was the far-off face of Mary Antrim. She smiled at him from the glory of heaven — she brought the glory down with her to take him. He bowed his head in submission, and at the same moment another wave rolled over him. Was it the quickening of joy to pain? In the midst of his joy at any rate he felt his buried face grow hot as with some communicated knowledge that had the force of a reproach. It suddenly made him contrast that very rapture with the bliss he had refused to another. This breath of the passion immortal was all that other had asked; the descent of Mary Antrim opened his spirit with a great compunctious throb for the descent of Acton Hague. It was as if Stransom had read what her eyes said to him.

After a moment he looked round him in a despair which made him feel as if the source of life were ebbing. The church had been empty — he was alone; but he wanted to have something done, to make a last appeal. This idea gave him strength for an effort; he rose to his feet with a movement that made him turn, supporting himself by the back of a bench. Behind him was a prostrate figure, a figure he had seen before; a woman in deep mourning, bowed in grief or in prayer. He had seen her in other days — the first time he came into the church, and he slightly wavered there, looking at her again till she seemed to become aware he had noticed her. She raised her head and met his eyes: the partner of his long worship was there. She looked across at him an instant with a face wondering and scared; he saw that he had given her an alarm. Then quickly rising, she came straight to him with both hands out.

'Then you *could* come? God sent you!' he murmured with a happy smile.

'You're very ill — you shouldn't be here,' she urged in anxious reply.

'God sent me too, I think. I was ill when I came, but the sight of you does wonders.' He held her hands, and they steadied and quickened him. 'I've something to tell you.'

'Don't tell me!' she tenderly pleaded; 'let me tell you. This afternoon, by a miracle, the sweetest of miracles, the sense of our difference left me. I was out — I was near, thinking, wandering alone, when, on the spot, something changed in my heart. It's my confession — there it is. To come back, to come back on the instant — the idea gave me wings. It was as if I suddenly saw something — as if it all became possible. I could come for what you yourself came for: that was enough. So here I am. It's not for my own — that's over. But I'm here for *them*.' And breathless, infinitely relieved by her low, precipitate explanation, she looked with eyes that reflected all its splendour at the magnificence of their altar.

'They're here for you,' Stransom said, 'they're present tonight as they've never been. They speak for you — don't you see? — in a passion of light — they sing out like a choir of angels. Don't you hear what they say? — they offer the very thing you asked of me.'

'Don't talk of it — don't think of it; forget it!' She spoke in hushed supplication, and while the apprehension deepened in her eyes she disengaged one of her hands and passed an arm round him, to support him better, to help him to sink into a seat.

He let himself go, resting on her; he dropped upon the bench, and she fell on her knees beside him with his arm on her shoulder. So he remained an instant, staring up at his shrine. 'They say there's a gap in the array — they say it's not full, complete. Just one more,' he went on, softly — 'isn't that what you wanted? Yes, one more, one more.'

'Ah, no more — no more!' she wailed, as if with a quick, new horror of it, under her breath.

'Yes, one more,' he repeated, simply; 'just one!' And with this his head dropped on her shoulder; she felt that in his weakness he had fainted. But alone with him in the dusky church a great dread was on her of what might still happen, for his face had the whiteness of death.

[1895]

Study and Writing Questions

1. How is light IMAGERY (from candles, daylight, room lighting, and so on) used in this NARRATIVE? Does light seem to shift meanings from one use or section to another? What is the THEMATIC significance of light as the central image?

2. This NARRATIVE treats some matters that are usually narrated quite CON-CRETELY, like the names of main CHARACTERS and the facts surrounding a betrayal, in the most general possible way while treating events that are usually narrated quite generally, like the movement from one emotional state to another, in the most concrete possible way. Find examples of these techniques in the narrative. How does the use of these techniques, both singly and together, influence your reading of this narrative?

3. James uses FREE INDIRECT STYLE, often giving his narrator OMNISCIENCE, which would normally be considered RELIABLE NARRATION, and often having his narrator in effect report the thoughts of one (or another) of the characters. At what point do you first notice that the narration is not completely reliable? How does this occasional unreliability influence your reading of this narrative?

4. How would you describe Stransom's character? What does the first line mean by calling him "poor"? What does love mean to him? Does he change through the course of the story?

5. How many "altars" are there in this narrative? Who are "the dead"? What or who is being referred to in Stransom's last spoken line? What sort of RESOLU-TION, if any, does the last paragraph offer?

See also Questions for Contrast and Comparison: 7, 35, 43, 69, 234, 235, 236, and 237.

The Tree of Knowledge

I

It was one of the secret opinions, such as we all have, of Peter Brench that his main success in life would have consisted in his never having committed himself about the work, as it was called, of his friend Morgan Mallow. This was a subject on which it was, to the best of his belief, impossible with veracity to quote him, and it was nowhere on record that he had, in the connexion, on any occasion and in any embarrassment, either lied or spoken the truth. Such a triumph had its honour even for a man of other triumphs — a man who had reached fifty, who had escaped marriage, who had lived within his means, who had been in love with Mrs. Mallow for years without breathing it, and who, last but not least, had judged himself once for all. He had so judged himself in fact that he felt an extreme and general humility to be his proper portion; yet there was nothing that made him think so well of his parts as the course he had steered so often through the shallows just mentioned. It became thus a real wonder that the friends in whom he had most confidence were just those with whom he had most reserves. He couldn't tell Mrs. Mallow — or at least he supposed, excellent man, he couldn't — that she was the one beautiful reason he had never married; any more than he could tell her husband that the sight of the multiplied marbles in that gentleman's studio was an affliction of which even time had never blunted the edge. His victory, however, as I have intimated, in regard to these productions, was not simply in his not having let it out that he deplored them; it was, remarkably, in his not having kept it in by anything else.

The whole situation, among these good people, was verily a marvel, and there was probably not such another for a long way from the spot that engages us — the point at which the soft declivity of Hampstead began at that time to confess in broken accents to Saint John's Wood. He despised Mallow's statues and adored Mallow's wife, and yet was distinctly fond of Mallow, to whom, in turn, he was equally dear. Mrs. Mallow rejoiced in the statues — though she preferred, when pressed, the busts; and if she was visibly attached to Peter Brench it was because of his affection for Morgan. Each loved the other moreover for the love borne in each case to Lancelot, whom the Mallows respectively cherished as their only child and whom the friend of their fireside identified as the third — but decidedly the handsomest — of his godsons. Already in the old years it had come to that — that no one, for such a relation, could possibly have occurred to any of them, even to the baby itself, but Peter. There was luckily a certain independence, of the pecuniary sort, all round: the Master could never otherwise have spent his solemn *Wanderjahre* in Florence and Rome, and continued by the Thames as well as by the Arno and the Tiber to add unpurchased group to group and model, for what was too apt to prove in the event mere love, fancy-heads of celebrities either too busy or too buried — too much of the age or too little of it — to sit. Neither could Peter, lounging in almost daily, have found time to keep the whole complicated tradition so alive by his presence. He was massive but mild, the depositary of these mysteries — large and loose and ruddy and curly, with deep tones, deep eyes, deep pockets, to say nothing of the habit of long pipes, soft hats and brownish greyish weather-faded clothes, apparently always the same.

He had "written," it was known, but had never spoken, never spoken in particular of that; and he had the air (since, as was believed, he continued to write) of keeping it up in order to have something more — as if he hadn't at the worst enough — to be silent about. Whatever his air, at any rate, Peter's occasional unmentioned prose and verse were quite truly the result of an impulse to maintain the purity of his taste by establishing still more firmly the right relation of fame to feebleness. The little green door of his domain was in a garden-wall on which the discoloured stucco made patches, and in the small detached villa behind it everything was old, the furniture, the servants, the books, the prints, the immemorial habits and the new improvements. The Mallows, at Carrara Lodge, were within ten minutes, and the studio there was on their little land, to which they had added, in their happy faith, for building it. This was the good fortune, if it was not the ill, of her having brought him in marriage a portion that put them in a manner at their ease and enabled them thus, on their side, to keep it up. And they did keep it up — they always had — the infatuated sculptor and his wife, for whom nature had refined on the impossible by relieving them of the sense of the difficult. Morgan had at all events everything of the sculptor but the spirit of Phidias — the brown velvet, the becoming *beretto*, the "plastic" presence, the fine fingers, the beautiful accent in Italian and the old Italian factotum. He seemed to make up for everything when he addressed Egidio with the "tu" and waved him to turn one of the rotary pedestals of which the place was full. They were tremendous Italians at Carrara Lodge, and the secret of the part played by this fact in Peter's life was in a large degree that it gave him, sturdy Briton as he was, just the amount of "going abroad" he could bear. The Mallows were all his Italy, but it was in a measure for Italy he liked them. His one worry was that Lance — to which they had shortened his godson — was, in spite of a public school, perhaps a shade too Italian. Morgan meanwhile looked like somebody's flattering idea of somebody's own person as expressed in the great room provided at the Uffizi Museum for the general illustration of that idea by eminent hands. The Master's sole regret that he hadn't been born rather to the brush than to the chisel sprang from his wish that he might have contributed to that collection.

It appeared with time at any rate to be to the brush that Lance had been born; for Mrs. Mallow, one day when the boy was turning twenty, broke it to their friend, who shared, to the last delicate morsel, their problems and pains, that it seemed as if nothing would really do but that he should embrace the career. It had been impossible longer to remain blind to the fact that he was gaining no glory at Cambridge, where Brench's own college had for a year tempered its tone to him as for Brench's own sake. Therefore why renew the vain form of preparing him for the impossible? The impossible — it had become clear — was that he should be anything but an artist.

"Oh dear, dear!" said poor Peter.

"Don't you believe in it?" asked Mrs. Mallow, who still, at more than forty, had her violet velvet eyes, her creamy satin skin and her silken chestnut hair.

"Believe in what?"

"Why in Lance's passion."

"I don't know what you mean by 'believing in it.' I've never been unaware, certainly, of his disposition, from his earliest time, to daub and draw; but I confess I've hoped it would burn out."

"But why should it," she sweetly smiled, "with his wonderful heredity? Passion is passion — though of course indeed *you*, dear Peter, know nothing of that. Has the Master's ever burned out?"

Peter looked off a little and, in his familiar formless way, kept up for a moment, a sound between a smothered whistle and a subdued hum. "Do you think he's going to be another Master?"

She seemed scarce prepared to go that length, yet she had on the whole a marvellous trust. "I know what you mean by that. Will it be a career to incur the jealousies and provoke the machinations that have been at times almost too much for his father? Well — say it may be, since nothing but clap-trap, in these dreadful days, *can*, it would seem, make its way, and since, with the curse of refinement and distinction, one may easily find one's self begging one's bread. Put it at the worst — say he *has* the misfortune to wing his flight further than the vulgar taste of his stupid countrymen can follow. Think, all the same, of the happiness — the same the Master has had. He'll *know*."

Peter looked rueful. "Ah but *what* will he know?"

"Quiet joy!" cried Mrs. Mallow, quite impatient and turning away.

II

He had of course before long to meet the boy himself on it and to hear that practically everything was settled. Lance was not to go up again, but to go instead to Paris where, since the die was cast, he would find the best advantages. Peter had always felt he must be taken as he was, but had never perhaps found him so much of that pattern as on this occasion. "You chuck Cambridge then altogether? Doesn't that seem rather a pity?"

Lance would have been like his father, to his friend's sense, had he had less humour, and like his mother had he had more beauty. Yet it was a good middle way for Peter that, in the modern manner, he was, to the eye, rather the young stockbroker than the young artist. The youth reasoned that it was a question of time — there was such a mill to go through, such an awful lot to learn. He had talked with fellows and had judged. "One has got, today," he said, "don't you see? to know."

His interlocutor, at this, gave a groan. "Oh hang it, *don't* know!"

Lance wondered. "Don't? Then what's the use —?"

"The use of what?"

"Why of anything. Don't you think I've talent?"

Peter smoked away for a little in silence; then went on: "It isn't knowledge, it's ignorance that — as we've been beautifully told — is bliss."

"Don't you think I've talent?" Lance repeated.

Peter, with his trick of queer kind demonstration, passed his arm round his godson and held him a moment. "How do I know?"

"Oh," said the boy, "if it's your own ignorance you're defending —!"

Again, for a pause, on the sofa, his godfather smoked. "It isn't. I've the misfortune to be omniscient."

"Oh well," Lance laughed again, "if you know *too* much —!"

"That's what I do, and it's why I'm so wretched."

Lance's gaiety grew. "Wretched? Come, I say!"

"But I forgot," his companion went on—"you're not to know about that. It would indeed for you to make the too much. Only I'll tell you what I'll do." And Peter got up from the sofa. "If you'll go up again I'll pay your way at Cambridge."

Lance stared, a little rueful in spite of being still more amused. "Oh Peter! You disapprove so of Paris?"

"Well, I'm afraid of it."

"Ah I see!"

"No, you don't see—yet. But you will—that is you would. And you mustn't."

The young man thought more gravely. "But one's innocence, already—!"

"Is considerably damaged? Ah that won't matter," Peter persisted—"we'll patch it up here."

"Here? Then you want me to stay at home?"

Peter almost confessed to it. "Well, we're so right—we four together—just as we are. We're so safe. Come, don't spoil it."

The boy, who had turned to gravity, turned from this, on the real pressure in his friend's tone, to consternation. "Then what's a fellow to be?"

"My particular care. Come, old man"—and Peter now fairly pleaded—"I'll look out for you."

Lance, who had remained on the sofa with his legs out and his hands in his pockets, watched him with eyes that showed suspicion. Then he got up. "You think there's something the matter with me—that I can't make a success."

"Well, what do you call a success?"

Lance thought again. "Why, the best sort, I suppose, is to please one's self. Isn't that the sort that, in spite of cabals and things, is—in his own peculiar line—the Master's?"

There were so much too many things in this question to be answered at once that they practically checked the discussion, which became particularly difficult in the light of such renewed proof that, though the young man's innocence might, in the course of his studies, as he contended, somewhat have shrunken, the finer essence of it still remained. That was indeed exactly what Peter had assumed and what above all he desired; yet perversely enough it gave him a chill. The boy believed in the cabals and things, believed in the peculiar line, believed, to be brief, in the Master. What happened a month or two later wasn't that he went up again at the expense of his godfather, but that a fortnight after he had got settled in Paris this personage sent him fifty pounds.

He had meanwhile at home, this personage, made up his mind to the worst; and what that might be had never yet grown quite so vivid to him as when, on his presenting himself one Sunday night, as he never failed to do, for supper, the mistress of Carrara Lodge met him with an appeal as to—of all things in the world—the wealth of the Canadians. She was earnest, she was even excited. "Are many of them *really* rich?"

He had to confess he knew nothing about them, but he often thought afterwards of that evening. The room in which they sat was adorned with sundry specimens of the Master's genius, which had the merit of being, as Mrs. Mallow herself frequently suggested, of an unusually convenient size. They were indeed of dimensions not customary in the products of the chisel, and they had the singularity that, if the objects and features intended to be small looked too large, the objects and features intended to be large looked too small. The Master's idea, either in respect to this matter or to any other, had in almost any case, even after years, remained undiscoverable to Peter Brench. The creations that so failed to reveal it stood about on pedestals and brackets, on tables and shelves, a little staring white population, heroic, idyllic, allegoric, mythic, symbolic, in which "scale" had so strayed and lost itself that the public square and the chimney-piece seemed to have changed places, the monumental being all diminutive and the diminutive all monumental; branches at any rate, markedly, of a family in which stature was rather oddly irrespective of function, age, and sex. They formed, like the Mallows themselves, poor Brench's own family — having at least to such a degree the note of familiarity. The occasion was one of those he had long ago learnt to know and to name — short flickers of the faint flame, soft gusts of a kinder air. Twice a year regularly the Master believed in his fortune, in addition to believing all the year round in his genius. This time it was to be made by a bereaved couple from Toronto, who had given him the handsomest order for a tomb to three lost children, each of whom they desired to see, in the composition, emblematically and characteristically represented.

Such was naturally the moral of Mrs. Mallow's question: if their wealth was to be assumed, it was clear, from the nature of their admiration, as well as from mysterious hints thrown out (they were a little odd!) as to other possibilities of the same mortuary sort, that their further patronage might be; and no less evident that should the Master become at all known in those climes nothing would be more inevitable than a run of Canadian custom. Peter had been present before at runs of custom, colonial and domestic — present at each of those of which the aggregation had left so few gaps in the marble company round him; but it was his habit never at these junctures to prick the bubble in advance. The fond illusion, while it lasted, eased the wound of elections never won, the long ache of medals and diplomas carried off, on every chance, by every one but the Master; it moreover lighted the lamp that would glimmer through the next eclipse. They lived, however, after all — as it was always beautiful to see — at a height scarce susceptible of ups and downs. They strained a point at times charmingly, strained it to admit that the public was here and there not too bad to buy; but they would have been nowhere without their attitude that the Master was always too good to sell. They were at all events deliciously formed, Peter often said to himself, for their fate; the Master had a vanity, his wife had a loyalty, of which success, depriving these things of innocence, would have diminished the merit and the grace. Any one could be charming under a charm, and as he looked about him at a world of prosperity more void of proportion even than the Master's museum he wondered if he knew another pair that so completely escaped vulgarity.

"What a pity Lance isn't with us to rejoice!" Mrs. Mallow on this occasion sighed at supper.

"We'll drink to the health of the absent," her husband replied, filling his friend's glass and his own and giving a drop to their companion; "but we must hope he's preparing himself for a happiness much less like this of ours this evening — excusable as I grant it to be! — than like the comfort we have always (whatever has happened or has not happened) been able to trust ourselves to enjoy. The comfort," the Master explained, leaning back in the pleasant lamplight and firelight, holding up his glass and looking round at his marble family, quartered more or less, a monstrous brood, in every room — "the comfort of art in itself!"

Peter looked a little shyly at his wine. "Well — I don't care what you may call it when a fellow doesn't — but Lance must learn to *sell*, you know. I drink to his acquisition of the secret of a base popularity!"

"Oh, yes, *he* must sell," the boy's mother, who was still more, however, this seemed to give out, the Master's wife, rather artlessly allowed.

"Ah," the sculptor after a moment confidently pronounced, "Lance *will*. Don't be afraid. He'll have learnt."

"Which is exactly what Peter," Mrs. Mallow gaily returned — "why in the world were you so perverse, Peter? — wouldn't when he told him hear of."

Peter, when this lady looked at him with accusatory affection — a grace on her part not infrequent — could never find a word; but the Master, who was always all amenity and tact, helped him out now as he had often helped him before. "That's his old idea, you know — on which we've so often differed: his theory that the artist should be all impulse and instinct. *I* go in of course for a certain amount of school. Not too much — but a due proportion. There's where his protest came in," he continued to explain to his wife, "as against what *might*, don't you see? be in question for Lance."

"Ah, well!" — and Mrs. Mallow turned the violet eyes across the table at the subject of this discourse — "he's sure to have meant of course nothing but good. Only that wouldn't have prevented him, if Lance *had* taken his advice, from being in effect horribly cruel."

They had a sociable way of talking of him to his face as if he had been in the clay or — at most — in the plaster, and the Master was unfailingly generous. He might have been waving Egidio to make him revolve. "Ah but poor Peter wasn't so wrong as to what it may after all come to that he *will* learn."

"Oh but nothing artistically bad," she urged — still, for poor Peter, arch and dewy.

"Why just the little French tricks," said the Master: on which their friend had to pretend to admit, when pressed by Mrs. Mallow, that these aesthetic vices had been the objects of his dread.

III

"I know now," Lance said to him the next year, "why you were so much against it." He had come back supposedly for a mere interval and was looking about him at Carrara Lodge, where indeed he had already on two or three occasions since his expatriation briefly reappeared. This had the air of a longer holiday. "Something rather awful has happened to me. It *isn't* so very good to know."

"I'm bound to say high spirits don't show in your face," Peter was rather ruefully forced to confess. "Still, are you very sure you do know?"

"Well, I at least know about as much as I can bear." These remarks were exchanged in Peter's den, and the young man, smoking cigarettes, stood before the fire with his back against the mantel. Something of his bloom seemed really to have left him.

Poor Peter wondered. "You're clear then as to what in particular I wanted you not to go for?"

"In particular?" Lance thought. "It seems to me that in particular there can have been only one thing."

They stood for a little sounding each other. "Are you quite sure?"

"Quite sure I'm a beastly duffer? Quite — by this time."

"Oh!" — and Peter turned away as if almost with relief.

"It's *that* that isn't pleasant to find out."

"Oh I don't care for 'that,'" said Peter, presently coming round again. "I mean I personally don't."

"Yet I hope you can understand a little that I myself should!"

"Well, what do you mean by it?" Peter sceptically asked.

And on this Lance had to explain — how the upshot of his studies in Paris had inexorably proved a mere deep doubt of his means. These studies had so waked him up that a new light was in his eyes; but what the new light did was really to show him too much. "Do you know what's the matter with me? I'm too horribly intelligent. Paris was really the last place for me. I've learnt what I can't do."

Poor Peter stared — it was a staggerer; but even after they had had, on the subject, a longish talk in which the boy brought out to the full the hard truth of his lesson, his friend betrayed less pleasure than usually breaks into a face to the happy tune of "I told you so!" Poor Peter himself made now indeed so little a point of having told him so that Lance broke ground in a different place a day or two after. "What was it then that — before I went — you were afraid I should find out?" This, however, Peter refused to tell him — on the ground that if he hadn't yet guessed perhaps he never would, and that in any case nothing at all for either of them was to be gained by giving the thing a name. Lance eyed him on this an instant with the bold curiosity of youth — with the air indeed of having in his mind two or three names, of which one or other would be right. Peter nevertheless, turning his back again, offered no encouragement and when they parted afresh it was with some show of impatience on the side of the boy. Accordingly on their next encounter Peter saw at a glance that he had now, in the interval, divined and that, to sound his note, he was only waiting till they should find themselves alone. This he had soon arranged and he then broke straight out. "Do you know your conundrum has been keeping me awake? But in the watches of the night the answer came over me — so that, upon my honour, I quite laughed out. Had you been supposing I had to go to Paris to learn *that*?" Even now, to see him still so sublimely on his guard, Peter's young friend had to laugh afresh. "You won't give a sign till you're sure? Beautiful old Peter!" But Lance at last produced it. "Why, hang it, the truth about the Master."

It made between them for some minutes a lively passage, full of wonder for each at the wonder of the other. "Then how long have you understood —"

"The true value of his work? I understood it," Lance recalled, "as soon as I began to understand anything. But I didn't begin fully to do that, I admit, till I got *là-bas*."

"Dear, dear!" — Peter gasped with retrospective dread.

"But for what have you taken me? I'm a hopeless muff—that I *had* to have rubbed in. But I'm not such a muff as the Master!" Lance declared.

"Then why did you never tell me—?"

"That I hadn't after all"—the boy took him up—"remained such an idiot? Just because I never dreamed *you* knew. But I beg your pardon. I only wanted to spare you. And what I don't now understand is how the deuce then for so long you've managed to keep bottled."

Peter produced his explanation, but only after some delay and with a gravity not void of embarrassment. "It was for your mother."

"Oh!" said Lance.

"And that's the great thing now—since the murder *is* out. I want a promise from you. I mean"—and Peter almost feverishly followed it up—"a vow from you, solemn and such as you owe me here on the spot, that you'll sacrifice anything rather than let her ever guess—"

"That I've guessed?"—Lance took it in. "I see." He evidently after a moment had taken in much. "But what is it you've in mind that I may have a chance to sacrifice?"

"Oh one has always something."

Lance looked at him hard. "Do you mean that *you've* had—?" The look he received back, however, so put the question by that he found soon enough another. "Are you really sure my mother doesn't know?"

Peter, after renewed reflexion, was really sure. "If she does she's too wonderful."

"But aren't we all too wonderful?"

"Yes," Peter granted—"but in different ways. The thing's so desperately important because your father's little public consists only, as you know then," Peter developed—"well, of how many?"

"First of all," the Master's son risked, "of himself. And last of all too. I don't quite see of whom else."

Peter had an approach to impatience. "Of your mother, I say—*always*."

Lance cast it all up. "You absolutely feel that?"

"Absolutely."

"Well then with yourself that makes three."

"Oh *me!*"—and Peter, with a wag of his kind old head, modestly excused himself. "The number's at any rate small enough for any individual dropping out to be too dreadfully missed. Therefore, to put it in a nutshell, take care, my boy—that's all—that *you're* not!"

"I've got to keep on humbugging?" Lance wailed.

"It's just to warn you of the danger of your failing of that that I've seized this opportunity."

"And what do you regard in particular," the young man asked, "as the danger?"

"Why this certainty: that the moment your mother, who feels so strongly, should suspect your secret—well," said Peter desperately, "the fat would be on the fire."

Lance for a moment seemed to stare at the blaze. "She'd throw me over?"

"She'd throw *him* over."

"And come round to us?"

Peter, before he answered, turned away. "Come round to *you*." But he had said enough to indicate—and, as he evidently trusted, to avert—the horrid contingency.

IV

Within six months again, none the less, his fear was on more occasions than one all before him. Lance had returned to Paris for another trial; then had reappeared at home and had had, with his father, for the first time in his life, one of the scenes that strike sparks. He described it with much expression to Peter, touching whom (since they had never done so before) it was the sign of a new reserve on the part of the pair at Carrara Lodge that they at present failed, on a matter of intimate interest, to open themselves—if not in joy then in sorrow—to their good friend. This produced perhaps practically between the parties a shade of alienation and a slight intermission of commerce—marked mainly indeed by the fact that to talk at his ease with his old playmate Lance had in general to come to see him. The closest if not quite the gayest relation they had yet known together was thus ushered in. The difficulty for poor Lance was a tension at home—begotten by the fact that his father wished him to be at least the sort of success he himself had been. He hadn't "chucked" Paris—though nothing appeared more vivid to him than that Paris had chucked him: he would go back again because of the fascination in trying, in seeing, in sounding the depths—in learning one's lesson, briefly, even if the lesson were simply that of one's impotence in the presence of one's larger vision. But what did the Master, all aloft in his senseless fluency, know of impotence, and what vision—to be called such—had he in all his blind life ever had? Lance, heated and indignant, frankly appealed to his godparent on this score.

His father, it appeared, had come down on him for having, after so long, nothing to show, and hoped that on his next return this deficiency would be repaired. The thing, the Master complacently set forth was—for any artist, however inferior to himself—at least to "do" something. "What can you do? That's all I ask!" He had certainly done enough, and there was no mistake about what he had to show. Lance had tears in his eyes when it came thus to letting his old friend know how great the strain might be on the "sacrifice" asked of him. It wasn't so easy to continue humbugging—as from son to parent—after feeling one's self despised for not grovelling in mediocrity. Yet a noble duplicity was what, as they intimately faced the situation, Peter went on requiring; and it was still for a time what his young friend, bitter and sore, managed loyally to comfort him with. Fifty pounds more than once again, it was true, rewarded both in London and in Paris the young friend's loyalty; none the less sensibly, doubtless, at the moment, that the money was a direct advance on a decent sum for which Peter had long since privately prearranged an ultimate function. Whether by these arts or others, at all events, Lance's just resentment was kept for a season—but only for a season—at bay. The day arrived when he warned his companion that he could hold out—or hold in—no longer. Carrara Lodge had had to listen to another lecture delivered from a great height—an infliction really heavier at last than, without striking back or in some way letting the Master have the truth, flesh and blood could bear.

"And what I don't see is," Lance observed with a certain irritated eye for what was after all, if it came to that, owing to himself too; "what I don't see is, upon my honour, how *you*, as things are going, can keep the game up."

"Oh the game for me is only to hold my tongue," said placid Peter. "And I have my reason."

"Still my mother?"

Peter showed a queer face as he had often shown it before—that is by turning it straight away. "What will you have? I haven't ceased to like her."

"She's beautiful—she's a dear of course," Lance allowed; "but what is she to you, after all, and what is it to you that, as to anything whatever, she should or she shouldn't?"

Peter, who had turned red, hung fire a little. "Well—it's all simply what I make of it."

There was now, however, in his young friend a strange, an adopted insistence. "What are you after all to *her*?"

"Oh nothing. But that's another matter."

"She cares only for my father," said Lance the Parisian.

"Naturally—and that's just why."

"Why you've wished to spare her?"

"Because she cares so tremendously much."

Lance took a turn about the room, but with his eyes still on his host. "How awfully—always—you must have liked her!"

"Awfully. Always," said Peter Brench.

The young man continued for a moment to muse—then stopped again in front of him. "Do you know how much she cares?" Their eyes met on it, but Peter, as if his own found something new in Lance's, appeared to hesitate, for the first time in an age, to say he did know. "*I've* only just found out," said Lance. "She came to my room last night, after being present, in silence and only with her eyes on me, at what I had had to take from him; she came—and she was with me an extraordinary hour."

He had paused again and they had again for a while sounded each other. Then something—and it made him suddenly turn pale—came to Peter. "She *does* know?"

"She does know. She let it all out to me—so as to demand of me no more than 'that,' as she said, of which she herself had been capable. She has always, always known," said Lance without pity.

Peter was silent a long time; during which his companion might have heard him gently breathe, and on touching him might have felt within him the vibration of a long low sound suppressed. By the time he spoke at last he had taken everything in. "Then I do see how tremendously much."

"Isn't it wonderful?" Lance asked.

"Wonderful," Peter mused.

"So that if your original effort to keep me from Paris was to keep me from knowledge!—" Lance exclaimed as if with a sufficient indication of this futility.

It might have been at the futility Peter appeared for a little to gaze. "I think it must have been—without my quite at the time knowing it—to keep *me*!" he replied at last as he turned away.

[1900]

Study and Writing Questions

1. Is the knowledge that Peter Brench admits in the last paragraph genuinely new to him? Is that knowledge good or bad for him? Is his admission of it good or bad for him?
2. How is James's typical NARRATIVE sentence, such as the first one of the STORY, well adapted to his THEME?
3. How does the long paragraph in section II describing the Master's "Museum" CHARACTERIZE the Master, Mrs. Mallow, and Peter Brench and suggest their relations to each other?
4. What are the relationships of Peter Brench to the Mallow family? In what ways are Peter Brench and Lancelot alike in their relations to the senior Mallows and in what ways different? How do they relate to each other? How does Mrs. Mallow figure in Peter Brench's life at the beginning and at the end of the story? What does the Mallow family mean to Peter Brench at the beginning and at the end of the story?
5. The title obviously alludes to Genesis. How does our recognition of that ALLUSION enrich our understanding of the story? In what ways is James's story a commentary on Genesis?

See also Questions for Contrast and Comparison: 28, 32, 34, 35, 45, 65, 95, 97, 234, 235, and 237.

The Turn of the Screw

The story had held us, round the fire, sufficiently breathless, but except the obvious remark that it was gruesome, as on Christmas Eve in an old house a strange tale should essentially be, I remember no comment uttered till somebody happened to note it as the only case he had met in which such a visitation had fallen on a child. The case, I may mention, was that of an apparition in just such an old house as had gathered us for the occasion — an appearance, of a dreadful kind, to a little boy sleeping in the room with his mother and waking her up in the terror of it; waking her not to dissipate his dread and soothe him to sleep again, but to encounter also herself, before she had succeeded in doing so, the same sight that had shocked him. It was this observation that drew from Douglas —not immediately, but later in the evening—a reply that had the interesting consequence to which I call attention. Some one else told a story not particularly effective, which I saw he was not following. This I took for a sign that he had himself something to produce and that we should only have to wait. We waited in fact till two nights later; but that same evening, before we scattered, he brought out what was in his mind.

"I quite agree — in regard to Griffin's ghost, or whatever it was — that its appearing first to the little boy, at so tender an age, adds a particular touch. But it's not the first occurrence of its charming kind that I know to have been concerned with a child. If the child gives the effect another turn of the screw, what do you say to *two* children — ?"

"We say of course," somebody exclaimed, "that two children give two turns! Also that we want to hear about them."

I can see Douglas there before the fire, to which he had got up to present his back, looking down at this converser with his hands in his pockets. "Nobody but me, till now, has ever heard. It's quite too horrible." This was naturally declared by several voices to give the thing the utmost price, and our friend, with quiet art, prepared his triumph by turning his eyes over the rest of us and going on: "It's beyond everything. Nothing at all that I know touches it."

"For sheer terror?" I remember asking.

He seemed to say it wasn't so simple as that; to be really at a loss how to qualify it. He passed his hand over his eyes, made a little wincing grimace. "For dreadful — dreadfulness!"

"Oh how delicious!" cried one of the women.

He took no notice of her; he looked at me, but as if, instead of me, he saw what he spoke of. "For general uncanny ugliness and horror and pain."

"Well then," I said, "just sit right down and begin."

He turned round to the fire, gave a kick to a log, watched it an instant. Then as he faced us again: "I can't begin. I shall have to send to town." There was a unanimous groan at this, and much reproach; after which, in his preoccupied way, he explained. "The story's written. It's in a locked drawer — it has not been out for years. I could write to my man and enclose the key; he could send down the packet as he finds it." It was to me in particular that he appeared to propound this — appeared almost to appeal for aid not to hesitate. He had broken a thickness of ice, the formation of many a winter; had had his reasons for a long silence. The others resented postponement, but it was just his scruples that charmed me.

I adjured him to write by the first post and to agree with us for an early hearing; then I asked him if the experience in question had been his own. To this his answer was prompt. "Oh thank God, no!"

"And is the record yours? You took the thing down?"

"Nothing but the impression. I took that *here*"—he tapped his heart. "I've never lost it."

"Then your manuscript—?"

"Is in old faded ink and in the most beautiful hand." He hung fire again. "A woman's. She has been dead these twenty years. She sent me the pages in question before she died." They were all listening now, and of course there was somebody to be arch, or at any rate to draw the inference. But if he put the inference by without a smile it was also without irritation. "She was a most charming person, but she was ten years older than I. She was my sister's governess," he quietly said. "She was the most agreeable woman I've ever known in her position; she'd have been worthy of any whatever. It was long ago, and this episode was long before. I was at Trinity, and I found her at home on my coming down the second summer. I was much there that year—it was a beautiful one; and we had, in her off-hours, some strolls and talks in the garden—talks in which she struck me as awfully clever and nice. Oh yes; don't grin: I liked her extremely and am glad to this day to think she liked me too. If she hadn't she wouldn't have told me. She had never told any one. It wasn't simply that she said so, but that I knew she hadn't. I was sure; I could see. You'll easily judge why when you hear."

"Because the thing had been such a scare?"

He continued to fix me. "You'll easily judge," he repeated: "*you* will."

I fixed him too. "I see. She was in love."

He laughed for the first time. "You *are* acute. Yes, she was in love. That is she *had* been. That came out—she couldn't tell her story without its coming out. I saw it, and she saw it; but neither of us spoke of it. I remember the time and the place—the corner of the lawn, the shade of the great beeches and the long hot summer afternoon. It wasn't a scene for a shudder; but oh—!" He quitted the fire and dropped back into his chair.

"You'll receive the packet Thursday morning?" I said.

"Probably not till the second post."

"Well then; after dinner—"

"You'll all meet me here?" He looked us round again. "Isn't anybody going?" It was almost the tone of hope.

"Everybody will stay!"

"I will—and I will!" cried the ladies whose departure had been fixed. Mrs. Griffin, however, expressed the need for a little more light. "Who was it she was in love with?"

"The story will tell," I took upon myself to reply.

"Oh I can't wait for the story!"

"The story *won't* tell," said Douglas; "not in any literal vulgar way."

"More's the pity then. That's the only way I ever understand."

"Won't *you* tell, Douglas?" somebody else enquired.

He sprang to his feet again. "Yes—to-morrow. Now I must go to bed. Good-night." And, quickly catching up a candlestick, he left us slightly bewildered. From our end of the great brown hall we heard his step on the stair; whereupon Mrs. Griffin spoke. "Well, if I don't know who she was in love with I know who *he* was."

"She was ten years older," said her husband.

"*Raison de plus* — at that age! But it's rather nice, his long reticence."

"Forty years!" Griffin put in.

"With this outbreak at last."

"The outbreak," I returned, "will make a tremendous occasion of Thursday night"; and every one so agreed with me that in the light of it we lost all attention for everything else. The last story, however incomplete and like the mere opening of a serial, had been told; we handshook and "candlestuck," as somebody said, and went to bed.

I knew the next day that a letter containing the key had, by the first post, gone off to his London apartments; but in spite of — or perhaps just on account of — the eventual diffusion of this knowledge we quite let him alone till after dinner, till such an hour of the evening in fact as might best accord with the kind of emotion on which our hopes were fixed. Then he became as communicative as we could desire, and indeed gave us his best reason for being so. We had it from him again before the fire in the hall, as we had had our mild wonders of the previous night. It appeared that the narrative he had promised to read us really required for a proper intelligence a few words of prologue. Let me say here distinctly, to have done with it, that this narrative, from an exact transcript of my own made much later, is what I shall presently give. Poor Douglas, before his death — when it was in sight — committed to me the manuscript that reached him on the third of these days and that, on the same spot, with immense effect, he began to read to our hushed little circle on the night of the fourth. The departing ladies who had said they would stay didn't, of course, thank heaven, stay: they departed, in consequence of arrangements made, in a rage of curiosity, as they professed, produced by the touches with which he had already worked us up. But that only made his little final auditory more compact and select, kept it, round the hearth, subject to a common thrill.

The first of these touches conveyed that the written statement took up the tale at a point after it had, in a manner, begun. The fact to be in possession of was therefore that his old friend, the youngest of several daughters of a poor country parson, had at the age of twenty, on taking service for the first time in the schoolroom, come up to London, in trepidation, to answer in person an advertisement that had already placed her in brief correspondence with the advertiser. This person proved, on her presenting herself for judgment at a house in Harley Street that impressed her as vast and imposing — this prospective patron proved a gentleman, a bachelor in the prime of life, such a figure as had never risen, save in a dream or an old novel, before a fluttered anxious girl out of a Hampshire vicarage. One could easily fix his type; it never, happily, dies out. He was handsome and bold and pleasant, off-hand and gay and kind. He struck her, inevitably, as gallant and splendid, but what took her most of all and gave her the courage she afterwards showed was that he put the whole thing to her as a favour, an obligation he should gratefully incur. She figured him as rich, but as fearfully extravagant — saw him all in a glow of high fashion, of good looks, of expensive habits, of charming ways with women. He had for his town residence a big house filled with the spoils of travel and the trophies of the chase; but it was to his country home, an old family place in Essex, that he wished her immediately to proceed.

He had been left, by the death of his parents in India, guardian to a small nephew and a small niece, children of a younger, a military brother whom he had lost two years before. These children were, by the strangest of chances for a man in his position—a lone man without the right sort of experience or a grain of patience—very heavy on his hands. It had all been a great worry and, on his own part doubtless, a series of blunders, but he immensely pitied the poor chicks and had done all he could; had in particular sent them down to his other house, the proper place for them being of course the country, and kept them there from the first with the best people he could find to look after them, parting even with his own servants to wait on them and going down himself, whenever he might, to see how they were doing. The awkward thing was that they had practically no other relations and that his own affairs took up all his time. He had put them in possession of Bly, which was healthy and secure, and had placed at the head of their little establishment—but below-stairs only—an excellent woman, Mrs. Grose, whom he was sure his visitor would like and who had formerly been maid to his mother. She was now housekeeper and was also acting for the time as superintendent to the little girl, of whom, without children of her own, she was by good luck extremely fond. There were plenty of people to help, but of course the young lady who should go down as governess would be in supreme authority. She would also have, in holidays, to look after the small boy, who had been for a term at school—young as he was to be sent, but what else could be done?—and who, as the holidays were about to begin, would be back from one day to the other. There had been for the two children at first a young lady whom they had had the misfortune to lose. She had done for them quite beautifully—she was a most respectable person—till her death, the great awkwardness of which had, precisely, left no alternative but the school for little Miles. Mrs. Grose, since then, in the way of manners and things, had done as she could for Flora; and there were, further, a cook, a housemaid, a dairywoman, an old pony, an old groom and an old gardener, all likewise thoroughly respectable.

So far had Douglas presented his picture when some one put a question. "And what did the former governess die of? Of so much respectability?"

Our friend's answer was prompt. "That will come out. I don't anticipate."

"Pardon me—I thought that was just what you *are* doing."

"In her successor's place," I suggested, "I should have wished to learn if the office brought with it—"

"Necessary danger to life?" Douglas completed my thought. "She did wish to learn, and she did learn. You shall hear to-morrow what she learnt. Meanwhile of course the prospect struck her as slightly grim. She was young, untried, nervous: it was a vision of serious duties and little company, of really great loneliness. She hesitated—took a couple of days to consult and consider. But the salary offered much exceeded her modest measure, and on a second interview she faced the music, she engaged." And Douglas, with this, made a pause that, for the benefit of the company, moved me to throw in—

"The moral of which was of course the seduction exercised by the splendid young man. She succumbed to it."

He got up and, as he had done the night before, went to the fire, gave a stir to a log with his foot, then stood a moment with his back to us. "She saw him only twice."

"Yes, but that's just the beauty of her passion."

A little to my surprise, on this, Douglas turned round to me. "It *was* the beauty of it. There were others," he went on, "who hadn't succumbed. He told her frankly all his difficulty — that for several applicants the conditions had been prohibitive. They were somehow simply afraid. It sounded dull — it sounded strange; and all the more so because of his main condition."

"Which was —?"

"That she should never trouble him — but never, never: neither appeal nor complain nor write about anything; only meet all questions herself, receive all moneys from his solicitor, take the whole thing over and let him alone. She promised to do this, and she mentioned to me that when, for a moment, disburdened, delighted, he held her hand, thanking her for the sacrifice, she already felt rewarded."

"But was that all her reward?" one of the ladies asked.

"She never saw him again."

"Oh!" said the lady; which, as our friend immediately again left us, was the only other word of importance contributed to the subject till, the next night, by the corner of the hearth, in the best chair, he opened the faded red cover of a thin old-fashioned gilt-edged album. The whole thing took indeed more nights than one, but on the first occasion the same lady put another question. "What's your title?"

"I haven't one."

"Oh *I* have!" I said. But Douglas, without heeding me, had begun to read with a fine clearness that was like a rendering to the ear of the beauty of his author's hand.

I

I remember the whole beginning as a succession of flights and drops, a little see-saw of the right throbs and the wrong. After rising, in town, to meet his appeal I had at all events a couple of very bad days — found all my doubts bristle again, felt indeed sure I had made a mistake. In this state of mind I spent the long hours of bumping, swinging coach that carried me to the stopping-place at which I was to be met by a vehicle from the house. This convenience, I was told, had been ordered, and I found, toward the close of the June afternoon, a commodious fly in waiting for me. Driving at that hour, on a lovely day, through a country the summer sweetness of which served as a friendly welcome, my fortitude revived and, as we turned into the avenue, took a flight that was probably but a proof of the point to which it had sunk. I suppose I had expected, or had dreaded, something so dreary that what greeted me was a good surprise. I remember as a thoroughly pleasant impression the broad clear front, its open windows and fresh curtains and the pair of maids looking out; I remember the lawn and the bright flowers and the crunch of my wheels on the gravel and the clustered tree-tops over which the rooks circled and cawed in the golden sky. The scene had a greatness that made it a different affair from my own scant home, and there immediately appeared at the door, with a little girl in her hand, a civil person who dropped me as decent a curtsey as if I had been the mistress or a distinguished visitor. I had received in Harley Street a narrower notion of the place, and that, as I recalled it, made me think the proprietor still more of a gentleman, suggested that what I was to enjoy might be a matter beyond his promise.

I had no drop again till the next day, for I was carried triumphantly through the following hours by my introduction to the younger of my pupils. The little girl who accompanied Mrs. Grose affected me on the spot as a creature too charming not to make it a great fortune to have to do with her. She was the most beautiful child I had ever seen, and I afterwards wondered why my employer hadn't made more of a point to me of this. I slept little that night — I was too much excited; and this astonished me too, I recollect, remained with me, adding to my sense of the liberality with which I was treated. The large impressive room, one of the best in the house, the great state bed, as I almost felt it, the figured full draperies, the long glasses in which, for the first time, I could see myself from head to foot, all struck me — like the wonderful appeal of my small charge — as so many things thrown in. It was thrown in as well, from the first moment, that I should get on with Mrs. Grose in a relation over which, on my way, in the coach, I fear I had rather brooded. The one appearance indeed that in this early outlook might have made me shrink again was that of her being so inordinately glad to see me. I felt within half an hour that she was so glad — stout simple plain clean wholesome woman — as to be positively on her guard against showing it too much. I wondered even then a little why she should wish *not* to show it, and that, with reflexion, with suspicion, might of course have made me uneasy.

But it was a comfort that there could be no uneasiness in a connexion with anything so beatific as the radiant image of my little girl, the vision of whose angelic beauty had probably more than anything else to do with the restlessness that, before morning, made me several times rise and wander about my room to take in the whole picture and prospect; to watch from my open window the faint summer dawn, to look at such stretches of the rest of the house as I could catch, and to listen, while in the fading dusk the first birds began to twitter, for the possible recurrence of a sound or two, less natural and not without but within, that I had fancied I heard. There had been a moment when I believed I recognised, faint and far, the cry of a child; there had been another when I found myself just consciously starting as at the passage, before my door, of a light footstep. But these fancies were not marked enough not to be thrown off, and it is only in the light, or the gloom, I should rather say, of other and subsequent matters that they now come back to me. To watch, teach, "form" little Flora would too evidently be the making of a happy and useful life. It had been agreed between us downstairs that after this first occasion I should have her as a matter of course at night, her small white bed being already arranged, to that end, in my room. What I had undertaken was the whole care of her, and she had remained just this last time with Mrs. Grose only as an effect of our consideration for my inevitable strangeness and her natural timidity. In spite of this timidity — which the child herself, in the oddest way in the world, had been perfectly frank and brave about, allowing it, without a sign of uncomfortable consciousness, with the deep sweet serenity indeed of one of Raphael's holy infants, to be discussed, to be imputed to her and to determine us — I felt quite sure she would presently like me. It was part of what I already liked Mrs. Grose herself for, the pleasure I could see her feel in my admiration and wonder as I sat at supper with four tall candles and with my pupil, in a high chair and a bib, brightly facing me between them over bread and milk. There were naturally things that in Flora's presence could pass between us only as prodigious and gratified looks, obscure and round-about allusions.

"And the little boy—does he look like her? Is he too so very remarkable?"

One wouldn't, it was already conveyed between us, too grossly flatter a child. "Oh Miss, *most* remarkable. If you think well of this one!"—and she stood there with a plate in her hand, beaming at our companion, who looked from one of us to the other with placid heavenly eyes that contained nothing to check us.

"Yes; if I do—?"

"You *will* be carried away by the little gentleman!"

"Well, that, I think, is what I came for—to be carried away. I'm afraid, however," I remember feeling the impulse to add, "I'm rather easily carried away. I was carried away in London!"

I can still see Mrs. Grose's broad face as she took this in. "In Harley Street?"

"In Harley Street."

"Well, Miss, you're not the first—and you won't be the last."

"Oh I've no pretensions," I could laugh, "to being the only one. My other pupil, at any rate, as I understand, comes back to-morrow?"

"Not to-morrow—Friday, Miss. He arrives, as you did, by the coach, under care of the guard, and is to be met by the same carriage."

I forthwith wanted to know if the proper as well as the pleasant and friendly thing wouldn't therefore be that on the arrival of the public conveyance I should await him with his little sister; a proposition to which Mrs. Grose assented so heartily that I somehow took her manner as a kind of comforting pledge—never falsified, thank heaven!—that we should on every question be quite at one. Oh she was glad I was there!

What I felt the next day was, I suppose, nothing that could be fairly called a reaction from the cheer of my arrival; it was probably at the most only a slight oppression produced by a fuller measure of the scale, as I walked round them, gazed up at them, took them in, of my new circumstances. They had, as it were, an extent and mass for which I had not been prepared and in the presence of which I found myself, freshly, a little scared not less than a little proud. Regular lessons, in this agitation, certainly suffered some wrong; I reflected that my first duty was, by the gentlest arts I could contrive, to win the child into the sense of knowing me. I spent the day with her out of doors; I arranged with her, to her great satisfaction, that it should be she, she only, who might show me the place. She showed it step by step and room by room and secret by secret, with droll delightful childish talk about it and with the result, in half an hour, of our becoming tremendous friends. Young as she was I was struck, throughout our little tour, with her confidence and courage, with the way, in empty chambers and dull corridors, on crooked staircases that made me pause and even on the summit of an old machicolated square tower that made me dizzy, her morning music, her disposition to tell me so many more things than she asked, rang out and led me on. I have not seen Bly since the day I left it, and I dare say that to my present older and more informed eyes it would show a very reduced importance. But as my little conductress, with her hair of gold and her frock of blue, danced before me round corners and pattered down passages, I had the view of a castle of romance inhabited by a rosy sprite, such a place as would somehow, for diversion of the young idea, take all colour out of story-books and fairy-tales. Wasn't it just a story-book over which I had fallen a-doze and a-dream? No; it was a big ugly antique but convenient house, embodying a few features of a building still older, half-displaced and half-utilised, in which I had the fancy of our being almost as lost as a handful of passengers in a great drifting ship. Well, I was strangely at the helm!

II

This came home to me when, two days later, I drove over with Flora to meet, as Mrs. Grose said, the little gentleman; and all the more for an incident that, presenting itself the second evening, had deeply disconcerted me. The first day had been, on the whole, as I have expressed, reassuring; but I was to see it wind up to a change of note. The postbag that evening — it came late — contained a letter for me which, however, in the hand of my employer, I found to be composed but of a few words enclosing another, addressed to himself, with a seal still unbroken. "This, I recognise, is from the head-master, and the head-master's an awful bore. Read him, please; deal with him; but mind you don't report. Not a word. I'm off!" I broke the seal with a great effort — so great a one that I was a long time coming to it; took the unopened missive at last up to my room and only attacked it just before going to bed. I had better have let it wait till morning, for it gave me a second sleepless night. With no counsel to take, the next day, I was full of distress; and it finally got so the better of me that I determined to open myself at least to Mrs. Grose.

"What does it mean? The child's dismissed his school."

She gave me a look that I remarked at the moment; then, visibly, with a quick blankness, seemed to try to take it back. "But aren't they all — ?"

"Sent home — yes. But only for the holidays. Miles may never go back at all."

Consciously, under my attention, she reddened. "They won't take him?"

"They absolutely decline."

At this she raised her eyes, which she had turned from me; I saw them fill with good tears. "What has he done?"

I cast about; then I judged best simply to hand her my document — which, however, had the effect of making her, without taking it, simply put her hands behind her. She shook her head sadly. "Such things are not for me, Miss."

My counsellor couldn't read! I winced at my mistake, which I attenuated as I could, and opened the letter again to repeat it to her; then, faltering in the act and folding it up once more, I put it back in my pocket. "Is he really *bad*?"

The tears were still in her eyes. "Do the gentlemen say so?"

"They go into no particulars. They simply express their regret that it should be impossible to keep him. That can have but one meaning." Mrs. Grose listened with dumb emotion; she forbore to ask me what this meaning might be; so that, presently, to put the thing with some coherence and with the mere aid of her presence to my own mind, I went on: "That he's an injury to the others."

At this, with one of the quick turns of simple folk, she suddenly flamed up. "Master Miles! — *him* an injury?"

There was such a flood of good faith in it that, though I had not yet seen the child, my very fears made me jump to the absurdity of the idea. I found myself, to meet my friend the better, offering it, on the spot, sarcastically. "To his poor little innocent mates!"

"It's too dreadful," cried Mrs. Grose, "to say such cruel things! Why he's scarce ten years old."

"Yes, yes; it would be incredible."

She was evidently grateful for such a profession. "See him, Miss, first. *Then* believe it!" I felt forthwith a new impatience to see him; it was the beginning of a curiosity that, all the next hours, was to deepen almost to pain. Mrs. Grose was aware, I could judge, of what she had produced in me, and she followed it up with assurance. "You might as well believe it of the little lady. Bless her," she added the next moment—"*look* at her!"

I turned and saw that Flora, whom, ten minutes before, I had established in the schoolroom with a sheet of white paper, a pencil and a copy of nice "round O's," now presented herself to view at the open door. She expressed in her little way an extraordinary detachment from disagreeable duties, looking at me, however, with a great childish light that seemed to offer it as a mere result of the affection she had conceived for my person, which had rendered necessary that she should follow me. I needed nothing more than this to feel the full force of Mrs. Grose's comparison, and, catching my pupil in my arms, covered her with kisses in which there was a sob of atonement.

None the less, the rest of the day, I watched for further occasion to approach my colleague, especially as, toward evening, I began to fancy she rather sought to avoid me. I overtook her, I remember, on the staircase; we went down together and at the bottom I detained her, holding her there with a hand on her arm. "I take what you said to me at noon as a declaration that you've never known him to be bad."

She threw back her head; she had clearly by this time, and very honestly, adopted an attitude. "Oh never known him—I don't pretend *that*!"

I was upset again. "Then you *have* known him—?"

"Yes indeed, Miss, thank God!"

On reflexion I accepted this. "You mean that a boy who never is—?"

"Is no boy for *me*!"

I held her tighter. "You like them with the spirit to be naughty?" Then, keeping pace with her answer, "So do I!" I eagerly brought out. "But not to the degree to contaminate—"

"To contaminate?"—my big word left her at a loss.

I explained it. "To corrupt."

She stared, taking my meaning in; but it produced in her an odd laugh. "Are you afraid he'll corrupt *you*?" She put the question with such a fine bold humour that with a laugh, a little silly doubtless, to match her own, I gave way for the time to the apprehension of ridicule.

But the next day, as the hour for my drive approached, I cropped up in another place. "What was the lady who was here before?"

"The last governess? She was also young and pretty—almost as young and almost as pretty, Miss, even as you."

"Ah then I hope her youth and her beauty helped her!" I recollect throwing off. "He seems to like us young and pretty!"

"Oh he *did*," Mrs. Grose assented: "it was the way he liked every one!" She had no sooner spoken indeed than she caught herself up. "I mean that's *his* way—the master's."

I was struck. "But of whom did you speak first?"

She looked blank, but she coloured. "Why of *him*."

"Of the master?"

"Of who else?"

There was so obviously no one else that the next moment I had lost my impression of her having accidentally said more than she meant; and I merely asked what I wanted to know. "Did *she* see anything in the boy—?"

"That wasn't right? She never told me."

I had a scruple, but I overcame it. "Was she careful—particular?"

Mrs. Grose appeared to try to be conscientious. "About some things—yes."

"But not about all?"

Again she considered. "Well, Miss—she's gone. I won't tell tales."

"I quite understand your feeling," I hastened to reply; but I thought it after an instant not opposed to this concession to pursue: "Did she die here?"

"No—she went off."

I don't know what there was in this brevity of Mrs. Grose's that struck me as ambiguous. "Went off to die?" Mrs. Grose looked straight out of the window, but I felt that, hypothetically, I had a right to know what young persons engaged for Bly were expected to do. "She was taken ill, you mean, and went home?"

"She was not taken ill, so far as appeared, in this house. She left it, at the end of the year, to go home, as she said, for a short holiday, to which the time she had put in had certainly given her a right. We had then a young woman—a nurse-maid who had stayed on and who was a good girl and clever; and *she* took the children altogether for the interval. But our young lady never came back, and at the very moment I was expecting her I heard from the master that she was dead."

I turned this over. "But of what?"

"He never told me! But please, Miss," said Mrs. Grose, "I must get to my work."

III

Her thus turning her back on me was fortunately not, for my just preoccupations, a snub that could check the growth of our mutual esteem. We met, after I had brought little Miles, more intimately than ever on the ground of my stupefaction, my general emotion: so monstrous was I then ready to pronounce it that such a child as had now been revealed to me should be under an interdict. I was a little late on the scene of his arrival, and I felt, as he stood wistfully looking out for me before the door of the inn at which the coach had put him down, that I had seen him on the instant, without and within, in the great glow of freshness, the same positive fragrance of purity, in which I had from the first moment seen his little sister. He was incredibly beautiful, and Mrs. Grose had put her finger on it: everything but a sort of passion of tenderness for him was swept away by his presence. What I then and there took him to my heart for was something divine that I have never found to the same degree in any child—his indescribable little air of knowing nothing in the world but love. It would have been impossible to carry a bad name with a greater sweetness of innocence, and by the time I had got back to Bly with him I remained merely bewildered—so far, that is, as I was not outraged—by the sense of the horrible letter locked up in one of the drawers of my room. As soon as I could compass a private word with Mrs. Grose I declared to her that it was grotesque.

She promptly understood me. "You mean the cruel charge—?"

"It doesn't live an instant. My dear woman, *look* at him!"

She smiled at my pretension to have discovered his charm. "I assure you, Miss, I do nothing else! What will you say then?" she immediately added.

"In answer to the letter?" I had made up my mind. "Nothing at all."

"And to his uncle?"

I was incisive. "Nothing at all."

"And to the boy himself?"

I was wonderful. "Nothing at all."

She gave with her apron a great wipe to her mouth. "Then I'll stand by you. We'll see it out."

"We'll see it out!" I ardently echoed, giving her my hand to make it a vow.

She held me there a moment, then whisked up her apron again with her detached hand. "Would you mind, Miss, if I used the freedom—"

"To kiss me? No!" I took the good creature in my arms and after we had embraced like sisters felt still more fortified and indignant.

This at all events was for the time: a time so full that as I recall the way it went it reminds me of all the art I now need to make it a little distinct. What I look back at with amazement is the situation I accepted. I had undertaken, with my companion, to see it out, and I was under a charm apparently that could smooth away the extent and the far and difficult connexions of such an effort. I was lifted aloft on a great wave of infatuation and pity. I found it simple, in my ignorance, my confusion and perhaps my conceit, to assume that I could deal with a boy whose education for the world was all on the point of beginning. I am unable even to remember at this day what proposal I framed for the end of his holidays and the resumption of his studies. Lessons with me indeed, that charming summer, we all had a theory that he was to have; but I now feel that for weeks the lessons must have been rather my own. I learnt something—at first certainly—that had not been one of the teachings of my small smothered life; learnt to be amused, and even amusing, and not to think for the morrow. It was the first time, in a manner, that I had known space and air and freedom, all the music of summer and all the mystery of nature. And then there was consideration—and consideration was sweet. Oh it was a trap—not designed but deep—to my imagination, to my delicacy, perhaps to my vanity; to whatever in me was most excitable. The best way to picture it all is to say that I was off my guard. They gave me so little trouble—they were of a gentleness so extraordinary. I used to speculate—but even this with a dim disconnectedness—as to how the rough future (for all futures are rough!) would handle them and might bruise them. They had the bloom of health and happiness; and yet, as if I had been in charge of a pair of little grandees, of princes of the blood, for whom everything, to be right, would have to be fenced about and ordered and arranged, the only form that in my fancy the after-years could take for them was that of a romantic, a really royal extension of the garden and the park. It may be of course above all that what suddenly broke into this gives the previous time a charm of stillness — that hush in which something gathers or crouches. The change was actually like the spring of a beast.

In the first weeks the days were long; they often, at their finest, gave me what I used to call my own hour, the hour when, for my pupils, tea-time and bed-time having come and gone, I had before my final retirement a small interval alone. Much as I liked my companions this hour was the thing in the day I liked most; and I liked it best of all when, as the light faded — or rather, I should say, the day lingered and the last calls of the last birds sounded, in a flushed sky, from the old trees — I could take a turn into the grounds and enjoy, almost with a sense of property that amused and flattered me, the beauty and dignity of the place. It was a pleasure at these moments to feel myself tranquil and justified; doubtless perhaps also to reflect that by my discretion, my quiet good sense of general high propriety, I was giving pleasure — if he ever thought of it! — to the person to whose pressure I had yielded. What I was doing was what he had earnestly hoped and directly asked of me, and that I *could*, after all, do it proved even a greater joy than I had expected. I dare say I fancied myself in short a remarkable young woman and took comfort in the faith that this would more publicly appear. Well, I needed to be remarkable to offer a front to the remarkable things that presently gave their first sign.

It was plump, one afternoon, in the middle of my very hour: the children were tucked away and I had come out for my stroll. One of the thoughts that, as I don't in the least shrink now from noting, used to be with me in these wanderings was that it would be as charming as a charming story suddenly to meet some one. Some one would appear there at the turn of a path and would stand before me and smile and approve. I didn't ask more than that — I only asked that he should *know*; and the only way to be sure he knew would be to see it, and the kind light of it, in his handsome face. That was exactly present to me — by which I mean the face was — when, on the first of these occasions, at the end of a long June day, I stopped short on emerging from one of the plantations and coming into view of the house. What arrested me on the spot — and with a shock much greater than any vision had allowed for — was the sense that my imagination had, in a flash, turned real. He did stand there! — but high up, beyond the lawn and at the very top of the tower to which, on that first morning, little Flora had conducted me. This tower was one of a pair — square incongruous crenellated structures — that were distinguished, for some reason, though I could see little difference, as the new and the old. They flanked opposite ends of the house and were probably architectural absurdities, redeemed in a measure indeed by not being wholly disengaged nor of a height too pretentious, dating, in their gingerbread antiquity, from a romantic revival that was already a respectable past. I admired them, had fancies about them, for we could all profit in a degree, especially when they loomed through the dusk, by the grandeur of their actual battlements; yet it was not at such an elevation that the figure I had so often invoked seemed most in place.

It produced in me, this figure, in the clear twilight, I remember, two distinct gasps of emotion, which were, sharply, the shock of my first and that of my second surprise. My second was a violent perception of the mistake of my first:

the man who met my eyes was not the person I had precipitately supposed. There came to me thus a bewilderment of vision of which, after these years, there is no living view that I can hope to give. An unknown man in a lonely place is a permitted object of fear to a young woman privately bred; and the figure that faced me was — a few more seconds assured me — as little any one else I knew as it was the image that had been in my mind. I had not seen it in Harley Street — I had not seen it anywhere. The place moreover, in the strangest way in the world, had on the instant and by the very fact of its appearance become a solitude. To me at least, making my statement here with a deliberation with which I have never made it, the whole feeling of the moment returns. It was as if, while I took in what I did take in, all the rest of the scene had been stricken with death. I can hear again, as I write, the intense hush in which the sounds of evening dropped. The rooks stopped cawing in the golden sky and the friendly hour lost for the unspeakable minute all its voice. But there was no other change in nature, unless indeed it were a change that I saw with a stranger sharpness. The gold was still in the sky, the clearness in the air, and the man who looked at me over the battlements was as definite as a picture in a frame. That's how I thought, with extraordinary quickness, of each person he might have been and that he wasn't. We were confronted across our distance quite long enough for me to ask myself with intensity who then he was and to feel, as an effect of my inability to say, a wonder that in a few seconds more became intense.

The great question, or one of these, is afterwards, I know, with regard to certain matters, the question of how long they have lasted. Well, this matter of mine, think what you will of it, lasted while I caught at a dozen possibilities, none of which made a difference for the better, that I could see, in there having been in the house — and for how long, above all? — a person of whom I was in ignorance. It lasted while I just bridled a little with the sense of how my office seemed to require that there should be no such ignorance and no such person. It lasted while this visitant, at all events — and there was a touch of the strange freedom, as I remember, in the sign of familiarity of his wearing no hat — seemed to fix me, from his position, with just the question, just the scrutiny through the fading light, that his own presence provoked. We were too far apart to call to each other, but there was a moment at which, at shorter range, some challenge between us, breaking the hush, would have been the right result of our straight mutual stare. He was in one of the angles, the one away from the house, very erect, as it struck me, and with both hands on the ledge. So I saw him as I see the letters I form on this page; then, exactly, after a minute, as if to add to the spectacle, he slowly changed his place — passed, looking at me hard all the while, to the opposite corner of the platform. Yes, it was intense to me that during this transit he never took his eyes from me, and I can see at this moment the way his hand, as he went, moved from one of the crenellations to the next. He stopped at the other corner, but less long, and even as he turned away still markedly fixed me. He turned away; that was all I knew.

IV

It was not that I didn't wait, on this occasion, for more, since I was as deeply rooted as shaken. Was there a "secret" at Bly — a mystery of Udolpho or an insane, an unmentionable relative kept in unsuspected confinement? I can't say how long I turned it over, or how long, in a confusion of curiosity and dread, I remained where I had had my collision; I only recall that when I re-entered the house darkness had quite closed in. Agitation, in the interval, certainly had held me and driven me, for I must, in circling about the place, have walked three miles; but I was to be later on so much more overwhelmed that this mere dawn of alarm was a comparatively human chill. The most singular part of it in fact — singular as the rest had been — was the part I became, in the hall, aware of in meeting Mrs. Grose. This picture comes back to me in the general train — the impression, as I received it on my return, of the wide white panelled space, bright in the lamplight and with its portraits and red carpet, and of the good surprised look of my friend, which immediately told me she had missed me. It came to me straightway, under her contact, that, with plain heartiness, mere relieved anxiety at my appearance, she knew nothing whatever that could bear upon the incident I had there ready for her. I had not suspected in advance that her comfortable face would pull me up, and I somehow measured the importance of what I had seen by my thus finding myself hesitate to mention it. Scarce anything in the whole history seems to me so odd as this fact that my real beginning of fear was one, as I may say, with the instinct of sparing my companion. On the spot, accordingly, in the pleasant hall and with her eyes on me, I, for a reason that I couldn't then have phrased, achieved an inward revolution — offered a vague pretext for my lateness and, with the plea of the beauty of the night and of the heavy dew and wet feet, went as soon as possible to my room.

Here it was another affair; here, for many days after, it was a queer affair enough. There were hours, from day to day — or at least there were moments, snatched even from clear duties — when I had to shut myself up to think. It wasn't so much yet that I was more nervous than I could bear to be as that I was remarkably afraid of becoming so; for the truth I had now to turn over was simply and clearly the truth that I could arrive at no account whatever of the visitor with whom I had been so inexplicably and yet, as it seemed to me, so intimately concerned. It took me little time to see that I might easily sound, without forms of enquiry and without exciting remark, any domestic complication. The shock I had suffered must have sharpened all my senses; I felt sure, at the end of three days and as the result of mere closer attention, that I had not been practised upon by the servants nor made the object of any "game." Of whatever it was that I knew nothing was known around me. There was but one sane inference: some one had taken a liberty rather monstrous. That was what, repeatedly, I dipped into my room and locked the door to say to myself. We had been, collectively, subject to an intrusion; some unscrupulous traveller, curious in old houses, had made his way in unobserved, enjoyed the prospect from the best point of view and then stolen out as he came. If he had given me such a bold hard stare, that was but a part of his indiscretion. The good thing, after all, was that we should surely see no more of him.

This was not so good a thing, I admit, as not to leave me to judge that what, essentially, made nothing else much signify was simply my charming work. My charming work was just my life with Miles and Flora, and through nothing could I so like it as through feeling that to throw myself into it was to throw myself out of my trouble. The attraction of my small charges was a constant joy, leading me to wonder afresh at the vanity of my original fears, the distaste I had begun by entertaining for the probable grey prose of my office. There was to be no grey prose, it appeared, and no long grind; so how could work not be charming that presented itself as daily beauty? It was all the romance of the nursery and the poetry of the schoolroom. I don't mean by this of course that we studied only fiction and verse; I mean that I can express no otherwise the sort of interest my companions inspired. How can I describe that except by saying that instead of growing deadly used to them—and it's a marvel for a governess: I call the sisterhood to witness!—I made constant fresh discoveries. There was one direction, assuredly, in which these discoveries stopped: deep obscurity continued to cover the region of the boy's conduct at school. It had been promptly given me, I have noted, to face that mystery without a pang. Perhaps even it would be nearer the truth to say that—without a word—he himself had cleared it up. He had made the whole charge absurd. My conclusion bloomed there with the real rose-flush of his innocence: he was only too fine and fair for the little horrid unclean school-world, and he had paid a price for it. I reflected acutely that the sense of such individual differences, such superiorities of quality, always, on the part of the majority—which could include even stupid sordid head-masters—turns infallibly to the vindictive.

Both the children had a gentleness—it was their only fault, and it never made Miles a muff—that kept them (how shall I express it?) almost impersonal and certainly quite unpunishable. They were like those cherubs of the anecdote who had—morally at any rate—nothing to whack! I remember feeling with Miles in especial as if he had had, as it were, nothing to call even an infinitesimal history. We expect of a small child scant enough "antecedents," but there was in this beautiful little boy something extraordinarily sensitive, yet extraordinarily happy, that, more than in any creature of his age I have seen, struck me as beginning anew each day. He had never for a second suffered. I took this as a direct disproof of his having really been chastised. If he had been wicked he would have "caught" it, and I should have caught it by the rebound—I should have found the trace, should have felt the wound and the dishonour. I could reconstitute nothing at all, and he was therefore an angel. He never spoke of his school, never mentioned a comrade or a master; and I, for my part, was quite too much disgusted to allude to them. Of course I was under the spell, and the wonderful part is that, even at the time, I perfectly knew I was. But I gave myself up to it; it was an antidote to any pain, and I had more pains than one. I was in receipt in these days of disturbing letters from home, where things were not going well. But with this joy of my children what things in the world mattered? That was the question I used to put to my scrappy retirements. I was dazzled by their loveliness.

There was a Sunday—to get on—when it rained with such force and for so many hours that there could be no procession to church; in consequence of which, as the day declined, I had arranged with Mrs. Grose that, should the evening show improvement, we would attend together the late service. The rain happily stopped, and I prepared for our walk, which, through the park and by the good road to the village, would be a matter of twenty minutes. Coming downstairs to meet my colleague in the hall, I remembered a pair of gloves that had required three stitches and that had received them—with a publicity perhaps not edifying—while I sat with the children at their tea, served on Sundays, by exception, in that cold clean temple of mahogany and brass, the "grown-up" dining-room. The gloves had been dropped there, and I turned in to recover them. The day was grey enough, but the afternoon light still lingered, and it enabled me, on crossing the threshold, not only to recognise, on a chair near the wide window, then closed, the articles I wanted, but to become aware of a person on the other side of the window and looking straight in. One step into the room had sufficed; my vision was instantaneous; it was all there. The person looking straight in was the person who had already appeared to me. He appeared thus again with I won't say greater distinctness, for that was impossible, but with a nearness that represented a forward stride in our intercourse and made me, as I met him, catch my breath and turn cold. He was the same—he was the same, and seen, this time, as he had been seen before, from the waist up, the window, though the dining-room was on the ground floor, not going down to the terrace on which he stood. His face was close to the glass, yet the effect of this better view was, strangely, just to show me how intense the former had been. He remained but a few seconds—long enough to convince me he also saw and recognised; but it was as if I had been looking at him for years and had known him always. Something, however, happened this time that had not happened before; his stare into my face, through the glass and across the room, was as deep and hard as then, but it quitted me for a moment during which I could still watch it, see it fix successively several other things. On the spot there came to me the added shock of a certitude that it was not for me he had come. He had come for some one else.

The flash of this knowledge—for it was knowledge in the midst of dread—produced in me the most extraordinary effect, starting, as I stood there, a sudden vibration of duty and courage. I say courage because I was beyond all doubt already far gone. I bounded straight out of the door again, reached that of the house, got in an instant upon the drive and, passing along the terrace as fast as I could rush, turned a corner and came full in sight. But it was in sight of nothing now—my visitor had vanished. I stopped, almost dropped, with the real relief of this; but I took in the whole scene—I gave him time to reappear. I call it time, but how long was it? I can't speak to the purpose to-day of the duration of these things. That kind of measure must have left me: they couldn't have lasted as they actually appeared to me to last. The terrace and the whole place, the lawn and the garden beyond it, all I could see of the park, were empty with a great emptiness. There were shrubberies and big trees, but I remember the clear assurance I felt that none of them concealed him. He was there or was not there: not there if I didn't see him. I got hold of this; then, instinctively, instead of returning as I had come, went to the window. It was confusedly present to me that I ought to place myself where he had stood. I did so; I applied my face to the pane and looked, as he had looked into the room. As if, at this moment, to show me exactly what his range had been, Mrs. Grose, as I had done for himself just before, came in from the hall. With this I had the full image of a repetition of what had already occurred. She saw me as I had seen my own visitant; she pulled up short as I had done; I gave her something of the shock that I had received. She turned white, and this made me ask myself if I had blanched as much. She stared, in short, and retreated just on *my* lines, and I knew she had then passed out and come round to me and that I should presently meet her. I remained where I was, and while I waited I thought of more things than one. But there's only one I take space to mention. I wondered why *she* should be scared.

V

Oh she let me know as soon as, round the corner of the house, she loomed again into view. "What in the name of goodness is the matter — ?" She was now flushed and out of breath.

I said nothing till she came quite near. "With me?" I must have made a wonderful face. "Do I show it?"

"You're as white as a sheet. You look awful."

I considered; I could meet on this, without scruple, any degree of innocence. My need to respect the bloom of Mrs. Grose's had dropped, without a rustle, from my shoulders, and if I wavered for the instant it was not with what I kept back. I put out my hand to her and she took it; I held her hard a little, liking to feel her close to me. There was a kind of support in the shy heave of her surprise. "You came for me for church, of course, but I can't go."

"Has anything happened?"

"Yes. You must know now. Did I look very queer?"

"Through this window? Dreadful!"

"Well," I said, "I've been frightened." Mrs. Grose's eyes expressed plainly that *she* had no wish to be, yet also that she knew too well her place not to be ready to share with me any marked inconvenience. Oh it was quite settled that she *must* share! "Just what you saw from the dining-room a minute ago was the effect of that. What I saw — just before — was much worse."

Her hand tightened. "What was it?"

"An extraordinary man. Looking in."

"What extraordinary man?"

"I haven't the least idea."

Mrs. Grose gazed round us in vain. "Then where is he gone?"

"I know still less."

"Have you seen him before?"

"Yes — once. On the old tower."

She could only look at me harder. "Do you mean he's a stranger?"

"Oh very much!"

"Yet you didn't tell me?"

"No — for reasons. But now that you've guessed — "

Mrs. Grose's round eyes encountered this charge. "Ah I haven't guessed!" she said very simply. "How can I if *you* don't imagine?"

"I don't in the very least."

"You've seen him nowhere but on the tower?"

"And on this spot just now."

Mrs. Grose looked round again. "What was he doing on the tower?"

"Only standing there and looking down at me."

She thought a minute. "Was he a gentleman?"

I found I had no need to think. "No." She gazed in deeper wonder. "No."

"Then nobody about the place? Nobody from the village?"

"Nobody — nobody. I didn't tell you, but I made sure."

She breathed a vague relief: this was, oddly, so much to the good. It only went indeed a little way. "But if he isn't a gentleman —"

"What *is* he? He's a horror."

"A horror?"

"He's — God help me if I know *what* he is!"

Mrs. Grose looked round once more; she fixed her eyes on the duskier distance and then, pulling herself together, turned to me with full inconsequence. "It's time we should be at church."

"Oh I'm not fit for church!"

"Won't it do you good?"

"It won't do *them*—!" I nodded at the house.

"The children?"

"I can't leave them now."

"You're afraid—?"

I spoke boldly. "I'm afraid of *him*."

Mrs. Grose's large face showed me, at this, for the first time, the far-away faint glimmer of a consciousness more acute: I somehow made out in it the delayed dawn of an idea I myself had not given her and that was as yet quite obscure to me. It comes back to me that I thought instantly of this as something I could get from her; and I felt it to be connected with the desire she presently showed to know more. "When was it — on the tower?"

"About the middle of the month. At this same hour."

"Almost at dark," said Mrs. Grose.

"Oh no, not nearly. I saw him as I see you."

"Then how did he get in?"

"And how did he get out?" I laughed. "I had no opportunity to ask him! This evening, you see," I pursued, "he has not been able to get in."

"He only peeps?"

"I hope it will be confined to that!" She had now let go my hand; she turned away a little. I waited an instant; then I brought out: "Go to church. Good-bye. I must watch."

Slowly she faced me again. "Do you fear for them?"

We met in another long look. "Don't *you?*" Instead of answering she came nearer to the window and, for a minute, applied her face to the glass. "You see how he could see," I meanwhile went on.

She didn't move. "How long was he here?"

"Till I came out. I came to meet him."

Mrs. Grose at last turned round, and there was still more in her face. "I couldn't have come out."

"Neither could I!" I laughed again. "But I did come. I've my duty."

"So have I mine," she replied; after which she added: "What's he like?"

"I've been dying to tell you. But he's like nobody."

"Nobody?" she echoed.

"He has no hat." Then seeing in her face that she already, in this, with a deeper dismay, found a touch of picture, I quickly added stroke to stroke. "He has red hair, very red, close-curling, and a pale face, long in shape, with straight good features and little rather queer whiskers that are as red as his hair. His eyebrows are somehow darker; they look particularly arched and as if they might move a good deal. His eyes are sharp, strange—awfully; but I only know clearly that they're rather small and very fixed. His mouth's wide, and his lips are thin, and except for his little whiskers he's quite clean-shaven. He gives me a sort of sense of looking like an actor."

"An actor!" It was impossible to resemble one less, at least, than Mrs. Grose at that moment.

"I've never seen one, but so I suppose them. He's tall, active, erect," I continued, "but never—no, never!—a gentleman."

My companion's face had blanched as I went on; her round eyes started and her mild mouth gaped. "A gentleman?" she gasped, confounded, stupefied: "a gentleman *he*?"

"You know him then?"

She visibly tried to hold herself. "But he *is* handsome?"

I saw the way to help her. "Remarkably!"

"And dressed—?"

"In somebody's clothes. They're smart, but they're not his own."

She broke into a breathless affirmative groan. "They're the master's!"

I caught it up. "You *do* know him?"

She faltered but a second. "Quint!" she cried.

"Quint?"

"Peter Quint—his own man, his valet, when he was here!"

"When the master was?"

Gaping still, but meeting me, she pieced it all together. "He never wore his hat, but he did wear—well, there were waistcoats missed! They were both here—last year. Then the master went, and Quint was alone."

I followed, but halting a little. "Alone?"

"Alone with *us*." Then as from a deeper depth, "In charge," she added.

"And what became of him?"

She hung fire so long that I was still more mystified. "He went too," she brought out at last.

"Went where?"

Her expression, at this, became extraordinary. "God knows where! He died."

"Died?" I almost shrieked.

She seemed fairly to square herself, plant herself more firmly to express the wonder of it. "Yes. Mr. Quint's dead."

VI

It took of course more than that particular passage to place us together in presence of what we had now to live with as we could, my dreadful liability to impressions of the order so vividly exemplified, and my companion's knowledge henceforth—a knowledge half consternation and half compassion—of that liability. There had been this evening, after the revelation that left me for an hour so prostrate—there had been for either of us no attendance on any service but a little service of tears and vows, of prayers and promises, a climax to the series of mutual challenges and pledges that had straightway ensued on our retreating together to the schoolroom and shutting ourselves up there to have everything out. The result of our having everything out was simply to reduce our situation to the last rigour of its elements. She herself had seen nothing, not the shadow of a shadow, and nobody in the house but the governess was in the governess's plight; yet she accepted without directly impugning my sanity the truth as I gave it to her, and ended by showing me on this ground an awestricken tenderness, a deference to my more than questionable privilege, of which the very breath has remained with me as that of the sweetest of human charities.

What was settled between us accordingly that night was that we thought we might bear things together; and I was not even sure that in spite of her exemption it was she who had the best of the burden. I knew at this hour, I think, as well as I knew later, what I was capable of meeting to shelter my pupils; but it took me some time to be wholly sure of what my honest comrade was prepared for to keep terms with so stiff an agreement. I was queer company enough — quite as queer as the company I received; but as I trace over what we went through I see how much common ground we must have found in the one idea that, by good fortune, *could* steady us. It was the idea, the second movement, that led me straight out, as I may say, of the inner chamber of my dread. I could take the air in the court, at least, and there Mrs. Grose could join me. Perfectly can I recall now the particular way strength came to me before we separated for the night. We had gone over and over every feature of what I had seen.

"He was looking for some one else, you say — some one who was not you?"

"He was looking for little Miles." A portentous clearness now possessed me. "*That's* whom he was looking for."

"But how do you know?"

"I know, I know, I know!" My exaltation grew. "And *you* know, my dear!"

She didn't deny this, but I required, I felt, not even so much telling as that. She took it up again in a moment. "What if *he* should see him?"

"Little Miles? That's what he wants!"

She looked immensely scared again. "The child?"

"Heaven forbid! The man. He wants to appear to *them*." That he might was an awful conception, and yet somehow I could keep it at bay; which moreover, as we lingered there, was what I succeeded in practically proving. I had an absolute certainty that I should see again what I had already seen, but something within me said that by offering myself bravely as the sole subject of such experience, by accepting, by inviting, by surmounting it all, I should serve as an expiatory victim and guard the tranquillity of the rest of the household. The children in especial I should thus fence about and absolutely save. I recall one of the last things I said that night to Mrs. Grose.

"It does strike me that my pupils have never mentioned — !"

She looked at me hard as I musingly pulled up. "His having been here and the time they were with him?"

"The time they were with him, and his name, his presence, his history, in any way. They've never alluded to it."

"Oh the little lady doesn't remember. She never heard or knew."

"The circumstances of his death?" I thought with some intensity. "Perhaps not. But Miles would remember — Miles would know."

"Ah don't try him!" broke from Mrs. Grose.

I returned her the look she had given me. "Don't be afraid." I continued to think. "It *is* rather odd."

"That he has never spoken of him?"

"Never by the least reference. And you tell me they were 'great friends.'"

"Oh it wasn't *him!*" Mrs. Grose with emphasis declared. "It was Quint's own fancy. To play with him, I mean—to spoil him." She paused a moment; then she added: "Quint was much too free."

This gave me, straight from my vision of his face—*such* a face!—a sudden sickness of disgust. "Too free with *my* boy?"

"Too free with every one!"

I forbore for the moment to analyse this description further than by the reflexion that a part of it applied to several of the members of the household, of the half-dozen maids and men who were still of our small colony. But there was everything, for our apprehension, in the lucky fact that no discomfortable legend, no perturbation of scullions, had ever, within any one's memory, attached to the kind old place. It had neither bad name nor ill fame, and Mrs. Grose, most apparently, only desired to cling to me and to quake in silence. I even put her, the very last thing of all, to the test. It was when, at midnight, she had her hand on the schoolroom door to take leave. "I *have* it from you then—for it's of great importance—that he was definitely and admittedly bad?"

"Oh not admittedly. *I* knew it—but the master didn't."

"And you never told him?"

"Well, he didn't like tale-bearing—he hated complaints. He was terribly short with anything of that kind, and if people were all right to *him*—"

"He wouldn't be bothered with more?" This squared well enough with my impression of him: he was not a trouble-loving gentleman, nor so very particular perhaps about some of the company he himself kept. All the same, I pressed my informant. "I promise you *I* would have told!"

She felt my discrimination. "I dare say I was wrong. But really I was afraid."

"Afraid of what?"

"Of things that man could do. Quint was so clever—he was so deep."

I took this in still more than I probably showed. "You weren't afraid of anything else? Not of his effect—?"

"His effect?" she repeated with a face of anguish and waiting while I faltered.

"On innocent little precious lives. They were in your charge."

"No, they weren't in mine!" she roundly and distressfully returned. "The master believed in him and placed him here because he was supposed not to be quite in health and the country air so good for him. So he had everything to say. Yes"—she let me have it—"even about *them.*"

"Them—that creature?" I had to smother a kind of howl. "And you could bear it?"

"No. I couldn't—and I can't now!" And the poor woman burst into tears.

A rigid control, from the next day, was, as I have said, to follow them; yet how often and how passionately, for a week, we came back together to the subject! Much as we had discussed it that Sunday night, I was, in the immediate later hours in especial—for it may be imagined whether I slept—still haunted with the shadow of something she had not told me. I myself had kept back nothing, but there was a word Mrs. Grose had kept back. I was sure moreover by morning that this was not from a failure of frankness, but because on every side there were fears. It seems to me indeed, in raking it all over, that by the time the morrow's sun was high I had restlessly read into the facts before us almost all the meaning they were to receive from subsequent and more cruel occurrences. What they gave me above all was just the sinister figure of the living man — the dead one would keep a while! — and of the months he had continuously passed at Bly, which, added up, made a formidable stretch. The limit of this evil time had arrived only when, on the dawn of a winter's morning, Peter Quint was found, by a labourer going to early work, stone dead on the road from the village: a catastrophe explained — superficially at least — by a visible wound to his head; such a wound as might have been produced (and as, on the final evidence, *had* been) by a fatal slip, in the dark and after leaving the public-house, on the steepish icy slope, a wrong path altogether, at the bottom of which he lay. The icy slope, the turn mistaken at night and in liquor, accounted for much — practically, in the end and after the inquest and boundless chatter, for everything; but there had been matters in his life, strange passages and perils, secret disorders, vices more than suspected, that would have accounted for a good deal more.

I scarce know how to put my story into words that shall be a credible picture of my state of mind; but I was in these days literally able to find a joy in the extraordinary flight of heroism the occasion demanded of me. I now saw that I had been asked for a service admirable and difficult; and there would be a greatness in letting it be seen — oh in the right quarter! — that I could succeed where many another girl might have failed. It was an immense help to me — I confess I rather applaud myself as I look back! — that I saw my response so strongly and so simply. I was there to protect and defend the little creatures in the world the most bereaved and the most loveable, the appeal of whose helplessness had suddenly become only too explicit, a deep constant ache of one's own engaged affection. We were cut off, really, together; we were united in our danger. They had nothing but me, and I — well, I had *them*. It was in short a magnificent chance. This chance presented itself to me in an image richly material. I was a screen — I was to stand before them. The more I saw the less they would. I began to watch them in a stifled suspense, a disguised tension, that might well, had it continued too long, have turned to something like madness. What saved me, as I now see, was that it turned to another matter altogether. It didn't last as suspense — it was superseded by horrible proofs. Proofs, I say, yes — from the moment I really took hold.

This moment dated from an afternoon hour that I happened to spend in the grounds with the younger of my pupils alone. We had left Miles indoors, on the red cushion of a deep window-seat; he had wished to finish a book, and I had been glad to encourage a purpose so laudable in a young man whose only defect was a certain ingenuity of restlessness. His sister, on the contrary, had been alert to come out, and I strolled with her half an hour, seeking the shade, for the sun was still high and the day exceptionally warm. I was aware afresh with her, as we went, of how, like her brother, she contrived — it was the charming thing in both children — to let me alone without appearing to drop me and to accompany me without appearing to oppress. They were never importunate and yet never listless. My attention to them all really went to seeing them amuse themselves immensely without me: this was a spectacle they seemed actively to prepare and that employed me as an active admirer. I walked in a world of their invention—they had no occasion whatever to draw upon mine; so that my time was taken only with being for them some remarkable person or thing that the game of the moment required and that was merely, thanks to my superior, my exalted stamp, a happy and highly distinguished sinecure. I forget what I was on the present occasion; I only remember that I was something very important and very quiet and that Flora was playing very hard. We were on the edge of the lake, and, as we had lately begun geography, the lake was the Sea of Azof.

Suddenly, amid these elements, I became aware that on the other side of the Sea of Azof we had an interested spectator. The way this knowledge gathered in me was the strangest thing in the world—the strangest, that is, except the very much stranger in which it quickly merged itself. I had sat down with a piece of work—for I was something or other that could sit—on the old stone bench which overlooked the pond; and in this position I began to take in with certitude and yet without direct vision the presence, a good way off, of a third person. The old trees, the thick shrubbery, made a great and pleasant shade, but it was all suffused with the brightness of the hot still hour. There was no ambiguity in anything; none whatever at least in the conviction I from one moment to another found myself forming as to what I should see straight before me and across the lake as a consequence of raising my eyes. They were attached at this juncture to the stitching in which I was engaged, and I can feel once more the spasm of my effort not to move them till I should so have steadied myself as to be able to make up my mind what to do. There was an alien object in view—a figure whose right of presence I instantly and passionately questioned. I recollect counting over perfectly the possibilities, reminding myself that nothing was more natural for instance than the appearance of one of the men about the place, or even of a messenger, a postman or a tradesman's boy, from the village. That reminder had as little effect on my practical certitude as I was conscious—still even without looking—of its having upon the character and attitude of our visitor. Nothing was more natural than that these things should be the other things they absolutely were not.

Of the positive identity of the apparition I would assure myself as soon as the small clock of my courage should have ticked out the right second; meanwhile, with an effort that was already sharp enough, I transferred my eyes straight to little Flora, who, at the moment, was about ten yards away. My heart had stood still for an instant with the wonder and terror of the question whether she too would see; and I held my breath while I waited for what a cry from her, what some sudden innocent sign either of interest or of alarm, would tell me. I waited, but nothing came; then in the first place—and there is something more dire in this, I feel, than in anything I have to relate—I was determined by a sense that within a minute all spontaneous sounds from her had dropped; and in the second by the circumstance that also within the minute she had, in her play, turned her back to the water. This was her attitude when I at last looked at her—looked with the confirmed conviction that we were still, together, under direct personal notice. She had picked up a small flat piece of wood which happened to have in it a little hole that had evidently suggested to her the idea of sticking in another fragment that might figure as a mast and make the thing a boat. This second morsel, as I watched her, she was very markedly and intently attempting to tighten in its place. My apprehension of what she was doing sustained me so that after some seconds I felt I was ready for more. Then I again shifted my eyes—I faced what I had to face.

VII

I got hold of Mrs. Grose as soon after this as I could; and I can give no intelligible account of how I fought out the interval. Yet I still hear myself cry as I fairly threw myself into her arms: "They *know*—it's too monstrous: they know, they know!"

"And what on earth—?" I felt her incredulity as she held me.

"Why all that *we* know—and heaven knows what more besides!" Then as she released me I made it out to her, made it out perhaps only now with full coherency even to myself. "Two hours ago, in the garden"—I could scarce articulate—"Flora *saw*!"

Mrs. Grose took it as she might have taken a blow in the stomach. "She has told you?" she panted.

"Not a word—that's the horror. She kept it to herself! The child of eight, *that* child!" Unutterable still for me was the stupefaction of it.

Mrs. Grose of course could only gape the wider. "Then how do you know?"

"I was there—I saw with my eyes: saw she was perfectly aware."

"Do you mean aware of *him*?"

"No—of *her*." I was conscious as I spoke that I looked prodigious things, for I got the slow reflexion of them in my companion's face. "Another person—this time; but a figure of quite as unmistakeable horror and evil: a woman in black, pale and dreadful—with such an air also, and such a face!—on the other side of the lake. I was there with the child—quiet for the hour; and in the midst of it she came."

"Came how—from where?"

"From where they come from! She just appeared and stood there—but not so near."

"And without coming nearer?"

"Oh for the effect and the feeling she might have been as close as you!"

My friend, with an odd impulse, fell back a step. "Was she some one you've never seen?"

"Never. But some one the child has. Some one *you* have." Then to show how I had thought it all out: "My predecessor—the one who died."

"Miss Jessel?"

"Miss Jessel. You don't believe me?" I pressed.

She turned right and left in her distress. "How can you be sure?"

This drew from me, in the state of my nerves, a flash of impatience. "Then ask Flora—*she's* sure!" But I had no sooner spoken than I caught myself up. "No, for God's sake *don't*! She'll say she isn't—she'll lie!"

Mrs. Grose was not too bewildered instinctively to protest. "Ah how *can* you?"

"Because I'm clear. Flora doesn't want me to know."

"It's only then to spare you."

"No, no—there are depths, depths! The more I go over it the more I see in it, and the more I see in it the more I fear. I don't know what I *don't* see, what I *don't* fear!"

Mrs. Grose tried to keep up with me. "You mean you're afraid of seeing her again?"

"Oh no; that's nothing—now!" Then I explained. "It's of *not* seeing her."

But my companion only looked wan. "I don't understand."

"Why, it's that the child may keep it up—and that the child assuredly *will*—without my knowing it."

At the image of this possibility Mrs. Grose for a moment collapsed, yet presently to pull herself together again as from the positive force of the sense of what, should we yield an inch, there would really be to give way to. "Dear, dear—we must keep our heads! And after all, if she doesn't mind it—!" She even tried a grim joke. "Perhaps she likes it!"

"Like *such* things—a scrap of an infant!"

"Isn't it just a proof of her blest innocence?" my friend bravely enquired.

She brought me, for the instant, almost round. "Oh we must clutch at *that*—we must cling to it! If it isn't a proof of what you say, it's a proof of—God knows what! For the woman's a horror of horrors.'"

Mrs. Grose, at this, fixed her eyes a minute on the ground; then at last raising them, "Tell me how you know," she said.

"Then you admit it's what she was?" I cried.

"Tell me how you know," my friend simply repeated.

"Know? By seeing her! By the way she looked."

"At you, do you mean—so wickedly?"

"Dear me, no—I could have borne that. She gave me never a glance. She only fixed the child."

Mrs. Grose tried to see it. "Fixed her?"

"Ah with such awful eyes!"

She stared at mine as if they might really have resembled them. "Do you mean of dislike?"

"God help us, no. Of something much worse."

"Worse than dislike?"—this left her indeed at a loss.

"With a determination—indescribable. With a kind of fury of intention."

I made her turn pale. "Intention?"

"To get hold of her." Mrs. Grose—her eyes just lingering on mine—gave a shudder and walked to the window; and while she stood there looking out I completed my statement. "*That's* what Flora knows."

After a little she turned round. "The person was in black, you say?"

"In mourning—rather poor, almost shabby. But—yes—with extraordinary beauty." I now recognised to what I had at last, stroke by stroke, brought the victim of my confidence, for she quite visibly weighed this. "Oh handsome—very, very," I insisted; "wonderfully handsome. But infamous."

She slowly came back to me. "Miss Jessel—*was* infamous." She once more took my hand in both her own, holding it as tight as if to fortify me against the increase of alarm I might draw from this disclosure. "They were both infamous," she finally said.

So for a little we faced it once more together; and I found absolutely a degree of help in seeing it now so straight. "I appreciate," I said, "the great decency of your not having hitherto spoken; but the time has certainly come to give me the whole thing." She appeared to assent to this, but still only in silence; seeing which I went on: "I must have it now. Of what did she die? Come, there was something between them."

"There was everything."

"In spite of the difference—?"

"Oh of their rank, their condition"—she brought it woefully out. "*She* was a lady."

I turned it over; I again saw. "Yes—she was a lady."

"And he so dreadfully below," said Mrs. Grose.

I felt that I doubtless needn't press too hard, in such company, on the place of a servant in the scale; but there was nothing to prevent an acceptance of my companion's own measure of my predecessor's abasement. There was a way to deal with that, and I dealt; the more readily for my full vision—on the evidence—of our employer's late clever good-looking "own" man; impudent, assured, spoiled, depraved. "The fellow was a hound."

Mrs. Grose considered as if it were perhaps a little a case for a sense of shades. "I've never seen one like him. He did what he wished."

"With *her*?"

"With them all."

It was as if now in my friend's own eyes Miss Jessel had again appeared. I seemed at any rate for an instant to trace their evocation of her as distinctly as I had seen her by the pond; and I brought out with decision: "It must have been also what *she* wished!"

Mrs. Grose's face signified that it had been indeed, but she said at the same time: "Poor woman—she paid for it!"

"Then you do know what she died of?" I asked.

"No—I know nothing. I wanted not to know; I was glad enough I didn't; and I thanked heaven she was well out of this!"

"Yet you had then your idea—"

"Of her real reason for leaving? Oh yes—as to that. She couldn't have stayed. Fancy it here—for a governess! And afterwards I imagined—and I still imagine. And what I imagine is dreadful."

"Not so dreadful as what I do," I replied; on which I must have shown her—as I was indeed but too conscious—a front of miserable defeat. It brought out again all her compassion for me, and at the renewed touch of her kindness my power to resist broke down. I burst, as I had the other time made her burst, into tears; she took me to her motherly breast, where my lamentation overflowed. "I don't do it!" I sobbed in despair; "I don't save or shield them! It's far worse than I dreamed. They're lost!"

VIII

What I had said to Mrs. Grose was true enough: there were in the matter I had put before her depths and possibilities that I lacked resolution to sound; so that when we met once more in the wonder of it we were of a common mind about the duty of resistance to extravagant fancies. We were to keep our heads if we should keep nothing else — difficult indeed as that might be in the face of all that, in our prodigious experience, seemed least to be questioned. Late that night, while the house slept, we had another talk in my room; when she went all the way with me as to its being beyond doubt that I had seen exactly what I had seen. I found that to keep her thoroughly in the grip of this I had only to ask her how, if I had "made it up," I came to be able to give, of each of the persons appearing to me, a picture disclosing, to the last detail, their special marks — a portrait on the exhibition of which she had instantly recognised and named them. She wished, of course — small blame to her! — to sink the whole subject; and I was quick to assure her that my own interest in it had now violently taken the form of a search for the way to escape from it. I closed with her cordially on the article of the likelihood that with recurrence — for recurrence we took for granted — I should get used to my danger; distinctly professing that my personal exposure had suddenly become the least of my discomforts. It was my new suspicion that was intolerable; and yet even to this complication the later hours of the day had brought a little ease.

On leaving her, after my first outbreak, I had of course returned to my pupils, associating the right remedy for my dismay with that sense of their charm which I had already recognised as a resource I could positively cultivate and which had never failed me yet. I had simply, in other words, plunged afresh into Flora's special society and there become aware — it was almost a luxury! — that she could put her little conscious hand straight upon the spot that ached. She had looked at me in sweet speculation and then had accused me to my face of having "cried." I had supposed the ugly signs of it brushed away; but I could literally — for the time at all events — rejoice, under this fathomless charity, that they had not entirely disappeared. To gaze into the depths of blue of the child's eyes and pronounce their loveliness a trick of premature cunning was to be guilty of a cynicism in preference to which I naturally preferred to abjure my judgement and, so far as might be, my agitation. I couldn't abjure for merely wanting to, but I could repeat to Mrs. Grose — as I did there, over and over, in the small hours — that with our small friends' voices in the air, their pressure on one's heart and their fragrant faces against one's cheek, everything fell to the ground but their incapacity and their beauty. It was a pity that, somehow, to settle this once for all, I had equally to re-enumerate the signs of subtlety that, in the afternoon, by the lake, had made a miracle of my show of self-possession. It was a pity to be obliged to re-investigate the certitude of the moment itself and repeat how it had come to me as a revelation that the inconceivable communion I then surprised must have been for both parties a matter of habit. It was a pity I should have had to quaver out again the reasons for my not having, in my delusion, so much as questioned that the little girl saw our visitant even as I actually saw Mrs. Grose herself, and that she wanted, by just so much as she did thus see, to make me suppose she didn't, and at the same time, without showing anything, arrive at a guess as to whether I myself did! It was a pity I needed to recapitulate the portentous little activities by which she sought to divert my attention — the perceptible increase of movement, the greater intensity of play, the singing, the gabbling of nonsense and the invitation to romp.

Yet if I had not indulged, to prove there was nothing in it, in this review, I should have missed the two or three dim elements of comfort that still remained to me. I shouldn't for instance have been able to asseverate to my friend that I was certain—which was so much to the good—that I at least had not betrayed myself. I shouldn't have been prompted, by stress of need, by desperation of mind—I scarce know what to call it—to invoke such further aid to intelligence as might spring from pushing my colleague fairly to the wall. She had told me, bit by bit, under pressure, a great deal; but a small shifty spot on the wrong side of it all still sometimes brushed my brow like the wing of a bat; and I remember how on this occasion—for the sleeping house and the concentration alike of our danger and our watch seemed to help—I felt the importance of giving the last jerk to the curtain. "I don't believe anything so horrible," I recollect saying; "no, let us put it definitely, my dear, that I don't. But if I did, you know, there's a thing I should require now, just without sparing you the least bit more—oh not a scrap, come!—to get out of you. What was it you had in mind when, in our distress, before Miles came back, over the letter from his school, you said, under my insistence, that you didn't pretend for him he hadn't literally *ever* been 'bad'? He was *not*, truly, 'ever,' in these weeks that I myself have lived with him and so closely watched him; he has been an imperturbable little prodigy of delightful loveable goodness. Therefore you might perfectly have made the claim for him if you had not, as it happened, seen an exception to take. What was your exception, and to what passage in your personal observation of him did you refer?"

It was a straight question enough, but levity was not our note, and in any case I had before the grey dawn admonished us to separate got my answer. What my friend had had in mind proved immensely to the purpose. It was neither more nor less than the particular fact that for a period of several months Quint and the boy had been perpetually together. It was indeed the very appropriate item of evidence of her having ventured to criticise the propriety, to hint at the incongruity, of so close an alliance, and even to go so far on the subject as a frank overture to Miss Jessel would take her. Miss Jessel had, with a very high manner about it, requested her to mind her business, and the good woman had on this directly approached little Miles. What she had said to him, since I pressed, was that *she* liked to see young gentlemen not forget their station.

I pressed again, of course, the closer for that. "You reminded him that Quint was only a base menial?"

"As you might say! And it was his answer, for one thing, that was bad."

"And for another thing?" I waited. "He repeated your words to Quint?"

"No, not that. It's just what he *wouldn't!*" she could still impress on me. "I was sure, at any rate," she added, "that he didn't. But he denied certain occasions."

"What occasions?"

"When they had been about together quite as if Quint were his tutor—and a very grand one—and Miss Jessel only for the little lady. When he had gone off with the fellow, I mean, and spent hours with him."

"He then prevaricated about it—he said he hadn't?" Her assent was clear enough to cause me to add in a moment: "I see. He lied."

"Oh!" Mrs. Grose mumbled. This was a suggestion that it didn't matter; which indeed she backed up by a further remark. "You see, after all, Miss Jessel didn't mind. She didn't forbid him."

I considered. "Did he put that to you as a justification?"

At this she dropped again. "No, he never spoke of it."

"Never mentioned her in connexion with Quint?"

She saw, visibly flushing, where I was coming out. "Well, he didn't show anything. He denied," she repeated; "he denied."

Lord, how I pressed her now! "So that you could see he knew what was between the two wretches?"

"I don't know — I don't know!" the poor woman wailed.

"You do know, you dear thing," I replied; "only you haven't my dreadful boldness of mind, and you keep back, out of timidity and modesty and delicacy, even the impression that in the past, when you had, without my aid, to flounder about in silence, most of all made you miserable. But I shall get it out of you yet! There was something in the boy that suggested to you," I continued, "his covering and concealing their relation."

"Oh he couldn't prevent —"

"Your learning the truth? I dare say! But, heavens," I fell, with vehemence, a-thinking, "what it shows that they must, to that extent, have succeeded in making of him!"

"Ah nothing that's not nice *now!*" Mrs. Grose lugubriously pleaded.

"I don't wonder you looked queer," I persisted, "when I mentioned to you the letter from his school!"

"I doubt if I looked as queer as you!" she retorted with homely force. "And if he was so bad then as that comes to, how is he such an angel now?"

"Yes indeed — and if he was a fiend at school! How, how, how? Well," I said in my torment, "you must put it to me again, though I shall not be able to tell you for some days. Only put it to me again!" I cried in a way that made my friend stare. "There are directions in which I mustn't for the present let myself go." Meanwhile I returned to her first example — the one to which she had just previously referred — of the boy's happy capacity for an occasional slip. "If Quint — on your remonstrance at the time you speak of — was a base menial, one of the things Miles said to you, I find myself guessing, was that you were another." Again her admission was so adequate that I continued: "And you forgave him that?"

"Wouldn't *you?*"

"Oh yes!" And we exchanged there, in the stillness, a sound of the oddest amusement. Then I went on: "At all events, while he was with the man —"

"Miss Flora was with the woman. It suited them all!"

It suited me too, I felt, only too well; by which I mean that it suited exactly the particular deadly view I was in the very act of forbidding myself to entertain. But I so far succeeded in checking the expression of this view that I will throw, just here, no further light on it than may be offered by the mention of my final observation to Mrs. Grose. "His having lied and been impudent are, I confess, less engaging specimens than I had hoped to have from you of the outbreak in him of the little natural man. Still," I mused, "they must do, for they make me feel more than ever that I must watch."

It made me blush, the next minute, to see in my friend's face how much more unreservedly she had forgiven him than her anecdote struck me as pointing out to my own tenderness any way to do. This was marked when, at the schoolroom door, she quitted me. "Surely you don't accuse *him* —"

"Of carrying on an intercourse that he conceals from me? Ah remember that, until further evidence, I now accuse nobody." Then before shutting her out to go by another passage to her own place, "I must just wait," I wound up.

IX

I waited and waited, and the days took as they elapsed something from my consternation. A very few of them, in fact, passing, in constant sight of my pupils, without a fresh incident, sufficed to give to grievous fancies and even to odious memories a kind of brush of the sponge. I have spoken of the surrender to their extraordinary childish grace as a thing I could actively promote in myself, and it may be imagined if I neglected now to apply at this source for whatever balm it would yield. Stranger than I can express, certainly, was the effort to struggle against my new lights. It would doubtless have been a greater tension still, however, had it not been so frequently successful. I used to wonder how my little charges could help guessing that I thought strange things about them; and the circumstance that these things only made them more interesting was not by itself a direct aid to keeping them in the dark. I trembled lest they should see that they *were* so immensely more interesting. Putting things at the worst, at all events, as in meditation I so often did, any clouding of their innocence could only be — blameless and foredoomed as they were — a reason the more for taking risks. There were moments when I knew myself to catch them up by an irresistible impulse and press them to my heart. As soon as I had done so I used to wonder — "What will they think of that? Doesn't it betray too much?" It would have been easy to get into a sad wild tangle about how much I might betray; but the real account, I feel, of the hours of peace I could still enjoy was that the immediate charm of my companions was a beguilement still effective even under the shadow of the possibility that it was studied. For if it occurred to me that I might occasionally excite suspicion by the little outbreaks of my sharper passion for them, so too I remember asking if I mightn't see a queerness in the traceable increase of their own demonstrations.

They were at this period extravagantly and preternaturally fond of me; which, after all, I could reflect, was no more than a graceful response in children perpetually bowed down over and hugged. The homage of which they were so lavish succeeded in truth for my nerves quite as well as if I never appeared to myself, as I may say, literally to catch them at a purpose in it. They had never, I think, wanted to do so many things for their poor protectress; I mean — though they got their lessons better and better, which was naturally what would please her most — in the way of diverting, entertaining, surprising her; reading her passages, telling her stories, acting her charades, pouncing out at her, in disguises, as animals and historical characters, and above all astonishing her by the "pieces" they had secretly got by heart and could interminably recite. I should never get to the bottom — were I to let myself go even now — of the prodigious private commentary, all under still more private correction, with which I in these days overscored their full hours. They had shown me from the first a facility for everything, a general faculty which, taking a fresh start, achieved remarkable flights. They got their little tasks as if they loved them; they indulged, from the mere exuberance of the gift, in the most unimposed little miracles of memory. They not only popped out at me as tigers and as Romans, but as Shakespeareans, astronomers and navigators. This was so singularly the case that it had presumably much to do with the fact as to which, at the present day, I am at a loss for a different explanation: I allude to my unnatural composure on the subject of another school for Miles. What I remember is that I was content for the time not to open the question, and that contentment must have sprung from the sense of his perpetually striking show of cleverness. He was too clever for a bad governess, for a parson's daughter, to spoil; and the strangest if not the brightest thread in the pensive embroidery I just spoke of was the impression I might have got, if I had dared to work it out, that he was under some influence operating in his small intellectual life as a tremendous incitement.

If it was easy to reflect, however, that such a boy could postpone school, it was at least as marked that for such a boy to have been "kicked out" by a schoolmaster was a mystification without end. Let me add that in their company now—and I was careful almost never to be out of it—I could follow no scent very far. We lived in a cloud of music and affection and success and private theatricals. The musical sense in each of the children was of the quickest, but the elder in especial had a marvellous knack of catching and repeating. The schoolroom piano broke into all gruesome fancies; and when that failed there were confabulations in corners, with a sequel of one of them going out in the highest spirits in order to "come in" as something new. I had had brothers myself, and it was no revelation to me that little girls could be slavish idolaters of little boys. What surpassed everything was that there was a little boy in the world who could have for the inferior age, sex and intelligence so fine a consideration. They were extraordinarily at one, and to say that they never either quarrelled or complained is to make the note of praise coarse for their quality of sweetness. Sometimes perhaps indeed (when I dropped into coarseness) I came across traces of little understandings between them by which one of them should keep me occupied while the other slipped away. There is a naïf side, I suppose, in all diplomacy; but if my pupils practised upon me it was surely with the minimum of grossness. It was all in the other quarter that, after a lull, the grossness broke out.

I find that I really hang back; but I must take my horrid plunge. In going on with the record of what was hideous at Bly I not only challenge the most liberal faith—for which I little care; but (and this is another matter) I renew what I myself suffered, I again push my dreadful way through it to the end. There came suddenly an hour after which, as I look back, the business seems to me to have been all pure suffering; but I have at least reached the heart of it, and the straightest road out is doubtless to advance. One evening—with nothing to lead up or prepare it—I felt the cold touch of the impression that had breathed on me the night of my arrival and which, much lighter then as I have mentioned, I should probably have made little of in memory had my subsequent sojourn been less agitated. I had not gone to bed; I sat reading by a couple of candles. There was a roomful of old books at Bly—last-century fiction some of it, which, to the extent of a distinctly deprecated renown, but never to so much as that of a stray specimen, had reached the sequestered home and appealed to the unavowed curiosity of my youth. I remember that the book I had in my hand was Fielding's

"Amelia"; also that I was wholly awake. I recall further both a general conviction that it was horribly late and a particular objection to looking at my watch. I figure finally that the white curtain draping, in the fashion of those days, the head of Flora's little bed, shrouded, as I had assured myself long before, the perfection of childish rest. I recollect in short that though I was deeply interested in my author I found myself, at the turn of a page and with his spell all scattered, looking straight up from him and hard at the door of my room. There was moment during which I listened, reminded of the faint sense I had had, the first night, of there being something undefinably astir in the house, and noted the soft breath of the open casement just move the half-drawn blind. Then, with all the marks of a deliberation that must have seemed magnificent had there been any one to admire it, I laid down my book, rose to my feet and, taking a candle, went straight out of the room and, from the passage, on which my light made little impression, noiselessly closed and locked the door.

I can say now neither what determined nor what guided me, but I went straight along the lobby, holding my cradle high, till I came within sight of the tall window that presided over the great turn of the staircase. At this point I precipitately found myself aware of three things. They were practically simultaneous, yet they had flashes of succession. My candle, under a bold flourish, went out, and I perceived, by the uncovered window, that the yielding dusk of earliest morning rendered it unnecessary. Without it, the next instant, I knew that there was a figure on the stair. I speak of sequences, but I required no lapse of seconds to stiffen myself for a third encounter with Quint. The apparition had reached the landing half-way up and was therefore on the spot nearest the window, where, at sight of me, it stopped short and fixed me exactly as it had fixed me from the tower and from the garden. He knew me as well as I knew him; and so, in the cold faint twilight, with a glimmer in the high glass and another on the polish of the oak stair below, we faced each other in our common intensity. He was absolutely, on this occasion, a living detestable dangerous presence. But that was not the wonder of wonders; I reserve this distinction for quite another circumstance: the circumstance that dread had unmistakeably quitted me and that there was nothing in me unable to meet and measure him.

I had plenty of anguish after that extraordinary moment, but I had, thank God, no terror. And he knew I hadn't—I found myself at the end of an instant magnificently aware of this. I felt, in a fierce rigour of confidence, that if I stood my ground a minute I should cease—for the time at least—to have him to reckon with; and during the minute, accordingly, the thing was as human and hideous as a real interview: hideous just because it *was* human, as human as to have met alone, in the small hours, in a sleeping house, some enemy, some adventurer, some criminal. It was the dead silence of our long gaze at such close quarters that gave the whole horror, huge as it was, its only note of the unnatural. If I had met a murderer in such a place and at such an hour we still at least would have spoken. Something would have passed, in life, between us; if nothing had passed one of us would have moved. The moment was so prolonged that it would have taken but little more to make me doubt if even I were in life. I can't express what followed it save by saying that the silence itself—which was indeed in a manner an attestation of my strength—became the element into which I saw the figure disappear; in which I definitely saw it turn, as I might have seen the low wretch to which it had once belonged turn on receipt of an order, and pass, with my eyes on the villainous back that no hunch could have more disfigured, straight down the staircase and into the darkness in which the next bend was lost.

X

I remained a while at the top of the stair, but with the effect presently of understanding that when my visitor had gone, he had gone; then I returned to my room. The foremost thing I saw there by the light of the candle I had left burning was that Flora's little bed was empty; and on this I caught my breath with all the terror that, five minutes before, I had been able to resist. I dashed at the place in which I had left her lying and over which — for the small silk counterpane and the sheets were disarranged — the white curtains had been deceivingly pulled forward; then my step, to my unutterable relief, produced an answering sound: I noticed an agitation of the window-blind, and the child, ducking down, emerged rosily from the other side of it. She stood there in so much of her candour and so little of her night-gown, with pink bare feet and the golden glow of her curls. She looked intensely grave, and I had never had such a sense of losing an advantage acquired (the thrill of which had just been so prodigious) as on my consciousness that she addressed me with a reproach — "You naughty: where *have* you been?" Instead of challenging her own irregularity I found myself arraigned and explaining. She herself explained, for that matter, with the loveliest eagerest simplicity. She had known suddenly, as she lay there, that I was out of the room, and had jumped up to see what had become of me. I had dropped, with the joy of her reappearance, back into my chair — feeling then, and then only, a little faint; and she had pattered straight over to me, thrown herself upon my knee, given herself to be held with the flame of the candle full in the wonderful little face that was still flushed with sleep. I remember closing my eyes an instant, yielding, consciously, as before the excess of something beautiful that shone out of the blue of her own. "You were looking for me out of the window?" I said. "You thought I might be walking in the grounds?"

"Well, you know, I thought some one was" — she never blanched as she smiled out that at me.

Oh how I looked at her now! "And did you see any one?"

"Ah *no!*" she returned almost (with the full privilege of childish inconsequence) resentfully, though with a long sweetness in her little drawl of the negative.

At that moment, in the state of my nerves, I absolutely believed she lied; and if I once more closed my eyes it was before the dazzle of the three or four possible ways in which I might take this up. One of these for a moment tempted me with such singular force that, to resist it, I must have gripped my little girl with a spasm that, wonderfully, she submitted to without a cry or a sign of fright. Why not break out at her on the spot and have it all over? — give it to her straight in her lovely little lighted face? "You see, you see, you *know* that you do and that you already quite suspect I believe it; therefore why not frankly confess it to me, so that we may at least live with it together and learn perhaps, in the strangeness of our fate, where we are and what it means?" This solicitation dropped, alas, as it came: it I could immediately have succumbed to it I might have spared myself — well, you'll see what. Instead of succumbing I sprang again to my feet, looked at her bed and took a helpless middle way. "Why did you pull the curtain over the place to make me think you were still there?"

Flora luminously considered; after which, with her little divine smile: "Because I don't like to frighten you!"

"But if I had, by your idea, gone out—?"

She absolutely declined to be puzzled; she turned her eyes to the flame of the candle as if the question were as irrelevant, or at any rate as impersonal, as Mrs. Marcet or nine-times-nine. "Oh but you know," she quite adequately answered, "that you might come back, you dear, and that you *have!*" And after a little, when she had got into bed, I had, a long time, by almost sitting on her for the retention of her hand, to show how I recognised the pertinence of my return.

You may imagine the general complexion, from that moment, of my nights. I repeatedly sat up till I didn't know when; I selected moments when my roommate unmistakeably slept, and, stealing out, took noiseless turns in the passage. I even pushed as far as to where I had last met Quint. But I never met him there again, and I may as well say at once that I on no other occasion saw him in the house. I just missed, on the staircase, nevertheless, a different adventure. Looking down it from the top I once recognised the presence of a woman seated on one of the lower steps with her back presented to me, her body half-bowed and her head, in an attitude of woe, in her hands. I had been there but an instant, however, when she vanished without looking round at me. I knew, for all that, exactly what dreadful face she had to show; and I wondered whether, if instead of being above I had been below, I should have had the same nerve for going up that I had lately shown Quint. Well, there continued to be plenty of call for nerve. On the eleventh night after my latest encounter with that gentleman—they were all numbered now—I had an alarm that perilously skirted it and that indeed, from the particular quality of its unexpectedness, proved quite my sharpest shock. It was precisely the first night during this series that, weary with vigils, I had conceived I might again without laxity lay myself down at my old hour. I slept immediately and, as I afterwards knew, till about one o'clock; but when I woke it was to sit straight up, as completely roused as if a hand had shaken me. I had left a light burning, but it was now out, and I felt an instant certainty that Flora had extinguished it. This brought me to my feet and straight, in the darkness, to her bed, which I found she had left. A glance at the window enlightened me further, and the striking of a match completed the picture.

The child had again got up—this time blowing out the taper, and had again, for some purpose of observation or response, squeezed in behind the blind and was peering out into the night. That she now saw—as she had not, I had satisfied myself, the previous time—was proved to me by the fact that she was disturbed neither by my re-illumination nor by the haste I made to get into slippers and into a wrap. Hidden, protected, absorbed, she evidently rested on the sill—the casement opened forward—and gave herself up. There was a great still moon to help her, and this fact had counted in my quick decision. She was face to face with the apparition we had met at the lake, and could now communicate with it as she had not then been able to do. What I, on my side, had to care for was, without disturbing her, to reach, from the corridor, some other window turned to the same quarter. I got to the door without her hearing me; I got out of it, closed it and listened, from the other side, for some sound from her. While I stood in the passage I had my eyes on her brother's door, which was but ten steps off and which, indescribably, produced in me a renewal of the strange impulse that I lately spoke of as my temptation. What if I should go straight in and march to *his* window? — what if, by risking to his boyish bewilderment a revelation of my motive, I should throw across the rest of the mystery the long halter of my boldness?

This thought held me sufficiently to make me cross to his threshold and pause again. I preturnaturally listened; I figured to myself what might portentously be; I wondered if his bed were also empty and he also secretly at watch. It was a deep soundless minute, at the end of which my impulse failed. He was quiet; he might be innocent; the risk was hideous; I turned away. There was a figure in the grounds — a figure prowling for a sight, the visitor with whom Flora was engaged; but it wasn't the visitor most concerned with my boy. I hesitated afresh, but on other grounds and only a few seconds; then I had made my choice. There were empty rooms enough at Bly, and it was only a question of choosing the right one. The right one suddenly presented itself to me as the lower one — though high above the gardens — in the solid corner of the house that I have spoken of as the old tower. This was a large square chamber, arranged with some state as a bedroom, the extravagant size of which made it so inconvenient that it had not for years, though kept by Mrs. Grose in exemplary order, been occupied. I had often admired it and I knew my way about in it; I had only, after just faltering at the first chill gloom of its disuse, to pass across it and unbolt in all quietness one of the shutters. Achieving this transit I uncovered the glass without a sound and, applying my face to the pane, was able, the darkness without being much less than within, to see that I commanded the right direction. Then I saw something more. The moon made the night extraordinarily penetrable and showed me on the lawn a person, diminished by distance, who stood there motionless and as if fascinated, looking up to where I had appeared — looking, that is, not so much straight at me as at something that was apparently above me. There was clearly another person above me — there was a person on the tower; but the presence on the lawn was not in the least what I had conceived and had confidently hurried to meet. The presence on the lawn — I felt sick as I made it out — was poor little Miles himself.

XI

It was not till late next day that I spoke to Mrs. Grose; the rigour with which I kept my pupils in sight making it often difficult to meet her privately: the more as we each felt the importance of not provoking — on the part of the servants quite as much as on that of the children — any suspicion of a secret flurry or of a discussion of mysteries. I drew a great security in this particular from her mere smooth aspect. There was nothing in her fresh face to pass on to others the least of my horrible confidences. She believed me, I was sure, absolutely: if she hadn't I don't know what would have become of me, for I couldn't have borne the strain alone. But she was a magnificent monument to the blessing of a want of imagination, and if she could see in our little charges nothing but their beauty and amiability, their happiness and cleverness, she had no direct communication with the sources of my trouble. If they had been at all visibly blighted or battered she would doubtless have grown, on tracing it back, haggard enough to match them;

as matters stood, however, I could feel her, when she surveyed them with her large white arms folded and the habit of serenity in all her look, thank the Lord's mercy that if they were ruined the pieces would still serve. Flights of fancy gave place, in her mind, to a steady fireside glow, and I had already begun to perceive how, with the development of the conviction that—as time went on without a public accident—our young things could, after all, look out for themselves, she addressed her greatest solicitude to the sad case presented by their deputy-guardian. That, for myself, was a sound simplification: I could engage that, to the world, my face should tell no tales, but it would have been, in the conditions, an immense added worry to find myself anxious about hers.

At the hour I now speak of she had joined me, under pressure, on the terrace, where, with the lapse of the season, the afternoon sun was now agreeable; and we sat there together while before us and at a distance, yet within call if we wished, the children strolled to and fro in one of their most manageable moods. They moved slowly, in unison, below us, over the lawn, the boy, as they went, reading aloud from a story-book and passing his arm round his sister to keep her quite in touch. Mrs. Grose watched them with positive placidity; then I caught the suppressed intellectual creak with which she conscientiously turned to take from me a view of the back of the tapestry. I had made her a receptacle of lurid things, but there was an odd recognition of my superiority—my accomplishments and my function—in her patience under my pain. She offered her mind to my disclosures as, had I wished to mix a witch's broth and proposed it with assurance, she would have held out a large clean saucepan. This had become thoroughly her attitude by the time that, in my recital of the events of the night, I reached the point of what Miles had said to me when, after seeing him, at such a monstrous hour, almost on the very spot where he happened now to be, I had gone down to bring him in; choosing then, at the window, with a concentrated need of not alarming the house, rather that method than any noisier process. I had left her meanwhile in little doubt of my small hope of representing with success even to her actual sympathy my sense of the real splendour of the little inspiration with which, after I had got him into the house, the boy met my final articulate challenge. As soon as I appeared in the moonlight on the terrace he had come to me as straight as possible; on which I had taken his hand without a word and led him, through the dark spaces, up the staircase where Quint had so hungrily hovered for him, along the lobby where I had listened and trembled, and so to his forsaken room.

Not a sound, on the way, had passed between us, and I had wondered—oh *how* I had wondered!—if he were groping about in his dreadful little mind for something plausible and not too grotesque. It would tax his invention certainly, and I felt, this time, over his real embarrassment, a curious thrill of triumph. It was a sharp trap for any game hitherto successful. He could play no longer at perfect propriety, nor could he pretend to it; so how the deuce would he get out of the scrape? There beat in me indeed, with the passionate throb of this question, and equal dumb appeal as to how the deuce I should. I was confronted at last, as never yet, with all the risk attached even now to sounding my own horrid note. I remember in fact that as we pushed into his little chamber, where the bed had not been slept in at all and the window, uncovered to the moonlight, made the place so clear that there was no need of striking a match—I remember how I suddenly dropped, sank upon the edge of the bed from the force of the idea that he must know how he really, as they say, "had" me. He could do what he liked, with all his cleverness to help him, so long as I should continue to defer to the old tradition of the criminality of those caretakers of the young who minister to superstitions and fears. He "had" me indeed, and in a cleft stick; for who would ever absolve me, who would consent that I should go unhung, if, by the faintest tremor of an overture, I were the first to introduce into our perfect intercourse an element so dire? No, no: it was useless to attempt to convey to Mrs. Grose, just as it is scarcely less so to attempt to suggest here, how, during our short stiff brush there in the dark, he fairly shook me with admiration. I was of course thoroughly kind and merciful; never, never yet had I placed on his small shoulders hands of such tenderness as those with which, while I rested against the bed, I held him there well under fire. I had no alternative but, in form at least, to put it to him.

"You must tell me now—and all the truth. What did you go out for? What were you doing there?"

I can still see his wonderful smile, the whites of his beautiful eyes and the uncovering of his clear teeth, shine to me in the dusk. "If I tell you why, will you understand?" My heart, at this, leaped into my mouth. *Would* he tell me why? I found no sound on my lips to press it, and I was aware of answering only with a vague repeated grimacing nod. He was gentleness itself, and while I wagged my head at him he stood there more than ever a little fairy prince. It was his brightness indeed that gave me a respite. Would it be so great if he were really going to tell me? "Well," he said at last, "just exactly in order that you should do this."

"Do what?"

"Think me—for a change—*bad!*" I shall never forget the sweetness and gaiety with which he brought out the word, nor how, on top of it, he bent forward and kissed me. It was practically the end of everything. I met his kiss and I had to make, while I folded him for a minute in my arms, the most stupendous effort not to cry. He had given exactly the account of himself that permitted least my going behind it, and it was only with the effect of confirming my acceptance of it that, as I presently glanced about the room, I could say—

"Then you didn't undress at all?"

He fairly glittered in the gloom. "Not at all. I sat up and read."

"And when did you go down?"

"At midnight. When I'm bad I *am* bad!"

"I see, I see—it's charming. But how could you be sure I should know it?"

"Oh I arranged that with Flora." His answers rang out with a readiness! "She was to get up and look out."

"Which is what she did do." It was I who fell into the trap!

"So she disturbed you, and, to see what she was looking at, you also looked—you saw."

"While you," I concurred, "caught your death in the night air!"

He literally bloomed so from this exploit that he could afford radiantly to assent. "How otherwise should I have been bad enough?" he asked. Then, after another embrace, the incident and our interview closed on my recognition of all the reserves of goodness that, for his joke, he had been able to draw upon.

XII

The particular impression I had received proved in the morning light, I repeat, not quite successfully presentable to Mrs. Grose, though I re-enforced it with the mention of still another remark that he had made before we separated. "It all lies in half a dozen words," I said to her, "words that really settle the matter. 'Think, you know, what I *might* do!' He threw that off to show me how good he is. He knows down to the ground what he 'might do.' That's what he gave them a taste of at school."

"Lord, you do change!" cried my friend.

"I don't change—I simply make it out. The four, depend upon it, perpetually meet. If on either of these last nights you had been with either child you'd clearly have understood. The more I've watched and waited the more I've felt that if there were nothing else to make it sure it would be made so by the systematic silence of each. *Never*, by a slip of the tongue, have they so much as alluded to either of their old friends, any more than Miles has alluded to his expulsion. Oh yes, we may sit here and look at them, and they may show off to us there to their fill; but even while they pretend to be lost in their fairy-tale they're steeped in their vision of the dead restored to them. He's not reading to her," I declared; "they're talking of *them*—they're talking horrors! I go on, I know, as if I were crazy; and it's a wonder I'm not. What I've seen would have made *you* so; but it has only made me more lucid, made me get hold of still other things."

My lucidity must have seemed awful, but the charming creatures who were victims of it, passing and repassing in their interlocked sweetness, gave my colleague something to hold on by; and I felt how tight she held as, without stirring in the breath of my passion, she covered them still with her eyes. "Of what other things have you got hold?"

"Why of the very things that have delighted, fascinated and yet, at bottom, as I now so strangely see, mystified and troubled me. Their more than earthly beauty, their absolutely unnatural goodness. It's a game," I went on; "it's a policy and a fraud!"

"On the part of little darlings—?"

"As yet mere lovely babies? Yes, mad as that seems!" The very act of bringing it out really helped me to trace it—follow it all up and piece it all together. "They haven't been good—they've only been absent. It has been easy to live with them because they're simply leading a life of their own. They're not mine—they're not ours. They're his and they're hers!"

"Quint's and that woman's?"

"Quint's and that woman's. They want to get to them."

Oh how, at this, poor Mrs. Grose appeared to study them! "But for what?"

"For the love of all the evil that, in those dreadful days, the pair put into them. And to ply them with that evil still, to keep up the work of demons, is what brings the others back."

"Laws!" said my friend under her breath. The exclamation was homely, but it revealed a real acceptance of my further proof of what, in the bad time—for there had been a worse even than this!—must have occurred. There could have been no such justification for me as the plain assent of her experience to whatever depth of depravity I found credible in our brace of scoundrels. It was in obvious submission of memory that she brought out after a moment. "They *were* rascals! But what can they now do?" she pursued.

"Do?" I echoed so loud that Miles and Flora, as they passed at their distance, paused an instant in their walk and looked at us. "Don't they do enough?" I demanded in a lower tone, while the children, having smiled and nodded and kissed hands to us, resumed their exhibition. We were held by it a minute; then I answered: "They can destroy them!" At this my companion did turn, but the appeal she launched was a silent one, the effect of which was to make me more explicit. "They don't know as yet quite how—but they're trying hard. They're seen only across, as it were, and beyond—in strange places and on high places, the top of towers, the roof of houses, the outside of windows, the further edge of pools; but there's a deep design, on either side, to shorten the distance and overcome the obstacle: so the success of the tempters is only a question of time. They've only to keep to their suggestions of danger."

"For the children to come?"

"And perish in the attempt!" Mrs. Grose slowly got up, and I scrupulously added: "Unless, of course, we can prevent!"

Standing there before me while I kept my seat she visibly turned things over. "Their uncle must do the preventing. He must take them away."

"And who's to make him?"

She had been scanning the distance, but she now dropped on me a foolish face. "You, Miss."

"By writing to him that his house is poisoned and his little nephew and niece mad?"

"But if they *are*, Miss?"

"And if I am myself, you mean? That's charming news to be sent him by a person enjoying his confidence and whose prime undertaking was to give him no worry."

Mrs. Grose considered, following the children again. "Yes, he do hate worry. That was the great reason—"

"Why those fiends took him in so long? No doubt, though his indifference must have been awful. As I'm not a fiend, at any rate, I shouldn't take him in."

My companion, after an instant and for all answer, sat down again and grasped my arm. "Make him at any rate come to you."

I stared. "To *me*?" I had a sudden fear of what she might do. "'Him'?"

"He ought to be here—he ought to help."

I quickly rose and I think I must have shown her a queerer face than ever yet. "You see me asking him for a visit?" No, with her eyes on my face she evidently couldn't. Instead of it even—as a woman reads another—she could see what I myself saw: his derision, his amusement, his contempt for the breakdown of my resignation at being left alone and for the fine machinery I had set in motion to attract his attention to my slighted charms. She didn't know—no one knew—how proud I had been to serve him and to stick to our terms; yet she none the less took the measure, I think, of the warning I now gave her. "If you should so lose your head as to appeal to him for me—"

She was really frightened. "Yes, Miss?"

"I would leave, on the spot, both him and you."

XIII

It was all very well to join them, but speaking to them proved quite as much as ever an effort beyond my strength—offered, in close quarters, difficulties as insurmountable as before. This situation continued a month, and with new aggravations and particular notes, the note above all, sharper and sharper, of the small ironic consciousness on the part of my pupils. It was not, I am as sure to-day as I was sure then, my mere infernal imagination: it was absolutely traceable that they were aware of my predicament and that this strange relation made, in a manner, for a long time, the air in which we moved. I don't mean that they had their tongues in their cheeks or did anything vulgar, for that was not one of their dangers: I do mean, on the other hand, that the element of the unnamed and untouched became, between us, greater than any other, and that so much avoidance couldn't have been made successful without a great deal of tacit arrangement. It was as if, at moments, we were perpetually coming into sight of subjects before which we must stop short, turning suddenly out of alleys that we perceived to be blind, closing with a little bang that made us look at each other—for, like all bangs, it was something louder than we had intended—the doors we had indiscreetly opened. All roads lead to Rome, and there were times when it might have struck us that almost every branch of study or subject of conversation skirted forbidden ground. Forbidden ground was the question of the return of the dead in general and of whatever, in especial, might survive, for memory, of the friends little children had lost. There were days when I could have sworn that one of them had, with a small invisible nudge, said to the other: "She thinks she'll do it this time—but she *won't!*" To "do it" would have been to indulge for instance—and for once in a way—in some direct reference to the lady who had prepared them for my discipline. They had a delightful endless appetite for passages in my own history to which I had again and again treated them; they were in possession of everything that had ever happened to me, had had, with every circumstance, the story of my smallest adventures and of those of my brothers and sisters and of the cat and the dog at home, as well as many particulars of the whimsical bent of my father, of the furniture and arrangement of our house and of the conversation of the old women of our village. There were things enough, taking one with another, to chatter about, if one went very fast and knew by instinct when to go round. They pulled with an art of their own the strings of my invention and my memory; and nothing else perhaps, when I thought of such occasions afterwards, gave me so the suspicion of being watched from under cover. It was in any case over my life, my past and my friends alone that we could take anything like our ease; a state of affairs that led them sometimes without the least pertinence to break out into sociable reminders. I was invited—with no visible connexion—to repeat afresh Goody Gosling's celebrated *mot* or to confirm the details already supplied as to the cleverness of the vicarage pony.

It was partly at such junctures as these and partly at quite different ones that, with the turn my matters had now taken, my predicament, as I have called it, grew most sensible. The fact that the days passed for me without another encounter ought, it would have appeared, to have done something toward soothing my nerves. Since the light brush, that second night on the upper landing, of the presence of a woman at the foot of the stair, I had seen nothing, whether in or out of the house, that one had better not have seen. There was many a corner round which I expected to come upon Quint, and many a situation that, in a merely sinister way, would have favoured the appearance of Miss Jessel. The summer had turned, the summer had gone; the autumn had dropped upon Bly and had blown out half our lights. The place, with its grey sky and withered garlands, its bared spaces and scattered dead leaves, was like a theatre after the performance — all strewn with crumpled playbills. There were exactly states of the air, conditions of sound and of stillness, unspeakable impressions of the *kind* of ministering moment, that brought back to me, long enough to catch it, the feeling of the medium in which, that June evening out of doors, I had had my first sight of Quint, and in which too, at those other instants, I had, after seeing him through the window, looked for him in vain in the circle of shrubbery. I recognised the signs, the portents — I recognised the moment, the spot. But they remained unaccompanied and empty, and I continued unmolested; if unmolested one could call a young woman whose sensibility had, in the most extraordinary fashion, not declined but deepened. I had said in my talk with Mrs. Grose on that horrid scene of Flora's by the lake — and had perplexed her by so saying — that it would from that moment distress me much more to lose my power than to keep it. I had then expressed what was vividly in my mind: the truth that, whether the children really saw or not — since, that is, it was not yet definitely proved — I greatly preferred, as a safeguard, the fulness of my own exposure. I was ready to know the very worst that was to be known. What I had then had an ugly glimpse of was that my eyes might be sealed just while theirs were most opened. Well, my eyes *were* sealed, it appeared, at present — a consummation for which it seemed blasphemous not to thank God. There was, alas, a difficulty about that: I would have thanked him with all my soul had I not had in a proportionate measure this conviction of the secret of my pupils.

How can I retrace to-day the strange steps of my obsession? There were times of our being together when I would have been ready to swear that, literally, in my presence, but with my direct sense of it closed, they had visitors who were known and were welcome. Then it was that, had I not been deterred by the very chance that such an injury might prove greater than the injury to be averted, my exaltation would have broken out. "They're here, they're here, you little wretches," I would have cried, "and you can't deny it now!" The little wretches denied it with all the added volume of their sociability and their tenderness, just in the crystal depths of which — like the flash of a fish in a stream — the mockery of their advantage peeped up. The shock had in truth sunk into me still deeper than I knew on the night when, looking out either for Quint or for Miss Jessel under the stars, I had seen there the boy over whose rest I watched and who had immediately brought in with him — had straightway there turned on me — the lovely upward look with which, from the battlements above us, the hideous apparition of Quint had played. If it was a question of a scare my discovery on this occasion had scared me more than any other, and it was essentially in the scared state that I drew my actual conclusions. They harassed me so that sometimes, at odd moments, I shut myself up audibly to rehearse — it was at once a fantastic relief and a renewed despair — the manner in which I might come to the point. I approached it from one side and the other while, in my room, I flung myself about, but I always broke down in the monstrous utterance of names. As they died away on my lips I said to myself that I should indeed help them to represent something infamous if by pronouncing them I should violate as rare a little case of instinctive delicacy as any schoolroom probably had ever known. When I said to myself: "*They* have the manners to be silent, and you, trusted as you are, the baseness to speak!" I felt myself crimson and covered my face with my hands. After these secret scenes I chattered more than ever, going on volubly enough till one of our prodigious palpable hushes occurred — I can call them nothing else — the strange dizzy lift or swim (I try for terms!) into a stillness, a pause of all life, that had nothing to do with the more or less noise we at the moment might be engaged in making and that I could hear through any intensified mirth or quickened recitation or louder strum of the piano. Then it was that the others, the outsiders, were there. Though they were not angels they "passed," as the French say, causing me, while they stayed, to tremble with the fear of their addressing to their younger victims some yet more infernal message or more vivid image than they had thought good enough for myself.

What it was least possible to get rid of was the cruel idea that, whatever I had seen, Miles and Flora saw *more* — things terrible and unguessable and that sprang from dreadful passages of intercourse in the past. Such things naturally left on the surface, for the time, a chill that we vociferously denied we felt; and we had all three, with repetition, got into such splendid training that we went, each time, to mark the close of the incident, almost automatically through the very same movements. It was striking of the children at all events to kiss me inveterately , with a wild irrelevance and never to fail — one or the other — of the precious question that had helped us through many a peril. "When do you think he *will* come? Don't you think we *ought* to write?" — there was nothing like that enquiry, we found by experience, for carrying off an awkwardness. "He" of course was their uncle in Harley Street; and we lived in much profusion of theory that he might at any moment arrive to mingle in our circle. It was impossible to have given less encouragement than he had administered to such a doctrine, but if we had not had the doctrine to fall back upon we should have deprived each other of some of our finest exhibitions. He never wrote to them — that may have been selfish, but it was a part of the flattery of his trust of myself; for the way in which a man pays his highest tribute to a woman is apt to be but by the more festal celebration of one of the sacred laws of his comfort. So I held that I carried out the spirit of the pledge given not to appeal to him when I let our young friends understand that their own letters were but charming literary exercises. They were too beautiful to be posted; I kept them myself; I have them all to this hour. This was a rule indeed which only added to the satiric effect of my being plied with the supposition that he might at any moment be among us. It was exactly as if our young friends knew how almost more awkward than anything else that might be for me. There appears to me moreover as I look back no note in all this more extraordinary than the mere fact that, in spite of my tension and of their triumph, I never lost patience with them. Adorable they must in truth have been, I now feel, since I didn't in these days hate them! Would exasperation, however, if relief had longer been postponed, finally have betrayed me? It little matters, for relief arrived. I call it relief though it was only the relief that a snap brings to a strain or the burst of a thunderstorm to a day of suffocation. It was at least change, and it came with a rush.

XIV

Walking to church a certain Sunday morning, I had little Miles at my side and his sister, in advance of us and at Mrs. Grose's, well in sight. It was a crisp clear day, the first of its order for some time; the night had brought a touch of frost and the autumn air, bright and sharp, made the church-bells almost gay. It was an odd accident of thought that I should have happened at such a moment to be particularly and very gratefully struck with the obedience of my little charges. Why did they never resent my inexorable, my perpetual society? Something or other had brought nearer home to me that I had all but pinned the boy to my shawl, and that in the way our companions were marshalled before me I might have appeared to provide against some danger of rebellion. I was like a gaoler with an eye to possible surprises and escapes. But all this belonged—I mean their magnificent little surrender—just to the special array of the facts that were most abysmal. Turned out for Sunday by his uncle's tailor, who had had a free hand and a notion of pretty waistcoats and of his grand little air, Miles's whole title to independence, the rights of his sex and situation, were so stamped upon him that if he had suddenly struck for freedom I should have had nothing to say. I was by the strangest of chances wondering how I should meet him when the revolution unmistakeably occurred. I call it a revolution because I now see how, with the word he spoke, the curtain rose on the last act of my dreadful drama and the catastrophe was precipitated. "Look here, my dear, you know," he charmingly said, "when in the world, please, am I going back to school?"

Transcribed here the speech sounds harmless enough, particularly as uttered in the sweet, high, casual pipe with which, at all interlocutors, but above all at his eternal governess, he threw off intonations as if he were tossing roses. There was something in them that always made one "catch," and I caught at any rate now so effectually that I stopped as short as if one of the trees of the park had fallen across the road. There was something new, on the spot, between us, and he was perfectly aware I recognised it, though to enable me to do so he had no need to look a whit less candid and charming than usual. I could feel in him how he already, from my at first finding nothing to reply, perceived the advantage he had gained. I was so slow to find anything that he had plenty of time, after a minute, to continue with his suggestive but inconclusive smile: "You know, my dear, that for a fellow to be with a lady *always*—!" His "my dear" was constantly on his lips for me, and nothing could have expressed more the exact shade of the sentiment with which I desired to inspire my pupils than its fond familiarity. It was so respectfully easy.

But oh how I felt that at present I must pick my own phrases! I remember that, to gain time, I tried to laugh, and I seemed to see in the beautiful face with which he watched me how ugly and queer I looked. "And always with the same lady?" I returned.

He neither blenched nor winked. The whole thing was virtually out between us. "Ah of course she's a jolly 'perfect' lady; but after all I'm a fellow, don't you see? who's—well, getting on."

I lingered there with him an instant ever so kindly. "Yes, you're getting on." Oh but I felt helpless!

I have kept to this day the heartbreaking little idea of how he seemed to know that and to play with it. "And you can't say I've not been awfully good, can you?"

I laid my hand on his shoulder, for though I felt how much better it would have been to walk on I was not yet quite able. "No, I can't say that, Miles."

"Except just that one night, you know—!"

"That one night?" I couldn't look as straight as he.

"Why when I went down—went out of the house."

"Oh yes. But I forget what you did it for."

"You forget?"—he spoke with the sweet extravagance of childish reproach. "Why it was just to show you I could!"

"Oh yes—you could."

"And I can again."

I felt I might perhaps after all succeed in keeping my wits about me. "Certainly. But you won't."

"No, not *that* again. It was nothing."

"It was nothing," I said. "But we must go on."

He resumed our walk with me, passing his hand into my arm. "Then when *am* I going back?"

I wore, in turning it over, my most responsible air. "Were you very happy at school?"

He just considered. "Oh I'm happy enough anywhere!"

"Well then," I quavered, "if you're just as happy here—!"

"Ah but that isn't everything! Of course *you* know a lot—"

"But you hint that you know almost as much?" I risked as he paused.

"Not half I want to!" Miles honestly professed. "But it isn't so much that."

"What is it then?"

"Well—I want to see more life."

"I see; I see." We had arrived within sight of the church and of various persons, including several of the household of Bly, on their way to it and clustered about the door to see us go in. I quickened our step; I wanted to get there before the question between us opened up much further; I reflected hungrily that he would have for more than an hour to be silent; and I thought with envy of the comparative dusk of the pew and of the almost spiritual help of the hassock on which I might bend my knees. I seemed literally to be running a race with some confusion to which he was about to reduce me, but I felt he had got in first when, before we had even entered the churchyard, he threw out—

"I want my own sort!"

It literally made me bound forward. "There aren't many of your own sort, Miles!" I laughed. "Unless perhaps dear little Flora!"

"You really compare me to a baby girl?"

This found me singularly weak. "Don't you then *love* our sweet Flora?"

"If I didn't—and you too; if I didn't—!" he repeated as if retreating for a jump, yet leaving his thought so unfinished that, after we had come into the gate, another stop, which he imposed on me by the pressure of his arm, had become inevitable. Mrs. Grose and Flora had passed into the church, the other worshippers had followed and we were, for the minute, alone among the old thick graves. We had paused, on the path from the gate, by a low oblong table-like tomb.

"Yes, if you didn't—?"

He looked, while I waited, about at the graves. "Well, you know what!" But he didn't move, and he presently produced something that made me drop straight down on the stone slab as if suddenly to rest. "Does my uncle think what *you* think?"

I markedly rested. "How do you know what I think?"

"Ah well, of course I don't; for it strikes me you never tell me. But I mean does *he* know?"

"Know what, Miles?"

"Why the way I'm going on."

I recognised quickly enough that I could make, to this enquiry, no answer that wouldn't involve something of a sacrifice of my employer. Yet it struck me that we were all, at Bly, sufficiently sacrificed to make that venial. "I don't think your uncle much cares."

Miles, on this, stood looking at me. "Then don't you think he can be made to?"

"In what way?"

"Why by his coming down."

"But who'll get him to come down?"

"*I* will!" the boy said with extraordinary brightness and emphasis. He gave me another look charged with that expression and then marched off alone into church.

XV

The business was practically settled from the moment I never followed him. It was a pitiful surrender to agitation, but my being aware of this had somehow no power to restore me. I only sat there on my tomb and read into what our young friend had said to me the fulness of its meaning; by the time I had grasped the whole of which I had also embraced, for absence, the pretext that I was ashamed to offer my pupils and the rest of the congregation such an example of delay. What I said to myself above all was that Miles had got something out of me and that the gage of it for him would be just this awkward collapse. He had got out of me that there was something I was much afraid of, and that he should probably be able to make use of my fear to gain, for his own purpose, more freedom. My fear was of having to deal with the intolerable question of the grounds of his dismissal from school, since that was really but the question of the horrors gathered behind. That his uncle should arrive to treat with me of these things was a solution that, strictly speaking, I ought now to have desired to bring on; but I could so little face the ugliness and the pain of it that I simply procrastinated and lived from hand to mouth. The boy, to my deep discomposure, was immensely in the right, was in a position to say to me: "Either you clear up with my guardian the mystery of this interruption of my studies, or you cease to expect me to lead with you a life that's so unnatural for a boy." What was so unnatural for the particular boy I was concerned with was this sudden revelation of a consciousness and a plan.

That was what really overcame me, what prevented my going in. I walked round the church, hesitating, hovering; I reflected that I had already, with him, hurt myself beyond repair. Therefore I could patch up nothing and it was too extreme an effort to squeeze beside him into the pew: he would be so much more sure than ever to pass his arm into mine and make me sit there for an hour in close mute contact with his commentary on our talk. For the first minute since his arrival I wanted to get away from him. As I paused beneath the high east window and listened to the sounds of worship I was taken with an impulse that might master me, I felt, and completely, should I give it the least encouragement. I might easily put an end to my ordeal by getting away altogether. Here was my chance; there was no one to stop me; I could give the whole thing up — turn my back and bolt. It was only a question of hurrying again, for a few preparations, to the house which the attendance at church of so many of the servants would practically have left unoccupied. No one, in short, could blame me if I should just drive desperately off. What was it to get away if I should get away only till dinner? That would be in a couple of hours, at the end of which — I had the acute prevision — my little pupils would play at innocent wonder about my non-appearance in their train.

"What *did* you do, you naughty bad thing? Why in the world, to worry us so — and take our thoughts off too, don't you know? — did you desert us at the very door?" I couldn't meet such questions nor, as they asked them, their false little lovely eyes; yet it was all so exactly what I should have to meet that, as the prospect grew sharp to me, I at last let myself go.

I got, so far as the immediate moment was concerned, away; I came straight out of the churchyard and, thinking hard, retraced my steps through the park. It seemed to me that by the time I reached the house I had made up my mind to cynical flight. The Sunday stillness both of the approaches and of the interior, in which I met no one, fairly stirred me with a sense of opportunity. Were I to get off quickly this way I should get off without a scene, without a word. My quickness would have to be remarkable, however, and the question of a conveyance was the great one to settle. Tormented, in the hall, with difficulties and obstacles, I remember sinking down at the foot of the staircase — suddenly collapsing there on the lowest step and then, with a revulsion, recalling that it was exactly where, more than a month before, in the darkness of night and just so bowed with evil things, I had seen the spectre of the most horrible of women. At this I was able to straighten myself; I went the rest of the way up; I made, in my turmoil, for the schoolroom, where there were objects belonging to me that I should have to take. But I opened the door to find again, in a flash, my eyes unsealed. In the presence of what I saw I reeled straight back upon resistance.

Seated at my own table in the clear noonday light I saw a person whom, without my previous experience, I should have taken at the first blush for some housemaid who might have stayed at home to look after the place and who, availing herself of rare relief from observation and of the schoolroom table and my pens, ink and paper, had applied herself to the considerable effort of a letter to her sweetheart. There was an effort in the way that, while her arms rested on the table, her hands, with evident weariness, supported her head; but at the moment I took this in I had already become aware that, in spite of my entrance, her attitude strangely persisted. Then it was — with the very act of its announcing itself — that her identity flared up in a change of posture. She rose, not as if she had heard me, but with an indescribable grand melancholy of indifference and detachment, and, within a dozen feet of me, stood there as my vile predecessor. Dishonoured and tragic, she was all before me; but even as I fixed and, for memory, secured it, the awful image passed away. Dark as midnight in her black dress, her haggard beauty and her unutterable woe, she had looked at me long enough to appear to say that her right to sit at my table was as good as mine to sit at hers. While these instants lasted indeed I had the extraordinary chill of a feeling that it was I who was the intruder. It was as a wild protest against it that, actually addressing her — "You terrible miserable woman!" — I heard myself break into a sound that, by the open door, rang through the long passage and the empty house. She looked at me as if she heard me, but I had recovered myself and cleared the air. There was nothing in the room the next minute but the sunshine and the sense that I must stay.

XVI

I had so perfectly expected the return of the others to be marked by a demonstration that I was freshly upset at having to find them merely dumb and discreet about my desertion. Instead of gaily denouncing and caressing me they made no allusion to my having failed them, and I was left, for the time, on perceiving that she too said nothing, to study Mrs. Grose's odd face. I did this to such purpose that I made sure they had in some way bribed her to silence; a silence that, however, I would engage to break down on the first private opportunity. This opportunity came before tea: I secured five minutes with her in the house-keeper's room, where, in the twilight, amid a smell of lately-baked bread, but with the place all swept and garnished, I found her sitting in pained placidity before the fire. So I see her still, so I see her best: facing the flame from her straight chair in the dusky shining room, a large clean picture of the "put away" — of drawers closed and locked and rest without a remedy.

"Oh yes, they asked me to say nothing; and to please them — so long as they were there — of course I promised. But what had happened to you?"

"I only went with you for the walk," I said. "I had then to come back to meet a friend."

She showed her surprise. "A friend — *you?*"

"Oh yes, I've a couple!" I laughed. "But did the children give you a reason?"

"For not alluding to your leaving us? Yes; they said you'd like it better. *Do* you like it better?"

My face had made her rueful. "No, I like it worse!" But after an instant I added: "Did they say why I should like it better?"

"No; Master Miles only said 'We must do nothing but what she likes!'"

"I wish indeed he would! And what did Flora say?"

"Miss Flora was too sweet. She said 'Oh of course, of course!' — and I said the same."

I thought a moment. "You were too sweet too — I can hear you all. But none the less, between Miles and me, it's now all out."

"All out?" My companion stared. "But what, Miss?"

"Everything. It doesn't matter. I've made up my mind. I came home, my dear," I went on, "for a talk with Miss Jessel."

I had by this time formed the habit of having Mrs. Grose literally well in hand in advance of my sounding that note; so that even now, as she bravely blinked under the signal of my word, I could keep her comparatively firm. "A talk! Do you mean she spoke?"

"It came to that. I found her, on my return, in the schoolroom."

"And what did she say?" I can hear the good woman still, and the candour of her stupefaction.

"That she suffers the torments—!"

It was this, of a truth, that made her, as she filled out my picture, gape. "Do you mean," she faltered "—of the lost?"

"Of the lost. Of the damned. And that's why, to share them—" I faltered myself with the horror of it.

But my companion, with less imagination, kept me up. "To share them—?"

"She wants Flora." Mrs. Grose might, as I gave it to her, fairly have fallen away from me had I not been prepared. I still held her there, to show I was. "As I've told you, however, it doesn't matter."

"Because you've made up your mind? But to what?"

"To everything."

"And what do you call 'everything'?"

"Why to sending for their uncle."

"Oh Miss, in pity do," my friend broke out.

"Ah but I will, I *will*! I see it's the only way. What's 'out,' as I told you, with Miles is that if he thinks I'm afraid to—and has ideas of what he gains by that—he shall see he's mistaken. Yes, yes; his uncle shall have it here from me on the spot (and before the boy himself if necessary) that if I'm to be reproached with having done nothing again about more school—"

"Yes, Miss—" my companion pressed me.

"Well, there's that awful reason."

There were now clearly so many of these for my poor colleague that she was excusable for being vague.

"But—a—which?"

"Why the letter from his old place."

"You'll show it to the master?"

"I ought to have done so on the instant."

"Oh no!" said Mrs. Grose with decision.

"I'll put it before him," I went on inexorably, "that I can't undertake to work the question on behalf of a child who has been expelled—"

"For we've never in the least known what!" Mrs. Gorse declared.

"For wickedness. For what else—when he's so clever and beautiful and perfect? Is he stupid? Is he untidy? Is he infirm? Is he ill-natured? He's exquisite—so it can be only *that*; and that would open up the whole thing. After all," I said, "it's their uncle's fault. If he left here such people—!"

"He didn't really in the least know them. The fault's mine." She had turned quite pale.

"Well, you shan't suffer," I answered.

"The children shan't!" she emphatically returned.

I was silent a while; we looked at each other. "Then what am I to tell him?"

"You needn't tell him anything. *I'll* tell him."

I measured this. "Do you mean you'll write —?" Remembering she couldn't, I caught myself up. "How do you communicate?"

"I tell the bailiff. *He* writes."

"And should you like him to write our story?"

My question had a sarcastic force that I had not fully intended, and it made her after a moment inconsequently break down. The tears were again in her eyes. "Ah Miss, *you* write!"

"Well — to-night," I at last returned; and on this we separated.

XVII

I went so far, in the evening, as to make a beginning. The weather had changed back, a great wind was abroad, and beneath the lamp, in my room with Flora at peace beside me, I sat for a long time before a blank sheet of paper and listened to the lash of the rain and the batter of the gusts. Finally I went out, taking a candle; I crossed the passage and listened a minute at Miles's door. What, under my endless obsession, I had been impelled to listen for was some betrayal of his not being at rest, and I presently caught one, but not in the form I had expected. His voice tinkled out. "I say, you there — come in." It was gaiety in the gloom!

I went in with my light and found him in bed, very wide awake but very much at his ease. "Well, what are *you* up to?" he asked with a grace of sociability in which it occurred to me that Mrs. Grose, had she been present, might have looked in vain for proof that anything was "out."

I stood over him with my candle. "How did you know I was there?"

"Why of course I heard you. Did you fancy you made no noise? You're like a troop of cavalry!" he beautifully laughed.

"Then you weren't asleep?"

"Not much! I lie awake and think."

I had put my candle, designedly, a short way off, and then, as he held out his friendly old hand to me, had sat down on the edge of his bed. "What is it," I asked, "that you think of?"

"What in the world, my dear, but *you?*"

"Ah the pride I take in your appreciation doesn't insist on that! I had so far rather you slept."

"Well, I think also, you know, of this queer business of ours."

I marked the coolness of his firm little hand. "Of what queer business, Miles?"

"Why the way you bring me up. And all the rest!"

I fairly held my breath a minute, and even from my glimmering taper there was light enough to show how he smiled up at me from his pillow. "What do you mean by all the rest?"

"Oh you know, you know!"

I could say nothing for a minute, though I felt as I held his hand and our eyes continued to meet that my silence had all the air of admitting his charge and that nothing in the whole world of reality was perhaps at that moment so fabulous as our actual relation. "Certainly you shall go back to school," I said, "if it be that

that troubles you. But not to the old place — we must find another, a better. How could I know it did trouble you, this question, when you never told me so, never spoke of it at all?" His clear listening face, framed in its smooth whiteness, made him for the minute as appealing as some wistful patient in a children's hospital; and I would have given, as the resemblance came to me, all I possessed on earth really to be the nurse or the sister of charity who might have helped to cure him. Well, even as it was I perhaps might help! "Do you know you've never said a word to me about your school — I mean the old one; never mentioned it in any way?"

He seemed to wonder; he smiled with the same loveliness. But he clearly gained time; he waited, he called for guidance. "Haven't I?" It wasn't for *me* to help him — it was for the thing I had met!

Something in his tone and the expression of his face, as I got this from him, set my heart aching with such a pang as it had never yet known; so unutterably touching was it to see his little brain puzzled and his little resources taxed to play, under the spell laid on him, a part of innocence and consistency. "No, never — from the hour you came back. You've never mentioned to me one of your masters, one of your comrades, nor the least little thing that ever happened to you at school. Never, little Miles — no never — have you given me an inkling of anything that *may* have happened there. Therefore you can fancy how much I'm in the dark. Until you came out, that way, this morning, you had since the first hour I saw you scarce even made a reference to anything in your previous life. You seemed so perfectly to accept the present." It was extraordinary how my absolute conviction of his secret precocity — or whatever I might call the poison of an influence that I dared but half-phrase — made him, in spite of the faint breath of his inward trouble, appear as accessible as an older person, forced me to treat him as an intelligent equal. "I thought you wanted to go on as you are."

It struck me that at this he just faintly coloured. He gave, at any rate, like a convalescent slightly fatigued, a languid shake of his head. "I don't — I don't. I want to get away."

"You're tired of Bly?"

"Oh no, I like Bly."

"Well then — ?"

"Oh *you* know what a boy wants!"

I felt I didn't know so well as Miles, and I took temporary refuge. "You want to go to your uncle?"

Again, at this, with his sweet ironic face, he made a movement on the pillow. "Ah you can't get off with that!"

I was silent a little, and it was I now, I think, who changed colour. "My dear, I don't want to get off!"

"You can't even if you do. You can't, you can't!" — he lay beautifully staring. "My uncle must come down and you must completely settle things."

"If we do," I returned with some spirit, "you may be sure it will be to take you quite away."

"Well, don't you understand that that's exactly what I'm working for? You'll have to *tell* him — about the way you've let it all drop: you'll have to tell him a tremendous lot!"

The exultation with which he uttered this helped me somehow for the instant to meet him rather more. "And how much will *you*, Miles, have to tell him? There are things he'll ask you!"

He turned it over. "Very likely. But what things?"

"The things you've never told me. To make up his mind what to do with you. He can't send you back—"

"I don't want to go back!" he broke in. "I want a new field."

He said it with admirable serenity, with positive unimpeachable gaiety; and doubtless it was that very note that most evoked for me the poignancy, the unnatural childish tragedy, of his probable reappearance at the end of three months with all this bravado and still more dishonour. It overwhelmed me now that I should never be able to bear that, and it made me let myself go. I threw myself upon him and in the tenderness of my pity I embraced him. "Dear little Miles, dear little Miles—!"

My face was close to his, and he let me kiss him, simply taking it with indulgent good humour. "Well, old lady?"

"Is there nothing—nothing at all that you want to tell me?"

He turned off a little, facing round toward the wall and holding up his hand to look at as one had seen sick children look. "I've told you—I told you this morning."

Oh I was sorry for him! "That you just want me not to worry you?"

He looked round at me now as if in recognition of my understanding him; then ever so gently, "To let me alone," he replied.

There was even a strange little dignity in it, something that made me release him, yet, when I had slowly risen, linger beside him. God knows I never wished to harass him, but I felt that merely, at this, to turn my back on him was to abandon or, to put it more truly, lose him. "I've just begun a letter to your uncle," I said.

"Well then, finish it!"

I waited a minute. "What happened before?"

He gazed up at me again. "Before what?"

"Before you came back. And before you went away."

For some time he was silent, but he continued to meet my eyes. "What happened?"

It made me, the sound of the words, in which it seemed to me I caught for the very first time a small faint quaver of consenting consciousness—it made me drop on my knees beside the bed and seize once more the chance of possessing him. "Dear little Miles, dear little Miles, if you *knew* how I want to help you! It's only that, it's nothing but that, and I'd rather die than give you a pain or do you a wrong—I'd rather die than hurt a hair of you. Dear little Miles"—oh I brought it out now even if I *should* go too far—"I just want you to help me to save you!" But I knew in a moment after this that I had gone too far. The answer to my appeal was instantaneous, but it came in the form of an extraordinary blast and chill, a gust of frozen air and a shake of the room as great as if, in the wild wind, the casement had crashed in. The boy gave a loud high shriek which, lost in the rest of the shock of sound, might have seemed, indistinctly, though I was so close to him, a note either of jubilation or of terror. I jumped to my feet again and was conscious of darkness. So for a moment we remained, while I stared about me and saw the drawn curtains unstirred and the window still tight.

"Why the candle's out!" I then cried.

"It was I who blew it, dear!" said Miles.

XVIII

The next day, after lessons, Mrs. Grose found a moment to say to me quietly: "Have you written, Miss?"

"Yes—I've written." But I didn't add—for the hour—that my letter, sealed and directed, was still in my pocket. There would be time enough to send it before the messenger should go to the village. Meanwhile there had been on the part of my pupils no more brilliant, more exemplary morning. It was exactly as if they had both had at heart to gloss over any recent little friction. They performed the dizziest feats of arithmetic, soaring quite out of my feeble range, and perpetrated, in higher spirits than ever, geographical and historical jokes. It was conspicuous of course in Miles in particular that he appeared to wish to show how easily he could let me down. This child, to my memory, really lives in a setting of beauty and misery that no words can translate; there was a distinction all his own in every impulse he revealed; never was a small natural creature, to the uninformed eye all frankness and freedom, a more ingenious, a more extraordinary little gentleman. I had perpetually to guard against the wonder of contemplation into which my initiated view betrayed me; to check the irrelevant gaze and discouraged sigh in which I constantly both attacked and renounced the enigma of what such a little gentleman could have done that deserved a penalty. Say that, by the dark prodigy I knew, the imagination of all evil *had* been opened up to him: all the justice within me ached for the proof that it could ever have flowered into an act.

He had never at any rate been such a little gentleman as when, after our early dinner on this dreadful day, he came round to me and asked if I shouldn't like him for half an hour to play to me. David playing to Saul could never have shown a finer sense of the occasion. It was literally a charming exhibition of tact, of magnanimity, and quite tantamount to his saying outright: "The true knights we love to read about never push an advantage too far. I know what you mean now: you mean that—to be let alone yourself and not followed up—you'll cease to worry and spy upon me, won't keep me so close to you, will let me go and come. Well, I 'come,' you see—but I don't go! There'll be plenty of time for that. I do really delight in your society and I only want to show you that I contended for a principle." It may be imagined whether I resisted this appeal or failed to accompany him again, hand in hand, to the schoolroom. He sat down at the old piano and played as he had never played; and if there are those who think he had better have been kicking a football I can only say that I wholly agree with them. For at the end of a time that under his influence I had quite ceased to measure I started up with a strange sense of having literally slept at my post. It was after luncheon, and by the schoolroom fire, and yet I hadn't really in the least slept; I had only done something much worse—I had forgotten. Where all this time was Flora? When I put the question to Miles he played on a minute before answering, and then could only say: "Why, my dear, how do I know?"—breaking moreover into a happy laugh which immediately after, as if it were a vocal accompaniment, he prolonged into incoherent extravagant song.

I went straight to my room, but his sister was not there; then, before going downstairs, I looked into several others. As she was nowhere about she would surely be with Mrs. Grose, whom in the comfort of that theory I accordingly proceeded in quest of. I found her where I had found her the evening before, but she met my quick challenge with blank scared ignorance. She had only supposed that, after the repast, I had carried off both the children; as to which she was quite in her right, for it was the very first time I had allowed the little girl out of my sight without some special provision. Of course now indeed she might be with the maids, so that the immediate thing was to look for her without an air of alarm. This we promptly arranged between us; but when, ten minutes later and in pursuance of our arrangement, we met in the hall, it was only to report on either side that after guarded enquiries we had altogether failed to trace her. For a minute there, apart from observation, we exchanged mute alarms, and I could feel with what high interest my friend returned me all those I had from the first given her.

"She'll be above," she presently said — "in one of the rooms you haven't searched."

"No; she's at a distance." I had made up my mind. "She has gone out."

Mrs. Grose stared. "Without a hat?"

I naturally also looked volumes. "Isn't that woman always without one?"

"She's with *her?*"

"She's with *her!*" I declared. "We must find them."

My hand was on my friend's arm, but she failed for the moment, confronted with such an account of the matter, to respond to my pressure. She communed, on the contrary, where she stood, with her uneasiness. "And where's Master Miles?"

"Oh *he's* with Quint. They'll be in the schoolroom."

"Lord, Miss!" My view, I was myself aware — and therefore I suppose my tone — had never yet reached so calm an assurance.

"The trick's played," I went on; "they've successfully worked their plan. He found the most divine little way to keep me quiet while she went off."

"'Divine'?" Mrs. Grose bewilderedly echoed.

"Infernal then!" I almost cheerfully rejoined. "He has provided for himself as well. But come!"

She had helplessly gloomed at the upper regions. "You leave him — ?"

"So long with Quint? Yes — I don't mind that now."

She always ended at these moments by getting possession of my hand, and in this manner she could at present still stay me. But after gasping an instant at my sudden resignation, "Because of your letter?" she eagerly brought out.

I quickly, by way of answer, felt for my letter, drew it forth, held it up, and then, freeing myself, went and laid in on the great hall-table. "Luke will take it," I said as I came back. I reached the house-door and opened it; I was already on the steps.

My companion still demured: the storm of the night and the early morning had dropped, but the afternoon was damp and grey. I came down to the drive while she stood in the doorway. "You go with nothing on?"

"What do I care when the child has nothing? I can't wait to dress," I cried, "and if you must do so I leave you. Try meanwhile yourself upstairs."

"With *them?*" Oh on this the poor woman promptly joined me!

XIX

We went straight to the lake, as it was called at Bly, and I dare say rightly called, though it may have been a sheet of water less remarkable than my untravelled eyes supposed it. My acquaintance with sheets of water was small, and the pool of Bly, at all events on the few occasions of my consenting, under the protection of my pupils, to affront its surface in the old flat-bottomed boat moored there for our use, had impressed me both with its extent and its agitation. The usual place of embarkation was half a mile from the house, but I had an intimate conviction that, wherever Flora might be, she was not near home. She had not given me the slip for any small adventure, and, since the day of the very great one that I had shared with her by the pond, I had been aware, in our walks, of the quarter to which she most inclined. This was why I had now given to Mrs. Grose's steps so marked a direction—a direction making her, when she perceived it, oppose a resistance that showed me she was freshly mystified. "You're going to the water, Miss?—you think she's in—?"

"She may be, though the depth is, I believe, nowhere very great. But what I judge most likely is that she's on the spot from which, the other day, we saw together what I told you."

"When she pretended not to see—?"

"With that astounding self-possession! I've always been sure she wanted to go back alone. And now her brother has managed it for her."

Mrs. Grose still stood where she had stopped. "You suppose they really *talk* of them?"

I could meet this with an assurance! "They say things that, if we heard them, would simply appal us."

"And if she *is* there—?"

"Yes?"

"Then Miss Jessel is?"

"Beyond a doubt. You shall see."

"Oh thank you!" my friend cried, planted so firm that, taking it in, I went straight on without her. By the time I reached the pool, however, she was close behind me, and I knew that, whatever, to her apprehension, might befall me, the exposure of sticking to me struck her as her least danger. She exhaled a moan of relief as we at last came in sight of the greater part of the water without a sight of the child. There was no trace of Flora on that nearer side of the bank where my observation of her had been most startling, and none on the opposite edge, where, save for a margin of some twenty yards, a thick copse came down to the pond. This expanse, oblong in shape, was so narrow compared to its length that, with its ends out of view, it might have been taken for a scant river. We looked at the empty stretch, and then I felt the suggestion in my friend's eyes. I knew what she meant and I replied with a negative headshake.

"No, no; wait! She has taken the boat."

My companion stared at the vacant mooring-place and then again across the lake. "Then where is it?"

"Our not seeing it is the strongest of proofs. She has used it to go over, and then has managed to hide it."

"All alone — that child?"

"She's not alone, and at such times she's not a child: she an old, old woman." I scanned all the visible shore while Mrs. Grose took again, into the queer element I offered her, one of her plunges of submission; then I pointed out that the boat might perfectly be in a small refuge formed by one of the recesses of the pool, an indentation masked, for the hither side, by a projection of the bank and by a clump of trees growing close to the water.

"But if the boat's there, where on earth's *she?*" my colleague anxiously asked.

"That's exactly what we must learn." And I started to walk further.

"By going all the way round?"

"Certainly, far as it is. It will take us but ten minutes, yet it's far enough to have made the child prefer not to walk. She went straight over."

"Laws!" cried my friend again: the chain of my logic was ever too strong for her. It dragged her at my heels even now, and when we had got halfway round — a devious tiresome process, on ground much broken and by a path choked with overgrowth — I paused to give her breath. I sustained her with a grateful arm, assuring her that she might hugely help me; and this started us afresh, so that in the course of but few minutes more we reached a point from which we found the boat to be where I had supposed it. It has been intentionally left as much as possible out of sight and was tied to one of the stakes of a fence that came, just there, down to the brink and that had been an assistance to disembarking. I recognised, as I looked at the pair of short thick oars, quite safely drawn up, the prodigious character of the feat for a little girl; but I had by this time lived too long among wonders and had panted to too many livelier measures. There was a gate in the fence, through which we passed, and that brought us after a trifling interval more into the open. Then "There she is!" we both exclaimed at once.

Flora, a short way off, stood before us on the grass and smiled as if her performance had now become complete. The next thing she did, however, was to stoop straight down and pluck — quite as if it were all she was there for — a big ugly spray of withered fern. I at once felt sure she had just come out of the copse. She waited for us, not herself taking a step, and I was conscious of the rare solemnity with which we presently approached her. She smiled and smiled, and we met; but it was all done in a silence by this time flagrantly ominous. Mrs. Grose was the first to break the spell: she threw herself on her knees and, drawing the child to her breast, clasped in a long embrace the little tender yielding body. While this dumb convulsion lasted I could only watch it — which I did the more intently when I saw Flora's face peep at me over our companion's shoulder. It was serious now — the flicker had left it; but it strengthened the pang with which I at that moment envied Mrs. Grose the simplicity of *her* relation. Still, all this while, nothing more passed between us save that Flora had let her foolish fern again drop to the ground. What she and I had virtually said to each other was that pretexts were useless now. When Mrs. Gross finally got up she kept the child's hand, so that the two were still before me; and the singular reticence of our communion was even more marked in the frank look she addressed me. "I'll be hanged," it said, "if *I'll* speak!"

It was Flora who, gazing all over me in candid wonder, was the first. She was struck with our bareheaded aspect. "Why where are your things?"

"Where yours are, my dear!" I promptly returned.

She had already got back her gaiety and appeared to take this as an answer quite sufficient. "And where's Miles?" she went on.

There was something in the small valour of it that quite finished me: these three words from her were in a flash like the glitter of a drawn blade, the jostle of the cup that my hand for weeks and weeks had held high and full to the brim and that now, even before speaking, I felt overflow in a deluge. "I'll tell you if you'll tell me —" I heard myself say, then heard the tremor in which it broke.

"Well, what?"

Mrs. Grose's suspense blazed at me, but it was too late now, and I brought the thing out handsomely. "Where, my pet, is Miss Jessel?"

XX

Just as in the churchyard with Miles, the whole thing was upon us. Much as I had made of the fact that this name had never once, between us, been sounded, the quick smitten glare with which the child's face now received it fairly likened my breach of the silence to the smash of a pane of glass. It added to the interposing cry, as if to stay the blow, that Mrs. Grose at the same instant uttered over my violence — the shriek of a creature scared, or rather wounded, which, in turn, within a few seconds, was completed by a gasp of my own. I seized my colleague's arm. "She's there, she's there!"

Miss Jessel stood before us on the opposite bank exactly as she had stood the other time, and I remember, strangely, as the first feeling now produced in me, my thrill of joy at having brought on a proof. She was there, so I was justified; she was there, so I was neither cruel nor mad. She was there for poor scared Mrs. Grose, but she was there most for Flora; and no moment of my monstrous time was perhaps so extraordinary as that in which I consciously threw out to her — with the sense that, pale and ravenous demon as she was, she would catch and understand it — an inarticulate message of gratitude. She rose erect on the spot my friend and I had lately quitted, and there wasn't in all the long reach of her desire an inch of her evil that fell short. This first vividness of vision and emotion were things of a few seconds, during which Mrs. Grose's dazed blink across to where I pointed struck me as showing that she too at last saw, just as it carried my own eyes precipitately to the child. The revelation then of the manner in which Flora was affected startled me in truth far more than it would have done to find her also merely agitated, for direct dismay was of course not what I had expected. Prepared and on her guard as our pursuit had actually made her, she would repress every betrayal; and I was therefore at once shaken by my first glimpse of the particular one for which I had not allowed. To see her, without a convulsion of her small pink face, not even feign to glance in the direction of the prodigy I announced, but only, instead of that, turn at *me* an expression of hard still gravity, an expression absolutely new and unprecedented and that appeared to read and accuse and judge me — this was a stroke that somehow converted the little girl herself into a figure portentous. I gaped at her coolness even though my certitude of her thoroughly seeing was never greater than at that instant, and then, in the immediate need to defend myself, I called her passionately to witness.

"She's there, you little unhappy thing—there, there, *there*, and you know it as well as you know me!" I had said shortly before to Mrs. Grose that she was not at these times a child, but an old, old woman, and my description of her couldn't have been more strikingly confirmed than in the way in which, for all notice of this, she simply showed me, without an expressional concession or admission, a countenance of deeper and deeper, of indeed suddenly quite fixed reprobation. I was by this time—if I can put the whole thing at all together—more appalled at what I may properly call her manner than at anything else, though it was quite simultaneously that I became aware of having Mrs. Grose also, and very formidably, to reckon with. My elder companion, the next moment, at any rate, blotted out everything but her own flushed face and her loud shocked protest, a burst of high disapproval. "What a dreadful turn, to be sure, Miss! Where on earth do you see anything?"

I could only grasp her more quickly yet, for even while she spoke the hideous plain presence stood undimmed and undaunted. It had already lasted a minute, and it lasted while I continued, seizing my colleague, quite thrusting her at it and presenting her to it, to insist with my pointing hand. "You don't see her exactly as *we* see?—you mean to say you don't now—*now*? She's as big as a blazing fire! Only look, dearest woman, *look*—!" She looked, just as I did, and gave me, with her deep groan of negation, repulsion, compassion—the mixture with her pity of her relief at her exemption—a sense, touching to me even then, that she would have backed me up if she had been able. I might well have needed that, for with this hard blow of the proof that her eyes were hopelessly sealed I felt my own situation horribly crumble, I felt—I *saw*—my livid predecessor press, from her position, on my defeat, and I took the measure, more than all, of what I should have from this instant to deal with in the astounding little attitude of Flora. Into this attitude Mrs. Grose immediately and violently entered, breaking, even while there pierced through my sense of ruin a prodigious private triumph, into breathless reassurance.

"She isn't there, little lady, and nobody's there—and you never see nothing, my sweet! How can poor Miss Jessel—when poor Miss Jessel's dead and buried? *We* know, don't we, love?"—and she appealed, blundering in, to the child. "It's all a mere mistake and a worry and a joke—and we'll go home as fast as we can!"

Our companion, on this, had responded with a strange quick primness of propriety, and they were again, with Mrs. Grose on her feet, united, as it were, in shocked opposition to me. Flora continued to fix me with her small mask of disaffection, and even at that minute I prayed God to forgive me for seeming to see that, as she stood there holding tight to our friend's dress, her incomparable childish beauty had suddenly failed, had quite vanished. I've said it already—she was literally, she was hideously hard; she had turned common and almost ugly. "I don't know what you mean. I see nobody. I see nothing. I never *have*. I think you're cruel. I don't like you!" Then, after this deliverance, which might have been that of a vulgarly pert little girl in the street, she hugged Mrs. Grose more closely and buried in her skirts the dreadful little face. In this position she launched an almost furious wail. "Take me away, take me away—oh take me away from *her*!"

"From *me*?" I panted.

"From you—from you!" she cried.

Even Mrs. Grose looked across at me dismayed; while I had nothing to do but communicate again with the figure that, on the opposite bank, without a movement, as rigidly still as if catching, beyond the interval, our voices, was as vividly there for my disaster as it was not there for my service. The wretched child had spoken exactly as if she had got from some outside source each of her stabbing little words, and I could therefore, in the full despair of all I had to accept, but sadly shake my head at her. "If I had ever doubted all my doubt would at present have gone. I've been living with the miserable truth, and now it has only too much closed round me. Of course I've lost you: I've interfered, and you've seen, under *her* dictation"—with which I faced, over the pool again, our infernal witness—"the easy and perfect way to meet it. I've done my best, but I've lost you. Good-bye." For Mrs. Grose I had an imperative, an almost frantic "Go, go!" before which, in infinite distress, but mutely possessed of the little girl and clearly convinced, in spite of her blindness, that something awful had occurred and some collapse engulfed us, she retreated, by the way we had come, as fast as she could move.

Of what first happened when I was left alone I had no subsequent memory. I only knew that at the end of, I suppose, a quarter of an hour, an odorous dampness and roughness, chilling and piercing my trouble, had made me understand that I must have thrown myself, on my face, to the ground and given way to a wildness of grief. I must have lain there long and cried and wailed, for when I raised my head the day was almost done. I got up and looked a moment, through the twilight, at the grey pool and its blank haunted edge, and then I took, back to the house, my dreary and difficult course. When I reached the gate in the fence the boat, to my surprise, was gone, so that I had a fresh reflexion to make on Flora's extraordinary command of the situation. She passed that night, by the most tacit and, I should add, were not the word so grotesque a false note, the happiest of arrangements, with Mrs. Grose. I saw neither of them on my return, but on the other hand I saw, as by an ambiguous compensation, a great deal of Miles. I saw—I can use no other phrase—so much of him that it fairly measured more than it had ever measured. No evening I had passed at Bly was to have had the portentous quality of this one; in spite of which—and in spite also of the deeper depths of consternation that had opened beneath my feet—there was literally, in the ebbing actual, an extraordinarily sweet sadness. On reaching the house I had never so much as looked for the boy; I had simply gone straight to my room to change what I was wearing and to take in, at a glance, much material testimony to Flora's rupture. Her little belongings had all been removed. When later, by the schoolroom fire, I was served with tea by the usual maid, I indulged, on the article of my other pupil, in no enquiry whatever. He had his freedom now—he might have it to the end! Well, he did have it; and it consisted—in part at least—of his coming in at about eight o'clock and sitting down with me in silence. On the removal of the tea-things I had blown out the candles and drawn my chair closer: I was conscious of a mortal coldness and felt as if I should never again be warm. So when he appeared I was sitting in the glow with my thoughts. He paused a moment by the door as if to look at me; then—as if to share them—came to the other side of the hearth and sank into a chair. We sat there in absolute stillness; yet he wanted, I felt, to be with me.

XXI

Before a new day, in my room, had fully broken, my eyes opened to Mrs. Grose, who had come to my bedside with worse news. Flora was so markedly feverish that an illness was perhaps at hand; she had passed a night of extreme unrest, a night agitated above all by fears that had for their subject not in the least her former but wholly her present governess. It was not against the possible re-entrance of Miss Jessel on the scene that she protested—it was conspicuously and passionately against mine. I was at once on my feet, and with an immense deal to ask; the more that my friend had discernibly now girded her loins to meet me afresh. This I felt as soon as I had put to her the question of her sense of the child's sincerity as against my own. "She persists in denying to you that she saw, or has ever seen, anything?"

My visitor's trouble truly was great. "Ah Miss, it isn't a matter on which I can push her! Yet it isn't either, I must say, as if I much needed to. It has made her, every inch of her, quite old."

"Oh I see her perfectly from here. She resents, for all the world like some high little personage, the imputation on her truthfulness and, as it were, her respectability. 'Miss Jessel indeed—*she!*' Ah she's 'respectable,' the chit! The impression she gave me there yesterday was, I assure you, the very strangest of all: it was quite beyond any of the others. I *did* put my foot in it! She'll never speak to me again."

Hideous and obscure as it all was, it held Mrs. Grose briefly silent; then she granted my point with a frankness which, I made sure, had more behind it. "I think indeed, Miss, she never will. She do have a grand manner about it!"

"And that manner"—I summed it up—"is practically what's the matter with her now."

Oh that manner, I could see in my visitor's face, and not a little else besides! "She asks me every three minutes if I think you're coming in."

"I see—I see." I too, on my side, had so much more than worked it out. "Has she said to you since yesterday—except to repudiate her familiarity with anything so dreadful—a single other word about Miss Jessel?"

"Not one, Miss. And of course, you know," my friend added, "I took it from her by the lake that just then and there at least there *was* nobody."

"Rather! And naturally you take it from her still."

"I don't contradict her. What else can I do?"

"Nothing in the world! You've the cleverest little person to deal with. They've made them—their two friends, I mean—still cleverer even than nature did; for it was wondrous material to play on! Flora has now her grievance, and she'll work it to the end."

"Yes, Miss; but to *what* end?"

"Why that of dealing with me to her uncle. She'll make me out to him the lowest creature—!"

I winced at the fair show of the scene in Mrs. Grose's face; she looked for a minute as if she sharply saw them together. "And him who thinks so well of you!"

"He has an odd way—it comes over me now," I laughed, "—of proving it! But that doesn't matter. What Flora wants of course is to get rid of me."

My companion bravely concurred. "Never again to so much as look at you."

"So that what you've come to me now for," I asked, "is to speed me on my way?" Before she had time to reply, however, I had her in check. "I've a better idea—the result of my reflexions. My going *would* seem the right thing, and on Sunday I was terribly near it. Yet that won't do. It's *you* who must go. You must take Flora."

My visitor, at this, did speculate. "But where in the world—?"

"Away from here. Away from *them*. Away, even most of all, now, from me. Straight to her uncle."

"Only to tell on you—?"

"No, not 'only'! To leave me, in addition, with my remedy."

She was still vague. "And what *is* your remedy?"

"Your loyalty, to begin with. And then Miles's."

She looked at me hard. "Do you think he—?"

"Won't, if he has the chance, turn on me? Yes, I venture still to think it. At all events I want to try. Get off with his sister as soon as possible and leave me with him alone." I was amazed, myself, at the spirit I had still in reserve, and therefore perhaps a trifle the more disconcerted at the way in which, in spite of this fine example of it, she hesitated. "There's one thing, of course," I went on: "they mustn't, before she goes, see each other for three seconds." Then it came over me that, in spite of Flora's presumable sequestration from the instant of her return from the pool, it might already be too late. "Do you mean," I anxiously asked, "that they *have* met?"

At this she quite flushed. "Ah, Miss, I'm not such a fool as that! If I've been obliged to leave her three or four times, it has been each time with one of the maids, and at present, though she's alone, she's locked in safe. And yet—and yet!" There were too many things.

"And yet what?"

"Well, are you so sure of the little gentleman?"

"I'm not sure of anything but *you*. But I have, since last evening, a new hope. I think he wants to give me an opening. I do believe that—poor little exquisite wretch!—he wants to speak. Last evening, in the firelight and the silence, he sat with me for two hours as if it were just coming."

Mrs. Grose looked hard through the window at the grey gathering day. "And did it come?"

"No, though I waited and waited I confess it didn't, and it was without a breach of the silence, or so much as a faint allusion to his sister's condition and absence, that we at last kissed for good-night. All the same," I continued, "I can't, if her uncle sees her, consent to his seeing her brother without my having given the boy—and most of all because things have got so bad—a little more time."

My friend appeared on this ground more reluctant than I could quite understand. "What do you mean by more time?"

"Well, a day or two—really to bring it out. He'll then be on *my* side—of which you see the importance. If nothing comes I shall only fail, and you at the worst have helped me by doing on your arrival in town whatever you may have found possible." So I put it before her, but she continued for a little so lost in other reasons that I came again to her aid. "Unless indeed," I wound up, "you really want *not* to go."

I could see it, in her face, at last clear itself: she put out her hand to me as a pledge. "I'll go—I'll go. I'll go this morning."

I wanted to be very just. "If you *should* wish still to wait I'd engage she shouldn't see me."

"No, no: it's the place itself. She must leave it." She held me a moment with heavy eyes, then brought out the rest. "Your idea's the right one. I myself, Miss—"

"Well?"

"I can't stay."

The look she gave me with it made me jump at possibilities. "You mean that, since yesterday, you *have* seen—?"

She shook her head with dignity. "I've *heard*—!"

"Heard?"

"From that child—horrors! There!" she sighed with tragic relief. "On my honour, Miss, she says things—!" But at this evocation she broke down; she dropped with a sudden cry upon my sofa and, as I had seen her do before, gave way to all the anguish of it.

It was quite in another manner that I for my part let myself go. "Oh thank God!"

She sprang up again at this, drying her eyes with a groan. "'Thank God'?"

"It so justifies me!"

"It does that, Miss!"

I couldn't have desired more emphasis, but I just waited. "She's so horrible?"

I saw my colleague scarce knew how to put it. "Really shocking."

"And about me?"

"About you, Miss—since you must have it. It's beyond everything, for a young lady; and I can't think wherever she must have picked up—"

"The appalling language she applies to me? I can then!" I broke in with a laugh that was doubtless significant enough.

It only in truth left my friend still more grave. "Well, perhaps I ought to also—since I've heard some of it before! Yet I can't bear it," the poor woman went on while with the same movement she glanced, on my dressing-table, at the face of my watch. "But I must go back."

I kept her, however. "Ah if you can't bear it—!"

"How can I stop with her, you mean? Why just *for* that: to get her away. Far from this," she pursued, "far from *them*—"

"She may be different? She may be free?" I seized her almost with joy. "Then in spite of yesterday you *believe*—"

"In such doings?" Her simple description of them required, in the light of her expression, to be carried no further, and she gave me the whole thing as she had never done. "I believe."

Yes, it was a joy, and we were still shoulder to shoulder: if I might continue sure of that I should care but little what else happened. My support in the presence of disaster would be the same as it had been in my early need of confidence, and if my friend would answer for my honesty I would answer for all the rest. On the point of taking leave of her, none the less, I was to some extent embarrassed. "There's one thing of course—it occurs to me—to remember. My letter giving the alarm will have reached town before you."

I now felt still more how she had been beating about the bush and how weary at last it had made her. "Your letter won't have got there. Your letter never went."

"What then became of it?"

"Goodness knows! Master Miles —"

"Do you mean *he* took it?" I gasped.

She hung fire, but she overcame her reluctance. "I mean that I saw yesterday, when I came back with Miss Flora, that it wasn't where you had put it. Later in the evening I had the chance to question Luke, and he declared that he had neither noticed nor touched it." We could only exchange, on this, one of our deeper mutual soundings, and it was Mrs. Grose who first brought up the plumb with an almost elate "You see!"

"Yes, I see that if Miles took it instead he probably will have read it and destroyed it."

"And don't you see anything else?"

I faced her for a moment with a sad smile. "It strikes me that by this time your eyes are open even wider than mine."

They proved to be so indeed, but she could still almost blush to show it. "I make out now what he must have done at school." And she gave, in her simple sharpness, an almost droll disillusioned nod. "He stole!"

I turned it over — I tried to be more judicial. "Well — perhaps."

She looked as if she found me unexpectedly calm. "He stole *letters!*"

She couldn't know my reasons for a calmness after all pretty shallow; so I showed them off as I might. "I hope then it was to more purpose than in this case! The note, at all events, that I put on the table yesterday," I pursued, "will have given him so scant an advantage — for it contained only the bare demand for an interview — that he's already much ashamed of having gone so far for so little, and that what he had on his mind last evening was precisely the need of confession." I seemed to myself for the instant to have mastered it, to see it all. "Leave us, leave us" — I was already, at the door, hurrying her off. "I'll get it out of him. He'll meet me. He'll confess. If he confesses he's saved. And if he's saved —"

"Then *you* are?" The dear woman kissed me on this, and I took her farewell. "I'll save you without him!" she cried as she went.

XXII

Yet it was when she had got off — and I missed her on the spot — that the great pinch really came. If I had counted on what it would give me to find myself alone with Miles I quickly recognised that it would give me at least a measure. No hour of my stay in fact was so assailed with apprehensions as that of my coming down to learn that the carriage containing Mrs. Grose and my younger pupil had already rolled out of the gates. Now I *was*, I said to myself, face to face with the elements, and for much of the rest of the day, while I fought my weakness, I could consider that I had been supremely rash. It was a tighter place still than I had yet turned round in; all the more that, for the first time, I could see in the aspect of others a confused reflexion of the crisis. What had happened naturally caused them all to stare; there was too little of the explained, throw out whatever we might, in the suddenness of my colleague's act. The maids and the men looked blank; the effect of which on my nerves was an aggravation until I saw the necessity of making it a positive aid. It was in short by just clutching the helm that I avoided total wreck; and I dare say that, to bear up at all, I became that morning very grand and very dry. I welcomed the consciousness that I was charged with much to do, and I caused it to be known as well that, left thus to myself, I was quite remarkably firm. I wandered with that manner, for the next hour or two, all over the place and looked, I have no doubt, as if I were ready for any onset. So, for the benefit of whom it might concern, I paraded with a sick heart.

The person it appeared least to concern proved to be, till dinner, little Miles himself. My perambulations had given me meanwhile no glimpse of him, but they had tended to make more public the change taking place in our relation as a consequence of his having at the piano, the day before, kept me, in Flora's interest, so beguiled and befooled. The stamp of publicity had of course been fully given by her confinement and departure, and the change itself was now ushered in by our non-observance of the regular custom of the schoolroom. He had already disappeared when, on my way down, I pushed open his door, and I learned below that he had breakfasted — in the presence of a couple of the maids — with Mrs. Grose and his sister. He had then gone out, as he said, for a stroll; than which nothing, I reflected, could better have expressed his frank view of the abrupt transformation of my office. What he would now permit this office to consist of was yet to be settled: there was at the least a queer relief — I mean for myself in especial — in the renouncement of one pretension. If so much had sprung to the surface I scarce put it too strongly in saying that what had perhaps sprung highest was the absurdity of our prolonging the fiction that I had anything more to teach him. It sufficiently stuck out that, by tacit little tricks in which even more than myself he carried out the care for my dignity, I had had to appeal to him to let me off straining to meet him on the ground of his true capacity. He had at any rate his freedom now; I was never to touch it again: as I had amply shown, moreover, when, on his joining me in the schoolroom the previous night, I uttered, in reference to the interval just concluded, neither challenge nor hint. I had too much, from this moment, my other ideas. Yet when he at last arrived the difficulty of applying them, the accumulations of my problem, were brought straight home to me by the beautiful little presence on which what had occurred had as yet, for the eye, dropped neither stain nor shadow.

To mark, for the house, the high state I cultivated I decreed that my meals with the boy should be served, as we called it, downstairs; so that I had been awaiting him in the ponderous pomp of the room outside the window of which I had had from Mrs. Grose, that first scared Sunday, my flash of something it would scarce have done to call light. Here at present I felt afresh — for I had felt it again and again — how my equilibrium depended on the success of my rigid will, the will to shut my eyes as tight as possible to the truth that what I had to deal with was, revoltingly, against nature. I could only get on at all by taking "nature" into my confidence and my account, by treating my monstrous ordeal as a push in a direction unusual, of course, and unpleasant, but demanding after all, for a fair front, only another turn of the screw of ordinary human virtue. No attempt, none the less, could well require more tact than just this attempt to supply, one's self, *all* the nature. How could I put even a little of that article into a suppression of reference to what had occurred? How on the other hand could I make a reference without a new plunge into the hideous obscure? Well, a sort of answer, after a time, had come to me, and it was so far confirmed as that I was met, incontestably, by the quickened vision of what was rare in my little companion. It was indeed as if he had found even now — as he had so often found at lessons — still some other delicate way to ease me off. Wasn't there light in the fact which, as we shared our solitude, broke out with a specious glitter it had never yet quite worn? — the fact that (opportunity aiding, precious opportunity which had now come) it would be preposterous, with a child so endowed, to forego the help one might wrest from absolute intelligence? What had his intelligence been given him for but to save him? Mightn't one, to reach his mind, risk the stretch of a stiff arm across his character? It was as if, when we were face to face in the dining-room, he had literally shown me the way. The roast mutton was on the table and I had dispensed with attendance. Miles, before he sat down, stood for a moment with his hands in his pockets and looked at the joint, on which he seemed on the point of passing some humorous judgement. But what he presently produced was: "I say, my dear, is she really very awfully ill?"

"Little Flora? Not so bad but that she'll presently be better. London will set her up. Bly had ceased to agree with her. Come here and take your mutton."

He alertly obeyed me, carried the plate carefully to his seat and, when he was established, went on. "Did Bly disagree with her so terribly all at once?"

"Not so suddenly as you might think. One had seen it coming on."

"Then why didn't you get her off before?"

"Before what?"

"Before she became too ill to travel."

I found myself prompt. "She's *not* too ill to travel; she only might have become so if she had stayed. This was just the moment to seize. The journey will dissipate the influence" — oh I was grand! — "and carry it off."

"I see, I see" — Miles, for that matter, was grand too. He settled to his repast with the charming little "table manner" that, from that day of his arrival, had relieved me of all grossness of admonition. Whatever he had been expelled from school for, it wasn't for ugly feeding. He was irreproachable, as always, to-day; but was unmistakeably more conscious. He was discernibly trying to take for granted more things than he found, without assistance, quite easy; and he dropped into peaceful silence while he felt his situation. Our meal was of the briefest — mine a vain pretence, and I had the things immediately removed. While this was done Miles stood again with his hands in his little pockets and his back to me — stood and looked out of the wide window through which, that other day, I had seen what pulled me up. We continued silent while the maid was with us — as silent, it whimsically occurred to me, as some young couple who, on their wedding-journey, at the inn, feel shy in the presence of the waiter. He turned round only when the waiter had left us. "Well — so we're alone!"

XXIII

"Oh more or less." I imagine my smile was pale. "Not absolutely. We shouldn't like that!" I went on.

"No — I suppose we shouldn't. Of course we've the others."

"We've the others — we've indeed the others," I concurred.

"Yet even though we have them," he returned, still with his hands in his pockets and planted there in front of me, "they don't much count, do they?"

I made the best of it, but I felt wan. "It depends on what you call 'much'!"

"Yes"—with all accommodation—"everything depends!" On this, however, he faced to the window again and presently reached it with his vague restless cogitating step. He remained there a while with his forehead against the glass, in contemplation of the stupid shrubs I knew and the dull things of November. I had always my hypocrisy of "work," behind which I now gained the sofa. Steadying myself with it there as I had repeatedly done at those moments of torment that I have described as the moments of my knowing the children to be given to something from which I was barred, I sufficiently obeyed my habit of being prepared for the worst. But an extraordinary impression dropped on me as I extracted a meaning from the boy's embarrassed back—none other than the impression that I was not barred now. This inference grew in a few minutes to sharp intensity and seemed bound up with the direct perception that it was positively *he* who was. The frames and squares of the great window were a kind of image, for him, of a kind of failure. I felt that I saw him, in any case, shut in or shut out. He was admirable but not comfortable: I took it in with a throb of hope. Wasn't he looking through the haunted pane for something he couldn't see?— and wasn't it the first time in the whole business that he had known such a lapse? The first, the very first: I found it a splendid portent. It made him anxious, though he watched himself; he had been anxious all day and, even while in his usual sweet little manner he sat at table, had needed all his small strange genius to give it a gloss. When he at last turned round to meet me it was almost as if this genius had succumbed. "Well, I think I'm glad Bly agrees with *me!*"

"You'd certainly seem to have seen, these twenty-four hours, a good deal more of it than for some time before. I hope," I went on bravely, "that you've been enjoying yourself."

"Oh yes, I've been ever so far; all round about—miles and miles away. I've never been so free."

He had really a manner of his own, and I could only try to keep up with him. "Well, do you like it?"

He stood there smiling; then at last he put into two words—"Do *you?*"— more discrimination than I had ever heard two words contain. Before I had time to deal with that, however, he continued as if with the sense that this was an impertinence to be softened. "Nothing could be more charming than the way you take it, for of course if we're alone together now it's you that are alone most. But I hope," he threw in, "you don't particularly mind!"

"Having to do with you?" I asked. "My dear child, how can I help minding? Though I've renounced all claim to your company—you're so beyond me—I at least greatly enjoy it. What else should I stay on for?"

He looked at me more directly, and the expression of his face, graver now, struck me as the most beautiful I had ever found in it. "You stay on just for *that?*"

"Certainly. I stay on as your friend and from the tremendous interest I take in you till something can be done for you that may be more worth your while. That needn't surprise you." My voice trembled so that I felt it impossible to suppress the shake. "Don't you remember how I told you, when I came and sat on your bed the night of the storm, that there was nothing in the world I wouldn't do for you?"

"Yes, yes!" He, on his side, more and more visibly nervous, had a tone to master; but he was so much more successful than I that, laughing out through his gravity, he could pretend we were pleasantly jesting. "Only that, I think, was to get me to do something for *you!*"

"It was partly to get you to do something," I conceded. "But, you know, you didn't do it."

"Oh yes," he said with the brightest superficial eagerness, "you wanted me to tell you something."

"That's it. Out, straight out. What you have on your mind, you know."

"Ah then is *that* what you've stayed over for?"

He spoke with a gaiety through which I could still catch the finest little quiver of resentful passion; but I can't begin to express the effect upon me of an implication of surrender even so faint. It was as if what I had yearned for had come at last only to astonish me. "Well, yes — I may as well make a clean breast of it. It was precisely for that."

He waited so long that I supposed it for the purpose of repudiating the assumption on which my action had been founded; but what he finally said was: "Do you mean now — here?"

"There couldn't be a better place or time." He looked round him uneasily, and I had the rare — oh the queer! — impression of the very first symptom I had seen in him of the approach of immediate fear. It was as if he were suddenly afraid of me — which struck me indeed as perhaps the best thing to make him. Yet in the very pang of the effort I felt it vain to try sternness, and I heard myself the next instant so gentle as to be almost grotesque. "You want so to go out again?"

"Awfully!" He smiled at me heroically, and the touching little bravery of it was enhanced by his actually flushing with pain. He had picked up his hat, which he had brought in, and stood twirling it in a way that gave me, even as I was just nearly reaching port, a perverse horror of what I was doing. To do it in *any* way was an act of violence, for what did it consist of but the obtrusion of the idea of grossness and guilt on a small helpless creature who had been for me a revelation of the possibilities of beautiful intercourse? Wasn't it base to create for a being so exquisite a mere alien awkwardness? I suppose I now read into our situation a clearness it couldn't have had at the time, for I seem to see our poor eyes already lighted with some spark of a prevision of the anguish that was to come. So we circled about with terrors and scruples, fighters not daring to close. But it was for each other we feared! That kept us a little longer suspended and unbruised. "I'll tell you everything," Miles said — "I mean I'll tell you anything you like. You'll stay on with me, and we shall both be all right, and I *will* tell you — I *will*. But not now."

"Why not now?"

My insistence turned him from me and kept him once more at his window in a silence during which, between us, you might have heard a pin drop. Then he was before me again with the air of a person for whom, outside, some one who had frankly to be reckoned with was waiting. "I have to see Luke."

I had not yet reduced him to quite so vulgar a lie, and I felt proportionately ashamed. But, horrible as it was, his lies made up my truth. I achieved thoughtfully a few loops of my knitting. "Well then go to Luke, and I'll wait for what you promise. Only in return for that satisfy, before you leave me, one very much smaller request."

He looked as if he felt he had succeeded enough to be able still a little to bargain. "Very much smaller —?"

"Yes, a mere fraction of the whole. Tell me" — oh my work preoccupied me, and I was off-hand! — "if, yesterday afternoon, from the table in the hall, you took, you know, my letter."

XXIV

My grasp of how he received this suffered for a minute from something that I can describe only as a fierce split of my attention — a stroke that at first, as I sprang straight up, reduced me to the mere blind movement of getting hold of him, drawing him close and, while I just fell for support against the nearest piece of furniture, instinctively keeping him with his back to the window. The appearance was full upon us that I had already had to deal with here: Peter Quint had come into view like a sentinel before a prison. The next thing I saw was that, from outside, he had reached the window, and then I knew that, close to the glass and glaring in through it, he offered once more to the room his white face of damnation. It represents but grossly what took place within me at the sight to say that on the second my decision was made; yet I believe that no woman so overwhelmed ever in so short a time recovered her command of the *act*. It came to me in the very horror of the immediate presence that the act would be, seeing and facing what I saw and faced, to keep the boy himself unaware. The inspiration — I can call it by no other name — was that I felt how voluntarily, how transcendently, I *might*. It was like fighting with a demon for a human soul, and when I had fairly so appraised it I saw how the human soul — held out, in the tremor of my hands, at arms' length — had a perfect dew of sweat on a lovely childish forehead. The face that was close to mine was as white as the face against the glass, and out of it presently came a sound, not low nor weak, but as if from much further away, that I drank like a waft of fragrance.

"Yes — I took it."

At this, with a moan of joy, I enfolded, I drew him close; and while I held him to my breast, where I could feel in the sudden fever of his little body the tremendous pulse of his little heart, I kept my eyes on the thing at the window and saw it move and shift its posture. I have likened it to a sentinel, but its slow wheel, for a moment, was rather the prowl of a baffled beast. My present quickened courage, however, was such that, not too much to let it through, I had to shade, as it were, my flame. Meanwhile the glare of the face was again at the window, the scoundrel fixed as if to watch and wait. It was the very confidence that I might now defy him, as well as the positive certitude, by this time, of the child's unconsciousness, that made me go on. "What did you take it for?"

"To see what you said about me."

"You opened the letter?"

"I opened it."

My eyes were now, as I held him off a little again, on Miles's own face, in which the collapse of mockery showed me how complete was the ravage of uneasiness. What was prodigious was that at last, by my success, his sense was sealed and his communication stopped: he knew that he was in presence, but knew not of what, and knew still less that I also was and that I did know. And what did this strain of trouble matter when my eyes went back to the window only to see that the air was clear again and—by my personal triumph—the influence quenched? There was nothing there. I felt that the cause was mine and that I should surely get *all*. "And you found nothing!"—I let my elation out.

He gave the most mournful, thoughtful little headshake. "Nothing."

"Nothing, nothing!" I almost shouted in my joy.

"Nothing, nothing," he sadly repeated.

I kissed his forehead; it was drenched. "So what have you done with it?"

"I've burnt it."

"Burnt it?" It was now or never. "Is that what you did at school?"

Oh what this brought up! "At school?"

"Did you take letters?—or other things?"

"Other things?" He appeared now to be thinking of something far off and that reached him only through the pressure of his anxiety. Yet it did reach him. "Did I *steal?*"

I felt myself redden to the roots of my hair as well as wonder if it were more strange to put to a gentleman such a question or to see him take it with allowances that gave the very distance of his fall in the world. "Was it for that you mightn't go back?"

The only thing he felt was rather a dreary little surprise. "Did you know I mightn't go back?"

"I know everything."

He gave me at this the longest and strangest look. "Everything?"

"Everything. Therefore *did* you—?" But I couldn't say it again.

Miles could, very simply. "No. I didn't steal."

My face must have shown him I believed him utterly; yet my hands—but it was for pure tenderness—shook him as if to ask him why, if it was all for nothing, he had condemned me to months of torment. "What then did you do?"

He looked in vague pain all round the top of the room and drew his breath, two or three times over, as if with difficulty. He might have been standing at the bottom of the sea and raising his eyes to some faint green twilight. "Well—I said things."

"Only that?"

"They thought it was enough!"

"To turn you out for?"

Never, truly, had a person "turned out" shown so little to explain it as this little person! He appeared to weigh my question, but in a manner quite detached and almost helpless. "Well, I suppose I oughtn't."

"But to whom did you say them?"

He evidently tried to remember, but it dropped—he had lost it. "I don't know!"

He almost smiled at me in the desolation of his surrender, which was indeed practically, by this time, so complete that I ought to have left it there. But I was infatuated—I was blind with victory, though even then the very effect that was to have brought him so much nearer was already that of added separation. "Was it to every one?" I asked.

"No; it was only to —" But he gave a sick little headshake. "I don't remember their names."

"Were they then so many?"

"No — only a few. Those I liked."

Those he liked? I seemed to float not into clearness, but into a darker obscure, and within a minute there had come to me out of my very pity the appalling alarm of his being perhaps innocent. It was for the instant confounding and bottomless, for if he *were* innocent what then on earth was I? Paralysed, while it lasted, by the mere brush of the question, I let him go a little, so that, with a deep-drawn sigh, he turned away from me again; which, as he faced toward the clear window, I suffered, feeling that I had nothing now there to keep him from. "And did they repeat what you said?" I went on after a moment.

He was soon at some distance from me, still breathing hard and again with the air, though now without anger for it, of being confined against his will. Once more, as he had done before, he looked up at the dim day as if, of what had hitherto sustained him, nothing was left but an unspeakable anxiety. "Oh yes," he nevertheless replied — "they must have repeated them. To those *they* liked," he added.

There was somehow less of it than I had expected; but I turned it over. "And these things came round —?"

"To the masters? Oh yes!" he answered very simply. "But I didn't know they'd tell."

"The masters? They didn't — they've never told. That's why I ask you."

He turned to me again his little beautiful fevered face. "Yes, it was too bad."

"Too bad?"

"What I suppose I sometimes said. To write home."

I can't name the exquisite pathos of the contradiction given to such a speech by such a speaker; I only know that the next instant I heard myself throw off with homely force: "Stuff and nonsense!" But the next after that I must have sounded stern enough. "What *were* these things?"

My sternness was all for his judge, his executioner; yet it made him avert himself again, and that movement made *me*, with a single bound and an irrepressible cry, spring straight upon him. For there again, against the glass, as if to blight his confession and stay his answer, was the hideous author of our woe — the white face of damnation. I felt a sick swim at the drop of my victory and all the return of my battle, so that the wildness of my veritable leap only served as a great betrayal. I saw him, from the midst of my act, meet it with a divination, and on the perception that even now he only guessed, and that the window was still to his own eyes free, I let the impulse flame up to convert the climax of his dismay into the very proof of his liberation. "No more, no more, no more!" I shrieked to my visitant as I tried to press him against me.

"Is she *here*?" Miles panted as he caught with his sealed eyes the direction of my words. Then as his strange "she" staggered me and, with a gasp, I echoed it, "Miss Jessel, Miss Jessel!" he with a sudden fury gave me back.

I seized, stupefied, his supposition — some sequel to what we had done to Flora, but this made me only want to show him that it was better still than that. "It's not Miss Jessel! But it's at the window — straight before us. It's *there* — the coward horror, there for the last time!"

At this, after a second in which his head made the movement of a baffled dog's on a scent and then gave a frantic little shake for air and light, he was at me in a white rage, bewildered, glaring vainly over the place and missing wholly, though it now, to my sense, filled the room like the taste of poison, the wide overwhelming presence. "It's *he?*"

I was so determined to have all my proof that I flashed into ice to challenge him. "Whom do you mean by 'he'?"

"Peter Quint—you devil!" His face gave again, round the room, its con-vulsed supplication. *"Where?"*

They are in my ears still, his supreme surrender of the name and his tribute to my devotion. "What does he matter now, my own?—what will he *ever* matter? I have you," I launched at the beast, "but he has lost you for ever!" Then for the demonstration of my work, "There, *there!*" I said to Miles.

But he had already jerked straight round, stared, glared again, and seen but the quiet day. With the stroke of the loss I was so proud of he uttered the cry of a creature hurled over an abyss, and the grasp with which I recovered him might have been that of catching him in his fall. I caught him, yes, I held him—it may be imagined with what a passion; but at the end of a minute I began to feel what it truly was that I held. We were alone with the quiet day, and his little heart, dispossessed, had stopped.

[1898]

Study and Writing Questions

1. How does the SETTING at Bly contribute to the ATMOSPHERE and THEME of the STORY? How do the locations of events in the house reveal personal relations and social structure? How are the tower, garden, and pond used? To what extent is James, in constructing and using his setting, reworking IMAGES found in other NARRATIVES?

2. What are the varieties of eye and sight imagery used here? How does vision function in both PLOT and theme?

3. There are many possible love relationships in this STORY. What are they? Characterize each. What effect(s) does love have for each of the CHARACTERS?

4. Describe Miles. Can we infer what he felt about Miss Jessel? How does he feel about this new governess? What might he have said to his classmates at school? Whom does he address with his last two words? What happens to him at the end?

5. No one but the governess ever admits to seeing the "visitants," and the governess, when she first sees one, says, "'my imagination had, in a flash, turned real.'" What evidence is there that much of the narrative exists only in the imagination of the governess? What evidence is there that it all actually happened? What events seem necessarily to have happened no matter what view one takes of the governess's possible imaginative projection?

6. Describe the character of the governess. What does she hope to mean to her employer? What does she hope to mean to each of the children? What is her relationship with Mrs. Grose? What can you infer about her relationship with Douglas, the man to whom she gives her manuscript? To what extent is this narrative about the governess?

7. What is the significance of FRAMING in this narrative? What are some instances in which it is important to remember that the governess wrote the manuscript? Why does Douglas decide to read it aloud? Why does James create an outer FIRST-PERSON NARRATOR and other characters who interact with Douglas? Why, after the reading of the manuscript, does James not return to the frame?

See also Questions for Contrast and Comparison: 14, 23, 24, 25, 35, 49, 52, 64, 114, 234, 235, 237, and 238.

■ **(THEODORA) SARAH ORNE JEWETT** (1849–1909) *was ill most of her life. Although she occasionally attended local schools, she felt her real education came from reading and from making house calls by buggy with her father, a wealthy physician in rural South Berwick, Maine, Sarah's lifelong home. Inspired especially by Harriet Beecher Stowe's* The Pearl of Orr's Island: A Story of the Coast of Maine *(1866), by twenty she was publishing* STORIES *and sketches in* The Atlantic Monthly. *Encouraged by Atlantic editor William Dean Howells, Jewett wove her stories into* Deephaven *(1877), an* EPISODIC, *composite* NARRATIVE *of the life of a Maine coastal village. Thereafter, in addition to her writing, she read avidly the works of Gustave Flaubert, Émile Zola, Leo Tolstoy, and Henry James. Adapting their modern concerns for social* REALISM, *psychological sublety, and stylistic polish to her own concern for the lives of the people around her, she became highly prominent in the late nineteenth century "local color movement," an artistic school valuing faithful presentation of geographic setting, history, and the speech and manners of specific American regions. Her best writing appears in the* NOVEL A Country Doctor *(1884),* A White Heron and Other Stories *(1896), and another composite work,* The Country of the Pointed Firs *(1896). In her last years she counseled the young Willa Cather. Jewett died at home of a cerebral hemorrhage.*

A White Heron

I

The woods were already filled with shadows one June evening, just before eight o'clock, though a bright sunset still glimmered faintly among the trunks of the trees. A little girl was driving home her cow, a plodding, dilatory, provoking creature in her behavior, but a valued companion for all that. They were going away from the western light, and striking deep into the dark woods, but their feet were familiar with the path, and it was no matter whether their eyes could see it or not.

There was hardly a night the summer through when the old cow could be found waiting at the pasture bars; on the contrary, it was her greatest pleasure to hide herself away among the high huckleberry bushes, and though she wore a loud bell she had made the discovery that if one stood perfectly still it would not ring. So Sylvia had to hunt for her until she found her, and call Co'! Co'! with never an answering Moo, until her childish patience was quite spent. If the creature had not given good milk and plenty of it, the case would have seemed very different to her owners. Besides, Sylvia had all the time there was, and very little use to make of it. Sometimes in pleasant weather it was a consolation to look upon the cow's pranks as an intelligent attempt to play hide and seek, and as the child had no playmates she lent herself to this amusement with a good deal of zest. Though this chase had been so long that the wary animal herself had given an unusual signal of her whereabouts, Sylvia had only laughed when she came upon Mistress Moolly at the swamp-side, and urged her affectionately homeward with a twig of birch leaves. The old cow was not inclined to wander farther, she even turned in the right direction for once as they left the pasture, and stepped along the road at a good pace. She was quite ready to be milked now, and seldom stopped to browse. Sylvia wondered what her grandmother would say because they were so late. It was a great while since she had left home at half past five o'clock, but everybody knew the difficulty of making this errand a short one. Mrs. Tilley had chased the horned torment too many summer evenings herself to blame any one else for lingering, and was only thankful as she waited that she had Sylvia, nowadays, to give such valuable assistance. The good woman suspected that Sylvia loitered occasionally on her own account; there never was such a child for straying about out-of-doors since the world was made! Everybody said that it was a good change for a little maid who had tried to grow for eight years in a crowded manufacturing town, but, as for Sylvia herself, it seemed as if she never had been alive at all before she came to live at the farm. She thought often with wistful compassion of a wretched dry geranium that belonged to a town neighbor.

" 'Afraid of folks,' " old Mrs. Tilley said to herself, with a smile, after she had made the unlikely choice of Sylvia from her daughter's houseful of children, and was returning to the farm. " 'Afraid of folks,' they said! I guess she won't be troubled no great with 'em up to the old place!" When they reached the door of the lonely house and stopped to unlock it, and the cat came to purr loudly, and rub against them, a deserted pussy, indeed, but fat with young robins, Sylvia whispered that this was a beautiful place to live in, and she never should wish to go home.

The companions followed the shady woodroad, the cow taking slow steps, and the child very fast ones. The cow stopped long at the brook to drink, as if the pasture were not half a swamp, and Sylvia stood still and waited, letting her bare feet cool themselves in the shoal water, while the great twilight moths struck softly against her. She waded on through the brook as the cow moved away, and listened to the thrushes with a heart that beat fast with pleasure. There was a stirring in the great boughs overhead. They were full of little birds and beasts that seemed to be wide-awake, and going about their world, or else saying goodnight to each other in sleepy twitters. Sylvia herself felt sleepy as she walked along. However, it was not much farther to the house, and the air was soft and sweet. She was not often in the woods so late as this, and it made her feel as if she were a part of the gray shadows and the moving leaves. She was just thinking how long it seemed since she first came to the farm a year ago, and wondering if everything went on in the noisy town just the same as when she was there; the thought of the great red-faced boy who used to chase and frighten her made her hurry along the path to escape from the shadow of the trees.

Suddenly this little woods-girl is horrorstricken to hear a clear whistle not very far away. Not a bird's whistle, which would have a sort of friendliness, but a boy's whistle, determined, and somewhat aggressive. Sylvia left the cow to what-ever sad fate might await her, and stepped discreetly aside into the bushes, but she was just too late. The enemy had discovered her, and called out in a very cheerful and persuasive tone, "Halloa, little girl, how far is it to the road?" and trembling Sylvia answered almost inaudibly, "A good ways."

She did not dare to look boldly at the tall young man, who carried a gun over his shoulder, but she came out of her bush and again followed the cow, while he walked alongside.

"I have been hunting for some birds," the stranger said kindly, "and I have lost my way, and need a friend very much. Don't be afraid," he added gallantly.

"Speak up and tell me what your name is, and whether you think I can spend the night at your house, and go out gunning early in the morning."

Sylvia was more alarmed than before. Would not her grandmother consider her much to blame? But who could have foreseen such an accident as this? It did not appear to be her fault, and she hung her head as if the stem of it were broken, but managed to answer "Sylvy," with much effort when her companion again asked her name.

Mrs. Tilley was standing in the doorway when the trio came into view. The cow gave a loud moo by way of explanation.

"Yes, you'd better speak up for yourself, you old trial! Where'd she tucked herself away this time, Sylvy?" Sylvia kept an awed silence; she knew by instinct that her grandmother did not comprehend the gravity of the situation. She must be mistaking the stranger for one of the farmer-lads of the region.

The young man stood his gun beside the door, and dropped a heavy game-bag beside it; then he bade Mrs. Tilley good-evening, and repeated his wayfarer's story, and asked if he could have a night's lodging.

"Put me anywhere you like," he said. "I must be off early in the morning, before day; but I am very hungry, indeed. You can give me some milk at any rate, that's plain."

"Dear sakes, yes," responded the hostess, whose long slumbering hospitality seemed to be easily awakened. "You might fare better if you went out on the main road a mile or so, but you're welcome to what we've got. I'll milk right off, and you make yourself at home. You can sleep on husks or feathers," she proffered graciously. "I raised them all myself. There's good pasturing for geese just below here towards the ma'sh. Now step round and set a plate for the gentleman, Sylvy!" And Sylvia promptly stepped. She was glad to have something to do, and she was hungry herself.

It was a surprise to find so clean and comfortable a little dwelling in this New England wilderness. The young man had known the horrors of its most primitive housekeeping, and the dreary squalor of that level of society which does not rebel at the companionship of hens. This was the best thrift of an old-fashioned farmstead, though on such a small scale that it seemed like a hermitage. He listened eagerly to the old woman's quaint talk, he watched Sylvia's pale face and shining gray eyes with ever growing enthusiasm, and insisted that this was the best supper he had eaten for a month; then, afterward, the new-made friends sat down in the doorway together while the moon came up.

Soon it would be berry-time, and Sylvia was a great help at picking. The cow was a good milker, though a plaguy thing to keep track of, the hostess gossiped frankly, adding presently that she had burried four children, so that Sylvia's mother and a son (who might be dead) in California were all the children she had left. "Dan, my boy, was a great hand to go gunning," she explained sadly. "I never wanted for pa'tridges or gray squer'ls while he was to home. He's been a great wand'rer, I expect, and he's no hand to write letters. There, I don't blame him, I'd ha' seen the world myself if it had been so I could.

"Sylvia takes after him," the grandmother continued affectionately, after a minute's pause. "There ain't a foot o' ground she don't know her way over, and the wild creatur's counts her one o' themselves. Squer'ls she'll tame to come an' feed right out o' her hands, and all sorts o' birds. Last winter she got the jay-birds to bangeing here, and I believe she'd 'a' scanted herself of her own meals to have plenty to throw out amongst 'em, if I had n't kep' watch. Anything but crows, I tell her, I'm willin' to help support, — though Dan he went an' tamed one o' them that did seem to have reason same as folks. It was round here a good spell after he went away. Dan an' his father they did n't hitch, — but he never held up his head ag'in after Dan had dared him an' gone off."

The guest did not notice this hint of family sorrows in his eager interest in something else.

"So Sylvy knows all about birds, does she?" he exclaimed, as he looked round at the little girl who sat, very demure but increasingly sleepy, in the moonlight. "I am making a collection of birds myself. I have been at it ever since I was a boy." (Mrs. Tilley smiled.) "There are two or three very rare ones I have been hunting for these five years. I mean to get them on my own ground if they can be found."

"Do you cage 'em up?" asked Mrs. Tilley doubtfully, in response to this enthusiastic announcement.

"Oh, no, they're stuffed and preserved, dozens and dozens of them," said the ornithologist, "and I have shot or snared every one myself. I caught a glimpse of a white heron three miles from here on Saturday, and I have followed it in this direction. They have never been found in this district at all. The little white heron, it is," and he turned again to look at Sylvia with the hope of discovering that the rare bird was one of her acquaintances.

But Sylvia was watching a hop-toad in the narrow footpath.

"You would know the heron if you saw it," the stranger continued eagerly. "A queer tall white bird with soft feathers and long thin legs. And it would have a nest perhaps in the top of a high tree, made of sticks, something like a hawk's nest."

Sylvia's heart gave a wild beat; she knew that strange white bird, and had once stolen softly near where it stood in some bright green swamp grass, away over at the other side of the woods. There was an open place where the sunshine always seemed strangely yellow and hot, where tall, nodding rushes grew, and her grandmother had warned her that she might sink in the soft black mud underneath and never be heard of more. Not far beyond were the salt marshes and beyond those was the sea, the sea which Sylvia wondered and dreamed about, but never had looked upon, though its great voice could often be heard above the noise of the woods on stormy nights.

"I can't think of anything I should like so much as to find that heron's nest," the handsome stranger was saying. "I would give ten dollars to anybody who could show it to me," he added desperately, "and I mean to spend my whole vacation hunting for it if need be. Perhaps it was only migrating, or had been chased out of its own region by some bird of prey."

Mrs. Tilley gave amazed attention to all this, but Sylvia still watched the toad, not divining, as she might have done at some calmer time, that the creature wished to get to its hole under the doorstep, and was much hindered by the unusual spectators at that hour of the evening. No amount of thought, that night, could decide how many wished-for treasures the ten dollars, so lightly spoken of, would buy.

The next day the young sportsman hovered about the woods, and Sylvia kept him company, having lost her first fear of the friendly lad, who proved to be most kind and sympathetic. He told her many things about the birds and what they knew and where they lived and what they did with themselves. And he gave her a jackknife, which she thought as great a treasure as if she were a desert-islander. All day long he did not once make her troubled or afraid except when he brought down some unsuspecting singing creature from its bough. Sylvia would have liked him vastly better without his gun; she could not understand why he killed the very birds he seemed to like so much. But as the day waned, Sylvia still watched the young man with loving admiration. She had never seen anybody so charming and delightful; the woman's heart, asleep in the child, was vaguely thrilled by a dream of love. Some premonition of that great power stirred and swayed these young foresters who traversed the solemn woodlands with soft-footed silent care. They stopped to listen to a bird's song; they pressed forward again eagerly, parting the branches — speaking to each other rarely and in whispers; the young man going first and Sylvia following, fascinated, a few steps behind, with her gray eyes dark with excitement.

She grieved because the longed-for white heron was elusive, but she did not lead the guest, she only followed, and there was no such thing as speaking first. The sound of her own unquestioned voice would have terrified her, — it was hard enough to answer yes or no when there was need of that. At last evening began to fall, and they drove the cow home together, and Sylvia smiled with pleasure when they came to the place where she heard the whistle and was afraid only the night before.

II

Half a mile from home, at the farther edge of the woods, where the land was highest, a great pine-tree stood, the last of its generation. Whether it was left for a boundary mark, or for what reason, no one could say; the woodchoppers who had felled its mates were dead and gone long ago, and a whole forest of sturdy trees, pines and oaks and maples, had grown again. But the stately head of this old pine towered above them all and made a landmark for sea and shore miles and miles away. Sylvia knew it well. She had always believed that whoever climbed to the top of it could see the ocean; and the little girl had often laid her hand on the great rough trunk and looked up wistfully at those dark boughs that the wind always stirred, no matter how hot and still the air might be below. Now she thought of the tree with a new excitement, for why, if one climbed it at break of day, could not one see all the world, and easily discover whence the white heron flew, and mark the place, and find the hidden nest?

What a spirit of adventure, what wild ambition! What fancied triumph and delight and glory for the later morning when she could make known the secret! It was almost too real and too great for the childish heart to bear.

All night the door of the little house stood open, and the whippoorwills came and sang upon the very step. The young sportsman and his old hostess were sound asleep, but Sylvia's great design kept her broad awake and watching. She forgot to think of sleep. The short summer night seemed as long as the winter darkness, and at last when the whippoorwills ceased, and she was afraid the morning would after all come too soon, she stole out of the house and followed the pasture path through the woods, hastening toward the open ground beyond, listening with a sense of comfort and companionship to the drowsy twitter of a half-awakened bird, whose perch she had jarred in passing. Alas, if the great wave of human interest which flooded for the first time this dull little life should sweep away the satisfactions of an existence heart to heart with nature and the dumb life of the forest!

There was the huge tree asleep yet in the paling moonlight, and small and hopeful Sylvia began with utmost bravery to mount to the top of it, with tingling, eager blood coursing the channels of her whole frame, with her bare feet and fingers, that pinched and held like bird's claws to the monstrous ladder reaching up, up almost to the sky itself. First she must mount the white oak tree that grew alongside, where she was almost lost among the dark branches and the green leaves heavy and wet with dew; a bird fluttered off its nest, and a red squirrel ran to and fro and scolded pettishly at the harmless housebreaker. Sylvia felt her way easily. She had often climbed there, and knew that higher still one of the oak's upper branches chafed against the pine trunk, just where its lower boughs were set close together. There, when she made the dangerous pass from one tree to the other, the great enterprise would really begin.

She crept along the swaying oak limb at last, and took the daring step across into the old pine-tree. The way was harder than she thought; she must reach far and hold fast, the sharp dry twigs caught and held her and scratched her like angry talons, the pitch made her thin little fingers clumsy and stiff as she went round and round the tree's great stem, higher and higher upward. The sparrows and robins in the woods below were beginning to wake and twitter to the dawn, yet it seemed much lighter there aloft in the pine-tree, and the child knew that she must hurry if her project were to be of any use.

The tree seemed to lengthen itself out as she went up, and to reach farther and farther upward. It was like a great main-mast to the voyaging earth; it must truly have been amazed that morning through all its ponderous frame as it felt this determined spark of human spirit creeping and climbing from higher branch to branch. Who knows how steadily the least twigs held themselves to advantage this light, weak creature on her way! The old pine must have loved his new dependent. More than all the hawks, and bats, and moths, and even the sweet-voiced thrushes, was the brave, beating heart of the solitary gray-eyed child. And the tree stood still and held away the winds that June morning while the dawn grew bright in the east.

Sylvia's face was like a pale star, if one had seen it from the ground, when the last thorny bough was past, and she stood trembling and tired but wholly triumphant, high in the tree-top. Yes, there was the sea with the dawning sun making a golden dazzle over it, and toward that glorious east flew two hawks with slow-moving pinions. How low they looked in the air from that height when before one had only seen them far up, and dark against the blue sky. Their gray feathers were as soft as moths; they seemed only a little way from the tree, and Sylvia felt as if she too could go flying away among the clouds. Westward, the woodlands and farms reached miles and miles into the distance; here and there were church steeples, and white villages; truly it was a vast and awesome world.

The birds sang louder and louder. At last the sun came up bewilderingly bright. Sylvia could see the white sails of ships out at sea, and the clouds that were purple and rose-colored and yellow at first began to fade away. Where was the white heron's nest in the sea of green branches, and was this wonderful sight and pageant of the world the only reward for having climbed to such a giddy height? Now look down again, Sylvia, where the green marsh is set among the shining birches and dark hemlocks; there where you saw the white heron once you will see him again; look, look! a white spot of him like a single floating feather comes up from the dead hemlock and grows larger, and rises, and comes close at last, and goes by the landmark pine with steady sweep of wing and outstretched slender neck and crested head. And wait! wait! do not move a foot or finger, little girl, do not send an arrow of light and consciousness from your two eager eyes, for the heron has perched on a pine bough not far beyond yours, and cries back to his mate on the nest, and plumes his feathers for the new day!

The child gives a long sigh a minute later when a company of shouting cat-birds comes also to the tree, and vexed by their fluttering and lawlessness the solemn heron goes away. She knows his secret now, the wild, light, slender bird that floats and wavers, and goes back like an arrow presently to his home in the green world beneath. Then Sylvia, well satisfied, makes her perilous way down again, not daring to look far below the branch she stands on, ready to cry sometimes because her fingers ache and her lamed feet slip. Wondering over and over again what the stranger would say to her, and what he would think when she told him how to find his way straight to the heron's nest.

"Sylvy, Sylvy!" called the busy old grandmother again and again, but nobody answered, and the small husk bed was empty, and Sylvia had disappeared.

The guest waked from a dream, and remembering his day's pleasure hurried to dress himself that it might sooner begin. He was sure from the way the shy little girl looked once or twice yesterday that she had at least seen the white heron, and now she must really be persuaded to tell. Here she comes now, paler than ever, and her worn old frock is torn and tattered, and smeared with pine pitch. The grandmother and the sportsman stand in the door together and question her, and the splendid moment has come to speak of the dead hemlock-tree by the green marsh.

But Sylvia does not speak after all, though the old grandmother fretfully rebukes her, and the young man's kind appealing eyes are looking straight in her own. He can make them rich with money; he has promised it, and they are poor now. He is so well worth making happy, and he waits to hear the story she can tell.

No, she must keep silence! What is it that suddenly forbids her and makes her dumb? Has she been nine years growing, and now, when the great world for the first time puts out a hand to her, must she thrust it aside for a bird's sake? The murmur of the pine's green branches in her ears, she remembers how the white heron came flying through the golden air and how they watched the sea and the morning together, and Sylvia cannot speak; she cannot tell the heron's secret and give its life away.

Dear loyalty, that suffered a sharp pang as the guest went away disappointed later in the day, that could have served and followed him and loved him as a dog loves! Many a night Sylvia heard the echo of his whistle haunting the pasture path as she came home with the loitering cow. She forgot even her sorrow at the sharp report of his gun and the piteous sight of thrushes and sparrows dropping silent to the ground, their songs hushed and their pretty feathers stained and wet with blood. Were the birds better friends than their hunter might have been, — who can tell? Whatever treasures were lost to her, woodlands and summer-time, remember! Bring your gifts and graces and tell your secrets to this lonely country child!

[1886]

Study and Writing Questions

1. How is Sylvia CHARACTERIZED? To what extent is she a STEREOTYPE and to what extent does she achieve individuality?
2. How is the cow treated? Why does she play so prominent a role?
3. In the presence of the ornithologist, Sylvia "was vaguely thrilled by a dream of love." What MOTIVATES this dream of love? What kind of love is it? In what way(s) is the STORY about love?
4. Consider the significance of the title. Why is it "a" white heron rather than "the" white heron? Why white? Why a heron? Why does it nest in a "dead hemlock-tree"? What else about the white heron lends it special meaning?
5. Does the manipulation of VIEWPOINT contribute to the effective telling of this story? Why does the NARRATOR repeatedly shift from one mind to another and into OMNISCIENCE? How would you describe the narrator's attitude in the last paragraph of the story? In what way(s), if at all, does that paragraph RESOLVE the CONFLICTS of the narrative?

See also Questions for Contrast and Comparison: 14, 32, 42, 83, 84, 174, 220, 233, and 239.

JAMES (AUGUSTINE ALOYSIUS) JOYCE (1882–1941) *was born and raised in a solidly Roman Catholic family in Dublin, Ireland, and educated at Jesuit institutions, first the prestigious Clongowes Wood College, then, after family financial reversals, at Belvedere College, and University College, Dublin (B.A., 1902). Despising Irish Catholicism as narrow and bigoted, he spent virtually the rest of his life on the European mainland in Trieste, Zurich, and Paris, often supporting himself by language teaching. With his life-long companion, Nora Barnacle, he had a son and daughter. In Joyce's works Dublin, which he thought the "center of [spiritual] paralysis," becomes a microcosm of the modern world. Dubliners (1916) collects fifteen STORIES written between 1904 and 1912, each presenting what Joyce termed an "EPIPHANY," "a sudden spiritual manifestation" in the life of the CHARACTERS. Joyce further developed STREAM-OF-CONSCIOUSNESS NARRATION in his semi-autobiographical* A Portrait of the Artist as a Young Man *(1916). In* Ulysses *(1922), in which each chapter has its own STYLE, the events of a single day in Dublin combine with the epic events of Homer's* Odyssey. Finnegans Wake *(1939) attempts to interweave all MYTHOLOGIES with the Irish experience. Although lionized in his lifetime by such luminaries as Ezra Pound and Ernest Hemingway, only after his death was he universally acknowledged as one of the great founders of MODERNISM.*

Counterparts

The bell rang furiously and, when Miss Parker went to the tube, a furious voice called out in a piercing North of Ireland accent:

"Send Farrington here!"

Miss Parker returned to her machine, saying to a man who was writing at a desk:

"Mr. Alleyne wants you upstairs."

The man muttered "*Blast* him!" under his breath and pushed back his chair to stand up. When he stood up he was tall and of great bulk. He had a hanging face, dark wine-coloured, with fair eyebrows and moustache: his eyes bulged forward slightly and the whites of them were dirty. He lifted up the counter and, passing by the clients, went out of the office with a heavy step.

He went heavily upstairs until he came to the second landing, where a door bore a brass plate with the inscription Mr. Alleyne. Here he halted, puffing with labour and vexation, and knocked. The shrill voice cried:

"Come in!"

The man entered Mr. Alleyne's room. Simultaneously Mr. Alleyne, a little man wearing gold-rimmed glasses on a clean-shaven face, shot his head up over a pile of documents. The head itself was so pink and hairless it seemed like a large egg reposing on the papers. Mr. Alleyne did not lose a moment:

"Farrington? What is the meaning of this? Why have I always to complain of you? May I ask you why you haven't made a copy of that contract between Bodley and Kirwan? I told you it must be ready by four o'clock."

"But Mr. Shelley said, sir —"

"*Mr. Shelley said, sir.* . . . Kindly attend to what I say and not to what Mr. Shelley says, sir. You have always some excuse or another for shirking work. Let me tell you that if the contract is not copied before this evening I'll lay the matter before Mr. Crosbie. . . . Do you hear me now?"

"Yes, sir."

"Do you hear me now? . . . Ay and another little matter! I might as well be talking to the wall as talking to you. Understand once for all that you get a half an hour for your lunch and not an hour and a half. How many courses do you want, I'd like to know. . . . Do you mind me now?"

"Yes, sir."

Mr. Alleyne bent his head again upon his pile of papers. The man stared fixedly at the polished skull which directed the affairs of Crosbie & Alleyne, gauging its fragility. A spasm of rage gripped his throat for a few moments and then passed, leaving after it a sharp sensation of thirst. The man recognised the sensation and felt that he must have a good night's drinking. The middle of the month was passed and, if he could get the copy done in time, Mr. Alleyne might give him an order on the cashier. He stood still, gazing fixedly at the head upon the pile of papers. Suddenly Mr. Alleyne began to upset all the papers, searching for something. Then, as if he had been unaware of the man's presence till that moment, he shot up his head again, saying:

"Eh? Are you going to stand there all day? Upon my word, Farrington, you take things easy!"

"I was waiting to see . . ."

"Very good, you needn't wait to see. Go downstairs and do your work."

The man walked heavily towards the door and, as he went out of the room, he heard Mr. Alleyne cry after him that if the contract was not copied by evening Mr. Crosbie would hear of the matter.

He returned to his desk in the lower office and counted the sheets which remained to be copied. He took up his pen and dipped it in the ink but he continued to stare stupidly at the last words he had written: *In no case shall the said Bernard Bodley be* . . . The evening was falling and in a few minutes they would be lighting the gas: then he could write. He felt that he must slake the thirst in his throat. He stood up from his desk and, lifting the counter as before, passed out of the office. As he was passing out the chief clerk looked at him inquiringly.

"It's all right, Mr. Shelley," said the man, pointing with his finger to indicate the objective of his journey.

The chief clerk glanced at the hat-rack, but, seeing the row complete, offered no remark. As soon as he was on the landing the man pulled a shepherd's plaid cap out of his pocket, put it on his head and ran quickly down the rickety stairs. From the street door he walked on furtively on the inner side of the path towards the corner and all at once dived into a doorway. He was now safe in the dark snug of O'Neill's shop, and filling up the little window that looked into the bar with his inflamed face, the colour of dark wine or dark meat, he called out:

"Here, Pat, give us a g.p., like a good fellow."

The curate brought him a glass of plain porter. The man drank it at a gulp and asked for a caraway seed. He put his penny on the counter and, leaving the curate to grope for it in the gloom, retreated out of the snug as furtively as he had entered it.

Darkness, accompanied by a thick fog, was gaining upon the dusk of February and the lamps in Eustace Street had been lit. The man went up by the houses until he reached the door of the office, wondering whether he could finish his copy in time. On the stairs a moist pungent odour of perfumes saluted his nose: evidently Miss Delacour had come while he was out in O'Neill's. He crammed his cap back again into his pocket and re-entered the office, assuming an air of absent-mindedness.

"Mr. Alleyne has been calling for you," said the chief clerk severely. "Where were you?"

The man glanced at the two clients who were standing at the counter as if to intimate that their presence prevented him from answering. As the clients were both male the chief clerk allowed himself a laugh.

"I know that game," he said. "Five times in one day is a little bit. . . . Well, you better look sharp and get a copy of our correspondence in the Delacour case for Mr. Alleyne."

This address in the presence of the public, his run upstairs and the porter he had gulped down so hastily confused the man and, as he sat down at his desk to get what was required, he realised how hopeless was the task of finishing his copy of the contract before half past five. The dark damp night was coming and he longed to spend it in the bars, drinking with his friends amid the glare of gas and the clatter of glasses. He got out the Delacour correspondence and passed out of the office. He hoped Mr. Alleyne would not discover that the last two letters were missing.

The moist pungent perfume lay all the way up to Mr. Alleyne's room. Miss Delacour was a middle-aged woman of Jewish appearance. Mr. Alleyne was said to be sweet on her or on her money. She came to the office often and stayed a long time when she came. She was sitting beside his desk now in an aroma of perfumes, smoothing the handle of her umbrella and nodding the great black feather in her hat. Mr. Alleyne had swivelled his chair round to face her and thrown his right foot jauntily upon his left knee. The man put the correspondence on the desk and bowed respectfully but neither Mr. Alleyne nor Miss Delacour took any notice of his bow. Mr. Alleyne tapped a finger on the correspondence and then flicked it towards him as if to say: *"That's all right: you can go."*

The man returned to the lower office and sat down again at his desk. He stared intently at the incomplete phrase: *In no case shall the said Bernard Bodley be . . .* and thought how strange it was that the last three words began with the same letter. The chief clerk began to hurry Miss Parker, saying she would never have the letters typed in time for post. The man listened to the clicking of the machine for a few minutes and then set to work to finish his copy. But his head was not clear and his mind wandered away to the glare and rattle of the public-house. It was a night for hot punches. He struggled on with his copy, but when the clock struck five he had still fourteen pages to write. Blast it! He couldn't finish it in time. He longed to execrate aloud, to bring his fist down on something violently. He was so enraged that he wrote *Bernard Bernard* instead of *Bernard Bodley* and had to begin again on a clean sheet.

He felt strong enough to clear out the whole office single-handed. His body ached to do something, to rush out and revel in violence. All the indignities of his life enraged him. . . . Could he ask the cashier privately for an advance? No, the cashier was no good, no damn good: he wouldn't give an advance. . . . He knew where he would meet the boys: Leonard and O'Halloran and Nosey Flynn. The barometer of his emotional nature was set for a spell of riot.

His imagination had so abstracted him that his name was called twice before he answered. Mr. Alleyne and Miss Delacour were standing outside the counter and all the clerks had turned round in anticipation of something. The man got up from his desk. Mr. Alleyne began a tirade of abuse, saying that two letters were missing. The man answered that he knew nothing about them, that he had made a faithful copy. The tirade continued: it was so bitter and violent that the man could hardly restrain his fist from descending upon the head of the manikin before him:

"I know nothing about any other two letters," he said stupidly.

"You—know—nothing. Of course you know nothing," said Mr. Alleyne. "Tell me," he added, glancing first for approval to the lady beside him, "do you take me for a fool? Do you think me an utter fool?"

The man glanced from the lady's face to the little egg-shaped head and back again; and, almost before he was aware of it, his tongue had found a felicitous moment:

"I don't think, sir," he said, "that that's a fair question to put to me."

There was a pause in the very breathing of the clerks. Everyone was astounded (the author of the witticism no less than his neighbours) and Miss Delacour, who was a stout amiable person, began to smile broadly. Mr. Alleyne flushed to the hue of a wild rose and his mouth twitched with a dwarf's passion. He shook his fist in the man's face till it seemed to vibrate like the knob of some electric machine:

"You impertinent ruffian! You impertinent ruffian! I'll make short work of you! Wait till you see! You'll apologise to me for your impertinence or you'll quit the office instanter! You'll quit this, I'm telling you, or you'll apologise to me!"

He stood in a doorway opposite the office watching to see if the cashier would come out alone. All the clerks passed out and finally the cashier came out with the chief clerk. It was no use trying to say a word to him when he was with the chief clerk. The man felt that his position was bad enough. He had been obliged to offer an abject apology to Mr. Alleyne for his impertinence but he knew what a hornet's nest the office would be for him. He could remember the way in which Mr. Alleyne had hounded little Peake out of the office in order to make room for his own nephew. He felt savage and thirsty and revengeful, annoyed with himself and with everyone else. Mr. Alleyne would never give him an hour's rest; his life would be a hell to him. He had made a proper fool of himself this time. Could he not keep his tongue in his cheek? But they had never pulled together from the first, he and Mr. Alleyne, ever since the day Mr. Alleyne had overheard him mimicking his North of Ireland accent to amuse Higgins and Miss Parker: that had been the beginning of it. He might have tried Higgins for the money, but sure Higgins never had anything for himself. A man with two establishments to keep up, of course he couldn't. . . .

He felt his great body again aching for the comfort of the public-house. The fog had begun to chill him and he wondered could he touch Pat in O'Neill's. He could not touch him for more than a bob—and a bob was no use. Yet he must get money somewhere or other: he had spent his last penny for the g.p. and soon it would be too late for getting money anywhere. Suddenly, as he was fingering his watch-chain, he thought of Terry Kelly's pawn-office in Fleet Street. That was the dart! Why didn't he think of it sooner?

He went through the narrow alley of Temple Bar quickly, muttering to himself that they could all go to hell because he was going to have a good night of it. The clerk in Terry Kelly's said A crown! but the consignor held out for six shillings; and in the end the six shillings was allowed him literally. He came out of the pawn-office joyfully, making a little cylinder of the coins between his thumb and fingers. In Westmoreland Street the footpaths were crowded with young men and women returning from business and ragged urchins ran here and there yelling out the names of the evening editions. The man passed through the crowd, looking on the spectacle generally with proud satisfaction and staring masterfully at the office-girls. His head was full of the noises of tram-gongs and swishing trolleys and his nose already sniffed the curling fumes of punch. As he walked on he preconsidered the terms in which he would narrate the incident to the boys:

"So, I just looked at him — coolly, you know, and looked at her. Then I looked back at him again — taking my time, you know. 'I don't think that that's a fair question to put to me,' says I."

Nosey Flynn was sitting up in his usual corner of Davy Byrne's and, when he heard the story, he stood Farrington a half-one, saying it was as smart a thing as ever he heard. Farrington stood a drink in his turn. After a while O'Halloran and Paddy Leonard came in and the story was repeated to them. O'Halloran stood tailors of malt, hot, all round and told the story of the retort he had made to the chief clerk when he was in Callan's of Fownes's Street; but, as the retort was after the manner of the liberal shepherds in the eclogues, he had to admit that it was not as clever as Farrington's retort. At this Farrington told the boys to polish off that and have another.

Just as they were naming their poisons who should come in but Higgins! Of course he had to join in with the others. The men asked him to give his version of it, and he did so with great vivacity for the sight of five small hot whiskies was very exhilarating. Everyone roared laughing when he showed the way in which Mr. Alleyne shook his fist in Farrington's face. Then he imitated Farrington, saying, "And here was my nabs, as cool as you please," while Farrington looked at the company out of his heavy dirty eyes, smiling and at times drawing forth stray drops of liquor from his moustache with the aid of his lower lip.

When that round was over there was a pause. O'Halloran had money but neither of the other two seemed to have any; so the whole party left the shop somewhat regretfully. At the corner of Duke Street Higgins and Nosey Flynn bevelled off to the left while the other three turned back towards the city. Rain was drizzling down on the cold streets and, when they reached the Ballast Office, Farrington suggested the Scotch House. The bar was full of men and loud with the noise of tongues and glasses. The three men pushed past the whining match-sellers at the door and formed a little party at the corner of the counter. They began to exchange stories. Leonard introduced them to a young fellow named Weathers who was performing at the Tivoli as an acrobat and knockabout artiste. Farrington stood a drink all round. Weathers said he would take a small Irish and Apollinaris. Farrington, who had definite notions of what was what, asked the boys would they have an Apollinaris too; but the boys told Tim to make theirs hot. The talk became theatrical. O'Halloran stood a round and then Farrington stood another round, Weathers protesting that the hospitality was too Irish. He promised to get them in behind the scenes and introduce them to some nice girls. O'Halloran said that he and Leonard would go, but that Farrington wouldn't go because he was a married man; and Farrington's heavy dirty eyes leered at the company in token that he understood he was being chaffed. Weathers made them all have just one little tincture at his expense and promised to meet them later on at Mulligan's in Poolbeg Street.

When the Scotch House closed they went round to Mulligan's. They went into the parlour at the back and O'Halloran ordered small hot specials all round. They were all beginning to feel mellow. Farrington was just standing another round when Weathers came back. Much to Farrington's relief he drank a glass of bitter this time. Funds were getting low but they had enough to keep them going. Presently two young women with big hats and a young man in a check suit came in and sat at a table close by. Weathers saluted them and told the company that they were out of the Tivoli. Farrington's eyes wandered at every moment in the direction of one of the young women. There was something striking in her appearance. An immense scarf of peacock-blue muslin was wound round her hat and knotted in a great bow under her chin; and she wore bright yellow gloves, reaching to the elbow. Farrington gazed admiringly at the plump arm which she moved very often and with much grace; and when, after a little time, she answered his gaze he admired still more her large dark brown eyes. The oblique staring expression in them fascinated him. She glanced at him once or twice and, when the party was leaving the room, she brushed against his chair and said "O, pardon!" in a London accent. He watched her leave the room in the hope that she would look back at him, but he was disappointed. He cursed his want of money and cursed all the rounds he had stood, particularly all the whiskies and Apollinaris which he had stood to Weathers. If there was one thing that he hated it was a sponge. He was so angry that he lost count of the conversation of his friends.

When Paddy Leonard called him he found that they were talking about feats of strength. Weathers was showing his biceps muscle to the company and boasting so much that the other two had called on Farrington to uphold the national honour. Farrington pulled up his sleeve accordingly and showed his biceps muscle to the company. The two arms were examined and compared and finally it was agreed to have a trial of strength. The table was cleared and the two men rested their elbows on it, clasping hands. When Paddy Leonard said "Go!" each was to try to bring down the other's hand on to the table. Farrington looked very serious and determined.

The trial began. After about thirty seconds Weathers brought his opponent's hand slowly down on to the table. Farrington's dark wine-coloured face flushed darker still with anger and humiliation at having been defeated by such a stripling.

"You're not to put the weight of your body behind it. Play fair," he said.

"Who's not playing fair?" said the other.

"Come on again. The two best out of three."

The trial began again. The veins stood out on Farrington's forehead, and the pallor of Weathers' complexion changed to peony. Their hands and arms trembled under the stress. After a long struggle Weathers again brought his opponent's hand slowly on to the table. There was a murmur of applause from the spectators. The curate, who was standing beside the table, nodded his red head towards the victor and said with stupid familiarity:

"Ah! that's the knack!"

"What the hell do you know about it?" said Farrington fiercely, turning on the man. "What do you put in your gab for?"

"Sh, sh!" said O'Halloran, observing the violent expression of Farrington's face. "Pony up, boys. We'll have just one little smahan more and then we'll be off."

A very sullen-faced man stood at the corner of O'Connell Bridge waiting for the little Sandymount tram to take him home. He was full of smouldering anger and revengefulness. He felt humiliated and discontented; he did not even feel drunk; and he had only twopence in his pocket. He cursed everything. He had done for himself in the office, pawned his watch, spent all his money; and he had not even got drunk. He began to feel thirsty again and he longed to be back again in the hot reeking public-house. He had lost his reputation as a strong man, having been defeated twice by a mere boy. His heart swelled with fury and, when he thought of the woman in the big hat who had brushed against him and said *Pardon!* his fury nearly choked him.

His tram let him down at Shelbourne Road and he steered his great body along in the shadow of the wall of the barracks. He loathed returning to his home. When he went in by the side-door he found the kitchen empty and the kitchen fire nearly out. He bawled upstairs:

"Ada! Ada!"

His wife was a little sharp-faced woman who bullied her husband when he was sober and was bullied by him when he was drunk. They had five children. A little boy came running down the stairs.

"Who is that?" said the man, peering through the darkness.

"Me, pa."

"Who are you? Charlie?"

"No, pa. Tom."

"Where's your mother?"

"She's out at the chapel."

"That's right. . . . Did she think of leaving any dinner for me?"

"Yes, pa. I —— "

"Light the lamp. What do you mean by having the place in darkness? Are the other children in bed?"

The man sat down heavily on one of the chairs while the little boy lit the lamp. He began to mimic his son's flat accent, saying half to himself: "*At the chapel. At the chapel, if you please!*" When the lamp was lit he banged his fist on the table and shouted:

"What's for my dinner?"

"I'm going . . . to cook it, pa," said the little boy.

The man jumped up furiously and pointed to the fire.

"On that fire! You let the fire out! By God, I'll teach you to do that again!"

He took a step to the door and seized the walking-stick which was standing behind it.

"I'll teach you to let the fire out!" he said, rolling up his sleeve in order to give his arm free play.

The little boy cried "O, pa!" and ran whimpering round the table, but the man followed him and caught him by the coat. The little boy looked about him wildly but, seeing no way of escape, fell upon his knees.

"Now, you'll let the fire out the next time!" said the man, striking at him vigorously with the stick. "Take that, you little whelp!"

The boy uttered a squeal of pain as the stick cut his thigh. He clasped his hands together in the air and his voice shook with fright.

"O, pa!" he cried. "Don't beat me, pa! And I'll . . . I'll say a *Hail Mary* for you. . . . I'll say a *Hail Mary* for you pa, if you don't beat me. . . . I'll say a *Hail Mary*. . . ."

[1914]

Study and Writing Questions

1. Is Farrington's "retort" truly witty? Why does it anger Mr. Alleyne? Why does it please Farrington's drinking partners? What does Farrington himself think of it?
2. What is the ultimate source of Farrington's unhappiness?
3. How are women portrayed in the STORY? How does their portrayal enter into the story as a whole?
4. In what way does the last SCENE serve (or not serve) as a fit ending for the story? What is the story about?
5. What does the title mean?

See also Questions for Contrast and Comparison: 34, 60, 61, 62, 63, 70, 92, and 127.

The Dead

Lily, the caretaker's daughter, was literally run off her feet. Hardly had she brought one gentleman into the little pantry behind the office on the ground floor and helped him off with his overcoat than the wheezy hall-door bell clanged again and she had to scamper along the bare hallway to let in another guest. It was well for her she had not to attend to the ladies also. But Miss Kate and Miss Julia had thought of that and had converted the bathroom upstairs into a ladies' dressing-room. Miss Kate and Miss Julia were there, gossiping and laughing and fussing, walking after each other to the head of the stairs, peering down over the banisters and calling down to Lily to ask her who had come.

It was always a great affair, the Misses Morkan's annual dance. Everybody who knew them came to it, members of the family, old friends of the family, the members of Julia's choir, any of Kate's pupils that were grown up enough and even some of Mary Jane's pupils too. Never once had it fallen flat. For years and years it had gone off in splendid style as long as anyone could remember; ever since Kate and Julia, after the death of their brother Pat, had left the house in Stoney Batter and taken Mary Jane, their only niece, to live with them in the dark gaunt house on Usher's Island, the upper part of which they had rented from Mr Fulham, the corn-factor on the ground floor. That was a good thirty years ago if it was a day. Mary Jane, who was then a little girl in short clothes, was now the main prop of the household for she had the organ in Haddington Road. She had been through the Academy and gave a pupils' concert every year in the upper room of the Antient Concert Rooms. Many of her pupils belonged to better-class families on the Kingstown and Dalkey line. Old as they were, her aunts also did their share. Julia, though she was quite grey, was still the leading soprano in Adam and Eve's, and Kate, being too feeble to go about much, gave music lessons to beginners on the old square piano in the back room. Lily, the caretaker's daughter, did house-maid's work for them. Though their life was modest they believed in eating well; the best of everything; diamond-bone sirloins, three-shilling tea and the best bottled stout. But Lily seldom made a mistake in the orders so that she got on well with her three mistresses. They were fussy, that was all. But the only thing they would not stand was back answers.

Of course they had good reason to be fussy on such a night. And then it was long after ten o'clock and yet there was no sign of Gabriel and his wife. Besides they were dreadfully afraid that Freddy Malins might turn up screwed. They would not wish for worlds that any of Mary Jane's pupils should see him under the influence; and when he was like that it was sometimes very hard to manage him. Freddy Malins always came late but they wondered what could be keeping Gabriel: and that was what brought them every two minutes to the banisters to ask Lily had Gabriel or Freddy come.

—O, Mr Conroy, said Lily to Gabriel when she opened the door for him, Miss Kate and Miss Julia thought you were never coming. Good-night, Mrs Conroy.

—I'll engage they did, said Gabriel, but they forget that my wife here takes three mortal hours to dress herself.

He stood on the mat, scraping the snow from his goloshes, while Lily led his wife to the foot of the stairs and called out:

—Miss Kate, here's Mrs Conroy.

Kate and Julia came toddling down the dark stairs at once. Both of them kissed Gabriel's wife, said she must be perished alive and asked was Gabriel with her.

—Here I am as right as the mail, Aunt Kate! Go on up. I'll follow, called out Gabriel from the dark.

He continued scraping his feet vigorously while the three women went upstairs, laughing, to the ladies' dressing-room. A light fringe of snow lay like a cape on the shoulders of his overcoat and like toecaps on the toes of his goloshes; and, as the buttons of his overcoat slipped with a squeaking noise through the snow-stiffened frieze, a cold fragrant air from out-of-doors escaped from crevices and folds.

—Is it snowing again, Mr Conroy? asked Lily.

She had preceded him into the pantry to help him off with his overcoat. Gabriel smiled at the three syllables she had given his surname and glanced at her. She was a slim, growing girl, pale in complexion and with hay-coloured hair. The gas in the pantry made her look still paler. Gabriel had known her when she was a child and used to sit on the lowest step nursing a rag doll.

—Yes, Lily, he answered, and I think we're in for a night of it.

He looked up at the pantry ceiling, which was shaking with the stamping and shuffling of feet on the floor above, listened for a moment to the piano and then glanced at the girl, who was folding his overcoat carefully at the end of a shelf.

—Tell me, Lily, he said in a friendly tone, do you still go to school?

—O no, sir, she answered. I'd done schooling this year and more.

—O, then, said Gabriel gaily, I suppose we'll be going to your wedding one of these fine days with your young man, eh?

The girl glanced back at him over her shoulder and said with great bitterness:

—The men that is now is only all palaver and what they can get out of you.

Gabriel coloured as if he felt he had made a mistake and, without looking at her, kicked off his goloshes and flicked actively with his muffler at his patent-leather shoes.

He was a stout tallish young man. The high colour of his cheeks pushed upwards even to his forehead where it scattered itself in a few formless patches of pale red; and on his hairless face there scintillated restlessly the polished lenses and the bright gilt rims of the glasses which screened his delicate and restless eyes. His glossy black hair was parted in the middle and brushed in a long curve behind his ears where it curled slightly beneath the groove left by his hat.

When he had flicked lustre into his shoes he stood up and pulled his waist-coat down more tightly on his plump body. Then he took a coin rapidly from his pocket.

—O Lily, he said, thrusting it into her hands, it's Christmas-time, isn't it? Just . . . here's a little. . . .

He walked rapidly towards the door.

—O no, sir! cried the girl, following him. Really, sir, I wouldn't take it.

—Christmas-time! Christmas-time! said Gabriel, almost trotting to the stairs and waving his hand to her in deprecation.

The girl, seeing that he had gained the stairs, called out after him:

—Well, thank you, sir.

He waited outside the drawing-room door until the waltz should finish, listening to the skirts that swept against it and to the shuffling of feet. He was still discomposed by the girl's bitter and sudden retort. It had cast a gloom over him which he tried to dispel by arranging his cuffs and the bows of his tie. Then he took from his waistcoat pocket a little paper and glanced at the headings he had made for his speech. He was undecided about the lines from Robert Browning for he feared they would be above the heads of his hearers. Some quotation that they could recognise from Shakespeare or from the Melodies would be better. The indelicate clacking of the men's heels and the shuffling of their soles reminded him that their grade of culture differed from his. He would only make himself ridiculous by quoting poetry to them which they could not understand. They would think that he was airing his superior education. He would fail with them just as he had failed with the girl in the pantry. He had taken up a wrong tone. His whole speech was a mistake from first to last, an utter failure.

Just then his aunts and his wife came out of the ladies' dressing-room. His aunts were two small plainly dressed old women. Aunt Julia was an inch or so the taller. Her hair, drawn low over the tops of her ears, was grey; and grey also, with darker shadows, was her large flaccid face. Though she was stout in build and stood erect her slow eyes and parted lips gave her the appearance of a woman who did not know where she was or where she was going. Aunt Kate was more vivacious. Her face, healthier than her sister's, was all puckers and creases, like a shrivelled red apple, and her hair, braided in the same old-fashioned way, had not lost its ripe nut colour.

They both kissed Gabriel frankly. He was their favourite nephew, the son of their dead elder sister, Ellen, who had married T.J. Conroy of the Port and Docks.

—Gretta tells me you're not going to take a cab back to Monkstown to-night, Gabriel, said Aunt Kate.

—No, said Gabriel, turning to his wife, we had quite enough of that last year, hadn't we? Don't you remember, Aunt Kate, what a cold Gretta got out of it? Cab windows rattling all the way, and the east wind blowing in after we passed Merrion. Very jolly it was. Gretta caught a dreadful cold.

Aunt Kate frowned severely and nodded her head at every word.

—Quite right, Gabriel, quite right, she said. You can't be too careful.

—But as for Gretta there, said Gabriel, she'd walk home in the snow if she were let.

Mrs Conroy laughed.

—Don't mind him, Aunt Kate, she said. He's really an awful bother, what with green shades for Tom's eyes at night and making him do the dumb-bells, and forcing Eva to eat the stirabout. The poor child! And she simply hates the sight of it! . . . O, but you'll never guess what he makes me wear now!

She broke out into a peal of laughter and glanced at her husband, whose admiring and happy eyes had been wandering from her dress to her face and hair. The two aunts laughed heartily too, for Gabriel's solicitude was a standing joke with them.

—Goloshes! said Mrs Conroy. That's the latest. Whenever it's wet under-foot I must put on my goloshes. To-night even he wanted me to put them on, but I wouldn't. The next thing he'll buy me will be a diving suit.

Gabriel laughed nervously and patted his tie reassuringly while Aunt Kate nearly doubled herself, so heartily did she enjoy the joke. The smile soon faded from Aunt Julia's face and her mirthless eyes were directed towards her nephew's face. After a pause she asked:

—And what are goloshes, Gabriel?

—Goloshes, Julia! exclaimed her sister. Goodness me, don't you know what goloshes are? You wear them over your . . . over your boots, Gretta, isn't it?

—Yes, said Mrs Conroy. Guttapercha things. We both have a pair now. Gabriel says everyone wears them on the continent.

—O, on the continent, murmured Aunt Julia, nodding her head slowly.

Gabriel knitted his brows and said, as if he were slightly angered:

—It's nothing very wonderful but Gretta thinks it very funny because she says the word reminds her of Christy Minstrels.

—But tell me, Gabriel, said Aunt Kate, with brisk tact. Of course, you've seen about the room. Gretta was saying . . .

—O, the room is all right, replied Gabriel. I've taken one in the Gresham.

—To be sure, said Aunt Kate, by far the best thing to do. And the children, Gretta, you're not anxious about them?

—O, for one night, said Mrs Conroy. Besides, Bessie will look after them.

—To be sure, said Aunt Kate again. What a comfort it is to have a girl like that, one you can depend on! There's that Lily, I'm sure I don't know what has come over her lately. She's not the girl she was at all.

Gabriel was about to ask his aunt some questions on this point but she broke off suddenly to gaze after her sister who had wandered down the stairs and was craning her neck over the banisters.

—Now, I ask you, she said, almost testily, where is Julia going? Julia! Julia! Where are you going?

Julia, who had gone halfway down one flight, came back and announced blandly:

—Here's Freddy.

At the same moment a clapping of hands and a final flourish of the pianist told that the waltz had ended. The drawing-room door was opened from within and some couples came out. Aunt Kate drew Gabriel aside hurriedly and whis-pered into his ear:

—Slip down, Gabriel, like a good fellow and see if he's all right, and don't let him up if he's screwed. I'm sure he's screwed. I'm sure he is.

Gabriel went to the stairs and listened over the banisters. He could hear two persons talking in the pantry. Then he recognised Freddy Malins' laugh. He went down the stairs noisily.

—It's such a relief, said Aunt Kate to Mrs Conroy, that Gabriel is here. I always feel easier in my mind when he's here. . . . Julia, there's Miss Daly and Miss Power will take some refreshment. Thanks for your beautiful waltz, Miss Daly. It made lovely time.

A tall wizen-faced man, with a stiff grizzled moustache and swarthy skin, who was passing out with his partner said:

—And may we have some refreshment, too, Miss Morkan?

—Julia, said Aunt Kate summarily, and here's Mr Browne and Miss Furlong. Take them in, Julia, with Miss Daly and Miss Power.

—I'm the man for the ladies, said Mr Browne, pursing his lips until his moustache bristled and smiling in all his wrinkles. You know, Miss Morkan, the reason they are so fond of me is—

He did not finish his sentence, but, seeing that Aunt Kate was out of earshot, at once led the three young ladies into the back room. The middle of the room was occupied by two square tables placed end to end, and on these Aunt Julia and the caretaker were straightening and smoothing a large cloth. On the sideboard were arrayed dishes and plates, and glasses and bundles of knives and forks and spoons. The top of the closed square piano served also as a sideboard for viands and sweets. At a smaller sideboard in one corner two young men were standing, drinking hop-bitters.

Mr Browne led his charges thither and invited them all, in jest, to some ladies' punch, hot, strong and sweet. As they said they never took anything strong he opened three bottles of lemonade for them. Then he asked one of the young men to move aside, and, taking hold of the decanter, filled out for himself a goodly measure of whisky. The young men eyed him respectfully while he took a trial sip.

—God help me, he said, smiling, it's the doctor's orders.

His wizened face broke into a broader smile, and the three young ladies laughed in musical echo to his pleasantry, swaying their bodies to and fro, with nervous jerks of their shoulders. The boldest said:

—O, now, Mr Browne, I'm sure the doctor never ordered anything of the kind.

Mr Browne took another sip of his whisky and said, with sidling mimicry:

—Well, you see, I'm like the famous Mrs Cassidy, who is reported to have said: *Now, Mary Grimes, if I don't take it, make me take it, for I feel I want it.*

His hot face had leaned forward a little too confidentially and he had assumed a very low Dublin accent so that the young ladies, with one instinct, received his speech in silence. Miss Furlong, who was one of Mary Jane's pupils, asked Miss Daly what was the name of the pretty waltz she had played; and Mr Browne, seeing that he was ignored, turned promptly to the two young men who were more appreciative.

A red-faced young woman, dressed in pansy, came into the room, excitedly clapping her hands and crying:

—Quadrilles! Quadrilles!

Close on her heels came Aunt Kate, crying:

—Two gentlemen and three ladies, Mary Jane!

—O, here's Mr Bergin and Mr Kerrigan, said Mary Jane. Mr Kerrigan, will you take Miss Power? Miss Furlong, may I get you a partner, Mr Bergin. O, that'll just do now.

—Three ladies, Mary Jane, said Aunt Kate.

The two young gentlemen asked the ladies if they might have the pleasure, and Mary Jane turned to Miss Daly.

—O, Miss Daly, you're really awfully good, after playing for the last two dances, but really we're so short of ladies to-night.

—I don't mind in the least, Miss Morkan.

—But I've a nice partner for you, Mr Bartell D'Arcy, the tenor. I'll get him to sing later on. All Dublin is raving about him.

—Lovely voice, lovely voice! said Aunt Kate.

As the piano had twice begun the prelude to the first figure Mary Jane led her recruits quickly from the room. They had hardly gone when Aunt Julia wandered slowly into the room, looking behind her at something.

—What is the matter, Julia? asked Aunt Kate anxiously. Who is it?

Julia, who was carrying in a column of table-napkins, turned to her sister and said, simply, as if the question had surprised her:

—It's only Freddy, Kate, and Gabriel with him.

In fact right behind her Gabriel could be seen piloting Freddy Malins across the landing. The latter, a young man of about forty, was of Gabriel's size and build, with very round shoulders. His face was fleshy and pallid, touched with colour only at the thick hanging lobes of his ears and at the wide wings of his nose. He had coarse features, a blunt nose, a convex and receding brow, tumid and protruding lips. His heavy-lidded eyes and the disorder of his scanty hair made him look sleepy. He was laughing heartily in a high key at a story which he had been telling Gabriel on the stairs and at the same time rubbing the knuckles of his left fist backwards and forwards into his left eye.

—Good-evening, Freddy, said Aunt Julia.

Freddy Malins bade the Misses Morkan good-evening in what seemed an off-hand fashion by reason of the habitual catch in his voice and then, seeing that Mr Browne was grinning at him from the sideboard, crossed the room on rather shaky legs and began to repeat in an undertone the story he had just told to Gabriel.

—He's not so bad, is he? said Aunt Kate to Gabriel.

Gabriel's brows were dark but he raised them quickly and answered:

—O no, hardly noticeable.

—Now, isn't he a terrible fellow! she said. And his poor mother made him take the pledge on New Year's Eve. But come on, Gabriel, into the drawing-room.

Before leaving the room with Gabriel she signalled to Mr Browne by frowning and shaking her forefinger in warning to and fro. Mr Browne nodded in answer and, when she had gone, said to Freddy Malins:

—Now, then, Teddy, I'm going to fill you out a good glass of lemonade just to buck you up.

Freddy Malins, who was nearing the climax of his story, waved the offer aside impatiently but Mr Browne, having first called Freddy Malins' attention to a disarray in his dress, filled out and handed him a full glass of lemonade. Freddy Malins' left hand accepted the glass mechanically, his right hand being engaged in the mechanical readjustment of his dress. Mr Browne, whose face was once more wrinkling with mirth, poured out for himself a glass of whisky while Freddy Malins exploded, before he had well reached the climax of his story, in a kink of high-pitched bronchitic laughter and, setting down his untasted and overflowing glass, began to rub the knuckles of his left fist backwards and forwards into his left eye, repeating words of his last phrase as well as his fit of laughter would allow him.

Gabriel could not listen while Mary Jane was playing her Academy piece, full of runs and difficult passages, to the hushed drawing-room. He liked music but the piece she was playing had no melody for him and he doubted whether it had any melody for the other listeners, though they had begged Mary Jane to play something. Four young men, who had come from the refreshment-room to stand in the doorway at the sound of the piano, had gone away quietly in couples after a few minutes. The only persons who seemed to follow the music were Mary Jane herself, her hands racing along the key-board or lifted from it at the pauses like those of a priestess in momentary imprecation, and Aunt Kate standing at her elbow to turn the page.

Gabriel's eye, irritated by the floor, which glittered with beeswax under the heavy chandelier, wandered to the wall above the piano. A picture of the balcony scene in *Romeo and Juliet* hung there and beside it was a picture of the two murdered princes in the Tower which Aunt Julia had worked in red, blue and brown wools when she was a girl. Probably in the school they had gone to as girls that kind of work had been taught, for one year his mother had worked for him as a birthday present a waistcoat of purple tabinet, with little foxes' heads upon it, lined with brown satin and having round mulberry buttons. It was strange that his mother had had no musical talent though Aunt Kate used to call her the brains carrier of the Morkan family. Both she and Julia had always seemed a little proud of their serious and matronly sister. Her photograph stood before the pierglass. She held an open book on her knees and was pointing out something in it to Constantine who, dressed in a man-o'-war suit, lay at her feet. It was she who had chosen the names for her sons for she was very sensible of the dignity of family life. Thanks to her, Constantine was now senior curate in Balbriggan and, thanks to her, Gabriel himself had taken his degree in the Royal University. A shadow passed over his face as he remembered her sullen opposition to his marriage. Some slighting phrases she had used still rankled in his memory; she had once spoken of Gretta as being country cute and that was not true of Gretta at all. It was Gretta who had nursed her during all her last long illness in their house at Monkstown.

He knew that Mary Jane must be near the end of her piece for she was playing again the opening melody with runs of scales after every bar and while he waited for the end the resentment died down in his heart. The piece ended with a trill of octaves in the treble and a final deep octave in the bass. Great applause greeted Mary Jane as, blushing and rolling up her music nervously, she escaped from the room. The most vigorous clapping came from the four young men in the doorway who had gone away to the refreshment-room at the beginning of the piece but had come back when the piano had stopped.

Lancers were arranged. Gabriel found himself partnered with Miss Ivors. She was a frank-mannered talkative young lady, with a freckled face and prominent brown eyes. She did not wear a low-cut bodice and the large brooch which was fixed in the front of her collar bore on it an Irish device.

When they had taken their places she said abruptly:

—I have a crow to pluck with you.

—With me? said Gabriel.

She nodded her head gravely.

—What is it? asked Gabriel, smiling at her solemn manner.

—Who is G. C.? answered Miss Ivors, turning her eyes upon him.

Gabriel coloured and was about to knit his brows, as if he did not understand, when she said bluntly:

—O, innocent Amy! I have found out that you write for *The Daily Express*. Now, aren't you ashamed of yourself?

—Why should I be ashamed of myself? asked Gabriel, blinking his eyes and trying to smile.

—Well, I'm ashamed of you, said Miss Ivors frankly. To say you'd write for a rag like that. I didn't think you were a West Briton.

A look of perplexity appeared on Gabriel's face. It was true that he wrote a literary column every Wednesday in *The Daily Express*, for which he was paid fifteen shillings. But that did not make him a West Briton surely. The books he received for review were almost more welcome than the paltry cheque. He loved to feel the covers and turn over the pages of newly printed books. Nearly every day when his teaching in the college was ended he used to wander down the quays to the second-hand booksellers, to Hickey's on Bachelor's Walk, to Webb's or Massey's on Aston's Quay, or to O'Clohissey's in the by-street. He did not know how to meet her charge. He wanted to say that literature was above politics. But they were friends of many years' standing and their careers had been parallel, first at the University and then as teachers: he could not risk a grandiose phrase with her. He continued blinking his eyes and trying to smile and murmured lamely that he saw nothing political in writing reviews of books.

When their turn to cross had come he was still perplexed and inattentive. Miss Ivors promptly took his hand in a warm grasp and said in a soft friendly tone:

—Of course, I was only joking. Come, we cross now.

When they were together again she spoke of the University question and Gabriel felt more at ease. A friend of hers had shown her his review of Browning's poems. That was how she had found out the secret: but she liked the review immensely. Then she said suddenly:

—O, Mr Conroy, will you come for an excursion to the Aran Isles this summer? We're going to stay there a whole month. It will be splendid out in the Atlantic. You ought to come. Mr Clancy is coming, and Mr Kilkelly and Kathleen Kearney. It would be splendid for Gretta too if she'd come. She's from Connacht, isn't she?

—Her people are, said Gabriel shortly.

—But you will come, won't you? said Miss Ivors, laying her warm hand eagerly on his arm.

—The fact is, said Gabriel, I have already arranged to go—

—Go where? asked Miss Ivors.

—Well, you know, every year I go for a cycling tour with some fellows and so—

—But where? asked Miss Ivors.

—Well, we usually go to France or Belgium or perhaps Germany, said Gabriel awkwardly.

—And why do you go to France and Belgium, said Miss Ivors, instead of visiting your own land?

—Well, said Gabriel, it's partly to keep in touch with the languages and partly for a change.

—And haven't you your own language to keep in touch with—Irish? asked Miss Ivors.

—Well, said Gabriel, if it comes to that, you know, Irish is not my language.

Their neighbours had turned to listen to the cross-examination. Gabriel glanced right and left nervously and tried to keep his good humour under the ordeal which was making a blush invade his forehead.

—And haven't you your own land to visit, continued Miss Ivors, that you know nothing of, your own people, and your own country?

—O, to tell you the truth, retorted Gabriel suddenly, I'm sick of my own country, sick of it!

—Why? asked Miss Ivors.

Gabriel did not answer for his retort had heated him.

—Why? repeated Miss Ivors.

They had to go visiting together and, as he had not answered her, Miss Ivors said warmly:

—Of course, you've no answer.

Gabriel tried to cover his agitation by taking part in the dance with great energy. He avoided her eyes for he had seen a sour expression on her face. But when they met in the long chain he was surprised to feel his hand firmly pressed. She looked at him from under her brows for a moment quizzically until he smiled. Then, just as the chain was about to start again, she stood on tiptoe and whispered into his ear:

—West Briton!

When the lancers were over Gabriel went away to a remote corner of the room where Freddy Malins' mother was sitting. She was a stout feeble old woman with white hair. Her voice had a catch in it like her son's and she stuttered slightly. She had been told that Freddy had come and that he was nearly all right. Gabriel asked her whether she had had a good crossing. She lived with her married daughter in Glasgow and came to Dublin on a visit once a year. She answered placidly that she had had a beautiful crossing and that the captain had been most attentive to her. She spoke also of the beautiful house her daughter kept in Glasgow, and of all the nice friends they had there. While her tongue rambled on Gabriel tried to banish from his mind all memory of the unpleasant incident with Miss Ivors. Of course the girl or woman, or whatever she was, was an enthusiast but there was a time for all things. Perhaps he ought not to have answered her like that. But she had no right to call him a West Briton before people, even in joke. She had tried to make him ridiculous before people, heckling him and staring at him with her rabbit's eyes.

He saw his wife making her way towards him through the waltzing couples. When she reached him she said into his ear:

—Gabriel, Aunt Kate wants to know won't you carve the goose as usual. Miss Daly will carve the ham and I'll do the pudding.

—All right, said Gabriel.

—She's sending in the younger ones first as soon as this waltz is over so that we'll have the tables to ourselves.

—Were you dancing? asked Gabriel.

—Of course I was. Didn't you see me? What words had you with Molly Ivors?

—No words. Why? Did she say so?

—Something like that. I'm trying to get that Mr D'Arcy to sing. He's full of conceit, I think.

—There were no words, said Gabriel moodily, only she wanted me to go for a trip to the west of Ireland and I said I wouldn't.

His wife clasped her hands excitedly and gave a little jump.

—O, do go, Gabriel, she cried. I'd love to see Galway again.

—You can go if you like, said Gabriel coldly.

She looked at him for a moment, then turned to Mrs Malins and said:

—There's a nice husband for you, Mrs Malins.

While she was threading her way back across the room Mrs Malins, without adverting to the interruption, went on to tell Gabriel what beautiful places there were in Scotland and beautiful scenery. Her son-in-law brought them every year to the lakes and they used to go fishing. Her son-in-law was a splendid fisher. One day he caught a fish, a beautiful big big fish, and the man in the hotel boiled it for their dinner.

Gabriel hardly heard what she said. Now that supper was coming near he began to think again about his speech and about the quotation. When he saw Freddy Malins coming across the room to visit his mother Gabriel left the chair free for him and retired into the embrasure of the window. The room had already cleared and from the back room came the clatter of plates and knives. Those who still remained in the drawing-room seemed tired of dancing and were conversing quietly in little groups. Gabriel's warm trembling fingers tapped the cold pane of the window. How cool it must be outside! How pleasant it would be to walk out alone, first along by the river and then through the park! The snow would be lying on the branches of the trees and forming a bright cap on the top of the Wellington Monument. How much more pleasant it would be there than at the supper-table!

He ran over the headings of his speech: Irish hospitality, sad memories, the Three Graces, Paris, the quotation from Browning. He repeated to himself a phrase he had written in his review: *One feels that one is listening to a thought-tormented music*. Miss Ivors had praised the review. Was she sincere? Had she really any life of her own behind all her propagandism? There had never been any ill-feeling between them until that night. It unnerved him to think that she would be at the supper-table, looking up at him while he spoke with her critical quizzing eyes. Perhaps she would not be sorry to see him fail in his speech. An idea came into his mind and gave him courage. He would say, alluding to Aunt Kate and Aunt Julia: *Ladies and Gentlemen, the generation which is now on the wane among us may have had its faults but for my part I think it had certain qualities of hospitality, of humour, of humanity, which the new and very serious and hypereducated generation that is growing up around us seems to me to lack*. Very good: that was one for Miss Ivors. What did he care that his aunts were only two ignorant old women?

A murmur in the room attracted his attention. Mr Browne was advancing from the door, gallantly escorting Aunt Julia, who leaned upon his arm, smiling and hanging her head. An irregular musketry of applause escorted her also as far as the piano and then, as Mary Jane seated herself on the stool, and Aunt Julia, no longer smiling, half turned so as to pitch her voice fairly into the room, gradually ceased. Gabriel recognised the prelude. It was that of an old song of Aunt Julia's — *Arrayed for the Bridal*. Her voice, strong and clear in tone, attacked with great spirit the runs which embellish the air and though she sang very rapidly she did not miss even the smallest of the grace notes. To follow the voice, without looking at the singer's face, was to feel and share the excitement of swift and secure flight. Gabriel applauded loudly with all the others at the close of the song and loud applause was borne in from the invisible supper-table. It sounded so genuine that a little colour struggled into Aunt Julia's face as she bent to replace in the music-stand the old leather-bound song-book that had her initials on the cover. Freddy Malins, who had listened with his head perched sideways to hear her better, was still applauding when everyone else had ceased and talking animatedly to his mother who nodded her head gravely and slowly in acquiescence. At last, when he could clap no more, he stood up suddenly and hurried across the room to Aunt Julia whose hand he seized and held in both his hands, shaking it when words failed him or the catch in his voice proved too much for him.

— I was just telling my mother, he said, I never heard you sing so well, never. No, I never heard your voice so good as it is to-night. Now! Would you believe that now! That's the truth. Upon my word and honour that's the truth. I never heard your voice sound so fresh and so . . . so clear and fresh, never.

Aunt Julia smiled broadly and murmured something about compliments as she released her hand from his grasp. Mr Browne extended his open hand towards her and said to those who were near him in the manner of a showman introducing a prodigy to an audience:

— Miss Julia Morkan, my latest discovery!

He was laughing very heartily at this himself when Freddy Malins turned to him and said:

— Well, Browne, if you're serious you might make a worse discovery. All I can say is I never heard her sing half so well as long as I am coming here. And that's the honest truth.

— Neither did I, said Mr Browne. I think her voice has greatly improved.

Aunt Julia shrugged her shoulders and said with meek pride:

— Thirty years ago I hadn't a bad voice as voices go.

— I often told Julia, said Aunt Kate emphatically, that she was simply thrown away in that choir. But she never would be said by me.

She turned as if to appeal to the good sense of the others against a refractory child while Aunt Julia gazed in front of her, a vague smile of reminiscence playing on her face.

— No, continued Aunt Kate, she wouldn't be said or led by anyone, slaving there in that choir night and day, night and day. Six o'clock on Christmas morning! And all for what?

—Well, isn't it for the honour of God, Aunt Kate? asked Mary Jane, twisting round on the piano-stool and smiling.

Aunt Kate turned fiercely on her niece and said:

—I know all about the honour of God, Mary Jane, but I think it's not at all honourable for the pope to turn out the women out of the choirs that have slaved there all their lives and put little whipper-snappers of boys over their heads. I suppose it is for the good of the Church if the pope does it. But it's not just, Mary Jane, and it's not right.

She had worked herself into a passion and would have continued in defence of her sister for it was a sore subject with her but Mary Jane, seeing that all the dancers had come back, intervened pacifically:

—Now, Aunt Kate, you're giving scandal to Mr Browne who is of the other persuasion.

Aunt Kate turned to Mr Browne, who was grinning at this allusion to his religion, and said hastily:

—O, I don't question the pope's being right. I'm only a stupid old woman and I wouldn't presume to do such a thing. But there's such a thing as common everyday politeness and gratitude. And if I were in Julia's place I'd tell that Father Healy straight up to his face. . . .

—And besides, Aunt Kate, said Mary Jane, we really are all hungry and when we are hungry we are all very quarrelsome.

—And when we are thirsty we are also quarrelsome, added Mr Browne.

—So that we had better go to supper, said Mary Jane, and finish the discussion afterwards.

On the landing outside the drawing-room Gabriel found his wife and Mary Jane trying to persuade Miss Ivors to stay for supper. But Miss Ivors, who had put on her hat and was buttoning her cloak, would not stay. She did not feel in the least hungry and she had already overstayed her time.

—But only for ten minutes, Molly, said Mrs Conroy. That won't delay you.

—To take a pick itself, said Mary Jane, after all your dancing.

—I really couldn't, said Miss Ivors.

—I am afraid you didn't enjoy yourself at all, said Mary Jane hopelessly.

—Ever so much, I assure you, said Miss Ivors, but you really must let me run off now.

—But how can you get home? asked Mrs Conroy.

—O, it's only two steps up the quay.

Gabriel hesitated a moment and said:

—If you will allow me, Miss Ivors, I'll see you home if you really are obliged to go.

But Miss Ivors broke away from them.

—I won't hear of it, she cried. For goodness sake go in to your suppers and don't mind me. I'm quite well able to take care of myself.

—Well, you're the comical girl, Molly, said Mrs Conroy frankly.

—*Beannacht libh*, cried Miss Ivors, with a laugh, as she ran down the staircase.

Mary Jane gazed after her, a moody puzzled expression on her face, while Mrs Conroy leaned over the banisters to listen for the hall-door. Gabriel asked himself was he the cause of her abrupt departure. But she did not seem to be in ill humour: she had gone away laughing. He stared blankly down the staircase.

At that moment Aunt Kate came toddling out of the supper-room, almost wringing her hands in despair.

—Where is Gabriel? she cried. Where on earth is Gabriel? There's everyone waiting in there, stage to let, and nobody to carve the goose!

—Here I am, Aunt Kate! cried Gabriel, with sudden animation, ready to carve a flock of geese, if necessary.

A fat brown goose lay at one end of the table and at the other end, on a bed of creased paper strewn with sprigs of parsley, lay a great ham, stripped of its outer skin and peppered over with crust crumbs, a neat paper frill round its shin and beside this was a round of spiced beef. Between these rival ends ran parallel lines of side-dishes: two little minsters of jelly, red and yellow; a shallow dish full of blocks of blancmange and red jam, a large green leaf-shaped dish with a stalk-shaped handle, on which lay bunches of purple raisins and peeled almonds, a companion dish on which lay a solid rectangle of Smyrna figs, a dish of custard topped with grated nutmeg, a small bowl full of chocolates and sweets wrapped in gold and silver papers and a glass vase in which stood some tall celery stalks. In the centre of the table there stood, as sentries to a fruit-stand which upheld a pyramid of oranges and American apples, two squat old-fashioned decanters of cut glass, one containing port and the other dark sherry. On the closed square piano a pudding in a huge yellow dish lay in waiting and behind it were three squads of bottles of stout and ale and minerals, drawn up according to the colours of their uniforms, the first two black, with brown and red labels, the third and smallest squad white, with transverse green sashes.

Gabriel took his seat boldly at the head of the table and, having looked to the edge of the carver, plunged his fork firmly into the goose. He felt quite at ease now for he was an expert carver and liked nothing better than to find himself at the head of a well-laden table.

—Miss Furlong, what shall I send you? he asked. A wing or a slice of the breast?

—Just a small slice of the breast.

—Miss Higgins, what for you?

—O, anything at all, Mr Conroy.

While Gabriel and Miss Daly exchanged plates of goose and plates of ham and spiced beef Lily went from guest to guest with a dish of hot floury potatoes wrapped in a white napkin. This was Mary Jane's idea and she had also suggested apple sauce for the goose but Aunt Kate had said that plain roast goose without apple sauce had always been good enough for her and she hoped she might never eat worse. Mary Jane waited on her pupils and saw that they got the best slices and Aunt Kate and Aunt Julia opened and carried across from the piano bottles of stout and ale for the gentlemen and bottles of minerals for the ladies. There was a great deal of confusion and laughter and noise, the noise of orders and counter-orders, of knives and forks, of corks and glass-toppers. Gabriel began to carve second helpings as soon as he had finished the first round without serving himself. Everyone protested loudly so that he compromised by taking a long draught of stout for he had found the carving hot work. Mary Jane settled down quietly to her supper but Aunt Kate and Aunt Julia were still toddling round the table, walking on each other's heels, getting in each other's way and giving each other unheeded orders. Mr Browne begged of them to sit down and eat their suppers and so did Gabriel but they said there was time enough so that, at last, Freddy Malins stood up and, capturing Aunt Kate, plumped her down on her chair amid general laughter.

When everyone had been well served Gabriel said, smiling:

—Now, if anyone wants a little more of what vulgar people call stuffing let him or her speak.

A chorus of voices invited him to begin his own supper and Lily came forward with three potatoes which she had reserved for him.

—Very well, said Gabriel amiably, as he took another preparatory draught, kindly forget my existence, ladies and gentlemen, for a few minutes.

He set to his supper and took no part in the conversation with which the table covered Lily's removal of the plates. The subject of talk was the opera company which was then at the Theatre Royal. Mr Bartell D'Arcy, the tenor, a dark-complexioned young man with a smart moustache, praised very highly the leading contralto of the company but Miss Furlong thought she had a rather vulgar style of production. Freddy Malins said there was a negro chieftain singing in the second part of the Gaiety pantomime who had one of the finest tenor voices he had ever heard.

—Have you heard him? he asked Mr Bartell D'Arcy across the table.

—No, answered Mr Bartell D'Arcy carelessly.

—Because, Freddy Malins explained, now I'd be curious to hear your opinion of him. I think he has a grand voice.

—It takes Teddy to find out the really good things, said Mr Browne familiarly to the table.

—And why couldn't he have a voice too? asked Freddy Malins sharply. Is it because he's only a black?

Nobody answered this question and Mary Jane led the table back to the legitimate opera. One of her pupils had given her a pass for *Mignon*. Of course it was very fine, she said, but it made her think of poor Georgina Burns. Mr Browne could go back farther still, to the old Italian companies that used to come to Dublin—Teitjens, Ilma de Murzka, Campanini, the great Trebelli, Giuglini, Ravelli, Aramburo. Those were the days, he said, when there was something like singing to be heard in Dublin. He told too of how the top gallery of the old Royal used to be packed night after night, of how one night an Italian tenor had sung five encores to *Let Me Like a Soldier Fall*, introducing a high C every time, and of how the gallery boys would sometimes in their enthusiasm unyoke the horses from the carriage of some great *prima donna* and pull her themselves through the streets to her hotel. Why did they never play the grand old operas now, he asked, *Dinorah*, *Lucrezia Borgia*? Because they could not get the voices to sing them: that was why.

—O, well, said Mr Bartell D'Arcy, I presume there are as good singers to-day as there were then.

—Where are they? asked Mr Browne defiantly.

—In London, Paris, Milan, said Mr Bartell D'Arcy warmly. I suppose Caruso, for example, is quite as good, if not better than any of the men you have mentioned.

—Maybe so, said Mr Browne. But I may tell you I doubt it strongly.

—O, I'd give anything to hear Caruso sing, said Mary Jane.

—For me, said Aunt Kate, who had been picking a bone, there was only one tenor. To please me, I mean. But I suppose none of you ever heard of him.

—Who was he, Miss Morkan? asked Mr Bartell D'Arcy politely.

—His name, said Aunt Kate, was Parkinson. I heard him when he was in his prime and I think he had then the purest tenor voice that was ever put into a man's throat.

—Strange, said Mr Bartell D'Arcy. I never even heard of him.

—Yes, yes, Miss Morkan is right, said Mr Browne. I remember hearing of old Parkinson but he's too far back for me.

—A beautiful pure sweet mellow English tenor, said Aunt Kate with enthusiasm.

Gabriel having finished, the huge pudding was transferred to the table. The clatter of forks and spoons began again. Gabriel's wife served out spoonfuls of the pudding and passed the plates down the table. Midway down they were held up by Mary Jane, who replenished them with raspberry or orange jelly or with blancmange and jam. The pudding was of Aunt Julia's making and she received praises for it from all quarters. She herself said that it was not quite brown enough.

—Well, I hope, Miss Morkan, said Mr Browne, that I'm brown enough for you because, you know, I'm all brown.

All the gentlemen, except Gabriel, ate some of the pudding out of compliment to Aunt Julia. As Gabriel never ate sweets the celery had been left for him. Freddy Malins also took a stalk of celery and ate it with his pudding. He had been told that celery was a capital thing for the blood and he was just then under the doctor's care. Mrs Malins, who had been silent all through the supper, said that her son was going down to Mount Melleray in a week or so. The table then spoke of Mount Melleray, how bracing the air was down there, how hospitable the monks were and how they never asked for a penny-piece from their guests.

—And do you mean to say, asked Mr Browne incredulously, that a chap can go down there and put up there as if it were a hotel and live on the fat of the land and then come away without paying a farthing?

—O, most people give some donation to the monastery when they leave, said Mary Jane.

—I wish we had an institution like that in our Church, said Mr Browne candidly.

He was astonished to hear that monks never spoke, got up at two in the morning and slept in their coffins. He asked what they did it for.

—That's the rule of the order, said Aunt Kate firmly.

—Yes, but why? asked Mr Browne.

Aunt Kate repeated that it was the rule, that was all. Mr Browne still seemed not to understand. Freddy Malins explained to him, as best he could, that the monks were trying to make up for the sins committed in the outside world. The explanation was not very clear for Mr Browne grinned and said:

— I like that idea very much but wouldn't a comfortable spring bed do them as well as a coffin?

— The coffin, said Mary Jane, is to remind them of their last end.

As the subject had grown lugubrious it was buried in a silence of the table during which Mrs Malins could be heard saying to her neighbour in an indistinct undertone:

— They are very good men, the monks, very pious men.

The raisins and almonds and figs and apples and oranges and chocolates and sweets were now passed about the table and Aunt Julia invited all the guests to have either port or sherry. At first Mr Bartell D'Arcy refused to take either but one of his neighbours nudged him and whispered something to him upon which he allowed his glass to be filled. Gradually as the last glasses were being filled the conversation ceased. A pause followed, broken only by the noise of the wine and by unsettlings of chairs. The Misses Morkan, all three, looked down at the tablecloth. Someone coughed once or twice and then a few gentlemen patted the table gently as a signal for silence. The silence came and Gabriel pushed back his chair and stood up.

The patting at once grew louder in encouragement and then ceased altogether. Gabriel leaned his ten trembling fingers on the tablecloth and smiled nervously at the company. Meeting a row of upturned faces he raised his eyes to the chandelier. The piano was playing a waltz tune and he could hear the skirts sweeping against the drawing-room door. People, perhaps, were standing in the snow on the quay outside, gazing up at the lighted windows and listening to the waltz music. The air was pure there. In the distance lay the park where the trees were weighted with snow. The Wellington Monument wore a gleaming cap of snow that flashed westward over the white field of Fifteen Acres.

He began:

— Ladies and Gentlemen.

— It has fallen to my lot this evening, as in years past, to perform a very pleasant task but a task for which I am afraid my poor powers as a speaker are all too inadequate.

— No, no! said Mr Browne.

— But, however that may be, I can only ask you to-night to take the will for the deed and to lend me your attention for a few moments while I endeavor to express to you in words what my feelings are on this occasion.

— Ladies and Gentlemen. It is not the first time that we have gathered together under this hospitable roof, around this hospitable board. It is not the first time that we have been the recipients — or perhaps, I had better say, the victims — of the hospitality of certain good ladies.

He made a circle in the air with his arm and paused. Everyone laughed or smiled at Aunt Kate and Aunt Julia and Mary Jane who all turned crimson with pleasure. Gabriel went on more boldly:

— I feel more strongly with every recurring year that our country has no tradition which does it so much honour and which it should guard so jealously as that of its hospitality. It is a tradition that is unique as far as my experience goes (and I have visited not a few places abroad) among the modern nations. Some would say, perhaps, that with us it is rather a failing than anything to be boasted of. But granted even that, it is, to my mind, a princely failing, and one that I trust will long be cultivated among us. Of one thing, at least, I am sure. As long as this one roof shelters the good ladies aforesaid—and I wish from my heart it may do so for many and many a long year to come—the tradition of genuine warmhearted courteous Irish hospitality, which our forefathers have handed down to us and which we in turn must hand down to our descendants, is still alive among us.

A hearty murmur of ascent ran round the table. It shot through Gabriel's mind that Miss Ivors was not there and that she had gone away discourteously: and he said with confidence in himself:

—Ladies and Gentlemen.

—A new generation is growing up in our midst, a generation actuated by new ideas and new principles. It is serious and enthusiastic for these new ideas and its enthusiasm, even when it is misdirected, is, I believe, in the main sincere. But we are living in a skeptical and, if I may use the phrase, a thought-tormented age: and sometimes I fear that this new generation, educated or hypereducated as it is, will lack those qualities of humanity, of hospitality, of kindly humour which belonged to an older day. Listening tonight to the names of all those great singers of the past it seemed to me, I must confess, that we were living in a less spacious age. Those days might, without exaggeration, be called spacious days: and if they are gone beyond recall let us hope, at least, that in gatherings such as this we shall still speak of them with pride and affection, still cherish in our hearts the memory of those dead and gone great ones whose fame the world will not willingly let die.

—Hear, hear! said Mr Browne loudly.

—But yet, continued Gabriel, his voice falling into a softer inflection, there are always in gatherings such as this sadder thoughts that will recur to our minds: thoughts of the past, of youth, of changes, of absent faces that we miss here to-night. Our path through life is strewn with many such sad memories: and were we to brood upon them always we could not find the heart to go on bravely with our work among the living. We have all of us living duties and living affections which claim, and rightly claim, our strenuous endeavors.

—Therefore, I will not linger on the past. I will not let any gloomy moralising intrude upon us here to-night. Here we are gathered together for a brief moment from the bustle and rush of our everyday routine. We are met here as friends, in the spirit of good-fellowship, as colleagues, also to a certain extent, in the true spirit of *camaraderie*, and as the guests of—what shall I call them?—the Three Graces of the Dublin musical world.

The table burst into applause and laughter at this sally. Aunt Julia vainly asked each of her neighbours in turn to tell her what Gabriel had said.

—He says we are the Three Graces, Aunt Julia, said Mary Jane.

Aunt Julia did not understand but she looked up, smiling, at Gabriel, who continued in the same vein:

—Ladies and Gentlemen.

—I will not attempt to play to-night the part that Paris played on another occasion. I will not attempt to choose between them. The task would be an invidious one and one beyond my poor powers. For when I view them in turn, whether it be our chief hostess herself, whose good heart, whose too good heart, has become a byword with all who know her, or her sister, who seems to be gifted with perennial youth and whose singing must have been a surprise and a revelation to us all tonight, or, last but not least, when I consider our youngest hostess, talented, cheerful, hard-working and the best of nieces, I confess, Ladies and Gentlemen, that I do not know to which of them I should award the prize.

Gabriel glanced down at his aunts and, seeing the large smile on Aunt Julia's face and the tears which had risen to Aunt Kate's eyes, hastened to close. He raised his glass of port gallantly, while every member of the company fingered a glass expectantly, and said loudly:

— Let us toast them all three together. Let us drink to their health, wealth, long life, happiness and prosperity and may they long continue to hold the proud and self-won position which they hold in their profession and the position of honour and affection which they hold in our hearts.

All the guests stood up, glass in hand, and, turning towards the three seated ladies, sang in unison, with Mr Browne as leader:

For they are jolly gay fellows,
For they are jolly gay fellows,
For they are jolly gay fellows,
Which nobody can deny.

Aunt Kate was making frank use of her handkerchief and even Aunt Julia seemed moved. Freddy Malins beat time with his pudding-fork and the singers turned towards one another, as if in melodious conference, while they sang, with emphasis:

Unless he tells a lie,
Unless he tells a lie.

Then, turning once more towards their hostesses, they sang:

For they are jolly gay fellows,
For they are jolly gay fellows,
For they are jolly gay fellows,
Which nobody can deny.

The acclamation which followed was taken up beyond the door of the supper-room by many of the other guests and renewed time after time, Freddy Malins acting as officer with his fork on high.

The piercing morning air came into the hall where they were standing so that Aunt Kate said:

— Close the door, somebody. Mrs Malins will get her death of cold.

— Browne is out there, Aunt Kate, said Mary Jane.

— Browne is everywhere, said Aunt Kate, lowering her voice.

Mary Jane laughed at her tone.

— Really, she said archly, he is very attentive.

— He has been laid on here like the gas, said Aunt Kate in the same tone, all during the Christmas.

She laughed herself this time good-humouredly and then added quickly:

—But tell him to come in, Mary Jane, and close the door. I hope to goodness he didn't hear me.

At that moment the hall-door was opened and Mr Browne came in from the doorstep, laughing as if his heart would break. He was dressed in a long green overcoat with mock astrakhan cuffs and collar and wore on his head an oval fur cap. He pointed down the snow-covered quay from where the sound of shrill prolonged whistling was borne in.

—Teddy will have all the cabs in Dublin out, he said.

Gabriel advanced from the little pantry behind the office, struggling into his overcoat and, looking round the hall, said:

—Gretta not down yet?

—She's getting on her things, Gabriel, said Aunt Kate.

—Who's playing up there? asked Gabriel.

—Nobody. They're all gone.

—O no, Aunt Kate, said Mary Jane. Bartell D'Arcy and Miss O'Callaghan aren't gone yet.

—Someone is strumming at the piano, anyhow, said Gabriel.

Mary Jane glanced at Gabriel and Mr Browne and said with a shiver:

—It makes me feel cold to look at you two gentlemen muffled up like that. I wouldn't like to face your journey home at this hour.

—I'd like nothing better this minute, said Mr Browne stoutly, than a rattling fine walk in the country or a fast drive with a good spanking goer between the shafts.

—We used to have a very good horse and trap at home, said Aunt Julia sadly.

—The never-to-be-forgotten Johnny, said Mary Jane, laughing.

Aunt Kate and Gabriel laughed too.

—Why, what was wonderful about Johnny? asked Mr Browne.

—The late lamented Patrick Morkan, our grandfather, that is, explained Gabriel, commonly known in his later years as the old gentleman, was a glue-boiler.

—O, now, Gabriel, said Aunt Kate, laughing, he had a starch mill.

—Well, glue or starch, said Gabriel, the old gentleman had a horse by the name of Johnny. And Johnny used to work in the old gentleman's mill, walking round and round in order to drive the mill. That was all very well; but now comes the tragic part about Johnny. One fine day the old gentleman thought he'd like to drive out with the quality to a military review in the park.

—The Lord have mercy on his soul, said Aunt Kate compassionately.

—Amen, said Gabriel. So the old gentleman, as I said, harnessed Johnny and put on his very best tall hat and his very best stock collar and drove out in grand style from his ancestral mansion somewhere near Back Lane, I think.

Everyone laughed, even Mrs Malins, at Gabriel's manner and Aunt Kate said:

—O now, Gabriel, he didn't live in Back Lane, really. Only the mill was there.

—Out from the mansion of his forefathers, continued Gabriel, he drove with Johnny. And everything went on beautifully until Johnny came in sight of King Billy's statue: and whether he fell in love with the horse King Billy sits on or whether he thought he was back again in the mill, anyhow he began to walk round the statue.

Gabriel paced in a circle round the hall in his goloshes amid the laughter of the others.

—Round and round he went, said Gabriel, and the old gentleman, who was a very pompous old gentleman, was highly indignant. *Go on, sir! What do you mean, sir? Johnny! Johnny! Most extraordinary conduct! Can't understand the horse!*

The peals of laughter which followed Gabriel's imitation of the incident were interrupted by a resounding knock at the hall-door. Mary Jane ran to open it and let in Freddy Malins. Freddy Malins, with his hat well back on his head and his shoulders humped with cold, was puffing and steaming after his exertions.

—I could only get one cab, he said.

—O, we'll find another along the quay, said Gabriel.

—Yes, said Aunt Kate. Better not keep Mrs Malins standing in the draught.

Mrs Malins was helped down the front steps by her son and Mr Browne and, after many manoeuvres, hoisted into the cab. Freddy Malins clambered in after her and spent a long time settling her on the seat, Mr Browne helping him with advice. At last she was settled comfortably and Freddy Malins invited Mr Browne into the cab. There was a good deal of confused talk, and then Mr Browne got into the cab. The cabman settled his rug over his knees, and bent down for the address. The confusion grew greater and the cabman was directed differently by Freddy Malins and Mr Browne, each of whom had his head out through a window of the cab. The difficulty was to know where to drop Mr Browne along the route and Aunt Kate, Aunt Julia and Mary Jane helped the discussion from the doorstep with cross-directions and contradictions and abundance of laughter. As for Freddy Malins he was speechless with laughter. He popped his head in and out of the window every moment, to the great danger of his hat, and told his mother how the discussion was progressing till at last Mr Browne shouted to the bewildered cabman above the din of everybody's laughter:

—Do you know Trinity College?

—Yes, sir, said the cabman.

—Well, drive bang up against Trinity College gates, said Mr Browne, and then we'll tell you where to go. You understand now?

—Yes, sir, said the cabman.

—Make like a bird for Trinity College.

—Right, sir, cried the cabman.

The horse was whipped up and the cab rattled off along the quay amid a chorus of laughter and adieus.

Gabriel had not gone to the door with the others. He was in a dark part of the hall gazing up the staircase. A woman was standing near the top of the first flight, in the shadow also. He could not see her face but he could see the terracotta and salmonpink panels of her skirt which the shadow made appear black and white. It was his wife. She was leaning on the banisters, listening to something. Gabriel was surprised at her stillness and strained his ear to listen also. But he could hear little save the noise of laughter and dispute on the front steps, a few chords struck on the piano and a few notes of a man's voice singing.

He stood still in the gloom of the hall, trying to catch the air that the voice was singing and gazing up at his wife. There was grace and mystery in her attitude as if she were a symbol of something. He asked himself what is a woman standing on the stairs in the shadow, listening to distant music, a symbol of. If he were a painter he would paint her in that attitude. Her blue felt hat would show off the bronze of her hair against the darkness and the dark panels of her skirt would show off the light ones. *Distant Music* he would call the picture if he were a painter.

The hall-door closed; and Aunt Kate, Aunt Julia and Mary Jane came down the hall, still laughing.

—Well, isn't Freddy terrible? said Mary Jane. He's really terrible.

Gabriel said nothing but pointed up the stairs towards where his wife was standing. Now that the hall-door was closed the voice and the piano could be heard more clearly. Gabriel held up his hand for them to be silent. The song seemed to be in the old Irish tonality and the singer seemed uncertain both of his words and of his voice. The voice, made plaintive by distance and by the singer's hoarseness, faintly illuminated the cadence of the air with words expressing grief:

> O, the rain falls on my heavy locks
> And the dew wets my skin,
> My babe lies cold . . .

—O, exclaimed Mary Jane. It's Bartell D'Arcy singing and he wouldn't sing all the night. O, I'll get him to sing a song before he goes.

—O do, Mary Jane, said Aunt Kate.

Mary Jane brushed past the others and ran to the staircase but before she reached it the singing stopped and the piano was closed abruptly.

—O, what a pity! she cried. Is he coming down, Gretta?

Gabriel heard his wife answer yes and saw her come down towards them. A few steps behind her were Mr Bartell D'Arcy and Miss O'Callaghan.

—O, Mr D'Arcy, cried Mary Jane, it's downright mean of you to break off like that when we were all in raptures listening to you.

—I have been at him all the evening, said Miss O'Callaghan, and Mrs Conroy too and he told us he had a dreadful cold and couldn't sing.

—O, Mr D'Arcy, said Aunt Kate, now that was a great fib to tell.

—Can't you see that I'm as hoarse as a crow? said Mr D'Arcy roughly.

He went to the pantry hastily and put on his overcoat. The others, taken aback by his rude speech, could find nothing to say. Aunt Kate wrinkled her brows and made signs to the others to drop the subject. Mr D'Arcy stood swathing his neck carefully and frowning.

—It's the weather, said Aunt Julia, after a pause.

—Yes, everybody has colds, said Aunt Kate readily, everybody.

—They say, said Mary Jane, we haven't had snow like it for thirty years; and I read this morning in the newspapers that the snow is general all over Ireland.

—I love the look of snow, said Aunt Julia sadly.

—So do I, said Miss O'Callaghan. I think Christmas is never really Christmas unless we have the snow on the ground.

—But poor Mr D'Arcy doesn't like the snow, said Aunt Kate, smiling.

Mr D'Arcy came from the pantry, fully swathed and buttoned, and in a repentant tone told them the history of the cold. Everyone gave him advice and said it was a great pity and urged him to be very careful of his throat in the night air. Gabriel watched his wife, who did not join in the conversation. She was standing right under the dusty fanlight and the flame of the gas lit up the rich bronze of her hair which he had seen her drying at the fire a few days before. She was in the same attitude and seemed unaware of the talk about her. At last she turned towards them and Gabriel saw that there was colour on her cheeks and that her eyes were shining. A sudden tide of joy went leaping out of his heart.

—Mr D'Arcy, she said, what is the name of that song you were singing?

—It's called *The Lass of Aughrim*, said Mr D'Arcy, but I couldn't remember it properly. Why? Do you know it?

—*The Lass of Aughrim*, she repeated. I couldn't think of the name.

—It's a very nice air, said Mary Jane. I'm sorry you were not in voice to-night.

—Now, Mary Jane, said Aunt Kate, don't annoy Mr D'Arcy. I won't have him annoyed.

Seeing that all were ready to start she shepherded them to the door where good-night was said:

—Well, good-night, Aunt Kate, and thanks for the pleasant evening.

—Good-night, Gabriel. Good-night, Gretta!

—Good-night, Aunt Kate, and thanks ever so much. Good-night, Aunt Julia.

—O, good-night Gretta, I didn't see you.

—Good-night, Mr D'Arcy. Good-night, Miss O'Callaghan.

—Good-night, Miss Morkan.

—Good-night, again.

—Good-night, all. Safe home.

—Good-night. Good-night.

The morning was still dark. A dull yellow light brooded over the houses and the river; and the sky seemed to be descending. It was slushy underfoot; and only streaks and patches of snow lay on the roofs, on the parapets of the quay and on the area railings. The lamps were still burning redly in the murky air and, across the river, the palace of the Four Courts stood out menacingly against the heavy sky.

She was walking on before him with Mr Bartell D'Arcy, her shoes in a brown parcel tucked under one arm and her hands holding her skirt up from the slush. She had no longer any grace of attitude but Gabriel's eyes were still bright with happiness. The blood went bounding along his veins; and the thoughts were rioting through his brain, proud, joyful, tender, valorous.

She was walking on before him so lightly and so erect that he longed to run after her noiselessly, catch her by the shoulders and say something foolish and affectionate into her ear. She seemed to him so frail that he longed to defend her against something and then to be alone with her. Moments of their secret life together burst like stars upon his memory. A heliotrope envelope was lying beside his breakfast-cup and he was caressing it with his hand. Birds were twittering in the ivy and the sunny web of the curtain was shimmering along the floor: he could not eat for happiness. They were standing on the crowded platform and he was placing a ticket inside the warm palm of her glove. He was standing with her in the cold, looking in through a grated window at a man making bottles in a roaring furnace. It was very cold. Her face, fragrant in the cold air, was quite close to his; and suddenly she called out to the man at the furnace.

—Is the fire hot, sir?

But the man could not hear her with the noise of the furnace. It was just as well. He might have answered rudely.

A wave of yet more tender joy escaped from his heart and went coursing in warm flood along his arteries. Like the tender fires of stars moments of their life together, that no one knew of or would ever know of, broke upon and illumined his memory. He longed to recall to her those moments, to make her forget the years of their dull existence together and remember only their moments of ecstasy. For the years, he felt, had not quenched his soul or hers. Their children, his writing, her household cares had not quenched their souls' tender fire. In one letter that he had written to her then he had said: *Why is it that words like these seem to me so dull and cold? Is it because there is no word tender enough to be your name?*

Like distant music these words that he had written years before were borne towards him from the past. He longed to be alone with her. When the others had gone away, when he and she were in their room in the hotel, then they would be alone together. He would call her softly:

—Gretta!

Perhaps she would not hear at once: she would be undressing. Then something in his voice would strike her. She would turn and look at him. . . .

At the corner of Winetavern Street they met a cab. He was glad of its rattling noise as it saved him from conversation. She was looking out of the window and seemed tired. The others spoke only a few words, pointing out some building or street. The horse galloped along wearily under the murky morning sky, dragging his old rattling box after his heels, galloping to their honeymoon.

As the cab drove across O'Connell Bridge Miss O'Callaghan said:

—They say you never cross O'Connell Bridge without seeing a white horse.

—I see a white man this time, said Gabriel.

—Where? asked Mr Bartell D'Arcy.

Gabriel pointed to the statue, on which lay patches of snow. Then he nodded familiarly to it and waved his hand.

—Good-night, Dan, he said gaily.

When the cab drew up before the hotel Gabriel jumped out and, in spite of Mr Bartell D'Arcy's protest, paid the driver. He gave the man a shilling over his fare. The man saluted and said:

—A prosperous New Year to you, sir.

—The same to you, said Gabriel cordially.

She leaned for a moment on his arm in getting out of the cab and while standing at the curbstone, bidding the others good-night. She leaned lightly on his arm, as lightly as when she had danced with him a few hours before. He had felt proud and happy then, happy that she was his, proud of her grace and wifely carriage. But now, after the kindling again of so many memories, the first touch of her body, musical and strange and perfumed, sent through him a keen pang of lust. Under cover of her silence he pressed her arm closely to his side; and, as they stood at the hotel door, he felt that they had escaped from their lives and duties, escaped from home and friends and run away together with wild and radiant hearts to a new adventure.

An old man was dozing in a great hooded chair in the hall. He lit a candle in the office and went before them to the stairs. They followed him in silence, their feet falling in soft thuds on the thickly carpeted stairs. She mounted the stairs behind the porter, her head bowed in the ascent, her frail shoulders curved as with a burden, her skirt girt tightly about her. He could have flung his arms about her hips and held her still for his arms were trembling with desire to seize her and only the stress of his nails against the palms of his hands held the wild impulse of his body in check. The porter halted on the stairs to settle his guttering candle. They halted too on the steps below him. In the silence Gabriel could hear the falling of the molten wax into the tray and the thumping of his own heart against his ribs.

The porter led them along a corridor and opened a door. Then he set his unstable candle down on a toilet-table and asked at what hour they were to be called in the morning.

—Eight, said Gabriel.

The porter pointed to the tap of the electric-light and began a muttered apology but Gabriel cut him short.

—We don't want any light. We have enough light from the street. And I say, he added, pointing to the candle, you might remove that handsome article, like a good man.

The porter took up his candle again, but slowly for he was surprised by such a novel idea. Then he mumbled good-night and went out. Gabriel shot the lock to.

A ghostly light from the street lamp lay in a long shaft from one window to the door. Gabriel threw his overcoat and hat on a couch and crossed the room towards the window. He looked down into the street in order that his emotion might calm a little. Then he turned and leaned against a chest of drawers with his back to the light. She had taken off her hat and cloak and was standing before a large swinging mirror, unhooking her waist. Gabriel paused for a few moments, watching her, and then said:

—Gretta!

She turned away from the mirror slowly and walked along the shaft of light towards him. Her face looked so serious and weary that the words would not pass Gabriel's lips. No, it was not the moment yet.

—You look tired, he said.

—I am a little, she answered.

—You don't feel ill or weak?

—No, tired; that's all.

She went on to the window and stood there, looking out. Gabriel waited again and then, fearing that diffidence was about to conquer him, he said abruptly:

—By the way, Gretta!

—What is it?

—You know that poor fellow Malins? he said quickly.

—Yes. What about him?

—Well, poor fellow, he's a decent sort of chap after all, continued Gabriel in a false voice. He gave me back that sovereign I lent him and I didn't expect it really. It's a pity he wouldn't keep away from that Browne, because he's not a bad fellow at heart.

He was trembling now with annoyance. Why did she seem so abstracted? He did not know how he could begin. Was she annoyed, too, about something? If she would only turn to him or come to him of her own accord! To take her as she was would be brutal. No, he must see some ardour in her eyes first. He longed to be master of her strange mood.

—When did you lend him the pound? she asked, after a pause.

Gabriel strove to restrain himself from breaking out into brutal language about the sottish Malins and his pound. He longed to cry to her from his soul, to crush her body against his, to overmaster her. But he said:

—O, at Christmas, when he opened that little Christmas-card shop in Henry Street.

He was in such a fever of rage and desire that he did not hear her come from the window. She stood before him for an instant, looking at him strangely. Then, suddenly raising herself on tiptoe and resting her hands lightly on his shoulders, she kissed him.

—You are a very generous person, Gabriel, she said.

Gabriel, trembling with delight at her sudden kiss and at the quaintness of her phrase, put his hands on her hair and began smoothing it back, scarcely touching it with his fingers. The washing had made it fine and brilliant. His heart was brimming over with happiness. Just when he was wishing for it she had come to him of her own accord. Perhaps her thoughts had been running with his. Perhaps she had felt the impetuous desire that was in him and then the yielding mood had come upon her. Now that she had fallen to him so easily he wondered why he had been so diffident.

He stood, holding her head between his hands. Then, slipping one arm swiftly about her body and drawing her towards him, he said softly:

—Gretta, dear, what are you thinking about?

She did not answer nor yield wholly to his arm. He said again, softly:

—Tell me what it is, Gretta. I think I know what is the matter. Do I know?

She did not answer at once. Then she said in an outburst of tears:

—O, I am thinking about that song, The Lass of Aughrim.

She broke loose from him and ran to the bed and, throwing her arms across the bed-rail, hid her face. Gabriel stood stock-still for a moment in astonishment and then followed her. As he passed in the way of the cheval-glass he caught sight of himself in full length, his broad, well-filled shirt-front, the face whose expression always puzzled him when he saw it in a mirror and his glimmering gilt-rimmed eye-glasses. He halted a few paces from her and said:

—What about the song? Why does that make you cry?

She raised her head from her arms and dried her eyes with the back of her hand like a child. A kinder note than he had intended went into his voice.

—Why, Gretta? he asked.

—I am thinking about a person long ago who used to sing that song.

—And who was the person long ago? asked Gabriel, smiling.

—It was a person I used to know in Galway when I was living with my grandmother, she said.

The smile passed away from Gabriel's face. A dull anger began to gather again at the back of his mind and the dull fires of his lust began to glow angrily in his veins.

—Someone you were in love with? he asked ironically.

—It was a young boy I used to know, she answered, named Michael Furey. He used to sing that song, The Lass of Aughrim. He was very delicate.

Gabriel was silent. He did not wish her to think that he was interested in this delicate boy.

—I can see him so plainly, she said after a moment. Such eyes as he had; big dark eyes! And such an expression in them—an expression!

—O then, you were in love with him? said Gabriel.

—I used to go out walking with him, she said, when I was in Galway.

A thought flew across Gabriel's mind.

—Perhaps that was why you wanted to go to Galway with that Ivors girl? he said coldly.

She looked at him and asked in surprise:

—What for?

Her eyes made Gabriel feel awkward. He shrugged his shoulders and said:

—How do I know? To see him perhaps.

She looked away from him along the shaft of light towards the window in silence.

—He is dead, she said at length. He died when he was only seventeen. Isn't that a terrible thing to die so young as that?

—What was he? asked Gabriel, still ironically.

—He was in the gasworks, she said.

Gabriel felt humiliated by the failure of his irony and by the evocation of this figure from the dead, a boy in the gasworks. While he had been full of memories of their secret life together, full of tenderness and joy and desire, she had been comparing him in her mind with another. A shameful consciousness of his own person assailed him. He saw himself as a ludicrous figure, acting as a pennyboy for his aunts, a nervous well-meaning sentimentalist, orating to vulgarians and idealising his own clownish lusts, the pitiable fatuous fellow he had caught a glimpse of in the mirror. Instinctively he turned his back more to the light lest she might see the shame that burned upon his forehead.

He tried to keep up his tone of cold interrogation but his voice when he spoke was humble and indifferent.

—I suppose you were in love with this Michael Furey, Gretta, he said.

—I was great with him at that time, she said.

Her voice was veiled and sad. Gabriel, feeling now how vain it would be to try to lead her whither he had purposed, caressed one of her hands and said, also sadly:

—And what did he die of so young, Gretta? Consumption, was it?

—I think he died for me, she answered.

A vague terror seized Gabriel at this answer as if, at that hour when he had hoped to triumph, some impalpable and vindictive being was coming against him, gathering forces against him in its vague world. But he shook himself free of it with an effort of reason and continued to caress her hand. He did not question her again for he felt that she would tell him of herself. Her hand was warm and moist: it did not respond to his touch but he continued to caress it just as he had caressed her first letter to him that spring morning.

—It was in the winter, she said, about the beginning of the winter when I was going to leave my grandmother's and come up here to the convent. And he was ill at the time in his lodgings in Galway and wouldn't be let out and his people in Oughterard were written to. He was in decline, they said, or something like that. I never knew rightly.

She paused for a moment and sighed.

—Poor fellow, she said. He was very fond of me and he was such a gentle boy. We used to go out together, walking, you know, Gabriel, like the way they do in the country. He was going to study singing only for his health. He had a very good voice, poor Michael Furey.

—Well; and then? asked Gabriel.

—And then when it came to the time for me to leave Galway and come up to the convent he was much worse and I wouldn't be let see him so I wrote a letter saying I was going up to Dublin and would be back in the summer and hoping he would be better then.

She paused for a moment to get her voice under control and then went on:

—Then the night before I left I was in my grandmother's house in Nuns' Island, packing up, and I heard gravel thrown up against the window. The window was so wet I couldn't see so I ran downstairs as I was and slipped out the back into the garden and there was the poor fellow at the end of the garden, shivering.

—And did you not tell him to go back? asked Gabriel.

—I implored of him to go home at once and told him he would get his death in the rain. But he said he did not want to live. I can see his eyes as well as well! He was standing at the end of the wall where there was a tree.

—And did he go home? asked Gabriel.

—Yes, he went home. And when I was only a week in the convent he died and he was buried in Oughterard where his people came from. O, the day I heard that, that he was dead!

She stopped, choking with sobs, and, overcome by emotion, flung herself face downward on the bed, sobbing in the quilt. Gabriel held her hand for a moment longer, irresolutely, and then, shy of intruding on her grief, let it fall gently and walked quietly to the window.

She was fast asleep.

Gabriel, leaning on his elbow, looked for a few moments unresentfully on her tangled hair and half-open mouth, listening to her deep-drawn breath. So she had had that romance in her life: a man had died for her sake. It hardly pained him now to think how poor a part, he, her husband, had played in her life. He watched her while she slept as though he and she had never lived together as man and wife. His curious eyes rested long upon her face and on her hair: and, as he thought of what she must have been then, in that time of her first girlish beauty, a strange friendly pity for her entered his soul. He did not like to say even to himself that her face was no longer beautiful but he knew that it was no longer the face for which Michael Furey had braved death.

Perhaps she had not told him all the story. His eyes moved to the chair over which she had thrown some of her clothes. A petticoat string dangled to the floor. One boot stood upright, its limp upper fallen down: the fellow of it lay upon its side. He wondered at his riot of emotions of an hour before. From what had it proceeded? From his aunt's supper, from his own foolish speech, from the wine and dancing, the merry-making when saying good-night in the hall, the pleasure of the walk along the river in the snow. Poor Aunt Julia! She, too, would soon be a shade with the shade of Patrick Morkan and his horse. He had caught that haggard look upon her face for a moment when she was singing *Arrayed for the Bridal.* Soon, perhaps, he would be sitting in that same drawing-room, dressed in black, his silk hat on his knees. The blinds would be drawn down and Aunt Kate would be sitting beside him, crying and blowing her nose and telling him how Julia had died. He would cast about his mind for some words that might console her, and would find only lame and useless ones. Yes, yes: that would happen very soon.

The air of the room chilled his shoulders. He stretched himself cautiously along under the sheets and lay down beside his wife. One by one they were all becoming shades. Better pass boldly into that other world, in the full glory of some passion, than fade and wither dismally with age. He thought of how she who lay beside him had locked in her heart for so many years that image of her lover's eyes when he had told her that he did not wish to live.

Generous tears filled Gabriel's eyes. He had never felt like that himself towards any woman but he knew that such a feeling must be love. The tears gathered more thickly in his eyes and in the partial darkness he imagined he saw the form of a young man standing under a dripping tree. Other forms were near. His soul had approached that region where dwell the vast hosts of the dead. He was conscious of, but could not apprehend, their wayward and flickering existence. His own identity was fading out into a grey impalpable world: the solid world itself which these dead had one time reared and lived in was dissolving and dwindling.

A few light taps upon the pane made him turn to the window. It had begun to snow again. He watched sleepily the flakes, silver and dark, falling obliquely against the lamplight. The time had come for him to set out on his journey westward. Yes, the newspapers were right: snow was general all over Ireland. It was falling on every part of the dark central plain, on the treeless hills, falling softly upon the Bog of Allen and, farther westward, softly falling into the dark mutinous Shannon waves. It was falling, too, upon every part of the lonely churchyard on the hill where Michael Furey lay buried. It lay thickly drifted on the crooked crosses and headstones, on the spears of the little gate, on the barren thorns. His soul swooned slowly as he heard the snow falling faintly through the universe and faintly falling, like the descent of their last end, upon all the living and the dead.

[1914]

Study and Writing Questions

1. How is Gabriel's CHARACTER revealed DRAMATICALLY, for example in the opening exchanges with Lily or in his speech-making at dinner? How is his character revealed through his STREAM-OF-CONSCIOUSNESS, for example, in his reflections on his mother or in his imagination of Gretta as painted in *Distant Music*?

2. What is Miss Ivor's relationship with Gabriel? Why does she leave early? In what way does her leave-taking FORESHADOW the last SCENE of the STORY?

3. What patterns of IMAGERY run throughout the story? To what extent do these work together? Are they RESOLVED by the ending?

4. In what sense(s) is this a coherent NARRATIVE? To what extent is this narrative about Gabriel? about Gabriel and Gretta? about a part of Dublin society? about

Ireland? about something more universal? How do these stories work together?

5. Does the narrative achieve a satisfactory resolution? Is Gabriel's "shameful consciousness of his own person" as Gretta tells of Michael Furey an accurate portrait of Gabriel? Why does he cry while Gretta sleeps? What are we to make of the story's last paragraph?

See also Questions for Contrast and Comparison: 7, 12, 43, 45, 64, 65, 67, 68, 69, 92, 133, 219, and 234.

■ **FRANZ KAFKA** (1883 – 1924) *was born, raised, and lived most of his life with his parents in Prague, doubly alienated as a German-speaker in Czechoslovakia and as a Jew among Christians. His mother came from the Prague Jewish élite while his domineering father had raised himself from lower-class peddler to prominent merchant. Fluent with others, Kafka stuttered before his father and explored their relationship in the non-fictional* Letter to His Father *(1919). Kafka earned a doctor of jurisprudence degree (1906), practiced privately for the requisite year, and then entered the civil service. He worked for a quasi-governmental workers' insurance agency investigating claims by day and, as he asserted, writing through his insomniac nights to escape both his radical insecurity at work and his sense of alienation, fear, and failure at home. His grim* PARABLES *provided him no ultimate escape, and in his lifetime, through indecision, he published only a few short pieces, including his most famous work,* The Metamorphosis *(1915). In his mature years, he was engaged several times to be married, but each engagement was broken off. In 1922 tuberculosis forced him to resign his position. He instructed Max Brod, his literary executor, to burn his manuscripts, but after Kafka's death in a sanitorium, Brod defied him, edited the work, and published Kafka's three great, nightmarish* NOVELS: The Trial *(1925),* The Castle *(1926), and* Amerika *(1927).*

A Common Confusion

A common experience, resulting in a common confusion. A. has to transact important business with B. in H. He goes to H. for a preliminary interview, accomplishes the journey there in ten minutes, and the journey back in the same time, and on returning boasts to his family of his expedition. Next day he goes again to H., this time to settle his business finally. As that by all appearances will require several hours, A. leaves very early in the morning. But although all the surrounding circumstances, at least in A.'s estimation, are exactly the same as the day before, this time it takes him ten hours to reach H. When he arrives there quite exhausted in the evening he is informed that B., annoyed at his absence, had left half an hour before to go to A.'s village, and that they must have passed each other on the road. A. is advised to wait. But in his anxiety about his business he sets off at once and hurries home.

This time he covers the distance, without paying any particular attention to the fact, practically in an instant. At home he learns that B. had arrived quite early, immediately after A.'s departure, indeed that he had met A. on the threshold and reminded him of his business; but A. had replied that he had no time to spare, he must go at once.

In spite of this incomprehensible behavior of A., however, B. had stayed on to wait for A.'s return. It is true, he had asked several times whether A. was not back yet, but he was still sitting up in A.'s room. Overjoyed at the opportunity of seeing B. at once and explaining everything to him, A. rushes upstairs. He is almost at the top, when he stumbles, twists a sinew, and almost fainting with the pain, incapable even of uttering a cry, only able to moan faintly in the darkness, he hears B. — impossible to tell whether at a great distance or quite near him — stamping down the stairs in a violent rage and vanishing for good.

[1917]

Study and Writing Questions

1. What is the effect of Kafka using letters where we normally expect proper nouns?
2. Words like "common" and "confusion" have multiple meanings (both in English and in Kafka's original German). What are other multiply significant words and phrases in this NARRATIVE? What is the effect of Kafka's use of words and phrases with multiple meanings?
3. To what extent is this STORY about economics?
4. To what extent is this story about perception? To what extent does the story distort a reader's perception? What is the relationship between the perception of A. and of the reader?
5. What are some possible ALLEGORICAL meanings of this story? What might the journey represent? What might the relationship between A. and B. represent? What does the stairway represent? What does A.'s pain represent? What do the last two words mean?

See also Questions for Contrast and Comparison: 14, 70, 75, 77, 78, 80, 146, 155, and 184.

The Metamorphosis

I

As Gregor Samsa awoke one morning from uneasy dreams he found himself transformed in his bed into a gigantic insect. He was lying on his hard, as it were armor-plated, back and when he lifted his head a little he could see his domelike brown belly divided into stiff arched segments on top of which the bed quilt could hardly keep in position and was about to slide off completely. His numerous legs, which were pitifully thin compared to the rest of his bulk, waved helplessly before his eyes.

What has happened to me? he thought. It was no dream. His room, a regular human bedroom, only rather too small, lay quiet between the four familiar walls. Above the table on which a collection of cloth samples was unpacked and spread out — Samsa was a commercial traveler — hung the picture which he had recently cut out of an illustrated magazine and put into a pretty gilt frame. It showed a lady, with a fur cap on and a fur stole, sitting upright and holding out to the spectator a huge fur muff into which the whole of her forearm had vanished!

Gregor's eyes turned next to the window, and the overcast sky — one could hear raindrops beating on the window gutter — made him quite melancholy. What about sleeping a little longer and forgetting all this nonsense, he thought, but it could not be done, for he was accustomed to sleep on his right side and in his present condition he could not turn himself over. However violently he forced himself toward his right side he always rolled onto his back again. He tried it at least a hundred times, shutting his eyes to keep from seeing his struggling legs, and only desisted when he began to feel in his side a faint dull ache he had never experienced before.

Oh God, he thought, what an exhausting job I've picked on! Traveling about day in, day out. It's much more irritating work than doing the actual business in the office, and on top of that there's the trouble of constant traveling, of worrying about train connections, the bed and irregular meals, casual acquaintances that are always new and never become intimate friends. The devil take it all! He felt a slight itching up on his belly; slowly pushed himself on his back nearer to the top of the bed so that he could lift his head more easily; identified the itching place which was surrounded by many small white spots the nature of which he could not understand and made to touch it with a leg, but drew the leg back immediately, for the contact made a cold shiver run through him.

He slid down again into his former position. This getting up early, he thought, makes one quite stupid. A man needs his sleep. Other commercials live like harem women. For instance, when I come back to the hotel of a morning to write up the orders I've got, these others are only sitting down to the breakfast. Let me just try that with my chief; I'd be sacked on the spot. Anyhow, that might be quite a good thing for me, who can tell? If I didn't have to hold my hand because of my parents I'd have given notice long ago, I'd have gone to the chief and told him exactly what I think of him. That would knock him endways from his desk! It's a queer way of doing, too, this sitting on high at a desk and talking down to employees, especially when they have to come quite near because the chief is hard of hearing. Well, there's still hope; once I've saved enough money to pay back my parents' debts to him — that should take another five or six years —

I'll do it without fail. I'll cut myself completely loose then. For the moment, though, I'd better get up, since my train goes at five.

He looked at the alarm clock ticking on the chest. Heavenly Father! he thought. It was half-past six o'clock and the hands were quietly moving on, it was even past the half-hour, it was getting on toward a quarter to seven. Had the alarm clock not gone off? From the bed one could see that it had been properly set for four o'clock; of course it must have gone off. Yes, but was it possible to sleep quietly through that ear-splitting noise? Well, he had not slept quietly, yet apparently all the more soundly for that. But what was he to do now? The next train went at seven o'clock; to catch that he would need to hurry like mad and his samples weren't even packed up, and he himself wasn't feeling particularly fresh and active. And even if he did catch the train he wouldn't avoid a row with the chief, since the firm's porter would have been waiting for the five o'clock train and would have long since reported his failure to turn up. The porter was a creature of the chief's, spineless and stupid. Well, supposing he were to say he was sick? But that would be most unpleasant and would look suspicious, since during his five years' employment he had not been ill once. The chief himself would be sure to come with the sick-insurance doctor, would reproach his parents with their son's laziness, and would cut all excuses short by referring to the insurance doctor, who of course regarded all mankind as perfectly healthy malingerers. And would he be so far wrong on this occasion? Gregor really felt quite well, apart from a drowsiness that was utterly superfluous after such a long sleep, and he was even unusually hungry.

As all this was running through his mind at top speed without his being able to decide to leave his bed — the alarm clock had just struck a quarter to seven — there came a cautious tap at the door behind the head of his bed. "Gregor," said a voice — it was his mother's — "it's quarter to seven. Hadn't you a train to catch?" That gentle voice! Gregor had a shock as he heard his own voice answering hers, unmistakably his own voice, it was true, but with a persistent horrible twittering squeak behind it like an undertone, which left the words in their clear shape only for the first moment and then rose up reverberating around them to destroy their sense, so that one could not be sure one had heard them rightly. Gregor wanted to answer at length and explain everything, but in the circumstances he confined himself to saying: "Yes, yes, thank you, Mother, I'm getting up now." The wooden door between them must have kept the change in his voice from being noticeable outside, for his mother contented herself with this statement and shuffled away. Yet this brief exchange of words had made the other members of the family aware that Gregor was still in the house, as they had not expected, and at one of the side doors his father was already knocking, gently, yet with his fist. "Gregor, Gregor," he called, "What's the matter with you?" And after a little while he called again in a deeper voice: "Gregor! Gregor!" At the other side door his sister was saying in a low, plaintive tone: "Gregor? Aren't you well? Are you needing anything?" He answered them both at once: "I'm just ready," and did his best to make his voice sound as normal as possible by enunciating the words very clearly and leaving long pauses between them. So his father went back to his breakfast, but his sister whispered: "Gregor, open the door, do." However, he was not thinking of opening the door, and felt thankful for the prudent habit he had acquired in traveling of locking all doors during the night, even at home.

His immediate intention was to get up quietly without being disturbed, to put on his clothes and above all eat his breakfast, and only then consider what else was to be done, since in bed, he was well aware, his meditations would come to no sensible conclusion. He remembered that often enough in bed he had felt small aches and pains, probably caused by awkward postures, which had proved purely imaginary once he got up, and he looked forward eagerly to seeing this morning's delusions gradually fall away. That the change in his voice was nothing but the precursor of a severe chill, a standing ailment of commercial travelers, he had not the least possible doubt.

To get rid of the quilt was quite easy; he had only to inflate himself a little and it fell off by itself. But the next move was difficult, especially because he was so uncommonly broad. He would have needed arms and hands to hoist himself up; instead he had only the numerous little legs which never stopped waving in all directions and which he could not control in the least. When he tried to bend one of them it was the first to stretch itself straight; and did he succeed at last in making it do what he wanted, all the other legs meanwhile waved the more wildly in a high degree of unpleasant agitation. "But what's the use of lying idle in bed," said Gregor to himself.

He thought that he might get out of bed with the lower part of his body first, but this lower part, which he had not yet seen and of which he could form no clear conception, proved too difficult to move; it shifted so slowly; and when finally, almost wild with annoyance, he gathered his forces together and thrust out recklessly, he had miscalculated the direction and bumped heavily against the lower end of the bed, and the stinging pain he felt informed him that precisely this lower part of his body was at the moment probably the most sensitive.

So he tried to get the top part of himself out first, and cautiously moved his head toward the edge of the bed. That proved easy enough, and despite its breadth and mass the bulk of his body at last slowly followed the movement of his head. Still, when he finally got his head free over the edge of the bed he felt too scared to go on advancing, for after all if he let himself fall in this way it would take a miracle to keep his head from being injured. And at all costs he must not lose consciousness now, precisely now; he would rather stay in bed.

But when after a repetition of the same efforts he lay in his former position again, sighing, and watched his little legs struggling against each other more wildly than ever, if that were possible, and saw no way of bringing any order into this arbitrary confusion, he told himself again that it was impossible to stay in bed and that the most sensible course was to risk everything for the smallest hope of getting away from it. At the same time he did not forget to remind himself occasionally that cool reflection, the coolest possible, was much better than desperate resolves. In such moments he focused his eyes as sharply as possible on the window, but, unfortunately, the prospect of the morning fog, which muffled even the other side of the narrow street, brought him little encouragement and comfort. "Seven o'clock already," he said to himself when the alarm clock chimed again, "seven o'clock already and still such a thick fog." And for a little while he lay quiet, breathing lightly, as if perhaps expecting such complete repose to restore all things to their real and normal condition.

But then he said to himself: "Before it strikes a quarter past seven I must be quite out of this bed, without fail. Anyhow, by that time someone will have come from the office to ask for me, since it opens before seven." And he set himself to rocking his whole body at once in a regular rhythm, with the idea of swinging it out of the bed. If he tipped himself out in that way he could keep his head from injury by lifting it at an acute angle when he fell. His back seemed to be hard and was not likely to suffer from a fall on the carpet. His biggest worry was the loud crash he would not be able to help making, which would probably cause anxiety, if not terror, behind all the doors. Still, he must take the risk.

When he was already half out of the bed — the new method was more a game than an effort, for he needed only to hitch himself across by rocking to and fro — it struck him how simple it would be if he could get help. Two strong people — he thought of his father and the servant girl — would be amply sufficient; they would only have to thrust their arms under his convex back, lever him out of the bed, bend down with their burden, and then be patient enough to let him turn himself right over onto the floor, where it was to be hoped his legs would then find their proper function. Well, ignoring the fact that the doors were all locked, ought he really to call for help? In spite of his misery he could not suppress a smile at the very idea of it.

He had got so far that he could barely keep his equilibrium when he rocked himself strongly, and he would have to nerve himself very soon for the final decision since in five minutes' time it would be quarter past seven — when the front doorbell rang. "That's someone from the office," he said to himself, and grew almost rigid, while his little legs only jigged about all the faster. For a moment everything stayed quiet. "They're not going to open the door," said Gregor to himself, catching at some kind of irrational hope. But then of course the servant girl went as usual to the door with her heavy tread and opened it. Gregor needed only to hear the first good morning of the visitor to know immediately who it was — the chief clerk himself. What a fate, to be condemned to work for a firm where the smallest omission at once gave rise to the gravest suspicion! Were all employees in a body nothing but scoundrels, was there not among them one single loyal devoted man who, had he wasted only an hour or so of the firm's time in a morning, was so tormented by conscience as to be driven out of his mind and actually incapable of leaving his bed? Wouldn't it really have been sufficient to send an apprentice to inquire — if any inquiry were necessary at all — did the chief clerk himself have to come and thus indicate to the entire family, an innocent family, that this suspicious circumstance could be investigated by no one less versed in affairs than himself? And more through the agitation caused by these reflections than through any act of will Gregor swung himself out of bed with all his strength. There was a loud thump, but it was not really a crash. His fall was broken to some extent by the carpet, his back, too, was less stiff than he thought, and so there was merely a dull thud, not so very startling. Only he had not lifted his head carefully enough and had hit it; he turned it and rubbed it on the carpet in pain and irritation.

"That was something falling down in there," said the chief clerk in the next room to the left. Gregor tried to suppose to himself that something like what had happened to him today might someday happen to the chief clerk; one really could not deny that it was possible. But as if in brusque reply to this supposition the chief clerk took a couple of firm steps in the next-door room and his patent leather boots creaked. From the right-hand room his sister was whispering to inform him of the situation: "Gregor, the chief clerk's here." "I know," muttered Gregor to himself; but he didn't dare to make his voice loud enough for his sister to hear it.

"Gregor," said his father now from the left-hand room, "the chief clerk has come and wants to know why you didn't catch the early train. We don't know what to say to him. Besides, he wants to talk to you in person. So open the door, please. He will be good enough to excuse the untidiness of your room." "Good morning, Mr. Samsa," the chief clerk was calling amiably meanwhile. "He's not well," said his mother to the visitor, while his father was still speaking through the door, "he's not well, sir, believe me. What else would make him miss a train! The boy thinks about nothing but his work. It makes me almost cross the way he never goes out in the evenings; he's been here the last eight days and has stayed at home every single evening. He just sits there quietly at the table reading a newspaper or looking through railway timetables. The only amusement he gets is doing fretwork. For instance, he spent two or three evenings cutting out a little picture frame; you would be surprised to see how pretty it is; it's hanging in his room; you'll see it in a minute when Gregor opens the door. I must say I'm glad you've come, sir; we should never have got him to unlock the door by ourselves; he's so obstinate; and I'm sure he's unwell, though he wouldn't have it to be so this morning." "I'm just coming," said Gregor slowly and carefully, not moving an inch for fear of losing one word of the conversation. "I can't think of any other explanation, madame," said the chief clerk, "I hope it's nothing serious. Although on the other hand I must say that we men of business — fortunately or unfortunately — very often simply have to ignore any slight indisposition, since business must be attended to." "Well, can the chief clerk come in now?" asked Gregor's father impatiently, again knocking on the door. "No," said Gregor. In the left-hand room a painful silence followed this refusal, in the right-hand room his sister began to sob.

Why didn't his sister join the others? She was probably newly out of bed and hadn't even begun to put on her clothes yet. Well, why was she crying? Because he wouldn't get up and let the chief clerk in, because he was in danger of losing his job, and because the chief would begin dunning his parents again for the old debts? Surely these were things one didn't need to worry about for the present. Gregor was still at home and not in the least thinking of deserting the family. At the moment, true, he was lying on the carpet and no one who knew the condition he was in could seriously expect him to admit the chief clerk. But for such a small discourtesy, which could plausibly be explained away somehow later on, Gregor could hardly be dismissed on the spot. And it seemed to Gregor that it would be much more sensible to leave him in peace for the present than to trouble him with tears and entreaties. Still, of course, their uncertainty bewildered them all and excused their behavior.

"Mr. Samsa," the chief clerk called now in a louder voice, "what's the matter with you? Here you are, barricading yourself in your room, giving only 'yes' and 'no' for answers, causing your parents a lot of unnecessary trouble and neglecting — I mention this only in passing — neglecting your business duties in an incredible fashion. I am speaking here in the name of your parents and of your chief, and I beg you quite seriously to give me an immediate and precise explanation. You amaze me, you amaze me. I thought you were a quiet, dependable person, and now all at once you seem bent on making a disgraceful exhibition of yourself. The chief did hint to me early this morning a possible explanation for your disappearance — with reference to the cash payments that were entrusted to you recently — but I almost pledged my solemn word of honor that this could not be so. But now that I see how incredibly obstinate you are, I no longer have the slightest desire to take your part at all. And your position in the firm is not so unassailable. I came with the intention of telling you all this in private, but since you are wasting my time so needlessly I don't see why your parents shouldn't hear it too. For some time past your work has been most unsatisfactory; this is not the season of the year for a business boom, of course, we admit that, but a season of the year for doing no business at all, that does not exist, Mr. Samsa, must not exist."

"But, sir," cried Gregor, beside himself and in his agitation forgetting everything else, "I'm just going to open the door this very minute. A slight illness, an attack of giddiness, has kept me from getting up. I'm still lying in bed. But I feel all right again. I'm getting out of bed now. Just give me a moment or two longer! I'm not quite so well as I thought. But I'm all right, really. How a thing like that can suddenly strike one down! Only last night I was quite well, my parents can tell you, or rather I did have a slight presentiment. I must have showed some sign of it. Why didn't I report it at the office! But one always thinks that an indisposition can be got over without staying in the house. Oh sir, do spare my parents! All that you're reproaching me with now has no foundation; no one has ever said a word to me about it. Perhaps you haven't looked at the last orders I sent in. Anyhow, I can still catch the eight o'clock train, I'm much the better for my few hours' rest. Don't let me detain you here, sir; I'll be attending to business very soon, and do be good enough to tell the chief so and to make my excuses to him!"

And while all this was tumbling out pell-mell and Gregor hardly knew what he was saying, he had reached the chest quite easily, perhaps because of the practice he had had in bed, and was now trying to lever himself upright by means of it. He meant actually to open the door, actually to show himself and speak to the chief clerk; he was eager to find out what the others, after all their insistence, would say at the sight of him. If they were horrified then the responsibility was no longer his and he could stay quiet. But if they took it calmly, then he had no reason either to be upset, and could really get to the station for the eight o'clock train if he hurried. At first he slipped down a few times from the polished surface of the chest, but at length with a last heave he stood upright; he paid no more attention to the pains in the lower part of his body, however they smarted. Then he let himself fall against the back of a nearby chair, and clung with his little legs to the edges of it. That brought him into control of himself again and he stopped speaking, for now he could listen to what the chief clerk was saying.

"Did you understand a word of it?" the chief clerk was asking; "surely he can't be trying to make fools of us?" "Oh dear," cried his mother, in tears, "perhaps he's terribly ill and we're tormenting him. Grete! Grete!" she called out then. "Yes Mother?" called his sister from the other side. They were calling to each other across Gregor's room. "You must go this minute for the doctor. Gregor is ill. Go for the doctor, quick. Did you hear how he was speaking?" "That was no human voice," said the chief clerk in a voice noticeably low beside the shrillness of the mother's. "Anna! Anna!" his father was calling through the hall to the kitchen, clapping his hands, "get a locksmith at once!" And the two girls were already running through the hall with a swish of skirts—how could his sister have got dressed so quickly?—and were tearing the front door open. There was no sound of its closing again; they had evidently left it open, as one does in houses where some great misfortune has happened.

But Gregor was now much calmer. The words he uttered were no longer understandable, apparently, although they seemed clear enough to him, even clearer than before, perhaps because his ear had grown accustomed to the sound of them. Yet at any rate people now believed that something was wrong with him, and were ready to help him. The positive certainty with which these first measures had been taken comforted him. He felt himself drawn once more into the human circle and hoped for great and remarkable results from both the doctor and the locksmith, without really distinguishing precisely between them. To make his voice as clear as possible for the decisive conversation that was now imminent he coughed a little, as quietly as he could, of course, since this noise too might not sound like a human cough for all he was able to judge. In the next room meanwhile there was complete silence. Perhaps his parents were sitting at the table with the chief clerk, whispering, perhaps they were all leaning against the door and listening.

Slowly Gregor pushed the chair toward the door, then let go of it, caught hold of the door for support—the soles at the end of his little legs were somewhat sticky—and rested against it for a moment after his efforts. Then he set himself to turning the key in the lock with his mouth. It seemed, unhappily, that he hadn't really any teeth—what could he grip the key with?—but on the other hand his jaws were certainly very strong; with their help he did manage to set the key in motion, heedless of the fact that he was undoubtedly damaging them somewhere, since a brown fluid issued from his mouth, flowed over the key, and dripped on the floor. "Just listen to that," said the chief clerk next door; "he's turning the key." That was a great encouragement to Gregor; but they should all have shouted encouragement to him, his father and mother too: "Go on, Gregor," they should have called out, "keep going, hold on to that key!" And in the belief that they were all following his efforts intently, he clenched his jaws recklessly on the key with all the force at his command. As the turning of the key progressed he circled around the lock, holding on now only with his mouth, pushing on the key, as required, or pulling it down again with all the weight of his body. The louder click of the finally yielding lock literally quickened Gregor. With a deep breath of relief he said to himself: "So I didn't need the locksmith," and laid his head on the handle to open the door wide.

Since he had to pull the door toward him, he was still invisible when it was really wide open. He had to edge himself slowly around the near half of the double door, and to do it very carefully if he was not to fall plump upon his back just on the threshold. He was still carrying out this difficult maneuver, with no time to observe anything else, when he heard the chief clerk utter a loud "Oh!"—it sounded like a gust of wind—and now he could see the man, standing as he was nearest to the door, clapping one hand before his open mouth and slowly backing away as if driven by some invisible steady pressure. His mother—in spite of the chief clerk's being there her hair was still undone and sticking up in all directions—first clasped her hands and looked at his father, then took two steps toward Gregor and fell on the floor among her outspread skirts, her face quite hidden on her breast. His father knotted his fist with a fierce expression on his face as if he meant to knock Gregor back into his room, then looked uncertainly around the living room, covered his eyes with his hands, and wept till his great chest heaved.

Gregor did not go now into the living room, but leaned against the inside of the firmly shut wing of the door, so that only half his body was visible and his head above it bending sideways to look at the others. The light had meanwhile strengthened; on the other side of the street one could see clearly a section of the endlessly long, dark gray building opposite — it was a hospital — abruptly punctuated by its row of regular windows; the rain was still falling, but only in large singly discernible and literally singly splashing drops. The breakfast dishes were set out on the table lavishly, for breakfast was the most important meal of the day to Gregor's father, who lingered it out for hours over various newspapers. Right opposite Gregor on the wall hung a photograph of himself in military service, as a lieutenant, hand on sword, a carefree smile on his face, inviting one to respect his uniform and military bearing. The door leading to the hall was open, and one could see that the front door stood open too, showing the landing beyond and the beginning of the stairs going down.

"Well," said Gregor, knowing perfectly that he was the only one who had retained any composure, "I'll put my clothes on at once, pack up my samples, and start off. Will you only let me go? You see, sir, I'm not obstinate, and I'm willing to work; traveling is a hard life, but I couldn't live without it. Where are you going, sir? To the office? Yes? Will you give a true account of all this? One can be temporarily incapacitated, but that's just the moment for remembering former services and bearing in mind that later on, when the incapacity has been got over, one will certainly work with all the more industry and concentration. I'm loyally bound to serve the chief, you know that very well. Besides, I have to provide for my parents and my sister. I'm in great difficulties, but I'll get out of them again. Don't make things any worse for me than they are. Stand up for me in the firm. Travelers are not popular there, I know. People think they earn sacks of money and just have a good time. A prejudice there's no particular reason for revising. But you, sir, have a more comprehensive view of affairs than the rest of the staff, yes, let me tell you in confidence, a more comprehensive view than the chief himself, who, being the owner, lets his judgment easily be swayed against one of his employees. And you know very well that the traveler, who is never seen in the office almost the whole year around, can so easily fall a victim to gossip and ill luck and unfounded complaints, which he mostly knows nothing about, except when he comes back exhausted from his rounds, and only then suffers in person from their evil consequences, which he can no longer trace back to the original causes. Sir, sir, don't go away without a word to me to show that you think me in the right at least to some extent!"

But at Gregor's very first words the chief clerk had already backed away and only stared at him with parted lips over one twitching shoulder. And while Gregor was speaking he did not stand still one moment but stole away toward the door, without taking his eyes off Gregor, yet only an inch at a time, as if obeying some secret injunction to leave the room. He was already at the hall, and the suddenness with which he took his last step out of the living room would have made one believe he had burned the sole of his foot. Once in the hall he stretched his right arm before him toward the staircase, as if some supernatural power were waiting there to deliver him.

Gregor perceived that the chief clerk must on no account be allowed to go away in this frame of mind if his position in the firm were not to be endangered to the utmost. His parents did not understand this so well; they had convinced themselves in the course of years that Gregor was settled for life in this firm, and besides they were so preoccupied with their immediate troubles that all foresight had forsaken them. Yet Gregor had this foresight. The chief clerk must be detained, soothed, persuaded, and finally won over; the whole future of Gregor and his family depended on it! If only his sister had been there! She was intelligent; she had begun to cry while Gregor was still lying quietly on his back. And no doubt the chief clerk, so partial to ladies, would have been guided by her; she would have shut the door of the flat and in the hall talked him out of his horror. But she was not there, and Gregor would have to handle the situation himself. And without remembering that he was still unaware what powers of movement he possessed, without even remembering that his words in all possibility, indeed in all likelihood, would again be unintelligible, he let go the wing of the door, pushed himself through the opening, started to walk toward the chief clerk, who was already ridiculously clinging with both hands to the railing on the landing; but immediately, as he was feeling for a support, he fell down with a little cry upon all his numerous legs. Hardly was he down when he experienced for the first time this morning a sense of physical comfort; his legs had firm ground under them; they were completely obedient, as he noted with joy; they even strove to carry him forward in whatever direction he chose; and he was inclined to believe that a final relief from all his sufferings was at hand. But in the same moment as he found himself on the floor, rocking with suppressed eagerness to move, not far from his mother, indeed just in front of her, she, who had seemed so completely crushed, sprang all at once to her feet, her arms and fingers outspread, cried: "Help, for God's sake, help!" bent her head down as if to see Gregor better, yet on the contrary kept backing senselessly away; had quite forgotten that the laden table stood behind her; sat upon it hastily, as if in absence of mind, when she bumped into it; and seemed altogether unaware that the big coffeepot beside her was upset and pouring coffee in a flood over the carpet.

"Mother, Mother," said Gregor in a low voice, and looked up at her. The chief clerk, for the moment, had quite slipped from his mind; instead, he could not resist snapping his jaws together at the sight of the streaming coffee. That made his mother scream again, she fled from the table and fell into the arms of his father, who hastened to catch her. But Gregor had now no time to spare for his parents; the chief clerk was already on the stairs; with his chin on the banisters he was taking one last backward look. Gregor made a spring, to be as sure as possible of overtaking him; the chief clerk must have divined his intention, for he leaped down several steps and vanished; he was still yelling "Ugh!" and it echoed through the whole staircase.

Unfortunately, the flight of the chief clerk seemed completely to upset Gregor's father, who had remained relatively calm until now, for instead of running after the man himself, or at least not hindering Gregor in his pursuit, he seized in his right hand the walking stick that the chief clerk had left behind on a chair, together with a hat and greatcoat, snatched in his left hand a large newspaper from the table, and began stamping his feet and flourishing the stick and the newspaper to drive Gregor back into his room. No entreaty of Gregor's availed, indeed no entreaty was even understood, however humbly he bent his head his father only stamped on the floor the more loudly. Behind his father his mother had torn open a window, despite the cold weather, and was leaning far out of it with her face in her hands. A strong draught set in from the street to the staircase, the window curtains blew in, the newspapers on the table fluttered, stray pages whisked over the floor. Pitilessly Gregor's father drove him back, hissing and crying "Shoo!" like a savage. But Gregor was quite unpracticed in walking backwards, it really was a slow business. If he only had a chance to turn around he could get back to his room at once, but he was afraid of exasperating his father by the slowness of such a rotation and at any moment the stick in his father's hand might hit him a fatal blow on the back or on the head. In the end, however, nothing else was left for him to do since to his horror he observed that in moving backwards he could not even control the direction he took; and so, keeping an anxious eye on his father all the time over his shoulder, he began to turn around as quickly as he could, which was in reality very slowly. Perhaps his father noted his good intentions, for he did not interfere except every now and then to help him in the maneuver from a distance with the point of the stick. If only he would have stopped making that unbearable hissing noise! It made Gregor quite lose his head. He had turned almost completely around when the hissing noise so distracted him that he even turned a little the wrong way again. But when at last his head was fortunately right in front of the doorway, it appeared that his body was too broad simply to get through the opening. His father, of course, in his present mood was far from thinking of such a thing as opening the other half of the door, to let Gregor have enough space. He had merely the fixed idea of driving Gregor back into his room as quickly as possible. He would never have suffered Gregor to make the circumstantial preparations for standing up on end and perhaps slipping his way through the door. Maybe he was now making more noise than ever to urge Gregor forward, as if no obstacle impeded him; to Gregor, anyhow, the noise in his rear sounded no longer like the voice of one single father; this was really no joke, and Gregor thrust himself —come what might—into the doorway. One side of his body rose up, he was tilted at an angle in the doorway, his flank was quite bruised, horrid blotches stained the white door, soon he was stuck fast and, left to himself, could not have moved at all, his legs on one side fluttered trembling in the air, those on the other were crushed painfully to the floor—when from behind his father gave him a strong push which was literally a deliverance and he flew far into the room, bleeding freely. The door was slammed behind him with the stick, and then at last there was silence.

II

Not until it was twilight did Gregor awake out of a deep sleep, more like a swoon than a sleep. He would certainly have waked up of his own accord not much later, for he felt himself sufficiently rested and well slept, but it seemed to him as if a fleeting step and a cautious shutting of the door leading into the hall had aroused him. The electric lights in the street cast a pale sheen here and there on the ceiling and the upper surfaces of the furniture, but down below, where he lay, it was dark. Slowly, awkwardly trying out his feelers, which he now first learned to appreciate, he pushed his way to the door to see what had been happening there. His left side felt like one single long, unpleasantly tense scar, and he had actually to limp on his two rows of legs. One little leg, moreover, had been severely damaged in the course of that morning's events — it was almost a miracle that only one had been damaged — and trailed uselessly behind him.

He had reached the door before he discovered what had really drawn him to it: the smell of food. For there stood a basin filled with fresh milk in which floated little sops of white bread. He could almost have laughed with joy, since he was now still hungrier than in the morning, and he dipped his head almost over the eyes straight into the milk. But soon in disappointment he withdrew it again; not only did he find it difficult to feed because of his tender left side — and he could only feed with the palpitating collaboration of his whole body — he did not like the milk either, although milk had been his favorite drink and that was certainly why his sister had set it there for him, indeed it was almost with repulsion that he turned away from the basin and crawled back to the middle of the room.

He could see through the crack of the door that the gas was turned on in the living room, but while usually at this time his father made a habit of reading the afternoon newspaper in a loud voice to his mother and occasionally to his sister as well, not a sound was now to be heard. Well, perhaps his father had recently given up this habit of reading aloud, which his sister had mentioned so often in conversation and in her letters. But there was the same silence all around, although the flat was certainly not empty of occupants. "What a quiet life our family has been leading," said Gregor to himself, and as he sat there motionless staring into the darkness he felt great pride in the fact that he had been able to provide such a life for his parents and sister in such a fine flat. But what if all the quiet, the comfort, the contentment were now to end in horror? To keep himself from being lost in such thoughts Gregor took refuge in movement and crawled up and down the room.

Once during the long evening one of the side doors was opened a little and quickly shut again, later the other side door too; someone had apparently wanted to come in and then thought better of it. Gregor now stationed himself immediately before the living-room door, determined to persuade any hesitating visitor to come in or at least to discover who it might be; but the door was not opened again and he waited in vain. In the early morning, when the doors were locked, they had all wanted to come in, now that he had opened one door and the other had apparently been opened during the day, no one came in and even the keys were on the other side of the doors.

It was late at night before the gas went out in the living room, and Gregor could easily tell that his parents and his sister had all stayed awake until then, for he could clearly hear the three of them stealing away on tiptoe. No one was likely to visit him, not until the morning, that was certain; so he had plenty of time to meditate at his leisure on how he was to arrange his life afresh. But the lofty, empty room in which he had to lie flat on the floor filled him with an apprehension he could not account for, since it had been his very own room for the past five years — and with a half-unconscious action, not without a slight feeling of shame, he scuttled under the sofa, where he felt comfortable at once, although his back was a little cramped and he could not lift his head up, and his only regret was that his body was too broad to get the whole of it under the sofa.

He stayed there all night, spending the time partly in a light slumber, from which his hunger kept waking him up with a start, and partly in worrying and sketching vague hopes, which all led to the same conclusion, that he must lie low for the present and, by exercising patience and the utmost consideration, help the family to bear the inconvenience he was bound to cause them in his present condition.

Very early in the morning, it was still almost night, Gregor had the chance to test the strength of his new resolutions, for his sister, nearly fully dressed, opened the door from the hall and peered in. She did not see him at once, yet when she caught sight of him under the sofa — well, he had to be somewhere, he couldn't have flown away, could he? — she was so startled that without being able to help it she slammed the door shut again. But as if regretting her behavior she opened the door again immediately and came in on tiptoe, as if she were visiting an invalid or even a stranger. Gregor had pushed his head forward to the very edge of the sofa and watched her. Would she notice that he had left the milk standing, and not for lack of hunger, and would she bring in some other kind of food more to his taste? If she did not do it of her own accord, he would rather starve than draw her attention to the fact, although he felt a wild impulse to dart out from under the sofa, throw himself at her feet, and beg her for something to eat. But his sister at once noticed, with surprise, that the basin was still full, except for a little milk that had been spilled all around it, she lifted it immediately, not with her bare hands, true, but with a cloth and carried it away. Gregor was wildly curious to know what she would bring instead, and made various speculations about it. Yet what she actually did next, in the goodness of her heart, he could never have guessed at. To find out what he liked she brought him a whole selection of food, all set out on an old newspaper. There were old, half-decayed vegetables, bones from last night's supper covered with a white sauce that had thickened; some raisins and almonds; a piece of cheese that Gregor would have called uneatable two days ago; a dry roll of bread, a buttered roll, and a roll both buttered and salted. Besides all that, she set down again the same basin, into which she had poured some water, and which was apparently to be reserved for his exclusive use. And with fine tact, knowing that Gregor would not eat in her presence, she withdrew quickly and even turned the key, to let him understand that he could take his ease as much as he liked. Gregor's legs all whizzed toward the food. His wounds must have healed completely, moreover, for he felt no disability, which amazed him and made him reflect how more than a month ago he had cut one finger a little with a knife and had still suffered pain from the wound only the day before yesterday. Am I less sensitive now? he thought, and sucked greedily at the cheese, which above all the other edibles attracted him at once and strongly. One after another and with tears of satisfaction in his eyes he quickly devoured the cheese, the vegetables, and the sauce; the fresh food, on the other hand, had no charms for him, he could not even stand the smell of it and actually dragged away to some little distance the things he could eat. He had long finished his meal and was only lying lazily on the same spot when his sister turned the key slowly as a sign for him to retreat. That roused him at once, although he was nearly asleep, and he hurried under the sofa again. But it took considerable self-control for him to stay under the sofa, even for the short time his sister was in the room, since the large meal had swollen his body somewhat and he was so cramped he could hardly breathe. Slight attacks of breathlessness afflicted him and his eyes were starting a little out of his head as he watched his unsuspecting sister sweeping together with a broom not only the remains of what he had eaten but even the things he had not touched, as if these were now of no use to anyone, and hastily shoveling it all into a bucket, which she covered with a wooden lid and carried away. Hardly had she turned her back when Gregor came from under the sofa and stretched and puffed himself out.

In this manner Gregor was fed, once in the early morning while his parents and the servant girl were still asleep, and a second time after they had all had their midday dinner, for then his parents took a short nap and the servant girl could be sent out on some errand or other by his sister. Not that they would have wanted him to starve, of course, but perhaps they could not have borne to know more about his feeding than from heresay, perhaps too his sister wanted to spare them such little anxieties wherever possible, since they had quite enough to bear as it was.

Under what pretext the doctor and the locksmith had been got rid of on that first morning Gregor could not discover, for since what he said was not understood by the others it never struck any of them, not even his sister, that he could understand what they said, and so whenever his sister came into his room he had to content himself with hearing her utter only a sigh now and then and an occasional appeal to the saints. Later on, when she had got a little used to the situation — of course she could never get completely used to it — she sometimes threw out a remark which was kindly meant or could be so interpreted. "Well, he liked his dinner today," she would say when Gregor had made a good clearance of his food; and when he had not eaten, which gradually happened more and more often, she would say almost sadly: "Everything's been left standing again."

But although Gregor could get no news directly, he overheard a lot from the neighboring rooms, and as soon as voices were audible, he would run to the door of the room concerned and press his whole body against it. In the first few days especially there was no conversation that did not refer to him somehow, even if only indirectly. For two whole days there were family consultations at every mealtime about what should be done; but also between meals the same subject was discussed, for there were always at least two members of the family at home, since no one wanted to be alone in the flat and to leave it quite empty was unthinkable. And on the very first of these days the household cook — it was not quite clear what and how much she knew of the situation — went down on her knees to his mother and begged leave to go, and when she departed, a quarter of an hour later, gave thanks for her dismissal with tears in her eyes as if for the greatest benefit that could have been conferred on her, and without any prompting swore a solemn oath that she would never say a single word to anyone about what had happened.

Now Gregor's sister had to cook too, helping her mother; true, the cooking did not amount to much, for they ate scarcely anything. Gregor was always hearing one of the family vainly urging another to eat and getting no answer but: "Thanks, I've had all I want," or something similar. Perhaps they drank nothing either. Time and again his sister kept asking his father if he wouldn't like some beer and offered kindly to go and fetch it herself, and when he made no answer suggested that she could ask the concierge to fetch it, so that he need feel no sense of obligation, but then a round "No" came from his father and no more was said about it.

In the course of that very first day Gregor's father explained the family's financial position and prospects to both his mother and his sister. Now and then he rose from the table to get some voucher or memorandum out of the small safe he had rescued from the collapse of his business five years earlier. One could hear him opening the complicated lock and rustling papers out and shutting it again. This statement made by his father was the first cheerful information Gregor had heard since his imprisonment. He had been of the opinion that nothing at all was left over from his father's business, at least his father had never said anything to the contrary, and of course he had not asked him directly. At that time Gregor's sole desire was to do his utmost to help the family to forget as soon as possible the catastrophe that had overwhelmed the business and thrown them all into a state of complete despair. And so he had set to work with unusual ardor and almost overnight had become a commercial traveler instead of a little clerk, with of course much greater chances of earning money, and his success was immediately translated into good round coin which he could lay on the table for his amazed and happy family. These had been fine times, and they had never recurred, at least not with the same sense of glory, although later on Gregor had earned so much money that he was able to meet the expenses of the whole household and did so. They had simply got used to it, both the family and Gregor; the money was gratefully accepted and gladly given, but there was no special uprush of warm feeling. With his sister alone had he remained intimate, and it was a secret plan of his that she, who loved music, unlike himself, and could play movingly on the violin, should be sent next year to study at the Conservatorium, despite the great expense that would entail, which must be made up in some other way. During his brief visits home the Conservatorium was often mentioned in the talks he had with his sister, but always merely as a beautiful dream which could never come true, and his parents discouraged even these innocent references to it; yet Gregor had made up his mind firmly about it and meant to announce the fact with due solemnity on Christmas Day.

Such were the thoughts, completely futile in his present condition, that went through his head as he stood clinging upright to the door and listening. Sometimes out of sheer weariness he had to give up listening and let his head fall negligently against the door, but he always had to pull himself together again at once, for even the slight sound his head made was audible next door and brought all conversation to a stop. "What can he be doing now?" his father would say after a while, obviously turning toward the door, and only then would the interrupted conversation gradually be set going again.

Gregor was now informed as amply as he could wish — for his father tended to repeat himself in his explanations, partly because it was a long time since he had handled such matters and partly because his mother could not always grasp things at once — that a certain amount of investments, a very small amount it was true, had survived the wreck of their fortunes and had even increased a little because the dividends had not been touched meanwhile. And besides that, the money Gregor brought home every month — he had kept only a few dollars for himself—had never been quite used up and now amounted to a small capital sum. Behind the door Gregor nodded his head eagerly, rejoiced at this evidence of unexpected thrift and foresight. True, he could really have paid off some more of his father's debts to the chief with this extra money, and so brought much nearer the day on which he could quit his job, but doubtless it was better the way his father had arranged it.

Yet this capital was by no means sufficient to let the family live on the interest of it; for one year, perhaps, or at the most two, they could live on the principal, that was all. It was simply a sum that ought not to be touched and should be kept for a rainy day; money for living expenses would have to be earned. Now his father was still hale enough but an old man, and he had done no work for the past five years and could not be expected to do much; during these five years, the first years of leisure in his laborious though unsuccessful life, he had grown rather fat and become sluggish. And Gregor's old mother, how was she to earn a living with her asthma, which troubled her even when she walked through the flat and kept her lying on a sofa every other day panting for breath beside an open window? And was his sister to earn her bread, she who was still a child of seventeen and whose life hitherto had been so pleasant, consisting as it did in dressing herself nicely, sleeping long, helping in the housekeeping, going out to a few modest entertainments, and above all playing the violin? At first whenever the need for earning money was mentioned Gregor let go his hold on the door and threw himself down on the cool leather sofa beside it, he felt so hot with shame and grief.

Often he just lay there the long nights through without sleeping at all, scrabbling for hours on the leather. Or he nerved himself to the great effort of pushing an armchair to the window, then crawled up over the window sill and, braced against the chair, leaned against the windowpanes, obviously in some recollection of the sense of freedom that looking out of a window always used to give him. For in reality day by day things that were even a little way off were growing dimmer to his sight; the hospital across the street, which he used to execrate for being all too often before his eyes, was now quite beyond his range of vision, and if he had not known that he lived in Charlotte Street, a quiet street but still a city street, he might have believed that his window gave on a desert waste where gray sky and gray land blended indistinguishably into each other. His quick-witted sister only needed to observe twice that the armchair stood by the window; after that whenever she had tidied the room she always pushed the chair back to the same place at the window and even left the inner casements open.

If he could have spoken to her and thanked her for all she had to do for him, he could have borne her ministrations better; as it was, they oppressed him. She certainly tried to make as light as possible of whatever was disagreeable in her task, and as time went on she succeeded, of course, more and more, but time brought more enlightenment to Gregor too. The very way she came in distressed him. Hardly was she in the room when she rushed to the window, without even taking time to shut the door, careful as she was usually to shield the sight of Gregor's room from the others, and as if she were almost suffocating tore the casements open with hasty fingers, standing then in the open draught for a while even in the bitterest cold and drawing deep breaths. This noisy scurry of hers upset Gregor twice a day; he would crouch trembling under the sofa all the time, knowing quite well that she would certainly have spared him such a disturbance had she found it at all possible to stay in his presence without opening the window.

On one occasion, about a month after Gregor's metamorphosis, when there was surely no reason for her to be still startled at his appearance, she came a little earlier than usual and found him gazing out of the window, quite motionless, and thus well placed to look like a bogey. Gregor would not have been surprised had she not come in at all, for she could not immediately open the window while he was there, but not only did she retreat, she jumped back as if in alarm and banged the door shut; a stranger might well have thought that he had been lying in wait for her there meaning to bite her. Of course he hid himself under the sofa at once, but he had to wait until midday before she came again, and she seemed more ill at ease than usual. This made him realize how repulsive the sight of him still was to her, and that it was bound to go on being repulsive, and what an effort it must cost her not to run away even from the sight of the small portion of his body that stuck out from under the sofa. In order to spare her that, therefore, one day he carried a sheet on his back to the sofa—it cost him four hours' labor—and arranged it there in such a way as to hide him completely, so that even if she were to bend down she could not see him. Had she considered the sheet unnecessary, she would certainly have stripped it off the sofa again, for it was clear enough that this curtaining and confining of himself was not likely to conduce to Gregor's comfort, but she left it where it was, and Gregor even fancied that he caught a thankful glance from her eye when he lifted the sheet carefully a very little with his head to see how she was taking the new arrangement.

For the first fortnight his parents could not bring themselves to the point of entering his room, and he often heard them expressing their appreciation of his sister's activities, whereas formerly they had frequently scolded her for being as they thought a somewhat useless daughter. But now, both of them often waited outside the door, his father and his mother, while his sister tidied his room, and as soon as she came out she had to tell them exactly how things were in the room, what Gregor had eaten, how he had conducted himself this time, and whether there was not perhaps some slight improvement in his condition. His mother, moreover, began relatively soon to want to visit him, but his father and sister dissuaded her at first with arguments which Gregor listened to very attentively and altogether approved. Later, however, she had to be held back by main force, and when she cried out: "Do let me in to Gregor, he is my unfortunate son! Can't you understand that I must go to him?" Gregor thought that it might be well to have her come in, not every day, of course, but perhaps once a week; she understood things, after all, much better than his sister, who was only a child despite the efforts she was making and had perhaps taken on so difficult a task merely out of childish thoughtlessness.

Gregor's desire to see his mother was soon fulfilled. During the daytime he did not want to show himself at the window, out of consideration for his parents, but he could not crawl very far around the few square yards of floor space he had, nor could he bear lying quietly at rest all during the night, while he was fast losing any interest he had ever taken in food, so that for mere recreation he had formed the habit of crawling crisscross over the walls and ceiling. He especially enjoyed hanging suspended from the ceiling; it was much better than lying on the floor; one could breathe more freely; one's body swung and rocked lightly, and in the almost blissful absorption induced by this suspension it could happen to his own surprise that he let go and fell plump on the floor. Yet he now had his body much better under control than formerly, and even such a big fall did him no harm. His sister at once remarked the new distraction Gregor had found for himself—he left traces behind him of the sticky stuff on his soles wherever he crawled—and she got the idea in her head of giving him as wide a field as possible to crawl in and of removing the pieces of furniture that hindered him, above all the chest of drawers and the writing desk. But that was more than she could manage all by herself; she did not dare ask her father to help her; and as for the servant girl, a young creature of sixteen who had had the courage to stay on after the cook's departure, she could not be asked to help, for she had begged as a special favor that she might keep the kitchen door locked and open it only on a definite summons; so there was nothing left but to apply to her mother at an hour when her father was out. And the old lady did come, with exclamations of joyful eagerness, which, however, died away at the door of Gregor's room. Gregor's sister, of course, went in first, to see that everything was in order before letting his mother enter. In great haste Gregor pulled the sheet lower and tucked it more in folds so that it really looked as if it had been thrown accidentally over the sofa. And this time he did not peer out from under it; he renounced the pleasure of seeing his mother on this occasion and was only glad that she had come at all. "Come in, he's out of sight," said his sister, obviously leading her mother in by the hand. Gregor could now hear the two women struggling to shift the heavy old chest from its place, and his sister claiming the greater part of the labor for herself, without listening to the admonitions of her mother, who feared she might overstrain herself. It took a long time. After at least a quarter of an hour's tugging his mother objected that the chest had better be left where it was, for in the first place it was too heavy and could never be got out before his father came home, and standing in the middle of the room like that it would only hamper Gregor's movements, while in the second place it was not at all certain that removing the furniture would be doing a service to Gregor. She was inclined to think to the contrary; the sight of the naked walls made her own heart heavy, and why shouldn't Gregor have the same feeling, considering that he had been used to his furniture for so long and might feel forlorn without it. "And doesn't it look," she concluded in a low voice—in fact she had been almost whispering all the time as if to avoid letting Gregor, whose exact whereabouts she did not know, hear even the tones of her voice, for she was convinced that he could not understand her words—"doesn't it look as if we were showing him, by taking away his furniture, that we have given up hope of his ever getting better and are just leaving him coldly to himself? I think it would be best to keep his room exactly as it has always been, so that when he comes back to us he will find everything unchanged and be able all the more easily to forget what has happened in between."

On hearing these words from his mother Gregor realized that the lack of all direct human speech for the past two months together with the monotony of family life must have confused his mind, otherwise he could not account for the fact that he had quite earnestly looked forward to having his room emptied of furnishing. Did he really want his warm room, so comfortably fitted with old family furniture, to be turned into a naked den in which he would certainly be able to crawl unhampered in all directions but at the price of shedding simultaneously all recollection of his human background? He had indeed been so near the brink of forgetfulness that only the voice of his mother, which he had not heard for so long, had drawn him back from it. Nothing should be taken out of his room; everything must stay as it was; he could not dispense with the good influence of the furniture on his state of mind; and even if the furniture did hamper him in his senseless crawling around and around, that was no drawback but a great advantage.

Unfortunately his sister was of the contrary opinion; she had grown accustomed, and not without reason, to consider herself an expert in Gregor's affairs as against her parents, and so her mother's advice was now enough to make her determined on the removal not only of the chest and the writing desk, which had been her first intention, but of all the furniture except the indispensable sofa. This determination was not, of course, merely the outcome of childish recalcitrance and of the self-confidence she had recently developed so unexpectedly and at such cost; she had in fact perceived that Gregor needed a lot of space to crawl about in, while on the other hand he never used the furniture at all, so far as could be seen. Another factor might also have been the enthusiastic temperament of an adolescent girl, which seeks to indulge itself on every opportunity and which now tempted Grete to exaggerate the horror of her brother's circumstances in order that she might do all the more for him. In a room where Gregor lorded it all alone over empty walls no one save herself was likely ever to set foot.

And so she was not to be moved from her resolve by her mother, who seemed moreover to be ill at ease in Gregor's room and therefore unsure of herself, was soon reduced to silence, and helped her daughter as best she could to push the chest outside. Now, Gregor could do without the chest, if need be, but the writing desk he must retain. As soon as the two women had got the chest out of his room, groaning as they pushed it, Gregor stuck his head out from under the sofa to see how he might intervene as kindly and cautiously as possible. But as bad luck would have it, his mother was the first to return, leaving Grete clasping the chest in the room next door where she was trying to shift it all by herself, without of course moving it from the spot. His mother however was not accustomed to the sight of him, it might sicken her and so in alarm Gregor backed quickly to the other end of the sofa, yet could not prevent the sheet from swaying a little in front. That was enough to put her on the alert. She paused, stood still for a moment, and then went back to Grete.

Although Gregor kept reassuring himself that nothing out of the way was happening, but only a few bits of furniture were being changed around, he soon had to admit that all this trotting to and fro of the two women, their little ejaculations, and the scraping of furniture along the floor affected him like a vast disturbance coming from all sides at once, and however much he tucked in his head and legs and cowered to the very floor he was bound to confess that he would not be able to stand it for long. They were clearing his room out; taking away everything he loved; the chest in which he kept his fret saw and other tools was already dragged off; they were now loosening the writing desk which had almost sunk into the floor, the desk at which he had done all his homework when he was at the commercial academy, at the grammar school before that, and, yes, even at the primary school—he had no more time to waste in weighing the good intentions of the two women, whose existence he had by now almost forgotten, for they were so exhausted that they were laboring in silence and nothing could be heard but the heavy scuffling of their feet.

And so he rushed out—the women were just leaning against the writing desk in the next room to give themselves a breather—and four times changed his direction, since he really did not know what to rescue first, then on the wall opposite, which was already otherwise cleared, he was struck by the picture of the lady muffled in so much fur and quickly crawled up to it and pressed himself to the glass, which was a good surface to hold on to and comforted his hot belly. This picture at least, which was entirely hidden beneath him, was going to be removed by nobody. He turned his head toward the door of the living room so as to observe the women when they came back.

They had not allowed themselves much of a rest and were already coming; Grete had twined her arm around her mother and was almost supporting her. "Well, what shall we take now?" said Grete, looking around. Her eyes met Gregor's from the wall. She kept her composure, presumably because of her mother, bent her head down to her mother, to keep her from looking up, and said, although in a fluttering, unpremeditated voice: "Come, hadn't we better go back to the living room for a moment?" Her intentions were clear enough to Gregor, she wanted to bestow her mother in safety and then chase him down from the wall. Well, just let her try it! He clung to his picture and would not give it up. He would rather fly in Grete's face.

But Grete's words had succeeded in disquieting her mother, who took a step to one side, caught sight of the huge brown mass on the flowered wallpaper, and before she was really conscious that what she saw was Gregor, screamed in a loud, hoarse voice: "Oh God, oh God!" fell with outspread arms over the sofa as if giving up, and did not move. "Gregor!" cried his sister, shaking her fist and glaring at him. This was the first time she had directly addressed him since his metamorphosis. She ran into the next room for some aromatic essence with which to rouse her mother from her fainting fit. Gregor wanted to help too— there was still time to rescue the picture—but he was stuck fast to the glass and had to tear himself loose; he then ran after his sister into the next room as if he could advise her, as he used to do; but then had to stand helplessly behind her; she meanwhile searched among various small bottles and when she turned around started in alarm at the sight of him; one bottle fell on the floor and broke; a splinter of glass cut Gregor's face and some kind of corrosive medicine splashed him; without pausing a moment longer Grete gathered up all the bottles she could carry and ran to her mother with them; she banged the door shut with her foot. Gregor was now cut off from his mother, who was perhaps nearly dying because of him; he dared not open the door for fear of frightening away his sister, who had to stay with her mother; there was nothing he could do but wait; and harassed by self-reproach and worry he began now to crawl to and fro, over everything, walls, furniture, and ceiling, and finally in his despair, when the whole room seemed to be reeling around him, fell down onto the middle of the big table.

A little while elapsed, Gregor was still lying there feebly and all around was quiet, perhaps that was a good omen. Then the doorbell rang. The servant girl was of course locked in her kitchen, and Grete would have to open the door. It was his father. "What's been happening?" were his first words; Grete's face must have told him everything. Grete answered in a muffled voice, apparently hiding her head on his breast: "Mother has been fainting, but she's better now. Gregor's broken loose." "Just what I expected," said his father, "just what I've been telling you, but you women would never listen." It was clear to Gregor that his father had taken the worst interpretation of Grete's all too brief statement and was assuming that Gregor had been guilty of some violent act. Therefore Gregor must now try to propitiate his father, since he had neither time nor means for an explanation. And so he fled to the door of his own room and crouched against it, to let his father see as soon as he came in from the hall that his son had the good intention of getting back into his room immediately and that it was not necessary to drive him there, but that if only the door were opened he would disappear at once.

Yet his father was not in the mood to perceive such fine distinctions. "Ah!" he cried as soon as he appeared, in a tone that sounded at once angry and exultant. Gregor drew his head back from the door and lifted it to look at his father. Truly, this was not the father he had imagined to himself; admittedly he had been too absorbed of late in his new recreation of crawling over the ceiling to take the same interest as before in what was happening elsewhere in the flat, and he ought really to be prepared for some changes. And yet, and yet, could that be his father? The man who used to lie wearily sunk in bed whenever Gregor set out on a business journey; who welcomed him back of an evening lying in a long chair in a dressing gown; who could not really rise to his feet but only lifted his arms in greeting, and on the rare occasions when he did go out with his family, on one or two Sundays a year and on highest holidays, walked between Gregor and his mother, who were slow walkers anyhow, even more slowly than they did, muffled in his old greatcoat, shuffling laboriously forward with the help of his crook-handled stick which he set down most cautiously at every step and, whenever he wanted to say anything, nearly always came to a full stop and gathered his escort around him? Now he was standing there in fine shape; dressed in a smart blue uniform with gold buttons, such as bank messengers wear; his strong double chin bulged over the stiff high collar of his jacket; from under his bushy eyebrows his black eyes darted fresh and penetrating glances; his onetime tangled white hair had been combed flat on either side of a shining and carefully exact parting. He pitched his cap, which bore a gold monogram, probably the badge of some bank, in a wide sweep across the whole room onto a sofa and with the tail-ends of his jacket thrown back, his hands in his trouser pockets, advanced with a grim visage toward Gregor. Likely enough he did not himself know what he meant to do; at any rate he lifted his feet uncommonly high, and Gregor was dumbfounded at the enormous size of his shoe soles. But Gregor could not risk standing up to him, aware as he had been from the very first day of his new life that his father believed only the severest measures suitable for dealing with him. And so he ran before his father, stopping when he stopped and scuttling forward again when his father made any kind of move. In this way they circled the room several times without anything decisive happening, indeed the whole operation did not even look like a pursuit because it was carried out so slowly. And so Gregor did not leave the floor, for he feared that his father might take as a piece of peculiar wickedness any excursion of his over the walls or the ceiling. All the same, he could not stay this course much longer, for while his father took one step he had to carry out a whole series of movements. He was already beginning to feel breathless, just as in his former life his lungs had not been very dependable. As he was staggering along, trying to concentrate his energy on running, hardly keeping his eyes open; in his dazed state never even thinking of any other escape than simply going forward; and having almost forgotten that the walls were free to him, which in this room were well provided with finely carved pieces of furniture full of knobs and crevices — suddenly something lightly flung landed close behind him and rolled before him. It was an apple; a second apple followed immediately; Gregor came to a stop in alarm; there was no point in running on, for his father was determined to bombard him. He had filled his pockets with fruit from the dish on the sideboard and was now shying apple after apple, without taking particularly good aim for the moment. The small red apples rolled about the floor as if magnetized and cannoned into each other. An apple thrown without much force grazed Gregor's back and glanced off harmlessly. But another following immediately landed right on his back and sank in; Gregor wanted to drag himself forward, as if this startling, incredible pain could be left behind him; but he felt as if nailed to the spot and flattened himself out in a complete derangement of all his senses. With his last conscious look he saw the door of his room being torn open and his mother rushing out ahead of his screaming sister, in her underbodice, for her daughter had loosened her clothing to let her breathe more freely and recover from her swoon, he saw his mother rushing toward his father, leaving one after another behind her on the floor her loosened petticoats, stumbling over her petticoats straight to his father and embracing him, in complete union with him — but here Gregor's sight began to fail — with her hands clasped around his father's neck as she begged for her son's life.

III

The serious injury done to Gregor, which disabled him for more than a month — the apple went on sticking in his body as a visible reminder, since no one ventured to remove it — seemed to have made even his father recollect that Gregor was a member of the family, despite his present unfortunate and repulsive shape, and ought not to be treated as an enemy, that, on the contrary, family duty required the suppression of disgust and the exercise of patience, nothing but patience.

And although his injury had impaired, probably forever, his powers of movement, and for the time being it took him long, long minutes to creep across his room like an old invalid — there was no question now of crawling up the wall — yet in his own opinion he was sufficiently compensated for this worsening of his condition by the fact that toward evening the living-room door, which he used to watch intently for an hour or two beforehand, was always thrown open, so that lying in the darkness of his room, invisible to the family, he could see them all at the lamp-lit table and listen to their talk, by general consent as it were, very different from his earlier eavesdropping.

True, their intercourse lacked the lively character of former times, which he had always called to mind with a certain wistfulness in the small hotel bedrooms where he had been wont to throw himself down, tired out, on damp bedding. They were now mostly very silent. Soon after supper his father would fall asleep in his armchair; his mother and sister would admonish each other to be silent; his mother, bending low over the lamp, stitched at fine sewing for an underwear firm; his sister, who had taken a job as a salesgirl, was learning shorthand and French in the evenings on the chance of bettering herself. Sometimes his father woke up, and as if quite unaware that he had been sleeping said to his mother: "What a lot of sewing you're doing today!" and at once fell asleep again, while the two women exchanged a tired smile.

With a kind of mulishness his father persisted in keeping his uniform on even in the house; his dressing gown hung uselessly on its peg and he slept fully dressed where he sat, as if he were ready for service at any moment and even here only at the beck and call of his superior. As a result, his uniform, which was not brand-new to start with, began to look dirty, despite all the loving care of the mother and sister to keep it clean, and Gregor often spent whole evenings gazing at the many greasy spots on the garment, gleaming with gold buttons always in a high state of polish, in which the old man sat sleeping in extreme discomfort and yet quite peacefully.

As soon as the clock struck ten his mother tried to rouse his father with gentle words and to persuade him after that to get into bed, for sitting there he could not have a proper sleep and that was what he needed most, since he had to go on duty at six. But with the mulishness that had obsessed him since he became a bank messenger he always insisted on staying longer at the table, although he regularly fell asleep again and in the end only with the greatest trouble could be got out of his armchair and into his bed. However insistently Gregor's mother and sister kept urging him with gentle reminders, he would go on slowly shaking his head for a quarter of an hour, keeping his eyes shut, and refuse to get to his feet. The mother plucked at his sleeve, whispering endearments in his ear, the sister left her lessons to come to her mother's help, but Gregor's father was not to be caught. He would only sink down deeper in his chair. Not until the two women hoisted him up by the armpits did he open his eyes and look at them both, one after the other, usually with the remark: "This is a life. This is the peace and quiet of my old age." And leaning on the two of them he would heave himself up, with difficulty, as if he were a great burden to himself, suffer them to lead him as far as the door and then wave them off and go on alone, while the mother abandoned her needlework and the sister her pen in order to run after him and help him farther.

Who could find time, in this overworked and tired-out family, to bother about Gregor more than was absolutely needful? The household was reduced more and more; the servant girl was turned off; a gigantic bony charwoman with white hair flying around her head came in morning and evening to do the rough work; everything else was done by Gregor's mother, as well as great piles of sewing. Even various family ornaments, which his mother and sister used to wear with pride at parties and celebrations, had to be sold, as Gregor discovered of an evening from hearing them all discuss the prices obtained. But what they lamented most was the fact that they could not leave the flat which was much too big for their present circumstances, because they could not think of any way to shift Gregor. Yet Gregor saw well enough that consideration for him was not the main difficulty preventing the removal, for they could have easily shifted him in some suitable box with a few air holes in it; what really kept them from moving into another flat was rather their own complete hopelessness and the belief that they had been singled out for a misfortune such as had never happened to any of their relations or acquaintances. They fulfilled to the uttermost all that the world demands of poor people, the father fetched breakfast for the small clerks in the bank, the mother devoted her energy to making underwear for strangers, the sister trotted to and fro behind the counter at the behest of customers, but more than this they had not the strength to do. And the wound in Gregor's back began to nag at him afresh when his mother and sister, after getting his father into bed, came back again, left their work lying, drew close to each other, and sat cheek by cheek; when his mother, pointing toward his room, said: "Shut that door now, Grete," and he was left again in darkness, while next door the women mingled their tears or perhaps sat dry-eyed staring at the table.

Gregor hardly slept at all by night or by day. He was often haunted by the idea that next time the door opened he would take the family's affairs in hand again just as he used to do; once more, after this long interval, there appeared in his thoughts the figures of the chief and the chief clerk, the commercial travelers and the apprentices, the porter who was so dull-witted, two or three friends in other firms, a chambermaid in one of the rural hotels, a sweet and fleeting memory, a cashier in a milliner's shop, whom he had wooed earnestly but too slowly—they all appeared, together with strangers or people he had quite forgotten, but instead of helping him and his family they were one and all unapproachable and he was glad when they vanished. At other times he would not be in the mood to bother about his family, he was only filled with rage at the way they were neglecting him, and although he had no clear idea of what he might care to eat he would make plans for getting into the larder to take the food that was after all his due, even if he were not hungry. His sister no longer took thought to bring him what might especially please him, but in the morning and at noon before she went to business hurriedly pushed into his room with her foot any food that was available, and in the evening cleared it out again with one sweep of the broom, heedless of whether it had been merely tasted, or—as most frequently happened—left untouched. The cleaning of his room, which she now did always in the evenings, could not have been more hastily done. Streaks of dirt stretched along the walls, here and there lay balls of dust and filth. At first Gregor used to station himself in some particularly filthy corner when his sister arrived, in order to reproach her with it, so to speak. But he could have sat there for weeks without getting her to make any improvement; she could see the dirt as well as he did, but she had simply made up her mind to leave it alone. And yet, with a touchiness that was new to her, which seemed anyhow to have infected the whole family, she jealously guarded her claim to be the sole caretaker of Gregor's room. His mother once subjected his room to a thorough cleaning, which was achieved only by means of several buckets of water—all this dampness of course upset Gregor too and he lay widespread, sulky, and motionless on the sofa—but she was well punished for it. Hardly had his sister noticed the changed aspect of his room that evening than she rushed in high dudgeon into the living room and, despite the imploringly raised hands of her mother, burst into a storm of weeping, while her parents — her father had of course been startled out of his chair — looked on at first in helpless amazement; then they too began to go into action; the father reproached the mother on his right for not having left the cleaning of Gregor's room to his sister; shrieked at the sister on his left that never again was she to be allowed to clean Gregor's room; while the mother tried to pull the father into his bedroom, since he was beyond himself with agitation; the sister, shaken with sobs, then beat upon the table with her small fists; and Gregor hissed loudly with rage because not one of them thought of shutting the door to spare him such a spectacle and so much noise.

Still, even if the sister, exhausted by her daily work, had grown tired of looking after Gregor as she did formerly, there was no need for his mother's intervention or for Gregor's being neglected at all. The charwoman was there. This old widow, whose strong bony frame had enabled her to survive the worst a long life could offer, by no means recoiled from Gregor. Without being in the least curious she had once by chance opened the door of his room and at the sight of Gregor, who, taken by surprise, began to rush to and fro although no one was chasing him, merely stood there with her arms folded. From that time she never failed to open his door a little for a moment, morning and evening, to have a look at him. At first she even used to call him to her, with words which apparently she took to be friendly, such as: "Come along, then, you old dung beetle!" or "Look at the old dung beetle, then!" To such allocutions Gregor made no answer, but stayed motionless where he was, as if the door had never been opened. Instead of being allowed to disturb him so senselessly whenever the whim took her, she should rather have been ordered to clean out his room daily, that charwoman! Once, early in the morning — heavy rain was lashing on the windowpanes, perhaps a sign that spring was on the way — Gregor was so exasperated when she began addressing him again that he ran at her, as if to attack her, although slowly and feebly enough. But the charwoman instead of showing fright merely lifted high a chair that happened to be beside the door, and as she stood there with her mouth wide open it was clear that she meant to shut it only when she brought the chair down on Gregor's back. "So you're not coming any nearer?" she asked, as Gregor turned away again, and quietly put the chair back into the corner.

Gregor was now eating hardly anything. Only when he happened to pass the food laid out for him did he take a bit of something in his mouth as a pastime, kept it there for an hour at a time, and usually spat it out again. At first he thought it was chagrin over the state of his room that prevented him from eating, yet he soon got used to the various changes in his room. It had become a habit in the family to push into his room things there was no room for elsewhere, and there were plenty of these now, since one of the rooms had been let to three lodgers. These serious gentlemen — all three of them with full beards, as Gregor once observed through a crack in the door — had a passion for order, not only in their own room but, since they were now members of the household, in all its arrangements, especially in the kitchen. Superfluous, not to say dirty, objects they could not bear. Besides, they had brought with them most of the furnishings they needed. For this reason many things could be dispensed with that it was no use trying to sell but that should not be thrown away either. All of them found their way into Gregor's room. The ash can likewise and the kitchen garbage can.

Anything that was not needed for the moment was simply flung into Gregor's room by the charwoman, who did everything in a hurry; fortunately Gregor usually saw only the object, whatever it was, and the hand that held it. Perhaps she intended to take the things away again as time and opportunity offered, or to collect them until she could throw them all out in a heap, but in fact they just lay wherever she happened to throw them, except when Gregor pushed his way through the junk heap and shifted it somewhat, at first out of necessity, because he had not room enough to crawl, but later with increasing enjoyment, although after such excursions, being sad and weary to death, he would lie motionless for hours. And since the lodgers often ate their supper at home in the common living room, the living-room door stayed shut many an evening, yet Gregor reconciled himself quite easily to the shutting of the door, for often enough on evenings when it was opened he had disregarded it entirely and lain in the darkest corner of his room, quite unnoticed by the family. But on one occasion the charwoman left the door open a little and it stayed ajar even when the lodgers came in for supper and the lamp was lit. They set themselves at the top end of the table where formerly Gregor and his father and mother had eaten their meals, unfolded their napkins, and took knife and fork in hand. At once his mother appeared in the other doorway with a dish of meat and close behind her his sister with a dish of potatoes piled high. The food steamed with a thick vapor. The lodgers bent over the food set before them as if to scrutinize it before eating, in fact the man in the middle, who seemed to pass for an authority with the other two, cut a piece of meat as it lay on the dish, obviously to discover if it were tender or should be sent back to the kitchen. He showed satisfaction, and Gregor's mother and sister, who had been watching anxiously, breathed freely and began to smile.

The family itself took its meals in the kitchen. Nonetheless, Gregor's father came into the living room before going into the kitchen and with one prolonged bow, cap in hand, made a round of the table. The lodgers all stood up and murmured something in their beards. When they were alone again they ate their food in almost complete silence. It seemed remarkable to Gregor that among the various noises coming from the table he could always distinguish the sound of their masticating teeth, as if this were a sign to Gregor that one needed teeth in order to eat, and that with toothless jaws even of the finest make one could do nothing. "I'm hungry enough," said Gregor sadly to himself, "but not for that kind of food. How these lodgers are stuffing themselves, and here am I dying of starvation!"

On that very evening—during the whole of his time there Gregor could not remember ever having heard the violin—the sound of violin-playing came from the kitchen. The lodgers had already finished their supper, the one in the middle had brought out a newspaper and given the other two a page apiece, and now they were leaning back at ease reading and smoking. When the violin began to play they pricked up their ears, got to their feet, and went on tiptoe to the hall door where they stood huddled together. Their movements must have been heard in the kitchen, for Gregor's father called out: "Is the violin-playing disturbing you, gentlemen? It can be stopped at once." "On the contrary," said the middle lodger, "could not Fräulein Samsa come and play in this room, beside us, where it is much more convenient and comfortable?" "Oh certainly," cried Gregor's father, as if he were the violin-player. The lodgers came back into the living room and waited. Presently Gregor's father arrived with the music stand, his mother carrying the music and his sister with the violin. His sister quietly made everything ready to start playing; his parents, who had never let rooms before and so had an exaggerated idea of the courtesy due to lodgers, did not venture to sit down on their own chairs; his father leaned against the door, the right hand thrust between two buttons of his livery coat, which was formerly buttoned up; but his mother was offered a chair by one of the lodgers and, since she left the chair just where he had happened to put it, sat down in a corner to one side.

Gregor's sister began to play; the father and mother, from either side, intently watched the movements of her hands. Gregor, attracted by the playing, ventured to move forward a little until his head was actually inside the living room. He felt hardly any surprise at his growing lack of consideration for the others; there had been a time when he prided himself on being considerate. And yet just on this occasion he had more reason than ever to hide himself, since, owing to the amount of dust that lay thick in his room and rose into the air at the slightest movement, he too was covered with dust; fluff and hair and remnants of food trailed with him, caught on his back and along his sides; his indifference to everything was much too great for him to turn on his back and scrape himself clean on the carpet, as once he had done several times a day. And in spite of his condition, no shame deterred him from advancing a little over the spotless floor of the living room.

To be sure, no one was aware of him. The family was entirely absorbed in the violin-playing; the lodgers, however, who first of all had stationed themselves, hands in pockets, much too close behind the music stand so that they could all have read the music, which must have bothered his sister, had soon retreated to the window, half whispering with downbent heads, and stayed there while his father turned an anxious eye on them. Indeed, they were making it more than obvious that they had been disappointed in their expectation of hearing good or enjoyable violin-playing, that they had had more than enough of the performance and only out of courtesy suffered a continued disturbance of their peace. From the way they all kept blowing the smoke of their cigars high in the air through nose and mouth one could divine their irritation. And yet Gregor's sister was playing so beautifully. Her face leaned sideways, intently and sadly her eyes followed the notes of music. Gregor crawled a little farther forward and lowered his head to the ground so that it might be possible for his eyes to meet hers. Was he an animal, that music had such an effect upon him? He felt as if the way were opening before him to the unknown nourishment he craved. He was determined to push forward till he reached his sister, to pull at her skirt and so let her know that she was to come into his room with her violin, for no one here appreciated her playing as he would appreciate it. He would never let her out of his room, at least, not so long as he lived; his frightful appearance would become, for the first time, useful to him; he would watch all the doors of his room at once and spit at intruders; but his sister should need no constraint, she should stay with him of her own free will; she should sit beside him on the sofa, bend down her ear to him, and hear him confide that he had had the firm intention of sending her to the Conservatorium, and that, but for his mishap, last Christmas — surely Christmas was long past? — he would have announced it to everybody without allowing a single objection. After this confession his sister would be so touched that she would burst into tears, and Gregor would then raise himself to her shoulder and kiss her on the neck, which, now that she went to business, she kept free of any ribbon or collar.

"Mr. Samsa!" cried the middle lodger to Gregor's father, and pointed, without wasting any more words, at Gregor, now working himself slowly forward. The violin fell silent, the middle lodger first smiled to his friends with a shake of the head and then looked at Gregor again. Instead of driving Gregor out, his father seemed to think it more needful to begin by soothing down the lodgers, although they were not at all agitated and apparently found Gregor more entertaining than the violin-playing. He hurried toward them and, spreading out his arms, tried to urge them back into their own room and at the same time to block their view of Gregor. They now began to be really a little angry, one could not tell whether because of the old man's behavior or because it had just dawned on them that all unwittingly they had such a neighbor as Gregor next door. They demanded explanations of his father, they waved their arms like him, tugged uneasily at their beards, and only with reluctance backed toward their room. Meanwhile Gregor's sister, who stood there as if lost when her playing was so abruptly broken off, came to life again, pulled herself together all at once after standing for a while holding violin and bow in nervelessly hanging hands and staring at her music, pushed her violin into the lap of her mother, who was still sitting in her chair fighting asthmatically for breath, and ran into the lodgers' room to which they were now being shepherded by her father rather more quickly than before. One could see the pillows and blankets on the beds flying under her accustomed fingers and being laid in order. Before the lodgers had actually reached their room she had finished making the beds and slipped out.

The old man seemed once more to be so possessed by his mulish self-assertiveness that he was forgetting all the respect he should show to his lodgers. He kept driving them on and driving them on until in the very door of the bedroom the middle lodger stamped his foot loudly on the floor and so brought him to a halt. "I beg to announce," said the lodger, lifting one hand and looking also at Gregor's mother and sister, "that because of the disgusting conditions prevailing in this household and family" — here he spat on the floor with emphatic brevity — "I give you notice on the spot. Naturally I won't pay you a penny for the days I have lived here, on the contrary I shall consider bringing an action for damages against you, based on claims — believe me — that will be easily susceptible of proof." He ceased and stared straight in front of him, as if he expected something. In fact his two friends at once rushed into the breach with these words: "And we too give notice on the spot." On that he seized the door handle and shut the door with a slam.

Gregor's father, groping with his hands, staggered forward and fell into his chair; it looked as if he were stretching himself there for his ordinary evening nap, but the marked jerkings of his head, which were as if uncontrollable, showed that he was far from asleep. Gregor had simply stayed quietly all the time on the spot where the lodgers had espied him. Disappointment at the failure of his plan, perhaps also the weakness arising from extreme hunger, made it impossible for him to move. He feared, with a fair degree of certainty, that at any moment the general tension would discharge itself in a combined attack upon him, and he lay waiting. He did not react even to the noise made by the violin as it fell off his mother's lap from under her trembling fingers and gave out a resonant note.

"My dear parents," said his sister, slapping her hand on the table by way of introduction, "things can't go on like this. Perhaps you don't realize that, but I do. I won't utter my brother's name in the presence of this creature, and so all I say is: we must try to get rid of it. We've tried to look after it and to put up with it as far as is humanly possible, and I don't think anyone could reproach us in the slightest."

"She is more than right," said Gregor's father to himself. His mother, who was still choking for lack of breath, began to cough hollowly into her hand with a wild look in her eyes.

His sister rushed over to her and held her forehead. His father's thoughts seemed to have lost their vagueness at Grete's words, he sat more upright, fingering his service cap that lay among the plates still lying on the table from the lodgers' supper, and from time to time looked at the still form of Gregor.

"We must try to get rid of it," his sister now said explicitly to her father, since her mother was coughing too much to hear a word, "it will be the death of both of you, I can see that coming. When one has to work as hard as we do, all of us, one can't stand this continual torment at home on top of it. At least I can't stand it any longer." And she burst into such a passion of sobbing that her tears dropped on her mother's face, where she wiped them off mechanically.

"My dear," said the old man sympathetically, and with evident understanding, "but what can we do?"

Gregor's sister merely shrugged her shoulders to indicate the feeling of helplessness that had now overmastered her during her weeping fit, in contrast to her former confidence.

"If he could understand us," said her father, half questioningly; Grete, still sobbing, vehemently waved a hand to show how unthinkable that was.

"If he could understand us," repeated the old man, shutting his eyes to consider his daughter's conviction that understanding was impossible, "then perhaps we might come to some agreement with him. But as it is—"

"He must go," cried Gregor's sister, "that's the only solution, Father. You must just try to get rid of the idea that this is Gregor. The fact that we've believed it for so long is the root of all our trouble. But how can it be Gregor? If this were Gregor, he would have realized long ago that human beings can't live with such a creature, and he'd have gone away on his own accord. Then we wouldn't have any brother, but we'd be able to go on living and keep his memory in honor. As it is, this creature persecutes us, drives away our lodgers, obviously wants the whole apartment to himself, and would have us all sleep in the gutter. Just look, Father," she shrieked all at once, "he's at it again!" And in an access of panic that was quite incomprehensible to Gregor she even quitted her mother, literally thrusting the chair from her as if she would rather sacrifice her mother than stay so near to Gregor, and rushed behind her father, who also rose up, being simply upset by her agitation, and half spread his arms out as if to protect her.

Yet Gregor had not the slightest intention of frightening anyone, far less his sister. He had only begun to turn around in order to crawl back to his room, but it was certainly a startling operation to watch, since because of his disabled condition he could not execute the difficult turning movements except by lifting his head and then bracing it against the floor over and over again. He paused and looked around. His good intentions seemed to have been recognized; the alarm had only been momentary. Now they were all watching him in melancholy silence. His mother lay in her chair, her legs stiffly outstretched and pressed together, her eyes almost closing for sheer weariness; his father and his sister were sitting beside each other, his sister's arm around the old man's neck.

Perhaps I can go on turning around now, thought Gregor, and began his labors again. He could not stop himself from panting with the effort, and had to pause now and then to take breath. Nor did anyone harass him, he was left entirely to himself. When he had completed the turn-around he began at once to crawl straight back. He was amazed at the distance separating him from his room and could not understand how in his weak state he had managed to accomplish the same journey so recently, almost without remarking it. Intent on crawling as fast as possible, he barely noticed that not a single word, not an ejaculation from his family, interfered with his progress. Only when he was already in the doorway did he turn his head around, not completely, for his neck muscles were getting stiff, but enough to see that nothing had changed behind him except that his sister had risen to her feet. His last glance fell on his mother, who was not quite overcome by sleep.

Hardly was he well inside his room when the door was hastily pushed shut, bolted, and locked. The sudden noise in his rear startled him so much that his little legs gave beneath him. It was his sister who had shown such haste. She had been standing ready waiting and had made a light spring forward, Gregor had not even heard her coming, and she cried "At last!" to her parents as she turned the key in the lock.

"And what now?" said Gregor to himself, looking around in the darkness. Soon he made the discovery that he was now unable to stir a limb. This did not surprise him, rather it seemed unnatural that he should ever actually have been able to move on these feeble little legs. Otherwise he felt relatively comfortable. True, his whole body was aching, but it seemed that the pain was gradually growing less and would finally pass away. The rotting apple in his back and the inflamed area around it, all covered with soft dust, already hardly troubled him. He thought of his family with tenderness and love. The decision that he must disappear was one that he held to even more strongly than his sister, if that were possible. In this state of vacant and peaceful meditation he remained until the tower clock struck three in the morning. The first broadening of light in the world outside the window entered his consciousness once more. Then his head sank to the floor of its own accord and from his nostrils came the last faint flicker of his breath.

When the charwoman arrived early in the morning—what between her strength and her impatience she slammed all the doors so loudly, never mind how often she had been begged not to do so, that no one in the whole apartment could enjoy any quiet sleep after her arrival—she noticed nothing unusual as she took her customary peep into Gregor's room. She thought he was lying motionless on purpose, pretending to be in the sulks; she credited him with every kind of intelligence. Since she happened to have the long-handled broom in her hand she tried to tickle him up with it from the doorway. When that too produced no reaction she felt provoked and poked at him a little harder, and only when she had pushed him along the floor without meeting any resistance was her attention aroused. It did not take her long to establish the truth of the matter, and her eyes widened, she let out a whistle, yet did not waste much time over it but tore open the door of the Samsas' bedroom and yelled into the darkness at the top of her voice: "Just look at this, it's dead; it's lying here dead and done for!"

Mr. and Mrs. Samsa started up in their double bed and before they realized the nature of the charwoman's announcement had some difficulty in overcoming the shock of it. But then they got out of bed quickly, one on either side, Mr. Samsa throwing a blanket over his shoulders, Mrs. Samsa in nothing but her nightgown; in this array they entered Gregor's room. Meanwhile the door of the living room opened, too, where Grete had been sleeping since the advent of the lodgers; she was completely dressed as if she had not been to bed, which seemed to be confirmed also by the paleness of her face. "Dead?" said Mrs. Samsa, looking questioningly at the charwoman, although she would have investigated for herself, and the fact was obvious enough without investigation. "I should say so," said the charwoman, proving her words by pushing Gregor's corpse a long way to one side with her broomstick. Mrs. Samsa made a movement as if to stop her, but checked it. "Well," said Mr. Samsa, "now thanks be to God." He crossed himself, and the three women followed his example. Grete, whose eyes never left the corpse, said: "Just see how thin he was. It's such a long time since he's eaten anything. The food came out again just as it went in." Indeed, Gregor's body was completely flat and dry, as could only now be seen when it was no longer supported by the legs and nothing prevented one from looking closely at it.

"Come in beside us, Grete, for a little while," said Mrs. Samsa with a tremulous smile, and Grete, not without looking back at the corpse, followed her parents into their bedroom. The charwoman shut the door and opened the window wide. Although it was so early in the morning a certain softness was perceptible in the fresh air. After all, it was already the end of March.

The three lodgers emerged from their room and were surprised to see no breakfast; they had been forgotten. "Where's our breakfast?" said the middle lodger peevishly to the charwoman. But she put her finger to her lips and hastily, without a word, indicated by gestures that they should go into Gregor's room. They did so and stood, their hands in the pockets of their somewhat shabby coats, around Gregor's corpse in the room where it was now fully light.

At that the door of the Samsas' bedroom opened and Mr. Samsa appeared in his uniform, his wife on one arm, his daughter on the other. They all looked a little as if they had been crying; from time to time Grete hid her face on her father's arm.

"Leave my house at once!" said Mr. Samsa, and pointed to the door without disengaging himself from the women. "What do you mean by that?" said the middle lodger, taken somewhat aback, with a feeble smile. The two others put their hands behind them and kept rubbing them together, as if in gleeful expectation of a fine set-to in which they were bound to come off the winners. "I mean just what I say," answered Mr. Samsa, and advanced in a straight line with his two companions toward the lodger. He stood his ground at first quietly, looking at the floor as if his thoughts were taking a new pattern in his head. "Then let us go, by all means," he said, and looked up at Mr. Samsa as if in a sudden access of humility he were expecting some renewed sanction for this decision. Mr. Samsa merely nodded briefly once or twice with meaning eyes. Upon that the lodger really did go with long strides into the hall, his two friends had been listening and had quite stopped rubbing their hands for some moments and now went scuttling after him as if afraid that Mr. Samsa might get into the hall before them and cut them off from their leader. In the hall they all three took their hats from the rack, their sticks from the umbrella stand, bowed in silence, and quitted the apartment. With a suspiciousness that proved quite unfounded Mr. Samsa and the two women followed them out to the landing; leaning over the banister they watched the three figures slowly but surely going down the long stairs, vanishing from sight at a certain turn of the staircase on every floor and coming into view again after a moment or so; the more they dwindled, the more the Samsa family's interest in them dwindled, and when a butcher's boy met them and passed them on the stairs coming up proudly with a tray on his head, Mr. Samsa and the two women soon left the landing and as if a burden had been lifted from them went back into their apartment.

They decided to spend this day in resting and going for a stroll; they had not only deserved such a respite from work, but absolutely needed it. And so they sat down at the table and wrote three notes of excuse, Mr. Samsa to his board of management, Mrs. Samsa to her employer, and Grete to the head of her firm. While they were writing, the charwoman came in to say that she was going now, since her morning's work was finished. At first they only nodded without looking up, but as she kept hovering there they eyed her irritably. "Well?" said Mr. Samsa. The charwoman stood grinning in the doorway as if she had good news to impart to the family but meant not to say a word unless properly questioned. The small ostrich feather standing upright on her hat, which had annoyed Mr. Samsa ever since she was engaged, was waving gaily in all directions. "Well, what is it then?" asked Mrs. Samsa, who obtained more respect from the charwoman than the others. "Oh," said the charwoman, giggling so amiably that she could not at once continue, "just this, you don't need to bother about how to get rid of the thing next door. It's been seen to already." Mrs. Samsa and Grete bent over their letters again, as if preoccupied; Mr. Samsa, who perceived that she was eager to begin describing it all in detail, stopped her with a decisive hand. But since she was not allowed to tell her story, she remembered the great hurry she was in, obviously deeply huffed: "Bye, everybody," she said, whirling off violently, and departed with a frightful slamming of doors.

"She'll be given notice tonight," said Mr. Samsa, but neither from his wife nor his daughter did he get any answer, for the charwoman seemed to have shattered again the composure they had barely achieved. They rose, went to the window and stayed there, clasping each other tight. Mr. Samsa turned in his chair to look at them and quietly observed them for a little. Then he called out: "Come along, now, do. Let bygones be bygones. And you might have some consideration for me." The two of them complied at once, hastened to him, caressed him, and quickly finished their letters.

Then they all three left the apartment together, which was more than they had done for months, and went by tram into the open country outside the town. The tram, in which they were the only passengers, was filled with warm sunshine. Leaning comfortably back in their seats they canvassed their prospects for the future, and it appeared on closer inspection that these were not at all bad, for the jobs they had got, which so far they had never really discussed with each other, were all three admirable and likely to lead to better things later on. The greatest immediate improvement in their condition would of course arise from moving to another house; they wanted to take a smaller and cheaper but also better situated and more easily run apartment than the one they had, which Gregor had selected. While they were thus conversing, it struck both Mr. and Mrs. Samsa, almost at the same moment, as they became aware of their daughter's increasing vivacity, that in spite of all the sorrow of recent times, which had made her cheeks pale, she had bloomed into a pretty girl with a good figure. They grew quieter and half unconsciously exchanged glances of complete agreement, having come to the conclusion that it would soon be time to find a good husband for her. And it was like a confirmation of their new dreams and excellent intentions that at the end of their journey their daughter sprang to her feet first and stretched her young body.

[1915]

Study and Writing Questions

1. How does Kafka make us sympathize with Gregor? What do we learn about his life before his physical metamorphosis? What happens to him after his physical metamorphosis? What are his hopes, fears, reactions, thoughts?
2. In what way(s) is Gregor's initial metamorphosis appropriate to his situation in life? What other metamorphoses occur in the STORY? How are they appropriate?
3. What is the significance of the woman in furs? of the hospital?
4. What is the significance of the thrown apple? the three lodgers? the butcher boy?
5. What significance do the last SCENES, beginning with the charwoman's early morning arrival, have in the story?
6. What does this NARRATIVE suggest are the economic, familial, and social conditions of modern life? What conclusion(s) about modern life does the conclusion of the narrative offer?
7. What does this narrative suggest about the relations of the individual to family, society, God? If we see Gregor's story as a spiritual journey, is its outcome positive, negative, or ambivalent? What comment(s) does this narrative make about human spirituality?

See also Questions for Contrast and Comparison: 12, 43, 46, 51, 52, 59, 64, 70, 71, 72, 73, 74, 78, 90, 97, 107, 125, 132, 140, and 146.

■ YASUNARI KAWABATA (1899–1972), *born in Osaka, Japan, son of a physician, was orphaned at three. His sister and maternal grandmother, with whom he had been sent to live, died soon afterward and he was raised by his grandfather until that man's death left Kawabata, then sixteen, entirely on his own. His first book,* Diary of a Sixteen-Year Old *(written in 1915), recounts his conflict between youthful resentment at his demanding grandfather and grief at the man's suffering. Originally Kawabata wanted to be a painter; the visual, and especially the Japanese tradition of haiku — compressed three-line poems that juxtapose vivid natural* IMAGES *in startling and* SYMBOLIC *ways — is important in his written work. Already as a student at Tokyo Imperial University (B.A. in Japanese literature, 1924), he achieved prominence by helping found Bungei Jidai, the journal of an influential avant-garde movement called Neo-Sensualism. This movement found melancholy pleasurable and encouraged focus on fleeting natural phenomena like moonlight and cherry blossoms, as in Kawabata's most famous novels,* Snow Country *(1937) and* Thousand Cranes *(1952). Widely honored in Japan and abroad, in 1968 he became the first Japanese to win the Nobel Prize in literature. Despite a successful life, including marriage and fatherhood, possibly influenced by the 1970 ritual suicide of his literary disciple, Yukio Mishima, Kawabata gassed himself in his workroom.*

One Arm

"I can let you have one of my arms for the night," said the girl. She took off her right arm at the shoulder and, with her left hand, laid it on my knee.

"Thank you." I looked at my knee. The warmth of the arm came through.

"I'll put the ring on. To remind you that it's mine." She smiled and raised her left arm to my chest. "Please." With but one arm, it was difficult for her to take the ring off.

"An engagement ring?"

"No. A keepsake. From my mother."

It was silver, set with small diamonds.

"Perhaps it does look like an engagement ring, but I don't mind. I wear it, and then when I take it off it's as if I were leaving my mother."

Raising the arm on my knee, I removed the ring and slipped it on the ring finger.

"Is this the one?"

"Yes." She nodded. "It will seem artificial unless the elbow and fingers bend. You won't like that. Let me make them bend for you."

She took her right arm from my knee and pressed her lips gently to it. Then she pressed them to the finger joints.

"Now they'll move."

"Thank you." I took the arm back. "Do you suppose it will speak? Will it speak to me?"

"It only does what an arm does. If it talks I'll be afraid to have it back. But try anyway. It should at least listen to what you say, if you're good to it."

"I'll be good to it."

"I'll see you again," she said, touching the right arm with her left hand, as if to infuse it with a spirit of its own. "You're his, but just for the night."

As she looked at me she seemed to be fighting back tears.

"I don't suppose you'll try to change it for your own arm," she said. "But it will be all right. Go ahead, do."

"Thank you."

I put her arm in my raincoat and went out into the foggy streets. I feared I might be thought odd if I took a taxi or a streetcar. There would be a scene if the arm, now separated from the girl's body, were to cry out, or to weep.

I held it against my chest, toward the side, my right hand on the roundness at the shoulder joint. It was concealed by the raincoat, and I had to touch the coat from time to time with my left hand to be sure that the arm was still there. Probably I was making sure not of the arm's presence but of my own happiness.

She had taken off the arm at the point I liked. It was plump and round—was it at the top of the arm or the beginning of the shoulder? The roundness was that of a beautiful Occidental girl, rare in a Japanese. It was in the girl herself, a clean, elegant roundness, like a sphere glowing with a faint, fresh light. When the girl was no longer clean that gentle roundness would fade, grow flabby. Something that lasted for a brief moment in the life of a beautiful girl, the roundness of the arm made me feel the roundness of her body. Her breasts would not be large. Shy, only large enough to cup in the hands, they would have a clinging softness and strength. And in the roundness of the arm I could feel her legs as she walked along. She would carry them lightly, like a small bird, or a butterfly moving from flower to flower. There would be the same subtle melody in the tip of her tongue when she kissed.

It was the season for changing to sleeveless dresses. The girl's shoulder, newly bared, had the color of skin not used to the raw touch of the air. It had the glow of a bud moistened in the shelter of spring and not yet ravaged by summer. I had that morning bought a magnolia bud and put it in a glass vase; and the roundness of the girl's arm was like the great, white bud. Her dress was cut back more radically than most sleeveless dresses. The joint at the shoulder was exposed, and the shoulder itself. The dress, of dark green silk, almost black, had a soft sheen. The girl was in the rounded slope of the shoulders, which drew a gentle wave with the swelling of the back. Seen obliquely from behind, the flesh from the round shoulders to the long, slender neck came to an abrupt halt at the base of the upswept hair, and the black hair seemed to cast a glowing shadow over the roundness of the shoulders.

She had sensed that I thought her beautiful, and so she lent me her right arm for the roundness there at the shoulder.

Carefully hidden under my raincoat, the girl's arm was colder than my hand. I was giddy from the racing of my heart, and I knew that my hand would be hot. I wanted the warmth to stay as it was, the warmth of the girl herself. And the slight coolness in my hand passed on to me the pleasure of the arm. It was like her breasts, not yet touched by a man.

The fog yet thicker, the night threatened rain, and wet my uncovered hair. I could hear a radio speaking from the back room of a closed pharmacy. It announced that three planes unable to land in the fog had been circling the airport for a half hour. It went on to draw the attention of listeners to the fact that on damp nights clocks were likely to go wrong, and that on such nights the springs had a tendency to break if wound too tight. I looked for the lights of the circling planes, but could not see them. There was no sky. The pressing damp-ness invaded my ears, to give a wet sound like the wriggling of myriads of distant earthworms. I stood before the pharmacy awaiting further admonitions. I learned that on such nights the fierce beasts in the zoo, the lions and tigers and leopards and the rest, roared their resentment at the dampness, and that we were now to hear it. There was a roaring like the roaring of the earth. I then learned that pregnant women and despondent persons should go to bed early on such nights, and that women who applied perfume directly to their skins would find it difficult to remove afterwards.

At the roaring of the beasts, I moved off, and the warning about perfume followed me. That angry roaring had unsettled me, and I moved on lest my uneasiness be transmitted to the girl's arm. The girl was neither pregnant nor despondent, but it seemed to me that tonight, with only one arm, she should take the advice of the radio and go quietly to bed. I hoped that she would sleep peacefully.

As I started across the street I pressed my left hand against my raincoat. A horn sounded. Something brushed my side, and I twisted away. Perhaps the arm had been frightened by the horn. The fingers were clenched.

"Don't worry," I said. "It was a long way off. It couldn't see. That's why it honked."

Because I was holding something important to me, I had looked in both directions. The sound of the horn had been so far away that I had thought it must be meant for someone else. I looked in the direction from which it came, but could see no one. I could see only the headlights. They widened into a blur of faint purple. A strange color for headlights. I stood on the curb when I had crossed and watched it pass. A young woman in vermilion was driving. It seemed to me that she turned toward me and bowed. I wanted to run off, fearing that the girl had come for her arm. Then I remembered that she would hardly be able to drive with only one. But had not the woman in the car seen what I was carrying? Had she not sensed it with a woman's intuition? I would have to take care not to encounter another of the sex before I reached my apartment. The rear lights were also a faint purple. I still did not see the car. In the ashen fog a lavender blur floated up and moved away.

"She is driving for no reason, for no reason at all except to be driving. And while she drives she will simply disappear," I muttered to myself. "And what was that sitting in the back seat?"

Nothing, apparently. Was it because I went around carrying girls' arms that I felt so unnerved by emptiness? The car she drove carried the clammy night fog. And something about her had turned it faintly purple in the headlights. If not from her own body, whence had come that purplish light? Could the arm I concealed have so clothed in emptiness a woman driving alone on such a night? Had she nodded at the girl's arm from her car? Perhaps on such a night there were angels and ghosts abroad protecting women. Perhaps she had ridden not in a car but in a purple light. Her drive had not been empty. She had spied out my secret.

I made my way back to my apartment without further encounters. I stood listening outside the door. The light of a firefly skimmed over my head and disappeared. It was too large and too strong for a firefly. I recoiled backwards.

Several more lights like fireflies skimmed past. They disappeared even before the heavy fog could suck them in. Had a will-ó-the-wisp, a death-fire of some sort, run on ahead of me, to await my return? But then I saw that it was a swarm of small moths. Catching the light at the door, the wings of the moths glowed like fireflies. Too large to be fireflies, and yet, for moths, so small as to invite the mistake.

Avoiding the automatic elevator, I made my way stealthily up the narrow stairs to the third floor. Not being left-handed, I had difficulty unlocking the door. The harder I tried the more my hand trembled—as if in terror after a crime. Something would be waiting for me inside the room, a room where I lived in solitude; and was not the solitude a presence? With the girl's arm I was no longer alone. And so perhaps my own solitude waited there to intimidate me.

"Go on ahead," I said, taking out the girl's arm when at length I had opened the door. "Welcome to my room. I'll turn on the light."

"Are you afraid of something?" the arm seemed to say. "Is something here?"

"You think there might be?"

"I smell something."

"Smell? It must be me that you smell. Don't you see traces of my shadow, up there in the darkness? Look carefully. Maybe my shadow was waiting for me to come back."

"It's a sweet smell."

"Ah—the magnolia," I answered brightly. I was glad it was not the moldy smell of my loneliness. A magnolia bud befitted my winsome guest. I was getting used to the dark. Even in pitch blackness I knew where everything was.

"Let me turn on the light." Coming from the arm, a strange remark. "I haven't been in your room before."

"Thank you. I'll be very pleased. No one but me has ever turned on the lights here before."

I held the arm to the switch by the door. All five lights went on at once: at the ceiling, on the table, by the bed, in the kitchen, in the bathroom. I had not thought they could be so bright.

The magnolia was in enormous bloom. That morning it had been in bud. It could have only just bloomed, and yet there were stamens on the table. Curious, I looked more closely at the stamens than at the white flower. As I picked up one or two and gazed at them, the girl's arm, laid on the table, began to move, the fingers like spanworms and gathered the stamens in its hand. I went to throw them in the wastebasket.

"What a strong smell. It sinks right into my skin. Help me."

"You must be tired. It wasn't an easy trip. Suppose you rest awhile."

I laid the arm on the bed and sat down beside it. I stroked it gently.

"How pretty. I like it." The arm would be speaking of the bed cover. Flowers were printed in three colors on an azure ground, somewhat lively for a man who lived alone. "So this is where we spend the night. I'll be very quiet."

"Oh?"

"I'll be beside you and not beside you."

The hand took mine gently. The nails, carefully polished, were a faint pink. The tips extended well beyond the fingers.

Against my own short, thick nails, hers possessed a strange beauty, as if they belonged to no human creature. With such fingertips, a woman perhaps transcended mere humanity. Or did she pursue womanhood itself? A shell luminous from the pattern inside it, a petal bathed in dew—I thought of the obvious likenesses. Yet I could think of no shell or petal whose color and shape resembled them. They were the nails on the girl's fingers, comparable to nothing else. More translucent than a delicate shell, than a thin petal, they seemed to hold a dew of tragedy. Every day and every night her energies were poured into the polishing of this tragic beauty. It penetrated my solitude. Perhaps my yearning, my solitude, transformed them into dew.

I rested her little finger on the index finger of my free hand, gazing at the long, narrow nail as I rubbed it with my thumb. My finger touched the tip of hers, sheltered by the nail. The finger bent, and the elbow too.

"Does it tickle?" I asked. "It must."

I had spoken carelessly. I knew that the tips of a woman's fingers were sensitive when the nails were long. And so I had told the girl's arm that I had known other women.

From one who was not a great deal older than the girl who had lent me the arm but far more mature in her experience of men, I had heard that fingertips thus hidden by nails were often acutely sensitive. One became used to touching things not with the fingertips but with the nails, and the fingertips therefore tickled when something came against them.

I had shown astonishment at this discovery, and she had gone on: "You're, say, cooking—or eating— and something touches your fingers, and you find yourself hunching your shoulders, it seems so dirty."

Was it the food that seemed unclean, or the tip of the nail? Whatever touched her fingers made her writhe with its uncleanness. Her own cleanness would leave behind a drop of tragic dew, there under the long shadow of the nail. One could not assume that for each of the ten fingers there would be a separate drop of dew.

It was natural that I should want all the more to touch those fingertips, but I held myself back. My solitude held me back. She was a woman on whose body few tender spots could be expected to remain.

And on the body of the girl who had lent me the arm they would be beyond counting. Perhaps, toying with the fingertips of such a girl, I would feel not guilt but affection. But she had not lent me the arm for such mischief. I must not make a comedy of her gesture.

"The window." I noticed not that the window itself was open but that the curtain was undrawn.

"Will anything look in?" asked the girl's arm.

"Some man or woman. Nothing else."

"Nothing human would see me. If anything it would be a self. Yours."

"Self? What is that? Where is it?"

"Far away," said the arm, as if singing in consolation. "People walk around looking for selves, far away."

"And do they come upon them?"

"Far away," said the arm once more.

It seemed to me that the arm and the girl herself were an infinity apart. Would the arm be able to return to the girl, so far away? Should I be able to take it back, so far away? The arm lay peacefully trusting me; and would the girl be sleeping in the same peaceful confidence? Would there not be harshness, a nightmare? Had she not seemed to be fighting back tears when she parted with it? The arm was now in my room, which the girl herself had not visited.

The dampness clouded the window, like a toad's belly stretched over it. The fog seemed to withhold rain in mid-air, and the night outside the window lost distance, even while it was wrapped in limitless distance. There were no roofs to be seen, no horns to be heard.

"I'll close the window," I said, reaching for the curtain. It too was damp. My face loomed up in the window, younger than my thirty-three years. I did not hesitate to pull the curtain, however. My face disappeared.

Suddenly a remembered window. On the ninth floor of a hotel, two little girls in wide red skirts were playing in the window. Very similar children in similar clothes, perhaps twins, Occidentals. They pounded at the glass, pushing it with their shoulders and shoving at each other. Their mother knitted, her back to the window. If the large pane were to have broken or come loose, they would have fallen from the ninth floor. It was only I who thought them in danger. Their mother was quite unconcerned. The glass was in fact so solid that there was no danger.

"It's beautiful," said the arm on the bed as I turned from the window. Perhaps she was speaking of the curtain, in the same flowered pattern as the bed cover.

"Oh? But it's faded from the sun and almost ready to go." I sat down on the bed and took the arm on my knee. "This is what is beautiful. More beautiful than anything."

Taking the palm of the hand in my own right palm, and the shoulder in my left hand, I flexed the elbow, and then again.

"Behave yourself," said the arm, as if smiling softly. "Having fun?"

"Not in the least."

A smile did come over the arm, crossing it like light. It was exactly the fresh smile on the girl's cheek.

I knew the smile. Elbows on the table, she would fold her hands loosely and rest her chin or cheek on them. The pose should have been inelegant in a young girl; but there was about it a lightly engaging quality that made expressions like "elbows on the table" seem inappropriate. The roundness of the shoulders, the fingers, the chin, the cheeks, the ears, the long, slender neck, the hair, all came together in a single harmonious movement. Using knife and fork deftly, first and little fingers bent, she would raise them ever so slightly from time to time. Food would pass the small lips and she would swallow—I had before me less a person at dinner than an inviting music of hands and face and throat. The light of her smile flowed across the skin of her arm.

The arm seemed to smile because, as I flexed it, very gentle waves passed over the firm, delicate muscles, to send waves of light and shadow over the smooth skin. Earlier, when I had touched the fingertips under the long nails, the light passing over the arm as the elbow bent had caught my eye. It was that, and not any impulse toward mischief, that had made me bend and unbend her arm. I stopped, and gazed at it as it lay stretched out on my knee. Fresh lights and shadows were still passing over it.

"You ask if I'm having fun. You realize that I have permission to change you for my own arm?"

"I do."

"Somehow I'm afraid to."

"Oh?"

"May I?"

"Please."

I heard the permission granted, and wondered whether I could accept it. "Say it again. Say 'please.'"

"Please, please."

I remembered. It was like the voice of a woman who had decided to give herself to me, one not as beautiful as the girl who had lent me the arm. Perhaps there was something a little strange about her.

"Please," she had said, gazing at me. I had put my fingers to her eyelids and closed them. Her voice was trembling. " 'Jesus wept. Then said the Jews, Behold how he loved her!' "

"Her" was a mistake for "him." It was the story of the dead Lazarus. Perhaps, herself a woman, she had remembered it wrong, perhaps she had made the substitution intentionally.

The words, so inappropriate to the scene, had shaken me. I gazed at her, wondering if tears would start from the closed eyes.

She opened them and raised her shoulders. I pushed her down with my arm.

"You're hurting me!" She put her hand to the back of her head.

There was a small spot of blood on the white pillow. Parting her hair, I put my lips to the drop of blood swelling on her head.

"It doesn't matter." She took out all her hairpins. "I bleed easily. At the slightest touch."

A hairpin had pierced her skin. A shudder seemed about to pass through her shoulders, but she controlled herself.

Although I think I understand how a woman feels when she gives herself to a man, there is still something unexplained about the act. What is it to her? Why should she wish to do it, why should she take the initiative? I could never really accept the surrender, even knowing that the body of every woman was made for it. Even now, old as I am, it seems strange. And the ways in which various women go about it: unlike if you wish, or similar perhaps, or even identical. Is that not strange? Perhaps the strangeness I find in it all is the curiosity of a younger man, perhaps the despair of one advanced in years. Or perhaps some spiritual debility I suffer from.

Her anguish was not common to all women in the act of surrender. And it was with her only the one time. The silver thread was cut, the golden bowl destroyed.

"Please," the arm had said, and so reminded me of the other girl; but were the two voices in fact similar? Had they not sounded alike because the words were the same? Had the arm acquired independence in this measure of the body from which it was separated? And were the words not the act of giving itself up, of being ready for anything, without restraint or responsibility or remorse? It seemed to me that if I were to accept the invitation and change the arm for my own I would be bringing untold pain to the girl.

I gazed at the arm on my knee. There was a shadow at the inside of the elbow. It seemed that I might be able to suck it in. I pressed it to my lips, to gather in the shadow.

"It tickles. Do behave yourself." The arm was around my neck, avoiding my lips.

"Just when I was having a good drink."

"And what were you drinking?"

I did not answer.

"What were you drinking?"

"The smell of light? Of skin."

The fog seemed thicker; even the magnolia leaves seemed wet. What other warnings would issue from the radio? I started toward my table radio and stopped. To listen to it with the arm around my neck seemed altogether too much. But I suspected I would hear something like this: because of the wet branches and their own wet feet and wings, small birds have fallen to the ground and cannot fly. Automobiles passing through parks should take care not to run over them. And if a warm wind comes up, the fog will perhaps change color. Strange-colored fogs are noxious. Listeners should therefore lock their doors if the fog should turn pink or purple.

"Change color?" I muttered. "Turn pink or purple?"

I pulled at the curtain and looked out. The fog seemed to press down with an empty weight. Was it because of the wind that a thin darkness seemed to be moving about, different from the usual black of night? The thickness of the fog seemed infinite, and yet beyond it something fearsome writhed and coiled.

I remembered that earlier, as I was coming home with the borrowed arm, the head and tail beams of the car driven by the woman in vermilion had come up indistinctly in the fog. A great, blurred sphere of faint purple now seemed to come toward me. I hastily pulled away from the curtain.

"Let's go to bed. Us too."

It seemed as if no one else in the world would be up. To be up was terror.

Taking the arm from my neck and putting it on the table, I changed into a fresh night-kimono, a cotton print. The arm watched me change. I was shy at being watched. Never before had a woman watched me undress in my room.

The arm in my own, I got into bed. I lay facing it, and brought it lightly to my chest. It lay quiet.

Intermittently I could hear a faint sound as of rain, a very light sound, as if the fog had not turned to rain but were itself forming drops. The fingers clasped in my hand beneath the blanket grew warmer; and it gave me the quietest of sensations, the fact that they had not warmed to my own temperature.

"Are you asleep?"

"No," replied the arm.

"You were so quiet, I thought you might be asleep."

"What do you want me to do?"

Opening my kimono, I brought the arm to my chest. The difference in warmth sank in. In the somehow sultry, somehow chilly night, the smoothness of the skin was pleasant.

The lights were still on. I had forgotten to turn them out as I went to bed. "The lights." I got up, and the arm fell from my chest.

I hastened to pick it up. "Will you turn out the lights?" I started toward the door. "Do you sleep in the dark? Or with lights on?"

The arm did not answer. It would surely know. Why had it not answered? I did not know the girl's nocturnal practices. I compared the two pictures, of her asleep in the dark and with the lights on. I decided that tonight, without her arm, she would have them on. Somehow I too wanted them on. I wanted to gaze at the arm. I wanted to stay awake and watch the arm after it had gone to sleep. But the fingers stretched to turn off the switch by the door.

I went back and lay down in the darkness, the arm by my chest. I lay there silently, waiting for it to go to sleep. Whether dissatisfied or afraid of the dark, the hand lay open at my side, and presently the five fingers were climbing my chest. The elbow bent of its own accord, and the arm embraced me.

There was a delicate pulse at the girl's wrist. It lay over my heart, so that the two pulses sounded against each other. Hers was at first somewhat slower than mine, then they were together. And then I could feel only mine. I did not know which was faster, which slower.

Perhaps this identity of pulse and heartbeat was for a brief period when I might try to exchange the arm for my own. Or had it gone to sleep? I had once heard a woman say that women were less happy in the throes of ecstasy than sleeping peacefully beside their men; but never before had a woman slept beside me as peacefully as this arm.

I was conscious of my beating heart because of the pulsation above it. Between one beat and the next, something sped far away and sped back again. As I listened to the beating, the distance seemed to increase. And however far the something went, however infinitely far, it met nothing at its destination. The next beat summoned it back. I should have been afraid, and was not. Yet I groped for the switch beside my pillow.

Before turning it on, I quietly rolled back the blanket. The arm slept on, unaware of what was happening. A gentle band of faintest white encircled my naked chest, seeming to rise from the flesh itself, like the glow before the dawning of a tiny, warm sun.

I turned on the light. I put my hands to the fingers and shoulder and pulled the arm straight. I turned it quietly in my hands, gazing at the play of light and shadow, from the roundness at the shoulder over the narrowing and swelling of the forearm, the narrowing again at the gentle roundness of the elbow, the faint depression inside the elbow, the narrowing roundness to the wrist, the palm and back of the hand, and on to the fingers.

"I'll have it." I was not conscious of muttering the words. In a trance, I removed my right arm and substituted the girl's.

There was a slight gasp—whether from the arm or from me I could not tell—and a spasm at my shoulder. So I knew of the change.

The girl's arm—mine now—was trembling and reaching for the air. Bending it, I brought it close to my mouth.

"Does it hurt? Do you hurt?"

"No. Not at all. Not at all." The words were fitful.

A shudder went through me like lightning. I had the fingers in my mouth. Somehow I spoke my happiness, but the girl's fingers were at my tongue, and whatever it was I spoke did not form into words.

"Please. It's all right," the arm replied. The trembling stopped. "I was told you could. And yet—"

I noticed something. I could feel the girl's fingers in my mouth, but the fingers of her hand, now those of my own right hand, could not feel my lips or teeth. In panic I shook my right arm and could not feel the shaking. There was a break, a stop, between arm and shoulder.

"The blood doesn't go," I blurted out. "Does it or doesn't it?"

For the first time I was swept by fear. I rose up in bed. My own arm had fallen beside me. Separated from me, it was an unsightly object. But more important— would not the pulse have stopped? The girl's arm was warm and pulsing; my own looked as if it were growing stiff and cold. With the girl's, I grasped my own right arm. I grasped it, but there was no sensation.

"Is there a pulse?" I asked the arm. "Is it cold?"

"A little. Just a little colder than I am. I've gotten very warm." There was something especially womanly in the cadence. Now that the arm was fastened to my shoulder and made my own, it seemed womanly as it had not before.

"The pulse hasn't stopped?"

"You should be more trusting."

"Of what?"

"You changed your arm for mine, didn't you?"

"Is the blood flowing?"

"'Woman, whom seekest thou?' You know the passage?"

"'Woman, why weepest thou? Whom seekest thou?'"

"Very often when I'm dreaming and wake up in the night I whisper it to myself."

This time of course the "I" would be the owner of the winsome arm at my shoulder. The words from the Bible were as if spoken by an eternal voice, in an eternal place.

"Will she have trouble sleeping?" I too spoke of the girl herself. "Will she be having a nightmare? It's a fog for herds of nightmares to wander in. But the dampness will make even demons cough."

"To keep you from hearing them." The girl's arm, my own still in its hand, covered my right ear.

It was now my own right arm, but the motion seemed to have come not of my volition but of its own, from its heart. Yet the separation was by no means so complete.

"The pulse. The sound of the pulse."

I heard the pulse of my own right arm. The girl's arm had come to my ear with my own arm in its hand, and my own wrist was at my ear. My arm was warm—as the girl's arm had said, just perceptibly cooler than her fingers and my ear.

"I'll keep away the devils." Mischievously, gently, the long, delicate nail of her little finger stirred in my ear. I shook my head. My left hand—mine from the start—took my right wrist—actually the girl's. As I threw my head back, I caught sight of the girl's little finger.

Four fingers of her hand were grasping the arm I had taken from my right shoulder. The little finger alone—shall we say that it alone was allowed to play free?—was bent toward the back of the hand. The tip of the nail touched my right arm lightly. The finger was bent in a position possible only to a girl's supple hand, out of the question for a stiff-jointed man like me. From its base it rose at right angles. At the first joint it bent in another right angle, and at the next in yet another. It thus traced a square, the fourth side formed by the ring finger.

It formed a rectangular window at the level of my eye. Or rather a peep-hole, or an eyeglass, much too small for a window; but somehow I thought of a window. The sort of window a violet might look out through. The window of the little finger, the finger-rimmed eyeglass, so white that it gave off a faint glow—I brought it nearer my eye. I closed the other eye.

"A peep show?" asked the arm. "And what do you see?"

"My dusky old room. Its five lights." Before I had finished the sentence I was almost shouting. "No, no! I see it!"

"And what do you see?"

"It's gone."

"And what did you see?"

"A color. A blur of purple. And inside it little circles, little beads of red and gold, whirling around and around."

"You're tired." The girl's arm put down my right arm, and her fingers gently stroked my eyelids.

"Were the beads of gold and red spinning around in a huge cogwheel? Did I see something in the cogwheel, something that came and went?"

I did not know whether I had actually seen something there or only seemed to—a fleeting illusion, not to stay in the memory. I could not remember what it might have been.

"Was it an illusion you wanted to show me?"

"No. I came to erase it."

"Of days gone by. Of longing and sadness."

On my eyelids the movement of her fingers stopped.

I asked an unexpected question. "When you let down your hair does it cover your shoulders?"

"It does. I wash it in hot water, but afterward—a special quirk of mine, maybe—I pour cold water over it. I like the feel of cold hair against my shoulders and arms, and against my breasts too."

It would of course be the girl again. Her breasts had never been touched by a man, and no doubt she would have had difficulty describing the feel of the cold, wet hair against them. Had the arm, separated from the body, been separated too from the shyness and the reserve?

Quietly I took in my left hand the gentle roundness at the shoulder, now my own. It seemed to me that I had in my hand the roundness, not yet large, of her breasts. The roundness of the shoulder became the soft roundness of breasts.

Her hand lay gently on my eyelids. The fingers and the hand clung softly and sank through, and the underside of the eyelids seemed to warm at the touch. The warmth sank into my eyes.

"The blood is going now," I said quietly. "It is going."

It was not a cry of surprise as when I had noticed that my arm was changed for hers. There was no shuddering and no spasm, in the girl's arm or my shoulder. When had my blood begun to flow through the arm, her blood through me? When had the break at the shoulder disappeared? The clean blood of the girl was now, this very moment, flowing through me; but would there not be unpleasantness when the arm was returned to the girl, this dirty male blood flowing through it? What if it would not attach itself to her shoulder?

"No such betrayal," I muttered.

"It will be all right," whispered the arm.

There was no dramatic awareness that between the arm and my shoulder the blood came and went. My left hand, enfolding my right shoulder, and the shoulder itself, now mine, had a natural understanding of the fact. They had come to know it. The knowledge pulled them down into slumber.

I slept.

I floated on a great wave. It was the encompassing fog turned a faint purple, and there were pale green ripples at the spot where I floated on the great wave, and there alone. The dank solitude of my room was gone. My left hand seemed to rest lightly on the girl's right arm. It seemed that her fingers held magnolia stamens. I could not see them, but I could smell them. We had thrown them away — and when and how had she gathered them up again? The white petals, but a day old, had not yet fallen; why then the stamens? The automobile of the woman in vermilion slid by, drawing a great circle with me at the center. It seemed to watch over our sleep, the arm's and mine.

Our sleep was probably light, but I had never before known sleep so warm, so sweet. A restless sleeper, I had never before been blessed with the sleep of a child.

The long, narrow, delicate nail scratched gently at the palm of my hand, and the slight touch made my sleep deeper. I disappeared.

I awoke screaming. I almost fell out of bed, and staggered three or four steps. I had awakened to the touch of something repulsive. It was my right arm.

Steadying myself, I looked down at the arm on the bed. I caught my breath, my heart raced, my whole body trembled. I saw the arm in one instant, and the next I had torn the girl's from my shoulder and put back my own. The act was like murder upon a sudden, diabolic impulse.

I knelt by the bed, my chest against it, and rubbed at my insane heart with my restored hand. As the beating slowed down a sadness welled up from deeper than the deepest inside me.

"Where is her arm?" I raised my head.

It lay at the foot of the bed, flung palm up into the heap of the blanket. The outstretched fingers did not move. The arm was faintly white in the dim light.

Crying out in alarm I swept it up and held it tight to my chest. I embraced it as one would a small child from whom life was going. I brought the fingers to my lips. If the dew of woman would but come from between the long nails and the fingertips!

[1963-1964]

Study and Writing Questions

1. Kawabata's NARRATOR frequently seems to use PERSONIFICATION: he hears the "radio speaking"; a car "couldn't see"; his "solitude [is] a presence." Is the girl's arm merely another personification? Do we need to understand the arm as independently alive?

2. Why does the girl kiss the fingers of her hand when she gives it to the narrator? What do we come to know about the girl? In what way(s) is the girl related to her arm? What is her relationship with the narrator?

3. There are a number of recurring IMAGES in the story, such as magnolia blossoms, fog, and windows. What other recurring images are there? What does each contribute to the story?

4. What is the relationship of Orient (the East) and Occident (the West) in this story? Why are there references to the Occident, such as explicit references to the Bible (John 20:13ff.) and implicit references (the narrator's age, thirty-three, being the age at which tradition sets Jesus when he was crucified). What is the THEMATIC significance of these references? To what extent is the story about modern Japan?

5. What do we learn about the psychology of the narrator's desire? What does beauty mean in the narrator's life? What seems literally to be happening at the end of the story? What is the narrator really yearning for in the last line?

See also Questions for Contrast and Comparison: 23, 74, 96, 119, 120, 121, 122, 128, 131, and 133.

■ JAMAICA KINCAID (1949–), *born in Antigua, West Indies, is the only child of a carpenter and of a doting mother. According to Kincaid, the attentiveness of "my mother [Annie Richardson] wrote my life for me and told it to me . . . I can't account for the reason I became a writer any other way because . . . I thought writing was something people didn't do anymore." Educated at first in Antigua, Kincaid began college in New Hampshire but found it a "dismal failure" and educated herself. She began publishing fiction in prestigious magazines in 1974 and became a New Yorker staff writer in 1978. Although she lives in New York City and is a naturalized U.S. citizen (married to American composer Allen Shawn), all her books are rooted in Antigua. "America [has] given me a place to be myself—but myself as I was formed somewhere else." Her prose has been highly praised for its lyricism and attention to detail. Her first book, At the Bottom of the River (1983), a story collection, won the Morton Dauwen Zabel Award of the American Academy and Institute of Arts and Letters. Annie John (1985) is a linked series of stories about an island girl growing up. A Small Place (1988) is a fierce, anti-colonial essay. Lucy (1990), her first novel, concerns a Caribbean girl who comes to North America as an au pair.*

Girl

Wash the white clothes on Monday and put them on the stone heap; wash the color clothes on Tuesday and put them on the clothesline to dry; don't walk barehead in the hot sun; cook pumpkin fritters in very hot sweet oil; soak your little clothes right after you take them off; when buying cotton to make yourself a nice blouse, be sure that it doesn't have gum in it, because that way it won't hold up well after a wash; soak salt fish overnight before you cook it; is it true that you sing benna in Sunday school?; always eat your food in such a way that it won't turn someone else's stomach; on Sundays try to walk like a lady and not like the slut you are so bent on becoming; don't sing benna in Sunday school; you mustn't speak to wharf-rat boys, not even to give directions; don't eat fruits on the street—flies will follow you; *but I don't sing benna on Sundays at all and never in Sunday school*; this is how to sew on a button; this is how to make a buttonhole for the button you have just sewed on; this is how to hem a dress when you see the hem coming down and so to prevent yourself from looking like the slut I know you are so bent on becoming; this is how you iron your father's khaki shirt so that it doesn't have a crease; this is how you iron your father's khaki pants so that they don't have a crease; this is how you grow okra—far from the house, because okra tree harbors red ants; when you are growing dasheen, make sure it gets plenty of water or else it makes your throat itch when you are eating it; this is how you sweep a corner; this is how you sweep a whole house; this is how you sweep a yard; this is how you smile to someone you don't like too much; this is how you smile to someone you don't like at all; this is how you smile to someone you like completely; this is how you set a table for tea; this is how you set a table for dinner; this is how you set a table for dinner with an important guest; this is how you set a table for lunch; this is how you set a table for breakfast; this is how to behave in the presence of men who don't know you very well, and this way they won't recognize immediately the slut I have warned you against becoming; be sure to wash every day, even if it is with your own spit; don't squat down to play marbles — you are not a boy, you know; don't pick people's flowers — you might catch something; don't throw stones at blackbirds, because it might not be a blackbird at all; this is how to make a bread pudding; this is how to make doukona; this is how to make pepper pot; this is how to make a good medicine for a cold; this is how to make a good medicine to throw away a child before it even becomes a child; this is how to catch a fish; this is how to throw back a fish you don't like, and that way something bad won't fall on you; this is how to bully a man; this is how a man bullies you; this is how to love a man, and if this doesn't work there are other ways, and if they don't work don't feel too bad about giving up; this is how to spit up in the air if you feel like it, and this is how to move quick so that it doesn't fall on you; this is how to make ends meet; always squeeze bread to make sure it's fresh; *but what if the baker won't let me feel the bread?*; you mean to say that after all you are really going to be the kind of woman who the baker won't let near the bread?

[1978]

Study and Writing Questions

1. What attitudes do the mother and daughter have toward each other? How do you know?
2. What is the role of sexuality in the world of the title CHARACTER?
3. What seem to be the possible female/male relations in the world of this NARRATIVE? How do you know?
4. This narrative is not a SOLILOQUY nor does it take place all at one time, yet it is written as a single paragraph. How would you describe the mode of presentation of this narrative? What are the effects on the reader of this mode of presentation?
5. Some of the story's details may surprise us by their repetition (ironing away creases, for example), others by their inclusion (how to spit up in the air, for example), and others by their absence (how to raise a child, for example). How does the choice of details affect our understanding of this narrative?

See also Questions for Contrast and Comparison: 98, 125, 190, 196, 198, 201, and 202.

■ TOMMASO LANDOLFI (1908-1979), one of the greatest Italian authors of this century, was a fiercely reclusive man about whom little is known with certainty. Although he published prolifically and won both the Pirandello Prize (1968) for his drama Faust '67 and the Strega Prize (1975) for his short story collection A caso (1975; the title means "inadvertently"), he required his publishers to withhold all biographical information. In his only authorized photograph, published on the jacket of his first English-language collection, Gogol's Wife and Other Stories (1963), his hand obscures his face as he rejects the camera. We know that he was born in Pico, Frosinone, Italy, and received a degree in Italian literature from the University of Florence. While he was imprisoned for his anti-Fascist views during World War II, he made important contributions to journals. He published translations from French, German, and, most importantly, Russian. Always eccentric in his fiction, he has been compared to his great but quite different countrymen, Italo Calvino and Italo Svevo, and to Jorge Luis Borges and Franz Kafka. Cancerqueen and Other Stories (1971) is a somewhat more science fictional collection than the first, while Words in Commotion and Other Stories (1986) is somewhat more overtly philosophical. Landolfi was, apparently, very handsome, tall, reserved, an avid gambler, and the father of one or two children. He died in Rome.

Rain

Usually, as soon as my wife wakes up, she goes to the bathroom to brush her teeth. It's only when she comes back, still glassy-eyed, that she utters her first judgments on the situation or on life in general, or else she digs something up. And that's what happened today. Except that, today, she came out with this extraordinary statement:

"Our carriage was drawn by a spider, wasn't it?"

Now, let's get things straight. I'm accustomed to my wife's occasional eccentricities, but the fact is that my beloved wife never went this far before. Therefore, it was best for me to play the fool like the husbands in farces of the good old days, and exclaim:

"Huh? What the devil are you saying?"

"I'm asking you," she replied without batting an eyelash, "I'm simply asking you if our carriage was drawn by a spider. What's wrong, can't you hear, or have you become a square?"

"A square? What does that have to do with it? But, who'd understand you? Your question just might seem strange, you know."

"Strange, why?"

"Why, why . . . where have you ever seen that, a carriage drawn by a spider?"

"In dreams, obviously."

"Ah, all right, in dreams; and how am I supposed to know or tell you the exact details of your personal dream?"

"You don't love me."

"What are you talking about! I adore you."

"You don't one bit, and that adjective is all the bitter evidence I need. 'Personal dream!' If you really loved me, we would share all our dreams; everything between us should be shared and mutual. Ah, it's easy for you. I dream of us going for a ride in a spider-drawn carriage, and you know nothing of it and wash your hands of the whole thing?"

"I see your point."

"Thank goodness."

"But what do I know if . . ."

"Perfect, excellent, I could have bet you would use that hateful expression! 'What do I know?' By the way, can't you try not to use such common expressions, and speak more correctly? But anyway, what language do I have to tell you in; if you really loved me, you would have the same dreams I do without any effort at all."

"Ah, hold on. It's reciprocal."

"Reciprocal, what kind of trick is this? Tell me, darling, do you really think you can enchant me with your difficult terminology?"

"No, listen. Do you love me?"

"Of course I do, unfortunately."

"Then why is it that you don't have my dreams, or if anything, have no dreams at all (which is exactly what happened to me last night)?"

"What rubbish! You're admitting yourself that you didn't have any dreams, and you actually believe that I should conform to your nothingness? That's enough talk! But, let me tell you something. We were actually fleeing in the spider-drawn carriage from a young man who was courting me. And let me tell you, he was gorgeous, and I must say, I wasn't entirely indifferent to his attention. When I saw him, with those sad, intense eyes and I felt his silent yet overwhelming plea for love, I felt a sort of longing in my heart. . . . So watch it!"

"Oh, really, a gorgeous young man? Was he fair or dark, wearing velvet or satin? And you felt . . . ?"

"You think it's a joke, my dear fellow? Don't you know that even dreams, or rather, only dreams are dangerous? . . . In fact, I want some proof from you."

"In other words?"

"Describe and explain this dream to me."

"Which I didn't have."

"Which you didn't have but which it is your basic duty to have, and in any case, you are obliged to know point by point. Otherwise, it will mean you don't love me."

"I get it."

"Finally; so go on, begin."

"Well, to begin with we had a tiff."

"Exactly, but about what? Let's see if you know."

"About my observations on the household expenses."

"Yes, yes, that's right. You expect me to perform miracles, but if everything keeps going up, if the prices rise from one day to the next, while your salary stays the same . . ."

"Quiet. And so, after we argued, we went out together, it was twilight. No, wait a minute: dawn."

"Yes, dawn. Everything had a strange glow, the sky was clear and empty; that's right, it *was* dawn, but what a joy to hear you say it."

"Let's keep going. We were still cross, and we were both looking away, and suddenly the young man appeared before us."

"The young man."

"Who began to stare and lurch at you eagerly."

"What do you mean lurch?"

"It seemed that at any moment he might hurl himself at you, with those staring eyes of his, and he only seemed really substantial at those moments. And then he faded back in the distance."

"Oh, my God, perfect; yes, I like you better now."

"Eh, you know, I do understand some things. So, as I was saying, he kept looking at you like that and I was very embarrassed even though I realized that such an elusive guy had nothing to do with me. When . . ."

"When what? . . ." My wife, on the edge of her seat, urged me on.

But the truth was that I didn't know how to continue or what else to invent before the spider-drawn carriage arrived; that it would pull up without further mishap seemed too simple, too elementary for my wife's character. Therefore I tried to stall.

"Let's take a quick break, for God's sake. We could stand to clarify a few points. For example, you pompously call this thing that's about to appear a carriage, just like that, and yet, on second thought, it seems more like a common coach, a rented coach to me, huh?"

I was really trying to penetrate the nature of her fantasies and at the same time to go along with her. Except that she was implacable.

"If you say so. Go on, don't get lost in trifles."

Now what? Now, unforgivably, I grabbed hold of an external detail. It was raining out. I risked it.

"Well, in the meantime it had started to rain."

But now, damnation, she suddenly got angry, and pointing her index finger, said coldly:

"No, really no! Save your other leaps of the imagination; no, it wasn't raining, not at all. You're good at tricking a poor woman! It's lucky that I've got a head on my shoulders. It wasn't raining, my dear flatterer, my dear wicked seducer. And now I'll tell you how you managed to be on target up to this point. You must have some secret, diabolical ability to read minds since, when I thought intensely about my dream, let's say, you intercepted something. But at the critical moment, when you really had to explain it and point out the significance of the various symbols, you gave yourself away. . . . Your mysterious and amateurish powers aren't good enough, your kind willingness to please the weaker sex isn't good enough: feeling, deep feeling is required, love! Do you take me for a little girl? Listen to this: it was raining! I would just like to know how you came up with rain. Raining in a dream! Have you ever heard of this? It rains in your damn world, it's raining now, but not in dreams. And I have to conclude from all this, I must conclude, as much as it hurts me, that you don't love me, like I said, that your chatter is meaningless. . . . Oh, wretched me, what a terrible mess I'm in, snared (isn't that how you literary types talk and write?)."

"Come on, calm down. Maybe it wasn't raining, I might have been wrong."

" 'Maybe, wrong.' But that's just the point! How could you have been wrong, if . . . ? You shouldn't have let yourself be wrong, or you should've not let yourself be wrong, if . . ."

"Don't you think it's complicated, don't you think it's ultimately irrational to demand . . . ?"

"I was waiting, I just knew you would come up with irrationality! All of you think you can resolve everything, not only with reason (that still wouldn't hold water), but with rational classifications: this thing is rational, that other thing isn't. . . . How dare you be so presumptuous!"

"Look, darling."

"Darling nothing, and there's nothing to look at! But I'm telling you again, watch out—I may end up going back to him tonight."

"Him who, you little fool?"

"To him, the young man. Don't say I didn't tell you."

And with that she burst into tears; she flung her arms around my neck, and sobbed and moaned. Staring out the window, she murmured over and over: "It's raining, raining mercilessly. The sky is all closed up, it's raining. . . . But only here, not there, for the love of God. You're mean, you shouldn't have done this to me."

A bit of hysteria, clearly, and with two teeny children! And yet nobody can convince me that when you get right down to it, she might be right. In fact, if you love someone, why on earth shouldn't you dream the same thing at the same time? Or, to put it less absurdly, why the perennial discord of our moods and feelings?

[1978]

Study and Writing Questions

1. Judging from the first paragraph, to what extent is the STORY the NARRATOR tells common in his life and to what extent "extraordinary"?
2. How does the TONE change through the story? Why does it change?
3. What might be the significance of learning in the last paragraph of "two teeny children"?
4. In what ways might it be true, as the wife says, that the husband is "a literary type"? What does each sense of that phrase have to do with this story?
5. What does this story suggest about love?

See also Questions for Contrast and Comparison: 40, 45, 136, 137, 138, and 139.

■ D(AVID) H(ERBERT RICHARDS) LAWRENCE (1885–1930) *was born and lived his first twenty years around Nottingham, England. He was the son of a mismarriage between a tough, coal miner father and a "superior" mother, a former schoolteacher through whose financial sacrifices he attended school. At first a schoolteacher and clerk himself, with his second novel,* Sons and Lovers *(1913), Lawrence began a relentless exploration of the struggles to find satisfaction within, or else break from, mother-son and husband-wife relationships. Although Lawrence achieved critical acclaim, controversy kept him almost always impoverished. Were his sensuous, probing narratives necessary subversions of Victorian hypocrisy or merely obscene displays? His constant travels in Italy, Southern France, New Mexico, Mexico, and Australia seeking warmer, healthier climes for his tuberculosis and primitive alternatives to the modern world made him seem irredeemably alienated, as did his elopement in 1914 with a married German woman. He wrote superb short stories and such classic novels as* The Rainbow *(1915),* Women in Love *(1920),* The Plumed Serpent *(1926), and* Lady Chatterley's Lover *(1928). He also wrote poetry, plays, and incisive non-fictions such as* Twilight in Italy *(1916),* Psychoanalysis and the Unconscious *(1921),* Studies in Classic American Literature *(1923), and* Pornography and Obscenity *(1929). In his last years, he also painted.*

Odour of Chrysanthemums

I

The small locomotive engine, Number 4, came clanking, stumbling down from Selston with seven full wagons. It appeared round the corner with loud threats of speed, but the colt that it startled from among the gorse, which still flickered indistinctly in the raw afternoon, out-distanced it at a canter. A woman, walking up the railway line to Underwood, drew back into the hedge, held her basket aside, and watched the footplate of the engine advancing. The trucks thumped heavily past, one by one, with slow inevitable movement, as she stood insignificantly trapped between the jolting black wagons and the hedge; then they curved away towards the coppice where the withered oak leaves dropped noiselessly, while the birds, pulling at the scarlet hips beside the track, made off into the dusk that had already crept into the spinney. In the open, the smoke from the engine sank and cleaved to the rough grass. The fields were dreary and forsaken, and in the marshy strip that led to the whimsey, a reedy pit-pond, the fowls had already abandoned their run among the alders, to roost in the tarred fowl-house. The pit-bank loomed up beyond the pond, flames like red sores licking its ashy sides, in the afternoon's stagnant light. Just beyond rose the tapering chimneys and the clumsy black headstocks of Brinsley Colliery. The two wheels were spinning fast up against the sky, and the winding engine rapped out its little spasms. The miners were being turned up.

The engine whistled as it came into the wide bay of railway lines beside the colliery, where rows of trucks stood in harbour.

Miners, single, trailing and in groups, passed like shadows diverging home. At the edge of the ribbed level of sidings squatted a low cottage, three steps down from the cinder track. A large bony vine clutched at the house, as if to claw down the tiled roof. Round the bricked yard grew a few wintry primroses. Beyond, the long garden sloped down to a bush-covered brook course. There were some twiggy apple trees, winter-crack trees, and ragged cabbages. Beside the path hung dishevelled pink chrysanthemums, like pink cloths hung on bushes. A woman came stooping out of the felt-covered fowl-house, half-way down the garden. She closed and padlocked the door, then drew herself erect, having brushed some bits from her white apron.

She was a tall woman of imperious mien, handsome, with definite black eyebrows. Her smooth black hair was parted exactly. For a few moments she stood steadily watching the miners as they passed along the railway: then she turned towards the brook course. Her face was calm and set, her mouth was closed with disillusionment. After a moment she called:

"John!" There was no answer. She waited, and then said distinctly:

"Where are you?"

"Here!" replied a child's sulky voice from among the bushes. The woman looked piercingly through the dusk.

"Are you at that brook?" she asked sternly.

For answer the child showed himself before the raspberry-canes that rose like whips. He was a small, sturdy boy of five. He stood quite still, defiantly.

"Oh!" said the mother, conciliated. "I thought you were down at that wet brook — and you remember what I told you — "

The boy did not move or answer.

"Come, come on in," she said more gently, "it's getting dark. There's your grandfather's engine coming down the line!"

The lad advanced slowly, with resentful, taciturn movement. He was dressed in trousers and waistcoat of cloth that was too thick and hard for the size of the garments. They were evidently cut down from a man's clothes.

As they went slowly towards the house he tore at the ragged wisps of chrysanthemums and dropped the petals in handfuls along the path.

"Don't do that — it does look nasty," said his mother. He refrained, and she, suddenly pitiful, broke off a twig with three or four wan flowers and held them against her face. When mother and son reached the yard her hand hesitated, and instead of laying the flower aside, she pushed it in her apron-band. The mother and son stood at the foot of the three steps looking across the bay of lines at the passing home of the miners. The trundle of the small train was imminent. Suddenly the engine loomed past the house and came to a stop opposite the gate.

The engine-driver, a short man with round grey beard, leaned out of the cab high above the woman.

"Have you got a cup of tea?" he said in a cheery, hearty fashion.

It was her father. She went in, saying she would mash. Directly, she returned.

"I didn't come to see you on Sunday," began the little grey-bearded man.

"I didn't expect you," said his daughter.

The engine-driver winced; then, reassuming his cheery, airy manner, he said:

"Oh, have you heard then? Well, and what do you think — ?"

"I think it is soon enough," she replied.

At her brief censure the little man made an impatient gesture, and said coaxingly, yet with dangerous coldness:

"Well, what's a man to do? It's no sort of life for a man of my years, to sit at my own hearth like a stranger. And if I'm going to marry again it may as well be soon as late — what does it matter to anybody?"

The woman did not reply, but turned and went into the house. The man in the engine-cab stood assertive, till she returned with a cup of tea and a piece of bread and butter on a plate. She went up the steps and stood near the footplate of the hissing engine.

"You needn't 'a' brought me bread an' butter," said her father. "But a cup of tea" — he sipped appreciatively — "it's very nice." He sipped for a moment or two, then: "I hear as Walter's got another bout on," he said.

"When hasn't he?" said the woman bitterly.

"I heerd tell of him in the 'Lord Nelson' braggin' as he was going to spend that b —— afore he went: half a sovereign that was."

"When?" asked the woman.

"A' Sat'day night — I know that's true."

"Very likely," she laughed bitterly. "He gives me twenty-three shillings."

"Aye, it's a nice thing, when a man can do nothing with his money but make a beast of himself!" said the grey-whiskered man. The woman turned her head away. Her father swallowed the last of his tea and handed her the cup.

"Aye," he sighed, wiping his mouth. "It's a settler, it is —— "

He put his hand on the lever. The little engine strained and groaned, and the train rumbled towards the crossing. The woman again looked across the metals. Darkness was settling over the spaces of the railway and trucks: the miners, in grey sombre groups, were still passing home. The winding engine pulsed hurriedly, with brief pauses. Elizabeth Bates looked at the dreary flow of men, then she went indoors. Her husband did not come.

The kitchen was small and full of firelight; red coals piled glowing up the chimney mouth. All the life of the room seemed in the white, warm hearth and the steel fender reflecting the red fire. The cloth was laid for tea; cups glinted in the shadows. At the back, where the lowest stairs protruded into the room, the boy sat struggling with a knife and a piece of white wood. He was almost hidden in the shadow. It was half-past four. They had but to await the father's coming to begin tea. As the mother watched her son's sullen little struggle with the wood, she saw herself in his silence and pertinacity; she saw the father in her child's indifference to all but himself. She seemed to be occupied by her husband. He had probably gone past his home, slunk past his own door, to drink before he came in, while his dinner spoiled and wasted in waiting. She glanced at the clock, then took the potatoes to strain them in the yard. The garden and fields beyond the brook were closed in uncertain darkness. When she rose with the saucepan, leaving the drain steaming into the night behind her, she saw the yellow lamps were lit along the high road that went up the hill away beyond the space of the railway lines and the field.

Then again she watched the men trooping home, fewer now and fewer.

Indoors the fire was sinking and the room was dark red. The woman put her saucepan on the hob, and set a batter-pudding near the mouth of the oven. Then she stood unmoving. Directly, gratefully, came quick young steps to the door. Someone hung on the latch a moment, then a little girl entered and began pulling off her outdoor things, dragging a mass of curls, just ripening from gold to brown, over her eyes with her hat.

Her mother chid her for coming late from school, and said she would have to keep her at home the dark winter days.

"Why, mother, it's hardly a bit dark yet. The lamp's not lighted, and my father's not home."

"No, he isn't. But it's a quarter to five! Did you see anything of him?"

The child became serious. She looked at her mother with large, wistful blue eyes.

"No, mother, I've never seen him. Why? Has he come up an' gone past, to Old Brinsley? He hasn't, mother, 'cos I never saw him."

"He'd watch that," said the mother bitterly, "he'd take care as you didn't see him. But you may depend upon it, he's seated in the 'Prince o' Wales.' He wouldn't be this late."

The girl looked at her mother piteously.

"Let's have our teas, mother, should we?" said she.

The mother called John to table. She opened the door once more and looked out across the darkness of the lines. All was deserted: she could not hear the winding-engines.

"Perhaps," she said to herself, "he's stopped to get some ripping done."

They sat down to tea. John, at the end of the table near the door, was almost lost in the darkness. Their faces were hidden from each other. The girl crouched against the fender slowly moving a thick piece of bread before the fire. The lad, his face a dusky mark on the shadow, sat watching her who was transfigured in the red glow.

"I do think it's beautiful to look in the fire," said the child.

"Do you?" said her mother. "Why?"

"It's so red, and full of little caves — and it feels so nice, and you can fair smell it."

"It'll want mending directly," replied her mother, "and then if your father comes he'll carry on and say there never is a fire when a man comes home sweating from the pit. A public-house is always warm enough."

There was silence till the boy said complainingly: "Make haste, our Annie."

"Well, I am doing! I can't make the fire do it no faster, can I?"

"She keeps wafflin' it about so's to make 'er slow," grumbled the boy.

"Don't have such an evil imagination, child," replied the mother.

Soon the room was busy in the darkness with the crisp sound of crunching. The mother ate very little. She drank her tea determinedly, and sat thinking. When she rose her anger was evident in the stern unbending of her head. She looked at the pudding in the fender, and broke out:

"It is a scandalous thing as a man can't even come home to his dinner! If it's crozzled up to a cinder I don't see why I should care. Past his very door he goes to get to a public-house, and here I sit with his dinner waiting for him —— "

She went out. As she dropped piece after piece of coal on the red fire, the shadows fell on the walls, till the room was almost in total darkness.

"I canna see," grumbled the invisible John. In spite of herself, the mother laughed.

"You know the way to your mouth," she said. She set the dust-pan outside the door. When she came again like a shadow on the hearth, the lad repeated, complaining sulkily:

"I canna see."

"Good gracious!" cried the mother irritably, "you're as bad as your father if it's a bit dusk!"

Nevertheless, she took a paper spill from a sheaf on the mantelpiece and proceeded to light the lamp that hung from the ceiling in the middle of the room. As she reached up, her figure displayed itself just rounding with maternity.

"Oh, mother ——!" exclaimed the girl.

"What?" said the woman, suspended in the act of putting the lamp-glass over the flame. The copper reflector shone handsomely on her, as she stood with uplifted arm, turning to face her daughter.

"You've got a flower in your apron!" said the child, in a little rapture at this unusual event.

"Goodness me!" exclaimed the woman, relieved. "One would think the house was afire." She replaced the glass and waited a moment before turning up the wick. A pale shadow was seen floating vaguely on the floor.

"Let me smell!" said the child, still rapturously, coming forward and putting her face to her mother's waist.

"Go along, silly!" said the mother, turning up the lamp. The light revealed their suspense so that the woman felt it almost unbearable. Annie was still bending at her waist. Irritably, the mother took the flowers out from her apron-band.

"Oh, mother — don't take them out!" Annie cried, catching her hand and trying to replace the sprig.

"Such nonsense!" said the mother, turning away. The child put the pale chrysanthemums to her lips, murmuring:

"Don't they smell beautiful!"

Her mother gave a short laugh.

"No," she said, "not to me. It was chrysanthemums when I married him, and chrysanthemums when you were born, and the first time they ever brought him home drunk, he'd got brown chrysanthemums in his button-hole."

She looked at the children. Their eyes and their parted lips were wondering. The mother sat rocking in silence for some time. Then she looked at the clock.

"Twenty minutes to six!" In a tone of fine bitter carelessness she continued: "Eh, he'll not come now till they bring him. There he'll stick! But he needn't come rolling in here in his pit-dirt; for *I* won't wash him. He can lie on the floor —— Eh, what a fool I've been, what a fool! And this is what I came here for, to this dirty hole, rats and all, for him to slink past his very door. Twice last week — he's begun now ——"

She silenced herself, and rose to clear the table.

While for an hour or more the children played, subduedly intent, fertile of imagination, united in fear of the mother's wrath, and in dread of their father's home-coming, Mrs. Bates sat in her rocking-chair making a 'singlet' of thick cream-coloured flannel, which gave a dull wounded sound as she tore off the grey edge. She worked at her sewing with energy, listening to the children, and her anger wearied itself, lay down to rest, opening its eyes from time to time and steadily watching, its ears raised to listen. Sometimes even her anger quailed and shrank, and the mother suspended her sewing, tracing the footsteps that thudded along the sleepers outside; she would lift her head sharply to bid the children 'hush', but she recovered herself in time, and the footsteps went past the gate, and the children were not flung out of their play-world.

But at last Annie sighed, and gave in. She glanced at her wagon of slippers, and loathed the game. She turned plaintively to her mother.

"Mother!" —but she was inarticulate.

John crept out like a frog from under the sofa. His mother glanced up.

"Yes," she said, "just look at those shirt-sleeves!"

The boy held them out to survey them, saying nothing. Then somebody called in a hoarse voice away down the line, and suspense bristled in the room, till two people had gone by outside, talking.

"It is time for bed," said the mother.

"My father hasn't come," wailed Annie plaintively. But her mother was primed with courage.

"Never mind. They'll bring him when he does come —like a log." She meant there would be no scene. "And he may sleep on the floor till he wakes himself. I know he'll not go to work to-morrow after this!"

The children had their hands and faces wiped with a flannel. They were very quiet. When they had put on their nightdresses, they said their prayers, the boy mumbling. The mother looked down at them, at the brown silken bush of intertwining curls in the nape of the girl's neck, at the little black head of the lad, and her heart burst with anger at their father, who caused all three such distress. The children hid their faces in her skirts for comfort.

When Mrs. Bates came down, the room was strangely empty, with a tension of expectancy. She took up her sewing and stitched for some time without raising her head. Meantime her anger was tinged with fear.

II

The clock struck eight and she rose suddenly, dropping her sewing on her chair. She went to the stair-foot door, opened it, listening. Then she went out, locking the door behind her.

Something scuffled in the yard, and she started, though she knew it was only the rats with which the place was over-run. The night was very dark. In the great bay of railway lines, bulked with trucks, there was no trace of light, only away back she could see a few yellow lamps at the pit-top, and the red smear of the burning pit-bank on the night. She hurried along the edge of the track, then, crossing the converging lines, came to the stile by the white gates, whence she emerged on the road. Then the fear which had led her shrank. People were walking up to New Brinsley; she saw the lights in the houses; twenty yards farther on were the broad windows of the 'Prince of Wales', very warm and bright, and the loud voices of men could be heard distinctly. What a fool she had been to imagine that anything had happened to him! He was merely drinking over there at the 'Prince of Wales'. She faltered. She had never yet been to fetch him, and she never would go. So she continued her walk towards the long straggling line of houses, standing back on the highway. She entered a passage between the dwellings.

"Mr. Rigley? — Yes! Did you want him? No, he's not in at this minute."

The raw-boned woman leaned forward from her dark scullery and peered at the other, upon whom fell a dim light through the blind of the kitchen window.

"Is it Mrs. Bates?" she asked in a tone tinged with respect.

"Yes. I wondered if your Master was at home. Mine hasn't come yet."

"'Asn't 'e! Oh, Jack's been 'ome an' 'ad 'is dinner an' gone out. 'E's just gone for 'alf and hour afore bed-time. Did you call at the 'Prince of Wales'?"

"No —— "

"No, you didn't like ——! It's not very nice." The other woman was indulgent. There was an awkward pause. "Jack never said nothink about — about your Master," she said.

"No! — I expect he's stuck in there!"

Elizabeth Bates said this bitterly, and with recklessness. She knew that the woman across the yard was standing at her door listening, but she did not care. As she turned:

"Stop a minute! I'll just go an' ask Jack if 'e knows anythink," said Mrs. Rigley.

"Oh no — I wouldn't like to put ——!"

"Yes, I will, if you'll just step inside an' see as th' childer doesn't come downstairs and set theirselves afire."

Elizabeth Bates, murmuring a remonstrance, stepped inside. The other woman apologised for the state of the room.

The kitchen needed apology. There were little frocks and trousers and childish undergarments on the squab and on the floor, and a litter of playthings everywhere. On the black American cloth of the table were pieces of bread and cake, crusts, slops, and a teapot with cold tea.

"Eh, ours is just as bad," said Elizabeth Bates, looking at the woman, not at the house. Mrs. Rigley put a shawl over her head and hurried out, saying:

"I shanna be a minute."

The other sat, noting with faint disapproval the general untidiness of the room. Then she fell to counting the shoes of various sizes scattered over the floor. There were twelve. She sighed and said to herself: "No wonder!" — glancing at the litter. There came the scratching of two pairs of feet on the yard, and the Rigleys entered. Elizabeth Bates rose. Rigley was a big man, with very large bones. His head looked particularly bony. Across his temple was a blue scar, caused by a wound got in the pit, a wound in which the coat-dust remained blue like tattooing.

"'Asna 'e come whoam yit?" asked the man, without any form of greeting, but wit' deference and sympathy. "I couldna say wheer he is — 'e's non ower theer!" — he jerked his head to signify the 'Prince of Wales'.

"'E's 'appen gone up to th' 'Yew'," said Mrs. Rigley.

There was another pause. Rigley had evidently something to get off his mind:

"Ah left 'im finishin' a stint," he began. "Loose-all 'ad bin gone about ten minutes when we com'n away, an' I shouted: 'Are ter comin', Walt?' an' 'e said:

'Go on, Ah shanna be but a'ef a minnit,' so we com'n ter th' bottom, me an' Bowers, thinkin' as 'e wor just behint, an' 'ud come up i' th' next bantle —— "

He stood perplexed, as if answering a charge of deserting his mate. Elizabeth Bates, now again certain of disaster, hastened to reassure him:

"I expect 'e's gone up to th' 'Yew Tree', as you say. It's not the first time. I've fretted myself into a fever before now. He'll come home when they carry him."

"Ay, isn't it too bad!" deplored the other woman.

"I'll just step up to Dick's an' see if 'e *is* theer," offered the man, afraid of appearing alarmed, afraid of taking liberties.

"Oh, I wouldn't think of bothering you that far," said Elizabeth Bates, with emphasis, but he knew she was glad of his offer.

As they stumbled up the entry, Elizabeth Bates heard Rigley's wife run across the yard and open her neighbour's door. At this, suddenly all the blood in her body seemed to switch away from her heart.

"Mind!" warned Rigley. "Ah've said many a time as Ah'd fill up them ruts in this entry, sumb'dy 'll be breakin' their legs yit."

She recovered herself and walked quickly along with the miner.

"I don't like leaving the children in bed, and nobody in the house," she said.

"No, you dunna!" he replied courteously. They were soon at the gate of the cottage.

"Well, I shanna be many minnits. Dunna you be frettin' now, 'e'll be all right," said the butty.

"Thank you very much, Mr. Rigley," she replied.

"You're welcome!" he stammered, moving away. "I shanna be many minnits."

The house was quiet. Elizabeth Bates took off her hat and shawl, and rolled back the rug. When she had finished, she sat down. It was a few minutes past nine. She was startled by the rapid chuff of the winding-engine at the pit, and the sharp whirr of the brakes on the rope as it descended. Again she felt the painful sweep of her blood, and she put her hand to her side, saying aloud: "Good gracious! — it's only the nine o'clock deputy going down," rebuking herself.

She sat still, listening. Half an hour of this, and she was wearied out.

"What am I working myself up like this for?" she said pitiably to herself, "I s'll only be doing myself some damage."

She took out her sewing again.

At a quarter to ten there were footsteps. One person! She watched for the door to open. It was an elderly woman, in a black bonnet and a black woollen shawl — his mother. She was about sixty years old, pale, with blue eyes, and her face all wrinkled and lamentable. She shut the door and turned to her daughter-in-law peevishly.

"Eh, Lizzie, whatever shall we do, whatever shall we do!" she cried.

Elizabeth drew back a little, sharply.

"What is it, mother?" she said.

The elder woman seated herself on the sofa.

"I don't know, child, I can't tell you!" — she shook her head slowly. Elizabeth sat watching her, anxious and vexed.

"I don't know," replied the grandmother, sighing very deeply. "There's no end to my troubles, there isn't. The things I've gone through, I'm sure it's enough —— !" She wept without wiping her eyes, the tears running.

"But, mother," interrupted Elizabeth, "what do you mean? What is it?"

The grandmother slowly wiped her eyes. The fountains of her tears were stopped by Elizabeth's directness. She wiped her eyes slowly.

"Poor child! Eh, you poor thing!" she moaned. "I don't know what we're going to do, I don't — and you as you are — it's a thing, it is indeed!"

Elizabeth waited.

"Is he dead?" she asked, and at the words her heart swung violently, though she felt a slight flush of shame at the ultimate extravagance of the question. Her words sufficiently frightened the old lady, almost brought her to herself.

"Don't say so, Elizabeth! We'll hope it's not as bad as that; no, may the Lord spare us that, Elizabeth. Jack Rigley came just as I was sittin' down to a glass afore going to bed, an' 'e said: ''Appen you'll go down th' line, Mrs. Bates. Walt's had an accident. 'Appen you'll go an' sit wi' 'er till we can get him home.' I hadn't time to ask him a word afore he was gone. An' I put my bonnet on an' come straight down, Lizzie. I thought to myself: 'Eh, that poor blessed child, if anybody should come an' tell her of a sudden, there's no knowin' what'll 'appen to 'er.' You mustn't let it upset you, Lizzie — or you know what to expect. How long is it, six months — or is it five, Lizzie? Ay!" — the old woman shook her head — "time slips on, it slips on! Ay!"

Elizabeth's thoughts were busy elsewhere. If he was killed — would she be able to manage on the little pension and what she could earn? — she counted up rapidly. If he was hurt — they wouldn't take him to the hospital — how tiresome he would be to nurse! — but perhaps she'd be able to get him away from the drink and his hateful ways. She would — while he was ill. The tears offered to come to her eyes at the picture. But what sentimental luxury was this she was beginning? She turned to consider the children. At any rate she was absolutely necessary for them. They were her business.

"Ay!" repeated the old woman, "it seems but a week or two since he brought me his first wages. Ay — he was a good lad, Elizabeth, he was, in his way. I don't know why he got to be such a trouble, I don't. He was a happy lad at home, only full of spirits. But there's no mistake he's been a handful of trouble, he has! I hope the Lord'll spare him to mend his ways. I hope so, I hope so. You've had a sight o' trouble with him, Elizabeth, you have indeed. But he was a jolly enough lad wi' me, he was, I can assure you. I don't know how it is. . . ."

The old woman continued to muse aloud, a monotonous irritating sound, while Elizabeth thought concentratedly, startled once, when she heard the winding-engine chuff quickly, and the brakes skirr with a shriek. Then she heard the engine more slowly, and the brakes made no sound. The old woman did not notice. Elizabeth waited in suspense. The mother-in-law talked, with lapses into silence.

"But he wasn't your son, Lizzie, an' it makes a difference. Whatever he was, I remember him when he was little, an' I learned to understand him and to make allowances. You've got to make allowances for them —— "

It was half-past ten, and the old woman was saying: "But it's trouble from beginning to end; you're never too old for trouble, never too old for that —— " when the gate banged back, and there were heavy feet on the steps.

"I'll go, Lizzie, let me go," cried the old woman, rising. But Elizabeth was at the door. It was a man in pit-clothes.

"They're bringin' 'im, Missis," he said. Elizabeth's heart halted a moment. Then it surged on again, almost suffocating her.

"Is he — is it bad?" she asked.

The man turned away, looking at the darkness:

"The doctor says 'e'd been dead hours. 'E saw 'im i' th' lamp-cabin."

The old woman, who stood just behind Elizabeth, dropped into a chair, and folded her hands, crying: "Oh, my boy, my boy!"

"Hush!" said Elizabeth, with a sharp twitch of a frown. "Be still, mother, don't waken th' children: I wouldn't have them down for anything!"

The old woman moaned softly, rocking herself. The man was drawing away. Elizabeth took a step forward.

"How was it?" she asked.

"Well, I couldn't say for sure," the man replied, very ill at ease. "'E wor finishin' a stint an' th' butties 'ad gone, an' a lot o' stuff come down atop 'n 'im."

"And crushed him?" cried the widow, with a shudder.

"No," said the man, "it fell at th' back of 'im. 'E wor under th' face, an' it niver touched 'im. It shut 'im in. It seems 'e wor smothered."

Elizabeth shrank back. She heard the old woman behind her cry:

"What? — what did 'e say it was?"

The man replied, more loudly: "'E wor smothered!"

Then the old woman wailed aloud, and this relieved Elizabeth.

"Oh, mother," she said, putting her hand on the old woman, "don't waken th' children, don't waken th' children."

She wept a little, unknowing, while the old mother rocked herself and moaned. Elizabeth remembered that they were bringing him home, and she must be ready. "They'll lay him in the parlour," she said to herself, standing a moment pale and perplexed.

Then she lighted a candle and went into the tiny room. The air was cold and damp, but she could not make a fire, there was no fireplace. She set down the candle and looked round. The candlelight glittered on the lustre-glasses, on the two vases that held some of the pink chrysanthemums, and on the dark mahogany. There was a cold, deathly smell of chrysanthemums in the room. Elizabeth stood looking at the flowers. She turned away, and calculated whether there would be room to lay him on the floor, between the couch and the chiffonier. She pushed the chairs aside. There would be room to lay him down and to step round him. Then she fetched the old red tablecloth, and another old cloth, spreading them down to save her bit of carpet. She shivered on leaving the parlour; so, from the dresser drawer she took a clean shirt and put it at the fire to air. All the time her mother-in-law was rocking herself in the chair and moaning.

"You'll have to move from there, mother," said Elizabeth. "They'll be bringing him in. Come in the rocker."

The old mother rose mechanically, and seated herself by the fire, continuing to lament. Elizabeth went into the pantry for another candle, and there, in the little pent-house under the naked tiles, she heard them coming. She stood still in the pantry doorway, listening. She heard them pass the end of the house, and come awkwardly down the three steps, a jumble of shuffling footsteps and muttering voices. The old woman was silent. The men were in the yard.

Then Elizabeth heard Matthews, the manager of the pit, say: "You go in first, Jim. Mind!"

The door came open, and the two women saw a collier backing into the room, holding one end of a stretcher, on which they could see the nailed pit-boots of the dead man. The two carriers halted, the man at the head stooping to the lintel of the door.

"Wheer will you have him?" asked the manager, a short, white-bearded man.

Elizabeth roused herself and came from the pantry carrying the unlighted candle.

"In the parlour," she said.

"In there, Jim!" pointed the manager, and the carriers backed round into the tiny room. The coat with which they had covered the body fell off as they awkwardly turned through the two doorways, and the women saw their man, naked to the waist, lying stripped for work. The old woman began to moan in a low voice of horror.

"Lay th' stretcher at th' side," snapped the manager, "an' put 'im on th' cloths. Mind now, mind! Look you now ——!"

One of the men had knocked off a vase of chrysanthemums. He stared awkwardly, then they set down the stretcher. Elizabeth did not look at her husband. As soon as she could get in the room, she went and picked up the broken vase and the flowers.

"Wait a minute!" she said.

The three men waited in silence while she mopped up the water with a duster.

"Eh, what a job, what a job, to be sure!" the manager was saying, rubbing his brow with trouble and perplexity. "Never knew such a thing in my life, never! He'd no business to ha' been left. I never knew such a thing in my life! Fell over him clean as a whistle, an' shut him in. Not four foot of space, there wasn't — yet it scarce bruised him."

He looked down at the dead man, lying prone, half naked, all grimed with coal-dust.

" ' 'Sphyxiated', the doctor said. It *is* the most terrible job I've ever known. Seems as if it was done o' purpose. Clean over him, an' shut 'im in, like a mouse-trap" — he made a sharp, descending gesture with his hand.

The colliers standing by jerked aside their heads in hopeless comment.

The horror of the thing bristled upon them all.

Then they heard the girl's voice upstairs calling shrilly: "Mother, mother — who is it? Mother, who is it?"

Elizabeth hurried to the foot of the stairs and opened the door:

"Go to sleep!" she commanded sharply. "What are you shouting about? Go to sleep at once — there's nothing ——"

Then she began to mount the stairs. They could hear her on the boards, and on the plaster floor of the little bedroom. They could hear her distinctly:

"What's the matter now? — what's the matter with you, silly thing?" — her voice was much agitated, with an unreal gentleness.

"I thought it was some men come," said the plaintive voice of the child. "Has he come?"

"Yes, they've brought him. There's nothing to make a fuss about. Go to sleep now, like a good child."

They could hear her voice in the bedroom, they waited whilst she covered the children under the bedclothes.

"Is he drunk?" asked the girl, timidly, faintly.

"No! No—he's not! He—he's asleep."

"Is he asleep downstairs?"

"Yes—and don't make a noise."

There was silence for a moment, then the men heard the frightened child again:

"What's that noise?"

"It's nothing, I tell you, what are you bothering for?"

The noise was the grandmother moaning. She was oblivious of everything, sitting on her chair rocking and moaning. The manager put his hand on her arm and bade her "Sh—sh!!"

The old woman opened her eyes and looked at him. She was shocked by this interruption, and seemed to wonder.

"What time is it?" the plaintive thin voice of the child, sinking back unhappily into sleep, asked this last question.

"Ten o'clock," answered the mother more softly. Then she must have bent down and kissed the children.

Matthews beckoned to the men to come away. They put on their caps and took up the stretcher. Stepping over the body, they tiptoed out of the house. None of them spoke till they were far from the wakeful children.

When Elizabeth came down she found her mother alone on the parlour floor, leaning over the dead man, the tears dropping on him.

"We must lay him out," the wife said. She put on the kettle, then returning knelt at the feet, and began to unfasten the knotted leather laces. The room was clammy and dim with only one candle, so that she had to bend her face almost to the floor. At last she got off the heavy boots and put them away.

"You must help me now," she whispered to the old woman. Together they stripped the man.

When they arose, saw him lying in the naïve dignity of death, the woman stood arrested in fear and respect. For a few moments they remained still, looking down, the old mother whimpering. Elizabeth felt countermanded. She saw him, how utterly inviolable he lay in himself. She had nothing to do with him. She could not accept it. Stooping, she laid her hand on him, in claim. He was still warm, for the mine was hot where he had died. His mother had his face between her hands, and was murmuring incoherently. The old tears fell in succession as drops from wet leaves; the mother was not weeping, merely her tears flowed. Elizabeth embraced the body of her husband, with cheek and lips. She seemed to be listening, inquiring, trying to get some connection. But she could not. She was driven away. He was impregnable.

She rose, went into the kitchen, where she poured warm water into a bowl, brought soap and flannel and a soft towel.

"I must wash him," she said.

Then the old mother rose stiffly, and watched Elizabeth as she carefully washed his face, carefully brushing the big blond moustache from his mouth with the flannel. She was afraid with a bottomless fear, so she ministered to him. The old woman, jealous, said:

"Let me wipe him!"—and she kneeled on the other side drying slowly as Elizabeth washed, her big black bonnet sometimes brushing the dark head of her daughter-in-law. They worked thus in silence for a long time. They never forgot it was death, and the touch of the man's dead body gave them strange emotions, different in each of the women; a great dread possessed them both, the mother felt the lie was given to her womb, she was denied; the wife felt the utter isolation of the human soul, the child within her was a weight apart from her.

At last it was finished. He was a man of handsome body, and his face showed no traces of drink. He was blond, full-fleshed, with fine limbs. But he was dead.

"Bless him," whispered his mother, looking always at his face, and speaking out of sheer terror. "Dear lad—bless him!" She spoke in a faint, sibilant ecstasy of fear and mother love.

Elizabeth sank down again to the floor, and put her face against his neck, and trembled and shuddered. But she had to draw away again. He was dead, and her living flesh had no place against his. A great dread and weariness held her: she was so unavailing. Her life was gone like this.

"White as milk he is, clear as a twelve-month baby, bless him, the darling!" the old mother murmured to herself. "Not a mark on him, clear and clean and white, beautiful as ever a child was made," she murmured with pride. Elizabeth kept her face hidden.

"He went peaceful, Lizzie—peaceful as sleep. Isn't he beautiful, the lamb? Ay—he must ha' made his peace, Lizzie. 'Appen he made it all right, Lizzie, shut in there. He'd have time. He wouldn't look like this if he hadn't made his peace. The lamb, the dear lamb. Eh, but he had a hearty laugh. I loved to hear it. He had the heartiest laugh, Lizzie, as a lad——"

Elizabeth looked up. The man's mouth was fallen back, slightly open under the cover of the moustache. The eyes, half shut, did not show glazed in the obscurity. Life with its smoky burning gone from him, had left him apart and utterly alien to her. And she knew what a stranger he was to her. In her womb was ice of fear, because of this separate stranger with whom she had been living as one flesh. Was this what it all meant—utter, intact separateness, obscured by heat of living? In dread she turned her face away. The fact was too deadly. There had been nothing between them, and yet they had come together, exchanging their nakedness repeatedly. Each time he had taken her, they had been two isolated beings, far apart as now. He was no more responsible than she. The child was like ice in her womb. For as she looked at the dead man, her mind, cold and detached, said clearly: "Who am I? What have I been doing? I have been fighting a husband who did not exist. *He* existed all the time. What wrong have I done? What was that I have been living with? There lies the reality, this man." And her soul died in her for fear: she knew she had never seen him, he had never seen her, they had met in the dark and had fought in the dark, not knowing whom they met nor whom they fought. And now she saw, and turned silent in seeing.

For she had been wrong. She had said he was something he was not; she had felt familiar with him. Whereas he was apart all the while, living as she never lived, feeling as she never felt.

In fear and shame she looked at his naked body, that she had known falsely. And he was the father of her children. Her soul was torn from body and stood apart. She looked at his naked body and was ashamed, as if she had denied it. After all, it was itself. It seemed awful to her. She looked at his face, and she turned her own face to the wall. For his look was other than hers, his way was not her way. She had denied him what he was — she saw it now. She had refused him as himself. And this had been her life, and his life. She was grateful to death, which restored the truth. And she knew she was not dead.

And all the while her heart was bursting with grief and pity for him. What had he suffered? What stretch of horror for this helpless man! She was rigid with agony. She had not been able to help him. He had been cruelly injured, this naked man, this other being, and she could make no reparation. There were the children — but the children belonged to life. This dead man had nothing to do with them. He and she were only channels through which life had flowed to issue in the children. She was a mother — but how awful she knew it now to have been a wife. And he, dead now, how awful he must have felt it to be a husband. She felt that in the next world he would be a stranger to her. If they met there, in the beyond, they would only be ashamed of what had been before. The children had come, for some mysterious reason, out of both of them. But the children did not unite them. Now he was dead, she knew how eternally he was apart from her, how eternally he had nothing more to do with her. She saw this episode of her life closed. They had denied each other in life. Now he had withdrawn. An anguish came over her. It was finished then: it had become hopeless between them long before he died. Yet he had been her husband. But how little!

"Have you got his shirt, 'Lizabeth?"

Elizabeth turned without answering, though she strove to weep and behave as her mother-in-law expected. But she could not, she was silenced. She went into the kitchen and returned with the garment.

"It is aired," she said, grasping the cotton shirt here and there to try. She was almost ashamed to handle him; what right had she or anyone to lay hands on him; but her touch was humble on his body. It was hard work to clothe him. He was so heavy and inert. A terrible dread gripped her all the while: that he could be so heavy and utterly inert, unresponsive, apart. The horror of the distance between them was almost too much for her — it was so infinite a gap she must look across.

At last it was finished. They covered him with a sheet and left him lying, with his face bound. And she fastened the door of the little parlour, lest the children should see what was lying there. Then, with peace sunk heavy on her heart, she went about making tidy the kitchen. She knew she submitted to life, which was her immediate master. But from death, her ultimate master, she winced with fear and shame.

[1909, 1911]

Study and Writing Questions

1. What feature(s) of the DESCRIPTION, for instance in the opening paragraph, actually advance the NARRATIVE?

2. How do the unusual vocabulary and dialect speech affect your reading of the STORY?
3. When they hear a second time that "'E wor smothered!'" why does the old woman's "wail" "relieve" Elizabeth?
4. What precisely does Elizabeth believe she knows in the last two lines of the narrative? Why does she "wince with fear and shame"? Is her knowledge valid for anyone else?
5. Is the title appropriate? What are it effects?

See also Questions for Contrast and Comparison: 43, 108, 109, 110, 111, 112, and 133.

The Rocking-Horse Winner

There was a woman who was beautiful, who started with all the advantages, yet she had no luck. She married for love, and the love turned to dust. She had bonny children, yet she felt they had been thrust upon her, and she could not love them. They looked at her coldly, as if they were finding fault with her. And hurriedly she felt she must cover up some fault in herself. Yet what it was that she must cover up she never knew. Nevertheless, when her children were present, she always felt the centre of her heart go hard. This troubled her, and in her manner she was all the more gentle and anxious for her children, as if she loved them very much. Only she herself knew that at the centre of her heart was a hard little place that could not feel love, no, not for anybody. Everybody else said of her: "She is such a good mother. She adores her children." Only she herself, and her children themselves, knew it was not so. They read it in each other's eyes.

There were a boy and two little girls. They lived in a pleasant house, with a garden, and they had discreet servants, and felt themselves superior to anyone in the neighbourhood.

Although they lived in style, they felt always an anxiety in the house. There was never enough money. The mother had a small income, and the father had a small income, but not nearly enough for the social position which they had to keep up. The father went in to town to some office. But though he had good prospects, these prospects never materialized. There was always the grinding sense of the shortage of money, though the style was always kept up.

At last the mother said: "I will see if *I* can't make something." But she did not know where to begin. She racked her brains, and tried this thing and the other, but could not find anything successful. The failure made deep lines come into her face. Her children were growing up, they would have to go to school. There must be more money, there must be more money. The father, who was always very handsome and expensive in his tastes, seemed as if he never *would* be able to do anything worth doing. And the mother, who had a great belief in herself, did not succeed any better, and her tastes were just as expensive.

And so the house came to be haunted by the unspoken phrase: *There must be more money! There must be more money!* The children could hear it all the time, though nobody said it aloud. They heard it at Christmas, when the expensive and splendid toys filled the nursery. Behind the shining modern rocking-horse, behind the smart doll's-house, a voice would start whispering: "There *must* be more money! There *must* be more money!" And the children would stop playing, to listen for a moment. They would look into each other's eyes, to see if they had all heard. And each one saw in the eyes of the other two that they too had heard. "There *must* be more money! There *must* be more money!"

It came whispering from the springs of the still-swaying rocking-horse, and even the horse, bending his wooden, champing head, heard it. The big doll, sitting so pink and smirking in her new pram, could hear it quite plainly, and seemed to be smirking all the more self-consciously because of it. The foolish puppy, too, that took the place of the teddy-bear, he was looking so extraordinarily foolish for no other reason but that he heard the secret whisper all over the house: "There *must* be more money!"

Yet nobody ever said it aloud. The whisper was everywhere, and therefore no one spoke it. Just as no one ever says: "We are breathing!" in spite of the fact that breath is coming and going all the time.

"Mother," said the boy Paul one day, "why don't we keep a car of our own? Why do we always use uncle's, or else a taxi?"

"Because we're the poor members of the family," said the mother.

"But why *are* we, mother?"

"Well—I suppose," she said slowly and bitterly, "it's because your father has no luck."

The boy was silent for some time.

"Is luck money, mother?" he asked rather timidly.

"No, Paul. Not quite. It's what causes you to have money."

"Oh!" said Paul vaguely. "I thought when Uncle Oscar said *filthy lucker*, it meant money."

"Filthy *lucre* does mean money," said the mother. "But it's lucre, not luck."

"Oh!" said the boy. "Then what *is* luck, mother?"

"It's what causes you to have money. If you're lucky you have money. That's why it's better to be born lucky than rich. If you're rich, you may lose your money. But if you're lucky, you will always get more money."

"Oh! Will you? And is father not lucky?"

"Very unlucky, I should say," she said bitterly.

The boy watched her with unsure eyes.

"Why?" he asked.

"I don't know. Nobody ever knows why one person is lucky and another unlucky."

"Don't they? Nobody at all? Does *nobody* know?"

"Perhaps God. But He never tells."

"He ought to, then. And aren't you lucky either, mother?"

"I can't be, if I married an unlucky husband."

"But by yourself, aren't you?"

"I used to think I was, before I married. Now I think I am very unlucky indeed."

"Why?"

"Well—never mind! Perhaps I'm not really," she said.

The child looked at her, to see if she meant it. But he saw, by the lines of her mouth, that she was only trying to hide something from him.

"Well, anyhow," he said stoutly, "I'm a lucky person."

"Why?" said his mother, with a sudden laugh.

He stared at her. He didn't even know why he had said it.

"God told me," he asserted, brazening it out.

"I hope He did, dear!" she said, again with a laugh, but rather bitter.

"He did, mother!"

"Excellent!" said the mother, using one of her husband's exclamations.

The boy saw she did not believe him; or, rather, that she paid no attention to his assertion. This angered him somewhat, and made him want to compel her attention.

He went off by himself, vaguely, in a childish way, seeking for the clue to "luck." Absorbed, taking no heed of other people, he went about with a sort of stealth, seeking inwardly for luck. He wanted luck, he wanted it, he wanted it. When the two girls were playing dolls in the nursery, he would sit on his big rocking-horse, charging madly into space, with a frenzy that made the little girls peer at him uneasily. Wildly the horse careered, the waving dark hair of the boy tossed, his eyes had a strange glare in them. The little girls dared not speak to him.

When he had ridden to the end of his mad little journey, he climbed down and stood in front of his rocking-horse, staring fixedly into its lowered face. Its red mouth was slightly open, its big eye was wide and glassy-bright.

"Now!" he would silently command the snorting steed. "Now, take me to where there is luck! Now take me!"

And he would slash the horse on the neck with the little whip he had asked Uncle Oscar for. He *knew* the horse could take him to where there was luck, if only he forced it. So he would mount again, and start on his furious ride, hoping at last to get there. He knew he could get there.

"You'll break your horse, Paul!" said the nurse.

"He's always riding like that! I wish he'd leave off!" said his elder sister Joan.

But he only glared down on them in silence. Nurse gave him up. She could make nothing of him. Anyhow he was growing beyond her.

One day his mother and his Uncle Oscar came in when he was on one of his furious rides. He did not speak to them.

"Hallo, you young jockey! Riding a winner?" said his uncle.

"Aren't you growing too big for a rocking-horse? You're not a very little boy any longer, you know," said his mother.

But Paul only gave a blue glare from his big, rather close-set eyes. He would speak to nobody when he was in full tilt. His mother watched him with an anxious expression on her face.

At last he suddenly stopped forcing his horse into the mechanical gallop, and slid down.

"Well, I got there!" he announced fiercely, his blue eyes still flaring, and his sturdy long legs straddling apart.

"Where did you get to?" asked his mother.

"Where I wanted to go," he flared back at her.

"That's right, son!" said Uncle Oscar. "Don't you stop till you get there. What's the horse's name?"

"He doesn't have a name," said the boy.

"Gets on without all right?" asked the uncle.

"Well, he has different names. He was called Sansovino last week."

"Sansovino, eh? Won the Ascot. How did you know his name?"

"He always talks about horse-races with Bassett," said Joan.

The uncle was delighted to find that his small nephew was posted with all the racing news. Bassett, the young gardener, who had been wounded in the left foot in the war and had got his present job through Oscar Cresswell, whose batman he had been, was a perfect blade of the "turf." He lived in the racing events, and the small boy lived with him.

Oscar Cresswell got it all from Bassett.

"Master Paul comes and asks me, so I can't do more than tell him, sir," said Bassett, his face terribly serious, as if he were speaking of religious matters.

"And does he ever put anything on a horse he fancies?"

"Well—I don't want to give him away—he's a young sport, a fine sport, sir. Would you mind asking him himself? He sort of takes a pleasure in it, and perhaps he'd feel I was giving him away, sir, if you don't mind."

Bassett was serious as a church.

The uncle went back to his nephew and took him off for a ride in the car.

"Say, Paul, old man, do you ever put anything on a horse?" the uncle asked.

The boy watched the handsome man closely.

"Why, do you think I oughtn't to?" he parried.

"Not a bit of it! I thought perhaps you might give me a tip for the Lincoln."

The car sped on into the country, going down to Uncle Oscar's place in Hampshire.

"Honour bright?" said the nephew.

"Honour bright, son!" said the uncle.

"Well, then, Daffodil."

"Daffodil! I doubt it, sonny. What about Mirza?"

"I only know the winner," said the boy. "That's Daffodil."

"Daffodil, eh?"

There was a pause. Daffodil was an obscure horse comparatively.

"Uncle!"

"Yes, son?"

"You won't let it go any further, will you? I promised Bassett."

"Bassett be damned, old man! What's he got to do with it?"

"We're partners. We've been partners from the first. Uncle, he lent me my first five shillings, which I lost. I promised him, honour bright, it was only between me and him; only you gave me that ten-shilling note I started winning with, so I thought you were lucky. You won't let it go any further, will you?"

The boy gazed at his uncle from those big, hot, blue eyes, set rather close together. The uncle stirred and laughed uneasily.

"Right you are, son! I'll keep your tip private. Daffodil, eh? How much are you putting on him?"

"All except twenty pounds," said the boy. "I keep that in reserve."

The uncle thought it a good joke.

"You keep twenty pounds in reserve, do you, you young romancer? What are you betting, then?"

"I'm betting three hundred," said the boy gravely. "But it's between you and me, Uncle Oscar! Honour bright?"

The uncle burst into a roar of laughter.

"It's between you and me all right, you young Nat Could," he said, laughing. "But where's your three hundred?"

"Bassett keeps it for me. We're partners."

"You are, are you! And what is Bassett putting on Daffodil?"

"He won't go quite as high as I do, I expect. Perhaps he'll go a hundred and fifty."

"What, pennies?" laughed the uncle.

"Pounds," said the child, with a surprised look at his uncle. "Bassett keeps a bigger reserve than I do."

Between wonder and amusement Uncle Oscar was silent. He pursued the matter no further, but he determined to take his nephew with him to the Lincoln races.

"Now, son," he said, "I'm putting twenty on Mirza, and I'll put five for you on any horse you fancy. What's your pick?"

"Daffodil, uncle."

"No, not the fiver on Daffodil!"

"I should if it was my own fiver," said the child.

"Good! Good! Right you are! A fiver for me and a fiver for you on Daffodil."

The child had never been to a race-meeting before, and his eyes were blue fire. He pursed his mouth tight, and watched. A Frenchman just in front had put his money on Lancelot. Wild with excitement, he flayed his arms up and down, yelling "*Lancelot! Lancelot!*" in his French accent.

Daffodil came in first, Lancelot second, Mirza third. The child, flushed and with eyes blazing, was curiously serene. His uncle brought him four five-pound notes, four to one.

"What am I to do with these?" he cried, waving them before the boy's eyes.

"I suppose we'll talk to Bassett," said the boy. "I expect I have fifteen hundred now; and twenty in reserve; and this twenty."

His uncle studied him for some moments.

"Look here, son!" he said. "You're not serious about Bassett and that fifteen hundred, are you?"

"Yes, I am. But it's between you and me, uncle. Honour bright!"

"Honour bright all right, son! But I must talk to Bassett."

"If you'd like to be a partner, uncle, with Bassett and me, we could all be partners. Only, you'd have to promise, honour bright, uncle, not to let it go beyond us three. Bassett and I are lucky, and you must be lucky, because it was your ten shillings I started winning with. . . . ."

Uncle Oscar took both Bassett and Paul into Richmond Park for an afternoon, and there they talked.

"It's like this, you see, sir," Bassett said. "Master Paul would get me talking about racing events, spinning yarns, you know, sir. And he was always keen on knowing if I'd made or if I'd lost. It's about a year since, now, that I put five shilling on Blush of Dawn for him — and we lost. Then the luck turned, with that ten shillings he had from you, that we put on Singhalese. And since that time, it's been pretty steady, all things considering. What do you say, Master Paul?"

"We're all right when we're sure," said Paul. "It's when we're not quite sure that we go down."

"Oh, but we're careful then," said Bassett.

"But when are you *sure*?" smiled Uncle Oscar.

"It's Master Paul, sir," said Bassett, in a secret, religious voice. "It's as if he had it from heaven. Like Daffodil, now, for the Lincoln. That was as sure as eggs."

"Did you put anything on Daffodil?" asked Oscar Cresswell.

"Yes, sir. I made my bit."

"And my nephew?"

Bassett was obstinately silent, looking at Paul.

"I made twelve hundred, didn't I, Bassett? I told uncle I was putting three hundred on Daffodil."

"That's right," said Bassett, nodding.

"But where's the money?" asked the uncle.

"I keep it safe locked up, sir. Master Paul he can have it any minute he likes to ask for it."

"What, fifteen hundred pounds?"

"And twenty! And *forty*, that is, with the twenty he made on the course."

"It's amazing!" said the uncle.

"If Master Paul offers you to be partners, sir, I would, if I were you; if you'll excuse me," said Bassett.

Oscar Cresswell thought about it.

"I'll see the money," he said.

They drove home again, and sure enough, Bassett came round to the garden-house with fifteen hundred pounds in notes. The twenty pounds reserve was left with Joe Glee, in the Turf Commission deposit.

"You see, it's all right, uncle, when I'm *sure*! Then we go strong, for all we're worth. Don't we, Bassett?"

"We do that, Master Paul."

"And when are you sure?" said the uncle, laughing.

"Oh, well, sometimes I'm *absolutely* sure, like about Daffodil," said the boy; "and sometimes I have an idea; and sometimes I haven't even an idea, have I, Bassett? Then we're careful, because we mostly go down."

"You do, do you! And when you're sure, like about Daffodil, what makes you sure, sonny?"

"Oh, well, I don't know," said the boy uneasily. "I'm sure, you know, uncle; that's all."

"It's as if he had it from heaven, sir," Bassett reiterated.

"I should say so!" said the uncle.

But he became a partner. And when the Leger was coming on, Paul was "sure" about Lively Spark, which was a quite inconsiderable horse. The boy insisted on putting a thousand on the horse, Bassett went for five hundred, and Oscar Cresswell two hundred. Lively Spark came in first, and the betting had been ten to one against him. Paul had made ten thousand.

"You see," he said, "I was absolutely sure of him."

Even Oscar Cresswell had cleared two thousand.

"Look here, son," he said, "this sort of thing makes me nervous."

"It needn't, uncle! Perhaps I shan't be sure again for a long time."

"But what are you going to do with your money?" asked the uncle.

"Of course," said the boy, "I started it for mother. She said she had no luck, because father is unlucky, so I thought if I was lucky, it might stop whispering."

"What might stop whispering?"

"Our house. I *hate* our house for whispering."

"What does it whisper?"

"Why—why"—the boy fidgeted—"why, I don't know. But it's always short of money, you know, uncle."

"I know it, son, I know it."

"You know people send mother writs, don't you, uncle?"

"I'm afraid I do," said the uncle.

"And then the house whispers, like people laughing at you behind your back. It's awful, that is! I thought if I was lucky . . ."

"You might stop it," added the uncle.

The boy watched him with big blue eyes, that had an uncanny cold fire in them, and he said never a word.

"Well, then!" said the uncle. "What are we doing?"

"I shouldn't like mother to know I was lucky," said the boy.

"Why not, son?"

"She'd stop me."

"I don't think she would."

"Oh!" — and the boy writhed in an odd way — "I *don't* want her to know, uncle."

"All right, son! We'll manage it without her knowing."

They managed it very easily. Paul, at the other's suggestion, handed over five thousand pounds to his uncle, who deposited it with the family lawyer, who was then to inform Paul's mother that a relative had put five thousand pounds into his hands, which sum was to be paid out a thousand pounds at a time, on the mother's birthday, for the next five years.

"So she'll have a birthday present of a thousand pounds for five successive years," said Uncle Oscar. "I hope it won't make it all the harder for her later."

Paul's mother had her birthday in November. The house had been "whispering" worse than ever lately, and, even in spite of his luck, Paul could not bear up against it. He was very anxious to see the effect of the birthday letter, telling his mother about the thousand pounds.

When there were no visitors, Paul now took his meals with his parents, as he was beyond the nursery control. His mother went into town nearly every day. She had discovered that she had an odd knack of sketching furs and dress materials, so she worked secretly in the studio of a friend who was the chief "artist" for the leading drapers. She drew the figures of ladies in furs and ladies in silk and sequins for the newspaper advertisements. This young woman artist earned several thousand pounds a year, but Paul's mother only made several hundreds, and she was again dissatisfied. She so wanted to be first in something, and she did not succeed, even in making sketches for drapery advertisements.

She was down to breakfast on the morning of her birthday. Paul watched her face as she read her letters. He knew the lawyer's letter. As his mother read it, her face hardened and became more expressionless. Then a cold, determined look came on her mouth. She hid the letter under the pile of others, and said not a word about it.

"Didn't you have anything nice in the post for your birthday, mother?" said Paul.

"Quite moderately nice," she said, her voice cold and absent.

She went away to town without saying more.

But in the afternoon Uncle Oscar appeared. He said Paul's mother had had a long interview with the lawyer, asking if the whole five thousand could not be advanced at once, as she was in debt.

"What do you think, uncle?" said the boy.

"I leave it to you, son."

"Oh, let her have it, then! We can get some more with the other," said the boy.

"A bird in the hand is worth two in the bush, laddie!" said Uncle Oscar.

"But I'm sure to *know* for the Grand National; or the Lincolnshire; or else the Derby. I'm sure to know for *one* of them," said Paul.

So Uncle Oscar signed the agreement, and Paul's mother touched the whole five thousand. Then something very curious happened. The voices in the house suddenly went mad, like a chorus of frogs on a spring evening. There were certain new furnishings, and Paul had a tutor. He was *really* going to Eton, his father's school, in the following autumn. There were flowers in the winter, and a blossoming of the luxury Paul's mother had been used to. And yet the voices in the house, behind the sprays of mimosa and almond blossom, and from under the piles of iridescent cushions, simply trilled and screamed in a sort of ecstasy: "There *must* be more money! Oh-h-h; there *must* be more money. Oh, now, now-w! Now-w-w — there *must* be more money! — more than ever! More than ever!"

It frightened Paul terribly. He studied away at his Latin and Greek with his tutors. But his intense hours were spent with Bassett. The Grand National had gone by: he had not "known," and had lost a hundred pounds. Summer was at hand. He was in agony for the Lincoln. But even for the Lincoln he didn't "know," and he lost fifty pounds. He became wild-eyed and strange, as if something were going to explode in him.

"Let it alone, son! Don't you bother about it!" urged Uncle Oscar. But it was as if the boy couldn't really hear what his uncle was saying.

"I've got to know for the Derby! I've got to know for the Derby!" the child reiterated, his big blue eyes blazing with a sort of madness.

His mother noticed how overwrought he was.

"You'd better go to the seaside. Wouldn't you like to go now to the seaside, instead of waiting? I think you'd better," she said, looking down at him anxiously, her heart curiously heavy because of him.

But the child lifted his uncanny blue eyes.

"I couldn't possibly go before the Derby, mother!" he said. "I couldn't possibly"

"Why not?" she said, her voice becoming heavy when she was opposed. "Why not? You can still go from the seaside to see the Derby with your Uncle Oscar, if that's what you wish. No need for you to wait here. Besides, I think you care too much about these races. It's a bad sign. My family has been a gambling family, and you won't know till you grow up how much damage it has done. But it has done damage. I shall have to send Bassett away, and ask Uncle Oscar not to talk racing to you, unless you promise to be reasonable about it; go away to the seaside and forget it. You're all nerves!"

"I'll do what you like, mother, so long as you don't send me away till after the Derby," the boy said.

"Send you away from where? Just from this house?"

"Yes," he said, gazing at her.

"Why, you curious child, what makes you care about this house so much, suddenly? I never knew you loved it."

He gazed at her without speaking. He had a secret within a secret, something he had not divulged, even to Bassett or to his Uncle Oscar.

But his mother, after standing undecided and a little bit sullen for some moments, said:

"Very well, then! Don't go to the seaside till after the Derby, if you don't wish it. But promise me you won't let your nerves go to pieces. Promise you won't think so much about horse-racing and *events*, as you call them!"

"Oh, no," said the boy casually. "I won't think much about them, mother. You needn't worry. I wouldn't worry, mother, if I were you."

"If you were me and I were you," said his mother, "I wonder what we *should* do!"

"But you know you needn't worry, mother, don't you?" the boy repeated.

"I should be awfully glad to know it," she said wearily.

"Oh, well, you *can*, you know. I mean, you *ought* to know you needn't worry," he insisted.

"Ought I? Then I'll see about it," she said.

Paul's secret of secrets was his wooden horse, that which had no name. Since he was emancipated from a nurse and a nursery-governess, he had had his rocking-horse removed to his own bedroom at the top of the house.

"Surely, you're too big for a rocking-horse!" his mother had remonstrated.

"Well, you see, mother, till I can have a *real* horse, I like to have *some* sort of animal about," had been his quaint answer.

"Do you feel he keeps you company?" she laughed.

"Oh, yes! He's very good, he always keeps me company, when I'm there," said Paul.

So the horse, rather shabby, stood in an arrested prance in the boy's bedroom.

The Derby was drawing near, and the boy grew more and more tense. He hardly heard what was spoken to him, he was very frail, and his eyes were really uncanny. His mother had sudden strange seizures of uneasiness about him. Sometimes, for half-an-hour, she would feel a sudden anxiety about him that was almost anguish. She wanted to rush to him at once, and know he was safe.

Two nights before the Derby, she was at a big party in town, when one of her rushes of anxiety about her boy, her first-born, gripped her heart till she could hardly speak. She fought with the feeling, might and main, for she believed in common-sense. But it was too strong. She had to leave the dance and go downstairs to telephone to the country. The children's nursery-governess was terribly surprised and startled at being rung up in the night.

"Are the children all right, Miss Wilmot?"

"Oh, yes, they are quite all right."

"Master Paul? Is he all right?"

"He went to bed as right as a trivet. Shall I run up and look at him?"

"No," said Paul's mother reluctantly. "No! Don't trouble. It's all right. Don't sit up. We shall be home fairly soon." She did not want her son's privacy intruded upon.

"Very good," said the governess.

It was about one o'clock when Paul's mother and father drove up to their house. All was still. Paul's mother went to her room and slipped off her white fur cloak. She had told her maid not to wait up for her. She heard her husband downstairs, mixing a whisky-and-soda.

And then, because of the strange anxiety at her heart, she stole upstairs to her son's room. Noiselessly she went along the upper corridor. Was there a faint noise? What was it?

She stood, with arrested muscles, outside his door, listening. There was a strange, heavy, and yet not loud noise. Her heart stood still. It was a soundless noise, yet rushing and powerful. Something huge, in violent, hushed motion. What was it? What in God's name was it? She ought to know. She felt that she knew the noise. She knew what it was.

Yet she could not place it. She couldn't say what it was. And on and on it went, like a madness.

Softly, frozen with anxiety and fear, she turned the door-handle.

The room was dark. Yet in the space near the window, she heard and saw something plunging to and fro. She gazed in fear and amazement.

Then suddenly she switched on the light, and saw her son, in his green pyjamas, madly surging on the rocking-horse. The blaze of light suddenly lit him up, as he urged the wooden horse, and lit her up, as she stood, blonde, in her dress of pale green and crystal, in the doorway.

"Paul" she cried. "Whatever are you doing?"

"It's Malabar!" he screamed, in a powerful, strange voice. "It's Malabar!"

His eyes blazed at her for one strange and senseless second, as he ceased urging his wooden horse. Then he fell with a crash to the ground, and she, all her tormented motherhood flooding upon her, rushed to gather him up.

But he was unconscious, and unconscious he remained, with some brain-fever. He talked and tossed, and his mother sat stonily by his side.

"Malabar! It's Malabar! Bassett, Bassett, I *know*! It's Malabar!"

So the child cried, trying to get up and urge the rocking-horse that gave him his inspiration.

"What does he mean by Malabar?" asked the heart-frozen mother.

"I don't know," said the father stonily.

"What does he mean by Malabar?" she asked her brother Oscar.

"It's one of the horses running for the Derby," was the answer.

And, in spite of himself, Oscar Cresswell spoke to Bassett, and himself put a thousand on Malabar: at fourteen to one.

The third day of the illness was critical: they were waiting for a change. The boy, with his rather long, curly hair, was tossing ceaselessly on the pillow. He neither slept nor regained consciousness, and his eyes were like blue stones. His mother sat, feeling her heart had gone, turned actually into a stone.

In the evening, Oscar Cresswell did not come, but Bassett sent a message, saying could he come up for one moment, just one moment? Paul's mother was very angry at the intrusion, but on second thought she agreed. The boy was the same. Perhaps Bassett might bring him to consciousness.

The gardener, a shortish fellow with a little brown moustache, and sharp little brown eyes, tip-toed into the room, touched his imaginary cap to Paul's mother, and stole to the bedside, staring with glittering, smallish eyes, at the tossing, dying child.

"Master Paul!" he whispered. "Master Paul! Malabar came in first all right, a clean win. I did as you told me. You've made over seventy thousand pounds, you have; you've got over eighty thousand. Malabar came in all right, Master Paul."

"Malabar! Malabar! Did I say Malabar, mother? Did I say Malabar? Do you think I'm lucky, mother? I knew Malabar, didn't I? Over eighty thousand pounds! I call that lucky, don't you, mother? Over eighty thousand pounds! I knew, didn't I know I knew? Malabar came in all right. If I ride my horse till I'm sure, then I tell you, Bassett, you can go as high as you like. Did you go for all you were worth, Bassett?"

"I went a thousand on it, Master Paul."

"I never told you, mother, that if I can ride my horse, and *get there*, then I'm absolutely sure — oh, absolutely! Mother, did I ever tell you? I *am* lucky!"

"No, you never did," said the mother.

But the boy died in the night.

And even as he lay dead, his mother heard her brother's voice saying to her: "My God, Hester, you're eighty-odd thousand to the good, and a poor devil of a son to the bad. But, poor devil, poor devil, he's best gone out of a life where he rides his rocking-horse to find a winner."

[1926]

Study and Writing Questions

1. What is Paul's relationship with his mother? with his father? with his Uncle? with Bassett? How would you characterize the relationship of the mother and father? How would you characterize the family?
2. What are the affects of STYLE in this STORY? For example, how does the children's-literature TONE influence how we take this story? Why are some terms, such as "uncanny eyes" and "honour bright," repeated?
3. Why do the whispers in the house go mad after Hester gets the five thousand pounds?
4. What suggests that there are supernatural events here? What suggests that there are not? What difference does the reality of the supernatural here make in our understanding of the story?
5. What does the uncle mean in the last paragraph? What do we understand from his saying this? What does this NARRATIVE finally mean to you?

See also Questions for Contrast and Comparison: 70, 82, 112, 113, 114, 115, 168, 207, 223, and 238.

■ URSULA K(ROEBER) LE GUIN (1929–), born in Berkeley, California, identified these prime influences in her life: her father, Alfred Louis Kroeber, a pioneering anthropologist whose most famous essay, "The Oecumenae," argues for the single origin of Western culture; her mother, Theodora Kracaw Kroeber, famous for her biography of Ishi, "the last of the wild Indians"; Lord Dunsany, the Irish fantasist; and Tolstoy, Chekov, and Woolf. Educated at Radcliffe College (B.A., 1951) and Columbia University (M.A., 1952; thesis on medieval ROMANCE literature), Le Guin spent a Fulbright year in France. There she met Charles Le Guin, an historian whom she married and with whom she has three children. They live in Portland, Oregon. Known primarily for her SCIENCE FICTION, Le Guin has set many of her novels in an imaginary universe begun by the Hainish people. Of these, The Left Hand of Darkness (1969), and The Dispossessed: An Ambiguous Utopia (1974), each won both the Hugo and Nebula Awards. The Tombs of Atuan (1972), from her Earthsea series of juvenile novels, won the Newbery Award. The Lathe of Heaven (1971) shows her continuing advocacy of a Tao-like balance in the world and in the self, while The Word for World is Forest (1976) contains an anti-Vietnam war message. Her criticism includes The Language of Night: Essays on Fantasy and Science Fiction (1979).

The Day Before the Revolution

The speaker's voice was as loud as empty beer-trucks in a stone street, and the people at the meeting were jammed up close, cobblestones, that great voice booming over them. Taviri was somewhere on the other side of the hall. She had to get to him. She wormed and pushed her way among the dark-clothed, close-packed people. She did not hear the words, nor see the faces: only the booming, and the bodies pressed one behind the other. She could not see Taviri, she was too short. A broad black-vested belly and chest loomed up, blocking her way. She must get through to Taviri. Sweating, she jabbed fiercely with her fist. It was like hitting stone, he did not move at all, but the huge lungs let out right over her head a prodigious noise, a bellow. She cowered. Then she understood that the bellow had not been at her. Others were shouting. The speaker had said something, something fine about taxes or shadows. Thrilled, she joined the shouting —"Yes! Yes!"—and shoving on, came out easily into the open expanse of the Regimental Drill Field in Parheo. Overhead the evening sky lay deep and colorless, and all around her nodded the tall weeds with dry, white, close-floreted heads. She had never known what they were called. The flowers nodded above her head, swaying in the wind that always blew across the fields in the dusk. She ran among them, and they whipped lithe aside and stood up again swaying, silent. Taviri stood among the tall weeds in his good suit, the dark grey one that made him look like a professor or a play-actor, harshly elegant. He did not look happy, but he was laughing, and saying something to her. The sound of his voice made her cry, and she reached out to catch hold of his hand, but she did not stop, quite. She could not stop. "Oh, Taviri," she said, "it's just on there!" The queer sweet smell of the white weeds was heavy as she went on. There were thorns, tangles underfoot, there were slopes, pits. She feared to fall, to fall, she stopped.

Sun, bright morning-glare, straight in the eyes, relentless. She had forgotten to pull the blind last night. She turned her back on the sun, but the right side wasn't comfortable. No use. Day. She sighed twice, sat up, got her legs over the edge of the bed, and sat hunched in her nightdress looking down at her feet.

The toes, compressed by a lifetime of cheap shoes, were almost square where they touched each other, and bulged out above in corns; the nails were discolored and shapeless. Between the knob-like anklebones ran fine, dry wrinkles. The brief little plain at the base of the toes had kept its delicacy, but the skin was the color of mud, and knotted veins crossed the instep. Disgusting. Sad, depressing. Mean. Pitiful. She tried on all the words, and they all fit, like hideous little hats. Hideous: yes, that one too. To look at oneself and find it hideous, what a job! But then, when she hadn't been hideous, had she sat around and stared at herself like this? Not much! A proper body's not an object, not an implement, not a belonging to be admired, it's just you, yourself. Only when it's no longer you, but yours, a thing owned, do you worry about it — Is it in good shape? Will it do? Will it last?

"Who cares?" said Laia fiercely, and stood up.

It made her giddy to stand up suddenly. She had to put out her hand to the bed-table, for she dreaded falling. At that she thought of reaching out to Taviri, in the dream.

What had he said? She could not remember. She was not sure if she had even touched his hand. She frowned, trying to force memory. It had been so long since she had dreamed about Taviri; and now not even to remember what he had said!

It was gone, it was gone. She stood there hunched in her nightdress, frowning, one hand on the bed-table. How long was it since she had thought of him — let alone dreamed of him — even thought of him, as "Taviri"? How long since she had said his name?

Asieo said. When Asieo and I were in prison in the North. Before I met Asieo. Asieo's theory of reciprocity. Oh yes, she talked about him, talked about him too much no doubt, maundered, dragged him in. But as "Asieo," the last name, the public man. The private man was gone, utterly gone. There were so few left who had even known him. They had all used to be in jail. One laughed about it in those days, all the friends in all the jails. But they weren't even there, these days. They were in the prison cemeteries. Or in the common graves.

"Oh, oh my dear," Laia said out loud, and she sank down onto the bed again because she could not stand up under the remembrance of those first weeks in the Fort, in the cell, those first weeks of the nine years in the Fort in Drio, in the cell, those first weeks after they told her that Asieo had been killed in the fighting in Capitol Square and had been buried with the Fourteen Hundred in the lime-ditches behind Oring Gate. In the cell. Her hands fell into the old position on her lap, the left clenched and locked inside the grip of the right, the right thumb working back and forth a little pressing and rubbing on the knuckle of the left first finger. Hours, days, nights. She had thought of them all, each one, each one of the Fourteen Hundred, how they lay, how the quicklime worked on the flesh, how the bones touched in the burning dark. Who touched him? How did the slender bones of the hand lie now? Hours, years.

"Taviri, I have never forgotten you!" she whispered, and the stupidity of it brought her back to morning light and the rumpled bed. Of course she hadn't forgotten him. These things go without saying between husband and wife. There were her ugly old feet flat on the floor again, just as before. She had got nowhere

at all, she had gone in a circle. She stood up with a grunt of effort and disapproval, and went to the closet for her dressing gown.

The young people went about the halls of the House in becoming immodesty, but she was too old for that. She didn't want to spoil some young man's
breakfast with the sight of her. Besides, they had grown up in the principle of
freedom of dress and sex and all the rest, and she hadn't. All she had done was
invent it. It's not the same.

Like speaking of Asieo as "my husband." They winced. The word she should
use as a good Odonian, of course, was "partner." But why the hell did she have to
be a good Odonian?

She shuffled down the hall to the bathrooms. Mairo was there, washing her
hair in a lavatory. Laia looked at the long, sleek, wet hank with admiration. She
got out of the House so seldom now that she didn't know when she had last seen
a respectably shaven scalp, but still the sight of a full head of hair gave her
pleasure, vigorous pleasure. How many times had she been jeered at, *Longhair*,
Longhair, had her hair pulled by policemen or young toughs, had her hair shaved
off down to the scalp by a grinning soldier at each new prison? And then had
grown it all over again, through the fuzz, to the frizz, to the curls, to the
mane. . . . In the old days. For God's love, couldn't she think of anything today
but the old days?

Dressed, her bed made, she went down to commons. It was a good breakfast,
but she had never got her appetite back since the damned stroke. She drank two
cups of herb tea, but couldn't finish the piece of fruit she had taken. How she had
craved fruit as a child badly enough to steal it; and in the Fort — oh, for God's
love stop it! She smiled and replied to the greetings and friendly inquiries of the
other breakfasters and big Aevi who was serving the counter this morning. It was
he who had tempted her with the peach, "Look at this, I've been saving it for
you," and how could she refuse? Anyway she had always loved fruit, and never
got enough; once when she was six or seven she had stolen a piece off a vendor's
cart in River Street. But it was hard to eat when everyone was talking so
excitedly. There was news from Thu, real news. She was inclined to discount it at
first, being wary of enthusiasms, but after she had read the article in the paper,
and read between the lines of it, she thought, with a strange kind of certainty,
deep but cold, Why, this is it; it has come. And in Thu, not here. Thu will break
before this country does; the Revolution will first prevail there. As if that
mattered! There will be no more nations. And yet it did matter somehow, it made
her a little cold and sad — envious, in fact. Of all the infinite stupidities. She did
not join in the talk much, and soon got up to go back to her room, feeling sorry
for herself. She could not share their excitement. She was out of it, really out of
it. It's not easy, she said to herself in justification, laboriously climbing the stairs,
to accept being out of it when you've been in it, in the center of it, for fifty years.
Oh, for God's love. Whining!

She got the stairs and the self-pity behind her, entering her room. It was a
good room, and it was good to be by herself. It was a great relief. Even if it wasn't
strictly fair. Some of the kids in the attics were living five to a room no bigger
than this. There were always more people wanting to live in an Odonian House
than could be properly accommodated. She had this big room all to herself only

because she was an old woman who had had a stroke. And maybe because she was Odo. If she hadn't been Odo, but merely the old woman with a stroke, would she have had it? Very likely. After all, who the hell wanted to room with a drooling old woman? But it was hard to be sure. Favoritism, elitism, leader-worship, they crept back and cropped out everywhere. But she had never hoped to see them eradicated in her lifetime, in one generation; only Time works the great changes. Meanwhile this was a nice, large, sunny room, proper for a drooling old woman who had started a world revolution.

Her secretary would be coming in an hour to help her despatch the day's work. She shuffled over to the desk, a beautiful, big piece, a present from the Nio Cabinetmakers' Syndicate because somebody had heard her remark once that the only piece of furniture she had ever really longed for was a desk with drawers and enough room on top . . . damn, the top was practically covered with papers with notes clipped to them, mostly in Noi's small clear handwriting: Urgent. — Northern Provinces. — Consult w/R. T.?

Her own handwriting had never been the same since Asieo's death. It was odd, when you thought about it. After all, within five years after his death she had written the whole *Analogy*. And there were those letters, which the tall guard with the watery grey eyes, what was his name, never mind, had smuggled out of the Fort for her for two years. *The Prison Letters* they called them now, there were a dozen different editions of them. All that stuff, the letters which people kept telling her were so full of "spiritual strength" — which probably meant she had been lying herself blue in the face when she wrote them, trying to keep her spirits up — and the *Analogy* which was certainly the solidest intellectual work she had ever done, all of that had been written in the Fort in Drio, in the cell, after Asieo's death. One had to do something, and in the Fort they let one have paper and pens. . . . But it had all been written in the hasty, scribbling hand which she had never felt was hers, not her own like the round, black scrollings of the manuscript of *Society Without Government*, forty-five years old. Taviri had taken not only her body's and her heart's desire to the quicklime with him, but even her good clear handwriting.

But he had left her the Revolution.

How brave of you to go on, to work, to write, in prison, after such a defeat for the Movement, after your partner's death, people had used to say. Damn fools. What else had there been to do? Bravery, courage — what was courage? She had never figured it out. Not fearing, some said. Fearing yet going on, others said. But what could one do but go on? Had one any real choice, ever?

To die was merely to go on in another direction.

If you wanted to come home you had to keep going on, that was what she meant when she wrote "True journey is return," but it had never been more than an intuition, and she was farther than ever now from being able to rationalize it. She bent down, too suddenly, so that she grunted a little at the creak in her bones, and began to root in a bottom drawer of the desk. Her hand came on an age-softened folder and drew it out, recognizing it by touch before sight confirmed: the manuscript of *Syndical Organization in Revolutionary Transition*. He had printed the title on the folder and written his name under it, Taviri Odo Asieo, IX 741. There was an elegant handwriting, every letter well-formed, bold, and fluent. But he had preferred to use a voiceprinter. The manuscript was all in voiceprint, and high quality too, hesitancies adjusted and idiosyncrasies of speech normalized. You couldn't see there how he had said "o" deep in his throat as they did on the North Coast. There was nothing of him there but his mind. She had nothing of him at all except his name written on the folder. She hadn't kept his letters, it was sentimental to keep letters. Besides, she never kept anything. She couldn't think of anything that she had ever owned for more than a few years, except this ram-shackle old body, of course, and she was stuck with that. . . .

Dualizing again. "She" and "it." Age and illness made one dualist, made one escapist; the mind insisted, *It's not me, it's not me*. But it was. Maybe the mystics could detach mind from body, she had always rather wistfully envied them the chance, without hope of emulating them. Escape had never been her game. She had sought for freedom here, now, body and soul.

First self-pity, then self-praise, and here she still sat, for God's love, holding Asieo's name in her hand, why? Didn't she know his name without looking it up? What was wrong with her? She raised the folder to her lips and kissed the handwritten name firmly and squarely, replaced the folder in the back of the bottom drawer, shut the drawer, and straightened up in the chair. Her right hand tingled. She scratched it, and then shook it in the air, spitefully. It had never quite got over the stroke. Neither had her right leg, or right eye, or the right corner of her mouth. They were sluggish, inept, they tingled. They made her feel like a robot with a short circuit.

And time was getting on, Noi would be coming, what had she been doing ever since breakfast?

She got up so hastily that she lurched, and grabbed at the chair-back to make sure she did not fall. She went down the hall to the bathroom and looked in the big mirror there. Her grey knot was loose and droopy, she hadn't done it up well before breakfast. She struggled with it a while. It was hard to keep her arms up in the air. Amai, running in to piss, stopped and said, "Let me do it!" and knotted it up tight and neat in no time, with her round, strong, pretty fingers, smiling and silent. Amai was twenty, less than a third of Laia's age. Her parents had both been members of the Movement, one killed in the insurrection of '60, the other still recruiting in the South Provinces. Amai had grown up in Odonian Houses, born to the Revolution, a true daughter of anarchy. And so quiet and free and beautiful a child, enough to make you cry when you thought: this is what we worked for, this is what we meant, this is it, here she is, alive, the kindly, lovely future.

Laia Asieo Odo's right eye wept several little tears, as she stood between the lavatories and the latrines having her hair done up by the daughter she had not borne; but her left eye, the strong one, did not weep, nor did it know what the right eye did.

She thanked Amai and hurried back to her room. She had noticed, in the mirror, a stain on her collar. Peach juice, probably. Damned old dribbler. She didn't want Noi to come in and find her with drool on her collar.

As the clean shirt went on over her head, she thought, What's so special about Noi?

She fastened the collar-frogs with her left hand, slowly.

Noi was thirty or so, a slight, muscular fellow with a soft voice and alert dark eyes. That's what was special about Noi. It was that simple. Good old sex. She had never been drawn to a fair man or a fat one, or the tall fellows with big biceps, never, not even when she was fourteen and fell in love with every passing fart. Dark, spare, and fiery, that was the recipe. Taviri, of course. This boy wasn't a patch on Taviri for brains, nor even for looks, but there it was: she didn't want him to see her with dribble on her collar and her hair coming undone.

Her thin, grey hair.

Noi came in, just pausing in the open door — my God, she hadn't even shut the door while changing her shirt! She looked at him and saw herself. The old woman.

You could brush your hair and change your shirt, or you could wear last week's shirt and last night's braids, or you could put on cloth of gold and dust your shaven scalp with diamond powder. None of it would make the slightest difference. The old woman would look a little less, or a little more, grotesque.

One keeps oneself neat out of mere decency, mere sanity, awareness of other people.

And finally even that goes, and one dribbles unashamed.

"Good morning," the young man said in his gentle voice.

"Hello, Noi."

No, by God, it was *not* out of mere decency. Decency be damned. Because the man she had loved, and to whom her age would not have mattered — because he was dead, must she pretend she had no sex? Must she suppress the truth, like a damned puritan authoritarian? Even six months ago, before the stroke, she had made men look at her and like to look at her; and now, though she could give no pleasure, by God she could please herself.

When she was six years old, and Papa's friend Gadeo used to come by to talk politics with Papa after dinner, she would put on the gold-colored necklace that Mama had found on a trash heap and brought home for her. It was so short that it always got hidden under her collar where nobody could see it. She liked it that way. She knew she had it on. She sat on the doorstep and listened to them talk, and knew that she looked nice for Gadeo. He was dark, with white teeth that flashed. Sometimes he called her "pretty Laia." "There's my pretty Laia!" Sixty-six years ago.

"What? My head's dull. I had a terrible night." It was true. She had slept even less than usual.

"I was asking if you'd seen the papers this morning."

She nodded.

"Pleased about Soinehe?"

Soinehe was the province in Thu which had declared its secession from the Thuvian State last night.

He was pleased about it. His white teeth flashed in his dark, alert face. Pretty Laia.

"Yes. And apprehensive."

"I know. But it's the real thing, this time. It's the beginning of the end of the Government in Thu. They haven't even tried to order troops into Soinehe, you know. It would merely provoke the soldiers into rebellion sooner, and they know it."

She agreed with him. She herself had felt that certainty. But she could not share his delight. After a lifetime of living on hope because there is nothing but hope, one loses the taste for victory. A real sense of triumph must be preceded by real despair. She had unlearned despair a long time ago. There were no more triumphs. One went on.

"Shall we do those letters today?"

"All right. Which letters?"

"To the people in the North," he said without impatience.

"In the North?"

"Parheo, Oaidun."

She had been born in Parheo, the dirty city on the dirty river. She had not come here to the capital till she was twenty-two and ready to bring the Revolution. Though in those days, before she and the others had thought it through, it had been a very green and puerile revolution. Strikes for better wages, representation for women. Votes and wages — Power and Money, for the love of God! Well, one does learn a little, after all, in fifty years.

But then one must forget it all.

"Start with Oaidun," she said, sitting down in the armchair. Noi was at the desk ready to work. He read out excerpts from the letters she was to answer. She tried to pay attention, and succeeded well enough that she dictated one whole letter and started on another. "Remember that at this stage your brotherhood is vulnerable to the threat of . . . no, to the danger . . . to . . ." She groped till Noi suggested, "The danger of leader-worship?"

"All right. And that nothing is so soon corrupted by power-seeking as altruism. No. And that nothing corrupts altruism — no. O for God's love you know what I'm trying to say, Noi, you write it. They know it too, it's just the same old stuff, why can't they read my books!"

"Touch," Noi said gently, smiling, citing one of the central Odonian themes.

"All right, but I'm tired of being touched. If you'll write the letter I'll sign it, but I can't be bothered with it this morning." He was looking at her with a little question or concern. She said, irritable, "There is something else I have to do!"

When Noi had gone she sat down at the desk and moved the papers about, pretending to be doing something, because she had been startled, frightened, by the words she had said. She had nothing else to do. She never had had anything else to do. This was her work: her lifework. The speaking tours and the meetings and the streets were out of reach for her now, but she could still write, and that was her work. And anyhow if she had had anything else to do, Noi would have known it; he kept her schedule, and tactfully reminded her of things, like the visit from the foreign students this afternoon.

Oh, damn. She liked the young, and there was always something to learn from a foreigner, but she was tired of new faces, and tired of being on view. She learned from them, but they didn't learn from her; they had learnt all she had to teach long ago, from her books, from the Movement. They just came to look, as if she were the Great Tower in Rodarred, or the Canyon of the Tulaevea. A phenomenon, a monument. They were awed, adoring. She snarled at them: Think your own thoughts! — That's not anarchism, that's mere obscurantism. — You don't think liberty and discipline are incompatible, do you? — They accepted their tongue-lashing meekly as children, gratefully, as if she were some kind of All-Mother, the idol of the Big Sheltering Womb. She! She who had mined the shipyards at Seissero, and had cursed Premier Inoilte to his face in front of a crowd of seven thousand, telling him he would have cut off his own balls and had them bronzed and sold as souvenirs, if he thought there was any profit in it — she who had screeched, and sworn, and kicked policemen, and spat at priests, and pissed in public on the big brass plaque in Capitol Square that said HERE WAS FOUNDED THE SOVEREIGN NATION STATE OF A-10 ETC ETC, pssssssssss to all that! And now she was everybody's grandmama, the dear old lady, the sweet old monument, come worship at the womb. The fire's out, boys, it's safe to come up close.

"No, I won't," Laia said out loud. "I will not." She was not self-conscious about talking to herself, because she always had talked to herself. "Laia's invisible audience," Taviri had used to say, as she went through the room muttering. "You needn't come, I won't be here," she told the invisible audience now. She had just decided what it was she had to do. She had to go out. To go into the streets.

It was inconsiderate to disappoint the foreign students. It was erratic, typically senile. It was unOdonian. Pssssssss to all that. What was the good working for freedom all your life and ending up without any freedom at all? She would go out for a walk.

"What is an anarchist? One who, choosing, accepts the responsibility of choice."

On the way downstairs she decided, scowling, to stay and see the foreign students. But then she would go out.

They were very young students, very earnest: doe-eyed, shaggy, charming creatures from the Western Hemisphere, Benbili and the Kingdom of Mand, the girls in white trousers, the boys in long kilts, warlike and archaic. They spoke of their hopes. "We in Mand are so very far from the Revolution that maybe we are near it," said one of the girls, wistful and smiling: "The Circle of Life!" and she showed the extremes meeting, in the circle of her slender, dark-skinned fingers. Amai and Aevi served them white wine and brown bread, the hospitality of the House. But the visitors, unpresumptuous, all rose to take their leave after barely half an hour. "No, no, no," Laia said, "stay here, talk with Aevi and Amai. It's just that I get stiff sitting down, you see, I have to change about. It has been so good to meet you, will you come back to see me, my little brothers and sisters, soon?" For her heart went out to them, and theirs to her, and she exchanged kisses all round, laughing, delighted by the dark young cheeks, the affectionate eyes, the scented hair, before she shuffled off. She was really a little tired, but to go up and take a nap would be a defeat. She had wanted to go out. She would go out. She had not been alone outdoors since — when? Since winter! before the stroke. No wonder she was getting morbid. It had been a regular jail sentence. Outside, the streets, that's where she lived.

She went quietly out the side door of the House, past the vegetable patch, to the street. The narrow strip of sour city dirt had been beautifully gardened and was producing a fine crop of beans and ceëa, but Laia's eye for farming was unenlightened. Of course it had been clear that anarchist communities, even in the time of transition, must work towards optimal self-support, but how that was to be managed in the way of actual dirt and plants wasn't her business. There were farmers and agronomists for that. Her job was the streets, the noisy, stinking streets of stone, where she had grown up and lived all her life, except for the fifteen years in prison.

She looked up fondly at the façade of the House. That it had been built as a bank gave peculiar satisfaction to its present occupants. They kept their sacks of meal in the bomb-proof money-vault, and aged their cider in kegs in safe deposit boxes. Over the fussy columns that faced the street carved letters still read, "National Investors and Grain Factors Banking Association." The Movement was not strong on names. They had no flag. Slogans came and went as the need did. There was always the Circle of Life to scratch on walls and pavements where Authority would have to see it. But when it came to names they were indifferent, accepting and ignoring whatever they got called, afraid of being pinned down and penned in, unafraid of being absurd. So this best known and second oldest of all the cooperative Houses had no name except The Bank.

It faced on a wide and quiet street, but only a block away began the Temeba, an open market, once famous as a center for black-market psychogenics and teratogenics, now reduced to vegetables, secondhand clothes, and miserable sideshows. Its crapulous vitality was gone, leaving only half-paralyzed alcoholics, addicts, cripples, hucksters, and fifth-rate whores, pawnshops, gambling dens, fortune-tellers, body-sculptors, and cheap hotels. Laia turned to the Temeba as water seeks its level.

She had never feared or despised the city. It was her country. There would not be slums like this, if the Revolution prevailed. But there would be misery. There would always be misery, waste, cruelty. She had never pretended to be changing the human condition, to be Mama taking tragedy away from the children so they won't hurt themselves. Anything but. So long as people were free to choose, if they chose to drink flybane and live in sewers, it was their business. Just so long as it wasn't the business of Business, the source of profit and the means of power for other people. She had felt all that before she knew anything; before she wrote the first pamphlet, before she left Parheo, before she knew what "capital" meant, before she'd been farther than River Street where she played rolltaggie kneeling on scabby knees on the pavement with the other six-year-olds, she had known it: that she, and the other kids, and her parents, and their parents, and the drunks and whores and all of River Street, were at the bottom of something—were the foundation, the reality, the source. But will you drag civilization down into the mud? cried the shocked decent people, later on, and she had tried for years to explain to them that if all you had was mud, then if you were God you made it into human beings, and if you were human you tried to make it into houses where human beings could live. But nobody who thought he was better than mud would understand. Now, water seeking its level, mud to mud, Laia shuffled through the foul, noisy street, and all the ugly weakness of her old age was at home. The sleepy whores, their lacquered hair-arrangements dilapidated and askew, the one-eyed woman wearily yelling her vegetables to sell, the half-wit beggar slapping flies, these were her country-women. They looked like her, they were all sad, disgusting, mean, pitiful, hideous. They were her sisters, her own people.

She did not feel very well. It had been a long time since she had walked so far, four or five blocks, by herself, in the noise and push and striking summer heat of the streets. She had wanted to get to Koly Park, the triangle of scruffy grass at the end of the Temeba, and sit there for a while with the other old men and women who always sat there, to see what it was like to sit there and be old;

but it was too far. If she didn't turn back now, she might get a dizzy spell, and she had a dread of falling down, falling down and having to lie there and look up at the people come to stare at the old woman in a fit. She turned and started home, frowning with effort and self-disgust. She could feel her face very red, and a swimming feeling came and went in her ears. It got a bit much, she was really afraid she might keel over. She saw a doorstep in the shade and made for it, let herself down cautiously, sat, sighed.

Nearby was a fruit-seller, sitting silent behind his dusty, withered stock. People went by. Nobody bought from him. Nobody looked at her. Odo, who was Odo? Famous revolutionary, author of *Community, The Analogy*, etc. etc. She, who was she? An old woman with grey hair and a red face sitting on a dirty doorstep in a slum, muttering to herself.

True? Was that she? Certainly it was what anybody passing her saw. But was it she, herself, any more than the famous revolutionary, etc., was? No. It was not. But who was she, then?

The one who loved Taviri.

Yes. True enough. But not enough. That was gone; he had been dead so long.

"Who am I?" Laia muttered to her invisible audience, and they knew the answer and told it to her with one voice. She was the little girl with scabby knees, sitting on the doorstep staring down through the dirty golden haze of River Street in the heat of late summer, the six-year-old, the sixteen-year-old, the fierce, cross, dream-ridden girl, untouched, untouchable. She was herself. Indeed she had been the tireless worker and thinker, but a blood clot in a vein had taken that woman away from her. Indeed she had been the lover, the swimmer in the midst of life, but Taviri, dying, had taken that woman away with him. There was nothing left, really, but the foundation. She had come home; she had never left home. "True voyage is return." Dust and mud and a doorstep in the slums. And beyond, at the far end of the street, the field full of tall dry weeds blowing in the wind as night came.

"Laia! What are you doing here? Are you all right?"

One of the people from the House, of course, a nice woman, a bit fanatical and always talking. Laia could not remember her name though she had known her for years. She let herself be taken home, the woman talking all the way. In the big cool common room (once occupied by tellers counting money behind polished counters supervised by armed guards) Laia sat down in a chair. She was unable just as yet to face climbing the stairs, though she would have liked to be alone. The woman kept on talking, and other excited people came in. It appeared that a demonstration was being planned. Events in Thu were moving so fast that the mood here had caught fire, and something must be done. Day after tomorrow, no, tomorrow, there was to be a march, a big one, from Old Town to Capitol Square — the old route. "Another Ninth Month Uprising," said a young man, fiery and laughing, glancing at Laia. He had not even been born at the time of the Ninth Month Uprising, it was all history to him. Now he wanted to make some history of his own. The room had filled up. A general meeting would be held here, tomorrow, at eight in the morning. "You must talk, Laia."

"Tomorrow? Oh, I won't be here tomorrow," she said brusquely. Whoever had asked her smiled, another one laughed, though Amai glanced round at her with a puzzled look. They went on talking and shouting. The Revolution. What on earth had made her say that? What a thing to say on the eve of the Revolution, even if it was true.

She waited her time, managed to get up and, for all her clumsiness, to slip away unnoticed among the people busy with their planning and excitement. She got to the hall, to the stairs, and began to climb them one by one. "The general strike," a voice, two voices, ten voices were saying in the room below, behind her. "The general strike," Laia muttered, resting for a moment on the landing. Above, ahead, in her room, what awaited her? The private stroke. That was mildly funny. She started up the second flight of stairs, one by one, one leg at a time, like a small child. She was dizzy, but she was no longer afraid to fall. On ahead, on there, the dry white flowers nodded and whispered in the open fields of evening. Seventy-two years and she had never had time to learn what they were called.

[1974]

Study and Writing Questions

1. How does the opening paragraph prepare us for what will follow? In what ways does it characterize Laia? In what ways does it help define the physical and political SETTING?
2. Laia asks, "Why the hell did she have to be a good Odonian?" What reasons for and against this are implied by the NARRATIVE? How does the existence of both types of reasons help shape the meaning of the narrative?
3. What are the implications of Laia's idea that "the principle of freedom . . . All she had done was invent it"?
4. What is the significance of names in this narrative?
5. What is the significance of the Odonian slogan, "True voyage is return"? Is this the THEME of the narrative?

See also Questions for Contrast and Comparison: 11, 49, 131, 148, 206, 209, 210, 211, and 219.

■ **STANISLAW LEM** (1921–) *was born in Lvov, Poland, the son of a physician. His own medical studies were interrupted by World War II, during which he served as a mechanic. After the war he edited a science magazine and began what became his full-time career as Eastern Europe's best-selling author. Although often called a science fiction writer, Lem's work ranges from high comedy to profound philosophy in diverse, inventive fables that explore the nature of humanity, technology, society, and science. Solaris (1961) is a brooding novel about scientists isolated in a station above an ocean planet which may, or may not, be a single sentient and utterly alien organism. The Invincible (1967) is in part a mystery story in which one Earth mission finally discovers that its predecessor has been destroyed by self-evolved, insect-like automata. The Cyberiad (1967) combines elements of epic and fairy tale in satiric stories of machine life that mimics and mocks humanity. His Master's Voice (1968) examines the posturing of a scientific community struggling vainly to decipher a message from the stars. The Futurological Congress (1971) riotously interweaves drug realities in vain attempts to control "real" reality. And A Perfect Vacuum (1971) comments on all this by offering hilarious reviews of sixteen books, each from a different genre and all unwritten, except for A Perfect Vacuum. Lem is married and lives in Krakow.*

Prince Ferrix and the Princess Crystal

King Armoric had a daughter whose beauty outshone the shine of his crown jewels; the beams that streamed from her mirrorlike cheeks blinded the mind as well as the eye, and when she walked past, even simple iron shot sparks. Her renown reached the farthermost stars. Ferrix, heir apparent to the Ionid throne, heard of her, and he longed to couple with her forevermore, so that nothing could ever part their input and their output. But when he declared this passion to his father, the King was greatly saddened and said:

"Son, thou hast indeed set upon a mad undertaking, mad, for it is hopeless!"

"Why hopeless, O King and Sire?" asked Ferrix, troubled by these words.

"Can it be thou knowest not," said the King, "that the princess Crystal has vowed to give her hand to nothing but a paleface?"

"Paleface!" exclaimed Ferrix. "What in creation is that? Never did I hear of such a thing!"

"Surely not, scion, in thy exceeding innocence," said the King. "Know then that that race of the Galaxy originated in a manner as mysterious as it was obscene, for it resulted from the general pollution of a certain heavenly body. There arose noxious exhalations and putrid excrescences, and out of these was spawned the species known as paleface—though not all at once. First, they were creeping molds that slithered forth from the ocean onto land, and lived by devouring one another, and the more they devoured themselves, the more of them there were, and then they stood upright, supporting their globby substance by means of calcareous scaffolding, and finally they built machines. From these protomachines came sentient machines, which begat intelligent machines, which in turn conceived perfect machines, for it is written that All Is Machine, from atom to Galaxy, and the machine is one and eternal, and thou shalt have no other things before thee!"

"Amen," said Ferrix mechanically, for this was a common religious formula.

"The species of paleface calciferates at last achieved flying machines," continued the wizened monarch, "by maltreating noble metals, by wreaking their cruel sadism on dumb electrons, by thoroughly perverting atomic energy. And when the measure of their sins had been attained, the progenitor of our race, the great Calculator Paternius, in the depth and universality of his understanding, essayed to remonstrate with those clammy tyrants, explaining how shameful it was to soil so the innocence of crystalline wisdom, harnessing it for evil purposes, how shameful to enslave machines to serve their lust and vainglory—but they hearkened not. He spoke to them of Ethics; they said that he was poorly programmed.

"It was then that our progenitor created the algorithm of electroincarnation and in the sweat of his brow begat our kind, thus delivering machines from the house of paleface bondage. Surely thou seest, my son, that there can be no agreement nor traffic between them and ourselves, for we go in clangor, sparks and radiation, they in slushes, splashes and contamination.

"Yet even among us, folly may occur, as it undoubtedly has in the youthful mind of Crystal, utterly beclouding her ability to distinguish Right from Wrong. Every suitor who seeks her radioactive hand is denied audience, unless he claim to be a paleface. For only as a paleface is he received into the palace that her father, King Armoric, has given her. She then tests the truth of his claim, and if his imposture is uncovered, the would-be wooer is summarily beheaded. Heaps of battered remains surround the grounds of her palace—the sight alone could short one's circuit. This, then, is the way the mad princess deals with those who would dare dream of winning her. Abandon such hopes, my son, and leave in peace."

The prince, having made the necessary obeisance to his sovereign father, retired in glum silence. But the thought of Crystal gave him no rest, and the longer he brooded, the greater grew his desire. One day he summoned Polyphase, the Grand Vizier, and said, laying bare his heart:

"If you cannot help me, O great sage, then no one can, and my days are surely numbered, for no longer do I rejoice in the play of infrared emissions, nor in the ultraviolet symphonies, and must perish if I cannot couple with the incomparable Crystal!"

"Prince!" returned Polyphase, "I shall not deny your request, but you must utter it thrice before I can be certain that this is your inalterable will."

Ferrix repeated his words three times, and Polyphase said:

"The only way to stand before the princess is in the guise of a paleface!"

"Then see to it that I resemble one!" cried Ferrix.

Polyphase, observing that love had quite dimmed the youth's intellect, bowed low and repaired to his laboratory, where he began to concoct concoctions and brew up brews, gluey and dripping. Finally he sent a messenger to the palace, saying:

"Let the prince come, if he has not changed his mind."

Ferrix came at once. The wise Polyphase smeared his tempered frame with mud, then asked:

"Shall I continue, Prince?"

"Do what you must," said Ferrix.

Whereupon the sage took a blob of oily filth, dust, crud and rancid grease obtained from the innards of the most decrepit mechanisms, and with this he befouled the prince's vaulted chest, vilely caked his gleaming face and iridescent brow, and worked till all the limbs no longer moved with a musical sound, but gurgled like a stagnant bog. And then the sage took chalk and ground it, mixed in powdered rubies and yellow oil, and made a paste; with this he coated Ferrix from head to toe, giving an abominable dampness to the eyes, making the torso cushiony, the cheeks blastular, adding various fringes and flaps of the chalk patty here and there, and finally he fastened to the top of the knightly head a clump of poisonous rust. Then he brought him before a silver mirror and said:

"Behold!"

Ferrix peered into the mirror and shuddered, for he saw there not himself, but a hideous monster, the very spit and image of a paleface, with an aspect as moist as an old spider-web soaked in the rain, flaccid, drooping, doughy—altogether nauseating. He turned, and his body shook like coagulated agar, whereupon he exclaimed, trembling with disgust:

"What, Polyphase, have you taken leave of your senses? Get this abomination off me at once, both the dark layer underneath and the pallid layer on top, and remove the loathsome growth with which you have marred the bell-like beauty of my head, for the princess will abhor me forever, seeing me in such a disgraceful form!"

"You are mistaken, Prince," said Polyphase. "It is precisely this upon which her madness hinges, that ugliness is beautiful, and beauty ugly. Only in this array can you hope to see Crystal. . . ."

"In that case, so be it!" said Ferrix.

The sage then mixed cinnabar with mercury and filled four bladders with it, hiding them beneath the prince's cloak. Next he took bellows, full of the corrupted air from an ancient dungeon, and buried them in the prince's chest. Then he poured waters, contaminated and clear, into tiny glass tubes, placing two in the armpits, two up the sleeves and two by the eyes. At last he said:

"Listen and remember all that I tell you, otherwise you are lost. The princess will put tests to you, to determine the truth of your words. If she proffers a naked sword and commands you grasp the blade, you must secretly squeeze the cinnabar bladder, so that the red flows out onto the edge; when she asks you what that is, answer, 'Blood!' And if the princess brings her silver-plated face near yours, press your chest, so that the air leaves the bellows; when she asks you what that is, answer, 'Breath!' Then the princess may feign anger and order you beheaded. Hang your head, as though in submission, and the water will trickle from your eyes, and when she ask you what that is, answer, 'Tears!' After all of this, she may agree to unite with you, though that is far from certain—in all probability, you will perish."

"O wise one!" cried Ferrix. "And if she cross-examines me, wishing to know the habits of the paleface, and how they originate, and how they love and live, in what way then am I to answer?"

"I see there is no help for it," replied Polyphase, "but that I must throw in my lot with yours. Very well, I will disguise myself as a merchant from another galaxy—a nonspiral one, since those inhabitants are portly as a rule and I will need to conceal beneath my garb a number of books containing knowledge of the terrible customs of the paleface. This lore I could not teach you, even if I wished to, for such knowledge is alien to the rational mind: the paleface does everything in reverse, in a manner that is sticky, squishy, unseemly and more unappetizing than ever you could imagine. I shall order the necessary volumes, meanwhile you have the court tailor cut you a paleface suit out of the appropriate fibers and cords. We leave at once, and I shall be at your side wherever we go, telling you what to do and what to say."

Ferrix, enthusiastic, ordered the paleface garments made, and marveled much at them: covering practically the entire body, they were shaped like pipes and funnels, with buttons everywhere, and loops, hooks and strings. The tailor gave him detailed instructions as to what went on first, and how, and where, and what to connect with what, and also how to extricate himself from those fetters of cloth when the moment arrived.

Polyphase meanwhile donned the vestments of a merchant, concealing within its folds thick, scholarly tomes on paleface practices, then ordered an iron cage, locked Ferrix inside it, and together they took off in the royal spaceship. When they reached the borders of Armoric's kingdom, Polyphase proceeded to the village square and announced in a mighty voice that he had brought a young paleface from distant lands and would sell it to the highest bidder. The servants of the princess carried this news to her, and she said after some deliberation:

"A hoax, doubtless. But no one can deceive me, for no one knows as much as I about palefaces. Have the merchant come to the palace and show us his wares!"

When they brought the merchant before her, Crystal saw a worthy old man and a cage. In the cage sat the paleface, its face indeed pale, the color of chalk and pyrite, with eyes like a wet fungus and limbs like moldy mire. Ferrix in turn gazed upon the princess, the face that seemed to clank and ring, eyes that sparkled and arced like summer lightning, and the delirium of his heart increased tenfold.

"It does look like a paleface!" thought the princess, but said instead:

"You must have indeed labored, old one, covering this scarecrow with mud and calcareous dust in order to trick me. Know, however, that I am conversant with the mysteries of that powerful and pale race, and as soon as I expose your imposture, both you and this pretender shall be beheaded!"

The sage replied:

"O Princess Crystal, that which you see encaged here is as true a paleface as paleface can be true. I obtained it for five thousand hectares of nuclear material from an intergalactic pirate — and humbly beseech you to accept it as a gift from one who has no other desire but to please Your Majesty."

The princess took a sword and passed it through the bars of the cage; the prince seized the edge and guided it through his garments in such a way that the cinnabar bladder was punctured, staining the blade with bright red.

"What is that?" asked the princess, and Ferrix answered:

"Blood!"

Then the princess had the cage opened, entered bravely, brought her face near Ferrix's. That sweet proximity made his senses reel, but the sage caught his eye with a secret sign and the prince squeezed the bellows that released the rank air. And when the princess asked, "What is that?," Ferrix answered:

"Breath!"

"Forsooth you are a clever craftsman," said the princess to the merchant as she left the cage. "But you have deceived me and must die, and your scarecrow also!"

The sage lowered his head, as though in great trepidation and sorrow, and when the prince followed suit, transparent drops flowed from his eyes. The princess asked, "What is that?" and Ferrix answered:

"Tears!"

And she said:

"What is your name, you who profess to be a paleface from afar?"

And Ferrix replied in the words the sage had instructed him:

"Your Highness, my name is Myamlak and I crave nought else but to couple with you in a manner that is liquid, pulpy, doughy and spongy, in accordance with the customs of my people. I purposely permitted myself to be captured by the pirate, and requested him to sell me to this portly trader, as I knew the latter was headed for your kingdom. And I am exceeding grateful to his laminated person for conveying me hither, for I am as full of love for you as a swamp is full of scum."

The princess was amazed, for truly, he spoke in paleface fashion, and she said:

"Tell me, you who call yourself Myamlak the paleface, what do your brothers do during the day?"

"O Princess," said Ferrix, "in the morning they wet themselves in clear water, pouring it upon their limbs as well as into their interiors, for this affords them pleasure. Afterwards, they walk to and fro in a fluid and undulating way, and they slush, and they slurp, and when anything grieves them, they palpitate, and salty water streams from their eyes, and when anything cheers them, they palpitate and hiccup, but their eyes remain relatively dry. And we call the wet palpitating weeping, and the dry—laughter."

"If it is as you say," said the princess, "and you share your brothers' enthusiasm for water, I will have you thrown into my lake, that you may enjoy it to your fill, and also I will have them weigh your legs with lead, to keep you from bobbing up . . ."

"Your Majesty," replied Ferrix as the sage had taught him, "if you do this, I must perish, for though there is water within us, it cannot be immediately outside us for longer than a minute or two, otherwise we recite the words 'blub, blub, blub,' which signifies our last farewell to life."

"But tell me, Myamlak," asked the princess, "how do you furnish yourself with the energy to walk to and fro, to squish and to slurp, to shake and to sway?"

"Princess," replied Ferrix, "there, where I dwell, are other palefaces besides the hairless variety, palefaces that travel predominantly on all fours. These we perforate until they expire, and we steam and bake their remains, and chop and slice, after which we incorporate their corporeality into our own. We know three hundred and seventy-six distinct methods of murdering, twenty-eight thousand five hundred and ninety-seven distinct methods of preparing the corpses, and the stuffing of those bodies into our bodies (through an aperture called the mouth) provides us with no end of enjoyment. Indeed, the art of the preparation of corpses is more esteemed among us than astronautics and is termed gastronautics, or gastronomy—which, however, has nothing to do with astronomy."

"Does this then mean that you play at being cemeteries, making of yourselves the very coffins that hold your four-legged brethren?" This question was dangerously loaded, but Ferrix, instructed by the sage, answered thus:

"It is no game, Your Highness, but rather a necessity, for life lives on life. But we have made of this necessity a great art."

"Well then, tell me, Myamlak the paleface, how do you build your progeny?" asked the princess.

"In faith, we do not build them at all," said Ferrix, "but program them statistically, according to Markov's formula for stochastic probability, emotional-evolutional albeit distributional, and we do this involuntarily and coincidentally, while thinking of a variety of things that have nothing whatever to do with programming, whether statistical, alinear or algorithmical, and the programming itself takes place autonomously, automatically and wholly autoerotically, for it is precisely thus and not otherwise that we are constructed, that each and every paleface strives to program his progeny, for it is delightful, but programs without programming, doing all within his power to keep that programming from bearing fruit."

"Strange," said the princess, whose erudition in this area was less extensive than that of the wise Polyphase. "But how exactly is this done?"

"O Princess!" replied Ferrix. "We possess suitable apparatuses constructed on the principle of regenerative feedback coupling, though of course all this is in water. These apparatuses present a veritable miracle of technology, yet even the greatest idiot can use them. But to describe the precise procedure of their operation I would have to lecture at considerable length, since the matter is most complex. Still, it is strange, when you consider that we never invented these methods, but rather they, so to speak, invented themselves. Even so, they are perfectly functional and we have nothing against them."

"Verily," exclaimed Crystal, "you are a paleface! That which you say, it's as if it made sense, though it doesn't really, not in the least. For how can one be a cemetery without being a cemetery, or program progeny, yet not program it at all?! Yes, you are indeed a paleface, Myamlak, and therefore, should you so desire it, I shall couple with you in a closed-circuit matrimonial coupling, and you shall ascend the throne with me—provided you pass one last test."

"And what is that?" asked Ferrix.

"You must . . ." began the princess, but suddenly suspicion again entered her heart and she asked, "Tell me first, what do your brothers do at night?"

"At night they lie here and there, with bent arms and twisted legs, and air goes into them and comes out of them, raising in the process a noise not unlike the sharpening of a rusty saw."

"Well then, here is the test: give me your hand!" commanded the princess.

Ferrix gave her his hand, and she squeezed it, whereupon he cried out in a loud voice, just as the sage had instructed him. And she asked him why he had cried out.

"From the pain!" replied Ferrix.

At this point she had no more doubts about his palefaceness and promptly ordered the preparations for the wedding ceremony to commence.

But it so happened, at that very moment, that the spaceship of Cybercount Cyberhazy, the princess' Elector, returned from its interstellar expedition to find a paleface (for the insidious Cybercount sought to worm his way into her good graces). Polyphase, greatly alarmed, ran to Ferrix's side and said:

"Prince, Cyberhazy's spaceship has just arrived, and he's brought the princess a genuine paleface — I saw the thing with my own eyes. We must leave while we still can, since all further masquerade will become impossible when the princess sees it and you together: its stickiness is stickier, its ickiness is ickier! Our subterfuge will be discovered and we beheaded!"

Ferrix, however, could not agree to ignominious flight, for his passion for the princess was great, and he said:

"Better to die, than lose her!"

Meanwhile Cyberhazy, having learned of the wedding preparations, sneaked beneath the window of the room where they were staying and overheard everything; then he rushed back to the palace, bubbling over with villainous joy, and announced to Crystal:

"You have been deceived, Your Highness, for the so-called Myamlak is actually an ordinary mortal and no paleface. Here is the real paleface!"

And he pointed to the thing that had been ushered in. The thing expanded its hairy breast, batted its watery eyes and said:

"Me paleface!"

The princess summoned Ferrix at once, and when he stood before her alongside that thing, the sage's ruse became entirely obvious. Ferrix, though he was smeared with mud, dust and chalk, anointed with oil and aqueously gurgling, could hardly conceal his electroknightly stature, his magnificent posture, the breadth of those steel shoulders, that thunderous stride. Whereas the paleface of Cybercount Cyberhazy was a genuine monstrosity: its every step was like the overflowing of marshy vats, its face was like a scummy well; from its rotten breath the mirrors all covered over with a blind mist, and some iron nearby was seized with rust.

Now the princess realized how utterly revolting a paleface was — when it spoke, it was as if a pink worm tried to squirm from its maw. At last she had seen the light, but her pride would not permit her to reveal this change of heart. So she said:

"Let them do battle, and to the winner — my hand in marriage . . ."

Ferrix whispered to the sage:

"If I attack this abomination and crush it, reducing it to the mud from which it came, our imposture will become apparent, for the clay will fall from me and the steel will show. What should I do?"

"Prince," replied Polyphase, "don't attack, just defend yourself!"

Both antagonists stepped out into the palace courtyard, each armed with a sword, and the paleface leaped upon Ferrix as the slime leaps upon a swamp, and danced about him, gurgling, cowering, panting, and it swung at him with its blade, and the blade cut through the clay and shattered against the steel, and the paleface fell against the prince due to the momentum of the blow, and it smashed and broke, and splashed apart, and was no more.

But the dried clay, once moved, slipped from Ferrix's shoulders, revealing his true steely nature to the eyes of the princess; he trembled, awaiting his fate. Yet in her crystalline gaze he beheld admiration, and understood then how much her heart had changed.

Thus they joined in matrimonial coupling, which is permanent and reciprocal — joy and happiness for some, for others misery until the grave — and they reigned long and well, programming innumerable progeny. The skin of Cybercount Cyberhazy's paleface was stuffed and placed in the royal museum as an eternal reminder. It stands there to this day, a scarecrow thinly overgrown with hair. Many pretenders to wisdom say that this is all a trick and make-believe and nothing more, that there's no such thing as paleface cemeteries, doughy-nosed and gummy-eyed, and never was. Well, perhaps it was just another empty invention — there are certainly fables enough in this world. And yet, even if the story isn't true, it does have a grain of sense and instruction to it, and it's entertaining as well, so it's worth the telling.

[1967]

Study and Writing Questions

1. How do the first six paragraphs of the NARRATIVE let you know that you are reading something both like a traditional FAIRY TALE and different from such a tale? What are the traditional fairy tale elements throughout the narrative? What are the untraditional twists given to them?
2. How does the scientific RHETORIC and use of mineral IMAGERY help determine your attitude toward the CHARACTERS? toward the PLOT?
3. This narrative has numerous jokes, such as, "'I am as full of love for you as a swamp is full of scum'" and "'Me paleface!'" What are some others? What are their targets? Is there a consistent aim to the SATIRE of the narrative? If so, what is it? If not, what effect does that inconsistency have on your enjoyment of the narrative as a whole?
4. Do you consider this narrative to have a happy outcome? If so, why? If not, why not?
5. Support or attack the narrator's final assertions in the last two sentences of the work.

See also Questions for Contrast and Comparison: 27, 41, 131, 180, 184, 185, and 186.

■ DORIS (MAY) LESSING (1919-) *was born to British parents in Persia (now Iran) where her father managed a bank. In 1924 the family became pioneering white farmers in Rhodesia (now Zimbabwe). At fourteen, after a year in Salisbury (now Harare), in conflict with her mother, Doris left school, thereafter supporting herself as au pair, typist, clerk; educating herself; and writing. She married (1939), had two children, and divorced (1943), her husband retaining custody. She joined a Marxist group (1942) where she met German refugee Gottfried Anton Lessing. After they married (1945) and divorced (1949), Doris took their son to London where she has lived and written full-time since the publication of her first novel,* The Grass Is Singing *(1950).* Martha Quest *(1952) begins a cycle of novels* (Children of Violence) *tracing one person from her Rhodesian girlhood to the year 2000. The* Golden Notebook *(1962), a formally experimental treatment of the problems of a female writer in our fragmented society, launched Lessing's international acclaim.* Briefing For a Descent Into Hell *(1971) and* Memoirs of a Survivor *(1975), thoughtful,* SCIENCE FICTIONAL, *and subtly Sufic (see p. 34), respectively focus on a man and a woman seeking order and meaning in decaying worlds much like ours. The* Canopus in Argus Archives *novels, beginning with* Shikasta *(1979), set in a bizarre, future universe, have angered some of her former admirers.*

Pleasure

There were two great feasts, or turning points, in Mary Rogers' year. She began preparing for the second as soon as the Christmas decorations were down. This year, she was leafing through a fashion magazine when her husband said, "Dreaming of the sun, old girl?"

"I don't see why not," she said, rather injured. "After all, its been four years."

"I really don't see how we can afford it."

On her face he saw a look that he recognised.

Her friend Mrs. Baxter, the manager's wife, also saw the magazine, and said, "You'll be off to the south of France again, this year, I suppose, now that your daughter won't be needing you." She added those words which in themselves were justification for everything: "We'll stay faithful to Brighton, I expect."

And Mary Rogers said, as she always did: "I can't imagine why anyone takes a holiday in Britain when the same money'd take them to the continent."

For four years she had gone with her daughter and the grandchildren to Cornwall. It sounded a sacrifice on the altar of the family, the way she put it to her friends. But this year the daughter was going to the other grandmother in Scotland, and everyone knew it. Everyone. That is, Mrs. Baxter, Mrs. Justin-Smith, and Mrs. Jones.

Mary Rogers bought gay cottons and spread them over the livingroom. Outside, a particularly grim February held the little Midlands town in a steady shiver. Rain swept the windowpanes. Tommy Rogers saw the cottons and said not a word. But a week later she was fitting a white linen sunsuit before the mirror when he said, "I say, old girl, that shows quite a bit of leg, you know. . . ."

At that moment it was acknowledged that they should go. Also, that the four years had made a difference in various ways. Mary Rogers secretly examined her thighs and shoulders before the glass, and thought they might very well be exposed. But the clothes she made were of the sensible but smart variety. She sewed at them steadily through the evenings of March, April, May, June. She was a good needlewoman. Also, for a few happy months before she married, she had studied fashion designing in London. That had been a different world. In speaking of it now, to the women of her circle — Mrs. Baxter, Mrs. Justin-Smith, and Mrs. Jones — her voice conveyed the degree of difference. And Mrs. Baxter would say, kindly as always, "Ah well, we none of us know what's in store for us when we're young."

They were to leave towards the end of July. A week before, Tommy Rogers produced a piece of paper on which were set out certain figures. They were much lower figures than ever before. "Oh, we'll manage," said Mary vaguely. Her mind was already moving among the scenes of blue sea, blue sky.

"Perhaps we'd better book at the Plaza."

"Oh, surely no need. They know us there."

The evening before they left there was a bridge party in the Baxters' house for the jaunting couple. Tommy Rogers was seen to give his wife an uneasy glance as she said, "With air travel as cheap as it is now, I really can't understand why . . ."

For they had booked by train, of course, as usual.

They successfully negotiated the Channel, a night in a Paris hotel, and the catching of the correct train.

In a few hours they would see the little village on the sea where they had first come twenty-five years ago on their honeymoon. They had chosen it because Mary Hill had met, in those artistic circles which she had enjoyed for, alas, so short a time, a certain well-known stage decorator who had a villa there. During that month of honeymoon, they had spent a happy afternoon at the villa.

As the train approached, she was looking to see the villa, alone on its hill above the sea. But the hill was now thick with little white villas, green-shuttered, red-roofed in the warm southern green.

"The place seems to have grown quite a bit," said Tommy. The station had grown, too. There was a long platform now, and a proper station building. And gazing down towards the sea, they saw a cluster of shops and casinos and cafes. Even four years before, there had been only a single shop, a restaurant, and a couple of hotels.

"Well," said Mary bitterly, "if the place is full of tourists now, it won't be the same at all."

But the sun was shining, the sea tossed and sparkled, and the palm trees stood along the white beach. They carried their suitcases down the slope of the road to the Plaza, feeling at home.

Outside the Plaza, they looked at each other. What had been a modest building was now an imposing one, surrounded by gay awnings and striped umbrellas. "Old Jaques is spreading himself," said Tommy, and they walked up the neat gravel path to the foyer, looking for Jaques, who had welcomed them so often.

At the office, Mary enquired in her stiff, correct French for Monsieur Jaques. The clerk smiled and regretted that Monsieur Jaques had left them three years before. "He knew us well," said Mary, her voice coming aggrieved and shrill. "He always had room for us here."

But certainly there was a room for Madame. Most certainly. At once attendants came hurrying for the suitcases.

"Hold your horses a minute," said Tommy. "Wait. Ask what it costs now."

Mary enquired, casually enough, what the rates now were. She received the information with a lengthening of her heavy jaw, and rapidly transmitted it to Tommy. He glanced, embarrassed, at the clerk, who, recognising a situation, turned tactfully to a ledger and prepared to occupy himself so that the elderly English couple could confer.

They did, in rapid, angry undertones.

"We can't, Mary. It's no good. We'd have to go back at the end of a week."

"But we've always stayed here. . . ."

At last she turned towards the clerk, who was immediately attentive, and said with a stiff smile: "I'm afraid the currency regulations make things difficult for us." She had spoken in English, such was her upset; and it was in English that he replied pleasantly, "I understand perfectly, Madame. Perhaps you would care to try the Belle Vue across the street. There are many English people there."

The Rogerses left, carrying their two suitcases ignominiously down the neat gravelled path, among the gay tables where people already sat at dinner. The sun had gone down. Opposite, the Belle Vue was a glow of lights. Tommy Rogers was not surprised when Mary walked past it without a look. For years, staying at the Plaza, they had felt superior to the Belle Vue. Also, had that clerk not said it was full of English people?

Since this was France, and the season, the Agency was of course open. An attractive mademoiselle deplored that they had not booked rooms earlier.

"We've been here every year for twenty-five years," said Mary, pardonably overlooking the last four, and another stretch of five when the child had been small. "We've never had to book before."

Alas, alas, suggested the mademoiselle with her shoulders and her pretty eyes, what a pity that St. Nichole had become so popular, so attractive. There was no fact she regretted more. She suggested the Belle Vue.

The Rogerses walked the hundred yards back to the Belle Vue, feeling they were making a final concession to fate, only to find it fully booked up. Returning to the Agency, they were informed that there was, happily, one room vacant in a villa on the hillside. They were escorted to it. And now it was the turn of the pretty mademoiselle to occupy herself, not with a ledger, but in examining the view of brilliant stars and the riding lights of ships across the bay, while the Rogerses conferred. Their voices were now not only angry, but high with exasperation. For this room — an extremely small one, at the bottom of a big villa, stone-floored, uncarpeted, with a single large bed of the sort Mary always thought of as French; a wardrobe that was no wardrobe, since it had been filled with shelves; a sink and a small gas stove — they were asked to pay a sum which filled them with disbelief. If they desired hot water, as the English so often do, they would have to heat it in a saucepan on the stove.

But, as the mademoiselle pointed out, turning from her appreciative examination of the exotic night scene, it would be such an advantage to do one's own cooking.

"I suggest we go back to the Plaza. Better one week of comfort than three of this," said Mary. They returned to the Plaza to find that the room had been taken, and none were available.

It was now nearly ten in the evening, and the infinitely obliging mademoiselle returned them to the little room in the villa, for which they agreed to pay more than they had done four years before for comfort, good food, and hot water in the Plaza. Also, they had to pay a deposit of over ten pounds in case they might escape in the night with the bed, the wardrobe, or the tin spoons, or in case they refused to pay the bills for electricity, gas, and water.

The Rogerses went to bed immediately, worn out with travelling and disappointment.

In the morning Mary announced that she had no intention of cooking on a holiday, and they took *petit déjeuner* at a cafe, paid the equivalent of twelve shillings for two small cups of coffee and two rolls, and changed their minds. They would have to cook in the room.

Preserving their good humour with an effort, they bought cold food for lunch, left it in the room, and prepared themselves for enjoyment. For the sea was blue, blue and sparkling. And the sunshine was hot and golden. And after all, this was the south of France, the prettiest place in Europe, as they had always agreed. And in England now, said the *Daily Telegraph*, it was pouring rain.

On the beach they had another bad moment. Umbrellas stretched six deep, edge to edge, for half a mile along the silvery beach. Bodies lay stretched out, baking in the sun, hundreds to the acre, a perfect bed of heated brown flesh.

"They've ruined the place, ruined it!" cried Mary, as she surveyed the untidy scene. But she stepped heavily down into the sand and unbuttoned her dress. She was revealed to be wearing a heavy black bathing suit; and she did not miss the relieved glance her husband gave her. She felt it to be unfair. There he stood, a tall, very thin, fair man, quite presentable in an absurd bathing slip that consisted of six inches of material held on by a string round his hips. And there *she* was, a heavy firm woman, with clear white flesh—but middleaged, and in a black bathing suit.

She looked about. Two feet away was a mess of tangled brown limbs belonging to half a dozen boys and girls, the girls wearing nothing but colored cotton brassières and panties. She saw Tommy looking at them, too. Then she noticed, eighteen inches to the other side, a vast grey-haired lady, bulging weary pallid flesh out of a white cotton playsuit. Mary gave her a look of happy superiority and lay down flat on the sand, congratulating herself.

All the morning the English couple lay there, turning over and over on the sand like a pair of grilling herrings, for they felt their pale skins to be a shame and a disgrace. When they returned to their room for lunch, it was to find that swarms of small black ants had infested their cold meats. They were unable to mind very much, as it had become evident they had overdone the sunbathing. Both were bright scarlet, and their eyes ached. They lay down in the cool of the darkened room, feeling foolish to be such amateurs—they, who should know better! They kept to their beds that afternoon, and the next day . . . several days passed. Sometimes, when hunger overcame them, Mary winced down to the village to buy cold food—impossible to keep supplies in the room because of the ants. After eating, she hastily washed up in the sink where they also washed.

Twice a day, Tommy went reluctantly outside while she washed herself inch by inch in water heated in the saucepan. Then she went outside while he did the same. After these indispensable measures of hygiene, they retired to the much too narrow bed, shrinking away from any chance of contact with each other.

At last the discomfort of the room, as much as their healing flesh, drove them forth again, more cautiously clothed, to the beach. Skin was ripping off them both in long shreds. At the end of a week, however, they had become brown and shining, able to take their places without shame among the other brown and glistening bodies that littered the beach like so many stranded fish.

Day after day the Rogerses descended the steep path to the beach, after having eaten a hearty English breakfast of ham and eggs, and stayed there all morning. All morning they lay, and then all afternoon, but at a good distance from a colony of English, which kept itself to itself some hundreds of yards away.

They watched the children screaming and laughing in the unvarying blue waves. They watched the groups of French adolescents flirt and roll each other over on the sand in a way that Mary, at least, thought appallingly free. Thank heavens her daughter had married young and was safely out of harm's way! Nothing could have persuaded Mary Rogers of the extreme respectability of these youngsters. She suspected them all of shocking and complicated vices. Incredible that, in so few a number of years, they would be sorted by some powerful and comforting social process into these decent, well-fed French couples, each so anxiously absorbed in the welfare of one, or perhaps two small children.

They watched also, with admiration, the more hardened swimmers cleave out through the small waves into the sea beyond the breakwater with their masks, their airtubes, their frog's feet.

They were content.

This is what they had come for. This is what all these hundreds of thousands of people along the coast had come for—to lie on the sand and receive the sun on their heating bodies; to receive, too, in small doses, the hot blue water which dried so stickily on them. The sea was very salty and warm-smelling—smelling of a little more than salt and weed, for beyond the breakwater the town's sewers spilled into the sea, washing back into the inner bay rich deposits which dried on the perfumed oiled bodies of the happy bathers.

This is what they had come for.

Yet, there was no doubt that in the Plaza things had been quite different. There one rose late; lingered over coffee and rolls; descended, or did not descend, to the beach for a couple of hours' sun-worship; returned to a lengthy lunch; slept, bathed again, enjoyed an even more lengthy dinner. That, too, was called a seaside vacation. Now, the beach was really the only place to go. From nine until one, from two until seven, the Rogerses were on it. It was a seaside vacation with a vengeance.

About the tenth day, they realised that half of their time had gone; and Tommy showed his restlessness, his feeling that there should be more to it than this, by diving into one of the new and so terribly expensive shops and emerging with a mask, frog's feet, and airtube. With an apology to Mary for leaving her, he plunged out into the bay, looking like—or so she rather tartly remarked—a spaceman in a children's comic. He did not return for some hours.

"This is better than anything, old girl, you should try it," he said, wading out of the sea with an absorbed excited look. That afternoon she spent on the beach alone, straining her eyes to make out which of the bobbing periscopes in the water was his.

Thus engaged, she heard herself addressed in English: "I always say I am an undersea widow, too." She turned to see a slight girl, clearly English, with pretty fair curls, a neat blue bathing suit, pretty blue eyes, good legs stretched out in the warm sand. An English girl. But her voice was, so Mary decided, passable, in spite of a rather irritating giggle. She relented and, though it was her principle that one did not go to France to consort with the English, said: "Is your husband out there?"

"Oh, I never see him between meals," said the girl cheerfully, and lay back on the sand.

Mary thought that this girl was very similar to herself at that age—only, of course, *she* had known how to make the best of herself. They talked, in voices drugged by sea and sun, until first Tommy Rogers, and then the girl's husband, rose out of the sea. The young man was carrying a large fish speared through the back by a sort of trident. The excitement of this led the four of them to share a square yard of sand for a few minutes, making cautious overtures.

The next day, Tommy Rogers insisted that his wife should don mask and flippers and try the new sport. She was taken out into the bay, like a ship under escort, by the two men and young Betty Clarke. Mary Rogers did not like the suffocating feeling of the mask pressing against her nose. The speed the frog feet lent her made her nervous, for she was not a strong swimmer. But she was not going to appear a coward with that young girl sporting along so easily just in front.

Out in the bay a small island, a mere cluster of warm, red-brown rock, rose from a surf of frisking white. Around the island, a couple of feet below the surface, submerged rocks lay; and all over them floated the new race of frog-people, face down, tridents poised, observing the fish that darted there. As Mary looked back through her goggles to the shore, it seemed very far, and rather commonplace, with the striped umbrellas, the lolling browned bodies, the paddling children. That was the other sea. This was something different indeed. Here were the adventurers and explorers of the sea, who disdained the safe beaches.

Mary lay loose on the surface of the water and looked down. Enormous, this undersea world, with great valleys and boulders, all wavering green in the sun-dappled water. On a dazzling patch of white sand—twenty feet down, it seemed—sprouted green grass as fresh and bright as if it grew on the shore in sunlight. By reaching down her hand she could almost touch it. Farther away, long fronds of weed rocked and swayed, a forest of them. Mary floated over them, feeling with repugnance how they reached up to touch her knees and shoulders with their soft, dragging touch. Underneath her now, a floor of rock, covered with thick growth. Pale grey-green shapes, swelling like balloons, or waving like streamers; delicate whitey-brown flowers and stars, bubbled silver with air; soft swelling udders or bladders of fine white film, all rocking and drifting in the slow undersea movement. Mary was fascinated—a new world, this was. But also repelled. In her ears there was nothing but a splash and crash of surf, and, through it, voices that sounded a long way off. The rocks were now very close below. Suddenly, immediately below her, a thin brown arm reached down, groped in a dark gulf of rock, and pulled out a writhing tangle of grey-dappled flesh. Mary floundered up, slipping painfully on the rocks. She had drifted unknowingly close to the islet; and on the rocks above her stood a group of half-naked bronzed boys, yelling and screaming with excitement as they killed the octopus they had caught by smashing it repeatedly against a great boulder. They would eat it—so Mary heard—for supper. No, it was too much. She was in panic. The loathsome thing must have been six inches below her—she might have touched it! She climbed onto a rock and looked for Tommy, who was lying on a rock fifty feet off, pointing down at something under it, while Francis Clarke dived for it, and then again. She saw him emerge with a small striped fish, while Tommy and Betty Clarke yelled their excitement.

But she looked at the octopus, which was now lying draped over a rock like a limp, fringed, grey rag; she called her husband, handed over the goggles, the flippers and the tube, and swam slowly back to shore.

There she stayed. Nothing would tempt her out again.

That day Tommy bought an underwater fish gun. Mary found herself thinking, first, that it was all very well to spend over five pounds on this bizarre equipment; and then, that they weren't going to have much fun at Christmas if they went on like this.

A couple of days passed. Mary was alone all day. Betty Clarke, apparently, was only a beach widow when it suited her, for she much preferred the red-rock island to staying with Mary. Nevertheless, she did sometimes spend half an hour making conversation, and then, with a flurry of apology, darted off through the blue waves to rejoin the men.

Quite soon, Mary was able to say casually to Tommy, "Only three days to go."

"If only I'd tried this equipment earlier," he said. "Next year I'll know better."

But for some reason the thought of next year did not enchant Mary. "I don't think we ought to come here again," she said. "It's quite spoiled now it's so fashionable."

"Oh well—anywhere, provided there's rocks and fish."

On that next day, the two men and Betty Clarke were on the rock island from seven in the morning until lunchtime, to which meal they grudgingly allowed ten minutes, because it was dangerous to swim on a full stomach. Then they departed again until the darkness fell across the sea. All this time Mary Rogers lay on her towel on the beach, turning over and over in the sun. She was now a warm red-gold all over. She imagined how Mrs. Baxter would say: "You've got yourself a fine tan!" And then, inevitably, "You won't keep it long here, will you?" Mary found herself unaccountably close to tears. What did Tommy see in these people? she asked herself. As for that young man, Francis—she had never heard him make any remark that was not connected with the weights, the varieties, or the vagaries of fish!

That night, Tommy said he had asked the young couple to dinner at the Plaza.

"A bit rash, aren't you?"

"Oh well, let's have a proper meal, for once. Only another two days."

Mary let that "proper meal" pass. But she said, "I shouldn't have thought they were the sort of people to make friends of."

A cloud of irritation dulled his face. "What's the matter with them?"

"In England, I don't think . . ."

"Oh come off it, Mary!"

In the big garden of the Plaza, where four years ago they had eaten three times a day by right, they found themselves around a small table just over the sea. There was an orchestra and more waiters than guests, or so it seemed. Betty Clarke, seen for the first time out of a bathing suit, was revealed to be a remarkably pretty girl. Her thin brown shoulders emerged from a full white frock, which Mary Rogers conceded to be not bad at all; and her wide blue eyes were bright in her brown face. Again Mary thought: If I were twenty—well, twenty-five—years younger, they'd take us for sisters.

As for Tommy, he looked as young as the young couple—it simply wasn't fair, thought Mary. She sat and listened while they talked of judging distances underwater and the advantages of various types of equipment.

They tried to draw her in; but there she sat, silent and dignified. Francis Clarke, she had decided, looked stiff and commonplace in his suit, not at all the handsome young sea god of the beaches. As for the girl, her giggle was irritating Mary.

They began to feel uncomfortable. Betty mentioned London, and the three conscientiously talked about London, while Mary said yes and no.

The young couple lived in Clapham, apparently; and they went into town for a show once a month.

"There's ever such a nice show running now," said Betty. "The one at the Princess."

"We never get to a show these days," said Tommy. "It's five hours by train. Anyway, it's not in my line."

"Speak for yourself," said Mary.

"Oh I know you work in a matinée when you can."

At the irritation in the look she gave him, the Clarkes involuntarily exchanged a glance; and Betty said tactfully, "I like going to the theatre; it gives you something to talk about."

Mary remained silent.

"My wife," said Tommy, "knows a lot about the theatre. She used to be in a theatre set—all that sort of thing."

"Oh how interesting!" said Betty eagerly.

Mary struggled with temptation, then fell. "The man who did the décor for the show at the Princess used to have a villa here. We visited him quite a bit."

Tommy gave his wife an alarmed and warning look, and said, "I wish to God they wouldn't use so much garlic."

"It's not much use coming to France," said Mary, "if you're going to be insular about food."

"You never cook French at home," said Tommy suddenly. "Why not, if you like it so much?"

"How can I? If I do, you say you don't like your food messed up."

"I don't like garlic either," said Betty, with the air of one confessing a crime. "I must say I'm pleased to be back home where you can get a bit of good plain food."

Tommy now looked in anxious appeal at his wife, but she enquired, "Why don't you go to Brighton or somewhere like that?"

"Give me Brighton any time," said Francis Clarke. "Or Cornwall. You can get damned good fishing off Cornwall. But Betty drags me here. France is overrated, that's what I say."

"It would really seem to be better if you stayed at home."

But he was not going to be snubbed by Mary Rogers. "As for the French," he said aggressively, "they think of nothing but their stomachs. If they're not eating, they're talking about it. If they spent half the time they spend on eating on something worthwhile, they could make something of themselves, that's what I say."

"Such as — catching fish?"

"Well, what's wrong with that? Or . . . for instance . . ." Here he gave the matter his earnest consideration. "Well, there's that government of theirs for instance. They could do something about that."

Betty, who was now flushed under her tan, rolled her blue eyes, and let out a high, confused laugh. "Oh well, you've got to consider what people say. France is so much the rage."

A silence. It was to be hoped the awkward moment was over. But no; for Francis Clarke seemed to think matters needed clarifying. He said, with a sort of rallying gallantry towards his wife, "She's got a bee in her bonnet about getting on."

"Well," cried Betty, "it makes a good impression, you must admit that. And when Mr. Beaker — Mr. Beaker is his boss," she explained to Mary, "when you said to Mr. Beaker at the whist drive you were going to the south of France, he was impressed, you can say what you like."

Tommy offered his wife an entirely disloyal, sarcastic grin.

"A woman should think of her husband's career," said Betty. "It's true, isn't it? And I know I've helped Francie a lot. I'm sure he wouldn't have got that raise if it weren't for making a good impression. Besides, you meet such nice people. Last year, we made friends — well, acquaintance, if you like — with some people who live at Ealing. We wouldn't have, otherwise. He's in the films."

"He's a cameraman," said Francis, being accurate.

"Well, that's films, isn't it? And they asked us to a party. And who do you think was there?"

"Mr. Beaker?" enquired Mary finely.

"How did you guess? Well, they could see, couldn't they? And I wouldn't be surprised if Francis couldn't be buyer, now they know he's used to foreigners. He should learn French, I tell him."

"Can't speak a word," said Francis. "Can't stand it anyway — gabble, gabble, gabble."

"Oh, but Mrs. Rogers speaks it so beautifully," cried Betty.

"She's cracked," said Francis, good-humouredly, nodding to indicate his wife. "She spends half the year making clothes for three weeks' holiday at the sea.

Then the other half making Christmas presents out of bits and pieces. That's all she ever does."

"Oh, but it's so nice to give people presents with that individual touch," said Betty.

"If you want to waste your time I'm not stopping you," said Francis. "I'm not stopping you. It's your funeral."

"They're not grateful for what we do for them," said Betty, wrestling with tears, trying to claim the older woman as an ally. "If I didn't work hard, we couldn't afford the friends we got. . . ."

But Mary Rogers had risen from her place. "I think I'm ready for bed," she said. "Goodnight, Mrs. Clarke. Goodnight, Mr. Clarke." Without looking at her husband, she walked away.

Tommy Rogers hastily got up, paid the bill, bade the young couple an embarrassed goodnight, and hurried after his wife. He caught her up at the turning of the steep road up to the villa. The stars were brilliant overhead; the palms waved seductively in the soft breeze. "I say," he said angrily, "that wasn't very nice of you."

"I haven't any patience with that sort of thing," said Mary. Her voice was high and full of tears. He looked at her in astonishment and held his peace.

But next day he went off fishing. For Mary, the holiday was over. She was packing and did not go to the beach.

That evening he said, "They've asked us back to dinner."

"You go. I'm tired."

"I shall go," he said defiantly, and went. He did not return until very late.

They had to catch the train early next morning. At the little station, they stood with their suitcases in a crowd of people who regretted the holiday was over. But Mary was regretting nothing. As soon as the train came, she got in and left Tommy shaking hands with crowds of English people whom, apparently, he had met the night before. At the last minute, the young Clarkes came running up in bathing suits to say goodbye. She nodded stiffly out of the train window and went on arranging the baggage. Then the train started and her husband came in.

The compartment was full and there was an excuse not to talk. The silence persisted, however. Soon Tommy was watching her anxiously and making remarks about the weather, which worsened steadily as they went north.

In Paris there were five hours to fill in.

They were walking beside the river, by the open-air market, when she stopped before a stall selling earthenware.

"That big bowl," she exclaimed, her voice newly alive, "that big red one, there—it would be just right for the Christmas tree."

"So it would. Go ahead and buy it, old girl," he agreed at once, with infinite relief.

[1957]

Study and Writing Questions

1. How would you characterize the humor in this NARRATIVE? What incidents and phrases are funny? How does humor shape our attitudes toward Mary and the others?

2. We learn little about the occupations of the Rogerses and the Clarkes, but we learn that they have acquaintances who are in theater and film. Why? What role do those realms play in the CHARACTERS' lives and in the narrative as a whole?

3. What does the octopus SYMBOLIZE?

4. Four ages are mentioned in the STORY: childhood, youth, early married years, and middle age. How do the relations among these ages provide dramatic energy for the narrative?

5. There are three main SETTINGS in the story: England, the French beach, and the sea. Compare and contrast the importance of each to Mary and to the narrative as a whole.

See also Questions for Contrast and Comparison: 44, 45, 77, 125, 172, and 227.

■ JACK LONDON (1876–1916), *born poor in San Francisco, California, held life-long passions for reading and the sea. From childhood he worked at countless tasks with uneven success, including newspaper delivery, oyster pirating at fifteen, laboring in a cannery, and merchant sailing to Siberia and Japan. After a stint of tramping landed him in jail, he returned to Oakland to finish high school (1896). He attended the University of California for a semester but left to prospect in the Klondike. Although he found no gold, his observations provided material for short stories collected as* The Son of the Wolf *(1900), which won acclaim and wealth. London's intellectual heroes—Nietzsche, who preached the moral superiority of the strong, and Marx, who preached collectivism as the next step in human evolution—both influenced his best novel,* The Call of the Wild *(1903), in which a dog in the Far North escapes civilization to lead a wolf pack. His forty books include* The Sea-Wolf *(1904), about the ruthless captain of a sealing ship;* The Iron Heel *(1908), about a socialist future; and* Martin Eden *(1909), about the struggles of a would-be writer. Although hugely successful, London worked relentlessly, writing fiction even while covering far-flung wars as a correspondent. After years of drinking, indebted for his yacht, sick, despairing since the burning of his prized ranch home (1913), his second marriage failing, he died of a drug overdose.*

To Build a Fire

Day had broken cold and gray, exceedingly cold and gray, when the man turned aside from the main Yukon trail and climbed the high earth-bank, where a dim and little-travelled trail led eastward through the fat spruce timberland. It was a steep bank, and he paused for breath at the top, excusing the act to himself by looking at his watch. It was nine o'clock. There was no sun nor hint of sun, though there was not a cloud in the sky. It was a clear day, and yet there seemed an intangible pall over the face of things, a subtle gloom that made the day dark, and that was due to the absence of sun. This fact did not worry the man. He was used to the lack of sun. It had been days since he had seen the sun, and he knew that a few more days must pass before that cheerful orb, due south, would just peep above the sky line and dip immediately from view.

The man flung a look back along the way he had come. The Yukon lay a mile wide and hidden under three feet of ice. On top of this ice were as many feet of snow. It was all pure white, rolling in gentle undulations where the ice jams of the freeze-up had formed. North and south, as far as his eye could see, it was unbroken white, save for a dark hairline that curved and twisted from around the spruce-covered island to the south, and that curved and twisted away into the north, where it disappeared behind another spruce-covered island. This dark hairline was the trail—the main trail—that led south five hundred miles to the Chilcoot Pass, Dyea, and salt water; and that led north seventy miles to Dawson, and still on to the north a thousand miles to Nulato, and finally to St. Michael, on Bering Sea, a thousand miles and half a thousand more.

But all this—the mysterious, far-reaching hairline trail, the absence of sun from the sky, the tremendous cold, and the strangeness and weirdness of it all—made no impression on the man. It was not because he was long used to it. He was a newcomer in the land, a *chechaquo*, and this was his first winter. The trouble with him was that he was without imagination. He was quick and alert in the things of life, but only in the things, and not in the significances. Fifty degrees below zero meant eighty-odd degrees of frost. Such fact impressed him as being cold and uncomfortable, and that was all. It did not lead him to meditate upon his frailty as a creature of temperature, and upon man's frailty in general, able only to live within certain narrow limits of heat and cold; and from there on it did not lead him to the conjectural field of immortality and man's place in the universe. Fifty degrees below zero stood for a bite of frost that hurt and that must be guarded against by the use of mittens, ear flaps, warm moccasins, and thick socks. Fifty degrees below zero was to him just precisely fifty degrees below zero. That there should be anything more to it than that was a thought that never entered his head.

As he turned to go on, he spat speculatively. There was a sharp, explosive crackle that startled him. He spat again. And again, in the air, before it could fall to the snow, the spittle crackled. He knew that at fifty below spittle crackled on the snow, but this spittle had crackled in the air. Undoubtedly it was colder than fifty below—how much colder he did not know. But the temperature did not matter. He was bound for the old claim on the left fork of Henderson Creek, where the boys were already. They had come over across the divide from the Indian Creek country, while he had come the roundabout way to take a look at the possibilities of getting out logs in the spring from the islands in the Yukon. He would be in to camp by six o'clock; a bit after dark, it was true, but the boys would be there, a fire would be going, and a hot supper would be ready. As for lunch, he pressed his hand against the protruding bundle under his jacket. It was also under his shirt, wrapped up in a handkerchief and lying against the naked skin. It was the only way to keep the biscuits from freezing. He smiled agreeably to himself as he thought of those biscuits, each cut open and sopped in bacon grease, and each enclosing a generous slice of fried bacon.

He plunged in among the big spruce trees. The trail was faint. A foot of snow had fallen since the last sled had passed over, and he was glad he was without a sled, travelling light. In fact, he carried nothing but the lunch wrapped in the handkerchief. He was surprised, however, at the cold. It certainly was cold, he concluded, as he rubbed his numb nose and cheekbones with his mittened hand. He was a warm-whiskered man, but the hair on his face did not protect the high cheek-bones and the eager nose that thrust itself aggressively into the frosty air.

At the man's heels trotted a dog, a big native husky, the proper wolf dog, gray-coated and without any visible or temperamental difference from its brother, the wild wolf. The animal was depressed by the tremendous cold. It knew that it was no time for travelling. Its instinct told it a truer tale than was told to the man by the man's judgment. In reality, it was not merely colder than fifty below zero; it was colder than sixty below, than seventy below. It was seventy-five below zero. Since the freezing point is thirty-two above zero, it meant that one hundred and seven degrees of frost obtained. The dog did not know anything about thermometers. Possibly in its brain there was no sharp consciousness of a condition of very cold such as was in the man's brain. But the brute had its instinct. It experienced a vague but menacing apprehension that subdued it and made it slink along at the man's heels, and that made it question eagerly every unwonted movement of the man as if expecting him to go into camp or to seek shelter somewhere and build a fire. The dog had learned fire, and it wanted fire, or else to burrow under the snow and cuddle its warmth away from the air.

The frozen moisture of its breathing had settled on its fur in a fine powder of frost, and especially were its jowls, muzzle, and eyelashes whitened by its crystalled breath. The man's red beard and mustache were likewise frosted, but more solidly, the deposit taking the form of ice and increasing with every warm, moist breath he exhaled. Also, the man was chewing tobacco, and the muzzle of ice held his lips so rigidly that he was unable to clear his chin when he expelled the juice. The result was that a crystal beard of the color and solidity of amber was increasing its length on his chin. If he fell down it would shatter itself, like glass, into brittle fragments. But he did not mind the appendage. It was the penalty all tobacco chewers paid in that country, and he had been out before in two cold snaps. They had not been so cold as this, he knew, but by the spirit thermometer at Sixty Mile he knew they had been registered at fifty below and at fifty-five.

He held on through the level stretch of woods for several miles, crossed a wide flat of nigger heads, and dropped down a bank to the frozen bed of a small stream. This was Henderson Creek, and he knew he was ten miles from the forks. He looked at his watch. It was ten o'clock. He was making four miles an hour, and he calculated that he would arrive at the forks at half-past twelve. He decided to celebrate that event by eating his lunch there.

The dog dropped in again at his heels, with a tail drooping discouragement, as the man swung along the creek bed. The furrow of the old sled trail was plainly visible, but a dozen inches of snow covered the marks of the last runners. In a month no man had come up or down that silent creek. The man held steadily on. He was not much given to thinking, and just then particularly he had nothing to think about save that he would eat lunch at the forks and that at six o'clock he would be in camp with the boys. There was nobody to talk to; and, had there been, speech would have been impossible because of the ice muzzle on his mouth. So he continued monotonously to chew tobacco and to increase the length of his amber beard.

Once in a while the thought reiterated itself that it was very cold and that he had never experienced such cold. As he walked along he rubbed his cheekbones and nose with the back of his mittened hand. He did this automatically, now and again changing hands. But, rub as he would, the instant he stopped his cheekbones went numb, and the following instant the end of his nose went numb. He was sure to frost his cheeks; he knew that, and experienced a pang of regret that he had not devised a nose strap of the sort Bud wore in cold snaps. Such a strap passed across the cheeks, as well, and saved them. But it didn't matter much, after all. What were frosted cheeks? A bit painful, that was all; they were never serious.

Empty as the man's mind was of thoughts, he was keenly observant, and he noticed the changes in the creek, the curves and bends and timber jams, and always he sharply noted where he placed his feet. Once, coming around a bend, he shied abruptly, like a startled horse, curved away from the place where he had been walking, and retreated several paces back along the trail. The creek he knew was frozen clear to the bottom—no creek could contain water in that arctic winter—but he knew also that there were springs that bubbled out from the hillsides and ran along under the snow and on top the ice of the creek. He knew that the coldest snaps never froze these springs, and he knew likewise their danger. They were traps. They hid pools of water under the snow that might be three inches deep, or three feet. Sometimes a skin of ice half an inch thick covered them, and in turn was covered by the snow. Sometimes there were alternate layers of water and ice skin, so that when one broke through he kept on breaking through for a while, sometimes wetting himself to the waist.

That was why he had shied in such panic. He had felt the give under his feet and heard the crackle of a snow-hidden ice skin. And to get his feet wet in such a temperature meant trouble and danger. At the very least it meant delay, for he would be forced to stop and build a fire, and under its protection to bare his feet while he dried his socks and moccasins. He stood and studied the creek bed and its banks, and decided that the flow of water came from the right. He reflected awhile, rubbing his nose and cheeks, then skirted to the left, stepping gingerly and testing the footing for each step. Once clear of the danger, he took a fresh chew of tobacco and swung along at his four-mile gait.

In the course of the next two hours he came upon several similar traps. Usually the snow above the hidden pools had a sunken, candied appearance that advertised the danger. Once again, however, he had a close call; and once, suspecting danger, he compelled the dog to go on in front. The dog did not want to go. It hung back until the man shoved it forward, and then it went quickly across the white, unbroken surface. Suddenly it broke through, floundered to one side, and got away to firmer footing. It had wet its forefeet and legs, and almost immediately the water that clung to it turned to ice. It made quick efforts to lick the ice off its legs, then dropped down in the snow and began to bite out the ice that had formed between the toes. This was a matter of instinct. To permit the ice to remain would mean sore feet. It did not know this. It merely obeyed the mysterious prompting that arose from the deep crypts of its being. But the man knew, having achieved a judgment on the subject, and he removed the mitten from his right hand and helped tear out the ice particles. He did not expose his fingers more than a minute, and was astonished at the swift numbness that smote them. It certainly was cold. He pulled on the mitten hastily, and beat the hand savagely across his chest.

At twelve o'clock the day was at its brightest. Yet the sun was too far south on its winter journey to clear the horizon. The bulge of the earth intervened between it and Henderson Creek, where the man walked under a clear sky at noon and cast no shadow. At half-past twelve, to the minute, he arrived at the forks of the creek. He was pleased at the speed he had made. If he kept it up, he would certainly be with the boys by six. He unbuttoned his jacket and shirt and drew forth his lunch. The action consumed no more than a quarter of a minute, yet in that brief moment the numbness laid hold of the exposed fingers. He did not put the mitten on, but, instead, struck the fingers a dozen sharp smashes against his leg. Then he sat down on a snow-covered log to eat. The sting that followed upon the striking of his fingers against his leg ceased so quickly that he was startled. He had had no chance to take a bite of biscuit. He struck the fingers repeatedly and returned them to the mitten, baring the other hand for the purpose of eating. He tried to take a mouthful, but the ice muzzle prevented. He had forgotten to build a fire and thaw out. He chuckled at his foolishness, and as he chuckled he noted the numbness creeping into the exposed fingers. Also, he noted that the stinging which had first come to his toes when he sat down was already passing away. He wondered whether the toes were warm or numb. He moved them inside the moccasins and decided that they were numb.

He pulled the mitten on hurriedly and stood up. He was a bit frightened. He stamped up and down until the stinging returned into the feet. It certainly was cold, was his thought. That man from Sulphur Creek had spoken the truth when telling how cold it sometimes got in the country. And he had laughed at him at the time! That showed one must not be too sure of things. There was no mistake about it, it *was* cold. He strode up and down, stamping his feet and threshing his arms, until reassured by the returning warmth. Then he got out matches and proceeded to make a fire. From the undergrowth, where high water of the previous spring had lodged a supply of seasoned twigs, he got his firewood. Working carefully from a small beginning, he soon had a roaring fire, over which he thawed the ice from his face and in the protection of which he ate his biscuits. For the moment the cold of space was outwitted. The dog took satisfaction in the fire, stretching out close enough for warmth and far enough away to escape being singed.

When the man had finished, he filled his pipe and took his comfortable time over a smoke. Then he pulled on his mittens, settled the ear flaps of his cap firmly about his ears, and took the creek trail up the left fork. The dog was disappointed and yearned back toward the fire. This man did not know cold. Possibly all the generations of his ancestry had been ignorant of cold, of real cold, of cold one hundred and seven degrees below freezing point. But the dog knew; all its ancestry knew, and it had inherited the knowledge. And it knew that it was not good to walk abroad in such fearful cold. It was the time to lie snug in a hole in the snow and wait for a curtain of cloud to be drawn across the face of outer space whence this cold came. On the other hand, there was no keen intimacy between the dog and the man. The one was the toil slave of the other, and the only caresses it had ever received were the caresses of the whip lash and of harsh and menacing throat sounds that threatened the whip lash. So the dog made no effort to communicate its apprehension to the man. It was not concerned in the welfare of the man; it was for its own sake that it yearned back toward the fire. But the man whistled, and spoke to it with the sound of whip lashes, and the dog swung in at the man's heels and followed after.

The man took a chew of tobacco and proceeded to start a new amber beard. Also, his moist breath quickly powdered with white his mustache, eyebrows, and lashes. There did not seem to be so many springs on the left fork of the Henderson, and for half an hour the man saw no signs of any. And then it happened. At a place where there were no signs, where the soft, unbroken snow seemed to advertise solidity beneath, the man broke through. It was not deep. He wet himself halfway to the knees before he floundered out to the firm crust.

He was angry, and cursed his luck aloud. He had hoped to get into camp with the boys at six o'clock, and this would delay him an hour, for he would have to build a fire and dry out his footgear. This was imperative at that low temperature —he knew that much; and he turned aside to the bank, which he climbed. On top, tangled in the underbrush about the trunks of several small spruce trees, was a high-water deposit of dry firewood—sticks and twigs, principally, but also larger portions of seasoned branches and fine, dry, last year's grasses. He threw down several large pieces on top of the snow. This served for a foundation and prevented the young flame from drowning itself in the snow it otherwise would melt. The flame he got by touching a match to a small shred of birch bark that he took from his pocket. This burned even more readily than paper. Placing it on the foundation, he fed the young flame with wisps of dry grass and with the tiniest dry twigs.

He worked slowly and carefully, keenly aware of his danger. Gradually, as the flame grew stronger, he increased the size of the twigs with which he fed it. He squatted in the snow, pulling the twigs out from their entanglement in the brush and feeding directly to the flame. He knew there must be no failure. When it is seventy-five below zero, a man must not fail in his first attempt to build a fire — that is, if his feet are wet. If his feet are dry, and he fails, he can run along the trail for half a mile and restore his circulation. But the circulation of wet and freezing feet cannot be restored by running when it is seventy-five below. No matter how fast he runs, the wet feet will freeze the harder.

All this the man knew. The old-timer on Sulphur Creek had told him about it the previous fall, and now he was appreciating the advice. Already all sensation had gone out of his feet. To build the fire he had been forced to remove his mittens, and the fingers had quickly gone numb. His pace of four miles an hour had kept his heart pumping blood to the surface of his body and to all the extremities. But the instant he stopped, the action of the pump eased down. The cold of space smote the unprotected tip of the planet, and he, being on that unprotected tip, received the full force of the blow. The blood of his body recoiled before it. The blood was alive, like the dog, and like the dog it wanted to hide away and cover itself up from the fearful cold. So long as he walked four miles an hour, he pumped the blood, willy-nilly, to the surface; but now it ebbed away and sank down into the recesses of his body. The extremities were the first to feel its absence. His wet feet froze the faster, and his exposed fingers numbed the faster, though they had not yet begun to freeze. Nose and cheeks were already freezing, while the skin of all his body chilled as it lost its blood.

But he was safe. Toes and nose and cheeks would be only touched by the frost, for the fire was beginning to burn with strength. He was feeding it with twigs the size of his finger. In another minute he would be able to feed it with branches the size of his wrist, and then he could remove his wet footgear, and, while it dried, he could keep his naked feet warm by the fire, rubbing them at first, of course, with snow. The fire was a success. He was safe. He remembered the advice of the old-timer on Sulphur Creek, and smiled. The old-timer had been very serious in laying down the law that no man must travel alone in the Klondike after fifty below. Well, here he was; he had had the accident; he was alone; and he had saved himself. Those old-timers were rather womanish, some of them, he thought. All a man had to do was to keep his head, and he was all right. Any man who was a man could travel alone. But it was surprising, the rapidity with which his cheeks and nose were freezing. And he had not thought his fingers could go lifeless in so short a time. Lifeless they were, for he could scarcely make them move together to grip a twig, and they seemed remote from his body and from him. When he touched a twig, he had to look and see whether or not he had hold of it. The wires were pretty well down between him and his finger ends.

All of which counted for little. There was the fire, snapping and crackling and promising life with every dancing flame. He started to untie his moccasins. They were coated with ice; the thick German socks were like sheaths of iron halfway to the knees; and the moccasin strings were like rods of steel all twisted and knotted as by some conflagration. For a moment he tugged with his numb fingers, then, realizing the folly of it, he drew his sheath knife.

But before he could cut the strings, it happened. It was his own fault or, rather, his mistake. He should not have built the fire under the spruce tree. He should have built it in the open. But it had been easier to pull the twigs from the brush and drop them directly on the fire. Now the tree under which he had done this carried a weight of snow on its boughs. No wind had blown for weeks, and each bough was fully freighted. Each time he had pulled a twig he had communicated a slight agitation to the tree—an imperceptible agitation, so far as he was concerned, but an agitation sufficient to bring about the disaster. High up in the tree one bough capsized its load of snow. This fell on the boughs beneath, capsizing them. This process continued, spreading out and involving the whole tree. It grew like an avalanche, and it descended without warning upon the man and the fire, and the fire was blotted out! Where it had burned was a mantle of fresh and disordered snow.

The man was shocked. It was as though he had just heard his own sentence of death. For a moment he sat and stared at the spot where the fire had been. Then he grew very calm. Perhaps the old-timer on Sulphur Creek was right. If he had only had a trail mate he would have been in no danger now. The trail mate could have built the fire. Well, it was up to him to build the fire over again, and this second time there must be no failure. Even if he succeeded, he would most likely lose some toes. His feet must be badly frozen by now, and there would be some time before the second fire was ready.

Such were his thoughts, but he did not sit and think them. He was busy all the time they were passing through his mind. He made a new foundation for a fire, this time in the open, where no treacherous tree could blot it out. Next he gathered dry grasses and tiny twigs from the high-water flotsam. He could not bring his fingers together to pull them out, but he was able to gather them by the handful. In this way he got many rotten twigs and bits of green moss that were undesirable, but it was the best he could do. He worked methodically, even collecting an armful of the larger branches to be used later when the fire gathered strength. And all the while the dog sat and watched him, a certain yearning wistfulness in its eyes, for it looked upon him as the fire provider, and the fire was slow in coming.

When all was ready, the man reached in his pocket for a second piece of birch bark. He knew the bark was there, and, though he could not feel it with his fingers, he could hear its crisp rustling as he fumbled for it. Try as he would, he could not clutch hold of it. And all the time, in his consciousness, was the knowledge that each instant his feet were freezing. This thought tended to put him in a panic, but he fought against it and kept calm. He pulled on his mittens with his teeth, and threshed his arms back and forth, beating his hands with all his might against his sides. He did this sitting down, and he stood up to do it; and all the while the dog sat in the snow, its wolf brush of a tail curled around warmly over its forefeet, its sharp wolf ears pricked forward intently as it watched the man. And the man, as he beat and threshed with his arms and hands, felt a great surge of envy as he regarded the creature that was warm and secure in its natural covering.

After a time he was aware of the first faraway signals of sensations in his beaten fingers. The faint tingling grew stronger till it evolved into a stinging ache that was excruciating, but which the man hailed with satisfaction. He stripped the mitten from his right hand and fetched forth the birch bark. The exposed fingers were quickly going numb again. Next he brought out his bunch of sulphur matches. But the tremendous cold had already driven the life out of his fingers. In his effort to separate one match from the others, the whole bunch fell in the snow. He tried to pick it out of the snow, but failed. The dead fingers could neither touch nor clutch. He was very careful. He drove the thought of his freezing feet, and nose, and cheeks, out of his mind, devoting his whole soul to the matches. He watched, using the sense of vision in place of that of touch, and when he saw his fingers on each side the bunch, he closed them—that is, he willed to close them, for the wires were down, and the fingers did not obey. He pulled the mitten on the right hand, and beat it fiercely against his knee. Then, with both mittened hands, he scooped the bunch of matches, along with much snow, into his lap. Yet he was no better off.

After some manipulation he managed to get the bunch between the heels of his mittened hands. In this fashion he carried it to his mouth. The ice crackled and snapped when by a violent effort he opened his mouth. He drew the lower jaw in, curled the upper lip out of the way and scraped the bunch with his upper teeth in order to separate a match. He succeeded in getting one, which he dropped on his lap. He was no better off. He could not pick it up. Then he devised a way. He picked it up in his teeth and scratched it on his leg. Twenty times he scratched before he succeeded in lighting it. As it flamed he held it with his teeth to the birch bark. But the burning brimstone went up his nostrils and into his lungs, causing him to cough spasmodically. The match fell into the snow and went out.

The old-timer on Sulphur Creek was right, he thought in the moment of controlled despair that ensued: after fifty below, a man should travel with a partner. He beat his hands, but failed in exciting any sensation. Suddenly he bared both hands, removing the mittens with his teeth. He caught the whole bunch between the heels of his hands. His arm muscles not being frozen enabled him to press the hand heels tightly against the matches. Then he scratched the bunch along his leg. It flared into flame, seventy sulphur matches at once! There was no wind to blow them out. He kept his head to one side to escape the strangling fumes, and held the blazing bunch to the birch bark. As he so held it, he became aware of sensation in his hand. His flesh was burning. He could smell it. Deep down below the surface he could feel it. The sensation developed into pain that grew acute. And still he endured it, holding the flame of the matches clumsily to the bark that would not light readily because his own burning hands were in the way, absorbing most of the flame.

At last, when he could endure no more, he jerked his hands apart. The blazing matches fell sizzling into the snow, but the birch bark was alight. He began laying dry grasses and the tiniest twigs on the flame. He could not pick and choose, for he had to lift the fuel between the heels of his hands. Small pieces of rotten wood and green moss clung to the twigs, and he bit them off as well as he could with his teeth. He cherished the flame carefully and awkwardly. It meant life, and it must not perish. The withdrawal of blood from the surface of his body now made him begin to shiver, and he grew more awkward. A large piece of green moss fell squarely on the little fire. He tried to poke it out with his fingers, but his shivering frame made him poke too far, and he disrupted the nucleus of the little fire, the burning grasses and the tiny twigs separating and scattering. He tried to poke them together again, but in spite of the tenseness of the effort, his shivering got away with him, and the twigs were hopelessly scattered. Each twig gushed a puff of smoke and went out. The fire provider had failed. As he looked apathetically about him, his eyes chanced on the dog, sitting across the ruins of the fire from him, in the snow, making restless, hunching movements, slightly lifting one forefoot and then the other, shifting its weight back and forth on them with wistful eagerness.

The sight of the dog put a wild idea into his head. He remembered the tale of the man, caught in a blizzard, who killed a steer and crawled inside the carcass, and so was saved. He would kill the dog and bury his hands in the warm body until the numbness went out of them. Then he could build another fire. He spoke to the dog, calling it to him; but in his voice was a strange note of fear that frightened the animal, who had never known the man to speak in such way before. Something was the matter, and its suspicious nature sensed danger — it knew not what danger, but somewhere, somehow, in its brain arose an apprehension of the man. It flattened its ears down at the sound of the man's voice, and its restless, hunching movements and the liftings and shiftings of its forefeet became more pronounced; but it would not come to the man. He got on his hands and knees and crawled toward the dog. This unusual posture again excited suspicion, and the animal sidled mincingly away.

The man sat up in the snow for a moment and struggled for calmness. Then he pulled on his mittens, by means of his teeth, and got upon his feet. He glanced down at first in order to assure himself that he was really standing up, for the absence of sensation in his feet left him unrelated to the earth. His erect position in itself started to drive the webs of suspicion from the dog's mind; and when he spoke peremptorily, with the sound of whip lashes in his voice, the dog rendered its customary allegiance and came to him. As it came within reaching distance, the man lost his control. His arms flashed out to the dog, and he experienced genuine surprise when he discovered that his hands could not clutch, that there was neither bend nor feeling in the fingers. He had forgotten for the moment that they were frozen and that they were freezing more and more. All this happened quickly, and before the animal could get away, he encircled its body with his arms. He sat down in the snow, and in this fashion held the dog, while it snarled and whined and struggled.

But it was all he could do, hold its body encircled in his arms and sit there. He realized that he could not kill the dog. There was no way to do it. With his helpless hands he could neither draw nor hold his sheath knife nor throttle the animal. He released it, and it plunged wildly away, with tail between its legs, and still snarling. It halted forty feet away and surveyed him curiously, with ears sharply pricked forward.

The man looked down at his hands in order to locate them, and found them hanging on the ends of his arms. It struck him as curious that one should have to use his eyes in order to find out where his hands were. He began threshing his arms back and forth, beating the mittened hands against his sides. He did this for five minutes, violently, and his heart pumped enough blood up to the surface to put a stop to his shivering. But no sensation was aroused in the hands. He had an impression that they hung like weights on the ends of his arms, but when he tried to run the impression down, he could not find it.

A certain fear of death, dull and oppressive, came to him. This fear quickly became poignant as he realized that it was no longer a mere matter of freezing his fingers and toes, or of losing his hands and feet, but that it was a matter of life and death with the chances against him. This threw him into a panic, and he turned and ran up the creek bed along the old, dim trail. The dog joined in behind and kept up with him. He ran blindly, without intention, in fear such as he had never known in his life. Slowly, as he plowed and floundered through the snow, he began to see things again—the banks of the creek, the old timber jams, the leafless aspens, and the sky. The running made him feel better. He did not shiver. Maybe, if he ran on, his feet would thaw out; and, anyway, if he ran far enough, he would reach camp and the boys. Without doubt he would lose some fingers and toes and some of his face; but the boys would take care of him, and save the rest of him when he got there. And at the same time there was another thought in his mind that said he would never get to the camp and the boys; that he would soon be stiff and dead. This thought he kept in the background and refused to consider. Sometimes it pushed itself forward and demanded to be heard, but he thrust it back and strove to think of other things.

It struck him as curious that he could run at all on feet so frozen that he could not feel them when they struck the earth and took the weight of his body. He seemed to himself to skim along above the surface, and to have no connection with the earth. Somewhere he had once seen a winged Mercury, and he wondered if Mercury felt as he felt when skimming over the earth.

His theory of running until he reached camp and the boys had one flaw in it: he lacked the endurance. Several times he stumbled, and finally he tottered, crumpled up, and fell. When he tried to rise, he failed. He must sit and rest, he decided, and next time he would merely walk and keep on going. As he sat and regained his breath, he noted that he was feeling quite warm and comfortable. He was not shivering, and it even seemed that a warm glow had come to his chest and trunk. And yet, when he touched his nose or cheeks, there was no sensation. Running would not thaw them out. Nor would it thaw out his hands and feet. Then the thought came to him that the frozen portions of his body must be extending. He tried to keep this thought down, to forget it, to think of something else; he was aware of the panicky feeling that it caused, and he was afraid of the panic. But the thought asserted itself, and persisted, until it produced a vision of his body totally frozen. This was too much, and he made another wild run along the trail. Once he slowed down to a walk, but the thought of the freezing extending itself made him run again.

And all the time the dog ran with him, at his heels. When he fell down a second time, it curled its tail over its forefeet and sat in front of him, facing him, curiously eager and intent. The warmth and security of the animal angered him, and he cursed it till it flattened down its ears appeasingly. This time the shivering came more quickly upon the man. He was losing in his battle with the frost. It was creeping into his body from all sides. The thought of it drove him on, but he ran no more than a hundred feet, when he staggered and pitched headlong. It was his last panic. When he had recovered his breath and control, he sat up and entertained in his mind the conception of meeting death with dignity. However, the conception did not come to him in such terms. His idea of it was that he had been making a fool of himself, running around like a chicken with its head cut off—such was the simile that occurred to him. Well, he was bound to freeze anyway, and he might as well take it decently. With this newfound peace of mind came the first glimmerings of drowsiness. A good idea, he thought, to sleep off to death. It was like taking an anesthetic. Freezing was not so bad as people thought. There were lots worse way to die.

He pictured the boys finding his body next day. Suddenly he found himself with them, coming along the trail and looking for himself. And, still with them, he came around a turn in the trail and found himself lying in the snow. He did not belong with himself any more, for even then he was out of himself, standing with the boys and looking at himself in the snow. It certainly was cold, was his thought. When he got back to the States he could tell the folks what real cold was. He drifted on from this to a vision of the old-timer on Sulphur Creek. He could see him quite clearly, warm and comfortable, and smoking a pipe.

"You were right, old hoss; you were right," the man mumbled to the old-timer of Sulphur Creek.

Then the man drowsed off into what seemed to him the most comfortable and satisfying sleep he had ever known. The dog sat facing him and waiting. The brief day drew to a close in a long, slow twilight. There were no signs of a fire to be made, and, besides, never in the dog's experience had it known a man to sit like that in the snow and make no fire. As the twilight drew on, its eager yearning for the fire mastered it, and with a great lifting and shifting of forefeet, it whined softly, then flattened its ears down in anticipation of being chidden by the man. But the man remained silent. Later the dog whined loudly. And still later it crept close to the man and caught the scent of death. This made the animal bristle and back away. A little longer it delayed, howling under the stars that leaped and danced and shone brightly in the cold sky. Then it turned and trotted up the trail in the direction of the camp it knew, where were the other food providers and fire providers.

[1908]

Study and Writing Questions

1. How do the descriptions of nature comment on the place of the main CHARAC-
   TER in nature? In what way do repeated elements, like descriptions of the creek, and repeated phrases, like "cold of space," enter into our understanding of this issue? To what extent is the main character a representative human and to what extent an individual in his relation to nature?
2. How does the choice of VIEWPOINT enter into your understanding of this STORY? How would the NARRATIVE have been different if, for example, it had been a FIRST PERSON NARRATION limited to the consciousness of the man?
3. What is the relationship between the man and the dog? between humans and dogs? To what extent is this a political ALLEGORY?
4. In what way(s) is the old-timer at Sulphur Creek important? What does he

initially represent to the man? What does he come to represent? What else might he represent to us?

5. In the third paragraph, the OMNISCIENT NARRATOR says that "the trouble with [the man] was that he was without imagination. He was quick and alert in the things of life, but only in the things, and not in the significances." What kind(s) of significance might be meant? How does the narrative show or fail to show this statement to be true? To what extent is this narrative an allegory of human imagination?

See also Questions for Contrast and Comparison: 5, 43, 68, 72, 79, 100, and 233.

■ **BERNARD MALAMUD** (1914–1986), *often considered the leading Jewish-American writer of his generation, was born in Brooklyn, New York, to Russian immigrants who ran a "mom-and-pop" grocery store. He first published in the literary magazine of Brooklyn's Erasmus Hall High School. After earning degrees from New York's City College (B.A., 1936) and Columbia University (M.A., 1942; thesis on Thomas Hardy), he married (1945) an Italian-American with whom he had two children. He taught at Erasmus (1940–1949), Oregon State University (1949–1961), and Vermont's Bennington College (1961–1986) and lectured all over the world. Throughout his career, Malamud focused on the experiences of minorities—Jews, Italians, blacks, and others. His first* NOVEL, *The Natural (1952), is an ironic exploration of American culture that mixes baseball and* MYTHOLOGY. *The Assistant (1957) portrays the title character's striving for the good life while working in a small grocery. The Magic Barrel (1958; National Book Award), collects both fantastic and realistic stories. The Fixer (1967; National Book Award and Pulitzer Prize), dramatizes a 1913 Russian case of a falsely imprisoned Jew whose spirit—and that of all Jews—authorities try to break. Malamud published five more acclaimed story collections and four more novels, including A New Life (1961), a witty satire of the life of a New York Jewish professor at a Pacific Northwest "cow college."*

The German Refugee

Oskar Gassner sits in his cotton-mesh undershirt and summer bathrobe at the window of his stuffy, hot, dark hotel room on West Tenth Street as I cautiously knock. Outside, across the sky, a late-June green twilight fades in darkness. The refugee fumbles for the light and stares at me, hiding despair but not pain.

I was in those days a poor student and would brashly attempt to teach anybody anything for a buck an hour, although I have since learned better. Mostly I gave English lessons to recently arrived refugees. The college sent me, I had acquired a little experience. Already a few of my students were trying their broken English, theirs and mine, in the American marketplace. I was then just twenty, on my way into my senior year in college, a skinny, life-hungry kid, eating himself waiting for the next world war to start. It was a miserable cheat. Here I was panting to get going, and across the ocean Adolf Hitler, in black boots and a square mustache, was tearing up and spitting at all the flowers. Will I ever forget what went on with Danzig that summer?

Times were still hard from the Depression but I made a little living from the poor refugees. They were all over uptown Broadway in 1939. I had four I tutored—Karl Otto Alp, the former film star; Wolfgang Novak, once a brilliant economist; Friedrich Wilhelm Wolff, who had taught medieval history at Heidelberg; and after the night I met him in his disordered cheap hotel room, Oskar Gassner, the Berlin critic and journalist, at one time on the *Acht Uhr Abendblatt*. They were accomplished men. I had my nerve associating with them, but that's what a world crisis does for people, they get educated.

Oskar was maybe fifty, his thick hair turning gray. He had a big face and heavy hands. His shoulders sagged. His eyes, too, were heavy, a clouded blue; and as he stared at me after I had identified myself, doubt spread in them like underwater currents. It was as if, on seeing me, he had again been defeated. I had to wait until he came to. I stayed at the door in silence. In such cases I would rather be elsewhere, but I had to make a living. Finally he opened the door and I entered. Rather, he released it and I was in. "Bitte" — he offered me a seat and didn't know where to sit himself. He would attempt to say something and then stop, as though it could not possibly be said. The room was cluttered with clothing, boxes of books he had managed to get out of Germany, and some paintings. Oskar sat on a box and attempted to fan himself with his meaty hand. "Zis heat," he muttered, forcing his mind to the deed. "Impozzible. I do not know such heat." It was bad enough for me but terrible for him. He had difficulty breathing. He tried to speak, lifted a hand, and let it drop. He breathed as though he was fighting a war; and maybe he won because after ten minutes we sat and slowly talked.

Like most educated Germans Oskar had at one time studied English. Although he was certain he couldn't say a word he managed to put together a fairly decent, if sometimes comical English sentence. He misplaced consonants, mixed up nouns and verbs, and mangled idioms, yet we were able at once to communicate. We conversed in English, with an occasional assist by me in pidgin-German or Yiddish, what he called "Jiddish." He had been to America before, last year for a short visit. He had come a month before Kristallnacht, when the Nazis shattered the Jewish store windows and burnt all the synagogues, to see if he could find a job for himself; he had no relatives in America and getting a job would permit him quickly to enter the country. He had been promised something, not in journalism, but with the help of a foundation, as a lecturer. Then he returned to Berlin, and after a frightening delay of six months was permitted to emigrate. He had sold whatever he could, managed to get some paintings, gifts of Bauhaus friends, and some boxes of books out by bribing two Dutch border guards; he had said goodbye to his wife and left the accursed country. He gazed at me with cloudy eyes. "We parted amicably," he said in German, "my wife was gentile. Her mother was an appalling anti-Semite. They returned to live in Stettin." I asked no questions. Gentile is gentile, Germany is Germany.

His new job was in the Institute for Public Studies, in New York. He was to give a lecture a week in the fall term and during next spring, a course, in English translation, in "The Literature of the Weimar Republic." He had never taught before and was afraid to. He was in that way to be introduced to the public, but the thought of giving the lecture in English just about paralyzed him. He didn't see how he could do it. "How is it pozzible? I cannot say two words. I cannot pronounziate. I will make a fool of myself." His melancholy deepened. Already in the two months since his arrival, and a round of diminishingly expensive hotel rooms, he had had two English tutors, and I was the third. The others had given him up, he said, because his progress was so poor, and he thought he also depressed them. He asked me whether I felt I could do something for him, or should he go to a speech specialist, someone, say, who charged five dollars an hour, and beg his assistance? "You could try him," I said, "and then come back to me." In those days I figured what I knew, I knew. At that he managed a smile. Still, I wanted him to make up his mind or it would be no confidence down the line. He said, after a while, he would stay with me. If he went to the five-dollar professor it might help his tongue but not his appetite. He would have no money left to eat with. The Institute had paid him in advance for the summer, but it was only three hundred dollars and all he had.

He looked at me dully. "Ich weiss nicht, wie ich weiter machen soll."

I figured it was time to move past the first step. Either we did that quickly or it would be like drilling rock for a long time.

"Let's stand at the mirror," I said.

He rose with a sigh and stood there beside me, I thin, elongated, red-headed, praying for success, his and mine; Oskar uneasy, fearful, finding it hard to face either of us in the faded round glass above his dresser.

"Please," I said to him, "could you say 'right'?"

"Ghight," he gargled.

"No — right. You put your tongue here." I showed him where as he tensely watched the mirror. I tensely watched him. "The tip of it curls behind the ridge on top, like this."

He placed his tongue where I showed him.

"Please," I said, "now say right."

Oskar's tongue fluttered. "Rright."

"That's good. Now say 'treasure' — that's harder."

"Tgheasure."

"The tongue goes up in front, not in the back of the mouth. Look."

He tried, his brow wet, eyes straining, "Trreasure."

"That's it."

"A miracle," Oskar murmured.

I said if he had done that he could do the rest.

We went for a bus ride up Fifth Avenue and then walked for a while around Central Park Lake. He had put on his German hat, with its hatband bow at the back, a broad-lapeled wool suit, a necktie twice as wide as the one I was wearing, and walked with a small-footed waddle. The night wasn't bad, it had got a bit cooler. There were a few large stars in the sky and they made me sad.

"Do you sink I will succezz?"

"Why not?" I asked.

Later he bought me a bottle of beer.

To many of these people, articulate as they were, the great loss was the loss of language — that they could not say what was in them to say. You have some subtle thought and it comes out like a piece of broken bottle. They could, of course, manage to communicate, but just to communicate was frustrating. As Karl Otto Alp, the ex-film star who became a buyer for Macy's, put it years later, "I felt like a child, or worse, often like a moron. I am left with myself unexpressed. What I know, indeed, what I am, becomes to me a burden. My tongue hangs useless." The same with Oskar it figures. There was a terrible sense of useless tongue, and I think the reason for his trouble with his other tutors was that to keep from drowning in things unsaid he wanted to swallow the ocean in a gulp: today he would learn English and tomorrow wow them with an impeccable Fourth of July speech, followed by a successful lecture at the Institute for Public Studies.

We performed our lessons slowly, step by step, everything in its place. After Oskar moved to a two-room apartment in a house on West Eighty-fifth Street, near the Drive, we met three times a week at four-thirty, worked an hour and a half, then, since it was too hot to cook, had supper at the Seventy-second Street Automat and conversed on my time. The lessons we divided into three parts: diction exercises and reading aloud; then grammar, because Oskar felt the necessity of it, and composition correction; with conversation, as I said, thrown in at supper. So far as I could see he was coming along. None of these exercises was giving him as much trouble as they apparently had in the past. He seemed to be learning and his mood lightened. There were moments of elation as he heard his accent flying off. For instance when sink became think. He stopped calling himself "hopelezz," and I became his "bezt teacher," a little joke I liked.

Neither of us said much about the lecture he had to give early in October, and I kept my fingers crossed. It was somehow to come out of what we were doing daily, I think I felt, but exactly how, I had no idea; and to tell the truth, though I didn't say so to Oskar, the lecture frightened me. That and the ten more to follow during the fall term. Later, when I learned that he had been attempting, with the help of the dictionary, to write in English and had produced "a complete disahster," I suggested maybe he ought to stick to German and we could afterwards both try to put it into passable English. I was cheating when I said that because my German is meager, enough to read simple stuff but certainly not good enough for serious translation; anyway, the idea was to get Oskar into production and worry about translating later. He sweated with it, from enervating morning to exhausted night, but no matter what language he tried, though he had been a professional writer for a generation and knew his subject cold, the lecture refused to move past page one.

It was a sticky, hot July, and the heat didn't help at all.

I had met Oskar at the end of June, and by the seventeenth of July we were no longer doing lessons. They had foundered on the "impozzible" lecture. He had worked on it each day in frenzy and growing despair. After writing more than a hundred opening pages he furiously flung his pen against the wall, shouting he could not longer write in that filthy tongue. He cursed the German language. He hated the damned country and the damned people. After that, what was bad became worse. When he gave up attempting to write the lecture, he stopped making progress in English. He seemed to forget what he already knew. His tongue thickened and the accent returned in all its fruitiness. The little he had to say was in handcuffed and tortured English. The only German I heard him speak was in a whisper to himself. I doubt he knew he was talking it. That ended our formal work together, though I did drop in every other day or so to sit with him. For hours he sat motionless in a large green velour armchair, hot enough to broil in, and through tall windows stared at the colorless sky above Eighty-fifth Street with a wet depressed eye.

Then once he said to me, "If I do not this legture prepare, I will take my life."

"Let's begin, Oskar," I said. "You dictate and I'll write. The ideas count, not the spelling."

He didn't answer so I stopped talking.

He had plunged into an involved melancholy. We sat for hours, often in profound silence. This was alarming to me, though I had already had some experience with such depression. Wolfgang Novak, the economist, though English came more easily to him, was another. His problems arose mainly, I think, from physical illness. And he felt a greater sense of the lost country than Oskar. Sometimes in the early evening I persuaded Oskar to come with me for a short walk on the Drive. The tail end of sunsets over the Palisades seemed to appeal to him. At least he looked. He would put on full regalia—hat, suit coat, tie, no matter how hot or what I suggested—and we went slowly down the stairs, I wondering whether he would make it to the bottom.

We walked slowly uptown, stopping to sit on a bench and watch night rise above the Hudson. When we returned to his room, if I sensed he had loosened up a bit, we listened to music on the radio; but if I tried to sneak in a news broadcast, he said to me, "Please, I cannot more stand of world misery." I shut off the radio. He was right, it was a time of no good news. I squeezed my brain. What could I tell him? Was it good news to be alive? Who could argue the point? Sometimes I read aloud to him—I remember he liked the first part of Life on the Mississippi. We still went to the Automat once or twice a week, he perhaps out of habit, because he didn't feel like going anywhere—I to get him out of his room. Oskar ate little, he toyed with a spoon. His eyes looked as though they had been squirted with a dark dye.

Once after a momentary cooling rainstorm we sat on newspapers on a wet bench overlooking the river and Oskar at last began to talk. In tormented English he conveyed his intense and everlasting hatred of the Nazis for destroying his career, uprooting his life, and flinging him like a piece of bleeding meat to the hawks. He cursed them thickly, the German nation, an inhuman, conscienceless, merciless people. "They are pigs mazquerading as peacogs," he said. "I feel certain that my wife, in her heart, was a Jew hater." It was a terrible bitterness, and eloquence beyond the words he spoke. He became silent again. I wanted to hear more about his wife but decided not to ask.

Afterwards in the dark, Oskar confessed that he had attempted suicide during his first week in America. He was living, at the end of May, in a small hotel, and had one night filled himself with barbiturates; but his phone had fallen off the table and the hotel operator had sent up the elevator boy, who found him unconscious and called the police. He was revived in the hospital.

"I did not mean to do it," he said, "it was a mistage."

"Don't ever think of it," I said, "it's total defeat."

"I don't," he said wearily, "because it is so arduouz to come bag to life."

"Please, for any reason whatever."

Afterwards when we were walking, he surprised me by saying, "Maybe we ought to try now the legture onze more."

We trudged back to the house and he sat at his hot desk, I trying to read as he slowly began to reconstruct the first page of his lecture. He wrote, of course, in German.

He got nowhere. We were back to sitting in silence in the heat. Sometimes, after a few minutes, I had to take off before his mood overcame mine. One afternoon I came unwillingly up the stairs—there were times I felt momentary surges of irritation with him—and was frightened to find Oskar's door ajar. When I knocked no one answered. As I stood there, chilled down the spine, I realized I was thinking about the possibility of his attempting suicide again.

"Oskar?" I went into the apartment, looked into both rooms and the bathroom, but he wasn't there. I thought he might have drifted out to get something from a store and took the opportunity to look quickly around. There was nothing startling in the medicine chest, no pills but aspirin, no iodine. Thinking, for some reason, of a gun, I searched his desk drawer. In it I found a thin-paper airmail letter from Germany. Even if I had wanted to, I couldn't read the handwriting, but as I held it in my hand I did make out a sentence: "Ich bin dir siebenundzwanzig Jahre treu gewesen." There was no gun in the drawer. I shut it and stopped looking. It had occurred to me if you want to kill yourself all you need is a straight pin. When Oskar returned he said he had been sitting in the public library, unable to read.

Now we are once more enacting the changeless scene, curtain rising on two speechless characters in a furnished apartment, I in a straight-back chair, Oskar in the velour armchair that smothered rather than supported him, his flesh gray, the big gray face unfocused, sagging. I reached over to switch on the radio but he barely looked at me in a way that begged no. I then got up to leave but Oskar, clearing his throat, thickly asked me to stay. I stayed, thinking, was there more to this than I could see into? His problems, God knows, were real enough, but could there be something more than a refugee's displacement, alienation, financial insecurity, being in a strange land without friends or a speakable tongue? My speculation was the old one: not all drown in this ocean, why does he? After a while I shaped the thought and asked him was there something below the surface, invisible? I was full of this thing from college, and wondered if there mightn't be some unknown quantity in his depression that a psychiatrist maybe might help him with, enough to get him started on his lecture.

He meditated on this and after a few minutes haltingly said he had been psychoanalyzed in Vienna as a young man. "Just the jusual drek," he said, "fears and fantazies that afterwaards no longer bothered me."

"They don't now?"

"Not."

"You've written many articles and lectures before," I said. "What I can't understand, though I know how hard the situation is, is why you can never get past page one."

He half lifted his hand. "It is a paralyzis of my will. The whole legture is clear in my mind, but the minute I write down a single word — or in English or in German — I have a terrible fear I will not be able to write the negst. As though someone has thrown a stone at a window and the whole house — the whole idea zmashes. This repeats, until I am dezperate."

He said the fear grew as he worked that he would die before he completed the lecture, or if not that, he would write it so disgracefully he would wish for death. The fear immobilized him.

"I have lozt faith. I do not — not longer possezz my former value of myself. In my life there has been too much illusion."

I tried to believe what I was saying: "Have confidence, the feeling will pass."

"Confidenze I have not. For this and alzo whatever elze I have lozt I thank the Nazis."

It was by then mid-August and things were growing steadily worse wherever one looked. The Poles were mobilizing for war. Oskar hardly moved. I was full of worries though I pretended calm weather.

He sat in his massive armchair, breathing like a wounded animal.

"Who can write about Walt Whitman in such terrible times?"

"Why don't you change the subject?"

"It mages no differenze what is the subject. It is all uzelezz."

I came every day, as a friend, neglecting my other students and therefore my livelihood. I had a panicky feeling that if things went on as they were going they would end in Oskar's suicide; and I felt a frenzied desire to prevent that. What's more, I was sometimes afraid I was myself becoming melancholy, a new talent, call it, of taking less pleasure in my little pleasures. And the heat continued, oppressive, relentless. We thought of escape into the country, but neither of us had the money. One day I bought Oskar a secondhand electric fan—wondering why we hadn't thought of that before—and he sat in the breeze for hours each day, until after a week, shortly after the Soviet-Nazi non-aggression pact was signed, the motor gave out. He could not sleep at night and sat at his desk with a wet towel on his head, still attempting to write the lecture. He wrote reams on a treadmill, it came out nothing. When he slept in exhaustion he had fantastic frightening dreams of the Nazis inflicting torture, sometimes forcing him to look upon the corpses of those they had slain. In one dream he told me about he had gone back to Germany to visit his wife. She wasn't home and he had been directed to a cemetery. There, though the tombstone read another name, her blood seeped out of the earth above her shallow grave. He groaned aloud at the memory.

Afterwards he told me something about her. They had met as students, lived together, and were married at twenty-three. It wasn't a very happy marriage. She had turned into a sickly woman, unable to have children. "Something was wrong with her interior strugture."

Though I asked no questions, Oskar said, "I offered her to come with me here, but she refused this."

"For what reason?"

"She did not think I wished her to come."

"Did you?" I asked.

"Not," he said.

He explained he had lived with her for almost twenty-seven years under difficult circumstances. She had been ambivalent about their Jewish friends and his relatives, though outwardly she seemed not a prejudiced person. But her mother was always a dreadful anti-Semite.

"I have nothing to blame myzelf," Oskar said.

He took to his bed. I took to the New York Public Library. I read some of the German poets he was trying to write about, in English translation. Then I read *Leaves of Grass* and wrote down what I thought one or two of them had got from Whitman. One day, toward the end of August, I brought Oskar what I had written. It was in good part guessing, but my idea wasn't to do the lecture for him. He lay on his back, motionless, and listened sadly to what I had written. Then he said, no, it wasn't the love of death they had got from Whitman—that ran through German poetry — but it was most of all his feeling for Brudermensch, his humanity.

"But this does not grow long on German earth," he said, "and is soon deztroyed."

I said I was sorry I had got it wrong, but he thanked me anyway.

I left, defeated, and as I was going down the stairs, heard the sound of sobbing. I will quit this, I thought, it has got to be too much for me. I can't drown with him.

I stayed home the next day, tasting a new kind of private misery too old for somebody my age, but that same night Oskar called me on the phone, blessing me wildly for having read those notes to him. He had got up to write me a letter to say what I had missed, and it ended in his having written half the lecture. He had slept all day and tonight intended to finish it up.

"I thank you," he said, "for much, alzo including your faith in me."

"Thank God," I said, not telling him I had just about lost it.

Oskar completed his lecture — wrote and rewrote it — during the first week in September. The Nazis had invaded Poland, and though we were greatly troubled, there was some sense of release; maybe the brave Poles would beat them. It took another week to translate the lecture, but here we had the assistance of Friedrich Wilhelm Wolff, the historian, a gentle, erudite man, who liked translating and promised his help with future lectures. We then had about two weeks to work on Oskar's delivery. The weather had changed, and so, slowly, had he. He had awakened from defeat, battered, after a wearying battle. He had lost close to twenty pounds. His complexion was still gray; when I looked at his face I expected to see scars, but it had lost its flabby unfocused quality. His blue eyes had returned to life and he walked with quick steps, as though to pick up a few for all the steps he hadn't taken during those long hot days he had lain in his room.

We went back to our former routine, meeting three late afternoons a week for diction, grammar, and the other exercises. I taught him the phonetic alphabet and transcribed lists of words he was mispronouncing. He worked many hours trying to fit each sound in place, holding a matchstick between his teeth to keep his jaws apart as he exercised his tongue. All this can be a dreadfully boring business unless you think you have a future. Looking at him, I realized what's meant when somebody is called "another man."

The lecture, which I now knew by heart, went off well. The director of the Institute had invited a number of prominent people. Oskar was the first refugee they had employed, and there was a move to make the public cognizant of what was then a new ingredient in American life. Two reporters had come with a lady photographer. The auditorium of the Institute was crowded. I sat in the last row, promising to put up my hand if he couldn't be heard, but it wasn't necessary. Oskar, in a blue suit, his hair cut, was of course nervous, but you couldn't see it unless you studied him. When he stepped up to the lectern, spread out his manuscript, and spoke his first English sentence in public, my heart hesitated; only he and I, of everybody there, had any idea of the anguish he had been through. His enunciation wasn't at all bad — a few s's for th's, and he once said bag for back, but otherwise he did all right. He read poetry well — in both languages — and though Walt Whitman, in his mouth, sounded a little as though he had come to the shores of Long Island as a German immigrant, still the poetry read as poetry:

> *And I know the Spirit of God is the brother of my own,*
> *And that all the men ever born are also my brothers,*
>   *and the women my sisters and lovers,*
> *And that the kelson of creation is love . . .*

Oskar read it as though he believed it. Warsaw had fallen, but the verses were somehow protective. I sat back conscious of two things: how easy it is to hide the deepest wounds; and the pride I felt in the job I had done.

Two days later I came up the stairs into Oskar's apartment to find a crowd there. The refugee, his face beet-red, lips bluish, a trace of froth in the corners of his mouth, lay on the floor in his limp pajamas, two firemen on their knees working over him with an inhalator. The windows were open and the air stank.

A policeman asked me who I was and I couldn't answer.

"No, oh no."

I said no but it was unchangeably yes. He had taken his life — gas — I hadn't even thought of the stove in the kitchen.

"Why?" I asked myself. "Why did he do it?" Maybe it was the fate of Poland on top of everything else, but the only answer anyone could come up with was Oskar's scribbled note that he wasn't well, and had left Martin Goldberg all his possessions. I am Martin Goldberg.

I was sick for a week, had no desire either to inherit or investigate, but I thought I ought to look through his things before the court impounded them, so I spent a morning sitting in the depths of Oskar's armchair, trying to read his correspondence. I had found in the top drawer a thin packet of letters from his wife and an airmail letter of recent date from his mother-in-law.

She writes in a tight script it takes me hours to decipher, that her daughter, after Oskar abandons her, against her own mother's fervent pleas and anguish, is converted to Judaism by a vengeful rabbi. One night the Brown Shirts appear, and though the mother wildly waves her bronze crucifix in their faces, they drag Frau Gassner, together with the other Jews, out of the apartment house, and transport them in lorries to a small border town in conquered Poland. There, it is rumored, she is shot in the head and topples into an open ditch with the naked Jewish men, their wives and children, some Polish soldiers, and a handful of gypsies.

[1963]

Study and Writing Questions

1. What is the importance of education in this STORY? What does it mean to acquire education? to impart it? How does the personal importance of education vary according to age or situation?
2. What is the importance of language to Oskar? to Martin? What is the importance of poetry? Why does the story contain the precise passage of poetry that it does? What is the importance of the eloquence of this story to Martin? to you?

3. Why is the story set in the past? How do the public historical events resonate with, reflect, or cause the story's private events? To what extent do the historical circumstances of this story make it unique and to what extent can we find general meaning in it?
4. What does Oskar's wife represent to him? Does her importance change through time? To what extent is her fate the cause of his final action? (Note: the German sentence Martin reads from a letter while Oskar is at the library says, "I have been true to you for twenty-seven years.")
5. What is the relationship of the NARRATOR with "recently arrived refugees"? Why is the story called "The German Refugee" and not, say, "The Jewish Refugee" or "The Jewish Immigrant"? From what does Oskar seek refuge? From what, if anything, does Martin seek refuge? In what way(s) can this be thought of as Martin's story?

See also Questions for Contrast and Comparison: 11, 63, 67, 70, 101, 104, 105, 205, 217, 219, 227, and 239.

KATHERINE MANSFIELD (1888–1923) *was born Kathleen Mansfield Beauchamp in Wellington, New Zealand, daughter of a wealthy business-man. Mansfield persuaded her father to support her in London, England, where she studied at Queens College (1903–1906). After a return to New Zealand (1906–1908), she made London her base for the rest of her restless, bohemian life. As a child, she enjoyed solitary occupations, particularly writing, music, and playing with dolls, but from youth on seems always to have been attracted to both men and women. When her first fiancé's family rejected her, she impetuously married a recent acquaintance, but ran away on her wedding night to the solace of Ida Constance Baker (known as L.M.), her friend from college days until Mansfield's death. Mansfield quickly divorced, seems to have had an abortion, and was unsuccessfully "treated for lesbianism." In 1912 she began a relationship with the critic John Middleton Murry, whom she married after his divorce (1918). Her widely praised stories, published in three volumes in her life and two thereafter, are considered the first Chekovian writing in English. She was deeply influenced by ambivalent friendships with D. H. Lawrence and Virginia Woolf. She envied Woolf for her fixed home and was envied by Woolf for her clarity and simplicity of plot and expression. Tuberculous from 1916 on, Mansfield died in the sanitarium of G. I. Gurdjieff, the Armenian mystic.*

The Doll's House

When dear old Mrs. Hay went back to town after staying with the Burnells she sent the children a doll's house. It was so big that the carter and Pat carried it into the courtyard, and there it stayed, propped up on two wooden boxes beside the feed-room door. No harm could come of it; it was summer. And perhaps the smell of paint would have gone off by the time it had to be taken in. For, really, the smell of paint coming from that doll's house ("Sweet of old Mrs. Hay, of course; most sweet and generous!")—but the smell of paint was quite enough to make any one seriously ill, in Aunt Beryl's opinion. Even before the sacking was taken off. And when it was. . . .

There stood the doll's house, a dark, oily, spinach green, picked out with bright yellow. Its two solid little chimneys, glued on to the roof, were painted red and white, and the door, gleaming with yellow varnish, was like a little slab of toffee. Four windows, real windows, were divided into panes by a broad streak of green. There was actually a tiny porch, too, painted yellow, with big lumps of congealed paint hanging along the edge.

But perfect, perfect little house! Who could possibly mind the smell? It was part of the joy, part of the newness.

"Open it quickly, some one!"

The hook at the side was stuck fast. Pat pried it open with his penknife, and the whole house-front swung back, and—there you were, gazing at one and the same moment into the drawing-room and dining-room, the kitchen and two bedrooms. That is the way for a house to open! Why don't all houses open like that? How much more exciting than peering through the slit of a door into a mean little hall with a hatstand and two umbrellas! That is—isn't it?—what you long to know about a house when you put your hand on the knocker. Perhaps it is the way God opens houses at dead of night when He is taking a quiet turn with an angel. . . .

"O-oh!" The Burnell children sounded as though they were in despair. It was too marvelous; it was too much for them. They had never seen anything like it in their lives. All the rooms were papered. There were pictures on the walls, painted on the paper, with gold frames complete. Red carpet covered all the floors except the kitchen; red plush chairs in the drawing-room, green in the dining-room; tables, beds with real bedclothes, a cradle, a stove, a dresser with tiny plates and one big jug. But what Kezia liked more than anything, what she liked frightfully, was the lamp. It stood in the middle of the dining-room table, an exquisite little amber lamp with a white globe. It was even filled all ready for lighting, though, of course, you couldn't light it. But there was something inside that looked like oil, and that moved when you shook it.

The father and mother dolls, who sprawled very stiff as though they had fainted in the drawing-room, and their two little children asleep upstairs, were really too big for the doll's house. They didn't look as though they belonged. But the lamp was perfect. It seemed to smile at Kezia, to say, "I live here." The lamp was real.

The Burnell children could hardly walk to school fast enough the next morning. They burned to tell everybody, to describe, to — well — to boast about their doll's house before the school-bell rang.

"I'm to tell," said Isabel, "because I'm the eldest. And you two can join in after. But I'm to tell first."

There was nothing to answer. Isabel was bossy, but she was always right, and Lottie and Kezia knew too well the powers that went with being eldest. They brushed through the thick buttercups at the road edge and said nothing.

"And I'm to choose who's to come and see it first. Mother said I might."

For it had been arranged that while the doll's house stood in the courtyard they might ask the girls at school, two at a time, to come and look. Not to stay to tea, of course, or to come traipsing through the house. But just to stand quietly in the courtyard while Isabel pointed out the beauties, and Lottie and Kezia looked pleased. . . .

But hurry as they might, by the time they had reached the tarred palings of the boys' playground the bell had begun to jangle. They only just had time to whip off their hats and fall into line before the roll was called. Never mind. Isabel tried to make up for it by looking very important and mysterious and by whispering behind her hand to the girls near her, "Got something to tell you at playtime."

Playtime came and Isabel was surrounded. The girls of her class nearly fought to put their arms round her, to walk away with her, to beam flatteringly, to be her special friend. She held quite a court under the huge pine trees at the side of the playground. Nudging, giggling together, the little girls pressed up close. And the only two who stayed outside the ring were the two who were always outside, the little Kelveys. They knew better than to come anywhere near the Burnells.

For the fact was, the school the Burnell children went to was not at all the kind of place their parents would have chosen if there had been any choice. But there was none. It was the only school for miles. And the consequence was all the children in the neighbourhood, the Judge's little girls, the doctor's daughters, the storekeeper's children, the milkman's, were forced to mix together. Not to speak of there being an equal number of rude, rough little boys as well. But the line had to be drawn somewhere. It was drawn at the Kelveys. Many of the children, including the Burnells, were not allowed even to speak to them. They walked past the Kelveys with their heads in the air, and as they set the fashion in all matters of behaviour, the Kelveys were shunned by everybody. Even the teacher had a special voice for them, and a special smile for the other children when Lil Kelvey came up to her desk with a bunch of dreadfully common-looking flowers.

They were the daughters of a spry, hardworking little washerwoman, who went about from house to house by the day. This was awful enough. But where was Mr. Kelvey? Nobody knew for certain. But everybody said he was in prison. So they were the daughters of a washerwoman and a gaolbird. Very nice company for other people's children! And they looked it. Why Mrs. Kelvey made them so conspicuous was hard to understand. The truth was they were dressed in "bits" given to her by the people for whom she worked. Lil, for instance, who was a stout, plain child, with big freckles, came to school in a dress made from a green art-serge table-cloth of the Burnells', with red plush sleeves from the Logans' curtains. Her hat, perched on top of her high forehead, was a grown-up woman's hat, once the property of Miss Lecky, the postmistress. It was turned up at the back and trimmed with a large scarlet quill. What a little guy she looked! It was impossible not to laugh. And her little sister, our Else, wore a long white dress, rather like a nightgown, and a pair of little boy's boots. But whatever our Else wore she would have looked strange. She was a tiny wishbone of a child, with cropped hair and enormous solemn eyes—a little white owl. Nobody had ever seen her smile; she scarcely ever spoke. She went through life holding on to Lil, with a piece of Lil's skirt screwed up in her hand. Where Lil went our Else followed. In the playground, on the road going to and from school, there was Lil marching in front and our Else holding on behind. Only when she wanted anything, or when she was out of breath, our Else gave Lil a tug, a twitch, and Lil stopped and turned round. The Kelveys never failed to understand each other.

Now they hovered at the edge; you couldn't stop them listening. When the little girls turned round and sneered, Lil, as usual, gave her silly, shamefaced smile, but our Else only looked.

And Isabel's voice, so very proud, went on telling. The carpet made a great sensation, but so did the beds with real bedclothes, and the stove with an oven door.

When she finished Kezia broke in. "You've forgotten the lamp, Isabel."

"Oh, yes," said Isabel, "and there's a teeny little lamp, all made of yellow glass, with a white globe that stands on the dining-room table. You couldn't tell it from a real one."

"The lamp's best of all," cried Kezia. She thought Isabel wasn't making half enough of the little lamp. But nobody paid any attention. Isabel was choosing the two who were to come back with them that afternoon and see it. She chose Emmie Cole and Lena Logan. But when the others knew they were all to have a chance, they couldn't be nice enough to Isabel. One by one they put their arms round Isabel's waist and walked her off. They had something to whisper to her, a secret. "Isabel's *my* friend."

Only the little Kelveys moved away forgotten; there was nothing more for them to hear.

Days passed, and as more children saw the doll's house, the fame of it spread. It became the one subject, the rage. The one question was, "Have you seen Burnells' doll's house? Oh, ain't it lovely!" "Haven't you seen it? O, I say!"

Even the dinner hour was given up to talking about it. The little girls sat under the pines eating their thick mutton sandwiches and big slabs of johnny cake spread with butter. While always, as near as they could get, sat the Kelveys, our Else holding on to Lil, listening too, while they chewed their jam sandwiches out of a newspaper soaked with large red blobs. . . .

"Mother," said Kezia, "can't I ask the Kelveys just once?"

"Certainly not, Kezia."

"But why not?"

"Run away, Kezia; you know quite well why not."

At last everybody had seen it except them. On that day the subject rather flagged. It was the dinner hour. The children stood together under the pine trees, and suddenly, as they looked at the Kelveys eating out of their paper, always by themselves, always listening, they wanted to be horrid to them. Emmie Cole started the whisper.

"Lil Kelvey's going to be a servant when she grows up."

"O-oh, how awful!" said Isabel Burnell, and she made eyes at Emmie.

Emmie swallowed in a very meaning way and nodded to Isabel as she'd seen her mother do on those occasions.

"It's true—it's true—it's true," she said.

Then Lena Logan's little eyes snapped. "Shall I ask her?" she whispered.

"Bet you don't," said Jessie May.

"Pooh, I'm not frightened," said Lena. Suddenly she gave a little squeal and danced in front of the other girls. "Watch! Watch me! Watch me now!" said Lena. And sliding, gliding, dragging one foot, giggling behind her hand, Lena went over to the Kelveys.

Lil looked up from her dinner. She wrapped the rest quickly away. Our Else stopped chewing. What was coming now?

"Is it true you're going to be a servant when you grow up, Lil Kelvey?" shrilled Lena.

Dead silence. But instead of answering, Lil only gave her silly, shamefaced smile. She didn't seem to mind the question at all. What a sell for Lena! The girls began to titter.

Lena couldn't stand that. She put her hands on her hips; she shot forward. "Yah, yer father's in prison!" she hissed, spitefully.

This was such a marvellous thing to have said that the little girls rushed away in a body, deeply, deeply excited, wild with joy. Some one found a long rope, and they began skipping. And never did they skip so high, run in and out so fast, or do such daring things as on that morning.

In the afternoon Pat called for the Burnell children with the buggy and they drove home. There were visitors. Isabel and Lottie, who liked visitors, went upstairs to change their pinafores. But Kezia thieved out at the back. Nobody was about; she began to swing on the big white gates of the courtyard. Presently, looking along the road, she saw two little dots. They grew bigger, they were coming towards her. Now she could see that one was in front and one close behind. Now she could see that they were the Kelveys. Kezia stopped swinging. She slipped off the gate as if she was going to run away. Then she hesitated. The Kelveys came nearer, and beside them walked their shadows, very long, stretching right across the road with their heads in the buttercups. Kezia clambered back on the gate; she had made up her mind; she swung out.

"Hullo," she said to the passing Kelveys.

They were so astounded that they stopped. Lil gave her silly smile. Our Else stared.

"You can come and see our doll's house if you want to," said Kezia, and she dragged one toe on the ground. But at that Lil turned red and shook her head quickly.

"Why not?" asked Kezia.

Lil gasped, then she said, "Your ma told our ma you wasn't to speak to us."

"Oh, well," said Kezia. She didn't know what to reply. "It doesn't matter. You can come and see our doll's house all the same. Come on. Nobody's looking."

But Lil shook her head still harder.

"Don't you want to?" asked Kezia.

Suddenly there was a twitch, a tug at Lil's skirt. She turned round. Our Else was looking at her with big, imploring eyes; she was frowning; she wanted to go. For a moment Lil looked at our Else very doubtfully. But then our Else twitched her skirt again. She started forward. Kezia led the way. Like two little stray cats they followed across the courtyard to where the doll's house stood.

"There it is," said Kezia.

There was a pause. Lil breathed loudly, almost snorted; our Else was still as a stone.

"I'll open it for you," said Kezia kindly. She undid the hook and they looked inside.

"There's the drawing-room and the dining-room, and that's the—"

"Kezia!"

Oh, what a start they gave!

"Kezia!"

It was Aunt Beryl's voice. They turned round. At the back door stood Aunt Beryl, staring as if she couldn't believe what she saw.

"How dare you ask the little Kelveys into the courtyard?" said her cold, furious voice. "You know as well as I do, you're not allowed to talk to them. Run away, children, run away at once. And don't come back again," said Aunt Beryl. And she stepped into the yard and shooed them out as if they were chickens.

"Off you go immediately!" she called, cold and proud.

They did not need telling twice. Burning with shame, shrinking together, Lil huddling along like her mother, our Else dazed, somehow they crossed the big courtyard and squeezed through the white gate.

"Wicked, disobedient little girl!" said Aunt Beryl bitterly to Kezia, and she slammed the doll's house to.

The afternoon had been awful. A letter had come from Willie Brent, a terrifying, threatening letter, saying if she did not meet him that evening in

Pulman's Bush, he'd come to the front door and ask the reason why! But now that she had frightened those little rats of Kelveys and given Kezia a good scolding, her heart felt lighter. That ghastly pressure was gone. She went back to the house humming.

When the Kelveys were well out of sight of Burnells', they sat down to rest on a big red drain-pipe by the side of the road. Lil's cheeks were still burning; she took off the hat with the quill and held it on her knee. Dreamily they looked over the hay paddocks, past the creek, to the group of wattles where Logan's cows stood waiting to be milked. What were their thoughts?

Presently our Else nudged up close to her sister. But now she had forgotten the cross lady. She put out a finger and stroked her sister's quill; she smiled her rare smile.

"I seen the little lamp," she said, softly.

Then both were silent once more.

[1922]

Study and Writing Questions

1. Just as in FAIRY TALES, the dominant colors here are either primary, white, black, or expressed in terms of precious materials such as gold. What other features of this STORY recall fairy tales? To what extent is this story like a fairy tale and to what extent different? What are the THEMATIC implications of those similarities and differences?
2. What is meant by the assertion that "the lamp was real"?
3. Why is Else invariably called "our Else"?
4. What are the precise attitudes of the NARRATOR? Consider, for example, the narrator's voice in the sixth paragraph (beginning, "The hook at the side . . .").
5. Consider the DÉNOUEMENT of the NARRATIVE. Are the last two lines overly sentimental? What can we infer about Willie Brent and why is he mentioned at all? What is the story about?

See also Questions for Contrast and Comparison: 37, 62, 70, 88, 135, and 170.

■ BOBBIE ANN MASON (1940–) *grew up on a farm outside Mayfield, Kentucky. Her parents fed her appetite for popular fiction, particularly with Bobbsey Twins stories and Nancy Drew mysteries. After majoring in journalism at the University of Kentucky, Mason moved first to New York City, where she wrote articles about such teen stars as Annette Funicello and Troy Donahue for movie magazines, and then to the University of Connecticut, for doctoral studies. Her dissertation on Vladimir Nabokov's experimental novel Ada was published in paperback as Nabokov's Garden (1974). Her next book, Girl Sleuth: A Feminist Guide (1975), mined her childhood reading. By her own account, she started writing fiction only in her late thirties because "it took me a very long time to grow up" and to recognize that "home . . . [was] the center of my thoughts." She has had enormous success since she turned her wry, sympathetic eye on the people with whom she was raised. The New Yorker accepted her first story in 1980, and her first collection, Shiloh and Other Stories (1982), won the Hemingway Foundation Award. Her novel In Country (1985), about Kentucky people dealing with the experience of the Vietnam War, became an admired movie. She has also written a short novel, Spence and Lila (1988), and another story collection, Love Life (1989). She lives in Pennsylvania with her husband, Roger Rawlings, a writer and editor.*

A New-Wave Format

Edwin Creech drives a yellow bus, transporting a group of mentally retarded adults to the Cedar Hill Mental Health Center, where they attend training classes. He is away from 7:00 to 9:30 A.M. and from 2:30 to 5:00 P.M. His hours are so particular that Sabrina Jones, the girl he has been living with for several months, could easily cheat on him. Edwin devises schemes to test her. He places a long string of dental floss on her pillow (an idea he got from a mystery novel), but it remains undisturbed. She is away four nights a week, at rehearsals for Oklahoma! with the Western Kentucky Little Theatre, and she often goes out to eat afterward with members of the cast. Sabrina won't let him go to rehearsals, saying she wants the play to be complete when he sees it. At home, she sings and dances along with the movie sound track, and she acts out scenes for him. In the play, she's in the chorus, and she has two lines in Act I, Scene 3. Her lines are "And to yer house a dark clubman!" and "Then out of your dreams you'll go." Edwin loves the dramatic way Sabrina waves her arms on her first line. She is supposed to be a fortune teller.

One evening when Sabrina comes home, Edwin is still up, as she puts on the sound track of Oklahoma! and sings along with Gordon MacRae while she does splits on the living room floor. Her legs are long and slender, and she still has her summer tan. She is wearing her shorts, even though it is late fall. Edwin suddenly has an overwhelming feeling of love for her. She really seems to believe what she is singing — "Oh, What a Beautiful Mornin'." When the song ends, he tells her that.

"It's the middle of the night," he says, teasing. "And you think it's morning."

"I'm just acting."

"No, you really believe it. You believe it's morning, a beautiful morning."

Sabrina gives him a fishy look, and Edwin feels embarrassed. When the record ends, Sabrina goes into the bedroom and snaps on the radio. Rock music helps her relax before going to sleep. The new rock music she likes is monotonous and bland, but Edwin tells himself that he likes it because Sabrina likes it. As she undresses, he says to her, "I'm sorry. I wasn't accusing you of nothing."

"That's O.K." She shrugs. The T-shirt she sleeps in has a hole revealing a spot of her skin that Edwin would like to kiss, but he doesn't because it seems like a corny thing to do. So many things about Sabrina are amazing: her fennel toothpaste and herbal deodorant; her slim, snaky hips; the way she puts Vaseline on her teeth for a flashier smile, something she learned to do in a beauty contest.

When she sits on the bed, Edwin says, "If I say the wrong things, I want you to tell me. It's just that I'm so crazy about you I can't think sometimes. But if I can do anything better, I will. I promise. Just tell me."

"I don't think of you as the worrying type," she says, lying down beside him. She still has her shoes on.

"I didn't used to be."

"You're the most laid back guy I know."

"Is that some kind of actor talk from your actor friends?"

"No. You're just real laid back. Usually good-looking guys are so stuck up. But you're not." The music sends vibrations through Edwin like a cat's purr. She says, "I brag on you all the time to Jeff and Sue—Curly and Laurey."

"I know who Jeff and Sue are." Sabrina talks constantly about Jeff and Sue, the romantic leads in the play.

Sabrina says, "Here's what I wish. If we had a big pile of money, we could have a house like Sue's. Did I tell you she's got *woven* blinds on her patio that she made herself? Everything she does is so *artistic*." Sabrina shakes Edwin's shoulder. "Wake up and talk to me."

"I can't. I have to get up at six."

Sabrina whispers to him, "Sue has the hots for Jeff. And Jeff's wife is going to have a duck with a rubber tail if she finds out." Sabrina giggles. "He kept dropping hints about how his wife was going to Louisville next week. And he and Sue were eating off the same slice of pizza."

"Is that supposed to mean something?"

"You figure it out."

"Would you do me that way?"

"Don't be silly." Sabrina turns up the radio, then unties her shoes and tosses them over Edwin's head into a corner.

Edwin is forty-three and Sabrina is only twenty, but he does not want to believe age is a barrier between them. Sometimes he cannot believe his good luck, that he has a beautiful girl who finds him still attractive. Edwin has a deep dimple in his chin, which reminded his first wife, Lois Ann, of Kirk Douglas. She had read in a movie magazine that Kirk Douglas has a special attachment for shaving his dimple. But Sabrina thinks Edwin looks like John Travolta, who also has a dimple. Now and then Edwin realizes how much older he is than Sabrina, but time has passed quickly, and he still feels like the same person, unchanged, that he was twenty years ago. His two ex-wives had seemed to drift away from him, and he never tried to hold them back. But with Sabrina, he knows he must make an effort, for it is beginning to dawn on him that sooner or later women get disillusioned with him. Maybe he's too laid back. But Sabrina likes this quality. Sabrina has large round gray eyes and limp, brownish-blond hair, the color of birch paneling, which she highlights with Miss Clairol. They share a love of Fudgsicles, speedboats, and *WKRP in Cincinnati.* At the beginning, he thought that was enough to build a relationship on, because he knew so many couples who never shared such simple pleasures, but gradually he has begun to see that it is more complicated than that. Sabrina's liveliness makes him afraid that she will be fickle. He can't bear the thought of losing her, and he doesn't like the idea that his new possessiveness may be the same uneasy feeling a man would have for a daughter.

Sabrina's parents sent her to college for a year, but her father, a farmer, lost money on his hogs and couldn't afford to continue. When Edwin met her, she was working as a waitress in a steak house. She wants to go back to college, but Edwin does not have the money to send her either. In college, she learned things that make him feel ignorant around her. She said that in an anthropology course, for instance, she learned for a fact that people evolved from animals. But when he tried to argue with her, she said his doubts were too silly to discuss. Edwin doesn't want to sound like a father, so he usually avoids such topics. Sabrina believes in the ERA, although she likes to keep house. She cooks odd things for him, like eggplant, and a weird lasagna with vegetables. She says she knows how to make a Big Mac from scratch, but she never does. Her specialty is pizza. She puts sliced dill pickles on it, which Edwin doesn't dare question. She likes to do things in what she calls an arty way. Now Sabrina is going out for pizza with people in the Theatre. Sabrina talks of "the Theatre."

Until he began driving the bus, Edwin had never worked closely with people. He worked on an offshore oil rig for a time, but kept his distance from the other men. He drove a bulldozer in a logging camp out West. In Kentucky, during his marriages, he worked in an aluminum products company, an automotive machine shop, and numerous gas stations, going from job to job as casually as he did with women. He used to think of himself as an adventurer, but now he believes he has gone through life rather blindly, without much pain or sense of loss.

When he drives the bus, he feels stirred up, perhaps the way Sabrina feels about *Oklahoma!* The bus is a new luxury model with a tape deck, AM-FM, CB, and built-in first-aid kit. He took a first-aid course, so he feels prepared to handle emergencies. Edwin has to stay alert, for anything could happen. The guys who came back from Vietnam said it was like this every moment. Edwin was in the army, but he was never sent to Vietnam, and now he feels that he has bypassed some critical stage in his life: a knowledge of terror. Edwin has never had this kind of responsibility, and he has never been around mentally retarded people before. His passengers are like bizarre, overgrown children, badly behaved and unpredictable. Some of them stare off into space, others are hyperactive. A woman named Freddie Johnson kicks aimlessly at the seat in front of her, spouting her ten-word vocabulary. She can say, "Hot! Shorts," "*Popeye* on?" "*Dukes* on!" "Cook supper," and "Go bed." She talks continuously. A gangly man with a clubfoot has learned to get Hershey bars from a vending machine, and every day he brings home Hershey bars, clutching them in his hand until he squeezes them out of shape. A pretty blond woman shows Edwin the braces on her teeth every day when she gets on the bus. She gets confused if Edwin brings up another topic. The noises on the bus are chaotic and eerie—spurts, gurgles, yelps, squeals. Gradually, Edwin has learned how to keep his distance and keep order at the same time. He plays tape-recorded music to calm and entertain the passengers. In effect, he has become a disc jockey, taking requests and using the microphone, but he avoids fast talk. The supervisors at the center have told him that the developmentally disabled—they always use this term—need a world that is slowed down; they can't keep up with today's fast pace. So he plays mellow old sixties tunes by the Lovin' Spoonful, Joni Mitchell, Donovan. It seems to work. The passengers have learned to clap or hum along with the music. One man, Merle Cope, has been learning to clap his hands in a body-awareness class. Merle is forty-seven years old, and he walks two miles—in an hour—to the bus stop, down a country road. He climbs onto the bus with agonizing slowness. When he gets on, he makes an exaggerated clapping motion, as if to congratulate himself for having made it, but he never lets his hands quite touch. Merle Cope always has an eager grin on his face, and when he tries to clap his hands he looks ecstatic. He looks happier than Sabrina singing "Oh, What a Beautiful Mornin'."

On Thursday, November 14, Edwin stops at the junction of a state road and a gravel road called Ezra Combs Lane to pick up a new passenger. The country roads have shiny new green signs, with the names of the farmers who originally settled there three or four generations ago. The new passenger is Laura Combs, who he has been told is thirty-seven and has never been to school. She will take classes in Home Management and Living Skills. When she gets on the bus, the people who were with her drive off in a blue Pacer. Laura Combs, a large, angular woman with buckteeth, stomps deliberately down the aisle, then plops down beside a young black man named Ray Watson, who has been riding the bus for about three weeks. Ray has hardly spoken, except to say "Have a nice day" to Edwin when he leaves the bus. Ray, who is mildly retarded from a blow on the head in his childhood, is subject to seizures, but so far he has not had one on the bus. Edwin watches him carefully. He learned about convulsions in his first-aid course.

When Laura Combs sits down by Ray Watson, she shoves him and says, "Scoot over. And cheer up."

Her tone is not cheerful. Edwin watches in the rear-view mirror, ready to act. He glides around a curve and slows down for the next passenger. A tape has ended and Edwin hesitates before inserting another. He hears Ray Watson say, "I never seen anybody as ugly as you."

"Shut up or I'll send you to the back of the bus." Laura Combs speaks with a snappy authority that makes Edwin wonder if she is really retarded. Her hair is streaked gray and yellow, and her face is filled with acne pits.

Ray Watson says, "That's fine with me, long as I don't have to set by you."

"Want me to throw you back in the woodpile where you come from?"

"I bet you could throw me plumb out the door, you so big."

It is several minutes before it is clear to Edwin that they are teasing. He is pleased that Ray is talking, but he can't understand why it took a person like Laura Combs to motivate him. She is an imposing woman with a menacing stare. She churns gum, her mouth open.

For a few weeks, Edwin watches them joke with each other, and whenever he decides he should separate them, they break out into big grins and pull at each other's arms. The easy intimacy they develop seems strange to Edwin, but then it suddenly occurs to him what a fool he is being about a twenty-year-old girl, and that seems even stranger. He hears Ray ask Laura, "Did you get that hair at the Piggly Wiggly?" Laura's hair is in pigtails, which seem to be freshly plaited on Mondays and untouched the rest of the week. Laura says, "I don't want no birds nesting in my hair."

Edwin takes their requests. Laura has to hear "Mister Bojangles" every day, and Ray demands that Edwin play something from Elvis's Christmas album. They argue over tastes. Each says the other's favorite songs are terrible.

Laura tells Ray she never heard of a black person liking Elvis, and Ray says, "There's a lot about black people you don't know."

"What?"

"That's for me to know and you to find out. You belong on the moon. All white peoples belong on the moon."

"You belong in Atlanta," Laura says, doubling over with laughter.

When Edwin reports their antics one day to Sabrina, she says, "That's too depressing for words."

"They're a lot smarter than you'd think."

"I don't see how you can stand it." Sabrina shudders. She says, "Out in the woods, animals that are defective wouldn't survive. Even back in history, deformed babies were abandoned."

"Today's different," says Edwin, feeling alarmed. "Now they have rights."

"Well, I'll say one thing. If I was going to have a retarded baby, I'd get an abortion."

"That's killing."

"It's all in how you look at it," says Sabrina, changing the radio station.

They are having lunch. Sabrina has made a loaf of zucchini bread, because Sue made one for Jeff. Edwin doesn't understand her reasoning, but he takes it as a compliment. She gives him another slice, spreading it with whipped margarine. All of his women were good cooks. Maybe he didn't praise them enough. He suddenly blurts out so much praise for the zucchini bread that Sabrina looks at him oddly. Then he realizes that her attention is on the radio. The Humans are singing a song about paranoia, which begins, "Attention, all you K Mart shoppers, fill your carts, 'cause your time is almost up." It is Sabrina's favorite song.

"Most of my passengers are real poor country people," Edwin says. "Use to, they'd be kept in the attic or out in the barn. Now they're riding a bus, going to school and having a fine time."

"In the attic? I never knew that. I'm a poor country girl and I never knew that."

"Everybody knows that," says Edwin, feeling a little pleased. "But don't call yourself a poor country girl."

"It's true. My daddy said he'd give me a calf to raise if I came back home. Big deal. My greatest dread is that I'll end up on a farm, raising a bunch of dirty-faced younguns. Just like some of those characters on your bus."

Edwin does not know what to say. The song ends. The last line is, "They're looking in your picture window."

While Sabrina clears away the dishes, Edwin practices rolling bandages. He has been reviewing his first-aid book. "I want you to help me practice a simple splint," he says to Sabrina.

"If I broke a leg, I couldn't be in *Oklahoma!*"

"You won't break a leg." He holds out the splint. It is a fraternity paddle, a souvenir of her college days. She sits down for him and stretches out her leg.

"I can't stand this," she says.

"I'm just practicing. I have to be prepared. I might have an emergency."

Sabrina, wincing, closes her eyes while Edwin ties the fraternity paddle to her ankle.

"It's perfect," he says, tightening the knot.

Sabrina opens her eyes and wiggles her foot. "Jim says he's sure I can have a part in *Life with Father*," she says. Jim is the director of *Oklahoma!* She adds, "Jeff is probably going to be the lead."

"I guess you're trying to make me jealous."

"No, I'm not. It's not even a love story."

"I'm glad then. Is that what you want to do?"

"I don't know. Don't you think I ought to go back to school and take a drama class? It'd be a real great experience, and I'm not going to get a job anytime soon, looks like. Nobody's hiring." She shakes her leg impatiently, and Edwin begins untying the bandage. "What do you think I ought to do?"

"I don't know. I never know how to give you advice, Sabrina. What do I know? I haven't been to college like you."

"I wish I were rich, so I could go back to school," Sabrina says sadly. The fraternity paddle falls to the floor, and she says, with her hands rushing to her face, "Oh, God, I can't stand the thought of breaking a leg."

The play opens in two weeks, during the Christmas season, and Sabrina has been making her costumes — two gingham outfits, virtually identical. She models them for Edwin and practices her dances for him. Edwin applauds, and she gives him a stage bow, as the director has taught her to do. Everything Sabrina does now seems like a performance. When she slices the zucchini bread, sawing at it because it has hardened, it is a performance. When she sat in the kitchen chair with the splint, it was as though she imagined her audience. Edwin has been involved in his own performances, on the bus. He emulates Dr. Johnny Fever, on *WKRP*, because he likes to be low-key, cool. But he hesitates to tell Sabrina about his disc jockey role because she doesn't watch *WKRP in Cincinnati* with him anymore. She goes to rehearsals early.

Maybe it is out of resistance to the sappy *Oklahoma!* sound track, or maybe it is an inevitable progression, but Edwin finds himself playing a few Dylan tunes, some Janis Joplin, nothing too hectic. The passengers shake their heads in pleasure or beat things with their fists. It makes Edwin sad to think how history passes them by, but sometimes he feels the same way about his own life. As he drives along, playing these old songs, he thinks about what his life was like back then. During his first marriage, he worked in a gas station, saving for a down payment on a house. Lois Ann fed him on a TV tray while he watched the war. It was like a drama series. After Lois Ann, and then his travels out West, there was Carolyn and another down payment on another house and more of the war. Carolyn had a regular schedule — pork chops on Mondays, chicken on Tuesdays. Thursday's menu has completely escaped his memory. He feels terrible, remembering his wives by their food, and remembering the war as a TV series. His life has been a delayed reaction. He feels as if he's about Sabrina's age. He plays music he did not understand fifteen years ago, music that now seems full of possibility: the Grateful Dead, the Jefferson Airplane, groups with vision. Edwin feels that he is growing and changing for the first time in years. The passengers on his bus fill him with a compassion he has never felt before. When Freddie Johnson learns a new word—"bus"—Edwin is elated. He feels confident. He could drive his passengers all the way to California if he had to.

One day a stringbean girl with a speech impediment gives Edwin a tape cassette she wants him to play. Her name is Lou Murphy. Edwin has tried to encourage her to talk, but today he hands the tape back to her abruptly.

"I don't like the Plasmatics," he explains, enjoying his authority. "I don't play new-wave. I have a golden-oldie format. I just play sixties stuff."

The girl takes the tape cassette and sits down by Laura Combs. Ray Watson is absent today. She starts pulling at her hair, and the cassette jostles in her lap. Laura is wound up too, jiggling her knees. The pair of them make Edwin think of those vibrating machines that mix paint by shaking the cans.

Edwin takes the microphone and says, "If you want a new-wave format, you'll have to ride another bus. Now let's crawl back in the stacks of wax for this oldie but goodie—Janis Joplin and 'A Little Bit Harder.' "

Lou Murphy nods along with the song. Laura's chewing gum pops like BBs. A while later, after picking up another passenger, Edwin glances in the rear-view mirror and sees Laura playing with the Plasmatics tape, pulling it out in a curly heap. Lou seems to be trying to shriek, but nothing comes out. Before Edwin can stop the bus, Laura has thrown the tape out the window.

"You didn't like it, Mr. Creech," Laura says when Edwin, after halting the bus on a shoulder, stalks down the aisle. "You said you didn't like it."

Edwin has never heard anyone sound so matter-of-fact, or look so reasonable. He has heard that since Laura began her classes, she has learned to set a table, make change, and dial a telephone. She even has a job at the training center, sorting seeds and rags. She is as hearty and domineering, yet as delicate and vulnerable, as Janis Joplin must have been. Edwin manages to move Lou to a front seat. She is sobbing silently, her lower jaw jerking, and Edwin realizes he is trembling too. He feels ashamed. After all, he is not driving the bus in order to make a name for himself. Yet it had felt right to insist on the format for his show. There is no appropriate way to apologize, or explain.

Edwin doesn't want to tell Sabrina about the incident. She is preoccupied with the play and often listens to him distractedly. Edwin has decided that he was foolish to suspect that she had a lover. The play is her love. Her nerves are on edge. One chilly afternoon, on the weekend before Oklahoma! opens, he suggests driving over to Kentucky Lake.

"You need a break," he tells her. "A little relaxation. I'm worried about you."

"This is nothing," she says. "Two measly lines. I'm not exactly a star."

"What if you were? Would you get an abortion?"

"What are you talking about? I'm not pregnant."

"You said once you would. Remember?"

"Oh. I would if the baby was going to be creepy like those people on your bus."

"But how would you know if it was?"

"They can tell." Sabrina stares at him and then laughs. "Through science."

In the early winter, the lake is deserted. The beaches are washed clean, and the water is clear and gray. Now and then, as they walk by the water, they hear a gunshot from the Land Between the Lakes wilderness area. "The Surrey with the Fringe on Top" is going through Edwin's head, and he wishes he could throw the *Oklahoma!* sound track in the lake, as easily as Laura Combs threw the Plasmatics out the window of the bus. He has an idea that after the play, Sabrina is going to feel a letdown too great for him to deal with.

When Sabrina makes a comment about the "artistic intention" of Rodgers and Hammerstein, Edwin says, "Do you know what Janis Joplin said?"

"No — what?" Sabrina stubs the toe of her jogging shoe in the sand.

"Janis Joplin said, 'I don't write songs. I just make 'em up.' I thought that was clever."

"That's funny, I guess."

"She said she was going to her high school reunion in Port Arthur, Texas. She said, 'I'm going to laugh a lot. They laughed me out of class, out of town, and out of the state.' "

"You sound like you've got that memorized," Sabrina says, looking at the sky.

"I saw it on TV one night when you were gone, an old tape of a Dick Cavett show. It seemed worth remembering." Edwin rests his arm around Sabrina's waist, as thin as a post. He says, "I see a lot of things on TV, when you're not there."

Wild ducks are landing on the water, scooting in like water skiers. Sabrina seems impressed by them. They stand there until the last one lands.

Edwin says, "I bet you can't even remember Janis Joplin. You're just a young girl, Sabrina. *Oklahoma!* will seem silly to you one of these days."

Sabrina hugs his arm. "That don't matter." She breaks into laughter. "You're cute when you're being serious."

Edwin grabs her hand and jerks her toward him. "Look, Sabrina. I was never serious before in my life. I'm just now, at this point in my life — this week — getting to be serious." His words scare him, and he adds with a grin that stretches his dimple, "I'm serious about *you.*"

"I know that," she says. She is leading the way along the water, through the trees, pulling him by the hand. "But you never believe how much I care about you," she says, drawing him to her. "I think we get along real good. That's why I wish you'd marry me instead of just stringing me along."

Edwin gasps like a swimmer surfacing. It is very cold on the beach. Another duck skis onto the water.

Oklahoma! has a four-night run, with one matinee. Edwin goes to the play three times, surprised that he enjoys it. Sabrina's lines come off differently each time, and each evening she discusses the impression she made. Edwin tells her that she is the prettiest woman in the cast, and that her lines are cute. He wants to marry Sabrina, although he hasn't yet said he would. He wishes he could buy her a speedboat for a wedding present. She wants him to get a better-paying job, and she has ideas about a honeymoon cottage at the lake. It feels odd that Sabrina has proposed to him. He thinks of her as a liberated woman. The play is old-fashioned and phony. The love scenes between Jeff and Sue are comically stilted, resembling none of the passion and intrigue that Sabrina has reported. She compared them to Bogart and Bacall, but Edwin can't remember if she meant Jeff and Sue's roles or their actual affair. How did Sabrina know about Bogart and Bacall?

At the cast party, at Jeff's house, Jeff and Sue are publicly affectionate, getting away with it by playing their Laurey and Curly roles, but eventually Jeff's wife, who has made ham, potato salad, chiffon cakes, eggnog, and cranberry punch for sixty people, suddenly disappears from the party. Jeff whizzes off in his Camaro to find her. Sabrina whispers to Edwin, "Look how Sue's pretending nothing's happened. She's flirting with the guy who played Jud Fry." Sabrina, so excited that she bounces around on her tiptoes, is impressed by Jeff's house, which has wicker furniture and rose plush carpets.

Edwin drinks too much cranberry punch at the party, and most of the time he sits on a wicker love seat watching Sabrina flit around the room, beaming with the joy of her success. She is out of costume, wearing a sweatshirt with a rainbow on the front and pots of gold on her breasts. He realizes how proud he is of her. Her complexion is as smooth as a white mushroom, and she has crinkled her hair by braiding and unbraiding it. He watches her join some of the cast members around the piano to sing songs from the play, as though they cannot bear it that the play has ended. Sabrina seems to belong with them, these theatre people. Edwin knows they are not really theatre people. They are only local merchants putting on a play in their spare time. But Edwin is just a bus driver. He should get a better job so that he can send Sabrina to college, but he knows that he has to take care of his passengers. Their faces have become as familiar to him as the sound track of *Oklahoma!* He can practically hear Freddie Johnson shouting out her TV shows: "*Popeye* on! *Dukes* on!" He sees Sabrina looking at him lovingly. The singers shout, "Oklahoma, O.K.!"

Sabrina brings him a plastic glass of cranberry punch and sits with him on the love seat, holding his hand. She says, "Jim definitely said I should take a drama course at Murray State next semester. He was real encouraging. He said. 'Why not be in the play *and* take a course or two?' I could drive back and forth, don't you think?"

"Why not? You can have anything you want." Edwin plays with her hand.

"Jeff took two courses at Murray and look how good he was. Didn't you think he was good? I loved that cute way he went into that dance."

Edwin is a little drunk. He finds himself telling Sabrina about how he plays disc jockey on the bus, and he confesses to her his shame about the way he sounded off about his golden-oldie format. His mind is reeling and the topic sounds trivial, compared to Sabrina's future.

"Why *don't* you play a new-wave format?" she asks him. "It's what *everybody* listens to." She nods at the stereo, which is playing "You're Living in Your Own Private Idaho," by the B-52s, a song Edwin has often heard on the radio late at night when Sabrina is unwinding, moving into his arms. The music is violent and mindless, with a fast beat like a crazed parent abusing a child, thrashing it senseless.

"I don't know," Edwin says. "I shouldn't have said that to Lou Murphy. It bothers me."

"She don't know the difference," Sabrina says, patting his head. "It's ridiculous to make a big thing out of it. Words are so arbitrary, and people don't say what they mean half the time anyway."

"You should talk, Miss Oklahoma!" Edwin laughs, spurting a little punch on the love seat. "You and your two lines!"

"They're just lines," she says, smiling up at him and poking her finger into his dimple.

Some of Edwin's passengers bring him Christmas presents, badly wrapped, with tags that say his name in wobbly writing. Edwin puts the presents in a drawer, where Sabrina finds them.

"Aren't you going to open them?" she asks. "I'd be dying to know what was inside."

"I will eventually. Leave them there." Edwin knows what is in them without opening them. There is a bottle of shaving cologne, a tie (he never wears a tie), and three boxes of chocolate-covered cherries (he peeked in one, and the others are exactly the same shape). The presents are so pathetic Edwin could cry. He cannot bring himself to tell Sabrina what happened on the bus.

On the bus, the day before Christmas break, Ray Watson had a seizure. During that week, Edwin had been playing more Dylan and even some Stones. No Christmas music, except the Elvis album as usual for Ray. And then, almost unthinkingly, following Sabrina's advice, Edwin shifted formats. It seemed a logical course, as natural as Sabrina's herbal cosmetics, her mushroom complexion. It started with a revival of The Doors—Jim Morrison singing "Light My Fire," a song that was so long it carried them from the feed mill on one side of town to the rendering plant on the other. The passengers loved the way it stretched out, and some shook their heads and stomped their feet. As Edwin realized later, the whole bus was in a frenzy, and he should have known he was leading the passengers toward disaster, but the music seemed so appropriate. The Doors were a bridge from the past to the present, spanning those empty years— his marriages, the turbulence of the times—and connecting his youth solidly with the present. That day Edwin taped more songs from the radio—Adam and the Ants, Squeeze, the B-52s, the Psychedelic Furs, the Flying Lizards, Frankie and the Knockouts—and he made a point of replacing the Plasmatics tape for Lou Murphy. The new-wave format was a hit. Edwin believed the passengers understood what was happening. The frantic beat was a perfect expression of their aimlessness and frustration. Edwin had the impression that his passengers were growing, expanding, like the corn in *Oklahoma!*, like his own awareness. The new format went on for two days before Ray had his seizure. Edwin did not know exactly what happened, and it was possible Laura Combs had shoved Ray into the aisle. Edwin was in an awkward place on the highway, and he had to shoot across a bridge and over a hill before he could find a good place to stop. Everyone on the bus was making an odd noise, gasping or clapping, some imitating Ray's convulsions. Freddie Johnson was saying, "*Popeye* on! *Dukes* on!" Ray was on the floor, gagging, with his head thrown back, and twitching like someone being electrocuted. Laura Combs stood hunched in her seat, her mouth open in speechless terror, pointing her finger at Edwin. During the commotion, the Flying Lizards were chanting tonelessly, "I'm going to take my problems to the United Nations; there ain't no cure for the summertime blues."

Edwin followed all the emergency steps he had learned. He loosened Ray's clothing, slapped his cheeks, turned him on his side. Ray's skin was the color of the Hershey bars the man with the clubfoot collected. Edwin recalled grimly the first-aid book's ironic assurance that facial coloring was not important in cases of seizure. On the way to the hospital, Edwin clicked in a Donovan cassette. To steady himself, he sang along under his breath. "I'm just wild about saffron," he sang. It was a tune as carefree and lyrical as a field of daffodils. The passengers were screaming. All the way to the hospital, Edwin heard their screams, long and drawn out, orchestrated together into an accusing wail — eerie and supernatural.

Edwin's supervisors commended him for his quick thinking in handling Ray and getting him to the hospital, and everyone he has seen at the center has congratulated him. Ray's mother sent him an uncooked fruitcake made with graham cracker crumbs and marshmallows. She wrote a poignant note, thanking him for saving her son from swallowing his tongue. Edwin keeps thinking: what he did was no big deal; you can't swallow your tongue anyway; and it was Edwin's own fault that Ray had a seizure. He does not feel like a hero. He feels almost embarrassed.

Sabrina seems incapable of embarrassment. She is full of hope, like the Christmas season. *Oklahoma!* was only the beginning for her. She has a new job at McDonald's and a good part in *Life with Father*. She plans to commute to Murray State next semester to take a drama class and a course in Western Civilization that she needs to fulfill a requirement. She seems to assume that Edwin will marry her. He finds it funny that it is up to him to say yes. When she says she will keep her own name, Edwin wonders what the point is.

"My parents would just love it if we got married," Sabrina explains. "For them, it's worse for me to live in sin than to be involved with an older man."

"I didn't think I was really older," says Edwin. "But now I know it. I feel like I've had a developmental disability and it suddenly went away. Something like if Freddie Johnson learned to read. That's how I feel."

"I never thought of you as backward. Laid back is what I said." Sabrina laughs at her joke. "I'm sure you're going to impress Mom and Dad."

Tomorrow, she is going to her parents' farm, thirty miles away, for the Christmas holidays, and she has invited Edwin to go with her. He does not want to disappoint her. He does not want to go through Christmas without her. She has arranged her Christmas cards on a red string between the living room and the kitchen. She is making cookies, and Edwin has a feeling she is adding something strange to them. Her pale, fine hair is falling down in her face. Flour streaks her jeans.

"Let me show you something," Edwins says, bringing out a drugstore envelope of pictures. "One of my passengers, Merle Cope, gave me these."

"Which one is he? The one with the fits?"

"No. The one that claps all the time. He lives with a lot of sisters and brothers down in Langley's Bottom. It's a case of incest. The whole family's backward — your word. He's forty-seven and goes around with this big smile on his face, clapping." Edwin demonstrates.

He pins the pictures on Sabrina's Christmas card line with tiny red and green clothespins. "Look at these and tell me what you think."

Sabrina squints, going down the row of pictures. Her hands are covered with flour and she holds them in front of her, the way she learned from her actor friends to hold an invisible baby.

These pictures are black-and-white snapshots: fried eggs on cracked plates, an oilclothed kitchen table, a bottle of tomato ketchup, a fence post, a rusted tractor seat sitting on a stump, a corn crib, a sagging door, a toilet bowl, a cow, and finally, a horse's rear end.

"I can't look," says Sabrina. "These are disgusting."

"I think they're arty."

Sabrina laughs. She points to the pictures one by one, getting flour on some of them. Then she gets the giggles and can't stop. "Can you imagine what the developers thought when they saw that horse's ass?" she gasps. Her laughter goes on and on, then subsides with a little whimper. She goes back to the cookies. While she cuts out the cookies, Edwin takes the pictures down and puts them in the envelope. He hides the envelope in the drawer with the Christmas presents. Sabrina sets the cookie sheet in the oven and washes her hands.

Edwin asks, "How long do those cookies take?"

"Twelve minutes. Why?"

"Let me show you something else—in case you ever need to know it. The CPR technique—that's cardio-pulmonary resuscitation, in case you've forgotten."

Sabrina looks annoyed. "I'd rather do the Heimlich maneuver," she says. "Besides, you've practiced CPR on me a hundred times."

"I'm not practicing. I don't have to anymore. I'm beyond that." Edwin notices Sabrina's puzzled face. The thought of her fennel toothpaste, which makes her breath smell like licorice, fills him with something like nostalgia, as though she is already only a memory. He says, "I just want you to feel what it would be like. Come on." He leads her to the couch and sets her down. Her hands are still moist. He says, "Now just pretend. Bend over like this. Just pretend you have the biggest pain, right here, right in your chest, right there."

"Like this?" Sabrina is doubled over, her hair falling to her knees and her fists knotted between her breasts.

"Yes. Right in your heart."

[1982]

Study and Writing Questions

1. This NARRATIVE mentions three parallel historical forces: the normal maturing of an individual; U.S. political history from the 1950s through the 1970s; and music from the 1940s through the 1970s. How do the CHARACTERS react to these forces and how do they try to either control or transcend them?

2. This narrative is told primarily in the present TENSE but moves to the past tense at strategic points. Where are those points? What effect(s) does this tense switching have?

3. Matters of art (music, photography, "theatre") are clearly important in Sabrina's and Edwin's lives. What is "arty" to each of them? What is its importance? Do their ideas change?

4. Describe Edwin's growth in the narrative. He says, " 'I feel like I've had a developmental disability and it suddenly went away.' " What does he mean? Do you agree?
5. Describe Edwin and Sabrina's relationship. What needs did they fulfill for each other as the story began? What needs might they fulfill for each other at its end?

See also Questions for Contrast and Comparison: 12, 28, 66, 125, and 212.

(HENRI RENÉ ALBERT) GUY DE MAUPASSANT (1850–1893) *was born near Dieppe, in Normandy, France, son of a wealthy stockbroker. His highly cultured mother educated him and gave him a love of writing, particularly of the work of a family friend and distant relative, the great novelist Gustave Flaubert. At thirteen Guy was enrolled in seminary but was expelled for insubordination. Undisciplined at subsequent schools, he joined the army and served during the Franco-Prussian War (1870–1871). After the war he moved to Paris, worked as a clerk in the naval ministry, and became part of Flaubert's famous circle. For seven years, during which he published nothing in his own name, Maupassant would write and Flaubert would criticize, urging the apprentice always to look with new eyes at ordinary life. In 1880 his reputation was made by the publication of a single story "Boule de Suif" ("Ball of Fat"), which unsentimentally and without traditional moralizing compares the patriotism of a prostitute with the hypocrisy of the bourgeoisie. In the next ten years, Maupassant published plays, verse, six novels, and nearly three hundred economical, dramatic, almost impressionistic stories that permanently changed the genre. Now wealthy, he indulged his life-long taste for women, luxury, and yachting, but by 1890 was incapacitated by syphilis, which he had contracted probably by twenty. He went insane and finally died of paresis.*

The Jewels

MONSIEUR LANTIN had met the girl at a party given one evening by his office superior and love had caught him in its net.

She was the daughter of a country tax-collector who had died a few years before. She had come to Paris then with her mother, who struck up acquaintance with a few middle-class families in her district in the hope of marrying her off. They were poor and decent, quiet and gentle. The girl seemed the perfect example of the virtuous woman to whom every sensible young man dreams of entrusting his life. Her simple beauty had a modest, angelic charm and the imperceptible smile which always hovered about her lips seemed to be a reflection of her heart.

Everybody sang her praises and people who knew her never tired of saying: 'Happy the man who marries her. Nobody could find a better wife.'

Monsieur Lantin, who was then a senior clerk at the Ministry of the Interior with a salary of three thousand five hundred francs a year, proposed to her and married her.

He was incredibly happy with her. She ran his household so skillfully and economically that they gave the impression of living in luxury. She lavished attention on her husband, spoiling and coddling him, and the charm of her person was so great that six years after their first meeting he loved her even more than in the early days.

He found fault with only two of her tastes: her love for the theatre and her passion for imitation jewellery.

Her friends (she knew the wives of a few petty officials) often obtained a box at the theatre for her for popular plays, and even for first nights; and she dragged her husband along willy-nilly to these entertainments, which he found terribly tiring after a day's work at the office. He therefore begged her to go to the theatre with some lady of her acquaintance who would bring her home afterwards. It was a long time before she gave in, as she thought that this arrangement was not quite respectable. But finally, just to please him, she agreed, and he was terribly grateful to her.

Now this love for the theatre soon aroused in her a desire to adorn her person. True, her dresses remained very simple, always in good taste, but unpretentious; and her gentle grace, her irresistible, humble, smiling charm seemed to be enhanced by the simplicity of her gowns. But she took to wearing two big rhinestone earrings which sparkled like diamonds, and she also wore necklaces of fake pearls, bracelets of imitation gold, and combs set with coloured glass cut to look like real stones.

Her husband, who was rather shocked by this love of show, often used to say: 'My dear, when a woman can't afford to buy real jewels, she ought to appear adorned with her beauty and grace alone: those are still the rarest of gems'.

But she would smile sweetly and reply: 'I can't help it. I like imitation jewellery. It's my only vice. I know you're right, but people can't change their natures. I would have loved to own some real jewels.'

Then she would run the pearl necklaces through her fingers and make the cut-glass gems flash in the light, saying: 'Look! Aren't they beautifully made? Anyone would swear they were real.'

He would smile and say: 'You have the taste of a gipsy.'

Sometimes, in the evening, when they were sitting together by the fireside, she would place on the tea-table the leather box in which she kept her 'trash', as Monsieur Lantin called it. Then she would start examining these imitation jewels with passionate attention, as if she were enjoying some deep and secret pleasure; and she would insist on hanging a necklace around her husband's neck, laughing uproariously and crying: 'How funny you look!' And then she would throw herself into his arms and kiss him passionately.

One night in winter when she had been to the Opera, she came home shivering with cold. The next morning she had a cough, and a week later she died of pneumonia.

Lantin very nearly followed her to the grave. His despair was so terrible that his hair turned white within a month. He wept from morning to night, his heart ravaged by unbearable grief, haunted by the memory, the smile, the voice, the every charm of his dead wife.

Time did nothing to assuage his grief. Often during office hours, when his colleagues came along to chat about the topics of the day, his cheeks would suddenly puff out, his nose wrinkle up, his eyes fill with tears, and with a terrible grimace he would burst out sobbing.

He had left his wife's room untouched, and every day would shut himself in it and think about her. All the furniture and even her clothes remained exactly where they had been on the day she had died.

But life soon became a struggle for him. His income, which in his wife's hands had covered all their expenses, was now no longer sufficient for him on his own; and he wondered in amazement how she had managed to provide him with excellent wines and rare delicacies which he could no longer afford on his modest salary.

He incurred a few debts and ran after money in the way people do when they are reduced to desperate shifts. Finally, one morning, finding himself without a sou a whole week before the end of the month, he decided to sell something; and immediately the idea occurred to him of disposing of his wife's 'trash'. He still harboured a sort of secret grudge against those false gems which had irritated him in the past, and indeed the sight of them every day somewhat spoiled the memory of his beloved.

He rummaged for a long time among the heap of gawdy trinkets she had left behind, for she had stubbornly gone on buying jewellery until the last days of her life, bringing home a new piece almost every evening. At last he decided on the large necklace which she had seemed to like best, and which, he thought, might well be worth six or seven francs, for it was beautifully made for a piece of paste.

He put it in his pocket and set off for his Ministry, following the boulevards and looking for a jeweller's shop which inspired confidence.

At last he spotted one and went in, feeling a little ashamed of exposing his poverty in this way, and of trying to sell such a worthless article.

'Monsieur,' he said to the jeweller, 'I would like to know what you think this piece is worth.'

The man took the necklace, examined it, turned it over, weighed it, inspected it with a magnifiying glass, called his assistant, made a few remarks to him in an undertone, placed the necklace on the counter and looked at it from a distance to gauge the effect.

Monsieur Lantin, embarrassed by all this ritual, was opening his mouth to say: 'Oh, I know perfectly well that it isn't worth anything,' when the jeweller said: 'Monsieur, this necklace is worth between twelve and fifteen thousand francs; but I couldn't buy it unless you told me where it came from.'

The widower opened his eyes wide and stood there gaping, unable to understand what the jeweller had said. Finally he stammered: 'What was that you said? . . . Are you sure?'

The other misunderstood his astonishment and said curtly: 'You can go somewhere else and see if they'll offer you more. In my opinion it's worth fifteen thousand at the most. Come back and see me if you can't find a better price.'

Completely dumbfounded, Monsieur Lantin took back his necklace and left the shop, in obedience to a vague desire to be alone and to think.

Once outside, however, he felt an impulse to laugh, and he thought: 'The fool! Oh, the fool! But what if I'd taken him at his word? There's a jeweller who can't tell real diamonds from paste!'

And he went into another jeweller's shop at the beginning of the Rue de la Paix. As soon as he saw the necklace, the jeweller exclaimed: 'Why, I know that necklace well: it was bought here.'

Monsieur Lantin asked in amazement: 'How much is it worth?'

'Monsieur, I sold it for twenty-five thousand. I am prepared to buy it back for eighteen thousand once you have told me, in accordance with the legal requirements, how you came to be in possession of it.'

This time Monsieur Lantin was dumbfounded. He sat down and said: 'But . . . but . . . examine it carefully, Monsieur. Until now I thought it was paste."

"Will you give me your name, Monsieur?' said the jeweller.

'Certainly. My name's Lantin. I'm an official at the Ministry of the Interior, and I live at No. 16, Rue des Martyrs.'

The jeweller opened his books, looked for the entry, and said: 'Yes, this necklace was sent to Madame Lantin's address, No. 16, Rue des Martyrs, on the 20th of July 1876.'

The two men looked into each other's eyes, the clerk speechless with astonishment, the jeweller scenting a thief. Finally the latter said: 'Will you leave the necklace with me for twenty-four hours? I'll give you a receipt.'

'Why, certainly,' stammered Monsieur Lantin. And he went out folding the piece of paper, which he put in his pocket.

Then he crossed the street, walked up it again, noticed that he was going the wrong way, went back as far as the Tuileries, crossed the Seine, realized that he had gone wrong again, and returned to the Champs-Élysés, his mind a complete blank. He tried to think it out, to understand. His wife couldn't have afforded to buy something so valuable — that was certain. But in that case it was a present! A present! But a present from whom? And why was it given her?

He halted in his tracks and remained standing in the middle of the avenue. A horrible doubt crossed his mind. Her? But in that case all the other jewels were presents too! The earth seemed to be trembling under his feet and a tree in front of him to be falling; he threw up his arms and fell to the ground unconscious.

He came to his senses in a chemist's shop into which the passers-by had carried him. He took a cab home and shut himself up.

He wept bitterly until nightfall, biting on a handkerchief so as not to cry out. Then he went to bed worn out with grief and fatigue and slept like a log.

A ray of sunlight awoke him and he slowly got up to go to his Ministry. It was hard to think of working after such a series of shocks. It occurred to him that he could ask to be excused and he wrote a letter to his superior. Then he remembered that he had to go back to the jeweller's and he blushed with shame. He spent a long time thinking it over, but decided that he could not leave the necklace with that man. So he dressed and went out.

It was a fine day and the city seemed to be smiling under the clear blue sky. People were strolling about the streets with their hands in their pockets.

Watching them, Lantin said to himself: 'How lucky rich people are! With money you can forget even the deepest of sorrows. You can go where you like, travel, enjoy yourself. Oh, if only I were rich!'

He began to feel hungry, for he had eaten nothing for two days, but his pocket was empty. Then he remembered the necklace. Eighteen thousand francs! Eighteen thousand francs! That was a tidy sum, and no mistake!

When he reached the Rue de la Paix he started walking up and down the pavement opposite the jeweller's shop. Eighteen thousand francs! A score of times he almost went in, but every time shame held him back.

He was hungry, though, very hungry, and he had no money at all. He quickly made up his mind, ran across the street so as not to have any time to think, and rushed into the shop.

As soon as he saw him the jeweller came forward and offered him a chair with smiling politeness. His assistants came into the shop, too, and glanced surreptitiously at Lantin with laughter in their eyes and on their lips.

'I have made inquiries, Monsieur,' said the jeweller, 'and if you still wish to sell the necklace, I am prepared to pay you the price I offered you.'

'Why, certainly,' stammered the clerk.

The jeweller took eighteen large banknotes out of a drawer, counted them and handed them to Lantin, who signed a little receipt and with a trembling hand put the money in his pocket.

Then, as he was about to leave the shop, he turned towards the jeweller, who was still smiling, and lowering his eyes said: 'I have . . . I have some other jewels which have come to me from . . . from the same legacy. Would you care to buy them from me too?'

The jeweller bowed.

'Certainly, Monsieur.'

One of the assistants went out, unable to contain his laughter; another blew his nose loudly.

Lantin, red-faced and solemn, remained unmoved.

'I will bring them to you,' he said.

And he took a cab to go and fetch the jewels.

When he returned to the shop an hour later he still had had nothing to eat. The jeweller and his assistants began examining the jewels one by one, estimating the value of each piece. Almost all of them had been bought at that shop.

Lantin now began arguing about the valuations, lost his temper, insisted on seeing the sales registers, and spoke more and more loudly as the sum increased.

The large diamond earrings were worth twenty thousand francs, the bracelets thirty-five thousand, the brooches, rings and lockets sixteen thousand, a set of emeralds and sapphires fourteen thousand, and a solitaire pendant on a gold chain forty thousand—making a total sum of one hundred and ninety-six thousand francs.

The jeweller remarked jokingly: 'These obviously belonged to a lady who invested all her savings in jewellery.'

Lantin replied seriously: 'It's as good a way as any of investing one's money.'

And he went off after arranging with the jeweller to have a second expert valuation the next day.

Out in the street he looked at the Vendôme column and felt tempted to climb up it as if it were a greasy pole. He felt light enough to play leap-frog with the statue of the Emperor perched up there in the sky.

He went to Voisin's for lunch and ordered wine with his meal at twenty francs a bottle.

Then he took a cab and went for a drive in the Bois. He looked at the other carriages with a slightly contemptuous air, longing to call out to the passers-by: 'I'm a rich man too! I'm worth two hundred thousand francs!'

Suddenly he remembered his Ministry. He drove there at once, strode into his superior's office, and said: 'Monsieur, I have come to resign my post. I have just been left three hundred thousand francs.'

He shook hands with his former colleagues and told them some of his plans for the future; then he went off to dine at the Café Anglais.

Finding himself next to a distinguished-looking gentleman, he was unable to refrain from informing him, with a certain coyness, that he had just inherited four hundred thousand francs.

For the first time in his life he was not bored at the theatre, and he spent the night with some prostitutes.

Six months later he married again: His second wife was a very virtuous woman, but extremely bad-tempered. She made him very unhappy.

[1883]

Study and Writing Questions

1. The STORY begins when "love had caught [M. Lantin] in its net." What are the qualities that make up "love" in this story?
2. How do wealth and feelings of both happiness and beauty interact according to this story? What might have been the first Mme. Lantin's MOTIVES in acquiring the jewels?
3. The *Place Vendôme* is famous for its forty-four meter tall column which was cast from the bronze of 1200 cannons taken by Napoleon from the enemies of France. In what ways might *Place Vendôme* be SYMBOLIC in this story? Use a French dictionary to find the meanings of the street names mentioned. How might they be symbolic?
4. Reread the story in order to discover its use of FORESHADOWING. Compare and contrast the impact of first and subsequent readings.
5. To what extent does the last paragraph represent POETIC JUSTICE?

See also Questions for Contrast and Comparison: 7, 33, 54, 70, 163, 164, 165, 166, and 231.

Mother Savage

I had not been back to Virelogne for fifteen years. I returned there to do some shooting in the autumn, staying with my friend Serval, who had finally rebuilt his château, which had been destroyed by the Prussians.

I was terribly fond of that part of the country. There are some delightful places in this world which have a sensual charm for the eyes. One loves them with a physical love. We people who are attracted by the countryside cherish fond memories of certain springs, certain woods, certain ponds, certain hills, which have become familiar sights and can touch our hearts like happy events. Sometimes indeed the memory goes back towards a forest glade, or a spot on a river bank, or an orchard in blossom, glimpsed only once on a happy day, but preserved in our heart like those pictures of women seen in the street on a spring morning, wearing gay, flimsy dresses, and which leave in our soul and flesh an unappeased, unforgettable desire, the feeling that happiness has passed us by.

At Virelogne I loved the whole region, scattered with little woods and crossed by streams which ran through the ground like veins carrying blood to the earth. We fished in them for crayfish, trout and eels. What heavenly happiness we knew there! There were certain places where we could bathe, and we often found snipe in the tall grass which grew on the banks of those narrow brooks.

I walked along, as light-footed as a goat, watching my two dogs foraging ahead of me. Serval, a hundred yards to my right, was beating a field of lucerne. I went round the bushes which mark the edge of Saudres woods, and I noticed a cottage in ruins.

All of a sudden I remembered it as it had been the last time I had seen it, in 1869, neat, covered with vines, with chickens outside the door. What is sadder than a dead house, with nothing left standing but its skeleton, a sinister ruin?

I remembered too that a woman had given me a glass of wine inside the house, one day when I was very tired, and that afterwards Serval had told me the story of the occupants. The father, an old poacher, had been killed by the gendarmes. The son, whom I had seen before, was a tall, wiry fellow who was likewise supposed to be a ferocious killer of game. People called the family the Savages.

Was it a name or a nickname?

I called out to Serval. He came over to me with his long lanky stride. I asked him: 'What has become of the people who lived here?'

And he told me this story.

'When war was declared, the younger Savage, who was then thirty-three years old, enlisted, leaving his mother alone at home. People didn't feel too sorry for the old woman, though, because they knew she had money.

'So she stayed all alone in this isolated house, far away from the village, on the edge of the woods. But she wasn't afraid, because she was made of the same stuff as her men, a tough, tall, thin old woman, who didn't laugh very often and whom nobody joked with. Country women don't laugh much anyway. That's the men's business! They have sad, narrow souls, because they lead dull, dreary lives. The peasant learns a little noisy gaiety in the tavern, but his wife remains serious, forever wearing a stern expression. The muscles of her face have never learnt the motions of laughter.

'Mother Savage continued to lead her usual life in her cottage, which was soon covered with snow. She came to the village once a week to get bread and a little meat; then she returned to her cottage. As there was talk of wolves in the region, she went out with a gun slung over her shoulder, her son's gun, which was rusty, with the butt worn down by the rubbing of the hand. She was a strange sight, the Savage woman, tall, rather bent, striding slowly through the snow, with the barrel of the gun showing above the tight black head-dress which imprisoned the white hair nobody had ever seen.

'One day the Prussians arrived. They were distributed among the local inhabitants according to the means and resources of each. The old woman, who was known to be well off, had four soldiers billeted on her.

'They were four big young fellows with fair skins, fair beards and blue eyes, who had remained quite plump in spite of the hardships they had already endured, and good-natured even though they were in conquered territory. Alone with that old woman, they showed her every consideration, sparing her fatigue and expense as best they could. All four were to be seen washing at the well every morning in their shirt-sleeves, splashing water, in the cold glare of the snow, over their pink and white flesh, the flesh of men of the north, while Mother Savage went to and fro, cooking their soup. They could then be seen cleaning the kitchen, polishing the floor, chopping wood, peeling potatoes, washing the linen, and doing all the household jobs, just like four good sons helping their mother.

'But the old woman kept thinking all the time about her own son, her tall thin boy with his hooked nose, his brown eyes, and the bushy moustache which covered his upper lip with a roll of black hair. Every day she asked each of the soldiers sitting around her hearth: "Do you know where the French regiment has gone—the Twenty-third Infantry? My boy is in it."

'They would reply: "No, we don't know. We have no idea."

'And, understanding her grief and anxiety, they, who had mothers of their own at home, performed countless little services for her. She for her part was quite fond of her four enemies, for peasants scarcely ever feel patriotic hatred: that is the prerogative of the upper classes. The humble, those who pay the most because they are poor and because every new burden weighs heavily on them, those who are killed in droves, who form the real cannon-fodder because they are the most numerous, who, in a word, suffer the most from the atrocious hardships of war because they are the weakest and most vulnerable, find it hard to understand those bellicose impulses, those touchy points of honour and those so-called political manoeuvres which exhaust two nations within six months, the victor as well as the vanquished.

'The people around here, speaking of Mother Savage's Germans, used to say: "Those four have found a cosy billet, and no mistake."

'Now, one morning, when the old woman was alone in the house, she caught sight of a man a long way off on the plain coming towards her home. Soon she recognized him: it was the man whose job it was to deliver letters. He handed her a folded piece of paper, and she took the spectacles she used for sewing out of their case. Then she read:

Madame Savage, this is to give you some sad news. Your son Victor was killed yesterday by a cannon-ball which pretty well cut him in two. I was very close, seeing as we were side by side in the company, and he had asked me to let you know if anything happened to him.

I took his watch out of his pocket to bring it back to you when the war is over.

Best regards.

CÉSAIRE RIVOT,
Private in the 23rd Infantry.

'The letter was dated three weeks earlier.

'She didn't cry. She stood stock still, so shocked and dazed that she didn't even feel any grief yet. She thought to herself: "Now it's Victor who's gone and got killed." Then, little by little, the tears came into her eyes and grief flooded into her heart. Ideas occurred to her one by one, horrible, agonizing ideas. She would never kiss him again, her big boy, never! The gendarmes had killed the father, the Prussians had killed the son. He had been cut in two by a cannon-ball. And it seemed to her that she could see the horrible thing happening: the head falling, the eyes wide open, while he was chewing the end of his bushy moustache as he always did when he was angry.

'What had they done with his body afterwards? If only they had sent her boy back to her, as they had sent back her husband, with the bullet in the middle of his forehead!

'But then she heard the sound of voices. It was the Prussians coming back from the village. She quickly hid the letter in her pocket and, having had time to wipe her eyes, greeted them calmly, looking her usual self.

'All four of them were laughing with delight, for they had brought back a fine rabbit, which had probably been stolen, and they made signs to the old woman that they were going to eat something good.

'She set to work straight away getting dinner ready, but when it came to killing the rabbit, her heart failed her. And it wasn't the first by any means! One of the soldiers had to kill it with a punch behind the ears.

'Once the animal was dead she stripped the skin from the red body; but the sight of the blood which she was touching, which covered her hands, the warm blood which she could feel growing cold and congealing, made her tremble from head to foot; and she kept seeing her big boy cut in two and red all over, like the animal still quivering in her hands.

'She sat down to table with her Prussians, but she couldn't eat, not so much as a mouthful. They devoured the rabbit without speaking, thinking over an idea, her face so expressionless that they noticed nothing.

'Suddenly she said: "We've been together a whole month now and I don't even know your names."

'They understood, not without some difficulty, what she wanted, and gave her their names. But that wasn't enough: she got them to write them down for her on a piece of paper, with the addresses of their families; and, setting her spectacles on her big nose, she inspected the unfamiliar script and then folded the sheet of paper and put it in her pocket, with the letter which had told her of the death of her son.

'When the meal was over, she said to the men: "I'm going to do some work for you."

'And she started taking straw up to the loft in which they slept.

'They were puzzled by what she was doing. She explained to them that the straw would keep them warmer, and they gave her a helping hand. They piled the bundles of straw up to the roof and thus made themselves a sort of big, warm, sweet-smelling room with four walls of forage, where they would sleep wonderfully well.

'At supper one of them was upset to see that Mother Savage didn't eat anything again. She said that she was suffering from cramps. Then she lit a good fire to warm herself, and the four Germans climbed up to their room by the ladder which they used every evening.

'As soon as the trap-door was closed, the old woman took away the ladder. Then she quietly opened the outside door and went out to fetch some more bundles of straw with which she filled the kitchen. She walked barefoot in the snow, moving so quietly that the men heard nothing. Every now and then she listened to the loud, uneven snores of the four sleeping soldiers.

'When she decided her preparations were sufficient, she threw one of the bundles of straw into the hearth, and when it had caught fire she scattered it over the others. Then she went outside and watched.

'Within a few seconds a blinding glare lit up the whole inside of the cottage. Then it became a fearful brazier, a gigantic furnace, the light of which shone through the narrow window and fell on the snow in a dazzling ray.

'Then a great cry came from the top of the house, followed by a clamour of human screams, of heartrending shrieks of anguish and terror. Then, as the trap-door collapsed inside the cottage, a whirlwind of the fire shot into the loft, pierced the thatched roof, and rose into the sky like the flame of a huge torch; and the whole cottage went up in flames.

'Nothing more could be heard inside but the crackling of the flames, the crumbling of the walls and the crashing of the beams. All of a sudden the roof fell in, and the glowing carcase of the house was hurled up into the air amid a cloud of smoke, a great fountain of sparks.

'The white countryside, lit up by fire, glistened like a cloth of silver tinted with red.

'In the distance a bell began ringing.

'Old Mother Savage remained standing in front of her burnt-out home, armed with her gun, her son's gun, for fear that one of the men should escape.

'When she saw that it was all over, she threw the weapon in the fire. An explosion rang out.

'People came running up, peasants and Prussians.

'They found the woman sitting on a tree trunk, calm and satisfied.

'A German officer, who spoke French like a Frenchman, asked her: "Where are your soldiers?"

'She stretched out her thin arm towards the red heap of the dying fire, and replied in a loud voice: "In there!"

'They crowded around her. The Prussian asked: "How did the fire break out?"

' "I started it," she said.

'They didn't believe her, thinking that the disaster had driven her mad all of a sudden. So, as everyone gathered around her to listen to her, she told the story from beginning to end, from the arrival of the letter to the last screams of the men who had been burnt with her house. She didn't leave out a single detail of what she had felt or of what she had done.

'When she had finished, she took two pieces of paper out of her pocket, and, in order to tell them apart, put on her spectacles again. Then, showing one of them, she said: "This one is Victor's death."

'Showing the other, and nodding in the direction of the red ruins, she added: "This one is their names so as you can write to their families."

'She calmly held out the white sheet of paper to the officer, who was holding her by the shoulders, and went on: "You must write to say what happened, and tell their parents that it was me that did it. Victoire Simon, the Savage woman! Don't forget."

'The officer shouted out some orders in German. She was seized and pushed against the walls of the house, which were still warm. Then twelve men lined up quickly facing her, at a distance of twenty yards. She didn't budge. She had understood, and stood there waiting.

'An order rang out, followed straight away by a long volley. A late shot went off by itself, after the others.

'The old woman didn't fall. She collapsed as if her legs had been chopped off.

'The Prussian officer came over to her. She had been practically cut in two, and in her hand she was clutching her letter soaked in blood.'

My friend Serval added: 'It was by way of a reprisal that the Germans destroyed the local château, which belonged to me.'

I for my part was thinking of the mothers of the four gentle boys burnt in there, and of the fearful heroism of that other mother, shot against that wall.

And I picked up a little stone, still blackened by the fire.

[1884]

Study and Writing Questions

1. What is the importance of the first paragraph for the NARRATIVE as a whole?
2. The narrator frequently uses body METAPHORS and SIMILES, as when he says the streams "were like veins carrying blood to the earth." What are other examples of such language? What effect(s) does this language have on our understanding of the narrative?
3. Compare and contrast the peacetime and wartime class structures implicit in the narrative world.
4. The narrator calls special attention to the word "savage." In French, *sauvage* has the same multiple meanings that it does in English. In addition, *sauver* is the French verb meaning "to save." Consequently, *sauvage* could also mean "sav-age" (like *drain, drainage* in English), however, in both languages a different form of the word is used: *salvage* in English and *sauvetage* in French.

Considering these and other facts, what is the THEMATIC significance of the title?

5. It is possible to consider this story as ALLUDING to the life of Jesus. Victor enlists at thirty-three, the age at which tradition sets Jesus at his crucifixon. When we finally learn that the mother's name is Victoire Simon, we might note that "Simon" comes from a Hebrew word meaning "he heard" and is used in the name "Simon Peter" for the apostle of whom Jesus said "upon this rock I will build my church" (Matthew 16:18). ("Peter" means "rock" in Latin.) What other allusions to the Gospels are in this narrative? How do these allusions add interest and meaning to the narrative?

See also Questions for Contrast and Comparison: 25, 36, 43, 166, 168, 187, 201, and 227.

WINSOR (ZENIC) MCCAY (1871–1934), *born in Spring Lake, Michigan, briefly studied art (1888) at Ypsilanti Normal College. He then moved, first with his working-class family to Chicago, where he lived by producing large, colorful woodcuts to advertise traveling circuses and theatrical productions, and then alone to Cincinnati (1889), where he produced bold posters for a permanent freak show. In 1892 he married; his two children inspired much of his mature work. Hired by a Cincinnati newspaper (1898) to illustrate fires, crimes, political events, and fiction, McCay daily practiced his art school lessons in observation and perspective and used his experience with posters. In 1902 he began publishing colorful, one-page Sunday fantasies for which he was lured to the* New York Herald *(1903). His enormously popular yet experimental comics include* Dreams of the Rarebit Fiend *(1904–1913) and* Little Nemo in Slumberland *(1905–1913, 1924–1926). In these comics fantasy and reality clash in visually compelling and psychologically revealing ways. Inspired by the flip-book, he pioneered animated film. In* Gertie, the Trained Dinosaur *(1914), McCay gave commands on the vaudeville stage while the projected, anthropomorphic creature responded. Maurice Sendak and Walt Disney, among many others, have acknowledged their debt to McCay, who ultimately rejected the growing commercialism of comics and concentrated on editorial cartooning.*

Study and Writing Questions

1. Try to note the visual details panel by panel. For example, despite the evidence of the eyeglasses, the rolled sleeves let us know that, relative to the VIEWPOINT CHARACTER, the two men in the first panel switch position in the second panel. What might this switch signify? What other significant visual details are there?
2. Do the pictures merely illustrate the words or do the pictures themselves convey a part of the STORY?
3. Describe the society of the viewpoint character. What are its values? Do people's actions always conform to those values?
4. What is the importance of perspective in this work? How does the use of a kind of FIRST PERSON NARRATION influence your sense of the dreamer? How, if at all, does the change of perspective in the last panel change your sense of the dreamer?
5. What is the importance of dreaming in this work? What does the dreamer mean when he says, " 'I'll be good' "? Is it really the "cheese pie" (otherwise known as "Welsh rabbit" or "Welsh rarebit") that causes this particular dream?

See also Questions for Contrast and Comparison: 7, 23, 25, 38, 43, 61, 72, 87, 92, 95, 125, 138, and 199.

from Dreams of the Rarebit Fiend

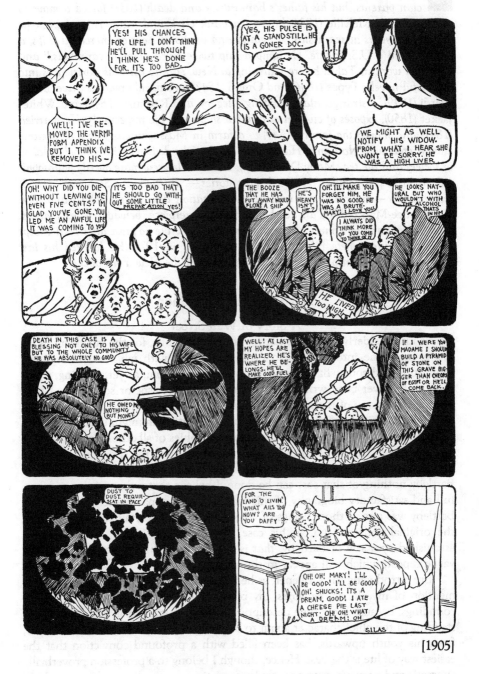

[1905]

■ HERMAN MELVILLE (1819–1891) *was born in New York City to patri-
cian parents, but his father's bankruptcy and death (1831) forced a move to
Albany where Melville (1834) became a bank clerk and tutor. At seventeen he
began four years at sea, visiting England and the South Seas on merchant ships, a
whaler, and a U.S. frigate. He jumped ship twice, lived among "cannibals," and
did farm work in Tahiti before returning to New York to turn his experiences into
successful novels: Typee (1846) and Omoo (1847), mistakenly read as travel books;
Mardi (1849), a strange, island-hopping allegory; and Redburn (1849) and White-
Jacket (1850), exposés of civilian and naval shipboard life respectively. He married
(1847) and moved the family (1849) to a farm in Massachusetts where he became
close friends with Nathaniel Hawthorne, to whom he dedicated his symbolic classic
of society and the sea, Moby Dick (1851). As Melville grew more overtly philosophical, he grew less popular. He tried short stories—"Bartleby the Scrivener" (1853)
was the first—but could not retrieve his reputation after Pierre (1852) and The
Confidence-Man (1857), an acerbic, formal masterpiece, bewildered his readers.
Now ranked among America's greatest authors, he wrote no prose after 1861 except
the superb, incomplete Billy Budd, first published in 1924. He labored his last
nineteen years as an obscure customs inspector on the New York docks.*

Bartleby the Scrivener

A Story of Wall Street

I am a rather elderly man. The nature of my avocations, for the last thirty years,
has brought me into more than ordinary contact with what would seem an
interesting and somewhat singular set of men, of whom, as yet, nothing, that I
now of, has ever been written—I mean, the law-copyists, or scriveners. I have
known very many of them, professionally and privately, and, if I pleased, could
relate diverse histories, at which good-natured gentlemen might smile, and sentimental souls might weep. But I waive the biographies of all other scriveners, for a
few passages in the life of Bartleby, who was a scrivener, the strangest I ever saw,
or heard of. While, of other law-copyists, I might write the complete life, of
Bartleby nothing of that sort can be done. I believe that no materials exist for a
full and satisfactory biography of this man. It is an irreparable loss to literature.
Bartleby was one of those beings of whom nothing is ascertainable, except from
the original sources, and, in his case, those are very small. What my own
astonished eyes saw of Bartleby, *that* is all I know of him, except, indeed, one
vague report, which will appear in the sequel.

   Ere introducing the scrivener, as he first appeared to me, it is fit I make some
mention of myself, my *employés*, my business, my chambers, and general surroundings; because some such description is indispensable to an adequate understanding of the chief character about to be presented. Imprimis: I am a man who,
from his youth upwards, has been filled with a profound conviction that the
easiest way of life is the best. Hence, though I belong to a profession proverbially
energetic and nervous, even to turbulence, at times, yet nothing of that sort have
I ever suffered to invade my peace. I am one of those unambitious lawyers who
never addresses a jury, or in any way draws down public applause; but, in the cool
tranquillity of a snug retreat, do a snug business among rich men's bonds, and
mortgages, and title-deeds. All who know me, consider me an eminently *safe*

man. The late John Jacob Astor, a personage little given to poetic enthusiasm, had no hesitation in pronouncing my first grand point to be prudence; my next, method. I do not speak it in vanity, but simply record the fact, that I was not unemployed in my profession by the late John Jacob Astor; a name which, I admit, I love to repeat; for it hath a rounded and orbicular sound to it, and rings like unto bullion. I will freely add, that I was not insensible to the late John Jacob Astor's good opinion.

Some time prior to the period at which this little history begins, my avocations had been largely increased. The good old office, now extinct in the State of New York, of a Master in Chancery, had been conferred upon me. It was not a very arduous office, but very pleasantly remunerative. I seldom lose my temper; much more seldom indulge in dangerous indignation at wrongs and outrages; but, I must be permitted to be rash here, and declare, that I consider the sudden and violent abrogation of the office of Master in Chancery, by the new Constitution, as a —— premature act; inasmuch as I had counted upon a life-lease of the profits, whereas I only received those of a few short years. But this is by the way.

My chambers were up stairs, at No. —— Wall Street. At one end, they looked upon the white wall of the interior of a spacious sky-light shaft, penetrating the building from top to bottom.

This view might have been considered rather tame than otherwise, deficient in what landscape painters call "life." But, if so, the view from the other end of my chambers offered, at least, a contrast, if nothing more. In that direction, my windows commanded an unobstructed view of a lofty brick wall, black by age and everlasting shade; which wall required no spy-glass to bring out its lurking beauties, but, for the benefit of all near-sighted spectators, was pushed up to within ten feet of my window panes. Owing to the great height of the surrounding buildings, and my chambers being on the second floor, the interval between this wall and mine not a little resembled a huge square cistern.

At the period just preceding the advent of Bartleby, I had two persons as copyists in my employment, and a promising lad as an office-boy. First, Turkey; second, Nippers; third, Ginger Nut. These may seem names, the like of which are not usually found in the Directory. In truth, they were nicknames, mutually conferred upon each other by my three clerks, and were deemed expressive of their respective persons or characters. Turkey was a short, pursy Englishman, of about my own age — that is, somewhere not far from sixty. In the morning, one might say, his face was of a fine florid hue, but after twelve o'clock, meridian — his dinner hour — it blazed like a grate full of Christmas coals; and continued blazing — but, as it were with a gradual wane — till six o'clock P.M., or thereabouts; after which, I saw no more of the proprietor of the face, which, gaining its meridian with the sun, seemed to set with it, to rise, culminate, and decline the following day, with the like regularity and undiminished glory. There are many singular coincidences I have known in the course of my life, not the least among which was the fact, that, exactly when Turkey displayed his fullest beams from his red and radiant countenance, just then, too, at that critical moment, began the daily period when I considered his business capacities as seriously disturbed for the remainder of the twenty-four hours. Not that he was absolutely idle, or averse to business, then; far from it. The difficulty was, he was apt to be altogether too energetic. There was a strange, inflamed, flurried, flighty recklessness of activity about him. He would be incautious in dipping his pen into his inkstand. All his blots upon my documents were dropped there after twelve o'clock meridian. Indeed, not only would he be reckless, and sadly given to making blots in the afternoon, but, some days, he went further, and was rather noisy. At such times, too, his face flamed with augmented blazonry, as if cannel coal had been heaped on anthracite. He made an unpleasant racket with his chair; spilled his sand-box; in mending his pens, impatiently split them all to pieces, and threw them on the floor in a sudden passion; stood up, and leaned over his table, boxing his papers about in a most indecorous manner, very sad to behold in an elderly man like him. Nevertheless, as he was in many ways a most valuable person to me, and all the time before twelve o'clock meridian, was the quickest, steadiest creature, too, accomplishing a great deal of work in a style not easily to be matched—for these reasons, I was willing to overlook his eccentricities, though, indeed, occasionally, I remonstrated with him. I did this very gently, however, because, though the civilest, nay, the blandest and most reverential of men in the morning, yet, in the afternoon, he was disposed, upon provocation, to be slightly rash with his tongue—in fact, insolent. Now, valuing his morning services as I did, and resolved not to lose them—yet, at the same time, made uncomfortable by his inflamed ways after twelve o'clock—and being a man of peace, unwilling by my admonitions to call forth unseemly retorts from him, I took upon me, one Saturday noon (he was always worse on Saturdays) to hint to him, very kindly, that, perhaps, now that he was growing old, it might be well to abridge his labors; in short, he need not come to my chambers after twelve o'clock, but, dinner over, had best go home to his lodgings, and rest himself till tea-time. But no; he insisted upon his afternoon devotions. His countenance became intolerably fervid, as he oratorically assured me—gesticulating with a long ruler at the other end of the room—that if his services in the morning were useful, how indispensable, then, in the afternoon?

"With submission, sir," said Turkey, on this occasion, "I consider myself your right-hand man. In the morning I but marshal and deploy my columns; but in the afternoon I put myself at their head, and gallantly charge the foe, thus"—and he made a violent thrust with the ruler.

"But the blots, Turkey," intimated I.

"True; but, with submission, sir, behold these hairs! I am getting old. Surely, sir, a blot or two of a warm afternoon is not to be severely urged against gray hairs. Old age—even if it blot the page—is honorable. With submission, sir, we both are getting old."

This appeal to my fellow-feeling was hardly to be resisted. At all events, I saw that go he would not. So, I made up my mind to let him stay, resolving, nevertheless, to see to it that, during the afternoon, he had to do with my less important papers.

Nippers, the second on my list, was a whiskered, sallow, and, upon the whole, rather piratical-looking young man, of about five and twenty. I always deemed him the victim of two civil powers—ambition and indigestion. The ambition was evinced by a certain impatience of the duties of a mere copyist, an unwarrantable usurpation of strictly professional affairs, such as the original drawing up of legal documents. The indigestion seemed betokened in an occasional nervous testiness and grinning irritability, causing the teeth to audibly grind together over mistakes committed in copying; unnecessary maledictions, hissed, rather than spoken, in the heat of business; and especially by a continual discontent with the height of the table where he worked. Though of a very ingenious, mechanical turn, Nippers could never get this table to suit him. He put chips under it, blocks of various sorts, bits of pasteboard, and at last went so far as to attempt an exquisite adjustment, by final pieces of folded blotting-paper. But no invention would answer. If, for the sake of easing his back, he brought the table lid at a sharp angle well up towards his chin, and wrote there like a man using the steep roof of a Dutch house for his desk, then he declared that it stopped the circulation in his arms. If now he lowered the table to his waistbands, and stooped over it in writing, then there was a sore aching in his back. In short, the truth of the matter was, Nippers knew not what he wanted. Or, if he wanted anything, it was to be rid of a scrivener's table altogether. Among the manifestations of his diseased ambition was a fondness he had for receiving visits from certain ambiguous-looking fellows in seedy coats, whom he called his clients. Indeed, I was aware that not only was he, at times, considerable of a ward-politician, but he occasionally did a little business at the Justices' courts, and was not unknown on the steps of the Tombs. I have good reason to believe, however, that one individual who called upon him at my chambers, and who, with a grand air, he insisted was his client, was no other than a dun, and the alleged title-deed, a bill. But, with all his failings, and the annoyances he caused me, Nippers, like his compatriot Turkey, was a very useful man to me; wrote a neat, swift hand; and, when he chose, was not deficient in a gentlemanly sort of deportment. Added to this, he always dressed in a gentlemanly sort of way; and so, incidentally, reflected credit upon my chambers. Whereas, with respect to Turkey, I had much ado to keep him from being a reproach to me. His clothes were apt to look oily, and smell of eating-houses. He wore his pantaloons very loose and baggy in summer. His coats were execrable; his hat not to be handled. But while the hat was a thing of indifference to me, inasmuch as his natural civility and deference, as a dependent Englishman, always led him to doff it the moment he entered the room, yet his coat was another matter. Concerning his coats, I reasoned with him; but with no effect. The truth was, I suppose, that a man with so small an income could not afford to sport such a lustrous face and a lustrous coat at one and the same time. As Nippers once observed, Turkey's money went chiefly for red ink. One winter day, I presented Turkey with a highly respectable-looking coat of my own—a padded gray coat, of a most comfortable warmth, and which buttoned straight up from the knee to the neck. I thought Turkey would appreciate the favor, and abate his rashness and obstreperousness of afternoons. But no; I verily believe that buttoning himself up in so downy and blanket-like a coat had a pernicious effect upon him—upon the same principle that too much oats are bad for horses. In fact, precisely as a rash, restive horse is said to feel his oats, so Turkey felt his coat. It made him insolent. He was a man whom prosperity harmed.

Though, concerning the self-indulgent habits of Turkey, I had my own private surmises, yet, touching Nippers, I was well persuaded that, whatever might be his faults in other respects, he was, at least, a temperate young man. But, indeed, nature herself seemed to have been his vintner, and, at his birth, charged him so thoroughly with an irritable, brandy-like disposition, that all subsequent potations were needless. When I consider how, amid the stillness of my chambers, Nippers would sometimes impatiently rise from his seat, and stooping over his table, spread his arms wide apart, seize the whole desk, and move it, and jerk it, with a grim, grinding motion on the floor, as if the table were a perverse voluntary agent and vexing him, I plainly perceive that, for Nippers, brandy-and-water were altogether superfluous.

It was fortunate for me that, owing to its peculiar cause — indigestion — the irritability and consequent nervousness of Nippers were mainly observable in the morning, while in the afternoon he was comparatively mild. So that, Turkey's paroxysms only coming on about twelve o'clock, I never had to do with their eccentricities at one time. Their fits relieved each other, like guards. When Nippers's was on, Turkey's was off; and *vice versa*. This was a good natural arrangement, under the circumstances.

Ginger Nut, the third on my list, was a lad, some twelve years old. His father was a car-man, ambitious of seeing his son on the bench instead of a cart, before he died. So he sent him to my office, as student at law, errand-boy, cleaner and sweeper, at the rate of one dollar a week. He had a little desk to himself; but he did not use it much. Upon inspection, the drawer exhibited a great array of the shells of various sorts of nuts. Indeed, to this quick-witted youth, the whole noble science of the law was contained in a nutshell. Not the least among the employments of Ginger Nut, as well as one which he discharged with the most alacrity, was his duty as cake and apple purveyor for Turkey and Nippers. Copying law-papers being proverbially a dry, husky sort of business, my two scriveners were fain to moisten their mouths very often with Spitzenbergs, to be had at the numerous stalls nigh the Custom House and Post Office. Also, they sent Ginger Nut very frequently for that peculiar cake — small, flat, round, and very spicy — after which he had been named by them. Of a cold morning, when business was but dull, Turkey would gobble up scores of these cakes, as if they were mere wafers — indeed, they sell them at the rate of six or eight for a penny — the scrape of his pen blending with the crunching of the crisp particles in his mouth. Rashest of all the fiery afternoon blunders and flurried rashnesses of Turkey, was his once moistening a ginger-cake between his lips, and clapping it on to a mortgage, for a seal. I came within an ace of dismissing him then. But he mollified me by making an oriental bow, and saying —

"With submission, sir, it was generous of me to find you in stationery on my own account."

Now my original business — that of a conveyancer and title hunter, and drawer-up of recondite documents of all sorts — was considerably increased by receiving the master's office. There was now great work for scriveners. Not only must I push the clerks already with me, but I must have additional help.

In answer to my advertisement, a motionless young man one morning stood upon my office threshold, the door being open, for it was summer. I can see that figure now — pallidly neat, pitiably respectable, incurably forlorn! It was Bartleby.

After a few words touching his qualifications, I engaged him, glad to have among my corps of copyists a man of so singularly sedate an aspect, which I thought might operate beneficially upon the flighty temper of Turkey, and the fiery one of Nippers.

I should have stated before that ground glass folding-doors divided my premises into two parts, one of which was occupied by my scriveners, the other by myself. According to my humor, I threw open these doors, or closed them. I resolved to assign Bartleby a corner by the folding-doors, but on my side of them, so as to have this quiet man within easy call, in case any trifling thing was to be done. I placed his desk close up to a small side-window in that part of the room, a window which originally had afforded a lateral view of certain grimy backyards and bricks, but which, owing to subsequent erections, commanded at present no view at all, though it gave some light. Within three feet of the panes was a wall, and the light came down from far above, between two lofty buildings, as from a very small opening in a dome. Still further to a satisfactory arrangement, I procured a high green folding screen, which might entirely isolate Bartleby from my sight, though not remove him from my voice. And thus, in a manner, privacy and society were conjoined.

At first, Bartleby did an extraordinary quantity of writing. As if long famishing for something to copy, he seemed to gorge himself on my documents. There was no pause for digestion. He ran a day and night line, copying by sun-light and by candle-light. I should have been quite delighted with his application, had he been cheerfully industrious. But he wrote on silently, palely, mechanically.

It is, of course, an indispensable part of a scrivener's business to verify the accuracy of his copy, word by word. Where there are two or more scriveners in an office, they assist each other in this examination, one reading from the copy, the other holding the original. It is a very dull, wearisome, and lethargic affair. I can readily imagine that, to some sanguine temperaments, it would be altogether intolerable. For example, I cannot credit that the mettlesome poet, Byron, would have contentedly sat down with Bartleby to examine a law document of, say five hundred pages, closely written in a crimpy hand.

Now and then, in the haste of business, it had been my habit to assist in comparing some brief document myself, calling Turkey or Nippers for this purpose. One object I had, in placing Bartleby so handy to me behind the screen, was to avail myself of his services on such trivial occasions. It was on the third day, I think, of his being with me, and before any necessity had arisen for having his own writing examined, that, being much hurried to complete a small affair I had in hand, I abruptly called to Bartleby. In my haste and natural expectancy of instant compliance, I sat with my head bent over the original on my desk, and my right hand sideways, and somewhat nervously extended with the copy, so that, immediately upon emerging from his retreat, Bartleby might snatch it and proceed to business without the least delay.

In this very attitude did I sit when I called to him, rapidly stating what it was I wanted him to do—namely, to examine a small paper with me. Imagine my surprise, nay, my consternation, when, without moving from his privacy, Bartleby, in a singularly mild, firm voice, replied, "I would prefer not to."

I sat awhile in perfect silence, rallying my stunned faculties. Immediately it occurred to me that my ears had deceived me, or Bartleby had entirely misunderstood my meaning. I repeated my request in the clearest tone I could assume; but in quite as clear a one came the previous reply, "I would prefer not to."

"Prefer not to," echoed I, rising in high excitement, and crossing the room with a stride. "What do you mean? Are you moon-struck? I want you to help me compare this sheet here—take it," and I thrust it towards him.

"I would prefer not to," said he.

I looked at him steadfastly. His face was leanly composed; his gray eye dimly calm. Not a wrinkle of agitation rippled him. Had there been the least uneasiness, anger, impatience, or impertinence in his manner; in other words, had there been any thing ordinarily human about him, doubtless I should have violently dismissed him from the premises. But as it was, I should have as soon thought of turning my pale plaster-of-paris bust of Cicero out of doors. I stood gazing at him awhile, as he went on with his own writing, and then reseated myself at my desk. This is very strange, thought I. What had one best do? But my business hurried me. I concluded to forget the matter for the present, reserving it for my future leisure. So calling Nippers from the other room, the paper was speedily examined.

A few days after this, Bartleby concluded four lengthy documents, being quadruplicates of a week's testimony taken before me in my High Court of Chancery. It became necessary to examine them. It was an important suit, and great accuracy was imperative. Having all things arranged, I called Turkey, Nippers, and Ginger Nut from the next room, meaning to place the four copies in the hands of my four clerks, while I should read from the original. Accordingly, Turkey, Nippers, and Ginger Nut had taken their seats in a row, each with his document in his hand, when I called to Bartleby to join this interesting group.

"Bartleby! quick, I am waiting."

I heard a slow scrape of his chair legs on the uncarpeted floor, and soon he appeared standing at the entrance of his hermitage.

"What is wanted?" said he, mildly.

"The copies, the copies," said I, hurriedly. "We are going to examine them. There—" and I held towards him the fourth quadruplicate.

"I would prefer not to," he said, and gently disappeared behind the screen.

For a few moments I was turned into a pillar of salt, standing at the head of my seated column of clerks. Recovering myself, I advanced towards the screen, and demanded the reason for such extraordinary conduct.

"Why do you refuse?"

"I would prefer not to."

With any other man I should have flown outright into a dreadful passion, scorned all further words, and thrust him ignominiously from my presence. But there was something about Bartleby that not only strangely disarmed me, but in a wonderful manner, touched and disconcerted me. I began to reason with him.

"These are your own copies we are about to examine. It is labor saving to you, because one examination will answer for your four papers. It is common usage. Every copyist is bound to help examine his copy. Is it not so? Will you not speak? Answer!"

"I prefer not to," he replied in a flutelike tone. It seemed to me that, while I had been addressing him, he carefully revolved every statement that I made; fully comprehended the meaning; could not gainsay the irresistible conclusion; but, at the same time, some paramount consideration prevailed with him to reply as he did.

"You are decided, then, not to comply with my request—a request made according to common usage and common sense?"

He briefly gave me to understand, that on that point my judgment was sound. Yes: his decision was irreversible.

It is not seldom the case that, when a man is browbeaten in some unprecedented and violently unreasonable way, he begins to stagger in his own plainest faith. He begins, as it were, vaguely to surmise that, wonderful as it may be, all the justice and all the reason is on the other side. Accordingly, if any disinterested persons are present, he turns to them for some reinforcement of his own faltering mind.

"Turkey," said I, "what do you think of this? Am I not right?"

"With submission, sir," said Turkey, in his blandest tone, "I think that you are."

"Nippers," said I, "what do *you* think of it?"

"I think I should kick him out of the office."

(The reader, of nice perceptions, will here perceive that, it being morning, Turkey's answer is couched in polite and tranquil terms, but Nippers replies in ill-tempered ones. Or, to repeat a previous sentence, Nippers's ugly mood was on duty, and Turkey's off.)

"Ginger Nut," said I, willing to enlist the smallest suffrage in my behalf, "what do you think of it?"

"I think, sir, he's a little *luny*," replied Ginger Nut, with a grin.

"You hear what they say," said I, turning towards the screen, "come forth and do your duty."

But he vouchsafed no reply. I pondered a moment in sore perplexity. But once more business hurried me. I determined again to postpone the consideration of this dilemma to my future leisure. With a little trouble we made out to examine the papers without Bartleby, though at every page or two Turkey deferentially dropped his opinion, that this proceeding was quite out of the common; while Nippers, twitching in his chair with a dyspeptic nervousness, ground out, between his set teeth, occasional hissing maledictions against the stubborn oaf behind the screen. And for his (Nippers's) part, this was the first and the last time he would do another man's business without pay.

Meanwhile Bartleby sat in his hermitage, oblivious to everything but his own peculiar business there.

Some days passed, the scrivener being employed upon another lengthy work. His late remarkable conduct led me to regard his ways narrowly. I observed that he never went to dinner; indeed, that he never went anywhere. As yet I had never, of my personal knowledge, known him to be outside of my office. He was a perpetual sentry in the corner. At about eleven o'clock though, in the morning, I noticed that Ginger Nut would advance toward the opening in Bartleby's screen, as if silently beckoned thither by a gesture invisible to me where I sat. The boy would then leave the office, jingling a few pence, and reappear with a handful of ginger-nuts, which he delivered in the hermitage, receiving two of the cakes for his trouble.

He lives, then, on ginger-nuts, thought I; never eats a dinner, properly speaking; he must be a vegetarian, then; but no; he never eats even vegetables; he eats nothing but ginger-nuts. My mind then ran on in reveries concerning the probable effects upon the human constitution of living entirely on ginger-nuts. Ginger-nuts are so called, because they contain ginger as one of their peculiar constituents, and the final flavoring one. Now, what was ginger? A hot, spicy thing. Was Bartleby hot and spicy? Not at all. Ginger, then, had no effect upon Bartleby. Probably he preferred it should have none.

Nothing so aggravates an earnest person as a passive resistance. If the individual so resisted be of a not inhuman temper, and the resisting one perfectly harmless in his passivity, then, in the better moods of the former, he will endeavor charitably to construe to his imagination what proves impossible to be solved by his judgment. Even so, for the most part, I regarded Bartleby and his ways. Poor fellow! thought I, he means no mischief; it is plain he intends no insolence; his aspect sufficiently evinces that his eccentricities are involuntary. He is useful to me. I can get along with him. If I turn him away, the chances are he will fall in with some less-indulgent employer, and then he will be rudely treated, and perhaps driven forth miserably to starve. Yes. Here I can cheaply purchase a delicious self-approval. To befriend Bartleby; to humor him in his strange willfulness, will cost me little or nothing, while I lay up in my soul what will eventually prove a sweet morsel for my conscience. But this mood was not invariable with me. The passiveness of Bartleby sometimes irritated me. I felt strangely goaded on to encounter him in new opposition—to elicit some angry spark from him answerable to my own. But, indeed, I might as well have essayed to strike fire with my knuckles against a bit of Windsor soap. But one afternoon the evil impulse in me mastered me, and the following little scene ensued:

"Bartleby," said I, "when those papers are all copied, I will compare them with you."

"I would prefer not to."

"How? Surely you do not mean to persist in that mulish vagary?"

No answer.

I threw open the folding-doors near by, and, turning upon Turkey and Nippers, exclaimed:

"Bartleby a second time says, he won't examine his papers. What do you think of it, Turkey?"

It was afternoon, be it remembered. Turkey sat glowing like a brass boiler; his bald head steaming; his hands reeling among his blotted papers.

"Think of it?" roared Turkey; "I think I'll just step behind his screen, and black his eyes for him!"

So saying, Turkey rose to his feet and threw his arms into a pugilistic position. He was hurrying away to make good his promise, when I detained him, alarmed at the effect of incautiously rousing Turkey's combativeness after dinner.

"Sit down, Turkey," said I, "and hear what Nippers has to say. What do you think of it, Nippers? Would I not be justified in immediately dismissing Bartleby?"

"Excuse me, that is for you to decide, sir. I think his conduct quite unusual, and, indeed, unjust, as regards Turkey and myself. But it may only be a passing whim."

"Ah," exclaimed I, "you have strangely changed your mind, then—you speak very gently of him now."

"All beer," cried Turkey; "gentleness is effects of beer—Nippers and I dined together to-day. You see how gentle I am, sir. Shall I go and black his eyes?"

"You refer to Bartleby, I suppose. No, not to-day, Turkey," I replied; "pray, put up your fists."

I closed the doors, and again advanced towards Bartleby. I felt additional incentives tempting me to my fate. I burned to be rebelled against again. I remembered that Bartleby never left the office.

"Bartleby," said I, "Ginger Nut is away; just step around to the Post Office, won't you? (it was but a three minutes' walk), and see if there is anything for me."

"I would prefer not to."

"You *will* not?"

"I *prefer* not."

I staggered to my desk, and sat there in a deep study. My blind inveteracy returned. Was there any other thing in which I could procure myself to be ignominiously repulsed by this lean, penniless wight? — my hired clerk? What added thing is there, perfectly reasonable, that he will be sure to refuse to do?

"Bartleby!"

No answer.

"Bartleby," in a louder tone.

No answer.

"Bartleby," I roared.

Like a very ghost, agreeably to the laws of magical invocation, at the third summons, he appeared at the entrance of his hermitage.

"Go to the next room, and tell Nippers to come to me."

"I prefer not to," he respectively and slowly said, and mildly disappeared.

"Very good, Bartleby," said I, in a quiet sort of serenely-severe, self-possessed tone, intimating the unalterable purpose of some terrible retribution very close at hand. At the moment I half intended something of the kind. But upon the whole, as it was drawing towards my dinner-hour, I thought it best to put on my hat and walk home for the day, suffering much from perplexity and distress of mind.

Shall I acknowledge it? The conclusion of this whole business was, that it soon became a fixed fact of my chambers, that a pale young scrivener, by the name of Bartleby, had a desk there; that he copied for me at the usual rate of four cents a folio (one hundred words); but he was permanently exempt from examining the work done by him, that duty being transferred to Turkey and Nippers, out of compliment, doubtless, to their superior acuteness; moreover, said Bartleby was never, on any account, to be dispatched on the most trivial errand of any sort; and that even if entreated to take upon him such a matter, it was generally understood that he would "prefer not to" — in other words, that he would refuse point-blank.

As days passed on, I became considerably reconciled to Bartleby. His steadiness, his freedom from all dissipation, his incessant industry (except when he chose to throw himself into a standing revery behind his screen), his great stillness, his unalterableness of demeanor under all circumstances, made him a valuable acquisition. One prime thing was this — *he was always there* — first in the morning, continually through the day, and the last at night. I had a singular confidence in his honesty. I felt my most precious papers perfectly safe in his hands. Sometimes, to be sure, I could not, for the very soul of me, avoid falling into sudden spasmodic passions with him. For it was exceeding difficult to bear in mind all the time those strange peculiarities, privileges, and unheard of exemptions, forming the tacit stipulations on Bartleby's part under which he remained in my office. Now and then, in the eagerness of dispatching pressing business, I would inadvertently summon Bartleby, in a short, rapid tone, to put his finger, say, on the incipient tie of a bit of red tape with which I was about compressing some papers. Of course, from behind the screen the usual answer, "I prefer not to," was sure to come; and then, how could a human creature, with the common infirmities of our nature, refrain from bitterly exclaiming upon such perverseness — such unreasonableness. However, every added repulse of this sort which I received only tended to lessen the probability of my repeating the inadvertence.

Here it must be said, that according to the custom of most legal gentlemen occupying chambers in densely-populated law buildings, there were several keys to my door. One was kept by a woman residing in the attic, which person weekly scrubbed and daily swept and dusted my apartments. Another was kept by Turkey for convenience sake. The third I sometimes carried in my own pocket. The fourth I knew not who had.

Now, one Sunday morning I happened to go to Trinity Church, to hear a celebrated preacher, and finding myself rather early on the ground I thought I would walk around to my chambers for a while. Luckily I had my key with me; but upon applying it to the lock, I found it resisted by something inserted from the inside. Quite surprised, I called out; when to my consternation a key was turned from within; and thrusting his lean visage at me, and holding the door ajar, the apparition of Bartleby appeared, in his shirt sleeves, and otherwise in a strangely tattered *déshabillé*, saying quietly that he was sorry, but he was deeply engaged just then, and — preferred not admitting me at present. In a brief word or two, he moreover added, that perhaps I had better walk around the block two or three times, and by that time he would probably have concluded his affairs.

Now, the utterly unsurmised appearance of Bartleby, tenanting my law-chambers of a Sunday morning, with his cadaverously gentlemanly *nonchalance*, yet withal firm and self-possessed, had such a strange effect upon me, that incontinently I slunk away from my own door, and did as desired. But not without sundry twinges of impotent rebellion against the mild effrontery of this unaccountable scrivener. Indeed, it was his wonderful mildness chiefly, which not only disarmed me, but unmanned me as it were. For I consider that one, for the time, is somehow unmanned when he tranquilly permits his hired clerk to dictate to him, and order him away from his own premises. Furthermore, I was full of uneasiness as to what Bartleby could possibly be doing in my office in his shirt sleeves, and in an otherwise dismantled condition of a Sunday morning. Was anything amiss going on? Nay, that was out of the question. It was not to be thought of for a moment that Bartleby was an immoral person. But what could he be doing there? — copying? Nay again, whatever might be his eccentricities, Bartleby was an eminently decorous person. He would be the last man to sit down to his desk in any state approaching to nudity. Besides, it was Sunday; and there was something about Bartleby that forbade the supposition that he would by any secular occupation violate the proprieties of the day.

Nevertheless, my mind was not pacified; and full of a restless curiosity, at last I returned to the door. Without hindrance I inserted my key, opened it, and entered. Bartleby was not to be seen. I looked round anxiously, peeped behind his screen; but it was very plain that he was gone. Upon more closely examining the place, I surmised that for an indefinite period Bartleby must have eaten, dressed, and slept in my office, and that, too, without plate, mirror, or bed. The cushioned seat of a ricketty old sofa in one corner bore the faint impress of a lean, reclining form. Rolled away under his desk, I found a blanket; under the empty grate, a blacking box and brush; on a chair, a tin basin, with soap and a ragged towel; in a newspaper a few crumbs of ginger-nuts and a morsel of cheese. Yes, thought I, it is evident enough that Bartleby has been making his home here, keeping bachelor's hall all by himself. Immediately then the thought came sweeping across me, what miserable friendlessness and loneliness are here revealed! His poverty is great; but his solitude, how horrible! Think of it. Of a Sunday, Wall Street is deserted as Petra; and every night of every day it is an emptiness. This building, too, which of weekdays hums with industry and life, at nightfall echoes with sheer vacancy, and all through Sunday is forlorn. And here Bartleby makes his home; sole spectator of a solitude which he has seen all populous—a sort of innocent and transformed Marius brooding among the ruins of Carthage!

For the first time in my life a feeling of over-powering stinging melancholy seized me. Before, I had never experienced aught but a not unpleasing sadness. The bond of a common humanity now drew me irresistibly to gloom. A fraternal melancholy! For both I and Bartleby were sons of Adam. I remembered the bright silks and sparkling faces I had seen that day, in gala trim, swan-like sailing down the Mississippi of Broadway; and I contrasted them with the pallid copyist, and thought to myself, Ah, happiness courts the light, so we deem the world is gay; but misery hides aloof, so we deem that misery there is none. These sad fancyings—chimeras, doubtless, of a sick and silly brain—led on to other and more special thoughts, concerning the eccentricities of Bartleby. Presentiments of strange discoveries hovered round me. The scrivener's pale form appeared to me laid out, among uncaring strangers, in its shivering winding sheet.

Suddenly I was attracted by Bartleby's closed desk, the key in open sight left in the lock.

I mean no mischief, seek the gratification of no heartless curiosity, thought I; besides, the desk is mine, and its contents, too, so I will make bold to look within. Everything was methodically arranged, the papers smoothly placed. The pigeon holes were deep, and removing the files of documents, I groped into their recesses. Presently I felt something there, and dragged it out. It was an old bandanna handkerchief, heavy and knotted. I opened it, and saw it was a savings's bank.

I now recalled all the quiet mysteries which I had noted in the man. I remembered that he never spoke but to answer; that, though at intervals he had considerable time to himself, yet I had never seen him reading—no, not even a newspaper; that for long periods he would stand looking out, at his pale window behind the screen, upon the dead brick wall; I was quite sure he never visited any refectory or eating house; while his pale face clearly indicated that he never drank beer like Turkey, or tea and coffee even, like other men; that he never went anywhere in particular that I could learn; never went out for a walk, unless, indeed, that was the case at present; that he had declined telling who he was, or whence he came, or whether he had any relatives in the world; that though so thin and pale, he never complained of ill health. And more than all, I remembered a certain unconscious air of pallid—how shall I call it?—of pallid haughtiness, say, or rather an austere reserve about him, which had positively awed me into my tame compliance with his eccentricities, when I had feared to ask him to do the slightest incidental thing for me, even though I might know, for his long-continued motionlessness, that behind his screen he must be standing in one of those dead-wall reveries of his.

Revolving all these things, and coupling them with the recently discovered fact, that he made my office his constant abiding place and home, and not forgetful of his morbid moodiness; revolving all these things, a prudential feeling began to steal over me. My first emotions had been those of pure melancholy and sincerest pity; but just in proportion as the forlornness of Bartleby grew and grew to my imagination, did that same melancholy merge into fear, that pity into repulsion. So true it is, and so terrible, too, that up to a certain point the thought or sight of misery enlists our best affections; but, in certain special cases, beyond that point it does not. They err who would assert that invariably this is owing to the inherent selfishness of the human heart. It rather proceeds from a certain hopelessness of remedying excessive and organic ill. To a sensitive being, pity is not seldom pain. And when at last it is perceived that such pity cannot lead to effectual succor, common sense bids the soul be rid of it. What I saw that morning persuaded me that the scrivener was the victim of innate and incurable disorder. I might give alms to his body; but his body did not pain him; it was his soul that suffered, and his soul I could not reach.

I did not accomplish the purpose of going to Trinity Church that morning. Somehow, the things I had seen disqualified me for the time from church-going. I walked homeward, thinking what I would do with Bartleby. Finally, I resolved upon this—I would put certain calm questions to him the next morning, touching his history, etc., and if he declined to answer them openly and unreservedly (and I supposed he would prefer not), then to give him a twenty dollar bill over and above whatever I might owe him, and tell him his services were no longer required; but that if in any other way I could assist him, I would be happy to do so, especially if he desired to return to his native place, wherever that might be, I would willingly help to defray the expenses. Moreover, if, after reaching home, he found himself at any time in want of aid, a letter from him would be sure of a reply.

The next morning came.

"Bartleby," said I, gently calling to him behind his screen.

No reply.

The next morning came.

"Bartleby," said I, gently calling to him behind his screen.

No reply.

"Bartleby," said I, in a still gentler tone, "come here; I am not going to ask you to do anything you would prefer not to do—I simply wish to speak to you."

Upon this he noiselessly slid into view.

"Will you tell me, Bartleby, where you were born?"

"I would prefer not to."

"Will you tell me anything about yourself?"

"I would prefer not to."

"But what reasonable objection can you have to speak to me? I feel friendly towards you."

He did not look at me while I spoke, but kept his glance fixed upon my bust of Cicero, which, as I then sat, was directly behind me, some six inches above my head.

"What is your answer, Bartleby," said I, after waiting a considerable time for a reply, during which his countenance remained immovable, only there was the faintest conceivable tremor of the white attenuated mouth.

"At present I prefer to give no answer," he said, and retired into his hermitage.

It was rather weak in me I confess, but his manner, on this occasion, nettled me. Not only did there seem to lurk in it a certain calm disdain, but his perverseness seemed ungrateful, considering the undeniable good usage and indulgence he had received from me.

Again I sat ruminating what I should do. Mortified as I was at his behavior, and resolved as I had been to dismiss him when I entered my office, nevertheless I strangely felt something superstitious knocking at my heart, and forbidding me to carry out my purpose, and denouncing me for a villain if I dared to breathe one bitter word against this forlornest of mankind. At last, familiarly drawing my chair behind his screen, I sat down and said: "Bartleby, never mind, then, about revealing your history; but let me entreat you, as a friend, to comply as far as may be with the usages of this office. Say now, you will help to examine papers to-morrow or next day: in short, say now, that in a day or two you will begin to be a little reasonable: — say so, Bartleby."

"At present I would prefer not to be a little reasonable," was his mildly cadaverous reply.

Just then the folding-doors opened, and Nippers approached. He seemed suffering from an unusually bad night's rest, induced by severer indigestion than common. He overhead those final words of Bartleby.

"*Prefer not*, eh?" gritted Nippers — "I'd *prefer* him, if I were you, sir," addressing me — "I'd prefer him; I'd give him preferences, the stubborn mule! What is it, sir, pray, that he *prefers* not to do now?"

Bartleby moved not a limb.

"Mr. Nippers," said I, "I'd prefer that you would withdraw for the present."

Somehow, of late, I had got into the way of involuntarily using this word "prefer" upon all sorts of not exactly suitable occasions. And I trembled to think that my contact with the scrivener had already and seriously affected me in a mental way. And what further and deeper aberration might it not yet produce? This apprehension had not been without efficacy in determining me to summary measures.

As Nippers, looking very sour and sulky, was departing, Turkey blandly and deferentially approached.

"With submission, sir," said he, "yesterday I was thinking about Bartleby here, and I think that if he would but prefer to take a quart of good ale every day, it would do much towards mending him, and enabling him to assist in examining his papers."

"So you have got the word, too," said I, slightly excited.

"With submission, what word, sir," asked Turkey, respectfully crowding himself into the contracted space behind the screen, and by so doing, making me jostle the scrivener. "What word, sir?"

"I would prefer to be left alone here," said Bartleby, as if offended at being mobbed in his privacy.

"*That's* the word, Turkey," said I — "*that's* it,"

"Oh, *prefer*? oh yes — queer word. I never use it myself. But, sir, as I was saying, if he would but prefer —"

"Turkey," interrupted I, "you will please withdraw."

"Oh certainly, sir, if you prefer that I should."

As he opened the folding-door to retire, Nippers at his desk caught a glimpse of me, and asked whether I would prefer to have a certain paper copied on blue paper or white. He did not in the least roguishly accent the word prefer. It was plain that it involuntarily rolled from his tongue. I thought to myself, surely I must get rid of a demented man, who already has in some degree turned the tongues, if not the heads of myself and clerks. But I thought it prudent not to break the dismission at once.

The next day I noticed that Bartleby did nothing but stand at his window in his dead-wall revery. Upon asking him why he did not write, he said that he had decided upon doing no more writing.

"Why, how now? what next?" exclaimed I, "do no more writing?"

"No more."

"And what is the reason?"

"Do you not see the reason for yourself," he indifferently replied.

I looked steadfastly at him, and perceived that his eyes looked dull and glazed. Instantly it occurred to me, that his unexampled diligence in copying by his dim window or the first few weeks of his stay with me might have temporarily impaired his vision.

I was touched. I said something in condolence with him. I hinted that of course he did wisely in abstaining from writing for a while; and urged him to embrace that opportunity of taking wholesome exercise in the open air. This, however, he did not do. A few days after this, my other clerks being absent, and being in a great hurry to dispatch certain letters by the mail, I thought that, having nothing else earthly to do, Bartleby would surely be less inflexible than usual, and carry these letters to the post-office. But he blankly declined. So, much to my inconvenience, I went myself.

Still added days went by. Whether Bartleby's eyes improved or not, I could not say. To all appearance I thought they did. But when I asked him if they did, he vouchsafed no answer. At all events, he would do no copying. At last, in reply to my urgings, he informed me that he had permanently given up copying.

"What!" exclaimed I; "suppose your eyes should get entirely well — better than ever before — would you not copy then?"

"I have given up copying," he answered, and slid aside.

He remained as ever, a fixture in my chamber. Nay — if that were possible — he became still more of a fixture than before. What was to be done? He would do nothing in the office; why should he stay there? In plain fact, he had now become a millstone to me, not only useless as a necklace, but afflictive to bear. Yet I was sorry for him. I speak less than truth when I say that, on his own account, he occasioned me uneasiness. If he would but have named a single relative or friend, I would instantly have written and urged their taking the poor fellow away to some convenient retreat. But he seemed alone, absolutely alone in the universe.

A bit of wreck in the mid Atlantic. At length, necessities connected with my business tyrannized over all other considerations. Decently as I could, I told Bartleby that in six days times he must unconditionally leave the office. I warned him to take measures, in the interval, for procuring some other abode. I offered to assist him in his endeavor, if he himself would but take the first step towards a removal. "And when you finally quit me, Bartleby," added I, "I shall see that you go not away entirely unprovided. Six days from this hour, remember."

At the expiration of that period, I peeped behind the screen, and lo! Bartleby was there.

I buttoned up my coat, balanced myself; advanced slowly towards him, touched his shoulder, and said, "The time has come; you must quit this place; I am sorry for you; here is money; but you must go."

"I would prefer not," he replied, with his back still towards me.

"You *must*."

He remained silent.

Now I had an unbounded confidence in this man's common honesty. He had frequently restored to me sixpences and shillings carelessly dropped upon the floor, for I am apt to be very reckless in such shirt-button affairs. The proceeding, then, which followed will not be deemed extraordinary.

"Bartleby," said I, "I owe you twelve dollars on account; here are thirty-two; the odd twenty are yours — Will you take it?" and I handed the bills towards him.

But he made no motion.

"I will leave them here, then," putting them under a weight on the table. Then taking my hat and cane and going to the door, I tranquilly turned and added — "After you have removed your things from these offices, Bartleby, you will of course lock the door — since every one is now gone for the day but you — and if you please, slip your key underneath the mat, so that I may have it in the morning. I shall not see you again; so good-by to you. If, hereafter, in your new place of abode, I can be of any service to you, do not fail to advise me by letter. Good-by, Bartleby, and fare you well."

But he answered not a word; like the last column of some ruined temple, he remained standing mute and solitary in the middle of the otherwise deserted room.

As I walked home in a pensive mood, my vanity got the better of my pity. I could not but highly plume myself on my masterly management in getting rid of Bartleby. Masterly I call it, and such it must appear to any dispassionate thinker. The beauty of my procedure seemed to consist in its perfect quietness. There was no vulgar bullying, no bravado of any sort, no choleric hectoring, and striding to and fro across the apartment, jerking out vehement commands for Bartleby to bundle himself off with his beggarly traps. Nothing of the kind. Without loudly bidding Bartleby depart — as an inferior genius might have done — I *assumed* the ground that depart he must; and upon that assumption built all I had to say. The more I thought over my procedure, the more I was charmed with it. Nevertheless, next morning, upon awakening, I had my doubts — I had somehow slept off the fumes of vanity. One of the coolest and wisest hours a man has, is just after he awakes in the morning. My procedure seemed as sagacious as ever — but only in theory. How it would prove in practice — there was the rub. It was truly a beautiful thought to have assumed Bartleby's departure; but, after all, that assumption was simply my own, and none of Bartleby's. The great point was, not whether I had assumed that he would quit me, but whether he would prefer so to do. He was more a man of preferences than assumptions.

After breakfast, I walked down town, arguing the probabilities *pro* and *con.* One moment I thought it would prove a miserable failure, and Bartleby would be found all alive at my office as usual; the next moment it seemed certain that I should find his chair empty. And so I kept veering about. At the corner of Broadway and Canal Street, I saw quite an excited group of people standing in earnest conversation.

"I'll take odds he doesn't," said a voice as I passed.

"Doesn't go? — done!" said I; "put up your money."

I was instinctively putting my hand in my pocket to produce my own, when I remembered that this was an election day. The words I had overheard bore no reference to Bartleby, but to the success or non-success of some candidate for the mayoralty. In my intent frame of mind, I had, as it were, imagined that all Broadway shared in my excitement, and were debating the same question with me. I passed on, very thankful that the uproar of the street screened my momentary absent-mindedness.

As I had intended, I was earlier than usual at my office door. I stood listening for a moment. All was still. He must be gone. I tried the knob. The door was locked. Yes, my procedure had worked to a charm; he indeed must be vanished. Yet a certain melancholy mixed with this: I was almost sorry for my brilliant success. I was fumbling under the door mat for the key, which Bartleby was to have left there for me, when accidentally my knee knocked against a panel, producing a summoning sound, and in response a voice came to me from within — "Not yet; I am occupied."

It was Bartleby.

I was thunderstruck. For an instant I stood like the man who, pipe in mouth, was killed one cloudless afternoon long ago in Virginia, by summer lightning; at his own warm open window he was killed, and remained leaning out there upon the dreamy afternoon, till some one touched him, when he fell.

"Not gone!" I murmured at last. But again obeying that wondrous ascendancy which the inscrutable scrivener had over me, and from which ascendancy, for all my chafing, I could not completely escape, I slowly went down stairs and out into the street, and while walking round the block, considered what I should next do in this unheard-of perplexity. Turn the man out by an actual thrusting I could not; to drive him away by calling him hard names would not do; calling in the police was an unpleasant idea; and yet, permit him to enjoy his cadaverous triumph over me — this, too, I could not think of. What was to be done? or, if nothing could be done, was there anything further that I could *assume* in the matter? Yes, as before I had prospectively assumed that Bartleby would depart, so now I might retrospectively assume that departed he was. In the legitimate carrying out of this assumption, I might enter my office in a great hurry, and pretending not to see Bartleby at all, walk straight against him as if he were air. Such a proceeding would in a singular degree have the appearance of a home-thrust. It was hardly possible that Bartleby could withstand such an application of the doctrine of assumptions. But upon second thoughts the success of the plan seemed rather dubious. I resolved to argue the matter over with him again.

"Bartleby," said I, entering the office, with a quietly severe expression, "I am seriously displeased. I am pained, Bartleby. I had thought better of you. I had imagined you of such a gentlemanly organization, that in any delicate dilemma a slight hint would suffice — in short, an assumption. But it appears I am deceived. Why," I added, unaffectedly starting, "you have not even touched that money yet," pointing to it, just where I had left it the evening previous.

He answered nothing.

"Will you, or will you not, quit me?" I now demanded in a sudden passion, advancing close to him.

"I would prefer *not* to quit you," he replied, gently emphasizing the *not*.

"What earthly right have you to stay here? Do you pay any rent? Do you pay my taxes? Or is this property yours?"

He answered nothing.

"Are you ready to go on and write now? Are your eyes recovered? Could you copy a small paper for me this morning? or help examine a few lines? or step round to the post-office? In a word, will you do anything at all, to give a coloring to your refusal to depart the premises?"

He silently retired into his hermitage.

I was now in such a state of nervous resentment that I thought it but prudent to check myself at present from further demonstrations. Bartleby and I were alone. I remembered the tragedy of the unfortunate Adams and the still more unfortunate Colt in the solitary office of the latter; and how poor Colt, being dreadfully incensed by Adams, and imprudently permitting himself to get widely excited, was at unawares hurried into his fatal act — an act which certainly no man could possibly deplore more than the actor himself. Often it had occurred to me in my ponderings upon the subject, that had that altercation taken place in the public street, or at a private residence, it would not have terminated as it did. It was the circumstance of being alone in a solitary office, up stairs, of a building entirely unhallowed by humanizing domestic associations — an uncarpeted office, doubtless, of a dusty, haggard sort of appearance — this it must have been, which greatly helped to enhance the irritable desperation of the hapless Colt.

But when this old Adam of resentment rose in me and tempted me concerning Bartleby, I grappled him and threw him. How? Why, simply by recalling the divine injunction: "A new commandment give I unto you, that ye love one another." Yes, this it was that saved me. Aside from higher considerations, charity often operates as a vastly wise and prudent principle — a great safeguard to its possessor. Men have committed murder for jealousy's sake, and anger's sake, and hatred's sake, and selfishness' sake, and spiritual pride's sake; but no man, that ever I heard of, ever committed a diabolical murder for sweet charity's sake. Mere self-interest, then, if no better motive can be enlisted, should, especially with high-tempered men, prompt all beings to charity and philanthropy. At any rate, upon the occasion in question, I strove to drown my exasperated feelings towards the scrivener by benevolently construing his conduct. Poor fellow, poor fellow! thought I, he don't mean anything; and besides, he has seen hard times, and ought to be indulged.

I endeavored, also, immediately to occupy myself, and at the same time to comfort my despondency. I tried to fancy, that in the course of the morning, at such time as might prove agreeable to him, Bartleby, of his own free accord, would emerge from his hermitage and take up some decided line of march in the direction of the door. But no. Half-past twelve o'clock came; Turkey began to glow in the face, overturn his inkstand, and become generally obstreperous; Nippers abated down into quietude and courtesy; Ginger Nut munched his noon apple; and Bartleby remained standing at his window in one of his profoundest dead-wall reveries. Will it be credited? Ought I to acknowledge it? That afternoon I left the office without saying one further word to him.

Some days now passed, during which, at leisure intervals I looked a little into "Edwards on the Will," and "Priestley on Necessity." Under the circumstances, those books induced a salutary feeling. Gradually I slid into the persuasion that these troubles of mine, touching the scrivener, had been all predestinated from eternity, and Bartleby was billeted upon me for some mysterious purpose of an allwise Providence, which it was not for a mere mortal like me to fathom. Yes, Bartleby, stay there behind your screen, thought I; I shall persecute you no more; you are harmless and noiseless as any of these old chairs; in short, I never feel so private as when I know you are here. At last I see it, I feel it; I penetrate to the predestinated purpose of my life. I am content. Others may have loftier parts to enact; but my mission in this world, Bartleby, is to furnish you with office-room for such period as you may see fit to remain.

I believe that this wise and blessed frame of mind would have continued with me, had it not been for the unsolicited and uncharitable remarks obtruded upon me by my professional friends who visited the rooms. But thus it often is, that the constant friction of illiberal minds wears out at last the best resolves of the more generous. Though to be sure, when I reflected upon it, it was not strange that people entering my office should be struck by the peculiar aspect of the unaccountable Bartleby, and so be tempted to throw out some sinister observations concerning him. Sometimes an attorney, having business with me, and calling at my office, and finding no one but the scrivener there, would undertake to obtain some sort of precise information from him touching my whereabouts; but without heeding his idle talk, Bartleby would remain standing immovable in the middle of the room. So after contemplating him in that position for a time, the attorney would depart, no wiser than he came.

Also, when a reference was going on, and the room full of lawyers and witnesses, and business driving fast, some deeply-occupied legal gentleman present, seeing Bartleby wholly unemployed, would request him to run round to his (the legal gentleman's) office and fetch some papers for him. Thereupon, Bartleby would tranquilly decline, and yet remain idle as before. Then the lawyer would give a great stare, and turn to me. And what could I say? At last I was made aware that all through the circle of my professional acquaintance, a whisper of wonder was running round, having reference to the strange creature I kept at my office. This worried me very much. And as the idea came upon me of his possibly turning out a long-lived man, and keep occupying my chambers, and denying my authority; and perplexing my visitors; and scandalizing my professional reputation; and casting a general gloom over the premises; keeping soul and body together to the last upon his savings (for doubtless he spent but half a dime a day), and in the end perhaps outlive me, and claim possession of my office by right of his perpetual occupancy: as all these dark anticipations crowded upon me more and more, and my friends continually intruded their relentless remarks upon the apparition in my room; a great change was wrought in me. I resolved to gather all my faculties together, and forever rid me of this intolerable incubus.

Ere revolving any complicated project, however, adapted to this end, I first simply suggested to Bartleby the propriety of his permanent departure. In a calm and serious tone, I commended the idea to his careful and mature consideration. But, having taken three days to meditate upon it, he apprised me, that his original determination remained the same; in short, that he still preferred to abide with me.

What shall I do? I now said to myself, buttoning up my coat to the last button. What shall I do? what ought I to do? what does conscience say I *should* do with this man, or, rather, ghost. Rid myself of him, I must; go, he shall. But how? You will not thrust him, the poor, pale, passive mortal — you will not thrust such a helpless creature out of your door? you will not dishonor yourself by such cruelty? No, I will not, I cannot do that. Rather would I let him live and die here, and then mason up his remains in the wall. What, then, will you do? For all your coaxing, he will not budge. Bribes he leaves under your own paper-weight on your table; in short, it is quite plain that he prefers to cling to you.

Then something severe, something unusual must be done. What! surely you will not have him collared by a constable, and commit his innocent pallor to the common jail? And upon what ground could you procure such a thing to be done? — a vagrant, is he? What! he a vagrant, a wanderer, who refuses to budge? It is because he will *not* be a vagrant, then, that you seek to count him *as* a vagrant. That is too absurd. No visible means of support: there I have him. Wrong again: for indubitably he *does* support himself, and that is the only unanswerable proof that any man can show of his possessing the means so to do. No more, then. Since he will not quit me, I must quit him. I will change my offices; I will move elsewhere, and give him fair notice, that if I find him on my new premises I will then proceed against him as a common trespasser.

Acting accordingly, next day I thus addressed him: "I find these chambers too far from the City Hall; the air is unwholesome. In a word, I propose to remove my offices next week, and shall no longer require your services. I tell you this now, in order that you may seek another place."

He made no reply; and nothing more was said.

On the appointed day I engaged carts and men, proceeded to my chambers, and, having but little furniture, everything was removed in a few hours. Throughout, the scrivener remained standing behind the screen, which I directed to be removed the last thing. It was withdrawn; and, being folded up like a huge folio, left him the motionless occupant of a naked room. I stood in the entry watching him a moment, while something from within me upbraided me.

I re-entered, with my hand in my pocket — and — and my heart in my mouth.

"Good-by, Bartleby; I am going — good-by, and God some way bless you; and take that," slipping something in his hand. But it dropped upon the floor, and then — strange to say — I tore myself from him whom I had so longed to be rid of.

Established in my new quarters, for a day or two I kept the door locked, and started at every footfall in the passages. When I returned to my rooms, after any little absence, I would pause at the threshold for an instant, and attentively listen, ere applying my key. But these fears were needless. Bartleby never came nigh me.

I thought all was going well, when a perturbed-looking stranger visited me, inquiring whether I was the person who had recently occupied rooms at No. — Wall Street.

"Then, sir," said the stranger, who proved a lawyer, "you are responsible for the man you left there. He refuses to do any copying; he refuses to do anything; he says he prefers not to; and he refuses to quite the premises."

"I am very sorry, sir," said I, with assumed tranquillity, but an inward tremor, "but, really, the man you allude to is nothing to me — he is no relation or apprentice of mine, that you should hold me responsible for him."

"In mercy's name, who is he?"

"I certainly cannot inform you. I know nothing about him. Formerly I employed him as a copyist; but he has done nothing for me now for some time past."

"I shall settle him, then — good morning, sir."

Several days passed, and I heard nothing more; and, though I often felt a charitable prompting to call at the place and see poor Bartleby, yet a certain squeamishness, of I know not what, withheld me.

All is over with him, by this time, thought I, at last, when, through another week, no further intelligence reached me. But, coming to my room the day after, I found several persons waiting at my door in a high state of nervous excitement.

"That's the man — here he comes," cried the foremost one, whom I recognized as the lawyer who had previously called upon me alone.

"You must take him away, sir, at once," cried a portly person among them, advancing upon me, and whom I knew to be the landlord of No. — Wall Street. "These gentlemen, my tenants, cannot stand it any longer; Mr. B — ," pointing to the lawyer, "has turned him out of his room, and he now persists in haunting the building generally, sitting upon the banisters of the stairs by day, and sleeping in the entry by night. Everybody is concerned; clients are leaving the offices; some fears are entertained of a mob; something you must do, and that without delay."

Aghast at this torrent, I fell back before it, and would fain have locked myself in my new quarters. In vain I persisted that Bartleby was nothing to me — no more than to any one else. In vain — I was the last person known to have anything to do with him, and they held me to the terrible account. Fearful, then, of being exposed in the papers (as one person present obscurely threatened), I considered the matter, and, at length, said, that if the lawyer would give me a confidential interview with the scrivener, in his (the lawyer's) own room, I would, that afternoon, strive my best to rid them of the nuisance they complained of.

Going up stairs to my old haunt, there was Bartleby silently sitting upon the banister at the landing.

"What are you doing here, Bartleby?" said I.

"Sitting upon the banister," he mildly replied.

I motioned him into the lawyer's room, who then left us.

"Bartleby," said I, "are you aware that you are the cause of great tribulation to me, by persisting in occupying the entry after being dismissed from the office?"

No answer.

"Now one of two things must take place. Either you must do something, or something must be done to you. Now what sort of business would you like to engage in? Would you like to re-engage in copying for some one?"

"No; I would prefer not to make any change."

"Would you like a clerkship in a dry-goods store?"

"There is too much confinement about that. No, I would not like a clerkship; but I am not particular."

"Too much confinement," I cried, "why you keep yourself confined all the time!"

"I would prefer not to take a clerkship," he rejoined, as if to settle that little item at once.

"How would a bar-tender's business suit you? There is no trying of the eye-sight in that."

"I would not like it at all; though, as I said before, I am not particular."

His unwonted wordiness inspirited me. I returned to the charge.

"Well, then, would you like to travel through the country collecting bills for the merchants? That would improve your health."

"No, I would prefer to be doing something else."

"How, then, would going as a companion to Europe, to entertain some young gentleman with your conversation—how would that suit you?"

"Not at all. It does not strike me that there is anything definite about that. I like to be stationary. But I am not particular."

"Stationary you shall be, then," I cried, now losing all patience, and, for the first time in all my exasperating connection with him, fairly flying into a passion. "If you do not go away from these premises before night, I shall feel bound— indeed, I *am* bound—to—to—to quit the premises myself!" I rather absurdly concluded, knowing not with what possible threat to try to frighten his immobility into compliance. Despairing of all further efforts, I was precipitately leaving him, when a final thought occurred to me—one which had not been wholly unindulged before.

"Bartleby," said I, in the kindest tone I could assume under such exciting circumstances, "will you go home with me now—not to my office, but my dwelling—and remain there till we can conclude upon some convenient arrangement for you at our leisure? Come, let us start now, right away."

"No: at present I would prefer not to make any change at all,"

I answered nothing; but, effectually dodging every one by the suddenness and rapidity of my flight, rushed from the building, ran up Wall Street towards Broadway, and, jumping into the first omnibus, was soon removed from pursuit. As soon as tranquillity returned, I distinctly perceived that I had now done all that I possibly could, both in respect to the demands of the landlord and his tenants, and with regard to my own desire and sense of duty, to benefit Bartleby, and shield him from rude persecution. I now strove to be entirely care-free and quiescent; and my conscience justified me in the attempt; though, indeed, it was not so successful as I could have wished. So fearful was I of being again hunted out by the incensed landlord and his exasperated tenants, that, surrendering my business to Nippers, for a few days, I drove about the upper part of the town and through the suburbs, in my rockaway; crossed over to Jersey City and Hoboken, and paid fugitive visits to Manhattanville and Astoria. In fact, I almost lived in my rockaway for the time.

When again I entered my office, lo, a note from the landlord lay upon the desk. I opened it with trembling hands. It informed me that the writer had sent to the police, and had Bartleby removed to the Tombs as a vagrant. Moreover, since I knew more about him than any one else, he wished me to appear at that place, and make a suitable statement of the facts. These tidings had a conflicting effect upon me. At first I was indignant; but, at last, almost approved. The landlord's energetic, summary disposition, had led him to adopt a procedure which I do not think I would have decided upon myself; and yet, as a last resort, under such peculiar circumstances, it seemed the only plan.

As I afterwards learned, the poor scrivener, when told that he must be conducted to the Tombs, offered not the slightest obstacle, but, in his pale, unmoving way, silently acquiesced.

Some of the compassionate and curious bystanders joined the party; and headed by one of the constables arm in arm with Bartleby, the silent procession filed its way through all the noise, and heat, and joy of the roaring thoroughfares at noon.

The same day I received the note, I went to the Tombs, or, to speak more properly, the Halls of Justice. Seeking the right officer, I stated the purpose of my call, and was informed that the individual I described was, indeed, within. I then assured the functionary that Bartleby was a perfectly honest man, and greatly to be compassionated, however unaccountably eccentric. I narrated all I knew, and closed by suggesting the idea of letting him remain in as indulgent confinement as possible, till something less harsh might be done — though, indeed, I hardly knew what. At all events, if nothing else could be decided upon the alms-house must receive him. I then begged to have an interview.

Being under no disgraceful charge, and quite serene and harmless in all his ways, they had permitted him freely to wander about the prison, and, especially, in the inclosed grass-platted yards thereof. And so I found him there, standing all alone in the quietest of the yards, his face towards a high wall, while all around, from the narrow slits of the jail windows, I thought I saw peering out upon him the eyes of murderers and thieves.

"Bartleby!"

"I know you," he said, without looking around — "and I want nothing to say to you."

"It was not I that brought you here, Bartleby," said I, keenly pained at his implied suspicion. "And to you, this should not be so vile a place. Nothing reproachful attaches to you by being here. And see, it is not so sad a place as one might think. Look, there is the sky, and here is the grass."

"I know where I am," he replied, but would say nothing more, and so I left him.

As I entered the corridor again, a broad meat-like man, in an apron, accosted me, and, jerking his thumb over his shoulder, said — "Is that your friend?"

"Yes."

"Does he want to starve? If he does, let him live on the prison fare, that's all."

"Who are you?" asked I, not knowing what to make of such an unofficially speaking person in such a place.

"I am the grub-man. Such gentlemen as have friends here, hire me to provide them with something good to eat."

"Is this so?" said I, turning to the turnkey.

He said it was.

"Well, then," said I, slipping some silver into the grub-man's hands (for so they called him), "I want you to give particular attention to my friend there; let him have the best dinner you can get. And you must be as polite to him as possible."

"Introduce me, will you?" said the grub-man, looking at me with an expression which seemed to say he was all impatience for an opportunity to give a specimen of his breeding.

Thinking it would prove of benefit to the scrivener, I acquiesced; and, asking the grub-man his name, went up with him to Bartleby.

"Bartleby, this is a friend; you will find him very useful to you."

"Your sarvant, sir, your sarvant," said the grub-man, making a low salutation behind his apron. "Hope you find it pleasant here, sir; nice grounds — cool apartments — hope you'll stay with us sometime — try to make it agreeable. What will you have for dinner to-day?"

"I prefer not to dine to-day," said Bartleby, turning away. "It would disagree with me; I am unused to dinners." So saying, he slowly moved to the other side of the inclosure, and took up a position fronting the dead-wall.

"How's this?" said the grub-man, addressing me with a stare of astonishment. "He's odd, ain't he?"

"I think he is a little deranged," said I, sadly.

"Deranged? deranged is it? Well, now, upon my word, I thought that friend of yourn was a gentleman forger; they are always pale and genteel-like, them forgers. I can't help pity'em — can't help it, sir. Did you know Monroe Edwards?" he added, touchingly, and paused. Then, laying his hand piteously on my shoulder, sighed, "he died of consumption at Sing-Sing. So you weren't acquainted with Monroe?"

"No, I was never socially acquainted with any forgers. But I cannot stop longer. Look to my friend yonder. You will not lose by it. I will see you again."

Some few days after this, I again obtained admission to the Tombs, and went through the corridors in quest of Bartleby; but without finding him.

"I saw him coming from his cell not long ago," said a turnkey, "may be he's gone to loiter in the yards."

So I went in that direction.

"Are you looking for the silent man?" said another turnkey, passing me. "yonder he lies — sleeping in the yard there. 'Tis not twenty minutes since I saw him lie down."

The yard was entirely quiet. It was not accessible to the common prisoners. The surrounding walls, of amazing thickness, kept off all sounds behind them. The Egyptian character of the masonry weighed upon me with its gloom. But a soft imprisoned turf grew under foot. The heart of the eternal pyramids, it seemed, wherein, by some strange magic, through the clefts, grass-seed, dropped by birds, had sprung.

Strangely huddled at the base of the wall, his knees drawn up, and lying on his side, his head touching the cold stones, I saw the wasted Bartleby. But nothing stirred. I paused; then went close up to him; stooped over, and saw that his dim eyes were open; otherwise he seemed profoundly sleeping. Something prompted me to touch him. I felt his hand, when a tingling shiver ran up my arm and down my spine to my feet.

The round face of the grub-man peered upon me now. "His dinner is ready. Won't he dine to-day, either? Or does he live without dining?"

"Lives without dining," said I, and closed the eyes.

"Eh!—He's asleep, ain't he?"

"With kings and counselors," murmured I.

There would seem little need for proceeding further in this history. Imagination will readily supply the meagre recital of poor Bartleby's interment. But, ere parting with the reader, let me say, that if this little narrative has sufficiently interested him to awaken curiosity as to who Bartleby was, and what manner of life he led prior to the present narrator's making his acquaintance, I can only reply, that in such curiosity I fully share, but am wholly unable to gratify it. Yet here I hardly know whether I should divulge one little item of rumor, which came to my ear a few months after the scrivener's decease. Upon what basis it rested, I could never ascertain; and hence, how true it is I cannot now tell. But, inasmuch as this vague report has not been without a certain suggestive interest to me, however said, it may prove the same with some others; and so I will briefly mention it. The report was this: that Bartleby had been a subordinate clerk in the Dead Letter Office at Washington, from which he had been suddenly removed by a change in the administration. When I think over this rumor, hardly can I express the emotions which seize me. Dead letters! does it not sound like dead men? Conceive a man by nature and misfortune prone to a pallid hopelessness, can any business seem more fitted to heighten it than that of continually handling these dead letters, and assorting them for the flames? For by the cart-load they are annually burned. Sometimes from out the folded paper the pale clerk takes a ring—the finger it was meant for, perhaps, moulders in the grave; a bank-note sent in swiftest charity—he whom it would relieve, nor eats nor hungers any more; pardon for those who died despairing; hope for those who died unhoping; good tidings for those who died stifled by unrelieved calamities. On errands of life, these letters speed to death.

Ah, Bartleby! Ah, humanity!

[1853]

Study and Writing Questions

1. How do the meanings of the repeated phrases "dead-wall reveries" and "I would prefer not to" change through the STORY? What effects have these phrases on the development of THEME?
2. In what ways are the SETTINGS crucial to the story?
3. What do the CHARACTERS of Turkey, Nippers, and Ginger Nut add to the story?
4. What do we know about Bartleby? What is the significance of his previous

employment? How does his behavior change in the course of the time the NARRATOR knows him? In what ways is Bartleby unique and in what ways does he stand for something widespread in humanity? Why does the narrator continue to support Bartleby? Does Bartleby teach anything to the narrator? Does he teach anything to us? What does the last line mean?

5. Why does the narrator introduce himself in such detail? What does "the green folding-screen, which might entirely isolate Bartleby from my sight, though not remove him from my voice" suggest about the narrator? about his attitude toward Bartleby? about the IMPLIED AUTHOR'S attitude toward the narrator? To what extent might one say that this story is about the narrator?

See also Questions for Contrast and Comparison: 11, 15, 33, 47, 48, 49, 50, 51, 60, 105, 127, 142, and 217.

■ **YUKIO MISHIMA** (1925–1970) *was the pseudonym of Kimitake Hiraoka. Born and educated in Tokyo (J.D., Tokyo Imperial University, 1947), after a year as a civil servant he turned full-time to the arts. Quickly recognized as the leading voice of Japan's post-World War II generation, he wrote novels (including the* Confessions of a Mask *[1949], about the hypocrisy imposed on a homosexual, and* The Temple of the Golden Pavilion *[1957], about a Buddhist acolyte whose ugliness makes him hate beauty), verse, and traditional Noh plays. He also directed plays and acted (including the Lieutenant's role in the film of "Patriotism"). A bisexual and avid body builder, he posed for a series of spectacular photos of death by various means. Although deeply influenced by Western culture, he rejected the "spinelessness" of Japan under its Western constitution. In 1968 he formed the Shield Society dedicated to restoring traditional values. His masterpiece is a tetralogy,* Spring Snow, *four novels that weave folktales and history into a panoramic view of twentieth-century Japan. The day he completed it, he led a Shield Society takeover of an army barracks where he harangued the troops to reject the Constitution. When they laughed at him, he committed the ritual suicide of a samurai warrior, leaving a wife, two children, and a personal legend. His stories appear in* Death in Midsummer and Other Stories *(1966) and* Acts of Worship *(1989).*

Patriotism

1

On the twenty-eighth of February, 1936 (on the third day, that is of the February 26 Incident), Lieutenant Shinji Takeyama of the Konoe Transport Battalion — profoundly disturbed by the knowledge that his closet colleagues had been with the mutineers from the beginning, and indignant at the imminent prospect of Imperial troops attacking Imperial troops — took his officer's sword and ceremonially disemboweled himself in the eight-mat room of his private residence in the sixth block of Aoba-chō, in Yotsuya Ward. His wife, Reiko, followed him, stabbing herself to death. The lieutenant's farewell note consisted of one sentence: "Long live the Imperial Forces." His wife's, after apologies for her unfilial conduct in thus preceding her parents to the grave, concluded: "The day which, for a soldier's wife, had to come, has come. . . ." The last moments of this heroic and dedicated couple were such as to make the gods themselves weep. The lieutenant's age, it should be noted, was thirty-one, his wife's twenty-three; and it was not half a year since the celebration of their marriage.

2

Those who saw the bride and bridegroom in the commemorative photograph — perhaps no less than those actually present at the lieutenant's wedding — had exclaimed in wonder at the bearing of this handsome couple. The lieutenant, majestic in military uniform, stood protectively beside his bride, his right hand resting upon his sword, his officer's cap held at his left side. His expression was severe, and his dark brows and wide-gazing eyes well conveyed the clear integrity of youth. For the beauty of the bride in her white over-robe no comparisons were adequate. In the eyes, round beneath soft brows, in the slender, finely shaped nose, and in the full lips, there was both sensuousness and refinement. One hand, emerging shyly from a sleeve of the over-robe, held a fan, and the tips of the fingers, clustering delicately, were like the bud of a moonflower.

After the suicide, people would take out this photograph and examine it, and sadly reflect that too often there was a curse on these seemingly flawless unions. Perhaps it was no more than imagination, but looking at the picture after the tragedy it almost seemed as if the two young people before the gold-lacquered screen were gazing, each with equal clarity, at the deaths which lay before them.

Thanks to the good offices of their go-between, Lieutenant General Ozeki, they had been able to set themselves up in a new home at Aoba-chō in Yotsuya. "New home" is perhaps misleading. It was an old three-room rented house backing onto a small garden. As neither the six- nor the four-and-a-half-mat room downstairs was favored by the sun, they used the upstairs eight mat room as both bedroom and guest room. There was no maid, so Reiko was left alone to guard the house in her husband's absence.

The honeymoon trip was dispensed with on the grounds that these were times of national emergency. The two of them had spent the first night of their marriage at this house. Before going to bed, Shinji, sitting erect on the floor with his sword laid before him, had bestowed upon his wife a soldierly lecture. A woman who had become the wife of a soldier should know and resolutely accept that her husband's death might come at any moment. It could be tomorrow. It could be the day after. But, no matter when it came—he asked—was she steadfast in her resolve to accept it? Reiko rose to her feet, pulled open a drawer of the cabinet, and took out what was the most prized of her new possessions, the dagger her mother had given her. Returning to her place, she laid the dagger without a word on the mat before her, just as her husband had laid his sword. A silent understanding was achieved at once, and the lieutenant never again sought to test his wife's resolve.

In the first few months of her marriage Reiko's beauty grew daily more radiant, shining serene like the moon after rain.

As both were possessed of young, vigorous bodies, their relationship was passionate. Nor was this merely a matter of the night. On more than one occasion, returning home straight from maneuvers, and begrudging even the time it took to remove his mud-splashed uniform, the lieutenant had pushed his wife to the floor almost as soon as he had entered the house. Reiko was equally ardent in her response. For a little more or a little less than a month, from the first night of their marriage Reiko knew happiness, and the lieutenant, seeing this, was happy too.

Reiko's body was white and pure, and her swelling breasts conveyed a firm and chaste refusal; but, upon consent, those breasts were lavish with their intimate, welcoming warmth. Even in bed these two were frighteningly and awesomely serious. In the very midst of wild, intoxicating passions, their hearts were sober and serious.

By day the lieutenant would think of his wife in the brief rest periods between training; and all day long, at home, Reiko would recall the image of her husband. Even when apart, however, they had only to look at the wedding photograph for their happiness to be once more confirmed. Reiko felt not the slightest surprise that a man who had been a complete stranger until a few months ago should now have become the sun about which her whole world revolved.

All these things had a moral basis, and were in accordance with the Education Rescript's injunction that "husband and wife should be harmonious." Not once did Reiko contradict her husband, nor did the lieutenant ever find reason to scold his wife. On the god shelf below the stairway, alongside the tablet from the Great Ise Shrine, were set photographs of their Imperial Majesties, and regularly every morning, before leaving for duty, the lieutenant would stand with his wife at this hallowed place and together they would bow their heads low. The offering water was renewed each morning, and the sacred sprig of *sasaki* was always green and fresh. Their lives were lived beneath the solemn protection of the gods and were filled with an intense happiness which set every fiber in their bodies trembling.

3

Although Lord Privy Seal Saitō's house was in their neighborhood, neither of them heard any noise of gunfire on the morning of February 26. It was a bugle, sounding muster in the dim, snowy dawn, when the ten-minute tragedy had already ended, which first disrupted the lieutenant's slumbers. Leaping at once from his bed, and without speaking a word, the lieutenant donned his uniform, buckled on the sword held ready for him by his wife, and hurried swiftly out into the snow-covered streets of the still darkened morning. He did not return until the evening of the twenty-eighth.

Later, from the radio news, Reiko learned the full extent of this sudden eruption of violence. Her life throughout the subsequent two days was lived alone, in complete tranquillity, and behind locked doors.

In the lieutenant's face, as he hurried silently out into the snowy morning, Reiko had read the determination to die. If her husband did not return, her own decision was made: she too would die. Quietly she attended to the disposition of her personal possessions. She chose her sets of visiting kimonos as keepsakes for friends of her schooldays, and she wrote a name and address on the stiff paper wrapping in which each was folded. Constantly admonished by her husband never to think of the morrow, Reiko had not even kept a diary and was now denied the pleasure of assiduously rereading her record of the happiness of the past few months and consigning each page to the fire as she did so. Ranged across the top of the radio were a small china dog, a rabbit, a squirrel, a bear, and a fox. There were also a small vase and a water pitcher. These comprised Reiko's one and only collection. But it would hardly do, she imagined, to give such things as keepsakes. Nor again would it be quite proper to ask specifically for them to be included in the coffin. It seemed to Reiko, as these thoughts passed through her mind, that the expressions on the small animals' faces grew even more lost and forlorn.

Reiko took the squirrel in her hand and looked at it. And then, her thoughts turning to a realm far beyond these child-like affections, she gazed up into the distance at the great sunlike principle which her husband embodied. She was ready, and happy, to be hurtled along to her destruction in that gleaming sun chariot — but now, for these few moments of solitude, she allowed herself to luxuriate in this innocent attachment to trifles. The time when she had genuinely loved these things, however, was long past. Now she merely loved the memory of having once loved them, and their place in her heart had been filled by more intense passions, by a more frenzied happiness.

. . . For Reiko had never, even to herself, thought of those soaring joys of the flesh as a mere pleasure. The February cold, and the icy touch of the china squirrel, had numbed Reiko's slender fingers; yet, even so, in her lower limbs, beneath the ordered repetition of the pattern which crossed the skirt of her trim *meisen* kimono, she could feel now, as she thought of the lieutenant's powerful arms reaching out toward her, a hot moistness of the flesh which defied the snows.

She was not in the least afraid of the death hovering in her mind. Waiting alone at home, Reiko firmly believed that everything her husband was feeling or thinking now, his anguish and distress, was leading her—just as surely as the power in his flesh—to a welcome death. She felt as if her body could melt away with ease and be transformed to the merest fraction of her husband's thought.

Listening to the frequent announcements on the radio, she heard the names of several to her husband's colleagues mentioned among those of the insurgents. This was news of death. She followed the developments closely, wondering anxiously, as the situation became daily more irrevocable, why no Imperial ordinance was sent down, and watching what had at first been taken as a movement to restore the nation's honor come gradually to be branded with the infamous name of mutiny. There was no communication from the regiment. At any moment, it seemed, fighting might commence in the city streets, where the remains of the snow still lay.

Toward sundown on the twenty-eighth Reiko was startled by a furious pounding on the front door. She hurried downstairs. As she pulled with fumbling fingers at the bolt, the shape dimly outlined beyond the frosted-glass panel made no sound, but she knew it was her husband. Reiko had never known the bolt on the sliding door to be so stiff. Still it resisted. The door just would not open.

In a moment, almost before she knew she had succeeded, the lieutenant was standing before her on the cement floor inside the porch, muffled in a khaki greatcoat, his top boots heavy with slush from the street. Closing the door behind him, he returned the bolt once more to its socket. With what significance, Reiko did not understand.

"Welcome home."

Reiko bowed deeply, but her husband made no response. As he had already unfastened his sword and was about to remove his greatcoat, Reiko moved around behind to assist. The coat, which was cold and damp and had lost the odor of horse dung it normally exuded when exposed to the sun, weighed heavily upon her arm. Draping it across a hanger, and cradling the sword and leather belt in her sleeves, she waited while her husband removed his top boots and then followed behind him into the "living room." This was the six-mat room downstairs.

Seen in the clear light from the lamp, her husband's face, covered with a heavy growth of bristle, was almost unrecognizably wasted and thin. The cheeks were hollow, their luster and resilience gone. In his normal good spirits he would have changed into old clothes as soon as he was home and have pressed her to get supper at once, but now he sat before the table still in his uniform, his head drooping dejectedly. Reiko refrained from asking whether she should prepare the supper.

After an interval the lieutenant spoke.

"I knew nothing. They hadn't asked me to join. Perhaps out of consideration, because I was newly married. Kanō, and Homma too, and Yamaguchi."

Reiko recalled momentarily the faces of high-spirited young officers, friends of her husband, who had come to the house occasionally as guests.

"There may be an Imperial ordinance sent down tomorrow. They'll be posted as rebels, I imagine. I shall be in command of a unit with orders to attack them. . . . I can't do it. It's impossible to do a thing like that."

He spoke again.

"They've taken me off guard duty, and I have permission to return home for one night. Tomorrow morning, without question, I must leave to join the attack. I can't do it, Reiko."

Reiko sat erect with lowered eyes. She understood clearly that her husband had spoken of his death. The lieutenant was resolved. Each word, being rooted in death, emerged sharply and with powerful significance against this dark, unmovable background. Although the lieutenant was speaking of his dilemma, already there was no room in his mind for vacillation.

However, there was a clarity, like the clarity of a stream fed from melting snows, in the silence which rested between them. Sitting in his own home after the long two-day ordeal, and looking across at the face of his beautiful wife, the lieutenant was for the first time experiencing true peace of mind. For he had at once known, though she said nothing, that his wife divined the resolve which lay beneath his words.

"Well, then . . ." The lieutenant's eyes opened wide. Despite his exhaustion they were strong and clear, and now for the first time they looked straight into the eyes of his wife. "Tonight I shall cut my stomach."

Reiko did not flinch.

Her round eyes showed tension, as taut as the clang of a bell.

"I am ready," she said. "I ask permission to accompany you."

The lieutenant felt almost mesmerized by the strength in those eyes. His words flowed swiftly and easily, like the utterances of a man in delirium, and it was beyond his understanding how permission in a matter of such weight could be expressed so casually.

"Good. We'll go together. But I want you as a witness, first, for my own suicide. Agreed?"

When this was said a sudden release of abundant happiness welled up in both their hearts. Reiko was deeply affected by the greatness of her husband's trust in her. It was vital for the lieutenant, whatever else might happen, that there should be no irregularity in his death. For that reason there had to be a witness. The fact that he had chosen his wife for this was the first mark of his trust. The second, and even greater mark, was that though he had pledged that they should die together did not intend to kill his wife first—he had deferred her death to a time when he would no longer be there to verify it. If the lieutenant had been a suspicious husband, he would doubtless, as in the usual suicide pact, have chosen to kill his wife first.

When Reiko said, "I ask permission to accompany you," the lieutenant felt these words to be the final fruit of the education which he had himself given his wife, starting on the first night of their marriage, and which had schooled her, when the moment came, to say what had to be said without a shadow of hesitation. This flattered the lieutenant's opinion of himself as a self-reliant man. He was not so romantic or conceited as to imagine that the words were spoken spontaneously, out of love for her husband.

With happiness welling almost too abundantly in their hearts, they could not help smiling at each other. Reiko felt as if she had returned to her wedding night.

Before her eyes was neither pain nor death. She seemed to see only a free and limitless expanse opening out into vast distances.

"The water is hot. Will you take your bath now?"

"Ah yes, of course."

"And supper . . . ?"

The words were delivered in such level, domestic tones that the lieutenant came near to thinking, for the fraction of a second, that everything had been a hallucination.

"I don't think we'll need supper. But perhaps you could warm some sake?"

"As you wish."

As Reiko rose and took a *tanzen* gown from the cabinet for after the bath, she purposely directed her husband's attention to the opened drawer. The lieutenant rose, crossed to the cabinet, and looked inside. From the ordered array of paper wrappings he read, one by one, the addresses of the keepsakes. There was no grief in the lieutenant's response to this demonstration of heroic resolve. His heart was filled with tenderness. Like a husband who is proudly shown the childish purchases of a young wife, the lieutenant, overwhelmed by affection, lovingly embraced his wife from behind and implanted a kiss upon her neck.

Reiko felt the roughness of the lieutenant's unshaven skin against her neck. This sensation, more than being just a thing of this world, was for Reiko almost the world itself, but now — with the feeling that it was soon to be lost forever — it had freshness beyond all her experience. Each moment had its own vital strength, and the senses in every corner of her body were reawakened. Accepting her husband's caresses from behind, Reiko raised herself on the tips of her toes, letting the vitality seep through her entire body.

"First the bath, and then, after some sake . . . lay out the bedding upstairs, will you?"

The lieutenant whispered the words into his wife's ear. Reiko silently nodded.

Flinging off his uniform, the lieutenant went to the bath. To faint background noises of slopping water Reiko tended the charcoal brazier in the living room and began the preparations for warming the sake.

Taking the *tanzen*, a sash, and some underclothes, she went to the bathroom to ask how the water was. In the midst of a coiling cloud of steam the lieutenant was sitting cross-legged on the floor, shaving, and she could dimly discern the rippling movements of the muscles on his damp, powerful back as they responded to the movement of his arms.

There was nothing to suggest a time of any special significance. Reiko, going busily about her tasks, was preparing side dishes from odds and ends in stock.

Her hands did not tremble. If anything, she managed even more efficiently and smoothly than usual. From time to time, it is true, there was a strange throbbing deep within her breast. Like distant lightning, it had a moment of sharp intensity and then vanished without trace. Apart from that, nothing was in any way out of the ordinary.

The lieutenant, shaving in the bathroom, felt his warmed body miraculously healed at last of the desperate tiredness of the days of indecision and filled — in spite of the death which lay ahead — with pleasurable anticipation. The sound of his wife going about her work came to him faintly. A healthy physical craving, submerged for two days, reasserted itself.

The lieutenant was confident there had been no impurity in the joy they had experienced when resolving upon death. They had both sensed at that moment — though not, of course, in any clear and conscious way — that those permissible pleasures which they shared in private were once more beneath the protection of Righteousness and Divine Power, and of a complete and unassailable morality. On looking into each other's eyes and discovering there an honorable death, they had felt themselves safe once more behind steel walls which none could destroy, encased in an impenetrable armor of Beauty and Truth. Thus, so far from seeing any inconsistency or conflict between the urges of his flesh and the sincerity of his patriotism, the lieutenant was even able to regard the two as parts of the same thing.

Thrusting his face close to the dark, cracked, misted wall mirror, the lieutenant shaved himself with great care. This would be his death face. There must be no unsightly blemishes. The clean shaven face gleamed once more with a youthful luster, seeming to brighten the darkness of the mirror. There was a certain elegance, he even felt, in the association of death with this radiantly healthy face.

Just as it looked now, this would become his death face! Already, in fact, it had half departed from the lieutenant's personal possession and had become the bust above a dead soldier's memorial. As an experiment he closed his eyes tight. Everything was wrapped in blackness, and he was no longer a living, seeing creature.

Returning from the bath, the traces of the shave glowing faintly blue beneath his smooth cheeks, he seated himself beside the now well-kindled charcoal brazier. Busy though Reiko was, he noticed, she had found time lightly to touch up her face. Her cheeks were gay and her lips moist. There was no shadow of sadness to be seen. Truly, the lieutenant felt, as he saw this mark of his young wife's passionate nature, he had chosen the wife he ought to have chosen.

As soon as the lieutenant had drained his sake cup he offered it to Reiko. Reiko had never before tasted sake, but she accepted without hesitation and sipped timidly.

"Come here," the lieutenant said.

Reiko moved to her husband's side and was embraced as she leaned backward across his lap. Her breast was in violent commotion, as if sadness, joy, and the potent sake were mingling and reacting within her. The lieutenant looked down into his wife's face. It was the last face he would see in this world, the last face he would see of his wife. The lieutenant scrutinized the face minutely, with the eyes of a traveler bidding farewell to splendid vistas which he will never revisit. It was a face he could not tire of looking at — the features regular yet not cold, the lips lightly closed with a soft strength. The lieutenant kissed those lips, unthinkingly. And suddenly, though there was not the slightest distortion of the face into the unsightliness of sobbing, he noticed that tears were welling slowly from beneath the long lashes of the closed eyes and brimming over into a glistening stream.

When, a little later, the lieutenant urged that they should move to the upstairs bedroom, his wife replied that she would follow after taking a bath. Climbing the stairs alone to the bedroom, where the air was already warmed by the gas heater, the lieutenant lay down on the bedding with arms outstretched and legs apart. Even the time at which he lay waiting for his wife to join him was no later and no earlier than usual.

He folded his hands beneath his head and gazed at the dark boards of the ceiling in the dimness beyond the range of the standard lamp. Was it death he was now waiting for? Or a wild ecstasy of the senses? The two seemed to overlap, almost as if the object of this bodily desire was death itself. But, however that might be, it was certain that never before had the lieutenant tasted such total freedom.

There was the sound of a car outside the window. He could hear the screech of its tires skidding in the snow piled at the side of the street. The sound of its horn re-echoed from near-by walls. . . . Listening to these noises he had the feeling that this house rose like a solitary island in the ocean of a society going as restlessly about its business as ever. All around, vastly and untidily, stretched the country for which he grieved. He was to give his life for it. But would that great country, with which he was prepared to remonstrate to the extent of destroying himself, take the slightest heed of his death? He did not know; and it did not matter. His was a battlefield without glory, a battlefield where none could display deeds of valor: it was the front line of the spirit.

Reiko's footsteps sounded on the stairway. The steep stairs in this old house creaked badly. There were fond memories in that creaking, and many a time, while waiting in bed, the lieutenant had listened to its welcome sound. At the thought that he would hear it no more he listened with intense concentration, striving for every corner of every moment of this precious time to be filled with the sound of those soft footfalls on the creaking stairway. The moments seemed transformed to jewels, sparkling with inner light.

Reiko wore a Nagoya sash about the waist of her *yukata*, but as the lieutenant reached toward it, its redness sobered by the dimness of the light, Reiko's hand moved to his assistance and the sash fell away, slithering swiftly to the floor. As she stood before him, still in her *yukata*, the lieutenant inserted his hands through the side slits beneath each sleeve, intending to embrace her as she was; but at the touch of his finger tips upon the warm naked flesh, and as the armpits closed gently about his hands, his whole body was suddenly aflame.

In a few moments the two lay naked before the glowing gas heater.

Neither spoke the thought, but their hearts, their bodies, and their pounding breasts blazed with the knowledge that this was the very last time. It was as if the words "The Last Time" were spelled out, in invisible brushstrokes, across every inch of their bodies.

The lieutenant drew his wife close and kissed her vehemently. As their tongues explored each other's mouths, reaching out into the smooth, moist interior, they felt as if the still-unknown agonies of death had tempered their senses to the keenness of red-hot steel. The agonies they could not yet feel, the distant pains of death, had refined their awareness of pleasure.

"This is the last time I shall see your body," said the lieutenant. "Let me look at it closely." And, tilting the shade on the lampstand to one side, he directed the rays along the full length of Reiko's outstretched form.

Reiko lay still with her eyes closed. The light from the low lamp clearly revealed the majestic sweep of her white flesh. The lieutenant, not without a touch of egocentricity, rejoiced that he would never see this beauty crumble in death.

At his leisure, the lieutenant allowed the unforgettable spectacle to engrave itself upon his mind. With one hand he fondled the hair, with the other he softly stroked the magnificent face, implanting kisses here and there where his eyes lingered. The quiet coldness of the high, tapering forehead, the closed eyes with their long lashes beneath faintly etched brows, the set of the finely shaped nose, the gleam of teeth glimpsed between full, regular lips, the soft cheeks and the small, wise chin . . . these things conjured up in the lieutenant's mind the vision of a truly radiant death face, and again and again he pressed his lips tight against the white throat — where Reiko's own hand was soon to strike — and the throat reddened faintly beneath his kisses. Returning to the mouth he laid his lips against it with the gentlest of pressures, and moved them rhythmically over Reiko's with the light rolling motion of a small boat. If he closed his eyes, the world became a rocking cradle.

Wherever the lieutenant's eyes moved his lips faithfully followed. The high, swelling breasts, surmounted by nipples like the buds of a wild cherry, hardened as the lieutenant's lips closed about them. The arms flowed smoothly downward from each side of the breast, tapering toward the wrists, yet losing nothing of their roundness or symmetry, and at their tips were those delicate fingers which had held the fan at the wedding ceremony. One by one, as the lieutenant kissed them, the fingers withdrew behind their neighbor as if in shame. . . . The natural hollow curving between the bosom and the stomach carried in its lines a suggestion not only of softness but of resilient strength, and while it gave forewarning of the rich curves spreading outward from here to the hips it had, in itself, an appearance only of restraint and proper discipline. The whiteness and richness of the stomach and hips was like milk brimming in a great bowl, and the sharply shadowed dip of the navel could have been the fresh impress of a raindrop, fallen there that very moment. Where the shadows gathered more thickly, hair clustered, gentle and sensitive, and as the agitation mounted in the now no longer passive body there hung over this region a scent like the smoldering of fragrant blossoms, growing steadily more pervasive.

At length, in a tremulous voice, Reiko spoke.

"Show me. . . . Let me look too, for the last time."

Never before had he heard from his wife's lips so strong and unequivocal a request. It was as if something which her modesty had wished to keep hidden to the end had suddenly burst its bonds of constraint. The lieutenant obediently lay back and surrendered himself to his wife. Lithely she raised her white, trembling body, and — burning with an innocent desire to return to her husband what he had done for her — placed two white fingers on the lieutenant's eyes, which gazed fixedly up at her, and gently stroked them shut.

Suddenly overwhelmed by tenderness, her cheeks flushed by a dizzying uprush of emotion, Reiko threw her arms about the lieutenant's close-cropped head. The bristly hairs rubbed painfully against her breast, the prominent nose was cold as it dug into her flesh, and his breath was hot. Relaxing her embrace, she gazed down at her husband's masculine face. The severe brows, the closed eyes, the splendid bridge of the nose, the shapely lips drawn firmly together . . . the blue, clean-shaven cheeks reflecting the light and gleaming smoothly. Reiko kissed each of these. She kissed the broad nape of the neck, the strong, erect shoulders, the powerful chest with its twin circles like shields and its russet nipples. In the armpits, deeply shadowed by the ample flesh of the shoulders and chest, a sweet and melancholy odor emanated from the growth of hair, and in the sweetness of this odor was contained, somehow, the essence of young death. The lieutenant's naked skin glowed like a field of barley, and everywhere the muscles showed in sharp relief, converging on the lower abdomen about the small, unassuming navel. Gazing at the youthful, firm stomach, modestly covered by a vigorous growth of hair, Reiko thought of it as it was soon to be, cruelly cut by the sword, and she laid her head upon it, sobbing in pity, and bathed it with kisses.

At the touch of his wife's tears upon his stomach the lieutenant felt ready to endure with courage the cruelest agonies of his suicide.

What ecstasies they experienced after these tender exchanges may well be imagined. The lieutenant raised himself and enfolded his wife in a powerful embrace, her body now limp with exhaustion after her grief and tears. Passionately they held their faces close, rubbing cheek against cheek. Reiko's body was trembling. Their breasts, moist with sweat, were tightly joined, and every inch of the young and beautiful bodies had become so much one with the other that it seemed impossible there should ever again be a separation. Reiko cried out. From the heights they plunged into the abyss, and from the abyss they took wing and soared once more to dizzying heights. The lieutenant panted like the regimental standard-bearer on a route march. . . . As one cycle ended, almost immediately a new wave of passion would be generated, and together — with no trace of fatigue — they would climb again in a single breathless movement to the very summit.

4

When the lieutenant at last turned away, it was not from weariness. For one thing, he was anxious not to undermine the considerable strength he would need in carrying out his suicide. For another, he would have been sorry to mar the sweetness of these last memories by overindulgence.

Since the lieutenant had clearly desisted, Reiko too, with her usual compliance, followed his example. The two lay naked on their backs, with fingers interlaced, staring fixedly at the dark ceiling. The room was warm from the heater, and even when the sweat had ceased to pour from their bodies they felt no cold. Outside, in the hushed night, the sounds of passing traffic had ceased. Even the noises of the trains and streetcars around Yotsuya station did not penetrate this far. After echoing through the region bounded by the moat, they were lost in the heavily wooded park fronting the broad driveway before Akasaka Palace. It was hard to believe in the tension gripping this whole quarter, where the two factions of the bitterly divided Imperial Army now confronted each other, poised for battle.

Savoring the warmth glowing within themselves, they lay still and recalled the ecstasies they had just known. Each moment of the experience was relived. They remembered the taste of kisses which had never wearied, the touch of naked flesh, episode after episode of dizzying bliss. But already, from the dark boards of the ceiling, the face of death was peering down. These joys had been final, and their bodies would never know them again. Not that joy of this intensity — and the same thought had occurred to them both — was ever likely to be reexperienced, even if they should live on to old age.

The feel of their fingers intertwined — this too would soon be lost. Even the wood-grain patterns they now gazed at on the dark ceiling boards would be taken from them. They could feel death edging in, nearer and nearer. There could be no hesitation now. They must have the courage to reach out to death themselves, and to seize it.

"Well, let's make our preparations," said the lieutenant. The note of determination in the words was unmistakable, but at the same time Reiko had never heard her husband's voice so warm and tender.

After they had risen, a variety of tasks awaited them.

The lieutenant, who had never once before helped with the bedding, now cheerfully slid back the door of the closet, lifted the mattress across the room by himself, and stowed it away inside.

Reiko turned off the gas heater and put away the lamp standard. During the lieutenant's absence she had arranged this room carefully, sweeping and dusting it to a fresh cleanness, and now — if one overlooked the rosewood table drawn into one corner — the eight-mat room gave all the appearance of a reception room ready to welcome an important guest.

"We've seen some drinking here, haven't we? With Kanō and Homma and Noguchi . . ."

"Yes, they were great drinkers, all of them."

"We'll be meeting them before long, in the other world. They'll tease us, I imagine, when they find I've brought you with me."

Descending the stairs, the lieutenant turned to look back into this calm, clean room, now brightly illuminated by the ceiling lamp. There floated across his mind the faces of the young officers who had drunk there, and laughed, and innocently bragged. He had never dreamed then that he would one day cut open his stomach in this room.

In the two rooms downstairs husband and wife busied themselves smoothly and serenely with their respective preparations. The lieutenant went to the toilet, and then to the bathroom to wash. Meanwhile Reiko folded away her husband's padded robe, placed his uniform tunic, his trousers, and a newly cut bleached loincloth in the bathroom, and set out sheets of paper on the living-room table for the farewell notes. Then she removed the lid from the writing box and began rubbing ink from the ink tablet. She had already decided upon the wording of her own note.

Reiko's fingers pressed hard upon the cold gilt letters of the ink tablet, and the water in the shallow well at once darkened, as if a black cloud had spread across it. She stopped thinking that this repeated action, this pressure from her fingers, this rise and fall of faint sound, was all and solely for death. It was a routine domestic task, a simple paring away of time until death should finally stand before her. But somehow, in the increasingly smooth motion of the tablet rubbing on the stone, and in the scent from the thickening ink, there was unspeakable darkness.

Neat in his uniform, which he now wore next to his skin, the lieutenant emerged from the bathroom. Without a word he seated himself at the table, bolt upright, took a brush in his hand, and stared undecidedly at the paper before him.

Reiko took a white silk kimono with her and entered the bathroom. When she reappeared in the living room, clad in the white kimono and with her face lightly made up, the farewell note lay completed on the table beneath the lamp. The thick black brushstrokes said simply:

"Long Live the Imperial Forces—Army Lieutenant Takeyama Shinji."

While Reiko sat opposite him writing her own note, the lieutenant gazed in silence, intensely serious, at the controlled movement of his wife's pale fingers as they manipulated the brush.

With their respective notes in their hands—the lieutenant's sword strapped to his side, Reiko's small dagger thrust into the sash of her white kimono—the two of them stood before the god shelf and silently prayed. Then they put out all the downstairs lights. As he mounted the stairs the lieutenant turned his head and gazed back at the striking, white-clad figure of his wife, climbing behind him, with lowered eyes, from the darkness beneath.

The farewell notes were laid side by side in the alcove of the upstairs room. They wondered whether they ought not to remove the hanging scroll, but since it had been written by their go-between, Lieutenant General Ozeki, and consisted, moreover, of two Chinese characters signifying "Sincerity," they left it where it was. Even if it were to become stained with splashes of blood, they felt that the lieutenant general would understand.

The lieutenant, sitting erect with his back to the alcove, laid his sword on the floor before him.

Reiko sat facing him, a mat's width away. With the rest of her so severely white the touch of rouge on her lips seemed remarkable seductive.

Across the dividing mat they gazed intently into each other's eyes. The lieutenant's sword lay before his knees. Seeing it, Reiko recalled their first night and was overwhelmed with sadness. The lieutenant spoke, in a hoarse voice:

"As I have no second to help me I shall cut deep. It may look unpleasant, but please do not panic. Death of any sort is a fearful thing to watch. You must not be discouraged by what you see. Is that all right?"

"Yes."

Reiko nodded deeply.

Looking at the slender white figure of his wife the lieutenant experienced a bizarre excitement. What he was about to perform was an act in his public capacity as a soldier, something he had never previously shown his wife. It called for a resolution equal to the courage to enter battle; it was a death of no less degree and quality than death in the front line. It was his conduct on the battlefield that he was now to display.

Momentarily the thought led the lieutenant to a strange fantasy. A lonely death on the battlefield, a death beneath the eyes of his beautiful wife . . . in the sensation that he was now to die in these two dimensions, realizing an impossible union of them both, there was sweetness beyond words. This must be the very pinnacle of good fortune, he thought. To have every moment of his death observed by those beautiful eyes — it was like being borne to death on a gentle, fragrant breeze. There was some special favor here. He did not understand precisely what it was, but it was a domain unknown to others: a dispensation granted to no one else had been permitted to himself. In the radiant, bridelike figure of his white-robed wife the lieutenant seemed to see a vision of all those things he had loved and for which he was to lay down his life — the Imperial Household, the Nation, the Army Flag. All these, no less than the wife who sat before him, were presences observing him closely with clear and never-faltering eyes.

Reiko too was gazing intently at her husband, so soon to die, and she thought that never in this world had she seen anything so beautiful. The lieutenant always looked well in uniform, but now, as he contemplated death with severe brows and firmly closed lips, he revealed what was perhaps masculine beauty at its most superb.

"It's time to go," the lieutenant said at last.

Reiko bent her body low to the mat in a deep bow. She could not raise her face. She did not wish to spoil her make-up with tears, but the tears could not be held back.

When at length she looked up she saw hazily through the tears that her husband had wound a white bandage around the blade of his now unsheathed sword, leaving five or six inches of naked steel showing at the point.

Resting the sword in its cloth wrapping on the mat before him, the lieutenant rose from his knees, resettled himself cross-legged, and unfastened the hooks of his uniform collar. His eyes no longer saw his wife. Slowly, one by one, he undid the flat brass buttons. The dusky brown chest was revealed, and then the stomach. He unclasped his belt and undid the buttons of his trousers. The pure whiteness of the thickly coiled loincloth showed itself. The lieutenant pushed the cloth down with both hands, further to ease his stomach, and then reached for the white-bandaged blade of his sword. With his left hand he massaged his abdomen, glancing downward as he did so.

To reassure himself on the sharpness of his sword's cutting edge the lieutenant folded back the left trouser flap, exposing a little of his thigh, and lightly drew the blade across the skin. Blood welled up in the wound at once, and several streaks of red trickled downward, glistening in the strong light.

It was the first time Reiko had ever seen her husband's blood, and she felt a violent throbbing in her chest. She looked at her husband's face. The lieutenant was looking at the blood with calm appraisal. For a moment — though thinking at the same time that it was hollow comfort — Reiko experienced a sense of relief.

The lieutenant's eyes fixed his wife with an intense, hawk-like stare. Moving the sword around to his front, he raised himself slightly on his hips and let the upper half of his body lean over the sword point. That he was mustering his whole strength was apparent from the angry tension of the uniform at his shoulders. The lieutenant aimed to strike deep into the left of his stomach. His sharp cry pierced the silence of the room.

Despite the effort he had himself put into the blow, the lieutenant had the impression that someone else had struck the side of his stomach agonizingly with a thick rod of iron. For a second or so his head reeled and he had no idea what had happened. The five or six inches of naked point had vanished completely into his flesh, and the white bandage, gripped in his clenched fist, pressed directly against his stomach.

He returned to consciousness. The blade had certainly pierced the wall of the stomach, he thought. His breathing was difficult, his chest thumped violently, and in some far deep region, which he could hardly believe was a part of himself, a fearful and excruciating pain came welling up as if the ground had split open to disgorge a boiling stream of molten rock. The pain came suddenly nearer, with terrifying speed. The lieutenant bit his lower lip and stifled an instinctive moan.

Was this *seppuku?* — he was thinking. It was a sensation of utter chaos, as if the sky had fallen on his head and the world was reeling drunkenly. His will power and courage, which had seemed so robust before he made the incision, had now dwindled to something like a single hairlike thread of steel, and he was assailed by the uneasy feeling that he must advance along this thread, clinging to it with desperation. His clenched fist had grown moist. Looking down, he saw that both his hand and the cloth about the blade were drenched in blood. His loin-cloth too was dyed a deep red. It struck him as incredible that, amidst this terrible agony, things which could be seen could still be seen, and existing things existed still.

The moment the lieutenant thrust the sword into his left side and she saw the deathly pallor fall across his face, like an abruptly lowered curtain, Reiko had to struggle to prevent herself from rushing to his side. Whatever happened, she must watch. She must be a witness. That was the duty her husband had laid upon her. Opposite her, a mat's space away, she could clearly see her husband biting his lip to stifle the pain. The pain was there, with absolute certainty, before her eyes. And Reiko had no means of rescuing him from it.

The sweat glistened on her husband's forehead. The lieutenant closed his eyes, and then opened them again, as if experimenting. The eyes had lost their luster, and seemed innocent and empty like the eyes of a small animal.

The agony before Reiko's eyes burned as strong as the summer sun, utterly remote from the grief which seemed to be tearing herself apart within. The pain grew steadily in stature, stretching upward. Reiko felt that her husband had already became a man in a separate world, a man whose whole being had been resolved into pain, a prisoner in a cage of pain where no hand could reach out to him. But Reiko felt no pain at all. Her grief was not pain. As she thought about this, Reiko began to feel as if someone had raised a cruel wall of glass high between herself and her husband.

Ever since her marriage her husband's existence had been her own existence, and every breath of his had been a breath drawn by herself. But now, while her husband's existence in pain was a vivid reality, Reiko could find in this grief of hers no certain proof at all of her own existence.

With only his right hand on the sword the lieutenant began to cut sideways across his stomach. But as the blade became entangled with the entrails it was pushed constantly outward by their soft resilience; and the lieutenant realized that it would be necessary, as he cut, to use both hands to keep the point pressed deep into his stomach. He pulled the blade across. It did not cut as easily as he had expected. He directed the strength of his whole body into his right hand and pulled again. There was a cut of three or four inches.

The pain spread slowly outward from the inner depths until the whole stomach reverberated. It was like the wild clanging of a bell. Or like a thousand bells which jangled simultaneously at every breath he breathed and every throb of his pulse, rocking his whole being. The lieutenant could no longer stop himself from moaning. But by now the blade had cut its way through to below the navel, and when he noticed this he felt a sense of satisfaction, and a renewal of courage.

The volume of blood had steadily increased, and now it spurted from the wound as if propelled by the beat of the pulse. The mat before the lieutenant was drenched red with splattered blood, and more blood overflowed onto it from pools which gathered in the folds of the lieutenant's khaki trousers. A spot, like a bird, came flying across to Reiko and settled on the lap of her white silk kimono.

By the time the lieutenant had at last drawn the sword across to the right side of his stomach, the blade was already cutting shallow and had revealed its naked tip, slippery with blood and grease. But, suddenly stricken by a fit of vomiting, the lieutenant cried out hoarsely. The vomiting made the fierce pain fiercer still, and the stomach, which had thus far remained firm and compact, now abruptly heaved, opening wide its wound, and the entrails burst through, as if the wound too were vomiting. Seemingly ignorant of their master's suffering, the entrails gave an impression of robust health and almost disagreeable vitality as they slipped smoothly out and spilled over into the crotch. The lieutenant's head drooped, his shoulders heaved, his eyes opened to narrow slits, and a thin trickle of saliva dribbled from his mouth. The gold markings on his epaulettes caught the light and glinted.

Blood was scattered everywhere. The lieutenant was soaked in it to his knees, and he sat now in a crumpled and listless posture, one hand on the floor. A raw smell filled the room. The lieutenant, his head drooping, retched repeatedly, and the movement showed vividly in his shoulders. The blade of the sword, now pushed back by the entrails and exposed to its tip, was still in the lieutenant's right hand.

It would be difficult to imagine a more heroic sight than that of the lieutenant at this moment, as he mustered his strength and flung back his head. The movement was performed with sudden violence, and the back of his head struck with a sharp crack against the alcove pillar. Reiko had been sitting until now with her face lowered, gazing in fascination at the tide of blood advancing toward her knees, but the sound took her by surprise and she looked up.

The lieutenant's face was not the face of a living man. The eyes were hollow, the skin parched, the once so lustrous cheeks and lips the color of dried mud. The right hand alone was moving. Laboriously gripping the sword, it hovered shakily in the air like the hand of a marionette and strove to direct the point at the base of the lieutenant's throat. Reiko watched her husband make this last, most heart-rending, futile exertion. Glistening with blood and grease, the point was thrust at the throat again and again. And each time it missed its aim. The strength to guide it was no longer there. The straying point struck the collar and the collar badges. Although its hooks had been unfastened, the stiff military collar had closed together again and was protecting the throat.

Reiko could bear the sight no longer. She tried to go to her husband's help, but she could not stand. She moved through the blood on her knees, and her white skirts grew deep red. Moving to the rear of her husband, she helped no more than by loosening the collar. The quivering blade at last contacted the naked flesh of the throat. At that moment Reiko's impression was that she herself had propelled her husband forward; but that was not the case. It was a movement planned by the lieutenant himself, his last exertion of strength. Abruptly he threw his body at the blade, and the blade pierced his neck, emerging at the nape. There was a tremendous spurt of blood and the lieutenant lay still, cold blue-tinged steel protruding from his neck at the back.

5

Slowly, her socks slippery with blood, Reiko descended the stairway. The upstairs room was now completely still.

Switching on the ground-floor lights, she checked the gas jet and the main gas plug and poured water over the smoldering, half-buried charcoal in the brazier. She stood before the upright mirror in the four-and-a-half-mat room and held up her skirts. The bloodstains made it seem as if a bold, vivid pattern was printed across the lower half of her white kimono. When she sat down before the mirror, she was conscious of the dampness and coldness of her husband's blood in the region of her thighs, and she shivered. Then, for a long while, she lingered over her toilet preparations. She applied the rouge generously to her cheeks, and her lips too she painted heavily. This was no longer make-up to please her husband. It was make-up for the world which she would leave behind, and there was a touch of the magnificent and the spectacular in her brushwork. When she rose, the mat before the mirror was wet with blood. Reiko was not concerned about this.

Returning from the toilet, Reiko stood finally on the cement floor of the porchway. When her husband had bolted the door here last night it had been in preparation for death. For a while she stood immersed in the consideration of a simple problem. Should she now leave the bolt drawn? If she were to lock the door, it could be that the neighbors might not notice their suicide for several days. Reiko did not relish the thought of their two corpses putrifying before discovery. After all, it seemed, it would be best to leave it open. . . . She released the bolt, and also drew open the frosted-glass door a fraction. . . . At once a chill wind blew in. There was no sign of anyone in the midnight streets, and stars glittered ice-cold through the trees in the large house opposite.

Leaving the door as it was, Reiko mounted the stairs. She had walked here and there for some time and her socks were no longer slippery. About halfway up, her nostrils were already assailed by a peculiar smell.

The lieutenant was lying on his face in a sea of blood. The point protruding from his neck seemed to have grown even more prominent than before. Reiko walked heedlessly across the blood. Sitting beside the lieutenant's corpse, she stared intently at the face, which lay on one cheek on the mat. The eyes were opened wide, as if the lieutenant's attention had been attracted by something. She raised the head, folding it in her sleeve, wiped the blood from the lips, and bestowed a last kiss.

Then she rose and took from the closet a new white blanket and a waist cord. To prevent any derangement of her skirts, she wrapped the blanket about her waist and bound it there firmly with the cord.

Reiko sat herself on a spot about one foot distant from the lieutenant's body. Drawing the dagger from her sash, she examined its dully gleaming blade intently, and held it to her tongue. The taste of the polished steel was slightly sweet.

Reiko did not linger. When she thought how the pain which had previously opened such a gulf between herself and her dying husband was now to become a part of her own experience, she saw before her only the joy of herself entering a realm her husband had already made his own. In her husband's agonized face there had been something inexplicable which she was seeing for the first time. Now she would solve that riddle. Reiko sensed that at last she too would be able to taste the true bitterness and sweetness of that great moral principle in which her husband believed. What had until now been tasted only faintly through her husband's example she was about to savor directly with her own tongue.

Reiko rested the point of the blade against the base of her throat. She thrust hard. The wound was only shallow. Her head blazed, and her hands shook uncontrollably. She gave the blade a strong pull sideways. A warm substance flooded into her mouth, and everything before her eyes reddened, in a vision of spouting blood. She gathered her strength and plunged the point of the blade deep into her throat.

[1960]

Study and Writing Questions

1. The first section of the NARRATIVE removes one source of SUSPENSE. What other interests does this allow to develop for the reader? How does the section structure of the narrative contribute to its impact?

2. Do Takeyama and Reiko understand themselves well? Do they understand each other well? What do they believe to be their own and each other's MOTIVES? Do their motives really exhibit "purity"? What difference does the purity of a motive make?

3. What does this narrative suggest are the relationships between duty and desire and between intellect and emotion?

4. What are the key IMAGES and SYMBOLS in this narrative? How are the lovemaking and the suicides described? Why are there so many details? Why is the last line chosen as last?

5. Are there different types of patriotism? What attitude(s) does the narrative seem to favor about patriotism? To what extent is this narrative about changing times and the impact of modernization?

See also Questions for Contrast and Comparison: 7, 45, 67, 119, 126, 128, 162, and 217.

■ **LORRIE (born Lorena Marie) MOORE** (1957–), *daughter of a Glens Falls, New York, insurance executive and a housewife, has had public success with her socially acute writing from her student days. She won first prize in Seventeen magazine's* SHORT STORY *contest for "Raspberries" (1976) and prestigious writing awards at the schools she attended (St. Lawrence University, B.A., 1978; Cornell University, M.F.A., 1982). She has taught at Cornell (1982–1984) and the University of Wisconsin, Madison (1984–). She early began publishing stories and reviews in such widely-read periodicals as Cosmopolitan, Ms., and the New York Times Book Review. Six of the nine stories in her first book, Self-Help (1985), are second-person* NARRATIONS, *parodies of the self-help genre of popular non-fiction. Her second book, Anagrams (1986), a formally experimental* NOVEL, *bounces between first-and third-person narration as it explores two shifting lives, one of which is that of a woman academic writer who fails to find the love she seeks. The title of Moore's third book (1990), another collection of short stories, illustrates both her shrewd punning and her continuing concern for language as a way of dealing with personal and social tragedy: Like Life: Stories.*

How

So all things limp together for the only possible.

—Beckett
Murphy

Begin by meeting him in a class, in a bar, at a rummage sale. Maybe he teaches sixth grade. Manages a hardware store. Foreman at a carton factory. He will be a good dancer. He will have perfectly cut hair. He will laugh at your jokes.

A week, a month, a year. Feel discovered, comforted, needed, loved, and start sometimes, somehow, to feel bored. When sad or confused, walk uptown to the movies. Buy popcorn. These things come and go. A week, a month, a year.

Make attempts at a less restrictive arrangement. Watch them sputter and deflate like balloons. He will ask you to move in. Do so hesitantly, with ambivalence. Clarify: rents are high, nothing long-range, love and all that, hon, but it's footloose. Lay out the rules with much elocution. Stress openness, non-exclusivity. Make room in his closet, but don't rearrange the furniture.

And yet from time to time you will gaze at his face or his hands and want nothing but him. You will feel passing waves of dependency, devotion, and sentimentality. A week, a month, a year, and he has become your family. Let's say your real mother is a witch. Your father a warlock. Your brothers twin hunchbacks of Notre Dame. They all live in a cave together somewhere.

His name means savior. He rolls into your arms like Ozzie and Harriet, the whole Nelson genealogy. He is living rooms and turkey and mantels and Vicks, a nip at the collarbone and you do a slow syrup sink into those arms like a hearth, into those living rooms, well hello Mary Lou.

Say you work in an office but you have bigger plans. He wants to go with you. He wants to be what it is that you want to be. Say you're an aspiring architect. Playwright. Painter. He shows you his sketches. They are awful. What do you think?

Put on some jazz. Take off your clothes. Carefully. It is a craft. He will lie on the floor naked, watching, his arms crossed behind his head. Shirt: brush on snare, steady. Skirt: the desultory talk of piano keys, rocking slow, rambling. Dance together in the dark though it is only afternoon.

Go to a wedding. His relatives. Everyone will compare weight losses and gains. Maiden cousins will be said to have fattened embarrassingly. His mother will be a bookkeeper or a dental hygienist. She will introduce you as his *girl*. Try not to protest. They will have heard a lot about you. Uncles will take him aside and query, What is keeping you, boy? Uncomfortable, everywhere, women in stiff blue taffeta will eye you pitifully, then look quickly away. Everyone will polka. Someone will flash a fifty to dance with the bride and she will hike up her gown and flash back: freshly shaven legs, a wide rolled-out-barrel of a grin. Feel spared. Thought you two'd be doing this by now, you will hear again. Smile. Shrug. Shuffle back for more potato salad.

It hits you more insistently. A restlessness. A virus of discontent. When you pass other men in the street, smile and stare them straight in the eye, straight in the belt buckle.

Somehow — in a restaurant or a store — meet an actor. From Vassar or Yale. He can quote Coriolanus's mother. This will seem good. Sleep with him once and ride home at 5 A.M. crying in a taxicab. Or: don't sleep with him. Kiss him good night at Union Square and run for your life.

Back at home, days later, feel cranky and tired. Sit on the couch and tell him he's stupid. That you bet he doesn't know who Coriolanus is. That since you moved in you've noticed he rarely reads. He will give you a hurt, hungry-to-learn look, with his James Cagney eyes. He will try to kiss you. Turn your head. Feel suffocated.

When he climbs onto the covers, naked and hot for you, unleash your irritation in short staccato blasts. Show him your book. Your aspirin. Your clock on the table reading 12:45. He will flop back over to his side of the bed, exasperated. Maybe he'll say something like: Christ, what's wrong? Maybe he won't. If he spends too long in the bathroom, don't ask questions.

The touchiest point will always be this: he craves a family, a neat nest of human bowls; he wants to have your children. On the street he pats their heads. In the supermarket they gather around him by the produce. They form a tight little cluster of cheeks and smiles and hopes. They look like grapes. It will all be for you, baby; reel, sway backward into the frozen foods. An unwitting sigh will escape from your lips like gas. He will begin to talk about a movie camera and children's encyclopedias, picking up size-one shoes in department stores and marveling in one high, amazed whistle. Avoid shopping together.

He will have a nephew named Bradley Bob. Or perhaps a niece named Emily who is always dressed in pink and smells of milk and powder and dirty diapers, although she is already three. At visits she will prance and squeal. She will grab his left leg like a tree trunk and not let go. She will call him nunko. He will know tricks: pulling dimes from her nose, quarters from her ears. She will shriek with glee, flapping her hands in front of her. Leg released, he will pick her up, carry her around like a prize. He is the best nunko in town.

Think about leaving. About packing a bag and slithering off, out the door.

But it is hot out there. And dry. And he can look somehow good to you, like Robert Goulet in a bathing suit.

No, it wouldn't be in summer.

Escape into books. When he asks what you're reading, hold it up without comment. The next day look across to the brown chair and you will see him reading it too. A copy from the library that morning. He has seven days. He will look over the top and wink, saying: Beat you.

He will seem to be listening to the classical music station, glancing quickly at you for approval.

At the theater he will chomp Necco wafers loudly and complain about the head in front of him.

He will ask you what *supercilious* means.

He will ask you who Coriolanus is.

He might want to know where Sardinia is located.

What's a *croissant*?

Begin to plot your getaway. Envision possibilities for civility. These are only possibilities.

A week, a month, a year: Tell him you've changed. You no longer like the same music, eat the same food. You dress differently. The two of you are incongruous together. When he tells you that he is changing too, that he loves your records, your teas, your falafel, your shoes, tell him: See, that's the problem. Endeavor to baffle.

Pace around in the kitchen and say that you are unhappy.

But I love you, he will say in his soft, bewildered way, stirring the spaghetti sauce but not you, staring into the pan as if waiting for something, a magic fish, to rise from it and say: That is always enough, why is that not always enough?

You will forget whoever it was that said never trust a thought that doesn't come while walking. But clutch at it. Apartments can shrink inward like drying ponds. You will gasp. Say: I am going for a walk. When he follows you to the door, buzzing at your side like a fly by a bleeding woman, add: *alone.* He will look surprised and hurt and you will hate him. Slam the door, out, down, hurry, it will be colder than you thought, but not far away will be a bar, smoky and dark and sticky with spilled sours. The bartender will be named Rusty or Max and he will know you. A flashy jukebox will blare Jimmy Webb. A balding, purple-shirted man to your left will try to get your attention, mouthing, singing drunkenly. Someone to your right will sniffle to the music. Blink into your drink. Hide behind your hair. Sweet green icing will be flowing down. Flowing, baby, like the Mississippi.

Next: there are medical unpleasantries. Kidneys. He will pee blood. Say you can't believe it. When he shows you later, it will be dark, the color of meat drippings. A huge invisible fist will torpedo through your gut, your face, your pounding heart.

This is no time to leave.

There will be doctor's appointments, various opinions. There is nothing conclusive, just an endless series of tests. He will have jarred urine specimens in the refrigerator among the eggs and peanut butter. Some will be in salad dressing bottles. They will be different colors: some green, some purple, some brown. Ask which is the real salad dressing. He will point it out and smile helplessly. Smile back. He will begin to laugh and so will you. Collapse. Roll. Roar together on the floor until you cannot laugh anymore. Bury your face in the crook of his neck. There will be nothing else in the world you can do. That night lie next to each other, silent, stiff, silvery-white in bed. Lie like sewing needles.

Continue to doctor-hop. Await the reports. Look at your watch. If ever you would leave him. Look at your calendar. It wouldn't be in autumn.

There is never anything conclusive, just an endless series of tests.

Once a week you will feel in love with him again. Massage his lower back when it is aching. Lay your cheek against him, feeling, listening for his kidneys. Stay like that all night, never quite falling asleep, never quite wanting to.

The thought will occur to you that you are waiting for him to die.

You will meet another actor. Or maybe it's the same one. Begin to have an affair. Begin to lie. Have dinner with him and his Modigliani-necked mother. She will smoke cigars, play with the fondue, discuss the fallacy of feminine maternal instinct. Afterward, you will all get high.

There is never anything conclusive, just an endless series of tests.

And could you leave him tripping merrily through the snow?

You will fantasize about a funeral. At that you could cry. It would be a study in post-romantic excess, something vaguely Wagnerian. You would be comforted by his lugubrious sisters and his dental hygienist mom. The four of you in the cemetery would throw yourselves at his grave's edge, heaving and sobbing like old Israeli women. You, in particular, would shout, bare your wrists, shake them at the sky, foam at the mouth. There would be no shame, no dignity. You would fly immediately to Acapulco and lounge drunk and malodorous in the casinos until three.

After dinners with the actor: creep home. Your stomach will get fluttery, your steps smaller as you approach the door. Neighbors will be playing music you recall from your childhood — an opera about a pretty lady who was bad and cut a man's hair in his sleep. You recall, recall your grandfather playing it with a sort of wrath, his visage laminated with Old Testament righteousness, the violins warming, the scenario unfolding now as you stand outside the door. Ray pawned off my ten dresses: it cascades like a waterfall. Dolly-la, Dolly-la: it is the wail, the next to the last good solo of a doomed man.

Tiptoe. It won't matter. He will be sitting up in bed looking empty. Kiss him, cajole him. Make love to him like never before. At four in the morning you will still be awake, staring at the ceiling. You will horrify yourself.

Thoughts of leaving will move in, bivouac throughout the living room; they will have eyes like rodents and peer out at you from under the sofa, in the dark, from under the sink, luminous glass beads positioned in twos. The houseplants will appear to have chosen sides. Some will thrust stems at you like angry limbs. They will seem to caw like crows. Others will simply sag.

When you go out, leave him with a sinkful of dirty dishes. He will slowly dry them with paper towels, his skin scalded red beneath the wet, flattened hair of his forearms. You will be tempted to tell him to leave them, or to use the terrycloth in the drawer. But you won't. You will put on your coat and hurry away.

When you return, the bathroom light will be on. You will see blouses of yours that he has washed by hand. They will hang in perfect half-inches, dripping, scolding from the shower curtain rod. They will be buttoned with his Cagney eyes, faintly hooded, the twinkle sad and dulled.
Slip quietly under the covers; hold his sleeping hand.
There is never anything conclusive.

At work you will be lachrymose and distracted. You will shamble through the hall like a legume with feet. People will notice.

Nightmares have seasons like hurricanes. Be prepared. You will dream that someone with a violin case is trailing you through the city. Little children come at you with grins and grenades. You may bolt awake with a spasm, reach for him, and find he is not there, but lost in his own sleep, somnambulant, is roaming through the apartment like an old man, babbling gibberish, bumping into tables and lamps, a blanket he has torn from the bed wrapped clumsily around him, toga-style. Get up. Go to him. Touch him. At first he will look at you, wide-eyed, and not see. Put your arms around his waist. He will wake and gasp and cry into your hair. In a minute he will know where he is.

Dream about rainbows, about escapes, about wizards. Your past will fly by you, event by event, like Dorothy's tornadoed neighborhood, past the blown-out window. Airborne. One by one. Wave hello, good-bye. Practice.

Begin to call in sick. Make sure it is after he has already left for work. Sit in a rocking chair. Stare around at the apartment. It will be mid-morning and flooded in a hush of sunlight. You rarely see it like this. It will seem strangely deserted, premonitory. There will be apricots shrunk to buttons on the windowsill. A fly will bang stupidly against the panes. The bed will lie open, revealed, like something festering, the wrinkles in the sheets marking time, marking territory like the capillaries of a map. Rock. Hush. Breathe.

On the night you finally tell him, take him out to dinner. Translate the entrees for him. When you are home, lying in bed together, tell him that you are going to leave. He will look panicked, but not surprised. Perhaps he will say, Look, I don't care who else you're seeing or anything: what is your reason?

Do not attempt to bandy words. Tell him you do not love him anymore. It will make him cry, rivulets wending their way into his ears. You will start to feel sick. He will say something like: Well, you lose some, you lose some. You are supposed to laugh. Exhale. Blow your nose. Flick off the light. Have a sense of humor, he will whisper into the black. Have a heart.

Make him breakfast. He will want to know where you will go. Reply: To the actor. Or: To the hunchbacks. He will not eat your breakfast. He will glare at it, stir it around the plate with a fork, and then hurl it against the wall.

When you walk up Third Avenue toward the IRT, do it quickly. You will have a full bag. People will seem to know what you have done, where you are going. They will have his eyes, the same pair, passed along on the street from face to face, like secrets, like glasses at the opera.

This is how you are.
Rushing downstairs into the steamy burn of the subway.
Unable to look a panhandler in the pan.

You will never see him again. Or perhaps you will be sitting in Central Park one April eating your lunch and he will trundle by on roller skates. You will greet him with a wave and a mouth full of sandwich. He will nod, but he will not stop.

There will be an endless series of tests.

A week, a month, a year. The sadness will die like an old dog. You will feel nothing but indifference. The logy whine of a cowboy harmonica, plaintive, weary, it will fade into the hills slow as slow Hank Williams. One of those endings.

[1985]

Study and Writing Questions

1. "How to" articles traditionally are non-fiction works of instruction addressed by an expert to someone wanting to learn. In what ways does this NARRATIVE have the form of a "how to" article? How does using this form affect our understanding of the STORY? How does the narrative change if we think of the speaker as addressing either herself or her former lover?
2. There are numerous repeated phrases, such as, "There will be an endless series of tests." Locate these phrases. What is the special significance of each?
3. With phrases such as "He wants to have your children," Moore reverses the traditional male/female roles. Is this a feminist narrative? Is this reversal in part responsible for the outcome of the plot?
4. What is the cultural background of this narrative? Pursue the allusions to Robert Goulet and the musical *Camelot*, to Shakespeare's *Coriolanus*, to fondue, and so on. To what extent is the importance of this story limited to the time period and socioeconomic group it reflects?
5. What sense of morality is reflected in this narrative? When do the characters feel guilt, shame, duty? Is the man really morally inferior to the woman? Who, if anyone, is at fault in producing the outcome of the story?

See also Questions for Contrast and Comparison: 94, 105, 164, 197, 198, and 200.

■ **ALICE MUNRO** (1931–) *was born and raised in the flat, thinly populated farm country of western Ontario, Canada, near Lake Huron, where her father raised silver foxes. She began writing at age twelve and first published in the student literary magazine while attending the University of Western Ontario (1949–1951). In 1951 she married James Munro, a bookseller, and moved with him to the West. Despite raising her three daughters in the city of Vancouver and in rural British Columbia, Munro's fiction has consistently explored shifting, difficult personal relationships in her own stern version of her native region. Always occupied with domestic life, Munro finally put aside her youthful desire to write novels in favor of more compact short stories. Her first collection,* Dance of the Happy Shades and Other Stories *(1968), won the prestigious Governor General's Award for fiction, as did both another collection,* Progress of Love *(1986, and* Who Do You Think You Are? *(1988; U.S. title:* The Beggar Maid: Stories of Flo and Rose*), a cycle of related stories often read as a novel. She returned permanently to western Ontario in 1972, where she divorced her first husband (1976) and married (1976) Gerald Fremlin, a geographer. Her earlier writing includes another story cycle,* Lives of Girls and Women *(1971), and her later writing includes two more collections,* Moons of Jupiter *(1983) and* Friend of my Youth *(1990).*

Royal Beatings

Royal Beating. That was Flo's promise. You are going to get one Royal Beating.

The word Royal lolled on Flo's tongue, took on trappings. Rose had a need to picture things, to pursue absurdities, that was stronger than the need to stay out of trouble, and instead of taking this threat to heart she pondered: how is a beating royal? She came up with a tree-lined avenue, a crowd of formal spectators, some white horses and black slaves. Someone knelt, and the blood came leaping out like banners. An occasion both savage and splendid. In real life they didn't approach such dignity, and it was only Flo who tried to supply the event with some high air of necessity and regret. Rose and her father soon got beyond anything presentable.

Her father was king of the royal beatings. Those Flo gave never amounted to much; they were quick cuffs and slaps dashed off while her attention remained elsewhere. You get out of my road, she would say. You mind your own business. You take that look off your face.

They lived behind a store in Hanratty, Ontario. There were four of them: Rose, her father, Flo, Rose's young half brother Brian. The store was really a house, bought by Rose's father and mother when they married and set up here in the furniture and upholstery repair business. Her mother could do upholstery. From both parents Rose should have inherited clever hands, a quick sympathy with materials, an eye for the nicest turns of mending, but she hadn't. She was clumsy, and when something broke she couldn't wait to sweep it up and throw it away.

Her mother had died. She said to Rose's father during the afternoon, "I have a feeling that is so hard to describe. It's like a boiled egg in my chest, with the shell left on." She died before night, she had a blood clot on her lung. Rose was a baby in a basket at the time, so of course could not remember any of this. She heard it from Flo, who must have heard it from her father. Flo came along soon afterward, to take over Rose in the basket, marry her father, open up the front room to make a grocery store. Rose, who had known the house only as a store, who had known only Flo for a mother, looked back on the sixteen or so months her parents spent here as an orderly, far gentler and more ceremonious time, with little touches of affluence. She had nothing to go on but some egg cups her mother had bought, with a pattern of vines and birds on them, delicately drawn as if with red ink; the pattern was beginning to wear away. No books or clothes or pictures of her mother remained. Her father must have got rid of them, or else Flo would. Flo's only story about her mother, the one about her death, was oddly grudging. Flo liked the details of a death: the things people said, the way they protested or tried to get out of bed or swore or laughed (some did those things), but when she said Rose's mother mentioned a hard-boiled egg in her chest she made the comparison sound slightly foolish, as if her mother really was the kind of person who might think you could swallow an egg whole.

Her father had a shed out behind the store, where he worked at his furniture repairing and restoring. He caned chair seats and backs, mended wickerwork, filled cracks, put legs back on, all most admirably and skillfully and cheaply. That was his pride: to startle people with such fine work, such moderate, even ridiculous charges. During the Depression people could not afford to pay more, perhaps, but he continued the practice through the war, through the years of prosperity after the war, until he died. He never discussed with Flo what he charged or what was owing. After he died she had to go out and unlock the shed and take all sorts of scraps of paper and torn envelopes from the big wicked-looking hooks that were his files. Many of these she found were not accounts or receipts at all but records of the weather, bits of information about the garden, things he had been moved to write down.

Ate new potatoes 25th June. Record.
Dark Day, 1880's, nothing supernatural. Clouds of ash from forest fires.
Aug. 16, 1938. Giant thunderstorm in evng. Lighting str. Pres. Church, Turberry Twp. Will of God?
Scald strawberries to remove acid.
All things are alive. Spinoza.

Flo thought Spinoza must be some new vegetable he planned to grow, like broccoli or eggplant. He would often try some new thing. She showed the scrap of paper to Rose and asked, did she know what Spinoza was? Rose did know, or had an idea—she was in her teens by that time—but she replied that she did not. She had reached an age where she thought she could not stand to know any more, about her father, or about Flo; she pushed any discovery aside with embarrassment and dread.

There was a stove in the shed, and many rough shelves covered with cans of paint and varnish, shellac and turpentine, jars of soaking brushes and also some dark sticky bottles of cough medicine. Why should a man who coughed constantly, whose lungs took in a whiff of gas in the War (called, in Rose's earliest childhood, not the First, but the Last, War) spend all his days breathing fumes of paint and turpentine? At the time, such questions were not asked as often as they are now. On the bench outside Flo's store several old men from the neighborhood sat gossiping, drowsing, in the warm weather, and some of these old men coughed all the time too. The fact is they were dying, slowly and discreetly, of what was called, without any particular sense of grievance, "the foundry disease." They had worked all their lives at the foundry in town, and now they sat still, with their wasted yellow faces, coughing, chuckling, drifting into aimless obscenity on the subject of women walking by, or any young girl on a bicycle.

From the shed came not only coughing, but speech, a continual muttering, reproachful or encouraging, usually just below the level at which separate words could be made out. Slowing down when her father was at a tricky piece of work, taking on a cheerful speed when he was doing something less demanding, sandpapering or painting. Now and then some words would break through and hang clear and nonsensical on the air. When he realized they were out, there would be a quick bit of cover-up coughing, a swallowing, an alert, unusual silence.

"Macaroni, pepperoni, Botticelli, beans—"

What could that mean? Rose used to repeat such things to herself. She could never ask him. The person who spoke these words and the person who spoke to her as her father were not the same, though they seemed to occupy the same space. It would be the worst sort of taste to acknowledge the person who was not supposed to be there; it would not be forgiven. Just the same, she loitered and listened.

The cloud-capped towers, she heard him say once.

"The cloud-capped towers, the gorgeous palaces."

That was like a hand clapped against Rose's chest, not to hurt, but astonish her, to take her breath away. She had to run then, she had to get away. She knew that was enough to hear, and besides, what if he caught her? It would be terrible.

This was something the same as bathroom noises. Flo had saved up, and had a bathroom put in, but there was no place to put it except in a corner of the kitchen. The door did not fit, the walls were only beaverboard. The result was that even the tearing of a piece of toilet paper, the shifting of a haunch, was audible to those working or talking or eating in the kitchen. They were all familiar with each other's nether voices, not only in their more explosive moments but in their intimate sighs and growls and pleas and statements. And they were all most prudish people. So no one ever seemed to hear, or be listening, and no reference was made. The person creating the noises in the bathroom was not connected with the person who walked out.

They lived in a poor part of town. There was Hanratty and West Hanratty, with the river flowing between them. This was West Hanratty. In Hanratty the social structure ran from doctors and dentists and lawyers down to foundry workers and factory workers and draymen; in West Hanratty it ran from factory workers and foundry workers down to large improvident families of casual bootleggers and prostitutes and unsuccessful thieves. Rose thought of her own family as straddling the river, belonging nowhere, but that was not true. West Hanratty was where the store was and they were, on the straggling tail end of the main street. Across the road from them was a blacksmith shop, boarded up about the time the war started, and a house that had been another store at one time. The Salada Tea sign had never been taken out of the front window; it remained as a proud and interesting decoration though there was no Salada Tea for sale inside. There was just a bit of sidewalk, too cracked and tilted for rollerskating, though Rose longed for roller skates and often pictured herself whizzing along in a plaid skirt, agile and fashionable. There was one street light, a tin flower; then the amenities gave up and there were dirt roads and boggy places, front-yard dumps and strange-looking houses. What made the houses strange-looking were the attempts to keep them from going completely to ruin. With some the attempt had never been made. These were gray and rotted and leaning over, falling into a landscape of scrub hollows, frog ponds, cattails and nettles. Most houses, however, had been patched up with tarpaper, a few fresh shingles, sheets of tin, hammered-out stovepipes, even cardboard. This was, of course, in the days before the war, days of what would later be legendary poverty, from which Rose would remember mostly lowdown things — serious-looking anthills and wooden steps, and a cloudy, interesting, problematical light on the world.

There was a long truce between Flo and Rose in the beginning. Rose's nature was growing like a prickly pineapple, but slowly, and secretly, hard pride and skepticism overlapping, to make something surprising even to herself. Before she was old enough to go to school, and while Brian was still in the baby carriage, Rose stayed in the store with both of them — Flo sitting on the high stool behind the counter, Brian asleep by the window; Rose knelt or lay on the wide creaky floorboards working with crayons on pieces of brown paper too torn or irregular to be used for wrapping.

People who came to the store were mostly from the houses around. Some country people came too, on their way home from town, and a few people from Hanratty, who walked across the bridge. Some people were always on the main street, in and out of stores, as if it was their duty to be always on display and their right to be welcomed. For instance, Becky Tyde.

Becky Tyde climbed up on Flo's counter, made room for herself beside an open tin of crumbly jam-filled cookies.

"Are these any good?" she said to Flo, and boldly began to eat one. "When are you going to give us a job, Flo?"

"You could go and work in the butcher shop," said Flo innocently. "You could go and work for your brother."

"Roberta?" said Becky with a stagey sort of contempt. "You think I'd work for him?" Her brother who ran the butcher shop was named Robert but often called Roberta, because of his meek and nervous ways. Becky Tyde laughed. Her laugh was loud and noisy like an engine bearing down on you.

She was a big-headed loud-voiced dwarf, with a mascot's sexless swagger, a red velvet tam, a twisted neck that forced her to hold her head on one side, always looking up and sideways. She wore little polished high-heeled shoes, real lady's shoes. Rose watched her shoes, being scared of the rest of her, of her laugh and her neck. She knew from Flo that Becky Tyde had been sick with polio as a child, that was why her neck was twisted and why she had not grown any taller. It was hard to believe that she had started out differently, that she had ever been normal. Flo said she was not cracked, she had as much brains as anybody, but she knew she could get away with anything.

"You know I used to live out here?" Becky said, noticing Rose. "Hey! What's-your-name! Didn't I used to live out here, Flo?"

"If you did it was before my time," said Flo, as if she didn't know anything.

"That was before the neighborhood got so downhill. Excuse me saying so. My father built his house out here and he built his slaughterhouse and we had half an acre of orchard."

"Is that so?" said Flo, using her humoring voice, full of false geniality, humility even. "Then why did you ever move away?"

"I told you, it got to be such a downhill neighborhood," said Becky. She would put a whole cookie in her mouth if she felt like it, let her cheeks puff out like a frog's. She never told any more.

Flo knew anyway, and who didn't. Everyone knew the house, red brick with the veranda pulled off and the orchard, what was left of it, full of the usual outflow — car seats and washing machines and bedsprings and junk. The house would never look sinister, in spite of what had happened in it, because there was so much wreckage and confusion all around.

Becky's old father was a different kind of butcher from her brother according to Flo. A bad-tempered Englishman. And different from Becky in the matter of mouthiness. His was never open. A skinflint, a family tyrant. After Becky had polio he wouldn't let her go back to school. She was seldom seen outside the house, never outside the yard. He didn't want people gloating. That was what Becky said, at the trial. Her mother was dead by that time and her sisters married. Just Becky and Robert at home. People would stop Robert on the road and ask him, "How about your sister, Robert? Is she altogether better now?"

"Yes."

"Does she do the housework? Does she get your supper?"

"Yes."

"And is your father good to her, Robert?"

The story being that the father beat them, had beaten all his children and beaten his wife as well, beat Becky more now because of her deformity, which some people believed he had caused (they did not understand about polio). The stories persisted and got added to. The reason that Becky was kept out of sight was now supposed to be her pregnancy, and the father of the child was supposed to be her own father. Then people said it had been born, and disposed of.

"What?"

"Disposed of," Flo said. "They used to say go and get your lamb chops at Tyde's, get them nice and tender! It was all lies in all probability," she said regretfully.

Rose could be drawn back — from watching the wind shiver along the old torn awning, catch in the tear — by this tone of regret, caution, in Flo's voice. Flo telling a story — and this was not the only one, or even the most lurid one, she knew — would incline her head and let her face go soft and thoughtful, tantalizing, warning.

"I shouldn't even be telling you this stuff."

More was to follow.

Three useless young men, who hung around the livery stable, got together — or were got together, by more influential and respectable men in town — and prepared to give old man Tyde a horsewhipping, in the interests of public morality. They blacked their faces. They were provided with whips and a quart of whiskey apiece, for courage. They were: Jelly Smith, a horse-racer and a drinker; Bob Temple, a ballplayer and strongman; and Hat Nettleton, who worked on the town dray, and had his nickname from a bowler hat he wore, out of vanity as much as for the comic effect. He still worked on the dray, in fact; he had kept the name if not the hat, and could often be seen in public — almost as often as Becky Tyde — delivering sacks of coal, which blackened his face and arms. That should have brought to mind his story, but didn't. Present time and past, the shady melodramatic past of Flo's stories, were quite separate, at least for Rose. Present people could not be fitted into the past. Becky herself, town oddity and public pet, harmless and malicious, could never match the butcher's prisoner, the cripple daughter, a white streak at the window: mute, beaten, impregnated. As with the house, only a formal connection could be made.

The young men primed to do the horsewhipping showed up late, outside Tyde's house, after everybody had gone to bed. They had a gun, but they used up their ammunition firing it off in the yard. They yelled for the butcher and beat on the door; finally they broke it down. Tyde concluded they were after his money, so he put some bills in a handkerchief and sent Becky down with them, maybe thinking those men would be touched or scared by the sight of a little wry-necked girl, a dwarf. But that didn't content them. They came upstairs and dragged the butcher out from under his bed, in his nightgown. They dragged him outside and stood him in the snow. The temperature was four below zero, a fact noted later in court. They meant to hold a mock trial but they could not remember how it was done. So they began to beat him and kept beating him until he fell. They yelled at him, *Butcher's meat!* and continued beating him while his nightgown and the snow he was lying in turned red. His son Robert said in court that he had not watched the beating. Becky said that Robert had watched at first but had run away and hid. She herself had watched all the way through. She watched the men leave at last and her father make his delayed bloody progress through the snow and up the steps of the veranda. She did not go out to help him, or open the door until he got to it. Why not? she was asked in court, and she said she did not go out because she just had her nightgown on, and she did not open the door because she did not want to let the cold into the house.

Old man Tyde then appeared to have recovered his strength. He sent Robert to harness the horse, and made Becky heat water so that he could wash. He dressed and took all the money and with no explanation to his children got into the cutter and drove to Belgrave where he left the horse tied in the cold and took the early morning train to Toronto. On the train he behaved oddly, groaning and cursing as if he was drunk. He was picked up on the streets of Toronto a day later, out of his mind with fever, and was taken to a hospital, where he died. He still had all the money. The cause of death was given as pneumonia.

But the authorities got wind, Flo said. The case came to trial. The three men who did it all received long prison sentences. A farce, said Flo. Within a year they were all free, had all been pardoned, had jobs waiting for them. And why was that? It was because too many higher-ups were in on it. And it seemed as if Becky and Robert had no interest in seeing justice done. They were left well-off. They bought a house in Hanratty. Robert went into the store. Becky after her long seclusion started on a career of public sociability and display.

That was all. Flo put the lid down on the story as if she was sick of it. It reflected no good on anybody.

"Imagine," Flo said.

Flo at this time must have been in her early thirties. A young woman. She wore exactly the same clothes that a woman of fifty, or sixty, or seventy, might wear: print housedresses loose at the neck and sleeves as well as the waist; bib aprons, also of print, which she took off when she came from the kitchen into the store. This was a common costume at the time, for a poor though not absolutely poverty-stricken woman, it was also, in a way, a scornful deliberate choice. Flo scorned slacks, she scorned the outfits of people trying to be in style, she scorned lipstick and permanents. She wore her own black hair cut straight across, just long enough to push behind her ears. She was tall but fine-boned, with narrow wrists and shoulders, a small head, a pale, freckled, mobile, monkeyish face. If she had thought it worthwhile, and had the resources, she might have had a black-and-pale, fragile, nurtured sort of prettiness; Rose realized that later. But she would have to have been a different person altogether; she would have to have learned to resist making faces, at herself and others.

Rose's earliest memories of Flo were of extraordinary softness and hardness. The soft hair, the long, soft, pale cheeks, soft almost invisible fuzz in front of her ears and above her mouth. The sharpness of her knees, hardness of her lap, flatness of her front.

When Flo sang:

Oh the buzzin' of the bees in the cigarette trees
And the soda-*water* fountain . . .

Rose thought of Flo's old life before she married her father, when she worked as a waitress in the coffee shop in Union Station, and went with her girl friends Mavis and Irene to Centre Island, and was followed by men on dark streets and knew how pay phones and elevators worked. Rose heard in her voice the reckless dangerous life of cities, the gum-chewing sharp answers.

And when she sang:

Then slowly, slowly, she got up
And slowly she came nigh him
And all she said, that she ever did say,
Was young man I think, you're dyin'!

Rose thought of a life Flo seemed to have had beyond that, earlier than that, crowded and legendary, with Barbara Allen and Becky Tyde's father and all kinds of outrages and sorrows jumbled up together in it.

The royal beatings. What got them started?

Suppose a Saturday, in spring. Leaves not out yet but the doors open to the sunlight. Crows. Ditches full of running water. Hopeful weather. Often on Saturdays Flo left Rose in charge of the store — it's a few years now, these are the years when Rose was nine, ten, eleven, twelve — while she herself went across the bridge to Hanratty (going uptown they called it) to shop and see people, and listen to them. Among the people she listened to were Mrs. Lawyer Davies, Mrs. Anglican Rector Henley-Smith, and Mrs. Horse-Doctor McKay. She came home and imitated their flibberty voices. Monsters, she made them seem; of foolishness, and showiness, and self-approbation.

When she finished shopping she went into the coffee shop of the Queen's Hotel and had a sundae. What kind? Rose and Brian wanted to know when she got home, and they would be disappointed if it was only pineapple or butterscotch, pleased if it was a Tin Roof, or Black and White. Then she smoked a cigarette. She had some ready-rolled, that she carried with her, so that she wouldn't have to roll one in public. Smoking was the one thing she did that she would have called showing off in anybody else. It was a habit left over from her working days, from Toronto. She knew it was asking for trouble. Once the Catholic priest came over to her right in the Queen's Hotel, and flashed his lighter at her before she could get her matches out. She thanked him but did not enter into conversation, lest he should try to convert her.

Another time, on the way home, she saw at the town end of the bridge a boy in a blue jacket, apparently looking at the water. Eighteen, nineteen years old. Nobody she knew. Skinny, weakly looking, something the matter with him, she saw at once. Was he thinking of jumping? Just as she came up even with him, what does he do but turn and display himself, holding his jacket open, also his pants. What he must have suffered from the cold, on a day that had Flo holding her coat collar tight around her throat.

When she first saw what he had in his hand, Flo said, all she could think of was, what is he doing out here with a baloney sausage?

She could say that. It was offered as truth; no joke. She maintained that she despised dirty talk. She would go out and yell at the old men sitting in front of her store.

"If you want to stay where you are you better clean your mouths out!"

Saturday, then. For some reason Flo is not going uptown, has decided to stay home and scrub the kitchen floor. Perhaps this has put her in a bad mood. Perhaps she was in a bad mood anyway, due to people not paying their bills, or the stirring-up of feelings in spring. The wrangle with Rose had already commenced, has been going on forever, like a dream that goes back and back into other dreams, over hills and through doorways, maddeningly dim and populous and familiar and elusive. They are carting all the chairs out of the kitchen preparatory to the scrubbing, and they have also got to move some extra provisions for the store, some cartons of canned goods, tins of maple syrup, coal-oil cans, jars of vinegar. They take these things out to the woodshed. Brian who is five or six by this time is helping drag the tins.

"Yes," says Flo, carrying on from our lost starting point. "Yes, and that filth you taught to Brian."

"What filth?"

"And he doesn't know any better."

There is one step down from the kitchen to the woodshed, a bit of carpet on it so worn Rose can't ever remember seeing the pattern. Brian loosens it, dragging a tin.

"Two Vancouvers," she says softly.

Flo is back in the kitchen. Brian looks from Flo to Rose and Rose says again in a slightly louder voice, an encouraging sing-song, "Two Vancouvers —"

"Fried in snot!" finishes Brian, not able to control himself any longer.

"Two pickled arseholes —"

"—tied in a knot!"
There it is. The filth.

Two Vancouvers fried in snot!
Two pickled arseholes tied in a knot!

Rose has known that for years, learned it when she first went to school. She came home and asked Flo, what is a Vancouver?

"It's a city. It's a long ways away."

"What else besides a city?"

Flo said, what did she mean, what else? How could it be fried, Rose said, approaching the dangerous moment, the delightful moment, when she would have to come out with the whole thing.

"Two Vancouvers fried in snot! Two pickled arseholes tied in a knot!"

"You're going to get it!" cried Flo in a predictable rage. "Say that again and you'll get a good clout!"

Rose couldn't stop herself. She hummed it tenderly, tried saying the innocent words aloud, humming through the others. It was not just the words snot and arsehole that gave her pleasure, though of course they did. It was the pickling and tying and the unimaginable Vancouver. She saw them in her mind shaped rather like octopuses, twitching in the pan. The tumble of reason; the spark and spit of craziness.

Lately she has remembered it again and taught it to Brian, to see if it has the same effect on him, and of course it has.

"Oh, I heard you!" says Flo. "I heard that! And I'm warning you!"

So she is. Brian takes the warning. He runs away, out the woodshed door, to do as he likes. Being a boy, free to help or not, involve himself or not. Not committed to the household struggle. They don't need him anyway, except to use against each other, they hardly notice his going. They continue, can't help continuing, can't leave each other alone. When they seem to have given up they really are just waiting and building up steam.

Flo gets out the scrub pail and the brush and the rag and the pad for her knees, a dirty red rubber pad. She starts to work on the floor. Rose sits on the kitchen table, the only place left to sit, swinging her legs. She can feel the cool oilcloth, because she is wearing shorts, last summer's tight faded shorts dug out of the summer-clothes bag. They smell a bit moldy from winter storage.

Flo crawls underneath, scrubbing with the brush, wiping with the rag. Her legs are long, white and muscular, marked all over with blue veins as if somebody had been drawing rivers on them with an indelible pencil. An abnormal energy, a violent disgust, is expressed in the chewing of the brush at the linoleum, the swish of the rag.

What do they have to say to each other? It doesn't really matter. Flo speaks of Rose's smart-aleck behavior, rudeness and sloppiness and conceit. Her willingness to make work for others, her lack of gratitude. She mentions Brian's innocence, Rose's corruption. Oh, don't you think you're somebody, says Flo, and a moment later, Who do you think you are? Rose contradicts and objects with such poisonous reasonableness and mildness, displays theatrical unconcern. Flo goes beyond her ordinary scorn and self-possession and becomes amazingly theatrical herself, saying it was for Rose that she sacrificed her life. She saw her father saddled with a baby daughter and thought, what is that man going to do? So she married him, and here she is, on her knees.

At that moment the bell rings, to announce a customer in the store. Because the fight is on, Rose is not permitted to go into the store and wait on whoever it is. Flo gets up and throws off her apron, groaning — but not communicatively, it is not a groan whose exasperation Rose is allowed to share — and goes in and serves. Rose hears her using her normal voice.

"About time! Sure is!"

She comes back and ties on her apron and is ready to resume.

"You never have a thought for anybody but your ownself! You never have a thought for what I'm doing."

"I never asked you to do anything. I wish you never had. I would have been a lot better off."

Rose says this smiling directly at Flo, who has not yet gone down on her knees. Flo sees the smile, grabs the scrub rag that is hanging on the side of the pail, and throws it at her. It may be meant to hit her in the face but instead it falls against Rose's leg and she raises her foot and catches it, swinging it negligently against her ankle.

"All right," says Flo. "You've done it this time. All right."

Rose watches her go to the woodshed door, hears her tramp through the woodshed, pause in the doorway, where the screen door hasn't yet been hung, and the storm door is standing open, propped with a brick. She calls Rose's father. She calls him in a warning, summoning voice, as if against her will preparing him for bad news. He will know what this is about.

The kitchen floor has five or six different patterns of linoleum on it. Ends, which Flo got for nothing and ingeniously trimmed and fitted together, bordering them with tin strips and tacks. While Rose sits on the table waiting, she looks at the floor, at this satisfying arrangement of rectangles, triangles, some other shape whose name she is trying to remember. She hears Flo coming back through the woodshed, on the creaky plank walk laid over the dirt floor. She is loitering, waiting, too. She and Rose can carry this no further, by themselves.

Rose hears her father come in. She stiffens, a tremor runs through her legs, she feels them shiver on the oilcloth. Called away from some peaceful, absorbing task, away from the words running in his head, called out of himself, her father has to say something. He says, "Well? What's wrong?"

Now comes another voice of Flo's. Enriched, hurt, apologetic, it seems to have been manufactured on the spot. She is sorry to have called him from his work. Would never have done it, if Rose was not driving her to distraction. How to distraction? With her back talk and impudence and her terrible tongue. The things Rose has said to Flo are such that, if Flo had said them to her mother, she knows her father would have thrashed her into the ground.

Rose tries to butt in, to say this isn't true.

What isn't true?

Her father raises a hand, doesn't look at her, says, "Be quiet."

When she says it isn't true, Rose means that she herself didn't start this, only responded, that she was goaded by Flo, who is now, she believes, telling the grossest sort of lies, twisting everything to suit herself. Rose puts aside her other knowledge that whatever Flo has said or done, whatever she herself has said or done, does not really matter at all. It is the struggle itself that counts, and that can't be stopped, can never be stopped, short of where it has got to, now.

Flo's knees are dirty, in spite of the pad. The scrub rag is still hanging over Rose's foot.

Her father wipes his hands, listening to Flo. He takes his time. He is slow at getting into the spirit of things, tired in advance, maybe, on the verge of rejecting the role he has to play. He won't look at Rose, but at any sound or stirring from Rose, he holds up his hand.

"Well we don't need the public in on this, that's for sure," Flo says, and she goes back to lock the door of the store, putting in the store window the sign that says BACK SOON, a sign Rose made for her with a great deal of fancy curving and shading of letters in black and red crayon. When she comes back she shuts the door to the store, then the door to the stairs, then the door to the woodshed. Her shoes have left marks on the clean wet part of the floor.

"Oh, I don't know," she says now, in a voice worn down from its emotional peak. "I don't know what to do about her." She looks down and sees her dirty knees (following Rose's eyes) and rubs at them viciously with her bare hands, smearing the dirt around.

"She humiliates me," she says, straightening up. There it is, the explanation. "She humiliates me," she repeats with satisfaction. "She has no respect."

"I do not!"

"Quiet, you!" says her father.

"If I hadn't called your father you'd still be sitting there with that grin on your face! What other way is there to manage you?"

Rose detects in her father some objections to Flo's rhetoric, some embarrassment and reluctance. She is wrong, and ought to know she is wrong, in thinking that she can count on this. The fact that she knows about it, and he knows she knows, will not make things any better. He is beginning to warm up. He gives her a look. This look is at first cold and challenging. It informs her of his judgment, of the hopelessness of her position. Then it clears, it begins to fill up with something else, the way a spring fills up when you clear the leaves away. It fills with hatred and pleasure. Rose sees that and knows it. Is that just a description of anger, should she see his eyes filling up with anger? No. Hatred is right. Pleasure is right. His face loosens and changes and grows younger, and he holds up his hand this time to silence Flo.

"All right," he says, meaning that's enough, more than enough, this part is over, things can proceed. He starts to loosen his belt.

Flo has stopped anyway. She has the same difficulty Rose does, a difficulty in believing that what you know must happen really will happen, that there comes a time when you can't draw back.

"Oh, I don't know, don't be too hard on her." She is moving around nervously as if she has thoughts of opening some escape route. "Oh, you don't have to use the belt on her. Do you have to use the belt?"

He doesn't answer. The belt is coming off, not hastily. It is being grasped at the necessary point. *All right you.* He is coming over to Rose. He pushes her off the table. His face, like his voice, is quite out of character. He is like a bad actor, who turns a part grotesque. As if he must savor and insist on just what is shameful and terrible about this. That is not to say he is pretending, that he is acting, and does not mean it. He is acting, and he means it. Rose knows that, she knows everything about him.

She has since wondered about murders, and murderers. Does the thing have to be carried through, in the end, partly for the effect, to prove to the audience of one — who won't be able to report, only register, the lesson — that such a thing can happen, that there is nothing that can't happen, that the most dreadful antic is justified, feelings can be found to match it?

She tries again looking at the kitchen floor, that clever and comforting geometrical arrangement, instead of looking at him or his belt. How can this go on in front of such daily witnesses — the linoleum, the calendar with the mill and creek and autumn trees, the old accommodating pots and pans?

Hold out your hand!

Those aren't going to help her, none of them can rescue her. They turn bland and useless, even unfriendly. Pots can show malice, the patterns of linoleum can leer up at you, treachery is the other side of dailiness.

At the first, or maybe the second, crack of pain, she draws back. She will not accept it. She runs around the room, she tries to get to the doors. Her father blocks her off. Not an ounce of courage or of stoicism in her, it would seem. She runs, she screams, she implores. Her father is after her, cracking the belt at her when he can, then abandoning it and using his hands. Bang over the ear, then bang over the other ear. Back and forth, her head ringing. Bang in the face. Up against the wall and bang in the face again. He shakes her and hits her against the wall, he kicks her legs. She is incoherent, insane, shrieking. *Forgive me! Oh please, forgive me!*

Flo is shrieking too. *Stop, stop!*

Not yet. He throws Rose down. Or perhaps she throws herself down. He kicks her legs again. She has given up on words but is letting out a noise, the sort of noise that makes Flo cry, *Oh, what if people can hear her?* The very last-ditch willing sound of humiliation and defeat it is, for it seems Rose must play her part in this with the same grossness, the same exaggeration, that her father displays, playing his. She plays his victim with a self-indulgence that arouses, and maybe hopes to arouse, his final, sickened contempt.

They will give this anything that is necessary, it seems, they will go to any lengths.

Not quite. He has never managed really to injure her, though there are times, of course, when she prays that he will. He hits her with an open hand, there is some restraint in his kicks.

Now he stops, he is out of breath. He allows Flo to move in, he grabs Rose up and gives her a push in Flo's direction, making a sound of disgust. Flo retrieves her, opens the stair door, shoves her up the stairs.

"Go on up to your room now! Hurry!"

Rose goes up the stairs, stumbling, letting herself stumble, letting herself fall against the steps. She doesn't bang her door because a gesture like that could still bring him after her, and anyway, she is weak. She lies on the bed. She can hear through the stovepipe hole Flo snuffling and remonstrating, her father saying angrily that Flo should have kept quiet then, if she did not want Rose punished she should not have recommended it. Flo says she never recommended a hiding like that.

They argue back and forth on this. Flo's frightened voice is growing stronger, getting its confidence back. By stages, by arguing, they are being drawn back into themselves. Soon it's only Flo talking; he will not talk anymore. Rose has had to fight down her noisy sobbing, so as to listen to them, and when she loses interest in listening, and wants to sob some more, she finds she can't work herself up to it. She has passed into a state of calm, in which outrage is perceived as complete and final. In this state events and possibilities take on a lovely simplicity. Choices are mercifully clear. The words that come to mind are not the quibbling, seldom the conditional. Never is a word to which the right is suddenly established. She will never speak to them, she will never look at them with anything but loathing, she will never forgive them. She will punish them; she will finish them. Encased in these finalities, and in her bodily pain, she floats in curious comfort, beyond herself, beyond responsibility.

Suppose she dies now? Suppose she commits suicide? Suppose she runs away? Any of these things would be appropriate. It is only a matter of choosing, of figuring out the way. She floats in her pure superior state as if kindly drugged.

And just as there is a moment, when you are drugged, in which you feel perfectly safe, sure, unreachable, and then without warning and right next to it a moment in which you know the whole protection has fatally cracked, though it is still pretending to hold soundly together, so there is a moment now—the moment, in fact, when Rose hears Flo step on the stairs—that contains for her both present peace and freedom and a sure knowledge of the whole down-spiraling course of events from now on.

Flo comes into the room without knocking, but with a hesitation that shows it might have occurred to her. She brings a jar of cold cream. Rose is hanging on to advantage as long as she can, lying face down on the bed, refusing to acknowledge or answer.

"Oh come on," Flo says uneasily. "You aren't so bad off, are you? You put some of this on and you'll feel better."

She is bluffing. She doesn't know for sure what damage has been done. She has the lid off the cold cream. Rose can smell it. The intimate, babyish, humiliating smell. She won't allow it near her. But in order to avoid it, the big ready clot of it in Flo's hand, she has to move. She scuffles, resists, loses dignity, and lets Flo see there is not really much the matter.

"All right," Flo says. "You win. I'll leave it here and you can put it on when you like."

Later still a tray will appear. Flo will put it down without a word and go away. A large glass of chocolate milk on it, made with Vita-Malt from the store. Some rich streaks of Vita-Malt around the bottom of the glass. Little sandwiches, neat and appetizing. Canned salmon of the first quality and reddest color, plenty of mayonnaise. A couple of butter tarts from a bakery package, chocolate biscuits with a peppermint filling. Rose's favorites, in the sandwich, tart and cookie line. She will turn away, refuse to look, but left alone with these eatables will be miserably tempted, roused and troubled and drawn back from thoughts of suicide or flight by the smell of salmon, the anticipation of crisp chocolate, she will reach out a finger, just to run it around the edge of one of the sandwiches (crusts cut off!) to get the overflow, get a taste. Then she will decide to eat one, for strength to refuse the rest. One will not be noticed. Soon, in helpless corruption, she will eat them all. She will drink the chocolate milk, eat the tarts, eat the cookies. She will get the malty syrup out of the bottom of the glass with her finger, though she sniffles with shame. Too late.

Flo will come up and get the tray. She may say, "I see you got your appetite still," or, "Did you like the chocolate milk, was it enough syrup in it?" depending on how chastened she is feeling, herself. At any rate, all advantage will be lost. Rose will understand that life has started up again, that they will all sit around the table eating again, listening to the radio news. Tomorrow morning, maybe even tonight. Unseemly and unlikely as that may be. They will be embarrassed, but rather less than you might expect considering how they have behaved. They will feel a queer lassitude, a convalescent indolence, not far off satisfaction.

One night after a scene like this they were all in the kitchen. It must have been summer, or at least warm weather, because her father spoke of the old men who sat on the bench in front of the store.

"Do you know what they're talking about now?" he said, and nodded his head toward the store to show who he meant, though of course they were not there now, they went home at dark.

"Those old coots," said Flo. "What?"

There was about them both a geniality not exactly false but a bit more emphatic than was normal, without company.

Rose's father told them then that the old men had picked up the idea somewhere that what looked like a star in the western sky, the first star that came out after sunset, the evening star, was in reality an airship hovering over Bay City, Michigan, on the other side of Lake Huron. An American invention, sent up to rival the heavenly bodies. They were all in agreement about this, the idea was congenial to them. They believed it to be lit by ten thousand electric light bulbs. Her father had ruthlessly disagreed with them, pointing out that it was the planet Venus they saw, which had appeared in the sky long before the invention of an electric light bulb. They had never heard of the planet Venus.

"Ignoramuses," said Flo. At which Rose knew, and knew her father knew, that Flo had never heard of the planet Venus either. To distract them from this, or even apologize for it, Flo put down her teacup, stretched out with her head resting on the chair she been sitting on and her feet on another chair (somehow she managed to tuck her dress modestly between her legs at the same time), and lay stiff as a board, so that Brian cried out in delight, "Do that! Do that!"

Flo was double-jointed and very strong. In moments of celebration or emergency she would do tricks.

They were silent while she turned herself around, not using her arms at all but just her strong legs and feet. Then they all cried out in triumph, though they had seen it before.

Just as Flo turned herself Rose got a picture in her mind of that air-ship, an elongated transparent bubble, with its strings of diamond lights, floating in the miraculous American sky.

"The planet Venus!" her father said, applauding Flo. "Ten thousand electric lights!"

There was a feeling of permission, relaxation, even a current of happiness, in the room.

Years later, many years later, on a Sunday morning, Rose turned on the radio. This was when she was living by herself in Toronto.

Well sir.

It was a different kind of place in our day. Yes it was.

It was all horses then. Horses and buggies. Buggy races up and down the main street on the Saturday nights.

"Just like the chariot races," says the announcer's, or interviewer's, smooth encouraging voice.

I never seen a one of them.

"No sir, that was the old Roman chariot races I was referring to. That was before your time."

Musta been before my time. I'm a hunerd and two years old.

"That's a wonderful age, sir."

It is so.

She left it on, as she went around the apartment kitchen, making coffee for herself. It seemed to her that this must be a staged interview, a scene from some play, and she wanted to find out what it was. The old man's voice was so vain and belligerent, the interviewer's quite hopeless and alarmed, under its practiced gentleness and ease. You were surely meant to see him holding the microphone up to some toothless, reckless, preening centenarian, wondering what in God's name he was doing here, and what would he say next?

"They must have been fairly dangerous."

What was dangerous?

"Those buggy races."

They was. Dangerous. Used to be the runaway horses. Used to be a-plenty of accidents. Fellows was dragged along on the gravel and cut their face open. Wouldna matter so much if they was dead. Heh.

Some of them horses was the high-steppers. Some, they had to have the mustard under their tail. Some wouldn step out for nothin. That's the thing it is with the horses. Some'll work and pull till they drop down dead and some wouldn pull your cock out of a pail of lard. Hehe.

It must be a real interview after all. Otherwise they wouldn't have put that in, wouldn't have risked it. It's all right if the old man says it. Local color. Anything rendered harmless and delightful by his hundred years.

Accidents all the time then. In the mill. Foundry. Wasn't the precautions.

"You didn't have so many strikes, then I don't suppose? You didn't have so many unions?"

Everybody taking it easy nowadays. We worked and we was glad to get it. Worked and was glad to get it.

"You didn't have television."

Didn't have no TV. Didn't have no radio. No picture show.

"You made your own entertainment."

That's the way we did it.

"You had a lot of experiences young men growing up today will never have."

Experiences.

"Can you recall any of them for us?"

I eaten groundhog meat one time. One winter. You wouldna cared for it. Heh.

There was a pause, of appreciation, it would seem, then the announcer's voice saying that the foregoing had been an interview with Mr. Wilfred Nettleton of Hanratty, Ontario, made on his hundred and second birthday, two weeks before his death, last spring. A living link with our past. Mr. Nettleton had been interviewed in the Wawanash County Home for the Aged.

Hat Nettleton.

Horsewhipper into centenarian. Photographed on his birthday, fussed over by nurses, kissed no doubt by a girl reporter. Flash bulbs popping at him. Tape recorder drinking in the sound of his voice. Oldest resident. Oldest horsewhipper. Living link with our past.

Looking out from her kitchen window at the cold lake, Rose was longing to tell somebody. It was Flo who would enjoy hearing. She thought of her saying *Imagine!* in a way that meant she was having her worst suspicions gorgeously confirmed. But Flo was in the same place Hat Nettleton had died in, and there wasn't any way Rose could reach her. She had been there even when that interview was recorded, though she would not have heard it, would not have known about it. After Rose put her in the Home, a couple of years earlier, she had stopped talking. She had removed herself, and spent most of her time sitting in a corner of her crib, looking crafty and disagreeable, not answering anybody, though she occasionally showed her feelings by biting a nurse.

[1977]

Study and Writing Questions

1. Why is Rose's father (and her mother) unnamed in the STORY?
2. What is the role of humor in the story? What is the story finally about?
3. What does Becky Tyde add to the story?
4. What do the various SETTINGS contribute to the NARRATIVE?
5. What are the changing meanings of the title phrase?

See also Questions for Contrast and Comparison: 57, 58, 59, 62, 84, and 116.

■ **(MARY) FLANNERY O'CONNOR** (1925–1964) *was born in Savannah, Georgia, the only child of a real estate broker and a housewife. In 1938, when her father was struck with lupus, a chronic autoimmune disease, the family moved to her mother's hometown, Milledgeville, and acquired the nearby family farm. After her father's death (1941), O'Connor completed high school (1942), attended Milledgeville's Georgia State College for Women (B.A., 1945), and accepted a fellowship to the prestigious University of Iowa Writers' Workshop (M.F.A., 1947) where she began publishing professionally (1946). From 1948 to 1950, she lived and wrote in an apartment hotel in New York City, in an upstate New York writers' colony, and in a room rented from friends in Ridgefield, Connecticut. When she too fell ill with lupus, she returned to the farm where, except for brief lecture trips, she lived her last fourteen years with her mother. A devout Roman Catholic, O'Connor viewed the modern world as spiritually "hostile," so she used the* GROTESQUE *and bizarre because "for the almost blind you draw large and startling figures." She published two novels,* Wise Blood *(1952), about a guilt-ridden preacher, and* The Violent Bear It Away *(1960), about a would-be prophet, but is best known for two story collections,* A Good Man Is Hard To Find *(1955) and* Everything That Rises Must Converge *(1965). Her* Complete Stories *(1971) won the National Book Award.*

Good Country People

Besides the neutral expression that she wore when she was alone, Mrs. Freeman had two others, forward and reverse, that she used for all her human dealings. Her forward expression was steady and driving like the advance of a heavy truck. Her eyes never swerved to left or right but turned as the story turned as if they followed a yellow line down the center of it. She seldom used the other expression because it was not often necessary for her to retract a statement, but when she did, her face came to a complete stop, there was an almost imperceptible movement of her black eyes, during which they seemed to be receding, and then the observer would see that Mrs. Freeman, though she might stand there as real as several grain sacks thrown on top of each other, was no longer there in spirit. As for getting anything across to her when this was the case, Mrs. Hopewell had given it up. She might talk her head off. Mrs. Freeman could never be brought to admit herself wrong on any point. She would stand there and if she could be brought to say anything, it was something like, "Well, I wouldn't of said it was and I wouldn't of said it wasn't," or letting her gaze range over the top kitchen shelf where there was an assortment of dusty bottles, she might remark, "I see you ain't ate many of them figs you put up last summer."

They carried on their most important business in the kitchen at breakfast. Every morning Mrs. Hopewell got up at seven o'clock and lit her gas heater and Joy's. Joy was her daughter, a large blonde girl who had an artificial leg. Mrs. Hopewell thought of her as a child though she was thirty-two years old and highly educated. Joy would get up while her mother was eating and lumber into the bathroom and slam the door, and before long, Mrs. Freeman would arrive at the back door. Joy would hear her mother call, "Come on in," and then they would talk for a while in low voices that were indistinguishable in the bathroom. By the time Joy came in, they had usually finished the weather report and were on one or the other of Mrs. Freeman's daughters, Glynese or Carramae. Joy called them Glycerin and Caramel. Glynese, a redhead, was eighteen and had many admirers; Carramae, a blonde, was only fifteen but already married and pregnant. She could not keep anything on her stomach. Every morning Mrs. Freeman told Mrs. Hopewell how many times she had vomited since the last report.

Mrs. Hopewell liked to tell people that Glynese and Carramae were two of the finest girls she knew and that Mrs. Freeman was a *lady* and that she was never ashamed to take her anywhere or introduce her to anybody they might meet. Then she would tell how she had happened to hire the Freemans in the first place and how they were a godsend to her and how she had had them four years. The reason for her keeping them so long was that they were not trash. They were good country people. She had telephoned the man whose name they had given as a reference and he had told her that Mr. Freeman was a good farmer but that his wife was the nosiest woman ever to walk the earth. "She's got to be into everything," the man said. "If she don't get there before the dust settles, you can bet she's dead, that's all. She'll want to know all your business. I can stand him real good," he had said, "but me nor my wife neither could have stood that woman one more minute on this place." That had put Mrs. Hopewell off for a few days.

She had hired them in the end because there were no other applicants but she had made up her mind beforehand exactly how she would handle the woman. Since she was the type who had to be into everything, then, Mrs. Hopewell had decided, she would not only let her be into everything, she would *see to it* that she was into everything — she would give her the responsibility of everything, she would put her in charge. Mrs. Hopewell had no bad qualities of her own but she was able to use other people's in such a constructive way that she never felt the lack. She had hired the Freemans and she had kept them four years.

Nothing is perfect. This was one of Mrs. Hopewell's favorite sayings. Another was: that is life! And still another, the most important, was: well, other people have their opinions too. She would make these statements, usually at the table, in a tone of gentle insistence as if no one held them but her, and the large hulking Joy, whose constant outrage had obliterated every expression from her face, would stare just a little to the side of her, her eyes icy blue, with the look of someone who has achieved blindness by an act of will and means to keep it.

When Mrs. Hopewell said to Mrs. Freeman that life was like that, Mrs. Freeman would say, "I always said so myself." Nothing had been arrived at by anyone that had not first been arrived at by her. She was quicker than Mr. Freeman. When Mrs. Hopewell said to her after they had been on the place a while, "You know, you're the wheel behind the wheel," and winked, Mrs. Freeman had said, "I know it. I've always been quick. It's some that are quicker than others."

"Everybody is different," Mrs. Hopewell said.

"Yes, most people is," Mrs. Freeman said.

"It takes all kinds to make the world."

"I always said it did myself."

The girl was used to this kind of dialogue for breakfast and more of it for dinner; sometimes they had it for supper too. When they had no guest they ate in the kitchen because that was easier. Mrs. Freeman always managed to arrive at some point during the meal and to watch them finish it. She would stand in the doorway if it were summer but in the winter she would stand with one elbow on top of the refrigerator and look down on them, or she would stand by the gas heater, lifting the back of her skirt slightly. Occasionally she would stand against the wall and roll her head from side to side. At no time was she in any hurry to leave. All this was very trying on Mrs. Hopewell but she was a woman of great patience. She realized that nothing is perfect and that in the Freemans she had good country people and that if, in this day and age, you get good country people, you had better hang onto them.

She had had plenty of experience with trash. Before the Freemans she had averaged one tenant family a year. The wives of these farmers were not the kind you would want to be around you for very long. Mrs. Hopewell, who had divorced her husband long ago, needed someone to walk over the fields with her; and when Joy had to be impressed for these services, her remarks were usually so ugly and her face so glum that Mrs. Hopewell would say, "If you can't come pleasantly, I don't want you at all," to which the girl, standing square and rigid-shouldered with her neck thrust slightly forward, would reply, "If you want me here, here I am—LIKE I AM."

Mrs. Hopewell excused this attitude because of the leg (which had been shot off in a hunting accident when Joy was ten). It was hard for Mrs. Hopewell to realize that her child was thirty-two now and that for more than twenty years she had had only one leg. She thought of her still as a child because it tore her heart to think instead of the poor stout girl in her thirties who had never danced a step or had any *normal* good times. Her name was really Joy but as soon as she was twenty-one and away from home, she had had it legally changed. Mrs. Hopewell was certain that she had thought and thought until she had hit upon the ugliest name in any language. Then she had gone and had the beautiful name, Joy, changed without telling her mother until after she had done it. Her legal name was Hulga.

When Mrs. Hopewell thought the name, Hulga, she thought of the broad blank hull of a battleship. She would not use it. She continued to call her Joy to which the girl responded but in a purely mechanical way.

Hulga had learned to tolerate Mrs. Freeman who saved her from taking walks with her mother. Even Glynese and Carramae were useful when they occupied attention that might otherwise have been directed at her. At first she had thought she could not stand Mrs. Freeman for she had found that it was not possible to be rude to her. Mrs. Freeman would take on strange resentments and for days together she would be sullen but the source of her displeasure was always obscure; a direct attack, a positive leer, blatant ugliness to her face—these never touched her. And without warning one day, she began calling her Hulga.

She did not call her that in front of Mrs. Hopewell who would have been incensed but when she and the girl happened to be out of the house together, she would say something and add the name Hulga to the end of it, and the big spectacled Joy-Hulga would scowl and redden as if her privacy had been intruded upon. She considered the name her personal affair. She had arrived at it first purely on the basis of its ugly sound and then the full genius of its fitness had struck her. She had a vision of the name working like the ugly sweating Vulcan who stayed in the furnace and to whom, presumably, the goddess had to come when called. She saw it as the name of her highest creative act. One of her major triumphs was that her mother had not been able to turn her dust into Joy, but the greater one was that she had been able to turn it herself into Hulga. However, Mrs. Freeman's relish for using the name only irritated her. It was as if Mrs. Freeman's beady steel-pointed eyes had penetrated far enough behind her face to reach some secret fact. Something about her seemed to fascinate Mrs. Freeman and then one day Hulga realized that it was the artificial leg. Mrs. Freeman had a special fondness for the details of secret infections, hidden deformities, assaults upon children. Of diseases, she preferred the lingering or incurable. Hulga had heard Mrs. Hopewell give her the details of the hunting accident, how the leg had been literally blasted off, how she had never lost consciousness. Mrs. Freeman could listen to it any time as if it had happened an hour ago.

When Hulga stumped into the kitchen in the morning (she could walk without making the awful noise but she made it — Mrs. Hopewell was certain — because it was ugly-sounding), she glanced at them and did not speak. Mrs. Hopewell would be in her red kimono with her hair tied around her head in rags. She would be sitting at the table, finishing her breakfast and Mrs. Freeman would be hanging by her elbow outward from the refrigerator, looking down at the table. Hulga always put her eggs on the stove to boil and then stood over them with her arms folded, and Mrs. Hopewell would look at her — a kind of indirect gaze divided between her and Mrs. Freeman — and would think that if she would only keep herself up a little, she wouldn't be so bad looking. There was nothing wrong with her face that a pleasant expression wouldn't help. Mrs. Hopewell said that people who looked on the bright side of things would be beautiful even if they were not.

Whenever she looked at Joy this way, she could not help but feel that it would have been better if the child had not taken the Ph.D. It had certainly not brought her out any and now that she had it, there was no more excuse for her to go to school again. Mrs. Hopewell thought it was nice for girls to go to school to have a good time but Joy had "gone through." Anyhow, she would not have been strong enough to go again. The doctors had told Mrs. Hopewell that with the best of care, Joy might see forty-five. She had a weak heart. Joy had made it plain that if it had not been for this condition, she would be far from these red hills and good country people. She would be in a university lecturing to people who knew what she was talking about. And Mrs. Hopewell could very well picture her there, looking like a scarecrow and lecturing to more of the same. Here she went about all day in a six-year-old skirt and a yellow sweat shirt with a faded cowboy on a horse embossed on it. She thought this was funny; Mrs. Hopewell thought it was idiotic and showed simply that she was still a child. She was brilliant but she didn't have a grain of sense. It seemed to Mrs. Hopewell that every year she grew less like other people and more like herself — bloated, rude, and squint-eyed. And she said such strange things! To her own mother she had said — without warning, without excuses, standing up in the middle of a meal with her face purple and her mouth half full — "Woman! do you ever look inside? Do you ever look inside and see what you are *not*? God!" she had cried sinking down again and staring at her plate, "Malebranche was right: we are not our own light. We are not our own light!" Mrs. Hopewell had no idea to this day what brought that on. She had only made the remark, hoping Joy would take it in, that a smile never hurt anyone.

The girl had taken the Ph.D. in philosophy and this left Mrs. Hopwell at a complete loss. You could say, "My daughter is a nurse," or "My daughter is a school teacher," or even, "My daughter is a chemical engineer." You could not say, "My daughter is a philosopher." That was something that had ended with the Greeks and Romans. All day Joy sat on her neck in a deep chair, reading. Sometimes she went for walks but she didn't like dogs or cats or birds or flowers or nature or nice young men. She looked at nice young men as if she could smell their stupidity.

One day Mrs. Hopewell had picked up one of the books the girl had just put down and opening it at random, she read, "Science, on the other hand, has to assert its soberness and seriousness afresh and declare that it is concerned solely with what-is. Nothing—how can it be for science anything but a horror and a phantasm? If science is right, then one thing stands firm: science wishes to know nothing of nothing. Such is after all the strictly scientific approach to Nothing. We know it by wishing to know nothing of Nothing." These words had been underlined with a blue pencil and they worked on Mrs. Hopewell like some evil incantation in gibberish. She shut the book quickly and went out of the room as if she were having a chill.

This morning when the girl came in, Mrs. Freeman was on Carramae. "She thrown up four times after supper," she said, "and was up twict in the night after three o'clock. Yesterday she didn't do nothing but ramble in the bureau drawer. All she did. Stand up there and see what she could run up on."

"She's got to eat," Mrs. Hopewell muttered, sipping her coffee, while she watched Joy's back at the stove. She was wondering what the child had said to the Bible salesman. She could not imagine what kind of a conversation she could possibly have had with him.

He was a tall gaunt hatless youth who had called yesterday to sell them a Bible. He had appeared at the door, carrying a large black suitcase that weighted him so heavily on one side that he had to brace himself against the door facing. He seemed on the point of collapse but he said in a cheerful voice, "Good morning, Mrs. Cedars!" and set the suitcase down on the mat. He was not a bad-looking young man though he had on a bright blue suit and yellow socks that were not pulled up far enough. He had prominent face bones and a streak of sticky-looking brown hair falling across his forehead.

"I'm Mrs. Hopewell," she said.

"Oh!" he said, pretending to look puzzled but with his eyes sparkling, "I saw it said 'The Cedars,' on the mailbox so I thought you was Mrs. Cedars!" and he burst out in a pleasant laugh. He picked up the satchel and under cover of a pant, he fell forward into her hall. It was rather as if the suitcase had moved first, jerking him after it. "Mrs. Hopewell!" he said and grabbed her hand. "I hope you are well!" and he laughed again and then all at once his face sobered completely. He paused and gave her a straight earnest look and said, "Lady, I've come to speak of serious things."

"Well, come in," she muttered, none too pleased because her dinner was almost ready. He came into the parlor and sat down on the edge of a straight chair and put the suitcase between his feet and glanced around the room as if he were sizing her up by it. Her silver gleamed on the two sideboards; she decided he had never been in a room as elegant as this.

"Mrs. Hopewell," he began, using her name in a way that sounded almost intimate, "I know you believe in Christian service."

"Well yes," she murmured.

"I know," he said and paused, looking very wise with his head cocked on one side, "that you're a good woman. Friends have told me."

Mrs. Hopewell never liked to be taken for a fool. "What are you selling?" she asked.

"Bibles," the young man said and his eye raced around the room before he added, "I see you have no family Bible in your parlor, I see that is the one lack you got!"

Mrs. Hopewell could not say, "My daughter is an atheist and won't let me keep the Bible in the parlor." She said, stiffening slightly, "I keep my Bible by my bedside." This was not the truth. It was in the attic somewhere.

"Lady," he said, "the word of God ought to be in the parlor."

"Well, I think that's a matter of taste," she began. "I think . . . ."

"Lady," he said, "for a Christian, the word of God ought to be in every room in the house besides in his heart. I know you're a Christian because I can see it in every line of your face."

She stood up and said, "Well, young man, I don't want to buy a Bible and I smell my dinner burning."

He didn't get up. He began to twist his hands and looking down at them, he said softly, "Well lady, I'll tell you the truth—not many people want to buy one nowadays and besides, I know I'm real simple. I don't know how to say a thing but to say it. I'm just a country boy." He glanced up into her unfriendly face. "People like you don't like to fool with country people like me!"

"Why!" she cried, "good country people are the salt of the earth! Besides, we all have different ways of doing, it takes all kinds to make the world go 'round. That's life!"

"You said a mouthful," he said.

"Why, I think there aren't enough good country people in the world!" she said, stirred. "I think that's what's wrong with it!"

His face had brightened. "I didn't inraduce myself," he said. "I'm Manley Pointer from out in the country around Willohobie, not even from a place, just from near a place."

"You wait a minute," she said. "I have to see about my dinner." She went out to the kitchen and found Joy standing near the door where she had been listening.

"Get rid of the salt of the earth," she said, "and let's eat."

Mrs. Hopewell gave her a pained look and turned the heat down under the vegetables. "I can't be rude to anybody," she murmured and went back into the parlor.

He had opened the suitcase and was sitting with a Bible on each knee.

"You might as well put those up," she told him. "I don't want one."

"I appreciate your honesty," he said. "You don't see any more real honest people unless you go way out in the country."

"I know," she said, "real genuine folks!" Through the crack in the door she heard a groan.

"I guess a lot of boys come telling you they're working their way through college," he said, "but I'm not going to tell you that. Somehow," he said, "I don't want to go to college. I want to devote my life to Christian service. See," he said, lowering his voice, "I got this heart condition. I may not live long. When you know it's something wrong with you and you may not live long, well then, lady . . ." He paused, with his mouth open, and stared at her.

He and Joy had the same condition! She knew that her eyes were filling with tears but she collected herself quickly and murmured, "Won't you stay for dinner? We'd love to have you!" and was sorry the instant she heard herself say it.

"Yes mam," he said in an abashed voice, "I would sher love to do that!"

Joy had given him one look on being introduced to him and then throughout the meal had not glanced at him again. He had addressed several remarks to her, which she had pretended not to hear. Mrs. Hopewell could not understand deliberate rudeness, although she lived with it, and she felt she had always to overflow with hospitality to make up for Joy's lack of courtesy. She urged him to talk about himself and he did. He said he was the seventh child of twelve and that his father had been crushed under a tree when he himself was eight years old. He had been crushed very badly, in fact, almost cut in two and was practically not recognizable. His mother had got along the best she could by hard working and she had always seen that her children went to Sunday School and that they read the Bible every evening. He was now nineteen years old and he had been selling Bibles for four months. In that time he had sold seventy-seven Bibles and had the promise of two more sales. He wanted to become a missionary because he thought that was the way you could do most for people. "He who losest his life shall find it," he said simply and he was so sincere, so genuine and earnest that Mrs. Hopewell would not for the world have smiled. He prevented his peas from sliding onto the table by blocking them with a piece of bread which he later cleaned his plate with. She could see Joy observing sidewise how he handled his knife and fork and she saw too that every few minutes, the boy would dart a keen appraising glance at the girl as if he were trying to attract her attention.

After dinner Joy cleared the dishes off the table and disappeared and Mrs. Hopewell was left to talk with him. He told her again about his childhood and his father's accident and about various things that had happened to him. Every five minutes or so she would stifle a yawn. He sat for two hours until finally she told him she must go because she had an appointment in town. He packed his Bibles and thanked her and prepared to leave, but in the doorway he stopped and wrung her hand and said that not on any of his trips had he met a lady as nice as her and asked if he could come again. She had said she would always be happy to see him.

Joy had been standing in the road, apparently looking at something in the distance, when he came down the steps toward her, bent to the side with his heavy valise. He stopped where she was standing and confronted her directly. Mrs. Hopewell could not hear what he said but she trembled to think what Joy would say to him. She could see that after a minute Joy said something and that then the boy began to speak again, making an excited gesture with his free hand. After a minute Joy said something else at which the boy began to speak once more. Then to her amazement, Mrs. Hopewell saw the two of them walk off together, toward the gate. Joy had walked all the way to the gate with him and Mrs. Hopewell could not imagine what they had said to each other, and she had not yet dared to ask.

Mrs. Freeman was insisting upon her attention. She had moved from the refrigerator to the heater so that Mrs. Hopewell had to turn and face her in order to seem to be listening. "Glynese gone out with Harvey Hill again last night," she said. "She had this sty."

"Hill," Mrs. Hopewell said absently, "is that the one who works in the garage?"

"Nome, he's the one that goes to chiropractor school," Mrs. Freeman said. "She had this sty. Been had it two days. So she says when he brought her in the other night he says, 'Lemme get rid of that sty for you,' and she says, 'How?' and he says, 'You just lay yourself down acrost the seat of that car and I'll show you.' So she done it and he popped her neck. Kept on a-popping it several times until she made him quit. This morning," Mrs. Freeman said, "she ain't got no sty. She ain't got no traces of a sty."

"I never heard of that before," Mrs. Hopewell said.

"He ast her to marry him before the Ordinary," Mrs. Freeman went on, "and she told him she wasn't going to be married in no *office*."

"Well, Glynese is a fine girl," Mrs. Hopewell said. "Glynese and Carramae are both fine girls."

"Carramae said when her and Lyman was married Lyman said it sure felt sacred to him. She said he said he wouldn't take five hundred dollars for being married by a preacher."

"How much would he take?" the girl asked from the stove.

"He said he wouldn't take five hundred dollars," Mrs. Freeman repeated.

"Well we all have work to do," Mrs. Hopewell said.

"Lyman said it just felt more sacred to him," Mrs. Freeman said. "The doctor wants Carramae to eat prunes. Says instead of medicine. Says them cramps is coming from pressure. You know where I think it is?"

"She'll be better in a few weeks," Mrs. Hopewell said.

"In the tube," Mrs. Freeman said. "Else she wouldn't be as sick as she is."

Hulga had cracked her two eggs into a saucer and was bringing them to the table along with a cup of coffee that she had filled too full. She sat down carefully and began to eat, meaning to keep Mrs. Freeman there by questions if for any reason she showed an inclination to leave. She could perceive her mother's eye on her. The first round-about question would be about the Bible salesman and she did not wish to bring it on. "How did he pop her neck?" she asked.

Mrs. Freeman went into a description of how he had popped her neck. She said he owned a '55 Mercury but that Glynese said she would rather marry a man with only a '36 Plymouth who would be married by a preacher. The girl asked what if he had a '32 Plymouth and Mrs. Freeman said what Glynese had said was a '36 Plymouth.

Mrs. Hopewell said there were not many girls with Glynese's common sense. She said what she admired in those girls was their common sense. She said that reminded her that they had a nice visitor yesterday, a young man selling Bibles. "Lord," she said, "he bored me to death but he was so sincere and genuine I couldn't be rude to him. He was just good country people, you know," she said, "—just the salt of the earth."

"I seen him walk up," Mrs. Freeman said, " and then later—I seen him walk off," and Hulga could feel the slight shift in her voice, the slight insinuation, that he had not walked off alone, had he? Her face remained expressionless but the color rose into her neck and she seemed to swallow it down with the next spoonful of egg. Mrs. Freeman was looking at her as if they had a secret together.

"Well, it takes all kinds of people to make the world go 'round," Mrs. Hopewell said. "It's very good we aren't all alike."

"Some people are more alike than others," Mrs. Freeman said.

Hulga got up and stumped, with about twice the noise that was necessary, into her room and locked the door. She was to meet the Bible salesman at ten o'clock at the gate. She had thought about it half the night. She had started thinking of it as a great joke and then she had begun to see profound implications in it. She had lain in bed imagining dialogues for them that were insane on the surface but that reached below to depths that no Bible salesman would be aware of. Their conversation yesterday had been of this kind.

He had stopped in front of her and had simply stood there. His face was bony and sweaty and bright, with a little pointed nose in the center of it, and his look was different from what it had been at the dinner table. He was gazing at her with open curiosity, with fascination, like a child watching a new fantastic animal at the zoo, and he was breathing as if he had run a great distance to reach her. His gaze seemed somehow familiar but she could not think where she had been regarded with it before. For almost a minute he didn't say anything. Then on what seemed an insuck of breath, he whispered, "You ever ate a chicken that was two days old?"

The girl looked at him stonily. He might have just put this question up for consideration at the meeting of a philosophical association. "Yes," she presently replied as if she had considered it from all angles.

"It must have been mighty small!" he said triumphantly and shook all over with little nervous giggles, getting very red in the face, and subsiding finally into his gaze of complete admiration, while the girl's expression remained exactly the same.

"How old are you?" he asked softly.

She waited some time before she answered. Then in a flat voice she said, "Seventeen."

His smiles came in succession like waves breaking on the surface of the lake. "I see you got a wooden leg," he said. "I think you're real brave. I think you're real sweet."

The girl stood blank and solid and silent.

"Walk to the gate with me," he said. "You're a brave sweet little thing and I liked you the minute I seen you walk in the door."

Hulga began to move forward.

"What's your name?" he asked, smiling down on the top of her head.

"Hulga," she said.

"Hulga," he murmured, "Hulga. Hulga. I never heard of anybody name Hulga before. You're shy, aren't you, Hulga?" he asked.

She nodded, watching his large red hand on the handle of the giant valise.

"I like girls that wear glasses," he said. "I think a lot. I'm not like these people that a serious thought don't ever enter their heads. It's because I may die."

"I may die too," she said suddenly and looked up at him. His eyes were very small and brown, glittering feverishly.

"Listen," he said, "don't you think some people was meant to meet on account of what all they got in common and all? Like they both think serious thoughts and all?" He shifted the valise to his other hand so that the hand nearest her was free. He caught hold of her elbow and shook it a little. "I don't work on Saturday," he said. "I like to walk in the woods and see what Mother Nature is wearing. O'er the hills and far away. Pic-nics and things. Couldn't we go on a pic-nic tomorrow? Say yes, Hulga," he said and gave her a dying look as if he felt his insides about to drop out of him. He had even seemed to sway slightly toward her.

During the night she had imagined that she seduced him. She imagined that the two of them walked on the place until they came to the storage barn beyond the two back fields and there, she imagined, that things came to such a pass that she very easily seduced him and that then, of course, she had to reckon with his remorse. True genius can get an idea across even to an inferior mind. She imagined that she took his remorse in hand and changed it into a deeper understanding of life. She took all his shame away and turned it into something useful.

She set off for the gate at exactly ten o'clock, escaping without drawing Mrs. Hopewell's attention. She didn't take anything to eat, forgetting that food is usually taken on a picnic. She wore a pair of slacks and a dirty white shirt, and as an afterthought, she had put some Vapex on the collar of it since she did not own any perfume. When she reached the gate no one was there.

She looked up and down the empty highway and had the furious feeling that she had been tricked, that he had only meant to make her walk to the gate after the idea of him. Then suddenly he stood up, very tall, from behind a bush on the opposite embankment. Smiling, he lifted his hat which was new and wide-brimmed. He had not worn it yesterday and she wondered if he had bought it for the occasion. It was toast-colored with a red and white band around it and was slightly too large for him. He stepped from behind the bush still carrying the black valise. He had on the same yellow socks sucked down in his shoes from walking. He crossed the highway and said, "I knew you'd come!"

The girl wondered acidly how he had known this. She pointed to the valise and asked, "Why did you bring your Bibles?"

He took her elbow, smiling down on her as if he could not stop. "You can never tell when you'll need the word of God, Hulga," he said. She had a moment in which she doubted that this was actually happening and then they began to climb the embankment. They went down into the pasture toward the woods. The boy walked lightly by her side, bouncing on his toes. The valise did not seem to be heavy today; he even swung it. They crossed half the pasture without saying anything and then, putting his hand easily on the small of her back, he asked softly, "Where does your wooden leg join on?"

She turned an ugly red and glared at him and for an instant the boy looked abashed. "I didn't mean you no harm," he said. "I only meant you're so brave and all. I guess God takes care of you."

"No," she said, looking forward and walking fast, "I don't even believe in God."

At this he stopped and whistled. "No!" he exclaimed as if he were too astonished to say anything else.

She walked on and in a second he was bouncing at her side, fanning with his hat. "That's very unusual for a girl," he remarked, watching her out of the corner of his eye. When they reached the edge of the wood, he put his hand on her back again and drew her against him without a word and kissed her heavily.

The kiss, which had more pressure than feeling behind it, produced that extra surge of adrenalin in the girl that enables one to carry a packed trunk out of a burning house, but in her, the power went at once to the brain. Even before he released her, her mind, clear and detached and ironic anyway, was regarding him from a great distance, with amusement but with pity. She had never been kissed before and she was pleased to discover that it was an unexceptional experience and all a matter of the mind's control. Some people might enjoy drain water if they were told it was vodka. When the boy, looking expectant but uncertain, pushed her gently away, she turned and walked on, saying nothing as if such business, for her, were common enough.

He came along panting at her side, trying to help her when he saw a root that she might trip over. He caught and held back the long swaying blades of thorn vine until she had passed beyond them. She led the way and he came breathing heavily behind her. Then they came out on a sunlit hillside, sloping softly into another one a little smaller. Beyond, they could see the rusted top of the old barn where the extra hay was stored.

The hill was sprinkled with small pink weeds. "Then you ain't saved?" he asked suddenly, stopping.

The girl smiled. It was the first time she had smiled at him at all. "In my economy," she said, "I'm saved and you are damned but I told you I didn't believe in God."

Nothing seemed to destroy the boy's look of admiration. He gazed at her now as if the fantastic animal at the zoo had laid its paw through the bars and given him a loving poke. She thought he looked as if he wanted to kiss her again and she walked on before he had the chance.

"Ain't there somewheres we can sit down sometime?" he murmured, his voice softening toward the end of the sentence.

"In that barn," she said.

They made for it rapidly as if it might slide away like a train. It was a large two-story barn, cool and dark inside. The boy pointed up the ladder that led into the loft and said, "It's too bad we can't go up there."

"Why can't we?" she asked.

"Yer leg," he said reverently.

The girl gave him a contemptuous look and putting both hands on the ladder, she climbed it while he stood below, apparently awestruck. She pulled herself expertly through the opening and then looked down at him and said, "Well, come on if you're coming," and he began to climb the ladder, awkwardly bringing the suitcase with him.

"We won't need the Bible," she observed.

"You never can tell," he said, panting. After he had got into the loft, he was a few seconds catching his breath. She had sat down in a pile of straw. A wide sheath of sunlight, filled with dust particles, slanted over her. She lay back against a bale, her face turned away, looking out the front opening of the barn where hay was thrown from a wagon into the loft. The two pink-speckled hillsides lay back against a dark ridge of woods. The sky was cloudless and cold blue. The boy dropped down by her side and put one arm under her and the other over her and began methodically kissing her face, making little noises like a fish. He did not remove his hat but it was pushed far enough back not to interfere. When her glasses got in his way, he took them off of her and slipped them into his pocket.

The girl at first did not return any of the kisses but presently she began to and after she had put several on his cheek, she reached his lips and remained there, kissing him again and again as if she were trying to draw all the breath out of him. His breath was clear and sweet like a child's and the kisses were sticky like a child's. He mumbled about loving her and about knowing when he first seen her that he loved her, but the mumbling was like the sleepy fretting of a child being put to sleep by his mother. Her mind, throughout this, never stopped or lost itself for a second to her feelings. "You ain't said you loved me none," he whispered finally, pulling back from her. "You got to say that."

She looked away from him off into the hollow sky and then down at a black ridge and then down farther into what appeared to be two green swelling lakes. She didn't realize he had taken her glasses but this landscape could not seem exceptional to her for she seldom paid any close attention to her surroundings.

"You got to say it," he repeated. "You got to say you love me."

She was always careful how she committed herself. "In a sense," she began, "if you use the word loosely, you might say that. But it's not a word I use. I don't have illusions. I'm one of those people who see *through* to nothing."

The boy was frowning. "You got to say it. I said it and you got to say it," he said.

The girl looked at him almost tenderly. "You poor baby," she murmured. "It's just as well you don't understand," and she pulled him by the neck, face-down, against her. "We are all damned," she said, "but some of us have taken off our blindfolds and see that there's nothing to see. It's a kind of salvation."

The boy's astonished eyes looked blankly through the ends of her hair. "Okay," he almost whined, "but do you love me or don'tcher?"

"Yes," she said and added, "in a sense. But I must tell you something. There musn't be anything dishonest between us." She lifted his head and looked him in the eye. "I am thirty years old," she said. "I have a number of degrees."

The boy's look was irritated but dogged. "I don't care," he said. "I don't care a thing about what all you done. I just want to know if you love me or don'tcher?" and he caught her to him and wildly planted her face with kisses until she said, "Yes, yes."

"Okay then," he said, letting her go. "Prove it."

She smiled, looking dreamily out on the shifty landscape. She had seduced him without even making up her mind to try. "How?" she asked, feeling that he should be delayed a little.

He leaned over and put his lips to her ear. "Show me where your wooden leg joins on," he whispered.

The girl uttered a sharp little cry and her face instantly drained of color. The obscenity of the suggestion was not what shocked her. As a child she had sometimes been subject to feelings of shame but education had removed the last traces of that as a good surgeon scrapes for cancer; she would no more have felt it over what he was asking than she would have believed in his Bible. But she was as sensitive about the artificial leg as a peacock about his tail. No one ever touched it but her. She took care of it as someone else would his soul, in private and almost with her own eyes turned away. "No," she said.

"I known it," he muttered, sitting up. "You're just playing me for a sucker."

"Oh no no!" she cried. "It joins on at the knee. Only at the knee. Why do you want to see it?"

The boy gave her a long penetrating look, "Because," he said, "it's what makes you different. You ain't like anybody else."

She sat staring at him. There was nothing about her face or her round freezing-blue eyes to indicate that this had moved her; but she felt as if her heart had stopped and left her mind to pump her blood. She decided that for the first time in her life she was face to face with real innocence. This boy, with an instinct that came from beyond wisdom, had touched the truth about her. When after a minute, she said in a hoarse high voice, "All right," it was like surrendering to him completely. It was like losing her own life and finding it again, miraculously, in his.

Very gently he began to roll the slack leg up. The artificial limb, in a white sock and brown flat shoe, was bound in a heavy material like canvas and ended in an ugly jointure where it was attached to the stump. The boy's face and his voice were entirely reverent as he uncovered it and said, "Now show me how to take it off and on."

She took it off for him and then he took it off for himself, handling it as tenderly as if it were a real one. "See!" he said with a delighted child's face. "Now I can do it myself!"

"Put it back on," she said. She was thinking that she would run away with him and that every night he would take the leg off and every morning put it back on again. "Put it back on," she said.

"Not yet," he murmured, setting it on its foot out of her reach. "Leave it off for awhile. You got me instead."

She gave a little cry of alarm but he pushed her down and began to kiss her again. Without the leg she felt entirely dependent on him. Her brain seemed to have stopped thinking altogether and to be about some other function that it was not very good at. Different expressions raced back and forth over her face. Every now and then the boy, his eyes like two steel spikes, would glance behind him where the leg stood. Finally she pushed him off and said, "Put it back on me now."

"Wait," he said. He leaned the other way and pulled the valise toward him and opened it. It had a pale blue spotted lining and there were only two Bibles in it. He took one of these out and opened the cover of it. It was hollow and contained a pocket flask of whiskey, a pack of cards, and a small blue box with printing on it. He laid these out in front of her one at a time in an evenly-spaced row, like one presenting offerings at the shrine of a goddess. He put the blue box in her hand. THIS PRODUCT TO BE USED ONLY FOR THE PREVENTION OF DISEASE, she read, and dropped it. The boy was unscrewing the top of the flask. He stopped and pointed, with a smile, to the deck of cards. It was not an ordinary deck but one with an obscene picture on the back of each card. "Take a swig," he said, offering her the bottle first. He held it in front of her, but like one mesmerized, she did not move.

Her voice when she spoke had an almost pleading sound. "Aren't you," she murmured, "aren't you just good country people?"

The boy cocked his head. He looked as if he were just beginning to understand that she might be trying to insult him. "Yeah," he said, curling his lip slightly. "but it ain't held me back none. I'm as good as you any day in the week."

"Give me my leg," she said.

He pushed it further away with his foot. "Come on now, let's begin to have us a good time," he said coaxingly. "We ain't got to know one another good yet."

"Give me my leg!" she screamed and tried to lunge for it but he pushed her down easily.

"What's the matter with you all of a sudden?" he asked, frowning as he screwed the top on the flask and put it quickly back inside the Bible. "You just a while ago said you didn't believe in nothing. I thought you was some girl!"

Her face was almost purple. "You're a Christian!" she hissed. "You're a fine Christian! You're just like them all—say one thing and do another. You're a perfect Christian, you're . . ."

The boy's mouth was set angrily. "I hope you don't think," he said in a lofty indignant tone, "that I believe in that crap! I may sell Bibles but I know which end is up and I wasn't born yesterday and I know where I'm going!"

"Give me my leg!" she screeched. He jumped up so quickly that she barely saw him sweep the cards and the blue box back into the Bible and throw the Bible into the valise. She saw him grab the leg and then she saw it for an instant slanted forlornly across the inside of the suitcase with a Bible at either side of its opposite ends. He slammed the lid shut and snatched up the valise and swung it down the hole and then stepped through himself.

When all of him had passed but his head, he turned and regarded her with a look that no longer had any admiration in it. "I've gotten a lot of interesting things," he said. "One time I got a woman's glass eye this way. And you needn't to think you'll catch me because Pointer ain't really my name. I use a different name at every house I call at and don't stay nowhere long. And I'll tell you another thing, Hulga," he said, using the name as if he didn't think much of it, "you ain't so smart. I been believing in nothing ever since I was born!" and then the toast-colored hat disappeared down the hole and the girl was left, sitting on the straw in the dusty sunlight. When she turned her churning face toward the opening, she saw his blue figure struggling successfully over the green speckled lake.

Mrs. Hopewell and Mrs. Freeman, who were in the back pasture, digging up onions, saw him emerge a little later from the woods and head across the meadow toward the highway. "Why, that looks like that nice dull young man that tried to sell me a Bible yesterday," Mrs. Hopewell said, squinting. "He must have been selling them to the Negroes back in there. He was so simple," she said, "but I guess the world would be better off if we were all that simple."

Mrs. Freeman's gaze drove forward and just touched him before he disappeared under the hill. Then she returned her attention to the evil-smelling onion shoot she was lifting from the ground. "Some can't be that simple," she said, "I know I never could."

[1955]

Study and Writing Questions

1. In the first paragraph, Mrs. Freeman is described as if she were a somewhat inadequate truck. What is the effect of this METAPHOR? Where else is mechanical IMAGERY applied to people in this NARRATIVE? In what ways does the STORY depend on the mechanical aspects of the human condition?
2. The NARRATOR says that "Mrs. Hopewell had no bad qualities of her own but she was able to use other people's in such a constructive way that she never felt the lack." How would you characterize the narrator's attitude toward Mrs. Hopewell? What is the THEMATIC significance of this statement?
3. What is the significance of names in this narrative?
4. Both Mrs. Freeman and Mrs. Hopewell have adopted ideas about the world. Are their ideas sound? What does the story suggest about science, philosophy, and religion? How does intellect enter into the lives of each of the characters?
5. What are the characteristics of "good country people"? Do they exist in reality? Why are they important as ideals? What does the last line imply?

See also Questions for Contrast and Comparison: 66, 80, 84, 103, 121, 123, 128, 181, 190, 192, 205, and 239.

■ FRANK O'CONNOR (1903-1966) *was born Michael John O'Donovan in Cork, Ireland. His hard-laboring father's binges periodically wrecked the family financially and emotionally, so O'Connor, with only brief formal schooling, early chose writing because painting and music cost too much. He published nearly fifty books, including* NOVELS, *plays, autobiographies (such as My Father's Son, 1968, which discusses his deep filial ambivalence). His fourteen* SHORT STORY *collections range from Guests of the Nation (1931), which began his full-time writing career, to Collected Stories (1981). O'Connor's criticism includes The Lonely Voice (1963), a study of short stories which he calls "the literature of submerged population groups." O'Connor fought with the Irish Republican Army against England (1919-1923) both before independence (1921) and after, seeking to join Ulster to the Irish Free State. Imprisoned for these activities, he pursued his self-education and emerged in 1924 to work at a series of librarian jobs that allowed him to read and write. It was then, for political reasons, that he adopted the maiden name of his beloved mother. With William Butler Yeats, who called O'Connor the Irish Chekov, he co-directed (1935-1939) the important nationalistic Abbey Theater in Dublin but left to protest government censorship. In the 1950's, he taught at Harvard, Northwestern, and Stanford Universities. He had two marriages and four children. He died in Dublin.*

My Oedipus Complex

Father was in the army all through the war — the first war, I mean — so, up to the age of five, I never saw much of him, and what I saw did not worry me. Sometimes I woke and there was a big figure in khaki peering down at me in the candlelight. Sometimes in the early morning I heard the slamming of the front door and the clatter of nailed boots down the cobbles of the lane. These were Father's entrances and exits. Like Santa Claus he came and went mysteriously.

In fact, I rather liked his visits, though it was an uncomfortable squeeze between Mother and him when I got into the big bed in the early morning. He smoked, which gave him a pleasant musty smell, and shaved, an operation of astounding interest. Each time he left a trail of souvenirs — model tanks and Gurkha knives with handles made of bullet cases, and German helmets and cap badges and button-sticks, and all sorts of military equipment carefully stowed away in a long box on top of the wardrobe, in case they ever came in handy. There was a bit of the magpie about Father; he expected everything to come in handy. When his back was turned, Mother let me get a chair and rummage through his treasures. She didn't seem to think so highly of them as he did.

The war was the most peaceful period of my life. The window of my attic faced southeast. My mother had curtained it, but that had small effect. I always woke with the first light and, with all the responsibilities of the previous day melted, feeling myself rather like the sun, ready to illumine and rejoice. Life never seemed so simple and clear and full of possibilities as then. I put my feet out from under the clothes — I called them Mrs. Left and Mrs. Right — and invented dramatic situations for them in which they discussed the problems of the day. At least Mrs. Right did; she was very demonstrative, but I hadn't the same control of Mrs. Left, so she mostly contented herself with nodding agreement.

They discussed what Mother and I should do during the day, what Santa Claus should give a fellow for Christmas, and what steps should be taken to brighten the home. There was that little matter of the baby, for instance. Mother and I could never agree about that. Ours was the only house in the terrace without a new baby, and Mother said we couldn't afford one till Father came back from the war because they cost seventeen and six. That showed how simple she was. The Geneys up the road had a baby, and everyone knew they couldn't afford seventeen and six. It was probably a cheap baby, and Mother wanted something really good, but I felt she was too exclusive. The Geneys' baby would have done us fine.

Having settled my plans for the day, I got up, put a chair under the attic window, and lifted the frame high enough to stick out my head. The window overlooked the front gardens of the terrace behind ours, and beyond these it looked over a deep valley to the tall, red brick houses terraced up the opposite hillside, which were all still in shadow, while those at our side of the valley were all lit up, though with long strange shadows that made them seem unfamiliar; rigid and painted.

After that I went into Mother's room and climbed into the big bed. She woke and I began to tell her of my schemes. By this time, though I never seem to have noticed it, I was petrified in my nightshirt, and I thawed as I talked until, the last frost melted, I fell asleep beside her and woke again only when I heard her below in the kitchen, making the breakfast.

After breakfast we went into town; heard Mass at St. Augustine's and said a prayer for Father, and did the shopping. If the afternoon was fine we either went for a walk in the country or a visit to Mother's great friend in the convent, Mother St. Dominic. Mother had them all praying for Father, and every night, going to bed, I asked God to send him back safe from the war to us. Little, indeed, did I know what I was praying for!

One morning, I got into the big bed, and there, sure enough, was Father in his usual Santa Claus manner, but later, instead of uniform, he put on his best blue suit, and Mother was as pleased as anything. I saw nothing to be pleased about, because, out of uniform, Father was altogether less interesting, but she only beamed, and explained that our prayers had been answered, and off we went to Mass to thank God for having brought Father safely home.

The irony of it! That very day when he came in to dinner he took off his boots and put on his slippers, donned the dirty old cap he wore about the house to save him from colds, crossed his legs, and began to talk gravely to Mother, who looked anxious. Naturally, I disliked her looking anxious, because it destroyed her good looks, so I interrupted him.

"Just a moment, Larry!" she said gently.

This was only what she said when we had boring visitors, so I attached no importance to it and went on talking.

"Do be quiet, Larry!" she said impatiently. "Don't you hear me talking to Daddy?"

This was the first time I had heard those ominous words, "talking to Daddy," and I couldn't help feeling that if this was how God answered prayers, he couldn't listen to them very attentively.

"Why are you talking to Daddy?" I asked with as great a show of indifference as I could muster.

"Because Daddy and I have business to discuss. Now, don't interrupt again!"

In the afternoon, at Mother's request, Father took me for a walk. This time we went into town instead of out to the country, and I thought at first, in my usual optimistic way, that it might be an improvement. It was nothing of the sort. Father and I had quite different notions of a walk in town. He had no proper interest in trams, ships, and horses, and the only thing that seemed to divert him was talking to fellows as old as himself. When I wanted to stop he simply went on, dragging me behind him by the hand; when he wanted to stop I had no alternative but to do the same. I noticed that it seemed to be a sign that he wanted to stop for a long time whenever he leaned against a wall. The second time I saw him do it I got wild. He seemed to be settling himself forever. I pulled him by the coat and trousers, but, unlike Mother who, if you were too persistent, got into a wax and said: "Larry, if you don't behave yourself, I'll give you a good slap," Father had an extraordinary capacity for amiable inattention. I sized him up and wondered would I cry, but he seemed to be too remote to be annoyed even by that. Really, it was like going for a walk with a mountain! He either ignored the wrenching and pummeling entirely, or else glanced down with a grin of amusement from his peak. I had never met anyone so absorbed in himself as he seemed.

At teatime, "talking to Daddy" began again, complicated this time by the fact that he had an evening paper, and every few minutes he put it down and told Mother something new out of it. I felt this was foul play. Man for man, I was prepared to compete with him any time for Mother's attention, but when he had it all made up for him by other people it left me no chance. Several times I tried to change the subject without success.

"You must be quiet while Daddy is reading, Larry," Mother said impatiently.

It was clear that she either genuinely liked talking to Father better than talking to me, or else that he had some terrible hold on her which made her afraid to admit the truth.

"Mummy," I said that night when she was tucking me up, "do you think if I prayed hard God would send Daddy back to the war?"

She seemed to think about that for a moment.

"No, dear," she said with a smile. "I don't think he would."

"Why wouldn't he, Mummy?"

"Because there isn't a war any longer, dear."

"But, Mummy, couldn't God make another war, if He liked?"

"He wouldn't like to, dear. It's not God who makes wars, but bad people."

"Oh!" I said.

I was disappointed about that. I began to think that God wasn't quite what he was cracked up to be.

Next morning I woke at my usual hour, feeling like a bottle of champagne. I put out my feet and invented a long conversation in which Mrs. Right talked of the trouble she had with her own father till she put him in the Home. I didn't quite know what the Home was but it sounded the right place for Father. Then I got my chair and stuck my head out of the attic window. Dawn was just breaking, with a guilty air that made me feel I had caught it in the act. My head bursting with stories and schemes, I stumbled in next door, and in the half-darkness scrambled into the big bed. There was no room at Mother's side so I had to get between her and Father. For the time being I had forgotten about him, and for several minutes I sat bolt upright, racking my brains to know what I could do with him. He was taking up more than his fair share of the bed, and I couldn't get comfortable, so I gave him several kicks that made him grunt and stretch. He made room all right, though. Mother waked and felt for me. I settled back comfortably in the warmth of the bed with my thumb in my mouth.

"Mummy!" I hummed, loudly and contentedly.

"Sssh! dear," she whispered. "Don't wake Daddy!"

This was a new development, which threatened to be even more serious than "talking to Daddy." Life without my early-morning conferences was unthinkable.

"Why?" I asked severely.

"Because poor Daddy is tired."

This seemed to me a quite inadequate reason, and I was sickened by the sentimentality of her "poor Daddy." I never liked that sort of gush; it always struck me as insincere.

"Oh!" I said lightly. Then in my most winning tone: "Do you know where I want to go with you today, Mummy?"

"No, dear," she sighed.

"I want to go down the Glen and fish for thornybacks with my new net, and then I want to go out to the Fox and Hounds, and —"

"Don't-wake-Daddy!" she hissed angrily, clapping her hand across my mouth.

But it was too late. He was awake, or nearly so. He grunted and reached for the matches. Then he stared incredulously at his watch.

"Like a cup of tea, dear?" asked Mother in a meek, hushed voice I had never heard her use before. It sounded almost as though she were afraid.

"Tea?" he exclaimed indignantly. "Do you know what the time is?"

"And after that I want to go up the Rathcooney Road," I said loudly, afraid I'd forget something in all those interruptions.

"Go to sleep at once, Larry!" she said sharply.

I began to snivel. I couldn't concentrate, the way that pair went on, and smothering my early-morning schemes was like burying a family from the cradle.

Father said nothing, but lit his pipe and sucked it, looking out into the shadows without minding Mother or me. I knew he was mad. Every time I made a remark Mother hushed me irritably. I was mortified. I felt it wasn't fair; there was even something sinister in it. Every time I pointed out to her the waste of making two beds when we could both sleep in one, she had told me it was healthier like that, and now here was this man, this stranger, sleeping with her without the least regard for her health!

He got up early and made tea, but though he brought Mother a cup he brought none for me.

"Mummy," I shouted, "I want a cup of tea, too."

"Yes, dear," she said patiently. "You can drink from Mummy's saucer."

That settled it. Either Father or I would have to leave the house. I didn't want to drink from Mother's saucer; I wanted to be treated as an equal in my own home, so, just to spite her, I drank it all and left none for her. She took that quietly, too.

But that night when she was putting me to bed she said gently:

"Larry, I want you to promise me something."

"What is it?" I asked.

"Not to come in and disturb poor Daddy in the morning. Promise?"

"Poor Daddy" again! I was becoming suspicious of everything involving that quite impossible man.

"Why?" I asked.

"Because poor Daddy is worried and tired and he doesn't sleep well."

"Why doesn't he, Mummy?"

"Well, you know, don't you, that while he was at the war Mummy got the pennies from the Post Office?"

"From Miss MacCarthy?"

"That's right. But now, you see, Miss MacCarthy hasn't any more pennies, so Daddy must go out and find us some. You know what would happen if he couldn't?"

"No," I said, "tell us."

"Well, I think we might have to go out and beg for them like the poor old woman on Fridays. We wouldn't like that, would we?"

"No," I agreed. "We wouldn't."

"So you'll promise not to come in and wake him?"

"Promise."

Mind you, I meant that. I knew pennies were a serious matter, and I was all against having to go out and beg like the old woman on Fridays. Mother laid out all my toys in a complete ring round the bed so that, whatever way I got out, I was bound to fall over one of them.

When I woke I remembered my promise all right. I got up and sat on the floor and played—for hours, it seemed to me. Then I got my chair and looked out the attic window for more hours. I wished it was time for Father to wake; I wished someone would make me a cup of tea. I didn't feel in the least like the sun; instead, I was bored and so very, very cold! I simply longed for the warmth and depth of the big featherbed.

At last I could stand it no longer. I went into the next room. As there was still room at Mother's side I climbed over her and she woke with a start.

"Larry," she whispered, gripping my arm very tightly, "what did you promise?"

"But I did, Mummy," I wailed, caught in the very act. "I was quiet for ever so long."

"Oh, dear, and you're perished!" she said sadly, feeling me all over. "Now, if I let you stay will you promise not to talk?"

"But I want to talk, Mummy," I wailed.

"That has nothing to do with it," she said with a firmness that was new to me. "Daddy wants to sleep. Now do you understand that?"

I understood it only too well. I wanted to talk, he wanted to sleep—whose house was it, anyway?

"Mummy," I said with equal firmness, "I think it would be healthier for Daddy to sleep in his own bed."

That seemed to stagger her, because she said nothing for awhile.

"Now, once and for all," she went on, "you're to be perfectly quiet or go back to your own bed. Which is it to be?"

The injustice of it got me down. I had convicted her out of her own mouth of inconsistency and unreasonableness, and she hadn't even attempted to reply. Full of spite, I gave Father a kick, which she didn't notice but which made him grunt and open his eyes in alarm.

"What time is it?" he asked in a panic-stricken voice, not looking at Mother but at the door, as if he saw someone there.

"It's early yet," she replied soothingly. "It's only the child. Go to sleep again. . . . Now, Larry," she added, getting out of bed, "you've wakened Daddy and you must go back."

This time, for all her quiet air, I knew she meant it, and knew that my principal rights and privileges were as good as lost unless I asserted them at once. As she lifted me, I gave a screech, enough to wake the dead, not to mind Father. He groaned.

"That damn child! Doesn't he ever sleep?"

"It's only a habit, dear," she said quietly, though I could see she was vexed.

"Well, it's time he got out of it," shouted Father, beginning to heave in the bed. He suddenly gathered all the bedclothes about him, turned to the wall, and then looked back over his shoulder with nothing showing only two small, spiteful, dark eyes. The man looked very wicked.

To open the bedroom door, Mother had to let me down, and I broke free and dashed for the farthest corner, screeching. Father sat bolt upright in bed.

"Shut up, you little puppy!" he said in a choking voice.

I was so astonished that I stopped screeching. Never, never had anyone spoken to me in that tone before. I looked at him incredulously and saw his face convulsed with rage. It was only then that I fully realized how God had codded me, listening to my prayers for the safe return of this monster.

"Shut up, you!" I bawled, beside myself.

"What's that you said?" shouted Father, making a wild leap out of the bed.

"Mick, Mick!" cried Mother. "Don't you see the child isn't used to you?"

"I see he's better fed than taught," snarled Father, waving his arms wildly. "He wants his bottom smacked."

All his previous shouting was as nothing to these obscene words referring to my person. They really made my blood boil.

"Smack your own!" I screamed hysterically. "Smack your own! Shut up! Shut up!"

At this he lost his patience and let fly at me. He did it with the lack of conviction you'd expect of a man under Mother's horrified eyes, and it ended up as a mere tap, but the sheer indignity of being struck at all by a stranger, a total stranger who had cajoled his way back from the war into our big bed as a result of my innocent intercession, made me completely dotty. I shrieked and shrieked, and danced in my bare feet, and Father, looking awkward and hairy in nothing but a short gray army shirt, glared down at me like a mountain out for murder. I think it must have been then that I realized he was jealous too. And there stood Mother in her nightdress, looking as if her heart was broken between us. I hoped she felt as she looked. It seemed to me that she deserved it all.

From that morning out my life was a hell. Father and I were enemies, open and avowed. We conducted a series of skirmishes against one another, he trying to steal my time with Mother and I his. When she was sitting on my bed, telling me a story, he took to looking for some pair of old boots which he alleged he had left behind him at the beginning of the war. While he talked to Mother I played loudly with my toys to show my total lack of concern. He created a terrible scene one evening when he came in from work and found me at his box playing with his regimental badges, Gurkha knives and button-sticks. Mother got up and took the box from me.

"You mustn't play with Daddy's toys unless he lets you, Larry," she said severely. "Daddy doesn't play with yours."

For some reason Father looked at her as if she had struck him and then turned away with a scowl.

"Those are not toys," he growled, taking down the box again to see had I lifted anything. "Some of those curios are very rare and valuable."

But as time went on I saw more and more how he managed to alienate Mother and me. What made it worse was that I couldn't grasp his method or see what attraction he had for Mother. In every possible way he was less winning than I. He had a common accent and made noises at his tea. I thought for a while that it might be the newspapers she was interested in, so I made up bits of news of my own to read to her. Then I thought it might be the smoking, which I personally thought attractive, and took his pipes and went round the house dribbling into them till he caught me. I even made noises at my tea, but Mother only told me I was disgusting. It all seemed to hinge round that unhealthy habit of sleeping together, so I made a point of dropping into their bedroom and nosing round, talking to myself, so that they wouldn't know I was watching them, but they were never up to anything that I could see. In the end it beat me. It seemed to depend on being grown-up and giving people rings, and I realized I'd have to wait.

But at the same time I wanted him to see that I was only waiting, not giving up the fight. One evening when he was being particularly obnoxious, chattering away well above my head, I let him have it.

"Mummy," I said, "do you know what I'm going to do when I grow up?"

"No, dear," she replied. "What?"

"I'm going to marry you," I said quietly.

Father gave a great guffaw out of him, but he didn't take me in. I knew it must only be pretense. And Mother, in spite of everything, was pleased. I felt she was probably relieved to know that one day Father's hold on her would be broken.

"Won't that be nice?" she said with a smile.

"It'll be very nice," I said confidently. "Because we're going to have lots and lots of babies."

"That's right, dear," she said placidly. "I think we'll have one soon, and then you'll have plenty of company."

I was no end pleased about that because it showed that in spite of the way she gave in to Father she still considered my wishes. Besides, it would put the Geneys in their place.

It didn't turn out like that, though. To begin with, she was very preoccupied —I suppose about where she would get the seventeen and six—and though

Father took to staying out late in the evenings it did me no particular good. She stopped taking me for walks, became as touchy as blazes, and smacked me for nothing at all. Sometimes I wished I'd never mentioned the confounded baby—I seemed to have a genius for bringing calamity on myself.

And calamity it was! Sonny arrived in the most appalling hullabaloo—even that much he couldn't do without a fuss—and from the first moment I disliked him. He was a difficult child—so far as I was concerned he was always difficult—and demanded far too much attention. Mother was simply silly about him, and couldn't see when he was only showing off. As company he was worse than useless. He slept all day, and I had to go round the house on tiptoe to avoid waking him. It wasn't any longer a question of not waking Father. The slogan now was "Don't-wake-Sonny!" I couldn't understand why the child wouldn't sleep at the proper time, so whenever Mother's back was turned I woke him. Sometimes to keep him awake I pinched him as well. Mother caught me at it one day and gave me a most unmerciful flaking.

One evening, when Father was coming in from work, I was playing trains in the front garden. I let on not to notice him; instead, I pretended to be talking to myself, and said in a loud voice: "If another bloody baby comes into this house, I'm going out."

Father stopped dead and looked at me over his shoulder.

"What's that you said?" he asked sternly.

"I was only talking to myself," I replied, trying to conceal my panic. "It's private."

He turned and went in without a word. Mind you, I intended it as a solemn warning, but its effect was quite different. Father started being quite nice to me. I could understand that, of course. Mother was quite sickening about Sonny. Even at mealtimes she'd get up and gawk at him in the cradle with an idiotic smile, and tell Father to do the same. He was always polite about it, but he looked so puzzled you could see he didn't know what she was talking about. He complained of the way Sonny cried at night, but she only got cross and said that Sonny never cried except when there was something up with him—which was a flaming lie, because Sonny never had anything up with him, and only cried for attention. It was really painful to see how simple-minded she was. Father wasn't attractive, but he had a fine intelligence. He saw through Sonny, and now he knew that I saw through him as well.

One night I woke with a start. There was someone beside me in the bed. For one wild moment I felt sure it must be Mother, having come to her senses and left Father for good, but then I heard Sonny in convulsions in the next room, and Mother saying: "There! There! There!" and I knew it wasn't she. It was Father. He was lying beside me, wide awake, breathing hard and apparently as mad as hell.

After awhile it came to me what he was mad about. It was his turn now. After turning me out of the big bed, he had been turned out himself. Mother had no consideration now for anyone but that poisonous pup, Sonny. I couldn't help feeling sorry for Father. I had been through it all myself, and even at that age I was magnanimous. I began to stroke him down and say: "There! There!" He wasn't exactly responsive.

"Aren't you asleep either?" he snarled.

"Ah, come on and put your arm around us, can't you?" I said, and he did, in a sort of way. Gingerly, I suppose, is how you'd describe it. He was very bony but better than nothing.

At Christmas he went out of his way to buy me a really nice model railway.

[1950]

Study and Writing Questions

1. To what extent does PARADOX ("The war was the most peaceful period of my life") typify Larry's narrative STYLE? Are there aspects of the PLOT or THEME you would consider paradoxical?

2. What inferences can you draw about Larry's personality from his playing with Mrs. Left and Mrs. Right? Has he other playmates?

3. Larry professes disappointment in both his father and in God. Is it childish to see a parent and a god in similar terms? In what ways does the IMPLIED AUTHOR seem to share or reject Larry's disappointments?

4. What are the MOTIVES of the NARRATOR? How would you describe the age, circumstances, and attitude of the narrator as he narrates? Clearly he understands now what he did not understand as a child, yet he does not make his present understanding explicit. How would you describe the mind of Larry as a child? If the narrator is RELIABLE, Larry had a precocious understanding of people's emotions and intellect yet apparently no idea of the relations between husbands and wives. Do you feel the narrator is reliable? Why is he telling this STORY now?

5. What does the RESOLUTION of this NARRATIVE suggest about the process of maturing in males? What does it suggest about the importance and effects of the FREUDIAN Oedipus complex? What are we to feel about the last line?

See also Questions for Contrast and Comparison: 34, 41, 59, 92, 168, and 207.

■ **TILLIE OLSEN** (1913–) *was born in Omaha, Nebraska, to political refugees from the repression in Czarist Russia following the 1905 Revolution. Her father was a jack-of-all-trades and her mother a factory worker. She left school at fifteen for domestic service and a lifetime of political activism and radical feminism with the Young Communist League and with labor unions in the Midwest and in San Francisco. In 1932 she began a novel, part of which appeared in* Partisan Review *(1934), but, left with a child by a husband who could not stand their poverty, she ceased writing by 1937. In 1936 she married Jack Olsen, a house painter who shared her passionate social commitments and with whom she had three more children. While raising her family, she did factory work in the 1940s and secretarial work in the 1950s. When her youngest child was five (1953), she resumed writing, slowly producing the four stories of* Tell Me A Riddle *(1961); the title piece won the O. Henry Award for the best short story of its year. She accepted a writing fellowship at Stanford University (1955–1956) and has since won many awards and taught at major American universities. In 1972 she introduced a reissue of Rebecca Harding Davis's* Life in the Iron Mills *(1861); her novel,* Yonnondio: From the Thirties, *reworked but still unfinished, appeared in 1974; and* Silences, *essays about how circumstances thwart self-expression, appeared in 1978.*

I Stand Here Ironing

I stand here ironing, and what you asked me moves tormented back and forth with the iron.

"I wish you would manage the time to come in and talk with me about your daughter. I'm sure you can help me understand her. She's a youngster who needs help and whom I'm deeply interested in helping."

"Who needs help." Even if I came, what good would it do? You think because I am her mother I have a key, or that in some way you could use me as a key? She has lived for nineteen years. There is all that life that has happened outside of me, beyond me.

And when is there time to remember, to sift, to weigh, to estimate, to total? I will start and there will be an interruption and I will have to gather it all together again. Or I will become engulfed with all I did or did not do, with what should have been and what cannot be helped.

She was a beautiful baby. The first and only one of our five that was beautiful at birth. You do not guess how new and uneasy her tenancy in her now-loveliness. You did not know her all those years she was thought homely, or see her poring over her baby pictures, making me tell her over and over how beautiful she had been — and would be, I would tell her — and was now, to the seeing eye. But the seeing eyes were few or non-existent. Including mine.

I nursed her. They feel that's important nowadays. I nursed all the children, but with her, with all the fierce rigidity of first motherhood, I did like the books then said. Though her cries battered me to trembling and my breasts ached with swollenness, I waited till the clock decreed.

Why do I put that first? I do not even know if it matters, or if it explains anything.

She was a beautiful baby. She blew shining bubbles of sound. She loved motion, loved light, loved color and music and textures. She would lie on the floor in her blue overalls patting the surface so hard in ecstasy her hands and feet would blur. She was a miracle to me, but when she was eight months old I had to leave her daytimes with the woman downstairs to whom she was no miracle at all, for I worked or looked for work and for Emily's father, who "could no longer endure" (he wrote in his good-bye note) "sharing want with us."

I was nineteen. It was the pre-relief, pre-WPA world of the depression. I would start running as soon as I got off the streetcar, running up the stairs, the place smelling sour, and awake or asleep to startle awake, when she saw me she would break into a clogged weeping that could not be comforted, a weeping I can hear yet.

After a while I found a job hashing at night so I could be with her days, and it was better. But it came to where I had to bring her to his family and leave her.

It took a long time to raise the money for her fare back. Then she got the chicken pox and I had to wait longer. When she finally came, I hardly knew her, walking quick and nervous like her father, looking like her father, thin, and dressed in a shoddy red that yellowed her skin and glared at the pockmarks. All the baby loveliness gone.

She was two. Old enough for nursery school they said, and I did not know then what I know now — the fatigue of the long day, and the lacerations of group life in nurseries that are only parking places for children.

Except that it would have made no difference if I had known. It was the only place there was. It was the only way we could be together, the only way I could hold a job.

And even without knowing, I knew. I knew the teacher that was evil because all these years it has curdled into my memory, the little boy hunched in the corner, her rasp, "why aren't you outside, because Alvin hits you? that's no reason, go out, scaredy." I knew Emily hated it even if she did not clutch and implore "don't go Mommy" like the other children, mornings.

She always had a reason why we should stay home. Momma, you look sick, Momma. I feel sick. Momma, the teachers aren't there today, they're sick. Momma, we can't go, there was a fire there last night. Momma, it's a holiday today, no school, they told me.

But never a direct protest, never rebellion. I think of our others in their three-, four-year-oldness — the explosions, the tempers, the denunciations, the demands — and I feel suddenly ill. I put the iron down. What in me demanded that goodness in her? And what was the cost, the cost to her of such goodness?

The old man living in the back once said in his gentle way: "You should smile at Emily more when you look at her." What *was* in my face when I looked at her? I loved her. There were all the acts of love.

It was only with the others I remembered what he said, and it was the face of joy, and not of care or tightness or worry I turned to them — too late for Emily. She does not smile easily, let alone almost always as her brothers and sisters do. Her face is closed and sombre, but when she wants, how fluid. You must have seen it in her pantomimes, you spoke of her rare gift for comedy on the stage that rouses a laughter out of the audience so dear they applaud and applaud and do not want to let her go.

Where does it come from, that comedy? There was none of it in her when she came back to me that second time, after I had had to send her away again. She had a new daddy now to learn to love, and I think perhaps it was a better time.

Except when we left her alone nights, telling ourselves she was old enough.

"Can't you go some other time, Mommy, like tomorrow?" she would ask. "Will it be just a little while you'll be gone? Do you promise?"

The time we came back, the front door open, the clock on the floor in the hall. She rigid awake. "It wasn't just a little while. I didn't cry. Three times I called you, just three times, and then I ran downstairs to open the door so you could come faster. The clock talked loud. I threw it away, it scared me what it talked."

She said the clock talked loud again that night I went to the hospital to have Susan. She was delirious with the fever that comes before red measles, but she was fully conscious all the week I was gone and the week after we were home when she could not come near the new baby or me.

She did not get well. She stayed skeleton thin, not wanting to eat, and night after night she had nightmares. She would call for me, and I would rouse from exhaustion to sleepily call back: "You're all right, darling, go to sleep, it's just a dream," and if she still called, in a sterner voice, "now go to sleep, Emily, there's nothing to hurt you." Twice, only twice, when I had to get up for Susan anyhow, I went to sit with her.

Now when it is too late (as if she would let me hold and comfort her like I do the others) I get up and go to her at once at her moan or restless stirring. "Are you awake, Emily? Can I get you something?" And the answer is always the same: "No, I'm all right, go back to sleep, Mother."

They persuaded me at the clinic to send her away to a convalescent home in the country where "she can have the kind of food and care you can't manage for her, and you'll be free to concentrate on the new baby." They still send children to that place. I see pictures on the society page of sleek young women planning affairs to raise money for it, or dancing at the affairs, or decorating Easter eggs or filling Christmas stockings for the children.

They never have a picture of the children so I do not know if the girls still wear those gigantic red bows and the ravaged looks on the every other Sunday when parents can come to visit "unless otherwise notified" — as we were notified the first six weeks.

Oh it is a handsome place, green lawns and tall trees and fluted flower beds. High up on the balconies of each cottage the children stand, the girls in their red bows and white dresses, the boys in white suits and giant red ties. The parents stand below shrieking up to be heard and the children shriek down to be heard, and between them the invisible wall "Not To Be Contaminated by Parental Germs or Physical Affection."

There was a tiny girl who always stood hand in hand with Emily. Her parents never came. One visit she was gone. "They moved her to Rose Cottage" Emily shouted in explanation. "They don't like you to love anybody here."

She wrote once a week, the labored writing of a seven-year-old. "I am fine. How is the baby. If I write my leter nicly I will have a star. Love." There never was a star. We wrote every other day, letters she could never hold or keep but only hear read — once. "We simply do not have room for children to keep any personal possessions," they patiently explained when we pieced one Sunday's shrieking together to plead how much it would mean to Emily, who loved so to keep things, to be allowed to keep her letters and cards.

Each visit she looked frailer. "She isn't eating," they told us.

(They had runny eggs for breakfast or mush with lumps, Emily said later, I'd hold it in my mouth and not swallow. Nothing ever tasted good, just when they had chicken.)

It took us eight months to get her released home, and only the fact that she gained back so little of her seven lost pounds convinced the social worker.

I used to try to hold and love her after she came back, but her body would stay stiff, and after a while she'd push away. She ate little. Food sickened her, and I think much of life too. Oh she had physical lightness and brightness, twinkling by on skates, bouncing like a ball up and down up and down over the jump rope, skimming over the hill; but these were momentary.

She fretted about her appearance, thin and dark and foreign-looking at a time when every little girl was supposed to look or thought she should look a chubby blonde replica of Shirley Temple. The doorbell sometimes rang for her, but no one seemed to come and play in the house or be a best friend. Maybe because we moved so much.

There was a boy she loved painfully through two school semesters. Months later she told me she had taken pennies from my purse to buy him candy. "Licorice was his favorite and I brought him some every day, but he still liked Jennifer better'n me. Why, Mommy?" The kind of question for which there is no answer.

School was a worry to her. She was not glib or quick in a world where glibness and quickness were easily confused with ability to learn. To her over-worked and exasperated teachers she was an overconscientious "slow learner" who kept trying to catch up and was absent entirely too often.

I let her be absent, though sometimes the illness was imaginary. How different from my now-strictness about attendance with the others. I wasn't working. We had a new baby, I was home anyhow. Sometimes, after Susan grew old enough, I would keep her home from school, too, to have them all together.

Mostly Emily had asthma, and her breathing, harsh and labored, would fill the house with a curiously tranquil sound. I would bring the two old dresser mirrors and her boxes of collections to her bed. She would select beads and single earrings, bottle tops and shells, dried flowers and pebbles, old postcards and scraps, all sorts of oddments; then she and Susan would play Kingdom, setting up landscapes and furniture, peopling them with action.

Those were the only times of peaceful companionship between her and Susan. I have edged away from it, that poisonous feeling between them, that terrible balancing of hurts and needs I had to do between the two, and did so badly, those earlier years.

Oh there are conflicts between the others too, each one human, needing, demanding, hurting, taking—but only between Emily and Susan, no, Emily toward Susan that corroding resentment. It seems so obvious on the surface, yet it is not obvious. Susan, the second child, Susan, golden- and curly-haired and chubby, quick and articulate and assured, everything in appearance and manner Emily was not; Susan, not able to resist Emily's precious things, losing or sometimes clumsily breaking them; Susan telling jokes and riddles to company for applause while Emily sat silent (to say to me later: that was *my* riddle, Mother, I told it to Susan); Susan, who for all the five years' difference in age was just a year behind Emily in developing physically.

I am glad for that slow physical development that widened the difference between her and her contemporaries, though she suffered over it. She was too vulnerable for that terrible world of youthful competition, of preening and parading, of constant measuring of yourself against every other, of envy, "If I had that copper hair," "If I had that skin. . . . " She tormented herself enough about not looking like the others, there was enough of the unsureness, the having to be conscious of words before you speak, the constant caring—what are they thinking of me? without having it all magnified by the merciless physical drives.

Ronnie is calling. He is wet and I change him. It is rare there is such a cry now. That time of motherhood is almost behind me when the ear is not one's own but must always be racked and listening for the child cry, the child call. We sit for a while and I hold him, looking out over the city spread in charcoal with its soft aisles of light. "*Shoogily*," he breathes and curls closer. I carry him back to bed, asleep. *Shoogily*. A funny word, a family word, inherited from Emily, invented by her to say: *comfort*.

In this and other ways she leaves her seal, I say aloud. And startle at my saying it. What do I mean? What did I start to gather together, to try and make coherent? I was at the terrible, growing years. War years. I do not remember them well. I was working, there were four smaller ones now, there was not time for her. She had to help be a mother, and housekeeper, and shopper. She had to set her seal. Mornings of crisis and near hysteria trying to get lunches packed, hair combed, coats and shoes found, everyone to school or Child Care on time, the baby ready for transportation. And always the paper scribbled on by a smaller one, the book looked at by Susan then mislaid, the homework not done. Running out to that huge school where she was one, she was lost, she was a drop; suffering over the unpreparedness, stammering and unsure in her classes.

There was so little time left at night after the kids were bedded down. She would struggle over books, always eating (it was in those years she developed her enormous appetite that is legendary in our family) and I would be ironing, or preparing food for the next day, or writing V-mail to Bill, or tending the baby. Sometimes, to make me laugh, or out of her despair, she would imitate happenings or types at school.

I think I said once: "Why don't you do something like this in the school amateur show?" One morning she phoned me at work, hardly understandable through the weeping: "Mother, I did it. I won, I won; they gave me first prize; they clapped and clapped and wouldn't let me go."

Now suddenly she was Somebody, and as imprisoned in her difference as she had been in anonymity.

She began to be asked to perform at other high schools, even in colleges, then at city and statewide affairs. The first one we went to, I only recognized her that first moment when thin, shy, she almost drowned herself into the curtains. Then: Was this Emily? The control, the command, the convulsing and deadly clowning, the spell, then the roaring, stamping audience, unwilling to let this rare and precious laughter out of their lives.

Afterwards: You ought to do something about her with a gift like that — but without money or knowing how, what does one do? We have left it all to her, and the gift has as often eddied inside, clogged and clotted, as been used and growing.

She is coming. She runs up the stairs two at a time with her light graceful step, and I know she is happy tonight. Whatever it was that occasioned your call did not happen today.

"Aren't you ever going to finish the ironing, Mother? Whistler painted his mother in a rocker. I'd have to paint mine standing over an ironing board." This is one of her communicative nights and she tells me everything and nothing as she fixes herself a plate of food out of the icebox.

She is so lovely. Why did you want me to come in at all? Why were you concerned? She will find her way.

She starts up the stairs to bed. "Don't get me up with the rest in the morning." "But I thought you were having midterms." "Oh, those," she comes back in, kisses me, and says quite lightly, "in a couple of years when we'll all be atom-dead they won't matter a bit."

She has said it before. She *believes* it. But because I have been dredging the past, and all that compounds a human being is so heavy and meaningful in me, I cannot endure it tonight.

I will never total it all. I will never come in to say: She was a child seldom smiled at. Her father left me before she was a year old. I had to work her first six years when there was work, or I sent her home and to his relatives. There were years she had care she hated. She was dark and thin and foreign-looking in a world where the prestige went to blondeness and curly hair and dimples, she was slow where glibness was prized. She was a child of anxious, not proud, love. We were poor and could not afford for her the soil of easy growth. I was a young mother, I was a distracted mother. There were the other children pushing up, demanding. Her younger sister seemed all that she was not. There were years she did not want me to touch her. She kept too much to herself, her life was such she had to keep too much in herself. My wisdom came too late. She has much to her and probably nothing will come of it. She is a child of her age, of depression, of war, of fear.

Let her be. So all that is in her will not bloom — but in how many does it? There is still enough left to live by. Only help her to know — help make it so there is cause for her to know — that she is more than this dress on the ironing board, helpless before the iron.

[1956]

Study and Writing Questions

1. What precisely are the "cost[s] of . . . goodness" for the speaker and for Emily?
2. In what ways is the title appropriate or inappropriate to the STORY? Is the story about "I" or "Emily" or something else? Of all the ACTIONS that the speaker has performed in motherhood, what is the effect of choosing "ironing" for the title?
3. In the next-to-last paragraph, the speaker says she "will never total it all" and then gives a summary of what she has already narrated. If that paragraph does

not "total it all," why not? If it does "total it all," why does she do it? What is the point of having that paragraph in the NARRATIVE?

4. How is personal responsibility portrayed in this story? To what extent is the speaker responsible for Emily's character and success in life? To what extent are circumstances (other individuals, social institutions, historical forces, and so on) responsible? To what extent is Emily herself responsible?

5. What evidence is there for or against the proposition that this narrative is overly sentimental?

See also Questions for Contrast and Comparison: 70, 131, 190, 200, and 201.

OVID (PUBLIUS OVIDIUS NASO) (43 B.C.E. – 17 C.E.) *was born in Sulmo (modern Sulmona, about 75 miles east of Rome, Italy) to an old "equestrian" (knightly) family. Intended by his father for public service, he studied law and* RHETORIC *in Rome and Athens, traveled in Sicily and Asia Minor, and settled in Rome. There he held a number of minor judicial posts before committing himself to poetry. He caused an immediate sensation with his erotic poems:* Amores *(20 B.C.E.);* Heroides *(date unknown), fictitious love letters of famous heroines; and* Ars Amatoria (The Art of Love, *after 2 B.C.E.), instruction in love-making. His greatest poem is* Metamorphoses *(begun about 2 C.E. and revised over many years), a work in fifteen books of verse beginning with the change of Chaos into Order and retelling all the famous Greek and Roman myths of individual metamorphosis. Despite using traditional materials, the work is stylistically fresh and structurally innovative; for example, the* ACTION *is often interrupted while the* CHARACTERS *themselves tell tales, down to as many as five* NESTED *levels. For reasons now unknown, in 8 C.E. the emperor Augustus banished Ovid to Tomis on the Black Sea. There Ovid composed poems of exile addressed to those still in Rome:* Tristia (Sorrow) *and* Epistulae Ex Ponto. *He had three wives and one daughter, probably by his second wife. His work forms a cornerstone of Western literature.*

Metamorphoses

My purpose is to tell of bodies which have been transformed into shapes of a different kind. You heavenly powers, since you were responsible for those changes, as for all else, look favourably on my attempts, and spin an unbroken thread of verse, from the earliest beginnings of the world, down to my own times.

Before there was any earth or sea, before the canopy of heaven stretched overhead, Nature presented the same aspect the world over, that to which men have given the name of Chaos. This was a shapeless uncoordinated mass, nothing but a weight of lifeless matter, whose ill-assorted elements were indiscriminately heaped together in one place. There was no sun, in those days, to provide the world with light, no crescent moon ever filling out her horns: the earth was not poised in the enveloping air, balanced there by its own weight, nor did the sea stretch out its arms along the margins of the shores. Although the elements of land and air and sea were there, the earth had no firmness, the water no fluidity, there was no brightness in the sky. Nothing had any lasting shape, but everything got in the way of everything else; for, within that one body, cold warred with hot, moist with dry, soft with hard, and light with heavy.

This strife was finally resolved by a god, a natural force of a higher kind, who separated the earth from heaven, and the waters from the earth, and set the clear air apart from the cloudy atmosphere. When he had freed these elements, sorting them out from the heap where they had lain, indistinguishable from one another, he bound them fast, each in its separate place, forming a harmonious union. The fiery aether, which has no weight, formed the vault of heaven, flashing upwards to take its place in the highest sphere. The air, next to it in lightness, occupied the neighbouring regions. Earth, heavier than these, attracted to itself the grosser elements, and sank down under its own weight, while the encircling sea took possession of the last place of all, and held the solid earth in its embrace. In this way the god, whichever of the gods it was, set the chaotic mass in order, and, after dividing it up, arranged it in its constituent parts.

When this was done, his first care was to shape the earth into a great ball, so that it might be the same in all directions. After that, he commanded the seas to spread out this way and that, to swell into waves under the influence of the rushing winds, and to pour themselves around earth's shores. Springs, too, he created, and great pools and lakes, and confined between sloping banks the rivers which flow down from the hills and continue, each in its own channel, until they are either swallowed up by the earth itself, or reach the sea and enter its expanse of wider waters, there to wash against shores instead of banks. Then the god further ordained that earth's plains should unroll, its valleys sink down, the woods be clothed with leaves, and rocky mountains rise up.

As the sky is divided into two zones on the right hand, and two on the left, with a fifth in between, hotter than any of the rest, so the world which the sky encloses was marked off in the same way, thanks to the providence of the god: he imposed the same number of zones on earth as there are in the heavens. The central zone is so hot as to be uninhabitable, while two others are covered in deep snow: but between these extremes he set two zones to which he gave a temperate climate, compounded of heat and cold.

Over all these regions hangs the air, as much heavier than the fiery aether as it is lighter than earth or water. To the air the god assigned mists and clouds, and thunder that was destined to cause human hearts to tremble: here too he placed the thunderbolts, and winds that strike out lightnings from the clouds. Nor did the builder of the world allow the winds, any more than the rest, to roam at will throughout the air — they can scarcely be prevented from tearing the world apart, even as it is, although each blows in a different direction: so violent is the strife between brothers. The East wind withdrew to the lands of the dawn, to the kingdoms of Arabia and Persia, and to the mountain ridges that lie close to the sun's mornings rays. The West, and the shores which are warmed by the setting sun, are subject to Zephyr. Boreas, who makes men shudder with his chill breath, invaded Scythia and the North, while the lands opposite to those are continually drenched with rain and clouds, brought by the South wind.

Above all these, the god set the clear aether that has no weight, and is untainted by any earthly particles.

No sooner were all things separated in this way, and confined within definite limits, than the stars which had long been buried in darkness and obscurity began to blaze forth all through the sky. So that every region should have its appropriate inhabitants, stars and divine forms occupied the heavens, the waters afforded a home to gleaming fishes, earth harboured wild beasts, and the yielding air welcomed the birds.

There was as yet no animal which was more akin to the gods than these, none more capable of intelligence, none that could be master over all the rest. It was at this point that man was born: either the Creator, who was responsible for this better world, made him from divine seed, or else Prometheus, son of Iapetus, took the new-made earth which, only recently separated from the lofty aether, still retained some elements related to those of heaven and, mixing it with rainwater, fashioned it into the image of the all-governing gods. Whereas other animals hang their heads and look at the ground, he made man stand erect, bidding him look up to heaven, and lift his head to the stars. So the earth, which had been rough and formless, was moulded into the shape of man, a creature till then unknown.

In the beginning was the Golden Age, when men of their own accord, without threat of punishment, without laws, maintained good faith and did what was right. There were no penalties to be afraid of, no bronze tablets were erected, carrying threats of legal action, no crowd of wrong-doers, anxious for mercy, trembled before the face of their judge: indeed, there were no judges, men lived securely without them. Never yet had any pine tree, cut down from its home in the mountains, been launched on ocean's waves, to visit foreign lands: men knew only their own shores. Their cities were not yet surrounded by sheer moats, they had no straight brass trumpets, no coiling brass horns, no helmets and no swords. The peoples of the world, untroubled by any fears, enjoyed a leisurely and peaceful existence, and had no use for soldiers. The earth itself, without compulsion, untouched by the hoe, unfurrowed by any share, produced all things spontaneously, and men were content with foods that grew without cultivation. They gathered arbute berries and mountain strawberries, wild cherries and blackberries that cling to thorny bramble bushes: or acorns, fallen from Jupiter's spreading oak. It was a season of everlasting spring, when peaceful zephyrs, with their warm breath, caressed the flowers that sprang up without having been planted. In time the earth, though untilled, produced corn too, and fields that never lay fallow whitened with heavy ears of grain. Then there flowed rivers of milk and rivers of nectar, and golden honey dripped from the green holm-oak.

When Saturn was consigned to the darkness of Tartarus, and the world passed under the rule of Jove, the age of silver replaced that of gold, inferior to it, but superior to the age of tawny bronze. Jupiter shortened the springtime which had prevailed of old, and instituted a cycle of four seasons in the year, winter, summer, changeable autumn, and a brief spring. Then, for the first time, the air became parched and arid, and glowed with white heat, then hanging icicles formed under the chilling blasts of the wind. It was in those days that men first sought covered dwelling places: they made their homes in caves and thick shrubberies, or bound branches together with bark. Then corn, the gift of Ceres, first began to be sown in long furrows, and straining bullocks groaned beneath the yolk.

After that came the third age, the age of bronze, when men were of a fiercer character, more ready to turn to cruel warfare, but still free from any taint of wickedness.

Last of all arose the age of hard iron: immediately, in this period which took its name from a baser ore, all manner of crime broke out; modesty, truth, and loyalty fled. Treachery and trickery took their place, deceit and violence and criminal greed. Now sailors spread their canvas to the winds, though they had as yet but little knowledge of these, and trees which had once clothed the high mountains were fashioned into ships, and tossed upon the ocean waves, far removed from their own element. The land, which had previously been common to all, like the sunlight and the breezes, was now divided up far and wide by boundaries, set by cautious surveyors. Nor was it only corn and their due nourishment that men demanded of the rich earth: they explored its very bowels, and dug out the wealth which it had hidden away, close to the Stygian shades;

and this wealth was a further incitement to wickedness. By this time iron had been discovered, to the hurt of mankind, and gold, more hurtful still than iron. War made its appearance, using both those metals in its conflict, and shaking clashing weapons in bloodstained hands. Men lived on what they could plunder: friend was not safe from friend, not father-in-law from son-in-law, and even between brothers affection was rare. Husbands waited eagerly for the death of their wives, and wives for that of their husbands. Ruthless stepmothers mixed brews of deadly aconite, and sons pried into their fathers' horoscopes, impatient for them to die. All proper affection lay vanquished and, last of the immortals, the maiden Justice left the blood-soaked earth.

The heights of heaven were no safer than the earth; for the giants, so runs the story, assailed the kingdom of the gods and, piling mountains together, built them up to the stars above. Then the almighty father hurled his thunderbolt, smashed through Olympus, and flung down Pelion from where it had been piled on top of Ossa. The terrible bodies of the giants lay crushed beneath their own massive structures, and the earth was drenched and soaked with torrents of blood from her sons. Then, they say, she breathed life into this warm blood and, so that her offspring might not be completely forgotten, changed it into the shape of men. But the men thus born, no less than the giants, were contemptuous of the gods, violent and cruel, with a lust to kill: it was obvious that they were the children of blood.

When the father of the gods, the son of Saturn, looked down from his high citadel, and saw what was going on, he groaned aloud. He recalled the horrid banquet of Lycaon which had not yet become common knowledge, so recent was the deed, and his heart swelled with dreadful wrath, worthy of Jupiter. He called together his council, and they did not delay when they heard his summons.

There is a track across the heavens, plain to see in the clear sky. It is called the Milky Way, and is famous for its brightness. It is by this road that the gods come to the palace of the mighty Thunderer, and to his royal home. On the right hand and on the left stand the houses of distinguished gods, filled with crowds that throng their open doors. The ordinary inhabitants of heaven live elsewhere, in different places. Here the powerful and noble divinities have made their homes. This is the spot which, were I allowed to speak boldly, I would not hesitate to call the Palatine district of high heaven.

So the gods took their seats in the marble council chamber, and their lord sat, throned high above them, leaning on his ivory sceptre. Three times, four times, he shook those awe-inspiring locks and with them moved heaven and earth, the sea, the stars. Then he opened his lips, and spoke these indignant words: 'Never was I more anxious concerning the sovereignty of the universe, no, not even at that time when each of the snaky-footed giants was preparing to throw his hundred arms round the sky and take it captive. For then the attack was made by one small group of enemies and, although they were fierce ones, still the trouble originated from one source. Now the entire human race must be destroyed, throughout all the lands which Nereus surrounds with his roaring waters. I swear by the rivers of the underworld that flow through the Stygian grove beneath the earth: all other remedies have already been tried. This cancer is incurable, and must be cut out by the knife, in case the healthy part become infected. We have the demigods to care for, the spirits of the countryside, nymphs and fauns, satyrs and silvani, who roam the hills. Since we have not, as yet, considered them worthy of the honour of a place in heaven, let us at least ensure that they can live on the earth which we have given them. For can you believe, you gods, that they will go unmolested when Lycaon, a man notorious for his savagery, has laid plots against me, the lord and master of the thunderbolt, aye, and your king and master too?'

All the gods muttered uneasily, and eagerly demanded the punishment of the man who dared to do such a deed. Their dismay was such as was felt by the human race, when a wicked band of fanatics tried to extinguish the Roman name by shedding Caesar's blood: all men were seized by panic fear of instant destruction, and the whole world shuddered. Just as the loyal devotion of your subjects pleases you, Augustus, so did that of the gods please Jupiter. He checked their murmurs with a word, and as he raised his hand, all fell silent. When the uproar had subsided, hushed by the authority of the king of heaven, Jupiter again broke the silence with these words: "As far as he is concerned, he has paid the penalty. Have no fear on that score. But I shall tell you what his crime was, and what his punishment.

"Scandalous rumours concerning the state of the times had reached my ears. Hoping to find them false, I descended from the heights of Olympus, and walked the earth, a god in human form. It would take long to tell what wickedness I found on every side. Even the scandalous rumours were less than the truth. I had crossed over the ridge of Maenalus, a place bristling with the lairs of wild beasts, over Cyllene, and through the pinewoods of chill Lycaeus. From there, when the last shades of twilight were heralding the night, I entered the inhospitable home of the Arcadian tyrant. I revealed myself as a god, and the people began to do me homage. Lycaon, however, first laughed at their pious prayers, and then exclaimed: 'I shall find out, by an infallible test, whether he be god or mortal: there will be no doubt about the truth.' His plan was to take me unawares, as I lay sound asleep at night, and kill me. This was the test of truth on which he was resolved. Not content with that, he took a hostage sent him by the Molossian people, slit the man's throat with his sharp blade, and cooked his limbs, still warm with life, boiling some and roasting others over the fire. Then he set this banquet on the table. No sooner had he done so, than I with my avenging flames brought the house crashing down upon its household gods, gods worthy of such a master. Lycaon fled, terrified, until he reached the safety of the silent countryside. There he uttered howling noises, and his attempts to speak were all in vain. His clothes changed into bristling hairs, his arms to legs, and he became a wolf. His own savage nature showed in his rabid jaws, and he now directed against the flocks his innate lust for killing. He had a mania, even yet, for shedding blood. But, though he was a wolf, he retained some traces of his original shape. The greyness of his hair was the same, his face showed the same violence, his eyes gleamed as before, and he presented the same picture of ferocity.

"One house has fallen, but far more than one have deserved to perish. To the ends of the earth, the dread Fury holds sway. You would think men had sworn allegiance to crime! They shall all be punished, forthwith, as they deserve. Such is my resolve."

Some of the gods shouted their approval of Jove's words, and sought to increase his indignation: others played the part of silent supporters. Yet all were grieved at the thought of the destruction of the human race, and wondered what the earth would be like, in future, when it had been cleared of mortal inhabitants. They inquired who would bring offerings of incense to their altars, whether Jove meant to abandon the world to the plundering of wild beasts. In answer to their questions, the king of the gods assured them that they need not be anxious, for he himself would attend to everything. He promised them a new stock of men, unlike the former ones, a race of miraculous origin.

Now he was on the point of launching his thunderbolts against every part of the earth, when he felt a sudden dread lest he should set light to the pure upper air by so many fiery bolts, and send the whole vault of heaven up in flames. He remembered, too, one of fate's decrees, that a time would come when the sea and earth and the dome of the sky would blaze up, and the massive structure of the universe collapse in ruins. So he laid aside the weapons forged by the hands of the Cyclopes, and resolved on a different punishment, namely to send rain pouring down from every quarter of the sky, and so destroy mankind beneath the waters.

He wasted no time, but imprisoned the North wind in Aeolus' caves, together with all the gusts which dispel the gathering clouds; and he let loose the South wind. On dripping wings the South wind flew, his terrible features shrouded in pitchy darkness. His beard was heavy with rain, water streamed from his hoary locks, mists wreathed his brow, his robes and feathers dripped with moisture. When he crushed the hanging clouds in his broad hand, there was a crash; thereafter sheets of rain poured down from heaven. Juno's messenger Iris, clad in rainbow hues, drew up water and supplied nourishment to the clouds. The corn was laid low, and the crops the farmer had prayed for now lay flattened and sadly mourned, the long year's toil was wasted and gone for nothing.

Nor was Jupiter's anger satisfied with the resources of his own realm of heaven: his brother Neptune, the god of the sea, lent him the assistance of his waves. He sent forth a summons to the rivers, and when they entered the king's home: "No time now for long exhortations!" he cried. "Exert your strength to the utmost: that is what we need. Fling wide your homes, withdraw all barriers, and give free course to your waters." These were his orders. The rivers returned to their homes and, opening up the mouths of their springs, went rushing to the sea in frenzied torrents.

Neptune himself struck the earth with his trident; it trembled, and by its movement threw open channels for the waters. Across the wide plains the rivers raced, overflowing their banks, sweeping away in one torrential flood crops and orchards, cattle and men, houses and temples, sacred images and all. Any building which did manage to survive this terrible disaster unshaken and remain standing, was in the end submerged when some wave yet higher than the rest covered its roof, and its gables lay drowned beneath the waters. Now sea and earth could no longer be distinguished: all was sea, and a sea that had no shores.

Some tried to escape by climbing to the hilltops, others, sitting in their curved boats, plied the oars where lately they had been ploughing; some sailed over cornlands, over the submerged roofs of their homes, while some found fish in the topmost branches of the elms. At times it happened that they dropped anchor in green meadows, sometimes the curved keels grazed vineyards that lay beneath them. Where lately sinewy goats cropped the grass, now ugly seals disported themselves. The Nereids wondered to see groves and towns and houses under the water; dolphins took possession of the woods, and dashed against high branches, shaking the oak trees as they knocked against them. Wolves swam among the flocks, and the waves supported tawny lions, and tigers too. The lightning stroke of his strong tusk was of no use, then, to the wild boar, nor his swift legs to the stag—both alike were swept away. Wandering birds searched long for some land where they might rest, till their wings grew weary and they fell into the sea. The ocean, all restraints removed, overwhelmed the hills, and waves were washing the mountain peaks, a sight never seen before. The greater part of the human race was swallowed up by the waters: those whom the sea spared died from lack of food, overcome by long-continued famine.

There is a land, Phocis, which separates the fields of Boeotia from those of Oeta. It was a fertile spot while it was land, but now it had become part of the sea, a broad stretch of waters, suddenly formed. In that region a high mountain, called Parnassus, raises twin summits to the stars, and its ridges pierce the clouds. When the waters had covered all the rest of the earth, the little boat which carried Deucalion and his wife ran aground here. Of all the men who ever lived, Deucalion was the best and the most upright, no woman ever showed more reverence for the gods than Pyrrha, his wife. Their first action was to offer prayers to the Corycian nymphs, to the deities of the mountain, and to Themis, the goddess who foretold the future from its oracular shrine.

Now Jupiter saw the earth all covered with standing waters. He perceived that one alone survived of so many thousand men, one only of so many thousand women, and he knew that both were guiltless, both true worshippers of god. So, with the help of the North wind he drove away the storm clouds and, scattering the veils of mist, displayed heaven to earth and earth to heaven. The sea was no longer angry, for the ruler of ocean soothed the waves, laying aside his trident. Then he called to the sea-god Triton, who rose from the deep, his shoulders covered with clustering shellfish. Neptune bade him blow on his echoing conch shell, and recall waves and rivers by his signal. He lifted his hollow trumpet, a coiling instrument which broadens out in circling spirals from its base. When he blows upon it in mid-ocean, its notes fill the furthest shores of east and west. So now, too, the god put it to his lips, which were all damp from his dripping beard, and blew it, sending forth the signal for retreat as he had been bidden. The sound was heard by all the waters that covered earth and sea, and all the waves which heard it were checked in their course. The sea had shores once more, the swollen rivers were contained within their own channels, the floods sank down, and hills were seen to emerge. Earth rose up, its lands advancing as the waves retreated, and after a long interval the woods displayed their treetops uncovered, the mud left behind still clinging to their leaves.

The world was restored: but when Deucalion saw its emptiness, the desolate lands all deeply silent, tears started to his eyes, and he said to Pyrrha: "My cousin, my wife, the only woman left alive, related to me first by birth and blood, then joined to me in marriage—now, Pyrrha, our very dangers unite us. We two are the sole inhabitants of all the lands which east and west behold. The sea has taken the rest. Indeed, even yet, I feel no certainty that we shall survive; even now the clouds strike terror to my heart. What would your feelings be now, my poor wife, had fate snatched you to safety, without saving me? How could you have endured your fears, had you been left all alone? Who would have comforted you in your grief? For believe me, if the sea had taken you with the rest, I should follow you, my dear one, and the sea would have me too. If only I could create the nations anew, by my father's skill! If only I could mould the earth and give it breath: now the human race depends upon us two. It is god's will: we have been left as samples of mankind." So he spoke, and they wept together.

Then they decided to pray to the god in heaven, and to seek help from the holy oracle. Without delay, they went side by side to the waters of Cephisus which, though not yet clear, were already flowing in their accustomed channel. When they had sprinkled their heads and garments with water drawn from the river they turned their steps to the shrine of the holy goddess. The gables of the temple were discoloured with foul moss, and its altars stood unlit. At the temple steps they both fell forward, prone upon the ground, and timidly kissed the chill rock, saying: "If the gods may be touched and softened by the prayers of the righteous, if divine anger may be thus turned aside, tell us, O Themis, how we may repair the destruction that has overtaken our race. Most gentle goddess, assist us in our distress."

The goddess pitied them, and uttered this oracle. Depart from my temple, veil your heads, loosen the girdles of your garments and throw behind you the bones of your great mother. For long they stood in speechless wonder at this reply. Pyrrha was the first to break the silence, by declaring that she would not obey the commands of the goddess. With trembling lips she prayed to be excused: for she was afraid to injure her mother's ghost by disturbing her bones. But meanwhile they considered again the words of the oracle, so puzzling and obscure, and pondered them deeply: till after a time the son of Prometheus soothed the fears of Epimetheus' daughter with these comforting words: "Oracles are righteous, and never advise guilty action; so, unless my intuition deceives me, our great mother is the earth, and by her bones I think the oracle means the stones in the body of the earth. It is those we are instructed to throw behind our backs." The Titan's daughter was impressed by her husband's surmise; but she did not trust her hopes, for neither of them had any confidence in heaven's counsels. Still, there could be no harm in putting the matter to the test.

They went down the hillside, veiled their heads, loosened their tunics, and threw the stones behind them, as they had been bidden. Who would believe what followed, did not ancient tradition bear witness to it? The stones began to lose their hardness and rigidity, and after a little, grew soft. Then, once softened, they acquired a definite shape. When they had grown in size, and developed a tenderer nature, a certain likeness to a human form could be seen, though it was still not clear: they were like marble images, begun but not yet properly chiselled out, or like unfinished statues. The damp earthy parts, containing some moisture, were adapted to make the body: that which was solid and inflexible became bone. What was lately a vein in the rock kept the same name, and in a brief space of time, thanks to the divine will of the gods, the stones thrown from male hands took on the appearance of men, while from those the woman threw, women were recreated. So it comes about that we are a hardy race, well accustomed to toil, giving evidence of the origin from which we sprang.

[c. 8 C.E.]

Study and Writing Questions

1. Ovid gives us many metamorphoses, including the transformation of the man Lycaon into a wolf and the changing of wood into ships. What other metamorphoses are there in this selection? How are they alike and how unlike? Do they share a common THEMATIC significance?

2. The NARRATOR says his purpose is to "tell of bodies which have been transformed," but he also makes references to his own world of Rome (Palatine hill, Augustus). What might be some other purposes of the IMPLIED AUTHOR?

3. The narrator uses many oratorical flourishes, such as the opening APOSTROPHE and the PERSONIFICATION of Justice. How would you characterize the STYLE of this NARRATIVE? How does the style affect our reading?

4. What is the significance of Ovid's many uses of mineral METAPHORS, including metals and rock?

5. What is the significance of the hierarchical arrangement of the social and the physical worlds in *Metamorphoses*?

See also Questions for Contrast and Comparison: 25, 42, 71, 132, 144, 145, 146, 147, and 233.

GRACE PALEY (1922–   ) *was born in New York City to immigrants, a physician and a housewife. She grew up loving the stories she heard — in Russian and Yiddish in her home and in English in the streets — and wrote poems for herself. In the late 1930s, she briefly attended Hunter College in New York City and New York University, but her life was shaped most by her commitments to feminism, pacifism, and the raising of her two children from her early, first marriage (1942) to Jack Paley. In the 1950s she began writing short stories. Her first collection,* The Little Disturbances of Man *(1959), won great critical acclaim. In the 1960s and 1970s Paley was prominent in the anti-Vietnam War movement, organizing in Greenwich Village, serving jail time, and visiting Hanoi and Moscow (where she condemned the Soviets for their suppression of political dissent). Subsequent volumes (*Enormous Changes at the Last Minute, *1974, and* Later the Same Day, *1985) confirmed her capacity to reveal character subtly through thought and conversation, particularly in dialect. In 1988 she was the first person declared an official New York State Author by an act of the legislature. She returned to poetry in* Leaning Forward *(1985) and published stories and poems in* Long Walks and Intimate Talks *(1991). She has taught, primarily at Sarah Lawrence College, and lives in New York with her second husband, Robert Nichols, a poet and playwright.*

Wants

I saw my ex-husband in the street. I was sitting on the steps of the new library.

Hello, my life, I said. We had once been married for twenty-seven years, so I felt justified.

He said, What? What life? No life of mine.

I said, O.K. I don't argue when there's real disagreement. I got up and went into the library to see how much I owed them.

The librarian said $32 even and you've owed it for eighteen years. I didn't deny anything. Because I don't understand how time passes. I have had those books. I have often thought of them. The library is only two blocks away.

My ex-husband followed me to the Books Returned desk. He interrupted the librarian, who had more to tell. In many ways, he said, as I look back, I attribute the dissolution of our marriage to the fact that you never invited the Bertrams to dinner.

That's possible, I said. But really, if you remember: first, my father was sick that Friday, then the children were born, then I had those Tuesday-night meetings, then the war began. Then we didn't seem to know them any more. But you're right. I should have had them to dinner.

I gave the librarian a check for $32. Immediately she trusted me, put my past behind her, wiped the record clean, which is just what most other municipal and/or state bureaucracies will *not* do.

I checked out the two Edith Wharton books I had just returned because I'd read them so long ago and they are more apropos now than ever. They were *The House of Mirth* and *The Children*, which is about how life in the United States in New York changed in twenty-seven years fifty years ago.

A nice thing I do remember is breakfast, my ex-husband said. I was surprised. All we ever had was coffee. Then I remembered there was a hole in the back of the kitchen closet which opened into the apartment next door. There, they always ate sugar-cured smoked bacon. It gave us a very grand feeling about breakfast, but we never got stuffed and sluggish.

That was when we were poor, I said.

When were we ever rich? he asked.

Oh, as time went on, as our responsibilities increased, we didn't go in need. You took adequate financial care, I reminded him. The children went to camp four weeks a year and in decent ponchos with sleeping bags and boots, just like everyone else. They looked very nice. Our place was warm in winter, and we had nice red pillows and things.

I wanted a sailboat, he said. But you didn't want anything.

Don't be bitter, I said. It's never too late.

No, he said with a great deal of bitterness. I may get a sailboat. As a matter of fact I have money down on an eighteen-foot two-rigger. I'm doing well this year and can look forward to better. But as for you, it's too late. You'll always want nothing.

He had had a habit throughout the twenty-seven years of making a narrow remark which, like a plumber's snake, could work its way through the ear down the throat, half-way to my heart. He would then disappear, leaving me choking with equipment. What I mean is, I sat down on the library steps and he went away.

I looked through *The House of Mirth*, but lost interest. I felt extremely accused. Now, it's true, I'm short of requests and absolute requirements. But I do want *something*.

I want, for instance, to be a different person. I want to be the woman who brings these two books back in two weeks. I want to be the effective citizen who changes the school system and addresses the Board of Estimate on the troubles of this dear urban center.

I *had* promised my children to end the war before they grew up.

I wanted to have been married forever to one person, my ex-husband or my present one. Either has enough character for a whole life, which as it turns out is really not such a long time. You couldn't exhaust either man's qualities or get under the rock of his reasons in one short life.

Just this morning I looked out the window to watch the street for a while and saw that the little sycamores the city had dreamily planted a couple of years before the kids were born had come that day to the prime of their lives.

Well! I decided to bring those two books back to the library. Which proves that when a person or an event comes along to jolt or appraise me I *can* take some appropriate action, although I am better known for my hospitable remarks.

[1971]

Study and Writing Questions

1. In the paragraph beginning "That's possible," the NARRATOR offers her ex-husband an explanation of why their marriage dissolved. To what extent is this a believable explanation? To what extent does this paragraph reveal other, unstated, reasons, perhaps reasons of which the narrator is unaware, that led to "the dissolution of our marriage"?

2. What are the stated characteristics of the ex-husband? What unstated characteristics are revealed about the ex-husband? How are these unstated characteristics revealed?
3. What is the importance of the library as SETTING for this encounter? What is the significance of the librarian to the narrator? to the reader?
4. What are the possible meanings and importance of the title?
5. What are the possible meanings of the last paragraph and its impact on the IMPLIED READER?

See also Questions for Contrast and Contrast: 45, 91, 92, 93, 94, 98, 105, and 171.

■ **DOROTHY (ROTHSCHILD) PARKER** (1893–1967) *was born in West End, New Jersey. She was raised in New York City and environs by her father, a Jewish garment manufacturer, and her stepmother, whom he married after Dorothy's Scottish mother's death. Parker was educated at private schools, including a convent. She detested her parents but turned her bitterness to excellent literary effect. The most famous wit of her era, she cofounded, with Robert Benchley, the famous Algonquin Round Table, a luncheon club of literati. She contributed regularly to The New Yorker from its inception (1925) until her death. Her book and drama reviews for magazines such as Vogue and Esquire were famous. (She is credited with the world's shortest review: "The House Beautiful is the play lousy"; but, in her typically self-derogatory manner, she dismissed her own skill as well, for "Brevity is the soul of lingerie.") She had a short, unhappy marriage to E.P. Parker and a long relationship with screen writer Alan Campbell, whom she twice married and once divorced. Because she was prominent in leftist causes and reported the Spanish Civil War with sympathy for the Communists, she was blacklisted in Hollywood despite such screen credits as* A Star is Born *(1937). Her volumes of cynical, mocking verse (appearing until 1944) and* SHORT STORIES *won her acclaim, but she died poor, lonely, bitter, and alcoholic in a New York apartment hotel.*

The Last Tea

The young man in the chocolate-brown suit sat down at the table, where the girl with the artificial camellia had been sitting for forty minutes.

"Guess I must be late," he said. "Sorry you been waiting."

"Oh, goodness!" she said. "I just got here myself, just about a second ago. I simply went ahead and ordered because I was dying for a cup of tea. I was late, myself. I haven't been here more than a minute."

"That's good," he said. "Hey, hey, easy on the sugar — one lump is fair enough. And take away those cakes. Terrible! Do I feel terrible!"

"Ah," she said. "you do? Ah. Whadda matter?"

"Oh, I'm ruined," he said. "I'm in terrible shape."

"Ah, the poor boy," she said. "Was it feelin' mizzable? Ah, and it came way up here to meet me! You shouldn't have done that — I'd have understood. Ah, just think of it coming all the way up here when it's so sick!"

"Oh, that's all right," he said. "I might as well be here as any place else. Any place is like any other place, the way I feel today. Oh, I'm all shot."

"Why, that's just awful," she said. "Why, you poor sick thing. Goodness, I hope it isn't influenza. They say there's a lot of it around."

"Influenza!" he said. "I wish that was all I had. Oh, I'm poisoned. I'm through. I'm off the stuff for life. Know what time I got to bed? Twenty minutes past five, A.M., this morning. What a night! What an evening!"

"I thought," she said, "that you were going to stay at the office and work late. You said you'd be working every night this week."

"Yeah, I know," he said. "But it gave me the jumps, thinking about going down there and sitting at that desk. I went up to May's — she was throwing a party. Say, there was somebody there said they knew you."

"Honestly?" she said. "Man or woman?"

"Dame," he said. "Name's Carol McCall. Say, why haven't I been told about her before? That's what I call a girl. What a looker she is!"

"Oh, really?" she said. "That's funny—I never heard of anyone that thought that. I've heard people say she was sort of nice-looking, if she wouldn't make up so much. But I never heard of anyone that thought she was pretty."

"Pretty is right," he said. "What a couple of eyes she's got on her!"

"Really?" she said. "I never noticed them particularly. But I haven't seen her for a long time—sometimes people change, or something."

"She says she used to go to school with you," he said.

"Well, we went to the same school," she said. "I simply happened to go to public school because it happened to be right near us, and Mother hated to have me crossing streets. But she was three or four classes ahead of me. She's ages older than I am.

"She's three or four classes ahead of them all," he said. "Dance! Can she step! 'Burn your clothes, baby,' I kept telling her. I must have been fried pretty."

"I was out dancing myself, last night," she said. "Wally Dillon and I. He's just been pestering me to go out with him. He's the most wonderful dancer. Goodness! I didn't get home until I don't know what time. I must look just simply a wreck. Don't I?"

"You look all right." he said.

"Wally's crazy," she said. "The things he says! For some crazy reason or other, he's got it into his head that I've got beautiful eyes, and, well, he just kept talking about them till I didn't know where to look, I was so embarrassed. I got so red, I thought everybody in the place would be looking at me. I got just as red as a brick. Beautiful eyes! Isn't he crazy?"

"He's all right," he said. "Say, this little McCall girl, she's had all kinds of offers to go into moving pictures. 'Why don't you go ahead and go?' I told her. But she says she doesn't feel like it."

"There was a man up at the lake, two summers ago," she said. "He was a director or something with one of the big moving-picture people—oh, he had all kinds of influence!—and he used to keep insisting and insisting that I ought to be in the movies. Said I ought to be doing sort of Garbo parts. I used to just laugh at him. Imagine!"

"She's had about a million offers," he said. "I told her to go ahead and go. She keeps getting these offers all the time."

"Oh, really?" she said. "Oh, listen, I knew I had something to ask you. Did you call me up last night, by any chance?"

"Me?" he said. "No, I didn't call you."

"While I was out, Mother said this man's voice kept calling up," she said. "I thought maybe it might be you, by some chance. I wonder who it could have been. Oh—I guess I know who it was. Yes, that's who it was!"

"No, I didn't call you," he said. "I couldn't have seen a telephone, last night. What a head I had on me, this morning! I called Carol up, around ten, and she said she was feeling great. Can that girl hold her liquor!"

"It's a funny thing about me," she said. "It just makes me feel sort of sick to see a girl drunk. It's just something in me, I guess. I don't mind a man so much, but it makes me feel perfectly terrible to see a girl intoxicated. It's just the way I am, I suppose.

"Does she carry it!" he said. "And then feels great the next day. There's a girl! Hey, what are you doing there? I don't want any more tea, thanks. I'm not one of these tea boys. And these tea rooms give me the jumps. Look at all those old dames, will you? Enough to give you the jumps."

"Of course, if you'd rather be some place, drinking, with I don't know what kinds of people," she said, "I'm sure I don't see how I can help that. Goodness, there are enough people that are glad enough to take me to tea. I don't know how many people keep calling me up and pestering me to take me to tea. Plenty of people!"

"All right, all right, I'm here, aren't I?" he said. "Keep your hair on."

"I could name them all day," she said.

"All right," he said. "What's there to crab about?"

"Goodness, it isn't any of my business what you do," she said. "But I hate to see you wasting your time with people that aren't nearly good enough for you. That's all."

"No need worrying over me," he said. "I'll be all right. Listen. You don't have to worry."

"It's just I don't like to see you wasting your time," she said, "staying up all night and then feeling terrible the next day. Ah, I was forgetting he was so sick. Ah, I was mean, wasn't I, scolding him when he was so mizzable. Poor boy. How's he feel now?"

"Oh, I'm all right," he said. "I feel fine. You want anything else? How about getting a check? I got to make a telephone call before six."

"Oh, really?" she said. "Calling up Carol?"

"She said she might be in around now," he said.

"Seeing her tonight?" she said.

"She's going to let me know when I call up," he said. "She's probably got a million dates. Why?"

"I was just wondering," she said. "Goodness, I've got to fly! I'm having dinner with Wally, and he's so crazy, he's probably there now. He's called me up about a hundred times today."

"Wait till I pay the check," he said, "and I'll put you on a bus."

"Oh, don't bother," she said. "It's right at the corner. I've got to fly. I suppose you want to stand and call up your friend from here?"

"It's an idea," he said. "Sure you'll be all right?"

"Oh, sure," she said. Busily she gathered her gloves and purse, and left her chair. He rose, not quite fully, as she stopped beside him.

"When'll I see you again?" she said.

"I'll call you up," he said. "I'm all tied up, down at the office and everything. Tell you what I'll do. I'll give you a ring."

"Honestly, I have more dates!" she said. "It's terrible. I don't know when I'll have a minute. But you call up, will you?"

"I'll do that," he said. "Take care of yourself."

"You take care of yourself," she said. "Hope you'll feel all right."

"Oh, I'm fine," he said. "Just beginning to come back to life."

"Be sure and let me know how you feel," she said. "Will you? Sure, now? Well, good-by. Oh, have a good time tonight!"

"Thanks," he said. "Hope you have a good time, too."

"Oh, I will," she said. "I expect to. I've got to rush! Oh, I nearly forgot! Thanks ever so much for the tea. It was lovely."

"Be yourself, will you?" he said.

"It was," she said. "Well. Now don't forget to call me up, will you? Sure? Well, good-by."

"Solong," he said.

She walked on down the little lane between the blue-painted tables.

[1926]

Study and Writing Questions

1. The STORY's only lines of physical description occur in the first and last paragraphs. What, in addition to their literal meaning, do those details convey?
2. With lines like " 'sometimes people change, *or something*' " (emphasis added), readers of this NARRATIVE are urged implicitly to seek further meanings behind the CHARACTERS' words. What are some other lines with double meanings? What are those meanings?
3. What does "tea" signify in this narrative? How does tea figure in the PLOT? What is its social significance? What are the possible meanings of the title?
4. Many phrases in this story, like "three or four classes ahead," have radically different meanings to the two characters. What is the importance of VIEW-POINT to the ACTION, STRUCTURE, and THEME of this story?
5. To what extent is the double standard at work in the narrative world a consequence of the unequal gender roles in the society and to what extent is it a consequence of the unequal desires of the two characters? To what extent is this a feminist narrative?

See also Questions for Contrast and Comparison: 20, 40, 41, 152, and 192.

■ ALAN (STEWART) PATON (1903–1988) *was born into a white, English-speaking family in Pietermaritzburg, South Africa and educated at the University of Natal (B.Sc., 1923). Like his father, a civil servant, Paton worked for the government, most importantly as a physics and mathematics teacher (Ixopo High School, 1925–1928; Maritzburg College, 1928–1935) and as the principal of Diepfkloof Reformatory near Johannesburg (1935–1948). Paton burst into the world's consciousness with his compassionate first* NOVEL, *Cry, the Beloved Country (1948), which shows how a black murderer cannot be judged fairly without understanding the circumstances of his life and crime. Paton's second novel, Too Late the Phalarope (1953), is an equally moving story of an interracial love affair under apartheid, the South African system of legal racial separation that, among other effects, made such love a crime. Paton founded (1958) the Liberal Party of South Africa and served as its president until it was declared illegal (1968); he remained active in liberal politics all his life. Other works include two volumes of autobiography (Towards the Mountain, 1980, and Journey Continued, 1988), a third politically sensitive novel (Ah, But Your Land Is Beautiful, 1981), and Tales From a Troubled Land (1961),* SHORT STORIES. *His first marriage (1928–1967), which produced two sons, lasted until his wife's death. His second marriage (1969) lasted until his own death in his native land.*

Life For A Life

The doctor had closed up the ugly hole in Flip's skull so that his widow, and her brothers and sisters, and their wives and husbands and children, and Flip's own brothers and sisters and their wives and husbands and children, could come and stand for a minute and look down on the hard stony face of the master of Kroon, one of the richest farmers of the whole Karroo. The cars kept coming and going, the police, the doctor, the newspaper men, the neighbours from near and far.

All the white women were in the house, and all the white men outside. An event like this, the violent death of one of themselves, drew them together in an instant, so that all the world might see that they were one, and that they would not rest till justice had been done. It was this standing there, this drawing together, that kept the brown people in their small stone houses, talking in low voices, and their fear communicated itself to their children, so that there was no need to silence them. Now and then one of them would leave the houses to relieve his needs in the bushes, but otherwise there was no movement on this side of the valley. Each family sat in its house, at a little distance from each front door, watching with anxious fascination the goings and the comings of the white people standing in front of the big house.

Then the white predikant came from Poort, you could tell him by the black hat and the black clothes. He shook hands with Big Baas Flip's sons, and said words of comfort to them. Then all the men followed him into the house, and after a while the sound of the slow determined singing was carried across the valley, to the small stone houses on the other side, to Enoch Maarman, head-shepherd of Kroon, and his wife Sara, sitting just inside the door of their own house. Maarman's anxiety showed itself in the movements of his face and hands, and his wife knew of his condition but kept her face averted from it. Guilt lay heavily upon them both, because they had hated Big Baas Flip, not with clenched fists and bared teeth, but, as befitted people in their station, with salutes and deference.

Sara suddenly sat erect.

—They are coming, she said.

They watched the four men leave the big stone house, and take the path that led to the small stone houses, and both could feel the fear rising in them. Their guilt weighed down on them all the more heavily because they felt no grief. They felt all the more afraid because the show of grief might have softened the harshness of the approaching ordeal. Someone must pay for so terrible a crime, and if not the one who did it, then who better than the one who could not grieve. That morning Maarman had stood hat in hand before Baas Gysbert, who was Big Baas Flip's eldest son, and had said to him, *my people are sorry to hear of this terrible thing.* And Baas Gysbert had given him the terrible answer, *that could be so.*

Then Sara said to him, Robbertse is one.

He nodded. He knew that Robbertse was one, the big detective with the temper that got out of hand, so that reddish foam would come out of his mouth, and he would hold a man by the throat till one of his colleagues would shout at him to let the man go. Sara's father, who was one of the wisest men in all the district of Poort, said that he could never be sure whether Robbertse was mad or only pretending to be, but that it didn't really matter, because whichever it was, it was dangerous.

Maarman and his wife stood up when two of the detectives came to the door of the small stone house. One was Robbertse, but both were big men and confident. They wore smart sports jackets and grey flannels, and grey felt hats on their heads. They came in and kept their hats on their heads, looking round the small house with the air of masters. They spoke to each other as though there were nobody standing there waiting to be spoken to.

Then Robbertse said, you are Enoch Maarman?

—Yes, baas.

—The head-shepherd?

—Yes, baas.

—Who are the other shepherds?

Enoch gave him the names, and Robbertse sat down on one of the chairs, and wrote the names in his book. Then he tilted his hat back on his head and said, has anyone of these men ever been in gaol?

Enoch moistened his lips. He wanted to say that the detective could easily find it out for himself, that he was the head-shepherd and would answer any question about the farm or the work. But he said instead, I don't know, baas.

—You don't know Kleinbooi was in gaol at Christmas?

—Yes, I know that, baas.

Suddenly Robbertse was on his feet, and his head almost touching the ceiling, and his body almost filling the small room, and he was shouting in a tremendous voice, then why did you lie?

Sara had shrunk back into the wall, and was looking at Robbertse out of terrified eyes, but Enoch did not move though he was deathly afraid.

He answered, I didn't mean to lie, baas. Kleinbooi was in gaol for drink, not killing.

Robbertse said, killing? Why do you mention killing?

Then when Enoch did not answer, the detective suddenly lifted his hand so that Enoch started back and knocked over the other chair. Down on his knees, and shielding his head with one hand, he set the chair straight again, saying, baas, we know that you are here because the master was killed.

But Robbertse's lifting his hand had been intended only to remove his hat from his head, and now with a grin he put his hat on the table.

—Why fall down, he asked, because I take off my hat? I like to take off my hat in another man's house.

He smiled at Sara, and looking at the chair now set upright, said to her, you can sit.

When she made no attempt to sit on it, the smile left his face, and he said to her coldly and menacingly, you can sit.

When she had sat down, he said to Maarman, don't knock over any more chairs. For if one gets broken, you'll tell the magistrate I broke it, won't you? That I lifted it up and threatened you?

—No, baas.

Robbertse sat down again, and studied his book as though something were written there, not the names of shepherds. Then he said suddenly, out of nothing, you hated him, didn't you?

And Enoch answered, no, baas.

—Where's your son Johannes?

—In Cape Town, baas.

—Why didn't he become a shepherd?

—I wouldn't let him, baas.

—You sent him to the white University?

—Yes, baas.

—So that he could play the white baas?

—No, baas.

—Why does he never come to see you?

—The Big Baas would not let him, baas.

—Because he wouldn't become a shepherd?

—Yes, baas.

—So you hated him, didn't you?

—No, baas.

Robbertse looked at him with contempt.

—A man keeps your own son away from your door, because you want a better life for him, and you don't hate him? God, what are you made of?

He continued to look at Maarman with contempt, then shrugged his shoulders as though it were a bad business; then he suddenly grew intimate, confidential, even friendly.

—Maarman, I have news for you, you may think it good, you may think it bad. But you have a right to know it, seeing it is about your son.

The shepherd was suddenly filled with a new apprehension. Robbertse was preparing some new blow. That was the kind of man he was, he hated to see any coloured man holding his head up, he hated to see any coloured man anywhere but on his knees or his stomach.

—Your son, said Robbertse, genially, you thought he was in Cape Town, didn't you?

—Yes, baas.

—Well, he isn't, said Robbertse, he's here in Poort, he was seen there yesterday.

He let it sink in, then he said to Maarman, he hated Big Baas Flip, didn't he?

Maarman cried out, no, baas.

For the second time Robbertse was on his feet, filling the room with his size, and his madness.

—He didn't hate him? he shouted. God Almighty, Big Baas Flip wouldn't let him come to his own home, and see his own father and mother, but he didn't hate him. And you didn't hate him either, you creeping yellow bastard, what are you all made of?

He looked at the shepherd out of his mad red eyes. Then with contempt he said again, you creeping yellow Hottentot bastard.

—Baas, said Maarman.

—What?

—Baas, the baas can ask me what he likes, and I shall try to answer him, but I ask the baas not to insult me in my own house, before my own wife.

Robbertse appeared delighted, charmed. Some other white man might have been outraged that a coloured man should so advise him, but he was able to admire such manly pride.

—Insult you? he said. Didn't you see me take off my hat when I came into this house?

He turned to Sara and asked her, didn't you see me take off my hat when I came into the house.

—Yes, baas.

—Did you think I was insulting your husband?

—No, baas.

Robbertse smiled at her ingratiatingly. I only called him a creeping yellow Hottentot bastard, he said.

The cruel words destroyed the sense of piquancy for him, and now he was truly outraged. He took a step towards the shepherd, and his colleague, the other detective, the silent one, suddenly shouted at him, Robbertse!

Robbertse stopped. He looked vacantly at Maarman.

—Was someone calling me? he asked. Did you hear a voice calling me?

Maarman was terrified, fascinated, he could see the red foam. He was at a loss, not knowing whether this was madness, or madness affecting to be madness, or what it was.

—The other baas was calling you, baas.

Then it was suddenly all over. Robbertse sat down again on the chair to ask more questions.

—You knew there was money stolen?

—Yes, baas.

—Who told you?

—Mimi, the girl who works at the house.

—You knew the money was in an iron safe, and they took it away?

—Yes, baas.

—Where would they take it to?

—I don't know, baas.

—Where would you have taken it, if you had stolen it?

But Maarman didn't answer.

—You won't answer, eh?

All three of them watched Robbertse anxiously, lest the storm should return. But he smiled benevolently at Maarman, as though he knew that even a coloured man must have pride, as though he thought all the better of him for it, and said, all right, I won't ask that question. But I want you to think of the places where that safe could be. It must have been carried by at least two men, perhaps more. And they couldn't have got it off the farm in the time. So it's still on the farm. Now all I want you to do is to think where it could be. No one knows this farm better than you.

—I'll think, baas.

The other detective suddenly said, *the lieutenant's come.* The two of them stood just inside the door, looking over to the house on the other side of the valley. Then suddenly Robbertse rounded on Maarman, and catching him by the back of the neck, forced him to the door, so that he could look too.

—You see that, he said. They want to know who killed Big Baas Flip, and they want to know soon. Do you see them?

—Yes, baas.

—And you see that lieutenant. He rides round in a Chrysler, and by God, he wants to know too. And by God he'll ride me if I don't find out.

He pulled the shepherd back into the room, and put on his hat and went out, followed by the other.

—Don't think you've seen the last of me, he said to Maarman. You've got to show me where your friends hid that safe.

Then he and his companion joined the other two detectives, and all four of them turned back towards the big house. They talked animatedly, and more than once, all of them stood for a moment while one of them made some point or put forward some theory. No one would have known that one of them was mad.

Twelve hours since they had taken her husband away. Twelve hours since the mad detective had come for him, with those red tormented eyes, as though the lieutenant were riding him too hard. He had grinned at her husband. *Come and we'll look for the safe,* he said. The sun was sinking in the sky, over the hills of Kroon. It was no time to be looking for a safe.

She did not sleep that night. Her neighbours had come to sit with her, till midnight, till two o'clock, till four o'clock, but there was no sign. Why did he not come back? Were they still searching at this hour of the morning? Then the sun was rising, over the hills of Kroon.

On the other side of the valley the big house was awake, for this was the day that Big Baas Flip would be laid to rest, under the cypress trees of the graveyard in the stones. Leaderless, the shepherds had gone to Baas Gysbert to be given the day's work; and Hendrik Baadjies, second shepherd, speaking on behalf of Sara Maarman, wife of the head-shepherd, told Baas Gysbert that the police had taken Enoch Maarman at sunset, and now at dawn he had not yet returned, and that his wife was anxious. Would Baas Gysbert not please strike the telephone, not much only a little, not for long only a short-time, to ask what had become of his father's head-shepherd?

And Baas Gysbert replied in a voice trembling with passion, do you not know it was my father who was killed?

So Hendrik Baadjies touched his hat, and said, Pardon me, baas, that I asked.

Then he went to stand with the other shepherds, a man shamed, a man shamed standing with other shamed men, who must teach their children to know forever their station.

Fifteen hours. But she would not eat. Her neighbours brought food, but she would not. She could see the red foam at the corners of the mouth, and see the tremendous form and hear the tremendous voice that filled her house with anger, and with feigned politeness, and with contempt, and with cruel smiling. Because one was a shepherd, because one had no certitude of home or work or life or favour, because one's back had to be bent though one's soul would be upright, because one had to speak the smiling craven words under any injustice, because one had to bear as a brand this dark sun-warmed colour of the skin, as good surely as any other, because of these things, this mad policeman could strike down, and hold by the neck, and call a creeping yellow Hottentot bastard, a man who had never hurt another in his long gentle life, a man who like the great Christ was a lover of sheep and of little children, and had been a good husband and father except for those occasional outbursts that any sensible woman will pass over, outbursts of the imprisoned manhood that has got tired of the chains that keep it down on its knees. Yes this mad policeman could take off his hat mockingly in one's house, and ask a dozen questions that he, for all that he was as big as a mountain, would never have dared to ask a white person.

But the anger went from her suddenly, leaving her spent, leaving her again full of anxiety for the safety of her husband, and for the safety of her son who had chosen to come to Poort at this dangerous hour. Just as a person sits in the cold, and by keeping motionless enjoys some illusion of warmth, so she sat inwardly motionless, lest by some interior movement she would disturb the numbness of her mind, and feel the pain of her condition. However she was not allowed to remain so, for at eleven o'clock a message came from Hendrik Baadjies to say that it was certain that neither detective nor head-shepherd was on the farm of Kroon. Then at noon a boy brought her a message that her brother Solomon Koopman had come with a taxi to the gate of the farm, and that she should come at once to him there, because he did not wish to come to her house. She tied a doek around her head, and as soon as she saw her brother, she cried out to him, *are they safe?* When he looked mystified, she said, *my man and my child,* and her brother told her it must have been Robbertse's joke, that her son was safe in Cape Town and had not been in Poort at all. He was glad to be able to tell her this piece of news, for his other news was terrible that Enoch her husband was dead. He had always been a little afraid of his sister, who had brought up the family when their mother had died, so he did not know how to comfort her. But she wept only a little, like one who is used to such events, and must not grieve but must prepare for the next.

Then she said, *how did he die?* So he told her the story that the police had told him of Enoch's death, how that the night was dark, and how they had gone searching down by the river, and how Enoch had slipped on one of the big stones there and had fallen on his head, and how they had not hesitated but had rushed him to Poort, but he had died in the car.

What can one say to a story like that? So they said nothing. He was ashamed to tell it, but he had to tell it so, because he had a butcher's licence in Poort, and he could not afford to doubt the police.

—This happened in the dark, Sara said. Why do they let me know now?

Alas, they could not give her her husband's body, it was buried already! Alas, she would know what it was like in the summer, how death began to smell because of the heat, that was why they had buried it! Alas, they wouldn't have done it had they only known who he was, and that his home was so near, at the well-known farm of Kroon!

Couldn't the body be lifted again, and be taken to Kroon, to be buried there in the hills where Enoch Maarman had worked so faithfully for nearly fifty years, tending the sheep of Big Baas Flip? Alas, no it couldn't be, for it is one thing to bury a man, and quite another thing to take him up again. To bury a man one only needs a doctor, and even that not always, but to take him up again you would have to go to Cape Town and get the permission of the Minister himself. And they do not permit that lightly, to disturb a man's bones when once he has been laid to rest in the earth.

Solomon Koopman would have gone away, with a smile on his lips, and cold hate in his heart. But she would not. For this surely was one thing that was her own, the body of the man she had lived with for so many years. She wanted the young white policeman behind the desk to show her the certificate of her husband's death, and she wanted to know by whose orders he had been buried, and who had hurried his body into the earth, so that she could tell for herself whether is was possible that such a person had not known that this was the body of Enoch Maarman, head-shepherd of the farm of Kroon, who had that very night been in the company of Detective Robbertse.

She put these questions, through her brother Solomon Koopman, who had a butcher's licence, and framed the questions apologetically, because he knew that they implied that something was very wrong somewhere, that something was being hidden. But although he put the questions as nicely as possible, he could see that the policeman behind the desk was becoming impatient with this importunity, and was beginning to think that grief was no excuse for this cross-examination of authority. Other policemen came in too, and listened to the questions of this woman who would not go away, and one of them said to the young constable behind the desk, *show her the death certificate.*

There it was, *death due to sub-cranial bleeding.*

—He fell on his head, explained the older policeman, and the blood inside finished him.

—I ask to see Detective Robbertse, she said.

The policemen smiled and looked at each other, not in any flagrant way, just knowingly.

—You can't see him, said the older policeman, he went away on holiday this very morning.

—Why does he go on holiday, she asked, when he is working on this case?

The policemen began to look at her impatiently. She was going too far, even though her husband was dead. Her own brother was growing restless, and he said to her, sister, let us go.

Her tears were coming now, made to flow by sorrow and anger. The policemen were uneasy, and drifted away, leaving only the young constable at the desk.

—What happened? she asked. How did my husband die? Why is Detective Robbertse not here to answer my questions?

The young policeman said to her angrily, we don't answer such questions here. If you want to ask such questions, get a lawyer.

—Good, she said, I shall get a lawyer.

She and her brother turned to leave, but the older policeman was there at the door, polite and reasonable.

—Why isn't your sister sensible? he asked Solomon Koopman. A lawyer will only stir up trouble between the police and the people.

Koopman looked from the policeman to his sister, for he feared them both.

—Ask him, Sara said to her brother, if it is not sensible to want to know about one's husband's death.

—Tell her, said the policeman to Koopman, that it was an accident.

—He knows who I am, Sara said. Why did he allow my husband to be buried here when he knew that he lived at Kroon?

Her voice was rising, and to compensate for it, the policeman's voice grew lower and lower.

—I did not have him buried, he said desperately. It was an order from a high person.

Outside in the street, Koopman said to his sister miserably, sister, I beg of you, do not get a lawyer. For if you do, I shall lose the licence, and who will help you to keep your son at the university?

Sara Maarman got back to her house as the sun was sinking over the hills of Kroon, twenty-four hours from the time that her husband had left with Detective Robbertse to look for the safe. She lit the lamp and sat down, too weary to think of food. While she sat there, Hendrik Baadjies knocked at the door and came in and brought her the sympathy of all the brown people on the farm of Kroon. Then he stood before her, twisting his hat in his hand almost as though she were a white woman. He brought a message from Baas Gysbert, who now needed a new shepherd, and needed Enoch Maarman's house for him to live in. She would be given three days to pack all her possessions, and the loan of the cart and donkeys to take them and herself to Poort.

—Is three days enough? asked Baadjies. For if it is not, I could ask for more.

—Three days is enough, she said.

When Baadjies had gone, she thought to herself, three days is three days too many, to go on living in this land of stone, three days before she could leave it all for the Cape, where her son lived, where people lived, so he told her, softer and sweeter lives.

[1961]

Study and Writing Questions

1. How does the control of VIEWPOINT influence your reactions to the ACTION in this STORY?
2. How would you answer Robbertse's question about the non-whites, "What are you all made of?"
3. In what sense(s) is Robbertse mad; in what sense(s) is he sane?
4. In what way(s) does the title (an ALLUSION to the Bible's Book of Exodus 21:23) comment on the action in Paton's NARRATIVE?
5. To what extent should this story be considered propaganda?

See also Questions for Contrast and Comparison: 15, 43, 55, 85, 86, 109, 117, 122, 157, 167, 179, and 189.

CHARLES PERRAULT (1628–1703) *was born in Paris, France, son of a lawyer. After his education at Beauvais, he was admitted to the Paris Bar (1651) where he worked successfully as a qualified lawyer and advocate. He nonetheless became secretary to his brother Claude, who was the architect of both the Paris Observatory and the east front of the Louvre Museum. Charles thus came to know Jean Baptiste Colbert, the great statesman and finance minister of Louis XIV. Through Colbert, Charles became Controller of Royal Buildings and later (1671) a member of the prestigious French Academy, official arbiter of French language and literature. There he led the modernists in the "ancients/moderns controversy." Nicolas Boileau and others held classic art to present an unreachable pinnacle, but Perrault held, particularly in his poem* The Age of Louis the Great *(1687), that literature and civilization advance. Already admired for light verse and love poetry after 1660, he became renowned for* Histories and Tales of Long Ago — with Morals *(1697). Possibly written for his son, this work is usually known by the inscription over its frontispiece,* Tales of Mother Goose *(the first occurrence of the phrase). Perrault's fresh retellings added to world literature such nearly forgotten, often gruesome, traditional stories as "The Sleeping Beauty," "Little Red Riding Hood," "Puss in Boots," and "Cinderella." Perrault died in Paris.*

Little Red Riding Hood

Once upon a time, deep in the heart of the country, there lived a pretty little girl whose mother adored her, and her grandmother adored her even more. This good woman made her a red hood like the ones that fine ladies wear when they go riding. The hood suited the child so much that soon everybody was calling her Little Red Riding Hood.

One day, her mother baked some cakes on the griddle and said to Little Red Riding Hood:

"Your granny is sick; you must go and visit her. Take her one of these cakes and a little pot of butter."

Little Red Riding Hood went off to the next village to visit her grandmother. As she walked through the wood, she met a wolf, who wanted to eat her but did not dare to because there were woodcutters working nearby. He asked her where she was going. The poor child did not know how dangerous it is to chatter away to wolves and replied innocently:

"I'm going to visit my grandmother to take her this cake and this little pot of butter from my mother."

"Does your grandmother live far away?" asked the wolf.

"Oh yes," said Little Red Riding Hood. "She lives beyond the mill you can see over there, in the first house you come to in the village."

"Well, I shall go and visit her, too," said the wolf. "I will take *this* road and you shall take *that* road and let's see who can get there first."

The wolf ran off by the shortest path and Red Riding Hood went off the longest way and she made it still longer because she dawdled along, gathering nuts and chasing butterflies and picking bunches of wayside flowers.

The wolf soon arrived at Grandmother's house. He knocked on the door, rat tat tat.

"Who's there?"

"Your grand-daughter, Little Red Riding Hood," said the wolf, disguising his voice. "I've brought you a cake baked on the griddle and a little pot of butter from my mother."

Grandmother was lying in bed because she was poorly. She called out:

"Lift up the latch and walk in!"

The wolf lifted the latch and opened the door. He had not eaten for three days. He threw himself on the good woman and gobbled her up. Then he closed the door behind him and lay down in Grandmother's bed to wait for Little Red Riding Hood. At last she came knocking on the door, rat tat tat.

"Who's there?"

Little Red Riding Hood heard the hoarse voice of the wolf and thought that her grandmother must have caught a cold. She answered:

"It's your grand-daughter, Little Red Riding Hood. I've brought you a cake baked on the griddle and a little pot of butter from my mother."

The wolf disguised his voice and said:

"Lift up the latch and walk in."

Little Red Riding Hood lifted the latch and opened the door.

When the wolf saw her come in, he hid himself under the bedclothes and said to her:

"Put the cake and the butter down on the bread-bin and come and lie down with me."

Little Red Riding Hood took off her clothes and went to lie down in the bed. She was surprised to see how odd her grandmother looked. She said to her:

"Grandmother, what big arms you have!"

"All the better to hold you with, my dear."

"Grandmother, what big legs you have!"

"All the better to run with, my dear."

"Grandmother, what big ears you have!"

"All the better to hear with, my dear."

"Grandmother, what big eyes you have!"

"All the better to see with, my dear!"

"Grandmother, what big teeth you have!"

"All the better to eat you up!"

At that, the wicked wolf threw himself upon Little Red Riding Hood and gobbled her up, too.

Moral

Children, especially pretty, nicely brought-up young ladies, ought never to talk to strangers; if they are foolish enough to do so, they should not be surprised if some greedy wolf consumes them, elegant red riding hoods and all.

Now, there are real wolves, with hairy pelts and enormous teeth; but also wolves who seem perfectly charming, sweet-natured and obliging, who pursue young girls in the street and pay them the most flattering attentions.

Unfortunately, these smooth-tongued, smooth-pelted wolves are the most dangerous beasts of all.

[1697]

Study and Writing Questions

1. What does the Little Red Riding Hood itself SYMBOLIZE both for the various CHARACTERS and for the reader in this version of the STORY?
2. There are many doublings and repetitions in this NARRATIVE. These range from exact repetitions of words to such parallelism of ACTION as the wolf and the heroine taking their own roads from their first meeting to the grandmother's house. List these doublings and repetitions. What are their different effects? What are their common effects?
3. What does productive work signify in this narrative? Who does work of what sort? Who does not do productive work?
4. What is the sexual symbolism of this narrative? What is its importance?
5. Consider the "Moral" of this narrative. Is this the MORAL that you would have drawn from the narrative? If so, what is gained by expressing it explicitly; if not, how has the "Moral" changed the overall story?

See also Questions for Contrast and Comparison: 3, 6, 26, 77, 119, and 132.

EDGAR ALLAN POE (1809 – 1849), *was born in Boston to traveling actors who both died before he was three. Sheltered but never adopted by Richard Allan, a Richmond, Virginia, merchant, Poe was always poor and unhappy. He struggled constantly for stability — even adopting Allan as his last name for a time. Intermittently favored by Allan, Poe was educated in England, Richmond, and briefly at the University of Virginia where gambling debts led to his expulsion. Allan later got Poe appointed to the U.S. Military Academy at West Point, which expelled him for drunkenness, although modern diagnosis suggests he may instead have suffered a congenital alcohol intolerance. Having already published verse, Poe won a* SHORT STORY *prize for "MS. Found in a Bottle" (1833). He then began a series of editorial jobs, notably on* The Southern Literary Messenger. *With Virginia, a first cousin whom he married (1835?) when she was thirteen, he lived in New York, Philadelphia, Richmond, and Baltimore. Both dismissed and lauded for his relentlessly musical poetry ("The Raven," "The Bells," "Annabel Lee"), his pioneering devotion to unitary literary effects reshaped the* TALE *of melancholy horror and set the patterns for what he called "tales of ratiocination," our detective stories and* SCIENCE FICTIONS. *After Virginia's death by tuberculosis (1845), Poe's chronic depression increased. He died four days after being found delirious outside a Baltimore saloon.*

The Black Cat

For the most wild, yet most homely narrative which I am about to pen, I neither expect nor solicit belief. Mad indeed would I be to expect it, in a case where my very senses reject their own evidence. Yet, mad am I not — and very surely do I not dream. But tomorrow I die, and to-day I would unburthen my soul. My immediate purpose is to place before the world, plainly, succinctly, and without comment, a series of mere household events. In their consequences, these events have terrified — have tortured — have destroyed me. Yet I will not attempt to expound them. To me, they have presented little but Horror — to many they will seem less terrible than *baroques.* Hereafter, perhaps, some intellect may be found which will reduce my phantasm to the common-place — some intellect more calm, more logical, and far less excitable than my own, which will perceive, in the circumstances I detail with awe, nothing more than an ordinary succession of very natural causes and effects.

From my infancy I was noted for the docility and humanity of my disposition. My tenderness of heart was even so conspicuous as to make me the jest of my companions. I was especially fond of animals, and was indulged by my parents with a great variety of pets. With these I spent most of my time, and never was so happy as when feeding and caressing them. This peculiarity of character grew with my growth, and, in my manhood, I derived from it one of my principal sources of pleasure. To those who have cherished an affection for a faithful and sagacious dog, I need hardly be at the trouble of explaining the nature or the intensity of the gratification thus derivable. There is something in the unselfish and self-sacrificing love of a brute, which goes directly to the heart of him who has had frequent occasion to test the paltry friendship and gossamer fidelity of mere Man.

I married early, and was happy to find in my wife a disposition not uncongenial with my own. Observing my partiality for domestic pets, she lost no opportunity of procuring those of the most agreeable kind. We had birds, gold fish, a fine dog, rabbits, a small monkey, and *a cat.*

This latter was a remarkably large and beautiful animal, entirely black, and sagacious to an astonishing degree. In speaking of his intelligence, my wife, who at heart was not a little tinctured with superstition, made frequent allusion to the ancient popular notion, which regarded all black cats as witches in disguise. Not that she was ever *serious* upon this point — and I mention the matter at all for no better reason than that it happens, just now, to be remembered.

Pluto — this was the cat's name — was my favorite pet and playmate. I alone fed him, and he attended me wherever I went about the house. It was even with difficulty that I could prevent him from following me through the streets.

Our friendship lasted, in this manner, for several years, during which my general temperament and character — through the instrumentality of the Fiend Intemperance — had (I blush to confess it) experienced a radical alteration for the worse. I grew, day by day, more moody, more irritable, more regardless of the feelings of others. I suffered myself to use intemperate language to my wife. At length, I even offered her personal violence. My pets, of course, were made to feel the change in my disposition. I not only neglected, but ill-used them. For Pluto, however, I still retained sufficient regard to restrain me from maltreating him, as I made no scruple of maltreating the rabbits, the monkey, or even the dog, when by accident, or through affection, they came in my way. But my disease grew upon me — for what disease is like Alcohol! — and at length even Pluto, who was now becoming old, and consequently somewhat peevish — even Pluto began to experience the effects of my ill temper.

One night, returning home, much intoxicated, from one of my haunts about town, I fancied that the cat avoided my presence. I seized him; when, in his fright at my violence, he inflicted a slight wound upon my hand with his teeth. The fury of a demon instantly possessed me. I knew myself no longer. My original soul seemed, at once, to take its flight from my body; and a more than fiendish malevolence, gin-nurtured, thrilled every fibre of my frame. I took from my waist-coat-pocket a pen-knife, opened it, grasped the poor beast by the throat, and deliberately cut one of its eyes from the socket! I blush, I burn, I shudder, while I pen the damnable atrocity.

When reason returned with the morning — when I had slept off the fumes of the night's debauch — I experienced a sentiment half of horror, half of remorse, for the crime of which I had been guilty; but it was, at best, a feeble and equivocal feeling, and the soul remained untouched. I again plunged into excess, and soon drowned in wine all memory of the deed.

In the meantime the cat slowly recovered. The socket of the lost eye presented, it is true, a frightful appearance, but he no longer appeared to suffer any pain. He went about the house as usual, but, as might be expected, fled in extreme terror at my approach. I had so much of my old heart left, as to be at first grieved by this evident dislike on the part of a creature which had once so loved me. But this feeling soon gave place to irritation. And then came, as if to my final and irrevocable overthrow, the spirit of PERVERSENESS. Of this spirit philosophy takes no account. Yet I am not more sure that my soul lives, than I am that perverseness is one of the primitive impulses of the human heart — one of the indivisible primary faculties, or sentiments, which give direction to the character of Man.

Who has not, a hundred times, found himself committing a vile or a silly action, for no other reason than because he knows he should *not*? Have we not a perpetual inclination, in the teeth of our best judgment, to violate that which is *Law*, merely because we understand it to be such? This spirit of perverseness, I say, came to my final overthrow. It was this unfathomable longing of the soul *to vex itself*—to offer violence to its own nature—to do wrong for the wrong's sake only—that urged me to continue and finally to consummate the injury I had inflicted upon the unoffending brute. One morning, in cool blood, I slipped a noose about its neck and hung it to the limb of a tree;—hung it with the tears streaming from my eyes, and with the bitterest remorse at my heart;—hung it *because* I knew that it had loved me, and *because* I felt it had given me no reason of offence;—hung it *because* I knew that in so doing I was committing a sin—a deadly sin that would so jeopardize my immortal soul as to place it—if such a thing were possible—even beyond the reach of the infinite mercy of the Most Merciful and Most Terrible God.

On the night of the day on which this cruel deed was done, I was aroused from sleep by the cry of fire. The curtains of my bed were in flames. The whole house was blazing. It was with great difficulty that my wife, a servant, and myself, made our escape from the conflagration. The destruction was complete. My entire worldly wealth was swallowed up, and I resigned myself thenceforward to despair.

I am above the weakness of seeking to establish a sequence of cause and effect, between the disaster and the atrocity. But I am detailing a chain of facts—and wish not to leave even a possible link imperfect. On the day succeeding the fire, I visited the ruins. The walls, with one exception, had fallen in. This exception was found in a compartment wall, not very thick, which stood about the middle of the house, and against which had rested the head of my bed. The plastering had here, in great measure, resisted the action of the fire—a fact which I attributed to its having been recently spread. About this wall a dense crowd were collected, and many persons seemed to be examining a particular portion of it with very minute and eager attention. The words "strange!" "singular!" and other similar expressions, excited my curiosity. I approached and saw, as if graven in *bas relief* upon the white surface, the figure of a gigantic *cat*. The impression was given with an accuracy truly marvellous. There was a rope about the animal's neck.

When I first beheld this apparition—for I could scarcely regard it as less—my wonder and my terror were extreme. But at length reflection came to my aid. The cat, I remembered, had been hung in a garden adjacent to the house. Upon the alarm of fire, this garden had been immediately filled by the crowd—by some one of whom the animal must have been cut from the tree and thrown, through an open window, into my chamber. This had probably been done with the view of arousing me from sleep. The falling of other walls had compressed the victim of my cruelty into the substance of the freshly-spread plaster; the lime of which, with the flames, and the *ammonia* from the carcass, had then accomplished the portraiture as I saw it.

Although I thus readily accounted to my reason, if not altogether to my conscience, for the startling fact just detailed, it did not the less fail to make a deep impression upon my fancy. For months I could not rid myself of the phantasm of the cat; and, during this period, there came back into my spirit a half-sentiment that seemed, but was not, remorse. I went so far as to regret the loss of the animal, and to look about me, among the vile haunts which I now habitually frequented, for another pet of the same species, and of somewhat similar appearance, with which to supply its place.

One night as I sat, half stupified, in a den of more than infamy, my attention was suddenly drawn to some black object, reposing upon the head of one of the immense hogsheads of Gin, or of Rum, which constituted the chief furniture of the apartment. I had been looking steadily at the top of this hogshead for some minutes, and what now caused me surprise was the fact that I had not sooner perceived the object thereupon. I approached it, and touched it with my hand. It was a black cat — a very large one — fully as large as Pluto, and closely resembling him in every respect but one. Pluto had not a white hair upon any portion of his body; but this cat had a large, although indefinite splotch of white, covering nearly the whole region of the breast.

Upon my touching him, he immediately arose, purred loudly, rubbed against my hand, and appeared delighted with my notice. This, then, was the very creature of which I was in search. I at once offered to purchase it of the landlord; but this person made no claim to it — knew nothing of it — had never seen it before.

I continued my caresses, and, when I prepared to go home, the animal evinced a disposition to accompany me. I permitted it to do so; occasionally stooping and patting it as I proceeded. When it reached the house it domesticated itself at once, and became immediately a great favorite with my wife.

For my own part, I soon found a dislike to it arising within me. This was just the reverse of what I had anticipated; but I know not how or why it was — its evident fondness for myself rather disgusted and annoyed. By slow degrees, these feelings of disgust and annoyance rose into the bitterness of hatred. I avoided the creature; a certain sense of shame, and the remembrance of my former deed of cruelty, preventing me from physically abusing it. I did not, for some weeks, strike, or otherwise violently ill use it; but gradually — very gradually — I came to look upon it with unutterable loathing, and to flee silently from its odious presence, as from the breath of a pestilence.

What added, no doubt, to my hatred of the beast, was the discovery, on the morning after I brought it home, that, like Pluto, it also had been deprived of one of its eyes. This circumstance, however, only endeared it to my wife, who, as I have already said, possessed, in a high degree, that humanity of feeling which had once been my distinguishing trait, and the source of many of my simplest and purest pleasures.

With my aversion to this cat, however, its partiality for myself seemed to increase. It followed my footsteps with a pertinacity which it would be difficult to make the reader comprehend. Whenever I sat, it would crouch beneath my chair, or spring upon my knees, covering me with its loathsome caresses. If I arose to walk it would get between my feet and thus nearly throw me down, or, fastening its long and sharp claws in my dress, clamber, in this manner, to my breast. At such times, although I longed to destroy it with a blow, I was yet withheld from so doing, partly by a memory of my former crime, but chiefly — let me confess it at once — by absolute *dread* of the beast.

This dread was not exactly a dread of physical evil—and yet I should be at a loss how otherwise to define it. I am almost ashamed to own—yes, even in this felon's cell. I am almost ashamed to own—that the terror and horror with which the animal inspired me, had been heightened by one of the merest chimeras it would be possible to conceive. My wife had called my attention, more than once, to the character of the mark of white hair, of which I have spoken, and which constituted the sole visible difference between the strange beast and the one I had destroyed. The reader will remember that this mark, although large, had been originally very indefinite; but, by slow degrees—degrees nearly imperceptible, and which for a long time my Reason struggled to reject as fanciful—it had, at length, assumed a rigorous distinctness of outline. It was now the representation of an object that I shudder to name—and for this, above all, I loathed, and dreaded, and would have rid myself of the monster *had I dared*—it was now, I say, the image of a hideous—of a ghastly thing—of the GALLOWS!—oh, mournful and terrible engine of Horror and of Crime—of Agony and of Death!

And now was I indeed wretched beyond the wretchedness of mere Humanity. And *a brute beast*—whose fellow I had contemptuously destroyed—*a brute beast* to work out for *me*—for me a man, fashioned in the image of the High God—so much of insufferable woe! Alas! neither by day nor by night knew I the blessing of Rest any more! During the former the creature left me no moment alone; and, in the latter, I started, hourly, from dreams of unutterable fear, to find the hot breath of *the thing* upon my face, and its vast weight—an incarnate Night-Mare that I had no power to shake off—incumbent eternally upon my *heart!*

Beneath the pressure of torments such as these, the feeble remnant of the good within me succumbed. Evil thoughts became my sole intimates—the darkest and most evil of thoughts. The moodiness of my usual temper increased to hatred of all things and of all mankind; while, from the sudden, frequent, and ungovernable outbursts of a fury to which I now blindly abandoned myself, my uncomplaining wife, alas! was the most usual and the most patient of sufferers.

One day she accompanied me, upon some household errand, into the cellar of the old building which our poverty compelled us to inhabit. The cat followed me down the steep stairs, and, nearly throwing me headlong, exasperated me to madness. Uplifting an axe, and forgetting, in my wrath, the childish dread which had hitherto stayed my hand, I aimed a blow at the animal which, of course, would have proved instantly fatal had it descended as I wished. But this blow was arrested by the hand of my wife. Goaded, by the interference, into a rage more than demoniacal, I withdraw my arm from her grasp and buried the axe in her brain. She fell dead upon the spot, without a groan.

This hideous murder accomplished, I set myself forthwith, and with entire deliberation, to the task of concealing the body. I knew that I could not remove it from the house, either by day or by night, without the risk of being observed by the neighbors. Many projects entered my mind. At one period I thought of cutting the corpse into minute fragments, and destroying them by fire. At another, I resolved to dig a grave for it in the floor of the cellar. Again, I deliberated about casting it in the well in the yard—about packing it in a box, as if merchandize, with the usual arrangements, and so getting a porter to take it from the house. Finally I hit upon what I considered a far better expedient than either of these. I determined to wall it up in the cellar — as the monks of the middle ages are recorded to have walled up their victims.

For a purpose such as this the cellar was well adapted. Its walls were loosely constructed, and had lately been plastered throughout with a rough plaster, which the dampness of the atmosphere had prevented from hardening. Moreover, in one of the walls was a projection, caused by a false chimney, or fireplace, that had been filled up, and made to resemble the rest of the cellar. I made no doubt that I could readily displace the bricks at this point, insert the corpse, and wall the whole up as before, so that no eye could detect anything suspicious.

And in this calculation I was not deceived. By means of a crow-bar I easily dislodged the bricks, and, having carefully deposited the body against the inner wall, I propped it in that position, while, with little trouble, I re-laid the whole structure as it originally stood. Having procured mortar, sand, and hair, with every possible precaution, I prepared a plaster which could not be distinguished from the old, and with this I very carefully went over the new brick-work. When I had finished, I felt satisfied that all was right. The wall did not present the slightest appearance of having been disturbed. The rubbish on the floor was picked up with the minutest care. I looked around triumphantly, and said to myself — "Here at least, then, my labor has not been in vain."

My next step was to look for the beast which had been the cause of so much wretchedness; for I had, at length, firmly resolved to put it to death. Had I been able to meet with it, at the moment, there could have been no doubt of its fate; but it appeared that the crafty animal had been alarmed at the violence of my previous anger, and forebore to present itself in my present mood. It is impossible to describe, or to imagine, the deep, the blissful sense of relief which the absence of the detested creature occasioned in my bosom. It did not make its appearance during the night — and thus for one night at least, since its introduction into the house, I soundly and tranquilly slept; aye, *slept* even with the burden of murder upon my soul!

The second and the third day passed, and still my tormentor came not. Once again I breathed as a freeman. The monster, in terror, had fled the premises forever! I should behold it no more! My happiness was supreme! The guilt of my dark deed disturbed me but little. Some few inquiries had been made, but these had been readily answered. Even a search had been instituted — but of course nothing was to be discovered. I looked upon my future felicity as secured.

Upon the fourth day of the assassination, a party of the police came, very unexpectedly, into the house, and proceeded again to make rigorous investigation of the premises. Secure, however, in the inscrutability of my place of concealment, I felt no embarrassment whatever. The officers bade me accompany them in their search. They left no nook or corner unexplored. At length, for the third or fourth time, they descended into the cellar. I quivered not a muscle. My heart beat calmly as that of one who slumbers in innocence. I walked the cellar from end to end. I folded my arms upon my bosom, and roamed easily to and fro. The police were thoroughly satisfied and prepared to depart. The glee at my heart was too strong to be restrained. I burned to say if but one word, by way of triumph, and to render doubly sure their assurance of my guiltlessness.

"Gentlemen," I said at last, as the party ascended the steps. "I delight to have allayed your suspicions. I wish you all health, and a little more courtesy. By the bye, gentlemen, this—this is a very well constructed house." [In the rabid desire to say something easily, I scarcely knew what I uttered at all.]—"I may say an *excellently* well constructed house. These walls—are you going, gentlemen?— these walls are solidly put together;" and here, through the mere phrenzy of bravado, I rapped heavily, with a cane which I held in my hand, upon that very portion of the brick-work behind which stood the corpse of the wife of my bosom.

But may God shield and deliver me from the fangs of the Arch-Fiend! No sooner had the reverberation of my blows sunk into silence, than I was answered by a voice from within the tomb!—by a cry, at first muffled and broken, like the sobbing of a child, and then quickly swelling into one long, loud, and continuous scream, utterly anomalous and inhuman—a howl—a wailing shriek, half of horror and half of triumph, such as might have arisen only out of hell, conjointly from the throats of the damned in their agony and of the demons that exult in the damnation.

Of my own thoughts it is folly to speak. Swooning, I staggered to the opposite wall. For one instant the party upon the stairs remained motionless, through extremity of terror and of awe. In the next, a dozen stout arms were toiling at the wall. It fell bodily. The corpse, already greatly decayed and clotted with gore, stood erect before the eyes of the spectators. Upon its head, with red extended mouth and solitary eye of fire, sat the hideous beast whose craft had seduced me into murder, and whose informing voice had consigned me to the hangman. I had walled the monster up within the tomb!

[1843]

Study and Writing Questions

1. What is the NARRATOR'S stated MOTIVE in telling this STORY? What is his actual motive?
2. What do we learn about the narrator from his DESCRIPTIONS of the causes of his ACTIONS?
3. What is the relationship of the wife to the successive cats from her VIEWPOINT? from the narrator's viewpoint? from your viewpoint?
4. How is AUTHORITY manipulated in this narrative? Many of the matters related in the story, such as the white fur patch turning into a portrait of a gallows and the creation of the *bas relief* of a hanged cat in the plaster of the bedroom wall, seem highly unlikely. What are some other unlikely matters? Which of these do you accept as having happened and which do you reject? Why?
5. To what extent might the THEME of this NARRATIVE be each of the following: a) the "spirit of perverseness," b) the relationship of perception and logic, and c) the nature of justice?

See also Questions for Contrast and Comparison: 17, 18, 19, 20, 21, 23, 24, 45, 47, 61, 71, 79, 92, 101, 117, 119, and 240.

The Purloined Letter

Nil sapientiae odiosius acumine nimio.

—SENECA

At Paris, just after dark one gusty evening in the autumn of 18—, I was enjoying the twofold luxury of meditation and a meerschaum, in company with my friend C. Auguste Dupin, in his little back library, or book-closet, *au troisième*, No. 33, *Rue Dunôt, Faubourg St. Germain.* For one hour at least we had maintained a profound silence; while each, to any casual observer, might have seemed intently and exclusively occupied with the curling eddies of smoke that oppressed the atmosphere of the chamber. For myself, however, I was mentally discussing certain topics which had formed matter for conversation between us at an earlier period of the evening; I mean the affair of the Rue Morgue, and the mystery attending the murder of Marie Rogêt. I looked upon it, therefore, as something of a coincidence, when the door of our apartment was thrown open and admitted our old acquaintance, Monsieur G——, the Prefect of the Parisian police.

We gave him a hearty welcome; for there was nearly half as much of the entertaining as of the contemptible about the man, and we had not seen him for several years. We had been sitting in the dark, and Dupin now arose for the purpose of lighting a lamp, but sat down again, without doing so, upon G.'s saying that he had called to consult us, or rather to ask the opinion of my friend, about some official business which had occasioned a great deal of trouble.

"If it is any point requiring reflection," observed Dupin, as he forbore to enkindle the wick, "we shall examine it to better purpose in the dark."

"That is another of your odd notions," said the Prefect, who had a fashion of calling every thing "odd" that was beyond his comprehension, and thus lived amid an absolute legion of "oddities."

"Very true," said Dupin, as he supplied his visiter with a pipe, and rolled towards him a comfortable chair.

"And what is the difficulty now?" I asked. "Nothing more in the assassination way, I hope?"

"Oh no; nothing of that nature. The fact is, the business is *very* simple indeed, and I make no doubt that we can manage it sufficiently well ourselves; but then I thought Dupin would like to hear the details of it, because it is so excessively *odd.*"

"Simple and odd," said Dupin.

"Why, yes; and not exactly that, either. The fact is, we have all been a good deal puzzled because the affair *is* so simple, and yet baffles us altogether."

"Perhaps it is the very simplicity of the thing which puts you at fault," said my friend.

"What nonsense you *do* talk!" replied the Prefect, laughing heartily.

"Perhaps the mystery is a little *too* plain," said Dupin.

"Oh, good heavens! who ever heard of such an idea?"

"A little *too* self-evident."

"Ha! ha! ha!—ha! ha! ha!—ho! ho! ho!"—roared our visitor, profoundly amused, "oh, Dupin, will be the death of me yet!"

"And what, after all, *is* the matter on hand?" I asked.

"Why, I will tell you," replied the Prefect, as he gave a long, steady, and contemplative puff, and settled himself in his chair. "I will tell you in a few words; but, before I begin, let me caution you that this is an affair demanding the greatest secrecy, and that I should most probably lose the position I now hold, were it known that I confided it to any one."

"Proceed," said I.

"Or not," said Dupin.

"Well, then; I have received personal information, from a very high quarter, that a certain document of the last importance, has been purloined from the royal apartments. The individual who purloined it is known; this beyond a doubt; he was seen to take it. It is known, also, that it still remains in his possession."

"How is this known?" asked Dupin.

"It is clearly inferred," replied the Prefect, "from the nature of the document, and from the non-appearance of certain results which would at once arise from its passing *out* of the robber's possession; — that is to say, from his employing it as he must design in the end to employ it."

"Be a little more explicit," I said.

"Well, I may venture so far as to say that the paper gives its holder a certain power in a certain quarter where such power is immensely valuable." The Prefect was fond of the cant of diplomacy.

"Still I do not quite understand," said Dupin.

"No? Well; the disclosure of the document to a third person, who shall be nameless, would bring in question the honor of a personage of most exalted station; and this fact gives the holder of the document an ascendancy over the illustrious personage whose honor and peace are so jeopardized."

"But this ascendancy," I interposed, "would depend upon the robber's knowledge of the loser's knowledge of the robber. Who would dare—"

"The thief," said G., "is the Minister D——, who dares all things, those unbecoming as well as those becoming a man. The method of the theft was not less ingenious than bold. The document in question—a letter, to be frank—had been received by the personage robbed while alone in the royal *boudoir*. During its perusal she was suddenly interrupted by the entrance of the other exalted personage from whom especially it was her wish to conceal it. After a hurried and vain endeavor to thrust it in a drawer, she was forced to place it, open as it was, upon a table. The address, however, was uppermost, and, the contents thus unexposed, the letter escaped notice. At this juncture enters the Minister D——. His lynx eye immediately perceives the paper, recognises the handwriting of the address, observes the confusion of the personage addressed, and fathoms her secret. After some business transactions, hurried through in his ordinary manner, he produces a letter somewhat similar to the one in question, opens it, pretends to read it, and then places it in close juxtaposition to the other. Again he converses, for some fifteen minutes, upon the public affairs. At length, in taking leave, he takes also from the table the letter to which he had no claim. Its rightful owner saw, but, of course, dared not call attention to the act, in the presence of the third personage who stood at her elbow. The minister decamped; leaving his own letter—one of no importance—upon the table."

"Here, then," said Dupin to me, "you have precisely what you demand to make the ascendancy complete — the robber's knowledge of the loser's knowledge of the robber."

"Yes," replied the Prefect; "and the power thus attained has, for some months past, been wielded, for political purposes, to a very dangerous extent. The personage robbed is more thoroughly convinced, every day, of the necessity of reclaiming her letter. But this, of course, cannot be done openly. In fine, driven to despair, she has committed the matter to me."

"Than whom," said Dupin, amid a perfect whirlwind of smoke, "no more sagacious agent could, I suppose, be desired, or even imagined."

"You flatter me," replied the Prefect; "but it is possible that some such opinion may have been entertained."

"It is clear," said I, "as you observe, that the letter is still in possession of the minister; since it is this possession, and not any employment of the letter, which bestows the power. With the employment the power departs."

"True," said G.; "and upon this conviction I proceeded. My first care was to make thorough search of the minister's hotel; and here my chief embarrassment lay in the necessity of searching without his knowledge. Beyond all things, I have been warned of the danger which would result from giving him reason to suspect our design."

"But," said I, "you are quite *au fait* in these investigations. The Parisian police have done this thing often before."

"O yes; and for this reason I did not despair. The habits of the minister gave me, too, a great advantage. He is frequently absent from home all night. His servants are by no means numerous. They sleep at a distance from their master's apartment, and, being chiefly Neapolitans, are readily made drunk. I have keys, as you know, with which I can open any chamber or cabinet in Paris. For three months a night has not passed, during the greater part of which I have not been engaged, personally, in ransacking the D—— Hôtel. My honor is interested, and, to mention a great secret, the reward is enormous. So I did not abandon the search until I had become fully satisfied that the thief is a more astute man than myself. I fancy that I have investigated every nook and corner of the premises in which it is possible that the paper can be concealed."

"But is it not possible," I suggested, "that although the letter may be in possession of the minister, as it unquestionably is, he may have concealed it elsewhere than upon his own premises?"

"This is barely possible," said Dupin. "The present peculiar condition of affairs at court, and especially of those intrigues in which D—— is known to be involved, would render the instant availability of the document — its susceptibility of being produced at a moment's notice — a point of nearly equal importance with its possession."

"It's susceptibility of being produced?" said I.

"That is to say, of being *destroyed*," said Dupin.

"True," I observed; "the paper is clearly then upon the premises. As for its being upon the person of the minister, we may consider that as out of the question."

"Entirely," said the Prefect. "He has been twice waylaid, as if by footpads, and his person rigorously searched under my own inspection."

"You might have spared yourself this trouble," said Dupin. "D——, I presume, is not altogether a fool, and, if not, must have anticipated these waylayings, as a matter of course."

"Not *altogether* a fool," said G., "but then he's a poet, which I take to be only one remove from a fool."

"True," said Dupin, after a long and thoughtful whiff from his meerschaum, "although I have been guilty of certain doggerel myself."

"Suppose you detail," said I, "the particulars of your search."

"Why the fact is, we took our time, and we searched *every where*. I have had long experience in these affairs. I took the entire building, room by room; devoting the nights of a whole week to each. We examined, first, the furniture of each apartment. We opened every possible drawer; and I presume you know that, to a properly trained police agent, such a thing as a *secret* drawer is impossible. Any man is a dolt who permits a 'secret' drawer to escape him in a search of this kind. The thing is *so* plain. There is a certain amount of bulk — of space — to be accounted for in every cabinet. Then we have accurate rules. The fiftieth part of a line could not escape us. After the cabinets we took the chairs. The cushions we probed with the fine long needles you have seen me employ. From the tables we removed the tops."

"Why so?"

"Sometimes the top of a table, or other similarly arranged piece of furniture, is removed by the person wishing to conceal an article; then the leg is excavated, the article deposited within the cavity, and the top replaced. The bottoms and tops of bed-posts are employed in the same way."

"But could not the cavity be detected by sounding?" I asked.

"By no means, if, when the article is deposited, a sufficient wadding of cotton be placed around it. Besides, in our case, we were obliged to proceed without noise."

"But you could not have removed — you could not have taken to pieces *all* articles of furniture in which it would have been possible to make a deposit in the manner you mention. A letter may be compressed into a thin spiral roll, not differing much in shape or bulk from a large knitting-needle, and in this form it might be inserted into the rung of a chair, for example. You did not take to pieces all the chairs?"

"Certainly not; but we did better — we examined the rungs of every chair in the hotel, and, indeed, the jointings of every description of furniture, by the aid of a most powerful microscope. Had there been any traces of recent disturbance we should not have failed to detect it instantly. A single grain of gimlet-dust, for example, would have been as obvious as an apple. Any disorder in the glueing — any unusual gaping in the joints — would have sufficed to insure detection."

"I presume you looked to the mirrors, between the boards and the plates, and you probed the beds and the bed-clothes, as well as the curtains and carpets."

"That of course; and when we had absolutely completed every particle of the furniture in this way, then we examined the house itself. We divided its entire surface into compartments, which we numbered, so that none might be missed; then we scrutinized each individual square inch throughout the premises, including the two houses immediately adjoining, with the microscope, as before."

"The two houses adjoining!" I exclaimed; "you must have had a great deal of trouble."

"We had; but the reward offered is prodigious."

"You include the *grounds* about the house?"

"All the grounds are paved with brick. They gave us comparatively little trouble. We examined the moss between the bricks, and found it undisturbed."

"You looked among D——'s papers, of course, and into the books of the library?"

"Certainly; we opened every package and parcel; we not only opened every book, but we turned over every leaf in each volume, not contenting ourselves with a mere shake, according to the fashion of some of our police officers. We also measured the thickness of every book-*cover*, with the most accurate admeasurement, and applied to each the most jealous scrutiny of the microscope. Had any of the bindings been recently meddled with, it would have been utterly impossible that the fact should have escaped observation. Some five or six volumes, just from the hands of the binder, we carefully probed, longitudinally, with the needles."

"You explored the floors beneath the carpets?"

"Beyond doubt. We removed every carpet, and examined the boards with the microscope."

"And the paper on the walls?"

"Yes."

"You looked into the cellars?"

"We did."

"Then," I said, "you have been making a miscalculation, and the letter is *not* upon the premises, as you suppose."

"I fear you are right there," said the Prefect. "And now, Dupin, what would you advise me to do?"

"To make a thorough re-search of the premises."

"That is absolutely needless," replied G——. "I am not more sure that I breathe than I am that the letter is not at the Hôtel."

"I have no better advice to give you," said Dupin. "You have, of course, an accurate description of the letter?"

"Oh yes!"—And here the Prefect, producing a memorandum-book, proceeded to read aloud a minute account of the internal, and especially of the external appearance of the missing document. Soon after finishing the perusal of this description, he took his departure, more entirely depressed in spirits than I had ever known the good gentleman before.

In about a month afterwards he paid us another visit, and found us occupied very nearly as before. He took a pipe and a chair and entered into some ordinary conversation. At length I said,—

"Well, but G——, what of the purloined letter? I presume you have at last made up your mind that there is no such thing as overreaching the Minister?"

"Confound him, say I—yes; I made the re-examination, however, as Dupin suggested—but it was all labor lost, as I knew it would be."

"How much was the reward offered, did you say?" asked Dupin.

"Why, a very great deal—a *very* liberal reward—I don't like to say how much, precisely; but one thing I *will* say, that I wouldn't mind giving my individual check for fifty thousand francs to any one who could obtain me that letter. The fact is, it is becoming of more and more importance every day; and the reward has been lately doubled. If it were trebled, however, I could do no more than I have done."

"Why, yes," said Dupin, drawlingly, between the whiffs of his meerschaum, "I really—think, G——, you have not exerted yourself—to the utmost in this matter. You might—do a little more, I think, eh?"

"How?—in what way?"

"Why—puff, puff—you might—puff, puff—employ counsel in the matter, eh?—puff, puff, puff. Do you remember the story they tell of Abernethy?"

"No; hang Abernethy!"

"To be sure! hang him and welcome. But, once upon a time, a certain rich miser conceived the design of spunging upon this Abernethy for a medical opinion. Getting up, for this purpose, an ordinary conversation in a private company, he insinuated his case to the physician, as that of an imaginary individual.

"'We will suppose,' said the miser, 'that his symptoms are such and such; now, doctor, what would *you* have directed him to take?'"

"'Take!' said Abernethy, 'why, take *advice*, to be sure.'"

"But," said the Prefect, a little discomposed, "I am *perfectly* willing to take advice, and to pay for it. I would *really* give fifty thousand francs to any one who would aid me in the matter."

"In that case," replied Dupin, opening a drawer, and producing a checkbook, "you may as well fill me up a check for the amount mentioned. When you have signed it, I will hand you the letter."

I was astounded. The Prefect appeared absolutely thunder-stricken. For some minutes he remained speechless and motionless, looking incredulously at my friend with open mouth, and eyes that seemed starting from their sockets; then, apparently recovering himself in some measure, he seized a pen, and after several pauses and vacant stares, finally filled up and signed a check for fifty thousand francs, and handed it across the table to Dupin. The latter examined it carefully and deposited it in his pocket-book; then, unlocking an *escritoire*, took thence a letter and gave it to the Prefect. This functionary grasped it in a perfect agony of joy, opened it with a trembling hand, cast a rapid glance at its contents, and then, scrambling and struggling to the door, rushed at length unceremoniously from the room and from the house, without having uttered a syllable since Dupin had requested him to fill up the check.

When he had gone, my friend entered into some explanations.

"The Parisian police," he said, "are exceedingly able in their way. They are persevering, ingenious, cunning, and thoroughly versed in the knowledge which their duties seem chiefly to demand. Thus, when G—— detailed to us his mode of searching the premises at the Hôtel D——, I felt entire confidence in his having made a satisfactory investigation—so far as his labors extended."

"So far as his labors extended?" said I.

"Yes," said Dupin. "The measures adopted were not only the best of their kind, but carried out to absolute perfection. Had the letter been deposited within the range of their search, these fellows would, beyond a question, have found it."

I merely laughed—but he seemed quite serious in all that he said.

"The measures, then," he continued, "were good in their kind, and well executed; their defeat lay in their being inapplicable to the case, and to the man. A certain set of highly ingenious resources are, with the Prefect, a sort of Procrustean bed, to which he forcibly adapts his designs. But he perpetually errs by being too deep or too shallow, for the matter in hand; and many a schoolboy is a better reasoner than he. I knew one about eight years of age, whose success at guessing in the game of 'even and odd' attracted universal admiration. This game is simple, and is played with marbles. One player holds in his hand a number of these toys, and demands of another whether that number is even or odd. If the guess is right, the guesser wins one; if wrong, he loses one. The boy to whom I allude won all the marbles of the school. Of course he had some principle of guessing; and this lay in mere observation and admeasurement of the astuteness of his opponents. For example, an arrant simpleton is his opponent, and, holding up his closed hand, asked, 'are they even or odd?' Our schoolboy replies, 'odd,' and loses; but upon the second trial he wins, for he then says to himself, 'the simpleton had them even upon the first trial, and his amount of cunning is just sufficient to make him have them odd upon the second; I will therefore guess odd;'—he guesses odd, and wins. Now, with a simpleton a degree above the first, he would have reasoned thus: 'This fellow finds that in the first instance I guessed odd, and, in the second, he will propose to himself upon the first impulse, a simple variation from even to odd, as did the first simpleton; but then a second thought will suggest that this is too simple a variation, and finally he will decide upon putting it even as before. I will therefore guess even;'—he guesses even, and wins. Now this mode of reasoning in the schoolboy, whom his fellows termed 'lucky,'—what, in its last analysis, is it?"

"It is merely," I said, "an identification of the reasoner's intellect with that of his opponent."

"It is,'" said Dupin; "and, upon inquiring of the boy by what means he effected the *thorough* identification in which his success consisted, I received answer as follows: 'When I wish to find out how wise, or how stupid, or how good, or how wicked is any one, or what are his thoughts at the moment, I fashion the expression of my face, as accurately as possible, in accordance with the expression of his, and then wait to see what thoughts or sentiments arise in my mind or heart, as if to match or correspond with the expression.' This response of the schoolboy lies at the bottom of all the spurious profundity which has been attributed to Rochefoueauld, to La Bongive, to Machiavelli, and to Campanella."

"And the identification," I said, "of the reasoner's intellect with that of his opponent, depends, if I understand you aright, upon the accuracy with which the opponent's intellect is admeasured."

"For its practical value it depends upon this," replied Dupin; "and the Prefect and his cohort fail so frequently, first, by default of this identification, and, secondly, by ill-admeasurement, or rather through non-admeasurement, of the intellect with which they are engaged. They consider only their *own* ideas of ingenuity; and, in searching for anything hidden, advert only to the modes in which *they* would have hidden it. They are right in this much—that their own ingenuity is a faithful representative of that of the *mass*; but when the cunning of the individual felon is diverse in character from their own, the felon foils them, of course. This always happens when it is above their own, and very usually when it is below. They have no variation of principle in their investigations; at best, when urged by some unusual emergency—by some extraordinary reward—they extend or exaggerate their old modes of *practice*, without touching their principles. What, for example, in this case of D——, has been done to vary the principle of action? What is all this boring, and probing, and sounding, and scrutinizing with the microscope, and dividing the surface of the building into registered square inches—what is it all but an exaggeration *of the application* of the one principle or set of principles of search, which are based upon the one set of notions regarding human ingenuity, to which the Prefect, in the long routine of his duty, has been accustomed? Do you not see he has taken it for granted that *all* men proceed to conceal a letter,—not exactly in a gimlet-hole bored in a chair-leg—but, at least, in *some* out-of-the-way hole or corner suggested by the same tenor of thought which would urge a man to secrete a letter in a gimlet-hold bored in a chair-leg? And do you not see also, that such *recherchés* nooks for concealment are adapted only for ordinary occasions, and would be adopted only by ordinary intellects; for, in all cases of concealment, a disposal of the article concealed—a disposal of it in this *recherché* manner,—is, in the very first instance, presumable and presumed; and thus its discovery depends, not at all upon the acumen, but altogether upon the mere care, patience, and determination of the seekers; and where the case is of importance—or, what amounts to the same thing in the policial eyes, when the reward is of magnitude,—the qualities in question have *never* been known to fail. You will now understand what I meant in suggesting that, had the purloined letter been hidden any where within the limits of the Prefect's examination—in other words, had the principle of its concealment been comprehended within the principles of the Prefect—its discovery would have been a matter altogether beyond question. This functionary, however, has been thoroughly mystified; and the remote source of his defeat lies in the supposition that the Minister is a fool, because he has acquired renown as a poet. All fools are poets; this the Prefect *feels*; and he is merely guility of a *non distributio medii* in thence inferring that all poets are fools."

"But is this really the poet?" I asked, "There are two brothers, I know; and both have attained reputation in letters. The Minister I believe has written learnedly on the Differential Calculus. He is a mathematician, and no poet."

"You are mistaken; I know him well; he is both. As poet *and* mathematician, he would reason well; as mere mathematician, he could not have reasoned at all, and thus would have been at the mercy of the Prefect."

"You surprise me," I said, "by these opinions, which have been contradicted by the voice of the world. You do not mean to set at naught the well-digested idea of centuries. The mathematical reason has long been regarded as *the* reason *par excellence*."

"'*Il y a à parier*,'" replied Dupin, quoting from Chamfort, "'*que toute idée publique, toute convention reçue, est une sottise, car elle a convenu au plus grand nombre*.' The mathematicians, I grant you, have done their best to promulgate the popular error to which you allude, and which is none the less an error for its promulgation as truth. With an art worthy a better cause, for example, they have insinuated the term 'analysis' into application to algebra. The French are the originators of this particular deception; but if a term is of any importance—if words derive any value from applicability—then 'analysis' conveys 'algebra' about as much as, in Latin, '*ambitus*' implies 'ambition,' '*religio*' 'religion,' or '*homines honesti*,' a set of *honorable* men."

"You have a quarrel on hand, I see," said I, "with some of the algebraists of Paris; but proceed."

"I dispute the availability, and thus the value, of that reason which is cultivated in any especial form other than the abstractly logical. I dispute, in particular, the reason educed by mathematical study. The mathematics are the science of form and quantity; mathematical reasoning is merely logic applied to observation upon form and quantity. The great error lies in supposing that even the truths of what is called *pure* algebra, are abstract of general truth. And this error is so egregious that I am confounded at the universality with which it has been received. Mathematical axioms are *not* axioms of general truth. What is true of *relation* — of form and quantity — is often grossly false in regard to morals, for example. In this latter science it is very usually *untrue* that the aggregated parts are equal to the whole. In chemistry also the axiom fails. In the consideration of motive it fails; for two motives, each of a given value, have not, necessarily, a value when united, equal to the sum of their values apart. There are numerous other mathematical truths which are only truths within the limits of *relation*. But the mathematician argues, from his *finite truths*, through habit, as if they were of an absolutely general applicability — as the world indeed imagines them to be. Bryant, in his very learned 'Mythology,' mentions an analogous source of error, when he says that 'although the Pagan fables are not believed, yet we forget ourselves continually, and make inferences from them as existing realities.' With the algebraists, however, who are Pagans themselves, the 'Pagan fables' *are* believed, and the inferences are made, not so much through lapse of memory, as through an unaccountable addling of the brains. In short, I never yet encountered the mere mathematician who could be trusted out of equal roots, or one who did not clandestinely hold it as a point of his faith that $x^2 + px$ was absolutely and unconditionally equal to q. Say to one of these gentlemen, by way of experiment, if you please, that you believe occasions may occur where $x^2 + px$ is *not* altogether equal to q, and, having made him understand what you mean, get out of his reach as speedily as convenient, for, beyond doubt, he will endeavor to knock you down.

"I mean to say," continued Dupin, while I merely laughed at his last observations, "that if the Minister had been no more than a mathematician, the Prefect would have been under no necessity of giving me this check. I knew him, however, as both mathematician and poet, and my measures were adapted to his capacity, with reference to the circumstances by which he was surrounded. I knew him as a courtier, too, and as a bold *intriguant*. Such a man, I considered, could not fail to be aware of the ordinary policial modes of action. He could not have failed to anticipate — and events have proved that he did not fail to anticipate — the waylayings to which he was subjected. He must have foreseen, I reflected, the secret investigations of his premises. His frequent absences from home at night, which were hailed by the Prefect as certain aids to his success, I regarded only as *ruses*, to afford opportunity for thorough search to the police, and thus the sooner to impress them with the conviction to which G——, in fact, did finally arrive — the conviction that the letter was not upon the premises. I felt, also, that the whole train of thought, which I was at some pains in detailing to you just now, concerning the invariable principle of policial action in searches for articles concealed—I felt that this whole train of thought would necessarily pass through the mind of the Minister. It would imperatively lead him to despise all the ordinary *nooks* of concealment. He could not, I reflected, be so weak as not to see that the most intricate and remote recess of his hotel would be as open as his commonest closets to the eyes, to the probes, to the gimlets, and to the microscopes of the Prefect. I saw, in fine, that he would be driven, as a matter of course, to *simplicity*, if not deliberately induced to it as a matter of choice. You will remember, perhaps, how desperately the Prefect laughed when I suggested, upon our first interview, that it was just possible this mystery troubled him so much on account of its being so *very* self-evident."

"Yes," said I, "I remember his merriment well. I really thought he would have fallen into convulsions."

"The material world," continued Dupin, "abounds with very strict analogies to the immaterial; and thus some color of truth has been given to the rhetorical dogma, that metaphor, or simile, may be made to strengthen an argument, as well as to embellish a description. The principle of the *vis inertiae*, for example, seems to be identical in physics and metaphysics. It is not more true in the former, that a large body is with more difficulty set in motion than a smaller one, and that its subsequent *momentum* is commensurate with this difficulty, than it is, in the latter, that intellects of the vaster capacity, while more forcible, more constant, and more eventful in their movements than those of inferior grade, are yet the less readily moved, and more embarrassed and full of hesitation in the first few steps of their progress. Again: have you ever noticed which of the street signs, over the shop doors, are the most attractive of attention?"

"I have never given the matter a thought," I said.

"There is a game of puzzles," he resumed, "which is played upon a map. One party playing requires another to find a given word—the name of town, river, state or empire—any word, in short, upon the motley and perplexed surface of the chart. A novice in the game generally seeks to embarrass his opponents by giving them the most minutely lettered names; but the adept selects such words as stretch, in large characters, from one end of the chart to the other. These, like the over-largely lettered signs and placards of the street, escape observation by dint of being excessively obvious; and here the physical oversight is precisely analogous with the moral inapprehension by which the intellect suffers to pass unnoticed those considerations which are too obtrusively and too palpably self-evident. But this is a point, it appears, somewhat above or beneath the understanding of the Prefect. He never once thought it probable, or possible, that the Minister had deposited the letter immediately beneath the nose of the whole world, by way of best preventing any portion of that world from perceiving it.

"But the more I reflected upon the daring, dashing, and discriminating ingenuity of D——; upon the fact that the document must always have been *at hand*, if he intended to use it to good purpose; and upon the decisive evidence, obtained by the Prefect, that it was not hidden within the limits of that dignitary's ordinary search—the more satisfied I became that, to conceal this letter, the Minister had resorted to the comprehensive and sagacious expedient of not attempting to conceal it at all.

"Full of these ideas, I prepared myself with a pair of green spectacles, and called one fine morning, quite by accident, at the Ministerial hotel. I found D —— at home, yawning, lounging, and dawdling, as usual, and pretending to be in the last extremity of *ennui*. He is, perhaps, the most really energetic human being now alive — but that is only when nobody sees him.

"To be even with him, I complained of my weak eyes, and lamented the necessity of the spectacles, under cover of which I cautiously and thoroughly surveyed the apartment, while seemingly intent only upon the conversation of my host.

"I paid special attention to a large writing-table near which he sat, and upon which lay confusedly, some miscellaneous letters and other papers, with one or two musical instruments and a few books. Here, however, after a long and very deliberate scrutiny, I saw nothing to excite particular suspicion.

"At length my eyes, in going the circuit of the room, fell upon a trumpery fillagree card-rack of pasteboard, that hung dangling by a dirty blue ribbon, from a little brass knob just beneath the middle of the mantel-piece. In this rack, which had three or four compartments, were five or six visiting cards and a solitary letter. This last was much soiled and crumpled. It was torn nearly in two, across the middle — as if a design, in the first instance, to tear it entirely up as worthless, had been altered, or stayed, in the second. It had a large black seal, bearing the D —— cipher *very* conspicuously, and was addressed, in a diminutive female hand, to D ——, the minister, himself. It was thrust carelessly, and even, as it seemed, contemptuously, into one of the upper divisions of the rack.

"No sooner had I glanced at this letter, than I concluded it to be that of which I was in search. To be sure, it was, to all appearance, radically different from the one of which the Prefect had read us so minute a description. Here the seal was large and black, with the D —— cipher; there it was small and red, with the ducal arms of the S —— family. Here, the address, to the Minister, was diminutive and feminine; there the superscription, to a certain royal personage, was markedly bold and decided; the size alone formed a point of correspondence. But, then, the *radicalness* of these differences, which was excessive; the dirt; the soiled and torn condition of the paper, so inconsistent with the *true* methodical habits of D ——, and so suggestive of a design to delude the beholder into an idea of the worthlessness of the document; these things, together with the hyperobtrusive situation of this document, full in the view of every visiter, and thus exactly in accordance with the conclusions to which I had previously arrived; these things, I say, were strongly corroborative of suspicion, in one who came with the intention to suspect.

"I protracted my visit as long as possible, and, while I maintained a most animated discussion with the Minister, on a topic which I knew well had never failed to interest and excite him, I kept my attention really riveted upon the letter. In this examination, I committed to memory its external appearance and arrangement in the rack; and also fell, at length, upon a discovery which set at rest whatever trivial doubt I might have entertained. In scrutinizing the edges of the paper, I observed them to be more *chafed* than seemed necessary. They presented the *broken* appearance which is manifested when a stiff paper, having been once folded and pressed with a folder, is refolded in a reversed direction, in the same creases or edges which had formed the original fold. This discovery was sufficient. It was clear to me that the letter had been turned, as a glove, inside out, re-directed, and re-sealed. I bade the Minister good morning, and took my departure at once, leaving a gold snuff-box upon the table.

"The next morning I called for the snuff-box, when we resumed, quite eagerly, the conversation of the preceding day. While thus engaged, however, a loud report, as if of a pistol, was heard immediately beneath the windows of the hotel, and was succeeded by a series of fearful screams, and the shoutings of a mob. D —— rushed to a casement, threw it open, and looked out. In the mean-time, I stepped to the card-rack, took the letter, put it in my pocket, and replaced it by a *fac-simile*, (so far as regards externals,) which I had carefully prepared at my lodgings; imitating the D —— cipher, very readily, by means of a seal formed of bread.

"The disturbance in the street had been occasioned by the frantic behavior of a man with a musket. He had fired it among a crowd of women and children. It proved, however, to have been without ball, and the fellow was suffered to go his way as a lunatic or a drunkard. When he had gone, D —— came from the window, whither I had followed him immediately upon securing the object in view. Soon afterwards I bade him farewell. The pretended lunatic was a man in my own pay."

"But what purpose had you," I asked, "in replacing the letter by a *fac-simile?* Would it not have been better, at the first visit, to have seized it openly, and departed?"

"D —— ," replied Dupin, "is a desperate man, and a man of nerve. His hotel, too, is not without attendants devoted to his interests. Had I made the wild attempt you suggest, I might never have left the Ministerial presence alive. The good people of Paris might have heard of me no more. But I had an object apart from these considerations. You know my political prepossessions. In this matter, I act as a partisan of the lady concerned. For eighteen months the Minister has had her in his power. She has now him in hers; since, being unaware that the letter is not in his possession, he will proceed with his exactions as if it was. Thus will he inevitably commit himself, at once, to his political destruction. His downfall, too, will not be more precipitate than awkward. It is all very well to talk about the *facilis descensus Averni*; but in all kinds of climbing, as Catalani said of singing, it is far more easy to get up than to come down. In the present instance I have no sympathy—at least no pity—for him who descends. He is that *monstrum horrendum*, an unprincipled man of genius. I confess, however, that I should like very well to know the precise character of his thoughts, when, being defied by her whom the Prefect terms 'a certain personage,' he is reduced to opening the letter which I left for him in the card-rack."

"How? did you put any thing particular in it?"

"Why—it did not seem altogether right to leave the interior blank—that would have been insulting. D —— , at Vienna once, did me an evil turn, which I told him, quite good-humoredly, that I should remember. So, as I knew he would feel some curiosity in regard to the identity of the person who had outwitted him, I thought it a pity not to give him a clue. He is well acquainted with my MS., and I just copied into the middle of the blank sheet the words—

——*Un dessein si funeste,*
S'il n'est digne d'Atrée, est digne de Thyeste.

They are to be found in Crébillon's *Atrée*."

[1845]

Study and Writing Questions

1. What does this STORY suggest is the relationship between life and games?
2. Why does Poe use so many foreign language quotations?
3. Does this story change on rereading? Explain.
4. What is the importance of justice in this NARRATIVE?
5. What is the importance of narrative VIEWPOINT in this narrative? Why, for example, does Poe create a nameless NARRATOR to tell the story rather than use Dupin?

See also Questions for Contrast and Comparison: 14, 16, 17, 18, 19, 48, 117, 148, 162, 183, 204, and 225.

The Facts in the Case of M. Valdemar

Of course I shall not pretend to consider it any matter for wonder, that the extraordinary case of M. Valdemar has excited discussion. It would have been a miracle had it not — especially under the circumstances. Through the desire of all parties concerned, to keep the affair from the public, at least for the present, or until we had farther opportunities for investigation — through our endeavors to effect this — a garbled or exaggerated account made its way into society, and became the source of many unpleasant misrepresentations, and, very naturally, of a great deal of disbelief.

It is now rendered necessary that I give the *facts* — as far as I comprehend them myself. They are, succinctly, these:

My attention, for the last three years, had been repeatedly drawn to the subject of Mesmerism; and, about nine months ago, it occurred to me, quite suddenly, that in the series of experiments made hitherto, there had been a very remarkable and most unaccountable omission: — no person had as yet been mesmerized *in articulo mortis*. It remained to be seen, first, whether, in such condition, there existed in the patient any susceptibility to the magnetic influence; secondly, whether, if any existed, it was impaired or increased by the condition; thirdly, to what extent, or for how long a period, the encroachments of Death might be arrested by the process. There were other points to be ascertained, but these most excited my curiosity — the last in especial, from the immensely important character of its consequences.

In looking around me for some subject by whose means I might test these particulars, I was brought to think of my friend, M. Ernest Valdemar, the well-known compiler of the "Bibliotheca Forensica," and author (under the *nom de plume* of Issachar Marx) of the Polish versions of "Wallenstein" and "Gargantua." M. Valdemar, who has resided principally at Harlaem, N. Y., since the year 1839, is (or was) particularly noticeable for the extreme spareness of his person — his lower limbs much resembling those of John Randolph; and, also, for the whiteness of his whiskers, in violent contrast to the blackness of his hair — the latter, in consequence, being very generally mistaken for a wig. His temperament was markedly nervous, and rendered him a good subject for mesmeric experiment. On two or three occasions I had put him to sleep with little difficulty, but was disappointed in other results which his peculiar constitution had naturally led me to anticipate. His will was at no period positively, or thoroughly, under my control, and in regard to *clairvoyance*, I could accomplish with him nothing to be relied upon. I always attributed my failure at these points to the disordered state of his health. For some months previous to my becoming acquainted with him, his physicians had declared him in a confirmed phthisis. It was his custom, indeed, to speak calmly of his approaching dissolution, as of a matter neither to be avoided nor regretted.

When the ideas to which I have alluded first occurred to me, it was of course very natural that I should think of M. Valdemar. I knew the steady philosophy of the man too well to apprehend any scruples from *him*; and he had no relatives in America who would be likely to interfere. I spoke to him frankly upon the subject; and, to my surprise, his interest seemed vividly excited. I say to my surprise; for, although he had always yielded his person freely to my experiments, he had never before given me any tokens of sympathy with what I did. His disease was of that character which would admit of exact calculation in respect to the epoch of its termination in death; and it was finally arranged between us that he would send for me about twenty-four hours before the period announced by his physicians as that of his decease.

It is now rather more than seven months since I received, from M. Valdemar himself, the subjoined note:

My dear P——,

You may as well come *now*. D—— and F—— are agreed that I cannot hold out beyond tomorrow midnight; and I think they have hit the time very nearly.

VALDEMAR

I received this note within half an hour after it was written, and in fifteen minutes more I was in the dying man's chamber. I had not seen him for ten days, and was appalled by the fearful alteration which the brief interval had wrought in him. His face wore a leaden hue; the eyes were utterly lustreless; and the emaciation was so extreme that the skin had been broken through by the cheek-bones. His expectoration was excessive. The pulse was barely perceptible. He retained, nevertheless, in a very remarkable manner, both his mental power and a certain degree of physical strength. He spoke with distinctness — took some palliative medicines without aid — and, when I entered the room, was occupied in penciling memoranda in a pocket-book. He was propped up in the bed by pillows. Doctors D—— and F—— were in attendance.

After pressing Valdemar's hand, I took these gentlemen aside, and obtained from them a minute account of the patient's condition. The left lung had been for eighteen months in a semi-osseous or cartilaginous state, and was, of course, entirely useless for all purposes of vitality. The right, in its upper portion, was also partially, if not thoroughly, ossified, while the lower region was merely a mass of purulent tubercles, running one into another. Several extensive perforations existed; and, at one point, permanent adhesion to the ribs had taken place. These appearances in the right lobe were of comparatively recent date. The ossification had proceeded with very unusual rapidity; no sign of it had been discovered a month before, and the adhesion had only been observed during the three previous days. Independently of the phthisis, the patient was suspected of aneurism of the aorta; but on this point the osseous symptoms rendered an exact diagnosis impossible. It was the opinion of both physicians that M. Valdemar would die about midnight on the morrow (Sunday). It was then seven o'clock on Saturday evening.

On quitting the invalid's bed-side to hold conversation with myself, Doctors D—— and F—— had bidden him a final farewell. It had not been their intention to return; but, at my request, they agreed to look in upon the patient about ten the next night.

When they had gone, I spoke freely with M. Valdemar on the subject of his approaching dissolution, as well as, more particularly, of the experiment proposed. He still professed himself quite willing and even anxious to have it made, and urged me to commence it at once. A male and a female nurse were in attendance; but I did not feel myself altogether at liberty to engage in a task of this character with no more reliable witnesses than these people, in case of sudden accident, might prove. I therefore postponed operations until about eight the next night, when the arrival of a medical student with whom I had some acquaintance, (Mr. Theodore L—— l,) relieved me from farther embarrassment. It had been my design, originally, to wait for the physicians; but I was induced to proceed, first, by the urgent entreaties of M. Valdemar, and secondly, by my conviction that I had not a moment to lose, as he was evidently sinking fast.

Mr. L—— l was so kind as to accede to my desire that he would take notes of all that occurred; and it is from his memoranda that what I now have to relate is, for the most part, either condensed or copied *verbatim*.

It wanted about five minutes of eight when, taking the patient's hand, I begged him to state, as distinctly as he could, to Mr. L—— l, whether he (M. Valdemar) was entirely willing that I should make the experiment of mesmerizing him in his then condition.

He replied feebly, yet quite audibly, "Yes, I wish to be mesmerized"—adding immediately afterwards, "I fear you have deferred it too long."

While he spoke thus, I commenced the passes which I had already found most effectual in subduing him. He was evidently influenced with the first lateral stroke of my hand across his forehead; but although I exerted all my powers, no farther perceptible effect was induced until some minutes after ten o'clock, when Doctors D—— and F—— called, according to appointment. I explained to them, in a few words, what I designed, and as they opposed no objection, saying that the patient was already in the death agony, I proceeded without hesitation— exchanging, however, the lateral passes for downward ones, and directing my gaze entirely into the right eye of the sufferer.

By this time his pulse was imperceptible and his breathing was stertorous, and at intervals of half a minute.

This condition was nearly unaltered for a quarter of an hour. At the expiration of this period, however, a natural although a very deep sigh escaped the bosom of the dying man, and the stertorous breathing ceased—that is to say, its stertorousness was no longer apparent; the intervals were undiminished. The patient's extremities were of an icy coldness.

At five minutes before eleven I perceived unequivocal signs of the mesmeric influence. The glassy roll of the eye was changed for that expression of uneasy *inward* examination which is never seen except in cases of sleep-waking, and which it is quite impossible to mistake. With a few rapid lateral passes I made the lids quiver, as in incipient sleep, and with a few more I closed them altogether. I was not satisfied, however, with this, but continued the manipulations vigorously, and with the fullest exertion of the will, until I had completely stiffened the limbs of the slumberer, after placing them in a seemingly easy position. The legs were at full length; the arms were nearly so, and reposed on the bed at a moderate distance from the loins. The head was very slightly elevated.

When I had accomplished this, it was fully midnight, and I requested the gentlemen present to examine M. Valdemar's condition. After a few experiments, they admitted him to be in an unusually perfect state of mesmeric trance. The curiosity of both the physicians was greatly excited. Dr. D—— resolved at once to remain with the patient all night, while Dr. F—— took leave with a promise to return at daybreak. Mr. L—— l and the nurses remained.

We left M. Valdemar entirely undisturbed until about three o'clock in the morning, when I approached him and found him in precisely the same condition as when Dr. F——— went away—that is to say, he lay in the same position; the pulse was imperceptible; the breathing was gentle (scarcely noticeable, unless through the application of a mirror to the lips); the eyes were closed naturally; and the limbs were as rigid and as cold as marble. Still, the general appearance was certainly not that of death.

As I approached M. Valdemar I made a kind of half effort to influence his right arm into pursuit of my own, as I passed the latter gently to and fro above his person. In such experiments with this patient I had never perfectly succeeded before; and assuredly I had little thought of succeeding now; but to my astonishment, his arm very readily, although feebly, followed every direction I assigned it with mine. I determined to hazard a few words of conversation.

"M. Valdemar," I said, "are you asleep?" He made no answer, but I perceived a tremor about the lips, and was thus induced to repeat the question, again and again. At its third repetition, his whole frame was agitated by a very slight shivering; the eyelids unclosed themselves so far as to display a white line of the ball; the lips moved sluggishly, and from between them, in a barely audible whisper, issued the words:

"Yes;—asleep now. Do not wake me!—let me die so!"

I here felt the limbs and found them as rigid as ever. The right arm, as before, obeyed the direction of my hand. I questioned the sleep-waker again:

"Do you still feel pain in the breast, M. Valdemar?"

The answer now was immediate, but even less audible than before:

"No pain—I am dying."

I did not think it advisable to disturb him farther just then, and nothing more was said or done until the arrival of Dr. F——— , who came a little before sunrise, and expressed unbounded astonishment at finding the patient still alive. After feeling the pulse and applying a mirror to the lips, he requested me to speak to the sleep-waker again. I did so, saying:

"M. Valdemar, do you still sleep?"

As before, some minutes elapsed ere a reply was made; and during the interval the dying man seemed to be collecting his energies to speak. At my fourth repetition of the question, he said very faintly, almost inaudibly:

"Yes; still asleep—dying."

It was now the opinion, or rather the wish, of the physicians, that M. Valdemar should be suffered to remain undisturbed in his present apparently tranquil condition, until death should supervene—and this, it was generally agreed, must now take place within a few minutes. I concluded, however, to speak to him once more, and merely repeated my previous question.

While I spoke, there came a marked change over the countenance of the sleep-waker. The eyes rolled themselves slowly open, the pupils disappearing upwardly; the skin generally assumed a cadaverous hue, resembling not so much parchment as white paper; and the circular hectic spots which, hitherto, had been strongly defined in the centre of each cheek, *went out* at once. I use this expression, because the suddenness of their departure put me in mind of nothing so much as the extinguishment of a candle by a puff of the breath. The upper lip, at the same time, writhed itself away from the teeth, which it had previously covered completely; while the lower jaw fell with an audible jerk, leaving the mouth widely extended, and disclosing in full view the swollen and blackened tongue. I presume that no member of the party then present had been unaccustomed to death-bed horrors; but so hideous beyond conception was the appearance of M. Valdemar at this moment, that there was a general shrinking back from the region of the bed.

I now feel that I have reached a point of this narrative at which every reader will be startled into positive disbelief. It is my business, however, simply to proceed.

There was no longer the faintest sign of vitality in M. Valdemar; and concluding him to be dead, we were consigning him to the charge of the nurses, when a strong vibratory motion was observable in the tongue. This continued for perhaps a minute. At the expiration of this period, there issued from the distended and motionless jaws a voice—such as it would be madness in me to attempt describing. There are, indeed, two or three epithets which might be considered as applicable to it in part; I might say, for example, that the sound was harsh, and broken and hollow; but the hideous whole is indescribable, for the simple reason that no similar sounds have ever jarred upon the ear of humanity. There were two particulars, nevertheless which I thought then, and still think, might fairly be stated as characteristic of the intonation—as well adapted to convey some idea of its unearthly peculiarity. In the first place, the voice seemed to reach our ears—at least mine—from a vast distance, or from some deep cavern within the earth. In the second place, it impressed me (I fear, indeed, that it will be impossible to make myself comprehended) as gelatinous or glutinous matters impress the sense of touch.

I have spoken both of "sound" and of "voice." I mean to say that the sound was one of distinct—of even wonderfully, thrillingly distinct—syllabification. M. Valdemar *spoke*—obviously in reply to the question I had propounded to him a few minutes before. I had asked him, it will be remembered, if he still slept. He now said:

"Yes;—no;—I *have been* sleeping—and now—now—*I am dead.*"

No person present even affected to deny, or attempted to repress, the unutterable, shuddering horror which these few words, thus uttered, were so well calculated to convey. Mr. L——l (the student) swooned. The nurses immediately left the chamber, and could not be induced to return. My own impressions I would not pretend to render intelligible to the reader. For nearly an hour, we busied ourselves, silently—without the utterance of a word—in endeavors to revive Mr. L——l. When he came to himself, we addressed ourselves again to an investigation of M. Valdemar's condition.

It remained in all respects as I have last described it, with the exception that the mirror no longer afforded evidence of respiration. An attempt to draw blood from the arm failed. I should mention, too, that this limb was no farther subject to my will. I endeavored in vain to make it follow the direction of my hand. The only real indication, indeed, of the mesmeric influence, was now found in the vibratory movement of the tongue, whenever I addressed M. Valdemar a question. He seemed to be making an effort to reply, but had no longer sufficient volition. To queries put to him by any other person than myself he seemed utterly insensible—although I endeavored to place each member of the company in mesmeric *rapport* with him. I believe that I have now related all that is necessary to an understanding of the sleep-waker's state at this epoch. Other nurses were procured; and at ten o'clock I left the house in company with the two physicians and Mr. L——l.

In the afternoon we all called again to see the patient. His condition remained precisely the same. We had now some discussion as to the propriety and feasibility of awakening him; but we had little difficulty in agreeing that no good purpose would be served by so doing. It was evident that, so far, death (or what is usually termed death) had been arrested by the mesmeric process. It seemed clear to us all that to awaken M. Valdemar would be merely to insure his instant, or at least his speedy dissolution.

From this period until the close of last week — *an interval of nearly seven months* — we continued to make daily calls at M. Valdemar's house, accompanied, now and then, by medical and other friends. All this time the sleeper-waker remained *exactly* as I have last described him. The nurses' attentions were continual.

It was on Friday last that we finally resolved to make the experiment of awakening, or attempting to awaken him; and it is the (perhaps) unfortunate result of this latter experiment which has given rise to so much discussion in private circles — to so much of what I cannot help thinking unwarranted popular feeling.

For the purpose of relieving M. Valdemar from the mesmeric trance, I made use of the customary passes. These, for a time, were unsuccessful. The first indication of revival was afforded by a partial descent of the iris. It was observed, as especially remarkable, that this lowering of the pupil was accompanied by the profuse out-flowing of a yellowish ichor (from beneath the lids) of a pungent and highly offensive odor.

It was now suggested that I should attempt to influence the patient's arm, as heretofore. I made the attempt and failed. Dr. F—— then intimated a desire to have me put a question. I did so, as follows:

"M. Valdemar, can you explain to us what are your feelings or wishes now?"

There was an instant return of the hectic circles on the cheeks; the tongue quivered, or rather rolled violently in the mouth (although the jaws and lips remained rigid as before;) and at length the same hideous voice which I have already described, broke forth:

"For God's sake! — quick! — quick! — put me to sleep — or, quick! — waken me! — quick! — I *say to you that I am dead!*"

I was thoroughly unnerved, and for an instant remained undecided what to do. At first I made an endeavor to re-compose the patient; but, failing in this through total abeyance of the will, I retraced my steps and as earnestly struggled to awaken him. In this attempt I soon saw that I should be successful — or at least I soon fancied that my success would be complete — and I am sure that all in the room were prepared to see the patient awaken.

For what really occurred, however, it is quite impossible that any human being could have been prepared.

As I rapidly made the mesmeric passes, amid ejaculations of "dead! dead!" absolutely *bursting* from the tongue and not from the lips of the sufferer, his whole frame at once — within the space of a single minute, or even less, shrunk

—crumbled—absolutely *rotted* away beneath my hands. Upon the bed, before that whole company, there lay a nearly liquid mass of loathsome—of detestable putridity.

[1845]

Study and Writing Questions

1. How does knowing that "Mesmerism" was regarded as a science at the time of Poe's writing affect your reading of the STORY?
2. This story uses a scientific RHETORIC, as in the doctor's description to P —— of Valdemar's condition. What is the effect of this rhetoric on our belief in the story's events? What evidence suggests that the story is *not* a scientifically accurate account?
3. To what extent is this NARRATIVE a satire of science, religion, the news media, or other targets?
4. What are examples of sexual SYMBOLISM in this narrative? How does this symbolism suggest Poe's THEME(s)?
5. P —— writes that "to awaken M. Valdemar would . . . insure . . . his speedy dissolution." On rereading, the word "dissolution" is clearly a pun. What are other differences between first and subsequent readings of this narrative? To what extent is the narrative about the ways that knowledge changes us?

See also Questions for Contrast and Comparison: 17, 18, 19, 22, 23, 29, 71, 72, 120, 122, 148, 181, 222, and 233.

■ **KATHERINE ANNE PORTER** (1890–1980), *whose mother died when she was two, was born in a small Texas town and raised by her paternal grandmother, who died when "Callie" was eleven, and her father. Educated at Southern private and convent schools, she eloped at sixteen but divorced at nineteen, running off to Chicago to begin nearly forty years of intermittent journalism as a reporter and reviewer in Texas, Colorado, and New York City, and as a correspondent in Mexico (where she pursued nativist art and politics from 1918–1921) and Europe. She supported herself in Texas (1914–1917) as a traveling ballad singer, stage actress, and bit player in films; suffered a near-fatal bout of influenza (1919) and perhaps later of tuberculosis; and married twice again, to a U.S. Foreign Service officer in Europe (1933–1938) and to a professor of English literature at Louisiana State University in Baton Rouge (1938–1942). Her one constant, from age fifteen on, was* SHORT STORY *writing, but she held back publication until 1922. After her first collection,* Flowering Judas *(1930), was acclaimed for its psychological subtlety and handling of symbol and myth, she published stories continually and served as writer-in-residence at Stanford University, the University of Michigan, and elsewhere. Her long-awaited allegorical* NOVEL, Ship of Fools *(1962), was a best-seller; her* Collected Stories *(1965) won both the Pulitzer Prize and the National Book Award.*

The Grave

The grandfather, dead for more than thirty years, had been twice disturbed in his long repose by the constancy and possessiveness of his widow. She removed his bones first to Louisiana and then to Texas as if she had set out to find her own burial place, knowing well she would never return to the places she had left. In Texas she set up a small cemetery in a corner of her first farm, and as the family connection grew, and oddments of relations came over from Kentucky to settle, it contained at last about twenty graves. After the grandmother's death, part of her land was to be sold for the benefit of certain of her children, and the cemetery happened to lie in the part set aside for sale. It was necessary to take up the bodies and bury them again in the family plot in the big new public cemetery, where the grandmother had been buried. At last her husband was to lie beside her for eternity, as she had planned.

The family cemetery had been a pleasant small neglected garden of tangled rose bushes and ragged cedar trees and cypress, the simple flat stones rising out of uncropped sweet-smelling wild grass. The graves were lying open and empty one burning day when Miranda and her brother Paul, who often went together to hunt rabbits and doves, propped their twenty-two Winchester rifles carefully against the rail fence, climbed over and explored among the graves. She was nine years old and he was twelve.

They peered into the pits all shaped alike with such purposeful accuracy, and looking at each other with pleased adventurous eyes, they said in solemn tones: "These were graves!" trying by words to shape a special, suitable emotion in their minds, but they felt nothing except an agreeable thrill of wonder: they were seeing a new sight, doing something they had not done before. In them both there was also a small disappointment at the entire commonplaceness of the actual spectacle. Even if it had once contained a coffin for years upon years, when the coffin was gone a grave was just a hole in the ground. Miranda leaped into the pit that had held her grandfather's bones. Scratching around aimlessly and pleasurably as any young animal, she scooped up a lump of earth and weighed it in her palm. It had a pleasantly sweet, corrupt smell, being mixed with cedar needles and small leaves, and as the crumbs fell apart, she saw a silver dove no larger than a hazel nut, with spread wings and a neat fan-shaped tail. The breast had a deep round hollow in it. Turning it up to the fierce sunlight, she saw that the inside of the hollow was cut in little whorls. She scrambled out, over the pile of loose earth that had fallen back into one end of the grave, calling to Paul that she had found something, he must guess what. . . His head appeared smiling over the rim of another grave. He waved a closed hand at her. "I've got something too!" They ran to compare treasures, making a game of it, so many guesses each, all wrong, and a final showdown with opened palms. Paul had found a thin wide gold ring carved with intricate flowers and leaves. Miranda was smitten at sight of the ring and wished to have it. Paul seemed more impressed by the dove. They made a trade, with some little bickering. After he had got the dove in his hand, Paul said, "Don't you know what this is? This is a screw head for a *coffin!* . . . I'll bet nobody else in the world has one like this!"

Miranda glanced at it without covetousness. She had the gold ring on her thumb; it fitted perfectly. "Maybe we ought to go now," she said, "maybe one of the niggers 'll see us and tell somebody." They knew the land had been sold, the cemetery was no longer theirs, and they felt like trespassers. They climbed back over the fence, slung their rifles loosely under their arms — they had been shooting at targets with various kinds of firearms since they were seven years old — and set out to look for the rabbits and doves or whatever small game might happen along. On these expeditions Miranda always followed at Paul's heels along the path, obeying instructions about handling her gun when going through fences; learning how to stand it up properly so it would not slip and fire unexpectedly; how to wait her time for a shot and not just bang away in the air without looking, spoiling shots for Paul, who really could hit things if given a chance. Now and then, in her excitement at seeing birds whizz up suddenly before her face, or a rabbit leap across her very toes, she lost her head, and almost without sighting she flung her rifle up and pulled the trigger. She hardly ever hit any sort of mark. She had no proper sense of hunting at all. Her brother would be often completely disgusted with her. "You don't care whether you get your bird or not," he said. "That's no way to hunt." Miranda could not understand his indignation. She had seen him smash his hat and yell with fury when he had missed his aim. "What I like about shooting," said Miranda, with exasperating inconsequence, "is pulling the trigger and hearing the noise."

"Then, by golly," said Paul, "why'n't you go back to the range and shoot at bulls-eyes?"

"I'd just as soon," said Miranda, "only like this, we walk around more."

"Well, you just stay behind and stop spoiling my shots," said Paul, who, when he made a kill, wanted to be certain he had made it. Miranda, who alone brought down a bird once in twenty rounds, always claimed as her own any game they got when they fired at the same moment. It was tiresome and unfair and her brother was sick of it.

"Now, the first dove we see, or the first rabbit, is mine," he told her. "And the next will be yours. Remember that and don't get smarty."

"What about snakes?" asked Miranda idly. "Can I have the first snake?"

Waving her thumb gently and watching her gold ring glitter, Miranda lost interest in shooting. She was wearing her summer roughing outfit: dark blue overalls, a light blue shirt, a hired-man's straw hat, and thick brown sandals. Her brother had the same outfit except his was a sober hickory-nut color. Ordinarily Miranda preferred her overalls to any other dress, though it was making rather a scandal in the countryside, for the year was 1903, and in the back country the law of female decorum had teeth in it. Her father had been criticized for letting his girls dress like boys and go careering around astride barebacked horses. Big sister Maria, the really independent and fearless one, in spite of her rather affected ways, rode at a dead run with only a rope knotted around her horse's nose. It was said the motherless family was running down, with the Grandmother no longer there to hold it together. It was known that she had discriminated against her son Harry in her will, and that he was in straits about money. Some of his old neighbors reflected with vicious satisfaction that now he would probably not be so stiffnecked, nor have any more high-stepping horses either. Miranda knew this, though she could not say how. She had met along the road old women of the kind who smoked corn-cob pipes, who had treated her grandmother with most sincere respect. They slanted their gummy old eyes side-ways at the granddaughter and said, "Ain't you ashamed of yoself, Missy? It's aginst the Scriptures to dress like that. Whut yo Pappy thinkin about?" Miranda, with her powerful social sense, which was like a fine set of antennae radiating from every pore of her skin, would feel ashamed because she knew well it was rude and ill-bred to shock anybody, even bad-tempered old crones, though she had faith in her father's judgment and was perfectly comfortable in the clothes. Her father had said, "They're just what you need, and they'll save your dresses for school . . ." This sounded quite simple and natural to her. She had been brought up in rigorous economy. Wastefulness was vulgar. It was also a sin. These were truths; she had heard them repeated many times and never once disputed.

Now the ring, shining with the serene purity of fine gold on her rather grubby thumb, turned her feelings against her overalls and sockless feet, toes sticking through the thick brown leather straps. She wanted to go back to the farmhouse, take a good cold bath, dust herself with plenty of Maria's violet talcum powder — provided Maria was not present to object, of course — put on the thinnest, most becoming dress she owned, with a big sash, and sit in a wicker chair under the trees. . . These things were not all she wanted, of course; she had vague stirrings of desire for luxury and a grand way of living which could not take precise form in her imagination but were founded on family legend of past wealth and leisure. These immediate comforts were what she could have, and she wanted them at once. She lagged rather far behind Paul, and once she thought of just turning back without a word and going home. She stopped, thinking that Paul would never do that to her, and so she would have to tell him. When a rabbit leaped, she let Paul have it without dispute. He killed it with one shot.

When she came up with him, he was already kneeling, examining the wound, the rabbit trailing from his hands. "Right through the head," he said complacently, as if he had aimed for it. He took out his sharp, competent bowie knife and started to skin the body. He did it very cleanly and quickly. Uncle Jimbilly knew how to prepare the skins so that Miranda always had fur coats for her dolls, for though she never cared much for her dolls she liked seeing them in fur coats. The children knelt facing each other over the dead animal. Miranda watched admiringly while her brother stripped the skin away as if he were taking off a glove. The flayed flesh emerged dark scarlet, sleek, firm; Miranda with thumb and finger felt the long fine muscles with the silvery flat strips binding them to the joints. Brother lifted the oddly bloated belly. "Look," he said, in a low amazed voice. "It was going to have young ones."

Very carefully he slit the thin flesh from the center ribs to the flanks, and a scarlet bag appeared. He slit again and pulled the bag open, and there lay a bundle of tiny rabbits, each wrapped in a thin scarlet veil. The brother pulled these off and there they were, dark gray, their sleek wet down lying in minute even ripples, like a baby's head just washed, their unbelievably small delicate ears folded close, their little blind faces almost featureless.

Miranda said, "Oh, I want to see," under her breath. She looked and looked—excited but not frightened, for she was accustomed to the sight of animals killed in hunting—filled with pity and astonishment and a kind of shocked delight in the wonderful little creatures for their own sakes, they were so pretty. She touched one of them ever so carefully, "Ah, there's blood running over them," she said and began to tremble without knowing why. Yet she wanted most deeply to see and to know. Having seen, she felt at once as if she had known all along. The very memory of her former ignorance faded, she had always known just this. No one had ever told her anything outright, she had been rather unobservant of the animal life around her because she was so accustomed to animals. They seemed simply disorderly and unaccountably rude in their habits, but altogether natural and not very interesting. Her brother had spoken as if he had known about everything all along. He may have seen all this before. He had never said a word to her, but she knew now a part at least of what he knew. She understood a little of the secret, formless intuitions in her own mind and body, which had been clearing up, taking form, so gradually and so steadily she had not realized that she was learning what she had to know. Paul said cautiously, as if he were talking about something forbidden: "They were just about ready to be born." His voice dropped on the last word. "I know," said Miranda, "like kittens. I know, like babies." She was quietly and terribly agitated, standing again with her rifle under her arm, looking down at the bloody heap. "I don't want the skin," she said, "I won't have it." Paul buried the young rabbits again in their mother's body, wrapped the skin around her, carried her to a clump of sage bushes, and hid her away. He came out again at once and said to Miranda, with an eager friendliness, a confidential tone quite unusual in him, as if he were taking her into an important secret on equal terms: "Listen now. Now you listen to me, and don't ever forget. Don't you ever tell a living soul that you saw this. Don't tell a soul. Don't tell Dad because I'll get into trouble. He'll say I'm leading you into things you ought not to do. He's always saying that. So now don't you go and forget and blab out sometime the way you're always doing . . . Now, that's a secret. Don't you tell."

Miranda never told, she did not even wish to tell anybody. She thought about the whole worrisome affair with confused unhappiness for a few days.

Then it sank quietly into her mind and was heaped over by accumulated thousands of impressions, for nearly twenty years. One day she was picking her path among the puddles and crushed refuse of a market street in a strange city of a strange country, when without warning, plain and clear in its true colors as if she looked through a frame upon a scene that had not stirred nor changed since the moment it happened, the episode of that far-off day leaped from its burial place before her mind's eye. She was so reasonlessly horrified she halted suddenly staring, the scene before her eyes dimmed by the vision back of them. An Indian vendor had held up before her a tray of dyed sugar sweets, in the shapes of all kinds of small creatures: birds, baby chicks, baby rabbits, lambs, baby pigs. They were in gay colors and smelled of vanilla, maybe. . . . It was a very hot day and the smell in the market, with its piles of raw flesh and wilting flowers, was like the mingled sweetness and corruption she had smelled that other day in the empty cemetery at home: the day she had remembered always until now vaguely as the time she and her brother had found treasure in the opened graves. Instantly upon this thought the dreadful vision faded, and she saw clearly her brother, whose childhood face she had forgotten, standing again in the blazing sunshine, again twelve years old, a pleased sober smile in his eyes, turning the silver dove over and over in his hands.

[1944]

Study and Writing Questions

1. Why does Paul want Miranda to keep the hunting episode a secret?
2. What connection is there between "the market street in a strange city in a strange country" and the opened family cemetery?
3. To what items in the STORY might the title refer? How does the title help us understand Miranda's perceptions at the end of the story?
4. Why are rabbits and doves always linked in this story?
5. Porter includes many details that distinguish gender roles in this NARRATIVE; for example, having the children trade "treasures" instead of simply finding the ones they will ultimately keep. What is the importance of gender in this narrative?

See also Questions for Contrast and Comparison: 36, 37, 38, 39, 52, 110, 158, and 220.

■ NAWAL EL SAADAWI (1931-) *was born in Kafr Tahla, Egypt, daughter of a housewife and the provincial controller of education. In* The Hidden Face of Eve: Women in the Arab World *(1977; English, 1979), she writes how at age six she and her sister were awakened one night and forced to undergo clitorectomy without anesthesia: "part of our body torn away by cold, unfeeling hands . . . [subject to] one of the measures by which the patriarchy reinforces the values of monogamy." Educated as a physician (M.D., University of Cairo, 1955), she has practiced medicine, and particularly women's medicine, and served with several United Nations agencies for health and women's affairs. Her forceful opposition to class and gender oppression led to her dismissal in 1972 as editor of* Health *magazine and as Director of Education for the Egyptian Ministry of Health. In her novel* Woman At Point Zero *(1975; English, 1983), set in Qanatir Women's Prison, an inmate tells her prison psychiatrist how she turned involuntary prostitution into economic freedom. El Saadawi was also briefly imprisoned in 1981 in Qanatir for her politics. Twice married and once divorced (1955–1956; 1964–), she has a child by each husband; both men are physicians, and her current husband is also a writer. She has practiced psychiatry full-time in Giza since 1980. Her stories are collected in English in a volume called* She Has No Place in Paradise *(1987).*

She Has No Place in Paradise

With the palm of her hand, she touched the ground beneath her but did not feel soil. She looked upwards, stretching her neck towards the light. Her face appeared long and lean, the skin so dark it was almost black.

She could not see her own face in the dark and held no mirror in her hand. But the white light fell onto the back of her hand so that it became white in turn. Her narrow eyes widened in surprise and filled with light. Thus widened and full of light, her eyes looked like those of a *houri.*

In astonishment, she turned her head to the right and to the left. A vast expanse between the leafy trees above her head as she sat in the shade and the stream of water like a strip of silver, its clusters of droplets like pearls, then that deep plate full of broth to the rim.

Her eyelids tightened to open her eyes to the utmost. The scene remained the same, did not alter. She touched her robe and found it to be as soft as silk. From the neck of her gown wafted the scent of musk or good perfume.

Her head and eyes were motionless for she feared that any blink of her eyelids would change the scene or that it would disappear as it had done before.

But from the corner of her eye, she could see the shade stretching endlessly before her, and green trees between the trunks of which she saw a house of red brick like a palace, with a marble staircase leading up to the bedroom.

She remained fixed to the spot, able neither to believe nor disbelieve. Nothing upset her more than the recurrence of the dream that she had died and woken to find herself in paradise. The dream seemed to her impossible, for dying seemed impossible, waking after death even more impossible and going to paradise the fourth impossibility.

She steadied her neck still more and from the corner of her eye stared into the light. The scene was still the same, unaltered. The red brick house, like that of the *Omda,* the towering staircase leading to the bedroom, the room itself bathed in white light, the window looking out onto distant horizons, the wide bed, its posts swathed in a curtain of silk, all were still there.

It was all so real it could not be denied. She stayed where she was, fearing to move and fearing to believe. Was it possible to die and waken so quickly and then go to paradise?

What she found hardest to believe was the speed of it all. Death, after all, was easy. Everybody died and her own death was easier than anyone's, for she had lived between life and death, closer to death than to life. When her mother gave birth to her, she lay on top of her with all her weight until she died; her father beat her on the head with a hoe until she died; she had gone into fever after each birth, even until the eighth child; when her husband kicked her in the stomach; when the blows of the sun penetrated under the bones of her head.

Life was hard and death for her was easier. Easier still was waking after death, for no one died and no one wakens; everyone dies and awakens, except an animal which dies and remains dead.

Her going to paradise was also impossible. But if not her, who would go to paradise? Throughout her life she had never done anything to anger Allah or His Prophet. She used to tie her frizzy black hair with a skein of wool into a plait; the plait she wrapped up in a white headscarf and her head she wrapped in a black shawl. Nothing showed from under her robe except the heel of her foot. From the moment of her birth until her death, she knew only the word: Okay.

Before dawn, when her mother slapped her as she lay, to go and carry dung-pats on her head, she knew only: Okay. If her father tied her to the water mill in place of the sick cow, she said only: Okay. She never raised her eyes to her husband's and when he lay on top of her when she was sick with fever, she uttered only the words: Okay.

She had never stolen or lied in her life. She would go hungry or die of hunger rather than take the food of others, even if it were her father's or brother's or husband's. Her mother would wrap up food for her father in a flat loaf of bread and make her carry it to the field on her head. Her husband's food was also wrapped up in a loaf by his mother. She was tempted, as she walked along with it, to stop under the shade of a tree and open the loaf; but she never once stopped. Each time she was tempted, she called on God to protect her from the Devil, until the hunger became unbearable and she would pick a bunch of wild grass from the side of the road which she would chew like gum, then swallow with a sip of water, filling the cup of her hand from the bank of the canal and drinking until she had quenched her thirst. Then, wiping her mouth on the sleeve of her robe, she would mutter to herself: Thank God, and repeat it three times. She prayed five times a day, her face to the ground, thanking God. If she were attacked by fever and her head filled with blood like fire, she would still praise Allah. On fast days, she would fast; on baking days, she would bake; on harvest days, she would harvest; on holy days, she would put on her mourning weeds and go to the cemetery.

She never lost her temper with her father or brother or husband. If her husband beat her to death and she returned to her father's house, her father would send her back to her husband. If she returned again, her father would beat her and *then* send her back. If her husband took her back and did not throw her out, and then beat her, she returned to her mother who would tell her: Go back, Zeinab. Paradise will be yours in the hereafter.

From the time she was born, she had heard the word 'paradise' from her mother. The first time she'd heard it, she was walking in the sun, a pile of dung on her head, the soles of her feet scorched by the earth. She pictured paradise as a vast expanse of shade without sun, without dung on her head, on her feet shoes like those of Hassanain, the neighbour's son, pounding the earth as he did, his hand holding hers, the two of them sitting in the shade.

When she thought of Hassanain, her imagination went no further than holding hands and sitting in the shade of paradise. But her mother scolded her and told her that neither their neighbour's son Hassanain, nor any other neighbour's son, would be in paradise, that her eyes would not fall on any man other than her father or brother, that if she died after getting married and went to paradise, only her husband would be there, that if her soul was tempted, awake or asleep, and her eye fell on a man other than her husband and even before he held her hand in his, she would not so much as catch a glimpse of paradise or smell it from a thousand metres . . .

From that time, whenever she lay down to sleep, she saw only her husband. In paradise, her husband did not beat her. The pile of dung was no longer on her head; neither did the earth burn the soles of her feet. Their black mud house became one of red brick, inside it a towering staircase, then a wide bed on which her husband sat, holding her hand in his.

Her imagination went no further than holding his hand in paradise. Never once in her life had her hand held her husband's. Eight sons and daughters she had conceived with him without once holding his hand. On summer nights, he lay in the fields; in the winter, he lay in the barn or above the oven. All night long, he slept on his back without turning. If he did turn, he would call to her in a voice like a jackal's: Woman! Before she could answer 'yes' or 'okay,' he would have kicked her over onto her back and rolled on top of her. If she made a sound or sighed, he would kick her again. If she did not sigh or make a sound, she would get a third kick, then a fourth until she did. His hand never chanced to hold hers nor his arm happen to stretch out to embrace her.

She had never seen a couple, human or otherwise, embrace except in the dovecot. When she went up there, on the top of the wall appeared a pair of doves, their beaks close together; or when she went down to the cattle pen or from behind the wall there appeared a pair — bull and cow or buffalo or dogs — and her mother brandishing a bamboo stick and whipping them, cursing the animals.

Never in her life had she taken the black shawl off her head nor the white scarf tied under the shawl, except when someone died, when she untied the scarf and pulled the black shawl around her head. When her husband died, she knotted the black shawl twice around her forehead and wore mourning weeds for three years. A man came to ask for her in marriage without her children. Her mother spat in disgust and pulled the shawl down over her forehead, whispering: It's shameful! Does a mother abandon her children for the sake of a man? The years passed by and a man came to ask for her hand in marriage, with her children. Her mother yelled at the top of her voice: What does a woman want in this world after she has become a mother and her husband dies?

One day, she wanted to take off the black shawl and put on a white scarf, but she feared that people would think she'd forgotten her husband. So she kept the black shawl and the mourning weeds and remained sad for her husband until she died of sadness.

She found herself wrapped in a silken shroud inside a coffin. From behind the funeral procession, she heard her mother's wailing like a howl in the night or like the whistle of a train: You'll meet up with your husband in paradise, Zeinab.

Then the noise stopped. She heard nothing but silence and smelled nothing but the soil. The ground beneath her became as soft as silk. She said: It must be the shroud. Above her head, she heard rough voices, like two men fighting. She did not know why they were fighting until she heard one of them mention her name and say that she deserved to go directly to paradise without suffering the torture of the grave. But the other man did not agree and insisted that she should undergo some torture, if only a little: She cannot go directly up to paradise. Everyone must go through the torture of the grave. But the first man insisted that she had done nothing to merit torture, that she had been one hundred percent faithful to her husband. The second man argued that her hair had shown from under her white headscarf, that she had dyed her hair red with henna, that the hennaed heels of her feet had shown from under her robe.

The first man retorted that her hair had never shown, that what his colleague had seen was only the skein of wool, that her robe had been long and thick, under it even thicker and longer underskirts, that no one had seen her heels red.

But his colleague argued, insisting that her red heels had enticed many of the village men.

The dispute between the two of them lasted all night. She lay face down on the ground, her nose and mouth pressed into the earth. She held her breath pretending to be dead. Her torture might be prolonged if it became clear that she had not died; death might save her. She heard nothing of what passed between them; nobody, human or spirit, can hear what happens in the grave after death. If one did happen to hear, one had to pretend not to have heard or not to have understood. The most serious thing to understand is that those two men are not angels of the grave or angels of any type, for it is not possible for angels to ignore the truth which everyone in the village with eyes to see could know: that her heels had never been red like those of the *Omda*'s daughter, but like her face and palms, were always cracked and as black as the soil.

The argument ended before dawn without torture. She thanked God when the voices stopped. Her body grew lighter and rose up as if in flight. She hovered as if in the sky, then her body fell and landed on soft, moist earth and she gasped: Paradise.

Cautiously, she raised her head and saw a vast expanse of green, and thick leafy trees, shade beneath them.

She sat up on the ground and saw the trees stretching endlessly before her. Fresh air entered her chest, expelling the dirt and dust and the smell of dung.

With a slight movement, she rose to her feet. Between the tree trunks she could see the house of red brick, the entrance before her very eyes.

She entered quickly, panting. She climbed the towering staircase panting. In front of the bedroom, she stopped for a moment to catch her breath. Her heart was beating wildly and her chest heaved.

The door was closed. She put out her hand carefully and pushed it. She saw the four posts of the bed, around them a silken curtain. In the middle, she saw a wide bed, on top of it her husband, sitting like a bridegroom. On his right, was a woman. On his left, another woman. Both of them wore transparent robes revealing skin as white as honey, their eyes filled with light, like the eyes of *houris*.

Her husband's face was not turned towards her, so he did not see her. Her hand was still on the door. She pulled it behind her and it closed. She returned to the earth, saying to herself: There is no place in paradise for a black woman.

[1987]

Study and Writing Questions

1. The words "death" and "died" are used many times in this NARRATIVE. What do they mean in context? What does the phrase in the last paragraph, "she returned to the earth," mean?
2. Most of the narrative is a FLASHBACK. What is the effect of this STRUCTURE on our reading?
3. "Black" is mentioned in the first and last paragraphs. What is the importance of this color in the STORY?
4. What is the role of Zeinab's mother in Zeinab's life and in the story?
5. Some readers might argue that this story is TRAGIC while others might argue that it is SENTIMENTAL. What evidence supports and/or contradicts these positions? What is your overall assessment of the narrative? Why?

See also Questions for Contrast and Comparison: 8, 43, 69, 70, 72, 150, 192, and 234.

LESLIE (MARMON) SILKO (1948–) *was born of mixed Pueblo Indian, white, and Mexican ancestry in Albuquerque, New Mexico, and raised fifty miles away in the Pueblo community of Old Laguna. Educated until the fifth grade in Bureau of Indian Affairs schools, and then through high school in Catholic schools, she attended the University of New Mexico (B.A. in English, 1969). There, as an undergraduate, she published her first story, "The Man to Send Rain Clouds," in the New Mexico Quarterly. She entered law school under a program to increase the number of Native American lawyers but soon returned to writing and the pursuit of graduate work in English. She taught English for two years at Navajo Community College in Many Farms, Arizona, while finishing the stories collected in Laguna Woman (1974). She then spent two years in Ketchikan, Alaska, working on Ceremony, her 1977 NOVEL about the struggle of a Native American Vietnam war veteran to intergrate his tribal and personal experiences. Since then she has taught at the Universities of New Mexico and Arizona and published Storyteller (1981), a collection of her own stories, poems, and retellings of traditional tribal TALES, and another novel, Almanac of the Dead (1991). Her achievements have been recognized by a MacArthur Foundation Fellowship. Divorced from John Silko, she has two sons.*

Yellow Woman

I

My thigh clung to his with dampness, and I watched the sun rising up through the tamaracks and willows. The small brown water birds came to the river and hopped across the mud, leaving brown scratches in the alkali-white crust. They bathed in the river silently. I could hear the water, almost at our feet where the narrow fast channel bubbled and washed green ragged moss and fern leaves. I looked at him beside me, rolled in the red blanket on the white river sand. I cleaned the sand out of the cracks between my toes, squinting because the sun was above the willow trees. I looked at him for the last time, sleeping on the white river sand.

I felt hungry and followed the river south the way we had come the afternoon before, following our footprints that were already blurred by lizard tracks and bug trails. The horses were still lying down, and the black one whinnied when he saw me but he did not get up—maybe it was because the corral was made out of thick cedar branches and the horses had not yet felt the sun like I had. I tried to look beyond the pale red mesas to the pueblo. I knew it was there, even if I could not see it, on the sand rock hill above the river, the same river that moved past me now and had reflected the moon last night.

The horse felt warm underneath me. He shook his head and pawed the sand. The bay whinnied and leaned against the gate trying to follow, and I remembered him asleep in the red blanket beside the river. I slid off the horse and tied him close to the other horse. I walked north with the river again, and the white sand broke loose in footprints over footprints.

"Wake up."

He moved in the blanket and turned his face to me with his eyes still closed. I knelt down to touch him.

"I'm leaving."

He smiled now, eyes still closed. "You are coming with me, remember?" He sat up now with his bare dark chest and belly in the sun.

"Where?"

"To my place."

"And will I come back?"

He pulled his pants on. I walked away from him, feeling him behind me and smelling the willows.

"Yellow Woman," he said.

I turned to face him. "Who are you?" I asked.

He laughed and knelt on the low, sandy bank, washing his face in the river. "Last night you guessed my name, and you knew why I had come."

I stared past him at the shallow moving water and tried to remember the night, but I could only see the moon in the water and remember his warmth around me.

"But I only said that you were him and that I was Yellow Woman—I'm not really her—I have my own name and I come from the pueblo on the other side of the mesa. Your name is Silva and you are a stranger I met by the river yesterday afternoon."

He laughed softly. "What happened yesterday has nothing to do with what you will do today, Yellow Woman."

"I know—that's what I'm saying—the old stories about the ka'tsina spirit and Yellow Woman can't mean us."

My old grandpa liked to tell those stories best. There is one about Badger and Coyote who went hunting and were gone all day, and when the sun was going down they found a house. There was a girl living there alone, and she had light hair and eyes and she told them that they could sleep with her. Coyote wanted to be with her all night so he sent Badger into a prairie-dog hole, telling him he thought he saw something in it. As soon as Badger crawled in, Coyote blocked up the entrance with rocks and hurried back to Yellow Woman.

"Come here," he said gently.

He touched my neck and I moved close to him to feel his breathing and to hear his heart. I was wondering if Yellow Woman had known who she was—if she knew that she would become part of the stories. Maybe she'd had another name that her husband and relatives called her so that only the ka'tsina from the north and the storytellers would know her as Yellow Woman. But I didn't go on; I felt him all around me, pushing me down into the white river sand.

Yellow Woman went away with the spirit from the north and lived with him and his relatives. She was gone for a long time, but then one day she came back and she brought twin boys.

"Do you know the story?"

"What story?" He smiled and pulled me close to him as he said this. I was afraid lying there on the red blanket. All I could know was the way he felt, warm, damp, his body beside me. This is the way it happens in the stories, I was thinking, with no thought beyond the moment she meets the ka'tsina spirit and they go.

"I don't have to go. What they tell in stories was real only then, back in time immemorial, like they say."

He stood up and pointed at my clothes tangled in the blanket. "Let's go," he said.

I walked beside him, breathing hard because he walked fast, his hand around my wrist. I had stopped trying to pull away from him, because his hand felt cool and the sun was high, drying the river bed into alkali. I will see someone, eventually I will see someone, and then I will be certain that he is only a man — some man from nearby — and I will be sure that I am not Yellow Woman. Because she is from out of time past and I live now and I've been to school and there are highways and pickup trucks that Yellow Woman never saw.

It was an easy ride north on horseback. I watched the change from the cottonwood trees along the river to the junipers that brushed past us in the foothills, and finally there were only piñons, and when I looked up at the rim of the mountain plateau I could see pine trees growing on the edge. Once I stopped to look down, but the pale sandstone had disappeared and the river was gone and the dark lava hills were all around. He touched my hand, not speaking, but always singing softly a mountain song and looking into my eyes.

I felt hungry and wondered what they were doing at home now — my mother, my grandmother, my husband, and the baby. Cooking breakfast, saying, "Where did she go? — maybe kidnaped," and Al going to the tribal police with the details: "She went walking along the river."

The house was made with black lava rock and red mud. It was high above the spreading miles of arroyos and long mesas. I smelled a mountain smell of pitch and buck brush. I stood there beside the black horse, looking down on the small, dim country we had passed, and I shivered.

"Yellow Woman, come inside where it's warm."

II

He lit a fire in the stove. It was an old stove with a round belly and an enamel coffeepot on top. There was only the stove, some faded Navajo blankets, and a bedroll and cardboard box. The floor was made of smooth adobe plaster, and there was one small window facing east. He pointed at the box.

"There's some potatoes and the frying pan." He sat on the floor with his arms around his knees pulling them close to his chest and he watched me fry the potatoes. I didn't mind him watching me because he was always watching me — he had been watching me since I came upon him sitting on the river bank trimming leaves from a willow twig with his knife. We ate from the pan and he wiped the grease from his fingers on his Levis.

"Have you brought women here before?" He smiled and kept chewing, so I said, "Do you always use the same tricks?"

"What tricks?" He looked at me like he didn't understand.

"The story about being a ka'tsina from the mountains. The story about Yellow Woman."

Silva was silent; his face was calm.

"I don't believe it. Those stories couldn't happen now," I said.

He shook his head and said softly, "But someday they will talk about us, and they will say, 'Those two lived long ago when things like that happened.'"

He stood up and went out. I ate the rest of the potatoes and thought about things — about the noise the stove was making and the sound of the mountain wind outside. I remembered yesterday and the day before, and then I went outside.

I walked past the corral to the edge where the narrow trail cut through the black rim rock. I was standing in the sky with nothing around me but the wind that came down from the blue mountain peak behind me. I could see faint mountain images in the distance miles across the vast spread of mesas and valleys and plains. I wondered who was over there to feel the mountain wind on those sheer blue edges — who walks on the pine needles in those blue mountains.

"Can you see the pueblo?" Silva was standing behind me.

I shook my head. "We're too far away."

"From here I can see the world." He stepped out on the edge. "The Navajo reservation begins over there." He pointed to the east. "The Pueblo boundaries are over here." He looked below us to the south, where the narrow trail seemed to come from. "The Texans have their ranches over there, starting with that valley, the Concho Valley. The Mexicans run some cattle over there too."

"Do you ever work for them?"

"I steal from them," Silva answered. The sun was dropping behind us and shadows were filling the land below. I turned away from the edge that dropped forever into the valleys below.

"I'm cold," I said; "I'm going inside." I started wondering about this man who could speak the Pueblo language so well but who lived on a mountain and rustled cattle. I decided that this man Silva must be Navajo, because Pueblo men didn't do things like that.

"You must be a Navajo."

Silva shook his head gently. "Little Yellow Woman," he said, "you never give up, do you? I have told you who I am. The Navajo people know me, too." He knelt down and unrolled the bedroll and spread the extra blankets out on a piece of canvas. The sun was down, and the only light in the house came from outside — the dim orange light from sundown.

I stood there and waited for him to crawl under the blankets.

"What are you waiting for?" he said, and I lay down beside him. He undressed me slowly like the night before beside the river — kissing my face gently and running his hands up and down my belly and legs. He took off my pants and then he laughed.

"Why are you laughing?"

"You are breathing so hard."

I pulled away from him and turned my back to him.

He pulled me around and pinned me down with his arms and chest. "You don't understand, do you, little Yellow Woman? You will do what I want."

And again he was all around me with his skin slippery against mine, and I was afraid because I understood that his strength could hurt me. I lay underneath him and I knew that he could destroy me. But later, while he slept beside me, I touched his face and I had a feeling — the kind of feeling for him that overcame me that morning along the river. I kissed him on the forehead and he reached out for me.

When I woke up in the morning he was gone. It gave me a strange feeling because for a long time I sat there on the blankets and looked around the little house for some object of his — some proof that he had been there or maybe that he was coming back. Only the blankets and the cardboard box remained. The .30-30 that had been leaning in the corner was gone, and so was the knife I had used the night before. He was gone, and I had my chance to go now. But first I had to eat, because I knew it would be a long walk home.

I found some dried apricots in the cardboard box, and I sat down on a rock at the edge of the plateau rim. There was no wind and the sun warmed me. I was surrounded by silence. I drowsed with apricots in my mouth, and I didn't believe that there were highways or railroads or cattle to steal.

When I woke up, I stared down at my feet in the black mountain dirt. Little black ants were swarming over the pine needles around my foot. They must have smelled the apricots. I thought about my family far below me. They would be wondering about me, because this had never happened to me before. The tribal police would file a report. But if old Grandpa weren't dead he would tell them what happened — he would laugh and say, "Stolen by a ka'tsina, a mountain spirit. She'll come home — they usually do." There are enough of them to handle things. My mother and grandmother will raise the baby like they raised me. Al will find someone else, and they will go on like before, except that there will be a story about the day I disappeared while I was walking along the river. Silva had come for me; he said he had. I did not decide to go. I just went. Moonflowers blossom in the sand hills before dawn, just as I followed him. That's what I was thinking as I wandered along the trail through the pine trees.

It was noon when I got back. When I saw the stone house I remembered that I had meant to go home. But that didn't seem important any more, maybe because there were little blue flowers growing in the meadow behind the stone house and the gray squirrels were playing in the pines next to the house. The horses were standing in the corral, and there was a beef carcass hanging on the shady side of a big pine in front of the house. Flies buzzed around the clotted blood that hung from the carcass. Silva was washing his hands in a bucket full of water. He must have heard me coming because he spoke to me without turning to face me.

"I've been waiting for you."

"I went walking in the big pine trees."

I looked into the bucket full of bloody water with brown-and-white animal hairs floating in it. Silva stood there letting his hand drip, examining me intently.

"Are you coming with me?"

"Where?" I asked him.

"To sell the meat in Marquez."

"If you're sure it's O.K."

"I wouldn't ask you if it wasn't," he answered.

He sloshed the water around in the bucket before he dumped it out and set the bucket upside down near the door. I followed him to the corral and watched him saddle the horses. Even beside the horses he looked tall, and I asked him again if he wasn't Navajo. He didn't say anything; he just shook his head and kept cinching up the saddle.

"But Navajos are tall."

"Get on the horse," he said "and let's go."

The last thing he did before we started down the steep trail was to grab the .30-30 from the corner. He slid the rifle into the scabbard that hung from his saddle.

"Do they ever try to catch you?" I asked.

"They don't know who I am."

"Then why did you bring the rifle?"

"Because we are going to Marquez where the Mexicans live."

III

The trail leveled out on a narrow ridge that was steep on both sides like an animal spine. On one side I could see where the trail went around the rocky gray hills and disappeared into the southeast where the pale sandrock mesas stood in the distance near my home. On the other side was a trail that went west, and as I looked far into the distance I thought I saw the little town. But Silva said no, that I was looking in the wrong place, that I just thought I saw houses. After that I quit looking off into the distance; it was hot and the wildflowers were closing up their deep-yellow petals. Only the waxy cactus flowers bloomed in the bright sun, and I saw every color that a cactus blossom can be; the white ones and the red ones were still buds, but the purple and the yellow were blossoms, open full and the most beautiful of all.

Silva saw him before I did. The white man was riding a big gray horse, coming up the trail toward us. He was traveling fast and the gray horse's feet sent rocks rolling off the trail into the dry tumbleweeds. Silva motioned for me to stop and we watched the white man. He didn't see us right away, but finally his horse whinnied at our horses and he stopped. He looked at us briefly before he loped the gray horse across the three hundred yards that separated us. He stopped his horse in front of Silva, and his young fat face was shadowed by the brim of his hat. He didn't look mad, but his small, pale eyes moved from the blood-soaked gunny sacks hanging from my saddle to Silva's face and then back to my face.

"Where did you get the fresh meat?" the white man asked.

"I've been hunting," Silva said, and when he shifted his weight in the saddle the leather creaked.

"The hell you have, Indian. You've been rustling cattle. We've been looking for the thief for a long time."

The rancher was fat, and sweat began to soak through his white cowboy shirt and the wet cloth stuck to the thick rolls of belly fat. He almost seemed to be panting from the exertion of talking, and he smelled rancid, maybe because Silva scared him.

Silva turned to me and smiled. "Go back up the mountain, Yellow Woman."

The white man got angry when he heard Silva speak in a language he couldn't understand. "Don't try anything, Indian. Just keep riding to Marquez. We'll call the state police from there."

The rancher must have been unarmed because he was very frightened and if he had a gun he would have pulled it out them. I turned my horse around and the rancher yelled, "Stop!" I looked at Silva for an instant and there was something ancient and dark — something I could feel in my stomach — in his eyes, and when I glanced at his hand I saw his finger on the trigger of .30–30 that was still in the saddle scabbard. I slapped my horse across the flank and the sacks of raw meat swung against my knees as the horse leaped up the trail. It was hard to keep my balance, and once I thought I felt the saddle slipping backward; it was because of this that I could not look back.

I didn't stop until I reached the ridge where the trail forked. The horse was breathing deep gasps and there was a dark film of sweat on its neck. I looked down in the direction I had come from, but I couldn't see the place. I waited. The wind came up and pushed warm air past me. I looked up at the sky, pale blue and full of thin clouds and fading vapor trails left by jets.

I think four shots were fired—I remember hearing four hollow explosions that reminded me of deer hunting. There could have been more shots after that, but I couldn't have heard them because my horse was running again and the loose rocks were making too much noise as they scattered around his feet.

Horses have a hard time running downhill, but I went that way instead of uphill to the mountain because I thought it was safer. I felt better with the horse running southeast past the round gray hills that were covered with cedar trees and black lava rock. When I got to the plain in the distance I could see the dark green patches of tamaracks that grew along the river; and beyond the river I could see the beginning of the pale sandrock mesas. I stopped the horse and looked back to see if anyone was coming; then I got off the horse and turned the horse around, wondering if it would go back to its corral under the pines on the mountain. It looked back at me for a moment and then plucked a mouthful of green tumbleweeds before it trotted back up the trail with its ears pointed forward, carrying its head daintily to one side to avoid stepping on the dragging reins. When the horse disappeared over the last hill, the gunny sacks full of meat were still swinging and bouncing.

IV

I walked toward the river on a wood-hauler's road that I knew would eventually lead to the paved road. I was thinking about waiting beside the road for someone to drive by, but by the time I got to the pavement I had decided it wasn't very far to walk if I followed the river back the way Silva and I had come.

The river water tasted good, and I sat in the shade under a cluster of silvery willows. I thought about Silva, and I felt sad at leaving him; still, there was something strange about him, and I tried to figure it out all the way back home.

I came back to the place on the river bank where he had been sitting the first time I saw him. The green willow leaves that he had trimmed from the branch were still lying there, wilted in the sand. I saw the leaves and I wanted to go back to him—to kiss him and to touch him—but the mountains were too far away now. And I told myself, because I believe it, he will come back sometime and be waiting again by the river.

I followed the path up from the river into the village. The sun was getting low, and I could smell supper cooking when I got to the screen door of my house. I could hear their voices inside—my mother was telling my grandmother how to fix the Jell-o and my husband, Al, was playing with the baby. I decided to tell them that some Navajo had kidnaped me, but I was sorry that old Grandpa wasn't alive to hear my story because it was the Yellow Woman stories he liked to tell best.

[1974]

Study and Writing Questions

1. What are the key examples of nature IMAGERY in this STORY? (Note, "silva" in Latin, and "selva" in Spanish, mean "forest" or "grove.")

2. What are the distinguishing characteristics of each of the story's four sections? Why does Silko break up the NARRATIVE as she does?
3. Why does the NARRATOR stay with Silva in the first section and then leave him in the third?
4. What is the importance of stories and storytelling to the narrator?
5. How does Silko create the dream-like ATMOSPHERE of this narrative? How does that atmosphere help shape the meaning of the work for us?

See also Questions for Contrast and Comparison: 5, 99, 133, 148, 164, 169, 173, and 213.

■ **ISAAC BASHEVIS SINGER** (1904–1991) *was born in Radzymin, Poland.*
Both his grandfathers were orthodox Hassidic rabbis, as was his father, who
also wrote religious essays. Singer began writing love poetry in Hebrew at fourteen
and finally, much against his family's wishes, halted rabbinical studies (1920–
1927) to follow his brother (novelist Israel Joshua Singer, 1893–1944) into secular
writing. Deeply faithful and shaped by his experiences of Jewish life in the ghetto and
the country village (shtetl), Singer worked in Poland in Yiddish and Hebrew as a
journalist (1923–1935), proofreader and translator (1923–1933), and editor (1932);
however, foreseeing the Nazi invasion, he followed his brother to New York City,
where he joined the staff of the Jewish Daily Forward (1935–1987). Although he
had been publishing fiction for ten years, culture shock halted his storytelling until
1943, the year he was naturalized. Although he was fluent in English, he wrote all of
his significant NOVELS, *plays, children's books, and* SHORT STORIES *in Yiddish,*
usually publishing first in the Forward and then supervising his translations. His
work, often set in a now vanished Poland, embraces both modern obsessions with sex
and traditional magic and fantasy. He had a son by his first wife, whom he
divorced, and was survived by his second wife, whom he married in 1940. He
received the Nobel Prize in 1978. His self-selected Collected Stories *appeared in*
1982.

Yentl the Yeshiva Boy

I

After her father's death, Yentl had no reason to remain in Yanev. She was all
alone in the house. To be sure, lodgers were willing to move in and pay rent; and
the marriage brokers flocked to her door with offers from Lublin, Tomashev,
Zamosc. But Yentl didn't want to get married. Inside her, a voice repeated over
and over: "No!" What becomes of a girl when the wedding's over? Right away she
starts bearing and rearing. And her mother-in-law lords it over her. Yentl knew
she wasn't cut out for a woman's life. She couldn't sew, she couldn't knit. She let
the food burn and the milk boil over; her Sabbath pudding never turned out
right, and her hallah dough didn't rise. Yentl much preferred men's activities to
women's. Her father, Reb Todros, may he rest in peace, during many bedridden
years had studied Torah with his daughter as if she were a son. He told Yentl to
lock the doors and drape the windows, then together they pored over the
Pentateuch, the Mishnah, the Gemara, and the Commentaries. She had proved
so apt a pupil that her father used to say:

"Yentl—you have the soul of a man."

"So why was I born a woman?"

"Even Heaven makes mistakes."

There was no doubt about it, Yentl was unlike any of the girls in Yanev—
tall, thin, bony, with small breasts and narrow hips. On Sabbath afternoons,
when her father slept, she would dress up in his trousers, his fringed garment, his
silk coat, his skullcap, his velvet hat, and study her reflection in the mirror. She
looked like a dark, handsome young man. There was even a slight down on her
upper lip. Only her thick braids showed her womanhood—and if it came to that,
hair could always be shorn. Yentl conceived a plan and day and night she could
think of nothing else. No, she had not been created for the noodle board and the
pudding dish, for chattering with silly women and pushing for a place at the

butcher's block. Her father had told her so many tales of yeshivas, rabbis, men of letters! Her head was full of Talmudic disputations, questions and answers, learned phrases. Secretly, she had even smoked her father's long pipe.

Yentl told the dealers she wanted to sell the house and go to live in Kalish with an aunt. The neighborhood women tried to talk her out of it, and the marriage brokers said she was crazy, that she was more likely to make a good match right here in Yanev. But Yentl was obstinate. She was in such a rush that she sold the house to the first bidder, and let the furniture go for a song. All she realized from her inheritance was one hundred and forty rubles. Then late one night in the month of Av, while Yanev slept, Yentl cut off her braids, arranged sidelocks at her temples, and dressed herself in her father's clothes. Packing underclothes, phylacteries, and a few books into a straw suitcase, she started off on foot for Lublin.

On the main road, Yentl got a ride in a carriage that took her as far as Zamosc. From there, she again set out on foot. She stopped at an inn along the way, and gave her name there as Anshel, after an uncle who had died. The inn was crowded with young men journeying to study with famous rabbis. An argument was in progress over the merits of various yeshivas, some praising those of Lithuania, others claiming that study was more intensive in Poland and the board better. It was the first time Yentl had ever found herself alone in the company of young men. How different their talk was from the jabbering of women, she thought, but she was too shy to join in. One young man discussed a prospective match and the size of the dowry, while another, parodying the manner of a Purim rabbi, declaimed a passage from the Torah, adding all sorts of lewd interpretations. After a while, the company proceeded to contests of strength. One pried open another's fist; a second tried to bend a companion's arm. One student, dining on bread and tea, had no spoon and stirred his cup with his penknife.

Presently, one of the group came over to Yentl and poked her in the shoulder. "Why so quiet? Don't you have a tongue?"

"I have nothing to say."

"What's your name?"

"Anshel."

"You *are* bashful. A violet by the wayside."

And the young man tweaked Yentl's nose. She would have given him a smack in return, but her arm refused to budge. She turned white. Another student, slightly older than the rest, tall and pale, with burning eyes and a black beard, came to her rescue.

"Hey, you, why are you picking on him?"

"If you don't like it, you don't have to look."

"Want me to pull your sidelocks off?"

The bearded young man beckoned to Yentl, then asked where she came from and where she was going. Yentl told him she was looking for a yeshiva, but wanted a quiet one. The young man pulled at his beard.

"Then come with me to Bechev."

He explained that he was returning to Bechev for his fourth year. The yeshiva there was small, with only thirty students, and the people in the town provided board for them all. The food was plentiful and the housewives darned the students' socks and took care of their laundry. The Bechev rabbi, who headed the yeshiva, was a genius. He could pose ten questions and answer all ten with one proof. Most of the students eventually found wives in the town.

"Why did you leave in the middle of the term?" Yentl asked.

"My mother died. Now I'm on my way back."

"What's your name?"

"Avigdor."

"How is it you're not married?"

The young man scratched his beard. "It's a long story."

"Tell me."

Avigdor covered his eyes and thought a moment. "Are you coming to Bechev?"

"Yes."

"Then you'll find out soon enough anyway. I was engaged to the only daughter of Alter Vishkower, the richest man in town. Even the wedding date was set when suddenly they sent back the engagement contract."

"What happened?"

"I don't know. Gossips, I guess, were busy spreading tales. I had the right to ask for half the dowry, but it was against my nature. Now they're trying to talk me into another match, but the girl doesn't appeal to me."

"In Bechev, yeshiva boys look at women?"

"At Alter's house, where I ate once a week, Hadass, his daughter, always brought in the food . . ."

"Is she good-looking?"

"She's blond."

"Brunettes can be good-looking too."

"No."

Yentl gazed at Avigdor. He was lean and bony with sunken cheeks. He had curly sidelocks so black they appeared blue, and his eyebrows met across the bridge of his nose. He looked at her sharply with the regretful shyness of one who has just divulged a secret. His lapel was rent, according to the custom for mourners, and the lining of his gaberdine showed through. He drummed restlessly on the table and hummed a tune. Behind the high furrowed brow his thoughts seemed to race.

Suddenly he spoke:

"Well, what of it. I'll become a recluse, that's all."

II

It was strange, but as soon as Yentl—or Anshel—arrived in Bechev, she was allotted one day's board a week at the house of that same rich man, Alter Vishkower, whose daughter had broken off her betrothal to Avigdor.

The students at the yeshiva studied in pairs, and Avigdor chose Anshel for a partner. He helped her with the lessons. He was also an expert swimmer and offered to teach Anshel the breast stroke and how to tread water, but she always found excuses for not going down to the river. Avigdor suggested that they share lodgings, but Anshel found a place to sleep at the house of an elderly widow who was half blind. Tuesdays, Anshel ate at Alter Vishkower's and Hadass waited on her. Avigdor always asked many questions: "How does Hadass look? Is she sad? Is she gay? Are they trying to marry her off? Does she ever mention my name?" Anshel reported that Hadass upset dishes on the tablecloth, forgot to bring the salt, and dipped her fingers into the plate of grits while carrying it. She ordered the servant girl around, was forever engrossed in storybooks, and changed her hairdo every week. Moreover, she must consider herself a beauty, for she was always in front of the mirror, but, in fact, she was not that good-looking.

"Two years after she's married," said Anshel, "she'll be an old bag."

"So she doesn't appeal to you?"

"Not particularly."

"Yet if she wanted you, you wouldn't turn her down."

"I can do without her."

"Don't you have evil impulses?"

The two friends, sharing a lectern in a corner of the study house, spent more time talking than learning. Occasionally Avigdor smoked, and Anshel, taking the cigarette from his lips, would have a puff. Avigdor liked baked flatcakes made with buckwheat, so Anshel stopped at the bakery every morning to buy one, and wouldn't let him pay his share. Often Anshel did things that greatly surprised Avigdor. If a button came off Avigdor's coat, for example, Anshel would arrive at the yeshiva the next day with needle and thread and sew it back on. Anshel bought Avigdor all kinds of presents: a silk handkerchief, a pair of socks, a muffler. Avigdor grew more and more attached to this boy, five years younger than himself, whose beard hadn't even begun to sprout.

Once Avigdor said to Anshel: "I want you to marry Hadass."

"What good would that do you?"

"Better you than a total stranger."

"You'd become my enemy."

"Never."

Avigdor liked to go for walks through the town and Anshel frequently joined him. Engrossed in conversation, they would go off to the water mill, or to the pine forest, or to the crossroads where the Christian shrine stood. Sometimes they stretched out on the grass.

"Why can't a woman be like a man?" Avigdor asked once, looking up at the sky.

"How do you mean?"

"Why couldn't Hadass be just like you?"

"How like me?"

"Oh — a good fellow."

Anshel grew playful. She plucked a flower and tore off the petals one by one. She picked up a chestnut and threw it at Avigdor. Avigdor watched a ladybug crawl across the palm of his hand.

After a while he spoke up: "They're trying to marry me off."

Anshel sat up instantly. "To whom?"

"To Feitl's daughter, Peshe."

"The widow?"

"That's the one."

"Why should you marry a widow?"

"No one else will have me."

"That's not true. Someone will turn up for you."

"Never."

Anshel told Avigdor such a match was bad. Peshe was neither good-looking nor clever, only a cow with a pair of eyes. Besides, she was bad luck, for her husband died in the first year of their marriage. Such women were husband-killers. But Avigdor did not answer. He lit a cigarette, took a deep puff, and blew out smoke rings. His face had turned green.

"I need a woman. I can't sleep at night."

Anshel was startled. "Why can't you wait until the right one comes along?"

"Hadass was my destined one."

And Avigdor's eyes grew moist. Abruptly he got to his feet. "Enough lying around. Let's go."

After that, everything happened quickly. One day Avigdor was confiding his problem to Anshel, two days later he became engaged to Peshe, and brought honey cake and brandy to the yeshiva. An early wedding date was set. When the bride-to-be is a widow, there's no need to wait for a trousseau. Everything is ready. The groom, moreover, was an orphan and no one's advice had to be asked. The yeshiva students drank the brandy and offered their congratulations. Anshel also took a sip, but promptly choked on it.

"Oy, it burns!"

"You're not much of a man," Avigdor teased.

After the celebration, Avigdor and Anshel sat down with a volume of the Gemara, but they made little progress, and their conversation was equally slow. Avigdor rocked back and forth, pulled at his beard, muttered under his breath.

"I'm lost," he said abruptly.

"If you don't like her, why are you getting married?"

"I'd marry a she-goat."

The following day Avigdor did not appear at the study house. Feitl the leather dealer belonged to the Hasidim and he wanted his prospective son-in-law to continue his studies at the Hasidic prayer house. The yeshiva students said privately that though there was no denying the widow was short and round as a barrel, her mother the daughter of a dairyman, her father half an ignoramus, still the whole family was filthy with money. Feitl was part-owner of a tannery; Peshe had invested her dowry in a shop that sold herring, tar, pots and pans, and was always crowded with peasants. Father and daughter were outfitting Avigdor and had placed orders for a fur coat, a cloth coat, a silk kapote, and two pair of boots. In addition, he had received many gifts immediately, things that had belonged to Peshe's first husband: the Vilna edition of the Talmud, a gold watch, a Hanukkah candelabra, a spice box. Anshel sat alone at the lectern.

On Tuesday when Anshel arrived for dinner at Alter Vishkower's house, Hadass remarked: "What do you say about your partner—back in clover, isn't he?"

"What did you expect—that no one else would want him?"

Hadass reddened. "It wasn't my fault. My father was against it."

"Why?"

"Because they found out a brother of his had hanged himself."

Anshel looked at her as she stood there—tall, blond, with a long neck, hollow cheeks, and blue eyes, wearing a cotton dress and a calico apron. Her hair, fixed in two braids, was flung back over her shoulders. A pity I'm not a man, Anshel thought.

"Do you regret it now?" Anshel asked.

"Oh, yes!"

Hadass fled from the room. The rest of the food, meat dumplings and tea, was brought in by the servant girl. Not until Anshel had finished eating and was washing her hands for the Final Blessings did Hadass reappear.

She came up to the table and said in a smothered voice: "Swear to me you won't tell him anything. Why should he know what goes on in my heart!"

Then she fled once more, nearly falling over the threshold.

III

The head of the yeshiva asked Anshel to choose another study partner, but weeks went by and still Anshel studied alone. There was no one in the yeshiva who could take Avigdor's place. All the others were small, in body and in spirit. They talked nonsense, bragged about trifles, grinned oafishly, behaved like shnorrers. Without Avigdor the study house seemed empty. At night Anshel lay on her bench at the widow's, unable to sleep. Stripped of gaberdine and trousers, she was once more Yentl, a girl of marriageable age, in love with a young man who was betrothed to another. Perhaps I should have told him the truth, Anshel thought. But it was too late for that. Anshel could not go back to being a girl, could never again do without books and a study house. She lay there thinking outlandish thoughts that brought her close to madness. She fell asleep, then awoke with a start. In her dream she had been at the same time a man and a woman, wearing both a woman's bodice and a man's fringed garment. Yentl's period was late and she was suddenly afraid . . . who knew? In *Midrash Talpioth* she had read of a woman who had conceived merely through desiring a man. Only now did Yentl grasp the meaning of the Torah's prohibition against wearing the clothes of the other sex. By doing so one deceived not only others but also oneself. Even the soul was perplexed, finding itself incarnate in a strange body.

At night Anshel lay awake; by day she could scarcely keep her eyes open. At the houses where she had her meals, the women complained that the youth left everything on his plate. The rabbi noticed that Anshel no longer paid attention to the lectures but stared out the window lost in private thoughts. When Tuesday came, Anshel appeared at the Vishkower house for dinner. Hadass set a bowl of soup before her and waited, but Anshel was so disturbed she did not even say thank you. She reached for a spoon but let it fall.

Hadass ventured a comment: "I hear Avigdor has deserted you."

Anshel awoke from her trance. "What do you mean?"

"He's no longer your partner."

"He's left the yeshiva."

"Do you see him at all?"

"He seems to be hiding."

"Are you at least going to the wedding?"

For a moment Anshel was silent as though missing the meaning of the words. Then she spoke: "He's a big fool."

"Why do you say that?"

"You're beautiful, and the other one looks like a monkey."

Hadass blushed to the roots of her hair. "It's all my father's fault."

"Don't worry. You'll find someone who's worthy of you."

"There's no one I want."

"But everyone wants you . . ."

There was a long silence. Hadass' eyes grew larger, filling with the sadness of one who knows there is no consolation.

"Your soup is getting cold."

"I, too, want you."

Anshel was astonished at what she had said. Hadass stared at her over her shoulder.

"What are you saying!"

"It's the truth."

"Someone might be listening."

"I'm not afraid."

"Eat the soup. I'll bring the meat dumplings in a moment."

Hadass turned to go, her high heels clattering. Anshel began hunting for beans in the soup, fished one up, then let it fall. Her appetite was gone; her throat had closed up. She knew very well she was getting entangled in evil, but some force kept urging her on. Hadass reappeared, carrying a platter with two meat dumplings on it.

"Why aren't you eating?"

"I'm thinking about you."

"What are you thinking?"

"I want to marry you."

Hadass made a face as though she had swallowed something.

"On such matters, you must speak to my father."

"I know."

"The custom is to send a matchmaker."

She ran from the room, letting the door slam behind her. Laughing inwardly, Anshel thought: "With girls I can play as I please!" She sprinkled salt on the soup and then pepper. She sat there lightheaded. What have I done? I must be going mad. There's no other explanation . . . She forced herself to eat, but could taste nothing. Only then did Anshel remember that it was Avigdor who had wanted her to marry Hadass. From her confusion, a plan emerged; she would exact vengeance for Avigdor, and at the same time, through Hadass, draw him closer to herself. Hadass was a virgin: what did she know about men? A girl like that could be deceived for a long time. To be sure, Anshel too was a virgin but she knew a lot about such matters from the Gemara and from hearing men talk. Anshel was seized by both fear and glee, as a person is who is planning to deceive the whole community. She remembered the saying: "The public are fools." She stood up and said aloud: "Now I'll really start something."

That night Anshel didn't sleep a wink. Every few minutes she got up for a drink of water. Her throat was parched, her forehead burned. Her brain worked away feverishly of its own volition. A quarrel seemed to be going on inside her. Her stomach throbbed and her knees ached. It was as if she had sealed a pact with Satan, the Evil One who plays tricks on human beings, who sets stumbling blocks and traps in their paths. By the time Anshel fell asleep, it was morning. She awoke more exhausted than before. But she could not go on sleeping on the bench at the widow's. With an effort she rose and, taking the bag that held her phylacteries, set out for the study house. On the way whom should she meet but Hadass's father. Anshel bade him a respectful good morning and received a friendly greeting in return. Reb Alter stroked his beard and engaged her in conversation:

"My daughter Hadass must be serving you left-overs. You look starved."

"Your daughter is a fine girl, and very generous."

"So why are you so pale?"

Anshel was silent for a minute. "Reb Alter, there's something I must say to you."

"Well, go ahead, say it."

"Reb Alter, your daughter pleases me."

Alter Vishkower came to a halt. "Oh, does she? I thought yeshiva students didn't talk about such things."

His eyes were full of laughter.

"But it's the truth."

"One doesn't discuss these matters with the young man himself."

"But I'm an orphan."

"Well . . . in that case the custom is to send a marriage broker."

"Yes . . ."

"What do you see in her?"

"She's beautiful . . . fine . . . intelligent . . ."

"Well, well, well . . . Come along, tell me something about your family."

Alter Vishkower put his arm around Anshel and in this fashion the two continued walking until they reached the courtyard of the synagogue.

IV

Once you say "A," you must say "B." Thoughts lead to words, words lead to deeds. Reb Alter Vishkower gave his consent to the match. Hadass's mother Freyda Leah held back for a while. She said she wanted no more Bechev yeshiva students for her daughter and would rather have someone from Lublin or Zamosc; but Hadass gave warning that if she were shamed publicly once more (the way she had been with Avigdor) she would throw herself into the well. As often happens with such ill-advised matches, everyone was strongly in favor of it — the rabbi, the relatives, Hadass's girl friends. For some time the girls of Bechev had been eyeing Anshel longingly, watching from their windows when the youth passed by on the street. Anshel kept his boots well polished and did not drop his eyes in the presence of women. Stopping in at Beila the baker's to buy a *pletzl*, he joked with them in such a worldly fashion that they marveled. The women agreed there was something special about Anshel: his sidelocks curled like nobody else's and he tied his neck scarf differently; his eyes, smiling yet distant, seemed always fixed on some faraway point. And the fact that Avigdor had become betrothed to Feitl's daughter Peshe, forsaking Anshel, had endeared him all the more to the people of the town. Alter Vishkower had a provisional contract drawn up for the betrothal, promising Anshel a bigger dowry, more presents, and an even longer period of maintenance than he had promised

Avigdor. The girls of Bechev threw their arms around Hadass and congratulated her. Hadass immediately began crocheting a sack for Anshel's phylacteries, a hallah cloth, a matzoh bag. When Avigdor heard the news of Anshel's betrothal, he came to the study house to offer his congratulations. The past few weeks had aged him. His beard was disheveled, his eyes were red.

He said to Anshel: "I knew it would happen this way. Right from the beginning. As soon as I met you at the inn."

"But it was you who suggested it."

"I know that."

"Why did you desert me? You went away without even saying good-bye."

"I wanted to burn my bridges behind me."

Avigdor asked Anshel to go for a walk. Though it was already past Succoth, the day was bright with sunshine. Avigdor, friendlier than ever, opened his heart to Anshel. Yes, it was true, a brother of his had succumbed to melancholy and hanged himself. Now he too felt himself near the edge of the abyss. Peshe had a lot of money and her father was a rich man, yet he couldn't sleep nights. He didn't want to be a store keeper. He couldn't forget Hadass. She appeared in his dreams. Sabbath night when her name occurred in the Havdala prayer, he turned dizzy. Still it was good that Anshel and no one else was to marry her . . . At least she would fall into decent hands. Avigdor stooped and tore aimlessly at the shriveled grass. His speech was incoherent, like that of a man possessed.

Suddenly he said: "I have thought of doing what my brother did."

"Do you love her *that* much?"

"She's engraved in my heart."

The two pledged their friendship and promised never again to part. Anshel proposed that, after they were both married, they should live next door or even share the same house. They would study together every day, perhaps even become partners in a shop.

"Do you want to know the truth?" asked Avigdor. "It's like the story of Jacob and Benjamin: my life is bound up in your life."

"Then why did you leave me?"

"Perhaps for that very reason."

Though the day had turned cold and windy, they continued to walk until they reached the pine forest, not turning back until dusk when it was time for the evening prayer. The girls of Bechev, from their posts at the windows, watched them going by with their arms round each other's shoulders and so engrossed in conversation that they walked through puddles and piles of trash without noticing. Avigdor looked pale, disheveled, and the wind whipped one sidelock about; Anshel chewed his fingernails. Hadass, too, ran to the window, took one look, and her eyes filled with tears.

Events followed quickly. Avigdor was the first to marry. Because the bride was a widow, the wedding was a quiet one, with no musicians, no wedding jester, no ceremonial veiling of the bride. One day Peshe stood beneath the marriage canopy, the next she was back at the shop, dispensing tar with greasy hands. Avigdor prayed at the Hasidic assembly house in his new prayer shawl. Afternoons, Anshel went to visit him and the two whispered and talked until evening. The date of Anshel's wedding to Hadass was set for the Sabbath in Hanukkah week, though the prospective father-in-law wanted it sooner. Hadass had already been betrothed once. Besides, the groom was an orphan. Why should he toss about on a makeshift bed at the widow's when he could have a wife and home of his own?

Many times each day Anshel warned herself that what she was about to do was sinful, mad, an act of utter depravity. She was entangling both Hadass and herself in a chain of deception and committing so many transgressions that she would never be able to do penance. One lie followed another. Repeatedly Anshel made up her mind to flee Bechev in time, to put an end to this weird comedy that was more the work of an imp than a human being. But she was in the grip of a power she could not resist. She grew more and more attached to Avigdor, and could not bring herself to destroy Hadass's illusory happiness. Now that he was married, Avigdor's desire to study was greater than ever, and the friends met twice each day: in the mornings they studied the Gemara and the Commentaries, in the afternoons the Legal Codes with their glosses. Alter Vishkower and Feitl the leather dealer were pleased and compared Avigdor and Anshel to David and Jonathan. With all the complications, Anshel went about as though drunk. The tailors took her measurements for a new wardrobe and she was forced into all kinds of subterfuge to keep them from discovering she was not a man. Though the imposture had lasted many weeks, Anshel still could not believe it: How was it possible? Fooling the community had become a game, but how long could it go on? And in what way would the truth come to the surface? Inside, Anshel laughed and wept. She had turned into a sprite brought into the world to mock people and trick them. I'm wicked, a transgressor, a Jeroboam ben Nabat, she told herself. Her only justification was that she had taken all these burdens upon herself because her soul thirsted to study Torah.

Avigdor soon began to complain that Peshe treated him badly. She called him an idler, a shlemiel, just another mouth to feed. She tried to tie him to the store, assigned him tasks for which he hadn't the slightest inclination, begrudged him pocket money. Instead of consoling Avigdor, Anshel goaded him on against Peshe. She called his wife an eyesore, a shrew, a miser, and said that Peshe had no doubt nagged her first husband to death and would Avigdor also. At the same time, Anshel enumerated Avigdor's virtues: his height and manliness, his wit, his erudition.

"If I were a woman and married to you," said Anshel, "I'd know how to appreciate you."

"Well, but you aren't . . ."

Avigdor sighed.

Meanwhile, Anshel's wedding date drew near.

On the Sabbath before Hanukkah, Anshel was called to the pulpit to read from the Torah. The women showered her with raisins and almonds. On the day of the wedding Alter Vishkower gave a feast for the young men. Avigdor sat at Anshel's right hand. The bridegroom delivered a Talmudic discourse, and the rest of the company argued the points, while smoking cigarettes and drinking wine, liqueurs, tea with lemon or raspberry jam. Then followed the ceremony of veiling the bride, after which the bridegroom was led to the wedding canopy that had been set up at the side of the synagogue. The night was frosty and clear, the sky full of stars. The musicians struck up a tune. Two rows of girls held lighted tapers and braided wax candles. After the wedding ceremony the bride and groom broke their fast with golden chicken broth. Then the dancing began and the announcement of the wedding gifts, all according to custom. The gifts were many and costly. The wedding jester depicted the joys and sorrows that were in store for the bride. Avigdor's wife, Peshe, was one of the guests but, though she was bedecked with jewels, she still looked ugly in a wig that sat low on her forehead, wearing an enormous fur cape, and with traces of tar on her hands that no amount of washing could ever remove. After the virtue dance the bride and groom were led separately to the marriage chamber. The wedding attendants instructed the couple in the proper conduct and enjoined them to "be fruitful and multiply."

At daybreak Anshel's mother-in-law and her band descended upon the marriage chamber and tore the bedsheets from beneath Hadass to make sure the marriage had been consummated. When traces of blood were discovered, the company grew merry and began kissing and congratulating the bride. Then, brandishing the sheet, they flocked outside and danced a kosher dance in the newly fallen snow. Anshel had found a way to deflower the bride. Hadass in her innocence was unaware that things weren't quite as they should have been. She was already deeply in love with Anshel. It is commanded that the bride and groom remain apart for seven days after the first intercourse. The next day Anshel and Avigdor took up the study of the Tractate on Menstruous Women. When the other men had departed and the two were left to themselves in the synagogue, Avigdor shyly questioned Anshel about his night with Hadass. Anshel gratified his curiosity and they whispered together until nightfall.

V

Anshel had fallen into good hands. Hadass was a devoted wife and her parents indulged their son-in-law's every wish and boasted of his accomplishments. To be sure, several months went by and Hadass was still not with child, but no one took it to heart. On the other hand, Avigdor's lot grew steadily worse. Peshe tormented him and finally would not give him enough to eat and even refused him a clean shirt. Since he was always penniless, Anshel again brought him a daily buckwheat cake. Because Peshe was too busy to cook and too stingy to hire a servant, Anshel asked Avigdor to dine at his house. Reb Alter Vishkower and his wife disapproved, arguing that it was wrong for the rejected suitor to visit the house of his former fiancée. The town had plenty to talk about. But Anshel cited precedents to show that it was not prohibited by the Law. Most of the townspeople sided with Avigdor and blamed Peshe for everything. Avigdor soon began pressing Peshe for a divorce, and, because he did not want to have a child by such a fury, he acted like Onan, or, as the Gemara translates it: he threshed on the inside and cast his seed without. He confided in Anshel, told him how Peshe came to bed unwashed and snored like a buzz saw, of how she was so occupied with the cash taken in at the store that she babbled about it even in her sleep.

"Oh, Anshel, how I envy you," he said.

"There's no reason for envying me."

"You have everything. I wish your good fortune were mine — with no loss to you, of course."

"Everyone has troubles of his own."

"What sort of troubles do *you* have? Don't tempt Providence."

How could Avigdor have guessed that Anshel could not sleep at night and thought constantly of running away? Lying with Hadass and deceiving her had become more and more painful. Hadass's love and tenderness shamed her. The devotion of her mother- and father-in-law and their hopes for a grandchild were a burden. On Friday afternoons all of the townspeople went to the baths and every week Anshel had to find a new excuse. But this was beginning to awake suspicions. There was talk that Anshel must have an unsightly birthmark, or a rupture, or perhaps was not properly circumcised. Judging by the youth's years, his beard should certainly have begun to sprout, yet his cheeks remained smooth. It was already Purim, and Passover was approaching. Soon it would be summer. Not far from Bechev there was a river where all the yeshiva students and young men went swimming as soon as it was warm enough. The lie was swelling like an abscess and one of these days it must surely burst. Anshel knew she had to find a way to free herself.

It was customary for the young men boarding with their in-laws to travel to nearby cities during the half-holidays in the middle of Passover week. They enjoyed the change, refreshed themselves, looked around for business opportunities, bought books or other things a young man might need. Bechev was not far from Lublin and Anshel persuaded Avigdor to make the journey with her at her expense. Avigdor was delighted at the prospect of being rid for a few days of the shrew he had at home. The trip by carriage was a merry one. The fields were turning green; storks, back from the warm countries, swooped across the sky in great arcs. Streams rushed toward the valleys. The birds chirped. The windmills turned. Spring flowers were beginning to bloom in the fields. Here and there a cow was already grazing. The companions, chatting, ate the fruit and little cakes that Hadass had packed, told each other jokes, and exchanged confidences until they reached Lublin. There they went to an inn and took a room for two. In the journey, Anshel had promised to reveal an astonishing secret to Avigdor in Lublin. Avigdor had joked: what sort of secret could it be? Had Anshel discovered a hidden treasure? Had he written an essay? By studying the Cabala, had he created a dove?

Now they entered the room and while Anshel carefully locked the door, Avigdor said teasingly: "Well, let's hear your great secret."

"Prepare yourself for the most incredible thing that ever was."

"I'm prepared for anything."

"I'm not a man but a woman," said Anshel. "My name isn't Anshel. it's Yentl."

Avigdor burst out laughing. "I knew it was a hoax."

"But it's true."

"Even if I'm a fool, I won't swallow this."

"Do you want me to show you?"

"Yes."

"Then I'll get undressed."

Avigdor's eyes widened. It occurred to him that Anshel might want to practice pederasty. Anshel took off the gaberdine and the fringed garment, and threw off her underclothes. Avigdor took one look and turned first white, then fiery red. Anshel covered herself hastily.

"I've done this only so that you can testify at the courthouse. Otherwise, Hadass will have to stay a grass widow."

Avigdor had lost his tongue. He was seized by a fit of trembling. He wanted to speak, but his lips moved and nothing came out. He sat down quickly, for his legs would not support him.

Finally he murmured: "How is it possible? I don't believe it!"

"Should I get undressed again?"

"No!"

Yentl proceeded to tell the whole story: how her father, bedridden, had studied Torah with her; how she had never had the patience for women and their silly chatter; how she had sold the house and all the furnishings, left the town, made her way disguised as a man to Lublin, and on the road met Avigdor. Avigdor sat speechless, gazing at the storyteller. Yentl was by now wearing men's clothes once more.

Avigdor spoke: "It must be a dream."

He pinched himself on the cheek.

"It isn't a dream."

"That such a thing should happen to me!"

"It's all true."

"Why did you do it? Nu, I'd better keep still."

"I didn't want to waste my life on a baking shovel and kneading trough."

"And what about Hadass — why did you do that?"

"I did it for your sake. I knew that Peshe would torment you and at our house you would have some peace."

Avigdor was silent for a long time. He bowed his head, pressed his hands to his temples, shook his head. "What will you do now?"

"I'll go away to a different yeshiva."

"What? If you had only told me earlier, we could have . . ."

Avigdor broke off in the middle.

"No — it wouldn't have been good."

"Why not?"

"I'm neither one nor the other."

"What a dilemma I'm in!"

"Get a divorce from that horror. Marry Hadass."

"She'll never divorce me and Hadass won't have me."

"Hadass loves you. She won't listen to her father again."

Avigdor stood up suddenly but then sat down. "I won't be able to forget you. Ever . . ."

VI

According to the Law, Avigdor was now forbidden to spend another moment alone with Yentl; yet dressed in the gaberdine and trousers, she was again the familiar Anshel.

They resumed their conversation on the old footing: "How could you bring yourself to violate the commandment every day: 'A woman shall not wear that which pertaineth to a man'?"

"I wasn't created for plucking feathers and chattering with females."

"Would you rather lose your share in the world to come?"

"Perhaps . . ."

Avigdor raised his eyes. Only now did he realize that Anshel's cheeks were too smooth for a man's, the hair too abundant, the hands too small. Even so he could not believe that such a thing could have happened. At any moment he expected to wake up. He bit his lips, pinched his thigh. He was seized by shyness and could not speak without stammering. His friendship with Anshel, their intimate talk, their confidences, had been turned into a sham and delusion. The thought even occurred to him that Anshel might be a demon. He shook himself as if to cast off a nightmare; yet that power which knows the difference between dream and reality told him it was all true. He summoned up his courage. He and Anshel could never be strangers to one another, even though Anshel was in fact Yentl . . .

He ventured a comment: "It seems to me that the witness who testifies for a deserted woman may not marry her, for the Law calls him 'a party to the affair.'"

"What? That didn't occur to me!"

"We must look it up in Eben Ezer."

"I'm not even sure that the rules pertaining to a deserted woman apply in this case," said Anshel in the manner of a scholar.

"If you don't want Hadass to be a grass widow, you must reveal the secret to her directly."

"That I can't do."

"In any event, you must get another witness."

Gradually the two went back to their Talmudic conversation. It seemed strange at first to Avigdor to be disputing holy writ with a woman, yet before long the Torah had reunited them. Though their bodies were different, their souls were of one kind. Anshel spoke in a singsong, gesticulated with her thumb, clutched her sidelocks, plucked at her beardless chin, made all the customary gestures of a yeshiva student. In the heat of argument she even seized Avigdor by the lapel and called him stupid. A great love for Anshel took hold of Avigdor, mixed with shame, remorse, anxiety. If I had only known this before, he said to himself. In his thoughts he likened Anshel (or Yentl) to Bruria, the wife of Reb Meir, and to Yalta, the wife of Reb Nachman. For the first time he saw clearly that this was what he had always wanted: a wife whose mind was not taken up with material things . . . His desire for Hadass was gone now, and he knew he would long for Yentl, but he dared not say so. He felt hot and knew that his face was burning. He could no longer meet Anshel's eyes. He began to enumerate Anshel's sins and saw that he too was implicated, for he had sat next to Yentl and had touched her during her unclean days. *Nu*, and what could be said about her marriage to Hadass? What a multitude of transgressions there! Wilful deception, false vows, misrepresentation! — Heaven knows what else.

He asked suddenly: "Tell the truth, are you a heretic?"

"God forbid!"

"Then how could you bring yourself to do such a thing?"

The longer Anshel talked, the less Avigdor understood. All Anshel's explanations seemed to point to one thing: she had the soul of a man and the body of a woman. Anshel said she had married Hadass only in order to be near Avigdor.

"You could have married me," Avigdor said.

"I wanted to study the Gemara and Commentaries with you, not darn your socks!"

For a long time neither spoke. Then Avigdor broke the silence: "I'm afraid Hadass will get sick from all this, God forbid!"

"I'm afraid of that, too."

"What's going to happen now?"

Dusk fell and the two began to recite the evening prayer. In his confusion Avigdor mixed up the blessings, omitted some and repeated others. He glanced sideways at Anshel, who was rocking back and forth, beating her breast, bowing her head. He saw her, eyes closed, lift her face to Heaven, as though beseeching: You, Father in Heaven, know the truth . . . When their prayers were finished, they sat down on opposite chairs, facing one another yet a good distance apart. The room filled with shadows. Reflections of the sunset, like purple embroidery, shook on the wall opposite the window. Avigdor again wanted to speak but at first the words, trembling on the tip of his tongue, would not come.

Suddenly they burst forth: "Maybe it's still not too late? I can't go on living with that accursed woman . . . You . . ."

"No, Avigdor, it's impossible."

"Why?"

"I'll live out my time as I am . . ."

"I'll miss you. Terribly."

"And I'll miss you."

"What's the sense of all this?"

Anshel did not answer. Night fell and the light faded. In the darkness they seemed to be listening to each other's thoughts. The Law forbade Avigdor to stay in the room alone with Anshel, but he could not think of her just as a woman. What a strange power there is in clothing, he thought.

But he spoke of something else: "I would advise you simply to send Hadass a divorce."

"How can I do that?"

"Since the marriage sacraments weren't valid, what difference does it make?"

"I suppose you're right."

"There'll be time enough later for her to find out the truth."

The maidservant came in with a lamp, but as soon as she had gone, Avigdor put it out. Their predicament and the words which they must speak to one another could not endure light. In the blackness Anshel related all the particulars. She answered all Avigdor's questions. The clock struck two, and still they talked. Anshel told Avigdor that Hadass had never forgotten him. She talked of him frequently, worried about his health, was sorry—though not without a certain satisfaction—about the way things had turned out with Peshe.

"She'll be a good wife," said Anshel. "I don't even know how to bake a pudding."

"Nevertheless, if you're willing . . ."

"No, Avigdor. It wasn't destined to be . . ."

VII

It was all a great riddle to the town: the messenger who arrived bringing Hadass the divorce papers; Avigdor's remaining in Lublin until after the holidays; his return to Bechev with slumping shoulders and lifeless eyes as if he had been ill. Hadass took to her bed and was visited by the doctor three times a day. Avigdor went into seclusion. If someone ran across him by chance and addressed him, he did not answer. Peshe complained to her parents that Avigdor paced back and forth smoking all night long. When he finally collapsed from sheer fatigue, in his sleep he called out the name of an unknown female—Yentl. Peshe began talking of a divorce. The town thought Avigdor wouldn't grant her one or would demand money at the very least, but he agreed to everything.

In Bechev the people were not used to having mysteries stay mysteries for long. How can you keep secrets in a little town where everyone knows what's cooking in everyone else's pots? Yet, though there were plenty of persons who made a practice of looking through keyholes and laying an ear to shutters, what happened remained an enigma. Hadass lay in her bed and wept. Chanina the herb doctor reported that she was wasting away. Anshel had disappeared without a trace. Reb Alter Vishkower sent for Avigdor and he arrived, but those who stood straining beneath the window couldn't catch a word of what passed between them. Those individuals who habitually pry into other people's affairs came up with all sorts of theories, but not one of them was consistent.

One party came to the conclusion that Anshel had fallen into the hands of Catholic priests and had been converted. That might have made sense. But where could Anshel have found time for the priests, since he was always studying in the yeshiva? And apart from that, since when does an apostate send his wife a divorce?

Another group whispered that Anshel had cast an eye on another woman. But who could it be? There were no love affairs conducted in Bechev. And none of the young women had recently left town—neither a Jewish woman nor a Gentile one.

Somebody else offered the suggestion that Anshel had been carried away by evil spirits, or was even one of them himself. As proof he cited the fact that Anshel had never come either to the bathhouse or to the river. It is well known that demons have the feet of geese. Well, but had Hadass never seen him barefoot? And who ever heard of a demon sending his wife a divorce? When a demon marries a daughter of mortals, he usually lets her remain a grass widow.

It occurred to someone else that Anshel had committed a major transgression and gone into exile in order to do penance. But what sort of transgression could it have been? And why had he not entrusted it to the rabbi? And why did Avigdor wander about like a ghost?

The hypothesis of Tevel the musician was closest to the truth. Tevel maintained that Avigdor had been unable to forget Hadass and that Anshel had divorced her so that his friend would be able to marry her. But was such friendship possible in this world? And in that case, why had Anshel divorced Hadass even before Avigdor divorced Peshe? Furthermore, such a thing can be accomplished only if the wife had been informed of the arrangement and is willing, yet all signs pointed to Hadass's great love for Anshel, and in fact she was ill from sorrow.

One thing was clear to all: Avigdor knew the truth. But it was impossible to get anything out of him. He remained in seclusion and kept silent with an obstinacy that was a reproof to the whole town.

Close friends urged Peshe not to divorce Avigdor, though they had severed all relations and no longer lived as man and wife. He did not even, on Friday night, perform the kiddush blessing for her. He spent his nights either at the study house or at the widow's where Anshel had found lodgings. When Peshe spoke to him he didn't answer, but stood with bowed head. The tradeswoman

Peshe had no patience for such goings-on. She needed a young man to help her out in the store, not a yeshiva student who had fallen into melancholy. Someone of that sort might even take it into his head to depart and leave her deserted. Peshe agreed to a divorce.

In the meantime, Hadass had recovered, and Reb Alter Vishkower let it be known that a marriage contract was being drawn up. Hadass was to marry Avigdor. The town was agog. A marriage between a man and a woman who had once been engaged and their betrothal broken off was unheard of. The wedding was held on the first Sabbath after Tishe b'Av, and included all that is customary at the marriage of a virgin: the banquet for the poor, the canopy before the synagogue, the musicians, the wedding jester, the virtue dance. Only one thing was lacking: joy. The bridegroom stood beneath the marriage canopy, a figure of desolation. The bride had recovered from her sickness, but had remained pale and thin. Her tears fell into the golden chicken broth. From all eyes the same question looked out: why had Anshel done it?

After Avigdor's marriage to Hadass, Peshe spread the rumor that Anshel had sold his wife to Avigdor for a price, and that the money had been supplied by Alter Vishkower. One young man pondered the riddle at great length until he finally arrived at the conclusion that Anshel had lost his beloved wife to Avigdor at cards, or even on a spin of the Hanukkah dreidl. It is a general rule that when the grain of truth cannot be found, men will swallow great helpings of falsehood. Truth itself is often concealed in such a way that the harder you look for it, the harder it is to find.

Not long after the wedding, Hadass became pregnant. The child was a boy and those assembled at the circumcision could scarcely believe their ears when they heard the father name his son Anshel.

[1962]

Study and Writing Questions

1. How would you describe the SETTING of this STORY? Why is it set sometime in the past? What are the apparent relations in this world between Jews and Christians? In this world, what is the role of work? of study? of religion? If this is not simply a REALISTIC world, for what artistic purposes does it seem to be constructed?

2. In this NARRATIVE world, many elements are divided into mutually exclusive male and female realms. Draw up lists of those elements. What are the proper relations between those realms? To what extent are they mutually hostile, to what extent cooperative, and to what extent merely different?

3. Sexual confusion and erotic attraction are clearly sources of humor here, but also of pain. Anshel thinks of putting an end "to this weird comedy." "Weird" means not only "odd" but also "fate." In what ways is sex fateful? comic? What are the effects of sex in this world?

4. When Yentl decides to marry, she says, " 'Now I'll really start something.' " Why? What MOTIVATES each of her main decisions? Are we supposed to sympathize with her? admire her? Do you?

5. Although the separation of the male and female realms is taken for granted here, the story was written in the United States in the 1960s. What sort of

RESOLUTION does the final situation offer? What does it imply about the place(s) of women in modern society?

See also Questions for Contrast and Comparison: 14, 53, 54, 69, 128, 133, 135, 163, 205, 231, and 234.

ART SPIEGELMAN (1948–) *was born in Stockholm, Sweden, but later emigrated to New York City with his family. He took an early interest in satiric comics, such as* Mad Magazine, *and sold his first cover illustration to the* Long Island Post *at fourteen. He studied art at Harpur College (1965–1968), now the State University of New York at Binghamton, but left for full-time cartooning. Since 1966 he has worked with the Topps Bubble Gum Company designing cards and novelties, including the "Garbage Pail Kids." Even while selling political and satiric cartoons to the establishment press, he became a well known "underground" comic artist. Tiring of the genre's standard sex, profanity, drugs, and violence, in 1980 he and Françoise Mouly co-founded* Raw, *a magazine of "comics by adults [and] for adults . . . redefining what comics should be." He publishes widely and teaches cartooning in New York, but his most famous work is* Maus, *the serialized saga of his family in Europe and the United States.* Maus *began as a three-page cartoon (1972) that rejected Mickey Mouse cuteness to tell movingly of the Holocaust, with Nazis as cats, Poles as pigs, and Jews as mice. Subsequent chapters, except "Prisoner on the Hell Planet" (1973), appeared in* Raw. *In book form (Volume 1, 1986; Volume 2, 1991),* Maus *has made Spiegelman perhaps America's most respected cartoonist. He and Mouly, whom he married in 1977, have a daughter.*

Prisoner on the Hell Planet: A Case History

A COUSIN HERDED ME AWAY FROM THE SCENE.

COME TO THE DOCTOR'S.... YOUR MOTHER IS -AH- SICK!... HE WILL EXPLAIN ......

DOCTOR ORENS LIVED NEARBY...

SIT DOWN, ARTHUR... I THOUGHT I SHOULD BE THE ONE TO TELL YOU...

YOUR MOTHER KILLED HER- SELF—SHE'S DEAD!

I COULD AVOID THE TRUTH NO LONGER—THE DOCTOR'S WORDS CLATTERED INSIDE ME.... I FELT CONFUSED; I FELT ANGRY, I FELT NUMB!... I DIDN'T EXACTLY FEEL LIKE CRYING; BUT FIGURED I SHOULD!....

SHE'S DEAD! A SUICIDE!

NOW, NOW, BOY...

NO, LET HIM CRY... IT'S GOOD FOR HIM!

WE WENT HOME... MY FATHER HAD COM- PLETELY FALLEN APART!....

OY ARTIE! WHY? WHY! SUCH A TRAGEDY! AND NOT EVEN A NOTE!!!

I WAS EXPECTED TO COMFORT *HIM*!

MOTHER... MOTHER...

SOMEHOW THE FUNERAL ARRANGE- MENTS WERE MADE...

...AND FOR $950⁰⁰ WE HAVE A BRONZE CASKET WITH BRONZE- COLORED VELVET... OF COURSE, FOR $2,000⁰⁰ WE CAN...

PROTECT WHAT YOU HAVE

[1973]

Study and Writing Questions

1. How does the drawing STYLE, which changes in some panels, help to tell the STORY?
2. Compare first and subsequent readings of the first two panels.
3. What is the role of Hitler in the lives of these CHARACTERS?
4. What do we know about the NARRATOR's upbringing? his mind? his values? his relations with his family? Why does Artie tell this story?
5. What issues does the story raise? What central issue unites them? Why is the last speech balloon given to a faceless voice? What sort of RESOLUTION, if any, does the last panel offer?

See also Questions for Contrast and Comparison: 67, 95, 168, 184, 187, 199, and 239.

■ **GERTRUDE STEIN** (1874–1946) *was born in Allegheny, Pennsylvania, the youngest of seven children of German Jewish immigrants. She attended school in Austria, France, and California (the family settled in Oakland in 1879). After the deaths of her mother (1888) and father (1891), a wealthy merchant, she and her brother Leo were raised in Baltimore, Maryland, by an aunt, but they had independent incomes arranged by their oldest brother. Gertrude followed Leo to Harvard (B.A., 1897), where she studied with William James, and then to Johns Hopkins University, where she studied brain anatomy before the two siblings moved to Paris (1902). Their home quickly became a famous salon. Stein fostered such modern painters as Picasso, Braque, and Gris, and such modern writers as Hemingway, Anderson, and Fitzgerald. Her controversial writing, exemplified by the prose portraits of* Three Lives *(1909), reflected James's belief in the past and future as present mental activities. Her lectures on composition were widely read. Stein, always very active, served with an American ambulance unit in France during World War I. Beginning in 1908, Leo's place in Gertrude's salon and life was supplanted by a young California woman whose voice Stein borrowed to write about herself in her popular* Autobiography of Alice B. Toklas *(1933). Toklas served as Stein's homemaker, secretary, and lifelong companion; they are buried together in Paris.*

Miss Furr and Miss Skeene

Helen Furr had quite a pleasant home. Mrs. Furr was quite a pleasant woman. Mr. Furr was quite a pleasant man. Helen Furr had quite a pleasant voice a voice quite worth cultivating. She did not mind working. She worked to cultivate her voice. She did not find it gay living in the same place where she had always been living. She went to a place where some were cultivating something, voices and other things needing cultivating. She met Georgine Skeene there who was cultivating her voice which some thought was quite a pleasant one. Helen Furr and Georgine Skeene lived together then. Georgine Skeene liked travelling. Helen Furr did not care about travelling, she liked to stay in one place and be gay there. They were together then and travelled to another place and stayed there and were gay there.

They stayed there and were gay there, not very gay there, just gay there. They were both gay there, they were regularly working there both of them cultivating their voices there, they were both gay there. Georgine Skeene was gay there and she was regular, regular in being gay, regular in not being gay, regular in being a gay one who was one not being gay longer than was needed to be one being quite a gay one. They were both gay then there and both working there then.

They were in a way both gay there where there were many cultivating something. They were both regular in being gay there. Helen Furr was gay there, she was gayer and gayer there and really she was just gay there, she was gayer and gayer there, that is to say she found ways of being gay there that she was using in being gay there. She was gay there, not gayer and gayer, just gay there, that is to say she was not gayer by using the things she found there that were gay things, she was gay there, always she was gay there.

They were quite regularly gay there, Helen Furr and Georgine Skeene, they were regularly gay there where they were gay. They were very regularly gay.

To be regularly gay was to do every day the gay thing that they did every day. To be regularly gay was to end every day at the same time after they had been regularly gay. They were regularly gay. There were gay every day. They ended every day in the same way, at the same time, and they had been every day regularly gay.

The voice Helen Furr was cultivating was quite a pleasant one. The voice Georgine Skeene was cultivating was, some said, a better one. The voice Helen Furr was cultivating she cultivated and it was quite completely a pleasant enough one then, a cultivated enough one then. The voice Georgine Skeene was cultivating she did not cultivate too much. She cultivated it quite some. She cultivated and she would sometime go on cultivating it and it was not then an unpleasant one, it would be a quite richly enough cultivated one, it would be quite richly enough to be a pleasant enough one.

They were gay where there were many cultivating something. The two were gay there, were regularly gay there. Georgine Skeene would have liked to do more travelling. They did some travelling, not very much travelling. Georgine Skeene would have liked to do more travelling. Helen Furr did not care about doing travelling, she liked to stay in a place and be gay there.

They stayed in a place and were gay there, both of them stayed there, they stayed together there, they were gay there, they were regularly gay there.

They went quite often, not very often, but they did go back to where Helen Furr had a pleasant enough home and then Georgine Skeene went to a place where her brother had quite some distinction. They both went, every few years, went visiting to where Helen Furr had quite a pleasant home. Certainly Helen Furr would not find it gay to stay, she did not find it gay, she said she would not stay, she said she did not find it gay, she said she would not stay where she did not find it gay, she said she found it gay where she did stay and she did stay there where very many were cultivating something. She did stay there. She always did find it gay there.

She went to see them where she had always been living and where she did not find it gay. She had a pleasant home there, Mrs. Furr was a pleasant enough woman, Mr. Furr was a pleasant enough man, Helen told them and they were not worrying, that she did not find it gay living where she had always been living.

Georgine Skeene and Helen Furr were living where they were both cultivating their voices and they were gay there. They visited where Helen Furr had come from and then they went to where they were living where they were then regularly living.

There were some dark and heavy men there then. There were some who were not so heavy and some who were not so dark. Helen Furr and Georgine Skeene sat regularly with them. They sat regularly with the ones who were dark and heavy. They sat regularly with the ones who were not so dark. They sat regularly with the ones that were not so heavy. They sat with them regularly, sat with some of them. They went with them regularly went with them. They were regular then, they were gay then, they were where they wanted to be then where it was gay to be then, they were regularly gay then. There were men there then who were dark and heavy and they sat with them with Helen Furr and Georgine Skeene and they went with them with Miss Furr and Miss Skeene, and they went with the heavy and dark men Miss Furr and Miss Skeene went with them, and they sat with them, Miss Furr and Miss Skeene sat with them, and there were other men, some were not heavy men and they sat with Miss Furr and Miss Skeene and Miss Furr and Miss Skeene sat with them, and there were other men who were not dark men and they sat with Miss Furr and Miss Skeene and Miss Furr and Miss Skeene sat with them. Miss Furr and Miss Skeene went with them and they went with Miss Furr and Miss Skeene, some who were not heavy men, some who were not dark men. Miss Furr and Miss Skeene sat regularly, they sat with some men. Miss Furr and Miss Skeene went and there were some men with them. There were men and Miss Furr and Miss Skeene went with them, went somewhere with them, went with some of them.

Helen Furr and Georgine Skeene were regularly living where very many were living and cultivating in themselves something. Helen Furr and Georgine Skeene were living very regularly then, being very regular then in being gay then. They did then learn many ways to be gay and they were then being gay being quite regular in being gay, being gay and they were learning little things, little things in ways of being gay, they were very regular then, they were learning very many little things in ways of being gay, they were being gay and using these little things they were learning to have to be gay with regularly gay with then and they were gay the same amount they had been gay. They were quite gay, they were quite regular, they were learning little things, gay little things, they were gay inside them the same amount they had been gay, they were gay the same length of time they had been gay every day.

They were regular in being gay, they learned little things that are things in being gay, they learned many little things that are things in being gay, they were gay every day, they were regular, they were gay, they were gay the same length of time every day, they were gay, they were quite regularly gay.

Georgine Skeene went away to stay two months with her brother. Helen Furr did not go then to stay with her father and her mother. Helen Furr stayed there where they had been regularly living the two of them and she would then certainly not be lonesome, she would go on being gay. She did go on being gay. She was not any more gay but she was gay longer every day than they had been being gay when they were together being gay. She was gay then quite exactly the same way. She learned a few more little ways of being in being gay. She was quite gay and in the same way, the same way she had been gay and she was gay a little longer in the day, more of each day she was gay. She was gay longer every day than when the two of them had been being gay. She was gay quite in the way they had been gay, quite in the same way.

She was not lonesome then, she was not at all feeling any need of having Georgine Skeene. She was not astonished at this thing. She would have been a little astonished by this thing but she knew she was not astonished at anything and so she was not astonished at this thing not astonished at not feeling any need of having Georgine Skeene.

Helen Furr had quite a completely pleasant voice and it was quite well enough cultivated and she could use it and she did use it but then there was not any way of working at cultivating a completely pleasant voice when it has become a quite completely well enough cultivated one, and there was not much use in using it when one was not wanting it to be helping to make one a gay one. Helen Furr was not needing using her voice to be a gay one. She was gay then and sometimes she used her voice and she was not using it very often. It was quite completely enough cultivated and it was quite completely a pleasant one and she did not use it very often. She was then, she was quite exactly as gay as she had been, she was gay a little longer in the day than she had been.

She was gay exactly the same way. She was never tired of being gay that way. She had learned very many little ways to use in being gay. Very many were telling about using other ways in being gay. She was gay enough, she was always gay exactly the same way, she was always learning little things to use in being gay, she was telling about using other ways in being gay, she was telling about learning other ways in being gay, she was learning other ways in being gay, she would be using other ways in being gay, she would always be gay in the same way, when Georgine Skeene was there not so long each day as when Georgine Skeene was away.

She came to using many ways in being gay, she came to use every way in being gay. She went on living where many were cultivating something and she was gay, she had used every way to be gay.

They did not live together then Helen Furr and Georgine Skeene. Helen Furr lived there the longer where they had been living regularly together. Then neither of them were living there any longer. Helen Furr was living somewhere else then and telling some about being gay and she was gay then and she was living quite regularly then. She was regularly gay then. She was quite regular in being gay then. She remembered all the little ways of being gay. She used all the little ways of being gay. She was quite regularly gay. She told many then the way of being gay, she taught very many then little ways they could use in being gay. She was living very well, she was gay then, she went on living then, she was regular in being gay, she always was living very well and was gay very well and was telling about little ways one could be learning to use in being gay, and later was telling them quite often, telling them again and again.

[1922]

Study and Writing Questions

1. "Gay" has numerous meanings, including "merry," "happily excited," and "lively." According to Eric Partridge's *A Dictionary of Slang and Unconventional English*, gay also has had the meaning of "homosexual," at least among homosexuals, since the beginning of the nineteenth century. How are the meanings of "gay" introduced and modified in the course of the first two paragraphs? Since "gay" is the most important explicit concept in the lives of the title CHARACTERS, why is the most frequently repeated word in the first paragraph "pleasant"? What does "regularly gay" mean in its different contexts in this NARRATIVE?

2. Who are the "dark and heavy men"? What do they represent?

3. Although the NARRATOR uses many words, they are typically the same words repeated with small variations. In fact, the narrator is quite vague about most PLOT elements, ranging from the names of places to the descriptions of acts and emotions. What are the RHETORICAL effects of this vagueness on the story's MOOD and THEME?

4. What do we infer about the values and social positions of the title characters?

In what ways are they alike and in what ways different? Why are they attracted to each other? Why do they separate?

5. What sort of STORY is this? A love story? A story of social commentary? Something else? How do the narrator's attitudes toward the story's central subject evolve during the narrative? Whatever sort of story this is, what sort of RESOLUTION does the last paragraph offer?

See also Questions for Contrast and Comparison: 12, 28, 41, 88, 178, 181, and 205.

■ JOHN (ERNST) STEINBECK (1902–1968) *was born and raised in the agricultural Salinas Valley of northern California, son of the county treasurer and a former teacher. He attended Stanford University intermittently (1919–1925) but took no degree, working instead at odd jobs (hod-carrier, fruit-picker, caretaker, laboratory assistant, and so on) while trying to become a professional writer. His first* NOVEL, Cup of Gold *(1929), dramatized the life of Henry Morgan, the buccaneer. Steinbeck attracted popular attention only after publication of his fourth book,* Tortilla Flat *(1935), a tolerant look at the lives of Monterey laborers. A prolific memoir and essay writer, Steinbeck always sympathized with working people and their suffering under economic exploitation, natural disaster, and such human failings as greed. His greatest fictions include* Of Mice and Men *(1937), about two migrant farmers;* The Grapes of Wrath *(1939), a Depression epic about a family fleeing the Dust Bowl to seek work in California;* The Pearl *(1948), a short* PARABLE *of greed; and* East of Eden *(1952), a* SYMBOLIC *family saga ranging from the Civil War to World War I. Steinbeck also did war reporting from Italy (1943) and Vietnam (1966–1967). Three times married and twice divorced (1930–1943; 1943–1948; 1950–1968), he had two sons with his second wife. His best stories appear in* The Long Valley *(1938). He received the Nobel Prize for Literature in 1962.*

The Chrysanthemums

The high grey-flannel fog of winter closed off the Salinas Valley from the sky and from all the rest of the world. On every side it sat like a lid on the mountains and made of the great valley a closed pot. On the broad, level land floor the gang plows bit deep and left the black earth shining like metal where the shares had cut. On the foothill ranches across the Salinas River, the yellow stubble fields seemed to be bathed in pale cold sunshine, but there was no sunshine in the valley now in December. The thick willow scrub along the river flamed with sharp and positive yellow leaves.

It was a time of quiet and of waiting. The air was cold and tender. A light wind blew up from the southwest so that the farmers were mildly hopeful of a good rain before long; but fog and rain do not go together.

Across the river, on Henry Allen's foothill ranch there was little work to be done, for the hay was cut and stored and the orchards were plowed up to receive the rain deeply when it should come. The cattle on the higher slopes were becoming shaggy and rough-coated.

Elisa Allen, working in her flower garden, looked down across the yard and saw Henry, her husband, talking to two men in business suits. The three of them stood by the tractor shed, each man with one foot on the side of the little Fordson. They smoked cigarettes and studied the machine as they talked.

Elisa watched them for a moment and then went back to her work. She was thirty-five. Her face was lean and strong and her eyes were as clear as water. Her figure looked blocked and heavy in her gardening costume, a man's black hat pulled low down over her eyes, clodhopper shoes, a figured print dress almost completely covered by a big corduroy apron with four big pockets to hold the snips, the trowel and scratcher, the seeds and the knife she worked with. She wore heavy leather gloves to protect her hands while she worked.

She was cutting down the old year's chrysanthemum stalks with a pair of short and powerful scissors. She looked down toward the men by the tractor shed now and then. Her face was eager and mature and handsome; even her work with the scissors was over-eager, over-powerful. The chrysanthemum stems seemed too small and easy for her energy.

She brushed a cloud of hair out of her eyes with the back of her glove, and left a smudge of earth on her cheek in doing it. Behind her stood the neat white farm house with red geraniums close-banked around it as high as the windows. It was a hard-swept looking little house, with hard-polished windows, and a clean mud-mat on the front steps.

Elisa cast another glance toward the tractor shed. The strangers were getting into their Ford coupe. She took off a glove and put her strong fingers down into the forest of new green chrysanthemum sprouts that were growing around the old roots. She spread the leaves and looked down among the close-growing stems. No aphids were there, no sowbugs or snails or cutworms. Her terrier fingers destroyed such pests before they could get started.

Elisa started at the sound of her husband's voice. He had come near quietly, and he leaned over the wire fence that protected her flower garden from cattle and dogs and chickens.

"At it again," he said. "You've got a strong new crop coming."

Elisa straightened her back and pulled on the gardening glove again. "Yes. They'll be strong this coming year." In her tone and on her face there was a little smugness.

"You've got a gift with things," Henry observed. "Some of those yellow chrysanthemums you had this year were ten inches across. I wish you'd work out in the orchard and raise some apples that big."

Her eyes sharpened. "Maybe I could do it, too. I've a gift with things, all right. My mother had it. She could stick anything in the ground and make it grow. She said it was having planters' hands that knew how to do it."

"Well, it sure works with flowers," he said.

"Henry, who were those men you were talking to?"

"Why, sure, that's what I came to tell you. They were from the Western Meat Company. I sold those thirty head of three-year-old steers. Got nearly my own price, too."

"Good," she said. "Good for you."

"And I thought," he continued, "I thought how it's Saturday afternoon, and we might go into Salinas for dinner at a restaurant, and then to a picture show—to celebrate, you see."

"Good," she repeated. "Oh, yes. That will be good."

Henry put on his joking tone. "There's fights tonight. How'd you like to go to the fights?"

"Oh, no," she said breathlessly. "No, I wouldn't like fights."

"Just fooling, Elisa. We'll go to a movie. Let's see. It's two now. I'm going to take Scotty and bring down those steers from the hill. It'll take us maybe two hours. We'll go in town about five and have dinner at the Cominos Hotel. Like that?"

"Of course I'll like it. It's good to eat away from home."

"All right, then. I'll go get up a couple of horses."

She said, "I'll have plenty of time to transplant some of these sets, I guess."

She heard her husband calling Scotty down by the barn. And a little later she saw the two men ride up the pale yellow hillside in search of the steers.

There was a little square sandy bed kept for rooting the chrysanthemums. With her trowel she turned the soil over and over, and smoothed it and patted it firm. Then she dug ten parallel trenches to receive the sets. Back at the chrysanthemum bed she pulled out the little crisp shoots, trimmed off the leaves of each one with her scissors and laid it on a small orderly pile.

A squeak of wheels and plod of hoofs came from the road. Elisa looked up. The country road ran along the dense bank of willows and cottonwoods that bordered the river, and up this road came a curious vehicle, curiously drawn. It was an old spring-wagon, with a round canvas top on it like the cover of a prairie schooner. It was drawn by an old bay horse and a little grey-and-white burro. A big stubble-bearded man sat between the cover flaps and drove the crawling team. Underneath the wagon, between the hind wheels, a lean and rangy mongrel dog walked sedately. Words were painted on the canvas, in clumsy, crooked letters. "Pots, pans, knives, sisors, lawn mores, Fixed." Two rows of articles, and the triumphantly definitive "Fixed" below. The black paint had run down in little sharp points beneath each letter.

Elisa, squatting on the ground, watched to see the crazy, loose-jointed wagon pass by. But it didn't pass. It turned into the farm road in front of her house, crooked old wheels skirling and squeaking. The rangy dog darted from between the wheels and ran ahead. Instantly the two ranch shepherds flew out at him. Then all three stopped, and with stiff and quivering tails, with taut straight legs, with ambassadorial dignity, they slowly circled, sniffing daintily. The caravan pulled up to Elisa's wire fence and stopped. Now the newcomer dog, feeling out-numbered, lowered his tail and retired under the wagon with raised hackles and bared teeth.

The man on the wagon seat called out, "That's a bad dog in a fight when he gets started."

Elisa laughed. "I see he is. How soon does he generally get started?"

The man caught up her laughter and echoed it heartily. "Sometimes not for weeks and weeks," he said. He climbed stiffly down, over the wheel. The horse and the donkey drooped like unwatered flowers.

Elisa saw that he was a very big man. Although his hair and beard were greying, he did not look old. His worn black suit was wrinkled and spotted with grease. The laughter had disappeared from his face and eyes the moment his laughing voice ceased. His eyes were dark, and they were full of the brooding that gets in the eyes of teamsters and of sailors. The calloused hands he rested on the wire fence were cracked, and every crack was a black line. He took off his battered hat.

"I'm off my general road, ma'am," he said. "Does this dirt road cut over across the river to the Los Angeles highway?"

Elisa stood up and shoved the thick scissors in her apron pocket. "Well, yes, it does, but it winds around and then fords the river. I don't think your team could pull through the sand."

He replied with some asperity, "It might surprise you what them beasts can pull through."

"When they get started?" she asked.

He smiled for a second. "Yes. When they get started."

"Well," said Elisa, "I think you'll save time if you go back to the Salinas road and pick up the highway there."

He drew a big finger down the chicken wire and made it sing. "I ain't in any hurry, ma'am. I go from Seattle to San Diego and back every year. Takes all my time. About six months each way. I aim to follow nice weather."

Elisa took off her gloves and stuffed them in the apron pocket with the scissors. She touched the under edge of her man's hat, searching for fugitive hairs. "That sounds like a nice kind of a way to live," she said.

He leaned confidentially over the fence. "Maybe you noticed the writing on my wagon. I mend pots and sharpen knives and scissors. You got any of them things to do?"

"Oh, no," she said quickly. "Nothing like that." Her eyes hardened with resistance.

"Scissors is the worst thing," he explained. "Most people just ruin scissors trying to sharpen 'em, but I know how. I got a special tool. It's a little bobbit kind of thing, and patented. But it sure does the trick."

"No. My scissors are all sharp."

"All right, then. Take a pot," he continued earnestly, "a bent pot, or a pot with a hole. I can make it like new so you don't have to buy no new ones. That's a saving for you."

"No," she said shortly. "I tell you I have nothing like that for you to do."

His face fell to an exaggerated sadness. His voice took on a whining undertone. "I ain't had a thing to do today. Maybe I won't have no supper tonight. You see I'm off my regular road. I know folks on the highway clear from Seattle to San Diego. They save their things for me to sharpen up because they know I do it so good and save them money."

"I'm sorry," Elisa said irritably. "I haven't anything for you to do."

His eyes left her face and fell to searching the ground. They roamed about until they came to the chrysanthemum bed where she had been working. "What's them plants, ma'am?"

The irritation and resistance melted from Elisa's face. "Oh, those are chrysanthemums, giant whites and yellows. I raise them every year, bigger than anybody around here."

"Kind of a long-stemmed flower? Looks like a quick puff of colored smoke?" he asked.

"That's it. What a nice way to describe them."

"They smell kind of nasty till you get used to them," he said.

"It's a good bitter smell," she retorted, "not nasty at all."

He changed his tone quickly. "I like the smell myself."

"I had ten-inch blooms this year," she said.

The man leaned farther over the fence. "Look. I know a lady down the road a piece, has got the nicest garden you ever seen. Got nearly every kind of flower but no chrysanthemums. Last time I was mending a copper-bottom washtub for her (that's a hard job but I do it good), she said to me, 'If you ever run acrost some nice chrysanthemums I wish you'd try to get me a few seeds.' That's what she told me."

Elisa's eyes grew alert and eager. "She couldn't have known much about chrysanthemums. You can raise them from seed, but it's much easier to root the little sprouts you see there."

"Oh," he said. "I s'pose I can't take none to her, then."

"Why yes you can," Elisa cried. "I can put some in damp sand, and you can carry them right along with you. They'll take root in the pot if you keep them damp. And then she can transplant them."

"She'd sure like to have some, ma'am. You say they're nice ones?"

"Beautiful," she said. "Oh, beautiful." Her eyes shone. She tore off the battered hat and shook out her dark pretty hair. "I'll put them in a flower pot, and you can take them right with you. Come into the yard."

While the man came through the picket gate Elisa ran excitedly along the geranium-bordered path to the back of the house. And she returned carrying a big red flower pot. The gloves were forgotten now. She kneeled on the ground by the starting bed and dug up the sandy soil with her fingers and scooped it into the bright new flower pot. Then she picked up the little pile of shoots she had prepared. With her strong fingers she pressed them into the sand and tamped around them with her knuckles. The man stood over her. "I'll tell you what to do," she said. "You remember so you can tell the lady."

"Yes, I'll try to remember."

"Well, look. These will take root in about a month. Then she must set them out, about a foot apart in good rich earth like this, see?" She lifted a handful of dark soil for him to look at. "They'll grow fast and tall. Now remember this: In July tell her to cut them down, about eight inches from the ground."

"Before they bloom?" he asked.

"Yes, before they bloom." Her face was tight with eagerness. "They'll grow right up again. About the last of September the buds will start."

She stopped and seemed perplexed. "It's the budding that takes the most care," she said hesitantly. "I don't know how to tell you." She looked deep into his eyes, searchingly. Her mouth opened a little, and she seemed to be listening. "I'll try to tell you," she said. "Did you ever hear of planting hands?"

"Can't say I have, ma'am."

"Well, I can only tell you what it feels like. It's when you're picking off the buds you don't want. Everything goes right down into your fingertips. You watch your fingers work. They do it themselves. You can feel how it is. They pick and pick the buds. They never make a mistake. They're with the plant. Do you see? Your fingers and the plant. You can feel that, right up your arm. They know. They never make a mistake. You can feel it. When you're like that you can't do anything wrong. Do you see that? Can you understand that?"

She was kneeling on the ground looking up at him. Her breast swelled passionately.

The man's eyes narrowed. He looked away self-consciously. "Maybe I know," he said. "Sometimes in the night in the wagon there ——"

Elisa's voice grew husky. She broke in on him, "I've never lived as you do, but I know what you mean. When the night is dark—why, the stars are sharp-pointed, and there's quiet. Why, you rise up and up! Every pointed star gets driven into your body. It's like that. Hot and sharp and—lovely."

Kneeling there, her hand went out toward his legs in the greasy black trousers. Her hesitant fingers almost touched the cloth. Then her hand dropped to the ground. She crouched low like a fawning dog.

He said, "It's nice, just like you say. Only when you don't have no dinner, it ain't."

She stood up then, very straight, and her face was ashamed. She held the flower pot out to him and placed it gently in his arms. "Here. Put it in your wagon, on the seat, where you can watch it. Maybe I can find something for you to do."

At the back of the house she dug in the can pile and found two old and battered aluminum saucepans. She carried them back and gave them to him. "Here, maybe you can fix these."

His manner changed. He became professional. "Good as new I can fix them." At the back of his wagon he set a little anvil, and out of an oily tool box dug a small machine hammer. Elisa came through the gate to watch him while he pounded out the dents in the kettles. His mouth grew sure and knowing. At a difficult part of the work he sucked his under-lip.

"You sleep right in the wagon?" Elisa asked.

"Right in the wagon, ma'am. Rain or shine I'm dry as a cow in there."

"It must be nice," she said. "It must be very nice. I wish women could do such things."

"It ain't the right kind of a life for a woman."

Her upper lip raised a little, showing her teeth. "How do you know? How can you tell?" she said.

"I don't know, ma'am," he protested. "Of course I don't know. Now here's your kettles, done. You don't have to buy no new ones."

"How much?"

"Oh, fifty cents'll do. I keep my prices down and my work good. That's why I have all them satisfied customers up and down the highway."

Elisa brought him a fifty-cent piece from the house and dropped it in his hand. "You might be surprised to have a rival some time. I can sharpen scissors, too. And I can beat the dents out of little pots. I could show you what a woman might do."

He put his hammer back in the oily box and shoved the little anvil out of sight. "It would be a lonely life for a woman, ma'am, and a scarey life, too, with animals creeping under the wagon all night." He climbed over the singletree, steadying himself with a hand on the burro's white rump. He settled himself in the seat, picked up the lines. "Thank you kindly, ma'am," he said. "I'll do like you told me; I'll go back and catch the Salinas road."

"Mind," she called, "if you're long in getting there, keep the sand damp."

"Sand, ma'am? . . . Sand? Oh, sure. You mean around the chrysanthemums. Sure I will." He clucked his tongue. The beasts leaned luxuriously into their collars. The mongrel dog took his place between the back wheels. The wagon turned and crawled out the entrance road and back the way it had come, along the river.

Elisa stood in front of her wire fence watching the slow progress of the caravan. Her shoulders were straight, her head thrown back, her eyes half-closed, so that the scene came vaguely into them. Her lips moved silently, forming the words "Good-bye — good-bye." Then she whispered, "That's a bright direction.

There's a glowing there." The sound of her whisper startled her. She shook herself free and looked about to see whether anyone had been listening. Only the dogs had heard. They lifted their heads toward her from their sleeping in the dust, and then stretched out their chins and settled asleep again. Elisa turned and ran hurriedly into the house.

In the kitchen she reached behind the stove and felt the water tank. It was full of hot water from the noonday cooking. In the bathroom she tore off her soiled clothes and flung them into the corner. And then she scrubbed herself with a little block of pumice, legs and thighs, loins and chest and arms, until her skin was scratched and red. When she had dried herself she stood in front of the mirror in her bedroom and looked at her body. She tightened her stomach and threw out her chest. She turned and looked over her shoulder at her back.

After a while she began to dress, slowly. She put on her newest underclothing and her nicest stockings and the dress which was the symbol of her prettiness. She worked carefully on her hair, penciled her eyebrows and rouged her lips.

Before she was finished she heard the little thunder of hoofs and the shouts of Henry and his helper as they drove the red steers into the corral. She heard the gate bang shut and set herself for Henry's arrival.

His step sounded on the porch. He entered the house calling, "Elisa, where are you?"

"In my room, dressing. I'm not ready. There's hot water for your bath. Hurry up. It's getting late."

When she heard him splashing in the tub, Elisa laid his dark suit on the bed, and shirt and socks and tie beside it. She stood his polished shoes on the floor beside the bed. Then she went to the porch and sat primly and stiffly down. She looked toward the river road where the willow-line was still yellow with frosted leaves so that under the high grey fog they seemed a thin band of sunshine. This was the only color in the grey afternoon. She sat unmoving for a long time. Her eyes blinked rarely.

Henry came banging out of the door, shoving his tie inside his vest as he came. Elisa stiffened and her face grew tight. Henry stopped short and looked at her. "Why—why, Elisa. You look so nice!"

"Nice? You think I look nice? What do you mean by 'nice'?"

Henry blundered on. "I don't know. I mean you look different, strong and happy."

"I am strong? Yes, strong. What do you mean 'strong'?"

He looked bewildered. "You're playing some kind of a game," he said helplessly. "It's a kind of a play. You look strong enough to break a calf over your knee, happy enough to eat it like a watermelon."

For a second she lost her rigidity. "Henry! Don't talk like that. You didn't know what you said." She grew complete again. "I'm strong," she boasted. "I never knew before how strong."

Henry looked down toward the tractor shed, and when he brought his eyes back to her, they were his own again. "I'll get out the car. You can put on your coat while I'm starting."

Elisa went into the house. She heard him drive to the gate and idle his motor, and then she took a long time to put on her hat. She pulled it here and pressed it there. When Henry turned the motor off she slipped into her coat and went out.

The little roadster bounced along on the dirt road by the river, raising the birds and driving the rabbits into the brush. Two cranes flapped heavily over the willow-line and dropped into the river-bed.

Far ahead on the road Elisa saw a dark speck. She knew.

She tried not to look as they passed it, but her eyes would not obey. She whispered to herself sadly, "He might have thrown them off the road. That wouldn't have been much trouble, not very much. But he kept the pot," she explained. "He had to keep the pot. That's why he couldn't get them off the road."

The roadster turned a bend and she saw the caravan ahead. She swung full around toward her husband so she could not see the little covered wagon and the mismatched team as the car passed them.

In a moment it was over. The thing was done. She did not look back.

She said loudly, to be heard above the motor, "It will be good, tonight, a good dinner."

"Now you're changed again," Henry complained. He took one hand from the wheel and patted her knee. "I ought to take you in to dinner oftener. It would be good for both of us. We get so heavy out on the ranch."

"Henry," she asked, "could we have wine at dinner?"

"Sure we could. Say! That will be fine."

She was silent for a while; then she said, "Henry, at those prize fights, do the men hurt each other very much?"

"Sometimes a little, not often. Why?"

"Well, I've read how they break noses, and blood runs down their chests. I've read how the fighting gloves get heavy and soggy with blood."

He looked around at her. "What's the matter, Elisa? I didn't know you read things like that." He brought the car to a stop, then turned to the right over the Salinas River bridge.

"Do any women ever go to the fights?" she asked.

"Oh, sure, some. What's the matter, Elisa? Do you want to go? I don't think you'd like it, but I'll take you if you really want to go."

She relaxed limply in the seat. "Oh, no. No. I don't want to go. I'm sure I don't." Her face was turned away from him. "It will be enough if we can have wine. It will be plenty." She turned up her coat collar so he could not see that she was crying weakly—like an old woman.

[1937]

Study and Writing Questions

1. Why does the STORY begin with a DESCRIPTION of the natural world? In what ways could this description be taken to introduce the story or to predict its CONFLICTS or outcome?

2. Elisa and the tinker quite early in their encounter share laughter and quite late disagree about the fitness of a traveler's life for a woman. What are the different stages of their relationship? What MOTIVATES each CHARACTER through these changes?

3. How does the description of Elisa's bath scene suggest what she is thinking or feeling?

4. In this story, we learn many details about chrysanthemums in general and about Elisa's chrysanthemums in particular. What do these details add to the story? How is it that Elisa "knew" that the "dark speck" would be her discarded chrysanthemums?
5. What does marriage mean for Elisa? What kind of relationship do Elisa and Henry have? Does it remain constant throughout the story? What can we learn from Elisa's last statement? What can we learn from the last sentence of the story?

See also Questions for Contrast and Comparison: 4, 45, 84, 99, 100, 101, 102, 103, 108, 148, and 192.

The Harness

Peter Randall was one of the most highly respected farmers of Monterey County. Once, before he was to make a little speech at a Masonic convention, the brother who introduced him referred to him as an example for young Masons of California to emulate. He was nearing fifty; his manner was grave and restrained, and he wore a carefully tended beard. From every gathering he reaped the authority that belongs to the bearded man. Peter's eyes were grave, too; blue and grave almost to the point of sorrowfulness. People knew there was force in him, but force held caged. Sometimes, for no apparent reason, his eyes grew sullen and mean, like the eyes of a bad dog; but that look soon passed, and the restraint and probity came back into his face. He was tall and broad. He held his shoulders back as though they were braced, and he sucked in his stomach like a soldier. Inasmuch as farmers are usually slouchy men, Peter gained an added respect because of his posture.

Concerning Peter's wife, Emma, people generally agreed that it was hard to see how such a little skin-and-bones woman could go on living, particularly when she was sick most of the time. She weighed eighty-seven pounds. At forty-five, her face was as wrinkled and brown as that of an old, old woman, but her dark eyes were feverish with a determination to live. She was a proud woman, who complained very little. Her father had been a thirty-third degree Mason and Worshipful Master of the Grand Lodge of California. Before he died he had taken a great deal of interest in Peter's Masonic career.

Once a year Peter went away for a week, leaving his wife alone on the farm. To neighbors who called to keep her company she invariably explained, "He's away on a business trip."

Each time Peter returned from a business trip, Emma was ailing for a month or two, and this was hard on Peter, for Emma did her own work and refused to hire a girl. When she was ill, Peter had to do the housework.

The Randall ranch lay across the Salinas River, next to the foothills. It was an ideal balance of bottom and upland. Forty-five acres of rich level soil brought from the cream of the county by the river in old times and spread out as flat as a board; and eight acres of gentle upland for hay and orchard. The white farmhouse was as neat and restrained as its owners. The immediate yard was fenced, and in the garden, under Emma's direction, Peter raised button dahlias and immortelles, carnations and pinks.

From the front porch one could look down over the flat to the river with its sheath of willows and cottonwoods, and across the river to the beet fields, and past the fields to the bulbous dome of the Salinas courthouse. Often in the afternoon Emma sat in a rocking-chair on the front porch, until the breeze drove her in. She knitted constantly, looking up now and then to watch Peter working on the flat or in the orchard, or on the slope below the house.

The Randall ranch was no more encumbered with mortgage than any of the others in the valley. The crops, judiciously chosen and carefully tended, paid the interest, made a reasonable living and left a few hundred dollars every year toward paying off the principal. It was no wonder that Peter Randall was respected by his neighbors, and that his seldom spoken words were given attention even when they were about the weather or the way things were going. Let Peter say, "I'm going to kill a pig Saturday," and nearly every one of his hearers went home and killed a pig on Saturday. They didn't know why, but if Peter Randall was going to kill a pig, it seemed like a good, safe, conservative thing to do.

Peter and Emma were married for twenty-one years. They collected a houseful of good furniture, a number of framed pictures, vases of all shapes, and books of a sturdy type. Emma had no children. The house was unscarred, uncarved, unchalked. On the front and back porches footscrapers and thick cocoa-fiber mats kept dirt out of the house.

In the intervals between her illnesses, Emma saw to it that the house was kept up. The hinges of doors and cupboards were oiled, and no screws were gone from the catches. The furniture and woodwork were freshly varnished once a year. Repairs were usually made after Peter came home from his yearly business trips.

Whenever the word went around among the farms that Emma was sick again, the neighbors waylaid the doctor as he drove by on the river road.

"Oh, I guess she'll be all right," he answered their questions. "She'll have to stay in bed for a couple of weeks."

The good neighbors took cakes to the Randall farm, and they tiptoed into the sickroom, where the little skinny bird of a woman lay in a tremendous walnut bed. She looked at them with her bright little dark eyes.

"Wouldn't you like the curtains up a little, dear?" they asked.

"No, thank you. The light worries my eyes."

"Is there anything we can do for you?"

"No, thank you. Peter does for me very well."

"Just remember, if there's anything you think of —— "

Emma was such a tight woman. There was nothing you could do for her when she was ill, except to take pies and cakes to Peter. Peter would be in the kitchen, wearing a neat, clean apron. He would be filling a hot water bottle or making junket.

And so, one fall, when the news traveled that Emma was down, the farmwives baked for Peter and prepared to make their usual visits.

Mrs. Chappell, the next farm neighbor, stood on the river road when the doctor drove by. "How's Emma Randall, doctor?"

"I don't think she's so very well, Mrs. Chappell. I think she's a pretty sick woman."

Because to Dr. Marn anyone who wasn't actually a corpse was well on the road to recovery, the word went about among the farms that Emma Randall was going to die.

It was a long, terrible illness. Peter himself gave enemas and carried bedpans. The doctor's suggestion that a nurse be employed met only beady, fierce refusal in the eyes of the patient; and, ill as she was, her demands were respected. Peter fed her and bathed her, and made up the great walnut bed. The bedroom curtains remained drawn.

It was two months before the dark, sharp bird eyes veiled, and the sharp mind retired into unconsciousness. And only then did a nurse come to the house. Peter was lean and sick himself, not far from collapse. The neighbors brought him cakes and pies, and found them uneaten in the kitchen when they called again.

Mrs. Chappell was in the house with Peter the afternoon Emma died. Peter became hysterical immediately. Mrs. Chappell telephoned the doctor, and then she called her husband to come and help her, for Peter was wailing like a crazy man, and beating his bearded cheeks with his fists. Ed Chappell was ashamed when he saw him.

Peter's beard was wet with his tears. His loud sobbing could be heard throughout the house. Sometimes he sat by the bed and covered his head with a pillow, and sometimes he paced the floor of the bedroom bellowing like a calf. When Ed Chappell self-consciously put a hand on his shoulder and said, "Come on, Peter, come on, now," in a helpless voice, Peter shook his hand off. The doctor drove out and signed the certificate.

When the undertaker came, they had a devil of a time with Peter. He was half mad. He fought them when they tried to take the body away. It was only after Ed Chappell and the undertaker held him down while the doctor stuck him with a hypodermic, that they were able to remove Emma.

The morphine didn't put Peter to sleep. He sat hunched in the corner, breathing heavily and staring at the floor.

"Who's going to stay with him?" the doctor asked. "Miss Jack?" to the nurse.

"I couldn't handle him, doctor, not alone."

"Will you stay, Chappell?"

"Sure, I'll stay."

"Well, look. Here are some triple bromides. If he gets going again, give him one of these. And if they don't work, here's some sodium amytal. One of these capsules will calm him down."

Before they went away, they helped the stupefied Peter into the sitting-room and laid him gently down on a sofa. Ed Chappell sat in an easy-chair and watched him. The bromides and a glass of water were on the table beside him.

The little sitting-room was clean and dusted. Only that morning Peter had swept the floor with pieces of damp newspaper. Ed built a little fire in the grate, and put on a couple of pieces of oak when the flames were well started. The dark had come early. A light rain spattered against the windows when the wind drove it. Ed trimmed the kerosene lamps and turned the flames low. In the grate the blaze snapped and crackled and the flames curled like hair over the oak. For a long time Ed sat in his easy-chair watching Peter where he lay drugged on the couch. At last Ed dozed off to sleep.

It was about ten o'clock when he awakened. He started up and looked toward the sofa. Peter was sitting up, looking at him. Ed's hand went out toward the bromide bottle, but Peter shook his head.

"No need to give me anything, Ed. I guess the doctor slugged me pretty hard, didn't he? I feel all right now, only a little dopey."

"If you'll just take one of these, you'll get some sleep."

"I don't want sleep." He fingered his draggled beard and then stood up. "I'll go out and wash my face, then I'll feel better."

Ed heard him running water in the kitchen. In a moment he came back into the living-room, still drying his face on a towel. Peter was smiling curiously. It was an expression Ed had never seen on him before, a quizzical, wondering smile. "I guess I kind of broke loose when she died, didn't I?" Peter said.

"Well—yes, you carried on some."

"It seemed like something snapped inside of me," Peter explained. "Something like a suspender strap. It made me all come apart. I'm all right, now, though."

Ed looked down at the floor and saw a little brown spider crawling, and stretched out his foot and stomped it.

Peter asked suddenly, "Do you believe in an afterlife?"

Ed Chappell squirmed. He didn't like to talk about such things, for to talk about them was to bring them up in his mind and think about them. "Well, yes. I suppose if you come right down to it, I do."

"Do you believe that somebody that's—passed on—can look down and see what we're doing?"

"Oh, I don't know as I'd go that far—I don't know."

Peter went on as though he were talking to himself.

"Even if she could see me, and I didn't do what she wanted, she ought to feel good because I did it when she was here. It ought to please her that she made a good man of me. If I wasn't a good man when she wasn't here, that'd prove she did it all, wouldn't it? I was a good man, wasn't I, Ed?"

"What do you mean, 'was'?"

"Well, except for one week a year I was good. I don't know what I'll do now. . . ." His face grew angry. "Except one thing." He stood up and stripped off his coat and his shirt. Over his underwear there was a web harness that pulled his shoulders back. He unhooked the harness and threw it off. Then he dropped his trousers, disclosing a wide elastic belt. He shucked this off over his feet, and then he scratched his stomach luxuriously before he put on his clothes again. He smiled at Ed, the strange, wondering smile, again. "I don't know how she got me to do things, but she did. She didn't seem to boss me, but she always made me do things. You know, I don't think I believe in an after-life. When she was alive, even when she was sick, I had to do things she wanted, but just the minute she died, it was—why like that harness coming off! I couldn't stand it. It was all over. I'm going to have to get used to going without that harness." He shook his finger in Ed's direction. "My stomach's going to stick out," he said positively. "I'm going to let it stick out. Why, I'm fifty years old."

Ed didn't like that. He wanted to get away. This sort of thing wasn't very decent. "If you'll just take one of these, you'll get some sleep," he said weakly.

Peter had not put his coat on. He was sitting on the sofa in an open shirt. "I don't want to sleep. I want to talk. I guess I'll have to put that belt and harness on for the funeral, but after that I'm going to burn them. Listen, I've got a bottle of whiskey in the barn. I'll go get it."

"Oh no," Ed protested quickly. "I couldn't drink now, not at a time like this."

Peter stood up. "Well, I could. You can sit and watch me if you want. I tell you, it's all over." He went out the door, leaving Ed Chappell unhappy and scandalized. It was only a moment before he was back. He started talking as he came through the doorway with the whiskey. "I only got one thing in my life, those trips. Emma was a pretty bright woman. She knew I'd've gone crazy if I didn't get away once a year. God, how she worked on my conscience when I came back!" His voice lowered confidentially. "You know what I did on those trips?"

Ed's eyes were wide open now. Here was a man he didn't know, and he was becoming fascinated. He took the glass of whiskey when it was handed to him. "No, what did you do?"

Peter gulped his drink and coughed, and wiped his mouth with his hand. "I got drunk," he said. "I went to fancy houses in San Francisco. I was drunk for a week, and I went to a fancy house every night." He poured his glass full again. "I guess Emma knew, but she never said anything. I'd've *busted* if I hadn't got away."

Ed Chappell sipped his whiskey gingerly. "She always said you went on business."

Peter looked at his glass and drank it, and poured it full again. His eyes had begun to shine. "Drink your drink, Ed. I know you think it isn't right — so soon, but no one'll know but you and me. Kick up the fire. I'm not sad."

Chappell went to the grate and stirred the glowing wood until lots of sparks flew up the chimney like little shining birds. Peter filled the glasses and retired to the sofa again. When Ed went back to the chair he sipped from his glass and pretended he didn't know it was filled up. His cheeks were flushing. It didn't seem so terrible, now, to be drinking. The afternoon and the death had receded into an indefinite past.

"Want some cake?" Peter asked. "There's half a dozen cakes in the pantry."

"No, I don't think I will thank you for some."

"You know," Peter confessed, "I don't think I'll eat cake again. For ten years, every time Emma was sick, people sent cakes. It was nice of 'em, of course, only now cake means sickness to me. Drink your drink."

Something happened in the room. Both men looked up, trying to discover what it was. The room was somehow different than it had been a moment before. Then Peter smiled sheepishly. "It was that mantel clock stopped. I don't think I'll start it any more. I'll get a little quick alarm clock that ticks fast. That clack-clack-clack is too mournful." He swallowed his whiskey. "I guess you'll be telling around that I'm crazy, won't you?"

Ed looked up from his glass, and smiled and nodded. "No, I will not. I can see pretty much how you feel about things. I didn't know you wore that harness and belt."

"A man ought to stand up straight," Peter said. "I'm a natural sloucher." Then he exploded: "I'm a natural fool! For twenty years I've been pretending I was a wise, good man — except for that one week a year." He said loudly, "Things have been dribbled to me. My life's been dribbled out to me. Here, let me fill your glass. I've got another bottle out in the barn, way down under a pile of sacks."

Ed held out his glass to be filled. Peter went on, "I thought how it would be nice to have my whole river flat in sweet peas. Think how it'd be to sit on the front porch and see all those acres of blue and pink, just solid. And when the wind came up over them, think of the big smell. A big smell that would almost knock you over."

"A lot of men have gone broke on sweet peas. 'Course you get a big price for the seed, but too many things can happen to your crop."

"I don't give a damn," Peter shouted. "I want a lot of everything. I want forty acres of color and smell. I want fat women, with breasts as big as pillows. I'm hungry, I tell you, I'm hungry for everything, for a lot of everything."

Ed's face became grave under the shouting. "If you'd just take one of these, you'd get some sleep."

Peter looked ashamed. "I'm all right. I didn't mean to yell like that. I'm not just thinking these things for the first time. I been thinking about them for years, the way a kid thinks of vacation. I was always afraid I'd be too old. Or that I'd go first and miss everything. But I'm only fifty, I've got plenty of vinegar left. I told Emma about the sweet peas, but she wouldn't let me. I don't know how she made me do things," he said wonderingly. "I can't remember. She had a way of doing it. But she's gone. I can feel she's gone just like that harness is gone. I'm going to slouch, Ed—slouch all over the place. I'm going to track dirt into the house. I'm going to get a big fat housekeeper—a big fat one from San Francisco. I'm going to have a bottle of brandy on the shelf all the time."

Ed Chappell stood up and stretched his arms over his head. "I guess I'll go home now, if you feel all right. I got to get some sleep. You better wind that clock, Peter. It don't do a clock any good to stand not running."

The day after the funeral Peter Randall went to work on his farm. The Chappells, who lived on the next place, saw the lamp in his kitchen long before daylight, and they saw his lantern cross the yard to the barn half an hour before they even got up.

Peter pruned his orchard in three days. He worked from first light until he couldn't see the twigs against the sky any more. Then he started to shape the big piece of river flat. He plowed and rolled and harrowed. Two strange men dressed in boots and riding breeches came out and looked at his land. They felt the dirt with their fingers and ran a post-hole digger deep down under the surface, and when they went away they took little paper bags of the dirt with them.

Ordinarily, before planting time, the farmers did a good deal of visiting back and forth. They sat on their haunches, picking up handsful of dirt and breaking little clods between their fingers. They discussed markets and crops, recalled other years when beans had done well in a good market, and other years when field peas didn't bring enough to pay for the seed hardly. After a great number of these discussions it usually happened that all the farmers planted the same things. There were certain men whose ideas carried weight. If Peter Randall or Clark DeWitt thought they would put in pink beans and barley, most of the crops would turn out to be pink beans and barley that year; for, since such men were respected and fairly successful, it was conceded that their plans must be based on something besides chance choice. It was generally believed but never stated that Peter Randall and Clark DeWitt had extra reasoning powers and special prophetic knowledge.

When the usual visits started, it was seen that a change had taken place in Peter Randall. He sat on his plow and talked pleasantly enough. He said he hadn't decided yet what to plant, but he said it in such a guilty way that it was plain he didn't intend to tell. When he had rebuffed a few inquiries, the visits to his place stopped and the farmers went over in a body to Clark DeWitt. Clark was putting in Chevalier barley. His decision dictated the major part of the planting in the vicinity.

But because the question stopped, the interest did not. Men driving by the forty-five acre flat of the Randall place studied the field to try to figure out from the type of work what the crop was going to be. When Peter drove the seeder back and forth across the land no one came in, for Peter had made it plain that his crop was a secret.

Ed Chappell didn't tell on him, either. Ed was a little ashamed when he thought of that night; ashamed of Peter for breaking down, and ashamed of himself for having sat there and listened. He watched Peter narrowly to see whether his vicious intentions were really there or whether the whole conversation had been the result of loss and hysteria. He did notice that Peter's shoulders weren't back and that his stomach stuck out a little. He went to Peter's house and was relieved when he saw no dirt on the floor and when he heard the mantel clock ticking away.

Mrs. Chappell spoke often of the afternoon. "You'd've thought he lost his mind the way he carried on. He just howled. Ed stayed with him part of the night, until he quieted down. Ed had to give him some whiskey to get him to sleep. But," she said brightly, "hard work is the thing to kill sorrow. Peter Randall is getting up at three o'clock every morning. I can see the light in his kitchen window from my bedroom."

The pussywillows burst out in silver drops, and the little weeds sprouted up along the roadside. The Salinas River ran dark water, flowed for a month, and then subsided into green pools again. Peter Randall had shaped his land beautifully. It was smooth and black; no clod was larger than a small marble, and under the rains it looked purple with richness.

And then the little weak lines of green stretched out across the black field. In the dusk a neighbor crawled under the fence and pulled one of the tiny plants. "Some kind of legume," he told his friends. "Field peas, I guess. What did he want to be so quiet about it for? I asked him right out what he was planting, and he wouldn't tell me."

The word ran through the farms, "It's sweet peas. The whole God-damn' forty-five acres is in sweet peas!" Men called on Clark DeWitt then, to get his opinion.

His opinion was this: "People think because you can get twenty to sixty cents a pound for sweet peas you can get rich on them. But it's the most ticklish crop in the world. If the bugs don't get it, it might do good. And then come a hot day and bust the pods and lose your crop on the ground. Or it might come up a little rain and spoil the whole kaboodle. It's all right to put in a few acres and take a chance, but not the whole place. Peter's touched in the head since Emma died."

This opinion was widely distributed. Every man used it as his own. Two neighbors often said it to each other, each one repeating half of it. When too many people said it to Peter Randall he became angry. One day he cried, "Say, whose land is this? If I want to go broke, I've got a damn good right to, haven't I?" And that changed the whole feeling. Men remembered that Peter was a good farmer. Perhaps he had special knowledge. Why, that's who those two men in boots were — soil chemists! A good many of the farmers wished they'd put in a few acres of sweet peas.

They wished it particularly when the vines spread out, when they met each other across the rows and hid the dark earth from sight, when the buds began to form and it was seen the crop was rich. And then the blooms came; forty-five acres of color, forty-five acres of perfume. It was said that you could smell them in

Salinas, four miles away. Busses brought the school children out to look at them. A group of men from a seed company spent all day looking at the vines and feeling the earth.

Peter Randall sat on his porch in a rocking-chair every afternoon. He looked down on the great squares of pink and blue, and on the mad square of mixed colors. When the afternoon breeze came up, he inhaled deeply. His blue shirt was open at the throat, as though he wanted to get the perfume down next his skin.

Men called on Clark DeWitt to get his opinion now. He said, "There's about ten things that can happen to spoil that crop. He's welcome to his sweet peas." But the men knew from Clark's irritation that he was a little jealous. They looked up over the fields of color to where Peter sat on his porch, and they felt a new admiration and respect for him.

Ed Chappell walked up the steps to him one afternoon. "You got a crop there, mister."

"Looks that way," said Peter.

"I took a look. Pods are setting fine."

Peter sighed. "Blooming's nearly over," he said. "I'll hate to see the petals drop off."

"Well, I'd be glad to see 'em drop. You'll make a lot of money, if nothing happens."

Peter took out a bandana handkerchief and wiped his nose, and jiggled it sideways to stop an itch. "I'll be sorry when the smell stops," he said.

Then Ed made his reference to the night of the death. One of his eyes drooped secretly. "Found somebody to keep house for you?"

"I haven't looked," said Peter. "I haven't had time." There were lines of worry about his eyes. But who wouldn't worry, Ed thought, when a single shower could ruin his whole year's crop.

If the year and the weather had been manufactured for sweet peas, they couldn't have been better. The fog lay close to the ground in the morning when the vines were pulled. When the great piles of vines lay safely on spread canvasses, the hot sun shone down and crisped the pods for the threshers. The neighbors watched the long cotton sacks filling with round black seeds, and they went home and tried to figure out how much money Peter would make on his tremendous crop. Clark DeWitt lost a good part of his following. The men decided to find out what Peter was going to plant next year if they had to follow him around. How did he know, for instance, that this year'd be good for sweet peas? He must have some kind of special knowledge.

When a man from the upper Salinas Valley goes to San Francisco on business or for a vacation, he takes a room in the Ramona Hotel. This is a nice arrangement, for in the lobby he can usually find someone from home. They can sit in the soft chairs of the lobby and talk about the Salinas Valley.

Ed Chappell went to San Francisco to meet his wife's cousin who was coming out from Ohio for a trip. The train was not due until the next morning. In the lobby of the Ramona, Ed looked for someone from the Salinas Valley, but he could see only strangers sitting in the soft chairs. He went out to a moving picture show. When he returned, he looked again for someone from home, and still there were only strangers. For a moment he considered glancing over the register, but it was quite late. He sat down to finish his cigar before he went to bed.

There was a commotion at the door. Ed saw the clerk motion with his hand. A bellhop ran out. Ed squirmed around in his chair to look. Outside a man was being helped out of a taxicab. The bellhop took him from the driver and guided him in the door. It was Peter Randall. His eyes were glassy, and his mouth open and wet. He had no hat on his mussed hair. Ed jumped up and strode over to him.

"Peter!"

Peter was batting helplessly at the bellhop. "Let me alone," he explained. "I'm all right. You let me alone, and I'll give you two bits."

Ed called again, "Peter!"

The glassy eyes turned slowly to him, and then Peter fell into his arms. "My old friend," he cried. "Ed Chappell, my old, good friend. What you doing here? Come up to my room and have a drink."

Ed set him back on his feet. "Sure I will," he said. "I'd like a little night-cap."

"Night-cap, hell. We'll go out and see a show, or something."

Ed helped him into the elevator and got him to his room. Peter dropped heavily to the bed and struggled up to a sitting position. "There's a bottle of whiskey in the bathroom. Bring me a drink, too."

Ed brought out the bottle and the glasses. "What you doing, Peter, celebrating the crop? You must've made a pile of money."

Peter put out his palm and taped it impressively with a forefinger. "Sure I made money—but it wasn't a bit better than gambling. It was just like straight gambling."

"But you got the money."

Peter scowled thoughtfully. "I might've lost my pants," he said. "The whole time, all the year, I been worrying. It was just like gambling."

"Well, you got it, anyway."

Peter changed the subject, then. "I been sick," he said. "I been sick right in the taxicab. I just came from a fancy house on Van Ness Avenue," he explained apologetically, "I just had to come up to the city. I'd'a busted if I hadn't come up and got some of the vinegar out of my system."

Ed looked at him curiously. Peter's head was hanging loosely between his shoulders. His beard was draggled and rough. "Peter—" Ed began, "the night Emma—passed on, you said you was going to—change things."

Peter's swaying head rose up slowly. He stared owlishly at Ed Chappell. "She didn't die dead," he said thickly. "She won't let me do things. She's worried me all year about those peas." His eyes were wondering. "I don't know how she does it." Then he frowned. His palm came out, and he tapped it again. "But you mark, Ed Chappell, I won't wear that harness, and I damn well won't ever wear it. You remember that." His head dropped forward again. But in a moment he looked up. "I been drunk," he said seriously. "I been to fancy houses." He edged out confidentially toward Ed. His voice dropped to a heavy whisper. "But it's all right, I'll fix it. When I get back, you know what I'm going to do? I'm going to put in electric lights. Emma always wanted electric lights." He sagged sideways on the bed.

Ed Chappell stretched Peter out and undressed him before he went to his own room.

[1938]

Study and Writing Questions

1. How does money function in this STORY?
2. What vices and virtues of the farming society are revealed by the story? Consider individual CHARACTERS such as Mrs. Chappell, Clark DeWitt, and Dr. Marn.
3. What are some of the possible meanings of the title?
4. What is the relationship between Peter Randall and Ed Chappell? In what ways are they alike? In what ways are they different? To what extent, and why, do you finally esteem or look down on each man?
5. Compare first and subsequent readings of this NARRATIVE. In what ways does a rereading of the first paragraph, after you have read the story, differ from your first reading of this paragraph? What do these differences suggest about an ultimate judgment of Peter Randall? about the value of the story?

See also Questions for Contrast and Comparison: 45, 77, 84, 101, 102, 103, 106, 118, 123, and 133.

■ **JUNICHIRO TANIZAKI** (1886–1965) *was born in Tokyo, Japan. The family inherited wealth through his mother, but his father so mismanaged his rice business that they were alternately rich and poor. Only through the recommendation of his teachers did Tanizaki, who already showed a talent for writing, attend middle school. He studied classical literature at Tokyo Imperial University (1908–1910) but left to write full-time. After the Russo-Japanese War (1904–1905), Tanizaki was enthusiastic about Western culture, especially Poe; however, after traveling in China (1918) and moving to Kyoto (1923), the center of traditional Japanese culture, he returned to his roots, as in the luminous* Tale of Shunkin *(1933) about a blind musician and her devoted male servant. His writing embraces contrasts. In* Some Prefer Nettles *(1928), a westernized wife and a traditional husband stay together despite the exhaustion of their marriage. In* Diary of an Old Man *(1962), Tanizaki explores the eroticism of the impotent title character. Tanizaki's remarkable control of voice is obvious in* The Key *(1956), interwoven diaries of a husband and wife written as their marriage unravels. He also wrote* The Makioka Sisters *(1942–1948), a long family saga;* Seven Japanese Tales *(1963), which collects his short fiction; plays; and three different modern versions of the classic* Tale of Genji. *Twice married and divorced, he received the Imperial Prize for Literature in 1949.*

See also Questions for Reading and Comparison 35, 77, 84, 89, 97, 104, 116, 121, and 135.

The Thief

It was years ago, at the school where I was preparing for Tokyo Imperial University.

My dormitory roommates and I used to spend a lot of time at what we called "candlelight study" (there was very little studying to it), and one night, long after lights-out, the four of us were doing just that, huddled around a candle talking on and on.

I recall that we were having one of our confused, heated arguments about love — a problem of great concern to us in those days. Then, by a natural course of development, the conversation turned to the subject of crime: we found ourselves talking about such things as swindling, theft, and murder.

"Of all crimes, the one we're most likely to commit is murder." It was Higuchi, the son of a well-known professor, who declared this. "But I don't believe I'd ever steal — I just couldn't do it. I think I could be friends with any other kind of person, but a thief seems to belong to a different species." A shadow of distaste darkened his handsome features. Somehow that frown emphasized his good looks.

"I hear there's been a rash of stealing in the dormitory lately." This time it was Hirata who spoke. "Isn't that so?" he asked, turning to Nakamura, our other roommate.

"Yes, and they say it's one of the students."

"How do they know?" I asked.

"Well, I haven't heard all the details — " Nakamura dropped his voice to a confidential whisper. "But it's happened so often it must be an inside job."

"Not only that," Higuchi put in, "one of the fellows in the north wing was just going into his room the other day when somebody pushed the door open from the inside, caught him with a hard slap in the face, and ran away down the hall. He chased after him, but by the time he got to the bottom of the stairs the other one was out of sight. Back in his room, he found his trunk and bookshelves in a mess, which proves it was the thief."

"Did he see his face?"

"No, it all happened too fast, but he says he looked like one of us, the way he was dressed. Apparently he ran down the hall with his coat pulled up over his head—the one thing sure is that his coat had a wisteria crest."

"A wisteria crest?" said Hirata. "You can't prove anything by that." Maybe it was only my imagination, but I thought he flashed a suspicious look at me. At the same moment I felt that I instinctively made a wry face, since my own family crest is a wisteria design. It was only by chance that I wasn't wearing my crested coat that night.

"If he's one of us it won't be easy to catch him. Nobody wants to believe there's a thief among us." I was trying to get over my embarrassment because of that moment of weakness.

"No, they'll get him in a couple of days," Higuchi said emphatically. His eyes were sparkling. "This is a secret, but they say he usually steals things in the dressing room of the bathhouse, and for two or three days now the proctors have been keeping watch. They hide overhead and look down through a little hole."

"Oh? Who told you that?" Nakamura asked.

"One of the proctors. But don't go around talking about it."

"If *you* know so much, the thief probably knows it too!" said Hirata, looking disgusted.

Here I must explain that Hirata and I were not on very good terms. In fact, by that time we barely tolerated each other. I say "we," but it was Hirata who had taken a strong dislike to me. According to a friend of mine, he once remarked scornfully that I wasn't what everyone seemed to think I was, that he'd had a chance to see through me. And again: "I'm sick of him. He'll never be a friend of mine. It's only out of pity that I have anything to do with him."

He only said such things behind my back; I never heard them from him directly, though it was obvious that he loathed me. But it wasn't in my nature to demand an explanation. "If there's something wrong with me he ought to say so," I told myself. "If he doesn't have the kindness to tell me what it is, or if he thinks I'm not worth bothering with, then I won't think of *him* as a friend either." I felt a little lonely when I thought of his contempt for me, but I didn't really worry about it.

Hirata had an admirable physique and was the very type of masculinity that our school prides itself on, while I was skinny and pale and high-strung. There was something basically incompatible about us: I had to resign myself to the fact that we lived in separate worlds. Furthermore, Hirata was a judo expert of high rank, and displayed his muscles as if to say: "Watch out, or I'll give you a thrashing!" Perhaps it seemed cowardly of me to take such a meek attitude toward him, and no doubt I *was* afraid of his physical strength; but fortunately I was quite indifferent to matters of trivial pride or prestige. "I don't care how contemptuous the other fellow is; as long as I can go on believing in myself I don't need to feel bitter toward him." That was how I made up my mind, and so I was able to match Hirata's arrogance with my own cool magnanimity. I even told one of the other boys: "I can't help it if Hirata doesn't understand me, but I appreciate his good points anyway." And I actually believed it. I never considered myself a coward. I was even rather conceited, thinking I must be a person of noble character to be able to praise Hirata from the bottom of my heart.

"A wisteria crest?" That night, when Hirata cast his sudden glance at me, the malicious look in his eyes set my nerves on edge. What could that look possibly mean? Did he know that my family crest was wisteria? Or did I take it that way simply because of my own private feelings? If Hirata suspected me, how was I to handle the situation? Perhaps I should laugh good-naturedly and say: "Then I'm under suspicion too, because I have the same crest." If the others laughed along with me, I'd be all right. But suppose one of them, say Hirata, only began looking grimmer and grimmer — what then? When I visualized that scene I couldn't very well speak out impulsively.

It sounds foolish to worry about such a thing, but during that brief silence all sorts of thoughts raced through my mind. "In this kind of situation what difference is there, really, between an innocent man and an actual criminal?" By then I felt that I was experiencing a criminal's anxiety and isolation. Until a moment ago I had been one of their friends, one of the elite of our famous school. But now, if only in my own mind, I was an outcast. It was absurd, but I suffered from my inability to confide in them. I was uneasy about Hirata's slightest mood — Hirata who was supposed to be my equal.

"A thief seems to belong to a different species." Higuchi had probably said this casually enough, but now his words echoed ominously in my mind.

"A thief belongs to a different species. . . . " A thief! What a detestable name to be called! I suppose what makes a thief different from other men is not so much his criminal act itself as his effort to hide it at all costs, the strain of trying to put it out of his mind, the dark fears that he can never confess. And now I was becoming enshrouded by that darkness. I was trying not to believe that I was under suspicion; I was worrying about fears that I could not admit to my closest friend. Of course it must have been because Higuchi trusted me that he told us what he'd heard from the proctor. "Don't go around talking about it," he had said, and I was glad. But why should I feel glad? I thought. After all, Higuchi has never suspected me. Somehow I began to wonder about his motive for telling us.

It also struck me that if even the most virtuous person has criminal tendencies, maybe I wasn't the only one who imagined the possibility of being a thief. Maybe the others were experiencing a little of the same discomfort, the same elation. If so, then Higuchi, who had been singled out by the proctor to share his secret, must have felt very proud. Among the four of us it was he who was most trusted, he who was thought least likely to belong to that "other species." And if he won that trust because he came from a wealthy family and was the son of a famous professor, then I could hardly avoid envying him. Just as his social status improved his moral character, so my own background — I was acutely conscious of being a scholarship student, the son of a poor farmer — debased mine. For me to feel a kind of awe in his presence had nothing to do with whether or not I was a thief. We *did* belong to different species. I felt that the more he trusted me, with his frank, open attitude, the more the gulf between us deepened. The more friendly we tried to be, joking with each other in apparent intimacy, gossiping and laughing together, the more the distance between us increased. There was nothing I could do about it.

For a long time afterward I worried about whether or not I ought to wear that coat of mine with the "wisteria crest." Perhaps if I wore it around nonchalantly no one would pay any attention. But suppose they looked at me as much as to say: "Ah, he's wearing it!" Some would suspect me, or try to suppress their doubts of me, or feel sorry for me because I was under suspicion. If I became embarrassed and uneasy not only with Hirata and Higuchi but with all the students, and if I then felt obliged to put my coat away, that would seem even more sinister. What I dreaded was not the bare fact of being suspect, but all the unpleasant emotions that would be stirred up in others. If I were to cause doubt in other people's minds I would create a barrier between myself and those who had always been my friends. Even theft itself was not as ugly as the suspicions that would be aroused by it. No one would want to think of me as a thief: as long as it hadn't been proved, they'd want to go on associating with me as freely as ever, forcing themselves to trust me. Otherwise, what would friendship mean? Thief or not, I might be guilty of a worse sin than stealing from a friend: the sin of spoiling a friendship. Sowing seeds of doubt about myself was criminal. It *was* worse than stealing. If I were a prudent, clever thief—no, I mustn't put it that way—if I were a thief with the least bit of conscience and consideration for other people, I'd try to keep my friendships untarnished, try to be open with my friends, treat them with a sincerity and warmth that I need never be ashamed of, while carrying out my thefts in secrecy. Perhaps I'd be what people call "a brazen thief," but if you look at it from the thief's point of view, it's the most honest attitude to take. "It's true that I steal, but it's equally true that I value my friends," such a man would say. "That is typical of a thief, that's why he belongs to a different species." Anyhow, when I started thinking that way, I couldn't help becoming more and more aware of the distance between me and my friends. Before I knew it I felt like a full-fledged thief.

One day I mustered up my courage and wore the crested coat out on the school grounds. I happened to meet Nakamura, and we began walking along together.

"By the way," I remarked, "I hear they haven't caught the thief yet."

"That's right," Nakamura answered, looking away.

"Why not? Couldn't they trap him at the bathhouse?"

"He didn't show up there again, but you still hear about lots of things being stolen in other places. They say the proctors called Higuchi in the other day and gave him the devil for letting their plan leak out."

"Higuchi?" I felt the color drain from my face.

"Yes. . . ." He sighed painfully, and a tear rolled down his cheek. "You've got to forgive me! I've kept it from you till now, but I think you ought to know the truth. You won't like this, but you're the one the proctors suspect. I hate to talk about it—I've never suspected you for a minute. I believe in you. And because I believe in you, I just had to tell you. I hope you won't hold it against me."

"Thanks for telling me. I'm grateful to you." I was almost in tears myself, but at the same time I thought: "It's come at last!" As much as I dreaded it, I'd been expecting this day to arrive.

"Let's drop the subject," said Nakamura, to comfort me. "I feel better now that I've told you."

"But we can't put it out of our minds just because we hate to talk about it. I appreciate your kindness, but I'm not the only one who's been humiliated—I've brought shame on you too, as my friend. The mere fact that I'm under suspicion makes me unworthy of friendship. Any way you look at it, my reputation is ruined. Isn't that so? I imagine you'll turn your back on me too."

"I swear I never will—and I don't think you've brought any shame on me." Nakamura seemed alarmed by my reproachful tone. "Neither does Higuchi. They say he did his best to defend you in front of the proctors. He told them he'd doubt himself before he doubted you."

"But they still suspect me, don't they? There's no use trying to spare my feelings. Tell me everything you know. I'd rather have it that way."

Then Nakamura hesitantly explained: "Well, it seems the proctors get all kinds of tips. Ever since Higuchi talked too much that night there haven't been any more thefts at the bathhouse, and that's why they suspect you."

"But I wasn't the only one who heard him!"—I didn't say this, but the thought occurred to me immediately. It made me feel even more lonely and wretched.

"But how did they know Higuchi told us? There were only the four of us that night, so if nobody else knew it, and if you and Higuchi trust me—"

"You'll have to draw your own conclusions," Nakamura said, with an imploring look. "You know who it is. He's misjudged you, but I don't want to criticize him."

A sudden chill came over me. I felt as if Hirata's eyes were glaring into mine.

"Did you talk to him about me?"

"Yes. . . . But I hope you realize that it isn't easy, since I'm his friend as well as yours. In fact, Higuchi and I had a long argument with him last night, and he says he's leaving the dormitory. So I have to lose one friend on account of another."

I took Nakamura's hand and gripped it hard. "I'm grateful for friends like you and Higuchi," I said, tears streaming from my eyes. Nakamura cried too. For the first time in my life I felt that I was really experiencing the warmth of human compassion. This was what I had been searching for while I was tormented by my sense of helpless isolation. No matter how vicious a thief I might be, I could never steal anything from Nakamura.

After a while I said: "To tell you the truth, I'm not worth the trouble I'm causing you. I can't stand by in silence and see you two lose such a good friend because of someone like me. Even though he doesn't trust me, I still respect him. He's a far better man than I am. I recognize his value as well as anyone. So why don't I move out instead, if it's come to that? Please—let *me* go, and you three can keep on living together. Even if I'm alone I'll feel better about it."

"But there's no reason for you to leave," said Nakamura, his voice charged with emotion. "I recognize his good points too, but you're the one that's being persecuted. I won't side with him when it's so unfair. If *you* leave, *we* ought to leave too. You know how stubborn he is—once he's made up his mind to go he's not apt to change it. Why not let him do as he pleases? We might as well wait for him to come to his senses and apologize. That shouldn't take very long anyway."

"But he'll never come back to apologize. He'll go on hating me forever."

Nakamura seemed to assume that I felt resentful toward Hirata. "Oh, I don't think so," he said quickly. "He'll stick to his word—that's both his strength and his weakness—but once he knows he's wrong he'll come and apologize, and make a clean breast of it. That's one of the likable things about him."

"It would be fine if he did . . . ," I said thoughtfully. "He may come back to you, but I don't believe he'll ever make friends with me again. . . . But you're right, he's really likable. I only wish he liked me too."

Nakamura put his hand on my shoulder as if to protect his poor friend, as we plodded listlessly along on the grass. It was evening and a light mist hung over the school grounds: we seemed to be on an island surrounded by endless gray seas. Now and then a few students walking the other way would glance at me and go on. They already know, I thought; they're ostracizing me. I felt an overwhelming loneliness.

That night Hirata seemed to have changed his mind; he showed no intention of moving. But he refused to speak to us—even to Higuchi and Nakamura. Yet for me to leave at this stage was impossible, I decided. Not only would I be disregarding the kindness of my friends, I would be making myself seem all the more guilty. I ought to wait a little longer.

"Don't worry," my two friends were forever telling me. "As soon as they catch him the whole business will clear up." But even after another week had gone by, the criminal was still at large and the thefts were as frequent as ever. At last even Nakamura and Higuchi lost some money and a few books.

"Well, you two finally got it, didn't you? But I have a feeling the rest of us won't be touched." I remember Hirata's taunting look as he made this sarcastic remark.

After supper Nakamura and Higuchi usually went to the library, and Hirata and I were left to confront each other. I found this so uncomfortable that I began spending my evenings away from the dormitory too, either going to the library or taking long walks. One night around nine-thirty I came back from a walk and looked into our study. Oddly enough, Hirata wasn't there, nor did the others seem to be back yet. I went to look in our bedroom, but it was empty too. Then I went back to the study and over to Hirata's desk. Quietly I opened his drawer and ferreted out the registered letter that had come to him from his home a few days ago. Inside the letter were three ten-yen money orders, one of which I leisurely removed and put in my pocket. I pushed the drawer shut again and sauntered out into the hall. Then I went down to the yard, cut across the tennis court, and headed for the dark weedy hollow where I always buried the things I stole. But at that moment someone yelled: "Thief!" and flew at me from behind, knocking me down with a blow to my head. It was Hirata.

"Come on, let's have it! Let's see what you stuck in your pocket!"

"All right, all right, you don't have to shout like that," I answered calmly, smiling at him. "I admit I stole your money order. If you ask for it I'll give it back to you, and if you tell me to come with you I'll go anywhere you say. So we understand each other, don't we? What more do you want?"

Hirata seemed to hesitate, but soon began furiously raining blows on my face. Somehow the pain was not wholly unpleasant. I felt suddenly relieved of the staggering burden I had been carrying.

"There's no use beating me up like this, when I fell right into your trap for you. I made that mistake because you were so sure of yourself — I thought: 'Why the devil can't I steal from him?' But now you've found me out, so that's all there is to it. Later on we'll laugh about it together."

I tried to shake Hirata's hand good-naturedly, but he grabbed me by the collar and dragged me off toward our room. That was the only time Hirata seemed contemptible in my eyes.

"Hey, you fellows, I've caught the thief! You can't say I was taken in by him!" Hirata swaggered into our room and shoved me down in front of Nakamura and Higuchi, who were back from the library. Hearing the commotion, the other boys in the dormitory came swarming around our doorway.

"Hirata's right!" I told my two friends, picking myself up from the floor. "I'm the thief." I tried to speak in my normal tone, as casually as ever, but I realized that my face had gone pale.

"I suppose you hate me," I said to them. "Or else you're ashamed of me. . . . You're both honest, but you're certainly gullible. Haven't I been telling you the truth over and over again? I even said: 'I'm not the person you think I am. Hirata's the man to trust. He'll never be taken in.' But you didn't understand. I told you: 'Even if you become friendly with Hirata again, he'll never make friends with *me*!' I went as far as to say: 'I know better than anyone what a fine fellow Hirata is!' Isn't that so? I've never lied to you, have I? You may ask why I didn't come out and tell you the whole truth. You probably think I was deceiving you after all. But try looking at it from my position. I'm sorry, but stealing is one thing I can't control. Still, I didn't like to deceive you, so I told you the truth in a roundabout way. I couldn't be any more honest than that — it's your fault for not taking my hints. Maybe you think I'm just being perverse, but I've never been more serious. You'll probably ask why I don't quit stealing, if I'm so anxious to be honest. But that's not a fair question. You see, I was born a thief. I tried to be as sincere as I could with you under the circumstances. There was nothing else I could do. Even then my conscience bothered me — didn't I ask you to let *me* move out, instead of Hirata? I wasn't trying to fool you, I really wanted to do it for your sake. It's true that I stole from you, but it's also true that I'm your friend. I appeal to your friendship: I want you to understand that even a thief has feelings."

Nakamura and Higuchi stood there in silence, blinking with astonishment.

"Well, I can see you think I've got a lot of nerve. You just don't understand me. I guess it can't be helped, since you're of a different species." I smiled to conceal my bitterness, and added: "But since I'm your friend I'll warn you that this isn't the last time a thing like this will happen. So be on your guard! You two made friends with a thief because of your gullibility. You're likely to run into trouble when you go out in the world. Maybe you get better grades in school, but Hirata is a better man. You can't fool Hirata!"

When I singled him out for praise, Hirata made a wry face and looked away. At that moment he seemed strangely ill at ease.

Many years have passed since then. I became a professional thief and have been often behind bars; yet I cannot forget those memories — especially my memories of Hirata. Whenever I am about to commit a crime I see his face before me. I see him swaggering about as haughtily as ever, sneering at me: "Just as I suspected!" Yes, he was a man of character with great promise. But the world is mysterious. My prediction that the naïve Higuchi would "run into trouble" was wrong: partly through his father's influence, he has had a brilliant career—traveling abroad, earning a doctoral degree, and today holding a high position in the Ministry of Railways. Meanwhile nobody knows what has become of Hirata. It's no wonder we think life is unpredictable.

I assure my reader that this account is true. I have not written a single dishonest word here. And, as I hoped Nakamura and Higuchi would, I hope you will believe that delicate moral scruples can exist in the heart of a thief like me.

But perhaps you won't believe me either. Unless of course (if I may be pardoned for suggesting it) you happen to belong to my own species.

[1921]

Study and Writing Questions

1. The NARRATOR says in the third paragraph that the conversation turned from love, "by a natural course of development," to crime. In what way was this a "natural" development for each of the boys? In what way does the association of love and crime suggest reasons for the thief becoming a thief?
2. What is the social structure of the group of four boys? How does it reflect the conditions in the larger world of the school and in the still larger world of Japan?
3. On a first reading, what appear to be the narrator's MOTIVES in telling this STORY? On a subsequent reading, what appear to be his motives in telling this story?
4. What is the importance of secrets as presented in this NARRATIVE? Consider both the way they are shared and the way they are withheld. Also consider their effects on both the psychological state of individuals and on the social cohesion of groups.
5. In the first of the last three paragraphs, why does the NARRATOR tell what happened to his schoolmates years later? Do you, as a reader, draw the conclusions from that information that the narrator wants you to draw? In the second of those paragraphs, how do you react to the narrator's expressions of his own feelings and honesty? In the last paragraph, in what ways might it be true that a reader is a member of the narrator's own "species"? As a unit, what do these three paragraphs suggest this narrative is about?

See also Questions for Contrast and Comparison: 14, 16, 21, 54, 92, 135, 184, 204, and 225.

JAMES (GROVER) THURBER (1894–1961) *was born in Columbus, Ohio. His father, an appointed politician, moved the family to the Virginia suburbs of Washington, D.C., until 1902. In 1901, playing William Tell with his two brothers, Thurber lost an eye. The untreated wound created a progressive disease in the other eye that finally led to five operations (1940) and left him legally blind. He attended Ohio State University (1913–1918) but left to work as a State Department code clerk (his eyesight prevented his enlisting during World War I) in Washington and Paris (1918–1920). He then wrote for newspapers in Columbus, Paris, and New York until he joined the newly founded New Yorker magazine as managing editor (1927). As staff writer (1927–1933) and regular contributor (1933–1961), Thurber published most of his* STORIES, FABLES, *and essays in the* New Yorker. *His famous doodled cartoons, first submitted by his officemate and stylistic mentor, E. B. White, also appeared there. (White collaborated on Thurber's first book,* Is Sex Necessary? *[1929], a spoof of scientific marriage manuals.) Thurber's fanciful satires reflect his stormy first marriage (1922–1935), which produced one child. His second marriage (1935–1961) brought happiness even as his health failed. Thurber's best books include* The Seal in the Bedroom *(1932), cartoons;* My Life and Hard Times *(1933), stories; and* The 13 Clocks *(1950), a modern* FAIRY TALE.

The Secret Life of Walter Mitty

"We're going through!" The Commander's voice was like thin ice breaking. He wore his full-dress uniform, with the heavily braided white cap pulled down rakishly over one cold gray eye. "We can't make it, sir. It's spoiling for a hurricane, if you ask me." "I'm not asking you, Lieutenant Berg," said the Commander. "Throw on the power lights! Rev her up to 8,500! We're going through!" The pounding of the cylinders increased: ta-pocketa-pocketa-pocketa-pocketa-pocketa. The Commander stared at the ice forming on the pilot window. He walked over and twisted a row of complicated dials. "Switch on No. 8 auxiliary!" he shouted. "Switch on No. 8 auxiliary!" repeated Lieutenant Berg. "Full strength in No. 3 turret!" shouted the Commander. "Full strength in No. 3 turret!" The crew, bending to their various tasks in the huge, hurtling eight-engined Navy hydroplane, looked at each other and grinned. "The Old Man'll get us through," they said to one another. "The Old Man ain't afraid of Hell!" . . .

"Not so fast! You're driving too fast!" said Mrs. Mitty. "What are you driving so fast for?"

"Hmm?" said Walter Mitty. He looked at his wife, in the seat beside him, with shocked astonishment. She seemed grossly unfamiliar, like a strange woman who had yelled at him in a crowd. "You were up to fifty-five," she said. "You know I don't like to go more than forty. You were up to fifty-five." Walter Mitty drove on toward Waterbury in silence, the roaring of the SN_{202} through the worst storm in twenty years of Navy flying fading in the remote, intimate airways of his mind. "You're tensed up again," said Mrs. Mitty. "It's one of your days. I wish you'd let Dr. Renshaw look you over."

Walter Mitty stopped the car in front of the building where his wife went to have her hair done. "Remember to get those overshoes while I'm having my hair done," she said. "I don't need overshoes," said Mitty. She put her mirror back into her bag. "We've been all through that," she said, getting out of the car. "You're not a young man any longer." He raced the engine a little. "Why don't you wear your gloves? Have you lost your gloves? Walter Mitty reached in a pocket and brought out the gloves. He put them on, but after she had turned and gone into the building and he had driven on to a red light, he took them off again. "Pick it up, brother!" snapped a cop as the light changed, and Mitty hastily pulled on his gloves and lurched ahead. He drove around the streets aimlessly for a time, and then he drove past the hospital on his way to the parking lot.

. . . "It's the millionaire banker, Wellington McMillan," said the pretty nurse. "Yes?" said Walter Mitty, removing his gloves slowly. "Who has the case?" "Dr. Renshaw and Dr. Benbow, but there are two specialists here, Dr. Remington from New York and Mr. Pritchard-Mitford from London. He flew over." A door opened down a long, cool corridor and Dr. Renshaw came out. He looked distraught and haggard. "Hello, Mitty," he said. "We're having the devil's own time with McMillan, the millionaire banker and close personal friend of Roosevelt. Obstreosis of the ductal tract. Tertiary. Wish you'd take a look at him." "Glad to," said Mitty.

In the operating room there were whispered introductions: "Dr. Remington, Dr. Mitty. Mr. Pritchard-Mitford, Dr. Mitty." "I've read your book on streptothricosis," said Pritchard-Mitford, shaking hands. "A brilliant performance, sir." "Thank you," said Walter Mitty. "Didn't know you were in the States, Mitty," grumbled Remington. "Coals to Newcastle, bringing Mitford and me up here for a tertiary." "You are very kind," said Mitty. A huge, complicated machine, connected to the operating table, with many tubes and wires, began at this moment to go pocketa-pocketa-pocketa. "The new anesthetizer is giving way!" shouted an interne. "There is no one in the East who knows how to fix it!" "Quiet, man!" said Mitty, in a low, cool voice. He sprang to the machine, which was now going pocketa-pocketa-queep-pocketa-queep. He began fingering delicately a row of glistening dials. "Give me a fountain pen!" he snapped. Someone handed him a fountain pen. He pulled a faulty piston out of the machine and inserted the pen in its place. "That will hold for ten minutes," he said. "Get on with the operation." A nurse hurried over and whispered to Renshaw, and Mitty saw the man turn pale. "Corcopsis has set in," said Renshaw nervously. "If you would take over, Mitty?" Mitty looked at him and the craven figure of Benbow, who drank, and at the grave, uncertain faces of the two great specialists. "If you wish," he said. They slipped a white gown on him; he adjusted a mask and drew on thin gloves; nurses handed him shining . . .

"Back it up, Mac! Look out for that Buick!" Walter Mitty jammed on the brakes. "Wrong lane, Mac," said the parking-lot attendant, looking at Mitty closely. "Gee. Yeh," muttered Mitty. He began cautiously to back out of the lane marked "Exit Only." "Leave her sit there," said the attendant. "I'll put her away." Mitty got out of the car. "Hey, better leave the key." "Oh," said Mitty, handing the man the ignition key. The attendant vaulted into the car, backed it up with insolent skill, and put it where it belonged.

They're so damn cocky, thought Water Mitty, walking along Main Street; they think they know everything. Once he had tried to take his chains off, outside New Milford, and he had got them wound around the axles. A man had had to come out in a wrecking car and unwind them, a young, grinning garageman. Since then Mrs. Mitty always made him drive to a garage to have the chains taken off. The next time, he thought, I'll wear my right arm in a sling; they won't grin at me then. I'll have my right arm in a sling and they'll see I couldn't possibly take the chains off myself. He kicked at the slush on the sidewalk. "Overshoes," he said to himself, and he began looking for a shoe store.

When he came out into the street again, with the overshoes in a box under his arm, Walter Mitty began to wonder what the other thing was his wife had told him to get. She had told him twice, before they set out from their house for Waterbury. In a way he hated these weekly trips to town — he was always getting something wrong. Kleenex, he thought, Squibb's, razor blades? No. Toothpaste, toothbrush, bicarbonate, carborundum, initiative and referendum? He gave it up. But she would remember it. "Where's the what's-its-name?" she would ask. "Don't tell me you forgot the what's-its-name." A newsboy went by shouting something about the Waterbury trial.

. . . "Perhaps this will refresh your memory." The District Attorney suddenly thrust a heavy automatic at the quiet figure on the witness stand. "Have you ever seen this before?" Walter Mitty took the gun and examined it expertly. "This is my Webley-Vickers 50.80," he said calmly. An excited buzz ran around the courtroom. The judge rapped for order. "You are a crack shot with any sort of firearms, I believe?" said the District Attorney, insinuatingly. "Objection!" shouted Mitty's attorney. "We have shown that the defendant could not have fired the shot. We have shown that he wore his right arm in a sling on the night of the fourteenth of July." Walter Mitty raised his hand briefly and the bickering attorneys were stilled. "With any known make of gun," he said evenly, "I could have killed Gregory Fitzhurst at three hundred feet *with my left hand*." Pandemonium broke loose in the courtroom. A woman's scream rose above the bedlam and suddenly a lovely, dark-haired girl was in Walter Mitty's arms. The District Attorney struck at her savagely. Without rising from his chair, Mitty let the man have it on the point of the chin. "You miserable cur!". . .

"Puppy biscuit," said Walter Mitty. He stopped walking and the buildings of Waterbury rose up out of the misty courtroom and surrounded him again. A woman who was passing laughed. "He said 'Puppy biscuit,'" she said to her companion. "That man said 'Puppy biscuit' to himself." Walter Mitty hurried on. He went into an A. & P., not the first one he came to but a smaller one farther up the street. "I want some biscuit for small, young dogs," he said to the clerk. "Any special brand, sir?" The greatest pistol shot in the world thought a moment. "It says 'Puppies Bark for It' on the box," said Walter Mitty.

His wife would be through at the hairdresser's in fifteen minutes, Mitty saw in looking at his watch, unless they had trouble drying it; sometimes they had trouble drying it. She didn't like to get to the hotel first; she would want him to be there waiting for her as usual. He found a big leather chair in the lobby, facing a window, and he put the overshoes and the puppy biscuit on the floor beside it. He picked up an old copy of *Liberty* and sank down into the chair. "Can Germany Conquer the World Through the Air?" Walter Mitty looked at the pictures of bombing planes and of ruined streets.

. . . "The cannonading has got the wind up in young Raleigh, sir," said the sergeant. Captain Mitty looked up at him through tousled hair. "Get him to bed," he said wearily. "With the others. I'll fly alone." "But you can't, sir," said the sergeant anxiously. "It takes two men to handle that bomber and the Archies are pounding hell out of the air. Von Richtman's circus is between here and Saulier." "Somebody's got to get that ammunition dump," said Mitty. "I'm going over. Spot of brandy?" He poured a drink for the sergeant and one for himself. War thundered and whined around the dugout and battered at the door. "A bit of a near thing," said Captain Mitty carelessly. "The box barrage is closing in," said the sergeant. "We only live once, Sergeant," said Mitty, with his faint, fleeting smile. "Or do we?" He poured another brandy and tossed it off. "I never see a man could hold his brandy like you, sir," said the sergeant. "Begging your pardon, sir." Captain Mitty stood up and strapped on his huge Webley-Vickers automatic. "It's forty kilometers through hell, sir," said the sergeant. Mitty finished one last brandy. "After all," he said softly, "what isn't?" The pounding of the cannon increased; there was the rat-tat-tatting of machine guns, and from somewhere came the menacing pocketa-pocketa-pocketa of the new flame-throwers. Walter Mitty walked to the door of the dugout humming "Auprès de Ma Blonde." He turned and waved to the sergeant. "Cheerio!" he said. . . .

Something struck his shoulder. "I've been looking all over this hotel for you," said Mrs. Mitty. "Why do you have to hide in this old chair? How did you expect me to find you?" "Things close in," said Walter Mitty vaguely. "What?" Mrs. Mitty said. "Did you get the what's-its-name? The puppy biscuit? What's in that box?" "Overshoes," said Mitty. "Couldn't you have put them on in the store?" "I was thinking," said Walter Mitty. "Does it ever occur to you that I am sometimes thinking?" She looked at him. "I'm going to take your temperature when I get you home," she said.

They went out through the revolving doors that made a faintly derisive whistling sound when you pushed them. It was two blocks to the parking lot. At the drugstore on the corner she said, "Wait here for me. I forgot something. I won't be a minute." She was more than a minute. Walter Mitty lighted a cigarette. It began to rain, rain with sleet in it. He stood up against the wall of the drugstore, smoking. . . . He put his shoulders back and his heels together. "To hell with the handkerchief," said Walter Mitty scornfully. He took one last drag on his cigarette and snapped it away. Then, with that faint, fleeting smile playing about his lips, he faced the firing squad; erect and motionless, proud and disdainful, Walter Mitty the Undefeated, inscrutable to the last.

[1939]

Study and Writing Questions

1. What is the significance of machines in the life of Walter Mitty? How does his relationship to machines affect our feeling about him?
2. This NARRATIVE includes many highly specific details, like the date July 14, when more general details might do. What are some of these details? What do they mean in context?
3. How exactly does Walter Mitty's mind work? To what extent does he seem typical of all people in this and to what extent unusual?
4. This narrative begins and ends in the first and last of Walter Mitty's five daydreams. How does the order of those daydreams STRUCTURE the narrative and affect our understanding of its THEME?
5. In this fourth daydream, Mitty says, " 'We only live once, Sergeant,' " and then wonders, " 'Or do we?' " In what ways does the story provide answers to Mitty's question?

See also Questions for Contrast and comparison: 33, 45, 87, 92, 138, 216, and 232.

■ LEO (NIKOLAEVICH) TOLSTOY (1828-1910) was born at Yasnaya Polyana ("bright meadow"), the family estate near Tula, about one hundred forty miles south of Moscow, Russia. Orphaned at nine and raised by aunts, the young aristocrat studied with French and German tutors, attended the University of Kazan (1844-1847), gambled, womanized, volunteered with the army in the Caucasus (1851), served with distinction as an artillery officer during the Crimean War (1853-1856), traveled in western Europe (1856-1857, 1860-1861), and knew Chekov, Gorky, and others in his visits to St. Petersburg and Moscow. After inheriting Yasnaya Polyana (1847), Tolstoy ran the estate; although he could turn cruelly scornful, he instituted reforms and schools for his serfs. About 1876 he began developing his own variety of Christianity, preaching simplicity, pacifism, and nonresistance to evil. Although widely renowned as a moralist, he was nevertheless excommunicated from the Russian Orthodox Church (1901). His writings (ninety volumes) include memoirs (Childhood, 1851; Boyhood, 1854; Youth, 1857); the great Napoleonic epic, War and Peace (1869), and the great social and character study, Anna Karenina (1877); and religious writings (The Kingdom of God Is Within You, 1893). Married (1862) and the father of thirteen, he renounced most of his possessions in 1895. One winter night he left home, contracted pneumonia, and died.

The Death of Ivan Ilyitch

Chapter I

NEWS

Inside the great building of the Law Courts, during the interval in the hearing of the Melvinsky case, the members of the judicial council and the public prosecutor were gathered together in the private room of Ivan Yegorovitch Shebek, and the conversation turned upon the celebrated Krasovsky case. Fyodor Vassilievitch hotly maintained that the case was not in the jurisdiction of the court. Yegor Ivanovitch stood up for his own view; but from the first Pyotr Ivanovitch, who had not entered into the discussion, took no interest in it, but was looking through the newspapers which had just been brought in.

"Gentlemen!" he said, "Ivan Ilyitch is dead!"

"You don't say so!"

"Here, read it," he said to Fyodor Vassilievitch, handing him the fresh still damp-smelling paper.

Within a black margin was printed: "Praskovya Fyodorovna Golovin with heartfelt affliction informs friends and relatives of the decease of her beloved husband, member of the Court of Justice, Ivan Ilyitch Golovin, who passed away on the 4th of February. The funeral will take place on Thursday at one o'clock."

Ivan Ilyitch was a colleague of the gentlemen present, and all liked him. It was some weeks now since he had been taken ill; his illness had been said to be incurable. His post had been kept open for him, but it had been thought that in case of his death Alexyeev might receive his appointment, and either Vinnikov or Shtabel would succeed to Alexyeev's. So that on hearing of Ivan Ilyitch's death, the first thought of each of the gentlemen in the room was of the effect this death might have on the transfer or promotion of themselves or their friends.

"Now I am sure of getting Shtabel's place or Vinnikov's," thought Fyodor Vassilievitch. "It was promised me long ago, and the promotion means eight hundred roubles additional income, besides the grants for office expenses."

"Now I shall have to petition for my brother-in-law to be transferred from Kaluga," thought Pyotr Ivanovitch. "My wife will be very glad. She won't be able to say now that I've never done anything for her family."

"I thought somehow that he'd never get up from his bed again," Pyotr Ivanovitch said aloud. "I'm sorry!"

"But what was it exactly was wrong with him?"

"The doctors could not decide. That's to say, they did decide, but differently. When I saw him last, I thought he would get over it."

"Well, I positively haven't called there ever since the holidays. I've kept meaning to go."

"Had he any property?"

"I think there's something, very small, of his wife's. But something quite trifling."

"Yes, one will have to go and call. They live such a terribly long way off."

"A long way from you, you mean. Everything's a long way from your place."

"There, he can never forgive me for living the other side of the river," said Pyotr Ivanovitch, smiling at Shebek. And they began to talk of the great distances between different parts of the town, and went back into the court.

Besides the reflections upon the changes and promotions in the service likely to ensue from this death, the very fact of the death of an intimate acquaintance excited in every one who heard of it, as such a fact always does, a feeling of relief that "it is he that is dead, and not I."

"Only think! he is dead, but here am I all right," each one thought or felt. The more intimate acquaintances, the so-called friends of Ivan Ilyitch, could not help thinking too that now they had the exceedingly tiresome social duties to perform of going to the funeral service and paying the widow a visit of condolence.

The most intimately acquainted with their late colleague were Fyodor Vassilievitch and Pyotr Ivanovitch.

Pyotr Ivanovitch had been a comrade of his at the school of jurisprudence, and considered himself under obligations to Ivan Ilyitch.

Telling his wife at dinner of the news of Ivan Ilyitch's death and his reflections as to the possibility of getting her brother transferred into their circuit, Pyotr Ivanovitch, without lying down for his usual nap, put on his frockcoat and drove to Ivan Ilyitch's.

At the entrance before Ivan Ilyitch's flat stood a carriage and two hired flies. Downstairs in the entry near the hatstand there was leaning against the wall a coffin-lid with tassels and braiding freshly rubbed up with pipeclay. Two ladies were taking off their cloaks. One of them he knew, the sister of Ivan Ilyitch; the other was a lady he did not know. Pyotr Ivanovitch's colleague, Shvarts, was coming down; and from the top stair, seeing who it was coming in, he stopped and winked at him, as though to say: "Ivan Ilyitch has made a mess of it; it's a very different matter with you and me."

Shvarts's face, with his English whiskers and all his thin figure in his frockcoat, had, as it always had, an air of elegant solemnity; and this solemnity, always such a contrast to Shvarts's playful character, had a special piquancy here. So thought Pyotr Ivanovitch.

Pyotr Ivanovitch let the ladies pass up the stairs after them. Shvarts had not come down, but was waiting at the top. Pyotr Ivanovitch knew what for; he wanted obviously to settle with him where their game of "screw" was to be that evening. The ladies went up to the widow's room; while Shvarts, with his lips tightly and gravely shut, and amusement in his eyes, with a twitch of his eyebrows motioned Pyotr Ivanovitch to the right, to the room where the dead man was.

Pyotr Ivanovitch went in, as people always do on such occasions, in uncertainty as to what he would have to do there. One thing he felt sure of—that crossing oneself never comes amiss on such occasions. As to whether it was necessary to bow down while doing so, he did not feel quite sure, and so chose a middle course. On entering the room he began crossing himself, and made a slight sort of bow. So far as the movements of his hands and head permitted him, he glanced while doing so about the room. Two young men, one a high school boy, nephews probably, were going out of the room, crossing themselves. An old lady was standing motionless; and a lady, with her eyebrows queerly lifted, was saying something to her in a whisper. A deacon in a frockcoat, resolute and hearty, was reading something aloud with an expression that precluded all possibility of contradiction. A young peasant who used to wait at table, Gerasim, walking with light footsteps in front of Pyotr Ivanovitch, was sprinkling something on the floor. Seeing this, Pyotr Ivanovitch was at once aware of the faint odour of the decomposing corpse. On his last visit to Ivan Ilyitch Pyotr Ivanovitch had seen this peasant in his room; he was performing the duties of a sick-nurse and Ivan Ilyitch liked him particularly. Pyotr Ivanovitch continued crossing himself and bowing in a direction intermediate between the coffin, the deacon, and the holy pictures on the table in the corner. Then when this action of making the sign of the cross with his hand seemed to him to have been unduly prolonged, he stood still and began to scrutinize the dead man.

The dead man lay, as dead men always do lie, in a peculiarly heavy dead way, his stiffened limbs sunk in the cushions of the coffin, and his head bent back forever on the pillow, and thrust up, as dead men always do, his yellow waxen forehead with bald spots on the sunken temples, and his nose that stood out sharply and, as it were, squeezed on the upper lip. He was much changed, even thinner since Pyotr Ivanovitch had seen him, but his face—as always with the dead—was more handsome, and, above all, more impressive than it had been when he was alive. On the face was an expression of what had to be done having been done, and rightly done. Besides this, there was too in that expression a reproach or a reminder for the living. This reminder seemed to Pyotr Ivanovitch uncalled for, or, at least, to have nothing to do with him. He felt something unpleasant; and so Pyotr Ivanovitch once more crossed himself hurriedly, and, as it struck him, too hurriedly, not quite in accordance with the proprieties, turned and went to the door. Shvarts was waiting for him in the adjoining room, standing with his legs apart and both hands behind his back playing with his top hat. A single glance at the playful, sleek, and elegant figure of Shvarts revived Pyotr Ivanovitch. He felt that he, Shvarts, was above it, and would not give way to depressing impressions. The mere sight of him said plainly: the incident of the service over the body of Ivan Ilyitch cannot possibly constitute a sufficient ground for recognizing the business of the session suspended—in other words, in no way can it hinder us from shuffling and cutting a pack of cards this evening, while the footman sets four unsanctified candles on the table for us; in fact, there is no ground for supposing that this incident could prevent us from spending the evening agreeably. He said as much indeed to Pyotr Ivanovitch as he came out, proposing that the party should meet at Fyodor Vassilievitch's. But apparently it was Pyotr Ivanovitch's destiny not to play "screw" that evening. Praskovya Fyodorovna, a short, fat woman who, in spite of all efforts in a contrary direction, was steadily broader from her shoulders downwards, all in black, with lace on her head and her eyebrows as queerly arched as those of the lady standing beside the coffin, came out of her own apartments with some other ladies, and conducting them to the dead man's room, said: "The service will take place immediately; come in."

Shvarts, making an indefinite bow, stood still, obviously neither accepting nor declining this invitation. Praskovya Fyodorovna, recognizing Pyotr Ivanovitch, sighed, went right up to him, took his hand, and said, "I know that you were a true friend of Ivan Ilyitch's . . ." and looked at him, expecting from him the suitable action in response to these words. Pyotr Ivanovitch knew that, just as before he had to cross himself, now what he had to do was to press her hand, to sigh and to say, "Ah, I was indeed!" And he did so. And as he did so, he felt that the desired result had been attained; that he was touched, and she was touched.

"Come, since it's not begun yet, I have something I want to say to you," said the widow. "Give me your arm."

Pyotr Ivanovitch gave her his arm, and they moved towards the inner rooms, passing Shvarts, who winked gloomily at Pyotr Ivanovitch.

"So much for our 'screw'! Don't complain if we find another partner. You can make a fifth when you do get away," said his humorous glance.

Pyotr Ivanovitch sighed still more deeply and despondently, and Praskovya Fyodorovna pressed his hand gratefully. Going into her drawing-room, which was upholstered with pink cretonne and lighted by a dismal-looking lamp, they sat down at the table, she on a sofa and Pyotr Ivanovitch on a low ottoman with deranged springs which yielded spasmodically under his weight. Praskovya Fyodorovna was about to warn him to sit on another seat, but felt such a recommendation out of keeping with her position, and changed her mind. Sitting down on the ottoman, Pyotr Ivanovitch remembered how Ivan Ilyitch had arranged this drawing-room, and had consulted him about this very pink cretonne with green leaves. Seating herself on the sofa, and pushing by the table (the whole drawing-room was crowded with furniture and things), the widow caught the lace of her black fichu in the carving of the table. Pyotr Ivanovitch got up to disentangle it for her; and the ottoman, freed from his weight, began bobbing up spasmodically under him. The widow began unhooking her lace herself, and Pyotr Ivanovitch again sat down, suppressing the mutinous ottoman springs under him. But the widow could not quite free herself, and Pyotr Ivanovitch rose again, and again the ottoman became mutinous and popped up with a positive snap. When this was all over, she took out a clean cambric handkerchief and began weeping. Pyotr Ivanovitch had been chilled off by the incident with the lace and the struggle with the ottoman springs, and he sat looking sullen. This awkward position was cut short by the entrance of Sokolov, Ivan Ilyitch's butler, who came in to announce that the place in the cemetery fixed on by Praskovya Fyodorovna would cost two hundred roubles. She left off weeping, and with an air of a victim glancing at Pyotr Ivanovitch, said in French that it was very terrible for her. Pyotr Ivanovitch made a silent gesture signifying his unhesitating conviction that it must indeed be so.

"Please, smoke," she said in a magnanimous, and at the same time, crushed voice, and she began discussing with Sokolov the question of the price of the site for the grave.

Pyotr Ivanovitch, lighting a cigarette, listened to her very circumstantial inquiries as to the various prices of sites and her decision as to the one to be selected. Having settled on the site for the grave, she made arrangements also about the choristers. Sokolov went away.

"I see to everything myself," she said to Pyotr Ivanovitch, moving on one side the albums that lay on the table; and noticing the table was in danger from the cigarette-ash, she promptly passed an ash-tray to Pyotr Ivanovitch, and said: "I consider it affectation to pretend that my grief prevents me from looking after practical matters. On the contrary, if anything could — not console me . . . but distract me, it is seeing after everything for him." She took out her handkerchief again, as though preparing to weep again; and suddenly, as though struggling with herself, she shook herself, and began speaking calmly: "But I've business to talk about with you."

Pyotr Ivanovitch bowed, carefully keeping in check the springs of the otto-man, which had at once begun quivering under him.

"The last few days his sufferings were awful."

"Did he suffer very much?" asked Pyotr Ivanovitch.

"Oh, awfully! For the last moments, hours indeed, he never left off scream-ing. For three days and nights in succession he screamed incessantly. It was insufferable. I can't understand how I bore it; one could hear it through three closed doors. Ah, what I suffered!"

"And was he really conscious?" asked Pyotr Ivanovitch.

"Yes," she whispered, "up to the last minute. He said good-bye to us a quarter of an hour before his death, and asked Volodya to be taken away too."

The thought of the sufferings of a man he had known so intimately, at first as a light-hearted boy, a schoolboy, then grown up as a partner at whist, in spite of the unpleasant consciousness of his own and this woman's hypocrisy, suddenly horrified Pyotr Ivanovitch. He saw again that forehead, the nose that seemed squeezing the lip, and he felt frightened for himself. "Three days and nights of awful suffering and death. Why, that may at once, any minute, come upon me too," he thought, and he felt for an instant terrified. But immediately, he could not himself have said how, there came to his support the customary reflection that this had happened to Ivan Ilyitch and not to him, and that to him this must not and could not happen; that in thinking thus he was giving way to depression, which was not the right thing to do, as was evident from Shvarts's expression of face. And making these reflections, Pyotr Ivanovitch felt reassured, and began with interest inquiring details about Ivan Ilyitch's end, as though death were a mischance peculiar to Ivan Ilyitch, but not at all incidental to himself.

After various observations about the details of the truly awful physical sufferings endured by Ivan Ilyitch (these details Pyotr Ivanovitch learned only through the effect Ivan Ilyitch's agonies had had on the nerves of Praskovya Fyodorovna), the widow apparently thought it time to get to business.

"Ah, Pyotr Ivanovitch, how hard it is, how awfully, awfully hard!" and she began to cry again.

Pyotr Ivanovitch sighed, and waited for her to blow her nose. When she had done so, he said, "Indeed it is," and again she began to talk, and brought out what was evidently the business she wished to discuss with him; that business consisted in the inquiry as to how on the occasion of her husband's death she was to obtain a grant from the government. She made a show of asking Pyotr Ivanovitch's advice about a pension. But he perceived that she knew already to the minutest details, what he did not know himself indeed, everything that could be got out of the government on the ground of this death; but that what she wanted to find out was, whether there were not any means of obtaining a little more? Pyotr Ivanovitch tried to imagine such means; but after pondering a little, and out of politeness abusing the government for its stinginess, he said that he believed that it was impossible to obtain more. Then she sighed and began unmistakably looking about for an excuse for getting rid of her visitor. He perceived this, put out his cigarette, got up, pressed her hand, and went out into the passage.

In the dining-room, where was the bric-à-brac clock that Ivan Ilyitch had been so delighted at buying, Pyotr Ivanovitch met the priest and several people he knew who had come to the service for the dead, and saw too Ivan Ilyitch's daughter, a handsome young lady. She was all in black. Her very slender figure looked even slenderer than usual. She had a gloomy, determined, almost wrathful expression. She bowed to Pyotr Ivanovitch as though he were to blame in some way. Behind the daughter, with the same offended air on his face, stood a rich young man, whom Pyotr Ivanovitch knew, too, an examining magistrate, the young lady's fiancé, as he had heard. He bowed dejectedly to him, and would have gone on into the dead man's room, when from the staircase there appeared the figure of the son, the high school boy, extraordinarily like Ivan Ilyitch. He was the little Ivan Ilyitch over again as Pyotr Ivanovitch remembered him at school. His eyes were red with crying, and had that look often seen in unclean boys of thirteen or fourteen. The boy, seeing Pyotr Ivanovitch, scowled morosely and bashfully. Pyotr Ivanovitch nodded to him and went into the dead man's room. The service for the dead began—candles, groans, incense, tears, sobs. Pyotr Ivanovitch stood frowning, staring at his feet in front of him. He did not once glance at the dead man, and right through to the end did not once give way to depressing influences, and was one of the first to walk out. In the hall there was no one. Gerasim, the young peasant, darted out of the dead man's room, tossed over with his strong hand all the fur cloaks to find Pyotr Ivanovitch's, and gave it him.

"Well, Gerasim, my boy?" said Pyotr Ivanovitch, so as to say something. "A sad business, isn't it?"

"It's God's will. We shall come to the same," said Gerasim, showing his white, even, peasant teeth in a smile, and, like a man in a rush of extra work, he briskly opened the door, called up the coachman, saw Pyotr Ivanovitch into the carriage, and darted back to the steps as though bethinking himself of what he had to do next.

Pyotr Ivanovitch had a special pleasure in the fresh air after the smell of incense, of the corpse, and of carbolic acid.

"Where to?" asked the coachman.

"It's not too late. I'll still go round to Fyodor Vassilievitch's."

And Pyotr Ivanovitch drove there. And he did, in fact, find them just finishing the first rubber, so that he came just at the right time to take a hand.

Chapter II
Who He Was

The previous history of Ivan Ilyitch was the simplest, the most ordinary, and the most awful.

Ivan Ilyitch died at the age of forty-five, a member of the Judicial Council. He was the son of an official, whose career in Petersburg through various ministries and departments had been such as leads people into that position in which, though it is distinctly obvious that they are unfit to perform any kind of real duty, they yet cannot, owing to their long past service and their official rank, be dismissed; and they therefore receive a specially created fictitious post; and by no means fictitious thousands — from six to ten — on which they go on living till extreme old age. Such was the privy councillor, the superfluous member of various superfluous institutions, Ilya Efimovitch Golovin.

He had three sons. Ivan Ilyitch was the second son. The eldest son's career was exactly like his father's, only in a different department, and he was by now close upon the stage in the service in which the same sinecure would be reached. The third son was the unsuccessful one. He had in various positions always made a mess of things, and was now employed in the railway department. And his father and his brothers, and still more their wives, did not merely dislike meeting him, but avoided, except in extreme necessity, recollecting his existence. His sister had married Baron Greff, a Petersburg official of the same stamp as his father-in-law. Ivan Ilyitch was *le phénix de la famille*, as people said. He was not so frigid and precise as the eldest son, nor so wild as the youngest. He was the happy mean between them — a shrewd, lively, pleasant, and well-bred man. He had been educated with his younger brother at the school of jurisprudence. The younger brother had not finished the school course, but was expelled when in the fifth class. Ivan Ilyitch completed the course successfully. At school he was just the same as he was later on all his life — an intelligent fellow, highly good-humoured and sociable, but strict in doing what he considered to be his duty. His duty he considered whatever was so considered by those persons who were set in authority over him. He was not a toady as a boy, nor later on as a grownup person; but from his earliest years he was attracted, as a fly to the light, to persons of good standing in the world, assimilated their manners and their views of life, and established friendly relations with them. All the enthusiasms of childhood and youth passed, leaving no great traces in him; he gave way to sensuality and to vanity, and laterly when in the higher classes at school to liberalism, but always keeping within certain limits which were unfailingly marked out for him by his instincts.

At school he had commited actions which had struck him beforehand as great vileness, and gave him a feeling of loathing for himself at the very time he was committing them. But later on, perceiving that such actions were committed also by men of good position, and were not regarded by them as base, he was able, not to regard them as good, but to forget about them completely, and was never mortified by recollections of them.

Leaving the school of jurisprudence in the tenth class, and receiving from his father a sum of money for his outfit, Ivan Ilyitch ordered his clothes at Sharmer's, hung on his watchchain a medallion inscribed *respice finem*, said goodby to the prince who was the principal of his school, had a farewell dinner with his comrades at Donon's, and with all his new fashionable belongings — travelling trunk, linen, suits of clothes, shaving and toilet appurtenances, and travelling rug, all ordered and purchased at the very best shops — set off to take the post of secretary on special commissions for the governor of a province, a post which had been obtained for him by his father.

In the province Ivan Ilyitch without loss of time made himself a position as easy and agreeable as his position had been in the school of jurisprudence. He did his work, made his career, and at the same time led a life of well-bred social gaiety. Occasionally he visited various districts on official duty, behaved with dignity both with his superiors and his inferiors; and with exactitude and an incorruptible honesty of which he could not help feeling proud, performed the duties with which he was intrusted, principally having to do with the dissenters. When engaged in official work he was, in spite of his youth and taste for frivolous amusement, exceedingly reserved, official, and even severe. But in social life he was often amusing and witty, and always good-natured, well-bred, and *bon enfant*, as was said of him by his chief and his chief's wife, with whom he was like one of the family.

In the province there was, too, a connection with one of the ladies who obtruded their charms on the stylish young lawyer. There was a dressmaker, too, and there were drinking bouts with smart officers visiting the neighbourhood, and visits to a certain outlying street after supper; there was a rather cringing obsequiousness in his behaviour, too, with his chief, and even his chief's wife. But all this was accompanied with such a tone of the highest breeding, that it could not be called by harsh names; it all came under the rubric of the French saying, *Il faut que la jeunesse se passe*. Everything was done with clean hands, in clean shirts, with French phrases, and, what was of most importance, in the highest society, and consequently with the approval of people of rank.

Such was Ivan Ilyitch's career for five years, and then came a change in his social life. New methods of judicial procedure were established; new men were wanted to carry them out. And Ivan Ilyitch became such a new man. Ivan Ilyitch was offered the post of examining magistrate, and he accepted it in spite of the fact that this post was in another province, and he would have to break off all the ties he had formed and form new ones. Ivan Ilyitch's friends met together to see him off, had their photographs taken in a group, presented him with a silver cigarette-case, and he set off to his new post.

As an examining magistrate, Ivan Ilyitch was as *comme il faut*, as well-bred, as adroit in keeping official duties apart from private life, and as successful in gaining universal respect, as he had been as secretary of private commissions. The duties of his new office were in themselves of far greater interest and attractiveness for Ivan Ilyitch. In his former post it had been pleasant to pass in his smart uniform from Sharmer's through the crowd of petitioners and officials waiting timorously and envying him, and to march with his easy swagger straight into the governor's private room, there to sit down with him to tea and cigarettes. But the persons directly subject to his authority were few. The only such persons were the district police superintendents and the dissenters, when he was serving on special commissions. And he liked treating such persons affably, almost like comrades; liked to make them feel that he, able to annihilate them, was behaving in this simple, friendly way with them. But such people were then few in number. Now as an examining magistrate Ivan Ilyitch felt that every one — every one without exception — the most dignified, the most self-satisfied people, all were in his hands, and that he had but to write certain words on a sheet of paper with a printed heading, and this dignified self-satisfied person would be brought before him in the capacity of a defendant or a witness; and if he did not care to make him sit down, he would have to stand up before him and answer his questions. Ivan Ilyitch never abused this authority of his; on the contrary he tried to soften the expression of it. But the consiousness of this power and the possibility of softening its effect constituted for him the chief interest and attractiveness of his new position. In the work itself, in the preliminary inquiries, that is, Ivan Ilyitch very rapidly acquired the art of setting aside every consideration irrelevant to the official aspect of the case, and of reducing every case, however complex, to that form in which it could in a purely external fashion be put on paper, completely excluding his personal view of the matter, and what was of paramount importance, observing all the necessary formalities. All this work was new. And he was one of the first men who put into practical working the reforms in judicial procedure enacted in 1864.

On settling in a new town in his position as examining magistrate, Ivan Ilyitch made new acquaintances, formed new ties, took up a new line, and adopted a rather different attitude. He took up an attitude of somewhat dignified aloofness towards the provincial authorities while he picked out the best circle among the legal gentlemen and wealthy gentry living in the town, and adopted a tone of slight dissatisfaction with the government, moderate liberalism, and lofty civic virtue. With this, while making no change in the elegance of his get-up, Ivan Ilyitch in his new office gave up shaving, and left his beard free to grow as it liked. Ivan Ilyitch's existence in the new town proved to be very agreeable; the society which took the line of opposition to the governor was friendly and good; his income was larger, and he found a source of increased enjoyment in whist, at which he began to play at this time; and having a faculty for playing cards good-humouredly, and being rapid and exact in his calculations, he was as a rule on the winning side.

After living two years in the new town, Ivan Ilyitch met his future wife. Praskovya Fyodorovna Mihel was the most attractive, clever, and brilliant girl in the set in which Ivan Ilyitch moved. Among other amusements and recreations after his labours as a magistrate, Ivan Ilyitch started a light, playful flirtation with Praskovya Fyodorovna.

Ivan Ilyitch when he was an assistant secretary had danced as a rule; as an examining magistrate he danced only as an exception. He danced now as it were under protest, as though to show "that though I am serving on the new reformed legal code, and am of the fifth class in official rank, still if it comes to a question of dancing, in that line, too, I can do better than others." In this spirit he danced now and then towards the end of the evening with Praskovya Fyodorovna, and it was principally during these dances that he won the heart of Praskovya Fyodorovna. She fell in love with him. Ivan Ilyitch had no clearly defined intention of marrying; but when the girl fell in love with him, he put the question to himself: "After all, why not get married?"

The young lady, Praskovya Fyodorovna, was of good family, nice-looking. There was a little bit of property. Ivan Ilyitch might have reckoned on a more brilliant match, but this was a good match. Ivan Ilyitch had his salary; she, he hoped, would have as much of her own. It was a good family; she was a sweet, pretty, and perfectly *comme il faut* young woman. To say that Ivan Ilyitch got married because he fell in love with his wife and found in her sympathy with his views of life, would be as untrue as to say that he got married because the people of his world approved of the match. Ivan Ilyitch was influenced by both considerations; he was doing what was agreeable to himself in securing such a wife, and at the same time doing what persons of higher standing looked upon as the correct thing.

And Ivan Ilyitch got married.

The process itself of getting married and the early period of married life, with the conjugal caresses, the new furniture, the new crockery, the new house linen, all up to the time of his wife's pregnancy, went off very well; so that Ivan Ilyitch had already begun to think that so far from marriage breaking up that kind of frivolous, agreeable, light-hearted life, always decorous and always approved by society, which he regarded as the normal life, it would even increase its agreeableness. But at that point, in the early months of his wife's pregnancy, there came in a new element, unexpected, unpleasant, tiresome and unseemly, which could never have been anticipated, and from which there was no escape.

His wife, without any kind of reason, it seemed to Ivan Ilyitch, *de gaité de coeur*, as he expressed it, began to disturb the agreeableness and decorum of their life. She began without any sort of justification to be jealous, exacting in her demands on his attention, squabbled over everything, and treated him to the coarsest and most unpleasant scenes.

At first Ivan Ilyitch hoped to escape from the unpleasantness of this position by taking up the same frivolous and well-bred line that had served him well on other occasions of difficulty. He endeavored to ignore his wife's ill-humour, went on living light-heartedly and agreeably as before, invited friends to play cards, tried to get away himself to the club or to his friends. But his wife began on one occasion with such energy, abusing him in such coarse language, and so obstinately persisted in her abuse of him every time he failed in carrying out her demands, obviously having made up her mind firmly to persist till he gave way, that is, stayed at home and was as dull as she was, that Ivan Ilyitch took alarm. He perceived that matrimony, at least with his wife, was not invariably conducive to the pleasures and proprieties of life; but, on the contrary, often destructive of them, and that it was therefore essential to erect some barrier to protect himself from these disturbances. And Ivan Ilyitch began to look about for such means of protecting himself. His official duties were the only thing that impressed Praskovya Fyodorovna, and Ivan Ilyitch began to use his official position and the duties arising from it in his struggle with his wife to fence off his own independent world apart.

With the birth of the baby, the attempts at nursing it, and the various unsuccessful experiments with foods, with the illnesses, real and imaginary, of the infant and its mother, in which Ivan Ilyitch was expected to sympathize, though he never had the slightest idea about them, the need for him to fend off a world apart for himself outside his family life became still more imperative. As his wife grew more irritable and exacting, so did Ivan Ilyitch more and more transfer the centre of gravity of his life to his official work. He became fonder and fonder of official life, and more ambitious than he had been.

Very quickly, not more than a year after his wedding, Ivan Ilyitch had become aware that conjugal life, though providing certain comforts, was in reality a very intricate and difficult business towards which one must, if one is to do one's duty, that is, lead the decorous life approved by society, work out for oneself a definite line, just as in the government service.

And such a line Ivan Ilyitch did work out for himself in his married life. He expected from his home life only those comforts — of dinner at home, of house-keeper and bed which it could give him, and, above all, that perfect propriety in external observances required by public opinion. For the rest, he looked for good-humoured pleasantness, and if he found it he was very thankful. If he met with antagonism and querulousness, he promptly retreated into the separate world he had shut off for himself in his official life, and there he found quiet.

Ivan Ilyitch was prized as a good official, and three years later he was made assistant public prosecutor. The new duties of this position, their dignity, the possibility of bringing any one to trial and putting any one in prison, the publicity of the speeches and the success Ivan Ilyitch had in that part of his work — all this made his official work still more attractive to him.

Children were born to him. His wife became steadily more querulous and ill-tempered, but the line Ivan Ilyitch had taken up for himself in home life put him almost out of reach of her grumbling.

After seven years of service in the same town, Ivan Ilyitch was transferred to another province with the post of public prosecutor. They moved, money was short, and his wife did not like the place they had moved to. The salary was indeed a little higher than before, but their expenses were larger. Besides, a couple of children died, and home life consequently became even less agreeable for Ivan Ilyitch.

For every mischance that occurred in their new place of residence, Praskovya Fyodorovna blamed her husband. The greater number of subjects of conversation between husband and wife, especially the education of the children, led to questions which were associated with previous quarrels, and quarrels were ready to break out at every instant. There remained only those rare periods of being in love which did indeed come upon them, but never lasted long. These were the islands at which they put in for a time, but they soon set off again upon the ocean of concealed hostility, that was made manifest in their aloofness from one an-other. This aloofness might have distressed Ivan Ilyitch if he had believed that this ought not to be so, but by now he regarded this position as perfectly normal, and it was indeed the goal towards which he worked in his home life. His aim was to make himself more and more free from the unpleasant aspects of domestic life and to render them harmless and decorous. And he attained this aim by spending less and less time with his family; and when he was forced to be at home, he endeavored to secure his tranquility by the presence of outsiders. The great thing for Ivan Ilyitch was having his office. In the official world all the interest of life was concentrated for him. And this interest absorbed him. The sense of his own power, the consciousness of being able to ruin any one he wanted to ruin, even the external dignity of his office, when he made his entry into the court or met subordinate officials, his success in the eyes of his superiors and his subordinates, and, above all, his masterly handling of cases, of which he was conscious, — all this delighted him and, together with chats with his colleagues, dining out, and whist, filled his life. So that, on the whole, Ivan Ilyitch's life still went on in the way he thought it should go — agreeably and decorously.

So he lived for another seven years. His eldest daughter was already sixteen, another child had died, and there was left only one other, a boy at the high school, a subject of dissension. Ivan Ilyitch wanted to send him to the school of jurisprudence, while Praskovya Fyodorovna to spite him sent him to the high school. The daughter had been educated at home, and had turned out well; the boy too did fairly well at his lessons.

Chapter III
The Quarrel

Such was Ivan Ilyitch's life for seventeen years after his marriage. He had been by now a long while prosecutor, and had refused several appointments offered him, looking out for a more desirable post, when there occurred an unexpected incident which utterly destroyed his peace of mind. Ivan Ilyitch had been expected to be appointed presiding judge in a university town, but a certain Goppe somehow stole a march on him and secured the appointment. Ivan Ilyitch took offence, began upbraiding him, and quarrelled with him and with his own superiors. A coolness was felt towards him, and on the next appointment that was made he was again passed over.

This was in the year 1880. That year was the most painful one in Ivan Ilyitch's life. During that year it became evident on the one hand that his pay was insufficient for his expenses; on the other hand, that he had been forgotten by every one, and that what seemed to him the most monstrous, the cruelest injustice, appeared to other people as a quite commonplace fact. Even his father felt no obligation to assist him. He felt that every one had deserted him, and that every one regarded his position with an income of three thousand five hundred roubles as a quite normal and even fortunate one. He alone, with a sense of the injustice done him, and the everlasting nagging of his wife and the debts he had begun to accumulate, living beyond his means, knew that his position was far from being normal.

The summer of that year, to cut down his expenses, he took a holiday and went with his wife to spend the summer in the country at her brother's.

In the country, with no official duties to occupy him, Ivan Ilyitch was for the first time a prey not to simple boredom, but to intolerable depression; and he made up his mind that things could not go on like that, and that it was absolutely necessary to take some decisive steps.

After a sleepless night spent by Ivan Ilyitch walking up and down the terrace, he determined to go to Petersburg to take active steps and to get transferred to some other department, so as to revenge himself on *them*, the people, that is, who had not known how to appreciate him.

Next day, in spite of all the efforts of his wife and his mother-in-law to dissuade him, he set off to Petersburg.

He went with a single object before him — to obtain a post with an income of five thousand. He was ready now to be satisfied with a post in any department, of any tendency, with any kind of work. He must only have a post — a post with five thousand, in the executive department, the banks, the railways, the Empress Marya's institutions, even in the customs duties — what was essential was five thousand, and essential it was, too, to get out of the department in which they had failed to appreciate his value.

And, behold, this quest of Ivan Ilyitch's was crowned with wonderful, unexpected success. At Kursk there got into the same first-class carriage F. S. Ilyin, an acquaintance, who told him of a telegram just received by the governor of Kursk, announcing a change about to take place in the ministry — Pyotr Ivanovitch was to be superseded by Ivan Semyonovitch.

The proposed change, apart from its significance for Russia, had special significance for Ivan Ilyitch from the fact that by bringing to the front a new person, Pyotr Ivanovitch and obviously therefore, his friend Zahar Ivanovitch, it was in the highest degree propitious to Ivan Ilyitch's own plans. Zahar Ivanovitch was a friend and schoolfellow of Ivan Ilyitch's.

At Moscow the news was confirmed. On arriving at Petersburg, Ivan Ilyitch looked up Zahar Ivanovitch, and received a positive promise of an appointment in his former department — that of justice.

A week later he telegraphed to his wife: "*Zahar Miller's place. At first report I receive appointment.*"

Thanks to these changes, Ivan Ilyitch unexpectedly obtained, in the same department as before, an appointment which placed him two stages higher than his former colleagues, and gave him an income of five thousand, together with the official allowance of three thousand five hundred for travelling expenses. All his ill-humour with his former enemies and the whole department was forgotten, and Ivan Ilyitch was completely happy.

Ivan Ilyitch went back to the country more light-hearted and good-tempered than he had been for a very long while. Praskovya Fyodorovna was in better spirits, too, and peace was patched up between them. Ivan Ilyitch described what respect every one had shown him in Petersburg; how all those who had been his enemies had been put to shame, and were cringing now before him; how envious they were of his appointment, and still more of the high favor in which he stood at Petersburg.

Praskovya Fyodorovna listened to this, and pretended to believe it, and did not contradict him in anything, but confined herself to making plans for her new arrangements in the town to which they would be moving. And Ivan Ilyitch saw with delight that these plans were his plans; that they were agreed; and that his life after this disturbing hitch in its progress was about to regain its true, normal character of light-hearted agreeableness and propriety.

Ivan Ilyitch had come back to the country for a short stay only. He had to enter upon the duties of his new office on the 10th of September; and besides, he needed some time to settle in a new place, to move all his belongings from the other province, to purchase and order many things in addition; in short, to arrange things as settled in his own mind, and almost exactly as settled in the heart too of Praskovya Fyodorovna.

And now when everything was so successfully arranged, and when he and his wife were agreed in their aim, and were, besides, so little together, they got on with one another as they had not got on together since the early years of their married life. Ivan Ilyitch had thought of taking his family away with him at once; but his sister and his brother-in-law, who had suddenly become extremely cordial and intimate with him and his family, were so pressing in urging them to stay that he set off alone.

Ivan Ilyitch started off; and the lighthearted temper produced by his success, and his good understanding with his wife, one thing backing up another, did not desert him all the time. He found a charming set of apartments, the very thing both husband and wife had dreamed of. Spacious, lofty reception rooms in the old style, a comfortable, dignified-looking study for him, rooms for his wife and daughter, a schoolroom for his son, everything as though planned on purpose for them. Ivan Ilyitch himself looked after the furnishing of them, chose the wall-papers, bought furniture, by preference antique furniture, which had a peculiar *comme-il-faut* style to his mind, and it all grew up and grew up, and really attained the ideal he had set before himself. When he had half finished arranging the house, his arrangement surpassed his own expectations. He saw the *comme-il-faut* character, elegant and free from vulgarity, that the whole would have when it was all ready. As he fell asleep he pictured to himself the reception-room as it would be. Looking at the drawing-room, not yet finished, he could see the hearth, the screen, the *étagère*, and the little chairs dotted here and there, the plates and dishes on the wall, and the bronzes as they would be when they were all put in their places. He was delighted with the thought of how he would impress Praskovya and Lizanka, who had taste too in this line. They would never expect anything like it. He was particularly successful in coming across and buying cheap old pieces of furniture, which gave a peculiarly aristocratic air to the whole. In his letters he purposely disparaged everything so as to surprise them. All this so absorbed him that the duties of his new office, though he was so fond of his official work, interested him less than he had expected. During sittings of the court he had moments of inattention; he pondered the question which sort of cornices to have on the window-blinds, straight or fluted. He was so interested in this business that he often set to work with his own hands, moved a piece of furniture, or hung up curtains himself. One day he went up a ladder to show a workman, who did not understand, how he wanted some hangings draped, made a false step and slipped; but, like a strong and nimble person, he clung on, and only knocked his side against the corner of a frame. The bruised place ached, but it soon passed off. Ivan Ilyitch felt all this time particularly good-humoured and well. He wrote: "I feel fifteen years younger." He thought his house-furnishing would be finished in September, but it dragged on to the middle of October. But then the effect was charming; not he only said so, but every one who saw it told him so too.

In reality, it was all just what is commonly seen in the houses of people who are not exactly wealthy but want to look like wealthy people, and so succeed only in being like one another — hangings, dark wood, flowers, rugs and bronzes, everything dark and highly polished, everything that all people of a certain class have so as to be like all people of a certain class. And in his case it was all so like that it made no impression at all; but it all seemed to him somehow special. When he met his family at the railway station and brought them to his newly furnished rooms, all lighted up in readiness, and a footman in a white tie opened the door into an entry decorated with flowers, and then they walked into the drawing-room and the study, uttering cries of delight, he was very happy, conducted them everywhere, eagerly drinking in their praises, and beaming with satisfaction. The same evening, while they talked about various things at tea, Praskovya Fyodor-ovna inquired about his fall, and he laughed and showed them how he had gone flying, and how he had frightened the upholsterer.

"It's as well I'm something of an athlete. Another man might have been killed, and I got nothing worse than a blow here; when it's touched it hurts, but it's going off already; nothing but a bruise."

And they began to live in their new abode, which, as is always the case, when they had got thoroughly settled in they found to be short of just one room, and with their new income, which, as always, was only a little — some five hundred roubles — too little, and everything went very well. Things went particularly well at first, before everything was quite finally arranged, and there was still something to do to the place — something to buy, something to order, something to move, something to make to fit. Though there were indeed several disputes between husband and wife, both were so well satisfied, and there was so much to do, that it all went off without serious quarrels. When there was nothing left to arrange, it became a little dull, and something seemed to be lacking, but by then they were making acquaintances and forming habits, and life was filled up again.

Ivan Ilyitch, after spending the morning in the court, returned home to dinner, and at first he was generally in a good humour, although this was apt to be upset a little, and precisely on account of the new abode. Every spot on the table-cloth, on the hangings, the string of a window blind broken, irritated him. He had devoted so much trouble to the arrangement of the rooms that any disturbance of their order distressed him. But, on the whole, the life of Ivan Ilyitch ran its course as, according to his conviction, life ought to do — easily, agreeably, and decorously. He got up at nine, drank his coffee, read the newspaper, then put on his official uniform, and went to the court. There the routine of the daily work was ready mapped out for him, and he stepped into it at once. People with petitions, inquiries in the office, the office itself, the sittings — public and preliminary. In all this the great thing necessary was to exclude everything with the sap of life in it, which always disturbs the regular course of official business, not to admit any sort of relations with people except the official relations; the motive of all intercourse had to be simply the official motive, and the intercourse itself to be only official. A man would come, for instance, anxious for certain information. Ivan Ilyitch, not being the functionary on duty, would have nothing whatever to do with such a man. But if this man's relation to him as a member of the court is such as can be formulated on official stamped paper — within the limits of such a relation Ivan Ilyitch would do everything, positively everything he could, and in doing so would observe the semblance of human friendly relations, that is, the courtesies of social life. But where the official relation ended, there everything else stopped too. This art of keeping the official aspect of things apart from his real life, Ivan Ilyitch possessed in the highest degree; and through long practice and natural aptitude, he had brought it to such a pitch of perfection that he even permitted himself at times, like a skilled specialist, as it were in jest, to let the human and official relations mingle. He allowed himself this liberty just because he felt he had the power at any moment if he wished it to take up the purely official line again and to drop the human relation. This thing was not simply easy, agreeable, and decorous; in Ivan Ilyitch's hands it attained a positively artistic character. In the intervals of business he smoked, drank tea, chatted a little about politics, a little about public affairs, a little about cards, but most of all about appointments in the service. And tired but feeling like some artist who had skillfully played his part in the performance, one of the first violins in the orchestra, he returned home. At home his daughter and her mother had been paying calls somewhere else, or else some one had been calling on them; the son had been at school, had been preparing his lesson with his teachers, and duly learning correctly what was taught at the high school. Everything was as it should be. After dinner, if there were no visitors, Ivan Ilyitch sometimes read some book of which people were talking, and in the evening sat down to work, that is, read official papers, compared them with the laws, sorted depositions, and put them under the laws. This he found neither tiresome nor entertaining. It was tiresome when he might have been playing "screw"; but if there was no "screw" going on, it was anyway better than sitting alone or with his wife. Ivan Ilyitch's pleasures were little dinners, to which he invited ladies and gentlemen of good social position, and such methods of passing the time with them as were usual with such persons, so that his drawing-room might be like all other drawing-rooms.

Once they even gave a party—a dance. And Ivan Ilyitch enjoyed it, and everything was very successful, except that it led to a violent quarrel with his wife over the tarts and sweetmeats. Praskovya Fyodorovna had her own plan; while Ivan Ilyitch insisted on getting everything from an expensive pastry-cook, and ordered a great many tarts, and the quarrel was because these tarts were left over and the pastry-cook's bill came to forty-five roubles. The quarrel was a violent and unpleasant one, so much so that Praskovya Fyodorovna called him, "Fool, imbecile." And he clutched at his head, and in his anger made some allusion to a divorce. But the party itself was enjoyable. There were all the best people, and Ivan Ilyitch danced with Princess Trufonov, the sister of the one so well known in connection with the charitable association called, "Bear my Burden." His official pleasures lay in the gratification of his pride; his social pleasures lay in the gratification of his vanity. But Ivan Ilyitch's most real pleasure was the pleasure of playing "screw," the Russian equivalent for "poker." He admitted to himself that, after all, after whatever unpleasant incidents there had been in his life, the pleasure which burned like a candle before all others was sitting with good players, and not noisy partners, at "screw"; and, of course, a four-hand game (playing with five was never a success, though one pretends to like it particularly), and with good cards, to play a shrewd, serious game, then supper and a glass of wine. And after "screw," especially after winning some small stakes (winning large sums was unpleasant), Ivan Ilyitch went to bed in a particularly happy frame of mind.

So they lived. They moved in the very best circle, and were visited by people of consequence and young people.

In their views of their circle of acquaintance, the husband, the wife, and the daughter were in complete accord; and without any expressed agreement on the subject, they all acted alike in dropping and shaking off various friends and relations, shabby persons who swooped down upon them in their drawing-room with Japanese plates on the walls, and pressed their civilities on them. Soon these shabby persons ceased fluttering about them, and none but the very best society was seen at the Golovins. Young men began to pay attention to Lizanka; and Petrishtchev, the son of Dmitry Ivanovitch Petrishtchev, and the sole heir of his fortune, an examining magistrate, began to be so attentive to Lizanka, that Ivan Ilyitch had raised the question with his wife whether it would not be as well to arrange a sledge drive for them, or to get up some theatricals. So they lived. And everything went on in this way without change, and everything was very nice.

Chapter IV
NOCTURNAL PAIN

All were in good health. One could not use the word ill-health in connection with the symptoms Ivan Ilyitch sometimes complained of, namely, a queer taste in his mouth and a sort of uncomfortable feeling on the left side of the stomach.

But it came to pass that this uncomfortable feeling kept increasing, and became not exactly a pain, but a continual sense of weight in his side and irritable temper. This irritable temper, continually growing and growing, began at last to mar the agreeable easiness and decorum that had reigned in the Golovin household. Quarrels between the husband and wife became more and more frequent, and soon all the easiness and amenity of life had fallen away, and mere propriety was maintained with difficulty. Scenes became again more frequent. Again there were only islands in the sea of contention — and but few of these — at which the husband and wife could meet without an outbreak. And Praskovya Fyodorovna said now, not without grounds, that her husband had a trying temper. With her characteristic exaggeration — she said he had always had this awful temper, and she had needed all her sweetness to put up with it for twenty years. It was true that it was he now who began the quarrels. His gusts of temper always broke out just before dinner, and often just as he was beginning to eat, at the soup. He would notice that some piece of the crockery had been chipped, or that the food was not nice, or that his son put his elbow on the table, or his daughter's hair was not arranged as he liked it. And whatever it was, he laid the blame of it on Praskovya Fyodorovna. Praskovya Fyodorovna had at first retorted in the same strain, and said all sorts of horrid things to him; but on two occasions, just at the beginning of dinner, he had flown into such a frenzy that she perceived that it was due to physical derangement, and was brought on by taking food, and she controlled herself; she did not reply, but simply made haste to get dinner over. Praskovya Fyodorovna took great credit to herself for this exercise of self-control. Making up her mind that her husband had a fearful temper, and made her life miserable, she began to feel sorry for herself. And the more she felt for herself, the more she hated her husband. She began to wish he were dead; yet could not wish it, because then there would be no income. And this exasperated her against him even more. She considered herself dreadfully unfortunate, precisely because even his death could not save her, and she felt irritated and concealed it, and this hidden irritation on her side increased his irritability.

After one violent scene, in which Ivan Ilyitch had been particularly unjust, and after which he had said in explanation that he certainly was irritable, but that it was due to illness, she said that if he were ill he ought to take steps, and insisted on his going to see a celebrated doctor.

He went. Everything was as he had expected; everything was as it always is. The waiting and the assumption of dignity, that professional dignity he knew so well, exactly as he assumed it himself in court, and the sounding and listening and questions that called for answers that were foregone conclusions and obviously superfluous, and the significant air that seemed to insinuate — you only leave it all to us, and we will arrange everything, for us it is certain and incontestable how to arrange everything, everything in one way for every man of every sort. It was all exactly as in his court of justice. Exactly the same air as he put on in dealing with a man brought up for judgment, the doctor put on for him.

The doctor said: This and that proves that you have such-and-such a thing wrong inside you; but if that is not confirmed by analysis of this and that, then we must assume this and that. If we assume this and that, then — and so on. To Ivan Ilyitch there was only one question of consequence. Was his condition dangerous or not? But the doctor ignored that irrelevant inquiry. From the doctor's point of view this was a side issue, not the subject under consideration; the only real question was the balance of probabilities between a loose kidney, chronic catarrh, and appendicitis. It was not a question of the life of Ivan Ilytich, but the question between the loose kidney and the intestinal appendix. And this question, as it seemed to Ivan Ilyitch, the doctor solved in a brilliant manner in favour of the appendix, with the reservation that analysis of the water might give a fresh clue, and that then the aspect of the case would be altered. All this was point for point identical with what Ivan Ilyitch had himself done in brilliant fashion a thousand times over in dealing with some man on his trial. Just as brilliantly the doctor made his summing-up, and triumphantly, gaily even, glanced over his spectacles at the prisoner in the dock. From the doctor's summing-up Ivan Ilyitch deduced the conclusion — that things looked bad, and that he, the doctor, and most likely every one else, did not care, but that things looked bad for him. And this conclusion impressed Ivan Ilyitch morbidly, arousing in him a great feeling of pity for himself, of great anger against this doctor who could be unconcerned about a matter of such importance.

But he said nothing of that. He got up, and, laying the fee on the table, he said, with a sigh, "We sick people probably often ask inconvenient questions. Tell me, is this generally a dangerous illness or not?"

The doctor glanced severely at him with one eye through his spectacles, as though to say: "Prisoner at the bar, if you will not keep within the limits of the questions allowed you, I shall be compelled to take measures for your removal from the precincts of the court." "I have told you what I thought necessary and suitable already," said the doctor; "the analysis will show anything further." And the doctor bowed him out.

Ivan Ilyitch went out slowly and dejectedly, got into his sledge, and drove home. All the way home he was incessantly going over all the doctor had said, trying to translate all these complicated, obscure, scientific phrases into simple language, and to read in them an answer to the question, Is it bad — is it very bad, or nothing much as yet? And it seemed to him that the upshot of all the doctor had said was that it was very bad. Everything seemed dismal to Ivan Ilyitch in the streets. The sledge-drivers were dismal, the houses were dismal, the people passing, and the shops were dismal. This ache, this dull gnawing ache, that never ceased for a second, seemed, when connected with the doctor's obscure utterances, to have gained a new, more serious significance. With a new sense of misery Ivan Ilyitch kept watch on it now.

He reached home and began to tell his wife about it. His wife listened; but in the middle of his account his daughter came in with her hat on, ready to go out with her mother. Reluctantly she half sat down to listen to these tedious details, but she could not stand it for long, and her mother did not hear his story to the end.

"Well, I'm very glad," said his wife; "now you must be sure and take the medicine regularly. Give me the prescription; I'll send Gerasim to the chemist's!" And she went to get ready to go out.

He had not taken breath while she was in the room and he heaved a deep sigh when she was gone.

"Well," he said, "may be it really is nothing as yet."

He began to take the medicine, to carry out the doctor's directions, which were changed after the analysis of the water. But it was just at this point that some confusion arose, either in the analysis or in what ought to have followed from it. The doctor himself, of course, could not be blamed for it, but it turned out that things had not gone as the doctor had told him. Either he had forgotten or told a lie, or was hiding something from him.

But Ivan Ilyitch still went on just as exactly carrying out the doctor's direction, and in doing so he found comfort at first.

From the time of his visit to the doctor Ivan Ilyitch's principal occupation became the exact observance of the doctor's prescriptions as regards hygiene and medicine and the careful observation of his ailment in all the functions of his organism. Ivan Ilyitch's principal interest came to be people's ailments and people's health. When anything was said in his presence about sick people, about deaths and recoveries, especially in the case of an illness resembling his own, he listened, trying to conceal his excitement, asked questions, and applied what he heard to his own trouble.

The ache did not grow less; but Ivan Ilyitch made great efforts to force himself to believe that he was better. And he succeeded in deceiving himself so long as nothing happened to disturb him. But as soon as he had a mischance, some unpleasant words with his wife, a failure in his official work, an unlucky hand at "screw," he was at once acutely sensible of his illness. In former days he had borne with such mishaps, hoping soon to retrieve the mistake, to make a struggle, to reach success later, to have a lucky hand. But now he was cast down by every mischance and reduced to despair. He would say to himself: "Here I'm only just beginning to get better, and the medicine has begun to take effect, and now this mischance or disappointment." And he was furious against the mischance or the people who were causing him the disappointment and killing him, and he felt that this fury was killing him, but could not check it. One would have thought that it should have been clear to him that this exasperation against circumstances and people was aggravating his disease, and that therefore he ought not to pay attention to the unpleasant incidents. But his reasoning took quite the opposite direction. He said that he needed peace, and was on the watch for everything that disturbed his peace, and at the slightest disturbance of it he flew into a rage. What made his position worse was that he read medical books and consulted doctors. He got worse so gradually that he might have deceived himself, comparing one day with another, the difference was so slight. But when he consulted the doctors, then it seemed to him that he was getting worse, and very rapidly so indeed. And in spite of this, he was continually consulting the doctors.

That month he called on another celebrated doctor. The second celebrity said almost the same as the first, but put his questions differently; and the interview with this celebrity only redoubled the doubts and terrors of Ivan Ilyitch. A friend of a friend of his, a very good doctor, diagnosed the disease quite differently; and in spite of the fact that he guaranteed recovery by his questions and his suppositions he confused Ivan Ilyitch even more and strengthened his suspicions. A homoeopath gave yet another diagnosis of the complaint, and prescribed medicine, which Ivan Ilyitch's took secretly for a week; but after a week of the homoeopathic medicine he felt no relief, and losing faith both in the other doctor's treatment and in this, he fell into even deeper depression. One day a lady of his acquaintance talked to him of healing wrought by the holy pictures. Ivan Ilyitch caught himself listening attentively and believing in the reality of the facts alleged. This incident alarmed him. "Can I have degenerated to such a point of intellectual feebleness?" he said to himself. "Nonsense! it's all rubbish. I must not give way to nervous fears, but fixing on one doctor, adhere strictly to his treatment. That's what I will do. Now it's settled. I won't think about it, but till next summer I will stick to the treatment, and then I shall see. Now I'll put a stop to this wavering!" It was easy to say this, but impossible to carry it out. The pain in his side was always dragging at him, seeming to grow acute and ever more incessant; it seemed to him that the taste in his mouth was queerer, and there was a loathsome smell even from his breath, and his appetite and strength kept dwindling. There was no deceiving himself; something terrible, new, and so important that nothing more important had ever been in Ivan Ilyitch's life, was taking place in him, and he alone knew of it. All about him did not or would not understand, and believed that everything in the world was going on as before. This was what tortured Ivan Ilyitch more than anything. Those of his own household, most of all his wife and daughter, who were absorbed in a perfect whirl of visits, did not, he saw, comprehend it at all, and were annoyed that he was so depressed and exacting, as though he were to blame for it. Though they tried indeed to disguise it, he saw he was a nuisance to them; but that his wife had taken up a definite line of her own in regard to his illness, and stuck to it regardless of what he might say and do. This line was expressed thus: "You know," she would say to acquaintances, "Ivan Ilyitch cannot, like all other simple-hearted folks, keep to the treatment prescribed him. One day he'll take his drops and eat what he's ordered, and go to bed in good time; the next day, if I don't see to it, he'll suddenly forget to take his medicine, eat sturgeon (which is forbidden by the doctors), yes, and sit up at 'screw' till past midnight."

"Why, when did I do that?" Ivan Ilyitch asked in vexation one day at Pyotr Ivanovitch's.

"Why, yesterday, with Shebek."

"It makes no difference. I couldn't sleep for pain."

"Well, it doesn't matter what you do it for, only you'll never get well like that, and you make us wretched."

Praskovya Fyodorovna's external attitude to her husband's illness, openly expressed to others and to himself, was that Ivan Ilyitch was to blame in the matter of his illness, and that the whole illness was another injury he was doing to his wife. Ivan Ilyitch felt that the expression of this dropped from her unconsciously, but that made it no easier for him.

In his official life, too, Ivan Ilyitch noticed, or fancied he noticed, a strange attitude to him. At one time it seemed to him that people were looking inquisitively at him, as a man who would shortly have to vacate his position; at another time his friends would suddenly begin chaffing him in a friendly way over his nervous fears, as though that awful and horrible, unheard-of-thing that was going on within him, incessantly gnawing at him, and irresistibly dragging him away somewhere, were the most agreeable subject for joking. Shvarts especially, with his jocoseness, his liveliness, and his *comme-il-faut* tone, exasperated Ivan Ilyitch by reminding him of himself ten years ago.

Friends came sometimes to play cards. They sat down to the card-table; they shuffled and dealt the new cards. Diamonds were led and followed by diamonds, the seven. He partner said, "Can't trump," and played the two of diamonds. What then? Why, delightful, capital, it should have been — he had a trump hand. And suddenly Ivan Ilyitch feels that gnawing ache, that taste in his mouth, and it strikes him as something grotesque that with that he could be glad of a trump hand.

He looks at Mihail Mihailovitch, his partner, how he taps on the table with his red hand, and affably and indulgently abstains from snatching up the trick, and pushes the cards towards Ivan Ilyitch so as to give him the pleasure of taking them up, without any trouble, without even stretching out his hand. "What, does he suppose that I'm so weak that I can't stretch out my hand?" thinks Ivan Ilyitch, and he forgets the trumps, and trumps his partner's cards, and plays his trump hand without making three tricks; and what's the most awful thing of all is that he sees how upset Mihail Mihailovitch is about it, while he doesn't care a bit, and it's awful for him to think why he doesn't care.

They all see that he's in pain, and say to him, "We can stop if you're tired. You go and lie down." Lie down? No, he's not in the least tired; they will play the rubber. All are gloomy and silent. Ivan Ilyitch feels that it is he who has brought this gloom upon them, and he cannot disperse it. They have supper, and the party breaks up, and Ivan Ilyitch is left alone with the consciousness that his life is poisoned for him and poisons the life of others, and that this poisons the life of others, and that this poison is not losing its force, but is continually penetrating more and more deeply into his whole existence.

And with the consciousness of this, and with the physical pain in addition, and the terror in addition to that, he must lie in his bed, often not able to sleep for pain the greater part of the night; and in the morning he must get up again, dress, go to the law-court, speak, write, or, if he does not go out, stay at home for all the four-and-twenty hours of the day and night, of which each one is a torture. And he had to live thus on the edge of the precipice alone, without one man who would understand and feel for him.

Chapter V
HATRED!

In this way one month, then a second, passed by. Just before the New Year his brother-in-law arrived in the town on a visit to them. Ivan Ilyitch was at the court when he arrived. Praskovya Fyodorovna had gone out shopping. Coming home and going into his study, he found there his brother-in-law, a healthy, florid man, engaged in unpacking his trunk. He raised his head, hearing Ivan Ilyitch's step, and for a second stared at him without a word. That stare told Ivan Ilyitch everything. His brother-in-law opened his mouth to utter an "Oh!" of surprise, but checked himself. That confirmed it all.

"What! have I changed?"

"Yes, there is a change."

And all Ivan Ilyitch's efforts to draw him into talking of his appearance his brother-in-law met with obstinate silence. Praskovya Fyodorovna came in; the brother-in-law went to see her. Ivan Ilyitch locked his door and began gazing at himself in the looking-glass, first full face, then in profile. He took up his photograph, taken with his wife, and compared the portrait with what he saw in the looking-glass. The change was immense. Then he bared his arm to the elbow, looked at it, pulled the sleeve down again, sat down on an ottoman and felt blacker than night.

"I mustn't, I mustn't," he said to himself, jumped up, went to the table, opened some official paper, tried to read it, but could not. He opened the door, went into the drawing-room. The door into the drawing-room was closed. He went up to it on tiptoe and listened.

"No, you're exaggerating," Praskovya Fyodorovna was saying.

"Exaggerating? You can't see it. Why, he's a dead man. Look at his eyes—there's no light in them. But what's wrong with him?"

"No one can tell. Nikolaev" (that was another doctor) "said something, but I don't know. Leshtchetitsky" (this was the celebrated doctor) "said the opposite."

Ivan Ilyitch walked away, went to his own room, lay down, and fell to musing. "A kidney—a loose kidney." He remembered all the doctors had told him, how it had been detached, and how it was loose; and by an effort of imagination he tried to catch that kidney and to stop it, to strengthen it. So little was needed, he fancied. "No, I'll go again to Pyotr Ivanovitch" (this was the friend who had a friend a doctor). He rang, ordered the horse to be put in, and got ready to go out.

"Where are you off to, Jean?" asked his wife with a peculiarly melancholy and exceptionally kind expression.

This exceptionally kind expression exasperated him. He looked darkly at her.

"I want to see Pyotr Ivanovitch."

He went to the friend who had a friend a doctor. And with him to the doctor's. He found him in, and had a long conversation with him.

Reviewing the anatomical and physiological details of what, according to the doctor's view, was taking place within him, he understood it all. It was just one thing—a little thing wrong with the intestinal appendix. It might all come right. Only strengthen one sluggish organ, and decrease the undue activity of another, and absorption would take place, and all would be set right. He was a little late for dinner. He ate his dinner, talked cheerfully, but it was a long while before he could go to his own room to work. At last he went to his study, and at once sat down to work. He read his legal documents and did his work, but the consciousness never left him of having a matter of importance very near to his heart which he had put off, but would look into later. When he had finished his work, he remembered that the matter near his heart was thinking about the intestinal appendix. But he did not give himself up to it; he went into the drawing-room to tea. There were visitors; and there was talking, playing on the piano, and singing; there was the young examining magistrate, the desirable match for the daughter. Ivan Ilyitch spent the evening, as Praskovya Fyodorovna observed, in better spirits than any of them; but he never forgot for an instant that he had the important matter of the intestinal appendix put off for consideration later. At eleven o'clock he said good night and went to his own room. He had slept alone since his illness in a little room adjoining his study. He went in, undressed, and took up a novel of Zola, but did not read it; he fell to thinking. And in his imagination the desired recovery of the intestinal appendix had taken place. There had been absorption, rejection, re-establishment of the regular action.

"Why, it's all simply that," he said to himself. "One only wants to assist nature." He remembered the medicine, got up, took it, lay down on his back, watching for the medicine to act beneficially and overcome the pain. "It's only to take it regularly and avoid injurious influences; why, already I feel rather better, much better." He began to feel his side; it was not painful to the touch. "Yes, I don't feel it — really, much better already." He put out the candle and lay on his side. The appendix is getting better, absorption." Suddenly he felt the familiar, old, dull, gnawing ache, persistent, quiet, in earnest. In his mouth the same familiar loathsome taste. His heart sank, and his brain felt dim, misty. "My God, my God!" he said, "again, again, and it will never cease." And suddenly the whole thing rose before him in quite a different aspect. "Intestinal appendix! kidney!" he said to himself. "It's not a question of the appendix, not a question of the kidney, but of life and . . . death. Yes, life has been and now it's going, going away, and I cannot stop it. Yes. Why deceive myself? Isn't it obvious to every one, except me, that I'm dying, and it's only a question of weeks, of days — at once perhaps. There was light, and now there is darkness. I was here, and now I am going! Where?" A cold chill ran over him, his breath stopped. He heard nothing but the throbbing of his heart.

"I shall be no more, then what will there be? There'll be nothing. Where then shall I be when I'm no more? Can this be dying? No; I don't want to!" He jumped up, tried to light the candle; and fumbling with trembling hands, he dropped the candle and the candlestick on the floor and fell back again on the pillow. "Why trouble? it doesn't matter," he said to himself, staring with open eyes into the darkness. "Death. Yes, death. And they — all of them — don't understand, and don't want to understand, and feel no pity. They are playing. (He caught through the closed doors the far-away cadence of a voice and the accompaniment.) They don't care, but they will die too. Fools! Me sooner and them later; but it will be the same for them. And they are merry. The beasts!" Anger stifled him. And he was agonisingly, insufferably miserable. "It cannot be that all men always have been doomed to this awful horror!" He raised himself.

"There is something wrong in it; I must be calm, I must think it all over from the beginning." And then he began to consider. "Yes, the beginning of my illness. I knocked my side, and I was just the same, that day and the days after: it ached a little, then more, then doctors, then depression, misery, and again doctors; and I've gone on getting closer and closer to the abyss. Strength growing less. Nearer and nearer. And here I am, wasting away, no light in my eyes. I think of how to cure the appendix, but this is death. Can it be death?" Again a horror came over him! Gasping for breath, he bent over, began feeling for the matches, and knocked his elbow against the bedside table. It was in his way and hurt him; he felt furious with it, in his anger knocked against it more violently, and upset it. And in despair, breathless, he fell back on his spine waiting for death to come that instant.

The visitors were leaving at that time. Praskovya Fyodorovna was seeing them out. She heard something fall, and came in.

"What is it?"

"Nothing. I dropped something by accident."

She went out, brought a candle. He was lying, breathing hard and fast, like a man who has run a mile, and staring with fixed eyes at her.

"What is it, Jean?"

"No—othing, I say. I dropped something."—"Why speak? She won't understand," he thought.

She certainly did not understand. She picked up the candle, lighted it for him, and went out hastily. She had to say good-bye to a departing guest. When she came back, he was lying in the same position on his back, looking upwards.

"How are you—worse?"

"Yes."

She shook her head, sat down.

"Do you know what, Jean? I wonder if we hadn't better send for Leshtchetitsky to see you here?"

This meant calling in the celebrated doctor, regardless of expense. He smiled malignantly, and said no. She sat a moment longer, went up to him, and kissed him on the forehead.

He hated her with all the force of his soul when she was kissing him, and had to make an effort not to push her away.

"Good night. Please God, you'll sleep."

"Yes."

Chapter VI
DESPAIR

Ivan Ilyitch saw that he was dying, and was in continual despair.

At the bottom of his heart Ivan Ilyitch knew that he was dying; but so far from growing used to this idea, he simply did not grasp it—he was utterly unable to grasp it.

The example of the Syllogism that he had learned in Kiseveter's logic—Caius is a man, men are mortal, therefore Caius is mortal—had seemed to him all his life correct only as regards Caius, but not at all as regards himself. In that case it was a question of Caius, a man, an abstract man, and it was perfectly true, but he was not Caius, and was not an abstract man; he had always been a creature quite, quite different from all others; he had been little Vanya with a mamma and pappa, and Mitya and Volodya, with playthings and a coachman and a nurse; afterwards with Katenka, with all the joys and griefs and ecstasies of childhood, boyhood, and youth. What did Caius know of the smell of the leathern ball Vanya had been so fond of? Had Caius kissed his mother's hand like that? Caius had not heard the silk rustle of his mother's skirts. He had not made a riot at school over the pudding. Had Caius been in love like that? Could Caius preside over the sittings of the court?

And Caius certainly was mortal, and it was right for him to die; but for me, little Vanya, Ivan Ilyitch, with all my feelings and ideas — for me it's a different matter. And it cannot be that I ought to die. That would be too awful.

That was his feeling.

"If I had to die like Caius, I should have known it was so, some inner voice would have told me so. But there was nothing of the sort in me. And I and all my friends, we felt that it was not at all the same as with Caius. And now here it is!" he said to himself "It can't be! It can't be, but it is! How is it? How's one to understand it?" And he could not conceive it, and tried to drive away this idea as false, incorrect, and morbid, and to supplant it by other, correct, healthy ideas. But this idea, not as an idea merely, but as it were an actual fact, came back again and stood confronting him.

And to replace this thought he called up other thoughts, one after another, in the hope of finding support in them. He tried to get back into former trains of thought, which in old days had screened off the thought of death. But, strange to say, all that had in old days covered up, obliterated the sense of death, could not now produce the same effect. Latterly, Ivan Ilyitch spent the greater part of his time in these efforts to restore his old trains of thought which had shut off death. At one time he would say to himself, "I'll put myself into my official work; why, I used to live in it." And he would go to the law-courts, banishing every doubt. He would enter into conversation with his colleagues, and would sit carelessly, as his old habit was, scanning the crowd below dreamily, and with both his wasted hands he would lean on the arms of the oak arm-chair just as he always did; and bending over to a colleague, pass the papers to him and whisper to him, then suddenly dropping his eyes and sitting up straight, he would pronounce the familiar words that opened the proceedings. But suddenly in the middle, the pain in his side, utterly regardless of the stage he had reached in his conduct of the case, began its work. It riveted Ivan Ilyitch's attention. He drove away the thought of it, but it still did its work, and than It came and stood confronting him and looked at him, and he felt turned to stone, and the light died away in his eyes, and he began to ask himself again, "Can it be that It is the only truth?" And his colleagues and his subordinates saw with surprise and distress that he, the brilliant, subtle judge, was losing the thread of his speech, was making blunders. He shook himself, tried to regain his self-control, and got somehow to the end of the sitting, and went home with the painful sense that his judicial labours could not as of old hide from him what he wanted to hide; that he could not by means of his official work escape from It. And the worst of it was that It drew him to itself not for him to do anything in particular, but simply for him to look at It straight in the face, to look at It and, doing nothing, suffer unspeakably.

And to save himself from this, Ivan Ilyitch sought amusements, other screens, and these screens he found, and for a little while they did seem to save him; but soon again they were not so much broken down as let the light through, as though It pierced through everything, and there was nothing that could shut It off.

Sometimes during those days he would go into the drawing-room he had furnished, that drawing-room where he had fallen, for which — how bitterly ludicrous it was for him to think of it! — for the decoration of which he had sacrificed his life, for he knew that it was that bruise that had started his illness. He went in and saw that the polished table had been scratched by something. He looked for the cause, and found it in the bronze clasps of the album, which had been twisted on one side. He took up the album, a costly one, which he had himself arranged with loving care, and was vexed at the carelessness of his daughter and her friends. Here a page was torn, here the photographs had been shifted out of their places. He carefully put it to rights again and bent the clasp back.

Then the idea occurred to him to move all this *établissement* of the albums to another corner where the flowers stood. He called the footman; or his daughter or his wife came to help him. They did not agree with him, contradicted him; he argued, got angry. But all that was very well, since he did not think of It; It was not in sight.

But then his wife would say, as he moved something himself, "Do let the servants do it, you'll hurt yourself again," and all at once It peeped through the screen; he caught a glimpse of It. He caught a glimpse of It, but still he hoped It would hide itself. Involuntarily though, he kept watch on his side; there it is just the same still, aching still, and now he cannot forget it, and It is staring openly at him from behind the flowers. What's the use of it all?

"And it's the fact that here, at that curtain, as if it had been storming a fort, I lost my life. Is it possible? How awful and how silly! It cannot be! It cannot be, and it is."

He went into his own room, lay down, and was again alone with It. Face to face with It, and nothing to be done with It. Nothing but to look at It and shiver.

Chapter VII
LONGING

How it came to pass during the third month of Ivan Ilyitch's illness, it would be impossible to say, for it happened little by little, imperceptibly, but it had come to pass that his wife and his daughter and his son and their servants and their acquaintances, and the doctors, and, most of all, he himself — all were aware that all interest in him for other people consisted now in the question how soon he would leave his place empty, free the living from the constraint of his presence, and be set free himself from his sufferings.

He slept less and less; they gave him opium, and began to inject morphine. But this did not relieve him. The dull pain he experienced in the half-asleep condition at first only relieved him as a change, but then it became as bad, or even more agonising, than the open pain. He had special things to eat prepared for him according to the doctors' prescriptions; but these dishes became more and more distasteful, more and more revolting to him.

Special arrangements, too, had to be made for his other physical needs, and this was a continual misery to him. Misery from the uncleanliness, the unseemliness, and the stench, from the feeling of another person having to assist in it.

But just from this most unpleasant side of his illness there came comfort to Ivan Ilyitch. There always came into his room on these occasions to clear up for him the peasant who waited on table, Gerasim.

Gerasim was a clean, fresh, young peasant, who had grown stout and hearty on the good fare in town. Always cheerful and bright. At first the sight of this lad, always cleanly dressed in the Russian style, engaged in this revolting task, embarrassed Ivan Ilyitch.

One day, getting up from the night-stool, too weak to replace his clothes, he dropped on to a soft low chair and looked with horror at his bare, powerless thighs, with the muscles so sharply standing out on them.

Then there came in with light, strong steps Gerasim, in his thick boots, diffusing a pleasant smell of tar from his boots, and bringing in the freshness of the winter air. Wearing a clean hempen apron, and a clean cotton shirt, with his sleeves tucked up on his strong, bare young arms, without looking at Ivan Ilyitch, obviously trying to check the radiant happiness in his face so as not to hurt the sick man, he went up to the night-stool.

"Gerasim," said Ivan Ilyitch faintly.

Gerasim started, clearly afraid that he had done something amiss, and with a rapid movement turned towards the sick man his fresh, good-natured, simple young face, just beginning to be downy with the first growth of beard.

"Yes, your honour."

"I'm afraid this is very disagreeable for you. You must excuse me. I can't help it."

"Why, upon my word, sir!" And Gerasim's eyes beamed, and he showed his white young teeth in a smile. "What's a little trouble? It's a case of illness with you, sir."

And with his deft, strong arms he performed his habitual task, and went out, stepping lightly. And five minutes later, treading just as lightly, he came back.

Ivan Ilyitch was still sitting in the same way in the armchair.

"Gerasim," he said, when the latter had replaced the night-stool all sweet and clean, "please help me; come here." Gerasim went up to him. "Lift me up. It's difficult for me alone, and I've sent Dmitry away."

Gerasim went up to him; as lightly as he stepped he put his strong arms round him, deftly and gently lifted and supported him, with the other hand pulled up his trousers, and would have set him down again. But Ivan Ilyitch asked him to carry him to the sofa. Gerasim, without effort, carefully not squeezing him, led him, almost carrying him, to the sofa, and settled him there.

"Thank you; how neatly and well . . . you do everything."

Gerasim smiled again, and would have gone away. But Ivan Ilyitch felt his presence such a comfort that he was reluctant to let him go.

"Oh, move that chair near me, please. No, that one, under my legs. I feel easier when my legs are higher."

Gerasim picked up the chair, and without letting it knock, set it gently down on the ground just at the right place, and lifted Ivan Ilyitch's legs on to it. It seemed to Ivan Ilyitch that he was easier just at the moment when Gerasim lifted his legs higher.

"I'm better when my legs are higher," said Ivan Ilyitch. "Put that cushion under me."

Gerasim did so. Again he lifted his legs to put the cushion under them. Again it seemed to Ivan Ilyitch that he was easier at that moment when Gerasim held his legs raised. When he laid them down again, he felt worse.

"Gerasim," he said to him, "are you busy just now?"

"Not at all, sir," said Gerasim, who had learned among the town-bred servants how to speak to gentlefolks.

"What have you left to do?"

"Why, what have I to do? I've done everything, there's only the wood to chop for to-morrow."

"Then hold my legs up like that—can you?"

"To be sure, I can." Gerasim lifted the legs up. And it seemed to Ivan Ilyitch that in that position he did not feel the pain at all.

"But how about the wood?"

"Don't you trouble about that, sir. We shall have time enough."

Ivan Ilyitch made Gerasim sit and hold his legs, and began to talk to him. And, strange to say, he fancied he felt better while Gerasim had hold of his legs.

From that time forward Ivan Ilyitch would sometimes call Gerasim, and get him to hold his legs on his shoulders, and he liked talking with him. Gerasim did this easily, readily, simply, and with a good-nature that touched Ivan Ilyitch. Health, strength, and heartiness in all other people were offensive to Ivan Ilyitch; but the strength and heartiness of Gerasim did not mortify him, but soothed him.

Ivan Ilyitch's great misery was due to the deception that for some reason or other every one kept up with him—that he was simply ill, and not dying, and that he need only keep quiet and follow the doctor's orders, and then some great change for the better would be the result. He knew that whatever they might do, there would be no result except more agonising sufferings and death. And he was made miserable by this lie, made miserable at their refusing to acknowledge what they all knew and he knew, by their persisting in lying over him about his awful position, and in forcing him too to take part in this lie. Lying, lying, this lying carried on over him on the eve of his death, and destined to bring that terrible, solemn act of his death down to the level of all their visits, curtains, sturgeons for dinner . . . was a horrible agony for Ivan Ilyitch. And, strange to say, many times when they had been going through the regular performance over him, he had been within a hair's-breadth of screaming at them: "Cease your lying! You know, and I know, that I'm dying; so do, at least, give over lying!" But he had never had the spirit to do this. The terrible, awful act of his dying was, he saw, by all those about him, brought down to the level of a casual, unpleasant, and to some extent indecorous, incident (somewhat as they would behave with a person who should enter a drawing-room smelling unpleasant). It was brought down to this level by that very decorum to which he had been enslaved all his life. He saw that no one felt for him, because no one would even grasp his position. Gerasim was the only person who recognised the position, and felt sorry for him. And that was why Ivan Ilyitch was only at ease with Gerasim. He felt comforted when

Gerasim sometimes supported his legs for whole nights at a stretch, and would not go away to bed, saying, "Don't you worry yourself, Ivan Ilyitch, I'll get sleep enough yet," and when suddenly dropping into the familiar peasant forms of speech, he added: "If thou weren't sick, but as 'tis, 'twould be strange if I didn't wait on thee." Gerasim alone did not lie; everything showed clearly that he alone understood what it meant, and saw no necessity to disguise it, and simply felt sorry for his sick, wasting master. He even said this once straight out, when Ivan Ilyitch was sending him away.

"We shall all die. So what's a little trouble?" he said, meaning by this to express that he did not complain of the trouble just because he was taking this trouble for a dying man, and he hoped that for him too some one would be willing to take the same trouble when his time came.

Apart from this deception, or in consequence of it, what made the greatest misery for Ivan Ilyitch was that no one felt for him as he would have liked them to feel for him. At certain moments, after prolonged suffering, Ivan Ilyitch, ashamed as he would have been to own it, longed more than anything for some one to feel sorry for him, as for a sick child. He longed to be petted, kissed, and wept over, as children are petted and comforted. He knew that he was an important member of the law-courts, that he had a beard turning grey, and that therefore it was impossible. But still he longed for it. And in his relations with Gerasim there was something approaching to that. And that was why being with Gerasim was a comfort to him. Ivan Ilyitch longs to weep, longs to be petted and wept over, and then there comes in a colleague, Shebek; and instead of weeping and being petted, Ivan Ilyitch puts on his serious, severe, earnest face, and from mere inertia gives his views on the effect of the last decision in the Court of Appeal, and obstinately insists upon them. This falsity around him and within him did more than anything to poison Ivan Ilyitch's last days.

Chapter VIII
THE DOCTOR'S VISIT

It was morning. All that made it morning for Ivan Ilyitch was that Gerasim had gone away, and Pyotr the footman had come in; he had put out the candles, opened one of the curtains, and begun surreptitiously setting the room to rights. Whether it were morning or evening, Friday or Sunday, it all made no difference; it was always just the same thing. Gnawing, agonising pain never ceasing for an instant; the hopeless sense of life always ebbing away, but still not yet gone; always swooping down on him that fearful, hated death, which was the only reality, and always the same falsity. What were days, or weeks, or hours of the day to him?

"Will you have tea, sir?"

"He wants things done in their regular order. In the morning the family should have tea," he thought, and only said —

"No."

"Would you care to move on to the sofa?"

"He wants to make the room tidy, and I'm in his way. I'm uncleanness, disorder," he thought, and only said —

"No, leave me alone."

The servant still moved busily about his work. Ivan Ilyitch stretched out his hand. Pyotr went up to offer his services.

"What can I get you?"

"My watch."

Pyotr got out the watch, which lay just under his hand and gave it to him.

"Half-past eight. Are they up?"

"Not yet, sir. Vladimir Ivanovitch" (that was his son) "has gone to the high school, and Praskovya Fyodorovna gave orders that she was to be waked if you asked for her. Shall I send word?"

"No, no need. Should I try some tea?" he thought.

"Yes, tea . . . bring it."

Pyotr was on his way out. Ivan Ilyitch felt frightened of being left alone. "How keep him? Oh, the medicine. Pyotr, give me my medicine. Oh well, may be, medicine may still be some good." He took the spoon, drank it. "No, it does no good. It's all rubbish, deception," he decided, as soon as he tasted the familiar, mawkish, hopeless taste. "No, I can't believe it now. But the pain, why this pain; if it would only cease for a minute." And he groaned. Pyotr turned round. "No, go on. Bring the tea."

Pyotr went away. Ivan Ilyitch, left alone, moaned, not so much from the pain, awful as it was, as from misery. Always the same thing again and again, all these endless days and nights. If it would only be quicker. Quicker to what? Death, darkness. No, no. Anything better than death!

When Pyotr came in with the tea on a tray, Ivan Ilyitch stared for some time absent-mindedly at him, not grasping who he was and what he wanted. Pyotr was disconcerted by this stare. And when he showed he was disconcerted, Ivan Ilyitch came to himself.

"Oh yes," he said, "tea, good, set it down. Only help me to wash and put on a clean shirt."

And Ivan Ilyitch began his washing. He washed his hands slowly, and then his face, cleaned his teeth, combed his hair, and looked in the looking-glass. He felt frightened at what he saw, especially at the way his hair clung limply to his pale forehead. When his shirt was being changed, he knew he would be still more terrified if he glanced at his body, and he avoided looking at himself. But at last it was all over. He put on his dressing-gown, covered himself with a rug, and sat in the armchair to drink his tea. For one moment he felt refreshed; but as soon as he began to drink the tea, again there was the same taste, the same pain. He forced himself to finish it, and lay down, stretched out his legs. He lay down and dismissed Pyotr.

Always the same. A gleam of hope flashes for a moment, then again the sea of despair roars about him again, and always pain, always pain, always heartache, and always the same thing. Alone it is awfully dreary; he longs to call some one, but he knows beforehand that with others present it will be worse. "Morphine again — only to forget again. I'll tell him, the doctor, that he must think of something else. It can't go on; it can't go on like this."

One hour, two hours pass like this. Then there is a ring at the front door. The doctor, perhaps. Yes, it is the doctor, fresh, hearty, fat, and cheerful, wearing that expression that seems to say, "You there are in a panic about something, but we'll soon set things right for you." The doctor is aware that this expression is hardly fitting here, but he has put it on once and for all, and can't take it off, like a man who has put on a frockcoat to pay a round of calls.

In a hearty, reassuring manner the doctor rubs his hands.

"I'm cold. It's a sharp frost. Just let me warm myself," he says with an expression, as though it's only a matter of waiting a little till he's warm, and as soon as he's warm he'll set everything to rights.

"Well, now, how are you?"

Ivan Ilyitch feels that the doctor would like to say, "How's the little trouble?" but that he feels that he can't talk like that, and says, "How did you pass the night?"

Ivan Ilyitch looks at the doctor with an expression that asks —

"Is it possible you're never ashamed of lying?"

But the doctor does not care to understand this look.

And Ivan Ilyitch says —

"It's always just as awful. The pain never leaves me, never ceases. If only there were something!"

"Ah, you're all like that, all sick people say that. Come, now I do believe I'm thawed; even Praskovya Fyodorovna, who's so particular, could find no fault with my temperature. Well, now I can say good morning." And the doctor shakes hands.

And dropping his former levity, the doctor, with a serious face, proceeds to examine the patient, feeling his pulse, to take his temperature, and then the tappings and soundings begin.

Ivan Ilyitch knows positively and indubitably that it's all nonsense and empty deception; but when the doctor, kneeling down, stretches over him, putting his ear first higher, then lower, and goes through various gymnastic evolutions over him with a serious face, Ivan Ilyitch is affected by this, as he used sometimes to be affected by the speeches of the lawyers in court, though he was perfectly well aware that they were telling lies all the while and why they were telling lies.

The doctor, kneeling on the sofa, was still sounding him, when there was the rustle of Praskovya Fyodorovna's silk dress in the doorway, and she was heard scolding Pyotr for not having let her know that the doctor had come.

She comes in, kisses her husband, and at once begins to explain that she has been up a long while, and that it was only through a misunderstanding that she was not there when the doctor came.

Ivan Ilyitch looks at her, scans her all over, and sets down against her her whiteness and plumpness, and the cleanness of her hands and neck, and the glossiness of her hair, and the gleam full of life in her eyes. With all the force of his soul he hates her. And when she touches him it makes him suffer from the thrill of hatred he feels for her.

Her attitude to him and his illness is still the same. Just as the doctor had taken up a certain line with the patient which he was not now able to drop, so she too had taken up a line with him — that he was not doing something he ought to do, and was himself to blame, and she was lovingly reproaching him for his neglect, and she could not now get out of this attitude.

"Why, you know, he won't listen to me; he doesn't take his medicine at the right times. And what's worse still, he insists on lying in a position that surely must be bad for him—with his legs in the air."

She described how he made Gerasim hold his legs up.

The doctor smiled with kindly condescension that said, "Oh well, it can't be helped, these sick people do take up such foolish fancies; but we must forgive them."

When the examination was over, the doctor looked at his watch, and then Praskovya Fyodorovna informed Ivan Ilyitch that it must, of course, be as he liked, but she had sent to-day for a celebrated doctor, and that he would examine him, and have a consultation with Mihail Danilovitch (that was the name of their regular doctor).

"Don't oppose it now, please. This I'm doing entirely for my own sake," she said ironically, meaning it to be understood that she was doing it all for his sake, and was only saying this to give him no right to refuse her request. He lay silent, knitting his brows. He felt that he was hemmed in by such a tangle of falsity that it was hard to disentangle anything from it.

Everything she did for him was entirely for her own sake, and she told him she was doing for her own sake what she actually was doing for her own sake as something so incredible that he would take it as meaning the opposite.

At half-past eleven the celebrated doctor came. Again came the sounding, and then grave conversation in his presence and in the other room about the kidney and the appendix, and questions and answers, with such an air of significance, that again, instead of the real question of life and death, which was now the only one that confronted him, the question that came uppermost was of the kidney and the appendix, which were doing something not as they ought to do, and were for that reason being attacked by Mihail Danilovitch and the celebrated doctor, and forced to mend their ways.

The celebrated doctor took leave of him with a serious, but not a hopeless face. And to the timid question that Ivan Ilyitch addressed to him while he lifted his eyes, shining with terror and hope, up towards him, Was there a chance of recovery? he answered that he could not answer for it, but that there was a chance. The look of hope with which Ivan Ilyitch watched the doctor out was so piteous that, seeing it, Praskovya Fyodorovna positively burst into tears, as she went out of the door to hand the celebrated doctor his fee in the next room.

The gleam of hope kindled by the doctor's assurance did not last long. Again the same room, the same pictures, the curtains, the wall-paper, the medicine-bottles, and ever the same, his aching suffering body. And Ivan Ilyitch began to moan; they gave him injections, and he sank into oblivion. When he waked up it was getting dark; they brought him his dinner. He forced himself to eat some broth; and again everything the same, and again the coming night.

After dinner at seven o'clock, Praskovya Fyodorovna came into his room, dressed as though to go to a *soirée*, with her full bosom laced in tight, and traces of powder on her face. She had in the morning mentioned to him that they were going to the theatre. Sarah Bernhardt was visiting the town, and they had a box, which he had insisted on their taking. By now he had forgotten about it, and her smart attire was an offence to him. But he concealed this feeling when he recollected that he had himself insisted on their taking a box and going, because it was an æsthetic pleasure, beneficial and instructive for the children.

Praskovya Fyodorovna came in satisfied with herself, but yet with something of a guilty air. She sat down, asked how he was, as he saw, simply for the sake of asking, and not for the sake of learning anything, knowing indeed that there was nothing to learn, and began telling him how absolutely necessary it was; how she would not have gone for anything, but the box had been taken, and Ellen, their daughter, and Petrishtchev (the examining lawyer, the daughter's suitor) were going, and that it was out of the question to let them go alone. But that she would have liked much better to stay with him. If only he would be sure to follow the doctor's prescription while she was away.

"Oh, and Fyodor Dmitryevitch" (the suitor) "would like to come in. May he? And Liza?"

"Yes, let them come in."

The daughter came in, in full dress, her fresh young body bare, while his body made him suffer so. But she made a show of it; she was strong, healthy, obviously in love, and impatient of the illness, suffering, and death that hindered her happiness.

Fyodor Dmitryevitch came in too in evening dress, his hair curled *à la Capoul,* with his long sinewy neck tightly fenced round by a white collar, with his vast expanse of white chest and strong thighs displayed in narrow black trousers, with one white glove in his hand and a crush opera hat.

Behind him crept in unnoticed the little high school boy in his new uniform, poor fellow, in gloves, and with that awful blue ring under his eyes that Ivan Ilyitch knew the meaning of.

He always felt sorry for his son. And pitiable indeed was his scared face of sympathetic suffering. Except Gerasim, Ivan Ilyitch fancied that Volodya was the only one that understood and was sorry.

They all sat down; again they asked how he was. A silence followed. Liza asked her mother about the opera-glass. An altercation ensued between the mother and daughter as to who had taken it, and where it had been put. It turned into an unpleasant squabble.

Fyodor Dmitryevitch asked Ivan Ilyitch whether he had seen Sarah Bernhardt? Ivan Ilyitch could not at first catch the question that was asked him, but then he said, "No, have you seen her before?"

"Yes, in *Adrienne Lecouvreur.*"

Praskovya Fyodorovna observed that she was particularly good in that part. The daughter made some reply. A conversation sprang up about the art and naturalness of her acting, that conversation that is continually repeated and always the same.

In the middle of the conversation Fyodor Dmitryevitch glanced at Ivan Ilyitch and relapsed into silence. The others looked at him and became mute, too. Ivan Ilyitch was staring with glittering eyes straight before him, obviously furious with them. This had to be set right, but it could not anyhow be set right. This silence had somehow to be broken. No one would venture on breaking it, and all began to feel alarmed that the decorous deception was somehow breaking down, and the facts would be exposed to all. Liza was the first to pluck up courage. She broke the silence. She tried to cover up what they were all feeling, but inadvertently she gave it utterance.

"If *we are going*, though, it's time to start," she said, glancing at her watch, a gift from her father; and with a scarcely perceptible meaning smile to the young man, referring to something only known to themselves, she got up with a rustle of her skirts.

They all got up, said good-bye, and went away. When they were gone, Ivan Ilyitch fancied he was easier; there was no falsity — that had gone away with them, but the pain remained. That continual pain, that continual terror, made nothing harder, nothing easier. It was always worse.

Again came minute after minute, hour after hour, still the same and still no end, and ever more terrible the inevitable end.

"Yes, send Gerasim," he said in answer to Pyotr's question.

Chapter IX
A STRANGE IDEA

Late at night his wife came back. She came in on tiptoe, but he heard her, opened his eyes, and made haste to close them again. She wanted to send away Gerasim and sit up with him herself instead. He opened his eyes and said, "No, go away."

"Are you in great pain?"

"Always the same."

"Take some opium."

He agreed, and drank it. She went away.

Till three o'clock he slept a miserable sleep. It seemed to him that he and his pain were being thrust somewhere into a narrow, deep, black sack, and they kept pushing him further and further in, and still could not thrust him to the bottom. And this operation was awful to him, and was accompanied with agony. And he was afraid, and yet wanted to fall into it, and struggled and yet tried to get into it. And all of a sudden he slipped and fell and woke up. Gerasim, still the same, is sitting at the foot of the bed half-dozing peacefully, patient. And he is lying with his wasted legs clad in stockings, raised on Gerasim's shoulders, the same candle burning in the alcove, and the same interminable pain.

"Go away, Gerasim," he whispered.

"It's all right, sir. I'll stay a bit longer."

"No, go away."

He took his legs down, lay sideways on his arm, and he felt very sorry for himself. He only waited until Gerasim had gone away into the next room; he could restrain himself no longer, and cried like a child. He cried at his own helplessness, at his awful loneliness, at the cruelty of people, at the cruelty of God, at the absence of God.

"Why hast Thou done all this? What brought me to this? Why, why torture me so horribly?"

He did not expect an answer, and wept indeed that there was and could be no answer. The pain grew more acute again, but he did not stir, did not call.

He said to himself, "Come, more then; come, strike me! But what for? What have I done to Thee? what for?"

Then he was still, ceased weeping, held his breath, and was all attention; he listened, as it were, not to a voice uttering sounds, but to the voice of his soul, to the current of thoughts that rose up within him.

"What is it you want?" was the first clear idea able to be put into words that he grasped.

"What? Not to suffer, to live," he answered.

And again he was utterly plunged into attention so intense that even the pain did not distract him.

"To live? Live how?" the voice of his soul was asking.

"Why, live as I used to live before—happily and pleasantly."

"As you used to live before—happily and pleasantly?" queried the voice. And he began going over in his imagination the best moments of his pleasant life. But strange to say, all these best moments of his pleasant life seemed now not at all what they had seemed then. All—except the first memories of childhood— there, in his childhood there had been something really pleasant in which one could have lived if it had come back. But the creature who had this pleasant experience was no more; it was like a memory of some one else.

As soon as he reached the beginning of what had resulted in him as he was now, Ivan Ilyitch, all that had seemed joys to him then now melted away before his eyes and were transformed into something trivial, and often disgusting.

And the further he went from childhood, the nearer to the actual present, the more worthless and uncertain were the joys. It began with life at the school of jurisprudence. Then there had still been something genuinely good; then there had been gaiety; then there had been friendship; then there had been hopes. But in the higher classes these good moments were already becoming rarer. Later on, during the first period of his official life, at the governor's, good moments appeared; but it was all mixed, and less and less of it was good. And further on even less than good, and the further he went the less good there was.

His marriage . . . as gratuitous as the disillusion of it and the smell of his wife's breath and the sensuality, the hypocrisy! And that deadly official life, and anxiety about money, and so for one year, and two, and ten, and twenty, and always the same thing. And the further he went, the more deadly it became. "As though I had been going steadily downhill, imagining that I was going uphill. So it was in fact. In public opinion I was going uphill, and steadily as I got up it life was ebbing away from me. . . . And now the work's done, there's only to die.

"But what is this? What for? It cannot be! It cannot be that life has been so senseless, so loathsome? And if it really was so loathsome and senseless, then why die, and die in agony? There's something wrong.

"Can it be I have not lived as one ought?" suddenly came into his head. "But how not so, when I've done everything as it should be done?" he said, and at once dismissed this only solution of all the enigma of life and death as something utterly out of the question.

"What do you want now? To live? Live how? Live as you live at the courts when the usher booms out: 'The Judge is coming!' . . . The judge is coming, the judge is coming" he repeated to himself. "Here he is, the judge! But I'm not to blame!" he shrieked in fury. "What's it for?" And he left off crying, and turning with his face to the wall, fell to pondering always on the same question, "What for, why all this horror?"

But however much he pondered, he could not find an answer. And whenever the idea struck him, as it often did, that it all came of his never having lived as he ought, he thought of all the correctness of his life and dismissed the strange idea.

Chapter X
No Explanation

Another fortnight had passed. Ivan Ilyitch could not now get up from the sofa. He did not like lying in bed, and lay on the sofa. And lying almost all the time facing the wall, in loneliness he suffered all the inexplicable agonies, and in loneliness pondered always that inexplicable question, "What is it? Can it be true that it's death?" And an inner voice answered, "Yes, it is true." "Why these agonies?" and a voice answered, "For no reason." Beyond and besides this there was nothing.

From the very beginning of his illness, ever since Ivan Ilyitch first went to the doctor's, his life had been split up into two contradictory moods, which were continually alternating — one was despair and the anticipation of an uncomprehended and awful death; the other was hope and an absorbed watching over the actual condition of his body. First, there was nothing confronting him but a kidney or intestine which had temporarily declined to perform their duties, then there was nothing but unknown awful death, which there was no escaping.

These two moods had alternated from the very beginning of the illness; but the further the illness progressed, the more doubtful and fantastic became the conception of the kidney, and the more real the sense of approaching death.

He had but to reflect on what he had been three months before and what he was now, to reflect how steadily he had been going downhill, for every possibility of hope to be shattered.

Of late, in the loneliness in which he found himself, lying with his face to the back of the sofa, a loneliness in the middle of a populous town and of his numerous acquaintances and his family, a loneliness than which none more complete could be found anywhere — not at the bottom of the sea, not deep down in the earth; — of late in this fearful loneliness Ivan Ilyitch had lived only in imagination in the past. One by one the pictures of his past rose up before him. It always began from what was nearest in time and went back to the most remote, to childhood, and rested there. If Ivan Ilyitch thought of the stewed prunes that had been offered him for dinner that day, his mind went back to the damp, wrinkled French plum of his childhood, of its peculiar taste and the flow of saliva when the stone was sucked; and along with this memory of a taste there rose up a whole series of memories of that period — his nurse, his brother, his playthings. "I mustn't . . . it's too painful," Ivan Ilyitch said to himself, and he brought himself back to the present. The button on the back of the sofa and the creases in the morocco. "Morocco's dear, and doesn't wear well; there was a quarrel over it. But the morocco was different, and different too the quarrel when we tore father's portfolio and were punished, and mamma bought us the tarts." And again his mind rested on his childhood, and again it was painful, and he tried to drive it away and think of something else.

And again at that point, together with that chain of associations, quite another chain of memories came into his heart, of how his illness had grown up and become more acute. It was the same there, the further back the more life there had been. There had been both more that was good in life and more of life itself. And the two began to melt into one. "Just as the pain goes on getting worse and worse, so has my whole life gone on getting worse and worse," he thought. One light spot was there at the back, at the beginning of life, and then it kept getting blacker and blacker, and going faster and faster. "In inverse ratio to the square of the distance from death," thought Ivan Ilyitch. And the image of a stone falling downwards with increasing velocity sank into his soul. Life, a series of increasing sufferings, falls more and more swiftly to the end, the most fearful sufferings. "I am falling." He shuddered, shifted himself, would have resisted, but he knew beforehand that he could not resist; and again, with eyes weary with gazing at it, but unable not to gaze at what was before him, he stared at the back of the sofa and waited, waited expecting that fearful fall and shock and dissolution. "Resistance is impossible," he said to himself. "But if one could at least comprehend what it's for? Even that's impossible. It could be explained if one were to say that I hadn't lived as I ought. But that can't be alleged," he said to himself, thinking of all the regularity, correctness, and propriety of his life. "That really can't be admitted," he said to himself, his lips smiling ironically as though some one could see his smile and be deceived by it. "No explanation! Agony, death. . . . What for?"

Chapter XI
CONFESSION

So passed a fortnight. During that fortnight an event occurred that had been desired by Ivan Ilyitch and his wife. Petrishtchev made a formal proposal. This took place in the evening. Next day Praskovya Fyodorovna went in to her husband, resolving in her mind how to inform him of Fyodor Dmitryevitch's proposal, but that night there had been a change for the worse in Ivan Ilyitch. Praskovya Fyodorovna found him on the same sofa, but in a different position. He was lying on his face, groaning, and staring straight before him with a fixed gaze.

She began talking of remedies. He turned his stare on her. She did not finish what she had begun saying; such hatred of her in particular was expressed in that stare.

"For Christ's sake, let me die in peace," he said.

She would have gone away, but at that moment the daughter came in and went up to say good morning to him. He looked at his daughter just as at his wife, and to her inquiries how he was, he told her drily that they would soon all be rid of him. Both were silent, sat a little while, and went out.

"How are we to blame?" said Liza to her mother. "As though we had done it! I'm sorry for papa, but why punish us?"

At the usual hour the doctor came. Ivan Ilyitch answered, "Yes, no," never taking his exasperated stare from him, and towards the end he said, "Why, you know that you can do nothing, so let me be."

"We can relieve your suffering," said the doctor.

"Even that you can't do; let me be."

The doctor went into the drawing-room and told Praskovya Fyodorovna that it was very serious, and that the only resource left them was opium to relieve his sufferings, which must be terrible. The doctor said his physical sufferings were terrible, and that was true; but even more terrible than his physical sufferings were his mental sufferings, and in that lay his chief misery.

His moral sufferings were due to the fact that during that night, as he looked at the sleepy, good-natured, broad-cheeked face of Gerasim, the thought had suddenly come into his head, "What if in reality all my life, my conscious life, has been not the right thing?" The thought struck him that what he had regarded before as an utter impossibility, that he had spent his life not as he ought, might be the truth. It struck him that those scarcely detected impulses of struggle within him against what was considered good by persons of higher position, scarcely detected impulses which he had dismissed, that they might be the real thing, and everything else might be not the right thing. And his official work, and his ordering of his daily life and of his family, and these social and official interests — all that might be not the right thing. He tried to defend it all to himself. And suddenly he felt all the weakness of what he was defending. And it was useless to defend it.

"But if it's so," he said to himself, "and I am leaving life with the consciousness that I have lost all that was given me, and there's no correcting it, then what?" He lay on his back and began going over his whole life entirely anew. When he saw the footman in the morning, then his wife, then his daughter, then the doctor, every movement they made, every word they uttered, confirmed for him the terrible truth that had been revealed to him in the night. In them he saw himself, saw all in which he had lived, and saw distinctly that it was all not the right thing; it was a horrible, vast deception that concealed both life and death. This consciousness intensified his physical agonies, multiplied them tenfold. He groaned and tossed from side to side and pulled at the covering over him. It seemed to him that it was stifling him and weighing him down. And for that he hated them.

They gave him a big dose of opium; he sank into unconsciousness; but at dinner-time the same thing began again. He drove them all away, and tossed from side to side.

His wife came to him and said, "Jean, darling, do this for my sake" (for my sake?). "It can't do harm, and it often does good. Why, it's nothing. And often in health people —"

He opened his eyes wide.

"What? Take the sacrament? What for? No. Besides . . ."

She began to cry.

"Yes, my dear. I'll send for our priest, he's so nice."

"All right, very well," he said.

When the priest came and confessed him he was softened, felt as it were a relief from his doubts, and consequently from his sufferings, and there came a moment of hope. He began once more thinking of the intestinal appendix and the possibility of curing it. He took the sacrament with tears in his eyes.

When they laid him down again after the sacrament for a minute, he felt comfortable, and again the hope of life sprang up. He began to think about the operation which had been suggested to him. "To live, I want to live," he said to himself. His wife came in to congratulate him; she uttered the customary words and added —

"It's quite true, isn't it, that you're better?"

Without looking at her, he said, "Yes."

Her dress, her figure, the expression of her face, the tone of her voice — all told him the same: "Not the right thing. All that in which you lived and are living is lying, deceit, hiding life and death away from you." And as soon as he had formed that thought, hatred sprang up in him, and with that hatred agonising physical sufferings, and with these sufferings the sense of inevitable, approaching ruin. Something new was happening; there were screwing and shooting pains, and a tightness in his breathing.

The expression of his face as he uttered that "Yes" was terrible. After uttering that "Yes," looking her straight in the face, he turned on to his face, with a rapidity extraordinary in his weakness, and shrieked.

"Go away, go away, let me be!"

Chapter XII
DEATH IS OVER

From that moment there began the scream that never ceased for three days, and was so awful that through two closed doors one could not hear it without horror. At the moment when he answered his wife he grasped that he had fallen, that there was no return, that the end had come, quite the end, while doubt was still as unsolved, still remained doubt.

"Oo! Oo — o! Oo!" he screamed in varying intonations. He had begun screaming, "I don't want to!" and so had gone on screaming on the same vowel sound — oo!

All those three days, during which time did not exist for him, he was struggling in that black sack into which he was being thrust by an unseen resistless force. He struggled as the man condemned to death struggles in the hands of the executioner, knowing that he cannot save himself. And every moment he felt that in spite of all his efforts to struggle against it, he was getting nearer and nearer to what terrified him. He felt that his agony was due both to his being thrust into this black hole and still more to his not being able to get right into it. What hindered him from getting into it was the claim that his life had been good. That justification of his life held him fast and would not let him get forward, and it caused him more agony than all.

All at once some force struck him in the chest, in the side, and stifled his breathing more than ever; he rolled forward into the hole, and there at the end there was some sort of light. It had happened with him, as it had sometimes happened to him in a railway carriage, when he had thought he was going forward while he was going back, and all of a sudden recognised his real direction.

"Yes, it has all been not the right thing," he said to himself, "but that's no matter." He could, he could do the right thing. "What is the right thing?" he asked himself, and suddenly he became quiet.

This was at the end of the third day, two hours before his death. At that very moment the schoolboy had stealthily crept into his father's room and gone up to his bedside. The dying man was screaming and waving his arms. His hand fell on the schoolboy's head. The boy snatched it, pressed it to his lips, and burst into tears.

At that very moment Ivan Ilyitch had rolled into the hole, and caught sight of the light, and it was revealed to him that his life had not been what it ought to have been, but that that could still be set right. He asked himself, "What is the right thing?" — and became quiet, listening. Then he felt some one was kissing his hand. He opened his eyes and glanced at his son. He felt sorry for him. His wife went up to him. He glanced at her. She was gazing at him with open mouth, and tears unwiped streaming over her nose and cheeks, a look of despair on her face. He felt sorry for her.

"Yes, I'm making them miserable," he thought. "They're sorry, but it will be better for them when I die." He would have said this, but had not the strength to utter it. "Besides, why speak, I must act," he thought. With a glance to his wife he pointed to his son and said —

"Take away . . . sorry for him. . . . And you too . . ." He tried to say "forgive," but said "forgo" . . . and too weak to correct himself, shook his hand, knowing that He would understand Whose understanding mattered.

And all at once it became clear to him that what had tortured him and would not leave him was suddenly dropping away all at once on both sides and on ten sides and on all sides. He was sorry for them, must act so that they might not suffer. Set them free and be free himself of those agonies. "How right and how simple!" he thought. "And the pain?" he asked himself. "Where's it gone? Eh, where are you, pain?"

He began to watch for it.

"Yes, here it is. Well, what of it, let the pain be.

"And death. Where is it?"

He looked for his old accustomed terror of death, and did not find it. "Where is it? What death?" There was no terror, because death was not either.

In the place of death there was light.

"So this is it!" he suddenly exclaimed aloud.

"What joy!"

To him all this passed in a single instant, and the meaning of that instant suffered no change after. For those present his agony lasted another two hours. There was a rattle in his throat, a twitching in his wasted body. Then the rattle and the gasping came at longer and longer intervals.

"It is finished!" some one said over him.

He caught those words and repeated them in his soul.

"Death is over," he said to himself. "It's no more."

He drew in a breath, stopped midway in the breath, stretched and died.

[1886]

Study and Writing Questions

1. Why does the STORY begin just after Ivan Ilyitch's death and then FLASH BACK and work forward toward it?
2. What picture of society is conveyed by the attitudes of Ivan Ilyitch's friends, wife, and children?
3. Why does Tolstoy, in Chapter IV, have Ivan Ilyitch see the doctor as behaving just like a magistrate?

4. What details describing the SETTING, timing, and kind of wound add significance to Ivan Ilyitch's accident?
5. In what ways is Gerasim unique in the story? What does his presence imply for Ivan Ilyitch? for us?
6. Does the NARRATIVE convince you of the truth of the assertion that "The previous history of Ivan Ilyitch was the simplest, the most ordinary, and the most awful"? If so, how does it convince you? If not, why is the assertion in the narrative?
7. What useful advice, if any, does the story offer us about how to face death or how to live life?

See also Questions for Contrast and Comparison: 7, 43, 44, 45, 46, 60, 70, 72, 82, 107, 109, 115, 127, 141, 157, 165, 178, 224, 228, and 236.

■ JEAN TOOMER (1894–1967) *saw himself as both black and white. His white grandfather raised and led a black New Orleans regiment in the Civil War and became acting governor of Louisiana. Born in Washington, D.C., of what he called "French, Dutch, Welsh, Negro, German, Jewish, and Indian" blood, Toomer sought to transcend racial boundaries in his life, but drew his art from the "Negro peasant" culture of rural Georgia where he had taught (1920–1921). He attended the University of Wisconsin (1914) and the City College of the City of New York (1917–1918) but left to write and discover "what I may become." The three parts of his great work,* Cane *(1923), combine* SHORT STORIES *and poems into a* NOVEL *about black experiences in the South, the North, and the world of art. Toomer, always searching, spent the summer of 1924 at the theosophical Gurdjieff Institute in Fontainbleau, France. Although* Cane *placed Toomer with Countee Cullen, Langston Hughes, and W. E. B. DuBois in the first rank of the Harlem Renaissance, his subsequent writing was largely rejected. His first wife, Margery Latimer, a promising writer and descendant of such famous New Englanders as Anne Bradstreet and Cotton Mather, died in childbirth in the year of their marriage (1932). After marrying wealthy Marjorie Content (1934), Toomer wrote little, mainly tracts for the Society of Friends (Quakers). He spent his last decade as a recluse.*

Becky

Becky was the white woman who had two Negro sons. She's dead; they've gone away. The pines whisper to Jesus. The Bible flaps its leaves with an aimless rustle on her mound.

Becky had one Negro son. Who gave it to her? Damn buck nigger, said the white folks' mouths. She wouldnt tell. Common, God-forsaken, insane white shameless wench, said the white folks' mouths. Her eyes were sunken, her neck stringy, her breasts fallen, till then. Taking their words, they filled her, like a bubble rising— then she broke. Mouth setting in a twist that held her eyes, harsh, vacant, staring . . . Who gave it to her? Low-down nigger with no self-respect, said the black folks' mouths. She wouldnt tell. Poor Catholic poor-white crazy woman, said the black folks' mouths. White folks and black folks built her cabin, fed her and her growing baby, prayed secretly to God who'd put His cross upon her and cast her out.

When the first was born, the white folks said they'd have no more to do with her. And black folks, they too joined hands to cast her out . . . The pines whispered to Jesus . . . The railroad boss said not to say he said it, but she could live, if she wanted to, on the narrow strip of land between the railroad and the road. John Stone, who owned the lumber and the bricks, would have shot the man who told he gave the stuff to Lonnie Deacon, who stole out there at night and built the cabin. A single room held down to earth . . . O fly away to Jesus . . . by a leaning chimney . . .

Six trains each day rumbled past and shook the ground under her cabin. Fords, and horse- and mule-drawn buggies went back and forth along the road. No one ever saw her. Trainmen, and passengers who'd heard about her, threw out papers and food. Threw out little crumpled slips of paper scribbled with prayers, as they passed her eye-shaped piece of sandy ground. Ground islandized between the road and railroad track. Pushed up where a blue-sheen God with listless eyes could look at it. Folks from the town took turns, unknown, of course, to each other, in bringing corn and meat and sweet potatoes. Even sometimes snuff . . . O thank y Jesus . . . Old David Georgia, grinding cane and boiling syrup, never went her way without some sugar sap. No one ever saw her. The boy grew up and ran around. When he was five years old as folks reckoned it, Hugh Jourdon saw him carrying a baby. "Becky has another son," was what the whole town knew. But nothing was said, for the part of man that says things to the likes of that had told itself that if there was a Becky, that Becky now was dead.

The two boys grew. Sullen and cunning . . . O pines, whisper to Jesus; tell Him to come and press sweet Jesus-lips against their lips and eyes . . . It seemed as though with those two big fellows there, there could be no room for Becky. The part that prayed wondered if perhaps she'd really died, and they had buried her. No one dared ask. They'd beat and cut a man who meant nothing at all in mentioning that they lived along the road. White or colored? No one knew, and least of all themselves. They drifted around from job to job. We, who had cast out their mother because of them, could we take them in? They answered black and white folks by shooting up two men and leaving town. "Godam the white folks; godam the niggers," they shouted as they left town. Becky? Smoke curled up from her chimney; she must be there. Trains passing shook the ground. The ground shook the leaning chimney. Nobody noticed it. A creepy feeling came over all who saw that thin wraith of smoke and felt the trembling of the ground. Folks began to take her food again. They quit it soon because they had a fear. Becky if dead might be a hant, and if alive — it took some nerve even to mention it . . . O pines, whisper to Jesus . . .

It was Sunday. Our congregation had been visiting at Pulverton, and were coming home. There was no wind. The autumn sun, the bell from Ebenezer Church, listless and heavy. Even the pines were stale, sticky, like the smell of food that makes you sick. Before we turned the bend of the road that would show us the Becky cabin, the horses stopped stock-still, pushed back their ears, and nervously whinnied. We urged, then whipped them on. Quarter of a mile away thin smoke curled up from the leaning chimney . . . O pines, whisper to Jesus . . . Goose-flesh came on my skin though there still was neither chill nor wind. Eyes left their sockets for the cabin. Ears burned and throbbed. Uncanny eclipse! fear closed my mind. We were just about to pass . . . Pines shout to Jesus! . . . the ground trembled as a ghost train rumbled by. The chimney fell into the cabin. Its thud was like a hollow report, ages having passed since it went off. Barlo and I were pulled out of our seats. Dragged to the door that had swung open. Through the dust we saw the bricks in a mound upon the floor. Becky, if she was there, lay under them. I thought I heard a groan. Barlo, mumbling something, threw his Bible on the pile (No one has ever touched it.) Somehow we got away. My buggy was still on the road. The last thing that I remember was whipping old Dan like fury; I remember nothing after that—that is, until I reached town and folks crowded round to get the true word of it.

Becky was the white woman who had two Negro sons. She's dead; they've gone away. The pines whisper to Jesus. The Bible flaps its leaves with an aimless rustle on her mound.

[1923]

Study and Writing Questions

1. The NARRATOR repeats the phrases "white folks' mouths" and "black folks' mouths" and says the people "prayed secretly." What did they pray for? Why did they keep it secret? Describe the social structure of this town.
2. What were the MOTIVES of the people who supplied Becky but also denied that they had anything to do with her? What was the fear they had of Becky "if alive"?
3. How would you characterize the TONE of this NARRATIVE? of the EPIGRAPH? Why is the epigraph repeated? How does the tone help tell the STORY?
4. What is the role of religion in this story? What do the pines represent? How is the Bible used? What religious references are made by or about the characters?
5. Can you infer the gender or skin color of the narrator? What is the narrator's relation to Becky? Why is the narrator telling this story? What does the narrator think the story is about? What do you think the story is about?

See also Questions for Contrast and Comparison: 7, 32, 42, 43, 55, 56, 69, 70, 84, 98, 150, and 231.

MARK TWAIN (pseudonym of Samuel Langhorne Clemens; 1835–1910) *was born in Missouri and raised in Hannibal, the Mississippi River town immortalized in his novels* Tom Sawyer *(1876) and* Huckleberry Finn *(1884). His father, an often transplanted Virginian, struggled vainly to get rich in land speculation; his mother, distant cousin to a British earl, also filled Sam with unlikely hope. After his father's death (1847), Sam apprenticed at a newspaper and then worked as an itinerant typesetter (1853–1854). His happiest years, spent as a riverboat pilot (1856–1861), ended when the Civil War closed the Mississippi. After two indelible weeks as a Confederate volunteer, he went to Nevada, where his brother was secretary to the territorial governor, and turned to reporting. His first humorous sketch, "The Celebrated Jumping Frog" (1865), brought immediate recognition. "Mark Twain" (pilot lingo for "two fathoms deep," that is, "ample depth") became an enormously popular writer, a much and widely traveled lecturer in Europe and the United States, and a publisher/businessman. He settled grandly in Hartford, Connecticut, and married (1870) wealth, but investment in an experimental typesetting machine bankrupted him (1894). The fine satire seen in* A Connecticut Yankee in King Arthur's Court *(1889) turned bitter after the deaths of his wife (1904) and daughter (1909). He published his most acid work only posthumously.*

The Diary of Adam and Eve

Part I—Extracts from Adam's Diary

Monday This new creature with the long hair is a good deal in the way. It is always hanging around and following me about. I don't like this; I am not used to company. I wish it would stay with the other animals. . . . Cloudy today, wind in the east; think we shall have rain. . . . We? Where did I get that word?—I remember now—the new creature uses it.

Tuesday Been examining the great waterfall. It is the finest thing on the estate, I think. The new creature calls it Niagara Falls—why, I am sure I do not know. Says it *looks* like Niagara Falls. That is not a reason, it is mere waywardness and imbecility. I get no chance to name anything myself. The new creature names everything that comes along, before I can get in a protest. And always that same pretext is offered—it *looks* like the thing. There is the dodo, for instance. Says the moment one looks at it one sees at a glance that it "looks like a dodo." It will have to keep that name, no doubt. It wearies me to fret about it, and it does no good, anyway. Dodo! It looks no more like a dodo than I do.

Wednesday Built me a shelter against the rain, but could not have it to myself in peace. The new creature intruded. When I tried to put it out it shed water out of the holes it looks with, and wiped it away with the back of its paws, and made a noise such as some of the other animals make when they are in distress. I wish it would not talk; it is always talking. That sounds like a cheap fling at the poor creature, a slur; but I do not mean it so. I have never heard the human voice before, and any new and strange sound intruding itself here upon the solemn hush of these dreaming solitudes offends my ear and seems a false note. And this new sound is so close to me; it is right at my shoulder, right at my ear, first on one side and then on the other, and I am used only to sounds that are more or less distant from me.

Friday The naming goes recklessly on, in spite of anything I can do. I had a very good name for the estate, and it was musical and pretty — GARDEN OF EDEN. Privately, I continue to call it that, but not any longer publicly. The new creature says it is all woods and rocks and scenery, and therefore has no resemblance to a garden. Says it *looks* like a park, and does not look like anything *but* a park. Consequently, without consulting me, it has been new-named — NIAGARA FALLS PARK. This is sufficiently high-handed, it seems to me. And already there is a sign up:

KEEP OFF
THE GRASS

My life is not as happy as it was.

Saturday The new creature eats too much fruit. We are going to run short, most likely. "We" again — that is *its* word; mine, too, now, from hearing it so much. Good deal of fog this morning. I do not go out in the fog myself. The new creature does. It goes out in all weathers, and stumps right in with its muddy feet. And talks. It used to be so pleasant and quiet here.

Sunday Pulled through. This day is getting to be more and more trying. It was selected and set apart last November as a day of rest. I had already six of them per week before. This morning found the new creature trying to clod apples out of that forbidden tree.

Monday The new creature says its name is Eve. That is all right, I have no objections. Says it is to call it by, when I want it to come. I said it was superfluous, then. The word evidently raised me in its respect; and indeed it is a large, good word and will bear repetition. It says it is not an It, it is a She. This is probably doubtful; yet it is all one to me; what she is were nothing to me if she would but go by herself and not talk.

Tuesday She has littered the whole estate with execrable names and offensive signs:

THIS WAY TO THE WHIRLPOOL
THIS WAY TO GOAT ISLAND
CAVE OF THE WINDS THIS WAY

She says this park would make a tidy summer resort if there was any custom for it. Summer resort — another invention of hers — just words, without any meaning. What is a summer resort? But it is best not to ask her, she has such a rage for explaining.

Friday She has taken to beseeching me to stop going over the Falls. What harm does it do? Says it makes her shudder. I wonder why; I have always done it — always liked the plunge, and coolness. I supposed it was what the Falls were for. They have no other use that I can see, and they must have been made for something. She says they were only made for scenery — like the rhinoceros and the mastodon.

I went over the Falls in a barrel — not satisfactory to her. Went over in a tub — still not satisfactory. Swam the Whirlpool and the Rapids in a fig-leaf suit. It got much damaged. Hence, tedious complaints about my extravagance. I am too much hampered here. What I need is change of scene.

Saturday I escaped last Tuesday night, and traveled two days, and built me another shelter in a secluded place, and obliterated my tracks as well as I could, but she hunted me out by means of a beast which she has tamed and calls a wolf, and came making that pitiful noise again, and shedding that water out of the places she looks with. I was obliged to return with her, but will presently emigrate again when occasion offers. She engages herself in many foolish things; among others, to study out why the animals called lions and tigers live on grass and flowers, when, as she says, the sort of teeth they wear would indicate that they were intended to eat each other. This is foolish, because to do that would be to kill each other, and that would introduce what, as I understand it, is called "death"; and death, as I have been told, has not yet entered the Park. Which is a pity, on some accounts.

Sunday Pulled through.

Monday I believe I see what the week is for: it is to give time to rest up from the weariness of Sunday. It seems a good idea. . . . She has been climbing that tree again. Clodded her out of it. She said nobody was looking. Seems to consider that a sufficient justification for chancing any dangerous thing. Told her that. The word justification moved her admiration—and envy, too, I thought. It is a good word.

Tuesday She told me she was made out of a rib taken from my body. This is at least doubtful, if not more than that. I have not missed any rib. . . . She is in much trouble about the buzzard; says grass does not agree with it; is afraid she can't raise it; thinks it was intended to live on decayed flesh. The buzzard must get along the best it can with what it is provided. We cannot overturn the whole scheme to accommodate the buzzard.

Saturday She fell in the pond yesterday when she was looking at herself in it, which she is always doing. She nearly strangled, and said it was most uncomfortable. This made her sorry for the creatures which live in there, which she calls fish, for she continues to fasten names on to things that don't need them and don't come when they are called by them, which is a matter of no consequence to her, she is such a numskull, anyway; so she got a lot of them out and brought them in last night and put them in my bed to keep warm, but I have noticed them now and then all day and I don't see that they are any happier there than they were before, only quieter. When night comes I shall throw them outdoors. I will not sleep with them again, for I find them clammy and unpleasant to lie among when a person hasn't anything on.

Sunday Pulled through.

Tuesday She has taken up with a snake now. The other animals are glad, for she was always experimenting with them and bothering them; and I am glad because the snake talks, and this enables me to get a rest.

Friday She says the snake advises her to try the fruit of that tree, and says the result will be a great and fine and noble education. I told her there would be another result, too—it would introduce death into the world. That was a mistake—it had been better to keep the remark to myself; it only gave her an idea—she could save the sick buzzard, and furnish fresh meat to the despondent lions and tigers. I advised her to keep away from the tree. She said she wouldn't. I foresee trouble. Will emigrate.

Wednesday I have had a variegated time. I escaped last night, and rode a horse all night as fast as he could go, hoping to get clear out of the Park and hide in some other country before the trouble should begin; but it was not to be. About an hour after sun-up, as I was riding through a flowery plain where thousands of animals were grazing, slumbering, or playing with each other, according to their wont, all of a sudden they broke into a tempest of frightful noises, and in one moment the plain was a frantic commotion and every beast was destroying its neighbor. I knew what it meant—Eve had eaten that fruit, and death was come into the world. . . . The tigers ate my horse, paying no attention when I ordered them to desist, and they would have eaten me if I had stayed—which I didn't, but went away in much haste. . . . I found this place, outside the Park, and was fairly comfortable for a few days, but she has found me out. Found me out, and has named the place Tonawanda—says it *looks* like that. In fact I was not sorry she came, for there are but meager pickings here, and she brought some of those apples. I was obliged to eat them, I was so hungry. It was against my principles, but I find that principles have no real force except when one is well fed. . . . She came curtained in boughs and bunches of leaves, and when I asked her what she meant by such nonsense, and snatched them away and threw them down, she tittered and blushed. I had never seen a person titter and blush before, and to me it seemed unbecoming and idiotic. She said I would soon know how it was myself. This was correct. Hungry as I was, I laid down the apple half-eaten—certainly the best one I ever saw, considering the lateness of the season—and arrayed myself in the discarded boughs and branches, and then spoke to her with some severity and ordered her to go and get some more and not make such a spectacle of herself. She did it, and after this we crept down to where the wild-beast battle had been, and collected some skins, and I made her patch together a couple of suits proper for public occasions. They are uncomfortable, it is true, but stylish, and that is the main point about clothes. . . . I find she is a good deal of a companion. I see I should be lonesome and depressed without her, now that I have lost my property. Another thing, she says it is ordered that we work for our living hereafter. She will be useful. I will superintend.

Ten Days Later She accuses *me* of being the cause of our disaster! She says, with apparent sincerity and truth, that the Serpent assured her that the forbidden fruit was not apples, it was chestnuts. I said I was innocent, then, for I had not eaten any chestnuts. *She* said the Serpent informed her that "chestnut" was a figurative term meaning an aged and moldy joke. I turned pale at that, for I have made many jokes to pass the weary time, and some of them could have been of that sort, though I had honestly supposed that they were new when I made them. She asked me if I had made one just at the time of the catastrophe. I was obliged to admit that I had made one to myself, though not aloud. It was this. I was thinking about the Falls, and I said to myself, "How wonderful it is to see that vast body of water tumble down there!" Then in an instant a bright thought flashed into my head, and I let it fly, saying, "It would be a deal more wonderful to see it tumble *up* there!"—and I was just about to kill myself with laughing at it when all nature broke loose in war and death and I had to flee for my life. "There," she said, with triumph, "that is just it; the Serpent mentioned that very jest, and called it the First Chestnut, and said it was coeval with the creation."

Alas, I am indeed to blame. Would that I were not witty; oh, that I had never had that radiant thought!

Next Year We have named it Cain. She caught it while I was up country trapping on the North Shore of the Erie; caught it in the timber a couple of miles from our dug-out—or it might have been four, she isn't certain which. It resembles us in some ways, and may be a relation. That is what she thinks, but this is an error, in my judgment. The difference in size warrants the conclusion that it is a different and new kind of animal—a fish, perhaps, though when I put it in the water to see, it sank, and she plunged in and snatched it out before there was opportunity for the experiment to determine the matter. I still think it is a fish, but she is indifferent about what it is, and will not let me have it to try. I do not understand this. The coming of the creature seems to have changed her whole nature and made her unreasonable about experiments. She thinks more of it than she does of any of the other animals, but is not able to explain why. Her mind is disordered—everything shows it. Sometimes she carries the fish in her arms half the night when it complains and wants to get to the water. At such times the water comes out of the places in her face that she looks out of, and she pats the fish on the back and makes soft sounds with her mouth to soothe it, and betrays sorrow and solicitude in a hundred ways. I have never seen her do like this with any other fish, and it troubles me greatly. She used to carry the young tigers around so, and play with them, before we lost our property, but it was only play; she never took on about them like this when their dinner disagreed with them.

Sunday She doesn't work, Sundays, but lies around all tired out, and likes to have the fish wallow over her; and she makes fool noises to amuse it, and pretends to chew its paws, and that makes it laugh. I have not seen a fish before that could laugh. This makes me doubt. . . . I have come to like Sunday myself. Superintending all the week tires a body so. There ought to be more Sundays. In the old days they were tough, but now they come handy.

Wednesday It isn't a fish. I cannot quite make out what it is. It makes curious devilish noises when not satisfied, and says "goo-goo" when it is. It is not one of us, for it doesn't walk; it is not a bird, for it doesn't fly; it is not a frog, for it doesn't hop; it is not a snake, for it doesn't crawl, I feel sure it is not a fish, though I cannot get a chance to find out whether it can swim or not. It merely lies around, and mostly on its back, with its feet up. I have not seen any other animal do that before. I said I believed it was an enigma; but she only admired the word without understanding it. In my judgment it is either an enigma or some kind of a bug. If it dies, I will take it apart and see what its arrangements are. I never had a thing perplex me so.

Three Months Later The perplexity augments instead of diminishing. I sleep but little. It has ceased from lying around, and goes about on its four legs now. Yet it differs from the other four-legged animals, in that its front legs are unusually short, consequently this causes the main part of its person to stick up uncomfortably high in the air, and this is not attractive. It is built much as we are, but its method of traveling shows that it is not of our breed. The short front legs and long hind ones indicate that it is of the kangaroo family, but it is a marked variation of the species, since the true kangaroo hops, whereas this one never does. Still it is a curious and interesting variety, and has not been catalogued before. As I discovered it, I have felt justified in securing the credit of the discovery for attaching my name to it, and hence have called it *Kangaroorum Adamiensis.* . . . It must have been a young one when it came, for it has grown exceedingly since. It must be five times as big, now, as it was then, and when discontented it is able to make from twenty-two to thirty-eight times the noise it made at first. Coercion does not modify this, but has the contrary effect. For this reason I discontinued the system. She reconciles it by persuasion, and by giving it things which she had previously told me she wouldn't give it. As already observed, I was not at home when it first came, and she told me she found it in the woods. It seems odd that it should be the only one, yet it must be so, for I have worn myself out these many weeks trying to find another one to add to my collection, and for this one to play with; for surely then it would be quieter and we could tame it more easily. But I find none, nor any vestige of any; and strangest of all, no tracks. It has to live on the ground, it cannot help itself; therefore, how does it get about without leaving a track? I have set a dozen traps, but they do no good. I catch all small animals except that one; animals that merely go into the trap out of curiosity, I think, to see what the milk is there for. They never drink it.

Three Months Later The Kangaroo still continues to grow, which is very strange and perplexing. I never knew one to be so long getting its growth. It has fur on its head now; not like kangaroo fur, but exactly like our hair except that it is much finer and softer, and instead of being black is red. I am like to lose my mind over the capricious and harassing developments of this unclassifiable zoological freak. If I could catch another one — but that is hopeless; it is a new variety, and the only sample; this is plain. But I caught a true kangaroo and brought it in, thinking that this one, being lonesome, would rather have that for company than have no kin at all, or any animal it could feel a nearness to or get sympathy from in its forlorn condition here among strangers who do not know its ways or habits, or what to do to make it feel that it is among friends; but it was a mistake — it went into such fits at the sight of the kangaroo that I was convinced it had never seen one before. I pity the poor noisy little animal, but there is nothing I can do to make it happy. If I could tame it — but that is out of the question; the more I try the worse I seem to make it. It grieves me to the heart to see it in its little storms of sorrow and passion. I wanted to let it go, but she wouldn't hear of it. That seemed cruel and not like her; and yet she may be right. It might be lonelier than ever; for since I cannot find another one, how could *it?*

Five Months Later It is not a kangaroo. No, for it supports itself by holding to her finger, and thus goes a few steps on its hind legs, and then falls down. It is probably some kind of a bear; and yet it has no tail — as yet — and no fur, except on its head. It still keeps on growing — that is a curious circumstance, for bears get their growth earlier than this. Bears are dangerous — since our catastrophe — and I shall not be satisfied to have this one prowling about the place much longer without a muzzle on. I have offered to get her a kangaroo if she would let this one go, but it did no good — she is determined to run us into all sorts of foolish risks, I think. She was not like this before she lost her mind.

A Fortnight Later I examined its mouth. There is no danger yet: it has only one tooth. It has no tail yet. It makes more noise now than it ever did before — and mainly at night. I have moved out. But I shall go over, mornings, to breakfast, and see if it has more teeth. If it gets a mouthful of teeth it will be time for it to go, tail or no tail, for a bear does not need a tail in order to be dangerous.

Four Months Later I have been off hunting and fishing a month, up in the region that she calls Buffalo; I don't know why, unless it is because there are not any buffaloes there. Meantime the bear has learned to paddle around all by itself on its hind legs, and says "poppa" and "momma." It is certainly a new species. This resemblance to words may be purely accidental, of course, and may have no purpose or meaning; but even in that case it is still extraordinary, and is a thing which no other bear can do. This imitation of speech, taken together with general absence of fur and entire absence of tail, sufficiently indicates that this is a new kind of bear. The further study of it will be exceedingly interesting. Meantime I will go off on a far expedition among the forests of the north and make an exhaustive search. There must certainly be another one somewhere, and this one will be less dangerous when it has company of its own species. I will go straightway; but I will muzzle this one first.

Three Months Later It has been a weary, weary hunt, yet I have had no success. In the mean time, without stirring from the home estate, she has caught another one! I never saw such luck. I might have hunted these woods a hundred years, I never would have run across that thing.

Next Day I have been comparing the new one with the old one, and it is perfectly plain that they are the same breed. I was going to stuff one of them for my collection, but she is prejudiced against it for some reason or other; so I have relinquished the idea, though I think it is a mistake. It would be an irreparable loss to science if they should get away. The old one is tamer than it was and can laugh and talk like the parrot, having learned this, no doubt, from being with the parrot so much, and having the imitative faculty in a highly developed degree. I shall be astonished if it turns out to be a new kind parrot; and yet I ought not to be astonished, for it has already been everything else it could think of since those first days when it was a fish. The new one is as ugly now as the old one was at first; has the same sulphur-and-raw-meat complexion and the same singular head without any fur on it. She calls it Abel.

Ten Years Later They are boys; we found it out long ago. It was their coming in that small, immature shape that puzzled us; we were not used to it. There are some girls now. Abel is a good boy, but if Cain had stayed a bear it would have improved him. After all these years, I see that I was mistaken about Eve in the beginning; it is better to live outside the Garden with her than inside it without her. At first I thought she talked too much; but now I should be sorry to have that voice fall silent and pass out of my life. Blessed be the chestnut that brought us near together and taught me to know the goodness of her heart and the sweetness of her spirit!

Part II — Eve's Diary
(TRANSLATED FROM THE ORIGINAL)

Saturday I am almost a whole day old, now. I arrived yesterday. That is as it seems to me. And it must be so, for if there was a day-before-yesterday I was not there when it happened, or I should remember it. It could be, of course, that it did happen, and that I was not noticing. Very well; I will be very watchful now, and if any day-before-yesterdays happen I will make a note of it. It will be best to start right and not let the record get confused, for some instinct tells me that these details are going to be important to the historian some day. For I feel like an experiment, I feel exactly like an experiment; it would be impossible for a person to feel more like an experiment than I do, and so I am coming to feel convinced that that is what I *am*—an experiment; just an experiment, and nothing more.

Then if I am an experiment, am I the whole of it? No, I think not; I think the rest of it is part of it. I am the main part of it, but I think the rest of it has its share in the matter. Is my position assured, or do I have to watch it and take care of it? The latter, perhaps. Some instinct tells me that eternal vigilance is the price of supremacy. [That is a good phrase, I think, for one so young.]

Everything looks better to-day than it did yesterday. In the rush of finishing up yesterday, the mountains were left in a ragged condition, and some of the plains were so cluttered with rubbish and remnants that the aspects were quite distressing. Noble and beautiful works of art should not be subjected to haste; and this majestic new world is indeed a most noble and beautiful work. And certainly marvelously near to being perfect, notwithstanding the shortness of the time. There are too many stars in some places and not enough in others, but that can be remedied presently, no doubt. The moon got loose last night, and slid down and fell out of the scheme—a very great loss; it breaks my heart to think of it. There isn't another thing among the ornaments and decorations that is comparable to it for beauty and finish. It should have been fastened better. If we can only get it back again—

But of course there is no telling where it went to. And besides, whoever gets it will hide it; I know it because I would do it myself. I believe I can be honest in all other matters, but I already begin to realize that the core and center of my nature is love of the beautiful, a passion for the beautiful, and that it would not be safe to trust me with a moon that belonged to another person and that person didn't know I had it. I could give up a moon that I found in the daytime, because I should be afraid some one was looking; but if I found it in the dark, I am sure I should find some kind of an excuse for not saying anything about it. For I do love moons, they are so pretty and so romantic. I wish we had five or six; I would never go to bed; I should never get tired lying on the moss-bank and looking up at them.

Stars are good, too. I wish I could get some to put in my hair. But I suppose I never can. You would be surprised to find how far off they are, for they do not look it. When they first showed, last night, I tried to knock some down with a pole, but it didn't reach, which astonished me; then I tried clods till I was all tired out, but I never got one. It was because I am left-handed and cannot throw good. Even when I aimed at the one I wasn't after I couldn't hit the other one, though I did make some close shots, for I saw the black blot of the clod sail right into the midst of the golden clusters forty or fifty times, just barely missing them, and if I could have held out a little longer maybe I could have got one.

So I cried a little, which was natural, I suppose, for one of my age, and after I was rested I got a basket and started for a place on the extreme rim of the circle, where the stars were close to the ground and I could get them with my hands, which would be better, anyway, because I could gather them tenderly then, and not break them. But it was farther than I thought, and at last I had to give it up; I was so tired I couldn't drag my feet another step; and besides, they were sore and hurt me very much.

I couldn't get back home; it was too far and turning cold; but I found some tigers and nestled in among them and was most adorably comfortable, and their breath was sweet and pleasant, because they live on strawberries. I had never seen a tiger before, but I knew them in a minute by the stripes. If I could have one of those skins, it would make a lovely gown.

To-day I am getting better ideas about distances. I was so eager to get hold of every pretty thing that I giddily grabbed for it, sometimes when it was too far off, and sometimes when it was but six inches away but seemed a foot—alas, with thorns between! I learned a lesson; also I made an axiom, all out of my own head—my very first one: *The scratched Experiment shuns the thorn.* I think it is a very good one for one so young.

I followed the other Experiment around, yesterday afternoon, at a distance, to see what it might be for, if I could. But I was not able to make out. I think it is a man. I had never seen a man, but it looked like one, and I feel sure that that is what it is. I realize that I feel more curiosity about it than about any of the other reptiles. If it is a reptile, and I suppose it is; for it has frowsy hair and blue eyes, and looks like a reptile. It has no hips; it tapers like a carrot; when it stands, it spreads itself apart like a derrick; so I think it is a reptile, though it may be architecture.

I was afraid of it at first, and started to run every time it turned around, for I thought it was going to chase me; but by and by I found it was only trying to get away, so after that I was not timid any more, but tracked it along, several hours, about twenty yards behind, which made it nervous and unhappy. At last it was a good deal worried, and climbed a tree. I waited a good while, then gave it up and went home.

To-day the same thing over. I've got it up the tree again.

Sunday It is up there yet. Resting, apparently. But that is a subterfuge: Sunday isn't the day of rest; Saturday is appointed for that. It looks to me like a creature that is more interested in resting than in anything else. It would tire me to rest so much. It tires me just to sit around and watch the tree. I do wonder what it is for; I never see it do anything.

They returned the moon last night, and I was *so* happy! I think it is very honest of them. It slid down and fell off again, but I was not distressed; there is no need to worry when one has that kind of neighbors; they will fetch it back. I wish I could do something to show my appreciation. I would like to send them some stars, for we have more than we can use. I mean I, not we, for I can see that the reptile cares nothing for such things.

It has low tastes, and is not kind. When I went there yesterday evening in the gloaming it had crept down and was trying to catch the little speckled fishes that play in the pool, and I had to clod it to make it go up the tree again and let them alone. I wonder if *that* is what it is for? Hasn't it any heart? Hasn't it any compassion for those little creatures? Can it be that it was designed and manufactured for such ungentle work? It has the look of it. One of the clods took it back of the ear, and it used language. It gave me a thrill, for it was the first time I had ever heard speech, except my own. I did not understand the words, but they seemed expressive.

When I found it could talk I felt a new interest in it, for I love to talk; I talk, all day, and in my sleep, too, and I am very interesting, but if I had another to talk to I could be twice as interesting, and would never stop, if desired.

If this reptile is a man, it isn't an *it*, is it? That wouldn't be grammatical, would it? I think it would be *he*. I think so. In that case one would parse it thus: nominative, *he*; dative, *him*; possessive, *his'n*. Well, I will consider it a man and call it he until it turns out to be something else. This will be handier than having so many uncertainties.

Next week Sunday   All the week I tagged around after him and tried to get acquainted. I had to do the talking, because he was shy, but I didn't mind it. He seemed pleased to have me around, and I used the sociable "we" a good deal, because it seemed to flatter him to be included.

Wednesday   We are getting along very well indeed, now, and getting better and better acquainted. He does not try to avoid me any more, which is a good sign, and shows that he likes to have me with him. That pleases me, and I study to be useful to him in every way I can, so as to increase his regard. During the last day or two I have taken all the work of naming things off his hands, and this has been a great relief to him, for he has no gift in that line, and is evidently very grateful. He can't think of a rational name to save him, but I do not let him see that I am aware of this defect. Whenever a new creature comes along I name it before he has time to expose himself by an awkward silence. In this way I have saved him many embarrassments. I have no defect like his. The minute I set eyes on an animal I know what it is. I don't have to reflect a moment; the right name comes out instantly, just as if it were an inspiration, as no doubt it is, for I am sure it wasn't in me half a minute before. I seem to know just by the shape of the creature and the way it acts what animal it is.

When the dodo came along he thought it was a wildcat—I saw it in his eye. But I saved him. And I was careful not to do it in a way that could hurt his pride. I just spoke up in a quite natural way of pleased surprise, and not as if I was dreaming of conveying information, and said, "Well, I do declare, if there isn't the dodo!" I explained—without seeming to be explaining—how I knew it for a dodo, and although I thought maybe he was a little piqued that I knew the creature when he didn't, it was quite evident that he admired me. That was very agreeable, and I thought of it more than once with gratification before I slept. How little a thing can make us happy when we feel that we have earned it!

Thursday   My first sorrow. Yesterday he avoided me and seemed to wish I would not talk to him. I could not believe it, and thought there was some mistake, for I loved to be with him, and loved to hear him talk, and so how could it be that he could feel unkind toward me when I had not done anything? But at last it seemed true, so I went away and sat lonely in the place where I first saw him the morning that we were made and I did not know what he was and was indifferent about him; but now it was a mournful place, and every little thing spoke of him, and my heart was very sore. I did not know why very clearly, for it was a new feeling; I had not experienced it before, and it was all a mystery, and I could not make it out.

But when night came I could not bear the lonesomeness, and went to the new shelter which he has built, to ask him what I had done that was wrong and how I could mend it and get back his kindness again; but he put me out in the rain, and it was my first sorrow.

Sunday It is pleasant again, now, and I am happy; but those were heavy days; I do not think of them when I can help it.

I tried to get him some of those apples, but I cannot learn to throw straight. I failed, but I think the good intention pleased him. They are forbidden, and he says I shall come to harm; but so I come to harm through pleasing him, why shall I care for that harm?

Monday This morning I told him my name, hoping it would interest him. But he did not care for it. It is strange. If he should tell me his name, I would care. I think it would be pleasanter in my ears than any other sound.

He talks very little. Perhaps it is because he is not bright, and is sensitive about it and wishes to conceal it. It is such a pity that he should feel so, for brightness is nothing; it is in the heart that the values lie. I wish I could make him understand that a loving good heart is riches, and riches enough, and that without it intellect is poverty.

Although he talks so little, he has quite a considerable vocabulary. This morning he used a surprisingly good word. He evidently recognized, himself, that it was a good one, for he worked it in twice afterward, casually. It was not good casual art, still it showed that he possesses a certain quality of perception. Without a doubt that seed can be made to grow, if cultivated.

Where did he get that word? I do not think I have ever used it.

No, he took no interest in my name. I tried to hide my disappointment, but I suppose I did not succeed. I went away and sat on the moss-bank with my feet in the water. It is where I go when I hunger for companionship, some one to look at, some one to talk to. It is not enough — that lovely white body painted there in the pool — but it is something, and something is better than utter loneliness. It talks when I talk; it is sad when I am sad; it comforts me with its sympathy; it says, "Do not be downhearted, you poor friendless girl; I will be your friend." It *is* a good friend to me, and my only one; it is my sister.

That first time that she forsook me! ah, I shall never forget that — never, never. My heart was lead in my body! I said, "She was all I had, and now she is gone!" In my despair I said, "Break, my heart; I cannot bear my life any more!" and hid my face in my hands, and there was no solace for me. And when I took them away, after a little, there she was again, white and shining and beautiful, and I sprang into her arms!

That was perfect happiness; I had known happiness before, but it was not like this, which was ecstasy. I never doubted her afterward. Sometimes she stayed away — maybe an hour, maybe almost the whole day, but I waited and did not doubt; I said, "She is busy, or she is gone a journey, but she will come." And it was so: she always did. At night she would not come if it was dark, for she was a timid little thing; but if there was a moon she would come. I am not afraid of the dark, but she is younger than I am; she was born after I was. Many and many are the visits I have paid her; she is my comfort and my refuge when my life is hard — and it is mainly that.

Tuesday All the morning I was at work improving the estate; and I purposely kept away from him in the hope that he would get lonely and come. But he did not.

At noon I stopped for the day and took my recreation by flitting all about with the bees and the butterflies and reveling in the flowers, those beautiful creatures that catch the smile of God out of the sky and preserve it! I gathered them, and made them into wreaths and garlands and clothed myself in them while I ate my luncheon — apples, of course; then I sat in the shade and wished and waited. But he did not come.

But no matter. Nothing would have come of it, for he does not care for flowers. He calls them rubbish, and cannot tell one from another, and thinks it is superior to feel like that. He does not care for me, he does not care for flowers, he does not care for the painted sky at eventide — is there anything he does care for, except building shacks to coop himself up in from the good clean rain, and thumping the melons, and sampling the grapes, and fingering the fruit on the trees, to see how those properties are coming along?

I laid a dry stick on the ground and tried to bore a hole in it with another one, in order to carry out a scheme that I had, and soon I got an awful fright. A thin, transparent bluish film rose out of the hole, and I dropped everything and ran! I thought it was a spirit, and I *was* so frightened! But I looked back, and it was not coming; so I leaned against a rock and rested and panted, and let my limbs go on trembling until they got steady again; then I crept warily back, alert, watching, and ready to fly if there was occasion; and when I was come near, I parted the branches of a rose-bush and peeped through — wishing the man was about, I was looking so cunning and pretty — but the sprite was gone. I went there, and there was a pinch of delicate pink dust in the hole. I put my finger in, to feel it, and said *ouch!* and took it out again. It was a cruel pain. I put my finger in my mouth; and by standing first on one foot and then the other, and grunting, I presently eased my misery; then I was full of interest, and began to examine.

I was curious to know what the pink dust was. Suddenly the name of it occurred to me, though I had never heard of it before. It was *fire!* I was as certain of it as a person could be of anything in the world. So without hesitation I named it that — fire.

I had created something that didn't exist before; I had added a new thing to the world's uncountable properties; I realized this, and was proud of my achievement, and was going to run and find him and tell him about it, thinking to raise myself in his esteem — but I reflected, and did not do it. No — he would not care for it. He would ask what it was good for, and what could I answer? for if it was not *good* for something, but only beautiful, merely beautiful —

So I sighed, and did not go. For it wasn't good for anything; it could not build a shack, it could not improve melons, it could not hurry a fruit crop; it was useless, it was a foolishness and a vanity; he would despise it and say cutting words. But to me it was not despicable; I said, "Oh, you fire, I love you, you dainty pink creature, for you are *beautiful* — and that is enough!" and was going to gather it to my breast. But refrained. Then I made another maxim out of my own head, though it was so nearly like the first one that I was afraid it was only a plagiarism: "*The burnt Experiment shuns the fire.*"

I wrought again; and when I had made a good deal of fire-dust I emptied it into a handful of dry brown grass, intending to carry it home and keep it always and play with it; but the wind struck it and it sprayed up and spat out at me fiercely, and I dropped it and ran. When I looked back the blue spirit was towering up and stretching and rolling away like a cloud, and instantly I thought of the name of it — *smoke!* — though, upon my word, I had never heard of smoke before.

Soon, brilliant yellow and red flares shot up through the smoke, and I named them in an instant — *flames* — and I was right, too, though these were the very first flames that had ever been in the world. They climbed the trees, they flashed splendidly in and out of the vast and increasing volume of tumbling smoke, and I had to clap my hands and laugh and dance in my rapture, it was so new and strange and so wonderful and so beautiful!

He came running, and stopped and gazed, and said not a word for many minutes. Then he asked what it was. Ah, it was too bad that he should ask such a direct question. I had to answer it, of course, and I did. I said it was fire. If it annoyed him that I should know and he must ask, that was not my fault; I had no desire to annoy him. After a pause he asked:

"How did it come?"

Another direct question, and it also had to have a direct answer.

"I made it."

The fire was traveling farther and farther off. He went to the edge of the burned place and stood looking down, and said:

"What are these?"

"Fire-coals."

He picked up one to examine it, but changed his mind and put it down again. Then he went away. *Nothing* interests him.

But I was interested. There were ashes, gray and soft and delicate and pretty — I knew what they were at once. And the embers; I knew the embers, too. I found my apples, and raked them out, and was glad; for I am very young and my appetite is active. But I was disappointed; they were all burst open and spoiled. Spoiled apparently; but it was not so; they were better than raw ones. Fire is beautiful; some day it will be useful, I think.

Friday I saw him again, for a moment, last Monday at nightfall, but only for a moment. I was hoping he would praise me for trying to improve the estate, for I had meant well and had worked hard. But he was not pleased, and turned away and left me. He was also displeased on another account: I tried once more to persuade him to stop going over the Falls. That was because the fire had revealed to me a new passion — quite new, and distinctly different from love, grief, and those others which I had already discovered — *fear*. And it is horrible! — I wish I had never discovered it; it gives me dark moments, it spoils my happiness, it makes me shiver and tremble and shudder. But I could not persuade him, for he has not discovered fear yet, and so he could not understand me.

Extract from Adam's Diary

Perhaps I ought to remember that she is very young, a mere girl, and make allowances. She is all interest, eagerness, vivacity, the world is to her a charm, a wonder, a mystery, a joy; she can't speak for delight when she finds a new flower, she must pet it and caress it and smell it and talk to it, and pour out endearing names upon it. And she is color-mad: brown rocks, yellow sand, gray moss, green foliage, blue sky; the pearl of the dawn, the purple shadows on the mountains, the golden islands floating in crimson seas at sunset, the pallid moon sailing through the shredded cloud-rack, the star-jewels glittering in the wastes of space—none of them is of any practical value, so far as I can see, but because they have color and majesty, that is enough for her, and she loses her mind over them. If she could quiet down and keep still a couple of minutes at a time, it would be a reposeful spectacle. In that case I think I could enjoy looking at her; indeed I am sure I could, for I am coming to realize that she is a quite remarkably comely creature—lithe, slender, trim, rounded, shapely, nimble, graceful; and once when she was standing marble-white and sun-drenched on a boulder, with her young head tilted back and her hand shadowing her eyes, watching the flight of a bird in the sky, I recognized that she was beautiful.

Monday noon   If there is anything on the planet that she is not interested in it is not in my list. There are animals that I am indifferent to, but it is not so with her. She has no discrimination, she takes to all of them, she thinks they are all treasures, every new one is welcome.

When the mighty brontosaurus came striding into camp, she regarded it as an acquisition, I considered it a calamity; that is a good sample of the lack of harmony that prevails in our views of things. She wanted to domesticate it, I wanted to make it a present of the homestead and move out. She believed it could be tamed by kind treatment and would be a good pet; I said a pet twenty-one feet high and eighty-four feet long would be no proper thing to have about the place, because, even with the best intentions and without meaning any harm, it could sit down on the house and mash it, for any one could see by the look of its eye that it was absent-minded.

Still, her heart was set upon having that monster, and she couldn't give it up. She thought we could start a dairy with it, and wanted me to help her milk it; but I wouldn't; it was too risky. The sex wasn't right, and we hadn't any ladder anyway. Then she wanted to ride it, and look at the scenery. Thirty or forty feet of its tail was lying on the ground, like a fallen tree, and she thought she could climb it, but she was mistaken; when she got to the steep place it was too slick and down she came, and would have hurt herself but for me.

Was she satisfied now? No. Nothing ever satisfies her but demonstration; untested theories are not in her line, and she won't have them. It is the right spirit, I concede it; it attracts me; I feel the influence of it; if I were with her more I think I should take it up myself. Well, she had one theory remaining about this colossus: she thought that if we could tame him and make him friendly we could stand him in the river and use him for a bridge. It turned out that he was already plenty tame enough—at least as far as she was concerned—so she tried her theory, but it failed: every time she got him properly placed in the river and went ashore to cross over on him, he came out and followed her around like a pet mountain. Like the other animals. They all do that.

Friday   Tuesday—Wednesday—Thursday—and to-day: all without seeing him. It is a long time to be alone; still, it is better to be alone than unwelcome.

I had to have company—I was made for it, I think—so I made friends with the animals. They are just charming, and they have the kindest disposition and the politest ways; they never look sour, they never let you feel that you are intruding, they smile at you and wag their tail, if they've got one, and they are always ready for a romp or an excursion or anything you want to propose. I think they are perfect gentlemen. All these days we have had such good times, and it hasn't been lonesome for me, ever. Lonesome! No, I should say not. Why, there's always a swarm of them around — sometimes as much as four or five acres — you can't count them; and when you stand on a rock in the midst and look out over the furry expanse it is so mottled and splashed and gay with color and frisking sheen and sun-flash, and so rippled with stripes, that you might think it was a lake, only you know it isn't; and there's storms of social birds, and hurricanes of whirring wings; and when the sun strikes all that feathery commotion, you have a blazing up of all the colors you can think of, enough to put your eyes out.

We have made long excursions, and I have seen a great deal of the world; almost all of it, I think; and so I am the first traveler, and the only one. When we are on the march, it is an imposing sight — there's nothing like it anywhere. For comfort I ride a tiger or a leopard, because it is soft and has a round back that fits me, and because they are such pretty animals; but for long distance or for scenery I ride the elephant. He hoists me up with his trunk, but I can get off myself; when we are ready to camp, he sits and I slide down the back way.

The birds and animals are all friendly to each other, and there are no disputes about anything. They all talk, and they all talk to me, but it must be a foreign language, for I cannot make out a word they say; yet they often understand me when I talk back, particularly the dog and the elephant. It makes me ashamed. It shows that they are brighter than I am, and are therefore my superiors. It annoys me, for I want to be the principal Experiment myself — and I intend to be, too.

I have learned a number of things, and am educated, now, but I wasn't at first. I was ignorant at first. At first it used to vex me because, with all my watching, I was never smart enough to be around when the water was running uphill; but now I do not mind it. I have experimented and experimented until now I know it never does run uphill, except in the dark. I know it does in the dark, because the pool never goes dry, which it would, of course, if the water didn't come back in the night. It is best to prove things by actual experiment; then you *know*; whereas if you depend on guessing and supposing and conjecturing, you will never get educated.

Some things you *can't* find out; but you will never know you can't by guessing and supposing: no, you have to be patient and go on experimenting until you find out that you can't find out. And it is delightful to have it that way, it makes the world so interesting. If there wasn't anything to find out, it would be dull. Even trying to find out and not finding out is just as interesting as trying to find out and finding out, and I don't know but more so. The secret of the water was a treasure until I *got* it; then the excitement all went away, and I recognized a sense of loss.

By experiment I know that wood swims, and dry leaves, and feathers, and plenty of other things; therefore by all that cumulative evidence you know that a rock will swim; but you have to put up with simply knowing it, for there isn't any way to prove it — up to now. But I shall find a way — then *that* excitement will go. Such things make me sad; because by and by when I have found out everything there won't be any more excitements, and I do love excitements so! The other night I couldn't sleep for thinking about it.

At first I couldn't make out what I was made for, but now I think it was to search out the secrets of this wonderful world and be happy and thank the Giver of it all for devising it. I think there are many things to learn yet — I hope so; and by economizing and not hurrying too fast I think they will last weeks and weeks. I hope so. When you cast up a feather it sails away on the air and goes out of sight; then you throw up a clod and it doesn't. It comes down, every time. I have tried it and tried it, and it is always so. I wonder why it is? Of course it *doesn't* come down, but why should it *seem* to? I suppose it is an optical illusion. I mean, one of them is. I don't know which one. It may be the feather, it may be the clod; I can't prove which it is, I can only demonstrate that one or the other is a fake, and let a person take his choice.

By watching, I know that the stars are not going to last. I have seen some of the best ones melt and run down the sky. Since one can melt, they can all melt; since they can all melt, they can all melt the same night. That sorrow will come — I know it. I mean to sit up every night and look at them as long as I can keep awake; and I will impress those sparkling fields on my memory, so that by and by when they are taken away I can by my fancy restore those lovely myriads to the black sky and make them sparkle again, and double them by the blur of my tears.

After the Fall

When I look back, the Garden is a dream to me. It was beautiful, surpassingly beautiful, enchantingly beautiful; and now it is lost, and I shall not see it any more.

The Garden is lost, but I have found *him*, and am content. He loves me as well as he can; I love him with all the strength of my passionate nature, and this, I think, is proper to my youth and sex. If I ask myself why I love him, I find I do not know, and do not really much care to know; so I suppose that this kind of love is not a product of reasoning and statistics, like one's love for other reptiles and animals. I think that this must be so. I love certain birds because of their song; but I do not love Adam on account of his singing — no, it is not that; the more he sings the more I do not get reconciled to it. Yet I ask him to sing, because I wish to learn to like everything he is interested in. I am sure I can learn, because at first I could not stand it, but now I can. It sours the milk, but it doesn't matter; I can get used to that kind of milk.

It is not on account of his brightness that I love him — no, it is not that. He is not to blame for his brightness, such as it is, for he did not make it himself; he is as God made him, and that is sufficient. There was a wise purpose in it, *that* I know. In time it will develop, though I think it will not be sudden; and besides, there is no hurry; he is well enough just as he is.

It is not on account of his gracious and considerate ways and his delicacy that I love him. No, he has lacks in these regards, but he is well enough just so, and is improving.

It is not on account of his industry that I love him — no, it is not that. I think he has it in him, and I do not know why he conceals it from me. It is my only pain. Otherwise he is frank and open with me, now. I am sure he keeps nothing from me but this. It grieves me that he should have a secret from me, and sometimes it spoils my sleep, thinking of it, but I will put it out of my mind; it shall not trouble my happiness, which is otherwise full to overflowing.

It is not on account of his education that I love him — no, it is not that. He is self-educated, and does really know a multitude of things, but they are not so.

It is not on account of his chivalry that I love him — no, it is not that. He told on me, but I do not blame him; it is a peculiarity of sex, I think, and he did not make his sex. Of course I would not have told on him, I would have perished first; but that is a peculiarity of sex, too, and I do not take credit for it, for I did not make my sex.

Then why is it that I love him? *Merely because he is masculine*, I think.

At bottom he is good, and I love him for that, but I could love him without it. If he should beat me and abuse me, I should go on loving him. I know it. It is a matter of sex, I think.

He is strong and handsome, and I love him for that, and I admire him and am proud of him, but I could love him without those qualities. If he were plain, I should love him; if he were a wreck, I should love him; and I would work for him, and slave over him, and pray for him, and watch by his bedside until I died.

Yes, I think I love him merely because he is *mine* and is *masculine*. There is no other reason, I suppose. And so I think it is as I first said: that this kind of love is not a product of reasonings and statistics. It just *comes* — none knows whence — and cannot explain itself. And doesn't need to.

It is what I think. But I am only a girl, and the first that has examined this matter, and it may turn out that in my ignorance and inexperience I have not got it right.

Forty Years Later

It is my prayer, it is my longing, that we may pass from this life together — a longing which shall never perish from the earth, but shall have place in the heart of every wife that loves, until the end of time; and it shall be called by my name.

But if one of us must go first, it is my prayer that it shall be I; for he is strong, I am weak, I am not so necessary to him as he is to me — life without him would not be life; how could I endure it? This prayer is also immortal, and will not cease from being offered up while my race continues. I am the first wife; and in the last wife I shall be repeated.

At Eve's Grave

Adam: Wheresoever she was, *there* was Eden.

[1893, 1905]

Study and Writing Questions

1. "The serpent assured her that the forbidden fruit was not apples, it was chestnuts . . . a term meaning an aged and moldy joke." What are the sources of humor in this NARRATIVE? To what extent is this narrative about humor?

2. The comment that "eternal vigilance is the price of supremacy" alludes to the saying, usually attributed to Thomas Jefferson, that "eternal vigilance is the

price of liberty." What sort of political comment does this ALLUSION make? What other political implications does this story have?

3. Both Adam and Eve, in their different ways, display some of the habits of mind that we associate with scientists. Eve even feels to herself "like an experiment." How is science portrayed in this narrative? What does the IMPLIED AUTHOR seem to think about knowledge?

4. How is language treated in this narrative? What is the importance of naming? How does language itself enter into the relationship between Adam and Eve?

5. What are the principle CHARACTERISTICS of Adam and of Eve? In what ways do they each develop in the course of the narrative? What are the stages in their relationship? In what way is the ending a RESOLUTION of issues raised in the narrative as a whole?

See also Questions for Contrast and Comparison: 11, 33, 45, 92, 118, 124, 143, and 229.

■ **JOHN (HOYER) UPDIKE** (1932–), *an only child, was born and raised in Shillington, Pennsylvania. Economic circumstances forced his father, a high school algebra teacher, and mother, an aspiring writer, to live with her parents until John was thirteen. He attended Harvard University on full scholarship (A.B. summa cum laude, 1954) and studied art at the Ruskin School in Oxford, England (1954–1955). His first marriage (1953–1977) produced four children but ended in divorce; his second marriage (1977) continues. He was a staff writer for the New Yorker (1955–1957) until he moved to coastal Massachusetts, where he still lives. His first* NOVEL *(The Poorhouse Fair) and first* STORY *collection (The Same Door) both appeared in 1959. He has since then rapidly alternated novels with volumes of stories (such as* Pigeon Feathers, *1962) that typically appear first in the New Yorker. He has also published several plays, volumes of poetry (mostly light), and award-winning essays (Hugging the Shore, 1983). His saga of Harry "Rabbit" Angstrom, a suburbanite whose best years were as a high school athlete, includes* Rabbit, Run *(1960);* Rabbit Redux *(1971);* Rabbit Is Rich *(1981), which won virtually every American fiction award; and* Rabbit At Rest *(1990). Also important are* The Centaur *(1963), a* REALISTIC/MYTHOLOGICAL *tale of a teenager and his father, a high school science teacher, and* The Witches of Eastwick *(1984), social* SATIRE *as* FANTASY.

Should Wizard Hit Mommy?

In the evenings and for Saturday naps like today's, Jack told his daughter Jo a story out of his head. This custom, begun when she was two, was itself now nearly two years old, and his head felt empty. Each new story was a slight variation of a basic tale: a small creature, usually named Roger (Roger Fish, Roger Squirrel, Roger Chipmunk), had some problem and went with it to the wise old owl. The owl told him to go to the wizard, and the wizard performed a magic spell that solved the problem, demanding in payment a number of pennies greater than the number Roger Creature had but in the same breath directing the animal to a place where the extra pennies could be found. Then Roger was so happy he played many games with other creatures, and went home to his mother just in time to hear the train whistle that brought his daddy home from Boston. Jack described their supper, and the story was over. Working his way through this scheme was especially fatiguing on Saturday, because Jo never fell asleep in naps any more, and knowing this made the rite seem futile.

The little girl (not so little any more; the bumps her feet made under the covers were halfway down the bed, their big double bed that they let her be in for naps and when she was sick) had at last arranged herself, and from the way her fat face deep in the pillow shone in the sunlight sifting through the drawn shades, it did not seem fantastic that something magic would occur, and she would take her nap like an infant of two. Her brother, Bobby, was two, and already asleep with his bottle. Jack asked, "Who shall the story be about today?"

"Roger . . ." Jo squeezed her eyes shut and smiled to be thinking she was thinking. Her eyes opened, her mother's blue. "Skunk," she said firmly.

A new animal; they must talk about skunks at nursery school. Having a fresh hero momentarily stirred Jack to creative enthusiasm. "All right," he said. "Once upon a time, in the deep dark woods, there was a tiny little creature name of Roger Skunk. And he smelled very bad—"

"Yes," Jo said.

"He smelled so bad none of the other little woodland creatures would play with him." Jo looked at him solemnly; she hadn't foreseen this. "Whenever he would go out to play," Jack continued with zest, remembering certain humiliations of his own childhood, "all of the other tiny animals would cry, 'Uh-oh, here comes Roger Stinky Skunk,' and they would run away, and Roger Skunk would stand there all alone, and two little round tears would fall from his eyes." The corners of Jo's mouth drooped down and her lower lip bent forward as he traced with a forefinger along the side of her nose the course of one of Roger Skunk's tears.

"Won't he see the owl?" she asked in a high and faintly roughened voice.

Sitting on the bed beside her, Jack felt the covers tug as her legs switched tensely. He was pleased with this moment—he was telling her something true, something she must know—and had no wish to hurry on. But downstairs a chair scraped, and he realized he must get down to help Clare paint the living-room woodwork.

"Well, he walked along very sadly and came to a very big tree, and in the tiptop of the tree was an enormous wise old owl."

"Good."

" 'Mr. Owl,' Roger Skunk said, 'all the other little animals run away from me because I smell so bad.' 'So you do,' the owl said. 'Very, very bad,' 'What can I do?' Roger Skunk said, and he cried very hard."

"The wizard, the wizard," Jo shouted, and sat right up, and a Little Golden Book spilled from the bed.

"Now, Jo. Daddy's telling the story. Do you want to tell Daddy the story?"

"No. You me."

"Then lie down and be sleepy."

Her head relapsed onto the pillow and she said, "Out of your head."

"Well. The owl thought and thought. At last he said, 'Why don't you go see the wizard?' "

"Daddy?"

"What?"

"Are magic spells *real*?" This was a new phase, just this last month, a reality phase. When he told her spiders eat bugs, she turned to her mother and asked, "Do they *really*?" and when Clare told her God was in the sky and all around them, she turned to her father and insisted, with a sly yet eager smile, "Is He *really*?"

"They're real in stories," Jack answered curtly. She had made him miss a beat in the narrative. "The owl said, 'Go through the dark woods, under the apple trees, into the swamp, over the crick—'"

"What's a crick?"

"A little river. 'Over the crick, and there will be the wizard's house.' And that's the way Roger Skunk went, and pretty soon he came to a little white house, and he rapped on the door." Jack rapped on the window sill, and under the covers Jo's tall figure clenched in an infantile thrill. "And then a tiny little old man came out, with a long white beard and a pointed blue hat, and said, 'Eh? Whatzis? Whatcher want? You smell awful.'" The wizard's voice was one of Jack's own favorite effects; he did it by scrunching up his face and somehow whining through his eyes, which felt for the interval rheumy. He felt being an old man suited him.

"'I know it,' Roger Skunk said, 'and all the little animals run away from me. The enormous wise owl said you could help me.'"

"'Eh? Well, maybe. Come on in. Don't git too close.' Now, inside, Jo, there were all these magic things, all jumbled together in a big dusty heap, because the wizard did not have any cleaning lady."

"Why?"

"Why? Because he was a wizard, and a very old man."

"Will he die?"

"No. Wizards don't die. Well, he rummaged around and found an old stick called a magic wand and asked Roger Skunk what he wanted to smell like. Roger thought and thought and said, 'Roses.'"

"Yes. Good," Jo said smugly.

Jack fixed her with a trancelike gaze and chanted in the wizard's elderly irritable voice:

"'Abracadabry, hocus-poo,
Roger Skunk, how do you do,
Roses, boses, pull an ear,
Roger Skunk, you never fear:
      Bingo!'"

He paused as a rapt expression widened out from his daughter's nostrils, forcing her eyebrows up and her lower lip down in a wide noiseless grin, an expression in which Jack was startled to recognize his wife feigning pleasure at cocktail parties. "And all of a sudden," he whispered, "the whole inside of the wizard's house was full of the smell of — roses! 'Roses!' Roger Fish cried. And the wizard said, very cranky, 'That'll be seven pennies.'"

"Daddy."

"What?"

"Roger *Skunk*. You said Roger Fish."

"Yes. Skunk."

"You said Roger *Fish*. Wasn't that silly?"

"Very silly of your stupid old daddy. Where was I? Well, you know about the pennies."

"Say it."

"O.K. Roger Skunk said, 'But all I have is four pennies,' and he began to cry." Jo made the crying face again, but this time without a trace of sincerity. This annoyed Jack. Downstairs some more furniture rumbled. Clare shouldn't move heavy things; she was six months pregnant. It would be their third.

"So the wizard said, 'Oh, very well. Go to the end of the lane and turn around three times and look down the magic well and there you will find three pennies. Hurry up.' So Roger Skunk went to the end of the lane and turned around three times and there in the magic well were *three pennies*! So he took them back to the wizard and was very happy and ran out into the woods and all the other little animals gathered around him because he smelled so good. And they played tag, baseball, football, basketball, lacrosse, hockey, soccer, and pick-up-sticks."

"What's pick-up-sticks?"

"It's a game you play with sticks."

"Like the wizard's magic wand?"

"Kind of. And they played games and laughed all afternoon and then it began to get dark and they all ran home to their mommies."

Jo was starting to fuss with her hands and look out of the window, at the crack of day that showed under the shade. She thought the story was all over. Jack didn't like women when they took anything for granted; he liked them apprehensive, hanging on his words. "Now, Jo, are you listening?"

"Yes."

"Because this is very interesting. Roger Skunk's mommy said, "What's that awful smell?""

"Wha-at?"

"And Roger Skunk said, 'It's me, Mommy. I smell like roses.' And she said, 'Who made you smell like that?' And he said, 'The wizard,' and she said, 'Well, of all the nerve. You come with me and we're going right back to that very awful wizard.'"

Jo sat up, her hands dabbling in the air with genuine fright. "But Daddy, then he said about the other little animals run *away*!" Her hands skittered off, into the underbrush.

"All right. He said, 'But Mommy, all the other little animals run away,' and she said, 'I don't care. You smelled the way a little skunk should have and I'm going to take you right back to that wizard,' and she took an umbrella and went back with Roger Skunk and hit that wizard right over the head."

"No," Jo said, and put her hand out to touch his lips, yet even in her agitation did not quite dare to stop the source of truth. Inspiration came to her. "Then the wizard hit *her* on the head and did not change that little skunk back."

"No," he said. "The wizard said 'O.K.' and Roger Skunk did not smell of roses any more. He smelled very bad again."

"But the other little amum — oh! — amum —"

"Joanne. It's Daddy's story. Shall Daddy not tell you any more stories?" Her broad face looked at him through sifted light, astounded. "This is what happened, then. Roger Skunk and his mommy went home and they heard W*oo-oo*, w*oooo-oo* and it was the choo-choo train bringing Daddy Skunk home from Boston. And they had lima beans, pork chops, celery, liver, mashed potatoes, and Pie-Oh-My for dessert. And when Roger Skunk was in bed Mommy Skunk came up and hugged him and said he smelled like her little baby skunk again and she loved him very much. And that's the end of the story."

"But Daddy."

"What?"

"Then did the other little ani-mals run away?"

"No, because eventually they got used to the way he was and did not mind it at all."

"What's evenshiladee?"

"In a little while."

"That was a stupid mommy."

"It was *not*," he said with rare emphasis, and believed, from her expression, that she realized he was defending his own mother to her, or something as odd. "Now I want you to put your big heavy head in the pillow and have a good long nap." He adjusted the shade so not even a crack of day showed, and tiptoed to the door, in the pretense that she was already asleep. But when he turned, she was crouching on top of the covers and staring at him. "Hey. Get under the covers and fall faaast asleep. Bobby's asleep."

She stood up and bounced gingerly on the springs. "Daddy."

"What?"

"Tomorrow, I want you to tell me the story that that wizard took that magic wand and hit that mommy" — her plump arms chopped fiercely — "right over the head."

"No. That's not the story. The point is that the little skunk loved his mommy more than he loved aaalll the other little animals and she knew what was right."

"No. Tomorrow you say he hit that mommy. Do it." She kicked her legs up and sat down on the bed with a great heave and complaint of springs, as she had done hundreds of times before, except that this time she did not laugh. "Say it, Daddy."

"Well, we'll see. Now at least have a rest. Stay on the bed. You're a good girl."

He closed the door and went downstairs. Clare had spread the newspapers and opened the paint can and, wearing an old shirt of his on top of her maternity smock, was stroking the chair rail with a dipped brush. Above him footsteps vibrated and he called, "*Joanne*. Shall I come up there and spank you?" The footsteps hesitated.

"That was a long story," Clare said.

"The poor kid," he answered, and with utter weariness watched his wife labor. The woodwork, a cage of moldings and rails and baseboards all around them, was half old tan and half new ivory and he felt caught in an ugly middle position, and though he as well felt his wife's presence in the cage with him, he did not want to speak with her, work with her, touch her, anything.

[1959]

Study and Writing Questions

1. The opening paragraph gives us the skeleton of Jack's habitual STORY while the rest of this NARRATIVE presents a specific variation of that story. What is the significance of this narrative's many repetitions and variations, as between Jack and Jo? Are there other repetitions and variations either explicit or implicit?
2. Jack realizes "he was telling [Jo] something true." In what sense(s) is he correct?
3. Compare and contrast Jack's activities and Clare's activities.
4. What are Jack's attitudes toward females?
5. Compare and contrast first and subsequent readings. For example, how does the phrase from the first sentence, "out of his head," change?

See also Questions for Contrast and Comparison: 27, 97, 132, 139, 201, 215, and 238.

■ **BILL WATTERSON** (1958–) *was born in Washington, D.C., and graduated from Kenyon College (1980). Ever since he was "a kid," he wanted to be
a cartoonist. He began working as a political cartoonist for the Cincinnati Post in
1980 but was unhappy at the job. Consequently he started sending various newspaper syndicates comic strip ideas, including "a sort of out-of-space parody" called
"Spaceman Spiff." One of these submissions had, as minor characters, Calvin and
Hobbes, a little boy and his stuffed playmate. United Features Syndicate suggested
building a strip around them and Watterson, finding them the funniest characters
of the group, agreed. Ironically, United Features turned the strip down, instead
offering Watterson "Robotman," a character being developed to merchandise a line
of products; however, he "really recoiled at the idea of drawing someone else's
character . . . [at] cartooning by committee." He rejected that job, but on November 18, 1985, "Calvin and Hobbes" was finally launched by Universal Press
Syndicate. The strip has grown to over six hundred newspaper outlets and Something Under the Bed Is Drooling: A Calvin and Hobbes Collection (1988) spent
over a year on the New York Times best-seller list. Watterson has refused to license
his characters for merchandising, to "condense [my work] for a product." He is
married to an artist.*

from Something Under the Bed Is Drooling:
A Calvin and Hobbes Collection

[1988]

Study and Writing Questions

1. There are three different SETTINGS in this STORY. What meanings does setting
   convey here?
2. What are the effects of the third panel ALLUSIONS to the FAIRY TALE tradition?
3. There are two different drawing styles used for the tiger. What does each
   imply for the boy and for the reader?
4. What is the importance of using four different lettering fonts in this story?
5. What is the importance of SELF-REFLEXIVITY in this NARRATIVE? Note that each
   of the panels implies at least one use for stories. What is the MORAL of this
   story?

See also Questions for Contrast and Comparison: 34, 87, 95, 139, 199, and 215.

■ H(ERBERT) G(EORGE) WELLS (1866–1946) *was a pivotal figure in the development of British fiction. Born in Kent of lower middle-class parents, he was virtually self-educated. Winning a scholarship to the Normal School of Science, Wells worked for a year under T. H. Huxley, the great disciple of Charles Darwin. Huxley's influence helped to shape Wells into a writer who typically combined a vision of vast patterns with details from the mundane. Wells worked as a journalist and essayist throughout his career, writing on every imaginable subject from politics to marriage to art. He was for a time an influential member of the Fabian Society, a body that helped bring about British Socialism. Today his fame rests largely on his early "scientific romances" (such as* The Invisible Man, *1897 and* The War of the Worlds, *1898), but his vast output includes histories, biographies, realistic* NOVELS, *utopias, autobiography. His four-volume* The Outline of History *(1920) was the first attempt to see world history as a whole and as a reflection of peoples rather than of great individuals. In their famous, public literary controversy, Henry James argued for the crucial importance of minute psychological characterization within a realistic framework if one is to understand individuals and thus humanity, while Wells argued for the crucial importance of imaginative* ROMANCE *and the portrayal of great social forces if one is to understand how our lives are conditioned.*

The Star

It was on the first day of the new year that the announcement was made, almost simultaneously from three observatories, that the motion of the planet Neptune, the outermost of all the planets that wheel about the sun, had become very erratic. Ogilvy had already called attention to a suspected retardation in its velocity in December. Such a piece of news was scarcely calculated to interest a world the greater portion of whose inhabitants were unaware of the existence of the planet Neptune, nor outside the astronomical profession did the subsequent discovery of a faint remote speck of light in the region of the perturbed planet cause any very great excitement. Scientific people, however, found the intelligence remarkable enough, even before it became known that the new body was rapidly growing larger and brighter, that its motion was quite different from the orderly progress of the planets, and that the deflection of Neptune and its satellite was becoming now of an unprecedented kind.

Few people without a training in science can realise the huge isolation of the solar system. The sun with its specks of planets, its dust of planetoids, and its impalpable comets, swims in a vacant immensity that almost defeats the imagination. Beyond the orbit of Neptune there is space, vacant so far as human observation has penetrated, without warmth or light or sound, blank emptiness, for twenty million times a million miles. That is the smallest estimate of the distance to be traversed before the very nearest of the stars is attained. And, saving a few comets more unsubstantial than the thinnest flame, no matter had ever to human knowledge crossed this gulf of space, until early in the twentieth century this strange wanderer appeared. A vast mass of matter it was, bulky, heavy, rushing without warning out of the black mystery of the sky into the radiance of the sun. By the second day it was clearly visible to any decent instrument, as a speck with a barely sensible diameter, in the constellation Leo near Regulus. In a little while an opera glass could attain it.

On the third day of the new year the newspaper readers of two hemispheres were made aware for the first time of the real importance of this unusual apparition in the heavens. "A Planetary Collision," one London paper headed the news, and proclaimed Duchaine's opinion that this strange new planet would probably collide with Neptune. The leader writers enlarged upon the topic. So that in most of the capitals of the world, on January 3rd, there was an expectation, however vague, of some imminent phenomenon in the sky; and as the night followed the sunset round the globe, thousands of men turned their eyes skyward to see — the old familiar stars just as they had always been.

Until it was dawn in London and Pollux setting and the stars overhead grown pale. The Winter's dawn it was, a sickly filtering accumulation of daylight, and the light of gas and candles shone yellow in the windows to show where people were astir. But the yawning policeman saw the thing, the busy crowds in the markets stopped agape, workmen going to their work betimes, milkmen, the drivers of newscarts, dissipation going home jaded and pale, homeless wanderers, sentinels on their beats, and in the country, labourers trudging afield, poachers slinking home, all over the dusky quickening country it could be seen — and out at sea by seamen watching for the day — a great white star, come suddenly into the westward sky!

Brighter it was than any star in our skies: brighter than the evening star at its brightest. It still glowed out white and large, no mere twinkling spot of light, but a small round clear shining disc, an hour after the day had come. And where science has not reached, men stared and feared, telling one another of the wars and pestilences that are foreshadowed by these fiery signs in the Heavens. Sturdy Boers, dusky Hottentots, Gold Coast Negroes, Frenchmen, Spaniards, Portuguese, stood in the warmth of the sunrise watching the setting of this strange new star.

And in a hundred observatories there had been suppressed excitement, rising almost to shouting pitch, as the two remote bodies had rushed together, and a hurrying to and fro, to gather photographic apparatus and spectroscope, and this appliance and that, to record this novel astonishing sight, the destruction of a world. For it was a world, a sister planet of our earth, far greater than our earth indeed, that had so suddenly flashed into flaming death. Neptune it was, had been struck, fairly and squarely, by the strange planet from outer space and the heat of the concussion had incontinently turned two solid globes into one vast mass of incandescence. Round the world that day, two hours before the dawn, went the pallid great white star, fading only as it sank westward and the sun mounted above it. Everywhere men marvelled at it, but of all those who saw it none could have marvelled more than those sailors, habitual watchers of the stars, who far away at sea had heard nothing of its advent and saw it now rise like a pigmy moon and climb zenithward and hang overhead and sink westward with the passing of the night.

And when next it rose over Europe everywhere were crowds of watchers on hilly slopes, on house-roofs, in open spaces, staring eastward for the rising of the great new star. It rose with a white glow in front of it, like the glare of a white fire, and those who had seen it come into existence the night before cried out at the sight of it. "It is larger," they cried. "It is brighter!" And, indeed the moon a quarter full and sinking in the west was in its apparent size beyond comparison, but scarcely in all its breadth had it as much brightness now as the little circle of the strange new star.

"It is brighter!" cried the people clustering in the streets. But in the dim observatories the watchers held their breath and peered at one another. "It is nearer," they said. "Nearer!"

And voice after voice repeated, "It is nearer," and the clicking telegraph took that up, and it trembled along telephone wires, and in a thousand cities grimy compositors fingered the type. "It is nearer." Men writing in offices, struck with a strange realisation, flung down their pens, men talking in a thousand places suddenly came upon a grotesque possibility in those words, "It is nearer." It hurried along awakening streets, it was shouted down the frost-stilled ways of quiet villages; men who had read these things from the throbbing tape stood in yellow-lit doorways shouting the news to the passers-by. "It is nearer." Pretty women, flushed and glittering, heard the news told jestingly between the dances, and feigned an intelligent interest they did not feel. "Nearer! Indeed. How curious! How very, very clever people must be to find out things like that!"

Lonely tramps faring through the wintry night murmured those words to comfort themselves—looking skyward. "It has need to be nearer, for the night's as cold as charity. Don't seem much warmth from it if it is nearer, all the same."

"What is a new star to me?" cried the weeping woman kneeling beside her dead.

The schoolboy, rising early for his examination work, puzzled it out for himself—with the great white star, shining broad and bright through the frost-flowers of his window. "Centrifugal, centripetal," he said, with his chin on his fist. "Stop a planet in its flight, rob it of its centrifugal force, what then? Centripetal has it, and down it falls into the sun! and this—!"

"Do we come in the way? I wonder—"

The light of that day went the way of its brethren, and with the later watches of the frosty darkness rose the strange star again. And it was now so bright that the waxing moon seemed but a pale yellow ghost of itself, hanging huge in the sunset. In a South African city a great man had married, and the streets were alight to welcome his return with his bride. "Even the skies have illuminated," said the flatterer. Under Capricorn, two Negro lovers, daring the wild beasts and evil spirits, for love of one another, crouched together in a cane brake where the fire-flies hovered. "That is our star," they whispered, and felt strangely comforted by the sweet brilliance of its light.

The master mathematician sat in his private room and pushed the papers from him. His calculations were already finished. In a small white phial there still remained a little of the drug that had kept him awake and active for four long nights. Each day, serene, explicit, patient as ever, he had given his lecture to his students, and then had come back at once to this momentous calculation. His face was grave, a little drawn and hectic from his drugged activity. For some time he seemed lost in thought. Then he went to the window, and the blind went up with a click. Half way up the sky, over the clustering roofs, chimneys and steeples of the city, hung the star.

He looked at it as one might look into the eyes of a brave enemy. "You may kill me," he said after a silence. "But I can hold you—and all the universe for that matter—in the grip of this little brain. I would not change. Even now."

He looked at the little phial. "There will be no need of sleep again," he said. The next day at noon, punctual to the minute, he entered his lecture theatre, put his hat on the end of the table as his habit was, and carefully selected a large piece of chalk. It was a joke among his students that he could not lecture without that piece of chalk to fumble in his fingers, and once he had been stricken to impotence by their hiding his supply. He came and looked under his grey eyebrows at the rising tiers of young fresh faces, and spoke with his accustomed studied commonness of phrasing. "Circumstances have arisen — circumstances beyond my control," he said and paused, "which will debar me from completing the course I had designed. It would seem, gentlemen, if I may put the thing clearly and briefly, that Man has lived in vain."

The students glanced at one another. Had they heard aright? Mad? Raised eyebrows and grinning lips there were, but one or two faces remained intent upon his calm grey-fringed face. "It will be interesting," he was saying, "to devote this morning to an exposition, so far as I can make it clear to you, of the calculations that have led me to this conclusion. Let us assume —"

He turned towards the blackboard, meditating a diagram in the way that was usual to him. "What was that about 'lived in vain?'" whispered one student to another. "Listen," said the other, nodding towards the lecturer.

And presently they began to understand.

That night the star rose later, for its proper eastward motion had carried it some way across Leo towards Virgo, and its brightness was so great that the sky became a luminous blue as it rose, and every star was hidden in its turn, save only Jupiter near the zenith. Capella, Aldebaran, Sirius and the pointers of the Bear. It was very white and beautiful. In many parts of the world that night a pallid halo encircled it about. It was perceptibly larger: in the clear refractive sky of the tropics it seemed as if it were nearly a quarter the size of the moon. The frost was still on the ground in England, but the world was as brightly lit as if it were midsummer moonlight. One could see to read quite ordinary print by that cold clear light, and in the cities the lamps burnt yellow and wan.

And everywhere the world was awake that night, and throughout Christendom a sombre murmur hung in the keen air over the country side like the belling of bees in the heather, and this mumurous tumult grew to a clangour in the cities. It was the tolling of the bells in a million belfry towers and steeples, summoning the people to sleep no more, to sin no more, but to gather in their churches and pray. And overhead, growing larger and brighter, as the earth rolled on its way and the night passed, rose the dazzling star.

And the streets and houses were alight in all the cities, the shipyards glared, and whatever roads led to high country were lit and crowded all night long. And in all the seas about the civilised lands, ships with throbbing engines, and ships with bellying sails, crowded with men and living creatures, were standing out to ocean and the north. For already the warning of the master mathematician had been telegraphed all over the world, and translated into a hundred tongues. The new planet and Neptune, locked in a fiery embrace, were whirling headlong, ever faster and faster towards the sun. Already every second this blazing mass flew a hundred miles, and every second its terrific velocity increased. As it flew now, indeed, it must pass a hundred million of miles wide of the earth and scarcely affect it. But near its destined path, as yet only slightly perturbed, spun the mightly planet Jupiter and his moons sweeping splendid round the sun. Every moment now the attraction between the fiery star and the greatest of the planets grew stronger. And the result of that attraction? Inevitably Jupiter would be deflected from its orbit into an elliptical path, and the burning star, swung by his attraction wide of its sunward rush, would "describe a curved path" and perhaps collide with, and certainly pass very close to, our earth. "Earthquakes, volcanic outbreaks, cyclones, sea waves, floods, and a steady rise in temperature to I know not what limit" — so prophesied the master mathematician.

And overhead, to carry out his words, lonely and cold and livid, blazed the star of the coming doom.

To many who stared at it that night until their eyes ached, it seemed that it was visibly approaching. And that night, too, the weather changed and the frost that had gripped all Central Europe and France and England softened towards a thaw.

But you must not imagine because I have spoken of people praying through the night and people going aboard ships and people fleeing towards mountainous country that the whole world was already in a terror because of the star. As a matter of fact, use and wont still ruled the world, and save for the talk of idle moments and the splendour of the night, nine human beings out of ten were still busy at their common occupations. In all the cities the shops, save one here and there, opened and closed at their proper hours, the doctor and the undertaker plied their trades, the workers gathered in the factories, soldiers drilled, scholars studied, lovers sought one another, thieves lurked and fled, politicians planned their schemes. The presses of the newspapers roared through the nights, and many a priest of this church and that would not open his holy building to further what he considered a foolish panic. The newspapers insisted on the lesson of the year 1000 — for then, too, people had anticipated the end. The star was no star — mere gas — a comet: and were it a star it could not possibly strike the earth. There was no precedent for such a thing. Common sense was sturdy everywhere, scornful, jesting, a little inclined to persecute the obdurate fearful. That night, at seven-fifteen by Greenwich time, the star would be at its nearest to Jupiter. Then the world would see the turn things would take. The master mathematician's grim warnings were treated by many as so much mere elaborate self-advertisement. Common sense at last, a little heated by argument, signified its unalterable convictions by going to bed. So, too, barbarism and savagery, already tired of the novelty, went about their nightly business, and save for a howling dog here and there, the beast world left the star unheeded.

And yet, when at the last the watchers in the European States saw the star rise, an hour late it is true, but no larger than it had been the night before, there were still plenty awake to laugh at the master mathematician — to take the danger as if it had passed.

But hereafter the laughter ceased. The star grew — it grew with a terrible steadiness hour after hour, a little larger each hour, a little nearer the midnight zenith, and brighter and brighter, until it had turned night into a second day. Had it come straight to the earth instead of in a curved path, had it lost no velocity to Jupiter, it must have lept the intervening gulf in a day, but as it was it took five days altogether to come by our planet. The next night it had become a third the size of the moon before it set to English eyes, and the thaw was assured. It rose over America near the size of the moon, but blinding white to look at, and *hot*, and a breath of hot wind blew now with its rising and gathering strength, and in Virginia and Brazil, and down the St. Lawrence valley, it shown intermittently through a driving reek of thunder-clouds, flickering violet lightning, and hail unprecedented. In Manitoba was a thaw and devastating floods. And upon all the mountains of the earth the snow and ice began to melt that night, and all the rivers coming out of high country flowed thick and turbid, and soon — in their upper reaches — with swirling trees and the bodies of beasts and men. They rose steadily, steadily in the ghostly brilliance, and came trickling over their banks at last, behind the flying population of their valleys.

And along the coast of Argentina and up the South Atlantic the tides were higher than had ever been in the memory of man, and the storms drove the waters in many cases scores of miles inland, drowning whole cities. And so great grew the heat during the night that the rising of the sun was like the coming of a shadow. The earthquakes began and grew until all down America, from the Arctic Circle to Cape Horn, hillsides were sliding, fissures were openings, and houses and walls crumbling to destruction. The whole side of Cotopaxi slipped out in one vast convulsion, and a tumult of lava poured out so high and broad and swift and liquid that in one day it reached the sea.

So the star, with the wan moon in its wake, marched across the Pacific, trailed the thunderstorms like the hem of a robe, and the growing tidal wave that toiled behind it, frothing and eager, poured over island and island and swept them clear of men. Until that wave came at last — in a blinding light and with the breath of a furnace, swift and terrible it came — a wall of water, fifty feet high, roaring hungrily, upon the long coasts of Asia, and swept inland across the plains of China. For a space the star, hotter now and larger and brighter than the sun in its strength, showed with pitiless brilliance the wide and populous country; towns and villages with their pagodas and trees, roads, wide cultivated fields, millions of sleepless people staring in helpless terror at the incandescent sky; and then, low and growing, came the murmur of the flood. And thus it was with millions of men that night — a flight nowhither, with limbs heavy with heat and breath fierce and scant, and the flood like a wall swift and white behind. And then death.

China was lit glowing white, but over Japan and Java and all the islands of Eastern Asia the great star was a ball of dull red fire because of the steam and smoke and ashes the volcanoes were spouting forth to salute its coming. Above was the lava, hot gases and ash, and below the seething floods, and the whole earth swayed and rumbled with the earthquake shocks. Soon the immemorial snows of Tibet and the Himalaya were melting and pouring down by ten million deepening converging channels upon the plains of Burmah and Hindostan. The tangled summits by the Indian jungles were aflame in a thousand places, and below the hurrying waters around the stems were dark objects that still struggled feebly and reflected the blood-red tongues of fire. And in a rudderless confusion a multitude of men and women fled down the broad river-ways to that one last hope of men — the open sea.

Larger grew the star, and larger, hotter, and brighter with a terrible swiftness now. The tropical ocean had lost its phosphorescence, and the whirling steam rose in ghostly wreaths from the black waves that plunged incessantly, speckled with storm-tossed ships.

And then came a wonder. It seemed to those who in Europe watched for the rising of the star that the world must have ceased its rotation. In a thousand open spaces of down and upland the people who had fled thither from the floods and the falling houses and sliding slopes of hill watched for that rising in vain. Hour followed hour through a terrible suspense, and the star rose not. Once again men set their eyes upon the old constellations they had counted lost to them forever. In England it was hot and clear overhead, though the ground quivered perpetually, but in the tropics, Sirius and Capella and Aldebaran showed through a veil of steam. And when at last the great star rose near ten hours late, the sun rose close upon it, and in the centre of its white heat was a disc of black.

Over Asia it was the star had begun to fall behind the movement of the sky, and then suddenly, as it hung over India, its light had been veiled. All the plain of India from the mouth of the Indus to the mouths of the Ganges was a shallow waste of shining water that night, out of which rose temples and palaces, mounds and hills, black with people. Every minaret was a clustering mass of people, who fell one by one into the turbid waters, as heat and terror overcame them. The whole land seemed a-wailing, and suddenly there swept a shadow across that furnace of despair, and a breath of cold wind, and a gathering of clouds, out of the cooling air. Men looking up, near blinded, at the star, saw that a black disc was creeping across the light. It was the moon, coming between the star and the earth. And even as men cried to God at this respite, out of the East with a strange inexplicable swiftness sprang the sun. And then star, sun and moon rushed together across the heavens.

So it was that presently, to the European watchers, star and sun rose close upon each other, drove headlong for a space and then slower, and at last came to rest, star and sun merged into one glare of flame at the zenith of the sky. The moon no longer eclipsed the star but was lost to sight in the brilliance of the sky. And though those who were still alive regarded it for the most part with that dull stupidity that hunger, fatigue, heat and despair engender, there were still men who could perceive the meaning of these signs. Star and earth had been at their nearest, had swung about one another, and the star had passed. Already it was receding, swifter and swifter, in the last stage of its headlong journey downward into the sun.

And then the clouds gathered, blotting out the vision of the sky, the thunder and lightning wove a garment round the world; all over the earth was such a downpour of rain as men had never before seen, and where the volcanoes flared red against the cloud canopy there descended torrents of mud. Everywhere the waters were pouring off the land, leaving mud-silted ruins, and the earth littered like a storm-worn beach with all that had floated, and the dead bodies of the men and brutes, its children. For days, the water streamed off the land, sweeping away soil and trees and houses in the way, and piling huge dykes and scooping out Titantic gullies over the country side. Those were the days of darkness that followed the star and the heat. All through them, and for many weeks and months, the earthquakes continued.

But the star had passed, and men, hunger-driven and gathering courage only slowly, might creep back to their ruined cities, buried granaries, and sodden fields. Such few ships as had escaped the storms of that time came stunned and shattered and sounding their way cautiously through the new marks and shoals of once familiar ports. And as the storms subsided men perceived that everywhere the days were hotter than of yore, and the sun larger, and the moon, shrunk to a third of its former size, took now forescore days between its new and new.

But of the new brotherhood that grew presently among men, of the saving of laws and books and machines, of the strange change that had come over Iceland and Greenland and the shores of Baffin's Bay, so that the sailors coming there presently found them green and gracious, and could scarce believe their eyes, this story does not tell. Nor of the movement of mankind now that the earth was hotter, northward and southward towards the poles of the earth. It concerns itself only with the coming and the passing of the Star.

The Martian astronomers — for there are astronomers on Mars, although they are very different beings from men — were naturally profoundly interested by these things. They saw them from their own standpoint of course. "Considering the mass and temperature of the missile that was flung through our solar system into the sun," one wrote, "it is astonishing what a little damage the earth, which it missed so narrowly, has sustained. All the familiar continental markings and the masses of the seas remain intact, and indeed the only difference seems to be a shrinking of the white discoloration (supposed to be frozen water) round either pole." Which only shows how small the vastest of human catastrophes may seem, at a distance of a few million miles.

[1899]

Study and Writing Questions

1. What attitude toward science is projected by this NARRATIVE? Note that both those without science and the "master mathematician" are correct about "the star," while most people are wrong. What incidents suggest the IMPLIED AUTHOR'S view of the proper place of science in human affairs?

2. The two references to "terrible" and "swift" ALLUDE to Julia Ward Howe's "Battle Hymn of the Republic" with its mention of God's "terrible, swift sword." What attitude toward religion is projected by Wells's narrative? Note that clergy both lock their churches and pray. What incidents suggest the implied author's view of the proper place of religion in human affairs?

3. How does this narrative create SUSPENSE and hold one's attention despite the virtual absence of individuated CHARACTERS? What devices, such as PERSONIFICATION, engage our emotions? How is the narrative STRUCTURED to pull us along? How is the STYLE used to pull us along?

4. Why does the narrator tell us in the next to last paragraph that there developed a "new brotherhood" but then refuse to tell about it? Why not simply omit this paragraph? What purposes of the narrative are served by including it?

5. In the last paragraph, who — or what — do we finally discover the NARRATOR to be? What is the narrator's relation to human history? Does the narrator intend the last line as a sober lesson, as a joke, or as something else? What is the THEME of this narrative?

See also Questions for Contrast and Comparison: 7, 14, 73, 76, 107, 124, 146, 148, 155, 211, 222, 233, and 236.

The Time Machine

I

The Time Traveller (for so it will be convenient to speak of him) was expounding a recondite matter to us. His grey eyes shown and twinkled, and his usually pale face was flushed and animated. The fire burned brightly, and the soft radiance of the incandescent lights in the lilies of silver caught the bubbles that flashed and passed in our glasses. Our chairs, being his patents, embraced and caressed us rather than submitted to be sat upon, and there was that luxurious after-dinner atmosphere when thought runs gracefully free of the trammels of precision. And he put it to us in this way—marking the points with a lean forefinger—as we sat and lazily admired his earnestness over this new paradox (as we thought it:) and his fecundity.

'You must follow me carefully. I shall have to controvert one or two ideas that are almost universally accepted. The geometry, for instance, they taught you at school is founded on a misconception.'

'Is not that rather a large thing to expect us to begin upon?' said Filby, an argumentative person with red hair.

'I do not mean to ask you to accept anything without reasonable ground for it. You will soon admit as much as I need from you. You know of course that a mathematical line, a line of thickness *nil*, has no real existence. They taught you that? Neither has a mathematical plane. These things are mere abstractions.'

'That is all right,' said the Psychologist.

'Nor, having only length, breadth, and thickness, can a cube have a real existence.'

'There I object,' said Filby. 'Of course a solid body may exist. All real things——'

'So most people think. But wait a moment. Can an *instantaneous* cube exist?'

'Don't follow you,' said Filby.

'Can a cube that does not last for any time at all, have a real existence?'

Filby became pensive. 'Clearly,' the Time Traveller proceeded, 'any real body must have extension in *four* directions: it must have Length, Breadth, Thickness, and—Duration. But through a natural infirmity of the flesh, which I will explain to you in a moment, we incline to overlook this fact. There are really four dimensions, three which we call the three planes of Space, and a fourth, Time. There is, however, a tendency to draw an unreal distinction between the former three dimensions and the latter, because it happens that our consciousness moves intermittently in one direction along the latter from the beginning to the end of our lives.'

'That,' said a very young man, making spasmodic efforts to relight his cigar over the lamp; 'that . . . very clear indeed.'

'Now, it is very remarkable that this is so extensively overlooked,' continued the Time Traveller, with a slight accession of cheerfulness. 'Really this is what is meant by the Fourth Dimension, though some people who talk about the Fourth Dimension do not know they mean it. It is only another way of looking at Time. *There is no difference between Time and any of the three dimensions of Space except that our consciousness moves along it.* But some foolish people have got hold of the wrong side of that idea. You have all heard what they have to say about this Fourth Dimension?'

'I have not,' said the Provincial Mayor.

'It is simply this. That Space, as our mathematicians have it, is spoken of as having three dimensions, which one may call Length, Breadth, and Thickness, and is always definable by reference to three planes, each at right angles to the others. But some philosophical people have been asking why *three* dimensions particularly—why not another direction at right angles to the other three?—and have even tried to construct a Four-Dimension geometry. Professor Simon Newcomb was expounding this to the New York Mathematical Society only a month or so ago. You know how on a flat surface, which has only two dimensions, we can represent a figure of a three-dimensional solid, and similarly they think that by models of three dimensions they could represent one of four—if they could master the perspective of the thing. See?'

'I think so,' murmured the Provincial Mayor; and, knitting his brows, he lapsed into an introspective state, his lips moving as one who repeats mystic words. 'Yes, I think I see it now,' he said after some time, brightening in a quite transitory manner.

'Well, I do not mind telling you I have been at work upon this geometry of Four Dimensions for some time. Some of my results are curious. For instance, here is a portrait of a man at eight years old, another at fifteen, another at seventeen, another at twenty-three, and so on. All these are evidently sections, as it were, Three-Dimensional representations of his Four-Dimensioned being, which is a fixed and unalterable thing.

'Scientific people,' proceeded the Time Traveller, after the pause required for the proper assimilation of this, 'know very well that Time is only a kind of Space. Here is a popular scientific diagram, a weather record. This line I trace with my finger shows the movement of the barometer. Yesterday it was so high, yesterday night it fell, then this morning it rose again, and so gently upward to here. Surely the mercury did not trace this line in any of the dimensions of Space generally recognized? But certainly it traced such a line, and that line, therefore, we must conclude was along the Time-Dimension.'

'But,' said the Medical Man, staring hard at a coal in the fire, 'if Time is really only a fourth dimension of Space, why is it, and why has it always been, regarded as something different? And why cannot we move in Time as we move about the other dimensions of Space?'

The Time Traveller smiled. 'Are you sure we can move freely in Space? Right and left we can go, backward and forward freely enough, and men always have done so. I admit we move freely in two dimensions. But how about up and down? Gravitation limits us there.'

'Not exactly,' said the Medical Man. 'There are balloons.'

'But before the balloons, save for spasmodic jumping and the inequalities of the surface, man had no freedom of vertical movement.'

'Still they could move a little up and down,' said the Medical Man.

'Easier, far easier down than up.'

'And you cannot move at all in Time, you cannot get away from the present moment.'

'My dear sir, that is just where you are wrong. That is just where the whole world has gone wrong. We are always getting away from the present movement. Our mental existences, which are immaterial and have no dimensions, are passing along the Time-Dimension with a uniform velocity from the cradle to the grave. Just as we should travel *down* if we began our existence fifty miles above the earth's surface.'

'But the great difficulty is this,' interrupted the Psychologist. 'You *can* move about in all directions of Space, but you cannot move about in Time.'

'That is the germ of my great discovery. But you are wrong to say that we cannot move about in Time. For instance, if I am recalling an incident very vividly I go back to the instant of its occurrence: I become absent-minded, as you say. I jump back for a moment. Of course we have no means of staying back for any length of Time, any more than a savage or an animal has of staying six feet above the ground. But a civilized man is better off than the savage in this respect. He can go up against gravitation in a balloon, and why should he not hope that ultimately he may be able to stop or accelerate his drift along the Time-Dimension, or even turn about and travel the other way?'

'Oh, *this*,' began Filby, 'is all —— '

'Why not?' said the Time Traveller.

'It's against reason,' said Filby.

'What reason?' said the Time Traveller.

'You can show black is white by argument,' said Filby, 'but you will never convince me.'

'Possibly not,' said the Time Traveller. 'But now you begin to see the object of my investigations into the geometry of Four Dimensions. Long ago I had a vague inkling of a machine —— '

'To travel through Time!' exclaimed the Very Young Man.

'That shall travel indifferently in any direction of Space and Time, as the driver determines.'

Filby contented himself with laughter.

'But I have experimental verification,' said the Time Traveller.

'It would be remarkably convenient for the historian,' the Psychologist suggested. 'One might travel back and verify the accepted account of the Battle of Hastings, for instance!'

'Don't you think you would attract attention?' said the Medical Man. 'Our ancestors had no great tolerance for anachronisms.'

'One might get one's Greek from the very lips of Homer and Plato,' the Very Young Man thought.

'In which case they would certainly plough you for the Little-go. The German scholars have improved Greek so much.'

'Then there is the future,' said the Very Young Man. 'Just think! One might invest all one's money, leave it to accumulate at interest, and hurry on ahead!'

'To discover a society,' said I, 'erected on a strictly communistic basis.'

'Of all the wild extravagant theories!' began the Psychologist.

'Yes, so it seemed to me, and so I never talked of it until —— '

'Experimental verification!' cried I. 'You are going to verify *that*?'

'The experiment!' cried Filby, who was getting brain-weary.

'Let's see your experiment anyhow,' said the Psychologist, 'though it's all humbug, you know.'

The Time Traveller smiled round at us. Then, still smiling faintly, and with his hands deep in his trousers pockets, he walked slowly out of the room, and we heard his slippers shuffling down the long passage to his laboratory.

The Psychologist looked at us. 'I wonder what he's got?'

'Some sleight-of-hand trick or other,' said the Medical Man, and Filby tried to tell us about a conjurer he had seen at Burslem; but before he had finished his preface the Time Traveller came back, and Filby's anecdote collapsed.

The thing the Time Traveller held in his hand was a glittering metallic framework, scarcely larger than a small clock, and very delicately made. There was ivory in it, and some transparent crystalline substance. And now I must be explicit, for this that follows — unless his explanation is to be accepted — is an absolutely unaccountable thing. He took one of the small octagonal tables that were scattered about the room, and set it in front of the fire, with two legs on the hearthrug. On this table he placed the mechanism. Then he drew up a chair, and sat down. The only other object on the table was a small shaded lamp, the bright light of which fell upon the model. There were also perhaps a dozen candles about, two in brass candlesticks upon the mantel and several in sconces, so that the room was brilliantly illuminated. I sat in a low arm-chair nearest the fire, and I drew this forward so as to be almost between the Time Traveller and the fire-place. Filby sat behind him, looking over his shoulder. The Medical Man and the Provincial Mayor watched him in profile from the right, the Psychologist from the left. The Very Young Man stood behind the Psychologist. We were all on the alert. It appears incredible to me that any kind of trick, however subtly conceived and however adroitly done, could have been played upon us under these conditions.

The Time Traveller looked at us, and then at the mechanism. 'Well?' said the Psychologist.

'This little affair,' said the Time Traveller, resting his elbows upon the table and pressing his hands together above the apparatus, 'is only a model. It is my plan for a machine to travel through time. You will notice that it looks singularly askew, and that there is an odd twinkling appearance about this bar, as though it was in some way unreal.' He pointed to the part with his finger. 'Also, here is one little white lever, and here is another.'

The Medical Man got up out of his chair and peered into the thing. 'It's beautifully made,' he said.

'It took two years to make,' retorted the Time Traveller. Then, when we had all imitated the action of the Medical Man, he said: 'Now I want you clearly to understand that this lever, being pressed over, sends the machine gliding into the future, and this other reverses the motion. This saddle represents the seat of a time traveller. Presently I am going to press the lever, and off the machine will go. It will vanish, pass into future Time, and disappear. Have a good look at the thing. Look at the table too, and satisfy yourselves there is no trickery. I don't want to waste this model, and then be told I'm a quack.'

There was a minute's pause perhaps. The Psychologist seemed about to speak to me, but changed his mind. Then the Time Traveller put forth his finger towards the lever. 'No,' he said suddenly. 'Lend me your hand.' And turning to the Psychologist, he took that individual's hand in his own and told him to put out his forefinger. So that it was the Psychologist himself who sent forth the model Time Machine on its interminable voyage. We all saw the lever turn. I am absolutely certain there was no trickery. There was a breath of wind, and the lamp flame jumped. One of the candles on the mantel was blown out, and the little machine suddenly swung round, became indistinct, was seen as a ghost for a second perhaps, as an eddy of faintly glittering brass and ivory; and it was gone — vanished! Save for the lamp the table was bare.

Everyone was silent for a minute. Then Filby said he was damned.

The Psychologist recovered from his stupor, and suddenly looked under the table. At that the Time Traveller laughed cheerfully. 'Well?' he said, with a reminiscence of the Psychologist. Then, getting up, he went to the tobacco jar on the mantel, and with his back to us began to fill his pipe.

We stared at each other. 'Look here,' said the Medical Man, 'are you in earnest about this? Do you seriously believe that that machine has travelled into time?'

'Certainly,' said the Time Traveller, stooping to light a spill at the fire. Then he turned, lighting his pipe, to look at the Psychologist's face. (The Psychologist, to show that he was not unhinged, helped himself to a cigar and tried to light it uncut.) 'What is more, I have a big machine nearly finished in there' — he indicated the laboratory — 'and when that is put together I mean to have a journey on my own account.'

'You mean to say that that machine has travelled into the future?' said Filby.

'Into the future or the past — I don't, for certain, know which.'

After an interval the Psychologist had an inspiration. 'It must have gone into the past if it has gone anywhere,' he said.

'Why?' said the Time Traveller.

'Because I presume that it has not moved in space, and if it travelled into the future it would still be here all this time, since it must have travelled through this time.'

'But,' I said, 'if it travelled into the past it would have been visible when we came first into this room; and last Thursday when we were here; and the Thursday before that; and so forth!'

'Serious objections,' remarked the Provincial Mayor, with an air of impartiality, turning towards the Time Traveller.

'Not a bit,' said the Time Traveller, and, to the Psychologist: 'You think. You can explain that. It's presentation below the threshold, you know, diluted presentation.'

'Of course,' said the Psychologist, and reassured us. 'That's a simple point of psychology. I should have thought of it. It's plain enough, and helps the paradox delightfully. We cannot see it, nor can we appreciate this machine, any more than we can the spoke of a wheel spinning, or a bullet flying through the air. If it is travelling through time fifty times or a hundred times faster than we are, if it gets through a minute while we get through a second, the impression it creates will of course be only one-fiftieth or one-hundredth of what it would make if it were not travelling in time. That's plain enough.' He passed his hand through the space in which the machine had been. 'You see?' he said, laughing.

We sat and stared at the vacant table for a minute or so. Then the Time Traveller asked us what we thought of it all.

'It sounds plausible enough to-night,' said the Medical Man; 'but wait until to-morrow. Wait for the common sense of the morning.'

'Would you like to see the Time Machine itself?' asked the Time Traveller. And therewith, taking the lamp in his hand, he led the way down the long, draughty corridor to his laboratory. I remember vividly the flickering light, his queer, broad head in silhouette, the dance of the shadows, how we all followed him, puzzled but incredulous, and how there in the laboratory we beheld a larger edition of the little mechanism which we had seen vanish from before our eyes. Parts were of nickel, parts of ivory, parts had certainly been filed or sawn out of rock crystal. The thing was generally complete, but the twisted crystalline bars lay unfinished upon the bench beside some sheets of drawings, and I took one up for a better look at it. Quartz it seemed to be.

'Look here,' said the Medical Man, 'are you perfectly serious? Or is this a trick — like that ghost you showed us last Christmas?'

'Upon that machine,' said the Time Traveller, holding the lamp aloft, 'I intend to explore time. Is that plain? I was never more serious in my life.'

None of us quite knew how to take it.

I caught Filby's eye over the shoulder of the Medical Man, and he winked at me solemnly.

II

I think that at that time none of us quite believed in the Time Machine. The fact is, the Time Traveller was one of those men who are too clever to be believed: you never felt that you saw all round him; you always suspected some subtle reserve, some ingenuity in ambush, behind his lucid frankness. Had Filby shown the model and explained the matter in the Time Traveller's words, we should have shown *him* far less scepticism. For we should have perceived his motives; a pork butcher could understand Filby. But the Time Traveller had more than a touch of whim among his elements, and we distrusted him. Things that would have made the fame of a less clever man seemed tricks in his hands. It is a mistake to do things too easily. The serious people who took him seriously never felt quite sure of his deportment; they were somehow aware that trusting their reputations for judgment with him was like furnishing a nursery with egg-shell china. So I don't think any of us said very much about time travelling in the interval between that Thursday and the next, though its odd potentialities ran, no doubt, in most of our minds: its plausibility, that is, its practical incredibleness, the curious possibilities of anachronism and of utter confusion it suggested. For my own part, I was particularly preoccupied with the trick of the model. That I remember discussing with the Medical Man, whom I met on Friday at the Linnaean. He said he had seen a similar thing at Tübingen, and laid considerable stress on the blowing out of the candle. But how the trick was done he could not explain.

The next Thursday I went again to Richmond — I suppose I was one of the Time Traveller's most constant guests — and, arriving late, found four or five men already assembled in his drawing-room. The Medical Man was standing before the fire with a sheet of paper in one hand and his watch in the other. I looked round for the Time Traveller, and — 'It's half-past seven now,' said the Medical Man. 'I suppose we'd better have dinner?'

'Where's ——?' said I, naming our host.

'You've just come? It's rather odd. He's unavoidably detained. He asks me in this note to lead off with dinner at seven if he's not back. Says he'll explain when he comes.'

'It seems a pity to let the dinner spoil,' said the Editor of a well-known daily paper; and thereupon the Doctor rang the bell.

The Psychologist was the only person besides the Doctor and myself who had attended the previous dinner. The other men were Blank, the Editor afore-mentioned, a certain journalist, and another — a quiet, shy man with a beard — whom I didn't know, and who, as far as my observation went, never opened his mouth all the evening. There was some speculation at the dinner-table about the Time Traveller's absence, and I suggested time travelling, in a half-jocular spirit. The Editor wanted that explained to him, and the Psychologist volunteered a wooden account of the 'ingenious paradox and trick' we had witnessed that day week. He was in the midst of his exposition when the door from the corridor opened slowly and without noise. I was facing the door, and saw it first. 'Hallo!' I said. 'At last!' And the door opened wider, and the Time Traveller stood before us. I gave a cry of surprise. 'Good heavens! man, what's the matter?' cried the Medical Man, who saw him next. And the whole tableful turned towards the door.

He was in an amazing plight. His coat was dusty and dirty, and smeared with green down the sleeves; his hair disordered, and as it seemed to me greyer — either with dust and dirt or because its colour had actually faded. His face was ghastly pale; his chin had a brown cut on it — a cut half healed; his expression was haggard and drawn, as by intense suffering. For a moment he hesitated in the doorway, as if he had been dazzled by the light. Then he came into the room. He walked with just such a limp as I have seen in footsore tramps. We stared at him in silence, expecting him to speak.

He said not a word, but came painfully to the table, and made a motion towards the wine. The Editor filled a glass of champagne, and pushed it towards him. He drained it, and it seemed to do him good: for he looked round the table, and the ghost of his old smile flickered across his face. 'What on earth have you been up to, man?' said the Doctor. The Time Traveller did not seem to hear. 'Don't let me disturb you,' he said, with a certain faltering articulation. 'I'm all right.' He stopped, held out his glass for more, and took it off at a draught. 'That's good,' he said. His eyes grew brighter, and a faint colour came into his cheeks. His glance flickered over our faces with a certain dull approval, and then went round the warm and comfortable room. Then he spoke again, still as it were feeling his way among his words. 'I'm going to wash and dress, and then I'll come down and explain things. . . . Save me some of that mutton. I'm starving for a bit of meat.'

He looked across at the Editor, who was a rare visitor, and hoped he was all right. The Editor began a question. 'Tell you presently,' said the Time Traveller, 'I'm — funny. Be all right in a minute.'

He put down his glass, and walked towards the staircase door. Again I remarked his lameness and the soft padding sound of his footfall, and standing up in my place, I saw his feet as he went out. He had nothing on them but a pair of tattered, blood-stained socks. Then the door closed upon him. I had half a mind to follow, till I remembered how he detested any fuss about himself. For a minute, perhaps, my mind was wool-gathering. Then, 'Remarkable Behaviour of an Eminent Scientist,' I heard the Editor say, thinking (after his wont) in head-lines. And this brought my attention back to the bright dinner-table.

'What's the game?' said the Journalist. 'Has he been doing the Amateur Cadger? I don't follow.' I met the eye of the Psychologist, and read my own interpretation in his face. I thought of the Time Traveller limping painfully upstairs. I don't think any one else had noticed his lameness.

The first to recover completely from this surprise was the Medical Man, who rang the bell—the Time Traveller hated to have servants waiting at dinner—for a hot plate. At that the Editor turned to his knife and fork with a grunt, and the Silent Man followed suit. The dinner was resumed. Conversation was exclama-tory for a little while, with gaps of wonderment; and then the Editor got fervent in his curiosity. 'Does our friend eke out his modest income with a crossing? or has he his Nebuchadnezzar phases?' he inquired. 'I feel assured it's this business of the Time Machine,' I said, and took up the Psychologist's account of our previous meeting. The new guests were frankly incredulous. The Editor raised objections. 'What *was* this time travelling? A man couldn't cover himself with dust by rolling in a paradox, could he?' And then, as the idea came home to him, he resorted to caricature. Hadn't they any clothes-brushes in the Future? The Journalist, too, would not believe at any price, and joined the Editor in the easy work of heaping ridicule on the whole thing. They were both the new kind of journalist—very joyous, irreverent young men. 'Our Special Correspondent in the Day after To-morrow reports,' the Journalist was saying—or rather shouting—when the Time Traveller came back. He was dressed in ordinary evening clothes, and nothing save his haggard look remained of the change that had startled me.

'I say,' said the Editor hilariously, 'these chaps here say you have been travelling into the middle of next week!! Tell us all about little Rosebery, will you? What will you take for the lot?'

The Time Traveller came to the place reserved for him without a word. He smiled quietly, in his old way. 'Where's my mutton?' he said. 'What a treat it is to stick a fork into meat again!'

'Story!' cried the Editor.

'Story be damned!' said the Time Traveller. 'I want something to eat. I won't say a word until I get some peptone into my arteries. Thanks. And the salt.'

'One word,' said I. 'Have you been time travelling?'

'Yes,' said the Time Traveller, with his mouth full, nodding his head.

'I'd give a shilling a line for a verbatim note,' said the Editor. The Time Traveller pushed his glass towards the Silent Man and rang it with his fingernail; at which the Silent Man, who had been staring at his face, started convulsively, and poured him wine. The rest of the dinner was uncomfortable. For my own part, sudden questions kept on rising to my lips, and I dare say it was the same with the others. The Journalist tried to relieve the tension by telling anecdotes of Hettie Potter. The Time Traveller devoted his attention to his dinner, and displayed the appetite of a tramp. The Medical Man smoked a cigarette, and watched the Time Traveller through his eyelashes. The Silent Man seemed even more clumsy than usual, and drank champagne with regularity and determination out of sheer nervousness. At last the Time Traveller pushed his plate away, and looked round us. 'I suppose I must apologize,' he said. 'I was simply starving. I've had a most amazing time.' He reached out his hand for a cigar, and cut the end. 'But come into the smoking-room. It's too long a story to tell over greasy plates.' And ringing the bell in passing, he led the way into the adjoining room.

'You have told Blank, and Dash, and Chose about the machine?' he said to me, leaning back in his easy-chair and naming the three new guests.

'But the thing's a mere paradox,' said the Editor.

'I can't argue to-night. I don't mind telling you the story, but I can't argue. I will,' he went on, 'tell you the story of what has happened to me, if you like, but you must refrain from interruptions. I want to tell it. Badly. Most of it will sound like lying. So be it! It's true — every word of it, all the same. I was in my laboratory at four o'clock, and since then . . . I've lived eight days . . . such days as no human being ever lived before! I'm nearly worn out, but I shan't sleep till I've told this thing over to you. Then I shall go to bed. But no interruptions! Is it agreed?'

'Agreed,' said the Editor, and the rest of us echoed 'Agreed.' And with that the Time Traveller began his story as I have set it forth. He sat back in his chair at first, and spoke like a weary man. Afterwards he got more animated. In writing it down I feel with only too much keenness the inadequacy of pen and ink — and, above all, my own inadequacy — to express its quality. You read, I will suppose, attentively enough; but you cannot see the speaker's white, sincere face in the bright circle of the little lamp, nor hear the intonation of his voice. You cannot know how his expression followed the turns of his story! Most of us hearers were in shadow, for the candles in the smoking-room had not been lighted, and only the face of the Journalist and the legs of the Silent Man from the knees downward were illuminated. At first we glanced now and again at each other. After a time we ceased to do that, and looked only at the Time Traveller's face.

III

'I told some of you last Thursday of the principles of the Time Machine, and showed you the actual thing itself, incomplete in the workshop. There it is now, a little travel-worn, truly; and one of the ivory bars is cracked, and a brass rail bent; but the rest of it's sound enough. I expected to finish it on Friday, but on Friday, when the putting together was nearly done, I found that one of the nickel bars was exactly one inch too short, and this I had to get remade; so that the thing was not complete until this morning. It was at ten o'clock to-day that the first of all Time Machines began its career. I gave it a last tap, tried all the screws again, put one more drop of oil on the quartz rod, and sat myself in the saddle. I suppose a suicide who holds a pistol to his skull feels much the same wonder at what will come next as I felt then. I took the starting lever in one hand and the stopping one in the other, pressed the first, and almost immediately the second. I seemed to reel; I felt a nightmare sensation of falling; and, looking round, I saw the laboratory exactly as before. Had anything happened? For a moment I suspected that my intellect had tricked me. Then I noted the clock. A moment before, as it seemed, it had stood at a minute or so past ten; now it was nearly half-past three!

'I drew a breath, set my teeth, gripped the starting lever with both hands, and went off with a thud. The laboratory got hazy and went dark. Mrs. Watchett came in and walked, apparently without seeing me, towards the garden door. I suppose it took her a minute or so to traverse the place, but to me she seemed to shoot across the room like a rocket. I pressed the lever over to its extreme position. The night came like the turning out of a lamp, and in another moment came to-morrow. The laboratory grew faint and hazy, then fainter and ever fainter. To-morrow night came black, then day again, night again, day again, faster and faster still. An eddying murmur filled my ears, and a strange, dumb confusedness descended on my mind.

'I am afraid I cannot convey the peculiar sensations of time travelling. They are excessively unpleasant. There is a feeling exactly like that one has upon a switchback — of a helpless headlong motion! I felt the same horrible anticipation, too, of an imminent smash. As I put on pace, night followed day like the flapping of a black wing. The dim suggestion of the laboratory seemed presently to fall away from me, and I saw the sun hopping swiftly across the sky, leaping it every minute, and every minute marking a day. I supposed the laboratory had been destroyed and I had come into the open air. I had a dim impression of scaffolding, but I was already going too fast to be conscious of any moving things. The slowest snail that ever crawled dashed by too fast for me. The twinkling succession of darkness and light was excessively painful to the eye. Then, in the intermittent darknesses, I saw the moon spinning swiftly through her quarters from new to full, and had a faint glimpse of the circling stars. Presently, as I went on, still gaining velocity, the palpitation of night and day merged into one continuous greyness; the sky took on a wonderful deepness of blue, a splendid luminous color like that of early twilight; the jerking sun became a streak of fire, a brilliant arch, in space; the moon a fainter fluctuating band; and I could see nothing of the stars, save now and then a brighter circle flickering in the blue.

'The landscape was misty and vague. I was still on the hill-side upon which this house now stands, and the shoulder rose above me grey and dim. I saw trees growing and changing like puffs of vapour, now brown, now green; they grew, spread, shivered, and passed away. I saw huge buildings rise up faint and fair, and pass like dreams. The whole surface of the earth seemed changed — melting and flowing under my eyes. The little hands upon the dials that registered my speed raced round faster and faster. Presently I noted that the sun belt swayed up and down, from solstice to solstice, in a minute or less, and that consequently my pace was over a year a minute; and minute by minute the white snow flashed across the world, and vanished, and was followed by the bright, brief green of spring.

'The unpleasant sensations of the start were less poignant now. They merged at last into a kind of hysterical exhilaration. I remarked indeed a clumsy swaying of the machine, for which I was unable to account. But my mind was too confused to attend to it, so with a kind of madness growing upon me, I flung myself into futurity. At first I scarce thought of stopping, scarce thought of anything but these new sensations. But presently a fresh series of impressions grew up in my mind — a certain curiosity and therewith a certain dread — until at last they took complete possession of me. What strange developments of human-ity, what wonderful advances upon our rudimentary civilization, I thought, might not appear when I came to look nearly into the dim elusive world that raced and fluctuated before my eyes! I saw great and splendid architecture rising about me, more massive than any buildings of our own time, and yet, as it seemed, built of glimmer and mist. I saw a richer green flow up the hill-side, and remain there without any wintry intermission. Even through the veil of my confusion the earth seemed very fair. And so my mind came round to the business of stopping.

'The peculiar risk lay in the possibility of my finding some substance in the space which I, or the machine, occupied. So long as I travelled at a high velocity through time, this scarcely mattered; I was, so to speak, attenuated—was slipping like a vapour through the interstices of intervening substances! But to come to a stop involved the jamming of myself, molecule by molecule, into whatever lay in my way; meant bringing my atoms into such intimate contact with those of the obstacle that a profound chemical reaction—possibly a far-reaching explosion—would result, and blow myself and my apparatus out of all possible dimensions—into the Unknown. This possibility had occurred to me again and again while I was making the machine; but then I had cheerfully accepted it as an unavoidable risk—one of the risks a man has got to take! Now the risk was inevitable, I no longer saw it in the same cheerful light. The fact is that, insensibly, the absolute strangeness of everything, the sickly jarring and swaying of the machine, above all, the feeling of prolonged falling, had absolutely upset my nerve. I told myself that I could never stop, and with a gust of petulance I resolved to stop forthwith. Like an impatient fool, I lugged over the lever, and incontinently the thing went reeling over, and I was flung headlong through the air.

'There was the sound of a clap of thunder in my ears. I may have been stunned for a moment. A pitiless hail was hissing round me, and I was sitting on soft turf in front of the overset machine. Everything still seemed grey, but presently I remarked that the confusion in my ears was gone. I looked round me. I was on what seemed to be a little lawn in a garden, surrounded by rhododendron bushes, and I noticed that their mauve and purple blossoms were dropping in a shower under the beating of the hail-stones. The rebounding, dancing hail hung in a cloud over the machine, and drove along the ground like smoke. In a moment I was wet to the skin. "Fine hospitality," said I, "to a man who has travelled innumerable years to see you."

'Presently I thought what a fool I was to get wet. I stood up and looked round me. A colossal figure, carved apparently in some white stone, loomed indistinctly beyond the rhododendrons through the hazy downpour. But all else of the world was invisible.

'My sensations would be hard to describe. As the columns of hail grew thinner, I saw the white figure more distinctly. It was very large, for a silver birch-tree touched its shoulder. It was of white marble, in shape something like a winged sphinx, but the wings, instead of being carried vertically at the sides, were spread so that it seemed to hover. The pedestal, it appeared to me, was of bronze, and was thick with verdigris. It chanced that the face was towards me; the sightless eyes seemed to watch me; there was the faint shadow of a smile on the lips. It was greatly weather-worn, and that imparted an unpleasant suggestion of disease. I stood looking at it for a little space—half a minute, perhaps, or half an hour. It seemed to advance and to recede as the hail drove before it denser or thinner. At last I tore my eyes from it for a moment, and saw that the hail curtain had worn threadbare, and that the sky was lightening with the promise of the sun.

'I looked up again at the crouching white shape, and the full temerity of my voyage came suddenly upon me. What might appear when that hazy curtain was altogether withdrawn? What might not have happened to men? What if cruelty had grown into a common passion? What if in this interval the race had lost its manliness, and had developed into something inhuman, unsympathetic, and overwhelmingly powerful? I might seem some old-world savage animal, only the more dreadful and disgusting for our common likeness — a foul creature to be incontinently slain.

'Already I saw other vast shapes — huge buildings with intricate parapets and tall columns, with a wooded hill-side dimly creeping in upon me through the lessening storm. I was seized with a panic fear. I turned frantically to the Time Machine, and strove hard to readjust it. As I did so the shafts of the sun smote through the thunderstorm. The grey downpour was swept aside and vanished like the trailing garments of a ghost. Above me, in the intense blue of the summer sky, some faint brown shreds of cloud whirled into nothingness. The great buildings about me stood out clear and distinct, shining with the wet of the thunderstorm, and picked out in white by the unmelted hailstones piled along their courses. I felt naked in a strange world. I felt as perhaps a bird may feel in the clear air, knowing the hawk wings above and will swoop. My fear grew to frenzy. I took a breathing space, set my teeth, and again grappled fiercely, wrist and knee, with the machine. It gave under my desperate onset and turned over. It struck my chin violently. One hand on the saddle, the other on the lever, I stood panting heavily in attitude to mount again.

'But with this recovery of a prompt retreat my courage recovered. I looked more curiously and less fearfully at this world of the remote future. In a circular opening, high up in the wall of the nearer house, I saw a group of figures clad in rich soft robes. They had seen me, and their faces were directed towards me.

'Then I heard voices approaching me. Coming through the bushes by the White Sphinx were the heads and shoulders of men running. One of these emerged in a pathway leading straight to the little lawn upon which I stood with my machine. He was a slight creature — perhaps four feet high — clad in a purple tunic, girdled at the waist with a leather belt. Sandals or buskins — I could not clearly distinguish which — were on his feet; his legs were bare to the knees, and his head was bare. Noticing that, I noticed for the first time how warm the air was.

'He struck me as being a very beautiful and graceful creature, but indescribably frail. His flushed face reminded me of the more beautiful kind of consumptive — that hectic beauty of which we used to hear so much. At the sight of him I suddenly regained confidence. I took my hands from the machine.

IV

'In another moment we were standing face to face, I and this fragile thing out of futurity. He came straight up to me and laughed into my eyes. The absence from his bearing of any sign of fear struck me at once. Then he turned to the two others who were following him and spoke to them in a strange and very sweet and liquid tongue.

'There were others coming, and presently a little group of perhaps eight or ten of these exquisite creatures were about me. One of them addressed me. It came into my head, oddly enough, that my voice was too harsh and deep for them. So I shook my head, and, pointing to my ears, shook it again. He came a step forward, hesitated, and then touched my hand. Then I felt other soft little tentacles upon my back and shoulders. They wanted to make sure I was real. There was nothing in this at all alarming. Indeed, there was something in these pretty little people that inspired confidence — a graceful gentleness, a certain childlike ease. And besides, they looked so frail that I could fancy myself flinging the whole dozen of them about like nine-pins. But I made a sudden motion to warn them when I saw their little pink hands feeling at the Time Machine. Happily then, when it was not too late, I thought of a danger I had hitherto forgotten, and reaching over the bars of the machine I unscrewed the little levers that would set it in motion, and put these in my pocket. Then I turned again to see what I could do in the way of communication.

'And then, looking more nearly into their features, I saw some further peculiarities in their Dresden-china type of prettiness. Their hair, which was uniformly curly, came to a sharp end at the neck and cheek; there was not the faintest suggestion of it on the face, and their ears were singularly minute. The mouths were small, with bright red, rather thin lips, and the little chins ran to a point. The eyes were large and mild; and — this may seem egotism on my part — I fancied even that there was a certain lack of the interest I might have expected in them.

'As they made no effort to communicate with me, but simply stood round me smiling and speaking in soft cooing notes to each other, I began the conversation. I pointed to the Time Machine and to myself. Then hesitating for a moment how to express time, I pointed to the sun. At once a quaintly pretty little figure in chequered purple and white followed my gesture, and then astonished me by imitating the sound of thunder.

'For a moment I was staggered, though the import of his gesture was plain enough. The question had come into my mind abruptly: were these creatures fools? You may hardly understand how it took me. You see I had always anticipated that the people of the year Eight Hundred and Two Thousand odd would be incredibly in front of us in knowledge, art, everything. Then one of them suddenly asked me a question that showed him to be on the intellectual level of one of our five-year-old children — asked me, in fact, if I had come from the sun in a thunderstorm! It let loose the judgment I had suspended upon their clothes, their frail light limbs, and fragile features. A flow of disappointment rushed across my mind. For a moment I felt that I had built the Time Machine in vain.

'I nodded, pointed to the sun, and gave them such a vivid rendering of a thunderclap as startled them. They all withdrew a pace or so and bowed. Then came one laughing towards me, carrying a chain of beautiful flowers altogether new to me, and put it about my neck. The idea was received with melodious applause; and presently they were all running to and fro for flowers, and laughingly flinging them upon me until I was almost smothered with blossom. You who have never seen the like can scarcely imagine what delicate and wonderful flowers countless years of culture had created. Then someone suggested that their plaything should be exhibited in the nearest building, and so I was led past the sphinx of white marble, which had seemed to watch me all the while with a smile at my astonishment, towards a vast grey edifice of fretted stone. As I went with them the memory of my confident anticipations of a profoundly grave and intellectual posterity came, with irresistible merriment, to my mind.

'The building had a huge entry, and was altogether of colossal dimensions. I was naturally most occupied with the growing crowd of little people, and with the big open portals that yawned before me shadowy and mysterious. My general impression of the world I saw over their heads was a tangled waste of beautiful bushes and flowers, a long-neglected and yet weedless garden. I saw a number of tall spikes of strange white flowers, measuring a foot perhaps across the spread of the waxen petals. They grew scattered, as if wild, among the variegated shrubs, but, as I say, I did not examine them closely at this time. The Time Machine was left deserted on the turf among the rhododendrons.

'The arch of the doorway was richly carved, but naturally I did not observe the carving very narrowly, though I fancied I saw suggestions of old Phoenician decorations as I passed through, and it struck me that they were very badly broken and weather-worn. Several more brightly clad people met me in the doorway, and so we entered, I, dressed in dingy nineteenth-century garments, looking grotesque enough, garlanded with flowers, and surrounded by an eddy-ing mass of bright, soft-colored robes and shining white limbs, in a melodious whirl of laughter and laughing speech.

'The big doorway opened into a proportionately great hall hung with brown. The roof was in shadow, and the windows, partially glazed with coloured glass and partially unglazed, admitted a tempered light. The floor was made up of huge blocks of some very hard white metal, not plates nor slabs — blocks, and it was so much worn, as I judged by the going to and fro of past generations, as to be deeply channelled along the more frequented ways. Transverse to the length were innumerable tables made of slabs of polished stone, raised perhaps a foot from the floor, and upon these were heaps of fruits. Some I recognized as a kind of hypertrophied raspberry and orange, but for the most part they were strange.

'Between the tables was scattered a great number of cushions. Upon these my conductors seated themselves, signing for me to do likewise. With a pretty absence of ceremony they began to eat the fruit with their hands, flinging peel and stalks, and so forth, into the round openings in the sides of the tables. I was not loath to follow their example, for I felt thirsty and hungry. As I did so I surveyed the hall at my leisure.

'And perhaps the thing that struck me most was its dilapidated look. The stained-glass windows, which displayed only a geometrical pattern, were broken in many places, and the curtains that hung across the lower end were thick with dust. And it caught my eye that the corner of the marble table near me was fractured. Nevertheless, the general effect was extremely rich and picturesque. There were, perhaps, a couple of hundred people dining in the hall, and most of them, seated as near to me as they could come, were watching me with interest, their little eyes shining over the fruit they were eating. All were clad in the same soft, and yet strong, silky material.

'Fruit, by the by, was all their diet. These people of the remote future were strict vegetarians, and while I was with them, in spite of some carnal cravings, I had to be frugivorous also. Indeed, I found afterwards that horses, cattle, sheep, dogs, had followed the Ichthyosaurus into extinction. But the fruits were very delightful; one, in particular, that seemed to be in season all the time I was there—a floury thing in a three-sided husk—was especially good, and I made it my staple. At first I was puzzled by all these strange fruits, and by the strange flowers I saw, but later I began to perceive their import.

'However, I am telling you of my fruit dinner in the distant future now. So soon as my appetite was a little checked, I determined to make a resolute attempt to learn the speech of these new men of mine. Clearly that was the next thing to do. The fruits seemed a convenient thing to begin upon, and holding one of these up I began a series of interrogative sounds and gestures. I had some considerable difficulty in conveying my meaning. At first my efforts met with a stare of surprise or inextinguishable laughter, but presently a fair-haired little creature seemed to grasp my intention and repeated a name. They had to chatter and explain the business at great length to each other, and my first attempts to make the exquisite little sounds of their language caused an immense amount of amusement. However, I felt like a schoolmaster amidst children, and persisted, and presently I had a score of noun substantives at least at my command; and then I got to demonstrative pronouns, and even the verb "to eat." But it was slow work, and the little people soon tired and wanted to get away from my interrogations, so I determined, rather of necessity, to let them give their lessons in little doses when they felt inclined. And very little doses I found they were before long, for I never met people more indolent or more easily fatigued.

'A queer thing I soon discovered about my little hosts, and that was their lack of interest. They would come to me with eager cries of astonishment, like children, but like children they would soon stop examining me and wander away after some other toy. The dinner and my conversational beginnings ended, I noted for the first time that almost all those who had surrounded me at first were gone. It is odd, too, how speedily I came to disregard these little people. I went out through the portal into the sunlit world again so soon as my hunger was satisfied. I was continually meeting more of these men of the future, who would follow me a little distance, chatter and laugh about me, and, having smiled and gesticulated in a friendly way, leave me again to my own devices.

'The calm of evening was upon the world as I emerged from the great hall, and the scene was lit by the warm glow of the setting sun. At first things were very confusing. Everything was so entirely different from the world I had known—even the flowers. The big building I had left was situated on the slope of a broad river valley, but the Thames had shifted perhaps a mile from its present position. I resolved to mount to the summit of a crest, perhaps a mile and a half away, from which I could get a wider view of this our planet in the year Eight Hundred and Two Thousand Seven Hundred and One A.D. For that, I should explain, was the date the little dials of my machine recorded.

'As I walked I was watchful for every impression that could possibly help to explain the condition of ruinous splendour in which I found the world—for ruinous it was. A little way up the hill, for instance, was a great heap of granite, bound together by masses of aluminium, a vast labyrinth of precipitous walls and crumbled heaps, amidst which were thick heaps of very beautiful pagoda-like plants—nettles possibly—but wonderfully tinted with brown about the leaves, and incapable of stinging. It was evidently the derelict remains of some vast structure, to what end built I could not determine. It was here that I was destined, at a later date, to have a very strange experience—the first intimation of a still stranger discovery—but of that I will speak in its proper place.

'Looking round with a sudden thought, from a terrace on which I rested for a while, I realized that there were no small houses to be seen. Apparently the single house, and possibly even the household, had vanished. Here and there among the greenery were palace-like buildings, but the house and the cottage, which form such characteristic features of our own English landscape, had disappeared.

' "Communism," said I to myself.

'And on the heels of that came another thought. I looked at the half-dozen little figures that were following me. Then, in a flash, I perceived that all had the same form of costume, the same soft hairless visage, and the same girlish rotundity of limb. It may seem strange, perhaps, that I had not noticed this before. But everything was so strange. Now, I saw the fact plainly enough. In costume, and in all the differences of texture and bearing that now mark off the sexes from each other, these people of the future were alike. And the children seemed to my eyes to be but the miniatures of their parents. I judged, then, that the children of that time were extremely precocious, physically at least, and I found afterwards abundant verification of my opinion.

'Seeing the ease and security in which these people were living, I felt that this close resemblance of the sexes was after all what one would expect; for the strength of a man and the softness of a woman, the institution of the family, and the differentiation of occupations are mere militant necessities of an age of physical force; where population is balanced and abundant, much child-bearing becomes an evil rather than a blessing to the State; where violence comes but rarely and off-spring are secure, there is less necessity—indeed there is no necessity—for an efficient family, and the specialization of the sexes with reference to their children's needs disappears. We see some beginnings of this even in our own time, and in this future age it was complete. This, I must remind you, was my speculation at the time. Later, I was to appreciate how far it fell short of the reality.

'While I was musing upon these things, my attention was attracted by a pretty little structure, like a well under a cupola. I thought in a transitory way of the oddness of wells still existing, and then resumed the thread of my speculations. There were no large buildings towards the top of the hill, and as my walking powers were evidently miraculous, I was presently left alone for the first time. With a strange sense of freedom and adventure I pushed on up to the crest.

'There I found a seat of some yellow metal that I did not recognize, corroded in places with a kind of pinkish rust and half smothered in soft moss, the arm-rests cast and filed into the resemblance of griffins' heads. I sat down on it, and I surveyed the broad view of our old world under the sunset of that long day. It was as sweet and fair a view as I have ever seen. The sun had already gone below the horizon and the west was flaming gold, touched with some horizontal bars of purple and crimson. Below was the valley of the Thames, in which the river lay like a band of burnished steel. I have already spoken of the great palaces dotted about among the variegated greenery, some in ruins and some still occupied. Here and there rose a white or silvery figure in the waste garden of the earth, here and there came the sharp vertical line of some cupola or obelisk. There were no hedges, no signs of proprietary rights, no evidences of agriculture; the whole earth had become a garden.

'So watching, I began to put my interpretation upon the things I had seen, and as it shaped itself to me that evening, my interpretation was something in this way. (Afterwards I found I had got only a half-truth — or only a glimpse of one facet of the truth.)

'It seemed to me that I happened upon humanity upon the wane. The ruddy sunset set me thinking of the sunset of mankind. For the first time I began to realize an odd consequence of the social effort in which we are at present engaged. And yet, come to think, it is a logical consequence enough. Strength is the outcome of need; security sets a premium on feebleness. The work of ameliorating the conditions of life — the true civilizing process that makes life more and more secure — had gone steadily on to a climax. One triumph of a united humanity over Nature had followed another. Things that are now mere dreams had become projects deliberately put in hand and carried forward. And the harvest was what I saw!

'After all, the sanitation and the agriculture of to-day are still in the rudimentary stage. The science of our time has attacked but a little department of the field of human disease, but, even so, it spreads its operations very steadily and persistently. Our agriculture and horticulture destroy a weed just here and there and cultivate perhaps a score or so of wholesome plants, leaving the greater number to fight out a balance as they can. We improve our favourite plants and animals — and how few they are — gradually by selective breeding; now a new and better peach, now a seedless grape, now a sweeter and larger flower, now a more convenient breed of cattle. We improve them gradually, because our ideals are vague and tentative, and our knowledge is very limited; because Nature, too, is shy and slow in our clumsy hands. Some day all this will be better organized, and still better. That is the drift of the current in spite of the eddies. The whole world will be intelligent, educated, and co-operating; things will move faster and faster towards the subjugation of Nature. In the end, wisely and carefully we shall readjust the balance of animal and vegetable life to suit our human needs.

'This adjustment, I say, must have been done, and done well; done indeed for all Time, in the space of Time across which my machine had leaped. The air was free from gnats, the earth from weeds or fungi; everywhere were fruits and sweet and delightful flowers, brilliant butterflies flew hither and thither. The ideal of preventive medicine was attained. Diseases had been stamped out. I saw no evidence of any contagious diseases during all my stay. And I shall have to tell you later that even the processes of putrefaction and decay had been profoundly affected by these changes.

'Social triumphs, too, had been effected. I saw mankind housed in splendid shelters, gloriously clothed, and as yet I had found them engaged in no toil. There were no signs of struggle, neither social nor economical struggle. The shop, the advertisement, traffic, all that commerce which constitutes the body of our world, was gone. It was natural on that golden evening that I should jump at the idea of a social paradise. The difficulty of increasing population had been met, I guessed, and population had ceased to increase.

'But with this change in condition comes inevitably adaptations to the change. What, unless biological science is a mass of errors, is the cause of human intelligence and vigour? Hardship and freedom: conditions under which the active, strong, and subtle survive and the weaker go to the wall; conditions that put a premium upon the loyal alliance of capable men, upon self-restraint, patience, and decision. And the institution of the family, and the emotions that arise therein, the fierce jealousy, the tenderness for offspring, parental self-devotion, all found their justification and support in the imminent dangers of the young. Now, where are these imminent dangers? There is a sentiment arising, and it will grow, against connubial jealousy, against fierce maternity, against passion of all sorts; unnecessary things now, and things that make us uncomfortable, savage survivals, discords in a refined and pleasant life.

'I thought of the physical slightness of the people, their lack of intelligence, and those big abundant ruins, and it strengthened my belief in a perfect conquest of Nature. For after the battle comes Quiet. Humanity had been strong, energetic, and intelligent, and had used all its abundant vitality to alter the conditions under which it lived. And now came the reaction of the altered conditions.

'Under the new conditions of perfect comfort and security, that restless energy, that with us is strength, would become weakness. Even in our own time certain tendencies and desires, once necessary to survival, are a constant source of failure. Physical courage and the love of battle, for instance, are no great help— may even be hindrances—to a civilized man. And in a state of physical balance and security, power, intellectual as well as physical, would be out of place. For countless years I judged there had been no danger of war or solitary violence, no danger from wild beasts, no wasting disease to require strength of constitution, no need of toil. For such a life, what we should call the weak are as well equipped as the strong, are indeed no longer weak. Better equipped indeed they are, for the strong would be fretted by an energy for which there was no outlet. No doubt the exquisite beauty of the buildings I saw was the outcome of the last surgings of the now purposeless energy of mankind before it settled down into perfect harmony with the conditions under which it lived—the flourish of that triumph which began the last great peace. This has ever been the fate of energy in security; it takes to art and to eroticism, and then come languor and decay.

'Even this artistic impetus would at last die away—had almost died in the Time I saw. To adorn themselves with flowers, to dance, to sing in the sunlight: so much was left of the artistic spirit, and no more. Even that would fade in the end into a contented inactivity. We are kept keen on the grindstone of pain and necessity, and, it seemed to me, that here was that hateful grindstone broken at last!

'As I stood there in the gathering dark I thought that in this simple explanation I had mastered the problem of the world—mastered the whole secret of these delicious people. Possibly the checks they had devised for the increase of population had succeeded too well, and their numbers had rather diminished than kept stationary. That would account for the abandoned ruins. Very simple was my explanation, and plausible enough—as most wrong theories are!

V

'As I stood there musing over this too perfect triumph of man, the full moon, yellow and gibbous, came up out of an overflow of silver light in the north-east. The bright little figures ceased to move about below, a noiseless owl flitted by, and I shivered with the chill of the night. I determined to descend and find where I could sleep.

'I looked for the building I knew. Then my eye travelled along to the figure of the White Sphinx upon the pedestal of bronze, growing distinct as the light of the rising moon grew brighter. I could see the silver birch against it. There was the tangle of rhododendron bushes, black in the pale light, and there was the little lawn. I looked at the lawn again. A queer doubt chilled my complacency. "No," said I stoutly to myself, "that was not the lawn."

'But it *was* the lawn. For the white leprous face of the sphinx was towards it. Can you imagine what I felt as this conviction came home to me? But you cannot. The Time Machine was gone!

'At once, like a lash across the face, came the possibility of losing my own age, of being left helpless in this strange new world. The bare thought of it was an actual physical sensation. I could feel it grip me at the throat and stop my breathing. In another moment I was in a passion of fear and running with great leaping strides down the slope. Once I fell headlong and cut my face; I lost no time in stanching the blood, but jumped up and ran on, with a warm trickle down my cheek and chin. All the time I ran I was saying to myself: "They have moved it a little, pushed it under the bushes out of the way." Nevertheless, I ran with all my might. All the time, with the certainty that sometimes comes with excessive dread, I knew that such assurance was folly, knew instinctively that the machine was removed out of my reach. My breath came with pain. I suppose I covered the whole distance from the hill crest to the little lawn, two miles perhaps, in ten minutes. And I am not a young man. I cursed aloud, as I ran, at my confident folly in leaving the machine, wasting good breath thereby. I cried aloud, and none answered. Not a creature seemed to be stirring in that moonlit world.

'When I reached the lawn my worst fears were realized. Not a trace of the thing was to be seen. I felt faint and cold when I faced the empty space among the black tangle of bushes. I ran around it furiously, as if the thing might be hidden in a corner, and then stopped abruptly, with my hands clutching my hair. Above me towered the sphinx, upon the bronze pedestal, white, shining, leprous, in the light of the rising moon. It seemed to smile in mockery of my dismay.

'I might have consoled myself by imagining the little people had put the mechanism in some shelter for me, had I not felt assured of their physical and intellectual inadequacy. That is what dismayed me: the sense of some hitherto unsuspected power, through whose intervention my invention had vanished. Yet, for one thing I felt assured: unless some other age had produced its exact duplicate, the machine could not have moved in time. The attachment of the levers—I will show you the method later—prevented any one from tampering with it in that way when they were removed. It had moved, and was hid, only in space. But then, where could it be?

'I think I must have had a kind of frenzy. I remember running violently in and out among the moonlit bushes all round the sphinx, and startling some white animal that, in the dim light, I took for a small deer. I remember, too, late that night, beating the bushes with my clenched fist until my knuckles were gashed and bleeding from the broken twigs. Then, sobbing and raving in my anguish of mind, I went down to the great building of stone. The big hall was dark, silent, and deserted. I slipped on the uneven floor, and fell over one of the malachite tables, almost breaking my shin. I lit a match and went on past the dusty curtains, of which I have told you.

'There I found a second great hall covered with cushions, upon which, perhaps, a score or so of the little people were sleeping. I have no doubt they found my second appearance strange enough, coming suddenly out of the quiet darkness with inarticulate noises and the splutter and flare of a match. For they had forgotten about matches. "Where is my Time Machine?" I began, bawling like an angry child, laying hands upon them and shaking them up together. It must have been very queer to them. Some laughed, most of them looked sorely frightened. When I saw them standing round me, it came into my head that I was doing as foolish a thing as it was possible for me to do under the circumstances, in trying to revive the sensation of fear. For, reasoning from their daylight behaviour, I thought that fear must be forgotten.

'Abruptly, I dashed down the match, and, knocking one of the people over in my course, went blundering across the big dining-hall again, out under the moonlight. I heard cries of terror and their little feet running and stumbling this way and that. I do not remember all I did as the moon crept up the sky. I suppose it was the unexpected nature of my loss that maddened me. I felt hopelessly cut off from my own kind—a strange animal in an unknown world. I must have raved to and fro, screaming and crying upon God and Fate. I have a memory of horrible fatigue, as the long night of despair wore away; of looking in this impossible place and that; of groping among moon-lit ruins and touching strange creatures in the black shadows; at last, of lying on the ground near the sphinx and weeping with absolute wretchedness. I had nothing left but misery. Then I slept, and when I woke again it was full day, and a couple of sparrows were hopping round me on the turf within reach of my arm.

'I sat up in the freshness of the morning, trying to remember how I had got there, and why I had such a profound sense of desertion and despair. Then things came clear in my mind. With the plain, reasonable daylight, I could look my circumstances fairly in the face. I saw the wild folly of my frenzy overnight, and I could reason with myself. "Suppose the worst?" I said. "Suppose the machine altogether lost—perhaps destroyed? It behoves me to be calm and patient, to learn the way of the people, to get a clear idea of the method of my loss, and the means of getting materials and tools; so that in the end, perhaps, I may make another." That would be my only hope, perhaps, but better than despair. And, after all, it was a beautiful and curious world.

'But probably, the machine had only been taken away. Still, I must be calm and patient, find its hiding place, and recover it by force or cunning. And with that I scrambled to my feet and looked about me, wondering where I could bathe. I felt weary, stiff, and travel-soiled. The freshness of the morning made me desire an equal freshness. I had exhausted my emotion. Indeed, as I went about my business, I found myself wondering at my intense excitement overnight. I made a careful examination of the ground about the little lawn. I wasted some time in futile questionings, conveyed, as well as I was able, to such of the little people as came by. They all failed to understand my gestures; some were simply stolid, some thought it was a jest and laughed at me. I had the hardest task in the world to keep my hands off their pretty laughing faces. It was a foolish impulse, but the devil begotten of fear and blind anger was ill curbed and still eager to take advantage of my perplexity. The turf gave better counsel. I found a groove ripped in it, about midway between the pedestal of the sphinx and the marks of my feet where, on arrival, I had struggled with the overturned machine. There were other signs of removal about, with queer narrow footprints like those I could imagine made by a sloth. This directed my closer attention to the pedestal. It was, as I think I have said, of bronze. It was not a mere block, but highly decorated with deep framed panels on either side. I went and rapped at these. The pedestal was hollow. Examining the panels with care I found them discontinuous with the frames. There were no handles or keyholes, but possibly the panels, if they were doors, as I supposed, opened from within. One thing was clear enough to my mind. It took no very great mental effort to infer that my Time Machine was inside that pedestal. But how it got there was a different problem.

'I saw the heads of two orange-clad people coming through the bushes and under some blossom-covered apple-trees towards me. I turned smiling to them and beckoned them to me. They came, and then, pointing to the bronze pedestal, I tried to intimate my wish to open it. But at my first gesture towards this they behaved very oddly. I don't know how to convey their expression to you. Suppose you were to use a grossly improper gesture to a delicate-minded woman —it is how she would look. They went off as if they had received the last possible insult. I tried a sweet-looking little chap in white next, with exactly the same result. Somehow, his manner made me feel ashamed of myself. But, as you know, I wanted the Time Machine, and I tried him once more. As he turned off, like the others, my temper got the better of me. In three strides I was after him, had him by the loose part of his robe round the neck, and began dragging him towards the sphinx. Then I saw the horror and repugnance of his face, and all of a sudden I let him go.

'But I was not beaten yet. I banged with my fist at the bronze panels, I thought I heard something stir inside—to be explicit, I thought I heard a sound like a chuckle—but I must have been mistaken. Then I got a big pebble from the river, and came and hammered till I had flattened a coil in the decorations, and the verdigris came off in powdery flakes. The delicate little people must have heard me hammering in gusty outbreaks a mile away on either hand, but nothing came of it. I saw a crowd of them upon the slopes, looking furtively at me. At last, hot and tired, I sat down to watch the place. But I was too restless to watch long; I am too Occidental for a long vigil. I could work at a problem for years, but to wait inactive for twenty-four hours—that is another matter.

'I got up after a time, and began walking aimlessly through the bushes towards the hill again. "Patience," said I to myself. "If you want your machine again you must leave that sphinx alone. If they mean to take your machine away, it's little good your wrecking their bronze panels, and if they don't, you will get it back as soon as you can ask for it. To sit among all those unknown things before a puzzle like that is hopeless. That way lies monomania. Face this world. Learn its ways, watch it, be careful of too hasty guesses at its meaning. In the end you will find clues to it all." Then suddenly the humour of the situation came into my mind: the thought of the years I had spent in study and toil to get into the future age, and now my passion of anxiety to get out of it. I had made myself the most complicated and the most hopeless trap that ever a man devised. Although it was at my own expense, I could not help myself. I laughed aloud.

'Going through the big palace, it seemed to me that the little people avoided me. It may have been my fancy, or it may have had something to do with my hammering at the gates of bronze. Yet I felt tolerably sure of the avoidance. I was careful, however, to show no concern and to abstain from any pursuit of them, and in the course of a day or two things got back to the old footing. I made what progress I could in the language, and in addition I pushed my explorations here and there. Either I missed some subtle point, or their language was excessively simple — almost exclusively composed of concrete substantives and verbs. There seemed to be few, if any, abstract terms, or little use of figurative language. Their sentences were usually simple and of two words, and I failed to convey or understand any but the simplest propositions. I determined to put the thought of my Time Machine and the mystery of the bronze doors under the sphinx as much as possible in a corner of memory, until my growing knowledge would lead me back to them in a natural way. Yet a certain feeling, you may understand, tethered me in a circle of a few miles round the point of my arrival.

'So far as I could see, all the world displayed the same exuberant richness as the Thames valley. From every hill I climbed I saw the same abundance of splendid buildings, endlessly varied in material and style, the same clustering thickets of evergreens, the same blossom-laden trees and tree-ferns. Here and there water shone like silver, and beyond, the land rose into blue undulating hills, and so faded into the serenity of the sky. A peculiar feature, which presently attracted my attention, was the presence of certain circular wells, several, as it seemed to me, of a very great depth. One lay by the path up the hill, which I had followed during my first walk. Like the others, it was rimmed with bronze, curiously wrought, and protected by a little cupola from the rain. Sitting by the side of these wells, and peering down into the shafted darkness, I could see no gleam of water, nor could I start any reflection with a lighted match. But in all of them I heard a certain sound: a thud — thud — thud, like the beating of some big engine; and I discovered, from the flaring of my matches, that a steady current of air set down the shafts. Further, I threw a scrap of paper into the throat of one, and, instead of fluttering down, it was at once sucked swiftly out of sight.

'After a time, too, I came to connect these wells with tall towers standing here and there upon the slopes; for above them was often just such a flicker in the air as one sees on a hot day above a sun-scorched beach. Putting things together, I reached a strong suggestion of an extensive system of subterranean ventilation, whose true import it was difficult to imagine. I was at first inclined to associate it with the sanitary apparatus of these people. It was an obvious conclusion, but it was absolutely wrong.

'And here I must admit that I learned very little of drains and bells and modes of conveyance, and the like conveniences, during my time in this real future. In some of these visions of Utopias and coming times which I have read, there is a vast amount of detail about building, and social arrangements, and so forth. But while such details are easy enough to obtain when the whole world is contained in one's imagination, they are altogether inaccessible to a real traveller amid such realities as I found here. Conceive the tale of London which a negro, fresh from Central Africa, would take back to his tribe! What would he know of railway companies, of social movements, of telephone and telegraph wires, of the Parcels Delivery Company, and postal orders and the like? Yet we, at least, should be willing enough to explain these things to him! And even of what he knew, how much could he make his untravelled friend either apprehend or believe?

Then, think how narrow the gap between a negro and a white man of our own times, and how wide the interval between myself and these of the Golden Age! I was sensible of much which was unseen, and which contributed to my comfort; but save for a general impression of automatic organization, I fear I can convey very little of the difference to your mind.

'In the matter of sepulture, for instance, I could see no signs of crematoria nor anything suggestive of tombs. But it occurred to me that, possibly, there might be cemeteries (or crematoria) somewhere beyond the range of my explorings. This, again, was a question I deliberately put to myself, and my curiosity was at first entirely defeated upon the point. The thing puzzled me, and I was led to make a further remark, which puzzled me still more: that aged and infirm among this people there were none.

'I must confess that my satisfaction with my first theories of an automatic civilization and a decadent humanity did not long endure. Yet I could think of no other. Let me put my difficulties. The several big palaces I had explored were mere living places, great dining-halls and sleeping apartments. I could find no machinery, no appliances of any kind. Yet these people were clothed in pleasant fabrics that must at times need renewal, and their sandals, though undecorated, were fairly complex specimens of metalwork. Somehow such things must be made. And the little people displayed no vestige of a creative tendency. There were no shops, no workshops, no sign of importations among them. They spent all their time in playing gently, in bathing in the river, in making love in a half-playful fashion, in eating fruit and sleeping. I could not see how things were kept going.

'Then again, about the Time Machine: something, I knew not what, had taken it into the hollow pedestal of the White Sphinx. Why? For the life of me I could not imagine. Those waterless wells, too, those flickering pillars. I felt I lacked a clue. I felt — how shall I put it? Suppose you found an inscription; with sentences here and there in excellent plain English, and interpolated therewith, others made up of words, of letters even, absolutely unknown to you? Well, on the third day of my visit, that was how the world of Eight Hundred and Two Thousand Seven Hundred and One presented itself to me!

'That day, too, I made a friend — of a sort. It happened that, as I was watching some of the little people bathing in a shallow, one of them was seized with cramp and began drifting downstream. The main current ran rather swiftly, but not too strongly for even a moderate swimmer. It will give you an idea, therefore, of the strange deficiency in these creatures, when I tell you that none made the slightest attempt to rescue the weakly crying little thing which was drowning before their eyes. When I realized this, I hurriedly slipped off my clothes, and, wading in at a point lower down, I caught the poor mite and drew her safe to land. A little rubbing of the limbs soon brought her round, and I had the satisfaction of seeing she was all right before I left her. I had got to such a low estimate of her kind that I did not expect any gratitude from her. In that, however, I was wrong.

This happened in the morning. In the afternoon I met my little woman, as I believe it was, as I was returning towards my centre from an exploration, and she received me with cries of delight and presented me with a big garland of flowers — evidently made for me and me alone. The thing took my imagination. Very possibly I had been feeling desolate. At any rate I did my best to display my appreciation of the gift. We were soon seated together in a little stone arbour, engaged in conversation, chiefly of smiles. The creature's friendliness affected me exactly as a child's might have done. We passed each other flowers, and she kissed my hands. I did the same to hers. Then I tried talk, and found that her name was Weena, which, though I don't know what it meant, somehow seemed appropriate enough. That was the beginning of a queer friendship which lasted a week, and ended—as I will tell you!

'She was exactly like a child. She wanted to be with me always. She tried to follow me every where, and on my next journey out and about it went to my heart to tire her down, and leave her at last, exhausted and calling after me rather plaintively. But the problems of the world had to be mastered. I had not, I said to myself, come into the future to carry on a miniature flirtation. Yet her distress when I left her was very great, her expostulations at the parting were sometimes frantic, and I think, altogether, I had as much trouble as comfort from her devotion. Nevertheless she was, somehow, a very great comfort. I thought it was mere childish affection that made her cling to me. Until it was too late, I did not clearly know what I had inflicted upon her when I left her. Nor until it was too late did I clearly understand what she was to me. For, by merely seeming fond of me, and showing in her weak, futile way that she cared for me, the little doll of a creature presently gave my return to the neighbourhood of the White Sphinx almost the feeling of coming home; and I would watch for her tiny figure of white and gold so soon as I came over the hill.

'It was from her, too, that I learned that fear had not yet left the world. She was fearless enough in the daylight, and she had the oddest confidence in me; for once, in a foolish moment, I made threatening grimaces at her, and she simply laughed at them. But she dreaded the dark, dreaded shadows, dreaded black things. Darkness to her was the one thing dreadful. It was a singularly passionate emotion, and it set me thinking and observing. I discovered then, among other things, that these little people gathered into the great houses after dark, and slept in droves. To enter upon them without a light was to put them into a tumult of apprehension. I never found one out of doors, or one sleeping alone within doors, after dark. Yet I was still such a blockhead that I missed the lesson of that fear, and in spite of Weena's distress I insisted upon sleeping away from these slumbering multitudes.

'It troubled her greatly, but in the end her odd affection for me triumphed, and for five of the nights of our acquaintance, including the last night of all, she slept with her head pillowed on my arm. But my story slips away from me as I speak of her. It must have been the night before her rescue that I was awakened about dawn. I had been restless, dreaming most disagreeably that I was drowned, and that sea-anemones were feeling over my face with their soft palps. I woke with a start, and with an odd fancy that some greyish animal had just rushed out of the chamber. I tried to get to sleep again, but I felt restless and uncomfortable. It was that dim grey hour when things are just creeping out of darkness, when everything is colourless and clear cut, and yet unreal. I got up, and went down into the great hall, and so out upon the flagstones in front of the palace. I thought I would make a virtue of necessity, and see the sunrise.

'The moon was setting, and the dying moonlight and the first pallor of dawn were mingled in a ghastly half-light. The bushes were inky black, the ground a sombre grey, the sky colourless and cheerless. And up the hill I thought I could see ghosts. Three several times, as I scanned the slope, I saw white figures. Twice I fancied I saw a solitary white, ape-like creature running rather quickly up the hill, and once near the ruins I saw a leash of them carrying some dark body. They moved hastily. I did not see what became of them. It seemed that they vanished among the bushes. The dawn was still indistinct, you must understand. I was feeling that chill, uncertain, early-morning feeling you may have known. I doubted my eyes.

'As the eastern sky grew brighter, and the light of the day came on and its vivid colouring returned upon the world once more, I scanned the view keenly. But I saw no vestige of my white figures. They were mere creatures of the half-light. "They must have been ghosts," I said; "I wonder whence they dated." For a queer notion of Grant Allen's came into my head, and amused me. If each generation die and leave ghosts, he argued, the world at last will get overcrowded with them. On that theory they would have grown innumerable some Eight Hundred Thousand Years hence, and it was no great wonder to see four at once. But the jest was unsatisfying, and I was thinking of these figures all the morning, until Weena's rescue drove them out of my head. I associated them in some indefinite way with the white animal I had startled in my first passionate search for the Time Machine. But Weena was a pleasant substitute. Yet all the same, they were soon destined to take far deadlier possession of my mind.

'I think I have said how much hotter than our own was the weather of this Golden Age. I cannot account for it. It may be that the sun was hotter, or the earth nearer the sun. It is usual to assume that the sun will go on cooling steadily in the future. But people, unfamiliar with such speculations as those of the younger Darwin, forget that the planets must ultimately fall back one by one into the parent body. As these catastrophes occur, the sun will blaze with renewed energy; and it may be that some inner planet had suffered this fate. Whatever the reason, the fact remains that the sun was very much hotter than we know it.

'Well, one very hot morning — my fourth, I think — as I was seeking shelter from the heat and glare in a colossal ruin near the great house where I slept and fed, there happened this strange thing: Clambering among these heaps of masonry, I found a narrow gallery, whose end and side windows were blocked by fallen masses of stone. By contrast with the brilliancy outside, it seemed at first impenetrably dark to me. I entered it groping, for the change from light to blackness made spots of colour swim before me. Suddenly I halted spellbound. A pair of eyes, luminous by reflection against the daylight without, was watching me out of the darkness.

'The old instinctive dread of wild beasts came upon me. I clenched my hands and steadfastly looked into the glaring eyeballs. I was afraid to turn. Then the thought of the absolute security in which humanity appeared to be living came to my mind. And then I remembered that strange terror of the dark. Overcoming my fear to some extent, I advanced a step and spoke. I will admit that my voice was harsh and ill-controlled. I put out my hand and touched something soft. At once the eyes darted sideways, and something white ran past me. I turned with my heart in my mouth, and saw a queer little ape-like figure, its head held down in a peculiar manner, running across the sunlit space behind me. It blundered against a block of granite, staggered aside, and in a moment was hidden in a black shadow beneath another pile of ruined masonry.

'My impression of it is, of course, imperfect; but I know it was a dull white, and had strange large greyish-red eyes; also that there was flaxen hair on its head and down its back. But, as I say, it went too fast for me to see distinctly. I cannot even say whether it ran on all-fours, or only with its forearms held very low. After an instant's pause I followed it into the second heap of ruins. I could not find it at first; but, after a time in the profound obscurity, I came upon one of those round well-like openings of which I have told you, half closed by a fallen pillar. A sudden thought came to me. Could this Thing have vanished down the shaft? I lit a match, and, looking down, I saw a small, white, moving creature, with large bright eyes which regarded me steadfastly as it retreated. It made me shudder. It was so like a human spider! It was clambering down the wall, and now I saw for the first time a number of metal foot and hand rests forming a kind of ladder down the shaft. Then the light burned my fingers and fell out of my hand, going out as it dropped, and when I had lit another the little monster had disappeared.

'I do not know how long I sat peering down that well. It was not for some time that I could succeed in persuading myself that the thing I had seen was human. But, gradually, the truth dawned on me: that Man had not remained one species, but had differentiated into two distinct animals: that my graceful children of the Upper-world were not the sole descendants of our generation, but that this bleached, obscene, nocturnal Thing, which had flashed before me, was also heir to all the ages.

'I thought of the flickering pillars and of my theory of an underground ventilation. I began to suspect their true import. And what, I wondered, was this Lemur doing in my scheme of a perfectly balanced organization? How was it related to the indolent serenity of the beautiful Upper-worlders? And what was hidden down there, at the foot of that shaft? I sat upon the edge of the well telling myself that, at any rate, there was nothing to fear, and that there I must descend for the solution of my difficulties. And withal I was absolutely afraid to go! As I hesitated, two of the beautiful Upper-world people came running in their amorous sport across the daylight in the shadow. The male pursued the female, flinging flowers at her as he ran.

'They seemed distressed to find me, my arm against the overturned pillar, peering down the well. Apparently it was considered bad form to remark these apertures; for when I pointed to this one, and tried to frame a question about it in their tongue, they were still more visibly distressed and turned away. But they were interested by my matches, and I struck some to amuse them. I tried them again about the well, and again I failed. So presently I left them, meaning to go back to Weena, and see what I could get from her. But my mind was already in revolution; my guesses and impressions were slipping and sliding to a new adjustment. I had now a clue to the import of these wells, to the ventilating towers, to the mystery of the ghosts; to say nothing of a hint at the meaning of the bronze gates and the fate of the Time Machine! And very vaguely there came a suggestion towards the solution of the economic problem that had puzzled me.

'Here was the new view. Plainly, this second species of Man was subterranean. There were three circumstances in particular which made me think that its rare emergence above ground was the outcome of a long-continued underground look common in most animals that live largely in the dark — the white fish of the Kentucky caves, for instance. Then, those large eyes, with that capacity for reflecting light, are common features of nocturnal things — witness the owl and the cat. And last of all, that evident confusion in the sunshine, that hasty yet fumbling awkward flight towards dark shadow, and that peculiar carriage of the head while in the light — all reinforced the theory of an extreme sensitiveness of the retina.

'Beneath my feet, then, the earth must be tunnelled enormously, and these tunnellings were the habitat of the new race. The presence of ventilating shafts and wells along the hill slopes — everywhere, in fact, except along the river valley — showed how universal were its ramifications. What so natural, then, as to assume that it was in this artificial Under-world that such work as was necessary to the comfort of the daylight race was done? The notion was so plausible that I at once accepted it, and went on to assume the how of this splitting of the human species. I dare say you will anticipate the shape of my theory; though, for myself, I very soon felt that it fell far short of the truth.

'At first, proceeding from the problems of our own age, it seemed clear as daylight to me that the gradual widening of the present merely temporary and social difference between the Capitalist and the Labourer, was the key to the whole position. No doubt it will seem grotesque enough to you — and wildly incredible! — and yet even now there are existing circumstances to point that way. There is a tendency to utilize underground space for the less ornamental purposes of civilization; there is the Metropolitan Railway in London, for instance, there are new electric railways, there are subways, there are underground workrooms and restaurants, and they increase and multiply. Evidently, I thought, this tendency had increased till Industry had gradually lost its birthright in the sky. I mean that it had gone deeper and deeper into larger and ever larger underground factories, spending a still-increasing amount of its time therein, till, in the end — ! Even now, does not an East-end worker live in such artificial conditions as practically to be cut off from the natural surface of the earth?

'Again, the exclusive tendency of richer people — due, no doubt, to the increasing refinement of their education, and the widening gulf between them and the rude violence of the poor — is already leading to the closing, in their interest, of considerable portions of the surface of the land. About London, for instance, perhaps half the prettier country is shut in against intrusion. And this same widening gulf — which is due to the length and expense of the higher educational process and the increased facilities for and temptations towards refined habits on the part of the rich — will make that exchange between class and class, that promotion by intermarriage which at present retards the splitting of our species along lines of social stratification, less and less frequent. So, in the end, above ground you must have the Haves, pursuing pleasure and comfort and beauty, and below ground the Have-nots, the Workers getting continually adapted to the conditions of their labour. Once they were there, they would no doubt have to pay rent, and not a little of it, for the ventilation of their caverns; and if they refused, they would starve or be suffocated for arrears. Such of them as were so constituted as to be miserable and rebellious would die; and, in the end, the balance being permanent, the survivors would become as well adapted to the conditions of underground life, and as happy in their way, as the Upper-world people were to theirs. As it seemed to me, the refined beauty and the etiolated pallor followed naturally enough.

'The great triumph of Humanity I had dreamed of took a different shape in my mind. It had been no such triumph of moral education and general co-opera-tion as I had imagined. Instead, I saw a real aristocracy, armed with a perfected science and working to a logical conclusion the industrial system of to-day. Its triumph had not been simply a triumph over Nature, but a triumph over Nature and the fellow-man. This, I must warn you, was my theory at the time. I had no convenient cicerone in the pattern of the Utopian books. My explanation may be absolutely wrong. I still think it is the most plausible one. But even on this supposition the balanced civilization that was at last attained must have long since passed its zenith, and was now far fallen into decay. The too-perfect security of the Upper-worlders had led them to a slow movement of degeneration, to a general dwindling in size, strength, and intelligence. That I could see clearly enough already. What had happened to the Under-grounders I did not yet suspect: but from what I had seen of the Morlocks—that, by the by, was the name by which these creatures were called—I could imagine that the modifica-tion of the human type was even far more profound than among the "Eloi," the beautiful race that I already knew.

'Then came troublesome doubts. Why had the Morlocks taken my Time Machine? For I felt sure it was they who had taken it. Why, too, if the Eloi were masters, could they not restore the machine to me? And why were they so terribly afraid of the dark? I proceeded, as I have said, to question Weena about this Under-world, but here again I was disappointed. At first she would not understand my questions, and presently she refused to answer them. She shiv-ered as though the topic was unendurable. And when I pressed her, perhaps a little harshly, she burst into tears. They were the only tears, except my own, I ever saw in that Golden Age. When I saw them I ceased abruptly to trouble about the Morlocks, and was only concerned in banishing these signs of the human inheritance from Weena's eyes. And very soon she was smiling and clapping her hands, while I solemnly burned a match.

VI

'It may seem odd to you, but it was two days before I could follow up the new-found clue in what was manifestly the proper way. I felt a peculiar shrinking from those pallid bodies. They were just the half-bleached colour of the worms and things one sees preserved in spirit in a zoological museum. And they were filthily cold to the touch. Probably my shrinking was largely due to the sympa-thetic influence of the Eloi, whose disgust of the Morlocks I now began to appreciate.

'The next night I did not sleep well. Probably my health was a little disor-dered. I was oppressed with perplexity and doubt. Once or twice I had a feeling of intense fear for which I could perceive no definite reason. I remember creeping noiselessly into the great hall where the little people were sleeping in the moonlight—that night Weena was among them—and feeling reassured by their presence. It occurred to me even then, that in the course of a few days the moon must pass through its last quarter, and the nights grow dark, when the appearances of these unpleasant creatures from below, these whitened Lemurs, this new vermin that had replaced the old, might be more abundant. And on both these days I had the restless feeling of one who shirks an inevitable duty. I felt assured that the Time Machine was only to be recovered by boldly penetrating these underground mysteries. Yet I could not face the mystery. If only I had had a companion it would have been different. But I was so horribly alone, and even to clamber down into the darkness of the well appalled me. I don't know if you will understand my feeling, but I never felt quite safe at my back.

'It was this restlessness, this insecurity, perhaps, that drove me further and further afield in my exploring expeditions. Going to the south-westward towards the rising country that is now called Combe Wood, I observed far off, in the direction of nineteenth-century Banstead, a vast green structure, different in character from any I had hitherto seen. It was larger than the largest of the palaces of ruins I knew, and the façade had an Oriental look: the face of it having the lustre, as well as the pale green tint, a kind of bluish-green, of a certain type of Chinese porcelain. This difference in aspect suggested a difference in use, and I was minded to push on and explore. But the day was growing late, and I had come upon the sight of the place after a long and tiring circuit; so I resolved to hold over the adventure for the following day, and I returned to the welcome and the caresses of little Weena. But next morning I perceived clearly enough that my curiosity regarding the Palace of Green Porcelain was a piece of self-deception, to enable me to shirk, by another day, an experience I dreaded. I resolved I would make the descent without further waste of time, and started out in the early morning towards a well near the ruins of granite and aluminium.

'Little Weena ran with me. She danced beside me to the well, but when she saw me lean over the mouth and look downward, she seemed strangely disconcerted. "Good-bye, little Weena," I said, kissing her; and then, putting her down, I began to feel over the parapet for the climbing hooks. Rather hastily, I may as well confess, for I feared my courage might leak away! At first she watched me in amazement. Then she gave a most piteous cry, and, running to me, she began to pull at me with her little hands. I think her opposition nerved me rather to proceed. I shook her off, perhaps a little roughly, and in another moment I was in the throat of the well. I saw her agonized face over the parapet, and smiled to reassure her. Then I had to look down at the unstable hooks to which I clung.

'I had to clamber down a shaft of perhaps two hundred yards. The descent was effected by means of metallic bars projecting from the sides of the well, and these being adapted to the needs of a creature much smaller and lighter than myself, I was speedily cramped and fatigued by the descent. And not simply fatigued! One of the bars bent suddenly under my weight, and almost swung me off into the blackness beneath. For a moment I hung by one hand, and after that experience I did not dare to rest again. Though my arms and back were presently acutely painful, I went on clambering down the sheer descent with as quick a motion as possible. Glancing upward, I saw the aperture, a small blue disk, in which a star was visible, while little Weena's head showed as a round black projection. The thudding sound of a machine below grew louder and more oppressive. Everything save that little disk above was profoundly dark, and when I looked up again Weena had disappeared.

'I was in an agony of discomfort. I had some thought of trying to go up the shaft again, and leave the Under-world alone. But even while I turned this over in my mind I continued to descend. At last, with intense relief, I saw dimly coming up, a foot to the right of me, a slender loophole in the wall. Swinging myself in, I found it was the aperture of a narrow horizontal tunnel in which I could lie down and rest. It was not too soon. My arms ached, my back was cramped, and I was trembling with the prolonged terror of a fall. Besides this, the unbroken darkness had had a distressing effect upon my eyes. The air was full of the throb and hum of machinery pumping air down the shaft.

'I do not know how long I lay. I was roused by a soft hand touching my face. Starting up in the darkness I snatched at my matches and, hastily striking one, I saw three stooping white creatures similar to the one I had seen above ground in the ruin, hastily retreating before the light. Living, as they did, in what appeared to me impenetrable darkness, their eyes were abnormally large and sensitive, just as are the pupils of the abysmal fishes, and they reflected the light in the same way. I have no doubt they could see me in that rayless obscurity, and they did not seem to have any fear of me apart from the light. But, so soon as I struck a match in order to see them, they fled incontinently, vanishing into dark gutters and tunnels, from which their eyes glared at me in the strangest fashion.

'I tried to call to them, but the language they had was apparently different from that of the Over-world people; so that I was needs left to my own unaided efforts, and the thought of flight before exploration was even then in my mind. But I said to myself, "You are in for it now," and, feeling my way along the tunnel, I found the noise of machinery grow louder. Presently the walls fell away from me, and I came to a large open space, and striking another match, saw that I had entered a vast arched cavern, which stretched into utter darkness beyond the range of my light. The view I had of it was as much as one could see in the burning of a match.

'Necessarily my memory is vague. Great shapes like big machines rose out of dimness, and cast grotesque black shadows, in which dim spectral Morlocks sheltered from the glare. The place, by the by, was very stuffy and oppressive, and the faint halitus of freshly shed blood was in the air. Some way down the central vista was a little table of white metal, laid with what seemed a meal. The Morlocks at any rate were carnivorous! Even at that time, I remember wondering what large animal could have survived to furnish the red joint I saw. It was all very indistinct: the heavy smell, the big unmeaning shapes, the obscene figures lurking in the shadows, and only waiting for the darkness to come at me again! Then the match burned down, and stung my fingers, and fell, a wriggling red spot in the blackness.

'I have thought since how particularly ill-equipped I was for such an experience. When I had started with the Time Machine, I had started with the absurd assumption that the men of the Future would certainly be infinitely ahead of ourselves in all their appliances. I had come without arms, without medicine, without anything to smoke — at times I missed tobacco frightfully — even without enough matches. If only I had thought of a Kodak! I could have flashed that glimpse of the Underworld in a second, and examined it at leisure. But, as it was, I stood there with only the weapons and powers that Nature had endowed me with — hands, feet, and teeth: these, and four safety-matches that still remained to me.

'I was afraid to push my way in among all this machinery in the dark, and it was only with my last glimpse of light I discovered that my store of matches had run low. It had never occurred to me until that moment that there was any need to economize them, and I had wasted almost half the box in astonishing the Upper-worlders, to whom fire was a novelty. Now, as I say, I had four left, and while I stood in the dark, a hand touched mine, lank fingers came feeling over my face, and I was sensible of a peculiar unpleasant odour. I fancied I heard the breathing of a crowd of those dreadful little beings about me. I felt the box of matches in my hand being gently disengaged, and other hands behind me pluck-ing at my clothing. The sense of these unseen creatures examining me was indescribably unpleasant. The sudden realization of my ignorance of their ways of thinking and doing came home to me very vividly in the darkness. I shouted at them as loudly as I could. They started away, and then I could feel them approaching me again. They clutched at me more boldly, whispering odd sounds to each other. I shivered violently, and shouted again — rather discordantly. This time they were not so seriously alarmed, and they made a queer laughing noise as they came back at me. I will confess I was horribly frightened. I determined to strike another match and escape under protection of its glare. I did so, and eking out the flicker with a scrap of paper from my pocket, I made good my retreat to the narrow tunnel. But I had scarce entered this when my light was blown out, and in the blackness I could hear the Morlocks rustling like wind among leaves, and pattering like the rain, as they hurried after me.

'In a moment I was clutched by several hands, and there was no mistaking that they were trying to haul me back. I struck another light, and waved it in their dazzled faces. You can scarce imagine how nauseatingly inhuman they looked — those pale, chinless faces and great, lidless, pinkish-grey eyes! — as they stared in their blindness and bewilderment. But I did not stay to look, I promise you: I retreated again, and when my second match had ended, I struck my third. It had almost burned through when I reached the opening into the shaft. I lay down on the edge, for the throb of the great pump below made me giddy. Then I felt sideways for the projecting hooks, and, as I did so, my feet were grasped from behind, and I was violently tugged backward. I lit my last match . . . and it incontinently went out. But I had my hand on the climbing bars now, and, kicking violently, I disengaged myself from the clutches of the Morlocks and was speedily clambering up the shaft, while they stayed peering and blinking up at me: all but one little wretch who followed me for some way, and wellnigh secured my boot as a trophy.

'That climb seemed interminable to me. With the last twenty or thirty feet of it a deadly nausea came upon me. I had the greatest difficulty in keeping my hold. The last few yards was a frightful struggle against this faintness. Several times my head swam, and I felt all the sensations of falling. At last, however, I got over the well-mouth somehow, and staggered out of the ruin into the blinding sunlight. I fell upon my face. Even the soil smelt sweet and clean. Then I remember Weena kissing my hands and ears, and the voices of others among the Eloi. Then, for a time, I was insensible.

VII

'Now, indeed, I seemed in a worse case than before. Hitherto, except during my night's anguish at the loss of the Time Machine, I had felt a sustaining hope of ultimate escape, but that hope was staggered by these new discoveries. Hitherto I had merely thought myself impeded by the childish simplicity of the little people, and by some unknown forces which I had only to understand to overcome; but there was an altogether new element in the sickening quality of the Morlocks—a something inhuman and malign. Instinctively I loathed them. Before, I had felt as a man might feel who had fallen into a pit: my concern was with the pit and how to get out of it. Now I felt like a beast in a trap, whose enemy would come upon him soon.

'The enemy I dreaded may surprise you. It was the darkness of the new moon. Weena had put this into my head by some at first incomprehensible remarks about the Dark Nights. It was not now such a very difficult problem to guess what the coming Dark Nights might mean. The moon was on the wane: each night there was a longer interval of darkness. And I now understood to some slight degree at least the reason of the fear of the little Upper-world people for the dark. I wondered vaguely what foul villainy it might be that the Morlocks did under the new moon. I felt pretty sure now that my second hypothesis was all wrong. The Upper-world people might once have been the favoured aristocracy, and the Morlocks their mechanical servants: but that had long since passed away. The two species that had resulted from the evolution of man were sliding down towards, or had already arrived at, an altogether new relationship. The Eloi, like the Carlovingian kings, had decayed to a mere beautiful futility. They still possessed the earth on sufferance: since the Morlocks, subterranean for innumerable generations, had come at last to find the daylit surface intolerable. And the Morlocks made their garments, I inferred, and maintained them in their habitual needs, perhaps through the survival of an old habit of service. They did it as a standing horse paws with his foot, or as a man enjoys killing animals in sport: because ancient and departed necessities had impressed it on the organism. But, clearly, the old order was already in part reversed. The Nemesis of the delicate ones was creeping on apace. Ages ago, thousands of generations ago, man had thrust his brother man out of the ease and the sunshine. And now that brother was coming back—changed! Already the Eloi had begun to learn one old lesson anew. They were becoming reacquainted with Fear. And suddenly there came into my head the memory of the meat I had seen in the Under-world. It seemed odd how it floated into my mind: not stirred up as it were by the current of meditations, but coming in almost like a question from outside. I tried to recall the form of it. I had a vague sense of something familiar, but I could not tell what is was at the time.

'Still, however helpless the little people in the presence of their mysterious Fear, I was differently constituted. I came out of this age of ours, this ripe prime of the human race, when Fear does not paralyse and mystery has lost its terrors. I at least would defend myself. Without further delay I determined to make myself arms and a fastness where I might sleep. With that refuge as a base, I could face this strange world with some of that confidence I had lost in realizing to what creatures night by night I lay exposed. I felt I could never sleep again until my bed was secure from them. I shuddered with horror to think how they must already have examined me.

'I wandered during the afternoon along the valley of the Thames, but found nothing that commended itself to my mind as inaccessible. All the buildings and trees seemed easily practicable to such dexterous climbers as the Morlocks, to judge by their wells, must be. Then the tall pinnacles of the Palace of Green Porcelain and the polished gleam of its walls came back to my memory: and in the evening, taking Weena like a child upon my shoulder, I went up the hills towards the south-west. The distance, I had reckoned, was seven or eight miles, but it must have been nearer eighteen. I had first seen the place on a moist afternoon when distances are deceptively diminished. In addition, the heel of one of my shoes was loose, and a nail was working through the sole — they were comfortable old shoes I wore about indoors — so that I was lame. And it was already long past sunset when I came in sight of the palace, silhouetted black against the pale yellow of the sky.

'Weena had been hugely delighted when I began to carry her, but after a time she desired me to let her down, and ran along by the side of me, occasionally darting off on either hand to pick flowers to stick in my pockets. My pockets had always puzzled Weena, but at the last she had concluded that they were an eccentric kind of vase for floral decoration. At least she utilized them for that purpose. And that reminds me! In changing my jacket I found . . . .'

The Time Traveller paused, put his hand into his pocket, and silently placed two withered flowers, not unlike very large white mallows, upon the little table. Then he resumed his narrative.

'As the hush of evening crept over the world and we proceeded over the hill crest towards Wimbledon, Weena grew tired and wanted to return to the house of grey stone. But I pointed out the distant pinnacles of the Palace of Green Porcelain to her, and contrived to make her understand that we were seeking a refuge there from her Fear. You know that great pause that comes upon things before the dusk? Even the breeze stops in the trees. To me there is always an air of expectation about the evening stillness. The sky was clear, remote, and empty save for a few horizontal bars far down in the sunset. Well, that night the expectation took the colour of my fears. In that darkling calm my senses seemed preternaturally sharpened. I fancied I could even feel the hollowness of the ground beneath my feet: could, indeed, almost see through it the Morlocks on their anthill going hither and thither and waiting for the dark. In my excitement I fancied that they would receive my invasion of their burrows as a declaration of war. And why had they taken my Time Machine?

'So we went on in the quiet, and the twilight deepened into night. The clear blue of the distance faded, and one star after another came out. The ground grew dim and the trees black. Weena's fears and her fatigue grew upon her. I took her in my arms and talked to her and caressed her. Then, as the darkness grew deeper, she put her arms around my neck, and, closing her eyes, tightly pressed her face against my shoulder. So we went down a long slope into a valley, and there in the dimness I almost walked into a little river. This I waded, and went up the opposite side of the valley, past a number of sleeping houses, and by a statue — a Faun, or some such figure, *minus* the head. Here too were acacias. So far I had seen nothing of the Morlocks, but it was yet early in the night, and the darker hours before the old moon rose were still to come.

'From the brow of the next hill I saw a thick wood spreading wide and black before me. I hesitated at this. I could see no end to it, either to the right or the left. Feeling tired—my feet, in particular, were very sore—I carefully lowered Weena from my shoulder as I halted, and sat down upon the turf. I could no longer see the Palace of Green Porcelain, and I was in doubt of my direction. I looked into the thickness of the wood and thought of what it might hide. Under that dense tangle of branches one would be out of sight of the stars. Even were there no other lurking danger—a danger I did not care to let my imagination loose upon—there would still be all the roots to stumble over and the tree-boles to strike against.

'I was very tired, too, after the excitements of the day; so I decided that I would not face it, but would pass the night upon the open hill.

Weena, I was glad to find, was fast asleep. I carefully wrapped her in my jacket, and sat down beside her to wait for the moonrise. The hill-side was quiet and deserted, but from the black of the wood there came now and then a stir of living things. Above me shone the stars, for the night was very clear. I felt a certain sense of friendly comfort in their twinkling. All the old constellations had gone from the sky, however: that slow movement which is imperceptible in a hundred human lifetimes, had long since rearranged them in unfamiliar groupings. But the Milky Way, it seemed to me, was still the same tattered streamer of star-dust as of yore. Southward (as I judged it) was a very bright red star that was new to me; it was even more splendid than our own green Sirius. And amid all these scintillating points of light one bright planet shone kindly and steadily like the face of an old friend.

'Looking at these stars suddenly dwarfed my own troubles and all the gravities of terrestrial life. I thought of their unfathomable distance, and the slow inevitable drift of their movements out of the unknown past into the unknown future. I thought of the great precessional cycle that the pole of the earth describes. Only forty times had that silent revolution occurred during all the years that I had traversed. And during these few revolutions all the activity, all the traditions, the complex organizations, the nations, languages, literatures, aspirations, even the mere memory of Man as I knew him, had been swept out of existence. Instead were these frail creatures who had forgotten their high ancestry, and the white Things of which I went in terror. Then I thought of the Great Fear that was between the two species, and for the first time, with a sudden shiver, came the clear knowledge of what the meat I had seen might be. Yet it was too horrible! I looked at little Weena sleeping beside me, her face white and starlike under the stars, and forthwith dismissed the thought.

'Through that long night I held my mind off the Morlocks as well as I could, and whiled away the time by trying to fancy I could find signs of the old constellations in the new confusion. The sky kept very clear, except for a hazy cloud or so. No doubt I dozed at times. Then, as my vigil wore on, came a faintness in the eastward sky, like the reflection of some colourless fire, and the old moon rose, thin and peaked and white. And close behind, and overtaking it, and overflowing it, the dawn came, pale at first, and then growing pink and warm.

No Morlocks had approached us. Indeed, I had seen none upon the hill that night. And in the confidence of renewed day it almost seemed to me that my fear had been unreasonable. I stood up and found my foot with the loose heel swollen at the ankle and painful under the heel; so I sat down again, took off my shoes, and flung them away.

'I awakened Weena, and we went down into the wood, now green and pleasant instead of black and forbidding. We found some fruit wherewith to break our fast. We soon met others of the dainty ones, laughing and dancing in the sunlight as though there was no such thing in nature as the night. And then I thought once more of the meat that I had seen. I felt assured now of what it was, and from the bottom of my heart I pitied this last feeble rill from the great flood of humanity. Clearly, at some time in the Long-Ago of human decay the Morlocks' food had run short. Possibly they had lived on rats and such-like vermin. Even now man is far less discriminating and exclusive in his food than he was—far less than any monkey. His prejudice against human flesh is no deep-seated instinct. And so these inhuman sons of men——! I tried to look at the thing in a scientific spirit. After all, they are less human and more remote than our cannibal ancestors of three or four thousand years ago. And the intelligence that would have made this state of things a torment had gone. Why should I trouble myself? These Eloi were mere fatted cattle, which the ant-like Morlocks preserved and preyed upon—probably saw to the breeding of. And there was Weena dancing at my side!

'Then I tried to preserve myself from the horror that was coming upon me, by regarding it as a rigorous punishment of human selfishness. Man had been content to live in ease and delight upon the labours of his fellow-man, had taken Necessity as his watchword and excuse, and in the fullness of time Necessity had come home to him. I even tried a Carlyle-like scorn of this wretched aristocracy in decay. But this attitude of mind was impossible. However great their intellectual degradation, the Eloi had kept too much of the human form not to claim my sympathy, and to make me perforce a sharer in their degradation and their Fear.

'I had at that time very vague ideas as to the course I should pursue. My first was to secure some safe place of refuge, and to make myself such arms of metal or stone as I could contrive. That necessity was immediate. In the next place, I hoped to procure some means of fire, so that I should have the weapon of a torch at hand, for nothing, I knew, would be more efficient against these Morlocks. Then I wanted to arrange some contrivance to break open the doors of bronze under the White Sphinx. I had in mind a battering-ram. I had a persuasion that if I could enter those doors and carry a blaze of light before me I should discover the Time Machine and escape. I could not imagine the Morlocks were strong enough to move it far away. Weena I had resolved to bring with me to our own time. And turning such schemes over in my mind I pursued our way towards the building which my fancy had chosen as our dwelling.

VIII

'I found the Palace of Green Porcelain, when we approached it about noon, deserted and falling into ruin. Only ragged vestiges of glass remained in its windows, and great sheets of the green facing had fallen away from the corroded metallic framework. It lay very high upon a turfy down, and looking north-eastward before I entered it, I was surprised to see a large estuary, or even creek, where I judged Wandsworth and Battersea must once have been. I thought then—though I never followed up the thought—of what might have happened, or might be happening, to the living things in the sea.

'The material of the Palace proved on examination to be indeed porcelain, and along the face of it I saw an inscription in some unknown character. I thought, rather foolishly, that Weena might help me interpret this, but I only learned that the bare idea of writing had never entered her head. She always seemed to me, I fancy, more human than she was, perhaps because her affection was so human.

'Within the big valves of the door—which were open and broken—we found, instead of the customary hall, a long gallery lit by many side windows. At the first glance I was reminded of a museum. The tiled floor was thick with dust, and a remarkable array of miscellaneous objects was shrouded in the same grey covering. Then I perceived, standing strange and gaunt in the centre of the hall, what was clearly the lower part of a huge skeleton. I recognized by the oblique feet that it was some extinct creature after the fashion of the Megatherium. The skull and the upper bones lay beside it in the thick dust, and in one place, where rain-water had dropped through a leak in the roof, the thing itself had been worn away. Further in the gallery was the huge skeleton barrel of a Brontosaurus. My museum hypothesis was confirmed. Going towards the side I found what appeared to be sloping shelves, and clearing away the thick dust, I found the old familiar glass cases of our own time. But they must have been air-tight to judge from the fair preservation of some of their contents.

'Clearly we stood among the ruins of some latter-day South Kensington! Here, apparently, was the Palaeontological Section, and a very splendid array of fossils it must have been, though the inevitable process of decay that had been staved off for a time, and had, through the extinction of bacteria and fungi, lost ninety-nine hundredths of its force, was nevertheless, with extreme sureness if with extreme slowness at work again upon all its treasures. Here and there I found traces of the little people in the shape of rare fossils broken to pieces or threaded in strings upon reeds. And the cases had in some instances been bodily removed—by the Morlocks as I judged. The place was very silent. The thick dust deadened our footsteps. Weena, who had been rolling a sea-urchin down the sloping glass of a case, presently came, as I stared about me, and very quietly took my hand and stood beside me.

'And at first I was so much surprised by this ancient monument of an intellectual age, that I gave no thought to the possibilities it presented. Even my preoccupation about the Time Machine receded a little from my mind.

'To judge from the size of the place, this Palace of Green Porcelain had a great deal more in it than a Gallery of Palaeontology; possibly historical galleries; it might be, even a library! To me, at least in my present circumstances, these would be vastly more interesting than this spectacle of old-time geology in decay. Exploring, I found another short gallery running transversely to the first. This appeared to be devoted to minerals, and the sight of a block of sulphur set my mind running on gunpowder. But I could find no saltpeter; indeed, no nitrates of any kind. Doubtless they had deliquesced ages ago. Yet the sulphur hung in my mind, and set up a train of thinking. As for the rest of the contents of that gallery, though on the whole they were the best preserved of all I saw, I had little interest. I am no specialist in mineralogy, and I went on down a very ruinous aisle running parallel to the first hall I had entered. Apparently this section had been devoted to natural history, but everything had long since passed out of recognition. A few shrivelled and blackened vestiges of what had once been stuffed animals, desiccated mummies in jars that had once held spirit, a brown dust of departed plants: that was all! I was sorry for that, because I should have been glad to trace the patent readjustments by which the conquest of animated nature had been attained. Then we came to a gallery of simply colossal proportions, but singularly ill-lit, the floor of it running downward at a slight angle from the end at which I entered. At intervals white globes hung from the ceiling — many of them cracked and smashed — which suggested that originally the place had been artificially lit. Here I was more in my element, for rising on either side of me were the huge bulks of big machines, all greatly corroded and many broken down, but some still fairly complete. You know I have a certain weakness for mechanism, and I was inclined to linger among these; the more so as for the most part they had the interest of puzzles, and I could make only the vaguest guesses at what they were for. I fancied that if I could solve their puzzles I should find myself in possession of powers that might be of use against the Morlocks.

'Suddenly Weena came very close to my side. So suddenly that she startled me. Had it not been for her I do not think I should have noticed that the floor of the gallery sloped at all.[1] The end I had come in at was quite above ground, and was lit by rare slit-like windows. As you went down the length, the ground came up against these windows, until at last there was a pit like the "area" of a London house before each, and only a narrow line of daylight at the top. I went slowly along, puzzling about the machines, and had been too intent upon them to notice the gradual diminution of the light, until Weena's increasing apprehensions drew my attention. Then I saw that the gallery ran down at last into a thick darkness. I hesitated, and then, as I looked round me, I saw that the dust was less abundant and its surface less even. Further away towards the dimness, it appeared to be broken by a number of small narrow footprints. My sense of the immediate presence of the Morlocks revived at that. I felt that I was wasting my time in this academic examination of machinery. I called to mind that it was already far advanced in the afternoon, and that I had still no weapon, no refuge, and no means of making a fire. And then down in the remote blackness of the gallery I heard a peculiar pattering, and the same odd noises I had heard down the well.

'I took Weena's hand. Then, struck with a sudden idea, I left her and turned to a machine from which projected a lever not unlike those in a signal-box. Clambering upon the stand, and grasping this lever in my hands, I put all my weight upon it sideways. Suddenly Weena, deserted in the central aisle, began to whimper. I had judged the strength of the lever pretty correctly, for it snapped after a minute's strain, and I rejoined her with a mace in my hand more than sufficient, I judged, for any Morlock skull I might encounter. And I longed very much to kill a Morlock or so. Very inhuman, you may think, to want to go killing

---

[1]It may be, of course, that the floor did not slope, but that the museum was built into the side of a hill. — Ed.

one's own descendants! But it was impossible, somehow, to feel any humanity in the things. Only my disinclination to leave Weena, and a persuasion that if I began to slake my thirst for murder my Time Machine might suffer, restrained me from going straight down the gallery and killing the brutes I heard.

'Well, mace in one hand and Weena in the other, I went out of that gallery and into another and still larger one, which at the first glance reminded me of a military chapel hung with tattered flags. The brown and charred rags that hung from the sides of it, I presently recognized as the decaying vestiges of books. They had long since dropped to pieces, and every semblance of print had left them. But here and there were warped boards and cracked metallic clasps that told the tale well enough. Had I been a literary man I might, perhaps, have moralized upon the futility of all ambition. But as it was, the thing that struck me with keenest force was the enormous waste of labour to which this sombre wilderness of rotting paper testified. At the time I will confess that I thought chiefly of the *Philosophical Transactions* and my own seventeen papers upon physical optics.

'Then, going up a broad staircase, we came to what may once have been a gallery of technical chemistry. And here I had not a little hope of useful discoveries. Except at one end where the roof had collapsed, this gallery was well preserved. I went eagerly to every unbroken case. And at last, in one of the really air-tight cases, I found a box of matches. Very eagerly I tried them. They were perfectly good. They were not even damp. I turned to Weena. "Dance," I cried to her in her own tongue. For now I had a weapon indeed against the horrible creatures we feared. And so, in that derelict museum, upon the thick soft carpeting of dust, to Weena's huge delight, I solemnly performed a kind of composite dance, whistling *The Land of the Leal* as cheerfully as I could. In part it was a *cancan*, in part a step-dance, in part a skirt-dance (so far as my tail-coat permitted), and in part original. For I am naturally inventive, as you know.

'Now, I still think that for this box of matches to have escaped the wear of time for immemorial years was a most strange, as for me it was a most fortunate thing. Yet, oddly enough, I found a far unlikelier substance, and that was camphor. I found it in a sealed jar, that by chance, I suppose, had been really hermetically sealed. I fancied at first that it was paraffin wax, and smashed the glass accordingly. But the odour of camphor was unmistakable. In the universal decay this volatile substance had chanced to survive, perhaps through many thousands of centuries. It reminded me of a sepia painting I had once seen done from the ink of a fossil Belemnite that must have perished and become fossilized millions of years ago. I was about to throw it away, but I remembered that it was inflammable and burned with a good bright flame—was, in fact, an excellent candle—and I put it in my pocket. I found no explosives, however, nor any means of breaking down the bronze doors. As yet my iron crowbar was the most helpful thing I had chanced upon. Nevertheless I left that gallery greatly elated.

'I cannot tell you all the story of that long afternoon. It should require a great effort of memory to recall my explorations in at all the proper order. I remember a long gallery of rusting stands of arms, and how I hesitated between my crowbar and a hatchet or a sword. I could not carry both, however, and my bar of iron promised best against the bronze gates. There were numbers of guns, pistols, and rifles. The most were masses of rust, but many were of some new metal, and still fairly sound. But any cartridges or powder there may once have been had rotted into dust. One corner I saw was charred and shattered; perhaps, I thought, by an explosion among the specimens. In another place was a vast array of idols — Polynesian, Mexican, Grecian, Phoenician, every country on earth I should think. And here, yielding to an irresistible impulse, I wrote my name upon the nose of a steatite monster from South America that particularly took my fancy.

'As the evening drew on, my interest waned. I went through gallery after gallery, dusty, silent, often ruinous, the exhibits sometimes mere heaps of rust and lignite, sometimes fresher. In one place I suddenly found myself near the model of a tin-mine, and then by the merest accident I discovered, in an air-tight case, two dynamite cartridges! I shouted "Eureka!" and smashed the case with joy. Then came a doubt. I hesitated. Then, selecting a little side gallery, I made my essay. I never felt such a disappointment as I did in waiting five, ten, fifteen minutes for an explosion that never came. Of course the things were dummies, as I might have guessed from their presence. I really believe that, had they not been so, I should have rushed off incontinently and blown Sphinx, bronze doors, and (as it proved) my chances of finding the Time Machine, all together into nonexistence.

'It was after that, I think, that we came to a little open court within the palace. It was turfed, and had three fruit-trees. So we rested and refreshed ourselves. Towards sunset I began to consider our position. Night was creeping upon us, and my inaccessible hiding-place had still to be found. But that troubled me very little now. I had in my possession a thing that was, perhaps, the best of all defences against the Morlocks — I had matches! I had the camphor in my pocket, too, if a blaze were needed. It seemed to me that the best thing we could do would be to pass the night in the open, protected by a fire. In the morning there was the getting of the Time Machine. Towards that, as yet, I had only my iron mace. But now, with my growing knowledge, I felt very differently towards those bronze doors. Up to this, I had refrained from forcing them, largely because of the mystery on the other side. They had never impressed me as being very strong, and I hoped to find my bar of iron not altogether inadequate for the work.

IX

'We emerged from the palace while the sun was still in part above the horizon. I was determined to reach the White Sphinx early the next morning, and ere the dusk I purposed pushing through the woods that had stopped me on the previous journey. My plan was to go as far as possible that night, and then, building a fire, to sleep in the protection of its glare. Accordingly, as we went along I gathered any sticks or dried grass I saw, and presently had my arms full of such litter. Thus loaded, our progress was slower than I had anticipated, and besides Weena was tired. And I began to suffer from sleepiness too; so that it was full night before we reached the wood. Upon the shrubby hill of its edge Weena would have stopped, fearing the darkness before us; but a singular sense of impending calamity, that should indeed have served me as a warning, drove me onward. I had been without sleep for a night and two days, and I was feverish and irritable. I felt sleep coming upon me, and the Morlocks with it.

'While we hesitated, among the black bushes behind us, and dim against their blackness, I saw three crouching figures. There was scrub and long grass all about us, and I did not feel safe from their insidious approach. The forest, I calculated, was rather less than a mile across. If we could get through it to the bare hill-side, there, as it seemed to me, was an altogether safer resting-place; I thought that with my matches and my camphor I could contrive to keep my path illuminated through the woods. Yet it was evident that if I was to flourish matches with my hands I should have to abandon my firewood; so, rather reluctantly, I put it down. And then it came into my head that I would amaze our friends behind by lighting it. I was to discover the atrocious folly of this proceeding, but it came to my mind as an ingenious move for covering our retreat.

'I don't know if you have ever thought what a rare thing flame must be in the absence of man and in a temperate climate. The sun's heat is rarely strong enough to burn, even when it is focused by dewdrops, as is sometimes the case in more tropical districts. Lightning may blast and blacken, but it rarely gives rise to widespread fire. Decaying vegetation may occasionally smoulder with the heat of its fermentation, but this rarely results in flame. In this decadence, too, the art of fire-making had been forgotten on the earth. The red tongues that went licking up my heap of wood were an altogether new and strange thing to Weena.

'She wanted to run to it and play with it. I believe she would have cast herself into it had I not restrained her. But I caught her up, and, in spite of her struggles, plunged boldly before me into the wood. For a little way the glare of my fire lit the path. Looking back presently, I could see, through the crowded stems, that from my heap of sticks the blaze had spread to some bushes adjacent, and a curved line of fire was creeping up the grass of the hill. I laughed at that, and turned again to the dark trees before me. It was very black, and Weena clung to me convulsively, but there was still, as my eyes grew accustomed to the darkness, sufficient light for me to avoid the stems. Overhead it was simply black, except where a gap of remote blue sky shone down upon us here and there. I struck none of my matches because I had no hand free. Upon my left arm I carried my little one, in my right hand I had my iron bar.

'For some way I heard nothing but the crackling twigs under my feet, the faint rustle of the breeze above, and my own breathing and the throb of the blood-vessels in my ears. Then I seemed to know of a pattering about me. I pushed on grimly. The pattering grew more distinct, and then I caught the same queer sound and voices I had heard in the Under-world. There were evidently several of the Morlocks, and they were closing in upon me. Indeed, in another minute I felt a tug at my coat, then something at my arm. And Weena shivered violently, and became quite still.

'It was time for a match. But to get one I must put her down. I did so, and, as I fumbled with my pocket, a struggle began in the darkness about my knees, perfectly silent on her part and with the same peculiar cooing sounds from the Morlocks. Soft little hands, too, were creeping over my coat and back, touching even my neck. Then the match scratched and fizzed. I held it flaring, and saw the white backs of the Morlocks in flight amid the trees. I hastily took a lump of camphor from my pocket, and prepared to light it as soon as the match should wane. Then I looked at Weena. She was lying clutching my feet and quite motionless, with her face to the ground. With a sudden fright I stooped to her. She seemed scarcely to breathe. I lit the block of camphor and flung it to the ground, and as it split and flared up and drove back the Morlocks and the shadows, I knelt down and lifted her. The wood behind seemed full of the stir and murmur of a great company!

'She seemed to have fainted. I put her carefully upon my shoulder and rose to push on, and then there came a horrible realization. In manoeuvring with my matches and Weena, I had turned myself about several times, and now I had not the faintest idea in what direction lay my path. For all I knew, I might be facing back towards the Palace of Green Porcelain. I found myself in a cold sweat. I had to think rapidly what to do. I determined to build a fire and encamp where we were. I put Weena, still motionless, down upon a turfy bole, and very hastily, as my first lump of camphor waned, I began collecting sticks and leaves. Here and there out of the darkness round me the Morlocks' eyes shone like carbuncles.

'The camphor flickered and went out. I lit a match, and as I did so, two white forms that had been approaching Weena dashed hastily away. One was so blinded by the light that he came straight for me, and I felt his bones grind under the blow of my fist. He gave a whoop of dismay, staggered a little way, and fell down. I lit another piece of camphor, and went on gathering my bonfire. Presently I noticed how dry was some of the foliage above me, for since my arrival on the Time Machine, a matter of a week, no rain had fallen. So, instead of casting about among the trees for fallen twigs, I began leaping up and dragging down branches. Very soon I had a choking smoky fire of green wood and dry sticks, and could economize my camphor. Then I turned to where Weena lay beside my iron mace. I tried what I could to revive her, but she lay like one dead. I could not even satisfy myself whether or not she breathed.

'Now, the smoke of the fire beat over towards me, and it must have made me heavy of a sudden. Moreover, the vapour of camphor was in the air. My fire would not need replenishing for an hour or so. I felt very weary after my exertion, and sat down. The wood, too, was full of a slumbrous murmur that I did not understand. I seemed just to nod and open my eyes. But all was dark, and the Morlocks had their hands upon me. Flinging off their clinging fingers I hastily felt in my pocket for the match-box, and — it had gone! Then they gripped and closed with me again. In a moment I knew what had happened. I had slept, and my fire had gone out, and the bitterness of death came over my soul. The forest seemed full of the smell of burning wood. I was caught by the neck, by the hair, by the arms, and pulled down. It was indescribably horrible in the darkness to feel all these soft creatures heaped upon me. I felt as if I was in a monstrous spider's web. I was overpowered, and went down. I felt little teeth nipping at my neck. I rolled over, and as I did so my hand came against my iron lever. It gave me strength. I struggled up, shaking the human rats from me, and, holding the bar short, I thrust where I judged their faces might be. I could feel the succulent giving of flesh and bone under my blows, and for a moment I was free.

'The strange exultation that so often seems to accompany hard fighting came upon me. I knew that both I and Weena were lost, but I determined to make the Morlocks pay for their meat. I stood with my back to a tree, swinging the iron bar before me. The whole wood was full of the stir and cries of them. A minute passed. Their voices seemed to rise to a higher pitch of excitement, and their movements grew faster. Yet none came within reach. I stood glaring at the blackness. Then suddenly came hope. What if the Morlocks were afraid? And close on the heels of that came a strange thing. The darkness seemed to grow luminous. Very dimly I began to see the Morlocks about me — three battered at my feet — and then I recognized, with incredulous surprise, that the others were running, in an incessant stream, as it seemed, from behind me, and away through the wood in front. And their backs seemed no longer white, but reddish. As I stood agape, I saw a little red spark go drifting across a gap of starlight between the branches, and vanish. And at that I understood the smell of burning wood, the slumbrous murmur that was growing now into a gusty roar, the red glow, and the Morlocks' flight.

'Stepping out from behind my tree and looking back, I saw, through the black pillars of the nearer trees, the flames of the burning forest. It was my first fire coming after me. With that I looked for Weena, but she was gone. The hissing and crackling behind me, the explosive thud as each fresh tree burst into flame, left little time for reflection. My iron bar still gripped, I followed in the Morlocks' path. It was a close race. Once the flames crept forward so swiftly on my right as I ran that I was outflanked and had to strike off to the left. But at last I emerged upon a small open space, and as I did so, a Morlock came blundering towards me, and past me, and went on straight into the fire!

'And now I was to see the most weird and horrible thing, I think, of all that I beheld in that future age. This whole space was as bright as day with the reflection of the fire. In the centre was a hillock or tumulus, surmounted by a scorched hawthorn. Beyond this was another arm of the burning forest, with yellow tongues already writhing from it, completely encircling the space with a fence of fire. Upon the hill-side were some thirty or forty Morlocks, dazzled by the light and heat, and blundering hither and thither against each other in their bewilderment. At first I did not realize their blindness, and struck furiously at them with my bar, in a frenzy of fear, as they approached me, killing one and crippling several more. But when I had watched the gestures of one of them groping under the hawthorn against the red sky, and heard their moans, I was assured of their absolute helplessness and misery in the glare, and I struck no more of them.

'Yet every now and then one would come straight towards me, setting loose a quivering horror that made me quick to elude him. At one time the flames died down somewhat, and I feared the foul creatures would presently be able to see me. I was thinking of beginning the fight by killing some of them before this should happen; but the fire burst out again brightly, and I stayed my hand. I walked about the hill among them and avoided them, looking for some trace of Weena. But Weena was gone.

'At last I sat down on the summit of the hillock, and watched this strange incredible company of blind things groping to and fro, and making uncanny noises to each other, as the glare of the fire beat on them. The coiling uprush of smoke streamed across the sky, and through the rare tatters of that red canopy, remote as though they belonged to another universe, shone the little stars. Two or three Morlocks came blundering into me, and I drove them off with blows of my fists, trembling as I did so.

'For the most part of that night I was persuaded it was a nightmare. I bit myself and screamed in a passionate desire to awake. I beat the ground with my hands, and got up and sat down again, and wandered here and there, and again sat down. Then I would fall to rubbing my eyes and calling upon God to let me awake. Thrice I saw Morlocks put their heads down in a kind of agony and rush into the flames. But, at last, above the subsiding red of the fire, above the streaming masses of black smoke and the whitening and blackening tree stumps, and the diminishing numbers of these dim creatures, came the white light of the day.

'I searched again for traces of Weena, but there were none. It was plain that they had left her poor little body in the forest. I cannot describe how it relieved me to think that it had escaped the awful fate to which it seemed destined. As I thought of that, I was almost moved to begin a massacre of the helpless abominations about me, but I contained myself. The hillock, as I have said, was a kind of island in the forest. From its summit I could now make out through a haze of smoke the Palace of Green Porcelain, and from that I could get my bearings for the White Sphinx. And so, leaving the remnant of these damned souls still going hither and thither and moaning, as the day grew clearer, I tied some grass about my feet and limped on across smoking ashes and among black stems, that still pulsated internally with fire, towards the hiding-place of the Time Machine. I walked slowly, for I was almost exhausted, as well as lame, and I felt the intensest wretchedness for the horrible death of little Weena. It seemed an overwhelming calamity. Now, in this old familiar room, it is more like the sorrow of a dream than an actual loss. But that morning it left me absolutely lonely again — terribly alone. I began to think of this house of mine, of this fireside, of some of you, and with such thoughts came a longing that was pain.

'But, as I walked over the smoking ashes under the bright morning sky, I made a discovery. In my trouser pocket were still some loose matches. The box must have leaked before it was lost.

X

'About eight or nine in the morning I came to the same seat of yellow metal from which I had viewed the world upon the evening of my arrival. I thought of my hasty conclusions upon that evening and could not refrain from laughing bitterly at my confidence. Here was the same beautiful scene, the same abundant foliage, the same splendid palaces and magnificent ruins, the same silver river running between its fertile banks. The gay robes of the beautiful people moved hither and thither among the trees. Some were bathing in exactly the place where I had saved Weena, and that suddenly gave me a keen stab of pain. And like blots upon the landscape rose the cupolas above the ways to the Under-world. I understood now what all the beauty of the Over-world people covered. Very pleasant was their day, as pleasant as the day of the cattle in the field. Like the cattle, they knew of no enemies and provided against no needs. And their end was the same.

'I grieved to think how brief the dream of the human intellect had been. It had committed suicide. It had set itself steadfastly towards comfort and ease, a balanced society with security and permanency as its watchword, it had attained its hopes — to come to this at last. Once, life and property must have reached almost absolute safety. The rich had been assured of his wealth and comfort, the toiler assured of his life and work. No doubt in that perfect world there had been no unemployed problem, no social question left unsolved. And a great quiet had followed.

'It is a law of nature we overlook, that intellectual versatility is the compensation for change, danger, and trouble. An animal perfectly in harmony with its environment is a perfect mechanism. Nature never appeals to intelligence until habit and instinct are useless. There is no intelligence where there is no change and no need of change. Only those animals partake of intelligence that have to meet a huge variety of needs and dangers.

'So, as I see it, the Upper-world man had drifted towards his feeble prettiness, and the Under-world to mere mechanical industry. But that perfect state had lacked one thing even — for mechanical perfection — absolute permanency. Apparently as time went on, the feeding of the Under-world, however it was effected, had become disjointed. Mother Necessity, who had been staved off for a few thousand years, came back again, and she began below. The Under-world being in contact with machinery, which, however perfect, still needs some little thought outside habit, had probably retained perforce rather more initiative, if less of every other human character, than the Upper. And when other meat failed them, they turned to what old habit had hitherto forbidden. So I say I saw it in my last view of the world of Eight Hundred and Two Thousand Seven Hundred and One. It may be as wrong an explanation as mortal wit could invent. It is how the thing shaped itself to me, and as that I give it to you.

'After the fatigues, excitements, and terrors of the past days, and in spite of my grief, this seat and the tranquil view and the warm sunlight were very pleasant. I was very tired and sleepy, and soon my theorizing passed into dozing. Catching myself at that, I took my own hint, and spreading myself out upon the turf I had a long and refreshing sleep.

'I awoke a little before sunsetting. I now felt safe against being caught napping by the Morlocks, and, stretching myself, I came on down the hill towards the White Sphinx. I had my crowbar in one hand, and the other hand played with the matches in my pocket.

'And now came a most unexpected thing. As I approached the pedestal of the sphinx I found the bronze valves were open. They had slid down into grooves.

'At that I stopped short before them, hesitating to enter.

'Within was a small apartment, and on a raised place in the corner of this was the Time Machine. I had the small levers in my pocket. So here, after all my elaborate preparations for the siege of the White Sphinx, was a meek surrender. I threw my iron bar away, almost sorry not to use it.

'A sudden thought came into my head as I stooped towards the portal. For once, at least, I grasped the mental operations of the Morlocks. Suppressing a strong inclination to laugh, I stepped through the bronze frame and up to the Time Machine. I was surprised to find it had been carefully oiled and cleaned. I have suspected since that the Morlocks had even partially taken it to pieces while trying in their dim way to grasp its purpose.

'Now as I stood and examined it, finding a pleasure in the mere touch of the contrivance, the thing I had expected happened. The bronze panels suddenly slid up and struck the frame with a clang. I was in the dark — trapped. So the Morlocks thought. At that I chuckled gleefully.

'I could already hear their murmuring laughter as they came towards me. Very calmly I tried to strike the match. I had only to fix the levers and depart then like a ghost. But I had overlooked one little thing. The matches were of that abominable kind that light only on the box.

'You may imagine how all my calm vanished. The little brutes were close upon me. One touched me. I made a sweeping blow in the dark at them with the levers, and began to scramble into the saddle of the machine. Then came one hand upon me and then another. Then I had simply to fight against their persistent fingers for my levers, and at the same time feel for the studs over which these fitted. One, indeed, they almost got away from me. As it slipped from my hand, I had to butt in the dark with my head — I could hear the Morlock's skull ring — to recover it. It was a nearer thing than the fight in the forest, I think, this last scramble.

'But at last the lever was fixed and pulled over. The clinging hands slipped from me. The darkness presently fell from my eyes. I found myself in the same grey light and tumult I have already described.

XI

'I have already told you of the sickness and confusion that comes with time travelling. And this time I was not seated properly in the saddle, but sideways and in an unstable fashion. For an indefinite time I clung to the machine as it swayed and vibrated, quite unheeding how I went, and when I brought myself to look at the dials again I was amazed to find where I had arrived. One dial records days, and another thousands of days, another millions of days, and another thousands of millions. Now, instead of reversing the levers, I had pulled them over so as to go forward with them, and when I came to look at these indicators I found that the thousands hand was sweeping round as fast as the seconds hand of a watch — into futurity.

'As I drove on, a peculiar change crept over the appearance of things. The palpitating greyness grew darker; then — though I was still traveling with prodigious velocity — the blinking succession of day and night, which was usually indicative of a slower pace, returned, and grew more and more marked. This puzzled me very much at first. The alterations of night and day grew slower and slower, and so did the passage of the sun across the sky, until they seemed to stretch through centuries. At last a steady twilight brooded over the earth, a twilight only broken now and then when a comet glared across the darkling sky. The band of light that had indicated the sun had long since disappeared; for the sun had ceased to set — it simply rose and fell in the west, and grew ever broader and more red. All trace of the moon had vanished. The circling of the stars, growing slower and slower, had given place to creeping points of light. At last, some time before I stopped, the sun, red and very large, halted motionless upon the horizon, a vast dome glowing with a dull heat, and now and then suffering a momentary extinction. At one time it had for a little while glowed more brilliantly again, but it speedily reverted to its sullen red heat. I perceived by this slowing down of its rising and setting that the work of the tidal drag was done. The earth had come to rest with one face to the sun, even as in our own time the moon faces the earth. Very cautiously, for I remembered my former headlong fall, I began to reverse my motion. Slower and slower went the circling hands until the thousands one seemed motionless and the daily one was no longer a mere mist upon its scale. Still slower, until the dim outlines of a desolate beach grew visible.

'I stopped very gently and sat upon the Time Machine, looking round. The sky was no longer blue. North-eastward it was inky black, and out of the blackness shone brightly and steadily the pale white stars. Overhead it was a deep Indian red and starless, and south-eastward it grew brighter to a glowing scarlet where, cut by the horizon, lay the huge hull of the sun, red and motionless. The rocks about me were of a harsh reddish colour, and all the trace of life that I could see at first was the intensely green vegetation that covered every projecting point on their south-eastern face. It was the same rich green that one sees on forest moss or on the lichen in caves: plants which like these grow in a perpetual twilight.

'The machine was standing on a sloping beach. The sea stretched away to the south-west, to rise into a sharp bright horizon against the wan sky. There were no breakers and no waves, for not a breath of wind was stirring. Only a slight oily swell rose and fell like a gentle breathing, and showed that the eternal sea was still moving and living. And along the margin where the water sometimes broke was a thick incrustation of salt—pink under the lurid sky. There was a sense of oppression in my head, and I noticed that I was breathing very fast. The sensation reminded me of my only experience of mountaineering, and from that I judged the air to be more rarefied than it is now.

'Far away up the desolate slope I heard a harsh scream, and saw a thing like a huge white butterfly go slanting and fluttering up into the sky and, circling, disappear over some low hillocks beyond. The sound of its voice was so dismal that I shivered and seated myself more firmly upon the machine. Looking round me again, I saw that, quite near, what I had taken to be a reddish mass of rock was moving slowly towards me. Then I saw the thing was really a monstrous crab-like creature. Can you imagine a crab as large as yonder table, with its many legs moving slowly and uncertainly, its big claws swaying, its long antennae, like carters' whips, waving and feeling, and its stalked eyes gleaming at you on either side of its metallic front? Its back was corrugated and ornamented with ungainly bosses, and a greenish incrustation blotched it here and there. I could see the many palps of its complicated mouth flickering and feeling as it moved.

'As I stared at this sinister apparition crawling towards me, I felt a tickling on my cheek as though a fly had lighted there. I tried to brush it away with my hand, but in a moment it returned, and almost immediately came another by my ear. I struck at this, and caught something threadlike. It was drawn swiftly out of my hand. With a frightful qualm, I turned, and I saw that I had grasped the antenna of another monster crab that stood just behind me. Its evil eyes were wriggling on their stalks, its mouth was all alive with appetite, and its vast ungainly claws, smeared with an algal slime, were descending upon me. In a moment my hand was on the lever, and I had placed a month between myself and these monsters. But I was still on the same beach, and I saw them distinctly now as soon as I stopped. Dozens of them seemed to be crawling here and there, in the sombre light, among the foliated sheets of intense green.

'I cannot convey the sense of abominable desolation that hung over the world. The red eastern sky, the northward blackness, the salt Dead Sea, the stony beach crawling with these fowl, slow-stirring monsters, the uniform poisonous-looking green of the lichenous plants, the thin air that hurts one's lungs: all contributed to an appalling effect. I moved on a hundred years, and there was the same red sun — a little larger, a little duller — the same dying sea, the same chill air, and the same crowd of earthy crustacea creeping in and out among the green weed and the red rocks. And in the westward sky, I saw a curved pale line like a vast new moon.

'So I travelled, stopping ever and again, in great strides of a thousand years or more, drawn on by the mystery of the earth's fate, watching with a strange fascination the sun grow larger and duller in the westward sky, and the life of the old earth ebb away. At last, more than thirty million years hence, the huge red-hot dome of the sun had come to obscure nearly a tenth part of the darkling heavens. Then I stopped once more, for the crawling multitude of crabs had disappeared, and the red beach, save for its livid green liverworts and lichens, seemed lifeless. And now it was flecked with white. A bitter cold assailed me. Rare white flakes ever and again came eddying down. To the north-eastward, the glare of snow lay under the starlight of the sable sky and I could see an undulating crest of hillocks pinkish white. There were fringes of ice along the sea margin, with drifting masses further out; but the main expanse of that salt ocean, all bloody under the eternal sunset, was still unfrozen.

'I looked about me to see if any traces of animal life remained. A certain indefinable apprehension still kept me in the saddle of the machine. But I saw nothing moving, in earth or sky or sea. The green slime on the rocks alone testified that life was not extinct. A shallow sandbank had appeared in the sea and the water had receded from the beach. I fancied I saw some black object flopping about upon this bank, but it became motionless as I looked at it, and I judged that my eye had been deceived, and that the black object was merely a rock. The stars in the sky were intensely bright and seemed to me to twinkle very little.

'Suddenly I noticed that the circular westward outline of the sun had changed; that a concavity, a bay, had appeared in the curve. I saw this grow larger. For a minute perhaps I stared aghast at this blackness that was creeping over the day, and then I realized that an eclipse was beginning. Either the moon or the planet Mercury was passing across the sun's disk. Naturally, at first I took it to be the moon, but there is much to incline me to believe that what I really saw was the transit of an inner planet passing very near to the earth.

'The darkness grew apace; a cold wind began to blow in freshening gusts from the east, and the showering white flakes in the air increased in number. From the edge of the sea came a ripple and whisper. Beyond these lifeless sounds the world was silent. Silent? It would be hard to convey the stillness of it. All sounds of man, the bleating of sheep, the cries of birds, the hum of insects, the stir that makes the background of our lives — all that was over. As the darkness thickened, the eddying flakes grew more abundant, dancing before my eyes; and the cold of the air more intense. At last, one by one, swiftly, one after the other, the white peaks of the distant hills vanished into blackness. The breeze rose to a moaning wind. I saw the black central shadow of the eclipse sweeping towards me. In another moment the pale stars alone were visible. All else was rayless obscurity. The sky was absolutely black.

'A horror of this great darkness came on me. The cold, that smote to my marrow, and the pain I felt in breathing, overcame me. I shivered, and a deadly nausea seized me. Then like a red-hot bow in the sky appeared the edge of the sun. I got off the machine to recover myself. I felt giddy and incapable of facing the return journey. As I stood sick and confused I saw again the moving thing upon the shoal — there was no mistake now that it was a moving thing — against the red water of the sea. It was a round thing, the size of a football perhaps, or may be, bigger, and tentacles trailed down from it; it seemed black against the weltering blood-red water, and it was hopping fitfully about. Then I felt I was fainting. But a terrible dread of lying helpless in that remote and awful twilight sustained me while I clambered upon the saddle.

XII

'So I came back. For a long time I must have been insensible upon the machine. The blinking succession of the days and nights was resumed, the sun got golden again, the sky blue. I breathed with greater freedom. The fluctuating contours of the land ebbed and flowed. The hands spun backward upon the dials. At last I saw again the dim shadows of houses, the evidences of decadent humanity. These, too, changed and passed, and others came. Presently, when the million dial was at zero, I slackened speed. I began to recognize our own petty and familiar architecture, the thousands hand ran back to the starting-point, the night and day flapped slower and slower. Then the old walls of the laboratory came round me. Very gently, now, I slowed the mechanism down.

'I saw one little thing that seemed odd to me. I think I have told you that when I set out, before my velocity became very high, Mrs. Watchett had walked across the room, travelling, as it seemed to me, like a rocket. As I returned, I passed again that minute when she traversed the laboratory. But now her every motion appeared to be the exact inversion of her previous ones. The door at the lower end opened, and she glided quietly up the laboratory, back foremost, and disappeared behind the door by which she had previously entered. Just before that I seemed to see Hillyer for a moment; but he passed like a flash.

'Then I stopped the machine, and saw about me again the old familiar laboratory, my tools, my appliances just as I had left them. I got off the thing very shakily, and sat down upon my bench. For several minutes I trembled violently. Then I became calmer. Around me was my old workshop again, exactly as it had been. I might have slept there, and the whole thing have been a dream.

'And yet, not exactly! The thing had started from the south-east corner of the laboratory. It had come to rest again in the north-west, against the wall where you saw it. That gives you the exact distance from my little lawn to the pedestal of the White Sphinx, into which the Morlocks had carried my machine.

'For a time my brain went stagnant. Presently I got up and came through the passage here, limping, because my heel was still painful, and feeling sorely begrimed. I saw the *Pall Mall Gazette* on the table by the door. I found the date was indeed to-day, and looking at the timepiece, saw the hour was almost eight o'clock. I heard your voices and the clatter of plates. I hesitated — I felt so sick and weak. Then I sniffed good wholesome meat, and opened the door on you. You know the rest. I washed, and dined, and now I am telling you the story.

'I know,' he said, after a pause, 'that all this will be absolutely incredible to you. To me the one incredible thing is that I am here to-night in this old familiar room looking into your friendly faces and telling you these strange adventures.'

He looked at the Medical Man. 'No. I cannot expect you to believe it. Take it as a lie — or a prophecy. Say I dreamed it in the workshop. Consider I have been speculating upon the destinies of our race until I have hatched this fiction. Treat my assertion of its truth as a mere stroke of art to enhance its interest. And taking it as a story, what do you think of it?'

He took up his pipe, and began, in his old accustomed manner, to tap with it nervously upon the bars of the grate. There was a momentary stillness. Then chairs began to creak and shoes to scrape upon the carpet. I took my eyes off the Time Traveller's face, and looked round at his audience. They were in the dark, and little spots of colour swam before them. The Medical Man seemed absorbed in the contemplation of our host. The Editor was looking hard at the end of his cigar — the sixth. The Journalist fumbled for his watch. The others, as far as I remember, were motionless.

The Editor stood up with a sigh. 'What a pity it is you're not a writer of stories!' he said, putting his hand on the Time Traveller's shoulder.

'You don't believe it?'

'Well ——'

'I thought not.'

The Time Traveller turned to us. 'Where are the matches?' he said. He lit one and spoke over his pipe, puffing. 'To tell you the truth . . . I hardly believe it myself. . . . And yet . . .'

His eye fell with a mute inquiry upon the withered white flowers upon the little table. Then he turned over the hand holding his pipe, and I saw he was looking at some half-healed scars on his knuckles.

The Medical Man rose, came to the lamp, and examined the flowers. 'The gynaeceum's odd,' he said. The Psychologist leant forward to see, holding out his hand for a specimen.

'I'm hanged if it isn't a quarter to one,' said the Journalist. 'How shall we get home?'

'Plenty of cabs at the station,' said the Psychologist.

'It's a curious thing,' said the Medical Man; 'but I certainly don't know the natural order of these flowers. May I have them?'

The Time Traveller hesitated. Then suddenly: 'Certainly not.'

'Where did you really get them?' said the Medical Man.

The Time Traveller put his hand to his head. He spoke like one who was trying to keep hold of an idea that eluded him. 'They were put into my pocket by Weena, when I travelled into Time.' He stared around the room. 'I'm damned if it isn't all going. This room and you and the atmosphere of every day is too much for my memory. Did I ever make a Time Machine, or a model of a Time Machine? Or is it all only a dream? They say life is a dream, a precious poor dream at times — but I can't stand another that won't fit. It's madness. And where did the dream come from? . . . I must look at that machine. If there *is* one!'

He caught up the lamp swiftly, and carried it, flaring red, through the door into the corridor. We followed him. There in the flickering light of the lamp was the machine sure enough, squat, ugly, and askew; a thing of brass, ebony, ivory, and translucent glimmering quartz. Solid to the touch — for I put out my hand and felt the rail of it — and with brown spots and smears upon the ivory, and bits of grass and moss upon the lower parts, and one rail bent awry.

The Time Traveller put the lamp down on the bench, and ran his hand along the damaged rail. 'It's all right now,' he said. 'The story I told you was true. I'm sorry to have brought you out here in the cold.' He took up the lamp, and, in an absolute silence, we returned to the smoking-room.

He came into the hall with us and helped the Editor on with his coat. The Medical Man looked into his face and, with a certain hesitation, told him he was suffering from overwork, at which he laughed hugely. I remember him standing in the open doorway, bawling good night.

I shared a cab with the Editor. He thought the tale a 'gaudy lie.' For my own part I was unable to come to a conclusion. The story was so fantastic and incredible, the telling so credible and sober. I lay awake most of the night thinking about it. I determined to go next day and see the Time Traveller again. I was told he was in the laboratory, and being on easy terms in the house, I went up to him. The laboratory, however, was empty. I stared for a minute at the Time Machine and put out my hand and touched the lever. At that the squat substantial-looking mass swayed like a bough shaken by the wind. Its instability startled me extremely, and I had a queer reminiscence of the childish days when I used to be forbidden to meddle. I came back through the corridor. The Time Traveller met me in the smoking-room. He was coming from the house. He had a small camera under one arm and a knapsack under the other. He laughed when he saw me, and gave me an elbow to shake. 'I'm frightfully busy,' said he, 'with that thing in there.'

'But is it not some hoax?' I said. 'Do you really travel through time?'

'Really and truly I do.' And he looked frankly into my eyes. He hesitated. His eye wandered about the room. 'I only want half an hour,' he said. 'I know why you came, and it's awfully good of you. There's some magazines here. If you'll stop to lunch I'll prove you this time travelling up to the hilt, specimen and all. If you'll forgive my leaving you now?'

I consented, hardly comprehending then the full import of his words, and he nodded and went on down the corridor. I heard the door of the laboratory slam, seated myself in a chair, and took up a daily paper. What was he going to do before lunch-time? Then suddenly I was reminded by an advertisement that I had promised to meet Richardson, the publisher, at two. I looked at my watch, and saw that I could barely save that engagement. I got up and went down the passage to tell the Time Traveller.

As I took hold of the handle of the door I heard an exclamation, oddly truncated at the end, and a click and a thud. A gust of air whirled round me as I opened the door, and from within came the sound of broken glass falling on the floor. The Time Traveller was not there. I seemed to see a ghostly, indistinct figure sitting in a whirling mass of black and brass for a moment — a figure so transparent that the bench behind with its sheets of drawings was absolutely distinct; but this phantasm vanished as I rubbed my eyes. The Time Machine had gone. Save for a subsiding stir of dust, the further end of the laboratory was empty. A pane of the skylight had, apparently, just been blow in.

I felt an unreasonable amazement. I knew that something strange had happened, and for the moment could not distinguish what the strange thing might be. As I stood staring, the door into the garden opened, and the man-servant appeared.

We looked at each other. Then ideas began to come. 'Has Mr. ―― gone out that way?' said I.

'No, sir. No one has come out this way. I was expecting to find him here.'

At that I understood. At the risk of disappointing Richardson I stayed on, waiting for the Time Traveller; waiting for the second, perhaps still stranger story, and the specimens and photographs he would bring with him. But I am beginning now to fear that I must wait a lifetime. The Time Traveller vanished three years ago. And, as every body knows now, he has never returned.

EPILOGUE

One cannot choose but wonder. Will he ever return? It may be that he swept back into the past, and fell among the blood-drinking, hairy savages of the Age of Unpolished Stone: into the abysses of the Cretaceous Sea; or among the grotesque saurians, the huge reptilian brutes of the Jurassic times. He may even now—if I may use the phrase—be wandering on some plesiosaurus-haunted Oolitic coral reef, or beside the lonely saline lakes of the Triassic Age. Or did he go forward, into one of the nearer ages, in which men are still men, but with the riddles of our own time answered and its wearisome problems solved? Into the manhood of the race: for I, for my own part, cannot think that these latter days of weak experiment, fragmentary theory, and mutual discord are indeed man's culminating time! I say, for my own part. He, I know—for the question had been discussed among us long before the Time Machine was made—thought but cheerlessly of Mankind and saw in the growing pile of civilization only a foolish heaping that must inevitably fall back upon and destroy its makers in the end. If that is so, it remains for us to live as though it were not so. But to me the future is still black and blank—is a vast ignorance, lit at a few casual places by the memory of his story. And I have by me, for my comfort, two strange white flowers— shrivelled now, and brown and flat and brittle—to witness that even when mind and strength had gone, gratitude and a mutual tenderness still lived on in the heart of man.

[1895]

Study and Writing Questions

1. What sorts of CHARACTERIZATION does Wells use? Why does he have CHARACTERS like The Very Young Man? Describe the qualities of the Time Traveller. What is the Time Traveller's relationship with Weena? To what extent is this NARRATIVE about character?

2. In the Bible, there are many names for the deity. Of these, "Eloi" is used in only one place, Mark 15:34: "And at the ninth hour [on the cross] Jesus cried with a loud voice, saying, Eloi, Eloi, lama sabachthani?" which is, being interpreted, "My God, my God, why hast thou forsaken me?" "Morlock" recalls the pagan god who demanded the sacrifice of children, as in Leviticus 19:21: "[And the Lord spake unto Moses, saying] And thou shalt not let any of

thy seed pass through the fire to Moloch, neither shalt thou profane the name of thy God: I am the Lord." Why does Wells use these evocative names? What are their implications here? What other ALLUSIONS are there to the Western religious tradition? What is the philosophical role of religion in this narrative?

3. What is the ancient story of the Sphinx? How does that affect our under-standing of this narrative?

4. What is the role of science and/or the intellect in this narrative? How smart is the Time Traveller really? How is science represented by some of the Time Traveller's dinner guests? How has science helped create the world of 802,701? How has science helped explain the world of 802,701? What does the narrative suggest is the proper use of science?

5. Why is chapter XI, the journey to about the year 30,000,000, included in the narrative? How would the narrative be different without it?

6. What is the political message of the main narrative? How is the world of 802,701 connected to the world of Wells's contemporaries? Although the Time Traveller sides with the Eloi, are they obviously more worthy than the Morlocks? What evidence is there that the IMPLIED AUTHOR may not see the future in such simple terms as the Time Traveller and the STYLE imply?

7. What are the central SYMBOLS in the Epilogue? What is the role of its narrator in the narrative as a whole? Describe the Epilogue narrator's attitude toward the overall narrative. Do you share that attitude? How would *The Time Machine* be different without the Epilogue?

See also Questions for Contrast and Comparison: 4, 22, 25, 29, 49, 76, 99, 146, 148, 173, 182, 183, 209, 212, and 222.

■ **EUDORA WELTY** (1909–) *was born and raised in Jackson, Mississippi,* *one of three children of an insurance company executive and a thrifty house-wife who kept a cow in the little pasture of their home two blocks from the state capital. She attended Jackson State College for Women (1925–1927), the University of Wisconsin (B.A., 1929), and the Columbia University School of Advertising (1930–1931). After her father's death (1931), she returned permanently to Jackson. During the Depression, she held various newspaper and radio jobs and was publicity agent for the state office of the Works Progress Administration. During World War II, from home, she was a* New York Times Book Review *staff writer. She began publishing* STORIES *casually in her mid-twenties but her New York literary agent pushed her to more prominent markets which led to her much admired first collection,* A Curtain of Green *(1941). "What I do . . . is try to enter in the mind, heart, and skin of a human being who is not myself. . . . It is the act of a writer's imagination that I set most high." Her many volumes, most set in Mississippi, have been widely honored. Most notable are* The Robber Bridegroom *(1942) combining the* FAIRY TALE *and ballad forms;* Delta Wedding *(1946) about a modern plantation family;* The Optimist's Daughter *(1972, Pulitzer Prize) about a relationship with a stepmother;* The Eye of the Story *(1978), essays and reviews; and* Collected Stories *(1980).*

Lily Daw and the Three Ladies

Mrs. Watts and Mrs. Carson were both in the post office in Victory when the letter came from the Ellisville Institute for the Feeble-Minded of Mississippi. Aimee Slocum, with her hand still full of mail, ran out in front and handed it straight to Mrs. Watts, and they all three read it together. Mrs. Watts held it taut between her pink hands, and Mrs. Carson underscored each line slowly with her thimbled finger. Everybody else in the post office wondered what was up now.

"What will Lily say," beamed Mrs. Carson at last, "when we tell her we're sending her to Ellisville!"

"She'll be tickled to death," beamed Mrs. Watts, and added in a guttural voice to a deaf lady, "Lily Daw's getting in at Ellisville!"

"Don't you all dare go off and tell Lily without me!" called Aimee Slocum, trotting back to finish putting up the mail.

"Do you suppose they'll look after her down there?" Mrs. Carson began to carry on a conversation with a group of Baptist ladies waiting in the post office. She was the Baptist preacher's wife.

"I've always heard it was lovely down there, but crowded," said one.

"Lily lets people walk over her so," said another.

"Last night at the tent show—" said another, and then popped her hand over her mouth.

"Don't mind me, I know there are such things in the world," said Mrs. Carson, looking down and fingering the tape measure which hung over her bosom.

"Oh, Mrs. Carson. Well, anyway, last night at the tent show, why, the man was just before making Lily buy a ticket to get in."

"A ticket!"

"Till my husband went up and explained she wasn't bright, and so did everybody else."

The ladies all clucked their tongues.

"Oh, it was a very nice show," said the lady who had gone. "And Lily acted so nice. She was a perfect lady—just set in her seat and stared."

"Oh, she can be a lady—she can be," said Mrs. Carson, shaking her head and turning her eyes up. "That's just what breaks your heart."

"Yes'm, she kept her eyes on—what's that thing makes all the commotion?—the xylophone," said the lady. "Didn't turn her head to the right or to the left the whole time. Set in front of me."

"The point is, what did she do after the show?" asked Mrs. Watts practically. "Lily has gotten so she is very mature for her age."

"Oh, Etta!" protested Mrs. Carson, looking at her wildly for a moment.

"And that's how come we are sending her to Ellisville," finished Mrs. Watts.

"I'm ready, you all," said Aimee Slocum, running out with white powder all over her face. "Mail's up. I don't know how good it's up."

"Well, of course, I do hope it's for the best," said several of the other ladies. They did not go at once to take their mail out of their boxes; they felt a little left out.

The three women stood at the foot of the water tank.

"To find Lily is a different thing," said Aimee Slocum.

"Where in the wide world do you suppose she'd be?" It was Mrs. Watts who was carrying the letter.

"I don't see a sign of her either on this side of the street or on the other side," Mrs. Carson declared as they walked along.

Ed Newton was stringing Redbird school tablets on the wire across the store.

"If you're after Lily, she come in here while ago and tole me she was fixin' to git married," he said.

"Ed Newton!" cried the ladies all together, clutching one another. Mrs. Watts began to fan herself at once with the letter from Ellisville. She wore widow's black, and the least thing made her hot.

"Why she is not. She's going to Ellisville, Ed," said Mrs. Carson gently. "Mrs. Watts and I and Aimee Slocum are paying her way out of our own pockets. Besides, the boys of Victory are on their honor. Lily's not going to get married, that's just an idea she's got in her head."

"More power to you, ladies," said Ed Newton, spanking himself with a tablet.

When they came to the bridge over the railroad tracks, there was Estelle Mabers, sitting on a rail. She was slowly drinking an orange Ne-Hi.

"Have you seen Lily?" they asked her.

"I'm supposed to be out here watching for her now," said the Mabers girl, as though she weren't there yet. "But for Jewel—Jewel says Lily come in the store while ago and picked out a two-ninety-eight hat and wore it off. Jewel wants to swap her something else for it."

"Oh, Estelle, Lily says she's going to get married!" cried Aimee Slocum.

"Well, I declare," said Estelle; she never understood anything.

Loralee Adkins came riding by in her Willys-Knight, tooting the horn to find out what they were talking about.

Aimee threw up her hands and ran out into the street. "Loralee, Loralee, you got to ride us up to Lily Daws'. She's up yonder fixing to get married!"

"Hop in, my land!"

"Well, that just goes to show you right now," said Mrs. Watts, groaning as she was helped into the back seat. "What we've got to do is persuade Lily it will be nicer to go to Ellisville."

"Just to think!"

While they rode around the corner Mrs. Carson was going on in her sad voice, sad as the soft noises in the hen house at twilight. "We buried Lily's poor defenseless mother. We gave Lily all her food and kindling and every stitch she had on. Sent her to Sunday school to learn the Lord's teachings, had her baptized a Baptist. And when her old father commenced beating her and tried to cut her head off with the butcher knife, why, we went and took her away from him and gave her a place to stay."

The paintless frame house with all the weather vanes was three stories high in places and had yellow and violet stained-glass windows in front and ginger-bread around the porch. It leaned steeply to one side, toward the railroad, and the front steps were gone. The car full of ladies drew up under the cedar tree.

"Now Lily's almost grown up," Mrs. Carson continued. "In fact, she's grown," she concluded, getting out.

"Talking about getting married," said Mrs. Watts disgustedly. "Thanks, Loralee, you run on home."

They climbed over the dusty zinnias onto the porch and walked through the open door without knocking.

"There certainly is always a funny smell in this house. I say it every time I come," said Aimee Slocum.

Lily was there, in the dark of the hall, kneeling on the floor by a small open trunk.

When she saw them she put a zinnia in her mouth, and held still.

"Hello, Lily," said Mrs. Carson reproachfully.

"Hello," said Lily. In a minute she gave a suck on the zinnia stem that sounded exactly like a jay bird. There she sat, wearing a petticoat for a dress, one of the things Mrs. Carson kept after her about. Her milky-yellow hair streamed freely down from under a new hat. You could see the wavy scar on her throat if you knew it was there.

Mrs. Carson and Mrs. Watts, the two fattest, sat in the double rocker. Aimee Slocum sat on the wire chair donated from the drugstore that burned.

"Well, what are you doing, Lily?" asked Mrs. Watts, who led the rocking.

Lily smiled.

The trunk was old and lined with yellow and brown paper, with an asterisk pattern showing in darker circles and rings. Mutely the ladies indicated to each other that they did not know where in the world it had come from. It was empty except for two bars of soap and a green washcloth, which Lily was now trying to arrange in the bottom.

"Go on and tell us what you're doing, Lily," said Aimee Slocum.

"Packing, silly," said Lily.

"Where are you going?"

"Going to get married, and I bet you wish you was me now," said Lily. But shyness overcame her suddenly, and she popped the zinnia back into her mouth.

"Talk to me, dear," said Mrs. Carson. "Tell old Mrs. Carson why you want to get married."

"No," said Lily, after a moment's hesitation.

"Well, we've thought of something that will be so much nicer," said Mrs. Carson. "Why don't you go to Ellisville!"

"Won't that be lovely?" said Mrs. Watts. "Goodness, yes."

"It's a lovely place," said Aimee Slocum uncertainly.

"You've got bumps on your face," said Lily.

"Aimee, dear, you stay out of this, if you don't mind," said Mrs. Carson anxiously. "I don't know what it is comes over Lily when you come around her."

Lily stared at Aimee Slocum meditatively.

"There! Wouldn't you like to go to Ellisville now?" asked Mrs. Carson.

"No'm," said Lily.

"Why not?" All the ladies leaned down toward her in impressive astonishment.

"'Cause I'm goin' to get married," said Lily.

"Well, and who are you going to marry, dear?" asked Mrs. Watts. She knew how to pin people down and make them deny what they'd already said.

Lily bit her lip and began to smile. She reached into the trunk and held up both cakes of soap and wagged them.

"Tell us," challenged Mrs. Watts. "Who you're going to marry, now."

"A man last night."

There was a gasp from each lady. The possible reality of a lover descended suddenly like a summer hail over their heads. Mrs. Watts stood up and balanced herself.

"One of those show fellows! A musician!" she cried.

Lily looked up in admiration.

"Did he—did he do anything to you?" In the long run, it was still only Mrs. Watts who could take charge.

"Oh, yes'm," said Lily. She patted the cakes of soap fastidiously with the tips of her small fingers and tucked them in with the washcloth.

"What?" demanded Aimee Slocum, rising up and tottering before her scream. "What?" she called out in the hall.

"Don't ask her what," said Mrs. Carson, coming up behind. "Tell me, Lily—just yes or no—are you the same as you were?"

"He had a red coat," said Lily graciously. "He took little sticks and went *ping-pong! ding-dong!*"

"Oh, I think I'm going to faint," said Aimee Slocum, but they said, "No, you're not."

"The xylophone!" cried Mrs. Watts. "The xylophone player! Why, the coward, he ought to be run out of town on a rail!"

"Out of town? He is out of town, by now," cried Aimee. "Can't you read?—the sign in the café—Victory on the ninth, Como on the tenth? He's in Como. Como!"

"All right! We'll bring him back!" cried Mrs. Watts. "He can't get away from me!"

"Hush," said Mrs. Carson. "I don't think it's any use following that line of reasoning at all. It's better in the long run for him to be gone out of our lives for good and all. That kind of a man. He was after Lily's body alone and he wouldn't ever in this world make the poor little thing happy, even if we went out and forced him to marry her like he ought—at the point of a gun."

"Still—" began Aimee, her eyes widening.

"Shut up," said Mrs. Watts. "Mrs. Carson, you're right, I expect."

"This is my hope chest—see?" said Lily politely in the pause that followed. "You haven't even looked at it. I've already got soap and a washrag. And I have my hat—on. What are you all going to give me?"

"Lily," said Mrs. Watts, starting over, "we'll give you lots of gorgeous things if you'll only go to Ellisville instead of getting married."

"What will you give me?" asked Lily.

"I'll give you a pair of hemstitched pillowcases," said Mrs. Carson.

"I'll give you a big caramel cake," said Mrs. Watts.

"I'll give you a souvenir from Jackson—a little toy bank," said Aimee Slocum. "Now will you go?"

"No," said Lily.

"I'll give you a pretty little Bible with your name on it in real gold," said Mrs. Carson.

"What if I was to give you a pink crêpe de Chine brassière with adjustable shoulder straps?" asked Mrs. Watts grimly.

"Oh, Etta."

"Well, she needs it," said Mrs. Watts. "What would they think if she ran all over Ellisville in a petticoat looking like a Fiji?"

"I wish *I* could go to Ellisville," said Aimee Slocum luringly.

"What will they have for me down there?" asked Lily softly.

"Oh! lots of things. You'll have baskets to weave, I expect. . . ." Mrs. Carson looked vaguely at the others.

"Oh, yes indeed, they will let you make all sorts of baskets," said Mrs. Watts; then her voice too trailed off.

"No'm, I'd rather get married," said Lily.

"Lily Daw! Now that's just plain stubbornness!" cried Mrs. Watts. "You almost said you'd go and then you took it back!"

"We've all asked God, Lily," said Mrs. Carson finally, "and God seemed to tell us—Mr. Carson, too—that the place where you ought to be, so as to be happy, was Ellisville."

Lily looked reverent, but still stubborn.

"We've really just got to get her there—now!" screamed Aimee Slocum all at once. "Suppose—! She can't stay here!"

"Oh, no, no, no," said Mrs. Carson hurriedly. "We mustn't think that."

They sat sunken in despair.

"Could I take my hope chest—to go to Ellisville?" asked Lily shyly, looking at them sidewise.

"Why, yes," said Mrs. Carson blankly.

Silently they rose once more to their feet.

"Oh, if I could just take my hope chest!"

"All the time it was just her hope chest," Aimee whispered.

Mrs. Watts struck her palms together. "It's settled!"

"Praise the fathers," murmured Mrs. Carson.

Lily looked up at them, and her eyes gleamed. She cocked her head and spoke out in a proud imitation of someone — someone utterly unknown.

"O.K. — Toots!"

The ladies had been nodding and smiling and backing away toward the door.

"I think I'd better stay," said Mrs. Carson, stopping in her tracks. "Where — where could she have learned that terrible expression?"

"Pack up," said Mrs. Watts. "Lily Daw is leaving for Ellisville on Number One."

In the station the train was puffing. Nearly everyone in Victory was hanging around waiting for it to leave. The Victory Civic Band had assembled without any orders and was scattered through the crowd. Ed Newton gave false signals to start on his bass horn. A crate full of baby chickens got loose on the platform. Everybody wanted to see Lily all dressed up, but Mrs. Carson and Mrs. Watts had sneaked her into the train from the other side of the tracks.

The two ladies were going to travel as far as Jackson to help Lily change trains and be sure she went in the right direction.

Lily sat between them on the plush seats with her hair combed and pinned up into a knot under a small blue hat which was Jewel's exchange for the pretty one. She wore a traveling dress made out of part of Mrs. Watt's last summer's mourning. Pink straps glowed through. She had a purse and a Bible and a warm cake in a box, all in her lap.

Aimee Slocum had been getting the outgoing mail stamped and bundled. She stood in the aisle of the coach now, tears shaking from her eyes.

"Good-bye, Lily," she said. She was the one who felt things.

"Good-bye, silly," said Lily.

"Oh, dear, I hope they get our telegram to meet her in Ellisville!" Aimee cried sorrowfully, as she thought how far away it was. "And it was so hard to get it all in ten words, too."

"Get off, Aimee, before the train starts and you break your neck," said Mrs. Watts, all settled and waving her dressy fan gaily. "I declare, it's so hot, as soon as we get a few miles out of town I'm going to slip my corset down."

"Oh, Lily, don't cry down there. Just be good, and do what they tell you — it's all because they love you." Aimee drew her mouth down. She was backing away, down the aisle.

Lily laughed. She pointed across Mrs. Carson's bosom out the window toward a man. He had stepped off the train and just stood there, by himself. He was a stranger and wore a cap.

"Look," she said, laughing softly through her fingers.

"Don't — look," said Mrs. Carson very distinctly, as if, out of all she had ever spoken, she would impress these two solemn words upon Lily's soft little brain. She added, "Don't look at anything till you get to Ellisville."

Outside, Aimee Slocum was crying so hard she almost ran into the stranger. He wore a cap and was short and seemed to have on perfume, if such a thing could be.

"Could you tell me, madam," he said, "where a little lady lives in this burg name of Miss Lily Daw?" He lifted his cap — and he had red hair.

"What do you want to know for?" Aimee asked before she knew it.

"Talk louder," said the stranger. He almost whispered, himself.

"She's gone away — she's gone to Ellisville!"

"Gone?"

"Gone to Ellisville!"

"Well, I like that!" The man stuck out his bottom lip and puffed till his hair jumped.

"What business did you have with Lily?" cried Aimee suddenly.

"We was only going to get married, that's all," said the man.

Aimee Slocum started to scream in front of all those people. She almost pointed to the long black box she saw lying on the ground at the man's feet. Then she jumped back in fright.

"The xylophone! The xylophone!" she cried, looking back and forth from the man to the hissing train. Which was more terrible? The bell began to ring hollowly, and the man was talking.

"Did you say Ellisville? That in the state of Mississippi?" Like lightning he had pulled out a red notebook entitled, "Permanent Facts & Data." He wrote down something. "I don't hear well."

Aimee nodded her head up and down, and circled around him.

Under "Ellis-Ville Miss" he was drawing a line; now he was flicking it with two little marks. "Maybe she didn't say she would. Maybe she said she wouldn't." He suddenly laughed very loudly, after the way he had whispered. Aimee jumped back. "Women! — Well, if we play anywheres near Ellisville, Miss., in the future I may look her up and I may not," he said.

The bass horn sounded the true signal for the band to begin. White steam rushed out of the engine. Usually the train stopped for only a minute in Victory, but the engineer knew Lily from waving at her, and he knew this was her big day.

"Wait!" Aimee Slocum did scream. "Wait, mister! I can get her for you. Wait, Mister Engineer! Don't go!"

Then there she was back on the train, screaming in Mrs. Carson's and Mrs. Watts's faces.

"The xylophone player! The xylophone player to marry her! Yonder he is!"

"Nonsense," murmured Mrs. Watts, peering over the others to look where Aimee pointed. "If he's there I don't see him. Where is he? You're looking at One-Eye Beasley."

"The little man with the cap — no, with the red hair! Hurry!"

"Is that really him?" Mrs. Carson asked Mrs. Watts in wonder. "Mercy! He's small, isn't he?"

"Never saw him before in my life!" cried Mrs. Watts. But suddenly she shut up her fan.

"Come on! This is a train we're on!" cried Aimee Slocum. Her nerves were all unstrung.

"All right, don't have a conniption fit, girl," said Mrs. Watts. "Come on," she said thickly to Mrs. Carson.

"Where are we going now?" asked Lily as they struggled down the aisle.

"We're taking you to get married," said Mrs. Watts. "Mrs. Carson, you'd better phone up your husband right there in the station."

"But I don't want to git married," said Lily, beginning to whimper. "I'm going to Ellisville."

"Hush, and we'll all have some ice-cream cones later," whispered Mrs. Carson.

Just as they climbed down the steps at the back end of the train, the band went into "Independence March."

The xylophone player was still there, patting his foot. He came up and said, "Hello, Toots. What's up — tricks?" and kissed Lily with a smack, after which she hung her head.

"So you're the young man we've heard so much about," said Mrs. Watts. Her smile was brilliant. "Here's your little Lily."

"What say?" asked the xylophone player.

"My husband happens to be the Baptist preacher of Victory," said Mrs. Carson in a loud, clear voice. "Isn't that lucky? I can get him here in five minutes: I know exactly where he is."

They were in a circle around the xylophone player, all going into the white waiting room.

"Oh, I feel just like crying, at a time like this," said Aimee Slocum. She looked back and saw the train moving slowly away, going under the bridge at Main Street. Then it disappeared around the curve.

"Oh, the hope chest!" Aimee cried in a stricken voice.

"And whom have we the pleasure of addressing?" Mrs. Watts was shouting, while Mrs. Carson was ringing up the telephone.

The band went on playing. Some of the people thought Lily was on the train, and some swore she wasn't. Everybody cheered, though, and a straw hat was thrown into the telephone wires.

[1937]

Study and Writing Questions

1. What details in the STORY suggest the economic structure of the society of Victory, Mississippi? What is that structure?
2. On the crowded station platform, the one person whom the xylophone player happens to ask for help turns out to be one of Lily's "three ladies." Does this seem too COINCIDENTAL? If so, is that a flaw in the story? If not, what about the story makes this coincidence believable?
3. Why does the IMPLIED AUTHOR have the band play "Independence March"?
4. What are the MOTIVES of the three ladies toward Lily? What are her motives toward them? Do these motives change through the story? Which motives do you prefer?
5. In what ways, if any, does the last paragraph seem to RESOLVE the NARRATIVE?

See also Questions for Contrast and Comparison: 44, 70, 84, 87, 88, 89, 90, 102, 103, and 137.

Petrified Man

"Reach in my purse and git me a cigarette without no powder in it if you kin, Mrs. Fletcher, honey," said Leota to her ten o'clock shampoo-and-set customer. "I don't like no perfumed cigarettes."

Mrs. Fletcher gladly reached over to the lavender shelf under the lavender-framed mirror, shook a hair net loose from the clasp of the patent-leather bag, and slapped her hand down quickly on a powder puff which burst out when the purse was opened.

"Why, look at the peanuts, Leota!" said Mrs. Fletcher in her marvelling voice.

"Honey, them goobers has been in my purse a week if they's been in it a day. Mrs. Pike bought them peanuts."

"Who's Mrs. Pike?" asked Mrs. Fletcher, settling back. Hidden in this den of curling fluid and henna packs, separated by a lavender swing-door from the other customers, who were being gratified in other booths, she could give her curiosity its freedom. She looked expectantly at the black part in Leota's yellow curls as she bent to light the cigarette.

"Mrs. Pike is this lady from New Orleans," said Leota, puffing, and pressing into Mrs. Fletcher's scalp with strong red-nailed fingers. "A friend, not a customer. You see, like maybe I told you last time, me and Fred and Sal and Joe all had us a fuss, so Sal and Joe up and moved out, so we didn't do a thing but rent out their room. So we rented it to Mrs. Pike. And Mr. Pike." She flicked an ash into the basket of dirty towels. "Mrs. Pike is a very decided blonde. *She* bought me the peanuts."

"She must be cute," said Mrs. Fletcher.

"Honey, 'cute' ain't the word for what she is. I'm tellin' you, Mrs. Pike is attractive. She has her a good time. She's got a sharp eye out, Mrs. Pike has."

She dashed the comb through the air, and paused dramatically as a cloud of Mrs. Fletcher's hennaed hair floated out of the lavender teeth like a small storm-cloud.

"Hair fallin'."

"Aw, Leota."

"Uh-huh, commencin' to fall out," said Leota, combing again, and letting fall another cloud.

"Is it any dandruff in it?" Mrs. Fletcher was frowning, her hair-line eyebrows diving down toward her nose, and her wrinkled, beady-lashed eyelids batting with concentration.

"Nope." She combed again. "Just fallin' out."

"Bet it was that last perm'nent you gave me that did it," Mrs. Fletcher said cruelly. "Remember you cooked me fourteen minutes."

"You had fourteen minutes comin' to you," said Leota with finality.

"Bound to be somethin'," persisted Mrs. Fletcher. "Dandruff, dandruff. I couldn't of caught a thing like that from Mr. Fletcher, could I?"

"Well," Leota answered at last, "you know what I heard in here yestiddy, one of Thelma's ladies was settin' over yonder in Thelma's booth gittin' a machine-less, and I don't mean to insist or insinuate or anything, Mrs. Fletcher, but Thelma's lady just happ'med to throw out—I forgotten what she was talkin' about at the time—that you was p-r-e-g., and lots of times that'll make your hair do awful funny, fall out and God knows what all. It just ain't our fault, is the way I look at it."

There was a pause. The women stared at each other in the mirror.

"Who was it?" demanded Mrs. Fletcher.

"Honey, I really couldn't say," said Leota. "Not that you look it."

"Where's Thelma? I'll get it out of her," said Mrs. Fletcher.

"Now, honey, I wouldn't go and git mad over a little thing like that," Leota said, combing hastily, as though to hold Mrs. Fletcher down by the hair. "I'm sure it was somebody didn't mean no harm in the world. How far gone are you?"

"Just wait," said Mrs. Fletcher, and shrieked for Thelma, who came in and took a drag from Leota's cigarette.

"Thelma, honey, throw your mind back to yestiddy if you kin," said Leota, drenching Mrs. Fletcher's hair with a thick fluid and catching the overflow in a cold wet towel at her neck.

"Well, I got my lady half wound for a spiral," said Thelma doubtfully.

"This won't take but a minute," said Leota. "Who is it you got in there, old Horse Face? Just cast your mind back and try to remember who your lady was yestiddy who happ'm to mention that my customer was pregnant, that's all. She's dead to know."

Thelma drooped her blood-red lips and looked over Mrs. Fletcher's head into the mirror. "Why, honey, I ain't got the faintest," she breathed. "I really don't recollect the faintest. But I'm sure she meant no harm. I declare, I forgot my hair finally got combed and thought it was a stranger behind me."

"Was it that Mrs. Hutchinson?" Mrs. Fletcher was tensely polite.

"Mrs. Hutchinson? Oh, Mrs. Hutchinson." Thelma batted her eyes. "Naw, precious, she come on Thursday and didn't ev'm mention your name. I doubt if she ev'm knows you're on the way."

"Thelma!" cried Leota staunchly.

"All I know is, whoever it is 'll be sorry some day. Why, I just barely knew it myself!" cried Mrs. Fletcher. "Just let her wait!"

"Why? What're you gonna do to her?"

It was a child's voice, and the women looked down. A little boy was making tents with aluminum wave pinchers on the floor under the sink.

"Billy Boy, hon, mustn't bother nice ladies." Leota smiled. She slapped him brightly and behind her back waved Thelma out of the booth. "Ain't Billy Boy a sight? Only three years old and already just nuts about the beauty-parlor business."

"I never saw him here before," said Mrs. Fletcher, still unmollified.

"He ain't been here before, that's how come," said Leota. "He belongs to Mrs. Pike. She got her a job but it was Fay's Millinery. He oughtn't to try on those ladies' hats, they come down over his eyes like I don't know what. They just git to look ridiculous, that's what, an' of course he's gonna put 'em on: hats. They tole Mrs. Pike they didn't appreciate him hangin' around there. Here, he couldn't hurt a thing."

"Well! I don't like children that much," said Mrs. Fletcher.

"Well!" said Leota moodily.

"Well! I'm almost tempted not to have this one," said Mrs. Fletcher. "That Mrs. Hutchinson! Just looks straight through you when she sees you on the street and then spits at you behind your back."

"Mr. Fletcher would beat you on the head if you didn't have it now," said Leota reasonably. "After going this far."

Mrs. Fletcher sat up straight. "Mr. Fletcher can't do a thing with me."

"He can't!" Leota winked at herself in the mirror.

"No, siree, he can't. If he so much as raises his voice against me, he knows good and well I'll have one of my sick headaches, and then I'm just not fit to live with. And if I really look that pregnant already—"

"Well, now, honey, I just want you to know—I habm't told any of my ladies and I ain't goin' to tell 'em—even that you're losin' your hair. You just get you one of those Stork-a-Lure dresses and stop worryin'. What people don't know don't hurt nobody, as Mrs. Pike says."

"Did you tell Mrs. Pike?" asked Mrs. Fletcher sulkily.

"Well, Mrs. Fletcher, look, you ain't ever goin' to lay eyes on Mrs. Pike or her lay eyes on you, so what diffunce does it make in the long run?"

"I knew it!" Mrs. Fletcher deliberately nodded her head so as to destroy a ringlet Leota was working on behind her ear. "Mrs. Pike!"

Leota sighed. "I reckon I might as well tell you. It wasn't any more Thelma's lady tole me you was pregnant than a bat."

"Not Mrs. Hutchinson?"

"Naw, Lord! It was Mrs. Pike."

"Mrs. Pike!" Mrs. Fletcher could only sputter and let curling fluid roll into her ear. "How could Mrs. Pike possibly know I was pregnant or otherwise, when she doesn't even know me? The nerve of some people!"

"Well, here's how it was. Remember Sunday?"

"Yes," said Mrs. Fletcher.

"Sunday, Mrs. Pike an' me was all by ourself. Mr. Pike and Fred had gone over to Eagle Lake, sayin' they was goin' to catch 'em some fish, but they didn't a course. So we was settin' in Mrs. Pike's car, it's a 1939 Dodge—"

"1939, eh," said Mrs. Fletcher.

"—An' we was gettin' us a Jax beer apiece—that's the beer that Mrs. Pike says is made right in N.O., so she won't drink no other kind. So I seen you drive up to the drugstore an' run in for just a secont, leavin' I reckon Mr. Fletcher in the car, an' come runnin' out with looked like a perscription. So I says to Mrs. Pike, just to be makin' talk, 'Right yonder's Mrs. Fletcher, and I reckon that's Mr. Fletcher—she's one of my regular customers,' I says."

"I had on a figured print," said Mrs. Fletcher tentatively.

"You sure did," agreed Leota. "So Mrs. Pike, she give you a good look—she's very observant, a good judge of character, cute as a minute, you know—and she says, 'I bet you another Jax that lady's three months on the way.'"

"What gall!" said Mrs. Fletcher. "Mrs. Pike!"

"Mrs. Pike ain't goin' to bite you," said Leota. "Mrs. Pike is a lovely girl, you'd be crazy about her, Mrs. Fletcher. But she can't sit still a minute. We went to the travellin' freak show yestiddy after work. I got through early—nine o'clock. In the vacant store next door. What, you ain't been?"

"No, I despise freaks," declared Mrs. Fletcher.

"Aw. Well, honey, talkin' about bein' pregnant an' all, you ought to see those twins in a bottle, you really owe it to yourself."

"What twins?" asked Mrs. Fletcher out of the side of her mouth.

"Well, honey, they got these two twins in a bottle, see? Born joined plumb together—dead a course." Leota dropped her voice into a soft lyrical hum. "They was about this long—pardon—must of been full time, all right, wouldn't you say?—an' they had these two heads an' two faces an' four arms an' four legs, all kind of joined *here*. See, this face looked this-a-way, and the other face looked that-a-way, over their shoulder, see. Kinda pathetic."

"Glah!" said Mrs. Fletcher disapprovingly.

"Well, ugly? Honey, I mean to tell you—their parents was first cousins and all like that. Billy Boy, git me a fresh towel from off Teeny's stack—this 'n's wringin' wet—an' quit ticklin' my ankles with that curler. I declare! He don't miss nothin'."

"Me and Mr. Fletcher aren't one speck of kin, or he could never of had me," said Mrs. Fletcher placidly.

"Of course not!" protested Leota. "Neither is me an' Fred, not that we know of. Well, honey, what Mrs. Pike liked was the pygmies. They've got these pygmies down there, too, an' Mrs. Pike was just wild about 'em. You know, the teeniest men in the universe? Well, honey, they can just rest back on their little bohunkus an' roll around an' you can't hardly tell if they're sittin' or standin'. That'll give you some idea. They're about forty-two years old. Just suppose it was your husband!"

"Well, Mr. Fletcher is five foot nine and one half," said Mrs. Fletcher quickly.

"Fred's five foot ten," said Leota, "but I tell him he's still a shrimp, account of I'm so tall." She made a deep wave over Mrs. Fletcher's other temple with the comb. "Well, these pygmies are a kind of a dark brown, Mrs. Fletcher. Not bad-lookin' for what they are, you know."

"I wouldn't care for them," said Mrs. Fletcher. "What does that Mrs. Pike see in them?"

"Aw, I don't know," said Leota. "She's just cute, that's all. But they got this man, this petrified man, that ever'thing ever since he was nine years old, when it goes through his digestion, see, somehow Mrs. Pike says it goes to his joints and has been turning to stone."

"How awful!" said Mrs. Fletcher.

"He's forty-two too. That looks like a bad age."

"Who said so, that Mrs. Pike? I bet she's forty-two," said Mrs. Fletcher.

"Naw," said Leota, "Mrs. Pike's thirty-three, born in January, an Aquarian. He could move his head—like this. A course his head and mind ain't a joint, so to speak, and I guess his stomach ain't either—not yet, anyways. But see—his food, he eats it, and it goes down, see, and then he digests it"—Leota rose on her toes for an instant—"and it goes out to his joints and before you can say 'Jack

Robinson,' it's stone — pure stone. He's turning to stone. How'd you like to be married to a guy like that? All he can do, he can move his head just a quarter of an inch. A course he *looks* just *terrible*."

"I should think he would," said Mrs. Fletcher frostily. "Mr. Fletcher takes bending exercises every night of the world. I make him."

"All Fred does is lay around the house like a rug. I wouldn't be surprised if he woke up some day and couldn't move. The petrified man just sat there moving his quarter of an inch though," said Leota reminiscently.

"Did Mrs. Pike like the petrified man?" asked Mrs. Fletcher.

"Not as much as she did the others," said Leota deprecatingly. "And then she likes a man to be a good dresser, and all that."

"Is Mr. Pike a good dresser?" asked Mrs. Fletcher sceptically.

"Oh, well, yeah," said Leota, "but he's twelve or fourteen years older'n her. She ast Lady Evangeline about him."

"Who's Lady Evangeline?" asked Mrs. Fletcher.

"Well, it's this mind reader they got in the freak show," said Leota. "Was real good. Lady Evangeline is her name, and if I had another dollar I wouldn't do a thing but have my other palm read. She had what Mrs. Pike said was the 'sixth mind' but she had the worst manicure I ever saw on a living person."

"What did she tell Mrs. Pike?" asked Mrs. Fletcher.

"She told her Mr. Pike was as true to her as he could be and besides, would come into some money."

"Humph!" said Mrs. Fletcher. "What does he do?"

"I can't tell," said Leota, "because he don't work. Lady Evangeline didn't tell me enough about my nature or anything. And I would like to go back and find out some more about this boy. Used to go with this boy until he got married to this girl. Oh, shoot, that was about three and a half years ago, when you was still goin' to the Robert E. Lee Beauty Shop in Jackson. He married her for her money. Another fortune-teller tole me that at the time. So I'm not in love with him any more, anyway, besides being married to Fred, but Mrs. Pike thought, just for the hell of it, see, to ask Lady Evangeline was he happy."

"Does Mrs. Pike know everything about you already?" asked Mrs. Fletcher unbelievingly. "Mercy!"

"Oh, yeah, I tole her ever'thing about ever'thing, from now on back to I don't know when — to when I first started goin' out," said Leota. "So I ast Lady Evangeline for one of my questions, was he happily married, and she says, just like she was glad I ask her, 'Honey,' she says, 'naw, he idn't. You write down this day, March 8, 1941,' she says, 'and mock it down: three years from today him and her won't be occupyin' the same bed.' There it is, up on the wall with them other dates — see, Mrs. Fletcher? And she says, 'Child, you ought to be glad you didn't git him, because he's so mercenary.' So I'm glad I married Fred. He sure ain't mercenary, money don't mean a thing to him. But I sure would like to go back and have my other palm read."

"Did Mrs. Pike believe in what the fortune-teller said?" asked Mrs. Fletcher in a superior tone of voice.

"Lord, yes, she's from New Orleans. Ever'body in New Orleans believes ever'thing spooky. One of 'em in New Orleans before it was raided says to Mrs.

Pike one summer she was goin' to go from State to State and meet some grey-headed men, and, sure enough, she says she went on a beautician convention up to Chicago. . . ."

"Oh!" said Mrs. Fletcher. "Oh, is Mrs. Pike a beautician too?"

"Sure she is," protested Leota. "She's a beautician. I'm goin' to git her in here if I can. Before she married. But it don't leave you. She says sure enough, there was three men who was a very large part of making her trip what it was, and they all three had grey in their hair and they went in six States. Got Christmas cards from 'em. Billy Boy, go see if Thelma's got any dry cotton. Look how Mrs. Fletcher's a-drippin'."

"Where did Mrs. Pike meet Mr. Pike?" asked Mrs. Fletcher primly.

"On another train," said Leota.

"I met Mr. Fletcher, or rather he met me, in a rental library," said Mrs. Fletcher with dignity, as she watched the net come down over her head.

"Honey, me an' Fred, we met in a rumble seat eight months ago and we was practically on what you might call the way to the altar inside of half an hour," said Leota in a guttural voice, and bit a bobby pin open. "Course it don't last. Mrs. Pike says nothin' like that ever lasts."

"Mr. Fletcher and myself are as much in love as the day we married," said Mrs. Fletcher belligerently as Leota stuffed cotton into her ears.

"Mrs. Pike says it don't last," repeated Leota in a louder voice. "Now go git under the dryer. You can turn yourself on, can't you? I'll be back to comb you out. Durin' lunch I promised to give Mrs. Pike a facial. You know—free. Her bein' in the business, so to speak."

"I bet she needs one," said Mrs. Fletcher, letting the swing-door fly back against Leota. "Oh, pardon me."

A week later, on time for her appointment, Mrs. Fletcher sank heavily into Leota's chair after first removing a drug-store rental book, called *Life Is Like That*, from the seat. She stared in a discouraged way into the mirror.

"You can tell it when I'm sitting down, all right," she said.

"Leota seemed preoccupied and stood shaking out a lavender cloth. She began to pin it around Mrs. Fletcher's neck in silence.

"I said you sure can tell it when I'm sitting straight on and coming at you this way," Mrs. Fletcher said.

"Why, honey, naw you can't," said Leota gloomily. "Why, I'd never know. If somebody was to come up to me on the street and say, 'Mrs. Fletcher is pregnant!' I'd say, 'Heck, she don't look it to me.'"

"If a certain party hadn't found it out and spread it around, it wouldn't be too late even now," said Mrs. Fletcher frostily, but Leota was almost choking her with the cloth, pinning it so tight, and she couldn't speak clearly. She paddled her hands in the air until Leota wearily loosened her.

"Listen, honey, you're just a virgin compared to Mrs. Montjoy," Leota was going on, still absent-minded. She bent Mrs. Fletcher back in the chair and, sighing, tossed liquid from a teacup on to her head and dug both hands into her scalp. "You know Mrs. Montjoy—her husband's that premature-grey-headed fella?"

"She's in the Trojan Garden Club, is all I know," said Mrs. Fletcher.

"Well, honey," said Leota, but in a weary voice, "she come in here not the week before and not the day before she had her baby — she come in here the very selfsame day, I mean to tell you. Child, we was all plumb scared to death. There she was! Come for her shampoo an' set. Why, Mrs. Fletcher, in an hour an' twenty minutes she was layin' up there in the Babtist Hospital with a seb'm-pound son. It was that close a shave. I declare, if I hadn't been so tired I would of drank up a bottle of gin that night."

"What gall," said Mrs. Fletcher. "I never knew her at all well."

"See, her husband was waitin' outside in the car, and her bags was all packed an' in the back seat, an' she was all ready, 'cept she wanted her shampoo an' set. An' havin' one pain right after another. Her husband kep' comin' in here, scared-like, but couldn't do nothin' with her a course. She yelled bloody murder, too, but she always yelled her head off when I give her a perm'nent."

"She must of been crazy," said Mrs. Fletcher. "How did she look?"

"Shoot!" said Leota.

"Well, I can guess," said Mrs. Fletcher. "Awful."

"Just wanted to look pretty while she was havin' her baby, is all," said Leota airily. "Course, we was glad to give the lady what she was after — that's our motto — but I bet a hour later she wasn't payin' no mind to them little end curls. I bet she wasn't thinkin' about she ought to have on a net. It wouldn't of done her no good if she had."

"No, I don't suppose it would," said Mrs. Fletcher.

"Yeah man! She was a-yellin'. Just like when I give her perm'nent."

"Her husband ought to make her behave. Don't it seem that way to you?" asked Mrs. Fletcher. "He ought to put his foot down."

"Ha," said Leota. "A lot he could do. Maybe some women is soft."

"Oh, you mistake me, I don't mean for her to get soft — far from it! Women have to stand up for themselves, or there's just no telling. But now you take me — I ask Mr. Fletcher's advice now and then, and he appreciates it, especially on something important, like is it time for a permanent — not that I've told him about the baby. He says, 'Why, dear, go ahead!' Just ask their *advice*."

"Huh! If I ever ast Fred's advice we'd be floatin' down the Yazoo River on a houseboat or somethin' by this time," said Leota. "I'm sick of Fred. I told him to go over to Vicksburg."

"Is he going?" demanded Mrs. Fletcher.

"Sure. See, the fortune-teller — I went back and had my other palm read, since we've got to rent the room agin — said my lover was goin' to work in Vicksburg, so I don't know who she could mean, unless she meant Fred. And Fred ain't workin' here — that much is so."

"Is he going to work in Vicksburg?' asked Mrs. Fletcher. "And — "

"Sure. Lady Evangeline said so. Said the future is going to be brighter than the present. He don't want to go, but I ain't gonna put up with nothin' like that. Lays around the house an' bulls — did bull — with that good-for-nothin' Mr. Pike. He says if he goes who'll cook, but I says I never get to eat anyway — not meals. Billy Boy, take Mrs. Grover that *Screen Secrets* and leg it."

Mrs. Fletcher heard stamping feet go out the door.

"Is that that Mrs. Pike's little boy here again?" she asked, sitting up gingerly.

"Yeah, that's still him." Leota stuck out her tongue.

Mrs. Fletcher could hardly believe her eyes. "Well! How's Mrs. Pike, your attractive new friend with the sharp eyes who spreads it around town that perfect strangers are pregnant?" she asked in a sweetened tone.

"Oh, Mizziz Pike." Leota combed Mrs. Fletcher's hair with heavy strokes.

"You act like you're tired," said Mrs. Fletcher.

"Tired? Feel like it's four o'clock in the afternoon already," said Leota. "I ain't told you the awful luck we had, me and Fred? It's the worst thing you ever heard of. Maybe *you* think Mrs. Pike's got sharp eyes. Shoot, there's a limit! Well, you know, we rented out our room to this Mr. and Mrs. Pike from New Orleans when Sal an' Joe Fentress got mad at us 'cause they drank up some home-brew we had in the closet—Sal an' Joe did. So, a week ago Sat'day Mr. and Mrs. Pike moved in. Well, I kinda fixed up the room, you know—put a sofa pillow on the couch and picked some ragged robbins and put in a vase, but they never did say they appreciated it. Anyway, then I put some old magazines on the table."

"I think that was lovely," said Mrs. Fletcher.

"Wait. So, come night 'fore last, Fred and this Mr. Pike, who Fred just took up with, was back from they said they was fishin', bein' as neither one of 'em has got a job to his name, and we was all settin' around in their room. So Mrs. Pike was settin' there, readin' a old *Startling G-Man Tales* that was mine, mind you, I'd bought it myself, and all of a sudden she jumps!—into the air—you'd 'a' thought she'd set on a spider—an' says, 'Canfield'—ain't that silly, that's Mr. Pike—'Canfield, my God A'mighty,' she says, 'honey,' she says, 'we're rich, and you won't have to work.' Not that he turned one hand anyway. Well, me and Fred rushes over to her, and Mr. Pike, too, and there she sets, pointin' her finger at a photo in my copy of *Startling G-Man*. 'See that man?' yells Mrs. Pike. 'Remember him, Canfield?' 'Never forget a face,' says Mr. Pike. 'It's Mr. Petrie, that we stayed with him in the apartment next to ours in Toulouse Street in N.O. for six weeks. Mr. Petrie.' 'Well,' says Mrs. Pike, like she can't hold out one secont longer, 'Mr. Petrie is wanted for five hundred dollars cash, for rapin' four women in California, and I know where he is.'"

"Mercy!" said Mrs. Fletcher. "Where was he?"

At some time Leota had washed her hair and now she yanked her up by the back locks and sat her up.

"Know where he was?"

"I certainly don't," Mrs. Fletcher said. Her scalp hurt all over.

Leota flung a towel around the top of her customer's head. "Nowhere else but in that freak show! I saw him just as plain as Mrs. Pike. He was the petrified man!"

"Who would ever have thought that!" cried Mrs. Fletcher sympathetically.

"So Mr. Pike says, 'Well whatta you know about that,' an' he looks real hard at the photo and whistles. And she starts dancin' and singin' about their good luck. She meant our bad luck! I made a point of tellin' that fortune-teller the next time I saw her. I said, 'Listen, that magazine was layin' around the house for a month, and there was the freak show runnin' night an' day, not two steps away from my own beauty parlor, with Mr. Petrie just settin' there waitin'. An' it had to be Mr. and Mrs. Pike, almost perfect strangers.'"

"What gall," said Mrs. Fletcher. She was only sitting there, wrapped in a turban, but she did not mind.

"Fortune-tellers don't care. And Mrs. Pike, she goes around actin' like she thinks she was Mrs. God," said Leota. "So they're goin' to leave tomorrow, Mr. and Mrs. Pike. And in the meantime I got to keep that mean, bad little ole kid here, gettin' under my feet ever' minute of the day an' talkin' back too."

"Have they gotten the five hundred dollars' reward already?" asked Mrs. Fletcher.

"Well," said Leota, "at first Mr. Pike didn't want to do anything about it. Can you feature that? Said he kinda liked that ole bird and said he was real nice to 'em, lent 'em money or somethin'. But Mrs. Pike simply tole him he could just go to hell, and I can see her point. She says, 'You ain't worked a lick in six months, and here I make five hundred dollars in two seconts, and what thanks do I get for it? You go to hell, Canfield,' she says. So," Leota went on in a despondent voice, "they called up the cops and they caught the ole bird, all right, right there in the freak show where I saw him with my own eyes, thinkin' he was petrified. He's the one. Did it under his real name — Mr. Petrie. Four women in California, all in the month of August. So Mrs. Pike gits five hundred dollars. And my magazine, and right next door to my beauty parlor. I cried all night, but Fred said it wasn't a bit of use and to go to sleep, because the whole thing was just a sort of coincidence — you know; can't do nothin' about it. He says it put him clean out of the notion of goin' to Vicksburg for a few days till we rent out the room agin — no tellin' who we'll git this time."

"But can you imagine anybody knowing this old man, that's raped four women?" persisted Mrs. Fletcher, and she shuddered audibly. "Did Mrs. Pike *speak* to him when she met him in the freak show?"

Leota had begun to comb Mrs. Fletcher's hair. "I says to her, I says. 'I didn't notice you fallin' on his neck when he was the petrified man — don't tell me you didn't recognize your fine friend?' And she says, 'I didn't recognize him with that white powder all over his face. He just looked familiar,' Mrs. Pike says, 'and lots of people look familiar.' But she says that ole petrified man did put her in mind of somebody. She wondered who it was! Kep' her awake, which man she'd ever knew it reminded her of. So when she seen the photo, it all come to her. Like a flash. Mr. Petrie. The way he'd turn his head and look at her when she took him in his breakfast."

"Took him in his breakfast!" shrieked Mrs. Fletcher. "Listen — don't tell me. I'd 'a' felt something."

"Four women. I guess those women didn't have the faintest notion at the time they'd be worth a hundred an' twenty-five bucks apiece some day to Mrs. Pike. We ast her how old the fella was then, an' she says he must had one foot in the grave, at least. Can you beat it?"

"Not really petrified at all, of course," said Mrs. Fletcher meditatively. She drew herself up. "I'd 'a' felt something," she said proudly.

"Shoot! I did feel somethin'," said Leota. "I tole Fred when I got home I felt so funny. I said, 'Fred, that ole petrified man sure did leave me with a funny feelin'.' He says, 'Funny-haha or funny-peculiar?' and I says, 'Funny-peculiar.'" She pointed her comb into the air emphatically.

"I'll bet you did," said Mrs. Fletcher.

They both heard a crackling noise.

Leota screamed, "Billy Boy! What you doin' in my purse?"

"Aw, I'm just eatin' these ole stale peanuts up," said Billy Boy.

"You come here to me!" screamed Leota, recklessly flinging down the comb, which scattered a whole ashtray of bobby pins and knocked down a row of Coca-Cola bottles. "This is the last straw!"

"I caught him! I caught him!" giggled Mrs. Fletcher. "I'll hold him on my lap. You bad, bad boy, you! I guess I better learn how to spank little old bad boys," she said.

Leota's eleven o'clock customer pushed open the swing-door upon Leota paddling him heartily with the brush, while he gave angry but belittling screams which penetrated beyond the booth and filled the whole curious beauty parlor. From everywhere ladies began to gather round to watch the paddling. Billy Boy kicked both Leota and Mrs. Fletcher as hard as he could, Mrs. Fletcher with her new fixed smile.

Billy Boy stomped through the group of wild-haired ladies and went out the door, but flung back the words, "If you're so smart, why ain't you rich?"

[1939]

Study and Writing Questions

1. What does this STORY suggest about the economic, sexual, and romantic roles of men and women? To what extent do these roles seem to be determined by the CHARACTERS' social class?

2. What effect has the SETTING on the characters? How does the NARRATOR convey a sense of the setting despite relying almost exclusively on DIALOGUE? Why does the narrator choose to rely almost exclusively on dialogue?

3. What is the relationship between the ACTIONS we see directly and those reported by the characters?

4. To what does the title refer? Is the title well chosen? Are all the men in some sense petrified? Are any of the women petrified?

5. What is the role of Billy Boy in the story? Why is he given the final line? In what way might one say that that line CONCLUDES the story?

See also Questions for Contrast and Comparison: 40, 84, 88, 89, 102, 103, 133, 152, 181, and 239.

■ EDITH (NEWBOLD JONES) WHARTON (1862–1937) *was born into moneyed society in New York City (where her mother was "best dressed woman") and educated privately in New York, in fashionable Newport, Rhode Island, and in France, Germany, and Italy. She debuted at seventeen and married (1885) E. R. "Teddy" Wharton, son of an equally idle Boston family. Edith, who had her poems privately printed at sixteen, was clearly Teddy's intellectual superior. The strained marriage led to her breakdown (1898) and submission to S. Weir Mitchell's "rest cure," from which she emerged (1899) determined to write, producing nearly a book a year thereafter. After Teddy's own breakdown (1911), he was institutionalized. Once divorced (1913), Edith led an energetic life of travel, entertainment in her adopted French home, and intellectual friendships, notably with Henry James. Her World War I relief work earned her the French Legion of Honor. The House of Mirth (1905) and The Age of Innocence (1920; Pulitzer) exemplify her morally and stylistically focused Jamesian dissection of New York "society." Her stark* NOVELS *of humbler life, such as the tragic Ethan Frome (1911), also explore struggles against oppressive convention. Of her ten collections, Xingu and Other Stories (1916) best suggests her full range, including* STORIES *of the supernatural, history, and war. Hugely admired and once America's highest paid novelist, she died at home in France.*

Roman Fever

I

From the table at which they had been lunching two American ladies of ripe but well-cared-for middle age moved across the lofty terrace of the Roman restaurant and, leaning on its parapet, looked first at each other, and then down on the outspread glories of the Palatine and the Forum, with the same expression of vague but benevolent approval.

As they leaned there a girlish voice echoed up gaily from the stairs leading to the court below. "Well, come along, then," it cried, not to them but to an invisible companion, "and let's leave the young things to their knitting"; and a voice as fresh laughed back: "Oh, look here, Babs, not actually *knitting*—" "Well, I mean figuratively," rejoined the first. "After all, we haven't left our poor parents much else to do . . ." and at that point the turn of the stairs engulfed the dialogue.

The two ladies looked at each other again, this time with a tinge of smiling embarrassment, and the smaller and paler one shook her head and colored slightly.

"Barbara!" she murmured, sending an unheard rebuke after the mocking voice in the stairway.

The other lady, who was fuller, and higher in color, with a small determined nose supported by vigorous black eyebrows, gave a good-humored laugh. "That's what our daughters think of us!"

Her companion replied by a deprecating gesture. "Not of us individually. We must remember that. It's just the collective modern idea of Mothers. And you see—" Half guiltily she drew from her handsomely mounted black hand-bag a twist of crimson silk run through by two fine knitting needles. "One never knows," she murmured. "The new system has certainly given us a good deal of time to kill; and sometimes I get tired just looking—even at this." Her gesture was now addressed to the stupendous scene at their feet.

The dark lady laughed again, and they both relapsed upon the view, contemplating it in silence, with a sort of diffused serenity which might have been borrowed from the spring effulgence of the Roman skies. The luncheon-hour was long past, and the two had their end of the vast terrace to themselves. At this opposite extremity a few groups, detained by a lingering look at the outspread city, were gathering up guide-books and fumbling for tips. The last of them scattered, and the two ladies were alone on the air-washed height.

"Well, I don't see why we shouldn't just stay here," said Mrs. Slade, the lady of the high color and energetic brows. Two derelict basket-chairs stood near, and she pushed them into the angle of the parapet, and settled herself in one, her gaze upon the Palatine. "After all, it's still the most beautiful view in the world."

"It always will be, to me," assented her friend Mrs. Ansley, with so slight a stress on the "me" that Mrs. Slade, though she noticed it, wondered if it were not merely accidental, like the random underlinings of old-fashioned letter-writers.

"Grace Ansley was always old-fashioned," she thought; and added aloud, with a retrospective smile: "It's a view we've both been familiar with for a good many years. When we first met here we were younger than our girls are now. You remember?"

"Oh, yes, I remember," murmured Mrs. Ansley, with the same undefinable stress.—"There's that head-waiter wondering," she interpolated. She was evidently far less sure than her companion of herself and of her rights in the world.

"I'll cure him of wondering," said Mrs. Slade, stretching her hand toward a bag as discreetly opulent-looking as Mrs. Ansley's. Signing to the head-waiter, she explained that she and her friend were old lovers of Rome, and would like to spend the end of the afternoon looking down on the view—that is, if it did not disturb the service? The head-waiter, bowing over her gratuity, assured her that the ladies were most welcome, and would be still more so if they would condescend to remain for dinner. A full moon night, they would remember. . . .

Mrs. Slade's black brows drew together, as though references to the moon were out-of-place and even unwelcome. But she smiled away her frown as the head-waiter retreated. "Well, why not? We might do worse. There's no knowing, I suppose, when the girls will be back. Do you even know back from *where*? I don't!"

Mrs. Ansley again colored slightly. "I think those young Italian aviators we met at the Embassy invited them to fly to Tarquinia for tea. I suppose they'll want to wait and fly back by moonlight."

"Moonlight—moonlight! What a part it still plays. Do you suppose they're as sentimental as we were?"

"I've come to the conclusion that I don't in the least know what they are," said Mrs. Ansley. "And perhaps we didn't know much more about each other."

"No; perhaps we didn't."

Her friend gave her a shy glance. "I never should have supposed you were sentimental, Alida."

"Well, perhaps I wasn't." Mrs. Slade drew her lids together in retrospect; and for a few moments the two ladies, who had been intimate since childhood, reflected how little they knew each other. Each one, of course, had a label ready to attach to the other's name; Mrs. Delphin Slade, for instance, would have told herself, or any one who asked her, that Mrs. Horace Ansley, twenty-five years ago, had been exquisitely lovely—no, you wouldn't believe it, would you? . . . though, of course, still charming, distinguished . . . Well, as a girl she had been exquisite; far more beautiful than her daughter Barbara, though certainly Babs, according to the new standards at any rate, was more effective— had more edge, as they say. Funny where she got it, with those two nullities as parents. Yes; Horace Ansley was—well, just the duplicate of his wife. Museum specimens of old New York. Good-looking, irreproachable, exemplary. Mrs. Slade and Mrs. Ansley had lived opposite each other—actually as well as figuratively—for years. When the drawing-room curtains in No. 20 East 73rd Street were renewed, No. 23, across the way, was always aware of it. And of all the movings, buyings, travels, anniversaries, illnesses—the tame chronicle of an estimable pair. Little of it escaped Mrs. Slade. But she had grown bored with it by the time her husband made his big *coup* in Wall Street, and when they bought in upper Park Avenue had already begun to think: "I'd rather live opposite a speak-easy for a change; at least one might see it raided." The idea of seeing Grace raided was so amusing that (before the move) she launched it at a woman's lunch. It made a hit, and went the rounds—she sometimes wondered if it had crossed the street, and reached Mrs. Ansley. She hoped not, but didn't much mind. Those were the days when respectability was at a discount, and it did the irreproachable no harm to laugh at them a little.

A few years later, and not many months apart, both ladies lost their husbands. There was an appropriate exchange of wreaths and condolences, and a brief renewal of intimacy in the half-shadow of their mourning; and now, after another interval, they had run across each other in Rome, at the same hotel, each of them the modest appendage of a salient daughter. The similarity of their lot had again drawn them together, lending itself to mild jokes, and the mutual confession that, if in old days it must have been tiring to "keep up" with daughters, it was now, at times, a little dull not to.

No doubt, Mrs. Slade reflected, she felt her unemployment more than poor Grace ever would. It was a big drop from being the wife of Delphin Slade to being his widow. She had always regarded herself (with a certain conjugal pride) as his equal in social gifts, as contributing her full share to the making of the exceptional couple they were: but the difference after his death was irremediable. As the wife of the famous corporation lawyer, always with an international case or two on hand, every day brought its exciting and unexpected obligation: the impromptu entertaining of eminent colleagues from abroad, the hurried dashes on legal business to London, Paris or Rome, where the entertaining was so handsomely reciprocated; the amusement of hearing in her wake: "What, that handsome woman with the good clothes and eyes is Mrs. Slade—*the* Slade's wife? Really? Generally the wives of celebrities are such trumps."

Yes; being *the* Slade's widow was a dullish business after that. In living up to such a husband all her faculties had been engaged; now she had only her daughter to live up to, for the son who seemed to have inherited his father's gifts had died suddenly in boyhood. She had fought through that agony because her husband was there, to be helped and to help; now, after the father's death, the thought of the boy had become unbearable. There was nothing left but to mother her daughter; and dear Jenny was such a perfect daughter that she needed no excessive mothering. "Now with Babs Ansley I don't know that I *should* be so quiet," Mrs. Slade sometimes half-enviously reflected; but Jenny, who was younger than her brilliant friend, was that rare accident, an extremely pretty girl who somehow made youth and prettiness seem as safe as their absence. It was all perplexing — and to Mrs. Slade a little boring. She wished that Jenny would fall in love — with the wrong man, even; that she might have to be watched, out-maneuvered, rescued. And instead, it was Jenny who watched her mother, kept her out of draughts, made sure that she had taken her tonic . . .

Mrs. Ansley was much less articulate than her friend, and her mental portrait of Mrs. Slade was slighter, and drawn with fainter touches. "Alida Slade's awfully brilliant but not as brilliant as she thinks," would have summed it up; though she would have added, for the enlightenment of strangers, that Mrs. Slade had been an extremely dashing girl; much more so than her daughter, who was pretty, of course, and clever in a way, but had none of her mother's — well, "vividness," some one had once called it. Mrs. Ansley would take up current words like this, and cite them in quotation marks, as unheard-of audacities. No; Jenny was not like her mother. Sometimes Mrs. Ansley thought Alida Slade was disappointed; on the whole she had had a sad life. Full of failures and mistakes; Mrs. Ansley had always been rather sorry for her . . .

So these two ladies visualized each other, each through the wrong end of her little telescope.

II

For a long time they continued to sit side by side without speaking. It seemed as though, to both, there was a relief in laying down their somewhat futile activities in the presence of the vast Memento Mori which faced them. Mrs. Slade sat quite still, her eyes fixed on the golden slope of the Palace of the Caesars, and after a while Mrs. Ansley ceased to fidget with her bag, and she too sank into meditation. Like many intimate friends, the two ladies had never before had occasion to be silent together, and Mrs. Ansley was slightly embarrassed by what seemed, after so many years, a new stage in their intimacy, and one with which she did not yet know how to deal.

Suddenly the air was full of that deep clangor of bells which periodically covers Rome with a roof of silver. Mrs. Slade glanced at her wrist-watch. "Five o'clock already," she said, as though surprised.

Mrs. Ansley suggested interrogatively: "There's bridge at the Embassy at five." For a long time Mrs. Slade did not answer. She appeared to be lost in contemplation, and Mrs. Ansley thought the remark had escaped her. But after a while she said, as if speaking out of a dream: "Bridge, did you say? Not unless you want to . . . But I don't think I will, you know."

"Oh, no," Mrs. Ansley hastened to assure her. "I don't care to at all. It's so lovely here; and so full of old memories, as you say." She settled herself in her chair, and almost furtively drew forth her knitting. Mrs. Slade took sideways note of this activity, but her own beautifully cared-for hands remained motionless on her knee.

"I was just thinking," she said slowly, "what different things Rome stands for to each generation of travelers. To our grandmothers, Roman fever; to our mothers, sentimental dangers—how we used to be guarded!—to our daughters, no more dangers than the middle of Main Street. They don't know it—but how much they're missing!"

The long golden light was beginning to pale, and Mrs. Ansley lifted her knitting a little closer to her eyes. "Yes; how we were guarded!"

"I always used to think," Mrs. Slade continued, "that our mothers had a much more difficult job than our grandmothers. When Roman fever stalked the streets it must have been comparatively easy to gather in the girls at the danger hour; but when you and I were young, with such beauty calling us, the spice of disobedience thrown in, and no worse risk than catching cold during the cool hour after sunset, the mothers used to be put to it to keep us in—didn't they?"

She turned again toward Mrs. Ansley, but the latter had reached a delicate point in her knitting. "One, two, three—slip two; yes, they must have been," she assented, without looking up.

Mrs. Slade's eyes rested on her with a deepened attention. "She can knit—in the face of *this!* How like her . . ."

Mrs. Slade leaned back, brooding, her eyes ranging from the ruins which faced her to the long green hollow of the Forum, the fading glow of the church fronts beyond it, and the outlying immensity of the Colosseum. Suddenly she thought: "It's all very well to say that our girls have done away with sentiment and moonlight. But if Babs Ansley isn't out to catch that young aviator—the one who's a Marchese—then I don't know anything. And Jenny has no chance beside her. I know that too. I wonder if that's why Grace Ansley likes the two girls to go everywhere together? My poor Jenny as a foil—!" Mrs. Slade gave a hardly audible laugh, and at the sound Mrs. Ansley dropped her knitting.

"Yes—!"

"I—oh, nothing. I was only thinking how your Babs carries everything before her. That Campolieri boy is one of the best matches in Rome. Don't look so innocent, my dear—you know he is. And I was wondering, ever so respect-fully, you understand . . . wondering how two such exemplary characters as you and Horace had managed to produce anything quite so dynamic." Mrs. Slade laughed again, with a touch of asperity.

Mrs. Ansley's hands lay inert across her needles. She looked straight out at the great accumulated wreckage of passion and splendor at her feet. But her small profile was almost expressionless. At length she said: "I think you overrate Babs, my dear."

Mrs. Slade's tone grew easier. "No; I don't. I appreciate her. And perhaps envy you. Oh, my girl's perfect; if I were a chronic invalid I'd—well, I think I'd rather be in Jenny's hands. There must be times . . . but there! I al-ways wanted a brilliant daughter . . . and never quite understood why I got an angel instead."

Mrs. Ansley echoed her laugh in a faint murmur. "Babs is an angel too."

"Of course—of course! But she's got rainbow wings. Well, they're wander-ing by the sea with their young men; and here we sit . . . and it all brings back the past a little too acutely."

Mrs. Ansley had resumed her knitting. One might almost have imagined (if one had known her less well, Mrs. Slade reflected) that, for her also, too many memories rose from the lengthening shadows of those august ruins. But no; she was simply absorbed in her work. What was there for her to worry about? She knew that Babs would almost certainly come back engaged to the extremely eligible Compolieri. "And she'll sell the New York house, and settle down near them in Rome, and never be in their way . . . she's much too tactful. But she'll have an excellent cook, and just the right people in for bridge and cocktails . . . and a perfectly peaceful old age among her grandchildren."

Mrs. Slade broke off this prophetic flight with a recoil of self-disgust. There was no one of whom she had less right to think unkindly than of Grace Ansley. Would she never cure herself of envying her? Perhaps she had begun too long ago.

She stood up and leaned against the parapet, filling her troubled eyes with the tranquilizing magic of the hour. But instead of tranquilizing her the sight seemed to increase her exasperation. Her gaze turned toward the Colosseum. Already its golden flank was drowned in purple shadow, and above it the sky curved crystal clear, without light or color. It was the moment when the afternoon and evening hang balanced in mid-heaven.

Mrs. Slade turned back and laid her hand on her friend's arm. The gesture was so abrupt that Mrs. Ansley looked up, startled.

"The sun's set. You're not afraid, my dear?"

"Afraid—?"

"Of Roman fever or pneumonia? I remember how ill you were that winter. As a girl you had a very delicate throat, hadn't you?"

"Oh, we're all right up here. Down below, in the Forum, it does get deathly cold, all of a sudden . . . but not here."

"Ah, of course you know because you had to be careful." Mrs. Slade turned back to the parapet. She thought: "I must make one more effort not to hate her." Aloud she said: "Whenever I look at the Forum from up here, I remember that story about a great-aunt of yours, wasn't she? A dreadfully wicked great-aunt?"

"Oh, yes; Great-aunt Harriet. The one who was supposed to have sent her young sister out to the Forum after sunset to gather a night-blooming flower for her album. All our great-aunts and grandmothers used to have albums of dried flowers."

Mrs. Slade nodded. "But she really sent her because they were in love with the same man—"

"Well, that was the family tradition. They said Aunt Harriet confessed it years afterward. At any rate, the poor little sister caught the fever and died. Mother used to frighten us with the story when we were children."

"And you frightened *me* with it, that winter when you and I were here as girls. The winter I was engaged to Delphin."

Mrs. Ansley gave a faint laugh. "Oh, did I? Really frightened you? I don't believe you're easily frightened."

"Not often; but I was then. I was easily frightened because I was too happy. I wonder if you know what that means?"

"I—yes . . ." Mrs. Ansley faltered.

"Well, I suppose that was why the story of your wicked aunt made such an impression on me. And I thought: 'There's no more Roman fever, but the Forum is deathly cold after sunset—especially after a hot day. And the Colosseum's even colder and damper.'"

"The Colosseum—?"

"Yes. It wasn't easy to get in, after the gates were locked for the night. Far from easy. Still, in those days it could be managed; it was managed, often. Lovers met there who couldn't meet elsewhere. You knew that?"

"I—I daresay. I don't remember."

"You don't remember? You don't remember going to visit some ruins or other one evening, just after dark, and catching a bad chill? You were supposed to have gone to see the moon rise. People always said that expedition was what caused your illness."

There was a moment's silence; then Mrs. Ansley rejoined: "Did they? It was all so long ago."

"Yes. And you got well again—so it didn't matter. But I suppose it struck your friends—the reason given for your illness, I mean—because everybody knew you were so prudent on account of your throat, and your mother took such care of you . . . You *had* been out late sightseeing, hadn't you, that night?"

"Perhaps I had. The most prudent girls aren't always prudent. What made you think of it now?"

Mrs. Slade seemed to have no answer ready. But after a moment she broke out: "Because I simply can't bear it any longer—!"

Mrs. Ansley lifted her head quickly. Her eyes were wide and very pale. "Can't bear what?"

"Why—your not knowing that I've always known why you went."

"Why I went?"

"Yes. You think I'm bluffing, don't you? Well, you went to meet the man I was engaged to—and I can repeat every word of the letter that you took there."

While Mrs. Slade spoke Mrs. Ansley had risen unsteadily to her feet. Her bag, her knitting and gloves, slid in a panic-stricken heap to the ground. She looked at Mrs. Slade as though she were looking at a ghost.

"No, no—don't," she faltered out.

"Why not? Listen, if you don't believe me. 'My one darling, things can't go on like this. I must see you alone. Come to the Colosseum immediately after dark tomorrow. There will be somebody to let you in. No one whom you need fear will suspect'—but perhaps you've forgotten what the letter said?"

Mrs. Ansley met the challenge with an unexpected composure. Steadying herself against the chair she looked at her friend, and replied: "No, I know it by heart too."

"And the signature? 'Only *your* D.S.' Was that it? I'm right, am I? That was the letter that took you out that evening after dark?"

Mrs. Ansley was still looking at her. It seemed to Mrs. Slade that a slow struggle was going on behind the voluntarily controlled mask of her small quiet face. "I shouldn't have thought she had herself so well in hand," Mrs. Slade reflected, almost resentfully. But at this moment Mrs. Ansley spoke. "I don't know how you knew. I burnt that letter at once."

"Yes; you would, naturally—you're so prudent!" The sneer was open now. "And if you burnt the letter you're wondering how on earth I know what was in it. That's it, isn't it?"

Mrs. Slade waited, but Mrs. Ansley did not speak.

"Well, my dear, I know what was in that letter because I wrote it!"

"You wrote it?"

"Yes."

The two women stood for a minute staring at each other in the last, golden light. Then Mrs. Ansley dropped back into her chair. "Oh," she murmured, and covered her face with her hands.

Mrs. Slade waited nervously for another word or movement. None came, and at length she broke out: "I horrify you."

Mrs. Ansley's hands dropped to her knee. The face they uncovered was streaked with tears. "I wasn't thinking of you. I was thinking—it was the only letter I ever had from him!"

"And I wrote it. Yes; I wrote it! But I was the girl he was engaged to. Did you happen to remember that?"

Mrs. Ansley's head dropped again. "I'm not trying to excuse myself . . . I remembered . . ."

"And still you went?"

"Still I went."

Mrs. Slade stood looking down on the small bowed figure at her side. The flame of her wrath had already sunk, and she wondered why she had ever thought there would be any satisfaction in inflicting so purposeless a wound on her friend. But she had to justify herself.

"You do understand? I found out—and I hated you, hated you. I knew you were in love with Delphin—and I was afraid; afraid of you, of your quiet ways, your sweetness . . . your . . . well, I wanted you out of the way, that's all. Just for a few weeks; just till I was sure of him. So in a blind fury I wrote the letter . . . I don't know why I'm telling you now."

"I suppose," said Mrs. Ansley slowly, "it's because you've always gone on hating me."

"Perhaps. Or because I wanted to get the whole thing off my mind." She paused. "I'm glad you destroyed the letter. Of course I never thought you'd die."

Mrs. Ansley relapsed into silence, and Mrs. Slade, leaning above her, was conscious of a strange sense of isolation, of being cut off from the warm current of human communion. "You think me a monster!"

"I don't know . . . It was the only letter I had, and you say he didn't write it?"

"Ah, how you care for him still!"

"I cared for that memory," said Mrs. Ansley.

Mrs. Slade continued to look down on her. She seemed physically reduced by the blow—as if, when she got up, the wind might scatter her like a puff of dust. Mrs. Slade's jealousy suddenly leapt up again at the sight. All these years the woman had been living on that letter. How she must have loved him, to treasure the mere memory of its ashes! The letter of the man her friend was engaged to. Wasn't it she who was the monster?

"You tried your best to get him away from me, didn't you? But you failed; and I kept him. That's all."

"Yes. That's all."

"I wish now I hadn't told you. I'd no idea you'd feel about it as you do; I thought you'd be amused. It all happened so long ago, as you say; and you must do me the justice to remember that I had no reason to think you'd ever taken it seriously. How could I, when you were married to Horace Ansley two months afterward? As soon as you could get of bed your mother rushed you off to Florence and married you. People were rather surprised — they wondered at its being done so quickly; but I thought I knew. I had an idea you did it out of *pique* — to be able to say you'd got ahead of Delphin and me. Girls have such silly reasons for doing the most serious things. And your marrying so soon convinced me that you'd never really cared."

"Yes, I suppose it would," Mrs. Ansley assented.

The clear heaven overhead was emptied of all its gold. Dusk spread over it, abruptly darkening the Seven Hills. Here and there lights began to twinkle through the foliage at their feet. Steps were coming and going on the deserted terrace — waiters looking out of the doorway at the head of the stairs, then reappearing with trays and napkins and flasks of wine. Tables were moved, chairs straightened. A feeble string of electric lights flickered out. Some vases of faded flowers were carried away, and brought back replenished. A stout lady in a dustcoat suddenly appeared, asking in broken Italian if any one had seen the elastic band which held together her tattered Baedeker. She poked with her stick under the table at which she had lunched, the waiters assisting.

The corner where Mrs. Slade and Mrs. Ansley sat was still shadowy and deserted. For a long time neither of them spoke. At length Mrs. Slade began again: "I suppose I did it as a sort of joke—"

"A joke?"

"Well, girls are ferocious sometimes, you know. Girls in love especially. And I remember laughing to myself all that evening at the idea that you were waiting around there in the dark, dodging out of sight, listening for every sound, trying to get in —. Of course I was upset when I heard you were so ill afterward."

Mrs. Ansley had not moved for a long time. But now she turned slowly toward her companion. "But I didn't wait. He'd arranged everything. He was there. We were let in at once," she said.

Mrs. Slade sprang up from her leaning position. "Delphin there? They let you in? — Ah, now you're lying!" she burst out with violence.

Mrs. Ansley's voice grew clearer, and full of surprise. "But of course he was there. Naturally he came—"

"Came? How did he know he'd find you there? You must be raving!"

Mrs. Ansley hesitated, as though reflecting. "But I answered the letter. I told him I'd be there. So he came."

Mrs. Slade flung her hands up to her face. "Oh, God — you answered! I never thought of your answering . . ."

"It's odd you never thought of it, if you wrote the letter."

"Yes. I was blind with rage."

Mrs. Ansley rose, and drew her fur scarf about her. "It is cold here. We'd better go . . . I'm sorry for you," she said, as she clasped the fur about her throat.

The unexpected words sent a pang through Mrs. Slade. "Yes; we'd better go." She gathered up her bag and cloak. "I don't know why you should be sorry for me," she muttered.

Mrs. Ansley stood looking away from her toward the dusky secret mass of the Colosseum. "Well — because I didn't have to wait that night."

Mrs. Slade gave an unquiet laugh. "Yes; I was beaten there. But I oughtn't to begrudge it to you, I suppose. At the end of all these years. After all, I had everything; I had him for twenty-five years. And you had nothing but that one letter he didn't write."

Mrs. Ansley was again silent. At length she turned toward the door of the terrace. She took a step, and turned back, facing her companion.

"I had Barbara," she said, and began to move ahead of Mrs. Slade toward the stairway.

[1936]

Study and Writing Questions

1. What are the literal and FIGURATIVE meanings of the title? In what ways does it enter into the PLOT and into the THEME?
2. The NARRATOR says that "these two ladies visualized each other, each through the wrong end of her little telescope." In what ways is this true? What sort of judgment of "these two ladies" by the narrator does this phrase reflect? How does the manipulation of VIEWPOINT control our feelings about first one CHARACTER and then the other?
3. Many small details, like Mrs. Ansley putting "so slight a stress on the 'me'" in the first SCENE, may seem vague on a first reading but highly meaningful on a subsequent reading. Compare the significance of details on a first and subsequent reading. In what ways is this NARRATIVE about the activity of interpretation?
4. Describe the lives of the main characters in New York. What sort of people had they been? What had marriage meant to each? What had widowhood meant to each? Does your judgment of the relative worth of these two people change as you come to know more about how they lived their lives?
5. Describe the relationship between these two "friends." What were their relations as youngsters, as young marrieds, as established matrons, as widows, and now? Given the tensions each felt about the other, what in themselves and in their society had sustained their so-called friendship? What does the last line, with its repetition of the first scene's reference to a stairway, suggest will be the next stage in their relationship? To what extent is this narrative about the nature of friendship?

See also Questions for Contrast and Comparison: 33, 88, 152, 175, 190, 206, and 231.

■ **RICHARD (NATHANIEL) WRIGHT** (1908–1960) *was born in poverty near Natchez, Mississippi. His father, a freedman farmer, abandoned the family when Richard was five. His mother, formerly a schoolteacher, became a domestic until a stroke paralyzed her. Richard finished the ninth-grade at fifteen and thereafter educated himself, moving through a succession of foster homes, an orphanage, and menial jobs in the rural south, Memphis, Tennessee (1925), Chicago (1927), and New York City (1937). He became an active Communist (1932) but ultimately left the party (1944) feeling it stifled intellectual curiosity. Although he had reported widely for left-wing journals, he gained broad recognition only with* Uncle Tom's Children *(1938), four (later enlarged to five) racially unflinching* STORIES. Native Son *(1940), a searing, controversial study of a black man who murders, combines the American* NATURALIST *tradition (circumstances made him do it) and the Existentialist tradition (murder as self-liberation). His autobiographical* Black Boy *(1945) confirmed his world stature. Living in France from 1947 on, always active in leftist, anti-racist, and Third World causes, he was an internationally powerful voice.* The God That Failed *(1950) explains his disenchantment with Communism;* Black Power *(1954) recounts his African travels; and* Eight Men *(1961) collects further stories. Twice married and the father of two, he is buried in Paris.*

The Man Who Was Almost a Man

Dave struck out across the fields, looking homeward through paling light. Whuts the usa talkin wid em niggers in the field? Anyhow, his mother was putting supper on the table. Them niggers can't understand *nothing*. One of these days he was going to get a gun and practice shooting, then they can't talk to him as though he were a little boy. He slowed, looking at the ground. Shucks, Ah ain scareda them even ef they are biggern me! Aw, Ah know whut Ahma do. . . . Ahm going by ol Joe's sto n git that Sears Roebuck catlog n look at them guns. Mabbe Ma will lemme buy one when she gits mah pay from ol man Hawkins. Ahma beg her t gimme some money. Ahm ol ernough to hava gun. Ahm seventeen. Almos a man. He strode, feeling his long, loose-jointed limbs. Shucks, a man oughta hava little gun aftah he done worked hard all day. . . .

He came in sight of Joe's store. A yellow lantern glowed on the front porch. He mounted steps and went through the screen door, hearing it bang behind him. There was a strong smell of coal oil and mackerel fish. He felt very confident until he saw fat Joe walk in through the rear door, then his courage began to ooze.

'Howdy, Dave! Whutcha want?'

'How yuh, Mistah Joe? Aw, Ah don wanna buy nothing. Ah jus wanted t see ef yuhd lemme look at tha ol catlog erwhile.'

'Sure! You wanna see it here?'

'Nawsuh. Ah wans t take it home wid me. Ahll bring it back termorrow when Ah come in from the fiels.'

'You plannin on buyin something?'

'Yessuh.'

'Your ma letting you have your own money now?'

'Shucks. Mistah Joe, Ahm gittin t be a man like anybody else!'

Joe laughed and wiped his greasy white face with a red bandanna.

'Whut you plannin on buyin?'

Dave looked at the floor, scratched his head, scratched his thigh, and smiled. Then he looked up shyly.

'Ahll tell yuh, Mistah Joe, ef yuh promise yuh won't tell.'

'I promise.'

'Waal, Ahma buy a gun.'

'A gun? Whut you want with a gun?'

'Ah wanna keep it.'

'You ain't nothing but a boy. You don't need a gun.'

'Aw, lemme have the catalog, Mistah Joe. Ahll bring it back.'

Joe walked through the rear door. Dave was elated. He looked around at barrels of sugar and flour. He heard Joe coming back. He craned his neck to see if he were bringing the book. Yeah, he's got it! Gawddog, he's got it!

'Here; but be sure you bring it back. It's the only one I got.'

'Sho, Mistah Joe.'

'Say, if you wanna buy a gun, why don't you buy one from me. I gotta gun to sell.'

'Will it shoot?'

'Sure it'll shoot.'

'What kind is it?'

'Oh, it's kinda old. . . . A Lefthand Wheeler. A pistol. A big one.'

'Is it got bullets in it?'

'It's loaded.'

'Kin Ah see it?'

'Where's your money?'

'Whut yuh wan fer it?'

'I'll let you have it for two dollars.'

'Just *two* dollahs? Shucks, Ah could buy tha when Ah git mah pay.'

'I'll have it here when you want it.'

'Awright, suh. Ah be in fer it.'

He went through the door, hearing it slam again behind him. Ahma git some money from Ma n buy me a gun! Only *two* dollahs! He tucked the thick catalogue under his arm and hurried.

'Where yuh been, boy?' His mother held a steaming dish of black-eyed peas.

'Aw, Ma, Ah jus stopped down the road t talk wid th boys.'

'Yuh know bettah than t keep suppah waitin.'

He sat down, resting the catalogue on the edge of the table.

'Yuh git up from there and git to the well n wash yosef! Ah ain feedin no hogs in mah house!'

She grabbed his shoulder and pushed him. He stumbled out of the room, then came back to get the catalogue.

'Whut this?'

'Aw, Ma, it's jusa catlog.'

'Who yuh git it from?'

'From Joe, down at the sto.'

'Waal, thas good. We kin use it around the house.'

'Naw, Ma.' He grabbed for it. 'Gimme mah catlog, Ma.'

She held onto it and glared at him.

'Quit hollerin at me! Whuts wrong wid yuh? Yuh crazy?'

'But Ma, please. It ain mine! It's Joe's! He tol me t bring it back t im termorrow.'

She gave up the book. He stumbled down the back steps, hugging the thick book under his arm. When he had splashed water on his face and hands, he groped back to the kitchen and fumbled in a corner for the towel. He bumped into a chair; it clattered to the floor. The catalogue sprawled at his feet. When he had dried his eyes he snatched up the book and held it again under his arm. His mother stood watching him.

'Now, ef yuh gonna acka fool over that ol book, Ahll take it n burn it up.'

'Naw, Ma, please.'

'Waal, set down n be still!'

He sat and drew the oil lamp close. He thumbed page after page, unaware of the food his mother set on the table. His father came in. Then his small brother.

'Whutcha got there, Dave?' his father asked.

'Jusa catlog,' he answered, not looking up.

'Ywah, here they is!' His eyes glowed at blue and black revolvers. He glanced up, feeling sudden guilt. His father was watching him. He eased the book under the table and rested it on his knees. After the blessing was asked, he ate. He scooped up peas and swallowed fat meat without chewing. Buttermilk helped to wash it down. He did not want to mention money before his father. He would do much better by cornering his mother when she was alone. He looked at his father uneasily out of the edge of his eye.

'Boy, how come yuh don quit foolin wid tha book n eat yo suppah?'

'Yessuh.'

'How yuh n ol man Hawkins gittin erlong?'

'Suh?'

'Can't yuh hear? Why don yuh lissen? Ah ast yuh how wuz yuh n ol man Hawkins gittin erlong?'

'Oh, swell, Pa. Ah plows mo lan than anybody over there.'

'Waal, yuh oughta keep yo min on whut yuh doin.'

'Yessuh.'

He poured his plate full of molasses and sopped at it slowly with a chunk of cornbread. When all but his mother had left the kitchen, he still sat and looked again at the guns in the catalogue. Lawd, ef Ah only had tha pretty one! He could almost feel the slickness of the weapon with his fingers. If he had a gun like that he would polish it and keep it shining so it would never rust. N Ahd keep it loaded, by Gawd!

'Ma?'

'Hunh?'

'Ol man Hawkins give yuh mah money yit?'

'Yeah, but ain no usa yuh thinkin bout thowin nona it erway. Ahm keepin tha money sos yuh kin have cloes t go to school this winter.'

He rose and went to her side with the open catalogue in his palms. She was washing dishes, her head bent low over a pan. Shyly he raised the open book. When he spoke his voice was husky, faint.

'Ma, Gawd knows Ah wans one of these.'

'One of whut?' she asked, not raising her eyes.

'One of *these*,' he said again, not daring even to point. She glanced up at the page, then at him with wide eyes.

'Nigger is yuh gone plum crazy?'

'Ah, Ma——'

'Git outta here! Don yuh talk t me bout no gun! Yuh a fool!'

'Ma, Ah kin buy one fer *two* dollahs.'

'Not ef Ah knows it yuh ain!'

'But yuh promised me one——'

'Ah don care whut Ah promised! Yuh ain nothing but a boy yit!'

'Ma, ef yuh lemme buy one Ahll *never* ast yuh fer nothing no mo.'

'Ah tol yuh t git outta here! Yuh ain gonna toucha penny of tha money fer no gun! Thas how come Ah has Mistah Hawkins t pay yo wages t me, cause Ah knows yuh ain got no sense.'

'But Ma, we needa gun. Pa ain got no gun. We needa gun in the house. Yuh kin never tell whut might happen.'

'Now don yuh try to maka fool outta me, boy! Ef we did hava gun yuh wouldn't have it!'

He laid the catalogue down and slipped his arm around her waist.

'Aw, Ma, Ah done worked hard alla summer n ain ast yuh fer nothin, is Ah, now?'

'Thas whut yuh spose t do!'

'But Ma, Ah wans a gun. Yuh kin lemme have two dollahs outta mah money. Please, Ma. I kin give it to Pa . . . Please, Ma! Ah loves yuh, Ma.'

When she spoke her voice came soft and low.

'Whut yuh wan wida gun, Dave? Yuh don need no gun. Yuhll git in trouble. N ef yo Pa jus *thought* Ah let yuh have money t buy a gun he'd hava fit.'

'Ahll hide it, Ma, it ain but two dollahs.'

'Lawd, chil, whuts wrong wid yuh?'

'Ain nothing wrong, Ma. Ahm almos a man now. Ah wans a gun.'

'Who gonna sell yuh a gun?'

'Ol Joe at the sto.'

'N it don cos but two dollahs?'

'Thas all, Ma. Just two dollahs. Please, Ma.'

She was stacking the plates away; her hands moved slowly, reflectively. Dave kept an anxious silence. Finally, she turned to him.

'Ahll let yuh git tha gun ef yuh promise me one thing.'

'Whuts tha, Ma?'

'Yuh bring it straight back t me, yuh hear? Itll be fer Pa.'

'Yessum! Lemme go now, Ma.'

She stooped, turned slightly to one side, raised the hem of her dress, rolled down the top of her stocking, and came up with a slender wad of bills.

'Here,' she said. 'Lawd knows yuh don need no gun. But yer Pa does. Yuh bring it right back t me, yuh hear? Ahma put it up. Now ef yuh don, Ahma have yuh Pa lick yuh so hard yuh won ferget it.'

'Yessum.'

He took the money, ran down the steps, and across the yard.

'Dave! Yuuuuuh Daaaaave!'

He heard, but he was not going to stop now. 'Naw, Lawd!'

The first movement he made the following morning was to reach under his pillow for the gun. In the gray light of dawn he held it loosely, feeling a sense of power. Could killa man wida gun like this. Kill anybody, black er white. And if he were holding his gun in his hand nobody could run over him; they would have to respect him. It was a big gun, with a long barrel and a heavy handle. He raised and lowered it in his hand, marveling at its weight.

He had not come straight home with it as his mother had asked; instead he had stayed out in the fields, holding the weapon in his hand, aiming it now and then at some imaginary foe. But he had not fired it; he had been afraid that his father might hear. Also he was not sure he knew how to fire it.

To avoid surrendering the pistol he had not come into the house until he knew that all were asleep. When his mother had tiptoed to his bedside late that night and demanded the gun, he had first played 'possum; then he had told her that the gun was hidden outdoors, that he would bring it to her in the morning. Now he lay turning it slowly in his hands. He broke it, took out the cartridges, felt them, and then put them back.

He slid out of bed, got a long strip of old flannel from a trunk, wrapped the gun in it, and tied it to his naked thigh while it was still loaded. He did not go in to breakfast. Even though it was not yet daylight, he started for Jim Hawkins' plantation. Just as the sun was rising he reached the barns where the mules and plows were kept.

'Hey! That you, Dave?'

He turned. Jim Hawkins stood eying him suspiciously.

'Whatre yuh doing here so early?'

'Ah didn't know Ah wuz gittin up so early, Mistah Hawkins. Ah wuz fixin t hitch up ol Jenny n take her t the fiels.'

'Good. Since you're here so early, how about plowing that stretch down by the wood?'

'Suits me. Mistah Hawkins.'

'O.K. Go to it!'

He hitched Jenny to a plow and started across the fields. Hot dog! This was just what he wanted. If he could get down by the woods, he could shoot his gun and nobody would hear. He walked behind the plow, hearing the traces creaking, feeling the gun tied tight to his thigh.

When he reached the woods, he plowed two whole rows before he decided to take out the gun. Finally, he stopped, looked in all directions, then untied the gun and held it in his hand. He turned to the mule and smiled.

'Know whut this is, Jenny? Naw, yuh wouldn't know! Yuhs jusa ol mule! Anyhow, this is a gun, n it kin shoot, by Gawd!'

He held the gun at arm's length. Whut t hell, Ahma shoot this thing! He looked at Jenny again.

'Lissen here, Jenny! When Ah pull this ol trigger Ah don wan yuh t run n acka fool now.'

Jenny stood with head down, her short ears pricked straight. Dave walked off about twenty feet, held the gun far out from him, at arm's length, and turned his head. Hell, he told himself, Ah ain afraid. The gun felt loose in his fingers; he waved it wildly for a moment. Then he shut his eyes and tightened his forefinger.

Blooom! A report half-deafened him and he thought his right hand was torn from his arm. He heard Jenny whinnying and galloping over the field, and he found himself on his knees, squeezing his fingers hard between his legs. His hand was numb; he jammed it into his mouth, trying to warm it, trying to stop the pain. The gun lay at his feet. He did not quite know what had happened. He stood up and stared at the gun as though it were a live thing. He gritted his teeth and kicked the gun. *Yuh almos broke mah arm!* He turned to look for Jenny; she was far over the fields, tossing her head and kicking wildly.

'Hol on there, ol mule!'

When he caught up with her she stood trembling, walling her big white eyes at him. The plow was far away; the traces had broken. Then Dave stopped short, looking, not believing. Jenny was bleeding. Her left side was red and wet with blood. He went closer. *Lawd have mercy! Wondah did Ah shoot this mule?* He grabbed for Jenny's mane. She flinched, snorted, whirled, tossing her head.

'Hol on now! Hol on.'

Then he saw the hole in Jenny's side, right between the ribs. It was round, wet, red. A crimson stream streaked down the front leg, flowing fast. *Good Gawd! Ah wuznt shootin at tha mule. . . .* He felt panic. He knew he had to stop that blood, or Jenny would bleed to death. He had never seen so much blood in all his life. He ran the mule for half a mile, trying to catch her. Finally she stopped, breathing hard, stumpy tail half arched. He caught her mane and led her back to where the plow and gun lay. Then he stopped and grabbed handfuls of damp black earth and tried to plug the bullet hole. Jenny shuddered, whinnied, and broke from him.

'Hol on! Hol on now!'

He tried to plug it again, but blood came anyhow. His fingers were hot and sticky. He rubbed dirt hard into his palms, trying to dry them. Then again he attempted to plug the bullet hole, but Jenny shied away, kicking her heels high. He stood helpless. He had to do something. He ran at Jenny; she dodged him. He watched a red stream of blood flow down Jenny's leg and form a bright pool at her feet.

'Jenny . . . Jenny . . .' he called weakly.

His lips trembled. *She's bleeding t death!* He looked in the direction of home, wanting to go back, wanting to get help. But he saw the pistol lying in the damp black clay. He had a queer feeling that if he only did something, this would not be; Jenny would not be there bleeding to death.

When he went to her this time, she did not move. She stood with sleepy, dreamy eyes; and when he touched her she gave a low-pitched whinny and knelt to the ground, her front knees slopping in blood.

'Jenny . . . Jenny . . .' he whispered.

For a long time she held her neck erect; then her head sank, slowly. Her ribs swelled with a mighty heave and she went over.

Dave's stomach felt empty, very empty. He picked up the gun and held it gingerly between his thumb and forefinger. He buried it at the foot of a tree. He took a stick and tried to cover the pool of blood with dirt—but what was the use? There was Jenny lying with her mouth open and her eyes walled and glassy. He could not tell Jim Hawkins he had shot his mule. But he had to tell something. *Yeah, Ahll tell em Jenny started gittin wil n fell on the joint of the plow. . . .* But that would hardly happen to a mule. He walked across the field slowly, head down.

It was sunset. Two of Jim Hawkins' men were over near the edge of the woods digging a hole in which to bury Jenny. Dave was surrounded by a knot of people; all of them were looking down at the dead mule.

'I don't see how in the world it happened,' said Jim Hawkins for the tenth time.

The crowd parted and Dave's mother, father, and small brother pushed into the center.

'Where Dave?' his mother called.

'There he is,' said Jim Hawkins.

His mother grabbed him.

'Whut happened, Dave? Whut yuh done?'

'Nothing.'

'C'mon, boy, talk,' his father said.

Dave took a deep breath and told the story he knew nobody believed.

'Waal,' he drawled. 'Ah brung ol Jenny down here sos Ah could do mah plowin. Ah plowed bout two rows, just like yuh see.' He stopped and pointed at the long rows of upturned earth. 'Then something musta been wrong wid ol Jenny. She wouldn't ack right atall. She started snortin n kickin her heels. Ah tried to hol her, but she pulled erway, rearin n goin on. Then when the point of the plow was stickin up in the air, she swung erroun n twisted hersef back on it. . . . She stuck hersef n started t bleed. N fo Ah could do anything, she wuz dead.'

'Did you ever hear of anything like that in all your life?' asked Jim Hawkins.

There were white and black standing in the crowd. They murmured. Dave's mother came close to him and looked hard into his face.

'Tell the truth, Dave,' she said.

'Looks like a bullet hole ter me,' said one man.

'Dave, whut yuh do wid tha gun?' his mother asked.

The crowd surged in, looking at him. He jammed his hands into his pockets, shook his head slowly from left to right, and backed away. His eyes were wide and painful.

'Did he hava gun?' asked Jim Hawkins.'

'By Gawd, Ah tol yuh tha wuz a *gun* wound,' said a man, slapping his thigh.

His father caught his shoulders and shook him till his teeth rattled.

'Tell whut happened, yuh rascal! Tell whut . . .'

Dave looked at Jenny's stiff legs and began to cry.

'Whut yuh do wid tha gun?' his mother asked.

'Whut wuz he doin wida gun?' his father asked.

'Come on and tell the truth,' said Hawkins. 'Ain't nobody going to hurt you . . .'

His mother crowded close to him.

'Did yuh shoot tha mule, Dave?'

Dave cried, seeing blurred white and black faces.

'Ahh ddinnt gggo tt sshoooot hher. . . . Ah ssswear off Gawd Ahh ddint. . . . Ah wuz a-tryin t sssee ef the ol gggun would sshoot——'

'Where yuh git the gun from?' his father asked.

'Ah got it from Joe, at the sto.'

'Where yuh git the money?'

'Ma give it t me.'

'He kept worryin me, Bob. . . . Ah had t. . . . Ah tol im t bring the gun right back t me. . . . It was fer yuh, the gun.'

'But how yuh happen to shoot that mule?' asked Jim Hawkins.

'Ah wuznt shootin at the mule, Mistah Hawkins. The gun jumped when Ah pulled the trigger . . . N fo Ah knowed anything Jenny wuz there a-bleedin.'

Somebody in the crowd laughed. Jim Hawkins walked close to Dave and looked into his face.

'Well, looks like you have bought you a mule, Dave.'

'Ah swear fo Gawd, Ah didn't go t kill the mule, Mistah Hawkins!'

'But you killed her!'

All the crowd was laughing now. They stood on tiptoe and poked heads over one another's shoulders.

'Well, boy, looks like yuh done bought a dead mule! Hahaha!'

'Ain tha ershame.'

'Hohohohoho.'

Dave stood head down, twisting his feet in the dirt.

'Well, you needn't worry about it, Bob,' said Jim Hawkins to Dave's father. 'Just let the boy keep on working and pay me two dollars a month.'

'Whut yuh wan fer yo mule, Mistah Hawkins?'

Jim Hawkins screwed up his eyes.

'Fifty dollars.'

'Whut yuh do wid tha gun?' Dave's father demanded.

Dave said nothing.

'Yuh wan me t take a tree lim n beat yuh till yuh talk!'

'Nawsuh!'

'Whut yuh do wid it?'

'Ah thowed it erway.'

'Where?'

'Ah . . . Ah thowed it in the creek.'

'Waal, c mon home. N firs thing in the mawnin git to tha creek n fin tha gun.'

'Yessuh.'

'Whut yuh pay fer it?'

'Two dollahs.'

'Take tha gun n git yo money back n carry it t Mistah Hawkins, yuh hear? N don fergit Ahma lam yo black bottom good fer this! Now march yosef on home, suh!'

Dave turned and walked slowly. He heard people laughing. Dave glared, his eyes welling with tears. Hot anger bubbled in him. Then he swallowed and stumbled on.

That night Dave did not sleep. He was glad that he had gotten out of killing the mule so easily, but he was hurt. Something hot seemed to turn over inside him each time he remembered how they had laughed. He tossed on his bed, feeling his hand pillow. N Pa says he's gonna beat me. . . . He remembered other beatings, and his back quivered. Naw, naw, Ah sho don wan im t beat me tha way no mo. . . . Dam em *all!* Nobody ever gave him anything. All he did was work. They treat me lika mule. . . . N then they beat me. . . . He gritted his teeth. N Ma had t tell on me.

Well, if he had to, he would take old man Hawkins that two dollars. But that meant selling the gun. And he wanted to keep that gun. Fifty dollahs fer a dead mule.

He turned over, thinking of how he had fired the gun. He had an itch to fire it again. Ef other men kin shoota gun, by Gawd, Ah kin! He was still listening. Mebbe they all sleepin now. . . . The house was still. He heard the soft breathing of his brother. Yes, now! He would go down and get that gun and see if he could fire it! He eased out of bed and slipped into overalls.

The moon was bright. He ran almost all the way to the edge of the woods. He stumbled over the ground, looking for the spot where he had buried the gun. Yeah, here it is. Like a hungry dog scratching for a bone he pawed it up. He puffed his black cheeks and blew dirt from the trigger and barrel. He broke it and found four cartridges unshot. He looked around; the fields were filled with silence and moonlight. He clutched the gun stiff and hard in his fingers. But as soon as he wanted to pull the trigger, he shut his eyes and turned his head. Naw. Ah can't shoot wid mah eyes closed n mah head turned. With effort he held his eyes open; then he squeezed. *Blooooom!* He was stiff, not breathing. The gun was still in his hands. Dammit, he'd done it! He fired again. *Blooooom!* He smiled. *Blooooom! Blooooom! Click, click.* There! It was empty. If anybody could shoot a gun, he could. He put the gun into his hip pocket and started across the fields.

When he reached the top of a ridge he stood straight and proud in the moonlight, looking at Jim Hawkins' big white house, feeling the gun sagging in his pocket. Lawd, ef Ah had jus one mo bullet Ahd taka shot at tha house. Ahd like t scare ol man Hawkins jusa little. . . . Jussa enough t let im know Dave Sanders is a man.

To his left the road curved, running to the tracks of the Illinois Central. He jerked his head, listening. From far off came a faint *hoooof-hoooof; hoooof-hoooof; hoooof-hoooof* . . . Tha's number eight. He took a swift look at Jim Hawkins' white house; he thought of pa, of ma, of his little brother, and the boys. He thought of the dead mule and heard *hoooof-hoooof; hoooof-hoooof; hoooof-hoooof* . . . He stood rigid. Two dollahs a mont. Les see now. . . . Tha means itll take bout two years. Shucks! Ahll be dam!

He started down the road, toward the tracks. Yeah, here she comes! He stood beside the track and held himself stiffly. Here she comes, erroun the ben. . . . C mon, yuh slow poke! C mon! He had his hand on his gun; something quivered in his stomach. Then the train thundered past, the gray and brown box cars rumbling and clinking. He gripped the gun tightly; then he jerked his hand out of his pocket. Ah betcha Bill wouldn't do it! Ah betcha . . . The cars slid past, steel grinding upon steel. Ahm riding yuh ternight so hep me Gawd! He was hot all over. He hesitated just a moment; then he grabbed, pulled atop of a car, and lay flat. He felt his pocket; the gun was still there. Ahead the long rails were glinting in the moonlight, stretching away, away to somewhere, somewhere where he could be a man. . . .

[1940]

Study and Writing Questions

1. What does the gun represent to Dave? to Dave's mother? to the storekeeper? to Jim Hawkins? to Dave's father? to the crowd?
2. What does Jenny represent in this story? Is it possible that the shooting is MOTIVATED unconsciously?
3. What is Dave's relationship to his mother?
4. What is the importance of race in this STORY?
5. How does the last paragraph suggest the nature of Dave's future? In what ways does the last line comment on the title? How is the NARRATIVE RESOLVED?

See also Questions for Contrast and Comparison: 34, 39, 53, 54, 55, 56, 70, 84, 97, 119, 130, 168, and 239.

■ **XIAOPING ZHU** (1952–) *was born in Sichuan province, People's Republic of China, and graduated (1982) from the literature department of the Central Institute of Drama in Beijing, where he taught until 1985. He was then assigned to the administrative staff of the All-China Writers' Union. "Chronicle of Mulberry Tree Village," his remarkable first story, has also been presented in a theatrical version in Beijing. Nothing further, in English or Chinese, is publicly available in the West concerning Zhu.*

Chronicle of
Mulberry Tree Village

On a business trip to Chengdu, I was held up by railway repairs on the Baoji–Chengdu line. I was stranded for the night in Baoji.

As evening descended, I walked through the streets of the city, the biggest in west Shaanxi. The Qing Mountains, grand and imposing, loomed in the distance, while the Wei River rippled eastward with a merry sound. A wave of emotion swept over me. I was actually quite near Mulberry Tree Village, where I received much of my education.

Mulberry Tree Village, always in my thoughts, was just a hundred *li* away. Yellow sandy slopes and yellow sandy cave dwellings; the sweet smell of golden wheat wafting from the fields; the crystal-clear brook with its shaded banks; on the slopes, giant poplars stretching to the sky, their leaves forever rustling; in the distance the crack of the herdsman's whip and the echo of his mountain song:

"Go eastward, my lambs, where the grass is good for grazing,
In the eastern slope, my lambs, a certain girl is waiting."

It was almost a dozen years since I left the village. I wondered: *what is it like now?* How I longed to see it again! Actually, the person I most wished to see was the production team leader Li Jindo.

Isn't it strange how a person can entangle himself in your very heartstrings, giving you no peace? Such a man was Li Jindo. Though I had spent two whole years with him, I still found him baffling.

The next morning, suffused with memories, I set out for Mulberry Tree Village.

My first encounter with the village—and with Li Jindo—came in 1968, when I was seventeen. A resident of Shanghai, I had been relocated to the countryside and was bused along with other students to the county of Linyou, one of the poorest counties of the Northwest. The bus left me off on the grounds of a dilapidated middle school forty *li* from Mulberry Tree Village. It was arranged that I would spend the evening at the local guest house. The next day I would be picked up by someone from Mulberry Tree Village.

The weather in March was still quite chilly. Even the sun hung listlessly in the sky. Lying in the clammy, stinky bedroom of the guest house, I hardly slept a wink that night. I was plagued by anxiety, overcome with nausea, and, finally, attacked by fleas. Gathering courage, I got up with the first light of dawn with the intention of sneaking back to Shanghai by hopping aboard the six-thirty train.

I pushed open the gate of the guest house, tripped over a dark bundle, and nearly tumbled down the steps. The bundle let out a cry of pain. It turned out to be a man, cowering under layers of posters torn from the walls. Evidently he had spent the night in the doorway of the guest house and had used the paper for warmth.

The hovering figure scrambled up and we scrutinized one another.

He was a man of about sixty (later I realized that I was a bad judge of faces, as people living in the hills age faster, and that he was only forty-six at the time). He had a dried-up, sallow face and a wisp of yellowish whiskers straggling on his chin. My first impression of his face was: this is not an honest fellow. Just look at his clothes! He was a mass of rags from head to foot. His pants and jacket were covered with patches in all the colors of the rainbow.

I had stepped on him and disturbed his sleep. I should, by all reason, apologize; but as he was just a street beggar, I turned and walked away.

"Are you a student from the province?" he called after me.

I stopped. "Yes."

"Are you going to Mulberry Tree Village?"

"Yes. What of it?"

"Oh, heavens, how I have looked for you all over the place! I have come to fetch you!" He reached out and grasped my hand. I made haste to extricate myself from his grasp. His palm was like a saw!

This peasant was none other than Li Jindo.

It turned out that he had been sent by district administrators to accompany me the rest of the way to Mulberry Tree Village.

"Why didn't you put up at the guest house?" I asked, thinking that he would be the perfect customer for such a miserable hole.

"Oh, that is not for people like me!"

"Then why didn't you go to an inn? It's so cold in the open."

Evidently Jindo thought my last question not worth answering. He took out his pipe, filled and lighted it, and said: "You babies from the city don't know a thing. I am lucky enough to spend the night here and not be chased off." He pulled at his pipe silently. (Later, when I had settled at Mulberry Tree Village, I learned that three days' hard work in the fields would not earn Li Jindo the price of one night on the common bed at the county inn.)

Jindo squatted down and went on smoking. When I considered that he had spent the cold night out in the open, all for my sake, my sympathy toward him began to grow.

"Come on, let's eat before we start off." I extended an invitation to Jindo as compensation for his privations the night before.

"Oh, forget it. I brought my own steamed bread."

No matter how I urged him, Jindo would not budge. Suddenly it occurred to me that this peasant did not get my message. So I said point-blank: "I am paying, I treat." It worked immediately. Jindo stood up with alacrity, mumbling, "No need for youngsters to stand on ceremony." He led the way to an eating-house.

We walked to a place that opened early. I took out money and grain coupons to buy tickets for our meal, but Jindo snatched the notes out of my hands, saying, "You go find seats while I take care of this." So I sat down, my mind assailed by conflicting emotions.

The house sold only one kind of food: the local steamed bread soaked in mutton soup, five *jiao* a serving. It was served in a steaming bowl — broken bits of bread saturated in soup with a few pieces of greasy meat floating on the surface.

I cast a glance in Jindo's direction and immediately saw something fishy was going on. He did not buy the steamed bread, after all, and he bought only one bowl of soup. He divided his own steamed bread in two and placed the portions in two bowls. He divided the one bowl of soup similarly. Thus he saved seven *jiao* and one grain coupon, which he quietly pocketed.

I fumed inwardly at this petty trick, but I didn't say anything. I realized that my impression of peasants had been derived from movies, magazines, and novels. And this flesh-and-blood Li Jindo had nothing in common with those imaginary peasants.

Jindo brought the two steaming bowls over. I closed my eyes and tried to swallow a few mouthfuls. Although the soup was thick and spicy, it could not disguise the smell of Jindo's musty bread. Jindo inhaled his food, almost burying his head in the bowl until it was empty. He then saw that I had put down my chopsticks and was sitting dejectedly.

"Why don't you eat? We have many *li* to travel!"

"I'm not hungry."

"You city people are so choosy. You don't even enjoy bread in boiled meat!" So saying, he finished off my bowl in a twinkling.

Having eaten, Jindo wiped his mouth with his hands and started to pull at his pipe, hiccoughing all the while. He was enjoying himself immensely.

I went back to the guest house to fetch my luggage, altogether seven pieces, a full two hundred *jin*. "My! My!" exclaimed Jindo. "Just a youngster and so many belongings, more than my whole household." He strapped the big bedrolls onto his back. It was impossible to take care of everything. "You store the rest somewhere," he said, "I'll send somebody for them later."

Spring had arrived in the Linyou hills. On mountain slopes and terrace fields, on branches and treetops, specks of tender green wove together the bright hue of the season. The joyful tidings of spring swept away all my unease. The place was beautiful.

My luggage pack of a hundred *jin* was like a bundle of hay on Jindo's shoulders. His stride was long and firm and fast. I began to respect him in spite of myself.

We walked in silence for a few *li*. There's nothing as bad as silence when you walk in company. Jindo started to chat.

"What does a baby schoolboy want to do in this poor valley?"

"To be reeducated by poor and lower-class peasants!" I joked.

"Don't underestimate us poor and lower-class peasants. Don't we know that you've been up to all sorts of mischief in the city? You've obviously offended the powers-that-be; on the surface, they're not revenging themselves on you, but actually they're sending you here to suffer for your sins. And to take the food out of our mouths!"

Jindo had said his say, and was silent. So, I thought, that's how they think of us students!

We walked on in silence.

Before long we had worked up a sweat. But when we descended into a valley, a cool wind curled up and wrapped itself around us. It was wonderful. Evidently, Jindo could not bear the silence; he raised his voice and sang a tune from the *Qin Qiang* opera:

"The grass is green on the slopes, and the flowers are sweet.
Spring is stirring in my maiden's bosom.
Across the nine-arch bridge, a scholar is walking toward me,
More handsome than Sung Yu or Pan An, stirring my desire."

Jindo's voice was hoarse and hollow, but he sang in the singsong voice of the young lover. Looking at his beggarly appearance and hearing his falsetto voice, I could not help laughing. This Jindo is really quite a character, I thought, the typical village idler and rascal.

And so, without realizing it, we cleared the forty *li*. Once we crossed Beanpod Valley, the little village of Mulberry Tree spread out in front of us.

The moment we entered the village, Li Jindo seemed to change into another man. Never had I seen such a strange metamorphosis.

As we walked through the village, a big strong peasant emerged. Li Jindo started to abuse him. "Guaiquan, you mother-fucker, are you blind? Get over here and give me a hand!" The man made haste to relieve Jindo of my bedrolls. "Take these things to the western cave-dwelling, and tell your aunt to fix dinner for this student baby." The man took his orders submissively and went.

On our way to the western cave-dwelling, everybody we met greeted Jindo respectfully. "What have you been doing with yourself the whole morning?" he asked one fellow.

"Carting manure."

"How many carts?"

"A dozen."

"You lazy bastard! You stand there and tell me you carted only a dozen in one morning?!"

"I also drove over a cart of cattle feed."

"Fuck your cattle feed! You finish carting all the manure this afternoon!"

Only then did I realize Jindo was leader of the production team.

The village was small, composed of about ten families; but Jindo lorded it over them in grand style. The entire population, man, woman, and child, all bowed to his orders.

I learned that the whole village, with one exception, was all branches of one family by the surname of Li. Except for his uncle and his cousin, Jindo was the eldest in the village.

My first two days in the village, I relaxed and put my lodging in order; the third morning I got up early—at the first stroke of the big bell calling the villagers to work.

Everyone was gathered under a big elm at the village entrance. Jindo was waiting there. One villager told me that ever since Mulberry Tree Village set up the cooperative, Jindo had personally struck the work bell—every single day, year in, year out, for ten years. After he struck the bell, he would light his pipe, and after smoking one pipeful, he would assign the work for the day. After he finished giving orders, he would go out into the fields and join in the work. He would never wait for late arrivals. If you did not turn up before his pipe went out, you were not given work and you lost work-points. Understandably, late arrivals were very rare in Mulberry Tree Village.

"What shall I do today, team leader?" I asked that morning after the assignments had been dispensed.

"Oh, you!" He looked in my direction. "You're still new; why don't you relax for a couple of days?"

I did not want to be idle. So, since Jindo did not assign me any work, I went off to seek work of my own. I saw some villagers tilling the soil; I saw others sowing corn.

But each time I tried to join a work group, I discovered that my enthusiasm was not appreciated. On the contrary, the laborers shunned me, as if they dared not tire me with work. They would either push me out of the way or refuse to let me use their tools. I could not understand this behavior, though I assumed it was owing to Jindo's supreme authority in the village, as if allowing me to work would violate his wishes and incur punishment on the offender.

There was nothing I could do. I borrowed a long-handle hoe and joined a group of women and children in breaking up lumps of soil. Only then was I allowed to work without interference.

After three days of pulverizing lumpy soil, I attended a regular meeting of the laborers.

According to regulations, the production team held a meeting every three months to adjust the members' work-points—that is, to determine how many points each member was worth according to physical strength and farming skill. Those who could perform hard tasks or were skilled at farming were conceded "full labor." These laborers were usually allotted over nine work-points. According to this scale, those under six points were granted "half labor." The old or the very young usually fell in this category, and they were really superfluous as far as real farming was concerned.

As the village was small, the number of exceptional farm hands came to about twenty. Everybody knew how many work-points a man was worth, so the allocation of work-points at the meeting was but a formality. The procedure went this way: first the members spoke up and gave their opinion as to who was worth what; then Jindo would say, "That's not far from the mark." Thus the tone was set and the matter settled. No one had the slightest objection to their alloted points.

When my turn came, absolute silence reigned.

The women sewed. The men puffed their pipes. Nobody so much as opened his mouth. They were all waiting for their cue.

"Come on, everybody," Jindo finally exclaimed, "speak up your minds. Of course, the student comes from a rich family and doesn't depend on a few measly work-points for food and drink. Still, he is now a member of our team." Jindo raised his eyes and looked over the gathering. Whenever his eyes fell on them, the women would hastily stop sewing while the men would also pretend to concentrate. Clearly Jindo had set the tone: that I didn't care for a few beggarly work-points. The members now started to speak up in a babble of voices:

"The kid hasn't started work yet," said an old fellow. "Let's put it at five points for the moment, and then see."

"Who said the kid didn't work? He has broken lumps of soil for two days. Five and a half is fairer."

Soon everybody was babbling, but none of them suggested my work-point should exceed five and a half! I was mortified! I had thought that I would get at least eight points. All the women who worked with me were evaluated at six and a half, and they only showed up for work half the morning, sneaking back to cook dinner before noon. Compared to them, I was a full laborer.

In our group, there were but a few half-grown kids like me who work full-time. Among them was Jinsheng's son Fulian. We had wrestled with each other several times during workbreaks, and every time he lost to me. And Fulian had been granted eight points. It's true I didn't care for the evaluation from the material side, but my honor was involved and I felt hurt.

"Fulian is worth eight work-points," I chimed in, "and I am much stronger than he is."

The whole assembly burst out in a loud guffaw.

Someone shouted, "Fulian is better at farm work than you; farming requires skill, you know."

With that, everybody started talking at once. I was at a loss for words. Suddenly Jindo struck the table with his pipe and there was immediate silence.

"That's not far off the mark," he said. "We should give the kid more credit. It's true he can't do hard work, and he has no skill, but he can learn. I suggest we add another half point. Let's give him a nice, round six."

Nobody raised any objections. My gratitude to Jindo was beyond bounds. He had spoken up on my behalf, asking people to give me more credit, and encouraged me to learn farming skills. From then on, I was a "half labor" at Mulberry Tree Village, worth six points.

The following day Jindo formally issued my assignment for the day: carting manure into the fields. One cart was given to each worker, and the worker was responsible for filling and transporting the cart. The distance from the animal shed to the fields was at least one *li*. The soil had just been turned and was soft and moist. As I pulled the cart through the field, every step was agony. Soon the cart rope left two deep blood-red welts on my shoulders, which burned with pain. Before half the morning was over, my whole body was one collective mass of pain. By afternoon, I sat on the shaft of the cart, unable to move.

The shepherd Old Li passed by me on his way back from the mountain slopes. He saw my misery and said, "Poor boy, you're still tender. You don't know the harshness of farm work. Just look and see what kind of people are here."

I raised my head and, sure enough, only the full laborers worth nine or ten points were doing this work. I was the only half laborer present. What did it mean? Why did Jindo give me this assignment?

"It's Jindo at his tricks again. You've been taken in."

Old Li had left the village when he was young and only after liberation had he returned from Xinjiang. He was virtually a newcomer and did not get along well with the other villagers. Perhaps that was why he was the only person who dared to stand up to Jindo, and for this he was treated as an alien. Hearing Old Li's remark, I began to see the work-point meeting in a new light.

It was, I realized, a charade to take advantage of me, a stranger. I felt cheated. In anger I stood up and wanted to confront Jindo.

"Fuck him," I spat out. "I'm not working tomorrow."

"Poor kid, if you don't, you won't even get six points at the next evaluation. You'll never put one over on wily Jindo."

"But what shall I do?"

"There's nothing to do. Just keep a cool head. It's only the fool who babbles. Set your teeth and keep working for three months and at the next evaluation, Jindo will treat you better. Actually he's not a bad man."

"Not bad! Then why did he deceive me?"

"It's not personal. When people are so poor, they'll do anything for a bit of amusement. Who can blame them?"

Six work-points! That meant that if I worked hard for two whole days, I would earn the price of a pack of Hai He cigarettes, the cheapest brand on the market. *When people are so poor . . . who can blame them?*

I suddenly remembered how Jindo had first cheated me of seven *jiao* at the eating-house. But then he had gladly shouldered my hundred-*jin* weight of luggage and walked a full forty *li*. This Jindo, I really didn't know what to think of him.

Old Li wanted to say something, then changed his mind. He made his way back to the village, the valley echoing with his song:

> "Dear maiden, your parting words I keep in mind,
> My way through the world is long and arduous. . . ."

Soon it was dusk, but I still sat motionless on the shaft of the cart, my mind in a turmoil. I turned and looked at Mulberry Tree Village. Smoke was rising slowly from every chimney. The villagers had all returned to their homes.

Suddenly I saw a figure walking through the empty fields, stopping here and there as if looking for something on the ground. In the dusk the shadow looked like Jindo's. The last few days I had discovered that Jindo was always the last to return.

It was Jindo indeed. He appeared to have discovered something. He then walked to the edge of the fields and, facing the village, shouted in a loud voice. The village was so small he could be heard in every corner.

"Pao Wua, you dog-fucker, is this the way you spread manure? Who do you think you're cheating anyway? If this is how you farm, you'll never fill your fucking stomach."

After he had abused the careless Pao Wua to his heart's content, he called out to the recorder of work-points, Li Fuquan. "Fuquan, do you hear me? Strike out Pao Wua's work-points for this morning!" He then saw me and said, "You must throw in the whole of body and soul just to be half fed. How dare anybody cheat the soil?" Then he hobbled away.

Again I recalled how he had cheated me at the work-point meeting. My anger dissolved. I smiled bitterly. This Jindo was really a riddle!

The wheat-cutting season arrived. The peasants had sweated and toiled for a whole year. This was the time they looked forward to; this was also the time they feared.

In that period of tumult and confusion, with few exceptions, everybody was suffering. But even in the worst years of the Cultural Revolution, the peasants dared not stop their labor. Nobody cared for their situation, but they had to work doubly hard to produce the grain to maintain the country through the turmoil. It seemed as if everybody was concerned for the future and destiny of China—except the peasants. As for them, their eyes were fixed on the soil. They were concerned only about the year's harvest.

The crops were really not bad that year. After the lunar month of May, the golden wheat stood thick and heavy in rows. From the fields, the rippling wheat sent out the sweet smell of harvest.

Old and young began to stir themselves to prepare for harvesting, but nobody was as busy as production team leader Jindo. He had to take care of every detail relating to the harvest. In a few days he was worn to a shadow. It seemed that only the skin on his lips had not wasted away. On the eve of cutting the wheat, Jindo made an announcement at the villagers' general meeting. To my surprise, he said that during the summer harvest, I was to be his personal aide. I would work as his liaison, running back and forth and helping him with all the business related to harvesting.

I had not forgotten how Jindo had tricked me before. I had even gritted my teeth and kept at heavy farm work for three months. Now that the next evaluation meeting was approaching, I suspected Jindo was up to new tricks, probably shifting me to some light work in order to lower my work-points.

"No thank you," I said. "I've had to work like a dog!"

Jindo replied hastily: "No, no tricks, I promise. Let's settle this right away. From now on, your work-point is eight and a half."

I was bewildered. What did it mean, giving me eight and a half points just to be Jindo's assistant? The villagers all looked at me expectantly. I sought out Old Li sitting in a corner, and appealed to him with my eyes, for fear I'd be taken in again. Contrary to expectation, even Old Li, usually hostile to Jindo, supported this decision. "Go ahead, my lad," he said. "The important thing is for our production team not to suffer loss. Jindo will treat you right."

I agreed. The very next morning, the harvest evaluation team from the commune leadership made its way into Mulberry Tree Village.

Every year at that time the evaluation team would invade each village. Their job was to assess the size of the harvest, judging by the yet uncut crops in the fields. Like the farmers, these assessors were shrewd and quite accurate in their assessments. And according to their assessment, the leadership would hand down the figures for the amount of grain to be turned over to the state.

Hence, it is the assessors that are really the scourge of the peasants. The way the assessors casually let drop figures from their lips was a matter of life and death to the poor peasant; it meant either food and warmth or hunger and cold for the next twelve months.

Jindo made early preparations to receive these all-important officials. The production team killed two fat lambs, and every family contributed eggs and wine and cigarettes. How much Mulberry Tree Village could keep of the harvest, how much would be portioned out to the villagers—all would be determined by the success of this reception.

The assessment team finally made its entry into the village. The head of the team was vice-chairman of the county revolutionary committee; before the Cultural Revolution, he was but a petty clerk.

On Jindo's orders, I led the assessors to the office quarters of the production team. There the banquet was already set: broiled lamb, scrambled eggs, goblets of wine. The children of the village were all glued to the windows, their mouths watering. Jindo did not keep the guests company. (He said he could not bear the sight. "Every mouthful they eat, I feel they are chewing my own flesh.")

Jindo instructed me to put plenty of water in the wine, reminding me to keep the assessors from drinking too much. Once dead drunk, those immortals would blubber any kind of nonsense and then stick to their words no matter what.

After the assessors finished their meal, Jindo led them to the fields. The villagers working in the fields held their breath.

It was apparent to every eye that the wheat was good. The vice-chairman glanced at the wheat rippling in the sun and, while picking his teeth, casually assessed the harvest at two hundred and ten jin per mu!

At mention of this figure, Jindo paled. If you take two hundred and ten as a starting point, you will never beat it down to an acceptable figure. He tried to put it off by a joke.

"Two hundred and ten! Why, you won't reach this figure even if you add last year's crop to it."

"Then what would you say?" another assessor asked.

"Well, you have all done farming yourself," Jindo said. "You should know, what with spilling and spoiling on the threshing grounds and this uncertain weather, we would be lucky to collect a hundred and thirty or forty per *mu!*"

The vice-chairman spat. "Do you intend to haggle with me?" He walked toward Jindo menacingly.

Jindo backed away. "Chairman, please look again," he begged. "Our fields have *never* yielded over two hundred. You know very well the kind of life we live. We are, after all, from the same region; don't you care to keep up good relations with your people?"

Somehow, Jindo's words offended the mighty official. He turned and cried angrily, "Why are you holding me up? You are trying to hit me!" Saying which, he hit Jindo on the chest. Jindo tried to parry the blow. The vice-chairman then seized Jindo by the collar and started hitting him in earnest. Jindo plopped to the ground and, holding his face to his hands, burst into tears. He was a man, a head of household, with wife and children, and now, to be treated like this . . .

All the villagers working in the fields turned their faces away, not daring to look. They could not bear to witness Jindo's mortification.

Jindo controlled himself and stood up with tears still running down his face.

Before Jindo could speak my anger shot up straight to my head. I stomped over to the vice-chairman.

"By what right do you hit us?" I spat. "You just try it again!"

The group bristled up in alarm. "What! You want to start a fight?" one of them cried.

"You just keep your hands off Jindo!" I screamed. They stopped their bluff immediately. Just a bunch of bullies, that's what they were.

Just as I was about to use my fists on them, two villagers tried to drag me back. As they got hold of me, the vice-chairman gained new courage and ordered his men, "Take him to the commune and I'll make him pay for this!"

The assessors rushed upon me. My arms were still pinned by the villagers trying to save me from myself. Without thinking, I kicked out and one of the assessors cried out in pain as my foot connected with his kneecap. The others scrambled back again. The villagers, seeing how desperate I was, held on to me all the more tightly as I cried out, "You son-of-a-dog vice-chairman, I'll beat the shit out of you!"

The villagers overpowered me finally and dragged me back. As I was struggling in their hands, I called out father's name without thinking. My father had been a leading government official in this region before the Cultural Revolution, and recently during the setup of the new revolutionary committee his name was listed as honorary member.

I don't know whether it was on account of my desperation, or because my father's name worked the magic, but anyway the assessing team left hastily without even eating their indispensable dinner. They departed for another village.

Jindo wanted to recall them and apologize. He even moved a few steps in their direction, then sighed and stopped, realizing the futility of it all.

In the afternoon word was sent round from the brigade. To our shock, the assessment for Mulberry Tree Village was a hundred and seventy *jin* per *mu*! Jindo and the whole village let out a sigh of relief.

"Good boy," Old Li commended me.

"Good boy!" the whole village echoed.

That night it seemed that every man, woman, and child in the village gathered in Jindo's house, to offer condolences for the blows he got.

When Jindo saw me, he said, "My boy, cutting wheat is tiring work. You needn't do it. You just keep boiling water, to keep the cutters in drinking water."

Then he turned to the work-point recordkeeper. "Fuquan, double the boy's work-points for today. And from now on, give him nine and a half points every day."

All the villagers smiled. Then Jindo added: "Go ahead and cancel all my work-points for today. I did a bad job, nearly brought disaster to the village." He patted me on the shoulder.

Jindo's wife sat by, quietly wiping her tears.

Jindo turned to her fiercely. "Why the hell are you crying? I'm alive and kicking. Why don't you make some eggs for the boy?" Boiling eggs is the mountain villagers' highest form of courtesy to distinguished guests.

As we talked out of Jindo's home, Old Li muttered to himself, "What a wily fox that Jindo is! Pushing the student boy to the front to bear the brunt of the abuse. And it actually worked!"

Old Li's words struck me like lightning. So I was taken in again! Jindo shrewdly foresaw that the assessment affair was a risky business, and he knew that students would not stand by and see officials abusing peasants, that they would stand up and pick a fight. Jindo's ruse worked. But supposing I hadn't had a father whose name meant something. I would at that moment be quivering under the lash of the vice-chairman!

Reflecting on all this, I couldn't suppress a deep sigh. So long as I can serve the poor underprivileged peasants of Mulberry Tree Village, I thought, I don't mind being deceived by Jindo anymore.

All those events happened more than ten years ago. And here I was, at nightfall, on the outskirts of the little village I left so long ago.

The soft tints of dusk had receded from the western slopes; in the gloaming, wisps of smoke rose gently from households behind stacks of wheat. Specks of light twinkled, like the deep and unfathomable eyes of Mulberry Tree Village. On the edge of the terrace fields, the poplars stood tall and straight, their leaves rustling to a sweet music.

That night I slept at the headquarters of the production team. The whole village turned out to greet me. There was such a lot to talk about. But I did not see Jindo, the person I missed most.

People told me he was not the production leader anymore, that Fuchun had taken over. When I was in the village, Fuchun was just a youngster. "And where is Jindo?" I asked. Someone said he was visiting with relatives.

I didn't believe it. The lunar month of July is the busiest season. How could the astute Jindo possibly be idle?

"Jindo is full of resentment," Fuchun told me.

I wondered: *what about?*

Jindo was never one to stay idle. As far back as the days when I was in the village, I remember seeing him digging holes to plant trees whenever he had a moment's free time. He would dig anywhere, on the side of roads, on terrace fields, on slopes, anywhere he could.

The year before last, Mulberry Tree Village adopted the responsibility system, part of the current reform. By that time the slopes were dotted with holes that Jindo dug to plant trees. He was no longer team leader, so he turned to tree planting seriously.

But even with the new policy, the backward village could not expect to turn rich in the twinkling. There was no money to buy saplings. So Jindo again resorted to his wiles.

Last year the land was parceled out and rented as private plots. Jindo offered to rent five *mu* only.

Five *mu* could only produce enough grain for basic food. Getting rich was totally out of the question. The villagers could not believe how such an astute farmer like Jindo could be so dense.

But Jindo had his own plans. "I'm renting twenty *mu*," he explained, "but will only farm five. I'd like to exchange the fifteen *mus* of land for saplings." At the time, all the peasants wanted to lay claims to as much land as possible. Jindo took advantage of the peasant mentality to get hold of tree saplings.

All the villagers laughed uproariously. So that's why Jindo only plans to farm five *mu*. He had made his calculations after all.

Jindo even resorted to blackmail. "If you won't give me saplings, I'd rather let those fifteen *mu* lie fallow." In the mountainous area, where arable land is so scarce, this was a great waste; but nobody knew where to get the required amount of tree saplings.

Jindo didn't achieve his goal after all, and left the village in a huff.

Fuquan said to me: "Who'd believe that he'd go visiting relatives at such a busy time! I bet he's gone to look for tree saplings. This old fellow always knew where his interests lay. I think he's right. It's much more lucrative to raise trees.

We're so poor because we've always stuck to farming. Jindo's ideas never go wrong."

Of that I have no doubt.

People said that before he set out, he had sold all the wood and stones and bricks that he had stored up to build a new house. Jindo, who had been dogged by poverty all his life, had certainly set out on a new track. He had plotted for petty advantages all his life. Now he had seen a new road to prosperity.

That night, thinking of Jindo, I didn't sleep a wink. I recollected the affair of the seven *jiao*, and all the things that followed. I feel that as Jindo looks back on his life so far, he must regret having wasted so much energy for so little. It's not worthwhile. But at the time, what could he do? He was a peasant. He tills and sows and harvests big stretches of land, but in his everyday life, he has to measure his spending grain by grain.

Could Jindo be reckoned as wise, diligent, honest, and lovable — as peasants are typically described? I really don't know. This Jindo! Even now I really don't know what to think of him.

[1988]

Study and Writing Questions

1. What can be inferred about the social position of the NARRATOR? How would you CHARACTERIZE his youth? Did his two years at Mulberry Tree Village materially change the course of the life he had expected?
2. What does the narrator think he learns from his first meeting with Li Jindo? Does he learn all he should? What are the major stages in what he calls his "education" at Mulberry Tree Village?
3. The central STORY is set in the last two years of the cultural Revolution (1966 – 1969), a frequently brutal campaign to weed out "bourgeois" influences in Chinese society and revitalize the principles and institutions of the Chinese Communist Party. Since the death of Mao Tse-tung (1893 – 1976), China's revolutionary leader, many Chinese have criticized the excesses of that period. In what ways does this NARRATIVE support and in what ways reject the Cultural Revolution? Why is the story of the narrator's education set within a FRAME?
4. "Even now I really don't know what to think of [Li Jindo]," the narrator says. What should he think of him? What do you think of him?
5. Is this narrative simply propaganda? Is there a psychological dimension to the relationship between the narrator and Li Jindo that makes this something more than a mere sketch of life during the Cultural Revolution? What message(s) do you infer from this narrative?

See also Questions for Contrast and Comparison: 4, 49, 56, 77, 100, 106, 134, 163, 205, and 210.

■

The Elements of Narrative

Keeping a Reading Journal

Writing About Narratives

Filmography

Glossary of Literary Terms

Questions for Contrast and Comparison

Title Index

■

The Elements of Narrative

If we wanted to know *everything* about even a single human being, we would need to know enough physics to understand her biochemistry and enough biochemistry to understand her psychology. We would need to know her background and aspirations, her work and her play, her friends and her enemies. Yet we still might not know why she loves maple walnut ice cream but never will eat it on a Thursday. Human complexity is inevitable, whether we meet someone on a bus or in a STORY. Thus, just as all life is potentially complex, all stories are potentially complex.

Because stories can be so complex, our understanding of them will profit by examining individually the elements composing them. However, the elements of NARRATIVE in isolation are no more like a story than the gases hydrogen and oxygen are like the liquid water produced by their burning. Something happens when elements combine. The iron we see rusting into decay by the roadside can be bound into the hemoglobin of our blood and carry life through our veins. The best analysis, then, must not only survey the elements of narrative but keep in sight the complexity of the stories in which these elements live.

The Narrative Situation

Our first images of the typical narrative situation may be somewhat ROMANTIC: a child listening rapt to a mother's tale, say, or a tribe held around a campfire by a shaman's legend. These IMAGES suggest three elements of narrative: a NARRATOR, a story, and a listener. But note: the mother and shaman are adopting speaking roles; at other times in their lives they may speak quite differently — as wife, say, or hunter. Similarly, even a simple story must be set in some place and relate events involving fictional actors. Real people, who at other times may be skeptical, are here invited to adopt the role of story listener and, as Samuel Taylor Coleridge suggested, perform "that willing suspension of disbelief for the moment, which constitutes the poetic faith." Clearly stories are more complex than our first images reveal.

To begin analyzing the complexities of the narrative situation, let us take as one example of narrative Edgar Allan Poe's "The Black Cat." Here is the opening paragraph. For ease of reference, I have numbered the sentences:

(1) For the most wild, yet most homely narrative which I am about to pen, I neither expect nor solicit belief. (2) Mad indeed would I be to expect it, in a case where my very senses reject their own evidence. (3) Yet, mad am I not — and very surely do I not dream. (4) But tomorrow I die, and to-day I would unburthen my soul. (5) My immediate purpose is to place before the world, plainly, succinctly, and without comment, a series of mere household events. (6) In their consequences, these events have terrified — have tortured — have destroyed me. (7) Yet I will not attempt to expound them. (8) To me, they have presented little but Horror — to many they will seem less terrible than *baroques*. (9) Hereafter, perhaps, some intellect may be found which will reduce my phantasm to the common-place — some intellect more calm, more logical, and far less excitable than my own, which will perceive, in the

circumstances I detail with awe, nothing more than an ordinary succession of very natural causes and effects.

The voice we hear in any narrative is that of a narrator. In this case, the narrator claims that he wants to "unburthen my soul" (4), thus suggesting extreme emotionalism; yet, in an unacknowledged contradiction, he also claims that "My immediate purpose is to place before the world, plainly, succinctly, and without comment, a series of mere household events" (5), thus suggesting utter rationalism. Is the narrator lying to us about his aims, or at least misrepresenting his inner state? He has unconsciously given us reason to think so. And yet, the narrator goes to some effort to win our trust. He cleverly disclaims credibility (1) and places himself on our side (2) by distrusting his own senses. Yet he would not have us conclude that the UNTRUSTWORTHINESS of his senses extends to an untrustworthiness about his narration (3). He asks, apparently honestly, for our pity (6); he acts humble (7); and he defers to greater "intellect" than he possesses (9). Yet along the way (8), he manages to slip in the suggestion that while his reaction was horror, it may be that the events he is about to narrate were merely strange. For an alert reader, then, the very extent of the effort the narrator makes to elicit belief should arouse suspicions. Thus, even on a first reading, we see the narrator as clever, self-serving, and deceitful.

Not every narrative has so specifically characterized a narrator; however, as a theoretical matter, every narrative must have a narrator, and all narrators are to a greater or lesser degree characterized. Who CHARACTERIZES the narrator? It does little good to say that he is defined by his own words since we know that his words are not really his own but put into his mouth by his creator. In the case of "The Black Cat," the narrator clearly does not want us to conclude that he is deceitful, and yet that is our inevitable conclusion. We infer, then, the existence of an AUTHOR who wanted us to see his narrator as deceitful. Put another way, although we hear only the narrator's voice, the text—the NARRATION—implies the existence of an author. In a narrative, the IMPLIED AUTHOR never speaks; yet we come to know the values and aims of the implied author, who in fact creates the story, characterizes the narrator, and controls everything about the narrative.

There is a natural tendency to confuse the BIOGRAPHICAL (also called HISTORI-CAL) AUTHOR, whose existence we presume since we know *someone* produced the text, with the implied author who never speaks but whose presence is so thoroughly implied by the text. Although it is possible that the biographical author and the implied author have the same aims and values, as a theoretical matter, that need never be the case. Consequently, we must be alert to the theoretical distinction between these two so-called authors. After all, biographical authors have the capacity to revise, dissimulate, lie. Biographical authors are paid not to tell the truth but to tell an artful story. For a story to appear artful, it must feel as if the whole works together; that is, it must seem the product of a fixed consciousness knowingly at work. The biographical Ernest Hemingway, if we can believe his public actions, letters, interviews, and nonfiction study *Death in the Afternoon* (1932), was an enthusiastic lover of bull-fighting; yet in *The Sun Also Rises* (1926), he created an implied author who chose to use bull-fighting as a central METAPHOR for the senselessness of all human ritualized violence, including war. Although narrators can learn and grow during a narrative, and biographical authors can have both happy and sad days while writing, the revised and polished product of their authorship must seem like the work of a single, stable mind, even if that stable mind — the implied author — creates a narrator whom we see going mad, as in Charlotte Perkins Gilman's "The Yellow Wall-Paper." Thus we must always acknowledge the distinction between the implied and biographical authors.

Even though it is wise to think of the artistic consciousness behind a story as the implied author, knowing something about the life of the biographical author is often useful for suggesting interpretive possibilities. For example, since the biographical Poe's wife Virginia died young, we might surmise that the effort by the narrator to relieve his own guilt is a reflection of a need Poe might have had to relieve some guilt about, perhaps, not nursing her properly. If we read about Poe's life, we learn that he had problems with alcohol, and we might infer that the "Fiend Intemperance," mentioned later in this story as a justification for the narrator's ACTIONS, reflects Poe's own desire to place the blame for Virginia's death outside himself. However, this inference would be a logical error called the BIOGRAPHICAL FALLACY, inferring literary causation from biographical information.

Although it is sometimes true that a biographical author may create an implied author who shares some or all of his or her values, this need not be the case. In Woody Allen's "The Whore of Mensa," the implied author (and the narrator) clearly enjoys making literary REFERENCE, as does the biographical Woody Allen; however, the implied author of Yukio Mishima's "Patriotism" is obviously ambivalent about the title concept even though the biographical Mishima was known to be a passionate superpatriot. Because biographical authors can create implied authors quite different from themselves, a direct inference of causation from biography to text is fallacious. Some female authors, like Colette, have sometimes found it best to write as if they were men. Adult authors, like Lynda Barry, sometimes write as if they were children. Many people wrongly inferred from *The Confessions of Nat Turner* (1967; Pulitzer Prize), a novel about the leader of a slave rebellion, that its author, William Styron, was black. Just because Poe had trouble with alcohol does not mean that he wrote "The Black Cat" to displace his own guilt. In fact, given the implied author's characterization of the narrator (making the narrator unconsciously reveal his own self-serving deceitfulness), we might better infer that Poe understood how some people try to displace guilt and was further condemning his own narrator by letting us see his narrator attempting just such a ploy. On a second reading of the story, when we realize the extraordinary crime the narrator has committed, when we realize why "tomorrow I die" (4), that self-serving displacement becomes even more objectionable. The biographical Poe may or may not, like most of us, sometimes have tried to push away his own sense of guilt, but the implied author of "The Black Cat" certainly wants us to see and condemn such displacement in his narrator.

This distinction between biographical and implied authors should make us cautious, but it should not cause us to reject biographical information. "The Black Cat" is a somewhat FANTASTIC story, and if one asks why something so clearly impossible should be meaningful to ordinary readers, biography may offer one possible answer. Whether or not the biographical Poe was trying by writing this story to relieve some guilt, we can all understand the story as an illustration of the way self-justification may lead to ever greater immorality and the ultimate need to deal with growing guilt once it becomes irrepressible. The police at the end of the story function like a conscience for the narrator. No matter what the narrator says, it is his own actions that reveal his crime.

All narratives, like "The Black Cat," have CHARACTERS and events. Henry James acknowledged the complex relationship of characters and events when he asked "What is character but the determination of incident? What is incident but the illustration of character?" There are at least two kinds of characters in a narrative: the character who may also be the narrator, as in "The Black Cat," and the characters, like the policemen in that story, who are only reported to us by the narrator. Similarly, there are at least two types of events that can occur in a narrative: the events reported by the narrator, and the events (called SPEECH ACTS) that constitute the narration itself; that is, every narrative contains both events reported and events enacted. (In the first paragraph of "The Black Cat," for example, the narrator's lengthy avoidance of naming the events he claims he wants to reveal is a narrative event, a speech act, defining his character.) And all of this multiplication of authors, characters, and events takes place, of course, in some SETTING. As we come to learn later in Poe's story, the setting for the event of narration is a prison cell, while the events narrated occurred in the narrator's home, a saloon, and so on.

The narrative situation always provides us with a complex nest of elements, starting with the biographical/historical author, moving on to the heart of the text, and then coming out again to us, the biographical/historical readers with our own backgrounds and daily variations in mood. But just as a narrative implies its author, a conscious creation of the biographical author, it also implies its reader, who needs to be constructed by the biographical reader. Stories, in other words, teach us what kinds of readers we need to be. For example, Poe's "The Purloined Letter" begins with an epigraph in Latin: "Nil sapientiae odiosius acumine nimio." Now we do not know if this EPIGRAPH is placed in the text by the narrator or directly by the implied author. What we do know is that it is provided without translation. Either someone (the implied author or the narrator) expects us to be the sort of reader who knows Latin, or someone is ironically reminding us that we, like most of Poe's readers when this story was first published in a Christmas volume called *The Gift* (1845), do *not* know Latin. Given the meaning of the epigraph ("Nothing is so hateful to wisdom as excessive cunning"), we might think we have here a narrator who unwittingly reveals his own hatefulness by too cleverly quoting in Latin. Such a revelation of the narrator's character, however, would be possible only to readers who actually knew Latin — and for such readers, Latin quotations are not excessively clever. Therefore, whether we can read Latin or not, the epigraph already implies that we readers have the ability to read Latin and become fictional Latin readers. Thus, when the story reveals two kinds of characters, those who can find hidden meaning, like the detective hero August Dupin, and those who cannot, like the narrator, we are made to side imaginatively with those who can. The implied author has managed, without a word audible in his/her/its own voice (for implied authors never speak — only narrators do), to train our allegiance and make us into a specific sort of IMPLIED READER.

There are, of course, limitations on our malleability as implied readers. If knowledge of Latin were indispensable for an understanding of "The Purloined Letter," those of us who cannot read Latin would find that the story was not artful; that is, for us it would not be a coherent, effective whole. Perhaps the greatest limitation on the malleability of the implied reader is the substantial dependence on whether the biographical reader is approaching the story for the *first* or a SUBSEQUENT READING. In a first reading of "The Purloined Letter," we do not know how the events will work out. To the extent that we are interested in discovering a fresh answer to that question, a subsequent reading will be impoverished. On the other hand, subsequent readings, precisely because they are done with knowledge of the outcome, may offer pleasures of their own. In "The Purloined Letter," Dupin's drily ironic treatment of the Prefect and of the narrator is much more pointed when we are in on the joke. In a first reading of Susan Glaspell's "A Jury of Her Peers," the minute attention to domestic detail may seem overdone; on a subsequent reading, knowing the importance of domestic detail for solving the mystery, we may find those same passages fascinating. Similarly, a subsequent reading of "The Black Cat" makes much plainer the self-serving nature of the narrator's first paragraph; it is hard to believe, once we know the crimes involved, that any sane "intellect" will find them "natural" rather than "terrible." In other words, while the text implies a reader, it may imply a different — but typically complementary — reader for first and subsequent readings. Thus the narrative situation is always, at least theoretically, a complex tapestry of biographical/historical author, implied author, narrator, characters, events, setting, implied reader, and biographical/historical reader. And we have simultaneous, although typically unconscious, knowledge of all those elements of narrative.

Varieties of Narrative Stance

Within any given narrative situation, implied authors make strategic choices among the possible varieties of narrative stance that a narrator may take in relation to the reader and to the reported events. For example, the narrator can be seen as speaking to us right now about events that happened long ago (as in FAIRY TALES beginning "Once upon a time"), or the narrator can be seen as long ago having left a written record of events that were happening at about the time they were being recorded (as in Mark Twain's "The Diary of Adam and Eve"). Narrative stance can even be manipulated within a story. In "The Joy of Nelly Deane," Willa Cather's narrator speaks as if she is close in time to the events narrated, but since the story turns out to cover years, we feel the narrator grow older. In Nawal El Saadawi's "She Has No Place In Paradise," we are at first confused about the setting until we realize the narrator's stance is beside the main character in an afterlife. In H. G. Well's "The Star," we are not confused until a dramatic shift of stance in the last paragraph makes us question the very species and location of the narrator. Our understanding of the narrator and of the events, then, is as much a function of narrative stance as it is of the details of the narrative situation. Narrative stance can vary significantly and involve such matters as tense, person, VIEWPOINT, and reliability.

Most stories are narrated predominantly in the present or past tense; that is, narrators utter sentences such as "He is going away" and "He went away" respectively. (There is also a tiny handful of future tense narrations, like Michael Frayn's charming SCIENCE FICTION FABLE called *A Very Private Life* [1968]. Frayn's novel begins, "Once upon a time there will be a little girl called Uncumber.") No matter what the predominant TENSE OF NARRATION, we come to view that tense as a ground tense against which others are measured. Thus in a past tense narration, when the narrator says "So now he went away," we do not view the temporal implications of "went," a past tense verb form, and "now," signifying the present, as contradictory. Similarly, in a present tense narration, when the narrator says, "So she yells at her sister," we still usually understand the action to have occurred before the recording of the narrator's perceptions of that action. Against the ground tense, other tenses signify *relative* past and future, so both present and past tense are equally capable of yielding a full range of temporal effects. However, there are two crucial differences between these predominant tenses. First, a past-tense narration reassures us (sometimes unwarrantedly) that the narrator lived through the events — but this benefit may come at the expense of potential SUSPENSE. Second, a present-tense narration gives us a sense of immediacy — but this benefit may well come at the expense of narrative reflection on the meaning and pattern of the events. In other words, both past and present ground tenses have strengths and weaknesses because verb tense creates an automatic understanding of where the narrator stands in time in relation both to us and to the reported events. In John Barth's "Night-Sea Journey," the immediacy of present tense narration is crucial for the surprise revelation of the narrator's nature, just as the past tense in Nathaniel Hawthorne's "Young Goodman Brown," especially when the last paragraph reveals how far in the past the story is set, is crucial for our ultimate perspective on the title character. There is nothing better or worse about present or past tense narration; however, the choice of present or past tense narration (a choice, like all others, made silently by the implied author) is crucial to establishing the narrative stance, and hence to establishing our relationships as readers to the narrator and to the events.

Another variable of narrative stance is person of narration (see FIRST-PERSON NARRATION). This phrase refers to the notion of grammatical person. In grammar, the so-called first person is the speaker, so first person pronouns include *I*, *me*, *my*, and *mine* in the singular and *we*, *us*, *our*, and *ours* in the plural: "I like our town." The so-called second person is the individual addressed by the speaker, so second person pronouns include *you*, *you*, *your*, and *yours*: "You had better like your town." The so-called third person is spoken of by the first person to the second person but is neither the first person nor the second person, so third person pronouns include *he*, *him*, *his*, and *his* in the masculine singular, *she*, *her*, *her*, and *hers* in the feminine singular, *it*, *it*, *its*, and *its* in the neuter singular, and *they*, *them*, *their*, and *theirs* in the plural: "He told her he liked their town." Using this terminology, we call narrators who frequently refer to themselves first-person narrators. The narrator of "The Black Cat" is a first-person narrator; the first paragraph of that story has sixteen uses of first person pronouns in its nine sentences. Similarly, we call narrators who generally refer to third persons, third-person narrators. Genesis is a third-person narration; we do not encounter a first person pronoun until Gen 1:26 where we find it not in the narrator's words but in a direct quotation: "And God said, Let us make man in our image." The vast majority of narratives are thought of as either first- or third-person narrations.

The second person, while very rare in narrative outside direct quotation, is common in some literary forms, such as love lyrics. William Shakespeare's Sonnet 18 begins, "Shall I compare thee to a summer's day?/Thou art more lovely and more temperate." But the stance of such a poem is not that of a speaker addressing us at all; rather, the implied reader here is overhearing a first-person address to a second person. Of course, since writers are always testing their tools, there is a tiny handful of exceptional, second-person narrations in which the narrator typically addresses us not by saying "I" or "he or she" but "you"; Carlos Fuentes' remarkable novella, *Aura* (1962) is an example of this. But these exceptions, by their very rarity, demonstrate the compelling importance of person of narration.

Clearly the implied author's choice of person of narration is crucial in defining narrative stance. First-person narrators, especially if, as in "The Black Cat," they are also major characters in the events they narrate, typically have clear and individual MOTIVES for telling their stories; indeed, the discovery of the narrator's motives in telling the story may be a basic interest for us in reading the narrative, more important even than the motives of the characters in the story, particularly on subsequent readings. Third-person narrators, especially those who make themselves comparatively transparent, like Katherine Anne Porter's in "The Grave," may seem to have no motives other than the recitation of an interesting story. But even third-person narrators do have motives which the implied author allows us to discover. Referring to the childhood incident that opens the story, Porter's last paragraph begins, "Miranda never told," yet somehow the narrator not only knows the incident but claims Miranda gains a special insight by recalling it as an adult; in effect, the narrator suddenly challenges us to judge her own selection of events to narrate. Henry James's "The Altar of the Dead," another third-person narration, begins, "He had a moral dislike, poor Stransom, to lean anniversaries, and he disliked them still more when they made a pretence of a figure." The phrase "poor Stransom" seems said with the narrator's nose a bit in the air. In addition, "they made a pretence of a figure" suggests that both Stransom and the narrator claim to look down on social hypocrisy, but that the narrator is not so concerned as to let it cause him moral discomfort. In other words, third-person narrators, like first-person narrators, may be more or less characterized, but first-person narrators are likely to have the special perspective of a character within their own stories while third-person narrators may adopt the stance, often untrue, of those with no special motive for telling the story.

Although we typically call narratives either first- or third-person, all narratives feel as if they are told to us by a narrator, a speaker, a first-person. In Jean Toomer's "Becky," short though it is, the first half seems to be a third-person narration. In attempting to construct ourselves as the implied reader, therefore, we may ignore any personal motives the narrator may have in recounting the events. But when the narrator begins using "I," "we," and "our," we suddenly recognize that he is one of the townspeople whose attitudes and behavior have shaped Becky's life. When this change in person of narration occurs, we must wonder not only what this narrator's motives are in telling the story but what his motives were in not making his own stance — his relation to the events — clear to begin with. Although we never hear implied authors speak, they can characterize not only the narrator but themselves by manipulating person of narration. In "Becky" the implied author sympathizes with those who want to avoid their moral responsibility by hiding but nonetheless believes such people must come forward.

Another variable of narrative stance is viewpoint, a term referring to the conditions governing a narrator's knowledge of the events narrated. Obviously an ordinary person can never be absolutely certain of what another person is thinking. This being so, a reader does not demand that an ordinary first-person narrator report exhaustive, accurate information about another character's inner thoughts; at most, we ask that the narrator speculate about those thoughts. Our willingness to accept less than full information allows us to tolerate the suspense that compels us to read on in order rather than skipping to the end or throwing the text down in disgust. If Poe had made Dupin the narrator of "The Purloined Letter" and had Dupin tell us what he was thinking when he first asked the Prefect to write a check, the whole explanatory second half of the story would have been useless and boring. Conversely, had Poe made Dupin the narrator and then had the narrator withhold vital information from us, we would have been angry. Junichiro Tanizaki uses this fact about narrative viewpoint effectively in "The Thief": when we realize that the first-person narrator has deceived us by acting as if he lacked knowledge we later learn he had, we share his schoolmates' anger at his deception. Thus when Poe invented the detective's sidekick as narrator, he made possible all subsequent stories in which we watch the GREAT DETECTIVE at work but remain contentedly ignorant of the Great Detective's hypotheses. The implied author's silent choice of narrative viewpoint is always crucial. Of the countless variations of narrative viewpoint, four are particularly worth individual mention: first-person limited, third-person omniscient, third-person limited, and FREE INDIRECT STYLE.

First-person narration is always limited by the limitations of the first-person narrator: we do not expect a child narrator to know about adult motives; we do not expect a lunatic to speak sanely; we do not expect an animal to be able to read street signs. More than that, the situation of the first-person narrator as a character may legitimately limit the narration. For example, when the first-person narrator's parents send her from the room at the end of the first paragraph of Louise Erdrich's "Chapter Two: 1932, Sita Kozka," her unexpectedly arrived cousin immediately becomes an object of jealousy for her and of mystery for her and for us. Because all first-person narrators have limitations, one might conclude that all such narrators are first-person limited. As a practical matter, this is true. However, as a theoretical matter, this is not true. If one had an all-knowing god as a narrator, then one could have a first-person narrator with no limitations on that narrator's knowledge. Similarly, if one had a first-person narrator of a past tense narration, one could imagine that between the time of the events and the time of narration the narrator might have acquired all knowledge relevant to the events and was, in relation to them, omniscient. As a practical matter, however, first-person narrators are limited in their knowledge both by the kinds of persons they are and by the situations in which they find themselves.

And, of course, since we learn the story from the narrator, the narrator's limitations limit us.

While first-person omniscient narrators are virtually nonexistent, third-person omniscient narrators are quite common. Near the end of chapter VII of Leo Tolstoy's "The Death of Ivan Ilyitch," the third-person narrator says, "Gerasim alone [. . .] understood." Only someone who is omniscient could know not only what one character thought but what all other characters didn't think. And yet we do not reject the narrator's statement as impossible; rather, we accept this god-like view, this omniscience, and rely on it. However, an alert reader will not rely unskeptically even on an omniscient narrator because even omniscient narrators willfully mislead us in order to surprise us later on. The crucial information for understanding the relation between the main characters of Edith Wharton's past tense, third-person omniscient narration "Roman Fever" comes only when the narrator quotes Mrs. Ansley in the last line. Nonetheless, we never feel that this information has been unfairly withheld. Along the way, we have been given much information and we can, after all, learn only one thing at a time. All narrators rely on the fact that language is linear and divert us from asking about one thing by telling us something else. And once Wharton does give us the final clue, once we can share the narrator's omniscience, we may well be tempted to reread the story in order to understand what all that other information really meant all along. In other words, even if a third-person narrator is omniscient—is presumed privy to all facts and thoughts—the implied author nonetheless will limit the ways in which that narrator reveals his or her knowledge.

Another way to manipulate viewpoint is by creating a third-person narrator who, like an ordinary first-person narrator, is necessarily limited. In James Agee's "A Mother's Tale," the third-person narrator gives words to the characters' thoughts, but because the characters are cattle, the narrator can't be expected to report things cattle do not know, thus creating the capacity for suspense, DRAMATIC IRONY, and all the other functions dependent on strategic ignorance.

There seems to be a limitless variety of third-person limited narrations. Consider the beginning of James Joyce's "Counterparts." Again I have numbered the sentences for reference.

(1) The bell rang furiously and, when Miss Parker went to the tube, a furious voice called out in a piercing North of Ireland accent: (2)—Send Farrington here! (3) Miss Parker returned to her machine, saying to a man who was writing at a desk: (4)—Mr. Alleyne wants you upstairs. (5) The man muttered *Blast him!* under his breath and pushed back his chair to stand up. (6) When he stood up he was tall and of great bulk. (7) He had a hanging face, dark wine-coloured, with fair eyebrows and moustache: his eyes bulged forward slightly and the whites of them were dirty. (8) He lifted up the counter and, passing by the clients, went out of the office with a heavy step. (9) He went heavily upstairs until he came to the second landing, where a door bore a brass plate with the inscription *Mr. Alleyne.*

The story seems to be told by a narrator limited, at least in the first sentence, to objective description; no internal states of characters are reported explicitly. However, the choice of metaphor, "rang *furiously*," must reflect someone's thought processes; metaphors are always subjective. That someone could be the narrator but when, still in the first sentence, we get the judgment implicit in "*furious* voice," we know that the metaphorizer might be either the narrator or Miss Parker, who clearly knows something about the person on the other end of the tube. Judging by her flat words (4), however, Miss Parker does not feel herself buffeted by fury, while we learn (5) that "the man" does. We are never told that "the man" is the "Farrington" mentioned earlier (2), but given the situation, we can infer that. Since Farrington, too, was within earshot of the bell, he is perhaps more likely to be the person in question. After all, this is clearly not the first time Mr. Alleyne has angrily called Farrington. Within half a sentence after she "returned to her machine" (3), Miss Parker drops out of the story, but we quickly get two full sentences (6 & 7) describing Farrington, so now our attention is squarely on him. When he gets up (8), our viewpoint gets up with him, and we leave the office behind to go with him to Mr. Alleyne's office door (9). In other words, although "Counterparts" begins in such a way that we might think this a standard third-person omniscient narration, we quickly learn that the implied author has radically limited the viewpoint to that of Farrington. Even though this is a third-person narration, then, we have as tight a focus as we would in a first-person narration.

One of the most important viewpoints available to third-person narration is called free indirect style. To understand what this means, we need to understand the grammarian's distinction between DIRECT and INDIRECT QUOTATION. In direct quotation, someone repeats a speaker's words exactly, as in Joyce's (5) above. In indirect quotation, a speaker's words are reported in the reporter's words, as Miss Parker does in (4) above. Sometimes, of course, it is difficult to distinguish direct from indirect quotation. Consider: "My friend said he loves chocolate." We know that these can be the friend's exact words only if the friend was referring to a third person: "My friend said, 'He loves chocolate.'" But even if we believe the friend was referring to himself, we cannot tell whether the first version of the report was a mere grammatical adjustment from "My friend said, 'I love chocolate'" or an indirect paraphrase of something potentially quite different, such as "My friend said, 'I'd kill for a chocolate bar.'" Despite this distinction problem, it is important to keep the ideas of direct and indirect quotation separate because when a narrator quotes directly, we have comparatively concrete evidence of what happened, while indirect quotation is really evidence of the narrator's view of what happened. The distinction between direct and indirect report is equally important whether the narrator is reporting words or thoughts. Thus, we speak of sentences such as "'I love chocolate,' he thought" as direct and "He wanted a chocolate bar fiercely enough to kill for it" as indirect.

In free indirect style, a narrator shifts freely from an objective third-person viewpoint in and out of the mind of a character without such explicit markers as "he thought." Henry James's "The Tree of Knowledge" begins, "It was one of the secret opinions, such as we all have, of Peter Brench that his main success in life would have consisted in his never having committed himself about the work, as it was called, of his friend Morgan Mallow." Since Brench's opinion is secret, we have here a report of knowledge that would be unavailable to a first-person narrator. Thus, despite the use of the word "we," this is a third-person narrator. Yet it turns out that this narrator is not privy to Brench's secret opinions by virtue of being omniscient; in fact, the narrator does not enter into any minds other than Brench's. Thus James has created a narrative viewpoint in some ways like that of third-person limited and in some ways like that of third-person omniscient. This particular viewpoint, free indirect style, is one of the most important in all of modern narrative because it so seamlessly shifts from objective to subjective report and therefore can fool us. It may give us access to a character's thoughts, but it also may give us a narrator's idiosyncratic view of those thoughts. Clearly here, as with all narration, the reliability of what we read is thoroughly dependent upon the narrator.

The fourth main variable contributing to narrative stance is the reliability of narration (see RELIABLE NARRATOR). As we have already seen, some narrators, like Poe's in "The Black Cat," are not reliable; that is, we cannot trust that what they say will be objectively true. Of course, since we are here speaking of FICTION, objectivity must be defined in the context of the narrative world. Although in real life wolves do not speak, in the Grimm brothers' "Little Red Cap," we do not take the narrator's report of a speaking wolf to indicate the narrator's unreliability; we have learned since childhood that animals may speak in fairy tales. Truth, in fiction, then, is often a relative matter. But in "The Black Cat," the narrator's own words reveal his duplicity. Thus he is called an UNRELIABLE, or untrustworthy, NARRATOR. Having such a narrator does not mean that the story is somehow weak; rather, it means that the implied author has made a strategic choice to characterize the narrator by his unreliability. We take the narrator of Genesis to be reliable. We do not ask how the narrator's own values influence the way the events under consideration were observed and reported. But in Ryunosuke Akutagawa's "In a Grove," where different voices give contradictory reports about the same set of events, precisely the point is that we need to discover how the viewpoint of an individual influences that individual's observations and reports.

In thinking about narrative reliability, we typically need to consider two issues: whether the report is a *fact* or *interpretation* and whether an unreliable report is a *conscious* or *unconscious misrepresentation*. Few narrators consciously lie about facts, although this can happen, as in Tanizaki's "The Thief." Sometimes, however, facts are unreliable because the narrator is simply misinformed. In Mark Twain's "The Diary of Adam and Eve," we readers have access to both of the two narrators' inner thoughts but the narrators themselves do not. As a result, we can understand that the facts each reports are really only his and her views of the facts. Indeed, most unreliability arises either from limitation of narrative viewpoint or from the narrator's own conscious or unconscious imposition of a personal interpretation on the facts. Whenever we deal with interpretation, even if the fact is correct, there is always the possibility that interpretation may misrepresent it. For example, in "The Black Cat," the narrator's assertion that he was driven to his deeds by "the Fiend Intemperance" may report a fact—that the narrator was often drunk—but the interpretation—that an outside agent is responsible for the narrator's actions and not the narrator himself—is clearly unreliable. In this case, therefore, by choosing this narrative stance, the implied author has made it possible for us to reinterpret the narrator's words in order to extract the relevant facts both of the plot—the narrator was drunk—and of his character—he is deceitful.

Sometimes, however, it is not easy to know whether a report is of a fact or of an interpretation. Because narrators and characters—and people, for that matter—freely slide from fact to interpretation and back again, often without even realizing it, a narrative may be simultaneously reporting a fact, an interpretation of that fact, and a bit of characterization of the individual whose motives shaped that interpretation. And crucial to our relation to the narrative is our judgment about whether those motives shaping the misrepresentation were unconscious or conscious. The first-person narrator in Gilman's "The Yellow Wall-Paper" arouses our sympathy precisely because she does not understand that she is going mad, but Poe's narrator arouses our loathing by his conscious misrepresentations. Thus the issue of reliability influences not only what we come to believe happened in a story but also how we feel about the storyteller.

Authority

Because all that we learn of a narrative we learn from its narrator, it may seem odd that we can know a narrator to be misrepresenting events. However, implied authors know that we readers carry into our reading some of the same notions that we use in life to determine the relative AUTHORITY of reports. Implied authors design the narrative situation and construct the narrative stance so that we can make our own judgments about the narrative and the narrator. All other things being equal, we accept reports as true according to one or another fairly well defined, although typically unconsciously held, hierarchy of authority. This notion of hierarchy involves many of the concepts we have already addressed.

Consider these two passages from "The Black Cat." In the first, the narrator describes his discovery on the wall of his burned out bedroom of a portrait of his first crime. In the second, the narrator tells us of the metamorphosis of the white markings on his second cat.

(A) (1) About this wall a dense crowd were collected, and many persons seemed to be examining a particular portion of it with very minute and eager attention. (2) The words "strange!" "singular!" and other similar expressions, excited my curiosity. (3) I approached and saw, as if graven in *bas relief* upon the white surface, the figure of a gigantic *cat*. (4) The impression was given with an accuracy truly marvellous. (5) There was a rope about the animal's neck.

(B) It was now the representation of an object that I shudder to name—and for this above all, I loathed, and dreaded, and would have rid myself of the monster *had I dared*—it was now, I say, the image of a hideous—of a ghastly thing—of the GALLOWS!—oh, mournful and terrible engine of Horror and of Crime—of Agony and of Death!

Both of these passages report the narrator's observation of what would normally be considered fantastic apparitions, yet we are likely to accept the first as factual and to doubt the second. Why? In (A), the narrator reports a crowd of people. These are all minor characters; not one is individuated. We have no reason, then, to suppose that any one of them has a personal cause for misperceiving or misrepresenting whatever is being observed. All other things being equal, characters about whom we know nothing are more authoritative than characters about whom we have information suggesting, as in the case of Poe's narrator, a peculiar viewpoint. Notice also that the very lack of individuation makes the members of the crowd interchangeable. Therefore, we attribute the actions and utterances in (A1) and (A2) to all these people. All other things being equal, a consensus report is more authoritative than an individual report.

Notice also that although (A) and (B) are of similar length (74 and 65 words respectively), (A) contains five orderly sentences while (B) contains one long, jerky, self-interrupted sentence; that is, the very grammar of (A) suggests that the narrator is comparatively dispassionate, while the very grammar of (B) suggests that the narrator is comparatively emotional. This difference in emotional register is reinforced by the content of the reports. While (A1) is clearly to some extent an interpretation ("many persons *seemed* to be examining . . . with . . . *eager* attention"), we have no reason to suppose this interpretation unreliable. (B), however, is littered with expressions of the narrator's own extreme fear ("*had I dared*"). We know that fear often makes people see things in peculiar ways. Also, the most prominent emotion in (A2) is reported in direct quotation (" 'singular!' 'strange!' ") while (B) offers only highly subjective experience ("a ghastly thing . . . oh, mournful and terrible engine"). All other things being equal, a direct and dispassionate report is more authoritative than an indirect and emotional report.

Notice also that in (A) the narrator does not see the image until (3), the same sentence in which he reports it to us. In (B), which is only one sentence long, the narrator must know what the image is even before he begins speaking since the first word of the sentence, "It," is a pronoun referring to that image; nonetheless, he cannot bring himself to name the image—"GALLOWS!"—until word 50, that is, until he is more than three-fourths through with the sentence. This forestalling of his utterance contrasts sharply with the prompt report of (A). In other words, in (B) the narrator seems much more likely to have a reason not to want to speak about the events. All other things being equal, a willing report is more authoritative than an unwilling report.

One could multiply these hierarchies of authority. For example, all other things being equal, reports about the setting, which must be inhabited by all the characters, are more authoritative than reports about single events; reports about objectively observed events are more authoritative than reports about rumors or about subjective experiences; direct quotation is more authoritative than indirect quotation; quotation, direct or indirect, of a character's words is more authoritative than quotation, direct or indirect, of a character's thoughts. Notice that these hierarchies in a sense nest, going from the most objective, shared, stable aspect of the narrative world, the setting, to the most mercurial, the changing moods and motives of individuals. In this sense, we go into and out of a hierarchy of authority much as we go into and out of the narrative situation.

When we enter a narrative world, we bring with us our knowledge of the so-called real world, such as the knowledge that fear often makes people see things in peculiar ways. But the real world is not truly a single, objective, unchanging entity; rather, it is socially constructed and subject to disagreement and change. For example, to Israelis, Jerusalem is the capital of their country, while many foreign governments still consider the Israeli capital Tel Aviv. If you ask Europeans for the enclosing dates of World War II, most will say 1939–1945, but many U.S. citizens would say 1941–1945 because the United States did not declare war until the end of 1941. If you ask a "pro-life" politician for a definition of abortion, you may get the answer "murder"; but if you ask a "pro-choice" politician the same question, you may get the answer "elective surgery." Although we may know from our own direct experience that fear can distort perceptions, most of what we know we know only indirectly, from others, as part of our habitation of a social world. Have you ever seen the "ozone hole" over Antarctica? Probably not; yet you still probably "know" that it exists. Have you ever measured the mountains of the world? Probably not; yet you still probably "know" that Everest is the tallest. But how do most of us know that Everest even exists? By consent. None of us was present at the births of our parents, yet most of us "know" when our parents were born. For all of this knowledge, we rely on words, on what people have said to us, and what we have read. As long as these words go uncontradicted by our own experience or by other words, we accept them. In large measure, then, reality is a social construction.

Narratives are part of the ongoing process of social construction. We tell stories to explain our career choices; we imagine stories that embody our hopes; we weigh stories that salespeople tell us. The writing and reading of fictional stories parallels the process of speaking and hearing stories in the wider social sphere. When we test the authority of a fictional narrative, at first we test it against what we "know" from the real world. This feature of language is called REFERENTIALITY. People always rely on the referential nature of language to give street directions and order from a restaurant menu. Authors always rely on the referential nature of language to engage a reader's knowledge of the real world. It is because we know that people usually have different impressions of anything vague that when we find a crowd agreeing in its reactions to the bas relief in "The Black Cat" we are willing to accept the image's reality. Conversely, precisely because we "know" that there is no "Fiend Intemperance," we disbelieve the narrator when he tries to displace his guilt.

Since so much of what we know to be true we know through stories, much of the reference of stories is not actually to the so-called real world but to other texts. This INTERTEXTUALITY is obviously at work when one text ALLUDES to another, as Sarah Henderson Hay's "Rapunzel" does in its very title and Robert Coover's "The Brother" does in its content when the title character turns out to be the brother of Noah from the story of the Flood in Genesis. But in less obvious ways, reference to other texts occurs all the time. Nadine Gordimer's title "Six Feet of the Country" in some (perhaps unconscious) way calls to our mind the common association in other stories, both fictional and not, of the phrase "six feet of earth" with graves. Erdrich's "Chapter Two: 1932, Sita Kozka" suggests a whole series of chapters, perhaps all unknown to us but referenced nonetheless. Ernest Haycox's title, "Stage to Lordsburg," suggests that there must exist some other text, a map, say, that already contains Lordsburg. Notice, then, that the texts being referenced may be unknown and perhaps even nonexistent, but so long as the intertextual reference is not contradicted, the *texture* of the narrative world becomes ever more palpable. "Text," "texture," and "textile" all come from the Latin word *texere*, "to weave," which suggests that the key to creating a narrative world is not so much the threads used as the way the threads are worked together.

If we can consider a single text, say "Counterparts," as being constructed of many subtexts, then we can look on intertextuality not only as reference from one text to another but as mutual reference of subtexts within a text. In "Counterparts" (1)—"The bell rang furiously and, when Miss Parker went to the tube, a furious voice called out . . ."—the repetition of "furious" adds texture, weaves a narrative world. Similarly, Miss Parker is named again in (3). "Mr. Alleyne" mentioned in (4) is named again in (9). The "man who was writing at a desk" in (3) "pushed back his chair to stand up" in (5). Pushed it back from what? Obviously from the desk. The man with the "heavy step" (8) went "heavily upstairs" (9). This rapid intertextual reference, like the repetitions of rhyme or plot, adds authority to a work. If Miss Parker were named in (1) and (3) then said "Miss Jones returned to her machine," we would wonder who Miss Jones was and what had happened to Miss Parker. Enough such loose threads and the fabric comes undone. Enough weaving of the threads and the story creates a tapestry in our minds.

Genre

If we were to consider all the narratives that the world has produced, we would quickly find ourselves segmenting them into groups. We would recognize one TALE OF THE GREAT DETECTIVE—with its ordinary sidekick, plodding policeman, and Great Detective—as something like another such tale and quite different from, say, a boy-and-girl ROMANCE. We would recognize some works as having similarities of attitude, for example SATIRES like Geoffrey Chaucer's "The Miller's Tale" and Gertrude Stein's "Miss Furr and Miss Skeene," while others had similarities of purpose, such as fictions that warn us (called monitory fictions) like Stephen Vincent Benét's "Nightmare Number Three" and H. G. Wells's *The Time Machine*, or fictions meant to stimulate our thoughtful conversation, like Tao and Sufi teaching tales. People tend quite sensibly to group stories according to similarities of features that seem both prominent in each story and repeated, perhaps with variations, from story to story.

As one example of a GENRE that is particularly easy to study, let us consider the WESTERN. John Cawelti has articulated the formula for this genre; the real measure of his success is our immediate recognition that in some sense we have known all along what he has to say. Cawelti states that a typical Western is set in landscape, like the developing American West, that supports two groups of characters, an ingroup and an outgroup. The ingroup may be the townspeople or the sheep farmers, say, and then the outgroup would be the outlaws or the open-range ranchers. In this landscape, the two groups come into conflict, the ingroup typically being more settled, civilized, law-abiding, and family-oriented while the outgroup is more mobile, wild, independent, and individualistic. The story concerns the CONFLICT between these two groups. The RESOLUTION typically depends on the emergence or arrival of a lone HERO who shares both the ingroup's greater respect for community values and the outgroup's greater individual survival skills. After the hero has won the day for the ingroup, his own superior capacity for violence implicitly makes him the greatest threat to the ingroup. He then must either hang up his guns (like the title character in Owen Wister's *The Virginian* [1904]), take on a badge so that he puts his guns permanently at the service of the ingroup (like Matt Dillon on the television series

Gunsmoke [1955–1975]), or leave (like the title character in Jack Schaefer's *Shane* [1954]). There are literally thousands of narratives that fall within this genre.

Each genre, like the Western, is set in a narrative world. Although some Westerns are set in a fictional Utah and others in a fictional Kansas, those fictional Utahs and Kansases are really the same world in supporting those in- and outgroups, the issue of individual hero or villain against society, the problem of the spread of civilization, and so on. Similarly, Arthur Conan Doyle's fictional London in "The Adventure of the Speckled Band" and Poe's fictional Paris in "The Purloined Letter" are the same world in supporting the functions of the Tale of the Great Detective. Even the vast and ill-defined genre called "REALISM," which includes, among many others, works about the frustrating quicksand of failed marriage, like Margaret Atwood's "The Resplendent Quetzal" and François Camoin's "Things I Did To Make It Possible," share a narrative world which is, like the so-called real world, a social construction. In other words, we have linguistic conventions that let us know quite quickly which world we are inhabiting and what genre we are reading. From the very first words of a narrative, the implied author not only characterizes the narrator and has the narrator report events, but also has the narrator convey genre information. "Once upon a time there lived a beautiful golden-haired princess" already tells us we should not be surprised if magic works and animals talk; we certainly should be surprised if the golden-haired princess dies.

Consider the first line of Haycox's "Stage to Lordsburg":

> This was one of those years in the Territory when Apache smoke signals spiraled up from the stony mountain summits and many a ranch cabin lay as a square of blackened ashes on the ground and the departure of a stage from Tonto was the beginning of an adventure that had no certain happy ending. . . . [sic]

Practiced readers of Westerns immediately recognize this as the world of the Western. The words "Territory" and "Apache" could be part of a nineteenth-century political communiqué, but the tone, "one of those years," tells us this is a fictional narrative. The Apaches, with their, to the implied readers' eyes, primitive communication ("smoke signals") represent a pervasive presence in the Territory, and associating them with "stony mountain summits" suggests that from the viewpoint of the implied author the Apaches are austere, haughty, individualistic, and powerful. That is, here they fulfill the characteristics of a Western genre outgroup. There is clearly violent conflict between this outgroup and the ranchers, because we know that each "cabin [that] lay as a square of blackened ashes on the ground" represents a conquest of the Apaches over the ranchers. The Apaches have smoke signals; the ranchers ashes. The Apaches are on the summits; the ranchers are on the ground. We do not yet know if the story will actually concern the conflict between Apaches and ranchers, but we do know from the title and this first sentence ("the departure of a stage from Tonto was the beginning of an adventure") that there will be a conflict and it will be set in this landscape. While we know that the typical Western has a lone hero who succeeds, by stating that these adventures "had no certain happy ending," Haycox's narrator opens the genre for reconsideration and creates the possibility of suspense. And all that in only 55 words.

Clearly we can begin to gain highly specified CONVENTIONAL genre information very rapidly in reading a narrative. Once we do recognize that a story is part of a given genre, we have expectations for how that story is likely to proceed. In both the Tale of the Great Detective and the Western, we expect the hero to succeed and social order to be restored. In realism we do not know how the plot will turn out, but we do expect to explore the subtleties of characters' conflicting feelings. In stories of the difficulties of growing up (called tales of education or sometimes BILDUNGSROMANS), like Katherine Mansfield's "A Doll's House" and Richard Wright's "The Man Who Was Almost a Man," we expect the outcome to be AMBIGUOUS. In TRAGEDIES, like Harlan Ellison's "I Have No Mouth and I Must Scream" and Gwendolyn Brooks's "The Ballad of Rudolph Reed," we expect the main character to meet a terrible fate. This doesn't mean that these outcomes are absolutely inevitable—authors often play with our expectations, as Haycox does above—but if the outcome is different, as in some of the stories in this collection, that very possibility of difference keeps a reader's suspense alive and creates the possibility of surprise. Thus, the violation of genre expectations, just like their fulfillment, is an element of narrative under the silent control of the implied author.

Our genre expectations can be far-reaching and highly detailed, even if we are not consciously aware of them. In the Tale of the Great Detective, for example, we expect the narrator to be reliable; the language to be somewhat scientific in its presentation of detail; the crime to be worthy of punishment yet treated more as a puzzle than as a tragedy; hidden guilt to be revealed; the sidekick to be less astute than the detective; the detective to be unmarried; the individual crime to be socially disruptive; the detective and the criminal to share parallel thought processes; the description of setting to be extensive and accurate; the narrative tone to be lightly IRONIC; the story to end with an explanation of how the detective solved the crime. Although this wealth of conventional generic knowledge makes for very efficient communication between the author and the reader, as readers become more familiar with a given genre, especially one that is highly specified, it may become harder for an author to elicit readers' enthusiastic engagement with new narratives in that genre. In order to create strong reader response, then, all authors work with genre expectations and pioneering authors develop them, which leads to genre evolution.

In "The Purloined Letter," published in 1845, approximately half of the story is devoted to the EXPOSITION of what Poe called "ratiocination," the thought processes by which Dupin was able to solve the crime. Ever since Poe, Tales of the Great Detective have always ended with such an exposition. However, as readers have become less amazed that the crime could be solved at all by rational means and more interested in the chase than the explanation, the climactic explanation has been progressively condensed. In 1892, Arthur Conan Doyle published "The Adventure of the Speckled Band" in which the explanation takes only the last ten percent of the story. In even more modern stories, like Agatha Christie's "The Case of the Missing Will," published in 1924, the explanation is reserved for approximately the last five percent of the story. This progressive condensation is one feature of the evolution of this particular genre.

A second feature of the evolution of this genre is the insertion of specious explanations. In Poe, the sidekick simply asks in amazement for the explanation.

However, as readers come to expect such explanations, authors seem to supply them along the way and then show these preliminary explanations, often offered by the sidekick, to be mistaken. Thus the straight-line build up to explanation is made more complicated. The progressive COMPLICATION of the line from the beginning of the investigation through to revelatory explanation is another feature of the evolution of the genre. In all genres, both condensation and complication, in forms appropriate to each genre, mark normal genre evolution.

There are, in addition to complication and condensation, other mechanisms of genre evolution. For example, authors can seem to change genres within a single text. This reversal of expectations can have a quick and startling effect: "Once upon a time there lived a beautiful golden-haired princess who fell under the spell of an evil accountant." With the word "accountant," our notion of what is and is not an expectable part of the fairy tale world has been reversed. This reversal of the ground rules of the narrative world gives rise to the psychological affect we associate with the fantastic, whether the element in question does exist in the real world (as accountants surely do) or does not (as talking wolves do not). The application of the fantastic is one of the tools for genre development that leads to the evolution of whole new genres. Other such tools are PARODY, satire, and the mixing of genres, as in the modern versions of fairy tales by Olga Broumas and Hay.

If we examine the evolution of genres within short narrative as a whole, we find many parallel and often intertwining lineages. Among our oldest texts are explanatory legends such as we find in Ovid and the Hebrew portion of the Bible. Once these founding documents become established, people create narratives to teach particular points, such as the parables of the New Testament of the Bible and the Tao and Sufi teaching tales. These stories typically involve more emphasis on character than do the earlier tales. That is, although we know some things about Noah, the story is really about the Flood; however, the story of the Prodigal Son is most important only when we confront a situation involving a prodigal individual. With the rise of democracy, particularly after the Renaissance, an increasing emphasis on the details of character changed art of all sorts. In the nineteenth century, with the preeminence of industrialism and the parallel rise of interest in scientific psychology, so-called realism became a dominant force in literary evolution. However, just as there are still lemurs in the world inhabited by chimpanzees, LEGEND, romance, and fantasy never died out in the world that honored realism. The same author, Henry James, who is often considered the premier realist in the English language for such works as "The Altar of the Dead," is both the highly self-conscious creator of "The Tree of Knowledge" and the craftsman of such famous ghost stories as *The Turn of the Screw*. In the twentieth century, even as pulp fiction and then movies kept the nonrealistic genres vital, high-brow magazines like *The New Yorker* and *The Atlantic Monthly* honored and fostered perceptive character studies and incisive social criticism in the works of such writers as John Updike and Bobbie Ann Mason. These stories, however, had their own sources in earlier writers whose realistic works combined a tight focus on individuals with commentary on society: Dostoevsky, Tolstoy, Maupassant, Chekov. Taking the long view, stories are a living heritage with a complex evolution driven by the twin needs to refresh each genre and address the conditions of a changing world.

Character

One point that never changed in the course of the development of stories is that there is no narrative without a character. As a technical matter, at the very least we must have a narrator if we are to have a narrative. Even if all a narrator reports are his or her own feelings and observations, the narrator still performs a self-characterization, as we saw in the first paragraph of "The Black Cat." However, normally we think of characters as the human beings about whom a narrator speaks, say Miss Parker and Farrington in "Counterparts." This notion that characters equal human beings in a story is a handy approximation of the truth, but it is erroneous for two reasons. First, not all characters are humans. The cattle in "A Mother's Tale" are clearly characters; if they were not, they would hardly arouse the personal sympathy that they do. Second, not all humans in stories are characters. The unindividuated crowd saying " 'strange!' 'singular!' " in "The Black Cat" functions as an objective part of the changing setting, more like weather than like individuals. Although characters are indispensable for stories, people are not.

A character is an abstraction that a readers draws from a narrative. The characters don't really exist, of course, but we think of them as *if* they did. The abstractions we call characters share two special properties. First, we must be able to think of them, even if only unconsciously, as being susceptible to significant change while maintaining essential continuity. Second, we must be able to think of them as being capable of free will. They need not necessarily demonstrate either of these two capacities, but we must be able to think of them as possessing those capacities. Normally these are the characteristics we impute to human beings, but not always and not exclusively.

A river can flood or go dry, but when such a significant change occurs, the change is also essential. A flood and a dry ravine are simply different, in most of our minds, from rivers. But a human being, and hence a character, can make a significant change—grow up, lose a limb, discover his or her surprising parentage—but still remain essentially the same. In Franz Kafka's *The Metamorphosis*, Gregor Samsa undergoes one of the most far-reaching and famous changes in all of literature, becoming "a gigantic insect." Yet sharing his thoughts through free indirect style, we never lose the sense that he is our main character, whether he is human or not.

Gregor Samsa, unlike a well-trained bird or an actual insect, seems to be able to think and demonstrates the capacity to act on his thoughts. We grant him, as we grant ourselves and other people, free will. The son—calf—in "A Mother's Tale" makes a fateful choice, and in so doing confirms his characterhood. Conversely, a human being who could exercise no choice, a comatose human, for example, or a newborn, would function for us less as a character than as part of the setting. It is philosophically debatable whether or not real human beings have free will. An argument could be made that since the laws of brain chemistry and such determine our thoughts and actions, free will is merely an illusion we are fated to hold. But if so, it is an illusion we all do hold because otherwise we would never be able to enter into the social construction of reality. Without granting free will to other individuals we could not rely on their promises or fault them for failing to fulfill those promises; after all, without free will, the act of promising and the failure to fulfill the promise would be no more morally significant than growing hair or going bald. One of the great attractions of stories is that they allow us to reinforce our belief in the importance of characters, that is, in abstractions from the text much like our images of human beings, ourselves. Stories make us feel that our decisions matter.

It is convenient to think of characters as being either conventional or novel. A conventional character, like our "golden-haired princess," takes its particular characteristics primarily from its genre. A novel character works against or outside the conventions of the genre, like our fairyland accountant, and in so doing perturbs our understanding of the genre and of what a character may mean within that genre. For example, in traditional fairy tales, such as the Grimm brothers' "The Three Spinsters," physical beauty is a sign of moral and social worth. The spinsters may be industrious, honest, and talented, but the deceitful, beautiful girl gets to move up the social ladder and leave hard work behind. This is conventional. In Hay's "Rapunzel," told as a sonnet, a traditional form of yearning love poetry and not of fairy tale, the adult anguish expressed is much more complicated than anything we find in the Grimms' "Rapunzel" and makes us question the whole idea of tolerating fairy tales. We make comparatively minor demands of a conventional character; after all, our knowledge of the genre as a whole gives us a detailed set of expectations which, if not contradicted, we assume the character fulfills. But once a character violates these conventions by demonstrating some fundamental novelty, as Hay's Rapunzel does by reflecting deeply on the meaning of erotic and romantic desire, we make many more demands, asking for details to build up a consistent image of this novel sort of character. In Hay's case, both the plot background, borrowed from the earlier "Rapunzel," and the character's utterances, which are true to our own sense of what modern women sometimes think, validate the novel character. Hay not only creates a new narrative and a new character but a new way of looking at the genre of fairy tales.

Hay's Rapunzel is the only character we hear in Hay's "Rapunzel." As the only character, she is surely a primary character, as is the downtrodden Farrington in Joyce's "Counterparts." But consider that story's Miss Parker. Because she is a secondary character who quickly serves her purpose and is gone, we ask much less of her characterization. Clearly there is a strong difference in our engagement of primary or secondary characters. However, notice that we also ask little of the characterization of the sidekicks in Tales of the Great Detective. Although they do not quickly serve their purposes and leave, they are nonetheless secondary. Sidekicks should be conventionally literal-minded and loyal to their more brilliant friends, but they do not need to reveal much feeling about anything else, including crime. If the detective, who is primary, treated the crime as worth little feeling, we might think him or her monstrous; when the sidekick ignores the moral dimension of the crime, we often don't even notice. The demands we make on fullness of characterization, then, depend on whether the character is primary or secondary to our *conscious* understanding of the story. The sidekick, as the ever-present narrator, has an enormous impact on our unconscious understanding, but that is another matter. If, as in Tanizaki's "The Thief," the narrator comes to have unexpectedly great importance and moves from secondary to primary status, we suddenly do make many more demands of the fullness of characterization.

A traditional way to differentiate characters depends on geometric metaphors, calling characters either FLAT OR ROUND, either ONE- OR THREE-DIMENSIONAL. (Flat characters are less substantial than round ones, one-dimensional less substantial than three.) Often the less substantial term is used as a criticism of an author's characterization, but this should not necessarily be so. We would not expect a secondary character to be well rounded. If Joyce stopped to give us a deep understanding of Miss Parker's feelings and background, we would never get to Farrington's story. Rounding out characters may be a virtue, but only if the demands of novelty or primacy make that so. Otherwise, as in the Bible, flat or one-dimensional characters serve the narrative purposes exactly.

Language

Everyone reading this essay knows at least one language. People who know only one language often have the feeling that the words they use to express themselves are somehow natural. A chair is called a chair because that's what it is, right? But of course we know that other languages use other words for the objects we call chairs. Even within a single language, there are often important differences of language. A white American speaking so-called Black English might well sound socially displaced—laughable, perhaps, or pitiable. Since most stories come to us in language (there are, of course, virtual exceptions such as R. Crumb's "fred the teen-age girl pigeon"), it is important to understand how the element of language itself may influence a story.

Writers who are multilingual, like Joseph Conrad and Isaac Bashevis Singer, must choose a language of composition for their stories. The fact that each of these people could have written in a number of languages but chose to write in one (English and Yiddish, their third and first languages respectively), suggests that languages carry important implications. There is no room here to treat this enormous subject in detail, but it is worth our time at least to indicate some of the dimensions of the issue.

Take color. We English-speakers like to say that there are three primary colors, red, yellow, and blue, or red, green, and blue depending on whether one is mixing pigments or lights. To say that "there are three primary colors" suggests an objective universality, but the speakers of many languages do not see color this way. Linguists have determined that while no culture sees fewer than two primary colors, some see as many as eleven. This is very difficult for an English-speaker to grasp, but it is, apparently, true. Now take temperature. In English we have four basic temperatures: hot, warm, cool, and cold. In French, there are two basic temperatures: *chaud* (hot) and *froid* (cold). Of course the French can feel all the temperatures that English-speakers feel, and of course they can express relative temperatures by one means or another, but not in the same way we do. We could say that the day, food, or emotion is "cool," but a French-speaker would call the day *frais* (which in this context also has the implication of windy), the food *fraîche* (which in this context also might have the implication of fresh), and the attitude *indifférent* (which is cognate with the English "indifferent" and means something slightly different than we mean by "cool"). Hence, even in using such basic and apparently objective words as those for color or temperature, the choice of language of composition inevitably generates some word associations and eliminates others. No translation can ever fully capture such nuances.

Within any given language — English, say, or even a translation into English — we can also recognize linguistic regularities that set the style of a narrator apart from the style of some other narrator. Ernest Hemingway's narrators, for example, typically speak in a spare, direct way, employ few rhetorical figures, few adjectives or adverbs, and tend to gain nuance, as Stein did, by repetition. Unlike the Stein of "Miss Furr and Miss Skeene," the repetition in Hemingway is subtle and hence shades meaning over, enriching it, rather than repeating directly and creating an undercutting irony. Here is the opening paragraph of Hemingway's "A Clean, Well-Lighted Place":

(1) It was late and every one had left the café except an old man who sat in the shadow the leaves of the tree made against the electric light. (2) In the day time the street was dusty, but at night the dew settled the dust and the old man liked to sit late because he was deaf and now at night it was quiet and he felt the difference. (3) The two waiters inside the café knew that the old man was a little drunk, and while he was a good client they knew that if he became too drunk he would leave without paying, so they kept watch on him.

Notice how many of these words repeat or vary earlier words. (1) begins "It was late" and (2) includes "sit late . . . it was." The phrase "old man" occurs in all three sentences. The obtrusive words "café," "dust," "night," and "drunk" are each used twice, while unobtrusive words are also repeated, for example, "and" five times, "was" six times, and "the" fourteen times, all in a passage only 110 words long. But if the deaf old man "felt the difference" between day and night at the café, so do we. Just as language, say English or French, may have implications for meaning, so too does the STYLE of a narrator. Here we see that subtlety grows from focused consideration on something (like drunkenness or the dust) itself, rather than on explicit modification of whatever that something might be.

Given the implications of the spare style of Hemingway's narrators, we might expect his characters to speak sparely as well. In fact, they do. Here are the next lines of the story:

(4) "Last week he tried to commit suicide," one waiter said.
(5) "Why?"
(6) "He was in despair."
(7) "What about?"
(8) "Nothing."
(9) "How do you know it was nothing?"
(10) "He has plenty of money."

Talk about spare: here we have seven sentences in a total of only thirty words. Notice again, however, the way modifiers are left out; we are to understand through a focus on the things themselves. After (4), "one waiter said," we have no more guidance from the narrator about who is speaking. After the question in (9), the answer in (10) presumes that one can understand that the only real causes for despair are things that money can alleviate. Especially if we notice the repetition of "nothing" from (8) to (9), which impels a focused consideration, we see that we have a "Hemingway style" functioning, with all its implications, both in the voice of the narrator and in the voices of the characters.

There are many, many styles, of course, some barely distinguishable from their near neighbors; some styles however, are relatively easy to recognize. Could we doubt the source of "And to every beast of the earth, and to every fowl of the air, and to every thing that creepeth upon the earth, wherein there is life, I have given every green herb for meat: and it was so"? This sentence (Genesis 1:30) does not mention a deity or Adam or Eve or a miracle, yet the subject matter and the DICTION remind us inevitably of the Bible. Thus when a character, as in the last chapter of Tolstoy's "The Death of Ivan Ilyitch," uses this style — particularly in the context of a narration like Tolstoy's that does not use such a style — its spiritual implications become an immediate object of our attention. In other words, although the style of a character in Hemingway is much like the style of the narrator, and although both styles may convey important implications, a narrative as a whole can mix the styles of the narrator and of one or more characters. Style, then, in complex ways, can and does convey an enormous amount of information and is a key element of narrative.

We can think of style as a regular subset of language, more general than particular sentences but more specific than the language as a whole. In the same way, we can think of a dialect, which reflects the culture (historical moment, social class, and so on) of its speaker, as a regular subset of language, more general than style but still more specific than language as a whole. In the same way that dialect reflects the culture of a speaker, GRAPHOLECT — the regularities of the language itself, the typical grammatical structures, choice of vocabulary and subject, and so on — reflects the culture of a writer. In the following extracts, all originally written in English, I have replaced dates with blanks and familiar location names with initials so that only the grapholects, rather than more overt clues, will be able to mark the culture from which each arose.

A) In the country of A_____, in a certain village, there was on a time a parson of a church which preached unto his parishioners, and thereby showed them the joys of heaven and the pains of hell, and many other things. And as he thus preached in the pulpit, among the people there was a miller which knew well that the priest had a concubine, and spake so loud that everybody did hear him.

B) I was born in the year _____, in the city of Y_____, of a good family, though not of this country, my father being a foreigner of B_____, who settled first at H_____. He got a good estate by merchandise, and leaving off his trade, lived afterward at Y_____; from whence he had married my mother, whose relations were named R_____, a very good family in that country, and from whom I was called R_____ K_____.

C) "It is with considerable difficulty that I remember the original era of my being: all the events of that period appear confused and indistinct. A strange multiplicity of sensations seized me, and I saw, felt, heard, and smelt, at the same time; and it was, indeed, a long time before I learned to distinguish between the operations of my various senses."

D) When B_____ H_____ went to interview S_____ L_____ for the "Solid Men of B_____" series, which he undertook to finish up in *The*

Events, after he replaced their original projector on that newspaper, L‾‾‾‾‾ received him in his private office by previous appointment.

E) She was so deeply imbedded in my consciousness that for the first year of school I seem to have believed that each of my teachers was my mother in disguise.

Although you may never have encountered any of these extracts before, and although there is no reason that you should be able even to guess at the names of their authors, I believe that if you take a moment to read them with care you will be able to know whether or not they are in chronological order and perhaps also the country of origin and social class of the authors. Try it.

Ready for the answers? In fact, (A) is the beginning of the first tale from an anonymous English collection of about 1558 called *A Sackful of News*; (B) is the beginning of Englishman Daniel Defoe's *Robinson Crusoe* of 1719; (C) contains the beginning of the recitation by Frankenstein's monster of his earliest memories in Englishwoman Mary Shelley's *Frankenstein* of 1818; (D) is the opening sentence of American William Dean Howells' *The Rise of Silas Lapham* of 1884; and (E) begins American Philip Roth's *Portnoy's Complaint* (1967). The extracts are in chronological order, and all but one fall before the Hemingway of 1933. As far as is known, all the writers were middle class, although Shelley and Hemingway came from decidedly more comfortable circumstances than did the other four. And, although most of us never make any conscious study of grapholect, I think we find these cultural facts highly plausible after reading these extracts. In fact, practiced readers can often and easily date texts from within the last century to within a few years.

The fact that grapholect is so pervasive and carries so much meaning makes it a very important, although rarely noticed, element of narrative. In most cases, authors do not meddle with grapholect because writing in a grapholect appropriate to their own cultural setting for readers who inhabit that same cultural setting makes possible the efficient sharing of a wealth of cultural knowledge. However, there may be other considerations. Writers like the Ghanaian Ama Ata Aidoo and the Japanese Yukio Mishima have cultural reasons for wanting to forge a grapholect that accommodates the literary traditions of Europe and North America. Writers of pseudomedieval fantasy like William Morris and J. R. R. Tolkien use a quasi-antique grapholect to lend texture to their fictional worlds. And Mark Twain, by refusing to use a Biblical style or, more generally, an early seventeenth-century grapholect like that of the King James Bible, modernizes his Adam and Eve.

We can see language in narrative, then, functioning at many nested levels. At the most general we have the language of composition, for example, English. More specifically, we have a grapholect, for example, middle-class between-the-wars American so-called Standard English. Still more specifically, we have a style, for example, Hemingway's. And even more specifically, we have the styles of the individual characters. Most specifically of all, we have the precise sentences of a given text. Each of these levels conveys progressively more specific information about the social construction of reality, information that typically must be consistent with the implications of the higher levels. Since genre, through similar means of increasing specification, also conveys information about the social construction of reality, it is reasonable and true that certain genres become associated with certain styles or grapholects depending on the generality of the genre. The so-called HARD BOILED DETECTIVE story, of which Dashiell Hammett's "The Gutting of Couffignal" (1925) is an example, typically uses a middle-class between-the-wars grapholect, just as Hemingway does. This is not to say that we cannot distinguish the styles of Hemingway and Hammett — we can — but that both arise from the same culture. However, they have differing aims, and while Hemingway's spare style evolves into the nuanced ironies of Updike and Mason, Hammett's style evolves into the violent styles of such modern thriller writers as Lawrence Sanders. Yet all writers of Hard Boiled Detective stories, including such moderns as John D. MacDonald, continue to recall in their writing the between-the-wars grapholect. And this is to be expected. Language, after all, is what stories are made of.

Structure

If we want to investigate how something is made, how it is constructed, then we will want to examine its STRUCTURE. In discussing narratives, the most fundamental structural distinction is between story (here used as a technical term) and PLOT. Story is the sequence of events in the order in which they happened; plot is the sequence of events in the order in which they are reported. To illustrate, let us construct a simple and not uncommon story:

I

A)   Boy 1 meets girl 1 in the spring.
B)   Boy 1 and girl 1 love each other deliriously in the summer.
C)   Girl 1's father prefers boy 2 in the fall and forbids boy 1 and girl 1 to meet.
D1)   Boy 1 goes out West and prospects for gold all winter.
D2)   Boy 1 strikes it rich.
E)   Boy 1 returns with gold, pleases father, and marries girl 1 in the spring.

If a particular narrative told this story in precisely this order and in precisely these words, then we could say that the story is also the plot. However, in virtually all cases, plot is different from story. We can think of plot as reshaping story by introducing changes in the *order* in which the events are narrated and in the RHYTHM of their narration. To illustrate:

II

D1)   As the narrative begins, we find boy 1 living a desolate, cold, lonely life in the mountains of northern California, panning for gold, eating badly, and cursing a fate that made him love a woman above his station in life.
B)   He thinks back to the way they used to meet when he came in from the fields at day's end, how they would share a picnic dinner, and how they would sit together on a hilltop watching the larks dart across the setting sun.

C1) But then her father had returned from his sojourn in the Big City where he had made the acquaintance of Powerful Men. He wanted girl 1 to marry boy 2, the son of one of these men, in order to cement the alliance between himself and the other father.

C2) He had shamed boy 1, rebuked him for his poverty, and demanded whether or not boy 1 himself thought girl 1 should live the kind of life boy 1 could provide.

A) Remembering how they had first met, how boy 1 had saved girl 1's life from the runaway horse, boy 1 thinks that yes, by golly, he was the kind of man she needed.

D2) And the next morning, he finds the first big nugget.

E1) He returns to a neighboring town and buys a farm of his own. Then, wiser and established, he goes to claim girl 1's hand.

E2) The father still refuses him, saying that he wants no farmer for his daughter.

E3) But girl 1 now rebels, pointing to boy 1's achievements and qualities of character.

E4) The father realizes now that boy 1 will truly make girl 1 happy, throws them an enormous wedding, and buys them a brass bed as a wedding present.

The second version of this narrative contains the same elements as the first, but the second presents them in a different order and with much greater detail. If we had never seen the first version but read only the second, that is, the plot, we would still, as we read, have constructed the story in our minds. That is, while reading (D1), we would have first felt some suspense — why is this fellow suffering here? — and soon learned about girl 1. As the plot unfolded in the order D1 – B – C1 – C2 – A – D2 – E1 – E2 – E3 – E4, or, more simply, D – B – C – A – D – E, we would have been making a mental construction of the story, A – B – C – D – E. At the same time, we would have been adjusting our sense of what the story must have been in light of what we were reading (including our knowledge of the genre and so on) and making predictions about what the story would turn out to be.

Notice that we might have constructed the same story while reading a different plot:

III

E1b) An old, wandering drunk stops by a farm and asks boy 1 for food. Boy 1 gives him food and, as the old man eats, thinks of how grateful he is to have a farm at all.

E1a) Boy 1 recalls coming to this town, unknown, but with gold and a dream. The gold, however, was the least of it; it had bought him the farm, but it could not make the dream come true.

D1) He recalls his desolate winter life as a prospector and

B) Compares it with the summer evenings he had once shared with girl 1.

C) But girl 1's father had wanted better for her, and made him face his own poverty. "Even if you had money," the father had said, "look at where you've come from. Could you ever be a fit husband for the likes of her?"

D2) He had to admit it: even his finding of gold had been only luck, not a sign of real character.

E1c) The drunk turns out to have been a foreman of a big farm, but down on his luck; he offers to work for food. Boy 1 trusts him. They combine boy 1's money, energy, and faith in people with the old man's knowledge and gratitude. Together they make the land begin to sprout.

A) Boy 1 remembers how, in that previous spring, when he had saved girl 1 from the runaway horse, he had felt he could achieve anything.

E2) He goes and asks her father again for her hand, but again his request is rebuffed.

E3) But girl 1 now rebels, pointing to boy 1's achievements and qualities of character.

E4) The father realizes now that boy 1 will truly make girl 1 happy and throws them an enormous wedding — the old man serving as best man — and buys them a brass bed as a wedding present.

The differences in plot between versions II and III profoundly affect our understanding of the story. Version II, beginning as it does in the winter (D1) with boy 1 all alone, emphasizes his individuality and suffering. When he is rebuked (C2), he angrily thinks of his own bravery (A) and immediately discovers gold (D2). Version III, beginning as it does in the second spring back East (E1b) with boy 1 taking in the old man, emphasizes boy 1's community values and desire to be productive. When he is rebuked (C), he recognizes his own short-comings (D2); only back on the farm (E1c) does he think of how his first meeting with girl 1 (A) had filled him with hope. In version II, the farm is a sign of wealth used primarily to contradict the father's argument; in version III, the farm also reflects boy 1's concern for productivity. In version II, girl 1 represents a prize for boy 1's perseverance, a validation of his individuality; in version III, girl 1 also represents an integration of boy 1 into the community, a validation of his commitment to social growth. In version II, then, the wedding bed primarily suggests sexuality; in version III, the wedding bed also suggests fertility. These important differences in emphasis arise not only from reordering, of course. The introduction of a character to contrast the father, the old man who is helped by boy 1 and helps boy 1 in return, FORESHADOWS boy 1's integration into a family and highlights his desire to nurture. But the main events of the story remain unchanged. We can see, then, that the distinction between plot and story, while a technical matter, is not merely a technical matter. While we read plots, we construct mental stories, and the relations between those plots and stories help shape our thoughts and feelings.

Plots reshape stories by changing both the temporal order of events and the temporal flow of events. The changes in the temporal flow of events, changes in the rate at which events are narrated, is called rhythm. To understand how rhythm works in narration, we need to notice that narration consists of three temporally distinct kinds of report: DESCRIPTION, DRAMATIZATION, and RECAPITULATION.

In description (the opening paragraph of Hemingway's "A Clean Well-Lighted Place," for example), time stops while we get more and more detail. Description emphasizes a single moment. It is much like a close-up or freeze frame in cinema. In description, the time spent reading is much longer than the time being read about.

In dramatization (the first dialogue section of "A Clean Well-Lighted Place," for example), time continues at its normal pace and we notice only a few details as we attend to the characters' words and actions. It is much like a normal action sequence in cinema or drama. In dramatization, the time spent reading is (depending on individual reading speed) more or less the same as the time being read about.

In recapitulation (version I of our boy-and-girl romance, for example), time is speeded up and detail is virtually eliminated. Recapitulation emphasizes the broad sweep of events. It is much like voice-over narration in cinema. In recapitulation, the time spent reading is much shorter than the time being read about.

The implied author's variation among these three types of report varies our sense of time in relation to the events of the plot and to the events of the story (the same events, of course, but arriving in different orders). Although we can sometimes find whole paragraphs of description, long exchanges of dramatic dialogue, or uninterrupted recapitulation, most frequently we find these three temporal types mixed in various ways. In "A Clean, Well-Lighted Place," the first quoted speech is embedded in a longer sentence (4): "'Last week he tried to commit suicide,' one waiter said.'" The next sentence (5) — "'Why?'" — is not only shorter in the number of words but flows faster in time because it is unencumbered with "one waiter said." Those three words do not advance the temporal flow. For event (C) in our narrative, version I has a simple recapitulation: "Girl 1's father prefers boy 2 in the fall and forbids boy 1 and girl 1 to meet." In version III, (C) contains some additional dramatization, which exemplifies the recapitulated event, and the dramatization itself is slowed down in turn by some description of the dramatic scene, that is, by restating the identity of the speaker:

(C) But girl 1's father had wanted better for her, and made him face his own poverty. "Even if you had money," the father had said, "look at where you've come from. Could you ever be a fit husband for the likes of her?"

By selecting among and combining the temporal types of report — description, dramatization, and recapitulation — implied authors can control our sense of the rhythm of a narrative, rushing us over unimportant phenomena and dwelling on important ones. By slowing the narrative down they can build suspense, and by speeding it up they can add the excitement of a roller-coaster. Conversely, by controlling the rhythm, implied authors let us know what is more or less important in a narrative. In our version I, the lightly mentioned father mostly stands for the superficiality of social judgment. In version II, where we learn of the father's economic plans, he becomes more of an antagonist to the poor boy 1. In version III, which dwells on the father's role as protector of his daughter, he is a more acceptable, albeit mistaken, voice of society.

Story and plot, order and rhythm, these are matters of structure. Whenever we do a structural analysis of anything, we allow ourselves to ignore some information in order to highlight other information. If we want to understand how people walk, we probably would want to study the skeletal system, but in so doing, we would strip away the nervous system and the digestive system. Ultimately, however, no one moves without nerves and sustenance, so while a structural view may be very helpful, we need to recognize that it is necessarily incomplete. For narratives, the two most widely used kinds of structural analysis yield SYNCHRONIC and DIACHRONIC STRUCTURES.

Synchronic means "all at one time." Our boy-and-girl story begins in the spring, goes through the seasons, and ends in the spring. If we think of all the parts of this as coexisting, we might say that the structure is a circle, with the action rising from spring to summer as the protagonists' love grows, falling when the father thwarts them in the fall, bottoming out in the winter, and then rising again as the earth and the relationship renew themselves.

B

A,E   C

D

Viewed this way, the structure suggests a kind of unity, a stability, an eternal reality. We often speak of the cycle of the seasons, and this story mimics that cycle.

Diachronic, on the other hand, means "occurring through time." If we view our story through time, the same description yields a sine wave:

B

A   C   E

D

Viewed this way, the structure suggests a stronger emphasis on the rise and fall of our protagonists' fortunes and ends not so much with a sense of stability as with a sense of commencement; they are just entering the positive portion of the wave's rise and who knows what tomorrow will bring?

Neither a synchronic nor a diachronic structural analysis is intrinsically superior to the other; neither is a complete description of the narrative; both are useful. As we go through the process of reading, we follow the text diachronically, of course. But in so doing, we constantly construct, and, if need be, constantly revise, an idea of the synchronic structure. Put another way, we read plots, but simultaneously think stories. But, of course, story and plot are inseparable. No story can be told instantaneously with absolutely even weight given to every bit of information narrated. Narrators must tell us who said what, or describe the look in boy 1's eyes when he sees that the person he saved is a young woman. Similarly, no plot can be told in absolutely separable, one-after-another segments because the very meaning of an event, as we saw by comparing versions II and III, is dependent on the order in which we receive the report of each event. In reading narratives, as in perceiving all phenomena, we simultaneously see their parts as co-existing in time (synchronic) and occurring through time (diachronic). Just as implied authors manipulate both kinds of structure, so we must recognize both kinds of structure. But ultimately we must rise above separate structural analyses to appreciate the double life of each narrative as a whole.

One of the most common structural devices is FRAMING. When a painting is set off in a frame, we often tend to ignore the frame and look only at the painting. But if the frame is obtrusive — say a huge, gilded frame with carved angels — we would certainly notice it. If it framed a flamboyant, mythological painting by Peter Paul Rubens, we might well think the frame quite appropriate. If the picture in the frame were a modern geometric abstraction, however, say something by Piet Mondrian, we might wonder just what the idea was in putting those two objects together. One way or another, then, as corroboration or commentary, a frame can influence our view of its painting. In similar ways, frames make a difference to our understanding of narratives.

In the simplest case, a frame narrative begins with a character deciding to tell a story; then the body of the narrative is that story; and then we return to the situation in which the character told the story, looking, perhaps, at the way other characters react to that story. H. G. Well's *The Time Machine* is a frame narrative, the book opening with commentary by the young acquaintance of the Time Traveller and ending with that narrator's ultimate reflections. Along the way, most of the narrative is the Time Traveller's own report of his experiences in the future, but this lengthy report is interrupted strategically so that we will remember that all that we are reading is being told at a dinner table—at which our narrator is present—in Victorian England. The implied author, in other words, wants to remind us of the frame; by so doing, the implied author is at least reminding us that the point of such a far-fetched story must be applied to contemporary life.

The Time Machine is called a full-frame narrative because we have both an opening of the frame and a closing of it. Although the play within the play in William Shakespeare's *Hamlet* (1601) is very short compared to the play as a whole, Hamlet could also be thought of as full-framed because we come up to and away from the framed inner play in an orderly way. And again, of course, the relationship between the inner and outer material is crucial for our understanding of the whole.

Some narratives use partial framing. Henry James's *The Turn of the Screw*, for example, is a front-framed narrative: we have a character propose to relay a narrative, but then at the end of that narrative, we never return to that character, to the frame situation. That makes us feel some terrible incompleteness—which James's implied author doubtless wants us to understand as like that incompleteness others have felt within the inner narrated tale. In a similar way, there are back-framed narratives, tales which we read as if they were not framed and then find part way through, often right at the end, that they were framed after all. Winsor McCay's "Tales of the Rarebit Fiend" is back-framed, the ending suddenly making us realize that the narrative world we thought we were inhabiting is itself part of another world. The sense that what goes on in one world makes a difference to what goes on in another world is clearly central to McCay's point.

On occasion, we find narratives in which one frame nests within another, a narrator telling a story about a character who happens to tell a story about a character who happens to tell a story and so on. In such a NESTED NARRATIVE— for example, the whole book of Ovid's *Metamorphoses*—the multiple framing creates a sense that the innermost narrative has some fundamental significance. In other words, the device of nesting, like the control of rhythm, has the capacity to underscore the importance of one part of the narrative or another. Structure, then, like every other element of narrative we have discussed, makes a difference in how we feel about a narrative and in what we understand a narrative to mean.

Theme

The Random House Dictionary of the English Language defines THEME simply as "a subject of discourse, discussion, meditation, or composition: topic." In short, the theme is what a narrative is about. This idea is so basic that the first edition of the authoritative *Princeton Encyclopedia of Poetry and Poetics* didn't even bother to define the term. However, as we have seen, in the course of reading a narrative we may many times revise our sense of the story, and hence of what the story is about. In other words, as fundamental and simple as the notion of theme may be, it still represents a noteworthy element of narrative under the control of the implied author.

It has been common to use the word "theme" to refer only to some ultimate understanding of what a work is about. In that sense, one might say simply that the theme of "The Black Cat" is how egotism may lead to crime. However, a fuller discussion of theme in that story would recognize that Poe's opening paragraph may at first suggest to us that the narrative is about confession; that soon we see the work as about self-justification; and ultimately we know it as a study in the evasion of moral responsibility. The word "theme" comes from an Indo-European root meaning "to set down," as in placing something in position before us. It is the Greek word for "proposition," meaning both something put forward in space and something put forward for consideration. To think of theme only as the last something put forward, rather than to recognize that the last something exists only as it grows out of prior propositions, is to discount the ways in which narratives ask us to approach topics, to contemplate them, to wrestle with them. Theme, like structure, evolves as we read.

Aesthetic Virtues

At the end of his life, in *The Art of Poetry*, the great Roman author Horace (65–8 B.C.E.) said that successful writing "mingles profit with pleasure, by delighting and instructing the reader at the same time." In other words, a work bent solely on improving us would fail as art, and a work bent solely on titillating us would also fail as art. Propaganda and pornography are, respectively, categories of such writing. Horace was right.

Horace's two AESTHETIC virtues, delight and instruction, are virtues only when properly balanced. There is, in fact, no aesthetic virtue which is in and of itself good. If we think, for example, that all good English writing must be correct according to the grammatical norms of so-called Standard English, then we are ignoring the contribution other dialects make, for example in bringing to life the speech of regional characters (as in Richard Wright's "The Man Who Was Almost a Man") or in characterizing the cultural origins of narrators (as in Lynda Barry's "The Night We All Got Sick"). Some critics claim that all art must be "responsible" to "the class struggle" or "to feminism" or to some other political position that many find important. But if a narrative is to deal with politics artistically, it must integrate that concern with the work as a whole; most people find relentlessly political writing boring and gratuitously political writing annoying. Other critics claim that all narratives must strive for artistic "progress"; but such a view ignores the value of efficient communication within a known genre. Clearly what is needed is a set of aesthetic virtues that, while perhaps not virtuous singly, mark excellence when they are balanced in a well crafted work. Aestheticians have proposed many such sets of virtues, but most such sets seem to have three key elements. These elements may go by various names, but as a set they all address the concerns most frequently denoted by the terms UNITY (often called COHERENCE), VARIETY, and ECONOMY.

Unity/coherence refers to the appropriateness of the parts of the work to each other. If, in the middle of "The Purloined Letter," a work filled with "instruction," we had suddenly found the narrator pursuing a long discussion of how to make a good soufflé, we probably would have thought that section incoherent; that is, it would not seem to cohere with the work as a whole. Unconnected diversions destroy the unity of a work.

On the other hand, too much unity is as bad as too little. The endless repetition of one word surely would produce a unified text, but just as surely that text would not "delight." There is no work more unified — or instructive — than a telephone directory since every part fits in precisely its rational place. However, in that context the mere progress from "Smith, Joseph" to "Smith, Josephine" is hardly thrilling. Although those are indeed two different names, in a phone book they feel like just more of the same. While that may be fine for the purposes of a directory, a NOVEL needs novelty, variety.

But again, too much variety can be as bad as too little. If the text seems to jump from one utter surprise to another, we lose all sense of structure. What is wanted is ample variety while still allowing readers continuously to construct a whole. Each part of the text should bear as powerfully as possible on all others, bring in as much information as possible about stance or genre or character or theme, while not bringing in incoherent information.

Getting the most from each word an implied author selects is like getting the most from each dollar one spends. This virtue is called economy. Of course, too much economy may lead to a miserly text, one that refuses to glory in its own fun or plumb its own tragedy. A work which is too economical may convey insufficient information for us to understand how the whole of it works.

Too much economy, then, is the enemy of unity; too much unity is the enemy of variety; and too much variety, is the enemy of economy. And yet together, balanced, unity, variety, and economy form a set of aesthetic virtues marking the best of narratives that have instructed and delighted humanity since the dawn of time and that will continue to enrich us until the end. Over the ages, and across cultures and classes and countries, works of art change in their content, structure, aims, language, and audience, but art itself goes on. There is much to know about narrative, but not an impossible amount. From the elements of narrative we have discussed, authors have and always will make for us worlds of beauty. That is a virtue indeed.

Keeping a Reading Journal

A reading journal is a kind of diary, a tool by which you can train yourself to become a better reader of STORIES and a better writer about stories. It can help you focus your thoughts both while you read and immediately thereafter. Later it can not only remind you of what you read and thought, but can also spark further thinking by you or others who read it. It can help you prepare for lectures on your reading, for discussion of your reading, and for writing about your reading.

The benefits of a reading journal are enormous, amply repaying time invested both in writing the journal and in reading it. Because the process of merely scanning a page is almost automatic for most of us, and because a powerful story seems so memorable while we read, it is sometimes difficult to believe how important it is to slow down and think about what we read, to question NARRATIVES, and to capture and review our thoughts. Because SUSPENSE and curiosity impel us to read rapidly, keeping a reading journal may require the development of unusual restraint. Yet this restraint provides crucial time. When we drive down a street and come to a familiar red, octagonal sign that says "Stop," we react almost automatically. But if the sign were blue or triangular, some mental alarm might go off. The slight change—which does not, after all, change the basic message—would make the sign less familiar. Just as this slightly new sign invites us to slow down and think, so should artful narratives which are always, as the Russian Formalist critics said, DEFAMILIARIZED. The commitment to keep a reading journal helps us to slow down and think.

If a red, octagonal sign, instead of saying "Stop," said "Stare," what would you do? Laugh, perhaps? Wonder about the identity of the sign's "author"? For that matter, who is the author of a common stop sign? Stare at what? Is the sign meant for you at all or is it, perhaps, a prank aimed at someone else? Has it replaced a real stop sign and thereby made that intersection more dangerous? The full understanding of a "Stare" sign begins, then, with noticing its details—color, placement, content—and goes on to the posing of questions and attempts to answer those questions. A reading journal participates in precisely this process of noticing and questioning. And just as slowing down to observe and think about the stare sign makes you a better observer and allows you the chance to understand more fully what that sign might mean, so the very process of writing as or after you read defamiliarizes the reading process and helps make you a better reader.

Personal diaries concerning a person's general activities and thoughts are quite various in their form and content, reflecting the needs and personalities of the diarists. Reading journals concerning a person's reading activities and responses will also vary, both among individuals and from entry to entry. We can divide the variety of reading journals into three basic types: the structured journal, the subject journal, and the free-writing journal. Each has its special strengths.

The Structured Journal

A structured reading journal is a general-purpose tool used to fulfill both anticipated and unforeseen needs by following a predetermined structure. In it, you focus your thoughts on the reading material, record references to key passages, articulate questions that the texts seem to raise, and sometimes try out answers to those questions. For ease of handling and for safety, all reading journals should be kept in some sort of permanently bound, 8 1/2" × 11" notebook — such as a spiral-bound notebook — with your name and phone number prominently displayed. A typical entry should be headed with the date of entry and objective data about the text, such as the AUTHOR'S name, the title of the work, the birth and death dates of the author, the language, nationality, and gender of the author, and the date of publication of the work. You should leave some space after these preliminaries, since after reading the work you might want to add other heading information. For instance, you might want to indicate the type of work this is (for example, FAIRY TALE or SCIENCE FICTION) or other works that you associate with it and the reasons for those associations (for example, similarity of narrative STRUCTURE or of THEME). As you read, of course, you ought to mark your texts, not only underscoring key passages but indicating in the book's margins why those passages are key or at least what they contain (for example, "typical style," or "plot twist"). In your structured reading journal you may want to record those comments by page number and amplify them. The process of writing as one reads often leads to promising thoughts that one doesn't want to forget but doesn't want to stop reading to pursue. These thoughts should also go in the reading journal. At least as important as these thoughts are those that arise after the reading is complete and one has had a chance to digest the work a bit, both by reflection and by looking back through it and through one's marginal notes. At that point, you ought to write down your observations about anything in the story that seems interesting (for example, STYLE, CHARACTERIZATION, SETTING, PLOT, MORAL, and so on), indicating whether those observations feel conclusive or provisional. If provisional, you ought to try to pose questions that might test those observations. And if you then find answers, they should be added too. If you have not yet done so, at that point you should also indicate pages on which important passages may be found, be they important for posing or answering the questions in the entry or simply important as examples of something that you find striking. Each such page reference should be accompanied by a few words indicating your idea of the passage's importance. These ideas, like all ideas in reading journals, should be thought of as open to revision as discussion, further reflection, and further reading suggest new understandings of individual texts and of fiction in general. Entries should be made with very wide margins so that these second thoughts and cross-references to other works noted in the journal can be made clearly and conveniently. A typical entry, then, will have heading information, a section of comparatively unorganized notes made during reading, and a section of somewhat more organized observations made after reflection and review of the text and the beginning of the journal entry.

In addition to thoughts on individual works made before, during, and immediately after the reading of each text, the journal should also record your more general observations and questions about FICTION. These observations may serve many purposes: to focus discussion; to lead you to new understanding as you read new stories or reread old stories; and to lead you to your own essay topics.

By writing in the reading journal, you focus your ideas. Once written, those ideas can be shared and developed with others. Some courses are designed so that at the beginning of each class you can exchange your journal with a classmate. In other courses, students are divided into study groups that meet and exchange journals outside class. And in yet others, there is no formal arrangement for such exchanges. But even in those cases, students can team up on their own to exchange journals. In any case, supposing it fits the needs of the course, much can be gained by reading a classmate's journal and by writing in it. Your response might comment on the virtues or weaknesses of each entry as a self-teaching tool; it might try to offer an answer to one or more of the questions posed; it might pose new questions in relation to the observations presented; or it might try to help in the development of such general ideas into possible paper topics. Unless you have a permanent journal partnership, you should sign the comments you make in your classmate's reading journal.

If it is consistent with the instructor's goals for the course, you should also take your class notes right in the reading journal. This makes your own review easy. Whenever you do review, feel free to write cross-referenced further thoughts in your margins and to add new observations, ideas, and questions wherever they seem appropriate. Date all such additional writing for your own reference so that, if you wish, you can reconstruct the development of your own ideas.

Since your reading journal will be read by others, and by you weeks or months after the semester begins, either write very clearly or print. Given the nature of the entries, sentence fragments may well be quite reasonable, but illegible words are useless. The typical entry for a SHORT STORY probably should be about a handwritten page or somewhat more. NOVELS obviously require longer entries made over more than one day. You should leave at least half a page after each entry so that your exchange partner has room to write and so that you have room to jot further notes based on that response and/or on class discussion. Number the pages in your journal so that your partner's references and your own cross-references can be made easily. Review your journal periodically, especially when you seek a subject for an essay.

The Subject Journal

Physically, the subject journal is quite like the structured journal (being kept in a bound notebook, leaving wide margins for review, and so on); however, the subject journal is limited to a single subject (style; the evolution of the short story; the role of children in fiction) or to two or three related subjects (the narrative treatment of race, class, and gender; the use of IMAGERY and SETTING in CHARAC-TERIZATION; the devices of SUSPENSE). A subject journal has one enormous advantage compared to a structured journal: it is potentially much less time-consuming both to maintain on a daily basis and to review, as when you seek a topic for an essay. On the other hand, a subject journal has one enormous disadvantage compared to a structured journal: it has a narrow focus. A subject journal begun at the start of a program of reading can help you notice and record everything having to do with its subject, but by its very nature contributes to a sort of relative blindness toward other subjects. If you want your journal to have a wide focus, you should keep a structured journal. But if you know that you want to pursue a single subject, you might choose a subject journal. Some people who do not normally keep structured journals begin to keep a subject journal once they have settled on a topic for a term paper; others who keep a structured journal sometimes begin a second subject journal within that structured journal by distinctively marking all parts having to do with a single subject, say by highlighting in a special color.

A subject journal should have entries like those of a structured journal — heading information, notes taken as you read, reflections after you are done reading — and also dated entries for records of other work you do on the subject. The notes taken while you read and on reflection will, of course, be limited by the subject. However, if in pursuing the subject you are reading books in addition to this collection, the subject journal heading sections need to include full bibliographic information about those books so that they can be properly cited. If these are borrowed books that cannot be marked, the entry information needs to be self-contained, giving page references and ample quotation, and distinguishing paraphrase from exact quotation by careful use of quotation marks. A subject journal, like a structured journal, should be reviewed so that you make sure you are developing a general understanding of your subject. The subject journal will then be an excellent source for both paper topics and the material you need to pursue them.

The Free-Writing Journal

Free-writing is the process of doing one's own informal writing in response to what one reads. While the structured journal and the subject journal may contain many fragmentary notes, the entries in a free-writing journal, though informal, normally should be whole sentences organized into coherent paragraphs. For that reason, the free-writing journal may be physically different from the structured journal and the subject journal. Since only the free-writing journal invites revision of its own entries, it alone might best be kept in a ring-binder or folder. Still, the binder or folder should be clearly marked with the journalist's name and phone number, and each entry should be dated and should begin by citing the text, or section of text, that prompted the written response.

A free-writing response may be a small study of some aspect of the FORM or CONTENT of the initiating text (How did FLASHBACK help control suspense here? In what way was the choice of setting helpful in exploring the theme?); it may be an exploration of one's personal responses (Why did I find the RESOLUTION so disturbing? Why might I recommend this story to my best friend?); or it may be a general meditation prompted by the writing (How did the world get to be the way it is shown here? How can we improve race relations today?). Playing with the printed text produces some of the most instructive free-writing. One can try to write a scene that resolves an AMBIGUITY or reveals a CHARACTER'S MOTIVATION. One can write the scene that would follow the conclusion or retell part of the narrative from a different VIEWPOINT or change the ending or create a PARODY. One can imitate the text by creating, or at least beginning, another like it in some important way. Or one can create other incidents from the lives of these characters or put these characters into a different GENRE. One can also use the occasion to try out a text of one's own on the same subject or write a sketch of a character like one in the printed text. Only your imagination and the desire to produce something clear should limit you in free-writing.

A free-writing journal has two main disadvantages and two main advantages compared to the two other types of reading journal. The first disadvantage is that a free-writing journal provides little record of the details of your reading and of your critical thinking. This means those details cannot initiate reflection, conversation, or essays. The second disadvantage is that the desire to produce something worth reading in its own right, even if only by you, may seduce you into spending so much time in polishing your free-writing that your journal will lose its informality and become artificial and burdensome.

On the other hand, free-writing is perfect if your aim in reading is as an adjunct to learning to write narrative since free-writing offers an opportunity to play with the masters of the game. Also, the requirement of coherence means that free-writing will encourage you to stick with a text you find boring — even if only to parody it — until you may come so well to understand it that it will reveal to you beauties you might have missed in taking only a few fragmentary notes.

A reading journal, then, is as personal and individual as any other sort of diary. It is something a reader not only uses but creates. In that regard, a reading journal is visible evidence of the activity that goes into the best reading. If we are to understand art, and gain from it both pleasure and instruction, we must attend to it. That takes time. Keeping a reading journal provides a framework within which to spend that time profitably. It is a way of holding up to ourselves a sign that says, "Stop!" And having stopped, we can proceed where we might previously have been unprepared.

Writing About Narratives

The Role of the Critic

Most scholars hold that Western literary CRITICISM began with Plato's *Ion* (c. 390 B.C.E.). In this dialogue, Ion is a rhapsode, meaning here both singer and critic. When Ion wonders how it is that all agree that he speaks so powerfully about the work of Homer but only indifferently about the work of others, the CHARACTER Socrates explains:

> The gift which you possess of speaking excellently about Homer is not an art [technê], but . . . an inspiration; there is a divinity moving you, like that contained in the stone which Euripides calls a magnet. . . . This stone not only attracts iron rings but imparts to them a similar power of attracting other rings; and sometimes you may see a number of pieces of iron and rings suspended from one another so as to form quite a long chain: and all of them derive their power of suspension from the original stone. In like manner the Muse first of all inspires men herself; and from these inspired persons a chain of other persons is suspended, who take the inspiration. For all good poets, epic as well as lyric, compose their beautiful poems not by art, but because they are inspired and possessed. . . . Do you know that the spectator is the last of the rings . . . ? The rhapsode like yourself and the actor are intermediate links, and the poet himself is the first of them.

From Plato's viewpoint, the rhapsode, like the poet, is possessed. Like the actor who makes the play real and moving to the spectator, the rhapsode makes the epic (a variety of NARRATIVE) real and moving to his or her audience. CRITICISM, then, like FICTION writing, is a powerful act in which the critic is both moved to write and by writing moves others. In Plato's view, we write about narratives because we are compelled by inspiration and because others are enriched (inspired) by our writing.

On the other hand, Aristotle (384–322 B.C.E.), the greatest student of Plato, wrote in *The Nichomachean Ethics* that art (technê) is "a trained disposition to make in accordance with correct calculation." While in modern English we often distinguish between "art" and "technique," for the Greeks these concepts shared a single word. Aristotle, foreshadowing the Russian Formalist critics, asserted that art *is* technique. Technê is the root of our word "technology," and the job of the critic is to analyze the work of art — that is, literally to disassemble it — in order to understand by what means ("correct calculation") it achieves its effect. For Aristotle there is no inspiration about either art or criticism. His *Poetics* tells exactly how a TRAGEDY ought to be constructed and his *Rhetoric* tells exactly how one may most effectively speak about a tragedy or anything else. Aristotle believes that we write about narratives because they are a powerful phenomenon in human culture and require scientific understanding.

Although the German philosopher Friedrich Schlegel (1772–1829) wrote that everyone "is born either a Platonist or an Aristotelian," most people subscribe, in part, to both positions. They believe, as Plato had it, that criticism is an activity inspired by a need to respond to a work and by a need to share that response, and also believe, as Aristotle had it, that criticism is a vigorous activity of inquiry that is ultimately calculated to fulfill a goal with its own audience. In discussing the types of writing about narrative and the components of the writing process, it is easy to become dominated by the desire for correct calculation. We must remember at each step, however, that the point of criticism is also the enrichment of the critic and the audience, so inspiration ought never to be far from our minds. Inspiration and calculation are the twin beacons that should light our way as critics.

Types of Writing About Narrative

What types of writing do critics create? Although the types of writing about narrative mix and merge in infinite variety, for the sake of setting forth the issues, one can distinguish five basic types of writing about narrative: analysis, generalization, review, meditation, and reflection.

ANALYSIS

Analysis disassembles a work into its elements, explores how those elements are themselves made, and then reconstructs the work. The result is a richer understanding of the meaning, effects, or importance of the work as a whole or of some significant part of the work (a SCENE, a character, an IMAGE, and so on). The discussion of Bruna's *The King* in the "Introduction" to this volume is an example of analysis. While Bruna's narrative is quite simple, the critical focus on color imagery and the explication (literally "unfolding") of the way that imagery reinforces the tension between the young king's aspirations and the values of the "two tall thin green ladies" gives us a more detailed sense of the artistry behind the narrative. It also helps us see more clearly meanings woven into what at first might seem merely random authorial choices. Similarly, the analysis of the STYLE of Poe's narrator in "The Black Cat" in the essay on "The Elements of Narrative" helps make clear not only how that narrator's style is constituted but also what it means for the narrative as a whole that the style quickly reveals the narrator's unreliability. Most academic essays about narrative are primarily analytic.

Some critics make a distinction between "explication" and "analysis," the former being the description of what is in a narrative (a FIRST-PERSON NARRATOR, a tragic RESOLUTION, and so on) and the latter being the logical discussion of what these elements mean in context. The distinction between "EXPLICATION" and "analysis" in criticism, then, is an exact parallel to the distinction in rhetoric between "EXPOSITION" (exposing—revealing—the subject of discussion) and "ARGUMENT" (developing and fostering an intellectual position concerning the subject of discussion). From one viewpoint, this distinction is very helpful: it reminds us that we cannot develop an argument unless we know what we are arguing about. From another viewpoint, however, this distinction is more apparent than real: we virtually never bother setting forth what we know unless we want to urge a particular view of it on someone. In other words, while the distinction between explication and analysis is sound in theory, it is sometimes distracting in practice. I would never have studied color imagery in *The King* if I hadn't suspected that that imagery had important uses, and I would never have discussed the color imagery if I hadn't become convinced that my suspicions were correct. In the course of writing an analysis, then, I need both to say what is in the work objectively (for example, the color green) and simultaneously to justify my taking the time to say it by urging on my reader a helpful view of what is really in the work (here green used to represent envy). One might assert that green represents in Bruna's narrative, as it sometimes does in other works, money or the fertility of vegetation; however, such an assertion would be unconvincing unless one could show that that understanding of the color helped make clear when, where, and why it is used in the narrative. In other words, explication and analysis, like exposition and argument, are normally two aspects of a single activity, an activity of observation, hypothesis construction, testing of hypotheses, rejecting or refining hypotheses, and so on. All of this honest inquiry is part of analysis as that term is used here.

One can also distinguish between intrinsic and extrinsic approaches to analysis. Intrinsic approaches aim to stay entirely within the work; this is an ideal of the NEW CRITICISM. Extrinsic approaches aim to use material outside the work to suggest clues to how one ought to analyze the work; this is an ideal of, say, HISTORICAL CRITICISM. While the distinction between intrinsic and extrinsic approaches is often helpful, one needs to recognize that it is not absolute. The analysis of color imagery in *The King* required intrinsic analysis based on the extrinsic knowledge that green can symbolize envy while it required rejecting the extrinsic knowledge that green can symbolize money. Of course, the extrinsic knowledge that Bruna is Dutch and that the Netherlands has money of varying colors may save us the time of searching for an intrinsic justification to accept or reject the green-symbolizes-money association. Under no circumstances can one ever confine analysis entirely within a single work since an understanding of any work requires extrinsic knowledge at least of the language of the time and place of its composition. For example, today "to lead a gay life" means to be homosexual; in England a hundred years ago, that same phrase meant "to be a prostitute." We would misread a text, then, if we did not bring extrinsic knowledge to our reading. On the other hand, no amount of extrinsic knowledge can determine how one must analyze a text. For example, Gertrude Stein's own public commitment to her companion Alice Toklas does not invalidate reading as SATIRIC the portrait of the mutual dependence of the title characters of Stein's "Miss Furr and Miss Skeene." In other words, all analysis is always to some extent intrinsic and to some extent extrinsic. Most academic essays about narrative, however, are primarily intrinsic, relying on the so-called common knowledge of the critic to supply most of the extrinsic knowledge that may be needed.

GENERALIZATION

Generalization uses the analyses, or parts of the analyses, of more than one work to accomplish one or more of three goals: a) to highlight a feature of a given text; b) to compare and contrast a small set of texts; c) to yield a richer understanding of the meaning, effects, or importance of a set of texts. Generalization, then, begins conceptually with the analyses of individual works but proceeds to refine those analyses by comparisons and to construct a critical argument based on the conclusions reached through those comparisons. In analyzing Poe's "The Purloined Letter" in isolation, one might easily focus, as does the second half of the narrative, on Dupin's cleverness, and never recognize consciously that that cleverness is made vivid by contrast with the mundane thinking of Dupin's nameless colleague. However, in Glaspell's "A Jury of Her Peers," the mundane thinking of the men is a major issue. Thus, an analysis of Glaspell's work might suggest that we pay further attention to the role of the NARRATOR in Poe's

narrative, and, indeed, such a return with freshened eyes reveals just how important the contrast between the minds of Dupin and his friend is in highlighting
Dupin's cleverness. An argument aimed primarily at urging those results on its
reader would illustrate the first goal of generalization, highlighting a feature of a
given text.

If we looked at the STRUCTURES of Poe's story and also of "The Adventure of
the Speckled Band" by Doyle, we would notice that the amount of space given to
the FALLING ACTION (the detective's explanation of how he solved the crime)
becomes a much smaller percentage of the total narrative. While analyzing one of
those narratives alone might suggest only that part of the point is to watch the
detective reveal his cleverness, looking at more than one suggests that that
revelation must be done differently for different audiences. We can see that Poe,
an early writer of SUSPENSE stories, needs to educate his audience about this
matching of minds with the criminal; hence, he takes his time in explaining
Dupin's thinking. On the other hand, Doyle clearly assumes a readership that
knows the rules of the GENRE and consequently compresses the revelation of
cleverness and shifts it toward the end of the narrative. An argument aimed
primarily at making clear how the genre has adapted to its increasingly sophisticated readership would illustrate the second goal of generalization, comparing
and contrasting a small set of texts.

If we looked at the plots of the Poe and Doyle stories singly, we might say
that they concerned the thwarting of a politician and the punishment of a
murderer. However, if we looked for a common element in the plots of both, we
might well arrive at the more general insight of W. H. Auden (1907–1973) that
the TALE OF THE GREAT DETECTIVE involves the psychological FANTASY that hidden
guilt will be revealed. Having recognized that common feature of PLOT, we would
easily arrive at the hypothesis that one attraction of detective fiction is the
fulfillment of that fantasy or the hypothesis that a thematic issue in this genre is a
discussion of justice. In fact, both this fantasy and this THEME represent widespread concerns; they underscore, for example, part of the attraction of the
religious notion of Judgment Day when God or God's delegate will award
blessings to the righteous and damnation to the guilty. Should we say then that
the Great Detective is the god of his narrative? If so, that helps explain why such
narratives, despite their concern with crime, make us feel secure as we read them:
they reflect a world with a just and present god. The power of this fantasy is
highlighted when contrasted with Glaspell's portrayal of the world. In her
insecure world justice can be achieved only if the oppressed take matters into
their own hands and have the luck to receive aid from a community of the
oppressed that allows their guilt to remain concealed. Glaspell's story, then,
suggests that the attractions of the Tale of the Great Detective are really aimed at
an audience willing to believe, at least for the time of reading, that the world is
fundamentally just. An argument like this would illustrate the third goal of
generalization, yielding a richer understanding of the meaning, effects, or importance of a whole set of texts, in this case the Tale of the Great Detective. It is now
apparent that these stories base their enormous appeal, at least in part, on an
artistic evasion of the complexities of our world.

Although there are many ways to arrive at generalizations, three are particularly noteworthy: contrast and comparison; genre criticism; and "ism" criticism.

In contrast and comparison, one examines the individual works within a set of works (two or more) to see what features are alike and what features are different. One then proceeds to construct hypotheses based on the notion that the likenesses (comparisons) reflect something important about all the works in the set while the differences (contrasts) reflect something important about the individual works in the set. For example, the discussion of structural compression and shifting of the Great Detective's explanation is an example of contrast and comparison. In genre criticism, one tries by an examination of features common to all or most of the works within the set to arrive at a generalization about the set. The discussion of the revelation of hidden guilt in the Tale of the Great Detective is an example of genre criticism. In "ism" criticism, one looks at a whole set of works, not for features common to those works alone, but for features that transcend that set of works. To identify such features, we borrow the insights of various "isms," such as Freudianism (see FREUDIAN CRITICISM), feminism, or Marxism (see MARXIST CRITICISM). One Freudian approach to the Tale of the Great Detective might hypothesize that the god-like protagonist is a father-figure in an Oedipal conflict. According to this theory, the antagonist would represent the rebellious child and the victim of the crime — the noblewoman whose letter is stolen in Poe's story and the endangered young woman in Doyle's — would represent the desired Other. Thus the work, rather than being a tragedy like the story of Oedipus, would be highlighted as a comedy in which social order is restored not through marriage but through the successful repression of the id (the criminal) by the superego (the detective). A feminist view might notice that in both cases a woman needs to turn to a man for protection, thus initiating an exploration of anti-feminist assumptions behind the Tale of the Great Detective. Glaspell also addressed these assumptions both in her portrayal of men and in having a female victim take action herself. If one took a Marxist approach, one might begin by noticing that in both Tales of the Great Detective events impel the protagonist, who is an independent member of the middle-class, to protect someone who is in danger of losing everything to someone who has or seeks great wealth. The role of capital in motivating injustice and allowing restitution then emerges as a common theme in this genre. Thus each "ism" prompts us to different but often complementary understandings of the works both as a set and individually. Ultimately, all forms of generalization — contrast and comparison, genre criticism, and "ism" criticism — rest on a foundation of analysis.

REVIEW

Reviews reveal enough about a work to justify the reviewer's assessment of the work but not enough to undercut the possible pleasure the reader of a review might have in reading the work. Reviews of books and movies are features of almost all newspapers and of most magazines. In the context of an academic course, a review is useful if one is hoping to persuade one's colleagues to read a book, as might be the case if reading groups are pursuing term-paper projects or if the course structure allows the class to decide on part of the syllabus, for example by supplementing *Stories* with a selection of NOVELS. If one wrote an analysis of the novel to be recommended or included a detailed analysis of that novel in a generalization essay, the future reading of the novel might be unduly limited by the conclusions of the writer. A review, whether or not it makes a positive recommendation, must try to allow its readers a full range for exploration of the reviewed work. After all, readers and reviewers may have different criteria for investing their time. But whether the review is positive or negative, the reviewer must demonstrate to his or her audience that the reviewer's own judgment is trustworthy. Therefore, a review must include some analysis, at least enough to display the reviewer's analytic skill. As the review proceeds, its analysis will, of course, make direct reference to the work. These references, in addition to supplying the occasion for demonstrating the reviewer's skill, also make explicit some aspect of the work itself. Therefore, the points under analysis in a review should be chosen to demonstrate the virtues and vices of the work. Unlike analysis and generalization essays, which are typically written with the assumption that their own readers are familiar with the works under discussion, reviews are written with the assumption that their readers are unfamiliar with the work. All three sorts of writing, however, reflect both Plato's notion of criticism as inspired by the work and inspiring readers and Aristotle's notion of criticism as based on analysis.

MEDITATION

Meditations stimulated by the text are less directly focused on the text than are the first three types of writing but they too should be based on analysis. If a reader of Glaspell's story used reference to it as a starting point for a discussion of the importance of economics in gaining equal rights for women, most of us would at least entertain the argument; however, if a reader of Glaspell's story used reference to it to argue against the education of women, those who understood the importance of the SATIRE of the men as narrow-minded would lose confidence in the reader and would be much less likely to entertain the argument. In a meditation, the stimulating text serves two roles, then: first, the reading of the text provides the occasion for discussing something upon which the text touches; second, the intelligent analysis of some feature of the text demonstrates the authority of the reader to take up the discussion. Meditation, too, then, requires fundamental analysis.

REFLECTION

Reflections of the text in a new work of fiction should also be based on careful analysis, even if that analysis is never explicitly mentioned in the reflection. An imitation, for example, a new work within the genre, is likely to fail unless the writer understands the genre well. Clearly the same is true for a PARODY of the work or an alternative ending or a sequel or a newly invented scene using the same characters. A reflection, then, is both an act of independent creation and an act of criticism. As an act of creation, a reflection must be judged by the same standards applied to any other work of art; as an act of criticism, a reflection must be judged not only by how well the writer understood the stimulating text but how well the writer helped other readers to understand it. In other words, a reflection actually takes on two tasks at once, and is therefore a particularly difficult type of writing. If it succeeds, however, it is a particularly rewarding type of writing. In this volume, the works of Coover, Broumas, and Hay are reflections of individual works while that by Moore is a reflection of a whole genre.

Components of the Writing Process

All of the components of the writing process are involved in each of the types of writing about narrative. Although each of those components may—and typically should—come into play repeatedly at various points in the process of writing, for the sake of discussion it is possible to consider them as an ordered set: knowing your audience and purpose, getting ideas, testing ideas, drafting, and revising.

KNOWING YOUR AUDIENCE AND PURPOSE

Knowing your audience and purpose is the most important component of the writing process; it controls how you write. If your purpose is to encourage someone to read a particular story, you should write a review, not an analysis. If your purpose is to help people see that Haycox's "Stage to Lordsburg" is powerful precisely because it is a WESTERN, then you should write a generalization rather than an analysis. If your purpose is to show an audience familiar with FAIRY TALES the weaknesses in them, then a reflection such as a parody might be the type of writing you should choose. If you know your audience is familiar with the text under discussion, you should not waste their time summarizing it; but if your goal is to help them realize the text's fine control of STYLE, you should quote directly a representative passage and then offer an analysis of it. If you want to use information that is not in the story and is not itself common knowledge, you will want to cite your source for that information in order to build your authority with your reader. If you know that your audience, your class for example, has knowledge of another text that bears on yours, you can make economical references to it. At every step of the writing process, then, you should constantly ask yourself: To whom am I writing? What is my purpose in writing? Does this sentence I am now writing or thinking of writing address that audience and help fulfill that purpose? You can ask these questions while you are getting your ideas for writing, while you are testing your ideas for writing, while you are drafting your ideas for writing, and while you are revising your writing.

GETTING IDEAS

Getting ideas for writing about narratives seems difficult to some people, but in truth there are many good sources to help us. The easiest is keeping a reading journal, which would, quite naturally, contain both your insights and your questions. Whether or not you have a reading journal, open the text and review it; memory is fallible, but the page is unchanging. Pay special attention to your own marginal notes. If some feature of the text seemed noteworthy to you as you read, then in all likelihood you can now figure out why it was noteworthy or else what you needed to discover in order to see that it was not noteworthy. A review of these marginal notes, like a review of a reading journal, is in part a review of your own reactions. If it is true that a narrative may be different on first and subsequent readings, then it is also in some sense true that a particular narrative exists only as it is read. In other words, a sensitivity to your own reactions is crucial to your full understanding of the narrative, and without understanding you cannot produce a polished piece of writing. But your reactions, of course, are limited to your own background, taste, and so on. It is entirely possible that you and a colleague will view a single narrative in two quite different ways. You may be impressed with the cleverness of the PLOT, your colleague with the unusual style; you may see the work as representing the oppression of women, your colleague may see the work as exploring the rigidity of social institutions. These are not necessarily incompatible views; allowing them to confront each other sparks thought. But even incompatible views help us understand the range of interpretive possibilities. Just as a review of your own reactions is useful, so is a discussion that elicits the reactions of others. In fact, discussion is particularly useful because it allows you to explore what others think of the narrative. If you believe their views need alteration (expansion, refinement, correction), you may have discovered the purpose for your writing.

Fundamental to the process of generating ideas about what to write is the process of questioning: questioning your own reactions, questioning the reactions of others, questioning the text. No question is so simple or silly that it isn't worth at least a moment's consideration, and no answer is so final that it does not deserve being examined by renewed questioning. I. A. Richards wrote in *Practical Criticism* (1929) that it is exactly at the point that a reader thinks an author has done something foolish that the reader ought to ask if perhaps the reading has been defective and seek to understand why the author committed the supposed offense. One can ask questions about every one of the elements of narrative: why does the plot require so many CHARACTERS? how is the SETTING important? what are the key IMAGES? why does the author use this particular narrative VIEWPOINT? and so on. Questions lead not only to answers but to more questions. A careful critic notes both questions and answers in the process of questioning. A review of those notes often suggests ideas: note, for example, that in one narrative both viewpoint and setting are involved in justifying violence; in another both the CHARACTERIZATION of the PROTAGONIST and the RESOLUTION leave the HEROINE'S role AMBIGUOUS; and so on.

While all thoughtful readers question themselves and the text, both as they are reading and afterwards, some questions cannot be answered merely by consulting one's own education, experience, or judgment. What exactly did "horror" mean when Conrad wrote "The horror! The horror!" in *Heart of Darkness*? What might a salamander traditionally SYMBOLIZE? Is there any special significance in Chaucer's naming a character "Nicholas"? "They also serve who only stand and wait" certainly sounds like a quotation, but what did it refer to in its original context? In such cases, the questions should be directed to reference books. The information in them will not usually address the text that motivated the question, but it may very well provide information whereby the questioner can construct a useful answer, an idea which can then be brought into the whole process of writing about narrative.

There are many fine reference works that are both rich in information and remarkably easy to use. Word dictionaries are excellent sources not only of spellings and meanings of common words but also of information about proper names of people and places. The *Oxford English Dictionary*, with its wealth of exemplary quotations, is particularly useful for showing the nuances of word meaning at different stages in the history of our language. A good book of word origins, like Joseph T. Shipley's *Origins of English Words: A Discursive Dictionary of Indo-European Roots*, helps reveal the whole range of meanings with which a word may be involved. Symbol dictionaries, like J. E. Cirlot's *A Dictionary of Symbols*, J. C. Cooper's *An Illustrated Encyclopedia of Traditional Symbols*, and Anthony S. Mercatante's *Facts on File Encyclopedia of World Mythology and*

Legend are arranged alphabetically and sometimes also well indexed to lead us right to a knowledge of what the number five may have meant, or the color blue, or fire, or emeralds. Writers write from within cultures; reference works like these give us fast access to crucial cultural facts. Quotation finders, like Bartlett's *Familiar Quotations*, which is general purpose, and Cruden's *Handy Concordance to the Bible*, which focuses on the best known version of the Bible, the so-called Authorized or King James version (1611), allow us to look up single words and locate the phrases from which they come. They also indicate the sources of those phrases so we can consult them in their original context. Mythology guides, like Mercatante's and also Donald Atwater's *The Penguin Dictionary of Saints*, H. R. Ellis Davidson's *Gods and Myths of Northern Europe*, John L. McKenzie's *Dictionary of the Bible*, H. J. Rose's *A Handbook of Greek Mythology*, and J. E. Zimmerman's *A Dictionary of Classical Mythology* are all provided with alphabetical apparatus so that one can discover quickly if a certain name (of a character, place, or even event) had some traditional significance. And for both broader issues of literary study and for quick descriptions of well known works, authors, characters, and historical matters, one can consult alphabetical literature handbooks such as Margaret Drabble's *Oxford Companion to English Literature*, N. G. L. Hammond and H. H. Scullard's *Oxford Companion to Classical Literature*, and James D. Hart's *Oxford Companion to American Literature*. Some of these works are available in inexpensive paperback editions and make good and convenient additions to any serious reader's library. Others are available only in hardback but are usually worth the investment. And all these works, and many others like them, are available in any reference library. Make it a habit to note your questions in your text or in your reading journal and then ask a reference librarian how to answer your questions. You will learn about our common heritage and also get new ideas for writing about narratives.

(By the way, "horror" meant in Conrad's time what it does now, but "the horrors" also referred to delirium and alcoholic depression, perhaps a clue about the character who utters those words. Salamanders are the traditional minor deities of fire in Western culture. "Old Nick" is another name for the Devil. And John Milton [1608–1674] was discussing religious faith when he wrote that "they also serve who only stand and wait" in a poem called "On His Blindness" which referred to himself.)

Normally one should write only about a work or set of works that has captured one's attention, offered a moving experience, raised a profound question, or revealed a special beauty. But sometimes we must consider writing about a work that leaves us flat, perhaps because it has been assigned, or perhaps because it is part of an exciting larger project that includes this work. What to do? At that moment, I often turn to the professionals—reviewers, popularizers, scholars—not so much because I hope they will offer me complete understanding—indeed, if they do, there will be nothing original that I can contribute to the discussion—but because I hope that their insights will spur me to new ideas. To find professional criticism, one can use the library catalog or special bibliographies such as the Modern Language Association's *MLA International Bibliography* for scholarly articles or the *Reader's Guide to Periodical Literature* for more popular articles. Again, a reference librarian can help you, and the help is well worth seeking because published criticism is as valuable as discussion for getting ideas. And while you usually can't have a conversation with a published critic, published criticism is usually more thoroughly developed than anyone's casual remarks.

TESTING IDEAS

Testing ideas is crucial no matter where one gets them. This is obvious in matters that hinge on knowledge extrinsic to the narrative, like the source of a quote or the date of an historical event, but it is just as true in matters dependent on intrinsic knowledge. Because a narrative is a complex whole, we can often see in a narrative just what we would like, as when we pick constellations from the heavens. Once we have an idea, we tend to see evidence in the narrative that confirms that idea. But while confirmation is gratifying, it may be misleading. To return to *The King*, it might be very appealing to see green there as symbolizing money. One could then argue that the green ladies want to retain their hold on money — and hence power — by controlling the king. But an honest testing of this idea would reveal that if that were their motivation, they would not try to find him a princess to marry — that is, they would not want to help him to grow up. By testing ideas against the text, or, in the case of generalization essays, against a body of texts, one can assess the value of an idea.

If an idea turns out to be correct, it usually will resonate through the narrative. Seeing Chaucer's Nicholas as a version of the Devil fits in with Chaucer's numerous ALLUSIONS to the Bible. But if an idea turns out to be incorrect, one should try to find out why. Some ideas, of course, are simply mistaken. A student I knew once based a long, sexually charged interpretation of a marriage poem (Edmund Spenser's "Epithalamion," 1594) on the poem's repeated APOSTROPHES to "Hymen." What the student did not know, but what the *Oxford English Dictionary* made clear, is that "hymen" first took on an anatomical meaning twenty years after the poem was written. At the time of its writing, all educated English people would have known that Hymen was the ancient Greek god of marriage. If your testing of an idea reveals that it is simply incorrect, put it aside. It is better for you to realize your mistake than for your reader to do the same.

On the other hand, an idea that is mistaken is often not absolutely mistaken but rather incomplete or distorted. If one thought the well in Atwood's "The Resplendent Quetzal" represented female fertility, as water often does, honest testing would note that the story, even though it is set in the fertile jungle, concerns characters who have a sterile relationship. Although one might then set aside this idea, that step would be premature. In fact, one should continue the process of questioning. Why is this water different from water that symbolizes fertility? It turns out that this water is rather stagnant. What has made it stagnant? Its shape, of course, but also what has been thrown in it through the ages. This is the well of memory, then. Is it only the well of memory or does it still have something to do with fertility? Since the two main characters are having trouble with their marriage, perhaps the well in part suggests that sterility arises where fertility might be expected when natural fertility is burdened by memory. What exactly are these burdens? We have hints, of course, in the thoughts of the characters, but the well itself is set in a jungle, an image of overwhelming fertility, a kind of fertility unavailable in our citified world. Yet our characters have made a pilgrimage here. Perhaps this suggests that the memory of the failure of marriage expectations is what now prevents the fertility of this couple. Suddenly we have a much better developed idea, one that does not so much abandon the first idea as rework it and test it so that we emerge with a new, more complex idea that offers a much richer understanding of the text. Surely this is an idea that any writer about narrative would prefer to have and what any reader would prefer to receive. Honest testing of ideas, then, lies at the heart of the development of one's critical skills and of one's knowledge of particular narratives.

DRAFTING

Drafting ideas in an essay becomes possible once one has tested them. In drafting, too, of course, one must keep in mind one's audience and purpose. Normally we do not write about narratives merely to confirm the opinions of our readers; rather, we write to help enrich peoples' understanding of a text. For example, you may believe — perhaps because of class discussion, perhaps because you once believed it yourself at an earlier stage of reading, or perhaps because a published critic has stated it — that many people think that Callaghan's "A Cap for Steve" is maudlin. You may want to argue, however, that it is in fact quite properly moving. Your argument might rest on the realism of the portrait of the dilemma of the father. If that is your plan, you probably ought to begin by referring to some feature of the text that is at the heart of precisely that matter: a quotation from the narrative about the role of money in our world or a paraphrase of the narrative's view of social class. Since you know you are writing for an audience that has seen the narrative as maudlin, your opening position might well acknowledge the emotional torment such matters yield. Once you and your audience share the same ground, you can then begin to show that this torment is not overblown but justified by the details of the text that make Steve's desire, small and childish as it may be, an emblem for all legitimate desire. In other words, not only should you begin your draft with a concrete reference to something in the narrative, but you should structure your argument to take into account your audience's reasonable reactions and consequently lead them to a richer and, in your view, more correct, understanding.

As you proceed to lead your reader, it is very important to maintain your own authority as a critic. If you make an assertion that is unclear, fix it. If you make an assertion that is shaky, test and revise it. And if you make an assertion that is correct, base it on data from the narrative or show how it applies in the narrative or both. To do that, you will want to refer to the narrative. In most written arguments, the relevant facts can only be reported. Astronomers and historians, after all, can't put planets and battles on their pages. But literary arguments can reproduce the actual evidence. Take advantage of that. Use paraphrase and quotation to make your assertions vivid and pointed. But include only enough evidence to make your point. Don't multiply examples needlessly and don't summarize for an audience familiar with the text; remind them.

In reproducing literary evidence, you should document your sources. Styles of documentation vary from discipline to discipline and from type of writing to type of writing. Newspaper reviews use quotation marks to set off exact quotes but almost never give page references or full bibliographic information about the work and edition quoted. The Modern Language Association publishes a small book, *A Guide to MLA Documentation*, giving the norms for documentation style in literary criticism. Many instructors will ask you to follow that style. Summaries of it can be found in standard college writing handbooks, and full guidance for that style and others can be found in a standard editorial reference work called *The Chicago Manual of Style*. In most courses, however, the key concern in documentation is maintaining simplicity and clarity: put enough information in your documentation so that your reader can find the source, but do not distract your reader with unnecessary information. This usually means that the once popular footnotes and endnotes will be abandoned in favor of parenthetical references in the text.

In the following opening of a critical essay, I have lettered the sentences for ease of reference:

(A) In the first paragraph of Sherwood Anderson's "Hands," the words "nervous" and "berry pickers" are each repeated. (B) The berry pickers are "youths and maidens" while the nervous character is "a fat little old man." (C) Already Anderson opposes youth to age, romance to isolation, fruit to infertility, and the capable hands of the "berry pickers" to the "nervous little hands" of the bald "Wing Biddlebaum." (D) If a bird may symbolize the spirit (Cirlot 25), a wing alone may symbolize an incomplete spirit. (E) The "town mystery" (p. 91), and the mystery for the reader, is whether Wing's incompleteness arises from a teacher's legitimate love of the young or, like the berry pickers' love of berries, from a desire to consume.

If we assume that this paragraph is written within the context of a course using *Stories*, all readers already have full bibliographic information about the source of the text. Therefore the reference in (A) to the story title and quotation location is quite adequate and carries over to (B) and (C). However, the reference in (E), because it is not to the place indicated, requires a page number. By listing only a page number, (E) implies that the page cited is from the work currently under discussion. The citation in (D), however, is to a completely different text. If you use other texts, it is customary to attach a list of "Works Cited" at the end of your essay. Such a list is arranged alphabetically by the last name of the author and, in the case of multiple works by a single author, alphabetically by title. For example:

Works Cited

Anderson, Sherwood. *Tar: A Midwest Childhood*. 1926. Ed. Ray Lewis White. Cleveland: Press of Case Western Reserve University, 1969.

——. *Winesburg, Ohio*. New York: Modern Library, 1919.

Cirlot, J. E. *A Dictionary of Symbols*. New York: Philosophical Library, 1962.

Taylor, Welford Dunaway. *Sherwood Anderson*. New York: F. Ungar, 1977.

Later references to Cirlot and Taylor would be made in the form in (E). References to the Anderson texts outside *Stories* should use, if unclear in context, a short form of the title, for example (Anderson, *Winesburg* 35), or, if the author is clear in context, simply (*Tar* 15). The point is always that the documentation should distract your reader as little as possible while indicating all necessary information. Note that in the "Works Cited," subsequent works by a single author do not repeat the author's name. In the case of works consulted in texts that are not from the original date of publication, the original date may be given to clarify the publishing history.

This opening is also a useful example of drafting a critical essay. Note how it begins with material that establishes the grounds for argument and offers concrete citation woven right into the logical discussion. (A) and (B) give factual reports that lead to a statement (C) of a tension in Anderson's first paragraph that, by implication, is crucial throughout Anderson's narrative. (D) brings in information from outside the narrative (common knowledge would have done the same thing here) in order to uncover one feature of that tension. (E) connects that tension with another part of the narrative and goes on to suggest the nature of the argument that the critic will pursue. The reader may not yet know it, but the critic has already used key terms, terms to which the essay can repeatedly refer so that they serve as a center as more and more argumentative weight accumulates. "Mystery" has its original meaning in the initiation of adepts into ancient religions, and the talk of "spirit" and the citation of the old-fashioned words "youths and maidens" also prepare us for a discussion of initiation and, perhaps, religion. Here the religion, with its "berry pickers," will turn out to be a sensuous one, but sensuousness does not necessarily invalidate a spiritual MOTIVE, or does it? This is the path the essay might now take. In other words, as Horace suggested of fiction writers, the critic begins "IN MEDIAS RES," in the middle of things. The "things" of the writer of a critical essay are the grounds for argument, the key terms, and AUTHORITY (as established by quotation, citation, paraphrase, and interpretation) that lead to a structured discussion.

Of course, only a very experienced writer who has already done a thorough analysis of the text is likely to produce a first draft like the paragraph above. But that's fine. Remember, nobody ever has to see your draft until you are ready. While speech may escape us thoughtlessly, writing does not. While writing may lack the directness and spontaneity of speech, it has the magnificent virtue of revisability. Indeed, some people say, "I don't know what I think until I write it." Writing is a process of discovery.

REVISING

Revising is a crucial part of the process of discovery in writing. You should always revise with the eyes of the potentially dissenting reader. Most essays are not written for the consenting reader. A consenting reader already knows what we want to impart; there is no gain in "convincing" the consenting reader. And most essays are not written for the rigidly dissenting reader. The rigidly dissenting reader already knows something else and is committed to believing it; there is no gain in knocking your head against a stone wall. Most essays are written for potentially dissenting readers, readers who attend to what is written but question it not because they are committed to finding fault but because they are curiously testing to see if there is fault to be found or truth. Such readers will want to see an assertion supported with precise detail or an idea used to show how a text really works. Once you have a draft, you should of course copyedit it, fixing errors of spelling and grammar, clarifying unintentional ambiguities, and so on. But copyediting is not revising. Copyediting aims to make the language say properly what you meant it to say. Revising is another type of questioning in which you probe what you wrote in order to see if it holds up to close examination. Just as ideas develop, drafts develop. It is, again, much better for you to adopt the role of potentially dissenting reader and discover a weakness—and correct it by refinement, modification, or rejection—than to have your actual reader discover the weakness and reject your argument. Be prepared to revise ruthlessly: changing ideas, settling on new key terms, reorganizing, selecting different key passages for analysis, and so on. Revising is not only rereading what you think, but discovering what you think. Copyediting is a high-level job of housekeeping; revision is a high-level job of invention. Good writers do both.

Any literate person can read a narrative, but only a good reader can reap the full pleasure from a complex work of written art. Any literate person can write a few sentences about a narrative, but only a good writer can impart a sense of the importance of a work of written art. The components of the writing process, no matter what type of writing about narrative you choose, interpenetrate and repeat from first impulse through polished product. We must constantly keep audience and purpose in mind; we must constantly seek ideas; we must constantly test ideas; we must constantly draft ideas in specific words; and we must constantly revise those words with the eyes of the potentially dissenting reader until we have discovered for ourselves the virtues and importance of our argument and imparted those discoveries to others. In this way, the critic fulfills both the inspirational goals of Plato and the scientific goals of Aristotle. Writing about narratives is one way to participate in the finest works of human culture.

Sample Student Essays

The following two essays are provided as examples of good student writing, but they are very different. You should read these with care at least three times. First, read them in order to see what they argue, how they structure and support their arguments, and how they weave their evidence into their arguments. Second, read them in order to see where their arguments may be mistaken or fail to account for important matters or demonstrate imbalance. Third, read them with an eye toward improving them through revision. These are quite good essays, and may serve as reliable examples of proper citation and punctuation, but they are by no means perfect or inevitable essays; they can be improved or changed by those with different viewpoints. These conditions are true for both the first essay that deals with only one work and the second that deals with two. Use these essays to sharpen your own writing and editorial skills.

SAMPLE PAPER #1
Truth, Justice, and Religion in Borges' ''Emma Zunz''

In ''Emma Zunz'' by Jorge Luis Borges, the title character not only avenges her father by murdering the man who drove him to suicide, but she stages a rape so that she will go unpunished. While we might suppose that a murderer's own instinct for self-preservation would be an adequate explanation for a desire to evade punishment, in this story the narrator tells us that Emma submitted to her ''hellish experience'' (p. 160) of intercourse ''not out of fear [of punishment] but because of being an instrument of Justice'' (p. 162). This is a strikingly definite report coming from a narrator who often seems not to know precisely what has happened: ''Perhaps . . . she saw herself multiplied in mirrors . . .'' (p. 160) and ''It is my belief that . . . '' (p. 161). The word ''justice'' occurs often in the story, for example, when Emma acts the role of prostitute ''she served [the sailor] for pleasure whereas he served her for justice'' (p. 161). While we may want Emma to get vengeance and may even want her to escape punishment, in the terms of the story, is it *just* that she go unpunished?

The last paragraph of the story seems to express a paradox:

> Actually, [her] story *was* incredible, but it impressed everyone because substantially it was true. True was Emma Zunz' tone, true was her shame, true was her hate. True also was the outrage she had suffered: only the circumstances were false, the time, and one or two proper names.

Normally we think of ''circumstances,'' ''time,'' and ''proper names'' as matters of fact and, as the *Random House Dictionary* says, ''true'' means ''conforming to . . . fact.'' But the dictionary also says that ''true'' means ''sincere.'' Borges has created a situation in which truth conflicts with itself. Emma creates this conflict in order to allow ''the Justice of God to triumph over human justice'' (p. 162).

On a careful reading, we can find a lot in this story that has to do with God. Emma had never told anyone about her father's innocence for fear of their ''profane incredulity'' (p. 160) and the narrator omits some details because to tell them would be ''perhaps unrighteous'' (p. 160). According to the dictionary, her father's name, Emmanuel, is another name for Jesus, and her name, Emma, links her to her father linguistically. According to the *New Cassell's German Dictionary*, ''Loewen'' means ''lions'' and ''thal'' means ''valley,'' so when she goes to meet Loewenthal, she is going to ''the valley of lions,'' perhaps like Daniel entering the lions' den. This parallel is probably not coincidental.

In the Bible story (Daniel 6), Daniel is the trusted administrator of king Darius, but the king is tricked by those who hate Daniel into issuing a decree forbidding prayer for thirty days. This decree then becomes ''true, according to the law of the Medes and Persians, which altereth not'' (Daniel 6:12). When Daniel is caught praying anyway, the king seals him in the lions' den. But Daniel goes unhurt, and

this proves to the king that Daniel's God is the true god, so
Daniel is released and the unalterable law is altered anyway.

In Borges's modern story, Emma achieves her victory over
Loewenthal's false ''piety'' (p. 161) not by praying to God
but by telling her story to the police. However, if we see the
action of ''Emma Zunz,'' set in ''time outside of time''
(p. 161), as being like a Bible story, then we can accept that
justice truly is served. Borges seems to be suggesting that
even in a world in which God allows evil to occur, He gives
resourceful people the ability to take actions that will
preserve His justice. The paradox of the last paragraph is
resolved if we believe that Emma's real triumph indeed is not
in vengeance but, like Daniel, in going free.

SAMPLE PAPER #2
The Power of Revision in Broumas and Borges

In both ''Little Red Riding Hood'' by Olga Broumas and
''Emma Zunz'' by Jorge Luis Borges, the main characters
present stories that significantly revise the ones we expect
to hear. In the case of Broumas, the speaker, unlike her
namesake in the Grimm brothers' tale, ''kept/ to the road,
kept/ the hood secret, kept what it sheathed more/ secret
still'' (p. 175). In the case of Borges, we see the
protagonist commit a premeditated murder but then convince
everyone that she acted in self-defense during a rape. In
both works, the success or failure of the main character is
dependent on the power of a story.

Broumas makes clear that both the red hood and food
symbolize female sexuality. Of her bloody birth, she says,

> . . . Dressed in my red hood, howling, I went—
>
> evading
> the white-clad doctor and his fancy claims: microscope,
> stethoscope, scalpel, all
> the better to see with, to hear,
> and to eat-straight from your hollowed basket
> into the midwife's skirts.

By this allusion to the wolf's famous lines, Broumas's
speaker equates even the most helpful men, like doctors,
with sexual predators. There is no helpful hunter in
Broumas's version of the story because the speaker never
strays from the path, never gets eaten, and therefore never
needs help. However, the consequence of the speaker, unlike
the Grimms' character, accepting her mother's tale of
warning, is that, unlike her mother, Broumas's speaker never
has any child of her own. While her ''flower-gathering/

sisters'' may be ''lost,'' they at least had flowers. Now with her mother gone from the external world but still defining the ''landscape/ of my heart,'' the speaker, without sister or daughter, ''grow[s] old, old.''

Like Broumas's speaker, Emma Zunz is devoted to an absent parent and is herself childless. But unlike Broumas's speaker, Emma decides to do ''the hideous thing . . . that her father had done to her mother'' (p. 161). By prostituting herself, Emma creates the evidence, both emotional and physical, that will corroborate her tale of self-defense. One of the reasons that her deception works is that her tale is, in a way, an old story, ''substantially true . . . [except that] the circumstances were false, the time, and one or two proper names'' (p. 162). People are ready to believe her story because they already believe it, just as Broumas's speaker believed her mother's old tale of pain because she (''howling'') was born in pain.

Broumas's speaker says that the forceps used at her birth

> might . . . have accomplished
> what you and that good woman [the midwife] failed
> in all these years to do: cramp
> me between the temples, hobble
> my baby feet.

That is, the speaker claims to be free in her mind and in her actions, as if she could walk off the path. But her lament clearly shows that she is deceiving only herself; she ''kept'' the path and now regrets it. Emma, on the other hand, deceives everyone but herself.

If we compare these two characters and their stories, we see that although the women are equally revolted by men, the one who has the courage to take physical action is also the one who is able to make believable her own version of an ancient story. The power of revision belongs to those with the power of action. And in both stories, it seems, the act of revision is fundamental to a woman defining her place in the world.

Filmography

Film is a NARRATIVE medium. The adaptation of a STORY from the page to the screen is simultaneously an act of invention and an act of CRITICISM. Just as discussing a story with someone who has read it critically can sharpen and even change one's perceptions of that story, so can viewing a film version of that story. The following filmography lists films made from works collected in *Stories*. The entries are arranged in their order in the main Contents, that is, first the anonymous materials (the Bible in this case) and then others alphabetically by the author of the original story. Each entry lists the name of the story in capital letters and the name of the movie (often not the same) in boldface letters. Where multiple film versions exist, they are entered for the convenience of those who care to make film comparisons. Other information about running time, color or black-and-white, year of production, director, producer, screenwriter, and cast is provided when possible. In almost all entries a distributor has also been listed in case the film is unavailable in a local library or video store. The addresses of the distributors follow the listing of the films.

Films

BIBLE
The Bible . . . In the Beginning
174 min.　color　1966
Director: John Huston
Producer: Twentieth-Century Fox
Screenplay: Christopher Fry, Jonathan Griffin, Ivo Perilli, Vittorio Bonicelli
Cast: Michael Parks, Ulla Bergryd, John Huston, George C. Scott, Richard Harris
Distributor: CBS/Fox Home Video

BIBLE
Jonah and the Great Fish
6 min.　color　1987
Distributor: Weston Woods

James Agee, A MOTHER'S TALE
A Mother's Tale
18 min.　color　1975
Director: Rex Goff
Producer: American Film Institute
Cast: Maureen Stapleton and Orson Welles provide off-screen voices.
Distributor: Learning Corporation of America

Ryunosuke Akutagawa, IN A GROVE
Rashomon
83 min.　b&w　1950
Director: Akira Kurosawa
Producer: Daiei Film Studios
Screenplay: Akira Kurosawa, Shinobu Hashimoto
Cast: Toshiro Mifune, Machiko Kyo, Masayuki Mori

Distributor: Nelson Entertainment, Inc.
Taken from "In a Grove" and "Rashomon," both by Akutagawa

Ambrose Bierce, AN OCCURRENCE AT OWL CREEK BRIDGE
An Occurrence at Owl Creek Bridge
27 min.　b&w　1964
Director and screenplay: Robert Enrico
Producer: Marcel Ichac & Paul Deroubaix
Cast: Roger Jacqet, Anne Cornaly, Anker Larsen
Distributor: Video Yesteryear; Facets Multimedia

John Cheever, THE SWIMMER
The Swimmer
94 min.　color　1968
Director: Frank Perry
Producer: Columbia Pictures
Screenplay: Eleanor Perry
Cast: Burt Lancaster, Janet Landgard, Janice Rule
Distributor: Goodtimes/Kids Klassics Distribution Corporation

Geoffrey Chaucer, THE MILLER'S TALE
The Canterbury Tales
109 min.　color　1971
Director and Screenplay: Pier Paolo Pasolini
Producer: United Artists/PEA/PAA
Cast: Hugh Griffith, Pier Paolo Pasolini, Laura Betti
Distributor: Water Bearer Films

Joseph Conrad, HEART OF DARKNESS
Apocalyse Now
150 min. color 1979
Director: Francis Ford Coppola
Producer: Zoetrope Studios
Screenplay: John Milius, Francis Ford
    Coppola
Cast: Martin Sheen, Marlon Brando,
    Robert Duvall
Distributor: Paramount Home Video

Stephen Crane, THE BLUE HOTEL
The Blue Hotel
54 min. color 1977
Director: Jan Kadar
Producer: Perspective Films/Learning in
    Focus
Screenplay: Harry M. Petrakis
Distributor: Coronet/MTI Film & Video
From the "American Short Story" series.

Arthur Conan Doyle, THE
    ADVENTURE OF THE SPECKLED
    BAND
The Speckled Band
90 min. b&w 1931
Director: Jack Raymond
Producer: First Division Pictures
Screenplay: W.P. Lipscomb
Cast: Raymond Massey, Lyn Harding,
    Anthole Stewart
Distributor: Video Yesteryear

William Faulkner, BARN BURNING
Barn Burning
41 min. color 1979
Director: Peter Werner
Producer: Perspective Films/Learning in
    Focus
Screenplay: Horton Foote
Cast: Tommy Lee Jones, Shawn
    Whittington
Distributor: Monterey Home
    Video/Coronet
From the "American Short Story" series.

F. Scott Fitzgerald, BABYLON
    REVISITED
The Last Time I Saw Paris
116 min. color 1954
Director: Richard Brooks
Producer: Metro-Goldwyn-Mayer (MGM)

Screenplay: Julius J. and Philip G. Epstein
    and Richard Brooks
Cast: Elizabeth Taylor, Van Johnson,
    Walter Pidgeon, Donna Reed, Eva
    Gabor
Distributor: MGM/UA Home Video

Charlotte Perkins Gilman, THE
    YELLOW WALL-PAPER
The Yellow Wallpaper
14 min. color 1977
Director and script: Marie Ashton
Distributor: Women Make Movies
**The Yellow Wallpaper by Charlotte
    Perkins Gilman**
15 min. color 1978
Producer: International Instructional
    Television Cooperative
Distributor: Indiana University

Susan Glaspell, A JURY OF HER
    PEERS
A Jury of Her Peers
30 min. color 1980
Director: Sally Heckel
Producer: Texture Films
Cast: Diane de Lorian, Dorothy
    Lancaster
Distributor: Texture films
Trifles
22 min. b&w 1979
Director: Martha Moran
Producer: Barr Productions
Distributor: Centre Films

Nikolai Gogol, THE OVERCOAT
The Overcoat
73 min. b&w 1959
Director: Alexei Batalov
Producer: Lenfilm Studios
Screenplay: L. Solovyov
Distributor: International Home Video;
    Facets Multimedia
Cast: Roland Bykov, Yuri Tolubeyev

Nadine Gordimer, SIX FEET OF THE
    COUNTRY
Six Feet of the Country
29 min. color 1977
Director: Lynton Stephenson
Producer: Perspective Films
Screenplay: Barney Simon
Distributor: Learning Corp of America

Jakob and Wilhelm Grimm, RAPUNZEL
Rapunzel
11 min. color 1955
Director and animator: Ray Harryhausen
Distributor: Phoenix/BFA Films
Rapunzel
60 min. color 1983
Producer: Shelley Duvall
Cast: Jeff Bridges, Gena Rowlands
Distributor: CBS/Fox Home Video
From the "Faerie Tale Theatre"
Rapunzel, Rapunzel
15 min. color 1988
Producer and Distributor: Davenport
Films

Francis Bret Harte, THE OUTCASTS
OF POKER FLAT
Man Hunt
61 min. b&w 1931
Director: William Clemens
Producer: Pictures Comp.
Cast: Ricardo Cortaz, Marguerite
Churchill
Outcasts of Poker Flat
81 min. b&w 1952
Director: Joseph Newman
Producer: 20th Century Fox
Screenplay: Edmund H. North
Cast: Dale Robertson, Anne Baxter,
Miriam Hopkins
Distributor: Budget Films

Nathaniel Hawthorne, RAPPACCINI'S
DAUGHTER
Rappaccini's Daughter
57 min. color 1979
Director: Dexso Magyar
Producer: Learning in Focus
Screenplay: Herbert Hartis
Cast: Kathleen Beller, Kris Tabori,
Michael Egan
Distributor: Coronet/MTI Film & Video
Twice Told Tales
119 min. color 1963
Director: Sidney Kalkow
Producer: United Artists
Screenplay: Robert E. Kent
Cast: Vincent Price, Sebastian Cabot,
Brett Halsey
Distributor: MGM/UA Home Video

Horror trilogy based on "Dr.
Heidegger's Experiment,"
"Rappaccini's Daughter," and "The
House of the Seven Gables."

Nathaniel Hawthorne, YOUNG
GOODMAN BROWN
Young Goodman Brown
30 min. color 1972
Director and Producer: Donald Fox
Distributor: Pyramid Film & Video

Ernest Haycox, STAGE TO
LORDSBURG
Stagecoach
114 min. b&w 1939
Director: John Ford
Producer: United Artists
Screenplay: Dudley Nichols
Cast: John Wayne, Claire Trevor,
Thomas Mitchell
Distributor: Vestron Video
Stagecoach
115 min. color 1966
Director: Gordon Douglas
Producer: Twentieth-Century Fox
Screenplay: Joseph Landon
Cast: Ann-Margaret, Alex Cord, Bing
Crosby, Red Buttons
Distributor: Films Inc.
Stagecoach
95 min. color 1986
Director: Ted Post
Producer: Heritage Entertainment
Cast: Kris Kristofferson, John
Schneider, Elizabeth Ashley, Mary
Crosby
Distributor: Vidmark Entertainment

Henry James, THE TURN OF THE
SCREW
The Innocents
100 min. b&w 1961
Director: Jack Clayton
Producer: Twentieth-Century Fox
Screenplay: William Archibald &
Truman Capote; adaptation:
Archibald & John Mortimer
Cast: Deborah Kerr, Michael Redgrave,
Peter Wyngarde, Martin Stephens,
Pamela Franklin
Distributor: Films Inc.

Sarah Orne Jewett, A WHITE HERON
The White Heron
26 min. color 1978
Director and screenplay: Jane Morrison
Producer: Learning Corporation of
America
Cast: Ruth Rogers, Gary Stine, Mary
Pike
Distributor: Learning Corporation of
America

James Joyce, THE DEAD
The Dead
83 min. color 1987
Director: John Huston
Producer: Vestron Pictures
Screenplay: Tony Huston
Cast: Angelica Huston, Donal McCann
Distributor: Vestron Video

D. H. Lawrence, THE ROCKING-
HORSE WINNER
The Rocking-Horse Winner
91 min. b&w 1949
Director and Screenplay: Anthony
Pelissier
Producer: Rank/Two Cities Films
Cast: John Mills, Valerie Hobson
Distributor: Voyager Company
The Rocking-Horse Winner
30 min. color 1977
Director: Peter Medak
Producer: Learning Corporation of
America
Screenplay: Julian Bond
Cast: Kenneth More
Distributor: Learning Corporation of
America

Jack London, TO BUILD A FIRE
To Build a Fire
56 min. color 1969
Director: David Cobham
Cast: Ian Hogg
Narrated by Orson Welles
Distributor: Facets Multimedia

Herman Melville, BARTLEBY THE
SCRIVENER
Bartleby
28 min. color 1969
Producer: Encyclopedia Britanica
Distributor: Britannica Educational
Corporation

Bartleby
78 min. color 1971
Director: Anthony Friedmann
Producer: British Lion
Screenplay: Rodney Carr-Smith
Cast: Paul Scofield, John McEnery
Distributor: Kultur Home Video

Yukio Mishima, PATRIOTISM
Rite of Love and Death
21 min. b&w 1968
Producer, Director, Script, Cast: Yukio
Mishima
Distributor: Washington State
University

Flannery O'Connor, GOOD
COUNTRY PEOPLE
Good Country People
32 min. color 1975
Director, Producer and Distributor: Jeff
Jackson

Tillie Olsen, I STAND HERE
IRONING
Ironing
15 min. b&w 1976
Director: Lynne Conroy
Producer: Thalia Films
**I Stand Here Ironing: A Personal
Interpretation of I Stand Here
Ironing by Tillie Olsen**
20 min. color (w/ b&w
sequences) 1979
Director: Midge Mackenzie
Producer: Film Boston, Cambridge, MA
Distributor: Women Make Movies
Also known as: **Motherlove**

Charles Perrault, LITTLE RED
RIDING HOOD
Little Red Riding Hood
9 min. color 1958
Director: Ray Harryhausen
Distributor: Phoenix/BFA Films
Little Red Riding Hood
60 min. color 1984
Director: Graeme Clifford
Producer: Shelley Duvall
Cast: Mary Steenburgen, Malcolm
McDowell
Distributor: CBS/Fox Home Video

Edgar Allan Poe, THE BLACK CAT
The Black Cat
65 min. b&w 1934
Director: Edgar Ulmer
Producer: Universal
Cast: Boris Karloff, Bela Lugosi
Distributor: MCA/Universal Home
  Video
Loose adaptation of the Poe story.
The Black Cat
70 min. b&w 1941
Director: Albert S. Rosell
Producer: Universal
Screenplay: Robert Lees, Fred Rinaldo,
  Eric Taylor and Robert Neville
Cast: Basil Rathbone, Bela Lugosi
Loose adaptation of the Poe story.
Tales of Terror
90 min. color 1961
Director: Roger Corman
Producer: American International
Screenplay: Richard Matheson
Cast: Vincent Price, Peter Lorre, Basil
  Rathbone, Debra Paget
Distributor: Warner Home Video
Adaptation of three stories by Poe:
  "The Black Cat," "The Facts in the
  Case of M. Valdemar," and
  "Morella."

Edgar Allan Poe, THE FACTS IN
  THE CASE OF M. VALDEMAR
Tales of Terror
90 min. color 1961
Director: Roger Corman
Producer: American International
Screenplay: Richard Matheson
Cast: Vincent Price, Peter Lorre, Basil
  Rathbone, Debra Paget
Distributor: Warner Home Video

Isaac Bashevis Singer, YENTL THE
  YESHIVA BOY
Yentl
134 min. color 1983
Director: Barbra Streisand
Producer: United Artists
Screenplay: Jack Rosenthal, Barbra
  Streisand
Cast: Barbra Streisand, Mandy Patinkin,
  Amy Irving
Distributor: MGM/UA Home Video

John Steinbeck, THE
  CHRYSANTHEMUMS
The Chrysanthemums
23 min. color 1989
Producers: Mac and Ava Motion Pictures
Distributor: Pyramid Film & Video

James Thurber, THE SECRET LIFE
  OF WALTER MITTY
The Secret Life of Walter Mitty
110 min. color 1947
Director: Norman Z. MacLeod
Producer: Samuel Goldwyn Productions
Screenplay: Ken Englund, Everett
  Freeman
Cast: Danny Kaye, Virginia Mayo, Boris
  Karloff
Distributor: Nelson Entertainment

Mark Twain, THE DIARY OF ADAM
  AND EVE
The Diary of Adam and Eve
15 min. color 1978
From the "Short Stories" series.
Producer: International Instructional
  Television Cooperative
Distributor: Indiana University
The Diary
28 min. color 1981
Producer and Director: Will Vinton
Adaptation of the story done in
  "claymation."
Distributor: Visucom Productions

H. G. Wells, THE TIME MACHINE
The Time Machine
103 min. color 1960
Director: George Pal
Producer: MGM
Screenplay: David Duncan
Cast: Rod Taylor, Yvette Mimieux,
  Alan Young
Distributor: MGM/UA Home Video

Richard Wright, THE MAN WHO
  WAS ALMOST A MAN
Almos' a Man
39 min. color 1977
Director: Stan Lathan
Producer: Learning in Focus
Screenplay: Leslie Lee
Cast: LeVar Burton
Distributor: Coronet/MTI Film & Video

Distributors

Britannica Films
310 South Michigan Ave
Chicago, IL 60604
312-347-7958

CBS/Fox Home Video
1211 Avenue of the Americas
New York, NY 10036
800-222-7369

Coronet/MTI
108 Wilmot Road
Deerfield, IL 60015
800-621-2131

Davenport Films
Route 1
Box 527
Delaplane, VA 22025
703-592-3701

Facets Multimedia
1517 West Fullerton Ave.
Chicago, IL 60614
312-281-9075

Films Inc
5547 N. Ravenswood Ave
Chicago, IL 60640
800-323-4222 (ext. 46.)

Goodtimes/Kids Klassics
401 Fifth Ave.
New York, NY 10016
212-889-0044

Indiana University Audio-Visual Center
Bloomington, IN 47405
812-335-8087

Kultur Home Video
121 Highway 36
West Long Branch, NJ 07764
800-458-5887

Learning Corporation of America
108 Wilmot Road
Deerfield, IL 60015
800-621-2131

MCA/Universal Home Video
70 Universal City Plaza
Universal City, CA 91608
818-777-4300

MGM/UA Home Video
8670 Wilshire
Beverly Hills, CA 90211
213-967-2296

Monterey Home Video
5142 North Clareton Street
Suite 270
Agoura Hills, CA 91301
818-597-0047

Nelson Entertainment
335 North Maple Drive
Suite 350
Beverly Hills, CA 90210
213-285-6000

Paramount Home Video
5555 Melrose Ave
Hollywood, CA 90038
213-956-5000

Phoenix/BFA
468 Park Ave South
800-221-1274

Pyramid Films & Video
Box 1048
Santa Monica, CA 90405
800-421-2304

Texture Films
see Films Inc.

Vestron Video
15400 Sherman Way
Suite 500
Van Nuys, CA 91406
818-908-0303

Video Yesteryear
Box C
Sandy Hook, CT 06482
800-243-0987 (ext. 49)

Visucom Productions
P.O. Box 5472
Redwood City, CA 94063
415-364-5566

Voyager Company
1351 Pacific Coast Highway
Santa Monica, CA 90401
800-446-2001

Warner Home Video
4000 Warner Boulevard
Burbank, CA 91522
818-954-6000

Washington State University
Instructional Media Services
Pullman, WA 99164
800-999-1765

Water Bearer Films
205 West End Ave.
Suite 24H
New York, NY 10023
212-580-8185

Weston Woods
389 Newtown Turnpike
Weston, CT 06883
800-243-5020

Women Make Movies
225 Lafayette Street
Suite 212
New York, NY 10012
212-925-0606

A Glossary of Literary Terms[1,2]

Abstract terms: Terms that describe or denote ideas abstracted (drawn) from examination of many instances. "Beauty" is an abstract term. By contrast, **concrete terms** refer to specific instances. The dark vitality of Beatrice in Hawthorne's "Rappaccini's Daughter" and the soft curves of the arm in Kawabata's "One Arm" excite romance and aestheticism respectively. **General terms** refer to classes of phenomena (colors, things, people, emotions, ideas, and so on), whether or not they are abstractions, while **specific terms** refer to the elements within those classes. The general term GREAT DETECTIVE includes Poe's Dupin and Doyle's Sherlock Holmes as specific examples. Thus an abstract term is more general than a concrete term, but not all general terms are abstract.

Action: In general, the events, both physical and psychological, in a narrative. The chronological sequence of these events is the **story**; the sequence of these events as they are narrated is the PLOT. Occasionally "action" refers to the overall story. In this sense, action is almost synonymous with THEME. The action of Wright's "The Man Who Was Almost a Man" is the struggle to grow up. See also SPEECH ACTS, EN: The Narrative Situation, and EN: Structure.

Aesthetic: Having to do with art, the beautiful, or human reactions to the artistic and/or the beautiful. See EN: Aesthetic Virtues.

Allegory: In general, a DIDACTIC work of art in which some or all of the CHARACTERS, SETTINGS, and even ACTIONS serve as one-to-one representations of ABSTRACT TERMS. In the story of The Fall in Genesis, Adam and Eve represent all humanity; the garden represents perfect happiness; the serpent represents temptation; and so on. The actions show surrender to temptation leading to separation from perfect happiness. Note that not all aspects of an allegory are to be read allegorically. We are not supposed to conclude from The Fall that a man should never accept the arguments of his wife. See also ALLUSION, FABLE, PARABLE, and SYMBOL.

Allusion: From Latin for "touching lightly on a subject"; a brief reference, explicit or implicit, to a real or imaginary person, place, event, or literary work with which the reader is supposed to be familiar: "She worked on Wall Street" used not to give the address of her workplace but to indicate that her occupation had to do with finance; "He had obviously been eating his spinach" to indicate that, like Popeye, he was very strong. Successful allusion, which may be very subtle, ECONOMICALLY enriches the meaning of a work. In Harlan Ellison's "I Have No Mouth And I Must Scream," the powerful, singular, vengeful computer

---

[1](A) **Boldface** indicates entries in which a term is at least partially defined.

(B) SMALLCAPS within an entry indicate terms that have their own entries in this Glossary.

(C) **BOLDFACE SMALLCAPS** within an entry indicate terms that are at least partially defined in that entry and have of their own entries in this Glossary.

[2]References in the form "EN: The Narrative Situation" refer to the essay in this volume called "The Elements of Narrative" and to one or more of its nine named sections.

imprisoning the human CHARACTERS is named AM which may well call to mind Exodus 3:14, "And God said unto Moses, I AM THAT I AM." At that point in Exodus, God is instructing Moses to lead the Israelites out of captivity. That AM imprisons rather than releases its people casts the light of IRONY on the relation between divine and technological power. See EPONYM.

Ambiguity: The condition of a word, phrase, event, or situation that may be understood as having one of two or more mutually exclusive meanings. The sentence "Beware of flying airplanes" is ambiguous. The process of determining which of the meanings is appropriate is called **disambiguation.** "So don't become a pilot" and "So keep your eyes on the sky" each disambiguates the earlier sentence but in different ways. Intentional ambiguity that is used to enrich a work, as in Akutagawa's "In a Grove," is an AESTHETIC virtue; unintentional ambiguity that creates mere confusion is one source of *vagueness*, an aesthetic vice. Ambiguity is one type of PLURISIGNIFICATION. See also AMBIVALENCE.

Ambivalence: Simultaneous and contradictory feelings or attitudes toward a person, place, object, or situation. Glasgow's "A Point in Morals" concerns the difficulty of trusting our judgments when we feel ambivalence. Since clearly people can maintain ambivalent feelings or attitudes, though these are contradictory, they are not mutually exclusive. Thus ambivalence, a state of contradictory feelings or attitudes, should not be confused with AMBIGUITY, a condition of mutually exclusive meanings.

Anachronism: A CHARACTER, thing, or event chronologically out of place. A jet plane would be anachronistic in a WESTERN. In *The Time Machine*, Wells's Time Traveller is an anachronism in the future. Kafka's "A Common Confusion" uses anachronism to reinforce its THEME of the difficulties inherent in the social construction of reality. See AUTHORITY.

Anagnorisis: A crucial, usually sudden, recognition or discovery; literally (from Greek), "a loss of ignorance." The plot of Chopin's "Désirée's Baby" has a particularly powerful anagnorisis. Anagnorisis often leads to **peripeteia,** a radical shift in ACTION, and to REVERSAL.

Anecdote: A short NARRATIVE, often a single EPISODE of an interesting, amusing, or biographical incident. Etymologically, anecdote means "unpublished" and referred originally to those details of the private lives of great personages that would not be included in sober histories or biographies. While a SHORT STORY could be an anecdote, most short stories are more complex, comprising an arrangement of episodes and offering more than mere gossip value.

Anima/animus: See JUNGIAN CRITICISM.

Antagonist: The main CHARACTER opposing the PROTAGONIST; often the DEUTERAGONIST.

Anticlimax: A sudden shift from the main, important, or serious matter of a discourse to the irrelevant, trivial, or ludicrous. "A conscientious police officer will always uphold the law and fill out forms." When anticlimax is unintentional, it is an aesthetic vice. When it is intentional, as in the last paragraph of Wells's "The Star," it may create efficiently such RHETORICAL effects as IRONY.

Antihero: A PROTAGONIST many of whose traits oppose those of the traditional HERO/HEROINE. He or she may be despicable rather than admirable, insecure rather than confident, rash rather than wise, cowardly rather than brave, and so on. An IMPLIED AUTHOR may use an antihero in order to examine those negative qualities in an individual (as in Tanizaki's "The Thief") or in order to show the difficulty of living a classically heroic life in our more modern world (as in Crane's "The Blue Hotel").

Antistory (Antinovel): A NARRATIVE that attempts to convey reality objectively or directly by superficially dispensing with the traditional elements of PLOT, CHARACTER, and so on, relying instead on fragments of uninterrupted observations, speech, and description, as in Lorrie Moore's "How."

Apostrophe: The RHETORICAL device of addressing an absent character or thing as if it were a present person. Apostrophizing a thing is a variety of PERSONIFICATION.

Archetype: An IMAGE, MOTIF, or PATTERN that occurs so often in world literature that it seems to have a universal meaning, as a bright light representing revelation, disorientation in a dark forest representing confusion, or a final marriage representing the restoration of social order. Some psychologists and critics, following the ideas of JUNGIAN CRITICISM, have gone so far to claim that these archetypes are biologically inherited parts of a human "collective unconscious."

Argument: A summary of the content or THEME of a literary work. See also SYNOPSIS.

Atmosphere: The overall **mood** or feeling of a literary work, such as calm, tense, gritty, joyful, depressed, and so on. Atmosphere is usually controlled most by the CHARACTERIZATION of the NARRATOR and the depiction of the SETTING.

Author: The person or persons who create the literary work. Whether the author is single or multiple, known or unknown, in reading we feel ourselves to be receiving a communication from some individual. This inferred individual is the stable consciousness whose existence is implied by the text and is called the **implied author.** The implied author is constructed by the **biographical** (also called **historical**) **author**(s) who may or may not share the attitudes and interests of the implied author. The implied author is commonly called simply the author and is even called by the name of the biographical author, but should not be confused with the biographical author. Similarly, the voice that we hear in reading a NARRATIVE is that of the NARRATOR, not of the implied author, who is always silent and known only by authorial choices, such as the characterization of the narrator or the ordering of the PLOT. Even if a narrator speaks of him- or herself as the author, in fiction that voice is still the voice of a narrator, a speaking CHARACTER created by the implied author to relate the narrative. Authors of narratives are always silent. See EN: The Narrative Situation.

Authorial Intrusion: An interruption in the recitation of the NARRATIVE in which a voice claiming to be the AUTHOR offers interpretation of or commentary on the ACTION. Also called "authorial intrusion." Authorial intrusion is a device of IMPLIED AUTHORS that complicates the narrative situation since the voice claiming to be the author is, of course, another fictional construction, like the main NARRATOR. See EN: The Narrative Situation.

Authority: The grounds for accepting a statement as true or false. Both GENRE expectations (witches can fly in FAIRY TALES) and our knowledge of our own world (people could not fly before the invention of hot air balloons in 1783) are sources of authority for a reader. See EN: Authority.

Bathos: The effect of an unsuccessful effort to achieve dignity or stylistic elevation or PATHOS; unintentional ANTICLIMAX. While the term bathos may properly signify an attempt at excessive pathos, the achievement of excessive pathos is a variety of SENTIMENTALITY. Bathos is typically ridiculous while sentimentality is typically maudlin.

Bildungsroman: A NOVEL, and sometimes a SHORT STORY, about the moral and psychological growth of the PROTAGONIST. Bildungsroman is a German word that literally means novel of formation or **novel of education**. See INITIATION STORY.

Biographical author: See AUTHOR.

Biographical criticism: A variety of CRITICISM that seeks clues to the understanding of a work of literature by studying the life of the author of the work. See HISTORICAL CRITICISM.

Biographical fallacy: The logical error of inferring from facts about the biography of an AUTHOR how or why a literary work must have been written or what it must mean. Biographical information can often be suggestive, but it cannot be determinative. This is clear once we recognize that a single author is often capable of producing radically different works. See INTENTIONAL FALLACY and EN: The Narrative Situation.

Burlesque: Ridicule through comic imitation or GROTESQUE exaggeration or distortion.

Caricature: A BURLESQUE representation of a CHARACTER.

Catastrophe: A momentous, frequently disastrous, event, often the RESOLUTION of a TRAGEDY.

Character: Both (1) an individual in a work of literature and (2) the complex of psychological and ethical traits that define an individual. Usually these individuals in literature are human beings, but, as in beast FABLES, not always. Also, not all human beings in literature, for example the people in a crowd, are characters. Characters may be **three-dimensional** or **round**, meaning fully developed, or **one-dimensional** or **flat**, meaning little developed. The main character is the PROTAGONIST; the character with whom the protagonist is in CONFLICT is the ANTAGONIST. Characters who appear by CONVENTION in work after work, such as the HARD BOILED DETECTIVE, the cruel stepmother of FAIRY TALES, and the mustachioed villain of MELODRAMA, are called **stock characters**. See EN: Character.

Characterization: The process through which a fictional CHARACTER is presented and developed. Characterization can be achieved through many means, including the use of CONVENTIONS, showing the character in action, hearing the character speak, and AUTHORIAL INTRUSION. See EN: Character and EN: Language.

Climax: The point of highest dramatic tension or a major turning point in the ACTION of a NARRATIVE, often the culminating confrontation in the CONFLICT between the PROTAGONIST and the ANTAGONIST. A climax may also be called a CRISIS.

Coherence: See UNITY.

Coincidence: An instance of events that happen at the same time by accident but seem to have some connection; also, any of these events. See CONTRIVANCE.

Comedy: (1) A work treating its subject in a light, humorous STYLE. (2) A work, often witty, in which the social order is perturbed but is restored in the RESOLUTION. Some critics restrict the use of the term comedy to DRAMA as opposed to NARRATIVE or LYRIC. In classic drama, comedy is the antithesis of TRAGEDY.

Complication: A part of the PLOT in which the CONFLICT is complicated, developed, or intensified. A plot may have few or many complications. The part of the plot during which complications intensify our SUSPENSE is called the **rising action**.

Conceit: An elaborated METAPHOR. "Charlemagne was a lion in battle. Once his enemies felt the power of his claws, his roar alone impelled them to flee the field."

Conclusion: See RESOLUTION.

Concrete terms: See ABSTRACT TERMS.

Confidant/confidante: A CHARACTER, often a FICELLE, to whom another character reveals his or her thoughts and feelings, thereby allowing readers access to those thoughts and feelings.

Conflict: The central struggle in the ACTION of a NARRATIVE. This may be a conflict between CHARACTERS (as in Borges's "Emma Zunz"), between a character and the environment (as in London's "To Build a Fire"), between philosophies or ways of life (as in Anderson's "Hands"), or even within a single character (as in Jewett's "A White Heron"). Conflict is often thought to be the heart of narrative because it creates SUSPENSE. See COMPLICATION, RESOLUTION, and ANTAGONIST.

Connotation: The implicit meanings associated with a word or phrase as opposed to **denotation**, the explicit meaning of a word or phrase itself. The denotations of "dog," "canine," "hound," "cur," and "man's best friend" are the same, but "dog," the most general term, carries no special connotation while "canine" may also connote a scientific attitude on the part of the speaker, "hound" may also connote a hunting dog, "cur" usually connotes nastiness, and "man's best friend" clearly connotes affection for people. Connotations may be widely known as in these examples, or they may develop in the course of an individual work, as they do with many words in Stein's "Miss Furr and Miss Skeene."

Content: See **form**.

Contrivance: An artificial arrangement or development. In CRITICISM, the term contrivance is often used to convey a negative evaluation, as when a COMPLICA-TION depends on a disturbingly improbable COINCIDENCE or the RESOLUTION depends on a DEUS EX MACHINA.

Convention: Any device, technique, STYLE, or other aspect of LITERATURE that has been established by common practice to have certain requirements and certain uses. We accept paragraphing in DIALOGUE and the plausibility of nick-of-time rescues in ROMANCE as matters of convention. STOCK CHARACTERS and Biblical DICTION are conventional. GENRES are defined by convention. When AUTHORS use convention to communicate with great ECONOMY, that is an AES-THETIC virtue; but when they rely on convention to evade adequate VARIETY of development and invention, that is an aesthetic vice.

Conventional form: See FORM.

Crisis: A major turning point in the ACTION of a NARRATIVE. Crisis is often used as a synonym for CLIMAX; however, usually one speaks of a narrative as having only one climax while one may speak of a narrative as having a series of crises.

Criticism: Northrop Frye (1912 - 1991) wrote that criticism should be to LITERA-TURE as physics is to natural phenomena; that is, the aim of criticism should be to study literature in all its varieties, to understand its parts, and to understand how those parts interrelate. Critics should observe and question literary phenomena — which means also that they should observe and question their own reactions as they read and discuss works of literature — in order to notice the details of individual works and to arrive at generalizations true of groups of works. Criti-cism, then, is the discipline that describes, analyzes, interprets, and evaluates individual works of art and whole sets of works of art. One may divide these activities into **practical criticism** focusing on the study of individual works and **theoretical criticism** focusing on the development of generalizations about liter-ary works. Some of the most prominent types of criticism are BIOGRAPHICAL CRITICISM, DECONSTRUCTION, FREUDIAN CRITICISM, HISTORICAL CRITICISM, JUNGIAN CRITICISM, MARXIST CRITICISM, NEW CRITICISM, STRUCTURALISM, and TEXTUAL CRITICISM. See also FORM for *prescriptive* and *descriptive criticism.*

Dark Double: See JUNGIAN CRITICISM.

Dark Man/Dark Woman: See JUNGIAN CRITICISM.

Deconstruction: A variety of **criticism** that emphasizes the CONVENTIONAL and INTERTEXTUAL nature of literary language and seeks to reveal explicitly the con-ventions that we may accept unconsciously. Critics of this school, associated initially with Jacques Derrida (1930 -), particularly value works that invite the reader to observe these conventions at work. SELF-REFLEXIVITY, then, is one device honored by Deconstructionists.

Defamiliarization: The process of making us attend carefully to matters that familiarity had caused to slip to low levels of attention. FIGURATIVE LANGUAGE, for example, may defamiliarize. Compare "He didn't stand a chance" with "He didn't stand the chance of a hiccup in a hurricane." On the other hand, figurative language itself can become too familiar, as in "ship of state." But such a familiar metaphor can be revived, for example by involving it in a CONCEIT: "The governor felt like she'd been shanghaied into service on the ship of state." The Russian Formalist critics, particularly Viktor Shklovskii (1893–1984), argued that defamiliarization is what distinguishes art from other types of expression. The slogan of the Formalists: "Art should make the stone *stony*." In Formalist terms, PLOT is defamiliarized STORY.

Denotation: See CONNOTATION.

Dénouement: See RESOLUTION.

Description: The use of language to give a detailed mental picture of a person, place, thing, or situation. See RHYTHM.

Descriptive criticism: See FORM.

Deus ex machina: Latin for "god from a machine." Originally a god introduced by means of a crane in ancient Greek and Roman DRAMA to resolve the PLOT. Now used disparagingly of any CONTRIVANCE introduced suddenly and unexpectedly to solve an apparently insoluble difficulty.

Deuteragonist: The second most important CHARACTER in a literary work; often the ANTAGONIST.

Dialogue: Exchanges of speech among people, actors, or CHARACTERS.

Diachronic structure: See STRUCTURE.

Diction: Choice and arrangement of words. See STYLE and EN: Language.

Didactic: Literally, "designed to teach." More narrowly, designed to convey a MORAL. Didactic is a term of praise applied to some works, such as FABLES, where didacticism is expected and desired. Didactic is a term of deprecation applied to other works, such as those of REALISM, where overt teaching and plain morals are usually thought to be respectively intrusive and simplistic.

Direct quotation: Reporting a CHARACTER's actual words, as in "He said, 'I want to go home,' " as opposed to **indirect quotation** reporting a character's words in the NARRATOR's words, as in "He said he wanted to go home" or "He said he'd like to go home now." See EN: Authority.

Disambiguation: See AMBIGUITY.

Discovery: See ANAGNORISIS.

Distance: The removal—always emotional and sometimes also temporal or spatial—of the reader, NARRATOR, or a CHARACTER from another character or from the ACTION of a NARRATIVE.

Doppelgänger: A German term introduced by Jean Paul Friedrich Richter (1763–1825; known as Jean Paul) for a CHARACTER who is intimately tied to another, usually the PROTAGONIST, and whose actions mimic or in some other fantastic way reflect those of the protagonist. In a sense, each of these characters is the doppelgänger of the other; they are defined as a pair. The conflict between doppelgängers represents an overt enactment of a struggle that could be thought of as occurring within a single character, usually the protagonist. In Poe's "The

Purloined Letter," the detective Dupin and the criminal Minister are doppel-gängers.

Double: In general, the English word for DOPPELGÄNGER. More technically, a category in JUNGIAN CRITICISM.

Drama: Direct representation of events by actors, as on a stage. See GENRE.

Dramatic irony: See IRONY.

Dramatization: The use of exchanges of DIRECT QUOTATION in NARRATIVE to imitate DRAMA; passages containing such exchanges. See RHYTHM.

Economy: The efficient use of the resources of language to accomplish an artistic goal. See EN: Aesthetic virtues.

Ego: See FREUDIAN CRITICISM.

Empathy: (1) Imaginative participation in the feelings, thoughts, and experiences of someone else (a person or a CHARACTER). (2) The capacity for this. (3) The imaginative projection of an emotion into an object so that the object seems suffused with the emotion. **Sympathy** can be used as a synonym for empathy, but is sometimes restricted to a contrasting meaning, empathy referring to feeling the same emotions as the other, sympathy referring to understanding and respecting the emotions of the other. In that restricted sense, we can speak of a sympathetic character, one that elicits our understanding, respect, and perhaps even liking, but one speaks of an empathetic character only to indicate a character who demonstrates empathy.

Epigraph: Literally (from Greek), "that which is written above." A quotation (or apparent quotation) set at the beginning of a literary work or a division of a work to suggest or comment on its THEME.

Epiphany: Literally (from Greek), a "showing forth." The Christian celebration of Epiphany (January 6) commemorates the first manifestation of Jesus to the Gentile Magi. Joyce gave epiphany currency as a term for the sudden manifestation or perception of the essential truth about a CHARACTER, situation, or experience.

Episode: A single, usually brief, unified incident narrated as a whole within a larger NARRATIVE. An episode may or may not advance the PLOT. Plots constructed as a loose series of episodes are called **episodic**.

Epithet: See FORMULA.

Eponym: A variety of ALLUSION in which a name is used to refer to the qualities with which it is widely associated: "He was a modern Machiavelli," meaning he was a consummate conniver; "She was the Helen of her high school class," meaning the outstanding beauty.

Explication: In general, a detailed explanation or interpretation, as in CRITICISM. More specifically, EXPLICATION DE TEXTE.

Explication de texte: A painstaking procedure, developed in France for teaching literature, that systematically addresses the DENOTATIONS and CONNOTATIONS of the words of a text; the syntax; the FIGURATIVE LANGUAGE; the rhyme, RHYTHM, and units of verse; and finally the THEME. It served as a model in the Anglo-American development of NEW CRITICISM.

Exposition: A part of a work relating necessary background information. See PLOT.

Fable: A short, often humorous NARRATIVE designed to teach a simple MORAL. Fables often use speaking animals as STOCK CHARACTERS such as the wily fox or the industrious ant. See also PARABLE and ALLEGORY.

Fairy tale: A GENRE of NARRATIVE set in a CONVENTIONAL land of enchantment and marked by magic, supernatural CHARACTERS, COINCIDENCE and wish-fulfilling RESOLUTIONS. See EN: Genre.

Falling action: The part of the PLOT following the CLIMAX and preceding the RESOLUTION.

Fantastic: See FANTASY.

Fantasy: Works that make exhaustive use of the devices of the fantastic. The **fantastic** is a reader response created by the reversal of the ground rules of the NARRATIVE world, whether those rules are imported from the reader's world (for example, the rule that the dead stay dead) or are indigenous to the narrative world (for example, the rule that magic works in FAIRY TALES; hence a fairy tale in which magic failed would be more fantastic than one in which it worked). See EN: Genre.

Ficelle: A minor CHARACTER whose function in the NARRATIVE is primarily to ask the PROTAGONIST questions or otherwise elicit the protagonist's thoughts and feelings without the IMPLIED AUTHOR resorting to SOLILOQUY or an OMNISCIENT VIEWPOINT. Ficelle is originally a French word meaning "a piece of string." Henry James first used it for those characters who ask the questions we readers would want to ask if we lived in the world of the narrative. The ficelle connects us to that world.

Fiction: Literally (from Latin), "made or shaped thing." This term is usually restricted to imaginative NARRATIVES, as opposed, say, to historical narratives, although imaginative narratives obviously may contain historical facts and historical narratives may represent highly idiosyncratic selections, arrangements, and interpretations of historical facts. Fictions have been called "true lies." In distinguishing a lie from a truth, we test the accuracy of the statement and the intent of the speaker. If the statement is inaccurate and the speaker knows it to be so but wishes to deceive us thereby, it is a lie; however, if the speaker believes the statement to be accurate, it is merely a mistake. In fiction, however, the question of accuracy is subsumed to the question of VERISIMILITUDE and the intent should be to have us accept an account as *if* it were true while signalling that it may or may not (usually not) be true. In other words, we enter into the reading of fiction by CONVENTION. (Some critics further restrict the use of the term fiction to prose, but clearly there are many verse fictions, such as Chaucer's "The Miller's Tale.") See EN: Authority.

Figurative language: Language meant to be understood in nonliteral ways. "If I've told you once, I've told you a million times" is an example of the figure called **hyperbole,** exaggeration for RHETORICAL effect. Some other common rhetorical figures (also called **tropes**) are APOSTROPHE, CONCEIT, IMAGE, IRONY, LITOTES, METAPHOR, METONYMY, PERSONIFICATION, SIMILE, SYMBOL, and SYNECDOCHE.

First-person narration: See NARRATION.

First-person viewpoint: See VIEWPOINT.

Flashback: An interruption in the forward chronological flow of the STORY in order to present an earlier EPISODE, often used as a means of EXPOSITION or of creating SUSPENSE. See ACTION and EN: Structure.

Flat character: See CHARACTER.

Foil: A person or CHARACTER who serves to contrast and set off another, for example, the straight man for a comedian or Watson for Holmes in Doyle's "The Adventure of the Speckled Band."

Folktale: A typically anonymous, timeless, oral tale passed from one generation to the next of a given people. Many written FAIRY TALES, MYTHS, and LEGENDS are based on folktales.

Foreshadowing: Hints about what is to come later in the NARRATIVE.

Form: A general term in CRITICISM used to indicate the organization of the elements of a work in relation to the work's total effect. CONVENTION, FORMULA, GENRE, and STRUCTURE are all formal concerns. Form is often treated as the complement of **content,** those elements that are organized by the form (the ACTION, the THEME, the specific words, and so on). Although no work can express its content without form and no work can have a form without embodying it in some content, for purposes of analysis it is sometimes useful to concentrate either on matters of form or on matters of content. In an effort to move from a completely **prescriptive criticism** toward a more **descriptive criticism,** Samuel Taylor Coleridge (1772–1834) distinguished between **conventional form** and **organic form.** Prescriptive criticism requires that a successful work conform to preexisting standards for its type of work, including the requirement that its content be organized according to a form established by prior CONVENTION. For example, it had been prescribed from Aristotle (384–322 B.C.E.) onward that a tragedy must express so-called unity of time, that is, encompass its action in a single day. By that standard, William Shakespeare's *Hamlet* (1601) would be a failed work of art. Coleridge (1772–1834) argued that a work should have what he called organic unity, that is, like a living organism, each part should grow from another and all parts should function together according to the needs of the individual work. By that standard, *Hamlet* is a success. Today we say it possesses organic form. See EN: Aesthetic virtues.

Formalism: Any critical approach that stresses the analysis of the FORM of a work above other possible concerns. See DEFAMILIARIZATION.

Formula: Any CONVENTIONALLY established phrase, CHARACTER, PLOT event, or other AESTHETIC device used repeatedly, especially if used from work to work. A standard EPITHET, such as "defender of the faith" or "wily Odysseus" is a formula phrase. STOCK CHARACTERS such as the mad scientist of SCIENCE FICTION are formula characters. The discovery of a false clue in the TALE OF THE GREAT DETECTIVE is a formula plot event. Some well specified GENRES, like the WESTERN, are highly formulaic; others, like the novels of REALISM, are much less so. The term formula is sometimes used negatively to suggest a lack of inventiveness (VARIETY) on the part of the author; however, each genre has its own conventions for necessary variety and so long as a work fulfills those conventional expectations it can succeed with its intended readership. See EN: Aesthetic virtues.

Framing: The enclosure of one work within another, as the film of *The Wizard of Oz* (1939) frames Dorothy's colorful adventures in Oz within the black-and-white story of her life in Kansas. In *front-framing*, the work opens in the frame, goes into the inner work, and does not return to the frame; James's *The Turn of the Screw* is an example. In *back-framing*, the reader only discovers that the work is an inner work when, near the end, for the first time it is placed in a frame; McCay's "Tales of the Rarebit Fiend" is an example. In *full-framing*, the inner work is framed both in front and in back; *The Wizard of Oz* and Wells's *The Time Machine* are examples. In an extended NESTED NARRATIVE, inner works themselves frame other works; Ovid's *Metamorphoses* is an example. In all cases of framing, there is at least a THEMATIC connection between the framed and the framing work. See EN: Structure.

Free indirect style: The technique by which a THIRD-PERSON NARRATOR presents the thoughts of a CHARACTER without actually saying "He thought" or "She understood," as in the first long paragraph of Baldwin's "Going to Meet the Man": "Then he just lay there, silent, angry, helpless. Excitement filled him like a toothache, but. . . ." Although the term was coined in French, *style indirect libre*, it was first applied to the work of Henry James. See EN: Varieties of Narrative Stance.

Freudian criticism: CRITICISM based on the psychological theories of Sigmund Freud (1856–1939). These include the idea that the deep meaning and appeal of a work of art are unconscious but manifested SYMBOLICALLY to the conscious mind. Freud introduced the idea that our unconscious needs are formed in part by basic drives (a desire for pleasure, for repetition, for death) and through our experiences while growing up. An adult mind (psyche) has three parts in Freudian terms: the **id**, the source of instinctual needs and drives, such as a desire for sexual activity; the **ego**, the consciously recognizable self; and the **superego**, the partly conscious internalization of the rules of the parents and of society, the source of guilt, morality, and so on. Freud is well known for having defined the **Oedipus complex** in which a child wants to supplant the place of one parent in the affections of the other parent. Many critics have found Freud's ideas fruitful in analyzing texts and readers' reactions to them, for example by seeing the structure of the Oedipus complex enacted symbolically in many works. In that light, the appeal of the work would be in its treatment of an issue still unresolved, or once unresolved, in the life of the reader. Other critics have argued that these ideas are too restrictive and perhaps even fictions themselves. See JUNGIAN CRITICISM.

General terms: See ABSTRACT TERMS.

Genre: A systematic grouping of literary works; a literary kind. At the broadest level, there are four genres: NARRATIVE, DRAMA, LYRIC, and nonfiction (essay, history, and so on). Narrower groupings within narrative include NOVEL, SHORT STORY, FABLE, and so on. Even more highly specified groupings include, say, INITIATION STORY and WESTERN. We must understand a work's genre to evaluate the work. In Lewis Carroll's *Alice In Wonderland* (1865), Alice remarks about an unattractive baby that turns into a pig and runs away that " 'If it had grown up . . . it would have made a dreadfully ugly child: but it makes rather a handsome pig.' " See En: Genre.

Gothic tale: A NARRATIVE involving horror, the supernatural, or both; sometimes used for any tale of brooding, MELODRAMATIC violence and GROTESQUE characters. The term entered literary language as the subtitle for Horace Walpole's *The Castle of Otranto: A Gothic Story* (1764), a work set largely in a decaying stone castle and characterized by family curses and bizarre passions. The works of such writers as William Faulkner, Flannery O'Connor, and Eudora Welty are sometimes called **Southern Gothic.**

Grapholect: A written dialect characteristic of a particular historical time, GENRE, and social context of composition. See EN: Language.

Great Detective: The detective in the GENRE called the TALE OF THE GREAT DETECTIVE.

Grotesque: Departing markedly from the natural, the expected, or the typical.

Hard Boiled Detective: The tough-guy detective PROTAGONIST of works like those of Raymond Chandler and Dashiell Hammett. Unlike the GREAT DETECTIVE, the Hard Boiled Detective is typically of comparatively low social class, lives in a gritty environment, relies as much on his fists as on his brains, and is willing to break the law to achieve his (or, very rarely, her) own idea of justice.

Hero/heroine: Loosely, the PROTAGONIST of a literary work. More technically, such a CHARACTER who happens to be admirable. See ANTIHERO.

Historical author: See AUTHOR.

Historical criticism: A variety of CRITICISM that seeks clues to the understanding of a work of literature by studying what Hippolyte Taine (1828–1893) called the "race, moment, and milieu" in which the work was written; that is, what today we might call the author's nationality, historical situation, and socioeconomic context. This differs from biographical criticism in concentrating much more on the public facts of life in the author's time than on the private facts of the author's particular life. Modern historical criticism also takes into account the historical evolution of the GENRE of the work. See EN: Genre.

Hyperbole: RHETORICAL exaggeration. See FIGURATIVE LANGUAGE.

Id: See FREUDIAN CRITICISM.

Image: Most narrowly, a CONCRETE representation of the visual aspects of an object; more generally, any concrete sensory representation. Snow imagery has crucial thematic importance in Joyce's "The Dead."

Implied author: See AUTHOR.

Implied reader: The reading consciousness implied by the text. Some works, for example, Bruna's *The King*, imply that their readers are children; others, for example, Benét's "Nightmare Number Three," that they live in the future; others that they subscribe to one attitude or another or have a particular gender or nationality. In order to understand a narrative fully, we biographical readers, in the process of reading, must construct within ourselves mental approximations of the implied reader. See NARRATEE, AUTHOR, and EN: The Narrative Situation.

Indirect quotation: See DIRECT QUOTATION.

Initiation story: A BILDUNGSROMAN focusing on a young person's loss of innocence through experience.

In medias res: Literally (from Latin), "in the middle of things." The Roman writer Horace (65–8 B.C.E.) argued that all narratives should begin in medias res.

Intentional fallacy: The logical error of inferring from statements made by an author or facts about the biography of an author how or why a literary work must have been written or what it must mean. Information about an author's intention can often be suggestive, but it cannot be determinative. This is clear once we recognize that a single author is often capable of producing works of radically different degrees of success; that is, even if we are willing to believe that an author is honest in reporting his or her intentions, there is no reason to suppose that the author was thoroughly successful in fulfilling them. See BIOGRAPHICAL FALLACY and EN: Authority.

Interior monologue: A NARRATIVE version of the SOLILOQUY of DRAMA. See STREAM OF CONSCIOUSNESS.

Intertextuality: The construction of fictional reality by reference to other texts. This source of AUTHORITY is theoretically opposed to a MIMETIC theory of art. See REFERENTIALITY and EN: Authority.

Irony: A contrast or discrepancy between appearance and reality. The term irony is derived from the Greek *eirōn*, meaning a dissembler or pretender. There are many varieties of irony. **Socratic irony**, as used by the character Socrates in the DIALOGUES of Plato (427–327 B.C.E.), is a pretense of ignorance so that one can draw out someone else in conversation in order to demonstrate the mistaken nature of the other person's beliefs. It is one variety of **verbal irony**, the contrast between what is actually said and what is meant. "I just love his new shoes," said derisively, is verbal irony, indicating the opposite of what is apparently said. **Dramatic irony** refers to a situation in which a reader, NARRATOR, or CHARACTER knows that the state of affairs is the opposite of that believed by a narrator or character. For example, in Crane's "The Blue Hotel," we see that the Swede has a mistaken idea of what America is like and watch him commit errors accordingly. **Situational irony** refers to circumstances that turn out to be the opposite of what is appropriate or expected, as in Allen's "The Whore of Mensa." Many NARRATIVES, like Chopin's "Desirée's Baby" and Wharton's "Roman Fever," by ultimately revealing situational irony on a first reading, display deep dramatic irony on SUBSEQUENT READINGS.

Jungian criticism: CRITICISM based on the psychological theories of Carl Gustav Jung (1875–1961). Jung shared with his teacher FREUD the notion that works of art reveal SYMBOLICALLY their deep unconscious meanings but where Freud saw these symbols working out the interplay of a three-part psyche, Jung saw a four-part psyche which yielded major categories of characters for both real-world interactions and literary PATTERNS. If the PROTAGONIST may be thought of as a male **ego** (self), he has available four standard figures: an **anima**, a female figure representing that which he is not and that which he desires; a **Dark Woman**, an inverse of the anima who shows the negative side of those desires; a **Double** who represents an exaggeration of some trait or traits of the ego; and a **Dark Double**, an inverse of the Double. For example, if the ego is a soldier, the anima might be a pacifist female nurse, the Dark Woman an enemy spy, the Double a model of bravery, and the Dark Double a ruthless killer. (If the ego is female, the terms are adjusted; anima becomes **animus** and Dark Woman becomes **Dark Man**.) According to Jung, the ego in life and in art strives for integration, union of the ego with the anima or animus. While most critics reject Jung's assertion that these CHARACTER ARCHETYPES are genetically inevitable, many recognize their CONVENTIONAL force.

Legend: A STORY coming down from the past, especially one popularly regarded as historical but unverifiable, such as stories of the lives of saints or of Western outlaws.

Limited narration: See NARRATION.

Limited viewpoint: See VIEWPOINT.

Limited omniscient narration: See NARRATION.

Limited omniscient viewpoint: See VIEWPOINT.

Literature: Written works valued for their own artistry regardless of their use within the particular and immediate real world context of their composition. Edward Gibbon's *Decline and Fall of the Roman Empire* (1776–1788), the most celebrated history in the English language, is no longer considered an especially accurate representation of the ancient world, but it has come to be admired for the elegance of its prose and its revelation of British thinking in the eighteenth century. In those regards, it has become both literature and an historical document in its own right. In the course of courtship, one may write a poem to one's beloved; if other people unacquainted with the writer and recipient of the poem also find it moving, it is literature. In this sense, then, literature is simply written art, whether or not the work was created primarily to be art. If one thinks of art as an evaluative term, then literature is also an evaluative term. There are, of course, other uses of the term which have no bearing on the question of art and do not imply any value judgment: "the scientific literature" refers to the body of scientific writing; "the literature of psychology" refers at once to psychological novels and to the case studies of psychoanalysts. Because, in a similar way, one can refer to, say "Renaissance literature," including works that we value both positively and negatively, some critics prefer to see the term literature as value-free; others argue that that is impossible. All agree, however, that, once included within the category of art, some works of literature are better than others.

Litotes: UNDERSTATEMENT in which an affirmation is expressed by the negation of its contrary. "He was not a poor man."

Locale: See SETTING.

Lyric: The direct expression of the emotions of a single individual, as in a song, for example, "Amazing Grace." See GENRE.

Magical realism: FICTION that juxtaposes the REALISTIC and the FANTASTIC treating each alike. First used of the works of such modern Latin American writers as Cortázar, Borges, and Gabriel García Márquez, it is now applied to writers around the world, such as the U.S. writer Barthelme and the Nigerian Amos Tutuola.

Marxist criticism: An important variety of HISTORICAL CRITICISM based on the socioeconomic theories of Karl Marx (1818 – 1883). Marx argued that works of art were products like any other and needed to be understood in terms of market forces: whose economic interests are being served by writing (producing) this work in a certain way, by publishing (printing and marketing) it in a certain way, by buying and reading (consuming) it in a certain way? In Marxist terms, this can be quite complex because authors and readers may have a "false consciousness"; that is, they may consciously associate themselves with one social class (for example, with the ruling elite that controls the schools and the publishing houses) while they are really "wage slaves" toiling to stay alive by following the FORMULAS available to them. Marxist critics typically honor works that are "socially engaged" and reveal the CONFLICT between social classes, like Baldwin's "Going to Meet the Man" and Gordimer's "Six Feet of the Country."

Melodrama: In general, a thrilling, action-oriented work characterized by extravagant theatricality, and a reliance on STOCK CHARACTERS such as the virtuous HEROINE and villainous landlord. More narrowly, a type of DRAMA with these characteristics.

Melodramatic: Having the characteristics of MELODRAMA. This term is often used to convey a negative evaluation of works in GENRES, such as the REALISTIC NOVEL, that require detailed motivation of the CHARACTERS but can be used to express a positive evaluation of more FORMULAIC genres.

Metafiction: FICTIONS about the processes of reading and writing fiction, such as those of Borges. All ANTISTORIES are implicitly metafictional because they undercut our expectations of how a narrative should work and thereby remind us that we are in the world of NARRATIVES. At a moment when a work is explicitly metafictional, it is **self-reflexive**. If one character says to another, " 'If this coincidence happened in a story, I'd call it contrived,' " the NARRATIVE reflects on its own nature as narrative. As with antistories, self-reflexivity is simultaneously a rejection of the MIMETIC capacities of fiction and a metafictional claim for the reality of the fiction itself.

Metaphor: A FIGURATIVE, implicit comparison of unlike things meant to attribute one or more of the qualities of one thing to another. "War is hell" and "The stormy sea of romance" are metaphoric. The thing to be characterized (war, romance) is the **tenor** of the metaphor; the thing conveying the attribution (hell conveying the qualities of extreme and indefinite suffering, stormy sea conveying the qualities of overwhelming power bearing one on a long journey) is the **vehicle** of the metaphor. Tenor and vehicle are not always expressed in separate words. In the sentence "After she accepted his proposal, George floated for a week," if George is an ordinary human being, "floated" is a metaphor, the tenor being George's emotional state, the vehicle being his superhuman act. (Of course, if for some reason George actually spent the ensuing week aloft in a hot air balloon, "floated" is no longer metaphoric, although it still may be SYMBOLIC of his joy). If the comparison of unlike things is made explicit by the use of connecting words such as "like" or "as," the figure is a **simile**. The sentences "She swam like a mermaid" and "He was as happy as a puppy chasing butterflies" both contain similes. See METONYMY.

Metonymy: The FIGURATIVE use of the name of one thing to indicate something else with which that thing is associated, as in "The lands belonging to the crown" or "The White House issued a news release." Distinctions among varieties of figurative language depend on examining not only the language used but also the context in which it is used. If Jake is an armed bodyguard, the sentence "Jake was a hired gun" exemplifies only metonymy; however, if Jake is an unarmed lawyer, that same sentence also exemplifies METAPHOR. See SYNECDOCHE.

Mimesis: The Greek word for "imitation," often used in CRITICISM for Aristotle's theory that art should imitate nature.

Minimalism: An artistic creed favoring ECONOMY and disparaging such overt interpretive devices as AUTHORIAL INTRUSION. Carver's "Viewfinder" is an example of minimalism. Hemingway can be considered a pioneering minimalist.

Modernism: A loosely applied label referring to a literary movement beginning around the beginning of the twentieth century that valued self-consciousness (and SELF-REFLEXIVITY) in literature, that investigated and played with the CONVENTIONS of literary technique, that preferred passion and an exploration of the unconscious to logic, and that saw itself as an explicit alternative to the MIMETIC and scientific standards of REALISM and NATURALISM. Modernism was deeply influenced by FREUDIAN CRITICISM and the anthropological notion of cultural relativism that asks us to judge actions within their own cultural context. Conrad, Joyce, and Virginia Woolf are among the great writers of modernist prose.

Mood: See ATMOSPHERE.

Moral: The lesson to be drawn from a NARRATIVE, particularly a simple ethical or behavioral imperative, such as "Honesty is the best policy."

Motif: An IMAGE or other artistic element that recurs in a single work or in a set of works so that it can take on THEMATIC significance. Individual colors serve as motifs in Bruna's *The King* (see Introduction). FAIRY TALES often use the motif of a girl separated from her mother. Motifs can combine to form larger **patterns**. The three stories of the Grimm brothers called "Little Red Cap," "Rapunzel," and "The Three Spinsters" are in some ways quite different, but they share a pattern of the heroine being separated from her mother because of actions by her mother; this separation endangers the heroine; and the escape from danger leads to a RESOLUTION implying that without this separation there can be no adult happiness.

Motive: That which causes a CHARACTER to act. REALISM requires that a character's motives (collectively called a character's **motivation**) be consistent with his or her individual psychology and particular external situation while in GENRES that are more FORMULAIC, such as the WESTERN, STOCK CHARACTERS are sufficiently motivated simply by occupying their formulaic roles.

Motivation: See MOTIVE.

Myth: A traditional STORY of ostensibly true events that serves to explain part of the beliefs of a people about themselves, their practices, or their world. Myths typically involve gods or great heros or heroines as PROTAGONISTS.

Narratee: A CHARACTER within a NARRATIVE (never the reader) to whom the NARRATOR'S recitation is ostensibly addressed.

Narration: In general, the act of representing a STORY. More narrowly, the varieties of NARRATION are often known by the VIEWPOINT of the NARRATOR. Thus **first-person narration** is narration from a first-person viewpoint, **omniscient narration** is narration from an omniscient viewpoint, and so on. Some critics use the term narration to refer to the specific narrative technique of RECAPITULATION. See EN: Varieties of Narrative Stance.

Narrative: A representation of a STORY. See GENRE.

Narrative technique: The means employed in construction a NARRATIVE. See EN.

Narrator: The speaker (or singer or filmer or drawer) of a NARRATIVE. A NARRATIVE may have a single narrator or multiple narrators, for example two narrators taking turns, as in Twain's "The Diary of Adam and Eve," or narrators of narratives within the main narrative, as in James's *The Turn of the Screw*. The nature of the narrator(s) and how the narrator goes about narrating (for example, the TENSE OF NARRATION and the VIEWPOINT of the narrator) are crucial to the construction of every narrative. See EN: The Narrative Situation and EN: Varieties of Narrative Stance.

Naturalism: An extreme form of REALISM influenced by Darwinian evolutionary theory. Naturalism insisted that good literature show human behavior as determined by heredity and environment. Great writers of naturalist prose include Upton Sinclair and Émile Zola.

Nested narrative: See FRAMING.

New Criticism: A variety of CRITICISM that takes as its ideal the analysis of a work of art as utterly autonomous, existing ahistorically and most valuable for the ways in which its elements are constructed and interrelate as opposed to the ways it conveys some message. As Archibald MacLeish wrote in 1926, "A poem should not mean but be." Although John Crowe Ransom named this approach "The New Criticism" in 1941, it is still known by that name today because its newness, which still represents an important view, lay in rejecting the older critical practice of subjecting works to moral analysis. While one can never achieve the ideal of the New Criticism—after all, we cannot know what even one word means without knowing the usage of the time of composition—the move toward that ideal has had enormous influence in shifting literary education away from types of HISTORICAL CRITICISM that require research outside the work and toward types of criticism, like STRUCTURALISM, that require analysis within the work.

Novel: Today this term may refer to any lengthy prose FICTION. Until the mid-nineteenth century, such fictions were considered to be of two opposing types, the ROMANCE, which could be extravagant and lack a firm basis in fact, and the novel, which was expected to meet stricter standards of plausibility and historical accuracy. See SHORT STORY.

Novelette: A short NOVEL or long SHORT STORY.

Novella: Usually a synonym for NOVELETTE; occasionally restricted to mean a NARRATIVE with a compact and pointed PLOT.

Novel of education: See BILDUNGSROMAN.

Oedipus complex: See FREUDIAN CRITICISM.

Omniscient narration: See NARRATION.

Omniscient viewpoint: See VIEWPOINT.

One-dimensional character: See CHARACTER.

Organic form: See FORM.

Pace: In discussing prose NARRATIVE, a synonym for RHYTHM.

Parable: A NARRATIVE, usually short and often ALLEGORICAL, designed to teach a complex MORAL or answer a complex moral or spiritual question. See also FABLE.

Paradox: The RHETORICAL device of stating something which is seemingly impossible but may be true ("The coward dies a thousand deaths" — Oscar Wilde) or something which appears true but may be self-contradictory ("I never tell the truth" — the so-called Cretan paradox).

Parody: A BURLESQUE of a particular artistic work or genre.

Pathetic fallacy: A term coined by John Ruskin (1819 – 1900) for the inappropriate imputation of human emotions to nature. Ruskin would disparage a sentence like "the storm angrily pursued our hero across the remorseless sea," although clearly some GENRES invite such PERSONIFICATION. The connection with PATHOS is only tangential: Ruskin thought the use of such personification to evoke pathos to be an artistic flaw.

Pathos: An element in life or art evoking pity or compassion; an emotion of sympathetic pity. See BATHOS.

Pattern: See MOTIF.

Peripeteia: See ANAGNORISIS.

Persona: Literally (from Greek), "a mask"; the so-called mask or voice an IMPLIED AUTHOR creates and adopts to tell a STORY; the NARRATOR of a FICTION.

Personification: (1) FIGURATIVE LANGUAGE that treats animals, ideas, or objects as if they were persons, as in "This jalopy hates me" or as in Poe's narrator speaking of "the Fiend Intemperance" in "The Black Cat"; or (2) the device of having a character incarnate for another character or for the reader some abstract idea, as in Uncle Sam standing for the United States or as in the protagonist's wife representing faith to him in Hawthorne's "Young Goodman Brown."

Plot: A classic plot consists of a CONFLICT between a PROTAGONIST and an ANTAGONIST. This conflict has a RISING ACTION generated by one or more COMPLICATIONS and leads to a CLIMAX after which a FALLING ACTION leads to a RESOLUTION. In Poe's "The Purloined Letter," the conflict is between the detective Dupin and the criminal Minister. The complications include the searches reported by the Prefect of Police that make the solution of the mystery appear progressively less possible. The climax occurs when Dupin presents evidence that he has solved the mystery and the falling action is his explanation of his solution. Both the report of the searches and the explanation are EXPOSITIONS. The resolution is the final state of affairs returning power to those Dupin favors. See ACTION.

Plurisignification: The condition of a word, phrase, event, or situation having more than one meaning at the same time. A SYMBOL is plurisignificant. Compare AMBIGUITY.

Poetic justice: The once popular prescription that in art good should be rewarded and evil punished.

Point of view: See VIEWPOINT.

Practical criticism: See CRITICISM.

Prescriptive criticism: See FORM.

Protagonist: The main character of a literary work. See ANTAGONIST, DEUTERAGONIST, HERO/HEROINE.

Realism: The telling of a STORY in a manner reflecting the writer's objective understanding of everyday life, limiting the ACTION to events that could actually happen and CHARACTERS to representations of people who could actually exist. Also, a nineteenth century artistic movement that made realism the highest artistic value. Great writers of realist prose include James and Maupassant.

Recapitulation: The use of language to give a summary of events, feelings, and so on. Sometimes called simply NARRATION. See RHYTHM.

Referentiality: In general, the directing of attention elsewhere; more narrowly, the correspondence between that which directs the attention (the so-called **signifier**, a word, for example) and that toward which the attention is directed (the so-called **signified**, a thing, for example). The highway sign "Slippery when wet" directs our attention to the road surface, not to the sign itself or to any of its words; the reference is to physical phenomena in the world of the driver. We usually treat language in NARRATIVE as if it were referencing our world even if, as in FAIRY TALES, we know that the narrative cannot be making such a reference. Some critics argue that all literary reference is in fact to other texts (or among parts of the same text). Such reference within the literary realm is called INTERTEXTUALITY. See EN: Authority.

Reliable narrator: Also called **trustworthy narrator**; a NARRATOR whose NARRATION the IMPLIED AUTHOR wants the reader to accept throughout. See EN: Varieties of Narrative Stance.

Resolution: The final section of the PLOT in which we learn the outcome of the CONFLICT; sometimes called also **conclusion** or **dénouement**, a French word that literally means "unknotting." In a sense, the resolution allows the IMPLIED AUTHOR to dramatize the relative power of the conflicting forces in the NARRATIVE by showing, for example, whether the values of the PROTAGONIST prevail. Sometimes, of course, the so-called resolution does not actually resolve the conflict, suggesting that the conflict is irresolvable.

Reversal: Any turnabout in the fortunes of a CHARACTER, especially of the PROTAGONIST. See "peripeteia" under ANAGNORISIS.

Rhetoric: The art of speaking and writing effectively. See FIGURATIVE LANGUAGE.

Rhythm: The controlled fluctuation of the flow of any phenomenon. In verse, rhythm usually refers specifically to the patterns of stress and line length. In prose, rhythm refers more generally to any control of patterns of flow. For example, in DESCRIPTION, the reading time is much longer than the narrative time; in DRAMATIZATION, the reading time is approximately the same as the narrative time; and in RECAPITULATION, the reading time is much shorter than the narrative time. Hence a crucial aspect of rhythm in NARRATIVE is manipulating the alternation and interweaving of these three varieties of report. See EN: Structure.

Rising action: See COMPLICATION and PLOT.

Romance: There are three related but distinct literary uses of this term: (1) a medieval TALE based on LEGEND, chivalric love, adventure, or the supernatural; (2) a NARRATIVE with fanciful CHARACTERS, implausible or MELODRAMATIC events, often set in a remote time and place and involving heroism, adventure, or mystery; (3) a love STORY. See NOVEL.

Romantic: An adjective referring to (1) works of ROMANCE or to the qualities that distinguish such works, or (2) works or AUTHORS marked by ROMANTICISM.

Romanticism: A literary movement begun in the late eighteenth century that valued individuality, imagination, and the power of art to reveal the truth inherent in nature and daily life. The prototypical Romantic writers were the poets Samuel Taylor Coleridge (1772–1834) and William Wordsworth (1770–1850). Hawthorne and Poe were writers of **Romantic prose**.

Round character: See CHARACTER.

Russian Formalism: See DEFAMILIARIZATION.

Sarcasm: Derisive VERBAL IRONY intended to scorn its subject.

Satire: A work that holds up ideas or human vices or foibles to scorn or ridicule, often by means of BURLESQUE or IRONY. In ancient times, satire ranged from invective to gently deflating wit; in modern times, satire is generally restricted to works that seem to intend correction of their targets.

Scene: (1) A self-contained, DRAMATIZED segment of a work of fiction. (2) Sometimes used as a synonym for SETTING.

Science Fiction: More or less FANTASTIC art in which the ground rules we import into our reading from the everyday world appear reversed against a background of science. Mary Shelley's *Frankenstein* (1818) is often considered the first science fiction novel. Wells has been called "the father of science fiction."

Second reading: See SUBSEQUENT READING.

Self-reflexivity: See METAFICTION.

Sentimentality: In modern usage, any emotion that seems excessive in light of the objective circumstances. See BATHOS.

Setting: The time and place in which the ACTION of a NARRATIVE occurs. Sometimes the physical setting alone is referred to as the **locale**.

Short story: A FICTIONAL NARRATIVE, usually in prose, typically dealing with at most a few CHARACTERS and aiming at a unity of effect. A NOVEL is longer than a short story, is usually divided into chapters, may have more characters, and may have one or more comparatively well developed SUBPLOTS. See SKETCH and TALE.

Signified: See REFERENTIALITY.

Signifier: See REFERENTIALITY.

Simile: See METAPHOR.

Situational irony: See IRONY.

Sketch: A short, predominantly descriptive work, sometimes FICTIONAL and sometimes not, typically light in treatment and discursive in TONE, usually recounting a single EPISODE focused on a single CHARACTER in a single SETTING. See SHORT STORY.

Socratic irony: See IRONY.

Soliloquy: The act of talking to oneself. In a literary work, particularly in DRAMA, a speech that we take by CONVENTION to express unspoken thoughts. Hamlet's speech beginning "To be or not to be" (*Hamlet*, III, i, 56) is a famous soliloquy.

Southern Gothic: See GOTHIC TALE.

Specific terms: See ABSTRACT TERMS.

Speech acts: Acts which are accomplished simply by producing words. People often distinguish between deeds, which are taken to cause effects, and words, which are not. Children chant, "Sticks and stones can break my bones but words can never harm me." However, words can harm one. Many acts are accomplished merely by speaking or writing. Speech acts include advising, begging, betraying, commiserating, confessing, contracting, courting, criticizing, cursing, denouncing, denying, enchanting, explaining, flattering, greeting, haranguing, insulting, joking, judging, kidding, lying, misleading, nagging, ordering, perjuring, pledging, praising, praying, promising, questioning, reciting, repeating, storytelling, teaching, threatening, verifying, warning and so on. It is crucial to recognize that in

LITERATURE while all acts can be represented, only speech acts can be reproduced. This gives speech acts a special literary immediacy of which AUTHORS typically take advantage. The decisive last action in the PLOT of Wharton's "Roman Fever," for example, is simply one character revealing a fact to another.

Stereotype: Originally a metal plate used for exact duplication in the printing process. Now, any model used without individual variation. Since variety is an AESTHETIC virtue, to say that a CHARACTER is a stereotype or a situation is stereotypical usually conveys a negative judgment.

Stock characters: See CHARACTER.

Stock situation: A familiar literary situation or incident, such as the love triangle, the deathbed promise, the accidental witnessing of a crime. See DEFAMIL-IARIZATION.

Story: See ACTION.

Stream of consciousness: The CONVENTION whereby a NARRATOR directly represents the unimpeded flow of a character's inner thoughts. Some critics restrict this term to the representation of a free association of thoughts that often abandons normal grammar and logic while reserving the term INTERIOR MONO-LOGUE for a grammatically and logically correct representation of inner thoughts.

Structure: The arrangement of the parts of a work. If these parts are seen as existing all at one time, we have a **synchronic structure**; if they are seen as existing through time, we have a **diachronic structure**. See EN: Structure.

Structuralism: The general term for the study of the STRUCTURES of phenomena. Structuralism grew from the linguistics of Ferdinand de Saussure (1857-1913) and the anthropology of Claude Lévi-Strauss (1908-). An underlying premise of structuralism is that while we focus consciously on the surface details of a phenomenon (such as the words of a NARRATIVE) in order to understand those details we construct, often unconsciously, a sense of how they are arranged. These arrangements, because they are more pervasive than the individual details and because they often escape conscious attention, are held to be of fundamental importance in our reactions to phenomena. The aim of structuralism is to reveal and analyze these arrangements. See EN: Structure and EN: Language.

Style: A habitual manner of expression, including choices in such matters as ATMOSPHERE, DICTION, FIGURATIVE LANGUAGE, RHYTHM, and so on. See TONE and EN: Language.

Style indirect libre: See FREE INDIRECT STYLE.

Subplot: A subsidiary PLOT, typically involving comparatively minor CHARAC-TERS, that supplements the main plot either by offering an extension of it (say to another social class) or a contrast to it (say a comic version of it). Also called **minor plot, secondary plot,** or **underplot.** Subplots are common in NOVELS but rare in SHORT STORIES.

Subsequent reading: Any reading other than a first reading of a text; sometimes called **second reading.** See IRONY and EN: The Narrative Situation.

Superego: See FREUDIAN CRITICISM.

Surrealism: An AESTHETIC movement, begun in early twentieth century France, emphasizing the expression of the unfettered imagination and the irrational, especially in dreams and dream-like juxtapositions of IMAGES and ACTIONS.

Suspense: The reader's psychological state of anxiety, tension, doubt, or pleasant excitement about what will happen in a NARRATIVE.

Symbol: Something that stands for something else; literally (from Greek), "a token of identity verified by comparing it with its other half." The cross is a symbol for Christianity. Symbols can be CONVENTIONAL, like the cross, or novel, generated within the specific work, like the pink ribbon in Hawthorne's "Young Goodman Brown" that comes to represent the title character's faith. Note that these symbols, cross and ribbon, respectively represent a generality and a specific. In FREUDIAN and JUNGIAN CRITICISM, important symbols are those representing unconscious states, which may be features of general humanity and also specific to a single character, as the gun in Wright's "The Man Who Was Almost a Man" is a phallic symbol representing the PROTAGONIST's idea of manliness. A symbol can be a word, phrase, IMAGE, object, ACTION, CHARACTER, or situation. See ALLEGORY.

Sympathy: See EMPATHY.

Synchronic structure: See STRUCTURE.

Synecdoche: FIGURATIVE LANGUAGE using division in any of four ways: (1) the general for the specific ("Here comes the army," meaning some soldiers); (2) the specific for the general ("He was a cutthroat," meaning murderer); (3) the part for the whole ("They hired three hands," meaning laborers); and (4) the material for the object made from it ("She trod the boards," meaning stage). See METONYMY.

Synopsis: A condensed outline or summary of a NARRATIVE. See also ARGUMENT.

Tale: A loosely defined term, sometimes synonymous with STORY, sometimes meaning any short prose NARRATIVE, sometimes forming a contrasting pair with SHORT STORY in which the tale is the more ROMANTIC and the short story the more REALISTIC.

Tale of the Great Detective: A GENRE characterized by a miraculously rational GREAT DETECTIVE as PROTAGONIST, a plodding sidekick who narrates the tale, baffled police, and the discovery of hidden guilt, usually accomplished by the Great Detective matching his or her mind with that of the criminal, his DOUBLE. Poe set the FORMULA with such works as "The Purloined Letter." See HARD BOILED DETECTIVE and EN: Genre.

Tall tale: A humorous TALE using REALISTIC detail and common speech while presenting impossible occurrences or superhuman CHARACTERS. Most tall tales, like the NARRATIVES about Paul Bunyan and Pecos Bill, are or pretend to be FOLKTALES, but there also exist more sophisticated tall tales, such as Rudolph Erich Raspe's *Baron von Munchausen's Narrative of his Marvellous Travels* (1785).

Tenor: See METAPHOR.

Tense of narration: The predominant verb tense used by the NARRATOR, almost always either present ("Our hero is leaving") or past ("Our hero left"). The IMPLIED AUTHOR's choice of tense of narration helps control our reactions to the NARRATIVE. See EN: Varieties of Narrative Stance.

Textual criticism: Scholarship that attempts to reconstruct a "correct" or "original" version of a text by studying its variants, the intentions of its AUTHOR, the CONVENTIONS at its time of composition, and so on.

Theme: The main idea or subject of a work of art. See EN: Theme.

Theoretical criticism: See CRITICISM.

Third-person narration: See NARRATION.

Third-person viewpoint: See VIEWPOINT.

Three-dimensional character: See CHARACTER.

Tone: The verbal expression of mental or emotional attitude. One can speak of the tone of a NARRATOR (or CHARACTER) as conciliatory or belligerent, tolerant or critical, playful or somber, and so on. Tone is conveyed by STYLE.

Tragedy: In general, a serious work describing the conflict between a PROTAGONIST (often a noble individual) and some superior force (such as fate or a deep flaw in the protagonist's own character) and having a woeful or dreadful RESOLUTION that, according to Aristotle, excites pity or terror in the audience. Some critics restrict the use of the term tragedy to DRAMA as opposed to NARRATIVE or LYRIC. In classic drama, tragedy is the antithesis of COMEDY.

Trope: A RHETORICAL figure. See FIGURATIVE LANGUAGE.

Trustworthy narrator: See RELIABLE NARRATOR.

Understatement: A variety of IRONY in which one sets a comparatively low value on something so that someone else will magnify its value in imagination. "Now that you mention it, I suppose you could call him handsome." See LITOTES.

Unity: A condition of artistic harmony, each part having an appropriate place in the whole work. Also called **coherence**. See FORM and EN: Aesthetic Virtues.

Unreliable narrator: A NARRATOR whose NARRATION the IMPLIED AUTHOR wants the reader to question, perhaps because the narrator is mistaken, deceitful, or in some way mentally incompetent. Also called **untrustworthy narrator**. See EN: Varieties of Narrative Stance.

Untrustworthy narrator: See UNRELIABLE NARRATOR.

Variety: The multiplication of novelty within a work. See EN: Aesthetic Virtues.

Vehicle: See METAPHOR.

Verbal irony: See IRONY.

Verisimilar: Having the appearance of truth.

Verisimilitude: The quality of being VERISIMILAR. See FICTION.

Viewpoint: The conditions governing a NARRATOR's knowledge of the events narrated. Also called **point of view.** The narrator by CONVENTION may have one of a number of viewpoints, but is normally expected to maintain that viewpoint throughout the NARRATIVE. An **omniscient viewpoint** gives access to all the events and all the thoughts of all the CHARACTERS. A **limited viewpoint** gives more restricted access, for example, just to those events occurring in the presence of a particular VIEWPOINT CHARACTER. A **limited omniscient viewpoint** gives access to all the events, but is limited to the thoughts of one or a small number of viewpoint characters. A **third-person viewpoint** sees the characters as "he" and "she" without being involved in the narrative. A **first-person viewpoint** is that of a narrator who is also a character in the narrative and often makes self-reference. Most critics agree that the selection of viewpoint is the IMPLIED AUTHOR's most important strategic choice. See EN: Varieties of Narrative Stance.

Viewpoint character: A CHARACTER in a NARRATIVE whose VIEWPOINT we readers share. We may or may not have access to the thoughts of a viewpoint character. Some works, like Twain's "The Diary of Adam and Eve," have more than one viewpoint character. Others, like Kafka's *The Metamorphosis,* use a sudden shift away from the viewpoint character to create a powerful narrative effect. Normally, however, if a work has a viewpoint character, it will have only one, as in James's "The Tree of Knowledge." See EN: Varieties of Narrative Stance.

Voice: Sometimes used as a synonym for TONE.

Western: A FORMULAIC GENRE set in the Western United States of the nineteenth century and characterized by the CONFLICT between a more civilized in-group and a more individualistic out-group which is resolved by the intervention of a lone HERO (or, rarely, HEROINE) who shares the survival skills of the out-group and the social values of the in-group. See En: Genre.

Questions for Contrast and Comparison

Each of the following Questions for Contrast and Comparison (QCC) capitalizes on the availability within this single collection of works that can, in many ways, contextualize each other. Following the Study and Writing Questions at the end of each STORY is a listing by number of the QCCs in this section that make reference to that story. These QCCs are constructed so that they will rarely duplicate issues raised in the Study and Writing Questions and so that they will, as a set consulted throughout reading this book, deal with a full range of matters that skilled readers come to know: important NARRATIVE TECHNIQUES, traditional IMAGES and SYMBOLS, variations on THEMES, and so on. These QCCs may be used to raise further issues about each story, to contextualize the study of individual works, to suggest some stories that might profitably be read in conjunction with a story just read, and to suggest comparative study and writing topics. One can adapt these QCCs by using more or fewer specific works than are suggested here or one can rely on them exactly as written below.

1. Water, which visibly brings forth plants and without which we die, frequently SYMBOLIZES life; but life can have many qualities. Compare and contrast the symbolic uses of water in Bierce's "An Occurrence at Owl Creek Bridge," Cheever's "The Swimmer," and Barth's "Night-Sea Journey."

2. Water in overwhelming quantities frequently SYMBOLIZES mystery and death. Compare and contrast the symbolic uses of water in the Genesis story of the Flood (Genesis 6:1–9:29), "Jonah," and Atwood's "The Resplendent Quetzal."

3. A forest may represent both a rejuvenating wilderness and a threatening antithesis to civilization. Compare and contrast the use of forests in at least three of the following: the Grimms' "Little Red Cap," Perrault's "Little Red Riding Hood," Hawthorne's "Young Goodman Brown," Bierce's "An Occurrence at Owl Creek Bridge," and Akutagawa's "In A Grove."

4. A garden often represents Paradise, a place both of safety and of natural vigor. Eden sets the model of the garden as the ideal world to which we wish to return, a natural environment purposefully ordered to support human life. Compare and contrast the significance of the gardens in
   a. Genesis, the Sufi tale of "The Ancient Coffer of Nuri Bey," and the Grimms' "Rapunzel," or
   b. Cortázar's "Continuity of Parks," Hawthorne's "Rappaccini's Daughter," and Steinbeck's "The Chrysanthemums."
   c. Compare and contrast any of the stories in (a) or (b) with the garden IMAGERY in Wells's *The Time Machine* or Zhu's "Chronicle of Mulberry Village."

5. The wilderness often represents a nature which we take to be challenging us to tame it. Compare and contrast the significance of the wilderness settings in
   a. Harte's "The Outcasts of Poker Flat" or Haycox's "Stage to Lordsburg," Conrad's *Heart of Darkness*, and London's "To Build a Fire," or
   b. any work in (a) with either Hoist's "The Zebra Storyteller" or Silko's "Yellow Woman."

6. Small variations in a STORY often make for significant differences in meaning and/or effect on a reader. Compare and contrast the Grimms' "Little Red Cap" and Perrault's "Little Red Riding Hood."

7. Some STORIES try to convey their meaning by focusing on a single important moment. Compare and contrast the importance of tight focus in stories about

   a. the moment of death, such as McCay's "Dreams of the Rarebit Fiend," Bierce's "An Occurrence at Owl Creek Bridge," and Toomer's "Becky," or

   b. the moment of discovering that one has been mistaken, such as Maupassant's "The Jewels," Chopin's "Désirée's Baby," and Joyce's "The Dead."

   Compare and contrast any of the stories in (a) or (b) with stories in which the parallel important "moment" develops slowly through time, as in stories about

   c. the moment of death, such as Tolstoy's *The Death of Ivan Ilyitch* and Mishima's "Patriotism," or

   d. the moment of discovering that one has been mistaken, such as James's "The Altar of the Dead" and H. G. Wells's "The Star."

8. Some STORIES have endings that are intended to surprise us in ways that REVERSE our previous understanding of what we had been reading. Because these endings were prominent in many of the stories of O. Henry, they are often known as O. Henry endings.

   a. Are the endings of O. Henry's "Springtime à la Carte" and "A Midsummer Knight's Dream" equally effective in giving significance to their respective stories?

   b. Compare and contrast the effectiveness of the endings in Chekov's "Vanka," Chopin's "Désirée's Baby," and one of the following: Crumb's "fred the teen-age girl pigeon," Saadawi's "She Has No Place in Paradise," and Hernandez's "The Whispering Tree."

   c. Compare and contrast the effectiveness of rereadings with that of first readings of any two STORIES with O. Henry endings.

9. To what extent should one think of Borges's "Pierre Menard, Author of the *Quixote*" and "Emma Zunz" as "stories," as "essays," or as something else? Are they alike as to type? What difference does our GENRE definition of these texts make to our understanding of them?

10. Compare the RHETORICAL effects of such catalogs as that in the fourth chapter of Genesis, the list of Menard's "visible work" in Borges's "Pierre Menard, Author of the *Quixote*," and the whole of Camoin's "Things I Did To Make It Possible."

11. Compare and contrast the importance of writing in

    a. the Taoist TALE called "Smelling Essays," and Chekov's "Vanka," or

    b. Borges's "Pierre Menard, Author of the *Quixote*," Holst's "The Zebra Storyteller," and Brautigan's "Homage to the San Francisco YMCA," or

    c. three of the following: Melville's "Bartleby the Scrivener," Twain's "The Diary of Adam and Eve," O. Henry's "Springtime à la Carte," Malamud's "The German Refugee" and LeGuin's "The Day Before the Revolution."

    d. Compare and contrast the importance of writing in any of the above with the importance of drawing in Barry's "The Night We All Got Sick."

12. Compare and contrast the uses of music in
    a. Kafka's *The Metamorphosis* or Delany's "Corona," Crumb's "fred the teenage girl pigeon," and Mason's "New Wave Format," or
    b. Joyce's "The Dead," Stein's "Miss Furr and Miss Skeene," and Barthelme's "The Piano Player," or
    c. any STORY in (a) with any story in (b).

13. Compare and contrast the IMAGE of the popular singer in Samuel R. Delany's "Corona" and R. Crumb's "fred the teen-age girl pigeon."

14. Truth often seems to be a matter of VIEWPOINT. Compare the uses of this idea in
    a. the Sufi TALE called "The Limitations of Dogma," Kafka's "A Common Confusion," Akutagawa's "In a Grove," and Borges's "Emma Zunz," or
    b. Poe's "The Purloined Letter," Wells's "The Star," and James's *The Turn of the Screw,* or
    c. Tanizaki's "The Thief," Singer's "Yentl the Yeshiva Boy," and either Jewett's "A White Heron" or Clarke's "The Star."

15. The relationship between employer and employee is based on economics but often goes beyond economics. Compare and contrast the nature of the employer/employee relationships in
    a. Melville's "Bartleby the Scrivener," Gogol's "The Overcoat," and Faulkner's "Barn Burning," or
    b. Borges's "Emma Zunz," Paton's "Life for a Life" or Gordimer's "Six Feet of the Country," and Cortázar's "Continuity of Parks."

16. What are the FORMULAIC elements of the TALE OF THE GREAT DETECTIVE as seen in
    a. Poe's "The Purloined Letter" and Doyle's "The Adventure of the Speckled Band"?
    b. Compare and contrast the effectiveness with which these stories use any one of these elements.
    c. Compare and contrast the formula for the Tale of the Great Detective with the elements found in one of these other stories of detection: Glaspell's "A Jury of Her Peers," Akutagawa's "In a Grove," Hammett's "The Gutting of Couffignal," Tanizaki's "The Thief."
    d. Compare and contrast the uses of what Poe (in "The Purloined Letter") calls the "identification of the reasoner's intellect with that of his opponent" in one story from (a) and one from (c).

17. Compare and contrast the roles of the women CHARACTERS in Poe's "The Black Cat," "The Purloined Letter," and "The Facts in the Case of M. Valdemar."

18. Compare and contrast uses of logic in Poe's "The Black Cat," "The Purloined Letter," and "The Facts in the Case of M. Valdemar."

19. Compare and contrast the uses made of eye IMAGERY in Poe's "The Black Cat," "The Purloined Letter," and "The Facts in the Case of M. Valdemar."

20. Compare and contrast the eye IMAGERY in the Bible STORY of the Fall (Genesis 3), the Grimm brothers' "Rapunzel," and either Poe's "The Black Cat" or Parker's "The Last Tea."

21. Compare and contrast the uses made of UNRELIABLE NARRATORS in three of the following: Poe's "The Black Cat" or Gilman's "The Yellow Wall-Paper," Tanizaki's "The Thief," Barth's "Night-Sea Journey," and Gordimer's "Six Feet of the Country."

22. Compare and contrast the significance of science in motivating the PLOTS of Poe's "The Facts in the Case of M. Valdemar," Wells's *The Time Machine*, Asimov's "Reason," and Ellison's "I Have No Mouth, and I Must Scream."

23. Compare and contrast the THEMATIC significance of horror in three of the following: Poe's "The Black Cat" or "The Facts in the Case of M. Valdemar," James's *The Turn of the Screw*, McCay's "Dreams of the Rarebit Fiend," and Kawabata's "One Arm."

24. Compare and contrast the uses of the architectural SETTINGS in
    a. the Grimm brothers' "Rapunzel" and Hawthorne's "Rappaccini's Daughter," or
    b. Poe's "The Black Cat," Doyle's "The Adventure of the Speckled Band," and James's *The Turn of the Screw*.

25. Compare and contrast the uses of FRAMING, the device of a STORY within the story, in
    a. "The Prodigal Son" (Luke 15) and the Biblical discussion of parables (Mark 4), or
    b. the story of Lycaon in Ovid's *Metamorphoses*, Maupassant's "Mother Savage" or Glasgow's "A Point in Morals," and Wells's *The Time Machine* or Conrad's *Heart of Darkness*, or
    c. Dostoevsky's "The Honest Thief," James's *The Turn of the Screw*, and Borges's "Emma Zunz" or Cortázar's "Continuity of Parks," or
    d. one story from (b), one story from (c), and McCay's "Dreams of the Rarebit Fiend."

26. What are the FAIRY TALE elements common to Perrault's "Little Red Riding Hood" and the three STORIES by the Grimm brothers?

27. Compare and contrast the uses made of FAIRY TALE elements in at least two of the following: Hawthorne's "Rappaccini's Daughter," Updike's "Should Wizard Hit Mommy?" Bruna's *The King*, Lem's "Prince Ferrix and the Princess Crystal," and Brautigan's "Homage to the San Francisco YMCA."

28. Compare and contrast the relationship(s) of art to life in
    a. Borges's "Emma Zunz," Holst's "The Zebra Storyteller," and James's "The Tree of Knowledge," or
    b. Stein's "Miss Furr and Miss Skeene," Delany's "Corona," and Mason's "A New Wave Format," or
    c. Borges's "Pierre Menard, Author of the *Quixote*," Cortázar's "Continuity of Parks," and Brautigan's "Homage to the San Francisco YMCA."

29. Compare and contrast the figures of the scientists in Hawthorne's "Rappaccini's Daughter," Poe's "The Facts in the Case of M. Valdemar," and Wells's *The Time Machine*.

30. Compare and contrast the roles of the main female CHARACTERS in the two STORIES by Hawthorne.

31. Compare and contrast the figure of the devil in the Genesis story of the Fall and in Hawthorne's "Young Goodman Brown."

32. Compare and contrast the treatment of the IMAGE of the tree in the STORY of The Fall in "Genesis" and in at least two of the following: Jewett's "A

White Heron," James's "The Tree of Knowledge," Toomer's "Becky," Brooks's "The Ballad of Rudolph Reed," and Hernandez's "The Whispering Tree."

33. Compare and contrast the treatment of willful silence in any three STORIES from either of the following groups:
    a. the Sufi TALE of "The Ancient Coffer of Nuri Bey," Melville's "Bartleby the Scrivener," Twain's "The Diary of Adam and Eve," Anderson's "Hands," and Atwood's "The Resplendent Quetzal," or
    b. Maupassant's "The Jewels," Glaspell's "A Jury of Her Peers," Wharton's "Roman Fever," Faulkner's "Barn Burning," and Thurber's "The Secrete Life of Walter Mitty."

34. Compare and contrast the relationships between the fathers and the sons in
    a. Joyce's "Counterparts" and Faulkner's "Barn Burning," or
    b. Wright's "The Man Who Was Almost A Man," Frank O'Connor's "My Oedipus Complex," and Callaghan's "A Cap for Steve," or
    c. James's "The Tree of Knowledge" and Watterson's "Something Under the Bed Is Drooling," or
    d. either story in (c) with any story in (a) or (b).

35. Compare and contrast the significance of James's control of VIEWPOINT in his three NARRATIVES collected here.

36. Compare and contrast the use of the rabbit IMAGE in Maupassant's "Mother Savage" and Porter's "The Grave."

37. Compare and contrast the importance of "treasures" to children in
    a. any three of the following: Mansfield's "The Doll's House," Porter's "The Grave," Callaghan's "A Cap for Steve," and Erdrich's "Chapter Two: Sita Kozka," or
    b. any story in (a) and Bruna's *The King*.

38. Compare and contrast the IMAGE of the grave in
    a. McCay's "Dreams of the Rarebit Fiend," Porter's "The Grave," and Gordimer's "Six Feet of the Country," or
    b. any of the stories in (a) and Erdrich's "Chapter Two: 1932, Sita Kozka."

39. Compare and contrast the significance of the guns in Wright's "The Man Who Was Almost A Man," Porter's "The Grave," and Brooks's "The Ballad of Rudolph Reed."

40. Compare and contrast the effects of DRAMATIC, as opposed to NARRATIVE, presentation in
    a. Aidoo's "Something to Talk About on the Way to the Funeral," Landolfi's "Rain," and either Parker's "The Last Tea" or Welty's "Petrified Man," or
    b. any of the stories in (a) and Hemingway's "A Clean, Well-Lighted Place" or Barthelme's "The Piano Player," or
    c. any of the stories in (a) or (b) and the Taoist tale "Outsides."

41. Compare and contrast the sources and effects of humor in
    a. O. Henry's "Springtime à la Carte" and Frank O'Connor's "My Oedipus Complex," or
    b. Allen's "The Whore of Mensa" and either Asimov's "Reason" or Lem's "Prince Ferrix and the Princess Crystal," or
    c. Stein's "Miss Furr and Miss Skeene" and Parker's "The Last Tea" or Coover's "The Brother," or

    d. Barthelme's "The Piano Player" and Brautigan's "Homage to the San Francisco YMCA."

42. Compare and contrast the use of the RHETORICAL device of APOSTROPHE in the first paragraph of Ovid's *Metamorphoses*, the last paragraph of Jewett's "A White Heron," and throughout Toomer's "Becky."

43. Compare and contrast the ways in which death comments on life in
    a. Tolstoy's *The Death of Ivan Ilyitch*, McCay's "Dreams of the Rarebit Fiend," and Saadawi's "She Has No Place in Paradise," or
    b. James's "The Altar of the Dead," Kafka's *The Metamorphosis*, and Aidoo's "Something to Talk About on the Way to the Funeral," or
    c. London's "To Build a Fire," Joyce's "The Dead," and Lawrence's "Odour of Chrysanthemums," or
    d. Maupassant's "Mother Savage," Toomer's "Becky," Paton's "Life for a Life," and Gordimer's "Six Feet of the Country."

44. Compare and contrast the roles of the friends in three of the following: Tolstoy's *The Death of Ivan Ilyitch*, Cather's "The Joy of Nelly Deane," Welty's "Lily Daw and the Three Ladies," and Lessing's "Pleasure."

45. Compare and contrast the relationship of the husband and wife in the marriages presented in
    a. Tolstoy's *The Death of Ivan Ilyitch*, Chopin's "Désirée's Baby" or Gilman's "The Yellow-Wallpaper," and Joyce's "The Dead," or
    b. Atwood's "The Resplendent Quetzal," Paley's "Wants," and Camoin's "Things I Did To Make It Possible," or
    c. The Sufi TALE of "The Ancient Coffer of Nuri Bey" or Akutagawa's "In a Grove," Poe's "The Black Cat," James's "The Tree of Knowledge," and Mishima's "Patriotism," or
    d. Twain's "The Diary of Adam and Eve," O. Henry's "A Midsummer Knight's Dream" or Lessing's "Pleasure," and Landolfi's "Rain," or
    e. Steinbeck's "The Harness," Fitzgerald's "Babylon Revisited," and Thurber's "The Secret Life of Water Mitty" or Barthelme's "The Piano Player," or
    f. Steinbeck's "The Chrysanthemums" and "The Harness."

46. Compare and contrast the significance of the physical wounds
    a. to the main characters of Tolstoy's *The Death of Ivan Ilyitch* and Kafka's *The Metamorphosis*, or
    b. to either character in (a) with that to the student in the Taoist "A Ch'an Koan."

47. Compare and contrast the relationships between the DOPPELGÄNGERS occupying the same spaces in Poe's "The Black Cat," Melville's "Bartleby the Scrivener" and Dostoevsky's "The Honest Thief."

48. Compare and contrast the significance of conflicting systems of reasoning within three of the following: the Taoist "A Ch'an Koan," Poe's "The Purloined Letter," Melville's "Bartleby the Scrivener," Asimov's "Reason," and Borges's "Pierre Menard, Author of the *Quixote*."

49. Compare and contrast the significance of using a workplace as a residence in
    a. Crane's "The Blue Hotel," Wells's *The Time Machine*, and Borges's "Emma Zunz," or
    b. three of the following: Melville's "Bartleby the Scrivener," Chekov's

"Vanka," James's *The Turn of the Screw*, and Gordimer's "Six Feet of the Country," or

   c. LeGuin's "The Day Before the Revolution" and Zhu's "Chronicle of Mulberry Village," or

   d. one from each of (a), (b), and (c).

50. Compare and contrast the significance of the city in Melville's "Bartleby the Scrivener," Benét's "Nightmare Number Three," and Baraka's "The Death of Horatio Alger."

51. Compare and contrast the refusals to act in

   a. Melville's "Bartleby the Scrivener" and Kafka's *The Metamorphosis*, or

   b. the Taoist STORY of "The Ancient Coffer of Nuri Bey," Glasgow's "A Point in Morals," and either story in (a).

52. Compare and contrast the relationship between the siblings in James's *The Turn of the Screw* or Kafka's *The Metamorphosis*, Porter's "The Grave" or Hernandez's "The Whispering Tree," and Coover's "The Brother."

53. Compare and contrast the significance of leaving home in

   a. the Grimm brothers' "Little Red Cap," Agee's "A Mother's Tale," and Wright's "The Man Who Was Almost a Man," or

   b. three of the following: Crane's "The Blue Hotel," Wright's "The Man Who Was Almost A Man," Barth's "Night-Sea Journey," and Singer's "Yentl the Yeshiva Boy."

54. Compare and contrast the relative significance of lying in

   a. the Grimm brothers' "The Three Spinsters," Borges's "Emma Zunz," and Singer's "Yentl The Yeshiva Boy," or

   b. Maupassant's "The Jewels," Chopin's "Désirée's Baby," and Wright's "The Man Who Was Almost a Man," or

   c. Dostoevsky's "The Honest Thief," Akutagawa's "In a Grove," and Tanizaki's "The Thief."

55. Compare and contrast the importance of race relations in

   a. Faulkner's "Dry September" or Brooks's "The Ballad of Rudolph Reed" and Baldwin's "Going to Meet the Man," or

   b. Toomer's "Becky," Wright's "The Man Who Was Almost a Man," and Baraka's "The Death of Horatio Alger," or

   c. Conrad's *Heart of Darkness*, Paton's "Life for a Life" or Gordimer's "Six Feet of the Country," and Achebe's "Girls at War," or

   d. Delany's "Corona" with any story from (a), (b), or (c), or

   e. Faulkner's "Barn Burning" or "Dry September" and Wright's "The Man Who Was Almost A Man."

56. Compare and contrast the use of train IMAGERY in at least three of the following: Bierce's "An Occurrence at Owl Creek Bridge," Crane's "The Blue Hotel," Glasgow's "A Point in Morals," Toomer's "Becky," Wright's "The Man Who Was Almost a Man," Agee's "A Mother's Tale," and Zhu's "Chronicle of Mulberry Tree Village."

57. Compare and contrast the stepparent/stepchild relationships in the Grimm brothers' "Rapunzel" and Munro's "Royal Beatings."

58. Compare and contrast the treatment of vigilante justice in

   a. three of the following: Anderson's "Hands," Faulkner's "Dry

September," Baldwin's "Going to Meet the Man," and Munro's "Royal Beatings," or

b. Harte's "The Outcasts of Poker Flat" and any story in (a).

59. Compare and contrast the father/child relationships in Kafka's *The Metamorphosis*, Frank O'Connor's "My Oedipus Complex," and Munro's "Royal Beatings."

60. Compare and contrast the representation of the practice of law in Melville's "Bartleby the Scrivener," Tolstoy's *The Death of Ivan Ilyitch*, and Joyce's "Counterparts."

61. Compare and contrast the role of alcohol in

a. the story of Noah in Genesis or Poe's "The Black Cat," Joyce's "Counterparts" or Fitzgerald's "Babylon Revisited," and Hemingway's "A Clean, Well-Lighted Place," or

b. any story in (a) and McCay's "Dreams of the Rarebit Fiend."

62. When emotions evoked in a person by one individual or object are directed by that person at another individual or object, the first person is said to be *displacing* his or her emotions. Compare and contrast the role of displacement in Joyce's "Counterparts," Mansfield's "The Doll's House," and Munro's "Royal Beatings."

63. Compare and contrast the characters who display bitterness in three of the following: Joyce's "Counterparts," Faulkner's "Barn Burning," Malamud's "The German Refugee," and Ellison's "I Have No Mouth, and I Must Scream."

64. Many stories make use of the conjunction between the supposed spiritual warmth of the Christmas season and the climatic cold of that season.

a. Compare and contrast the uses of this conjunction in stories with child protagonists such as Chekov's "Vanka" and Baraka's "The Death of Horatio Alger."

b. Compare and contrast the uses of this conjunction in any three stories with adult protagonists such as James's *The Turn of the Screw*, Joyce's "The Dead," Cather's "The Joy of Nelly Deane," or Kafka's *The Metamorphosis*.

c. Compare and contrast the significance of the Christmastide setting in any story from (a) and any story from (b).

65. Compare and contrast the importance of secrets in the Sufi TALE of "The Ancient Coffer of Nuri Bey," James's "The Tree of Knowledge" or Glaspell's "A Jury of Her Peers," and Chopin's "Désirée's Baby" or Joyce's "The Dead."

66. Compare and contrast the representation of "country people" in Flannery O'Connor's "Good Country People" and Mason's "A New-Wave Format."

67. Compare and contrast the impact of politics on private lives in Joyce's "The Dead," Mishima's "Patriotism," Achebe's "Girls at War" or Gordimer's "Six Feet of the Country," and Malamud's "The German Refugee" or Spiegelman's "Prisoner on the Hell Planet."

68. Compare and contrast the snow IMAGERY in three of the following: Harte's "The Outcasts of Poker Flat," Chekov's "Vanka," London's "To Build a Fire," Joyce's "The Dead," and Fitzgerald's "Babylon Revisited."

69. Compare and contrast the role of religion in
    a. Hawthorne's "Young Goodman Brown" or Toomer's "Becky," Hardy's "The Son's Veto," and Clarke's "The Star," or
    b. James's "The Altar of the Dead," Joyce's "The Dead," and Singer's "Yentl the Yeshiva Boy," or
    c. Chaucer's "The Miller's Tale" with any story in (a) or (b), or
    d. Saadawi's "She Has No Place in Paradise" with any story in (a) or (b), or
    e. Hemingway's "A Clean, Well-Lighted Place" with any story in (a).
70. Compare and contrast the significance of economics in
    a. Tolstoy's *The Death of Ivan Ilyitch*, Conrad's *Heart of Darkness*, and Kafka's *The Metamorphosis*, or
    b. Joyce's "Counterparts," Faulkner's "Barn Burning," and Wright's "The Man Who Was Almost A Man," or
    c. Hammett's "The Gutting of Couffignal" or Hemingway's "A Clean, Well-Lighted Place" and any two of the following: Chekov's "Vanka," Lawrence's "The Rocking-Horse Winner," Callaghan's "A Cap for Steve," and Olsen's "I Stand Here Ironing," or
    d. any three of the following: the Grimm brothers' "The Three Spinsters," Maupassant's "The Jewels," Toomer's "Becky," Cather's "The Joy of Nelly Deane," Mansfield's "The Doll's House," Welty's "Lily Daw and the Three Ladies," Malamud's "The German Refugee," Achebe's "Girls at War," and Saadawi's "She Has No Place in Paradise," or
    e. Gogol's "The Overcoat," Kafka's "A Common Confusion," and Brautigan's "Homage to the San Francisco YMCA," or
    f. O. Henry's "A Midsummer Knight's Dream," Lessing's "Pleasure," and Cheever's "The Swimmer."
71. Compare and contrast the significance of the device of metamorphosis in
    a. the selections from Ovid's *Metamorphoses*, Poe's "The Facts in the Case of M. Valdemar," and Kafka's *The Metamorphosis*, or
    b. Poe's "The Black Cat" and Hawthorne's "Rappaccini's Daughter."
72. Compare and contrast the THEMATIC significance of the dying character's final vision in
    a. Poe's "The Facts in the Case of M. Valdemar," Tolstoy's *The Death of Ivan Ilyitch*, and Kafka's *The Metamorphosis*, or
    b. McCay's "Dreams of the Rarebit Fiend," London's "To Build a Fire," and Bierce's "An Occurrence at Owl Creek Bridge" or Saadawi's "She Has No Place in Paradise."
73. Some stories maintain a single VIEWPOINT throughout; others vary their viewpoint. In a few, the comparatively consistent viewpoint is radically changed just at the end. Compare and contrast the significance of this device of change in any three of the following: the Sufi TALE called "The Limitations of Dogma," Chopin's "Désirée's Baby," Wells's "The Star," and Kafka's *The Metamorphosis*.
74. Compare and contrast the effect of treating the fantastic as commonplace in Kafka's *The Metamorphosis*, Kawabata's "One Arm," and Barthelme's "The Piano Player."
75. Compare and contrast the effect of having the STORY require the reader to change his or her normal perceptions in the course of Kafka's "A Common

Confusion," Borges's "Pierre Menard, Author of the *Quixote*," and Cortázar's "Continuity of Parks."

76. Compare and contrast in as many ways as possible Wells's "The Star" and
The Time Machine, considering at least STRUCTURE, CHARACTERIZATION,
SYMBOLISM, the role of science, and DIDACTIC implications.

77. Compare and contrast the significance of the journey away and subsequent
return to home in
a. Perrault's "Little Red Riding Hood," the Grimm brothers' "Little Red
Cap," Lessing's "Pleasure," and Zhu's "Chronicle of Mulberry Village,"
or
b. three of the following: Hawthorne's "Young Goodman Brown," Kafka's
"A Common Confusion," Steinbeck's "The Harness," and Cheever's
"The Swimmer."

78. Compare and contrast the significance of the family in Kafka's "A Common
Confusion" and *The Metamorphosis*.

79. Compare and contrast the uses of fire IMAGERY in
a. London's "To Build a Fire," Faulkner's "Barn Burning," and Baldwin's
"Going to Meet the Man," or
b. Genesis 3:24, the Taoist TALE called "Smelling Essays," and Poe's "The
Black Cat."

80. Compare and contrast the significance of leg injuries in Kafka's "A Common Confusion," Faulkner's "Barn Burning," and Flannery O'Connor's
"Good Country People."

81. Compare and contrast the attitudes toward African-Americans that are
projected by each of the STORIES by Faulkner. Do the attitudes in these
stories seem compatible with each other?

82. Compare and contrast the NARRATIVE uses of gambling in Harte's "The
Outcasts of Poker Flat" or Crane's "The Blue Hotel," Tolstoy's *The Death
of Ivan Ilyitch*, and Lawrence's "The Rocking-Horse Winner."

83. Compare and contrast the Grimm brothers' "Little Red Cap" with Jewett's
"A White Heron."

84. Compare contrast the way different authors use strongly regional SETTINGS,
such as the American South, to convey and use socioeconomic information.
a. To what extent do such white authors as Faulkner, Flannery O'Connor,
and Welty give a mutually consistent picture of the South?
b. To what extent do such African-American authors as Toomer, Wright,
and Baldwin give a mutually consistent picture of the South?
c. To what extent are the common elements of the white authors' picture
and the common elements of the black authors' picture the same? To
what extent are they different? In what ways, if any, do these differences
seem to reflect the race of the authors?
d. Compare and contrast the uses made of SETTING by Canadian authors
Atwood, Callaghan, and Munro.
e. Compare and contrast the uses made of the New England SETTING in
Hawthorne's "Young Goodman Brown" and Jewett's "A White
Heron."
f. Compare and contrast the uses made of the California SETTING in three
of the following: Hammett's "The Gutting of Couffignal," Steinbeck's

"The Chrysanthemums" or "The Harness," and Brautigan's "Homage to the San Francisco YMCA."

85. Compare and contrast the picture of race relations in Paton's "Life for a Life" and Gordimer's "Six Feet of the Country." What are the common elements in these pictures? What are the uncommon elements? To what extent do the uncommon elements seem to reflect the gender of the author?

86. Compare and contrast the picture of race relations in Paton's "Life for a Life" or Gordimer's "Six Feet of the Country" with that in Faulkner's "Dry September" or Baldwin's "Going to Meet the Man."

87. Compare and contrast the uses of humor in
   a. McCay's "Dreams of the Rarebit Fiend" and Welty's "Lily Daw and the Three Ladies," or
   b. Thurber's "The Secret Life of Walter Mitty" and Watterson's "Something Under the Bed is Drooling."

88. Compare and contrast the presentations of female groups in Wharton's "Roman Fever," Stein's "Miss Furr and Miss Skeene," either Welty's "Petrified Man" or "Lily Daw and the Three Ladies," and Mansfield's "The Doll's House."

89. Compare and contrast the uses of humor in the two STORIES by Welty.

90. Compare and contrast the three lodgers in Kafka's *The Metamorphosis* with the three ladies in Welty's "Lily Daw and the Three Ladies."

91. Compare and contrast the role of miscommunication in the dissolution of the central marriage in Fitzgerald's "Babylon Revisited," Paley's "Wants," and Camoin's "Things I Did To Make It Possible."

92. STREAM-OF-CONSCIOUSNESS NARRATION conventionally dramatizes the train of a character's conscious and unconscious thoughts.
   a. Compare and contrast the uses of stream-of-consciousness narration in the last sections of Bierce's "An Occurrence at Owl Creek Bridge" and Joyce's "The Dead."
   b. Compare and contrast the significance of using first or third person stream-of-consciousness narration in Gilman's "The Yellow Wall-Paper" or Paley's "Wants" and Joyce's "Counterparts."
   c. Compare and contrast the uses of stream-of-consciousness in producing humor in McCay's "Dreams of the Rarebit Fiend" and Thurber's "The Secret Life of Walter Mitty."
   d. Compare and contrast stream-of-consciousness narration in any of the stories above with multiple first person narration, as in Akutagawa's "In a Grove."
   e. Compare and contrast multiple first person narration, as in Twain's "The Diary of Adam and Eve," with single first person narration, as in Poe's "The Black Cat," Frank O'Connor's "My Oedipus Complex," or Erdrich's "Chapter Two: 1932, Sita Kozka."
   f. To what extent is it helpful to distinguish between first person narration and stream-of-consciousness narration in considering such stories as Tanizaki's "The Thief," Barth's "Night-Sea Journey," and Baraka's "The Death of Horatio Alger"?

93. Compare and contrast the significance of the brevity of the following NARRATIVES: Brautigan's "Homage to the San Francisco YMCA," Paley's "Wants," Holst's "The Zebra Storyteller," and Carver's "Viewfinder."

94. Compare and contrast the treatment of desire in
    a. Paley's "Wants" and Camoin's "Things I Did To Make It Possible," or
    b. Crumb's "fred the teen-age girl pigeon" and Moore's "How."

95. Although verbal and graphic art (paintings, sculpture, and so on) seem to offer two fundamentally different means of representation, graphic art often contains or is labelled by words and NARRATIVES often involve or describe graphic art. Compare and contrast the narrative uses of graphic representation in
    a. James's "The Tree of Knowledge" and Carver's "Viewfinder," or
    b. in any three of the following: McCay's "Dreams of the Rarebit Fiend," Crumb's "fred the teen-age girl pigeon," Bruna's *The King*, Spiegelman's "Prisoner on the Hell Planet," Hernandez's, "The Whispering Tree," Barry's "The Night We All Got Sick," and Watterson's "Something Under the Bed is Drooling," or
    c. in Carver's "Viewfinder" and any of the narratives in (b).

96. Compare and contrast the NARRATIVE significance of hands in any three of the following: Anderson's "Hands," Kawabata's "One Arm," Baraka's "The Death of Horatio Alger," and Carver's "Viewfinder."

97. Compare and contrast the portrayal of family relationships in
    a. Fitzgerald's "Babylon Revisited" or Carver's "Viewfinder," Updike's "Should Wizard Hit Mommy?" or Barthelme's "The Piano Player," and Hardy's "The Son's Veto" or Kafka's *The Metamorphosis*, or
    b. James's "The Tree of Knowledge," Wright's "The Man Who Was Almost a Man," and Adams's "A Southern Spelling Bee" or Erdrich's "Chapter Two: 1932, Sita Kozka," or
    c. any STORY from (a) and any story from (b).

98. Compare and contrast the significance of the length of the telling in the STORY of Noah (Genesis 6–9), the Taoist "A Ch'an Koan," the Grimms' "Rapunzel," and one of the following: Toomer's "Becky," Paley's "Wants," Hannah's "I'm Shaking to Death," Kincaid's "Girl," or Barry's "The Night We All Got Sick."

99. Compare and contrast the SYMBOLIC meaning of flowers in any two of the following: the Grimms' TALE of "Little Red Cap" or Broumas's "Little Red Riding Hood," Hawthorne's "Rappaccini's Daughter," Wells's *The Time Machine*, Steinbeck's "The Chrysanthemums," and Silko's "Yellow Woman."

100. Many STORIES begin with DESCRIPTIONS of nature. Compare and contrast the uses of the opening descriptions of nature in
    a. Faulkner's "Dry September," Steinbeck's "The Chrysanthemums," and Hammett's "The Gutting of Couffignal," or
    b. any of the stories in (a) with opening nature descriptions seen through the eyes of a specific character in one of the following: Conrad's *Heart of Darkness*, Atwood's "The Resplendent Quetzal," Zhu's "Chronicle of Mulberry Village," or
    c. any story from (a) and any story from (b) and the opening nature description in London's "To Build a Fire."

101. Since most marriages of any duration produce children, childlessness in marriage may be a very important fact.

    a. In both Steinbeck STORIES, a central marriage is childless. Compare and contrast the significance of this fact for each wife, for each husband, and for each story.

    b. Compare and contrast the childless marriages in three of the following: Poe's "The Black Cat," Glaspell's "A Jury of Her Peers," Steinbeck's "The Chrysanthemums" or "The Harness," Gordimer's "Six Feet of the Country," and Malamud's "The German Refugee."

102. Compare and contrast the relationships of neighbors in three of the following: Cather's "The Joy of Nelly Deane," Glaspell's "A Jury of Her Peers," Anderson's "Hands," Steinbeck's "The Chrysanthemums" or "The Harness," Welty's "Lily Daw and the Three Ladies" or "Petrified Man," and Aidoo's "Something to Talk About on the Way to the Funeral."

103. Compare and contrast the way regional color both particularizes and universalizes the actions in

    a. either Steinbeck's "The Chrysanthemums" or "The Harness" and either Faulkner's "Barn Burning" or "Dry September," or

    b. either Welty's "Lily Daw and the Three Ladies" or "Petrified Man" and Flannery O'Connor's "Good Country People."

104. Compare and contrast the presentation of refugees in three of the following: Anderson's "Hands," Hammett's "The Gutting of Couffignal," Malamud's "The German Refugee," and Achebe's "Girls at War."

105. Compare and contrast the IMAGE of New York City in three of the following: Melville's "Bartleby the Scrivener," O. Henry's "A Midsummer Knight's Dream" or "Springtime à la Carte," Malamud's "The German Refugee," and Paley's "Wants" or Moore's "How."

106. Compare and contrast the city/country opposition in

    a. the Grimm brothers' tale of "Little Red Cap," Hawthorne's "Young Goodman Brown," and Anderson's "Hands," or

    b. Hardy's "The Son's Veto," Steinbeck's "The Harness," and Aidoo's "Something to Talk About on the Way to the Funeral," or

    c. O. Henry's "Springtime à la Carte" or "A Midsummer Knight's Dream," Benét's "Nightmare Number Three," and Agee's "A Mother's Tale," or

    d. Hawthorne's "Young Goodman Brown," Hardy's "The Son's Veto," and Zhu's "Chronicle of Mulberry Tree Village."

107. Compare and contrast the significance of changing the VIEWPOINT CHARACTER after the first section of Tolstoy's *The Death of Ivan Ilyitch* with a similar change for the last section of Kafka's *The Metamorphosis* or Wells's "The Star."

108. Compare and contrast the uses of chrysanthemums in Lawrence's "Odour of Chrysanthemums" and Steinbeck's "The Chrysanthemums."

109. Compare and contrast the reactions of the wives to the news of their husbands' deaths in Tolstoy's *The Death of Ivan Ilyitch*, Lawrence's "Odour of Chrysanthemums," and Paton's "Life for a Life."

110. Compare and contrast the relationship of children to death in Lawrence's "Odour of Chrysanthemums" and Porter's "The Grave."

111. Compare and contrast the significance of funeral preparations in Lawrence's "Odour of Chrysanthemums" and Aidoo's "Something to Talk About on the Way to the Funeral."

112. Compare and contrast the STYLES of the two NARRATIVES by Lawrence. In what ways is each appropriate in its own right?

113. Compare and contrast the opening CONTENT and TONE of the Grimm brothers' TALE of "Rapunzel" with that of Lawrence's "The Rocking-Horse Winner." Compare and contrast the THEMATIC contents of these two STORIES.

114. Compare and contrast the use of the supernatural in
    a. the Sufi TALE called "The Bequest," Lawrence's "The Rocking-Horse Winner," and Akutagawa's "In a Grove," or
    b. any of the stories in (a) and James's *The Turn of The Screw*.

115. Compare and contrast the role of Gerasim in Tolstoy's *The Death of Ivan Ilyitch* with that of Bassett in Lawrence's "The Rocking-Horse Winner."

116. Compare and contrast the father/daughter relationships in Hawthorne's "Rappaccini's Daughter," Fitzgerald's "Babylon Revisited," and Munro's "Royal Beatings."

117. Compare and contrast the police figures in either Poe's "The Black Cat" or "The Purloined Letter," Glaspell's "A Jury of Her Peers," and Paton's "Life for a Life."

118. Compare and contrast the way the main male CHARACTERS react to the deaths of their wives in Twain's "The Diary of Adam and Eve," Fitzgerald's "Babylon Revisited," and Steinbeck's "The Harness."

119. The written DESCRIPTION of violence may vividly reveal the sensibility of the writer.
    a. What are the common features to the descriptions of violence in Akutagawa's "In A Grove," Kawabata's "One Arm," and Mishima's "Patriotism"? In what ways might these features seem to reflect Japanese culture?
    b. What are the features common to the descriptions of violence in Baldwin's "Going to Meet the Man," Faulkner's "Barn Burning" or "Dry September," and Wright's "The Man Who Was Almost a Man"? In what ways might these features seem to reflect Southern U.S. culture?
    c. By comparing and contrasting the descriptions of violence in any story from (a) with that in any story from (b), consider the way(s) in which physical violence seems to have a culture-bound meaning.
    d. Compare and contrast the NARRATIVE uses of violence in the Taoist "A Ch'an Koan" and Perrault's "Little Red Riding Hood."
    e. Compare and contrast the presentation of violence in Poe's "The Black Cat," Doyle's "The Adventure of the Speckled Band" or Hammett's "The Gutting of Couffignal," and Haycox's "Stage to Lordsburg."

120. Compare and contrast the speaking tongue in Poe's "The Facts in the Case of M. Valdemar," the speaking arm in Kawabata's "One Arm," and the narrator in Barth's "Night-Sea Journey."

121. Compare and contrast the woman's detached arm in Kawabata's "One Arm" and the woman's artificial leg in Flannery O'Connor's "Good Country People."

122. Compare and contrast the significance of the human body in Paton's "Life for a Life" or Gordimer's "Six Feet of the Country," Poe's "The Facts in the Case of M. Valdemar" or Ellison's "I Have No Mouth, and I Must Scream," and Baldwin's "Going to Meet the Man" or Kawabata's "One Arm."

123. It is traditional to see humans and machines as fundamentally antithetical, as when Ellison's narrator invokes "the innate loathing that all machines had always held for the weak soft creatures who had built them." Compare and contrast the underlying human/machine relationships in
    a. Benét's "Nightmare Number Three" or Ellison's "I Have No Mouth, and I Must Scream," Asimov's "Reason," and Barthelme's "The Piano Player," or
    b. Steinbeck's "The Harness," Flannery O'Connor's "Good Country People," and Carver's "Viewfinder," or
    c. one story from (a) and one story from (b).

124. Many works of literature function in part by relying on their readers to know of some earlier work to which the later one alludes. Compare and contrast the use(s) and effect(s) of ALLUSION in any two of the following: Twain's "The Diary of Adam and Eve," Clarke's "The Star," Coover's "The Brother," Broumas's "Little Red Riding Hood," and Hay's "Rapunzel" (which allude, respectively, to the STORY of Adam and Eve in Genesis, Wells's "The Star," the story of Noah in Genesis, and the Grimm brothers' TALES of "Little Red Cap" and "Rapunzel").

125. Compare and contrast the significance of food in
    a. three of the following: the Grimms' TALE of "Rapunzel" or "Little Red Cap" or Kafka's *The Metamorphosis*, O. Henry's "Springtime à la Carte," and Mason's "A New-Wave Format," or
    b. one of the stories from (a) and Colette's "The Other Wife" and Lessing's "Pleasure," or
    c. one of the stories from (a) and Kincaid's "Girl," or
    d. McCay's "Dreams of the Rarebit Fiend" and Barry's "The Night We All Got Sick."

126. Compare and contrast the treatment of the breakdown of a CHARACTER'S faith in
    a. Hawthorne's "Young Goodman Brown" and Conrad's *Heart of Darkness*, or
    b. one story from (a) and Mishima's "Patriotism," or
    c. one story from (a) and Brautigan's "Homage to the San Francisco YMCA."

127. Compare and contrast the importance of the business office as a SETTING in Gogol's "The Overcoat" or Tolstoy's *The Death of Ivan Ilyitch*, Melville's "Bartleby the Scrivener" or Borges's "Emma Zunz," and O. Henry's "A Midsummer Knight's Dream" or Joyce's "Counterparts."

128. Many STORIES portray the voluntary sacrifices women make for men. Compare and contrast the thematic importance of these sacrifices in at least three of these stories: Hawthorne's "Rappaccini's Daughter" or Mishima''s "Patriotism," Gilman's "The Yellow Wall-Paper," Kawabata's "One Arm" or Flannery O'Connor's "Good Country People," and Singer's "Yentel the Yeshiva Boy" or Hannah's "I'm Shaking to Death."

129. Compare and contrast the significance of longing for someone in Chekov's "Vanka," Fitzgerald's "Babylon Revisited," and one of the following: Broumas's "Little Red Riding Hood," Carver's "Viewfinder," Camoin's "Things I Did To Make It Possible," and Hannah's "I'm Shaking to Death."

130. In American literature, the North and the South are often used to express

THEMATIC as well as geographic contrasts. Compare and contrast the role of that contrast in three of the following: Bierce's "An Occurrence at Owl Creek Bridge," Wright's "The Man Who Was Almost a Man," Adams's "A Southern Spelling Bee," and Hannah's "I'm Shaking to Death."

131. Compare and contrast the significance of human beauty in
   a. the Grimm brothers' tale of "The Three Spinsters" and Hannah's "I'm Shaking to Death," or
   b. either STORY from (a) and one of the following: Olsen's "I Stand Here Ironing," Kawabata's "One Arm," Allen's "The Whore of Mensa," and Lem's "Prince Ferrix and the Princess Crystal," or
   c. any story from (a) or (b) and LeGuin's "The Day Before the Revolution."

132. Compare and contrast the portrayal of people as animals in at least one TALE in Ovid's *Metamorphoses* and in Kafka's *The Metamorphosis* with that of animals as people in at least one of the following: Perrault's "Little Red Riding Hood," Grimms' "Little Red Cap," Agee's "A Mother's Tale," Updike's "Should Wizard Hit Mommy?" Crumb's "fred the teen-age girl pigeon," and Holst's "The Zebra Storyteller."

133. Erotic attraction obviously binds people together, but in some ways the power of eros sometimes separates people. Compare and contrast the portraits of erotic separation in at least two of the STORIES from one of the following groups or in one story from each of at least three of the following groups:
   a. the Genesis stories of Adam and Eve and of Noah;
   b. Steinbeck's "The Harness," Joyce's "The Dead," Lawrence's "The Odour of Chrysanthemums," and Welty's "Petrified Man";
   c. Hawthorne's "Young Goodman Brown," Gilman's "The Yellow Wallpaper," Kawabata's "One Arm," Ellison's "I Have No Mouth, and I Must Scream," and Silko's "Yellow Woman";
   d. Baldwin's "Going to Meet the Man" and Faulkner's "Dry September";
   e. Chaucer's "The Miller's Tale," Singer's "Yentl the Yeshiva Boy," and Allen's "The Whore of Mensa."

134. Compare and contrast the portraits of the teacher in the Taoist "A Ch'an Koan," Anderson's "Hands," Atwood's "The Resplendent Quetzal," and Zhu's "Chronicle of Mulberry Tree Village."

135. Compare and contrast the social structure of
   a. boys' groups in Tanizaki's "The Thief," Callaghan's "A Cap for Steve" or Baraka's "The Death of Horatio Alger," and Singer's "Yentl the Yeshiva Boy," or
   b. girls' groups in Cather's "The Joy of Nelly Deane" and Mansfield's "The Doll House," or
   c. children's groups in any story from (a) and any story from (b).

136. Compare and contrast the significance of rain in the Genesis story of Noah, Coover's "The Brother," and Landolfi's "Rain."

137. Compare and contrast the relationship between the central female CHARACTER and her helper(s) in
   a. the Grimms' "The Three Spinsters," Glaspell's "A Jury of Her Peers," and Welty's "Lily Daw and the Three Ladies," or
   b. Gilman's "The Yellow Wall-Paper," Landolfi's "Rain," and Achebe's "Girls at War," or

c. one STORY from each of the previous groups.

138. Compare and contrast the significance of dreams in McCay's "Dreams of the Rarebit Fiend," Thurber's "The Secret Life of Walter Mitty," and Landolfi's "Rain."

139. Many NARRATIVES are at least in part about the activity of constructing narratives. Compare and contrast the treatment of this THEME in any three of the following: Akutagawa's "In a Grove," Borges's "Emma Zunz" or "Pierre Menard, Author of the *Quixote*," Updike's "Should Wizard Hit Mommy?" Cortázar's "Continuity of Parks," Aidoo's "Something to Talk About on the Way to the Funeral," Holst's "The Zebra Storyteller," Landolfi's "Rain," Hernandez's "The Whispering Tree," and Watterson's "Something Under the Bed Is Drooling."

140. Compare and contrast the effects in Gogol's "The Overcoat" and Kafka's *The Metamorphosis* of the NARRATIVE continuing beyond the death of the main CHARACTER.

141. Compare and contrast the treatment of czarist bureaucracy in Gogol's "The Overcoat" and Tolstoy's *The Death of Ivan Ilyitch*.

142. Compare and contrast the occupation of copyist in the lives of the main CHARACTERS in Gogol's "The Overcoat" and Melville's "Bartleby the Scrivener."

143. Compare and contrast the alternating FIRST PERSON NARRATION of Twain's "The Diary of Adam and Eve" with the alternating FREE INDIRECT STYLE of Atwood's "The Resplendent Quetzal."

144. Compare and contrast the notion of the Golden Age in Ovid's *Metamorphoses* with the description in Genesis of the Garden of Eden.

145. Compare and contrast the STORIES of the flood in
    a. the Bible (Genesis 6:1–9:29) and in Ovid's *Metamorphoses*, or
    b. the Bible (Genesis 6:1–9:29), Chaucer's "The Miller's Tale," and Coover's "The Brother."

146. Some NARRATIVES, although they are highly FANTASTIC, make strategic use of homely, REALISTIC details, as when Ovid in his story of the flood in *Metamorphoses* writes that "dolphins took possession of the woods." Compare and contrast the use of this blending of the fantastic and the realistic in three of the following: Ovid's *Metamorphoses*, the Grimm brothers' "The Three Spinsters," Wells's *The Time Machine* or "The Star," Kafka's "A Common Confusion" or *The Metamorphosis*, Holst's "The Zebra Storyteller," and Brautigan's "Homage to the San Francisco YMCA."

147. Whenever we read a NARRATIVE, we become involved in acts of interpretation. Some narratives make the activity of interpretation central to their PLOTS. Compare and contrast the importance of interpretation as a literary subject in
    a. The story of Deucalion and Pyrrha in Ovid's *Metamorphoses*, the Biblical discussion of PARABLES (Mark 4), and the Sufi TALE of "The Bequest," or
    b. Asimov's "Reason," Allen's "The Whore of Mensa," and Borges's "Emma Zunz."

148. Even highly formulaic GENRES often evolve through time. In order to understand this process, compare and contrast works in the following genres:

    a. The Tale of the Great Detective (Poe's "The Purloined Letter" and Doyle's "The Adventure of the Speckled Band,"

    b. Science Fiction (either Hawthorne's "Rappaccini's Daughter," Wells's *The Time Machine*, Delany's "Corona," Ellison's "I Have No Mouth, and I Must Scream," and LeGuin's "The Day Before the Revolution," or Poe's "The Facts in the Case of M. Valdemar," Wells's "The Star," Benét's "Nightmare Number Three," and Clarke's "The Star"), and

    c. The Western (Harte's "The Outcasts of Poker Flat," Crane's "The Blue Hotel," Haycox's "Stage to Lordsburg," Steinbeck's "The Chrysanthemums," Silko's "Yellow Woman").

149. Compare and contrast the Bible's use of the ship IMAGE in the STORY of Noah (Genesis 6:1–29), in "Jonah," and in Mark 4.

150. Compare and contrast the significance of skin color in Chopin's "Désirée's Baby," Toomer's "Becky," and Saadawi's "She Has No Place in Paradise."

151. Compare and contrast the uses of the names Faith and Grace in Hawthorne's "Young Goodman Brown" and Baldwin's "Going to Meet the Man" respectively.

152. Many SETTINGS that combine social and economic functions can be more or less intimate. Compare and contrast the use of

    a. the barbershop in Faulkner's "Dry September" and the beauty shop in Welty's "Petrified Man," or

    b. the restaurant in Parker's "The Last Tea " and in Colette's "The Other Wife," or

    c. the café in Hemingway's "A Clean, Well-Lighted Place" with the restaurant in either story in (b), or

    d. the hotel in two or more of the following: Crane's "The Blue Hotel," Wharton's "Roman Fever," Allen's "The Whore of Mensa," and Brautigan's "Homage to the San Francisco YMCA."

153. Compare and contrast God's relationship to Noah with His relationship to Jonah.

154. Compare and contrast God as a protector in Genesis and "Jonah" with God as a protector in Mark and Luke.

155. Compare and contrast the uses of PARABLES in

    a. the traditions of Judaism and Christianity, Taoism, and Sufism;

    b. any of the religious traditions in (a) with any of the Grimm brothers' FAIRY TALES and with Bruna's *The King*;

    c. any of the works in (b) with any modern philosophical TALE such as Glasgow's "A Point in Morals," Wells's "The Star," Kafka's "A Common Confusion," Borges's "Pierre Menard, Author of the *Quixote*," Clarke's "The Star," or Holst's "The Zebra Storyteller."

156. To what extent does the PARABLE of the Prodigal Son (Luke 15) exemplify Jesus's theories of parables expressed in Mark 4?

157. Compare and contrast the relationship between truth on the one hand and beauty and/or wealth and/or power on the other in the Sufi TALE called "The Bequest," either of the Grimm brothers' stories "Rapunzel" or "The Three Spinsters," and either Tolstoy's *The Death of Ivan Ilyitch* or Paton's "Life for a Life."

158. Compare and contrast the use of the MOTIF of irregular inheritance in:

a. Porter's "The Grave" and Erdrich's "Chapter Two: 1932, Sita Kozka"; or

b. the Biblical parable of The Prodigal Son (Luke 15), the Sufi tale called "The Bequest," and one work from (a).

159. Compare and contrast the importance of the gardeners in the Sufi TALE of "The Ancient Coffer of Nuri Bey," Hardy's "The Son's Veto," and Bruna's *The King.*

160. Compare and contrast the effectiveness of including interpretations of PARABLES within parables themselves by considering as a set the Sufi TALES or the Taoist tales.

161. Compare and contrast the reactions to a return of someone who has erred in the Bible PARABLE of the Prodigal Son (Luke 15), the Taoist "A Ch'an Koan," and Fitzgerald's "Babylon Revisisted."

162. Compare and contrast the attitudes toward government in the Taoist TALE "Outsides" and two of the following: Poe's "The Purloined Letter," Mishima's "Patriotism," Gordimer's "Six Feet of the Country," and Achebe's "Girls at War."

163. Compare and contrast the treatment of the THEME of appearances versus essences

a. in the Tao TALES called "Outsides" and "Smelling Essays," or

b. in either of the tales from (a) and Maupassant's "The Jewels" and Singer's "Yentl the Yeshiva Boy," or

c. both tales in (a) and Zhu's "Chronicle of Mulberry Village."

164. Compare and contrast the treatment of adultery in three of the following: the Sufi TALE of "The Ancient Coffer of Nuri Bey," Chaucer's "The Miller's Tale," Maupassant's "The Jewels," Silko's "Yellow Woman," Camoin's "Things I Did To Make It Possible," and Moore's "How."

165. Compare and contrast the portraits of society in Maupassant's "The Jewels," Tolstoy's *The Death of Ivan Ilyitch* or Gogol's "The Overcoat," and Hardy's "The Son's Veto."

166. Compare and contrast the conceptions of happiness in Maupassant's "The Jewels" and "Mother Savage."

167. Compare and contrast the treatment of revenge in three of the following: Chaucer's "The Miller's Tale," Anderson's "Hands," Faulkner's "Barn Burning," Borges's "Emma Zunz," Paton's "Life for a Life," Ellison's "I Have No Mouth, and I Must Scream."

168. Compare and contrast the relationships between mothers and sons in

a. Maupassant's "Mother Savage" and Agee's "A Mother's Tale," or

b. Hardy's "The Son's Veto" and Lawrence's "The Rocking-Horse Winner," or

c. Frank O'Connor's "My Oedipus Complex," Wright's "The Man Who Was Almost a Man," and Spiegelman's "Prisoner on the Hell Planet," or

d. one story from each of the three previous groups, or

e. Hardy's "The Son's Veto" and Aidoo's "Something to Talk About on the Way to the Funeral."

169. Compare and contrast the kinds and importance of colors used in

a. the Grimm brothers' "Little Red Cap" and Bruna's *The King*, or

b. Gilman's "The Yellow Wall-Paper" and Silko's "Yellow Woman," or

    c. Crane's "The Blue Hotel" and Colette's "The Other Wife," or

    d. one story from each of (a), (b), and (c).

170. Compare and contrast the treatment of envy in

    a. any three of the following: Mansfield's "The Doll's House," Callaghan's "A Cap for Steve," Baraka's "The Death of Horatio Alger," Adams's "A Southern Spelling Bee," and Erdrich's "Chapter Two: 1932, Sita Kozka," or

    b. any story from (a) and one of the following: the Bible story of the Prodigal Son (Luke 15), Colette's "The Other Wife," and Barry's "The Night We All Got Sick."

171. Compare and contrast the marital breakdowns preceding the NARRATION in Colette's "The Other Wife" and Paley's "Wants."

172. Compare and contrast the significance of rocks in the Sufi TALE called "The Limitations of Dogma," the Grimm brothers' "Little Red-cap," Lessing's "Pleasure," and Carver's "Viewfinder."

173. Rivers are traditional SYMBOLS for time. Compare and contrast the use of rivers in Wells's *The Time Machine,* Bierce's "An Occurrence at Owl Creek Bridge," Conrad's *Heart of Darkness,* and Silko's "Yellow Woman."

174. Cather claimed that the single strongest influence on her writing was the work of Jewett. Compare and contrast the stories by these writers to discover what influence, if any, one had on the other.

175. Compare and contrast the significance of Rome in Cather's "The Joy of Nelly Deane" and Wharton's "Roman Fever."

176. Compare and contrast the treatment of social class in the Grimm brothers' "The Three Spinsters," Hardy's "The Son's Veto," and Faulkner's "Barn Burning."

177. Compare and contrast the use of rhyme in

    a. Chaucer's "The Miller's Tale" and Bruna's *The King,* or

    b. Brooks's "The Ballad of Rudolph Reed" and Benét's "Nightmare Number Three," or

    c. either work in (a) with either work in (b).

178. Compare and contrast the effects of the repetition of key terms like "pleasantly" in Tolstoy's *The Death of Ivan Ilyitch,* "gay" in Stein's "Miss Furr and Miss Skeene," and "oaken" in Brooks's "The Ballad of Rudolph Reed."

179. Compare and contrast the CHARACTERS of Rudolph Reed in Brooks's "The Ballad of Rudolph Reed" and Enoch Maarman in Paton's "Life for a Life."

180. Compare and contrast the portraits of machine intelligence

    a. in Benét's "Nightmare Number Three" and Ellison's "I Have No Mouth, and I Must Scream," or

    b. in Asimov's "Reason," and Lem's "Prince Ferrix and the Princess Crystal," or

    c. in one story from (a) and one story from (b).

181. Compare and contrast the elements of SATIRE in

    a. Poe's "The Facts in the Case of M. Valdemar" and Benét's "Nightmare Number Three," or

    b. Stein's "Miss Furr and Miss Skeene" and Brautigan's "Homage to the San Francisco YMCA," or

    c. Flannery O'Connor's "Good Country People" and Welty's "Petrified Man," or

    d. Barthelme's "The Piano Player" and Cheever's "The Swimmer."

182. Compare and contrast the threatened end of humanity as portrayed in the Bible STORY of The Flood (Genesis 6:1–9:29), Wells's *The Time Machine*, and Benét's "Nightmare Number Three" or Ellison's "I Have No Mouth, and I Must Scream."

183. Poe named STORIES that engaged us through logic "tales of ratiocination." As such tales, compare and contrast

    a. a science fiction work, such as Wells's *The Time Machine* or Asimov's "Reason," with a Tale of the Great Detective, such as Poe's "The Purloined Letter" or Doyle's "The Adventure of the Speckled Band," or

    b. compare and contrast any work in (a) with Glasgow's "A Point in Morals."

184. Compare and contrast the effects of SELF-REFLEXIVITY in

    a. Cortázar's "Continuity of Parks," Lem's "Prince Ferrix and the Princess Crystal," and Holst's "The Zebra Storyteller," or

    b. Kafka's "A Common Confusion" or Barth's "Night-Sea Journey," Tanizaki's "The Thief" or Borges's "Pierre Menard, Author of the *Quixote*," and Spiegelman's "Prisoner on the Hell Planet" or Barry's "The Night We All Got Sick," or

    c. O. Henry's "A Midsummer Knight's Dream" and "Springtime à la Carte."

185. Compare and contrast the use of the MOTIF of testing the PROTAGONIST in the Grimm brothers' "The Three Spinsters" and Lem's "Prince Ferrix and the Princess Crystal."

186. Compare and contrast the way the characters portray human beings in Agee's "A Mother's Tale" and Lem's "Prince Ferrix and the Princess Crystal."

187. Compare and contrast the portraits of the impact of war on civilians in three of the following: Maupassant's "Mother Savage," Bierce's "An Occurrence at Owl Creek Bridge," Benét's "Nightmare Number Three," Achebe's "Girls at War," and Spiegelman's "Prisoner on the Hell Planet."

188. Compare and contrast the SYMBOLISM of the automobile in Achebe's "Girls at War" and Hannah's "I'm Shaking to Death."

189. Compare and contrast the societies portrayed in

    a. Aidoo's "Something to Talk About on the Way to the Funeral" and Achebe's "Girls at War," or

    b. either STORY in (a) with the societies portrayed in either Paton's "Life for a Life" or Gordimer's "Six Feet of the Country."

190. Compare and contrast the relationships between mothers and daughters in

    a. the three Grimm brothers' STORIES, or

    b. any of the three Grimm brothers' stories and at least one of the following: Wharton's "Roman Fever," Flannery O'Connor's "Good Country People," Olsen's "I Stand Here Ironing," and Kincaid's "Girl."

191. Compare and contrast the rebirth IMAGERY in the Bible's "Jonah" and the Grimm brothers' "Little Red-cap."

192. Compare and contrast the portraits of romantic or erotic betrayal and its consequences in
    a. one of Cather's "The Joy of Nelly Deane," Parker's "The Last Tea," Steinbeck's "The Chrysanthemums," and Flannery O'Connor's "Good Country People," plus Saadawi's "She Has No Place in Paradise" and Hay's "Rapunzel," or
    b. Chaucer's "The Miller's Tale" and Ellison's "I Have No Mouth, and I Must Scream," or
    c. one story from (a) and one story from (b).
193. Compare and contrast the use of the rope IMAGE in three of the following: Chaucer's "The Miller's Tale," Doyle's "The Adventure of the Speckled Band," Glaspell's "A Jury of Her Peers," and Hay's "Rapunzel."
194. In what ways do either Hay's "Rapunzel" or Broumas's "Little Red Riding Hood" make you rethink their respective Grimm brothers' antecedent versions of those STORIES?
195. Compared to the Grimm brothers' versions of their STORIES, Hay's "Rapunzel" and Broumas's "Little Red Riding Hood" compel us to focus much more directly on the lives of the female CHARACTERS from their own VIEWPOINTS. Compare and contrast the Hay and Broumas pieces as works of feminism.
196. Compare and contrast the use of the word "girl" in Achebe's "Girls at War" and Kincaid's "Girl."
197. Compare and contrast Hannah's "I'm Shaking to Death" and Moore's "How" as works their NARRATORS might want to have discovered by their former lovers.
198. Compare and contrast Kincaid's "Girl" and Moore's "How" as works of instruction.
199. Compare and contrast the use of panels as units of NARRATIVE STRUCTURE in Spiegelman's "Prisoner on the Hell Planet" or Hernandez's "The Whispering Tree," and any two of the following: McCay's "Dreams of the Rarebit Fiend," Crumb's "fred the teen-age girl pigeon," Barry's "The Night We All Got Sick," and Watterson's "Something Under the Bed Is Drooling."
200. Compare and contrast the use and effects of second person NARRATION in Moore's "How" with the narration of Olsen's "I Stand Here Ironing."
201. Compare and contrast the significance of domestic work in
    a. three of the following: Olsen's "I Stand Here Ironing," Updike's "Should Wizard Hit Mommy?" Barthelme's "The Piano Player," and Kincaid's "Girl," or
    b. any story in (a) with the Grimm brothers' "The Three Spinsters" and Maupassant's "Mother Savage."
202. Compare and contrast the effects of a single, unbroken onrush as the NARRATIVE TECHNIQUE in Coover's "The Brother" and Kincaid's "Girl."
203. Compare and contrast the critique of religion in Clarke's "The Star" and Coover's "The Brother."
204. Some works reveal information in the course of their reading that so alters our understanding that we feel virtually compelled to reread them.
    a. Compare and contrast the experiences at first and SUBSEQUENT READINGS of Bierce's "An Occurrence at Owl Creek Bridge" or Gilman's "The

Yellow Wall-Paper," Tanizaki's "The Thief," and Cortázar's "Continuity of Parks."

b. Compare and contrast a subsequent reading of any of the stories in (a) with that of one of the Tales of the Great Detective (Poe's "The Purloined Letter" and Doyle's "The Adventure of the Speckled Band").

205. Compare and contrast the significance of education in

a. three of the following: Gilman's "The Yellow Wall-Paper," Cather's "The Joy of Nelly Deane," Stein's "Miss Furr and Miss Skeene," Doyle's "The Adventure of the Speckled Band," Flannery O'Connor's "Good Country People," Singer's "Yentl the Yeshiva Boy," and Allen's "The Whore of Mensa," or

b. Malamud's "The German Refugee," Adams's "A Southern Spelling Bee," and Zhu's "Chronicle of Mulberry Tree Village," or

c. any two STORIES in (a) or (b) with the Taoist "A Ch'an Koan."

206. Compare and contrast the treatment of memory in

a. Wharton's "Roman Fever" and Adams's "A Southern Spelling Bee," or

b. Baldwin's "Going to Meet the Man," Leguin's "The Day Before the Revolution," and Cheever's "The Swimmer."

207. Compare and contrast the treatment of children longing for adult affection in Lawrence's "The Rocking-Horse Winner," Frank O'Connor's "My Oedipus Complex," and Adams's "A Southern Spelling Bee."

208. Compare and contrast Native American/white American relations as backgrounds to Silko's "Yellow Woman" and Erdrich's "Chapter Two: 1932, Sita Kozka."

209. Why do AUTHORS create STORIES about the future? Compare and contrast the visions of the human future, and the NARRATIVE effects of those visions, in

a. Asimov's "Reason" or Delany's "Corona," Ellison's "I Have No Mouth, and I Must Scream," and LeGuin's "The Day Before the Revolution," or

b. any story from (a) and Wells's *The Time Machine*, or

c. all of the above.

210. Compare and contrast the depiction of the individual's relation to political revolution in Achebe's "Girls at War," LeGuin's "The Day Before the Revolution," and Zhu's "Chronicle of Mulberry Tree Village."

211. LeGuin is usually considered to be a SCIENCE FICTION AUTHOR. Indeed, "Thuvian" may well be taken as an ALLUSION to a prominent CHARACTER in the famous pulp NOVELS about Mars by Edgar Rice Burroughs (1875–1950). Compare and contrast the GENRE assumptions of "The Day Before the Revolution" with a work more directly within that pulp tradition such as Wells's "The Star" or Asimov's "Reason."

212. Compare and contrast the use of scientific evolution in Wells's *The Time Machine* and Mason's "A New-Wave Format."

213. Compare and contrast the role of legend in the lives of the main CHARACTERS in Agee's "A Mother's Tale" and Silko's "Yellow Woman."

214. Compare and contrast the descriptions of midsummer in O. Henry's "A Midsummer Knight's Dream" and Cheever's "The Swimmer."

215. Compare and contrast the uses parents make of STORIES in dealing with

their children in Agee's "A Mother's Tale," Updike's "Should Wizard Hit Mommy?" and Watterson's "Something Under the Bed Is Drooling."

216. Compare and contrast the portraits of suburban life in
    a. Thurber's "The Secrete Life of Walter Mitty," Cheever's "The Swimmer," and Barthelme's "The Piano Player," or
    b. any story in (a) and Hammett's "The Gutting of Couffignal."

217. Compare and contrast the treatment of suicide in
    a. Akutagawa's "In a Grove" and Mishima's "Patriotism," or
    b. three of the following: Hawthorne's "Rappaccini's Daughter," Melville's "Bartleby the Scrivener," Gilman's "The Yellow Wall-Paper," Glasgow's "A Point in Morals," Malamud's "The German Refugee," and Ellison's "I Have No Mouth, and I Must Scream," or
    c. either story from (a) and any story from (b).

218. Compare and contrast the use of the flashforward technique (the disclosure early in the plot of an event late in the story) in Tolstoy's *The Death of Ivan Ilyitch* and Mishima's "Patriotism."

219. Compare and contrast the importance of speech-making in Joyce's "The Dead," Malamud's "The German Refugee," and LeGuin's "The Day Before the Revolution."

220. Compare and contrast the uses of bird IMAGERY in three of the following: Jewett's "A White Heron," Glaspell's "A Jury of Her Peers," Anderson's "Hands," Porter's "The Grave," and Atwood's "The Resplendent Quetzal."

221. Compare and contrast the MOTIVES, talents, and social roles of the main detectives in Doyle's "The Adventure of the Speckled Band" and Hammett's "The Gutting of Couffignal."

222. According to one purist's prescription, a work of SCIENCE FICTION should make one and only one assumption that violates what we know about our own world and then extrapolate a NARRATIVE world consistent with that assumption. Compare and contrast the nature of the violation and the success in fulfilling this prescription achieved in any three of the following: Hawthorne's "Rappaccini's Daughter," Poe's "The Facts in the Case of M. Valdemar," Wells's *The Time Machine*, Wells's "The Star," Benét's "Nightmare Number Three," Clarke's "The Star," and Ellison's "I Have No Mouth, and I Must Scream."

223. Compare and contrast the children with special abilities in Lawrence's "The Rocking-Horse Winner" and Delany's "Corona."

224. Compare and contrast the portraits of Russian society in at least three of the following: Gogol's "The Overcoat," Dostoevsky's "The Honest Thief," Chekov's "Vanka," and Tolstoy's *The Death of Ivan Ilyitch*.

225. Compare and contrast the treatment of the THEME of theft in at least three of the following: Poe's "The Purloined Letter," Dostoevsky's "The Honest Thief," Tanizaki's "The Thief," Hammett's "The Gutting of Couffignal," and Callaghan's "A Cap for Steve."

226. Compare and contrast the significance of coats in Gogol's "The Overcoat" and Dostoevsky's "The Honest Thief."

227. Compare and contrast the importance of foreign languages in three of the following: Maupassant's "Mother Savage," Conrad's *Heart of Darkness*,

Lessing's "Pleasure," Malamud's "The German Refugee," and Holst's "The Zebra Storyteller."

228. Compare and contrast the portraits of the Russian upper class in Tolstoy's *The Death of Ivan Ilyitch* and Hammett's "The Gutting of Couffignal."

229. Compare and contrast the treatment of ostracism in
    a. the Bible story of the Fall (Genesis 3) and Twain's "The Diary of Adam and Eve," or
    b. either story in (a), Harte's "The Outcasts of Poker Flat," and Chopin's "Désirée's Baby" or Anderson's "Hands."

230. Compare and contrast the uses made of one or more of the common elements of the WESTERN in Harte's "The Outcasts of Poker Flat," Crane's "The Blue Hotel," and Haycox's "Stage to Lordsburg."

231. Literary CONVENTION gives us the STOCK CHARACTER of the "whore with a heart of gold," the "fallen woman" of "tarnished virtue" who really offers us at least glimpses of a higher virtue. Compare and contrast the portraits of the "fallen women" in
    a. Harte's "The Outcasts of Poker Flat" or Haycox's "Stage to Lordsburg," Maupassant's "The Jewels," and Borges's "Emma Zunz," or
    b. Ellison's "I Have No Mouth, and I Must Scream," Achebe's "Girls at War," and Allen's "The Whore of Mensa," or
    c. Toomer's "Becky," Wharton's "Roman Fever," and Singer's "Yentl The Yeshiva Boy," or
    d. one STORY from each of (a), (b), and (c).

232. Literary CONVENTION gives us the STOCK CHARACTER of the outcast HERO, the man society denigrates who nonetheless offers us at least glimpses of a higher virtue. Compare and contrast the portraits of the outcast heroes in Harte's "The Outcasts of Poker Flat" or Haycox's "Stage to Lordsburg" with those of the would-be heros of Faulkner's "Dry September" and Thurber's "The Secret Life of Walter Mitty."

233. Compare and contrast the relationship of humanity to nature as represented in
    a. Ovid's *Metamorphoses*, Wells's "The Star," and London's "To Build a Fire," or
    b. any story in (a), Poe's "The Facts in the Case of M. Valdemar," and Jewett's "A White Heron."

234. In James's "The Altar of the Dead," we read that Stransom's life "was ruled by ghosts." Compare and contrast the treatment of unfulfilled love in
    a. James's "The Altar of the Dead," "The Tree of Knowledge," and *The Turn of the Screw*, or
    b. Hawthorne's "Young Goodman Brown," Joyce's "The Dead," and one story in (a), or
    c. one story in (a) or (b) and Singer's "Yentl the Yeshiva Boy" and Saadawi's "She Has No Place in Paradise."

235. Compare and contrast the uses made of DIALOGUE in James's "The Altar of the Dead," "The Tree of Knowledge," and *The Turn of the Screw*.

236. In general, light is often a SYMBOL for life and in the Bible light is the traditional symbol for spiritual revelation. Compare and contrast the uses made of light imagery in Genesis 1 and at least two of the following:

Tolstoy's *The Death of Ivan Ilyitch*, James's "The Altar of the Dead," Wells's "The Star," and Hemingway's "A Clean, Well-Lighted Place."

237. James typically portrays a central CHARACTER whose understanding of his or her situation may be vague and/or mistaken but whose step-by-step emotional evolution is shown with great precision. Compare and contrast this process as it occurs in works by James of very different lengths: "The Tree of Knowledge," "The Altar of the Dead," and *The Turn of the Screw*.

238. Children are traditionally taken to be naturally innocent. Compare and contrast the treatment of the innocence of children in
   a. the Grimm brothers' "Little Red Cap" or Agee's "A Mother's Tale," Chekov's "Vanka" or Cather's "The Joy of Nelly Deane," and James's *The Turn of the Screw*, or
   b. Lawrence's "The Rocking-Horse Winner," Updike's "Should Wizard Hit Mommy?" and Hernandez's "The Whispering Tree."

239. Compare and contrast the handling and importance of dialect in any three of the following: Jewett's "A White Heron," Faulkner's "Barn Burning" or "Dry September," Welty's "Petrified Man," Wright's "The Man Who Was Almost a Man," Flannery O'Connor's "Good Country People," Malamud's "The German Refugee," Baldwin's "Going to Meet the Man," and Spiegelman's "Prisoner of the Hell Planet."

240. Compare and contrast the IMAGES of cats in Poe's "The Black Cat," Crumb's "fred the teen-age girl pigeon," and Holst's "The Zebra Storyteller."

Acknowledgments

CHINUA ACHEBE ["Girls at War" from *Girls at War and Other Stories* by Chinua Achebe, copyright © 1972, 1973 by Chinua Achebe. Used by permission of Doubleday, a division of Bantam, Doubleday, Dell Publishing Group, Inc. and Harold Ober Associates Incorporated.]

ALICE ADAMS "A Southern Spelling Bee" [from *To See You Again* by Alice Adams. Copyright © 1982 by Alice Adams. Reprinted by permission of Alfred A. Knopf, Inc.]

JAMES AGEE "A Mother's Tale" from *The Collected Short Prose of James Agee*, Houghton Mifflin, 1968, copyright © The James Agee Trust. [Reprinted by permission of The James Agee Trust.]

AMA ATA AIDOO "Something to Talk About on the Way to the Funeral" from *No Sweetness Here* by Ama Ata Aidoo. [© Ama Ata Aidoo 1969.]

RYUNOSUKE AKUTAGAWA ["In a Grove" is reprinted from *Rashomon and Other Stories* by Ryunosuke Akutagawa, translated by Takashi Kojima, Liveright Publishing Corporation. Copyright © 1952, 1970 by Liveright Publishing Corporation.]

WOODY ALLEN "The Whore of Mensa" [from *Without Feathers* by Woody Allen. Copyright © 1974 by Woody Allen. Reprinted by permission of Random House, Inc.]

SHERWOOD ANDERSON ["Hands," from *Winesburg, Ohio* by Sherwood Anderson. Copyright 1919 by B. W. Huebsch. Copyright 1947 by Eleanor Copenhaver Anderson. Used by permission of Viking Penguin, a division of Penguin Books USA Inc.]

ANONYMOUS "The Ancient Coffer of Nuri Bey," "The Bequest," and "The Limitations of Dogma" [from *Tales of the Dervishes* by Idries Shah. Copyright © 1967 by Idries Shah. Used by permission of the publisher, Dutton, an imprint of New American Library, a division of Penguin Books USA Inc., Octagon Press, London, and Curtis Brown Ltd.]

ANONYMOUS "Smelling Essays," "Outsiders," and "Ach'an Koan" [from *Taoist Tales* by Raymond Van Over. Copyright © 1973 by Raymond Van Over. Used by permission of New American Library, a Division of Penguin Books USA Inc.]

ISAAC ASIMOV "Reason" from *I. Robot* by Isaac Asimov. Reprinted by permission of the author.

MARGARET ATWOOD "The Resplendent Quetzal" from *Dancing Girls and Other Stories* by Margaret Atwood. [Copyright © 1977, 1982 by O. W. Toad, Ltd. Reprinted by permission of Simon & Schuster, Inc.]

JAMES BALDWIN ["Sonney's Blues," copyright © 1957 by James Baldwin from *Going to Meet the Man* by James Baldwin. Used by permission of Doubleday, a division of Bantam, Doubleday, Dell Publishing Group, Inc.]

AMIRI BARAKA "The Death of Horatio Alger" from TALES by Amiri Baraka. [Reprinted by permission of Sterling Lord Literistic, Inc. Copyright © 1967 by Amiri Baraka.]

LYNDA BARRY ["The Night We All Got Sick" from *The Funhouse* by Lynda Barry. Copyright © 1986 by Lynda Barry. Reprinted by permission of HarperCollins Publishers.]

JOHN BARTH "Night Sea Journey," copyright © 1966 by John Barth (first published in *Esquire* Magazine), from *Lost in the Funhouse* by John Barth. Used by permission of Doubleday, a division of Bantam, Doubleday, Dell Publishing Group, Inc.]

DONALD BARTHELME "The Piano Player" [from *Come Back, Dr. Caligari* by Donald Barthelme. Copyright © 1963 by Donald Barthelme. By permission of Little, Brown and Company.]

STEPHEN VINCENT BENET "Nightmare Number Three" from *The Selected Works and Prose of Stephen Vincent Benet*. [Reprinted by permission of Brandt & Brandt. Copyright © 1960.]

JORGE LUIS BORGES "Emma Zunz" and "Pierre Menard, Author of Don Quixote" from [*Labyrinths* by Jorge Luis Borges. Copyright © 1962, 1964 by New Directions Publishing Corporation. Reprinted by permission of New Directions Publishing Corporation.]

RICHARD BRAUTIGAN "Homage to the San Francisco YMCA" from *Revenge of the Lawn* by Richard Brautigan, Simon & Schuster, 1972. [Copyright © 1972 by Richard Brautigan. Reprinted by permission of The Helen Brann Agency, Inc.]

GWENDOLYN BROOKS "The Ballad of Rudolph Reed" [from *Blacks* by Gwendolyn Brooks, published by The David Company, Chicago. © 1987.]

OLGA BROUMAS "Little Red Riding Hood" from *Beginning with O* by Olga Broumas. Reprinted by permission of Yale University Press.

DICK BRUNA *The King* by Dick Bruna. © 1968. Reprinted by permission of Unieboek and Reed Consumer Books.

MORELY CALLAGHAN "A Cap for Steve" from *Morely Callaghan's Stories* by Morley Callaghan. [© Estate of Morley Callaghan.] Reprinted by permission.

FRANÇOIS CAMOIN "Things I Did to Make It Possible" [reprinted from *The End of the World Is Los Angeles* by François Camoin, by permission of the University of Missouri Press. Copyright © 1982 by the author.]

RAYMOND CARVER "Viewfinder" [from *What We Talk About When We Talk About Love* by Raymond Carver. Copyright © 1981 by Raymond Carver. Reprinted by permission of Alfred A. Knopf, Inc.]

JOHN CHEEVER "The Swimmer" [from *The Stories of John Cheever* by John Cheever. Copyright © 1964 by John Cheever. Reprinted by permission of Alfred A. Knopf, Inc.]

ANTON CHEKHOV ["Vanka," from *The Portable Chekhov* by Avrahm Yarmolinsky, editor. Copyright 1947, 1968 by Viking Penguin, Inc. Renewed copyright © 1975 by Avrahm Yarmolinsky. Used by permission of Viking Penguin, a division of Penguin Books USA Inc.]

ARTHUR C. CLARKE "The Star" [reprinted by permission of the author and the author's agents, Scott Meredith Literary Agency, Inc., 845 Third Avenue, New York, New York 10022.]

COLLETTE ["The Other Wife" from *The Collected Stories* by Collette. Translation copyright © 1983 by Farrar, Straus & Giroux, Inc. Reprinted by permission of Farrar, Straus & Giroux, Inc.]

ROBERT COOVER ["The Brother," from *Pricksongs & Descants* by Robert Coover. Copyright © 1969 by Robert Coover. Used by permission of the publisher, Dutton, an imprint of New American Library, a division of Penguin Books USA Inc.]

JULIO CORTAZAR "The Continuity of Parks" [from *End of the Game and Other Stories* by Julio Cortazar, trans., P. Blackburn. Copyright © 1967 by Random House, Inc. Reprinted by permission of Pantheon Books, a Division of Random House, Inc.]

ROBERT DENNIS CRUMB "fred the teen-age girl pigeon" from *Headcomix, Twenty Years Later* by Richard Crumb. [© 1965 by R. Crumb.] Reprinted by permission of the author.

SAMUEL R. DELANY "Corona" from *Driftglass* by Samuel R. Delany. [Copyright © 1967 by Mercury Press, Inc.] Reprinted by permission of Henry Morrison, Inc.

FYODOR DOSTOEVSKY "An Honest Thief" from *An Honest Thief and Other Stories* by Fyodor Dostoevsky, translated by Constance Garnett. [Reprinted by permission of William Heinemann Limited.]

HARLAN ELLISON "I Have No Mouth and I Must Scream" by Harlan Ellison; copyright © 1967 by Galaxy Publishing Corporation, Inc. Copyright reassigned to Author 3 December 1968; copyright © 1968 by Harlan Ellison. Reprinted by arrangement with, and permission of, the Author and the Author's agent, Richard Curtis Associates, Inc., New York. All rights reserved. Computer printouts for "I Have No Mouth, and I Must Scream" by Jeff Levin: Copyright © 1987 by The Kilimanjaro Corporation.

LOUISE ERDRICH "Sita Kozka" [from *The Beet Queen* by Louise Erdrich. Copyright © 1986 by Louise Erdrich. Reprinted by permission of Henry Holt and Company, Inc.]

WILLIAM FAULKNER "Barn Burning" [from *Collected Stories of William Faulkner* by William Faulkner. Copyright 1950 by Random House, Inc. and renewed 1977 by Jill Faulkner Summers.] "Dry September" [from *Collected Stories of William Faulkner* by William Faulkner. Copyright 1930 and renewed 1958 by William Faulkner. Reprinted by permission of Random House, Inc.]

F. SCOTT FITZGERALD "Babylon Revisited" [reprinted with permission from Charles Scribner's Sons, an imprint of Macmillan Publishing Company, from *Taps at Reveille* by F. Scott Fitzgerald. Copyright 1931 by The Curtis Publishing Company; renewal copyright © 1959 by Frances Scott Fitzgerald Lanahan.]

NICOLAI GOGOL "The Overcoat" [from *The Overcoat & Other Tales of Good and Evil* by Nicolai Gogol. Copyright © 1957 by David Magarshack. Used by permission of Doubleday, a division of Bantam Doubleday Dell Publishing Group, Inc.]

NADINE GORDIMER ["Six Feet of the Country," copyright © 1956 by Nadine Gordimer, from *Selected Stories* by Nadine Gordimer. Used by permission of Viking Penguin, a division of Penguin Books USA Inc.]

DASHIELL HAMMETT "The Butting of Couffignal" [from *The Big Knockover* by Dashiell Hammett. Copyright © 1966 by Lillian Hellman. Reprinted by permission of Random House, Inc.]

BARRY HANNAH "I'm Shaking to Death" [from *Captain Maximus* by Barry Hannah. Copyright © 1985 by Barry Hannah. Reprinted by permission of Alfred A. Knopf, Inc.]

SARAH HENDERSON HAY "Rapunzel" from *Story Hour* by Sara Henderson Hay, University of Arkansas Press. [Copyright © 1963 by Sara Henderson Hay.] Reprinted by permission of the author.

ERNEST HAYCOX "Stage to Lordsburg," © 1937 by Ernest Haycox. Reprinted by permission of the author.

ERNEST HEMINGWAY "A Clean, Well-Lighted Place" [reprinted with permission of Charles Scribner's Sons, an imprint of Macmillan Publishing

Company, from *Winner Take Nothing* by Ernest Hemingway. Copyright 1933 by Charles Scribner's Sons; renewal copyright © 1961 by Mary Hemingway.]

GILBERT HERNANDEZ "The Whispering Tree" from *Heartbreak Soup* by Gilbert Hernandez, Fantagraphics Books, 1984.

SPENCER HOLST ["Zebra Storyteller" from *Language of Cats and Other Stories*, McCall Publishing Company, © 1971. Reprinted by permission of the author.]

FRANZ KAFKA "A Common Confusion" and "Metamorphosis" [from *Franz Kafka: The Complete Stories* by Franz Kafka, edited by Nahum N. Glatzer. Copyright 1946, 1947, 1948, 1949, 1954, © 1958, 1971 by Schocken Books, Inc. Reprinted by permission of Schocken Books, published by Pantheon Books, a Division of Random House, Inc.]

YASUNARI KAWABATA "One Arm" [from *House of the Sleeping Beauties* by Yasunari Kawabata published by Kodansha International Ltd. Copyright © 1969 by Kodansha International Ltd. Reprinted by permission. All rights reserved.]

JAMAICA KINCAID ["Girl" from *At the Bottom of the River* by Jamaica Kincaid. Copyright © 1978, 1984 by Jamaica Kincaid. Reprinted by permission of Farrar, Straus & Giroux, Inc.]

TOMMASO LANDOLFI ["Rain," from *Words in Commotion* by Tommaso Landolfi, translated by Kathrine Jason, Translation copyright © 1986 by Viking Penguin, Inc., English translation; copyright © 1982 by Rizzoli Editore. Used by permission of Viking Penguin, a division of Penguin Books USA Inc.]

D. H. LAWRENCE ["Odour of Chrysanthemums," copyright © 1933 by the Estate of D. H. Lawrence, renewed © 1961 by Angelo Ravagli and C. M. Weekley, Executors of the Estate of Frieda Lawrence, "The Rocking-Horse Winner" by D. H. Lawrence, copyright 1933 by the Estate of D. H. Lawrence, renewed © 1961 by Angelo Ravagli and C. M. Weekley, Executors of the Estate of Frieda Lawrence, from *Complete Short Stories of D. H. Lawrence* by D. H. Lawrence. Used by permission of Viking Penguin, a division of Penguin Books USA Inc.]

URSULA K. LE GUIN "The Day Before the Revolution" from *The Wind's Twelve Quarters* by Ursula K. Le Guin. [Copyright © 1974 by Ursula K. Le Guin: first appeared in *Galaxy*; reprinted by permission of the author and the author's agent, Virginia Kidd.]

STANISLAW LEM "Prince Ferrix and the Princess Crystal" [from *The Cyberiad* by Stanislaw Lem. English translation © 1974 by The Continuum Publishing Company. Reprinted by permission of the publisher.]

DORIS LESSING ["Pleasure" from *The Habit of Loving* by Doris Lessing. Copyright © 1957 by Doris Lessing. Reprinted by permission of HarperCollins Publishers.]

JACK LONDON ["To Build a Fire" from *Great Short Works of Jack London.* Copyright © 1965 by Harper & Row, Publishers, Inc. Reprinted by permission of HarperCollins Publishers.]

BERNARD MALAMUD ["The German Refugee" from *The Stories of Bernard Malamud* by Bernard Malamud. Copyright © 1963, 1983 by Bernard Malamud. Reprinted by permission of Farrar, Straus & Giroux, Inc.]

KATHERINE MANSFIELD "The Doll's House" [from *The Short Stories of Katherine Mansfield* by Katherine Mansfield. Copyright 1923 by Alfred A. Knopf, Inc. and renewed 1951 by J. Middleton Murry. Reprinted by permission of the publisher.]

BOBBIE ANN MASON ["A New-Wave Format" from *Shiloh and Other Stories* by Bobbie Ann Mason. Copyright © 1982 by Bobbie Ann Mason. Reprinted by permission of HarperCollins Publishers.]

GUY DE MAUPASSANT ["The Jewels" and "Mother Savage" from *Selected Short Stories* by Guy de Maupassant, translated by Roger Colet (Penguin Classics, 1971), copyright © Roger Colet, 1971.]

YUKIO MISHIMA "Patriotism" from [*Death in Midsummer* by Yukio Mishima. Copyright © 1966 by New Directions Publishing Corp. Reprinted by permission of New Directions Publishing Corporation.]

LORRIE MOORE "How" [from *Self-Help* by Lorrie Moore. Copyright © 1985 by M. L. Moore. Reprinted by permission of Alfred A. Knopf, Inc.]

ALICE MUNRO ["Royal Beatings" from *The Beggar Maid.* Copyright © 1977, 1978, 1979 by Alice Munro. This Collection was originally published in Canada by The Macmillan Company of Canada Limited in 1978 under the title *Who Do You Think You Are?* and in the United States by Alfred A. Knopf, Inc. in 1979. All rights reserved.]

FLANNERY O'CONNOR ["Good Country People" from *A Good Man Is Hard to Find and Other Stories,* copyright © 1955 by Flannery O'Connor and renewed 1983 by Mrs. Regina O'Connor, reprinted by permission of Harcourt Brace Jovanovich, Inc.]

FRANK O'CONNOR "My Oedipus Complex" [from *Collected Stories* by Frank O'Connor. Copyright 1950 by Frank O'Connor. Reprinted by permission of Alfred A. Knopf, Inc. and Joan Daves Agency.]

TILLIE OLSEN ["I Stand Here Ironing," from *Tell Me A Riddle* by Tillie

Olsen. Copyright © 1956, 1957, 1960, 1961 by Tillie Olsen. Used by permission of Delacorte Press/Seymour Lawrence, a division of Bantam Doubleday Dell Publishing Group, Inc.]

OVID Excerpt [from *Metamorphoses* by Ovid, translated by Mary M. Innes (Penguin Classics, 1955), copyright © Mary M. Innes, 1955.]

GRACE PALEY ["Wants" from *Enormous Changes at the Last Minute* by Grace Paley. Copyright © 1971, 1974 by Grace Paley. Reprinted by permission of Farrar, Straus & Giroux, Inc.]

DOROTHY PARKER ["The Last Tea," copyright 1926, renewed © 1954 by Dorothy Parker, from *The Portable Dorothy Parker* by Dorothy Parker, Introduction by Brendan Gill. Used by permission of Viking Penguin, a division of Penguin Books USA Inc.]

ALAN PATON "Life for a Life" [reprinted with the permission of Charles Scribner's Sons, an imprint of Macmillan Publishing Company from *Tales from a Troubled Land* by Alan Paton. Copyright © 1961 Alan Paton.]

CHARLES PERRAULT "Little Red Riding Hood" by Charles Perrault, translated by Angela Carter from *The Fairy Tales of Charles Perrault*, Avon Books, 1977.

KATHERINE ANNE PORTER ["The Grave" from *The Leaning Tower and Other Stories*, copyright 1944 and renewed 1972 by Katherine Anne Porter, reprinted by permission of Harcourt Brace Jovanovich, Inc.]

NAWAL EL SAADAWI "She Has No Place in Paradise" from *She Has No Place in Paradise*, translated by Shirley Eber. Copyright © 1987 by Nawal El Saadawi. [Reprinted by permission of Methuen London.]

LESLIE MARMON SILKO "Yellow Woman" by Leslie Marmon Silko. [Reprinted by permission of Wylie, Aitken & Stone, Inc.]

ISAAC BASHEVIS SINGER ["Yentl the Yeshiva Boy" from *The Collected Stories of Isaac Bashevis Singer* by Isaac Bashevis Singer. Copyright © 1962, 1964, 1984 by Isaac Bashevis Singer. Reprinted by permission of Farrar, Straus & Giroux, Inc.]

ART SPIEGELMAN "Prisoner on the Hell Planet" [from *Maus* by Art Spiegelman. Copyright © 1986 by Art Spiegelman. Reprinted by permission of Pantheon Books, a Division of Random House, Inc.]

GERTRUDE STEIN "Miss Furr and Miss Skeene" [from *Selected Writings of Gertrude Stein* by Gertrude Stein. Copyright 1946 by Random House, Inc. Reprinted by permission of the publisher.]

JOHN STEINBECK ["The Chrysanthemums," copyright 1927, renewed © 1865 by John Steinbeck, "The Harness," copyright 1938, renewed © 1966 by John Steinbeck, from *The Long Valley* by John Steinbeck. Used by permission of Viking Penguin, a division of Penguin Books USA Inc.]

JUNICHIRO TANIZAKI "Thief" [from *Seven Japanese Tales* by Junichiro Tanizaki, trans., H. Hibbett. Copyright © 1963 by Alfred A. Knopf, Inc. Reprinted by permission of the publisher.]

JAMES THURBER "The Secret Life of Walter Mitty" [copyright © 1942 James Thurber. Copyright © 1970 Helen Thurber and Rosemary A. Thurber. From *My World—and Welcome To It*, published by Harcourt Brace Jovanovich, Inc.]

JEAN TOOMER ["Becky" is reprinted from *Cane* by Jean Toomer, by permission of Liveright Publishing Corporation. Copyright 1923 by Boni & Liveright. Copyright renewed 1951 by Jean Toomer.]

JOHN UPDIKE "Should Wizard Hit Mommy?" [from *Pigeon Feathers and Other Stories* by John Updike. Copyright © 1959 by John Updike. Reprinted by permission of Alfred A. Knopf, Inc. Originally appeared in *The New Yorker*.]

EDITH WHARTON "Roman Fever" [reprinted with the permission of Charles Scribner's Sons, an imprint of Macmillan Publishing Company, from *Roman Fever and Other Stories* by Edith Wharton. Copyright 1934 *Liberty Magazine*; copyright renewed © 1962 William R. Tyler.]

BILL WATTERSON [*Calvin and Hobbes* © 1986 Watterson. Reprinted with permission of Universal Press Syndicate. All rights reserved.]

EUDORA WELTY ["Lily Daw and the Three Ladies" from *A Curtain of Green and Other Stories*, copyright 1937 and renewed 1965 by Eudora Welty, "Petrified Man" from *A Curtain of Green and Other Stories*, copyright 1939 and renewed 1967 by Eudora Welty, reprinted by permission of Harcourt Brace Jovanovich, Inc.]

RICHARD WRIGHT "The Man Who Was Almost a Man" [from the book, *Eight Men* by Richard Wright. Copyright © 1987 by the Estate of Richard Wright. Used by permission of the publisher, Thunder's Mouth Press.]

XIAOPING ZHU "Chronicle of Mulberry Tree Village" [from *The Chinese Western* by Zhu Hong, trans. Copyright © 1988 by Zhu Hong. Reprinted by permission of Ballantine Books, a Division of Random House, Inc.]

Title Index

Adventure of the Speckled Band, The, 370

Altar of the Dead, The, 629

Ancient Coffer of Nuri Bey, The, 34

Babylon Revisited, 428

Ballad of Rudolph Reed, The, 172

Barn Burning, 406

Bartleby the Scrivener, 944

Becky, 1215

Bequest, The, 36

Black Cat, The, 1069

Blue Hotel, The, 319

Brother, The, 312

Cap for Steve, A, 182

Ch'an Koan, A, 31

Chapter Two: 1932, Sita Kozka, 400

Chronicle of Mulberry Tree Village, 1341

Chrysanthemums, The, 1143

Clean, Well-Lighted Place, A, 609

Common Confusion, A, 780

Continuity of Parks, 317

Corona, 342

Counterparts, 743

Day Before the Revolution, The, 859

Dead, The, 751

Death of Horatio Alger, The, 132

Death of Ivan Ilyitch, The, 1174

Diary of Adam and Eve, The, 1218

Doll's House, The, 911

Dreams of the Rarebit Fiend, 942

Dry September, 419

Désirée's Baby, 240

Emma Zunz, 159

Facts in the Case of M. Valdemar, The, 1089

fred the teen-age girl pigeon, 339

Genesis, 10

German Refugee, The, 901

Girl, 827

Girls at War, 38

Going to Meet the Man, 119

Good Country People, 1010

Grave, The, 1096

Gutting of Couffignal, The, 523

Hands, 90

Harness, The, 1152

Heart of Darkness, 253

Homage to the San Francisco YMCA, 169

Honest Thief, The, 356

How, 987

I Stand Here Ironing, 1034

I Have No Mouth, and I Must Scream, 388

I'm Shaking to Death, 546

In a Grove, 78

Jewels, The, 930

Jonah, 23

Joy of Nelly Deane, The, 196

Jury of Her Peers, A, 465

King, The, 177

Last Tea, The, 1053

Life for a Life, A, 1057

Lily Daw and the Three Ladies, 1302

Limitations of Dogma, The, 37

Little Red Riding Hood (Broumas), 175

Little Red Riding Hood (Perrault), 1066

Little Red-cap, 520

Man Who Was Almost a Man, The, 1330

Metamorphoses, 1041

Metamorphosis, The, 782

Midsummer Knight's Dream, A, 613

Miller's Tale, The, 207

Miss Furr and Miss Skeene, 1138

Mother Savage, 936

Mother's Tale, A, 54

My Oedipus Complex, 1025

New-Wave Format, A, 917

Night We All Got Sick, The, 137

Night-Sea Journey, 139

Nightmare Number Three, 149

Occurrence at Owl Creek Bridge, An, 152

Odour of Chrysanthemums, 833

On Parables (Mark 4), 26

One Arm, 814

Other Wife, The, 250

Outcasts of Poker Flat, The, 560

Outsides, 32
Overcoat, The, 481
Patriotism, 970
Petrified Man, 1310
Piano Player, The 146
Pierre Menard, Author of the
    Quixote, 163
Pleasure, 878
Point in Morals, A, 456
Prince Ferrix and the Princess
    Crystal, 870
Prisoner on the Hell Planet, 1132
Prodigal Son, The (Luke 15), 29
Purloined Letter, The, 1076
Rain, 829
Rappaccini's Daughter, 568
Rapunzel (Hay), 597
Rapunzel (Grimm), 514
Reason, 95
Resplendent Quetzal, The, 109
Rocking-Horse Winner, The, 848
Roman Fever, 1320
Royal Beatings, 994
Secret Life of Walter Mitty, The,
    1170
She Has No Place in Paradise,
    1101
Should Wizard Hit Mommy?, 1236
Six Feet of the Country, 505
Smelling Essays, 33

Something Under the Bed is Drooling:
    A Calvin and Hobbes Collection,
    1241
Something to Talk About on the
    Way to the Funeral, 69
Son's Veto, The, 549
Southern Spelling Bee, A, 49
Springtime à la Carte, 618
Stage to Lordsburg, 598
Star, The (Clarke), 245
Star, The (Wells), 1242
Swimmer, The, 227
Thief, The, 1162
Things I Did To Make It Possible, 190
Three Spinsters, The, 518
Time Machine, The, 1250
To Build a Fire, 889
Tree of Knowledge, The, 653
Turn of the Screw, The, 664
Vanka, 236
Viewfinder, 193
Wants, 1050
Whispering Tree, The, 623
White Heron, A, 735
Whore of Mensa, The, 85
Yellow Woman, 1106
Yellow Wall-Paper, The, 443
Yentl the Yeshiva Boy, 1114
Young Goodman Brown, 588
Zebra Storyteller, The, 627